# THE CRITICAL TRADITION

## Classic Texts and Contemporary Trends

# THE CRITICAL TRADITION

## Classic Texts and Contemporary Trends

*Edited by*

# David H. Richter

*Queens College*
*of the City University of New York*

A BEDFORD BOOK · ST. MARTIN'S PRESS · NEW YORK

**For Bedford Books**

*Publisher:* Charles H. Christensen
*Associate Publisher:* Joan E. Feinberg
*Managing Editor:* Elizabeth M. Schaaf
*Developmental Editor:* Stephen A. Scipione
*Copyeditor:* Linda Howe
*Text design:* Claire Seng-Niemoeller
*Cover design:* Michael Mauceri, Independent Design

*For information, write:* St. Martin's Press, Inc.
175 Fifth Avenue, New York, NY 10010

*Editorial Offices:* Bedford Books of St. Martin's Press
29 Winchester Street, Boston, MA 02116

ISBN: 0–312–00344–7

## Acknowledgments

Dante Alighieri, "Letter to Can Grande della Scala," reprinted from *Literary Criticism of Dante Alighieri*, translated and edited by Robert S. Haller, by permission of the University of Nebraska Press. Copyright © 1973 by the University of Nebraska Press.

Aristotle, *Poetics*, reprinted from *Aristotle's Poetics: A Translation and Commentary for Students of Literature* by Leon Golden and O. B. Hardison, Jr., by permission of the publisher, Florida State University Press/University Presses of Florida, Tallahassee.

Houston A. Baker, Jr., "Generational Shifts and the Recent Criticism of Afro-American Literature," reprinted by permission from *Black American Literature Forum* 15:1 (Spring 1981). Copyright © 1981 by Indiana State University.

Mikhail Bakhtin, excerpt from "Discourse in the Novel," from *The Dialogic Imagination: Four Essays*, edited by Michael Holquist, translated by Caryl Emerson and Michael Holquist, published by the University of Texas Press. Copyright © 1981. Reprinted by permission of the University of Texas Press. "Discourse in Dostoevsky," from *Problems of Dostoevsky's Poetics* by Mikhail Bakhtin, translated by Caryl Emerson, published by the University of Minnesota Press, Minneapolis. Copyright © 1984 by the University of Minnesota. Reprinted by permission.

Roland Barthes, "From Work to Text," from *Image — Music — Text* by Roland Barthes. Copyright © 1977 by Roland Barthes. Reprinted by permission of Hill and Wang, a division of Farrar, Straus and Giroux, Inc.

Nina Baym, "Melodramas of Beset Manhood," from *American Quarterly* 33. Copyright © 1981 the Trustees of the University of Pennsylvania. Reprinted by permission of the author and the publisher.

Simone de Beauvoir, "Of Women in Five Authors," from *The Second Sex* by Simone de Beauvoir, translated and edited by H. M. Parshley. Copyright © 1952 by Alfred A. Knopf, Inc. Reprinted by permission of Alfred A. Knopf, Inc.

*Acknowledgments and copyrights are continued at the back of the book on pages 1441–1444, which constitute an extension of the copyright page.*

# Preface

*The Critical Tradition* might seem a paradoxical title, since it would be hard to name a field that has overthrown its traditions more thoroughly in the past two decades than literary theory and criticism. In the late 1960s, criticism in North America consisted primarily of New Critical explications of canonical texts — and everyone knew which texts were canonical. Biographical analysis in the Freudian manner was fashionable, and a few ambitious souls were combining archetypal criticism with the literary cosmography of Northrop Frye. But structuralism and phenomenology as methods of literary study were just coming over the horizon. Jacques Derrida, who published his *Grammatology* in Paris in 1967, had not yet brought deconstruction across the Atlantic, and Yale was thought of as the university of Cleanth Brooks. Social and historical scholars in North America discreetly avoided any mention of the name of Karl Marx, and only a few ideologues of the New Left were prepared to debate his ideas. The enfante terrible of feminist literary criticism was Kate Millett, whose *Sexual Politics* was much discussed. The notion that the poem was created in part or whole by the reader was a gleam in the eyes of Stanley Fish and Wolfgang Iser, but there was still definitely a text in this class.

At the time, the political and social turbulence of that era seemed to leave the academic study of literature untouched, whatever challenges might have been posed to history, sociology, and other more immediately relevant fields. But it is now clear that since the late 1960s, North America — and the entire English-speaking world — has undergone a phase of intellectual colonization reminiscent of the sixteenth-century voyages of discovery, as wave after wave of European thought has found readers and shaped disciples within the human sciences in general and critical theory in particular. And the ideas of theorists such as Jacques Lacan, Hans Robert Jauss, Louis Althusser, Mikhail Bakhtin, Claude Lévi-Strauss, and Michel Foucault, once the intellectual property of a few specialists, have become common ground for the profession of letters as a whole. That such issues would be the profession's common ground constitutes a second revolution no less profound in its implications. Two decades ago, literary theory, like paleography or textual editing, was a specialist's field at the margins of the profession; today all scholars and teachers must be initiated into new theoretical approaches. Some will have original ideas to propound, but the majority must come to terms with the revolution in theory merely to enter the discourse of the profession, to comprehend and respond to the latest articles on Donne or Dickinson, Kafka or Camus.

These two revolutions have not made the "critical tradition" irrelevant; rather, they have forced the profession to redefine that tradition. In "Tradition and the Individual Talent," T. S. Eliot hypothesized that the masterpieces of imaginative literature form an "ideal order," which is subtly altered upon the entry of the genuinely original work. Much the same can be said of the critical tradition; as new literary theories have entered current discourse, it has been forced to broaden its horizons. The writings of Derrida, to choose one contemporary theorist out of many, cannot be understood apart from the theories of structuralism and semiotics against which he reacted; and Derrida presumes in addition, among much else, a knowledge of Plato, Kant, Hegel, Nietzsche, and Heidegger. Contemporary feminist theory, like that of Elaine Showalter and Hélène Cixous, must be understood against the backdrop of Virginia Woolf, Simone de Beauvoir, and other forebears who served either as sources of inspiration or as antagonists.

If the critical tradition shifts and expands as new writers enter the discourse and older ones move from the margin to the center, it also contracts. The differences between New Critics like Allen Tate, John Crowe Ransom, and Cleanth Brooks no longer seem so profound as they once did, and the New Criticism itself seems merely one part of a larger formalist movement in the earlier part of the century that comprehended such disparate theorists as Victor Shklovsky, Mikhail Bakhtin, Roman Jakobson, and R. S. Crane. At the same time, original thinkers like Kenneth Burke, who once were seen against the context of New Criticism, now assume their individual places in the critical pantheon. And an entire tradition of rhetorical theory going back to classical times, whose centrality depended on that of the New Criticism, has been displaced.

In view of all these changes, it no longer seemed possible to do justice to the critical tradition merely by supplementing the anthologies of two decades ago with new collections. There was clearly a pressing need for a comprehensive new anthology of literary theory and criticism that would provide an overview of the history of criticism since Plato, trace major trends in modern and contemporary literary theory, and convey a sense of the current range of literary argumentation and methodology — an anthology, moreover, that would not only come to terms with the revolution in critical thought of the past two decades but would also put that revolution into the context of the evolving tradition out of which the present ferment has arisen. There *is* a critical tradition and to ignore it is to misconstrue what the innovations of the present are all about. Furthermore, the new anthology would need to deal with the reciprocal relationship of theory and practice. As Goethe said, theories without facts are empty; facts without theories are dry. Many readers find it difficult to absorb the implications of theory without examples of critical practice, nor can intricate theories be grasped merely from their practical applications.

To the extent possible in one volume, *The Critical Tradition* integrates past and present, theory and practice. The volume is organized in two parts. Part I presents a history of criticism through selections by thirty-five major critics from Plato to Susan Sontag. Part II is divided into nine sections dealing with contemporary theory. Seven address "schools" of criticism — Marxism, psychological criticism, formalism, structuralism and semiotics, poststructuralism, feminism, and reader-response criticism — modes of critical thought that have developed over time. Each section emphasizes the *range* of thought within each school and the interplay between critical theory and practice. The section on psychoanalytic criticism, for example, contains essays by Freud, Jung, and Lacan, along with theoretical and practical criticism by writers such as Northrop Frye and Peter Brooks, who have turned to depth psychology in analyzing literary texts. The final two sections provide readings on critical issues much debated at present: the literary canon — the list of texts deemed important — and the forces that shape it; and the vexed question of interpretation — whether poetic interpretation is defined and delimited by authorial intention, and, if so, why interpretations of texts differ as widely as they do. The emphasis in Part II falls less on the sixty-six individual selections than on the nine intellectual currents they exemplify.

The aim of *The Critical Tradition* is not to remake the canon of criticism but to recognize the changes that have occurred. To this end, the contents have been chosen in consultation with many experts in critical theory. Complete essays and chapters rather than snippets from longer pieces have been included wherever possible. Superior contemporary translations have been procured (for example, Leon Golden's version of Aristotle's *Poetics* or Burton Raffel's free rendering of Horace's *Ars Poetica*) instead of older specimens in the public domain. In the selections illustrating critical practice, the clearest example of each method was selected; the table of contents includes Bakhtin on Dostoevsky, Wayne Booth on Austen, Tzvetan Todorov on Henry James, Fredric Jameson on Conrad, Derrida and Lacan on Poe, Fish on Milton's sonnets, and Barbara Johnson on Melville. This extensive range of material is inescapable, as no single text has inspired the most original theorists' finest work.

## "THE DULL DUTY OF AN EDITOR"

Because the critical tradition contains such varied ideas in such complex relation-ships, extensive apparatus — what Alexander Pope disdained as "dull duty" — has been provided to make the works collected here easier to assimilate. *The Critical Tradition* begins with an introduction that explores the ways in which theorists have tried to chart the terrain of criticism. This introduction describes the ineluctible fourfold classification of critical theories from M. H. Abrams's *The Mirror and the Lamp*, evaluates the powers and limitations of the Abrams map, its general biases and unspoken assumptions, and then discusses three other ways of mapping critical tasks and methods.

In Part I of *The Critical Tradition*, each reading is prefaced with an extensive headnote that places the text within the context of the author's life and works, explores the key issues of each reading and its relationship with other readings, and occasionally analyzes troublesome twists in the argumentation. For the readings by contemporary academic theorists and critics composing Part II, the biographical headnotes before each selection are necessarily briefer, but each of the nine sections is prefaced by a substantial introduction. These introductions, addressed to the serious reader, cover the origins, the general approach, and the variations in theory and practice of each of the seven movements, and provide equivalent coverage for the two issues under debate. Individual readings are analyzed primarily to mark out their place within larger critical trends. The introductions try to navigate between the Scylla of commentary that expresses only the prejudices of the editor and the Charybdis of neutralist mumbling addressed to nobody and expressing nothing. The intent was to provide an even-handed overview of each critical movement or issue showing both its powers and its limitations. Finally, following the headnotes to Part I and the introductions to Part II, selected bibliographies direct the interested reader to further works by and about the authors and their critical approaches. The texts in both parts are annotated to save the reader's time in tracking down allusions, to highlight the cross-references between one text and another, and to fill in the argument where the text has been abridged.

Although Part II sorts sixty-three critics into nine "schools" and "debates," it need hardly be said that even centrally placed "members" of a "school" swear no allegiance to its doctrines; despite the "fallacies" and "heresies" of the New Critics, there were no recorded excommunications. The problem is that some theorists belong under more than one category; Wayne Booth, for example, is a formalist who writes reader-response criticism, while Roland Barthes was a structuralist who became a poststructuralist. Still others, like Mikhail Bakhtin, are transitional figures who bridge two categories without belonging precisely to either. Therefore, an additional table of contents that places theorists in alternative categories has been provided for Part II. The book concludes with an index to proper names and major critical terms, which, together with the cross-references in the annotations, should aid the reader in understanding the shifting skeins of influence upon which the critical tradition is built. "Let us now be told no more," as Samuel Johnson said with both weariness and pride, "of 'the dull duty of an editor.'"

## ACKNOWLEDGMENTS

Though the title page might suggest a solo performance, no book of the size and complexity of *The Critical Tradition* is created alone; at every stage, from conception through final corrections, I have depended on the assistance and collaboration of a great many others. At Bedford Books of St. Martin's Press, first and foremost were Chuck Christensen and Joan Feinberg, who believed in the project and encouraged its completion, Steve Scipione, who worked out the myriad details together with me over several years, and Elizabeth Schaaf, whose fine production crew has turned the book into an aesthetically pleasing object. I am deeply indebted to Laura Wadenpfuhl, whose splendid initiative and business judgment were invaluable in the long and exacting task of acquiring permissions and who also made penetrating comments on various versions of the manuscript.

I am also thankful to the literary critics and theorists who have provided helpful suggestions and pointed comments on the choice of contents and the editorial materials. They include William Cain of Wellesley College; Frederick Crews of the University of California, Berkeley; Elizabeth Flynn of Michigan Technological University; Steven Goldsmith of the University of California, Berkeley; Stephen Greenblatt of the University of California, Berkeley; Susan Gubar of Indiana University, Bloomington; David Halliburton of Stanford University; Michael Hancher of the University of Minnesota; Barbara Leah Harmon of Wellesley College; Norman N. Holland of the University of Florida, Gainesville; Lawrence Lipking of Northwestern University; Steven Mailloux of Syracuse University; Michael Meyer of the University of Connecticut, Storrs; Nancy K. Miller of the Graduate Center, City University of New York; Michael Murrin of the University of Chicago; Mary Poovey of Johns Hopkins University; Herman Rapaport of the University of Iowa; William Sheidley of the University of Connecticut, Storrs; Elaine Showalter of Princeton University; Barbara Herrnstein Smith of Duke University; James Sosnoski of Miami University, Ohio; Patricia Meyer Spacks of Yale University; Susan Suleiman of Harvard University; Brook Thomas of the University of California, Irvine; Jane Tompkins of Duke University; David Wagenknecht of Boston University; and David Willbern of the State University of New York, Buffalo. I would particularly like to thank James Phelan of Ohio State University, whose perceptive commentary on the entire manuscript forced me to clarify or rethink many of my entrenched opinions, and whose unfailing generosity and tact made his suggestions easy to take.

In addition to these participants in formal reviewing procedures, the table of contents and sections of the manuscript have been read informally by friends, whose suggestions I have shamelessly incorporated. These include Don Bialostosky of the University of Toledo, Brian Corman of the University of Toronto, William J. Harris of the State University of New York, Stony Brook, Donald McQuade of the University of California, Berkeley, and my colleagues at Queens College: Barbara Bowen, Susan Harris, William Kelly, Richard McCoy, Anthony J. O'Brien, and Barbara Shollar. Institutions have also played their part: the research for *The Critical Tradition* was carried on at the Klapper and Rosenthal Libraries of Queens College, the Library of Columbia University, the New York Public Library, the Mina Rees Library of the Graduate Center of the City University of New York, the Robarts Library of the University of Toronto, and the British Library. The index was collated on the IBM PS-70 with the generous assistance of Marc Eichen, Sal Saieva, and Mendel Gottesman of the Queens College Academic Computing Center.

In closing, I must recall those who taught me literary theory at the University of Chicago, including Wayne Booth, Elder Olson, and Norman Maclean, in whose literary criticism courses I sat with varying degrees of comprehension. At times I hear also the ghostly voices of R. S. Crane and Richard P. McKeon, and of Shelly

Sacks, who taught me the uses of theory. From the hundreds of students in the undergraduate and graduate literary criticism courses at Queens College over the last fifteen years, I have learned what was clear and what opaque about the theoretical texts we studied together. I have tried to put some of that knowledge to work in this book, but I plan to continue learning from them. And I dedicate this book to my son Gabriel, for whom all of Western philosophy is but a footnote to Play-Doh.

# Contents

*Part Two*

# CONTEMPORARY TRENDS IN LITERARY CRITICISM   551

## 1. MARXIST CRITICISM ——————————————— 553

## 2. PSYCHOLOGICAL CRITICISM ——————————— 637

# INTRODUCTION

*Everybody . . . would be willing to admit, as a general proposition, that the critical faculty is lower than the inventive. But is it true that criticism is really, in itself, a baneful and injurious employment?*
— MATTHEW ARNOLD, *The Function of Criticism*
*at the Present Time* (1864)

*What if criticism is a science as well as an art?*
— NORTHROP FRYE, *The Function of Criticism*
*at the Present Time* (1949)

*Criticism is not literature, and the pleasure of criticism is not the pleasure of literature.*
*. . . But experience suggests that the two pleasures go together, and the pleasure of criticism makes literature and its pleasure the more readily accessible.*
— LIONEL TRILLING, Preface to *Literary Criticism:*
*An Introductory Reader* (1970)

*To put criticism at a Platonic remove from its object — to consider it as referring to literature without being literary — is to demoralize it as surely as art was demoralized (in theory) by the Platonic notion of its remove from the archetype. . . . Criticism can be pastoral: it can do a job, it can annotate or write helpful (and even virtuoso) commentaries on texts. But it can also write texts of its own.*
— GEOFFREY HARTMAN, *Criticism in the Wilderness* (1980)

In the Socratic dialogues of the early fourth century B.C., Plato raised skeptical questions about the value of art and literature that have provoked responses from artists and philosophers from Aristotle's day to our own. In striving to rescue poetry from the exile to which Socrates had condemned it, the defenders of literature have had to recast the questions Plato answered with such assurance. We are still asking the same questions today: What is the nature of the work of art? What are its sources in the artist, in the literary scene, in the society for which it is produced? What are its properties, uses, powers, and value? How is the nature of literature circumscribed by the properties of language itself, by the gender of the writer or the reader, by the intrinsic limitations of the human mind? What are literature's effects on individuals and on communities? Questions like these remain at the heart of the critical tradition. They have inspired an ongoing conversation that is continually modified by new voices from different cultural matrices, which join in with other critical languages, other norms, other views of the world.

The proliferation in the past two decades of new critical theories and practices is a sign that the inquiring and speculative spirit of that critical tradition is thriving as never before. But the very abundance of voices and vocabularies can be intimidating to the newcomer seeking to enter the conversation. The discussion that follows is intended as a guide to some of the various maps of the critical terrain and to various ways in which ideas about the nature of literature and the tasks of criticism have been organized. Learning this terrain is the surest way to take one's own bearings and find one's own voice.

## MAPPING CRITICAL THEORIES:
## THE TRADITIONAL CLASSIFICATION

In his influential treatise on romantic views of art, *The Mirror and the Lamp* (1953), the literary historian M. H. Abrams distinguished between four different types of literary theories, and the map he drew is still valuable as a place to start thinking about the history of criticism.

Historically, the first type, the *mimetic* theories of classical antiquity, focused on the relationship between the outside world and the work of art. These theories posited that poetry could best be understood as an imitation, a representation, a copy of the physical world.

The second type, the *rhetorical*, emphasized the relationship between the work of art and its audience — either how the literary work should be formed to please and instruct its audience, or what that audience should be like in order to appreciate literature correctly. These theories held that to attain its proper effect, the poem must be shaped by both the poet's innate talent and the rules of art. Such theories, most popular during the later classical period, the Middle Ages, and the Renaissance, began to decline toward the end of the eighteenth century.

The third type, called *expressive* by Abrams, stressed the relationship between the work of art and the artist, particularly the special faculties of mind and soul that the artist brings to the act of creation. These theories proliferated during the late eighteenth and most of the nineteenth centuries.[1]

The fourth type, which developed around the beginning of the twentieth century, played down the connections of the work of art with the exterior world, the audience, and the artist. These *formal* theories stressed the purely aesthetic relationship between the parts of a work of literature, analyzing its "themes" or "motifs"

---

[1]Although it is possible to specify when mimetic, rhetorical, and expressive theories flourished, it must be understood that all three continue to be influential. Even when theory is not progressing along certain lines, the old questions are asked of new texts. Thus the movie reviewer who wonders whether *Platoon* accurately depicts battle conditions in Vietnam is as much a mimetic critic as Aristotle.

as if a literary text were a form of classical music or an abstract painting, and strove for a quasi-scientific objectivity. Such theories probably prevail today, since thousands of teachers and scholars who might deny allegiance to any theory actually adhere to formalist principles. In their explicit claims to possessing the highest truth about literature, however, formal theories now face a great deal of competition.

One version of the Abrams map might look like Figure 1. The world of criticism is not as clear or as neat as this diagram suggests. Abrams himself points out that a label such as "mimetic" or "expressive" indicates only the primary orientation of a theory: "Any reasonable theory takes account of all four elements." A mimetic theorist (such as Aristotle) might have much to say about how works of art affect an audience or about the artist, but his views often derive directly from his mimetic principles. When Aristotle suggests in *Poetics*, Chapter IV, for example, that poets of noble character took up the art of tragedy and those of baser character created comedy, his rationale is that nobler poets are better able to understand and then to imitate in poetic language the noble characters of tragedy. In this sense, Aristotle's mimetic orientation comes through even when he takes up the problem of poetic creativity.

Abrams's notion of critical orientation helps us to distinguish the disparate rationales behind the same piece of conventional wisdom. A mimetic critic, for instance, might enjoin an aspiring poet to observe human nature well, the more accurately to imitate human actions in his poetry. A rhetorical critic might advise the poet in the very same words, but in order to prompt the poet to discover what pleases the various classes and age groups that comprise his audience. As the notes

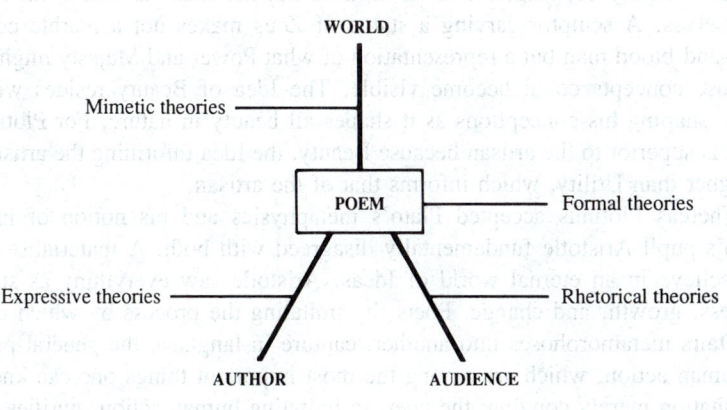

**Figure 1**

to Part One of this collection show, the various dicta of Plato and Aristotle, shorn of their mimetic logic, reappear in the works of rhetorical, expressive, and objective critics to bolster markedly different arguments.

Each of these four orientations covers a great deal of ground, and the fact that two critics are both mimetic in orientation does not guarantee that they agree. Quite the contrary: whereas critics with different principles merely tend to miss each other's points, those who share a theoretical orientation are likely to clash in an interesting and violent way. A brief consideration of Plato, (p. 17) Aristotle (p. 38), and Plotinus (p. 107), three of the more influential mimetic critics, can reveal how some of these disagreements take shape.

## DIFFERENCES WITHIN THEORETICAL ORIENTATIONS

Plato's view of art derives from a complicated metaphysics and a relatively simple notion of imitation. Imitation, for Plato, is the creation of an *eidolon*. The artist makes an "image" — a degraded copy — of the external world, which is analogous to the image formed in a mirror (it lasts longer than a mirror image, but, not being eternal, the difference is not significant). Plato's worldview is *idealist*, which means that he takes the material world, the world of the senses, to be a copy of an eternal world of Ideas. Works of art, in their turn, are copies of material things, and hence copies of copies. For Plato, art is therefore an activity inferior to artisanship — the making of useful objects — first, because art copies rather than creates a material object, and second, because an artist needs only the knowledge of the appearances of things, not of their real nature. Plato also worried that imitation might weaken the individual spirit by arousing passion and corrupt the body politic through its distance from the truth.

Six centuries later, the Neoplatonic philosopher Plotinus developed a mimetic theory of art that generally conformed with that of Plato but drew vastly different conclusions about the value of art. In the idealism of Plotinus, although imitation is still basically copying, the artist imitates not the material world but the Ideas themselves. A sculptor carving a statue of Zeus makes not a marble copy of a flesh-and-blood man but a representation of what Power and Majesty might be like if those concepts could become visible. The Idea of Beauty resides within the artist, shaping his conceptions as it shapes all beauty in nature. For Plotinus, the artist is superior to the artisan because Beauty, the Idea informing the artist's craft, is higher than Utility, which informs that of the artisan.

Whereas Plotinus accepted Plato's metaphysics and his notion of imitation, Plato's pupil Aristotle fundamentally disagreed with both. A materialist who did not believe in an eternal world of Ideas, Aristotle saw everything as subject to process, growth, and change. Poets, by imitating the process by which one state of affairs metamorphoses into another, capture in language the general principles of human action, which are among the most important things one can know. Nor is imitation merely copying: the poet, in imitating human action, purifies it of the dross of the accidental and the incidental, unifies it into a plot, beautifies it with expressive language, and molds it into a concrete whole with the capacity to command the emotions. Those feelings, aroused and guided by a complex imitation, can cleanse rather than weaken the individual, and can serve the state rather than harming it by draining off passions and frustrations that might lead to political instability.

Just as mimetic thinkers could agree that art was primarily a matter of imitation but differ about what the world was like, what aspect of that world the artists imitated, and what sort of process imitation actually was, so rhetorical theorists also had their differences about the ends and means of artistic production. The main question for them was how to construct a work of art so that it would affect an audience properly. Horace (p. 66), one of the earliest and most influential of the rhetorical theorists, thought that poems should "either delight, or instruct, or if possible accomplish both ends at once," but later critics subtly redrew his specifications. For moralists like Dante (p. 118) or Samuel Johnson (p. 223), the more significant purpose was instruction, delight being merely a means to that didactic end. Others, Sir Philip Sidney (p. 131) and John Dryden (p. 160), gave delight a more equal role. Although many theorists took "delight" and "instruction" as general and indivisible qualities to be sought in poetry, others elaborately classified the arts according to the varieties of pleasure and benefit that should reside in each.

And for which audience should the poet write? Horace's audience is apparently limited to the upper classes — the *senatores* and *equites* of the early Roman Empire. Dryden's debaters in *Essay of Dramatic Poesy* posit national audiences with specific national characteristics. Sidney assumes a universal contemporary audience (although that universe may be implicitly restricted to gentlemen). And in Samuel Johnson's analysis, Shakespeare's greatness inheres in affecting people of other countries and later eras. In the eighteenth century, when the question of taste had become an important one in literary theory, Horace's problem, the adaptation of work to audience, had, in effect, been inverted. For critics like David Hume (p. 209), the most important issue was not how poems should be shaped to please audiences but why some members of the audience were better adapted to appreciate the arts than others.

In similar fashion, expressive theorists concurred that art manifested the artist's sensibility even as they disputed the source of that sensibility. Many nineteenth-century romantics agreed that the key faculty was the imagination — although they differed sharply on how that faculty worked. Later expressive theorists found the source of poetry in the artist's *un*conscious mind. For one group of psychological critics, the followers of Sigmund Freud, a poem, like a dream, was the imagined fulfillment of an individual artist's unconscious wish; for another group, the followers of Carl Gustav Jung, all art evinced archetypal imagery common to the entire human race. For critics like Northrop Frye (p. 677), the artist expresses the "dream of mankind," which is contained not in the collective unconscious but in a literary tradition that speaks through us all. For sociohistorical critics, followers of Karl Marx or Hippolyte Taine, artists inadvertently expressed the ideologies of their times, conveying their understanding of the world in ways determined by their position within the class struggle and their moment in history.

In the twentieth century, formalists have differed about both what sort of form should be sought and where it could be found. The "New Critics" discovered form in a dialectical thrust and counterthrust of themes; neo-Aristotelians in a complex linkage of plot, language, technique, and purpose; and structuralists and semioticians in repeated patterns of language. And just as in the eighteenth century, there is a split between those critics investigating the various principles of form within literature and those exploring the reader's capacity to discover form or to *supply* it when it is not to be found.

These variations and developments within major critical orientations seem to embody the behavior of biological organisms that proliferate to fill up a new ecological niche. Once a mode like *expressive* criticism had become established, it was almost inevitable that every aspect of the poet's psyche, conscious and unconscious, would be held up to scrutiny as a source of the creative spirit. A more difficult question is why changes in critical orientation occur — why mimetic criticism gave way to rhetorical or rhetorical to expressive.

Such epochs seem to be analogous to scientific revolutions, described by Thomas Kuhn in *The Structure of Scientific Revolutions* (1962). Over one or two generations, the previous "paradigm," a vast structure of assumptions, principles, and methods, gives way and is replaced by another for a variety of reasons — new facts that need explaining, new theories that cannot be reconciled with the present paradigm, a scientific community that has lost intellectual cohesion over its basic principles. The causes of such "revolutions" in critical tradition, where Kuhn's model is less exact, might include the creation of new literary works and styles, shifts in the canon (the informal list of the literature of the past that is held to be significant), developments in the other arts, in philosophy, and in other humanistic disciplines, and changes in politics and society.

## CHANGES IN THEORETICAL PARADIGMS

The first critical revolution was the displacement of the Sophists, who saw literature as essentially a function of language, by Plato and his doctrine of imitation. Because the writings of the Sophists have largely failed to survive, too little is known about that revolution to hazard any explanation of Plato's triumph.

The second major change, from mimetic to rhetorical criticism, might have developed partly from a misreading of Aristotle's *Poetics*, a document of enormous authority, if one more respected than understood. (Critics quoted — or misquoted — Aristotle while ignoring his central ideas, methods, and principles as late as the age of Dryden and Johnson.) Though the *Poetics* views art as the imitation of human action, the product is not a simple copy. It differs from the natural process it represents in its form, its material (language instead of action itself), its technique, and its purpose. These four "causes," as Aristotle termed them, all contribute equally in defining the special character of a particular work of art. But one of them — purpose — is, so to speak, more equal than the rest, since it largely dictates the others. Purpose, for Aristotle, refers to the *potential* capacity of a work to move human beings in a certain way, not its *actual* effect on an audience.

One can easily imagine, however, how internal *purpose* could be altered to external *effect*, and how the four-cause structure of Aristotelian imitation might be simplified to the means/end argument we find in Horace. There were surely external reasons as well. The development in late republican Rome of a publishing industry (using hand-copying), serving a far-flung and disparate literary audience, may have fostered a critical scene different from that of post-Periclean Athens, where the poet's audience was the tight-knit coterie within the polis.

The revolution from rhetorical to expressive criticism may also have been partly the result of social change. The reading public grew enormously in the eighteenth century as formerly illiterate classes became avid consumers of literature. The new cadres of less-educated readers made *taste* an issue in criticism as it had never been before. As theorists investigating taste examined the inner experience of readers, they found that the faculties behind good taste, the capacities that made ideal readers — delicate imagination, good sense, wide experience — were the same as those that made the best poets. Creation and appreciation were more closely allied than one might have supposed, for the audience passively reenacted what the poets had actively created. Poetic creativity was therefore a refined but not a mysterious process: it could be investigated and understood.

The twentieth-century shift from expressive to formal criticism was not a total revolution: biographical, psychological, sociological, and myth criticism continued to develop alongside the several varieties of formalism. But in a sense, formalism grew out of the *exhaustion* of expressive criticism. Literature, once thought to grow organically from the artistic imagination, which, as Samuel Taylor Coleridge (p. 299) said, was "coexistent with the conscious will," was increasingly seen as deriving from forces beyond the artist's control (milieu, class, unconscious drives, the collective unconscious). The poet appeared to be less an agent and more a mere catalyst in the act of creation,[2] while at the same time, poetry, like music, painting, and sculpture, became increasingly abstract. And in the demotic twentieth century, audience reaction has seemed an even less plausible guide to art than in the eighteenth. The eighteenth-century split between refined and popular art, which had been partially repaired during the Victorian era, re-emerged in the 1890s to become an ongoing fixture of twentieth-century culture.

As a result, criticism was left with almost nowhere to go. With the principle of imitation stymied by the vogue of abstraction, the fashion of the impersonal artist nullifying the romantic appeal to expression, and the fragmented and unreliable audience undermining rhetorical criticism, the only avenue left was an appeal to pure form. These developments seem to have been felt all over Europe and America after World War I, and they culminated in a variety of formalist movements: Russian formalism, structuralism, the New Criticism, neo-Aristotelianism. Another

---

[2]The cult of impersonality in poetry and of the poet as the catalyst will be found in the criticism of T. S. Eliot (p. 463), one of the founders of the New Criticism.

factor, exterior to art and criticism, was the development of the modern university within which departments of literature, structured like those of the natural and social sciences, may have sought for a comparably "objective" and "scientific" mode of literary study, which the varieties of formalism could supply.[3]

During the most recent critical revolution, which began in the years since Abrams drew his map, many poststructuralist theorists have attempted to see literature as the "free play of signifiers." Words — the signifiers — have thus been detached from their meanings — the signified. Instead of testifying to the truth and beauty in the world, instead of expressing the personality (or impersonality) of the author, instead of moving or teaching, language now expresses only the circularity of meaning; it contemplates only itself. The text is no longer the poem isolated at the center of the diagram. Rather, textuality — the condition of inscription within language — is implicated in all of our knowledge of the world, of reading, of expression. History is not to be viewed as the inferior of poetry, as Aristotle thought, nor its master, as Karl Marx (p. 565) suggested; history cannot even be opposed to poetry, for both are equally texts. We have returned full circle to the position of the Sophists, for whom language was all. A key question for the future of theory is whether textuality — the topics of language and discourse — will remain at the center of critical study.

## OTHER MAPS

The discussion has stayed within the context of Abrams's map of the spectrum of critical theory, which is useful as far as it goes. But maps have a way of reducing the number of dimensions, inevitably distorting even as they clarify the actual landscape.

The points of Abrams's compass should not be taken as natural, self-evident, or unquestionable. Like any other theoretical construct, Abrams's map includes areas of blindness as well as insight, and its limitations derive from its unstated assumptions. By differentiating between "rhetorical" and "objective" theories, for example, Abrams seems to presume that the text can have a meaning apart from what it means to its readers. In practice, however, many formalist critics have relied heavily for their analysis on what an "ideal" or "potential" reader would make of the text. Nor can Abrams's map comfortably accommodate forms of criticism (Marxist and otherwise) that view the text, author, and reader as determined, collectively or separately, by the processes of history. (Abrams may think that an author expresses his or her age, but while this will do for some forms of historical criticism, it will not adequately characterize most modern Marxist thought.)

Another limitation of the Abrams map — or at least of how many readers have employed it — is the specious linearity it imposes upon the history of criticism. It seems to imply that mimetic thought was confined to classical antiquity and that

[3]Cf. Richard Ohmann, *English in America* (New York: Oxford University Press, 1976), and Gerald Graff, *Professing Literature: An Institutional History* (Chicago: University of Chicago Press, 1987).

everyone shifted from rhetorical to expressive criticism around the end of the eighteenth century. Not only did rhetorical criticism continue to be practiced throughout the nineteenth and twentieth centuries, but (as the late Robert Marsh has shown) one essential pattern of romantic criticism flourished during what is typically considered the neoclassical period. The prestige of the Abrams map should not mask the importance of other theorists and critics (like James "Hermes" Harris, or Walter Scott) whose work challenges its implicit notion of historical succession.

One way of transcending the limitations of the Abrams map is by formulating other maps whose limitations are different. The Abrams map groups literary theories in terms of the critical *principle* on which each rests. Both R. S. Crane (p. 807) and Norman Friedman have, at different times, constructed a different sort of map to clarify the interrelationships of critical *tasks* and the variety of approaches to a given literary work. The form of these maps is not a group of adjacent territories but a series of concentric circles, with the work itself in the middle. A single composite map combining the essential features of both might look something like Figure 2.

This map is one way of visualizing the relationship of various modes of literary interpretation to one another. Its bias is its suggestion that a poem is determined most intimately by the requirements of form, both its own organic shape and the institutional shapes that culture bequeaths to art. (For example, the terseness of a sonnet — its fourteen-line structure — is a formal issue.) Overdetermination is always a distinct possibility, but as long as form accounts adequately for an aspect of a given work, no explanation need be sought elsewhere.

But when form is exhausted, one must turn to the poet himself, both to his conscious life (biographical interpretation) and his unconscious fantasies and defenses (psychological interpretation). The circle is broader here, too, because what biographical and psychological interpretation reveals will cover the whole of the artist's work. Still broader modes of interpretation, sociological and historical, will link that work with others written by authors of the same class in the same era — or explain the differences in works written from different class perspectives and at different times. Broadest of all (and hence least explanatory of any given work) are interpretations based on human universals. One such universal is the collective unconscious, of Carl Gustav Jung (p. 656), whose *archetypes* are said to run through all imaginative literature and art. Another is the ethical wisdom that can give works of literature long-term significance across cultural boundaries.[4]

Yet another map embodying the critical tasks was drawn by Paul Hernadi (see Figure 3).[5] Like the concentric map derived from Friedman and Crane, Hernadi's "compass" diagrams critical tasks and philosophical disciplines that are theoretically available at any time rather than sketching a historical succession of critical

[4]For further discussion of this "concentric" map of critical theory, see R. S. Crane, "Questions and Answers in the Teaching of Literary Texts," in *The Idea of the Humanities*, 2 vols. (Chicago: University of Chicago Press, 1966); and Norman Friedman, "Pluralism Exemplified: *Great Expectations* and *The Great Gatsby*" in *Form and Meaning in Fiction* (Athens: University of Georgia Press, 1975).

[5]This map appears in Paul Hernadi's "Literary Theory: A Compass for Critics," *Critical Inquiry* 3 (1976): 382.

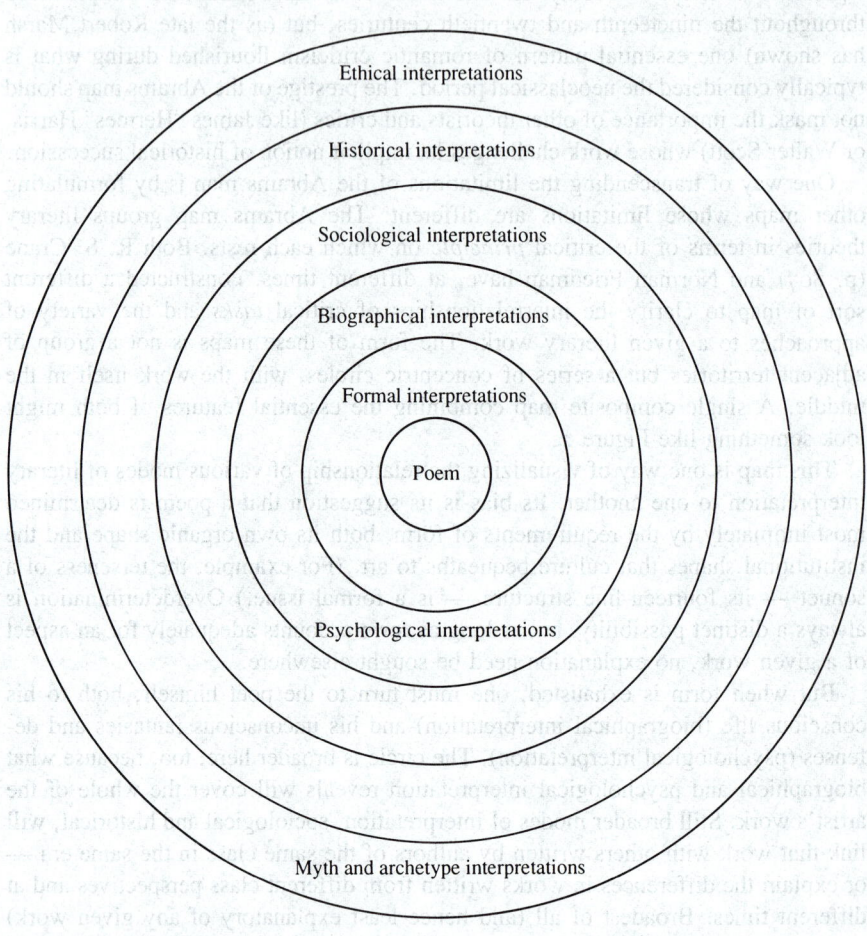

Ethical interpretations

Historical interpretations

Sociological interpretations

Biographical interpretations

Formal interpretations

Poem

Psychological interpretations

Myth and archetype interpretations

**Figure 2**

principles. But in a sense, Hernadi's map includes Abrams's. On an east-west axis, it locates the text between its genesis in the author and its impact on the reader; on a north-south axis, it places the work between the signification system of language, in which it is inscribed, and the world of signifieds to which it relates. Three of the four points of Hernadi's compass, in other words, are equivalent to Abrams's *author, audience*, and *world*; the fourth point, *language*, is new. Where Hernadi resembles both Crane and Friedman is in the third dimension of the map, which measures the degree of orientation toward text-centered, literary-critical tasks in terms of the distance outward from the central *text* toward the periphery.

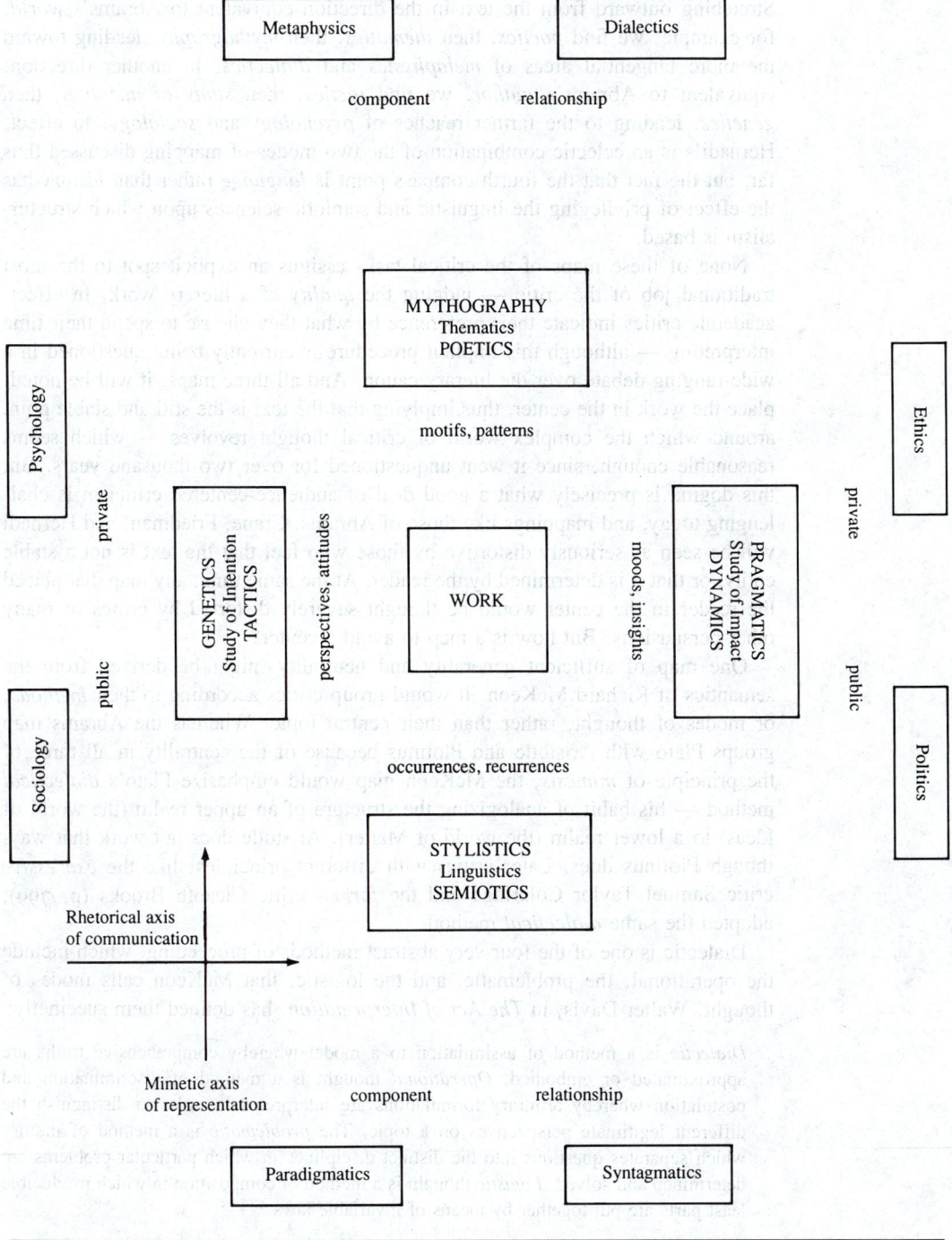

Figure 3

Stretching outward from the text in the direction equivalent to Abrams's *world*, for example, we find *poetics*, then *thematics*, then *mythography*, leading toward the more tangential areas of *metaphysics* and *dialectics*. In another direction, equivalent to Abrams's *author*, we find *tactics*, then *study of intention*, then *genetics*, leading to the farther reaches of *psychology* and *sociology*. In effect, Hernadi's is an eclectic combination of the two modes of mapping discussed thus far, but the fact that the fourth compass point is *language* rather than *history* has the effect of privileging the linguistic and semiotic sciences upon which structuralism is based.

None of these maps of the critical tasks assigns an explicit spot to the most traditional job of the critic — judging the *quality* of a literary work. In effect, academic critics indicate their preference by what they choose to spend their time interpreting — although this implicit procedure is currently being questioned in a wide-ranging debate over the literary canon. And all three maps, it will be noted, place the work in the center, thus implying that the text is the still and stable point around which the complex world of critical thought revolves — which seems reasonable enough, since it went unquestioned for over two thousand years. But this dogma is precisely what a good deal of audience-centered criticism is challenging today, and mappings like those of Abrams, Crane, Friedman, and Hernadi will be seen as seriously distortive by those who feel that the text is not a stable entity, or that it is determined by the reader. At the same time, any map that placed the reader in the center would be thought severely distorted by critics of many other persuasions. But how is a map to avoid a center?

One map of sufficient generality and neutrality might be derived from the semantics of Richard McKeon. It would group critics according to their *methods*, or modes of thought, rather than their central topic. Whereas the Abrams map groups Plato with Aristotle and Plotinus because of the centrality in all three of the principle of *mimesis*, the McKeon map would emphasize Plato's *dialectical* method — his habit of analogizing the structure of an upper realm (the world of Ideas) to a lower realm (the world of Matter). Aristotle does not work that way, though Plotinus does. Later critics with different principles, like the *expressive* critic Samuel Taylor Coleridge and the *formal* critic Cleanth Brooks (p. 799), adopted the same *dialectical* method.

Dialectic is one of the four very abstract methods of proceeding, which include the operational, the problematic, and the logistic, that McKeon calls modes of thought. Walter Davis, in *The Act of Interpretation*, has defined them succinctly:

> *Dialectic* is a method of assimilation to a model whereby comprehensive truths are approximated or embodied. *Operational* thought is a method of discrimination and postulation whereby arbitrary formulations are interpreted in order to distinguish the different legitimate perspectives on a topic. The *problematic* is a method of inquiry which separates questions into the distinct disciplines in which particular problems are determined and solved. *Logistic* thought is a method of composition in which irreducible least parts are put together by means of invariable laws.[6]

[6]Walter A. Davis, *The Act of Interpretation: A Critique of Literary Reason* (Chicago: University of

Dialectical thinkers, such as Plato and Georg Friedrich Hegel (p. 341), see the world as a bound and interconnected whole, with a lower realm (defined by terms like "becoming" or mere "consciousness") and an upper realm (that of "being" or "self-consciousness"). Such a pattern runs through all of reality, and each aspect of life — religion, politics, ethics, aesthetics — can be analyzed in the same way using analogous terms.

But where dialectical thought is intrinsically interdisciplinary, problematic thought is discipline-bound. Problematic thinkers, such as Aristotle and John Dewey (p. 484), see the world as containing a number of irreconcilable things, and therefore find no single method that will answer all questions, no single set of terms that can be used to grapple with all problems. The initial task of problematic thinking is to separate disciplines according to their scope, determining their bounds and establishing a method of inquiry according to the nature of the discipline itself.

Like dialectical thinkers, operational thinkers take a holistic view of the universe, but for them, the whole is determined not by the nature of things but by the way people view them and talk about them. There is no higher realm of being or truth: The way people see things is all there is. The role of operational thought, in Cicero or in Kenneth Burke (p. 500), is to clarify discourse, to reduce the ambiguities that arise from using common language to describe disparate perspectives.

Like problematic thinkers, logistic thinkers avoid the holistic; but unlike them, they have a single method, which is associated with but not limited to modern science: breaking down phenomena into their least parts and then discovering the laws by which those parts are interrelated. This method is clearest in sciences like chemistry and physics, which are concerned with particles and forces, but a logistic approach has also been made to politics (by Niccolò Machiavelli), ethics (by René Descartes and Thomas Hobbes), and social structure (by Claude Lévi-Strauss, p. 869).

Applied to literature, dialectical thought often takes poetry to be a mode of thinking, while problematic thought often takes it to be a mode of making. Operational thought considers literature as one of many forms of discourse; logistic thought considers literature as data in its scientific analysis of the parts of a text, confident that parts make up a whole. Another map might be created, in other words, gathering *dialectical* thinkers (like Plato, Plotinus, Coleridge, and Hegel)

---

Chicago Press, 1978), 93–94. McKeon's grid is too complex to do justice to here, since it contains three other dimensions as well: a dialectical thinker might have comprehensive, simple, reflexive, or actional *principles*. There are also quadripartite distinctions for a thinker's *organization* and *interpretation*. The result is sixteen categories that generate 256 possible positions. McKeon's own mode of thought is, of course, operationalist — his grid is a way of talking about the relation among modes of discourse. Richard McKeon's clearest exposition of his semantics occurs in an essay called "Philosophic Semantics and Philosophic Discovery," widely circulated among his students but unpublished at his death; see his article, "Philosophy and Method" in *Journal of Philosophy* 48 (1951); 653–81; and "Imitation and Poetry" in his book *Thought, Action and Passion* (Chicago: University of Chicago Press, 1954). See also the exposition of McKeon in Walter A. Davis, "Critical Theory and Philosophic Method" in *The Act of Interpretation*, 88–119.

into one group, *problematic* thinkers (like Aristotle and Dewey) into another, *logistic* thinkers (like Freud, p. 650, or Lévi-Strauss) into a third, and *operational* thinkers (like Alexander Pope, p. 197, and Kenneth Burke) into a fourth. This map would be more historically complicated than Abrams's since competing modes of thought would operate within a given age, but it would suggest some important linkages across the centuries that should not be ignored.[7]

It is useful to be able to refer to four maps rather than one, but in the long run, all maps are inadequate and none is wholly innocent. That is, any map, no matter how apparently objective and pluralistic, is certain to contain implicit assumptions congenial to some theorists and anathema to others. Maps are like Ludwig Wittgenstein's ladder in the *Tractatus Logico-Philosophicus* (1922): We can climb only with their assistance, but once we have ascended, we throw them to the ground. Once we outgrow the maps we are given, we learn to do without them or make our own.

Traditional literature courses typically impose a method and an order on the disparate texts of one period or one author. In contrast, a course in critical theory will often call into question the very myths of order the traditions of culture have handed down. The study of critical theory tends to raise the ultimate questions about literature and its relation to life without establishing an ultimate order, because the clash of one principle, one method, one logic with another cannot be evaded. To the extent that these oppositions are genuinely understood, we are unlikely to end by resolving their differences into a tidy and harmonious chorus. We can, however, set the voices at play, engage them in contrapuntal dialogue with each other, and enter that dialogue ourselves. And in discoursing with some of the most probing minds that have trained their gaze upon literature, we become participants in an ancient and exalted conversation.

[7]Applied to the critical revolution of the past two decades, the McKeon map might suggest that operational thought, hitherto one element among many, moved into the vanguard, as once dialectical Marxists began (after Louis Althusser) to consider history as a text rather than a force, as once logistical psychoanalysts began (after Jacques Lacan) to think of the unconscious as a mode of discourse rather than a hidden space. Similarly, the Derridean revolution consists, as Paul de Man has explicitly stated, in the displacement of grammar (in Ferdinand De Saussure's logistical approach) by rhetoric.

# Part One

# CLASSIC TEXTS IN LITERARY CRITICISM

# Plato

## ca. 427–347 B.C.

"All of Western philosophy is but a footnote to Plato," Alfred North Whitehead once said, and it is true in the sense that most of the historically significant issues with which philosophy has been concerned — the nature of being, the question of how we know things, the purposes of right action, the structure of an ordered society, the meaning of love and beauty — were issues that he raised. Later philosophers, including Plato's great pupil, Aristotle, have disagreed not only with his results but also with his ways of setting up the questions, and their argument with Plato makes up much of the history of thought. Nor have later thinkers always merely disagreed with and revised Plato: Century after century has witnessed a renaissance of his system of thought, most notably in the Neoplatonists of the second century A.D., the Cambridge Platonists of the latter seventeenth century, and the idealists of the romantic movement. Later thinkers, including Plotinus (p. 107), Sidney (p. 131), and Shelley (p. 321), directly take up Plato's challenge, but his shadow falls, as Whitehead said, over all of Western thought.

For contemporary readers the most difficult concept in Plato's thought is his *idealism* — the doctrine of a permanent realm of eternal Forms that shape our mutable material world. In a philosophy class students might be asked to contrast the "Idea of the Desk" — the concept of a thing to write on that also holds one's papers — with the physical object in the classroom. The former is timeless and pure, while the latter is time-bound: It came into being, exists for a time, will soon vanish. Nor is the material desk a *perfect* desk: Its very materiality precludes it. Presumably, the Idea of the Desk must have preceded the material desk and caused it, in effect, to be created. A carpenter who is not merely copying an existing desk must be working from some inner awareness of this Idea.

This approach is a time-honored way of introducing Plato's ideas, but it tends to lead our thought downward, to wondering, for example, whether there is a Platonic Idea of a pencil-shaving or of manure. Actually, despite their vulgarity, these are perfectly sound Platonic questions. The usual solution is to assume that formless things — mud, sawdust, and so on — have no Forms because they are in fact formless matter. The real problem is that the explanation removes Plato's ideas from common human thought. Few of us are acquainted, other than in theory, with the ideas of things like desks. Nor is it apparent at first glance that the Idea of a Desk is a higher or better thing than a material desk; it is certainly much harder to do one's work on.

It may be more helpful to think of a geometry class, where one operates with perfect circles, right angles, and parallel lines, and where one learns to prove theorems — or eternal truths — about them. It is understood that the diagrams drawn to illustrate the theorems, however neatly done, are imperfect representations of the lines and angles of the theorem. Here, on a mathematical level, one is working with the Ideal and the Material, and it is the Ideal — the proof, not the diagram — which counts. This may be why the door to Plato's school, the Academy, had a warning on it: "Let no one ignorant of geometry enter here." The mathematics prerequisite, so to speak, had a good reason: Those who had already wrestled with the Idea of the Right Triangle in proving the Pythagorean theorem were prepared to understand the higher ideas of Truth, Goodness and, Beauty, that Plato believed shape all human knowledge, right action, artistic endeavor, and love.

Plato developed his idealism in reaction against the notions of the Sophists. They have a poor reputation today — the word *sophistry* testifies to that — but the original Sophists were not a set of quibblers but a diverse group of teachers of what we would now call rhetoric and composition, the language arts. Some of the major Sophists, like Gorgias and Lysias, are known today because Plato used them as debating opponents for his spokesman, Socrates. The Sophists claimed that their science of language could lead to the knowledge of truth and virtue. Against this, Plato thought it dangerous to suppose that the highest realities — Truth, Goodness, and Beauty — had the flickering impermanence of human words, and his world of ideas may derive from his fear that, like language, even matter could be shaped to cheat and deceive.

Because Plato mistrusted writing, he did not set down his philosophy in the usual form of a set of treatises but rather in dialogues.[1] Their liveliness and depth remain unequalled, but their form creates problems of both interpretation (at times we may wonder whether Socrates is being serious or ironic, at other times whether he *always* speaks directly for Plato) and consistency (a position held in one dialogue may be renounced in another). Both issues emerge in the *Republic*, Book X, and in *Ion*.

### *REPUBLIC,* BOOK X

Book X is the most influential discussion of art in the Platonic canon. Its central thesis — that poets have no place in Plato's perfect state save as writers of hymns to the gods and songs in praise of great leaders — has stung devotees of the arts for the last two thousand years.

Book X is at the end of the *Republic*, the longest of the dialogues, which opens with the issue of whether Might makes Right. This harsh question leads Socrates and his two friends to consider the question, What is Justice? Socrates's hypothesis is that Justice is knowing one's place and performing its duties — but how can one know and act properly in the Athenian polis? This question leads Socrates to fashion a model state, a republic governed by a natural elite of guardians, in which it would be possible, as it is not in Athens, to understand one's place and its

[1]Indeed, in the Seventh Letter, Plato claims that he never wrote his philosophy down at all, because it could not be written down. The usual interpretation of this claim is that the published dialogues represent philosophy *in action* rather than as doctrine; another possibility is that Plato meant the dialogues to *stimulate* philosophy — to cause *us* to philosophize — by reasoning and arguing with their positions.

duties. But how should the guardians be educated to rule? They must learn a great many other things, but at the center of their training is philosophy. And it is in answering *this* question — of what does philosophy consist? — that Socrates presents his hierarchical portrait of the physical and mental universe: the myth of the divided line. In simplified form, the diagram Socrates draws looks like this:

| MODES OF BEING | MODES OF MENTAL ACTIVITY |
|---|---|
| Ideas | Knowing |
| Mathematical Forms | Understanding |
| Material Things | Opinion |
| Images | Conjecture |

The first horizontal line separates the eternal world of true Being from the world of Becoming, the material things that are begotten, born, and die. The vertical line separates modes of existence from the modes of thought appropriate to them. For Plato the word *know* applies only to Ideas, but about material animals, plants, and human artifacts we can at best hold correct opinions, and with respect to mere images we can only hazard guesses.

In this context, the discussion of art in Book X is logically sound. First of all, Plato identifies art as imitation, positing that what artists do (as they have claimed in the centuries before and after Plato) is hold the mirror up to nature: They copy the appearances of men, animals, and objects in the physical world. But if this is the case, then the artistic object is merely an image, slightly but not more meaningfully permanent than a reflection in a pool of water. And the intelligence that went into its creation need involve nothing more than conjecture. (Notice that Socrates is not being redundant when he twice proves the inferiority of art: The first time he proves the inferiority of the *mode of being* of art; the second, its inferiority as a *mode of mental activity*.) As a result, art cannot be justified as an activity worthy in its own right. The poets may stay as servants of the state if they teach piety and virtue, but the pleasures of art are condemned as inherently corrupting to citizens and guardians alike.

## ION

Much of the *Ion* is reasonably consistent with the *Republic*, and a good deal more entertaining if we allow ourselves to enjoy the spectacle of Socrates exposing the vanity and pretensions of the none-too-bright performer for whom the dialogue is named. (The moment when Ion declares that he is the greatest general in Athens as well as its greatest rhapsode is made richer if one remembers that at the purported time of the discourse, Athens was fighting for its survival in the Peloponnesian War.) Here, as in the *Republic*, Socrates exposes the inferiority of art as a way of knowing.

Where *Ion* differs from the *Republic* is in the suggestion contained in the image of the magnet as a metaphor of divine inspiration. Just as a magnet attracts iron and passes that attraction along, so the muse inspires the artist, who inspires the interpreter, who inspires the audience. The chain runs from the god to Homer to Ion to the applauding citizens. If this view of art is true, then it is divine, not inferior stuff.

Reconciling this notion of art with the contrary position in *Republic*, Book X, has been attempted in a number of different ways. One way is to suppose that Plato changed his mind, but that would mean trying to discover which, the *Ion* or the *Republic*, is the later dialogue (we have only conjectural datings) and deciding whether his first or second thoughts were the more trustworthy.

Another possibility is to suppose that the *Ion* is an essentially ironic (as well as humorous) dialogue, and that Socrates does not seriously respect inspiration. The Greek word translated as "inspiration" is *enthousiasmós*, and its literal meaning is closer to "demonic possession" than to the English derivative "enthusiasm." It is hard to believe that the rationalistic Plato could commend such a state. But on the other side, Socrates *does* praise such an experience elsewhere, in the *Phaedrus*, the principal dialogue on love and beauty, where poetry finds its place along with prophecy and love as forms of divine madness, the gods' most precious gifts to humanity. There Socrates claims that the state of *enthousiasmós* allows a dim but gripping memory of the Ideas, the eternal Forms of Truth, Goodness and Beauty, which the soul experienced directly prior to its incarnation. This doctrine is narrated as a myth, but it is surely not ironic in context.

Perhaps most plausibly, the discrepancies between *Ion* and *Republic* may be ascribed to their different contexts. In *Republic* Socrates is imagining a perfect state, one that must be designed to run without benefit of chance, luck, or divine intervention. Its rulers must therefore act rightly out of permanently dependable knowledge, not occasional inspiration. In the *Ion* Socrates is discoursing about the actual world, where poets may be generally foolish and ignorant, but can sometimes be heard to speak holy truths in tongues given them by the gods.

### Selected Bibliography

Cavarnos, Constantine. *Plato's Theory of Fine Art*. Athens: Astir, 1973.

Else, Gerald F. *Plato and Aristotle on Poetry*. Chapel Hill: University of North Carolina Press, 1986.

Friedländer, Paul. *Plato*. New York: Pantheon, 1958–69.

Gadamer, Hans-Georg. "Plato und die Dichter" in *Platos Dialektische Ethik und andere Studien*. Hamburg: F. Meiner, 1968.

Greene, William Chase. "Plato's View of Poetry," *Harvard Studies in Classical Philology* 29 (1918): 1–75.

Grube, G. M. A. *Plato's Thought*. London: Methuen, 1935.

Gulley, Norman. *Plato's Theory of Knowledge*. London: Methuen, 1962.

Havelock, Eric. *Preface to Plato*. Cambridge: Harvard University Press, 1963.

Lodge, Rupert C. *Plato's Theory of Art*. New York: Humanities Press, 1953.

Murdoch, Iris. *The Fire and the Sun: Why Plato Banished the Artists*. Oxford: Clarendon Press, 1972.

Oates, Whitney J. *Plato's View of Art*. New York: Scribner, 1972.

Partee, Morriss Henry. *Plato's Poetics: The Authority of Beauty*. Salt Lake City: University of Utah Press, 1981.

Shorey, Paul. *What Plato Said*. Chicago: University of Chicago Press, 1933.

Sinaiko, Herman J. *Love, Knowledge and Discourse in Plato*. Chicago: University of Chicago Press, 1965.

Taylor, A. E. *Plato*. 1929; Ann Arbor: University of Michigan Press, 1960.

# *Republic*, Book X

Of the many excellences which I perceive in the order of our State, there is none which upon reflection pleases me better than the rule about poetry.

To what do you refer?

To our refusal to admit the imitative kind of poetry, for it certainly ought not to be received; as I see far more clearly now that the parts of the soul have been distinguished.

What do you mean?

Speaking in confidence, for you will not denounce me to the tragedians and the rest of the imitative tribe, all poetical imitations are ruinous to the understanding of the hearers, unless as an antidote they possess the knowledge of the true nature of the originals.

Explain the purport of your remark.

Well, I will tell you, although I have always from my earliest youth had an awe and love of Homer which even now makes the words falter on my lips, for he seems to be the great captain and teacher of the whole of that noble tragic company; but a man is not to be reverenced more than the truth, and therefore I will speak out.

Very good, he said.

Listen to me then, or rather, answer me.

Put your question.

Translated by Benjamin Jowett. The speakers are Socrates and Glaucon.

Can you give me a general definition of imitation? for I really do not myself understand what it professes to be.

A likely thing, then, that I should know.

There would be nothing strange in that, for the duller eye may often see a thing sooner than the keener.

Very true, he said; but in your presence, even if I had any faint notion, I could not muster courage to utter it. Will you inquire yourself?

Well then, shall we begin the inquiry at this point, following our usual method: Whenever a number of individuals have a common name, we assume that there is one corresponding idea or form: — do you understand me?

I do.

Let us take, for our present purpose, any instance of such a group; there are beds and tables in the world — many of each, are there not?

Yes.

But there are only two ideas or forms of such furniture — one the idea of a bed, the other of a table.

True.

And the maker of either of them makes a bed or he makes a table for our use, in accordance with the idea — that is our way of speaking in this and similar instances — but no artificer makes the idea itself: how could he?

Impossible.

And there is another artificer — I should like to know what you would say of him.

Who is he?

One who is the maker of all the works of all other workmen.

What an extraordinary man!

Wait a little, and there will be more reason for your saying so. For this is the craftsman who is able to make not only furniture of every kind, but all that grows out of the earth, and all living creatures, himself included; and besides these he can make earth and sky and the gods, and all the things which are in heaven or in the realm of Hades under the earth.

He must be a wizard and no mistake.

Oh! you are incredulous, are you? Do you mean that there is no such maker or creator, or that in one sense there might be a maker of all these things but in another not? Do you see that there is a way in which you could make them all yourself?

And what way is this? he asked.

An easy way enough; or rather, there are many ways in which the feat might be quickly and easily accomplished, none quicker than that of turning a mirror round and round — you would soon enough make the sun and the heavens, and the earth and yourself, and other animals and plants, and furniture and all the other things of which we were just now speaking, in the mirror.

Yes, he said; but they would be appearances only.

Very good, I said, you are coming to the point now. And the painter too is, as I conceive, just such another — a creator of appearances, is he not?

Of course.

But then I suppose you will say that what he creates is untrue. And yet there is a sense in which the painter also creates a bed? Is there not?

Yes, he said, but here again, an appearance only.

And what of the maker of the bed? Were you not saying that he too makes, not the idea which according to our view is the real object denoted by the word bed, but only a particular bed?

Yes, I did.

Then if he does not make a real object he cannot make what *is*, but only some semblance of existence; and if anyone were to say that the work of the maker of the bed, or of any other workman, has real existence, he could hardly be supposed to be speaking the truth.

Not, at least, he replied, in the view of those who make a business of these discussions.

No wonder, then, that his work too is an indistinct expression of truth.

No wonder.

Suppose now that by the light of the examples just offered we inquire who this imitator is?

If you please.

Well then, here we find three beds: one existing in nature, which is made by God, as I think that we may say — for no one else can be the maker?

No one, I think.

There is another which is the work of the carpenter?

Yes.

And the work of the painter is a third?

Yes.

Beds, then, are of three kinds, and there are three artists who superintend them: God, the maker of the bed, and the painter?

Yes, there are three of them.

God, whether from choice or from necessity, made one bed in nature and one only; two or more such beds neither ever have been nor ever will be made by God.

Why is that?

Because even if He had made but two, a third would still appear behind them of which they again both possessed the form, and that would be the real bed and not the two others.

Very true, he said.

God knew this, I suppose, and He desired to be the real maker of a real bed, not a kind of bed, and therefore He created a bed which is essentially and by nature one only.

So it seems.

Shall we, then, speak of Him as the natural author or maker of the bed?

Yes, he replied; inasmuch as by the natural process of creation, He is the author of this and of all other things.

And what shall we say of the carpenter — is not he also the maker of a bed?

Yes.

But would you call the painter an artificer and maker?

Certainly not.

Yet if he is not the maker, what is he in relation to the bed?

I think, he said, that we may fairly designate him as the imitator of that which the others make.

Good, I said; then you call him whose product is third in the descent from nature, an imitator?

Certainly, he said.

And so if the tragic poet is an imitator, he too is thrice removed from the king and from the truth; and so are all other imitators.

That appears to be so.

Then about the imitator we are agreed. And what about the painter? — Do you think he tries to imitate in each case that which originally exists in nature, or only the creation of artificers?

The latter.

As they are or as they appear? you have still to determine this.

What do you mean?

I mean to ask whether a bed really becomes different when it is seen from different points of view, obliquely or directly or from any other point of view? Or does it simply appear different, without being really so? And the same of all things.

Yes, he said, the difference is only apparent.

Now let me ask you another question: Which is the art of painting designed to be — an imitation of things as they are, or as they appear — of appearance or of reality?

Of appearance, he said.

Then the imitator is a long way off the truth, and can reproduce all things because he lightly touches on a small part of them, and that part an image. For example: A painter will paint a cobbler, carpenter, or any other artisan, though he knows nothing of their arts; and, if he is a good painter, he may deceive children or simple persons when he shows them his picture of a carpenter from a distance, and they will fancy that they are looking at a real carpenter.

Certainly.

And surely, my friend, this is how we should regard all such claims: Whenever any one informs us that he has found a man who knows all

the arts, and all things else that anybody knows, and every single thing with a higher degree of accuracy than any other man — whoever tells us this, I think that we can only retort that he is a simple creature who seems to have been deceived by some wizard or imitator whom he met, and whom he thought all-knowing, because he himself was unable to analyze the nature of knowledge and ignorance and imitation.

Most true.

And next, I said, we have to consider tragedy and its leader, Homer; for we hear some persons saying that these poets know all the arts; and all things human; where virtue and vice are concerned, and indeed all divine things too; because the good poet cannot compose well unless he knows his subject, and he who has not this knowledge can never be a poet. We ought to consider whether here also there may not be a similar illusion. Perhaps they may have come across imitators and been deceived by them; they may not have remembered when they saw their works that these were thrice removed from the truth, and could easily be made without any knowledge of the truth, because they are appearances only and not realities? Or, after all, they may be in the right, and good poets do really know the things about which they seem to the many to speak so well?

The question, he said, should by all means be considered.

Now do you suppose that if a person were able to make the original as well as the image, he would seriously devote himself to the image-making branch? Would he allow imitation to be the ruling principle of his life, as if he had nothing higher in him?

I should say not.

But the real artist, who had real knowledge of those things which he chose also to imitate, would be interested in realities and not in imitations; and would desire to leave as memorials of himself works many and fair; and, instead of being the author of encomiums, he would prefer to be the theme of them.

Yes, he said, that would be to him a source of much greater honor and profit.

Now let us refrain, I said, from calling Homer or any other poet to account regarding those arts to which his poems incidentally refer: We will not ask them, in case any poet has been a doctor and not a mere imitator of medical parlance, to show what patients have been restored to health by a poet, ancient or modern, as they were by Asclepius; or what disciples in medicine a poet has left behind him, like the Asclepiads. Nor shall we press the same question upon them about the other arts. But we have a right to know respecting warfare, strategy, the administration of States, and the education of man, which are the chiefest and noblest subjects of his poems, and we may fairly ask him about them. "Friend Homer," then we say to him, "if you are only in the second remove from truth in what you say of virtue, and not in the third — not an image maker, that is, by our definition, an imitator — and if you are able to discern what pursuits make men better or worse in private or public life, tell us what State was ever better governed by your help? The good order of Lacedaemon is due to Lycurgus, and many other cities great and small have been similarly benefited by others; but who says that you have been a good legislator to them and have done them any good? Italy and Sicily boast of Charondas, and there is Solon who is renowned among us; but what city has anything to say about you?" Is there any city which he might name?

I think not, said Glaucon; not even the Homerids themselves pretend that he was a legislator.

Well, but is there any war on record which was carried on successfully owing to his leadership or counsel?

There is not.

Or is there anything comparable to those clever improvements in the arts, or in other operations, which are said to have been due to men of practical genius such as Thales the Milesian or Anacharsis the Scythian?

There is absolutely nothing of the kind.

But, if Homer never did any public service, was he privately a guide or teacher of any? Had he in his lifetime friends who loved to associate with him, and who handed down to posterity a Homeric way of life, such as was established by Pythagoras who was especially beloved for this reason and whose followers are to this day conspicuous among others by what they term the Pythagorean way of life?

Nothing of the kind is recorded of him. For surely, Socrates, Creophylus, the companion of Homer, that child of flesh, whose name always makes us laugh, might be more justly ridiculed for his want of breeding, if what is said is true, that Homer was greatly neglected by him in his own day when he was alive?

Yes, I replied, that is the tradition. But can you imagine, Glaucon, that if Homer had really been able to educate and improve mankind — if he had been capable of knowledge and not been a mere imitator — can you imagine, I say, that he would not have attracted many followers, and been honored and loved by them? Protagoras of Abdera, and Prodicus of Ceos, and a host of others, have only to whisper to their contemporaries: "You will never be able to manage either your own house or your own State until you appoint us to be your ministers of education" — and this ingenious device of theirs has such an effect in making men love them that their companions all but carry them about on their shoulders. And is it conceivable that the contemporaries of Homer, or again of Hesiod, would have allowed either of them to go about as rhapsodists, if they had really been able to help mankind forward in virtue? Would they not have been as unwilling to part with them as with gold, and have compelled them to stay at home with them? Or, if the master would not stay, then the disciples would have followed him about everywhere, until they had got education enough?

Yes, Socrates, that, I think, is quite true.

Then must we not infer that all these poetical individuals, beginning with Homer, are only imitators, who copy images of virtue and the other themes of their poetry, but have no contact with the truth? The poet is like a painter who, as we have already observed, will make a likeness of a cobbler though he understands nothing of cobbling; and his picture is good enough for those who know no more than he does, and judge only by colors and figures.

Quite so.

In like manner the poet with his words and phrases[1] may be said to lay on the colors of the several arts, himself understanding their nature

---

[1]Or, "with his nouns and verbs." [Tr.]

only enough to imitate them; and other people, who are as ignorant as he is, and judge only from his words, imagine that if he speaks of cobbling, or of military tactics, or of anything else, in meter and harmony and rhythm, he speaks very well — such is the sweet influence which melody and rhythm by nature have. For I am sure that you know what a poor appearance the works of poets make when stripped of the colors which art puts upon them, and recited in simple prose. You have seen some examples?

Yes, he said.

They are like faces which were never really beautiful, but only blooming, seen when the bloom of youth has passed away from them?

Exactly.

Come now, and observe this point: The imitator or maker of the image knows nothing, we have said, of true existence; he knows appearances only. Am I not right?

Yes.

Then let us have a clear understanding, and not be satisfied with half an explanation.

Proceed.

Of the painter we say that he will paint reins, and he will paint a bit?

Yes.

And the worker in leather and brass will make them?

Certainly.

But does the painter know the right form of the bit and reins? Nay, hardly even the workers in brass and leather who make them; only the horseman who knows how to use them — he knows their right form.

Most true.

And may we not say the same of all things?

What?

That there are three arts which are concerned with all things: one which uses, another which makes, a third which imitates them?

Yes.

And the excellence and beauty and rightness of every structure, animate or inanimate, and of every action of man, is relative solely to the use for which nature or the artist has intended them.

True.

Then beyond doubt it is the user who has the greatest experience of them, and he must report to the maker the good or bad qualities which develop themselves in use; for example, the flute player will tell the flute maker which of his flutes is satisfactory to the performer; he will tell him how he ought to make them, and the other will attend to his instructions?

Of course.

So the one pronounces with knowledge about the goodness and badness of flutes, while the other, confiding in him, will make them accordingly?

True.

The instrument is the same, but about the excellence or badness of it the maker will possess a correct belief, since he associates with one who knows, and is compelled to hear what he has to say; whereas the user will have knowledge?

True.

But will the imitator have either? Will he know from use whether or not that which he paints is correct or beautiful? or will he have right opinion from being compelled to associate with another who knows and gives him instructions about what he should paint?

Neither.

Then an imitator will no more have true opinion than he will have knowledge about the goodness or badness of his models?

I suppose not.

The imitative poet will be in a brilliant state of intelligence about the theme of his poetry?

Nay, very much the reverse.

And still he will go on imitating without knowing what makes a thing good or bad, and may be expected therefore to imitate only that which appears to be good to the ignorant multitude?

Just so.

Thus far then we are pretty well agreed that the imitator has no knowledge worth mentioning of what he imitates. Imitation is only a kind of play or sport, and the tragic poets, whether they write in iambic or in heroic verse,[2] are imitators in the highest degree?

Very true.

And now tell me, I conjure you — this imitation is concerned with an object which is thrice removed from the truth?

[2]Dramatists wrote in iambic verse and epic poets in dactylic hexameters — "heroic" verse. [Ed.]

Certainly.

And what kind of faculty in man is that to which imitation makes its special appeal?

What do you mean?

I will explain: The same body does not appear equal to our sight when seen near and when seen at a distance?

True.

And the same objects appear straight when looked at out of the water, and crooked when in the water; and the concave becomes convex, owing to the illusion about colors to which the sight is liable. Thus every sort of confusion is revealed within us; and this is that weakness of the human mind on which the art of painting in light and shadow, the art of conjuring, and many other ingenious devices impose, having an effect upon us like magic.

True.

And the arts of measuring and numbering and weighing come to the rescue of the human understanding — there is the beauty of them — with the result that the apparent greater or less, or more or heavier, no longer have the mastery over us, but give way before the power of calculation and measuring and weighing?

Most true.

And this, surely, must be the work of the calculating and rational principle in the soul?

To be sure.

And often when this principle measures and certifies that some things are equal, or that some are greater or less than others, it is, at the same time, contradicted by the appearance which the objects present?

True.

But did we not say that such a contradiction is impossible — the same faculty cannot have contrary opinions at the same time about the same thing?

We did; and rightly.

Then that part of the soul which has an opinion contrary to measure can hardly be the same with that which has an opinion in accordance with measure?

True.

And the part of the soul which trusts to measure and calculation is likely to be the better one?

Certainly.

And therefore that which is opposed to this is probably an inferior principle in our nature?

No doubt.

This was the conclusion at which I was seeking to arrive when I said that painting or drawing, and imitation in general, are engaged upon productions which are far removed from truth, and are also the companions and friends and associates of a principle within us which is equally removed from reason, and that they have no true or healthy aim.

Exactly.

The imitative art is an inferior who from intercourse with an inferior has inferior offspring.

Very true.

And is this confined to the sight only, or does it extend to the hearing also, relating in fact to what we term poetry?

Probably the same would be true of poetry.

Do not rely, I said, on a probability derived from the analogy of painting; but let us once more go directly to that faculty of the mind with which imitative poetry has converse, and see whether it is good or bad.

By all means.

We may state the question thus: Imitation imitates the actions of men, whether voluntary or involuntary, on which, as they imagine, a good or bad result has ensued, and they rejoice or sorrow accordingly. Is there anything more?

No, there is nothing else.

But in all this variety of circumstances is the man at unity with himself — or rather, as in the instance of sight there was confusion and opposition in his opinions about the same things, so here also is there not strife and inconsistency in his life? Though I need hardly raise the question again, for I remember that all this has been already admitted; and the soul has been acknowledged by us to be full of these and ten thousand similar oppositions occurring at the same moment?

And we were right, he said.

Yes, I said, thus far we were right; but there was an omission which must now be supplied.

What was the omission?

Were we not saying that a good man, who has the misfortune to lose his son or anything else which is most dear to him, will bear the loss with more equanimity than another?

Yes, indeed.

But will he have no sorrow, or shall we say that although he cannot help sorrowing, he will moderate his sorrow?

The latter, he said, is the truer statement.

Tell me: will he be more likely to struggle and hold out against his sorrow when he is seen by his equals, or when he is alone in a deserted place?

The fact of being seen will make a great difference, he said.

When he is by himself he will not mind saying many things which he would be ashamed of anyone hearing, and also doing many things which he would not care to be seen doing?

True.

And doubtless it is the law and reason in him which bids him resist; while it is the affliction itself which is urging him to indulge his sorrow?

True.

But when a man is drawn in two opposite directions, to and from the same object, this, as we affirm, necessarily implies two distinct principles in him?

Certainly.

One of them is ready to follow the guidance of the law?

How do you mean?

The law would say that to be patient under calamity is best, and that we should not give way to impatience, as the good and evil in such things are not clear, and nothing is gained by impatience; also, because no human thing is of serious importance, and grief stands in the way of that which at the moment is most required.

What is most required? he asked.

That we should take counsel about what has happened, and when the dice have been thrown, according to their fall, order our affairs in the way which reason deems best; not, like children who have had a fall, keeping hold of the part struck and wasting time in setting up a howl, but always accustoming the soul forthwith to apply a remedy, raising up that which is sickly and fallen, banishing the cry of sorrow by the healing art.

Yes, he said, that is the true way of meeting the attacks of fortune.

Well then, I said, the higher principle is ready to follow this suggestion of reason?

Clearly.

But the other principle, which inclines us to recollection of our troubles and to lamentation, and can never have enough of them, we may call irrational, useless, and cowardly?

Indeed, we may.

Now does not the principle which is thus inclined to complaint, furnish a great variety of materials for imitation? Whereas the wise and calm temperament, being always nearly equable, is not easy to imitate or to appreciate when imitated, especially at a public festival when a promiscuous crowd is assembled in a theater. For the feeling represented is one to which they are strangers.

Certainly.

Then the imitative poet who aims at being popular is not by nature made, nor is his art intended, to please or to affect the rational principle in the soul; but he will appeal rather to the lachrymose and fitful temper, which is easily imitated?

Clearly.

And now we may fairly take him and place him by the side of the painter, for he is like him in two ways: first, inasmuch as his creations have an inferior degree of truth — in this, I say, he is like him; and he is also like him in being the associate of an inferior part of the soul; and this is enough to show that we shall be right in refusing to admit him into a State which is to be well ordered, because he awakens and nourishes this part of the soul, and by strengthening it impairs the reason. As in a city when the evil are permitted to wield power and the finer men are put out of the way, so in the soul of each man, as we shall maintain, the imitative poet implants an evil constitution, for he indulges the irrational nature which has no discernment of greater and less, but thinks the same thing at one time great and at another small — he is an imitator of images and is very far removed from the truth.

Exactly.

But we have not yet brought forward the heaviest count in our accusation: The power which poetry has of harming even the good (and there are very few who are not harmed) is surely an awful thing?

Yes, certainly, if the effect is what you say.

Hear and judge: The best of us, as I conceive, when we listen to a passage of Homer or one of the tragedians, in which he represents some hero who is drawling out his sorrows in a long oration, or singing, and smiting his breast — the best of us, you know, delight in giving way to sympathy, and are in raptures at the excellence of the poet who stirs our feelings most.

Yes, of course I know.

But when any sorrow of our own happens to us, then you may observe that we pride ourselves on the opposite quality — we would fain be quiet and patient; this is considered the manly part, and the other which delighted us in the recitation is now deemed to be the part of a woman.

Very true, he said.

Now can we be right in praising and admiring another who is doing that which any one of us would abominate and be ashamed of in his own person?

No, he said, that is certainly not reasonable.

Nay, I said, quite reasonable from one point of view.

What point of view?

If you consider, I said, that when in misfortune we feel a natural hunger and desire to relieve our sorrow by weeping and lamentation, and that this very feeling which is starved and suppressed in our own calamities is satisfied and delighted by the poets; the better nature in each of us, not having been sufficiently trained by reason or habit, allows the sympathetic element to break loose because the sorrow is another's; and the spectator fancies that there can be no disgrace to himself in praising and pitying anyone who, while professing to be a brave man, gives way to untimely lamentation; he thinks that the pleasure is a gain, and is far from wishing to lose it by rejection of the whole poem. Few persons ever reflect, as I should imagine, that the contagion must pass from others to themselves. For the pity which has been nourished and strengthened in the misfortunes of others is with difficulty repressed in our own.

How very true!

And does not the same hold also of the ridiculous? There are jests which you would be ashamed to make yourself, and yet on the comic stage, or indeed in private, when you hear them, you are greatly amused by them, and are not at all disgusted at their unseemliness; the case of pity is repeated; there is a principle in human nature which is disposed to raise a laugh, and this, which you once restrained by reason because you were afraid of being thought a buffoon, is now let out again; and having stimulated the risible faculty at the theater, you are betrayed unconsciously to yourself into playing the comic poet at home.

Quite true, he said.

And the same may be said of lust and anger and all the other affections, of desire and pain and pleasure, which are held to be inseparable from every action — in all of them poetry has a like effect; it feeds and waters the passions instead of drying them up; she lets them rule, although they ought to be controlled if mankind are ever to increase in happiness and virtue.

I cannot deny it.

Therefore, Glaucon, I said, whenever you meet with any of the eulogists of Homer declaring that he has been the educator of Hellas, and that he is profitable for education and for the ordering of human things, and that you should take him up again and again and get to know him and regulate your whole life according to him, we may love and honor those who say these things — they are excellent people, as far as their lights extend; and we are ready to acknowledge that Homer is the greatest of poets and first of tragedy writers; but we must remain firm in our conviction that hymns to the gods and praises of famous men are the only poetry which ought to be admitted into our State. For if you go beyond this and allow the honeyed Muse to enter, either in epic or lyric verse, not law and the reason of mankind, which by common consent have ever been deemed best, but pleasure and pain will be the rulers in our State.

That is most true, he said.

And now since we have reverted to the subject of poetry, let this our defense serve to show the reasonableness of our former judgment in sending away out of our State an art having the tendencies which we have described; for reason constrained us. But that she may not impute to us any harshness or want of politeness, let us tell her that there is an ancient quarrel between philosophy and poetry; of which there are many proofs, such as the saying of "the yelping hound howling at her lord," or of one "mighty in the vain talk of fools," and "the mob of sages circumventing Zeus," and the "subtle thinkers who are beggars after all,"[3] and there are innumerable other signs of ancient enmity between them. Notwithstanding this, let us assure the poetry which aims at pleasure, and the art of imitation, that if she will only prove her title to exist in a well-ordered State we shall be delighted to receive her — we are very conscious of her charms; but it would not be right on that account to betray the truth. I dare say, Glaucon, that you are as much charmed by her as I am, especially when she appears in Homer?

Yes, indeed, I am greatly charmed.

Shall I propose, then, that she be allowed to return from exile, but upon this condition only — that she make a defense of herself in some lyrical or other meter?

Certainly.

And we may further grant to those of her defenders who are lovers of poetry and yet not poets the permission to speak in prose on her behalf: let them show not only that she is pleasant but also useful to States and to human life, and we will listen in a kindly spirit; for we shall

[3]Socrates is alluding to various proverbs, otherwise unknown, denigrating both poets and philosophers. [Ed.]

surely be the gainers if this can be proved, that there is a use in poetry as well as a delight?

Certainly, he said, we shall be the gainers.

If her defense fails, then, my dear friend, like other persons who are enamored of something, but put a restraint upon themselves when they think their desires are opposed to their interests, so too must we after the manner of lovers give her up, though not without a struggle. We too are inspired by that love of such poetry which the education of noble States has implanted in us, and therefore we shall be glad if she appears at her best and truest; but so long as she is unable to make good her defense, this argument of ours shall be a charm to us, which we will repeat to ourselves while we listen to her strains; that we may not fall away into the childish love of her which captivates the many. At all events we are well aware that poetry, such as we have described, is not to be regarded seriously as attaining to the truth; and he who listens to her, fearing for the safety of the city which is within him, should be on his guard against her seductions and make our words his law.

Yes, he said, I quite agree with you.

Yes, I said, my dear Glaucon, for great is the issue at stake, greater than appears, whether a man is to be good or bad. And what will any one be profited if under the influence of honor or money or power, aye, or under the excitement of poetry, he neglect justice and virtue?

Yes, he said; I have been convinced by the argument, as I believe that anyone else would have been.

# Ion

Translated by Lane Cooper.

SOCRATES: Welcome, Ion! And whence come you now to pay us a visit? From your home in Ephesus?

ION: No, Socrates, I come from Epidaurus and the festival of Asclepius.[1]

[1]Greek god of medicine; his festival, like that of other minor divinities connected with Apollo, was the occasion for artistic performances and competitions. [Ed.]

SOCRATES: What! Do the citizens of Epidaurus, in honoring the god, have a contest between rhapsodes[2] too?

ION: Indeed they do. They have every sort of musical competition.

[2]Professionals who delivered recitations of poetry, especially of Homer and the other epic poets. [Ed.]

SOCRATES: So? And did you compete? And how did you succeed?

ION: We carried off first prize, Socrates.

SOCRATES: Well done! See to it, now, that we win the Panathenaea also.

ION: It shall be so, God willing.

SOCRATES: I must say, Ion, I am often envious of you rhapsodists in your profession. Your art requires of you always to go in fine array, and look as beautiful as you can, and meanwhile you must be conversant with many excellent poets, and especially with Homer, the best and most divine of all. You have to understand his thought, and not merely learn his lines. It is an enviable lot! In fact, one never could be a rhapsode if one did not comprehend the utterances of the poet, for the rhapsode must become an interpreter of the poet's thought to those who listen, and to do this well is quite impossible unless one knows just what the poet is saying. All that, of course, will excite one's envy.

ION: What you say is true, Socrates; to me, at all events, this aspect of the art has given the most concern. And I judge that I, of all men, have the finest things to say on Homer, that neither Metrodorus of Lampsacus, nor Stesimbrotus of Thasos, nor Glaucon, nor anyone else who ever lived, had so many reflections, or such fine ones, to present on Homer as have I.

SOCRATES: That is pleasant news, Ion, for obviously you will not begrudge me a display of your talent.

ION: Not at all. And, Socrates, it really is worthwhile to hear how well I have embellished Homer. In my opinion I deserve to be crowned with a wreath of gold by the Homeridae.[3]

SOCRATES: Another time I shall find leisure to hear your recitation. At the moment do but answer me so far. Are you skilled in Homer only, or in Hesiod and Archilochus as well?

ION: No, only in regard to Homer; to me that seems enough.

SOCRATES: Is there any point on which both Homer and Hesiod say the same thing?

ION: Indeed, I think so; there are many cases of it.

SOCRATES: In those cases, then, would you interpret what Homer says better than what Hesiod says?

ION: In the cases where they say the same, Socrates, I should do equally well with both.

SOCRATES: But what about the cases where they do not say the same? For example, take the art of divination; Homer and Hesiod both speak of it.

ION: Quite so.

SOCRATES: Well then, where they say the same on the art of divination, and where they differ on it, would you interpret better what these two poets say, or would one of the diviners, one of the good ones, do so?

ION: One of the diviners.

SOCRATES: But suppose you were a diviner. If you were competent to explain the passages where they agree, would you not be competent to explain as well the passages where they differ?

ION: Manifestly, yes.

SOCRATES: How is it, then, that you are skilled in Homer, but not in Hesiod or the other poets? Does Homer treat of matters different from those that all the other poets treat of? Wasn't his subject mainly war, and hasn't he discussed the mutual relations of men good and bad, or the general run as well as special craftsmen, the relations of the gods to one another and to men, as they forgather, the phenomena of the heavens and occurrences in the underworld, and the birth of gods and heroes? Are not these the subjects Homer dealt with in his poetry?

ION: What you say is true, Socrates.

SOCRATES: And what about the other poets? Haven't they dealt with these same themes?

ION: Yes, but, Socrates, not in the same way.

SOCRATES: How so? In a worse way than he?

ION: Far worse.

SOCRATES: He in a better way?

ION: Better indeed, I warrant you.

SOCRATES: Well now, Ion darling, tell me. When several persons are discussing number, and one of them talks better than the rest, there will be someone who distinguishes the good speaker?

ION: I agree.

SOCRATES: It will be the same one who distinguishes those who are speaking badly, or will it be another?

---

[3]A group of poets who claimed descent from Homer, or more generally in this case, the admirers of Homer. [Ed.]

ION: No doubt the same.

SOCRATES: And this will be the one who knows the art of numbers?

ION: Yes.

SOCRATES: Tell me. When several are discussing diet, and what foods are wholesome, and one of them speaks better than the rest, will a given person see the excellence of the best speaker, and another the inferiority of the worse, or will the same man distinguish both?

ION: Obviously, I think, the same.

SOCRATES: Who is he? What is he called?

ION: The doctor.

SOCRATES: We may therefore generalize, and say: When several persons are discussing a given subject, the man who can distinguish the one who is talking well on it, and the one who is talking badly, will always be the same. Or, if he does not recognize the one who is talking badly, then, clearly, neither will he recognize the one who is talking well, granted that the subject is the same.

ION: That is so.

SOCRATES: Then the same man will be skilled with respect to both?

ION: Yes.

SOCRATES: Now you assert that Homer and the other poets, among them Hesiod and Archilochus, all treat of the same subjects, yet not all in the same fashion, but the one speaks well, and the rest of them speak worse.

ION: And what I say is true.

SOCRATES: Then you, if you can recognize the poet who speaks well, could also recognize the poets who speak worse, and see that they speak worse.

ION: So it seems.

SOCRATES: Well then, my best of friends, when we say that Ion has equal skill in Homer and all other poets, we shall not be mistaken. It must be so, since you yourself admit that the same man will be competent to judge of all who speak of the same matters, and that the poets virtually all deal with the same subjects.

ION: Then what can be the reason, Socrates, for my behavior? When anyone discusses any other poet, I pay no attention, and can offer no remark of any value. I frankly doze. But whenever anyone mentions Homer, immediately I am awake, attentive, and full of things to say.

SOCRATES: The riddle is not hard to solve, my friend. No, it is plain to everyone that not from art and knowledge comes your power to speak concerning Homer. If it were art that gave you power, then you could speak about all the other poets as well. There is an art of poetry as a whole? Am I not right?

ION: Yes.

SOCRATES: And is not the case the same with any other art you please, when you take it as a whole? The same method of inquiry holds for all the arts? Do you want some explanation, Ion, of what I mean by that?

ION: Yes, Socrates, upon my word I do. It gives me joy to listen to you wise men.

SOCRATES: I only wish you were right in saying that, Ion. But "wise men"! That means you, the rhapsodists and actors, and the men whose poems you chant, while I have nothing else to tell besides the truth, after the fashion of the ordinary man. For example, take the question I just now asked you. Observe what a trivial and commonplace remark it was that I uttered, something anyone might know, when I said that the inquiry is the same whenever one takes an art in its entirety. Let us reason the matter out. There is an art of painting taken as a whole?

ION: Yes.

SOCRATES: And there are and have been many painters, good and bad?

ION: Yes indeed.

SOCRATES: Now, take Polygnotus, son of Aglaophon. Have you ever seen a man with the skill to point out what is good and what is not in the works of Polygnotus, but without the power to do so in the works of other painters? A man who, when anybody shows the works of other painters, dozes off, is at a loss, has nothing to suggest, but when he has to express a judgment on one particular painter, say Polygnotus or anyone else you choose, wakes up, and is attentive, and is full of things to say?

ION: No, on my oath, I never saw the like.

SOCRATES: Or, again, take sculpture. Have you ever seen a man with the skill to judge the finer works of Daedalus, son of Metion, or of Epeus, son of Panopeus, or of Theodorus of

Samos, or the works of any other single sculptor, but, confronted by the works of other sculptors, is at a loss, and dozes off, without a thing to say?

ION: No, on my oath, I never saw one.

SOCRATES: Yet further, as I think, the same is true of playing on the flute, and on the harp, and singing to the harp, and rhapsody. You never saw a man with the skill to judge of Olympus, of Thamyras, or of Orpheus, or of Phemius, the rhapsodist at Ithaca, but is at a loss, has no remark to make concerning Ion the Ephesian, and his success or failure in reciting.

ION: On that I cannot contradict you, Socrates. But of this thing I am conscious, that I excel all men in speaking about Homer, and on him have much to say, and that everybody else avers I do it well, but on the other poets I do not. Well then, see what that means.

SOCRATES: I do see, Ion, and in fact will proceed to show you what to my mind it betokens. As I just now said, this gift you have of speaking well on Homer is not an art; it is a power divine, impelling you like the power in the stone Euripides called the magnet, which most call "stone of Heraclea." This stone does not simply attract the iron rings, just by themselves; it also imparts to the rings a force enabling them to do the same thing as the stone itself, that is, to attract another ring, so that sometimes a chain is formed, quite a long one, of iron rings, suspended from one another. For all of them, however, their power depends upon that loadstone. Just so the Muse. She first makes men inspired, and then through these inspired ones others share in the enthusiasm, and a chain is formed, for the epic poets, all the good ones, have their excellence, not from art, but are inspired, possessed, and thus they utter all these admirable poems. So is it also with the good lyric poets; as the worshiping Corybantes[4] are not in their senses when they dance, so the lyric poets are not in their senses when they make these lovely lyric poems. No, when once they launch into harmony and rhythm, they are seized with the Bacchic transport, and

are possessed — as the bacchants, when possessed, draw milk and honey from the rivers, but not when in their senses. So the spirit of the lyric poet works, according to their own report. For the poets tells us, don't they, that the melodies they bring us are gathered from rills that run with honey, out of glens and gardens of the Muses, and they bring them as the bees do honey, flying like the bees? And what they say is true, for a poet is a light and winged thing, and holy, and never able to compose until he has become inspired, and is beside himself, and reason is no longer in him. So long as he has this in his possession, no man is able to make poetry or to chant in prophecy. Therefore, since their making is not by art, when they utter many things and fine about the deeds of men, just as you do about Homer, but is by lot divine — therefore each is able to do well only that to which the Muse has impelled him — one to make dithyrambs, another panegyric odes, another choral songs, another epic poems, another iambs. In all the rest, each one of them is poor, for not by art do they utter these, but by power divine, since if it were by art that they knew how to treat one subject finely, they would know how to deal with all the others too. Herein lies the reason why the deity has bereft them of their senses, and uses them as ministers, along with soothsayers and godly seers; it is in order that we listeners may know that it is not they who utter these precious revelations while their mind is not within them, but that it is the god himself who speaks, and through them becomes articulate to us. The most convincing evidence of this statement is offered by Tynnichus of Chalcis. He never composed a single poem worth recalling, save the song of praise which everyone repeats, wellnigh the finest of all lyrical poems, and absolutely what he called it, an "Invention of the Muses." By this example above all, it seems to me, the god would show us, lest we doubt, that these lovely poems are not of man or human workmanship, but are divine and from the gods, and that the poets are nothing but interpreters of the gods, each one possessed by the divinity to whom he is in bondage. And to prove this, the deity on purpose sang the loveliest of all lyrics through the most

[4]Female worshippers of Dionysus whose rites drove them to frenzy; cf. Euripides's The Bacchae. [Ed.]

miserable poet. Isn't it so, Ion? Don't you think that I am right?[5]

ION: You are indeed, I vow! Socrates, your words in some way touch my very soul, and it does seem to me that by dispensation from above good poets convey to us these utterances of the gods.

SOCRATES: Well, and you rhapsodists, again, interpret the utterances of the poets?

ION: There also you are right.

SOCRATES: Accordingly, you are interpreters of interpreters?

ION: Undeniably.

SOCRATES: Wait now, Ion; tell me this. And answer frankly what I ask you. Suppose you are reciting epic poetry well, and thrill the spectators most deeply. You are chanting, say, the story of Odysseus as he leaped up to the dais, unmasked himself to the suitors, and poured the arrows out before his feet, or of Achilles rushing upon Hector, or one of the pitiful passages, about Andromache, or Hecuba, or Priam. When you chant these, are you in your senses? Or are you carried out of yourself, and does not your soul in an ecstasy conceive herself to be engaged in the actions you relate, whether they are in Ithaca, or Troy, or wherever the story puts them?

ION: How vivid, Socrates, you make your proof for me! I will tell you frankly that whenever I recite a tale of pity, my eyes are filled with tears, and when it is one of horror or dismay, my hair stands up on end with fear, and my heart goes leaping.

SOCRATES: Well now, Ion, what are we to say of a man like that? There he is, at a sacrifice or festival, got up in holiday attire, adorned with golden chaplets, and he weeps, though he has lost nothing of his finery. Or he recoils with fear, standing in the presence of more than twenty thousand friendly people, though nobody is stripping him or doing him damage. Shall we say that the man is in his senses?

[5] In the preceding speech, the language spoken by Socrates takes on the rhythms of the dithyramb — the traditional hymn to Dionysus — as though he himself were in an inspired state. [Ed.]

ION: Never, Socrates, upon my word. That is strictly true.

SOCRATES: Now then, are you aware that you produce the same effects in most of the spectators too?

ION: Yes, indeed, I know it very well. As I look down at them from the stage above, I see them, every time, weeping, casting terrible glances, stricken with amazement at the deeds recounted. In fact, I have to give them very close attention, for if I set them weeping, I myself shall laugh when I get my money, but if they laugh, it is I who have to weep at losing it.

SOCRATES: Well, do you see that the spectator is the last of the rings I spoke of, which receive their force from one another by virtue of the loadstone? You, the rhapsodist and actor, are the middle ring, and the first one is the poet himself. But it is the deity who, through all the series, draws the spirit of men wherever he desires, transmitting the attractive force from one into another. And so, as from the loadstone, a mighty chain hangs down, of choric dancers, masters of the chorus, undermasters, obliquely fastened to the rings which are suspended from the Muse. One poet is suspended from one Muse, another from another; we call it being "possessed," but the fact is much the same, since he is *held*. And from these primary rings, the poets, others are in turn suspended, some attached to this one, some to that, and are filled with inspiration, some by Orpheus, others by Musaeus. But the majority are possessed and held by Homer, and, Ion, you are one of these, and are possessed by Homer. And whenever anyone chants the work of any other poet, you fall asleep, and haven't a thing to say, but when anybody gives tongue to a strain of this one, you are awake at once, your spirit dances, and you have much to say, for not by art or science do you say of Homer what you say, but by dispensation from above and by divine possession. So the worshiping Corybantes have a lively feeling for that strain alone which is of the deity by whom they are possessed, and for that melody are well supplied with attitudes and utterances, and heed no others. And so it is with you, Ion. When anyone mentions Homer, you are ready, but about the other poets you are at a loss. You ask me why you are ready about Homer and not about the rest. Because it is not by art but by lot divine that you are eloquent in praise of Homer.

ION: Well put, I grant you, Socrates. And yet I should be much surprised if by your argument you succeeded in convincing me that I am possessed or mad when I praise Homer. Nor do I think that you yourself would find me so if you heard me speaking upon Homer.

SOCRATES: And indeed I wish to hear you, but not until you have answered me as follows. On what point in Homer do you speak well? Not on all points, I take it.

ION: I assure you, Socrates, I do it on every point, without exception.

SOCRATES: Yet not, I fancy, on those matters of which you happen to be ignorant, but Homer tells of?

ION: And the matters Homer tells of, and I do not know, what are they?

SOCRATES: Why, does not Homer in many passages speak of arts, and have much to say about them? About driving a chariot, for instance; if I can recollect the lines, I'll repeat them to you.

ION: No, let me do it, for I know them.

SOCRATES: Then recite for me what Nestor says to Antilochus, his son, where he warns him to be careful at the turning post, in the lay of the horse race in honor of Patroclus.

ION:

Thyself lean slightly in the burnished car
To the left of them, then call upon the off horse
With goad and voice; with hand give him free rein.
And at the post let the near horse come so close
That the nave of the well-wrought wheel shall seem
To graze the stone. Which yet beware to strike![6]

SOCRATES: That will do. Now, Ion, in these lines, which will be more capable of judging whether Homer speaks aright or not, a doctor or a charioteer?

ION: The charioteer, no doubt.

SOCRATES: Because that is his art, or for some other reason?

ION: No, because it is his art.

[6] *Iliad* 23:335. [Tr.]

SOCRATES: Each separate art, then, has had assigned to it by the deity the power of knowing a particular occupation? I take it that what we know by the pilot's art we do not know by the art of medicine as well.

ION: No indeed.

SOCRATES: And what we know by medical art we do not know by the builder's art as well.

ION: No indeed.

SOCRATES: Well, and so it is with all the arts? What we know by one of them, we do not know by another? But before you answer that, just tell me this. Do you allow a distinction between arts? One differs from another?

ION: Yes.

SOCRATES: Now with me the mark of differentiation is that one art means the knowledge of one kind of thing, another art the knowledge of another, and so I give them their respective names. Do you do that?

ION: Yes.

SOCRATES: If they meant simply knowledge of the same things, why should we distinguish one art from another? Why call them different, when both would give us the same knowledge? For example, take these fingers. I know that there are five of them, and you know the same as I about them. Suppose I asked you if we knew this same matter, you and I, by the same art, that of arithmetic, or by different arts. I fancy you would hold that we knew it by the same?

ION: Yes.

SOCRATES: Then tell me now what just a little while ago I was on the point of asking you. Does that seem true to you of all the arts — that, necessarily, the same art makes us know the same, another art not the same, but, if it really is another art, it must make us know something else?

ION: That is my opinion, Socrates.

SOCRATES: Well then, if one does not possess a given art, one will not be capable of rightly knowing what belongs to it in word or action?

ION: That is true.

SOCRATES: Then, in the lines which you recited, which will have the better knowledge whether Homer speaks aright or not, you or a charioteer?

ION: The charioteer.

SOCRATES: Doubtless because you are a rhapsode, and not a charioteer?

ION: Yes.

SOCRATES: The rhapsode's art is different from the charioteer's?

ION: Yes.

SOCRATES: If it is another art, then, it is a knowledge also about other matters.

ION: Yes.

SOCRATES: Now what about the passage in which Homer tells how Hecamede, Nestor's concubine, gave the wounded Machaon the broth to drink? The passage runs something like this:

She grated goat's-milk cheese in Pramnian wine,
With brazen grater, adding onion as a relish to the brew.[7]

On the question whether Homer here speaks properly or not, is it for the art of the physician, or the rhapsode's art, to discriminate aright?

ION: The art of the physician.

SOCRATES: What of this? The passage in which Homer says:

She plunged to the bottom like a leaden sinker
Which, mounted on the horntip from a field ox,
Speeds its way bringing mischief to voracious fish.[8]

What shall we say? Is it rather for the art of fishing, or the rhapsode's art, to decide on what the verses mean, and whether they are good or not?

ION: Obviously, Socrates, it is for the art of fishing.

SOCRATES: Reflect now. Suppose that you were questioning, and asked me, "Now, Socrates, you find it is for these several arts to judge in Homer, severally, what appertains to each of them. Come then, pick me out the passages concerning the diviner, and the diviner's art, the kind of things that appertain to him, regarding which he must be able to discern whether the poetry is good or bad?" Observe how easily and truly I can answer you. The poet does, in fact, treat of this matter in the *Odyssey* too — for example, when a scion of Melampus, the diviner Theoclymenus, says to the wooers:

Ah, wretched men, what bane is this ye suffer?
    Shrouded in night
Are your heads and your faces and your limbs
    below,
And kindled is the voice of wailing, and cheeks
    are wet with tears.
And the porch is full of ghosts; the hall is full of
    them,
Hastening hellward beneath the gloom, and the sun
Has perished out of heaven, and an evil mist infolds
    the world.[9]

And he treats of it in many places in the *Iliad* — for instance, in the lay of the battle at the wall. There he says:

For, as they were eager to pass over, a bird approached them,
An eagle of lofty flight, skirting the host on the left,
And in its talons bearing a monstrous blood-red serpent,
Still alive and struggling; nor had it yet forgot the joy of battle.
Writhing back, it smote the bird that held it, upon the breast
Beside the neck, and the bird did cast it from him,
In the agony of pain, to the earth,
And dropped it in the middle of the throng.
And, with a cry, himself went flying on the gusty wind.[10]

These passages, I contend, and others like them, appertain to the diviner to examine and to judge.

ION: And, Socrates, you are right.

SOCRATES: And you are right too, Ion, when you say so. Come now, you do for me what I have done for you. From both the *Odyssey* and *Iliad* I picked out for you the passages belonging to the doctor, the diviner, and the fisherman; now you likewise, since you are better versed than I in Homer, pick out for me the sort of passages, Ion, that concern the rhapsode and the rhapsode's art, the passages it befits the rhapsode, above all other men, to examine and to judge.

ION: *All* passages, Socrates, is what I say.

SOCRATES: Surely, Ion, you don't mean *all!* Are you really so forgetful? Indeed, it would ill become a man who is a rhapsode to forget.

---

[7]*Iliad* 11:639–640. [Tr.]
[8]*Iliad* 24:80–82. [Tr.]

[9]*Odyssey* 20:351–56. [Tr.]
[10]*Iliad* 12:200–208. [Tr.]

ION: Why? What am I forgetting?

SOCRATES: Don't you remember how you stated that the art of the rhapsode was different from the charioteer's?

ION: I remember.

SOCRATES: Well, and you admitted also that, being different, it had another field of knowledge?

ION: Yes.

SOCRATES: Well then, by your own account the art of rhapsody wil not know everything, nor the rhapsode either.

ION: The exceptions, Socrates, are doubtless only such matters as that.

SOCRATES: In "such matters" you must include approximately all the other arts. Well, as the rhapsode does not know the subject matter of them all, what sort of matters *will* he know?

ION: The kind of thing, I judge, that a man would say, and a woman would say, and a slave and a free man, a subject and a ruler — the suitable thing for each.

SOCRATES: You mean, the rhapsode will know better what the ruler of a ship in a storm at sea should say than will the pilot?

ION: No, in that case the pilot will know better.

SOCRATES: But suppose it is the ruler of a sick man. Will the rhapsode know better what the ruler should say than will the doctor?

ION: No, not in that case, either.

SOCRATES: But you say, "the kind of speech that suits a slave."

ION: Yes.

SOCRATES: You mean, for instance, if the slave is a cowherd, it is not he who will know what one should say to quiet angry cattle, but the rhapsode?

ION: Surely not.

SOCRATES: Well, "the kind of speech that suits a woman" — one who spins — about the working up of wool?

ION: No.

SOCRATES: Well, the rhapsodist will know "the kind of speech that suits a man" — a general exhorting his soldiers?

ION: Yes! that is the sort of thing the rhapsodist will know.

SOCRATES: What! Is the rhapsode's art the general's?

ION: At all events I ought to know the kind of speech a general should make.

SOCRATES: Indeed, you doubtless have the talents of a general, Ion! And suppose you happened to have skill in horsemanship, along with skill in playing on the lyre, you would know when horses were well or badly ridden, but if I asked you, "By which art, Ion, do you know that horses are well managed — is it because you are a horseman, or because you play the lyre?" What answer would you give me?

ION: I should say, "It is by my skill as horseman."

SOCRATES: Then, too, if you were picking out good players on the lyre, you would admit that you discerned them by your art in playing the lyre, and not by your art as horseman?

ION: Yes.

SOCRATES: But when you know of military matters, do you know them because you are competent as a general, or as a rhapsode?

ION: I cannot see a bit of difference.

SOCRATES: What, no difference, you say? You mean to call the art of the rhapsode and the art of the general a single art, or two?

ION: To me, there is a single art.

SOCRATES: And so, whoever is an able rhapsode is going to be an able general as well?

ION: Unquestionably, Socrates.

SOCRATES: And then, whoever happens to be an able general is an able rhapsode too.

ION: No, I do not think that holds.

SOCRATES: But you think the other does? That whoever is an able rhapsode is an able general too?

ION: Absolutely!

SOCRATES: Well, and you are the ablest rhapsodist in Greece?

ION: Yes, Socrates, by far.

SOCRATES: And the ablest general, Ion? The ablest one in Greece?

ION: You may be sure of it, for, Socrates, I learned this also out of Homer.

SOCRATES: Then, Ion, how in heaven's name is this? You are at once the ablest general and ablest rhapsodist among the Greeks, and yet you go about Greece performing as a rhapsode, but not as general. What think you? The Greeks are in great need of a rhapsode adorned with a wreath of gold, and do not need a general at all?[11]

ION: It is because my native city, Socrates, is under your dominion, and your military rule, and has no need whatever of a general. As for yours and Lacedaemon, neither would choose me for general; you think yourselves sufficient to yourselves.

SOCRATES: Excellent Ion, you know who Apollodorus is, of Cyzicus, don't you?

ION: What might he be?

SOCRATES: The man whom the Athenians at various times have chosen for their general, although he is an alien. The same is true of Phanosthenes of Andros, and Heraclides of Clazomenae, also aliens, who nevertheless, when they had shown their competence, were raised to the generalship by the city, and put in other high positions. And Ion of Ephesus, will she not elect him general, and accord him honors, if his worth becomes apparent? Why, you inhabitants of Ephesus are originally Athenians, are you not, and Ephesus is a city inferior to none? But the

[11]The dialogue occurs during the Peloponnesian War, which Athens eventually lost to Sparta.

fact is, Ion, that if you are right, if it really is by art and knowledge that you are able to praise Homer, then you do me wrong. You assure me that you have much fine knowledge about Homer, and you keep offering to display it, but you are deceiving me. Far from giving the display, you will not even tell me what subject it is on which you are so able, though all this while I have been entreating you to tell. No, you are just like Proteus; you twist and turn, this way and that, assuming every shape, until finally you elude my grasp and reveal yourself as a general. And all in order not to show how skilled you are in the lore concerning Homer! So if you are an artist, and, as I said just now, if you only promised me a display on Homer in order to deceive me, then you are at fault. But if you are not an artist, if by lot divine you are possessed by Homer, and so, knowing nothing, speak many things and fine about the poet, just as I said you did, then you do no wrong. Choose, therefore, how you will be called by us, whether we shall take you for a man unjust, or for a man divine.

ION: The difference, Socrates, is great. It is far lovelier to be deemed divine.

SOCRATES: This lovelier title, Ion, shall be yours, to be in our minds divine, and not an artist, in praising Homer.

# Aristotle
## 384–322 B.C.

Unlike his teacher Plato, who was a native-born Athenian aristocrat, Aristotle was a *metic* — a foreigner with a green card, as it were — the son of a doctor from Thrace. Aristotle's origins may help explain why Plato's idealism had so little ultimate appeal for him. As a skilled biologist from Macedonia, an impoverished military state, Aristotle may have been loath to dismiss physical reality as an illusion. Certainly for Aristotle the universal *processes* of nature, the eternal laws of change were not mere signs of the mutable, inferior character of the world of Becoming compared with the unalterable world of Ideas. They possessed immense significance.

Aristotle spent many years in Plato's Academy, learning its philosophy and its methods of argumentation, but his own school, the Lyceum, rejected Plato's idealism in favor of a materialism that investigated every aspect of the physical world. If Plato is the father of Western philosophy, Aristotle is the father of most of the sciences. Although Aristotle was often wildly wrong about details (Galileo's disproof of his speculations on gravity is the most famous instance), his systematizing of thought made science as we know it possible.

Aristotle's immense philosophical output may be divided into treatises on three types of science: the *theoretical* sciences, like logic or physics, which aimed at improving thought itself — one's general ideas on a particular subject; the *practical* sciences, like ethics and politics, whose goal lay in the realm of human action; and the *productive* sciences, like rhetoric and poetics, whose purpose was in making something. Here already, one can see a major difference from Plato, whose *Republic* combined speculation on metaphysics, ethics, politics, music, poetry, and much else. For Plato, thought was *holistic*: all was ultimately One and could be known through one dialectical method. For Aristotle, the world was not One but Many, and investigating it meant adapting one's methods and principles to the subject under consideration. This is the *problematic* method, and it is rare in the history of philosophy, where most thinkers have preferred universal dialectic to institutionalized improvisation. At the same time, Aristotle's mode of organization has clearly prevailed over Plato's in the structure of the modern university, where specialized departments of physics, psychology, literature, and music pursue their disparate disciplines by different methodologies.

Textual scholars believe the *Poetics* to be what is technically termed an *esoteric* treatise — it was circulated privately, within the Lyceum — rather than an *exoteric* one meant for general publication. It can be compared to teacher's lecture notes, brief and pointed, but meant to be filled out with further examples and arguments during presentation. Where the text seems dogmatic or disconnected or downright obscure, we should be tolerant — this was not the form in which Aristotle's students received it. There are other sources of obscurity, of course, the usual gaps that appear in transmitting and translating a verbal text more than two thousand years old. In Chapter 6, for example, Aristotle tells us that he will "speak hereafter of comedy" but never returns to the subject. It has been presumed for centuries that the treatise on comedy was a second book of the *Poetics* that had been lost forever. Recently a manuscript has turned up containing what some scholars believe to be fragments of the lost *Poetics II*, but whether the fragments are genuinely Aristotelian or not is still undecided.

## ORGANIZATION AND METHOD

As a treatise on productive science, the *Poetics* takes as its topic the making of a work of art, specifically a dramatic or epic tragedy. Although the *Poetics* was later misread as a how-to manual, Aristotle was only presenting the general *principles* of dramatic construction as they applied to the poetry and theater of his age; he was not dispensing tips for the practicing tragedian. Later critics attacked the drama of their day for not conforming to Aristotle's rules, often without understanding the reasons behind his general statements or the highly empirical basis of the *Poetics*. It would be as much a mistake to fault Aristotle for not being able to anticipate every development in the drama over the last two millennia.

Productive science relies on Aristotle's method of four-cause analysis, in which an artifact is defined by its shape (the formal cause), its composition (the material cause), its manner of construction (the efficient cause), and its end or purpose (the final cause).[1] Thus, in the poetics of hammers, that tool might be defined by its shape (a long handle to give leverage, a flat striking surface), its materials (hard metal for the head, light but strong wood or plastic for the handle), its manner of construction (the relation and attachments of the parts), and its purpose (pounding nails). In defining a dramatic or epic tragedy, the same method of definition is used. Here the material is language, rhythm, and harmony; the form is the imitation of a serious action; the manner is dramatic or narrative (as the case may be); and the end is the *katharsis* of pity and fear (about which more will be said later). The first four chapters of the *Poetics* discuss the causes of tragedy (among the other arts) and prepare the reader for the famous definition of tragedy in Chapter 6.

(Note that Aristotle never formally defines more general categories like *poetry* or *drama*. For him these are not legitimate genres. They are not definable because they do not have all their causes in common. Those things called poetry are similar in formal and material causes; those called drama in formal, material, and efficient causes; but because they do not have similar final causes, they remain congeries of many things rather than one definite species. Aristotle is a genre critic, in other words, not by choice but because of the demands of his systematic method.)

Having defined tragedy, Aristotle analyzes its qualitative parts (plot, character, thought, diction, song, and spectacle), and then examines each part successively, beginning with the most important — plot. Nearly half of the *Poetics* is devoted to the analysis of plot, and here again the same four-cause organization is used.

---

[1]The method of analysis is itself discussed in the *Posterior Analytics*, one of Aristotle's major treatises on logic.

Aristotle considers plot *form* (its general character, length, relation to history, the course of the action, and so on), plot *materials* (devices like recognition and reversal or the tragic deed), and plot *handling*. All these technical issues are explained ultimately in terms of the *purpose* of plot, the *katharsis*. In Chapter 13, he argues deductively that *hamartia* — the tragic protagonist's character flaw — derives directly from the nature of the tragic emotions of pity and fear. Later he moves from plot to the formal and material aspects of character, thought, and so on. Throughout, his method is rigorous, though what remains of the *Poetics* is not complete and there are occasional interruptions or interpolations (like Chapter 12).

## ARISTOTELIAN IMITATION

Although Aristotle, like Plato, considers poetry a form of mimetic art, he surprisingly does not think that art itself is necessarily or essentially imitative. (Thus without having experienced abstract art or even discussing it, he does not preclude its possibility.)[2] Another surprise is the title of the treatise, since the word *poētikēs* in Greek means "things that are made or crafted." The point is that for Aristotle, poetic art is not, as Plato thought, merely copying: it is a creative act.

One reason poetics cannot be simple copying is that art involves the translation of reality into another medium. Just as the portrait sculptor translates the human countenance into clay or stone, the poet translates action into language. Nor can the poet merely translate his materials raw. Even if he does not invent his plots but takes them, as many Greek tragedians did, from the historical or mythological record, he selectively reshapes the action to make it more universal, and thus more powerfully tragic. Divesting the historical action of the accidental and the incidental,[3] he pares away unnecessary prologue until he has a probable sequence of actions leading inexorably to the protagonist's doom. If this is done well, the bare summary of a tragic plot should have something of the tragic effect. After he has constructed the plot, he must compose it verbally using extraordinary, "embellished" language and compose it visually for the stage. The whole process is a complex one — of making, not of mere imitation — that requires keeping the ultimate end in constant view.

For Plato, that artists were not always faithful to the truth counted against them; for Aristotle, artists must disregard incidental facts to search for deeper *universal* truths. For Plato, Pygmalion's statue, which came to life, would be the transcendent

---

[2]In the sentence where Aristotle tells us that poetry "is" a form of imitation, he uses not the usual verb *eimi* ("be") but rather *tugkhano*, "happen to be."

[3]"Poetry is a more serious and a more philosophical thing than history, for poetry involves the universal, history the particular." This is a crucial passage in the *Poetics*. The issue for Aristotle seems to be that we can learn more from the universal principles that poets must abstract in creating their plots than from the messy, contingent realities the historian is forced to deal with. This is the paradox behind the saying "Truth is stranger than fiction." Precisely — the poets who create fictions must jettison the strange accidents that shape the events of this world.

triumph of art; for Aristotle, a statue that was merely true to life would not be art at all.


## KATHARSIS

One of the most controversial passages in the *Poetics* is contained in the passage on the final cause of tragedy: The play, "through incidents arousing pity and fear effects their *katharsis*."[4] But what does *katharsis* mean and what is "katharted"? Three possible translations of *katharsis* are "clarification," "purification," and "purgation"; and what is clarified, purified, or purged must be either the "incidents" or the emotions of "pity and fear."

According to the classical scholar Leon Golden, *katharsis* means "clarification," and it is the tragic *incidents* that are clarified: The process of poetic imitation, by stripping all accident and contingency from the tragic fall of the noble protagonist reveals as clearly as possible how such things can happen. Tragedy here has an educative function. The "purification" theory, which has a long history beginning with the Renaissance theorists Lodovico Castelvetro and Francesco Robortello, suggests that tragedy has the function of tempering (or hardening) the emotions by revealing to the audience the proper objects of pity and fear.

The oldest theory holds that *katharsis* means "purgation," the violent driving-out of the emotions of pity and fear. This theory is supported by the only other instance in which Aristotle uses *katharsis* in the context of the arts, in a passage from the *Politics*:

> Music should be studied . . . for the sake of . . . many benefits. . . . [one of which is] purgation (the word purgation we use at present without any explanation, but when hereafter we speak of poetry we will treat the subject with more precision). For feelings such as pity and fear, or, again, enthusiasm, exist very strongly in some souls, and have more or less influence over all. Some persons fall into a religious frenzy, whom we see . . . when they have used the sacred melodies, restored as though they had found healing and purgation. Those who are influenced by pity or fear, and every emotional nature, must have a like experience, and others in so far as each is susceptible to such emotions, and all are in a manner purged and their souls lightened and delighted. (*Politics* 1341$^b$ 35 to 1342$^a$ 15)

Aristotle thought that the *Poetics* would clarify the *Politics* rather than the other way around, but the context of this passage is clear enough: Unpleasant feelings may be relieved through music or poetry. When the experience is over, the soul is "lightened and delighted." After seeing a performance of *Oedipus the King* or *King Lear*, spectators are no longer gripped by pity and fear; rather they are exhausted, cleansed, emptied of emotion. The primary meaning of the word *katharsis*, preserved in the English cognate "cathartic," is the action of a powerful laxative. A

---

[4]Editor's literal translation.

doctor's son, Aristotle perhaps could not resist using a familiar medical metaphor for the experience.

## Selected Bibliography

Butcher, S. H. *Aristotle's Theory of Poetry and Fine Art*. New York: Macmillan, 1902.

Cooper, Lane. *The Poetics of Aristotle: Its Meaning and Influence*. 1923; New York: Cooper Square, 1963.

Else, Gerald F. *Aristotle's Poetics: The Argument*. Cambridge: Harvard University Press, 1957.

————. *Plato and Aristotle on Poetry*. Chapel Hill: University of North Carolina Press, 1986.

Fergusson, Francis. "On the *Poetics*," *Tulane Drama Review* 4 (1960): 23–32.

House, Humphrey. *The Poetics of Aristotle in England*. London: R. Hart-Davis, 1956.

Lucas, F. L. *Tragedy: Serious Drama in Relation to Aristotle's Poetics*. New York: Macmillan, 1958.

Modrak, Deborah. *Aristotle: The Power of Perception*. Chicago: University of Chicago Press, 1987.

Olson, Elder. *Aristotle's Poetics and English Literature*. Chicago: University of Chicago Press, 1965.

————. "The Poetic Method of Aristotle: Its Powers and Limitations." In *On Value Judgments in the Arts and Other Essays*. Chicago: University of Chicago Press, 1976.

# Poetics

**I**

Let us discuss the art of poetry, itself, and its species, describing the character of each of them, and how it is necessary to construct plots if the poetic composition is to be successful and, furthermore, the number and kind of parts to be found in the poetic work, and as many other matters as are relevant. Let us follow the order of nature, beginning with first principles.

Now epic poetry, tragedy, comedy, dithyrambic poetry, and most forms of flute and lyre playing all happen to be, in general, imitations, but they differ from each other in three ways: either because the imitation is carried on by different means or because it is concerned with different kinds of objects or because it is presented, not in the same, but in a different manner.

Translated by Leon Golden.

For just as some artists imitate many different objects by using color and form to represent them (some through art, others only through habit), other artists imitate through sound, as indeed, in the arts mentioned above; for all these accomplish imitation through rhythm and speech and harmony, making use of these elements separately or in combination. Flute playing and lyre playing, for example, use harmony and rhythm alone; and this would also be true of any other arts (for example, the art of playing the shepherd's pipe) that are similar in character to these. Dancers imitate by using rhythm without harmony, since they imitate characters, emotions, and actions by rhythms that are arranged into dance-figures.

The art that imitates by words alone, in prose and in verse, and in the latter case, either combines various meters or makes use of only one, has been nameless up to the present time. For we cannot assign a common name to the mimes of Sophron and Xenarchus and the Socratic dialogues; nor would we have a name for such an imitation if someone should accomplish it through trimeters or elegiacs or some other such meter, except that the public at large by joining the term "poet" to a meter gives writers such names as "elegiac poets" and "epic poets." Here the public classifies all those who write in meter as poets and completely misses the point that the capacity to produce an imitation is the essential characteristic of the poet. The public is even accustomed to apply the name "poet" to those who publish a medical or scientific treatise in verse, although Homer has nothing at all in common with Empedocles except the meter. It is just to call Homer a poet, but we must consider Empedocles a physicist rather than a poet.

And in the same way, if anyone should create an imitation by combining all the meters as Chairemon did when he wrote *The Centaur*, a rhapsody composed by the use of all the meters, he must also be designated a poet. Concerning these matters let us accept the distinctions we have just made.

There are some arts that use all the means that have been discussed, namely, rhythm and song and meter, as in the writing of dithyrambs and nomic poetry[1] and in tragedy and comedy. A difference is apparent here in that some arts use all the various elements at the same time, whereas others use them separately. These, then, are what I call the differences in the artistic means through which the imitation is accomplished.

## 2

Artists imitate men involved in action and these must either be noble or base since human character regularly conforms to these distinctions, all of us being different in character because of some quality of goodness or evil. From this it follows that the objects imitated are either better than or

worse than or like the norm. We find confirmation of this observation in the practice of our painters. For Polygnotus represents men as better, Pauson as worse, and Dionysius as like the norm.[2] It is clear that each of the above-mentioned forms of imitation will manifest differences of this type and will be different through its choosing, in this way, a different kind of object to imitate. Even in dancing, flute-playing, and lyre-playing it is possible for these differences to exist, and they are seen also in prose, and in verse that does not make use of musical accompaniment, as is shown by the fact that Cleophon represents men like the norm, Homer as better, and both Hegemon the Thasian (who was the first writer of parodies) and Nicochares, the author of the *Deiliad*, as worse.[3] The same situation is found in dithyrambic and nomic poetry,[4] as we see in the way Timotheus and Philoxenus handled the Cyclops theme.[5] It is through the same distinction in objects that we differentiate comedy from tragedy, for the former takes as its goal the representation of men as worse, the latter as better, than the norm.

## 3

There is, finally, a third factor by which we distinguish imitations, and that is the manner in which the artist represents the various types of object. For, using the same means and imitating the same kinds of object, it is possible for the poet on different occasions to narrate the story (either speaking in the person of one of his characters as Homer does or in his own person with-

[1]The dithyramb was originally a choral ode sung in honor of Dionysus, whereas nomic poetry was originally concerned with texts taken from the epic and was presented with a flute or lyre accompaniment. [Tr.]

[2]Polygnotus was one of the great painters of the fifth century B.C. Neither Pauson nor Dionysius are identified with certainty. [Tr.]

[3]Not much is known about the poets other than Homer mentioned here. Cleophon was a dramatic or epic writer; a small fragment of a parody of Hegemon of Thasos is preserved in Athenaeus; we have no further certain information about Nicochares. [Tr.]

[4]There is a lacuna in the text at this point where the name of another writer of nomic poetry was probably mentioned. [Tr.]

[5]Timotheus was a dithyrambic poet who lived in Miletus from 450 to 360 B.C.; Philoxenus was a dithyrambic poet who lived in Cythera from 436 to 380 B.C. [Tr.]

out changing roles)[6] or to have the imitators performing and acting out the entire story.

As we said at the beginning, imitations are to be distinguished under these three headings: means, object, and manner. Thus, in one way, Sophocles is the same kind of imitative artist as Homer, since they both imitate noble men; but in another sense, he resembles Aristophanes, since they both imitate characters as acting and dramatizing the incidents of the story. It is from this, some tell us, that these latter kinds of imitations are called "dramas" because they present characters who "dramatize" the incidents of the plot.

By the way, it is also for this reason that the Dorians claim to be the originators of both tragedy and comedy. The Megarians — both those in Megara itself, who assert that comedy arose when democracy was established among them, and those Megarians in Sicily, who point out that their poet Epicharmus far antedates Chionides and Magnes[7] — claim to have originated comedy; in addition, some of the Dorians in the Peloponnesus claim to be the originators of tragedy. As proof of their contentions, they cite the technical terms they use for these art forms; for they say that they call the towns around their city *komai*, but that the Athenians call their towns *demoi*. By this they argue that the root of the name "comedian" is not derived from *komazein* [the word for "reveling"] but from *komai* [their word for the towns] that the comic artists visited in their wanderings after they had been driven in disgrace from the city. In support of their claim to be the originators of "drama," they point out that the word for "doing" is *dran* in their dialect,

[6]The translation given of this phrase is based on the traditional text, which has been accepted by Butcher, Hardy, and Kassel. On philosophical and linguistic grounds, Bywater prefers to emend the text of the passage so that it reads as follows: "Given both the same means and the same kind of object for imitation, one may either (1) speak at one moment in narrative and at another in an assumed character, as Homer does; or (2) one may remain the same throughout, without any such change; or (3) the imitators may represent the whole story dramatically, as though they were actually doing the things described." [Tr.]

[7]Not much is known, in addition to what Aristotle tells us in the *Poetics*, about these three comic writers who lived in the early part of the fifth century B.C. [Tr.]

whereas Athenians use the word *prattein* for this concept.

Concerning the number and kind of distinctions that characterize "imitations," let us accept what has been said above.

## 4

Speaking generally, the origin of the art of poetry is to be found in two natural causes. For the process of imitation is natural to mankind from childhood on: Man is differentiated from other animals because he is the most imitative of them, and he learns his first lessons through imitation, and we observe that all men find pleasure in imitations. The proof of this point is what actually happens in life. For there are some things that distress us when we see them in reality, but the most accurate representations of these same things we view with pleasure — as, for example, the forms of the most despised animals and of corpses. The cause of this is that the act of learning is not only most pleasant to philosophers but, in a similar way, to other men as well, only they have an abbreviated share in this pleasure. Thus men find pleasure in viewing representations because it turns out that they learn and infer what each thing is — for example, that this particular object is that kind of object; since if one has not happened to see the object previously, he will not find any pleasure in the imitation qua imitation but rather in the workmanship or coloring or something similar.

Since imitation is given to us by nature, as are harmony and rhythm (for it is apparent that meters are parts of the rhythms), men, having been naturally endowed with these gifts from the beginning and then developing them gradually, for the most part, finally created the art of poetry from their early improvisations.

Poetry then diverged in the directions of the natural dispositions of the poets. Writers of greater dignity imitated the noble actions of noble heroes; the less dignified sort of writers imitated the actions of inferior men, at first writing invectives as the former writers wrote hymns and encomia. We know of no "invective" by poets before Homer, although it is probable that there were many who wrote such poems; but it is possible to attribute them to authors who came after Homer — for example, the *Margites* of Homer himself, and other such poems. In these poems, the fitting meter came to light, the one that now bears the name "iambic" [i.e., invective] because it was originally used by men to satirize each other. Thus, of our earliest writers, some were heroic and some iambic poets. And just as Homer was especially the poet of noble actions (for he not only handled these well but he also made his imitations dramatic), so also he first traced out the form of comedy by dramatically presenting not invective but the ridiculous. For his *Margites* has the same relation to comedy as the *Iliad* and *Odyssey* have to tragedy. But when tragedy and comedy began to appear, poets were attracted to each type of poetry according to their individual natures, one group becoming writers of comedies in place of iambics, and the other, writers of tragedies instead of epics because these genres were of greater importance and more admired than the others.

Now then, the consideration of whether or not tragedy is by now sufficiently developed in its formal elements, judged both in regard to its essential nature and in regard to its public performances, belongs to another discussion. What is relevant is that it arose, at first, as an improvisation (both tragedy and comedy are similar in this respect) on the part of those who led the dithyrambs, just as comedy arose from those who led the phallic songs that even now are still customary in many of our cities. Tragedy, undergoing many changes (since our poets were developing aspects of it as they emerged), gradually progressed until it attained the fulfillment of its own nature. Aeschylus was the first to increase the number of actors from one to two; he also reduced the role of the chorus and made the dialogue the major element in the play. Sophocles increased the number of actors to three and introduced scene painting. Then tragedy acquired its magnitude. Thus by developing away from a satyr-play of short plots and absurd diction, tragedy achieved, late in its history, a dignified level. Then the iambic meter took the place of the tetrameter. For the poets first used the trochaic tetrameter because their poetry was satyric and very closely associated with dance; but when

dialogue was introduced, nature itself discovered the appropriate meter. For the iambic is the most conversational of the meters — as we see from the fact that we speak many iambs when talking to each other, but few [dactylic] hexameters, and only when departing from conversational tone. Moreover, the number of episodes was increased. As to the other elements by which, we are told, tragedy was embellished, we must consider them as having been mentioned by us. For it would probably be an enormous task to go through each of these elements one by one.

**5**

As we have said, comedy is an imitation of baser men. These are characterized not by every kind of vice but specifically by "the ridiculous," which is a subdivision of the category of "deformity." What we mean by "the ridiculous" is some error or ugliness that is painless and has no harmful effects. The example that comes immediately to mind is the comic mask, which is ugly and distorted but causes no pain.

Now then, the successive changes in the history of tragedy and the men who brought them about have been recorded; but the analogous information about the history of comedy is lacking because the genre was not treated, at the beginning, as a serious art form. It was only recently that the archons began to grant choruses to the comic poets; until then, the performers were all volunteers. And it was only after comedy had attained some recognizable form that we began to have a record of those designated as "comic poets." Who introduced masks or prologues, who established the number of actors, and many other matters of this type, are unknown. The creation of plots came first from Sicily, where it is attributed to Epicharmus and Phormis; and it was first Crates among the Athenian poets who departed from iambic [or invective] poetry and began to write speeches and plots of a more universal nature.

Now epic poetry follows the same pattern as tragedy insofar as it is the imitation of noble subjects presented in an elevated meter. But epic differs from tragedy in that it uses a single meter, and its manner of presentation is narrative. And further, there is a difference in length. For tragedy attempts, as far as possible, to remain within one circuit of the sun or, at least, not depart from this by much. Epic poetry, however, has no limit in regard to time, and differs from tragedy in this respect; although at first the poets proceeded in tragedy in the same way as they did in epic. Some of the parts of a poem are common to both tragedy and epic, and some belong to tragedy alone. Therefore, whoever can judge what is good and bad in tragedy can also do this in regard to epic. For whatever parts epic poetry has, these are also found in tragedy; but, as we have said, not all of the parts of tragedy are found in epic poetry.

**6**

We shall speak about the form of imitation that is associated with hexameter verse and about comedy later.[8] Let us now discuss tragedy, bringing together the definition of its essence that has emerged from what we have already said. Tragedy is, then, an imitation of a noble and complete action, having the proper magnitude;[9] it employs language that has been artistically enhanced by each of the kinds of linguistic adornment, applied separately in the various parts of the play; it is presented in dramatic, not narrative form, and achieves, through the representation of pitiable and fearful incidents, the catharsis of such pitiable and fearful incidents. I mean by "language that has been artistically enhanced," that which is accompanied by rhythm and harmony and song; and by the phrase "each of the kinds of linguistic adornment applied separately in the vaious parts of the play," I mean that some parts

are accomplished by meter alone and others, in turn, through song.

And since [in drama] agents accomplish the imitation by acting the story out, it follows, first of all, that the arrangement of the spectacle should be, of necessity, some part of the tragedy as would be melody and diction, also; for these are the means through which the agents accomplish the imitation. I mean by diction the act, itself, of making metrical compositions, and by melody, what is completely obvious. Since the imitation is of an action and is accomplished by certain agents, the sort of men these agents are is necessarily dependent upon their "character" and "thought." It is, indeed, on the basis of these two considerations that we designate the quality of actions, because the two natural causes of human action are thought and character. It is also in regard to these that the lives of all turn out well or poorly. For this reason we say that tragic plot is an imitation of action.

Now I mean by the plot the arrangement of the incidents, and by character that element in accordance with which we say that agents are of a certain type; and by thought I mean that which is found in whatever things men say when they prove a point or, it may be, express a general truth. It is necessary, therefore, that tragedy as a whole have six parts in accordance with which, as a genre, it achieves its particular quality. These parts are plot, character, diction, thought, spectacle, and melody. Two of these parts come from the means by which the imitation is carried out; one from the manner of its presentation, and three from the objects of the imitation. Beyond these parts there is nothing left to mention. Not a few poets, so to speak, employ these parts; for indeed, every drama [theoretically] has spectacle, character, plot, diction, song, and thought.

The most important of these parts is the arrangement of the incidents; for tragedy is not an imitation of men, per se, but of human action and life and happiness and misery. Both happiness and misery consist in a kind of action; and the end of life is some action, not some quality.[10]

---

[8]Aristotle discusses the epic in Chs. 23 and 24, but the section of the *Poetics* dealing with comedy seems to have been written but lost. Various Aristotelian scholars (including Lane Cooper and Elder Olson) have attempted to reconstruct what a poetics of comedy would be like. [Ed.]

[9]There is no word in the Greek text for "proper" but I have followed the practice of several other translators who add a modifier to the term "magnitude" where it is logically warranted. The term "representation" has also been added to the final clause of this sentence because of Aristotle's insistence that the pleasure of tragedy is achieved *through imitation* (Ch. XIV, ll. 15–16). See L. Golden, "Catharsis," *TAPA* 93 (1962): 58. [Tr.]

[10]The text is corrupt here. The translation follows an emendation suggested by Vahlen and accepted by Bywater and Hardy. [Tr.]

Now according to their characters men have certain qualities; but according to their actions they are happy or the opposite. Poets do not, therefore, create action in order to imitate character; but character is included on account of the action. Thus the end of tragedy is the presentation of the individual incidents and of the plot; and the end is, of course, the most significant thing of all. Furthermore, without action tragedy would be impossible, but without character it would still be possible. This point is illustrated both by the fact that the tragedies of many of our modern poets are characterless, and by the fact that many poets, in general, experience this difficulty. Also, to take an example from our painters, Zeuxis illustrates the point when compared to Polygnotus; for Polygnotus is good at incorporating character into his painting, but the work of Zeuxis shows no real characterization at all. Furthermore, if someone arranges a series of speeches that show character and are well-constructed in diction and thought, he will not, by this alone, achieve the end of tragedy; but far more will this be accomplished by the tragedy that employs these elements rather inadequately but, nevertheless, has a satisfactory plot and arrangement of incidents. In addition to the arguments already given, the most important factors by means of which tragedy exerts an influence on the soul are parts of the plot, the reversal, and the recognition. We have further proof of our view of the importance of plot in the fact that those who attempt to write tragedies are able to perfect diction and character before the construction of the incidents, as we see, for example, in nearly all of our early poets.

The first principle, then, and to speak figuratively, the soul of tragedy, is the plot; and second in importance is character. A closely corresponding situation exists in painting. For if someone should paint by applying the most beautiful colors, but without reference to an overall plan, he would not please us as much as if he had outlined the figure in black and white. Tragedy, then, is an imitation of an action; and it is, on account of this, an imitation of men acting.

Thought is the third part of tragedy and is the ability to say whatever is pertinent and fitting to the occasion, which, in reference to the composition of speeches, is the essential function of the arts of politics and rhetoric. As proof of this we point out that our earlier poets made their characters speak like statesmen, and our contemporary poets make them speak like rhetoricians. Now character is that part of tragedy which shows an individual's purpose by indicating, in circumstances where it is not clear, what sort of things he chooses or rejects. Therefore those speeches do not manifest character in which there is absolutely nothing that the speaker chooses or rejects. Thought we find in those speeches in which men show that something is or is not, or utter some universal proposition.

The fourth literary part is diction, and I mean by diction, as has already been said, the expression of thoughts through language which, indeed, is the same whether in verse or prose.

Of the remaining parts, melody is the greatest of the linguistic adornments; and spectacle, to be sure, attracts our attention but is the least essential part of the art of poetry. For the power of tragedy is felt even without a dramatic performance and actors. Furthermore, for the realization of spectacle, the art of the costume designer is more effective than that of the poet.

7

Now that we have defined these terms, let us discuss what kind of process the arrangement of incidents must be, since this is the first and most important element of tragedy. We have posited that tragedy is the imitation of a complete and whole action having a proper magnitude. For it is possible for something to be a whole and yet not have any considerable magnitude. To be a whole is to have a beginning and a middle and an end. By a "beginning" I mean that which is itself not, by necessity, after anything else but after which something naturally is or develops. By an "end" I mean exactly the opposite: that which is naturally after something else, either necessarily or customarily, but after which there is nothing else. By a "middle" I mean that which is itself after something else and which has something else after it. It is necessary, therefore, that well-constructed plots not begin by chance, anywhere, nor end anywhere, but that they conform to the distinctions that have been made above.

Furthermore, for beauty to exist, both in regard to a living being and in regard to any object that is composed of separate parts, not only must there be a proper arrangement of the component elements, but the object must also be of a magnitude that is not fortuitous. For beauty is determined by magnitude and order; therefore, neither would a very small animal be beautiful (for one's view of the animal is not clear, taking place, as it does, in an almost unperceived length of time), nor is a very large animal beautiful (for then one's view does not occur all at once, but, rather, the unity and wholeness of the animal are lost to the viewer's sight as would happen, for example, if we should come across an animal a thousand miles in length). So that just as it is necessary in regard to bodies and animals for there to be a proper magnitude — and this is the length that can easily be perceived at a glance — thus, also, there must be a proper length in regard to plots, and this is one that can be easily taken in by the memory. The limit of length in regard to the dramatic contests and in terms of the physical viewing of the performance is not a matter related to the art of poetry. For if it were necessary for a hundred tragedies to be played, they would be presented by timing them with water clocks as we are told happened on some occasions in the past. The limit, however, that is set in regard to magnitude by the very nature of the subject itself is that whatever is longer (provided it remains quite clear) is always more beautiful. To give a general rule, we say that whatever length is required for a change to occur from bad fortune to good or from good fortune to bad through a series of incidents that are in accordance with probability or necessity, is a sufficient limit of magnitude.

## 8

A plot is a unity not, as some think, merely if it is concerned with one individual, for in some of the many and infinitely varied things that happen to any one person, there is no unity. Thus, we must assert, there are many actions in the life of a single person from which no overall unity of action emerges. For this reason all those poets seem to have erred who have written a *Heracleid* and a *Theseid* and other poems of this type; for they think that since Heracles was one person it is appropriate for his story to be one story. But Homer, just as he was superior in other respects, also seems to have seen this point well, whether through his technical skill or his native talent, since in making the *Odyssey* he did not include all the things that ever happened to Odysseus. (For example, it happened that Odysseus was wounded on Parnassus and that he feigned madness at the time of the call to arms; but between these two events there is no necessary or probable relation.) Homer, rather, organized the *Odyssey* around one action of the type we have been speaking about and did the same with the *Iliad*. Necessarily, then, just as in other forms of imitation, one imitation is of one thing, so also, a plot, since it is an imitation of an action, must be an imitation of an action that is one and whole. Moreover, it is necessary that the parts of the action be put together in such a way that if any one part is transposed or removed, the whole will be disordered and disunified. For that whose presence or absence has no evident effect is not part of the whole.

*only an incident not whole life*

## 9

It is apparent from what we have said that it is not the function of the poet to narrate events that have actually happened, but rather, events such as might occur and have the capability of occurring in accordance with the laws of probability or necessity. For the historian and the poet do not differ by their writing in prose or verse (the works of Herodotus might be put into verse but they would, nonetheless, remain a form of history both in their metrical and prose versions). The difference, rather, lies in the fact that the historian narrates events that have actually happened, whereas the poet writes about things as they might possibly occur. Poetry, therefore, is more philosophical and more significant than history, for poetry is more concerned with the uni-

*universal all*

versal, and history more with the individual. By the universal I mean what sort of man turns out to say or do what sort of thing according to probability or necessity — this being the goal poetry aims at, although it gives individual names to the characters whose actions are imitated. By the individual I mean a statement telling, for example, "what Alcibiades did or experienced."

Now then, this point has already been made clear in regard to comedy; for the comic poets, once they have constructed the plot through probable incidents, assign any names that happen to occur to them, and they do not follow the procedure of the iambic poets who write about specific individuals. In regard to tragedy, however, our poets cling to the names of the heroes of the past on the principle that whatever is clearly capable of happening is readily believable. We cannot be sure that whatever has not yet happened is possible; but it is apparent that whatever has happened is also capable of happening for, if it were not, it could not have occurred. Nevertheless in some tragedies one or two of the names are well known and the rest have been invented for the occasion; in others not even one is well-known, for example, Agathon's *Antheus*,[11] since in this play both the incidents and the names have been invented, and nonetheless they please us. Thus we must not seek to cling exclusively to the stories that have been handed down and about which our tragedies are usually written. It would be absurd, indeed, to do this since the well-known plots are known only to a few, but nevertheless please everyone. It is clear then from these considerations that it is necessary for the poet to be more the poet of his plots than of his meters, insofar as he is a poet because he is an imitator and imitates human actions. If the poet happens to write about things that have actually occurred, he is no less the poet for that. For nothing prevents some of the things that have actually occurred from belonging to the class of

the probable or possible, and it is in regard to this aspect that he is the poet of them.

Of the simple plots and actions the episodic are the worst; and I mean by episodic a plot in which the episodes follow each other without regard for the laws of probability or necessity. Such plots are constructed by the inferior poets because of their own inadequacies, and by the good poets because of the actors. For since they are writing plays that are to be entered in contests (and so stretch the plot beyond its capacity) they are frequently forced to distort the sequence of action.

Since the imitation is not only a complete action but is also of fearful and pitiable incidents, we must note that these are intensified when they occur unexpectedly, yet because of one another. For there is more of the marvelous in them if they occur this way than if they occurred spontaneously and by chance. Even in regard to coincidences, those seem to be most astonishing that appear to have some design associated with them. We have an example of this in the story of the statue of Mitys in Argos killing the man who caused Mitys' death by falling upon him as he was a spectator at a festival.[12] The occurrence of such an event, we feel, is not without meaning and thus we must consider plots that incorporate incidents of this type to be superior ones.

**10**

Plots are divided into the simple and the complex, for the actions of which the plots are imitations are naturally of this character. An action that is, as has been defined, continuous and unified I call simple when its change of fortune arises without reversal and recognition, and complex when its change of fortune arises through recognition or reversal or both. Now these aspects of the plot must develop directly from the construction of the plot itself, so that they occur from prior events either out of necessity or according to the laws of probability. For it makes

---

[11]Agathon was a late fifth-century B.C. tragic poet whose work has not survived except in fragments. He appears, prominently, in Plato's *Symposium*. [Tr.]

[12]I have followed Butcher's, Hardy's, and Bywater's interpretation of this passage. Others, however, understand the phrase to mean "when he was looking at the statue." [Tr.]

quite a difference whether they occur *because* of those events or merely *after* them.

## 11

Reversal is the change of fortune in the action of the play to the opposite state of affairs, just as has been said; and this change, we argue, should be in accordance with probability and necessity. Thus, in the *Oedipus* the messenger comes to cheer Oedipus and to remove his fears in regard to his mother; but by showing him who he actually is he accomplishes the very opposite effect. And in *Lynceus*, Lynceus is being led away to die and Danaus is following to kill him; but it turns out, because of the action that has taken place, that Danaus dies and Lynceus is saved. Recognition, as the same indicates, is a change from ignorance to knowledge, bringing about either a state of friendship or one of hostility on the part of those who have been marked out for good fortune or bad. The most effective recognition is one that occurs together with reversal, for example, as in the *Oedipus*. There are also other kinds of recognition for, indeed, what we have said happens, in a way, in regard to inanimate things, even things of a very causal kind; and it is possible, further, to "recognize" whether someone has or has not done something. But the type of recognition that is especially a part of the plot and the action is the one that has been mentioned. For such a recognition and reversal will evoke pity or fear, and we have defined tragedy as an imitation of actions of this type; and furthermore, happiness and misery will appear in circumstances of this type. Since this kind of recognition is of persons, some recognitions that belong to this class will merely involve the identification of one person by another when the identity of the second person is clear; on other occasions it will be necessary for there to be a recognition on the part of both parties: for example, Iphigenia is recognized by Orestes from her sending of the letter; but it is necessary that there be another recognition of him on her part.

Now then, these are two parts of the plot, reversal and recognition, and there is also a third part, suffering. Of these, reversal and recognition have been discussed; the incident of suffering results from destructive or painful action such as death on the stage, scenes of very great pain, the infliction of wounds, and the like.

## 12

The parts of tragedy that we must view as formal elements we have discussed previously; looking at the quantitative aspect of tragedy and the parts into which it is divided in this regard, the following are the distinctions to be made: prologue, episode, exode, and the choral part, which is divided into parode and stasimon. These are commonly found in all plays, but only in a few are found songs from the stage and *kommoi*. The prologue is the complete section of a tragedy before the parode of the chorus; an episode is the complete section of a tragedy between complete choric songs; the exode is the complete section of a tragedy after which there is no song of the chorus. Of the choral part, the parode is the entire first speech of the chorus, the stasimon is a song of the chorus without anapests and trochees, and a *kommos* is a lament sung in common by the chorus and the actors. The parts of tragedy that we must view as formal elements we have discussed previously; the above distinctions have been made concerning the quantitative aspect of tragedy, and the parts into which it is divided in this regard.

## 13

What goals poets must aim at, which difficulties they must be wary of when constructing their plots, and how the proper function of tragedy is accomplished are matters we should discuss after the remarks that have just been made.

Since the plots of the best tragedies must be complex, not simple, and the plot of a tragedy must be an imitation of pitiable and fearful incidents (for this is the specific nature of the imitation under discussion), it is clear, first of all, that unqualifiedly good human beings must not appear to fall from good fortune to bad; for that is neither pitiable nor fearful; it is, rather, repellent. Nor must an extremely evil man appear to move from bad fortune to good fortune for that is the most untragic situation of all because it has none of the necessary requirements of tragedy; it both violates our human sympathy and contains nothing of the pitiable or fearful in it. Furthermore, a villainous man should not appear to fall from good fortune to bad. For, although such a plot would be in accordance with our human sympathy, it would not contain the necessary elements of pity and fear; for pity is aroused by someone who undeservedly falls into misfortune, and fear is evoked by our recognizing that it is someone like ourselves who encounters this misfortune (pity, as I say, arising for the former reason, fear for the latter). Therefore the emotional effect of the situation just mentioned will be neither pitiable nor fearful. What is left, after our considerations, is someone in between these extremes. This would be a person who is neither perfect in virtue and justice, nor one who falls into misfortune through vice and depravity; but rather, one who succumbs through some miscalculation. He must also be a person who enjoys great reputation and good fortune, such as Oedipus, Thyestes, and other illustrious men from similar families. It is necessary, furthermore, for the well-constructed plot to have a single rather than a double construction, as some urge, and to illustrate a change of fortune not from bad fortune to good but, rather, the very opposite, from good fortune to bad, and for this to take place not because of depravity but through some great miscalculation on the part of the type of person we have described (or a better rather than a worse one).

A sign of our point is found in what actually happens in the theater. For initially, our poets accepted any chance plots; but now the best tragedies are constructed about a few families, for example, about Alcmaeon, Oedipus, Orestes, Meleager, Thyestes, Telephon, and any others who were destined to experience, or to commit, terrifying acts. For as we have indicated, artistically considered, the best tragedy arises from this kind of plot. Therefore, those critics make the very mistake that we have been discussing who blame Euripides because he handles the material in his tragedies in this way, and because many of his plots end in misfortune. For this is, indeed, the correct procedure, as we have said. The very great proof of this is that on the stage and in the dramatic contests such plays appear to be the most tragic, if they are properly worked out; and Euripides, even if in other matters he does not manage things well, nevertheless appears to be the most tragic of the poets. The second ranking plot, one that is called first by some, has a double structure of events, as in the *Odyssey*, ending in opposite ways for the better and worse characters. It seems to be first on account of the inadequacy of the audience. For our poets trail along writing to please the tastes of the audience. But this double structure of events involves a pleasure that is not an appropriate pleasure of tragedy but rather of comedy. For in comedy, whoever are the greatest enemies in the story — for example, Orestes and Aegisthus — becoming friends at the end, go off together, and no one is killed by anyone.

## 14

Pity and fear can arise from the spectacle and also from the very structure of the plot, which is the superior way and shows the better poet. The poet should construct the plot so that even if the action is not performed before spectators, one who merely hears the incidents that have occurred both shudders and feels pity from the way they turn out. That is what anyone who hears the plot of the *Oedipus* would experience. The achievement of this effect through the spectacle does not have much to do with poetic art and really belongs to the business of producing the play. Those who use the spectacle to create not the fearful but only the monstrous have no share in the creation of tragedy; for we should not seek every pleasure from tragedy but only the one proper to it.

Since the poet should provide pleasure from pity and fear through imitation, it is apparent that this function must be worked into the incidents. Let us try to understand what type of occurrences appear to be terrifying and pitiable. It is, indeed, necessary that any such action occur either between those who are friends or enemies to each other, or between those who have no relationship, whatsoever, to each other. If an enemy takes such an action against an enemy, there is nothing pitiable in the performance of the act or in the intention to perform it, except the suffering itself. Nor would there be anything pitiable if neither party had any relationship with the other. But whenever the tragic incidents occur in situations involving strong ties of affection — for example, if a brother kills or intends to kill a brother or a son a father or a mother a son or a son a mother or commits some equally terrible act — there will be something pitiable. These situations, then, are the ones to be sought. Now, it is not possible for a poet to alter completely the traditional stories. I mean, for example, the given fact that Clytemnestra dies at the hands of Orestes, and Eriphyle at the hands of Alcmaeon; but it is necessary for the poet to be inventive and skillful in adapting the stories that have been handed down. Let us define more clearly what we mean by the skillful adaptation of a story. It is possible for the action to occur, as our early poets handled it, with the characters knowing and understanding what they are doing, as indeed Euripides makes Medea kill her children. It is also possible to have the deed done with those who accomplish the terrible deed in ignorance of the identity of their victim, only later recognizing the relationship as in Sophocles' *Oedipus*. The incident, here, is outside the plot, but we find an example of such an incident in the play itself, in the action of Astydamas's *Alcmaeon* or of Telegonus in the *Wounded Odysseus*;[13] and there is further a third type in addition to these that involves someone who intends to commit some fatal act through ignorance of his relationship to another person but recognizes this relationship before doing it. Beyond these possibilities, there is no other way to have an action take place. For it is necessary either to do the deed or not and either knowingly or in ignorance.

Of these possibilities, the case in which one knowingly is about to do the deed and does not is the worst; for it is repellent and not tragic because it lacks the element of suffering. Therefore, no one handles a situation this way, except rarely; for example, in the *Antigone*, Haemon is made to act in this way toward Creon. To do the deed knowingly is the next best way. Better

than this is the case where one does the deed in ignorance and after he has done it recognizes his relationship to the other person. For the repellent aspect is not present, and the recognition is startling. But the most effective is the final type, for example, in the *Cresphontes*, where Merope is going to kill her son and does not, but, on the contrary, recognizes him, and in the *Iphigenia*, where a sister is involved in a similar situation with a brother, and in the *Helle*, where a son who is about to surrender his mother recognizes her.[14]

It is for this reason that, as we have said previously, tragedies are concerned with a few families. For proceeding not by art, but by trial and error, poets learned how to produce the appropriate effect in their plots. They are compelled, therefore, to return time and again to that number of families in which these terrifying events have occurred. We have now spoken sufficiently about the construction of the incidents and of what type the plot must be.

## 15

In regard to character, there are four points to be aimed at. First and foremost, character should be good. If a speech or action has some choice connected with it, it will manifest character, as has been said, and the character will be good if the choice is good. Goodness is possible for each class of individuals. For, both a woman and a slave have their particular virtues even though the former of these is inferior to a man, and the latter is completely ignoble.[15] Second, character must be appropriate. For it is possible for a person to be manly in terms of character, but it is

[13]Astydamas was a fourth-century B.C. poet; the *Wounded Odysseus* may have been a play by Sophocles. [Tr.]

[14]The *Cresphontes* and the *Iphigenia*, the former no longer extant, are plays by Euripedes. We have no further information concerning the *Helle*. [Tr.]

[15]Aristotle's word for "good" here, *chrēstēn*, means "valuable" rather than "noble." Aristotle is distinguishing between the intrinsic value of personages (he considered women and slaves to be inferior beings) and the instrumental value of their ethical choices to the drama in which they figure. Aristotle's point is that character must serve the ends of the drama, and that *motiveless* choice, which has no effect on the action — like Menelaus's cowardice in Euripides' *Orestes* — is to be avoided. [Ed.]

not appropriate for a woman to exhibit either this quality or the intellectual cleverness that is associated with men. The third point about character is that it should be like reality, for this is different from making character virtuous and making it appropriate, as we have defined these terms. The fourth aspect of character is consistency. For even if it is an inconsistent character who is the subject of the imitation (I refer to the model that suggested the kind of character being imitated), it is nevertheless necessary for him to be consistently inconsistent. We have an example of unnecessarily debased character in the figure of Menelaus in the *Orestes*, of unsuitable and inappropriate character in the lament of Odysseus in the *Scylla* and the speech of Melanippe, and of inconsistency of character in *Iphigenia at Aulis* where the heroine's role as a suppliant does not fit in with her character as it develops later in the play.

In character, as in the construction of the incidents, we must always seek for either the necessary or the probable, so that a given type of person says or does certain kinds of things, and one event follows another according to necessity or probability. Thus, it is apparent that the resolutions of the plots should also occur through the plot itself and not by means of the deus ex machina, as in the *Medea*, and also in regard to the events surrounding the department of the fleet in the *Iliad*. The deus ex machina must be reserved for the events that lie outside the plot, either those that happened before it that are not capable of being known by men, or those that occur after that need to be announced and spoken of beforehand. For we grant to the gods the power of seeing all things. There should, then, be nothing improbable in the action; but if this is impossible, it should be outside the plot as, for example, in Sophocles' *Oedipus*.

Because tragedy is an imitation of the nobler sort of men it is necessary for poets to imitate good portrait painters. For even though they reproduce the specific characteristics of their subjects and represent them faithfully, they also paint them better than they are. Thus, also, the poet imitating men who are prone to anger or who are indifferent or who are disposed in other such ways in regard to character makes them good as well, even though they have such characteristics, just as Agathon[16] and Homer portray Achilles.

It is necessary to pay close attention to these matters and, in addition, to those that pertain to the effects upon an audience that follow necessarily from the nature of the art of poetry. For, indeed, it is possible frequently to make mistakes in regard to these. We have spoken sufficiently about these matters in our published works.

## 16

What we mean by "recognition" we have indicated previously. Of the kinds of recognition that occur, there is one, first of all, that is least artistic, which poets mainly use through the poverty of their inspiration. This is the form of recognition that is achieved through external signs; some of these are birthmarks, for example, "the spearhead which the Earth-born are accustomed to bear," or the "stars" such as Carcinus wrote about in his *Thyestes*. Then there are characteristics that we acquire after birth. Of these some are found on the body, for example, scars; and others are external to the body, such as necklaces, and as another example, the ark through which the recognition is accomplished in the *Tyro*. It is also possible to employ these recognitions in better and worse ways; for example, Odysseus was recognized through his scar in one way by the nurse and in another way by the swineherds. Now those recognitions are less artistic that depend on signs as proof, as well as all that are similar to these; but those that derive from the reversal of action, as in the Bath Scene of the *Odyssey*, are better.

In second place come those recognitions that have been contrived for the occasion by the poet and are therefore inartistic. For example, the way Orestes in the *Iphigenia* makes known that he is Orestes; for Iphigenia made herself known through the letter, but he himself says what the poet wishes him to say but not what the plot requires. Therefore this type of recognition is rather close to the error that has already been

[16]I have followed Butcher, Hardy, and Bywater in reading the name of the tragic poet here. Other scholars accept a manuscript reading of the word meaning "good." [Tr.]

mentioned; for it would have been just as possible for him to carry tokens with him. Another example of this type of recognition is the use of the "voice of the shuttle" in the *Tereus* of Sophocles.

The third type arises from our being stimulated by something that we see to remember an event that has an emotional significance for us. This type of recognition occurs in the *Cyprioe* of Dicaeogenes where the sight of the painting brings forth tears, and also in the story of Alcinous where Odysseus hears the lyre player and, reminded of his past fortunes, weeps; in both instances, it was by their emotional reactions that the characters were recognized.

The fourth type of recognition occurs through reasoning, for example, in the *Choëphoroe* it is achieved by the deduction: Someone like me has come; there is no one resembling me except Orestes; he, therefore, has come. Another recognition of this type was suggested by Polyidus the Sophist in regard to Iphigenia; for it was reasonable for Orestes to infer that, since his sister was sacrificed, he was also going to be sacrificed. Again, in the *Tydeus* of Theodectes, the deduction is made that he who had come to find a son was, himself, to perish. Another example is in the *Phinidae* where the women, when they had seen the place, inferred their destiny: that since they had been exposed there, they were fated to die there.

There is also a type of composite recognition from false reasoning on the part of another character,[17] for example, in the story of Odysseus, the False Messenger; for he said that he would know the bow that he had not seen, but it is false reasoning to suppose through this that he *would* recognize it again (as if he had seen it before).[18]

The best recognition is the one that arises from the incidents themselves, striking us, as they do, with astonishment through the very probability of their occurrence as, for example, in the action of the *Oedipus* of Sophocles and in the *Iphigenia*, where it is reasonable for the heroine to wish to dispatch a letter. Such recognitions alone are accomplished without contrived signs and necklaces. The second-best type of recognition is the one that is achieved by reasoning.

**17**

In constructing plots and working them out with diction, the poet must keep the action as much as possible before his eyes. For by visualizing the events as distinctly as he can, just as if he were present at their actual occurrence, he will discover what is fitting for his purpose, and there will be the least chance of incongruities escaping his notice. A sign of this is found in the criticism that is made of Carcinus. For Amphiarus is coming back from the temple, a point that would have escaped the audience's notice if it had not actually seen it; and on the stage, the play failed because the audience was annoyed at this incongruity.[19]

As much as is possible the poet should also work out the action with gestures. For, given poets of the same natural abilities, those are most persuasive who are involved in the emotions they imitate; for example, one who is distressed conveys distress, and one who is enraged conveys anger most truly. Therefore, the art of poetry is more a matter for the well-endowed poet than for the frenzied one. For poets marked by the former characteristic can easily change character, whereas those of the latter type are possessed.

In regard to arguments, both those that already are in existence and those he himself invents, the poet should first put them down in universal form and then extend them by adding episodes. I mean that the poet should take a general view of the action of the play, like, for example, the following general view of the *Iphigenia*: A young girl had been sacrificed and had disappeared in a way that was obscure to the sacrificers. She settled in another country in which it was the custom to sacrifice strangers to the goddess, and she came

---

[17] I have followed Bywater in accepting an emendation meaning "another" in place of the manuscript reading "audience" followed by Kassel and Hardy. [Tr.]

[18] In this passage, Bywater notes that, "both text and interpretation here are in the highest degree doubtful." I have followed his interpretation of this difficult passage. Except for the *Choëphoroe*, we do not have any information about the plays mentioned in the previous paragraph. [Tr.]

[19] Carcinus was a fifth-century B.C. tragic poet; nothing further is known of the play mentioned here. [Tr.]

to hold the priesthood for this sacrifice. Later, it turned out that the brother of the priestess came to this country (the fact that the god, for some reason, commanded him to come is outside the argument; the purpose of his coming is outside of the plot). When he came he was seized, and on the point of being sacrificed he made himself known, either as Euripides handled the situation or as Polyidus arranged it, by his saying, in a very reasonable way, that not only had it been necessary for his sister to be sacrificed but also for him; and from this came his deliverance. After this, when the names have already been assigned, it is necessary to complete the episodes. The episodes must be appropriate, as, for example, the madness of Orestes through which he was captured and his deliverance through purification.

In drama, the episodes are short, but epic achieves its length by means of them. For the argument of the *Odyssey* is not long: A certain man is away from home for many years, closely watched by Poseidon but otherwise completely alone. His family at home continually faces a situation where his possessions are being squandered by the suitors who plot against his son. Storm-driven, he arrives home and, having made certain people acquainted with him, he attacks the suitors and, while destroying his enemies, is himself saved. This is the essence of the story; everything else is episode.

## 18

In every tragedy, we find both the complication and the resolution of the action. Frequently some matters outside the action together with some within it comprise the complication, and the rest of the play consists of the resolution. By complication I mean that part of the play from the beginning up to the first point at which the change occurs to good or to bad fortune. By resolution I mean the part of the play from the beginning of the change in fortune to the end of the play. For example, in the *Lynceus* of Theodectes, the complication comprises everything done before the action of the play begins and the seizing of the child, and, in turn, of the parents;

the resolution comprises all that happens from the accusation of murder to the end of the play.[20]

There are four kinds of tragedy (for that number of parts has been mentioned): the complex, which consists wholly in reversal and recognition; the tragedies of suffering, for example, the *Ajaxes* and *Ixions* that have been written; the tragedies of character, for example, the *Phthiotian Women* and the *Peleus*.[21] And a fourth type [the tragedy of spectacle], for example, is The *Daughters of Phorcis* and *Prometheus*[22] and those plays that take place in Hades. Now it is necessary to attempt, as much as possible, to include all elements in the play, but if that is not possible, then as many as possible and certainly the most important ones. This is especially so now, indeed, when the public unjustly criticizes our poets. For although there have been poets who were outstanding in regard to each kind of tragedy, the public now demands that one man be superior to the particular virtue of each of his predecessors.

It is correct to speak of a tragedy as different from or similar to another one on the basis of its plot more than anything else: that is, in regard to an action having the same complication and resolution. Many poets are skillful in constructing their complications, but their resolutions are poor. It is, however, necessary for both elements to be mastered.

The poet, as has frequently been said, must remember not to make a tragedy out of an epic body of incidents (by which I mean a multiple plot), [as would be the case], for example, if someone should construct a plot out of the entire *Iliad*. For, there, because of the length, the parts take on the appropriate magnitude, but the same plot used in the drama turns out quite contrary

[20]The text is in dispute here. Bywater, following a suggestion of Susemihl, translates the passage 1456ᵃ, 7–10, at this point in the text. Butcher, Hardy, and Kassel retain the traditional reading that I have followed in my translation. [Tr.]

[21]*The Phthiotian Women* and *Peleus*, neither now extant, were probably written by Sophocles. The *Lynceus*, mentioned above and at l. 7 in Ch. 11, is also no longer extant. [Tr.]

[22]*The Daughters of Phorcis* and *Prometheus* are both by Aeschylus; Bywater identifies them as lost satyr-plays and does not connect the latter play with the famous *Prometheus Bound*. [Tr.]

to one's expectations. A sign of this is that so many as have written about the entire destruction of Troy (and not of sections of it, as Euripides) or about the entire story of Niobe (and not just a part, as Aeschylus) either completely fail on stage or do badly, since even Agathon failed for this reason alone. But in their reversals and in their simple plots, these poets aim with marvelous accuracy at the effects that they wish for: that is, whatever is tragic and touches our human sympathy. This occurs whenever a clever but evil person is deceived, as Sisyphus, or a brave but unjust man is defeated. Such an event is probable, as Agathon says, because it is probable for many things to occur contrary to probability.

It is necessary to consider the chorus as one of the actors and as an integral part of the drama; its involvement in the action should not be in Euripides' manner but in Sophocles'. In the hands of our later poets, the songs included in the play are no more a part of that particular plot than they are of any other tragedy. They have been sung, therefore, as inserted pieces from the time Agathon first introduced this practice. And yet what difference does it make whether one sings an inserted song or adopts a speech or a whole episode from one play into another?

**19**

We have already spoken about other matters; it remains for us to discuss diction and thought. Concerning thought, let it be taken as given what we have written in the *Rhetoric*, for this is more appropriately a subject of that discipline. All those matters pertain to thought that must be presented through speech; and they may be subdivided into proof and refutation and the production of emotional effects, for example, pity or fear or anger or other similar emotions. Indications of the importance or insignificance of anything also fall under this heading. It is clear that we must employ thought also in actions in the same ways [as in speech] whenever we aim at the representation of the pitiable, the terrible, the significant, or the probable, with the exception of this one difference — that the effects arise in the case of the incidents without verbal explanation, whereas in the speech they are produced

by the speaker and arise because of the speech. For what would be the function of the speaker if something should appear in the way that is required without being dependent on the speech?

Concerning diction one kind of study involves the forms of diction that are investigated by the art of elocution and are the concern of the individual who considers this his guiding art, for example, what a command is and what a prayer is, what a statement is, and threat and question and answer and any other such matters. For in regard to the knowledge or ignorance of these matters, no censure worth taking seriously can be made against the art of poetry. Why should any one accept as an error Protagoras's censure of Homer on the grounds that when he said, "Sing, O goddess, of the wrath . . ." he gave a command, although he really wished to utter a prayer. For Protagoras says to order someone to do something or not is a command. Let us, therefore, disregard such a consideration as being a principle of some other art, not the art of poetry.

**20**

The following parts comprise the entire scope of diction: letter, syllable, connective, noun, verb, inflection and sentence. A letter is an indivisible sound; not every such sound is a letter, however, but only one from which a compound sound can be constructed. For I would call none of the individual sounds uttered by wild animals letters. The subdivisions of this category of "letters" are vowel, semivowel, and mute. A vowel is a sound that is audible without the contact of any of the physical structures of the mouth,[23] a semivowel is a sound that is audible with the contact of some of the physical structures of the mouth, for example, the S and R sounds; and a mute is a letter produced by the contact of the physical structures of the mouth, but inaudible in itself, although it becomes audible when it is accom-

[23] I have followed Butcher and Hardy in seeing this passage as a reference to the physical means of producing speech. Bywater disputes this interpretation and argues that the ambiguous term *prosbole* does not refer to the impact of the physical structures of the mouth but to the addition of one letter to another. [Tr.]

panied by letters that are sounded, for example, the *G* and *D* sounds. These letters differ in the positions taken by the mouth to produce them, in the places in the mouth where they are produced, in aspiration and smoothness, in being long or short and, furthermore, in having an acute, grave, or middle [circumflex] pitch accent. The detailed investigation concerning these matters belongs to the study of metrics.

A syllable is a nonsignificant sound constructed from a mute and a vowel. For, indeed, *GR* without an *A* is a syllable and also with it, for example, *GRA*. However, it is the business of the art of metrics also to investigate distinctions in this area.[24]

A connective is a nonsignificant sound that neither hinders nor promotes the creation of one significant sound from many sounds and that it is not appropriate to place at the beginning of a speech that stands independently, for example, *men, dē, toi, de*. Or it is a nonsignificant sound that is naturally able to make one significant sound from a number of sounds, for example, *amphi, peri*, and others like them. There is also a kind of connective that is a nonsignificant sound that shows the beginning, end, or division of a sentence and that may naturally be placed at either end or in the middle of a sentence.

A noun is a compound significant sound, not indicating time, no part of which is significant by itself. For in compound nouns we do not consider each part of the compound as being significant in itself; for example, in the name "Theodore" the root *dor* [gift] has no significance.

A verb is a compound significant sound indicating time, no part of which is significant by itself in the same way as has been indicated in regard to nouns. For "man" or "white" do not tell us anything about "when"; but "he goes" or "he has gone" indicate the present and the past.

Inflection is a characteristic of a noun or verb signifying the genitive or dative relation, or other similar ones, or indicating the singular or plural, that is, man or men, or is concerned with matters that fall under the art of elocution, for example,

questions and commands; for the phrases, "Did he go?" or "Go!" involve inflections of the verb in regard to these categories.

A speech is a compound, significant sound some of whose parts are significant by themselves. For not every speech is composed of verbs and nouns but it is possible to have a speech without verbs (for example, the definition of man). However, part of the speech will always have some significance, for example, "Cleon" in the phrase "Cleon walks." A speech is a unity in two ways. Either it signifies one thing or it is a unity through the joining together of many speeches. For example, the *Iliad* is a unity by the process of joining together many speeches, and the definition of man by signifying one thing.

**21**

Nouns are either simple, by which I mean constructed solely from nonsignificant elements, for example *gē* [earth], or compound. This latter category is divided into nouns that are constructed from both significant and nonsignificant elements (except that neither element is significant within the compound word itself) and nouns that are composed solely out of significant elements. Nouns may also be made up of three, four, or more parts, for example, many of the words in the Massilian vocabulary, such as Hermocaicoxanthus. . . .[25]

Every word is either standard, or is a strange word, or is a metaphor, or is ornamental, or is a coined word, or is lengthened, or contracted, or is altered in some way. I mean by standard, words that everyone uses, and by a strange word, one that foreigners use. Thus, it is apparent, the same word can be both strange and ordinary but not, of course, to the same persons. The word *sigunon* [spear] is ordinary for the Cyprians and strange to us.

Metaphor is the transference of a name from the object to which it has a natural application; this transference can take place from genus to species or species to genus or from species to

[24]The passage that begins here is corrupt and contains many difficulties of interpretation. [Tr.]

[25]There is a lacuna in the text here. Some editors accept Diel's conjecture, "praying to father Zeus," as the completion of this line. [Tr.]

species or by analogy. I mean by from genus to species, for example, "This ship of mine stands there." For to lie at anchor is a species of standing. An example of the transference from species to genus, "Odysseus has truly accomplished a myriad of noble deeds." For a myriad is the equivalent of "many," for which the poet now substitutes this term. An example of the transference from species to species is "having drawn off life with a sword" and also "having cut with unyielding bronze." For here to draw off is to cut and to cut is called to draw off, for both are subdivisions of "taking away."

I mean by transference by analogy the situation that occurs whenever a second element is related to a first as a fourth is to a third. For the poet will then use the fourth in place of the second or the second in place of the fourth, and sometimes poets add the reference to which the transferred term applies. I mean, for example, that a cup is related to Dionysus as a shield is to Ares. The poet will, therefore, speak of the cup as the shield of Dionysus and the shield as the cup of Ares. The same situation occurs in regard to the relation of old age to life and evening to day. A poet will say that evening is the old age of day, or however Empedocles expressed it, and that old age is the evening of life or the sunset of life. In some situations, there is no regular name in use to cover the analogous relation, but nevertheless the related elements will be spoken of by analogy; for example, to scatter seed is to sow, but the scattering of the sun's rays has no name. But the act of sowing in regard to grain bears an analogous relation to the sun's dispersing of its rays, and so we have the phrase "sowing the god-created fire."

It is also possible to use metaphor in a different way by applying the transferred epithet and then denying some aspect that is proper to it — for example, if one should call the shield not the cup of Ares but the wineless cup.[26] A coined word is one that is not in use among foreigners but is the invention of the poet. There seem to be some words of this type, for example, horns

[*kerata*] called "sprouters" [*ernuges*], and a priest [*iereus*] called "supplicator" [*arētēr*].

A word may be lengthened or contracted. It is lengthened if it makes use of a longer vowel than is usual for it, or a syllable is inserted in it; and it is contracted if any element is removed from it. An example of lengthening is *poleōs* to *poleōs* and *Pēleidou* to *Pēlēiadeō*; an example of contraction is *krī* and *dō* and *ops* in "*mia ginetai amphoterōn ops.*"

A word is altered whenever a poet utilizes part of the regular name for the object he is describing and invents part anew, for example, in the phrase "*deksiteron kata mazon*" the use of *deksiteron* in place of *deksion*.[27]

Nouns are subdivided into masculine, feminine, and neuter. Those are masculine that end in nu, rho, and sigma and in the two letters psi and ksi that are constructed in combination with sigma. Those nouns are feminine that end in the vowels that are always long, the eta and omega, and that end (in regard to the vowels subject to lengthening) in the lengthened alpha. Thus it turns out that there are an equal number of terminations for masculine and feminine nouns since psi and ksi are subdivisions of sigma. No noun ends in a mute nor in a short vowel. Only three end in iota, *meli, kommi, peperi*, and five end in upsilon. Neuter nouns end in these vowels and in nu and sigma.

## 22

Diction achieves its characteristic virtue in being clear but not mean. The clearest style results from the use of standard words; but it is also mean, as can be seen in the poetry of Cleophon and Sthenelus. A really distinguished style varies ordinary diction through the employment of unusual words. By unusual I mean strange words and metaphor and lengthened words and everything that goes beyond ordinary diction. But if someone should write exclusively in such forms the result would either be a riddle or a barbarism. A riddle will result if someone writes exclusively

---

[26]Editors have noted that a definition of the term "ornamental word" belongs in the text at this point, although it is missing from the manuscripts. [Tr.]

[27]The phrase quoted comes from the *Iliad* 5:393 and means "at her right breast." Two words meaning "right" are quoted to illustrate Aristotle's point here. [Tr.]

in metaphor; and a barbarism will result if there is an exclusive use of strange words. For it is in the nature of a riddle for one to speak of a situation that actually exists in an impossible way. Now it is not possible to do this by the combination of strange words; but it can be done by metaphor, for example, "I saw a man who welded bronze on another man by fire," and other metaphors like this. A statement constructed exclusively from strange words is a barbarism.

It is therefore necessary to use a combination of all these forms. The employment of strange words and metaphor and ornamental words and the other forms of speech that have been mentioned will prevent the diction from being ordinary and mean; and the use of normal speech will keep the diction clear. The lengthening and contraction of words and alterations in them contribute in no small measure to the diction's clarity and its elevation above ordinary diction. For because such words are different they will prevent the diction from being ordinary through their contrast with the ordinary expression; and because they have a share in the customary word, they will keep the diction clear.

Thus, the criticism is not well-taken on the part of those who censure this way of using language and who mock the poet, as the elder Euclid did, on the grounds that it is easy to write poetry if you are allowed to lengthen forms as much as you want; Euclid composed a satiric verse in the very words he used, *Epicharēn eidon Marathōnade badizonta* and *ouk an g'eramenos ton ekeinou elleboron.*[28]

Now then, the employment of the technique of lengthening in excess is ridiculous, and moderation is a quality that is commonly needed in all aspects of diction. For, indeed, if one employs metaphors and strange words and other forms in an inappropriate way and with intended absurdity, he can also accomplish the same effect. When the ordinary words are inserted in the verse, it can be seen how great a difference the appropriate use of lengthening makes in epic poetry. If someone should also change the strange words and metaphors and other forms to ordinary words, he would see the truth of what we have said. For example, Aeschylus and Euripides wrote the same iambic line, but Euripides changed one word and instead of using a standard one employed a strange one; his line thus has an elegance to it, whereas the other is mean. For Aeschylus wrote in his *Philoctetes*:

*phagediana hē mou sarkas esthiei podos*
[this cancerous sore eats the flesh of my leg].

Euripides in place of "eats" substitutes *thoinatai* [feasts upon]. A similar situation would occur in the line

*nun de m'eōn oligos te kai outidanos kai aeikēs*[29]

if someone should substitute the ordinary words

*nun de m'eōn mikros te kai asthenikos kai aeidēs*

or if we changed the line

*diphron aeikelion katatheis oligēn te trapezan*[30]

to

*diphron moxtheῤon katatheis mikran te trapezan*

or for *ēiones booōsin*, we substituted *ēiones krazousin*.[31] Furthermore, Ariphrades mocked the tragedians because no one would use their style in conversation; for example, the word order *dōmatōn apo* in place of *apo dōmatōn*, and the word *sethen*, and the phrase *egō de nin*, and the word order *Achilleōs peri* in place of *peri Achilleōs*, and many other similar expressions. For he missed the point that the virtue of all these expressions is that they create an unusual element in the diction by their not being in ordinary speech.

It is a matter of great importance to use each of the forms mentioned in a fitting way, as well

---

[28]This passage offers a number of difficulties in text and interpretation. The essential point is that the prosaic lines quoted can be technically turned into verse if enough licenses are allowed. The first phrase may be translated "I saw Epichares going to Marathon." The text of the second phrase is corrupt and does not have a clear meaning as it stands. [Tr.]

[29]A passage quoted from *Odyssey* 9:515, meaning "someone small, worthless, and unseemly." [Tr.]

[30]A passage quoted from *Odyssey* 20:259 meaning "having set down [for him] an unseemly chair and a small table." [Tr.]

[31]A passage quoted from *Iliad* 17:265 meaning "the shores cry out." [Tr.]

as compound words and strange ones, but by far the most important matter is to have skill in the use of metaphor. This skill alone it is not possible to obtain from another, and it is, in itself, a sign of genius. For the ability to construct good metaphors implies the ability to see essential similarities.

In regard to words, compounds are especially suitable for dithyrambs, strange words for heroic verse, and metaphors for iambic verse; in heroic verse all the forms mentioned are serviceable; but in iambic verse, because as much as possible it imitates conversation, only those words are appropriate that might be used in prose.

Of this nature are standard words, metaphors, and ornamental words.

Now, then, concerning tragedy and the imitation that is carried out in action, let what has been said suffice.

## 23

Concerning that form of verse imitation that is narrative, it is necessary to construct the plot as in tragedy in a dramatic fashion, and concerning a single action that is whole and complete (having a beginning, middle, and end) so that, like a single integrated organism, it achieves the pleasure natural to it.

The composition of incidents should not be similar to that found in our histories, in which it is necessary to show not one action but one period of time and as many things as happened in this time, whether they concern one man or many, and whether or not each of these things is related to the others. For just as there occurred in the same period of time a sea battle at Salamis and a battle with the Carthaginians in Sicily, but these did not at all lead to a common goal, thus also in the sequence of time, occasionally one event happens after another without there being a common goal to join them.

However, almost all the poets commit this error. Also in this, then, Homer would appear to be of exceptional skill in relation to other poets, as we have already said, since he did not attempt to write about the complete war, although it had a beginning and end; for that would have been a very large subject and could not have been taken

in easily in a single view; or even if its magnitude were moderate, the story still would be tangled because of the diversity of incidents. But note how although treating only one part of the war, he also introduces many of the other episodes in the war, for example, the catalogue of ships and others, by which he gives variety to his poem. Others write about one man and about one period and one action with diverse parts, for example, the poet who wrote the *Cypria* and the *Little Iliad*. Therefore from the *Iliad* and *Odyssey* one or two tragedies apiece are constructed; but from the *Cypria* many tragedies are constructed and from the *Little Iliad* eight, for example, *The Award of the Arms, Philoctetes, Neoptolemus, Eurypylus, The Beggar, The Laconian Woman, The Sack of Troy, The Return Voyage*, and a *Sinon*, and a *Women of Troy*.[32]

## 24

Moreover, it is necessary for epic poetry to exhibit the same characteristic forms as tragedy; for it is either simple or complex, displays character or suffering, and is composed of the same parts, with the exception of song and spectacle. In epic, there is also a necessity for reversals, recognitions, and the depiction of suffering. Here too, thought and diction must be handled with skill. Homer used all these elements first and in a proper way. For each of his poems is well-constructed; the *Iliad* is simple and exhibits suffering, whereas the *Odyssey* is complex (for there is recognition throughout) and shows character. In addition to these matters, Homer outstrips all others in diction and thought.

Epic differs from tragedy in regard to the length of the plot, and the meter. The sufficient limit of length has been mentioned, for we have noted that it must be possible to take in the plot's beginning and end in one view. This would occur if the plots were shorter than those of the old epics but would extend to the length of the number of tragedies that are designated for one performance. For the purpose of extending its

[32]Butcher and Kassel bracket the names of the last two plays as being later additions to the original text of the *Poetics*. [Tr.]

length, epic poetry has a very great capacity that is specifically its own, since it is not possible in tragedy to imitate many simultaneous lines of action but only that performed by the actors on the stage. But because of the narrative quality of epic it is possible to depict many simultaneous lines of action that, if appropriate, become the means of increasing the poem's scope. This has an advantage in regard to the elegance of the poem and in regard to varying the interest of the audience and for constructing a diverse sequence of episodes. For the rapid overloading of tragedies with the same kind of incident is what makes tragedies fail.

The heroic meter has been found appropriate to epic through practical experience. If someone should write a narrative imitation in another meter, or in a combination of meters, we would feel it to be inappropriate. For the heroic is the stateliest and most dignified meter, and therefore it is especially receptive to strange words and metaphors, for narrative poetry in this regard is exceptional among the forms of imitation; the iambic and the trochaic tetrameter are expressive of motion, the latter being a dance meter and the former displaying the quality of action. Furthermore, it makes a very strange impression if someone combines these meters as Chairemon did. Therefore, no one has written a long poem in a meter other than the heroic; but, as we said, nature herself teaches us to choose the appropriate meter.

Homer deserves praise for many qualities and, especially, because alone of the poets he is not ignorant of the requirements of his craft. For it is necessary for the poet himself to speak in his own person in the poem as little as possible, because he is not fulfilling his function as an imitator when he appears in this way. Now the other poets are themselves active performers throughout the poem, and they perform their imitative function infrequently and in regard to only a few objects. Homer, on the other hand, when he has made a brief prelude immediately brings in a man or woman or some other character; and all his figures are expressive of character, and none lacks it.

Now then, it is necessary in tragedy to create the marvelous, but the epic admits, even more, of the irrational, on which the marvelous especially depends, because the audience does not see the person acting. The whole business of the pursuit of Hector would appear ridiculous on the stage with some men standing about and not pursuing and Achilles nodding at them to keep them back; but in the narrative description of epic, this absurdity escapes notice.

The marvelous is pleasant, and the proof of this is that everyone embellishes the stories he tells as if he were adding something pleasant to his narration. Homer has especially taught others how it is necessary to lie, and this is through the employment of false reasoning. For whenever one event occurs or comes into existence and is naturally accompanied by a second event, men think that whenever this second event is present the first one must also have occurred or have come into existence. This, however, is a fallacy. Therefore, if the first event mentioned is false but there is another event that must occur or come into existence when the first event occurs, we feel compelled to join the two events in our thought. For our mind, through knowing that the second event is true, falsely reasons that the first event must have occurred or have come into existence also. There is an example of this type of fallacy in the Bath Scene in the *Odyssey*.

The use of impossible probabilities is preferable to that of unpersuasive possibilities. We must not construct plots from irrational elements, and we should especially attempt not to have anything irrational at all in them; but if this is not possible, the irrational should be outside the plot (as in Oedipus's ignorance of how Laius died); it should not be in the drama itself, as occurs in the *Electra* concerning those who bring news of the Pythian games, or in the *Mysians*, concerning the man who has come from Tegea to Mysia without speaking. To say that without the use of such incidents the plot would have been ruined is ridiculous. For it is necessary, right from the beginning, not to construct such plots.

If the poet takes such a plot and if it appears to admit of a more probable treatment, the situation is also absurd,[33] since it is clear that even

[33]Butcher and Hardy, following a different punctuation of

the improbable elements in the *Odyssey* concerning the casting ashore of Odysseus would not be bearable if a poor poet had written them. Here the poet conceals the absurdity by making it pleasing through his other skillful techniques. It is necessary to intensify the diction only in those parts of the poem that lack action and are unexpressive of character and thought. For too brilliant a diction conceals character and thought.

## 25

Concerning the number and character of the problems that lead to censure in poetry and the ways in which this censure must be met, the following considerations would be apparent to those who study the question. Since the poet is an imitator, like a painter or any maker of likenesses, he must carry out his imitations on all occasions in one of three possible ways. Thus, he must imitate the things that were in the past, or are now, or that people say and think to be or those things that ought to be. The poet presents his imitation in standard diction, as well as in strange words and metaphors and in many variations of diction, for we grant this license to poets. In addition to this, there is not the same standard of correctness for politics and poetry, nor for any other art and poetry. In regard to poetry itself, two categories of error are possible, one essential, and one accidental. For if the poet chose to imitate but imitated incorrectly through lack of ability[34] the error is an essential one; but if he erred by choosing an incorrect representation of the object (for example, representing a horse putting forward both right hooves) or made a technical error, for example, in regard to medicine or any other art, or introduced impossibilities of any sort, the mistake is an accidental, not an essential, one.

As a result, we must meet the criticisms of the problems encountered in poetry by taking these points into consideration. First, in regard to the problems that are related to the essential nature of art: if impossibilities have been represented, an error has been made; but it may be permissible to do this if the representation supports the goal of the imitation (for the goal of an imitation has been discussed) and if it makes the section in which it occurs, or another part of the poem, more striking. An example of such a situation is the pursuit of Hector in the *Iliad*. If, indeed, the goal of the imitation admits of attainment as well, or better, when sought in accordance with technical requirements, then it is incorrect to introduce the impossible. For, if it is at all feasible, no error should be committed at all. Further, we must ascertain whether an error originates from an essential or an accidental aspect of the art. For it is a less important matter if the artist does not know that a hind does not have horns than if he is unskillful in imitating one. In addition, the criticism that a work of art is not a truthful representation can be met by the argument that it represents the situation as it should be. For example, Sophocles said that he himself created characters such as should exist, whereas Euripides created ones such as actually do exist. If neither of the above is the case, the criticism must be met by reference to men's opinions, for example, in the myths that are told about the gods. For, perhaps, they do not describe a situation that is better than actuality, nor a true one, but they are what Xenophanes said of them — in accordance, at any rate, with men's opinions. Perhaps the situation described by the artist is not better than actuality but was one that actually existed in the past, for example, the description of the arms that goes, "The spears were standing upright on their butt spikes"; for once this was customary, as it is now among the Illyrians. Now to judge the nobility or ignobility of any statement made or act performed by anyone, we must not only make an investigation into the thing itself that has been said or done, considering whether it is noble or ignoble, but we must also consider the one who does the act or says the words in regard to whom, when, by

the text, interpret this passage to mean that it is possible to admit some element of the irrational to the plot; others feel that the Greek text does not make adequate sense as it stands. I have followed Bywater's punctuation and interpretation of this passage. [Tr.]

[34]There is a lacuna in the text here that I have filled by translating Bywater's suggested reading, *hēmarte de di'*. [Tr.]

what means, and for what purpose he speaks or acts — for example, whether the object is to achieve a greater good or to avoid a greater evil.

We must meet some kinds of criticism by considering the diction, for example, by reference to the use of a strange word, as in the phrase, *oureas men prōton*.[35] The word *oureas* here could cause some difficulty because perhaps the poet does not mean mules but guards. Dolon's statement, "I who was badly formed,"[36] has a similar difficulty involved in it; for he does not mean that he was misshapen in body but that he was ugly, because the Cretans use *eueidēs* [of fair form] to denote "handsome." A difficulty might arise in the phrase "mix the drink purer,"[37] which does not mean stronger, as if for drunkards, but faster. Difficulties arise in thoughts that are expressed in metaphors, for example, "All the gods and men slept the entire night through," which is said at the same time as "When truly he turned his gaze upon the Trojan plain, and hears the sound of flutes and pipes." "All" is used here metaphorically in place of "many," since "all" is some division of "many." The phrase "alone, she has no share"[38] shows a similar use of metaphor, since the best-known one is "alone." A problem may arise from the use of accent; Hippias the Thasian solved such a problem in the phrase, *didomen de oi* and similarly, in the phrase, *to men hoi katapythetai ombrō*.[39] Some difficulties are solved through punctuation, for example, in Empedocles' statement that "Suddenly things became mortal that had previously learned to be immortal and things unmixed before mixed."[40] Some problems are solved by

reference to ambiguities, for example, "more than two-thirds of night has departed" because "more" is ambiguous here.[41] Some difficulties are met by reference to customary usages in our language. Thus, we call "wine" the mixture of water and wine; and it is with the same justification that the poet writes of "a greave of newly wrought tin"; and iron workers are called *chalkeas*, literally, copper smiths; and it is for this reason that Ganymede is called the wine pourer of Zeus, although the gods do not drink wine. This would also be justified through metaphor.

Whenever a word seems to signify something contradictory, we must consider how many different meanings it might have in the passage quoted; for example, in the phrase "the bronze spear was held there," we must consider how many different senses of "to be held" are possible, whether by taking it in this way or that one might best understand it. The procedure is opposite to the one that Glaucon mentions in which people make an unreasonable prior assumption and, having themselves made their decree, they draw their conclusions, and then criticize the poet as if he had said whatever they think he has said if it is opposed to their thoughts. We have had this experience in regard to discussion of the character Icarius.[42] People assume that he was a Spartan; but then it appears ridiculous that Telemachus did not meet him in Sparta when he visited there. Perhaps the situation is as the Cephallenians would have it, for they say that Odysseus married amongst them and that there was an Icadius involved, but no Icarius. Thus, it is probable that the difficulty has arisen through a mistake.

Speaking generally, the impossible must be justified in regard to the requirements of poetry, or in regard to what is better than actuality, or what, in the opinion of men, is held to be true.

---

[35]Quoted from *Iliad* 1:50. The phrase means "first of all, the mules." [Tr.]

[36]Quoted from *Iliad* 10:316. [Tr.]

[37]Quoted from *Iliad*, 11:202. [Tr.]

[38]Quoted from *Iliad* 18:489. [Tr.]

[39]The problem here is that words that are spelled the same way, when given different accents, change their meaning. In the first phrase quoted, *didomen* can be either a present indicative or an infinitive used as an imperative, depending on the way in which it is accented; in the second phrase, *ou* can be either a relative pronoun or a negative adverb, depending on the way in which it is accented. [Tr.]

[40]The problem treated here is the effect that punctuation has on the meaning of a sentence. Thus, by means of different

punctuations the word "before" in Empedocles' statement could be referred either to the phrase that precedes it, "things unmixed," or to the word that follows it, "mixed." [Tr.]

[41]The word "more" has a form in Greek that can also be translated as "full." [Tr.]

[42]In Homer, Icarius is Penelope's father. [Tr.]

In regard to the art of poetry, we must prefer a persuasive impossibility to an unpersuasive possibility. Perhaps it is impossible[43] for the kind of men Zeuxis painted to exist; but they illustrate what is better than the actual. For whatever is a model must express superior qualities. The irrational must be justified in regard to what men say and also on the grounds that it is, sometimes, not at all irrational. For it is reasonable that some things occur contrary to reason.

We must consider contradictions in the same way as the refutation of arguments is carried on: that is, with reference to whether the same object is involved, and in the same relationship, and in the same sense, so that the poet, indeed, has contradicted himself in regard to what he himself says or what a sensible person might assume. There is justifiable censure for the presence of irrationality and depravity where, there being no necessity for them, the poet makes no use of them, as Euripides' handling of Aegeus in the *Medea* (in regard to the irrational) or in the same poet's treatment of the character of Menelaus in the *Orestes* (in regard to depravity). Criticisms of poetry, then, derive from five sources: either that the action is impossible or that it is irrational or that is is morally harmful or that it is contradictory or that it contains technical errors. The answers to these criticisms must be sought from the solutions, twelve in number, that we have discussed.

**26**

The problem of whether epic or tragedy is the better type of imitation might be raised. For if whatever is less common is better, that art would be superior that is directed at the more discriminating audience; and it is very clear that the art that imitates every detail is common. For on the grounds that the audience does not see the point unless they themselves add something, the actors make quite a commotion; for example, the poorer sort of flute players roll about the stage if they must imitate a discus throw and drag their leader

about if they are playing the *Scylla*. Now tragedy is considered to be of the same character that our older actors attribute to their successors; for, indeed, Mynescus called Callippides an ape on the grounds of overacting, and such an opinion was also held about Pindarus. As these two types of actor are related to each other, so the whole art of tragedy is thought to be related to epic by some people, who then conclude that epic is oriented toward a reasonable audience that does not at all require gestures, but that tragedy is disposed toward a less sophisticated audience. If, then, tragedy is directed toward a more common audience, it would be clear that it is the inferior art form.

Now then, first, this accusation is made against the art of acting, not poetry, since it is possible to overdo gestures both in epic recitations as Sosistratus did, and in song competitions as Mnasitheus the Opuntian did. Then, too, not every movement is to be rejected, if dancing indeed is not to be condemned, but only the movements of the ignoble, a point that was criticized in Callippides and now in others, since, it was charged, they were not representing freeborn women. Further, tragedy even without action achieves its function just as epic does; for its character is apparent simply through reading. If, then, tragedy is better in other respects, this defect is not essential to it. We argue, next, that it *is* better since it contains all of the elements that epic has (for it is even possible to use epic meter in tragedy) and, further, it has no small share in music and in spectacle, through which pleasure is very distinctly evoked. Tragedy also provides a vivid experience in reading as well as in actual performance. Further, in tragedy the goal of the imitation is achieved in a shorter length of time (for a more compact action is more pleasant than one that is much diluted). I mean, for example, the situation that would occur if someone should put Sophocles' *Oedipus* into an epic as long as the *Iliad*. Further, the imitation of an epic story is less unified than that of tragedy (a proof of this is that a number of tragedies can be derived from any one epic). So that if epic poets write a story with a single plot, that plot is either presented briefly and appears to lack full

---

[43]Translating *kai ei adunaton*, suggested by Vahlen to fill a lacuna in the text at this point. [Tr.]

development, or, if it follows the accustomed length of epic, it has a watered-down quality (I mean, for example, if the epic should be composed of very many actions in the same way as the *Iliad* and *Odyssey* have many such elements that also have magnitude in themselves). And yet these poems are constructed in the best possible way and are, as much as possible, the imitations of a single action.

If, then, tragedy is superior in all these areas and, further, in accomplishing its artistic effect (for it is necessary that these genres create not any chance pleasure, but the one that has been discussed as proper to them), it is apparent that tragedy, since it is better at attaining its end, is superior to epic.

Now then, we have expressed our view of tragedy and epic, both in general, and in their various species, and of the number and differences in their parts, as well as of some of the causes of their effectiveness or ineffectiveness, and the criticisms that can be directed against them, and the ways in which these criticisms must be answered. . . .[44]

[44]One of our manuscripts, Riccardianus 46, continues the text briefly at this point. The continuation seems to read, "Now as to iambic poetry and comedy. . . ." [Tr.]

# Horace

65–8 B.C.

Quintus Horatius Flaccus was the son of a freed slave but received an excellent education in the private academies of Rome. Following the assassination of Julius Caesar, Horace fought in the ill-fated army of Marcus Brutus but was allowed to return to Rome at the amnesty. He served for a time as a clerk in government offices, but his talent as a poet and satirist came to the attention of Virgil, who introduced him to the renowned Roman patron Maecenas. Maecenas provided Horace with encouragement and money, and ultimately, the farm in the Sabine hills to which he retired.

The *Ars Poetica*, also known as the *Epistle to the Pisos*, was composed as a letter of advice in verse to the two sons of Lucius Calpurnius Piso, both of whom had poetic ambitions. Because it is a verse letter, it lacks the careful composition and exhaustive organization of a treatise on the art of poetry; Horace's aim was to blend witty reminders and sage maxims in an entertaining way.

Like Pope's *Essay on Criticism*, the *Ars Poetica* contains dozens of lines and phrases that passed into the Latin language (and to an extent into English) as proverbs or catch phrases. We still speak of "purple patches" in prose, a phrase Horace coined. *Bonus dormitat Homerus* is the familiar "even Homer sometimes nods." *Parturiunt montes, nascetur ridiculus mus* (the mountains labor, giving birth to a ridiculous mouse) has become an adage for any pretentious activity. (The meaning of some of Horace's maxims have become garbled over the years: *Ut pictura poesis* [a poem is like a picture] was Horace's way of saying that some poems repay close scrutiny while others appeal through their broad outlines; it has been misinterpreted to suggest that Horace saw spatial form in poetry.)

To a reader expecting system, the organization of the *Ars Poetica* can be baffling. It is traditionally divided into three parts: lines 1–41 are on *poesis* or subject matter; lines 42–294 on *poema* or technique; and lines 295–476 on *poeta* or the poet. But in fact, Horace's wildfire ideas always outrace any system or organization that can be devised, and the reader should be prepared for rapid and unexpected transitions from one topic to another.

In the Middle Ages and the Renaissance, the *Ars Poetica* was often regarded as a commentary on Aristotle's *Poetics*. Though undoubtedly Horace had read Aristotle and occasionally echoes some of his remarks, the two thinkers have little in common. Where Aristotle suggests that tragedy uses iambic meter because it is closest to natural human speech, Horace offers two other rationales: literary tradition and the fact that iambics are better able to drown out a noisy and inattentive audience. Aristotle's explanation derives from his principle of *mimesis*, Horace's from his understanding of the expectations and the physical boisterousness of the *audience*.

Although Horace pays lip service to *mimesis* from time to time, what is really important to him is audience response. The poet should stick to traditional subjects, he tells us, but treat them in a new way. Poetic language should be novel, but not too novel — and the only way of judging the mean here is by closely observing the audience and the literary marketplace. Regardless of his innate genius, the poet must learn his art, especially the conventions that guide his audience in their expectations. Some of these, like the use of iambics in drama, may be more than mere conventions: They may reflect enduring aspects of human nature. Others, like Horace's dictum that a tragedy should have neither more nor less than five acts, were pure formalities. From Horace's point of view, such a distinction makes no difference, and indeed, he does not differentiate between rules and conventions. All alike need to be observed if the poet is to succeed in gaining a hearing from a fastidious and often captiously critical audience.

At the center of the *Ars Poetica* is Horace's statement of the ultimate aim of poetry: *aut prodesse aut delectare*, to teach or to delight — or both if possible, because the poet's audience, made up of diverse types, will require both: the *equites*, the knightly class, insist upon amusement, while the *senatores* want profitable lessons. The poet must understand their demands — and even those of the middle classes, the "sellers of bean and chestnut-meal" who applaud what is simple and exciting.

Like Aristotle, Horace assumes that different genres have their proper subject matter, technical devices, and effects; for example, that tragedy will concern dire events, be written in the highest style, and cause the audience to weep. But while for Aristotle, genres come into existence as if by the laws of nature and are scientifically comprehensible as emergent outgrowths of natural human impulses, for Horace genres do not have to make sense: They are just *there*. They exist, by accident as far as he is concerned, as predefined parts of the literary scene into which the poet comes, and the poet learns their rules as any prudent traveler in a strange country would learn the laws.

Unlike Plato and Aristotle, Horace is very much the worldly philosopher, and it is possible to misunderstand and cheapen the values by which he operates. Though Horace tells us that the successful author "makes money for the Sosii" — the Roman family that ran an operation copying manuscripts much in demand — he is not a prostitute producing verses to order. It is not vulgar commercial success Horace worships. For Horace, the author's reward is not money but fame. His ambition is to be read and praised, his terror to be ignored or laughed at. For Horace the poet was not a private man, but a public servant, like a successful statesman or ruler; both wore their laurels with pride, and their rewards came from the same public source.

## Selected Bibliography

Brink, C. O. *Horace on Poetry*. Cambridge: Cambridge University Press, 1963.
D'Alton, J. F. *Horace and His Age*. London: Longmans Green, 1917.
Dettmer, Helena. *Horace: A Study in Structure*. Hildesheim and New York: Olms-Weidmann, 1983.

Goad, Caroline. *Horace in the English Literature of the Eighteenth Century*. New Haven: Yale University Press, 1918.

Hack, R. K. "The Doctrine of Literary Forms." *Harvard Studies in Classical Philology* 27 (1916): 1–65.

Herrick, Marvin T. *The Fusion of Horatian and Aristotelian Literary Criticism*. Urbana: University of Illinois Press, 1946.

Perrot, Jacques. *Horace*. New York: New York University Press, 1964.

Showerman, Grant. *Horace and His Influence*. London: Longmans Green, 1922.

Stack, Frank. *Pope and Horace: Studies in Imitation*. Cambridge and New York: Cambridge University Press, 1985.

West, David. *Reading Horace*. Edinburgh: Edinburgh University Press, 1967.

Wood, Allen G. *Literary Satire and Theory: A Study of Horace, Boileau, and Pope*. New York: Garland, 1985.

# The Art of Poetry

A painter who puts a horse's mane
on a man's neck — who pulls feathers
from canaries and doves and parrots and owls
and grows them on a sheep's back — who lets
the upper half of a beautiful woman come
to a bad end, wriggling like a black
fish: if he let you see her, friends,
could you keep your laughter down?
And books are like pictures, and any book
written as that canvas was slopped,
empty-brained, like a sick man's nocturnal
editions, will read like a portrait of a one-footed
    hero,
maybe blessed with a head at the top,
even resembling *Homo sapiens*
perhaps.

"Poets, like painters, can do as they like,
have always done what they pleased."

True: And as poet I need, and as critic I permit
    freedom — but not to let Africa lie down with
    Europe,
not to have snakes sleeping with birds,
lambs making love to tigers. Give an inflated ass
a windy plan, and an Olympian hope,
and he sews on purple patches

Translated by Burton Raffel.

of brilliant scenic descriptions,
a shady grove, Diana's peaceful altar,
and a lazy stream
in a pleasant meadow
tinkling clear,
or the mighty Rhine,
or the glorious arch of a rainbow —
though no one was visiting Diana,
there were no streams,
no rivers,
no rain for the poet's bow.
No.
But maybe you can design a cypress
in the wind? For a portrait — paid in cash —
of a *sailor swimming to shore*, his ship
ground in the rocks? The potter's wheel
starts on a wine jar: whoops, a pitcher.
What?
Oh let it be what it wants to,
but let it be what it is,
just what it is; please.

Most poets, leaders and led, chase a will-o'-the-
    wisp
of abstract Right. Thus:
    I aim at concision, I hit on darkness;
    I aim to be smooth, my lines go slack;
    the eloquent idealist rants and raves;
    the timid, the gutless, crawl like beetles;

seekers after novelty hang dolphins in
        trees,
    float a boar in the sea:
    rare effects,
    marvelous:
    ugh.
Even if critics can't bite you
you can be hangdog dull, Witness painters
who draw exquisite nails,
sculptors who can curl bronze
like a Roman barber, but can't paint pictures,
can't turn out statues that stand and stare back.
Not for me: who wants to walk around
with split and dripping nostrils and have people
    praise
your fine black hair, your deep dark eyes?
Writers!
Write what you can, and
think: can you really? really?
Words will flow, order and ideas
will feed at your hand,
if you pick what is yours.


Order: is: I think:
just this:
Saying, now, what now needs said;
not saying, now, everything that can be left un-
    said for some other more appropriate time.
Take one part, hold back on another;
and blend words like pigment, slowly,
cautiously; be proud if some clean metal
comes up out of the slag heap,
some tired phrase shines.
Invent words, if new ideas need them;
don't look over your shoulder, the graybeards
won't like you whatever you do.
Freemen are right to relish freedom but not
to roll in it,
arrogant.
New words are good words, no matter who
    makes them,
if Greek gets poured into Latin, but drop by drop.
Who the hell is Plautus, to have
what Virgil and Varius cannot?[1]

---

[1]Horace's point is that Plautus, a century earlier, had
made new Latin words out of good Greek ones, but his
contemporaries Virgil and Varius were being criticized for
the same artistic license. [Ed.]

And who needs to envy me, if I coin
some new ones,
when Cato made bushels, and Ennius,
and left our Latin richer?
Words from living mouths
slide easily into poetry.
Forests turn and change, grow leaves,
drop leaves; so old words die, while
new ones run like boys.
Death will take us all, in the end: no matter
if Neptune shelters or sinks our ships,
or some enemy fleet; if the soggy marsh,
where boats ran, spills out, is tilled
and feeds cities; if the once-wild river
is tamed, cherishing trees
instead of drowning them —
Everything mortal dies; beautiful
language is easily broken.
Dead words shall live
and live words shall die,
and only the mouths of men can decide;
only what's said is said
and therefore alive. And therefore correct.

Homer made meters for war
and kings and the deeds of great men.
(Who sang the first songs of sorrow, and of love,
and the two together, is a scholar's argument
unsettled still.) Angry Archilochus
put his rage into iambs; and comedy,
and tragedy, walked in his shoes, shaping talk
for the stage.
(And an actor must be heard.)
And the songs we sing are sung for the Gods,
and the sons of the Gods,
and for Olympic winners,
and for fast horses,
and the painful love of young men,
and the freedom of wine.
And why am I a poet, and praised,
if not because I see differences,
and know them, and mark them
just as they are? To blush at wisdom
is to lie; I'd rather learn.
Thus:
Comic themes need comic verse;
Thyestes' gory supper can't stand
a vulgar tone, a comic tint.
Everything in its place,

I say. And still,
comedy can rail, swell, puff in anger; and
tragic heroes,
poor exiles,
must always forget their yard-long language,
to melt indifferent audiences.
Poems can be oh so beautiful
and dull: poets need charm, too,
to seduce our minds. We smile
when we see smiling, weep at tears:
ask me to sob when you can sob yourself —
then tragic heroes are tragic
to me. Not when words are mouthed
at me, never digested, square
in round red lips. I sleep, I laugh,
then. Let sad eyes weep,
angry ones burn,
sly ones wink,
harsh ones frown.

And in fact we are born
ready-makable, flexible in every emotion
to the touch of Nature's hands — and once
formed, ah, we show our lessons, our new-
    shaped minds,
with our tongues.
Let words jar with face or fortune
and Romans rich and poor will howl with laugh-
    ter.
A God speaks so, a hero
differently, or a ripe old man,
or a young man hot with passion;
so a patrician lady, so a pushy nurse;
so a footloose merchant, or a
farmer in his green furrows;
a man of Colchus or of Assyria,
of Thebes, or Argos. Different. Describe
either what is and has been
or what might well be.
Writers: Writers:
If Achilles
lives in your words, let him be brave,
angry, unbending, fierce, scoffing
at laws which were made for ordinary men;
arms are the thing, and himself.
Let Medea be a fearless witch, give Ino her tears,
make Ixion a dirty thief, Io a wanderer, Orestes
sorrowful. Or when you take your name
in your hands and invent

unknown people, let them come from your brain
in one piece, seamless, the same
from start to finish.
But literary property that belongs
to everybody
is the hardest
to invent well: poets who carve up
songs of ancient Troy,
constructing well-shaped plays,
work harder than poets who make it all up
as it falls on the page. Old stories
are yours for the working — *if* you walk some-
    where
off the beaten path and
forget the exact words of tradition and
*never* use the names without the substance
and spirit. But if you begin:
"O Muse, I sing Priam's fate and glorious war!"
oh Lord, where can you go, after such vigorous
boasting? The mountains will labor
and out will come
a shivering mouse.
But Homer, Homer, who dares nothing
he cannot be sure of doing: "Sing,
Muse, the man who, once Troy was down,
saw the ways of many men, and knew
their cities." His plan is not to use fire
to make smoke, but to turn smoke into light
and dazzle us with the dazzling sight of
        Antiphates
        and Scylla
        and Charybdis
        and the Cyclops.
And Homer hurries to the core, the reality:
he neither pegs Diomedes' return to the death of
    Meleager,
nor the Trojan War to Leda's double egg and
    Helen's birth.
No: Homer's reader soars *in medias res*,[2]
right where things happen, and in the way they
    happened
and we know they happened,
and nothing impossible to mention is mentioned,
only what the poet can polish and present
alive. Fictions are carefully crafted,
invention and history so blended

2"Into the middle of things." [Ed.]

that it does not matter whether middle or beginning
or end, everything is part of one single whole.

Listen: Do you understand
what we want of you,
poets? Are you listening?
If you want audiences to clap their hands instead
  of sitting on them,
to beat their hands, to bang their hands,
then watch men, learn men
and manners
and how a man ripens,
and changes, and grows. Boys
barely able to answer questions
walk like bipeds, they love other boys
to play with, they scream,
they smile, they change
hour by hour. Boys
grown almost men, but beardless, play
with horses and dogs
(no longer with tutors),
love grass and meadows and melt
to vice like slender candles, glower
at all guardians, produce
nothing, spend
everything, want
anything, enjoy
desperately, hate
soon — what they once loved. Men
full-grown chase after friends
and friends' friends,
cautious in risking
anything. And men
grown old suffer, rich
but afraid to spend, not daring to eat,
sick of living but sicker
at death's first breath, cold
and slow, endlessly
timid, greedy for time but trembling,
short-tempered, intolerant,
able to see only what they once saw,
bitter to boys and men
still growing old.
Flowers bring fruit as they come,
take sweetness with them as they go.
Writers: Keep senility
for the senile, adolescence
for boys, and let your audience

trust you to show that apples are
apples, pears pears.

What's on the stage is either what is
or what is said to be
though performed elsewhere.
What is heard, not seen, is weaker
in the mind than what the eyes record
faithfully as it happens. Yet
judge
for yourself what the eyes
must not see, leave to the ears
what belongs out of sight:
Actors' tongues can stir an audience
almost as well as actors' bodies:
Keep Medea in the darkness
as she butchers her sons, and Atreus
brewing human guts, and Procne
running for her raped life,
becoming a bird, and Cadmus
turning into a snake. What I cannot believe
I will loathe: let me believe
and I love.

Let a play end
    not sooner
    not later
but at the end
and be played
    so
    again.
Let Gods be Gods, not Gordian
knot untiers: unless the knot is truly Gordian
hard. Only three characters may
speak, not four.[3]
Let the chorus seem
like a living man, not
stand trilling irrelevant tunes
while the actors rest.
Let the chorus work for good
and for the good, and against
the angry, and let it help
the law-abiding and preach
abstinence, simplicity, justice and right

[3]Latin and Greek plays had more than three characters,
but by convention, no more than three speaking actors in
addition to the chorus were allowed on stage at the same
time. See Aristotle's *Poetics*, Ch. 4. [Ed.]

and the open gates of peace.
Let the chorus
keep its peace
and pray for the unlucky
and against the proud.

As for music:
Not the brass flute,
invented this morning to blare like a trumpet,
but the simple reed with simple stops:
This slender flute sounded the key
and kept the chorus in tune
and blew gently across a few rows
of patient listeners — few because
too many cannot be
      modest,
        decent,
cannot sit quietly together.
Rome first staggered the world, then swelled
to fill it up; spilling wine
in their Own Great Name,
Romans now feast like wild pigs,
swilling loud. And how
could clods and bankers
be quietly mixed, crooks and senators?
So musicians gave up being quiet,
grave, turned into strolling players,
sneered, leered,
pulled their sacred gowns like balloons
across the stage; the sober lyre was strung like a
    banjo;
actors learned a bright melodramatic bray; and
    our once-wise chorus
began to read tea-leaves like other
gypsies.

Playwrights (fighting for nothing more than
a goat) pushed a pack of naked satyrs
into the public eye, but tried
to stay sober and in all things
ennoble the stage, and audiences sat seduced,
coaxed,
titillated even in their drunken satisfaction,
ready to piss on Zeus. Naked satyrs
are good for a laugh: yes: but keep them, in the
    name of all that's holy,
away from gods, and keep gods (and heroes)
out of whorehouses, let them sound
a little less like dirty deities

floating up into empty space
    with empty spaces
      in their faces.
Tragedy and barroom ballads don't mix:
Senators' wives, dancing in festival streets,
are careful to hold their hems high. My friends:
If I wrote parts for satyrs
I'd let them speak some noble Latin, too,
and I'd have nobles speaking nobly,
slobs like slobs, professors like
professors, apes like apes.
I'd weave verse out of everyday stuff,
but I'd weave it —
and it would seem so easy
that anyone might try, and would, and would
sweat like a constipated horse,
trying.
It's all in the knowing how,
and when,
and where.
A rock is only a rock
if you can't cut diamonds out of it.
Wood fauns
running lightly on a stage
should never carry switchblades
or whistle at girls.
There are people, still, who have land,
and horses, and who know their father's name,
and care about these things,
and can be offended,
and have no interest in what pleases the bubble-
    gum buyers,
the soda-pop-crowd.

Fine: Now what about the rules
for writing poetry? We've got them:
Iambics, trochaics, spondees (a nice invention
and a new one), and we've got good Latin poets
who like one better than the other, or who like
    one
too much, and hang it like wet blankets
across sagging lines. (Are you listening,
Ennius?) Not everyone knows the rules:
too many of our poets
get away with too much.
Writers: So what?
When another Roman slops on a page
should I slop too,
and hope for the best?

Or, never slop, and never venture,
and never gain?
No one wins races by being afraid to run.
Read the Greeks.
Read them again.
And so what if Plautus was praised?
Did he deserve it? Shouldn't you
know the good from the stupid
for yourself? Train your ears?

Thespis (says the old tale) was the first to write
     tragedies,
he loaded his poems
onto carts, and carried them here and there
to be acted, to be sung,
by worshippers with wine-smeared faces.
And then Aeschylus invented actors' masks,
and noble costumes, and covered the stage
with boards, and taught players
to talk like gods, to stalk
like kings. And comedy was born,
and came to be famous, then fell,
from too much freedom, into
disgrace, and needed law to correct it,
and a law was framed, and the chorus
withered away, too used to smut and slander.

Our poets tried everything,
in time, dared to be different from Homer,
sang Latin things, Roman things;
some of them sang cheerful,
some sang sad,
many, many sang well.
And Rome would rule the world
of letters, too, if our poets —
all our poets, friends,
all — could stop to blot
and erase. My friends: Lock your desk
on uncorrected lines; poems
written nine times over are nothing,
ten is the beginning. Democritus
can prefer inspiration to perspiration,
he can keep sane poetry out of his poets' heaven,
but why let your nails curl black,
your beard hang dirty, why hide in foul corners
and stink like an uncombed goat?
(Democritus? Who's Democritus?)
Can you get to be a poet by hurting the barbers'
     business

or forgetting to purge poetry
and madness
away?


Ass, I'm an
ass, letting spring
purge me sweet:
bile is pure essence of verse
distilled. But is it worth
distilling?
No.
So let me play grindstone
instead of cutting edge:
at least a grindstone sharpens steel.
I will professor poetry, myself professing
nothing
(professors are well paid,
these days): dig here,
poets; drink this;
stand just so;
push the discipline button — whoosh!
— and then try if
vice
is nicer.
I'm serious: good sense
is everything, in art. Plato
is the best guide
to the best poems
of all: words wag on the stick
of substance.
Understand what your country asks of you
and your friends,
and how to love your father, your brother,
your new neighbor,
and what a senator owes
his country,
and a judge,
and how a general issues orders —
and you can create them living, breathing,
on the page.
Draw them as they are,
see them as they are,
let them talk as they talk.
A touch of reality
goes down better than the sound of sweet music,
even when the story is stale
and the point pointless.
Pretty Polly can sing all day

for no pennies: be in tune
with the turning world.

The Greeks sang for applause, and honor,
only applause, and honor,
and the gods gave them music.
But Romans grow up like accountants:
    "Tell me, son of Atticus:
    if there are five ounces
    and one is taken away
    how much is left?
    Tell me, at once:
    long division need not be
    quite so long."

    "A third of a pound."

    "Marvelous! You'll audit
    your own accounts,
    you will. Fine, fine.
    — But then, if we add
    an ounce? How much
    then?"

    "Half a pound."

Does anyone think poems worth rubbing with oil
    of cedar,
worth cherishing in cypress chests,
can come from minds
rusted with this money-grubbing
shit?
Poets should write for our profit,
delight us,
or neatly frame us a thought,
pass on good counsel.
Or both,
or all at once.
Whichever,
say it quickly, so he who runs
can listen, and hear, and learn,
and be better for learning.
A bursting head
opens like a bladder
and leaks away.
Imagine only what is almost
true, to delight us: Don't demand that we believe
whatever your cracked brain conceives for the
    stage,

don't feed an infant to Lamia and
let her swallow and chew,
then show him, squalling, whole,
pulled from her belly.
Ripe old wisdom balks at empty
display, and dandies won't dance
when the music's too slow.
Tame sense with a dash of sugar,
stroke your reader's cheek
while you box his ears:
Then everyone reads you,
your royalties mount like gushing oil,
foreigners run for your latest title
and read you long after you're dust.
Make your own memorial!

You'll make mistakes: we all do: sometimes
sin is forgiveable, sometimes
a plucked string goes YAW-YAW-YACK
instead of singing what you thought you'd sung,
sometimes
        A♯
        comes out
            when you've planned
        A♭
and even archers
miss
sometimes.
But the forest excuses a few misshapen trees:
Give me more good lines than bad
and I'll read you cheerfully,
in spite of bad luck
or a bit of bad judgment
and carelessness.
So? Writers:
A drunken clerk
copying over and over the same mistake
can be forgiven once, twice, three times,
maybe, but not forever.
A harper makes us wince
when he mucks up a passage
once,
but we laugh if he stumbles in the same place
over and over.
So a hardened poetic
sinner, forever irresponsible, sings
to my ears like famous Choerilus, to whom
I offer only laughter
even when (by accident?)

he turns out a gorgeous phrase;
I scowl,
too, when even Homer
nods, though Morpheus can't really be kept away
from a really long poem.
Poems are like pictures: stand
and stare and some look better
close up, some better
at a distance. There are things that shine
better in the dark; things that shine
only in bright light (where even critics
can screw up their eyes and — with awful
    sight —
see): things
pleasant the first time, others
pleasant again and again. My friend, older of my
    young friends:
You're shaped by your father's knowing voice
and you know, and you think, and
you understand, but
Listen:
        Remember this:
            In some things you've got to be good:
            flawed poets, medium-rare
            of talent, only halfway up the flag-
                pole,
            just aren't all right.
Some lawyers know their stuff
and can't turn it on like Messala (whose voice
    rolls like honey),
can't ever know what Cascellus knows (which is
    everything),
and yet they're all right.
Not poets. No one,
no god, no publisher,
cares about mediocre poets.
        It's like jangling drummers
        banging Beethoven's Fifth
        when the party's gay
        and everyone wants to sing.

        It's like a tablecloth soaked in perfume
        and strawberries blessed with poppy seeds.
        No one wants to eat such extravagant crap.
        The food is better left alone

        and so is the party.
And so are the poems
of mediocre poets: slip anywhere

and you're face down in the mud.
If you can't handle a short sword
you stay out of duels;
if you can't throw and you can't catch
you stay off the ball field
and sit still
and just watch
if you don't want rows and rows of spectators
laughing at your idiocies.
But EVERYONE writes poems,
Just e-v-e-r-y-o-n-e.

Why not?
Free and white (or black: it doesn't matter)
and twenty-one (or eighteen) (or less):
sure, and his father's well-known,
and his mother's virtuous,
and his grandfather left him an income,
and he's never been in jail.
O Lord.

But, my friends, my wise young friends,
not you: you'll speak
when wisdom speaks to you, act
when Jove tells you to;
you know, I know you know.
But if you do write —
anything,
ever —
read it to Mecius first (a first-rate critic)
and to your father
and to me,
and then lock it up for nine full years,
lock it up tight.
Anything that's safe in your desk
can be repaired, canceled,
amended; once it's published
it's gone out to the world
and can never come back.

Orpheus, with the gods speaking in his voice,
kept cannibals from their feasts,
held back tigers and raving lions;
Amphion builder of Thebes could move
stones with his lyre, could pray them
into place.
Ancient wisdom, which knew public
from private, knew what was holy
and what was not, and

told men that every woman they wanted
was not to be had; made rules for marriage;
built great cities;
carved law onto wood.
Fame and honor descended
on holy poets
and poems.
Homer
and then Tyrtaeus
inspired heroes.
The oracles spoke in rhyme
and ordered our lives,
and kings were courted with music, with song,
and festivals sung into being
— and I tell you this, friends,
to remind you what song
and Apollo
can do.

Art or Nature: which egg
opens into poetry? I could argue too,
but in fact how much can you do
if all you have is your effort?
What good is genius that can't scan or spell or
    parse?
It takes the two to tango
well.
Runners with everyone at their heels
have worked like horses
before the race, have sweated and shivered,
refrained when wine was offered,
refrained when women were offered.
The harper who sings for thousands
at the Pythian games started
nowhere, and sat awestruck at his teacher's
flying hands. But today?
    "Poems? I write ɛκsτRoARdinry poems"
— and that does it,
today.
    "Why should I get left out?
    Why should I be disgraced,
    admitting what I don't know,
    what I never learned?"
Like sideshow barkers
or peddlers at a fair
a poet who owns half a province
and has hundreds of interest-paying debtors
lets flatterers praise him
for profit.

Suppose a Roman
    who knows peas from onions
    steak from lamb chops
        and owns enough land to bail a friend
        with zero credit at the bank
        and who can hire lawyers
        for friends in trouble:
Can a man so rich, so blessed, tell, today,
an honest friend from a fake?
If you like to give presents, if you ever gave
    presents, if you intend to give presents, if you
    might ever want to give presents,
keep all your friends away when you read poems
in public, or they'll gush:
        "How charming!
        How fine!
        How true!
        How very very true!"
They'll faint with excitement, turn
pale with fear, weep
like a rainstorm (or ooze it out drop by drop),
leap
for joy, beat
time with their feet.
Like hired mourners, who grieve
more than widows and orphans, flatterers
praise beyond words: no honest man
could meet them on equal ground.
So emperors and kings fill cup after cup,
torture with wine, to find
a friend really a friend!
Writers: Poets: Foxes
in clever fur should never cheat you
with praise: Try Quintilius,
instead, and he'll tell you which lines
are bad, and why, and how to repair them
if repair is possible.
Try to tell him you've done your best
already, try to tell him how many times
you've tried, he'll still tell you which lines
are bad, and why, and how to repair them,
if repair is possible.
Try to argue, to show
how right you are, how wrong
Quintilius, and Quintilius
smiles and bows and lets you
strut unmatchable
on your imaginary pedestal.
Every honest man

with an ear
will tell you the same: A clinker
is a clinker
is a clinker.
And he'll tell you when you've raised
your voice too high, when
you've stumbled, wanting to dance
the most elegant dance
ever danced. If you've written darkness,
he'll call for light; if you've put six meanings
where only one will work, he'll ask for clarity;
he'll wince where you've wandered
and tumbled and coughed — in a word,
every honest man will seem like Aristarchus,
never worrying about your precious poetic ego
or the size of your mistakes (refuse to boggle at
   a minnow
and you might have to swallow a whale).
Mad poets are different: Admitted: Wise men
close their ears
and their doors, when a madman comes to
   read —
as welcome as a malignant itch
or a plague of yellow jaundice
or a moonstruck gorilla with sonnets in his arms.
Boys throw stones, when he walks declaiming
(but the foolish run after him):
head in the clouds, belching poems
like a sooty chimney, he staggers
up one aimless street, down another,
tumbling into ditches, into wells (like a hunter
watching birds instead of his feet),
yelling, "Help! Help!
     Oh your arms, citizens,
     your arms!"
— for hours,
but left where he lies,
no one willing to lend him
a hand. Suppose some fool
went to him, lowered a rope, told him politely
to climb, I'd ask just one question:

"Did he fall, or
did he jump?
Does he *want* to be saved?"
And I'd tell him about Empedocles, a Sicilian,
a poet, and mad, who wanted to become
a God
and leaped into burning Aetna,
eyes open.
Let poets die
when they want to;
it's as bad to save a poet against his will
as to kill one
unwilling to die. Who knows
how often he's fallen into a well
before,
or when he's pulled out
if
he'll stay out
forever, or leap to a hero's grave
all over again?
And who knows, indeed,
when a bad poet goes on making bad poems,
why he goes on and on and on and on and on
and on?
Maybe he's punishing himself for pissing
on his father's ashes, or for wrecking
a temple wall — but everyone knows
he's M-A-D, pure mad.
Like a bear in a cage, if he could break his bars
he'd roar poems without mercy
and drive off anyone who heard him,
the knowing, the unknowing — anyone.
And like a bear, let him fold you in his rapturous
arms
and his poems will choke you to death —
worse than a bear, a bloodsucking leech
who bites and sucks till your skin
is an empty bag, all your blood
drained dry.
(Do I hear one now?
Run for your life!)

# Longinus

## First Century A.D.

One of the most controversial aspects of "On the Sublime" has been its author-ship. The oldest manuscript, from the tenth century, calls the author "Dionysius Longinus." The name is too apt to be true. Each of its two halves belongs to a great Greco-Roman philosopher, Dionysius of Halicarnassus (who wrote under Augustus Caesar) and Cassius Longinus (who died nearly three centuries later, in A.D. 273). But neither of these men is a plausible candidate to have written "On the Sublime." The literary opinions of Longinus are inconsistent with those of Dionysius, while Cassius Longinus, who wrote during the most brutally chaotic period of the Empire, is unlikely to have penned Chapter 44, which discusses the causes of literary decline in an era of universal peace.

The style and historical allusions suggest a date during the quiet reigns of Nerva and Trajan, toward the end of the first century. The quotation in Chapter 4 from the Old Testament book of Genesis would be an extraordinary allusion for a pagan author to make, and it has been suggested that Longinus may have been either a Hellenized Jew (perhaps of the circle of Philo Judaeus[1]) or a Greek with Jewish connections.

Unlike Plato, who concerned hmself with common features of artistic works in general, Longinus is interested in a special quality, sublimity or elevation, which is possessed by some works but not others. Unlike Aristotle, whose poetics dealt with the particular characteristics of different literary forms, Longinus's sublimity is a quality that transcends generic boundaries. It can be found in drama or epic or lyric — or even in rhetoric or history or theology. Longinus's approach might be called "qualitative criticism," and it constitutes the third enduring method of literary theory, with descendants from Burke to Bakhtin. "On the Sublime" is related in one sense to the rhetorical criticism of Horace and others — its principal topics seem to be author, work, and audience — but where Horace differentiated between a high, a middle, and a low style, Longinus is concerned only with the first. And Longinus is far more methodical in exploring his more limited subject than Horace.

The argument of "On the Sublime" can be easily outlined. In Chapters 1 and 2 Longinus defines the Sublime as that quality within a discourse that produces "not persuasion but transport" (*ekstasis*) within the audience. He then questions whether there is such an art — whether it is purely a matter of inspiration or whether there are basic principles at work. Much of the actual argument itself has been lost, but from the rest of the essay, which presents five components of the art, it is clear on which side Longinus comes down. In Chapters 3 through 7, Longinus discusses the traps that lie on all sides of the target, those faults in literature that result from trying for the sublime and missing the mark. There are faults of commission, such

---

[1]Philo may be the "philosopher" in Ch. 44 whom Longinus attempts to confute.

as trying too hard (bombast, pedantry, hysteria), and there are faults of omission, such as frigidity of tone.

In Chapter 8, Longinus outlines the remainder of his essay, which successively treats the five sources (beyond language itself) of the Sublime. First are high thoughts (Chapters 9–15) and second, strong passions (not included but promised in a separate treatise), both of which are innate within the artist. Next are rhetorical figures (Chapters 16–29), then noble diction (Chapters 30–38 and 43), and finally, elevated composition (Chapters 39–42), all of which are the product of art and must be learned.

Just as important as Longinus's systematic method is the clarity and vigor with which he pursues it. He always has an apt quotation ready to exemplify a literary fault or grace, and for a judicial critic, there is nothing mean-spirited about his tone or temper.

Longinus's treatise "On the Sublime" was not influential in its own time. Its importance dates only from the Renaissance; it was published by Francesco Robortello in 1554 and translated by Nicolas Boileau in 1674. Soon thereafter it became common property, and poet-critics like John Dryden drew upon its central issues. During the eighteenth century, the Sublime was considered to be of great significance in opposition to the beautiful (a dichotomy treated by Edmund Burke, Immanuel Kant, and many others), and Longinus's brilliance as a critic was much appreciated. In his *Essay on Criticism*, Alexander Pope conveys the typical Augustan sentiments about the author of "On the Sublime":

> Thee, bold Longinus! all the Nine inspire,
> And bless their critic with a poet's fire:
> An ardent judge, who, zealous in his trust,
> With warmth gives sentence, yet is always just;
> Whose own example strengthens all his laws;
> And is himself that great Sublime he draws.

But Longinus was more admired than imitated in the eighteenth century — except on one occasion by Pope, who wrote a travesty of "On the Sublime" in "The Art of Sinking in Poetry," explaining (with delicious examples from contemporary works) the sources of the quality of Bathos. In the nineteenth century, his overt influence and reputation declined somewhat, perhaps owing to his antidemocratic political beliefs, but his method of qualitative criticism was paradoxically revived in thinkers like Matthew Arnold (*The Study of Poetry*), Walter Pater, and most recently Mikhail Bakhtin.

## Selected Bibliography

Apfel, Henrietta Veit. *Literary Quotation and Allusion in Demetrius' Peri hermeneias and Longinus' Peri hypsos.* New York: Columbia University Library, 1935.

Brody, Jules. *Boileau and Longinus.* Geneva: Droz, 1953.

Davidson, Hugh M. "The Literary Arts of Longinus and Boileau." In *Studies in Seventeenth-*

Century French Literature. Edited by Jean Demonest. Ithaca: Cornell University Press, 1962.

Henn, T. R. Longinus and English Criticism. Cambridge: Cambridge University Press, 1934.

Marin, Demetrio St. Bibliography of the Essay on the Sublime. N.p. 1967.

Olson, Elder. "The Argument of Longinus's On the Sublime." In On Value Judgments in the Arts and Other Essays. Chicago: University of Chicago Press, 1976.

Rosenberg, Alfred. Longinus in England. Berlin: Meyer und Müller, 1937.

Russell, D. A., ed. "Longinus" on the Sublime. Oxford: Clarendon Press, 1964.

# On the Sublime

I

You will remember, my dear Postumius Terentianus, that when we examined together the treatise of Caecilius on the Sublime, we found that it fell below the dignity of the whole subject, while it failed signally to grasp the essential points, and conveyed to its readers but little of that practical help which it should be a writer's principal aim to give. In every systematic treatise two things are required. The first is a statement of the subject; the other, which although second in order ranks higher in importance, is an indication of the methods by which we may attain our end. Now Caecilius seeks to show the nature of the sublime by countless instances as though our ignorance demanded it, but the consideration of the means whereby we may succeed in raising our own capacities to a certain pitch of elevation he has, strangely enough, omitted as unnecessary. 2. However, it may be that the man ought not so much to be blamed for his shortcomings as praised for his happy thought and his enthusiasm. But since you have urged me, in my turn, to write a brief essay on the sublime for your special gratification, let us consider whether the views I have formed contain anything which will be of use to public men. You will yourself, my friend, in accordance with your nature and with what is fitting, join me in appraising each detail with the utmost regard for truth; for he answered well who, when asked in what qualities we re-

semble the gods, declared that we do so in benevolence and truth. 3. As I am writing to you, my good friend, who are well versed in literary studies, I feel almost absolved from the necessity of premising at any length that sublimity is a certain distinction and excellence in expression, and that it is from no other source than this that the greatest poets and writers have derived their eminence and gained an immortality of renown. 4. The effect of elevated language upon an audience is not persuasion but transport. At every time and in every way imposing speech, with the spell it throws over us, prevails over that which aims at persuasion and gratification. Our persuasions we can usually control, but the influences of the sublime bring power and irresistible might to bear, and reign supreme over every hearer. Similarly, we see skill in invention, and due order and arrangement of matter, emerging as the hard-won result not of one thing nor of two, but of the whole texture of the composition, whereas Sublimity flashing forth at the right moment scatters everything before it like a thunderbolt, and at once displays the power of the orator in all its plenitude. But enough; for these reflections, and others like them, you can, I know well, my dear Terentianus, yourself suggest from your own experience.

2

First of all, we must raise the question whether there is such a thing as an art of the sublime or lofty. Some hold that those are entirely in error

Translated by W. Rhys Roberts.

who would bring such matters under the precepts of art. A lofty tone, says one, is innate, and does not come by teaching; nature is the only art that can compass it. Works of nature are, they think, made worse and altogether feebler when wizened by the rules of art. 2. But I maintain that this will be found to be otherwise if it be observed that, while nature as a rule is free and independent in matters of passion and elevation, yet is she wont not to act at random and utterly without system. Further, nature is the original and vital underlying principle in all cases, but system can define limits and fitting seasons, and can also contribute the safest rules for use and practice. Moreover, the expression of the sublime is more exposed to danger when it goes its own way without the guidance of knowledge — when it is suffered to be unstable and unballasted — when it is left at the mercy of mere momentum and ignorant audacity. It is true that it often needs the spur, but it is also true that it often needs the curb. 3. Demosthenes expresses the view, with regard to human life in general, that good fortune is the greatest of blessings, while good counsel, which occupies the second place, is hardly inferior in importance, since its absence contributes inevitably to the ruin of the former. This we may apply to diction, nature occupying the position of good fortune, art that of good counsel. Most important of all, we must remember that the very fact that there are some elements of expression which are in the hands of nature alone, can be learnt from no other source than art. If, I say, the critic of those who desire to learn were to turn these matters over in his mind, he would no longer, it seems to me, regard the discussion of the subject as superfluous or useless.

**3**

Quell they the oven's far-flung splendour-glow!
Ha, let me but one hearth-abider mark —
One flame-wreath torrent-like I'll whirl on high;
I'll burn the roof, to cinders shrivel it —
Nay, now my chant is not of noble strain.[1]

Such things are not tragic but pseudo-tragic — "flame-wreaths," and "belching to the sky," and

[1] Aeschylus, *Oreithia*. [Ed.]

Boreas represented as a "flute-player," and all the rest of it. They are turbid in expression and confused in imagery rather than the product of intensity, and each one of them, if examined in the light of day, sinks little by little from the terrible into the contemptible. But since even in tragedy, which is in its very nature stately and prone to bombast, tasteless tumidity is unpardonable, still less, I presume, will it harmonize with the narration of fact. 2. And this is the ground on which the phrases of Gorgias of Leontini are ridiculed when he describes Xerxes as the "Zeus of the Persians" and vultures as "living tombs." So is it with some of the expressions of Callisthenes which are not sublime but high-flown, and still more with those of Cleitarchus, for the man is frivolous and blows, as Sophocles has it,

On pigmy hautboys: mouthpiece have they none.

Other examples will be found in Amphicrates and Hegesias and Matris, for often when these writers seem to themselves to be inspired they are in no true frenzy but are simply trifling. 3. Altogether, tumidity seems particularly hard to avoid. The explanation is that all who aim at elevation are so anxious to escape the reproach of being weak and dry that they are carried, as by some strange law of nature, into the opposite extreme. They put their trust in the maxim that "failure in a great attempt is at least a noble error." 4. But evil are the swellings, both in the body and in diction, which are inflated and unreal, and threaten us with the reverse of our aim; for nothing, say they, is drier than a man who has the dropsy. While tumidity desires to transcend the limits of the sublime, the defect which is termed puerility is the direct antithesis of elevation, for it is utterly low and mean and in real truth the most ignoble vice of style. What, then, is this puerility? Clearly, a pedant's thoughts, which begin in learned trifling and end in frigidity. Men slip into this kind of error because, while they aim at the uncommon and elaborate and most of all at the attractive, they drift unawares into the tawdry and affected. 5. A third, and closely allied, kind of defect in matters of passion is that which Theodorus used to call *parenthyrsus*. By this is meant unseasonable and empty passion, where no passion is required, or immoderate, where moderation is needed. For men are often carried away, as if by intoxication, into displays of emotion which are not caused by the nature of the subject, but are purely personal and wearisome. In consequence they seem to hearers who are in no wise affected to act in an ungainly way. And no wonder; for they are beside themselves, while their hearers are not. But the question of the passions we reserve for separate treatment.

## 4

Of the second fault of which we have spoken — frigidity — Timaeus supplies many examples. Timaeus was a writer of considerable general ability, who occasionally showed that he was not incapable of elevation of style. He was learned and ingenious, but very prone to criticize the faults of others while blind to his own. Through his passion for continually starting novel notions, he often fell into the merest childishness. 2. I will set down one or two examples only of his manner, since the greater number have been already appropriated by Caecilius. In the course of a eulogy on Alexander the Great, he describes him as "the man who gained possession of the whole of Asia in fewer years than it took Isocrates to write his *Panegyric* urging war against the Persians." Strange indeed is the comparison of the man of Macedon with the rhetorician. How plain it is, Timaeus, that the Lacedaemonians, thus judged, were far inferior to Isocrates in prowess, for they spent thirty years in the conquest of Messene, whereas he composed his *Panegyric* in ten. 3. Consider again the way in which he speaks of the Athenians who were captured in Sicily. "They were punished because they had acted impiously towards Hermes and mutilated his images, and the infliction of punishment was chiefly due to Hermocrates the son of Hermon, who was descended, in the paternal line, from the outraged god." I am surprised, beloved Terentianus, that he does not write with regard to the despot Dionysius that "Dion and Heracleides deprived him of his sovereignty because he had acted impiously towards Zeus and Heracles." 4. But why speak of Timaeus when even those heroes of literature, Xenophon and Plato, though trained in the school of Socrates, nevertheless sometimes forget themselves for the

sake of such paltry pleasantries? Xenophon writes in the *Polity of the Lacedaemonians*: "You would find it harder to hear their voice than that of busts of marble, harder to deflect their gaze than that of statues of bronze; you would deem them more modest than the very maidens in their eyes."[2]

It was worthy of an Amphicrates and not of a Xenophon to call the pupils of our eyes "modest maidens." Good heavens, how strange it is that the pupils of the whole company should be believed to be modest notwithstanding the common saying that the shamelessness of individuals is indicated by nothing so much as the eyes! "Thou sot, that hast the eyes of a dog," as Homer has it.[3] 5. Timaeus, however, has not left even this piece of frigidity to Xenophon, but clutches it as though it were hid treasure. At all events, after saying of Agathocles that he abducted his cousin, who had been given in marriage to another man, from the midst of the nuptial rites, he asks, "Who could have done this had he not had wantons, in place of maidens, in his eyes?" 6. Yes, and Plato (usually so divine) when he means simply *tablets* says, "They shall write and preserve *cypress memorials* in the temples."[4]

And again, "As touching walls, Megillus, I should hold with Sparta that they be suffered to lie asleep in the earth and not summoned to arise."[5] The expression of Herodotus to the effect that beautiful women are "eye-smarts" is not much better.[6] This, however, may be condoned in some degree since those who use this particular phrase in his narrative are barbarians and in their cups, but not even in the mouths of such characters is it well that an author should suffer, in the judgment of posterity, from an unseemly exhibition of triviality.

## 5

All these ugly and parasitical growths arise in literature from a single cause, that pursuit of novelty in the expression of ideas which may be

[2]Xenophon, *On the Government of the Lacedaimonians* 3:5. [Tr.]
[3]Homer, *Iliad* 1:225. [Tr.]
[4]Plato, *Laws* 5:741c. [Tr.]
[5]Plato, *Laws* 6:778d [Tr.]
[6]Herodotus, *History* 5:18. [Tr.]

regarded as the fashionable craze of the day. Our defects usually spring, for the most part, from the same sources as our good points. Hence, while beauties of expression and touches of sublimity, and charming elegances withal, are favorable to effective composition, yet these very things are the elements and foundation, not only of success, but also of the contrary. Something of the kind is true also of variations and hyperboles and the use of the plural number, and we shall show subsequently the dangers to which these seem severally to be exposed. It is necessary now to seek and to suggest means by which we may avoid the defects which attend the steps of the sublime.

**6**

The best means would be, my friend, to gain, first of all, clear knowledge and appreciation of the true sublime. The enterprise is, however, an arduous one. For the judgment of style is the last and crowning fruit of long experience. Nonetheless, if I must speak in the way of precept, it is not impossible perhaps to acquire discrimination in these matters by attention to some such hints as those which follow.

**7**

You must know, my dear friend, that it is with the sublime as in the common life of man. In life nothing can be considered great which it is held great to despise. For instance, riches, honors, distinctions, sovereignties, and all other things which possess in abundance the external trappings of the stage, will not seem, to a man of sense, to be supreme blessings, since the very contempt of them is reckoned good in no small degree, and in any case those who could have them, but are high-souled enough to disdain them, are more admired than those who have them. So also in the case of sublimity in poems and prose writings, we must consider whether some supposed examples have not simply the appearance of elevation with many idle accretions, so that when analyzed they are found to be mere vanity — objects which a noble nature will rather despise than admire. 2. For, as if instinctively, our soul is uplifted by the true sub-lime; it takes a proud flight, and is filled with joy and vaunting, as though it had itself produced what it has heard. 3. When therefore, a thing is heard repeatedly by a man of intelligence, who is well versed in literature, and its effect is not to dispose the soul to high thoughts, and it does not leave in the mind more food for reflection than the words seem to convey, but falls, if examined carefully through and through, into disesteem, it cannot rank as true sublimity because it does not survive a first hearing. For that is really great which bears a repeated examination, and which it is difficult or rather impossible to withstand, and the memory of which is strong and hard to efface. 4. In general, consider those examples of sublimity to be fine and genuine which please all and always. For when men of different pursuits, lives, ambitions, ages, languages, hold identical views on one and the same subject, then that verdict which results, so to speak, from a concert of discordant elements makes our faith in the object of admiration strong and unassailable.

**8**

There are, it may be said, five principal sources of elevated language. Beneath these five varieties there lies, as though it were a common foundation, the gift of discourse, which is indispensable. First and most important is the power of forming great conceptions, as we have elsewhere explained in our remarks on Xenophon. Secondly, there is vehement and inspired passion. These two components of the sublime are for the most part innate. Those which remain are partly the product of art. The due formation of figures deals with two sorts of figures, first those of thought and secondly those of expression. Next there is noble diction, which in turn comprises choice of words, and use of metaphors, and elaboration of language. The fifth cause of elevation — one which is the fitting conclusion of all that have preceded it — is dignified and elevated composition. Come now, let us consider what is involved in each of these varieties, with this one remark by way of preface, that Caecilius has omitted some of the five divisions, for example, that of passion. 2. Surely he is quite mistaken if he does so on the ground that these two, sublimity and passion, are a unity, and if it seems to him that they are by nature one and inseparable. For some passions are found which are far removed from sublimity and are of a low order, such as pity, grief and fear; and on the other hand there are many examples of the sublime which are independent of passion, such as the daring words of Homer with regard to the Aloadae, to take one out of numberless instances,

> Yea, Ossa in fury they strove to upheave on Olympus on high,
> With forest-clad Pelion above, that thence they might step to the sky.[7]

And so of the words which follow with still greater force:

> Ay, and the deed had they done.

3. Among the orators, too, eulogies and ceremonial and occasional addresses contain on every side examples of dignity and elevation, but are for the most part void of passion. This is the reason why passionate speakers are the worst eulogists, and why, on the other hand, those who are apt in encomium are the least passionate. 4. If, on the other hand, Caecilius thought that passion never contributes at all to sublimity, and if it was for this reason that he did not deem it worthy of mention, he is altogether deluded. I would affirm with confidence that there is no tone so lofty as that of genuine passion, in its right place, when it bursts out in a wild gust of mad enthusiasm and as it were fills the speaker's words with frenzy.

## 9

Now the first of the conditions mentioned, namely elevation of mind, holds the foremost rank among them all. We must, therefore, in this case also, although we have to do rather with an endowment than with an acquirement, nurture our souls (as far as that is possible) to thoughts sublime, and make them always pregnant, so to say, with noble inspiration. 2. In what way, you may ask, is this to be done? Elsewhere I have written as follows: "Sublimity is the echo of a great soul." Hence also a bare idea, by itself and without a spoken word, sometimes excites admiration just because of the greatness of soul implied. Thus the silence of Ajax in the Underworld is great and more sublime than words.[8] 3. First, then, it is absolutely necessary to indicate the source of this elevation, namely, that the truly eloquent must be free from low and ignoble thoughts. For it is not possible that men with mean and servile ideas and aims prevailing throughout their lives should produce anything that is admirable and worthy of immortality. Great accents we expect to fall from the lips of those whose thoughts are deep and grave. 4. Thus it is that stately speech comes naturally to the proudest spirits. [You will remember the answer of] Alexander to Parmenio when he said "For my part I had been well content."[9] . . .

. . . the distance from earth to heaven; and this might well be considered the measure of Homer no less than of Strife. 5. How unlike to this the expression which is used of Sorrow by Hesiod, if indeed the *Shield* is to be attributed to Hesiod:

> Rheum from her nostrils was trickling.[10]

The image he has suggested is not terrible but rather loathsome. Contrast the way in which Homer magnifies the higher powers:

> And far as a man with his eyes through the sea-line haze may discern,
> On a cliff as he sitteth and gazeth away o'er the wine-dark deep,
> So far at a bound do the loud-neighing steeds of the Deathless leap.[11]

He makes the vastness of the world the measure of their leap. The sublimity is so overpowering as naturally to prompt the exclamation that if the divine steeds were to leap thus twice in succession they would pass beyond the confines of the world. 6. How transcendent also are the images in the Battle of the Gods:

---

[7]Homer, *Odyssey* 11:315–16. [Tr.]

[8]Homer, *Odyssey* 11:543. [Tr.]
[9]From Arrian's *Anabasis of Alexander*. A lacuna in the manuscript follows. [Ed.]
[10]Hesiod, *The Shield of Heracles*, 267. [Tr.]
[11]Homer, *Iliad* 5:770–72. [Tr.]

Far round wide heaven and Olympus echoed his
   clarion of thunder;
And Hades, king of the realm of shadows, quaked
   thereunder.
And he sprang from his throne, and he cried aloud
   in the dread of his heart
Lest o'er him earth-shaker Poseidon should cleave
   the ground apart,
And revealed to Immortals and mortals should
   stand those awful abodes,
Those mansions ghastly and grim, abhorred of the
   very Gods.[12]

You see, my friend, how the earth is torn
from its foundations, Tartarus itself is laid bare,
the whole world is upturned and parted asunder,
and all things together — heaven and hell, things
mortal and things immortal — share in the conflict and the perils of that battle!

7. But although these things are awe-inspir-
ing, yet from another point of view, if they be
not taken allegorically, they are altogether impious, and violate our sense of what is fitting.
Homer seems to me, in his legends of wounds
suffered by the gods, and of their feuds, repris-
als, tears, bonds, and all their manifold passions,
to have made, as far as lay within his power,
gods of the men concerned in the Siege of Troy,
and men of the gods. But whereas we mortals
have death as the destined haven of our ills if
our lot is miserable, he portrays the gods as
immortal not only in nature but also in misfortune. 8. Much superior to the passages respecting
the Battle of the Gods are those which represent
the divine nature as it really is — pure and great
and undefiled; for example, what is said of Poseidon in a passage fully treated by many before
ourselves:

Her far-stretching ridges, her forest-trees, quaked
   in dismay,
And her peaks, and the Trojans' town, and the
   ships of Achaia's array,
Beneath his immortal feet, as onward Poseidon
   strode.
Then over the surges he drave: leapt sporting before
   the God
Sea-beasts that uprose all around from the depths,
   for their king they knew,

And for rapture the sea was disparted, and onward
   the car-steeds flew.[13]

9. Similarly, the legislator of the Jews, no ordinary man, having formed and expressed a worthy
conception of the might of the Godhead, writes
at the very beginning of his Laws, "God said,"
— what? "Let there be light, and there was light;
let there be land, and there was land."[14] 10.
Perhaps I shall not seem tedious, my friend, if I
bring forward one passage more from Homer —
this time with regard to the concerns of *men* —
in order to show that he is wont himself to enter
into the sublime actions of his heroes. In his
poem the battle of the Greeks is suddenly veiled
by mist and baffling night. Then Ajax, at his
wits' end, cries:

Zeus, Father, yet save thou Achaia's sons from
   beneath the gloom,
And make clear day, and vouchsafe unto us with
   our eyes to see!
So it be but in light, destroy us![15]

That is the true attitude of an Ajax. He does not
pray for life, for such a petition would have ill
beseemed a hero. But since in the hopeless darkness he can turn his valor to no noble end, he
chafes at his slackness in the fray and craves the
boon of immediate light, resolved to find a death
worthy of his bravery, even though Zeus should
fight in the ranks against him. 11. In truth, Homer in these cases shares the full inspiration of
the combat, and it is neither more nor less than
true of the poet himself that

Mad rageth he as Arês the shaker of spears, or as
   mad flames leap
Wild-wasting from hill unto hill in the folds of a
   forest deep,
And the foam-froth fringeth his lips.[16]

He shows, however, in the Odyssey (and this
further observation deserves attention on many
grounds) that, when a great genius is declining,
the special token of old age is the love of mar-

---

[12]Homer, *Iliad* 20:61–65. [Tr.]

[13]Homer, *Iliad* 13:18–19, 27–29. The second line belongs
at the beginning of the last quotation; it is *Iliad* 20:60. [Ed.]
[14]Genesis 1:3, slightly misquoted. [Ed.]
[15]Homer, *Iliad* 17:645–47. [Tr.]
[16]Homer, *Iliad* 15:605–7. [Tr.]

velous tales. 12. It is clear from many indications that the Odyssey was his second subject. A special proof is the fact that he introduces in that poem remnants of the adventures before Ilium as episodes, so to say, of the Trojan War. And indeed, he there renders a tribute of mourning and lamentation to his heroes as though he were carrying out a long-cherished purpose. In fact, the Odyssey is simply an epilogue to the Iliad:

> There lieth Ajax the warrior wight, Achilles is there,
> There is Patroclus, whose words had weight as a God he were;
> There lieth mine own dear son.[17]

13. It is for the same reason, I suppose, that he has made the whole structure of the Iliad, which was written at the height of his inspiration, full of action and conflict, while the Odyssey for the most part consists of narrative, as is characteristic of old age. Accordingly, in the Odyssey Homer may be likened to a sinking sun, whose grandeur remains without its intensity. He does not in the Odyssey maintain so high a pitch as in those poems of Ilium. His sublimities are not evenly sustained and free from the liability to sink; there is not the same profusion of accumulated passions, nor the supple and oratorical style, packed with images drawn from real life. You seem to see henceforth the ebb and flow of greatness, and a fancy roving in the fabulous and incredible, as though the ocean were withdrawing into itself and were being laid bare within its own confines. 14. In saying this I have not forgotten the tempests in the Odyssey and the story of the Cyclops and the like. If I speak of old age, it is nevertheless the old age of Homer. The fabulous element, however, prevails throughout this poem over the real. The object of this digression has been, as I said, to show how easily great natures in their decline are sometimes diverted into absurdity, as in the incident of the wine-skin and of the men who were fed like swine by Circe (*whining porkers*, as Zoilus called them), and of Zeus like a nestling nurtured by the doves, and of the hero who was without food for ten days

upon the wreck, and of the incredible tale of the slaying of the suitors.[18] For what else can we term these things than veritable dreams of Zeus? 15. These observations with regard to the Odyssey should be made for another reason — in order that you may know that the genius of great poets and prose-writers, as their passion declines, finds its final expression in the delineation of character. For such are the details which Homer gives, with an eye to characterization, of life in the home of Odysseus; they form as it were a comedy of manners.

**10**

Let us next consider whether we can point to anything further that contributes to sublimity of style. Now, there inhere in all things by nature certain constituents which are part and parcel of their substance. It must needs be, therefore, that we shall find one source of the sublime in the systematic selection of the most important elements, and the power of forming, by their mutual combination, what may be called one body. The former process attracts the hearer by the choice of the ideas, the latter by the aggregation of those chosen. For instance, Sappho everywhere chooses the emotions that attend delirious passion from its accompaniments in actual life. Wherein does she demonstrate her supreme excellence? In the skill with which she selects and binds together the most striking and vehement circumstances of passion:

> 2. Peer of Gods he seemeth to me, the blissful
> Man who sits and gazes at thee before him,
> Close beside thee sits, and in silence hears thee
> Silverly speaking,
>
> Laughing love's low laughter. Oh this, this only
> Stirs the troubled heart in my breast to tremble!
> For should I but see thee a little moment,
> Straight is my voice hushed;
>
> Yea, my tongue is broken, and through and through me

---

[17]Homer, *Odyssey* 3:109–11. [Tr.]

[18]Five incidents from the *Odyssey*. The Cyclops at 9:192; Aiolos's wineskin at 10:17; the metamorphosis at 10:237; Zeus's doves at 12:62; Odysseus's fast at 12:447; the slaying of the suitors at 22:79–380. [Ed.]

'Neath the flesh impalpable fire runs tingling;
Nothing see mine eyes, and a noise of roaring
   Waves in my ear sounds;
Sweat runs down in rivers, a tremor seizes
All my limbs, and paler than grass in autumn,
Caught by pains of menacing death, I falter,
   Lost in the love-trance.

3. Are you not amazed how at one instant she summons, as though they were all alien from herself and dispersed, soul, body, ears, tongue, eyes, color? Uniting contradictions, she is, at one and the same time, hot and cold, in her senses and out of her mind, for she is either terrified or at the point of death. The effect desired is that not one passion only should be seen in her, but a concourse of the passions. All such things occur in the case of lovers, but it is, as I said, the selection of the most striking of them and their combination into a single whole that has produced the singular excellence of the passage. In the same way Homer, when describing tempests, picks out the most appalling circumstances. 4. The author of the *Arimaspeia* thinks to inspire awe in the following way:

A marvel exceeding great is this withal to my
   soul —
Men dwell on the water afar from the land, where
   deep seas roll.
Wretches are they, for they reap but a harvest of
   travail and pain,
Their eyes on the stars ever dwell, while their
   hearts abide in the main.
Often, I ween, to the Gods are their hands upraised
   on high,
And with hearts in misery heavenward-lifted in
   prayer do they cry.

It is clear, I imagine, to everybody that there is more elegance than terror in these words. 5. But what says Homer? Let one instance be quoted from among many:

And he burst on them like as a wave swift-rushing
   beneath black clouds,
Heaved huge by the winds, bursts down on a ship,
   and the wild foam shrouds
From the stem to the stern her hull, and the storm-
   blast's terrible breath
Roars in the sail, and the heart of the shipmen
   shuddereth

In fear, for that scantly upborne are they now from the clutches of death.[19]

6. Aratus has attempted to convert this same expression to his own use:

And a slender plank averteth their death.

Only, he has made it trivial and neat instead of terrible. Furthermore, he has put bounds to the danger by saying *A plank keeps off death*. After all, it *does* keep it off. Homer, however, does not for one moment set a limit to the terror of the scene, but draws a vivid picture of men continually in peril of their lives, and often within an ace of perishing with each successive wave. Moreover, he has in the words ὑπὲκ θανάτοιο, forced into union, by a kind of unnatural compulsion, prepositions not usually compounded.[20] He has thus tortured his line into the similitude of the impending calamity, and by the constriction of the verse has excellently figured the disaster, and almost stamped upon the expression the very form and pressure of the danger, ὑπὲκ θανάτοιο φέρονται. 7. This is true also of Archilochus in his account of the shipwreck, and of Demosthenes in the passage which begins "It was evening," where he describes the bringing of the news.[21] The salient points they selected, one might say, according to merit and massed them together, inserting in the midst nothing frivolous, mean, or trivial. For these faults mar the effect of the whole, just as though they introduced chinks or fissures into stately and co-ordered edifices, whose walls are compacted by their reciprocal adjustment.

## II

An allied excellence to those already set forth is that which is termed *amplification*. This figure is employed when the narrative or the course of a forensic argument admits, from section to section, of many starting points and many pauses,

---

[19]Homer, *Iliad* 15:624–28. [Tr.]
[20]The point is that Homer has created an unusual compound word — *hypek*, out of *hyper* ("up") and *ek* ("out of"): "up out of death." [Ed.]
[21]Demosthenes, *On the Crown*, 169. [Tr.]

and elevated expressions follow, one after the other, in an unbroken succession and in an ascending order. 2. And this may be effected either by way of the rhetorical treatment of commonplaces, or by way of intensification (whether events or arguments are to be strongly presented), or by the orderly arrangement of facts or of passions; indeed, there are innumerable kinds of amplification. Only, the orator must in every case remember that none of these methods by itself, apart from sublimity, forms a complete whole, unless indeed where pity is to be excited or an opponent to be disparaged. In all other cases of amplification, if you take away the sublime, you will remove as it were the soul from the body. For the vigor of the amplification at once loses its intensity and its substance when not resting on a firm basis of the sublime. 3. Clearness, however, demands that we should define concisely how our present precepts differ from the point under consideration a moment ago, namely the marking-out of the most striking conceptions and the unification of them; and wherein, generally, the sublime differs from amplification.

## 12

Now the definition given by the writers on rhetoric does not satisfy me. Amplification is, say they, discourse which invests the subject with grandeur. This definition, however, would surely apply in equal measure to sublimity and passion and figurative language, since they too invest the discourse with a certain degree of grandeur. The point of distinction between them seems to me to be that sublimity consists in elevation, while amplification embraces a multitude of details. Consequently, sublimity is often comprised in a single thought, while amplification is universally associated with a certain magnitude and abundance. 2. Amplification (to sum the matter up in a general way) is an aggregation of all the constituent parts and topics of a subject, lending strength to the argument by dwelling upon it, and differing herein from proof that, while the latter demonstrates the matter under investigation. . . .

With his vast riches Plato swells, like some sea, into a greatness which expands on every

side. 3. Wherefore it is, I suppose, that the orator in his utterance shows, as one who appeals more to the passions, all the glow of a fiery spirit. Plato, on the other hand, firm-planted in his pride and magnificent stateliness, cannot indeed be accused of coldness, but he has not the same vehemence. 4. And it is in these same respects, my dear friend Terentianus, that it seems to me (supposing always that we Greeks are allowed to have an opinion upon the point) that Cicero differs from Demosthenes in elevated passages. For the latter is characterized by sublimity which is for the most part rugged, Cicero by profusion. Our orator,[22] owing to the fact that in his vehemence — aye, and in his speed, power and intensity — he can as it were consume by fire and carry away all before him, may be compared to a thunderbolt or flash of lightning. Cicero, on the other hand, it seems to me, after the manner of a widespread conflagration, rolls on with all-devouring flames, having within him an ample and abiding store of fire, distributed now at this point now at that, and fed by an unceasing succession. 5. This, however, you will be better able to decide; but the great opportunity of Demosthenes' high-pitched elevation comes where intense utterance and vehement passion are in question, and in passages in which the audience is to be utterly enthralled. The profusion of Cicero is in place where the hearer must be flooded with words, for it is appropriate to the treatment of commonplaces, and to perorations for the most part and digressions, and to all descriptive and declamatory passages, and to writings on history and natural science, and to many other departments of literature.

## 13

To return from my digression. Although Plato thus flows on with noiseless stream, he is nonetheless elevated. You know this because you have read the *Republic* and are familiar with his manner. "Those," says he, "who are destitute of wisdom and goodness and are ever present at carousals and the like are carried on the down-

---

[22]Demosthenes. He is "our" orator because Longinus is a Greek writing to a Roman. [Ed.]

ward path, it seems, and wander thus throughout their life. They never look upwards to the truth, nor do they lift their heads, nor enjoy any pure and lasting pleasure, but like cattle they have their eyes ever cast downwards and bent upon the ground and upon their feeding-places, and they graze and grow fat and breed, and through their insatiate desire of these delights they kick and butt with horns and hoofs of iron and kill one another in their greed."[23]

2. This writer shows us, if only we were willing to pay him heed, that another way (beyond anything we have mentioned) leads to the sublime. And what, and what manner of way, may that be? It is the imitation and emulation of previous great poets and writers. And let this, my dear friend, be an aim to which we steadfastly apply ourselves. For many men are carried away by the spirit of others as if inspired, just as it is related of the Pythian priestess when she approaches the tripod, where there is a rift in the ground which (they say) exhales divine vapor. By heavenly power thus communicated she is impregnated and straightway delivers oracles in virtue of the afflatus. Similarly from the great natures of the men of old there are borne in upon the souls of those who emulate them (as from sacred caves) what we may describe as *effluences*, so that even those who seem little likely to be possessed are thereby inspired and succumb to the spell of the others' greatness. 3. Was Herodotus alone a devoted imitator of Homer? No, Stesichorus even before his time, and Archilochus, and above all Plato, who from the great Homeric source drew to himself innumerable tributary streams. And perhaps we should have found it necessary to prove this, point by point, had not Ammonius and his followers selected and recorded the particulars. 4. This proceeding is not plagiarism; it is like taking an impression from beautiful forms or figures or other works of art. And it seems to me that there would not have been so fine a bloom of perfection on Plato's philosophical doctrines, and that he would not in many cases have found his way to poetical subject matter and modes of expression, unless he

had with all his heart and mind struggled with Homer for the primacy, entering the lists like a young champion matched against the man whom all admire, and showing perhaps too much love of contention and breaking a lance with him as it were, but deriving some profit from the contest nonetheless. For, as Hesiod says, "This strife is good for mortals."[24] And in truth that struggle for the crown of glory is noble and best deserves the victory in which even to be worsted by one's predecessors brings no discredit.

**14**

Accordingly it is well that we ourselves also, when elaborating anything which requires lofty expression and elevated conception, should shape some idea in our minds as to how perchance Homer would have said this very thing, or how it would have been raised to the sublime by Plato or Demosthenes or by the historian Thucydides. For those personages, presenting themselves to us and inflaming our ardor and as it were illumining our path, will carry our minds in a mysterious way to the high standards of sublimity which are imaged within us. 2. Still more effectual will it be to suggest this question to our thoughts, "What sort of hearing would Homer, had he been present, or Demosthenes have given to this or that when said by me, or how would they have been affected by the other?" For the ordeal is indeed a severe one, if we presuppose such a tribunal and theater for our own utterances, and imagine that we are undergoing a scrutiny of our writings before these great heroes, acting as judges and witnesses. 3. A greater incentive still will be supplied if you add the question, "In what spirit will each succeeding age listen to me who have written thus?" But if one shrinks from the very thought of uttering aught that may transcend the term of his own life and time, the conceptions of his mind must necessarily be incomplete, blind, and as it were untimely born, since they are by no means brought to the perfection needed to ensure a futurity of fame.

[23]Plato. *Republic* 9:586a. [Tr.]

[24]Hesiod, *Works and Days*, 24. [Tr.]

**15**

Images, moreover, contribute greatly, my young friend, to dignity, elevation, and power as a pleader. In this sense some call them mental representations. In a general way the name of *image* or *imagination* is applied to every idea of the mind, in whatever form it presents itself, which gives birth to speech. But at the present day the word is predominantly used in cases where, carried away by enthusiasm and passion, you think you see what you describe, and you place it before the eyes of your hearers. 2. Further, you will be aware of the fact that an image has one purpose with the orators and another with the poets, and that the design of the poetical image is enthrallment, of the rhetorical — vivid description. Both, however, seek to stir the passions and the emotions.

> Mother — 'beseech thee, hark not thou on me
> Yon maidens gory-eyed and snaky-haired!
> Lo there — lo there! — they are nigh — they leap
>     on me![25]

And:

> Ah! she will slay me! whither can I fly?[26]

In these scenes the poet himself saw Furies, and the image in his mind he almost compelled his audience also to behold. 3. Now, Euripides is most assiduous in giving the utmost tragic effect to these two emotions — fits of love and madness. Herein he succeeds more, perhaps, than in any other respect, although he is daring enough to invade all the other regions of the imagination. Notwithstanding that he is by nature anything but elevated, he forces his own genius, in many passages, to tragic heights, and everywhere in the matter of sublimity it is true of him (to adopt Homer's words) that

> The tail of him scourgeth his ribs and his flanks to
>     left and to right,
> And he lasheth himself into frenzy, and spurreth
>     him on to the fight.[27]

4. When the Sun hands the reins to Phaethon, he says

> "Thou, driving, trespass not on Libya's sky,
> Whose heat, by dews untempered, else shall split
> Thy car asunder."

And after that,

> "Speed onward toward the Pleiads seven thy
>     course."
> thus far the boy heard; then he snatched the reins:
> He lashed the flanks of that wing-wafted team;
> Loosed rein; and they through folds of cloudland
>     soared.
> Hard after on a fiery star his sire
> Rode, counselling his son — "Ho! thither drive!
> Hither thy car turn — hither!"

Would you not say that the soul of the writer enters the chariot at the same moment as Phaethon and shares in his dangers and in the rapid flight of his steeds? For it could never have conceived such a picture had it not been borne in no less swift career on that journey through the heavens. The same is true of the words which Euripides attributes to his Cassandra:

> O chariot-loving Trojans.

5. Aeschylus, too, ventures on images of a most heroic stamp. An example will be found in his *Seven Against Thebes*, where he says

> For seven heroes, squadron-captains fierce,
> Over a black-rimmed shield have slain a bull,
> And, dipping in the bull's blood each his hand,
> By Ares and Enyo, and by Panic
> Lover of blood, have sworn.[28]

In mutual fealty they devoted themselves by that joint oath to a relentless doom. Sometimes, however, he introduces ideas that are rough-hewn and uncouth and harsh; and Euripides, when stirred by the spirit of emulation, comes perilously near the same fault, even in spite of his own natural bent. 6. Thus in Aeschylus the palace of Lycurgus at the coming of Dionysus is strangely represented as *possessed*:

---

[25]Euripides, *Orestes*, 255–57. [Tr.]

[26]Euripides, *Iphigeneia in Tauris*, 291. [Tr.] The three following quotations are from lost plays. [Ed.]

[27]Homer, *Iliad* 20:170–71. [Tr.]

[28]Aeschylus, *Seven Against Thebes*, 42–46. [Tr.] The following quotation is from a lost play. [Ed.]

A frenzy thrills the hall; the roofs are bacchant
With ecstasy:

an idea which Euripides has echoed, in other words, it is true, and with some abatement of its crudity, where he says:

The whole mount shared their bacchic ecstasy.[29]

7. Magnificent are the images which Sophocles has conceived of the death of Oedipus, who makes ready his burial amid the portents of the sky.[30] Magnificent, too, is the passage where the Greeks are on the point of sailing away and Achilles appears above his tomb to those who are putting out to sea — a scene which I doubt whether anyone has depicted more vividly than Simonides. But it is impossible to cite all the examples that present themselves. 8. It is no doubt true that those which are found in the poets contain, as I said, a tendency to exaggeration in the way of the fabulous and that they transcend in every way the credible, but in oratorical imagery the best feature is always its reality and truth. Whenever the form of a speech is poetical and fabulous and breaks into every kind of impossibility, such digressions have a strange and alien air. For example, the clever orators forsooth of our day, like the tragedians, see Furies, and — fine fellows that they are — cannot even understand that Orestes when he cries

Unhand me — of mine Haunting Fiends thou art —
Dost grip my waist to hurl me into hell![31]

has these fancies because he is mad. 9. What, then, can oratorical imagery effect? Well, it is able in many ways to infuse vehemence and passion into spoken words, while more particularly when it is combined with the argumentative passages it not only persuades the hearer but actually makes him its slave. Here is an example. "Why, if at this very moment," says Demosthenes, "a loud cry were to be heard in front of the courts, and we were told that the prison-house lies open and the prisoners are in full flight, no one, whether he be old or young, is so heedless as

not to lend aid to the utmost of his power; aye, and if anyone came forward and said that yonder stands the man who let them go, the offender would be promptly put to death without a hearing."[32] 10. In the same way, too, Hyperides on being accused, after he had proposed the liberation of the slaves subsequently to the great defeat, said "This proposal was framed, not by the orator, but by the battle of Chaeroneia." The speaker has here at one and the same time followed a train of reasoning and indulged a flight of imagination. He has, therefore, passed the bounds of mere persuasion by the boldness of his conception. 11. By a sort of natural law in all such matters we always attend to whatever possesses superior force; whence it is that we are drawn away from demonstration pure and simple to any startling image within whose dazzling brilliancy the argument lies concealed. And it is not unreasonable that we should be affected in this way, for when two things are brought together, the more powerful always attracts to itself the virtue of the weaker. 12. It will be enough to have said this much with regard to examples of the sublime in thought, when produced by greatness of soul, imitation, or imagery.

**16**

Here, however, in due order comes the place assigned to Figures; for they, if handled in the proper manner, will contribute, as I have said, in no mean degree to sublimity. But since to treat thoroughly of them all at the present moment would be a great, or rather an endless task, we will now, with the object of proving our proposition, run over a few only of those which produce elevation of diction. 2. Demosthenes is bringing forward a reasoned vindication of his public policy. What was the natural way of treating the subject? It was this. "You were not wrong, you who engaged in the struggle for the freedom of Greece. You have domestic warrant for it. For the warriors of Marathon did no wrong, nor they of Salamis, nor they of Plataea."[33] When, however, as though suddenly in-

[29]Euripides, *The Bacchae*, 726. [Tr.]
[30]Sophocles, *Oedipus at Colonus*, 1586. [Tr.]
[31]Euripides, *Orestes*, 264–65. [Tr.]

[32]Demosthenes, *Contra Timocrates*, 208. [Tr.]
[33]Demosthenes, *On the Crown*, 208. [Tr.]

spired by heaven and as it were frenzied by the god of Prophecy, he utters his famous oath by the champions of Greece ("assuredly ye did no wrong; I swear it by those who at Marathon stood in the forefront of the danger"), in the public view by this one Figure of Adjuration, which I here term *Apostrophe*, he deifies his ancestors. He brings home the thought that we ought to swear by those who have thus nobly died as we swear by gods, and he fills the mind of the judges with the high spirit of those who there bore the brunt of the danger, and he has transformed the natural course of the argument into transcendent sublimity and passion and that secure belief which rests upon strange and prodigious oaths. He instills into the minds of his hearers the conviction — which acts as a medicine and an antidote — that they should, uplifted by these eulogies, feel no less proud of the fight against Philip than of the triumph at Marathon and Salamis. By all these means he carries his hearers clean away with him through the employment of a single figure. 3. It is said, indeed, that the germ of the oath is found in Eupolis:

For, by the fight I won at Marathon,
No one shall vex my soul and rue it not.

But it is not sublime to swear by a person in any chance way; the sublimity depends upon the place and the manner and the circumstances and the motive. Now in the passage of Eupolis there is nothing but the mere oath, addressed to the Athenians when still prosperous and in no need of comfort. Furthermore, the poet in his oath has not made divinities of the men in order so to create in his hearers a worthy conception of their valor, but he has wandered away from those who stood in the forefront of the danger to an inanimate thing — the fight. In Demosthenes the oath is framed for vanquished men, with the intention that Chaeroneia should no longer appear a failure to the Athenians. He gives them at one and the same time, as I remarked, a demonstration that they have done no wrong, an example, the sure evidence of oaths, a eulogy, an exhortation. 4. And since the orator was likely to be confronted with the objection, "You are speaking of the *defeat* which has attended your administration, and yet you swear by *victories*," in what follows

he consequently measures even individual words, and chooses them unerringly, showing that even in the revels of the imagination sobriety is required. "Those," he says, "who stood in the forefront of the danger at Marathon, and those who fought by sea at Salamis and Artemisium, and those who stood in the ranks at Plataea." Nowhere does he use the word "conquered," but at every turn he has evaded any indication of the result, since it was fortunate and the opposite of what happened at Chaeroneia. So he at once rushes forward and carries his hearer off his feet. "All of whom," says he, "were accorded a public burial by the state, Aeschines, and not *the successful only*."

17

I ought not, my dear friend, to omit at this point an observation of my own, which shall be most concisely stated. It is that, by a sort of natural law, figures bring support to the sublime, and on their part derive support in turn from it in a wonderful degree. Where and how, I will explain. The cunning use of figures is peculiarly subject to suspicion, and produces an impression of ambush, plot, fallacy. This is so when the plea is addressed to a judge with absolute powers, and particularly to despots, kings, and leaders in positions of superiority. Such a one at once feels resentment if, like a foolish boy, he is tricked by the paltry figures of the oratorical craftsman. Construing the fallacy into a personal affront, sometimes he becomes quite wild with rage, or if he controls his anger, steels himself utterly against persuasive words. Wherefore a figure is at its best when the very fact that it is a figure escapes attention. 2. Accordingly, sublimity and passion form an antidote and a wonderful help against the mistrust which attends upon the use of figures. The art which craftily employs them lies hid and escapes all future suspicion, when once it has been associated with beauty and sublimity. A sufficient proof is the passage already adduced, "By the men of Marathon I swear." By what means has the orator here concealed the figure? Clearly, by the very excess of light. For just as all dim lights are extinguished in the blaze of the sun, so do the artifices of rhetoric fade from view when bathed in the pervading splendor of sublimity. 3. Something like this happens also in the art of painting. For although light and shade, as depicted in colors, lie side by side upon the same surface, light nevertheless meets the vision first, and not only stands out, but also seems far nearer. So also with the manifestations of passion and the sublime in literature. They lie nearer to our minds through a sort of natural kinship and through their own radiance, and always strike our attention before the figures, whose art they throw into the shade and as it were keep in concealment.

**18**

But what are we next to say of questions and interrogations? Is it not precisely by the visualizing qualities of these figures that Demosthenes strives to make his speeches far more effective and impressive? "Pray tell me — tell me, you sir — do you wish to go about and inquire of one another, Is there any news? Why, what greater news could there be than this, that a Macedonian is subduing Greece? Is Philip dead? No; but he is ill. Dead or ill, what difference to you? Should anything happen to him, you will speedily create another Philip." Again he says, "Let us sail against Macedonia. Where shall we find a landing-place? someone asks. The war itself will discover the weak places in Philip's position."[34] All this, if stated plainly and directly, would have been altogether weaker. As it is, the excitement, and the rapid play of question and answer, and the plan of meeting his own objections as though they were urged by another, have by the help of the figure made the language used not only more elevated but also more convincing. 2. For an exhibition of passion has a greater effect when it seems not to be studied by the speaker himself but to be inspired by the occasion; and questions asked and answered by oneself simulate a natural outburst of passion. For just as those who are interrogated by others experience a sudden excitement and answer the inquiry incisively and with the utmost candor, so

the figure of question and answer leads the hearer to suppose that each deliberate thought is struck out and uttered on the spur of the moment, and thus beguiles his reason. We may further quote that passage of Herodotus which is regarded as one of the most elevated: "If thus. . . ."

**19**

The words issue forth without connecting links and are poured out as it were, almost outstripping the speaker himself. "Locking their shields," says Xenophon, "they thrust fought slew fell."[35] 2. And so with the words of Eurylochus:

> We passed, as thou badst, Odysseus, midst twilight
>   of oak-trees round.
> There amidst of the forest-glens a beautiful palace
>   we found.[36]

For the lines detached from one another, but nonetheless hurried along, produce the impression of an agitation which interposes obstacles and at the same time adds impetuosity. This result Homer has produced by the omission of conjunctions.

**20**

A powerful effect usually attends the union of figures for a common object, when two or three mingle together as it were in partnership, and contribute a fund of strength, persuasiveness, beauty. Thus, in the speech against Meidias, examples will be found of *asyndeton*, interwoven with instances of *anaphora* and *diatyposis*.[37] "For the smiter can do many things (some of which the sufferer cannot even describe to another) by attitude, by look, by voice."[38] 2. Then, in order that the narrative may not, as it advances, continue in the same groove (for continuance betokens tranquillity, while passion — the transport and commotion of the soul — sets order at defiance) straightway he hurries off to

[34]Demosthenes, *Philippics* 1:10, 44. [Tr.]

[35]Xenophon, *Hellenica* 4:3, 19. [Tr.]
[36]Homer, *Odyssey* 10:251–52. [Tr.]
[37]Asyndeton is the omission of conjunctions between clauses; anaphora the repetition of words beginning clauses or sentences; diatyposis is vivid description. [Tr.]
[38]Demosthenes, *Against Meidias*, 72. [Tr.]

other *Asyndeta* and *Repetitions*. "By attitude, by look, by voice, when he acts with insolence, when he acts like an enemy, when he smites with his fists, when he smites you like a slave." By these words the orator produces the same effect as the assailant — he strikes the mind of the judges by the swift succession of blow on blow. 3. Starting from this point again, as suddenly as a gust of wind, he makes another attack. "When smitten with blows of fists," he says, "when smitten upon the cheek. These things stir the blood, these drive men beyond themselves, when unused to insult. No one can, in describing them, convey a notion of the indignity they imply." So he maintains throughout, though with continual variation, the essential character of the *Repetitions* and *Asyndeta*. In this way, with him, order is disorderly, and on the other hand, disorder contains a certain element of order.

**21**

Come now, add, if you please, in these cases connecting particles after the fashion of the followers of Isocrates. Furthermore, this fact too must not be overlooked that the smiter may do many things, first by attitude, then by look, then again by the mere voice. You will feel, if you transcribe the passage in this orderly fashion, that the rugged impetuosity of passion, once you make it smooth and equable by adding the copulatives, falls pointless and immediately loses all its fire. 2. Just as the binding of the limbs of runners deprives them of their power of rapid motion, so also passion, when shackled by connecting links and other appendages, chafes at the restriction, for it loses the freedom of its advance and its rapid emission as though from an engine of war.

**22**

*Hyperbata*, or *inversions*, must be placed under the same category. They are departures in the order of expressions or ideas from the natural sequence; and they bear, it may be said, the very stamp and impress of vehement emotion. Just as

those who are really moved by anger, or fear, or indignation, or jealousy, or any other emotion (for the passions are many and countless, and none can give their number), at times turn aside, and when they have taken one thing as their subject often leap to another, foisting in the midst some irrelevant matter, and then again wheel round to their original theme, and driven by their vehemence, as by a veering wind, now this way now that with rapid changes, transform their expressions, their thoughts, the order suggested by a natural sequence, into numberless variations of every kind; so also among the best writers it is by means of *hyperbaton* that imitation approaches the effects of nature. For art is perfect when it seems to be nature, and nature hits the mark when she contains art hidden within her. We may illustrate by the words of Dionysius of Phocaea in Herodotus. "Our fortunes lie on a razor's edge, men of Ionia; for freedom or for bondage, and that the bondage of runaway slaves. Now, therefore, if you choose to submit to hardships you will have toil for the moment, but you will be able to overcome your foes."[39] 2. Here the natural order would have been: "Men of Ionia, now is the time for you to meet hardships; for our fortunes lie on a razor's edge." But the speaker postpones the words "Men of Ionia." He starts at once with the danger of the situation, as though in such imminent peril he had no time at all to address his hearers. Moreover, he inverts the order of ideas. For instead of saying that they ought to endure hardships, which is the real object of his exhortation, he first assigns the reason because of which they ought to endure hardships, in the words "our fortunes lie on a razor's edge." The result is that what he says seems not to be premeditated but to be prompted by the necessities of the moment. 3. In a still higher degree Thucydides is most bold and skillful in disjoining from one another by means of transpositions things that are by nature intimately united and indivisible. Demosthenes is not so masterful as Thucydides, but of all writers he most abounds in this kind of figure, and through his use of hyperbata makes a great impression of vehem-

[39]Herodotus, *History* 6:11. [Tr.]

ence, yes and of unpremeditated speech, and moreover draws his hearers with him into all the perils of his long inversions. 4. For he will often leave in suspense the thought which he has begun to express, and meanwhile he will heap, into a position seemingly alien and unnatural, one thing upon another parenthetically and from any external source whatsoever, throwing his hearer into alarm lest the whole structure of his words should fall to pieces, and compelling him in anxious sympathy to share the peril of the speaker; and then unexpectedly, after a long interval, he adds the long-awaited conclusion at the right place, namely the end, and produces a far greater effect by this very use, so bold and hazardous, of hyperbaton. Examples may be spared because of their abundance.

**23**

The figures which are termed *polyptota* — accumulations, and variations, and climaxes — are excellent weapons of public oratory, as you are aware, and contribute to elegance and to every form of sublimity and passion. Again, how greatly do changes of cases, tenses, persons, numbers, genders, diversify and enliven exposition. 2. Where the use of numbers is concerned, I would point out that style is not adorned only or chiefly by those words which are, as far as their forms go, in the singular but in meaning are, when examined, found to be plural: as in the lines

> A countless crowd forthright
> Far-ranged along the beaches were clamoring
> "Thunny in sight!"

The fact is more worthy of observation that in certain cases the use of the plural (for the singular) falls on the ear with still more imposing effect and impresses us by the very sense of multitude which the number conveys. 3. Such are the words of Oedipus in Sophocles:

> O nuptials, nuptials,
> Ye gendered me, and, having gendered, brought
> To light the selfsame seed, and so revealed
> Sires, brothers, sons, in one — all kindred
>   blood! —

> Brides, mothers, wives, in one! — yea, whatso deeds
> Most shameful among humankind are done.[40]

The whole enumeration can be summed up in a single proper name — on the one side Oedipus, on the other Jocasta. Nonetheless, the expansion of the number into the plural helps to pluralize the misfortunes as well. There is a similar instance of multiplication in the line:

> Forth Hectors and Sarpedons marching came,

and in that passage of Plato concerning the Athenians which we have quoted elsewhere. 4. "For no Pelopes, nor Cadmi, nor Aegypti and Danai, nor the rest of the crowd of born foreigners dwell with us, but ours is the land of pure Greeks, free from foreign admixture," etc.[41] For naturally a theme seems more imposing to the ear when proper names are thus added, one upon the other, in troops. But this must only be done in cases in which the subject admits of amplification or redundancy or exaggeration or passion — one or more of these — since we all know that a richly caparisoned style is extremely pretentious.

**24**

Further (to take the converse case) particulars which are combined from the plural into the singular are sometimes most elevated in appearance. "Thereafter," says Demosthenes, "all Peloponnesus was at variance."[42] "And when Phrynichus had brought out a play entitled the *Capture of Miletus*, the whole theater burst into tears."[43] For the compression of the number from multiplicity into unity gives more fully the feeling of a single body. 2. In both cases the explanation of the elegance of expression is, I think, the same. Where the words are singular, to make them plural is the mark of unlooked-for passion; and where they are plural, the rounding of a number of things into a fine-sounding singular is surprising owing to the converse change.

[40]Sophocles, *Oedipus the King*, 1403–7. [Tr.]
[41]Plato, *Menexinus*, 245d. [Tr.]
[42]Demosthenes, *On the Crown*, 18. [Tr.]
[43]Herodotus, *History* 6:21. [Tr]

**25**

If you introduce things which are past as present and now taking place, you will make your story no longer a narration but an actuality. Xenophon furnishes an illustration. "A man," says he, "has fallen under Cyrus's horse, and being trampled strikes the horse with his sword in the belly. He rears and unseats Cyrus, who falls."[44] This construction is specially characteristic of Thucydides.

**26**

In like manner the interchange of persons produces a vivid impression, and often makes the hearer feel that he is moving in the midst of perils:

> Thou hadst said that with toil unspent, and all
> unwasted of limb,
> They closed in the grapple of war, so fiercely they
> rushed to the fray;[45]

and the line of Aratus.

> Never in that month launch thou forth amid lashing
> seas.

2. So also Herodotus: "From the city of Elephantine thou shalt sail upwards, and then shalt come to a level plain; and after crossing this tract, thou shalt embark upon another vessel and sail for two days, and then shalt thou come to a great city whose name is Meroe."[46] Do you observe, my friend, how he leads you in imagination through the region and makes you *see* what you hear? All such cases of direct personal address place the hearer on the very scene of action. 3. So it is when you seem to be speaking, not to all and sundry, but to a single individual:

> But Tydeides — thou wouldst not have known him,
> for whom that hero fought.[47]

You will make your hearer more excited and more attentive, and full of active participation, if you keep him on the alert by words addressed to himself.

**27**

There is further the case in which a writer, when relating something about a person, suddenly breaks off and converts himself into that self-same person. This species of figure is a kind of outburst of passion:

> Then with a far-ringing shout to the Trojans Hector
> cried,
> Bidding them rush on the ships, bidding leave the
> spoils blood-dyed —
> And whomso I mark from the galleys aloof on the
> farther side,
> I will surely devise his death.[48]

The poet assigns the task of narration, as is fit, to himself, but the abrupt threat he suddenly, with no note of warning, attributes to the angered chief. It would have been frigid had he inserted the words, "Hector said so and so." As it is, the swift transition of the narrative has outstripped the swift transitions of the narrator. 2. Accordingly this figure should be used by preference when a sharp crisis does not suffer the writer to tarry but constrains him to pass at once from one person to another. An example will be found in Hecataeus: "Ceyx treated the matter gravely, and straightway bade the descendants of Heracles depart; for I am not able to succor you. In order, therefore, that ye may not perish yourselves and injure me, get you gone to some other country." 3. Demosthenes in dealing with Aristogeiton has, somewhat differently, employed this variation of person to betoken the quick play of emotion. "And will none of you," he asks, "be found to be stirred by loathing or even by anger at the violent deeds of this vile and shameless fellow, who — you whose license of speech, most abandoned of men, is not confined by barriers nor by doors, which might perchance be opened!"[49] With the sense thus incomplete, he suddenly breaks off and in his anger almost tears asunder a single expression into two persons — "he who,

---

[44]Xenophon, *Cyropaedia* 7.i:37. [Tr.]
[45]Homer, *Iliad* 15:697–98. [Tr.]
[46]Herodotus, *History* 2:29. [Tr.]
[47]Homer, *Iliad* 5:85. [Tr.]

[48]Homer, *Iliad* 15:346–49. [Tr.]
[49]Demosthenes, *Contra Aristogeitus* 1:27. [Tr.]

O thou most abandoned!" Thus, although he has turned aside his address and seems to have left Aristogeiton, yet through passion he directs it upon him with far greater force. 4. Similarly with the words of Penelope:

> Herald, with what behest art thou come from the suitor-band?
> To give to the maids of Odysseus the godlike their command
> To forsake their labors, and yonder for them the banquet to lay?
> I would that of all their wooing this were the latest day,
> That this were the end of your banquets, your uttermost revelling-hour,
> Ye that assemble together and all our substance devour,
> The wise Telemachus' sore, as though ye never had heard,
> In the days overpast of your childhood, your fathers' praising word,
> How good Odysseus was.[50]

## 28

As to whether or not periphrasis contributes to the sublime, no one, I think, will hesitate. For just as in music the so-called accompaniments bring out the charm of the melody, so also periphrasis often harmonizes with the normal expression and adds greatly to its beauty, especially if it has a quality which is not inflated and dissonant but pleasantly tempered. 2. Plato will furnish an instance in proof at the opening of his Funeral Oration. "In truth they have gained from us their rightful tribute, in the enjoyment of which they proceed along their destined path, escorted by their country publicly, and privately each by his kinsmen."[51] Death he calls "their destined path," and the tribute of accustomed rites he calls "being escorted publicly by their fatherland." Is it in a slight degree only that he has magnified the conception by the use of these words? Has he not rather, starting with unadorned diction, made it musical, and shed over it like a harmony the melodious rhythm which comes from periphrasis? 3. And Xenophon says, "You regard toil as the guide to a joyous life. You have garnered in your souls the goodliest of all possessions and the fittest for warriors. For you rejoice in praise more than in all else."[52] In using, instead of "you are willing to toil," the words "you deem toil the guide to a joyous life," and in expanding the rest of the sentence in like manner, he has annexed to his eulogy a lofty idea. 4. And so with that inimitable phrase of Herodotus: "The goddess afflicted with an unsexing malady those Scythians who had pillaged the temple."[53]

## 29

A hazardous business, however, eminently hazardous is periphrasis, unless it be handled with discrimination; otherwise it speedily falls flat, with its odor of empty talk and its swelling amplitude. This is the reason why Plato (who is always strong in figurative language, and at times unseasonably so) is taunted because in his Laws he says that "neither gold nor silver treasure should be allowed to establish itself and abide in the city."[54] The critic says that, if he had been forbidding the possession of cattle, he would obviously have spoken of ovine and bovine treasure. 2. But our parenthetical disquisition with regard to the use of figures as bearing upon the sublime has run to sufficient length, my dear Terentianus; for all these things lend additional passion and animation to style, and passion is as intimately allied with sublimity as sketches of character with entertainment.

## 30

Since, however, it is the case that, in discourse, thought and diction are for the most part developed one through the other, come let us proceed to consider any branches of the subject of diction which have so far been neglected. Now it is, no doubt, superfluous to dilate to those who know it well upon the fact that the choice of proper

[50]Homer, *Odyssey* 4:681–89. [Tr.]
[51]Plato, *Menexinus*, 236d. [Tr.]

[52]Xenophon, *Cyropaedia* I:v.12. [Tr.]
[53]Herodotus, *History* I:105. [Tr.]
[54]Plato, *Laws*, 801b. [Tr.]

and striking words wonderfully attracts and enthralls the hearer, and that such a choice is the leading ambition of all orators and writers, since it is the direct agency which ensures the presence in writings, as upon the fairest statues, of the perfection of grandeur, beauty, mellowness, dignity, force, power, and any other high qualities there may be, and breathes into dead things a kind of living voice. All this it is, I say, needless to mention, for beautiful words are in very truth the peculiar light of thought. 2. It may, however, be pointed out that stately language is not to be used everywhere, since to invest petty affairs with great and high-sounding names would seem just like putting a full-sized tragic mask upon an infant boy. But in poetry and. . . .

**31**

. . . full of vigor and racy; and so is Anacreon's line, "That Thracian mare no longer do I heed." In this way, too, that original expression of Theopompus merits praise. Owing to the correspondence between word and thing it seems to me to be highly expressive; and yet Caecilius for some unexplained reason finds fault with it. "Philip," says Theopompus, "had a genius for *stomaching* things." Now a homely expression of this kind is sometimes much more telling than elegant language, for it is understood at once since it is drawn from common life, and the fact that it is familiar makes it only the more convincing. So the words "stomaching things" are used most strikingly of a man who, for the sake of attaining his own ends, patiently and with cheerfulness endures things shameful and vile. 2. So with the words of Herodotus. "Cleomenes," he says, "went mad, and with a small sword cut the flesh of his own body into strips, until he slew himself by making mincemeat of his entire person." And, "Pythes fought on shipboard, until he was utterly hacked to pieces."[55] These phrases graze the very edge of vulgarity, but they are saved from vulgarity by their expressiveness.

**32**

Further, with regard to the number of metaphors to be employed, Caecilius seems to assent to the view of those who lay it down that not more than two, or at the most three, should be ranged together in the same passage. Demosthenes is, in fact, the standard in this as in other matters. The proper time for using metaphors is when the passions roll like a torrent and sweep a multitude of them down their resistless flood. 2. "Men," says he, "who are vile flatterers, who have maimed their own fatherlands each one of them, who have toasted away their liberty first to Philip and now to Alexander, who measure happiness by their belly and their lowest desires, and who have overthrown that liberty and that freedom from despotic mastery which to the Greeks of an earlier time were the rules and standards of good."[56] Here the orator's wrath against the traitors throws a veil over the number of the tropes. 3. In the same spirit, Aristotle and Theophrastus point out that the following phrases serve to soften bold metaphors — "as if," and "as it were," and "if one may so say," and "if one may venture such an expression"; for the qualifying words mitigate, they say, the audacity of expression. 4. I accept that view, but still for number and boldness of metaphors I maintain, as I said in dealing with figures, that strong and timely passion and noble sublimity are the appropriate palliatives. For it is the nature of the passions, in their vehement rush, to sweep and thrust everything before them, or rather to demand hazardous turns as altogether indispensable. They do not allow the hearer leisure to criticize the number of the metaphors because he is carried away by the fervor of the speaker. 5. Moreover, in the treatment of commonplaces and in descriptions there is nothing so impressive as a number of tropes following close one upon the other. It is by this means that in Xenophon the anatomy of the human tabernacle is magnificently depicted, and still more divinely in Plato. Plato says that its head is a citadel; in the midst, between the head and the breast, is built the neck like some isthmus. The vertebrae, he says, are fixed be-

---

[55] Herodotus, *History* 6:75; 7:181. [Tr.]

[56] Demosthenes, *On the Crown*, 296. [Tr.]

neath like pivots. Pleasure is a bait which tempts men to ill, the tongue the test of taste; the heart is the knot of the veins and the wellspring of the blood that courses round impetuously, and it is stationed in the guardhouse of the body. The passages by which the blood races this way and that he names alleys. He says that the gods, contriving succor for the beating of the heart (which takes place when dangers are expected, and when wrath excites it, since it then reaches a fiery heat), have implanted the lungs, which are soft and bloodless and have pores within, to serve as a buffer, in order that the heart may, when its inward wrath boils over, beat against a yielding substance and so escape injury. The seat of the desires he compared to the women's apartments in a house, that of anger to the men's. The spleen he called the napkin of the inward parts, whence it is filled with secretions and grows to a great and festering bulk. After this, the gods canopied the whole with flesh, putting forward the flesh as a defense against injuries from without, as though it were a hair-cushion. The blood he called the fodder of the flesh. "In order to promote nutrition," he continues, "they irrigated the body, cutting conduits as in gardens, in order that, with the body forming a set of tiny channels, the streams of the veins might flow as from a never-failing source." When the end comes, he says that the cables of the soul are loosed like those of a ship, and she is allowed to go free.[57] 6. Examples of a similar nature are to be found in a never-ending series. But those indicated are enough to show that figurative language possesses great natural power, and that metaphors contribute to the sublime; and at the same time that it is impassioned and descriptive passages which rejoice in them to the greatest extent. 7. It is obvious, however, even though I do not dwell upon it, that the use of tropes, like all other beauties of expression, is apt to lead to excess. On this score Plato himself is much criticized, since he is often carried away by a sort of frenzy of words into strong and harsh metaphors and into inflated allegory. "For it is not readily observed," he says, "that a city ought to be mixed

like a bowl, in which the mad wine seethes when it has been poured in, though when chastened by another god who is sober, falling thus into noble company, it makes a good and temperate drink."[58] For to call water "a sober god," and mixing "chastening," is — the critics say — the language of a poet, and one who is in truth far from sober. 8. Fastening upon such defects, however, Caecilius ventured, in his writings in praise of Lysias, to make the assertion that Lysias was altogether superior to Plato. In so doing he gave way to two blind impulses of passion. Loving Lysias better even than himself, he nevertheless hates Plato more perfectly than he loves Lysias. In fact, he is carried away by the spirit of contention, and even his premises are not, as he thought, admitted. For he prefers the orator as faultless and immaculate to Plato as one who has often made mistakes. But the truth is not of this nature, nor anything like it.

## 33

Come, now, let us take some writer who is really immaculate and beyond reproach. Is it not worthwhile, on this very point, to raise the general question whether we ought to give the preference, in poems and prose writings, to grandeur with some attendant faults, or to success which is moderate but altogether sound and free from error? Aye, and further, whether a greater number of excellences, or excellences higher in quality, would in literature rightly bear away the palm? For these are inquiries appropriate to a treatise on the sublime, and they imperatively demand a settlement. 2. For my part, I am well aware that lofty genius is far removed from flawlessness; for invariable accuracy incurs the risk of pettiness, and in the sublime, as in great fortunes, there must be something which is overlooked. It may be necessarily the case that low and average natures remain as a rule free from failing and in greater safety because they never run a risk or seek to scale the heights, while great endowments prove insecure because of their very greatness. 3. In the second place, I am not ignorant

---

[57] Plato, *Timaeus*, 65c–85b. [Tr.]

[58] Plato, *Laws*, 773c. [Tr.]

that it naturally happens that the worse side of human character is always the more easily recognized, and that the memory of errors remains indelible, while that of excellences quickly dies away. 4. I have myself noted not a few errors on the part of Homer and other writers of the greatest distinction, and the slips they have made afford me anything but pleasure. Still I do not term them willful errors, but rather oversights of a random and casual kind, due to neglect and introduced with all the heedlessness of genius. Consequently I do not waver in my view that excellences higher in quality, even if not sustained throughout, should always on a comparison be voted the first place, because of their sheer elevation of spirit if for no other reason. Granted that Apollonius in his *Argonautica* shows himself a poet who does not trip, and that in his pastorals Theocritus is, except in a few externals, most happy, would you not, for all that, choose to be Homer rather than Apollonius? 5. Again: does Eratosthenes in the *Erigone* (a little poem which is altogether free from flaw) show himself a greater poet than Archilochus with the rich and disorderly abundance which follows in his train and with that outburst of the divine spirit within him which it is difficult to bring under the rules of law? Once more: in lyric poetry would you prefer to be Bacchylides rather than Pindar? And in tragedy to be Ion of Chios rather than — Sophocles? It is true that Bacchylides and Ion are faultless and entirely elegant writers of the polished school, while Pindar and Sophocles, although at times they burn everything before them as it were in their swift career, are often extinguished unaccountably and fail most lamentably. But would anyone in his senses regard all the compositions of Ion put together as an equivalent for the single play of the *Oedipus*?

**34**

If successful writing were to be estimated by number of merits and not by the true criterion, thus judged Hyperides would be altogether superior to Demosthenes. For he has a greater variety of accents than Demosthenes and a greater number of excellences, and like the pentathlete he falls just below the top in every branch. In all the contests he has to resign the first place to his rivals, while he maintains that place as against all ordinary persons. 2. Now Hyperides not only imitates all the strong points of Demosthenes with the exception of his composition, but he has embraced in a singular degree the excellences and graces of Lysias as well. For he talks with simplicity, where it is required, and does not adopt like Demosthenes one unvarying tone in all his utterances. He possesses the gift of characterization in a sweet and pleasant form and with a touch of piquancy. There are innumerable signs of wit in him — the most polished raillery, high-bred ease, supple skill in the contests of irony, jests not tasteless or rude after the well-known Attic manner but naturally suggested by the subject, clever ridicule, much comic power, biting satire with well-directed fun, and what may be termed an inimitable charm investing the whole. He is excellently fitted by nature to excite pity; in narrating a fable he is facile, and with his pliant spirit he is also most easily turned toward a digression (as for instance in his rather poetical presentation of the story of Leto), while he has treated his Funeral Oration in the epideictic vein with probably unequalled success. 3. Demosthenes, on the other hand, is not an apt delineator of character, he is not facile, he is anything but pliant or epideictic, he is comparatively lacking in the entire list of excellences just given. Where he forces himself to be jocular and pleasant, he does not excite laughter but rather becomes the subject of it, and when he wishes to approach the region of charm, he is all the farther removed from it. If he had attempted to write the short speech about Phryne or about Athenogenes, he would have all the more commended Hyperides to our regard. 4. The good points of the latter, however, many though they be, are wanting in elevation; they are the staid utterances of a sober-hearted man and leave the hearer unmoved, no one feeling terror when he reads Hyperides. But Demosthenes draws — as from a store — excellences allied to the highest sublimity and perfected to the utmost, the tone of lofty speech, living passions, copiousness, readiness, speed (where it is legitimate), and that power and vehemence of his which forbid approach. Having, I say, absorbed bodily within himself these mighty gifts which we may deem heaven-sent (for it would not be right to term them *human*), he thus with the noble qualities which are his own routs all comers even where the qualities he does not possess are concerned, and overpowers with thunder and with lightning the orators of every age. One could sooner face with unflinching eyes a descending thunderbolt than meet with steady gaze his bursts of passion in their swift succession.

## 35

But in the case of Plato and Lysias there is, as I said, a further point of difference. For not only in the degree of his excellences, but also in their number, Lysias is much inferior to Plato; and at the same time he surpasses him in his faults still more than he falls below him in his excellences. 2. What fact, then, was before the eyes of those superhuman writers who, aiming at everything that was highest in composition, contemned an all-pervading accuracy? This besides many other things, that Nature has appointed us men to be no base or ignoble animals; but when she ushers us into life and into the vast universe as into some great assembly, to be as it were spectators of the mighty whole and the keenest aspirants for honor, forthwith she implants in our souls the unconquerable love of whatever is elevated and more divine than we. 3. Wherefore not even the entire universe suffices for the thought and contemplation within the reach of the human mind, but our imaginations often pass beyond the bounds of space, and if we survey our life on every side and see how much more it everywhere abounds in what is striking, and great, and beautiful, we shall soon discern the purpose of our birth. 4. This is why, by a sort of natural impulse, we admire not the small streams, useful and pellucid though they be, but the Nile, the Danube or the Rhine, and still more the Ocean. Nor do we view the tiny flame of our own kindling (guarded in lasting purity as its light ever is) with greater awe than the celestial fires though they are often shrouded in darkness; nor do we deem it a greater marvel than the craters of Etna, whose eruptions throw up stones from its depths and great masses of rock, and at times pour forth rivers of that pure and unmixed subterranean fire. 5. In all such matters we may say that what is useful or necessary men regard as commonplace, while they reserve their admiration for that which is astounding.

## 36

Now as regards the manifestations of the sublime in literature, in which grandeur is never, as it sometimes is in nature, found apart from utility and advantage, it is fitting to observe at once that, though writers of this magnitude are far removed from faultlessness, they nonetheless all rise above what is mortal; that all other qualities prove their possessors to be men, but sublimity raises them near the majesty of God; and that, while immunity from errors relieves from censure, it is grandeur that excites admiration. 2. What need to add thereto that each of these supreme authors often redeems all his failures by a single sublime and happy touch, and (most important of all) that if one were to pick out and mass together the blunders of Homer, Demosthenes, Plato, and all the rest of the greatest writers, they would be found to be a very small part, nay an infinitesimal fraction, of the triumphs which those heroes achieve on every hand? This is the reason why the judgment of all posterity — a verdict which envy itself cannot convict of perversity — has brought and offered those meeds of victory which up to this day it guards intact and seems likely still to preserve,

> Long as earth's waters shall flow, and her tall trees burgeon and bloom.

3. In reply, however, to the writer who maintains that the faulty Colossus is not superior to the Spearman of Polycleitus, it is obvious to remark among many other things that in art the utmost exactitude is admired, grandeur in the works of nature; and that it is by nature that man is a being gifted with speech. In statues likeness to man is the quality required; in discourse we demand, as I said, that which transcends the human. 4. Nevertheless — and the counsel about to be given reverts to the beginning of our memoir — since freedom from failings is for the most part the successful result of art, and excellence

(though it may be unevenly sustained) the result of sublimity, the employment of art is in every way a fitting aid to nature; for it is the conjunction of the two which tends to ensure perfection.

Such are the decisions to which we have felt bound to come with regard to the questions proposed; but let every man cherish the view which pleases him best.

## 37

Closely related to Metaphors (for we must return to our point) are comparisons and similes, differing only in this respect. . . . .

## 38

. . . such Hyperboles as: "unless you carry your brains trodden down in your heels."[59] It is necessary, therefore, to know where to fix the limit in each case; for an occasional overshooting of the mark ruins the hyperbole, and such expressions, when strained too much, lose their tension, and sometimes swing round and produce the contrary effect. 2. Isocrates, for example, fell into unaccountable puerility owing to the ambition which made him desire to describe everything with a touch of amplification. The theme of his *Panegyric* is that Athens surpasses Lacedaemon in benefits conferred upon Greece, and yet at the very outset of his speech he uses these words: "Further, language has such capacity that it is possible thereby to debase things lofty and invest things small with grandeur, and to express old things in a new way, and to discourse in ancient fashion about what has newly happened."[60] "Do you then, Isocrates," it may be asked, "mean in that way to interchange the facts of Lacedaemonian and Athenian history?" For in his eulogy of language he has, we may say, published to his hearers a preamble warning them to distrust himself. 3. Perhaps, then, as we said in dealing with figures generally, those hyperboles are best in which the very fact that they are hyperboles escapes attention. This happens when, through stress of strong emotion, they are uttered in con-

nection with some great crisis, as is done by Thucydides in the case of those who perished in Sicily. "The Syracusans," he says, "came down to the water's edge and began the slaughter of those chiefly who were in the river, and the water at once became polluted, but nonetheless it was swallowed although muddy and mixed with blood, and to most it was still worth fighting for."[61] That a draught of blood and mud should still be worth fighting for, is rendered credible by the intensity of the emotion at a great crisis. 4. So with the passage in which Herodotus tells of those who fell at Thermopylae. "On this spot," he says, "the barbarians buried them as they defended themselves with daggers — those of them who had daggers still left — and with hands and mouths."[62] Here you may be inclined to protest against the expressions "fight with their very mouths" against men in armor, and "being buried" with darts. At the same time the narrative carries conviction; for the event does not seem to be introduced for the sake of the hyperbole, but the hyperbole to spring naturally from the event. 5. For (as I never cease to say) the deeds and passions which verge on transport are a sufficient lenitive and remedy for every audacity of speech. This is the reason why the quips of comedy, although they may be carried to the extreme of absurdity, are plausible because they are so amusing. For instance,

Smaller his field was than a Spartan letter.

For mirth, too, is an emotion, an emotion which has its root in pleasure. 6. Hyperboles are employed in describing things small as well as great, since exaggeration is the common element in both cases. And, in a sense, ridicule is an amplification of the paltriness of things.

## 39

The fifth of those elements contributing to the sublime which we mentioned, my excellent friend, at the beginning, still remains to be dealt with, namely the arrangement of the words in a certain order. In regard to this, having already in

[59]Demosthenes (?), *On Halonesius*, 45. [Tr.]
[60]Isocrates, *Panegyric*, 8. [Tr.]

[61]Thucydides, *Peloponnesian War* 7:84. [Tr.]
[62]Herodotus, *History* 7:225. [Tr.]

two treatises sufficiently stated such results as our inquiry could compass, we will add, for the purpose of our present undertaking, only what is absolutely essential, namely the fact that harmonious arrangement is not only a natural source of persuasion and pleasure among men but also a wonderful instrument of lofty utterance and of passion. 2. For does not the flute instill certain emotions into its hearers and as it were make them beside themselves and full of frenzy, and supplying a rhythmical movement constrain the listener to move rhythmically in accordance therewith and to conform himself to the melody, although he may be utterly ignorant of music? Yes, and the tones of the harp, although in themselves they signify nothing at all, often cast a wonderful spell, as you know, over an audience by means of the variations of sounds, by their pulsation against one another, and by their mingling in concert. 3. And yet these are mere semblances and spurious copies of persuasion, not (as I have said) genuine activities of human nature. Are we not, then, to hold that composition (being a harmony of that language which is implanted by nature in man and which appeals not to the hearing only but to the soul itself), since it calls forth manifold shapes of words, thoughts, deeds, beauty, melody, all of them born at our birth and growing with our growth, and since by means of the blending and variation of its own tones it seeks to introduce into the minds of those who are present the emotion which affects the speaker, and since it always brings the audience to share in it and by the building of phrase upon phrase raises a sublime and harmonious structure: are we not, I say, to hold that harmony by these selfsame means allures us and invariably disposes us to stateliness and dignity and elevation and every emotion which it contains within itself, gaining absolute mastery over our minds? But it is folly to dispute concerning matters which are generally admitted, since experience is proof sufficient. 4. An example of a conception which is usually thought sublime and is really admirable is that which Demosthenes associates with the decree: "This decree caused the danger which then beset the city to pass by just as a cloud."[63]

[63]Demosthenes, *On the Crown*, 188. [Tr.]

But it owes its happy sound no less to the harmony than to the thought itself. For the thought is expressed throughout in dactylic rhythms, and these are most noble and productive of sublimity; and therefore it is that they constitute the heroic, the finest meter that we know. For if you derange the words of the sentence and transpose them in whatever way you will, as for example "This decree just as a cloud caused the danger of the time to pass by"; nay, if you cut off a single syllable only and say "caused to pass by as a cloud," you will perceive to what an extent harmony is in unison with sublimity. For the very words "just as a cloud" begin with a long rhythm, which consists of four metrical beats; but if one syllable is cut off and we read "as a cloud," we immediately maim the sublimity by the abbreviation. Conversely, if you elongate the word and write "caused to pass by just as if a cloud," it means the same thing, but no longer falls with the same effect upon the ear, inasmuch as the abrupt grandeur of the passage loses its energy and tension through the lengthening of the concluding syllables.

**40**

Among the chief causes of the sublime in speech, as in the structure of the human body, is the collocation of members, a single one of which if severed from another possesses in itself nothing remarkable, but all united together make a full and perfect organism. So the constituents of grandeur, when separated from one another, carry with them sublimity in distraction this way and that, but when formed into a body by association and when further encircled in a chain of harmony they become sonorous by their very rotundity; and in periods sublimity is, as it were, a contribution made by a multitude. 2. We have, however, sufficiently shown that many writers and poets who possess no natural sublimity and are perhaps even wanting in elevation have nevertheless, although employing for the most part common and popular words with no striking associations of their own, by merely joining and fitting these together, secured dignity and distinction and the appearance of freedom from meanness. Instances will be furnished by Philistus among many others, by Aristophanes in certain passages, by Euripides in most. 3. In the last-mentioned author, Heracles, after the scene in which he slays his children, uses the words:

Full-fraught am I with woes — no space for more.[64]

The expression is a most ordinary one, but it has gained elevation through the aptness of the structure of the line. If you shape the sentence in a different way, you will see this plainly, the fact being that Euripides is a poet in virtue of his power of composition rather than of his invention. 4. In the passage which describes Dirce torn away by the bull:

Whitherso'er he turned
Swift wheeling round, he haled and hurled withal
Dame, rock, oak, intershifted ceaselessly,

the conception itself is a fine one, but it has been rendered more forcible by the fact that the harmony is not hurried or carried as it were on rollers, but the words act as buttresses for one another and find support in the pauses, and issue finally in a well-grounded sublimity.

## 41

There is nothing in the sphere of the sublime that is so lowering as broken and agitated movement of language, such as is characteristic of pyrrhics and trochees and dichorees, which fall altogether to the level of dance-music.[65] For all over-rhythmical writing is at once felt to be affected and finical and wholly lacking in passion owing to the monotony of its superficial polish. 2. And the worst of it all is that, just as petty lays draw their hearer away from the point and compel his attention to themselves, so also overrhythmical style does not communicate the feeling of the words but simply the feeling of the rhythm. Sometimes, indeed, the listeners knowing beforehand the due terminations stamp their feet in

[64]Euripides, *Heracles,* 1245. [Tr.] The subsequent passage is from a lost play. [Ed.]
[65]A pyrrhic foot was made up of two short syllables; a trochee was a long syllable followed by a short; a dichoric foot had four syllables arranged long-short-long-short. These variants on the nobler dactyls and iambs were thought to lower the tone. [Ed.]

time with the speaker, and as in a dance give the right step in anticipation. 3. In like manner those words are destitute of sublimity which lie too close together, and are cut up into short and tiny syllables, and are held together as if with wooden bolts by sheer inequality and ruggedness.

## 42

Further, excessive concision of expression tends to lower the sublime, since grandeur is marred when the thought is brought into too narrow a compass. Let this be understood not of proper compression, but of what is absolutely petty and cut into segments. For concision curtails the sense, but brevity goes straight to the mark. It is plain that, vice versa, prolixities are frigid, for so is everything that resorts to unseasonable length.

## 43

Triviality of expression is also apt to disfigure sublimity. In Herodotus, for example, the tempest is described with marvelous effect in all its details, but the passage surely contains some words below the dignity of the subject. The following may serve as an instance — "when the sea seethed."[66] The word "seethed" detracts greatly from the sublimity because it is an ill-sounding one. Further, "the wind," he says, "grew fagged," and those who clung to the spars met "an unpleasant end."[67] The expression "grew fagged" is lacking in dignity, being vulgar; and the word "unpleasant" is inappropriate to so great a disaster. 2. Similarly, when Theopompus had dressed out in marvelous fashion the descent of the Persian king upon Egypt, he spoilt the whole by some petty words. "For which of the cities (he says) or which of the tribes in Asia did not send envoys to the Great King? Which of the products of the earth or of the achievements of art was not, in all its beauty or preciousness, brought as an offering to his presence? Consider the multitude of costly coverlets and mantles, in purple or white or embroidery; the multitude of

[66]Herodotus, *History* 7:188. [Tr.]
[67]Herodotus, *History* 7:191; 8:13. [Tr.]

pavilions of gold furnished with all things useful; the multitude, too, of tapestries and costly couches. Further, gold and silver plate richly wrought, and goblets and mixing bowls, some of which you might have seen set with precious stones, and others finished with care and at great price. In addition to all this, countless myriads of Greek and barbaric weapons, and beasts of burden beyond all reckoning and victims fattened for slaughter, and many bushels of condiments, and many bags and sacks and sheets of papyrus and all other useful things, and an equal number of pieces of salted flesh from all manner of victims, so that the piles of them were so great that those who were approaching from a distance took them to be hills and eminences confronting them." 3. He runs off from the more elevated to the more lowly, whereas he should, on the contrary, have risen higher and higher. With his wonderful description of the whole outfit he mixes bags and condiments and sacks, and conveys the impression of a confectioner's shop! For just as if, in the case of those very adornments, between the golden vessels and the jeweled mixing bowls and the silver plate and the pavilions of pure gold and the goblets, a man were to bring and set in the midst paltry bags and sacks, the proceeding would have been offensive to the eye, so do such words when introduced out of season constitute deformities and as it were blots on the diction. 4. He might have described the scene in broad outline just as he says that hills blocked their way, and with regard to the preparations generally have spoken of "wagons and camels and the multitude of beasts of burden carrying everything that ministers to the luxury and enjoyment of the table," or have used some such expression as "piles of all manner of grain and things which conduce preeminently to good cookery and comfort of body," or if he must necessarily put it in so uncompromising a way, he might have said that "all the dainties of cooks and caterers were there." 5. In lofty passages we ought not to descend to sordid and contemptible language unless constrained by some overpowering necessity, but it is fitting that we should use words worthy of the subject and imitate nature the artificer of man, for she has not placed in full view our grosser parts or the means of

purging our frame, but has hidden them away as far as was possible, and as Xenophon says, has put their channels in the remotest background, so as not to sully the beauty of the entire creature. 6. But enough; there is no need to enumerate, one by one, the things which produce triviality. For since we have previously indicated those qualities which render style noble and lofty, it is evident that their opposites will for the most part make it low and base.

## 44

It remains however (as I will not hesitate to add, in recognition of your love of knowledge) to clear up, my dear Terentianus, a question which a certain philosopher has recently mooted. "I wonder," he says, "as no doubt do many others, how it happens that in our time there are men who have the gift of persuasion to the utmost extent, and are well fitted for public life, and are keen and ready, and particularly rich in all the charms of language, yet there no longer arise really lofty and transcendent natures unless quite exceptionally. So great and worldwide a dearth of high utterance attends our age." 2. "Can it be," he continued, "that we are to accept the trite explanation that democracy is the kind nursing-mother of genius, and that literary power may be said to share its rise and fall with democracy and democracy alone? For freedom, it is said, has power to feed the imaginations of the lofty-minded and to inspire hope, and where it prevails there spreads abroad the eagerness of mutual rivalry and the emulous pursuit of the foremost place. 3. Moreover, owing to the prizes which are open to all under popular government, the mental excellences of the orator are continually exercised and sharpened, and as it were rubbed bright, and shine forth (as it is natural they should) with all the freedom which inspires the doings of the state. Today," he went on, "we seem in our boyhood to learn the lessons of a righteous servitude, being all but enswathed in its customs and observances, when our thoughts are yet young and tender, and never tasting the fairest and most productive source of eloquence (by which," he added, "I mean freedom), so that we emerge in no other guise than that of sublime flatterers." 4. This is the reason, he maintained, why no slave ever becomes an orator, although all other faculties may belong to menials. In the slave there immediately burst out signs of fettered liberty of speech, of the dungeon as it were, of a man habituated to buffetings. 5. "For the day of slavery," as Homer has it, "takes away half our manhood."[68] "Just as," he proceeded, "the cages (if what I hear is true) in which are kept the Pygmies, commonly called *nani*, not only hinder the growth of the creatures confined within them, but actually attenuate them through the bonds which beset their bodies, so one has aptly termed all servitude (though it be most righteous) the cage of the soul and a public prisonhouse." 6. I answered him thus: "It is easy, my good sir, and characteristic of human nature, to find fault with the age in which one lives. But consider whether it may not be true that it is not the world's peace that ruins great natures, but far rather this war illimitable which holds our desires in its grasp, aye, and further still those passions which occupy as with troops our present age and utterly harry and plunder it. For the love of money, (a disease from which we all now suffer sorely) and the love of pleasure make us their thralls, or rather, as one may say, drown us body and soul in the depths, the love of riches being a malady which makes men petty, and the love of pleasure one which makes them most ignoble. 7. On reflection I cannot discover how it is possible for us, if we value boundless wealth so highly, or (to speak more truly) deify it, to avoid allowing the entrance into our souls of the evils which are inseparable from it. For vast and unchecked wealth is accompanied, in close conjunction and step for step as they say, by extravagance, and as soon as the former opens the gates of cities and houses, the latter immediately enters and abides. And when time has passed the pair build nests in the lives of men, as the wise say, and quickly give themselves to the rearing of offspring, and breed ostentation, and vanity, and luxury, no spurious progeny of theirs, but only too legitimate. If these children of wealth are permitted to come to maturity, straightway they beget in the soul inexorable masters — insolence, and lawlessness, and shamelessness. 8. This must necessarily happen, and men will no longer lift up their eyes or have any further regard for fame, but the ruin of such lives will gradually reach its complete consummation and sublimities of soul fade and wither away and become contemptible, when men are lost in admiration of their own mortal parts and omit to exalt that which is immortal. 9. For a man who has once accepted a bribe for a judicial decision cannot be an unbiased and upright judge of what is just and honorable (since to the man who is venal his own interests must seem honorable and just), and the same is true where the entire life of each of us is ordered by bribes, and huntings after the death of others, and the laying of ambushes for legacies, while gain from any and every source we purchase — each one of us — at the price of life itself, being the slaves of pleasure. In an age which is ravaged by plagues so sore, is it possible for us to imagine that there is still left an unbiased and incorruptible judge of works that are great and likely to reach posterity, or is it not rather the case that all are influenced in their decisions by the passion for gain? 10. Nay, it is perhaps better for men like ourselves to be ruled than to be free, since our appetites, if let loose without restraint upon our neighbors like beasts from a cage, would set the world on fire with deeds of evil. 11. Summing up, I maintained that among the banes of the natures which our age produces must be reckoned that half-heartedness in which the life of all of us with few exceptions is passed, for we do not labor or exert ourselves except for the sake of praise and pleasure, never for those solid benefits which are a worthy object of our own efforts and the respect of others. 12. But " 'tis best to leave these riddles unresolved,"[69] and to proceed to what next presents itself, namely the subject of the Passions, about which I previously undertook to write in a separate treatise. These form, as it seems to me, a material part of discourse generally and of the Sublime itself. . . .

---

[68]Homer, *Odyssey* 17:322. [Tr.]

[69]Euripides, *Electra*, 379. [Tr.]

# Plotinus
## 204?–270 A.D.

Plotinus, the greatest of the Neoplatonists, was born of Roman parents in the Egyptian city of Lycopolis. To one who has read Plato, Plotinus's ideas will be alternately familiar and strange. What is familiar is his metaphysics, the structure of the universe. Like Plato, Plotinus posits an Ideal world (which he calls *ekei*, "There"), as the paradigm for the physical world here below. What is strange is encountering these ideas unaccompanied by the classical clarity of Plato. Like other Neoplatonists Plotinus derives not only from Plato but also from the Gnostics of Alexandria and the Eastern Mystery cults of Dionysus or Mithras. He gives the impression of an improbable combination of Plato and Zen: This is inaccurate historically, but there is an oriental flavor to his thought.

Plotinus's thought is based on the higher Ideas, which he views in a complex hierarchy. At the top is The One, the principle of existence itself, Plotinus's God-term. The One gives rise to the Intellectual-Principle, by which things are knowable and differentiable; the Intellectual-Principle is the basis of beauty in the universe. Similarly the Intellectual-Principle gives rise to the All-Soul, which is the paradigm for consciousness here below. In his treatise "On the Intellectual Beauty," Plotinus explains that the Greek gods Ouranos, Kronos, and Zeus are myths of these three basic Ideas, though the Ideas give birth one to the other not through temporal but through logical priority. Below the All-Soul is the Nature-Principle, and it is this that gives rise to matter in all its diverse forms.

Plotinus is not primarily an aesthetician, and when he discusses art, he generally thinks first about painting and sculpture rather than about poetry. Nevertheless, his ideas are a useful adjunct to Plato's because, unlike Plato, Plotinus is basically sympathetic to art. For Plotinus as for Plato, the artist imitates but does not *necessarily* copy the things of this world. The artist may represent his grasp of an Idea within the medium of his art: "Thus Phidias wrought the [Olympian] *Zeus* upon no model among things of sense but by apprehending what form Zeus must take if he chose to become manifest to sight." Art at its best can be a way of knowing the Ideas. In fact, it is the artist's grasp of higher things that lends quality to his work.

This does not mean, however, that the artist should be a mathematician or a philosopher, for art does not derive from reason. Like Benedetto Croce (p. 446) at the beginning of the twentieth century, Plotinus insists that the work of art exists primarily as the intuition of the artist and is known prior to reason. (Plotinus calls it "one totality . . . a unity working out into detail . . . a distinct image, . . . not an aggregate of discursive reasoning and detailed willing.") Beauty exists in its highest degree only There, in lesser degree as the intuition within the soul of the artist, and in still lesser degree ("insofar as it has subdued the resistance of the material") in the concrete and physical work the artist makes. But even natural beauty is primarily a quality of soul: Even beautiful women, Plotinus suggests, are beautiful only insofar as their flesh projects a beautiful spirit.

The most mystical part of "On the Intellectual Beauty" is found in sections 10 and 11, where Plotinus discusses a series of spiritual exercises that help to bring the world of There within the self. To do this, he says, is to be "a man filled with a god — possessed by Apollo or by one of the Muses — he need no longer look outside for his vision of the divine being; it is but finding the strength to see divinity within." In the *Ion* Plato discussed *enthousiasmós*, or inspiration, as a form of possession given to favored mortals; for Plotinus this mystical state of unity with the Divine lies within the reach of everyone.

In the first stage of mystical union, the Divine invades the subject as a glorified self-image. In its final stages, the self fades out completely as the subject becomes completely identified with divine power and will. This process may suggest why egoism and temperament are so often found in the incomplete artist, and why the most supreme creators — Shakespeare, Rembrandt, Mozart — seem to show in their art not mere personality but rather a transcendent objectivity and clarity.

### Selected Bibliography

Armstrong, A. H. *The Architecture of the Intelligible Universe in the Philosophy of Plotinus*. Cambridge: Cambridge University Press, 1940.

Asti Vera, Carlos. *Arte y realidad en la estetica de Plotino*. San Antonio de Padua: Ediciones Castaneda, 1978.

Atkinson, M. J. *A Commentary on Plotinus*. New York: Oxford University Press, 1983.

Blumenthal, H. J. *Plotinus's Psychology: His Doctrines of the Embodied Soul*. The Hague: Nijhoff, 1971.

Deck, John N. *Nature, Contemplation and the One*. Toronto: University of Toronto Press, 1967.

Harris, R. Baines. *The Structure of Being: A Neoplatonic Approach*. Norfolk: International Society for Neoplatonic Studies, 1982.

Inge, William R. *The Philosophy of Plotinus*. 1918; Hamden, Conn.: Greenwood, 1968.

Mead, G. R. S. *The Spiritual World of Plotinus*. London: Quest, 1920.

O'Daly, Gerard. *Plotinus's Philosophy of the Self*. New York: Barnes and Noble, 1973.

Underhill, Evelyn. *The Mysticism of Plotinus*. *Quarterly Review* 231 (1919): 479–97.

# On the Intellectual Beauty

I

It is a principle with us that one who has attained to the vision of the Intellectual Beauty and grasped the beauty of the Authentic Intellect will be able also to come to understand the Father and Transcendent of that Divine Being. It con-

Translated by Stephen McKenna.

cerns us, then, to try to see and say, for ourselves and as far as such matters may be told, how the Beauty of the divine Intellect and of the Intellectual Kosmos may be revealed to contemplation.

Let us go to the realm of magnitudes: Suppose two blocks of stone lying side by side: one is unpatterned, quite untouched by art; the other has been minutely wrought by the craftsman's hands into some statue of god or man, a Grace or a Muse, or if a human being, not a portrait but a creation in which the sculptor's art has concentrated all loveliness.

Now it must be seen that the stone thus brought under the artist's hand to the beauty of form is beautiful not as stone — for so the crude block would be as pleasant — but in virtue of the form or idea introduced by the art. This form is not in the material; it is in the designer before ever it enters the stone; and the artificer holds it not by his equipment of eyes and hands but by his participation in his art. The beauty, therefore, exists in a far higher state in the art; for it does not come over integrally into the work; that original beauty is not transferred; what comes over is a derivative and a minor: and even that shows itself upon the statue not integrally and with entire realization of intention but only in so far as it has subdued the resistance of the material.[1]

Art, then, creating in the image of its own nature and content, and working by the Idea or Reason-Principle of the beautiful object it is to produce, must itself be beautiful in a far higher and purer degree since it is the seat and source of that beauty, indwelling in the art, which must naturally be more complete than any comeliness of the external. In the degree in which the beauty is diffused by entering into matter, it is so much the weaker than that concentrated in unity; everything that reaches outwards is the less for it, strength less strong, heat less hot, every power less potent, and so beauty less beautiful.

Then again every prime cause must be, within itself, more powerful than its effect can be: the musical does not derive from an unmusical source but from music; and so the art exhibited in the material work derives from an art yet higher.

Still the arts are not to be slighted on the ground that they create by imitation of natural objects; for, to begin with, these natural objects are themselves imitations; then we must recognize that they give no bare reproduction of the

thing seen but go back to the Ideas from which Nature itself derives, and, furthermore, that much of their work is all their own; they are holders of beauty and add where nature is lacking. Thus Pheidias wrought the Zeus upon no model among things of sense but by apprehending what form Zeus must take if he chose to become manifest to sight.[2]

**2**

But let us leave the arts and consider those works produced by Nature and admitted to be naturally beautiful which the creations of art are charged with imitating, all reasoning life and unreasoning things alike, but especially the consummate among them, where the moulder and maker has subdued the material and given the form he desired. Now what is the beauty here?[3] It has nothing to do with the blood or the menstrual process: either there is also a color and form apart from all this or there is nothing unless sheer ugliness or (at best) a bare recipient, as it were the mere Matter of beauty.

Whence shone forth the beauty of Helen, battle-sought; or of all those women like in loveliness to Aphrodite; or of Aphrodite herself; or of any human being that has been perfect in beauty; or of any of these gods manifest to sight, or unseen but carrying what would be beauty if we saw?

In all these is it not the Idea, something of that realm but communicated to the produced from within the producer just as in works of art, we held, it is communicated from the arts to their creations? Now we can surely not believe that, while the made thing and the Idea thus impressed upon Matter are beautiful, yet the Idea not so alloyed but resting still with the creator — the Idea primal, immaterial, firmly a unity — is not Beauty.

If material extension were in itself the ground

---

[1] Ideal Beauty fades as it descends from the Idea into the art into the artist into the world. But compare this passage with John Dewey (p. 484), who views artistic expression as coming out of the artist's struggle with the resistance of the material. [Ed.]

[2] Here Plotinus distinguishes his position from Plato's in the *Republic*, where the artist was said to imitate material objects, not ideas. [Ed.]

[3] Plotinus continues his argument that Beauty resides in ideal form rather than in matter or in the process of origin. [Ed.]

of beauty, then the creating principle, being without extension, could not be beautiful: but beauty cannot be made to depend upon magnitude since, whether in a large object or a small, the one Idea equally moves and forms the mind by its inherent power. A further indication is that as long as the object remains outside us we know nothing of it; it affects us by entry; but only as an Idea can it enter through the eyes which are not of scope to take an extended mass: we are, no doubt, simultaneously possessed of the magnitude which, however, we take in not as mass but by an elaboration upon the presented form.

Then again the principle producing the beauty must be, itself, ugly, neutral or beautiful: ugly, it could not produce the opposite; neutral, why should its product be the one rather than the other? The Nature, then, which creates things so lovely must be itself of a far earlier beauty; we, undisciplined in discernment of the inward, knowing nothing of it, run after the outer, never understanding that it is the inner which stirs us; we are in the case of one who sees his own reflection but not realizing whence it comes goes in pursuit of it.

But that the thing we are pursuing is something different and that the beauty is not in the concrete object is manifest from the beauty there is in matters of study, in conduct and custom; briefly in soul or mind. And it is precisely here that the greater beauty lies, perceived whenever you look to the wisdom in a man and delight in it, not wasting attention on the face, which may be hideous, but passing all appearance by and catching only at the inner comeliness, the truly personal; if you are still unmoved and cannot acknowledge beauty under such conditions, then looking to your own inner being you will find no beauty to delight you and it will be futile in that state to seek the greater vision, for you will be questing it through the ugly and impure.

This is why such matters are not spoken of to everyone; you, if you are conscious of beauty within, remember.

**3**

Thus there is in the Nature-Principle itself an Ideal archetype of the beauty that is found in material forms and, of that archetype again, the still more beautiful archetype in Soul, source of that in Nature. In the proficient soul this is brighter and of more advanced loveliness: adorning the soul and bringing to it a light from that greater light which is beauty primally, its immediate presence sets the soul reflecting upon the quality of this prior, the archetype which has no such entries, and is present nowhere but remains in itself alone, and thus is not even to be called a Reason-Principle but is the creative source of the very first Reason-Principle, which is the Beauty to which Soul serves as Matter.

This prior, then, is the Intellectual-Principle, the veritable, abiding and not fluctuant since not taking intellectual quality from outside itself. By what image thus, can we represent it? We have nowhere to go but to what is less. Only from itself can we take an image of it; that is, there can be no representation of it, except in the sense that we represent gold by some portion of gold — purified, either actually or mentally, if it be impure — insisting at the same time that this is not the total thing gold, but merely the particular gold of a particular parcel. In the same way we learn in this matter from the purified Intellect in ourselves or, if you like, from the gods and the glory of the Intellect in them.

For assuredly all the gods are august and beautiful in a beauty beyond our speech. And what makes them so? Intellect; and especially Intellect operating within them (the divine sun and stars) to visibility. It is not through the loveliness of their corporeal forms: even those that have body are not gods by that beauty; it is in virtue of Intellect that they, too, are gods, and as gods beautiful. They do not veer between wisdom and folly: in the immunity of Intellect unmoving and pure, they are wise always, all-knowing, taking cognizance not of the human but of their own being and of all that lies within the contemplation of Intellect. Those of them whose dwelling is in the heavens are ever in this meditation — what task prevents them? — and from afar they look, too, into that further heaven by a lifting of the head. The Gods belonging to that higher Heaven itself, they whose station is upon it and in it, see and know in virtue of their omnipresence to it. For all There is heaven; earth is heaven, and sea heaven; and animal and plant and man; all is the heavenly content of that heaven: and the Gods in it, despising neither men nor anything else that is there where all is of the heavenly order, traverse all that country and all space in peace.

## 4

To "live at ease" is There;[4] and to these divine beings verity is mother and nurse, existence and sustenance; all that is not of process but of authentic being they see, and themselves in all: for all is transparent, nothing dark, nothing resistant; everything being is lucid to every other in breadth and depth; light runs through light. And each of them contains all within itself, and at the same time sees all in every other, so that everywhere there is all, and all is all and each all, and infinite the glory. Each of them is great; the small is great; the sun, There, is all the stars; and every star, again, is all the stars and sun. While some one manner of being is dominant in each, all are mirrored in every other.

Movement There is pure (as self-caused) for the moving principle is not a separate thing to complicate it as it speeds.

So, too, Repose is not troubled, for there is no admixture of the unstable; and the Beauty is all beauty since it is not merely resident (as an attribute or addition) in some beautiful object. Each There walks upon no alien soul; its place is its essential self; and, as each moves, so to speak, toward what is Above, it is attended by the very ground from which it starts: there is no distinguishing between the Being and the Place; all is Intellect, the Principle and the ground on which it stands, alike. Thus we might think that our visible sky (the ground or place of the stars), lit, as it is, produces the light which reaches us from it, though of course this is really produced by the stars (as it were, by the Principles of light alone not also by the ground as the analogy would require).

In our realm all is part rising from part and nothing can be more than partial; but There each being is an eternal product of a whole and is at once a whole and an individual manifesting as

[4] Just as "There" is Plotinus's term for the transcendent realm within and beyond matter, "Here" or "our realm" is the world of matter and time. [Ed.]

part but, to the keen vision There, known for the whole it is.

The myth of Lynceus seeing into the very deeps of the earth tells us of those eyes in the divine. No weariness overtakes this vision which yet brings no such satiety as would call for its ending; for there never was a void to be filled so that, with the fullness and the attainment of purpose, the sense of sufficiency be induced: nor is there any such incongruity within the divine that one Being there could be repulsive to another: and of course all There are unchangeable. This absence of satisfaction means only a satisfaction leading to no distaste for that which produces it; to see is to look the more, since for them to continue in the contemplation of an infinite self and of infinite objects is but to acquiesce in the bidding of their nature.

Life, pure, is never a burden; how then could there be weariness There where the living is most noble? That very life is wisdom, not a wisdom built up by reasonings but complete from the beginning, suffering no lack which could set it inquiring, a wisdom primal, unborrowed, not something added to the Being, but its very essence. No wisdom, thus, is greater; this is the authentic knowing, assessor to the divine Intellect as projected into manifestation simultaneously with it; thus, in the symbolic saying, Justice is assessor to Zeus.

(Perfect wisdom) for all the Principles of this order, dwelling There, are as it were visible images projected from themselves, so that all becomes an object of contemplation to contemplators immeasurably blessed. The greatness and power of the wisdom There we may know from this, that it embraces all the real Beings, and has made all and all follow it, and yet that it is itself those beings, which sprang into being with it, so that all is one and the essence There is wisdom. If we have failed to understand, it is that we have thought of knowledge as a mass of theorems and an accumulation of propositions, though that is false even for our sciences of the sense-realm. But in case this should be questioned, we may leave our own sciences for the present, and deal with the knowing in the Supreme at which Plato glances where he speaks of "that knowledge which is not a stranger in something strange to it" — though in what sense, he leaves us to examine and declare, if we boast ourselves worthy of the discussion. This is probably our best starting point.

## 5

All that comes to be, work of nature or of craft, some wisdom has made: everywhere a wisdom presides at a making.

No doubt the wisdom of the artist may be the guide of the work; it is sufficient explanation of the wisdom exhibited in the arts; but the artist himself goes back, after all, to that wisdom in Nature which is embodied in himself; and this is not a wisdom built up of theorems but one totality, not a wisdom consisting of manifold detail coordinated into a unity but rather a unity working out into detail.

Now, if we could think of this as the primal wisdom, we need look no further, since, at that, we have discovered a principle which is neither a derivative nor a "stranger in something strange to it." But if we are told that, while this Reason-Principle is in Nature, yet Nature itself is its source, we ask how Nature came to possess it; and, if Nature derived it from some other source, we ask what that other source may be; if, on the contrary, the principle is self-sprung, we need look no further: but if (as we assume) we are referred to the Intellectual-Principle, we must make clear whether the Intellectual-Principle engendered the wisdom: if we learn that it did, we ask whence: if from itself, then inevitably, it is itself Wisdom.

The true Wisdom, then (found to be identical with the Intellectual-Principle) is Real Being; and Real Being is Wisdom; it is wisdom that gives value to Real Being; and Being is Real in virtue of its origin in wisdom. It follows that all forms of existence not possessing wisdom are, indeed, Beings in right of the wisdom which went to their forming, but, as not in themselves possessing it, are not Real Beings.

We cannot therefore think that the divine Beings of that sphere, or the other supremely blessed There, need look to our apparatus of science: all of that realm (the very Beings themselves), all is noble image, such images as we may conceive to lie within the soul of the wise — but There not as inscription but as authentic existence. The ancients had this in mind when they declared the Ideas to be Beings, Essentials.

## 6

Similarly, as it seems to me, the wise of Egypt — whether in precise knowledge or by a prompting of nature — indicated the truth where, in their effort toward philosophical statement, they left aside the writing forms that take in the detail of words and sentences — those characters that represent sounds and convey the propositions of reasoning — and drew pictures instead, engraving in the temple inscriptions a separate image for every separate item: thus they exhibited the mode in which the Supreme goes forth.

For each manifestation of knowledge and wisdom is a distinct image, an object in itself, an immediate unity, not an aggregate of discursive reasoning and detailed willing. Later, from this wisdom in unity there appears, in another form of being, an image, already less compact, which announces the original in an outward stage and seeks the causes by which things are such that the wonder rises how a generated world can be so excellent.

For one who knows must declare his wonder that this Wisdom, while not itself containing the causes by which Being exists and takes such excellence, yet imparts them to the entities produced in Being's realm. This excellence, whose necessity is scarcely or not at all manifest to search, exists, if we could but find it out, before all searching and reasoning.

What I say may be considered in one chief thing, and thence applied to all the particular entities:

## 7

Consider the universe: we are agreed that its existence and its nature come to it from beyond itself; are we, now, to imagine that its maker first thought it out in detail — the earth, and its necessary situation in the middle; water and, again, its position as lying upon the earth; all the other elements and objects up to the sky in due place and order; living beings with their appropriate forms as we know them, their inner organs and their outer limbs — and that having thus appointed every item beforehand, he then set about the execution?

Such designing was not even possible; how could the plan for a universe come to one that had never looked outward? Nor could he work on material gathered from elsewhere as our craftsmen do, using hands and tools; feet and hands are of the later order.

One way, only, remains: all things must exist in something else; of that prior — since there is no obstacle, all being continuous within the realm of reality — there has suddenly appeared a sign, an image, whether given forth directly or through the ministry of soul or of some phase of soul, matters nothing for the moment: thus the entire aggregate of existence springs from the divine world, in greater beauty There because There unmingled but mingled here.

From the beginning to end all is gripped by the Forms of the Intellectual Realm: Matter itself is held by the Ideas of the elements and to these Ideas are added other Ideas and others again, so that it is hard to work down to crude Matter beneath all that sheathing of Idea. Indeed since Matter itself is, in its degree, an Idea — the lowest — all this universe is Idea and there is nothing that is not Idea as the archetype was. And all is made silently, since nothing had part in the making but Being and Idea — a further reason why creation went without toil. The Exemplar was the Idea of an All, and so an All must come into being.

Thus nothing stood in the way of the Idea, and even now it dominates, despite all the clash of things: the creation is not hindered on its way even now; it stands firm in virtue of being All. To me, moreover, it seems that if we ourselves were archetypes, Ideas, veritable Being, and the Idea with which we construct here were our veritable Essence, then our creative power too would toillessly effect its purpose: as man now stands, he does not produce in his work a true image of himself: become man, he has ceased to be the All; ceasing to be man — we read — "he soars aloft and administers the Kosmos entire"; restored to the All he is maker of the All.

But — to our immediate purpose — it is possible to give a reason why the earth is set in the midst and why it is round and why the ecliptic runs precisely as it does, but, looking to the creating principle, we cannot say that because this was the way, therefore things were so planned: we can say only that because the All is what it is, therefore there is a total of good; the causing principle, we might put it, reached the conclusion before all formal reasoning and not from any premises, not by sequence or plan but before either, since all of that order is later, all reason, demonstration, persuasion.

Since there is a Source, all the created must spring from it and in accordance with it; and we are rightly told not to go seeking the causes impelling a Source to produce, especially when this is the perfectly sufficient Source and identical with the Term: a Source which is Source and Term must be the All-Unity, complete in itself.

**8**

This then is Beauty primally: it is entire and omnipresent as an entirety; and therefore in none of its parts or members lacking in beauty; beautiful thus beyond denial. Certainly it cannot be anything (be, for example, Beauty) without being wholly that thing; it can be nothing which it is to possess partially or in which it utterly fails (and therefore it must entirely be Beauty entire).

If this principle were not beautiful, what other could be? Its prior does not deign to be beautiful; that which is the first to manifest itself — Form and object of vision to the intellect — cannot but be lovely to see. It is to indicate this that Plato, drawing on something well within our observation, represents the Creator as approving the work he has achieved: the intention is to make us feel the lovable beauty of the autotype and of the Divine Idea; for to admire a representation is to admire the original upon which it was made.

It is not surprising if we fail to recognize what is passing within us: lovers, and those in general that admire beauty here, do not stay to reflect that it is to be traced, as of course it must be, to the Beauty There. That the admiration of the Demiurge is to be referred to the Ideal Exemplar is deliberately made evident by the rest of the passage: "He admired; and determined to bring the work into still closer likeness with the Exemplar": he makes us feel the magnificent beauty of the Exemplar by telling us that the Beauty sprung from this world is, itself, a copy from That.[5]

And indeed if the divine did not exist, the transcendently beautiful, in a beauty beyond all thought, what could be lovelier than the things we see? Certainly no reproach can rightly be brought against this world save only that it is not That.

**9**

Let us, then, make a mental picture of our universe: each member shall remain what it is, distinctly apart; yet all is to form, as far as possible, a complete unity so that whatever comes into view shall show as if it were the surface of the orb over all, bringing immediately with it the vision, on the one plane, of the sun and of all the stars with earth and sea and all living things as if exhibited upon a transparent globe.

Bring this vision actually before your sight, so that there shall be in your mind the gleaming representation of a sphere, a picture holding all the things of the universe moving or in repose or (as in reality) some at rest, some in motion. Keep this sphere before you, and from it imagine another, a sphere stripped of magnitude and of spatial differences; cast out your inborn sense of Matter, taking care not merely to attenuate it: call on God, maker of the sphere whose image you now hold, and pray Him to enter. And may He come bringing His own Universe with all the Gods that dwell in it — He who is the one God and all the gods, where each is all, blending into a unity, distinct in powers but all one god in virtue of that one divine power of many facets.

More truly, this is the one God who is all the gods; for, in the coming to be of all those, this, the one, has suffered no diminishing. He and all have one existence, while each again is distinct. It is distinction by state without interval: there is no outward form to set one here and another there and to prevent any from being an entire

identity; yet there is no sharing of parts from one to another. Nor is each of those divine wholes a power in fragment, a power totaling to the sum of the measurable segments: the divine is one all-power, reaching out to infinity, powerful to infinity: and so great is God that his very members are infinites. What place can be named to which He does not reach?

Great, too, is this firmament of ours and all the powers constellated within it, but it would be greater still, unspeakably, but that there is inbound in it something of the petty power of body; no doubt the powers of fire and other bodily substances might themselves be thought very great, but in fact, it is through their failure in the true power that we see them burning, destroying, wearing things away, and slaving toward the production of life; they destroy because they are themselves in process of destruction, and they produce because they belong to the realm of the produced.

The power in that other world has merely Being and Beauty of Being. Beauty without Being could not be, nor Being voided of Beauty: abandoned of Beauty, Being loses something of its essence. Being is desirable because it is identical with Beauty; and Beauty is loved because it is Being. How then can we debate which is the cause of the other, where the nature is one? The very figment of Being needs some imposed image of Beauty to make it passable, and even to ensure its existence; it exists to the degree in which it has taken some share in the beauty of Idea; and the more deeply it has drawn on this, the less imperfect it is, precisely because the nature which is essentially the beautiful has entered into it the more intimately.

**10**

This is why Zeus, although the oldest of the gods and their sovereign, advances first (in the Phaidros myth) toward that vision, followed by gods and demigods and such souls as are of strength to see.[6] That Being appears before them from some unseen place and rising loftily over them

---

[5]The Demiurge is the creator of the world in Plato's *Timaeus*, 40. [Ed.]

[6]This is part of the myth of the soul in Plato's *Phaedrus*, 246e. [Ed.]

pours its light upon all things, so that all gleams in its radiance; it upholds some beings, and they see; the lower are dazzled and turn away, unfit to gaze upon that sun, the trouble falling the more heavily on those most remote.

Of those looking upon that Being and its content, and able to see, all take something but not all the same vision always: intently gazing, one sees the fount and principle of Justice, another is filled with the sight of Moral Wisdom, the original of that quality as found, sometimes at least, among men, copied by them in their degree from the divine virtue which, covering all the expanse, so to speak, of the Intellectual Realm is seen, last attainment of all, by those who have known already many splendid visions.

The gods see, each singly and all as one. So, too, the souls; they see all There in right of being sprung, themselves, of that universe and therefore including all from beginning to end and having their existence There if only by that phase which belongs inherently to the Divine, though often too they are There entire, those of them that have not incurred separation.

This vision Zeus takes and it is for such of us, also, as share his love and appropriate our part in the Beauty There, the final object of all seeing, the entire beauty upon all things; for all There sheds radiance, and floods those that have found their way thither so that they too become beautiful; thus it will often happen that men climbing heights where the soil has taken a yellow glow will themselves appear so, borrowing color from the place on which they move. The color flowering on that other height we speak of is Beauty; or rather all There is light and beauty, through and through, for the beauty is no mere bloom upon the surface.

To those that do not see entire, the immediate impression is alone taken into account; but those drunken with this wine, filled with the nectar, all their soul penetrated by this beauty, cannot remain mere gazers: no longer is there a spectator outside gazing on an outside spectacle; the clear-eyed hold the vision within themselves, though, for the most part, they have no idea that it is within but look toward it as to something beyond them and see it is an object of vision caught by the direction of the will.

All that one sees as a spectacle is still external; one must bring the vision within and see no longer in that mode of separation but as we know ourselves; thus a man filled with a god — possessed by Apollo or by one of the Muses — need no longer look outside for his vision of the divine being; it is but finding the strength to see divinity within.[7]

## II

Similarly any one, unable to see himself, but possessed by that God, has but to bring that divine-within before his consciousness and at once he sees an image of himself, himself lifted to a better beauty: now let him ignore that image, lovely though it is, and sink into a perfect self-identity, no such separation remaining; at once he forms a multiple unity with the God silently present; in the degree of his power and will, the two become one; should he turn back to the former duality, still he is pure and remains very near to the God; he has but to look again and the same presence is there.

This conversion brings gain: at the first stage, that of separation, a man is aware of self; but retreating inward, he becomes possessor of all; he puts sense away behind him in dread of the separated life and becomes one in the Divine; if he plans to see in separation, he sets himself outside.

The novice must hold himself constantly under some image of the Divine Being and seek in the light of a clear conception; knowing thus, in a deep conviction, whither he is going — into what a sublimity he penetrates — he must give himself forthwith to the inner and, radiant with the Divine Intellections (with which he is now one), be no longer the seer, but, as that place has made him, the seen.

Still, we will be told, one cannot be in beauty and yet fail to see it. The very contrary: to see the divine as something external is to be outside of it; to become it is to be most truly in beauty: since sight deals with the external, there can here

---

[7]Here Plotinus gives a very different account of inspiration than Plato in the *Ion*: the source of *enthousiasmós* is within, not outside the poet. [Ed.]

be no vision unless in the sense of identification with the object.

And this identification amounts to a self-knowing, a self-consciousness, guarded by the fear of losing the self in the desire of a too wide awareness.

It must be remembered that sensations of the ugly and evil impress us more violently than those of what is agreeable and yet leave less knowledge as the residue of the shock: sickness makes the rougher mark, but health, tranquilly present, explains itself better; it takes the first place, it is the natural thing, it belongs to our being; illness is alien, unnatural and thus makes itself felt by its very incongruity, while the other conditions are native and we take no notice. Such being our nature, we are most completely aware of ourselves when we are most completely identified with the object of our knowledge.

This is why in that other sphere, when we are deepest in that knowledge by intellection, we are aware of none; we are expecting some impression on sense, which has nothing to report since it has seen nothing and never could in that order see anything. The unbelieving element is sense; it is the other, the Intellectual-Principle, that sees; and if this too doubted, it could not even credit its own existence, for it can never stand away and with bodily eyes apprehend itself as a visible object.

## 12

We have told how this vision is to be procured, whether by the mode of separation or in identity: now, seen in either way, what does it give to report?

The vision has been of God in travail of a beautiful offspring, God engendering a universe within himself in a painless labor and — rejoiced in what he has brought into being, proud of his children — keeping all closely by Him, for the pleasure He has in his radiance and in theirs.

Of this offspring — all beautiful, but most beautiful those that have remained within — only one has become manifest without; from him (Zeus, sovereign over the visible universe) the youngest born, we may gather, as from some image, the greatness of the Father and of the Brothers that remain within the Father's house.

Still the manifested God cannot think that he has come forth in vain from the father; for through him another universe has arisen, beautiful as the image of beauty, and it could not be lawful that Beauty and Being should fail of a beautiful image.

This second Kosmos at every point copies the archetype: it has life and being in copy, and has beauty as springing from that diviner world. In its character of image it holds, too, that divine perpetuity without which it would only at times be truly representative and sometimes fail like a construction of art; for every image whose existence lies in the nature of things must stand during the entire existence of the archetype.

Hence it is false to put an end to the visible sphere as long as the Intellectual endures, or to found it upon a decision taken by its maker at some given moment.

That teaching shirks the penetration of such a making as is here involved: it fails to see that as long as the Supreme is radiant there can be no failing of its sequel but, that existing, all exists. And — since the necessity of conveying our meaning compels such terms — the Supreme has existed forever and forever will exist.

## 13

The God fettered (as in the Kronos Myth) to an unchanging identity leaves the ordering of this universe to his son (to Zeus), for it could not be in his character to neglect his rule within the divine sphere, and, as though sated with the Authentic-Beauty, seek a lordship too recent and too poor for his might. Ignoring this lower world, Kronos (Intellectual-Principle) claims for his own father (Ouranios, the Absolute, or One) with all the upward-tending between them: and he counts all that tends to the inferior, beginning from his son (Zeus, the All-Soul), as ranking beneath him. Thus he holds a midposition determined on the one side by the differentiation implied in the severance from the very highest and, on the other, by that which keeps him apart from the link between himself and the lower: he stands between a greater father and an inferior son. But since that father is too lofty to be thought of under the name of Beauty, the second God remains the primally beautiful.[8]

Soul also has beauty, but is less beautiful than Intellect as being its image and therefore, though beautiful in nature, taking increase of beauty by looking to that original. Since then the All-Soul

---

[8]Plotinus presents the traditional succession of the Greek gods — Ouranos, Kronos, and Zeus — as an allegory of the philosophical relationship between the One, the Intellectual-Principle, and the All-Soul, which generates the Nature-Principle. The transcendent idea of Intellectual Beauty thus mediates between the incomprehensible One and the forms of beauty we can apprehend in matter. [Ed.]

---

— to use the more familiar term — since Aphrodite herself is so beautiful, what name can we give to that other? If Soul is so lovely in its own right, of what quality must that prior be? And since its being is derived, what must that power be from which the Soul takes the double beauty, the borrowed and the inherent?

We ourselves possess beauty when we are true to our own being; our ugliness is in going over to another order; our self-knowledge, that is to say, is our beauty; in self-ignorance we are ugly.

Thus beauty is of the Divine and comes Thence only.

Do these considerations suffice to a clear understanding of the Intellectual Sphere or must we make yet another attempt by another road?

# Dante Alighieri
## 1265–1321

Dante Alighieri was born in Florence, the son of Alighiero Alighieri of the lesser nobility. His mother died when Dante was quite young, and his father, whom Dante mentions seldom and then only formally, remarried and produced a large second family. Dante was well educated, probably by the Franciscans; his rhetoric tutor was Brunetto Latini. Around 1285, Dante married Gemma Donati, by whom he had two sons and two daughters. Gemma's influence on his life pales, however, beside the radiance of another Florentine noblewoman, Bice Portinari, whom Dante dubbed "Beatrice," the bringer of blessing. Dante's contacts with Beatrice (who married Simone dei Bardi) were undoubtedly few and platonic in the years before her death in 1290, but she became his lifelong Muse and his guide through Paradise in the *Commedia*.

Although Dante experimented with verse in his twenties (under the influence of the poet Guido Cavalcanti), his life was devoted to public affairs: He fought in 1289 in the battle of Campaldino, spoke in the Florentine assembly, and became one of the six priors of Florence. While Dante was away from Florence on a diplomatic mission in 1300, factional warfare broke out; a rival party came to power and convicted Dante in absentia of graft and corruption in office. Under sentence of death if he returned, Dante spent the rest of his life abroad, where he learned "how salt is the bread of exile and how steep the stairs of another." Except for the *Vita Nuova,* which was written in Florence in 1292, most of Dante's works are the product of his exile, including the *Convivio* ("The Banquet," 1304–8), the *De Monarchia* (1308), and his masterpiece the *Commedia* (1306–14) — "Divina" was added by its readers. Dante's literary life was spent wandering between Verona (where his patrons included Can Grande della Scala) and other intellectual centers such as Bologna and Paris. He finally settled in Ravenna, where he died in 1321.

Dante's letter to Can Grande is the most familiar exposition of medieval semiotic theory; the ideas are not original with Dante, but have a long and distinguished history. In the sixth century, St. Augustine had claimed in *Of the Value of Belief* that the Old Testament was to be interpreted as "history, etiology, analogy and allegory." During the Middle Ages, the Hebrew bible was interpreted not only as the literal history of the Israelites, but as prefiguring events in the life of Christ. And in the thirteenth century, St. Thomas Aquinas's *Summa Theologica* had codified this mode of interpreting scripture:

> That first signification whereby words signify things belongs to the first sense, the historical. . . . That signification whereby things signified by words have themselves also a signification is called the spiritual sense. . . . Now this spiritual sense has a threefold division. . . . So far as the things of the Old Law signify the things of the New Law, there is the allegorical sense. . . . So far as the things done in Christ . . . are signs of what we ought to do, there is the moral sense. . . . But so far as they signify what relates to eternal glory, there is the anagogical sense.

Dante's principal innovation, if indeed it is an innovation, is in applying these principles of symbolic meaning to something other than sacred scripture — to his *Commedia,* a poetical work written in the "vulgar" language of common speech. Some contemporary medievalists (the followers of D. W. Robertson) have suggested that this multivalent mode of reading was part of the freight of medieval literacy, and that even apparently secular texts (like Chaucer's *Canterbury Tales,* or Boccaccio's *Decameron*) were automatically read in this manner. Whether this was actually the case is controversial, but certainly with the coming of the Renaissance, this mode of reading began to fade away, and the notion that all literature was potentially ambiguous — indeed, that the mark of literature was ambiguity and multiplicity of interpretation — would not return until Northrop Frye (p. 677) and William Empson in the middle of the twentieth century.

## Selected Bibliography

Alighieri, Dante. *The Divine Comedy.* Translated and with a commentary by Charles S. Singleton. Princeton: Princeton University Press, 1970–75.

Dunbar, Helen Flanders. *Symbolism in Medieval Thought.* New Haven: Yale University Press, 1929.

Hollander, Robert. *Allegory in Dante's Commedia.* Princeton: Princeton University Press, 1969.

Kirkpatrick, Robin. *Dante's Paradiso and the Limitations of Modern Criticism: A Study of Style and Poetic Theory.* Cambridge: Cambridge University Press, 1978.

Pietrobono, Luigi. "L'epistola a Can Grande." *Giornale dantesco* 4 (1939): 3–51.

Saley, John V. *Dante and the English Romantics.* New York: Columbia University Library, 1960.

Singleton, Charles S. *Dante Studies.* 2 vols. Cambridge: Harvard University Press, 1954–58.

Toynbee, Paget Jackson. *Dante in English Literature from Chaucer to Cary.* 2 vols. London: Methuen, 1909.

# From the
# *Letter to Can Grande della Scala*

5. As the Philosopher says in the second book of the *Metaphysics,* "As a thing is with respect to being, so it is with respect to truth";[1] and the reason for this is that the truth concerning a thing, which consists in the truth as its subject, is the perfect image of the thing as it is. And so, of all

Translated by Robert S. Haller.
[1]Aristotle, *Metaphysics* 2.1 [Tr.]

things which have being, some are such that they have absolute being in themselves, others such that their being is dependent upon a relationship with something else: they exist at the same time with something which is their correlative, as is the case with father and son, master and servant, double and half, the whole and the parts, and many other such things. Because such things depend for their being upon another thing, it follows that their truth would depend upon the truth of the other; not knowing the "half," its "double" could not be understood, and so with the other cases.

6. Therefore, if one should wish to present an introduction to a part of a work, it is necessary to present some conception of the whole work of which it is a part. For this reason I, who wish to present something in the form of an introduction to the above-mentioned part of the whole *Comedy*,[2] have decided to preface it with some discussion of the whole work, in order to make the approach to the part easier and more complete. There are six questions, then, which should be asked at the beginning about any doctrinal work: what is its subject, its form, its agent, its end, the title of the book, and its branch of philosophy. In three cases the answers to these questions will be different for the part of the work I propose to give you than for the whole, that is, in the cases of its subject, form, and title, while in the other three, as will be clear upon inspection, they will be the same. Thus these first three should be specifically asked in a discussion of the whole work, after which the way will be clear for an introduction to the part. Let us, then, ask the last three questions not only about the whole but also about the offered part itself.

7. For the clarification of what I am going to say, then, it should be understood that there is not just a single sense in this work: it might rather be called *polysemous*, that is, having several senses. For the first sense is that which is contained in the letter, while there is another which is contained in what is signified by the letter. The first is called literal, while the second is called allegorical, or moral or anagogical. And in order to make this manner of treatment clear, it can be applied to the following verses: "When Israel went out of Egypt, the house of Jacob from a barbarous people, Judea was made his sanctuary, Israel his dominion."[3] Now if we look at the letter alone, what is signified to us is the departure of the sons of Israel from Egypt during the time of Moses; if at the allegory, what is signified

to us is our redemption through Christ; if at the moral sense, what is signified to us is the conversion of the soul from the sorrow and misery of sin to the state of grace; if at the anagogical, what is signified to us is the departure of the sanctified soul from bondage to the corruption of this world into the freedom of eternal glory. And although these mystical senses are called by various names, they may all be called allegorical, since they are all different from the literal or historical. For allegory is derived from the Greek *alleon,* which means in Latin *alienus* ("belonging to another") or *diversus* ("different").

8. This being established, it is clear that the subject about which these two senses play must also be twofold. And thus it should first be noted what the subject of the work is when taken according to the letter, and then what its subject is when understood allegorically. The subject of the whole work, then, taken literally, is the state of souls after death, understood in a simple sense; for the movement of the whole work turns upon this and about this. If on the other hand the work is taken allegorically, the subject is man, in the exercise of his free will, earning or becoming liable to the rewards or punishments of justice.

9. And the form is twofold: the form of the treatise and the form of the treatment. The form of the treatise is threefold, according to its three kinds of divisions. The first division is that which divides the whole work into three canticles. The second is that which divides each canticle into cantos. The third, that which divides the cantos into rhymed units. The form or manner of treatment is poetic, fictive, descriptive, digressive, and transumptive, and it as well consists in definition, division, proof, refutation, and the giving of examples.

10. The title of the work is, "Here begins the Comedy of Dante Alighieri, a Florentine by birth but not in character." To understand the title, it must be known that comedy is derived from *comos,* "a village," and from *oda,* "a song," so that a comedy is, so to speak, "a rustic song." Comedy, then, is a certain genre of poetic narrative differing from all others. For it differs from tragedy in its matter, in that tragedy is tranquil and conducive to wonder at the beginning, but foul and conducive to horror at the end, or ca-

---

[2]His *Divine Comedy.* [Ed.]

[3]Psalm 113:1–2 (114:1–2 in the King James version). [Tr.]

tastrophe, for which reason it is derived from *tragos,* meaning "goat," and *oda,* making it, as it were, a "goat song," that is, foul as a goat is foul. This is evident in Seneca's tragedies. Comedy, on the other hand, introduces a situation of adversity, but ends its matter in prosperity, as is evident in Terence's comedies. And for this reason some writers have the custom of saying in their salutations, by way of greeting, "a tragic beginning and a comic ending to you." And, as well, they differ in their manner of speaking. Tragedy uses an elevated and sublime style, while comedy uses an unstudied and low style, which is what Horace implies in the *Art of Poetry* where he allows comic writers occasionally to speak like the tragic, and also the reverse of this:

Yet sometimes even comedy elevates its voice,
and angry Chremes rages in swelling tones;
and in tragedy Telephus and Peleus often lament
in prosaic speeches. . . .[4]

So from this it should be clear why the present work is called the *Comedy.* For, if we consider the matter, it is, at the beginning, that is, in Hell, foul and conducive to horror, but at the end, in Paradise, prosperous, conducive to pleasure, and welcome. And if we consider the manner of speaking, it is unstudied and low, since its speech is the vernacular, in which even women communicate. There are, besides these, other genres of poetic narrative, such as pastoral verse, elegy, satire, and the hymn of thanksgiving, as could also be gathered from Horace in his *Art of Poetry.* But there is no purpose to discussing these at this time.

11. Now it can be explained in what manner the part I have offered you may be assigned a subject. For if the subject of the whole work, on the literal level, is the state of souls after death, in an absolute, not in a restricted sense, then the subject of this part is the same state, but restricted to the state of blessed souls after death. And if the subject of the whole work, considered allegorically, is man, through exercise of free will, earning or becoming liable to the rewards or punishments of justice, then it is evident that the subject in this part is restricted to man's becoming eligible, to the extent he has earned them, for the rewards of justice.

12. And in the same manner the form of this part follows from the form ascribed to the whole. For if the form of the whole treatise is threefold, then the form in this part is twofold, that is, the division into cantos and into rhymed units. This part could not have the first division as its form, since this part itself is [a product] of the first division.

13. The title of the book also follows; for while the title of the whole book is, as was said earlier, "Here begins the Comedy, etc.," the title of this part is, "Here begins the third canticle of Dante's *Comedy,* etc., which is called *Paradise.*"

14. Having settled these three questions, where the answer was different for the part than for the whole, it remains to deal with the other three, where the answers will not be different for either the part or the whole. The agent, then, in the whole and in the part, is he who has been mentioned above; and he is clearly so throughout.

15. The end of the whole and of the part could be multiple, that is, both immediate and ultimate. But, without going into details, it can be briefly stated that the end of the whole as of the part is to remove those living in this life from the state of misery and to lead them to the state of happiness.

16. The branch of philosophy which determines the procedure of the work as a whole and in this part is moral philosophy, or ethics, inasmuch as the whole and this part have been conceived for the sake of practical results, not for the sake of speculation. So even if some parts or passages are treated in the manner of speculative philosophy, this is not for the sake of the theory, but for a practical purpose, following that principle which the Philosopher advances in the second book of the *Metaphysics,* that "practical men sometimes speculate about things in their particular and temporal relations."[5]

[4]Horace, *Art of Poetry,* 93–96. [Tr.] See Horace, p. 70. [Ed.]

[5]Aristotle, *Metaphysics* 2.1. [Ed.]

# Giovanni Boccaccio

## 1313–1375

The father of Italian prose was born the illegitimate son of a well-to-do Florentine merchant-banker. Boccaccio, who claims to have written poetry at the age of seven, was nevertheless apprenticed to his father's trade and wasted six years in "bondage" to commerce and canon law until his desperate father agreed to let him pursue liberal studies. In 1341, while visiting the court of Naples, he met Maria, a natural daughter of King Robert of Anjou, whom he was to call Fiammetta in his works. Fiammetta was to Boccaccio what Laura was to Petrarch and Beatrice to Dante: the focus of his earthly desire, heavenly ideals, and poetic inspiration.

Most of Boccaccio's early works are poetry in the courtly love tradition, like the elaborate *Amoroso Visione,* in which the initial letters of each stanza acrostically spell out three further canzone dedicated to Maria. To English-speaking readers Boccaccio's verse is not well known except as the source of Geoffrey Chaucer's *Knight's Tale* (from Boccaccio's *Teseide*, ca. 1341) and his *Troilus and Criseyde* (from the *Filostrato*, ca. 1344–50).

During the plague years of the late 1340s, Boccaccio wrote his masterwork, the *Decameron* (published in 1353), an anthology of a hundred sharply crafted stories and folktales, which he began to collect and write out at Fiammetta's instigation. The stories, sometimes nobly pathetic, sometimes grossly bawdy or farcical, have given pleasure to millions for the past six centuries. The philosophical worldview of the stories replays the medieval hierarchies of Aquinas and Dante, but their anticlericalism — and the secular spirit of character and act — seems to belong to the humanistic Renaissance. Like his good friend Petrarch (whom he sponsored during the French poet's sojourn in Florence), Boccaccio straddles the medieval and Renaissance worlds, and also like Petrarch, he contributed to the revival of classical learning by endowing a chair of Greek and by helping copy and restore Greek manuscripts.

Boccaccio's Latin work on mythology, *De Genealogiis* (1366) belongs to the end of his life, after his reputed conversion and his entry into the Church as a lay brother in 1362. His discussion of poetry in that work is fully consistent with the scholastic doctrines of polysemy already seen in Dante, but there is a more humanistic tone to Boccaccio's rendering of them. Boccaccio insists that the poets' work needs to be interpreted as moral and anagogical allegory in order to reveal the truth that is hidden behind the veil of fiction: Just as the Old Testament prefigures the New, and just as Jesus hid his truth in parables, so the pagan poets, like Homer and Virgil, have purposes beyond their literal narratives that justify their falsehood. Where Boccaccio goes beyond Dante is in his sense that poetry originates in a divine fervor. Here we seem to be hearing an echo of Plato's *Ion* and his idea of *enthousiasmós* — the muse-inspired madness that is magnetically transmitted from poet to rhapsode to audience. But this must be a distant echo resounding faintly through Latin authors, since Boccaccio lived and died before the full rediscovery of Greek learning that would have allowed him to read for himself the works of Plato.

### Selected Bibliography

Bergin, Thomas G. *Boccaccio*. New York: Viking Press, 1981.

Chubb, T. C. *The Life of Giovanni Boccaccio*. 1930; Port Washington, N.Y.: Kennikat Press, 1969.

Gathercole, Patricia M. *Tension in Boccaccio: Boccaccio and the Fine Arts*. University, Mich.: Romance Monographs, 1975.

Osgood, C. G. *Boccaccio on Poetry*. Princeton: Princeton University Press, 1930.

Smarr, Janet Levarie. *Boccaccio and Fiammetta: The Narrator as Lover*. Urbana: University of Illinois Press, 1986.

Woodbridge, Elisabeth. "Boccaccio's Defense of Poetry." *PMLA* 13 (1898): 333–49.

Wright, Herbert Gladstone. *Boccaccio in England from Chaucer to Tennyson*. London: Athlone, 1957.

# The Definition of Poetry

## Its Origin and Function

This poetry, which ignorant triflers cast aside, is a sort of fervid and exquisite invention, with fervid expression, in speech or writing, of that which the mind has invented. It proceeds from the bosom of God, and few, I find, are the souls in whom this gift is born; indeed so wonderful a gift it is that true poets have always been the rarest of men. This fervor of poesy is sublime in its effects: it impels the soul to a longing for utterance; it brings forth strange and unheard-of creations of the mind;[1] it arranges these meditations in a fixed order, adorns the whole composition with unusual interweaving of words and thoughts; and thus it veils truth in a fair and fitting garment of fiction. Further, if in any case the invention so requires, it can arm kings, marshal them for war, launch whole fleets from their docks, nay, counterfeit sky, land, sea, adorn young maidens with flowery garlands, portray human character in its various phases, awake the idle, stimulate the dull, restrain the rash, subdue the criminal, and distinguish excellent men with their proper meed of praise: these, and many other such, are the effects of poetry. Yet if any man who has received the gift of poetic fervor shall imperfectly fulfill its function here described, he is not, in my opinion, a laudable poet. For, however deeply the poetic impulse stirs the mind to which it is granted, it very rarely accomplishes anything commendable if the instruments by which its concepts are to be wrought out are wanting — I mean, for example, the precepts of grammar and rhetoric, an abundant knowledge of which is opportune.[2] I grant that many a man already writes his mother tongue admirably, and indeed has performed each of the various duties of poetry as such; yet over and above this, it is necessary to know at least the principles of the other Liberal Arts, both moral and natural, to possess a strong and abundant vocabulary, to behold the monuments and relics

Translated by Charles Osgood.

[1] Boccaccio's notion that the poet is not an imitator, but a free creator of worlds otherwise unknown seems to be original with him. [Ed.]

[2] Boccaccio mentions grammar and rhetoric, two-thirds of the standard medieval curriculum called the trivium, but omits logic. [Ed.]

of the Ancients, to have in one's memory the histories of the nations, and to be familiar with the geography of various lands, of seas, rivers and mountains.

Furthermore, places of retirement, the lovely handiwork of Nature herself, are favorable to poetry, as well as peace of mind and desire for worldly glory; the ardent period of life also has very often been of great advantage. If these conditions fail, the power of creative genius frequently grows dull and sluggish.

Now since nothing proceeds from this poetic fervor, which sharpens and illumines the powers of the mind, except what is wrought out by art, poetry is generally called an art. Indeed the word poetry has not the origin that many carelessly suppose, namely *poio, pois,* which is but Latin *fingo, fingis;* rather it is derived from a very ancient Greek word *poetes,* which means in Latin exquisite discourse (*exquisita locutio*).[3] For the first men who, thus inspired, began to employ an exquisite style of speech, such, for example, as song in an age hitherto unpolished, to render this unheard of discourse sonorous to their hearers, let it fall in measured periods; and lest by its brevity it fail to please, or, on the other hand, become prolix and tedious, they applied to it the standard of fixed rules, and restrained it within a definite number of feet and syllables. Now the product of this studied method of speech they no longer called by the more general term poesy, but poem. Thus as I said above, the name of the art, as well as its artificial product, is derived from its effect.

Now though I allege that this science of poetry has ever streamed forth from the bosom of God

upon souls while even yet in their tenderest years, these enlightened cavillers will perhaps say that they cannot trust my words. To any fair-minded man the fact is valid enough from its constant recurrence. But for these dullards I must cite witnesses to it. If, then, they will read what Cicero, a philosopher rather than a poet, says in his oration delivered before the senate in behalf of Aulus Licinius Archias, perhaps they will come more easily to believe me. He says: "And yet we have it on the highest and most learned authority, that while other arts are matters of science and formula and technique, poetry depends solely upon an inborn faculty, is evoked by a purely mental activity, and is infused with a strange supernal inspiration."[4]

But not to protract this argument, it is now sufficiently clear to reverent men that poetry is a practical art, springing from God's bosom and deriving its name from its effect, and that it has to do with many high and noble matters that constantly occupy even those who deny its existence. If my opponents ask when and in what circumstances, the answer is plain: the poets would declare with their own lips under whose help and guidance they compose their inventions when, for example, they raise flights of symbolic steps to heaven, or make thick-branching trees spring aloft to the very stars, or go winding about mountains to their summits. Haply, to disparage this art of poetry now unrecognized by them, these men will say that it is rhetoric which the poets employ. Indeed, I will not deny it in part, for rhetoric has also its own inventions. Yet, in truth, among the disguises of fiction rhetoric has no part, for whatever is composed as under a veil, and thus exquisitely wrought, is poetry and poetry alone.

[3]Boccaccio's limitations in Greek have allowed him to follow Isidore of Seville — bad etymology and all — in this whole passage, as did writers before him who knew no Greek. [Tr.]

[4]Cicero, *Pro Archias,* 18. [Tr.]

# Pierre de Ronsard
## 1524–1585

The "prince of poets," as his contemporaries called him, was born at Couture, the son of King Francis I's *maître d'hôtel du roi*. Ronsard was educated at the College de Navarre in Paris and subsequently employed by the Duc d'Orléans on diplomatic missions, but as the result of an illness, he became totally deaf and was forced to leave politics for a career in letters. He spent seven years at the Collège Coqueret, where there formed the nucleus of the seven Renaissance writers known as the Pléiade, which would establish French as a literary vernacular language as Dante had established Italian. In addition to Ronsard the Pléiade included Jean Du Bellay, Jean-Antoine de Baïf, Rémy Belleau, Pontus de Tyard, Étienne Jodelle, and the college's principal, Jean Daurat.

Ronsard's poetic fame rests most firmly on the lyric poetry he published in his late twenties, the *Odes* (1550) and the *Amours de Cassandre* (1552). These works inaugurated his favorable reception at court, which was to continue uninterrupted through the reigns of four monarchs who rewarded Ronsard so liberally with benefices that he published his verses without demanding any profit for himself. But as with many lyric poets, his later works, like the epic *La Franciade* (1572), lack the vigor and fancy of his more youthful productions, and the revisions he undertook of his earlier poems altered them mostly for the worse. He died in 1585 at the priory of Saint-Cosme at Tours.

Ronsard's *Abrégé de l'art de poétique français* (1565) is, like Horace's *Ars Poetica*, a letter addressed to an aspiring artist by an established one. Ronsard's is addressed to Alphonse Delbene, a younger poet of Italian extraction; hence the reference to "your father" and his use of "the Italian language," and hence the explanations of the peculiarities of French. Horace supplies not only the form, but much of the matter of Ronsard's *Brief*: Ronsard quotes Horace when he suggests that the fledgling poet "file" his verses and when he warns him to begin his poem *in medias res*. And like Horace, Ronsard considers poetics a branch of rhetoric: He even organizes his essay according to the three branches of medieval rhetoric — *inventio, dispositio, elocutio*. But Horace is not his only source: He has also read Aristotle and Longinus and is familiar with the medieval tradition of allegorizing the classical poets.

In the interstices of these borrowings, however, one can glimpse Ronsard himself and detect the vital spirit of the Renaissance that he embodied. One can picture the Renaissance expansion of world commerce and industry and hear Ronsard's excitement when he recommends that Delbene visit ships in the harbor and the steamy workshops of tradesmen so as to

store up many good and lively semblances . . . to enrich and beautify your work. For just as one may not call a body fair, comely, or gifted unless it be made up of blood, veins, arteries and tendons . . . . so Poetry cannot be charming, alive or perfect without excellent inventions, descriptions, comparisons, which are the nerve and life of books.

Another aspect of the Renaissance — the centralization of life around the prince and his court — emerges in Ronsard's complaint that "it is often necessary to yield to the opinion of some . . . young courtier, who will often have . . . little knowledge of good and true poetry." Most of all, one sees the Renaissance joy in the rediscovery of the classics and Ronsard's sense of the calling of poetry as a fraternity of kindred spirits, cooperating, reading, and criticizing one another's efforts as they compete for the prize of immortality.

## Selected Bibliography

Armstrong, Elizabeth. *Ronsard and the Age of Gold*. London: Cambridge University Press, 1968.

Bishop, Morris. *Ronsard: Prince of Poets*. New York: Oxford University Press, 1940.

Cave, Terence C. *Ronsard the Poet*. London: Methuen, 1973.

Lewis, D. B. Wyndham. *Ronsard*. New York: Coward-McCann, 1944.

McGowan, Margaret. *Ideal Forms in the Age of Ronsard*. Berkeley: University of California Press, 1985.

Raymond, Marcel. *L'influence de Ronsard sur la poésie française*. 2 vols. Paris: Champion, 1927.

Silver, Isidore. *Ronsard and the Hellenic Renaissance in France*. St. Louis: Washington University Press, 1961.

# A Brief on the Art of French Poetry

Although the art of Poetry can be neither learned nor taught by precept, it being a thing more experiential than traditional, yet, insofar as human art, attainment, and labor will permit, I wish to lay down some rules by which one day you may be able to reach the first order of skill in this happy calling, by my means, who confess myself reasonably learned in it. Always you will hold the Muses in reverence, in singular veneration, and not have them serve for any purpose dishonorable, ridiculous, or libelous; but you are to keep them beloved and sacramental, the daughters of Jupiter, which is to say, of God, who in his sacred grace, first through them made known to ignorant peoples the excellence of his majesty. For poetry was in the earliest time only an allegorical theology, to carry into men's coarse brains, by charming and prettily colored fables, the secret truths which they could not comprehend if openly declared. The Athenian Eumolpus, Linus the instructor of Hercules, Orpheus, Homer, Hesiod invented this excellent profession. So poets were called divine, not so much for the godlike soul which made them wonderful above others, as for the communion which they had with oracles, prophets, diviners, sibyls, interpreters of dreams, for of what these knew the poets had learned the superior part: to what the oracles said in few words, these elevated persons gave expansion, color, commentary, being for the people what the sibyls and diviners were but for themselves. A long time afterward appeared in the same country the second school of poets, whom I call human, as being more filled with artifice and labor than with divine inspiration. As an example of the latter, the Roman poets swarmed in abundance, with so many puffed out and artificial books that they brought

Translated by James Harry Smith.

to bookstores more burden than honor, except for five or six, whose understanding of their art, accompanied by perfect craftsmanship, has always held my admiration.

But since the Muses are not willing to reside in a soul unless it be kindly, saintly, virtuous, you should act always with kindness, never with meanness, sullenness, or chagrin; moved by a fine spirit, let nothing enter your soul which is not superhuman, divine. You are to bear in highest regard conceptions which are elevated, grand, beautiful — not those that lie round the earth. For the principal thing is invention, which comes as much from goodness of nature as from the lessons of the good ancient authors. If you attempt a great work, you should show yourself religious and God-fearing, beginning the poem either with his name or with another which will represent some effect of his majesty, as in the example of the Greek poets, "Sing, O Goddess, the wrath," "Tell me of the man, O Muse," "With Zeus let us begin," "Beginning from thee O Phoebus," and of the Latin, "Great Mother of Rome," "Muse, relate to me the causes."[1] For the Muses, Apollo, Mercury, Pallas, Venus, and other such deities represent to us no other thing than powers of God, to which the earliest men gave various names, in accord with the different effects of his incomparable majesty. And it must also show you that nothing can be good or perfect, if the beginning not come of God. Then, you are to study the writings of the good poets, and learn by heart as many of them as you can. You are to take great pains to correct and file your verses, and are not to excuse faults in them any more than a good gardener neglects his poles when he sees them overburdened with branches useless or of little account. You are to hold sweet converse with the other poets of your time: you will honor the oldest among them as your fathers, those your age, as your brothers, the younger, as the children. And you will show to your fellow poets your writings, for you should let nothing see the light which has not first been viewed and reviewed by your friends whom you think the

best qualified on the matter; to the end that by such relationships and familiarities of your minds, with the learning and the talent that you have, you will arrive with ease at the height of all honor, having for local example the virtues of your father, who not only has surpassed in his, the Italian language, those in highest reputation in his time, but even has made the victory doubtful between himself and those who write today with most purity and learning the old language of the Romans.

But since you have denied recognition to Greek and Latin as mediums of composition, and only French remains, which ought to be the more readily commended to you, as it is your native language, I shall say a few things that seem expedient, and without losing you in a large and tedious forest, I shall conduct you straightway, and by the path which I have found shortest, so that you may easily overtake those who first set out on the road, and may find yourself not outstripped to any extent at all.

In the manner in which Latin verse has its feet, as you know, we have in our French poetry a certain measure of syllables, according to the kind of poem to be written; and this cannot be trespassed without offense to the law of our verse, the particular measures and numbers of which I treat more amply farther on. We have also a *cæsure* on the vowel *e*, which is done away whenever it is encountered with another vowel or a diphthong, provided that the vowel which follows *e* not have the force of a consonant.[2] In imitation of my precepts you will appoint the verses, masculine and feminine, as well as it be possible for you to do, to approach nearest music and the harmony of instruments, in the favor of which poetry seems to have been born: for poetry without instruments, or without the grace of one or more voices, is in no wise charming, any more than instruments unenlivened by a pleasing voice. If you happen to have composed the two first verses masculine in ending, make the next two feminine, and proceed in this manner for the remainder of your elegy or *chanson,* that the musicians may the more easily

[1]The opening phrases, respectively, of Homer's *Iliad,* his *Odyssey,* the 17th Idyll of Theocritus, an unidentified ode, Lucretius's *De rerum natura,* and Virgil's *Aeneid.* [Ed.]

[2]In other words, the vowel *e* is elided before other vowels. [Ed.]

harmonize with it. As to lyric verse, you will build the first couplet as you desire, but the others must follow the plan of the first. If you make use of Greek and Roman proper names, you will, insofar as your tongue permits, give them French terminations; there are many which cannot so be changed. You ought not to disdain our old Latin words, but to choose them with prudence.

You will frequent the practitioners of all trades, seamanship, hunting, falconry, and especially those that owe the perfection in their craft to the furnace: goldsmiths, foundrymen, blacksmiths, metallurgists; and from them you will store up many good and lively semblances, along with the very names of the instruments, to enrich and beautify your work. For just as one may not call a body fair, comely, or gifted, unless it be made up of blood, veins, arteries, and tendons, and, above all, have a purely natural color, so Poetry cannot be charming, alive, or perfect without excellent inventions, descriptions, comparisons, which are the nerve and the life of books, which can force the centuries to leave them, in universal remembrance, victorious over time.

You are to learn to choose dexterously, and to appropriate to your work the most significant words of the dialects of our France, when those of your nation are not sufficiently proper or significant, not troubling yourself whether they be of Gascony, Poitou, Normandy, Manche, Lyonnais, or another province, provided only that they be good, and that they properly express what you want to say; without affecting too much the speech of the court, which is many times quite mediocre to be the language of courtly ladies and of gentlemen, who pursue more the practice of arms than of well-chosen speech. You will observe that the Greek language would never have been so scattered and so full of dialects and varieties of words as it is, had not the majority of the republics that flourished in that time selfishly desired that their learned citizens write in their own particular dialects. And because of that there has come down an infinity of dialects, phrases, and manners of speaking, which even today carry on their foreheads the marks of their native countries, which are held indifferently

good by the learned pens that write of that time. For a country can never be so entirely perfect that it may not borrow some something from its neighbor. And I doubt not that if there remained in France the Dukes of Burgundy, Picardy, Normandy, Brittany, Champaign, Gascony, they would yet desire the extreme honor of their subjects' writing in a provincial dialect. For princes must be no less eager to widen the bounds of their realms than, on the example of the Romans, to extend the language of their countries through all nations. But today, France under one king, we are compelled, if we wish to come to any honor, to speak the courtier's language; or our labor, however learned it may be, is liable to be estimated of little value, or may be totally scorned. And since the goods and favors come in from this source, it is often necessary to yield to the opinion of some court lady or some young courtier, who will often have as little knowledge of good and true poetry as they have skill in arms and other of the more honorable exercises.

## OF INVENTION[3]

Since I have mentioned invention before, it seems to me that it would be timely here to refresh your memory by a short notice of it. Invention is nothing other than the natural virtue of an imagination, conceiving the ideas and forms of all things that can be imagined, whether of heaven or of earth, living or inanimate, for the purpose of afterwards representing, describing, imitating: for just as the aim of the orator is to persuade, so that of the poet is to imitate, invent, and represent — things which are, or which may be — in a resemblance to truth. And it must not be doubted that after one has invented boldly and well, a "disposition" of verse which is effective will follow, for disposition follows invention, in all cases, just as the shadow does a body. When I bid you invent fair things and great, I do not mean inventions fantastic and melancholic; these do not more correspond to one another than do the broken dreams of one in a frenzy, or terribly tormented by a fever, to an

[3]The titles of the three following sections are those of the three great divisions of medieval rhetoric. [Ed.]

imagination bruised or injured, in which a thousand monstrous forms, without order or connection, are represented. But your inventions, on which I cannot give you rules, as they are of the spirit, must be well ordered and appointed. And although they seem to pass those of the vulgar, they must nevertheless be such as can easily be conceived and understood by everyone.

## OF DISPOSITION

As invention depends upon the refined state of the mind, so disposition depends upon sound invention, consisting in an elegant and consummate placing and ordering of the things invented; it does not permit what appertains to one place to be put in another, but, operating by artifice, study, and application, it disposes and sets each matter to its proper point. For examples of it you may take the ancient authors and those of the moderns who have during the last fifteen years illuminated our literature, now justly proud in this glorious achievement. Happy demigods, they who cultivate their own earth, nor strive after another, from which they could only return thankless and unhappy, unrecompensed, unhonored. The first to dare abandon the ancient Greek and Roman languages for the greater glory of their own truly must be good sons, not ungrateful citizens; worthy to be signalized in a public statue, wherein from age to age men shall encounter a lasting memorial of them and of their greatness: not that other languages should be ignored; for I counsel you to know them perfectly, and from them, as from an old treasure found under the earth, enrich your own nation. For it is very difficult to write well in the vernacular if one be not perfectly, or at least fairly, learned in those more honored and more famous languages.

## OF ELOCUTION

Elocution is a propriety and splendor of words, properly chosen and adorned, in varying lengths of sentence, which make the verse glitter like precious stones on the fingers of some great lord. Under elocution I put choice of words, which Virgil and Horace so conscientiously observed. For you ought to strive to be well supplied with words, and to call the most appropriate and significant that you can to serve as the sinew and force of your song, which will shine in proportion as the words be significant, and chosen with judgment. You are not to forget the comparisons, the descriptions of places, streams, forests, mountains, of night, and of sunrise, of midday, of the winds, the sea, of gods and goddesses, with their proper attributes, dress, cars, horses: guiding yourself in this by imitation of Homer, whom you are to observe as a divine example, from whom you are to draw, as from life, the most perfect lineaments for your picture.

## OF POETRY IN GENERAL

You are to know that great poems never begin at the first point of the action, nor are so completed as that the reader, taken with the delight of it, may not still wish the end farther off; but the good literary craftsmen begin in the middle, and knowing so well how to join the beginning to the middle, and the middle to the end, make of the pieces so produced a body entire and perfect. Never begin a poem on a large scale unless its subject stretch back before the memory of men; and invoke the Muse, who remembers everything, being a goddess, to sing to you things of which men can remember nothing. The others, little poems, may be begun abruptly, the lyric odes, for example, in the composition of which I advise you to train yourself first, taking care above all against being more the versifier than the poet: for fable and fictions have furnished the material for the good poets, those who have been recommended to posterity from as far back as memory goes; and mere verse is but the aim of the ignorant versifier, who thinks that he has made great headway in his work when he has composed a great many rhyming verses which so smell of prose that I am amazed how our French publishers can print such drugs, to the confusion of authors, and of our nation as a whole. I should inform you of the proper subjects for each particular kind of poem, if you had not already read the *arts of poetry* of Horace and of Aristotle, in which I know you are fairly well versed.

I counsel you to avoid epithets relating to

objects of nature, as they do not advance at all the sense of what you want to say; for example, *the flowing river, the green bough,* and infinite others. You should seek out epithets which mean something, not merely fill up your verse form, or trifle with your sense. Take this verse for an example:

The vaulted sky encloses all the earth.

I have said "vaulted," and not "burning," "clear," "high," or "azure," because a vault appertains to the embracing and enclosing a thing. You may well say,

The small boat goes along the running wave,

because the course of the water makes the boat to run. The Romans have been very cautious observers of this rule, Virgil and Horace among the others. The Greeks, as in all things pertaining to verse, have been freer about it, and have not regarded it so closely. You are also to avoid the manner of composition of the Italians in your language, who commonly put four or five epithets one after the other in the same verse, as for example, "dear, comely, angelic, rich gifts." You can see that such epithets are more to puff up and paint the verse than to fill any need in it. Content yourself with one epithet, or at most, with two, unless some time for amusement you

make five or six, but if you follow my advice in the matter, that will happen as infrequently as you can manage.

## OF RHYME

Rhyme is the correspondence and cadence of syllables, falling at the ends of the verses, which I wish you to observe as well for masculine as for feminine, in the two complete, perfect syllables, or at least in the masculine, provided that it be resonant, and of a sound perfect and entire. Examples of the feminine: *France, Esperance, despence, negligence, familiere, foumiliere, premiere, chere, mere.* Examples of the masculine: *surmonter, monter, donter, sauter, Juppiter.* Always you are to be more attentive to good invention and to the words, than to the rhyme, which comes easily enough of itself after some little practice and experience.[4]

[4]Ronsard's *Brief* goes on to take up various technical matters. The titles of the remaining sections indicate sufficiently their absorption with French phonetics and orthography. De La Voyelle E [On the Vowel E]. De L'H [On the H — a semisilent letter in French]. Des Vers Alexandrins [On Hexameter Couplets]. Des Vers Communs [On Popular Verse]. Des Autres Vers en Général [On Other Verse Generally]. Des Personnes des Verbes François et de L'Ortographie [On Person in French Verbs and On Spelling]. [Ed.]

# Sir Philip Sidney
## 1554–1586

As a skilled courtier, scholar, soldier, and poet, Philip Sidney was the pattern of the English Renaissance gentleman. After attending Shrewsbury School and Christ Church College at Oxford, and making a grand tour of the continent, he established himself at Elizabeth's court, where he joined the faction led by one of the queen's favorites, his uncle Robert Dudley, Earl of Leicester. Sidney ended his short life as military governor in Flanders during the Dutch wars. His heroic death at the battle of Zutphen was the stuff of legend: Sidney is said to have courteously declined water and medical attention in favor of a lowlier fellow soldier, a deed that made him a model of the chivalric ideal. But notwithstanding his nobility of birth and spirit, Sidney's unique talents and personality would have procured him success and fame. His *Arcadia* (1593), a romance alternating prose with poetry, established a tradition for the English pastoral; it was a best-seller for over two centuries and was crucial to the development of the English novel. And his *Apology for Poetry*, written in 1583 and published in 1595, was the first significant piece of literary criticism in the English language. (The essay is also known as *The Defence of Poetry*, the title of a slightly earlier version.)

The occasion of *An Apology for Poetry* was to refute *The Schoole of Abuse* (1579), a moralistic attack on poetry written by Puritan minister Stephen Gosson and dedicated (without leave) to Sidney himself. In constructing his *apologia* — Greek for a legal defense — Sidney addressed himself less to Gosson than to Plato, whose *Republic* provides most of the ammunition the Puritan divine expended against poetry. Sidney's *Apology* is structured according to the principles of medieval rhetoric like a good legal brief, with an introduction that draws the reader into the case while offering reassurance of the ethical rightness of the speaker, a central argumentative section, a set of answers to objections, and a glowing peroration. The contemporary reader must have patience, however, with the slow Senecan amble of Sidney's sentences. They were formed before muscularity became the mainstay of English prose. The reader who gets lost will be glad of another characteristic of Renaissance prose: Sidney signals all his transitions with a rapid and elegant summary of the preceding section.

Sidney opens the systematic section of the *Apology* with a definition of poetry, which he calls "an art of imitation, for so Aristotle termeth it in his word *mimesis*, that is to say, a representing, counterfeiting, or figuring forth. . . ." The definition suggests an affinity with Aristotle that is more apparent than real, for Sidney concludes with the Horatian phrase ". . . with this end, to teach and delight." Like many Renaissance theorists, Sidney appeals to mimesis not because it is a crucial principle, but in order to set limits to his subject. He wants to differentiate that class of poetry he will discuss, fictions based on human action, from hymns and psalms on the one hand and philosophy or history or natural science written in verse on the other. The distinction is needed: The two latter types of poetry were not under attack as were fictions. But the end, "to teach and delight," is the pivotal phrase.

Sidney's world, like Plato's, is structured hierarchically and holistically. Like Plato also, he sees the sciences and arts all directed to a single end, "the mistress-knowledge, by the Greeks called *architectonike,* which stands . . . in the knowledge of a man's self, in the ethic and politic consideration, with the end of well doing and not of well knowing only." Horsemanship — the art Sidney begins his *Apology* by mentioning — is no end in itself but serves the art of the soldier, just as the soldier's art serves the statesman's; the ultimate goal is right action.

The arts are judged by their distance from that architectonic goal: the closer, the higher. Thus divinity, Sidney concedes, must be the highest of the sciences, and with this no merely earthly art, including poetry, can compete. It is only against the other major sublunary disciplines — law, history, and philosophy — that Sidney pits the poets. Which of these arts will best serve to make men better? Once the question is so phrased, poetry excels. For law at best keeps us from evil: Its function is not to make us good. Ethical philosophy will help us with fine moral distinctions, but philosophy, although it teaches us what virtue is, will not *move* us to virtuous action. History occasionally teaches sound moral lessons — yet just as often its examples are immoral: how the evil triumphed or the virtuous were slain. Only poetry always provides poetic justice to move us to virtuous action, and by the pleasure it gives, move us to go on reading it. Poetry does not merely teach and delight; for Sidney it delights *in order to* teach.

Sidney's aesthetic principle, then, is Horatian, while his metaphysics owes much to Plato. Because of this, whenever he quotes and glosses Aristotle, he subtly alters and distorts his meaning. On page 142, for instance, Sidney argues for the poets and against the claims of history by quoting *Poetics*, Chapter 9, that "poetry is *philosophoteron* and *spoudaioteron,* that is to say, it is more philosophical and more studiously serious than history. . . . because poesy dealeth with *katholou*, that is to say, with the universal consideration, and the history with *kathekaston*, the particular. . . ." The quotation is accurate as far as it goes, but within the same paragraph, Sidney loses track of the distinction between the universal and the particular, substituting one more consistent with his basic Platonism between the *ideal* and the *real*. ("But if the question be . . . whether it be better to have it set down as it should be, or as it was, then certainly is more doctrinable [instructive] the feigned Cyrus in Xenophon than the true Cyrus in Justin. . . .")

The central argument in Sidney is based on poetry's "works and parts" — Elizabethan English for its *effects* and *genres*. After he has shown the superiority of poetry to law, history, and philosophy, he reviews the major genres of poetry to show that they are all instructive, or at least not injurious.

That done, Sidney runs through Gosson's four major objections to poetry in *The Schoole of Abuse*. The first, that there are more fruitful arts than poetry, his main argument has already disposed of. The second is an objection to fiction in general: that poets by the very nature of their trade must be liars. Here Sidney claims benefit of poetic license: that "the poet nothing affirmeth"; fictions are not asserted or received as verifiable truth and therefore can never deceive, as the statements of the historian or the scientist might.

The third objection, that "poetry abuseth man's wit," Sidney turns on its head. He admits that immoral poetry and fictions exist, but these constitute an abuse of the art, not a reflection of its deepest nature. In fact, the possible damage poetry may do, if its ends are perverted, is a reflection of poetry's importance — just as the improper use of the art of medicine will lead to illness and death. The fourth, that the poets were banished from Plato's republic, Sidney refutes with arguments ad hominem — that Plato, as a philosopher, was naturally in competition with the poets. While Sidney also expresses shock at Plato's frank discussions of homoerotic love (in the *Phaedrus* and the *Symposium*), in truth he wants Plato on his side, not on Gosson's, and his most serious argument here is that Plato banished poetry not because it was evil in its nature but only to avoid its possible abuses — such as the teaching of falsehoods about the nature of God. He thus assimilates the last objection to the previous one.

For many, the most interesting section of the *Apology for Poetry* is Sidney's digression on the arts in contemporary England, which he considered to be in a bad way. Applying the strict standards of Renaissance poetics to home-grown English verse and drama, Sidney finds most of his fellow poets admirable for their natural genius but lamentably ignorant about the rules and regulations that Horatian aesthetics had down the centuries evolved for literary art. Several of Sidney's accusations about the English theater — its neglect of the three unities of time, place, and action; mixing of comic scenes into tragedy, polluting genres that ought to be kept pure; indecorous portrayal of violence on the stage — will be debated nearly a century later in Dryden's *Essay of Dramatic Poesy* (p. 163) and laid to rest after another century in Johnson's "Preface to *Shakespeare*" (p. 229). What Sidney thought to be immutable laws of art came to be seen, more and more, as mere conventions, useful in their day but no longer valid.

Today Sidney and his strictures on the artist's need for study and practice may seem pedantic unless we remember what was always before the well-traveled Sidney's eyes: how recently England had emerged from provincial barbarism into the sunlight of Elizabethan courtliness, and how much the English still needed to learn from the older cultures of Europe and the classical world. This international spirit was one of Sidney's many legacies to his country.

## Selected Bibliography

Devereux, James A. "The Meaning of Delight in Sidney's Defense of Poesy." *Studies in the Literary Imagination* 15 (1982): 85–97.

Levao, Ronald. *Renaissance Minds and Their Fictions: Cusanus, Sidney, Shakespeare.* Berkeley: University of California Press, 1985.

McCoy, Richard C. *Sir Philip Sidney: Rebellion in Arcadia.* New Brunswick: Rutgers University Press, 1979.

Mason, H. A. "An Introduction to Literary Criticism by Way of Sidney's Apologie for Poetrie." *Cambridge Quarterly* 12, no. 2–3 (1984): 79–173.

Myrick, Kenneth Orne. *Sir Philip Sidney as a Literary Craftsman*. Cambridge: Harvard University Press, 1935.

Robinson, Forrest Glen. *The Shape of Things Known: Sidney's Apology in Its Philosophical Tradition*. Cambridge: Harvard University Press, 1972.

Spingarn, J. E. *A History of Literary Criticism in the Renaissance*. New York: Columbia University Press, 1912.

Stump, Donald V. "Sidney's Concept of Tragedy in the Apology and the Arcadia." *Studies in Philology* 79 (1982): 78–99.

Ulreich, John C., Jr. "Poets Only Deliver: Sidney's Conception of Mimesis." *Studies in the Literary Imagination* 15 (1982): 67–84.

Weiner, Andrew D. *Sir Philip Sidney and the Poetics of Protestantism*. Minneapolis: University of Minnesota Press, 1978.

# An Apology for Poetry

When the right virtuous Edward Wotton and I were at the Emperor's Court together, we gave ourselves to learn horsemanship of John Pietro Pugliano, one that with great commendation had the place of an esquire in his stable. And he, according to the fertileness of the Italian wit, did not only afford us the demonstration of his practice, but sought to enrich our minds with the contemplations there which he thought most precious. But with none I remember mine ears were at any time more loaden, than when (either angered with slow payment, or moved with our learnerlike admiration) he exercised his speech in the praise of his faculty. He said soldiers were the noblest estate of mankind, and horsemen the noblest of soldiers. He said they were the masters of war and ornaments of peace; speedy goers and strong abiders; triumphers both in camps and courts. Nay, to so unbelieved a point he proceeded, as that no earthly thing bred such wonder to a prince as to be a good horseman. Skill of government was but a *pedenteria*[1] in comparison. Then would he add certain praises, by telling what a peerless beast a horse was, the only serviceable courtier without flattery, the beast of most beauty, faithfulness, courage, and such

more, that, if I had not been a piece of a logician before I came to him, I think he would have persuaded me to have wished myself a horse. But thus much at least with his no few words he drove into me, that self-love is better than any gilding to make that seem gorgeous wherein ourselves are parties. Wherein, if Pugliano's strong affection and weak arguments will not satisfy you, I will give you a nearer example of myself, who (I know not by what mischance) in these my not old years and idlest times having slipped into the title of a poet, am provoked to say something unto you in the defense of that my unelected vocation, which if I handle with more good will than good reasons, bear with me, since the scholar is to be pardoned that followeth the steps of his master. And yet I must say that, as I have just cause to make a pitiful defense of poor Poetry, which from almost the highest estimation of learning is fallen to be the laughingstock of children, so have I need to bring some more available proofs, since the former is by no man barred of his deserved credit, the silly latter hath had even the names of philosophers used to the defacing of it, with great danger of civil war among the Muses.

And first, truly, to all them that professing learning inveigh against poetry may justly be

---

[1]Pedantry: useless book-learning. [Ed.]

objected, that they go very near to ungratefulness, to seek to deface that which, in the noblest nations and languages that are known, hath been the first light-giver to ignorance, and first nurse, whose milk by little and little enabled them to feed afterwards of tougher knowledges. And will they now play the hedgehog that, being received into the den, drove out his host, or rather the vipers, that with their birth kill their parents? Let learned Greece in any of her manifold sciences be able to show me one book before Musaeus, Homer, and Hesiod, all three nothing else but poets. Nay, let any history be brought that can say any writers were there before them, if they were not men of the same skill, as Orpheus, Linus, and some other are named, who, having been the first of that country that made pens deliverers of their knowledge to their posterity, may justly challenge to be called their fathers in learning, for not only in time they had this priority (although in itself antiquity be venerable) but went before them, as causes to draw with their charming sweetness the wild untamed wits to an admiration of knowledge, so, as Amphion was said to move stones with his poetry to build Thebes, and Orpheus to be listened to by beasts — indeed stony and beastly people.[2] So among the Romans were Livius Andronicus, and Ennius. So in the Italian language the first that made it aspire to be a treasure-house of science were the poets Dante, Boccaccio, and Petrarch. So in our English were Gower and Chaucer.

After whom, encouraged and delighted with their excellent foregoing, others have followed, to beautify our mother tongue, as well in the same kind as in other arts. This did so notably show itself that the philosophers of Greece durst not a long time appear to the world but under the masks of poets. So Thales, Empedocles, and Parmenides sang their natural philosophy in verses; so did Pythagoras and Phocylides their moral counsels; so did Tyrtaeus in war matters, and Solon in matters of policy: or rather, they, being poets, did exercise their delightful vein in those points of highest knowledge, which before them lay hid to the world. For that wise Solon

was directly a poet it is manifest, having written in verse the notable fable of the Atlantic Island, which was continued by Plato.

And truly, even Plato, whosoever well considereth shall find that in the body of his work, though the inside and strength were philosophy, the skin as it were and beauty depended most of poetry: for all standeth upon dialogues, wherein he feigneth many honest burgesses of Athens to speak of such matters, that, if they had been set on the rack, they would never have confessed them, besides his poetical describing the circumstances of their meetings, as the well ordering of a banquet, the delicacy of a walk, with interlacing mere tales, as Gyges' ring, and others, which who knoweth not to be flowers of poetry did never walk into Apollo's garden.[3]

And even historiographers (although their lips sound of things done, and verity be written in their foreheads) have been glad to borrow both fashion and perchance weight of poets. So Herodotus entitled his history by the name of the nine Muses;[4] and both he and all the rest that followed him either stole or usurped of poetry their passionate describing of passions, the many particularities of battles, which no man could affirm, or, if that be denied me, long orations put in the mouths of great kings and captains, which it is certain they never pronounced. So that, truly, neither philosopher nor historiographer could at the first have entered into the gates of popular judgments, if they had not taken a great passport of poetry, which in all nations at this day, where learning flourisheth not, is plain to be seen, in all which they have some feeling of poetry. In Turkey, besides their lawgiving divines, they have no other writers but poets. In our neighbor country Ireland, where truly learning goeth very bare, yet are their poets held in a devout reverence. Even among the most barbarous and simple Indians where no writing is, yet have they their poets, who make and sing songs,

[2]Sidney's notion of poetry's power derives from Horace's *Art of Poetry*. See p. 75. [Ed.]

[3]The myth of Gyges' ring appears in *Republic,* Book 2, and other myths appear in other dialogues; Plato also occasionally writes prose that modulates into dithyrambic verse, as in the *Ion* and the *Phaedrus.* [Ed.]

[4]Each of the nine books of Herodotus's *History* is titled with the name of one of the Muses. [Ed.]

which they call *areytos,* both of their ancestors' deeds and praises of their gods — a sufficient probability that, if ever learning come among them, it must be by having their hard dull wits softened and sharpened with the sweet delights of poetry. For until they find a pleasure in the exercises of the mind, great promises of much knowledge will little persuade them that know not the fruits of knowledge. In Wales, the true remnant of the ancient Britons, as there are good authorities to show the long time they had poets, which they called bards, so through all the conquests of Romans, Saxons, Danes, and Normans, some of whom did seek to ruin all memory of learning from among them, yet do their poets, even to this day, last; so as it is not more notable in soon beginning than in long continuing. But since the authors of most of our sciences were the Romans, and before them the Greeks, let us a little stand upon their authorities, but even so far as to see what names they have given unto this now scorned skill.

Among the Romans a poet was called *vates,* which is as much as a diviner, foreseer, or prophet, as by his conjoined words *vaticinium* and *vaticinari* is manifest: so heavenly a title did that excellent people bestow upon this heart-ravishing knowledge. And so far were they carried into the admiration thereof, that they thought in the chanceable hitting upon any such verses great foretokens of their following fortunes were placed. Whereupon grew the word of *sortes Virgilianae*[5] when, by sudden opening Virgil's book, they lighted upon any verse of his making: whereof the histories of the emperors' lives are full, as of Albinus, the governor of our island, who in his childhood met with this verse, "*Arma amens capio nec sat rationis in armis*";[6] and in his age performed it: which, although it were a very vain and godless superstition, as also it was to think that spirits were commanded by such verses — whereupon this word charms, derived of *carmina,*[7] "cometh" — so yet serveth it to show the great reverence those wits were held in. And altogether not without ground, since both the Oracles of Delphos and Sibylla's prophecies were wholly delivered in verses. For that same exquisite observing of number and measure in words, and that high flying liberty of conceit proper to the poet, did seem to have some divine force in it.

And may not I presume a little further, to show the reasonableness of this word *vates,* and say that the holy David's Psalms are a divine poem? If I do, I shall not do it without the testimony of great learned men, both ancient and modern. But even the name Psalms will speak for me, which, being interpreted, is nothing but "songs"; then that it is fully written in meter, as all learned Hebricians agree, although the rules be not yet fully found; lastly and principally, his handling his prophecy, which is merely poetical. For what else is the awaking his musical instruments, the often and free changing of persons, his notable *prosopopeias,*[8] when he maketh you, as it were, see God coming in his majesty, his telling of the beasts' joyfulness, and hills' leaping, but a heavenly poesy, wherein almost he showeth himself a passionate lover of that unspeakable and everlasting beauty to be seen by the eyes of the mind, only cleared by faith? But truly now having named him, I fear me I seem to profane that holy name, applying it to poetry, which is among us thrown down to so ridiculous an estimation. But they that with quiet judgments will look a little deeper into it, shall find the end and working of it such, as, being rightly applied, deserveth not to be scourged out of the church of God.

But now, let us see how the Greeks named it, and how they deemed of it. The Greeks called him "a poet," which name hath, as the most excellent, gone through other languages. It cometh of this word *poiein,* which is "to make": wherein, I know not whether by luck or wisdom, we Englishmen have met with the Greeks in calling him a *maker:* which name, how high and incomparable a title it is, I had rather were known by marking the scope of other sciences than by my partial allegation.

[5]The Virgilian lots: a method of fortune-telling using a random passage from the *Aeneid.* [Ed.]

[6]"Insane, I seize my weapons; there's no sense in weapons. . . ." *Aeneid* 2:314. [Ed.]

[7]Songs. [Ed.]

[8]Personifications. [Ed.]

There is no art delivered to mankind that hath not the works of nature for his principal object, without which they could not consist, and on which they so depend, as they become actors and players, as it were, of what nature will have set forth. So doth the astronomer look upon the stars, and, by that he seeth, setteth down what order nature hath taken therein. So do the geometrician and arithmetician in their diverse sorts of quantities. So doth the musician in times tell you which by nature agree, which not. The natural philosopher thereon hath his name, and the moral philosopher standeth upon the natural virtues, vices, and passions of man; and "follow nature" (saith he) "therein, and thou shalt not err." The lawyer saith what men have determined; the historian what men have done. The grammarian speaketh only of the rules of speech; and the rhetorician and logician, considering what in nature will soonest prove and persuade, thereon give artificial rules, which still are compassed within the circle of a question according to the proposed matter. The physician weigheth the nature of a man's body, and the nature of things helpful or hurtful unto it. And the metaphysic, though it be in the second and abstract notions, and therefore be counted supernatural, yet doth he indeed build upon the depth of nature. Only the poet, disdaining to be tied to any such subjection, lifted up with the vigor of his own invention, doth grow in effect another nature, in making things either better than nature bringeth forth, or, quite anew, forms such as never were in nature, as the Heroes, Demigods, Cyclopes, Chimeras, Furies, and such like: so as he goeth hand in hand with nature, not enclosed within the narrow warrant of her gifts, but freely ranging only within the zodiac of his own wit.

Nature never set forth the earth in so rich tapestry as divers poets have done — neither with pleasant rivers, fruitful trees, sweet-smelling flowers, nor whatsoever else may make the too much loved earth more lovely. Her world is brazen, the poets only deliver a golden. But let those things alone, and go to man — for whom as the other things are, so it seemeth in him her uttermost cunning is employed — and know whether she have brought forth so true a lover as Theagenes, so constant a friend as Pylades, so valiant a man as Orlando, so right a prince as Xenophon's Cyrus, so excellent a man every way as Virgil's Aeneas. Neither let this be jestingly conceived, because the works of the one be essential, the other in imitation or fiction; for any understanding knoweth the skill of the artificer standeth in that idea or foreconceit of the work, and not in the work itself. And that the poet hath that idea is manifest, by delivering them forth in such excellency as he hath imagined them. Which delivering forth also is not wholly imaginative, as we are wont to say by them that build castles in the air: but so far substantially it worketh, not only to make a Cyrus, which had been but a particular excellency, as nature might have done, but to bestow a Cyrus upon the world, to make many Cyruses, if they will learn aright why and how that maker made him.

Neither let it be deemed too saucy a comparison to balance the highest point of man's wit with the efficacy of nature; but rather give right honor to the heavenly Maker of that maker, who, having made man to his own likeness, set him beyond and over all the works of that second nature: which in nothing he showeth so much as in poetry, when with the force of a divine breath he bringeth things forth far surpassing her doings, with no small argument to the incredulous of that first accursed fall of Adam, since our erected wit maketh us know what perfection is, and yet our infected will keepeth us from reaching unto it. But these arguments will by few be understood, and by fewer granted. Thus much (I hope) will be given me, that the Greeks with some probability of reason gave him the name above all names of learning. Now let us go to a more ordinary opening of him, that the truth may be more palpable: and so I hope, though we get not so unmatched a praise as the etymology of his names will grant, yet his very description, which no man will deny, shall not justly be barred from a principal commendation.

Poesy therefore is an art of imitation, for so Aristotle termeth it in his word *mimesis*,[9] that is to say, a representing, counterfeiting, or figuring forth — to speak metaphorically, a speaking pic-

[9]Aristotle, *Poetics,* Ch. I; see p. 42. [Ed.]

ture; with this end, to teach and delight.[10] Of this have been three several kinds. The chief, both in antiquity and excellency, were they that did imitate the inconceivable excellencies of God. Such were David in his Psalms; Solomon in his Song of Songs, in his Ecclesiastes, and Proverbs; Moses and Deborah in their Hymns; and the writer of Job, which, beside other, the learned Emanuel Tremellius and Franciscus Junius do entitle the poetical part of the Scripture. Against these none will speak that hath the Holy Ghost in due holy reverence.

In this kind, though in a full wrong divinity, were Orpheus, Amphion, Homer in his *Hymns,* and many other, both Greeks and Romans, and this poesy must be used by whosoever will follow St. James's counsel in singing psalms when they are merry, and I know is used with the fruit of comfort by some, when, in sorrowful pangs of their death-bringing sins, they find the consolation of the never-leaving goodness.

The second kind is of them that deal with matters, philosophical: either moral, as Tyrtaeus, Phocylides, and Cato; or natural, as Lucretius and Virgil's *Georgics;* or astronomical, as Manilius and Pontanus; or historical, as Lucan; which who mislike, the fault is in their judgments quite out of taste, and not in the sweet food of sweetly uttered knowledge. But because this second sort is wrapped within the fold of the proposed subject, and takes not the course of his own invention, whether they properly be poets or no let grammarians dispute; and go to the third, indeed right poets, of whom chiefly this question ariseth, betwixt whom and these second is such a kind of difference as betwixt the meaner sort of painters, who counterfeit only such faces as are set before them, and the more excellent, who, having no law but wit, bestow that in colors upon you which is fittest for the eye to see, as the constant though lamenting look of Lucretia, when she punished in herself another's fault.

Wherein he painteth not Lucretia whom he never saw, but painteth the outward beauty of such a virtue. For these third be they which most properly do imitate to teach and delight, and to imitate borrow nothing of what is, hath been, or shall be; but range, only reined with learned discretion, into the divine consideration of what may be, and should be. These be they that, as the first and most noble sort may justly be termed *vates,* so these are waited on in the excellentest languages and best understandings, with the fore-described name of poets; for these indeed do merely make to imitate, and imitate both to delight and teach, and delight to move men to take that goodness in hand, which without delight they would fly as from a stranger, and teach, to make them know that goodness whereunto they are moved: which being the noblest scope to which ever any learning was directed, yet want there not idle tongues to bark at them. These be subdivided into sundry more special denominations. The most notable be the heroic, lyric, tragic, comic, satiric, iambic, elegiac, pastoral, and certain others, some of these being termed according to the matter they deal with, some by the sorts of verses they liked best to write in; for indeed the greatest part of poets have appareled their poetical inventions in that numbrous kind of writing which is called verse — indeed but appareled, verse being but an ornament and no cause to poetry, since there have been many most excellent poets that never versified, and now swarm many versifiers that need never answer to the name of poets. For Xenophon, who did imitate so excellently as to give us *effigiem iusti imperii,* "the portraiture of a just empire," under name of Cyrus (as Cicero saith of him), made therein an absolute heroical poem.[11]

So did Heliodorus in his sugared invention of that picture of love in *Theagenes and Chariclea;* and yet both these writ in prose: which I speak to show that it is not rhyming and versing that maketh a poet — no more than a long gown maketh an advocate, who though he pleaded in armor should be an advocate and no soldier.[12] But it is that feigning notable images of virtues, vices, or what else, with that delightful teaching, which must be the right describing note to know a poet by, although indeed the senate of poets

---

[10]Horace, *Art of Poetry;* see p. 74. [Ed.]

[11]Sidney is praising Xenophon's *Cyropaedia,* or *Education of Cyrus.* [Ed.]

[12]Cf. Aristotle, *Poetics,* Ch. 9; see p. 48. [Ed.]

hath chosen verse as their fittest raiment, meaning, as in matter they passed all in all, so in manner to go beyond them — not speaking (table talk fashion or like men in a dream) words as they chanceably fall from the mouth, but peising each syllable of each word by just proportion according to the dignity of the subject.

Now therefore it shall not be amiss first to weigh this latter sort of poetry by his works, and then by his parts,[13] and, if in neither of these anatomies he be condemnable, I hope we shall obtain a more favorable sentence. This purifying of wit, this enriching of memory, enabling of judgment, and enlarging of conceit, which commonly we call learning, under what name soever it come forth, or to what immediate end soever it be directed, the final end is to lead and draw us to as high a perfection as our degenerate souls, made worse by their clayey lodgings, can be capable of. This, according to the inclination of the man, bred many formed impressions. For some that thought this felicity principally to be gotten by knowledge and no knowledge to be so high and heavenly as acquaintance with the stars, gave themselves to astronomy; others, persuading themselves to be demigods if they knew the causes of things, became natural and supernatural philosophers; some an admirable delight drew to music; and some the certainty of demonstration to the mathematics. But all, one and other, having this scope — to know, and by knowledge to lift up the mind from the dungeon of the body to the enjoying his own divine essence. But when by the balance of experience it was found that the astronomer looking to the stars might fall into a ditch, that the inquiring philosopher might be blind in himself, and the mathematician might draw forth a straight line with a crooked heart, then, lo, did proof, the overruler of opinions, make manifest that all these are but serving sciences, which, as they have each a private end in themselves, so yet are they all directed to the highest end of the mistress-knowledge, by the Greeks called *architectonike*,[14] which stands (as

I think) in the knowledge of a man's self, in the ethic and politic consideration, with the end of well doing and not of well knowing only — even as the saddler's next end is to make a good saddle, but his farther end to serve a nobler faculty, which is horsemanship; so the horseman's to soldiery, and the soldier not only to have the skill, but to perform the practice of a soldier. So that, the ending end of all earthly learning being virtuous action, those skills, that most serve to bring forth that, have a most just title to be princes over all the rest. Wherein we can show the poet's nobleness, by setting him before his other competitors, among whom as principal challengers step forth the moral philosophers, whom, me thinketh, I see coming towards me with a sullen gravity, as though they could not abide vice by daylight, rudely clothed for to witness outwardly their contempt of outward things, with books in their hands against glory, whereto they set their names, sophistically speaking against subtlety, and angry with any man in whom they see the foul fault of anger. These men casting largesse as they go of definitions, divisions, and distinctions, with a scornful interrogative do soberly ask whether it be possible to find any path so ready to lead a man to virtue as that which teacheth what virtue is — and teacheth it not only by delivering forth his very being, his causes, and effects, but also by making known his enemy, vice (which must be destroyed), and his cumbersome servant, passion (which must be mastered), by showing the generalities that containeth it, and the specialities that are derived from it; lastly, by plain setting down, how it extendeth itself out of the limits of a man's own little world to the government of families, and maintaining of public societies.

The historian scarcely giveth leisure to the moralist to say so much, but that he, laden with old mouse-eaten records, authorizing himself (for the most part) upon other histories, whose greatest authorities are built upon the notable foundation of hearsay; having much ado to accord differing writers and to pick truth out of partiality; better acquainted with a thousand years ago than with the present age, and yet better knowing how this world goeth than how his own wit runneth; curious for antiquities and inquisitive of

[13]"Works" and "parts" are, in modern English, effects and genres. [Ed.]

[14]In Aristotle, the controlling principle of something. For Sidney, the ultimate end of knowledge is the Greek ideal of *sophrosyne:* self-knowledge and self-mastery. [Ed.]

novelties; a wonder to young folks and a tyrant in table talk, denieth, in a great chafe, that any man for teaching of virtue, and virtuous actions, is comparable to him. "I am '*lux vitae, temporum magistra, vita memoriae, nuntia vetustatis,*'" &c.[15]

The philosopher (saith he)

teacheth a disputative virtue, but I do an active. His virtue is excellent in the dangerless Academy of Plato, but mine showeth forth her honorable face in the battles of Marathon, Pharsalia, Poitiers, and Agincourt. He teacheth virtue by certain abstract considerations, but I only bid you follow the footing of them that have gone before you. Old-aged experience goeth beyond the fine-witted philosopher, but I give the experience of many ages. Lastly, if he make the song book, I put the learner's hand to the lute; and if he be the guide, I am the light.

Then would he allege you innumerable examples, conferring story by story, how much the wisest senators and princes have been directed by the credit of history, as Brutus, Alphonsus of Aragon, and who not, if need be? At length the long line of their disputation maketh a point in this, that the one giveth the precept, and the other the example.

Now, whom shall we find (since the question standeth for the highest form in the school of learning) to be moderator? Truly, as me seemeth, the poet; and if not a moderator, even the man that ought to carry the title from them both, and much more from all other serving sciences. Therefore compare we the poet with the historian, and with the moral philosopher; and, if he go beyond them both, no other human skill can match him. For as for the Divine, with all reverence it is ever to be excepted, not only for having his scope as far beyond any of these as eternity exceedeth a moment, but even for passing each of these in themselves.

And for the lawyer, though Jus be the daughter of justice, and justice the chief of virtues, yet because he seeketh to make men good rather

*formidine poenae* than *virtutis amore,*[16] or, to say righter, doth not endeavor to make men good, but that their evil hurt not others, having no care, so he be a good citizen, how bad a man he be: therefore, as our wickedness maketh him necessary, and necessity maketh him honorable, so is he not in the deepest truth to stand in rank with these who all endeavor to take naughtiness away, and plant goodness even in the secretest cabinet of our souls. And these four are all that any way deal in that consideration of men's manners, which being the supreme knowledge, they that best breed it deserve the best commendation.

The philosopher therefore and the historian are they which would win the goal, the one by precept, the other by example. But both, not having both, do both halt. For the philosopher, setting down with thorny argument the bare rule, is so hard of utterance, and so misty to be conceived, that one that hath no other guide but his shall wade in him till he be old before he shall find sufficient cause to be honest. For his knowledge standeth so upon the abstract and general, that happy is that man who may understand him, and more happy that can apply what he doth understand.

On the other side, the historian, wanting the precept, is to tied, not to what should be but to what is, to the particular truth of things and not to the general reason of things, that his example draweth no necessary consequence, and therefore a less fruitful doctrine.

Now doth the peerless poet perform both: for whatsoever the philosopher saith should be done, he giveth a perfect picture of it in someone by whom he presupposeth it was done; so as he coupleth the general notion with the particular example. A perfect picture I say, for he yieldeth to the powers of the mind an image of that whereof the philosopher bestoweth but a wordish description: which doth neither strike, pierce, nor possess the sight of the soul so much as that other doth.

For as in outward things, to a man that had never seen an elephant or a rhinoceros, who should tell him most exquisitely all their shapes,

---

[15]"The light of life, the master of the times, the life of memory, the messenger of antiquity." Cicero, *On Oratory* 2.9:36. [Ed.]

[16]Rather through fear of punishment than through love of virtue. [Ed.]

color, bigness, and particular marks, or of a gorgeous palace the architecture, with declaring the full beauties might well make the hearer able to repeat, as it were by rote, all he had heard, yet should never satisfy his inward conceits with being witness to itself of a true lively knowledge: but the same man, as soon as he might see those beasts well painted, or the house well in model, should straightways grow, without need of any description, to a judicial comprehending of them: so no doubt the philosopher with his learned definition — be it of virtue, vices, matters of public policy or private government — replenisheth the memory with many infallible grounds of wisdom, which, notwithstanding, lie dark before the imaginative and judging power, if they be not illuminated or figured forth by the speaking picture of poesy.

Tully taketh much pains, and many times not without poetical helps, to make us know the force love of our country hath in us. Let us but hear old Anchises speaking in the midst of Troy's flames, or see Ulysses in the fullness of all Calypso's delights bewail his absence from barren and beggarly Ithaca. Anger, the Stoics say, was a short madness: let but Sophocles bring you Ajax on a stage, killing and whipping sheep and oxen, thinking them the army of Greeks, with their chieftains Agamemnon and Menelaus, and tell me if you have not a more familiar insight into anger than finding in the schoolmen his genus and difference. See whether wisdom and temperance in Ulysses and Diomedes, valor in Achilles, friendship in Nisus and Euryalus, even to an ignorant man carry not an apparent shining, and, contrarily, the remorse of conscience in Oedipus, the soon repenting pride of Agamemnon, the self-devouring cruelty in his father Atreus, the violence of ambition in the two Theban brothers, the sour-sweetness of revenge in Medea, and, to fall lower, the Terentian Gnatho and our Chaucer's Pandar so expressed that we now use their names to signify their trades; and finally, all virtues, vices, and passions so in their own natural seats laid to the view, that we seem not to hear of them, but clearly to see through them. But even in the most excellent determination of goodness, what philosopher's counsel can so readily direct a prince, as the feigned Cyrus in Xenophon; or a virtuous man in all fortunes, as Aeneas in Virgil; or a whole commonwealth, as the way of Sir Thomas More's *Utopia*? I say the way, because where Sir Thomas More erred, it was the fault of the man and not of the poet, for that way of patterning a commonwealth was most absolute, though he perchance hath not so absolutely performed it. For the question is, whether the feigned image of poesy or the regular instruction of philosophy hath the more force in teaching: wherein if the philosophers have more rightly showed themselves philosophers than the poets have attained to the high top of their profession, as in truth, *"mediocribus esse poetis, / Non dii, non homines, non concessere columnae"*;[17] it is, I say again, not the fault of the art, but that by few men that art can be accomplished.

Certainly, even our Saviour Christ could as well have given the moral commonplaces of uncharitableness and humbleness as the divine narration of Dives and Lazarus; or of disobedience and mercy, as that heavenly discourse of the lost child and the gracious father; but that his through-searching wisdom knew the estate of Dives burning in hell, and of Lazarus being in Abraham's bosom, would more constantly (as it were) inhabit both the memory and judgment. Truly, for myself, meseems I see before my eyes the lost child's disdainful prodigality, turned to envy a swine's dinner: which by the learned divines are thought not historical acts, but instructing parables. For conclusion, I say the philosopher teacheth, but he teacheth obscurely, so as the learned only can understand him; that is to say, he teacheth them that are already taught. But the poet is the food for the tenderest stomachs, the poet is indeed the right popular philosopher, whereof Aesop's tales give good proof: whose pretty allegories, stealing under the formal tales of beasts, make many, more beastly than beasts, begin to hear the sound of virtue from these dumb speakers.

But now may it be alleged that, if this imagining of matters be so fit for the imagination, then must the historian needs surpass, who brin-

17"No one, / no god, no publisher / cares about mediocre poets." Horace, *Art of Poetry*; see p. 75. [Ed.]

geth you images of true matters, such as indeed were done, and not such as fantastically or falsely may be suggested to have been done. Truly, Aristotle himself, in his discourse of poesy, plainly determineth this question, saying that poetry is *philosophoteron* and *spoudaioteron,* that is to say, it is more philosophical and more studiously serious than history. His reason is, because poesy dealeth with *katholou*, that is to say, with the universal consideration, and the history with *kathekaston,* the particular: "now," saith he, "the universal weighs what is fit to be said or done, either in likelihood or necessity (which the poesy considereth in his imposed names), and the particular only marks whether Alcibiades did, or suffered, this or that."[18] Thus far Aristotle: which reason of his (as all his) is most full of reason. For indeed, if the question were whether it were better to have a particular act truly or falsely set down, there is no doubt which is to be chosen, no more than whether you had rather have Vespasian's picture right as he was, or at the painter's pleasure nothing resembling. But if the question be for your own use and learning, whether it be better to have it set down as it should be, or as it was, then certainly is more doctrinable the feigned Cyrus in Xenophon than the true Cyrus in Justin, and the feigned Aeneas in Virgil than the right Aeneas in Dares Phrygius.[19]

As to a lady that desired to fashion her countenance to the best grace, a painter should more benefit her to portrait a most sweet face, writing Canidia upon it, than to paint Canidia as she was, who, Horace sweareth, was foul and ill favored.

If the poet do his part aright, he will show you in Tantalus, Atreus, and such like, nothing that is not to be shunned; in Cyrus, Aeneas, Ulysses, each thing to be followed; where the historian, bound to tell things as things were, cannot be liberal (without he will be poetical) of

a perfect pattern, but, as in Alexander or Scipio himself, show doings, some to be liked, some to be misliked. And then how will you discern what to follow but by your own discretion, which you had without reading Quintus Curtius? And whereas a man may say, though in universal consideration of doctrine the poet prevaileth, yet that the history, in his saying such a thing was done, doth warrant a man more in that he shall follow.

The answer is manifest: that if he stand upon that *was* — as if he should argue, because it rained yesterday, therefore it should rain today — then indeed it hath some advantage to a gross conceit; but if he know an example only informs a conjectured likelihood, and so go by reason, the poet doth so far exceed him, as he is to frame his example to that which is most reasonable, be it in warlike, politic, or private matters; where the historian in his bare *was* hath many times that which we call fortune to overrule the best wisdom. Many times he must tell events whereof he can yield no cause: or, if he do, it must be poetical. For that a feigned example hath as much force to teach as a true example (for as for to move, it is clear, since the feigned may be tuned to the highest key of passion), let us take one example wherein a poet and a historian do concur.

Herodotus and Justin do both testify that Zopyrus, King Darius's faithful servant, seeing his master long resisted by the rebellious Babylonians, feigned himself in extreme disgrace of his king: for verifying of which, he caused his own nose and ears to be cut off, and so flying to the Babylonians, was received, and for his known valor so far credited, that he did find means to deliver them over to Darius. Much like matter doth Livy record of Tarquinius and his son. Xenophon excellently feigneth such another stratagem performed by Abradates in Cyrus's behalf. Now would I fain know, if occasion be presented unto you to serve your prince by such an honest dissimulation, why you do not as well learn it of Xenophon's fiction as of the other's verity — and truly so much the better, as you shall save your nose by the bargain; for Abradates did not counterfeit so far. So then the best of the historian is subject to the poet; for whatsoever action, or

[18]Aristotle, *Poetics,* Ch. 9; see pp. 49–50. [Ed.]

[19]A slippage of terms characteristic of Sidney has just occurred. Aristotle's distinction between the universal and the particular has just become a distinction between the ideal and the real, which will support Sidney's defense of the moral function of poetry. [Ed.]

faction, whatsoever counsel, policy, or war stratagem the historian is bound to recite, that may the poet (if he list) with his imitation make his own, beautifying it both for further teaching, and more delighting, as it pleaseth him, having all, from Dante's heaven to his hell, under the authority of his pen. Which if I be asked what poets have done so, as I might well name some, yet say I, and say again, I speak of the art, and not of the artificer.

Now, to that which commonly is attributed to the praise of histories, in respect of the notable learning is gotten by marking the success, as though therein a man should see virtue exalted and vice punished — truly that commendation is peculiar to poetry, and far off from history. For indeed poetry ever setteth virtue so out in her best colors, making Fortune her well-waiting handmaid, that one must needs be enamored of her. Well may you see Ulysses in a storm, and in other hard plights; but they are but exercises of patience and magnanimity, to make them shine the more in the near-following prosperity. And of the contrary part, if evil men come to the stage, they ever go out (as the tragedy writer answered to one that misliked the show of such persons) so manacled as they little animate folks to follow them. But the historian, being captived to the truth of a foolish world, is many times a terror from well doing, and an encouragement to unbridled wickedness.

For see we not valiant Miltiades rot in his fetters: the just Phocion and the accomplished Socrates put to death like traitors; the cruel Severus live prosperously; the excellent Severus miserably murdered; Sylla and Marius dying in their beds; Pompey and Cicero slain then when they would have thought exile a happiness?

See we not virtuous Cato driven to kill himself, and rebel Caesar so advanced that his name yet, after 1,600 years, lasteth in the highest honor? And mark but even Caesar's own words of the forenamed Sylla (who in that only did honestly, to put down his dishonest tyranny). *Literas nescivit,*[20] as if want of learning caused him to do well. He meant it not by poetry, which,

not content with earthly plagues, deviseth new punishments in hell for tyrants, nor yet by philosophy, which teacheth *Occidendos esse;*[21] but no doubt by skill in history, for that indeed can afford your Cypselus, Periander, Phalaris, Dionysius, and I know not how many more of the same kennel, that speed well enough to their abominable injustice or usurpation. I conclude, therefore, that he excelleth history, not only in furnishing the mind with knowledge, but in setting it forward to that which deserveth to be called and accounted good: which setting forward, and moving to well doing, indeed setteth the laurel crown upon the poet as victorious, not only of the historian, but over the philosopher, howsoever in teaching it may be questionable.

For suppose it be granted (that which I suppose with great reason may be denied) that the philosopher, in respect of his methodical proceeding, doth teach more perfectly than the poet, yet do I think that no man is so much *philophilosophos*[22] as to compare the philosopher, in moving, with the poet.

And that moving is of a higher degree than teaching, it may by this appear, that it is wellnigh the cause and the effect of teaching. For who will be taught, if he be not moved with desire to be taught, and what so much good doth that teaching bring forth (I speak still of moral doctrine) as that it moveth one to do that which it doth teach? For, as Aristotle saith, it is not *gnosis* but *praxis*[23] must be the fruit. And how *praxis* cannot be, without being moved to practice, it is no hard matter to consider.

The philosopher showeth you the way, he informeth you of the particularities, as well of the tediousness of the way, as of the pleasant lodging you shall have when your journey is ended, as of the many by-turnings that may divert you from your way. But this is to no man but to him that will read him, and read him with attentive studious painfulness; which constant desire whosoever hath in him, hath already passed half the hardness of the way, and therefore is beholding to the philosopher but for the other half. Nay

[20]He did not know literature. [Ed.]

[21]They must be put to death. [Ed.]
[22]A lover of philosophy. [Ed.]
[23]Not abstract knowledge but action. [Ed.]

truly, learned men have learnedly thought that where once reason hath so much over-mastered passion as that the mind hath a free desire to do well, the inward light each mind hath in itself is as good as a philosopher's book; seeing in nature we know it is well to do well, and what is well and what is evil, although not in the words of art which philosophers bestow upon us. For out of natural conceit the philosophers drew it; but to be moved to do that which we know, or to be moved with desire to know, *Hoc opus, hic labor est.*[24]

Now therein of all sciences (I speak still of human, and according to the humane conceits) is our poet the monarch. For he doth not only show the way, but giveth so sweet a prospect into the way, as will entice any man to enter into it. Nay, he doth, as if your journey should lie through a fair vineyard, at the first give you a cluster of grapes, that, full of that taste, you may long to pass further. He beginneth not with obscure definitions, which must blur the margent[25] with interpretations, and load the memory with doubtfulness; but he cometh to you with words set in delightful proportion, either accompanied with, or prepared for, the well-enchanting skill of music; and with a tale forsooth he cometh unto you, with a tale which holdeth children from play, and old men from the chimney corner. And, pretending no more, doth intend the winning of the mind with wickedness to virtue: even as the child is often brought to take most wholesome things by hiding them in such other as have a pleasant taste: which, if one should begin to tell them the nature of aloes or rhubarb they should receive, would sooner take their physic at their ears than at their mouth. So is it in men (most of which are childish in the best things, till they be cradled in their graves): glad they will be to hear the tales of Hercules, Achilles, Cyrus, and Aeneas; and, hearing them, must needs hear the right description of wisdom, valor, and justice; which, if they had been barely, that is to say

philosophically, set out, they would swear they be brought to school again.

That imitation whereof poetry is, hath the most conveniency to nature of all other, insomuch that, as Aristotle saith, those things which in themselves are horrible, as cruel battles, unnatural monsters, are made in poetical imitation delightful. Truly, I have known men, that even with reading *Amadis de Gaule* (which God knoweth wanteth much of a perfect poesy) have found their hearts moved to the exercise of courtesy, liberality, and especially courage.

Who readeth Aeneas carrying old Anchises on his back, that wisheth not it were his fortune to perform so excellent an act? Whom do not the words of Turnus move, the tale of Turnus having planted his image in the imagination? — *"Fugientem haec terra videbit? / Usque adeone mori miserum est?"*[26] Where the philosophers, as they scorn to delight, so must they be content little to move, saving wrangling whether virtue be the chief or the only good, whether the contemplative or the active life do excel: which Plato and Boethius well knew, and therefore made Mistress Philosophy very often borrow the masking raiment of Poesy. For even those hardhearted evil men who think virtue a school name, and know no other good but *indulgere genio,*[27] and therefore despise the austere admonitions of the philosopher, and feel not the inward reason they stand upon, yet will be content to be delighted — which is all the good fellow poet seemeth to promise — and so steal to see the form of goodness, which seen they cannot but love ere themselves be aware, as if they took a medicine of cherries. Infinite proofs of the strange effects of his poetical invention might be alleged; only two shall serve, which are so often remembered as I think all men know them.

The one of Menenius Agrippa, who, when the whole people of Rome had resolutely divided themselves from the Senate, with apparent show of utter ruin, though he were (for that time) an excellent orator, came not among them upon trust of figurative speeches or cunning insinuations,

---

[24]"That is the labor, that is the task." Virgil, *Aeneid* 6: 129. [Ed.]

[25]The margins of the page, where the notes to a text were then placed. [Ed.]

[26]"And shall the land see me fleeing? And after all, is death so sad a thing?" *Aeneid* 12:645–46. [Ed.]

[27]To indulge one's nature. [Ed.]

and much less with farfetched maxims of philosophy, which (especially if they were Platonic) they must have learned geometry before they could well have conceived; but forsooth he behaves himself like a homely and familiar poet. He telleth them a tale, that there was a time when all the parts of the body made a mutinous conspiracy against the belly, which they thought devoured the fruits of each other's labor: they concluded they would let so unprofitable a spender starve. In the end, to be short (for the tale is notorious, and as notorious that it was a tale), with punishing the belly they plagued themselves. This applied by him wrought such effect in the people, as I never read that ever words brought forth but then so sudden and so good an alteration; for upon reasonable conditions a perfect reconcilement ensued. The other is of Nathan the Prophet, who, when the holy David had so far forsaken God as to confirm adultery with murder, when he was to do the tenderest office of a friend, in laying his own shame before his eyes, sent by God to call again so chosen a servant, how doth he it but by telling of a man whose beloved lamb was ungratefully taken from his bosom? — the application most divinely true, but the discourse itself feigned. Which made David (I speak of the second and instrumental cause) as in a glass to see his own filthiness, as that heavenly Psalm of Mercy well testifieth.

By these, therefore, examples and reasons, I think it may be manifest that the poet, with that same hand of delight, doth draw the mind more effectually than any other art doth: and so a conclusion not unfitly ensueth, that, as virtue is the most excellent resting place for all worldly learning to make his end of, so poetry, being the most familiar to teach it, and most princely to move towards it, in the most excellent work is the most excellent workman. But I am content not only to decipher him by his works (although works in commendation or dispraise must ever hold an high authority), but more narrowly will examine his parts: so that, as in a man, though all together may carry a presence full of majesty and beauty, perchance in some one defectious piece we may find a blemish. Now in his parts, kinds, or species (as you list to term them), it is to be noted that some poesies have coupled to-

gether two or three kinds, as tragical and comical, whereupon is risen the tragicomical. Some, in the like manner, have mingled prose and verse, as Sannazzaro and Boethius. Some have mingled matters heroical and pastoral. But that cometh all to one in this question, for, if severed they be good, the conjunction cannot be hurtful. Therefore, perchance forgetting some, and leaving some as needless to be remembered, it shall not be amiss in a word to cite the special kinds, to see what faults may be found in the right use of them.

Is it then the pastoral poem which is misliked? For perchance where the hedge is lowest they will soonest leap over. Is the poor pipe disdained, which sometime out of Melibaeus's mouth can show the misery of people under hard lords or ravening soldiers, and again, by Tityrus, what blessedness is derived to them that lie lowest from the goodness of them that sit highest; sometimes, under the pretty tales of wolves and sheep, can include the whole considerations of wrongdoing and patience; sometimes show that contention for trifles can get but a trifling victory; where perchance a man may see that even Alexander and Darius, when they strave who should be cock of this world's dunghill, the benefit they got was that the afterlivers may say, "*Haec memini et victum frustra contendere Thirsin: / Ex illo Coridon, Coridon est tempore nobis*"?[28]

Or is it the lamenting elegiac, which in a kind heart would move rather pity than blame, who bewails with the great philosopher Heraclitus the weakness of mankind and the wretchedness of the world; who surely is to be praised, either for compassionate accompanying just causes of lamentation, or for rightly pointing out how weak be the passions of woefulness? Is it the bitter but wholesome iambic, which rubs the galled mind, in making shame the trumpet of villainy with bold and open crying out against naughtiness? Or the satiric, who "*omne vafer vitium ridenti tangit amico*";[29] who sportingly never leaveth

---

[28]"I remember those things, and that conquered Thyrsis strove then in vain; Since then Corydon is for us Corydon." Virgil, *Eclogues* 7:69–70. [Ed.]

[29]"The rogue touches every vice while making his friend laugh." Persius, *Satires* 1:116–17. [Ed.]

until he make a man laugh at folly, and, at length ashamed, to laugh at himself, which he cannot avoid, without avoiding the folly; who, while "*circum praecordia ludit,*"[30] giveth us to feel how many headaches a passionate life bringeth us to; how, when all is done, "*est Ulubris animus si nos non deficit aequus?*"[31]

No, perchance it is the comic, whom naughty play-makers and stage-keepers have justly made odious. To the argument of abuse I will answer after. Only thus much now is to be said, that the comedy is an imitation of the common errors of our life, which he representeth in the most ridiculous and scornful sort that may be, so as it is impossible that any beholder can be content to be such a one.

Now, as in geometry the oblique must be known as well as the right, and in arithmetic the odd as well as the even, so in the actions of our life who seeth not the filthiness of evil wanteth a great foil to perceive the beauty of virtue. This doth the comedy handle so in our private and domestical matters, as with hearing it we get as it were an experience, what is to be looked for of a niggardly Demea, of a crafty Davus, of a flattering Gnatho, of a vainglorious Thraso; and not only to know what effects are to be expected, but to know who be such, by the signifying badge given them by the comedian. And little reason hath any man to say that men learn evil by seeing it so set out; since, as I said before, there is no man living but, by the force truth hath in nature, no sooner seeth these men play their parts, but wisheth them in *pistrinum;*[32] although perchance the sack of his own faults lie so behind his back that he seeth not himself dance the same measure; whereto yet nothing can more open his eyes than to find his own actions contemptibly set forth. So that the right use of comedy will (I think) by nobody be blamed, and much less of the high and excellent tragedy, that openeth the greatest wounds, and showeth forth the ulcers that are covered with tissue; that maketh kings fear to be tyrants, and tyrants manifest their tyrannical humors; that, with stirring the affects of admiration and commiseration, teacheth the uncertainty of this world, and upon how weak foundations gilden roofs are builded; that maketh us know, "*Qui sceptra saevus duro imperio regit, / Timet timentes, metus in auctorem redit.*"[33]

But how much it can move, Plutarch yieldeth a notable testimony of the abominable tyrant Alexander Phераeus, from whose eyes a tragedy, well made and represented, drew abundance of tears, who, without all pity, had murdered infinite numbers, and some of his own blood, so as he, that was not ashamed to make matters for tragedies, yet could not resist the sweet violence of a tragedy.

And if it wrought no further good in him, it was that he, in despite of himself, withdrew himself from hearkening to that which might mollify his hardened heart. But it is not the tragedy they do mislike; for it were too absurd to cast out so excellent a representation of whatsoever is most worthy to be learned. Is it the lyric that most displeaseth, who with his tuned lyre, and well-accorded voice, giveth praise, the reward of virtue, to virtuous acts, who gives moral precepts, and natural problems, who sometimes raiseth up his voice to the height of the heavens, in singing the lauds of the immortal God? Certainly, I must confess my own barbarousness, I never heard the old song of Percy and Douglas that I found not my heart moved more than with a trumpet; and yet is it sung but by some blind crowder, with no rougher voice than rude style; which, being so evil appareled in the dust and cobwebs of that uncivil age, what would it work, trimmed in the gorgeous eloquence of Pindar? In Hungary I have seen it the manner at all feasts, and other such meetings, to have songs of their ancestors' valor; which that right soldierlike nation think the chiefest kindlers of brave courage. The incomparable Lacedaemonians did not only carry that kind of music ever with them to the field, but even at home, as such songs were made, so were they

---

[30]"He plays about the heartstrings." From the passage above. [Ed.]

[31]"Happiness is to be found, even in Ulubrae [a dead city], so long as we don't lose our sense of proportion." Horace, *Epistles* I.11:30. [Ed.]

[32]A treadmill for slaves. [Ed.]

[33]"The savage ruler who wields the sceptre with a hard hand / Fears the timid, and thus fear returns to its author." Seneca, *Oedipus,* 705–6. [Ed.]

all content to be the singers of them, when the lusty men were to tell what they did, the old men what they had done, and the young men what they would do. And where a man may say that Pindar many times praiseth highly victories of small moment, matters rather of sport than virtue; as it may be answered, it was the fault of the poet, and not of the poetry, so indeed the chief fault was in the time and custom of the Greeks, who set those toys at so high a price that Philip of Macedon reckoned a horse race won at Olympus among his three fearful felicities. But as the inimitable Pindar often did, so is that kind most capable and most fit to awake the thoughts from the sleep of idleness, to embrace honorable enterprises.

There rests the heroical, whose very name (I think) should daunt all backbiters; for by what conceit can a tongue be directed to speak evil of that which draweth with it no less champions than Achilles, Cyrus, Aeneas, Turnus, Tydeus, and Rinaldo? Who doth not only teach and move to a truth, but teacheth and moveth to the most high and excellent truth; who maketh magnanimity and justice shine throughout all misty fearfulness and foggy desires; who, if the saying of Plato and Tully[34] be true, that who could see virtue would be wonderfully ravished with the love of her beauty — this man sets her out to make her more lovely in her holiday apparel, to the eye of any that will deign not to disdain until they understand. But if anything be already said in the defense of sweet Poetry, all concurreth to the maintaining the heroical, which is not only a kind, but the best and most accomplished kind of poetry.[35] For as the image of each action stirreth and instructeth the mind, so the lofty image of such worthies most inflameth the mind with desire to be worthy, and informs with counsel how to be worthy. Only let Aeneas be worn in the tablet of your memory, how he governeth himself in the ruin of his country, in the preserving his old father, and carrying away his religious

ceremonies, in obeying the god's commandment to leave Dido, though not only all passionate kindness, but even the human consideration of virtuous gratefulness, would have craved other of him; how in storms, how in sports, how in war, how in peace, how a fugitive, how victorious, how besieged, how besieging, how to strangers, how to allies, how to enemies, how to his own; lastly, how in his inward self, and how in his outward government, and I think, in a mind not prejudiced with a prejudicating humor, he will be found in excellency fruitful, yea, even as Horace saith, "*melius Chrysippo et Crantore.*"[36]

But truly I imagine it falleth out with these poet-whippers, as with some good women, who often are sick, but in faith they cannot tell where. So the name of poetry is odious to them, but neither his cause nor effects, neither the sum that contains him nor the particularities descending from him, give any fast handle to their carping dispraise.

Since then poetry is of all human learning the most ancient and of most fatherly antiquity, as from whence other learnings have taken their beginnings; since it is so universal that no learned nation doth despise it, nor no barbarous nation is without it; since both Roman and Greek gave divine names unto it, the one of *prophesying*, the other of *making,* and that indeed that name of *making* is fit for him, considering that whereas other arts retain themselves within their subject, and receive, as it were, their being from it, the poet only bringeth his own stuff, and doth not learn a conceit out of a matter, but maketh matter for a conceit; since neither his description nor his end containeth any evil, the thing described cannot be evil; since his effects be so good as to teach goodness and to delight the learners; since therein (namely in moral doctrine, the chief of all knowledges) he doth not only far pass the historian, but, for instructing, is well-nigh comparable to the philosopher, and, for moving, leaves him behind him; since the Holy Scripture (wherein there is no uncleanness) hath whole

[34]Cicero. [Ed.]

[35]It was characteristic of Renaissance criticism to favor epic over tragedy — unlike Aristotle, who in *Poetics*, Ch. 26, had favored the concise tragedy over the full-blown epic. [Ed.]

[36]"Better than Chrysippus and Crantor." Horace, *Epistles* I.2:4. Horace claims that Homer teaches virtue better than the above-mentioned two philosophers. [Ed.]

parts in it poetical, and that even our Saviour Christ vouchsafed to use the flowers of it; since all his kinds are not only in their united forms but in their severed dissections fully commendable; I think (and think I think rightly) the laurel crown appointed for triumphing captains doth worthily (of all other learnings) honor the poet's triumph. But because we have ears as well as tongues, and that the lightest reasons that may be will seem to weigh greatly, if nothing be put in the counter-balance, let us hear, and, as well as we can, ponder, what objections may be made against this art, which may be worthy either of yielding or answering.

First, truly I note not only in these *mysomousoi,* "poet-haters," but in all that kind of people who seek a praise by dispraising others, that they do prodigally spend a great many wandering words in quips and scoffs, carping and taunting at each thing, which, by stirring the spleen, may stay the brain from a thorough beholding the worthiness of the subject.

Those kind of objections, as they are full of very idle easiness, since there is nothing of so sacred a majesty but that an itching tongue may rub itself upon it, so deserve they no other answer, but, instead of laughing at the jest, to laugh at the jester. We know a playing wit can praise the discretion of an ass, the comfortableness of being in debt, and the jolly commodity of being sick of the plague. So of the contrary side, if we will turn Ovid's verse, *"Ut lateat virtus proximitate mali,"* that "good lie hid in nearness of the evil," Agrippa will be as merry in showing the vanity of science as Erasmus was in commending of folly. Neither shall any man or matter escape some touch of these smiling railers. But for Erasmus and Agrippa, they had another foundation than the superficial part would promise. Marry, these other pleasant faultfinders, who will correct the verb before they understand the noun, and confute others' knowledge before they confirm their own, I would have them only remember that scoffing cometh not of wisdom; so as the best title in true English they get with their merriments is to be called good fools, for so have our grave forefathers ever termed that humorous kind of jesters. But that which giveth greatest scope to their scorning humors is rhyming and versing. It is already said (and, as I think truly said) it is not rhyming and versing that maketh poesy. One may be a poet without versing, and a versifier without poetry. But yet presuppose it were inseparable (as indeed it seemeth Scaliger judgeth) truly it were an inseparable commendation.[37] For if *oratio* next to *ratio,* "speech" next to "reason," be the greatest gift bestowed upon mortality, that cannot be praiseless which doth most polish that blessing of speech; which considers each word, not only (as a man may say) by his forcible quality, but by his best measured quantity, carrying even in themselves a harmony (without, perchance, number, measure, order, proportion be in our time grown odious). But lay aside the just praise it hath, by being the only fit speech for music (music, I say, the most divine striker of the senses), thus much is undoubtedly true, that if reading be foolish without remembering, memory being the only treasurer of knowledge, those words which are fittest for memory are likewise most convenient for knowledge.

Now, that verse far exceedeth prose in the knitting up of the memory, the reason is manifest — the words (besides their delight, which hath a great affinity to memory) being so set as one word cannot be lost but the whole work fails; which accuseth itself, calleth the remembrance back to itself, and so most strongly confirmeth it. Besides, one word so, as it were, begetting another, as, be it in rhyme or measured verse, by the former a man shall have a near guess to the follower: lastly, even they that have taught the art of memory have showed nothing so apt for it as a certain room divided into many places well and thoroughly known. Now, that hath the verse in effect perfectly, every word having his natural seat, which seat must needs make the words remembered. But what needeth more in a thing so known to all men? Who is it that ever was a scholar that doth not carry away some verses of Virgil, Horace, or Cato, which in his youth he learned, and even to his old age serve him for hourly lessons? But the fitness it hath for

---

[37]In his *Poetics,* Julius Caesar Scaliger claimed that what the poet made was verses; Aristotle identified the poet's primary product as the imitation of a human action. [Ed.]

memory is notably proved by all delivery of arts: wherein for the most part, from grammar to logic, mathematic, physic, and the rest, the rules chiefly necessary to be borne away are compiled in verses. So that, verse being in itself sweet and orderly, and being best for memory, the only handle of knowledge, it must be in jest that any man can speak against it. Now then go we to the most important imputations laid to the poor poets. For aught I can yet learn, they are these. First, that there being many other more fruitful knowledges, a man might better spend his time in them than in this. Secondly, that it is the mother of lies. Thirdly, that it is the nurse of abuse, infecting us with many pestilent desires, with a siren's sweetness drawing the mind to the serpent's tale of sinful fancy — and herein, especially, comedies give the largest field to ear (as Chaucer saith) — how both in other nations and in ours, before poets did soften us, we were full of courage, given to martial exercises, the pillars of manlike liberty, and not lulled asleep in shady idleness with poets' pastimes. And lastly, and chiefly, they cry out with an open mouth, as if they outshot Robin Hood, that Plato banished them out of his commonwealth.[38] Truly, this is much, if there be much truth in it. First, to the first, that a man might better spend his time is a reason indeed: but it doth (as they say) but *petere principium*:[39] for if it be, as I affirm, that no learning is so good as that which teacheth and moveth to virtue, and that none can both teach and move thereto so much as poetry, then is the conclusion manifest that ink and paper cannot be to a more profitable purpose employed. And certainly, though a man should grant their first assumption, it should follow (methinks) very unwillingly, that good is not good because better is better. But I still and utterly deny that there is sprung out of earth a more fruitful knowledge. To the second therefore, that they should be the principal liars, I answer paradoxically, but truly, I think truly, that of all writers under the sun the poet is the least liar, and, though he would, as a poet can scarcely be a liar. The astronomer, with

[38]Plato, *Republic* 10; see p. 29. [Ed.]
[39]To beg the question — assume what one needs to prove. [Ed.]

his cousin the geometrician, can hardly escape, when they take upon them to measure the height of the stars.

How often, think you, do the physicians lie, when they aver things good for sicknesses, which afterwards send Charon a great number of souls drowned in a potion before they come to his ferry? And no less of the rest, which take upon them to affirm. Now, for the poet, he nothing affirms, and therefore never lieth. For, as I take it, to lie is to affirm that to be true which is false; so as the other artists, and especially the historian, affirming many things, can, in the cloudy knowledge of mankind, hardly escape from many lies. But the poet (as I said before) never affirmeth. The poet never maketh any circles about your imagination, to conjure you to believe for true what he writes. He citeth not authorities of other histories, but even for his entry calleth the sweet Muses to inspire into him a good invention; in truth, no laboring to tell you what is, or is not, but what should or should not be. And therefore, though he recount things not true, yet because he telleth them not for true, he lieth not — without we will say that Nathan lied in his speech, before alleged, to David; which as a wicked man durst scarce say, so think I none so simple would say that Aesop lied in the tales of his beasts: for who thinks that Aesop writ it for actually true were well worthy to have his name chronicled among the beasts he writeth of.

What child is there that, coming to a play, and seeing *Thebes* written in great letters upon an old door, doth believe that it is Thebes? If then a man can arrive, at that child's age, to know that the poets' persons and doings are but pictures what should be, and not stories what have been, they will never give the lie to things not affirmatively but allegorically and figuratively written. And therefore, as in history, looking for truth, they go away full fraught with falsehood, so in poesy, looking for fiction, they shall use the narration but as an imaginative ground plot of a profitable invention.

But hereto is replied, that the poets give names to men they write of, which argueth a conceit of an actual truth, and so, not being true, proves a falsehood. And doth the lawyer lie then, when under the names of John a Stile and John a Noakes he puts his case? But that is easily answered. Their naming of men is but to make their picture the more lively, and not to build any history; painting men, they cannot leave men nameless. We see we cannot play at chess but that we must give names to our chessmen; and yet, methinks, he were a very partial champion of truth that would say we lied for giving a piece of wood the reverend title of a bishop. The poet nameth Cyrus or Aeneas no other way than to show what men of their fames, fortunes, and estates should do.

Their third is, how much it abuseth men's wit, training it to wanton sinfulness and lustful love: for indeed that is the principal, if not the only, abuse I can hear alleged. They say the comedies rather teach than reprehend amorous conceits. They say the lyric is larded with passionate sonnets, the elegiac weeps the want of his mistress, and that even to the heroical Cupid hath ambitiously climbed. Alas, Love, I would thou couldst as well defend thyself as thou canst offend others. I would those on whom thou dost attend could either put thee away, or yield good reason why they keep thee. But grant love of beauty to be a beastly fault (although it be very hard, since only man, and no beast, hath that gift to discern beauty); grant that lovely name of Love to deserve all hateful reproaches (although even some of my masters the philosophers spent a good deal of their lamp-oil in setting forth the excellency of it); grant, I say, whatsoever they will have granted; that not only love, but lust, but vanity, but (if they list) scurrility, possesseth many leaves of the poets' books: yet think I, when this is granted, they will find their sentence may with good manners put the last words foremost, and not say that poetry abuseth man's wit, but that man's wit abuseth poetry.

For I will not deny but that man's wit may make poesy, which should be *eikastike*, which some learned have defined, "figuring forth good things," to be *phantastike*, which doth, contrariwise, infect the fancy with unworthy objects, as the painter, that should give to the eye either some excellent perspective, or some fine picture, fit for building or fortification, or containing in it some notable example, as Abraham sacrificing his son Isaac, Judith killing Holofernes, David fighting with Goliath, may leave those, and please an ill-pleased eye with wanton shows of better hidden matters. But what, shall the abuse of a thing make the right use odious? Nay truly, though I yield that poesy may not only be abused, but that being abused, by the reason of his sweet charming force, it can do more hurt than any other army of words, yet shall it be so far from concluding that the abuse should give reproach to the abused, that contrariwise it is a good reason, that whatsoever, being abused, doth most harm, being rightly used (and upon the right use each thing conceiveth his title), doth most good.

Do we not see the skill of physic (the best rampire to our often-assaulted bodies), being abused, teach poison, the most violent destroyer? Doth not knowledge of law, whose end is to even and right all things, being abused, grow the crooked fosterer of horrible injuries? Doth not (to go to the highest) God's word abused breed heresy, and his name abused become blasphemy? Truly, a needle cannot do much hurt, and as truly (with leave of ladies be it spoken) it cannot do much good. With a sword thou mayest kill thy father, and with a sword thou mayest defend thy prince and country. So that, as in their calling poets the fathers of lies they say nothing, so in this their argument of abuse they prove the commendation.

They allege herewith, that before poets began to be in price our nation hath set their heart's delight upon action, and not upon imagination, rather doing things worthy to be written, than writing things fit to be done. What that beforetime was, I think scarcely Sphinx can tell, since no memory is so ancient that hath the precedence of poetry. And certain it is that, in our plainest homeliness, yet never was the Albion nation without poetry. Marry, this argument, though it be leveled against poetry, yet is it indeed a chainshot against all learning, or bookishness, as they commonly term it. Of such mind were certain Goths, of whom it is written that, having in the spoil of a famous city taken a fair library, one hangman, belike, fit to execute the fruits of their wits, who had murdered a great number of bodies, would have set fire to it. "No," said another very gravely, "take heed what you do, for while they are busy about these toys, we shall with more leisure conquer their countries."

This indeed is the ordinary doctrine of ignorance, and many words sometimes I have heard spent in it: but because this reason is generally against all learning, as well as poetry, or rather, all learning but poetry; because it were too large a digression to handle, or at least too superfluous (since it is manifest that all government of action is to be gotten by knowledge, and knowledge best by gathering many knowledges, which is reading), I only, with Horace, to him that is of that opinion, "*iubeo stultum esse libenter*";[40] for as for poetry itself, it is the freest from this objection. For poetry is the companion of the camps.

I dare undertake, Orlando Furioso, or honest King Arthur, will never displease a soldier: but the quiddity of *ens* and *prima materia*[41] will hardly agree with a corselet. And therefore, as I said in the beginning, even Turks and Tartars are delighted with poets. Homer, a Greek, flourished before Greece flourished. And if to a slight conjecture a conjecture may be opposed, truly it may seem, that, as by him their learned men took almost their first light of knowledge, so their active men received their first motions of courage. Only Alexander's example may serve, who by Plutarch is accounted of such virtue, that fortune was not his guide but his footstool; whose acts speak for him, though Plutarch did not — indeed the Phoenix of warlike princes. This Alexander left his schoolmaster, living Aristotle, behind him, but took dead Homer with him. He put the philosopher Callisthenes to death for his seeming philosophical, indeed mutinous, stubbornness, but the chief thing he ever was heard to wish for was that Homer had been alive. He well found he received more bravery of mind by the pattern of Achilles than by hearing the definition of fortitude: and therefore, if Cato misliked Fulvius for carrying Ennius with him to the field,

it may be answered that, if Cato misliked it, the noble Fulvius liked it, or else he had not done it: for it was not the excellent Cato Uticensis (whose authority I would much more have reverenced), but it was the former, in truth a bitter punisher of faults, but else a man that had never well sacrificed to the Graces. He misliked and cried out upon all Greek learning, and yet, being eighty years old, began to learn it, belike fearing that Pluto understood not Latin. Indeed, the Roman laws allowed no person to be carried to the wars but he that was in the soldier's roll, and therefore, though Cato misliked his unmustered persons, he misliked not his work. And if he had, Scipio Nasica, judged by common consent the best Roman, loved him. Both the other Scipio brothers, who had by their virtues no less surnames than of Asia and Afric, so loved him that they caused his body to be buried in their sepulcher. So as Cato's authority being but against his person, and that answered with so far greater than himself, is herein of no validity. But now indeed my burden is great; now Plato's name is laid upon me, whom I must confess, of all philosophers I have ever esteemed most worthy of reverence, and with great reason, since of all philosophers he is the most poetical. Yet if he will defile the fountain out of which his flowing streams have proceeded, let us boldly examine with what reasons he did it. First truly, a man might maliciously object that Plato, being a philosopher, was a natural enemy of poets. For indeed, after the philosophers had picked out of the sweet mysteries of poetry the right discerning true points of knowledge, they forthwith, putting it in method, and making a school art of that which the poets did only teach by a divine delightfulness, beginning to spurn at their guides, like ungrateful 'prentices, were not content to set up shops for themselves, but sought by all means to discredit their masters; which by the force of delight being barred them, the less they could overthrow them, the more they hated them. For indeed, they found for Homer seven cities strove who should have him for their citizen; where many cities banished philosophers as not fit members to live among them. For only repeating certain of Euripides' verses, many Athenians had

---

[40]"I ask him to be a fool as much as he likes." Horace, *Satires* I.1:63. [Ed.]

[41]The whatness of being and primal matter. Sidney uses scholastic terms here. [Ed.]

their lives saved of the Syracusians, when the Athenians themselves thought many philosophers unworthy to live.

Certain poets, as Simonides and Pindarus, had so prevailed with Hiero the First, that of a tyrant they made him a just king; where Plato could do so little with Dionysius, that he himself of a philosopher was made a slave. But who should do thus, I confess, should requite the objections made against poets with like cavillation against philosophers; as likewise one should do that should bid one read *Phaedrus* or *Symposium* in Plato, or the discourse of love in Plutarch, and see whether any poet do authorize abominable filthiness, as they do. Again, a man might ask out of what commonwealth Plato did banish them. In sooth, thence where he himself alloweth community of women. So as belike this banishment grew not for effeminate wantonness, since little should poetical sonnets be hurtful when a man might have what woman he listed. But I honor philosophical instructions, and bless the wits which bred them: so as they be not abused, which is likewise stretched to poetry.

St. Paul himself, who yet, for the credit of poets, allegeth twice two poets, and one of them by the name of a prophet, setteth a watchword upon philosophy — indeed upon the abuse. So doth Plato upon the abuse, not upon poetry. Plato found fault that the poets of his time filled the world with wrong opinions of the gods, making light tales of that unspotted essence, and therefore would not have the youth depraved with such opinions. Herein may much be said; let this suffice: the poets did not induce such opinions, but did imitate those opinions already induced. For all the Greek stories can well testify that the very religion of that time stood upon many and many-fashioned gods, not taught so by the poets, but followed according to their nature of imitation. Who list may read in Plutarch the discourses of Isis and Osiris, of the cause why oracles ceased, of the divine providence, and see whether the theology of that nation stood not upon such dreams which the poets indeed superstitiously observed, and truly (since they had not the light of Christ) did much better in it than the philosophers, who, shaking off superstition, brought in atheism. Plato therefore (whose authority I had much rather justly construe than unjustly resist) meant not in general of poets, in those words of which Julius Scaliger saith, "*Qua authoritate barbari quidam atque hispidi abuti velint ad poetas e republica exigendos*";[42] but only meant to drive out those wrong opinions of the Deity (whereof now, without further law, Christianity hath taken away all the hurtful belief), perchance (as he thought) nourished by the then esteemed poets. And a man need go no further than to Plato himself to know his meaning: who, in his dialogue called *Ion,* giveth high and rightly divine commendation to poetry. So as Plato, banishing the abuse, not the thing, not banishing it, but giving due honor unto it, shall be our patron and not our adversary. For indeed I had much rather (since truly I may do it) show their mistaking of Plato (under whose lion's skin they would make an asslike braying against poesy) than go about to overthrow his authority; whom, the wiser a man is, the more just cause he shall find to have in admiration; especially since he attributeth unto poesy more than myself do, namely, to be a very inspiring of a divine force, far above man's wit, as in the afore-named dialogue is apparent.

Of the other side, who would show the honors have been by the best sort of judgments granted them, a whole sea of examples would present themselves: Alexanders, Caesars, Scipios, all favorers of poets; Laelius, called the Roman Socrates, himself a poet, so as part of *Heautontimorumenos*[43] in Terence was supposed to be made by him, and even the Greek Socrates, whom Apollo confirmed to be the only wise man, is said to have spent part of his old time in putting Aesop's fables into verses. And therefore, full evil should it become his scholar Plato to put such words in his master's mouth against poets. But what need more? Aristotle writes the *Art of Poesy*: and why, if it should not be written? Plutarch teacheth the use to be gathered of them, and how, if they should not be read? And who reads Plutarch's either history or philosophy, shall find he trimmeth both their garments with

[42]"Barbarous and rude men would abuse this authority to drive poets out of the republic." Scaliger, *Poetics* I:2. [Ed.]
[43]*The Self-Tormentor.* [Ed.]

guards of poesy. But I list not to defend poesy with the help of her underling historiography. Let it suffice that it is a fit soil for praise to dwell upon; and what dispraise may set upon it, is either easily overcome, or transformed into just commendation. So that, since the excellencies of it may be so easily and so justly confirmed, and the low-creeping objections so soon trodden down; it not being an art of lies, but of true doctrine; not of effeminateness, but of notable stirring of courage; not of abusing man's wit, but of strengthening man's wit; not banished, but honored by Plato; let us rather plant more laurels for to engarland our poets' heads (which honor of being laureate, as besides them only triumphant captains wear, is a sufficient authority to show the price they ought to be had in) than suffer the ill-favoring breath of such wrong-speakers once to blow upon the clear springs of poesy.

But since I have run so long a career in this matter, methinks, before I give my pen a full stop, it shall be but a little more lost time to inquire why England (the mother of excellent minds) should be grown so hard a stepmother to poets, who certainly in wit ought to pass all other, since all only proceedeth from their wit, being indeed makers of themselves, not takers of others. How can I but exclaim, "*Musa, mihi causas memora, quo numine laeso!*"[44] Sweet Poesy, that hath anciently had kings, emperors, senators, great captains, such as, besides a thousand others, David, Adrian, Sophocles, Germanicus, not only to favor poets, but to be poets; and of our nearer times can present for her patrons a Robert, king of Sicily, the great King Francis of France, King James of Scotland; such cardinals as Bembus and Bibbiena: such famous preachers and teachers as Beza and Melancthon; so learned philosophers as Fracastorius and Scaliger; so great orators as Pontanus and Muretus; so piercing wits as George Buchanan; so grave counselors as, besides many, but before all, that Hospital of France, than whom (I think) that realm never brought forth a more accomplished judgment, more firmly builded upon virtue — I

say, these, with numbers of others, not only to read others' poesies, but to poetize for others' reading — that poesy, thus embraced in all other places, should only find in our time a hard welcome in England, I think the very earth lamenteth it, and therefore decketh our soil with fewer laurels than it was accustomed. For heretofore poets have in England also flourished, and, which is to be noted, even in those times when the trumpet of Mars did sound loudest. And now that an overfaint quietness should seem to strew the house for poets, they are almost in as good reputation as the mountebanks at Venice. Truly even that, as of the one side it giveth great praise to poesy, which like Venus (but to better purpose) hath rather be troubled in the net with Mars than enjoy the homely quiet of Vulcan; so serves it for a piece of a reason why they are less grateful to idle England, which now can scarce endure the pain of a pen. Upon this necessarily followeth, that base men with servile wits undertake it, who think it enough if they can be rewarded of the printer. And so as Epaminondas is said, with the honor of his virtue, to have made an office, by his exercising it, which before was contemptible, to become highly respected, so these, no more but setting their names to it, by their own disgracefulness disgrace the most graceful poesy. For now, as if all the Muses were got with child, to bring forth bastard poets, without any commission they do post over the banks of Helicon, till they make the readers more weary than post-horses, while, in the meantime, they, "*queis meliore luto finxit praecordia Titan,*"[45] are better content to suppress the outflowing of their wit, than, by publishing them, to be accounted knights of the same order. But I that, before ever I durst aspire unto the dignity, am admitted into the company of the paper-blurrers, do find the very true cause of our wanting estimation is want of desert, taking upon us to be poets in despite of Pallas. Now, wherein we want desert were a thankworthy labor to express: but if I knew, I should have mended myself. But I, as I never desired the title, so have I neglected the means to come by it. Only, overmastered by some

---

[44]"Tell me the reason, Muse: what was the injury to her divinity?" Virgil, *Aeneid* I:8. [Ed.]

[45]"Whom the Titan has formed out of finer clay." Juvenal, *Satires* 14:35. [Ed.]

thoughts, I yielded an inky tribute unto them. Marry, they that delight in poesy itself should seek to know what they do, and how they do, and, especially, look themselves in an unflattering glass of reason, if they be inclinable unto it. For poesy must not be drawn by the ears; it must be gently led, or rather it must lead; which was partly the cause that made the ancient-learned affirm it was a divine gift, and no human skill; since all other knowledges lie ready for any that hath strength of wit; a poet no industry can make, if his own genius be not carried unto it; and therefore is it an old proverb, *Orator fit, poeta nascitur.*[46] Yet confess I always that as the fertilest ground must be manured, so must the highest-flying wit have a Daedalus to guide him. That Daedalus, they say, both in this and in other, hath three wings to bear itself up into the air of due commendation: that is, art, imitation, and exercise. But these, neither artificial rules nor imitative patterns, we much cumber ourselves withal. Exercise indeed we do, but that very forebackwardly: for where we should exercise to know, we exercise as having known: and so is our brain delivered of much matter which never was begotten by knowledge. For, there being two principal parts — matter to be expressed by words and words to express the matter — in neither we use art or imitation rightly. Our matter is *quodlibet*[47] indeed, though wrongly performing Ovid's verse, "*Quicquid conabar dicere, versus erat*":[48] never marshaling it into an assured rank, that almost the readers cannot tell where to find themselves.

Chaucer, undoubtedly, did excellently in his *Troilus and Cressida;* of whom, truly, I know not whether to marvel more, either that he in that misty time could see so clearly, or that we in this clear age walk so stumblingly after him. Yet had he great wants, fit to be forgiven in so reverent antiquity. I account the *Mirror of Magistrates* meetly furnished of beautiful parts, and in the Earl of Surrey's *Lyrics* many things tasting of a noble birth, and worthy of a noble mind.

The *Shepherd's Calendar* hath much poetry in his eclogues, indeed worthy the reading, if I be not deceived. That same framing of his style to an old rustic language I dare not allow, since neither Theocritus in Greek, Virgil in Latin, nor Sannazzaro in Italian did affect it. Besides these, do I not remember to have seen but few (to speak boldly) printed, that have poetical sinews in them: for proof whereof, let but most of the verses be put in prose, and then ask the meaning; and it will be found that one verse did but beget another, without ordering at the first what should be at the last; which becomes a confused mass of words, with a tingling sound of rhyme, barely accompanied with reason.

Our tragedies and comedies (not without cause cried out against), observing rules neither of honest civility nor of skillful poetry, excepting *Gorboduc* (again, I say, of those that I have seen), which notwithstanding, as it is full of stately speeches and well-sounding phrases, climbing to the height of Seneca's style, and as full of notable morality, which it doth most delightfully teach, and so obtain the very end of poesy, yet in truth it is very defectious in the circumstances, which grieveth me, because it might not remain as an exact model of all tragedies. For it is faulty both in place and time, the two necessary companions of all corporal actions.[49] For where the stage should always represent but one place, and the uttermost time presupposed in it should be, both by Aristotle's precept and common reason, but one day, there is both many days, and many places, inartificially[50] imagined. But if it be so in *Gorboduc*, how much more in all the rest, where you shall have Asia of the one side, and Afric of the other, and so many other underkingdoms, that the player, when he cometh in, must ever begin with telling where he is, or else the tale will not be conceived? Now ye shall have three ladies walk to gather flowers and then we must believe the stage to be a garden. By and by we hear news of shipwreck in the same place, and

---

[46]The orator is made; the poet is born. [Ed.]

[47]An impromptu performance. [Ed.]

[48]"Whatever I tried to say was verse." Ovid, *Tristia* IV. 10:26. [Ed.]

[49]*Gorboduc* fails to satisfy the unities of place and time, which Sidney ascribes to Aristotle. [Ed.]

[50]Unartistically. [Ed.]

then we are to blame if we accept it not for a rock.

Upon the back of that comes out a hideous monster, with fire and smoke, and then the miserable beholders are bound to take it for a cave. While in the meantime two armies fly in, represented with four swords and bucklers, and then what hard heart will not receive it for a pitched field? Now, of time they are much more liberal, for ordinary it is that two young princes fall in love. After many traverses, she is got with child, delivered of a fair boy; he is lost, groweth a man, falls in love, and is ready to get another child; and all this in two hours' space: which, how absurd it is in sense, even sense may imagine, and art hath taught, and all ancient examples justified, and, at this day, the ordinary players in Italy will not err in. Yet will some bring in an example of *Eunuchus*[51] in Terence, that containeth matter of two days, yet far short of twenty years. True it is, and so was it to be played in two days, and so fitted to the time it set forth. And though Plautus hath in one place done amiss, let us hit with him, and not miss with him. But they will say, How then shall we set forth a story, which containeth both many places and many times? And do they not know that a tragedy is tied to the laws of poesy, and not of history; not bound to follow the story, but, having liberty, either to feign a quite new matter, or to frame the history to the most tragical conveniency? Again, many things may be told which cannot be showed, if they know the difference betwixt reporting and representing. As, for example, I may speak (though I am here) of Peru, and in speech digress from that to the description of Calicut; but in action I cannot represent it without Pacolet's horse. And so was the manner the ancients took, by some nuncius[52] to recount things done in former time or other place. Lastly, if they will represent an history, they must not (as Horace saith) begin *ab ovo*,[53] but they must come to the principal point of that one action

which they will represent. By example this will be best expressed. I have a story of young Polydorus, delivered for safety's sake, with great riches, by his father Priam to Polymnestor, king of Thrace, in the Trojan war time. He, after some years, hearing the overthrow of Priam, for to make the treasure his own, murdereth the child. The body of the child is taken up by Hecuba. She, the same day, findeth a slight to be revenged most cruelly of the tyrant. Where now would one of our tragedy writers begin, but with the delivery of the child? Then should he sail over into Thrace, and so spend I know not how many years, and travel numbers of places. But where doth Euripides? Even with the finding of the body, leaving the rest to be told by the spirit of Polydorus. This need no further to be enlarged; the dullest wit may conceive it. But besides these gross absurdities, how all their plays be neither right tragedies, nor right comedies, mingling kings and clowns, not because the matter so carrieth it, but thrust in clowns by head and shoulders, to play a part in majestical matters, with neither decency nor discretion, so as neither the admiration and commiseration, nor the right sportfulness, is by their mongrel tragicomedy obtained. I know Apuleius did somewhat so, but that is a thing recounted with space of time, not represented in one moment: and I know the ancients have one or two examples of tragicomedies, as Plautus hath *Amphitrio*. But, if we mark them well, we shall find that they never, or very daintily, match hornpipes and funerals. So falleth it out that, having indeed no right comedy, in that comical part of our tragedy we have nothing but scurrility, unworthy of any chaste ears, or some extreme show of doltishness, indeed fit to lift up a loud laughter, and nothing else: where the whole tract of a comedy should be full of delight, as the tragedy should be still maintained in a well-raised admiration. But our comedians think there is no delight without laughter; which is very wrong, for though laughter may come with delight, yet cometh it not of delight, as though delight should be the cause of laughter; but well may one thing breed both together. Nay, rather in themselves they have, as it were, a kind of contrariety: for delight we scarcely do but in things that have a conveniency to ourselves or to

---

[51]Actually the *Self-Tormentor*, not the *Eunuch*. [Ed.]

[52]Messenger. [Ed.]

[53]"From the egg"; Horace praises Homer for not beginning his tale of the Trojan war with the egg from which Helen was hatched. See the *Art of Poetry*, p. 70. [Ed.]

the general nature: laughter almost ever cometh of things most disproportioned to ourselves and nature. Delight hath a joy in it, either permanent or present. Laughter hath only a scornful tickling.

For example, we are ravished with delight to see a fair woman, and yet are far from being moved to laughter. We laugh at deformed creatures, wherein certainly we cannot delight. We delight in good chances, we laugh at mischances; we delight to hear the happiness of our friends, or country, at which he were worthy to be laughed at that would laugh. We shall, contrarily, laugh sometimes to find a matter quite mistaken and go down the hill against the bias, in the mouth of some such men, as for the respect of them one shall be heartily sorry, yet he cannot choose but laugh; and so is rather pained than delighted with laughter. Yet deny I not but that they may go well together. For as in Alexander's picture well set out we delight without laughter, and in twenty mad antics we laugh without delight, so in Hercules, painted with his great beard and furious countenance, in woman's attire, spinning at Omphale's commandment, it breedeth both delight and laughter. For the representing of so strange a power in love procureth delight: and the scornfulness of the action stirreth laughter. But I speak to this purpose, that all the end of the comical part be not upon such scornful matters as stirreth laughter only, but, mixed with it, that delightful teaching which is the end of poesy. And the great fault even in that point of laughter, and forbidden plainly by Aristotle, is that they stir laughter in sinful things, which are rather execrable than ridiculous; or in miserable, which are rather to be pitied than scorned.[54] For what is it to make folks gape at a wretched beggar, or a beggarly clown; or, against the law of hospitality, to jest at strangers, because they speak not English so well as we do? What do we learn, since it is certain *Nil habet infelix paupertas durius in se, / Quam quod ridiculos homines facit*?[55] But rather a busy loving courtier, a

heartless threatening Thraso, a self-wise-seeming schoolmaster, an awry-transformed traveler — these if we saw walk in stage names, which we play naturally, therein were delightful laughter, and teaching delightfulness: as in the other, the tragedies of Buchanan do justly bring forth a divine admiration. But I have lavished out too many words of this play matter. I do it because, as they are excelling parts of poesy, so is there none so much used in England, and none can be more pitifully abused; which, like an unmannerly daughter showing a bad education, causeth her mother poesy's honesty to be called in question. Other sorts of poetry almost have we none, but that lyrical kind of songs and sonnets: which, Lord, if he gave us so good minds, how well it might be employed, and with how heavenly fruit, both private and public, in singing the praises of the immortal beauty, the immortal goodness of that God who giveth us hands to write and wits to conceive; of which we might well want words, but never matter; of which we could turn our eyes to nothing, but we should ever have new budding occasions. But truly many of such writings as come under the banner of unresistible love, if I were a mistress, would never persuade me they were in love; so coldly they apply fiery speeches, as men that had rather read lovers' writings, and so caught up certain swelling phrases (which hang together like a man which once told me the wind was at northwest, and by south, because he would be sure to name winds enough), than that in truth they feel those passions, which easily (as I think) may be betrayed by that same forcibleness or *energia* (as the Greeks call it) of the writer. But let this be a sufficient though short note, that we miss the right use of the material point of poesy.

Now, for the outside of it, which is words, or (as I may term it) diction, it is even well worse. So is that honey-flowing matron eloquence appareled, or rather disguised, in a courtesanlike painted affectation: one time with so farfetched words, they may seem monsters, but must seem strangers, to any poor Englishman; another time, with coursing of a letter, as if they were bound to follow the method of a dictionary; another time, with figures and flowers, extremely winter-starved. But I would this fault were only peculiar

---

[54]Sidney may be thinking of Ch. 5 of the *Poetics,* but this is not Aristotle's point there. [Ed.]

[55]"The worst thing about poverty is that it makes people ridiculous." Juvenal, *Satires* 2:152–53. [Ed.]

to versifiers, and had not as large possession among prose-printers, and (which is to be marveled) among many scholars, and (which is to be pitied) among some preachers. Truly I could wish, if at least I might be so bold to wish in a thing beyond the reach of my capacity, the diligent imitators of Tully and Demosthenes (most worthy to be imitated) did not so much keep Nizolian paper books of their figures and phrases, as by attentive translation (as it were) devour them whole, and make them wholly theirs. For now they cast sugar and spice upon every dish that is served to the table, like those Indians, not content to wear earrings at the fit and natural place of the ears, but they will thrust jewels through their nose and lips, because they will be sure to be fine.

Tully, when he was to drive out Catiline, as it were with a thunderbolt of eloquence, often used that figure of repetition, *"Vivit. Vivit? Imo in Senatum venit,"*&c.[56] Indeed, inflamed with a well-grounded rage, he would have his words (as it were) double out of his mouth, and so do that artificially which we see men do in choler naturally. And we, having noted the grace of those words, hale them in sometime to a familiar epistle, when it were too much choler to be choleric. Now for similitudes in certain printed discourses, I think all herberists, all stories of beasts, fowls, and fishes are rifled up, that they come in multitudes to wait upon any of our conceits; which certainly is as absurd a surfeit to the ears as is possible: for the force of a similitude not being to prove anything to a contrary disputer, but only to explain to a willing hearer; when that is done, the rest is a most tedious prattling, rather overswaying the memory from the purpose whereto they were applied, than any whit informing the judgment, already either satisfied, or by similitudes not to be satisfied. For my part, I do not doubt, when Antonius and Crassus, the great forefathers of Cicero in eloquence, the one (as Cicero testifieth of them) pretended not to know art, the other not to set by it, because with a plain sensibleness they might win credit of popular ears; which credit is the nearest step to persuasion; which persuasion is the chief mark of oratory — I do not doubt (I say) that but they used these knacks very sparingly; which, who doth generally use, any man may see doth dance to his own music; and so be noted by the audience more careful to speak curiously than to speak truly.

Undoubtedly (at least to my opinion undoubtedly) I have found in divers small-learned courtiers a more sound style than in some professors of learning: of which I can guess no other cause, but that the courtier, following that which by practice he findeth fittest to nature, therein (though he know it not) doth according to art, though not by art: where the other, using art to show art, and not to hide art (as in these cases he should do), flieth from nature, and indeed abuseth art.

But what? Methinks I deserve to be pounded for straying from poetry to oratory: but both have such an affinity in this wordish consideration, that I think this digression will make my meaning receive the fuller understanding — which is not to take upon me to teach poets how they should do, but only, finding myself sick among the rest, to show some one or two spots of the common infection grown among the most part of writers: that, acknowledging ourselves somewhat awry, we may bend to the right use both of matter and manner; whereto our language giveth us great occasion, being indeed capable of any excellent exercising of it. I know some will say it is a mingled language. And why not so much the better, taking the best of both the other? Another will say in wanteth grammar. Nay truly, it hath that praise, that it wanteth grammar: for grammar it might have, but it needs it not; being so easy of itself, and so void of those cumbersome differences of cases, genders, moods, and tenses, which I think was a piece of the Tower of Babylon's curse, that a man should be put to school to learn his mother tongue. But for the uttering sweetly and properly the conceits of the mind, which is the end of speech, that hath it equally with any other tongue in the world: and is particularly happy in compositions of two or three words together, near the Greek, far beyond the Latin: which is one of the greatest beauties can be in a language.

[56]"He lives. Does he live? He even comes into the Senate." [Ed.]

Now, of versifying there are two sorts, the one ancient, the other modern: the ancient marked the quantity of each syllable, and according to that framed his verse; the modern observing only number (with some regard of the accent), the chief life of it standeth in that like sounding of the words, which we call rhyme. Whether of these be the most excellent, would bear many speeches. The ancient (no doubt) more fit for music, both words and tune observing quantity, and more fit lively to express divers passions, by the low and lofty sound of the well-weighed syllable. The latter likewise, with his rhyme, striketh a certain music to the ear: and, in fine, since it doth delight, though by another way, it obtains the same purpose: there being in either sweetness, and wanting in neither majesty. Truly the English, before any other vulgar language I know, is fit for both sorts: for, for the ancient, the Italian is so full of vowels that it must ever be cumbered with elisions; the Dutch so, of the other side, with consonants, that they cannot yield the sweet sliding fit for a verse; the French, in his whole language, hath not one word that hath his accent in the last syllable saving two, called *antepenultima;* and little more hath the Spanish: and, therefore, very gracelessly may they use dactyls. The English is subject to none of these defects.

Now, for the rhyme, though we do not observe quantity, yet we observe the accent very precisely: which other languages either cannot do, or will not do so absolutely. That *caesura,* or breathing place in the midst of the verse, neither Italian nor Spanish have, the French, and we, never almost fail of. Lastly, even the very rhyme itself the Italian cannot put in the last syllable, by the French named the "masculine rhyme," but still in the next to the last, which the French call the "female," or the next before that, which the Italians term *sdrucciola.* The example of the former is *buono:suono,* of the *sdrucciola, femina:semina.* The French, of the other side, hath both the male, as *bon:son,* and the female, as *plaise:taise,* but the *sdrucciola* he hath not: where the English hath all three, as *due:true, father:rather, motion:potion,* with much more which might be said, but that I find

already the triflingness of this discourse is much too much enlarged. So that since the ever-praiseworthy poesy is full of virtue-breeding delightfulness, and void of no gift that ought to be in the noble name of learning; since the blames laid against it are either false or feeble; since the cause why it is not esteemed in England is the fault of poet-apes, not poets; since, lastly, our tongue is most fit to honor poesy, and to be honored by poesy; I conjure you all that have had the evil luck to read this ink-wasting toy of mine, even in the name of the nine Muses, no more to scorn the sacred mysteries of poesy, no more to laugh at the name of *poets,* as though they were next inheritors to fools, no more to jest at the reverent title of a *rhymer;* but to believe, with Aristotle, that they were the ancient treasurers of the Grecians' divinity; to believe, with Bembus,[57] that they were first bringers-in of all civility; to believe, with Scaliger, that no philosopher's precepts can sooner make you an honest man than the reading of Virgil; to believe, with Clauserus, the translator of Cornutus, that it pleased the heavenly Deity, by Hesiod and Homer, under the veil of fables, to give us all knowledge, logic, rhetoric, philosophy, natural and moral, and *Quid non?*;[58] to believe, with me, that there are many mysteries contained in poetry, which of purpose were written darkly, lest by profane wits it should be abused; to believe, with Landino, that they are so beloved of the gods that whatsoever they write proceeds of a divine fury; lastly, to believe themselves, when they tell you they will make you immortal by their verses.

Thus doing, your name shall flourish in the printers' shops; thus doing, you shall be of kin to many a poetical preface; thus doing, you shall be most fair, most rich, most wise, most all; you shall dwell upon superlatives. Thus doing, though you be "*libertino patre natus,*" you shall suddenly grow "*Herculea proles,*" "*si quid mea carmina possunt.*"[59] Thus doing, your soul shall

---

[57]Pietro Bembo (1470–1547), Italian scholar and critic. [Ed.]

[58]What not? [Ed.]

[59]"Thus doing, though you be 'the son of a freed slave,'

be placed with Dante's Beatrix, or Virgil's Anchises. But if (fie of such a but) you be born so near the dull-making cataract of Nilus that you cannot hear the planetlike music of poetry, if you have so earth-creeping a mind that it cannot lift itself up to look to the sky of poetry, or rather,

by a certain rustical disdain, will become such a mome as to be a momus of poetry; then, though I will not wish unto you the ass's ears of Midas, nor to be driven by a poet's verses (as Bubonax was) to hang himself, nor to be rhymed to death, as is said to be done in Ireland; yet thus much curse I must send you, in the behalf of all poets, that while you live, you live in love, and never get favor for lacking skill of a sonnet, and, when you die, your memory die from the earth for want of an epitaph.

you shall suddenly grow 'Herculean offspring,' 'if my poems can do anything.'" The quotations are from Horace, Ovid, and Virgil. [Ed.]

# John Dryden

## 1631–1700

Best known as the poet laureate of Charles II and James II, and as the satirical author of *Mac Flecknoe* (1682) and the political allegory *Absalom and Achitophel* (1681), Dryden was also one of the most successful of the Restoration dramatists, famous for comedies like *Marriage à-la-Mode* (1673); for tragedies like *All for Love* (1678); and for operatic melodramas, now long out of fashion, called "heroic plays." *An Essay of Dramatic Poesy* (1668) derives from Dryden's practical experience in all areas of the theater.

The *Essay* is neither a Platonic dialogue nor a treatise, but rather a formal debate on the drama among four speakers: Crites, Eugenius, Lisideius, and Neander. Although no one supposes that any such debate actually took place, the speakers have traditionally been identified with contemporary personages. Crites, whose name suggests his captiously critical air, may be Sir Robert Howard, Dryden's brother-in-law and sometime collaborator, with whom Dryden had publicly quarreled over the issue of rhyme in drama. Eugenius, which means "well-born," is probably Charles Sackville, Lord Buckhurst, Dryden's patron before his laureateship and an eminent Cavalier poet in his own right. Lisideius is Sir Charles Sedley (the name is a Latinized anagram of Sedley). And Neander (Greek for "new man") is Dryden himself, of middle-class origins. By using the debate form, Dryden gives the other side equal time (or nearly) but manages to reserve some of the best arguments for himself.

Like Jonathan Swift's *Battle of the Books*, the *Essay of Dramatic Poesy* might be thought of as one volley of the international controversy in the late seventeenth century over the relative value of the ancient and modern writers. Conservative thinkers like Swift felt that the ancients — Homer, Virgil, Juvenal — could never be surpassed, while others, enthusiastic about the advances in learning since the Renaissance, felt that by building upon the foundations of the past, the present might progress beyond it. ("Dwarfs who stand on the shoulders of giants may see farther than the giants themselves," said Isaac Newton, Dryden's contemporary and fellow Modern.) This context helps explain the debate between Crites and Eugenius on the merits of classical and modern drama.

But there was another even more topical concern. The London theaters, closed for twenty years during the Civil War and the Protectorate of Cromwell, had reopened only six years before, in 1662. The drama was beginning to revive, but the traditions of the Elizabethan and Jacobean stage had lapsed during the interregnum. It remained to be seen on what model the English stage would return. Would the new drama be built on the native Tudor-Stuart model and look to Shakespeare, Jonson, and Fletcher as exemplars? Or would the English stage imitate Racine and Corneille, who had created the elegant but rather formal drama of France, where Charles II and his cavaliers had spent most of the interregnum?

Underlying these topical concerns are a set of more abstract issues that divided Renaissance and neoclassical critics. One was the status of the so-called Three Unities of Time, Place, and Action, a set of rules for drama supposedly derived from Aristotle and Horace.[1] Under Unity of Time, it was claimed that the plot of a drama might take up no more than a single day from the first incident to the last; ideally, according to Pierre Corneille, the plot of a drama should last no longer than the dramatic representation itself — two hours or so. Under Unity of Place, it was asserted that the plot should be laid in a single city, ideally in a single room. Unity of Action meant that everything in a drama should further a single plot and that subplots, like that of Gloucester and his sons in *King Lear*, were to be avoided.

A second issue was that of generic integrity: comedy and tragedy were considered mutually exclusive, and characters and speeches appropriate to the one would not be appropriate to the other. The gravediggers in *Hamlet* or Iago's bawdy jokes in *Othello* would thus be inappropriate. A third issue was that of decorum: All acts of violence, especially deaths, should be performed offstage and revealed to the audience through narration. These matters were arguably a part of both Greek and Roman dramatic practice, though only Horace comments on them.

As the debate is joined between Crites and Eugenius, and between Lisideius and Neander, the reader is forced to dwell on an all-subsuming question: What is the status of the Three Unities, Generic Integrity, and Stage Decorum? Are they rules of art that hold for the ages or are they merely artistic conventions? Beyond this there is the further question: If there is no real difference between conventions and rules, then how do artistic styles change? If conventions may be irresponsibly disregarded, how can art function without them?

*An Essay of Dramatic Poesy*, like Aristotle's *Poetics*, hinges on a definition, this time of a *play*, which Lisideius defines as "a just and lively image of human nature, representing its passions and humours, and the changes of fortune to which it is subject; for the delight and instruction of mankind." The derivation from Horace and the *Ars Poetica* appears clearly in the last clause. Crites objects that the definition is "*a genere et fine,*" that it states only general class and purpose, implying that it is too broad, since it could serve as a definition of a novel or poem as well.

Crites is correct but has missed the main ambiguity in the definition: The combatants have differing interpretations of the key words "just" and "lively." For Crites, an image is "just" when it has been constructed according to correct rules; for Neander, when it gives a faithful impression of the original. For Lisideius,

---

[1]Unity of Action is the only unity that is taken directly and unequivocally from Aristotle's *Poetics* (Ch. 8). Unity of Time may derive from one passage in *Poetics*, Ch. 5 ("Tragedy endeavors as far as possible to confine itself to a single revolution of the sun or to exceed this but slightly"), which is contradicted by another passage in *Poetics*, Ch. 7 ("The proper magnitude is comprised within such limits that the sequence of events, according to the law of probability or necessity, will admit of a change from bad fortune to good or from good to bad"). Unity of Place does not appear in Aristotle or Horace, but one could claim that it follows as a corollary from the Unities of Time and Action: A single action occurring within a single day could not possibly, in the days before automobiles and airplanes, take place over a very widespread area.

"lively" takes its older meaning of *lifelike*; for Neander it means something more like *spirited*.

Another confusion seems to arise over just what "mankind" is: While some of the debaters seem to be absolutists, Neander is a critical relativist who feels that the French and the English will be delighted and instructed by very different sorts of things. This is not to suggest that the debaters are quarreling over the meaning of terms; on the contrary their apparent unanimity on the definition masks genuine disagreements over what drama ought to be.

In the final debate, Crites and Neander square off directly over the use of rhymed verse in the drama, with Crites attacking the practice and Neander defending it. In this section, Neander concedes half his ground by admitting the inappropriateness of rhyme in comedy. (In fact, Dryden was later to recant his position and write his tragedies, including the popular *All for Love*, in blank verse.) Here as elsewhere, however, Neander applies his audience-centered criteria, arguing that rhyme may be used in tragic drama if it is used well and thereby gains the acceptance of the public, while Crites puts forth a pseudo-mimetic argument that the characters of a drama may not speak poetry since their counterparts in real life spoke prose.[2]

For many readers, the most fascinating section of the *Essay of Dramatic Poesy* is Neander's comparative discussion of Shakespeare, Jonson, and Fletcher, and his explication of Jonson's *Epicoene, or The Silent Woman*. Abstract argument recedes as a major poet responds to his great exemplars. It is interesting to see how tastes have changed — that Shakespeare was not so certainly the greatest of the Elizabethan dramatists in Dryden's day as he is today. It is also enlightening to watch the principles of rhetorical criticism applied by a sensitive critic, who was also his age's most versatile practicing playwright.

## Selected Bibliography

Bredvold, Louis I. *The Intellectual Milieu of John Dryden*. Ann Arbor: University of Michigan Press, 1934.

Cole, Elmer Joseph. *The Consistency of John Dryden's Literary Criticism in Theory and Practice*. Albuquerque: New Mexico University Press, 1970.

Eliot, T. S. *John Dryden: The Poet, the Dramatist, the Critic; Three Essays*. New York: Haskell House, 1966.

Hume, Robert D. *Dryden's Criticism*. Ithaca: Cornell University Press, 1970.

Huntley, Frank Livingstone. *On Dryden's Essay of Dramatic Poesy*. Ann Arbor: University of Michigan Press, 1951.

Mishra, J. B. *John Dryden: His Theory and Practice of Drama*. New Delhi: Bahri Publications, 1978.

Pechter, Edward. *Dryden's Classical Theory of Literature*. London and New York: Cambridge University Press, 1975.

[2]Neither Aristotle nor Horace had so argued, certainly, and it is not clear where such literal-minded mimesis would stop. Should the characters in *Julius Caesar* have spoken in Latin because their historical originals did?

Trowbridge, Hoyt. "The Place of Rules in Dryden's Criticism." *Modern Philology* 44 (1946): 84–96.

Watson, George. *John Dryden: Of Dramatic Poesy and Other Critical Essays.* 2 vols. London: J. Dent, 1962.

# An Essay of Dramatic Poesy

It was that memorable day,[1] in the first summer of the late war, when our Navy engaged the Dutch: a day wherein the two most mighty and best appointed fleets which any age had ever seen, disputed the command of the greater half of the globe, the commerce of nations, and the riches of the universe. While these vast floating bodies, on either side, moved against each other in parallel lines, and our countrymen, under the happy conduct of his Royal Highness,[2] went breaking, by little and little, into the line of the enemies, the noise of the cannon from both navies reached our ears about the City; so that all men, being alarmed with it, and in a dreadful suspense of the event, which they knew was then deciding, every one went following the sound as his fancy led him; and leaving the town almost empty, some took towards the Park, some cross the river, others down it; all seeking the noise in the depth of silence.

Amongst the rest, it was the fortune of Eugenius, Crites, Lisideius and Neander,[3] to be in company together: three of them persons whom their wit and quality have made known to all the town: and whom I have chose to hide under these borrowed names, that they may not suffer by so ill a relation as I am going to make of their discourse.

Taking then a barge which a servant of Lisideius had provided for them, they made haste to shoot the bridge, and left behind them that great fall of waters which hindered them from hearing what they desired: after which, having disengaged themselves from many vessels which rode at anchor in the Thames, and almost blocked up the passage towards Greenwich, they ordered the watermen to let fall their oars more gently; and then every one favouring his own curiosity with a strict silence, it was not long ere they perceived the air to break about them like the noise of distant thunder, or of swallows in a chimney: those little undulations of sound, though almost vanishing before they reached them, yet still seeming to retain somewhat of their first horror which they had betwixt the fleets: after they had attentively listened till such time as the sound by little and little went from them; Eugenius lifting up his head, and taking notice of it, was the first who congratulated to the rest that happy omen of our nation's victory: adding, that we had but this to desire in confirmation of it, that we might hear no more of that noise which was now leaving the English coast. When the rest had concurred in the same opinion, Crites, a person of a sharp judgement, and somewhat too delicate a taste in wit, which the world have mistaken in him for ill nature, said, smiling to us, that if the concernment of this battle had not been so exceeding great, he could scarce have wished the victory at the price he knew he must pay for it, in being subject to the reading and hearing of so many ill verses as he was sure would be made on that subject. Adding, that no argument could scape some of those eternal rhymers, who watch a battle with more diligence than the ravens and birds of prey; and the worst of them surest to be first in upon the quarry, while the better able, either out of modesty writ not at all, or set that due value upon their poems, as to let them be often desired and long expected! There are some of those impertinent people of whom you speak,

[1] June 3, 1665. [Ed.]

[2] James, Duke of York, the Lord Admiral, afterward James II. [Ed.]

[3] For the traditional ascriptions of these names, see p. 160. [Ed.]

answered Lisideius, who to my knowledge are already so provided, either way, that they can produce not only a panegyric upon the victory, but, if need be, a funeral elegy on the Duke: wherein after they have crowned his valour with many laurels, they will at last deplore the odds under which he fell, concluding that his courage deserved a better destiny. All the company smiled at the conceit of Lisideius; but Crites, more eager than before, began to make particular exceptions against some writers, and said the public magistrate ought to send betimes to forbid them; and that it concerned the peace and quiet of all honest people, that ill poets should be as well silenced as seditious preachers. In my opinion, replied Eugenius, you pursue your point too far; for as to my own particular, I am so great a lover of poesy, that I could wish them all rewarded who attempt but to do well, at least I would not have them worse used than one of their brethren was by Sylla the dictator: *Quem in concione vidimus* (says Tully) *cum ei libellum malus poeta de populo subjecisset, quod epigramma in eum fecisset tantummodo alternis versibus longiusculis, statim ex iis rebus quas tunc vendebat jubere ei praemium tribui, sub ea conditione ne quid postea scriberet.*[4] I could wish with all my heart, replied Crites; that many whom we know were as bountifully thanked upon the same condition, that they would never trouble us again. For amongst others, I have a mortal apprehension of two poets, whom this victory with the help of both her wings will never be able to escape;[5] 'tis easy to guess whom you intend, said Lisideius, and without naming them, I ask you if one of them does not perpetually pay us with clenches[6] upon words and a certain clownish kind of raillery? If now and then he does not offer at a catachresis[7] or Clevelandism, wresting and torturing a word into another meaning: in fine, if he be not one of those whom the French would call *un mauvais buffon*; one who is so much a well-willer to the satire, that he intends at least, to spare no man; and though he cannot strike a blow to hurt any, yet he ought to be punished for the malice of the action; as our witches are justly hanged because they think themselves to be such: and suffer deservedly for believing they did mischief, because they meant it. You have described him, said Crites, so exactly, that I am afraid to come after you with my other extremity of poetry: he is one of those who having had some advantage of education and converse, knows better than the other what a poet should be, but puts it into practice more unluckily than any man; his style and matter are everywhere alike; he is the most calm, peaceable writer you ever read: he never disquiets your passions with the least concernment, but still leaves you in as even a temper as he found you; he is a very Leveller in poetry, he creeps along with ten little words in every line,[8] and helps out his numbers with *For to*, and *Unto*, and all the pretty expletives he can find, till he drags them to the end of another line; while the sense is left tired half way behind it: he doubly starves all his verses, first for want of thought, and then of expression; his poetry neither has wit in it, nor seems to have it; like him in Martial.

Pauper videri Cinna vult, et est pauper:[9]

He affects plainness, to cover his want of imagination: when he writes the serious way, the highest flight of his fancy is some miserable antithesis, or seeming contradiction; and in the comic he is still reaching at some thin conceit, the ghost of a jest, and that too flies before him, never to be caught; these swallows which we see before us on the Thames, are the just resem-

---

[4] "We have seen how, at a public meeting, when a bad poet among the people offered him an epigram made on himself, written in limping elegiacs, Sulla ordered that he be paid a reward from the booty on sale, provided that he never write again." Cicero, *Pro Archia Poeta* 10:25. [Ed.]

[5] It has been conjectured that Dryden's two poets were Richard Wild and Richard Flecknoe, respectively, who wrote on the battle. But the poets' faults seem to correspond to the two criteria of value in the subsequent definition of a play: The former poet's language fails to be just; the latter's, to be lively. [Ed.]

[6] Puns. [Ed.]

[7] Abuse of language. John Cleveland (1613–58) tortured language in this way. [Ed.]

[8] Cf. Pope, *An Essay on Criticism*: "And ten low words oft creep in one dull line." [Ed.]

[9] "Cinna wishes to seem poor — and he is poor." Martial, *Epigrams* 8:19. [Ed.]

blance of his wit: you may observe how near the water they stoop, how many proffers they make to dip, and yet how seldom they touch it: and when they do, 'tis but the surface: they skim over it but to catch a gnat, and then mount into the air and leave it. Well gentlemen, said Eugenius, you may speak your pleasure of these authors; but though I and some few more about the town may give you a peaceable hearing, yet assure yourselves, there are multitudes who would think you malicious and them injured: especially him whom you first described; he is the very Withers[10] of the City: they have bought more editions of his works than would serve to lay under all their pies at the Lord Mayor's Christmas. When his famous poem first came out in the year 1660, I have seen them reading it in the midst of change-time; nay so vehement they were at it, that they lost their bargain by the candles' ends: but what will you say, if he has been received amongst great persons; I can assure you he is, this day, the envy of one, who is lord in the art of quibbling; and who does not take it well, that any man should intrude so far into his province. All I would wish, replied Crites, is, that they who love his writings, may still admire him, and his fellow poet, *qui Bavium non odit*,[11] etc. is curse sufficient. And farther, added Lisideius, I believe there is no man who writes well, but would think he had hard measure, if their admirers should praise anything of his: *Nam quos contemnimus eorum quoque laudes contemnimus*.[12] There are so few who write well in this age, said Crites, that methinks any praises should be welcome; they neither rise to the dignity of the last age, nor to any of the Ancients; and we may cry out of the writers of this time, with more reason than Petronius of his, *Pace vestra liceat dixisse, primi omnium eloquentiam perdidistis*:[13] you have debauched the true old poetry so far, that nature, which is the soul of it, is not in any of your writings.

If your quarrel (said Eugenius) to those who now write, be grounded only on your reverence to antiquity, there is no man more ready to adore those great Greeks and Romans than I am: but on the other side, I cannot think so contemptibly of the age in which I live or so dishonourably of my own country, as not to judge we equal the Ancients in most kinds of poesy, and in some surpass them; neither know I any reason why I may not be as zealous for the reputation of our age, as we find the Ancients themselves were in reference to those who lived before them. For you hear your Horace saying,

> Indignor quidquam reprehendi, non quia crasse
> compositum, illepideve putetur, sed quia nuper.

And after,

> Si meliora dies, ut vina, poemata reddit,
> scire velim pretium chartis quotus arroget annus?[14]

But I see I am engaging in a wide dispute, where the arguments are not like to reach close on either side; for poesy is of so large an extent, and so many both of the Ancients and Moderns have done well in all kinds of it, that in citing one against the other, we shall take up more time this evening, than each man's occasions will allow him: therefore I would ask Crites to what part of poesy he would confine his arguments, and whether he would defend the general cause of the Ancients against the Moderns, or oppose any age of the Moderns against this of ours?[15]

Crites a little while considering upon this demand, told Eugenius that if he pleased, he would limit their dispute to Dramatic Poesy; in which he thought it not difficult to prove, either that the Ancients were superior to the Moderns, or the last age to this of ours.

Eugenius was somewhat surprised, when he heard Crites make choice of the subject; for aught

---

[10]George Withers (1588–1667) was a Puritan poet. [Ed.]

[11]"Let whoever does not hate Bavius [love your songs, Maevius]." Virgil, *Eclogues* 3:90. [Ed.]

[12]"We despise the praise of those whom we despise." [Ed.]

[13]"If you will allow me to say so, you have killed the old eloquence." Petronius, *Satyricon*, 2. [Ed.]

[14]"I get angry when something is attacked, not for being coarse or clumsy, but for being new." and "If like wine, poems improve with age, how many years does it take for a poem to be ripe?" Horace, *Epistles* II.1:76–177 and 34–35. [Ed.]

[15]The periods in dispute are classical and modern literature — a traditional argument known as the *querelle des anciens et des modernes* — and within the modern age, the Elizabethan era and the contemporary period. [Ed.]

I see, said he, I have undertaken a harder province than I imagined; for though I never judged the plays of the Greek or Roman poets comparable to ours; yet on the other side those we now seen acted, come short of many which were written in the last age: but my comfort is if we are overcome, it will be only by our own countrymen: and if we yield to them in this one part of poesy, we more surpass them in all the other; for in the epic or lyric way it will be hard for them to show us one such amongst them, as we have many now living, or who lately were. They can produce nothing so courtly writ, or which expresses so much the conversation of a gentleman, as Sir John Suckling; nothing so even, sweet, and flowing as Mr. Waller, nothing so majestic, so correct as Sir John Denham; nothing so elevated, so copious, and full of spirit, as Mr. Cowley; as for the Italian, French, and Spanish plays, I can make it evident, that those who now write, surpass them; and that the drama is wholly ours.

All of them were thus far of Eugenius' opinion, that the sweetness of English verse was never understood or practised by our fathers. Even Crites himself did not much oppose it: and every one was willing to acknowledge how much our poesy is improved, by the happiness of some writers yet living; who first taught us to mould our thoughts into easy and significant words, to retrench the superfluities of expression, and to make our rhyme so properly a part of the verse, that it should never mislead the sense, but itself be led and governed by it.

Eugenius was going to continue this discourse, when Lisideius told him that it was necessary, before they proceeded further, to take a standing measure of their controversy; for how was it possible to be decided who writ the best plays, before we know what a play should be? but, this once agreed on by both parties, each might have recourse to it, either to prove his own advantages, or to discover the failings of his adversary.

He had no sooner said this, but all desired the favour of him to give the definition of a play; and they were the more importunate, because neither Aristotle, nor Horace, nor any other, who had writ of that subject, had ever done it.

Lisideius, after some modest denials, at last confessed he had a rude notion of it; indeed rather a description than a definition, but which served to guide him in his private thoughts, when he was to make a judgement of what others writ: that he conceived a play ought to be, a just and lively image of human nature, representing its passions and humours, and the changes of fortune to which it is subject; for the delight and instruction of mankind.

This definition, though Crites raised a logical objection against it; that it was only *a genere et fine*,[16] and so not altogether perfect; was yet well received by the rest: and after they had given order to the watermen to turn their barge, and row softly, that they might take the cool of the evening in their return, Crites, being desired by the company to begin, spoke on behalf of the Ancients, in this manner:

If confidence presage a victory, Eugenius, in his own opinion, has already triumphed over the Ancients. Nothing seems more easy to him, than to overcome those whom it is our greatest praise to have imitated well: for we do not only build upon their foundations; but by their models. Dramatic poesy had time enough, reckoning from Thespis (who first invented it) to Aristophanes, to be born, to grow up, and to flourish in maturity. It has been observed of arts and sciences, that in one and the same century they have arrived to great perfection; and no wonder, since every age has a kind of universal genius, which inclines those that live in it to some particular studies: the work then being pushed on by many hands, must of necessity go forward.

Is it not evident, in these last hundred years (when the study of philosophy[17] has been the business of all the virtuosi in Christendom) that almost a new nature has been revealed to us? that more errors of the school have been detected, more useful experiments in philosophy have been made, more noble secrets in optics, medicine, anatomy, astronomy, discovered, than in all

[16]"By genus and end": Crites is complaining that the definition is not restrictive enough, since it will serve to define poetry and prose fiction as well as drama. In fact, the problem is that the meaning of central terms — "just," "lively," and "representing" — is slippery. [Ed.]

[17]Natural philosophy; science. [Ed.]

those credulous and doting ages from Aristotle to us? so true it is that nothing spreads more fast than science, when rightly and generally cultivated.

Add to this the more than common emulation that was in those times of writing well; which though it be found in all ages and all persons that pretend to the same reputation; yet poesy being then in more esteem than now it is, had greater honours decreed to the professors of it; and consequently the rivalship was more high between them; they had judges ordained to decide their merit, and prizes to reward it: and historians have been diligent to record of Aeschylus, Euripides, Sophocles, Lycophron, and the rest of them, both who they were that vanquished in these wars of the theatre, and how often they were crowned: while the Asian kings, and Grecian commonwealths scarce afforded them a nobler subject than the unmanly luxuries of a debauched court, or giddy intrigues of a factious city. *Alit aemulatio ingenia* (says Paterculus) *et nunc invidia, nunc admiratio incitationem accendit*: Emulation is the spur of wit, and sometimes envy, sometimes admiration quickens our endeavours.[18]

But now since the rewards of honour are taken away, that virtuous emulation is turned into direct malice; yet so slothful, that it contents itself to condemn and cry down others, without attempting to do better. 'Tis a reputation too unprofitable, to take the necessary pains for it; yet wishing they had it, that desire is incitement enough to hinder others from it. And this, in short, Eugenius, is the reason, why you have now so few good poets; and so many severe judges. Certainly, to imitate the Ancients well, much labour and long study is required: which pains, I have already shown, our poets would want encouragement to take, if yet they had ability to go through the work. Those Ancients have been faithful imitators and wise observers of that nature which is so torn and ill represented in our plays; they have handed down to us a perfect resemblance of her; which we, like ill copiers, neglecting to look on, have rendered monstrous, and disfig-

ured. But, that you may know how much you are indebted to those your masters, and be ashamed to have so ill requited them, I must remember you that all the rules by which we practise the drama at this day, (either such as relate to the justness and symmetry of the plot; or the episodical ornaments, such as descriptions, narrations, and other beauties, which are not essential to the play) were delivered to us from the observations which Aristotle made, of those poets, who either lived before him, or were his contemporaries: we have added nothing of our own, except we have the confidence to say our wit is better; of which none boast in this our age, but such as understand not theirs. Of that book which Aristotle has left us περι τῆς Ποιητικῆς[19] Horace's *Art of Poetry* is an excellent comment, and, I believe, restores to us that second book of his concerning comedy, which is wanting in him.

Out of these two have been extracted the famous rules which the French call, *Des Trois Unités*, or, the three unities, which ought to be observed in every regular play; namely, of time, place, and action.[20]

The unity of time they comprehend in twenty-four hours, the compass of a natural day; or as near it as can be contrived. And the reason of it is obvious to every one; that the time of the feigned action, or fable of the play, should be proportioned as near as can be to the duration of that time in which it is represented; since therefore all plays are acted on the theatre in a space of time much within the compass of twenty-four hours, that play is to be thought the nearest imitation of nature, whose plot or action is confined within that time; and, by the same rule which concludes this general proportion of time, it fol-

---

[18]Velleius Paterculus, in the *Historia Romana* I:17. [Ed.]

[19]The *Poetics*. [Ed.]

[20]The unity of Place is not explicitly mentioned in the *Poetics* but it is implied by the constraints of the unities of Time and Action. If a tragedy "is confined to one revolution of the sun" then its single action cannot occur at widely separated places, given the limits of premodern transportation. But while Aristotle treats the unity of action as an essential matter of art, he treats the limitations of time in tragedy as a stage convention, with the length of plays regulated by such extraneous matters as dramatic competitions. [Ed.]

lows, that all the parts of it are (as near as may be) to be equally sub-divided; namely, that one act take not up the supposed time of half a day, which is out of proportion to the rest, since the other four are then to be straitened within the compass of the remaining half. For it is unnatural that one act, which being spoke or written, is not longer than the rest, should be supposed longer by the audience. 'Tis therefore the poet's duty, to take care that no act should be imagined to exceed the time in which it is represented on the stage; and that the intervals and inequalities of time be supposed to fall out between the acts.

This rule of time how well it has been observed by the Ancients, most of their plays will witness. You see them in their tragedies (wherein to follow this rule, is certainly most difficult) from the very beginning of their plays, falling close into that part of the story which they intend for the action or principal object of it; leaving the former part to be delivered by narration: so that they set the audience, as it were, at the post where the race is to be concluded: and, saving them the tedious expectation of seeing the poet set out and ride the beginning of the course, they suffer you not to behold him, till he is in sight of the goal, and just upon you.

For the second unity, which is that of place, the Ancients meant by it, that the scene ought to be continued through the play, in the same place where it was laid in the beginning: for the stage, on which it is represented, being but one and the same place, it is unnatural to conceive it many; and those far distant from one another. I will not deny but by the variation of painted scenes, the fancy (which in these cases will contribute to its own deceit) may sometimes imagine it several places, with some appearance of probability; yet it still carries the greater likelihood of truth, if those places be supposed so near each other, as in the same town or city; which may all be comprehended under the larger denomination of one place: for a greater distance will bear no proportion to the shortness of time, which is allotted in the acting, to pass from one of them to another; for the observation of this, next to the Ancients, the French are to be most commended. They tie themselves so strictly to the unity of place, that you never see in any of their plays, a scene changed in the middle of an act: if the act begins in a garden, a street, or chamber, 'tis ended in the same place; and that you may know it to be the same, the stage is so supplied with persons that it is never empty all the time: he who enters second has business with him who was on before; and before the second quits the stage, a third appears who has business with him.

This Corneille[21] calls *La liaison des scènes*, the continuity or joining of the scenes; and 'tis a good mark of a well contrived play when all the persons are known to each other, and every one of them has some affairs with all the rest.

As for the third unity, which is that of action, the Ancients meant no other by it than what the logicians do by their Finis, the end or scope of any action: that which is the first in intention, and last in execution. Now the poet is to aim at one great and complete action, to the carrying on of which all things in his play, even the very obstacles, are to be subservient; and the reason of this is as evident as any of the former.

For two actions equally laboured and driven on by the writer, would destroy the unity of the poem; it would be no longer one play, but two: not but that there may be many actions in a play, as Ben Jonson has observed in his *Discoveries*; but they must be all subservient to the great one, which our language happily expresses in the name of under-plots: such as in Terence's *Eunuch* is the difference and reconcilement of Thais and Phaedria, which is not the chief business of the play, but promotes the marriage of Charea and Chremes's sister, principally intended by the poet. There ought to be but one action, says Corneille, that is one complete action which leaves the mind of the audience in a full repose. But this cannot be brought to pass but by many other imperfect actions which conduce to it, and hold the audience in a delightful suspense of what will be.

If by these rules (to omit many other drawn from the precepts and practice of the Ancients) we should judge our modern plays, 'tis probable, that few of them would endure the trial. That which should be the business of a day, takes up

---

[21] In the *Discours des trois unités* (1660). [Ed.]

in some of them an age; instead of one action they are the epitomes of a man's life; and for one spot of ground (which the stage should represent) we are sometimes in more countries than the map can show us.

But if we will allow the Ancients to have contrived well, we must acknowledge them to have written better; questionless we are deprived of a great stock of wit in the loss of Menander among the Greek poets, and of Caecilius, Afranius, and Varius, among the Romans: we may guess at Menander's excellency by the plays of Terence, who translated some of them: and yet wanted so much of him that he was called by C. Caesar the half-Menander; and may judge of Varius, by the testimonies of Horace, Martial, and Velleius Paterculus. 'Tis probable that these, could they be recovered, would decide the controversy; but so long as Aristophanes and Plautus are extant; while the tragedies of Euripides, Sophocles, and Seneca are in our hands, I can never see one of those plays which are now written, but it increases my admiration of the Ancients; and yet I must acknowledge further, that to admire them as we ought, we should understand them better than we do. Doubtless many things appear flat to us, the wit of which depended on some custom or story which never came to our knowledge, or perhaps on some criticism in their language, which being so long dead, and only remaining in their books, 'tis not possible they should make us understand perfectly. To read Macrobius, explaining the propriety and elegancy of many words in Virgil, which I had before passed over without consideration, as common things, is enough to assure me that I ought to think the same of Terence; and that in the purity of his style (which Tully so much valued that he ever carried his works about him) there is yet left in him great room for admiration, if I knew but where to place it. In the mean time I must desire you to take notice, that the greatest man of the last age (Ben Jonson) was willing to give place to them in all things. He was not only a professed imitator of Horace, but a learned plagiary of all the others. You track him everywhere in their snow. If Horace, Lucan, Petronius Arbiter, Seneca, and Juvenal, had their own from him, there are few serious thoughts which are

new in him. You will pardon me therefore if I presume he loved their fashion when he wore their clothes. But since I have otherwise a great veneration for him, and you, Eugenius, prefer him above all other poets, I will use no farther argument to you than his example. I will produce before you Father Ben, dressed in all the ornaments and colours of the Ancients, you will need no other guide to our party if you follow him; and whether you consider the bad plays of our age, or regard the good plays of the last, both the best and worst of the modern poets will equally instruct you to admire the Ancients.

Crites had no sooner left speaking, but Eugenius, who had waited with some impatience for it, thus began:

I have observed in your speech that the former part of it is convincing as to what the Moderns have profited by the rules of the Ancients, but in the latter you are careful to conceal how much they have excelled them. We own all the helps we have from them, and want neither veneration nor gratitude while we acknowledge that to overcome them we must make use of the advantages we have received from them; but to these assistances we have joined our own industry; for (had we sat down with a dull imitation of them) we might then have lost somewhat of the old perfection, but never acquired any that was new. We draw not therefore after their lines, but those of nature; and having the life before us, besides the experience of all they knew, it is no wonder if we hit some airs and features which they have missed. I deny not what you urge of arts and sciences, that they have flourished in some ages more than others; but your instance in philosophy makes for me; for if natural causes be more known now than in the time of Aristotle, because more studied, it follows that poesy and other arts may with the same pains arrive still nearer to perfection, and, that granted, it will rest for you to prove that they wrought more perfect images of human life than we; which, seeing in your discourse you have avoided to make good, it shall now be my task to show you some part of their defects, and some few excellencies of the Moderns; and I think there is none among us can imagine I do it enviously, or with purpose to detract from them; for what interest of fame or profit can the living lose by the reputation of the dead? On the other side, it is a great truth which Velleius Paterculus affirms, *Audita visis libentius laudamus; et praesentia invidia, praeterita admiratione prosequimur; et his nos obrui, illis instrui credimus:*[22] That praise or censure is certainly the most sincere which unbribed posterity shall give us.

Be pleased then in the first place to take notice, that the Greek poesy, which Crites has affirmed to have arrived to perfection in the reign of the Old Comedy,[23] was so far from it, that the distinction of it into acts was not known to them; or if it were, it is yet so darkly delivered to us that we cannot make it out.

All we know of it is from the singing of their chorus, and that too is so uncertain that in some of their plays we have reason to conjecture they sung more than five times. Aristotle indeed divides the integral parts of a play into four.[24] First, the protasis or entrance, which gives light only to the characters of the persons, and proceeds very little into any part of the action: secondly, the epitasis, or working up of the plot where the play grows warmer; the design or action of it is drawing on, and you see something promising that it will come to pass: thirdly, the catastasis, called by the Romans, status, the heighth, and full growth of the play: we may call it properly the counterturn, which destroys that expectation, embroils the action in new difficulties, and leaves you far distant from that hope in which it found you, as you may have observed in a violent stream resisted by a narrow passage: it runs round to an eddy, and carries back the waters with more swiftness than it brought them on. Lastly, the catastrophe, which the Grecians called λύσις, the French *le dénouement*, and we the discovery or unravelling of the plot: there you see all things settling again upon their first foundations, and the obstacles which hindered the design or action of the play once removed, it ends with that resemblance of truth and nature, that the audience are satisfied with the conduct of it. Thus this great man delivered to us the image of a play, and I must confess it is so lively that from thence much light has been derived to the forming it more perfectly into acts and scenes; but what poet first limited to five the number of the acts I know not; only we see it so firmly established in the time of Horace, that he gives it for a rule in comedy; *Neu brevior quinto, neu sit productior actu:*[25] So that you see the Grecians cannot be said to have consummated this art; writing rather by entrances than by acts, and having rather a general indigested notion of a play, than knowing how and where to bestow the particular graces of it.

But since the Spaniards at this day allow but three acts, which they call *jornadas*, to a play, and the Italians in many of theirs follow them, when I condemn the Ancients, I declare it is not altogether because they have not five acts to every play, but because they have not confined themselves to one certain number; 'tis building an house without a model: and when they succeeded in such undertakings, they ought to have sacrificed to Fortune, not to the Muses.

Next, for the plot, which Aristotle called τὸ μύθος, and often τῶν πραγμάτων σύνθεσις,[26] and from him the Romans *fabula*, it has already been judiciously observed by a late writer, that in their tragedies it was only some tale derived from Thebes or Troy, or at least something that happened in those two ages; which was worn so threadbare by the pens of all the epic poets, and even by tradition itself of the talkative Greeklings (as Ben Jonson calls them) that before it came upon the stage, it was already known to all the audience: and the people so soon as ever they heard the name of Oedipus, knew as well as the poet, that he had killed his father by a mistake, and committed incest with his mother, before the

---

[22]"We praise more freely what we have heard about than what we have seen; we view the present with envy and the past with admiration; and we believe we are injured by the present and taught by the past." *Historia Romana* 2:92. [Ed.]

[23]The time of Aristophanes. [Ed.]

[24]Aristotle's discussion of the quantitative parts of tragedy occurs in *Poetics*, Ch. 12, where he differentiates the prologue, episode, exode, and choral ode. Later, in Ch. 18, he divides the play into the complication and the denouement. Neither of these corresponds to Eugenius's distinctions here. [Ed.]

[25]"Let no play be shorter or longer than five acts." Horace, *Art of Poetry*, 189. [Ed.]

[26]The synthesis of the actions. [Ed.]

play; that they were now to hear of a great plague, an oracle, and the ghost of Laius: so that they sat with a yawning kind of expectation, till he was to come with his eyes pulled out, and speak a hundred or more verses in a tragic tone, in complaint of his misfortunes. But one Oedipus, Hercules, or Medea, had been tolerable; poor people they scaped not so good cheap: they had still the *chapon bouillé*[27] set before them, till their appetites were cloyed with the same dish, and the novelty being gone, the pleasure vanished: so that one main end of dramatic poesy in its definition, which was to cause delight, was of consequence destroyed.

In their comedies, the Romans generally borrowed their plots from the Greek poets; and theirs was commonly a little girl stolen or wandered from her parents, brought back unknown to the city, there got with child by some lewd young fellow; who, by the help of his servant, cheats his father, and when her time comes, to cry *Juno Lucina fer opem*;[28] one or other sees a little box or cabinet which was carried away with her, and so discovers her to her friends, if some God do not prevent it, by coming down in a machine,[29] and taking the thanks of it to himself.

By the plot you may guess much of the characters of the persons. An old father who would willingly before he dies see his son well married; his debauched son, kind in his nature to his mistress, but miserably in want of money; a servant or slave, who has so much wit to strike in with him, and help to dupe his father, a braggadochio captain, a parasite, and a lady of pleasure.

As for the poor honest maid, on whom the story is built, and who ought to be one of the principal actors in the play, she is commonly a mute in it. She has the breeding of the old Elizabeth way, which was for maids to be seen and not to be heard; and it is enough you know she is willing to be married, when the fifth act requires it.

These are plots built after the Italian mode of houses, you see through them all at once; the characters are indeed the imitations of nature, but so narrow as if they had imitated only an eye or an hand, and did not dare to venture on the lines of a face, or the proportion of a body.

But in how straight a compass soever they have bounded their plots and characters, we will pass it by, if they have regularly pursued them, and perfectly observed those three unities of time, place, and action: the knowledge of which you say is derived to us from them. But in the first place give me leave to tell you, that the unity of place, however it might be practised by them, was never any of their rules. We neither find it in Aristotle, Horace, or any who have written of it, till in our age the French poets first made it a precept of the stage.[30] The unity of time, even Terence himself (who was the best and most regular of them) has neglected. His *Heautontimoroumenos* or *Self-Punisher* takes up visibly two days; says Scaliger, the two first acts concluding the first day, the three last the day ensuing; and Euripides, in tying himself to one day, has committed an absurdity never to be forgiven him: for in one of his tragedies he has made Theseus go from Athens to Thebes, which was about forty English miles, under the walls of it to give battle, and appear victorious in the next act; and yet from the time of his departure to the return of the Nuntius, who gives the relation of his victory, Aethra and the chorus have but thirty-six verses; which is not for every mile a verse.

The like error is as evident in Terence's *Eunuch*, when Laches, the old man, enters by mistake into the house of Thais, where betwixt his exit and the entrance of Pythias, who comes to give ample relation of the disorders he has raised within, Parmeno who was left upon the stage, has not above five lines to speak: *C'est bien employer un temps si court*,[31] says the French poet, who furnished me with one of the observations; and almost all their tragedies will afford us examples of the like nature.

[27] Boiled capon. [Ed.]

[28] "Juno goddess of childbirth, help me!" Terence, *Andria* 3.1.15. [Ed.]

[29] The *deus ex machina* of Horace's stricture. [Ed.]

[30] Eugenius forgets that the quintessentially English Philip Sidney condemns *Gorboduc* as "faulty in both place and time." See p. 154. [Ed.]

[31] "It's a good use of so short a time." Here and elsewhere, Dryden is paraphrasing Corneille's *Discours des trois unités*. [Ed.]

'Tis true, they have kept the continuity, or as you called it, *liaison des scènes* somewhat better: two do not perpetually come in together, talk and go out together; and other two succeed them, and do the same throughout the act, which the English call by the name of single scenes; but the reason is, because they have seldom above two or three scenes, properly so called, in every act; for it is to be accounted a new scene, not only every time the stage is empty, but every person who enters, though to others, makes it so; because he introduces a new business. Now the plots of their plays being narrow, and the persons few, one of their acts was written in a less compass than one of our well wrought scenes, and yet they are often deficient even in this. To go no further than Terence, you find in the *Eunuch* Antipho entering single in the midst of the third act, after Chremes and Pythias were gone off. In the same play you have likewise Dorias beginning the fourth act alone; and after she has made a relation of what was done at the soldiers' entertainment (which by the way was very inartificial) because she was presumed to speak directly to the audience, and to acquaint them with what was necessary to be known, but yet should have been so contrived by the poet as to have been told by persons of the drama to one another (and so by them to have come to the knowledge of the people) she quits the stage, and Phaedria enters next, alone likewise. He also gives you an account of himself, and of his returning from the country, in monologue, to which unnatural way of narration Terence is subject in all his plays: In his *Adelphi* or Brothers, Syrus and Demea enter; after the scene was broken by the departure of Sostrata, Geta and Canthara; and indeed you can scarce look into any of his comedies, where you will not presently discover the same interruption.

But as they have failed both in laying of their plots, and in the management, swerving from the rules of their own art, by misrepresenting nature to us, in which they have ill-satisfied one intention of a play, which was delight, so in the instructive part they have erred worse: instead of punishing vice and rewarding virtue, they have often shown a prosperous wickedness, and an unhappy piety. They have set before us a bloody image of revenge in *Medea*, and given her dragons to convey her safe from punishment. A Priam and Astyanax murdered, and Cassandra ravished, and the lust and murder ending in the victory of him who acted them. In short, there is no indecorum in any of our modern plays, which if I would excuse, I could not shadow with some authority from the Ancients.

And one farther note of them let me leave you. Tragedies and comedies were not writ then as they are now, promiscuously, by the same person; but he who found his genius bending to the one, never attempted the other way. This is so plain, that I need not instance to you, that Aristophanes, Plautus, Terence, never any of them writ a tragedy; Aeschylus, Euripides, Sophocles, and Seneca, never meddled with comedy: the sock and buskin were not worn by the same poet: having then so much care to excel in one kind, very little is to be pardoned them if they miscarried in it; and this would lead me to the consideration of their wit, had not Crites given me sufficient warning not to be too bold in my judgement of it; because the languages being dead, and many of the customs and little accidents on which it depended, lost to us, we are not competent judges of it. But though I grant that here and there we may miss the application of a proverb or a custom, yet a thing well said will be wit in all languages; and though it may lose something in the translation, yet to him who reads it in the original, 'tis still the same; he has an idea of its excellency, though it cannot pass from his mind into any other expression or words than those in which he finds it. When Phaedria, in the *Eunuch*, had a command from his mistress to be absent two days; and encouraging himself to go through with it, said; *Tandem ego non illa caream, si opus sit, vel totum triduum?* Parmeno to mock the softness of his master, lifting up his hands and eyes, cries out as it were in admiration; *Hui! universum triduum!*[32] the elegancy of which *universum*, though it cannot be rendered in our language, yet leaves an impression on our souls: but this happens seldom in him, in Plautus of-

---

[32]"But cannot I manage to do without her, if I have to, for three whole days. . . . Alas, three entire days!" Terence, *Eunuch* 2.1.17–18. [Ed.]

tener; who is infinitely too bold in his metaphors and coining words; out of which many times his wit is nothing, which questionless was one reason why Horace falls upon him so severely in those verses:

Sed proavi nostri Plautinos et numeros, et
laudavere sales, nimium patienter utrumque
ne dicam stolide.[33]

For Horace himself was cautious to obtrude a new word on his readers, and makes custom and common use the best measure of receiving it into our writings.

Multa renascentur quae nunc cecidere, cadentque
quae nunc sunt in honore vocabula, si volet usus,
quem penes, arbitrium est, et jus, et norma lo-
quendi.[34]

The not observing this rule is that which the world has blamed in our satirist Cleveland; to express a thing hard and unnaturally, is his new way of elocution. 'Tis true, no poet but may sometimes use a catachresis, Virgil does it;

Mistaque ridenti colocasia fundet acantho.

In his Eclogue of Pollio, and in his 7th Æneid.

Mirantur et undae,
miratur nemus, insuetum fulgentia longe,
scuta virum fluvio, pictasque, innare carinas.

And Ovid once so modestly, that he asks leave to do it;

Si verbo audacia detur
haud metuam summi dixisse Palatia coeli.[35]

<hr>

[33]"And so what if Plautus was praised? / Did he deserve it? Shouldn't you / know the good from the stupid by yourself?" Horace, *Art of Poetry*, 270–72; see p. 73. [Ed.]

[34]"Everything mortal dies; beautiful / language is easily broken. / Dead words shall live / and live words shall die / and only the mouths of men can decide; / only what's said is said / and therefore alive. And therefore correct." Horace, *Art of Poetry*, 70–72; see p. 69. [Ed.]

[35]"The Egyptian bean, mixed with smiling acanthus, will flourish." (Virgil, *Eclogues* 4:20); "The waves and the woods wonder, shocked by the men's shining shields and by the painted ships." (Virgil, *Aeneid* 8:91–93); "If I were bold, I would not hesitate to call it the Palace of Heaven" (Ovid, *Metamorphoses* 1:175–76). [Ed.]

Calling the court of Jupiter by the name of Augustus's palace, though in another place he is more bold, where he says, *et longas visent capitolia pompas.*[36] But to do this always, and never be able to write a line without it, though it may be admired by some few pedants, will not pass upon those who know that wit is best conveyed to us in the most easy language; and is most to be admired when a great thought comes dressed in words so commonly received that it is understood by the meanest apprehensions, as the best meat is the most easily digested: but we cannot read a verse of Cleveland's without making a face at it, as if every word were a pill to swallow. He gives us many times a hard nut to break our teeth, without a kernel for our pains. So that there is this difference between his satires and Doctor Donne's, that the one gives us deep thoughts in common language, though rough cadence; the other gives us common thoughts in abstruse words: 'tis true, in some places his wit is independent of his words, as in that of the *Rebel Scot*:

Had Cain been Scot God would have changed his
doom;
Not forced him wander, but confined him home,

*Si sic omnia dixisset!*[37] This is wit in all languages: 'tis like Mercury, never to be lost or killed; and so that other:

For beauty like white-powder makes no noise,
And yet the silent hypocrite destroys.

You see the last line is highly metaphorical, but it is so soft and gentle that it does not shock us as we read it.

But, to return from whence I have digressed, to the consideration of the Ancients' writing and their wit, (of which by this time you will grant us in some measure to be fit judges,) though I see many excellent thoughts in Seneca, yet he, of them who had a genius most proper for the stage, was Ovid; he had a way of writing so fit to stir up a pleasing admiration and concernment, which are the objects of a tragedy, and to show

<hr>

[36]"And Capitols view the long processions." Ovid, *Metamorphoses* 1:561. [Ed.]

[37]"If only he had always spoken thus!" [Ed.]

the various movements of a soul combating between two different passions, that, had he lived in our age, or in his own could have writ with our advantages, no man but must have yielded to him; and therefore I am confident the *Medea* is none of his: for, though I esteem it for the gravity and sententiousness of it, which he himself concludes to be suitable to a tragedy, *Omne genus scripti gravitate tragaedia vincit*,[38] yet it moves not my soul enough to judge that he, who in the epic way wrote things so near the drama, as the story of Myrrha, of Caunus and Biblis, and the rest, should stir up no more concernment where he most endeavoured it. The masterpiece of Seneca I hold to be that scene in the *Troades*, where Ulysses is seeking for Astyanax to kill him. There you see the tenderness of a mother, so represented in Andromache, that it raises compassion to a high degree in the reader, and bears the nearest resemblance of anything in the tragedies of the Ancients, to the excellent scenes of passion in Shakespeare, or in Fletcher. For love-scenes you will find few among them, their tragic poets dealt not with that soft passion, but with lust, cruelty, revenge, ambition, and those bloody actions they produced; which were more capable of raising horror than compassion in an audience: leaving love untouched, whose gentleness would have tempered them, which is the most frequent of all the passions, and which being the private concernment of every person, is soothed by viewing its own image in a public entertainment.

Among their comedies, we find a scene or two of tenderness, and that where you would least expect it, in Plautus; but to speak generally, their lovers say little, when they see each other, but *anima mea, vita mea*; ζωὴ καὶ ψυχὴ,[39] as the women in Juvenal's time used to cry out in the fury of their kindness. Any sudden gust of passion (as an ecstasy of love in an unexpected meeting) cannot better be expressed than in a word and a sigh, breaking one another. Nature is dumb on such occasions, and to make her

speak, would be to represent her unlike herself. But there are a thousand other concernments of lovers, as jealousies, complaints, contrivances and the like, where not to open their minds at large to each other, were to be wanting to their own love, and to the expectation of the audience who watch the movements of their minds, as much as the changes of their fortunes. For the imaging of the first is properly the work of a poet, the latter he borrows from the historian.

Eugenius was proceeding in that part of his discourse, when Crites interrupted him. I see, said he, Eugenius and I are never like to have this question decided betwixt us; for he maintains the Moderns have acquired a new perfection in writing; I can only grant they have altered the mode of it. Homer described his heroes men of great appetites, lovers of beef broiled upon the coals, and good fellows; contrary to the practice of the French romances, whose heroes neither eat, nor drink, nor sleep, for love. Virgil makes Aeneas a bold avower of his own virtues,

Sum pius Aeneas fama super aethera notus;[40]

which in the civility of our poets is the character of a fanfaron or Hector: for with us the knight takes occasion to walk out, or sleep, to avoid the vanity of telling his own story, which the trusty squire is ever to perform for him. So in their love scenes, of which Eugenius spoke last, the Ancients were more hearty, we more talkative: they writ love as it was then the mode to make it, and I will grant thus much to Eugenius, that perhaps one of their poets, had he lived in our age,

Si foret hoc nostrum fato delapsus in aevum,[41]

(as Horace says of Lucilius) he had altered many things; not that they were not natural before, but that he might accommodate himself to the age in which he lived; yet in the mean time we are not to conclude anything rashly against those great men, but preserve to them the dignity of masters, and give that honour to their memories, (*Quos*

---

[38]"Tragedy surpasses in gravity all other kinds of writing." Ovid, *Tristia* 2:381. [Ed.]

[39]"My soul, my life, life and soul." Cf. Juvenal, *Satires* 6:195. [Ed.]

[40]"I am pious Aeneas, renowned above the heavens." Virgil, *Aeneid* 1:378–89. [Ed.]

[41]"If Fate had dropped him into this era of ours." Horace, *Satires* I.9:68. [Ed.]

*libitina sacravit*[42];) part of which we expect may be paid to us in future times.

This moderation of Crites, as it was pleasing to all the company, so it put an end to that dispute; which, Eugenius, who seemed to have the better of the argument, would urge no farther: but Lisideius after he had acknowledged himself of Eugenius's opinion concerning the Ancients, yet told him he had forborne, till his discourse were ended, to ask him why he preferred the English plays above those of other nations? and whether we ought not to submit our stage to the exactness of our next neighbours?

Though, said Eugenius, I am at all times ready to defend the honour of my country against the French, and to maintain, we are as well able to vanquish them with our pens as our ancestors have been with their swords, yet, if you please, added he, looking upon Neander, I will commit this cause to my friend's management; his opinion of our plays is the same with mine: and besides, there is no reason, that Crites and I, who have now left the stage, should re-enter so suddenly upon it; which is against the laws of comedy.

If the question had been stated, replied Lisideius, who had writ best, the French or English forty years ago, I should have been of your opinion, and adjudged the honour to our own nation; but since that time (said he, turning towards Neander) we have been so long together bad Englishmen, that we had not leisure to be good poets; Beaumont, Fletcher, and Jonson (who were only capable of bringing us to that degree of perfection which we have) were just then leaving the world; as if in an age of so much horror, wit and those milder studies of humanity, had no farther business among us. But the Muses, who ever follow peace, went to plant in another country; it was then, that the great Cardinal of Richelieu began to take them into his protection; and that, by his encouragement, Corneille and some other Frenchmen reformed their theatre, (which before was as much below ours as it now surpasses it and the rest of Europe); but because Crites, in his discourse for the Ancients, has

prevented me, by observing many rules of the stage, which the Moderns have borrowed from them, I shall only, in short, demand of you, whether you are not convinced that of all nations the French have best observed them? In the unity of time you find them so scrupulous, that it yet remains a dispute among their poets, whether the artificial day of twelve hours more or less, be not meant by Aristotle, rather than the natural one of twenty-four; and consequently whether all plays ought not to be reduced into that compass? This I can testify, that in all their dramas writ within these last twenty years and upwards, I have not observed any that have extended the time to thirty hours: in the unity of place they are full as scrupulous, for many of their critics limit it to that very spot of ground where the play is supposed to begin; none of them exceed the compass of the same town or city.

The unity of action in all their plays is yet more conspicuous, for they do not burden them with under-plots, as the English do, which is the reason why many scenes of our tragi-comedies carry on a design that is nothing of kin to the main plot; and that we see two distinct webs in a play, like those in ill-wrought stuffs; and two actions, that is, two plays carried on together, to the confounding of the audience, who, before they are warm in their concernments for one part, are diverted to another; and by that means espouse the interest of neither. From hence likewise it arises that the one half of our actors are not known to the other. They keep their distances as if they were Montagues and Capulets, and seldom begin an acquaintance till the last scene of the fifth act, when they are all to meet upon the stage. There is no theatre in the world has anything so absurd as the English tragi-comedy, 'tis a drama of our own invention, and the fashion of it is enough to proclaim it so; here a course of mirth, there another of sadness and passion; and a third of honour, and a duel. Thus in two hours and a half we run through all the fits of Bedlam. The French afford you as much variety on the same day, but they do it not so unseasonably, or *mal à propos* as we. Our poets present you the play and the farce together, and our stages still retain somewhat of the original civility of the Red Bull;

---

[42]"Whom the Goddess of funerals has sanctified." Horace, *Epistles* II.1:9. [Ed.]

Atque ursum et pugiles media inter carmina pos-
cunt.[43]

The end of tragedies or serious plays, says
Aristotle, is to beget admiration, compassion, or
concernment;[44] but are not mirth and compassion
things incompatible? and is it not evident that the
poet must of necessity destroy the former by
intermingling of the latter? that is, he must ruin
the sole end and object of his tragedy to introduce
somewhat that is forced in to it; and is not of the
body of it. Would you not think that physician
mad, who having prescribed a purge, should immediately order you to take restringents?

But to leave our plays, and return to theirs, I
have noted one great advantage they have had in
the plotting of their tragedies; that is, they are
always grounded upon some known history: according to that of Horace, *ex noto fictum carmen
sequar*[45]; and in that they have so imitated the
Ancients, that they have surpassed them. For the
Ancients, as was observed before, took for the
foundation of their plays some poetical fiction,
such as under that consideration could move but
little concernment in the audience, because they
already knew the event of it. But the French goes
farther;

Atque ita mentitur; sic veris falsa remiscet,
primo ne medium, medio ne discrepet imum.[46]

He so interweaves truth with probable fiction,
that he puts a pleasing fallacy upon us; mends
the intrigues of fate, and dispenses with the severity of history, to reward that virtue which has
been rendered to us there unfortunate. Sometimes
the story has left the success so doubtful, that
the writer is free, by the privilege of a poet, to
take that which of two or more relations will best
suit with his design. As for example, in the death

of Cyrus, whom Justin and some others report
to have perished in the Scythian war, but Xenophon affirms to have died in his bed of extreme
old age. Nay more, when the event is past dispute, even then we are willing to be deceived,
and the poet, if he contrives it with appearance
of truth, has all the audience of his party; at least
during the time his play is acting: so naturally
we are kind to virtue, when our own interest is
not in question, that we take it up as the general
concernment of mankind. On the other side, if
you consider the historical plays of Shakespeare,
they are rather so many chronicles of kings, or
the business many times of thirty or forty years,
cramped into a representation of two hours and
an half, which is not to imitate or paint nature,
but rather to draw her in miniature, to take her
in little, to look upon her through the wrong end
of a perspective, and receive her images not only
much less, but infinitely more imperfect than the
life: this, instead of making a play delightful,
renders it ridiculous.

Quodcumque ostendis mihi sic, incredulus odi.[47]

For the spirit of man cannot be satisfied but
with truth, or at least verisimility; and a poem is
to contain, if not τὰ ἔτυμα, yet ἐτύμοισιν
ὁμοῖα,[48] as one of the Greek poets has expressed
it.

Another thing in which the French differ from
us and from the Spaniards, is that they do not
embarrass, or cumber themselves with too much
plot: they only represent so much of a story as
will constitute one whole and great action sufficient for a play; we, who undertake more, do but
multiply adventures; which, not being produced
from one another, as effects from causes, but
barely following, constitute many actions in the
drama, and consequently make it many plays.

But by pursuing closely one argument, which
is not cloyed with many turns, the French have
gained more liberty for verse, in which they
write: they have leisure to dwell on a subject
which deserves it; and to represent the passions

[43]"They ask for a bear and boxers in the middle of the
play." Horace, *Epistles* II.1:185–86. [Ed.]

[44]Aristotle mentions pity and fear, which may correspond
to "compassion" and "concernment." [Ed.]

[45]"I'd weave verse out of everyday stuff." Horace, *Art of
Poetry*, 240; see p. 72. [Ed.]

[46]"Fictions are carefully crafted, / invention and history
so blended / that it does not matter whether middle or beginning / or end, everything is part of one single whole." Horace,
*Art of Poetry*, 151–52; see pp. 70–71. [Ed.]

[47]"What I cannot believe / I will loathe." Horace, *Art of
Poetry*, 188; see p. 71. [Ed.]

[48]"The truth"; "things like the truth." Homer, *Odyssey*
19:203. [Ed.]

(which we have acknowledged to be the poet's work) without being hurried from one thing to another, as we are in the plays of Calderón, which we have seen lately upon our theatres, under the name of Spanish plots.[49] I have taken notice but of one tragedy of ours, whose plot has that uniformity and unity of design in it which I have commended in the French; and that is *Rollo*, or rather, under the name of *Rollo*, the story of Bassianus and Geta in Herodian; there indeed the plot is neither large nor intricate, but just enough to fill the minds of the audience, not to cloy them. Besides, you see it founded upon the truth of history, only the time of the action is not reducible to the strictness of the rules; and you see in some places a little farce mingled, which is below the dignity of the other parts; and in this all our poets are extremely peccant, even Ben Jonson himself in *Sejanus* and *Catiline* has given us this oleo of a play: this unnatural mixture of comedy and tragedy, which to me sounds just as ridiculously as the history of David with the merry humours of Golia. In *Sejanus* you may take notice of the scene betwixt Livia and the physician, which is a pleasant satire upon the artificial helps of beauty. In *Catiline* you may see the parliament of women; the little envies of them to one another; and all that passes betwixt Curio and Fulvia, scenes admirable in their kind, but of an ill mingle with the rest.

But I return again to the French writers who, as I have said, do not burden themselves too much with plot, which has been reproached to them by an ingenious person of our nation as a fault, for he says they commonly make but one person considerable in a play; they dwell on him, and his concernments, while the rest of the persons are only subservient to set him off. If he intends this by it, that there is one person in the play who is of greater dignity than the rest, he must tax, not only theirs, but those of the Ancients, and which he would be loth to do, the best of ours; for 'tis impossible but that one person must be more conspicuous in it than any other, and consequently the greatest share in the action must devolve on him. We see it so in the

management of all affairs; even in the most equal aristocracy, the balance cannot be so justly poised, but someone will be superior to the rest, either in parts, fortune, interest, or the consideration of some glorious exploit, which will reduce the greatest part of business into his hands.

But, if he would have us to imagine that in exalting one character the rest of them are neglected, and that all of them have not some share or other in the action of the play, I desire him to produce any of Corneille's tragedies, wherein every person (like so many servants in a well governed family) has not some employment, and who is not necessary to the carrying on of the plot, or at least to your understanding it.

There are indeed some protatic[50] persons in the Ancients, whom they make use of in their plays, either to hear, or give the relation: but the French avoid this with great address, making their narrations only to, or by such, who are some way interested in the main design. And now I am speaking of relations, I cannot take a fitter opportunity to add this in favour of the French, that they often use them with better judgement and more *à propos* than the English do. Not that I commend narrations in general, but there are two sorts of them; one of those things which are antecedent to the play, and are related to make the conduct of it more clear to us, but, 'tis a fault to choose such subjects for the stage as will force us on that rock; because we see they are seldom listened to by the audience, and that is many times the ruin of the play: for, being once let pass without attention, the audience can never recover themselves to understand the plot; and indeed it is somewhat unreasonable that they should be put to so much trouble as, that to comprehend what passes in their sight, they must have recourse to what was done, perhaps, ten or twenty years ago.

But there is another sort of relations, that is, of things happening in the action of the play, and supposed to be done behind the scenes, and this is many times both convenient and beautiful: for, by it the French avoid the tumult, to which we are subject in England, by representing duels,

---

[49]Dryden himself was to adapt Calderon in *An Evening's Love* (1668). [Ed.]

[50]Introductory: like the Watchman in Aeschylus's *Agamemnon*. [Ed.]

battles, and the like, which renders our stage too like the theatres where they fight prizes. For what is more ridiculous than to represent an army with a drum and five men behind it; all which, the hero of the other side is to drive in before him, or to see a duel fought, and one slain with two or three thrusts of the foil, which we know are so blunted, that we might give a man an hour to kill another in good earnest with them.

I have observed that in all our tragedies, the audience cannot forbear laughing when the actors are to die; 'tis the most comic part of the whole play. All passions may be lively[51] represented on the stage, if to the well-writing of them the actor supplies a good commanded voice, and limbs that move easily, and without stiffness; but there are many actions which can never be imitated to a just height: dying especially is a thing which none but a Roman gladiator could naturally perform on the stage when he did not imitate or represent, but do it; and therefore it is better to omit the representation of it.

The words of a good writer which describe it lively, will make a deeper impression of belief in us than all the actor can insinuate into us, when he seems to fall dead before us; as a poet in the description of a beautiful garden, or a meadow, will please our imagination more than the place itself can please our sight. When we see death represented we are convinced it is but fiction; but when we hear it related, our eyes (the strongest witnesses) are wanting, which might have undeceived us; and we are all willing to favour the sleight when the poet does not too grossly impose on us. They therefore who imagine these relations would make no concernment in the audience, are deceived, by confounding them with the other, which are of things antecedent to the play; those are made often in cold blood (as I may say) to the audience; but these are warmed with our concernments, which were before awakened in the play. What the philosophers say of motion, that, when it is once begun, it continues of itself, and will do so to eternity without some stop put to it,[52] is clearly true on this occasion; the soul being already moved with the characters and fortunes of those imaginary persons, continues going of its own accord, and we are no more weary to hear what becomes of them when they are not on the stage, than we are to listen to the news of an absent mistress. But it is objected, that if one part of the play may be related, then why not all? I answer, some parts of the action are more fit to be represented, some to be related. Corneille says judiciously, that the poet is not obliged to expose to view all particular actions which conduce to the principal: he ought to select such of them to be seen which will appear with the greatest beauty, either by the magnificence of the show, or the vehemence of passions which they produce, or some other charm which they have in them, and let the rest arrive to the audience by narration. 'Tis a great mistake in us to believe the French present no part of the action on the stage: every alteration or crossing of a design, every new sprung passion, and turn of it, is a part of the action, and much the noblest, except we conceive nothing to be action till the players come to blows; as if the painting of the hero's mind were not more properly the poet's work than the strength of his body. Nor does this anything contradict the opinion of Horace, where he tells us,

Segnius irritant animos demissa per aurem,
quam quae sunt oculis subjecta fidelibus. —

For he says immediately after,

Non tamen intus
digna geri promes in scenam, multaque tolles
ex oculis, quae mox narret facundia praesens.

Among which many he recounts some.

Nec pueros coram populo Medea trucidet,
aut in avem Progne mutetur, Cadmus in anguem,
etc.[53]

[51]In a lifelike manner. [Ed.]

[52]Dryden is not quoting Newton's first law of motion before it was announced; he is probably echoing Descartes's *Principia Philosophiae*, which had just been translated into English. [Ed.]

[53]"What is heard, not seen, is weaker / in the mind that what the eyes record / faithfully as it happens. Yet I judge / for yourself what the eyes / must not see, leave to the ears / what belongs out of sight: . . . / Keep Medea in the darkness / as she butchers her sons, and Atreus / brewing human guts / and Procne / running for her raped life, / becoming a bird,

That is, those actions which by reason of their cruelty will cause aversion in us, or by reason of their impossibility unbelief, ought either wholly to be avoided by a poet, or only delivered by narration. To which, we may have leave to add such as to avoid tumult, (as was before hinted) or to reduce the plot into a more reasonable compass of time, or for defect of beauty in them, are rather to be related than presented to the eye. Examples of all these kinds are frequent, not only among all the Ancients, but in the best received of our English poets. We find Ben Jonson using them in his *Magnetic Lady*, where one comes out from dinner, and relates the quarrels and disorders of it to save the indecent appearance of them on the stage, and to abbreviate the story: and this in express imitation of Terence, who had done the same before him in his *Eunuch*, where Pythius makes the like relation of what had happened within at the soldiers' entertainment. The relations likewise of Sejanus's death, and the prodigies before it are remarkable; the one of which was hid from sight to avoid the horror and tumult of the representation; the other to shun the introducing of things impossible to be believed. In that excellent play, *The King and no King*, Fletcher goes yet farther; for the whole unravelling of the plot is done by narration in the fifth act, after the manner of the Ancients; and it moves great concernment in the audience, though it be only a relation of what was done many years before the play. I could multiply other instances, but these are sufficient to prove that there is no error in choosing a subject which requires this sort of narrations; in the ill-management of them, there may.

But I find I have been too long in this discourse since the French have many other excellencies not common to us; as that you never see any of their plays end with a conversion, or simple change of will, which is the ordinary way which our poets use to end theirs. It shows little art in the conclusion of a dramatic poem, which they who have hindered the felicity during the four acts, desist from it in the fifth without some powerful cause to take them off their design; and though I deny not but such reasons may be found, yet it is a path that is cautiously to be trod, and the poet is to be sure he convinces the audience that the motive is strong enough. As for example, the conversion of the usurer in *The Scornful Lady*, seems to me a little forced; for being a usurer, which implies a lover of money to the highest degree of covetousness (and such the poet has represented him) the account he gives for the sudden change is that he has been duped by the wild young fellow, which in reason might render him more wary another time, and make him punish himself with harder fare and coarser clothes to get up again what he had lost: but that he should look on it as a judgement, and so repent, we may expect to hear in a sermon, but I should never endure it in a play.

I pass by this; neither will I insist on the care they take, that no person after his first entrance shall ever appear, but the business which brings him upon the stage shall be evident: which rule if observed, must needs render all the events in the play more natural; for there you see the probability of every accident, in the cause that produced it; and that which appears chance in the play will seem so reasonable to you, that you will there find it almost necessary; so that in the exit of the actor you have a clear account of his purpose and design in the next entrance: (though, if the scene be well wrought, the event will commonly deceive you) for there is nothing so absurd, says Corneille, as for an actor to leave the stage, only because he has no more to say.

I should now speak of the beauty of their rhyme, and the just reason I have to prefer that way of writing in tragedies before ours in blank verse; but because it is partly received by us, and therefore not altogether peculiar to them, I will say no more of it in relation to their plays. For our own I doubt not but it will exceedingly beautify them, and I can see but one reason why it should not generally obtain, that is, because our poets write so ill in it. This indeed may prove a more prevailing argument than all others which are used to destroy it, and therefore I am only troubled when great and judicious poets, and those who are acknowledged such, have writ or spoke against it; as for others they are to be

and Cadmus / turning into a snake." Horace, *Art of Poetry*, 180–87; see p. 71. [Ed.]

answered by that one sentence of an ancient author.

> Sed ut primo ad consequendos eos quos priores ducimus accendimur, itaubi aut praeteriri, aut aequari eos posse desperavimus, studium cum spesenescit: quod, scilicet, assequi non potest, sequi desinit; praeteritoque eo in quo eminere non possumus, aliquid in quo nitamur conquirimus.[54]

Lisideius concluded in this manner; and Neander after a little pause thus answered him.

I shall grant Lisideius, without much dispute, a great part of what he has urged against us; for I acknowledge that the French contrive their plots more regularly, and observe the laws of comedy, and decorum of the stage (to speak generally) with more exactness than the English. Farther, I deny not but he has taxed us justly in some irregularities of ours which he has mentioned; yet, after all, I am of opinion that neither our faults nor their virtues are considerable enough to place them above us.

For the lively imitation of nature being in the definition of a play, those which best fulfill that law ought to be esteemed superior to the others. 'Tis true, those beauties of the French poesy are such as will raise perfection higher where it is, but are not sufficient to give it where it is not: they are indeed the beauties of a statue, but not of a man, because not animated with the soul of poesy, which is imitation of humour and passions: and this Lisideius himself, or any other, however biased to their party, cannot but acknowledge, if he will either compare the humours of our comedies, or the characters of our serious plays with theirs. He who will look upon theirs which have been written till these last ten years or thereabouts, will find it an hard matter to pick out two or three passable humours amongst them. Corneille himself, their archpoet, what has he produced except *The Liar*, and you know how it was cried up in France; but when it came upon the English stage, though

well translated, and that part of Dorant acted to so much advantage as I am confident it never received in its own country, the most favourable to it would not put it in competition with many of Fletcher's or Ben Jonson's. In the rest of Corneille's comedies you have little humour; he tells you himself his way is first to show two lovers in good intelligence with each other; in the working up of the play to embroil them by some mistake, and in the latter end to clear it, and reconcile them.

But of late years Molière, the younger Corneille, Quinault, and some others, have been imitating afar off the quick turns and graces of the English stage. They have mixed their serious plays with mirth, like our tragi-comedies, since the death of Cardinal Richelieu, which Lisideius and many others not observing, have commended that in them for a virtue which they themselves no longer practise. Most of their new plays are like some of ours, derived from the Spanish novels. There is scarce one of them without a veil, and a trusty Diego,[55] who drolls much after the rate of the *Adventures*. But their humours, if I may grace them with that name, are so thin sown that never above one of them comes up in any play. I dare take upon me to find more variety of them in some one play of Ben Jonson's than in all theirs together: as he who has seen the *Alchemist*, *The Silent Woman*, or *Bartholomew Fair*, cannot but acknowledge with me.

I grant the French have performed what was possible on the ground-work of the Spanish plays; what was pleasant before, they have made regular; but there is not above one good play to be writ on all those plots; they are too much alike to please often, which we need not the experience of our own stage to justify. As for their new way of mingling mirth with serious plot, I do not with Lisideius condemn the thing, though I cannot approve their manner of doing it. He tell us we cannot so speedily recollect ourselves after a scene of great passion and concernment, as to pass to another of mirth and humour, and to enjoy it with any relish: but why should he imagine the soul of man more heavy than his senses? Does

---

[54]"At first we burn to excel those whom we think our leaders, but when we despair of surpassing them or even equalling them, our enthusiasm weakens with our hope; when it cannot overtake, it ceases to follow; putting away what we cannot excel in, we seek another outlet for our efforts." Velleius Paterculus, *Historia Romana* I:17. [Ed.]

[55]Neander is alluding to a comic servant, Diego, in Samuel Tuke's *Adventures of Five Hours*. [Ed.]

not the eye pass from an unpleasant object to a pleasant in a much shorter time than is required to this? and does not the unpleasantness of the first commend the beauty of the latter? The old rule of logic might have convinced him, that contraries when placed near, set off each other. A continued gravity keeps the spirit too much bent; we must refresh it sometimes, as we bait in a journey, that we may go on with greater ease. A scene of mirth mixed with tragedy has the same effect upon us which our music has betwixt the acts, which we find a relief to us from the best plots and language of the stage, if the discourses have been long. I must therefore have stronger arguments ere I am convinced, that compassion and mirth in the same subject destroy each other, and in the mean time cannot but conclude, to the honour of our nation, that we have invented, increased and perfected a more pleasant way of writing for the stage than was ever known to the Ancients or Moderns of any nation, which is tragi-comedy.

And this leads me to wonder why Lisideius and many others should cry up the barrenness of the French plots above the variety and copiousness of the English. Their plots are single, they carry on one design which is pushed forward by all the actors, every scene in the play contributing and moving towards it. Our plays besides the main design, have upper-plots or by-concernments, of less considerable persons, and intrigues, which are carried on with the motion of the main plot: as they say the orb of the fixed stars, and those of the planets, though they have motions of their own, are whirled about by the motion of the *primum mobile*, in which they are contained: that similitude expresses much of the English stage, for if contrary motions may be found in nature to agree; if a planet can go east and west at the same time, one way by virtue of his own motion, the other by the force of the first mover, it will not be difficult to imagine how the under-plot, which is only different, not contrary to the great design, may naturally be conducted along with it.

Eugenius[56] has already shown us, from the confession of the French poets, that the unity of action is sufficiently preserved if all the imperfect actions of the play are conducing to the main design: but when those pretty intrigues of a play are so ill ordered, that they have no coherence with the other, I must grant that Lisideius has reason to tax that want of due connexion; for co-ordination in a play is as dangerous and unnatural as in a state. In the mean time he must acknowledge our variety, if well ordered, will afford a greater pleasure to the audience.

As for his other argument, that by pursuing one single theme they gain an advantage to express and work up the passions, I wish any example he could bring from them would make it good: for I confess their verses are to me the coldest I have ever read. Neither indeed is it possible for them, in the way they take, so to express passion, as that the effects of it should appear in the concernment of an audience, their speeches being so many declamations, which tire us with the length; so that instead of persuading us to grieve for their imaginary heroes, we are concerned for our own trouble, as we are in tedious visits of bad company; we are in pain till they are gone. When the French stage came to be reformed by Cardinal Richelieu, those long harangues were introduced, to comply with the gravity of a churchman. Look upon the *Cinna* and the *Pompey*, they are not so properly to be called plays, as long discourses of reason of state: and *Polyeucte* in matters of religion is as solemn as the long stops upon our organs. Since that time it is grown into a custom, and their actors speak by the hourglass, like our parsons; nay, they account it the grace of their parts, and think themselves disparaged by the poet, if they may not twice or thrice in a play entertain the audience with a speech of an hundred lines. I deny not but this may suit well enough with the French; for as we, who are a more sullen people, come to be diverted at our plays; so they who are of an airy and gay temper come thither to make themselves more serious. And this I conceive to be one reason why comedies are more pleasing to us, and tragedies to them. But to speak generally, it cannot be denied that short speeches and replies are more apt to move the passions, and beget concernment in us than the other: for it is unnat-

[56]Crites; see p. 168. [Ed.]

ural for any one in a gust of passion to speak long together, or for another in the same condition, to suffer him, without interruption. Grief and passion are like floods raised in little brooks by a sudden rain; they are quickly up, and if the concernment be poured unexpectedly in upon us, it overflows us. But a long sober shower gives them leisure to run out as they came in, without troubling the ordinary current. As for comedy, repartee is one of its chiefest graces; the greatest pleasure of the audience is a chase of wit kept up on both sides, and swiftly managed. And this our forefathers, if not we, have had in Fletcher's plays, to a much higher degree of perfection than the French poets can, reasonably, hope to reach.

There is another part of Lisideius's discourse, in which he has rather excused our neighbours than commended them; that is, for aiming only to make one person considerable in their plays. 'Tis very true what he has urged, that one character in all plays, even without the poet's care, will have advantage of all the others; and that the design of the whole drama will chiefly depend on it. But this hinders not that there may be more shining characters in the play: many persons of a second magnitude, nay, some so very near, so almost equal to the first, that greatness may be opposed to greatness, and all the persons be made considerable, not only by their quality, but their action. 'Tis evident that the more the persons are, the greater will be the variety of the plot. If then the parts are managed so regularly that the beauty of the whole be kept entire, and that the variety become not a perplexed and confused mass of accidents, you will find it infinitely pleasing to be led in a labyrinth of design, where you see some of your way before you, yet discern not the end till you arrive at it. And that all this is practicable, I can produce for examples many of our English plays: as *The Maid's Tragedy*, *The Alchemist*, *The Silent Woman*: I was going to have named *The Fox*, but that the unity of design seems not exactly observed in it; for there appear two actions in the play; the first naturally ending with the fourth act; the second forced from it in the fifth: which yet is the less to be condemned in him, because the disguise of Volpone, though it suited not with his character as a crafty or covetous person, agreed well enough with that of a voluptuary: and by it the poet gained the end at which he aimed, the punishment of vice, and the reward of virtue, both which that disguise produced. So that to judge equally of it, it was an excellent fifth act, but not so naturally proceeding from the former.

But to leave this, and pass to the latter part of Lisideius's discourse, which concerns relations, I must acknowledge with him, that the French have reason to hide that part of the action which would occasion too much tumult on the stage, and to choose rather to have it made known by narration to the audience. Farther I think it very convenient, for the reasons he has given, that all incredible actions were removed; but, whether custom has so insinuated itself into our countrymen, or nature has so formed them to fierceness, I know not; but they will scarcely suffer combats and other objects of horror to be taken from them. And indeed, the indecency of tumults is all which can be objected against fighting. For why may not our imagination as well suffer itself to be deluded with the probability of it, as with any other thing in the play? For my part, I can with as great ease persuade myself that the blows are given in good earnest, as I can, that they who strike them are kings or princes, or those persons which they represent. For objects of incredibility I would be satisfied from Lisideius, whether we have any so removed from all appearance of truth as are those of Corneille's *Andromède*? A play which has been frequented the most of any he has writ? If the Perseus, or the son of an heathen god, the Pegasus and the monster were not capable to choke a strong belief, let him blame any representation of ours hereafter. Those indeed were objects of delight; yet the reason is the same as to the probability: for he makes it not a ballet or masque, but a play, which is to resemble truth. But for death, that it ought not to be represented, I have besides the arguments alleged by Lisideius, the authority of Ben Jonson, who has forborne it in his tragedies; for both the death of Sejanus and Catiline are related: though in the latter I cannot but observe one irregularity of that great poet: he has removed the scene in the same act, from Rome to Catiline's army, and from thence again to Rome; and besides, has allowed a very inconsiderable time, after Catiline's speech, for the striking of the battle, and the return of Petreius, who is to relate the event of it to the Senate: which I should not animadvert on him, who was otherwise a painful observer of τὸ πρέπον, or the decorum of the stage, if he had not used extreme severity in his judgement on the incomparable Shakespeare for the same fault. To conclude on this subject of relations, if we are to be blamed for showing too much of the action, the French are as faulty for discovering too little of it: a mean betwixt both should be observed by every judicious writer, so as the audience may neither be left unsatisfied by not seeing what is beautiful, or shocked by beholding what is either incredible or indecent. I hope I have already proved in this discourse, that though we are not altogether so punctual as the French, in observing the laws of comedy; yet our errors are so few and little, and those things wherein we excel them so considerable, that we ought of right to be preferred before them. But what will Lisideius say if they themselves acknowledge they are too strictly bounded by those laws, for breaking which he has blamed the English? I will allege Corneille's words, as I find them in the end of his Discourse of the three unities; *Il est facile aux speculatifs d'estre severes*, etc. ''Tis easy for speculative persons to judge severely; but if they would produce to public view ten or twelve pieces of this nature, they would perhaps give more latitude to the rules than I have done, when by experience they had known how much we are limited and constrained by them, and how many beauties of the stage they banished from it.' To illustrate a little what he has said; by their servile observations of the unities of time and place, and integrity of scenes, they have brought on themselves that dearth of plot, and narrowness of imagination, which may be observed in all their plays. How many beautiful accidents might naturally happen in two or three days, which cannot arrive with any probability in the compass of twenty-four hours? There is time to be allowed also for maturity of design, which amongst great and prudent persons, such as are often represented in tragedy, cannot, with any likelihood of truth, be brought to pass at so short a warning. Farther, by tying themselves strictly to the unity of place, and unbroken scenes, they are forced many times to omit some beauties which cannot be shown where the act began; but might, if the scene were interrupted, and the stage cleared for the persons to enter in another place; and therefore the French poets are often forced upon absurdities: for if the act begins in a chamber, all the persons in the play must have some business or other to come thither, or else they are not to be shown that act, and sometimes their characters are very unfitting to appear there; as, suppose it were the king's bedchamber, yet the meanest man in the tragedy must come and dispatch his business there, rather than in the lobby or courtyard, (which is fitter for him) for fear the stage should be cleared, and the scenes broken. Many times they fall by it into a greater inconvenience; for they keep their scenes unbroken, and yet change the place; as in one of their newest plays where the act begins in the street. There a gentleman is to meet his friend; he sees him with his man, coming out from his father's house; they talk together, and the first goes out: the second, who is a lover, has made an appointment with his mistress; she appears at the window, and then we are to imagine the scene lies under it. This gentleman is called away, and leaves his servant with his mistress: presently her father is heard from within; the young lady is afraid the serving-man should be discovered, and thrusts him into a place of safety, which is supposed to be her closet. After this, the father enters to the daughter, and now the scene is in a house: for he is seeking from one room to another for this poor Philipin, or French Diego, who is heard from within, drolling and breaking many a miserable conceit on the subject of his sad condition. In this ridiculous manner the play goes forward, the stage being never empty all the while: so that the street, the window, the two houses, and the closet, are made to walk about, and the persons to stand still. Now what, I beseech you, is more easy than to write a regular French play, or more difficult than to write an irregular English one, like those of Fletcher, or of Shakespeare?

If they content themselves as Corneille did, with some flat design, which, like an ill riddle, is found out ere it be half proposed, such plots we can make every way regular as easily as they: but whenever they endeavour to rise to any quick turns and counterturns of plot, as some of them have attempted, since Corneille's plays have been less in vogue, you see they write as irregularly as we, though they cover it more speciously. Hence the reason is perspicuous, why no French plays, when translated, have, or ever can, succeed on the English stage. For, if you consider the plots, our own are fuller of variety; if the writing, ours are more quick and fuller of spirit: and therefore 'tis a strange mistake in those who decry the way of writing plays in verse, as if the English therein imitated the French. We have borrowed nothing from them; our plots are weaved in English looms: we endeavour therein to follow the variety and greatness of characters which are derived to us from Shakespeare and Fletcher. The copiousness and well-knitting of the intrigues we have from Jonson, and for the verse itself we have English precedents of elder date than any of Corneille's plays (not to name our old comedies before Shakespeare, which were all writ in verse of six feet, or Alexandrines, such as the French now use). I can show in Shakespeare, many scenes of rhyme together, and the like in Ben Jonson's tragedies: in *Catiline* and *Sejanus* sometimes thirty or forty lines; I mean besides the chorus, or the monologues, which by the way, showed Ben no enemy to this way of writing, especially if you read his *Sad Shepherd*, which goes sometimes on rhyme, sometimes on blank verse, like an horse who eases himself on trot and amble. You find him likewise commending Fletcher's pastoral of *The Faithful Shepherdess*; which is for the most part rhyme, though not refined to that purity to which it hath since been brought. And these examples are enough to clear us from a servile imitation of the French.

But to return whence I have digressed, I dare boldly affirm these two things of the English drama: first, that we have many plays of ours as regular as any of theirs; and which, besides, have more variety of plot and characters: and secondly, that in most of the irregular plays of Shakespeare or Fletcher (for Ben Jonson's are for the most part regular) there is a more masculine fancy and greater spirit in the writing, than there is in any of the French. I could produce even in Shakespeare's and Fletcher's works, some plays which are almost exactly formed; as *The Merry Wives of Windsor*, and *The Scornful Lady*: but because (generally speaking) Shakespeare, who writ first, did not perfectly observe the laws of comedy, and Fletcher, who came nearer to perfection, yet through carelessness made many faults, I will take the pattern of a perfect play from Ben Jonson, who was a careful and learned observer of the dramatic laws, and from all his comedies I shall select *The Silent Woman*; of which I will make a short examen, according to those rules which the French observe.

As Neander was beginning to examine *The Silent Woman*, Eugenius, earnestly regarding him; I beseech you, Neander, said he, gratify the company and me in particular so far, as before you speak of the play, to give us a character of the author; and tell us frankly your opinion, whether you do not think all writers, both French and English, ought to give place to him?

I fear, replied Neander, that in obeying your commands I shall draw some envy on myself. Besides, in performing them, it will be first necessary to speak somewhat of Shakespeare and Fletcher, his rivals in poesy, and one of them, in my opinion, at least is equal, perhaps his superior.

To begin with Shakespeare; he was the man who of all modern, and perhaps ancient poets, had the largest and most comprehensive soul. All the images of nature were still present to him, and he drew them not laboriously, but luckily: when he describes anything, you more than see it, you feel it too. Those who accuse him to have wanted learning, give him the greater commendation: he was naturally learned; he needed not the spectacles of books to read nature; he looked inwards, and found her there. I cannot say he is everywhere alike; were he so, I should do him injury to compare him with the greatest of mankind. He is many times flat, insipid; his comic wit degenerating into clenches, his serious swelling into bombast. But he is always great, when some great occasion is presented to him: no man can say he ever had a fit subject for his wit, and did not then raise himself as high above the rest of poets,

Quantum lenta solent inter viburna cupressi.[57]

The consideration of this made Mr. Hales of Eton say that there was no subject of which any poet ever writ, but he would produce it much better done in Shakespeare; and however others are now generally preferred before him, yet the age wherein he lived, which had contemporaries with him, Fletcher and Jonson, never equalled them to him in their esteem. And in the last king's Court, when Ben's reputation was at highest, Sir John Suckling, and with him the greater part of the courtiers, set our Shakespeare far above him.

Beaumont and Fletcher of whom I am next to speak, had with the advantage of Shakespeare's wit, which was their precedent, great natural gifts, improved by study, Beaumont especially being so accurate a judge of plays, that Ben Jonson while he lived, submitted all his writings to his censure, and 'tis thought, used his judgement in correcting, if not contriving all his plots. What value he had for him, appears by the verse he writ to him; and therefore I need speak no farther of it. The first play that brought Fletcher and him in esteem was their *Philaster*, for before that, they had written two or three very unsuccessfully: as the like is reported of Ben Jonson, before he writ *Every Man in His Humour*. Their plots were generally more regular than Shakespeare's, especially those which were made before Beaumont's death; and they understood and imitated the conversation of gentlemen much better; whose wild debaucheries, and quickness of wit in repartees, no poet before them could paint as they have done. Humour which Ben Jonson derived from particular persons, they made it not their business to describe. They represented all the passions very lively, but above all, love. I am apt to believe the English language in them arrived to its highest perfection; what words have since been taken in, are rather superfluous than ornamental. Their plays are now the most pleasant and frequent entertainments of the stage, two of theirs being acted through the year for one of Shakespeare's or Jonson's: the reason is, because there is a certain gaiety in their comedies, and pathos in their more serious plays, which suits generally with all men's humours. Shakespeare's language is likewise a little obsolete, and Ben Jonson's wit comes short of theirs.

As for Jonson, to whose character I am now arrived, if we look upon him while he was himself, (for his last plays were but his dotages) I think him the most learned and judicious writer which any theatre ever had. He was a most severe judge of himself as well as others. One cannot say he wanted wit, but rather that he was frugal of it. In his works you find little to retrench or alter. Wit and language, and humour also in some measure we had before him; but something of art was wanting to the drama till he came. He managed his strength to more advantage than any who preceded him. You seldom find him making love in any of his scenes, or endeavouring to move the passions; his genius was too sullen and saturnine to do it gracefully, especially when he knew he came after those who had performed both to such an height. Humour was his proper sphere, and in that he delighted most to represent mechanic[58] people. He was deeply conversant in the Ancients, both Greek and Latin, and he borrowed boldly from them. There is scarce a poet or historian among the Roman authors of those times whom he has not translated in *Sejanus* and *Catiline*. But he has done his robberies so openly, that one may see he fears not to be taxed by any law. He invades authors like a monarch, and what would be theft in other poets, is only victory in him. With the spoils of these writers he so represents old Rome to us, in its rites, ceremonies and customs, that if one of their poets had written either of his tragedies, we had seen less of it than in him. If there was any fault in his language, 'twas that he weaved it too closely and laboriously, in his comedies especially: perhaps too, he did a little too much Romanize our tongue, leaving the words which he translated

<hr>

[57]"As cypresses usually do among bending osiers." Virgil, *Eclogues* 1:25. [Ed.]

[58]Low, vulgar. [Ed.]

almost as much Latin as he found them: wherein though he learnedly followed their language, he did not enough comply with the idiom of ours. If I would compare him with Shakespeare, I must acknowledge him the more correct poet, but Shakespeare the greater wit. Shakespeare was the Homer, or father of our dramatic poets; Jonson was the Virgil, the pattern of elaborate writing. I admire him, but I love Shakespeare. To conclude of him, as he has given us the most correct plays, so in the precepts which he has laid down in his *Discoveries*, we have as many and profitable rules for perfecting the stage as any wherewith the French can furnish us.

Having thus spoken of the author, I proceed to the examination of his comedy, *The Silent Woman*.

## EXAMEN OF THE SILENT WOMAN

To begin first with the length of the action, it is so far from exceeding the compass of a natural day, that it takes not up an artificial one. 'Tis all included in the limits of three hours and an half, which is no more than is required for the presentment on the stage. A beauty perhaps not much observed; if it had, we should not have looked on the Spanish translation of *Five Hours* with so much wonder. The scene of it is laid in London; the latitude of place is almost as little as you can imagine, for it lies all within the compass of two houses, and after the first act, in one.[59] The continuity of scenes is observed more than in any of our plays, except his own *Fox* and *Alchemist*. They are not broken above twice or thrice at most in the whole comedy, and in the two best of Corneille's plays, the *Cid* and *Cinna*, they are interrupted once. The action of the play is entirely one; the end or aim of which is the settling Morose's estate on Dauphine. The intrigue of it is the greatest and most noble of any pure unmixed comedy in any language: you see in it many persons of various characters and humours, and all delightful; as first, Morose, or an old man, to whom all noise but his own talking

is offensive. Some who would be thought critics, say this humour of his is forced: but to remove that objection, we may consider him first to be naturally of a delicate hearing, as many are to whom all sharp sounds are unpleasant; and secondly, we may attribute much of it to the peevishness of his age, or the wayward authority of an old man in his own house, where he may make himself obeyed; and to this the poet seems to allude in his name, Morose. Beside this, I am assured from divers persons, that Ben Jonson was actually acquainted with such a man, one altogether as ridiculous as he is here represented. Others say it is not enough to find one man of such an humour; it must be common to more, and the more common the more natural. To prove this, they instance in the best of comical characters, Falstaff. There are many men resembling him; old, fat, merry, cowardly, drunken, amorous, vain, and lying. But to convince these people, I need but tell them, that humour is the ridiculous extravagance of conversation, wherein one man differs from all others. If then it be common, or communicated to many, how differs it from other men's? or what indeed causes it to be ridiculous so much as the singularity of it? As for Falstaff, he is not properly one humour, but a miscellany of humours or images, drawn from so many several men; that wherein he is singular is his wit, or those things he says, *praeter expectatum*, unexpected by the audience; his quick evasions when you imagine him surprised, which as they are extremely diverting of themselves, so receive a great addition from his person; for the very sight of such an unwieldy old debauched fellow is a comedy alone. And here having a place so proper for it, I cannot but enlarge somewhat upon this subject of humour into which I am fallen. The Ancients had little of it in their comedies; for the τὸ γελοῖον,[60] of the Old Comedy, of which Aristophanes was chief, was not so much to imitate a man, as to make the people laugh at some odd conceit, which had commonly somewhat of unnatural or obscene in it. Thus when you see Socrates brought upon the stage you are not to imagine him made ridiculous by

[59]There are actually six different locations, and the action of the play takes up more than twelve hours, or more than an "artificial" day. [Ed.]

[60]The ridiculous. [Ed.]

the imitation of his actions, but rather by making him perform something very unlike himself, something so childish and absurd, as by comparing it with the gravity of the true Socrates, makes a ridiculous object for the spectators. In their New Comedy which succeeded, the poets sought indeed to express the ἦθος, as in their tragedies the πάθος of mankind.[61] But this ἦθος contained only the general characters of men and manners; as old men, lovers, serving-men, courtesans, parasites, and such other persons as we see in their comedies; all which they made alike: that is, one old man or father; one lover, one courtesan so like another, as if the first of them had begot the rest of every sort: *ex homine hunc natum dicas*.[62] The same custom they observed likewise in their tragedies. As for the French, though they have the word *humeur* among them, yet they have small use of it in their comedies, or farces; they being but ill imitations of the *ridiculum*, or that which stirred up laughter in the Old Comedy. But among the English 'tis otherwise, whereby humour is meant some extravagant habit, passion, or affection, particular (as I said before) to some one person, by the oddness of which, he is immediately distinguished from the rest of men; which being lively and naturally represented, most frequently begets that malicious pleasure in the audience which is testified by laughter, as all things which are deviations from customs are ever the aptest to produce it, though by the way this laughter is only accidental, as the person represented is fantastic or bizarre. But pleasure is essential to it, as the imitation of what is natural. The description of these humours, drawn from the knowledge and observation of particular persons, was the peculiar genius and talent of Ben Jonson; to whose play I now return.

Besides Morose, there are at least nine or ten different characters and humours in *The Silent Woman*, all which persons have several concernments of their own, yet are all used by the poet, to the conducting of the main design to perfec-

tion. I shall not waste time in commending the writing of this play, but I will give you my opinion, that there is more wit and acuteness of fancy in it than in any of Ben Jonson's. Besides, that he has here described the conversation of gentlemen in the persons of Truewit, and his friends, with more gaiety, air and freedom, than in the rest of his comedies. For the contrivance of the plot, 'tis extreme elaborate, and yet withal easy; for the λύσις, or untying of it, 'tis so admirable, that when it is done, no one of the audience would think the poet could have missed it; and yet it was concealed so much before the last scene, that any other way would sooner have entered into your thoughts. But I dare not take upon me to commend the fabric of it, because it is altogether so full of art, that I must unravel every scene in it to commend it as I ought. And this excellent contrivance is still the more to be admired, because 'tis comedy where the persons are only of common rank, and their business private, not elevated by passions or high concernments as in serious plays. Here everyone is a proper judge of all he sees; nothing is represented but that with which he daily converses: so that by consequence all faults lie open to discovery, and few are pardonable. 'Tis this which Horace has judiciously observed:

Creditur ex medio quia res arcessit habere
sudoris minimum, sed habet Comedia tanto
plus oneris, quanto veniae minus. — [63]

But our poet, who was not ignorant of these difficulties, has made use of all advantages, as he who designs a large leap takes his rise from the highest ground. One of these advantages is that which Corneille has laid down as the greatest which can arrive to any poem, and which he himself could never compass above thrice in all his plays, viz., the making choice of some signal and long-expected day, whereon the action of the play is to depend. This day was that designed by Dauphine for the settling of his uncle's estate upon him; which to compass he contrives to marry him. That the marriage had been plotted

[61]*Ethos* in Aristotle is "character": *pathos* is "suffering" — in particular the tragic deed. [Ed.]

[62]"You'd say the spit and image." Terence, *Eunuch*, 460. [Ed.]

[63]"One might think that Comedy takes less work because its matter comes from daily life, but it takes more because less allowance is made." Horace, *Epistles* II.1:168–70. [Ed.]

by him long beforehand is made evident by what he tells Truewit in the second act, that in one moment he had destroyed what he had been raising many months.

There is another artifice of the poet, which I cannot here omit, because by the frequent practice of it in his comedies, he has left it to us almost as a rule, that is, when he has any character or humour wherein he would show a *coup de maistre*, or his highest skill; he recommends it to your observation by a pleasant description of it before the person first appears. Thus, in *Bartholomew Fair* he gives you the pictures of Numps and Cokes, and in this those of Daw, Lafoole, Morose, and the Collegiate Ladies; all which you hear described before you see them. So that before they come upon the stage you have a longing expectation of them, which prepares you to receive them favourably; and when they are there, even from their first appearance you are so far acquainted with them, that nothing of their humour is lost to you.

I will observe yet one thing further of this admirable plot; the business of it rises in every act. The second is greater than the first, the third than the second, and so forward to the fifth. There too you see, till the very last scene, new difficulties arising to obstruct the action of the play; and when the audience is brought into despair that the business can naturally be effected, then, and not before, the discovery is made. But that the poet might entertain you with more variety all this while, he reserves some new characters to show you, which he opens not till the second and third act. In the second Morose, Daw, the Barber and Otter; in the third the Collegiate Ladies, all which he moves afterwards in by-walks, or under-plots, as diversions to the main design, lest it should grow tedious, though they are still naturally joined with it, and somewhere or other subservient to it. Thus, like a skilful chess-player, by little and little he draws out his men, and makes his pawns of use to his greater persons.

If this comedy, and some others of his, were translated into French prose (which would now be no wonder to them, since Molière has lately given them plays out of verse which have not displeased them) I believe the controversy would soon be decided betwixt the two nations, even making them the judges. But we need not call our heroes to our aid. Be it spoken to the honour of the English, our nation can never want in any age such who are able to dispute the empire of wit with any people in the universe. And though the fury of a civil war, and power, for twenty years together, abandoned to a barbarous race of men, enemies of all good learning, had buried the muses under the ruins of monarchy, yet with the restoration of our happiness, we see revived poesy lifting up its head, and already shaking off the rubbish which lay so heavy on it. We have seen since his majesty's return, many dramatic poems which yield not to those of any foreign nation, and which deserve all laurels but the English. I will set aside flattery and envy. It cannot be denied but we have had some little blemish either in the plot or writing of all those plays which have been made within these seven years: (and perhaps there is no nation in the world so quick to discern them, or so difficult to pardon them, as ours:) yet if we can persuade ourselves to use the candour of that poet, who (though the most severe of critics) has left us this caution by which to moderate our censures;

— Ubi plura nitent in carmine non ego paucis offendar maculis.[64]

If in consideration of their many and great beauties, we can wink at some slight, and little imperfections; if we, I say, can be thus equal to ourselves, I ask no favour from the French. And if I do not venture upon any particular judgement of our late plays, 'tis out of the consideration which an ancient writer gives me; *Vivorum, ut magna admiratio, ita censura difficilis*: betwixt the extremes of admiration and malice, 'tis hard to judge uprightly of the living. Only I think it may be permitted me to say, that as it is no lessening to us to yield to some plays, and those not many of our own nation in the last age, so can it be no addition to pronounce of our present poets that they have far surpassed all the Ancients, and the modern writers of other countries.

---

[64]"Give me more good lines than bad / and I'll read you cheerfully." Horace, *Art of Poetry*, 352; see p. 74. [Ed.]

This, my Lord, was the substance of what was then spoke on that occasion; and Lisideius, I think, was going to reply, when he was prevented thus by Crites: "I am confident," said he, "that the most material things that can be said have been already urged on either side; if they have not, I must beg of Lisideius that he will defer his answer till another time: for I confess I have a joint quarrel to you both, because you have concluded, without any reason given for it, that rhyme is proper for the stage. I will not dispute how ancient it hath been among us to write this way; perhaps our ancestors knew no better till Shakespeare's time. I will grant it was not altogether left by him, and that Fletcher and Ben Jonson used it frequently in their Pastorals, and sometimes in other plays. Farther, I will not argue whether we received it originally from our own countrymen, or from the French; for that is an inquiry of as little benefit, as theirs who, in the midst of the great Plague, were not so solicitous to provide against it as to know whether we had it from the malignity of our own air, or by transportation from Holland. I have therefore only to affirm, that it is not allowable in serious plays; for comedies, I find you already concluding with me. To prove this, I might satisfy myself to tell you, how much in vain it is for you to strive against the stream of the people's inclination; the greatest part of which are prepossessed so much with those excellent plays of Shakespeare, Fletcher, and Ben Jonson, which have been written out of rhyme, that except you could bring them such as were written better in it, and those too by persons of equal reputation with them, it will be impossible for you to gain your cause with them, who will still be judges. This it is to which, in fine, all your reasons must submit. The unanimous consent of an audience is so powerful, that even Julius Cæsar (as Macrobius reports of him), when he was perpetual dictator, was not able to balance it on the other side. But when Laberius, a Roman Knight, at his request contended in the Mime with another poet, he was forced to cry out, *Etiam favente me victus es, Laberi.*[65] But I will not on this occasion take the advantage of the greater number, but only urge such reasons against rhyme, as I find in the writings of those who have argued for the other way. First then, I am of opinion, that rhyme is unnatural in a play, because dialogue there is presented as the effect of sudden thought: for a play is the imitation of Nature; and since no man without premeditation speaks in rhyme, neither ought he to do it on the stage. This hinders not but the fancy may be there elevated to an higher pitch of thought than it is in ordinary discourse; for there is a probability that men of excellent and quick parts may speak noble things *ex tempore*: but those thoughts are never fettered with the numbers or sound of verse without study, and therefore it cannot be but unnatural to present the most free way of speaking in that which is the most constrained. For this reason, says Aristotle, 'tis best to write tragedy in that kind of verse which is the least such, or which is nearest prose: and this amongst the Ancients was the iambic, and with us is blank verse, or the measure of verse kept exactly without rhyme. These numbers therefore are fittest for a play; the others for a paper of verses, or a poem; blank verse being as much below them, as rhyme is improper for the Drama. And if it be objected that neither are blank verses made *ex tempore*, yet, as nearest nature, they are still to be preferred. But there are two particular exceptions, which many besides myself have had to verse; by which it will appear yet more plainly how improper it is in plays. And the first of them is grounded on that very reason for which some have commended rhyme; they say, the quickness of repartees in argumentative scenes receives an ornament from verse. Now what is more unreasonable than to imagine that a man should not only light upon the wit, but the rhyme too, upon the sudden? This nicking of him who spoke before both in sound and measure, is so great an happiness, that you must at least suppose the persons of your play to be born poets: *Arcades omnes, et cantare pares, et respondere parati:*[66] they must have arrived to the degree of *quicquid conabar dicere*;[67] to make verses almost whether they will

[65]"Even with me favoring you, you are beaten, Laberius." Macrobius, *Saturnalia* 2:7. [Ed.]

[66]"All Arcadians, prepared to sing and to respond." Virgil, *Eclogues* 7:4–5. [Ed.]

[67]"To say whatever I tried to say." [Ed.]

or no. If they are any thing below this, it will look rather like the design of two, than the answer of one: it will appear that your actors hold intelligence together; that they perform their tricks like fortune-tellers, by confederacy. The hand of art will be too visible in it, against that maxim of all professions, *Ars est celare artem*, that it is the greatest perfection of art to keep itself undiscovered. Nor will it serve you to object, that however you manage it, 'tis still known to be a play; and, consequently, the dialogue of two persons understood to be the labour of one poet. For a play is still an imitation of Nature; we know we are to be deceived, and we desire to be so; but no man ever was deceived but with a probability of truth; for who will suffer a gross lie to be fastened on him? Thus we sufficiently understand, that the scenes which represent cities and countries to us are not really such, but only painted on boards and canvas; but shall that excuse the ill painture or designment of them? Nay, rather ought they not to be laboured with so much the more diligence and exactness, to help the imagination? since the mind of man does naturally tend to, and seek after truth; and therefore the nearer any thing comes to the imitation of it, the more it pleases.

"Thus, you see, your rhyme is uncapable of expressing the greatest thoughts naturally, and the lowest it cannot with any grace: for what is more unbefitting the majesty of verse, than to call a servant, or bid a door be shut in rhyme? And yet this miserable necessity you are forced upon. But verse, you say, circumscribes a quick and luxuriant fancy, which would extend itself too far on every subject, did not the labour which is required to well-turned and polished rhyme, set bounds to it. Yet this argument, if granted, would only prove that we may write better in verse, but not more naturally. Neither is it able to evince that; for he who wants judgment to confine his fancy in blank verse, may want it as much in rhyme: and he who has it will avoid errors in both kinds. Latin verse was as great a confinement to the imagination of those poets, as rhyme to ours; and yet you find Ovid saying too much on every subject. *Nescivit* (says Seneca) *quod bene cessit relinquere*:[68] of which he

gives you one famous instance in his description of the deluge:

*Omnia pontus erat, deerant quoque litora ponto.*
Now all was sea, nor had that sea a shore.

Thus Ovid's fancy was not limited by verse, and Virgil needed not verse to have bounded his.

"In our own language we see Ben Jonson confining himself to what ought to be said, even in the liberty of blank verse; and yet Corneille, the most judicious of the French poets, is still varying the same sense an hundred ways, and dwelling eternally on the same subject, though confined by rhyme. Some other exceptions I have to verse; but being these I have named are for the most part already public, I conceive it reasonable they should first be answered."

"It concerns me less than any," said Neander (seeing he had ended), "to reply to this discourse; because when I should have proved that verse may be natural in plays, yet I should always be ready to confess, that those which I have written in this kind come short of that perfection which is required. Yet since you are pleased I should undertake this province, I will do it, though with all imaginable respect and deference, both to that person from whom you have borrowed your strongest arguments, and to whose judgment, when I have said all, I finally submit. But before I proceed to answer your objections, I must first remember you, that I exclude all Comedy from my defence; and next that I deny not but blank verse may be also used; and content myself only to assert, that in serious plays where the subject and characters are great, and the plot unmixed with mirth, which might allay or divert these concernments which are produced, rhyme is there as natural and more effectual than blank verse.

"And now having laid down this as a foundation, to begin with Crites, I must crave leave to tell him, that some of his arguments against rhyme reach no farther than, from the faults or defects of ill rhyme, to conclude against the use of it in general. May not I conclude against blank

---

[68] "He does not know when to leave well enough alone."

Marcus Seneca, spoken of Ovid, in *Controversiae*. But the quotation and praise of the line from Ovid's *Metamorphoses* is by Lucius Seneca in *Quaestiones Naturales*. [Ed.]

verse by the same reason? If the words of some poets who write in it, are either ill chosen, or ill placed, which makes not only rhyme, but all kind of verse in any language unnatural, shall I, for their vicious affectation, condemn those excellent lines of Fletcher, which are written in that kind? Is there any thing in rhyme more constrained than this line in blank verse, *I heaven invoke, and strong resistance make?* where you see both the clauses are placed unnaturally, that is, contrary to the common way of speaking, and that without the excuse of a rhyme to cause it: yet you would think me very ridiculous, if I should accuse the stubbornness of blank verse for this, and not rather the stiffness of the poet. Therefore, Crites, you must either prove that words, though well chosen, and duly placed, yet render not rhyme natural in itself; or that, however natural and easy the rhyme may be, yet it is not proper for a play. If you insist on the former part, I would ask you, what other conditions are required to make rhyme natural in itself, besides an election of apt words, and a right disposing of them? For the due choice of your words expresses your sense naturally, and the due placing them adapts the rhyme to it. If you object that one verse may be made for the sake of another, though both the words and rhyme be apt, I answer, it cannot possibly so fall out; for either there is a dependence of sense betwixt the first line and the second, or there is none: if there be that connection, then in the natural position of the words the latter line must of necessity flow from the former; if there be no dependence, yet still the due ordering of words makes the last line as natural in itself as the other: so that the necessity of a rhyme never forces any but bad or lazy writers to say what they would not otherwise. 'Tis true, there is both care and art required to write in verse. A good poet never concludes upon the first line, till he has sought out such a rhyme as may fit the sense, already prepared to heighten the second: many times the close of the sense falls into the middle of the next verse, or farther off, and he may often prevail himself of the same advantages in English which Virgil had in Latin; he may break off in the hemistich,[69] and begin another line. Indeed,

the not observing these two last things, makes plays which are writ in verse so tedious: for though, most commonly, the sense is to be confined to the couplet, yet nothing that does *perpetuo tenore fluere*, run in the same channel, can please always. 'Tis like the murmuring of a stream, which not varying in the fall, causes at first attention, at last drowsiness. Variety of cadences is the best rule; the greatest help to the actors, and refreshment to the audience.

"If then verse may be made natural in itself, how becomes it improper to a play? You say the stage is the representation of Nature, and no man in ordinary conversation speaks in rhyme. But you foresaw when you said this, that it might be answered — neither does any man speak in blank verse, or in measure without rhyme. Therefore you concluded, that which is nearest Nature is still to be preferred. But you took no notice that rhyme might be made as natural as blank verse, by the well placing of the words, &c. All the difference between them, when they are both correct, is, the sound in one, which the other wants; and if so, the sweetness of it, and all the advantage resulting from it, which are handled in the Preface to *The Rival Ladies*,[70] will yet stand good. As for that place of Aristotle, where he says, plays should be writ in that kind of verse which is nearest prose, it makes little for you; blank verse being properly but measured prose. Now measure alone, in any modern language, does not constitute verse; those of the Ancients in Greek and Latin consisted in quantity of words, and a determinate number of feet. But when, by the inundation of the Goths and Vandals into Italy, new languages were brought in, and barbarously mingled with the Latin, of which the Italian, Spanish, French, and ours (made out of them and the Teutonic) are dialects, a new way of poesy was practised; new, I say, in those countries, for in all probability it was that of the conquerors in their own nations. This new way consisted in measure or number of feet, and rhyme; the sweetness of rhyme, and observation of accent, supplying the place of quantity in words, which could neither exactly be observed by those Barbarians, who knew not the rules of

[69]Halfway through the hexameter verse. [Ed.]

[70]Dryden's *The Rival Ladies* (1664) was partly in rhyme; his preface had defended the practice. [Ed.]

it, neither was it suitable to their tongues, as it had been to the Greek and Latin. No man is tied in modern poesy to observe any farther rule in the feet of his verse, but that they be dissyllables; whether spondee, trochee, or iambic, it matters not; only he is obliged to rhyme. Neither do the Spanish, French, Italian, or Germans, acknowledge at all, or very rarely, any such kind of poesy as blank verse amongst them. Therefore, at most 'tis but a poetic prose, a *sermo pedestris*; and as such, most fit for comedies, where I acknowledge rhyme to be improper. Farther; as to that quotation of Aristotle, our couplet verses may be rendered as near prose as blank verse itself, by using those advantages I lately named, as breaks in a hemistich, or running the sense into another line, thereby making art and order appear as loose and free as nature: or not tying ourselves to couplets strictly, we may use the benefit of the Pindaric way practised in *The Siege of Rhodes*;[71] where the numbers vary, and the rhyme is disposed carelessly, and far from often chiming. Neither is that other advantage of the Ancients to be despised, of changing the kind of verse when they please, with the change of the scene, or some new entrance; for they confine not themselves always to iambics, but extend their liberty to all lyric numbers, and sometimes even to hexameter. But I need not go so far to prove that rhyme, as it succeeds to all other offices of Greek and Latin verse, so especially to this of plays, since the custom of all nations at this day confirms it, all the French, Italian, and Spanish tragedies are generally writ in it; and sure the universal consent of the most civilized parts of the world ought in this, as it doth in other customs, to include the rest.

"But perhaps you may tell me, I have proposed such a way to make rhyme natural, and consequently proper to plays, as is unpracticable; and that I shall scarce find six or eight lines together in any play, where the words are so placed and chosen as is required to make it natural. I answer, no poet need constrain himself at all times to it. It is enough he makes it his general

rule; for I deny not but sometimes there may be a greatness in placing the words otherwise; and sometimes they may sound better, sometimes also the variety itself is excuse enough. But if, for the most part, the words be placed as they are in the negligence of prose, it is sufficient to denominate the way practicable; for we esteem that to be such, which in the trial oftener succeeds than misses. And thus far you may find the practice made good in many plays: where you do not, remember still, that if you cannot find six natural rhymes together, it will be as hard for you to produce as many lines in blank verse, even among the greatest of our poets, against which I cannot make some reasonable exception.

"And this, Sir, calls to my remembrance the beginning of your discourse, where you told us we should never find the audience favourable to this kind of writing, till we could produce as good plays in rhyme, as Ben Jonson, Fletcher, and Shakespeare, had writ out of it. But it is to raise envy to the living, to compare them with the dead. They are honoured, and almost adored by us, as they deserve; neither do I know any so presumptuous of themselves as to contend with them. Yet give me leave to say thus much, without injury to their ashes; that not only we shall never equal them, but they could never equal themselves, were they to rise and write again. We acknowledge them our fathers in wit; but they have ruined their estates themselves, before they came to their children's hands. There is scarce an humour, a character, or any kind of plot, which they have not blown upon. All comes sullied or wasted to us: and were they to entertain this age, they could not make so plenteous treatments out of such decayed fortunes. This therefore will be a good argument to us, either not to write at all, or to attempt some other way. There is no bays to be expected in their walks: *tentanda via est, qua me quoque possum tollere humo*.[72]

"This way of writing in verse they have only left free to us; our age is arrived to a perfection in it, which they never knew; and which (if we may guess by what of theirs we have seen in

[71]An operatic entertainment (1656) by Sir William Davenant, prototype of the Restoration heroic play and influenced by Abraham Cowley's pindarics. [Ed.]

[72]"I too must find a way to raise myself from the earth." Virgil, *Georgics* 3:8–9. [Ed.]

verse, as *The Faithful Shepherdess*, and *Sad Shepherd*)[73] 'tis probable they never could have reached. For the genius of every age is different; and though ours excel in this, I deny not but that to imitate Nature in that perfection which they did in prose, is a greater commendation than to write in verse exactly. As for what you have added, that the people are not generally inclined to like this way; if it were true, it would be no wonder, that betwixt the shaking off an old habit, and the introducing of a new, there should be difficulty. Do we not see them stick to Hopkins' and Sternhold's psalms, and forsake those of David, I mean Sandys his translation of them? If by the people you understand the multitude, οἱ πολλοί, 'tis no matter what they think; they are sometimes in the right, sometimes in the wrong: their judgment is a mere lottery. *Est ubi plebs recte putat, est ubi peccat.*[74] Horace says it of the vulgar, judging poesy. But if you mean the mixed audience of the populace and the noblesse, I dare confidently affirm that a great part of the latter sort are already favourable to verse; and that no serious plays written since the King's return have been more kindly received by them, than *The Siege of Rhodes*, the *Mustapha*, *The Indian Queen*, and *Indian Emperor*.[75]

"But I come now to the inference of your first argument. You said the dialogue of plays is presented as the effect of sudden thought, but no man speaks suddenly, or *ex tempore*, in rhyme; and you inferred from thence, that rhyme, which you acknowledge to be proper to epic poesy, cannot equally be proper to dramatic, unless we could suppose all men born so much more than poets, that verses should be made in them, not by them.

"It has been formerly urged by you, and confessed by me, that since no man spoke any kind of verse *ex tempore*, that which was nearest Nature was to be preferred. I answer you, therefore,

by distinguishing betwixt what is nearest to the nature of Comedy, which is the imitation of common persons and ordinary speaking, and what is nearest the nature of a serious play: this last is indeed the representation of Nature, but 'tis Nature wrought up to an higher pitch. The plot, the characters, the wit, the passions, the descriptions, are all exalted above the level of common converse, as high as the imagination of the poet can carry them, with proportion to verisimility. Tragedy, we know, is wont to image to us the minds and fortunes of noble persons, and to portray these exactly; heroic rhyme is nearest Nature, as being the noblest kind of modern verse.

*Indignatur enim privatis et prope socco*
*Dignis carminibus narrari cœna Thyestæ,*[76]

says Horace: and in another place,

*Effutire leves indigna tragœdia versus.*[77]

Blank verse is acknowledged to be too low for a poem, nay more, for a paper of verses; but if too low for an ordinary sonnet, how much more for Tragedy, which is by Aristotle, in the dispute betwixt the epic poesy and the dramatic, for many reasons he there alleges, ranked above it?

"But setting this defence aside, your argument is almost as strong against the use of rhyme in poems as in plays; for the epic way is every where interlaced with dialogue, or discoursive scenes; and therefore you must either grant rhyme to be improper there, which is contrary to your assertion, or admit it into plays by the same title which you have given it to poems. For though Tragedy be justly preferred above the other, yet there is a great affinity between them, as may easily be discovered in that definition of a play which Lisideius gave us. The *genus* of them is the same, a just and lively image of human nature, in its actions, passions, and traverses of fortune: so is the end, namely, for the delight and benefit of mankind. The characters and persons are still the same, viz. the greatest of both sorts; only the manner of acquainting us

---

[73]By Beaumont and Fletcher, and Ben Jonson, respectively. [Ed.]

[74]"Sometimes the people are right and sometimes wrong." Horace, *Epistles* 2.1:63. [Ed.]

[75]*Mustapha* (1665) was by Roger Boyle, Earl of Orrery; *The Indian Queen* (1664) by Dryden and Sir Robert Howard; *The Indian Emperor* (1665) by Dryden. [Ed.]

[76]"It is inappropriate to relate the banquet of Thyestes in light verse." Horace, *Art of Poetry*, 90–91; see p. 69. [Ed.]

[77]"It is inappropriate for tragedy to babble in light verse." Horace, *Art of Poetry*, 231; see p. 72. [Ed.]

with those actions, passions, and fortunes, is different. Tragedy performs it *viva voce*, or by action, in dialogue; wherein it excels the Epic Poem, which does it chiefly by narration, and therefore is not so lively an image of human nature. However, the agreement betwixt them is such, that if rhyme be proper for one, it must be for the other. Verse, 'tis true, is not the effect of sudden thought; but this hinders not that sudden thought may be represented in verse, since those thoughts are such as must be higher than Nature can raise them without premeditation, especially to a continuance of them, even out of verse; and consequently you cannot imagine them to have been sudden either in the poet or in the actors. A play, as I have said, to be like Nature, is to be set above it; as statues which are placed on high are made greater than the life, that they may descend to the sight in their just proportion.

"Perhaps I have insisted too long on this objection; but the clearing of it will make my stay shorter on the rest. You tell us, Crites, that rhyme appears most unnatural in repartees, or short replies: when he who answers, it being presumed he knew not what the other would say, yet makes up that part of the verse which was left incomplete, and supplies both the sound and measure of it. This, you say, looks rather like the confederacy of two, than the answer of one.

"This, I confess, is an objection which is in every one's mouth, who loves not rhyme: but suppose, I beseech you, the repartee were made only in blank verse, might not part of the same argument be turned against you? for the measure is as often supplied there, as it is in rhyme; the latter half of the hemistich as commonly made up, or a second line subjoined as a reply to the former; which any one leaf in Jonson's plays will sufficiently clear to you. You will often find in the Greek tragedians, and in Seneca, that when a scene grows up into the warmth of repartees, which is the close fighting of it, the latter part of the trimeter is supplied by him who answers; and yet it was never observed as a fault in them by any of the ancient or modern critics. The case is the same in our verse, as it was in theirs; rhyme to us being in lieu of quantity to them. But if no latitude is to be allowed a poet, you take from

him not only his licence of *quidlibet audendi*,[78] but you tie him up in a straiter compass than you would a philosopher. This is indeed *Musas colere severiores*.[79] You would have him follow Nature, but he must follow her on foot; you have dismounted him from his Pegasus. But you tell us, this supplying the last half of a verse, or adjoining a whole second to the former, looks more like the design of two, than the answer of one. Supposing we acknowledge it: how comes this confederacy to be more displeasing to you, than in a dance which is well contrived? You see there the united design of many persons to make up one figure: after they have separated themselves in many petty divisions, they rejoin one by one into a gross: the confederacy is plain amongst them, for chance could never produce any thing so beautiful; and yet there is nothing in it, that shocks your sight. I acknowledge the hand of art appears in repartee, as of necessity it must in all kinds of verse. But there is also the quick and poynant brevity of it (which is an high imitation of Nature in those sudden gusts of passion) to mingle with it; and this, joined with the cadency and sweetness of the rhyme, leaves nothing in the soul of the hearer to desire. 'Tis an art which appears; but it appears only like the shadowings of painture, which being to cause the rounding of it, cannot be absent; but while that is considered, they are lost: so while we attend to the other beauties of the matter, the care and labour of the rhyme is carried from us, or at least drowned in its own sweetness, as bees are sometimes buried in their honey. When a poet has found the repartee, the last perfection he can add to it, is to put it into verse. However good the thought may be, however apt the words in which 'tis couched, yet he finds himself at a little unrest, while rhyme is wanting: he cannot leave it till that comes naturally, and then is at ease, and sits down contented.

"From replies, which are the most elevated thoughts of verse, you pass to the most mean

[78]"Daring anything." Horace, *Art of Poetry*, 10; see p. 68. [Ed.]

[79]"To worship the severer muses." Martial, *Epigrams* 9.11:17. [Ed.]

ones, those which are common with the lowest of household conversation. In these, you say, the majesty of verse suffers. You instance in the calling of a servant, or commanding a door to be shut, in rhyme. This, Crites, is a good observation of yours, but no argument: for it proves no more but that such thoughts should be waived, as often as may be, by the address of the poet. But suppose they are necessary in the places where he uses them, yet there is no need to put them into rhyme. He may place them in the beginning of a verse, and break it off, as unfit, when so debased, for any other use; or granting the worst, that they require more room than the hemistich will allow, yet still there is a choice to be made of the best words, and least vulgar (provided they be apt) to express such thoughts. Many have blamed rhyme in general, for this fault, when the poet with a little care might have redressed it. But they do it with no more justice, than if English Poesy should be made ridiculous for the sake of the Water Poet's rhymes.[80] Our language is noble, full, and significant; and I know not why he who is master of it may not clothe ordinary things in it as decently as the Latin, if he use the same diligence in his choice of words. *Delectus verborum origo est eloquentiae.*[81] It was the saying of Julius Cæsar, one so curious in his, that none of them can be changed but for a worse. One would think, *unlock the door*, was a thing as vulgar as could be spoken; and yet Seneca could make it sound high and lofty in his Latin:

*Reserate clusos regii postes laris.*[82]
Set wide the palace gates.

"But I turn from this exception, both because it happens not above twice or thrice in any play that those vulgar thoughts are used; and then too, were there no other apology to be made, yet the necessity of them which is alike in all kind of writing, may excuse them. Besides that the great eagerness and precipitation with which they are spoken makes us rather mind the substance than the dress; that for which they are spoken, rather than what is spoken. For they are always the effect of some hasty concernment, and something of consequence depends on them.

"Thus, Crites, I have endeavoured to answer your objections; it remains only that I should vindicate an argument for verse, which you have gone about to overthrow. It had formerly been said, that the easiness of blank verse renders the poet too luxuriant, but that the labour of rhyme bounds and circumscribes an overfruitful fancy; the sense there being commonly confined to the couplet, and the words so ordered that the rhyme naturally follows them, not they the rhyme. To this you answered, that it was no argument to the question in hand; for the dispute was not which way a man may write best, but which is most proper for the subject on which he writes.

"First, give me leave, Sir, to remember you, that the argument against which you raised this objection, was only secondary: it was built on this hypothesis, that to write in verse was proper for serious plays. Which supposition being granted (as it was briefly made out in that discourse, by showing how verse might be made natural), it asserted, that this way of writing was an help to the poet's judgment, by putting bounds to a wild overflowing fancy. I think, therefore, it will not be hard for me to make good what it was to prove. But you add, that were this let pass, yet he who wants judgment in the liberty of his fancy, may as well show the defect of it when he is confined to verse; for he who has judgment will avoid errors, and he who has it not, will commit them in all kinds of writing.

"This argument, as you have taken it from a most acute person,[83] so I confess it carries much weight in it: but by using the word judgment here indefinitely, you seem to have put a fallacy upon us. I grant, he who has judgment, that is, so profound, so strong, so infallible a judgment, that he needs no helps to keep it always poised and upright, will commit no faults either in

---

[80] John Taylor (1580–1653), boatman on the Thames and facetious poet. [Ed.]

[81] "Choice of words is the fount of eloquence." Cicero, *Brutus* 72:253, misquoted. [Ed.]

[82] Seneca, *Hippolytus*, 863. [Ed.]

[83] From Sir Robert Howard's preface to *Four New Plays* (1665). [Ed.]

rhyme or out of it. And on the other extreme, he who has a judgment so weak and crazed that no helps can correct or amend it, shall write scurvily out of rhyme, and worse in it. But the first of these judgments is no where to be found, and the latter is not fit to write at all. To speak therefore of judgment as it is in the best poets; they who have the greatest proportion of it, want other helps than from it, within. As for example, you would be loth to say, that he who was endued with a sound judgment had no need of History, Geography, or Moral Philosophy, to write correctly. Judgment is indeed the master-workman in a play; but he requires many subordinate hands, many tools to his assistance. And verse I affirm to be one of these; 'tis a rule and line by which he keeps his building compact and even, which otherwise lawless imagination would raise either irregularly or loosely. At least, if the poet commits errors with this help, he would make greater and more without it: 'tis, in short, a slow and painful, but the surest kind of working. Ovid, whom you accuse for luxuriancy in verse, had perhaps been farther guilty of it, had he writ in prose. And for your instance of Ben Jonson, who, you say, writ exactly without the help of rhyme; you are to remember, 'tis only an aid to a luxuriant fancy, which his was not: as he did

not want imagination, so none ever said he had much to spare. Neither was verse then refined so much to be an help to that age, as it is to ours. Thus then the second thoughts being usually the best, as receiving the maturest digestion from judgment, and the last and most mature product of those thoughts being artful and laboured verse, it may well be inferred, that verse is a great help to a luxuriant fancy; and this is what that argument which you opposed was to evince."

Neander was pursuing this discourse so eagerly, that Eugenius had called to him twice or thrice, ere he took notice that the barge stood still, and that they were at the foot of Somerset Stairs, where they had appointed it to land. The company were all sorry to separate so soon, though a great part of the evening was already spent; and stood a while looking back on the water, which the moon-beams played upon, and made it appear like floating quick-silver: at last they went up through a crowd of French people, who were merrily dancing in the open air, and nothing concerned for the noise of guns which had alarmed the town that afternoon. Walking thence together to the Piazze, they parted there; Eugenius and Lisideius to some pleasant appointment they had made, and Crites and Neander to their several lodgings.

# Alexander Pope
## 1688–1744

Born into a Roman Catholic family in the year the last Catholic monarch of England, James II, was forced to abdicate his throne, Alexander Pope was legally barred from a university education and from many careers. From his wet nurse he caught a severe case of spinal tuberculosis, which left him dwarfed, twisted, and delicate of constitution. Nevertheless, with the private education provided by his father, a well-to-do merchant of London just retired to Windsor Forest, Pope crafted himself into the prodigy and soon into the poet of eighteenth-century England, its laureate in all but name. His translations of the *Iliad* and the *Odyssey* (1720 and 1725) not only made him a fortune in royalties, they set the poetic standard for the age; his *Essay on Man* (1733) became its optimistic and rationalistic creed. What has best survived, however, are his satires, delicate fantasies like *The Rape of the Lock* (1714), or vitriolic diatribes like *An Epistle to Dr. Arbuthnot* (1735) and the *Dunciad* (1728–43).

The *Essay on Criticism*, published in 1711 and written possibly as early as 1707, belongs to Pope's earliest years, when he "lisp'd in numbers, and the numbers came." It would be astonishing for any nineteen-year-old, however learned, to make an original contribution to literary theory, and in fact, the *Essay on Criticism* is original only in that it is addressed to critics rather than to poets. But since Pope considered it the critic's first duty to endeavor to comprehend fully and disinterestedly the poem's form, matter, and end, the *Essay* easily and often shifts its focus from qualities of criticism to qualities of poetry. Pope's central ideas are the standard poetic notions of the Augustan Age, drawn from a variety of classical and Renaissance sources — from Horace and Quintilian to Boileau and Dryden — but these well-worn truths he imbues with a clarity and brilliance of expression.

The central and recurring image of the *Essay on Criticism* is that of the eternal war between critics, who judge according to a rigid system of regulations, and poets, hemmed in by such rules and longing to soar. By and large, although Pope presents the poets' perspective, he sides with the critics. While he insists that "some beauties yet no precepts can declare / For there's a happiness as well as care," and admits that poets can through genius "snatch a grace beyond the reach of art," he also warns them that remorseless criticism will justly clip their wings should they depart from the precedent of the rules and practices of the ancients. The critics come in for a lashing in Part II, where they are attacked for partial readings, partial both in the sense that their praise and blame depend on the congruence of their party politics with that of the poet, and in the sense that they take only a single aspect of a poem into account without understanding its end or how it relates to the chosen means. Pope's demonstrations of prosody and imagery here have become classic citations.

Pope's tendency to use his central terms in a variety of related but distinct ways can be confusing. "Nature" is sometimes used to signify the objective world of creation and other times to mean human nature or the instinctual basis of our humanity. "Art" can be opposed to "Nature" in any of the following senses: It can be the world of human invention, as opposed to that of divine creation; it can be technique and craft, as opposed to creative instinct; it can be the rules behind a skill, as opposed to the skill itself; it can be (as in its usual modern meaning) the class of objects created by human intelligence and creativity. "Wit" is even more ambiguous than "Art" and "Nature" and can partake of either realm: It may mean "sense," or "intelligence" or "verbal facility" or "genius" or "creative power," or it may signify a person with any of these qualities — or just an educated person in general. These shifts, which are not announced, can create an immense and bewildering compression of meaning. When Pope claims that nature is "at once the source, and end, and test of Art," he may be using both Nature and Art in three different senses. Context is a guide here, and fortunately, the context is enhanced by Pope's tendency to repeat each of his ideas at least once before moving on to the next.

What may be more problematic for the reader is Pope's tendency to draw a distinction only to collapse it later on. Like Sidney, Pope suggests that the poet requires natural genius, a knowledge of the rules of art, and an education based on the classics to provide models for imitation. But art and nature, creation and imitation, turn out to be false dichotomies. The rules of art remain "Nature still, but Nature methodiz'd"; Virgil discovers that imitating Nature and imitating Homer are "the same." Pope in 1711 is content to leave such contradictions unresolved as poetic paradoxes; in later hands, like those of David Hume and Immanuel Kant, these issues will recur as evidence of inward mental structures common to humanity.

## Selected Bibliography

Empson, William. "'Wit' in the *Essay on Criticism.*" *Hudson Review* 2 (1950): 559–77.

Fenner, Arthur, Jr. "The Unity of Pope's *Essay on Criticism.*" *Philological Quarterly* 39 (1960): 435–56.

Griffin, Dustin. *Alexander Pope: The Poet in the Poems.* Princeton: Princeton University Press, 1978.

Hooker, E. N. "Pope on Wit: The Essay on Criticism." *Hudson Review* 2 (1950): 84–100.

Stack, Frank. *Pope and Horace: Studies in Imitation.* Cambridge and New York: Cambridge University Press, 1985.

Warren, Austin. *Pope as Critic and Humanist.* Princeton: Princeton University Press, 1929.

Wood, Allen G. *Literary Satire and Theory: A Study of Horace, Boileau, and Pope.* New York: Garland, 1985.

# An Essay on Criticism

*— Si quid novisti rectius istis,*
*Candidus imperti; si non, his utere mecum.*[1]

## PART I

'Tis hard to say, if greater want of skill
Appear in writing or in judging ill;
But of the two less dangerous is the offense
To tire our patience than mislead our sense.
Some few in that, but numbers err in this,
Ten censure wrong for one who writes amiss;
A fool might once himself alone expose,
Now one in verse makes many more in prose.

'Tis with our judgments as our watches, none
Go just alike, yet each believes his own.
In poets as true genius is but rare,
True taste as seldom is the critic's share;
Both must alike from Heaven derive their light,
These born to judge, as well as those to write.
Let such teach others who themselves excel,
And censure freely who have written well.
Authors are partial to their wit,[2] 'tis true.
But are not critics to their judgment too?

Yet if we look more closely, we shall find
Most have the seeds of judgment in their mind:
Nature affords at least a glimmering light;
The lines, though touched but faintly, are drawn
    right.
But as the slightest sketch, if justly traced,
Is by ill coloring but the more disgraced,
So by false learning is good sense defaced:
Some are bewildered in the maze of schools,[3]
And some made coxcombs Nature meant but
    fools.
In search of wit these lose their common sense,
And then turn critics in their own defense:
Each burns alike, who can, or cannot write,
Or with a rival's or an eunuch's spite.
All fools have still an itching to deride,
And fain would be upon the laughing side.

If Maevius[4] scribble in Apollo's spite,
There are who judge still worse than he can
    write.
Some have at first for wits, then poets passed,
Turned critics next, and proved plain fools at
    last.
Some neither can for wits nor critics pass,
As heavy mules are neither horse nor ass.
Those half-learn'd witlings, numerous in our
    isle,
As half-formed insects on the banks of Nile;[5]
Unfinished things, one knows not what to call,
Their generation's so equivocal:
To tell[6] them would a hundred tongues require,
Or one vain wit's, that might a hundred tire.

But you who seek to give and merit fame,
And justly bear a critic's noble name,
Be sure yourself and your own reach to know,
How far your genius, taste, and learning go;
Launch not beyond your depth, but be discreet,
And mark that point where sense and dullness
    meet.
Nature to all things fixed the limits fit,
And wisely curbed proud man's pretending wit.
As on the land while here the ocean gains,
In other parts it leaves wide sandy plains;
Thus in the soul while memory prevails,
The solid power of understanding fails;
Where beams of warm imagination play,
The memory's soft figures melt away.
One science[7] only will one genius fit,
So vast is art, so narrow human wit.[8]
Not only bounded to peculiar arts,
But oft in those confined to single parts.
Like kings we lose the conquests gained before,
By vain ambition still to make them more;
Each might his several province well command,
Would all but stoop to what they understand.

---

[1]"If you know better maxims, impart them to me; if not, use these with me." Horace, *Epistles* 6:1. [Ed.]

[2]Artistic genius. [Ed.]

[3]Scholastic learning. [Ed.]

[4]A legendarily bad poet, known only through contemptuous references by both Virgil and Horace. [Ed.]

[5]Insects were supposed to be spontaneously generated by river mud and other similar matter. [Ed.]

[6]Count. [Ed.]

[7]Branch of knowledge. [Ed.]

[8]Here, mental power. [Ed.]

First follow Nature, and your judgment frame
By her just standard, which is still the same;
Unerring Nature, still divinely bright,
One clear, unchanged, and universal light,
Life, force, and beauty must to all impart,
At once the source, and end, and test of art.
Art from that fund each just supply provides,
Works without show, and without pomp presides.
In some fair body thus the informing soul
With spirits feeds, with vigor fills the whole,
Each motion guides, and every nerve sustains;
Itself unseen, but in the effects remains.
Some, to whom Heaven in wit has been profuse,
Want as much more to turn it to its use;
For wit[9] and judgment often are at strife,
Though meant each other's aid, like man and
    wife.
'Tis more to guide than spur the Muse's steed,[10]
Restrain his fury than provoke his speed;
The wingéd courser, like a generous horse,
Shows most true mettle when you check his
    course.
    Those rules of old discovered, not devised,
Are Nature still, but Nature methodized;
Nature, like liberty, is but restrained
By the same laws which first herself ordained.
    Hear how learn'd Greece her useful rules in-
    dites,
When to repress and when indulge our flights:
High on Parnassus'[11] top her sons she showed,
And pointed out those arduous paths they trod;
Held from afar, aloft, the immortal prize,
And urged the rest by equal steps to rise.
Just precepts thus from great examples given,
She drew from them what they derived from
    Heaven.
The generous critic fanned the poet's fire,
And taught the world with reason to admire.
Then criticism the Muse's handmaid proved,
To dress her charms, and make her more beloved:
But following wits from that intention strayed,
Who could not win the mistress, wooed the maid;
Against the poets their own arms they turned,

Sure to hate most the men from whom they
    learned.
So modern 'pothecaries, taught the art
By doctors' bills to play the doctor's part,
Bold in the practice of mistaken rules,
Prescribe, apply, and call their masters fools.[12]
Some on the leaves of ancient authors prey,
Nor time nor moths e'er spoiled so much as they.
Some dryly plain, without invention's aid,
Write dull receipts[13] how poems may be made.
These leave the sense their learning to display,
And those explain the meaning quite away.
    You then whose judgment the right course
    would steer,
Know well each ancient's proper character;
His fable, subject, scope in every page;
Religion, country, genius of his age:
Without all these at once before your eyes,
Cavil you may, but never criticize.
Be Homer's works your study and delight,
Read them by day, and meditate by night;
Thence form your judgment, thence your maxims
    bring,
And trace the Muses upward to their spring.
Still with itself compared, his text peruse;
And let your comment be the Mantuan Muse,[14]
    When first young Maro in his boundless mind
A work to outlast immortal Rome designed,
Perhaps he seemed above the critic's law,
And but from Nature's fountains scorned to
    draw;
But when to examine every part he came,
Nature and Homer were, he found, the same.
Convinced, amazed, he checks the bold design, ⎫
And rules as strict his labored work confine  ⎬
As if the Stagirite[15] o'erlooked each line.   ⎭
Learn hence for ancient rules a just esteem;
To copy Nature is to copy them.
    Some beauties yet no precepts can declare,
For there's a happiness as well as care.[16]

---

Music resembles poetry, in each  
Are nameless graces which no methods teach,  
And which a master hand alone can reach.  
If, where the rules not far enough extend  
(Since rules were made but to promote their end)  
Some lucky license answers to the full  
The intent proposed, that license is a rule.  
Thus Pegasus, a nearer way to take,  
May boldly deviate from the common track.  
From vulgar bounds with brave disorder part,  
And snatch a grace beyond the reach of art,  
Which without passing through the judgment,  
    gains  
The heart, and all its end at once attains.  
In prospects thus, some objects please our eyes,  
Which out of Nature's common order rise,  
The shapeless rock, or hanging precipice.  
Great wits sometimes may gloriously offend,  
And rise to faults true critics dare not mend;  
But though the ancients thus their rules invade  
(As kings dispense with laws themselves have  
    made)  
Moderns, beware! or if you must offend  
Against the precept, ne'er transgress its end;  
Let it be seldom, and compelled by need;  
And have at least their precedent to plead.  
The critic else proceeds without remorse,  
Seizes your fame, and puts his laws in force.  
    I know there are, to whose presumptuous  
    thoughts  
Those freer beauties, even in them, seem faults.  
Some figures monstrous and misshaped appear,  
Considered singly, or beheld too near,  
Which, but proportioned to their light or place,  
Due distance reconciles to form and grace.[17]  
A prudent chief not always must display  
His powers in equal ranks and fair array,  
But with the occasion and the place comply,  
Conceal his force, nay seem sometimes to fly.  
Those oft are stratagems which errors seem,  
Nor is it Homer nods, but we that dream.[18]

Still green with bays each ancient altar stands  
Above the reach of sacrilegious hands,  
Secure from flames, from envy's fiercer rage,  
Destructive war, and all-involving age.  
See, from each clime the learn'd their incense  
    bring!  
Here in all tongues consenting paeans ring!  
In praise so just let every voice be joined,  
And fill the general chorus of mankind.  
Hail, bards triumphant! born in happier days,  
Immortal heirs of universal praise!  
Whose honors with increase of ages grow,  
As streams roll down, enlarging as they flow;  
Nations unborn your mighty names shall sound,  
And worlds applaud that must not yet be found!  
Oh, may some spark of your celestial fire,  
The last, the meanest of your sons inspire  
(That on weak wings, from far, pursues your  
    flights,  
Glows while he reads, but trembles as he writes)  
To teach vain wits a science little known,  
To admire superior sense, and doubt their own!

## PART II

Of all the causes which conspire to blind  
Man's erring judgment, and misguide the mind,  
What the weak head with strongest bias rules,  
Is pride, the never-failing vice of fools.  
Whatever Nature has in worth denied,  
She gives in large recruits of needful pride;  
For as in bodies, thus in souls, we find  
What wants in blood and spirits swelled with  
    wind:  
Pride, where wit fails, steps in to our defense,  
And fills up all the mighty void of sense.  
If once right reason drives that cloud away,  
Truth breaks upon us with resistless day.  
Trust not yourself: but your defects to know,  
Make use of every friend — and every foe.  
    A little learning is a dangerous thing;  
Drink deep, or taste not the Pierian spring.[19]  
There shallow draughts intoxicate the brain,  
And drinking largely sobers us again.  
Fired at first sight with what the Muse imparts,  
In fearless youth we tempt the heights of arts,

[17]Pope alludes to the "ut pictura poesis" passage in Horace's *Art of Poetry* which stresses that some poems, like some paintings, need to be looked at from afar, not scrutinized in detail. [Ed.]

[18]Where Horace claims in the *Art of Poetry* to be "indignant even when it is the great Homer who falls asleep on the job," Pope suggests that the critic rather than the poet may be at fault. [Ed.]

[19]Pieria, near Mt. Olympus, was sacred to the Muses. [Ed.]

While from the bounded level of our mind
Short views we take, nor see the lengths behind;
But more advanced, behold with strange surprise
New distant scenes of endless science rise!
So pleased at first the towering Alps we try,
Mount o'er the vales, and seem to tread the sky,
The eternal snows appear already past,
And the first clouds and mountains seem the last;
But, those attained, we tremble to survey
The growing labors of the lengthened way,
The increasing prospect tires our wandering eyes,
Hills peep o'er hills, and Alps on Alps arise!

   A perfect judge will read each work of wit
With the same spirit that its author writ:
Survey the whole, nor seek slight faults to find
Where Nature moves, and rapture warms the
   mind;
Nor lose, for that malignant dull delight,
The generous pleasure to be charmed with wit.
But in such lays as neither ebb nor flow,
Correctly cold, and regularly low,
That, shunning faults, one quiet tenor keep,
We cannot blame indeed — but we may sleep.
In wit, as nature, what affects our hearts
Is not the exactness of peculiar parts;
'Tis not a lip, or eye, we beauty call,
But the joint force and full result of all.
Thus when we view some well-proportioned
   dome[20]
(The world's just wonder, and even thine, O
   Rome!),
No single parts unequally surprise,
All comes united to the admiring eyes:
No monstrous height, or breadth, or length ap-
   pear;
The whole at once is bold and regular.

   Whoever thinks a faultless piece to see,
Thinks what ne'er was, nor is, nor e'er shall be.
In every work regard the writer's end,
Since none can compass more than they intend;
And if the means be just, the conduct true,
Applause, in spite of trivial faults, is due.
As men of breeding, sometimes men of wit,
To avoid great errors must the less commit,
Neglect the rules each verbal critic lays,
For not to know some trifles is a praise.

Most critics, fond of some subservient art,
Still make the whole depend upon a part:
They talk of principles, but notions prize,
And all to one loved folly sacrifice.

   Once on a time La Mancha's knight,[21] they
   say,
A certain bard encountering on the way,
Discoursed in terms as just, with looks as sage,
As e'er could Dennis,[22] of the Grecian stage;
Concluding all were desperate sots and fools
Who durst depart from Aristotle's rules.
Our author, happy in a judge so nice,
Produced his play, and begged the knight's ad-
   vice;
Made him observe the subject and the plot,
The manners, passions, unities; what not?
All which exact to rule were brought about,
Were but a combat in the lists left out.
"What! leave the combat out?" exclaims the
   knight.
"Yes, or we must renounce the Stagirite."
"Not so, by Heaven!" he answers in a rage,
"Knights, squires, and steeds must enter on the
   stage."
"So vast a throng the stage can ne'er contain."
"Then build a new, or act it in a plain."

   Thus critics of less judgment than caprice,
Curious,[23] not knowing, not exact, but nice,
Form short ideas, and offend in arts
(As most in manners), by a love to parts.

   Some to conceit[24] alone their taste confine,
And glittering thoughts struck out at every line;
Pleased with a work where nothing's just or fit,
One glaring chaos and wild heap of wit.
Poets, like painters, thus unskilled to trace
The naked nature and the living grace,
With gold and jewels cover every part,
And hide with ornaments their want of art.
   True wit is Nature to advantage dressed,

[20]Of St. Peter's Basilica. [Ed.]

[21]Don Quixote. The episode is not in Cervantes but in a sequel written under the name of Alonzo Fernandez de Avellaneda and translated into English around 1705. [Ed.]
[22]John Dennis (1657–1734), a playwright and critic who had argued for the application of classical rules to the English stage. [Ed.]
[23]Pedantically careful; "nice" in the same line means "overrefined." [Ed.]
[24]Figures of speech. [Ed.]

What oft was thought, but ne'er so well ex-
pressed;
Something whose truth convinced at sight we
find,
That gives us back the image of our mind.
As shades more sweetly recommend the light,
So modest plainness sets off sprightly wit;
For works may have more wit than does them
good,
As bodies perish through excess of blood.
  Others for language all their care express,
And value books, as women men, for dress.
Their praise is still — the style is excellent;
The sense they humbly take upon contént.[25]
Words are like leaves; and where they most
abound,
Much fruit of sense beneath is rarely found.
False eloquence, like the prismatic glass,
Its gaudy colors spreads on every place;
The face of Nature we no more survey,
All glares alike, without distinction gay.
But true expression, like the unchanging sun,
Clears and improves whate'er it shines upon;
It gilds all objects, but it alters none.
Expression is the dress of thought, and still
Appears more decent as more suitable.
A vile conceit in pompous words expressed
Is like a clown in regal purple dressed:
For different styles with different subjects sort,
As several garbs with country, town, and court.
Some by old words to fame have made pretense,
Ancients in phrase, mere moderns in their sense.
Such labored nothings, in so strange a style,
Amaze the unlearn'd, and make the learned
smile;
Unlucky as Fungoso[26] in the play,
These sparks with awkward vanity display
What the fine gentleman wore yesterday;
And but so mimic ancient wits at best,
As apes our grandsires in their doublets dressed.
In words as fashions the same rule will hold,
Alike fantastic if too new or old:
Be not the first by whom the new are tried,
Nor yet the last to lay the old aside.

But most by numbers[27] judge a poet's song,
And smooth or rough with them is right or
wrong.
In the bright Muse though thousand charms con-
spire,
Her voice is all these tuneful fools admire,
Who haunt Parnassus but to please their ear,
Not mend their minds; as some to church repair,
Not for the doctrine, but the music there.
These equal syllables alone require,
Though oft the ear the open vowels tire,
While expletives their feeble aid do join,
And ten low words oft creep in one dull line:
While they ring round the same unvaried chimes,
With sure returns of still expected rhymes;
Where'er you find "the cooling western breeze,"
In the next line, it "whispers through the trees";
If crystal streams "with pleasing murmurs
creep,"
The reader's threatened (not in vain) with
"sleep";
Then, at the last and only couplet fraught
With some unmeaning thing they call a thought,
A needless Alexandrine[28] ends the song
That, like a wounded snake, drags its slow length
along.
Leave such to tune their own dull rhymes, and
know
What's roundly smooth or languishingly slow;
And praise the easy vigor of a line
Where Denham's strength and Waller's sweet-
ness join.
True ease in writing comes from art, not chance,
As those move easiest who have learned to
dance.
'Tis not enough no harshness gives offense,
The sound must seem an echo to the sense.
Soft is the strain when Zephyr gently blows,
And the smooth stream in smoother numbers
flows;
But when loud surges lash the sounding shore,
The hoarse, rough verse should like the torrent
roar.
When Ajax strives some rock's vast weight to
throw,

[25]On faith. [Ed.]
[26]A character in Ben Jonson's *Every Man out of His
Humour* (1599). [Ed.]

[27]Prosody. [Ed.]
[28]Line of iambic hexameter, usually broken in the middle.
[Ed.]

The line too labors, and the words move slow;
Not so when swift Camilla[29] scours the plain,
Flies o'er the unbending corn, and skims along
    the main.
Hear how Timotheus'[30] varied lays surprise,
And bid alternate passions fall and rise!
While at each change the son of Libyan Jove
Now burns with glory, and then melts with love;
Now his fierce eyes with sparkling fury glow,
Now sighs steal out, and tears begin to flow:
Persians and Greeks like turns of nature found
And the world's victor stood subdued by sound!
The power of music all our hearts allow,
And what Timotheus was is Dryden now.

    Avoid extremes; and shun the fault of such
Who still are pleased too little or too much.
At every trifle scorn to take offense:
That always shows great pride, or little sense.
Those heads, as stomachs, are not sure the best,
Which nauseate all, and nothing can digest.
Yet let not each gay turn thy rapture move;
For fools admire, but men of sense approve:
As things seem large which we through mists
    descry,
Dullness is ever apt to magnify.

    Some foreign writers, some our own despise;
The ancients only, or the moderns prize.
Thus wit, like faith, by each man is applied
To one small sect, and all are damned beside.
Meanly they seek the blessing to confine,
And force that sun but on a part to shine,
Which not alone the southern wit sublimes,
But ripens spirits in cold northern climes;
Which from the first has shone on ages past,
Enlights the present, and shall warm the last;
Though each may feel increases and decays,
And see now clearer and now darker days,
Regard not then if wit be old or new,
But blame the false and value still the true.

    Some ne'er advance a judgment of their own,

But catch the spreading notion of the town;
They reason and conclude by precedent,
And own stale nonsense which they ne'er invent.
Some judge of authors' names, not works, and
    then
Nor praise nor blame the writings, but the men.
Of all this servile herd the worst is he
That in proud dullness joins with quality,
A constant critic at the great man's board,
To fetch and carry nonsense for my lord.
What woeful stuff this madrigal would be
In some starved hackney sonneteer or me!
But let a lord once own the happy lines,
How the wit brightens! how the style refines!
Before his sacred name flies every fault,
And each exalted stanza teems with thought!

    The vulgar thus through imitation err;
As oft the learn'd by being singular;
So much they scorn the crowd, that if the throng
By chance go right, they purposely go wrong.
So schismatics the plain believers quit,
And are but damned for having too much wit.
Some praise at morning what they blame at night,
But always think the last opinion right.
A Muse by these is like a mistress used,
This hour she's idolized, the next abused;
While their weak heads like towns unfortified,
'Twixt sense and nonsense daily change their
    side.
Ask them the cause; they're wiser still, they say;
And still tomorrow's wiser than today.
We think our fathers fools, so wise we grow;
Our wiser sons, no doubt, will think us so.
Once school divines[31] this zealous isle o'er-
    spread;
Who knew most sentences was deepest read.
Faith, Gospel, all seemed made to be disputed,
And none had sense enough to be confuted.
Scotists and Thomists now in peace remain
Amidst their kindred cobwebs in Duck Lane.[32]
If faith itself has different dresses worn,
What wonder modes in wit should take their
    turn?
Oft, leaving what is natural and fit,
The current folly proves the ready wit;

[29]Camilla was an Amazonian warrior allied to Turnus in Virgil's *Aeneid*. [Ed.]

[30]Pope retells the story of Dryden's *Alexander's Feast*: how Alexander the Great's bard, Timotheus, was able to subdue the conqueror of the world through his art. The "son of Libyan Jove" is Alexander, who claimed descent from Ammon after conquering Egypt. [Ed.]

[31]Scholastic theologians. [Ed.]
[32]Street of used bookstores. [Ed.]

And authors think their reputation safe,
Which lives as long as fools are pleased to laugh.
  Some valuing those of their own side or mind,
Still make themselves the measure of mankind:
Fondly[33] we think we honor merit then,
When we but praise ourselves in other men.
Parties in wit attend on those of state,
And public faction doubles private hate.
Pride, Malice, Folly against Dryden rose,
In various shapes of parsons, critics, beaux;
But sense survived, when merry jests were past;
For rising merit will buoy up at last.
Might he return and bless once more our eyes,
New Blackmores and new Milbourns must
  arise.[34]
Nay, should great Homer lift his awful head,
Zoilus[35] again would start up from the dead.
Envy will merit, as its shade, pursue,
But like a shadow, proves the substance true;
For envied wit, like Sol eclipsed, makes known
The opposing body's grossness, not its own.
When first that sun too powerful beams displays,
It draws up vapors which obscure its rays;
But even those clouds at last adorn its way,
Reflect new glories, and augment the day.
  Be thou the first true merit to befriend;
His praise is lost who stays till all commend.
Short is the date, alas! of modern rhymes,
And 'tis but just to let them live betimes.
No longer now that golden age appears,
When patriarch wits survived a thousand years:
Now length of fame (our second life) is lost,
And bare threescore is all even that can boast;
Our sons their fathers' failing language see,
And such as Chaucer is shall Dryden be.[36]
So when the faithful pencil has designed
Some bright idea of the master's mind,
Where a new world leaps out at his command,
And ready Nature waits upon his hand;
When the ripe colors soften and unite,
And sweetly melt into just shade and light;

When mellowing years their full perfection give,
And each bold figure just begins to live,
The treacherous colors the fair art betray,
And all the bright creation fades away!
  Unhappy wit, like most mistaken things,
Atones not for that envy which it brings.
In youth alone its empty praise we boast,
But soon the short-lived vanity is lost;
Like some fair flower the early spring supplies,
That gaily blooms, but even in blooming dies,
What is this wit, which must our cares employ?
The owner's wife, that other men enjoy;
Then most our trouble still when most admired,
And still the more we give, the more required;
Whose fame with pains we guard, but lose with
  ease,
Sure some to vex, but never all to please;
'Tis what the vicious fear, the virtuous shun,
By fools 'tis hated, and by knaves undone!
  If wit so much from ignorance undergo,
Ah, let not learning too commence its foe!
Of old those met rewards who could excel,
And such were praised who but endeavored well;
Though triumphs were to generals only due,
Crowns were reserved to grace the soldiers too.
Now they who reach Parnassus' lofty crown
Employ their pains to spurn some others down;
And while self-love each jealous writer rules,
Contending wits become the sport of fools;
But still the worst with most regret commend,
For each ill author is as bad a friend.
To what base ends, and by what abject ways,
Are mortals urged through sacred[37] lust of praise!
Ah, ne'er so dire a thirst of glory boast,
Nor in the critic let the man be lost!
Good nature and good sense must ever join;
To err is human, to forgive divine.
  But if in noble minds some dregs remain
Nor yet purged off, of spleen and sour disdain,
Discharge that rage on more provoking crimes,
Nor fear a dearth in these flagitious[38] times.
No pardon vile obscenity should find,
Though wit and art conspire to move your mind;
But dullness with obscenity must prove
As shameful sure as impotence in love.

[33]Foolishly. [Ed.]
[34]Richard Blackmore had attacked Dryden's dramas,
Luke Milbourn his translation of the *Aeneid*. [Ed.]
[35]Zoilus was a severe critic of Homer of the fourth century
B.C. [Ed.]
[36]The Middle English in which Chaucer wrote had become unintelligible by Pope's time. [Ed.]

[37]Accursed. [Ed.]
[38]Wicked. [Ed.]

In the fat age of pleasure, wealth, and ease
Sprung the rank weed, and thrived with large
   increase:
When love was all an easy monarch's[39] care,
Seldom at council, never in a war;
Jilts[40] ruled the state, and statesmen farces writ;
Nay, wits had pensions, and young lords had wit;
The fair sat panting at a courtier's play,
And not a mask[41] went unimproved away;
The modest fan was lifted up no more,
And virgins smiled at what they blushed before.
The following license of a foreign reign[42]
Did all the dregs of bold Socinus drain;
Then unbelieving priests reformed the nation,
And taught more pleasant methods of salvation;
Where Heaven's free subjects might their rights
   dispute,
Lest God himself should seem too absolute;
Pulpits their sacred satire learned to spare,
And Vice admired to find a flatterer there!
Encouraged thus, wit's Titans braved the skies,
And the press groaned with licensed blasphe-
   mies.
These monsters, critics! with your darts engage,
Here point your thunder, and exhaust your rage!
Yet shun their fault, who, scandalously nice,
Will needs mistake an author into vice;
All seems infected that the infected spy,
As all looks yellow to the jaundiced eye.

## PART III

Learn then what morals Critics ought to show,
For 'tis but half a judge's task to know.
'Tis not enough Taste, Judgment, Learning join;
In all you speak let Truth and Candour shine;
That not alone what to your Sense is due
All may allow, but seek your friendship too.

Be silent always when you doubt your Sense,
And speak, tho' sure, with seeming diffidence.
Some positive persisting fops we know,

Who if once wrong will needs be always so;
But you with pleasure own your errors past,
And make each day a critique on the last.

'Tis not enough your counsel still be true;
Blunt truths more mischief than nice falsehoods
   do.
Men must be taught as if you taught them not,
And things unknown proposed as things forgot.
Without good breeding truth is disapprov'd;
That only makes superior Sense belov'd.

Be niggards of advice on no pretence,
For the worst avarice is that of Sense.
With mean complacence ne'er betray your trust,
Nor be so civil as to prove unjust.
Fear not the anger of the wise to raise;
Those best can bear reproof who merit praise.

'Twere well might critics still this freedom
   take,
But Appius[43] reddens at each word you speak,
And stares tremendous, with a threat'ning eye,
Like some fierce tyrant in old tapestry.
Fear most to tax an honourable fool,
Whose right it is, uncensured to be dull:
Such without Wit, are poets when they please,
As without Learning they can take degrees.[44]
Leave dangerous truths to unsuccessful satires,
And flattery to fulsome dedicators;
Whom, when they praise, the world believes no
   more
Than when they promise to give scribbling o'er.
'Tis best sometimes your censure to restrain,
And charitably let the dull be vain;
Your silence there is better than your spite,
For who can rail so long as they can write?
Still humming on their drowsy course they keep,
And lash'd so long, like tops, are lash'd asleep.
False steps but help them to renew the race,
As, after stumbling, jades will mend their pace.
What crowds of these, impenitently bold,
In sounds and jingling syllables grown old,
Still run on poets, in a raging vein,
Ev'n to the dregs and squeezings of the brain,
Strain out the last dull dropping of their sense,
And rhyme with all the rage of impotence!

[39]Charles II (reigned 1660–85). [Ed.]

[40]Charles's mistresses. [Ed.]

[41]Women wearing a vizard mask, whose concealment allowed one to behave immorally without scandal. [Ed.]

[42]The reign of William III (1689–1701), who came from Holland. Socinus, in the next line, was the name of two Renaissance Italian theologians whose doctrines denied the divinity of Christ and the efficacy of the Atonement. [Ed.]

[43]See n. 22. Dennis wrote an unsuccessful play, *Appius and Virginia* (1709). [Ed.]

[44]Sons of peers were allowed to take degrees at Oxford and Cambridge without meeting the usual requirements. [Ed.]

Such shameless bards we have; and yet 'tis true
There are as mad abandon'd critics too.
The bookful blockhead ignorantly read,
With loads of learned lumber in his head,
With his own tongue still edifies his ears,
And always list'ning to himself appears.
All books he reads, and all he reads assails,
From Dryden's Fables down to Durfey's Tales.[45]
With him most authors steal their works, or buy;
Garth did not write his own Dispensary.[46]
Name a new play, and he's the poet's friend;
Nay, show'd his faults — but when would poets mend?
No place so sacred from such fops is barr'd,
Nor is Paul's church more safe than Paul's churchyard:[47]
Nay, fly to altars, there they'll talk you dead;
For fools rush in where angels fear to tread.
Distrustful sense with modest caution speaks,
It still looks home, and short excursions makes;
But rattling nonsense in full volleys breaks
And never shock'd, and never turn'd aside,
Bursts out, resistless, with a thund'ring tide.

But where's the man who counsel can bestow,
Still pleas'd to teach, and yet not proud to know?
Unbiass'd or by favour or by spite;
Not dully prepossess'd nor blindly right;
Tho' learn'd, well bred, and tho' well bred sincere;
Modestly bold, and humanly severe;
Who to a friend his faults can freely show,
And gladly praise the merit of a foe;
Bless'd with a taste exact, yet unconfin'd,
A knowledge both of books and humankind;
Gen'rous converse; a soul exempt from pride;
And love to praise, with reason on his side?
Such once were critics; such the happy few
Athens and Rome in better ages knew.
The mighty Stagyrite first left the shore,
Spread all his sails, and durst the deeps explore;
He steer'd securely, and discover'd far,

Led by the light of the Mæonian star.[48]
Poets, a race long unconfin'd and free,
Still fond and proud of savage liberty,
Receiv'd his laws, and stood convinc'd 'twas fit
Who conquer'd Nature should preside o'er Wit.
Horace still charms with graceful negligence,
And without method talks us into sense;
Will, like a friend, familiarly convey
The truest notions in the easiest way.
He who, supreme in judgment as in wit,
Might boldly censure as he boldly writ,
Yet judg'd with coolness, though he sung with fire;
His precepts teach but what his works inspire.
Our critics take a contrary extreme,
They judge with fury, but they write with phlegm;
Nor suffers Horace more in wrong translations
By Wits, than Critics in as wrong quotations.
See Dionysius[49] Homer's thoughts refine,
And call new beauties forth from ev'ry line!
Fancy and art in gay Petronius[50] please,
The Scholar's learning with the courtier's ease.
In grave Quintilian's[51] copious work we find
The justest rules and clearest method join'd.
Thus useful arms in magazines we place,
All ranged in order, and disposed with grace;
But less to please the eye then arm the hand,
Still fit for use, and ready at command.
Thee, bold Longinus! all the Nine[52] inspire,
And bless their critic with a poet's fire:
An ardent judge, who, zealous in his trust,
With warmth gives sentence, yet is always just;
Whose own example strengthens all his laws,
And is himself that great sublime he draws.
Thus long succeeding critics justly reign'd,
License repress'd, and useful laws ordain'd:
Learning and Rome alike in empire grew,
And arts still follow'd where her eagles flew;
From the same foes at last both felt their doom,

[48]Homer, whose birthplace, according to tradition, was Maeonia. [Ed.]

[49]Dionysius of Halicarnassus (first century B.C.), literary critic and historian. [Ed.]

[50]Petronius Arbiter (?–65 A.D.), author of the *Satyricon*. [Ed.]

[51]Quintilian (35–95), rhetorician and author of *Institutio Oratoria*. [Ed.]

[52]The nine Muses. [Ed.]

[45]Thomas Durfey (1653–1723), author of popular songs, tales, plays, and other entertainments. [Ed.]

[46]Samuel Garth (1661–1719), physician-poet who wrote a didactic poem called "The Dispensary." [Ed.]

[47]Where booksellers plied their trade. [Ed.]

And the same age saw learning fall and Rome.
With tyranny then superstition join'd,
As that the body, this enslaved the mind;
Much was believ'd, but little understood,
And to be dull was construed to be good;
A second deluge learning thus o'errun,
And the monks finish'd what the Goths begun.

At length Erasmus, that great injur'd name,
(The glory of the priesthood and the shame!)
Stemm'd the wild torrent of a barb'rous age,
And drove those holy Vandals off the stage.

But see! each Muse in Leo's[53] golden days
Starts from her trance, and trims her wither'd
  bays.
Rome's ancient genius, o'er its ruins spread,
Shakes off the dust, and rears his rev'rend head.
Then sculpture and her sister arts revive;
Stones leap'd to form, and rocks began to live;
With sweeter notes each rising temple rung;
A Raphael painted and a Vida[54] sung:
Immortal Vida! on whose honour'd brow
The poet's bays and critic's ivy grow:
Cremona now shall ever boast thy name,
As next in place to Mantua,[55] next in fame!

But soon by impious arms from Latium
  chased,
Their ancient bounds the banish'd Muses pass'd;
Thence arts o'er all the northern world advance,
But critic learning flourish'd most in France;
The rules a nation born to serve obeys,
And Boileau[56] still in right of Horace sways.

But we, brave Britons, foreign laws despised,
And kept unconquer'd and uncivilized;
Fierce for the liberties of wit, and bold,
We still defied the Romans, as of old.
Yet some there were, among the sounder few
Of those who less presumed and better knew,
Who durst assert the juster ancient cause,
And here restor'd Wit's fundamental laws.
Such was the Muse whose rules and practice tell
"Nature's chief masterpiece is writing well."[57]
Such was Roscommon,[58] not more learn'd than
  good,
With manners gen'rous as his noble blood;
To him the wit of Greece and Rome was known,
And every author's merit but his own.
Such late was Walsh[59] — the Muse's judge and
  friend,
Who justly knew to blame or to commend;
To failings mild but zealous for desert,
The clearest head, and the sincerest heart.
This humble praise, lamented Shade! receive;
This praise at least a grateful Muse may give:
The Muse whose early voice you taught to sing,
Prescribed her heights, and pruned her tender
  wing,
(Her guide now lost), no more attempts to rise,
But in low numbers short excursions tries;
Content if hence th' unlearn'd their wants may
  view,
The learn'd reflect on what before they knew;
Careless of censure, nor too fond of fame;
Still pleas'd to praise, yet not afraid to blame;
Averse alike to flatter or offend;
Not free from faults, nor yet too vain to mend.

[53]Leo X, originally Giovanni de' Medici (1475–1521), whose pontificate was "golden" from the artistic commissions given out. [Ed.]

[54]Marco Girolamo Vida (1480–1566), Italian critic, poet, and author of *De arte poetica*. [Ed.]

[55]Birthplace of Virgil. [Ed.]

[56]Nicolas Boileau-Despréaux (1636–1711), French poet and critic, whose *Art poétique* is one of the sources of Pope's ideas. [Ed.]

[57]From Buckingham's "Essay on Poetry." [Ed.]

[58]Wentworth Dillon, Earl of Roscommon (1633–85), poet, critic, and translator of Horace. [Ed.]

[59]William Walsh (1663–1708), Pope's friend, who had advised the young poet that he could make his mark by striving for correctness. [Ed.]

# David Hume

## 1711–1776

David Hume was one of the major figures of the Scottish Enlightenment, a
group of skeptical, empiricist thinkers that also included the economist Adam
Smith and the political philosophers Adam Ferguson and Francis Hutcheson.
Hume's earliest work, the *Treatise of Human Nature* (1739), upon its appearance,
as Hume put it, "fell dead-born from the press." It is, however, the centerpiece of
all the philosopher's thought: His more successful later works, the *Enquiry Concerning Human Understanding* (1748), the *Enquiry Concerning the Principles of
Morals* (1752), and his political essays all find their origin here.

Hume's last published work, the posthumous *Dialogues on Natural Religion*
(1779), was a brilliantly ironic dramatic performance in which the skeptical Philo
— a character identifiable with Hume himself — defeats two opponents, one
propounding the mysteries of revealed religion, the other a deistical "natural
religion" of the sort found in Pope's *Essay on Man*. In his private life, Hume was
an infidel and an atheist. James Boswell, Samuel Johnson's biographer, was present
at Hume's death, and he reports that the philosopher died calmly and quietly
without any belief in God or in the comforts of religion. This was something
remarkable in his time: When the pious Johnson heard Boswell tell of this, he
scoffed and refused to believe it.

Hume wrote few essays on the principles of art and aesthetics, except where
they intersected his central interest in the workings of the human mind. The essay
*Of the Standard of Taste* (published in 1757 as part of *Four Dissertations*) is an
attempt to refine the century's growing interest in the psychology of the audience's
response to literature and the other arts. (This is Horatian rhetorical criticism stood
on its head: Instead of discussing the qualities poems should have, given the
characteristics of an audience, the aestheticians of taste discuss the qualities that
readers should possess, given a body of classic literature.) Hume, in other words,
is interested in the same issue as Pope in his *Essay on Criticism*: What makes a
good reader? But where Pope simply assumes that one reader or critic's assessment
of a work of art can be rationally said to be better than another's, Hume subjects
such questions to strict philosophical scrutiny.

The first twelve paragraphs of Hume's essay are written in his most subtle style
and repay close examination. Hume begins by separating "taste" from "opinion."
We hold opinions upon matters of fact; we have taste with regard to the arts.
Furthermore, when we differ in our opinions, it is likely to be over generalities
rather than particulars. (For example, two people might disagree over whether the
United States ought to be called a democracy or a republic, though they might
agree entirely about how laws are made and carried out.) When our sentiments
differ on a matter of taste, however, according to Hume we tend to agree on the
generalities but disagree over how to apply them. We will agree, for example, that
elegance is a virtue in writing and coldness a fault; but the work you are damning
for its chilliness of spirit, I may be applauding for its elegant form.

So far, so good. But now Hume embarks upon what looks like a digression into moral questions. "Those who found morality on sentiment more than on reason" (and Hume is one of these) tend to link up ethics with aesthetics here as an area in which we agree on our general principles but disagree on particular cases. We may agree that courage is a virtue and that rashness and cowardice are vices, but whether an individual act was courageous or rash may depend on who is doing the labeling.

The purpose of the digression becomes clear in the sixth paragraph: "It is natural for us to seek a standard of taste; a rule by which the various sentiments of men may be reconciled. . . ." In the field of ethics the need for a standard is obvious; indeed, societies set up massive institutions, courts of law and equity, to make sure that there is a clear standard of conduct, to reconcile our moral sentiments or, at least, to decide in favor of one sentiment and against another. And so it must be in aesthetics: We would seek a standard of taste — if such a standard is possible.

But *is* it possible? We all know the proverb *de gustibus non est disputandum*: there is no disputing about tastes. The argument for this position, which Hume endeavors to refute, runs as follows. Opinions and judgments are objective: They refer to something outside themselves and can thus be proven right or wrong. If a person looks at a painting and guesses that it measures three feet by five, we can take a tape measure and discover whether the guess is right or wrong. But sentiments are different. A sentiment is subjective: It states a relation between the perceiving subject and an object outside. The relation exists in the human consciousness, and we cannot second-guess it from outside. If a man looks at a painting and experiences it as beautiful, he cannot be wrong. If another man looks at the same painting and experiences it as ugly, he too is right. Beauty, as the saying goes, lies in the eye of the beholder. If the beholders disagree, there exists no intersubjective standard that can mediate between them, no standard of taste.

The obvious way out of this would be to deny that beauty is merely subjective. If beauty were a quality within things themselves, then it would be possible in principle to compare two works of art objectively. (Plato, for instance, takes Beauty to be an Idea in which any work of art or nature participates to greater or lesser extent. For Plato there is clearly an objective standard of taste.) But Hume has already foreclosed this escape by claiming that sentiments of taste are essentially different from opinions on matters of fact. Any standard of taste will have to be a subjective standard.

Hume's first step toward such a solution is to point out that wide and varied as our disagreements on taste are, they are not so wide as they look. We may differ as to whether Shakespeare or Milton is the greater poet, but we don't differ over whether Shakespeare's sonnets are greater than the jingles in greeting cards. We may differ as to whether Rembrandt is greater than Michelangelo, yet we don't differ over whether a Rembrandt is more beautiful than a lump of mud. When two geniuses are at nearly the same level, we find it difficult to adjudicate their respective claims; if anybody defended the superiority of the greeting-card lyric or the lump of mud, we would assume he or she was either not being serious or not to be taken seriously. But to do this is to assume the existence of a standard of taste that is capable of making at least the coarsest of judgments.

Hume also appeals to the existence of rules of art. Whatever their value, such rules are not provable a priori, like a mathematical theorem. They are empirical rules, codifications of the "experience and . . . observation of the common sentiments of human nature." We cannot deny that such common sentiments exist; otherwise, how would we account for the way classic works of art have moved humanity from generation to generation? But the key point is that such "common sentiments" exist because there is a definable "human nature." Humankind, despite our wide variation, is cut to a pattern, and so a norm can be defined. There are thus "general principles of approbation and blame" deriving from the "operations of the mind. Some particular forms or qualities from the original structures of the internal fabric [of the brain], are calculated to please, and others displease; and if they fail of their effect in any particular instance, it is from some apparent defect or imperfection in the organ."

In effect Hume's aesthetic norm is like the norm of human vision. The norm is a standard of perfection for the organism, but it is not the average: Most of us do not have 20/20 vision, and most of us do not possess the standard of taste. And just as we would defer, in our attempts to read a distant sign, to someone with better vision, we should defer in our sentiments to those closer to the standard of taste.

From the thirteenth through the twenty-second paragraph, Hume attempts to define the qualities that the man of taste needs and the corresponding defects that keep most of us from attaining perfect aesthetic vision. He concludes that the man who combines exquisite sensitivity with freedom from prejudice, long experience, the habit of comparison, and massive good sense is the rare character who will embody the standard of taste.

But how does one find such a character and how does one tell a true claimant to the standard of taste from an imposter? We would seem to be back in the same skeptical swamp where we started. But though problems still remain, we have in fact advanced some real way. For the issue of whether A or B is in accord with the existing standard of taste is now a factual question, not one of judgment. And critic X can be compared with critic Y in terms of the five qualities that Hume finds make good readers. For instance, a sensitive reader will see subtleties in a poem that a less sensitive reader will ignore unless they are pointed out. And experience, freedom from prejudice, and general good sense are reasonably objectifiable qualities. Good critics, like good artists, make themselves known to us by appealing to what is best in our common human nature.

The penultimate section of Hume's essay suggests areas where the writ of the standard fails to run, places where the differing sentiments of men may *not* be reconcilable. One area is the generation gap. As Hume says, "At twenty, Ovid may be the favorite author; Horace at forty; and perhaps Tacitus at fifty." A second moot area is nationality. Though they may understand the nature of his greatness, few Americans can take the unaffected pleasure in reading Racine that the French can — nor do the French ever seem to comprehend what the English-speaking world sees in Shakespeare.

The final question Hume takes up is that of the factors by which the passage of time alters our perspectives on literature. Some changes, like advances in science or a shift in the dominant religion, cause no problems. We take no less pleasure in Homer because his scientific ideas have been superseded or because his characters worship pagan gods. On the other hand, changes in morality from his time to ours may be problematic. The brutality of Achilles and the casual way Odysseus breaks his oaths for personal advantage may affront our modern sensibilities — and Hume thinks we would not be wrong to be upset. The other manifestation that can upset the otherwise tolerant Hume is religious superstition; he objects to Catholic propaganda in Racine and Corneille, and even more to the easy mixture of the religious and the secular in medieval authors like Boccaccio and Petrarch. These are not the most important sections of *The Standard of Taste* but it is interesting to see what made Hume the infidel wince.

### Selected Bibliography

Brunet, Olivier. *Philosophie et esthetique chez David Hume*. Paris: A.-G. Nizet, 1965.

Brunius, Teddy. *David Hume on Criticism*. Stockholm: Almqvist and Wiksell, 1952.

Mall, Ram Adhar. *Naturalism and Criticism*. The Hague: Nijhoff, 1975.

Mossner, E. C. *The Life of David Hume*. Edinburgh: Nelson, 1954.

Murphy, Richard T. *Hume and Husserl: Towards Radical Subjectivism*. The Hague and Boston: M. Nijhoff, 1980.

Smith, N. K. *The Philosophy of David Hume*. London: Macmillan, 1941.

Wilbanks, Jan. *Hume's Theory of Imagination*. The Hague: Mouton, 1968.

# Of the Standard of Taste

The great variety of taste, as well as of opinion, which prevails in the world, is too obvious not to have fallen under everyone's observation. Men of the most confined knowledge are able to remark a difference of taste in the narrow circle of their acquaintance, even where the persons have been educated under the same government, and have early imbibed the same prejudices. But those, who can enlarge their view to contemplate distant nations and remote ages, are still more surprised at the great inconsistence and contrariety. We are apt to call barbarous whatever departs widely from our own taste and apprehension: but soon find the epithet of reproach retorted on us. And the highest arrogance and self-conceit is at last startled, on observing an equal assurance on all sides, and scruples, amidst such a contest of sentiment, to pronounce positively in its own favor.

As this variety of taste is obvious to the most careless inquirer; so will it be found, on examination, to be still greater in reality than in appearance. The sentiments of men often differ with regard to beauty and deformity of all kinds, even while their general discourse is the same. There are certain terms in every language, which import blame, and others praise; and all men, who use the same tongue, must agree in their application of them. Every voice is united in applauding elegance, propriety, simplicity, spirit in writing; and in blaming fustian, affectation, coldness, and a false brilliancy: but when critics come to particulars, this seeming unanimity vanishes; and it is found, that they had affixed a very different meaning to their expressions. In all matters of opinion and science, the case is opposite: The difference among men is there oftener found to lie in generals than in particulars; and to be less in reality than in appearance. An explanation of the terms commonly ends the controversy; and the disputants are surprised to find, that they had been quarreling, while at bottom they agreed in their judgment.

Those who found morality on sentiment, more than on reason are inclined to comprehend ethics under the former observation, and to maintain, that, in all questions, which regard conduct and manners, the difference among men is really greater than at first sight it appears. It is indeed obvious that writers of all nations and all ages concur in applauding justice, humanity, magnanimity, prudence, veracity; and in blaming the opposite qualities. Even poets and other authors, whose compositions are chiefly calculated to please the imagination, are yet found, from Homer down to Fénelon,[1] to inculcate the same moral precepts, and to bestow their applause and blame on the same virtues and vices. This great unanimity is usually ascribed to the influence of plain reason; which, in all these cases, maintains similar sentiments in all men, and prevents those controversies, to which the abstract sciences are so much exposed. So far as the unanimity is real, this account may be admitted as satisfactory: but we must also allow that some part of the seeming harmony in morals may be accounted for from the very nature of language. The word *virtue*, with its equivalent in every tongue, implies praise; as that of *vice* does blame: And no one, without the most obvious and grossest impropriety, could affix reproach to a term, which in general acceptation is understood in a good sense; or bestow applause, where the idiom requires disapprobation. Homer's general precepts, where he delivers any such, will never be controverted; but it is obvious, that, when he draws particular pictures of manners, and represents heroism in Achilles and prudence in Ulysses, he intermixes a much greater degree of ferocity in the former, and of cunning and fraud in the latter, than Fénelon would admit of. The sage Ulysses in the Greek poet seems to delight in lies and fictions, and often employs them without any necessity or even advantage: But his more scrupulous son, in the French epic writer, exposes himself to the most imminent perils, rather than depart from the most exact line of truth and veracity.

The admirers and followers of the Alcoran[2] insist on the excellent moral precepts interspersed throughout that wild and absurd performance. But it is to be supposed, that the Arabic words, which correspond to the English, equity, justice, temperance, meekness, charity, were such as, from the constant use of that tongue, must always be taken in a good sense; and it would have argued the greatest ignorance, not of morals, but of language, to have mentioned them with any epithets, besides those of applause and approbation. But would we know, whether the pretended prophet had really attained a just sentiment of morals? Let us attend to his narration; and we shall soon find, that he bestows praise on such instances of treachery, inhumanity, cruelty, revenge, bigotry, as are utterly incompatible with civilized society. No steady rule of right seems there to be attained to; and every action is blamed or praised, so far only as it is beneficial or hurtful to the true believers.

The merit of delivering true general precepts in ethics is indeed very small. Whoever recommends any moral virtues, really does no more than is implied in the terms themselves. That people, who invented the word *charity*, and used it in a good sense, inculcated more clearly and much more efficaciously, the precept, "be charitable," than any pretended legislator or prophet, who should insert such a maxim in his writings. Of all expressions, those, which, together with

---

[1]François de Salignac de la Mothe Fénelon, who wrote a novel, *Telemaque* (1699) as a continuation of Book 4 of Homer's *Odyssey*. [Ed.]

[2]The Koran. [Ed.]

their other meaning, imply a degree either of blame or approbation, are the least liable to be perverted or mistaken.

It is natural for us to seek a standard of taste; a rule by which the various sentiments of men may be reconciled; at least, a decision afforded, confirming one sentiment, and condemning another.

There is a species of philosophy, which cuts off all hopes of success in such an attempt, and represents the impossibility of ever attaining any standard of taste. The difference, it is said, is very wide between judgment and sentiment. All sentiment is right; because sentiment has a reference to nothing beyond itself, and is always real, wherever a man is conscious of it. But all determinations of the understanding are not right; because they have a reference to something beyond themselves, to wit, real matter of fact; and are not always conformable to that standard. Among a thousand different opinions which different men may entertain of the same subject, there is one, and but one, that is just and true; and the only difficulty is to fix and ascertain it. On the contrary, a thousand different sentiments, excited by the same object, are all right: because no sentiment represents what is really in the object. It only marks a certain conformity or relation between the object and the organs or faculties of the mind; and if that conformity did not really exist, the sentiment could never possibly have being. Beauty is no quality in things themselves: it exists merely in the mind which contemplates them; and each mind perceives a different beauty. One person may even perceive deformity, where another is sensible of beauty; and every individual ought to acquiesce in his own sentiment, without pretending to regulate those of others. To seek the real beauty, or real deformity, is as fruitless an inquiry, as to pretend to ascertain the real sweet or real bitter. According to the disposition of the organs, the same object may be both sweet and bitter; and the proverb has justly determined it to be fruitless to dispute concerning tastes. It is very natural, and even quite necessary, to extend this axiom to mental, as well as bodily taste; and thus common sense, which is so often at variance with philosophy, especially with the skeptical kind, is

found, in one instance at least, to agree in pronouncing the same decision.

But though this axiom, by passing into a proverb, seems to have attained the sanction of common sense; there is certainly a species of common sense which opposes it, at least serves to modify and restrain it. Whoever would assert an equality of genius and elegance between Ogilby[3] and Milton, or Bunyan and Addison, would be thought to defend no less an extravagance, than if he had maintained a molehill to be as high as Tenerife,[4] or a pond as extensive as the ocean. Though there may be found persons, who give the preference to the former authors, no one pays attention to such a taste; and we pronounce without scruple the sentiment of these pretended critics to be absurd and ridiculous. The principle of the natural equality of tastes is then totally forgot, and while we admit it on some occasions, where the objects seem near an equality, it appears an extravagant paradox, or rather a palpable absurdity, where objects so disproportioned are compared together.

It is evident that none of the rules of composition are fixed by reasoning *a priori*, or can be esteemed abstract conclusions of the understanding, from comparing those habitudes and relations of ideas, which are eternal and immutable. Their foundation is the same with that of all the practical sciences, experience; nor are they anything but general observations, concerning what has been universally found to please in all countries and in all ages. Many of the beauties of poetry and even of eloquence are founded on falsehood and fiction, on hyperboles, metaphors, and an abuse or perversion of terms from their natural meaning. To check the sallies of the imagination, and to reduce every expression to geometrical truth and exactness, would be the most contrary to the laws of criticism; because it would produce a work, which, by universal ex-

[3]John Ogilby (1600–76), a Scottish poet who, like Milton, but less successfully, tried his hand at epic. In Hume's day the comparison of Bunyan with Addison was as clear as that of Ogilby with Milton: The former in both pairings was considered a far inferior popular writer. Two hundred years later, Hume's preference for Addison seems less self-explanatory. [Ed.]

[4]A mountain in the Canary Islands. [Ed.]

perience, has been found the most insipid and disagreeable. But though poetry can never submit to exact truth, it must be confined by rules of art, discovered to the author either by genius or observation. If some negligent or irregular writers have pleased, they have not pleased by their transgressions of rule or order, but in spite of these transgressions: They have possessed other beauties, which were conformable to just criticism; and the force of these beauties has been able to overpower censure, and give the mind a satisfaction superior to the disgust arising from the blemishes. Ariosto[5] pleases; but not by his monstrous and improbable fictions, by his bizarre mixture of the serious and comic styles, by the want of coherence in his stories, or by the continual interruptions of his narration. He charms by the force and clearness of his expression, by the readiness and variety of his inventions, and by his natural pictures of the passions, especially those of the gay and amorous kind: And however his faults may diminish our satisfaction, they are not able entirely to destroy it. Did our pleasure really arise from those parts of his poem, which we denominate faults, this would be no objection to criticism in general: It would only be an objection to those particular rules of criticism, which would establish such circumstances to be faults, and would represent them as universally blamable. If they are found to please, they cannot be faults; let the pleasure, which they produce, be ever so unexpected and unaccountable.

But though all the general rules of art are founded only on experience and on the observation of the common sentiments of human nature, we must not imagine, that, on every occasion, the feelings of men will be conformable to these rules. Those finer emotions of the mind are of a very tender and delicate nature, and require the concurrence of many favorable circumstances to make them play with facility and exactness, according to their general and established principles. The least exterior hindrance to such small springs, or the least internal disorder, disturbs their motion, and confounds the operation of the whole machine. When we would make an ex-

periment of this nature, and would try the force of any beauty or deformity, we must choose with care a proper time and place, and bring the fancy to a suitable situation and disposition. A perfect serenity of mind, a recollection of thought, a due attention to the object; if any of these circumstances be wanting, our experiment will be fallacious, and we shall be unable to judge of the catholic and universal beauty. The relation, which nature has placed between the form and the sentiment, will at least be more obscure; and it will require greater accuracy to trace and discern it. We shall be able to ascertain its influence not so much from the operation of each particular beauty, as from the durable admiration, which attends those works, that have survived all the caprices of mode and fashion, all the mistakes of ignorance and envy.

The same Homer, who pleased at Athens and Rome two thousand years ago, is still admired at Paris and at London. All the changes of climate, government, religion, and language, have not been able to obscure his glory. Authority or prejudice may give a temporary vogue to a bad poet or orator; but his reputation will never be durable or general. When his compositions are examined by posterity or by foreigners, the enchantment is dissipated, and his faults appear in their true colors. On the contrary, a real genius, the longer his works endure, and the more wide they are spread, the more sincere is the admiration which he meets with. Envy and jealousy have too much place in a narrow circle; and even familiar acquaintance with his person may diminish the applause due to his performances: but when these obstructions are removed, the beauties, which are naturally fitted to excite agreeable sentiments, immediately display their energy; and while the world endures, they maintain their authority over the minds of men.

It appears then, that, amidst all the variety and caprice of taste, there are certain general principles of approbation or blame, whose influence a careful eye may trace in all operations of the mind. Some particular forms or qualities, from the original structures of the internal fabric, are calculated to please, and others displease; and if they fail of their effect in any particular instance, it is from some apparent defect or im-

[5]Ludovico Ariosto was the author of the fanciful epic, *Orlando Furioso* (1516). [Ed.]

perfection in the organ. A man in a fever would not insist on his palate as able to decide concerning flavors; nor would one, affected with the jaundice, pretend to give a verdict with regard to colors. In each creature, there is a sound and defective state; and the former alone can be supposed to afford us a true standard of taste and sentiment. If, in the sound state of the organ, there be an entire or a considerable uniformity of sentiment among men, we may thence derive an idea of the perfect beauty; in like manner as the appearance of objects in daylight, to the eye of a man in health, is denominated their true and real color, even while color is allowed to be merely a phantasm of the senses.

Many and frequent are the defects in the internal organs which prevent or weaken the influence of those general principles, on which depends our sentiment of beauty or deformity. Though some objects, by the structure of the mind, be naturally calculated to give pleasure, it is not to be expected, that in every individual the pleasure will be equally felt. Particular incidents and situations occur, which either throw a false light on the objects, or hinder the true from conveying to the imagination the proper sentiment and perception.

One obvious cause, why many feel not the proper sentiment of beauty, is the want of that delicacy of imagination, which is requisite to convey a sensibility of those finer emotions. This delicacy everyone pretends to: everyone talks of it; and would reduce every kind of taste or sentiment to its standard. But as our intention in this essay is to mingle some light of the understanding with the feeling of sentiment, it will be proper to give a more accurate definition of delicacy, than has hitherto been attempted. And not to draw our philosophy from too profound a source, we shall have recourse to a noted story in *Don Quixote*.

"It is with good reason," says Sancho to the squire with the great nose, "that I pretend to have a judgment in wine: this is a quality hereditary in our family. Two of my kinsmen were once called to give their opinion of a hogshead, which was supposed to be excellent, being old and of a good vintage. One of them tastes it; considers it; and after mature reflection pronounces the wine to be good, were it not for a small taste of leather, which he perceived in it. The other, after using the same precautions, gives also his verdict in favor of the wine; but with the reserve of a taste of iron, which he could easily distinguish. You cannot imagine how much they were both ridiculed for their judgment. But who laughed in the end? On emptying the hogshead, there was found at the bottom, an old key with a leathern thong tied to it."

The great resemblance between mental and bodily taste will easily teach us to apply this story. Though it be certain that beauty and deformity, more than sweet and bitter, are not qualities in objects, but belong entirely to the sentiment, internal or external; it must be allowed, that there are certain qualities in objects, which are fitted by nature to produce those particular feelings. Now as these qualities may be found in a small degree, or may be mixed and confounded with each other, it often happens, that the taste is not affected with such minute qualities, or is not able to distinguish all the particular flavors, amidst the disorder, in which they are presented. Where the organs are so fine, as to allow nothing to escape them; and at the same time so exact as to perceive every ingredient in the composition: this we call delicacy of taste, where we employ these terms in the literal or metaphorical sense. Here then the general rules of beauty are of use; being drawn from established models, and from the observation of what pleases or displeases, when presented singly and in a high degree: and if the same qualities, in a continued composition and in a smaller degree, affect not the organs with a sensible delight or uneasiness, we exclude the person from all pretensions to this delicacy. To produce these general rules or avowed patterns of composition is like finding the key with the leathern thong; which justified the verdict of Sancho's kinsmen, and confounded those pretended judges who had condemned them. Though the hogshead had never been emptied, the taste of the one was still equally delicate, and that of the other equally dull and languid: but it would have been more difficult to have proved the superiority of the former, to the conviction of every bystander. In like manner, though the beauties of writing had never been methodized, or reduced to general principles; though no excellent models had ever been acknowledged; the different degrees of taste would still have subsisted, and the judgment of one man been preferable to that of another; but it would not have been so easy to silence the bad critic, who might always insist upon his particular sentiment, and refuse to submit to his antagonist. But when we show him an avowed principle of art; when we illustrate this principle by examples, whose operation, from his own particular taste, he acknowledges to be comformable to the principle; when we prove, that the same principle may be applied to the present case, where he did not perceive or feel its influence: he must conclude, upon the whole, that the fault lies in himself, and that he wants the delicacy, which is requisite to make him sensible of every beauty and every blemish, in any composition or discourse.

It is acknowledged to be the perfection of every sense or faculty, to perceive with exactness its most minute objects, and allow nothing to escape its notice and observation. The smaller the objects are, which become sensible to the eye, the finer is that organ, and the more elaborate its make and composition. A good palate is not tried by strong flavors; but by a mixture of small ingredients, where we are still sensible of each part, notwithstanding its minuteness and its confusion with the rest. In like manner, a quick and acute perception of beauty and deformity must be the perfection of our mental taste; nor can a man be satisfied with himself while he suspects, that any excellence or blemish in a discourse has passed him unobserved. In this case, the perfection of the man, and the perfection of the sense or feeling, are found to be united. A very delicate palate, on many occasions, may be a great inconvenience both to a man himself and to his friends: but a delicate taste of wit or beauty must always be a desirable quality; because it is the source of all the finest and most innocent enjoyments, of which human nature is susceptible. In this decision the sentiments of all mankind are agreed. Wherever you can ascertain a delicacy of taste, it is sure to meet

with approbation; and the best way of ascertaining it is to appeal to those models and principles, which have been established by the uniform consent and experience of nations and ages.

But though there be naturally a wide difference in point of delicacy between one person and another, nothing tends further to increase and improve this talent, than practice in a particular art, and the frequent survey or contemplation of a particular species of beauty. When objects of any kind are first presented to the eye or imagination, the sentiment, which attends them, is obscure and confused; and the mind is, in a great measure, incapable of pronouncing concerning their merits or defects. The taste cannot perceive the several excellences of the performance; much less distinguish the particular character of each excellency, and ascertain its quality and degree. If it pronounce the whole in general to be beautiful or deformed, it is the utmost that can be expected; and even this judgment, a person, so unpracticed, will be apt to deliver with great hesitation and reserve. But allow him to acquire experience in those objects, his feeling becomes more exact and nice: he not only perceives the beauties and defects of each part, but marks the distinguishing species of each quality, and assigns it suitable praise or blame. A clear and distinct sentiment attends him through the whole survey of the objects; and he discerns that very degree and kind of approbation or displeasure, which each part is naturally fitted to produce. The mist dissipates, which seemed formerly to hang over the object: the organ acquires greater perfection in its operations; and can pronounce, without danger of mistake, concerning the merits of every performance. In a word, the same address and dexterity, which practice gives to the execution of any work, is also acquired by the same means, in the judging of it.

So advantageous is practice to the discernment of beauty, that, before we can give judgment on any work of importance, it will even be requisite, that that very individual performance be more than once perused by us, and be surveyed in different lights with attention and deliberation. There is a flutter or hurry of thought which attends the first perusal of any piece, and which confounds the genuine sentiment of beauty. The relation of the parts is not discerned: the true characters of style are little distinguished: the several perfections and defects seem wrapped up in a species of confusion, and present themselves indistinctly to the imagination. Not to mention, that there is a species of beauty, which, as it is florid and superficial, pleases at first; but being found incompatible with a just expression either of reason or passion, soon palls upon the taste, and is then rejected with disdain, at least rated at much lower value.

It is impossible to continue in the practice of contemplating any order of beauty, without being frequently obliged to form comparisons between the several species and degrees of excellence, and estimating their proportion to each other. A man, who has had no opportunity of comparing the different kinds of beauty, is indeed totally unqualified to pronounce an opinion with regard to any object presented to him. By comparison alone we fix the epithets of praise or blame, and learn how to assign the due degree of each. The coarsest daubing contains a certain luster of colors and exactness of imitation, which are so far beauties, and would affect the mind of a peasant or Indian with the highest admiration. The most vulgar ballads are not entirely destitute of harmony or nature; and none but a person, familiarized to superior beauties, would pronounce their numbers harsh, or narration uninteresting. A great inferiority of beauty gives pain to a person conversant in the highest excellence of the kind, and is for that reason pronounced a deformity: as the most finished object, with which we are acquainted, is naturally supposed to have reached the pinnacle of perfection, and to be entitled to the highest applause. One accustomed to see, and examine, and weigh the several performances, admired in different ages and nations, can only rate the merits of a work exhibited to his view, and assign its proper rank among the productions of genius.

But to enable a critic the more fully to execute this undertaking, he must preserve his mind free from all prejudice, and allow nothing to enter into his consideration, but the very object which is submitted to his examination. We may observe, that every work of art, in order to produce its due effect on the mind, must be surveyed in a certain point of view, and cannot be fully relished by persons, whose situation, real or imaginary, is not conformable to that which is required by the performance. An orator addresses himself to a particular audience, and must have a regard to their particular genius, interest, opinions, passions, and prejudices; otherwise he hopes in vain to govern their resolutions, and inflame their affections. Should they even have entertained some prepossessions against him, however unreasonable, he must not overlook this disadvantage; but, before he enters upon the subject, must endeavor to conciliate their affection, and acquire their good graces. A critic of a different age or nation, who should peruse this discourse, must have all these circumstances in his eye, and must place himself in the same situation as the audience, in order to form a true judgment of the oration. In like manner, when any work is addressed to the public, though I should have a friendship or enmity with the author, I must depart from this situation; and considering myself as a man in general, forget, if possible, my individual being and my peculiar circumstances. A person influenced by prejudice, complies not with this condition; but obstinately maintains his natural position, without placing himself in that point of view, which the performance supposes. If the work be addressed to persons of a different age or nation, he makes no allowance for their peculiar views and prejudices; but, full of the manners of his own age and country, rashly condemns what seemed admirable in the eyes of those for whom alone the discourse was calculated. If the work be executed for the public, he never sufficiently enlarges his comprehension, or forgets his interest as a friend or enemy, as a rival or commentator. By this means, his sentiments are perverted; nor have the same beauties and blemishes the same influence upon him, as if he had imposed a proper violence on his imagination, and had forgotten himself for a moment. So far his taste evidently departs from the true standard; and of consequence loses all credit and authority.

It is well known, that in all questions, submitted to the understanding, prejudice is destructive of sound judgment, and perverts all operations of the intellectual faculties: it is no less contrary to good taste; nor has it less influence to corrupt our sentiment of beauty. It belongs to good sense to check its influence in both cases; and in this respect, as well as in many others, reason, if not an essential part of taste, is at least requisite to the operations of this latter faculty. In all the nobler productions of genius, there is a mutual relation and correspondence of parts; nor can either the beauties or blemishes be perceived by him, whose thought is not capacious enough to comprehend all those parts, and compare them with each other, in order to perceive the consistence and uniformity of the whole. Every work of art has also a certain end or purpose, for which it is calculated; and is to be deemed more or less perfect, as it is more or less fitted to attain this end. The object of eloquence is to persuade, of history to instruct, of poetry to please by means of the passions and the imagination. These ends we must carry constantly in our view, when we peruse any performance; and we must be able to judge how far the means employed are adapted to their respective purposes. Besides every kind of composition, even the most poetical, is nothing but a chain of propositions and reasonings; not always, indeed, the justest and most exact, but still plausible and specious, however disguised by the coloring of the imagination. The persons introduced in tragedy and epic poetry, must be represented as reasoning, and thinking, and concluding, and acting, suitably to their character and circumstances; and without judgment, as well as taste and invention, a poet can never hope to succeed in so delicate an undertaking. Not to mention, that the same excellence of faculties which contributes to the improvement of reason, the same clearness of conception, the same exactness of distinction, the same vivacity of apprehension, are essential to the operations of true taste, and are its infallible concomitants. It seldom, or never happens, that a man of sense, who has experience in any art, cannot judge of its beauty; and it is no less rare to meet with a man who has a just taste without a sound understanding.

Thus, though the principles of taste be universal, and, nearly, if not entirely the same in all men; yet few are qualified to give judgment on any work of art, or establish their own sentiment as the standard of beauty. The organs of internal sensation are seldom so perfect as to allow the general principles their full play, and produce a feeling correspondent to those principles. They either labor under some defect, or are vitiated by some disorder; and by that means, excite a sentiment, which may be pronounced erroneous. When the critic has no delicacy, he judges without any distinction, and is only affected by the grosser and more palpable qualities of the object: the finer touches pass unnoticed and disregarded. Where he is not aided by practice, his verdict is attended with confusion and hesitation. Where no comparison has been employed, the most frivolous beauties, such as rather merit the name of defects, are the objects of his admiration. Where he lies under the influence of prejudice, all his natural sentiments are perverted. Where good sense is wanting, he is not qualified to discern the beauties of design and reasoning, which are the highest and most excellent. Under some or other of these imperfections, the generality of men labor; and hence a true judge in the finer arts is observed, even during the most polished ages, to be so rare a character: strong sense, united to delicate sentiment, improved by practice, perfected by comparison, and cleared of all prejudice, can alone entitle critics to this valuable character; and the joint verdict of such, wherever they are to be found, is the true standard of taste and beauty.

But where are such critics to be found? By what marks are they to be known? How distinguish them from pretenders? These questions are embarrassing; and seem to throw us back into the same uncertainty, from which, during the course of this essay, we have endeavored to extricate ourselves.

But if we consider the matter aright, these are questions of fact, not of sentiment. Whether any particular person be endowed with good sense and a delicate imagination, free from prejudice, may often be the subject of dispute, and be liable to great discussion and inquiry: But that such a character is valuable and estimable will be agreed in by all mankind. Where these doubts occur, men can do no more than in other disputable questions, which are submitted to the understanding: they must produce the best arguments, that their invention suggests to them; they must acknowledge a true and decisive standard to exist somewhere, to wit, real existence and matter of fact; and they must have indulgence to such as differ from them in their appeals to this standard. It is sufficient for our present purpose, if we have proved, that the taste of all individuals is not upon an equal footing, and that some men in general, however difficult to be particularly pitched upon, will be acknowledged by universal sentiment to have a preference above others.

But in reality the difficulty of finding, even in particulars, the standard of taste, is not so great as it is represented. Though in speculation, we may readily avow a certain criterion in science and deny it in sentiment, the matter is found in practice to be much more hard to ascertain in the former case than in the latter. Theories of abstract philosophy, systems of profound theology, have prevailed during one age: in a successive period, these have been universally exploded: their absurdity has been detected: other theories and systems have supplied their place, which again gave place to their successors: and nothing has been experienced more liable to the revolutions of chance and fashion than these pretended decisions of science. The case is not the same with beauties of eloquence and poetry. Just expressions of passion and nature are sure, after a little time, to gain public applause, which they maintain forever. Aristotle, and Plato, and Epicurus, and Descartes, may successively yield to each other: but Terence and Virgil maintain a universal, undisputed empire over the minds of men. The abstract philosophy of Cicero has lost its credit: the vehemence of his oratory is still the object of our admiration.

Though men of delicate taste be rare, they are easily to be distinguished in society, by the soundness of their understanding and the superiority of their faculties above the rest of mankind. The ascendant, which they acquire, gives a prevalence to that lively approbation, with which they receive any productions of genius, and renders it generally predominant. Many men, when left to themselves, have but a faint and dubious perception of beauty, who yet are capable of relishing any fine stroke, which is pointed out to them. Every convert to the admiration of the real poet or orator is the cause of some new conversion. And though prejudices may prevail for a time, they never unite in celebrating any rival to the true genius, but yield at last to the force of nature and just sentiment. Thus, though a civilized nation may easily be mistaken in the choice of their admired philosopher, they never have been found long to err, in their affection for a favorite epic or tragic author.

But notwithstanding all our endeavors to fix a standard of taste, and reconcile the discordant apprehensions of men, there still remain two sources of variation, which are not sufficient indeed to confound all the boundaries of beauty and deformity, but will often serve to produce a difference in the degrees of our approbation or blame. The one is the different humors of particular men; the other, the particular manners and opinions of our age and country. The general principles of taste are uniform in human nature: where men vary in their judgments, some defect or perversion in the faculties may commonly be remarked; proceeding either from prejudice, from want of practice, or want of delicacy; and there is just reason for approving one taste, and condemning another. But where there is such a diversity in the internal frame or external situation as is entirely blameless on both sides, and leaves no room to give one the preference above the other; in that case a certain degree of diversity in judgment is unavoidable, and we seek in vain for a standard, by which we can reconcile the contrary sentiments.

A young man, whose passions are warm, will be more sensibly touched with amorous and tender images, than a man more advanced in years, who takes pleasure in wise, philosophical reflections concerning the conduct of life and moderation of the passions. At twenty, Ovid may be the favorite author; Horace at forty; and perhaps Tacitus at fifty. Vainly would we, in such cases, endeavor to enter into the sentiments of others, and divest ourselves of those propensities, which are natural to us. We choose our favorite author as we do our friend, from a conformity of humor and disposition. Mirth or passion, sentiment or reflection; whichever of these most predominates in our temper, it gives us a peculiar sympathy with the writer who resembles us.

One person is more pleased with the sublime; another with the tender; a third with raillery. One has a strong sensibility to blemishes, and is extremely studious of correctness: another has a more lively feeling of beauties, and pardons twenty absurdities and defects for one elevated or pathetic stroke. The ear of this man is entirely turned toward conciseness and energy; that man is delighted with a copious, rich, and harmonious expression. Simplicity is affected by one; ornament by another. Comedy, tragedy, satire, odes, have each its partisans, who prefer that particular species of writing to all others. It is plainly an error in a critic, to confine his approbation to one species or style of writing, and condemn all the rest. But it is almost impossible not to feel a predilection for that which suits our particular turn and disposition. Such preferences are innocent and unavoidable, and can never reasonably be the object of dispute, because there is no standard, by which they can be decided.

For a like reason, we are more pleased, in the course of our reading, with pictures and characters, that resemble objects which are found in our own age or country, than with those which describe a different set of customs. It is not without some effort, that we reconcile ourselves to the simplicity of ancient manners, and behold princesses carrying water from the spring, and kings and heroes dressing their own victuals. We may allow in general, that the representation of such manners is no fault in the author, nor deformity in the piece; but we are not so sensibly touched with them. For this reason, comedy is not easily transferred from one age or nation to another. A Frenchman or Englishman is not pleased with the *Andria* of Terence, or *Clitia* of Machiavel; where the fine lady, upon whom all the play turns, never once appears to the spectators, but is always kept behind the scenes, suitably to the reserved humor of the ancient Greeks and modern Italians. A man of learning and reflection can make allowance for these peculiarities of manners; but a common audience can never divest themselves so far of their usual ideas and sentiments, as to relish pictures which in no wise resemble them.

But here there occurs a reflection, which may, perhaps, be useful in examining the celebrated controversy concerning ancient and modern learning; where we often find the one side excusing any seeming absurdity in the ancients from the manners of the age, and the other refusing to admit this excuse, or at least, admitting it only as an apology for the author, not for the performance. In my opinion, the proper boundaries in this subject have seldom been fixed between the contending parties. Where any innocent peculiarities of manners are represented, such as those above mentioned, they ought certainly to be admitted; and a man, who is shocked with them, gives an evident proof of false delicacy and refinement. The poet's monument more durable than brass must fall to the ground like common brick or clay, were men to make no allowance for the continual revolutions of manners and customs, and would admit of nothing but what was suitable to the prevailing fashion. Must we throw aside the pictures of our ancestors, because of their ruffs and farthingales? But where the ideas of morality and decency alter from one age to another, and where vicious manners are described, without being marked with the proper characters of blame and disapprobation; this must be allowed to disfigure the poem, and to be a real deformity. I cannot, nor is it proper I should, enter into such sentiments; and however I may excuse the poet, on account of the manners of his age, I never can relish the composition. The want of humanity and of decency, so conspicuous in the characters drawn by several of the ancient poets, even sometimes by Homer and the Greek tragedians, diminishes considerably the merit of their noble performances, and gives modern authors an advantage over them. We are not interested in the fortunes and sentiments of such rough heroes: we are displeased to find the limits of vice and virtue so much confounded: and whatever indulgence we may give to the writer on account of his prejudices, we cannot prevail on ourselves to enter into his sentiments, or bear an affection to characters, which we plainly discover to be blamable.

The case is not the same with moral principles, as with speculative opinions of any kind. These are in continual flux and revolution. The son embraces a different system from the father. Nay, there scarcely is any man, who can boast of great constance and uniformity in this particular. Whatever speculative errors may be found in the polite writings of any age or country, they detract but little from the value of those compositions. There needs but a certain turn of thought or imagination to make us enter into all the opinions, which then prevailed, and relish the sentiments or conclusions derived from them. But a very violent effort is requisite to change our judgment of manners, and excite sentiments of approbation or blame, love or hatred, different from those to which the mind from long custom has been familiarized. And where a man is confident of the rectitude of that moral standard, by which he judges, he is justly jealous of it, and will not pervert the sentiments of his heart for a moment, in complaisance to any writer whatsoever.

Of all speculative errors, those, which regard religion, are the most excusable in compositions of genius; nor is it ever permitted to judge of the civility or wisdom of any people, or even of single persons, by the grossness or refinement of their theological principles. The same good sense, that directs men in the ordinary occurrences of life, is not harkened to in religious matters, which are supposed to be placed altogether above the cognizance of human reason. On this account, all the absurdities of the pagan system of theology must be overlooked by every critic, who would pretend to form a just notion of ancient poetry; and our posterity, in their turn, must have the same indulgence to their forefathers. No religious principles can ever be imputed as a fault to any poet, while they remain merely principles, and take no such strong possession of his heart, as to lay him under the imputation of bigotry or superstition. Where that happens, they confound the sentiments of morality, and alter the natural boundaries of vice and virtue. They are therefore eternal blemishes, according to the principle above mentioned; nor are the prejudices and false opinions of the age sufficient to justify them.

It is essential to the Roman Catholic religion to inspire a violent hatred of every other worship, and to represent all pagans, Mahometans, and heretics as the objects of divine wrath and vengeance. Such sentiments, though they are in reality very blamable, are considered as virtues by the zealots of that communion, and are represented in their tragedies and epic poems as a kind of divine heroism. This bigotry has disfigured two very fine tragedies of the French theater, *Polyeucte* and *Athalie*;[6] where an intemperate zeal for particular modes of worship is set off with all the pomp imaginable, and forms the predominant character of the heroes. "What is this," says the sublime Joad to Josabet, finding her in discourse with Mathan, the priest of Baal, "does the daughter of David speak to this traitor? Are you not afraid, lest the earth should open and pour forth flames to devour you both? Or lest these holy walls should fall and crush you together? What is his purpose? Why comes that enemy of God hither to poison the air, which we breathe, with his horrid presence?" Such sentiments are received with great applause on the theater of Paris; but at London the spectators would be full as much pleased to hear Achilles tell Agamemnon, that he was a dog in his forehead, and a deer in his heart, or Jupiter threaten Juno with a sound drubbing, if she will not be quiet.

Religious principles are also a blemish in any polite composition, when they rise up to superstition, and intrude themselves into every sentiment, however remote from any connection with religion. It is no excuse for the poet, that the customs of his country had burthened life with so many religious ceremonies and observances, that no part of it was exempt from that yoke. It must forever be ridiculous in Petrarch to compare his mistress Laura, to Jesus Christ. Nor is it less ridiculous in that agreeable libertine, Boccace, very seriously to give thanks to God Almighty and the ladies, for their assistance in defending him against his enemies.

[6]Plays by Corneille and Racine, respectively. The dialogue Hume quotes is from the latter. [Ed.]

# Samuel Johnson
## 1709–1784

Samuel Johnson, the "Great Cham of Literature," is the magisterial personality that dominates the late eighteenth century in England with his insistent moralism, his unflappable common sense, and his tragic vision of life. The only son of a provincial book dealer, whose formal education came to an end after an impecunious year at Oxford, Johnson made himself into the most broadly learned man of his age.

He arrived in London in 1737, just around the time the system of patrician patronage (which had supported John Dryden so well) was giving way to the one familiar today, in which authors bargain with publishers for their material support. In his thirties, Johnson joined the army of hack writers who eked out their living by producing for the Grub Street booksellers the journalism, travel books, occasional essays, translations, and histories for which the new middle-class reading public hankered. From 1747 to 1755, in sickness and sorrow, Johnson labored virtually alone on his massive *Dictionary of the English Language;* its appearance made Johnson's reputation, became the standard dictionary for over half a century, and helped to standardize the chaotic English tongue. He wrote major works in every important literary genre of his age: They include satirical poems like "London" (1739) and "The Vanity of Human Wishes" (1749); the fable *Rasselas* (1759); the tragedy *Irene* (1749); weekly essays for *The Rambler* (1750–52), *The Adventurer* (1753–54), and *The Idler* (1758–60); an authoritative edition of Shakespeare (1763); and a massive series of biographical and critical essays, *Lives of the Poets*, on all the significant English writers of the seventeenth and eighteenth centuries (1779–81).

Johnson's criticism, like that of Sidney and Dryden and most of his own contemporaries, derives its principles from Horace: He conceives of the literary work as a piece of rhetoric to be judged by the impact it makes upon the audience. But those trying to place Johnson within the broad spectrum of rhetorical criticism should note that he takes the didactic purpose of literature far more seriously than either Horace or Dryden, and that his insistence on the universal character of poetry differentiates him from such Platonizing critics as Sidney.

"The end of writing is to instruct; the end of poetry is to instruct by pleasing," he declared in his Preface to *Shakespeare,* and this *locus classicus* dominates the rest of his theory. Didacticism is surely the keynote in his essay on the novel in *The Rambler,* No. 4 (1750). While Johnson admits that literature should imitate life, and that the novel is therefore an improvement over the romance, he sees no reason why writers should not be selective about what aspects of life they choose to imitate. The plots of novels should end with poetic justice, and in presenting characters, novelists should strive to exhibit "the most perfect idea of virtue" in their heroes, not to present characters at once fascinating and deeply flawed. The date of the essay suggests that Johnson may have been reacting specifically to

Fielding's *Tom Jones* (1749) and its scapegrace hero, but the viewpoint he presents is not topical, and it was one with which his entire age was in sympathy.

If the aim of poetry is "to instruct by pleasing," then we might inquire how that is brought about. The answer, also found in the Preface to *Shakespeare*, runs briefly thus: "Nothing can please many, and please long, but just representations of general nature." Poetry must be deeply true to life, not because art is a matter of imitation, but because the truth of accurate representation holds us longer than any artful fancy could: "The pleasures of sudden wonder are soon exhausted, and the mind can only repose on the stability of truth."

Precisely what Johnson means by "general nature" is glossed in *Rasselas,* Chapter 10, where Imlac tells the Prince that "the business of the poet is to examine not the individual but the species; to remark general properties and large appearances: he does not number the streaks of the tulip. . . . He . . . must neglect the minuter discriminations, which one may have remarked, and another have neglected, for those characteristics which are alike obvious to vigilance and carelessness." Johnson's insistence on the universality of poetry is very similar to Aristotle's, but his point is Horatian: If the literary work is to please a universal audience it must deal broadly with the world we all know, not with special issues of interest to a few.

From Johnson's universalizing perspective, the old topics of rhetorical criticism — the three unities, generic integrity, decorum of the stage — finally recede to the status of mere conventions, and conventions that were not those of Shakespeare's era. With all due reverence to the venerable antiquity of these doctrines, Johnson refutes their assumptions so thoroughly that it becomes difficult to see how they influenced so many for so long. At every point, Johnson insists that "there is always an appeal open from criticism to nature," and the old dogmas wither in the brutal spotlight of Johnson's common sense. The unities of time and place, he says, derive from "the supposed necessity of making the drama credible"; but in fact, no one in the audience believes for an instant that the things happening on stage are actually occurring. The audience's enjoyment indeed depends upon their sense that they are watching fiction. Critics have claimed that by mixing comic with tragic scenes, the passions are interrupted and the drama is deprived of emotional force. This reasoning, Johnson insinuates, is "so specious [attractive] that it is received as true even by those who in daily experience feel it to be false." To critics who object to the apparent indecorum of Shakespeare presenting King Claudius of Denmark as a drunkard, Johnson scoffs that "these are the petty cavils of petty minds."

Those who are accustomed to believe that Shakespeare could do no wrong may be surprised by Johnson's strictly judicial appraisal of the bard's faults and virtues. Johnson's didactic streak, in fact, is offended by Shakespeare's amorality, and Shakespeare's greatness is rescued only by his surpassing universality and trueness to life. In his stray judgments on Shakespeare, however, Johnson can be very shrewd — as when he states that Shakespeare's "tragedy seems to be skill, his comedy to be instinct."

The pleasures of reading Johnson's criticism are not merely intellectual. In his hands criticism becomes literature, delighting as well as instructing, and the source of the pleasure is Johnson's unique personality. We value his wisdom as much as his learning, and his tragic vision as much as his ebullient combativeness. He speaks of readers "willing to be thought wicked, if they may be allowed to be wits," and of writers who "are willing to hope from posterity what the present age refuses, and flatter themselves that the regard which is yet denied by envy, will be at last bestowed by time." He refers to the way "the common satiety of life sends us all in quest" of fantastic but worthless novelties; and reminds us that love "is only one of many passions, and . . . has no great influence upon the sum of life." It is then that we sense the presence of the very human sage who felt so deeply "The Vanity of Human Wishes."

## Selected Bibliography

Bate, Walter Jackson. *The Achievement of Samuel Johnson*. Chicago: University of Chicago Press, 1978.

Battersby, James L. *Rational Praise and Natural Lamentation: Johnson, Lycidas and Principles of Criticism*. Rutherford, N.J.: Fairleigh Dickinson University Press, 1980.

Damrosch, Leopold. *The Uses of Johnson's Criticism*. Charlottesville: University Press of Virginia, 1976.

Fussell, Paul. *Samuel Johnson and the Life of Writing*. New York: Norton, 1986.

Hagstrum, Jean H. *Samuel Johnson's Literary Criticism*. 1952; Chicago: University of Chicago Press, 1967.

Jenkins, Ralph Eugene. *Some Sources of Samuel Johnson's Literary Criticism*. Austin: University of Texas Press, 1969.

Keast, W. R. "Theoretical Foundations of Johnson's Criticism." In *Critics and Criticism: Ancient and Modern*, edited by R. S. Crane. Chicago: University of Chicago Press, 1952.

Stock, R. D. *Samuel Johnson and Neoclassical Dramatic Theory: The Literary Content of the "Preface to Shakespeare."* Lincoln: University of Nebraska Press, 1973.

# The Rambler, No. 4

*Simul et jucunda et idonea dicere vitæ.*
— HORACE, *Ars Poetica*, 334
*And join both profit and delight in one* — CREECH

The works of fiction, with which the present generation seems more particularly delighted, are such as exhibit life in its true state, diversified only by accidents that daily happen in the world, and influenced by passions and qualities which are really to be found in conversing with mankind.

This kind of writing may be termed not improperly the comedy of romance, and is to be conducted nearly by the rules of comic poetry. Its province is to bring about natural events by easy means, and to keep up curiosity without the help of wonder: it is therefore precluded from the machines and expedients of the heroic romance, and can neither employ giants to snatch away a lady from the nuptial rites, nor knights to bring her back from captivity; it can neither bewilder its personages in deserts, nor lodge them in imaginary castles.

I remember a remark made by Scaliger[1] upon Pontanus, that all his writings are filled with the same images; and that if you take from him his lilies and his roses, his satyrs and his dryads, he will have nothing left that can be called poetry. In like manner almost all the fictions of the last age will vanish, if you deprive them of a hermit and a wood, a battle and a shipwreck.

Why this wild strain of imagination found reception so long in polite and learned ages, it is not easy to conceive; but we cannot wonder that while readers could be procured, the authors were willing to continue it; for when a man had by practice gained some fluency of language, he had no further care than to retire to his closet, let loose his invention, and heat his mind with incredibilities; a book was thus produced without fear of criticism, without the toil of study, without knowledge of nature, or acquaintance with life.

The task of our present writers is very different; it requires, together with that learning which is to be gained from books, that experience which can never be attained by solitary diligence, but must arise from general converse and accurate observation of the living world. Their performances have, as Horace expresses it, *plus oneris quantum veniæ minus,* little indulgence, and therefore more difficulty.[2] They are engaged in portraits of which every one knows the original, and can detect any deviation from exactness of resemblance. Other writings are safe, except from the malice of learning, but these are in danger from every common reader; as the slipper ill executed was censured by a shoemaker who happened to stop in his way at the Venus of Apelles.[3]

But the fear of not being approved as just copiers of human manners, is not the most important concern that an author of this sort ought to have before him. These books are written chiefly to the young, the ignorant, and the idle, to whom they serve as lectures of conduct, and

introductions into life. They are the entertainment of minds unfurnished with ideas, and therefore easily susceptible of impressions; not fixed by principles, and therefore easily following the current of fancy; not informed by experience, and consequently open to every false suggestion and partial account.

That the highest degree of reverence should be paid to youth, and that nothing indecent should be suffered to approach their eyes or ears, are precepts extorted by sense and virtue from an ancient writer, by no means eminent for chastity of thought. The same kind, though not the same degree, of caution, is required in every thing which is laid before them, to secure them from unjust prejudices, perverse opinions, and incongruous combinations of images.

In the romances formerly written, every transaction and sentiment was so remote from all that passes among men, that the reader was in very little danger of making any applications to himself; the virtues and crimes were equally beyond his sphere of activity; and he amused himself with heroes and with traitors, deliverers and persecutors, as with beings of another species, whose actions were regulated upon motives of their own, and who had neither faults nor excellencies in common with himself.

But when an adventurer is levelled with the rest of the world, and acts in such scenes of the universal drama, as may be the lot of any other man; young spectators fix their eyes upon him with closer attention, and hope, by observing his behaviour and success, to regulate their own practices, when they shall be engaged in the like part.

For this reason these familiar histories may perhaps be made of greater use than the solemnities of professed morality, and convey the knowledge of vice and virtue with more efficacy than axioms and definitions. But if the power of example is so great as to take possession of the memory by a kind of violence, and produce effects almost without the intervention of the will, care ought to be taken, that, when the choice is unrestrained, the best examples only should be exhibited; and that which is likely to operate so strongly, should not be mischievous or uncertain in its effects.

[1]Julius Caesar Scaliger, *Poetics* 5:4. [Ed.]
[2]Horace, *Epistles* II.1:70. [Ed.]
[3]Pliny, *Natural History* 35:84–85. [Ed.]

The chief advantage which these fictions have over real life is, that their authors are at liberty, though not to invent, yet to select objects, and to cull from the mass of mankind, those individuals upon which the attention ought most to be employed; as a diamond, though it cannot be made, may be polished by art, and placed in such a situation, as to display that lustre which before was buried among common stones.

It is justly considered as the greatest excellency of art, to imitate nature; but it is necessary to distinguish those parts of nature, which are most proper for imitation: greater care is still required in representing life, which is so often discoloured by passion, or deformed by wickedness. If the world be promiscuously described, I cannot see of what use it can be to read the account; or why it may not be as safe to turn the eye immediately upon mankind as upon a mirror which shows all that presents itself without discrimination.

It is therefore not a sufficient vindication of a character, that it is drawn as it appears; for many characters ought never to be drawn: nor of a narrative, that the train of events is agreeable to observation and experience; for that observation which is called knowledge of the world, will be found much more frequently to make men cunning than good. The purpose of these writings is surely not only to show mankind, but to provide that they may be seen hereafter with less hazard; to teach the means of avoiding the snares which are laid by Treachery for Innocence, without infusing any wish for that superiority with which the betrayer flatters his vanity; to give the power of counteracting fraud, without the temptation to practise it; to initiate youth by mock encounters in the art of necessary defence, and to increase prudence without impairing virtue.

Many writers, for the sake of following nature, so mingle good and bad qualities in their principal personages, that they are both equally conspicuous; and as we accompany them through their adventures with delight, and are led by degrees to interest ourselves in their favour, we lose the abhorrence of their faults, because they do not hinder our pleasure, or, perhaps, regard them with some kindness, for being united with so much merit.

There have been men indeed splendidly wicked, whose endowments threw a brightness on their crimes, and whom scarce any villainy made perfectly detestable, because they never could be wholly divested of their excellencies; but such have been in all ages the great corrupters of the world, and their resemblance ought no more to be preserved, than the art of murdering without pain.

Some have advanced, without due attention to the consequences of this notion, that certain virtues have their correspondent faults, and therefore that to exhibit either apart is to deviate from probability. Thus men are observed by Swift to be "grateful in the same degree as they are resentful." This principle, with others of the same kind, supposes man to act from a brute impulse, and pursue a certain degree of inclination, without any choice of the object; for, otherwise, though it should be allowed that gratitude and resentment arise from the same constitution of the passions, it follows not that they will be equally indulged when reason is consulted; yet, unless that consequence be admitted, this sagacious maxim becomes an empty sound, without any relation to practice or to life.

Nor is it evident, that even the first motions to these effects are always in the same proportion. For pride, which produces quickness of resentment, will obstruct gratitude, by unwillingness to admit that inferiority which obligation implies; and it is very unlikely that he who cannot think he receives a favour, will acknowledge or repay it.

It is of the utmost importance to mankind, that positions of this tendency should be laid open and confuted; for while men consider good and evil as springing from the same root, they will spare the one for the sake of the other, and in judging, if not of others at least of themselves, will be apt to estimate their virtues by their vices. To this fatal error all those will contribute, who confound the colours of right and wrong, and, instead of helping to settle their boundaries, mix them with so much art, that no common mind is able to disunite them.

In narratives where historical veracity has no place, I cannot discover why there should not be exhibited the most perfect idea of virtue; of virtue not angelical, nor above probability, for what we cannot credit, we shall never imitate, but the highest and purest that humanity can reach, which, exercised in such trials as the various revolutions of things shall bring upon it, may, by conquering some calamities, and enduring others, teach us what we may hope, and what we can perform. Vice, for vice is necessary to be shown, should always disgust; nor should the graces of gaiety, or the dignity of courage, be so united with it, as to reconcile it to the mind. Wherever it appears, it should raise hatred by the malignity of its practices, and contempt by the meanness of its stratagems: for while it is supported by either parts or spirit, it will be seldom heartily abhorred. The Roman tyrant was content to be hated, if he was but feared; and there are thousands of the readers of romances willing to be thought wicked, if they may be allowed to be wits. It is therefore to be steadily inculcated, that virtue is the highest proof of understanding, and the only solid basis of greatness; and that vice is the natural consequence of narrow thoughts; that it begins in mistake, and ends in ignominy.

## Rasselas, Chapter 10

### IMLAC'S HISTORY CONTINUED

"Wherever I went, I found that Poetry was considered as the highest learning, and regarded with a veneration somewhat approaching to that which man would pay to the Angelick Nature. And it yet fills me with wonder, that, in almost all countries, the most ancient poets are considered as the best: whether it be that every other kind of knowledge is an acquisition gradually attained, and poetry is a gift conferred at once; or that the first poetry of every nation surprised them as a novelty, and retained the credit by consent which it received by accident at first: or whether the province of poetry is to describe Nature and Passion, which are always the same, and the first writers took possession of the most striking objects for description, and the most probable occurrences for fiction, and left nothing to those that followed them, but transcription of the same events, and new combinations of the same images. Whatever be the reason, it is commonly observed that the early writers are in possession of nature, and their followers of art: that the first excel in strength and invention, and the latter in elegance and refinement.

"I was desirous to add my name to this illustrious fraternity. I read all the poets of Persia and Arabia, and was able to repeat by memory the volumes that are suspended in the mosque of Mecca. But I soon found that no man was ever great by imitation. My desire of excellence impelled me to transfer my attention to nature and to life. Nature was to be my subject, and men to be my auditors: I could never describe what I had not seen: I could not hope to move those with delight or terrour, whose interests and opinions I did not understand.

"Being now resolved to be a poet, I saw every thing with a new purpose; my sphere of attention was suddenly magnified: no kind of knowledge was to be overlooked. I ranged mountains and desarts for images and resemblances, and pictured upon my mind every tree of the forest and flower of the valley. I observed with equal care the crags of the rock and the pinnacles of the palace. Sometimes I wandered along the mazes of the rivulet, and sometimes watched the changes of the summer clouds. To a poet nothing can be useless. Whatever is beautiful, and whatever is dreadful, must be familiar to his imagination: he must be conversant with all that is awfully vast or elegantly little. The plants of the garden, the animals of the wood, the minerals of the earth, and meteors of the sky, must all concur to store his mind with inexhaustible variety: for every idea is useful for the inforcement or decoration of moral or religious truth; and he, who knows most, will have most power of diversifying his scenes, and of gratifying his reader with remote allusions and unexpected instruction.

"All the appearances of nature I was therefore careful to study, and every country which I have surveyed has contributed something to my poetical powers."

"In so wide a survey, said the prince, you must surely have left much unobserved. I have lived, till now, within the circuit of these mountains, and yet cannot walk abroad without the sight of something which I had never beheld before, or never heeded."

"The business of a poet, said Imlac, is to examine, not the individual, but the species; to remark general properties and large appearances: he does not number the streaks of the tulip, or describe the different shades in the verdure of the forest. He is to exhibit in his portraits of nature such prominent and striking features, as recal the original to every mind; and must neglect the minuter discriminations, which one may have remarked, and another have neglected, for those characteristicks which are alike obvious to vigilance and carelesness.

"But the knowledge of nature is only half the task of a poet; he must be acquainted likewise with all the modes of life. His character requires that he estimate the happiness and misery of every condition; observe the power of all the passions in all their combinations, and trace the changes of the human mind as they are modified by various institutions and accidental influences of climate or custom, from the spriteliness of infancy to the despondence of decrepitude. He must divest himself of the prejudices of his age or country; he must consider right and wrong in their abstracted and invariable state; he must disregard present laws and opinions, and rise to general and transcendental truths, which will always be the same: he must therefore content himself with the slow progress of his name; contemn the applause of his own time, and commit his claims to the justice of posterity. He must write as the interpreter of nature, and the legislator of mankind, and consider himself as presiding over the thoughts and manners of successive generations; as a being superiour to time and place. His labour is not yet at an end: he must know many languages and many sciences; and, that his stile may be worthy of his thoughts, must, by incessant practice, familiarize to himself every delicacy of speech and grace of harmony."

# From *Preface to Shakespeare*

That praises are without reason lavished on the dead, and that the honours due only to excellence are paid to antiquity, is a complaint likely to be always continued by those, who, being able to add nothing to truth, hope for eminence from the heresies of paradox; or those, who, being forced by disappointment upon consolatory expedients, are willing to hope from posterity what the present age refuses, and flatter themselves that the regard which is yet denied by envy, will be at last bestowed by time.

Antiquity, like every other quality that attracts the notice of mankind, has undoubtedly votaries that reverence it, not from reason, but from prejudice. Some seem to admire indiscriminately whatever has been long preserved, without considering that time has sometimes cooperated with chance; all perhaps are more willing to honour past than present excellence; and the mind contemplates genius through the shades of age, as the eye surveys the sun through artificial opacity. The great contention of criticism is to find the faults of the moderns, and the beauties of the ancients. While an author is yet living we estimate his powers by his worst performance, and when he is dead we rate them by his best.

To works, however, of which the excellence is not absolute and definite, but gradual and comparative; to works not raised upon principles demonstrative and scientific, but appealing wholly to observation and experience, no other test can be applied than length of duration and continuance of esteem. What mankind have long possessed they have often examined and compared, and if they persist to value the possession, it is because frequent comparisons have confirmed opinion in its favour. As among the works of nature no man can properly call a river deep or a mountain high, without the knowledge of many mountains and many rivers; so in the productions of genius, nothing can be styled excellent till it has been compared with other works of the same kind. Demonstration immediately displays its power, and has nothing to hope or fear from the flux of years; but works tentative and experimental must be estimated by their proportion to the general and collective ability of man, as it is discovered in a long succession of endeavours. Of the first building that was raised, it might be with certainty determined that it was round or square, but whether it was spacious or lofty must have been referred to time. The Pythagorean scale of numbers was at once discovered to be perfect; but the poems of Homer we yet know not to transcend the common limits of human intelligence, but by remarking, that nation after nation, and century after century, has been able to do little more than transpose his incidents, new name his characters, and paraphrase his sentiments.

The reverence due to writings that have long subsisted arises therefore not from any credulous confidence in the superior wisdom of past ages, or gloomy persuasion of the degeneracy of mankind, but is the consequence of acknowledged and indubitable positions, that what has been longest known has been most considered, and what is most considered is best understood.

The Poet, of whose works I have undertaken the revision, may now begin to assume the dignity of an ancient, and claim the privilege of established fame and prescriptive veneration. He has long outlived his century, the term commonly fixed as the test of literary merit. Whatever advantages he might once derive from personal allusions, local customs, or temporary opinions, have for many years been lost; and every topic of merriment or motive of sorrow, which the modes of artificial life afforded him, now only obscure the scenes which they once illuminated. The effects of favour and competition are at an end; the tradition of his friendships and his enmities has perished; his works support no opinion with arguments, nor supply any faction with invectives; they can neither indulge vanity nor gratify malignity, but are read without any other reason than the desire of pleasure, and are therefore praised only as pleasure is obtained; yet, thus unassisted by interest or passion, they have passed through variations of taste and changes of manners, and, as they devolved from one generation to another, have received new honours at every transmission.

But because human judgement, though it be gradually gaining upon certainty, never becomes infallible; and approbation, though long continued, may yet be only the approbation of prejudice or fashion; it is proper to inquire, by what peculiarities of excellence Shakespeare has gained and kept the favour of his countrymen.

Nothing can please many, and please long, but just representations of general nature. Particular manners can be known to few, and therefore few only can judge how nearly they are copied. The irregular combinations of fanciful invention may delight a while, by that novelty of which the common satiety of life sends us all in quest; but the pleasures of sudden wonder are soon exhausted, and the mind can only repose on the stability of truth.

Shakespeare is above all writers, at least above all modern writers, the poet of nature; the poet that holds up to his readers a faithful mirror of manners and of life. His characters are not modified by the customs of particular places, unpractised by the rest of the world; by the peculiarities of studies or professions, which can operate but upon small numbers; or by the accidents of transient fashions or temporary opinions: they are the genuine progeny of common humanity, such as the world will always supply, and observation will always find. His persons act and speak by the influence of those general passions and principles by which all minds are agitated, and the whole system of life is continued in motion. In the writings of other poets a character is too often an individual; in those of Shakespeare it is commonly a species.

It is from this wide extension of design that so much instruction is derived. It is this which fills the plays of Shakespeare with practical axioms and domestic wisdom. It was said of Euripides, that every verse was a precept; and it may be said of Shakespeare, that from his works may be collected a system of civil and economical prudence. Yet his real power is not shown in the splendour of particular passages, but by the progress of his fable, and the tenor of his dialogue; and he that tries to recommend him by select quotations, will succeed like the pedant in *Hierocles,* who, when he offered his house to sale, carried a brick in his pocket as a specimen.

It will not easily be imagined how much Shakespeare excels in accommodating his sentiments to real life, but by comparing him with other authors. It was observed of the ancient schools of declamation, that the more diligently they were frequented, the more was the student disqualified for the world, because he found nothing there which he should ever meet in any other place. The same remark may be applied to every stage but that of Shakespeare. The theatre, when it is under any other direction, is peopled by such characters as were never seen conversing in a language which was never heard, upon topics which will never arise in the commerce of mankind. But the dialogue of this author is often so evidently determined by the incident which produces it, and is pursued with so much ease and simplicity, that it seems scarcely to claim the merit of fiction, but to have been gleaned by diligent selection out of common conversation, and common occurrences.

Upon every other stage the universal agent is love, by whose power all good and evil is distributed, and every action quickened or retarded. To bring a lover, a lady and a rival into the fable; to entangle them in contradictory obligations, perplex them with oppositions of interest, and harass them with violence of desires inconsistent with each other; to make them meet in rapture and part in agony; to fill their mouths with hyperbolical joy and outrageous sorrow; to distress them as nothing human ever was distressed; to deliver them as nothing human ever was delivered, is the business of a modern dramatist. For this probability is violated, life is misrepresented, and language is depraved. But love is only one of many passions, and as it has no great influence upon the sum of life, it has little operation in the dramas of a poet, who caught his ideas from the living world, and exhibited only what he saw before him. He knew, that any other passion, as it was regular or exorbitant, was a cause of happiness or calamity.

Characters thus ample and general were not easily discriminated and preserved, yet perhaps no poet ever kept his personages more distinct from each other. I will not say with Pope[1] that every speech may be assigned to the proper speaker, because many speeches there are which have nothing characteristical; but perhaps, though some may be equally adapted to every person, it will be difficult to find any that can be properly transferred from the present possessor to another claimant. The choice is right, when there is reason for choice.

Other dramatists can only gain attention by hyperbolical or aggravated characters, by fabulous and unexampled excellence or depravity, as the writers of barbarous romances invigorated the reader by a giant and a dwarf; and he that should form his expectations of human affairs from the play, or from the tale, would be equally deceived. Shakespeare has no heroes; his scenes are occupied only by men, who act and speak as the reader thinks that he should himself have spoken or acted on the same occasion. Even where the agency is supernatural the dialogue is level with life. Other writers disguise the most natural passions and most frequent incidents; so that he who contemplates them in the book will not know them in the world: Shakespeare approximates the remote, and familiarizes the wonderful; the event which he represents will not happen, but if it were possible, its effects would probably be such as he has assigned; and it may be said, that he has not only shown human nature as it acts in real exigencies, but as it would be found in trials, to which it cannot be exposed.

This therefore is the praise of Shakespeare, that his drama is the mirror of life; that he who has mazed his imagination, in following the phantoms which other writers raise up before him, may here be cured of his delirious ecstasies,

[1]In Pope's preface to his 1725 edition of Shakespeare. [Ed.]

by reading human sentiment in human language; by scenes from which a hermit may estimate the transactions of the world, and a confessor predict the progress of the passions.

His adherence to general nature has exposed him to the censure of critics, who form their judgements upon narrower principles. Dennis and Rhymer think his Romans not sufficiently Roman; and Voltaire censures his kings as not completely royal.[2] Dennis is offended, that Menenius, a senator of Rome, should play the buffoon; and Voltaire perhaps thinks decency violated when the Danish usurper is represented as a drunkard. But Shakespeare always makes nature predominate over accident; and if he preserves the essential character, is not very careful of distinctions superinduced and adventitious. His story requires Romans or kings, but he thinks only on men. He knew that Rome, like every other city, had men of all dispositions; and wanting a buffoon, he went into the senate-house for that which the senate-house would certainly have afforded him. He was inclined to show a usurper and a murderer not only odious but despicable; he therefore added drunkenness to his other qualities, knowing that kings love wine like other men, and that wine exerts its natural power upon kings. These are the petty cavils of petty minds; a poet overlooks the casual distinction of country and condition, as a painter, satisfied with the figure, neglects the drapery.

The censure which he has incurred by mixing comic and tragic scenes, as it extends to all his works, deserves more consideration. Let the fact be first stated, and then examined.

Shakespeare's plays are not in the rigorous and critical sense either tragedies or comedies, but compositions of a distinct kind; exhibiting the real state of sublunary nature, which partakes of good and evil, joy and sorrow, mingled with endless variety of proportion and innumerable modes of combination; and expressing the course of the world, in which the loss of one is the gain of another; in which, at the same time, the reveller is hasting to his wine, and the mourner burying his friend; in which the malignity of one is sometimes defeated by the frolic of another; and many mischiefs and many benefits are done and hindered without design.

Out of this chaos of mingled purposes and casualties the ancient poets, according to the laws which custom had prescribed, selected some the crimes of men, and some their absurdities; some the momentous vicissitudes of life, and some the lighter occurrences; some the terrors of distress, and some the gaieties of prosperity. Thus rose the two modes of imitation, known by the names of *tragedy* and *comedy,* compositions intended to promote different ends by contrary means, and considered as so little allied, that I do not recollect among the Greeks or Romans a single writer who attempted both.

Shakespeare has united the powers of exciting laughter and sorrow not only in one mind but in one composition. Almost all his plays are divided between serious and ludicrous characters, and, in the successive evolutions of the design, sometimes produce seriousness and sorrow, and sometimes levity and laughter.

That this is a practice contrary to the rules of criticism will be readily allowed; but there is always an appeal open from criticism to nature. The end of writing is to instruct; the end of poetry is to instruct by pleasing. That the mingled drama may convey all the instruction of tragedy or comedy cannot be denied, because it includes both in its alternations of exhibition, and approaches nearer than either to the appearance of life, by showing how great machinations and slender designs may promote or obviate one another, and the high and the low co-operate in the general system by unavoidable concatenation.

It is objected, that by this change of scenes the passions are interrupted in their progression, and that the principal event, being not advanced by a due gradation of preparatory incidents, wants at last the power to move, which constitutes the perfection of dramatic poetry. This reasoning is so specious, that it is received as true even by those who in daily experience feel it to be false. The interchanges of mingled scenes seldom fail to produce the intended vicissitudes

[2]Johnson refers to John Dennis's *Essay on the Genius and Writings of Shakespeare* (1713); Thomas Rymer's *A Short View of Tragedy* (1692); and Voltaire's *Dissertation sur la tragédie ancienne et moderne* (1749) and *Appel à toutes les nations de l'Europe* (1761). [Ed.]

of passion. Fiction cannot move so much, but that the attention may be easily transferred; and though it must be allowed that pleasing melancholy be sometimes interrupted by unwelcome levity, yet let it be considered likewise, that melancholy is often not pleasing, and that the disturbance of one man may be the relief of another; that different auditors have different habitudes; and that, upon the whole, all pleasure consists in variety.

The players, who in their edition[3] divided our author's works into comedies, histories, and tragedies, seem not to have distinguished the three kinds, by any very exact or definite ideas.

An action which ended happily to the principal persons, however serious or distressful through its intermediate incidents, in their opinion constituted a comedy. This idea of a comedy continued long amongst us, and plays were written, which, by changing the catastrophe, were tragedies today and comedies tomorrow.

Tragedy was not in those times a poem of more general dignity or elevation than comedy; it required only a calamitous conclusion, with which the common criticism of that age was satisfied, whatever lighter pleasure it afforded in its progress.

History was a series of actions, with no other than chronological succession, independent on each other, and without any tendency to introduce or regulate the conclusion. It is not always very nicely distinguished from tragedy. There is not much nearer approach to unity of action in the tragedy of *Antony and Cleopatra,* than in the history of *Richard the Second.* But a history might be continued through many plays; as it had no plan, it had no limits.

Through all these denominations of the drama, Shakespeare's mode of composition is the same; an interchange of seriousness and merriment, by which the mind is softened at one time, and exhilarated at another. But whatever be his purpose, whether to gladden or depress, or to conduct the story, without vehemence or emotion, through tracts of easy and familiar dialogue, he never fails to attain his purpose; as he commands us, we laugh or mourn, or sit silent with quiet expectation, in tranquillity without indifference.

When Shakespeare's plan is understood, most of the criticisms of Rhymer and Voltaire vanish away. The play of *Hamlet* is opened, without impropriety, by two sentinels; Iago bellows at Brabantio's window, without injury to the scheme of the play, though in terms which a modern audience would not easily endure; the character of Polonius is seasonable and useful; and the grave-diggers themselves may be heard with applause.

Shakespeare engaged in the dramatic poetry with the world open before him; the rules of the ancients were yet known to few; the public judgement was unformed; he had no example of such fame as might force him upon imitation, nor critics of such authority as might restrain his extravagance. He therefore indulged his natural disposition, and his disposition, as Rhymer has remarked, led him to comedy. In tragedy he often writes with great appearance of toil and study, what is written at last with little felicity; but in his comic scenes, he seems to produce without labour, what no labour can improve. In tragedy he is always struggling after some occasion to be comic, but in comedy he seems to repose, or to luxuriate, as in a mode of thinking congenial to his nature. In his tragic scenes there is always something wanting, but his comedy often surpasses expectation or desire. His comedy pleases by the thoughts and the language, and his tragedy for the greater part by incident and action. His tragedy seems to be skill, his comedy to be instinct.

The force of his comic scenes has suffered little diminution from the changes made by a century and a half, in manners or in words. As his personages act upon principles arising from genuine passion, very little modified by particular forms, their pleasures and vexations are communicable to all times and to all places; they are natural, and therefore durable; the adventitious peculiarities of personal habits, are only superficial dies, bright and pleasing for a little while, yet soon fading to a dim tint, without any remains of former lustre; but the discriminations of true passion are the colours of nature; they

---

[3]John Heminges and Henry Condell, who edited the First Folio in 1623. [Ed.]

pervade the whole mass, and can only perish with the body that exhibits them. The accidental compositions of heterogeneous modes are dissolved by the chance which combined them; but the uniform simplicity of primitive qualities neither admits increase, nor suffers decay. The sand heaped by one flood is scattered by another, but the rock always continues in its place. The stream of time, which is continually washing the dissoluble fabrics of other poets, passes without injury by the adamant of Shakespeare.

If there be, what I believe there is, in every nation, a style which never becomes obsolete, a certain mode of phraseology so consonant and congenial to the analogy and principles of its respective language as to remain settled and unaltered; this style is probably to be sought in the common intercourse of life, among those who speak only to be understood, without ambition of elegance. The polite are always catching modish innovations, and the learned depart from established forms of speech, in hope of finding or making better; those who wish for distinction forsake the vulgar, when the vulgar is right; but there is a conversation above grossness and below refinement, where propriety resides, and where this poet seems to have gathered his comic dialogue. He is therefore more agreeable to the ears of the present age than any other author equally remote, and among his other excellencies deserves to be studied as one of the original masters of our language.

These observations are to be considered not as unexceptionably constant, but as containing general and predominant truth. Shakespeare's familiar dialogue is affirmed to be smooth and clear, yet not wholly without ruggedness or difficulty; as a country may be eminently fruitful, though it has spots unfit for cultivation. His characters are praised as natural, though their sentiments are sometimes forced, and their actions improbable; as the earth upon the whole is spherical, though its surface is varied with protuberances and cavities.

Shakespeare with his excellencies has likewise faults, and faults sufficient to obscure and overwhelm any other merit. I shall show them in the proportion in which they appear to me, without envious malignity or superstitious veneration. No question can be more innocently discussed than a dead poet's pretensions to renown; and little regard is due to that bigotry which sets candour higher than truth.

His first defect is that to which may be imputed most of the evil in books or in men. He sacrifices virtue to convenience, and is so much more careful to please than to instruct, that he seems to write without any moral purpose. From his writings indeed a system of social duty may be selected, for he that thinks reasonably must think morally; but his precepts and axioms drop casually from him; he makes no just distribution of good or evil, nor is always careful to show in the virtuous a disapprobation of the wicked; he carries his persons indifferently through right and wrong, and at the close dismisses them without further care, and leaves their examples to operate by chance. This fault the barbarity of his age cannot extenuate; for it is always a writer's duty to make the world better, and justice is a virtue independent on time or place.

The plots are often so loosely formed, that a very slight consideration may improve them, and so carelessly pursued, that he seems not always fully to comprehend his own design. He omits opportunities of instructing or delighting which the train of his story seems to force upon him, and apparently rejects those exhibitions which would be more affecting, for the sake of those which are more easy.

It may be observed, that in many of his plays the latter part is evidently neglected. When he found himself near the end of his work, and in view of his reward, he shortened the labour to snatch the profit. He therefore remits his efforts where he should most vigorously exert them, and his catastrophe is improbably produced or imperfectly represented.

He had no regard to distinction of time or place, but gives to one age or nation, without scruple, the customs, institutions, and opinions of another, at the expense not only of likelihood, but of possibility. These faults Pope has endeavoured, with more zeal than judgement, to transfer to his imagined interpolators. We need not wonder to find Hector quoting Aristotle,[4] when

---

[4]In *Troilus and Cressida*, II.ii.166–67. [Ed.]

we see the loves of Theseus and Hippolyta combined with the Gothic mythology of fairies. Shakespeare, indeed, was not the only violator of chronology, for in the same age Sidney, who wanted not the advantages of learning, has, in his *Arcadia,* confounded the pastoral with the feudal times, the days of innocence, quiet and security, with those of turbulence, violence, and adventure.

In his comic scenes he is seldom very successful, when he engages his characters in reciprocations of smartness and contests of sarcasm; their jests are commonly gross, and their pleasantry licentious; neither his gentlemen nor his ladies have much delicacy, nor are sufficiently distinguished from his clowns by any appearance of refined manners. Whether he represented the real conversation of his time is not easy to determine; the reign of Elizabeth is commonly supposed to have been a time of stateliness, formality and reserve; yet perhaps the relaxations of that severity were not very elegant. There must, however, have been always some modes of gaiety preferable to others, and a writer ought to choose the best.

In tragedy his performance seems constantly to be worse, as his labour is more. The effusions of passion which exigence forces out are for the most part striking and energetic; but whenever he solicits his invention, or strains his faculties, the offspring of his throes is tumour, meanness, tediousness, and obscurity.

In narration he affects a disproportionate pomp of diction, and a wearisome train of circumlocution, and tells the incident imperfectly in many words, which might have been more plainly delivered in few. Narration in dramatic poetry is naturally tedious, as it is unanimated and inactive, and obstructs the progress of the action; it should therefore always be rapid, and enlivened by frequent interruption. Shakespeare found it an encumbrance, and instead of lightening it by brevity, endeavoured to recommend it by dignity and splendour.

His declamations or set speeches are commonly cold and weak, for his power was the power of nature; when he endeavoured, like other tragic writers, to catch opportunities of amplification, and instead of inquiring what the occasion demanded, to show how much his stores of knowledge could supply, he seldom escapes without the pity or resentment of his reader.

It is incident to him to be now and then entangled with an unwieldy sentiment, which he cannot well express, and will not reject; he struggles with it a while, and if it continues stubborn, comprises it in words such as occur, and leaves it to be disentangled and evolved by those who have more leisure to bestow upon it.

Not that always where the language is intricate the thought is subtle, or the image always great where the line is bulky; the equality of words to things is very often neglected, and trivial sentiments and vulgar ideas disappoint the attention, to which they are recommended by sonorous epithets and swelling figures.

But the admirers of this great poet have never less reason to indulge their hopes of supreme excellence, than when he seems fully resolved to sink them in dejection, and mollify them with tender emotions by the fall of greatness, the danger of innocence, or the crosses of love. He is not long soft and pathetic without some idle conceit, or contemptible equivocation. He no sooner begins to move, than he counteracts himself; and terror and pity, as they are rising in the mind, are checked and blasted by sudden frigidity.

A quibble is to Shakespeare, what luminous vapours are to the traveller; he follows it at all adventures, it is sure to lead him out of his way, and sure to engulf him in the mire. It has some malignant power over his mind, and its fascinations are irresistible. Whatever be the dignity or profundity of his disquisition, whether he be enlarging knowledge or exalting affection, whether he be amusing attention with incidents, or enhancing it in suspense, let but a quibble spring up before him, and he leaves his work unfinished. A quibble is the golden apple for which he will always turn aside from his career, or stoop from his elevation. A quibble, poor and barren as it is, gave him such delight, that he was content to purchase it, by the sacrifice of reason, propriety and truth. A quibble was to him the fatal Cleopatra for which he lost the world, and was content to lose it.

It will be thought strange, that, in enumerating the defects of this writer, I have not yet mentioned his neglect of the unities; his violation of those laws which have been instituted and established by the joint authority of poets and of critics.

For his other deviations from the art of writing, I resign him to critical justice, without making any other demand in his favour, than that which must be indulged to all human excellence; that his virtues be rated with his failings: but, from the censure which his irregularity may bring upon him, I shall, with due reverence to that learning which I must oppose, adventure to try how I can defend him.

His histories, being neither tragedies nor comedies, are not subject to any of their laws; nothing more is necessary to all the praise which they expect, than that the changes of action be so prepared as to be understood, that the incidents be various and affecting, and the characters consistent, natural and distinct. No other unity is intended, and therefore none is to be sought.

In his other works he has well enough preserved the unity of action. He has not, indeed, an intrigue regularly perplexed and regularly unravelled; he does not endeavour to hide his design only to discover it, for this is seldom the order of real events, and Shakespeare is the poet of nature: but his plan has commonly what Aristotle requires, a beginning, a middle, and an end;[5] one event is concatenated with another, and the conclusion follows by easy consequence. There are perhaps some incidents that might be spared, as in other poets there is much talk that only fills up time upon the stage; but the general system makes gradual advances, and the end of the play is the end of expectation.

To the unities of time and place he has shown no regard, and perhaps a nearer view of the principles on which they stand will diminish their value, and withdraw from them the veneration which, from the time of Corneille,[6] they have very generally received, by discovering that they have given more trouble to the poet, than pleasure to the auditor.

The necessity of observing the unities of time and place arises from the supposed necessity of making the drama credible. The critics hold it impossible, that an action of months or years can be possibly believed to pass in three hours; or that the spectator can suppose himself to sit in the theatre, while ambassadors go and return between distant kings, while armies are levied and towns besieged, while an exile wanders and returns, or till he whom they saw courting his mistress, shall lament the untimely fall of his son. The mind revolts from evident falsehood, and fiction loses its force when it departs from the resemblance of reality.

From the narrow limitation of time necessarily arises the contraction of place. The spectator, who knows that he saw the first act at Alexandria, cannot suppose that he sees the next at Rome, at a distance to which not the dragons of Medea could, in so short a time, have transported him; he knows with certainty that he has not changed his place; and he knows that place cannot change itself; that what was a house cannot become a plain; that what was Thebes can never be Persepolis.

Such is the triumphant language with which a critic exults over the misery of an irregular poet, and exults commonly without resistance or reply. It is time therefore to tell him, by the authority of Shakespeare, that he assumes, as an unquestionable principle, a position which, while his breath is forming it into words, his understanding pronounces to be false. It is false, that any representation is mistaken for reality; that any dramatic fable in its materiality was ever credible, or, for a single moment, was ever credited.

The objection arising from the impossibility of passing the first hour at Alexandria, and the next at Rome, supposes, that when the play opens, the spectator really imagines himself at Alexandria, and believes that his walk to the theatre has been a voyage to Egypt, and that he lives in the days of Antony and Cleopatra. Surely he that imagines this may imagine more. He that can take the stage at one time for the palace of the Ptolemies, may take it in half an hour for the promontory of Actium. Delusion, if delusion be admitted, has no certain limitation; if the spectator can be once persuaded, that his old acquain-

[5]Aristotle, *Poetics*, Ch. 7; see pp. 47–48. [Ed.]
[6]Pierre Corneille's *Discours des trois unités* was published in 1660. For other discussions of the three unities, see the selections from Sidney and Dryden. [Ed.]

tance are Alexander and Caesar, that a room illuminated with candles is the plain of Pharsalia, or the bank of Granicus, he is in a state of elevation above the reach of reason, or of truth, and from the heights of empyrean poetry, may despise the circumscriptions of terrestrial nature. There is no reason why a mind thus wandering in ecstasy should count the clock, or why an hour should not be a century in that calenture[7] of the brains that can make the stage a field.

The truth is, that the spectators are always in their senses, and know, from the first act to the last, that the stage is only a stage, and that the players are only players. They came to hear a certain number of lines recited with just gesture and elegant modulation. The lines relate to some action, and an action must be in some place; but the different actions that complete a story may be in places very remote from each other; and where is the absurdity of allowing that space to represent first Athens, and then Sicily, which was always known to be neither Sicily nor Athens, but a modern theatre?

By supposition, as place is introduced time may be extended; the time required by the fable elapses for the most part between the acts; for, of so much of the action as is represented, the real and poetical duration is the same. If, in the first act, preparations for war against Mithridates are represented to be made in Rome, the event of the war may without absurdity, be represented, in the catastrophe, as happening in Pontus; we know that there is neither war, nor preparation for war; we know that we are neither in Rome nor Pontus; that neither Mithridates nor Lucullus are before us. The drama exhibits successive imitations of successive actions, and why may not the second imitation represent an action that happened years after the first; if it be so connected with it, that nothing but time can be supposed to intervene. Time is, of all modes of existence, most obsequious to the imagination; a lapse of years is as easily conceived as a passage of hours. In contemplation we easily contract the time of real actions, and therefore willingly permit it to be contracted when we only see their imitation.

It will be asked, how the drama moves, if it is not credited. It is credited with all the credit due to a drama. It is credited, whenever it moves, as a just picture of a real original; as representing to the auditor what he would himself feel, if he were to do or suffer what is there feigned to be suffered or to be done. The reflection that strikes the heart is not, that the evils before us are real evils, but that they are evils to which we ourselves may be exposed. If there be any fallacy, it is not that we fancy the players, but that we fancy ourselves unhappy for a moment; but we rather lament the possibility than suppose the presence of misery, as a mother weeps over her babe, when she remembers that death may take it from her. The delight of tragedy proceeds from our consciousness of fiction; if we thought murders and treasons real, they would please no more.

Imitations produce pain or pleasure, not because they are mistaken for realities, but because they bring realities to mind. When the imagination is recreated by a painted landscape, the trees are not supposed capable to give us shade, or the fountains coolness; but we consider, how we should be pleased with such fountains playing beside us, and such woods waving over us. We are agitated in reading the history of *Henry the Fifth,* yet no man takes his book for the field of Agincourt. A dramatic exhibition is a book recited with concomitants that increase or diminish its effect. Familiar comedy is often more powerful in the theatre, than on the page; imperial tragedy is always less. The humour of Petruchio may be heightened by grimace; but what voice or what gesture can hope to add dignity or force to the soliloquy of Cato?

A play read, affects the mind like a play acted. It is therefore evident, that the action is not supposed to be real, and it follows that between the acts a longer or shorter time may be allowed to pass, and that no more account of space or duration is to be taken by the auditor of a drama, than by the reader of a narrative, before whom may pass in an hour the life of a hero, or the revolutions of an empire.

Whether Shakespeare knew the unities, and rejected them by design, or deviated from them by happy ignorance, it is, I think, impossible to

[7]Disorder. [Ed]

decide, and useless to inquire. We may reasonably suppose, that, when he rose to notice, he did not want the counsels and admonitions of scholars and critics, and that he at last deliberately persisted in a practice, which he might have begun by chance. As nothing is essential to the fable, but unity of action, and as the unities of time and place arise evidently from false assumptions, and, by circumscribing the extent of the drama, lessen its variety, I cannot think it much to be lamented, that they were not known by him, or not observed: nor, if such another poet could arise, should I very vehemently reproach him, that his first act passed at Venice, and his next in Cyprus. Such violations of rules merely positive, become the comprehensive genius of Shakespeare, and such censures are suitable to the minute and slender criticism of Voltaire:

> Non usque adeo permiscuit imis
> Longus summa dies, ut non, si voce Metelli
> Serventur leges, malint a Cœsare tolli.[8]

Yet when I speak thus slightly of dramatic rules, I cannot but recollect how much wit and learning may be produced against me; before such authorities I am afraid to stand, not that I think the present question one of those that are to be decided by mere authority, but because it is to be suspected, that these precepts have not been so easily received but for better reasons than I have yet been able to find. The result of my inquiries, in which it would be ludicrous to boast of impartiality, is, that the unities of time and place are not essential to a just drama, that though they may sometimes conduce to pleasure, they are always to be sacrificed to the nobler beauties of variety and instruction; and that a play, written with nice observation of critical rules, is to be contemplated as an elaborate curiosity, as the product of superfluous and ostentatious art, by which is shown, rather what is possible, than what is necessary.

He that, without diminution of any other excellence, shall preserve all the unities unbroken,

deserves the like applause with the architect, who shall display all the orders of architecture in a citadel, without any deduction from its strength; but the principal beauty of a citadel is to exclude the enemy; and the greatest graces of a play, are to copy nature and instruct life.

Perhaps, what I have here not dogmatically but deliberately written, may recall the principles of the drama to a new examination. I am almost frightened at my own temerity; and when I estimate the fame and the strength of those that maintain the contrary opinion, am ready to sink down in reverential silence; as Æneas withdrew from the defence of Troy, when he saw Neptune shaking the wall, and Juno heading the besiegers.[9]

Those whom my arguments cannot persuade to give their approbation to the judgement of Shakespeare, will easily, if they consider the condition of his life, make some allowance for his ignorance.

Every man's performances, to be rightly estimated, must be compared with the state of the age in which he lived, and with his own particular opportunities; and though to the reader a book be not worse or better for the circumstances of the author, yet as there is always a silent reference of human works to human abilities, and as the inquiry, how far man may extend his designs, or how high he may rate his native force, is of far greater dignity than in what rank we shall place any particular performance, curiosity is always busy to discover the instruments, as well as to survey the workmanship, to know how much is to be ascribed to original powers, and how much to casual and adventitious help. The palaces of Peru or Mexico were certainly mean and incommodious habitations, if compared to the houses of European monarchs; yet who could forbear to view them with astonishment, who remembered that they were built without the use of iron?

The English nation, in the time of Shakespeare, was yet struggling to emerge from barbarity. The philology of Italy had been transplanted hither in the reign of Henry the Eighth;

---

[8]"So long a time has not passed that the laws themselves would not prefer to be broken by Caesar than supported by Metellus." Lucan, *Pharsalia* 3:138–40. [Ed.]

[9]Virgil, *Aeneid* 2:610–15. [Ed.]

and the learned languages had been successfully cultivated by Lilly, Linacre and More; by Pole, Cheke, and Gardiner; and afterwards by Smith, Clerk, Haddon, and Ascham.[10] Greek was now taught to boys in the principal schools; and those who united elegance with learning, read, with great diligence, the Italian and Spanish poets. But literature was yet confined to professed scholars, or to men and women of high rank. The public was gross and dark; and to be able to read and write, was an accomplishment still valued for its rarity.

Nations, like individuals, have their infancy. A people newly awakened to literary curiosity, being yet unacquainted with the true state of things, knows not how to judge of that which is proposed as its resemblance. Whatever is remote from common appearance is always welcome to vulgar, as to childish credulity; and of a country unenlightened by learning, the whole people is the vulgar. The study of those who then aspired to plebeian learning was laid out upon adventures, giants, dragons, and enchantments. *The Death of Arthur*[11] was the favourite volume.

The mind, which has feasted on the luxurious wonders of fiction, has no taste of the insipidity of truth. A play which imitated only the common occurrences of the world, would upon the admirers of *Palmerin* and *Guy of Warwick,* have made little impression; he that wrote for such an audience was under the necessity of looking round for strange events and fabulous transactions, and that incredibility, by which maturer knowledge is offended, was the chief recommendation of writings, to unskilful curiosity.

Our author's plots are generally borrowed from novels, and it is reasonable to suppose, that he chose the most popular, such as were read by many, and related by more; for his audience

could not have followed him through the intricacies of the drama, had they not held the thread of the story in their hands.

The stories, which we now find only in remoter authors, were in his time accessible and familiar. The fable of *As you like it*, which is supposed to be copied from Chaucer's *Gamelyn*,[12] was a little pamphlet of those times; and old Mr. Cibber[13] remembered the tale of *Hamlet* in plain English prose, which the critics have now to seek in *Saxo Grammaticus*.[14]

His English histories he took from English chronicles and English ballads; and as the ancient writers were made known to his countrymen by versions, they supplied him with new subjects; he dilated some of Plutarch's lives into plays, when they had been translated by North.[15]

His plots, whether historical or fabulous, are always crowded with incidents, by which the attention of a rude people was more easily caught than by sentiment or argumentation; and such is the power of the marvellous even over those who despise it, that every man finds his mind more strongly seized by the tragedies of Shakespeare than of any other writer; others please us by particular speeches, but he always makes us anxious for the event, and has perhaps excelled all but Homer in securing the first purpose of a writer, by exciting restless and unquenchable curiosity, and compelling him that reads his work to read it through.

The shows and bustle with which his plays abound, have the same original. As knowledge advances, pleasure passes from the eye to the ear, but returns, as it declines, from the ear to the eye. Those to whom our author's labours were exhibited had more skill in pomps or processions than in poetical language, and perhaps wanted some visible and discriminated events, as comments on the dialogue. He knew how he should most please; and whether his practice is more agreeable to nature, or whether his

[10]Johnson's honor roll of Renaissance humanists includes William Lily, the author of a Latin grammar; Thomas Linacre, a Greek scholar; Thomas More, author of *Utopia* and other Latin works; Reginald Pole and Stephen Gardiner, scholar–statesmen who served Henry VIII and Mary Tudor; Sir John Cheke, who taught Greek at Cambridge; Sir Thomas Smith and Walter Haddon taught at Cambridge; John Clerk was Wolsey's chaplain; Roger Ascham was tutor to Elizabeth and the author of *Toxophilus*. [Ed.]

[11]Sir Thomas Malory's *Morte D'Arthur*. [Ed.]

[12]A tale once attributed to Chaucer. [Ed.]

[13]Colley Cibber (1671–1757). The book referred to is *History of Hamblet* published in 1608, too late to be the source of Shakespeare's play. [Ed.]

[14]Saxo Grammaticus's *Historia Danica* (1514). [Ed.]

[15]In 1579. [Ed.]

example has prejudiced the nation, we still find that on our stage something must be done as well as said, and inactive declamation is very coldly heard, however musical or elegant, passionate or sublime.

Voltaire expresses his wonder, that our author's extravagances are endured by a nation, which has seen the tragedy of *Cato*. Let him be answered, that Addison speaks the language of poets, and Shakespeare, of men. We find in *Cato* innumerable beauties which enamour us of its author, but we see nothing that acquaints us with human sentiments or human actions; we place it with the fairest and the noblest progeny which judgement propagates by conjunction with learning, but *Othello* is the vigorous and vivacious offspring of observation impregnated by genius. *Cato* affords a splendid exhibition of artificial and fictitious manners, and delivers just and noble sentiments, in diction easy, elevated and harmonious, but its hopes and fears communicate no vibration to the heart; the composition refers us only to the writer; we pronounce the name of *Cato*, but we think on Addison.

The work of a correct and regular writer is a garden accurately formed and diligently planted, varied with shades, and scented with flowers; the composition of Shakespeare is a forest, in which oaks extend their branches, and pines tower in the air, interspersed sometimes with weeds and brambles, and sometimes giving shelter to myrtles and to roses; filling the eye with awful pomp, and gratifying the mind with endless diversity. Other poets display cabinets of precious rarities, minutely finished, wrought into shape, and polished unto brightness. Shakespeare opens a mine which contains gold and diamonds in unexhaustible plenty, though clouded by incrustations, debased by impurities, and mingled with a mass of meaner minerals.

It has been much disputed, whether Shakespeare owed his excellence to his own native force, or whether he had the common helps of scholastic education, the precepts of critical science, and the examples of ancient authors.

There has always prevailed a tradition, that Shakespeare wanted learning, that he had no regular education, nor much skill in the dead languages. Jonson, his friend, affirms, that "he had

small Latin, and no Greek";[16] who, besides that he had no imaginable temptation to falsehood, wrote at a time when the character and acquisitions of Shakespeare were known to multitudes. His evidence ought therefore to decide the controversy, unless some testimony of equal force could be opposed.

Some have imagined, that they have discovered deep learning in many imitations of old writers; but the examples which I have known urged, were drawn from books translated in his time; or were such easy coincidences of thought, as will happen to all who consider the same subjects; or such remarks on life or axioms of morality as float in conversation, and are transmitted through the world in proverbial sentences.

I have found it remarked, that, in this important sentence, "Go before, I'll follow," we read a translation of, *I prae, sequar*. I have been told, that when Caliban, after a pleasing dream, says, "I cry'd to sleep again," the author imitates Anacreon, who had, like every other man, the same wish on the same occasion.

There are a few passages which may pass for imitations, but so few, that the exception only confirms the rule; he obtained them from accidental quotations, or by oral communication, and as he used what he had, would have used more if he had obtained it.

The *Comedy of Errors* is confessedly taken from the *Menæchmi* of Plautus; from the only play of Plautus which was then in English.[17] What can be more probable, than that he who copied that, would have copied more; but that those which were not translated were inaccessible?

Whether he knew the modern languages is uncertain. That his plays have some French scenes proves but little; he might easily procure them to be written, and probably, even though he had known the language in the common degree, he could not have written it without assistance. In the story of *Romeo and Juliet* he is observed to have followed the English translation, where it deviates from the Italian; but this

[16]In the verses prefaced to the First Folio. [Ed.]
[17]The 1595 translation of *Menaechmi* by W. W. probably postdates Shakespeare's *Comedy of Errors*. [Ed.]

on the other part proves nothing against his knowledge of the original. He was to copy, not what he knew himself, but what was known to his audience.

It is most likely that he had learned Latin sufficiently to make him acquainted with construction, but that he never advanced to an easy perusal of the Roman authors. Concerning his skill in modern languages, I can find no sufficient ground of determination; but as no imitations of French or Italian authors have been discovered, though the Italian poetry was then high in esteem, I am inclined to believe, that he read little more than English, and chose for his fables only such tales as he found translated.

That much knowledge is scattered over his works is very justly observed by Pope, but it is often such knowledge as books did not supply. He that will understand Shakespeare, must not be content to study him in the closet, he must look for his meaning sometimes among the sports of the field, and sometimes among the manufactures of the shop.

There is however proof enough that he was a very diligent reader, nor was our language then so indigent of books, but that he might very liberally indulge his curiosity without excursion into foreign literature. Many of the Roman authors were translated, and some of the Greek; the reformation had filled the kingdom with theological learning; most of the topics of human disquisition had found English writers; and poetry had been cultivated, not only with diligence, but success. This was a stock of knowledge sufficient for a mind so capable of appropriating and improving it.

But the greater part of his excellence was the product of his own genius. He found the English stage in a state of the utmost rudeness; no essays either in tragedy or comedy had appeared, from which it could be discovered to what degree of delight either one or other might be carried. Neither character nor dialogue were yet understood. Shakespeare may be truly said to have introduced them both amongst us, and in some of his happier scenes to have carried them both to the utmost height.

By what gradations of improvement he proceeded, is not easily known; for the chronology of his works is yet unsettled. Rowe is of opinion, that

> perhaps we are not to look for his beginning, like those of other writers, in his least perfect works; art had so little, and nature so large a share in what he did, that for ought I know, [says he] the performances of his youth, as they were the most vigorous, were the best.[18]

But the power of nature is only the power of using to any certain purpose the materials which diligence procures, or opportunity supplies. Nature gives no man knowledge, and when images are collected by study and experience, can only assist in combining or applying them. Shakespeare, however favoured by nature, could impart only what he had learned; and as he must increase his ideas, like other mortals, by gradual acquisition, he, like them, grew wiser as he grew older, could display life better, as he knew it more, and instruct with more efficacy, as he was himself more amply instructed.

There is a vigilance of observation and accuracy of distinction which books and precepts cannot confer; from this almost all original and native excellence proceeds. Shakespeare must have looked upon mankind with perspicacity, in the highest degree curious and attentive. Other writers borrow their characters from preceding writers, and diversify them only by the accidental appendages of present manners; the dress is a little varied, but the body is the same. Our author had both matter and form to provide; for except the characters of Chaucer, to whom I think he is not much indebted, there were no writers in English, and perhaps not many in other modern languages, which showed life in its native colours.

The contest about the original benevolence or malignity of man had not yet commenced. Speculation had not yet attempted to analyse the mind, to trace the passions to their sources, to unfold the seminal principles of vice and virtue, or sound the depths of the heart for the motives of action. All those inquiries, which from that time that human nature became the fashionable

[18]Nicholas Rowe, *Some Account of the Life &c of Mr. William Shakespeare* (1709). [Ed.]

study, have been made sometimes with nice discernment, but often with idle subtlety, were yet unattempted. The tales, with which the infancy of learning was satisfied, exhibited only the superficial appearances of action, related the events but omitted the causes, and were formed for such as delighted in wonders rather than in truth. Mankind was not then to be studied in the closet; he that would know the world, was under the necessity of gleaning his own remarks, by mingling as he could in its business and amusements.

Boyle congratulated himself upon his high birth, because it favoured his curiosity, by facilitating his access. Shakespeare had no such advantage; he came to London a needy adventurer, and lived for a time by very mean employments. Many works of genius and learning have been performed in states of life, that appear very little favourable to thought or to inquiry; so many, that he who considers them is inclined to think that he sees enterprise and perseverance predominating over all external agency, and bidding help and hindrance vanish before them. The genius of Shakespeare was not to be depressed by the weight of poverty, not limited by the narrow conversation to which men in want are inevitably condemned; the incumbrances of his fortune were shaken from his mind, "as dewdrops from a lion's mane."[19]

Though he had so many difficulties to encounter, and so little assistance to surmount them, he has been able to obtain an exact knowledge of many modes of life, and many casts of native dispositions; to vary them with great multiplicity; to mark them by nice distinctions; and to show them in full view by proper combinations. In this part of his performances he had none to imitate, but has himself been imitated by all succeeding writers; and it may be doubted, whether from all his successors more maxims of theoretical knowledge, or more rules of practical prudence, can be collected, than he alone has given to his country.

Nor was his attention confined to the actions of men; he was an exact surveyor of the inanimate world; his descriptions have always some peculiarities, gathered by contemplating things as they really exist. It may be observed, that the oldest poets of many nations preserve their reputation, and that the following generations of wit, after a short celebrity, sink into oblivion. The first, whoever they be, must take their sentiments and descriptions immediately from knowledge; the resemblance is therefore just, their descriptions are verified by every eye, and their sentiments acknowledged by every breast. Those whom their fame invites to the same studies, copy partly them, and partly nature, till the books of one age gain such authority, as to stand in the place of nature to another, and imitation, always deviating a little, becomes at last capricious and casual. Shakespeare, whether life or nature be his subject, shows plainly, that he has seen with his own eyes; he gives the image which he receives, not weakened or distorted by the intervention of any other mind; the ignorant feel his representations to be just, and the learned see that they are complete.

Perhaps it would not be easy to find any author, except Homer, who invented so much as Shakespeare, who so much advanced the studies which he cultivated, or effused so much novelty upon his age or country. The form, the characters, the language, and the shows of the English drama are his. He seems, says Dennis,

to have been the very original of our *English* tragical harmony, that is, the harmony of blank verse, diversified often by dissyllable and trissyllable terminations. For the diversity distinguishes it from heroic harmony, and by bringing it nearer to common use makes it more proper to gain attention, and more fit for action and dialogue. Such verse we make when we are writing prose; we make such verse in common conversation.[20]

I know not whether this praise is rigorously just. The dissyllable termination, which the critic rightly appropriates to the drama, is to be found, though, I think, not in *Gorboduc* which is confessedly before our author; yet in *Hieronimo*,[21] of which the date is not certain, but which there

---

[19]*Troilus and Cressida,* III.iii.224. [Ed.]

[20]In *Essay on the Genius and Writings of Shakespeare*, II:4–5. [Ed.]
[21]Thomas Kyd's *Spanish Tragedy* (1592). [Ed.]

is reason to believe at least as old as his earliest plays. This however is certain, that he is the first who taught either tragedy or comedy to please, there being no theatrical piece of any older writer, of which the name is known, except to antiquaries and collectors of books, which are sought because they are scarce, and would not have been scarce, had they been much esteemed.

To him we must ascribe the praise, unless Spenser may divide it with him, of having first discovered to how much smoothness and harmony the English language could be softened. He has speeches, perhaps sometimes scenes, which have all the delicacy of Rowe, without his effeminacy. He endeavours indeed commonly to strike by the force and vigour of his dialogue, but he never executes his purpose better, than when he tries to soothe by softness.

Yet it must be at last confessed that as we owe every thing to him, he owes something to us; that, if much of his praise is paid by perception and judgement, much is likewise given by custom and veneration. We fix our eyes upon his graces, and turn them from his deformities, and endure in him what we should in another loathe or despise. If we endured without praising, respect for the father of our drama might excuse us; but I have seen, in the book of some modern critic, a collection of anomalies, which show that he has corrupted language by every mode of depravation, but which his admirer has accumulated as a monument of honour.

He has scenes of undoubted and perpetual excellence, but perhaps not one play, which, if it were now exhibited as the work of a contemporary writer, would be heard to the conclusion. I am indeed far from thinking, that his works were wrought to his own ideas of perfection; when they were such as would satisfy the audience, they satisfied the writer. It is seldom that authors, though more studious of fame than Shakespeare, rise much above the standard of their own age; to add a little to what is best will always be sufficient for present praise, and those who find themselves exalted into fame, are willing to credit their encomiasts, and to spare the labour of contending with themselves.

It does not appear, that Shakespeare thought his works worthy of posterity, that he levied any ideal tribute upon future times, or had any further prospect, than of present popularity and present profit. When his plays had been acted, his hope was at an end; he solicited no addition of honour from the reader. He therefore made no scruple to repeat the same jests in many dialogues, or to entangle different plots by the same knot of perplexity, which may be at least forgiven him, by those who recollect, that of Congreve's four comedies, two are concluded by a marriage in a mask, by a deception, which perhaps never happened, and which, whether likely or not, he did not invent.[22]

So careless was this great poet of future fame, that, though he retired to ease and plenty, while he was yet little "declined into the vale of years,"[23] before he could be disgusted with fatigue, or disabled by infirmity, he made no collection of his works, nor desired to rescue those that had been already published from the depravations that obscured them, or secure to the rest a better destiny, by giving them to the world in their genuine state.

[22]*The Old Bachelor* and *Love for Love*. [Ed.]
[23]*Othello*, III.iii.269–70. [Ed.]

# Immanuel Kant
## 1724–1804

It is an irony of the history of philosophy that the most revolutionary thinker of the eighteenth century, an unwitting founder of the romantic movement, should have lived a life whose restriction and regularity were the stuff of legend. Immanuel Kant, son of a saddlemaker, was born and educated in the Prussian seaport of Königsberg, became professor of philosophy at the university, and died without traveling more than forty miles from his birthplace. His self-discipline was so stringent and his routine so invariable that Königsbergers reputedly set their watches by him: He was awakened daily at five A.M., read for two hours, lectured to his students for two hours, wrote for two hours, and then went to a restaurant for his midday meal, where, at the height of his fame, crowds of strangers would gather to see and hear him.

Kant began his career as a scientist rather than a metaphysician (his collected works include treatises on earthquakes and lunar volcanos), and he may have turned to philosophy to determine for himself the boundaries between the physical questions that may result in positive knowledge and the moral and aesthetic questions that can only produce further speculation.

In his *Critique of Pure Reason* (1781), Kant shifted the entire basis of our understanding of perception by showing how the mind, previously considered a passive receptor of objective sense data, instead actively *creates* the sensual world of which we are conscious. But because each mind has essentially the same equipment and performs the same operations, and because these creative operations occur prior to consciousness, we are able — in fact, we are forced — to experience the world of the senses as though it were objectively present. This theory of the mind has had immense influence on critical theory. (See the headnote for Samuel Taylor Coleridge on p. 299 for a fuller discussion of Kant's theory of perception.) In his *Critique of Judgment* (1790), Kant takes a similar tack. Just as the sensual world is the product of our subjective mental processes rather than of objective features, so our judgments of beauty are also subjective. The beauty of a work of art or a natural landscape exists nowhere but in the eye of the beholder. Yet because of their special qualities, aesthetic judgments seem to have an objective character and to reflect universal rather than individual concerns.

Kant has an unenviable reputation as one of the most perversely difficult of philosophers. His language tends to be abstract, it is true, but he proceeds slowly and delights in giving examples. The major problem readers often have with the *Critique of Judgment* involves their misunderstanding of the exact nature of the questions Kant is trying to answer. He is not trying, as Plato might have done, to define the essence of Beauty, since for him, such essences have no meaning. Nor is he concerned, as Aristotle was, to note what features good works of art have in common. His interest is in the mind, not in the object: He is more of a psychologist than a metaphysician. His overriding question might be paraphrased as follows: When a person looks at a flower or listens to a symphony and experiences it as beautiful, what propositions does that moment of aesthetic judgment strictly entail? When someone looks at Velasquez's *Las Meninas* and exclaims in aesthetic delight, what mental experience is implicit in that exclamation? Kant analyzes that mental experience in a vigorous and systematic way, by running it through his list of categories (Quality, Quantity, Relation, Modality).

The first issue is Quality: What sort of mental process underlies the judgment that a work of art or of nature is beautiful? Here Kant distinguishes beauty from two other types of judgments, those of utility and ethical goodness. Something is useful when it is good for an individual (though it may not benefit anybody else); ethically good things — virtuous actions — are universally beneficial, since it is to each person's collective advantage that everyone act justly. But to judge something as beautiful, is to approve of it *freely,* without considering individual or collective interests. (Obviously some works of art — like a Frank Lloyd Wright house — can be functional as well as beautiful, but the judgment of beauty, strictly speaking, has nothing to do with function.) Personal satisfaction in a thing of beauty, therefore, is entirely *disinterested.*

The second issue is Quantity. Some judgments we make — that something is *pleasant*, for example — are *singular*: We apply them purely as individuals. Someone might enjoy raspberries but without any sense that others should agree; if a friend says he detests raspberries, a rational reaction is "All the more for me!" Other judgments are *universal*: We apply them as individuals but with a sense that our judgment holds for all humankind. Ethical judgments are universal in this sense. If we are morally outraged at, for example, the Iranian persecution of the Baha'i faith, our judgment is combined with a sense that everyone ought to agree with us. According to Kant, the judgment of taste is *universal*, like moral judgments, not *singular*, like the judgment that something is pleasant; for to judge a thing as beautiful is also to *impute* that judgment implicitly to everyone else. Kant is not saying that aesthetic judgments are *in practice* universal, that everyone in fact agrees about what is and is not beautiful; he knew as well as Hume that human tastes differ enormously. His point is only that the *disinterested* quality of our sense of beauty makes us feel that, since there is nothing peculiar about us or our situation, everyone similarly placed ought to make the same judgment.

The third issue in the judgment of taste has to do with the "relations of purposes" inherent in it, which is the closest Kant comes to talking about the nature of beauty. His contemporaries had proposed that beauty was a matter of simple charm (Winckelmann) or the contemplation of perfection (Wolff). Kant disagreed: For him the central experience in a beautiful object is "the form of purposiveness without purpose" (*Zweckmässigkeit ohne Zweck*). That is, works of art and natural beauty evince relationships of parts to whole or means to end that are *like* artifacts that have purposes. The intricacy of the interaction of themes in a Bach fugue or the pattern of petals in a chrysanthemum is like the patterned intricacy of a precisely tooled machine; but the machine is made to serve another end — an exterior purpose — while the formal purposiveness in the fugue or the flower is an end in itself. However, Kant is never talking about what is objectively *in* the object we find beautiful. He is talking about the psychological experience of judgment and this sense of purposiveness-without-purpose as something that takes hold within us.

Kant's thesis under his final category, Modality, seems to follow from all that has gone before: Taste is an *exemplary* judgment. By this Kant means that our aesthetic feelings do not seem to be merely random; rather, they feel as though they were the *necessary* consequence of a rule, but one we cannot state. Our sense of beauty seems to be formed prior to conceptual knowledge, and its basis seems to be common sense. As a result, there can be (indeed, must be) disagreements about taste. But, as the proverb states, there cannot be *disputations* about taste, since there are no general, a priori principles to which we can rationally appeal.

In the second book, Kant takes up another common topic of late eighteenth-century aesthetics: the differences between the beautiful and the sublime. Consistently, Kant's interest is in psychological processes rather than in realities; he is less concerned to explain what things we consider sublime than to help us understand the motions of the mind when we experience it. Motion is important here, for the sublime is psychologically *dynamic*, while the beautiful is a matter of restful contemplation.

The movement of the mind that constitutes the sublime resembles one or the other of two mental acts: cognition or desire. But herein lies the paradox. We judge something to be sublime precisely when cognition fails — when in looking up into the starry sky, for instance, we experience a height, or depth, or magnitude that defies reason or is beyond our power to comprehend. On the other hand, it may be that the principles of rational desire are overthrown. When we contemplate something horrible and dangerous, like rocky cliffs or a storm at sea, and yet manage to stifle the imaginative desire to flee, we also experience the sublime. This means that the sublime depends on human reason, with its attendant limitations. An angelic or divine mind could experience the beautiful, as Kant defines it, but an omnipotent and omniscient God could not find his own handiwork sublime.

In Section 49, near the end of the *Critique of Judgment*, Kant shifts his interest from the (chiefly) eighteenth-century issue of *taste* to the quintessentially romantic issue of *genius*, from the psychological qualities involved in the reception of beauty to those involved in its creation.[1] His discussion not developed at great length or in detail, but one can see in it many of the ideas that later German critics, such as Schiller, were to take up and that students of German philosophy, such as Coleridge, were to import into the English tradition.

[1] Kant here also shifts his attention away from the beauty of nature to that of art. Where Hume's essay on taste had taken the response of the spectator to *art* (especially poetry) as the typical moment of aesthetic judgment, Kant instead presented taste as in terms of the response to nature ("flowers" he says "are typical free beauties"). Perhaps this is because in nature the forms of animals, plants, and landscapes seem clearly ends in themselves and our response to them almost unconditioned by social motives.

Here we begin with Kant's presentation of the imagination as the primary mental faculty in genius, and one that is primarily *creative and intuitive* rather than *rational and cognitive*. The imagination indulges in the free play of spirit, breaking the laws that bind rational thought (though it follows laws of its own) and "creating another nature . . . out of the material that actual nature gives it." Genius consists of the ability to seize and make concrete this free play of spirit and then to embody it in a material that will make it universally communicable. In this final process, the imagination must work unfettered yet somehow under the control of the understanding. This enables the creator to get *outside* the creative process in order to assess the product of the imagination as it would appear to the spirit of another. Artists must therefore be at once creators and consumers: They must approach their creations from the outside, via their faculty of taste, to shape and mold them into proper form.

But on the other side, the consumer of art must also be, potentially, at least, a producer, because the product of the artist's free play is what Kant calls an *aesthetical idea*. Unlike a *rational idea*, an aesthetical idea calls up the faculty of cognition only to defeat it by employing more thought in the representation than we can clearly grasp. To comprehend aesthetical ideas embodied in a poem or painting requires the free play of the listener or viewer's imagination as well.

In a sense, however, Kant had appealed to this free play of the spirit even in the earlier sections of the *Critique of Judgment* — particularly when he defined beauty as a product of the subjective sense of purposiveness (rational structure) cut loose from purpose itself. How could it be anything but a free play of the mind, untrammeled by the usually utilitarian (or ethical) notions of purpose, that could succeed in thus divorcing form from goal.

## Selected Bibliography

Cassirer, H. W. *Commentary on Kant's Critique of Judgment*. London: Methuen, 1938.

Cohen, Ted, and Paul Guyer, eds. *Essays in Kant's Aesthetics*. Chicago: University of Chicago Press, 1982.

Coleman, Francis X. J. *The Harmony of Reason: A Study in Kant's Aesthetics*. Pittsburgh: University of Pittsburgh Press, 1974.

Crawford, Donald W. *Kant's Aesthetic Theory*. Madison: University of Wisconsin Press, 1974.

Guyer, Paul. *Kant and the Claims of Taste*. Cambridge: Harvard University Press, 1979.

Jaspers, Karl. *Kant*. Munich: R. Piper, 1975.

McCloskey, Mary A. *Kant's Aesthetic*. Basingstoke, Hampshire: Macmillan, 1987.

Richardson, Robert Allan. *Aesthetics and Freedom: A Critique of Kant's Analysis of Beauty*. New Haven: Yale University Press, 1969.

Rogerson, Kenneth F. *Kant's Aesthetics: The Roles of Form and Expression*. Lanham, Md.: University Press of America, 1986.

Schaper, Eva. *Studies in Kant's Aesthetics*. Edinburgh: University of Edinburgh Press, 1979.

Zimmerman, R. L. "Kant: The Aesthetic Judgment." *Journal of Aesthetics and Art Criticism* 21 (1963): 333–44.

# From *Critique of Judgment*

## First Book.
## Analytic of the Beautiful

### FIRST MOMENT. OF THE JUDGMENT OF TASTE,[1] ACCORDING TO QUALITY

### *1. The Judgment of Taste Is Aesthetical*

In order to distinguish whether anything is beautiful or not, we refer the representation, not by the understanding to the object for cognition, but by the imagination (perhaps in conjunction with the understanding) to the subject and its feeling of pleasure or pain. The judgment of taste is therefore not a judgment of cognition, and is consequently not logical but aesthetical, by which we understand that whose determining ground can be *no other than subjective*. Every reference of representations, even that of sensations, may be objective (and then it signifies the real element of an empirical representation), save only the reference to the feeling of pleasure and pain, by which nothing in the object is signified, but through which there is a feeling in the subject as it is affected by the representation.

To apprehend a regular, purposive building by means of one's cognitive faculty (whether in a clear or a confused way of representation) is something quite different from being conscious of this representation as connected with the sensation of satisfaction. Here the representation is altogether referred to the subject and to its feeling of life, under the name of the feeling of pleasure or pain. This establishes a quite separate faculty

Translated by J. H. Bernard.

[1]The definition of "taste" which is laid down here is that it is the faculty of judging of the beautiful. But the analysis of judgments of taste must show what is required in order to call an object beautiful. The moments to which this judgment has regard in its reflection I have sought in accordance with the guidance of the logical functions of judgment (for in a judgment of taste a reference to the understanding is always involved). I have considered the moment of quality first because the aesthetical judgment upon the beautiful first pays attention to it. [Au.]

of distinction and of judgment, adding nothing to cognition, but only comparing the given representation in the subject with the whole faculty of representations, of which the mind is conscious in the feeling of its state. Given representations in a judgment can be empirical (consequently, aesthetical); but the judgment which is formed by means of them is logical, provided they are referred in the judgment to the object. Conversely, if the given representations are rational, but are referred in a judgment simply to the subject (to its feeling), the judgment is so far always aesthetical.

### *2. The Satisfaction Which Determines the Judgment of Taste Is Disinterested*

The satisfaction which we combine with the representation of the existence of an object is called "interest." Such satisfaction always has reference to the faculty of desire, either as its determining ground or as necessarily connected with its determining ground. Now when the question is if a thing is beautiful, we do not want to know whether anything depends or can depend on the existence of the thing, either for myself or for anyone else, but how we judge it by mere observation (intuition or reflection). If anyone asks me if I find that palace beautiful which I see before me, I may answer: I do not like things of that kind which are made merely to be stared at. Or I can answer like that Iroquois Sachem, who was pleased in Paris by nothing more than by the cook shops. Or again, after the manner of Rousseau, I may rebuke the vanity of the great who waste the sweat of the people on such superfluous things. In fine, I could easily convince myself that if I found myself on an uninhabited island without the hope of ever again coming among men, and could conjure up just such a splendid building by my mere wish, I should not even give myself the trouble if I had a sufficiently comfortable hut. This may all be admitted and approved, but we are not now talking of this. We wish only to know if this mere representation of the object is accompanied in me with satisfaction, however indifferent I may be as regards the existence of the object of this representation. We easily see that, in saying it is *beautiful* and in showing that I have taste, I am concerned, not with that in which I depend on the existence of the object, but with that which I make out of this representation in myself. Everyone must admit that a judgment about beauty, in which the least interest mingles, is very partial and is not a pure judgment of taste. We must not be in the least prejudiced in favor of the existence of the things, but be quite indifferent in this respect, in order to play the judge in things of taste.

We cannot, however, better elucidate this proposition, which is of capital importance, than by contrasting the pure disinterested[2] satisfaction in judgments of taste with that which is bound up with an interest, especially if we can at the same time be certain that there are no other kinds of interest than those which are to be now specified.

### 3. The Satisfaction in the Pleasant Is Bound Up with Interest

*That which pleases the senses in sensation is "pleasant."* Here the opportunity presents itself of censuring a very common confusion of the double sense which the word "sensation" can have, and of calling attention to it. All satisfaction (it is said or thought) is itself sensation (of a pleasure). Consequently everything that pleases is pleasant because it pleases (and according to its different degrees or its relations to other pleasant sensations it is *agreeable, lovely, delightful, enjoyable,* etc.) But if this be admitted, then impressions of sense which determine the inclination, fundamental propositions of reason which

[2]A judgment upon an object of satisfaction may be quite *disinterested*, but yet very *interesting*, i.e., not based upon an interest, but bringing an interest with it; of this kind are all pure moral judgments. Judgments of taste, however, do not in themselves establish any interest. Only in society is it *interesting* to have taste; the reason of this will be shown in the sequel. [Au.]

determine the will, mere reflective forms of intuition which determine the judgment, are quite the same as regards the effect upon the feeling of pleasure. For this would be pleasantness in the sensation of one's state; and since in the end all the operations of our faculties must issue in the practical and unite in it as their goal, we could suppose no other way of estimating things and their worth than that which consists in the gratification that they promise. It is of no consequence at all how this is attained, and since then the choice of means alone could make a difference, men could indeed blame one another for stupidity and indiscretion, but never for baseness and wickedness. For thus they all, each according to his own way of seeing things, seek one goal, that is, gratification.

If a determination of the feeling of pleasure or pain is called sensation, this expression signifies something quite different from what I mean when I call the representation of a thing (by sense, as a receptivity belonging to the cognitive faculty) sensation. For in the latter case the representation is referred to the object, in the former simply to the subject, and is available for no cognition whatever, not even for that by which the subject *cognizes* itself.

In the above elucidation we understand by the word "sensation" an objective representation of sense; and, in order to avoid misinterpretation, we shall call that which must always remain merely subjective and can constitute absolutely no representation of an object by the ordinary term "feeling." The green color of the meadows belongs to *objective* sensation, as a perception of an object of sense; the pleasantness of this belongs to *subjective* sensation by which no object is represented, i.e., to feeling, by which the object is considered as an object of satisfaction (which does not furnish a cognition of it).

Now that a judgment about an object by which I describe it as pleasant expresses an interest in it, is plain from the fact that by sensation it excites a desire for objects of that kind; consequently the satisfaction presupposes, not the mere judgment about it, but the relation of its existence to my state, so far as this is affected by such an object. Hence we do not merely say of the pleasant, *it pleases,* but, *it gratifies.* I give to it no mere asssent, but inclination is aroused by it; and in the case of what is pleasant in the most lively fashion there is no judgment at all upon the character of the object, for those persons who always lay themselves out for enjoyment (for that is the word describing intense gratification) would fain dispense with all judgment.

### 4. The Satisfaction in the Good Is Bound Up with Interest

Whatever by means of reason pleases through the mere concept is *good.* That which pleases only as a means we call *good for something* (the useful), but that which pleases for itself is *good in itself.* In both there is always involved the concept of a purpose, and consequently the relation of reason to the (at least possible) volition, and thus a satisfaction in the *presence* of an object or an action, i.e., some kind of interest.

In order to find anything good, I must always know what sort of a thing the object ought to be, i.e., I must have a concept of it. But there is no need of this to find a thing beautiful. Flowers, free delineations, outlines intertwined with one another without design and called conventional foliage, have no meaning, depend on no definite concept, and yet they please. The satisfaction in the beautiful must depend on the reflection upon an object, leading to any concept (however indefinite), and it is thus distinguished from the pleasant, which rests entirely upon sensation.

It is true, the pleasant seems in many cases to be the same as the good. Thus people are accustomed to say that all gratification (especially if it lasts) is good in itself, which is very much the same as to say that lasting pleasure and the good are the same. But we can soon see that this is merely a confusion of words, for the concepts which properly belong to these expressions can in no way be interchanged. The pleasant, which, as such, represents the object simply in relation to sense, must first be brought by the concept of a purpose under principles of reason, in order to call it good, as an object of the will. But that there is involved a quite different relation to sat-isfaction in calling that which gratifies at the same time *good* may be seen from the fact that, in the case of the good, the question always is whether it is mediately or immediately good (useful or good in itself); but on the contrary in the case of the pleasant, there can be no question about this at all, for the word always signifies something which pleases immediately. (The same is applicable to what I call beautiful.)

Even in common speech men distinguish the pleasant from the good. Of a dish which stimulates the taste by spices and other condiments we say unhesitatingly that it is pleasant, though it is at the same time admitted not to be good; for though it immediately *delights* the senses, yet mediately, i.e., considered by reason which looks to the after results, it displeases. Even in the judging of health we may notice this distinction. It is immediately pleasant to everyone possessing it (at least negatively, i.e., as the absence of all bodily pains). But in order to say that it is good, it must be considered by reason with reference to purposes, viz., that it is a state which makes us fit for all our business. Finally, in respect of happiness, everyone believes himself entitled to describe the greatest sum of the pleasantness of life (as regards both their number and their duration) as a true, even as the highest, good. However, reason is opposed to this. Pleasantness is enjoyment. And if we were concerned with this alone, it would be foolish to be scrupulous as regards the means which procure it for us, or to care whether it is obtained passively by the bounty of nature or by our own activity and work. But reason can never be persuaded that the existence of a man who merely lives for *enjoyment* (however busy he may be in this point of view) has a worth in itself, even if he at the same time is conducive as a means to the best enjoyment of others and shares in all their gratifications by sympathy. Only what he does, without reference to enjoyment, in full freedom and independently of what nature can procure for him passively, gives an absolute worth to his presence in the world as the existence of a person; and happiness, with the whole abundance of its pleasures, is far from being an unconditioned good.[3]

[3]An obligation to enjoyment is a manifest absurdity. Thus

However, notwithstanding all this difference between the pleasant and the good, they both agree in this that they are always bound up with an interest in their object; so are not only the pleasant (§ 3), and the mediate good (the useful) which is pleasing as a means toward pleasantness somewhere, but also that which is good absolutely and in every aspect, viz., moral good, which brings with it the highest interest. For the good is the object of will (i.e., of a faculty of desire determined by reason). But to wish for something and to have a satisfaction in its existence, i.e., to take an interest in it, are identical.

## 5. Comparison of the Three Specifically Different Kinds of Satisfaction

The pleasant and the good have both a reference to the faculty of desire, and they bring with them, the former a satisfaction pathologically conditioned (by impulses, *stimuli*), the latter a pure practical satisfaction which is determined not merely by the representation of the object but also by the represented connection of the subject with the existence of the object. It is not merely the object that pleases, but also its existence. On the other hand, the judgment of taste is merely *contemplative;* i.e., it is a judgment which, indifferent as regards the existence of an object, compares its character with the feeling of pleasure and pain. But this contemplation itself is not directed to concepts; for the judgment of taste is not a cognitive judgment (either theoretical or practical), and thus is not *based* on concepts, nor has it concepts as its *purpose*.

The pleasant, the beautiful, and the good designate then three different relations of representations to the feeling of pleasure and pain, in reference to which we distinguish from one another objects or methods of representing them. And the expressions corresponding to each, by which we mark our complacency in them, are not the same. That which *gratifies* a man is called

pleasant; that which merely *pleases* him is *beautiful*; that which is *esteemed* or *approved* by him, i.e., that to which he accords an objective worth, is *good*. Pleasantness concerns irrational animals also, but beauty only concerns men, i.e., animal, but still rational, beings — not merely *qua* rational (e.g., spirits), but *qua* animal also — and the good concerns every rational being in general. This is a proposition which can only be completely established and explained in the sequel. We may say that, of all these three kinds of satisfaction, that of taste in the beautiful is alone a disinterested and *free* satisfaction; for no interest, either of sense or of reason, here forces our assent. Hence we may say of satisfaction that it is related in the three aforesaid cases to *inclination,* to *favor,* or to *respect*. Now *favor* is the only free satisfaction. An object of inclination and one that is proposed to our desire by a law of reason leave us no freedom in forming for ourselves anywhere an object of pleasure. All interest presupposes or generates a want, and, as the determining ground of assent, it leaves the judgment about the object no longer free.

As regards the interest of inclination in the case of the pleasant, everyone says that hunger is the best sauce, and everything that is eatable is relished by people with a healthy appetite; and thus a satisfaction of this sort shows no choice directed by taste. It is only when the want is appeased that we can distinguish which of many men has or has not taste. In the same way there may be manners (conduct) without virtue, politeness without good will, decorum without modesty, etc. For where the moral law speaks there is no longer, objectively, a free choice as regards what is to be done; and to display taste in its fulfillment (or in judging of another's fulfillment of it) is something quite different from manifesting the moral attitude of thought. For this involves a command and generates a want, while moral taste only plays with the objects of satisfaction, without attaching itself to one of them.

*Explanation of the Beautiful Resulting from the First Moment*

*Taste* is the faculty of judging of an object or a method of representing it by an *entirely disin-*

---

the obligation to all actions which have merely enjoyment for their aim can only be a pretended one, however spiritually it may be conceived (or decked out), even if it is a mystical, or so-called heavenly, enjoyment. [Au.]

*terested* satisfaction or dissatisfaction. The object of such satisfaction is called *beautiful*.[4]

## SECOND MOMENT. OF THE JUDGMENT OF TASTE, ACCORDING TO QUANTITY

### 6. The Beautiful Is That Which Apart from Concepts Is Represented as the Object of a Universal Satisfaction

This explanation of the beautiful can be derived from the preceding explanation of it as the object of an entirely disinterested satisfaction. For the fact of which everyone is conscious, that the satisfaction is for him quite disinterested, implies in his judgment a ground of satisfaction for all men. For since it does not rest on any inclination of the subject (nor upon any other premeditated interest), but since the person who judges feels himself quite *free* as regards the satisfaction which he attaches to the object, he cannot find the ground of this satisfaction in any private conditions connected with his own subject, and hence it must be regarded as grounded on what he can presuppose in every other person. Consequently he must believe that he has reason for attributing a similar satisfaction to everyone. He will therefore speak of the beautiful as if beauty were a characteristic of the object and the judgment logical (constituting a cognition of the object by means of concepts of it), although it is only aesthetical and involves merely a reference of the representation of the object to the subject. For it has this similarity to a logical judgment that we can presuppose its validity for all men. But this universality cannot arise from concepts; for from concepts there is no transition to the feeling of pleasure or pain (except in pure practical laws, which bring an interest with them such

as is not bound up with the pure judgment of taste). Consequently the judgment of taste, accompanied with the consciousness of separation from all interest, must claim validity for every man, without this universality depending on objects. That is, there must be bound up with it a title to subjective universality.

### 7. Comparison of the Beautiful with the Pleasant and the Good by Means of the Above Characteristic

As regards the pleasant, everyone is content that his judgment, which he bases upon private feeling and by which he says of an object that it pleases him, should be limited merely to his own person. Thus he is quite contented that if he says, "Canary wine is pleasant," another man may correct his expression and remind him that he ought to say, "It is pleasant *to me*." And this is the case not only as regards the taste of the tongue, the palate, and the throat, but for whatever is pleasant to anyone's eyes and ears. To one, violet color is soft and lovely; to another, it is washed out and dead. One man likes the tone of wind instruments, another that of strings. To strive here with the design of reproving as incorrect another man's judgment which is different from our own, as if the judgments were logically opposed, would be folly. As regards the pleasant, therefore, the fundamental proposition is valid: *Everyone has his own taste* (the taste of sense).

The case is quite different with the beautiful. It would (on the contrary) be laughable if a man who imagined anything to his own taste thought to justify himself by saying: "The object (the house we see, the coat that person wears, the concert we hear, the poem submitted to our judgment) is beautiful *for me*." For he must not call it *beautiful* if it merely pleases him. Many things may have for him charm and pleasantness — no one troubles himself at that — but if he gives out anything as beautiful, he supposes in others the same satisfaction; he judges not merely for himself, but for everyone, and speaks of beauty as if it were a property of things. Hence he says "the *thing* is beautiful"; and he does not count on the agreement of others with this his judgment

[4]Ueberweg points out (*History of Philosophy, II*, 528, English translation) that Mendelssohn had already called attention to the disinterestedness of our satisfaction in the beautiful. "It appears," says Mendelssohn, "to be a particular mark of the beautiful, that it is contemplated with quiet satisfaction, that it pleases, even though it be not in our possession, and even though we be never so far removed from the desire to put it to our use." But, of course, as Ueberweg remarks, Kant's conception of disinterestedness extends far beyond the idea of merely not desiring to possess the object. [Tr.]

of satisfaction, because he has found this agreement several times before, but he *demands* it of them. He blames them if they judge otherwise and he denies them taste, which he nevertheless requires from them. Here, then, we cannot say that each man has his own particular taste. For this would be as much as to say that there is no taste whatever, i.e., no aesthetical judgment which can make a rightful claim upon everyone's assent.

At the same time we find as regards the pleasant that there is an agreement among men in their judgments upon it in regard to which we deny taste to some and attribute it to others, by this not meaning one of our organic senses, but a faculty of judging in respect of the pleasant generally. Thus we say of a man who knows how to entertain his guests with pleasures (of enjoyment for all the senses), so that they are all pleased, he has taste." But here the universality is only taken comparatively; and there emerge rules which are only *general* (like all empirical ones), and not *universal*, which latter the judgment of taste upon the beautiful undertakes or lays claim to. It is a judgment in reference to sociability, so far as this rests on empirical rules. In respect of the good it is true that judgments make rightful claim to validity for everyone; but the good is represented only *by means of a concept* as the object of a universal satisfaction, which is the case neither with the pleasant nor with the beautiful.

## 8. The Universality of the Satisfaction Is Represented in a Judgment of Taste Only as Subjective

This particular determination of the universality of an aesthetical judgment, which is to be met with in a judgment of taste, is noteworthy, not indeed for the logician, but for the transcendental philosopher. It requires no small trouble to discover its origin, but we thus detect a property of our cognitive faculty which without this analysis would remain unknown.

First, we must be fully convinced of the fact that in a judgment of taste (about the beautiful) the satisfaction in the object is imputed to *every-one,* without being based on a concept (for then it would be the good). Further, this claim to universal validity so essentially belongs to a judgment by which we describe anything as *beautiful* that, if this were not thought in it, it would never come into our thoughts to use the expression at all, but everything which pleases without a concept would be counted as pleasant. In respect of the latter, everyone has his own opinion; and no one assumes in another agreement with his judgment of taste, which is always the case in a judgment of taste about beauty. I may call the first the taste of sense, the second the taste of reflection, so far as the first lays down mere private judgments and the second judgments supposed to be generally valid (public), but in both cases aesthetical (not practical) judgments about an object merely in respect of the relation of its representation to the feeling of pleasure and pain. Now here is something strange. As regards the taste of sense, not only does experience show that its judgment (of pleasure or pain connected with anything) is not valid universally, but everyone is content not to impute agreement with it to others (although actually there is often found a very extended concurrence in these judgments). On the other hand, the taste of reflection has its claim to the universal validity of its judgments (about the beautiful) rejected often enough, as experience teaches, although it may find it possible (as it actually does) to represent judgments which can demand this universal agreement. In fact it imputes this to everyone for each of its judgments of taste, without the persons that judge disputing as to the possibility of such a claim, although in particular cases they cannot agree as to the correct application of this faculty.

Here we must, in the first place, remark that a universality which does not rest on concepts of objects (not even on empirical ones) is not logical but aesthetical; i.e., it involves no objective quantity of the judgment, but only that which is subjective. For this I use the expression *general validity,* which signifies the validity of the reference of a representation, not to the cognitive faculty, but to the feeling of pleasure and pain for every subject. (We can avail ourselves also of the same expression for the logical quantity of the judgment, if only we prefix "objective" to "universal validity," to distinguish it from that which is merely subjective and aesthetical.)

A judgment with *objective universal validity* is also always valid subjectively; i.e., if the judgment holds for everything contained under a given concept, it holds also for everyone who represents an object by means of this concept. But from a *subjective universal validity*, i.e., aesthetical and resting on no concept, we cannot infer that which is logical because that kind of judgment does not extend to the object. But, therefore, the aesthetical universality which is ascribed to a judgment must be of a particular kind, because it does not unite the predicate of beauty with the concept of the object, considered in its whole logical sphere, and yet extends it to the whole sphere of judging persons.

In respect of logical quantity, all judgments of taste are *singular* judgments. For because I must refer the object immediately to my feeling of pleasure and pain, and that not by means of concepts, they cannot have the quantity of objective generally valid judgments. Nevertheless, if the singular representation of the object of the judgment of taste, in accordance with the conditions determining the latter, were transformed by comparison into a concept, a logically universal judgment could result therefrom. E.g., I describe by a judgment of taste the rose that I see as beautiful. But the judgment which results from the comparison of several singular judgments, "Roses in general are beautiful," is no longer described simply as aesthetical, but as a logical judgment based on an aesthetical one. Again the judgment, "The rose is pleasant" (to use) is, although aesthetical and singular, not a judgment of taste but of sense. It is distinguished from the former by the fact that the judgment of taste carries with it an *aesthetic quantity* of universality, i.e., of validity for everyone, which cannot be found in a judgment about the pleasant. It is only judgments about the good which, although they also determine satisfaction in an object, have logical and not merely aesthetical universality, for they are valid of the object as cognitive of it, and thus are valid for everyone.

If we judge objects merely according to concepts, then all representation of beauty is lost.

Thus there can be no rule according to which anyone is to be forced to recognize anything as beautiful. We cannot press [upon others] by the aid of any reasons or fundamental propositions our judgment that a coat, a house, or a flower is beautiful. People wish to submit the object to their own eyes, as if the satisfaction in it depended on sensation; and yet, if we then call the object beautiful, we believe that we speak with a universal voice, and we claim the assent of everyone, although on the contrary all private sensation can only decide for the observer himself and his satisfaction.

We may see now that in the judgment of taste nothing is postulated but such a *universal voice,* in respect of the satisfaction without the intervention of concepts, and thus the *possibility* of an aesthetical judgment that can, at the same time, be regarded as valid for everyone. The judgment of taste itself does not *postulate* the agreement of everyone (for that can only be done by a logically universal judgment because it can adduce reasons); it only *imputes* this agreement to everyone, as a case of the rule in respect of which it expects, not confirmation by concepts, but assent from others. The universal voice is, therefore, only an idea (we do not yet inquire upon what it rests). It may be uncertain whether or not the man who believes that he is laying down a judgment of taste is, as a matter of fact, judging in conformity with that idea; but that he refers his judgment thereto, and consequently that it is intended to be a judgment of taste, he announces by the expression "beauty." He can be quite certain of this for himself by the mere consciousness of the separating off everything belonging to the pleasant and the good from the satisfaction which is left; and this is all for which he promises himself the agreement of everyone — a claim which would be justifiable under these conditions, provided only he did not often make mistakes, and thus lay down an erroneous judgment of taste. . . .

*Explanation of the Beautiful Resulting from the Second Moment*

The *beautiful* is that which pleases universally without requiring a concept.

## THIRD MOMENT. OF JUDGMENTS OF TASTE, ACCORDING TO THE RELATION OF THE PURPOSES WHICH ARE BROUGHT INTO CONSIDERATION IN THEM

### *10. Of Purposiveness in General*

If we wish to explain what a purpose is according to its transcendental determinations (without presupposing anything empirical like the feeling of pleasure), we say that the purpose is the object of a concept, insofar as the concept is regarded as the cause of the object (the real ground of its possibility); and the causality of a *concept* in respect of its *object* is its purposiveness (*forma finalis*). Where then not merely the cognition of an object but the object itself (its form and existence) is thought as an effect only possible by means of the concept of this latter, there we think a purpose. The representation of the effect is here the determining ground of its cause and precedes it. The consciousness of the causality of a representation, for *maintaining* the subject in the same state, may here generally denote what we call pleasure; while on the other hand pain is that representation which contains the ground of the determination of the state of representations into their opposite of restraining or removing them.[5]

The faculty of desire, so far as it is determinable to act only through concepts, i.e., in conformity with the representation of a purpose, would be the will. But an object, or a state of mind, or even an action is called purposive, although its possibility does not necessarily presuppose the representation of a purpose, merely because its possibility can be explained and conceived by us only so far as we assume for its ground a causality according to purposes, i.e., in accordance with a will which has regulated it according to the representation of a certain rule. There can be, then, purposiveness without purpose, so far as we do not place the causes of this form in a will, but yet can only make the expla-

nation of its possibility intelligible to ourselves by deriving it from a will. Again, we are not always forced to regard what we observe (in respect of its possibility) from the point of view of reason. Thus we can at least observe a purposiveness according to form, without basing it on a purpose (as the material of the *nexus finalis*), and remark it in objects, although only by reflection.

### *11. The Judgment of Taste Has Nothing at Its Basis but the Form of the Purposiveness of an Object (or of Its Mode of Representation)*

Every purpose, if it be regarded as a ground of satisfaction, always carries with it an interest — as the determining ground of the judgment — about the object of pleasure. Therefore no subjective purpose can lie at the basis of the judgment of taste. But also the judgment of taste can be determined by no representation of an objective purpose, i.e., of the possibility of the object itself in accordance with principles of purposive combination, and consequently by no concept of the good, because it is an aesthetical and not a cognitive judgment. It therefore has to do with no *concept* of the character and internal or external possibility of the object by means of this or that cause, but merely with the relation of the representative powers to one another, so far as they are determined by a representation.

Now this relation in the determination of an object as beautiful is bound up with the feeling of pleasure, which is declared by the judgment of taste to be valid for everyone; hence a pleasantness merely accompanying the representation can as little contain the determining ground of the judgment as the representation of the perfection of the object and the concept of the good can. Therefore it can be nothing else than the subjective purposiveness in the representation of an object without any purpose (either objective or subjective), and thus it is the mere form of purposiveness in the representation by which an object is *given* to us, so far as we are conscious of it, which constitutes the satisfaction that we without a concept judge to be universally communicable; and, consequently, this is the determining ground of the judgment of taste.

[5]Mr. Herbert Spencer expresses much more concisely what Kant has in his mind here. "Pleasure . . . is a feeling which we seek to bring into consciousness and retain there; pain is . . . . a feeling which we seek to get out of consciousness and to keep out." *Principles of Psychology,* 125. [Tr.]

### 12. The Judgment of Taste Rests on A Priori Grounds

To establish *a priori* the connection of the feeling of a pleasure or pain as an effect, with any representation whatever (sensation or concept) as its cause, is absolutely impossible, for that would be a particular causal relation which (with objects of experience) can always only be cognized *a posteriori* and through the medium of experience itself. We actually have, indeed, in the *Critique of Practical Reason*, derived from universal moral concepts *a priori* the feeling of respect (as a special and peculiar modification of feeling which will not strictly correspond either to the pleasure or the pain that we get from empirical objects). But there we could go beyond the bounds of experience and call in a causality which rested on a supersensible attribute of the subject, viz., freedom. And even there, properly speaking, it was not this *feeling* which we derived from the idea of the moral as cause, but merely the determination of the will. But the state of mind which accompanies any determination of the will is in itself a feeling of pleasure and identical with it, and therefore does not follow from it as its effect. This last must only be assumed if the concept of the moral as a good precede the determination of the will by the law, for in that case the pleasure that is bound up with the concept could not be derived from it as from a mere cognition.

Now the case is similar with the pleasure in aesthetical judgments, only that here it is merely contemplative and does not bring about an interest in the object, while on the other hand in the moral judgment it is practical.[6] The consciousness of the mere formal purposiveness in the play of the subject's cognitive powers, in a representation through which an object is given, is the pleasure itself, because it contains a determining ground of the activity of the subject in respect of the excitement of its cognitive powers, and therefore an inner causality (which is purposive) in respect of cognition in general, without however being limited to any definite cognition, and consequently contains a mere form of the subjective purposiveness of a representation in an aesthetical judgment. This pleasure is in no way practical, neither like that arising from the pathological ground of pleasantness, nor that from the intellectual ground of the presented good. But yet it involves causality, viz., of *maintaining* without further design the state of the representation itself and the occupation of the cognitive powers. We *linger* over the contemplation of the beautiful because this contemplation strengthens and reproduces itself, which is analogous to (though not of the same kind as) that lingering which takes place when a physical charm in the representation of the object repeatedly arouses the attention, the mind being passive. . . .

### 16. The Judgment of Taste, by Which an Object Is Declared to Be Beautiful Under the Condition of a Definite Concept, Is Not Pure

There are two kinds of beauty: free beauty (*pulchritudo vaga*), or merely dependent beauty (*pulchritudo adhaerens*). The first presupposes no concept of what the object ought to be; the second does presuppose such a concept and the perfection of the object in accordance therewith. The first is called the (self-subsistent) beauty of this or that thing; the second, as dependent upon a concept (conditioned beauty), is ascribed to objects which come under the concept of a particular purpose.

Flowers are free natural beauties. Hardly anyone but a botanist knows what sort of a thing a flower ought to be; and even he, though recognizing in the flower the reproductive organ of the plant, pays no regard to this natural purpose if he is passing judgment on the flower by taste. There is, then, at the basis of this judgment no

---

[6]Cf. *Metaphysic of Morals*, Introduction I. "The pleasure which is necessarily bound up with the desire (of the object whose representation affects feeling) may be called *practical* pleasure, whether it be cause or effect of the desire. On the contrary, the pleasure which is not necessarily bound up with the desire of the object, and which, therefore, is at bottom not a pleasure in the existence of the object of the representation, but clings to the representation only, may be called mere contemplative pleasure or *passive satisfaction*. The feeling of the latter kind of pleasure we call *taste*." [Tr.]

perfection of any kind, no internal purposiveness, to which the collection of the manifold is referred. Many birds (such as the parrot, the humming bird, the bird of paradise) and many seashells are beauties in themselves, which do not belong to any object determined in respect of its purpose by concepts, but please freely and in themselves. So also delineations *à la grecque*, foliage for borders or wall papers, mean nothing in themselves; they represent nothing — no object under a definite concept — and are free beauties. We can refer to the same class what are called in music phantasies (i.e., pieces without any theme), and in fact all music without words.

In the judging of a free beauty (according to the mere form), the judgment of taste is pure. There is presupposed no concept of any purpose which the manifold of the given object is to serve, and which therefore is to be represented in it. By such a concept the freedom of the imagination which disports itself in the contemplation of the figure would be only limited.

But human beauty (i.e., of a man, a woman, or a child), the beauty of a horse, or a building (be it church, palace, arsenal, or summer house), presupposes a concept of the purpose which determines what the thing is to be, and consequently a concept of its perfection; it is therefore adherent beauty. Now as the combination of the pleasant (in sensation) with beauty, which properly is only concerned with form, is a hindrance to the purity of the judgment of taste, so also is its purity injured by the combination with beauty of the good (viz., that manifold which is good for the thing itself in accordance with its purpose).

We could add much to a building which would immediately please the eye if only it were not to be a church. We could adorn a figure with all kinds of spirals and light but regular lines, as the New Zealanders do with their tattooing, if only it were not the figure of a human being. And again this could have much finer features and a more pleasing and gentle cast of countenance provided it were not intended to represent a man, much less a warrior.

Now the satisfaction in the manifold of a thing in reference to the internal purpose which determines its possibility is a satisfaction grounded on a concept; but the satisfaction in beauty is such as presupposes no concept, but is immediately bound up with the representation through which the object is given (not through which it is thought). If now the judgment of taste in respect of the beauty of a thing is made dependent on the purpose in its manifold, like a judgment of reason, and thus limited, it is no longer a free and pure judgment of taste.

It is true that taste gains by this combination of aesthetical with intellectual satisfaction, inasmuch as it becomes fixed; and though it is not universal, yet in respect to certain purposively determined objects it becomes possible to prescribe rules for it. These, however, are not rules of taste, but merely rules for the unification of taste with reason, i.e., of the beautiful with the good, by which the former becomes available as an instrument of design in respect of the latter. Thus the tone of mind which is self-maintaining and of subjective universal validity is subordinated to the way of thinking which can be maintained only by painful resolve, but is of objective universal validity. Properly speaking, however, perfection gains nothing by beauty, or beauty by perfection; but when we compare the representation by which an object is given to us with the object (as regards what it ought to be) by means of a concept, we cannot avoid considering along with it the sensation in the subject. And thus when both states of mind are in harmony our *whole faculty* of representative power gains.

A judgment of taste, then, in respect of an object with a definite internal purpose, can only be pure if either the person judging has no concept of this purpose or else abstracts from it in his judgment. Such a person, although forming an accurate judgment of taste in judging of the object as free beauty, would yet by another who considers the beauty in it only as a dependent attribute (who looks to the purpose of the object) be blamed and accused of false taste, although both are right in their own way — the one in reference to what he has before his eyes, the other in reference to what he has in his thought. By means of this distinction we can settle many disputes about beauty between judges of taste, by showing that the one is speaking of free, the other of dependent, beauty — that the first is making a pure, the second an applied, judgment of taste. . . .

*Explanation of the Beautiful*
*Derived from This Third Moment*

*Beauty* is the form of the *purposiveness* of an object, so far as this is perceived in it *without any representation of a purpose*.[7]

## FOURTH MOMENT. OF THE JUDGMENT OF TASTE, ACCORDING TO THE MODALITY OF THE SATISFACTION IN THE OBJECT

### 18. What the Modality in a Judgment of Taste Is

I can say of every representation that it is at least *possible* that (as a cognition) it should be bound up with a pleasure. Of a representation that I call *pleasant* I say that it *actually* excites pleasure in me. But the *beautiful* we think as having a *necessary* reference to satisfaction. Now this necessity is of a peculiar kind. It is not a theoretical objective necessity, in which case it would be cognized a priori that everyone *will feel* this satisfaction in the object called beautiful by me. It is not a practical necessity, in which case, by concepts of a pure rational will serving as a rule for freely acting beings, the satisfaction is the necessary result of an objective law and only indicates that we absolutely (without any further design) ought to act in a certain way. But the

[7]It might be objected to this explanation that there are things in which we see a purposive form without cognizing any purpose in them, like the stone implements often gotten from old sepulchral tumuli with a hole in them, as if for a handle. These, although they plainly indicate by their shape a purposiveness of which we do not know the purpose, are nevertheless not described as beautiful. But if we regard a thing as a work of art, that is enough to make us admit that its shape has reference to some design and definite purpose. And hence there is no immediate satisfaction in the contemplation of it. On the other hand a flower, e.g., a tulip, is regarded as beautiful, because in perceiving it we find a certain purposiveness which, in our judgment, is referred to no purpose at all. [Au.]

necessity which is thought in an aesthetical judgment can only be called exemplary, i.e., a necessity of the assent of *all* to a judgment which is regarded as the example of a universal rule that we cannot state. Since an aesthetical judgment is not an objective cognitive judgment, this necessity cannot be derived from definite concepts and is therefore not apodictic. Still less can it be inferred from the universality of experience (of a complete agreement of judgments as to the beauty of a certain object). For not only would experience hardly furnish sufficiently numerous vouchers for this, but also, on empirical judgments, we can base no concept of the necessity of these judgments.

### 19. The Subjective Necessity, Which We Ascribe to the Judgment of Taste, Is Conditioned

The judgment of taste requires the agreement of everyone, and he who describes anything as beautiful claims that everyone *ought* to give his approval to the object in question and also describe it as beautiful. The *ought* in the aesthetical judgment is therefore pronounced in accordance with all the data which are required for judging, and yet is only conditioned. We ask for the agreement of everyone else, because we have for it a ground that is common to all; and we could count on this agreement, provided we were always sure that the case was correctly subsumed under that ground as rule of assent.

### 20. The Condition of Necessity Which a Judgment of Taste Asserts Is the Idea of a Common Sense

If judgments of taste (like cognitive judgments) had a definite objective principle, then the person who lays them down in accordance with this latter would claim an unconditioned necessity for his judgment. If they were devoid of all principle, like those of the mere taste of sense, we would not allow them in thought any necessity whatever. Hence they must have a subjective principle which determines what pleases or displeases only by feeling and not by concepts, but yet with universal validity. But such a principle could only be regarded as a *common sense,* which is essentially different from common understanding which people sometimes call common sense (*sensus communis*); for the latter does not judge by feeling but always by concepts, although ordinarily only as by obscurely represented principles.

Hence it is only under the presupposition that there is a common sense (by which we do not understand an external sense, but the effect resulting from the free play of our cognitive powers) — it is only under this presupposition, I say, that the judgment of taste can be laid down. . . .

*Explanation of the Beautiful*
*Resulting from the Fourth Moment*

The *beautiful* is that which without any concept is cognized as the object of a *necessary* satisfaction.

## GENERAL REMARK ON THE FIRST SECTION OF THE ANALYTIC

If we seek the result of the preceding analysis, we find that everything runs up into this concept of taste — that it is a faculty for judging an object in reference to the imagination's *free conformity to law.* Now, if in the judgment of taste the imagination must be considered in its freedom, it is in the first place not regarded as reproductive, as it is subject to the laws of association, but as productive and spontaneous (as the author of arbitrary forms of possible intuition). And although in the apprehension of a given object of sense it is tied to a definite form of this object and so far has no free play (such as that of poetry), yet it may readily be conceived that the object can furnish it with such a form containing a collection of the manifold as the imagination itself, if it were left free, would project in accordance with the *conformity to law of the understanding* in general. But that the *imaginative power* should be *free* and yet *of itself conformed to law,* i.e., bringing autonomy with it, is a contradiction. The understanding alone gives the law. If, however, the imagination is compelled to proceed according to a definite law,

its product in respect of form is determined by concepts as to what it ought to be. But then, as is above shown, the satisfaction is not that in the beautiful, but in the good (in perfection, at any rate in mere formal perfection), and the judgment is not a judgment of taste. Hence it is a conformity to law without a law; and a subjective agreement of the imagination and understanding — without such an objective agreement as there is when the representation is referred to a definite concept of an object — can subsist along with the free conformity to law of the understanding (which is also called purposiveness without purpose) and with the peculiar feature of a judgment of taste.

Now geometrically regular figures, such as a circle, a square, a cube, etc., are commonly adduced by critics of taste as the simplest and most indisputable examples of beauty, and yet they are called regular because we can only represent them by regarding them as mere presentations of a definite concept which prescribes the rule of the figure (according to which alone it is possible). One of these two must be wrong, either that judgment of the critic which ascribes beauty to the said figures, or ours which regards purposiveness apart from a concept as requisite for beauty.

Hardly anyone will say that a man must have taste in order that he should find more satisfaction in a circle than in a scrawled outline, in an equilateral and equiangular quadrilateral than in which is oblique, irregular, and as it were deformed, for this belongs to the ordinary understanding and is not taste at all. Where, e.g., our design is to judge of the size of an area or to make intelligible the relation of the parts of it, when divided, to one another and to the whole, then regular figures and those of the simplest kind are needed, and the satisfaction does not rest immediately on the aspect of the figure, but on its availability for all kinds of possible designs. A room whose walls form oblique angles, or a parterre of this kind, even every violation of symmetry in the figure of animals (e.g., being one-eyed), of buildings, or of flower beds, displeases because it contradicts the purpose of the thing, not only practically in respect of a definite use of it, but also when we pass judgment on it as regards any possible design. This is not the case in the judgment of taste, which when pure combines satisfaction or dissatisfaction — without any reference to its use or to a purpose — with the mere *consideration* of the object.

The regularity which leads to the concept of an object is indeed the indispensable condition (*conditio sine qua non*) for grasping the object in a single representation and determining the manifold in its form. This determination is a purpose in respect of cognition, and in reference to this it is always bound up with satisfaction (which accompanies the execution of every, even problematical, design). There is here, however, merely the approval of the solution satisfying a problem, and not a free and indefinite purposive entertainment of the mental powers with what we call beautiful, where the understanding is at the service of imagination, and not *vice versa*.

In a thing that is only possible by means of design — a building, or even an animal — the regularity consisting in symmetry must express the unity of the intuition that accompanies the concept of purpose, and this regularity belongs to cognition. But where only a free play of the representative powers (under the condition, however, that the understanding is to suffer no shock thereby) is to be kept up, in pleasure gardens, room decorations, all kinds of tasteful furniture, etc., regularity that shows constraint is avoided as much as possible. Thus in the English taste in gardens or in bizarre taste in furniture, the freedom of the imagination is pushed almost near to the grotesque, and in this separation from every constraint of rule we have the case where taste can display its greatest perfection in the enterprises of the imagination.

All stiff regularity (such as approximates to mathematical regularity) has something in it repugnant to taste; for our entertainment in the contemplation of it lasts for no length of time, but it rather, insofar as it has not expressly in view cognition or a definite practical purpose, produces weariness. On the other hand, that with which imagination can play in an unstudied and purposive manner is always new to us, and one does not get tired of looking at it. Marsden, in his description of Sumatra, makes the remark that the free beauties of nature surround the spectator everywhere and thus lose their attraction for him.[8] On the other hand, a pepper garden, where the stakes on which this plant twines itself form parallel rows, had much attractiveness for him if he met with it in the middle of a forest. And he hence infers that wild beauty, apparently irregular, only pleases as a variation from the regular beauty of which one has seen enough. But he need only have made the experiment of spending one day in a pepper garden to have been convinced that, if the understanding has put itself in accordance with the order that it always needs by means of regularity, the object will not entertain for long — nay, rather it will impose a burdensome constraint upon the imagination. On the other hand, nature, which there is prodigal in its variety even to luxuriance, that is subjected to no constraint of artificial rules, can supply constant food for taste. Even the song of birds, which we can bring under no musical rule, seems to have more freedom, and therefore more for taste, than a song of a human being which is produced in accordance with all the rules of music; for we very much sooner weary of the latter if it is repeated often and at length. Here, however, we probably confuse our participation in the mirth of a little creature that we love with the beauty of its song, for if this were exactly imitated by man (as sometimes the notes of the nightingale are), it would seem to our ear quite devoid of taste.

Again, beautiful objects are to be distinguished from beautiful views of objects (which often on account of their distance cannot be more clearly cognized). In the latter case taste appears, not so much in what the imagination *apprehends* in this field, as in the impulse it thus gets to *fiction,* i.e., in the peculiar fancies with which the mind entertains itself, while it is continually being aroused by the variety which strikes the eye. An illustration is afforded, e.g., by the sight of the changing shapes of a fire on the hearth or of a rippling brook; neither of these has beauty,

[8] W. Marsden, *The History of Sumatra* (London, 1783), p. 113. [Tr.]

but they bring with them a charm for the imagination because they entertain it in free play.

# Second Book.
## Analytic of the Sublime

### 23. Transition from the Faculty Which Judges of the Beautiful to That Which Judges of the Sublime

The beautiful and the sublime agree in this that both please in themselves. Further, neither presupposes a judgment of sense nor a judgment logically determined, but a judgment of reflection. Consequently the satisfaction belonging to them does not depend on a sensation, as in the case of the pleasant, nor on a definite concept, as in the case of the good; but it is nevertheless referred to concepts, although indeterminate ones. And so the satisfaction is connected with the mere presentation of the object or with the faculty of presentation, so that in the case of a given intuition this faculty or the imagination is considered as in agreement with the *faculty of concepts* of understanding or reason, regarded as promoting these latter. Hence both kinds of judgments are *singular*, and yet announce themselves as universally valid for every subject; although they lay claim merely to the feeling of pleasure, and not to any cognition of the object.

But there are also remarkable differences between the two. The beautiful in nature is connected with the form of the object, which consists in having definite boundaries. The sublime, on the other hand, is to be found in a formless object, so far as in it or by occasion of it *boundlessness* is represented, and yet its totality is also present to thought. Thus the beautiful seems to be regarded as the presentation of an indefinite concept of understanding, the sublime as that of a like concept of reason. Therefore the satisfaction in the one case is bound up with the representation of *quality*, in the other with that of *quantity*. And the latter satisfaction is quite different in kind from the former, for the beautiful directly brings with it a feeling of the furtherance of life, and thus is compatible with charms and with the play of the imagination. But the feeling of the sublime is a pleasure that arises only indirectly; viz., it is produced by the feeling of a momentary checking of the vital powers and a consequent stronger outflow of them, so that it seems to be regarded as emotion — not play, but earnest in the exercise of the imagination. Hence it is incompatible with physical charm; and as the mind is not merely attracted by the object but is ever being alternately repelled, the satisfaction in the sublime does not so much involve a positive pleasure as admiration or respect, which rather deserves to be called negative pleasure.

But the inner and most important distinction between the sublime and beautiful is, certainly, as follows. (Hence, as we are entitled to do, we only bring under consideration in the first instance the sublime in natural objects, for the sublime of art is always limited by the conditions of agreement with nature.) Natural beauty (which is independent) brings with it a purposiveness in its form by which the object seems to be, as it were, preadapted to our judgment, and thus constitutes in itself an object of satisfaction. On the other hand, that which excites in us, without any reasoning about it, but in the mere apprehension of it, the feeling of the sublime may appear, as regards its form, to violate purpose in respect of the judgment, to be unsuited to our presentative faculty, and as it were to do violence to the imagination; and yet it is judged to be only the more sublime.

Now we may see from this that, in general, we express ourselves incorrectly if we call any *object of nature* sublime, although we can quite correctly call many objects of nature beautiful. For how can that be marked by an expression of approval which is apprehended in itself as being a violation of purpose? All that we can say is that the object is fit for the presentation of a sublimity which can be found in the mind, for no sensible form can contain the sublime properly so-called. This concerns only ideas of the reason which, although no adequate presentation is possible for them, by this inadequateness that admits of sensible presentation are aroused and summoned into the mind. Thus the wide ocean, disturbed by the storm, cannot be called sublime. Its aspect is horrible; and the mind must be already filled with manifold ideas if it is to be determined by such an intuition to a feeling itself sublime, as it is incited to abandon sensibility and to busy itself with ideas that involve higher purposiveness.

Independent natural beauty discovers to us a technique of nature which represents it as a system in accordance with laws, the principle of which we do not find in the whole of our faculty of understanding. That principle is the principle of purposiveness, in respect of the use of our judgment in regard to phenomena, which requires that these must not be judged as merely belonging to nature in its purposeless mechanism, but also as belonging to something analogous to art. It therefore actually extends, not indeed our cognition of natural objects, but our concept of nature, which is now not regarded as mere mechanism but as art. This leads to profound investigations as to the possibility of such a form. But in what we are accustomed to call sublime there is nothing at all that leads to particular objective principles and forms of nature corresponding to them; so far from it that, for the most part, nature excites the ideas of the sublime in its chaos or in its wildest and most irregular disorder and desolation, provided size and might are perceived. Hence, we see that the concept of the sublime is not nearly so important or rich in consequences as the concept of the beautiful; and that, in general, it displays nothing purposive in nature itself, but only in that possible use of our intuitions of it by which there is produced in us a feeling of a purposiveness quite independent of nature. We must seek a ground external to ourselves for the beautiful of nature, but seek it for the sublime merely in ourselves and in our attitude of thought, which introduces sublimity into the representation of nature. This is a very needful preliminary remark, which quite separates the ideas of the sublime from that of a purposiveness of *nature* and makes the theory of the sublime a mere appendix to the aesthetical judging of that purposiveness, because by means of it no particular form is represented in nature, but there is only developed a purposive use which the imagination makes of its representation.

### 24. Of the Divisions of an Investigation into the Feeling of the Sublime

As regards the division of the moments of the aesthetical judging of objects in reference to the feeling of the sublime, the Analytic can proceed according to the same principle as was adopted in the analysis of judgments of taste. For as an act of the aesthetical reflective judgment, the satisfaction in the sublime must be represented just as in the case of the beautiful — according to *quantity* as universally valid, according to *quality* as devoid of *interest*, according to *relation* as subjective purposiveness, and according to *modality* as necessary. And so the method here will not diverge from that of the preceding section, unless indeed we count it a difference that in the case where the aesthetical judgment is concerned with the form of the object we began with the investigation of its quality, but here, in view of the formlessness which may belong to what we call sublime, we will begin with quantity, as the first moment of the aesthetical judgment as to the sublime. The reason for this may be seen from the preceding paragraph.

But the analysis of the sublime involves a division not needed in the case of the beautiful, viz., a division into the *mathematically* and the *dynamically sublime*.

For the feeling of the sublime brings with it as its characteristic feature a *movement* of the mind bound up with the judging of the object, while in the case of the beautiful taste presupposes and maintains the mind in *restful* contemplation. Now this movement ought to be judged as subjectively purposive (because the sublime pleases us), and thus it is referred through the imagination either to the *faculty of cognition* or *of desire*. In either reference the purposiveness of the given representation ought to be judged only in respect of this *faculty* (without purpose or interest), but in the first case, it is ascribed to the object as a *mathematical* determination of the imagination, in the second as *dynamical*. And hence we have this twofold way of representing the sublime.

## A. OF THE MATHEMATICALLY SUBLIME

### 25. Explanation of the Term Sublime

We call that *sublime* which is *absolutely great*. But to be great and to be a great something are quite different concepts (*magnitudo* and *quantitas*). In like manner to say simply (*simpliciter*) that anything is *great* is quite different from saying that it is *absolutely great* (*absolute, non comparative magnum*). The latter is *what is great beyond all comparison*. What now is meant by the expression that anything is great or small or of medium size? It is not a pure concept of understanding that is thus signified; still less is it an intuition of sense; and just as little as it a concept of reason, because it brings with it no principle of cognition. It must therefore be a concept of judgment or derived from one, and a subjective purposiveness of the representation in reference to the judgment must lie at its basis. That anything is a magnitude (*quantum*) may be cognized from the thing itself, without many comparison of it with other things, viz., if there is a multiplicity of the homogeneous constituting one thing. But to cognize *how great* it is always requires some other magnitude as a measure. But because the judging of magnitude depends, not merely on multiplicity (number), but also on the magnitude of the unit (the measure), and since, to judge of the magnitude of this latter again requires another as measure with which it may be compared, we see that the determination of the magnitude of phenomena can supply no absolute concept whatever of magnitude, but only a comparative one.

If now I say simply that anything is great, it appears that I have no comparison in view, at least none with an objective measure, because it is thus not determined at all how great the object is. But although the standard of comparison is merely subjective, yet the judgment nonetheless claims universal assent; "this man is beautiful" and "he is tall" are judgments, not limited merely to the judging subject, but, like theoretical judgments, demanding the assent of everyone.

In a judgment by which anything is designated simply as great, it is not merely meant that the object has a magnitude, but that this magnitude is superior to that of many other objects of the same kind, without, however, any exact determination of this superiority. Thus there is always at the basis of our judgment a standard which we assume as the same for everyone; this, however, is not available for any logical (mathematically definite) judging of magnitude, but only for aesthetical judging of the same, because it is a merely subjective standard lying at the basis of the reflective judgment upon magnitude. It may be empirical, as, e.g., the average size of the men known to us, of animals of a certain kind, trees, houses, mountains, etc. Or it may be a standard given *a priori* which, through the defects of the judging subject, is limited by the subjective conditions of presentation *in concreto*, as, e.g., in the practical sphere, the greatness of a certain virtue or of the public liberty and justice in a country, or, in the theoretical sphere, the greatness of the accuracy or the inaccuracy of an observation or measurement that has been made, etc.

Here it is remarkable that, although we have no interest whatever in an object — i.e., its existence is indifferent to us — yet its mere size, even if it is considered as formless, may bring a satisfaction with it that is universally communicable and that consequently involves the consciousness of a subjective purposiveness in the use of our cognitive faculty. This is not indeed a satisfaction in the object (because it may be formless), as in the case of the beautiful, in which the reflective judgment finds itself purposively determined in reference to cognition in general, but a satisfaction in the extension of the imagination by itself.

If (under the above limitation) we say simply of an object "it is great," this is no mathematically definite judgment, but a mere judgment of reflection upon the representation of it, which is subjectively purposive for a certain use of our cognitive powers in the estimation of magnitude; and we always then bind up with the representation a kind of respect, as also a kind of contempt, for what we simply call "small." Further, the judging of things as great or small extends to everything, even to all their characteristics; thus we describe beauty as great or small. The reason of this is to be sought in the fact that whatever we present in intuition according to the precept of the judgment (and thus represent aesthetically) is always a phenomenon, and thus a quantum.

But if we call anything, not only great, but absolutely great in every point of view (great beyond all comparison), i.e., sublime, we soon see that it is not permissible to seek for an adequate standard of this outside itself, but merely in itself. It is a magnitude which is like itself alone. It follows hence that the sublime is not to be sought in the things of nature, but only in our ideas; but in which of them it lies must be reserved for the "Deduction."

The foregoing explanation can be thus expressed: *The sublime is that in comparison with which everything else is small.* Here we easily see that nothing can be given in nature, however great it is judged by us to be, which could not, if considered in another relation, be reduced to the infinitely small; and conversely there is nothing so small which does not admit of extension by our imagination to the greatness of a world if compared with still smaller standards. Telescopes have furnished us with abundant material for making the first remark, microscopes for the second. Nothing, therefore, which can be an object of the senses is, considered on this basis, to be called sublime. But because there is in our imagination a striving toward infinite progress and in our reason a claim for absolute totality, regarded as a real idea, therefore this very inadequateness for that idea in our faculty for estimating the magnitude of things of sense excites in us the feeling of a supersensible faculty. And it is not the object of sense, but the use which the judgment naturally makes of certain objects on behalf of this latter feeling that is absolutely great, and in comparison every other use is small. Consequently it is the state of mind produced by a certain representation with which the reflective judgment is occupied, and not the object, that is to be called sublime.

We can therefore append to the preceding formulas explaining the sublime this other: *The sublime is that, the mere ability to think which shows a faculty of the mind surpassing every standard of sense. . . .*

### 27. Of the Quality of the Satisfaction in Our Judgments upon the Sublime

The feeling of our incapacity to attain to an idea *which is a law for us* is *respect*. Now the idea of the comprehension of every phenomenon that can be given us in the intuition of a whole is an idea prescribed to us by a law of reason, which recognizes no other measure, definite, valid of everyone, and invariable, than the absolute whole. But our imagination, even in its greatest efforts, in respect of that comprehension which we expect from it of a given object in a whole of intuition (and thus with reference to the presentation of the idea of reason) exhibits its own limits and inadequacy, although at the same time it shows that its destination is to make itself adequate to this idea regarded as a law. Therefore the feeling of the sublime in nature is respect for our own destination, which, by a certain subreption, we attribute to an object of nature (conversion of respect for the idea of humanity in our own subject into respect for the object). This makes intuitively evident the superiority of the rational determination of our cognitive faculties to the greatest faculty of our sensibility.

The feeling of the sublime is therefore a feeling of pain arising from the want of accordance between the aesthetical estimation of magnitude formed by the imagination and the estimation of the same formed by reason. There is at the same time a pleasure thus excited, arising from the correspondence with rational ideas of this very judgment of the inadequacy of our greatest faculty of sense, in so far as it is a law for us to strive after these ideas. In fact it is for us a law (of reason) and belongs to our destination to estimate as small, in comparison with ideas of reason, everything which nature, regarded as an object of sense, contains that is great for us; and that which arouses in us the feeling of this supersensible destination agrees with that law. Now the greatest effort of the imagination in the presentation of the unit for the estimation of magnitude indicates a reference to something *absolutely great,* and consequently a reference to the law of reason, which bids us take this alone as our highest measure of magnitude. Therefore the inner perception of the inadequacy of all sensible standards for rational estimation of magnitude indicates a correspondence with rational laws; it involves a pain, which arouses in us the feeling of our supersensible destination, according to which it is purposive and therefore pleasurable to find every standard of sensibility inadequate to the ideas of understanding.

The mind feels itself *moved* in the representation of the sublime in nature, while in aesthetical judgments about the beautiful it is in *restful* contemplation. This movement may (especially in its beginning) be compared to a vibration, i.e., to a quickly alternating attraction toward, and repulsion from, the same object. The transcendent (toward which the imagination is impelled in its apprehension of intuition) is for the imagination like an abyss in which it fears to lose itself; but for the rational idea of the supersensible it is not transcendent, but in conformity with law to bring about such an effort of the imagination, and consequently here there is the same amount of attraction as there was of repulsion for the mere sensibility. But the judgment itself always remains in this case only aesthetical, because, without having any determinate concept of the object at its basis, it merely represents the subjective play of the mental powers (imagination and reason) as harmonious through their very contrast. For just as imagination and *understanding,* in judging of the beautiful, generate a subjective purposiveness of the mental powers by means of their harmony, so in this case imagination and *reason* do so by means of their conflict. That is, they bring about a feeling that we possess pure self-subsistent reason, or a faculty for the estimation of magnitude, whose superiority can be made intuitively evident only by the inadequacy of that faculty imagination which is itself unbounded in the presentation of magnitudes (of sensible objects).

The measurement of a space (regarded as apprehension) is at the same time a description of it, and thus an objective movement in the act of imagination and a progress. On the other hand, the comprehension of the manifold in the unity — not of thought but of intuition — and consequently the comprehension of the successively apprehended elements in one glance is a regress which annihilates the condition of time in this progress of the imagination and makes *coexistence* intuitible. It is therefore (since the time series is a condition of the internal sense and of an intuition) and subjective movement of the imagination, by which it does violence to the internal sense; this must be the more noticeable, the greater the quantum in which the imagination comprehends in one intuition. The effort, therefore, to receive in one single intuition a measure for magnitude that requires a considerable time to apprehend is a kind of representation which, subjectively considered, is contrary to purpose; but objectively, as requisite for the estimation of magnitude, it is purposive. Thus that very violence which is done to the subject through the imagination is judged as purposive *in reference to the whole determination* of the mind.

The *quality* of the feeling of the sublime is that it is a feeling of pain in reference to the faculty by which we judge aesthetically of an object, which pain, however, is represented at the same time as purposive. This is possible through the fact that the very incapacity in question discovers the consciousness of an unlimited faculty of the same subject, and that the mind can only judge of the latter aesthetically by means of the former.

In the logical estimation of magnitude, the impossibility of ever arriving at absolute totality, by means of the progress of the measurement of things of the sensible world in time and space, was cognized as objective, i.e., as an impossibility of *thinking* the infinite as entirely given, and not as merely subjective or that there was only an incapacity to *grasp* it. For there we have not to do with the degree of comprehension in an intuition, regarded as a measure, but everything depends on a concept of number. But in aesthetical estimation of magnitude, the concept of number must disappear or be changed, and the comprehension of the imagination in reference to the unit of measure (thus avoiding the concepts of a law of the successive production of concepts of magnitude) is alone purposive for it. If now a magnitude almost reaches the limit of our faculty of comprehension in an intuition, and yet the imagination is invited by means of numerical magnitudes (in respect of which we are conscious that our faculty is unbounded) to aesthetical comprehension in a greater unit, then we mentally feel ourselves confined aesthetically within bounds. But nevertheless the pain in regard to the necessary extension of the imagination for accordance with that which is unbounded in our faculty of reason, viz., the idea of the absolute whole, and consequently the very unpurposiveness of the faculty of imagination for rational ideas and the arousing of them, are represented as purposive. Thus it is that the aesthetical judgment itself is subjectively purposive for the reason as the source of ideas, i.e., as the source of an intellectual comprehension for which all aesthetical comprehension is small, and there accompanies the reception of an object as sublime a pleasure, which is only possible through the medium of a pain.

## B. OF THE DYNAMICALLY SUBLIME IN NATURE

### 28. Of Nature Regarded as Might

*Might* is that which is superior to great hindrances. It is called *dominion* if it is superior to the resistance of that which itself possesses might. Nature, considered in an aesthetical judgment as might that has no dominion over us, is *dynamically sublime*.

If nature is to be judged by us as dynamically sublime, it must be represented as exciting fear (although it is not true conversely that every object which excites fear is regarded in our aesthetical judgment as sublime). For in aesthetical judgments (without the aid of concepts) superiority to hindrances can only be judged according to the greatness of the resistance. Now that which we are driven to resist is an evil and, if we do not find our faculties a match for it, is an object of fear. Hence nature can be regarded by the aesthetical judgment as might, and conse-

quently as dynamically sublime, only so far as it is considered an object of fear.

But we can regard an object as *fearful* without being afraid *of* it, viz., if we judge of it in such a way that we merely *think* a case in which we would wish to resist it and yet in which all resistance would be altogether vain. Thus the virtuous man fears God without being afraid of Him, because to wish to resist Him and His commandments he thinks is a case that *he* need not apprehend. But in every such case that he thinks as not impossible, he cognizes Him as fearful.

He who fears can form no judgment about the sublime in nature, just as he who is seduced by inclination and appetite can form no judgment about the beautiful. The former flies from the sight of an object which inspires him with awe, and it is impossible to find satisfaction in a terror that is seriously felt. Hence the pleasurableness arising from the cessation of an uneasiness is *a state of joy*. But this, on account of the deliverance from danger which is involved, is a state of joy when conjoined with the resolve that we shall no more be exposed to the danger; we cannot willingly look back upon our sensations of danger, much less seek the occasion for them again.

Bold, overhanging, and as it were threatening rocks; clouds piled up in the sky, moving with lightning flashes and thunder peals; volcanoes in all their violence of destruction; hurricanes with their track of devastation; the boundless ocean in a state of tumult; the lofty waterfall of a mighty river, and such like — these exhibit our faculty of resistance as insignificantly small in comparison with their might. But the sight of them is the more attractive, the more fearful it is, provided only that we are in security; and we willingly call these objects sublime, because they raise the energies of the soul above their accustomed height and discover in us a faculty of resistance of a quite different kind, which gives us courage to measure ourselves against the apparent almightiness of nature.

Now, in the immensity of nature and in the insufficiency of our faculties to take in a standard proportionate to the aesthetical estimation of the magnitude of its *realm,* we find our own limitation, although at the same time in our rational faculty we find a different, nonsensuous standard, which has that infinity itself under it as a unity, in comparison with which everything in nature is small, and thus in our mind we find a superiority to nature even in its immensity. And so also the irresistibility of its might, while making us recognize our own physical impotence, considered as beings of nature, discloses to us a faculty of judging independently of and a superiority over nature, on which is based a kind of self-preservation entirely different from that which can be attacked and brought into danger by external nature. Thus humanity in our person remains unhumiliated, though the individual might have to submit to this dominion. In this way nature is not judged to be sublime in our aesthetical judgments insofar as it excites fear, but because it calls up that power in us (which is not nature) of regarding as small the things about which we are solicitous (goods, health, and life), and of regarding its might (to which we are no doubt subjected in respect of these things) as nevertheless without any dominion over us and our personality to which we must bow where our highest fundamental propositions, and their assertion or abandonment, are concerned. Therefore nature is here called sublime merely because it elevates the imagination to a presentation of those cases in which the mind can make felt the proper sublimity of its destination, in comparison with nature itself.

This estimation of ourselves loses nothing through the fact that we might regard ourselves as safe in order to feel this inspiriting satisfaction and that hence, as there is no seriousness in the danger, there might be also (as might seem to be the case) just as little seriousness in the sublimity of our spiritual faculty. For the satisfaction here concerns only the *destination* of our faculty which discloses itself in such a case, so far as the tendency to this destination lies in our nature, while its development and exercise remain incumbent and obligatory. And in this there is truth and reality, however conscious the man may be of his present actual powerfulness, when he turns his reflection to it.

No doubt this principle seems to be too far-fetched and too subtly reasoned, and consequently seems to go beyond the scope of an aesthetical judgment; but observation of men proves the opposite and shows that it may lie at the root of the most ordinary judgments, although we are not always conscious of it. For what is that which is, even to the savage, an object of the greatest admiration? It is a man who shrinks from nothing, who fears nothing, and therefore does not yield to danger, but rather goes to face it vigorously with the most complete deliberation. Even in the most highly civilized state this peculiar veneration for the soldier remains, though only under the condition that he exhibit all the virtues of peace, gentleness, compassion, and even a becoming care for his own person; because even by these it is recognized that his mind is unsubdued by danger. Hence whatever disputes there may be about the superiority of the respect which is to be accorded them, in the comparison of a statesman and a general, the aesthetical judgment decides for the latter. War itself, if it is carried on with order and with a sacred respect for the rights of citizens, has something sublime in it, and makes the disposition of the people who carry it on thus only the more sublime, the more numerous are the dangers to which they are exposed and in respect of which they behave with courage. On the other hand, a long peace generally brings about a predominant commercial spirit and, along with it, low selfishness, cowardice, and effeminacy, and debases the disposition of the people.

It appears to conflict with this solution of the concept of sublime, so far as sublimity is ascribed to might, that we are accustomed to represent God as presenting Himself in His wrath and yet in His sublimity, in the tempest, the storm, the earthquake, etc.; and that it would be foolish and criminal to imagine a superiority of our minds over these works of His and, as it seems, even over the designs of such might. Hence it would appear that no feeling of the sublimity of our own nature, but rather subjection, abasement, and a feeling of complete powerlessness, is a fitting state of mind in the presence of such an object; and this is generally bound up with the idea of it during natural phenomena of this kind. In religion in general, prostration, adoration with bent head, with contrite, anxious demeanor and voice, seems to be the only fitting behavior in presence of the Godhead, and hence most peoples have adopted and still observe it. But this state of mind is far from being necessarily bound up with the idea of the *sublimity* of a religion and its object. The man who is actually afraid, because he finds reasons for fear in himself, while conscious by his culpable disposition of offending against a might whose will is irresistible and at the same time just, is not in the frame of mind for admiring the divine greatness. For this a mood of calm contemplation and a quite free judgment are needed. Only if he is conscious of an upright disposition pleasing to God do those operations of might serve to awaken in him the idea of the sublimity of this Being, for then he recognizes in himself a sublimity of disposition conformable to His will; and thus he is raised above the fear of such operations of nature, which he no longer regards as outbursts of His wrath. Even humility, in the shape of a stern judgment upon his own faults — which otherwise, with a consciousness of good intentions, could be easily palliated from the frailty of human nature — is a sublime state of mind, consisting in a voluntary subjection of himself to the pain of remorse, in order that the causes of this may be gradually removed. In this way religion is essentially distinguished from superstition. The latter establishes in the mind, not reverence for the sublime, but fear and apprehension of the all-powerful Being to whose will the terrified man sees himself subject, without according Him any high esteem. From this nothing can arise but a seeking of favor and flattery, instead of a religion which consists in a good life.[9]

Sublimity, therefore, does not reside in anything of nature, but only in our mind, in so far as we can become conscious that we are superior to nature within, and therefore also to nature without us (so far as it influences us). Everything that excites this feeling in us, e.g., the *might* of

nature which calls forth our forces, is called then (although improperly) sublime. Only by supposing this idea in ourselves and in reference to it are we capable of attaining to the idea of the sublimity of that Being which produces respect in us, not merely by the might that it displays in nature, but rather by means of the faculty which resides in us of judging it fearlessly and of regarding our destination as sublime in respect of it. . . .

## 49. *Of the Faculties of the Mind That Constitute Genius*

We say of certain products of which we expect that they should at least in part appear as beautiful art, they are without *spirit*,[10] although we find nothing to blame in them on the score of taste. A poem may be very neat and elegant, but without spirit. A history may be exact and well arranged, but without spirit. A festal discourse may be solid and at the same time elaborate, but without spirit. Conversation is often not devoid of entertainment, but it is without spirit; even of a woman we say that she is pretty, an agreeable talker, and courteous, but without spirit. What then do we mean by spirit?

*Spirit,* in an aesthetical sense, is the name given to the animating principle of the mind. But that by means of which this principle animates the soul, the material which it applies to that purpose, is what puts the mental powers purposively into swing, i.e., into such a play as maintains itself and strengthens the mental powers in their exercise.

Now I maintain that this principle is no other than the faculty of presenting *aesthetical ideas*. And by an aesthetical idea I understand that representation of the imagination which occasions much thought, without however any definite thought, i.e., any *concept,* being capable of being adequate to it; it consequently cannot be completely compassed and made intelligible by language. We easily see that it is the counterpart (pendant) of a *rational idea,* which conversely is

[9]In the *Philosophical Theory of Religion,* Pt. I (Abbott's trans., p. 360), Kant, as here, divides "all religions into two classes — *favor-seeking* religion (mere worship) and *moral* religion, that is, the religion *of a good life*"; and he concludes that "amongst all the public religions that have ever existed the Christian alone is moral." [Tr.]

[10]In English we would rather say "without soul," but I prefer to translate "*Geist*" consistently by "spirit," to avoid the confusion of it with "*Seele*." [Tr.]

a concept to which no *intuition* (or representation of the imagination) can be adequate.

The imagination (as a productive faculty of cognition) is very powerful in creating another nature, as it were, out of the material that actual nature gives it. We entertain ourselves with it when experience becomes too commonplace, and by it we remold experience, always indeed in accordance with analogical laws, but yet also in accordance with principles which occupy a higher place in reason (laws, too, which are just as natural to us as those by which understanding comprehends empirical nature). Thus we feel our freedom from the law of association (which attaches to the empirical employment of imagination), so that the material supplied to us by nature in accordance with this law can be worked up into something different which surpasses nature.

Such representations of the imagination we may call *ideas,* partly because they at least strive after something which lies beyond the bounds of experience and so seek to approximate to a presentation of concepts of reason (intellectual ideas), thus giving to the latter the appearance of objective reality, but especially because no concept can be fully adequate to them as internal intuitions. The poet ventures to realize to sense,[11] rational ideas of invisible beings, the kingdom of the blessed, hell, eternity, creation, etc.; or even if he deals with things of which there are examples in experience — e.g., death, envy and all vices, also love, fame, and the like — he tries, by means of imagination, which emulates the play of reason in its quests after a maximum, to go beyond the limits of experience and to present them to sense with a completeness of which there is no example in nature. This is properly speaking the art of the poet, in which the faculty of aesthetical ideas can manifest itself in its entire strength. But this faculty, considered in itself, is properly only a talent (of the imagination).

If now we place under a concept a representation of the imagination belonging to its presentation, but which occasions in itself more thought than can ever be comprehended in a definite concept and which consequently aesthetically enlarges the concept itself in an unbounded fashion, the imagination is here creative, and it brings the faculty of intellectual ideas (the reason) into movement; i.e., by a representation more thought (which indeed belongs to the concept of the object) is occasioned than can in it be grasped or made clear.

Those forms which do not constitute the presentation of a given concept itself but only, as approximate representations of the imagination, express the consequences bound up with it and its relationship to other concepts, are called (aesthetical) *attributes* of an object whose concept as a rational idea cannot be adequately presented. Thus Jupiter's eagle with the lightning in its claws is an attribute of the mighty king of heaven, as the peacock is of his magnificent queen. They do not, like *logical attributes,* represent what lies in our concepts of the sublimity and majesty of creation, but something different, which gives occasion to the imagination to spread itself over a number of kindred representations that arouse more thought than can be expressed in a concept determined by words. They furnish an *aesthetical idea,* which for that rational idea takes the place of logical presentation; and thus, as their proper office, they enliven the mind by opening out to it the prospect into an illimitable field of kindred representations. But beautiful art does this not only in the case of painting or sculpture (in which the term "attribute" is commonly employed); poetry and rhetoric also get the spirit that animates their works simply from the aesthetical attributes of the object, which accompany the logical and stimulate the imagination, so that it thinks more by their aid, although in an undeveloped way, than could be comprehended in a concept and therefore in a definite form of words. For the sake of brevity, I must limit myself to a few examples only.

When the great King[12] in one of his poems expresses himself as follows:

[11]Ventures to make real for the senses. [Ed.]

[12]"Yes, let us end without sadness and let us die without regrets, in leaving the world filled with our good deeds. So the day-star, at the end of its course, sheds a gentle light on the horizon; and the last rays that it darts into the air are the last sighs which it gives to the world." [Ed.] Barni quotes

Oui, finissons sans trouble et mourons sans regrets,
En laissant l'univers comblé de nos bienfaits.
Ainsi l'astre du jour au bout de sa carriere,
Répand sur l'horizon une douce lumière;
Et les derniers rayons qu'il darde dans les airs,
Sont les derniers soupirs qu'il donne à l'univers;

he quickens his rational idea of a cosmopolitan disposition at the end of life by an attribute which the imagination (in remembering all the pleasures of a beautiful summer day that are recalled at its close by a serene evening) associates with that representation, and which excites a number of sensations and secondary representations for which no expression is found. On the other hand, an intellectual concept may serve conversely as an attribute for a representation of sense, and so can quicken this latter by means of the idea of the supersensible, but only by the aesthetical element, that subjectively attaches to the concept of the latter, being here employed. Thus, for example, a certain poet says, in his description of a beautiful morning:

> The sun arose
> As calm from virtue springs.

The consciousness of virtue, if we substitute it in our thoughts for a virtuous man, diffuses in the mind a multitude of sublime and restful feelings, and a boundless prospect of a joyful future, to which no expression that is measured by a definite concept completely attains.[13]

In a word, the aesthetical idea is a representation of the imagination associated with a given

concept, which is bound up with such a multiplicity of partial representations in its free employment that for it no expression marking a definite concept can be found; and such a representation, therefore, adds to a concept much ineffable thought, the feeling of which quickens the cognitive faculties, and with language, which is the mere letter, binds up spirit also.

The mental powers, therefore, whose union (in a certain relation) constitutes genius are imagination and understanding. In the employment of the imagination for cognition, it submits to the constraint of the understanding and is subject to the limitation of being conformable to the concept of the latter. On the contrary, in an aesthetical point of view it is free to furnish unsought, over and above that agreement with a concept, abundance of undeveloped material for the understanding, to which the understanding paid no regard in its concept but which it applies, though not objectively for cognition, yet subjectively to quicken the cognitive powers and therefore also indirectly to cognitions. Thus genius properly consists in the happy relation between these faculties, which no science can teach and no industry can learn, by which ideas are found for a given concept; and, on the other hand, we thus find for these ideas the expression by means of which the subjective state of mind brought about by them, as an accompaniment of the concept, can be communicated to others. The latter talent is, properly speaking, what is called spirit; for to express the ineffable element in the state of mind implied by a certain representation and to make it universally communicable — whether the expression be in speech or painting or statuary — this requires a faculty of seizing the quickly passing play of imagination and of unifying it in a concept (which is even on that account original and discloses a new rule that could not have been inferred from any preceding principles of examples) that can be communicated without any constraint of rules.

If, after this analysis, we look back to the explanation given above of what is called genius, we find: first, that it is a talent for art, not for science, in which clearly known rules must go beforehand and determine the procedure. Sec-

---

these lines as occurring in one of Frederick the Great's French poems: "Epitre au maréchal Keith, sur les vaines terreurs de la mort et les frayeurs d'une autre vie" [Letter to Marshal Keith on the Pointless Terror of Death and Fears of Another Life]; but I have not been able to verify his reference. Kant here translates them into German. [Tr.]

[13]Perhaps nothing more sublime was ever said and no sublimer thought ever expressed than the famous inscription on the Temple of Isis (Mother Nature): "I am all that is and that was and that shall be, and no mortal hath lifted my veil." Segner availed himself of this idea in a *suggestive* vignette prefixed to his *Natural Philosophy*, in order to inspire beforehand the pupil whom he was about to lead into that temple with a holy awe, which should dispose his mind to serious attention. [Au.] J. A. de Segner (1704–1777) was Professor of Natural Philosophy at Göttingen and the author of several scientific works of repute. [Tr.]

ondly, as an artistic talent it presupposes a definite concept of the product as the purpose, and therefore understanding; but it also presupposes a representation (although an indeterminate one) of the material, i.e., of the intuition, for the presentment of this concept, and, therefore a relation between the imagination and the understanding. Thirdly, it shows itself, not so much in the accomplishment of the proposed purpose in a presentment of a definite concept, as in the enunciation or expression of aesthetical ideas which contain abundant material for that very design; and consequently it represents the imagination as free from all guidance of rules and yet as purposive in reference to the presentment of the given concept. Finally, in the fourth place, the unsought, undesigned subjective purposiveness in the free accordance of the imagination with the legality of the understanding presupposes such a proportion and disposition of these faculties as no following of rules, whether of science or of mechanical imitation, can bring about, but which only the nature of the subject can produce.

In accordance with these suppositions, genius is the examplary originality of the natural gifts of a subject in the *free* employment of his cognitive faculties. In this way the product of a genius (as regards what is to be ascribed to genius and not to possible learning or schooling) is an example, not to be imitated (for then that which in it is genius and constitutes the spirit of the work would be lost), but to be followed by another genius, whom it awakens to a feeling of his own originality and whom it stirs so to exercise his art in freedom from the constraint of rules, that thereby a new rule is gained for art; and thus his talent shows itself to be exemplary. But because a genius is a favorite of nature and must be regarded by us as a rare phenomenon, his example produces for other good heads a school, i.e., a methodical system of teaching according to rules, so far as these can be derived from the peculiarities of the products of his spirit. For such persons beautiful art is so far imitation, to which nature through the medium of a genius supplied the rule.

But this imitation becomes a mere *aping* if the scholar *copies* everything down to the deformities, which the genius must have let pass only because he could not well remove them without weakening his idea. This mental characteristic is meritorious only in the case of a genius. A certain *audacity* in expression — and in general many a departure from common rules — becomes him well, but it is in no way worthy of imitation; it always remains a fault in itself which we must seek to remove, though the genius is, as it were, privileged to commit it, because the inimitable rush of his spirit would suffer from overanxious carefulness. *Mannerism* is another kind of aping, viz., of mere *peculiarity* (originality) in general, by which a man separates himself as far as possible from imitators, without however possessing the talent to be at the same time *exemplary*. There are indeed in general two ways (*modi*) in which such a man may put together his notions of expressing himself; the one is called a *manner* (*modus aestheticus*), the other a *method* (*modus logicus*). They differ in this, that the former has no other standard than the *feeling* of unity in the presentment, but the latter follows definite *principles*; hence the former alone avails for beautiful art. But an artistic product is said to show *mannerism* only when the exposition of the artist's idea is *founded* on its very singularity and is not made appropriate to the idea itself. The ostentatious (*précieux*), contorted, and affected manner adopted to differentiate oneself from ordinary persons (though devoid of spirit) is like the behavior of a man of whom we say that he hears himself talk, or who stands and moves about as if he were on a stage in order to be stared at; this always betrays a bungler.

# Friedrich von Schiller

## 1759–1805

Friedrich von Schiller, who chafed at being thought the *second* greatest poet, dramatist, and thinker of the early phase of the German romantic movement, was the son of an army doctor who had risen to the rank of captain and married the daughter of an innkeeper. He was educated through the patronage of the Duke of Württemberg at his military school and trained in his father's career of military medicine. While still in school he published lyric poetry, and at eighteen wrote his most romantic tragedy, *Die Räuber* (published in 1781 and performed the next year). Despite the fame *Die Räuber* brought him, Schiller's artistic career took a long time to become established; his patron disapproved of and discouraged his literary ambitions, the more so as his drama became infected with liberal politics.

Schiller escaped to another province and wrote the domestic tragedy of *Kabale und Liebe* (1784) and the political drama *Don Carlos* (1787), plays that are familiar to operagoers from Verdi's *Luisa Miller* and *Don Carlo*. For most of the 1780s Schiller worked in provincial capitals like Mannheim and Dresden without securing a satisfactory position. At Weimar in 1787, however, he turned from the drama of Spanish politics — in *Don Carlos* — to its history, and began a study of the Dutch struggle against Spanish rule in the sixteenth century and the subsequent Thirty Years War that destroyed the Spanish empire. As a result, he won the patronage of the Duchess of Weimar and Goethe's recommendation to a professorship, and was able to marry Charlotte von Lengefeld.

In the 1790s, Schiller moved from history to philosophy, absorbing the then new theories of Immanuel Kant and turning his hand to the aesthetic questions that Kant's *Critique of Judgment* had raised. His criticism includes *On Tragic Art* (1792), *Letters on Aesthetic Development* (1795) and *On Naive and Sentimental Poetry* (published in the journal *Die Horen* in 1795–96 and collected in 1800).

Following his work on poetic theory, Schiller returned to its practice, and in the late 1790s published his major ballads. At the end of his life, however, he went back to his first love, the theater, writing a series of grandly tragic plays that developed out of his studies of the past and out of his political vision of a free society. Drawing on his history of the Thirty Years War, Schiller developed a trilogy about the upstart general Wallenstein (1798–99), which he followed with *The Maid of Orleans* (1801), *The Bride of Messina* (1803) and *Wilhelm Tell* (1804). In chronic ill-health for the last several decades of his life, Schiller died at Weimar in 1805.

Schiller's motivation for writing *On Naive and Sentimental Poetry* is closely linked to his ambivalent feelings — a combination of envy and admiration — about his great contemporary, Goethe. Schiller was struck by how different he was from Goethe: He wrote with painful hesitations, Goethe with ease; he was chronically ill, Goethe vigorous; he was from the middle classes and social encounters were difficult for him, while Goethe had an aristocrat's easy manners. Since Goethe was evidently a great master of letters, what was Schiller? In a letter to his friend Wilhelm von Humboldt, Schiller said: "We shall be differently categorized, but in my most courageous moments I am convinced that our categories will not be subordinated to one another, but instead will be jointly assimilated to a higher ideal concept of the species." So long as Schiller thought of human nature as one thing, as Kant's notions in the *Critique of Judgment* would incline one to do, either he or Goethe would have to be the closer to its ideal, but the dichotomy he sees between the *naive* and the *sentimental* implicitly allowed both poets to be supreme, each in his category, Goethe as the type of the naive genius, Schiller himself as the type of the sentimental.

The central distinction between naive and sentimental poetry turns on the poet's basic temperament, and the relation of that temperament to nature, which was regarded by Schiller as an ideal. the naive poets (Schiller's chief examples are Homer and Shakespeare) *are* nature itself: Their character is that of a child, with a child's sweetness and simplicity, and with a child's cruelty.

> The childlike character that the genius imposes upon his works he likewise displays in his private life and morals. He is *chaste*, for this nature always is; but he is not *prudish*, for only decadence is prudish. He is *intelligent*, for nature can never be otherwise; but he is not *cunning*, for only art can be so. He is *true* to his characters and his inclinations, but not so much because he possesses principles as because nature, despite all fluctuations, always returns to its former state. . . . He is *modest*, . . . because genius always remains a mystery to itself, but he is not fearful because he does not know the dangers of the path he travels. The genres of naive poetry are the classic genres of epic, tragedy, and comedy.

If the naive poets *are* nature, the sentimental poets, in contract, *love* nature — love it as something they feel they lack, as something that complements their character. The genres of sentimental poetry take shape from the poet's response to this lack. If the sentimental poet takes up the subject of the world as it is, alienated from nature, the real contrary to the ideal, then the poetry will be some form of *satire* — *punitive* (like that of Juvenal or Swift) if the poet "dwells in the realm of the will," conscious of the need to make things better; or *playful* (like that of the Horace and Sterne) if the poet dwells in the "realm of the understanding," where the world's problems can be contemplated without battling over them.

On the other hand, the poet may write about the ideal rather than the real; the result is *elegiac* poetry. The true *elegy* is produced when the subject is the ideal of the past compared with the fallen present. (Here Schiller's primary example is the German poet Klopstock, but he also mentions James Thomson's *The Seasons* and Edward Young's *Night Thoughts* — a masterpiece of the English "graveyard school"). Or the poet may produce an *idyll* (as in Rousseau's *Julie, ou la Nouvelle Héloïse*) if the ideal is presented *as though* it were contemporary.

Since both the naive and the sentimental have associated temperaments and genres, it is possible for a sentimental master to work in a naive genre (as Virgil's and Milton's work in the epic demonstrates). Goethe is analyzed here as the reverse case, a naive genius taking up (in *The Sorrows of Young Werther* and *Wilhelm*

*Meister's Apprenticeship*) sentimental themes and genres: "fanatically unhappy love, sensitivity to nature, feeling for religion . . . the gloomy, formless, melancholic Ossianic world." "This task," Schiller concedes, "appears to be completely new and of quite unique difficulty, for in the ancient and naive world a *theme* of this kind did not occur, whereas in the modern the *poet* would be lacking." Goethe's subject — Werther — is "a personality who embraces the ideal with burning feeling and abandons actuality in order to contend with an insubstantial infinitude, who seeks continuously outside himself for that which he destroys within himself, to whom only his dreams are real." He himself is of all modern poets the most childlike and naive, the "least removed from the sensuous truth of things."

Schiller's ideas in *On Naive and Sentimental Poetry* spring from those of Kant but have a tendency to bring a historical dimension into idealist aesthetics, as the poet's work responds to his age and synthesizes its approach to the eternal nature from which all springs. As such, he is one of the links between the thinking of Kant and the later trends in German idealism that culminate in Hegel.

### Selected Bibliography

Grossmann, Walter. "The Idea of Cultural Evolution in Schiller's *Aesthetic Education*." *Germanic Review* 34 (1959): 39–49.

Hermand, Jost. "Schillers Abhandlung über naive und sentimentalische Dichtung im Lichte der deutschen Popularphilosophie der 18. Jahrhunderts." *PMLA* 79 (1964): 428–41.

Jones, Michael T. "Twilight of the Gods: The Greeks in Schiller and Lukács." *Germanic Review* 59 (1984): 49–56.

Lloyd, Tom "Madame Roland and Schiller's Aesthetics." *Prose Studies* 9 (1986): 39–53.

Lukács, Georg. "Schillers Theorie der modernen Literatur." In *Goethe und Seinen Zeit*. Bern: A. Francke, 1947.

Miller, R. D. *A Study of Schiller's 'Letters on the Aesthetic Education of Man.'* Harrogate, Eng.: Duchy, 1986.

Schaper, Eva. "Towards the Aesthetic: A Journey with Friedrich Schiller." *British Journal of Aesthetics* 25 (1985): 153–68.

Sharpe, Leslie. "Schiller's Fragment "Tragödie und Komödie."" *Modern Language Review* 81 (1986): 116–17.

Wilm, Emil Carl. *The Philosophy of Schiller in Its Historic Relations*. Boston: Luce and Co., 1912.

# From *On Naive and Sentimental Poetry*

The poet, I said either *is* nature or he will *seek* her. The former is the naive, the latter the sentimental poet.

Translated by Julius Elias.

The poetic spirit is immortal and inalienable in mankind, it cannot be lost except together with humanity or with the capacity for it. For even if man should separate himself by the freedom of his fantasy and his understanding from the simplicity, truth and necessity of nature, yet not only does the way back to her remain open always, but also a powerful and ineradicable impulse, the moral, drives him ceaselessly back to her, and it is precisely with this impulse that the poetic faculty stands in the most intimate relationship.

Even now, nature is the sole flame at which the poetic spirit nourishes itself; from her alone it draws its whole power, to her alone it speaks even in the artificial man entoiled by civilization. All other modes of expression are alien to the poetic spirit; hence, generally speaking, all so-called works of wit are quite misnamed poetic; although, for long, misled by the reputation of French literature, we have mistaken them as such. It is still nature, I say, even now in the artificial condition of civilization, in virtue of which the poetic spirit is powerful; but now it stands in quite another relation to nature.

So long as man is pure — not, of course, crude — nature, he functions as an undivided sensuous unity and as a unifying whole. Sense and reason, passive and active faculties, are not separated in their activities, still less do they stand in conflict with one another. His perceptions are not the formless play of chance, his thoughts not the empty play of the faculty of representation; the former proceed out of the law of *necessity,* the latter out of *actuality.* Once man has passed into the state of civilization and art has laid her hand upon him, that *sensuous* harmony in his is withdrawn, and he can now express himself only as a *moral* unity, i.e., as striving after unity. The correspondence between his feeling and thought which in his first condition *actually* took place, exists now only *ideally*; it is no longer within him, but outside of him, as an idea still to be realized, no longer as a fact in his life. If one now applies the notion of poetry, which is nothing but *giving mankind its most complete possible expression,* to both conditions, the result in the earlier state of natural simplicity is the completest possible *imitation of actuality* — at that stage man still functions with all his powers simultaneously as a harmonious unity and hence the whole of his nature is expressed completely in actuality; whereas now, in the state of civilization where that harmonious cooperation of his whole nature is only an idea,

it is the elevation of actuality to the ideal or, amounting to the same thing, the *representation of the ideal,* that makes for the poet. And these two are likewise the only possible modes in which poetic genius can express itself at all. They are, as one can see, extremely different from one another, but there is a higher concept under which both can be subsumed, and there should be no surprise if this concept should coincide with the idea of humanity.

This is not the place further to pursue these thoughts, which can only be expounded in full measure in a separate disquisition. But anyone who is capable of making a comparison, based on the spirit and not just on the accidental forms, between ancient and modern poets,[1] will be able readily to convince himself of the truth of the matter. The former move us by nature, by sensuous truth, by living presence; the latter by ideas.

This path taken by the modern poets is, moreover, that along which man in general, the individual as well as the race, must pass. Nature sets him at one with himself, art divides and cleaves him in two, through the ideal he returns to unity. But because the ideal is an infinitude to which he never attains, the civilized man can never become perfect in *his* own wise, while the natural men can in his. He must therefore fall infinitely short of the latter in perfection, if one heeds only the relation in which each stands to his species and to his maximum capacity. But if one compares the species with one another, it becomes evident that the goal to which man in civilization *strives* is infinitely preferable to that which he *attains* in nature. For the one obtains its value by the absolute achievement of a finite, the other by approximation to an infinite greatness. But

[1] It is perhaps not superfluous to remark that if here the new poets are set over against the ancients, the difference of manner rather than of time is to be understood. We possess in modern times, even most recently, naive works of poetry in all classes, even if no longer of the purest kind and, among the old Latin, even among the Greek poets, there is no lack of sentimental ones. Not only in the same poet, even in the same work one often encounters both species combined, as, for example, in *Werthers Leiden,* and such creations will always produce the greater effects. [Au.]

only the latter possesses *degrees* and displays a *progress,* hence the relative worth of a man who is involved in civilization is in general never determinable, even though the same man considered as an individual necessarily finds himself at a disadvantage compared with one in whom nature functions in her utter perfection. But insofar as the ultimate object of mankind is not otherwise to be attained than by that progress, and man cannot progress other than by civilizing himself and hence passing over into the first category, there cannot therefore be any question to which of the two the advantage accrues with reference to that ultimate object.

The very same as has been said of the two different forms of humanity can likewise be applied to those species of poet corresponding to them.

Perhaps on this account one should not compare ancient with modern — naive with sentimental — poets either at all, or only by reference to some higher concept common to both (there is in fact such a concept). For clearly, if one has first abstracted the concept of those species one-sidedly from the ancient poets, nothing is easier, but nothing also more trivial, than to depreciate the moderns by comparison. If one calls poetry only that which in every age has affected simple nature uniformly, the result cannot be other than to deny the modern poets their title just where they achieve their most characteristic and sublimest beauty, since precisely here they speak only to the adherent of civilization and have nothing to say to simple nature.[2] Anyone whose temperament is not already prepared to pass beyond actuality into the realm of ideas will find the richest content empty appearance, and the loftiest flights of the poet exaggeration. It would not occur to a reasonable person to want to compare any modern with Homer where Homer excels, and it sounds ridiculous enough to find Milton or Klopstock honored with the title of a modern Homer. But just as little could any ancient poet, and least of all Homer, support the comparison with a modern poet in those aspects which most characteristically distinguish him. The former, I might put it, is powerful through the art of finitude; the latter by the art of the infinite.

And for the very reason that the strength of the ancient artist (for what has been said here of the poet can, allowing for self-evident qualifications, be extended to apply to the fine arts generally) subsists in finitude, the great advantage arises which the plastic art of antiquity maintains over that of modern times, and in general the unequal value relationship in which the modern art of poetry and modern plastic art stand to both species of art in antiquity. A work addressed to the eye can achieve perfection only in finitude; a work addressed to the imagination can achieve it also through the infinite. In plastic art works the modern is little aided by his superiority in ideas; here he is obliged to *determine in space in the most precise way* the representation of his imagination and hence to compete with the ancient artists in precisely that quality in which they indisputably excel. In poetic works it is otherwise, and even if the ancient poets are victorious too in the simplicity of forms and in whatever is sensuously representable and *corporeal,* the modern can nonetheless leave them behind in richness of material in whatever is insusceptible of representation and ineffable, in a word, in whatever in the work of art is called *spirit.*

Since the naive poet only follows simple nature and feeling, and limits himself solely to imitation of actuality, he can have only a single relationship to his subject and in *this* respect there is for him no choice in his treatment. The varied impression of naive poetry depends (provided that one puts out of mind everything which in it

---

[2]Molière, as a naive poet, is said to have left it in every case to the opinion of his chambermaid what should stand or fall in his comedies; it might also be wished that the masters of the French buskin had occasionally tried the same experiment with their tragedies. But I would not advise that a similar experiment be undertaken with Klopstock's *Odes,* with the finest passages in the *Messiade,* in *Paradise Lost,* in *Nathan the Wise,* or in many other pieces. Yet what am I saying? — the test has really been undertaken, and Molière's chambermaid chops logic back and forth in our critical literature, philosophical and belletristic journals and travel accounts, on poetry, art and the like, as easily, if in poorer taste, on German soil than on French, as only becomes the servants' hall of German literature. [Au.]

belongs to the content, and considers that impression only as the pure product of the poetic treatment) it depends, I say, solely upon the various degrees of one and the same mode of feeling; even the variety of external forms cannot effect any alteration in the quality of that aesthetic impression. The form may be lyric or epic, dramatic or narrative: We can indeed be moved to a weaker or stronger degree, but (as soon as the matter is abstracted) never heterogeneously. Our feeling is uniformly the same, entirely composed of *one* element, so that we cannot differentiate within it. Even the difference of language and era changes nothing in this regard, for just this pure unity of its origin and of its effect is a characteristic of naive poetry.

The case is quite otherwise with the sentimental poet. He *reflects* upon the impression that objects make upon him, and only in that reflection is the emotion grounded which he himself experiences and which he excites in us. The object here is referred to an idea and his poetic power is based solely upon this referral. The sentimental poet is thus always involved with two conflicting representations and perceptions — with actuality as a limit and with his idea as

infinitude; and the mixed feelings that he excites will always testify to this dual source.[3] Since in this case there is a plurality of principles it depends which of the two will *predominate* in the perception of the poet and in his representation, and hence a variation in the treatment is possible. For now the question arises whether he will tend more toward actuality or toward the ideal — whether he will realize the former as an object of antipathy or the latter as an object of sympathy. His presentation will, therefore, be either *satirical* or it will be (in a broader connotation of the word which will become clearer later) *elegiac*; every sentimental poet will adhere to one of these two modes of perception.

[3]Anyone who observes the impression that naive poetry makes on him and is able to separate from it that part which is due to the content will find this impression always joyous, always pure, always serene, even in the case of very pathetic objects; with sentimental poetry it will always be somewhat solemn and intense. This is because with naive accounts, regardless of their subject matter, we always rejoice in our imagination in the truth, in the living presence of the object, and seek nothing further beyond these; whereas with the sentimental we have to reconcile the representation of imagination with an idea of reason and hence always fluctuate between two different conditions. [Au.]

# Madame de Staël

## 1766–1817

Born into a society that even today seems to exclude women systematically from many cultural and intellectual pursuits, Anne-Louise-Germaine Necker, Baronne de Staël-Holstein was the first French woman to become a writer of international importance. She was well placed to do so as the daughter of Jacques Necker, the Swiss banker and financier who was finance minister to Louis XVI from 1776 to 1781 and again at the fateful calling of the Estates General in 1788. Her mother, Suzanne Curchod, was an intellectual in her own right, a clergyman's daughter to whom the historian Edward Gibbon had in his youth been engaged.

Madame de Staël's *Essay on Fiction* dates from 1795, just after her return from exile in England, and its primary examples — Richardson and Fielding — are taken from English literature rather than from that of her native country. The ideas in the essay, like much written during this period, represent an awkward transitional phase between enlightenment and romantic thinking. Parts of the essay sound like an apology for fiction in line with Sidney's *Apology for Poetry* by insisting upon the greater power of the novel over history to make a sustained moral impression upon us. He is not mentioned by name, but her primary antagonist seems to be Samuel Johnson, for although she adroitly concedes what she must, she parries his major attacks in *The Rambler, No. 4*, on the immorality of fiction.

Instead of agreeing that the subject proper to art is general nature, she insists upon the importance of *nuance,* the specific and particular emotional quality within events that makes them real for us. (The reality achieved by the elaboration of details does not, on the other hand, strike her as artistically interesting.) Even more directly she defends the object of Johnson's odium, Fielding's *Tom Jones,* for possessing "a broader morality than any similar kind of work" geared "to show the doubtfulness of judgments based upon appearances and the superiority of natural — and, so to speak — instinctive qualities over those based only upon superiority conventionality."

If Madame de Staël defends Fielding as a moral educator — which would be Sidney's or Dryden's or Johnson's criterion as well — her ethical values, and specifically her preference for nature and instinct over social convention, bring her closer to being the first spokeswoman for Romanticism. If, like a woman of the enlightenment salons, she spoke for Truth, she also felt, like the major Romantics, that the highest truth was that of feeling and that such a truth needed nurturing. She defended the growing literature of passionate eloquence, from Pope's "Eloisa to Abelard" to Goethe's *Werther,* as serving a significant function in reconciling especially gifted individuals — sensitive, passionate, and isolated from society — to their place in the world. A generation later, Shelley, who was born the year de Staël published her essay on fiction, would term these sensitive beings — whose passions are Aeolian harps on which the world plays — the "unacknowledged legislators of the world."

## Selected Bibliography

Andrews, Wayne. *Germaine: A Portrait of Madame de Staël*. New York: Atheneum, 1963.
Duffy, Bella. *Madame de Staël*. Boston: Roberts Brothers, 1887.
Folkenflik, Vivian, ed. and trans. *An Extraordinary Woman: Selected Writings of Germaine de Staël*. New York: Columbia University Press, 1987.
Forsberg, Roberta. *Madame de Staël and the English*. New York: Astra Books, 1967.
Gutwirth, Madelyn. *Madame de Staël, novelist: The Emergence of the Artist as Woman*. Urbana: University of Illinois Press, 1978.
Luppé, Robert de. *Les Idées littéraires de Madame de Staël et l'heritage des lumières*. Paris: J. Vrin, 1969.
Postgate, Helen B. Smith. *Madame de Staël*. New York: Twayne, 1968.
Van Tieghem, Paul, ed. *De la littérature, considérée dans ses rapports avec les institutions sociales. Edition critique*. 3 vols. Geneva: Droz, 1959.
Winegarten, Renee. *Madame de Staël*. Leamington Spa, Eng., and Dover N.H.: Berg, 1985.

# Essay on Fiction

The pleasure it affords is not the sole benefit of fiction. When it reaches only the reader's eyes, it can do nothing but amuse, but when it moves the heart, it can have a great influence upon all human conceptions. So this ability is perhaps the most powerful means of guidance or enlightenment. Man has only two distinct faculties, reason and imagination; all the others, even sentiment, are dependent upon or made up of them. The domain of fiction, like that of the imagination, is thus widespread. Far from being hindered by the passions, it makes use of them. Philosophy ought to be an invisible power that guides fiction's effects, but if it becomes obvious it destroys its magic.

In speaking of fiction, then, I shall consider it at once in respect to its purpose and its fascination because this genre can afford pleasure without utility but never utility without pleasure. Fiction is designed to captivate. The more we should like its effect to be moral and philosophical, the more necessary it is to adorn it with all that can stir people and to lead to the goal without revealing it in advance.

Translated by Morroe Berger.

Fiction may be divided into three groups: (1) supernatural or allegorical inventions, (2) inventions based upon historical events, (3) events at once entirely invented and imitated, in which nothing is true but everything is believable.

This subject might require a rather extended treatise, for it could embrace most works of literature. But I have sought only to demonstrate that novels that show life as it is — with insight, eloquence, depth, and morality — must be the most useful of all forms of fiction, and I have excluded from this essay everything unrelated to this purpose.

The third and final part of this essay will consider the usefulness of what I have called pure fiction, in which everything is invented and imitated, and nothing is true but everything is believable. Tragedies whose theme is entirely a product of the imagination are excluded from this class because they portray an exalted character, an extraordinary social rank and condition. The verisimilitude of these plays rests upon rather rare occurrences whose moral is applicable to only a small number of people. Dramas, comedies, have in the theatre a place corresponding to that of the novel in other works of fiction, for they, too, take their themes from private life and real events. But the conventions of the theatre deprive us of the author's elaboration of the moral to be drawn from specific events. It seems to me that only the modern novel can achieve the effect of exactness of circumstantial detail that can be derived from the portrayal of our ordinary feelings. A special class has been created called the philosophical novel. All novels ought to be philosophical, since they all should have a moral goal. But when they relate the entire story to a leading idea, they lose verisimilitude in the train of events and thus perhaps lead less certainly to the moral goal. Each chapter becomes a kind of allegory in which the events are nothing but an illustration of the maxim that follows. *Candide, Zadig,* and *Memmon,*[1] fascinating as they are in other ways, would have a more widespread effect if, first, they were not supernatural, if they presented realities instead of symbols, and if, as I have already said, the entire story did not inevitably lead to the same moral.

Novels like those of Richardson and Fielding stay close to human life by following its slow movement toward climax, its gradual unfoldment, and its lack of logical sequence, and yet they also regularly alternate between pointing out the moral lessons of experience and the benefits of virtue. These events are invented, but the sentiments are so natural that the reader often thinks that it is he himself he is reading about under another name.

The art of writing novels does not have the reputation it merits because a host of poor authors have worn us down with their insipid works in this genre, in which perfection requires the most elevated genius but mediocrity is within everyone's reach. The countless number of insipid novels have almost exhausted the very emotion they portray; one fears to rediscover in his own past even the slightest connection with the circumstances they describe. It has taken nothing less than the authority of the great masters to restore the reputation of this genre against the writers who degraded it. Other authors have debased it even further by injecting disgusting scenes of vice.

There is, however, a justifiable reason for the fact that the general public holds the talent for writing novels in less esteem than it merits. It is that novels are regarded as dedicated to portraying only love — the most violent, universal, genuine of all the emotions but one that, exercising its power only upon the young, does not arouse our interest in other stages of life. Undoubtedly we may regard every profound and tender feeling to be in the nature of love. The destiny of women and the happiness of men not summoned to govern empires often depends, in their later life, upon the place they allowed the power of love in their youth. Yet at a certain age they completely forget the impression it left upon them. They assume another disposition, totally absorbed by other purposes and other emotions. And the themes of novels should be extended to these new concerns. It seems to me that a new realm thus opens itself to authors who have the talent to portray it and can intimately understand all the emotions of the human heart. Ambition, pride, avarice, vanity, might be the main subjects of novels whose incidents would be fresher and whose situations would be as varied as those arising from love. It may be said that such a portrayal of the emotions can be found in works of history, and that it would be better to seek it there. But history does not reach down into the life of ordinary people and to feelings and personalities that have no effect upon public affairs. History does not have a sustained moral influence upon us. Truth is often hidden. Moreover, the gradual unfolding of events, which alone can make a deep impression upon us, would slow down the quick pace necessary to historical narration and give dramatic form to a work that ought to have an entirely different kind of value. History, in a word, cannot make its lesson perfectly clear, whether because we cannot always prove that their inner feelings punished the wicked in the midst of their prosperity and rewarded the virtuous in their misfortune, or because the fate of man is not confined to this life. Lessons for moral development, based upon the rewards of virtue, do not always emerge from a reading of history.

The great historians, and especially Tacitus,

[1] By Voltaire. [Tr.]

certainly try to attach a moral significance to the events they relate — for example, to make us envy Germanicus as he is dying and to detest Tiberius at the pinnacle of success. But they can portray only those feelings warranted by the facts. And what emerges from the reading of history is more the exalting influence of talent, the brilliance of fame, and the privileges of power than that quiet morality, refined and gentle, on which individual happiness and human relationships depend. It would be absurd of me to depreciate the value of history and to prefer fiction to it, for inventions themselves derive from experience, and all the subtle nuances that novels bring out derive from philosophy and the fruitful conceptions that the great drama of public affairs presents. But there is only morality in history taken en masse, for its uniformities stem from the recurrence of probabilities. The lessons of history regularly apply, therefore, to multitudes and not to individuals. These lessons are appropriate to nations because in their broad aspects they are unchanging.

Novels, on the contrary, can portray personalities and feelings with such intensity and detail that no other kind of literature can produce so profound an aversion to vice and love of virtue. The morality of novels depends more upon the unfolding of the inner emotions of the heart than upon the events they relate. A practical lesson may be drawn not from the arbitrary event the author invents to avenge crime; rather, indelible impressions remain of the truth of the pictures drawn, the gradual unfolding of a chain of errors, the willingess of sacrifice, and the sympathy for misfortune. Everything is so believable in these novels that one is easily convinced it could very well have happened just that way. A novel is not a story of the past but often seems to be one of the future.

It has been maintained that novels give a false conception of mankind. That is true of the poor ones, as it is of paintings that copy nature poorly. But when a novel is good, nothing gives such an intimate understanding of the human heart as these representations of all the events of private life and of the feelings they generate; and nothing so stimulates thought, which finds much more to learn in specific examples than in general ideas. Mémoires might achieve the same goal, were it not for the fact that, like history, they deal only with famous men and public affairs. Novels would be useless if most men had enough wit and sincerity to give a faithful and colorful account of what they had experienced in life; yet even such sincere accounts would not combine all the advantages of novels. It would be necessary to add to the truth a kind of dramatic effect, which does not dilute it but makes it stand out the more by compressing it. This is the technique of the painter who, far from falsifying his subjects, represents them more vividly. Nature may often reveal their elements on the same level, hiding their contrasts. By copying nature too slavishly, therefore, one would not succeed in portraying it. The most exact account is always an imitative truth; like a painting, it demands its own harmony. A true story, though noteworthy for its *nuances,* emotions, and characters, could not arouse interest without the help of the talent necessary to create fiction.

But while admiring the talent that probes the recesses of the human heart, it is nevertheless impossible to endure the minute details with which even the most famous novels are burdened. The author thinks they add to the credibility of the picture, but he does not realize that everything that reduces interest destroys the single truth of fiction: the impression it produces. If one were to represent on the stage everything that happens in private life, the dramatic illusion would be absolutely destroyed. The novel, too, has its dramatic rules. Fiction ought not to be filled with useless detail. If a glance, a motion, or an unnoticed event is useful in portraying a personality or in revealing a sentiment, the simpler the technique the better. But the precise details of an ordinary event diminish its credibility rather than adding to it. Reduced by details to a narrow conception of truth, we escape the illusion and soon weary of ever finding in such fiction either the facts of history or the fascination of the novel.

The capacity to affect us emotionally is the great power of fiction. Virtually all moral truths can be made perceptible by putting them into action. Virtue has so great an influence upon our happiness and unhappiness that most classes of people can be said to depend upon it. There are stern philosophers who condemn all the emotions and would like morality to prevail through the mere statement of the obligations it calls for; but nothing is less suited to the nature of mankind than such an opinion. Virtue must be animated to struggle effectively against the passions, to create an exalted feeling so that we may be attracted to sacrifice — in brief, to beautify misfortune so that it will be preferred to sinful pleasures. Fiction that really moves us to noble emotions makes them habitual with us. It leads us unwittingly to make a pledge to ourselves that we would be ashamed to go back on. But the more genuine is this capacity to move us, the more important it is to extend its influence to the emotions of people of all ages and to the obligations of all classes. Love is the main theme of novels, and other dispositions are treated as secondary. By following another pattern, one might discover a multitude of new themes. *Tom Jones* has a broader morality than any similar kind of work. In this novel love is presented only as one of the means to emphasize the philosophical effect. The real purpose of *Tom Jones,* one of the most useful and justly famous novels, is to show the doubtfulness of judgments based upon appearances and the superiority of natural — and, so to speak, instinctive — qualities over those based only upon superficial conventionality.[2]

There is always a great objection to novels about love. It is that they portray this emotion in such a way as to stimulate it; and, it is said, there are times when this danger outweighs every sort of benefit. But this drawback does not pertain to novels that deal with the other emotions. By describing even the most obscure signs of a dangerous inclination from their very outset, one can deter oneself and others from it. Ambition, pride, and avarice often exist unknown even to those who yield to them. Love is stimulated by its portrayal. But the best way to combat the other passions is to reveal them.

Even if purely philosophical works could, like novels, allow for all the *nuances* of actions, there would still be a great advantage in the *genre* in which morality is dramatized: the power to inspire feelings of indignation, exaltation, sweet

melancholy — that is, the results of various romantic situations and a kind of supplement to one's own experience. This impression resembles that produced by real events witnessed by the readers. Always directed toward the same end, however, the impression produced by fiction does not confuse us so much as the disconnected picture of events around us does. There are, in short, men upon whom the sense of duty has no influence who might nevertheless be saved from evil by developing in them the capacity to be moved by emotion.

There are some writings, such as the letters of Abélard, works by Pope, *Werther,* the *Portuguese Letters,* etc., and a unique work, *The New Héloise,*[3] whose chief merit is eloquence of emotion. Though their theme may often be moral, what stands out above everything else in them is all-powerfulness of the feelings. Such works of fiction are in a class by themselves. In a hundred years we find only one mind, one genius, that can create them. So they cannot become a type, or a goal. Yet should one prohibit these miracles of language, these deep impressions that gratify all the emotions of people with strong feelings? There are only a few enthusiastic readers of such works, which always benefit those who admire them. Let these passionate and sensitive souls enjoy such works — they cannot make themselves heard. The feelings that move them are hardly understood. Ceaselessly condemned, they might believe themselves alone in the world and might soon come to abhor their own character that isolates them from others, did not some impassioned and melancholy works enable them to hear a voice in the desert of life and to find in solitude some rays of happiness that elude them in society. This pleasure in withdrawal gives them peace from the vain efforts of disappointed hope. As the whole world seethes far from such an unfortunate individual, an eloquent and tender piece of writing remains close to him, like the most faithful friend who best understands him.

[3]These references are to Abélard's letters to Héloise; Alexander Pope; Goethe's *Sorrows of Werther; Letters of a Portuguese Nun,* published in French in 1669 and purporting to be letters from Marianna Alcaforado to her French lover; and Rousseau's *Julie, or The New Héloise.* [Tr.]

[2]De Staël seems to be replying here to the strictures of Johnson's *The Rambler,* No. 4. [Ed.]

# William Wordsworth

## 1770–1850

William Wordsworth was born in Cockermouth, Cumberlandshire, the son of an attorney who was steward to a noble lord, and raised in the Lake District in northwest England among hills and lakes and their rustic inhabitants and sojourners, whom he would celebrate in his poetry. Though orphaned at thirteen, Wordsworth managed to attend St. John's College, Cambridge. Taking his degree in 1791, Wordsworth spent a year on the Continent absorbing the sights and the spirit of the French Revolution in its most idealistic phase. On his return to England, Wordsworth wrote *Descriptive Sketches* and met an admirer of that volume, Samuel Taylor Coleridge, who was to be a major poetical and intellectual influence. Together, Wordsworth and Coleridge (mostly Wordsworth) wrote *Lyrical Ballads* (1798), the premier volume of English romanticism. Although the critics were harsh ("This will never do," Francis Jeffrey began in his notorious attack), the public was not, and a second edition was published in 1800, to which Wordsworth contributed a preface, his single major piece of literary criticism, reprinted here.[1]

Most of Wordsworth's best poetry was written in a single decade, 1797–1807, not only *Lyrical Ballads* but *Poems in Two Volumes* (1807) including the "Intimations of Immortality" Ode, and *The Prelude* (1805, published 1850). By his forties, when he published *The Excursion* (1814) he was in decline, though he continued to write long into his eighth decade. In old age he had become an institution, and Queen Victoria appointed him poet laureate in 1843.

The Preface to *Lyrical Ballads* is a transitional work between the rhetorical/mimetic literary theory of the eighteenth century and the expressive theories of the nineteenth. As an argument it is at odds with itself. Part of the confusion derives from Wordsworth's revisions: Most of the original 1800 version of the Preface adheres to a mode of thought (though not, of course, a thesis) that Samuel Johnson would readily have understood, while the 1802 version and subsequent editions ally the essay with later expressive theories of literature.

The occasion of the Preface was Wordsworth's desire to defend two of the revolutionary aspects of *Lyrical Ballads:* their use of a plain style and their rustic subject matter. He does so by attacking the poetic diction of the latter eighteenth century as artificial and meaningless. His memorable analysis of Thomas Gray's "Sonnet on the Death of Mr. Richard West" demonstrates how little of that brief poem actually functions in making its elegiac impression.

When he discusses the subject and style of *Lyrical Ballads,* however, Wordsworth calls on the values the eighteenth century already revered. Why did he

---

[1]Reprinted here is the 1802 version of the Preface to *Lyrical Ballads,* which includes the *What is a poet?* section, among other revisions.

choose to write about "humble and rustic life"? Because there "the essential passions of the heart find a better soil in which they can attain their maturity, are under less restraint," and because "the manners of rural life . . . are more easily comprehended, and are more durable." This recalls Johnson's dictum that the poet who wishes to become a classic should choose to imitate "general nature" rather than topical but evanescent manners. Why did Wordsworth choose to write in the plain style, and what is the role of the reader? "My purpose was to imitate, and, as far as possible, to adopt the very language of men. . . . to keep the reader in the company of flesh and blood, persuaded that by so doing I shall interest him." At the same time, he hopes to "enlighten the understanding" of the reader and "strengthen and purify" his affections. It sounds as if Wordsworth, however revolutionary his style and subject matter, were defending his poetic practice in the most traditional terms as an attempt to "please many and please long" by providing "just representations of general nature."

Wordsworth thus far seems to be claiming that in *Lyrical Ballads* he was imitating the manners, passions, and actions of rustic Englishmen for the delight and instruction of his audience, but the sections added in 1802 suggest a very different approach to poetry: That poetry is created less by representing what is in the outside world than by attending to the voice within. These passages focus on the poet and the genesis of poetry. But once he had defined poetry as "the spontaneous overflow of powerful feelings," it becomes necessary to explain how the feelings of his preferred humble rustics, such as Goody Blake and Harry Gill, can overflow from a university-educated son of a country lawyer. Wordsworth's solution is to posit for the poet a special internal makeup. The poet is "endowed with more lively sensibility, more enthusiasm and tenderness . . . a greater knowledge of human nature and a more comprehensive soul than are supposed to be common among mankind." Most important, the poet can express "those thoughts and feelings which," voluntarily or not, "arise in him without immediate external excitement." At times the poet can "let himself slip into an entire delusion and even confound and identify his own feelings with" those of the people he describes. The poet is thus able to internalize something he has seen and experienced and call it up in himself as though he were participating in it.

As he discusses the process of poetic imagination and composition, Wordsworth erodes the mimetic/rhetorical framework with which he has begun by claiming that the feeling will not be precisely the same when it is imaginatively "recollected in tranquillity" as in immediate experience: It will be purified, on the one hand, but it will "fall short" of reality on the other. The validity of the feeling the poet conveys therefore is not measurable by its accuracy, as a mimetic theory would suggest; it must be measured by a subjective, internal measure: The poet's "faith that no words, which *his* fancy or imagination can suggest, will be to be compared with those which are the emanations of reality and truth."

Wordsworth's theories of poetic diction would be criticized by his friend Coleridge (in *Biographia Literaria,* Ch. 17), his theory of poetic process and imagination refined and replaced by more sophisticated versions, and his vision of the high status and purposes of poetry superseded by the celestial ascending rhetoric of Shelley. But in the Preface to *Lyrical Ballads* Wordsworth created the first and one of the most lasting apologies for the romantic movement in poetry and for the expressive theory of literature that underpinned its other beliefs.

## Selected Bibliography

Barstow, Marjorie Latta. *Wordsworth's Theory of Poetic Diction*. New Haven: Yale University Press, 1917.

Hirsch, E. D. *Wordsworth and Schelling*. New Haven: Yale University Press, 1960.

Jackson, Wallace. *The Probable and the Marvelous: Blake, Wordsworth and the Eighteenth-Century Critical Tradition*. Athens: University of Georgia Press, 1978.

Jones, Henry John Franklin. *The Egotistical Sublime: A History of Wordsworth's Imagination*. London: Chatto and Windus, 1960.

Knapp, Steven. *Personification and the Sublime: Milton to Coleridge*. Cambridge: Harvard University Press, 1985.

Peacock, M. L., Jr. *Critical Opinions of William Wordsworth*. Baltimore: Johns Hopkins University Press, 1950.

Smith, Nowell C., ed. *Wordsworth's Literary Criticism*. Bristol, Eng.: Bristol Classical Press, 1980.

Thorpe, C. D. "The Imagination: Coleridge versus Wordsworth." *Philological Quarterly* 18 (1939): 1–18.

Wlecke, Albert O. *Wordsworth and the Sublime*. Berkeley: University of California Press, 1973.

# Preface to *Lyrical Ballads*

The first volume of these poems has already been submitted to general perusal. It was published, as an experiment, which, I hoped, might be of some use to ascertain, how far, by fitting to metrical arrangement a selection of the real language of men in a state of vivid sensation, that sort of pleasure and that quantity of pleasure may be imparted, which a poet may rationally endeavour to impart.

I had formed no very inaccurate estimate of the probable effect of those poems: I flattered myself that they who should be pleased with them would read them with more than common pleasure: and, on the other hand, I was well aware, that by those who should dislike them they would be read with more than common dislike. The result has differed from my expectation in this only, that I have pleased a greater number, than I ventured to hope I should please.

For the sake of variety, and from a consciousness of my own weakness, I was induced to request the assistance of a friend, who furnished me with the poems of the *Ancient Mariner,* the "Foster-Mother's Tale," the *Nightingale,* and the poem entitled *Love.* I should not, however, have requested this assistance, had I not believed that the poems of my friend would in a great measure have the same tendency as my own, and that, though there would be found a difference, there would be found no discordance in the colours of our style; as our opinions on the subject of poetry do almost entirely coincide.

Several of my friends are anxious for the success of these poems from a belief, that, if the views with which they were composed were indeed realized, a class of poetry would be produced, well adapted to interest mankind permanently, and not unimportant in the multiplicity, and in the quality of its moral relations: and on this account they have advised me to prefix a systematic defence of the theory, upon which the poems were written. But I was unwilling to undertake the task, because I knew that on this occasion the reader would look coldly upon my arguments, since I might be suspected of having been principally influenced by the selfish and foolish hope of *reasoning* him into an approbation of these particular poems: and I was still more unwilling to undertake the task, because, adequately to display my opinions, and fully to enforce my arguments, would require a space wholly disproportionate to the nature of a preface. For to treat the subject with the clearness and coherence, of which I believe it susceptible, it would be necessary to give a full account of the present state of the public taste in this country, and to determine how far this taste is healthy or depraved; which, again, could not be determined, without pointing out, in what manner language and the human mind act and react on each other, and without retracing the revolutions, not of literature alone, but likewise of society itself. I have therefore altogether declined to enter regularly upon this defence; yet I am sensible, that there would be some impropriety in abruptly obtruding upon the public, without a few words of introduction, poems so materially different from those, upon which general approbation is at present bestowed.

It is supposed, that by the act of writing in verse an author makes a formal engagement that he will gratify certain known habits of association; that he not only thus apprizes the reader that certain classes of ideas and expressions will be found in his book, but that others will be carefully excluded. This exponent or symbol held forth by metrical language must in different eras of literature have excited very different expectations: for example, in the age of Catullus, Terence, and Lucretius and that of Statius or Claudian; and in our own country, in the age of Shakespeare and Beaumont and Fletcher, and that of Donne and Cowley, or Dryden, or Pope. I will not take upon me to determine the exact import of the promise which by the act of writing in verse an author, in the present day, makes to his reader; but I am certain, it will appear to many persons that I have not fulfilled the terms of an engagement thus voluntarily contracted. They who have been accustomed to the gaudiness and inane phraseology of many modern writers, if they persist in reading this book to its conclusion, will, no doubt, frequently have to struggle with feelings of strangeness and awkwardness: they will look round for poetry, and will be induced to inquire by what species of courtesy these attempts can be permitted to assume that title. I hope therefore the reader will not censure me, if I attempt to state what I have proposed to myself to perform; and also (as far as the limits of a preface will permit), to explain some of the chief reasons which have determined me in the choice of my purpose: that at least he may be spared any unpleasant feeling of disappointment, and that I myself may be protected from the most dishonourable accusation which can be brought against an author, namely, that of an indolence which prevents him from endeavouring to ascertain what is his duty, or, when his duty is ascertained, prevents him from performing it.

The principal object, then, which I proposed to myself in these poems was to choose incidents and situations from common life and to relate or describe them, throughout, as far as was possible, in a selection of language really used by men; and, at the same time, to throw over them a certain colouring of imagination, whereby ordinary things should be presented to the mind in an unusual way; and, further, and above all, to make these incidents and situations interesting by tracing in them, truly though not ostentatiously, the primary laws of our nature: chiefly, as far as regards the manner in which we associate ideas in a state of excitement. Low and rustic life was generally chosen, because in that condition, the essential passions of the heart find a better soil in which they can attain their maturity, are less under restraint, and speak a plainer and more emphatic language; because in that condition of life our elementary feelings co-exist in a state of greater simplicity, and, consequently, may be more accurately contemplated, and more forcibly communicated; because the manners of rural life germinate from those elementary feelings; and, from the necessary character of rural occupations, are most easily comprehended; and are more durable; and lastly, because in that condition the passions of men are incorporated with the beautiful and permanent forms of nature. The language, too, of these men is adopted (purified indeed from what appear to be its real defects, from all lasting and rational causes of dislike or disgust) because such men hourly communicate with the best objects from which the best part of language is originally derived; and because, from their rank in society and the sameness and narrow circle of their intercourse, being less under the influence of social vanity they convey their feelings and notions in simple and unelaborated expressions. Accordingly, such a language, arising out of repeated experience and regular feelings, is a more permanent, and a far more philosophical language, than that which is frequently substituted for it by poets, who think that they are conferring honour upon themselves and their art, in proportion as they separate themselves from the sympathies of men, and indulge in arbitrary and capricious habits of expression, in order to furnish food for fickle tastes, and fickle appetites, of their own creation.

I cannot, however, be insensible of the present outcry against the triviality and meanness both of thought and language, which some of my contemporaries have occasionally introduced into their metrical compositions; and I acknowledge, that this defect, where it exists, is more dishonourable to the writer's own character than false refinement or arbitrary innovation, though I should contend at the same time that it is far less pernicious in the sum of its consequences. From such verses the poems in these volumes will be found distinguished at least by one mark of difference, that each of them has a worthy *purpose*. Not that I mean to say, that I always began to write with a distinct purpose formally conceived; but I believe that my habits of meditation have so formed my feelings, as that my descriptions of such objects as strongly excite those feelings, will be found to carry along with them a *purpose*. If in this opinion I am mistaken, I can have little right to the name of a poet. For all good poetry is the spontaneous overflow of powerful feelings: but though this be true, poems to which any value can be attached, were never produced on any variety of subjects but by a man, who being possessed of more than usual organic sensibility, had also thought long and deeply. For our continued influxes of feeling are modified and directed by our thoughts, which are indeed the representatives of all our past feelings; and, as by contemplating the relation of these general representatives to each other we discover what is really important to men, so, by the repetition and continuance of this act, our feelings will be connected with important subjects, till at length, if we be originally possessed of much sensibility, such habits of mind will be produced, that, by obeying blindly and mechanically the impulses of those habits, we shall describe objects, and utter sentiments, of such a nature and in such connection with each other, that the understanding of the being to whom we address ourselves, if he be in a healthful state of association, must necessarily be in some degree enlightened, and his affections ameliorated.

I have said that each of these poems has a purpose. I have also informed my reader what this purpose will be found principally to be: namely to illustrate the manner in which our feelings and ideas are associated in a state of excitement. But, speaking in language somewhat more appropriate, it is to follow the fluxes and refluxes of the mind when agitated by the great and simple affections of our nature. This object I have endeavoured in these short essays to attain by various means; by tracing the maternal passion through many of its more subtle windings, as in the poems of the *Idiot Boy* and the *Mad Mother*; by accompanying the last struggles of a human being, at the approach of death, cleaving in solitude to life and society, as in the poem of the "Forsaken Indian"; by showing, as in the stanzas entitled "We Are Seven," the perplexity and obscurity which in childhood attend our notion of death, or rather our utter inability to admit that notion; or by displaying the strength of fraternal, or to speak more philosophically, of moral attachment when early associated with the great and beautiful objects of nature, as in *The Brothers*; or, as in the incident of "Simon Lee," by placing my reader in the way of receiving from ordinary moral sensations another and more salutary impression than we are accustomed to receive from them. It has also been part of my general purpose to attempt to sketch characters under the influence of less impassioned feelings, as in the "Two April Mornings," "The Fountain," *The Old Man Travelling, The Two Thieves,* etc. characters of which the elements are simple, belonging rather to nature than to manners, such as exist now, and will probably always exist, and which from their constitution may be distinctly and profitably contemplated. I will not abuse the indulgence of my reader by dwelling longer upon this subject; but it is proper that I should mention one other circumstance which distinguishes these poems from the popular poetry of the day; it is this, that the feeling therein developed gives importance to the action and situation, and not the action and situation to the feeling. My meaning will be rendered perfectly intelligible by referring my reader to the poems entitled "Poor Susan" and the "Childless Father," particularly to the last stanza of the latter poem.

I will not suffer a sense of false modesty to prevent me from asserting, that I point my reader's attention to this mark of distinction, far less for the sake of these particular poems than from the general importance of the subject. The subject is indeed important! For the human mind is capable of being excited without the application of gross and violent stimulants; and he must have a very faint perception of its beauty and dignity who does not know this, and who does not further know, that one being is elevated above another, in proportion as he possesses this capability. It has therefore appeared to me, that to endeavour to produce or enlarge this capability is one of the best services in which, at any period, a writer can be engaged; but this service, excellent at all times, is especially so at the present day. For a multitude of causes, unknown to former times, are now acting with a combined force to blunt the discriminating powers of the mind, and unfitting it for all voluntary exertion to reduce it to a state of almost savage torpor. The most effective of these causes are the great national events which are daily taking place, and the increasing accumulation of men in cities, where the uniformity of their occupations produces a craving for extraordinary incident, which the rapid communication of intelligence hourly

gratifies.[1] To this tendency of life and manners the literature and theatrical exhibitions of the country have conformed themselves. The invaluable works of our elder writers, I had almost said the works of Shakespeare and Milton, are driven into neglect by frantic novels, sickly and stupid German tragedies, and deluges of idle and extravagant stories in verse.[2] — When I think upon this degrading thirst after outrageous stimulation, I am almost ashamed to have spoken of the feeble effort with which I have endeavoured to counteract it; and, reflecting upon the magnitude of the general evil, I should be oppressed with no dishonourable melancholy, had I not a deep impression of certain inherent and indestructible qualities of the human mind, and likewise of certain powers in the great and permanent objects that act upon it which are equally inherent and indestructible; and did I not further add to this impression a belief, that the time is approaching when the evil will be systematically opposed, by men of greater powers, and with far more distinguished success.

Having dwelt thus long on the subjects and aim of these poems, I shall request the reader's permission to apprize him of a few circumstances relating to their *style*, in order, among other reasons, that I may not be censured for not having performed what I never attempted. The reader will find that personifications of abstract ideas rarely occur in these volumes; and, I hope, are utterly rejected as an ordinary device to elevate the style, and raise it above prose. I have proposed to myself to imitate, and, as far as is possible, to adopt the very language of men; and assuredly such personifications do not make any natural or regular part of that language. They are, indeed, a figure of speech occasionally prompted by passion, and I have made use of them as such; but I have endeavoured utterly to reject them as a mechanical device of style, or as a family language which writers in metre seem

[1]Wordsworth refers to the French Revolution and the war between England and France that followed. [Ed.]
[2]Wordsworth alludes to the vogue of the Gothic novel, which stretched from the early 1790s until about 1825. [Ed.]

to lay claim to by prescription. I have wished to keep my reader in the company of flesh and blood, persuaded that by so doing I shall interest him. I am, however, well aware that others who pursue a different track may interest him likewise; I do not interfere with their claim, I only wish to prefer a different claim of my own. There will also be found in these volumes little of what is usually called poetic diction; I have taken as much pains to avoid it as others ordinarily take to produce it; this I have done for the reason already alleged, to bring my language near to the language of men, and further, because the pleasure which I have proposed to myself to impart is of a kind very different from that which is supposed by many persons to be the proper object of poetry. I do not know how without being culpably particular I can give my reader a more exact notion of the style in which I wished these poems to be written than by informing him that I have at all times endeavoured to look steadily at my subject, consequently, I hope that there is in these poems little falsehood of description, and that my ideas are expressed in language fitted to their respective importance. Something I must have gained by this practice, as it is friendly to one property of all good poetry, namely, good sense; but it has necessarily cut me off from a large portion of phrases and figures of speech which from father to son have long been regarded as the common inheritance of poets. I also have thought it expedient to restrict myself still further, having abstained from the use of many expressions, in themselves proper and beautiful, but which have been foolishly repeated by bad poets, till such feelings of disgust are connected with them as it is scarcely possible by any art of association to overpower.

If in a poem there should be found a series of lines, or even a single line, in which the language, though naturally arranged and according to the strict laws of metre, does not differ from that of prose, there is a numerous class of critics, who, when they stumble upon these prosaisms as they call them, imagine that they have made a notable discovery, and exult over the poet as over a man ignorant of his own profession. Now

these men would establish a canon of criticism which the reader will conclude he must utterly reject, if he wishes to be pleased with these volumes. And it would be a most easy task to prove to him, that not only the language of a large portion of every good poem, even of the most elevated character, must necessarily, except with reference to the metre, in no respect differ from that of good prose, but likewise that some of the most interesting parts of the best poems will be found to be strictly the language of prose, when prose is well written. The truth of this assertion might be demonstrated by innumerable passages from almost all the poetical writings, even of Milton himself. I have not space for much quotation; but, to illustrate the subject in a general manner, I will here adduce a short composition of Gray, who was at the head of those who by their reasonings have attempted to widen the space of separation betwixt prose and metrical composition, and was more than any other man curiously elaborate in the structure of his own poetic diction.

> In vain to me the smiling mornings shine,
> And reddening Phoebus lifts his golden fire:
> The birds in vain their amorous descant join,
> Or cheerful fields resume their green attire:
> These ears alas! for other notes repine;
> *A different object do these eyes require;*
> *My lonely anguish melts no heart but mine;*
> *And in my breast the imperfect joys expire;*
> Yet Morning smiles the busy race to cheer,
> And new-born pleasure brings to happier men;
> The fields to all their wonted tribute bear;
> To warm their little loves the birds complain.
> *I fruitless mourn to him that cannot hear*
> *And weep the more because I weep in vain.*[3]

It will easily be perceived that the only part of this sonnet which is of any value is the lines printed in italics: it is equally obvious, that, except in the rhyme, and in the use of the single word "fruitless" for fruitlessly, which is so far a defect, the language of these lines does in no respect differ from that of prose.

By the foregoing quotation I have shown that

[3]Thomas Gray, "Sonnet on the Death of Richard West." [Ed.]

the language of prose may yet be well adapted to poetry; and I have previously asserted that a large portion of the language of every good poem can in no respect differ from that of good prose. I will go further. I do not doubt that it may be safely affirmed, that there neither is, nor can be, any essential difference between the language of prose and metrical composition. We are fond of tracing the resemblance between poetry and painting, and, accordingly, we call them sisters: but where shall we find bonds of connection sufficiently strict to typify the affinity betwixt metrical and prose composition? They both speak by and to the same organs; the bodies in which both of them are clothed may be said to be of the same substance, their affections are kindred and almost identical, not necessarily differing even in degree; poetry[4] sheds no tears "such as Angels weep," but natural and human tears; she can boast of no celestial ichor that distinguishes her vital juices from those of prose; the same human blood circulates through the veins of them both.

If it be affirmed that rhyme and metrical arrangement of themselves constitute a distinction which overturns what I have been saying on the strict affinity of metrical language with that of prose, and paves the way for other artificial distinctions which the mind voluntarily admits, I answer that the language of such poetry as I am recommending is, as far as is possible, a selection of the language really spoken by men; that this selection, wherever it is made with true taste and feeling, will of itself form a distinction far greater than would at first be imagined, and will entirely separate the composition from the vulgarity and meanness of ordinary life; and, if metre be superadded thereto, I believe that a dissimilitude will be produced altogether suffi-

cient for the gratification of a rational mind. What other distinction would we have? Whence is it to come? And where is it to exist? Not, surely, where the poet speaks through the mouths of his characters: it cannot be necessary here, either for elevation of style, or any of its supposed ornaments: for, if the poet's subject be judiciously chosen, it will naturally, and upon fit occasion, lead him to passions the language of which, if selected truly and judiciously, must necessarily be dignified and variegated, and alive with metaphors and figures. I forbear to speak of an incongruity which would shock the intelligent reader, should the poet interweave any foreign splendour of his own with that which the passion naturally suggests: it is sufficient to say that such addition is unnecessary. And, surely, it is more probable that those passages, which with propriety abound with metaphors and figures, will have their due effect, if, upon other occasions where the passions are of a milder character, the style also be subdued and temperate.

But, as the pleasure which I hope to give by the poems I now present to the reader must depend entirely on just notions upon this subject, and, as it is in itself of the highest importance to our taste and moral feelings, I cannot content myself with these detached remarks. And if, in what I am about to say, it shall appear to some that my labour is unnecessary, and that I am like a man fighting a battle without enemies, I would remind such persons, that, whatever may be the language outwardly holden by men, a practical faith in the opinions which I am wishing to establish is almost unknown. If my conclusions are admitted, and carried as far as they must be carried if admitted at all, our judgments concerning the works of the greatest poets both ancient and modern will be far different from what they are at present, both when we praise, and when we censure: and our moral feelings influencing, and influenced by these judgments will, I believe, be corrected and purified.

Taking up the subject, then, upon general grounds, I ask what is meant by the word poet? What is a poet? To whom does he address himself? And what language is to be expected from him? He is a man speaking to men: a man, it is true, endued with more lively sensibility, more

---

[4]I here use the word "poetry" (though against my own judgment) as opposed to the word prose, and synonymous with metrical composition. But much confusion has been introduced into criticism by this contradistinction of poetry and prose, instead of the more philosophical one of poetry and matter of fact, or science. The only strict antithesis to prose is metre; nor is this, in truth, a *strict* antithesis, because lines and passages of metre so naturally occur in writing prose, that it would be scarcely possible to avoid them, even were it desirable. [Au.]

enthusiasm and tenderness, who has a greater knowledge of human nature, and a more comprehensive soul, than are supposed to be common among mankind; a man pleased with his own passions and volitions, and who rejoices more than other men in the spirit of life that is in him; delighting to contemplate similar volitions and passions as manifested in the goings-on of the universe, and habitually impelled to create them where he does not find them. To these qualities he has added a disposition to be affected more than other men by absent things as if they were present; an ability of conjuring up in himself passions, which are indeed far from being the same as those produced by real events, yet (especially in those parts of the general sympathy which are pleasing and delightful) do more nearly resemble the passions produced by real events, than any thing which, from the motions of their own minds merely, other men are accustomed to feel in themselves; whence, and from practice, he has acquired a greater readiness and power in expressing what he thinks and feels, and especially those thoughts and feelings which, by his own choice, or from the structure of his own mind, arise in him without immediate external excitement.

But, whatever portion of this faculty we may suppose even the greatest poet to possess, there cannot be a doubt but that the language which it will suggest to him, must, in liveliness and truth, fall far short of that which is uttered by men in real life, under the actual pressure of those passions, certain shadows of which the poet thus produces, or feels to be produced, in himself. However exalted a notion we would wish to cherish of the character of a poet, it is obvious, that, while he describes and imitates passions, his situation is altogether slavish and mechanical, compared with the freedom and power of real and substantial action and suffering. So that it will be the wish of the poet to bring his feelings near to those of the persons whose feelings he describes, nay, for short spaces of time perhaps, to let himself slip into an entire delusion, and even confound and identify his own feelings with theirs; modifying only the language which is thus suggested to him, by a consideration that he describes for a particular purpose, that of giving pleasure. Here, then, he will apply the principle on which I have so much insisted, namely, that of selection; on this he will depend for removing what would otherwise be painful or disgusting in the passion; he will feel that there is no necessity to trick out or to elevate nature: and, the more industriously he applies this principle, the deeper will be his faith that no words, which *his* fancy or imagination can suggest, will be to be compared with those which are the emanations of reality and truth.

But it may be said by those who do not object to the general spirit of these remarks, that, as it is impossible for the poet to produce upon all occasions language as exquisitely fitted for the passion as that which the real passion itself suggests, it is proper that he should consider himself as in the situation of a translator, who deems himself justified when he substitutes excellences of another kind for those which are unattainable by him; and endeavours occasionally to surpass his original, in order to make some amends for the general inferiority to which he feels that he must submit. But this would be to encourage idleness and unmanly despair. Further, it is the language of men who speak of what they do not understand; who talk of poetry as of a matter of amusement and idle pleasure; who will converse with us as gravely about a *taste* for poetry, as they express it, as if it were a thing as indifferent as a taste for rope-dancing, or frontiniac or sherry. Aristotle, I have been told, hath said, that poetry is the most philosophic of all writing:[5] it is so: its object is truth, not individual and local, but general, and operative; not standing upon external testimony, but carried alive into the heart by passion; truth which is its own testimony, which gives strength and divinity to the tribunal to which it appeals, and receives them from the same tribunal. Poetry is the image of man and nature. The obstacles which stand in the way of the fidelity of the biographer and historian, and of their consequent utility, are incalculably greater than those which are to be encountered by the poet who has an adequate notion of the dignity of his art. The poet writes under one

[5]Aristotle, *Poetics,* Ch. 9. One notes that Wordsworth misquotes Aristotle by hearsay. [Ed.]

restriction only, namely, that of the necessity of giving immediate pleasure to a human being possessed of that information which may be expected from him, not as a lawyer, a physician, a mariner, an astronomer or a natural philosopher, but as a man. Except this one restriction, there is no object standing between the poet and the image of things; between this, and the biographer and historian there are a thousand.

Nor let this necessity of producing immediate pleasure be considered as a degradation of the poet's art. It is far otherwise. It is an acknowledgment of the beauty of the universe, an acknowledgment the more sincere because it is not formal, but indirect; it is a task light and easy to him who looks at the world in the spirit of love: further, it is a homage paid to the native and naked dignity of man, to the grand elementary principle of pleasure, by which he knows, and feels, and lives, and moves. We have no sympathy but what is propagated by pleasure: I would not be misunderstood; but wherever we sympathize with pain it will be found that the sympathy is produced and carried on by subtle combinations with pleasure. We have no knowledge, that is, no general principles drawn from the contemplation of particular facts, but what has been built up by pleasure, and exists in us by pleasure alone. The man of science, the chemist and mathematician, whatever difficulties and disgusts they may have had to struggle with, know and feel this. However painful may be the objects with which the anatomist's knowledge is connected, he feels that his knowledge is pleasure; and where he has no pleasure he has no knowledge. What then does the poet? He considers man and the objects that surround him as acting and reacting upon each other, so as to produce an infinite complexity of pain and pleasure; he considers man in his own nature and in his ordinary life as contemplating this with a certain quantity of immediate knowledge, with certain convictions, intuitions, and deductions which by habit become of the nature of intuitions; he considers him as looking upon this complex scene of ideas and sensations, and finding every where objects that immediately excite in him sympathies which, from the necessities of his nature, are accompanied by an overbalance of enjoyment.

To this knowledge which all men carry about with them, and to these sympathies in which without any other discipline than that of our daily life we are fitted to take delight, the poet principally directs his attention. He considers man and nature as essentially adapted to each other, and the mind of man as naturally the mirror of the fairest and most interesting qualities of nature. And thus the poet, prompted by this feeling of pleasure which accompanies him through the whole course of his studies, converses with general nature with affections akin to those, which, through labour and length of time, the man of science has raised up in himself, by conversing with those particular parts of nature which are the objects of his studies. The knowledge both of the poet and the man of science is pleasure; but the knowledge of the one cleaves to us as a necessary part of our existence, our natural and unalienable inheritance; the other is a personal and individual acquisition, slow to come to us, and by no habitual and direct sympathy connecting us with our fellow-beings. The man of science seeks truth as a remote and unknown benefactor; he cherishes and loves it in his solitude: the poet, singing a song in which all human beings join with him, rejoices in the presence of truth as our visible friend and hourly companion. Poetry is the breath and finer spirit of all knowledge; it is the impassioned expression which is in the countenance of all science. Emphatically may it be said of the poet, as Shakespeare hath said of man, "that he looks before and after." He is the rock of defence of human nature; an upholder and preserver, carrying every where with him relationship and love. In spite of difference of soil and climate, of language and manners, of laws and customs, in spite of things silently gone out of mind and things violently destroyed, the poet binds together by passion and knowledge the vast empire of human society, as it is spread over the whole earth, and over all time. The objects of the poet's thoughts are every where; though the eyes and senses of man are, it is true, his favourite guides, yet he will follow wheresoever he can find an atmosphere of sensation in which to move his wings. Poetry is the first and last of all knowledge — it is as immortal as the heart of man. If the labours of men of science should ever create any material revolution, direct or indirect, in our condition, and in the impressions which we habitually receive, the poet will sleep then no more than at present, but he will be ready to follow the steps of the man of science, not only in those general indirect effects, but he will be at his side, carrying sensation into the midst of the objects of the science itself. The remotest discoveries of the chemist, the botanist, or mineralogist, will be as proper objects of the poet's art as any upon which it can be employed, if the time should ever come when these things shall be familiar to us, and the relations under which they are contemplated by the followers of these respective sciences shall be manifestly and palpably material to us as enjoying and suffering beings. If the time should ever come when what is now called science, thus familiarized to men, shall be ready to put on, as it were, a form of flesh and blood, the poet will lend his divine spirit to aid the transfiguration, and will welcome the being thus produced, as a dear and genuine inmate of the household of man. — It is not, then, to be supposed that any one, who holds that sublime notion of poetry which I have attempted to convey, will break in upon the sanctity and truth of his pictures by transitory and accidental ornaments, and endeavour to excite admiration of himself by arts, the necessity of which must manifestly depend upon the assumed meanness of his subject.

What I have thus far said applies to poetry in general; but especially to those parts of composition where the poet speaks through the mouths of his characters; and upon this point it appears to have such weight that I will conclude, there are few persons, of good sense, who would not allow that the dramatic parts of composition are defective, in proportion as they deviate from the real language of nature, and are coloured by a diction of the poet's own, either peculiar to him as an individual poet, or belonging simply to poets in general, to a body of men who, from the circumstance of their compositions being in metre, it is expected will employ a particular language.

It is not, then, in the dramatic parts of composition that we look for this distinction of language; but still it may be proper and necessary where the poet speaks to us in his own person and character. To this I answer by referring my reader to the description which I have before given of a poet. Among the qualities which I have enumerated as principally conducing to form a poet, is implied nothing differing in kind from other men, but only in degree. The sum of what I have there said is, that the poet is chiefly distinguished from other men by a greater promptness to think and feel without immediate external excitement, and a greater power in expressing such thoughts and feelings as are produced in him in that manner. But these passions and thoughts and feelings are the general passions and thoughts and feelings of men. And with what are they connected? Undoubtedly with our moral sentiments and animal sensations, and with the causes which excite these; with the operations of the elements and the appearances of the visible universe; with storm and sunshine, with the revolutions of the seasons, with cold and heat, with loss of friends and kindred, with injuries and resentments, gratitude and hope, with fear and sorrow. These, and the like, are the sensations and objects which the poet describes, as they are the sensations of other men, and the objects which interest them. The poet thinks and feels in the spirit of the passions of men. How, then, can his language differ in any material degree from that of all other men who feel vividly and see clearly? It might be *proved* that it is impossible. But supposing that this were not the case, the poet might then be allowed to use a peculiar language, when expressing his feelings for his own gratification, or that of men like himself. But poets do not write for poets alone, but for men. Unless therefore we are advocates for that admiration which depends upon ignorance, and that pleasure which arises from hearing what we do not understand, the poet must descend from this supposed height, and, in order to excite rational sympathy, he must express himself as other men express themselves. To this it may be added, that while he is only selecting from the real language of men, or, which amounts to the same thing, composing accurately in the spirit of such selection, he is treading upon safe ground, and we know what we are to expect from him. Our feelings are the same with respect to metre; for, as it may be proper to remind the reader, the distinction of metre is regular and uniform, and not like that which is produced by what is usually called poetic diction, arbitrary, and subject to infinite caprices upon which no calculation whatever can be made. In the one case, the reader is utterly at the mercy of the poet respecting what imagery or diction he may choose to connect with the passion, whereas, in the other, the metre obeys certain laws, to which the poet and reader both willingly submit because they are certain, and because no interference is made by them with the passion but such as the concurring testimony of ages has shown to heighten and improve the pleasure which co-exists with it.

It will now be proper to answer an obvious question, namely, why, professing these opinions, have I written in verse? To this, in addition to such answer as is included in what I have already said, I reply in the first place, because, however I may have restricted myself, there is still left open to me what confessedly constitutes the most valuable object of all writing whether in prose or verse, the great and universal passions of men, the most general and interesting of their occupations, and the entire world of nature, from which I am at liberty to supply myself with endless combinations of forms and imagery. Now, supposing for a moment that whatever is interesting in these objects may be as vividly described in prose, why am I to be condemned, if to such description I have endeavoured to superadd the charm which, by the consent of all nations, is acknowledged to exist in metrical language? To this, by such as are unconvinced by what I have already said, it may be answered, that a very small part of the pleasure given by poetry depends upon the metre, and that it is injudicious to write in metre, unless it be accompanied with the other artificial distinctions of style with which metre is usually accompanied, and that by such deviation more will be lost from the shock which will be thereby given to the reader's associations, than will be counterbalanced by any pleasure which he can derive from the general power of numbers. In answer to those who still contend for the necessity of accompanying metre with certain appropriate colours of style in order to the accomplishment of its appropriate end, and who also, in my opinion, greatly underrate the power of metre in itself, it might perhaps, as far as relates to these poems, have been almost sufficient to observe, that poems are extant, written upon more humble subjects, and in a more naked and simple style than I have aimed at, which poems have continued to give pleasure from generation to generation. Now, if nakedness and simplicity be a defect, the fact here mentioned affords a strong presumption that poems somewhat less naked and simple are capable of affording pleasure at the present day; and, what I wished *chiefly* to attempt, at present, was to justify myself for having written under the impression of this belief.

But I might point out various causes why, when the style is manly, and the subject of some importance, words metrically arranged will long continue to impart such a pleasure to mankind as he who is sensible of the extent of that pleasure will be desirous to impart. The end of poetry is to produce excitement in co-existence with an overbalance of pleasure. Now, by the supposition, excitement is an unusual and irregular state of the mind; ideas and feelings do not in that state succeed each other in accustomed order. But, if the words by which this excitement is produced are in themselves powerful, or the images and feelings have an undue proportion of pain connected with them, there is some danger that the excitement may be carried beyond its proper bounds. Now the co-presence of something regular, something to which the mind has been accustomed in various moods and in a less excited state, cannot but have great efficacy in tempering and restraining the passion by an intertexture of ordinary feeling, and of feeling not strictly and necessarily connected with the passion. This is unquestionably true, and hence, though the opinion will at first appear paradoxical, from the tendency of metre to divest language in a certain degree of its reality, and thus to throw a sort of half consciousness of unsubstantial existence over the whole composition, there can be little doubt but that more pathetic situations and sentiments, that is, those which have a greater proportion of pain connected with them, may be endured in metrical composition, especially in rhyme, than in prose. The metre of the old ballads is very artless; yet they contain many passages which would illustrate this opinion, and, I hope, if the following poems be attentively perused, similar instances will be found in them. This opinion may be further illustrated by appealing to the reader's own experience of the reluctance with which he comes to the reperusal of the distressful parts of *Clarissa Harlowe,* or the *Gamester.*[6] While Shakespeare's writings, in the most pathetic scenes, never act upon us as pathetic beyond the bounds of pleasure — an effect which, in a much greater degree than might at first be imagined, is to be ascribed to small, but continual and regular impulses of pleasurable surprise from the metrical arrangement. — On the other hand (what it must be allowed will much more frequently happen) if the poet's words should be incommensurate with the passion, and inadequate to raise the reader to a height of desirable excitement, then, (unless the poet's choice of his metre has been grossly injudicious) in the feelings of pleasure which the reader has been accustomed to connect with metre in general, and in the feeling, whether cheerful or melancholy, which he has been accustomed to connect with that particular movement of metre, there will be found something which will greatly contribute to impart passion to the words, and to effect the complex end which the poet proposes to himself.

If I had undertaken a systematic defence of the theory upon which these poems are written, it would have been my duty to develop the various causes upon which the pleasure received from metrical language depends. Among the chief of these causes is to be reckoned a principle which must be well known to those who have made any of the arts the object of accurate reflection; I mean the pleasure which the mind derives from the perception of similitude in dissimilitude. This principle is the great spring of the activity of our minds, and their chief feeder. From this principle the direction of the sexual appetite, and all the passions connected with it take their origin: it is the life of our ordinary conversation; and upon the accuracy with which similitude in dissimilitude, and dissimilitude in similitude are perceived, depend our taste and our moral feelings. It would not have been a useless employment to have applied this principle to the consideration of metre, and to have shown that metre is hence enabled to afford much pleasure, and to have pointed out in what manner that pleasure is produced. But my limits will not permit me to enter upon this subject, and I must content myself with a general summary.

I have said that poetry is the spontaneous overflow of powerful feelings: it takes its origin from emotion recollected in tranquillity: the emotion is contemplated till by a species of reaction the tranquillity gradually disappears, and an emotion, kindred to that which was before the subject of contemplation, is gradually produced, and does itself actually exist in the mind. In this mood successful composition generally begins, and in a mood similar to this it is carried on; but the emotion, of whatever kind and in whatever degree, from various causes is qualified by various pleasures, so that in describing any passions whatsoever, which are voluntarily described, the mind will upon the whole be in a state of enjoyment. Now, if nature be thus cautious in preserving in a state of enjoyment a being thus employed, the poet ought to profit by the lesson thus held forth to him, and ought especially to take care, that whatever passions he communicates to his reader, those passions, if his reader's mind be sound and vigorous, should always be accompanied with an overbalance of pleasure. Now the music of harmonious metrical language, the sense of difficulty overcome, and the blind association of pleasure which has been previously received from works of rhyme or metre of the same or similar construction, an indistinct perception perpetually renewed of language closely resembling that of real life, and yet, in the circumstance of metre, differing from it so widely, all these imperceptibly make up a complex feeling of delight, which is of the most important use in tempering the painful feeling which will always be found intermingled with powerful descriptions of the deeper passions. This effect is always produced in pathetic and impassioned poetry; while, in lighter composi-

[6] Samuel Richardson's *Clarissa* (1747–48) and Edward Moore's *The Gamester* (1753). [Ed.]

tions, the ease and gracefulness with which the poet manages his numbers are themselves confessedly a principal source of the gratification of the reader. I might perhaps include all which it is *necessary* to say upon this subject by affirming, what few persons will deny, that, of two descriptions, either of passions, manners, or characters, each of them equally well executed, the one in prose and the other in verse, the verse will be read a hundred times where the prose is read once. We see that Pope by the power of verse alone, has contrived to render the plainest common sense interesting, and even frequently to invest it with the appearance of passion. In consequence of these convictions I related in metre the tale of *Goody Blake and Harry Gill,* which is one of the rudest of this collection. I wished to draw attention to the truth that the power of the human imagination is sufficient to produce such changes even in our physical nature as might almost appear miraculous. The truth is an important one; the fact (for it is a *fact*) is a valuable illustration of it. And I have the satisfaction of knowing that it has been communicated to many hundreds of people who would never have heard of it, had it not been narrated as a ballad, and in a more impressive metre than is usual in ballads.

Having thus explained a few of the reasons why I have written in verse, and why I have chosen subjects from common life, and endeavoured to bring my language near to the real language of men, if I have been too minute in pleading my own cause, I have at the same time been treating a subject of general interest; and it is for this reason that I request the reader's permission to add a few words with reference solely to these particular poems, and to some defects which will probably be found in them. I am sensible that my associations must have sometimes been particular instead of general, and that, consequently, giving to things a false importance, sometimes from diseased impulses I may have written upon unworthy subjects; but I am less apprehensive on this account, than that my language may frequently have suffered from those arbitrary connexions of feelings and ideas with particular words and phrases, from which no man can altogether protect himself. Hence I

have no doubt, that, in some instances, feelings even of the ludicrous may be given to my readers by expressions which appeared to me tender and pathetic. Such faulty expressions, were I convinced they were faulty at present, and that they must necessarily continue to be so, I would willingly take all reasonable pains to correct. But it is dangerous to make these alterations on the simple authority of a few individuals, or even of certain classes of men; for where the understanding of an author is not convinced, or his feelings altered, this cannot be done without great injury to himself: for his own feelings are his stay and support, and, if he sets them aside in one instance, he may be induced to repeat this act till his mind loses all confidence in itself, and becomes utterly debilitated. To this it may be added, that the reader ought never to forget that he is himself exposed to the same errors as the poet, and perhaps in a much greater degree: for there can be no presumption in saying, that it is not probable he will be so well acquainted with the various stages of meaning through which words have passed, or with the fickleness or stability of the relations of particular ideas to each other; and above all, since he is so much less interested in the subject, he may decide lightly and carelessly.

Long as I have detained my reader, I hope he will permit me to caution him against a mode of false criticism which has been applied to poetry in which the language closely resembles that of life and nature. Such verses have been triumphed over in parodies of which Dr. Johnson's stanza is a fair specimen.

I put my hat upon my head,
And walked into the Strand,
And there I met another man
Whose hat was in his hand.

Immediately under these lines I will place one of the most justly admired stanzas of the "Babes in the Wood."

These pretty Babes with hand in hand
Went wandering up and down;
But never more they saw the Man
Approaching from the Town.

In both these stanzas the words, and the order of the words, in no respect differ from the most unimpassioned conversation. There are words in both, for example, "the Strand," and "the Town," connected with none but the most familiar ideas; yet the one stanza we admit as admirable, and the other as a fair example of the superlatively contemptible. Whence arises this difference? Not from the metre, not from the language, not from the order of the words; but the *matter* expressed in Dr. Johnson's stanza is contemptible. The proper method of treating trivial and simple verses to which Dr. Johnson's stanza would be a fair parallelism is not to say, this is a bad kind of poetry, or this is not poetry; but this wants sense; it is neither interesting in itself, nor can *lead* to any thing interesting; the images neither originate in that sane state of feeling which arises out of thought, nor can excite thought or feeling in the reader. This is the only sensible manner of dealing with such verses: Why trouble yourself about the species till you have previously decided upon the genus? Why take pains to prove that an ape is not a Newton when it is self-evident that he is not a man?

I have one request to make of my reader, which is, that in judging these poems he would decide by his own feelings genuinely, and not by reflection upon what will probably be the judgment of others. How common is it to hear a person say, "I myself do not object to this style of composition or this or that expression, but to such and such classes of people it will appear mean or ludicrous." This mode of criticism, so destructive of all sound unadulterated judgment, is almost universal: I have therefore to request, that the reader would abide independently by his own feelings, and that if he finds himself affected he would not suffer such conjectures to interfere with his pleasure.

If an author by any single composition has impressed us with respect for his talents, it is useful to consider this as affording a presumption, that, on other occasions where we have been displeased, he nevertheless may not have written ill or absurdly; and, further, to give him so much credit for this one composition as may induce us to review what has displeased us with more care than we should otherwise have be-

stowed upon it. This is not only an act of justice, but in our decisions upon poetry especially, may conduce in a high degree to the improvement of our own taste: for an *accurate* taste in poetry and in all the other arts, as Sir Joshua Reynolds has observed,[7] is an *acquired* talent, which can only be produced by thought and a long continued intercourse with the best models of composition. This is mentioned, not with so ridiculous a purpose as to prevent the most inexperienced reader from judging for himself (I have already said that I wish him to judge for himself), but merely to temper the rashness of decision, and to suggest, that, if poetry be a subject on which much time has not been bestowed, the judgment may be erroneous; and that in many cases it necessarily will be so.

I know that nothing would have so effectually contributed to further the end which I have in view as to have shown of what kind the pleasure is, and how that pleasure is produced, which is confessedly produced by metrical composition essentially different from that which I have here endeavoured to recommend: for the reader will say that he has been pleased by such composition; and what can I do more for him? The power of any art is limited; and he will suspect, that, if I propose to furnish him with new friends, it is only upon condition of his abandoning his old friends. Besides, as I have said, the reader is himself conscious of the pleasure which he has received from such composition, composition to which he has peculiarly attached the endearing name of poetry; and all men feel an habitual gratitude, and something of an honourable bigotry for the objects which have long continued to please them: we not only wish to be pleased, but to be pleased in that particular way in which we have been accustomed to be pleased. There is a host of arguments on these feelings; and I should be the less able to combat them successfully, as I am willing to allow, that, in order entirely to enjoy the poetry which I am recommending, it would be necessary to give up much of what is ordinarily enjoyed. But, would my limits have permitted me to point out how this

[7]Wordsworth refers to Joshua Reynolds's *Discourses* on art, probably a passage in Discourse 12 (*Works*, 2:95). [Ed.]

pleasure is produced, I might have removed many obstacles, and assisted my reader in perceiving that the powers of language are not so limited as he may suppose; and that it is possible that poetry may give other enjoyments, of a purer, more lasting, and more exquisite nature. This part of my subject I have not altogether neglected; but it has been less my present aim to prove, that the interest excited by some other kinds of poetry is less vivid, and less worthy of the nobler powers of the mind, than to offer reasons for presuming, that, if the object which I have proposed to myself were adequately attained, a species of poetry would be produced, which is genuine poetry; in its nature well adapted to interest mankind permanently, and likewise important in the multiplicity and quality of its moral relations.

From what has been said, and from a perusal of the poems, the reader will be able clearly to perceive the object which I have proposed to myself: he will determine how far I have attained this object; and, what is a much more important question, whether it be worth attaining; and upon the decision of these two questions will rest my claim to the approbation of the public.

# Samuel Taylor Coleridge

## 1772–1834

Coleridge's father, a parson in rural Devonshire, died when his son was nine years old. Thereafter Coleridge was educated at Christ's Hospital school as a charity student and then at Jesus College, Cambridge, which he left in 1794 without a degree. He became involved with Robert Southey's protosocialist pantisocracy scheme and in 1795 married Southey's sister-in-law, Sara Fricker, with whom he was deeply unhappy. That same year he was introduced to William Wordsworth, and the two "lake poets" collaborated on the seminal romantic work of *Lyrical Ballads* (1798), in which Coleridge published "The Rime of the Ancient Mariner." Although he had experimented with opium as early as 1797, Coleridge did not become fully addicted until 1803 and remained so until 1816, when Dr. James Gillman attempted, with some success, to wean him gradually from the drug. Coleridge published *Christabel and Other Poems,* including the title poem "Christabel" and "Kubla Khan," in 1816, and his critical testament, *Biographia Literaria,* in 1817. The latter, together with some of Coleridge's Shakespeare lectures, comprises some of the richest critical theory the English romantic movement produced.

Coleridge based his ideas about the nature of imagination and art on his reading in the late 1790s of Kant and Kant's student Schelling. To understand fully what Coleridge intends in the *Biographia Literaria* requires a short detour into the history of the philosophy of mind.

## KANT AND THE MIND

Immanuel Kant's most difficult and important work is probably the *Critique of Pure Reason,* in which his central concern is the way the mind operates. Since we are necessarily unaware of many of the operations of the mind, Kant is forced to focus on the most fleeting of our sensations; in fact he must generate a large-scale set of abstract notions in order to account for the mental output of which we are aware. The debate about mind that Kant joined in the eighteenth century was in some ways much like the debate in post–World War II psychology between the behaviorists and the mentalists.

Nearly a century before Kant, John Locke, in the *Essay Concerning Human Understanding* (1690), had attempted to establish the ultimate behaviorist position. Locke posited that the mind is a *tabula rasa,* a blank slate upon which experience writes. All ideas are derived from two sources: sense experience and the ability of the mind to contemplate itself. Locke tried to show that one could explain the most complex notions of the mind as aggregations of simple ideas. All the mind has to be able to *do,* by and large, is to place current sensations in memory and recall them on demand, to form simple ideas by associating and comparing current with past sense data, and to be able to associate and compare the simple ideas that result to build up more complex ones. In Locke's notion, the mind is like a computer with data inputs (the senses), an information storage/retrieval system, and some very simple programs, endlessly iterated, to process and compare the data.

Locke's picture of the mind as a simple machine influenced the thought of the entire eighteenth century (the novelist Laurence Sterne based *Tristram Shandy* on the workings and misworkings of Lockean associationism). But over the course of the century, Locke's system came to seem less and less adequate to account for the world as we know it. One problem was that Locke's philosophy assumed a sharp distinction between the inner world of mind and the outer world of matter. But since, as the philosopher George Berkeley argued, we know the world of matter only through mind, skeptics might doubt the very existence of the material world.

Another problem (raised by David Hume) concerned causality, surely the most important of the simple ideas by which we make sense of the phenomenal world. When we say that event A caused event B, we minimally mean that A is included in the ground of being of B. But when we see (on a billiard table, for example) the red ball hit the white ball (A) and the white ball move into the pocket (B), it is not clear that we know this much. What we know is that two events show spatial contiguity (the balls touched) and temporal succession (B followed A). But spatial contiguity and temporal succession do not add up to causality. If a baseball player was to scratch his nose and then hit a home run, would the scratching be thought the *cause* of the homer? Hume suggested that we attribute causality only where we have seen consistency of behavior. Only if there were a pattern in which nose-scratching led to home runs would we say that the former caused the latter; only on the basis of long experience with billiard balls do we say that the motion of the red ball causes that of the white. But this adds only subjective mental *habit* to the objective spatiotemporal contact we had before, and we seem just as far as ever from what we mean by *cause*.

Berkeley questioned the existence of the physical world that provides Locke's sense data and experience, and Hume raised doubts about whether the behavioristic mind Locke had assumed could effectually process its data in the way we know it does. The problem, it was becoming clear, was that the human mind had to be more complicated in its workings than Locke had thought. In fact, in order to account for what the mind can do, Kant was forced to attribute a great many more features of our sense of reality to the subjective mind.

For Kant, the external world consists of *noumena,* things whose existence we have to assume but about which we can form no clear idea. As the noumena impinge upon our senses, the mind actively (not passively as Locke claimed) processes the data into "representations." First the datum is marked with our identity — as *ours*. Then it is labeled for space and time — which for Kant were features of mind rather than of matter. Then it is run through the Kantian categories of the understanding and marked for quality, quantity, substance, relation, and so on. The noumena enter the mind; what emerges is phenomena, the world as it appears to us. For Kant, then, the phenomenal world is not *given*; it is *created* by us at every conscious moment through the processing system he calls the productive imagination. Since all minds contain the same mechanisms, we all perceive phenomena consistently and in roughly the same ways: The features of the outside world appear objectively real to us, although they are largely produced by the subjective workings of the mind.

## COLERIDGE ON THE IMAGINATION

The above is a more elaborate explanation of what Coleridge is trying to say in a single enigmatic sentence of Chapter 13 of the *Biographia Literaria*. "The primary IMAGINATION I hold to be the living Power and prime Agent of all human Perception, and as a repetition in the finite mind of the eternal act of creation in the infinite I AM." What Kant had called the *productive* imagination, Coleridge renamed the *primary*: that mental faculty by which we *create* the world of our perceptions at each moment of consciousness. Just as God created the *noumena,* man creates the *phenomena*.

If the primary imagination is responsible for perception, the *secondary* imagination is responsible for art. It is, Coleridge says, "an echo" of the primary, and like an echo it is similar to but weaker than what it echoes. Like the primary imagination, it is a creative faculty, but even when the imagination operates it may not wholly displace the phenomenal world. Unlike the primary imagination, the power of the secondary imagination varies from individual to individual. Where the primary imagination creates the perceptual world without our desiring it, the secondary is "coexistent with," and at least partially responsive to, "the conscious will." It operates by dissolving, diffusing, dissipating the perceptual world and creating another world in its place — or at least minimally reshaping the perceptual world into a more idealized and unified picture. The more complete the process of dissolution and recreation, the more fantastic the art form produced; the less complete, the more realistic. Coleridge has thus accounted for the differences between his poetry and that of his friend Wordsworth.

At the end of Chapter 13, Coleridge differentiates between fancy and imagination. Imagination — the secondary imagination described above — is a fully creative activity that, in effect, produces a new perceptual world. Fancy, on the other hand, is an inferior activity, since it operates entirely within the usual perceptual world; it is an activity describable in purely Lockean terms as the willful conjunction of ideas that are normally distinct (like placing an elephant's head on the body of a camel).

## COLERIDGE ON POEMS AND POETRY

In Chapter 14 Coleridge differentiates between *poem* and *poetry* — which are almost but not quite related as product is to process. The procedure by which Coleridge defines "poem" is laborious but not entirely lucid. The confusion largely stems from an internal conflict. On the one hand Coleridge wants to evaluate as he defines, to define the *legitimate* as opposed to the *mere* poem; on the other hand, he also knows well that the word *poem* is generally used to apply to any composition in verse — good, bad, or indifferent. In trying to have it both ways, Coleridge muddies his argument. First, he grudgingly concedes that mere rhyming mnemonics "may be given the name of poem." But the real process of definition is more involved.

In Coleridge's definition there are two criteria: "object" or purpose and "superficial form." A poem has as its immediate purpose "pleasure not truth" and is thus differentiated from history or science. And it is written in verse: rhyme or meter or both conjointly. In effect, Coleridge specifies the following outline for major genres of poetry and prose:

|  | IMMEDIATE OBJECT | |
|---|---|---|
|  | PLEASURE | TRUTH |
| SUPERFICIAL FORM: | | |
| RHYME AND/OR METER | Poem | Mnemonic |
| PROSE | Novel | History or science |

This outline seems mechanical enough — but then Coleridge asks a revealing question: If we turned a work of prose fiction into verse, would that make it a poem? The superficial answer would be "yes," but Coleridge says it would not: "Nothing can permanently please, which does not contain in itself the reason why it is so, and not otherwise." In a genuine poem, the linguistic and ideological content justifies the "perpetual and distinct attention to each part" that meter excites in us. A novel versified might look like a poem, but it would be dreadful in effect, since its texture would not be tightly woven enough to bear up under the sort of attention we would give it *as verse*. In legitimate poems, on the other hand, form and content, structure and texture, are interconnected: They are designed to stand the intense scrutiny that meter provokes.

The broad principle to which Coleridge appeals is that of *organic form*; he discusses it at greater length in "Shakespeare's Judgment Equal to His Genius," where he contrasts the merely *mechanical* form that it is possible to impose upon materials with the *organic* form that grows out of the nature of the materials themselves. The "superficial" form in a genuine poem is, in fact, not superficial at all: It is an integral part of the poem's design.

Having defined "poem," Coleridge turns to "poetry," which to him is not a collective term for poems but an independent category. Poetry, he says, may be written in prose rather than in verse; and it may occur in works whose immediate object is truth rather than pleasure. More positively, his definition of poetry has "been in part anticipated in some of the remarks on the Fancy and Imagination": Less coyly, poetry is the verbal product of the "poetic genius" — the secondary imagination as defined in Chapter 13.

Long poems, Coleridge asserts, cannot be all poetry; conversely, much that is poetry is not in the form of a poem. In fact, so disparate are the two definitions that one might wonder why there needs to be *any* poetry whatever in the poem. The definitions only appear to be disconnected, however. What links them is Coleridge's concept of "organic form." If organic form is implicit in his definition of "poem," it is even more obvious that the distinction between organic and mechanical form is essentially that between imagination and fancy. Organicism is an essential characteristic of the workings of the secondary imagination in recreating an idealized, unified, and coherent fictive universe.

## Selected Bibliography

Barth, J. Robert. *The Symbolic Imagination: Coleridge and the Romantic Tradition*. Princeton: Princeton University Press, 1977.

Christensen, Jerome. *Coleridge's Blessed Machine of Language*. Ithaca: Cornell University Press, 1981.

Corrigan, Timothy. *Coleridge, Language and Criticism*. Athens: University of Georgia Press, 1982.

Fogle, R. H. *The Idea of Coleridge's Criticism*. Berkeley: University of California Press, 1962.

Hamilton, Paul. *Coleridge's Poetics*. Oxford: Blackwell, 1983.

Harding, Anthony John. *Coleridge and the Inspired Word*. Kingston, Ont.: McGill-Queen's University Press, 1985.

Marks, Emerson. *Coleridge on the Language of Verse*. Princeton: Princeton University Press, 1981.

McKenzie, Gordon. *Organic Unity in Coleridge*. Berkeley: University of California Press, 1939.

Read, Herbert Edward. *Coleridge as a Critic*. London: Faber and Faber, 1949.

Richards, Ivor Armstrong. *Coleridge on Imagination*. 3d ed. London: Routledge and Kegan Paul, 1962.

Sharma, L. S. *Coleridge: His Contribution to English Criticism*. New Delhi: Arnold-Heinemann, 1981.

Thorpe, C. D. "Coleridge as Aesthetician and Critic." *Journal of the History of Ideas* 1 (1944): 387–414.

# Shakespeare's Judgment Equal to His Genius

The object which I was proceeding to attain in my last lecture was to prove that independently of his peculiar merits, which are hereafter to be developed, Shakespeare appears, from his poems

"Shakespeare's Judgment" was delivered as a lecture, probably around 1808. The text is compiled from Coleridge's notebooks. [Ed.]

alone, apart from his great works, to have possessed all the conditions of a true poet, and by this proof to do away, as far as may [be] in my power, the popular notion that he was a great dramatist by a sort of instinct, immortal in his own despite, and sinking below men of second- or third-rate character when he attempted aught beside the drama — even as bees construct their cells and manufacture their honey to admirable perfection, but would in vain attempt to build a nest. Now this mode of reconciling a compelled sense of inferiority with a feeling of pride, began in a few pedants, who having read that Sophocles was the great model of tragedy, and Aristotle the infallible dictator, and finding that the *Lear, Hamlet, Othello,* and the rest, were neither in imitation of Sophocles, nor in obedience to Aristotle — and not having (with one or two exceptions) the courage to affirm that the delight which their country received from generation to generation, in defiance of the alterations of circumstances and habits, was wholly groundless — it was a happy medium and refuge, to talk of Shakespeare as a sort of beautiful *lusus naturae,*[1] a delightful monster, — wild, indeed, without taste or judgment, but like the inspired idiots so much venerated in the East, uttering, amid the strangest follies, the sublimest truths. In nine places out of ten in which I find his awful name mentioned, it is with some epithet of "wild," "irregular," "pure child of nature," etc., etc., etc. If all this be true, we must submit to it; tho' to a thinking mind it cannot but be painful to find any excellence, merely human, thrown out of all human analogy, and thereby leaving us neither rules for imitation, nor motives to imitate. But if false, it is a dangerous falsehood; for it affords a refuge to secret self-conceit, — enables a vain man at once to escape his reader's indignation by general swoln panegyrics on Shakespeare, merely by his *ipse dixit*[2] to treat what he has not intellect enough to comprehend, or soul to feel, as contemptible, without assigning any reason, or referring his opinion to any demonstrated principle; and so has left Shakespeare as a sort of Tartarian Dalai Lama, adored indeed, and his very excrescences prized as relics, but with no authority, no real influence. I grieve that every late voluminous edition of his works would enable me to substantiate the present charge with a variety of facts one tenth of which would of themselves exhaust the time allotted to me. Every

[1]Freak of nature. [Ed.]
[2]Authority. [Ed.]

critic, who has or has not made a collection of black letter books — in itself a useful and respectable amusement — puts on the seven-league boots of self-opinion and strides at once from an illustrator into a supreme judge, and blind and deaf, fills his three-ounce phial at the waters of Niagara — and determines positively the greatness of the cataract to be neither more nor less than his three-ounce phial has been able to receive.

Not only a multitude of individuals but even whole nations [are] so enslaved to the habits of their education and immediate circumstances as not to judge disinterestedly even on those subjects, the very pleasure from which consists in their disinterestedness — subjects of taste and *belles lettres.* Instead of deciding concerning their own modes and customs by any rule of reason, nothing appears natural, becoming, or beautiful but what coincides with the accidents of their education. In this narrow circle individuals may attain exquisite discrimination, as the French critics have in their own literature, but a true critic can no man be without placing himself on some central point in which he can command the whole; i.e., some general rule, which, [as] founded in reason, or faculties common to all men, must therefore apply to all men.

This will not produce despotism, but on the contrary true tolerance. He will indeed require, as the spirit and substance of a work, something true in human nature, and independent of circumstances; but in the mode of applying it, he will estimate genius and judgement according to the felicity with which this imperishable soul has clothed and adapted itself to the age, place, and existing manners.

The error is reversing this by considering the circumstances as perpetual, to the neglect of the animating power.

The subject of the present lecture is no less than a question submitted to your understandings, emancipated from national prejudice: Are the plays of *Shakespeare* works of rude uncultivated genius, in which the splendor of the parts compensates, if aught can compensate, for the barbarous shapelessness and irregularity of the whole? To which not only the French critics, but even his own English admirers, say [yes]. Or is the form equally admirable with the matter, the judgment of the great poet not less deserving of our wonder than his genius? Or to repeat the question in other words, is Shakespeare a great dynamic poet on account only of those beauties and excellencies which he possesses in common with the ancients, but with diminished claims to our love and honor to the full extent of his difference from them? Or are these very differences additional proofs of poetic wisdom, at once results and symbols of living power as contrasted with lifeless mechanism, of free and rival originality as contradistinguished from servile imitation, or more accurately, [from] a blind copying of effects instead of a true imitation of the essential principles? Imagine not I am about to oppose genius to rules. No! the comparative value of these rules is the very cause to be tried. The spirit of poetry, like all other living powers, must of necessity circumscribe itself by rules, were it only to unite power with beauty. It must embody in order to reveal itself; but a living body is of necessity an organized one, — and what is organization, but the connection of parts to a whole, so that each part is at once end and means! This is no discovery of criticism; it is a necessity of the human mind — and all nations have felt and obeyed it, in the invention of metre and measured sounds as the vehicle and involucrum of poetry, itself a fellow-growth from the same life, even as the bark is to the tree.

No work of true genius dare want its appropriate form; neither indeed is there any danger of this. As it must not, so neither can it, be lawless! For it is even this that constitutes it genius — the power of acting creatively under laws of its own origination. How then comes it that not only single Zoili,[3] but whole nations have combined in unhesitating condemnation of our great dramatist, as a sort of African nature, fertile in beautiful monsters, as a wild heath where islands of fertility look greener from the surrounding waste, where the loveliest plants now shine out among unsightly weeds and now are choked by their parasitic growth, so intertwined that we cannot disentangle the weed without snapping the flower. In this statement I have had no reference to the vulgar abuse of Voltaire, save as far as his charges are coincident with the decisions of his commentators and (so they tell you) his almost idolatrous admirers. The true ground of the mistake, as has been well remarked by a continental critic,[4] lies in the confounding mechanical regularity with organic form. The form is mechanic when on any given material we impress a predetermined form, not necessarily arising out of the properties of the material, as when to a mass of wet clay we give whatever shape we wish it to retain when hardened. The organic form, on the other hand, is innate; it shapes as it develops itself from within, and the fullness of its development is one and the same with the perfection of its outward form. Such is the life, such the form. Nature, the prime genial artist, inexhaustible in diverse powers, is equally inexhaustible in forms. Each exterior is the physiognomy of the being within, its true image reflected and thrown out from the concave mirror. And even such is the appropriate excellence of her chosen poet, of our own Shakespeare, himself a nature humanized, a genial understanding directing self-consciously a power and an implicit wisdom deeper than consciousness.

[3]Zoilus was a captious critic of Homer around the fourth century B.C. [Ed.]

[4]August Wilhelm von Schlegel, from whose writings many of Coleridge's ideas derive. [Ed.]

# From *Biographia Literaria*

## *From Chapter 13*

The IMAGINATION then, I consider either as primary, or secondary. The primary IMAGINATION I hold to be the living Power and prime Agent of all human Perception, and as a repetition in the finite mind of the eternal act of creation in the infinite I AM. The secondary Imagination I consider as an echo of the former, co-existing with the conscious will, yet still as identical with the primary in the *kind* of its agency, and differing only in *degree,* and in the *mode* of its operation. It dissolves, diffuses, dissipates, in order to re-create; or where this process is rendered impossible, yet still at all events it struggles to idealize and to unify. It is essentially *vital,* even as all objects (*as* objects) are essentially fixed and dead.

FANCY, on the contrary, has no other counters to play with, but fixities and definites. The Fancy is indeed no other than a mode of Memory emancipated from the order of time and space; while it is blended with, and modified by that empirical phenomenon of the will, which we express by the word CHOICE. But equally with the ordinary memory the Fancy must receive all its materials ready made from the law of association.

## *Chapter 14*

*Occasion of the Lyrical Ballads, and the objects originally proposed — Preface to the second edition — The ensuing controversy, its causes and acrimony — Philosophic definitions of a poem and poetry with scholia.*

During the first year that Mr. Wordsworth and I were neighbours,[1] our conversations turned frequently on the two cardinal points of poetry, the power of exciting the sympathy of the reader by a faithful adherence to the truth of nature, and the power of giving the interest of novelty by the modifying colors of imagination. The sudden charm, which accidents of light and shade, which

moon-light or sun-set diffused over a known and familiar landscape, appeared to represent the practicability of combining both. These are the poetry of nature. The thought suggested itself (to which of us I do not recollect) that a series of poems might be composed of two sorts. In the one, the incidents and agents were to be, in part at least, supernatural; and the excellence aimed at was to consist in the interesting of the affections by the dramatic truth of such emotions, as would naturally accompany such situations, supposing them real. And real in *this* sense they have been to every human being who, from whatever source of delusion, has at any time believed himself under supernatural agency. For the second class, subjects were to be chosen from ordinary life; the characters and incidents were to be such, as will be found in every village and its vicinity, where there is a meditative and feeling mind to seek after them, or to notice them, when they present themselves.

In this idea originated the plan of the "Lyrical Ballads"; in which it was agreed, that my endeavours should be directed to persons and characters supernatural, or at least romantic; yet so as to transfer from our inward nature a human interest and a semblance of truth sufficient to procure for these shadows of imagination that willing suspension of disbelief for the moment, which constitutes poetic faith. Mr. Wordsworth, on the other hand, was to propose to himself as his object, to give the charm of novelty to things of every day, and to excite a feeling analogous to the supernatural, by awakening the mind's attention from the lethargy of custom, and directing it to the loveliness and the wonders of the world before us; an inexhaustible treasure, but for which, in consequence of the film of familiarity and selfish solicitude we have eyes, yet see not, ears that hear not, and hearts that neither feel nor understand.

With this view I wrote "The Ancient Mariner," and was preparing among other poems, "The Dark Ladie," and the "Christabel," in which I should have more nearly realized my

---

[1]In 1797. [Ed.]

ideal, than I had done in my first attempt. But Mr. Wordsworth's industry had proved so much more successful, and the number of his poems so much greater, that my compositions, instead of forming a balance, appeared rather an interpolation of heterogeneous matter. Mr. Wordsworth added two or three poems written in his own character, in the impassioned, lofty, and sustained diction, which is characteristic of his genius. In this form the "Lyrical Ballads" were published; and were presented by him, as an *experiment*, whether subjects, which from their nature rejected the usual ornaments and extracolloquial style of poems in general, might not be so managed in the language of ordinary life as to produce the pleasureable interest, which it is the peculiar business of poetry to impart. To the second edition he added a preface of considerable length; in which, notwithstanding some passages of apparently a contrary import, he was understood to contend for the extension of this style to poetry of all kinds, and to reject as vicious and indefensible all phrases and forms of style that were not included in what he (unfortunately, I think, adopting an equivocal expression) called the language of *real* life. From this preface, prefixed to poems in which it was impossible to deny the presence of original genius, however mistaken its direction might be deemed, arose the whole long-continued controversy. For from the conjunction of perceived power with supposed heresy I explain the inveteracy and in some instances, I grieve to say, the acrimonious passions, with which the controversy has been conducted by the assailants.

Had Mr. Wordsworth's poems been the silly, the childish things, which they were for a long time described as being; had they been really distinguished from the compositions of other poets merely by meanness of language and inanity of thought; had they indeed contained nothing more than what is found in the parodies and pretended imitations of them; they must have sunk at once, a dead weight, into the slough of oblivion, and have dragged the preface along with them. But year after year increased the number of Mr. Wordsworth's admirers. They were found too not in the lower classes of the reading public, but chiefly among young men of strong sensibility and meditative minds; and their admiration (inflamed perhaps in some degree by opposition) was distinguished by its intensity, I might almost say, by its *religious* fervor. These facts, and the intellectual energy of the author, which was more or less consciously felt, where it was outwardly and even boisterously denied, meeting with sentiments of aversion to his opinions, and of alarm at their consequences, produced an eddy of criticism, which would of itself have borne up the poems by the violence, with which it whirled them round and round. With many parts of this preface, in the sense attributed to them, and which the words undoubtedly seem to authorize, I never concurred; but on the contrary objected to them as erroneous in principle, and as contradictory (in appearance at least) both to other parts of the same preface, and to the author's own practice in the greater number of the poems themselves. Mr. Wordsworth in his recent collection has, I find, degraded this prefatory disquisition to the end of his second volume, to be read or not at the reader's choice. But he has not, as far as I can discover, announced any change in his poetic creed. At all events, considering it as the source of a controversy, in which I have been honored more than I deserve by the frequent conjunction of my name with his, I think it expedient to declare once for all, in what points I coincide with his opinions, and in what points I altogether differ. But in order to render myself intelligible I must previously, in as few words as possible, explain my ideas, first, of a POEM; and secondly, of POETRY itself, in *kind*, and in *essence*.

The office of philosophical *disquisition* consists in just *distinction*; while it is the privilege of the philosopher to preserve himself constantly aware, that distinction is not division. In order to obtain adequate notions of any truth, we must intellectually separate its distinguishable parts; and this is the technical *process* of philosophy. But having so done, we must then restore them in our conceptions to the unity, in which they actually co-exist; and this is the *result* of philosophy. A poem contains the same elements as a prose composition; the difference therefore must consist in a different combination of them, in consequence of a different object being proposed. According to the difference of the object will be the difference of the combination. It is possible, that the object may be merely to facilitate the recollection of any given facts or observations by artificial arrangement; and the composition will be a poem, merely because it is distinguished from prose by metre, or by rhyme, or by both conjointly. In this, the lowest sense, a man might attribute the name of a poem to the well-known enumeration of the days in the several months;

Thirty days hath September,
April, June, and November, &c.

and others of the same class and purpose. And as a particular pleasure is found in anticipating the recurrence of sounds and quantities, all compositions that have this charm super-added, whatever be their contents, *may* be entitled poems.

So much for the superficial *form*. A difference of object and contents supplies an additional ground of distinction. The immediate purpose may be the communication of truths; either of truth absolute and demonstrable, as in works of science; or of facts experienced and recorded, as in history. Pleasure, and that of the highest and most permanent kind, may *result* from the *attainment* of the end; but it is not itself the immediate end. In other works the communication of pleasure may be the immediate purpose; and though truth, either moral or intellectual, ought to be the *ultimate* end, yet this will distinguish the character of the author, not the class to which the work belongs. Blest indeed is that state of society, in which the immediate purpose would be baffled by the perversion of the proper ultimate end; in which no charm of diction or imagery could exempt the Bathyllus even of an Anacreon, or the Alexis of Virgil, from disgust and aversion![2]

But the communication of pleasure may be the immediate object of a work not metrically composed; and that object may have been in a high degree attained, as in novels and romances. Would then the mere superaddition of metre, with or without rhyme, entitle *these* to the name

of poems? The answer is, that nothing can permanently please, which does not contain in itself the reason why it is so, and not otherwise. If metre be superadded, all other parts must be made consonant with it. They must be such, as to justify the perpetual and distinct attention to each part, which an exact correspondent recurrence of accent and sound are calculated to excite. The final definition then, so deduced, may be thus worded. A poem is that species of composition, which is opposed to works of science, by proposing for its *immediate* object pleasure, not truth; and from all other species (having *this* object in common with it) it is discriminated by proposing to itself such delight from the *whole,* as is compatible with a distinct gratification from each component *part*.

Controversy is not seldom excited in consequence of the disputants attaching each a different meaning to the same word; and in few instances has this been more striking, than in disputes concerning the present subject. If a man chooses to call every composition a poem, which is rhyme, or measure, or both, I must leave his opinion uncontroverted. The distinction is at least competent to characterize the writer's intention. If it were subjoined, that the whole is likewise entertaining or affecting, as a tale, or as a series of interesting reflections, I of course admit this as another fit ingredient of a poem, and an additional merit. But if the definition sought for be that of a *legitimate* poem, I answer, it must be one, the parts of which mutually support and explain each other; all in their proportion harmonizing with, and supporting the purpose and known influences of metrical arrangement. The philosophic critics of all ages coincide with the ultimate judgement of all countries, in equally denying the praises of a just poem, on the one hand, to a series of striking lines or distiches, each of which, absorbing the whole attention of the reader to itself, disjoins it from its context, and makes it a separate whole, instead of an harmonizing part; and on the other hand, to an unsustained composition, from which the reader collects rapidly the general result, unattracted by the component parts. The reader should be carried forward, not merely or chiefly by the mechanical impulse of curiosity, or by a restless

---

[2]Anacreon's Ode 29 to Bathyllus, and Virgil's *Eclogue* 2. [Ed.]

desire to arrive at the final solution; but by the pleasureable activity of mind excited by the attractions of the journey itself. Like the motion of a serpent, which the Egyptians made the emblem of intellectual power; or like the path of sound through the air; at every step he pauses and half recedes, and from the retrogressive movement collects the force which again carries him onward. "Præcipitandus est *liber* spiritus," says Petronius Arbiter most happily.[3] The epithet, *liber,* here balances the preceding verb; and it is not easy to conceive more meaning condensed in fewer words.

But if this should be admitted as a satisfactory character of a poem, we have still to seek for a definition of poetry. The writings of PLATO, and Bishop TAYLOR, and the "Theoria Sacra" of BURNET, furnish undeniable proofs that poetry of the highest kind may exist without metre, and even without the contra-distinguishing objects of a poem. The first chapter of Isaiah (indeed a very large portion of the whole book) is poetry in the most emphatic sense; yet it would be not less irrational than strange to assert, that pleasure, and not truth, was the immediate object of the prophet. In short, whatever *specific* import we attach to the word, poetry, there will be found involved in it, as a necessary consequence, that a poem of any length neither can be, or ought to be, all poetry. Yet if an harmonious whole is to be produced, the remaining parts must be preserved *in keeping* with the poetry; and this can be no otherwise effected than by such a studied selection and artificial arrangement, as will partake of *one,* though not a *peculiar* property of poetry. And this again can be no other than the property of exciting a more continuous and equal attention than the language of prose aims at, whether colloquial or written.

My own conclusions on the nature of poetry, in the strictest use of the word, have been in part anticipated in the preceding disquisition on the fancy and imagination. What is poetry? is so nearly the same question with, what is a poet? that the answer to the one is involved in the solution of the other. For it is a distinction re-

sulting from the poetic genius itself, which sustains and modifies the images, thoughts, and emotions of the poet's own mind.

The poet, described in *ideal* perfection, brings the whole soul of man into activity, with the subordination of its faculties to each other, according to their relative worth and dignity. He diffuses a tone and spirit of unity, that blends, and (as it were) *fuses,* each into each, by that synthetic and magical power, to which we have exclusively appropriated the name of imagination. This power, first put in action by the will and understanding, and retained under their irremissive, though gentle and unnoticed, controul (*laxis effertur habenis*)[4] reveals itself in the balance or reconciliation of opposite or discordant qualities: of sameness, with difference; of the general, with the concrete; the idea, with the image; the individual, with the representative; the sense of novelty and freshness, with old and familiar objects; a more than usual state of emotion, with more than usual order; judgement ever awake and steady self-possession, with enthusiasm and feeling profound or vehement; and while it blends and harmonizes the natural and the artificial, still subordinates art to nature; the manner to the matter; and our admiration of the poet to our sympathy with the poetry. "Doubtless," as Sir John Davies observes of the soul (and his words may with slight alteration be applied, and even more appropriately, to the poetic IMAGINATION)

Doubtless this could not be, but that she turns
    Bodies to spirit by sublimation strange,
As fire converts to fire the things it burns,
    As we our food into our nature change.

From their gross matter she abstracts their forms,
    And draws a kind of quintessence from things;
Which to her proper nature she transforms,
    To bear them light on her celestial wings.

Thus does she, when from individual states
    She doth abstract the universal kinds;
Which then re-clothed in divers names and fates
    Steal access through our senses to our minds.[5]

[4]"Carried on with slackened reins." Petrarch, *Epistola Barbato Sulmonensi,* 39. [Ed.]

[5]Sir John Davies, *Nosce Teipsum: Of the Soule of Man and the Immortality Thereof,* 4:11–13. [Ed.]

[3]"The free spirit must be hurried onward." Petronius, *Satyricon,* 118. [Ed.]

Finally, GOOD SENSE is the BODY of poetic genius, FANCY its DRAPERY, MOTION its LIFE, and IMAGINATION the SOUL that is everywhere, and in each; and forms all into one graceful and intelligent whole.

## Chapter 17

*Examination of the tenets peculiar to Mr. Wordsworth — Rustic life (above all, low and rustic life) especially unfavorable to the formation of a human diction — The best parts of language the product of philosophers, not of clowns or shepherds — Poetry essentially ideal and generic — The language of Milton as much the language of real life, yea, incomparably more so than that of the cottager.*

As far then as Mr. Wordsworth in his preface contended, and most ably contended, for a reformation in our poetic diction, as far as he has evinced the truth of passion, and the *dramatic* propriety of those figures and metaphors in the original poets, which, stripped of their justifying reasons, and converted into mere artifices of connection or ornament, constitute the characteristic falsity in the poetic style of the moderns; and as far as he has, with equal acuteness and clearness, pointed out the process by which this change was effected, and the resemblances between that state into which the reader's mind is thrown by the pleasureable confusion of thought from an unaccustomed train of words and images; and that state which is induced by the natural language of empassioned feeling; he undertook a useful task, and deserves all praise, both for the attempt and for the execution. The provocations to this remonstrance in behalf of truth and nature were still of perpetual recurrence before and after the publications of this preface. I cannot likewise but add, that the comparison of such poems of merit, as have been given to the public within the last ten or twelve years, with the majority of those produced previously to the appearance of that preface, leave no doubt on my mind, that Mr. Wordsworth is fully justified in believing his efforts to have been by no means ineffectual. Not only in the verses of those who have professed their admiration of his genius, but even of those who have distinguished themselves by hostility to his theory, and depreciation of his writings,

are the impressions of his principles plainly visible. It is possible, that with these principles others may have been blended, which are not equally evident; and some which are unsteady and subvertible from the narrowness or imperfection of their basis. But it is more than possible, that these errors of defect or exaggeration, by kindling and feeding the controversy may have conduced not only to the wider propagation of the accompanying truths, but that, by their frequent presentation to the mind in an excited state, they may have won for them a more permanent and practical result. A man will borrow a part from his opponent the more easily, if he feels himself justified in continuing to reject a part. While there remain important points in which he can still feel himself in the right, in which he still finds firm footing for continued resistance, he will gradually adopt those opinions, which were the least remote from his own convictions, as not less congruous with his own theory than with that which he reprobates. In like manner with a kind of instinctive prudence, he will abandon by little and little his weakest posts, till at length he seems to forget that they had ever belonged to him, or affects to consider them at most as accidental and "petty annexments," the removal of which leaves the citadel unhurt and unendangered.

My own differences from certain supposed parts of Mr. Wordsworth's theory ground themselves on the assumption, that his words had been rightly interpreted, as purporting that the proper diction for poetry in general consists altogether in a language taken, with due expectations, from the mouths of men in real life, a language which actually constitutes the natural conversation of men under the influence of natural feelings. My objection is, first, that in *any* sense this rule is applicable only to *certain* classes of poetry; secondly, that even to these classes it is not applicable, except in such a sense, as hath never by any one (as far as I know or have read) been denied or doubted; and lastly, that as far as, and in that degree in which it is *practicable*, yet as a *rule* it is useless, if not injurious, and therefore either need not, or ought not to be practised. The poet informs his reader, that he had generally chosen *low and rustic* life; but not *as* low and rustic, or in order to repeat that pleasure of doubtful moral effect, which persons of elevated rank and of superior refinement oftentimes derive from a happy *imitation* of the rude unpolished manners and discourse of their inferiors. For the pleasure so derived may be traced to three exciting causes. The first is the naturalness, in *fact,* of the things represented. The second is the apparent naturalness of the *representation,* as raised and qualified by an imperceptible infusion of the author's own knowledge and talent, which infusion does, indeed, constitute it an *imitation* as distinguished from a mere *copy*. The third cause may be found in the reader's conscious feeling of his superiority awakened by the contrast presented to him; even as for the same purpose the kings and great barons of yore retained sometimes *actual* clowns and fools, but more frequently shrewd and witty fellows in that *character*. These, however, were not Mr. Wordsworth's objects. *He* chose low and rustic life, "because in that condition the essential passions of the heart find a better soil, in which they can attain their maturity, are less under restraint, and speak a plainer and more emphatic language; because in that condition of life our elementary feelings coexist in a state of greater simplicity, and consequently may be more accurately contemplated, and more forcibly communicated; because the manners of rural life germinate from those elementary feelings; and from the necessary character of rural occupations are more easily comprehended, and are more durable; and lastly, because in that condition the passions of men are incorporated with the beautiful and permanent forms of nature."

Now it is clear to me, that in the most interesting of the poems, in which the author is more or less dramatic, as "the Brothers," "Michael," "Ruth," "the Mad Mother," &c., the persons introduced are by no means taken *from low or rustic life* in the common acceptation of those words; and it is not less clear, that the sentiments and language, as far as they can be conceived to have been really transferred from the minds and conversation of such persons, are attributable to causes and circumstances not necessarily connected with "their occupations and abode." The thoughts, feelings, language, and manners of the shepherd-farmers in the vales of Cumberland and Westmoreland, as far as they are actually adopted in those poems, may be accounted for from causes, which will and do produce the same results in *every* state of life, whether in town or country. As the two principal I rank that INDEPENDENCE, which raises a man above servitude, or daily toil for the profit of others, yet not above the necessity of industry and a frugal simplicity of domestic life; and the accompanying unambitious, but solid and religious, EDUCATION, which has rendered few books familiar, but the Bible, and the liturgy or hymn book. To this latter cause, indeed, which is so far *accidental,* that it is the blessing of particular countries and a particular age, not the product of particular places or employments, the poet owes the show of probability, that his personages might really feel, think, and talk with any tolerable resemblance to his representation. It is an excellent remark of Dr. Henry More's (Enthusiasmus triumphatus, Sec. 35), that "a man of confined education, but of good parts, by constant reading of the Bible will naturally form a more winning and commanding rhetoric than those that are learned; the intermixture of tongues and of artificial phrases debasing *their* style."

It is, moreover, to be considered that to the formation of healthy feelings, and a reflecting mind, *negations* involve impediments not less formidable than sophistication and vicious intermixture. I am convinced, that for the human soul to prosper in rustic life a certain vantage-ground is pre-requisite. It is not every man that is likely to be improved by a country life or by country labors. Education, or original sensibility, or both, must pre-exist, if the changes, forms, and incidents of nature are to prove a sufficient stimulants. And where these are not sufficient, the mind contracts and hardens by want of stimulants: and the man becomes selfish, sensual, gross, and hard-hearted. Let the management of the POOR LAWS in Liverpool, Manchester, or Bristol be compared with the ordinary dispensation of the poor rates in agricultural villages, where the *farmers* are the overseers and guardians of the poor. If my own experience have not been particularly unfortunate, as well as that of the many respectable country clergymen with whom I have conversed on the subject, the result would engender more than scepticism concerning the desireable influences of low and rustic life in and for itself. Whatever may be concluded on the other side, from the stronger local attachments and enterprising spirit of the Swiss, and other mountaineers, applies to a particular mode of pastoral life, under forms of property that permit and beget manners truly republican, not to rustic life in general, or to the absence of artificial cultivation. On the contrary the mountaineers, whose manners have been so often eulogized, are in general better educated and greater readers than men of equal rank elsewhere. But where this is not the case, as among the peasantry of North Wales, the ancient mountains, with all their terrors and all their glories, are pictures to the blind, and music to the deaf.

I should not have entered so much into detail upon this passage, but here seems to be the point, to which all the lines of difference converge as to their source and centre. (I mean, as far as, and in whatever respect, my poetic creed *does* differ from the doctrines promulged in this preface.) I adopt with full faith the principle of Aristotle, that poetry as poetry is essentially[6]

[6]Say not that I am recommending abstractions; for these class-characteristics which constitute the instructiveness of a character, are so modified and particularized in each person of the Shakespearean Drama, that life itself does not excite more distinctly that sense of individuality which belongs to real existence. Paradoxical as it may sound, one of the essential properties of Geometry is not less essential to dramatic excellence; and Aristotle has accordingly required of the poet an involution of the universal in the individual. The chief differences are, that in Geometry it is the universal truth, which is uppermost in the consciousness; in poetry the individual form, in which the truth is clothed. With the ancients, and not less with the elder dramatists of England and France, both comedy and tragedy were considered as kinds of poetry. They neither sought in comedy to make us laugh merely; much less to make us laugh by wry faces, accidents of jargon, *slang* phrases for the day, or the clothing of common-place morals drawn from the shops or mechanic occupations of their characters. Nor did they condescend in tragedy to wheedle away the applause of the spectators, by representing before them facsimiles of their own mean selves in all their existing meanness, or to work on the sluggish sympathies by a pathos not a whit more respectable than the maudlin tears of drunkenness. Their tragic scenes were meant to *affect* us indeed; but yet within the bounds of pleasure, and in union

*ideal,* that it avoids and excludes all *accident;* that its apparent individualities of rank, character, or occupation must be *representative* of a class; and that the *persons* of poetry must be clothed with *generic* attributes, with the *common* attributes of the class: not with such as one gifted individual might *possibly* possess, but such as from his situation it is most probable before-hand that he *would* possess. If my premises are right and my deductions legitimate, it follows that there can be no *poetic* medium between the swains of Theocritus and those of an imaginary golden age.

The characters of the vicar and the shepherd-mariner in the poem of "The Brothers," that of the shepherd of Greenhead Ghyll in the "Michael," have all the verisimilitude and representative quality, that the purposes of poetry can require. They are persons of a known and abiding class, and their manners and sentiments the natural product of circumstances common to the class. Take "Michael" for instance:

An old man stout of heart, and strong of limb:
His bodily frame had been from youth to age
Of an unusual strength: his mind was keen,
Intense, and frugal, apt for all affairs,
And in his shepherd's calling he was prompt
And watchful more than ordinary men.
Hence he had learnt the meaning of all winds,
Of blasts of every tone; and oftentimes
When others heeded not, he heard the South
Make subterraneous music, like the noise
Of bagpipers on distant Highland hills.
The shepherd, at such warning, of his flock
Bethought him, and he to himself would say,
The winds are now devising work for me!
And truly at all times the storm, that drives
The traveller to a shelter, summon'd him
Up to the mountains. He had been alone
Amid the heart of many thousand mists,

with the activity both of our understanding and imagination. They wished to transport the mind to a sense of its possible greatness, and to implant the germs of that greatness, during the temporary oblivion of the worthless "thing we are," and of the peculiar state in which each man *happens* to be, suspending our individual recollections and lulling them to sleep amid the music of nobler thoughts.

FRIEND, Pages 251, 252. [Au.]

That came to him and left him on the heights.
So liv'd he, till his eightieth year was pass'd.
And grossly that man errs, who should suppose
That the green vallies, and the streams and rocks,
Were things indifferent to the shepherd's thoughts.
Fields, where with chearful spirits he had breath'd
The common air; the hills, which he so oft
Had climb'd with vigorous steps; which had im-
    press'd
So many incidents upon his mind
Of hardship, skill or courage, joy or fear;
Which, like a book, preserved the memory
Of the dumb animals, whom he had sav'd,
Had fed or shelter'd, linking to such acts,
So grateful in themselves, the certainty
Of honorable gain; these fields, these hills
Which were his living being, even more
Than his own blood — what could they less? had
    laid
Strong hold on his affections, were to him
A pleasureable feeling of blind love,
The pleasure which there is in life itself.

On the other hand, in the poems which are pitched at a lower note, as the "Harry Gill," "Idiot Boy," the *feelings* are those of human nature in general; though the poet has judiciously laid the *scene* in the country, in order to place *himself* in the vicinity of interesting images, without the necessity of ascribing a sentimental perception of their beauty to the persons of his drama. In the "Idiot Boy," indeed, the mother's character is not so much a real and native product of a "situation where the essential passions of the heart find a better soil, in which they can attain their maturity and speak a plainer and more emphatic language," as it is an impersonation of an instinct abandoned by judgement. Hence the two following charges seem to me not wholly groundless: at least, they are the only plausible objections, which I have heard to that fine poem. The one is, that the author has not, in the poem itself, taken sufficient care to preclude from the reader's fancy the disgusting images of *ordinary morbid idiocy,* which yet it was by no means his intention to represent. He has even by the "burr, burr, burr," uncounteracted by any preceding description of the boy's beauty, assisted in recalling them. The other is, that the idiocy of the *boy* is so evenly balanced by the folly of the *mother,* as

to present to the general reader rather a laughable burlesque on the blindness of anile dotage, than an analytic display of maternal affection in its ordinary workings.

In the "Thorn" the poet himself acknowledges in a note the necessity of an introductory poem, in which he should have pourtrayed the character of the person from whom the words of the poem are supposed to proceed: a superstitious man moderately imaginative, of slow faculties and deep feelings, "a captain of a small trading vessel, for example, who, being past the middle age of life, had retired upon an annuity, or small independent income, to some village or country town of which he was not a native, or in which he had not been accustomed to live. Such men having nothing to do become credulous and talkative from indolence." But in a poem, still more in a lyric poem (and the Nurse in Shakespeare's Romeo and Juliet alone prevents me from extending the remark even to dramatic *poetry,* if indeed the Nurse itself can be deemed altogether a case in point) it is not possible to imitate truly a dull and garrulous discourser, without repeating the effects of dullness and garrulity. However this may be, I dare assert, that the parts (and these form the far larger portion of the whole) which might as well or still better have proceeded from the poet's own imagination, and have been spoken in his own character, are those which have given, and which will continue to give, universal delight; and that the passages exclusively appropriate to the supposed narrator, such as the last couplet of the third stanza;[7] the seven last lines of the tenth;[8] and the five following

7"I've measured it from side to side;
    'Tis three feet long, and two feet wide." [Au.]
8"Nay, rack your brain — 'tis all in vain,
    I'll tell you every thing I know;
    But to the Thorn, and to the Pond
    Which is a little step beyond,
    I wish that you would go:
    Perhaps when you are at the place,
    You something of her tale may trace.

    I'll give you the best help I can:
    Before you up the mountain go,
    Up to the dreary mountain-top,
    I'll tell you all I know.

stanzas, with the exception of the four admirable lines at the commencement of the fourteenth, are felt by many unprejudiced and unsophisticated hearts, as sudden and unpleasant sinkings from the height to which the poet had previously lifted

them, and to which he again re-elevates both himself and his reader.

If then I am compelled to doubt the theory, by which the choice of *characters* was to be directed, not only *a priori,* from grounds of reason, but both from the few instances in which the poet himself *need* be supposed to have been governed by it, and from the comparative inferiority of those instances; still more must I hesitate in my assent to the sentence which immediately follows the former citation; and which I can neither admit as particular fact, or as general rule. "The language too of these men is adopted (purified indeed from what appear to be its real defects, from all lasting and rational causes of dislike or disgust) because such men hourly communicate with the best objects from which the best part of language is originally derived; and because, from their rank in society and the sameness and narrow circle of their intercourse, being less under the action of social vanity, they convey their feelings and notions in simple and unelaborated expressions." To this I reply; that a rustic's language, purified from all provincialism and grossness, and so far reconstructed as to be made consistent with the rules of grammar (which are in essence no other than the laws of universal logic, applied to psychological materials) will not differ from the language of any other man of common-sense, however learned or refined he may be, except as far as the notions, which the rustic has to convey, are fewer and more indiscriminate. This will become still clearer, if we add the consideration (equally important though less obvious) that the rustic, from the more imperfect developement of his faculties, and from the lower state of their cultivation, aims almost solely to convey *insulated facts,* either those of his scanty experience or his traditional belief; while the educated man chiefly seeks to discover and express those *connections* of things, or those relative *bearings* of fact to fact, from which some more or less general law is deducible. For *facts* are valuable to a wise man, chiefly as they lead to the discovery of the indwelling *law,* which is the true *being* of things, the sole solution of their modes of existence, and in the knowledge of which consists our dignity and our power.

---

'Tis now some two-and-twenty years
Since she (her name is Martha Ray)
Gave, with a maiden's true good will,
Her company to Stephen Hill;
And she was blithe and gay,
And she was happy, happy still
Whene'er she thought of Stephen Hill.

And they had fix'd the wedding-day,
The morning that must wed them both;
But Stephen to another maid
Had sworn another oath;
And, with this other maid, to church
Unthinking Stephen went —
Poor Martha! on that woeful day
A pang of pitiless dismay
Into her soul was sent;
A fire was kindled in her breast,
Which might not burn itself to rest.

They say, full six months after this,
While yet the summer leaves were green,
She to the mountain-top would go,
And there was often seen.
'Tis said a child was in her womb,
As now to any eye was plain;
She was with child, and she was mad,
Yet often she was sober sad
From her exceeding pain.
Oh me! ten thousand times I'd rather
That he had died, that cruel father!

. . . . . . . . . . . . .

Last Christmas when we talked of this,
Old farmer Simpson did maintain,
That in her womb the infant wrought
About its mother's heart, and brought
Her senses back again:
And, when at last her time drew near,
Her looks were calm, her senses clear.

No more I know, I wish I did,
And I would tell it all to you:
For what became of this poor child
There's none that ever knew:
And if a child was born or no,
There's no one that could ever tell;
And if 'twas born alive or dead,
There's no one knows, as I have said:
But some remember well,
That Martha Ray about this time
Would up the mountain often climb." [Au.]

---

As little can I agree with the assertion, that from the objects with which the rustic hourly communicates the best part of language is formed. For first, if to communicate with an object implies such an acquaintance with it, as renders it capable of being discriminately reflected on; the distinct knowledge of an uneducated rustic would furnish a very scanty vocabulary. The few things, and modes of action, requisite for his bodily conveniences, would alone be individualized; while all the rest of nature would be expressed by a small number of confused general terms. Secondly, I deny that the words and combinations of words derived from the objects, with which the rustic is familiar, whether with distinct or confused knowledge, can be justly said to form the *best* part of language. It is more than probable, that many classes of the brute creation possess discriminating sounds, by which they can convey to each other notices of such objects as concern their food, shelter, or safety. Yet we hesitate to call the aggregate of such sounds a language, otherwise than metaphorically. The best part of human language, properly so called, is derived from reflection on the acts of the mind itself. It is formed by a voluntary appropriation of fixed symbols to internal acts, to processes and results of imagination, the greater part of which have no place in the consciousness of uneducated man; though in civilized society, by imitation and passive remembrance of what they hear from their religious instructors and other superiors, the most uneducated share in the harvest which they neither sowed nor reaped. If the history of the phrases in hourly currency among our peasants were traced, a person not previously aware of the fact would be surprised at finding so large a number, which three or four centuries ago were the exclusive property of the universities and the schools; and, at the commencement of the Reformation, had been transferred from the school to the pulpit, and thus gradually passed into common life. The extreme difficulty, and often the impossibility, of finding words for the simplest moral and intellectual processes in the languages of uncivilized tribes has proved perhaps the weightiest obstacle to the progress of our most zealous and adroit missionaries. Yet these tribes are surrounded by the same nature as our peasants are; but in still more impressive forms; and they are, moreover, obliged to *particularize* many more of them. When, therefore, Mr. Wordsworth adds, "accordingly, such a language" (meaning, as before, the language of rustic life purified from provincialism) "arising out of repeated experience and regular feelings, is a more permanent, and a far more philosophical language, than that which is frequently substituted for it by poets, who think they are conferring honor upon themselves and their art in proportion as they indulge in arbitrary and capricious habits of expression:" it may be answered, that the language, which he has in view, can be attributed to rustics with no greater right, than the style of Hooker or Bacon to Tom Brown or Sir Roger L'Estrange.[9] Doubtless, if what is peculiar to each were omitted in each, the result must needs be the same. Further, that the poet, who uses an illogical diction, or a style fitted to excite only the low and changeable pleasure of wonder by means of groundless novelty, substitutes a language of *folly* and *vanity,* not for that of the *rustic,* but for that of *good sense* and *natural feeling.*

Here let me be permitted to remind the reader, that the positions, which I controvert, are contained in the sentences — "*a selection of the* REAL *language of men;*" — "*the language of these men*" (i.e., men in low and rustic life) "*I propose to myself to imitate, and, as far as is possible, to adopt the very language of men.*" "*Between the language of prose and that of metrical composition, there neither is, nor can be any essential difference.*" It is against these exclusively that my opposition is directed.

I object, in the very first instance, to an equivocation in the use of the word "real." Every man's language varies, according to the extent of his knowledge, the activity of his faculties, and the depth or quickness of his feelings. Every man's language has, first, its *individualities;* sec-

---

[9]Richard Hooker was the sixteenth-century author of *Ecclesiastical Polity*; Francis Bacon wrote philosophy and essays at the beginning of the seventeenth century. Tom Brown and Roger L'Estrange were popular writers of the late seventeenth and early eighteenth centuries. [Ed.]

ondly, the common properties of the *class* to which he belongs; and thirdly, words and phrases of *universal* use. The language of Hooker, Bacon, Bishop Taylor, and Burke differs from the common language of the learned class only by the superior number and novelty of the thoughts and relations which they had to convey. The language of Algernon Sidney differs not at all from that, which every well-educated gentleman would wish to write, and (with due allowances for the undeliberateness, and less connected train, of thinking natural and proper to conversation) such as he would wish to talk. Neither one nor the other differ half so much from the general language of cultivated society, as the language of Mr. Wordsworth's homeliest composition differs from that of a common peasant. For "real" therefore, we must substitute *ordinary, or lingua communis*. And this, we have proved, is no more to be found in the phraseology of low and rustic life than in that of any other class. Omit the peculiarities of each, and the result of course must be common to all. And assuredly the omissions and changes to be made in the language of rustics, before it could be transferred to any species of poem, except the drama or other professed imitation, are at least as numerous and weighty, as would be required in adapting to the same purpose the ordinary language of tradesmen and manufacturers. Not to mention, that the language so highly extolled by Mr. Wordsworth varies in every county, nay in every village, according to the accidental character of the clergyman, the existence or non-existence of schools; or even, perhaps, as the exciseman, publican, or barber, happen to be, or not to be, zealous politicians, and readers of the weekly newspaper *pro bono publico*.[10] Anterior to cultivation, the lingua communis of every country, as Dante has well observed, exists every where in parts, and no where as a whole.

[10]For the public good. [Ed.]

Neither is the case rendered at all more tenable by the addition of the words, *in a state of excitement*. For the nature of a man's words, where he is strongly affected by joy, grief, or anger, must necessarily depend on the number and quality of the general truths, conceptions and images, and of the words expressing them, with which his mind had been previously stored. For the property of passion is not to *create*; but to set in increased activity. At least, whatever new connections of thoughts or images, or (which is equally, if not more than equally, the appropriate effect of strong excitement) whatever generalizations of truth or experience, the heat of passion may produce; yet the terms of their conveyance must have pre-existed in his former conversations, and are only collected and crowded together by the unusual stimulation. It is indeed very possible to adopt in a poem the unmeaning repetitions, habitual phrases, and other blank counters, which an unfurnished or confused understanding interposes at short intervals, in order to keep hold of his subject, which is still slipping from him, and to give him time for recollection; or in mere aid of vacancy, as in the scanty companies of a country stage the same player pops backwards and forwards, in order to prevent the appearance of empty spaces, in the procession of Macbeth, or Henry VIIIth. But what assistance to the poet, or ornament to the poem, these can supply, I am at a loss to conjecture. Nothing assuredly can differ either in origin or in mode widely from the *apparent* tautologies of intense and turbulent feeling, in which the passion is greater and of longer endurance than to be exhausted or satisfied by a single representation of the image or incident exciting it. Such repetitions I admit to be a beauty of the highest kind; as illustrated by Mr. Wordsworth himself from the song of Deborah. "*At her feet he bowed, he fell, he lay down; at her feet he bowed, he fell; where he bowed, there he fell down dead.*"[11]

[11]Judges 5:27. [Ed.]

# John Keats

## 1795–1821

John Keats was born in London, the son of a livery stableman who had married the stable-owner's daughter. He was educated in a private school at Enfield by Charles Cowden Clarke, later a friend to many of the second generation of romantic poets, who encouraged Keats's love of reading and writing. Orphaned at fourteen with his mother's capital tied up in a chancery suit, Keats was apprenticed by his guardian to an apothecary-surgeon, and he studied medicine at Guy's Hospital in London until he was twenty-one. In London, Keats met Leigh Hunt, who gathered him into a politically radical circle of artists that included the poet Percy Bysshe Shelley, the essayist Thomas Hazlitt, and the painter Benjamin Haydon. As soon as he was of age, Keats abandoned the medical profession to become a poet.

Keats's first books, *Poems* (1817) and *Endymion* (1818), were attacked, mainly by conservative enemies of Hunt. Stimulated more by his own scrutiny than by outside criticism, Keats refined his style and in 1819 wrote "The Eve of St. Agnes," "Lamia," the six Odes (on Psyche, Indolence, the Nightingale, the Grecian Urn, Melancholy, and Autumn), and "La Belle Dame sans Merci" — the quintessential lyrics of English romanticism. In that year Keats also knew he was racing the clock: He had returned from a walking tour in the autumn of 1818 with an ulcerated throat and had enough medical training to foresee his own death from tuberculosis. Keats worked furiously at his fragmentary epic, *The Fall of Hyperion*, but in February 1820 he began to cough up blood and had serious hemorrhages later in the spring. That summer he left for the milder climate of Rome, but it was already too late. He died there on February 23, 1821, and is buried in the Protestant Cemetery.

Keats wrote no developed body of critical theory; his ideas — picked up from the intellectual atmosphere of the romantics and completely unstructured by schools — appear as brilliant fragments in his personal letters to friends.

The letter to Benjamin Bailey reflects Keats's most idealistic phase. In it, Keats asserts that the product of the sensual intuition seems superior to the product of the rational intellect, and that what the imagination produces and records as Beauty is not illusion but "truth" — an authentic reality — "whether it existed before or not" in the material sense. Keats's first example of the authenticity of imagination — Adam's dream — comes from *Paradise Lost,* and seems to be a merely literary manifestation. But his second, when he asks Bailey to recall the way imagination reconstitutes the content of an old memory from a tiny stimulus, yet recaptures it more beautifully than it actually occurred, has become a major touchstone of romantic aesthetics.

The same is true of the letter to his brothers George and Thomas Keats. Here we find Keats's classic definition of *negative capability*: "when man is capable of being in uncertainties, Mysteries, doubts, without any irritable reaching after fact & reason." The meaning of the phrase is clear enough, but its significance takes some teasing out from the context. Keats begins by contrasting two painful but beautiful works of art: Benjamin West's painting, *Death on the Pale Horse* and Shakespeare's *King Lear*. Keats is only moderately pleased by the former, which lacks the intensity of Shakespeare's tragedy. The intensity of *Lear* seems to come from the "depth of speculation excited" in the audience that contemplates it. Shakespeare's work presents a vision of the pain and evil of life without attempting to comprehend and explain it; its raw presentation demands the intellectual and emotional participation of the viewer. But the West picture has already been processed through the artist's mind, and thus leaves less for the audience to do. Shakespeare possesses immense negative capability; West and the poet Coleridge (in the example at the end of the letter) are artists of a different kind. Keats's idea here may connect with Schiller's distinction between "naive" and "sentimental" writers; the naive Shakespeare presents the emotional object directly for the reader's consideration, whereas the sentimental West presents it filtered through his own private consciousness.

### Selected Bibliography

Bate, Walter Jackson. *Negative Capability.* Cambridge: Harvard University Press, 1939.
Ende, Stuart A. *Keats and the Sublime.* New Haven: Yale University Press, 1976.
Sharp, Ronald A. *Keats, Skepticism, and the Religion of Beauty.* Athens: University of Georgia Press, 1979.
Tate, Priscilla Weston. *From Innocence through Experience: Keats's Myth of the Poet.* Salzburg: Institut für Englische Sprache und Literatur, 1974.
Thekla, Sister. *The Disinterested Heart: The Philosophy of John Keats.* Newport Pagnell, Eng.: Greek Orthodox Monastery of the Assumption, 1973.
Thorpe, Clarence Dewitt. *The Mind of John Keats.* New York: Oxford University Press, 1926.

# From a *Letter to Benjamin Bailey*

[November 22, 1817]

My dear Bailey,

... O I wish I was as certain of the end of all your troubles as that of your momentary start about the authenticity of the Imagination. I am certain of nothing but of the holiness of the Heart's affections and the truth of Imagination — What the imagination seizes as Beauty must be truth[1] — whether it existed before or not — for I have the same Idea of all our Passions as of Love they are all in their sublime, creative of essential Beauty — In a Word, you may know my favorite Speculation by my first Book and the little song I sent in my last[2] — which is a representation from the fancy of the probable mode of operating in these Matters — The Imagination may be compared to Adam's dream[3] — he awoke and found it truth. I am the more

[1]Cf. the last two lines of "Ode on a Grecian Urn": in both cases, "truth" seems to mean something like "authentic reality" rather than "verifiable fact." [Ed.]

[2]"O Sorrow" from *Endymion.* [Ed.]
[3]Milton, *Paradise Lost,* 8:460–90. [Ed.]

zealous in this affair, because I have never yet been able to perceive how any thing can be known for truth by consequitive reasoning — and yet it must be — Can it be that even the greatest Philosopher ever arrived at his goal without putting aside numerous objections — However it may be, O for a Life of Sensations rather than of Thoughts! It is "a Vision in the form of Youth" a Shadow of reality to come — and this consideration has further convinced me for it has come as auxiliary to another favorite Speculation of mine, that we shall enjoy ourselves here after by having what we called happiness on Earth repeated in a finer tone and so repeated — And yet such a fate can only befall those who delight in sensation rather than hunger as you do after Truth — Adam's dream will do here and seems to be a conviction that Imagination and its empyreal reflection is the same as human Life and its spiritual repetition. But as I was saying — the simple imaginative Mind may have its rewards in the repetition of its own silent Working coming continually on the spirit with a fine suddenness — to compare great things with small — have you never by being surprised with an old Melody — in a delicious place — by a delicious voice, felt over again your very speculations and surmises at the time it first operated on your soul — do you not remember forming to yourself the singer's face more beautiful than it was possible and yet with the elevation of the Moment you did not think so — even then you were mounted on the Wings of Imagination so high — that the Prototype must be here after — that delicious face you will see — What a time! I am continually running away from the subject — sure this cannot be exactly the case with a complex Mind — one that is imaginative and at the same time careful of its fruits — who would exist partly on sensation partly on thought — to whom it is necessary that years should bring the philosophic Mind[4] — such an one I consider

[4]Keats is quoting Wordsworth's "Intimations of Immortality" ode. [Ed.]

your's and therefore it is necessary to your eternal Happiness that you not only drink this old Wine of Heaven which I shall call the redigestion of our most ethereal Musings on Earth; but also increase in knowledge and know all things. I am glad to hear you are in a fair Way for Easter — you will soon get through your unpleasant reading and then! — but the world is full of troubles and I have not much reason to think myself pesterd with many — I think Jane or Marianne[5] has a better opinion of me than I deserve — for really and truly I do not think my Brothers illness connected with mine — you know more of the real Cause than they do — nor have I any chance of being rack'd as you have been — you perhaps at one time thought there was such a thing as Worldly Happiness to be arrived at, at certain periods of time marked out — you have of necessity from your disposition been thus led away — I scarcely remember counting upon any Happiness — I look not for it if it be not in the present hour — nothing startles me beyond the Moment. The setting sun will always set me to rights — or if a Sparrow come before my Window I take part in its existince and pick about the Gravel. The first thing that strikes me on hearing a Misfortune having befalled another is this. Well it cannot be helped. — he will have the pleasure of trying the resources of his spirit, and I beg now my dear Bailey that hereafter should you observe any thing cold in me not to put it to the account of heartlessness but abstraction — for I assure you I sometimes feel not the influence of a Passion or Affection during a whole week — and so long this sometimes continues I begin to suspect myself and the genuiness of my feelings at other times — thinking them a few barren Tragedy-tears. . . .

Your affectionate friend
John Keats —

[5]Jane and Marianne Reynolds, friends of Keats. [Ed.]

# From a *Letter to George and Thomas Keats*

[December 21, 27 (?), 1817]

My dear Brothers

I must crave your pardon for not having written ere this. . . . I spent Friday evening with Wells[1] & went the next morning to see *Death on the Pale horse*. It is a wonderful picture, when West's age[2] is considered; But there is nothing to be intense upon; no women one feels mad to kiss; no face swelling into reality. the excellence of every Art is its intensity, capable of making all disagreeables evaporate, from their being in close relationship with Beauty & Truth — Examine King Lear & you will find this examplified throughout; but in this picture we have unpleasantness without any momentous depth of speculation excited, in which to bury its repulsiveness — The picture is larger than Christ rejected — I dined with Haydon[3] the sunday after you left, & had a very pleasant day, I dined too (for I have been out too much lately) with Horace Smith & met his two Brothers with Hill & Kingston & one Du Bois,[4] they only served to convince me, how superior humour is to wit in respect to enjoyment — These men say things which make one start, without making one feel, they are all alike; their manners are alike; they all know fashionables; they have a mannerism in their very

eating & drinking, in their mere handling a Decanter — They talked of Kean[5] & his low company — Would I were with that company instead of yours said I to myself! I know such like acquaintance will never do for me & yet I am going to Reynolds, on wednesday — Brown & Dilke[6] walked with me & back from the Christmas pantomime. I had not a dispute but a disquisition with Dilke, on various subjects; several things dovetailed in my mind, & at once it struck me, what quality went to form a Man of Achievement especially in Literature & which Shakespeare posessed so enormously — I mean *Negative Capability*, that is when man is capable of being in uncertainties, Mysteries, doubts, without any irritable reaching after fact & reason — Coleridge, for instance, would let go by a fine isolated verisimilitude caught from the Penetralium[7] of mystery, from being incapable of remaining content with half knowledge. This pursued through Volumes would perhaps take us no further than this, that with a great poet the sense of Beauty overcomes every other consideration, or rather obliterates all consideration.

Shelley's poem[8] is out & there are words about its being objected too, as much as Queen Mab was. Poor Shelley I think he has his Quota of good qualities, in sooth la!! Write soon to your most sincere friend & affectionate Brother

John

[1]Charles Wells, who had gone to school with Thomas Keats. [Ed.]

[2]Benjamin West (1738–1820) was seventy-nine when he painted *Death on the Pale Horse*. [Ed.]

[3]Benjamin Haydon, a painter who was a good friend of Keats's. [Ed.]

[4]Literary figures of the day. [Ed.]

[5]Edmund Kean, the Shakespearean actor. [Ed.]

[6]John Hamilton Reynolds, Charles Armitage Brown, and Charles Wentworth Dilke were literary friends of Keats. [Ed.]

[7]Inner sanctum. [Ed.]

[8]*Laon and Cythna* (1817). [Ed.]

# Percy Bysshe Shelley

## 1792–1822

The most radical English poet since Milton, Percy Bysshe Shelley wrote in proud rebellion against his conservative and aristocratic roots: His grandfather was a landowning baronet, his father a member of Parliament. Shelley was educated at Eton and Oxford, from which he was sent down at the age of eighteen for publishing a tract advocating atheism. In London, he came under the influence of the philosopher William Godwin, whose *Political Justice* questioned the foundations of the English state. Though already married to Harriet Westbrook, Shelley fell in love with Godwin's daughter Mary, and in 1814 eloped with her to France; they were able to marry only after Harriet's suicide, in 1816. In financial straits and anathematized by the British public for his political opinions as well as his sexual immorality, Shelley moved to Italy the next year. There he wrote his most impressive works: *Prometheus Unbound* (1819), *The Masque of Anarchy* (1819), *Epipsychidion* (1821), and *Adonais* (1821). He had just embarked on his most ambitious poem, *The Triumph of Life,* when he drowned in July of 1822 in a boating accident in the Gulf of Spezia.

Like Sir Philip Sidney's "Apology for Poetry," Shelley's "Defence of Poetry" (written in 1821, though not published until 1840) is a reply to Plato's attacks on mimetic art in *Republic* X. It should not be surprising that in the period after Kant and his successors, Shelley's riposte would depend on the notion of mental faculties and their powers. He thus begins the "Defence" with the parallel dialectical oppositions of *tò logizeín* and *tò poieîn*, reason and imagination, analysis and synthesis. His purpose is to refute Plato's attack on the mimetic artist as inferior to the artisan in knowledge and understanding by insisting that the poetic faculty is equal and complementary to logical reason.

The reader who scans "A Defence of Poetry" in search of a systematic approach to romantic critical theory, however, will be disappointed. Although the essay begins austerely enough with what appears to be a set of logical distinctions, philosophical rigor is soon abandoned. Indeed, some readers may find Shelley's prose disjointed and contradictory, apparently unplanned in organization, at times almost incoherent. But if we set aside system and rigor and attend instead to Shelley's ideals and imagery, the essay yields an inspiring vision, rather like that at the conclusion of "Adonais," of how the romantic poets saw themselves and the place of poetry in human society. Perhaps the first and third sections of "A Defence of Poetry" (pp. 323–327 and 337–340) should be read as we read a lyric, through key metaphors.

The first of these metaphors likens the mind to an Aeolian lyre, struck to melody by the wind of its "external and internal impressions." Shelley develops this metaphor further: The mind produces not just melody but harmony as well, and the spontaneous song of the child is an expression of delight in this harmony, an effect the child prolongs by recalling its cause. It is here, deep in human nature, that Shelley locates the impulse to produce art, for poetry is nothing but the adult analogy to this process.

Toward the end of the "Defence," in discussing the haphazard nature of poetic inspiration Shelley likens the mind of the poet to "a fading coal, which some invisible influence, like an inconstant wind, awakens to transitory brightness." Again, the external world is like a wind, forcible but insubstantial, while the mind is like a physical object that can make light or heat or melody. Perhaps nothing suggests Shelley's deep affinity to Plato more than this; it is as if the mind and its ideas are real while the external physical world is not.

Shelley is most Platonic in opposition to his master. Where Plato ejected the poets from his Republic, Shelley makes them its masters, calling them "the unacknowledged legislators of the World." He begins with the idea that "every original language near to its source is in itself the chaos of a cyclic [i.e., epic] poem." We might think of poetry as a special use of language that arranges a harmony between sound and meaning, but all language does that. Whoever creates any new word or names any unnamed feature of the sensual world is, in effect, a poet. Language is everywhere a network of living, dying, and dead metaphors, statements of the likenesses between one aspect of experience and another. We talk of "the iron curtain," we play the game of "cat's cradle": Both are poetic metaphors. And language embalms metaphors in its etymologies: At one time the verb *transgress* literally signified "straying from the herd." In shaping language, the poets — these innovators of language, who are not necessarily identical with the canonized poets from Homer to Shelley himself — have in effect shaped human thought, and thus molded society and human relations.

But it is not enough for Shelley to find a poetic act somewhere behind any use of language. He claims that poetry, in any age removed from the primitive *source* of language, recaptures for humanity, by metaphor and harmony, the immediacy of life and experience, an immediacy that is lost by the use of logical, analytical thought and language. For Shelley, the world is veiled from human participation by dead thought and language, and it is the poets alone who are able to penetrate and "lift the veil from the hidden beauty of the world."

In the course of this argument the words *poetry* and *poet* shift their ground away from pure aesthetics. A poet is anyone who can synthesize a vision of the world and express that apprehended synthesis in language. Thus the great philosophers, Plato among them, are revealed to be nothing other than poets. And conversely, since poets' visions are necessarily of the eternal truths of the human spirit, Shakespeare, Dante, and Milton must be seen as "philosophers of the very loftiest power."

The development of these general ideas is interrupted by a long middle section (pp. 327–337), which was inspired less by Plato than by "The Four Ages of Poetry" (1820), a pamphlet by Shelley's friend, the satirist Thomas Love Peacock. Perhaps influenced by the Italian philosopher Giambattista Vico, Peacock posited a cyclical theory of the history of Western civilization: Both history and poetry had by then gone through two cycles with four phases in each.

Each cycle begins with an "age of iron," like the archaic period or the Middle

Ages, when the poet is essentially a bard paid to flatter in verse the exploits of military chieftains. There follows an "age of gold," a tough but harmonious civilization, like Periclean Athens or Elizabethan England, which produces the finest poetry, the Homers and the Shakespeares. From then on, however, the increasing encroachment of scientific knowledge limits the scope of poetry. There arrives an "age of silver," a polished and classicizing civilization that gives rise to the Virgils and the Miltons and Popes. Finally comes the decadence of the "age of brass," in which poetry is mere nostalgic archaism, like the later Roman Empire — or the English romantic period. At last, the destruction of civilization itself — the fall of the Roman Empire in the first cycle — puts an end to the decay and allows a new age of iron to begin. The bulk of the "Defence of Poetry" is a reply to Peacock's attack on romantics and romanticism, which takes the form of a progressive (rather than a cyclical) theory of history and of the poetry that grew up alongside (and in Shelley's view helped to form) political institutions.

## Selected Bibliography

Bloom, Harold. *Shelley's Mythmaking*. New Haven: Yale University Press, 1959.

Damm, Robert F. *A Tale of Human Power: Art and Life in Shelley's Poetic Theory*. Oxford, Ohio: Miami University Press, 1970.

Grabo, C. H. *The Magic Plant: The Growth of Shelley's Thought*. Chapel Hill: University of North Carolina Press, 1936.

Notopoulos, J. A. *The Platonism of Shelley*. Durham: Duke University Press, 1949.

Schulze, Earl J. *Shelley's Theory of Poetry: A Reappraisal*. The Hague: Mouton, 1966.

Shawcross, John, ed. *Shelley's Literary and Philosophical Criticism*. London: H. Frowde, 1909.

Solve, Melvin T. *Shelley: His Theory of Poetry*. Chicago: University of Chicago Press, 1927.

# A Defence of Poetry

## or Remarks Suggested by an Essay Entitled "The Four Ages of Poetry"

According to one mode of regarding those two classes of mental action, which are called reason and imagination, the former may be considered as mind contemplating the relations borne by one thought to another, however produced; and the latter, as mind acting upon those thoughts so as to colour them with its own light, and composing from them, as from elements, other thoughts, each containing within itself the principle of its own integrity. The one is the τὸ ποιεῖν,[1] or the principle of synthesis, and has for its objects those forms which are common to universal nature and existence itself; the other is the τὸ λογιζειν,[2] or principle of analysis, and its action regards the relations of things, simply as relations; considering thoughts, not in their integral unity, but as the algebraical representations which conduct to certain general results. Reason

[1]Making. [Ed.]
[2]Reasoning. [Ed.]

is the enumeration of quantities already known; imagination is the perception of the value of those quantities, both separately and as a whole. Reason respects the differences, and imagination the similitudes of things. Reason is to Imagination as the instrument to the agent, as the body to the spirit, as the shadow to the substance.

Poetry, in a general sense, may be defined to be "the expression of the Imagination": and poetry is connate with the origin of man. Man is an instrument over which a series of external and internal impressions are driven, like the alternations of an ever-changing wind over an Æolian lyre, which move it by their motion to ever-changing melody. But there is a principle within the human being, and perhaps within all sentient beings, which acts otherwise than in the lyre, and produces not melody alone, but harmony, by an internal adjustment of the sounds or motions thus excited to the impressions which excite them. It is as if the lyre could accommodate its chords to the motions of that which strikes them, in a determined proportion of sound; even as the musician can accommodate his voice to the sound of the lyre. A child at play by itself will express its delight by its voice and motions; and every inflexion of tone and every gesture will bear exact relation to a corresponding antitype in the pleasurable impressions which awakened it; it will be the reflected image of that impression; and as the lyre trembles and sounds after the wind has died away, so the child seeks, by prolonging in its voice and motions the duration of the effect, to prolong also a consciousness of the cause. In relation to the objects which delight a child, these expressions are, what poetry is to higher objects. The savage (for the savage is to ages what the child is to years) expresses the emotions produced in him by surrounding objects in a similar manner; and language and gesture, together with plastic or pictorial imitation, become the image of the combined effect of those objects, and of his apprehension of them. Man in society, with all his passions and his pleasures, next becomes the object of the passions and pleasures of man; an additional class of emotions produces an augmented treasure of expressions; and language, gesture, and the imitative arts, become at once the representation and the me-dium, the pencil and the picture, the chisel and the statue, the chord and the harmony. The social sympathies, or those laws from which as from its elements society results, begin to develope themselves from the moment that two human beings coexist; the future is contained within the present as the plant within the seed; and equality, diversity, unity, contrast, mutual dependence, become the principles alone capable of affording the motives according to which the will of a social being is determined to action, inasmuch as he is social; and constitute pleasure in sensation, virtue in sentiment, beauty in art, truth in reasoning, and love in the intercourse of kind. Hence men, even in the infancy of society, observe a certain order in their words and actions, distinct from that of the objects and the impressions represented by them, all expression being subject to the laws of that from which it proceeds. But let us dismiss those more general considerations which might involve an enquiry into the principles of society itself, and restrict our view to the manner in which the imagination is expressed upon its forms.

In the youth of the world, men dance and sing and imitate natural objects, observing in these actions, as in all others, a certain rhythm or order. And, although all men observe a similar, they observe not the same order, in the motions of the dance, in the melody of the song, in the combinations of language, in the series of their imitations of natural objects. For there is a certain order or rhythm belonging to each of these classes of mimetic representation, from which the hearer and the spectator receive an intenser and purer pleasure than from any other: the sense of an approximation to this order has been called taste, by modern writers. Every man in the infancy of art, observes an order which approximates more or less closely to that from which this highest delight results: but the diversity is not sufficiently marked, as that its gradations should be sensible, except in those instances where the predominance of this faculty of approximation to the beautiful (for so we may be permitted to name the relation between this highest pleasure and its cause) is very great. Those in whom it exists in excess are poets, in the most universal sense of the word; and the pleasure resulting from the manner in which they express the influence of society or nature upon their own minds, communicates itself to others, and gathers a sort of reduplication from that community. Their language is vitally metaphorical; that is, it marks the before unapprehended relations of things, and perpetuates their apprehension, until the words which represent them, become through time signs for portions or classes of thoughts instead of pictures of integral thoughts; and then if no new poets should arise to create afresh the associations which have been thus disorganized, language will be dead to all the nobler purposes of human intercourse. These similitudes or relations are finely said by Lord Bacon to be "the same footsteps of nature impressed upon the various subjects of the world"[3] — and he considers the faculty which perceives them as the storehouse of axioms common to all knowledge. In the infancy of society every author is necessarily a poet, because language itself is poetry; and to be a poet is to apprehend the true and the beautiful, in a word the good which exists in the relation, subsisting, first between existence and perception, and secondly between perception and expression. Every original language near to its source is in itself the chaos of a cyclic poem: the copiousness of lexicography and the distinctions of grammar are the works of a later age, and are merely the catalogue and the form of the creations of Poetry.

But Poets, or those who imagine and express this indestructible order, are not only the authors of language and of music, of the dance and architecture and statuary and painting: they are the institutors of laws, and the founders of civil society and the inventors of the arts of life and the teachers, who draw into a certain propinquity with the beautiful and the true that partial apprehension of the agencies of the invisible world which is called religion. Hence all original religions are allegorical, or susceptible of allegory, and like Janus have a double face of false and true. Poets, according to the circumstances of the age and nation in which they appeared, were called in the earlier epochs of the world legislators or prophets: a poet essentially comprises and unites both these characters.[4] For he not only beholds intensely the present as it is, and discovers those laws according to which present things ought to be ordered, but he beholds the future in the present, and his thoughts are the germs of the flower and the fruit of latest time. Not that I assert poets to be prophets in the gross sense of the word, or that they can foretell the form as surely as they foreknow the spirit of events: such is the pretence of superstition which would make poetry an attribute of prophecy, rather than prophecy an attribute of poetry. A Poet participates in the eternal, the infinite, and the one; as far as relates to his conceptions, time and place and number are not. The grammatical forms which express the moods of time, and the difference of persons and the distinction of place are convertible with respect to the highest poetry without injuring it as poetry, and the choruses of Æschylus, and the book of Job, and Dante's Paradise would afford, more than any other writings, examples of this fact, if the limits of this essay did not forbid citation. The creations of sculpture, painting, and music, are illustrations still more decisive.

Language, colour, form, and religious and civil habits of action are all the instruments and materials of poetry; they may be called poetry by that figure of speech which considers the effect as a synonime of the cause. But poetry in a more restricted sense expresses those arrangements of language, and especially metrical language, which are created by that imperial faculty, whose throne is curtained within the invisible nature of man. And this springs from the nature itself of language, which is a more direct representation of the actions and passions of our internal being, and is susceptible of more various and delicate combinations, than colour, form, or motion, and is more plastic and obedient to the controul of that faculty of which it is the creation. For language is arbitrarily produced by the Imagination and has relation to thoughts alone; but all other materials, instruments and conditions of art, have relations among each other, which limit

---

[3]Francis Bacon, *The Advancement of Learning*, 3:1. [Ed.]

[4]Cf. Philip Sidney, *An Apology for Poetry*; see p. 136. [Ed.]

and interpose between conception and expression. The former is as a mirror which reflects, the latter as a cloud which enfeebles, the light of which both are mediums of communication. Hence the fame of sculptors, painters and musicians, although the intrinsic powers of the great masters of these arts, may yield in no degree to that of those who have employed language as the hieroglyphic of their thoughts, has never equalled that of poets in the restricted sense of the term; as two performers of equal skill will produce unequal effects from a guitar and a harp. The fame of legislators and founders of religions, so long as their institutions last, alone seems to exceed that of poets in the restricted sense; but it can scarcely be a question whether, if we deduct the celebrity which their flattery of the gross opinions of the vulgar usually conciliates, together with that which belonged to them in their higher character of poets, any excess will remain.

We have thus circumscribed the meaning of the word Poetry within the limits of that art which is the most familiar and the most perfect expression of the faculty itself. It is necessary however to make the circle still narrower, and to determine the distinction between measured and unmeasured language; for the popular division into prose and verse is inadmissible in accurate philosophy.

Sounds as well as thoughts have relation both between each other and towards that which they represent, and a perception of the order of those relations has always been found connected with a perception of the order of the relations of thoughts. Hence the language of poets has ever affected a certain uniform and harmonious recurrence of sound, without which it were not poetry, and which is scarcely less indispensable to the communication of its influence, than the words themselves, without reference to that peculiar order. Hence the vanity of translation; it were as wise to cast a violet into a crucible that you might discover the formal principle of its colour and odour, as seek to transfuse from one language into another the creations of a poet. The plant must spring again from its seed or it will bear no flower — and this is the burthen of the curse of Babel.

An observation of the regular mode of the recurrence of this harmony in the language of poetical minds, together with its relation to music, produced metre, or a certain system of traditional forms of harmony of language. Yet it is by no means essential that a poet should accommodate his language to this traditional form, so that the harmony which is its spirit, be observed. The practise is indeed convenient and popular, and to be preferred, especially in such composition as includes much form and action: but every great poet must inevitably innovate upon the example of his predecessors in the exact structure of his peculiar versification. The distinction between poets and prose writers is a vulgar error. The distinction between philosophers and poets has been anticipated. Plato was essentially a poet — the truth and splendour of his imagery and the melody of his language is the most intense that it is possible to conceive. He rejected the measure of the epic, dramatic, and lyrical forms, because he sought to kindle a harmony in thoughts divested of shape and action, and he forbore to invent any regular plan of rhythm which would include, under determinate forms, the varied pauses of his style. Cicero sought to imitate the cadence of his periods but with little success. Lord Bacon was a poet.[5] His language has a sweet and majestic rhythm, which satisfies the sense, no less than the almost superhuman wisdom of his philosophy satisfies the intellect; it is a strain which distends, and then bursts the circumference of the hearer's mind, and pours itself forth together with it into the universal element with which it has perpetual sympathy. All the authors of revolutions in opinion are not only necessarily poets as they are inventors, nor even as their words unveil the permanent analogy of things by images which participate in the life of truth; but as their periods are harmonious and rhythmical and contain in themselves the elements of verse; being the echo of the eternal music. Nor are those supreme poets, who have employed traditional forms of rhythm on account of the form and action of their subjects, less capable of perceiving and teaching the truth of things, than those who have omitted

[5] See the *Filium Labyrinthi* and the *Essay on Death* particularly. [Au.]

that form. Shakespeare, Dante and Milton (to confine ourselves to modern writers) are philosophers of the very loftiest power.

A poem is the very image of life expressed in its eternal truth. There is this difference between a story and a poem, that a story is a catalogue of detached facts, which have no other bond of connexion than time, place, circumstance, cause and effect; the other is the creation of actions according to the unchangeable forms of human nature, as existing in the mind of the creator, which is itself the image of all other minds. The one is partial, and applies only to a definite period of time, and a certain combination of events which can never again recur; the other is universal, and contains within itself the germ of a relation to whatever motives or actions have place in the possible varieties of human nature. Time, which destroys the beauty and the use of the story of particular facts, stript of the poetry which should invest them, augments that of Poetry, and for ever develops new and wonderful applications of the eternal truth which it contains. Hence epitomes have been called the moths of just history; they eat out the poetry of it. The story of particular facts is as a mirror which obscures and distorts that which should be beautiful: Poetry is a mirror which makes beautiful that which is distorted.

The parts of a composition may be poetical, without the composition as a whole being a poem. A single sentence may be considered as a whole though it be found in a series of unassimilated portions; a single word even may be a spark of inextinguishable thought. And thus all the great historians, Herodotus, Plutarch, Livy, were poets; and although the plan of these writers, especially that of Livy, restrained them from developing this faculty in its highest degree, they make copious and ample amends for their subjection, by filling all the interstices of their subjects with living images.

Having determined what is poetry, and who are poets, let us proceed to estimate its effects upon society.

Poetry is ever accompanied with pleasure: all spirits on which it falls, open themselves to receive the wisdom which is mingled with its delight. In the infancy of the world, neither poets themselves nor their auditors are fully aware of the excellence of poetry: for it acts in a divine and unapprehended manner, beyond and above consciousness; and it is reserved for future generations to contemplate and measure the mighty cause and effect in all the strength and splendour of their union. Even in modern times, no living poet ever arrived at the fulness of his fame; the jury which sits in judgement upon a poet, belonging as he does to all time, must be composed of his peers: it must be impanelled by Time from the selectest of the wise of many generations. A Poet is a nightingale, who sits in darkness and sings to cheer its own solitude with sweet sounds; his auditors are as men entranced by the melody of an unseen musician, who feel that they are moved and softened, yet know not whence or why. The poems of Homer and his contemporaries were the delight of infant Greece; they were the elements of that social system which is the column upon which all succeeding civilization has reposed. Homer embodied the ideal perfection of his age in human character; nor can we doubt that those who read his verses were awakened to an ambition of becoming like to Achilles, Hector and Ulysses: the truth and beauty of friendship, patriotism and persevering devotion to an object, were unveiled to the depths in these immortal creations: the sentiments of the auditors must have been refined and enlarged by a sympathy with such great and lovely impersonations, until from admiring they imitated, and from imitation they identified themselves with the objects of their admiration. Nor let it be objected, that these characters are remote from moral perfection, and that they can by no means be considered as edifying patterns for general imitation. Every epoch under names more or less specious has defied its peculiar errors; Revenge is the naked Idol of the worship of a semi-barbarous age; and Self-deceit is the veiled Image of unknown evil before which luxury and satiety lie prostrate. But a poet considers the vices of his contemporaries as the temporary dress in which his creations must be arrayed, and which cover without concealing the eternal proportions of their beauty. An epic or dramatic personage is understood to wear them around his soul, as he may the antient armour or the modern uniform around his body; whilst it is easy to conceive a dress more graceful than either. The beauty of the internal nature cannot be so far concealed by its accidental vesture, but that the spirit of its form shall communicate itself to the very disguise, and indicate the shape it hides from the manner in which it is worn. A majestic form and graceful motions will express themselves through the most barbarous and tasteless costume. Few poets of the highest class have chosen to exhibit the beauty of their conceptions in its naked truth and splendour; and it is doubtful whether the alloy of costume, habit, etc., be not necessary to temper this planetary music for mortal ears.

The whole objection however of the immorality of poetry rests upon a misconception of the manner in which poetry acts to produce the moral improvement of man. Ethical science arranges the elements which poetry has created, and propounds schemes and proposes examples of civil and domestic life: nor is it for want of admirable doctrines that men hate, and despise, and censure, and deceive, and subjugate one another. But Poetry acts in another and diviner manner. It awakens and enlarges the mind itself by rendering it the receptable of a thousand unapprehended combinations of thought. Poetry lifts the veil from the hidden beauty of the world, and makes familiar objects be as if they were not familiar; it reproduces all that it represents, and the impersonations clothed in its Elysian light stand thenceforward in the minds of those who have once contemplated them, as memorials of that gentle and exalted content which extends itself over all thoughts and actions with which it coexists. The great secret of morals is Love; or a going out of our own nature, and an identification of ourselves with the beautiful which exists in thought, action, or person, not our own. A man, to be greatly good, must imagine intensely and comprehensively; he must put himself in the place of another and of many others; the pains and pleasures of his species must become his own. The great instrument of moral good is the imagination; and poetry administers to the effect by acting upon the cause. Poetry enlarges the circumference of the imagination by replenishing it with thoughts of ever new delight, which have the power of attracting and assimilating of their own nature all other thoughts, and which form new intervals and interstices whose void for ever craves fresh food. Poetry strengthens that faculty which is the organ of the moral nature of man, in the same manner as exercise strengthens a limb. A Poet therefore would do ill to embody his own conceptions of right and wrong, which are usually those of his place and time, in his poetical creations, which participate in neither. By this assumption of the inferior office of interpreting the effect, in which perhaps after all he might acquit himself but imperfectly, he would resign the glory in a participation in the cause. There was little danger that Homer, or any of the eternal poets, should have so far misunderstood themselves as to have abdicated this throne of their widest dominion. Those in whom the poetical faculty, though great, is less intense, as Euripides, Lucan, Tasso, Spenser, have frequently affected a moral aim, and the effect of their poetry is diminished in exact proportion to the degree in which they compel us to advert to this purpose.

Homer and the cyclic poets were followed at a certain interval by the dramatic and lyrical Poets of Athens, who flourished contemporaneously with all that is most perfect in the kindred expressions of the poetical faculty; architecture, painting, music, the dance, sculpture, philosophy, and we may add the forms of civil life. For although the scheme of Athenian society was deformed by many imperfections which the poetry existing in Chivalry and Christianity have erased from the habits and institutions of modern Europe; yet never at any other period has so much energy, beauty, and virtue, been developed; never was blind strength and stubborn form so disciplined and rendered subject to the will of man, or that will less repugnant to the dictates of the beautiful and the true, as during the century which preceded the death of Socrates. Of no other epoch in the history of our species have we records and fragments stamped so visibly with the image of the divinity in man. But it is Poetry alone, in form, in action, or in language, which has rendered this epoch memorable above all others, and the storehouse of examples to everlasting time. For written poetry existed at that epoch simultaneously with the other arts, and it is an idle enquiry to demand which gave and which received the light, which all as from a common focus have scattered over the darkest periods of succeeding time. We know no more of cause and effect than a constant conjunction of events: Poetry is ever found to coexist with whatever other arts contribute to the happiness and perfection of man. I appeal to what has already been established to distinguish between the cause and the effect.

It was at the period here adverted to, that the Drama had its birth; and however a succeeding writer may have equalled or surpassed those few great specimens of the Athenian drama which have been preserved to us, it is indisputable that the art itself never was understood or practised according to the true philosophy of it, as at Athens. For the Athenians employed language, action, music, painting, the dance, and religious institutions, to produce a common effect in the representation of the highest idealisms of passion and of power; each division in the art was made perfect in its kind by artists of the most consummate skill, and was disciplined into a beautiful proportion and unity one towards another. On the modern stage a few only of the elements capable of expressing the image of the poet's conception are employed at once. We have tragedy without music and dancing; and music and dancing without the highest impersonations of which they are the fit accompaniment, and both without religion and solemnity. Religious institution has indeed been usually banished from the stage. Our system of divesting the actor's face of a mask, on which the many expressions appropriated to his dramatic character might be moulded into one permanent and unchanging expression, is favourable only to a partial and inharmonious effect; it is fit for nothing but a monologue, where all the attention may be directed to some great master of ideal mimicry. The modern practice of blending comedy with tragedy, though liable to great abuse in point of practise, is undoubtedly an extension of the dramatic circle; but the comedy should be as in King Lear, universal, ideal, and sublime. It is perhaps the intervention of this principle which determines the balance in favour of King Lear against the Œdipus Tyrannus or the Agamemnon, or, if you will the trilogies with which they are connected;[6] unless the intense power of the choral poetry, especially that of the latter, should be considered as restoring the equilibrium. King Lear, if it can sustain this comparison, may be judged to be the most perfect specimen of the dramatic art existing in the world; in spite of the narrow conditions to which the poet was subjected by the ignorance of the philosophy of the Drama which has prevailed in modern Europe. Calderón in his religious Autos[7] has attempted to fulfil some of the high conditions of dramatic representation neglected by Shakespeare; such as the establishing a relation between the drama and religion, and the accommodating them to music and dancing; but he omits the observation of conditions still more important, and more is lost than gained by a substitution of the rigidly-defined and ever-repeated idealisms of a distorted superstition for the living impersonations of the truth of human passion.

But we digress. — The Author of the Four Ages of Poetry[8] has prudently omitted to dispute on the effect of the Drama upon life and manners. For, if I know the knight by the device of his shield, I have only to inscribe Philoctetes or Agamemnon or Othello[9] upon mine to put to flight the giant sophisms which have enchanted him, as the mirror of intolerable light, though on the arm of one of the weakest of the Paladins, could blind and scatter whole armies of necromancers and pagans. The connexion of scenic exhibitions with the improvement or corruption of the manners of men, has been universally recognized: in other words, the presence or absence of poetry in its most perfect and universal form has been found to be connected with good and evil in conduct and habit. The corruption which has

---

[6]The *Agamemnon* by Aeschylus is the first play of the *Oresteia* trilogy. Sophocles' *Oedipus Tyrannos* is not part of an extant trilogy, though he wrote plays connected with the Oedipus story twenty years earlier (*Antigone*) and twenty years later (*Oedipus at Colonus*). [Ed.]

[7]The *autos* of the Spanish dramatist Calderón (1600–1681) were short religious allegorical dramas. [Ed.]

[8]Shelley's friend, Thomas Love Peacock (1785–1866). [Ed.]

[9]Tragic protagonists of Sophocles, Aeschylus, and Shakespeare, respectively. [Ed.]

been imputed to the drama as an effect, begins, when the poetry employed in its constitution, ends: I appeal to the history of manners whether the periods of the growth of the one and the decline of the other have not corresponded with an exactness equal to any other example of moral cause and effect.

The drama at Athens, or wheresoever else it may have approached to its perfection, coexisted with the moral and intellectual greatness of the age. The tragedies of the Athenian poets are as mirrors in which the spectator beholds himself, under a thin disguise of circumstance, stript of all but that ideal perfection and energy which every one feels to be the internal type of all that he loves, admires, and would become. The imagination is enlarged by a sympathy with pains and passions so mighty, that they distend in their conception the capacity of that by which they are conceived; the good affections are strengthened by pity, indignation, terror and sorrow; and an exalted calm is prolonged from the satiety of this high exercise of them into the tumult of familiar life; even crime is disarmed of half its horror and all its contagion by being represented as the fatal consequence of the unfathomable agencies of nature; error is thus divested of its wilfulness; men can no longer cherish it as the creation of their choice. In a drama of the highest order there is little food for censure or hatred; it teaches rather self-knowledge and self-respect. Neither the eye nor the mind can see itself, unless reflected upon that which it resembles. The drama, so long as it continues to express poetry, is as a prismatic and many-sided mirror, which collects the brightest rays of human nature and divides and reproduces them from the simplicity of these elementary forms, and touches them with majesty and beauty, and multiplies all that it reflects, and endows it with the power of propagating its like wherever it may fall.

But in periods of the decay of social life, the drama sympathizes with that decay. Tragedy becomes a cold imitation of the form of the great masterpieces of antiquity, divested of all harmonious accompaniment of the kindred arts; and often the very form misunderstood: or a weak attempt to teach certain doctrines, which the writer considers as moral truths; and which are usually no more than specious flatteries of some gross vice or weakness with which the author in common with his auditors are infected. Hence what has been called the classical and domestic drama. Addison's "Cato" is a specimen of the one; and would it were not superfluous to cite examples of the other! To such purposes Poetry cannot be made subservient. Poetry is a sword of lightning, ever unsheathed, which consumes the scabbard that would contain it. And thus we observe that all dramatic writings of this nature are unimaginative in a singular degree; they affect sentiment and passion: which, divested of imagination, are other names for caprice and appetite. The period in our own history of the grossest degradation of the drama is the reign of Charles II when all forms in which poetry had been accustomed to be expressed became hymns to the triumph of kingly power over liberty and virtue. Milton stood alone illuminating an age unworthy of him. At such periods the calculating principle pervades all the forms of dramatic exhibition, and poetry ceases to be expressed upon them. Comedy loses its ideal universality: wit succeeds to humour; we laugh from self-complacency and triumph instead of pleasure; malignity, sarcasm and contempt, succeed to sympathetic merriment; we hardly laugh, but we smile. Obscenity, which is ever blasphemy against the divine beauty in life, becomes, from the very veil which it assumes, more active if less disgusting: it is a monster for which the corruption of society for ever brings forth new food, which it devours in secret.

The drama being that form under which a greater number of modes of expression of poetry are susceptible of being combined than any other, the connexion of poetry and social good is more observable in the drama than in whatever other form: and it is indisputable that the highest perfection of human society has ever corresponded with the highest dramatic excellence; and that the corruption or the extinction of the drama in a nation where it has once flourished, is a mark of a corruption of manners, and an extinction of the energies which sustain the soul of social life. But, as Machiavelli says of political institutions, that life may be preserved and renewed, if men should arise capable of bringing back the drama to its principles. And this is true with respect to poetry in its most extended sense: all language, institution and form, require not only to be produced but to be sustained: the office and character of a poet participates in the divine nature as regards providence, no less than as regards creation.

Civil war, the spoils of Asia, and the fatal predominance first of the Macedonian, and then of the Roman arms were so many symbols of the extinction or suspension of the creative faculty in Greece. The bucolic writers, who found patronage under the lettered tyrants of Sicily and Egypt, were the latest representatives of its most glorious reign. Their poetry is intensely melodious; like the odour of the tuberose, it overcomes and sickens the spirit with excess of sweetness; whilst the poetry of the preceding age was as a meadow-gale of June which mingles the fragrance of all the flowers of the field, and adds a quickening and harmonizing spirit of its own which endows the sense with a power of sustaining its extreme delight. The bucolic and erotic delicacy in written poetry is correlative with that softness in statuary, music, and the kindred arts, and even in manners and institutions which distinguished the epoch to which we now refer. Nor is it the poetical faculty itself, or any misapplication of it, to which this want of harmony is to be imputed. An equal sensibility to the influence of the senses and the affections is to be found in the writings of Homer and Sophocles: the former especially has clothed sensual and pathetic images with irresistible attractions. Their superiority over these succeeding writers consists in the presence of those thoughts which belong to the inner faculties of our nature, not in the absence of those which are connected with the external; their incomparable perfection consists in an harmony of the union of all. It is not what the erotic writers have, but what they have not, in which their imperfection consists. It is not inasmuch as they were Poets, but inasmuch as they were not Poets, that they can be considered with any plausibility as connected with the corruption of their age. Had that corruption availed so as to extinguish in them the sensibility to pleasure, passion and natural scenery, which is imputed to them as an imperfection, the last triumph of evil would have been atchieved. For the end of social corruption is to destroy all sensibility to pleasure; and therefore it is corruption. It begins at the imagination and the intellect as at the core, and distributes itself thence as a paralyzing venom, through the affections into the very appetites, until all become a torpid mass in which sense hardly survives. At the approach of such a period, Poetry ever addresses itself to those faculties which are the last to be destroyed, and its voice is heard, like the footsteps of Astræa, departing from the world.[10] Poetry ever communicates all the pleasure which men are capable of receiving: it is ever still the light of life; the source of whatever of beautiful, or generous, or true can have place in an evil time. It will readily be confessed that those among the luxurious citizens of Syracuse and Alexandria who were delighted with the poems of Theocritus, were less cold, cruel and sensual than the remnant of their tribe. But corruption must have utterly destroyed the fabric of human society before Poetry can ever cease. The sacred links of that chain have never been entirely disjoined, which descending through the minds of many men is attached to those great minds, whence as from a magnet the invisible effluence is sent forth, which at once connects, animates and sustains the life of all. It is the faculty which contains within itself the seeds at once of its own and of social renovation. And let us not circumscribe the effects of the bucolic and erotic poetry within the limits of the sensibility of those to whom it was addressed. They may have perceived the beauty of those immortal compositions, simply as fragments and isolated portions: those who are more finely organized, or born in a happier age, may recognize them as episodes to that great poem, which all poets, like the co-operating thoughts of one great mind, have built up since the beginning of the world.

The same revolutions within a narrower sphere had place in antient Rome; but the actions and forms of its social life never seem to have been perfectly saturated with the poetical element. The Romans appear to have considered the

[10]Astraea was the goddess of justice who fled Earth for Heaven once the reign of Zeus began. [Ed.]

Greeks as the selectest treasuries of the selectest forms of manners and of nature, and to have abstained from creating in measured language, sculpture, music or architecture, anything which might bear a particular relation to their own condition, whilst it should bear a general one to the universal constitution of the world. But we judge from partial evidence; and we judge perhaps partially. Ennius, Varro, Pacuvius, and Accius, all great poets, have been lost. Lucretius is in the highest, and Virgil in a very high sense, a creator. The chosen delicacy of the expressions of the latter is as a mist of light which conceals from us the intense and exceeding truth of his conceptions of nature. Livy is instinct with poetry. Yet Horace, Catullus, Ovid, and generally the other great writers of the Virgilian age, saw man and nature in the mirror of Greece. The institutions also and the religion of Rome were less poetical than those of Greece, as the shadow is less vivid than the substance. Hence poetry in Rome, seemed to follow rather than accompany the perfection of political and domestic society. The true Poetry of Rome lived in its institutions; for whatever of beautiful, true and majestic they contained could have sprung only from the faculty which creates the order in which they consist. The life of Camillus, the death of Regulus; the expectation of the Senators, in their godlike state, of the victorious Gauls; the refusal of the Republic to make peace with Hannibal after the battle of Cannae, were not the consequences of a refined calculation of the probable personal advantage to result from such a rhythm and order in the shews of life, to those who were at once the poets and the actors of these immortal dramas. The imagination beholding the beauty of this order, created it out of itself according to its own idea: the consequence was empire, and the reward ever-living fame. These things are not the less poetry, *quia carent vate sacro*.[11] They are the episodes of the cyclic poem written by Time upon the memories of men. The Past, like an inspired rhapsodist, fills the theatre of everlasting generations with their harmony.

At length the antient system of religion and manners had fulfilled the circle of its revolution. And the world would have fallen into utter anarchy and darkness, but that there were found poets among the authors of the Christian and Chivalric systems of manners and religion, who created forms of opinion and action never before conceived; which, copied into the imaginations of men, became as generals to the bewildered armies of their thoughts. It is foreign to the present purpose to touch upon the evil produced by these systems: except that we protest, on the ground of the principles already established, that no portion of it can be imputed to the poetry they contain.

It is probable that the astonishing poetry of Moses, Job, David, Solomon and Isaiah had produced a great effect upon the mind of Jesus and his disciples. The scattered fragments preserved to us by the biographers of this extraordinary person, are all instinct with the most vivid poetry. But his doctrines seem to have been quickly distorted. At a certain period after the prevalence of a system of opinions founded upon those promulgated by him, the three forms into which Plato had distributed the faculties of mind underwent a sort of apotheosis, and became the object of the worship of the civilized world. Here it is to be confessed that "Light seems to thicken," and

> The crow makes wing to the rooky wood,
> Good things of day begin to droop and drowze,
> And night's black agents to their preys do rouze.[12]

But mark how beautiful an order has sprung from the dust and blood of this fierce chaos! how the World, as from a resurrection, balancing itself on the golden wings of knowledge and of hope, has reassumed its yet unwearied flight into the Heaven of time. Listen to the music, unheard by outward ears, which is as a ceaseless and invisible wind, nourishing its everlasting course with strength and swiftness.

The poetry in the doctrines of Jesus Christ, and the mythology and institutions of the Celtic[13]

---

[11]"Because they lack a sacred prophet/poet." Horace, *Odes* IV.9:28. [Ed.]

[12]Shakespeare, *Macbeth*, III.ii.50–53. [Ed.]
[13]Shelley uses "Celtic" to refer to Germanic tribes (like those Caesar fought), not the aboriginal inhabitants of the British Isles. [Ed.]

conquerors of the Roman empire, outlived the darkness and the convulsions connected with their growth and victory, and blended themselves into a new fabric of manners and opinion. It is an error to impute the ignorance of the dark ages to the Christian doctrines or the predominance of the Celtic nations. Whatever of evil their agencies may have contained sprung from the extinction of the poetical principle, connected with the progress of despotism and superstition. Men, from causes too intricate to be here discussed, had become insensible and selfish: their own will had become feeble, and yet they were its slaves, and thence the slaves of the will of others: lust, fear, avarice, cruelty and fraud, characterised a race amongst whom no one was to be found capable of *creating* in form, language, or institution. The moral anomalies of such a state of society are not justly to be charged upon any class of events immediately connected with them, and those events are most entitled to our approbation which could dissolve it most expeditiously. It is unfortunate for those who cannot distinguish words from thoughts, that many of these anomalies have been incorporated into our popular religion.

It was not until the eleventh century that the effects of the poetry of the Christian and Chivalric systems began to manifest themselves. The principle of equality had been discovered and applied by Plato in his Republic, as the theoretical rule of the mode in which the materials of pleasure and of power produced by the common skill and labour of human beings ought to be distributed among them. The limitations of this rule were asserted by him to be determined only by the sensibility of each, or the utility to result to all. Plato, following the doctrines of Timæus and Pythagoras, taught also a moral and intellectual system of doctrine comprehending at once the past, the present, and the future condition of man. Jesus Christ divulged the sacred and eternal truths contained in these views to mankind, and Christianity, in its abstract purity, became the exoteric expression of the esoteric doctrines of the poetry and wisdom of antiquity. The incorporation of the Celtic nations with the exhausted population of the South, impressed upon it the figure of the poetry existing in their mythology

and institutions. The result was a sum of the action and reaction of all the causes included in it; for it may be assumed as a maxim that no nation or religion can supersede any other without incorporating into itself a portion of that which it supersedes. The abolition of personal and domestic slavery, and the emancipation of women from a great part of the degrading restraints of antiquity were among the consequences of these events.

The abolition of personal slavery is the basis of the highest political hope that it can enter into the mind of man to conceive. The freedom of women produced the poetry of sexual love. Love became a religion, the idols of whose worship were ever present. It was as if the statues of Apollo and the Muses had been endowed with life and motion and had walked forth among their worshippers; so that earth became peopled by the inhabitants of a diviner world. The familiar appearance and proceedings of life became wonderful and heavenly; and a paradise was created as out of the wrecks of Eden. And as this creation itself is poetry, so its creators were poets; and language was the instrument of their art: "Galeotto fù il libro, e chi lo scrisse."[14] The Provençal Trouveurs, or inventors, preceded Petrarch, whose verses are as spells, which unseal the inmost enchanted fountains of the delight which is in the grief of Love. It is impossible to feel them without becoming a portion of that beauty which we contemplate: it were superfluous to explain how the gentleness and the elevation of mind connected with these sacred emotions can render men more amiable, more generous, and wise, and lift them out of the dull vapours of the little world of self. Dante understood the secret things of love even more than Petrarch. His *Vita Nuova* is an inexhaustible fountain of purity of sentiment and language: it is the idealized history of that period, and those intervals of his life

---

[14]"That book was a Galeotto [legend of Sir Galahad], and so was he that wrote it." Dante, *Inferno* 5:137. The quotation is spoken by Francesca di Rimini, an adulterous wife Dante meets in Hell, who recounts how her affair with Paolo Malatesta began over a book of chivalric romance. Galahad introduced his uncle Lancelot to Queen Guinevere and so began their adulterous liaison; hence "Galeotto" in Italian can mean a go-between. [Ed.]

which were dedicated to love. His apotheosis of Beatrice in Paradise and the gradations of his own love and her loveliness, by which as by steps he feigns himself to have ascended to the throne of the Supreme Cause, is the most glorious imagination of modern poetry. The acutest critics have justly reversed the judgement of the vulgar, and the order of the great acts of the "Divine Drama," in the measure of the admiration which they accord to the Hell, Purgatory and Paradise. The latter is a perpetual hymn of everlasting love. Love, which found a worthy poet in Plato alone of all the antients, has been celebrated by a chorus of the greatest writers of the renovated world; and the music has penetrated the caverns of society, and its echoes still drown the dissonance of arms and superstition. At successive intervals, Ariosto, Tasso, Shakespeare, Spenser, Calderón, Rousseau, and the great writers of our own age, have celebrated the dominion of love, planting as it were trophies in the human mind of that sublimest victory over sensuality and force. The true relation borne to each other by the sexes into which human kind is distributed has become less misunderstood; and if the error which confounded diversity with inequality of the powers of the two sexes has become partially recognized in the opinions and institutions of modern Europe, we owe this great benefit to the worship of which Chivalry was the law, and poets the prophets.

The poetry of Dante may be considered as the bridge thrown over the stream of time, which unites the modern and antient world. The distorted notions of invisible things which Dante and his rival Milton have idealized, are merely the mask and the mantle in which these great poets walk through eternity enveloped and disguised. It is a difficult question to determine how far they were conscious of the distinction which must have subsisted in their minds between their own creeds and that of the people. Dante at least appears to wish to mark the full extent of it by placing Riphæus, whom Virgil calls *justissimus unus,* in Paradise[15] and observing a most heretical caprice in his distribution of rewards and punishments. And Milton's poem contains within itself a philosophical refutation of that system of which, by a strange and natural antithesis, it has been a chief popular support. Nothing can exceed the energy and magnificence of the character of Satan as expressed in Paradise Lost. It is a mistake to suppose that he could ever have been intended for the popular personification of evil. Implacable hate, patient cunning, and a sleepless refinement of device to inflict the extremest anguish on an enemy, these things are evil; and although venial in a slave are not to be forgiven in a tyrant; although redeemed by much that ennobles his defeat in one subdued, are marked by all that dishonours his conquest in the victor. Milton's Devil as a moral being is as far superior to his God as one who perseveres in some purpose which he has conceived to be excellent in spite of adversity and torture, is to one who in the cold security of undoubted triumph inflicts the most horrible revenge upon his enemy, not from any mistaken notion of inducing him to repent of a perseverance in enmity, but with the alleged design of exasperating him to deserve new torments. Milton has so far violated the popular creed (if this shall be judged to be a violation) as to have alleged no superiority of moral virtue to his God over his Devil. And this bold neglect of a direct moral purpose is the most decisive proof of the supremacy of Milton's genius. He mingled as it were the elements of human nature, as colours upon a single pallet, and arranged them into the composition of his great picture according to the laws of epic truth; that is, according to the laws of that principle by which a series of actions of the external universe and of intelligent and ethical beings is calculated to excite the sympathy of succeeding generations of mankind. The Divina Commedia and Paradise Lost have conferred upon modern mythology a systematic form; and when change and time shall have added one more superstition to the mass of those which have arisen and decayed upon the earth, commentators will be learnedly employed in elucidating the religion of ancestral Europe, only not utterly forgotten because it will have been stamped with the eternity of genius.

Homer was the first, and Dante the second

---

[15]"The one who is most just." Virgil, *Aeneid* 2:426. Dante finds him, to his surprise (since he was a pagan), in Paradise (*Paradiso* 20:67–69). [Ed.]

epic poet: that is, the second poet the series of whose creations bore a defined and intelligible relation to the knowledge, and sentiment, and religion, and political conditions of the age in which he lived, and of the ages which followed it, developing itself in correspondence with their developement. For Lucretius had limed the wings of his swift spirit in the dregs of the sensible world; and Virgil, with a modesty which ill became his genius, had affected the fame of an imitator even whilst he created anew all that he copied; and none among the flock of mock-birds, though their notes were sweet, Apollonius Rhodius, Quintus Calaber Smyrnaeus, Nonnus, Lucan, Statius, or Claudian, have sought even to fulfil a single condition of epic truth. Milton was the third Epic Poet. For if the title of epic in its highest sense be refused to the Æneid, still less can it be conceded to the Orlando Furioso, the Gerusalemme Liberata, the Lusiad, or the Fairy Queen.

Dante and Milton were both deeply penetrated with the antient religion of the civilized world; and its spirit exists in their poetry probably in the same proportion as its forms survived in the unreformed worship of modern Europe. The one preceded and the other followed the Reformation at almost equal intervals. Dante was the first religious reformer, and Luther surpassed him rather in the rudeness and acrimony, than in the boldness of his censures of papal usurpation. Dante was the first awakener of entranced Europe; he created a language in itself music and persuasion out of a chaos of inharmonious barbarisms. He was the congregator of those great spirits who presided over the resurrection of learning; the Lucifer[16] of that starry flock which in the thirteenth century shone forth from republican Italy, as from a heaven, into the darkness of the benighted world. His very words are instinct with spirit; each is as a spark, a burning atom of inextinguishable thought; and many yet lie covered in the ashes of their birth, and pregnant with a lightning which has yet found no conductor. All high poetry is infinite; it is as the first acorn, which contained all oaks potentially.

[16]Shelley intends here the literal sense of "bearer of light." [Ed.]

Veil after veil may be undrawn, and the inmost naked beauty of the meaning never exposed. A great Poem is a fountain for ever overflowing with the waters of wisdom and delight; and after one person and one age has exhausted all its divine effluence which their peculiar relations enable them to share, another and yet another succeeds, and new relations are ever developed, the source of an unforeseen and an unconceived delight.

The age immediately succeeding to that of Dante, Petrarch, and Boccaccio, was characterized by a revival of painting, sculpture, music, and architecture. Chaucer caught the sacred inspiration, and the superstructure of English literature is based upon the materials of Italian invention.

But let us not be betrayed from a defence into a critical history of Poetry and its influence on Society. Be it enough to have pointed out the effects of poets, in the large and true sense of the word, upon their own and all succeeding times and to revert to the partial instances cited as illustrations of an opinion the reverse of that attempted to be established in the Four Ages of Poetry.

But poets have been challenged to resign the civic crown to reasoners and mechanists on another plea. It is admitted that the exercise of the imagination is most delightful, but it is alleged that that of reason is more useful. Let us examine as the grounds of this distinction, what is here meant by Utility. Pleasure or good in a general sense, is that which the consciousness of a sensitive and intelligent being seeks, and in which when found it acquiesces. There are two kinds of pleasure, one durable, universal, and permanent; the other transitory and particular. Utility may either express the means of producing the former or the latter. In the former sense, whatever strengthens and purifies the affections, enlarges the imagination, and adds spirit to sense, is useful. But the meaning in which the Author of the Four Ages of Poetry seems to have employed the word utility is the narrower one of banishing the importunity of the wants of our animal nature, the surrounding men with security of life, the dispersing the grosser delusions of superstition, and the conciliating such a degree of mutual forbearance among men as may consist with the motives of personal advantage.

Undoubtedly the promoters of utility in this limited sense, have their appointed office in society. They follow the footsteps of poets, and copy the sketches of their creations into the book of common life. They make space, and give time. Their exertions are of the highest value so long as they confine their administration of the concerns of the inferior powers of our nature within the limits due to the superior ones. But whilst the sceptic destroys gross superstitions, let him spare to deface, as some of the French writers have defaced, the eternal truths charactered upon the imaginations of men. Whilst the mechanist abridges, and the political œconomist combines, labour, let them beware that their speculations, for want of correspondence with those first principles which belong to the imagination, do not tend, as they have in modern England, to exasperate at once the extremes of luxury and want. They have exemplified the saying, "To him that hath, more shall be given; and from him that hath not, the little that he hath shall be taken away."[17] The rich have become richer, and the poor have become poorer; and the vessel of the state is driven between the Scylla and Charybdis of anarchy and despotism. Such are the effects which must ever flow from an unmitigated exercise of the calculating faculty.

It is difficult to define pleasure in its highest sense; the definition involving a number of apparent paradoxes. For, from an inexplicable defect of harmony in the constitution of human nature, the pain of the inferior is frequently connected with the pleasures of the superior portions of our being. Sorrow, terror, anguish, despair itself are often the chosen expressions of an approximation to the highest good. Our sympathy in tragic fiction depends on this principle; tragedy delights by affording a shadow of the pleasure which exists in pain. This is the source also of the melancholy which is inseparable from the sweetest melody. The pleasure that is in sorrow is sweeter than the pleasure of pleasure itself. And hence the saying, "It is better to go to the house of mourning, than to the house of mirth."[18] Not that this highest species of pleasure is necessarily linked with pain. The delight of love and friendship, the extacy of the admiration of nature, the joy of the perception and still more of the creation of poetry is often wholly unalloyed.

The production and assurance of pleasure in this highest sense is true utility. Those who produce and preserve this pleasure are Poets or poetical philosophers.

The exertions of Locke, Hume, Gibbon, Voltaire, Rousseau,[19] and their disciples, in favour of oppressed and deluded humanity, are entitled to the gratitude of mankind. Yet it is easy to calculate the degree of moral and intellectual improvement which the world would have exhibited, had they never lived. A little more nonsense would have been talked for a century or two; and perhaps a few more men, women, and children, burnt as heretics. We might not at this moment have been congratulating each other on the abolition of the Inquisition in Spain. But it exceeds all imagination to conceive what would have been the moral condition of the world if neither Dante, Petrarch, Boccaccio, Chaucer, Shakespeare, Calderón, Lord Bacon, nor Milton, had ever existed; if Raphael and Michael Angelo had never been born; if the Hebrew poetry had never been translated; if a revival of the study of Greek literature had never taken place; if no monuments of antient sculpture had been handed down to us; and if the poetry of the religion of the antient world had been extinguished together with its belief. The human mind could never, except by the intervention of these excitements, have been awakened to the invention of the grosser sciences, and that application of analytical reasoning to the aberrations of society, which it is now attempted to exalt over the direct expression of the inventive and creative faculty itself.

We have more moral, political and historical wisdom, than we know how to reduce into practise; we have more scientific and œconomical knowledge than can be accommodated to the just

[17]Matthew 25:29. [Ed.]

[18]Ecclesiastes 7:2. [Ed.]

[19]I follow the classification adopted by the author of the Four Ages of Poetry. But Rousseau was essentially a poet. The others, even Voltaire, were mere reasoners. [Au.]

distribution of the produce which it multiplies. The poetry in these systems of thought, is concealed by the accumulation of facts and calculating processes. There is no want of knowledge respecting what is wisest and best in morals, government, and political œconomy, or at least, what is wiser and better than what men now practise and endure. But we let "*I dare not* wait upon *I would,* like the poor cat i' the adage."[20] We want the creative faculty to imagine that which we know; we want the generous impulse to act that which we imagine; we want the poetry of life: our calculations have outrun conception; we have eaten more than we can digest. The cultivation of those sciences which have enlarged the limits of the empire of man over the external world, has, for want of the poetical faculty, proportionally circumscribed those of the internal world; and man, having enslaved the elements, remains himself a slave. To what but a cultivation of the mechanical arts in a degree disproportioned to the presence of the creative faculty, which is the basis of all knowledge, is to be attributed the abuse of all invention for abridging and combining labour, to the exasperation of the inequality of mankind? From what other cause has it arisen that the discoveries which should have lightened, have added a weight to the curse imposed on Adam? Poetry, and the principle of Self, of which money is the visible incarnation, are the God and the Mammon of the world.

The functions of the poetical faculty are twofold; by one it creates new materials of knowledge, and power and pleasure; by the other it engenders in the mind a desire to reproduce and arrange them according to a certain rhythm and order which may be called the beautiful and the good. The cultivation of poetry is never more to be desired than at periods when, from an excess of the selfish and calculating principle, the accumulation of the materials of external life exceed the quantity of the power of assimilating them to the internal laws of human nature. The body has then become too unwieldy for that which animates it.

Poetry is indeed something divine. It is at once the centre and circumference of knowledge; it is that which comprehends all science, and that to which all science must be referred. It is at the same time the root and blossom of all other systems of thought: it is that from which all spring, and that which adorns all; and that which, if blighted, denies the fruit and the seed, and withholds from the barren world the nourishment and the succession of the scions of the tree of life. It is the perfect and consummate surface and bloom of things; it is as the odour and the colour of the rose to the texture of the elements which compose it, as the form and the splendour of unfaded beauty to the secrets of anatomy and corruption. What were Virtue, Love, Patriotism, Friendship &c. — what were the scenery of this beautiful Universe which we inhabit — what were our consolations on this side of the grave — and what were our aspirations beyond it — if Poetry did not ascend to bring light and fire from those eternal regions where the owl-winged faculty of calculation dare not ever soar? Poetry is not like reasoning, a power to be exerted according to the determination of the will. A man cannot say, "I will compose poetry." The greatest poet even cannot say it: for the mind in creation is as a fading coal which some invisible influence, like an inconstant wind, awakens to transitory brightness: this power arises from within, like the colour of a flower which fades and changes as it is developed, and the conscious portions of our natures are unprophetic either of its approach or its departure. Could this influence be durable in its original purity and force, it is impossible to predict the greatness of the results: but when composition begins, inspiration is already on the decline, and the most glorious poetry that has ever been communicated to the world is probably a feeble shadow of the original conception of the poet. I appeal to the greatest Poets of the present day, whether it be not an error to assert that the finest passages of poetry are produced by labour and study. The toil and the delay recommended by critics can be justly interpreted to mean no more than a careful observation of the inspired moments, and an artificial connexion of the spaces between their suggestions by the intertexture of conventional expressions; a necessity only imposed by a limitedness of the poetical faculty

[20]Shakespeare, *Macbeth,* I.vii:44–45. [Ed.]

itself. For Milton conceived the Paradise Lost as a whole before he executed it in portions. We have his own authority also for the Muse having "dictated" to him the "unpremeditated song,"[21] and let this be an answer to those who would allege the fifty-six various readings of the first line of the Orlando Furioso. Compositions so produced are to poetry what mosaic is to painting. This instinct and intuition of the poetical faculty is still more observable in the plastic and pictorial arts: a great statue or picture grows under the power of the artist as a child in the mother's womb, and the very mind which directs the hands in formation is incapable of accounting to itself for the origin, the gradations, or the media of the process.

Poetry is the record of the best and happiest moments of the happiest and best minds. We are aware of evanescent visitations of thought and feeling sometimes associated with place or person, sometimes regarding our own mind alone, and always arising unforeseen and departing unbidden, but elevating and delightful beyond all expression: so that even in the desire and the regret they leave, there cannot but be pleasure, participating as it does in the nature of its object. It is as it were the interpenetration of a diviner nature through our own; but its footsteps are like those of a wind over a sea, which the coming calm erases, and whose traces remain only as on the wrinkled sand which paves it. These and corresponding conditions of being are experienced principally by those of the most delicate sensibility and the most enlarged imagination; and the state of mind produced by them is at war with every base desire. The enthusiasm of virtue, love, patriotism, and friendship is essentially linked with these emotions; and whilst they last, self appears as what it is, an atom to a Universe. Poets are not only subject to these experiences as spirits of the most refined organization, but they can colour all that they combine with the evanescent hues of this etherial world; a word, a trait in the representation of a scene or a passion, will touch the enchanted chord, and reanimate, in those who have ever experienced these emo-

tions, the sleeping, the cold, the buried image of the past. Poetry thus makes immortal all that is best and most beautiful in the world; it arrests the vanishing apparitions which haunt the interlunations of life, and veiling them or in language or in form sends them forth among mankind, bearing sweet news of kindred joy to those with whom their sisters abide — abide, because there is no portal of expression from the caverns of the spirit which they inhabit into the universe of things. Poetry redeems from decay the visitations of the divinity in man.

Poetry turns all things to loveliness; it exalts the beauty of that which is most beautiful, and it adds beauty to that which is most deformed: it marries exultation and horror, grief and pleasure, eternity and change; it subdues to union under its light yoke all irreconcilable things. It transmutes all that it touches, and every form moving within the radiance of its presence is changed by wondrous sympathy to an incarnation of the spirit which it breathes; its secret alchemy turns to potable gold the poisonous waters which flow from death through life; it strips the veil of familiarity from the world, and lays bare the naked and sleeping beauty which is the spirit of its forms.

All things exist as they are perceived: at least in relation to the percipient. "The mind is its own place, and of itself can make a heaven of hell, a hell of heaven."[22] But poetry defeats the curse which binds us to be subjected to the accident of surrounding impressions. And whether it spreads its own figured curtain or withdraws life's dark veil from before the scene of things, it equally creates for us a being within our being. It makes us the inhabitants of a world to which the familiar world is a chaos. It reproduces the common universe of which we are portions and percipients, and it purges from our inward sight the film of familiarity which obscures from us the wonder of our being. It compels us to feel that which we perceive, and to imagine that which we know. It creates anew the universe after it has been annihilated in our minds by the recurrence of impressions blunted by reiteration. It justifies that

[21]Milton, *Paradise Lost*, 9:21–24. [Ed.]

[22]Milton, *Paradise Lost*, 1:254–55. [Ed.]

bold and true word of Tasso — *Non merita nome di creatore, se non Iddio ed il Poeta.*[23]

A Poet, as he is the author to others of the highest wisdom, pleasure, virtue and glory, so he ought personally to be the happiest, the best, the wisest, and the most illustrious of men. As to his glory, let Time be challenged to declare whether the fame of any other institutor of human life be comparable to that of a poet. That he is the wisest, the happiest, and the best, inasmuch as he is a poet, is equally incontrovertible: the greatest poets have been men of the most spotless virtue, of the most consummate prudence, and, if we could look into the interior of their lives, the most fortunate of men: and the exceptions, as they regard those who possessed the poetic faculty in a high yet inferior degree, will be found on consideration to confirm rather than destroy the rule. Let us for a moment stoop to the arbitration of popular breath, and usurping and uniting in our own persons the incompatible characters of accuser, witness, judge and executioner, let us decide without trial, testimony, or form, that certain motives of those who are "there sitting where we dare not soar"[24] are reprehensible. Let us assume that Homer was a drunkard, that Virgil was a flatterer, that Horace was a coward, that Tasso was a madman, that Lord Bacon was a peculator, that Raphael was a libertine, that Spenser was a poet laureate.[25] It is inconsistent with this division of our subject to cite living poets, but Posterity has done ample justice to the great names now referred to. Their errors have been weighed and found to have been dust in the balance: if their sins "were as scarlet, they are now white as snow"; they have been washed in the blood of the mediator and the redeemer Time. Observe in what a ludicrous chaos the imputations of real or fictitious crime have been confused in the contemporary calumnies against poetry and poets; consider how little

is, as it appears — or appears, as it is; look to your own motives, and judge not, lest ye be judged.

Poetry, as has been said, in this respect differs from logic, that it is not subject to the controul of the active powers of the mind, and that its birth and recurrence has no necessary connexion with consciousness or will. It is presumptuous to determine that these are the necessary conditions of all mental causation, when mental effects are experienced insusceptible of being referred to them. The frequent recurrence of the poetical power, it is obvious to suppose, may produce in the mind an habit of order and harmony correlative with its own nature and with its effects upon other minds. But in the intervals of inspiration, and they may be frequent without being durable, a poet becomes a man, and is abandoned to the sudden reflux of the influences under which others habitually live. But as he is more delicately organized than other men, and sensible to pain and pleasure, both his own and that of others, in a degree unknown to them, he will avoid the one and pursue the other with an ardour proportioned to this difference. And he renders himself obnoxious to calumny, when he neglects to observe the circumstances under which these objects of universal pursuit and flight have disguised themselves in one another's garments.

But there is nothing necessarily evil in this error, and thus cruelty, envy, revenge, avarice, and the passions purely evil, have never formed any portion of the popular imputations on the lives of poets.

I have thought it most favourable to the cause of truth to set down these remarks according to the order in which they were suggested to my mind by a consideration of the subject itself, instead of following that of the treatise that excited me to make them public. Thus although devoid of the formality of a polemical reply; if the view they contain be just, they will be found to involve a refutation of the Four Ages of Poetry, so far at least as regards the first division of the subject. I can readily conjecture what should have moved the gall of the learned and intelligent author of that paper; I confess myself like him unwilling to be stunned by the Theseids of the hoarse Codri of the day. Bavius and

[23]"Nobody merits the title of Creator save God and the Poet." The line is quoted thus in Serassi's *Life of Torquato Tasso*. [Ed.]

[24]Milton, *Paradise Lost,* 4:829. [Ed.]

[25]Poet laureate may seem an odd member of this sequence, unless we remember that the current laureate was Robert Southey, a personal and political enemy of Shelley's. [Ed.]

Mævius undoubtedly are, as they ever were, insufferable persons.[26] But it belongs to a philosophical critic to distinguish rather than confound.

The first part of these remarks has related to Poetry in its elements and principles; and it has been shewn, as well as the narrow limits assigned them would permit, that what is called poetry, in a restricted sense, has a common source with all other forms of order and of beauty according to which the materials of human life are susceptible of being arranged, and which is poetry in an universal sense.

The second part will have for its object an application of these principles to the present state of the cultivation of Poetry, and a defence of the attempt to idealize the modern forms of manners and opinion, and compel them into a subordination to the imaginative and creative faculty.[27] For the literature of England, an energetic developement of which has ever preceded or accompanied a great and free developement of the national will, has arisen as it were from a new birth. In spite of the low-thoughted envy which would undervalue contemporary merit, our own will be a memorable age in intellectual achievements, and we live among such philosophers and poets as surpass beyond comparison any who have appeared since the last national struggle for civil and religious liberty. The most unfailing herald, companion, and follower of the awakening of a great people to work a beneficial change in opinion or institution, is Poetry. At such periods there is an accumulation of the power of communicating and receiving intense and impassioned conceptions respecting man and nature. The persons in whom this power resides, may often, as far as regards many portions of their nature, have little apparent correspondence with that spirit of good of which they are the ministers. But even whilst they deny and abjure, they are yet compelled to serve, the Power which is seated upon the throne of their own soul. It is impossible to read the compositions of the most celebrated writers of the present day without being startled with the electric life which burns within their words. They measure the circumference and sound the depths of human nature with a comprehensive and all-penetrating spirit, and they are themselves perhaps the most sincerely astonished at its manifestations, for it is less their spirit than the spirit of the age. Poets are the hierophants of an unapprehended inspiration, the mirrors of the gigantic shadows which futurity casts upon the present, the words which express what they understand not; the trumpets which sing to battle, and feel not what they inspire: the influence which is moved not, but moves. Poets are the unacknowledged legislators of the World.

[26]Codrus, Bavius, and Maevius are traditional examples of bad poets cited by Juvenal, Horace, and Virgil. [Ed.]

[27]The "second part" was never written. [Ed.]

# Georg Wilhelm Friedrich Hegel

1770–1831

The central philosopher of modern nationalism was born the son of a civil servant in Stuttgart. Hegel is not known to have been a remarkable child. As a boy he played cards, learned to take snuff, and made a vast, painstakingly arranged collection of clippings and extracts from sources as varied as the classics and local newspapers. Hegel studied theology at Tübingen University without having much interest in it or, for that matter, much commitment to the mystical content of Christianity. After taking his Ph.D., he wrote (in advance of the demythologizer David Friedrich Strauss) a biography of Jesus, which considers him not as the son of God but as a human professor of ethics and religion whose contribution was to restore to Judaism the classical harmony between God and Man. Two friends from Tübingen assisted Hegel's early career: The poet Friedrich Hölderlin helped him to good posts as a private tutor, and the philosopher Friedrich von Schelling got him a course of lectures at the university at Jena.

There, in the first years of the nineteenth century, he developed his central ideas about mind, art, and the state. These years were dominated by the epoch-making figure of Napoleon, who carved the map of Europe with his sword, and whom Hegel saw as one of the "world-historical individuals" — his term for people who embodied the spirit of an age, and whose greatness came from the confluence of their private wills with the ineluctible movement of history. When Napoleon took Jena in a great battle in 1806, Hegel's sympathies were with the emperor rather than with the German states, which he saw as desperately in need of the same political reform and consolidation, through blood and iron, that the Revolution and Napoleon had given France. His political ideas became the watchwords of the second German Reich, of Bismarck and the Hohenzollern emperors.

But the battle — and the decade of war — had made Jena an uncomfortable place for the philosopher. Despite the publication of his revolutionary *Phenomenology of Spirit* (1807), Hegel was nearly bankrupt. He edited a newspaper and then took a post in Nuremberg as rector of a secondary school, the Aegidien-Gymnasium. There, at forty-two, he married a local girl of nineteen, who bore him two sons and with whom he had a happy and affectionate relationship.

Hegel continued his work at Nuremberg and, on the publication of his *Logic* (1812–16), was offered three secure professorships. Hegel went first to Heidelberg, where he brought out his *Encyclopaedia of the Philosophical Sciences* (1817). The following year, he accepted the chair of philosophy in Berlin, where he published his essay on *Philosophy of Right* (1821) as a guide to the burgeoning Prussian state and where he taught for the rest of his life.

By the late 1820's, Hegel had become the founder of a school of philosophy with a host of disciples and imitators. He was decorated by the king of Prussia and made rector of his university. Then in 1831, at the height of his fame, he died suddenly during a cholera epidemic. His death expanded rather than erased his influence, however. Most of his major works were derived from his class lectures at Berlin, and many of them were compiled after his death from his notes and those of his students. These works were issued in nineteen volumes between 1832 and 1847; they include *The Philosophy of History, The Philosophy of Religion* and *Aesthetics*.

Hegel's philosophy in its broadest sense presents the metamorphoses of the Spirit of the World from the beginning of history, when Man differentiated himself from the rest of Nature, to modern times. *The Phenomenology of Spirit* describes this evolution of mind from its most primitive stage, mere consciousness of an outside world, through the intermediate stages of consciousness-of-self, reason, spirit, and religion, to the ultimate realm of Absolute Knowledge.

Like Plato, Hegel is a holistic thinker. His later treatises on various subjects, like his posthumous lectures on politics, religion, and art, did not constitute a departure from the philosophy of mind in *The Phenomenology*. Rather, they showed how the spiritual evolution described in *The Phenomenology* had worked itself out in different areas of human experience. In each area, Hegel regarded the primitive oriental mode as engaged with substance at the expense of spirit, the intermediate classic mode as characterized by a harmony between body and spirit, and the modern mode as the culminating triumph of spirit over substance.

In politics, for example, Hegel saw the spiritual metamorphosis as the historical development of freedom. Politics originated in the alienation of man from nature, which required taming by collective action. The first solution was the patriarchal family, where all power and right are invested in the father, and the father is free to kill his wife or children if they disobey him. In the oriental world, patriarchal power was collectivized in the despotism of the ruler, who was a father to his subjects. In the empires of China and Persia, only one man was free: the emperor. This patriarchal form of government gave way to the democracy and aristocracy of Greece and Rome, where a whole class of people could be free, but whose freedom was based on the subjugation of slaves and foreigners. In the postclassical age — what Hegel called the German World — he foresaw the day when all men could be free, not as patriarchs or oriental despots or slave-owning aristocrats, but as mutual participants in an orderly freedom under law as subjects of an enlightened monarch.

In terms of religion, Hegel saw the faiths of the Orient — of China and India — as spiritually coherent with their despotic politics. The ancestor worship of China is its most obvious and direct manifestation. The later Confucian notion that the emperor rules under the mandate of T'ien, or Heaven, is only a slight deviation, since it reifies the magical forces of nature as operating through that individual. The Indian religions, Hinduism and Buddhism, represent the opposite reaction. Religion is an escape, through fantasies of reincarnation and nirvana, from a despotism that, left intact on earth, is ignored as irrelevant or devalued as Maya (Illusion). Judaism too created a patriarchal God (like that of China) who was viewed as existing behind and transcending Nature (like the deities of India).

For Hegel the Greek religion was the next stage. Where the Orientals had portrayed spirit overwhelmed by substance, the Greeks found a balance between the two. Their gods were anthropomorphic and human in their spiritual nature as well as in their physical forms. Having humanized the gods that lurked behind natural phenomena, the Greeks were free to trust nature. This confidence allowed them to develop a politics of trust in themselves rather than one of subjection to a semidivine despot. Christianity, the religion of the modern world, tips the balance from substance toward spirit. It combines the patriarchal despot inherited from Judaism (God the Creator) with an anthropomorphic deity (Jesus); but it adds the Holy Spirit, who incarnates the divine in the spirit of each man and ends the divorce of man from nature.

Each of these historical transformations is mediated by Hegel's "transcendental dialectic" — a well-known feature of his reasoning usually summarized by the triad of thesis, antithesis, and synthesis. An aspect of life becomes a thesis when it is abstracted from the background of nature and made into an absolute. Each Absolute calls into being its Other, the antithesis, which it negates and which in turn negates it. At length the conflict is mediated by a higher transcendent being that can resolve the negations and contradictions. The Judaic god, for example, is absolutized as God the Creator. He is thus defined by, and in opposition to, his creation, nature, including man, and is therefore outside nature and time, inhuman and incomprehensible. At the same time, nature and man are defined as barren of the divine. Thesis and antithesis negate each other. The synthesis mediating and transcending these negations was provided in Christianity through God the Son, who is human and natural as well as divine. Hegel's dialectic was later adopted by Karl Marx, who used it to support a materialistic theory of economics and society rather than an idealist approach to the spiritual evolution of man.

Hegel's ideas on art must be seen in the context of both his dialectical method and his thinking on the histories of politics and religion, for in *The Phenomenology*, art is an aspect of religion (and vice versa) rather than a separate spiritual mode, and the collective expression of a society rather than of an individual voice. Although he was generally a follower of Kant's idealism, Hegel rejected Kant's aesthetic with its basis in natural beauty and its insistence on the purposelessness of the beautiful object. For Hegel, nature is beautiful only by analogy with art, and art is supremely useful to man, not as mere pleasure but for "its ability to represent in *sensuous form* the highest ideas, bringing them thus nearer to . . . the senses and to feeling." In the long run, perhaps in the last stage of human evolution toward absolute knowledge, art would be superseded by the more direct apprehension of ideas through philosophy. But far from being deceptive, as Plato thought, art serves to free "the true meaning of appearances from the show and deception of this bad and transient world."

If art is "the sensuous semblance of the Idea," then it has two distinct ways of evolving: in the history of its forms — the modes of substance the Idea inhabits — and through the history of the spirit itself. The latter gives Hegel his distinction between symbolic, classic, and romantic art. Each has its defects and virtues. Symbolic art (we should call it allegorical art) is typically the art of the oriental world, where substance is present in abundance but where the "spiritual idea has not yet found its adequate form." It can convey the sublime, as the pyramids do, although it has a spiritual quality that excludes the human, or it can merely degenerate into the grotesque. In classical art, as in Greek religion and politics, substance and spirit exist in full harmony in sculptures that express spiritual ideas "through the bodily form of man." But classic art, although perfect in its way, is limited to the contemplation of the merely human. Only romantic art can portray the greater spirituality of the divine. Here, though, the spirit outruns substance, giving the audience the sense of a meaning that extends beyond the power of matter to convey it.

In a second classification of artistic genres and forms, Hegel discusses the particular arts, categorizing them according to their relation to these movements of historical evolution. Architecture, the most massively physical of the arts, whose products dwarf the spectator, is clearly linked with the symbolic art of the oriental world while sculpture is obviously linked with the classic world. The romantic arts of the modern world are painting, music, and poetry, for they owe the least to substance and the most to spirit. Painting, like sculpture, is graphic, but a painting imposes a subjective point of view that sculpture — designed to be viewed in the round — cannot. And painting can represent whatever can be imagined — thoughts and feelings as well as plastic forms. Music is even more spiritual since it is insubstantial, but it still requires players and performance. Poetry alone is totally free of the requirements of substance.

Elsewhere, Hegel classifies poetic forms, viewing epic as the most objective and lyric as the most subjective of the poetic arts, and drama as the synthesis of the two. Like Aristotle, Hegel regarded tragedy as the highest of the arts, particularly because he felt that, at its best (as in Sophocles' *Antigone*), the tragic agon could be viewed not as a material struggle but as a battle for primacy between two ideas — an example of Hegel's own vision of spiritual evolution through the conflict of thesis and antithesis.

## Selected Bibliography

Bungay, Stephen. *Beauty and Truth: A Study of Hegel's Aesthetics*. Oxford and New York: Oxford University Press, 1984.

Horn, András. *Kunst und Freiheit: Eine kritische Interpretation der Hegelische Asthetik*. The Hague: Martinus Nijhoff, 1969.

Kaminsky, Jack. *Hegel on Art: An Interpretation of Hegel's Aesthetics*. Albany: State University of New York Press, 1962.

Kaufmann, Walter. *Hegel: Reinterpretation, Texts, and Commentary*. Garden City, N.Y.: Doubleday, 1965.

Kedney, John Steinfort. *Hegel's Aesthetics: A Critical Exposition*. Chicago: B. C. Griggs, 1892.

Knox, Israel. *The Aesthetic Theories of Kant, Hegel and Schopenhauer*. New York: Columbia University Press, 1936.

Stace, W. T. *The Philosophy of Hegel*. London: Macmillan, 1924.

Steinkraus, W., K. L. Schmitz, and J. O'Malley, eds. *Art and Logic in Hegel's Philosophy.*
  Atlantic Highlands, N.J.: Humanities Press, 1980.
Sussman, Henry. *The Hegelian Aftermath: Readings in Hegel, Kierkegaard, Freud, Proust,
  and James.* Baltimore: Johns Hopkins University Press, 1982.
Teyssèdre, Bernard. *L'esthétique de Hegel.* Paris: Presses universitaires de France, 1958.

# Introduction to the Philosophy of Art

## THE MEANING OF ART

The appropriate expression for our subject is the Philosophy of Art, or, more precisely, the Philosophy of Fine Arts. By this expression we wish to exclude the beauty of nature. In common life we are in the habit of speaking of beautiful color, a beautiful sky, a beautiful river, beautiful flowers, beautiful animals, and beautiful human beings. But quite aside from the question, which we wish not to discuss here, how far beauty may be predicated of such objects, or how far natural beauty may be placed side by side with artistic beauty, we must begin by maintaining that artistic beauty is higher than the beauty of nature. For the beauty of art is beauty born — and born again — of the spirit. And as spirit and its products stand higher than nature and its phenomena, by so much the beauty that resides in art is superior to the beauty of nature.

To say that spirit and artistic beauty stand higher than natural beauty, is to say very little, for "higher" is a very indefinite expression, which states the difference between them as quantitative and external. The "higher" quality of spirit and of artistic beauty does not at all stand in a merely relative position to nature. Spirit only is the true essence and content of the world, so that whatever is beautiful is truly beautiful only when it partakes of this higher essence and is produced by it. In this sense natural beauty appears only as a reflection of the beauty that belongs to spirit; it is an imperfect and incomplete expression of the spiritual substance.

Translated by Joseph Loewenberg.

Confining ourselves to artistic beauty, we must first consider certain difficulties. The first that suggests itself is the question whether art is at all worthy of a philosophic treatment. To be sure, art and beauty pervade, like a kindly genius, all the affairs of life, and joyously adorn all its inner and outer phases, softening the gravity and the burden of actual existence, furnishing pleasure for idle moments, and, where it can accomplish nothing positive, driving evil away by occupying its place. Yet, although art wins its way everywhere with its pleasing forms, from the crude adornment of the savages to the splendour of the temple with its marvellous wealth of decoration, art itself appears to fall outside the real aims of life. And though the creations of art cannot be said to be directly disadvantageous to the serious purposes of life, nay, on occasion actually further them by holding evil at bay, on the whole, art belongs to the relaxation and leisure of the mind, while the substantial interests of life demand its exertion. At any rate, such a view renders art a superfluity, though the tender and emotional influence which is wrought upon the mind by occupation with art is not thought necessarily detrimental, because effeminate.

There are others, again, who, though acknowledging art to be a luxury, have thought it necessary to defend it by pointing to the practical necessities of the fine arts and to the relation they bear to morality and piety. Very serious aims have been ascribed to art. Art has been recommended as a mediator between reason and sensuousness, between inclination and duty, as the reconcilor of all these elements constantly warring with one another. But it must be said that, by making art serve two masters, it is not rendered thereby more worthy of a philosophic treatment. Instead of being an end in itself, art is degraded into a means of appealing to higher aims, on the one hand, and to frivolity and idleness on the other.

Art considered as means offers another difficulty which springs from its form. Granting that art can be subordinated to serious aims and that the results which it thus produces will be significant, still the means used by art is deception, for beauty is appearance, its form is its life; and one must admit that a true and real purpose should not be achieved through deception. Even if a good end is thus, now and then, attained by art its success is rather limited, and even then deception cannot be recommended as a worthy means; for the means should be adequate to the dignity of the end, and truth can be produced by truth alone and not by deception and semblance.

It may thus appear as if art were not worthy of philosophic consideration because it is supposed to be merely a pleasing pastime; even when it pursues more serious aims it does not correspond with their nature. On the whole, it is conceived to serve both grave and light interests, achieving its results by means of deception and semblance.

As for the worthiness of art to be philosophically considered, it is indeed true that art can be used as a casual amusement, furnishing enjoyment and pleasure, decorating our surroundings, lending grace to the external conditions of life, and giving prominence to other objects through ornamentation. Art thus employed is indeed not an independent or free, but rather a subservient art. That art might serve other purposes and still retain its pleasure-giving function, is a relation which it has in common with thought. For science, too, in the hands of the servile understanding is used for finite ends and accidental means, and is thus not self-sufficient, but is determined by outer objects and circumstances. On the other hand, science can emancipate itself from such service and can rise in free independence to the pursuit of truth, in which the realization of its own aims is its proper function.

Art is not genuine art until it has thus liberated itself. It fulfils its highest task when it has joined the same sphere with religion and philosophy and has become a certain mode of bringing to consciousness and expression the divine meaning of things, the deepest interests of mankind, and the most universal truths of the spirit. Into works of art the nations have wrought their most profound ideas and aspirations. Fine Art often constitutes the key, and with many nations it is the only key, to an understanding of their wisdom and religion. This character art has in common with religion and philosophy. Art's peculiar feature, however, consists in its ability to represent in *sensuous form* even the highest ideas, bringing them thus nearer to the character of natural phenomena, to the senses, and to feeling. It is the height of a supra-sensuous world into which *thought* reaches, but it always appears to immediate consciousness and to present experience as an alien *beyond*. Through the power of philosophic thinking we are able to soar above what is merely *here,* above sensuous and finite experience. But spirit can heal the breach between the supra-sensuous and the sensuous brought on by its own advance; it produces out of itself the world of fine art as the first reconciling medium between what is merely external, sensuous, and transient, and the world of pure thought, between nature with its finite reality and the infinite freedom of philosophic reason.

Concerning the unworthiness of art because of its character as appearance and deception, it must be admitted that such criticism would not be without justice, if appearance could be said to be equivalent to falsehood and thus to something that ought not to be. Appearance is essential to reality; truth could not be, did it not shine through appearance. Therefore not appearance in general can be objected to, but merely the particular kind of appearance through which art seeks to portray truth. To charge the appearance in which art chooses to embody its ideas as deception, receives meaning only by comparison with the external world of phenomena and its immediate materiality, as well as with the inner world of sensations and feelings. To these two worlds we are wont, in our empirical work-a-day life, to attribute the value of actuality, reality, and truth, in contrast to art, which is supposed to be lacking such reality and truth. But, in fact, it is just the whole sphere of the empirical inner and outer world that is not the world of true reality; indeed it may be called a mere show and a cruel deception in a far stricter sense than in the case of art. Only beyond the immediacy of sense and of external objects is genuine reality to be found. Truly real is but the fundamental essence and the underlying substance of nature and of spirit, and the universal element in nature and in spirit is precisely what art accentuates and makes visible. This essence of reality appears also in the common outer and inner world, but it appears in the form of a chaos of contingencies, distorted by the immediateness of sense perception, and by the capriciousness and conditions, events, characters, etc. Art frees the true meaning of appearances from the show and deception of this bad and transient world, and invests it with a higher reality and a more genuine being than the things of ordinary life.

## THE CONTENT AND IDEAL OF ART

The content of art is spiritual, and its form is sensuous; both sides art has to reconcile into a united whole. The first requirement is that the content, which art is to represent, must be worthy of artistic representation; otherwise we obtain only a bad unity, since a content not capable of artistic treatment is made to take on an artistic form, and a matter prosaic in itself is forced into a form quite opposed to its inherent nature.

The second requirement demands of the content of art that it shall be no abstraction. By this is not meant that it must be concrete, as the sensuous is alleged to be concrete in contrast to everything spiritual and intellectual. For everything that is genuinely true, in the realm of thought as well as in the domain of nature, is concrete, and has, in spite of universality, nevertheless, a particular and subjective character. By saying, for example, that God is simply One, the Supreme Being as such, we express thereby nothing but a lifeless abstraction of an understanding devoid of reason. Such a God, as indeed he is not conceived in his concrete truth, can furnish no content for art, least of all for plastic art. Thus the Jews and the Turks have not been able to represent their God, who is still more abstract, in the positive manner in which the Christians have represented theirs. For in Christianity God is conceived in his truth, and therefore concrete, as a person, as a subject, and, more precisely still, as Spirit. What he is as spirit appears to the religious consciousness as a Trinity of persons, which at the same time is One. Here the essence of God is the reconciled unity of universality and particularity, such unity alone being concrete. Hence, as a content in order to be true must be concrete in this sense, art demands the same concreteness; because a mere abstract idea, or an abstract universal, cannot manifest itself in a particular and sensuous unified form.

If a true and therefore concrete content is to have its adequate sensuous form and shape, this sensuous form must — this being the third requirement — also be something individual, completely concrete, and one. The nature of concreteness belonging to both the content and the representation of art, is precisely the point in which both can coincide and correspond to each other. The natural shape of the human body, for example, is a sensuous concrete object, which is perfectly adequate to represent the spiritual in its concreteness; the view should therefore be abandoned that an existing object from the external world is accidentally chosen by art to express a spiritual idea. Art does not seize upon this or that form either because it simply finds it or because it can find no other, but the concrete spiritual content itself carries with it the element of external, real, yes, even sensuous, representation. And this is the reason why a sensuous concrete object, which bears the impress of an essentially spiritual content, addresses itself to the inner eye; the outward shape whereby the content is rendered visible and imaginable aims at an existence only in our heart and mind. For this reason alone are content and artistic shape harmoniously wrought. The mere sensuously concrete external nature as such has not this purpose for its only origin. The gay and variegated plumage of the birds shines unseen, and their song dies away unheard; the torch-thistle which blossoms only for a night withers without having been admired in the wilds of southern forests; and these forests, groves of the most beautiful and luxuriant vegetation, with the most odorous and fragrant perfumes, perish and waste, no more enjoyed. The work of art is not so unconsciously self-immersed, but it is essentially a question, an address to the responsive soul, an appeal to the heart and to the mind.

Although the sensuous form in which art clothes its content is not accidental, yet it is not the highest form whereby the spiritually concrete may be grasped. A higher mode than representation through a sensuous form, is thought. True and rational thinking, though in a relative sense abstract, must not be one-sided, but concrete. How far a definite content can be adequately treated by art and how far it needs, according to its nature, a higher and more spiritual form, is a distinction which we see at once, if, for example, the Greek gods are compared with God as conceived in accordance with Christian notions. The Greek god is not abstract but individual, closely related to the natural human form. The Christian God is also a concrete personality, but he is purely spiritual, and can be known only as spirit and in spirit. His sphere of existence is therefore essentially inner knowledge, and not the outer natural shape through which he can be represented but imperfectly and not in the whole depth of his essence.

But the task of art is to represent a spiritual idea to direct contemplation in sensuous form, and not in the form of thought or of pure spirituality. The value and dignity of such representation lies in the correspondence and unity of the two sides, of the spiritual content and its sensuous embodiment, so that the perfection and excellency of art must depend upon the grade of inner harmony and union with which the spiritual idea and the sensuous form interpenetrate.

The requirement of the conformity of spiritual idea and sensuous form might at first be interpreted as meaning that any idea whatever would suffice, so long as the concrete form represented this idea and no other. Such a view, however, would confound the ideal of art with mere correctness, which consists in the expression of any meaning in its appropriate form. The artistic ideal is not to be thus understood. For any content whatever is capable, according to the standard of its own nature, of adequate representation, but yet it does not for that reason lay claim to artistic

beauty in the ideal sense. Judged by the standard of ideal beauty, even such correct representation will be defective. In this connection we may remark that the defects of a work of art are not to be considered simply as always due to the incapacity of the artist; defectiveness of form has also its root in defectiveness of content. Thus, for instance, the Chinese, Indians, Egyptians, in their artistic objects, their representations of the gods, and their idols, adhered to formlessness, or to a vague and inarticulate form, and were not able to arrive at genuine beauty, because their mythological ideas, the content and conception of their works of art, were as yet vague and obscure. The more perfect in form works of art are, the more profound is the inner truth of their content and thought. And it is not merely a question of the greater or lesser skill with which the objects of external nature are studied and copied, for, in certain stages of artistic consciousness and artistic activity, the misrepresentation and distortion of natural objects are not unintentional technical inexpertness and incapacity, but conscious alteration, which depends upon the content that is in consciousness, and is, in fact, demanded by it. We may thus speak of imperfect art, which, in its own proper sphere, may be quite perfect both technically and in other respects. When compared with the highest idea and ideal of art, it is indeed defective. In the highest art alone are the idea and its representation in perfect congruity, because the sensuous form of the idea is in itself the adequate form, and because the content, which that form embodies, is itself a genuine content.

The higher truth of art consists, then, in the spiritual having attained a sensuous form adequate to its essence. And this also furnishes the principle of division for the philosophy of art. For the Spirit, before it wins the true notion or meaning of its absolute essence, has to develop through a series of stages which constitute its very life. To this universal evolution there corresponds a development of the phases of art, under the form of which the Spirit — as artist — attains to a comprehension of its own meaning.

This evolution within the spirit of art has two sides. The development is, in the first place, a spiritual and universal one, insofar as a gradual series of definite conceptions of the universe — of nature, man, and God — finds artistic representation. In the second place, this universal development of art, embodying itself in sensuous form, determines definite modes of artistic expression and a totality of necessary distinctions within the sphere of art. These constitute the particular arts.

We have now to consider three definite relations of the spiritual idea to its sensuous expression.

## SYMBOLIC ART

Art begins when the spiritual idea, being itself still indefinite and obscure and ill-comprehended, is made the content of artistic forms. As indefinite, it does not yet have that individuality which the artistic ideal demands; its abstractness and one-sidedness thus render its shape defective and whimsical. The first form of art is therefore rather a mere search after plasticity than a capacity of true representation. The spiritual idea has not yet found its adequate form, but is still engaged in striving and struggling after it. This form we may, in general, call the *symbolic* form of art; in such form the abstract idea assumes a shape in natural sensuous matter which is foreign to it; with this foreign matter the artistic creation begins, from which, however, it seems unable to free itself. The objects of external nature are reproduced unchanged, but at the same time the meaning of the spiritual idea is attached to them. They thus receive the vocation of expressing it, and must be interpreted as if the spiritual idea were actually present in them. It is indeed true that natural objects possess an aspect which makes them capable of representing a universal meaning, but in symbolic art a complete correspondence is not yet possible. In it the correspondence is confined to an abstract quality, as when, for example, a lion is meant to stand for strength.

This abstract relation brings also to consciousness the foreignness of the spiritual idea to natural phenomena. And the spiritual idea, having no other reality to express its essence, expatiates in all these natural shapes, seeks itself in their unrest and disproportion, but finds them inadequate to it. It then exaggerates these natural phenomena and shapes them into the huge and the boundless. The spiritual idea revels in them, as it were, seethes and ferments in them, does violence to them, distorts and disfigures them into grotesque shapes, and endeavors by the diversity, hugeness, and splendor of such forms to raise the natural phenomena to the spiritual level. For here it is the spiritual idea which is more or less vague and nonplastic, while the objects of nature have a thoroughly definite form.

The incongruity of the two elements to each other makes the relation of the spiritual idea to objective reality a negative one. The spiritual as a wholly inner element and as the universal substance of all things, is conceived unsatisfied with all externality, and in its *sublimity* it triumphs over the abundance of unsuitable forms. In this conception of sublimity the natural objects and the human shapes are accepted and left unaltered, but at the same time recognized as inadequate to their own inner meaning; it is this inner meaning which is glorified far and above every worldly content.

These elements constitute, in general, the character of the primitive artistic pantheism of the Orient, which either invests even the lowest objects with absolute significance, or forces all phenomena with violence to assume the expression of its world-view. This art becomes therefore bizarre, grotesque, and without taste, or it represents the infinite substance in its abstract freedom turning away with disdain from the illusory and perishing mass of appearances. Thus the meaning can never be completely molded into the expression, and, notwithstanding all the aspiration and effort, the incongruity between the spiritual idea and the sensuous form remains insuperable. This is, then, the first form of art — symbolic art with its endless quest, its inner struggle, its sphinxlike mystery, and its sublimity.

## CLASSICAL ART

In the second form of art, which we wish to designate as the *classical,* the double defect of symbolic art is removed. The symbolic form is imperfect, because the spiritual meaning which it seeks to convey enters into consciousness in but an abstract and vague manner, and thus the congruity between meaning and form must always remain defective and therefore abstract. This double aspect disappears in the classical type of art; in it we find the free and adequate embodiment of the spiritual idea in the form most suitable to it, and with it meaning and expression are in perfect accord. It is classical art, therefore, which first affords the creation and contemplation of the completed ideal, realizing it as a real fact in the world.

But the congruity of idea and reality in classical art must not be taken in the formal sense of the agreement of a content with its external form; otherwise every photograph of nature, every picture of a countenance, landscape, flower, scene, etc., which constitutes the aim of a representation, would, through the conformity of content and form, be at once classical. The peculiarity of classical art, on the contrary, consists in its content being itself a concrete idea, and, as such, a concrete spiritual idea, for only the spiritual is a truly classical content. For a worthy object of such a content, Nature must be consulted as to whether she contains anything to which a spiritual attribute really belongs. It must be the World-Spirit itself that *invented* the proper form for the concrete spiritual ideal; the subjective mind — in this case the spirit of art — has only *found* it, and given it natural plastic existence in accordance with free individual spirituality. The form in which the idea, as spiritual and individual, clothes itself when revealed as a temporal phenomenon, is the *human form*. To be sure, personification and anthropomorphism have frequently been decried as a degradation of the spiritual; but art, insofar as its task is to bring before direct contemplation the spiritual in sensuous form, must advance to such anthropomorphism, for only in its body can mind appear in an adequately sensuous fashion. The migration of souls[1] is, in this respect, an abstract notion, and physiology should make it one of its fundamental principles that life has necessarily, in its evolu-

tion, to advance to the human shape as the only sensuous phenomenon appropriate to the mind.

The human body as portrayed by classical art is not represented in its mere physical existence, but solely as the natural and sensuous form and garb of mind; it is therefore divested of all the defects that belong to the merely sensuous and of all the finite contingencies that appertain to the phenomenal. But if the form must be thus purified in order to express the appropriate content, and, furthermore, if the conformity of meaning and expression is to be complete, the content which is the spiritual idea must be perfectly capable of being expressed through the bodily form of man, without projecting into another sphere beyond the physical and sensuous representation. The result is that Spirit is characterized as a particular form of mind, namely, as human mind, and not as simply absolute and eternal; but the absolute and eternal Spirit must be able to reveal and express itself in a manner far more spiritual.

This latter point brings to light the defect of classical art, which demands its dissolution and its transition to a third and higher form, to wit, the *romantic* form of art.

## ROMANTIC ART

The romantic form of art destroys the unity of the spiritual idea and its sensuous form, and goes back, though on a higher level, to the difference and opposition of the two, which symbolic art left unreconciled. The classical form of art attained, indeed, the highest degree of perfection which the sensuous process of art was capable of realizing; and, if it shows any defects, the defects are those of art itself, due to the limitation of its sphere. This limitation has its root in the general attempt of art to represent in sensuous concrete form the infinite and universal Spirit, and in the attempt of the classical type of art to blend so completely spiritual and sensuous existence that the two appear in mutual conformity. But in such a fusion of the spiritual and sensuous aspects Spirit cannot be portrayed according to its true essence, for the true essence of Spirit is its infinite subjectivity; and its absolute internal meaning does not lend itself to a full and free

---

[1]Hegel means the transmigration of souls into the bodies of other animals; this notion is "abstract" because it presumes that the soul has an ideal reality that allows it to be put into any earthly envelope. [Ed.]

expression in the confinement of the bodily form as its only appropriate existence.

Now, romantic art dissolves the inseparable unity which is the ideal of the classical type, because it has won a content which goes beyond the classical form of art and its mode of expression. This content — if familiar ideas may be recalled — coincides with what Christianity declares to be true of God as Spirit, in distinction to the Greek belief in gods which constitutes the essential and appropriate subject for classical art. The concrete content of Hellenic art implies the unity of the human and divine nature, a unity which, just because it is merely *implied* and *immediate,* permits of a representation in an immediately visible and sensuous mold. The Greek god is the object of naïve contemplation and sensuous imagination; his shape is, therefore, the bodily shape of man; the circle of his power and his essence is individual and confined. To man the Greek god appears as a being and a power with whom he may *feel* a kinship and unity, but this kinship and unity are not reflected upon or raised into definite knowledge. The higher stage is the *knowledge* of this unconscious unity, which underlies the classical form of art and which it has rendered capable of complete plastic embodiment. The elevation of what is unconscious and implied into self-conscious knowledge brings about an enormous difference; it is the infinite difference which, for example, separates man from the animal. Man is an animal, but, even in his animal functions, does not rest satisfied with the potential and the unconscious as the animal does, but becomes conscious of them, reflects upon them, and raises them — as, for instance, the process of digestion — into self-conscious science. And it is thus that man breaks through the boundary of his merely immediate and unconscious existence, so that, just because he knows himself to be animal, he ceases in virtue of such knowledge to be animal, and, through such self-knowledge only, can characterize himself as mind or spirit.

If in the manner just described the unity of the human and divine nature is raised from an *immediate* to a *conscious* unity, the true mold for the reality of this content is no longer the sensuous, immediate existence of the spiritual, the bodily frame of man, but self-conscious and internal contemplation. For this reason Christianity, in depicting God as Spirit — not as particularized individual mind, but as absolute and universal Spirit — retires from the sensuousness of imagination into the sphere of inner being, and makes this, and not the bodily form, the material and mold of its content; and thus the unity of the human and divine nature is a conscious unity, capable of realization only by spiritual knowledge. The new content, won by this unity, is not dependent upon sensuous representation; it is now exempt from such immediate existence. In this way, however, romantic art becomes art which transcends itself, carrying on this process of self-transcendence within its own artistic sphere and artistic form.

Briefly stated, the essence of romantic art consists in the artistic object being the free, concrete, spiritual idea itself, which is revealed in its spirituality to the inner, and not the outer, eye. In conformity with such a content, art can, in a sense, not work for sensuous perception, but must aim at the inner mood, which completely fuses with its object, at the most subjective inner shrine, at the heart, the feeling, which, as spiritual feeling, longs for freedom within itself and seeks and finds reconciliation only within the inner recesses of the spirit. This *inner* world is the content of romantic art, and as such an inner life, or as its reflection, it must seek embodiment. The inner life thus triumphs over the outer world — indeed, so triumphs over it that the outer world itself is made to proclaim its victory, through which the sensuous appearance sinks into worthlessness.

On the other hand, the romantic type of art, like every other, needs an external mode of expression. But the spiritual has now retired from the outer mode into itself, and the sensuous externality of form assumes again, as it did in symbolic art, an insignificant and transient character. The subjective, finite mind and will, the particularity and caprice of the individual, of character, action or of incident and plot, assume likewise the character they had in symbolic art. The external side of things is surrendered to accident and committed to the excesses of the imagination, whose caprice now mirrors existence as it is, now chooses to distort the objects of the outer world into a bizarre and grotesque medley, for the external form no longer possesses a meaning and significance, as in classical art, on its own account and for its own sake. Feeling is now everything. It finds its artistic reflection, not in the world of external things and their forms, but in its own expression; and in every incident and accident of life, in every misfortune, grief, and even crime, feeling preserves or regains its healing power of reconciliation.

Hence, the indifference, incongruity, and antagonism of spiritual idea and sensuous form, the characteristics of symbolic art, reappear in the romantic type, but with this essential difference. In the romantic realm, the spiritual idea, to whose defectiveness was due the defective forms of symbolic art, now reveals itself in its perfection within mind and feeling. It is by virtue of the higher perfection of the idea that it shuns any adequate union with an external form, since it can seek and attain its true reality and expression best within itself.

This, in general terms, is the character of the symbolic, classical, and romantic forms of art, which stand for the three relations of the spiritual idea to its expression in the realm of art. They consist in the aspiration after, and the attainment and transcendence of, the ideal as the true idea of beauty.

## THE PARTICULAR ARTS

But, now, there inhere in the idea of beauty different modifications which art translates into sensuous forms. And we find a fundamental principle by which the several particular arts may be arranged and defined — that is, the species of art contain in themselves the same essential differences which we have found in the three general types of art. External objectivity, moreover, into which these types are molded by means of a sensuous and particular material, renders them independent and separate means of realizing different artistic functions, as far as each type finds its definite character in some one definite external material whose mode of portrayal determines its

adequate realization.[2] Furthermore, the general types of art correspond to the several particular arts, so that they (the particular arts) belong each of them *specifically* to *one* of the general types of art. It is these particular arts which give adequate and artistic external being to the general types.

## ARCHITECTURE

The first of the particular arts with which, according to their fundamental principle, we have to begin, is architecture. Its task consists in so shaping external inorganic nature that it becomes homogeneous with mind, as an artistic outer world. The material of architecture is matter itself in its immediate externality as a heavy mass subject to mechanical laws, and its forms remain the forms of inorganic nature, but are merely arranged and ordered in accordance with the abstract rules of the understanding, the rules of symmetry. But in such material and in such forms the ideal as concrete spirituality cannot be realized; the reality which is represented in them remains, therefore, alien to the spiritual idea, as something external which it has not penetrated or with which it has but a remote and abstract relation. Hence the fundamental type of architecture is the *symbolical* form of art. For it is architecture that paves the way, as it were, for the adequate realization of the God, toiling and wrestling in his service with external nature, and seeking to extricate it from the chaos of finitude, and the abortiveness of chance. By this means it levels a space for the God, frames his external surroundings, and builds him his temple as the place for inner contemplation and for reflection upon the eternal objects of the spirit. It raises an enclosure around those gathered together, as a defense against the threatening of the wind, against rain, the thunderstorm, and wild beasts, and re-

[2]Hegel's point is that while the art forms of architecture, sculpture, and poetry have intrinsic correspondences with the symbolic, the classical, and the romantic modalities of art, respectively, there nevertheless exist classical and romantic forms of architecture, symbolic and romantic forms of sculpture, symbolic and classic forms of poetry. [Ed.]

veals the will to assemble, though externally, yet in accordance with the artistic form. A meaning such as this, the art of architecture is able to mold into its material and its forms with more or less success, according as the determinate nature of the content which it seeks to embody is more significant or more trivial, more concrete or more abstract, more deeply rooted within its inner being or more dim and superficial. Indeed, it may even advance so far as to endeavor to create for such meaning an adequate artistic expression with its material and forms, but in such an attempt it has already overstepped the bounds of its own sphere, and inclines towards sculpture, the higher phase of art. For the limit of architecture lies precisely in this, that it refers to the spiritual as an internal essence in contrast with the external forms of its art, and thus whatever is endowed with mind and spirit must be indicated as something other than itself.

## SCULPTURE

Architecture, however, has purified the inorganic external world, has given it symmetric order, has impressed upon it the seal of mind, and the temple of the God, the house of his community, stands ready. Into this temple now enters the God himself. The lightning-flash of individuality strikes the inert mass, permeates it, and a form no longer merely symmetrical, but infinite and spiritual, concentrates and molds its adequate bodily shape. This is the task of sculpture. Inasmuch as in it the inner spiritual element, which architecture can no more than hint at, completely abides with the sensuous form and its external matter, and as both sides are so merged into each other that neither predominates, sculpture has the *classical* form of art as its fundamental type. In fact, the sensuous realm itself can command no expression which could not be that of the spiritual sphere, just as, conversely, no spiritual content can attain perfect plasticity in sculpture which is incapable of being adequately presented to perception in bodily form. It is sculpture which arrests for our vision the spirit in its bodily frame, in immediate unity with it, and in an attitude of peace and repose; and the form in turn is ani-

mated by the content of spiritual individuality. Therefore the external sensuous matter is here not wrought, either according to its mechanical quality alone, as heavy mass, or in forms peculiar to inorganic nature, or as indifferent to color, etc., but in ideal forms of the human shape, and in the whole of the spatial dimensions. In this last respect sculpture should be credited with having first revealed the inner and spiritual essence in its eternal repose and essential self-possession. To such repose and unity with itself corresponds only that external element which itself persists in unity and repose. Such an element is the form taken in its abstract spatiality. The spirit which sculpture represents is that which is solid in itself, not variously broken up in the play of contingencies and passions; nor does its external form admit of the portrayal of such a manifold play, but it holds to this one side only, to the abstraction of space in the totality of its dimensions.

## THE DEVELOPMENT OF THE ROMANTIC ARTS

After architecture has built the temple and the hand of sculpture has placed inside it the statue of the God, then this sensuously visible God faces in the spacious halls of his house the *community*. The community is the spiritual, self-reflecting element in this sensuous realm, it is the animating subjectivity and inner life. A new principle of art begins with it. Both the content of art and the medium which embodies it in outward form now demand particularization, individualization, and the subjective mode of expressing these. The solid unity which the God possesses in sculpture breaks up into the plurality of inner individual lives, whose unity is not sensuous, but essentially ideal.

And now God comes to assume the aspect which makes him truly spiritual. As a hither-and-thither, as an alteration between the unity within himself and his realization in subjective knowledge and individual consciousness, as well as in the common and unified life of the man individuals, he is genuinely Spirit — the Spirit in his community. In his community God is released from the abstractness of a mysterious self-identity, as well as from the naïve imprisonment in a bodily shape, in which he is represented by sculpture. Here he is exalted into spirituality, subjectivity, and knowledge. For this reason the higher content of art is now this spirituality in its absolute form. But since what chiefly reveals itself in this stage is not the serene repose of God in himself, but rather his appearance, his being, and his manifestation to others, the objects of artistic representation are now the most varied subjective expressions of life and activity for their own sake, as human passions, deeds, events, and, in general, the wide range of human feeling, will, and resignation. In accordance with this content, the sensuous element must differentiate and show itself adequate to the expression of subjective feeling. Such different media are furnished by color, by the musical sound, and finally by the sound as the mere indication of inner intuitions and ideas; and thus as different forms of realizing the spiritual content of art by means of these media we obtain painting, music, and poetry. The sensuous media employed in these arts being individualized and in their essence recognized as ideal, they correspond most effectively to the spiritual content of art, and the union between spiritual meaning and sensuous expression develops, therefore, into greater intimacy than was possible in the case of architecture and sculpture. This intimate unity, however, is due wholly to the subjective side.

Leaving, then, the symbolic spirit and architecture and the classical ideal of sculpture behind, these new arts in which form and content are raised to an ideal level borrow their type from the *romantic* form of art, whose mode of expression they are most eminently fitted to voice. They form, however, a totality of arts, because the romantic type is the most concrete in itself.

## PAINTING

The first art in this totality, which is akin to sculpture, is painting. The material which it uses for its content and for the sensuous expression of that content is visibility as such, in so far as it is individualized, viz., specified as color. To be sure, the media employed in architecture and sculpture are also visible and colored, but they are not, as in painting, visibility as such, not the simple light which contrasts itself with darkness and in combination with it becomes color. This visibility as a subjective and ideal attribute, requires neither, like architecture, the abstract mechanical form of mass which we find in heavy matter, nor, like sculpture, the three dimensions of sensuous space, even though in concentrated and organic plasticity, but the visibility which appertains to painting has its differences on a more ideal level, in the particular kind of color; and thus painting frees art from the sensuous completeness in space peculiar to material things only, by confining itself to a plane surface.

On the other hand, the content also gains in varied particularization. Whatever can find room in the human heart, as emotion, idea, and purpose, whatever it is able to frame into a deed, all this variety of material can constitute the many-colored content of painting. The whole range of particular existence, from the highest aspirations of the mind down to the most isolated objects of nature, can obtain a place in this art. For even finite nature, in its particular scenes and aspects, can here appear, if only some allusion to a spiritual element makes it akin to thought and feeling.

## MUSIC

The second art in which the romantic form finds realization, on still a higher level than in painting, is music. Its material, though still sensuous, advances to a deeper subjectivity and greater specification. The idealization of the sensuous, music brings about by negating space. In music the indifferent extension of space whose appearance painting admits and consciously imitates is concentrated and idealized into a single point. But in the form of a motion and tremor of the material body within itself, this single point becomes a concrete and active process within the idealization of matter. Such an incipient ideality of matter which no longer appears under the spatial form, but as temporal ideality, is sound — the sensuous acknowledged as ideal, whose abstract visibility is transformed into audibility.

Sound, as it were, exempts the ideal from its absorption in matter.

This earliest animation and inspiration of matter furnishes the medium for the inner and intimate life of the spirit, as yet on an indefinite level; it is through the tones of music that the heart pours out its whole scale of feelings and passions. Thus as sculpture constitutes the central point between architecture and the arts of romantic subjectivity, so music forms the center of the romantic arts, and represents the point of transition between abstract spatial sensuousness, which belongs to painting, and the abstract spirituality of poetry. Within itself music has, like architecture, an abstract quantitative relation, as a contrast to its inward and emotional quality; it also has as its basis a permanent law to which the tones with their combinations and successions must conform.[3]

## POETRY

For the third and most spiritual expression of the romantic form of art, we must look to poetry. Its characteristic peculiarity lies in the power with which it subjugates to the mind and to its ideas the sensuous element from which music and painting began to set art free. For sound, the one external medium of which poetry avails itself, is in it no longer a feeling of the tone itself, but is a sign which is, by itself, meaningless. This sign, moreover, is a sign of an idea which has become concrete, and not merely of indefinite feeling and of its *nuances* and grades. By this means the tone becomes the *word,* an articulate voice, whose function it is to indicate thoughts and ideas. The negative point to which music had advanced now reveals itself in poetry as the completely concrete point, as the spirit or the self-consciousness of the individual, which spontaneously unites the infinite space of its ideas with the time-element of sound. But this sensuous element which, in music, was still in immediate union with inner feelings and moods, is, in poetry, divorced from

the content of consciousness, for in poetry the mind determines this content on its own account and for the sake of its ideas, and while it employs sound to express them, yet sound itself is reduced to a symbol without value or meaning. From this point of view sound may just as well be considered a mere letter, for the audible, like the visible, is now relegated to a mere suggestion of mind. Thus the genuine mode of poetic representation is the inner perception and the poetic imagination itself. And since all types of art share in this mode, poetry runs through them all, and develops itself independently in each. Poetry, then, is the universal art of the spirit which has attained inner freedom, and which does not depend for its realization upon external sensuous matter, but expatiates only in the inner space and inner time of the ideas and feelings. But just in this, its highest phase, art oversteps the bounds of its own sphere by abandoning the harmoniously sensuous mode of portraying the spirit and by passing from the poetry of imagination into the prose of thought.

## SUMMARY

Such, then, is the organic totality of the several arts; the external art of architecture, the objective art of sculpture, and the subjective arts of painting, music, and poetry. The higher principle from which these are derived we have found in the types of art, the symbolic, the classical, and the romantic, which form the universal phases of the idea of beauty itself. Thus symbolic art finds its most adequate reality and most perfect application in architecture, in which it is self-complete, and is not yet reduced, so to speak, to the inorganic medium for another art. The classical form of art, on the other hand; attains its most complete realization in sculpture, while it accepts architecture only as forming an inclosure round its products and is as yet not capable of developing painting and music as absolute expressions of its meaning. The romantic type of art, finally, seizes upon painting, music, and poetry as its essential and adequate modes of expression. Poetry, however, is in conformity with all types of the beautiful and extends over them all, because its characteristic element is the aesthetic imagi-

---

[3]Hegel refers to the mathematical basis of the diatonic scale and the laws of harmony and counterpoint that derive from it. [Ed.]

nation, and imagination is necessary for every product of art, to whatever type it may belong.

Thus what the particular arts realize in individual artistic creations are, according to the philosophic conception, simply the universal types of the self-unfolding idea of beauty. Out of the external realization of this idea arises the wide Pantheon of art, whose architect and builder is the self-developing spirit of beauty, for the completion of which, however, the history of the world will require its evolution of countless ages.

# Ralph Waldo Emerson

## 1803–1882

Emerson was the son of a Unitarian minister of Boston; he was educated at Boston Latin School and Harvard University, and, after a brief and unhappy stint as a schoolmaster, returned to Cambridge to attend Harvard Divinity School. In 1826 he was licensed to preach and in 1829 was ordained as minister of the Second Church of Boston, where the Mathers had preached over a century before. In the same year he married Ellen Tucker, a young heiress who died of tuberculosis within sixteen months, leaving Emerson a widower with a legacy of over a thousand dollars a year and no pressing need to earn a living.

In the watershed year 1832, Emerson resigned his position at the Second Church because he had ceased to believe in the validity of the sacrament of the Lord's Supper and could no longer administer it. He embarked on an extended European tour, where he met the poets Wordsworth and Coleridge, and (most important for his intellectual development) Thomas Carlyle, who was to publicize Emerson in Britain and in return was publicized by Emerson in America.

In 1834, Emerson settled in the village of Concord, Massachusetts, where he married Lydia Jackson and settled down to the quiet and orderly intellectual life that would continue for nearly fifty years. Although he believed in the theory that hard manual labor should be combined with scholarship, he found that work in the fields sapped his energies for his study. He also tried vegetarianism for a while but gave it up, since it seemed to be doing him no particular good. He wrote sermons at his farm and delivered them in enormously popular lectures on tours of Boston and the Northeast.

His first work, *Nature* (1836), though influenced by the mystical theology of Emmanuel Swedenborg, was essentially an American restatement of the idealistic and pantheist philosophy of Carlyle's *Sartor Resartus* (1834). It became the unofficial bible of the "Symposium" — an informal and occasional gathering of the American Transcendentalists, who included Bronson Alcott, Margaret Fuller, and Henry David Thoreau. His lectures appeared in print as *Essays* (1841), *Essays, Second Series* (1844), *Representative Men* (1850), and *The Conduct of Life* (1860). Like most Unitarians, Emerson was antislavery, as his journals of the 1850s reveal, but he steered clear of the abolitionist movement until it was too late for him to influence its course. After the Civil War, his writing declined as his once-prodigious memory began to fail, and the Sage of Concord gradually sank into senility at least a decade before his death.

"The Poet" is from Emerson's second series of *Essays,* and like many of his effusions, it preaches rather than analyzes its topic. "The Poet" quickly expands from its ostensible subject to include many of Emerson's central ideas, which strongly resemble the mystical views of Plotinus. Where Plotinus's god-term was "The One," Emerson's is the "Over-Soul," a pantheistic spiritual entity wherein everything living is united, the ultimate source of truth, goodness, and beauty.

The universe itself, in its materiality, is merely a physical symbol, an emblem, of the Over-Soul. And the parts are as the whole: Each element in the material world is symbolic of spiritual truths.

Hence the centrality of the poet to Emerson's metaphysic, for the poet is, when working at full power, the individual who can transcend individuality, who through the professional manipulation of symbols and figures understands best the highest truths about the relationship between matter and spirit, which are to each other as the signifier is to the signified. Emerson consistently deals with poetry, as it was understood by Kant and Coleridge, as the product of the creative imagination. In this sense, any great spiritual thinker is a poet. Emerson's poet is not, however, the maker of *poems,* linguistic forms in measured language. His essay embodies instead, even more than Shelley's "Defence of Poetry," a heaven-ascending compendium of romantic ideas about the poet as idealist.

### Selected Bibliography

Foerster, Norman. *American Criticism: A Study in Literary Theory from Poe to the Present.* 1928; New York: Russell and Russell, 1962.

Hopkins, Vivian C. *Spires of Form: A Study of Emerson's Aesthetic Theory.* New York: Russell and Russell, 1965.

Matthiessen, F. O. *American Renaissance: Art and Expression in the Age of Emerson and Whitman.* New York: Oxford University Press, 1941.

Maulsby, David Lee. *Emerson: His Contribution to Literature.* Folcroft, Pa.: Folcroft Library Editions, 1973.

Michaud, Régis. *L'esthétique d'Emerson: La nature, l'art, l'histoire.* Paris: F. Alcan, 1927.

Paul, Sherman. *Emerson's Angle of Vision.* Cambridge: Harvard University Press, 1952.

Porte, Joel. *Representative Man: Emerson in His Time.* New York: Oxford University Press, 1979.

Van Leer, David. *Emerson's Epistemology: The Argument of the Essays.* New York: Cambridge University Press, 1976.

Yoder, R. A. *Emerson and the Orphic Poet in America.* Berkeley: University of California Press, 1978.

# The Poet

*A moody child and wildly wise*
*Pursued the game with joyful eyes,*
*Which chose, like meteors, their way,*
*And rived the dark with private ray:*
*They overleapt the horizon's edge,*
*Searched with Apollo's privilege;*
*Through man, and woman, and sea, and star*
*Saw the dance of nature forward far;*
*Through worlds, and races, and terms, and times*

*Saw musical order, and pairing rhymes.*[1]

*Olympian bards who sung*
*Divine ideas below,*
*Which always find us young,*
*And always keep us so.*[2]

[1]From Emerson's poem, "The Poet." [Ed.]
[2]From Emerson's "Ode to Beauty," lines 61–64. [Ed.]

Those who are esteemed umpires of taste are often persons who have acquired some knowledge of admired pictures or sculptures, and have an inclination for whatever is elegant; but if you inquire whether they are beautiful souls, and whether their own acts are like fair pictures, you learn that they are selfish and sensual. Their cultivation is local, as if you should rub a log of dry wood in one spot to produce fire, all the rest remaining cold. Their knowledge of the fine arts is some study of rules and particulars, or some limited judgment of color or form, which is exercised for amusement or for show. It is a proof of the shallowness of the doctrine of beauty as it lies in the minds of our amateurs, that men seem to have lost the perception of the instant dependence of form upon soul. There is no doctrine of forms in our philosophy. We were put into our bodies, as fire is put into a pan to be carried about; but there is no accurate adjustment between the spirit and the organ, much less is the latter the germination of the former. So in regard to other forms, the intellectual men do not believe in any essential dependence of the material world on thought and volition. Theologians think it a pretty air-castle to talk of the spiritual meaning of a ship or a cloud, of a city or a contract, but they prefer to come again to the solid ground of historical evidence; and even the poets are contented with a civil and conformed manner of living, and to write poems from the fancy, at a safe distance from their own experience. But the highest minds of the world have never ceased to explore the double meaning, or shall I say the quadruple or the centuple of much more manifold meaning, of every sensuous fact; Orpheus, Empedocles, Heraclitus, Plato, Plutarch, Dante, Swedenborg, and the masters of sculpture, picture and poetry. For we are not pans and barrows, nor even porters of the fire and torch-bearers, but children of the fire, made of it, and only the same divinity transmuted and at two or three removes, when we know least about it. And this hidden truth, that the fountains whence all this river of Time and its creatures floweth are intrinsically ideal and beautiful, draws us to the consideration of the nature and functions of the Poet, or the man of Beauty; to the means and materials he uses, and to

the general aspect of the art in the present time.

The breadth of the problem is great, for the poet is representative. He stands among partial men for the complete man, and apprises us not of his wealth, but of the common wealth. The young man reveres men of genius, because, to speak truly, they are more himself than he is. The receive of the soul as he also receives, but they more. Nature enhances her beauty, to the eye of loving men, from their belief that the poet is beholding her shows at the same time. He is isolated among his contemporaries by truth and by his art, but with this consolation in his pursuits, that they will draw all men sooner or later. For all men live by truth and stand in need of expression. In love, in art, in avarice, in politics, in labor, in games, we study to utter our painful secret. The man is only half himself, the other half is his expression.

Notwithstanding this necessity to be published, adequate expression is rare. I know not how it is that we need an interpreter, but the great majority of men seem to be minors, who have not yet come into possession of their own, or mutes, who cannot report the conversation they have had with nature. There is no man who does not anticipate a supersensual utility in the sun and stars, earth and water. These stand and wait to render him a peculiar service. But there is some obstruction or some excess of phlegm in our constitution, which does not suffer them to yield the due effect. Too feeble fall the impressions of nature on us to make us artists. Every touch should thrill. Every man should be so much an artist that he could report in conversation what had befallen him. Yet, in our experience, the rays or appulses have sufficient force to arrive at the senses, but not enough to reach the quick and compel the reproduction of themselves in speech. The poet is the person in whom these powers are in balance, the man without impediment, who sees and handles that which others dream of, traverses the whole scale of experience, and is representative of man, in virtue of being the largest power to receive and to impart.

For the universe has three children, born at one time, which reappear under different names in every system of thought, whether they be called cause, operation and effect; or, more poetically, Jove, Pluto, Neptune; or, theologically, the Father, the Spirit and the Son; but which we will call here the Knower, the Doer and the Sayer. These stand respectively for the love of truth, for the love of good, and for the love of beauty. These three are equal. Each is that which he is, essentially, so that he cannot be surmounted or analyzed, and each of these three has the power of the others latent in him and his own, patent.

The poet is the sayer, the namer, and represents beauty. He is a sovereign, and stands on the center. For the world is not painted or adorned, but is from the beginning beautiful; and God has not made some beautiful things, but Beauty is the creator of the universe. Therefore the poet is not any permissive potentate, but is emperor in his own right. Criticism is infested with a cant of materialism, which assumes that manual skill and activity is the first merit of all men, and disparages such as say and do not, overlooking the fact that some men, namely poets, are natural sayers, sent into the world to the end of expression, and confounds them with those whose province is action but who quit it to imitate the sayers. But Homer's words are as costly and admirable to Homer as Agamemnon's victories are to Agamemnon. The poet does not wait for the hero or the sage, but, as they act and think primarily, so he writes primarily what will and must be spoken, reckoning the others, though primaries also, yet, in respect to him, secondaries and servants; as sitters or models in the studio of a painter, or as assistants who bring building-materials to an architect.

For poetry was all written before time was, and whenever we are so finely organized that we can penetrate into that region where the air is music, we hear those primal warblings and attempt to write them down, but we lose ever and anon a word or a verse and substitute something of our own, and thus miswrite the poem. The men of more delicate ear write down these cadences more faithfully, and these transcripts, though imperfect, become the songs of the nations. For nature is as truly beautiful as it is good, or as it is reasonable, and must as much appear as it must be done, or be known. Words and deeds are quite indifferent modes of the divine energy. Words are also actions, and actions are a kind of words.

The sign and credentials of the poet are that he announces that which no man foretold. He is the true and only doctor; he knows and tells; he is the only teller of news, for he was present and privy to the appearance which he describes. He is a beholder of ideas and an utterer of the necessary and causal. For we do not speak now of men of poetical talents, or of industry and skill in meter, but of the true poet. I took part in a conversation the other day concerning a recent writer of lyrics, a man of subtle mind, whose head appeared to be a music-box of delicate tunes and rhythms, and whose skill and command of language we could not sufficiently praise. But when the question arose whether he was not only a lyrist but a poet, we were obliged to confess that he is plainly a contemporary, not an eternal man. He does not stand out of our low limitations, like a Chimborazo[3] under the line, running up from a torrid base through all the climates of the globe, with belts of the herbage of every latitude on its high and mottled sides; but this genius is the landscape-garden of a modern house, adorned with fountains and statues, with well-bred men and women standing and sitting in the walks and terraces. We hear, through all the varied music, the ground-tone of conventional life. Our poets are men of talents who sing, and not the children of music. The argument is secondary, the finish of the verses is primary.

For it is not meters, but a meter-making argument that makes a poem, — a thought so passionate and alive that like the spirit of a plant or an animal it has an architecture of its own, and adorns nature with a new thing. The thought and the form are equal in the order of time, but in the order of genesis the thought is prior to the form. The poet has a new thought; he has a whole new experience to unfold; he will tell us how it was with him, and all men will be the richer in his fortune. For the experience of each new age requires a new confession, and the world seems

[3]A mountain in Ecuador, near the equator ("under the line"). [Ed.]

always waiting for its poet. I remember when I was young how much I was moved one morning by tidings that genius had appeared in a youth who sat near me at table. He had left his work and gone rambling none knew whither, and had written hundreds of lines, but could not tell whether that which was in him was therein told; he could tell nothing but that all was changed, — man, beast, heaven, earth and sea. How gladly we listened! how credulous! Society seemed to be compromised. We sat in the aurora of a sunrise which was to put out all the stars. Boston seemed to be at twice the distance it had the night before, or was much farther than that. Rome, — what was Rome? Plutarch and Shakespeare were in the yellow leaf, and Homer no more should be heard of. It is much to know that poetry has been written this very day, under this very roof, by your side. What! that wonderful spirit has not expired! These stony moments are still sparkling and animated! I had fancied that the oracles were all silent, and nature had spent her fires; and behold! all night, from every pore, these fine auroras have been streaming. Every one has some interest in the advent of the poet, and no one knows how much it may concern him. We know that the secret of the world is profound, but who or what shall be our interpreter, we know not. A mountain ramble, a new style of face, a new person, may put the key into our hands. Of course the value of genius to us is in the veracity of its report. Talent may frolic and juggle; genius realizes and adds. Mankind in good earnest have availed so far in understanding themselves and their work, that the foremost watchman on the peak announces his news. It is the truest word ever spoken, and the phrase will be the fittest, most musical, and the unerring voice of the world for that time.

All that we call sacred history attests that the birth of a poet is the principal event in chronology. Man, never so often deceived, still watches for the arrival of a brother who can hold him steady to a truth until he has made it his own. With what joy I begin to read a poem which I confide in as an inspiration! And now my chains are to be broken; I shall mount above these clouds and opaque airs in which I live, — opaque, though they seem transparent, — and

from the heaven of truth I shall see and comprehend my relations. That will reconcile me to life and renovate nature, to see trifles animated by a tendency, and to know what I am doing. Life will no more be a noise; now I shall see men and women, and know the signs by which they may be discerned from fools and satans. This day shall be better than my birthday: then I became an animal; now I am invited into the science of the real. Such is the hope, but the fruition is postponed. Oftener it falls that this winged man, who will carry me into the heaven, whirls me into mists, then leaps and frisks about with me as it were from cloud to cloud, still affirming that he is bound heavenward; and I, being myself a novice, am slow in perceiving that he does not know the way into the heavens, and is merely bent that I should admire his skill to rise like a fowl or a flying fish, a little way from the ground or the water; but the all-piercing, all-feeding and ocular air of heaven that man shall never inhabit. I tumble down again soon into my old nooks, and lead the life of exaggerations as before, and have lost my faith in the possibility of any guide who can lead me thither where I would be.

But, leaving these victims of vanity, let us, with new hope, observe how nature, by worthier impulses, has insured the poet's fidelity to his office of announcement and affirming, namely by the beauty of things, which becomes a new and higher beauty when expressed. Nature offers all her creatures to him as a picture-language. Being used as a type, a second wonderful value appears in the object, far better than its old value; as the carpenter's stretched cord, if you hold your ear close enough, is musical in the breeze. "Things more excellent than every image," says Jamblichus,[4] "are expressed through images." Things admit of being used as symbols because nature is a symbol, in the whole, and in every part. Every line we can draw in the sand has expression; and there is no body without its spirit or genius. All form is an effect of character; all condition, of the quality of the life; all harmony, of health; and for this reason a perception of beauty should be sympathetic, or proper only to

[4]Iamblichus was a fourth-century Neoplatonist. [Ed.]

the good. The beautiful rests on the foundations of the necessary. The soul makes the body, as the wise Spenser teaches: —

> So every spirit, as it is more pure,
> And hath in it the more of heavenly light,
> So it the fairer body doth procure
> To habit in, and it more fairly dight,
> With cheerful grace and amiable sight.
> For, of the soul, the body form doth take,
> For soul is form, and doth the body make.[5]

Here we find ourselves suddenly not in a critical speculation but in a holy place, and should go very warily and reverently. We stand before the secret of the world, there where Being passes into Appearance and Unity into Variety.

The Universe is the externization of the soul. Wherever the life is, that bursts into appearance around it. Our science is sensual, and therefore superficial. The earth and the heavenly bodies, physics and chemistry, we sensually treat, as if they were self-existent; but these are the retinue of that Being we have. "The mighty heaven," said Proclus, "exhibits, in its transfigurations, clear images of the splendor of intellectual perceptions; being moved in conjunction with the unapparent periods of intellectual natures."[6] Therefore science always goes abreast with the just elevation of the man, keeping step with religion and metaphysics; or the state of science is an index of our self-knowledge. Since every thing in nature answers to a moral power, if any phenomenon remains brute and dark it is because the corresponding faculty in the observer is not yet active.

No wonder then, if these waters be so deep, that we hover over them with a religious regard. The beauty of the fable proves the importance of the sense; to the poet, and to all others; or, if you please, every man is so far a poet as to be susceptible of these enchantments of nature; for all men have the thoughts whereof the universe is the celebration. I find that the fascination resides in the symbol. Who loves nature? Who does not? It is only poets, and men of leisure

[5]Edmund Spenser, "An Hymne in Honour of Beautie," 19:127–34. [Ed.]

[6]A fifth-century Neoplatonist. [Ed.]

and cultivation, who live with her? No; but also hunters, farmers, grooms and butchers, though they express their affection in their choice of life and not in their choice of words. The writer wonders what the coachman or the hunter values in riding, in horses and dogs. It is not superficial qualities. When you talk with him he holds these at as slight a rate as you. His worship is sympathetic; he has no definitions, but he is commanded in nature by the living power which he feels to be there present. No imitation or playing of these things would content him; he loves the earnest of the north wind, of rain, of stone and wood and iron. A beauty not explicable is dearer than a beauty which we can see to the end of. It is nature the symbol, nature certifying the supernatural, body overflowed by life which he worships with coarse but sincere rites.

The inwardness and mystery of this attachment drive men of every class to the use of emblems. The schools of poets and philosophers are not more intoxicated with their symbols than the populace with theirs. In our political parties, compute the power of badges and emblems. See the great ball which they roll from Baltimore to Bunker Hill! In the political processions, Lowell goes in a loom, and Lynn in a shoe, and Salem in a ship. Witness the cider-barrel, the log-cabin, the hickory-stick, the palmetto, and all the cognizances of party. See the power of national emblems. Some stars, lilies, leopards, a crescent, a lion, an eagle, or other figure which came into credit God knows how, on an old rag of bunting, blowing in the wind on a fort at the ends of the earth, shall make the blood tingle under the rudest or the most conventional exterior. The people fancy they hate poetry, and they are all poets and mystics!

Beyond the universality of the symbolic language we are apprised of the divineness of this superior use of things, whereby the world is a temple whose walls are covered with emblems, pictures and commandments of the Deity, — in this, that there is no fact in nature which does not carry the whole sense of nature; and the distinctions which we make in events and in affairs, of low and high, honest and base, disappear when nature is used as a symbol. Thought makes everything fit for use. The vocabulary of an omniscient man would embrace words and images excluded from polite conversation. What would be base, or even obscene, to the obscene, becomes illustrious, spoken in a new connection of thought. The piety of the Hebrew prophets purges their grossness. The circumcision is an example of the power of poetry to raise the low and offensive. Small and mean things serve as well as great symbols. The meaner the type by which a law is expressed, the more pungent it is, and the more lasting in the memories of men; just as we choose the smallest box or case in which any needful utensil can be carried. Bare lists of words are found suggestive to an imaginative and excited mind, as it is related of Lord Chatham that he was accustomed to read in Bailey's Dictionary when he was preparing to speak in Parliament. The poorest experience is rich enough for all the purposes of expressing thought. Why covet a knowledge of new facts? Day and night, house and garden, a few books, a few actions, serve us as well as would all trades and all spectacles. We are far from having exhausted the significance of the few symbols we use. We can come to use them yet with a terrible simplicity. It does not need that a poem should be long. Every word was once a poem. Every new relation is a new word. Also we use defects and deformities to a sacred purpose, so expressing our sense that the evils of the world are such only to the evil eye. In the old mythology, mythologists observe, defects are ascribed to divine natures, as lameness to Vulcan, blindness to Cupid, and the like, — to signify exuberances.

For as it is dislocation and detachment from the life of God that makes things ugly, the poet, who re-attaches things to nature and the Whole, — re-attaching even artificial things and violation of nature, to nature, by a deeper insight, — disposes very easily of the most disagreeable facts. Readers of poetry see the factory-village and the railway, and fancy that the poetry of the landscape is broken up by these; for these works of art are not yet consecrated in their reading; but the poet sees them fall within the great Order not less than the beehive or the spider's geometrical web. Nature adopts them very fast into her vital circles, and the gliding train of cars she loves like her own. Besides, in a centered mind,

it signifies nothing how many mechanical inventions you exhibit. Though you add millions, and never so surprising, the fact of mechanics has not gained a grain's weight. The spiritual fact remains unalterable, by many or by few particulars; as no mountain is of any appreciable height to break the curve of the sphere. A shrewd country-boy goes to the city for the first time, and the complacent citizen is not satisfied with his little wonder. It is not that he does not see all the fine houses and know that he never saw such before, but he disposes of them as easily as the poet finds place for the railway. The chief value of the new fact is to enhance the great and constant fact of Life, which can dwarf any and every circumstance, and to which the belt of wampum and the commerce of America are alike.

The world being thus put under the mind for verb and noun, the poet is he who can articulate it. For though life is great, and fascinates and absorbs; and though all men are intelligent of the symbols through which it is named; yet they cannot originally use them. We are symbols and inhabit symbols; workmen, work, and tools, words and things, birth and death, all are emblems but we sympathize with the symbols, and being infatuated with the economical uses of things, we do not know that they are thoughts. The poet, by an ulterior intellectual perception, gives them a power which makes their old use forgotten, and puts eyes and a tongue into every dumb and inanimate object. He perceives the independence of the thought on the symbol, the stability of the thought, the accidency and fugacity of the symbol. As the eyes of Lyncaeus were said to see through the earth, so the poet turns the world to glass, and shows us all things in their right series and procession. For through that better perception he stands one step nearer to things, and sees the flowing or metamorphosis; perceives that thought is multiform; that within the form of every creature is a force compelling it to ascend into a higher form; and following with his eyes the life, uses the forms which express that life, and so his speech flows with the flowing of nature. All the facts of the animal economy, sex, nutriment, gestation, birth, growth, are symbols of the passage of the world into the soul of man, to suffer there a change and reappear a new and higher fact. He uses forms according to the life, and not according to the form. This is true science. The poet alone knows astronomy, chemistry, vegetation and animation, for he does not stop at these facts, but employs them as signs. He knows why the plain or meadow or space was strown with these flowers we call suns and moons and stars; why the great deep is adorned with animals, with men, and gods; for in every word he speaks he rides on them as the horses of thought.

By virtue of this science the poet is the Namer or Language-maker, naming things sometimes after their appearance, sometimes after their essence, and giving to every one its own name and not another's, thereby rejoicing the intellect, which delights in detachment or boundary. The poets made all the words, and therefore language is the archives of history, and, if we must say it, a sort of tomb of the muses. For though the origin of most of our words is forgotten, each word was at first a stroke of genius, and obtained currency because for the moment it symbolized the world to the first speaker and to the hearer. The etymologist finds the deadest word to have been once a brilliant picture. Language is fossil poetry. As the limestone of the continent consists of infinite masses of the shells of animalcules, so language is made up of images or tropes, which now, in their secondary use, have long ceased to remind us of their poetic origin. But the poet names the thing because he sees it, or comes one step nearer to it than any other. This expression or naming is not art, but a second nature, grown out of the first, as a leaf out of a tree. What we call nature is a certain self-regulated motion or change; and nature does all things by her own hands, and does not leave another to baptize her but baptizes herself; and this through the metamorphosis again. I remember that a certain poet[7] described it to me thus: —

> Genius is the activity which repairs the decays of things, whether wholly or partly of a material and finite kind. Nature, through all her kingdoms, insures herself. Nobody cares for planting the poor

fungus; so she shakes down from the gills of one agaric countless spores, any one of which, being preserved, transmits new billions of spores tomorrow or next day. The new agaric of this hour has a chance which the old one had not. This atom of seed is thrown into a new place, not subject to the accidents which destroyed its parent two rods off. She makes a man; and having brought him to ripe age, she will no longer run the risk of losing this wonder at a blow, but she detaches from him a new self, that the kind may be safe from accidents to which the individual is exposed. So when the soul of the poet has come to ripeness of thought, she detaches and sends away from it its poems or songs, — a fearless, sleepless, deathless progeny, which is not exposed to the accidents of the weary kingdom of time; a fearless, vivacious offspring, clad with wings (such was the virtue of the soul out of which they came) which carry them fast and far, and infix them irrecoverably into the hearts of men. These wings are the beauty of a poet's soul. The songs, thus flying immortal from their mortal parent, are pursued by clamorous flights of censures, which swarm in far greater numbers and threaten to devour them; but these last are not winged. At the end of a very short leap they fall plump down and rot, having received from the souls out of which they came no beautiful wings. But the melodies of the poet ascend and leap and pierce into the deeps of infinite time.

So far the bard taught me, using his freer speech. But nature has a higher end, in the production of new individuals, than security, namely *ascension,* or the passage of the soul into higher forms. I knew in my younger days the sculptor who made the statue of the youth which stands in the public garden. He was, as I remember, unable to tell directly what made him happy or unhappy, but by wonderful indirections he could tell. He rose one day, according to his habit, before the dawn, and saw the morning break, grand as the eternity out of which it came, and for many days after, he strove to express this tranquillity, and lo! his chisel had fashioned out of marble the form of a beautiful youth, Phosphorus,[8] whose aspect is such that it is said all persons who look on it become silent. The poet also resigns himself to his mood, and that thought

---

[7]The following passage is Emerson's own adaptation of Plato's *Phaedrus*. [Ed.]

[8]The morning star. [Ed.]

which agitated him is expressed, but *alter idem,*[9] in a manner totally new. The expression is organic, or the new type which things themselves take when liberated. As, in the sun, objects paint their images on the retina of the eye, so they, sharing the aspiration of the whole universe, tend to paint a far more delicate copy of their essence in his mind. Like the metamorphosis of things into higher organic forms is their change into melodies. Over everything stands its daemon or soul, and, as the form of the thing is reflected by the eye, so the soul of the thing is reflected by a melody. The sea, the mountain-ridge, Niagara, and every flower-bed, pre-exist, or superexist, in precantations, which sail like odors in the air, and when any man goes by with an ear sufficiently fine, he overhears them and endeavors to write down the notes without diluting or depraving them. And herein is the legitimation of criticism, in the mind's faith that the poems are a corrupt version of some text in nature with which they ought to be made to tally. A rhyme in one of our sonnets should not be less pleasing than the iterated nodes of a seashell, or the resembling difference of a group of flowers. The pairing of the birds is an idyl, not tedious as our idyls are; a tempest is a rough ode, without falsehood or rant; a summer, with its harvest sown, reaped and stored, is an epic song, subordinating how many admirably executed parts. Why should not the symmetry and truth that modulate these, glide into our spirits, and we participate the invention of nature?

This insight, which expresses itself by what is called Imagination, is a very high sort of seeing, which does not come by study, but by the intellect being where and what it sees; by sharing the path or circuit of things through forms, and so making them translucid to others. The path of things is silent. Will they suffer a speaker to go with them? A spy they will not suffer; a lover, a poet, is the transcendency of their own nature, — him they will suffer. The condition of true naming, on the poet's part, is his resigning himself to the divine *aura* which breathes through forms, and accompanying that.

[9]The same thing in another way. [Ed.]

It is a secret which every intellectual man quickly learns, that beyond the energy of his possessed and conscious intellect he is capable of a new energy (as of an intellect doubled on itself), by abandonment to the nature of things; that beside his privacy of power as an individual man, there is a great public power on which he can draw, by unlocking, at all risks, his human doors, and suffering the ethereal tides to roll and circulate through him; then he is caught up into the life of the Universe, his speech is thunder, his thought is law, and his words are universally intelligible as the plants and animals. The poet knows that he speaks adequately then only when he speaks somewhat wildly, or "with the flower of the mind"; not with the intellect used as an organ, but with the intellect released from all service and suffered to take its direction from its celestial life; or as the ancients were wont to express themselves, not with intellect alone but with the intellect inebriated by nectar. As the traveler who has lost his way throws his reins on his horse's neck and trusts to the instinct of the animal to find his road, so must we do with the divine animal who carries us through this world. For if in any manner we can stimulate this instinct, new passages are opened for us into nature; the mind flows into and through things hardest and highest, and the metamorphosis is possible.

This is the reason why bards love wine, mead, narcotics, coffee, tea, opium, the fumes of sandalwood and tobacco, or whatever other procurers of animal exhilaration. All men avail themselves of such means as they can, to add this extraordinary power to their normal powers; and to this end they prize conversation, music, pictures, sculpture, dancing, theaters, traveling, war, mobs, fires, gaming, politics, or love, or science, or animal intoxication, — which are several coarser or finer *quasi*-mechanical substitutes for the true nectar, which is the ravishment of the intellect by coming nearer to the fact. These are auxiliaries to the centrifugal tendency of a man, to his passage out into free space, and they help him to escape the custody of that body in which he is pent up, and of that jail-yard of individual relations in which he is enclosed. Hence a great number of such as were professionally expressers of Beauty, as painters, poets, musicians and actors, have been more than others wont to lead a life of pleasure and indulgence; all but the few who received the true nectar; and, as it was a spurious mode of attaining freedom, as it was an emancipation not into the heavens but into the freedom of baser places, they were punished for that advantage they won, by a dissipation and deterioration. But never can any advantage be taken of nature by a trick. The spirit of the world, the great calm presence of the Creator, comes not forth to the sorceries of opium or of wine. The sublime vision comes to the pure and simple soul in a clean and chaste body. That is not an inspiration, which we owe to narcotics, but some counterfeit excitement and fury. Milton says that the lyric poet may drink wine and live generously, but the epic poet, he who shall sing of the gods and their descent unto men, must drink water out of a wooden bowl. For poetry is not "Devil's wine," but God's wine. It is with this as it is with toys. We fill the hands and nurseries of our children with all manner of dolls, drums and horses; withdrawing their eyes from the plain face and suficing objects of nature, the sun and moon, the animals, the water and stones, which should be their toys. So the poet's habit of living should be set on a key so low that the common influences should delight him. His cheerfulness should be the gift of the sunlight; the air should suffice for his inspiration, and he should be tipsy with water. That spirit which suffices quiet hearts, which seems to come forth to such from every dry knoll of sere grass, from every pine stump and half-imbedded stone on which the dull March sun shines, comes forth to the poor and hungry, and such as are of simple taste. If thou fill thy brain with Boston and New York, with fashion and covetousness, and wilt stimulate thy jaded senses with wine and French coffee, thou shalt find no radiance of wisdom in the lonely waste of the pine woods.

If the imagination intoxicates the poet, it is not inactive in other men. The metamorphosis excites in the beholder an emotion of joy. The use of symbols has a certain power of emancipation and exhilaration for all men. We seem to be touched by a wand which makes us dance and run about happily, like children. We are like persons who come out of a cave or cellar into the open air. This is the effect on us of tropes, fables, oracles and all poetic forms. Poets are thus liberating gods. Men have really got a new sense, and found within their world another world, or nest of worlds; for, the metamorphosis once seen, we divine that it does not stop. I will not now consider how much this makes the charm of algebra and the mathematics, which also have their tropes, but it is felt in every definition; as when Aristotle defines *space* to be an immovable vessel in which things are contained; — or when Plato defines a *line* to be a flowing point; or *figure* to be bound of solid; and many the like. What a joyful sense of freedom we have when Vitruvius announces the old opinion of artists that no architect can build any house well who does not know something of anatomy. When Socrates, in Charmides, tells us that the soul is cured of its maladies by certain incantations, and that these incantations are beautiful reasons, from which temperance is generated in souls; when Plato calls the world an animal, and Timaeus affirms that the plants also are animals; or affirms a man to be a heavenly tree, growing with his root, which is his head, upward; and, as George Chapman, following him, writes,

So in our tree of man, whose nervie root
  Springs in his top; —

when Orpheus speaks of hoariness as "that white flower which marks extreme old age"; when Proclus calls the universe the statue of the intellect; when Chaucer, in his praise of "Gentilesse," compares good blood in mean condition to fire, which, though carried to the darkest house betwixt this and the mount of Caucasus, will yet hold its natural office and burn as bright as if twenty thousand men did it behold; when John saw, in the Apocalypse, the ruin of the world through evil, and the stars fall from heaven as the fig tree casteth her untimely fruit; when Aesop reports the whole catalogue of common daily relations through the masquerade of birds and beasts; — we take the cheerful hint of the immortality of our essence and its versatile habit and escapes, as when the gypsies say of themselves "it is in vain to hang them, they cannot die."

The poets are thus liberating gods. The ancient British bards had for the title of their order, "Those who are free throughout the world." They are free, and they make free. An imaginative book renders as much more service at first, by stimulating us through its tropes, than afterward when we arrive at the precise sense of the author. I think nothing is of any value in books excepting the transcendental and extraordinary. If a man is inflamed and carried away by his thought, to that degree that he forgets the authors and the public and heeds only this one dream which holds him like an insanity, let me read his paper, and you may have all the arguments and histories and criticism. All the value which attaches to Pythagoras, Paracelsus, Cornelius Agrippa, Cardan, Kepler, Swedenborg, Schelling, Oken, or any other who introduces questionable facts into his cosmogony, as angels, devils, magic, astrology, palmistry, mesmerism, and so on, is the certificate we have of departure from routine, and that here is a new witness. That also is the best success in conversation, the magic of liberty, which puts the world like a ball in our hands. How cheap even the liberty then seems; how mean to study, when an emotion communicates to the intellect the power to sap and upheave nature; how great the perspective! nations, times, systems, enter and disappear like threads in tapestry of large figure and many colors; dream delivers us to dream, and while the drunkenness lasts we will sell our bed, our philosophy, our religion, in our opulence.

There is good reason why we should prize this liberation. The fate of the poor shepherd, who, blinded and lost in the snowstorm, perishes in a drift within a few feet of his cottage door, is an emblem of the state of man. On the brink of the waters of life and truth, we are miserably dying. The inaccessibleness of every thought but that we are in, is wonderful. What if you come near to it; you are as remote when you are nearest as when you are farthest. Every thought is also a prison; every heaven is also a prison. Therefore we love the poet, the inventor, who in any form, whether in an ode or in an action or in looks and behavior, has yielded us a new thought. He unlocks our chains and admits us to a new scene.

This emancipation is dear to all men, and the power to impart it, as it must come from greater depth and scope of thought, is a measure of intellect. Therefore all books of the imagination endure, all which ascend to that truth that the writer sees nature beneath him, and uses it as his exponent. Every verse or sentence possessing this virtue will take care of its own immortality. The religions of the world are the ejaculations of a few imaginative men.

But the quality of the imagination is to flow, and not to freeze. The poet did not stop at the color or the form, but read their meaning; neither may he rest in this meaning, but he makes the same objects exponents of his new thought. Here is the difference betwixt the poet and the mystic, that the last nails a symbol to one sense, which was a true sense for a moment, but soon becomes old and false. For all symbols are fluxional; all language is vehicular and transitive, and is good, as ferries and horses are, for conveyance, not as farms and houses are, for homestead. Mysticism consists in the mistake of an accidental and individual symbol for an universal one. The morning-redness happens to be the favorite meteor to the eyes of Jacob Behmen,[10] and comes to stand to him for truth and faith; and, he believes, should stand for the same realities to every reader. But the first reader prefers as naturally the symbol of a mother and child, or a gardener and his bulb, or a jeweler polishing a gem. Either of these, or of a myriad more, are equally good to the person to whom they are significant. Only they must be held lightly, and be very willingly translated into the equivalent terms which others use. And the mystic must be steadily told, — All that you say is just as true without the tedious use of that symbol as with it. Let us have a little algebra, instead of this trite rhetoric, — universal signs, instead of these village symbols, — and we shall both be gainers. The history of hierarchies seems to show that all religious error consisted in making the symbol too stark and solid, and was at last nothing but an excess of the organ of language.

Swedenborg, of all men in the recent ages, stands eminently for the translator of nature into

[10]Emerson probably means German mystic Jakob Böhme (1575–1624). [Ed.]

thought. I do not know the man in history to whom things stood so uniformly for words. Before him the metamorphosis continually plays. Everything on which his eye rests, obeys the impulses of moral nature. The figs become grapes whilst he eats them. When some of his angels affirmed a truth, the laurel twig which they held blossomed in their hands. The noise which at a distance appeared like gnashing and thumping, on coming nearer was found to be the voice of disputants. The men in one of his visions, seen in heavenly light, appeared like dragons, and seemed in darkness; but to each other they appeared as men, and when the light from heaven shone into their cabin, they complained of the darkness, and were compelled to shut the window that they might see.

There was this perception in him which makes the poet or seer an object of awe and terror, namely that the same man or society of men may wear one aspect to themselves and their companions, and a different aspect to higher intelligences. Certain priests, whom he describes as conversing very learnedly together, appeared to the children who were at some distance, like dead horses; and many the like misappearances. And instantly the mind inquires whether these fishes under the bridge, yonder oxen in the pasture, those dogs in the yard, are immutably fishes, oxen and dogs, or only so appear to me, and perchance to themselves appear upright men; and whether I appear as a man to all eyes. The Brahmins and Pythagoras propounded the same question, and if any poet has witnessed the transformation he doubtless found it in harmony with various experiences. We have all seen changes as considerable in wheat and caterpillars. He is the poet and shall draw us with love and terror, who sees through the flowing vest the firm nature, and can declare it.

I look in vain for the poet whom I describe. We do not with sufficient plainness or sufficient profoundness address ourselves to life, nor dare we chaunt our own times and social circumstance. If we filled the day with bravery, we should not shrink from celebrating it. Time and nature yield us many gifts, but not yet the timely man, the new religion, the reconciler, whom all things await. Dante's praise is that he dared to write his autobiography in colossal cipher, or into universality. We have had no genius in America, with tyrannous eye, which knew the value of our incomparable materials, and saw, in the barbarism and materialism of the times, another carnival of the same gods whose picture he so much admires in Homer; then in the Middle Age; then in Calvinism. Banks and tariffs, the newspaper and caucus, Methodism and Unitarianism, are flat and dull to dull people, but rest on the same foundations of wonder as the town of Troy and the temple of Delphi, and are as swiftly passing away. Our log-rolling, our stumps and their politics, our fisheries, our Negroes and Indians, our boats and our repudiations, the wrath of rogues and the pusillanimity of honest men, the northern trade, the southern planting, the western clearing, Oregon and Texas, are yet unsung. Yet America is a poem in our eyes; its ample geography dazzles the imagination, and it will not wait long for meters. If I have not found that excellent combination of gifts in my countrymen which I seek, neither could I aid myself to fix the idea of the poet by reading now and then in Chalmers's collection of five centuries of English poets. These are wits more than poets, though there have been poets among them. But when we adhere to the ideal of the poets, we have our difficulties even with Milton and Homer. Milton is too literary, and Homer too literal and historical.

But I am not wise enough for a national criticism, and must use the old largeness a little longer, to discharge my errand from the muse to the poet concerning his art.

Art is the path of the creator to his work. The paths or methods are ideal and eternal, though few men ever see them; not the artist himself for years, or for a lifetime, unless he come into the conditions. The painter, the sculptor, the composer, the epic rhapsodist, the orator, all partake one desire, namely to express themselves symmetrically and abundantly, not dwarfishly and fragmentarily. They found or put themselves in certain conditions, as, the painter and sculptor before some impressive human figures; the orator into the assembly of the people; and the others in such scenes as each has found exciting to his intellect; and each presently feels the new desire.

He hears a voice, he sees a beckoning. Then he is apprised, with wonder, what herds of daemons hem him in. He can no more rest; he says, with the old painter, "By God it is in me and must go forth of me." He pursues a beauty, half seen, which flies before him. The poet pours out verses in every solitude. Most of the things he says are conventional, no doubt; but by and by he says something which is original and beautiful. That charms him. He would say nothing else but such things. In our way of talking we say "That is yours, this is mine"; but the poet knows well that it is not his; that it is as strange and beautiful to him as to you; he would fain hear the like eloquence at length. Once having tasted this immortal ichor, he cannot have enough of it, and as an admirable creative power exists in these intellections, it is of the last importance that these things get spoken. What a little of all we know is said! What drops of all the sea of our science are baled up! and by what accident it is that these are exposed, when so many secrets sleep in nature! Hence the necessity of speech and song; hence these throbs and heart-beatings in the orator, at the door of the assembly, to the end namely that thought may be ejaculated as Logos, or Word.

Doubt not, O poet, but persist. Say "It is in me, and shall out." Stand there, balked and dumb, stuttering and stammering, hissed and hooted, stand and strive, until at last rage draw out of thee that *dream*-power which every night shows thee is thine own; a power transcending all limit and privacy, and by virtue of which a man is the conductor of the whole river of electricity. Nothing walks, or creeps, or grows, or exists, which must not in turn arise and walk before him as exponent of his meaning. Comes he to that power, his genius is no longer exhaustible. All the creatures by pairs and by tribes pour into his mind as into a Noah's ark, to come forth again to people to a new world. This is like the stock of air for our respiration or for the combustion of our fireplace; not a measure of gallons, but the entire atmosphere if wanted. And therefore the rich poets, as Homer, Chaucer, Shakespeare, and Raphael, have obviously no limits to their works except the limits of their lifetime, and resemble a mirror carried through the street, ready to render an image of every created thing.

O poet! a new nobility is conferred in groves and pastures, and not in castles or by the sword-blade any longer. The conditions are hard, but equal. Thou shalt leave the world, and know the muse only. Thou shalt not know any longer the times, customs, graces, politics, or opinions of men, but shall take all from the muse. For the time of towns is tolled from the world by funereal chimes, but in nature the universal hours are counted by succeeding tribes of animals and plants, and by growth of joy on joy. God wills also that thou abdicate a manifold and duplex life, and that thou be content that others speak for thee. Others shall be thy gentlemen and shall represent all courtesy and wordly life for thee; others shall do the great and resounding actions also. Thou shalt lie close hid with nature, and canst not be afforded to the Capitol or the Exchange. The world is full of renunciations and apprenticeships, and this is thine; thou must pass for a fool and a churl for a long season. This is the screen and sheath in which Pan has protected his well-beloved flower, and thou shalt be known only to thine own, and they shall console thee with tenderest love. And thou shalt not be able to rehearse the names of thy friends in thy verse, for an old shame before the holy ideal. And this is the reward; that the ideal shall be real to thee, and the impressions of the actual world shall fall like summer rain, copious, but not troublesome to thy invulnerable essence. Thou shalt have the whole land for thy park and manor, the sea for thy bath and navigation, without tax and without envy; the woods and the rivers thou shalt own, and thou shalt possess that wherein others are only tenants and boarders. Thou true land-lord! sea-lord! air-lord! Wherever snow falls or water flows, or birds fly, wherever day and night meet in twilight, wherever the blue heaven is hung by clouds or sown with stars, wherever are forms with transparent boundaries, wherever are outlets into celestial space, wherever is danger, and awe, and love, — there is Beauty, plenteous as rain, shed for thee, and though thou shouldst walk the world over, thou shalt not be able to find a condition inopportune or ignoble.

# Edgar Allan Poe
## 1809–1849

Edgar Allan Poe was born in Boston, the son of touring actors. Poe's father deserted his mother just after Edgar's birth, and his mother, who continued to travel to support herself, died before he was three. Poe was raised in the home of John Allan, a merchant of Richmond, Virginia, who had him educated in England. Poe attended the University of Virginia in 1826, but his drinking and gambling at the expense of his projected literary career precipitated a quarrel with his foster father that never healed. In 1827, Poe tried the army, and in an attempt at reconciliation was admitted three years later to West Point through Allan's influence, but he was expelled in 1831 for drunkenness and inattention to duty. Poe returned to Baltimore after his expulsion and commenced a literary career, writing poetry with a characteristic note of romantic melancholy and working as editor for the *Southern Literary Messenger*. In Baltimore he stayed with his aunt, Maria Clemm, whose thirteen-year-old daughter, Virginia, he married in 1836. Although Poe worked for a number of newspapers and magazines in Richmond, Philadelphia, and New York over the next twelve years, he advanced little in his profession, owing to his alcohol addiction.

During this time, however, he perfected his poetic style in brief, moody, hyperromantic lyrics that would influence Baudelaire and the French symbolist poets. He also invented the "tale of ratiocination," the ancestor of the modern detective story, and refined the lengthy Gothic novel into the short tale of terror.

Poe's wife died of hunger and tuberculosis in 1847, and Poe himself was deteriorating physically from prolonged poverty and alcoholism. In 1849 he made a last effort to rehabilitate himself, returning to Richmond and becoming engaged to a widow who had been his childhood sweetheart. On the way to a business meeting in Philadelphia, however, he stopped off in Baltimore for a drink and was found five days later in the final stages of delirium tremens; he died soon after.

If we consider only Poe's self-destructive impulsiveness, we may be surprised by the coolness and rational calculation he advocates in "The Philosophy of Composition." This essay, which appeared in *Graham's Magazine* for April 1846, purports to recount the steps Poe had followed in composing "The Raven" the year before. Poe begins in orthodox Aristotelian fashion by selecting the primary desired effect, in this case melancholy, and then considers how he may evoke that effect. First he settles on a melancholy refrain with suitable sonority: the word "Nevermore." Next, he asks what subject matter is most clearly designed to evoke such a feeling and concludes that "the death . . . of a beautiful woman, is, unquestionably, the most poetical topic in the world — and equally is it beyond doubt that the lips best suited for such topic are those of a bereaved lover." The composition then proceeds, as Poe explains, from the necessity of working the subject and the language together. Is this an accurate account of how Poe actually composed "The Raven"? Most commentators are dubious about Poe's biographical claims. But even if Poe has revised events for the sake of his aesthetic theory, his notion that poets should rationally calculate effects and causes rather than romantically trusting their impulsive effusions was worth exploring in his day.

Poe's surprisingly antiromantic theory of art did not differentiate between poetry and prose. If there was a difference between prose and poetry, in fact, Poe gave the advantage to prose. In a review of Hawthorne's *Twice-Told Tales* (*Graham's Magazine,* May 1842), Poe insisted that poetry requires rhythm, and that "the artificialities of this rhythm are an inseparable bar to the development of all points of thought or expression which have their basis in *Truth.*" On the other hand, "the author who aims at the purely beautiful in a prose tale is laboring at great disadvantage. For Beauty can be better treated in the poem." But otherwise Poe makes arguments about the calculation of effects in prose narrative similar to those he was to make about "The Raven":

> A skilful literary artist has constructed a tale. If wise, he has not fashioned his thoughts to accommodate his incidents; but having conceived, with deliberate care, a certain unique or single *effect* to be wrought out, he then invents such incidents — he then combines such events as may best aid him in establishing this preconceived effect . . . .
> In the whole composition there should be no word written, of which the tendency, direct or indirect, is not to the one pre-established design.

## Selected Bibliography

Alterton, Margaret. *Origins of Poe's Critical Theory.* Iowa City: University of Iowa Press, 1925.

Conron, John Joseph. *Poe and the Theory of the Short Story.* Ann Arbor: UMI Press, 1970.

Davidson, Edward H. *Poe: A Critical Study.* Cambridge: Harvard University Press, 1957.

Gregorzewski, Carla. *Edgar Allan Poe und die Anfänge einer originär amerikanschen Ästhetik.* Heidelberg: Winter, 1982.

Halliburton, David. *Edgar Allan Poe: A Phenomenological View:* Princeton: Princeton University Press, 1973.

Jacobs, R. D. *Poe: Journalist and Critic.* Baton Rouge: Louisiana State University Press, 1969.

Marks, E. R. "Poe as a Literary Theorist: A Reappraisal." *American Literature* 33 (1961): 296–306.

Parks, Edd W. *Edgar Allan Poe as a Literary Critic.* Athens: University of Georgia Press, 1964.

# The Philosophy of Composition

Charles Dickens, in a note now lying before me, alluding to an examination I once made of the mechanism of *Barnaby Rudge,* says — "By the way, are you aware that Godwin wrote his *Caleb Williams* backward? He first involved his hero in a web of difficulties, forming the second volume, and then, for the first, cast about him for some mode of accounting for what had been done."

I cannot think this the *precise* mode of procedure on the part of Godwin — and indeed what he himself acknowledges, is not altogether in accordance with Mr. Dickens's idea — but the author of *Caleb Williams* was too good an artist not to perceive the advantage derivable from at least a somewhat similar process. Nothing is more clear than that every plot, worth the name, must be elaborated to its *dénouement* before anything be attempted with the pen. It is only with the *dénouement* constantly in view that we can give a plot its indispensable air of consequence, or causation, by making the incidents, and especially the tone at all points, tend to the development of the intention.

There is a radical error, I think, in the usual mode of constructing a story. Either history affords a thesis — or one is suggested by an incident of the day — or, at best, the author sets himself to work in the combination of striking events to form merely the basis of his narrative — designing, generally, to fill in with description, dialogue, or authorial comment, whatever crevices of fact, or action, may, from page to page, render themselves apparent.

I prefer commencing with the consideration of an *effect*. Keeping originality *always* in view — for he is false to himself who ventures to dispense with so obvious and so easily attainable a source of interest — I say to myself, in the first place, "Of the innumerable effects, or impressions, of which the heart, the intellect, or (more generally) the soul is susceptible, what one shall I, on the present occasion, select?" Having chosen a novel, first, and secondly a vivid effect, I consider whether it can be best wrought by incident or tone — whether by ordinary incidents and peculiar tone, or the converse, or by peculiarity both of incident and tone — afterward looking about me (or rather within) for such combinations of event, or tone, as shall best aid me in the construction of the effect.

I have often thought how interesting a magazine paper might be written by any author who would — that is to say who could — detail, step by step, the processes by which any one of his compositions attained its ultimate point of completion. Why such a paper has never been given to the world, I am much at a loss to say — but,

perhaps, the authorial vanity has had more to do with the omission than any one other cause. Most writers — poets in especial — prefer having it understood that they compose by a species of fine frenzy — an ecstatic intuition — and would positively shudder at letting the public take a peep behind the scenes, at the elaborate and vacillating crudities of thought — at the true purposes seized only at the last moment — at the innumerable glimpses of idea that arrived not at the maturity of full view — at the fully matured fancies discarded in despair as unmanageable — at the cautious selections and rejections — at the painful erasures and interpolations — in a word, at the wheels and pinions — the tackle for scene-shifting — the step-ladders and demon-traps — the cock's feathers, and red paint, and the black patches, which, in ninety-nine cases out of the hundred, constitute the properties of the literary *histrio*.[1]

I am aware, on the other hand, that the case is by no means common, in which an author is at all in condition to retrace the steps by which his conclusions have been attained. In general, suggestions, having arisen pell-mell, are pursued and forgotten in a similar manner.

For my own part, I have neither sympathy with the repugnance alluded to, nor at any time the least difficulty in recalling to mind the progressive steps of any of my compositions; and, since the interest of an analysis, or reconstruction, such as I have considered a *desideratum,* is quite independent of any real or fancied interest in the thing analyzed, it will not be regarded as a breach of decorum on my part to show the *modus operandi* by which some one of my own works was put together. I select *The Raven,* as most generally known. It is my design to render it manifest that no one point in its composition is referrible either to accident or intuition — that the work proceeded, step by step, to its completion with the precision and rigid consequence of a mathematical problem.

Let us dismiss, as irrelevant to the poem, *per se,* the circumstance — or say the necessity — which, in the first place, gave rise to the intention

[1]Actor. [Ed.]

of composing *a* poem that should suit at once the popular and the critical taste.

We commence, then, with this intention.

The initial consideration was that of extent. If any literary work is too long to be read at one sitting, we must be content to dispense with the immensely important effect derivable from unity of impression — for, if two sittings be required, the affairs of the world interfere, and every thing like totality is at once destroyed. But since, *ceteris paribus,* no poet can afford to dispense with *any thing* that may advance his design, it but remains to be seen whether there is, in extent, any advantage to counterbalance the loss of unity which attends it. Here I say no, at once. What we term a long poem is, in fact, merely a succession of brief ones — that is to say, of brief poetical effects. It is needless to demonstrate that a poem is such, only inasmuch as it intensely excites, by elevating the soul; and all intense excitements are, though a physical necessity, brief. For this reason, at least one half of the *Paradise Lost* is essentially prose — a succession of poetical excitements interspersed, *inevitably,* with corresponding depressions — the whole being deprived, through the extremeness of its length, of the vastly important artistic element, totality, or unity, of effect.

It appears evident, then, that there is a distinct limit, as regards length, to all works of literary art — the limit of a single sitting — and that, although in certain classes of prose composition, such as *Robinson Crusoe* (demanding no unity) this limit may be advantageously overpassed, it can never properly be overpassed in a poem. Within this limit, the extent of a poem may be made to bear mathematical relation to its merit — in other words, to the excitement or elevation — again in other words, to the degree of the true poetical effect which it is capable of inducing; for it is clear that the brevity must be in direct ratio of the intensity of the intended effect: — this, with one proviso — that a certain degree of duration is absolutely requisite for the production of any effect at all.

Holding in view these considerations, as well as that degree of excitement which I deemed not above the popular, while not below the critical, taste, I reached at once what I conceived the proper *length* for my intended poem — a length of about one hundred lines. It is, in fact, a hundred and eight.

My next thought concerned the choice of an impression, or effect, to be conveyed; and here I may as well observe that, throughout the construction, I kept steadily in view the design of rendering the work *universally* appreciable. I should be carried too far out of my immediate topic were I to demonstrate a point upon which I have repeatedly insisted, and which, with the poetical, stands not in the slightest need of demonstration — the point, I mean, that Beauty is the sole legitimate province of the poem. A few words, however, in elucidation of my real meaning, which some of my friends have evinced a disposition to misrepresent. That pleasure which is at once the most intense, the most elevating, and the most pure, is, I believe, found in the contemplation of the beautiful. When, indeed, men speak of Beauty, they mean, precisely, not a quality, as is supposed, but an effect — they refer, in short, just to that intense and pure elevation of *soul* — *not* of intellect, or of heart — upon which I have commented, and which is experienced in consequence of contemplating "the beautiful." Now I designate Beauty as the province of the poem, merely because it is an obvious rule of Art that effects should be made to spring from direct causes — that objects should be attained through means best adapted for their attainment — no one as yet having been weak enough to deny that the peculiar elevation alluded to is *most readily* attained in the poem. Now the object, Truth, or the satisfaction of the intellect, and the object Passion, or the excitement of the heart, are, although attainable, to a certain extent, in poetry, far more readily attainable in prose. Truth, in fact, demands a precision, and Passion a *homeliness* (the truly passionate will comprehend me) which are absolutely antagonistic to that Beauty which, I maintain, is the excitement, or pleasurable elevation, of the soul. It by no means follows from any thing here said, that passion, or even truth, may not be introduced, and even profitably introduced, into a poem — for they may serve in elucidation, or aid the general effect, as do discords in music, by contrast — but the true artist will always contrive, first, to tone them into proper subservience to the predominant aim, and, secondly, to enveil them, as far as possible, in that Beauty which is the atmosphere and the essence of the poem.

Regarding, then, Beauty as my province, my next question referred to the *tone* of its highest manifestation — and all experience has shown that this tone is one of *sadness*. Beauty of whatever kind, in its supreme development, invariably excites the sensitive soul to tears. Melancholy is thus the most legitimate of all the poetical tones.

The length, the province, and the tone, being thus determined, I betook myself to ordinary induction, with the view of obtaining some artistic piquancy which might serve me as a key-note in the construction of the poem — some pivot upon which the whole structure might turn. In carefully thinking over all the usual artistic effects — or more properly *points,* in the theatrical sense — I did not fail to perceive immediately that no one had been so universally employed as that of the *refrain*. The universality of its employment sufficed to assure me of its intrinsic value, and spared me the necessity of submitting it to analysis. I considered it, however, with regard to its susceptibility of improvement, and soon saw it to be in a primitive condition. As commonly used, the *refrain,* or burden, not only is limited to lyric verse, but depends for its impression upon the force of monotone — both in sound and thought. The pleasure is deduced solely from the sense of identity — of repetition. I resolved to diversify, and so heighten, the effect, by adhering, in general, to the monotone of sound, while I continually varied that of thought: that is to say, I determined to produce continuously novel effects, by the variation of the *application* of the refrain — the refrain itself remaining, for the most part, unvaried.

These points being settled, I next bethought me of the *nature* of my refrain. Since its application was to be repeatedly varied, it was clear that the refrain itself must be brief, for there would have been an insurmountable difficulty in frequent variations of application in any sentence of length. In proportion to the brevity of the sentence, would, of course, be the facility of the variation. This led me at once to a single word as the best refrain.

The question now arose as to the *character* of the word. Having made up my mind to a refrain, the division of the poem into stanzas way, of course, a corollary: the refrain forming the close of each stanza. That such a close, to have force, must be sonorous and susceptible of protracted emphasis, admitted no doubt; and these considerations inevitably led me to the long *o* as the most sonorous vowel, in connection with *r* as the most producible consonant.

The sound of the refrain being thus determined, it became necessary to select a word embodying this sound, and at the same time in the fullest possible keeping with that melancholy which I had predetermined as the tone of the poem. In such a search it would have been absolutely impossible to overlook the word "Nevermore." In fact, it was the very first which presented itself.

The next *desideratum* was a pretext for the continuous use of the one word "Nevermore." In observing the difficulty which I at once found in inventing a sufficiently plausible reason for its continuous repetition, I did not fail to perceive that this difficulty arose solely from the pre-assumption that the word was to be so continuously or monotonously spoken by a *human* being — I did not fail to perceive, in short, that the difficulty lay in the reconciliation of this monotony with the exercise of reason on the part of the creature repeating the word. Here, then, immediately arose the idea of a *non-reasoning* creature capable of speech; and, very naturally, a parrot, in the first instance, suggested itself, but was superseded forthwith by a Raven, as equally capable of speech, and infinitely more in keeping with the intended *tone*.

I had now gone so far as the conception of a Raven — the bird of ill omen — monotonously repeating the one word, "Nevermore" at the conclusion of each stanza, in a poem of melancholy tone, and in length about one hundred lines. Now, never losing sight of the object *supremeness,* or perfection, at all points, I asked myself — "Of all melancholy topics, what, according to the *universal* understanding of mankind, is the *most* melancholy?" "Death" — was the obvious reply. "And when," I said, "is this most melancholy of topics most poetical?" From what I have already explained at some length, the answer, here also, is obvious — "When it most closely allies itself to *Beauty*." The death, then, of a beautiful woman, is, unquestionably, the most poetical topic in the world — and equally is it beyond doubt that the lips best suited for such topic are those of a bereaved lover.

I had now to combine the two ideas, of a lover lamenting his deceased mistress, and a Raven continuously repeating the word "Nevermore." I had to combine these, bearing in mind my design of varying, at every turn, the *application* of the word repeated; but the only intelligible mode of such combination is that of imagining the Raven employing the word in answer to the queries of the lover. And here it was that I saw at once the opportunity afforded for the effect on which I had been depending — that is to say, the effect of the *variation of application*. I saw that I could make the first query propounded by the lover — the first query to which the Raven should reply "Nevermore" — that I could make this first query a commonplace one — the second less so — the third still less, and so on — until at length the lover, startled from his original *nonchalance* by the melancholy character of the word itself — by its frequent repetition — and by a consideration of the ominous reputation of the fowl that uttered it — is at length excited to superstition, and wildly propounds queries of a far different character — queries whose solution he has passionately at heart — propounds them half in superstition and half in that species of despair which delights in self-torture — propounds them not altogether because he believes in the prophetic or demoniac character of the bird (which, reason assures him, is merely repeating a lesson learned by rote) but because he experiences a phrenzied pleasure in so modeling his questions as to receive from the *expected* "Nevermore" the most delicious because the most intolerable of sorrow. Perceiving the opportunity thus afforded me — or, more strictly, thus forced upon me in the progress of the construction — I first established in mind the climax, or concluding query — that query to which "Nevermore" should be in the last place an answer — that in reply to which this word "Nevermore" should involve the utmost conceivable amount of sorrow and despair.

Here then the poem may be said to have its beginning — at the end, where all works of art should begin — for it was here, at this point of my preconsiderations, that I first put pen to paper in the composition of the stanza:

"Prophet," said I, "thing of evil! prophet still if bird or devil!
By that heaven that bends above us — by that God we both adore,
Tell this soul with sorrow laden, if within the distant Aidenn,
It shall clasp a sainted maiden whom the angels name Lenore —
Clasp a rare and radiant maiden whom the angels name Lenore."
     Quoth the Raven, "Nevermore."

I composed this stanza, at this point, first, that by establishing the climax, I might the better vary and graduate, as regards seriousness and importance, the preceding queries of the lover; and secondly, that I might definitely settle the rhythm, the meter, and the length and general arrangement of the stanza, — as well as graduate the stanzas which were to precede, so that none of them might surpass this in rhythmical effect. Had I been able, in the subsequent composition, to construct more vigorous stanzas, I should without scruple, have purposely enfeebled them, so as not to interfere with the climacteric effect.

And here I may as well say a few words of the versification. My first object (as usual) was originality. The extent to which this has been neglected, in versification, is one of the most unaccountable things in the world. Admitting that there is little possibility of variety in mere *rhythm,* it is still clear that the possible varieties of meter and stanza are absolutely infinite — and yet, *for centuries, no man, in verse, has ever done, or ever seemed to think of doing, an original thing.* The fact is, that originality (unless in minds of very unusual force) is by no means a matter, as some suppose, of impulse or intuition. In general, to be found, it must be elaborately sought, and although a positive merit of the highest class, demands in its attainment less of invention than negation.

Of course, I pretend to no originality in either the rhythm or meter of *The Raven*. The former is trochaic — the latter is octameter acatalectic, alternating with heptameter catalectic repeated in the refrain of the fifth verse, and terminating with tetrameter catalectic. Less pedantically — the feet employed throughout (trochees) consist of a long syllable followed by a short: the first line of the stanza consists of eight of these feet — the second of seven and a half (in effect two-thirds) — the third of eight — the fourth of seven and a half — the fifth the same — the sixth three and a half. Now, each of these lines, taken individually, has been employed before; and what originality *The Raven* has, is in their *combination into stanza;* nothing even remotely approaching this combination has ever been attempted. The effect of this originality of combination is aided by other unusual, and some altogether novel effects, arising from an extension of the application of the principles of rhyme and alliteration.

The next point to be considered was the mode of bringing together the lover and the Raven — and the first branch of this consideration was the *locale*. For this the most natural suggestion might seem to be forest, or the fields — but it has always appeared to me that a close *circumscription of space* is absolutely necessary to the effect of insulated incident: — it has the force of a frame to a picture. It has an indisputable moral power in keeping concentrated the attention, and, of course, must not be confounded with mere unity of place.

I determined, then, to place the lover in his chamber — in a chamber rendered sacred to him by memories of her who had frequented it. The room is represented as richly furnished — this in mere pursuance of the ideas I have already explained on the subject of Beauty, as the sole true poetical thesis.

The *locale* being thus determined, I had now to introduce the bird — and the thought of introducing him through the window, was inevitable. The idea of making the lover suppose, in the first instance, that the flapping of the wings of the bird against the shutter, is a "tapping" at the door, originated in a wish to increase, by prolonging, the reader's curiosity, and in a desire to admit the incidental effect arising from the lover's throwing open the door, finding all dark, and thence adopting the half-fancy that it was the spirit of his mistress that knocked.

I made the night tempestuous, first, to account for the Raven's seeking admission, and secondly, for the effect of contrast with the (physical) serenity within the chamber.

I made the bird alight on the bust of Pallas, also for the effect of contrast between the marble and the plumage — it being understood that the bust was absolutely *suggested* by the bird — the bust of *Pallas* being chosen, first, as most in keeping with the scholarship of the lover, and secondly, for the sonorousness of the word, *Pallas,* itself.

About the middle of the poem, also, I have availed myself of the force of contrast, with a view of deepening the ultimate impression. For example, an air of the fantastic — approaching as nearly to the ludicrous as was admissible — is given to the Raven's entrance. He comes in "with many a flirt and flutter."

Not the *least obeisance made he* — not a moment
    stopped or stayed he,
But *with mien of lord or lady,* perched above my
    chamber door.

In the two stanzas which follow, the design is more obviously carried out: —

Then this ebony bird beguiling my sad fancy into
    smiling
By the *grave and stern decorum of the countenance
    it wore,*
"Though thy *crest be shorn and shaven* thou," I
    said, "art sure no craven,
Ghastly grim and ancient Raven wandering from
    the nightly shore —
Tell me what thy lordly name is on the Night's
    Plutonian shore?"
        Quoth the Raven, "Nevermore."
Much I marvelled *this ungainly fowl* to hear dis-
    course so plainly
Though its answer little meaning — little relevancy
    bore;

For we cannot help agreeing that no living human
    being
*Ever yet was blessed with seeing bird above his*
    *chamber door —*
*Bird or beast upon the sculptured bust above his*
    *chamber door,*
      With such name as "Nevermore."

The effect of the *dénouement* being thus provided for, I immediately drop the fantastic for a
tone of the most profound seriousness — this
tone commencing in the stanza directly following
the one last quoted, with the line,

But the Raven, sitting lonely on that placid bust,
    spoke only, etc.

From this epoch the lover no longer jests —
no longer sees any thing even of the fantastic in
the Raven's demeanor. He speaks of him as a
"grim, ungainly, ghastly, gaunt, and ominous
bird of yore," and feels the "fiery eyes" burning
into his "bosom's core." This revolution of
thought, or fancy, on the lover's part, is intended
to induce a similar one on the part of the reader
— to bring the mind into a proper frame for the
*dénouement* — which is now brought about as
rapidly and as *directly* as possible.

With the *dénouement* proper — with the Rav-
en's reply, "Nevermore," to the lover's final demand if he shall meet his mistress in another
world — the poem, in its obvious phase, that of
a simple narrative, may be said to have its completion. So far, every thing is within the limits
of the unaccountable — of the real. A raven,
having learned by rote the single word "Nevermore," and having escaped from the custody of
its owner, is driven at midnight, through the
violence of a storm, to seek admission at a window from which a light still gleams — the cham-
ber-window of a student, occupied half in poring
over a volume, half in dreaming of a beloved
mistress deceased. The casement being thrown
open at the fluttering of the bird's wings, the bird
itself perches on the most convenient seat out of
the immediate reach of the student, who, amused
by the incident and the oddity of the visitor's
demeanor, demands of it, in jest and without
looking for a reply, its name. The raven addressed, answers with its customary word, "Nevermore" — a word which finds immediate echo
in the melancholy heart of the student, who,
giving utterance aloud to certain thoughts suggested by the occasion, is again startled by the
fowl's repetition of "Nevermore." The student
now guesses the state of the case, but is impelled,
as I have before explained, by the human thirst
for self-torture, and in part by superstition, to
propound such queries to the bird as will bring
him, the lover, the most of the luxury of sorrow,
through the anticipated answer "Nevermore."
With the indulgence, to the extreme, of this self-
torture, the narration, in what I have termed its
first or obvious phase, has a natural termination,
and so far there has been no overstepping of the
limits of the real.

But in subjects so handled, however skilfully,
or with however vivid an array of incident, there
is always a certain hardness or nakedness, which
repels the artistical eye. Two things are invariably required — first, some amount of complexity,
or more properly, adaptation; and, secondly,
some amount of suggestiveness — some undercurrent, however indefinite, of meaning. It is this
latter, in especial, which imparts to a work of art
so much of the *richness* (to borrow from colloquy
a forcible term) which we are too fond of confounding with the *ideal*. It is the *excess* of the
suggested meaning — it is the rendering this the
upper instead of the under current of the theme
— which turns into prose (and that of the very
flattest kind) the so-called poetry of the so-called
transcendentalists.

Holding these opinions, I added the two concluding stanzas of the poem — their suggestiveness being thus made to pervade all the narrative
which has preceded them. The undercurrent of
meaning is rendered first apparent in the lines —

"Take thy beak from out *my heart,* and take thy
    form from off my door!"
      Quoth the Raven, "Nevermore!"

It will be observed that the words, "from out
my heart," involve the first metaphorical expression in the poem. They, with the answer, "Nevermore," dispose the mind to seek a moral in all
that has been previously narrated. The reader
begins now to regard the Raven as emblematical
— but it is not until the very last line of the very
last stanza, that the intention of making him em-

blematical of *Mournful and Never-ending Remembrance* is permitted distinctly to be seen:

> And the Raven, never flitting, still is sitting, still is sitting,
> On the pallid bust of Pallas, just above my chamber door;

And his eyes have all the seeming of a demon's that is dreaming,
And the lamplight o'er him streaming throws his shadow on the floor;
And my soul *from out that shadow* that lies floating on the floor
Shall be lifted — nevermore.

# Matthew Arnold

## 1822–1888

Matthew Arnold was born at Laleham, Middlesex, but in 1828 moved to Rugby, where his father Dr. Thomas Arnold, the sage and humane spirit of *Tom Brown's School Days,* had been appointed headmaster. Arnold went to Winchester, then to Rugby, to Balliol College of Oxford, and then to a fellowship at Oriel. In 1851 Arnold left academia, became an inspector of schools (a position he held for thirty-five years), and married Frances Lucy Wightman. His chief volumes of poetry were *Empedocles on Etna* (1852), *Poems* (1853), *Poems, Second Series* (1855), *Merope, a Tragedy* (1858), and *New Poems* (1867). His chief critical publications were *Essays in Criticism,* First Series (1865), *Culture and Anarchy* (1869), *Literature and Dogma* (1873), and *Essays in Criticism,* Second Series (1888). Arnold was elected professor of poetry at Oxford in 1857 and held the position for ten years. He died unexpectedly in 1888.

Some passages in Arnold's criticism have struck commentators as Aristotelian, notably a section from his preface to *Poems* (1853), which insists that human action, rather than the consciousness of the poet, is the true subject of poetry:

> What are the eternal objects of poetry, among all nations and at all times? They are actions; human actions; possessing an inherent interest in themselves, and which are to be communicated in an interesting manner by the art of the poet. Vainly will the latter imagine that he has everything in his own power; that he can make an intrinsically inferior action . . . delightful . . . by his treatment of it . . . . I fearlessly assert that *Hermann and Dorothea, Childe Harold, Jocelyn, The Excursion,* leave the reader cold in comparison with the effect produced on him by the latter books of the *Iliad,* by the *Oresteia,* or by the episode of Dido . . . .

If to know and to cite Aristotle is to be Aristotelian, then Arnold was one of the most loyal Aristotelians the nineteenth century produced. Indeed, in both of the essays included here, Arnold quotes or alludes to *Poetics,* Chapter 9, that poetry is a higher thing than history, because poetry is *philosophoteron kai spoudaioteron,* the more philosophical and more nobly serious human activity.

But in fact, Arnold's conception of literature is far from the gist and method of the *Poetics.* For Aristotle the poem's only duty is to be good in the way of its kind, and he resolutely differentiated between the genres of poetry and between poetry and all other forms of creativity. Aristotle's sense of the discreteness of activities and the primacy of form over content — both intellectual and spiritual — would be totally foreign to Arnold's way of thinking. For Arnold, form as an issue in itself never comes up.

Even the word "criticism" in "The Function of Criticism at the Present Time" is far broader than *literary* criticism: It denominates literature itself as a "criticism of life." Literature and literary criticism alike engage in a comprehensive critique of the entire culture. And while Arnold seems at times to be discussing literature as such, art is never for art's sake: Literature is of interest to him primarily as an index to and a banner of the society that produced it. In this sense Arnold is as holistic a critic as Plato in *Republic,* Book X. In another sense, however, Arnold entirely inverts Plato, for he views art as one possible salvation for an inhumane society rather than as a potential source of pollution in a utopia. Instead of being, as in Plato, a distorting mirror of reality, art for Arnold is one way of increasing the accuracy of one's spiritual vision — and a corrective for the illusions of political propaganda.

In one passage of "The Function of Criticism," for example, Arnold quotes some of the dithyrambically optimistic oratory of contemporary parliamentarians Charles Adderley and John Arthur Roebuck, who viewed Victorian society as not merely perfectible but as nearly perfected. Arnold responds not with a quotation from the classics but rather with a sordid newspaper paragraph about a "shocking child murder" committed at Nottingham by a workhouse girl named Wragg. Arnold asks us to imagine "the workhouse, the dismal Mapperly hills . . . gloom, the smoke, the cold, the strangled illegitimate child . . . . And that final touch — short, bleak and inhuman: 'Wragg is in custody.'" The passage is astonishing in a work of literary criticism. In a way, though, it is the center of the essay. This quotation represents the lowest level at which literature — the imaginative recreation of human existence — can be "criticism of life": minimally, by ironically exploding the pretences of current ideology. But criticism of life has other phases. At its best literature can reawaken in us a sense of what it would mean to be fully human — a reawakening that Arnold sensed was needed more than ever in his mechanical age.

Because of what literature is capable of at its best, Arnold is concerned that we recognize what is best and not mistake cheaper merchandise for the genuine article. This form of elitism inspired "The Study of Poetry" and its doctrine of "touchstones" — lines of poetry that supposedly characterize the highest flights of the human spirit. When we hear a line of poetry, Arnold recommends that we compare it immediately to those lines in literature that are most sublime: "*In la sua voluntade è nostra pace*" from Dante's *Paradiso,* or "Absent thee from felicity awhile" from *Hamlet.*

As a method of literary criticism, "touchstonery" had been exploded a century before, in Johnson's *Preface to Shakespeare:* "He that tries to recommend [Shakespeare] by select quotations, will succeed like the pedant in Hierocles, who, when he offered his house to sale, carried a brick in his pocket as a specimen." One problem with touchstonery is obvious: It valorizes the single, sublime line to the neglect of every other aspect of literature: plot, characterization, consistency of tone, originality of thought. Less obviously, perhaps, it devalues genres other than epic and tragedy. Within Arnold's essay itself it is clear that the comic genius of Chaucer must be placed below the soberer Milton, even below François Villon. The brilliant eighteenth-century wits who devoted themselves to satire and comedy fall, by Arnold's standard, below the salt.

While it would be hard to defend Arnold's touchstones as a mode of literary analysis, it is important to understand their historical significance as well as the general importance of the sublime in Arnold's thought. Arnold's age was also that of Charles Darwin and Herbert Spencer and David Friedrich Strauss. With science beginning to undermine the tenets of revealed religion, with philosophy becoming either too abstruse or too pragmatic to provide consolation and solace, Arnold felt that poetry could provide the new Word for which humanity was listening. "More and more," Arnold prophesies, "mankind will discover that we have to turn to poetry to interpret life for us, to console us, to sustain us. Without poetry, our science will appear incomplete; most of what now passes with us for religion and philosophy will be replaced by poetry." Culture would be grounded in literature, and Arnold was determined that if the culture was not to decline or vanish, that foundation would have to be revelatory of humanity's highest spiritual aspirations.

Arnold expected that the trends he saw would continue or accelerate, but as is usual with human affairs, this did not precisely happen. Revealed religion revived in the decade of Arnold's death, and the pendulum has swung back and forth several times since then. In a few regions of America, Darwinian evolution is on the defensive, at least in the public schools, and one might as easily fear the possibility that religion might subvert science in the popular mind. But what has come to pass in the last few decades — a culture grounded not in poetry but in television and dedicated not to the sublime but to the lowest common denominator — might well have been Arnold's worst nightmare.

## Selected Bibliography

Boutellier, Victor N. *Imaginative Reason: The Continuity of Arnold's Critical Effort*. Bern: Franke, 1977.

Buckley, Vincent. *Poetry and Morality: Studies in the Criticism of Matthew Arnold, T. S. Eliot, and F. R. Leavis*. London: Chatto and Windus, 1959.

Carroll, Joseph. *The Cultural Theory of Matthew Arnold*. Berkeley: University of California Press, 1982.

Eells, John Shepard. *The Touchstones of Matthew Arnold*. New York: Bookman Associates, 1955.

Garrod, Heathcote William. *Poetry and the Criticism of Life*. New York: Russell and Russell, 1963.

Knickerbocker, William S. "Matthew Arnold's Theory of Poetry." *Sewanee Review* 33 (1925): 440–50.

Perkins, David, "Arnold and the Function of Literature." *ELH* 18 (1951): 287–309.

Stange, G. Robert. *Matthew Arnold: The Poet as Humanist*. Princeton: Princeton University Press, 1967.

Trilling, Lionel. *Matthew Arnold*. New York: Norton, 1939.

Wills, Anthony Aldwin. *Matthew Arnold's Literary and Religious Thought*. Stanford: Stanford University Press, 1968.

# The Function of Criticism at the Present Time

Many objections have been made to a proposition which, in some remarks of mine on translating Homer, I ventured to put forth; a proposition about criticism, and its importance at the present day. I said: "Of the literature of France and Germany, as of the intellect of Europe in general, the main effort, for now many years, has been a critical effort; the endeavour, in all branches of knowledge, theology, philosophy, history, art, science, to see the object as in itself it really is." I added, that owing to the operation of English literature of certain causes, "almost the last thing for which one would come to English literature is just that very thing which now Europe most desires, — criticism"; and that the power and value of English literature was thereby impaired. More than one rejoinder declared that the importance I here assigned to criticism was excessive, and asserted the inherent superiority of the creative effort of the human spirit over its critical effort. And the other day, having been led by an excellent notice of Wordsworth[1] published in the *North British Review,* to turn again to his biography, I found, in the words of this great man, whom I, for one, must always listen to with the profoundest respect, a sentence passed on the critic's business, which seems to justify every possible disparagement of it. Wordsworth says in one of his letters:

The writers in these publications [the Reviews], while they prosecute their inglorious employment, can not be supposed to be in a state of mind very favourable for being affected by the finer influences of a thing so pure as genuine poetry.[2]

And a trustworthy reporter of his conversation quotes a more elaborate judgment to the same effect:

Wordsworth holds the critical power very low, infinitely lower than the inventive; and he said today that if the quantity of time consumed in writing critiques on the works of others were given to original composition, of whatever kind it might be, it would be much better employed; it would make a man find out sooner his own level, and it would do infinitely less mischief. A false or malicious criticism may do much injury to the minds of others, a stupid invention, either in prose or verse, is quite harmless.[3]

It is almost too much to expect of poor human nature, that a man capable of producing some effect in one line of literature, should, for the greater good of society, voluntarily doom himself to impotence and obscurity in another. Still less is this to be expected from men addicted to the composition of the "false or malicious criticism", of which Wordsworth speaks. However, everybody would admit that a false or malicious criticism had better never have been written. Everybody, too, would be willing to admit, as a general proposition, that the critical faculty is lower than the inventive. But is it true that criticism is really, in itself, a baneful and injurious employment; is it true that all time given to writing critiques on the works of others would be much better employed if it were given to original composition, of whatever kind this may be? Is it true that

---

[1] I cannot help thinking that a practice, common in England during the last century, and still followed in France, of printing a notice of this kind, — a notice by a competent critic, — to serve as an introduction to an eminent author's works, might be revived among us with advantage. To introduce all succeeding editions of Wordsworth, Mr. Sharp's notice (it is permitted, I hope, to mention his name) might, it seems to me, excellently serve; it is written from the point of view of an admirer, nay, of a disciple, and that is right; but then the disciple must be also, as in this case he is, a critic, a man of letters, not, as too often happens, some relation or friend with no qualification for his task except affection for his author. [Au.] J. C. Shairp's "Wordsworth: The Man and Poet" appeared in *North British Review* 61 (1864): 1–54. [Ed.]

[2] Letter of January 12, 1816, to Bernard Barton in *The Letters of William and Dorothy Wordsworth* (ed. Ernest de Selincourt, revised by Mary Moorman and Alan G. Hill), 3: 269. [Ed.]

[3] William Knight, *Life of William Wordsworth* (1889) 3: 438. [Ed.]

Johnson had better have gone on producing more *Irenes* instead of writing his *Lives of the Poets;* nay, it is certain that Wordsworth himself was better employed in making his Ecclesiastical Sonnets than when he made his celebrated Preface, so full of criticism, and criticism of the works of others? Wordsworth was himself a great critic, and it is to be sincerely regretted that he has not left us more criticism; Goethe was one of the greatest of critics, and we may sincerely congratulate ourselves that he has left us so much criticism. Without wasting time over the exaggeration which Wordsworth's judgment on criticism clearly contains, or over an attempt to trace the causes, — not difficult I think to be traced, — which may have led Wordsworth to this exaggeration, a critic may with advantage seize an occasion for trying his own conscience, and for asking himself of what real service, at any given moment, the practice of criticism either is, or may be made, to his own mind and spirit, and to the minds and spirits of others.

The critical power is of lower rank than the creative. True; but in assenting to this proposition, one or two things are to be kept in mind. It is undeniable that the exercise of a creative power, that a free creative activity, is the highest function of man; it is proved to be so by man's finding in it his true happiness. But it is undeniable, also, that men may have the sense of exercising this free creative activity in other ways than in producing great works of literature or art; if it were not so, all but a very few men would be shut out from the true happiness of all men. They may have it in well-doing, they may have it in learning, they may have it even in criticizing. This is one thing to be kept in mind. Another is, that the exercise of the creative power in the production of great works of literature or art, however high this exercise of it may rank, is not at all epochs and under all conditions possible; and that therefore labour may be vainly spent in attempting it, which might with more fruit be used in preparing for it, in rendering it possible. This creative power works with elements, with materials; what if it has not those materials, those elements, ready for its use? In that case it must surely wait till they are ready. Now in literature, — I will limit myself to literature, for it is about literature that the question arises, — the elements with which the creative power works are ideas; the best ideas, on every matter which literature touches, current at the time. At any rate we may lay it down as certain that in modern literature no manifestation of the creative power not working with these can be very important or fruitful. And I say *current* at the time, not merely accessible at the time; for creative literary genius does not principally show itself in discovering new ideas; that is rather the business of the philosopher: the grand work of literary genius is a work of synthesis and exposition, not of analysis and discovery; its gift lies in the faculty of being happily inspired by a certain intellectual and spiritual atmosphere, by a certain order of ideas, when it finds itself in them; of dealing divinely with these ideas, presenting them in the most effective and attractive combinations, — making beautiful works with them, in short. But it must have the atmosphere, it must find itself amidst the order of ideas, in order to work freely; and these it is not so easy to command. This is why great creative epochs in literature are so rare; this is why there is so much that is unsatisfactory in the productions of many men of real genius; because of the creation of a masterwork of literature two powers must concur, the power of the man and the power of the moment, and the man is not enough without the moment; the creative power has, for its happy exercise, appointed elements, and those elements are not in its own control.

Nay, they are more within the control of the critical power. It is the business of the critical power, as I said in the words already quoted, "in all branches of knowledge, theology, philosophy, history, art, science, to see the object as in itself it really is." Thus it tends, at last, to make an intellectual situation of which the creative power can profitably avail itself. It tends to establish an order of ideas, if not absolutely true, yet true by comparison with that which it displaces; to make the best ideas prevail. Presently these new ideas reach society, the touch of truth is the touch of life, and there is a stir and growth everywhere; out of this stir and growth come the creative epochs of literature.

Or, to narrow our range, and quit these considerations of the general march of genius and of society, considerations which are apt to become too abstract and impalpable, — everyone can see that a poet, for instance, ought to know life and the world before dealing with them in poetry; and life and the world being, in modern times, very complex things, the creation of a modern poet, to be worth much, implies a great critical effort behind it; else it must be a comparatively poor, barren, and short-lived affair. This is why Byron's poetry had so little endurance in it, and Goethe's so much; both Byron and Goethe had a great productive power, but Goethe's was nourished by a great critical effort providing the true materials for it, and Byron's was not; Goethe knew life and the world, the poet's necessary subjects, much more comprehensively and thoroughly than Byron. He knew a great deal more of them, and he knew them much more as they really are.

It has long seemed to me that the burst of creative activity in our literature, through the first quarter of this century, had about it, in fact, something premature; and that from this cause its productions are doomed, most of them, in spite of the sanguine hopes which accompanied and do still accompany them, to prove hardly more lasting than the productions of far less splendid epochs. And this prematureness comes from its having proceeded without having its proper data, without sufficient materials to work with. In other words, the English poetry of the first quarter of this century, with plenty of energy, plenty of creative force, did not know enough. This makes Byron so empty of matter, Shelley so incoherent, Wordsworth even, profound as he is, yet so wanting in completeness and variety. Wordsworth cared little for books, and disparaged Goethe. I admire Wordsworth, as he is, so much that I cannot wish him different; and it is vain, no doubt, to imagine such a man different from what he is, to suppose that he could have been different. But surely the one thing wanting to make Wordsworth an even greater poet than he is, — his thought richer, and his influence of wider application, — was that he should have read more books, among them, no doubt, those of that Goethe whom he disparaged without reading him.

But to speak of books and reading may easily lead to a misunderstanding here. It was not really books and reading that lacked to our poetry at this epoch; Shelley had plenty of reading, Coleridge had immense reading. Pindar and Sophocles — as we all say so glibly, and often with so little discernment of the real import of what we are saying — had not many books; Shakespeare was no deep reader. True; but in the Greece of Pindar and Sophocles, in the England of Shakespeare, the poet lived in a current of ideas in the highest degree animating and nourishing to the creative power; society was, in the fullest measure, permeated by fresh thought, intelligent and alive; and this state of things is the true basis for the creative power's exercise, — in this it finds its data, its materials, truly ready for its hand; all the books and reading in the world are only valuable as they are helps to this. Even when this does not actually exist, books and reading may enable a man to construct a kind of semblance of it in his own mind, a world of knowledge and intelligence in which he may live and work: this is by no means an equivalent, to the artist, for the nationally diffused life and thought of the epochs of Sophocles or Shakespeare, but, besides that it may be a means of preparation for such epochs, it does really constitute, if many share in it, a quickening and sustaining atmosphere of great value. Such an atmosphere the many-sided learning and the long and widely combined critical effort of Germany formed for Goethe, when he lived and worked. There was no national glow of life and thought there as in the Athens of Pericles, or the England of Elizabeth. That was the poet's weakness. But there was a sort of equivalent for it in the complete culture and unfettered thinking of a large body of Germans. That was his strength. In the England of the first quarter of this century, there was neither a national glow of life and thought, such as we had in the age of Elizabeth, nor yet a culture and a force of learning and criticism, such as were to be found in Germany. Therefore the creative power of poetry wanted, for success in the highest sense, materials and a basis; a thorough interpretation of the world was necessarily denied to it.

At first sight it seems strange that out of the

immense stir of the French Revolution and its age should not have come a crop of works of genius equal to that which came out of the stir of the great productive time of Greece, or out of that of the Renascence, with its powerful episode the Reformation. But the truth is that the stir of the French Revolution took a character which essentially distinguished it from such movements as these. These were, in the main, disinterestedly intellectual and spiritual movements; movements in which the human spirit looked for its satisfaction in itself and in the increased play of its own activity: the French Revolution took a political, practical character. The movement which went on in France under the old régime, from 1700 to 1789, was far more really akin than that of the Revolution itself to the movement of the Renascence; the France of Voltaire and Rousseau told far more powerfully upon the mind of Europe than the France of the Revolution. Goethe reproached this last expressly with having "thrown quiet culture back."[4] Nay, and the true key to how much in our Byron, even in our Wordsworth, is this! — that they had their source in a great movement of feeling, not in a great movement of mind. The French Revolution, however, — that object of so much blind love and so much blind hatred, — found undoubtedly its motive-power in the intelligence of men and not in their practical sense; — this is what distinguishes it from the English Revolution of Charles the First's time; this is what makes it a more spiritual event than our Revolution, an event of much more powerful and worldwide interest, though practically less successful; — it appeals to an order of ideas which are universal, certain, permanent. 1789 asked of a thing, Is it rational? 1642 asked of a thing, Is it legal? or, when it went furthest, Is it according to conscience? This is the English fashion; a fashion to be treated, within its own sphere, with the highest respect; for its success, within its own sphere, has been prodigious. But what is law in one place, is not law in another; what is law here today, is not law even here tomorrow; and as for conscience, what is binding on one man's conscience is not binding on another's; the old woman who threw her stool at the head of the surpliced minister in St. Giles's Church at Edinburgh[5] obeyed an impulse to which millions of the human race may be permitted to remain strangers. But the prescriptions of reason are absolute, unchanging, of universal validity; *to count by tens is the easiest way of counting,* — that is a proposition of which every one, from here to the Antipodes, feels the force; at least, I should say so, if we did not live in a country where it is not impossible that any morning we may find a letter in *The Times* declaring that a decimal coinage is an absurdity.[6] That a whole nation should have been penetrated with an enthusiasm for pure reason, and with an ardent zeal for making its prescriptions triumph, is a very remarkable thing, when we consider how little of mind, or anything so worthy and quickening as mind, comes into the natives which alone, in general, impel great masses of men. In spite of the extravagant direction given to this enthusiasm, in spite of the crimes and follies in which it lost itself, the French Revolution derives from the force, truth, and universality of the ideas which it took for its law, and from the passion with which it could inspire a multitude for these ideas, a unique and still living power; it is — it will probably long remain — the greatest, the most animating event in history. And, as no sincere passion for the things of the mind, even though it turns out in many respects an unfortunate passion, is ever quite thrown away and quite barren of good, France has reaped from hers one fruit — the natural and legitimate fruit, though not precisely the grand fruit she expected: she is the country in Europe where *the people* is most alive.

But the mania for giving an immediate political and practical application to all these fine ideas of the reason was fatal. Here an Englishman is in his element: on this theme we can all go on for hours. And all we are in the habit of saying on it has undoubtedly a great deal of truth. Ideas cannot be too much prized in and for themselves, cannot be too much lived with; but to

[4] In Goethe's "The Four Seasons: Spring." [Ed.]

[5] Jenny Geddes did this on July 23, 1637. [Ed.]
[6] A decimal coinage bill was introduced and withdrawn in 1863. [Ed.]

transport them abruptly into the world of politics and practice, violently to revolutionize this world to their bidding, — that is quite another thing. There is the world of ideas and there is the world of practice; the French are often for suppressing the one and the English the other; but neither is to be suppressed. A member of the House of Commons said to me the other day: "That a thing is an anomaly, I consider to be no objection to it whatever." I venture to think he was wrong; that a thing is an anomaly *is* an objection to it, but absolutely and in the sphere of ideas: it is not necessarily, under such and such circumstances, or at such and such a moment, an objection to it in the sphere of politics and practice. Joubert has said beautifully: "C'est la force et la droit qui règlent toutes choses dans le monde; la force en attendant le droit." (Force and right are the governors of this world; force till right is ready.)[7] *Force till right is ready;* and till right is ready, force, the existing order of things, is justified, is the legitimate ruler. But right is something moral, and implies inward recognition, free assent of the will; we are not ready for right, — *right,* so far as we are concerned, *is not ready,* until we have attained this sense of seeing it and willing it. The way in which for us it may change and transform force, the existing order of things, and become, in its turn, the legitimate ruler of the world, should depend on the way in which, when our time comes, we see it and will it. Therefore for other people enamoured of their own newly discerned right, to attempt to impose it upon us as ours, and violently to substitute their right for our force, is an act of tyranny, and to be resisted. It sets at nought the second great half of our maxim, *force till right is ready.* This was the grand error of the French Revolution; and its movement of ideas, by quitting the intellectual sphere and rushing furiously into the political sphere, ran, indeed, a prodigious and memorable course, but produced no such intellectual fruit as the movement of ideas of the Renascence, and created, in opposition to itself, what I may call an *epoch of concentration.* The great force of that epoch of concentration was

England; and the great voice of that epoch of concentration was Burke. It is the fashion to treat Burke's writings on the French Revolution as superannuated and conquered by the event; as the eloquent but unphilosophical tirades of bigotry and prejudice. I will not deny that they are often disfigured by the violence and passion of the moment, and that in some directions Burke's view was bounded, and his observation therefore at fault; but on the whole, and for those who can make the needful corrections, what distinguishes these writings in their profound, permanent, fruitful, philosophical truth; they contain the true philosophy of an epoch of concentration, dissipate the heavy atmosphere which its own nature is apt to engender round it, and make its resistance rational instead of mechanical.

But Burke is so great because, almost alone in England, he brings thought to bear upon politics, he saturates politics with thought; it is his accident that his ideas were at the service of an epoch of concentration, not of an epoch of expansion; it is his characteristic that he so lived by ideas, and had such a source of them welling up within him, that he could float even an epoch of concentration and English Tory politics with them. It does not hurt him that Dr. Price and the Liberals were enraged with him; it does not even hurt him that George the Third and the Tories were enchanted with him. His greatness is that he lived in a world which neither English Liberalism nor English Toryism is apt to enter; — the world of ideas, not the world of catchwords and party habits. So far is it from being really true of him that he "to party gave up what was meant for mankind," that at the very end of his fierce struggle with the French Revolution, after all his invectives against its false pretensions, hollowness, and madness, with his sincere conviction of its mischievousness, he can close a memorandum on the best means of combating it, some of the last pages he ever wrote, — the *Thoughts on French Affairs,* in December 1791, — with these striking words:

The evil is stated, in my opinion, as it exists. The remedy must be where power, wisdom, and information, I hope, are more united with good intentions than they can be with me. I have done with this subject, I believe, for ever. It has given

[7]Jean Joubert, *Pensées* (1877), 2: 178. [Ed.]

me many anxious moments for the last two years. *If a great change is to be made in human affairs, the minds of men will be fitted to it; the general opinions and feelings will draw that way. Every fear, every hope will forward it; and then they who persist in opposing this mighty current in human affairs, will appear rather to resist the decrees of Providence itself, than the mere designs of men. They will not be resolute and firm, but perverse and obstinate.*

That return of Burke upon himself has always seemed to me one of the finest things in English literature, or indeed in any literature. That is what I call living by ideas; when one side of a question has long had your earnest support, when all your feelings are engaged, when you hear all round you no language but one, when your party talks this language like a steam-engine and can imagine no other, — still to be able to think, still to be irresistibly carried, if so it be, by the current of thought to the opposite side of the question, and, like Balaam, to be unable to speak anything *but what the Lord has put in your mouth.*[8] I know nothing more striking, and I must add that I know nothing more un-English.

For the Englishman in general is like my friend the Member of Parliament, and believes, point-blank, that for a thing to be an anomaly is absolutely no objection to it whatever. He is like the Lord Auckland of Burke's day, who, in a memorandum on the French Revolution, talks of "certain miscreants, assuming the name of philosophers, who have presumed themselves capable of establishing a new system of society." The Englishman has been called a political animal, and he values what is political and practical so much that ideas easily become objects of dislike in his eyes, and thinkers "miscreants," because ideas and thinkers have rashly meddled with politics and practice. This would be all very well if the dislike and neglect confined themselves to ideas transported out of their own sphere, and meddling rashly with practice; but they are inevitably extended to ideas as such, and to the whole life of intelligence; practice is everything, a free play of the mind is nothing. The notion of the free play of the mind upon all

[8]Numbers 22:38. [Ed.]

subjects being a pleasure in itself, being an object of desire, being an essential provider of elements without which a nation's spirit, whatever compensations it may have for them, must, in the long run, die of inanition, hardly enters into an Englishman's thoughts. It is noticeable that the word *curiosity,* which in other languages is used in a good sense, to mean, as a high and fine quality of man's nature, just this disinterested love of a free play of the mind on all subjects, for its own sake, — it is noticeable, I say, that this word has in our language no sense of the kind, no sense but a rather bad and disparaging one. But criticism, real criticism, is essentially the exercise of this very quality; it obeys an instinct prompting it to know the best that is known and thought in the world, irrespectively of practice, politics, and everything of the kind; and to value knowledge and thought as they approach this best, without the intrusion of any other considerations whatever. This is an instinct for which there is, I think, little original sympathy in the practical English nature, and what there was of it has undergone a long benumbing period of blight and suppression in the epoch of concentration which followed the French Revolution.

But epochs of concentration cannot well endure for ever; epochs of expansion, in the due course of things, follow them. Such an epoch of expansion seems to be opening in this country. In the first place all danger of a hostile forcible pressure of foreign ideas upon our practice has long disappeared; like the traveller in the fable, therefore, we begin to wear our cloak a little more loosely. Then, with a long peace, the ideas of Europe steal gradually and amicably in, and mingle, though in infinitesimally small quantities at a time, with our own notions. Then, too, in spite of all that is said about the absorbing and brutalizing influence of our passionate material progress, it seems to me indisputable that this progress is likely, though not certain, to lead in the end to an apparition of intellectual life; and that man, after he has made himself perfectly comfortable and has now to determine what to do with himself next, may begin to remember that he has a mind, and that the mind may be made the source of great pleasure. I grant it is mainly the privilege of faith, at present, to discern this end to our railways, our business, and our fortune-making; but we shall see if, here as elsewhere, faith is not in the end the true prophet. Our ease, our travelling, and our unbounded liberty to hold just as hard and securely as we please to the practice to which our notions have given birth, all tend to beget an inclination to deal a little more freely with these notions themselves, to canvass them a little, to penetrate a little into their real nature. Flutterings of curiosity, in the foreign sense of the word, appear amongst us, and it is in these that criticism must look to find its account. Criticism first; a time of true creative activity, perhaps, — which, as I have said, must inevitably be preceded amongst us by a time of criticism, — hereafter, when criticism has done its work.

It is of the last importance that English criticism should clearly discern what rule for its course, in order to avail itself of the field now opening to it, and to produce fruit for the future, it ought to take. The rule may be summed up in one word, — *disinterestedness*. And how is criticism to show disinterestedness? By keeping aloof from practice; by resolutely following the law of its own nature, which is to be a free play of the mind on all subjects which it touches; by steadily refusing to lend itself to any of those ulterior, political, practical considerations about ideas which plenty of people will be sure to attach to them, which perhaps ought often to be attached to them, which in this country at any rate are certain to be attached to them quite sufficiently, but which criticism has really nothing to do with. Its business is, as I have said, simply to know the best that is known and thought in the world, and by in its turn making this known, to create a current of true and fresh ideas. Its business is to do this with inflexible honesty, with due ability; but its business is to do no more, and to leave alone all questions of practical consequences and applications, questions which will never fail to have due prominence given to them. Else criticism, besides being really false to its own nature, merely continues in the old rut which it has hitherto followed in this country, and will certainly miss the chance now given to it. For what is at present the bane of criticism in this country? It is that practical considerations cling to it and stifle it; it subserves interests not its own; our organs of criticism are organs of men and parties having practical ends to serve, and with them those practical ends are the first thing and the play of mind the second; so much play of mind as is compatible with the prosecution of those practical ends is all that is wanted. An organ like the *Revue des Deux Mondes,* having for its main function to understand and utter the best that is known and thought in the world, existing, it may be said, as just an organ for a free play of the mind, we have not; but we have the *Edinburgh Review,* existing as an organ of the old Whigs, and for as much play of the mind as may suit its being that; we have the *Quarterly Review,* existing as an organ of the Tories, and for as much play of mind as may suit its being that; we have the *British Quarterly Review,* existing as an organ of the political Dissenters, and for as much play of mind as may suit its being that; we have *The Times,* existing as an organ of the common, satisfied, well-to-do Englishman, and for as much play of mind as may suit its being that. And so on through all the various fractions, political and religious, of our society; every fraction has, as such, its organ of criticism, but the notions of combining all fractions in the common pleasure of a free disinterested play of mind meets with no favour. Directly this play of mind wants to have more scope, and to forget the pressure of practical considerations a little, it is checked, it is made to feel the chain; we saw this the other day in the extinction, so much to be regretted, of the *Home and Foreign Review;* perhaps in no organ of criticism in this country was there so much knowledge, so much play of mind; but these could not save it: the *Dublin Review* subordinates play of mind to the practical business of English and Irish Catholicism, and lives. It must needs be that men should act in sects and parties, that each of these sects and parties should have its organ, and should make this organ subserve the interests of its action; but it would be well, too, that there should be a criticism, not the minister of these interests, not their enemy, but absolutely and entirely independent of them. No other criticism will ever attain any real authority or make any real way towards its end, — the creating a current of true and fresh ideas.

It is because criticism has so little kept in the pure intellectual sphere, has so little detached itself from practice, has been so directly polemical and controversial, that it has so ill accomplished, in this country, its best spiritual work; which is to keep man from a self-satisfaction which is retarding and vulgarizing, to lead him towards perfection, by making his mind dwell upon what is excellent in itself, and the absolute beauty and fitness of things. A polemical practical criticism makes men blind even to the ideal imperfection of their practice, makes them willingly assert its ideal perfection, in order the better to secure it against attack; and clearly this is narrowing and baneful for them. If they were reassured on the practical side, speculative considerations of ideal perfection they might be brought to entertain, and their spiritual horizon would thus gradually widen. Mr. Adderley says to the Warwickshire farmers:

> Talk of the improvement of breed! Why, the race we ourselves represent, the men and women, the old Anglo-Saxon race, are the best breed in the whole world . . . . The absence of a too enervating climate, too unclouded skies, and a too luxurious nature, has produced so vigorous a race of people, and has rendered us so superior to all the world.

Mr. Roebuck says to the Sheffeld cutlers:

> I look around me and ask what is the state of England? Is not property safe? Is not every man able to say what he likes? Can you not walk from one end of England to the other in perfect security? I ask you whether, the world over or in past history, there is anything like it? Nothing. I pray that our unrivalled happiness may last.[9]

Now obviously there is a peril for poor human nature in words and thoughts of each exuberant self-satisfaction, until we find ourselves safe in the streets of the Celestial City.

[9]These speeches were reported in the London *Times* on September 17, 1863, and August 19, 1864, respectively. [Ed.]

Das wenige verschwindet leicht dem Blicke
Der vorwärts sieht, wie viel noch übrig
   bleibt — [10]

says Goethe; the little that is done seems nothing when we look forward and see how much we have yet to do. Clearly this is a better line of reflection for weak humanity, so long as it remains on this earthly field of labour and trial.

But neither Mr. Adderley nor Mr. Roebuck is by nature inaccessible to considerations of this sort. They only lose sight of them owing to the controversial life we all lead, and the practical form which all speculation takes with us. They have in view opponents whose aim is not ideal, but practical; and in their zeal to uphold their own practice against these innovators, they go so far as even to attribute to this practice an ideal perfection. Somebody has been wanting to introduce a six-pound franchise, or to abolish church-rates, or to collect agricultural statistics by force, or to diminish local self-government. How natural, in reply to such proposals, very likely improper or ill-timed, to go a little beyond the mark and to say stoutly: "Such a race of people as we stand, so superior to all the world! The old Anglo-Saxon race, the best breed in the whole world! I pray that our unrivalled happiness may last! I ask you whether, the world over or in past history, there is anything like it?" And so long as criticism answers this dithyramb by insisting that the old Anglo-Saxon race would be still more superior to all others if it had no church-rates, or that our unrivalled happiness would last yet longer with a six-pound franchise, so long will the strain, "The best breed in the whole world!" swell louder and louder, everything ideal and refining will be lost out of sight, and both the assailed and their critics will remain in a sphere, to say the truth, perfectly unvital, a sphere in which spiritual progression is impossible. But let criticism leave church-rates and the franchise alone, and in the most candid spirit, without a single lurking thought of practical innovation, confront with our dithyramb this paragraph on which I stumbled in a newspaper immediately after reading Mr. Roebuck:

[10]Goethe, *Iphigenia on Tauris,* I.ii.91–92. [Ed.]

A shocking child murder has just been committed at Nottingham. A girl named Wragg left the workhouse there on Saturday morning with her young illegitimate child. The child was soon afterwards found dead on Mapperly Hills, having been strangled. Wragg is in custody.[11]

Nothing but that; but, in juxtaposition with the absolute eulogies of Mr Adderley and Mr Roebuck, how eloquent, how suggestive are those few lines! "Our old Anglo-Saxon breed, the best in the whole world!" — how much that is harsh and ill-favoured there is in this best! *Wragg!* If we are to talk of ideal perfection, of "the best in the whole world," has anyone reflected what a touch of grossness in our race, what an original shortcoming in the more delicate spiritual perceptions, is shown by the natural growth amongst us of such hideous names, — Higginbottom, Stiggins, Bugg! In Ionia and Attica they were luckier in this respect than "the best race in the world"; by the Ilissus there was no Wragg, poor thing! And "our unrivalled happiness"; — what an element of grimness, bareness, and hideousness mixes with it and blurs it; the workhouse, the dismal Mapperly Hills, — how dismal those who have seen them will remember; — the gloom, the smoke, the cold, the strangled illegitimate child! "I ask you whether, the world over or in past history, there is anything like it?" Perhaps not, one is inclined to answer; but at any rate, in that case, the world is very much to be pitied. And the final touch, — short, bleak, and inhuman: *Wragg is in custody.* The sex lost in the confusion of our unrivalled happiness; or (shall I say?) the superfluous Christian name lopped off by the straightforward vigour of our old Anglo-Saxon breed! There is profit for the spirit in such contrasts as this; criticism serves the cause of perfection by establishing them. By eluding sterile conflict, by refusing to remain in the sphere where alone narrow and relative conceptions have any worth and validity, criticism may diminish its momentary importance, but only in this way has it a chance of gaining admittance for those wider and more perfect conceptions to which all its duty is really owed. Mr Roebuck will have a poor opinion of an adversary who replies to his defiant songs of triumph only by murmuring under his breath, *Wragg is in custody;* but in no other way will these songs of triumph be induced gradually to moderate themselves, to get rid of what in them is excessive and offensive, and to fall into a softer and truer key.

It will be said that it is a very subtle and indirect action which I am thus prescribing for criticism, and that, by embracing in this manner the Indian virtue of detachment and abandoning the sphere of practical life, it condemns itself to a slow and obscure work. Slow and obscure it may be, but it is the only proper work of criticism. The mass of mankind will never have any ardent zeal for seeing things as they are; very inadequate ideas will always satisfy them. On these inadequate ideas reposes, and must repose, the general practice of the world. That is as much as saving that whoever sets himself to see things as they are will find himself one of a very small circle; but it is only by this small circle resolutely doing its own work that adequate ideas will ever get current at all. The rush and roar of practical life will always have a dizzying and attracting effect upon the most collected spectator, and tend to draw him into its vortex; most of all will this be the case where that life is so powerful as it is in England. But it is only by remaining collected, and refusing to lend himself to the point of view of the practical man, that the critic can do the practical man any service; and it is only by the greatest sincerity in pursuing his own course, and by at last convincing even the practical man of his sincerity, that he can escape misunderstandings which perpetually threaten him.

For the practical man is not apt for fine distinctions, and yet in these distinctions truth and the highest culture greatly find their account. But it is not easy to lead a practical man — unless you reassure him as to your practical intentions, you have no chance of leading him — to see that a thing which he has always been used to look at from one side only, which he greatly values, and which, looked at from that side, quite deserves, perhaps, all the prizing and admiring which he bestows upon it, — that this thing,

[11]The crime was committed on September 10, 1864. Elizabeth Wragg was sentenced to twenty years in prison in March of the following year. [Ed.]

looked at from another side, may appear much less beneficent and beautiful, and yet retain all its claims to our practical allegiance. Where shall we find language innocent enough, how shall we make the spotless purity of our intentions evident enough, to enable us to say to the political Englishman that the British Constitution itself, which, seen from the practical side, looks such a magnificent organ of progress and virtue, seen from the speculative side, — which its compromises, its love of facts, its horror of theory, its studied avoidance of clear thoughts, — that, seen from this side, our august Constitution sometimes looks, — forgive me, shade of Lord Somers! — a colossal machine for the manufacture of Philistines? How is Cobbett to say this and not be misunderstood, blackened as he is with the smoke of a lifelong conflict in the field of political practice? how is Mr. Carlyle to say it and not be misunderstood, after his furious raid into this field with his *Latter-day Pamphlets?* how is Mr. Ruskin, after his pugnacious political economy? I say, the critic must keep out of the region of immediate practice in the political, social, humanitarian sphere, if he wants to make a beginning for that more free speculative treatment of things, which may perhaps one day make its benefits felt even in this sphere, but in a natural and thence irresistible manner.

Do what he will, however, the critic will still remain exposed to frequent misunderstandings, and nowhere so much as in this country. For here people are particularly indisposed even to comprehend that without this free disinterested treatment of things, truth and the highest culture are out of the question. So immersed are they in practical life, so accustomed to take all their notions from this life and its processes, that they are apt to think that truth and culture themselves can be reached by the processes of this life, and that it is an impertinent singularity to think of reaching them in any other. "We are all *terrae filii*,"[12] cries their eloquent advocate; "all Philistines together. Away with the notion of proceeding by any other course than the course dear to the Philistines; let us have a social movement,

let us organize and combine a party to pursue truth and new thought, let us call it *the liberal party,* and let us all stick to each other, and back each other up. Let us have no nonsense about independent criticism, and intellectual delicacy, and the few and the many. Don't let us trouble ourselves about foreign thought; we shall invent the whole thing for ourselves as we go along: if one of us speaks well, applaud him; if one of us speaks ill, applaud him too; we are all in the same movement, we are all liberals, we are all in pursuit of truth." In this way the pursuit of truth becomes really a social, practical, pleasurable affair, almost requiring a chairman, a secretary, and advertisements; with the excitement of an occasional scandal, with a little resistance to give the happy sense of difficulty overcome; but, in general, plenty of bustle and very little thought. To act is so easy, as Goethe says; to think is so hard! It is true that the critic has many temptations to go with the stream, to make one of the party movement, one of these *terrae filii;* it seems ungracious to refuse to be a *terrae filius,* when so many excellent people are; but the critic's duty is to refuse, or, if resistance is vain, at least to cry with Obermann: *Périssons en résistant.*[13]

How serious a matter it is to try and resist, I had ample opportunity of experiencing when I ventured some time ago to criticize the celebrated first volume of Bishop Colenso.[14] The echoes of the storm which was then raised I still, from time

[12]Children of earth. [Ed.]

[13]"Let us perish while resisting." Étienne de Sénancour, *Obermann* (1804). [Ed.]

[14]So sincere is my dislike to all personal attack and controversy, that I abstain from reprinting, at this distance of time from the occasion which called them forth, the essays in which I criticized Dr. Colenso's book; I feel bound, however, after all that has passed, to make here a final declaration of my sincere impenitence for having published them. Nay, I cannot forbear repeating yet once more, for his benefit and that of his readers, this sentence from my original remarks upon him: *There is truth of science and truth of religion; truth of science does not become truth of religion till it is made religious.* And I will add; Let us have all the science there is from the men of science; from the men of religion let us have religion. [Au.] The essays in which Arnold criticized John William Colenso's *The Pentateuch and the Book of Judges Critically Examined* (1863) were "The Bishop and the Philosopher" and "Dr. Stanley's Lectures on the Jewish Church," published in 1863. [Ed.]

to time, hear grumbling round me. That storm arose out of a misunderstanding almost inevitable. It is a result of no little culture to attain to a clear perception that science and religion are two wholly different things; the multitude will for ever confuse them; but happily that is of no great real importance, for while the multitude imagines itself to live by its false science, it does really live by its true religion. Dr. Colenso, however, in his first volume did all he could to strengthen the confusion,[15] and to make it dangerous. He did this with the best intentions, I freely admit, and with the most candid ignorance that this was the natural effect of what he was doing; but, says Joubert, "Ignorance, which in matters of morals extenuates the crime, is itself, in intellectual matters, a crime of the first order."[16] I criticized Bishop Colenso's speculative confusion. Immediately there was a cry raised: "What is this? here is a liberal attacking a liberal. Do not you belong to the movement? are not you a friend of truth? Is not Bishop Colenso in pursuit of truth? then speak with proper respect of his book. Dr. Stanley is another friend of truth, and you speak with proper respect of his book; why make these invidious differences? both books are excellent, admirable, liberal; Bishop Colenso's perhaps the most so, because it is the boldest, and will have the best practical consequences for the liberal cause. Do you want to encourage to the attack of a brother liberal his, and your, and our implacable enemies, the *Church and State Review* or the *Record,* — the High Church rhinoceros and the Evangelical hyaena? Be silent, therefore; or rather speak, speak as loud as ever you can, and go into ecstasies over the eighty and odd pigeons."

But criticism cannot follow this coarse and indiscriminate method. It is unfortunately possible for a man in pursuit of truth to write a book which reposes upon a false conception. Even the practical consequences of a book are to genuine criticism no recommendation of it, if the book is, in the highest sense, blundering. I see that a lady who herself, too, is in pursuit of truth, and who writes with great ability, but a little too much, perhaps, under the influence of the practical spirit of the English liberal movement, classes Bishop Colenso's book and M. Renan's[17] together, in her survey of the religious state of Europe, as facts of the same order, works, both of them, of "great importance"; "great ability, power, and skill"; Bishop Colenso's, perhaps, the most powerful; at least, Miss Cobbe gives special expression[18] to her gratitude that to Bishop Colenso "has been given the strength to grasp, and the courage to teach, truths of such deep import." In the same way, more than one popular writer has compared him to Luther. Now it is just this kind of false estimate which the critical spirit is, it seems to me, bound to resist. It is really the strongest possible proof of the low ebb at which, in England, the critical spirit is, that while the critical hit in the religious literature of Germany is Dr. Strauss's book,[19] in that of France M. Renan's book, the book of Bishop Colenso is the critical hit in the religious literature of England. Bishop Colenso's book reposes on a total misconception of the essential elements of the religious problem, as that problem is now presented for solution. To criticism, therefore, which seeks to have the best that is known and thought on this problem, it is, however well meant, of no importance whatever. Mr. Renan's book attempts a new synthesis of the elements furnished to us by the Four Gospels. It attempts, in my opinion, a synthesis, perhaps premature, perhaps impossible, certainly not successful. Up to the present time, at any rate, we must acquiesce in Fleury's sentence on such recastings of the Gospel story: *Quiconque s'imagine la pouvoir mieux écrire, ne l'entend pas.*[20] M. Renan had himself passed by anticipation a like sentence on his own work, when he said: "If a new pres-

---

[15]It has been said I make it "a crime against literary criticism and the higher culture to attempt to inform the ignorant." Need I point out that the ignorant are not informed by being confirmed in a confusion? [Au.]

[16]Joubert, *Pensées,* 2: 311. [Ed.]

[17]Ernest Renan, *La Vie de Jesus* (1863). [Ed.]

[18]Frances Power Cobbe in *Broken Lights: An Inquiry into the Present Condition and Future Prospects of Religious Faith* (1864). [Ed.]

[19]David Friedrich Strauss's *Leben Jesus* (1835). [Ed.]

[20]"Whoever imagines himself able to write it better, does not understand it." Claude Fleury, *Ecclesiastical History* (1722). [Ed.]

entation of the character of Jesus were offered to me, I would not have it; its very clearness would be, in my opinion, the best proof of its insufficiency." His friends may with perfect justice rejoin that at the sight of the Holy Land, and of the actual scene of the Gospel story, all the current of M. Renan's thoughts may have naturally changed, and a new casting of that story irresistibly suggested itself to him; and that this is just a case for applying Cicero's maxim: Change of mind is not inconsistency — *nemo doctus unquam mutationem consilii inconstantiam dixit esse.*[21] Nevertheless, for criticism, M. Renan's first thought must still be the truer one, as long as his new casting so fails more fully to commend itself, more fully (to use Coleridge's happy phrase about the Bible) to *find* us. Still M. Renan's attempt is, for criticism, of the most real interest and importance, since, with all its difficulty, a fresh synthesis of the New Testament *data,* — not a making war on them, in Voltaire's fashion, not a leaving them out of mind, in the world's fashion, but the putting a new construction upon them, the taking them from under the old, adoptive, traditional, unspiritual point of view and placing them under a new one, — is the very essence of the religious problem, as now presented; and only by efforts in this direction can it receive a solution.

Again, in the same spirit in which she judges Bishop Colenso, Miss Cobbe, like so many earnest liberals of our practical race, both here and in America, herself sets vigorously about a positive reconstruction of religion, about making a religion of the future out of hand, or at least setting about making it; we must not rest, she and they are always thinking and saying, in negative criticism, we must be creative and constructive; hence we have such works as her recent *Religious Duty,* and works still more considerable, perhaps, by others, which will be in everyone's mind. These works often have much ability; they often spring out of sincere convictions, and a sincere wish to do good; and they sometimes, perhaps, do good. Their fault is (if I may be permitted to say so) one which they have a

common with the British College of Health, in the New Road. Everyone knows the British College of Health; it is that building with the lion and the statue of the Goddess Hygeia before it; as least I am sure about the lion, though I am not absolutely certain about the Goddess Hygeia. This building does credit, perhaps, to the resources of Dr. Morrison and his disciples; but it falls a good deal short of one's idea of which a British College of Health ought to be. In England, where we hate public interference and love individual enterprise, we have a whole crop of places like the British College of Health; the grand name without the grand thing. Unluckily, creditable to individual enterprise as they are, they tend to impair our taste by making us forget what more grandiose, noble, or beautiful character properly belongs to a public institution. The same may be said of the religions of the future of Miss Cobbe and others. Creditable, like the British College of Health, to the resources of their authors, they yet tend to make us forget what more grandiose, noble, or beautiful character properly belongs to religious constructions. The historic religions, with all their faults, have had this; it certainly belongs to the religious sentiment, when it truly flowers, to have this; and we impoverish our spirit if we allow a religion of the future without it. What then is the duty of criticism here? To take the practical point of view, to applaud the liberal movement and all its works, — its New Road religions of the future into the bargain, — for their general utility's sake? By no means; but to be perpetually dissatisfied with these works, while they perpetually fall short of a high and perfect ideal.

For criticism, these are elementary laws; but they never can be popular, and in this country they have been very little followed, and one meets with immense obstacles in following them. That is a reason for asserting them again and again. Criticism must maintain its independence of the practical spirit and its aims. Even with well-meant efforts of the practical spirit it must express dissatisfaction, if in the sphere of the ideal they seem impoverishing and limiting. It must not hurry on to the goal because of its practical importance. It must be patient, and know how to wait; and flexible, and know how

[21]Cicero, *To Atticus* 16.17:3. [Ed.]

to attain itself to things and how to withdraw from them. It must be apt to study and praise elements that for the fulness of spiritual perfection are wanted, even though they belong to a power which in the practical sphere may be maleficent. It must be apt to discern the spiritual shortcomings or illusions of powers that in the practical sphere may be beneficent. And this without any notion of favouring or injuring, in the practical sphere, one power or the other; without any notion of playing off, in this sphere, one power against the other. When one looks, for instance, at the English Divorce Court, — an institution which perhaps has its practical conveniences, but which in the ideal sphere is so hideous; an institution which neither makes divorce impossible nor makes it decent, which allows a man to get rid of his wife, or a wife of her husband, but makes them drag one another first, for the public edification, through a mire of unutterable infamy, — when one looks at this charming institution, I say, with its crowded benches, its newspaper-reports, and its money-compensations, this institution in which the gross unregenerate British Philistine has indeed stamped an image of himself, — one may be permitted to find the marriage-theory of Catholicism refreshing and elevating. Or when Protestantism, in virtue of its supposed rational and intellectual origin, gives the law to criticism too magisterially, criticism may and must remind it that its pretensions, in this respect, are illusive and do it harm; that the Reformation was a moral rather than an intellectual event; that Luther's theory of grace no more exactly reflects the mind of the spirit than Bossuet's philosophy of history[22] reflects it; and that there is no more antecedent probability of the Bishop of Durham's stock of ideas being agreeable to perfect reason than of Pope Pius the Ninth's. But criticism will not on that account forget the achievements of Protestantism in the practical and moral sphere; nor that, even in the intellectual sphere, Protestantism, though in a blind and stumbling manner,

carried forward the Renascence, while Catholicism threw itself violently across its path.

I lately heard a man of thought and energy[23] contrasting the want of ardour and movement which he now found amongst young men in this country with what he remembered in his own youth, twenty years ago. "What reformers we were then!" he exclaimed; "what a zeal we had! how we canvassed every institution in Church and State, and were prepared to remodel them all on first principles!" He was inclined to regret, as a spiritual flagging, the lull which he saw. I am disposed rather to regard it as a pause in which the turn to a new mode of spiritual progress is being accomplished; everything was long seen, by the young and ardent amongst us, in inseparable connection with politics and practical life; we have pretty well exhausted the benefits of seeing things in this connection, we have got all that can be got by so seeing them. Let us try a more disinterested mode of seeing them; let us betake ourselves more to the serener life of the mind and spirit. This life, too, may have its excesses and dangers; but they are not for us at present. Let us think of quietly enlarging our stock of true and fresh ideas, and not, as soon as we get an idea or half an idea, be running out with it into the street, and trying to make it rule there. Our ideas will, in the end, shape the world all the better for maturing a little. Perhaps in fifty years' time it will in the English House of Commons be an objection to an institution that it is an anomaly, and my friend the Member of Parliament will shudder in his grave. But let us in the meanwhile rather endeavour that in twenty years' time it may, in English literature, be an objection to a proposition that it is absurd. That will be a change so vast, that the imagination almost fails to grasp it. *Ab integro saeclorum nascitur ordo*.[24]

If I have insisted so much on the course which criticism must take where politics and religion are concerned, it is because, where these burning

<hr />

[22]Jacques-Bénigne Bossuet, *Discourse on Universal History* (1681). [Ed.]

[23]Charles Thomas Baring, Bishop of Durham (1861–79). [Ed.]

[24]"Order is born from the renewal of the ages." Virgil, *Eclogues* 4:5. [Ed.]

matters are in question, it is most likely to go astray. I have wished, above all, to insist on the attitude which criticism should adopt towards everything; on its right tone and temper of mind. Then comes the question as to the subject-matter which criticism should most seek. Here, in general, its course is determined for it by the idea which is the law of its being; the idea of a disinterested endeavour to learn and propagate the best that is known and thought in the world, and thus to establish a current of fresh and true ideas. By the very nature of things, as England is not all the world, much of the best that is known and thought in the world cannot be of English growth, must be foreign; by the nature of things, again, it is just this that we are least likely to know, while English thought is streaming in upon us from all sides, and takes excellent care that we shall not be ignorant of its existence; the English critic, therefore, must dwell much on foreign thought, and with particular heed on any part of it, which, while significant and fruitful in itself, is for any reason specially likely to escape him. Again, judging is often spoken of as the critic's one business, and so in some sense it is; but the judgment which almost insensibly forms itself in a fair and clear mind, along with fresh knowledge, is the valuable one; and thus knowledge, and ever fresh knowledge, must be the critic's great concern for himself; and it is by communicating fresh knowledge, and letting his own judgment pass along with it, — but insensibly, and in the second place not the first, as a sort of companion and clue, not as an abstract lawgiver, — that he will generally do most good to his readers. Sometimes, no doubt, for the sake of establishing an author's place in literature, and his relation to a central standard (and if this is not done, how are we to get at our *best in the world*?) criticism may have to deal with a subject-matter so familiar that fresh knowledge is out of the question, and then it must be all judgment; an enunciation and detailed application of principles. Here the great safeguard is never to let oneself become abstract, always to retain an intimate and lively consciousness of the truth of what one is saying, and, the moment this fails us, to be sure that something is wrong. Still,

under all circumstances, this mere judgment and application of principles is, in itself, not the most satisfactory work to the critic; like mathematics, it is tautological, and cannot well give us, like fresh learning, the sense of creative activity.

But stop, someone will say; all this talk is of no practical use to us whatever; this criticism of yours is not what we have in our minds when we speak of criticism; when we speak of critics and criticism, we mean critics and criticism of the current English literature of the day; when you offer to tell criticism its function, it is to this criticism that we expect you to address yourself. I am sorry for it, for I am afraid I must disappoint these expectations. I am bound by my own definition of criticism: *a disinterested endeavour to learn and propagate the best that is known and thought in the world.* How much of current English literature comes into this "best that is known and thought in the world"? Not very much, I fear; certainly less, at this moment, than of the current literature of France or Germany. Well, then, am I to alter my definition of criticism, in order to meet the requirements of a number of practising English critics, who, after all, are free in their choice of a business? That would be making criticism lend itself just to one of those alien practical considerations, which, I have said, are so fatal to it. One may say, indeed, to those who have to deal with the mass — so much better disregarded — of current English literature, that they may at all events endeavour, in dealing with this, to try it, so far as they can, by the standard of the best that is known and thought in the world; one may say, that to get anywhere near this standard, every critic should try and possess one great literature, at least, besides his own; and the more unlike his own; the better. But, after all, the criticism I am really concerned with, — the criticism which alone can much help us for the future, the criticism which, throughout Europe, is at the present day meant, when so much stress is laid on the importance of criticism and the critical spirit, — is a criticism which regards Europe as being, for intellectual and spiritual purposes, one great confederation, bound to a joint action and working to a common result; and whose members have, for their proper outfit, a knowledge of Greek, Roman, and Eastern antiquity, and of one another. Special, local, and temporary advantages being put out of account, that modern nation will in the intellectual and spiritual sphere make most progress, which most thoroughly carries out this programme. And what is that but saying that we too, all of us, as individuals, the more thoroughly we carry it out, shall make the more progress?

There is so much inviting us! — what are we to take? what will nourish us in growth towards perfection? That is the question which, with the immense field of life and of literature lying before him, the critic has to answer; for himself first, and afterwards for others. In this idea of the critic's business the essays brought together in the following pages have had their origin; in this idea, widely different as are their subjects, they have, perhaps, their unity.

I conclude with what I said at the beginning: to have the sense of creative activity is the great happiness and the great proof of being alive, and it is not denied to criticism to have it; but then criticism must be sincere, simple, flexible, ardent, ever widening its knowledge. Then it may

have, in no contemptible measure, joyful sense of creative activity; a sense which a man of insight and conscience will prefer to what he might derive from a poor, starved, fragmentary, inadequate creation. And at some epochs no other creation is possible.

Still, in full measure, the sense of creative activity belongs only to genuine creation; in literature we must never forget that. But what true man of letters ever can forget it? It is no such common matter for a gifted nature to come into possession of a current of true and living ideas, and to produce amidst the inspiration of them, that we are likely to underrate it. The epochs of Aeschylus and Shakespeare make us feel their pre-eminence. In an epoch like those is, no doubt, the true life of a literature; there is the promised land, towards which criticism can only beckon. That promised land it will not be ours to enter, and we shall die in the wilderness: but to have desired to enter it, to have saluted it from afar, is already, perhaps, the best distinction among contemporaries; it will certainly be the best title to esteem with posterity.

# From *The Study of Poetry*

The future of poetry is immense, because in poetry, where it is worthy of its high destinies, our race, as time goes on, will find an ever surer and surer stay. There is not a creed which is not shaken, not an accredited dogma which is not shown to be questionable, not a received tradition which does not threaten to dissolve. Our religion has materialized itself in the fact, in the supposed fact; it has attached its emotion to the fact, and now the fact is failing it. But for poetry the idea is everything; the rest is a world of illusion, of divine illusion. Poetry attaches its emotion to the idea; the idea *is* the fact. The strongest part of our religion today is its unconscious poetry.[1]

Let me be permitted to quote these words of my own, as uttering the thought which should, in my opinion, go with us and govern us in all our study of poetry. In the present work it is the course of one great contributory stream to the world-river of poetry that we are invited to follow. We are here invited to trace the stream of English poetry. But whether we set ourselves, as here, to follow only one of the several streams that make the mighty river of poetry, or whether we seek to know them all, our governing thought should be the same. We should conceive of poetry worthily, and more highly than it has been the custom to conceive of it. We should conceive of it as capable of higher uses, and called to higher destinies, than those which in general men have assigned to it hitherto. More and more man-

[1] From the Introduction to *The Hundred Greatest Men* (1879). [Ed.]

kind will discover that we have to turn to poetry to interpret life for us, to console us, to sustain us. Without poetry, our science will appear incomplete; and most of what now passes with us for religion and philosophy will be replaced by poetry. Science, I say, will appear incomplete without it. For finely and truly does Wordsworth call poetry "the impassioned expression which is in the countenance of all science"[2]; and what is a countenance without its expression? Again, Wordsworth finely and truly calls poetry "the breath and finer spirit of all knowledge": our religion, parading evidences such as those on which the popular mind relies now; our philosophy, pluming itself on its reasonings about causation and finite and infinite being; what are they but the shadows and dreams and false shows of knowledge? The day will come when we shall wonder at ourselves for having trusted to them, for having taken them seriously; and the more we perceive their hollowness, the more we shall prize "the breath and finer spirit of knowledge" offered to us by poetry.

But if we conceive thus highly of the destinies of poetry, we must also set our standard for poetry high, since poetry, to be capable of fulfilling such high destinies, must be poetry of a high order of excellence. We must accustom ourselves to a high standard and to a strict judgment. Sainte-Beuve relates that Napoleon one day said, when somebody was spoken of in his presence as a charlatan: "Charlatan as much as you please; but where is there *not* charlatanism?" — "Yes," answers Sainte-Beuve, "in politics, in the art of governing mankind, that is perhaps true. But in the order of thought, in art, the glory, the eternal honour, is that charlatanism shall find no entrance; herein lies the inviolableness of that noble portion of man's being." It is admirably said, and let us hold fast to it. In poetry, which is thought and art in one, it is the glory, the eternal honour, that charlatanism shall find no entrance; that this noble sphere be kept inviolate and inviolable. Charlatanism is for confusing or obliterating the distinctions between excellent and inferior, sound and unsound or only half-sound, true and untrue

or only half-true. It is charlatanism, conscious or unconscious, whenever we confuse or obliterate these. And in poetry, more than anywhere else, it is unpermissible to confuse or obliterate them. For in poetry the distinction between excellent and inferior, sound and unsound or only half-sound, true and untrue or only half-true, is of paramount importance. It is of paramount importance because of the high destinies of poetry. In poetry, as a criticism of life under the conditions fixed for such a criticism by the laws of poetic truth and poetic beauty, the spirit of our race will find, we have said, as time goes on and as other helps fail, its consolation and stay. But the consolation and stay will be of power in proportion to the power of the criticism of life. And the criticism of life will be of power in proportion as the poetry conveying it is excellent rather than inferior, sound rather than unsound or half-sound, true rather than untrue or half-true.

The best poetry is what we want; the best poetry will be found to have a power of forming, sustaining, and delighting us, as nothing else can. A clearer, deeper sense of the best in poetry, and of the strength and joy to be drawn from it, is the most precious benefit which we can gather from a poetical collection such as the present. And yet in the very nature and conduct of such a collection there is inevitably something which tends to obscure in us the consciousness of what our benefit should be, and to distract us from the pursuit of it. We should therefore steadily set it before our minds at the outset, and should compel ourselves to revert constantly to the thought of it as we proceed.

Yes; constantly, in reading poetry, a sense for the best, the really excellent, and of the strength and joy to be drawn from it, should be present in our minds and should govern our estimate of what we read. But this real estimate, the only true one, is liable to be superseded, if we are not watchful, by two other kinds of estimate, the historic estimate and the personal estimate, both of which are fallacious. A poet or a poem may count to us historically, they may count to us on grounds personal to ourselves, and they may count to us really. They may count to us historically. The course of development of a nation's

[2]In "Preface to *Lyrical Ballads*"; see p. 292. [Ed.]

language, thought, and poetry, is profoundly interesting; and by regarding a poet's work as a stage in this course of development we may easily bring ourselves to make it of more importance as poetry than in itself it really is, we may come to use a language of quite exaggerated praise in criticizing it; in short, to overrate it. So arises in our poetic judgments the fallacy caused by the estimate which we may call historic. Then, again, a poet or a poem may count to us on grounds personal to ourselves. Our personal affinities, likings, and circumstances have great power to sway our estimates of this or that poet's work, and to make us attach more importance to it as poetry than in itself it really possesses, because to us it is, or has been, of high importance. Here also we overrate the object of our interest, and apply to it a language of praise which is quite exaggerated. And thus we get the source of a second fallacy in our poetic judgments — the fallacy caused by an estimate which we may call personal.

Both fallacies are natural. It is evident how naturally the study of the history and development of a poetry may incline a man to pause over reputations and works once conspicuous but now obscure, and to quarrel with a careless public for skipping, in obedience to mere tradition and habit, from one famous name or work in its natural poetry to another, ignorant of what it misses, and of the reason for keeping what it keeps, and of the whole process of growth in its poetry. The French have become diligent students of their own early poetry, which they long neglected; the study makes many of them dissatisfied with their so-called classical poetry, the court-tragedy of the seventeenth century, a poetry which Pellisson long ago reproached with its want of the true poetic stamp, with its *politesse stérile et rampante,* but which nevertheless has reigned in France as absolutely as if it had been the perfection of classical poetry indeed. The dissatisfaction is natural; yet a lively and accomplished critic, M. Charles d'Héricault, the editor of Clément Marot, goes too far when he says that "the cloud of glory playing round a classic is a mist as dangerous to the future of a literature as it is intolerable for the purposes of history."

"It hinders," he goes on, "it hinders us from seeing more than one single point, the culminating and exceptional point; the summary, fictitious and arbitrary, of a thought and of a work. It substitutes a halo for a physiognomy, it puts a statue where there was once a man, and, hiding from us all trace of the labour, the attempts, the weaknesses, the failures, it claims not study but veneration; it does not show us how the thing is done, it imposes upon us a model. Above all, for the historian this creation of classic personages is inadmissible; for it withdraws the poet from his time, from his proper life, it breaks historical relationships, it blinds criticism by conventional admiration, and renders the investigation of literary origins unacceptable. It gives us a human personage no longer, but a God seated immovable amidst His perfect work, like Jupiter on Olympus; and hardly will it be possible for the young student, to whom such work is exhibited at such a distance from him, to believe that it did not issue ready made from that divine head."

All this is brilliantly and tellingly said, but we must plead for a distinction. Everything depends on the reality of a poet's classic character. If he is a dubious classic, let us sift him; if he is a false classic, let us explode him. But if he is a real classic, if his work belongs to the class of the very best (for this is the true and right meaning of the word *classic, classical*), then the great thing for us is to feel and enjoy his work as deeply as ever we can, and to appreciate the wide difference between it and all work which has not the same high character. This is what is salutary, this is what is formative; this is the great benefit to be got from the study of poetry. Everything which interferes with it, which hinders it, is injurious. True, we must read our classic with open eyes, and not with eyes blinded with superstition; we must perceive when his work comes short, when it drops out of the class of the very best, and we must rate it, in such cases, at its proper value. But the use of this negative criticism is not in itself, it is entirely in its enabling us to have a clearer sense and a deeper enjoyment of what is truly excellent. To trace the labour, the attempts, the weaknesses, the failures of a genuine classic, to acquaint oneself with his time and his life and his historical relationships, is mere literary dilettantism unless it has that clear sense and deeper enjoyment for its end. It may be said that the more we know about a classic the better we shall enjoy him; and, if we lived as long as Methuselah and had all of us heads of perfect clearness and wills of perfect steadfastness, this might be true in fact as it is plausible in theory. But the case here is much the same as the case with the Greek and Latin studies of our schooldays. The elaborate philological groundwork which we require them to lay is in theory an admirable preparation for appreciating the Greek and Latin authors worthily. The more thoroughly we lay the groundwork, the better we shall be able, it may be said, to enjoy the authors. True, if time were not so short, and schoolboys' wits not so soon tired and their power of attention exhausted; only, as it is, the elaborate philological preparation goes on, but the authors are little known and less enjoyed. So with the investigator of "historic origins" in poetry. He ought to enjoy the true classic all the better for his investigations; he often is distracted from the enjoyment of the best, and with the less good he overbusies himself, and is prone to overrate it in proportion to the trouble which it has cost him.

The idea of tracing historic origins and historical relationships cannot be absent from a compilation like the present. And naturally the poets to be exhibited in it will be assigned to those persons for exhibition who are known to prize them highly, rather than to those who have no special inclination towards them. Moreover, the very occupation with an author, and the business of exhibiting him, disposes us to affirm and amplify his importance. In the present work, therefore, we are sure of frequent temptation to adopt the historic estimate, or the personal estimate, and to forget the real estimate; which latter, nevertheless, we must employ if we are to make poetry yield us its full benefit. So high is that benefit, the benefit of clearly feeling and of deeply enjoying the really excellent, the truly classic in poetry, that we do well, I say, to set it fixedly before our minds as our object in studying poets and poetry, and to make the desire of at-

taining it the one principle to which, as the *Imitation*[3] says, whatever we may read or come to know, we always return. *Cum multa legeris et cognoveris, ad unum semper oportet redire principium.*

The historic estimate is likely in especial to affect our judgment and our language when we are dealing with ancient poets; the personal estimate when we are dealing with poets our contemporaries, or at any rate modern. The exaggerations due to the historic estimate are not in themselves, perhaps, of very much gravity. Their report hardly enters the general ear; probably they do not always impose even on the literary men who adopt them. But they lead to a dangerous abuse of language. So we hear Caedmon, amongst our own poets, compared to Milton. I have already noticed the enthusiasm of one accomplished French critic for "historic origins." Another eminent French critic, M. Vitet, comments upon that famous document of the early poetry of his nation, the *Chanson de Roland*. It is indeed a most interesting document. The *joculator* or *jongleur* Taillefer, who was with William the Conqueror's army at Hastings, marched before the Norman troops, so said the tradition, singing "of Charlemagne and of Roland and of Oliver, and of the vassals who died at Roncevaux"; and it is suggested that in the *Chanson de Roland* by one Turoldus or Théroulde, a poem preserved in a manuscript of the twelfth century in the Bodleian Library at Oxford, we have certainly the matter, perhaps even some of the words, of the chant which Taillefer sang. The poem has vigour and freshness; it is not without pathos. But M. Vitet is not satisfied with seeing in it a document of some poetic value, and of a very high historic and linguistic value; he sees in it a grand and beautiful work, a monument of epic genius. In its general design he finds the grandiose conception, in its details he finds the constant union of simplicity with greatness, which are the marks, he truly says, of the genuine epic, and distinguish it from the artificial epic of literary ages. One thinks of Homer; this is the

---

[3]Thomas à Kempis, *The Imitation of Christ*. [Ed.]

sort of praise which is given to Homer, and justly given. Higher praise there cannot well be, and it is the praise due to epic poetry of the highest order only and to no other. Let us try, then, the *Chanson de Roland* at its best. Roland, mortally wounded, lays himself down under a pine-tree, with his face turned towards Spain and the enemy —

De plusurs choses a remembrer li prist,
De tantes teres cume li bers cunquist,
De dulce France, des humes de sun lign,
De Carlemagne sun seignor ki l'nurrit.[4]

That is primitive work, I repeat, with an undeniable poetic quality of its own. It deserves such praise, and such praise is sufficient for it. But now turn to Homer —

Ὣς φάτο· τοὺς δ' ἤδη κατέχεν φυσίζοος αἶα
ἐν Λακεδαίμονι αὖθι, φίλῃ ἐν πατρίδι γαίῃ.[5]

We are here in another world, another order of poetry altogether; here is rightly due such supreme praise as that which M. Vitet gives to the *Chanson de Roland*. If our words are to have any meaning, if our judgments are to have any solidity, we must not heap that supreme praise upon poetry of an order immeasurably inferior.

Indeed there can be no more useful help for discovering what poetry belongs to the class of the truly excellent, and can therefore do us most good, than to have always in one's mind lines and expressions of the great masters, and to apply them as a touchstone to other poetry. Of course we are not to require this other poetry to resemble them; it may be very dissimilar. But if we have any tact we shall find them, when we have lodged them well in our minds, an infallible touchstone for detecting the presence or absence of high poetic quality, and also the degree of this quality, in all other poetry which we may place beside

them. Short passages, even single lines, will serve our turn quite sufficiently. Take the two lines which I have just quoted from Homer, the poet's comment on Helen's mention of her brothers; — or take his

Ἀ δειλώ, τί σφῶϊ δόμεν Πηλῆϊ ἄνακτι
θνητῷ; ὑμεῖς δ' ἐστόν ἀγήρω τ' ἀθανάτω τε.
ἦ ἵνα δυστήνοισι μετ' ἀνδράσιν ἄλγε' ἔχητον;[6]

the address of Zeus to the horses of Peleus; — or take finally his

Καὶ σέ, γέρον, τὸ πρὶν μὲν ἀκούομεν ὄλβιον εἶναι·[7]

the words of Achilles to Priam, a suppliant before him. Take that incomparable line and a half of Dante, Ugolino's tremendous words —

Io no piangeva; sì dentro impietrai.
Piangevan elli . . .[8]

take the lovely words of Beatrice to Virgil —

Io son fatta da Dio, sua mercè, tale,
Che la vostra miseria non mi tange,
Nè fiamma d' esto incendio non m' assale . . .[9]

take the simple, but perfect, single line —

In la sua volontade è nostra pace.[10]

Take of Shakespeare a line or two of Henry the Fourth's expostulation with sleep —

Wilt thou upon the high and giddy mast
Seal up the ship-boy's eyes, and rock his brains
In cradle of the rude imperious surge . . .[11]

and take, as well, Hamlet's dying request to Horatio —

[4]"Then began he to call many things to remembrance, — all the lands which his valour conquered, and pleasant France, and the men of his lineage, and Charlemagne his liege lord who nourished him." — *Chanson de Roland,* iii.939–42. [Au.]

[5]"So said she; they long since in Earth's soft arms were reposing,/There, in their own dear land, their fatherland, Lacedaemon." *Iliad,* iii. 243, 244 (translated by Dr Hawtrey). [Au.]

[6]"Ah, unhappy pair, why gave we you to King Peleus, to a mortal? but ye are without old age, and immortal. Was it that with men born in misery ye might have sorrow?" — *Iliad,* xvii. 443–45. [Au.]

[7]"Nay, and thou too, old man, in former days wast, as we hear, happy." — *Iliad,* xxiv. 543. [Au.]

[8]"I wailed not, so of stone grew I within; — *they* wailed." — *Inferno,* xxxiii. 39, 40. [Au.]

[9]"Of such sort hath God, thanked be His mercy, made me, that your misery toucheth me not, neither doth the flame of this fire strike me." — *Inferno,* ii. 91–93. [Au.]

[10]"In His will is our peace." — *Paradiso,* iii. 85. [Au.]

[11]Shakespeare, *2 Henry IV,* III.i.18–20. [Ed.]

If thou didst ever hold me in thy heart,
Absent thee from felicity awhile,
And in this harsh world draw thy breath in pain
To tell my story . . . .[12]

Take of Milton that Miltonic passage —

Darken'd so, yet shone
Above them all the archangel; but his face
Deep scars of thunder had intrench'd, and care
Sat on his faded cheek . . .[13]

add two such lines as —

And courage never to submit or yield
And what is else not to be overcome . . . .[14]

and finish with the exquisite close to the loss of
Proserpine, the loss

. . . which cost Ceres all that pain
To seek her through the world.[15]

These few lines, if we have tact and can use
them, are enough even of themselves to keep
clear and sound our judgments about poetry, to
save us from fallacious estimates of it, to conduct
us to a real estimate.

The specimens I have quoted differ widely
from one another, but they have in common this:
the possession of the very highest poetical quality. If we are thoroughly penetrated by their
power, we shall find that we have acquired a
sense enabling us, whatever poetry may be laid
before us, to feel the degree in which a high
poetical quality is present or wanting there. Critics give themselves great labour to draw out what
in the abstract constitutes the characters of a high
quality of poetry. It is much better simply to
have recourse to concrete examples; — to take
specimens of poetry of the high, the very highest
quality, and to say: The characters of a high
quality of poetry are what is expressed *there*.
They are far better recognized by being felt in
the verse of the master, than by being perused in
the prose of the critic. Nevertheless if we are
urgently pressed to give some critical account of
them, we may safely, perhaps, venture on laying

down, not indeed how and why the characters
arise, but where and in what they arise. They are
in the matter and substance of the poetry, and
they are in its manner and style. Both of these,
the substance and matter on the one hand, the
style and manner on the other, have a mark, an
accent, of high beauty, worth, and power. But if
we are asked to define this mark and accent in
the abstract, our answer must be: No, for we
should thereby be darkening the question, not
clearing it. The mark and accent are as given by
the substance and matter of that poetry, by the
style and manner of that poetry, and of all other
poetry which is akin to it in quality.

Only one thing we may add as to the substance
and matter of poetry, guiding ourselves by Aristotle's profound observation that the superiority
of poetry over history consists in its possessing
a higher truth and a higher seriousness (φιλο-
σοφώτερον καὶ σπουδαιότερον).[16] Let us add,
therefore, to what we have said, this: that the
substance and matter of the best poetry acquire
their special character from possessing, in an
eminent degree, truth and seriousness. We may
add yet further, what is in itself evident, that to
the style and manner of the best poetry their
special character, their accent, is given by their
diction, and, even yet more, by their movement.
And though we distinguish between the two characters, the two accents, of superiority, yet they
are nevertheless vitally connected one with the
other. The superior character of truth and seriousness, in the matter and substance of the best
poetry, is inseparable from the superiority of diction and movement marking its style and manner.
The two superiorities are closely related, and are
in steadfast proportion one to the other. So far
as high poetic truth and seriousness are wanting
to a poet's matter and substance, so far also, we
may be sure, will a high poetic stamp of diction
and movement be wanting to his style and manner. In proportion as this high stamp of diction
and movement, again, is absent from a poet's
style and manner, we shall find, also, that high
poetic truth and seriousness are absent from his
substance and matter.

---

[12]Shakespeare, *Hamlet*, V.ii.357–60. [Ed.]
[13]Milton, *Paradise Lost*, 1:599–602. [Ed.]
[14]Milton, *Paradise Lost*, 1:108–9. [Ed.]
[15]Milton, *Paradise Lost*, 4:271–72. [Ed.]

[16]Aristotle, *Poetics*, Book 9.

So stated, these are but dry generalities; their whole force lies in their application. And I could wish every student of poetry to make the application of them for himself. Made by himself, the application would impress itself upon his mind far more deeply than if made by me. Neither will my limits allow me to make any full application of the generalities above propounded; but in the hope of bringing out, at any rate, some significance in them, and of establishing an important principle more firmly by their means, I will, in the space which remains to me, follow rapidly from the commencement the course of our English poetry with them in my view.

# Friedrich Nietzsche

1844–1900

Friedrich Wilhelm Nietzsche was born in 1844, the son of a Saxon pastor. He was educated at the universities of Bonn and Leipzig, took his degrees in philology, and was appointed professor at the University of Basel in 1869. The selection included here is from Nietzsche's first book, *The Birth of Tragedy from the Spirit of Music* (1872). *The Birth of Tragedy* is unusual among Nietzsche's works in having a sustained and coherent argument: In his later works, he intentionally became more and more aphoristic, conveying his thought in brief flashes and ironic hints. Because he died relatively young of complications from tertiary syphilis and because of nervous breakdowns in the decade before his death, some of his critics have suggested that he was incapable of sustained argument almost from the outset of his career. This is unfair to Nietzsche, who, like Plato, was in rebellion against the stultifying philosophical treatise. His aim was to stimulate thought in others, and for this he was willing to risk being misunderstood. As a result, he has been misunderstood as few philosophers ever have been. Nietzsche was neither nationalistic nor racist nor anti-Semitic, for example, so it is hideously ironic that less than a generation after his death, his ideas, perverted almost beyond recognition, were adopted as the pet philosophy of the Nazi regime.

If there is any central theme in Nietzsche's philosophy it is his opposition to the complacent Victorian faith in progress through a rationalistic reordering of society. He saw as basic to human nature darker motives (like the will-to-power) than his utilitarian contemporaries were willing to acknowledge, but he also saw the possibility of self-sacrifice and transcendence. These themes appear most strongly in his ecstatic tract, *Thus Spake Zarathustra* (1883–92), along with *The Joyful Wisdom* (1882) and *Beyond Good and Evil* (1886). Nietzsche profoundly distrusted the Victorian myths of progress; like Dostoevsky, he was a reactionary whose insights into the obscene hunger of the human soul strikingly prefigured the discoveries of Freud.

## APOLLO AND DIONYSUS

Nietzsche's essay begins with two opposed symbolic images: Apollo and Dionysus, dream and intoxication, plastic arts and music. The obvious question is why they should divide the aesthetic world between them. This dichotomy is best understood if we see Nietzsche as a follower — with many qualifications — of Arthur Schopenhauer. Schopenhauer's monumental treatise, *The World as Will and Idea* (1819), had posited that human life reverberates between the extremes of boredom and longing — most often the latter, given the competition among the many hungry wills inhabiting the universe. To be alive, Nietzsche agreed, was to be in a state of want: The image of Tantalus, forever groping at the desired food and drink beyond his grasp, was for Nietzsche an image of humankind. Existence was, in a word, tragic.

Nietzsche saw art as civilization's most effective means of coping with this tragedy of existence. Art works by taming dream and intoxication, two primitive methods of coping with the hungry will. In dream the hunger is satiated; in intoxication the self is obliterated. In dream (as Freud and many others had noted) we retreat into a fantasy world in which our desires are all fulfilled, as they cannot be in reality. In intoxication we do not lose our desires so much as we lose *ourselves:* When drunk, our sense of self — our awareness of an inside and an outside, of a consciousness differentiated from the Other — fades away as the ego is annihilated.

## THE BIRTH, AND DEATH, AND REBIRTH, OF TRAGEDY

Most of Nietzsche's treatise is a historical essay on the development of Greek tragedy out of the religious ritual of Dionysus. It is startling to think that he developed this notion by an intuitive leap from a few hints in the classics, long before classical research established the religious origins and the ritual nature of the drama.

In the beginning was music, a chorus of dancing satyrs rhythmically, musically expressing their devotion to the god of intoxication, each Greek citizen losing his individuality within the satyr chorus. The choric dance then begins to include song, takes on language and, with it, the plastic images of Apollonian dream. For Nietzsche the essence of tragedy is now already present, before anything like a play exists, in the "Dionysiac chorus which again and again discharges itself in Apollonian images." Later still the god himself is impersonated by the choral leader, who becomes in effect the first actor. From here to the enactment of story and the addition of the second and third actors — to the drama of Aeschylus and Sophocles — it is only a short step: mere complications.

For Nietzsche, tragedy reaches its height with Aeschylus and Sophocles. Its essence in the fusion of Apollonian and Dionysiac impulses begins to be destroyed almost immediately thereafter. Nietzsche's villains are the individualism of Euripides and the rationalism of Socrates, which were consistent with the lyrics of Apollo but not with the music of Dionysus. Individualism and rationalism infected Greek civilization and the Roman and Western European civilizations that followed. Tragedy now began to explore the causes of the errors of highly placed individuals rather than expressing the essence of all human life. Even music itself began in the nineteenth century to become plastic and descriptive — Apollonian rather than Dionysian in character. This perversion of the tragic hit bottom, for Nietzsche, in the Italian opera.

The antidote for all this Nietzsche found in the music-dramas of Richard Wagner, who by 1871 had already written *Tristan und Isolde* and *Die Meistersinger* and had just produced *Das Rheingold* and *Die Walküre,* the first two segments of his massive cycle based on the *Nibelungenlied.* In Wagner's use of myth and universal types, and above all in his return of the leading role to the communal spirit of music rather than the individuation of the Apollonian image, Nietzsche saw the possibility for a rebirth of the healing qualities of art that had been lost when Greek tragedy declined. This enthusiasm with Wagner was to be short-lived. By the second edition of *The Birth of Tragedy,* Nietzsche had broken with Wagner, disgusted by his nationalism and the sickly spiritualism of his last opera, *Parsifal.* Nevertheless, Nietzsche's aesthetic ideas, his notions about the place of the tragic in human life, remain profoundly moving.

## Selected Bibliography

Danto, Arthur. *Nietzsche as a Philosopher.* New York: Macmillan, 1965.

Donadio, Stephen. *Nietzsche, Henry James, and the Artistic Will.* New York: Oxford University Press, 1976.

Gilman, Sander L. *Nietzschean Parody: An Introduction to Reading Nietzsche.* Bonn: Bouvier Verlag, 1976.

Jaspers, Karl. *Nietzsche: An Introduction to the Understanding of His Philosophical Activity.* Tucson: University of Arizona Press, 1965.

Kaufmann, Walter. *Nietzsche: Philosopher, Psychologist, Antichrist.* 3d ed. Princeton: Princeton University Press, 1968.

Ludovici, Anthony. *Nietzsche and Art.* Boston: J. W. Luce, 1912.

Megill, Allan. *Prophets of Extremity: Nietzsche, Heidegger, Foucault, Derrida.* Berkeley: University of California Press, 1985.

Nehamas, Alexander. *Nietzsche: Life as Literature.* Cambridge: Harvard University Press, 1985.

Silk, M. S. *Nietzsche on Tragedy.* Cambridge and New York: Cambridge University Press, 1981.

# From *The Birth of Tragedy from the Spirit of Music*

## I

Much will have been gained for esthetics once we have succeeded in apprehending directly — rather than merely *ascertaining* — that art owes its continuous evolution to the Apollonian-Dionysiac duality, even as the propagation of the species depends on the duality of the sexes, their constant conflicts and periodic acts of reconciliation. I have borrowed my adjectives from the Greeks, who developed their mystical doctrines of art through plausible *embodiments,* not through purely conceptual means. It is by those two art-sponsoring deities, Apollo and Dionysos, that we are made to recognize the tremendous split, as regards both origins and objectives, between the plastic, Apollonian arts and the nonvisual art of music inspired by Dionysos. The two creative tendencies developed alongside one another, usually in fierce opposition, each by its taunts forcing the other to more energetic production, both perpetuating in a discordant concord that agon[1] which the term *art* but feebly denominates: until at last, by the thaumaturgy of an Hellenic act of will, the pair accepted the

Translated by Francis Golffing.

[1]Tragic struggle. [Ed.]

yoke of marriage and, in this condition, begot Attic tragedy, which exhibits the salient features of both parents.

To reach a closer understanding of both these tendencies, let us begin by viewing them as the separate art realms of *dream* and *intoxication*, two physiological phenomena standing toward one another in much the same relationship as the Apollonian and Dionysiac. It was in a dream, according to Lucretius, that the marvelous gods and goddesses first presented themselves to the minds of men. That great sculptor, Phidias, beheld in a dream the entrancing bodies of more-than-human beings, and likewise, if anyone had asked the Greek poets about the mystery of poetic creation, they too would have referred him to dreams and instructed him much as Hans Sachs instructs us in *Die Meistersinger:*

My friend, it is the poet's work
Dreams to interpret and to mark.
Believe me that man's true conceit
In a dream becomes complete:
All poetry we ever read
Is but true dreams interpreted.[2]

The fair illusion of the dream sphere, in the production of which every man proves himself an accomplished artist, is a precondition not only of all plastic art, but even, as we shall see presently, of a wide range of poetry. Here we enjoy an immediate apprehension of form, all shapes speak to us directly, nothing seems indifferent or redundant. Despite the high intensity with which these dream realities exist for us, we still have a residual sensation that they are illusions; at least such has been my experience — and the frequency, not to say normality, of the experience is borne out in many passages of the poets. Men of philosophical disposition are known for their constant premonition that our everyday reality, too, is an illusion, hiding another, totally different kind of reality. It was Schopenhauer who considered the ability to view at certain times all men and things as mere phantoms or dream images to be the true mark of philosophic talent. The person who is responsive to the stimuli of art behaves toward the reality of dream much the

way the philosopher behaves toward the reality of existence: he observes exactly and enjoys his observations, for it is by these images that he interprets life, by these processes that he rehearses it. Nor is it by pleasant images only that such plausible connections are made: the whole divine comedy of life, including its somber aspects, its sudden balkings, impish accidents, anxious expectations, moves past him, not quite like a shadow play — for it is he himself, after all, who lives and suffers through these scenes — yet never without giving a fleeting sense of illusion; and I imagine that many persons have reassured themselves amidst the perils of dream by calling out, "It is a dream! I want it to go on." I have even heard of people spinning out the causality of one and the same dream over three or more successive nights. All these facts clearly bear witness that our innermost being, the common substratum of humanity, experiences dreams with deep delight and a sense of real necessity. This deep and happy sense of the necessity of dream experiences was expressed by the Greeks in the image of Apollo. Apollo is at once the god of all plastic powers and the soothsaying god. He who is etymologically the "lucent" one, the god of light, reigns also over the fair illusion of our inner world of fantasy. The perfection of these conditions in contrast to our imperfectly understood waking reality, as well as our profound awareness of nature's healing powers during the interval of sleep and dream, furnishes a symbolic analogue to the soothsaying faculty and quite generally to the arts, which make life possible and worth living. But the image of Apollo must incorporate that thin line which the dream image may not cross, under penalty of becoming pathological, of imposing itself on us as crass reality: a discreet limitation, a freedom from all extravagant urges, the sapient tranquillity of the plastic god. His eye must be sunlike, in keeping with his origin. Even at those moments when he is angry and ill-tempered there lies upon him the consecration of fair illusion. In an eccentric way one might say of Apollo what Schopenhauer says, in the first part of *The World as Will and Idea,* of man caught in the veil of Maya:[3] "Even as on an immense, raging

---

[2]Richard Wagner, *The Mastersingers of Nuremberg,* III.i.99–104. [Ed.]

[3]Illusion. [Ed.]

sea, assailed by huge wave crests, a man sits in a little rowboat trusting his frail craft, so, amidst the furious torments of this world, the individual sits tranquilly, supported by the *principium individuationis* and relying on it." One might say that the unshakable confidence in that principle has received its most magnificent expression in Apollo, and that Apollo himself may be regarded as the marvelous divine image of the *principium individuationis*,[4] whose looks and gestures radiate the full delight, wisdom, and beauty of "illusion."

In the same context Schopenhauer has described for us the tremendous awe which seizes man when he suddenly begins to doubt the cognitive modes of experience, in other words, when in a given instance the law of causation seems to suspend itself. If we add to this awe the glorious transport which arises in man, even from the very depths of nature, at the shattering of the *principium individuationis,* then we are in a position to apprehend the essence of Dionysiac rapture, whose closest analogy is furnished by physical intoxication. Dionysiac stirrings arise either through the influence of those narcotic portions of which all primitive races speak in their hymns, or through the powerful approach of spring, which penetrates with joy the whole frame of nature. So stirred, the individual forgets himself completely. It is the same Dionysiac power which in medieval Germany drove ever increasing crowds of people singing and dancing from place to place; we recognize in these St. John's and St. Vitus' dancers the bacchic choruses of the Greeks, who had their precursors in Asia Minor and as far back as Babylon and the orgiastic Sacaea.[5] There are people who, either from lack of experience or out of sheer stupidity, turn away from such phenomena, and, strong in the sense of their own sanity, label them either mockingly or pityingly "endemic diseases." These benighted souls have no idea how cadaverous and ghostly their "sanity" appears as the intense throng of Dionysiac revelers sweeps past them.

Not only does the bond between man and man come to be forged once more by the magic of the Dionysiac rite, but nature itself, long alienated or subjugated, rises again to celebrate the reconciliation with her prodigal son, man. The earth offers its gifts voluntarily, and the savage beasts of mountain and desert approach in peace. The chariot of Dionysos is bedecked with flowers and garlands; panthers and tigers stride beneath his yoke. If one were to convert Beethoven's "Paean to Joy"[6] into a painting, and refuse to curb the imagination when that multitude prostrates itself reverently in the dust, one might form some apprehension of Dionysiac ritual. Now the slave emerges as a freeman; all the rigid, hostile walls which either necessity or despotism has erected between men are shattered. Now that the gospel of universal harmony is sounded, each individual becomes not only reconciled to his fellow but actually at one with him — as though the veil of Maya had been torn apart and there remained only shreds floating before the vision of mystical Oneness. Man now expresses himself through song and dance as the member of a higher community; he has forgotten how to walk, how to speak, and is on the brink of taking wing as he dances. Each of his gestures betokens enchantment; through him sounds a supernatural power, the same power which makes the animals speak and the earth render up milk and honey. He feels himself to be godlike and strides with the same elation and ecstasy as the gods he has seen in his dreams. No longer the *artist,* he has himself become a *work of art*: the productive power of the whole universe is now manifest in his transport, to the glorious satisfaction of the primordial One. The finest clay, the most precious marble — man — is here kneaded and hewn, and the chisel blows of the Dionysiac world artist are accompanied by the cry of the Eleusinian mystagogues: "Do you fall on your knees, multitudes, do you divine your creator?"[7]

---

[4] "The principle of individuation": that which differentiates the Self from the Other, the ego from the outside world. [Ed.]

[5] The Babylonian "day of the false king" — a kind of Saturnalia. [Ed.]

[6] The setting of Schiller's "Ode to Joy" takes up most of the final movement of the Ninth Symphony. [Ed.]

[7] The Eleusinian Mysteries were a cult devoted to the goddess Persephone which celebrated the coming of winter and the return of spring; the quotation is from Schiller's "Ode to Joy." [Ed.]

## III

In order to comprehend this we must take down the elaborate edifice of Apollonian culture stone by stone until we discover its foundations. At first the eye is struck by the marvelous shapes of the Olympian gods who stand upon its pediments, and whose exploits, in shining bas-relief, adorn its friezes. The fact that among them we find Apollo as one god among many, making no claim to a privileged position, should not mislead us. The same drive that found its most complete representation in Apollo generated the whole Olympian world, and in this sense we may consider Apollo the father of that world. But what was the radical need out of which that illustrious society of Olympian beings sprang?

Whoever approaches the Olympians with a different religion in his heart, seeking moral elevation, sanctity, spirituality, loving-kindness, will presently be forced to turn away from them in ill-humored disappointment. Nothing in these deities reminds us of asceticism, high intellect, or duty: we are confronted by luxuriant, triumphant *existence,* which deifies the good and the bad indifferently. And the beholder may find himself dismayed in the presence of such overflowing life and ask himself what potion these heady people must have drunk in order to behold, in whatever direction they looked, Helen laughing back at them, the beguiling image of their own existence. But we shall call out to this beholder, who has already turned his back: Don't go! Listen first to what the Greeks themselves have to say of this life, which spreads itself before you with such puzzling serenity. An old legend has it that King Midas hunted a long time in the woods for the wise Silenus, companion of Dionysos, without being able to catch him. When he had finally caught him the king asked him what he considered man's greatest good. The daemon remained sullen and uncommunicative until finally, forced by the king, he broke into a shrill laugh and spoke: "Ephemeral wretch, begotten by accident and toil, why do you force me to tell you what it would be your greatest boon not to hear? What would be best for you is quite beyond your reach: not to have been born, not to *be,* to be *nothing.* But the second best is to die soon."

What is the relation of the Olympian gods to this popular wisdom? It is that of the entranced vision of the martyr to his torment.

Now the Olympian magic mountain[8] opens itself before us, showing us its very roots. The Greeks were keenly aware of the terrors and horrors of existence; in order to be able to live at all they had to place before them the shining fantasy of the Olympians. Their tremendous distrust of the titanic forces of nature: *Moira,*[9] mercilessly enthroned beyond the knowable world; the vulture which fed upon the great philanthropist Prometheus; the terrible lot drawn by wise Oedipus; the curse on the house of Atreus which brought Orestes to the murder of his mother: that whole Panic[10] philosophy, in short, with its mythic examples, by which the gloomy Etruscans perished, the Greeks conquered — or at least hid from view — again and again by means of this artificial Olympus. In order to live at all the Greeks had to construct these deities. The Apollonian need for beauty had to develop the Olympian hierarchy of joy by slow degrees from the original titanic hierarchy of terror, as roses are seen to break from a thorny thicket. How else could life have been borne by a race so hypersensitive, so emotionally intense, so equipped for suffering? The same drive which called art into being as a completion and consummation of existence, and as a guarantee of further existence, gave rise also to the Olympian realm which acted as a transfiguring mirror to the Hellenic will. The gods justified human life by living it themselves — the only satisfactory theodicy[11] ever invented. To exist in the clear sunlight of such deities was now felt to be the highest good, and the only real grief suffered by Homeric man was inspired by the thought of leaving that sunlight, especially when the departure seemed imminent. Now it became possible to stand the wisdom of Silenus on its head and proclaim that it was the worst evil for man to die soon, and

[8]The Zauberberg was the mountain where Venus lived, to which the troubador Tannhäuser was attracted in the medieval legend. Nietzsche uses it as a symbol for a fantasy world. [Ed.]

[9]Destiny. [Ed.]

[10]Relating to Pan, the god of Nature. [Ed.]

[11]Explanation of divine activity. [Ed.]

second worst for him to die at all. Such laments as arise now arise over short-lived Achilles, over the generations ephemeral as leaves, the decline of the heroic age. It is not unbecoming to even the greatest hero to yearn for an afterlife, though it be as a day laborer. So impetuously, during the Apollonian phase, does man's will desire to remain on earth, so identified does he become with existence, that even his lament turns to a song of praise.

It should have become apparent by now that the harmony with nature which we late-comers regard with such nostalgia, and for which Schiller has coined the cant term *naïve*,[12] is by no means a simple and inevitable condition to be found at the gateway to every culture, a kind of paradise. Such a belief could have been endorsed only by a period for which Rousseau's Emile was an artist and Homer just such an artist nurtured in the bosom of nature. Whenever we encounter "naïveté" in art, we are face to face with the ripest fruit of Apollonian culture — which must always triumph first over titans, kill monsters, and overcome the somber contemplation of actuality, the intense susceptibility to suffering, by means of illusions strenuously and zestfully entertained. But how rare are the instances of true naïveté, of that complete identification with the beauty of appearance! It is this achievement which makes Homer so magnificent — Homer, who, as a single individual, stood to Apollonian popular culture in the same relation as the individual dream artist to the oneiric capacity of a race and of nature generally. The naïveté of Homer must be viewed as a complete victory of Apollonian illusion. Nature often uses illusions of this sort in order to accomplish its secret purposes. The true goal is covered over by a phantasm. We stretch out our hands to the latter, while nature, aided by our deception, attains the former. In the case of the Greeks it was the will wishing to behold itself in the work of art, in the transcendence of genius; but in order so to behold itself its creatures had first to view themselves as glorious, to transpose themselves to a higher sphere, without having that sphere of pure contemplation either challenge them or upbraid them

[12]See Schiller, "On Naive and Sentimental Poetry," p. 274. [Ed.]

with insufficiency. It was in that sphere of beauty that the Greeks saw the Olympians as their mirror images; it was by means of that esthetic mirror that the Greek will opposed suffering and the somber wisdom of suffering which always accompanies artistic talent. As a monument to its victory stands Homer, the naïve artist.

## IV

We can learn something about the naïve artist through the analogy of dream. We can imagine the dreamer as he calls out to himself, still caught in the illusion of his dream and without disturbing it, "This is a dream, and I want to go on dreaming," and we can infer, on the one hand, that he takes deep delight in the contemplation of his dream, and, on the other, that he must have forgotten the day, with its horrible importunity, so to enjoy his dream. Apollo, the interpreter of dreams, will furnish the clue to what is happening here. Although of the two halves of life — the waking and the dreaming — the former is generally considered not only the more important but the only one which is truly lived, I would, at the risk of sounding paradoxical, propose the opposite view. The more I have come to realize in nature those omnipotent formative tendencies and, with them, an intense longing for illusion, the more I feel inclined to the hypothesis that the original Oneness, the ground of Being, ever-suffering and contradictory, time and again has need of rapt vision and delightful illusion to redeem itself. Since we ourselves are the very stuff of such illusions, we must view ourselves as the truly nonexistent, that is to say, as a perpetual unfolding in time, space, and causality — what we label "empiric reality." But if, for the moment, we abstract from our own reality, viewing our empiric existence, as well as the existence of the world at large, as the *idea* of the original Oneness, produced anew each instant, then our dreams will appear to us as illusions of illusions, hence as a still higher form of satisfaction of the original desire for illusion. It is for this reason that the very core of nature takes such a deep delight in the naïve artist and the naïve work of art, which likewise is merely the illusion of an illusion. Raphael, himself one of those immortal "naïve" artists, in a symbolic canvas has illustrated that reduction of illusion to further illusion which is the original act of the naïve artist and at the same time of all Apollonian culture. In the lower half of his *Transfiguration,* through the figures of the possessed boy, the despairing bearers, the helpless, terrified disciples, we see a reflection of original pain, the sole ground of being: "illusion" here is a reflection of eternal contradiction, begetter of all things. From this illusion there rises, like the fragrance of ambrosia, a new illusory world, invisible to those enmeshed in the first: a radiant vision of pure delight, a rapt seeing through wide-open eyes. Here we have, in a great symbol of art, both the fair world of Apollo and its substratum, the terrible wisdom of Silenus, and we can comprehend intuitively how they mutually require one another. But Apollo appears to us once again as the apotheosis of the *principium individuationis,* in whom the eternal goal of the original Oneness, namely its redemption through illusion, accomplishes itself. With august gesture the god shows us how there is need for a whole world of torment in order for the individual to produce the redemptive vision and to sit quietly in his rocking rowboat in mid-sea, absorbed in contemplation.

If this apotheosis of individuation is to be read in normative terms, we may infer that there is one norm only: the individual — or, more precisely, the observance of the limits of the individual: *sophrosyne.* As a moral deity Apollo demands self-control from his people and, in order to observe such self-control, a knowledge of self. And so we find that the esthetic necessity of beauty is accompanied by the imperatives, "Know thyself," and "Nothing too much." Conversely, excess and *hubris* come to be regarded as the hostile spirits of the non-Apollonian sphere, hence as properties of the pre-Apollonian era — the age of Titans — and the extra-Apollonian world, that is to say the world of the barbarians. It was because of his Titanic love of man that Prometheus had to be devoured by vultures; it was because of his extravagant wisdom which succeeded in solving the riddle of the Sphinx that Oedipus had to be cast into a whirlpool of crime: in this fashion does the Delphic god interpret the Greek past.

The effects of the Dionysiac spirit struck the Apollonian Greeks as titanic and barbaric; yet they could not disguise from themselves the fact that they were essentially akin to those deposed Titans and heroes. They felt more than that: their whole existence, with its temperate beauty, rested upon a base of suffering and *knowledge* which had been hidden from them until the reinstatement of Dionysos uncovered it once more. And lo and behold! Apollo found it impossible to live without Dionysos. The elements of titanism and barbarism turned out to be quite as fundamental as the Apollonian element. And now let us imagine how the ecstatic sounds of the Dionysiac rites penetrated ever more enticingly into that artificially restrained and discreet world of illusion, how this clamor expressed the whole outrageous gamut of nature — delight, grief, knowledge — even to the most piercing cry; and then let us imagine how the Apollonian artist with his thin, monotonous harp music must have sounded beside the demoniac chant of the multitude! The muses presiding over the illusory arts paled before an art which enthusiastically told the truth, and the wisdom of Silenus cried "Woe!" against the serene Olympians. The individual, with his limits and moderations, forgot himself in the Dionysiac vortex and became oblivious to the laws of Apollo. Indiscreet extravagance revealed itself as truth, and contradiction, a delight born of pain, spoke out of the bosom of nature. Wherever the Dionysiac voice was heard, the Apollonian norm seemed suspended or destroyed. Yet it is equally true that, in those places where the first assault was withstood, the prestige and majesty of the Delphic god appeared more rigid and threatening than before. The only way I am able to view Doric art and the Doric state[13] is as a perpetual military encampment of the Apollonian forces. An art so defiantly austere, so ringed about with fortifications — an education so military and exacting — a polity so ruthlessly cruel — could endure only in a continual state of resistance against the titanic and barbaric menace of Dionysos.

Up to this point I have developed at some length a theme which was sounded at the begin-

[13]Sparta. [Ed.]

ning of this essay: how the Dionysiac and Apollonian elements, in a continuous chain of creations, and enhancing the other, dominated the Hellenic mind; how from the Iron Age, with its battles of Titans and its austere popular philosophy, there developed under the aegis of Apollo the Homeric world of beauty; how this "naïve" splendor was then absorbed once more by the Dionysiac torrent, and how, face to face with this new power, the Apollonian code rigidified into the majesty of Doric art and contemplation. If the earlier phase of Greek history may justly be broken down into four major artistic epochs dramatizing the battle between the two hostile principles, then we must inquire further (lest Doric art appear to us as the acme and final goal of all these striving tendencies) what was the true end toward which that evolution moved. And our eyes will come to rest on the sublime and much lauded achievement of the dramatic dithyramb and Attic tragedy, as the common goal of both urges; whose mysterious marriage, after long discord, ennobled itself with such a child, at once Antigone and Cassandra.[14]

## V

We are now approaching the central concern of our inquiry, which has as its aim an understanding of the Dionysiac-Apollonian spirit, or at least an intuitive comprehension of the mystery which made this conjunction possible. Our first question must be: where in the Greek world is the new seed first to be found which was later to develop into tragedy and the dramatic dithyramb? Greek antiquity gives us a pictorial clue when it represents in statues, on cameos, etc., Homer and Archilochus side by side as ancestors and torchbearers of Greek poetry, in the certainty that only these two are to be regarded as truly original minds, from whom a stream of fire flowed onto the entire later Greek world. Homer, the hoary dreamer, caught in utter abstraction, prototype of the Apollonian naïve artist, stares in amazement at the passionate head of Archilochus, soldierly servant of the Muses, knocked about by fortune.

[14]The dutiful Antigone may represent the Apollonian principle, the possessed Cassandra the Dionysiac. [Ed.]

All that more recent esthetics has been able to add by way of interpretation is that here the "objective" artist is confronted by the first "subjective" artist. We find this interpretation of little use, since to us the subjective artist is simply the bad artist, and since we demand above all, in every genre and range of art, a triumph over subjectivity, deliverance from the self, the silencing of every personal will and desire; since, in fact, we cannot imagine the smallest genuine art work lacking objectivity and disinterested contemplation. For this reason our esthetic must first solve the following problem: how is the lyrical poet at all possible as artist — he who, according to the experience of all times, always says "I" and recites to us the entire chromatic scale of his passions and appetites? It is this Archilochus who most disturbs us, placed there beside Homer, with the stridor of his hate and mockery, the drunken outbursts of his desire. Isn't he — the first artist to be called subjective — for that reason the veritable nonartist? How, then, are we to explain the reverence in which he was held as a poet, the honor done him by the Delphic oracle, that seat of "objective" art, in a number of very curious sayings?

Schiller has thrown some light on his own manner of composition by a psychological observation which seems inexplicable to himself without, however, giving him pause. Schiller confessed that, prior to composing, he experienced not a logically connected series of images but rather a *musical mood*. "With me emotion is at the beginning without clear and definite ideas; those ideas do not arise until later on. A certain musical disposition of mind comes first, and after follows the poetical idea." If we enlarge on this, taking into account the most important phenomenon of ancient poetry, by which I mean that union — nay identity — everywhere considered natural, between musician and poet (alongside which our modern poetry appears as the statue of a god without a head), then we may, on the basis of the esthetics adumbrated earlier, explain the lyrical poet in the following manner. He is, first and foremost, a Dionysiac artist, become wholly identified with the original Oneness, its pain and contradiction, and producing a replica of that Oneness as music, if music may legitimately be seen as a repetition of the world; however, this music becomes visible to him again, as in a dream similitude, through the Apollonian dream influence. That reflection, without image or idea, of original pain in music, with its redemption through illusion, now produces a second reflection as a single simile or example. The artist had abrogated his subjectivity earlier, during the Dionysiac phase: the image which now reveals to him his oneness with the heart of the world is a dream scene showing forth vividly, together with original pain, the original delight of illusion. The "I" thus sounds out of the depth of being; what recent writers on esthetics speak of as "subjectivity" is a mere figment. When Archilochus, the first lyric poet of the Greeks, hurls both his frantic love and his contempt at the daughters of Lycambes, it is not his own passion that we see dancing before us in an orgiastic frenzy: we see Dionysos and the maenads, we see the drunken reveler Archilochus, sunk down in sleep — as Euripides describes him for us in the *Bacchae,* asleep on a high mountain meadow, in the midday sun — and now Apollo approaches him and touches him with his laurel. The sleeper's enchantment through Dionysiac music now begins to emit sparks of imagery, poems which, at their point of highest evolution, will bear the name of tragedies and dramatic dithyrambs.

The sculptor, as well as his brother, the epic poet, is committed to the pure contemplation of images. The Dionysiac musician, himself imageless, is nothing but original pain and reverberation of the image. Out of this mystical process of un-selving, the poet's spirit feels a whole world of images and similitudes arise, which are quite different in hue, causality, and pace from the images of the sculptor or narrative poet. While the last lives in those images and only in them, with joyful complacence, and never tires of scanning them down to the most minute features, while even the image of angry Achilles is no more for him than an *image* whose irate countenance he enjoys with a dreamer's delight in appearance — so that this mirror of appearance protects him from complete fusion with his characters — the lyrical poet, on the other hand, himself becomes his images, his images are objectified versions of himself. Being the active

center of that world he may boldly speak in the first person, only his "I" is not that of the actual waking man, but the "I" dwelling, truly and eternally, in the ground of being. It is through the reflections of that "I" that the lyric poet beholds the ground of being. Let us imagine, next, how he views himself too among these reflections — as nongenius, that is, as his own subject matter, the whole teeming crowd of his passions and intentions directed toward a definite goal; and when it now appears as though the poet and the nonpoet joined to him were one, and as though the former were using the pronoun "I," we are able to see through this appearance, which has deceived those who have attached the label "subjective" to the lyrical poet. The man Archilochus, with his passionate loves and hates, is really only a vision of genius, a genius who is no longer merely Archilochus but the genius of the universe, expressing its pain through the similitude of Archilochus the man. Archilochus, on the other hand, the subjectively willing and desiring human being, can never be a poet. Nor is it at all necessary for the poet to see only the phenomenon of the man Archilochus before him as a reflection of Eternal Being: the world of tragedy shows us to what extent the vision of the poet can remove itself from the urgent, immediate phenomenon.

Schopenhauer, who was fully aware of the difficulties the lyrical poet creates for the speculative esthetician, thought that he had found a solution, which, however, I cannot endorse. It is true that he alone possessed the means, in his profound philosophy of music, for solving this problem; and I think I have honored his achievement in these pages, I hope in his own spirit. Yet in the first part of *The World as Will and Idea* he characterizes the essence of song as follows:

The consciousness of the singer is filled with the subject of will, which is to say with his own willing. That willing may either be a released, satisfied willing (joy), or, as happens more commonly, an inhibited willing (sadness). In either case there is affect here: passion, violent commotion. At the same time, however, the singer is moved by the contemplation of nature surrounding him to experience himself as the subject of pure, unwilling ideation, and the unshakable tranquillity of that ideation becomes contrasted with the urgency of his willing, its limits, and its lacks. It is the experience of this contrast, or tug of war, which he expresses in his song. While we find ourselves in the lyrical condition, pure ideation approaches us, as it were, to deliver us from the urgencies of willing; we obey, yet obey for moments only. Again and again our willing, our memory of personal objectives, distracts us from tranquil contemplation, while, conversely, the next scene of beauty we behold will yield us up once more to pure ideation. For this reason we find in song and in the lyrical mood a curious mixture of willing (our personal interest in *purposes*) and pure contemplation (whose subject matter is furnished by our surroundings); relations are sought and imagined between these two sets of experiences. Subjective mood — the affection of the will — communicates its color to the purely viewed surroundings, and vice versa. All authentic song reflects a state of mind mixed and divided in this manner.

Who can fail to perceive in this description that lyric poetry is presented as an art never completely realized, indeed a hybrid whose essence is made to consist in an uneasy mixture of will and contemplation, i.e., the esthetic and the nonesthetic conditions? We, on our part, maintain that the distinction between subjective and objective, which even Schopenhauer still uses as a sort of measuring stick to distinguish the arts, has no value whatever in esthetics; the reason being that the subject — the striving individual bent on furthering his egoistic purposes — can be thought of only as an enemy to art, never as its source. But to the extent that the subject is an artist he is already delivered from individual will and has become a medium through which the True Subject celebrates His redemption in illusion. For better or worse, one thing should be quite obvious to all of us: the entire comedy of art is not played for our own sakes — for our betterment or education, say — nor can we consider ourselves the true originators of that art realm; while on the other hand we have every right to view ourselves as esthetic projections of the veritable creator and derive such dignity as we possess from our status as art works. Only as an esthetic product can the world be justified to all eternity — although our consciousness of our own significance does scarcely exceed the consciousness a painted soldier might have of the

battle in which he takes part. Thus our whole knowledge of art is at bottom illusory, seeing that as mere *knowers* we can never be fused with that essential spirit, at the same time creator and spectator, who has prepared the comedy of art for his own edification. Only as the genius in the act of creation merges with the primal architect of the cosmos can he truly know something of the eternal essence of art. For in that condition he resembles the uncanny fairy tale image which is able to see itself by turning its eyes. He is at once subject and object, poet, actor, and audience.

## XIV

Let us now imagine Socrates' great Cyclops' eye — that eye which never glowed with the artist's divine frenzy — turned upon tragedy. Bearing in mind that he was unable to look with any pleasure into the Dionysiac abysses, what could Socrates see in that tragic art which to Plato seemed noble and meritorious? Something quite abstruse and irrational, full of causes without effects and effects seemingly without causes, the whole texture so checkered that it must be repugnant to a sober disposition, while it might act as dangerous tinder to a sensitive and impressionable mind. We are told that the only genre of poetry Socrates really appreciated was the Aesopian fable. This he did with the same smiling complaisance with which honest Gellert sings the praise of poetry in his fable of the bee and the hen:

> I exemplify the use of poetry:
> To convey to those who are a bit backward
> The truth in a simile.[15]

The fact is that for Socrates tragic art failed even to "convey the truth," although it did address itself to those who were "a bit backward," which is to say to nonphilosophers: a double reason for leaving it alone.[16] Like Plato, he reckoned it among the beguiling arts which represent the agreeable, not the useful, and in consequence

[15]Christian Fürchtegott Gellert (1715–69), poet and novelist of the German Enlightenment; the quotation is from *Poems and Fables* (1746–48). [Ed.]

[16]Nietzsche alludes to Socrates' final assessment of poetry in Plato's *Republic*. Book X; see p. 19. [Ed.]

exhorted his followers to abstain from such unphilosophical stimulants. His success was such that the young tragic poet Plato burned all his writings in order to qualify as a student of Socrates. And while strong native genius might now and again manage to withstand the Socratic injunction, the power of the latter was still great enough to force poetry into entirely new channels.

A good example of this is Plato himself. Although he did not lag behind the naïve cynicism of his master in the condemnation of tragedy and of art in general, nevertheless his creative gifts forced him to develop an art form deeply akin to the existing forms which he had repudiated. The main objection raised by Plato to the older art (that it was the imitation of an imitation and hence belonged to an even lower order of empiric reality) must not, at all costs, apply to the new genre; and so we see Plato intent on moving beyond reality and on rendering the idea which underlies it. By a detour Plato the thinker reached the very spot where Plato the poet had all along been at home, and from which Sophocles, and with him the whole poetic tradition of the past, protested such a charge. Tragedy had assimilated to itself all the older poetic genres. In a somewhat eccentric sense the same thing can be claimed for the Platonic dialogue, which was a mixture of all the available styles and forms and hovered between narrative, lyric, drama, between prose and poetry, once again breaking through the old law of stylistic unity. The Cynic philosophers went even farther in that direction, seeking, by their utterly promiscuous style and constant alternation between verse and prose, to project their image of the "raving Socrates" in literature, as they sought to enact it in life. The Platonic dialogue was the lifeboat in which the shipwrecked older poetry saved itself, together with its numerous offspring. Crowded together in a narrow space, and timidly obeying their helmsman Socrates, they moved forward into a new era which never tired of looking at this fantastic spectacle. Plato has furnished for all posterity the pattern of a new art form, the novel, viewed as the Aesopian fable raised to its highest power; a form in which poetry played the same subordinate role with regard to dialectic philosophy as

that same philosophy was to play for many centuries with regard to theology. This, then, was the new status of poetry, and it was Plato who, under the pressure of daemonic Socrates, had brought it about.

It is at this point that philosophical ideas begin to entwine themselves about art, forcing the latter to cling closely to the trunk of dialectic. The Apollonian tendency now appears disguised as logical schematism, just as we found in the case of Euripides a corresponding translation of the Dionysiac affect into a naturalistic one. Socrates, the dialectical hero of the Platonic drama, shows a close affinity to the Euripidean hero, who is compelled to justify his actions by proof and counterproof, and for that reason is often in danger of forfeiting our tragic compassion. For who among us can close his eyes to the optimistic element in the nature of dialectics, which sees a triumph in every syllogism and can breathe only in an atmosphere of cool, conscious clarity? Once that optimistic element had entered tragedy, it overgrew its Dionysiac regions and brought about their annihilation and, finally, the leap into genteel domestic drama. Consider the consequences of the Socratic maxims: "Virtue is knowledge; all sins arise from ignorance; only the virtuous are happy" — these three basic formulations of optimism spell the death of tragedy. The virtuous hero must henceforth be a dialectician; virtue and knowledge, belief and ethics, be necessarily and demonstrably connected; Aeschylus' transcendental concept of justice be reduced to the brash and shallow principle of poetic justice with its regular *deus ex machina*.

What is the view taken of the chorus in this new Socratic-optimistic stage world, and of the entire musical and Dionysiac foundation of tragedy? They are seen as accidental features, as reminders of the origin of tragedy, which can well be dispensed with — while we have in fact come to understand that the chorus is the cause of tragedy and the tragic spirit. Already in Sophocles we find some embarrassment with regard to the chorus, which suggests that the Dionysiac floor of tragedy is beginning to give way. Sophocles no longer dares to give the chorus the major role in the tragedy but treats it as almost on the same footing as the actors, as though it had been raised from the *orchestra* onto the *scene*. By so doing he necessarily destroyed its meaning, despite Aristotle's endorsement of this conception of the chorus. This shift in attitude, which Sophocles displayed not only in practice but also, we are told, in theory, was the first step toward the total disintegration of the chorus: a process whose rapid phases we can follow in Euripides, Agathon, and the New Comedy. Optimistic dialectics took up the whip of its syllogisms and drove music out of tragedy. It entirely destroyed the meaning of tragedy — which can be interpreted only as a concrete manifestation of Dionysiac conditions, music made visible, an ecstatic dream world.

Since we have discovered an anti-Dionysiac tendency antedating Socrates, its most brilliant exponent, we must now ask, "Toward what does a figure like Socrates point?" Faced with the evidence of the Platonic dialogues, we are certainly not entitled to see in Socrates merely an agent of disintegration. While it is clear that the immediate result of the Socratic strategy was the destruction of Dionysiac drama, we are forced, nevertheless, by the profundity of the Socratic experience to ask ourselves whether, in fact, art and Socratism are diametrically opposed to one another, whether there is really anything inherently impossible in the idea of a Socratic artist?

It appears that this despotic logician had from time to time a sense of void, loss, unfulfilled duty with regard to art. In prison he told his friends how, on several occasions, a voice had spoken to him in a dream, saying "Practice music, Socrates!"[17] Almost to the end he remained confident that his philosophy represented the highest art of the muses, and would not fully believe that a divinity meant to remind him of "common, popular music." Yet in order to unburden his conscience he finally agreed, in prison, to undertake that music which hitherto he had held in low esteem. In this frame of mind he composed a poem on Apollo and rendered several Aesopian fables in verse. What prompted him to these exercises was something very similar to that warning voice of his daimonion: an

Apollonian perception that, like a barbarian king, he had failed to comprehend the nature of a divine effigy, and was in danger of offending his own god through ignorance. These words heard by Socrates in his dream are the only indication that he ever experienced any uneasiness about the limits of his logical universe. He may have asked himself: "Have I been too ready to view what was unintelligible to me as being devoid of meaning? Perhaps there is a realm of wisdom, after all, from which the logician is excluded? Perhaps art must be seen as the necessary complement of rational discourse?"

## XIX

The best way to characterize the core of Socratic culture is to call it the culture of the opera. It is in this area that Socratism has given an open account of its intentions — a rather surprising one when we compare the evolution of the opera with the abiding Apollonian and Dionysiac truths. First I want to remind the reader of the genesis of the *stilo rappresentativo*[18] and of recitative. How did it happen that this operatic music, so wholly external and incapable of reverence, was enthusiastically greeted by an epoch which, not so very long ago, had produced the inexpressibly noble and sacred music of Palestrina? Can anyone hold the luxury and frivolity of the Florentine court and the vanity of its dramatic singers responsible for the speed and intensity with which the vogue of opera spread? I can explain the passion for a semimusical declamation, at the same period and among the same people who had witnessed the grand architecture of Palestrina's harmonies (in the making of which the whole Christian Middle Ages had conspired), only by reference to an extra-artistic tendency. To the listener who desires to hear the words above the music corresponds the singer

[17]In Plato's *Phaedo*. [Ed.]

[18]A term characterizing the opera created in the late sixteenth century by the Florentine musical society known as the *Camerata*, in which dramatic recitative alternates with florid arias expressing emotion. Operas in the current repertory written in the *stilo rappresentativo* include Monteverdi's *L'Incoronazione di Poppaea* and Purcell's *Dido and Aeneas*. [Ed.]

who speaks more than he sings, emphasizing the verbal pathos in a kind of half-song. By this emphasis he aids the understanding of the words and gets rid of the remaining half of music. There is a danger that now and again the music will preponderate, spoiling the pathos and clarity of his declamation, while conversely he is always under the temptation to discharge the music of his voice in a virtuoso manner. The pseudopoetic librettist furnishes him ample opportunity for this display in lyrical interjections, repetitions of words and phrases, etc., where the singer may give himself up to the purely musical element without consideration for the text. This constant alternation, so characteristic of the *stilo rappresentativo,* between emotionally charged, only partly sung declamation and wholly musical interjections, this rapid shift of focus between concept and imagination, on the one hand, and the musical response of the listener, on the other, is so completely unnatural, equally opposed to the Dionysiac and the Apollonian spirit, that one must conclude the origin of recitative to have lain outside any artistic instinct. Viewed in these terms, the recitative may be characterized as a mixture of epic and lyric declamation. And yet, since the components are so wholly disparate, the resulting combination is neither harmonious nor constant, but rather a superficial and mosaic-like conglutination, not without precedent in the realm of nature and experience. However, the inventors of recitative took a very different view of it. They, and their age with them, thought they had discovered the secret of ancient music, that secret which alone could account for the amazing feats of an Orpheus or an Amphion or, indeed, for Greek tragedy. They thought that by that novel style they had managed to resuscitate ancient Greek music in all its power; and, given the popular conception of the Homeric world as the primordial world, it was possible to embrace the illusion that one had at last returned to the paradisaical beginnings of mankind, in which music must have had that supreme purity, power, and innocence of which the pastoral poets wrote so movingly. Here we have touched the nerve center of opera, that genuinely modern genre. In it, art satisfies a strong need, but one that can hardly be called esthetic: a hankering for the idyll, a belief in the primordial existence of pure, artistically sensitive man. Recitative stood for the rediscovered language of that archetypal man, opera for the rediscovered country of that idyllic and heroically pure species, who in all their actions followed a natural artistic bent — who, no matter what they had to say, sang at least part of it, and who when their emotions were ever so little aroused burst into full song. It is irrelevant to our inquiry that the humanists of the time used the new image of the paradisaical artist to combat the old ecclesiastical notion of man as totally corrupt and damned; that opera thus represented the opposition dogma of man as essentially good, and furnished an antidote to that pessimism which, given the terrible instability of the epoch, naturally enlisted its strongest and most thoughtful minds. What matters here is our recognition that the peculiar attraction and thus the success of this new art form must be attributed to its satisfaction of a wholly unesthetic need: it was optimistic; it glorified man in himself; it conceived of man as originally good and full of talent. This principle of opera has by degrees become a menacing and rather appalling claim, against which we who are faced with present-day socialist movements cannot stop our ears. The "noble savage" demands his rights: what a paradisaical prospect!

There is still a further point in support of my contention that opera is built on the same principles as our Alexandrian culture. Opera is the product of the man of theory, the critical layman, not the artist. This constitutes one of the most disturbing facts in the entire history of art. Since the demand, coming from essentially unmusical people, was for a clear understanding of the words, a renascence of music could come about only through the discovery of a type of music in which the words lorded it over the counterpoint as a master over his servant. For were not the words nobler than the accompanying harmonic system, as the soul is nobler than the body? It was with precisely that unmusical clumsiness that the combinations of music, image, and word were treated in the beginning of opera, and in this spirit the first experiments in the new genre were carried out, even in the noble lay circles of Florence, by the poets and singers patronized by those circles. Inartistic man produces his own brand of art, precisely by virtue of his artistic impotence. Having not the faintest conception of the Dionysiac profundity of music, he transforms musical enjoyment into a rationalistic rhetoric of passion in the *stilo rappresentativo,* into a voluptuous indulgence of vocal virtuoso feats; lacking imagination, he must employ engineers and stage designers; being incapable of understanding the true nature of the artist, he invents an "artistic primitive" to suit his taste, i.e., a man who, when his passions are aroused, breaks into song and recites verses. He projects himself into a time when passion sufficed to produce songs and poems — as though mere emotion had ever been able to create art. There lies at the root of opera a fallacious conception of the artistic process, the idyllic belief that every sensitive man is at bottom an artist. In keeping with this belief, opera is the expression of dilettantism in art, dictating its rules with the cheerful optimism of the theorist.

If we were to combine the two tendencies conspiring at the creation of opera into one, we might speak of an idyllic tendency of opera. Here it would be well to refer back to Schiller's account. Nature and ideal, according to Schiller, are objects of grief when the former is felt to be lost, the latter to be beyond reach. But both may become objects of joy when they are represented as actual. Then the first will produce the elegy, in its strict sense, and the second the idyll, in its widest sense. I would like to point out at once the common feature of these two conceptions in the origin of opera: here the ideal is never viewed as unattained nor nature as lost. Rather, a primitive period in the history of man is imagined, in which he lay at the heart of nature and in this state of nature attained immediately the ideal of humanity through Edenic nobility and artistry. From this supposedly perfect primitive we are all said to derive; indeed, we are still his faithful replicas. All we need do in order to recognize ourselves in that primitive is to jettison some of our later achievements, such as our superfluous learning and excess culture. The educated man of the Renaissance used the operatic imitation of Greek tragedy to lead him back to that concord of nature and ideal, to an idyllic reality. He used ancient tragedy the way Dante used Virgil, to

lead him to the gates of Paradise,[19] but from there on he went ahead on his own, moving from an imitation of the highest Greek art form to a "restitution of all things," to a re-creation of man's original art world. What confidence and bonhomie these bold enterprises betokened, arising as they did in the very heart of theoretical culture! The only explanation lies in the comforting belief of the day that "essential man" is the perennially virtuous operatic hero, the endlessly piping or singing shepherd, who, if he should ever by chance lose himself for a spell, would inevitably recover himself intact; in the optimism that rises like a perfumed, seductive cloud from the depths of Socratic contemplation.

Opera, then, does not wear the countenance of eternal grief but rather that of joy in an eternal reunion. It expresses the complacent delight in an idyllic reality, or such, at least, as can be viewed as real at any moment. Perhaps people will one day come to *realize* that this supposititious reality is at bottom no more than a fantastic and foolish trifling, which should make anyone who pits against it the immense seriousness of genuine nature and of the true origins of man exclaim in disgust: "Away with that phantom!" And yet it would be self-delusion to think that, trivial as it is, opera can be driven off with a shout, like an apparition. Whoever wants to destroy opera must gird himself for battle with that Alexandrian cheerfulness that has furnished opera its favorite conceptions and whose natural artistic expression it is. As for art proper, what possible benefit can it derive from a form whose origins lie altogether outside the esthetic realm, a form which from a semimoral sphere has trespassed on the domain of art and can only at rare moments deceive us as to its hybrid origin? What sap nourishes this operatic growth if not that of true art? Are we not right in supposing that its idyllic seductions and Alexandrian blandishments may sophisticate the highest, the truly serious task of art (to deliver the eye from the horror of night, to redeem us by virtue of the healing balm of illusion, from the spastic motions

---

[19]In the *Divina Commedia* the pagan Virgil guided Dante through Hell and Purgatory, but handed him over to Beatrice at the gates of Paradise.[Ed.]

of the will) into an empty and frivolous amusement? What becomes of the enduring Apollonian and Dionysiac truths in such a mixture of styles as we find in the *stilo rappresentativo;* where music acts the part of the servant, the text that of the master; where music is likened to the body, the text to the soul; where the ultimate goal is at best a periphrastic tone painting, similar to that found in the new Attic dithyramb; where music has abrogated its true dignity as the Dionysiac mirror of the universe and seems content to be the slave of appearance, to imitate the play of phenomenal forms, and to stimulate an artificial delight by dallying with lines and proportions? To a careful observer this pernicious influence of opera on music recapitulates the general development of modern music. The optimism that presided at the birth of opera and of the society represented by opera has succeeded with frightening rapidity in divesting music of its grand Dionysiac meanings and stamping it with the trivial character of a *divertissement,*[20] a transformation only equaled in scope by that of Aeschylean man into jovial Alexandrian man.

If we have been justified in suggesting a connection between the disappearance of the Dionysiac spirit and the spectacular, yet hitherto unexplained, degeneration of the Greek species, with what high hopes must we greet the auspicious signs of the opposite development in our own era, namely the gradual reawakening of the Dionysiac spirit! The divine power of Heracles cannot languish for ever in the service of Omphale.[21] Out of the Dionysiac recesses of the German soul has sprung a power which has nothing in common with the presuppositions of Socratic culture and which that culture can neither explain nor justify. Quite the contrary, the culture sees it as something to be dreaded and abhorred, something infinitely potent and hostile. I refer to German music, in its mighty course from Bach to Beethoven, and from Beethoven to Wagner. How can the petty intellectualism of our day deal with this monster that has risen out of the infinite

deeps? There is no formula to be found, in either the reservoir of operatic filigree and arabesque or the abacus of the fugue and contrapuntal dialectics, that will subdue this monster, make it stand and deliver. What a spectacle to see our estheticians beating the air with the butterfly nets of their pedantic slogans, in vain pursuit of that marvelously volatile musical genius, their movements sadly belying their standards of "eternal" beauty and grandeur! Look at these patrons of music for a moment at close range, as they repeat indefatigably: "Beauty! Beauty!" and judge for yourselves whether they really look like the beautiful darlings of nature, or whether it would not be more correct to say that they have assumed a disguise for their own coarseness, as esthetic pretext for their barren and jejune sensibilities — take the case of Otto Jahn.[22] But liars and prevaricators ought to watch their step in the area of German music. For amidst our degenerate culture music is the only pure and purifying flame, towards which and away from which all things move in a Heracleitean double motion.[23] All that is now called culture, education, civilization will one day have to appear before the incorruptible judge, Dionysos.

Let us now recall how the new German philosophy was nourished from the same sources, how Kant and Schopenhauer succeeded in destroying the complacent acquiescence of intellectual Socratism,[24] how by their labors an infinitely more profound and serious consideration of questions of ethics and art was made possible — a conceptualized form, in fact, of Dionysiac wisdom. To what does this miraculous union between German philosophy and music point if not to a new mode of existence, whose precise nature we can divine only with the aid of Greek analogies? For us, who stand on the watershed between two different modes of existence, the

[20]Diversion. [Ed.]
[21]In the legend, in atonement for killing Iphitus, Heracles was forced to wear women's clothes and learn to spin at the direction of Queen Omphale. [Ed.]

[22]Otto Jahn (1813–69), a classicist and archeologist, was a contemporary of Nietzsche. [Ed.]
[23]Heracleitus, who believed that all matter was in flux, thought nevertheless that changes in one direction for one aspect of the universe were balanced by changes in the opposite direction for another. [Ed.]
[24]Nietzsche is suggesting that Kant and Schopenhauer made aesthetics a matter of pure intuition, replacing the rationalist aesthetics common since Horace. [Ed.]

Greek example is still of inestimable value, since it embodies the violent transition to a classical, rationalistic form of suasion; only, we are living through the great phases of Hellenism in reverse order and seem at this very moment to be moving backward from the Alexandrian age into an age of tragedy. And we can't help feeling that the dawn of a new tragic age is for the German spirit only a return to itself, a blessed recovery of its true identity. For an unconscionably long time powerful forces from the outside have compelled the German spirit, which had vegetated in bar-baric formlessness, to subserve their forms. But at long last the German spirit may stand before the other nations, free of the leading strings of Romance culture — provided that it continues to be able to learn from the nation from whom to learn at all is a high and rare thing, the Greeks. And was there ever a time when we needed these supreme teachers more urgently than now, as we witness the rebirth of tragedy and are in danger of not knowing either whence it comes or whither it goes?

# Henry James
## 1843–1916

Born in America, partly formed by the French, and late in life naturalized a British subject, Henry James was a relentless experimentalist with technique and subject matter who brought a new sophistication to the art of fiction. His father, Henry James, Sr., an independently wealthy gentleman, was a philosopher and religious mystic who valued eccentricity in himself and in his offspring. Henry and his equally well-known elder brother, William, were educated at schools in England, France, Switzerland, and Germany as well as in their birthplace, New York City; their father believed that his sons could become themselves only by avoiding attachments to any master, school, place, or nation, and he also loathed the pragmatism and professionalism of the American educational system. The paradoxical result was that both Henry and William became ardent professionals — William a psychologist and philosopher, Henry a novelist and critic.

James began publishing stories in his twenties but did not find his true voice until he left America for good in 1875 to live in Paris and then settle in London. The fiction of his first period is often some variation on the "international theme" — the moral and spiritual gap between America and Europe. *The American* (1877), *Daisy Miller* (1878), and *Portrait of a Lady* (1881) made his reputation; today these works (especially the last) seem to mark a transition between the social chronicle of the nineteenth century and the twentieth century novel of psychological realism. The novels of his middle years, like *The Princess Casamassima* (1886) and *The Tragic Muse* (1890), were less successful, and James's attempt to conquer the London stage with *Guy Domville* (1895) ended in disaster. James withdrew from London to the retirement of Lamb House in Rye, where he produced the three ambiguous and highly nuanced masterworks of his late period, *The Wings of the Dove* (1902), *The Ambassadors* (1903), and *The Golden Bowl* (1904). In the next decade, James turned from fiction to memoir, but the outbreak of World War I disturbed the quiet of his last years. As an expression of solidarity with the British cause during America's long neutrality, James applied for citizenship (granted in 1915) and worked at war relief, the exertions of which broke his own health. He died on February 26, 1916.

"The Art of Fiction" (1884) seems to promise a manual of techniques, but this is precisely what James is least willing to provide. The title in fact is not James's own but was taken from a lecture by Walter Besant, which proposed that "laws of fiction may be laid down and taught with as much precision and exactness as the laws of harmony, perspective, and proportion." While generously granting everything he can to Besant's claims, James — who had been trained as a painter — essentially disagrees that regulations and conventions in fiction comparable to those in painting and music could exist. "If there are exact sciences, there are also exact arts, and the grammar of painting is so much more definite that it makes the difference." And James might have said, *Vive la différence,* for most of the distinctions that had become current in the short history of the criticism of fiction struck him as mechanical and empty.

Even before the English novel existed as such, William Congreve in his preface to *Incognita* (1692) had contrasted the romance and the novel. Later critics differentiated novels of incident from novels of character. For James, these notions might make talking about the novel easier but would only make excellence in writing more difficult. "What is character," he asks, "but the determination of incident? What is incident but the illustration of character?" For James, the novel is intended to convey the felt impression of life — a seamless web of action and motive that could not be reduced to simple formulas. The only Besantine dictum James wholeheartedly endorses is the recommendation that the prospective novelist keep a notebook to record impressions.

Although James rejects all of Besant's particular recommendations, he agrees that fiction is indeed an art. Today, after Joyce and Woolf and James himself, this contention would seem to need no proof. But the Victorian novel had been created mainly by entertainers who made few claims for themselves and their trade, and the British public was used to retreating into three-volume narratives that guaranteed adventure and escape, a love story with a happy ending, and poetic justice for all. In "The Art of Fiction" James positions himself against this stultifying formula. He is also concerned to champion his own style of writing fiction, which was more subtle and inward than was common. More generally, however, he wants the novelist to have the freedom to experiment not just with subject matter and point of view but with moral issues that disturb and disquiet.

Since James sets himself squarely against the philistines, we might expect him, in the 1880s, to embrace either the naturalism of Émile Zola or the pure "art for art's sake" aestheticism of Walter Pater. In fact he enters neither camp. James holds to fairly traditional notions of realism; beauty of form is not to be pursued merely for its own sake but in the process of conveying a complex and authentic experience that rests on the contingencies of life. "Do not listen," he warns, "to those who would . . . persuade you that this heavenly messenger wings her way outside of life altogether, breathing a superfine air and turning away her head from the truth of things." But at the same time, James does not, like Zola, expect the artist to present social conditions in a scientifically accurate way; he claimed, in fact, that Zola's deterministic philosophy "vitiated" his portraiture.

Ultimately, James's impatience with rules and formulas for fiction derives from a postromantic, expressive theory of art. "The deepest quality of a work of art will always be the quality of the mind of the producer. In proportion as that intelligence is fine will the novel . . . partake of the substance of beauty and truth." James's most heartfelt recommendation to the aspiring artist is not to watch his handling of point-of-view but to remain open to experience, to "be one of the people on whom nothing is lost." A fine intelligence will, he is confident, find or invent the techniques needed to realize the imagined vision, while a mechanical mind, using all the arts, will never produce something worthy of lasting fame.

### Selected Bibliography

Beach, Joseph Warren. *The Method of Henry James*. Philadelphia: A. Saifer, 1954.

Cameron, J. M. "History, Realism, and the Work of Henry James." *English Studies in Canada* 10 (1984): 299–316.

Daugherty, Sarah B. *The Literary Criticism of Henry James*. Athens: Ohio University Press, 1981.

Edel, Leon. *The Prefaces of Henry James*. Paris: Jouvé, 1931.

Hughes, Herbert Leland. *Theory and Practice in Henry James*. Ann Arbor: Edwards Bros., 1926.

Jackson, Wendell P. "Theory of the Creative Process in the 'Prefaces' of Henry James." In *Amid Visions and Revisions: Poetry and Criticism on Literature and the Arts*, ed., Burney J. Hillis. Baltimore: Morgan State University Press, 1985, pp. 59–64.

James, Henry. *The Art of the Novel: Critical Prefaces*. Introduction by R. P. Blackmur. New York: Scribner, 1934.

Roberts, Morris. *Henry James's Criticism*. Cambridge: Harvard University Press, 1929.

Veeder, William. "Image as Argument: Henry James and the Style of Criticism." *Henry James Review* 6 (1985): 172–81.

# The Art of Fiction

I should not have affixed so comprehensive a title to these few remarks, necessarily wanting in any completeness upon a subject the full consideration of which would carry us far, did I not seem to discover a pretext for my temerity in the interesting pamphlet lately published under this name by Mr. Walter Besant.[1] Mr. Besant's lecture at the Royal Institution — the original form of his pamphlet — appears to indicate that many persons are interested in the art of fiction, and are not indifferent to such remarks, as those who practice it may attempt to make about it. I am therefore anxious not to lose the benefit of this favorable association, and to edge in a few words under cover of the attention which Mr. Besant is sure to have excited. There is something very encouraging in his having put into form certain of his ideas on the mystery of story-telling.

It is a proof of life and curiosity — curiosity on the part of the brotherhood of novelists as well as on the part of their readers. Only a short

time ago it might have been supposed that the English novel was not what the French call *discutable*. It had no air of having a theory, a conviction, a consciousness of itself behind it — of being the expression of an artistic faith, the result of choice and comparison. I do not say it was necessarily the worse for that: it would take much more courage than I possess to intimate that the form of the novel as Dickens and Thackeray (for instance) saw it had any taint of incompleteness. It was, however, *naïf* (if I may help myself out with another French word); and evidently if it be destined to suffer in any way for having lost its *naïveté* it has now an idea of making sure of the corresponding advantages. During the period I have alluded to there was a comfortable, good-humored feeling abroad that a novel is a novel, as a pudding is a pudding and that our only business with it could be to swallow it. But within a year or two, for some reason or other, there have been signs of returning animation — the era of discussion would appear to have been to a certain extent opened. Art lives upon discussion, upon experiment, upon curiosity, upon

[1]Victorian man of letters (1836–1901). Besant's lecture on the art of fiction was delivered on April 25, 1884. [Ed.]

variety of attempt, upon the exchange of views and the comparison of standpoints; and there is a presumption that those times when no one has anything particular to say about it, and has no reason to give for practice or preference, though they may be times of honor, are not times of development — are times, possibly even, a little of dullness. The successful application of any art is a delightful spectacle, but the theory too is interesting; and though there is a great deal of the latter without the former I suspect there has never been a genuine success that has not had a latent core of conviction. Discussion, suggestion, formulation, these things are fertilizing when they are frank and sincere. Mr. Besant has set an excellent example in saying what he thinks, for his part, about the way in which fiction should be written, as well as about the way in which it should be published; for his view of the "art," carried on into an appendix, covers that too. Other laborers in the same field will doubtless take up the argument, they will give it the light of their experience, and the effect will surely be to make our interest in the novel a little more what it had for some time threatened to fail to be — a serious, active, inquiring interest, under protection of which this delightful study may, in moments of confidence, venture to say a little more what it thinks of itself.

It must take itself seriously for the public to take it so. The old superstition about fiction being "wicked"[2] has doubtless died out in England; but the spirit of it lingers in a certain oblique regard directed toward any story which does not more or less admit that it is only a joke. Even the most jocular novel feels in some degree the weight of the proscription that was formerly directed against literary levity: the jocularity does not always succeed in passing for orthodoxy. It is still expected, though perhaps people are ashamed to say it, that a production which is after all only a "make-believe" (for what else is a "story"?) shall be in some degree apologetic — shall renounce the pretension of attempting really to represent life. This, of course, any sensible, wide-awake story declines to do, for it quickly perceives that

the tolerance granted to it on such a condition is only an attempt to stifle it disguised in the form of generosity. The old evangelical hostility to the novel, which was as explicit as it was narrow, and which regarded it as little less favorable to our immortal part than a stage play, was in reality far less insulting. The only reason for the existence of a novel is that it does attempt to represent life. When it relinquishes this attempt, the same attempt that we see on the canvas of the painter, it will have arrived at a very strange pass. It is not expected of the picture that it will make itself humble in order to be forgiven; and the analogy between the art of the painter and the art of the novelist is, so far as I am able to see, complete. Their inspiration is the same, their process (allowing for the different quality of the vehicle) is the same, their success is the same. They may learn from each other, they may explain and sustain each other. Their cause is the same, and the honor of one is the honor of another. The Mahometans think a picture an unholy thing, but it is a long time since any Christian did, and it is therefore the more odd that in the Christian mind the traces (dissimulated though they may be) of a suspicion of the sister art should linger to this day. The only effectual way to lay it to rest is to emphasize the analogy to which I just alluded — to insist on the fact that as the picture is reality, so the novel is history. That is the only general description (which does it justice) that we may give of the novel. But history also is allowed to represent life; it is not, any more than painting, expected to apologize. The subject-matter of fiction is stored up likewise in documents and records, and if it will not give itself away, as they say in California, it must speak with assurance, with the tone of the historian. Certain accomplished novelists have a habit of giving themselves away which must often bring tears to the eyes of people who take their fiction seriously. I was lately struck, in reading over many pages of Anthony Trollope, with his want of discretion in this particular. In a digression, a parenthesis or an aside, he concedes to the reader that he and this trusting friend are only "making believe." He admits that the events he narrates have not really happened, and that he can give his narrative any turn the reader

2Cf. Johnson's strictures in *The Rambler*, No. 4, p. 225. [Ed.]

may like best.[3] Such a betrayal of a sacred office seems to me, I confess, a terrible crime; it is what I mean by the attitude of apology, and it shocks me every whit as much in Trollope as it would have shocked me in Gibbon or Macaulay. It implies that the novelist is less occupied in looking for the truth (the truth, of course I mean, that he assumes, the premises that we grant him, whatever they may be) than the historian, and in doing so it deprives him at a stroke of all his standing room. To represent and illustrate the past, the actions of men, is the task of either writer, and the only difference that I can see is, in proportion as he succeeds, to the honor of the novelist, consisting as it does in his having more difficulty in collecting his evidence, which is so far from being purely literary. It seems to me to give him a great character, the fact that he has at once so much in common with the philosopher and the painter; this double analogy is a magnificent heritage.

It is of all this evidently that Mr. Besant is full when he insists upon the fact that fiction is one of the *fine* arts, deserving in its turn of all the honors and emoluments that have hitherto been reserved for the successful profession of music, poetry, painting, architecture. It is impossible to insist too much on so important a truth, and the place that Mr. Besant demands for the work of the novelist may be represented, a trifle less abstractly, by saying that he demands not only that it shall be reputed artistic, but that it shall be reputed very artistic indeed. It is excellent that he should have struck this note, for his doing so indicates that there was need of it, that his proposition may be to many people a novelty. One rubs one's eyes at the thought; but the rest of Mr. Besant's essay confirms the revelation. I suspect in truth that it would be possible to confirm it still further, and that one would not be far wrong in saying that in addition to the people to whom it has never occurred that a novel ought to be artistic, there are a great many others who, if this principle were urged upon them,

would be filled with an indefinable mistrust. They would find it difficult to explain their repugnance, but it would operate strongly to put them on their guard. "Art," in our Protestant communities, where so many things have got so strangely twisted about, is supposed in certain circles to have some vaguely injurious effect upon those who make it an important consideration, who let it weigh in the balance. It is assumed to be opposed in some mysterious manner to morality, to amusement, to instruction. When it is embodied in the work of the painter (the sculptor is another affair!) you know what it is: it stands there before you, in the honesty of pink and green and a gilt frame; you can see the worst of it at a glance, and you can be on your guard. But when it is introduced into literature it becomes more insidious — there is danger of its hurting you before you know it. Literature should be either instructive or amusing, and there is in many minds an impression that these artistic preoccupations, the search for form, contribute to neither end, interfere indeed with both. They are too frivolous to be edifying, and too serious to be diverting; and they are moreover priggish and paradoxical and superfluous. That I think, represents the manner in which the latent thought of many people who read novels as an exercise in skipping would explain itself if it were to become articulate. They would argue, of course, that a novel ought to be "good," but they would interpret this term in a fashion of their own, which indeed would vary considerably from one critic to another. One would say that being good means representing virtuous and aspiring characters, placed in prominent positions; another would say that it depends on a "happy ending," on a distribution at the last of prizes, pensions, husbands, wives, babies, millions, appended paragraphs, and cheerful remarks. Another still would say that it means being full of incident and movement, so that we shall wish to jump ahead, to see who was the mysterious stranger, and if the stolen will was ever found, and shall not be distracted from this pleasure by any tiresome analysis or "description." But they would all agree that the "artistic" idea would spoil some of their fun. One would hold it accountable for all the description, another would see it revealed

---

[3]James may be thinking about such addresses to the reader as the opening of Ch. 51 in *Barchester Towers,* where the narrator worries aloud about the difficulty of writing endings. [Ed.]

in the absence of sympathy. Its hostility to a happy ending would be evident, and it might even in some cases render any ending at all impossible. The "ending" of a novel is, for many persons, like that of a good dinner, a course of dessert and ices, and the artist in fiction is regarded as a sort of meddlesome doctor who forbids agreeable aftertastes. It is therefore true that this conception of Mr. Besant's of the novel as a superior form encounters not only a negative but a positive indifference. It matters little that as a work of art it should really be as little or as much of its essence to supply happy endings, sympathetic characters, and an objective tone, as if it were a work of mechanics: the association of ideas, however incongruous, might easily be too much for it if an eloquent voice were not sometimes raised to call attention to the fact that it is at once as free and as serious a branch of literature as any other.

Certainly this might sometimes be doubted in presence of the enormous number of works of fiction that appeal to the credulity of our generation, for it might easily seem that there could be no great character in a commodity so quickly and easily produced. It must be admitted that good novels are much compromised by bad ones, and that the field at large suffers discredit from overcrowding. I think, however, that this injury is only superficial, and that the superabundance of written fiction proves nothing against the principle itself. It has been vulgarized, like all other kinds of literature, like everything else today, and it has proved more than some kinds accessible to vulgarization. But there is as much difference as there ever was between a good novel and a bad one: the bad is swept with all the daubed canvases and spoiled marble into some unvisited limbo, or infinite rubbish-yard beneath the back-windows of the world, and the good subsists and emits its light and stimulates our desire for perfection. As I shall take the liberty of making but a single criticism of Mr. Besant, whose tone is so full of the love of his art, I may as well have done with it at once. He seems to me to mistake in attempting to say so definitely beforehand what sort of an affair the good novel will be. To indicate the danger of such an error as that has been the purpose of these few pages; to suggest that certain traditions on the subject, applied *a priori*, have already had much to answer for, and that the good health of an art which undertakes so immediately to reproduce life must demand that it be perfectly free. It lives upon exercise, and the very meaning of exercise is freedom. The only obligation to which in advance we may hold a novel, without incurring the accusation of being arbitrary, is that it be interesting. That general responsibility rests upon it, but it is the only one I can think of. The ways in which it is at liberty to accomplish this result (of interesting us) strike me as innumerable, and such as can only suffer from being marked out or fenced in by prescription. They are as various as the temperament of man, and they are successful in proportion as they reveal a particular mind, different from others. A novel is in its broadest definition a personal, a direct impression of life: that, to begin with, constitutes its value, which is greater or less according to the intensity of the impression. But there will be no intensity at all, and therefore no value, unless there is freedom to feel and say. The tracing of a line to be followed, of a tone to be taken, of a form to be filled out, is a limitation of that freedom and a suppression of the very thing that we are most curious about. The form, it seems to me, is to be appreciated after the fact: then the author's choice has been made, his standard has been indicated; then we can follow lines and directions and compare tones and resemblances. Then in a word we can enjoy one of the most charming of pleasures, we can estimate quality, we can apply the test of execution. The execution belongs to the author alone; it is what is most personal to him, and we measure him by that. The advantage, the luxury, as well as the torment and responsibility of the novelist, is that there is no limit to what he may attempt as an executant — no limit to his possible experiments, efforts, discoveries, successes. Here it is especially that he works, step by step, like his brother of the brush, of whom we may always say that he has painted his picture in a manner best known to himself. His manner is his secret, not necessarily a jealous one. He cannot disclose it as a general thing if he would; he would be at a loss to teach it to others. I say this with a due recollection of having insisted on the community of method of the artist who paints a picture and the artist who writes a novel. The painter *is* able to teach the rudiments of his practice, and it is possible, from the study of good work (granted the aptitude), both to learn how to paint and to learn how to write. Yet it remains true, without injury to the *rapprochement,* that the literary artist would be obliged to say to his pupil much more than the other, "Ah, well, you must do it as you can!" It is a question of degree, a matter of delicacy. If there are exact sciences, there are also exact arts, and the grammar of painting is so much more definite that it makes the difference.

I ought to add, however, that if Mr. Besant says at the beginning of his essay that the "laws of fiction may be laid down and taught with as much precision and exactness as the laws of harmony, perspective, and proportion," he mitigates what might appear to be an extravagance by applying his remark to "general" laws, and by expressing most of these rules in a manner with which it would certainly be unaccommodating to disagree. That the novelist must write from his experience, that his "characters must be real and such as might be met with in actual life"; that "a young lady brought up in a quiet country village should avoid descriptions of garrison life," and "a writer whose friends and personal experiences belong to the lower middle-class should carefully avoid introducing his characters into society"; that one should enter one's notes in a common-place book; that one's figures should be clear in outline; that making them clear by some trick of speech or of carriage is a bad method, and "describing them at length" is a worse one; that English Fiction should have a "conscious moral purpose"; that "it is almost impossible to estimate too highly the value of careful workmanship — that is, of style"; that "the most important point of all is the story," that "the story is everything": these are principles with most of which it is surely impossible not to sympathize. That remark about the lower middle-class writer and his knowing his place is perhaps rather chilling; but for the rest I should find it difficult to dissent from any one of these recommendations. At the same time, I should find it difficult positively to assent to them, with the exception, perhaps, of the injunction as to entering one's notes in a common-place book. They scarcely seem to me to have the quality that Mr. Besant attributes to the rules of the novelist — the "precision and exactness" of "the laws of harmony, perspective, and proportion." They are suggestive, they are even inspiring, but they are not exact, though they are doubtless as much so as the case admits of: which is a proof of that liberty of interpretation for which I just contended. For the value of these different injunctions — so beautiful and so vague — is wholly in the meaning one attaches to them. The characters, the situation, which strike one as real will be those that touch and interest one most, but the measure of reality is very difficult to fix. The reality of Don Quixote or of Mr. Micawber is a very delicate shade; it is a reality so colored by the author's vision that, vivid as it may be, one would hesitate to propose it as a model: one would expose one's self to some very embarrassing questions on the part of a pupil. It goes without saying that you will not write a good novel unless you possess the sense of reality; but it will be difficult to give you a recipe for calling that sense into being. Humanity is immense, and reality has a myriad forms; the most one can affirm is that some of the flowers of fiction have the odor of it, and others have not; as for telling you in advance how your nosegay should be composed, that is another affair. It is equally excellent and inconclusive to say that one must write from experience; to our suppositious aspirant such a declaration might savor of mockery. What kind of experience is intended, and where does it begin and end? Experience is never limited, and it is never complete; it is an immense sensibility, a kind of huge spider-web of the finest silken threads suspended in the chamber of consciousness, and catching every air-borne particle in its tissue. It is the very atmosphere of the mind; and when the mind is imaginative — much more when it happens to be that of a man of genius — it takes to itself the faintest hints of life, it converts the very pulses of the air into revelations. The young lady living in a village has only to be a damsel upon whom nothing is lost to make it quite unfair (as it seems to me) to declare to her that she shall have nothing to say about the military. Greater miracles have been seen than that, imagination assisting, she should speak the truth about some of these gentlemen. I remember an English novelist, a woman of genius, telling me that she was much commended for the impression she had managed to give in one of her tales of the nature and way of life of the French Protestant youth.[4] She had been asked where she learned so much about this recondite being, she had been congratulated on her peculiar opportunities. These opportunities consisted in her having once, in Paris, as she ascended a staircase, passed an open door where, in the household of a *pasteur,*[5] some of the young Protestants were seated at table round a finished meal. The glimpse made a picture; it lasted only a moment, but that moment was experience. She had got her direct personal impression, and she turned out her type. She knew what youth was, and what Protestantism; she also had the advantage of having seen what it was to be French, so that she converted these ideas into a concrete image and produced a reality. Above all, however, she was blessed with the faculty which when you give it an inch takes an ell, and which for the artist is a much greater source of strength than any accident of residence or of place in the social scale. The power to guess the unseen from the seen, to trace the implication of things, to judge the whole piece by the pattern, the condition of feeling life in general so completely that you are well on your way to knowing any particular corner of it — this cluster of gifts may almost be said to constitute experience, and they occur in country and in town, and in the most differing stages of education. If experience consists of impressions, it may be said that impressions *are* experience, just as (have we not seen it?) they are the very air we breathe. Therefore, if I should certainly say to a novice, "Write from experience and experience only," I should feel that this was rather a tantalizing monition if I were not careful immediately to add, "Try to be one of the people on whom nothing is lost!"

I am far from intending by this to minimize

[4]Probably *The Story of Elizabeth* by Anne Thackeray, Lady Ritchie. [Ed.]
[5]Minister. [Ed.]

the importance of exactness — of truth of detail. One can speak best from one's own taste, and I may therefore venture to say that the air of reality (solidity of specification) seems to me to be the supreme virtue of a novel — the merit on which all its other merits (including that conscious moral purpose of which Mr. Besant speaks) helplessly and submissively depend. If it be not there they are all as nothing, and if these be there, they owe their effect to the success with which the author has produced the illusion of life. The cultivation of this success, the study of this exquisite process, form, to my taste, the beginning and the end of the art of the novelist. They are his inspiration, his despair, his reward, his torment, his delight. It is here in very truth that he competes with life; it is here that he competes with his brother the painter in *his* attempt to render the look of things, the look that conveys their meaning, to catch the color, the relief, the expression, the surface, the substance of the human spectacle. It is in regard to this that Mr. Besant is well inspired when he bids him take notes. He cannot possibly take too many, he cannot possibly take enough. All life solicits him, and to "render" the simplest surface, to produce the most momentary illusion is a very complicated business. His case would be easier, and the rule would be more exact, if Mr. Besant had been able to tell him what notes to take. But this, I fear, he can never learn in any manual; it is the business of his life. He has to take a great many in order to select a few, he has to work them up as he can, and even the guides and philosophers who might have most to say to him must leave him alone when it comes to the applications of precepts, as we leave the painter in communion with his palette. That his characters "must be clear in outline," as Mr. Besant says — he feels that down to his boots; but how he shall make them so is a secret between his good angel and himself. It would be absurdly simple if he could be taught that a great deal of "description" would make them so, or that on the contrary the absence of description and the cultivation of dialogue, or the absence of dialogue and the multiplication of "incident," would rescue him from his difficulties. Nothing, for instance, is more possible than that he be of a turn of mind for which this odd, literal opposition of description and dialogue, incident and description, has little meaning and light. People often talk of these things as if they had a kind of internecine distinctness, instead of melting into each other at every breath, and being intimately associated parts of one general effort of expression. I cannot imagine composition existing in a series of blocks, nor conceive, in any novel worth discussing at all, of a passage of description that is not in its intention narrative, a passage of dialogue that is not in its intention descriptive, a touch of truth of any sort that does not partake of the nature of incident, or an incident that derives its interest from any other source than the general and only source of the success of a work of art — that of being illustrative. A novel is a living thing, all one and continuous, like any other organism, and in proportion as it lives will it be found. I think, that in each of the parts there is something of each of the other parts. The critic who over the close texture of a finished work shall pretend to trace a geography of items will mark some frontiers as artificial, I fear, as any that have been known to history. There is an old-fashioned distinction between the novel of character and the novel of incident which must have cost many a smile to the intending fabulist who was keen about his work. It appears to me as little to the point as the equally celebrated distinction between the novel and the romance — to answer as little to any reality. There are bad novels and good novels, as there are bad pictures and good pictures; but that is the only distinction in which I see any meaning, and I can as little imagine speaking of a novel of character as I can imagine speaking of a picture of character. When one says picture one says of character, when one says novel one says of incident, and the terms may be transposed at will. What is character but the determination of incident? What is incident but the illustration of character? What is either a picture or a novel that is *not* of character? What else do we seek in it and find in it? It is an incident for a woman to stand up with her hand resting on a table and look out at you in a certain way; or if it be not an incident I think it will be hard to say what it is. At the same time it is an expression of character. If you

say you don't see it (character in *that* — *allons donc!*[6]), this is exactly what the artist who has reasons of his own for thinking he *does* see it undertakes to show you. When a young man makes up his mind that he has not faith enough after all to enter the church as he intended, that is an incident, though you may not hurry to the end of the chapter to see whether perhaps he doesn't change once more. I do not say that these are extraordinary or startling incidents. I do not pretend to estimate the degree of interest proceeding from them, for this will depend upon the skill of the painter. It sounds almost puerile to say that some incidents are intrinsically much more important than others, and I need not take this precaution after having professed my sympathy for the major ones in remarking that the only classification of the novel that I can understand is into that which has life and that which has it not.

The novel and the romance, the novel of incident and that of character — these clumsy separations appear to me to have been made by critics and readers for their own convenience, and to help them out of some of their occasional queer predicaments, but to have little reality or interest for the producer, from whose point of view it is of course that we are attempting to consider the art of fiction. The case is the same with another shadowy category which Mr. Besant apparently is disposed to set up — that of the "modern English novel"; unless indeed it be that in this matter he has fallen into an accidental confusion of standpoints. It is not quite clear whether he intends the remarks in which he alludes to it to be didactic or historical. It is as difficult to suppose a person intending to write a modern English as to suppose him writing an ancient English novel: that is a label which begs the question. One writes the novel, one paints the picture, of one's language and of one's time, and calling it modern English will not, alas! make the difficult task any easier. No more, unfortunately, will calling this or that work of one's fellow-artist a romance — unless it be, of course, simply for the pleasantness of the thing, as for

[6]Go on with you! [Ed.]

instance when Hawthorne gave this heading to his story of *Blithedale*. The French, who have brought the theory of fiction to remarkable completeness, have but one name for the novel, and have not attempted smaller things in it, that I can see, for that. I can think of no obligation to which the "romancer" would not be held equally with the novelist; the standard of execution is equally high for each. Of course it is of execution that we are talking — that being the only point of a novel that is open to contention. This is perhaps too often lost sight of, only to produce interminable confusions and cross-purposes. We must grant the artist his subject, his idea, his *donnée:*[7] our criticism is applied only to what he makes of it. Naturally I do not mean that we are bound to like it or find it interesting: in case we do not our course is perfectly simple — to let it alone. We may believe that of a certain idea even the most sincere novelist can make nothing at all, and the event may perfectly justify our belief; but the failure will have been a failure to execute, and it is in the execution that the fatal weakness is recorded. If we pretend to respect the artist at all, we must allow him his freedom of choice, in the face, in particular cases, of innumerable presumptions that the choice will not fructify. Art derives a considerable part of its beneficial exercise from flying in the face of presumptions, and some of the most interesting experiments of which it is capable are hidden in the bosom of common things. Gustave Flaubert has written a story about the devotion of a servant-girl to a parrot,[8] and the production, highly finished as it is, cannot on the whole be called a success. We are perfectly free to find it flat, but I think it might have been interesting; and I, for my part, am extremely glad he should have written it; it is a contribution to our knowledge of what can be done — or what cannot. Ivan Turgenev has written a tale about a deaf and dumb serf and a lap-dog,[9] and the thing is touching, loving, a little masterpiece. He struck the note of life where Gustave Flaubert missed it — he flew in the face of a presumption and achieved a victory.

[7]What is given. [Ed.]
[8]*A Simple Heart* [Ed.]
[9]*Mumu* [Ed.]

Nothing, of course, will ever take the place of the good old fashion of "liking" a work of art or not liking it: the most improved criticism will not abolish that primitive, that ultimate test. I mention this to guard myself from the accusation of intimating that the idea, the subject, of a novel or a picture, does not matter. It matters, to my sense, in the highest degree, and if I might put up a prayer it would be that artists should select none but the richest. Some, as I have already hastened to admit, are much more remunerative than others, and it would be a world happily arranged in which persons intending to treat them should be exempt from confusions and mistakes. This fortunate condition will arrive only, I fear, on the same day that critics become purged from error. Meanwhile, I repeat, we do not judge the artist with fairness unless we say to him,

"Oh, I grant you your starting-point, because if I did not I should seem to prescribe to you, and heaven forbid I should take that responsibility. If I pretend to tell you what you must not take, you will call upon me to tell you then what you must take; in which case I shall be prettily caught. Moreover, it isn't till I have accepted your data that I can begin to measure you. I have the standard, the pitch; I have no right to tamper with your flute and then criticize your music. Of course I may not care for your idea at all; I may think it silly, or stale, or unclean; in which case I wash my hands of you altogether. I may content myself with believing that you will not have succeeded in being interesting, but I shall, of course, not attempt to demonstrate it, and you will be as indifferent to me as I am to you. I needn't remind you that there are all sorts of tastes: who can know it better? Some people, for excellent reasons, don't like to read about carpenters; others, for reasons even better, don't like to read about courtesans. Many object to Americans. Others (I believe they are mainly editors and publishers) won't look at Italians. Some readers don't like quiet subjects; others don't like bustling ones. Some enjoy a complete illusion, others the consciousness of large concessions. They choose their novels accordingly, and if they don't care about your idea they won't, *a fortiori,* care about your treatment."

So that it comes back very quickly, as I have said, to the liking: in spite of M. Zola, who reasons less powerfully than he represents, and who will not reconcile himself to this absoluteness of taste, thinking that there are certain things that people ought to like, and that they can be made to like. I am quite at a loss to imagine anything (at any rate in this matter of fiction) that people *ought* to like or to dislike. Selection will be sure to take care of itself, for it has a constant motive behind it. That motive is simply experience. As people feel life, so they will feel the art that is most closely related to it. This closeness of relation is what we should never forget in talking of the effort of the novel. Many people speak of it as a factitious, artificial form, a product of ingenuity, the business of which is to alter and arrange the things that surround us, to translate them into conventional, traditional moulds. This, however, is a view of the matter which carries us but a very short way, condemns the art to an eternal repetition of a few familiar *clichés*, cuts short its development, and leads us straight up to a dead wall. Catching the very note and trick, the strange irregular rhythm of life, that is the attempt whose strenuous force keeps Fiction upon her feet. In proportion as in what she offers us we see life *without* rearrangement do we feel that we are touching the truth; in proportion as we see it *with* rearrangement do we feel that we are being put off with a substitute, a compromise and convention. It is not uncommon to hear an extraordinary assurance of remark in regard to this matter of rearranging, which is often spoken of as if it were the last word of art. Mr. Besant seems to me in danger of falling into the great error with his rather unguarded talk about "selection." Art is essentially selection, but it is a selection whose main care is to be typical, to be inclusive. For many people art means rose-colored window-panes, and selection means picking a bouquet for Mrs. Grundy.[10] They will tell you glibly that artistic considerations have nothing to do with the disagreeable, with the ugly; they will rattle off shallow commonplaces about the province of art and the limits of art till

you are moved to some wonder in return as to the province and the limits of ignorance. It appears to me that no one can ever have made a seriously artistic attempt without becoming conscious of an immense increase — a kind of revelation — of freedom. One perceives in that case — by the light of a heavenly ray — that the province of art is all life, all feeling, all observation, all vision. As Mr. Besant so justly intimates, it is all experience. That is a sufficient answer to those who maintain that it must not touch the sad things of life, who stick into its divine unconscious bosom little prohibitory inscriptions on the end of sticks, such as we see in public gardens — "It is forbidden to walk on the grass; it is forbidden to touch the flowers; it is not allowed to introduce dogs or to remain after dark; it is requested to keep to the right." The young aspirant in the line of fiction whom we continue to imagine will do nothing without taste, for in that case his freedom would be of little use to him; but the first advantage of his taste will be to reveal to him the absurdity of the little sticks and tickets. If he have taste, I must add, of course he will have ingenuity, and my disrespectful reference to that quality just now was not meant to imply that it is useless in fiction. But it is only a secondary aid; the first is a capacity of receiving straight impressions.

Mr. Besant has some remarks on the question of "the story" which I shall not attempt to criticize, though they seem to me to contain a singular ambiguity, because I do not think I understand them. I cannot see what is meant by talking as if there were a part of a novel which is the story and part of it which for mystical reasons is not — unless indeed the distinction be made in a sense in which it is difficult to suppose that any one should attempt to convey anything. "The story," if it represents anything, represents the subject, the idea, the *donnée* of the novel; and there is surely no "school" — Mr. Besant speaks of a school — which urges that a novel should be all treatment and no subject. There must assuredly be something to treat; every school is intimately conscious of that. This sense of the story being the idea, the starting-point, of the novel, is the only one that I see in which it can be spoken of as something different from its

[10]Personification of prudery. [Ed.]

organic whole; and since in proportion as the work is successful the idea permeates and penetrates it, informs and animates it, so that every word and every punctuation-point contribute directly to the expression, in that proportion do we lose our sense of the story being a blade which may be drawn more or less out of its sheath. The story and the novel, the idea and the form, are the needle and thread, and I never heard of a guild of tailors who recommended the use of the thread without the needle, or the needle without the thread. Mr. Besant is not the only critic who may be observed to have spoken as if there were certain things in life which constitute stories, and certain others which do not. I find the same odd implication in an entertaining article in the *Pall Mall Gazette*, devoted, as it happens, to Mr. Besant's lecture. "The story is the thing!" says this graceful writer, as if with a tone of opposition to some other idea. I should think it was, as every painter who, as the time for "sending in" his picture looms in the distance, finds himself still in quest of a subject — as every belated artist not fixed about his theme will heartily agree. There are some subjects which speak to us and others which do not, but he would be a clever man who should undertake to give a rule — an *index expurgatorius* — by which the story and the no-story should be known apart. It is impossible (to me at least) to imagine any such rule which shall not be altogether arbitrary. The writer in the *Pall Mall* opposes the delightful (as I suppose) novel of *Margot la Balafrée* to certain tales in which "Bostonian nymphs" appear to have "rejected English dukes for psychological reasons."[11] I am not acquainted with the romance just designated, and can scarcely forgive the *Pall Mall* critic for not mentioning the name of the author, but the title appears to refer to a lady who may have received a scar in some heroic adventure. I am inconsolable at not being acquainted with this episode, but am utterly at a loss to see why it is a story when the rejection (or acceptance) of a duke is not, and why a reason, psychological or other, is not a subject when a cicatrix is. They are all particles of the

multitudinous life with which the novel deals, and surely no dogma which pretends to make it lawful to touch the one and unlawful to touch the other will stand for a moment on its feet. It is the special picture that must stand or fall, according as it seem to possess truth or to lack it. Mr. Besant does not, to my sense, light up the subject by intimating that a story must, under penalty of not being a story, consist of "adventures." Why of adventures more than of green spectacles? He mentions a category of impossible things, and among them he places "fiction without adventure." Why without adventure, more than without matrimony, or celibacy, or parturition, or cholera, or hydropathy, or Jansenism? This seems to me to bring the novel back to the hapless little *rôle* of being an artificial, ingenious thing — bring it down from its large, free character of an immense and exquisite correspondence with life. And what *is* adventure, when it comes to that and by what sign is the listening pupil to recognize it? It is an adventure — an immense one — for me to write this little article; and for a Bostonian nymph to reject an English duke is an adventure only less stirring, I should say, than for an English duke to be rejected by a Bostonian nymph. I see dramas within dramas in that, and innumerable points of view. A psychological reason is, to my imagination, an object adorably pictorial; to catch the tint of its complexion — I feel as if that idea might inspire one to Titianesque efforts. There are few things more exciting to me, in short, than a psychological reason, and yet, I protest, the novel seems to me the most magnificent form of art. I have just been reading, at the same time, the delightful story of *Treasure Island*, by Mr. Robert Louis Stevenson and, in a manner less consecutive, the last tale from M. Edmond de Goncourt, which is entitled *Chérie*. One of these works treats of murders, mysteries, islands of dreadful renown, hairbreadth escapes, miraculous coincidences and buried doubloons. The other treats of a little French girl who lived in a fine house in Paris, and died of wounded sensibility because no one would marry her. I call *Treasure Island* delightful, because it appears to me to have succeeded wonderfully in what it attempts; and I venture to bestow no epithet upon *Chérie*, which strikes me

[11]Henry James's own *An International Episode* (1879). [Ed.]

as having failed deplorably in what it attempts — that is in tracing the development of the moral consciousness of a child. But one of these productions strikes me as exactly as much of a novel as the other, and as having a "story" quite as much. The moral consciousness of a child is as much a part of life as the islands of the Spanish Main, and the one sort of geography seems to me to have those "surprises" of which Mr. Besant speaks quite as much as the other. For myself (since it comes back in the last resort, as I say, to the preference of the individual), the picture of the child's experience has the advantage that I can at successive steps (an immense luxury, near to the "sensual pleasure" of which Mr. Besant's critic in the *Pall Mall* speaks) say Yes or No, as it may be, to what the artist puts before me. I have been a child in fact, but I have been on a quest for a buried treasure only in supposition, and it is a simple accident that with M. de Goncourt I should have for the most part to say No. With George Eliot, when she painted that country with a far other intelligence, I always said Yes.

The most interesting part of Mr. Besant's lecture is unfortunately the briefest passage — his very cursory allusion to the "conscious moral purpose" of the novel. Here again it is not very clear whether he be recording a fact or laying down a principle; it is a great pity that in the latter case he should not have developed his idea. This branch of the subject is of immense importance, and Mr. Besant's few words point to considerations of the widest reach, not to be lightly disposed of. He will have treated the art of fiction but superficially who is not prepared to go every inch of the way that these considerations will carry him. It is for this reason that at the beginning of these remarks I was careful to notify the reader that my reflections on so large a theme have no pretension to be exhaustive. Like Mr. Besant, I have left the question of the morality of the novel till the last, and at the last I find I have used up my space. It is a question surrounded with difficulties, as witness the very first that meets us, in the form of a definite question, on the threshold. Vagueness, in such a discussion, is fatal, and what is the meaning of your morality and your conscious moral purpose? Will you not define your terms and explain how (a novel being a picture) a picture can be either moral or immoral? You wish to paint a moral picture or carve a moral statue: will you not tell us how you would set about it? We are discussing the Art of Fiction; questions of art are questions (in the widest sense) of execution; questions of morality are quite another affair, and will you not let us see how it is that you find it so easy to mix them up? These things are so clear to Mr. Besant that he has deduced from them a law which he sees embodied in English Fiction, and which is "a truly admirable thing and a great cause for congratulation." It is a great cause for congratulation indeed when such thorny problems become as smooth as silk. I may add that in so far as Mr. Besant perceives that in point of fact English Fiction has addressed itself preponderantly to these delicate questions he will appear to many people to have made a vain discovery. They will have been positively struck, on the contrary, with the moral timidity of the usual English novelist; with his (or with her) aversion to face the difficulties with which on every side the treatment of reality bristles. He is apt to be extremely shy (whereas the picture that Mr. Besant draws is a picture of boldness), and the sign of his work, for the most part, is a cautious silence on certain subjects. In the English novel (by which of course I mean the American as well), more than in any other there is a traditional difference between that which people know and that which they agree to admit that they know, that which they see and that which they speak of, that which they feel to be a part of life and that which they allow to enter into literature. There is the great difference, in short, between what they talk of in conversation and what they talk of in print. The essence of moral energy is to survey the whole field, and I should directly reverse Mr. Besant's remark and say not that the English novel has a purpose, but that it has a diffidence. To what degree a purpose in a work of art is a source of corruption I shall not attempt to inquire; the one that seems to me least dangerous is the purpose of making a perfect work. As for our novel, I may say lastly on this score that as we find it in England today it strikes me as addressed in a large degree to "young people," and that this in itself constitutes a presumption that it will be rather shy. There are certain things which it is generally agreed not to discuss, not even to mention, before young people. That is very well, but the absence of discussion is not a symptom of the moral passion. The purpose of the English novel — "a truly admirable thing, and a great cause for congratulation" — strikes me therefore as rather negative.

There is one point at which the moral sense and the artistic sense lie very near together; that is in the light of the very obvious truth that the deepest quality of a work of art will always be the quality of the mind of the producer. In proportion as that intelligence is fine will the novel, the picture, the statue partake of the substance of beauty and truth. To be constituted of such elements is, to my vision, to have purpose enough. No good novel will ever proceed from a superficial mind; that seems to me an axiom which, for the artist in fiction, will cover all needful moral ground: If the youthful aspirant take it to heart it will illuminate for him many of the mysteries of "purpose." There are many other useful things that might be said to him, but I have come to the end of my article, and can only touch them as I pass. The critic in the *Pall Mall Gazette,* whom I have already quoted, draws attention to the danger, in speaking of the art of fiction, of generalizing. The danger that he has in mind is rather, I imagine, that of particularizing, for there are some comprehensive remarks which, in addition to those embodied in Mr. Besant's suggestive lecture, might without fear of misleading him be addressed to the ingenuous student. I should remind him first of the magnificence of the form that is open to him, which offers to sight so few restrictions and such innumerable opportunities. The other arts, in comparison, appear confined and hampered; the various conditions under which they are exercised are so rigid and definite. But the only condition that I can think of attaching to the composition of the novel is, as I have already said, that it be sincere. This freedom is a splendid privilege, and the first lesson of the young novelist is to learn to be worthy of it.

"Enjoy it as it deserves [I should say to him]; take possession of it, explore it to its utmost extent, publish it, rejoice in it. All life belongs to you, and do not listen either to those who would shut you up into corners of it and tell you that it is only here and there that art inhabits, or to those who would persuade you that this heavenly messenger wings her way outside of life altogether, breathing a superfine air, and turning away her head from the truth of things. There is no impression of life, no manner of seeing it and feeling it, to which the plan of the novelist may not offer a place; you have only to remember that talents so dissimilar as those of Alexandre Dumas and Jane Austen, Charles Dickens and Gustave Flaubert have worked in this field with equal glory. Do not think too much about optimism and pessimism; try and catch the color of life itself. In France today we see a prodigious effort (that of Émile Zola, to whose solid and serious work no explorer of the capacity of the novel can allude without respect), we see an extraordinary effort vitiated by a spirit of pessimism on a narrow basis. M. Zola is magnificent, but he strikes an English reader as ignorant; he has an air of working in the dark; if he had as much light as energy, his results would be of the highest value. As for the aberrations of a shallow optimism, the ground (of English fiction especially) is strewn with their brittle particles as with broken glass. If you must indulge in conclusions, let them have the taste of a wide knowledge. Remember that your first duty is to be as complete as possible — to make as perfect a work. Be generous and delicate and pursue the prize."

# Leo Tolstoy

## 1828–1910

Born on his mother's estate of Yasnaya Polyana, Count Leo Nikolaievich Tolstoy was educated privately and at Kazan University. After a dissipated youth spent drinking and hunting in the country and womanizing in Moscow, Tolstoy began to question the meaning of life, leaving records of his self-examinations in a series of diaries that he kept to the end of his days. Partly with the intent of reforming himself, Tolstoy enlisted in the army in 1850, and it was during the boredom of guard duty in the Caucasus that he began to write autobiographical sketches, which were published starting in 1852. In 1856 he left the service and took two extended European tours; these had the paradoxical effect of confirming him in his essential Russianness.

In 1861 Tolstoy returned to Yasnaya Polyana, where he set up and ran a successful progressive school for his peasants, recently emancipated from serfdom. He married Sofia Behr the following year, published his first major novel, *The Cossacks,* in 1863, and began to plan out his great epic of Napoleonic Russia, *War and Peace,* which was finally completed in 1869. His more concentrated psychological tragedy, *Anna Karenina,* was published in 1877.

That year Tolstoy experienced a major spiritual crisis in which he desperately sought the ultimate basis of moral action. He found it in quietism, a doctrine of nonresistance to evil, and in the rejection of self-gratification in favor of social responsibility. These doctrines govern Tolstoy's later fiction, including his classic novella, *The Death of Ivan Ilych* (1886) and his underrated late novel, *Resurrection* (1899). This later fiction is more explicitly didactic than the fiction Tolstoy wrote prior to his conversion, but his penetrating observation of human nature and his natural gifts as a storyteller remain intact.

Tolstoy's morality required absolute truth, without any of the myths that underlie most popular religion, and his demythologizing of Christianity resulted in his excommunication by the Orthodox church. This, along with his renunciation of his private property (which was divided among his wife and thirteen children), may have been responsible for his being the first major czarist author to be fully accepted by the Soviets. He died at the age of eighty-two and was buried at Yasnaya Polyana.

*What Is Art?* may be, as Ernest J. Simmons, a scholar of Russian literature, has said, "the most immodest contribution to aesthetics ever written." Composed at white heat in 1897, it is the fruit of Tolstoy's speculations since the 1850s about the nature of art. Except for Tolstoy's biographers, few commentators have been charitable to *What Is Art?,* partly because Tolstoy himself is so dismissive of all previous aesthetic thought and partly because the conclusions to which he comes put most of the masterpieces of painting, music, and literature (including Tolstoy's own) into the vast category of bad art. In fact, Tolstoy's notions about art have an admirable consistency, and they are important if only because they voice a theory one needs to learn how to argue with.

Tolstoy begins by rejecting most of the central aesthetic principles of the nineteenth century. He is mystified by Hegel's idea that art is a necessary road to Absolute Spirit, and equally mystified by philosophers' use of the idea of beauty. The various definitions of beauty either lead in a circle (e.g., "beauty is that which pleases without exciting desire") or culminate in the notion of taste, which is unsatisfactory because people's tastes differ, so that any aesthetic based on taste would have to be specific to a particular class, and hence, insufficiently universal. At this point, Tolstoy presents his own idea of art:

> To evoke in oneself a feeling that one has once experienced and having evoked it in oneself then by means of movements, lines, colors, sounds or forms expressed in words, so to transmit that feeling that others experience the same feeling — that is the activity of art.

> Art is a human activity consisting in this, that one man consciously by means of certain external signs, hands on to others feelings he has lived through, and that others are infected by these feelings and also experience them.

> Art is not, as the metaphysicians say, the manifestation of some mysterious Idea of beauty or God; it is not, as the aesthetic physiologists say, a game in which man lets off his excess of stored-up energy; it is not the expression of man's emotions by external signs; it is not the production of pleasing objects; and, above all, it is not pleasure; but it is a means of union among men joining them together in the same feelings, and indispensable for the life and progress towards well-being of individuals and humanity. (Ch. 5)

If art is a form of infection, then there are two criteria for value, one internal and the other external. The internal criterion is *efficacy*: The best art will be that which infects us most strongly, and this, Tolstoy said, depends upon "(1) the greater or lesser individuality of the feeling transmitted; (2) on the greater or lesser clearness with which the feeling is transmitted; (3) on the sincerity of the artist" (Ch. 15).

More significant to Tolstoy was the external criterion for quality of art: the subject matter, which would determine the specific feelings that were communicated. The better the feelings according to some criterion of value, the better the art. Tolstoy does not pause to justify which are the best feelings. He merely suggests that every society has what he calls a "religious ideal," which becomes the repository of its most cherished values. (Tolstoy emphatically does not mean the ideal of any specific *organized* religion, since he was inveterately hostile to all religious cults as coming between man and God.) This value system Tolstoy locates in "Christianity in its true meaning" — what is today called the Judeo-Christian tradition of human brotherhood.

Once he has located the values which art should infect us with, Tolstoy is forced to distinguish invidiously between the upper class art of his time, whose infectious feelings were those to which the upper classes are devoted — pride, sensuality, and ennui — and universal art, which serves *"to unite men with God and with one another."*

Here he distinguishes once more between the "higher, positive" kind of true art, which actively transmits the message of human brotherhood (and he gives a list that includes Dickens's *A Christmas Carol* and Eliot's *Adam Bede*), and a "lower, negative kind," which conveys universal feelings, if not the feeling of universality (the list here includes *Don Quixote* and Molière's comedies).

Had Tolstoy stopped here, he might have found general agreement with his thesis, but he also felt compelled to point out the negative consequence of his theory, which is that most of the artistic works beloved of the intelligentsia are, in his terms, bad art. Shakespeare's plays, for example, in that his characters speak a language never spoken by normal people and unintelligible to the normal people of the present day, work to divide rather than unite humankind. The same would be true of music, like Beethoven's Ninth Symphony, since, regardless of its explicit message, the medium in which it is expressed is such as to be unintelligible to most people. (A simple folksong or a lullaby would for Tolstoy be considered better art.) If Tolstoy was brutal, he was also consistent enough to consign most of his own works to the dustbin: He repudiated *War and Peace* and *Anna Karenina* as bad art, and excepted from the general condemnation only two of his stories: "God Sees the Truth but Waits" and "A Captive in the Caucasus."

The difficulties with *What Is Art?* have less to do with consistency than with the theory's external plausibility and internal coherence. It is questionable, for instance, whether feelings of pride, sensuality and ennui are found only among the upper classes or whether modern culture has not made them universal. Similarly, Tolstoy's assumption that a folksong is more universal than a Beethoven symphony needs to be examined: The folksong, like the symphony, is informed by a Western scale and strophic form that may not be intelligible to a different musical culture (Indonesians, for example, or Hopi Indians). On the other side, Tolstoy (who was not musical) tended to overestimate the amount of cultural training required to appreciate a symphony. Internally, there are difficulties with the "infection" theory that Tolstoy did not anticipate. For one thing, the criterion of *sincerity* of feeling is one that cannot be tested: We know what a work has communicated to us but cannot know whether it is the same thing the artist experienced or indeed whether the artist experienced anything at all. In fact, the central notion implicit in Tolstoy's infection metaphor — the idea that art instills identical feelings into its whole audience — is equally untestable, since we cannot cross-compare the feelings of everyone who has experienced and will experience a specific work. These problems do not devastate Tolstoy's theory: They are objections that can be answered. But it is interesting to note what different questions arise when a moral critique of art (begun by Plato) is couched, as Tolstoy's version is, in the postromantic aesthetic tradition that art is a form not of imitation but of self-expression.

### Selected Bibliography

Bayley, John. *Tolstoy and the Novel*. London: Chatto and Windus, 1966.
Farrell, James T. *Literature and Morality*. New York: Vanguard Press, 1947.
Garrod, H. W. *Tolstoi's Theory of Art*. Oxford: Clarendon Press, 1935.
Jones, Malcolm, ed. *New Essays on Tolstoy*. Cambridge and New York: Cambridge University Press, 1978.

Macy, John A. "Tolstoi's Moral Theory of Art." *Century Magazine* 62 (1901): 298–307.

Maude, Aylmer. *Tolstoi on Art and Its Critics.* London: H. Milford, 1925.

Perosa, Sergio. "James, Tolstoy, and the Novel." *Revue de Littérature Comparée* 53 (1983): 359–68.

Steiner, George. *Tolstoy or Dostoevsky: An Essay in Contrast.* London: Faber and Faber, 1960.

Tolstoy, Lev Nikolaievich. *What Is Art?* Translated by Aylmer Maude. New York: T. Y. Crowell, 1898.

Troyat, Henri. *Tolstoy.* Garden City, N.Y.: Doubleday, 1967.

# From *What Is Art?*

How in the subject-matter of art are we to decide what is good and what is bad?

Art like speech is a means of communication and therefore of progress, that is, of the movement of humanity forward toward perfection. Speech renders accessible to men of the latest generations all the knowledge discovered by the experience and reflection both of preceding generations and of the best and foremost men of their own times; art renders accessible to men of the latest generations all the feelings experienced by their predecessors and also those felt by their best and foremost contemporaries. And as the evolution of knowledge proceeds by truer and more necessary knowledge dislodging and replacing what was mistaken and unnecessary, so the evolution of feeling proceeds by means of art — feelings less kind and less necessary for the well-being of mankind being replaced by others kinder and more needful for that end. That is the purpose of art. And speaking now of the feelings which are its subject-matter, the more art fulfills that purpose the better the art, and the less it fulfills it the worse the art.

The appraisement of feelings (that is, the recognition of one or other set of feelings as more or less good, more or less necessary for the well-being of mankind) is effected by the religious perception of the age.

In every period of history and in every human society there exists an understanding of the meaning of life, which represents the highest level to which men of that society have attained — an understanding indicating the highest good at which that society aims. This understanding is the religious perception of the given time and society. And this religious perception is always clearly expressed by a few advanced men and more or less vividly perceived by members of the society generally. Such a religious perception and its corresponding expression always exists in every society. If it appears to us that there is no religious perception in our society, this is not because there really is none, but only because we do not wish to see it. And we often wish not to see it because it exposes the fact that our life is inconsistent with that religious perception.

Religious perception in a society is like the direction of a flowing river. If the river flows at all it must have a direction. If a society lives, there must be a religious perception indicating the direction in which, more or less consciously, all its members tend.

And so there always has been, and is, a religious perception in every society. And it is by the standard of this religious perception that the feelings transmitted by art have always been appraised. It has always been only on the basis of this religious perception of their age, that men have chosen from amid the endlessly varied spheres of art that art which transmitted feelings making religious perception operative in actual life. And such art has always been highly valued and encouraged, while art transmitting feelings

Translated by Aylmer Maude.

already outlived, flowing from the antiquated religious perceptions of a former age, has always been condemned and despised. All the rest of art transmitting those most diverse feelings by means of which people commune with one another was not condemned and was tolerated if only it did not transmit feelings contrary to religious perception. Thus for instance among the Greeks, art transmitting feelings of beauty, strength, and courage (Hesiod, Homer, Phidias) was chosen, approved, and encouraged, while art transmitting feelings of rude sensuality, despondency, and effeminacy, was condemned and despised. Among the Jews, art transmitting feelings of devotion and submission to the God of the Hebrews and to His will (the epic of Genesis, the prophets, the Psalms) was chosen and encouraged, while art transmitting feelings of idolatry (the Golden Calf) was condemned and despised. All the rest of art — stories, songs, dances, ornamentation of houses, of utensils, and of clothes — which was not contrary to religious perception, was neither distinguished nor discussed. Thus as regards its subject matter has art always and everywhere been appraised and thus it should be appraised, for this attitude toward art proceeds from the fundamental characteristics of human nature, and those characteristics do not change.

I know that according to an opinion current in our times religion is a superstition humanity has outgrown, and it is therefore assumed that no such thing exists as a religious perception common to us all by which art in our time can be appraised. I know that this is the opinion current in the pseudo-cultured circles of today. People who do not acknowledge Christianity in its true meaning because it undermines their social privileges, and who therefore invent all kinds of philosophic and aesthetic theories to hide from themselves the meaninglessness and wrongfulness of their lives, cannot think otherwise. These people intentionally, or sometimes unintentionally, confuse the notion of a religious cult with the notion of religious perception, and think that by denying the cult they get rid of the perception. But even the very attacks on religion and the attempts to establish an idea of life contrary to the religious perception of our times, most clearly demonstrate the existence of a religious perception condemning the lives that are not in harmony with it.

If humanity progresses, that is, moves forward, there must inevitably be a guide to the direction of that movement. And religions have always furnished that guide. All history shows that the progress of humanity is accomplished no otherwise than under the guidance of religion. But if the race cannot progress without the guidance of religion — and progress is always going on, and consequently goes on also in our own times — then there must be a religion of our times. So that whether it pleases or displeases the so-called cultured people of to-day, they must admit the existence of religion — not of a religious cult, Catholic, Protestant or another, but of religious perception — which even in our times is the guide always present where there is any progress. And if a religious perception exists amongst us, then the feelings dealt with by our art should be appraised on the basis of that religious perception; and as has been the case always and everywhere, art transmitting feelings flowing from the religious perception of our time should be chosen from amid all the indifferent art, should be acknowledged, highly valued, and encouraged, while art running counter to that perception should be condemned and despised, and all the remaining, indifferent, art should neither be distinguished nor encouraged.

The religious perception of our time in its widest and most practical application is the consciousness that our well-being, both material and spiritual, individual and collective, temporal and eternal, lies in the growth of brotherhood among men — in their loving harmony with one another. This perception is not only expressed by Christ and all the best men of past ages, it is not only repeated in most varied forms and from most diverse sides by the best men of our times, but it already serves as a clue to all the complex labour of humanity, consisting as this labor does on the one hand in the destruction of physical and moral obstacles to the union of men, and on the other hand in establishing the principles common to all men which can and should unite them in one universal brotherhood. And it is on the basis of this perception that we should appraise all the phenomena of our life and among the rest our art also: choosing from all its realms and highly prizing and encouraging whatever transmits feelings flowing from this religious perception, rejecting whatever is contrary to it, and not attributing to the rest of art an importance that does not properly belong to it.

The chief mistake made by people of the upper classes at the time of the so-called Renaissance — a mistake we will still perpetuate — was not that they ceased to value and attach importance to religious art (people of that period could not attach importance to it because, like our own upper classes, they could not believe in what the majority considered to be religion), but their mistake was that they set up in place of the religious art that was lacking, an insignificant art which aimed merely at giving pleasure, that is, they began to choose, to value, and to encourage, in place of religious art, something which in any case did not deserve such esteem and encouragement.

One of the Fathers of the Church said that the great evil is not that men do not know God, but that they have set up instead of God, that which is not God. So also with art. The great misfortune of the people of the upper classes of our time is not so much that they are without a religious art as that, instead of a supreme religious art chosen from all the rest as being specially important and valuable, they have chosen a most insignificant and, usually, harmful art, which aims at pleasing certain people and which therefore, if only by its exclusive nature, stands in contradiction to that Christian principle of universal union which forms the religious perception of our time. Instead of religious art, an empty and often vicious art is set up, and this hides from men's notice the need of that true religious art which should be present in life to improve it.

It is true that art which satisfies the demands of the religious perception of our time is quite unlike former art, but notwithstanding this dissimilarity, to a man who does not intentionally hide the truth from himself, what forms the religious art of our age is very clear and definite. In former times when the highest religious perception united only some people (who even if they formed a large society were yet but one society among others — Jews, or Athenian or Roman citizens), the feelings transmitted by the art of that time flowed from a desire for the might, greatness, glory, and prosperity, of that society, and the heroes of art might be people who contributed to that prosperity by strength, by craft, by fraud, or by cruelty (Ulysses, Jacob, David, Samson, Hercules, and all the heroes). But the religious perception of our times does not select any one society of men; on the contrary it demands the union of all — absolutely of all people without exception — and above every other virtue it sets brotherly love of all men. And therefore the feelings transmitted by the art of our time not only cannot coincide with the feelings transmitted by former art, but must run counter to them.

Christian, truly Christian, art has been so long in establishing itself, and has not yet established itself, just because the Christian religious perception was not one of those small steps by which humanity advances regularly, but was an enormous revolution which, if it has not already altered, must inevitably alter the entire conception of life of mankind, and consequently the whole internal organization of that life. It is true that the life of humanity, like that of an individual, moves regularly; but in that regular movement come, as it were, turning-points which sharply divide the preceding from the subsequent life. Christianity was such a turning-point; such at least it must appear to us who live by the Christian perception of life. Christian perception gave another, a new, direction to all human feelings, and therefore completely altered both the content and the significance of art. The Greeks could make use of Persian art and the Romans could use Greek art, or, similarly, the Jews could use Egyptian art — the fundamental ideals were one and the same. Now the ideal was the greatness and prosperity of the Greeks, now that of the Romans. The same art was transferred to other conditions and served new nations. But the Christian ideal changed and reversed everything, so that, as the Gospel puts it, "That which was exalted among men has become an abomination in the sight of God."[1] The ideal is no longer the

[1]Luke 16:15. [Ed.]

greatness of Pharaoh or of a Roman emperor, not the beauty of a Greek nor the wealth of Phœnicia, but humility, purity, compassion, love. The hero is no longer Dives, but Lazarus the beggar; not Mary Magdalene in the day of her beauty but in the day of her repentance; not those who acquire wealth but those who have abandoned it; not those who dwell in palaces but those who dwell in catacombs and huts; not those who rule over others, but those who acknowledge no authority but God's. And the greatest work of art is no longer a cathedral of victory[2] with statues of conquerors, but the representation of a human soul so transformed by love that a man who is tormented and murdered, yet pities and loves his persecutors.

And the change is so great that men of the Christian world find it difficult to resist the inertia of the heathen art to which they have been accustomed all their lives. The subject matter of Christian religious art is so new to them, so unlike the subject matter of former art, that it seems to them as though Christian art were a denial of art, and they cling desperately to the old art. But this old art, having no longer in our day any source in religious perception, has lost its meaning, and we shall have to abandon it whether we wish to or not.

The essence of the Christian perception consists in the recognition by every man of his sonship to God and of the consequent union of men with God and with one another, as is said in the Gospel (John 17:21).[3] Therefore the subject matter of Christian art is of a kind that feeling can unite men with God and with one another.

The expression *unite men with God and with one another* may seem obscure to people accustomed to the misuse of these words that is so customary, but the words have a perfectly clear meaning nevertheless. They indicate that the Christian union of man (in contradiction to the partial, exclusive, union of only certain men) is that which unites all without exception.

Art, all art, has this characteristic, that it unites people. Every art causes those to whom the artist's feeling is transmitted to unite in soul with the artist and also with all who receive the same impression. But non-Christian art while uniting some people, makes that very union a cause of separation between these united people and others; so that union of this kind is often a source not merely of division but even of enmity towards others. Such is all patriotic art, with its anthems, poems, and monuments; such is all Church art, that is, the art of certain cults, with their images, statues, processions, and other local ceremonies. Such art is belated and non-Christian, uniting the people of one cult only to separate them yet more sharply from the members of other cults, and even to place them in relations of hostility to one another. Christian art is such only as tends to unite all without exception, either by evoking in them the perception that each man and all men stand in a like relation toward God and toward their neighbor, or by evoking in them identical feelings, which may even be the very simplest, provided that they are not repugnant to Christianity and are natural to every one without exception.

Good Christian art of our time may be unintelligible to people because of imperfections in its form or because men are inattentive to it, but it must be such that all men can experience the feelings it transmits. It must be the art not of some one group of people, or of one class, or of one nationality, or of one religious cult; that is, it must not transmit feelings accessible only to a man educated in a certain way, or only to an aristocrat, or a merchant, or only to a Russian, or a native of Japan, or a Roman Catholic, or a Buddhist, and so on, but it must transmit feelings accessible to every one. Only art of this kind can in our time be acknowledged to be good art, worthy of being chosen out from all the rest of art and encouraged.

Christian art, that is, the art of our time, should be catholic in the original meaning of the word, that is, universal, and therefore it should unite all men. And only two kinds of feeling unite all men: first, feelings flowing from a perception of our sonship to God and of the brotherhood of man; and next, the simple feelings of

[2]There is in Moscow a magnificent cathedral of our Saviour, erected to commemorate the defeat of the French in the war of 1812. [Tr.]

[3]"That they may all be one; even as thou, Father, art in me, and I in Thee, that they also may be in us." [Tr.]

common life accessible to every one without exception — such as feelings of merriment, of pity, of cheerfulness, of tranquility, and so forth. Only these two kinds of feelings can now supply material for art good in its subject matter.

And the action of these two kinds of art apparently so dissimilar, is one and the same. The feelings flowing from the perception of our sonship to God and the brotherhood of man — such as a feeling of sureness in truth, devotion to the will of God, self-sacrifice, respect for and love of man — evoked by Christian religious perception; and the simplest feelings, such as a softened or a merry mood caused by a song or an amusing jest intelligible to every one, or by a touching story, or a drawing, or a little doll: both alike produce one and the same effect — the loving union of man with man. Sometimes people who are together, if not hostile to one another, are at least estranged in mood and feeling, till perhaps a story, a performance, a picture, or even a building, but oftenest of all music, unites them all as by an electric flash, and in place of their former isolation or even enmity they are conscious of union and mutual love. Each is glad that another feels what he feels; glad of the communion established not only between him and all present, but also with all now living who will yet share the same impression; and more than that, he feels the mysterious gladness of a communion which, reaching beyond the grave, unites us with all men of the past who have been moved by the same feelings and with all men of the future who will yet be touched by them. And this effect is produced both by religious art which transmits feelings of love of God and one's neighbour, and by universal art transmitting the very simplest feelings common to all men.

The art of our time should be appraised differently from former art chiefly in this, that the art of our time, that is, Christian art (basing itself on a religious perception which demands the union of man), excludes from the domain of art good in its subject matter, everything transmitting exclusive feelings which do not unite men but divide them. It relegates such work to the category of art that is bad in its subject matter; while on the other hand it includes in the category of art that is good in subject matter a section not formerly admitted as deserving of selection and respect, namely, universal art transmitting even the most trifling and simple feelings if only they are accessible to all men without exception, and therefore unite them. Such art cannot but be esteemed good in our time, for it attains the end which Christianity the religious perception of our time, sets before humanity.

Christian art either evokes in men feelings which through love of God and of one's neighbor draw them to closer and ever closer union and make them ready for, and capable of, such union; or evokes in them feelings which show them that they are already united in the joys and sorrows of life. And therefore the Christian art of our time can be and is of two kinds: first, art transmitting feelings flowing from a religious perception of man's position in the world in relation to God and to his neighbor — religious art in the limited meaning of the term; and secondly, art transmitting the simplest feelings of common life, but such always as are accessible to all men in the whole world — the art of common life — the art of the people — universal art. Only these two kinds of art can be considered good art in our time.

The first, religious art — transmitting both positive feelings of love of God and one's neighbor, and negative feelings of indignation and horror at the violation of love — manifests itself chiefly in the form of words, and to some extent also in painting and sculpture: the second kind, universal art, transmitting feelings accessible to all, manifests itself in words, in painting, in sculpture, in dances, in architecture, and most of all in music.

If I were asked to give modern examples of each of these kinds of art, then as examples of the highest art flowing from love of God and man (both of the higher, positive, and of the lower, negative kind), in literature I should name *The Robbers* by Schiller; Victor Hugo's *Les Pauvres Gens* and *Les Misérables*; the novels and stories of Dickens — *The Tale of Two Cities, The Christmas Carol, The Chimes,* and others — *Uncle Tom's Cabin;* Dostoevsky's works — especially his *Memoirs from the House of Death* — and *Adam Bede* by George Eliot.

In modern painting, strange to say, works of

this kind, directly transmitting the Christian feeling of love of God and of one's neighbor, are hardly to be found, especially among the works of the celebrated painters. There are plenty of pictures treating of the Gospel stories; these however, while depicting historical events with great wealth of detail, do not and cannot transmit religious feelings not possessed by their painters. There are many pictures treating of the personal feelings of various people, but of pictures representing great deeds of self-sacrifice and Christian love there are very few, and what there are are principally by artists who are not celebrated, and they are for the most part not pictures but merely sketches. Such for instance is the drawing by Kramskoy (worth many of his finished pictures), showing a drawing-room with a balcony past which troops are marching in triumph on their return from the war. On the balcony stands a wet-nurse holding a baby, and a boy. They are admiring the procession of the troops, but the mother, covering her face with a handkerchief, has fallen back on the sofa sobbing. Such also is the picture by Walter Langley to which I have already referred, and such again is a picture by the French artist Morlon, depicting a lifeboat hastening in a heavy storm to the relief of a steamer that is being wrecked. Approaching these in kind are pictures which represent the hard-working peasant with respect and love. Such are the pictures by Millet and particularly his drawing, *The Man with the Hoe,* also pictures in this style by Jules Breton, Lhermitte, Defregger, and others. As examples of pictures evoking indignation and horror at the violation of love of God and man, Gay's picture *Judgment* may serve, and also Leizen-Mayer's *Signing the Death Warrant.* But there are very few of this kind also. Anxiety about the technique and the beauty of the picture for the most part obscures the feeling. For instance, Gérôme's *Pollice Verso* expresses, not so much horror at what is being perpetrated as attraction by the beauty of the spectacle.[4]

To give examples from the modern art of our

[4]In this picture the spectators in the Roman Amphitheater are turning down their thumbs to show that they wish the vanquished gladiator to be killed. [Tr.]

upper classes, of art of the second kind: good universal art, or even of the art of a whole people, is yet more difficult, especially in literature and music. If there are some works which by their inner contents might be assigned to this class (such as *Don Quixote,* Molière's comedies, *David Copperfield* and *The Pickwick Papers* by Dickens, Gogol's and Pushkin's tales, and some things of Maupassant's), these works for the most part — owing to the exceptional nature of the feelings they transmit, and the superfluity of special details of time and locality, and above all on account of the poverty of their subject matter in comparison with examples of universal ancient art (such, for instance, as the story of Joseph) — are comprehensible only to people of their own circle. That Joseph's brethren, being jealous of his father's affection, sell him to the merchants; that Potiphar's wife wishes to tempt the youth; that having attained to highest station he takes pity on his brothers, including Benjamin the favorite — these and all the rest are feelings accessible alike to a Russian peasant, a Chinese, an African, a child, or an old man, educated or uneducated; and it is all written with such restraint, is so free from any superfluous detail, that the story may be told to any circle and will be equally comprehensible and touching to everyone. But not such are the feelings of Don Quixote or of Molière's heroes (though Molière is perhaps the most universal, and therefore the most excellent, artist of modern times), nor of Pickwick and his friends. These feelings are not common to all men but very exceptional, and therefore to make them contagious the authors have surrounded them with abundant details of time and place. And this abundance of detail makes the stories difficult of comprehension to all who do not live within reach of the conditions described by the author.

The author of the novel of Joseph did not need to describe in detail, as would be done nowadays, the blood-stained coat of Joseph, the dwelling and dress of Jacob, the pose and attire of Potiphar's wife, and how adjusting the bracelet on her left arm she said, "Come to me," and so on, because the content of feeling in this novel is so strong that all details except the most essential — such as that Joseph went out into another room to weep — are superfluous and would only hinder the transmission of emotion. And therefore this novel is accessible to all men, touches people of all nations and classes young and old, and has lasted to our times and will yet last for thousands of years to come. But strip the best novels of our time of their details and what will remain?

It is therefore impossible in modern literature to indicate works fully satisfying the demands of universality. Such works as exist are to a great extent spoilt by what is usually called "realism," but would be better termed "provincialism," in art.

In music the same occurs as in verbal art, and for similar reasons. In consequence of the poorness of the feeling they contain, the melodies of the modern composers are amazingly empty and insignificant. And to strengthen the impression produced by these empty melodies the new musicians pile complex modulations on each trivial melody, not only in their own national manner, but also in the way characteristic of their own exclusive circle and particular musical school. Melody — every melody — is free and may be understood of all men; but as soon as it is bound up with a particular harmony, it ceases to be accessible except to people trained to such harmony, and it becomes strange, not only to common men of another nationality, but to all who do not belong to the circle whose members have accustomed themselves to certain forms of harmonization. So that music, like poetry, travels in a vicious circle. Trivial and exclusive melodies, in order to make them attractive, are laden with harmonic, rhythmic, and orchestral complications and thus become yet more exclusive, and far from being universal are not even national, that is, they are not comprehensible to the whole people, but only to some people.

In music, besides marches and dances by various composers which satisfy the demands of universal art, one can indicate very few works of this class: Bach's famous violin *aria*, Chopin's nocturne in E flat major, and perhaps a dozen bits (not whole pieces, but parts) selected from the works of Haydn, Mozart, Schubert, Beethoven, and Chopin.[5]

[5]While offering as examples of art those that seem to me

Although in painting the same thing is repeated as in poetry and in music — namely, that in order to make them more interesting, works weak in conception are surrounded by minutely studied accessories of time and place which give them a temporary and local interest but make them less universal — still in painting more than in other spheres of art may be found works satisfying the demands of universal Christian art; that is to say, there are more works expressing feelings in which all men may participate.

In the arts of painting and sculpture, all pictures and statues in so-called genre style, representations of animals, landscapes, and caricatures with subjects comprehensible to every one, and also all kinds of ornaments, are universal in subject matter. Such productions in painting and sculpture are very numerous (for instance, china dolls), but for the most part such objects (for instance, ornaments of all kinds) are either not considered to be art or are considered to be art of low quality. In reality all such objects if only they transmit a true feeling experienced by the artist and comprehensible to every one (however insignificant it may seem to us to be), are works of real, good, Christian, art.

I fear it will here be urged against me that having denied that the conception of beauty can supply a standard for works of art, I contradict myself by acknowledging ornaments to be works of good art. The reproach is unjust, for the subject matter of all kinds of ornamentation consists not in the beauty but in the feeling (of admiration at, and delight in, the combination of lines and colors) which the artist has experienced and with

best, I attach no special importance to my selection: for, besides being insufficiently informed in all branches of art, I belong to the class of people whose taste has been perverted by false training. And therefore my old, inured habits may cause me to err, and I may mistake for absolute merit the impression a work produced upon me in my youth. My only purpose in mentioning examples of works of this or that class is to make my meaning clearer and to show how, with my present views, I understand excellence in art in relation to its subject matter. I must moreover mention that I consign my own artistic productions to the category of bad art, excepting the story *God Sees the Truth but Waits*, which seeks a place in the first class, and *A Prisoner of the Caucasus*, which belongs to the second. [Au.]

which he infects the spectator. Art remains what it was and what it must be: nothing but the infection by one man of another or of others with the feelings experienced by the artist. Among these feelings is the feeling of delight at what pleases the sight. Objects pleasing the sight may be such as please a small or a large number of people, or such as please all men — and ornaments for the most part are of the latter kind. A landscape representing a very unusual view, or a genre picture of a special subject, may not please every one, but ornaments, from Yakútsk ornaments to Greek ones, are intelligible to every one and evoke a similar feeling of admiration in all, and therefore this despised kind of art should in Christian society be esteemed far above exceptional, pretentious, pictures and sculptures.

So that in relation to feelings conveyed, there are only two kinds of good Christian art, all the rest of art not comprised in these two divisions should be acknowledged to be bad art, deserving not to be encouraged but to be driven out, denied, and despised, as being art not uniting but dividing people. Such in literary art are all novels and poems which transmit ecclesiastical or patriotic feelings, and also exclusive feelings pertaining only to the class of the idle rich: such as aristocratic honor, satiety, spleen, pessimism, and refined and vicious feelings flowing from sex-love — quite incomprehensible to the great majority of mankind.

In painting we must similarly place in the class of bad art all ecclesiastical, patriotic, and exclusive pictures; all pictures representing the amusements and allurements of a rich and idle life; all so-called symbolic pictures in which the very meaning of the symbol is comprehensible only to those of a certain circle; and above all pictures with voluptuous subjects — all that odious female nudity which fills all the exhibitions and galleries. And to this class belongs almost all the chamber and opera music of our times — beginning especially with Beethoven (Schumann, Berlioz, Liszt, Wagner) — by its subject matter devoted to the expression of feelings accessible only to people who have developed in themselves an unhealthy nervous irritation evoked by this exclusive, artificial, and complex music.

"What! the *Ninth Symphony* not a good work of art!" I hear exclaimed by indignant voices.

And I reply: Most certainly it is not. All that I have written I have written with the sole purpose of finding a clear and reasonable criterion by which to judge the merits of works of art. And this criterion, coinciding with the indications of plain and sane sense, indubitably shows me that that symphony of Beethoven's is not a good work of art. Of course to people educated in the worship of certain productions and of their authors, to people whose taste has been perverted just by being educated in such a worship, the acknowledgment that such a celebrated work is bad, is amazing and strange. But how are we to escape the indications of reason and common sense?

Beethoven's *Ninth Symphony* is considered a great work of art. To verify its claim to be such I must first ask myself whether this work transmits the highest religious feeling? I reply in the negative, since music in itself cannot transmit those feelings; and therefore I ask myself next: Since this work does not belong to the highest kind of religious art, has it the other characteristic of the good art of our time — the quality of uniting all men in one common feeling — does it rank as Christian universal art? And again I have no option but to reply in the negative; for not only do I not see how the feelings transmitted by this work could unite people not specially trained to submit themselves to its complex hypnotism, but I am unable to imagine to myself a crowd of normal people who could understand anything of this long, confused, and artificial production, except short snatches which are lost in a sea of what is incomprehensible. And therefore, whether I like it or not, I am compelled to conclude that this work belongs to the rank of bad art. It is curious to note in this connexion, that attached to the end of this very symphony is a poem of Schiller's[6] which (though somewhat obscurely) expresses this very thought, namely that feeling (Schiller speaks only of the feeling of gladness) unites people and evokes love in them. But though this poem is sung at the end

---

[6]The "Ode to Joy." [Ed.]

of the symphony, the music does not accord with the thought expressed in the verses; for the music is exclusive and does not unite all men, but unites only a few, dividing them off from the rest of mankind.

And just in this same way, in all branches of art, many and many works considered great by the upper classes of our society will have to be judged. By this one sure criterion we shall have to judge the celebrated *Divine Comedy* and *Jerusalem Delivered*; and a great part of Shakespeare's and Goethe's work, and in painting every representation of miracles, including Raphael's *Transfiguration,* etc.

Whatever the work may be and however it may have been extolled, we have first to ask whether this work is one of real art, or a counterfeit. Having acknowledged, on the basis of the indication of its infectiousness even to a small class of people, that a certain production belongs to the realm of art, it is necessary on this basis to decide the next question. Does this work belong to the category of bad exclusive art opposed to religious perception, or of Christian art uniting people? And having acknowledged a work to belong to real Christian art, we must then, according to whether it transmits feelings flowing from love of God and man, or merely the simple feelings uniting all men, assign it a place in the ranks of religious art, or in those of universal art.

Only on the basis of such verification shall we find it possible to select from the whole mass of what in our society claims to be art, those works which form real, important, necessary, spiritual food, and to separate them from all the harmful and useless art and from the counterfeits of art which surround us. Only on the basis of such verification shall we be able to rid ourselves of the pernicious results of harmful art and avail ourselves of that beneficent action which is the purpose of true and good art, and which is indispensable for the spiritual life of man and of humanity.

# Benedetto Croce

## 1866–1952

Benedetto Croce, for decades Italy's symbol of intellect and conscience, was born in the Abruzzi hills, the elder son of an ancient and wealthy Neapolitan family. He was educated in private boarding schools in Naples, where he became a fervid reader of fiction and a dilettante of literary journalism. At seventeen, on vacation on the island of Ischia, his parents and sister were killed in an earthquake, and Croce himself was dug out after spending half a day buried by debris. His appointed guardians placed him at the University of Rome, but Croce, scarred internally as well as externally, dropped out without taking a degree. He worked his way out of his severe depression through his interest in Neapolitan culture and folklore.

Around 1892, he came under the influence of Antonio Labriola, professor of ethics at Rome, and despite qualms about the impracticality of a career devoted to mere learning, Croce pursued the study of philosophy for the rest of his life. In 1895, influenced by Labriola, he began a Marxist phase and connected himself with European socialist movements; but in the course of his investigation of Marx and his intellectual roots, Croce developed a critique of Marxism (1900) that cured him of his commitment. Although he was initially trained in positivism, the predominant doctrine at the time of his education, and found German philosophy ridiculously abstract, Croce was drawn to Hegelian idealism. In 1902 he published the *Aesthetic,* which remains his most significant production and was the foundation of his later works on logic, ethics, and history. As a result of his major writings in the first decade of this century, Croce was made a senator of the Italian kingdom for life.

Despite his Germanic style of philosophy, Croce was a patriot during World War I. After the war, he served briefly as minister of education (1920–21), but was frustrated by the failure of the assembly to pass the educational reforms he sponsored. With the rise of Mussolini in 1922, Croce left government but had the satisfaction of seeing his reforms pushed through by his successor and friend, Giovanni Gentile. Initially no enemy of Mussolini, Croce soon became disenchanted, and in 1925 published an "anti-Fascist manifesto" that was a standing embarrassment to the government. His home was raided by gangs, and he sent his family to Capri to avoid harassment in Naples. But Croce himself was too famous internationally to be silenced: For the next eighteen years, he was banned from public mention, but his works were allowed to appear. At the collapse of Mussolini's government in 1943, Croce became the leader of the Liberal Party and the principal spokesman in the assembly of southern (i.e., Allied-held) Italy. He was one of the main architects of the postwar Italian constitution but refused offers to become head of the government or president of the Republic. After World War II, Croce again became minister of education briefly before returning to private life as a professor of history and philosophy. A severe stroke in 1950 slowed his apparently inexhaustible production of publications, but he continued to read and to dictate his essays until his death in 1952.

Croce is usually termed a neo-idealist. His aesthetic derives essentially from Hegel, although it corrects Hegel's tendency to view art as a declining spiritual field that will be replaced by transcendental philosophy. But Hegel's notion that art furnishes "the sensuous semblance of the idea" is not far removed from Croce's concept of the "lyrical intuition." For Croce, art is a form of knowledge; and while reason gives us knowledge of the universal, our intuition gives us knowledge of the particular. Works of art are "lyrical" or "pure" intuitions because they are immaterial. Unlike the intuition that gives us knowledge of the phenomenal world, they are entirely constructed by the mind, rather than adapted by the mind from matter. They are also pure because they are ideal, untainted by contingency.

Croce essentially identifies intuition with expression: One is a complex of feeling and thought, while the other is the image that derives from it; but for Croce they are the interior and exterior views of the same thing. Logically, one cannot have an intuition without a corresponding expression: It would be as if someone said he had a poem inside him he could not write. He can say so, but others are entitled to doubt whether the poem is really there. The reason we may think we have intuitions we cannot express is that most of our intuitions (like our memories) are vague and cloudy; when we come to actualize them we realize this and put the fault down to poor technique. What differentiates artists from the rest of us is that artists' intuitions are clearer than ours, and become clearer still in the process of expression.

Given Croce's idealism, the act of communication is relatively insignificant. If the intuition/expression exists in the artist's mind, then the work of art exists; its actualization as matter, as words on paper or paint on canvas, is a comparatively trivial issue, one that, for Croce, has nothing to do with aesthetics. In Croce's aesthetic the poem comes into existence when the poet silently recites its words, the painting when the artist has fully visualized it, the song when the composer has heard its melody in his or her head. Communication is crucial, of course, to the appreciation of the work of art by anyone other than the artist. And here technique becomes important. For the audience, the process works backward: We move from the actualization to the expression until we have apprehended the lyrical intuition with which the artist began.

It is important to recall that these three steps are presented in a *logical*, but not necessarily a *temporal* order. Croce is not under the illusion that a work comes into being full blown in the artist's head and only then is transferred to some material form. Poets have their drafts and painters their sketches, and Croce is well aware that artists constantly refine and reshape their work, that they move, in his terms, from the act of expression to that of communication and back again.

One consequence of Croce's theory is that the beauty of nature, that of human beings as well as landscapes, becomes difficult to explain unless one is willing (as Croce is not) to posit a divine creator given to actualizing lyrical intuitions. For

Croce the sense of natural beauty is not prior to but rather derivative of the sense of art. This may not seem historically likely.

As a pure complex of thought and feeling, Croce's lyrical intuition is insusceptible to categorizing of any sort. Therefore, genre distinctions such as those between comedy and tragedy, or lyric, epic, and drama are for Croce purely accidental, since they depend on the material form chosen for the actualization of the intuition. As categories, they may help rational creatures like librarians and may be useful in criticism, but in terms of the *aesthetic* question of our immediate experience of art, they are meaningless.

Even more obviously, art is not any of the rational sciences: philosophy, history, natural science, or rhetoric. Hegel may have felt that it was the destiny of literature to be superseded by philosophy, just as Pythagoras felt that music would become mathematics, but for the post-Hegelian Croce, the pursuit of the universal and the pursuit of "unreflective intuition" are entirely different aims.

It may be less clear why, in Croce's view, art has nothing to do with the "play of the imagination" or provocation of "pleasure" or "immediacy of feeling." Here one must tread warily. The imagination is indeed the faculty that produces lyrical intuitions, but the faculty in art is not at play, as it is in a daydream, but is operating according to a disciplined framework. Pleasure is a by-product of art but not its essential function. And while feeling is surely one of the essential components of the lyrical intuition, the emotions of art operate at second hand: They are contemplated rather than experienced directly.

Croce's mode of criticism follows from his premise that works of art are the unique mental products of an individual artist. The critic should merely assist the audience in seeing the integrity and clarity of the individual work of art. As Croce says, "there is really no other way than to follow out the individualizing method to the very end: to treat works of art not in relation to social history but as being each one a world in itself, each one, in its hour, receiving the inflow of the whole of history, transfigured and elevated by the power of fancy into the individuality of the work of art which is a creation, not a reflection, and a monument, not a document." In his critical practice, Croce tends to indicate in a broadly humanistic tradition the lines of force and of feeling that inform a given work. He is impressionistic in the best sense. The critic in the Anglo-American tradition who took Croce most seriously was A. C. Bradley, whose *Shakespearean Tragedy* (1904) remains very readable and helpful today.

### Selected Bibliography

Brown, M. E. *Neo-Idealist Aesthetics: Croce — Gentile — Collingwood.* Detroit: Wayne State University Press, 1966.
Carr, H. Wildon. *The Philosophy of Benedetto Croce: The Problem of Art and History.* London: Macmillan, 1917.
D'Angelo, Paolo. *L'estetica di Benedetto Croce.* Rome: Laterza, 1982.
De Gennaro, Angelo. *The Philosophy of Benedetto Croce: An Introduction.* New York: Philosophical Library, 1961.

Orsini, Gian Napoleone Giordano. *Benedetto Croce: Philosopher of Art and Literary Critic*. Carbondale: Southern Illinois University Press, 1961.

Palmer, L. M., and H. S. Harris, eds. *Thought, Action, and Intuition as a Symposium on the Philosophy of Benedetto Croce*. Hildesheim and New York: G. Olms, 1975.

Sprigge, Cecil. *Benedetto Croce: Man and Thinker*. New Haven: Yale University Press, 1952.

Wasiolek, Edward. "Croce and Contextualist Criticism." *Modern Philology* 57 (1959): 44–54.

Wellek, René. *Four Critics: Croce, Valery, Lukács, and Ingarden*. Seattle: University of Washington Press, 1981.

# From *Aesthetica in Nuce*[1]

## WHEREIN CONSISTS ART OR POETRY

If one examines some poetical work with the intent of arriving at what it is that makes us describe it as poetical, two elements are immediately recognized as being constant and necessary in a poem: a complex of images, and a feeling which inspires this. Let us recall, for example, a passage of Virgil's Aeneid which we will have learned by heart at school (III. 294 . . .). Aeneas recounts how on learning that the ruler of the place where he had landed was the Trojan Helenus with Andromache as his consort, he in his wonder and surprise became inflamed with a strong desire to see that surviving son of Priam and to learn of the mighty events that had overtaken him. He meets Andromache outside the city walls, near the waters of a stream renamed Simoens, celebrating funeral rites before the green turf of an empty grave, and two altars placed there in honor of Hector and Astyanax. She is astounded at the sight of him, stumbles, and in broken words asks him if he be a living man or a shade; and not less shaken is the questioner Aeneas than she, in her grief and abashment, as she recalls how she survived battle and outrage, was cast for by lot and assigned as slave and concubine to Pyrrhus, then rejected by Pyrrhus and allotted by him to be the slave bride of the slave Helenus, after which Pyrrhus was slain by the hand of Orestes and Helenus, liberated, became king. Then Aeneas with his men enters the city and is welcomed by the son of Priam in that little Troy, that miniature Pergamus, built in the likeness of the great one, beside a new Xanthus; and there Aeneas kisses the lintel of a new Scaean gate. All these, and further episodes here omitted, are images of persons, things, attitudes, gestures, sayings, mere images which are nowise offered as history, historical judgment, nor are taken or considered as such. But through them all runs a feeling which is ours as much as that of the poet, a human feeling of poignant memories, shuddering horror, melancholy, homesickness, tender-heartedness, indeed of something both puerile and pious which transpires in that pointless reconstruction of things lost, those toys of religious piety, the *parva Troia, Pergama simulata magnis, arens Xanti cognomine rivus*:[2] something not to be expressed in logical terms, but which poetry, and poetry alone, can, in its own way, fully recount. Here then, in the first and abstract analysis are two elements, but they are not to be thought of as two strands, not even as two closely interwoven

Translated by Cecil Sprigge.

[1] I borrow this title which Hamann once used for an Essay. The present piece was written as the article on *Aesthetics* in the *Encyclopaedia Britannica*, 14th ed. [Au.] The title means "Aesthetics in a Nutshell." [Ed.]

[2] A little Troy, a Pergamus / that mimes the great one, and a dried-up stream / that takes its name from Xanthus. [Ed.]

strands, because in effect the feeling has been wholly converted into images, the complex of images which we have recalled; it is a feeling which has been contemplated and therewith resolved and surpassed. Poetry, then, is neither feeling, nor image, nor the sum of these two, but is "contemplation of feeling," "lyrical intuition," or, what comes to the same, "pure intuition," pure, that is to say, of any historical or critical assessment of the reality or unreality of the images entering into the fabric, pure palpitation of life as ideal quality. Doubtless in poetry other things can be found besides these two elements or moments and their synthesis, but such other things are either intermingled but extraneous elements, (reflections, exhortations, controversies, allegories etc.), or else they are just these very feelings and images, or feeling-images, released from the link which connected them, taken materially, reconstituted as they were previously to the poetic creation. In the first eventuality they are nonpoetic elements which have simply been introduced and superadded, in the second they are elements which have been unpoeticized by an unpoetic or no longer poetic reader who has caused the poetry to evaporate, either because he could not abide in poetry's ideal sphere, or because he was engaged upon the legitimate business of historical investigation, or else upon some other practical concerns for the purpose of which poetry is reduced to, or rather employed as, a document or instrument.

What has here been said of "poetry" can be said equally of all the other "arts" as customarily enumerated, painting, sculpture, architecture, music. Whenever the question is that of the eligibility of some spiritual production to be considered as art, the dilemma will arise: either this is a lyrical intuition, or else it is something else, maybe very respectable, but not art. If, as some theorists have had it, the art of painting is an imitation or reproduction of objects, data, then it would be not art but something mechanical and practical. If, following other theories, the painter's task were to blend lines and lights and colors with a zealous pursuit of novelty of effect, then he would be not an artist but a technical inventor. If music consisted similarly in combinations of

tones, then Leibniz's and Father Kircher's paradox could be put into effect (the composition of musical scores by the unmusical), and the fears expressed by Proudhon in regard to poetry and by Stuart Mill in regard to music, lest, the totality of possible combinations of words or notes having been exhausted, the poetical and the musical should lose their place in the world, would have a basis. Undoubtedly, both in poetry and in these other arts, extraneous elements obtain an entrance, whether *a parte objecti* or *a parte subjecti,* whether, that is, in faulty execution or in the aesthetically defective appreciation of works by those who view them or hear them; whence it comes that the critics of those arts advise us to rule out or give no heed to what they call the "literary" elements in painting, sculpture, and music, and the critic of poetry demands our attention for the "poetry" and frowns upon the allurements of mere literature. Now he who has an understanding for poetry makes straight for the poetical heart of the poem, and feels its rhythm vibrate in his own heart, or else, if he fails to hear such a heartbeat, he denies the presence of poetry, no matter how much else that is admirable for skill and wit, for nobility of intention, quickness of intelligence, agreeableness of effects, may be found standing in the work in its stead. He who has no understanding of poetry follows the lure of these things, and his error is not that he admires them, but that he admires them as poetry.

## THE DISTINCTION OF ART FROM NON-ART

Defined as lyrical or pure intuition, art is implicitly distinguished from all the other forms of spiritual production. The distinctions in question are made explicit in the following negations:

1. Art is not philosophy. For philosophy is the logical understanding of the universal categories of being, but art is the unreflective intuition of being. Philosophy surpasses and resolves the image, while art abides within the sphere of image and has here its reign. But art, it will be said, may not behave irrationally nor disregard

logic. Quite right; art is neither irrational nor illogical; yet the reason and logic of art are quite other than dialectical or conceptual reason and logic. It was to draw attention to this peculiarity and originality that the names "Logica Sensitiva" and "Aesthetica" were coined. As often as a "logical" character is claimed for art, there is either a play on words confounding the conceptual with the aesthetic logic, or a use of the former to symbolize the latter.

2. Art is not history. History must critically distinguish between reality and unreality, between factual reality and imagined reality, between the reality of action and that of desire. But art does not reach to such distinctions, remaining, as we said, in the sphere of pure image. Whether Helenus, Andromache, Aeneas had historical existence is of no significance for the poetic quality of the Aeneid. However, the historical criterion, it has been objected, is not extraneous to art, seeing that art observes the law of verisimilitude. We answer that this last word is here no better than a metaphor enlisted, rather clumsily, to denote the coherency of images with one another. For if the images were not thus coherent, they could not exert their power as images (any more than the *delphinus in silvis* and the *aper in fluctibus*[3] of Horace), unless perhaps as a quaint eccentricity of the imagination.

3. Art is not natural science, nor is it mathematics. For natural science is an abstracting classification exerted upon historical reality, while mathematics is an operation with abstractions, not a contemplation. If a likeness has sometimes been traced between the works of mathematicians and of poets, this rests merely upon an outward and generic analogy, while the mathematic or geometric element sometimes alleged to be harbored in the inner essence of the arts is an unconscious metaphor for the constructive, cohesive, unifying power of the poetic spirit as it fashions for itself a body of images.

4. Art is not the play of the imagination, passing on from image to image under the spur of desire for variety, relaxation, distraction, or for entertainment by the interesting appearances of things agreeable, moving, or pathetic. In art, the imagination is disciplined by the single task of converting tumultuous feeling into clear intuition. Indeed there have been various proposals to abandon here the word "imagination" in favor of (poetic or creative) "fancy." For imagination is in itself alien to poetry: witness the unpoetical character of the works of Anne Radcliffe or Dumas *père*.[4]

5. Art is not immediacy of feeling. Andromache at the sight of Aeneas becomes *amens — diriguit visu in medio — labitur — longo vix tandem tempore fatur*. As she speaks, *longos ciebat incassum fletus*. But it is not the poet who thus raves, gazes fixedly, stumbles, struggles to utter hard-found words, breaks into long lament. The poet, having made of these commotions the argument of his poem, utters harmonious verses. Doubtless the feelings in their immediacy are, as it is commonly said, "expressed." If they were not expressed, if they were not (besides all else) sensible and bodily facts or, as the positivists and the neo-critical school used to say, "psychophysical phenomena," they would not be concrete things, would not exist. Andromache, after all, expressed herself in the manner described. But such "expression," albeit conscious, can rank as expression only by metaphorical license, when compared with the spiritual or aesthetic expression which alone truly expresses, that is to say gives to the feeling a theoretical form and converts it into language, song, shape. It is in the difference between feeling as contemplated (poetry, in fact), and feeling as enacted or undergone, that lies the catharsis, the liberation from the affections, the calming property which has been attributed to art; and to this corresponds the aesthetic condemnation of works of art if or insofar as immediate feeling breaks into them or uses them as an outlet. The same difference accounts for that other character (once again,

---

[3] A dolphin in a forest-picture and the wild boar in a sea-piece. Horace, *Art of Poetry*, 30; see p. 68. [Ed.]

[4] Ann Radcliffe (1764–1823) wrote Gothic novels of which the most famous is *The Mysteries of Udolpho*; Alexandre Dumas the elder (1802–70) wrote adventure stories, including *The Three Musketeers* and *The Count of Monte Cristo*. [Ed.]

properly speaking, synonymous with poetic expressiveness), the "infinity" of art which differentiates it from feeling or immediate passion which are finite, and this is also described as the "universal" or "cosmic" character of poetry. For when feeling, instead of entering in its travail into the living of life, is held in contemplation, it becomes thereby diffused far and wide through the domain of the soul, the domain of the world. And infinite then are its resonances: joy and grief, pleasure and pain, effort and relaxation, gravity and lightness, and all the rest, find in it their link each with the other, and pass by delicate shades each into the other, so that each feeling, though keeping its individual features, its original and dominant motive, yet eludes restriction or exhaustion in this. An image of comedy, if the comedy be poetic, has about it something that is not comic, as we see with Don Quixote or Falstaff, while an image of dreadfulness is never, in poetry, lacking in some comforting elevation, some goodness and love.

6. Art is not didactic and rhetorical, for these words betoken the art which has been overtaken and subdued and limited by a practical purpose, whatever that may be — whether, didactically, to implant in minds a certain philosophic, historical, or scientific truth, or, rhetorically, to sway minds to feel and by consequence to act in a certain particular manner. In oratory, expression loses its "infinity" and independence, and becoming the means to an end, is dissolved into that end. That is how Schiller is led to speak of the "non-determinant" character of art by contrast with the office of oratory which is to "determine" or to "move." Here we have an explanation of the quite proper distrust which is felt for "political poetry," sometimes described as necessarily bad poetry, though this is true only if it fails to rise above the "political" level to a poetic serenity and humanity.

7. If art is not to be confounded with that form of practical action which seems nearest to it, the didactic and rhetorical, still less is it to be confounded with other forms of action designed to produce certain effects of pleasure, sensual delight, or convenience, or for that matter of virtuousness or pious uplift. It behoves art to exclude the meretricious, but also the well-intentioned, as being both, in their different ways, unaesthetic and indigestible for the poetic mind. Flaubert remarked that obscene books are deficient in *vérité*,[5] but Voltaire used his wit upon certain *Poésies sacrées,* so called because *"personne n'y touche."*[6]

## ART IN ITS RELATIONS

The foregoing explicitly formulated "negations" are, as it will be easily understood, equally well formulated as "relations," it being impossible to conceive of the various and distinct forms of spiritual activity as separate, operating in isolation, providing each one solely for itself. There is no call for us to develop here a complete systematic exposition of the forms or spiritual categories in their order and dialectic. But limiting our remarks to art, we will simply say that the category of art, like any other, implies, and is implied by, conditions, and is conditioned by all the others in their turn. How could the aesthetic synthesis of poetry take place without a precedent disturbance of the mind? (*Si vis me flere dolendum est:*[7] et cetera.) And that precedent state of mind which we have called feeling, what else is it if not the spirit which has thought, willed, acted, and which thinks, desires, suffers, rejoices, labors within itself? Poetry is as a ray of sunshine clothing that mist with its light, outlining the hidden features of things. For that reason, it is no task for empty spirits, closed minds; and those artists who in their mistaken devotion to pure art, art for art's sake, shut out the stir of life and the throes of thought, turn out to be altogether unproductive of anything more than imitations or incoherent impressionism.

The foundation of all poetry is therefore the human personality, and since the human personality fulfils itself morally, the foundation of all poetry is the moral conscience. This does not mean that the artist requires to be a deep thinker and an acute critic, nor that he must be a moral

[5]Truth. [Ed.]

[6]*Sacred Poetry,* so called because "nobody touches it." [Ed.]

[7]"If you wish me to weep you must grieve yourself." Croce quotes from Horace's *Art of Poetry;* see p. 69. [Ed.]

paragon or hero. It means that he must be sufficiently a participant in the world of thought and of action, by way either of personal experience or of sympathy with the experience of others, to live the human drama in its fullness. As a practical man he may err, he may stain his purity and incur blame. But he must needs have alive in him, in some form or other, the sentiment of purity and impurity, righteousness and guilt, good and evil. He may not be endowed with marked courage as a man of action, he may even show himself wavering and timid, but he must at any rate be sensitive to the dignity of courage. Many artistic inspirations spring not from the artist's practical personality but from his feeling for what he is not but ought to be, what he admires when he sees it, and would fain be himself. Many, and those perhaps the finest, of the pages of heroic and warlike poetry, are the work of authors who could never have learned to wield an arm.

By this we do not mean that a moral personality is sufficient equipment for the poet and artist. To be *vir bonus*[8] is not sufficient equipment even for oratory: the orator must be also *dicendi peritus*.[9] There can be no poetry without the poetic art, that form of theoretical synthesis which was defined above, the gift without which all the rest is no more than a pile of logs which cannot be set aflame for want of a torch. And yet the figure of the pure poet, pure artist, cultivator of pure beauty, untouched by human concerns, is not a figure but a caricature.

What demonstrates that poetry both implies and is implied by the other forms of the spirit, both conditions and is conditioned by them, is the fact that logical thought cannot subsist without the help of the poetic fancy in giving a contemplative form to the travail of the feelings, an intuitive expression to dim impressions, itself becoming representation and language (a language of which the words may be speech, song, color, or some other medium). Logical thought is not itself language, but is never without language, of which language it is poetry that has been the creator. Logical thought by the use of

concepts sorts out the representations of poetry, dominates them, which would be impossible were they not already there as its potential subjects. Likewise, save for the critical discernments of thought there could be no action, nor consequently any goodness of action, as conscience and duty. No man, however seemingly absorbed in logical and critical and scientific study, or in practical interests, or the fulfillment of duty, lacks his little fund of fancy and poetry deep in his heart. Even the pedant Wagner, *famulus*[10] to Faust, confessed that he too often went through *grillenhafte Stunden*.[11] Indeed without such a fund one would not be a man, a thinking and acting agent, at all. But, disregarding such an extreme and therefore absurd hypothesis, it suffices to say that where the fund is scanty, there is proportionate superficiality and aridity in thought, and proportionate coldness in action.

## THE AESTHETIC SCIENCE, OR SCIENCE OF ART, AND ITS PHILOSOPHICAL CHARACTER

The concept of Art expounded above is, in a way, the common concept, as it appears with more or less clarity in current discussion, serving as a point of reference, more or less explicit, in all such discussions, which perpetually gravitate back to it. It performs this service not only in our own times, but in all times, as a collection of the sayings of writers, poets, artists, laymen, and even of the common man, if properly interpreted, could easily show. In spite of this it is necessary to dispel any mistaken supposition that this concept Exists as an innate idea. It is not an innate idea, but it is an operative *a priori*. Such an *a priori* is not something in itself, but has its being solely in the single productions which it generates. Just as the *a priori* of Art, Poetry, Beauty has no existence as an idea to be perceived and admired in itself in some region beyond the skies, but is present solely in the numberless works of poetry, art, beauty which it has shapen and still shapes, so too, similarly, the logical *a priori* of Art is to be found nowhere

[8]A good man. [Ed.]

[9]Skilled at speaking. [Ed.]

[10]Assistant. [Ed.]

[11]Whimsical hours. [Ed.]

else than in the particular judgments which it has formed and forever forms, the confutations, demonstrations, theories wrought by it, the problems and groups of problems resolved. All the definitions, distinctions, negations, relations expounded above have their history, all have been elaborated in the course of the centuries, and have come to us as the product of that slow, varied, and laborious process. The Aesthetic Science, or Science of Art, has not for its task, then, as sometimes appears from the pages of educational handbooks, the fixation, once for all, of a definition of art, to be developed with a fully exhaustive wealth of attendant concepts, but has simply to provide a continuously renewed and improved systematization of the problems which from age to age arise out of men's ponderings on art. This is precisely equivalent to saying that the task is to resolve difficulties, to criticize errors, out of which errors there thus comes the stimulus and the material for a perpetual progress of thought.

From this it is evident that no exposition of Aesthetics, and least of all a summary exposition like the present, can pretend to treat exhaustively the infinite problems thrown up, or henceforth to be thrown up, in the history of Aesthetics. It can only recall and deal with certain ones, first and foremost those which even now persist stubbornly in the discussions of ordinary educated people. What is here said implies an "etcetera" printed at the conclusion, to send the reader on a continuance of the exploration on the lines suggested to him, whether he chooses to pore over the discussions of past times, or to attend to the more or less novel debates of the present, which almost every hour branch out and proliferate in aspects of fresh appearance.

Another observation will not be out of place. Aesthetics is indeed a particular philosophic discipline having for its origin a particular and distinct category of the spirit. But as a philosophical discipline it can never detach itself from the main stem of philosophy. For its problems are those of the relation between art and the other spiritual forms, problems of difference and of identity. It is, in reality, the whole of philosophy displayed with a more special emphasis on the side of art. The cry has often gone up for an Aesthetic which should be able to stand on its own, uninvolved

in any general philosophic conception, fitting in equally well with various general conceptions or with all: but this is a contradictory and therefore an impracticable demand. Those too who have proclaimed some nonphilosophical doctrine of aesthetics, whether naturalistic, inductive, physical, physiological, or psychological, when they began to put their program into execution, surreptitiously introduced a general philosophical conception, which might be positivism, naturalism, or even materialism. Whoever regards these as fallacious or outworn philosophies, can spare himself the trouble of confuting the aesthetic or pseudo-aesthetic doctrines built upon them (and in turn serving them as foundations). He will not regard the problems pertinent to them as being still open and calling for discussion, or anyway for close discussion. To take an example: if the doctrine of psychological association (which put mechanical workings in the place of the *a priori* synthesis) has spent its force, this brings with it not only the demise of logical associationism, but also that of aesthetic associationism with its association of "content" and "form" or of "two representations," which by contrast with what Campanella[12] called the *tactus intrinsecus* making its contact *cum magna suavitate,* stood for a *tactus extrinsecus* in which the terms, as soon as they had touched, *discedebant.* Similarly, with the obsolescence of biological and evolutionist explanations of logical and ethical values, the analogous derivation of aesthetic values fell to the ground. The demonstration that empirical methods cannot help toward an understanding of reality, brings with it that of the hopelessness of an attempt to build an Aesthetic on the classification of aesthetic data and the deduction of laws therefrom.

## INTUITION AND EXPRESSION

If we start with defining a work of art as a "lyrical image," the problem quickly presents itself: What is the relation of "intuition" to "expres-

[12]Tommaso Campanella (1568–1639), Italian philosopher, author of *De sensu rerum* (1620); the Latin phrases quoted may be translated as, respectively, "intrinsic touch"; "with great smoothness"; "extrinsic touch"; "dissolved." [Ed.]

sion," and what is the mode of passage from the one to the other. Substantially this is the same problem which makes an appearance, in other parts of philosophy, as that of the relation between inward and outward, spirit and matter, soul and body, or again, in the Philosophy of Practice, between intention and will, will and action, and so forth.

In such terms the problem is insoluble, for once inward is severed from outward, spirit from body, will from action, intuition from expression, there is no way of passing from the former terms to the latter save by reuniting them in a third term, which has sometimes been called God, sometimes the Unknowable. The dualism must needs lead either to a Transcendence or to Agnosticism. Now when problems prove insoluble in the terms in which they are propounded, the only course is to criticize the terms themselves, to look into how they have originated and into the logical justification of that origin. Our enquiry will lead to this conclusion: these terms have their origin not as derivations from a philosophic principle, but as the effect of an empirical and naturalistic classification which formed these two classes of inward and outward (disregarding the fact that the inward must always be also outward, while the outward is inconceivable without its inwardness), and similarly the classes of souls and bodies, images and expressions. But notoriously things which have been distinguished empirically and materially, and not philosophically, or formally, can never be brought together in a higher synthesis. The soul is the soul inasmuch as it is the body, the will is will inasmuch as it moves legs and arms, thus becoming action. Intuition is, in its very operation, expression. An image not expressed as word, song, line, coloring, sculpture, architecture — or at the very least as a word murmured, a song hummed to oneself, a line, a color viewed in fancy so as to give its tone to the whole soul, the organism — is a nonexistent image, of which the existence may indeed be asserted, but cannot be affirmed, since an affirmation would necessarily have to be supported by the demonstration that it was somehow embodied and expressed.

The penetrating philosophical doctrine of the identity of intuition and expression is, moreover, at one with ordinary common sense, which mocks at those who say they have thoughts but cannot express them, or claim to have conceived a great pictorial work of art which they cannot put on the canvas. *Rem tene verba sequentur:*[13] if the *verba* are lacking, the *res* too must be wanting.

The identity of which we are speaking is discoverable in all the spheres of the spirit, but is perhaps, in the sphere of art, specially conspicuous. To watch the creation of a work of art is to watch, as it were, the mystery of the creation of the world: hence the influence exerted by the aesthetic science upon philosophy as a whole, which it guides toward the conception of Unity-Totality. Aesthetics, when it rejects abstract spiritualism, and the dualism resulting from that abstraction, in the life of art, bases itself upon (but at the same time lays the basis for) idealism or absolute spiritualism.

## EXPRESSION AND COMMUNICATION

Such objections as are raised against the identification of intuition with expression usually arise out of a psychological illusion. It appears to us that we are perpetually in possession of a vast wealth of lively and concrete images, when all that we possess is but signs and names. Or they may arise from a faulty analysis of certain cases, as when it is thought that some artists achieve merely a fragmentary expression of a whole world of images which they possess in their soul, whereas in truth they have nothing more in their soul than just those fragments, accompanied not by the supposed world of images but at the most by an aspiration or confused effort to attain it, to attain, that is, a larger and grander image, in which they may or may not be successful.

But another origin for such objections lies in the confounding of expression with something which really is distinct from the image and its expression: with communication. Communication is the business of fixing the intuition-expression in an object which we will allow ourselves to call, metaphorically, material or physical, even though in reality we have to deal not with the material and physical but with a

[13]Hold onto the thing and the word will follow. [Ed.]

spiritual operation. We will take this liberty because the demonstration that the so-called physical is unreal, and has to be resolved into the spiritual, is of prime importance for philosophy as a whole, but touches only indirectly upon the elucidation of aesthetic problems. For brevity's sake, then, we will here use this metaphor or symbol of matter and nature.

The poem, we must see, is there already in its entirety when the poet has expressed it in words uttered to himself. When he goes on to raise his voice to utter it to others, or procures that others shall commit it to memory and chant it to each other as in a *schola cantorum*,[14] or shall record it in writing and printing, this is a new stage of great social and cultural importance having not an aesthetic but a practical character. Likewise with the painter, who paints upon canvas or upon wood, but could not paint at all, did not the intuited image, the line and color as they have taken shape in the fancy, precede, at every stage of the work, from the first stroke of the brush or sketch of the outline to the finishing touches, these manual actions. And when it happens that some stroke of the brush runs ahead of the image, then the artist, in his final revision, erases and corrects it.

It is, no doubt, very difficult to perceive the frontier between expression and communication in actual fact, for the two processes usually alternate rapidly and are almost intermingled. But the distinction is ideally clear and must be strongly maintained. Neglect of it, or wavering inattention, are at the origin of confusions between art and technics. The technical does not enter into art, but pertains to the concept of communication. By it, generally speaking, we signify a cognition or complex of cognitions suited and arranged for the uses of practical action, meaning, in the case of art, that practical action which constructs means and instruments for recording and communicating works of art: cognitions concerning the preparation of canvases, panels, wall surfaces, pigments, varnishes, or concerning the acquisition of good pronunciation or vocal delivery, and so on. Books on such technical cognitions are not books on Aesthetics and cannot constitute parts or sections of them, if the concepts are thought out in full consequentiality and the words properly used in correspondence with them. For we need not pause to argue about the mere word, when "technique" is used, for example, in the sense of "inner technique" and thus as a synonym for the work of the artist, the formation of the intuition-expression, or in the sense of "discipline," the indispensable continuity with the historical tradition from which no one may sever himself though no one may rest satisfied by simple attachment to it. The confounding of art and the technical, the substitution of the technical for the artistic, is a frequent recourse of impotent artists who hope by dint of the practical, that is of practical devices and inventions, to discover the strength and reliance which they cannot muster in themselves.

## ARTISTIC OBJECTS: THE THEORY OF THE PARTICULAR ARTS AND OF NATURAL BEAUTY

Thus, guided by technical skill, the work of communication, devoted to the preservation and publication of artistic images, produces the material objects which, metaphorically, we call "artistic" or "works of art": paintings, sculptures, buildings, and on a more complex level literary and musical scripts, and nowadays gramophones with their records, whereby it is possible to reproduce voices and sounds. But these voices and sounds, these pictorial, sculptural, architectural signs, are works of art which exist nowhere else than in the souls which create or recreate them.

The impression of a paradox in this truth as to the nonexistence of objects or things of beauty, may be lessened by recalling the analogous case of Economics. It is well known that there are no commodities which naturally and physically possess utility. There are needs, and there is labor, and the adjective "useful" is drawn from these and metaphorically applied, in economics, to physical things. An economist who sought to deduce the economic value of things from their

---

[14]Singing school. [Ed.]

physical qualities would commit a crude *ignoratio elenchi*.[15]

However crude, the fallacy has been committed, and in Aesthetics the error still flourishes as a doctrine of the particular arts and of their respective limits, that is, of the aesthetic character proper to each. The limits so set upon the arts are merely technical or physical, corresponding to the consistency of the artistic objects: sounds and tones, objects colored, carved, and sculptured, objects constructed without apparent reference to natural bodies (whence poetry, music, painting, sculpture, architecture, and so on). The question as to the artistic character of each of these arts, as to each one's potentiality and the confines of this, as to what sort of images can be expressed in sounds, what in tones, colors, lines, and so forth, is like a question put to the economist as to which physically constituted things should be priced and which should go unpriced, and what should be the ratio of the prices, whereas it is clear that physical constitution enters not into the matter at all, and that each thing may be wanted and sought and marked with the higher or the highest price according to needs and circumstances.

Having rashly ventured on this slippery surface, even the great Lessing was driven to such strange conclusions as that poetry is concerned with "actions" and sculpture with "bodies,"[16] and no less a man than Richard Wagner talked irresponsibly of an all-embracing art, the Opera, which would aggregate the potentialities of the single arts. But the artistically sensitive man will in a poet's single line discover the musical, the pictorial, the sculptural, the architectonic, and in a picture too he will find all this, for a picture is always of the soul, not merely of the eyes, and in the soul it is present not only as color but also as sound, as word, nay even as silence (which is in its way sound and word). When one seeks to grasp the musical, the picturesque, or whatever quality it may be, in isolation, they become elusive and shade into one another, merging in

unity. And thus, no matter how common be the current usage of those separate words, it becomes evident that there is one Art, and it is not divided into arts. Though one, it is infinitely various, but varying not with the technical concepts of the arts, but with the infinite variety of artistic personalities and their states of mind.

The problem of natural beauty arises with the confusion between artistic creations and the instruments of communication or "artistic things." Let us ignore the question raised by some theorists whether there be in nature other poetic and artistic beings besides men — it should in any case be answered in the affirmative, both out of due regard for the songbirds, and also, still more, in virtue of the idealist conception of the world as all life and spirituality, though we, as in the fairy story, have lost that blade of grass which, held in the mouth, gave the power of understanding the speech of beasts and plants. The real meaning of "natural beauty" is that certain persons, things, places are, by the effect which they exert upon one, comparable with poetry, painting, sculpture, and the other arts. And there is no difficulty about admitting these "natural artistic things," for the process of poetic communication can be conducted by means of naturally given objects as well as by means of artificially produced objects. It is the fancy of the lover that creates the woman who is for him beautiful, and personifies her in Laura.[17] It is the pilgrim's fancy that creates a sublime or enchanting landscape and fixes it in the scenery of a lake or mountain. These poetic creations are sometimes diffused throughout a more or less wide social circle, whence those female "professional beauties" admired by all, and the "views" at the sight of which everyone displays a more or a less sincere rapture. True, such formations are impermanent. Sometimes a witticism dispels the enchantment, or people get tired of them, or fashion changes capriciously. Unlike works of art, they are unsusceptible of authoritative interpretation. The Gulf of Naples, viewed from one of the finest villas on the Vomero, once acquired

---

[15]Logical fallacy. [Ed.]

[16]Gotthold Ephraim Lessing (1729–81), German dramatist and critic in his theoretical treatise *Laocöon* (1766). [Ed.]

[17]The subject of Petrarch's sonnets. [Ed.]

by a Russian lady, was described by that same lady after some years of inescapable familiarity with it, as *une cuvette bleue*.[18] She came so to hate that blueness rimmed with green, that she sold the villa. The image of the *cuvette bleue* was incidentally a poetic creation. We will not argue with it.

## LITERARY AND ARTISTIC GENRES AND AESTHETIC CATEGORIES

Broader and worse consequences in literary and artistic criticism and history have followed from a theory of different but analogous origin, the theory of the literary and artistic kinds or *genres*. Once again, a classification, in itself legitimate and useful, is made to serve as a foundation. The theory we have just been discussing was founded on the technical or physical assortment of artistic objects; that which we are now discussing is founded upon the classification of works of art, according to their content or sentimental motive, into tragic, comic, lyric, heroic, amorous, idyllic, romantic, and such divisions and subdivisions. There is indeed a practical utility, when preparing an edition of the works of a poet, in grouping the lyrical pieces in one volume, the dramas in a second, longer poems in a third, narratives in a fourth and so on, and it is positively unavoidable when talking and writing about those works to recall them, or groups of them, by such labels. Illegitimate, on the other hand, we must once again declare to be any inference from these classificatory expedients to the aesthetic laws of composition or the aesthetic criteria of judgment. We thereby rule out such arguments as those which infer from the classifications in question that a tragedy may or may not legitimately have such and such a theme, or set of characters, or mode of development, or scope — all those arguments which instead of seeking out and pronouncing upon the poetic essence of a work, inquire whether it is a tragedy or a poem, and whether it conforms to the "laws" of one or of another such "genre." Criterions of this latter sort held the criticism of the Renais-

[18]A blue washbasin. [Ed.]

sance and of the French classical age in a bondage (witness the disputes of those times about the *Commedia* of Dante, the poems of Ariosto and Tasso, the *Pastor Fido* of Guarini, the *Cid* of Corneille, the dramas of the Lope de Vega), liberation from which was largely accountable for the great advance of literary criticism in the nineteenth century. The decay of these mistaken criteria has not to the same extent profited the artists. Irrespectively of how they are viewed in theory, in practice the artistically gifted man experiences the chains of this bondage, and indeed forges them into an instrument of power, while the ungifted find means of converting their very freedom into a new sort of servitude.

Some have thought that, of these literary classifications, one series at least deserved to be retained and given philosophic rank, namely the differentiation of "lyric," "epic," and "dramatic" which they proposed to interpret as three moments in the process of objectivization; the outpouring of the *ego* in the lyric being followed by the detachment of feeling which the *ego* effects in epic narration, and, further on, by the *ego's* generation of its own mouthpieces, the *dramatis personae,* in drama. But the lyric is no such outpouring: it is not a cry or a wail but is precisely the objectivization whereby the *ego* contemplates, narrates, dramatizes itself for itself, and the lyrical spirit forms the poetry of the epic and the dramatic work, the three being distinguishable only by exterior characteristics. A wholly poetical work like *Macbeth* or *Antony and Cleopatra* is verily a lyric in which the characters and scenes constitute its various tones and consecutive strophes.

In the old-fashioned systems of Aesthetic, and in present-day works on the same model, much is made of the "categories of the beautiful," the sublime, the tragic, the comic, the pleasing, the humorous, and so on, which merely psychological and empirical concepts the philosophers, particularly the Germans, proceeded to treat as philosophical concepts. Indeed, they developed them by that dialectical method which is suitable to pure or speculative concepts and to those alone, tracing a fanciful course of development which culminated now in the Beautiful, now in the Tragic, now in the Humorous — an idle game. Let us instead take those concepts for what they have already been shown to be. We will then remark how they substantially correspond to the concepts or the literary and artistic genres, from which origin, indeed, principally through the agency of the treatises known as "Institutions in the Art of Letters," they found their way into philosophy. As psychological and empirical concepts they have no part in Aesthetics. Taken as a whole, they stand simply for the totality of the feelings which are the perpetual material of artistic intuition, arranged in empirical groups and assortments.

## RHETORIC, GRAMMAR, AND THE PHILOSOPHY OF LANGUAGE

Errors can always be shown to have sprung out of some aspect of truth, through the arbitrary combination of things which taken in themselves were legitimate. This will once again become evident when we proceed to examine certain other erroneous doctrines which have played an important part in the past and still play some part. In teaching the art of letters, it is perfectly legitimate to make use of differentiations between the simple and the figurative style, between direct and metaphorical, or different sorts of metaphorical utterance. It is perfectly legitimate to observe that in such a place plain utterance and in such another metaphorical utterance is suitable, that elsewhere a given metaphor is incoherent or overelaborate, and that here the figure of "preterition" is called for, there that of "hyperbole" or "irony." But the merely didactic and practical origin of these distinctions gets forgotten; there arises a philosophic theory of form as distinguishable into "plain" and "ornate," "logical" and "affective," or whatever it may be, whereby Rhetoric gets transported into the field of Aesthetic and the genuine concept of expression is vitiated. In reality, expression is never logical but always affective, lyrical, fanciful, and always (but one can equally say, never) metaphorical, and always proper. It is never plain so as to be in need of covering and never ornate so as to be in need of liberation from the extraneous, but is always *simplex munditiis,* bright with its own light. Logical thought, or science, too, in

expressing itself, becomes feeling and fancy, whence a work of philosophy, history, science, may be beautiful as well as true, and is in any case judged by aesthetic as well as logical standards; and sometimes a book is said to be erroneous as theory, criticism, or historical assertion, yet, by reason of the feeling which animates and is expressed by it, of value as a work of art. The ferment of truth which was at work in the distinction between logical and metaphorical form, between the dialectical and the rhetorical, was the need for constructing a science of Aesthetics alongside of the science of Logic. But it was a mistake to try and distinguish the two sciences in the field of expression, which belongs solely to one of them.

No less legitimately, in the sphere of linguistic instruction, the practice developed in antiquity of differentiating expressions as periods, propositions, and words, and words themselves as belonging to different classes, each of these being analyzed in their inflections and composition out of roots and suffixes, syllables and sounds or letters. Here is the origin of alphabets, grammars, and vocabularies, and analogously, of the metrical arts for the use of poetry, and of grammars of music and painting for music and the figurative and architectonic arts. Antiquity itself, however, failed to prevent an illicit transference *ab intellectu ad rem,*[19] one of those shifts from the level of abstractions and the empirical to reality and the philosophical, which we have observed in other cases. Thus it was that language came to be conceived as the aggregation of words, words as the aggregation of syllables, roots, suffixes: whereas it is the *continuum* of speech (one might say the organism) which is the *prius,*[20] and words, syllables, roots, are the anatomical lay-out, the product of the abstracting intellect, not the original and real fact of the matter, but a *posterius.* But when Grammar, like Rhetoric, had been introduced into the bosom of Aesthetics, then "expression" had to share the ground with the "means" of expression, and this was a mere duplication, because the means of expression are expression itself, dissected by the

[19]From mind to matter. [Ed.]
[20]Prior principle. [Ed.]

grammarians. From this error, and from the associated error as to "plain" form and "ornate" form, derives a mistaken view about the Philosophy of Language. For the Philosophy of Language is not, as is misleadingly suggested, a philosophical Grammar, but stands above grammar, nor can it give philosophical shape to the classifications of the grammarians, but on the contrary, when these get in the way, it eliminates them. It is all one with the Philosophy of poetry and art, the science of intuition-expression, or Aesthetics, and it embraces language in its whole scope, including phonic and articulate language in its integral reality as lively and complete expression.

## THE CLASSIC AND THE ROMANTIC

The problems which we have recalled belong rather to the past (a past of many centuries) than to the present. For those misjudged positions and faulty solutions survive nowadays rather as things mechanically repeated in school books than as opinions current in general discourse and culture. Yet from the old roots new shoots push forth ever and anon, and must be carefully pruned and excised, such as that theory of styles which is applied by Wölfflin and others in the history of art, and extended by Strich[21] and others to the history of poetry, a veritable new invasion of rhetorical abstractions in the field of aesthetic judgement and history.

But the principal contemporary problem which Aesthetics must take in hand is one which harks back to the crisis in art and art criticism which occurred in the romantic age. It is possible indeed to point to certain precedents and parallels in earlier ages, for instance to Hellenistic art, late Roman literature, and in more modern times the Baroque art and poetry which followed on those of the Renaissance. There was however a particular origination, a particular configuration and

[21]Heinrich Wölfflin (1864–1945), German aesthetician and art historian, author of *Principles of Art History* (1915); Fritz Strich (1882–1963), German/Swiss literary historian whose studies of the history of style in German literature in the period of Goethe and Schiller were written under the influence of Wölfflin's aesthetics.

grandiosity about the crisis of the romantic age with its contrapositions of naive poetry and sentimental poetry and of classical art and romantic art, dividing, by the use of these concepts, the one and only Art into two inwardly diverse arts, and taking sides with the latter term as that which in consonance with modern times upheld the primacy, in art, of sentiment, passion, imagination. This, on one side, was a well-justified reaction against the satirical or frivolous, unfeeling, unfanciful, poetically shallow literature composed to the prescription of the French rationalists and classicists. Yet on another side Romanticism was a revolt not against Classicism but against the classic, against the idea of calm and infinity in the artistic image, against the catharsis of art, and in favor of the turmoil of passion, in its very resistance to the processes of purification. This was well understood by Goethe, who was at once a poet of passion and of serenity, and thus classical in his poet-hood. Goethe pronounced against the romantic poetry, describing it as "hospital poetry." Later, it was supposed that the illness had run its course and that Romanticism had expired. But it was only certain forms, and certain contents, and not the soul of Romanticism, not the overforcing of art into an immediate expression of the passions and the impressions, which had expired. Changing its name to "realism," "verism," "symbolism," "artistic style," "impressionism," "sensualism," "imaginism," "decadentism," and, in the extreme forms of the present day, "expressionism" or "futurism," the same thing went on and flourished. The concept of art itself is in these doctrines disturbed and confounded with one or other of the concepts of non-art. They are in fact directed against art, as is shown by the detestation of the extreme wing of the school in question for museums, for libraries, for the whole art of the past, for the very idea of an art the existence of which is bound up in the art which in the course of history has come into being. It is easy to see the links binding the movement in its present guise with industrialism and with the psychology which is encouraged by this. Its art seeks not to express and thereby to rise superior to the practical life of modern times, which is non-art, into the infinity and universality of contemplation, but to be the shouting, gesticulating, polychromatic side of this life itself. Meanwhile, of course, the true poets and artists, as rare now as they always were, carry on working on the old, the one and only artistic principle, expressing what they feel in harmonious form, while the appreciators of art, who (they too) are rarer than is commonly thought, continue to judge by that principle. The inclination to destroy the idea of art is however specially characteristic of our times, taking its origin from the *proton pseudos*[22] which confounds spiritual or aesthetic expression with natural or practical expression. Whereas the beautiful creation which art elaborates, builds, traces, colors, and molds is altogether different from that which throngs and breaks out from the passages of the senses, tumultuously. The present task of Aesthetics is the restoration and defence of the classical against the romantic; of the synthetic, formal, and theoretical moment which is of the essence of art, against that affective moment which it is art's business to resolve into itself, but which in our days is in rebellion against art seeking itself to occupy the throne. For sure, *portae Inferi non praevalebunt*[23] against the inexhaustible energy of the creative spirit. Nevertheless the effort of these "gates of Hell" to prevail disturbs the aesthetic judgment, the life of art, and, accordingly, thought and morality.

## CRITICISM AND HISTORY OF ART AND LITERATURE

There is another group of questions which, though there is a convenience in their being commonly included in treatises of Aesthetics, belong essentially to logic and the theory of history — those which concern aesthetic judgment and the history of poetry and the arts. The demonstration rendered by Aesthetics that the aesthetic activity, or art, is one of the forms of the spirit, a value, a category, and not as various schools have had it, an empirical concept applicable to certain orders of utilitarian or miscellaneous facts, has, by thus fixing the autonomy of aesthetic value, firmly demonstrated that the aesthetic is the predicate of a special judgment, the aesthetic judgment, and is the argument of a special history, the history of poetry and the arts.

The questions which arise concerning the aesthetic judgment and the history of art and literature, are substantially those same questions as to method which are found in all the fields of history, though here assuming the special form of problems of art. Thus it is asked whether the aesthetic judgment is absolute or relative. But every historical judgment, the aesthetic — which affirms the reality and the quality of aesthetic facts — as much as any other, is at the same time both absolute and relative. It is absolute in its employment of a category of universal truth, but relative in that its construct is historically conditioned. In the historical judgment the category thus becomes individualized while the individual becomes absolute. The sensistic, hedonistic, and utilitarian aestheticists who used to deny the absoluteness of the aesthetic judgment were in fact denying the quality, the reality, the autonomy of art. Again, it is asked whether the knowledge of past ages, of the whole history of a given moment, is needful for the passing of an aesthetic judgment. Certainly it is necessary; poetic creation has to presuppose all the other spirit which it converts into lyrical image, and the single aesthetic creation must presuppose all the other creations, such as passions, sentiments, customs, of a given historical moment. Both the "historicists" who advocate a merely historical judgment of art and the "aestheticists" who in contrast with these advocate a merely aesthetic judgment are evidently at fault, the former when they wish to see in art all the other histories (those for example of social conditions, or of the life of the author) without seeing, preeminent among these, that of art itself; and the second in wanting to judge the work of art outside of history, depriving it of its genuine meaning and substituting for this a work of fancy or of arbitrary comparison. Finally there is a sort of skepticism as to the very possibility of entering into a relation of understanding with the art of the past, a skepticism which if allowed at all ought to extend itself to every other part of history (intellectual, political, religious, moral), but can be confuted by a *reductio ad absurdum,* in that

[22]Primal falsehood. [Ed.]
[23]The gates of Hell shall not prevail. [Ed.]

even so-called modern or contemporary art and history are of the "past" along with those of remoter times; and none can be rendered "present" save in the soul which responds to them, the intelligence which understands them. That there should be artistic works and epochs which remain obscure to us means only that at this moment there are wanting the conditions for experiencing them anew in our souls and understanding them — which is no less true in respect of the ideas, customs, and actions of countless peoples and ages. Humanity, just like an individual, remembers a few things and forgets many others, but may revive the memory of these when the course of spiritual development requires it.

And there is one more question as to the form which is suitable for the history of art and literature. Today the prevailing form is still that which was mainly devised by the romantic age — the exposition of the history of works of art in terms of the social ideas and aspirations of an epoch, so that the work of art appears as the aesthetic expression of these. Art is thus brought into close relation with social history, whence comes a tendency to overlook and almost to suffocate the peculiar and individual accent of any work of art, that which renders it clearly different from any other. All art comes thus to be viewed as social documentation. True, in practice this method is tempered by what might be called the method of "individualization," or emphasis upon the particular character of single works. But the combination of the two methods has the defects inseparable from eclecticism. To get clear of these there is really no other way than to follow out the individualizing method to the very end: to treat works of art not in relation to social history but as being each one a world in itself, each one, in its hour, receiving the inflow of the whole of history, transfigured and elevated by the power of fancy into the individuality of the work of art which is a creation, not a reflection, and a monument, not a document. As a document of the Middle Ages the work of Dante is equaled or outclassed by many works of poor poetry or nonpoetry, and so too the work of Shakespeare as a document of the Elizabethan age. Some have objected that the history of art and literature would, if this advice were followed, be resolved into a disconnected series of essays and monographs. But connectedness is ensured by the whole of human history, of which poetic personalities are a part, a very conspicuous part. The appearance of Shakespeare's poetry is no less important than the Reformation or the French Revolution. Just because they are a part of it, poetic personalities should not be merged and lost to sight in history, that is in the other parts of history, but should retain their own proper and original outline and character.

# T. S. Eliot

## 1888–1965

Thomas Stearns Eliot, America's most influential literary expatriate since Henry James, was born in St. Louis, Missouri, where his father was a businessman and his mother a locally renowned poet. He was educated at private schools in St. Louis and in Milton, Massachusetts, before entering Harvard, where he studied with the philosophers Bertrand Russell and George Santayana (from whom he may have derived the idea of the "objective correlative"), and the literary critic Irving Babbitt, from whom he absorbed an inveterate hostility to romanticism. Eliot graduated from Harvard College in 1909 and spent most of the next five years in England working toward the Ph.D. in philosophy. He actually wrote his dissertation, on the English neo-idealist F. H. Bradley, but never returned to take his final orals. In 1914, he accepted a traveling fellowship to the University of Marburg but was stranded in England by the outbreak of World War I, stayed at Merton College, Oxford, and gradually came to make England his home. In 1915 he married Vivien Haigh-Wood, a beautiful and intelligent woman whose infidelities, emotional demands, and nervous instability made home life a misery for him; he eventually left her in 1933, and they lived apart until her death fourteen years later.

Eliot's poetic career seems to have dated from a year spent in France (1910–11), where his encounter with the French symbolists, especially Jules Laforgue, helped him to find his own voice. His first volume, *Prufrock and Other Observations* (1917), was a major contribution to the modernist movement in poetry, characterized by the combination of hard clear images, mysterious and transcendent symbols, and an almost classical restraint of subjective feeling. In *The Waste Land* (1922), Eliot produced modernism's epic of decay: an elegy upon the desiccation and near-death of the poet's own spirit with an odd Buddhistic conclusion ambiguously suggesting the hope of renewal and resurrection. The poem, written rapidly while Eliot was recovering from a nervous breakdown in a Swiss sanatorium, was tightened drastically by his friend Ezra Pound. Eliot found a more conventional source of solace and hope in his conversion to Anglo-Catholicism in 1927. Later poems included *Journey of the Magi* (1927), *Ash Wednesday* (1930), *Old Possum's Book of Practical Cats* (1939; adapted into *Cats,* an international theatrical success in the 1980s), and *Four Quartets* (1943). Eliot was also a successful playwright whose dry, menacing dialogue influenced postwar dramatists such as Harold Pinter. *The Cocktail Party* (1950), his most successful play, made Eliot a good deal of money from both the London and New York productions, though *Murder in the Cathedral* (1935), a verse tragedy on St. Thomas à Becket, may be the most durable and interesting of his dramas.

While he was gaining his reputation as a poet and playwright, Eliot worked first as a teacher of French and Latin, then as a clerk at Lloyds Bank, until he was made an editor at the publishing firm of Faber and Faber — which also subsidized the *Criterion,* a little magazine Eliot edited, and in which he published much of his critical writing. Eliot's criticism has been attacked as dry and pedantic, but at the time it was highly influential. Theoretical pieces like "Tradition and the Individual Talent" were manifestos of literary modernism. But Eliot may have been more important as a tastemaker than as a theorist: His essays on Jacobean playwrights such as Philip Massinger and Thomas Middleton helped put a vanished generation of English drama back on the stage, while those on the metaphysical poets heralded a revival of interest in such then-neglected names as John Donne and George Herbert and such virtually forgotten figures as Thomas Traherne and Lancelot Andrewes.

Most of Eliot's major poetry and criticism was written before the end of World War II, though it could be argued that his most pleasant days were spent after the war, as an honored elder statesman of letters. In 1948 he was awarded both the Nobel Prize for literature and the British Order of Merit. At the age of 69 he married his secretary, Valerie Fletcher, who shared his last happy years. He died in 1965 and was buried in East Coker, the Somerset village from which his ancestors had emigrated to America.

Eliot's literary theory does not appear full-blown in any single book. His most celebrated passages usually occur within an appreciation of an author or a text, and to put all of them together would require reprinting quite a number of different essays. His famous definition of an "objective correlative," so important for the development of the New Criticism, appears in an essay on *Hamlet*:

> The only way of expressing emotion in the form of art is by finding an "objective correlative"; in other words a set of objects, a situation, a chain of events which shall be the formula of that *particular* emotion; such that when the external facts, which must terminate in sensory experience, are given, the emotion is immediately evoked.

His theory of the dissociation of sensibility comes in the course of an essay on the metaphysical poets:

> . . . Something . . . had happened to the mind of England between the time of Donne or Lord Herbert of Cherbury and the time of Tennyson and Browning; it is the difference between the intellectual poet and the reflective poet. Tennyson and Browning are poets, and they think; but they do not feel their thought as immediately as the odour of a rose. A thought to Donne was an experience; it modified his sensibility. When a poet's mind is perfectly equipped for its work, it is constantly amalgamating disparate experience; the ordinary man's experience is chaotic, irregular, fragmentary. The latter falls in love, or reads Spinoza, and these two experiences have nothing to do with each other, or with the noise of the typewriter or the smell of cooking; in the mind of the poet these experiences are always forming new wholes.

In context, the first quotation is designed to explain what is special about *Hamlet* — it is a play that is problematic precisely because the external causes of feeling do not match the internal effects; the second is designed to explain the characteristic tone of seventeenth-century poetry to readers whose notions of the poetic have been corrupted, in Eliot's view, by the dissociation of sensibility that set in with Milton and Dryden. Both of these ideas, however, also have direct bearing on the poetics of the modernism that Eliot practiced. The doctrine of the objective correlative would lead to the sort of imagism practiced by both Eliot and Pound in their earliest poems, while the modernists, just as much as Donne, were interested in exploring a varied range of the sensibilities. In addition to the heart's feelings, Eliot went on, "one must look into the cerebral cortex, the nervous system, and the digestive tracts."

"Tradition and the Individual Talent" is much more openly a manifesto for modernism. In a voice that vacillates between a leaderly "we" and a modest "I," Eliot is clearly calling for a new "programme" for the *métier* of poetry. If the essay is a relatively difficult one, it is because of the ambiguities at the heart of what Eliot means by his two central terms, "tradition," which the poet is asked to cultivate, and "personality," which the poet must sacrifice.

Many creative writers are wary of immersing themselves in the tradition of English and American poetry because they fear that their own voices are not strong enough for the encounter and are likely to be lost in the process. Eliot argues the opposite: that a poet cannot become himself, cannot understand his own place in time, his own modernness, without an understanding of the past. As a result, the historical sense is "indispensable to anyone who would continue to be a poet beyond his twenty-fifth year" — Keats's age when he died. It is easy to understand the value Eliot places on tradition and on the historical sense that allows the poet to contemplate the current significance of the past.

What seems a bit mystical, however, is Eliot's claim that there is an "ideal order" in literary tradition. "The existing monuments form an ideal order among themselves, which is modified by the introduction of the new (the really new) work of art among them. The existing order is complete before the new work arrives; for order to persist after the supervention of novelty, the *whole* existing order must be, if ever so slightly, altered; and so the relations, proportions, values of each work of art toward the whole are readjusted; and this is conformity between the old and the new." Since Eliot never makes clear what the basis of the "ideal order" is — how this order is *ordered* — it remains unclear how the order can be perfect and complete both before and after the introduction of a new work. Nor is it clear of what this order is composed. It is not merely an anthology of celebrated texts, the current canon, but Eliot does not discuss how far removed a work can be from current fashion and yet remain within the tradition or how far down into popular culture the tradition reaches.

The difficulty with the issue of personality is not fuzziness but the apparent contradictions with other Eliot criticism. In "Tradition" Eliot seems to be suggesting that art is, or at least ought to be, essentially impersonal: that the tradition writes itself, as it were, using the poet as a catalyst for converting emotion and thought into poetry. But in an essay on Philip Massinger in 1920, Eliot suggests that personality is necessary for high art: "Marlowe's and Jonson's comedies . . . were, as great literature is, the transformation of a personality into a personal work of art. . . . Massinger is not simply a smaller personality: his personality hardly exists. He did not, out of his own personality, build a world of art, as Shakespeare and Marlowe and Jonson built."

A careful reading finds a paradox here, but no real self-contradiction. Eliot (like Proust in *Contre Sainte-Beuve*) repudiates the postromantic notion that the self an artist expresses is the habitual self one presents in society to intimates, friends, and acquaintances. He postulates another deeper self that is responsible for the artist's unique vision of reality, and that lends that vision authority and general truth. The former "personality" is what the artist escapes from into art; the latter is the source of that art. These two definitions of "personality," which incidentally correspond to the "you" and "I" in that schizoid lyric, "The Love Song of J. Alfred Prufrock," are what Eliot puns on throughout the last section of "Tradition and the Individual Talent."

### Selected Bibliography

Allan, Mowbray. *T. S. Eliot's Impersonal Theory of Poetry.* Lewisburg, Pa.: Bucknell University Press, 1974.

Austin, Allen. *T. S. Eliot: The Literary and Social Criticism.* Bloomington: Indiana University Press, 1971.

Brombert, Victor. *The Criticism of T. S. Eliot.* New Haven: Yale University Press, 1949.

Freed, Lewis. *T. S. Eliot: Aesthetics and History.* La Salle, Ill.: Open Court, 1962.

Frye, Northrop. *T. S. Eliot.* New York: Grove Press, 1963.

Lee, Brian. *Theory and Personality: The Significance of T. S. Eliot's Criticism.* London: Athlone Press, 1979.

Lu, Fei-Pai. *T. S. Eliot: The Dialectical Structure of His Theory of Poetry.* Chicago: University of Chicago Press, 1966.

Lucy, Sean. *T. S. Eliot and the Idea of Tradition.* London: Cohen and West, 1960.

Matthiessen, F. O. *The Achievement of T. S. Eliot.* New York: Oxford University Press, 1947.

Menand, Louis. *Discovering Modernism: T. S. Eliot and His Context.* New York: Oxford University Press, 1987.

Spurr, David. *Conflicts in Consciousness: T. S. Eliot's Poetry and Criticism.* Urbana: University of Illinois Press, 1983.

# Tradition and the Individual Talent

## I

In English writing we seldom speak of tradition, though we occasionally apply its name in deploring its absence. We cannot refer to "the tradition" or to "a tradition"; at most, we employ the adjective in saying that the poetry of so-and-so is "traditional" or even "too traditional." Seldom, perhaps, does the word appear except in a phrase of censure. If otherwise, it is vaguely approbative, with the implication, as to the work approved, of some pleasing archaeological reconstruction. You can hardly make the word agreeable in English ears without this comfortable reference to the reassuring science of archaeology.

Certainly the word is not likely to appear in our appreciations of living or dead writers. Every nation, every race, has not only its own creative, but its own critical turn of mind; and is even more oblivious of the shortcomings and limitations of its critical habits than of those of its creative genius. We know, or think we know, from the enormous mass of critical writing that has appeared in the French language the critical method or habit of the French; we only conclude (we are such unconscious people) that the French are "more critical" than we, and sometimes even plume ourselves a little with the fact, as if the French were the less spontaneous. Perhaps they are; but we might remind ourselves that criticism is as inevitable as breathing, and that we should be none the worse for articulating what passes in our minds when we read a book and feel an emotion about it, for criticizing our own minds in their work of criticism. One of the facts that might come to light in this process is our tendency to insist, when we praise a poet, upon those aspects of his work in which he least resembles anyone else. In these aspects or parts of his work we pretend to find what is individual, what is the peculiar essence of the man. We dwell with satisfaction upon the poet's difference from his predecessors, especially his immediate predecessors; we endeavor to find something that can be isolated in order to be enjoyed. Whereas if we approach a poet without this prejudice we shall often find that not only the best, but the most individual parts of his work may be those in which the dead poets, his ancestors, assert their immortality most vigorously. And I do not mean the impressionable period of adolescence, but the period of full maturity.

Yet if the only form of tradition, of handing down, consisted in following the ways of the immediate generation before us in a blind or timid adherence to its successes, "tradition" should positively be discouraged. We have seen many such simple currents soon lost in the sand; and novelty is better than repetition. Tradition is a matter of much wider significance. It cannot be inherited, and if you want it you must obtain it by great labor. It involves, in the first place, the historical sense, which we may call nearly indispensable to anyone who would continue to be a poet beyond his twenty-fifth year; and the historical sense involves a perception, not only of the pastness of the past, but of its presence; the historical sense compels a man to write not merely with his own generation in his bones, but with a feeling that the whole of the literature of Europe from Homer and within it the whole of the literature of his own country has a simultaneous existence and composes a simultaneous order. This historical sense, which is a sense of the timeless as well as of the temporal and of the timeless and of the temporal together, is what makes a writer traditional. And it is at the same time what makes a writer most acutely conscious of his place in time, of his own contemporaneity.

No poet, no artist of any art, has his complete meaning alone. His significance, his appreciation is the appreciation of his relation to the dead poets and artists. You cannot value him alone; you must set him, for contrast and comparison, among the dead. I mean this as a principle of aesthetic, not merely historical, criticism. The necessity that he shall conform, that he shall cohere, is not one-sided; what happens when a new work of art is created is something that happens simultaneously to all the works of art which preceded it. The existing monuments form an ideal order among themselves, which is modified by the introduction of the new (the really new) work of art among them. The existing order is complete before the new work arrives; for order to persist after the supervention of novelty, the whole existing order must be, if ever so slightly, altered; and so the relations, proportions, values of each work of art toward the whole are readjusted; and this is conformity between the old and the new. Whoever has approved this idea of order, of the form of European, of English literature will not find it preposterous that the past should be altered by the present as much as the present is directed by the past. And the poet who is aware of this will be aware of great difficulties and responsibilities.

In a peculiar sense he will be aware also that he must inevitably be judged by the standards of the past. I say judged, not amputated, by them; not judged to be as good as, or worse or better than, the dead; and certainly not judged by the canons of dead critics. It is a judgment, a comparison, in which two things are measured by each other. To conform merely would be for the new work not really to conform at all; it would not be new, and would therefore not be a work of art. And we do not quite say that the new is more valuable because it fits in; but its fitting in is a test of its value — a test, it is true, which can only be slowly and cautiously applied, for we are none of us infallible judges of conformity. We say: It appears to conform, and is perhaps individual, or it appears individual, and may conform; but we are hardly likely to find that it is one and not the other.

To proceed to a more intelligible exposition of the relation of the poet to the past: he can neither take the past a lump, an indiscriminate bolus, nor can he form himself wholly on one or two private admirations, nor can he form himself wholly upon one preferred period. The first course is inadmissible, the second is an important experience of youth, and the third is a pleasant and highly desirable supplement. The poet must be very conscious of the main current, which does not at all flow invariably through the most distinguished reputations. He must be quite aware of the obvious fact that art never improves, but that the material of art is never quite the same. He must be aware that the mind of Europe — the mind of his own country — a mind which he learns in time to be much more important than his own private mind — is a mind which changes, and that this change is a development which abandons nothing en route, which does not superannuate either Shakespeare, or Homer, or the rock drawing of the Magdalenian draftsmen.[1] That this development, refinement perhaps, complication certainly, is not, from the point of view of the artist, any improvement. Perhaps not even an improvement from the point of view of the psychologist or not to the extent which we imagine; perhaps only in the end based upon a complication in economics and machinery. But the difference between the present and the past is that the conscious present is an awareness of the past in a way and to an extent which the past's awareness of itself cannot show.

Someone said: "The dead writers are remote from us because we *know* so much more than they did." Precisely, and they are that which we know.

[1]The Cro-Magnon cave men. [Ed.]

I am alive to a usual objection to what is clearly part of my program for the métier of poetry. The objection is that the doctrine requires a ridiculous amount of erudition (pedantry), a claim which can be rejected by appeal to the lives of poets in any pantheon. It will even be affirmed that much learning deadens or perverts poetic sensibility. While, however, we persist in believing that a poet ought to know as much as will not encroach upon his necessary receptivity and necessary laziness, it is not desirable to confine knowledge to whatever can be put into a useful shape for examinations, drawing rooms, or the still more pretentious modes of publicity. Some can absorb knowledge, the more tardy must sweat for it. Shakespeare acquired more essential history from Plutarch than most men could from the whole British Museum. What is to be insisted upon is that the poet must develop or procure the consciousness of the past and that he should continue to develop this consciousness throughout his career.

What happens is a continual surrender of himself as he is at the moment to something which is more valuable. The progress of an artist is a continual self-sacrifice, a continual extinction of personality.

There remains to define this process of depersonalization and its relation to the sense of tradition. It is in this depersonalization that art may be said to approach the condition of science. I, therefore, invite you to consider, as a suggestive analogy, the action which takes place when a bit of finely filiated platinum is introduced into a chamber containing oxygen and sulfur dioxide.

## II

Honest criticism and sensitive appreciation are directed not upon the poet but upon the poetry. If we attend to the confused cries of the newspaper critics and the susurrus of popular repetition that follows, we shall hear the names of poets in great numbers; if we seek not blue-book knowledge but the enjoyment of poetry, and ask for a poem, we shall seldom find it. I have tried to point out the importance of the relation of the poem to other poems by other authors, and suggested the conception of poetry as a living whole of all the poetry that has ever been written. The other aspect of this impersonal theory of poetry is the relation of the poem to its author. And I hinted, by an analogy, that the mind of the mature poet differs from that of the immature one not precisely in any valuation of "personality," not being necessarily more interesting, or having "more to say," but rather by being a more finely perfected medium in which special, or very varied, feelings are at liberty to enter into new combinations.

The analogy was that of the catalyst. When the two gases previously mentioned are mixed in the presence of a filament of platinum, they form sulfurous acid. This combination takes place only if the platinum is present; nevertheless the newly formed acid contains no trace of platinum, and the platinum itself is apparently unaffected; has remained inert, neutral, and unchanged. The mind of the poet is the shred of platinum. It may partly or exclusively operate upon the experience of the man himself; but, the more perfect the artist, the more completely separate in him will be the man who suffers and the mind which creates; the more perfectly will the mind digest and transmute the passions which are its material.

The experience, you will notice, the elements which enter the presence of the transforming catalyst, are of two kinds: emotions and feelings. The effect of a work of art upon the person who enjoys it is an experience different in kind from any experience not of art. It may be formed out of one emotion, or may be a combination of several; and various feelings, inhering for the writer in particular words or phrases or images, may be added to compose the final result. Or great poetry may be made without the direct use of any emotion whatever: composed out of feelings solely. Canto XV of the *Inferno* (Brunetto Latini) is a working up of the emotion evident in the situation; but the effect, though single as that of any work of art, is obtained by considerable complexity of detail. The last quatrain gives an image, a feeling attaching to an image, which "came," which did not develop simply out of what precedes, but which was probably in suspension in the poet's mind until the proper combination arrived for it to add itself to.[2] The poet's mind is in fact a receptacle for seizing and storing up numberless feelings, phrases, images, which remain there until all the particles which can unite to form a new compound are present together.

If you compare several representative passages of the greatest poetry you see how great is the variety of types of combination, and also how completely any semiethical criterion of "sublimity" misses the mark. For it is not the "greatness," the intensity, of the emotions, the components, but the intensity of the artistic process, the pressure, so to speak, under which the fusion takes place, that counts. The episode of Paolo and Francesca employs a definite emotion, but the intensity of the poetry is something quite different from whatever intensity in the supposed experience it may give the impression of. It is no more intense, furthermore, than Canto XXVI, the voyage of Ulysses, which has not the direct dependence upon an emotion. Great variety is possible in the process of transmutation of emotion: the murder of Agamemnon, or the agony of Othello, gives an artistic effect apparently closer to a possible original than the scenes from Dante. In the *Agamemnon*, the artistic emotion approximates to the emotion of an actual spectator; in *Othello* to the emotion of the protagonist himself. But the difference between art and the event is always absolute; the combination which is the murder of Agamemnon is probably as complex as that which is the voyage of Ulysses. In either case there has been a fusion of elements. The ode of Keats contains a number of feelings which have nothing particular to do with the nightingale, but which the nightingale, partly, perhaps, because of its attractive name, and partly because of its reputation, served to bring together.

The point of view which I am struggling to attack is perhaps related to the metaphysical theory of the substantial unity of the soul: for my

---

[2]"And seemed like one of those who over the flat / And open course in the fields beside Verona / Run for the green cloth; and he seemed, at that, / Not like a loser but like the winning runner." Dante, *Inferno* 15:121–24. [Ed.]

meaning is, that the poet has, not a "personality" to express, but a particular medium, which is only a medium and not a personality, in which impressions and experiences combine in peculiar and unexpected ways. Impressions and experiences which are important for the man may take no place in the poetry, and those which become important in the poetry may play quite a negligible part in the man, the personality.

I will quote a passage which is unfamiliar enough to be regarded with fresh attention in the light — or darkness — of these observations:

And now methinks I could e'en chide myself
For doting on her beauty, though her death
Shall be revenged after no common action.
Does the silkworm expend her yellow labors
For thee? For thee does she undo herself?
Are lordships sold to maintain ladyships
For the poor benefit of a bewildering minute?
Why does yon fellow falsify highways,
And put his life between the judge's lips,
To refine such a thing — keeps horse and men
To beat their valors for her? . . .[3]

In this passage (as is evident if it is taken in its context) there is a combination of positive and negative emotions: an intensely strong attraction toward beauty and an equally intense fascination by the ugliness which is contrasted with it and which destroys it. This balance of contrasted emotion is in the dramatic situation to which the speech is pertinent, but that situation alone is inadequate to it. This is, so to speak, the structural emotion, provided by the drama. But the whole effect, the dominant tone, is due to the fact that a number of floating feelings, having an affinity to this emotion by no means superficially evident, have combined with it to give us a new art emotion.

It is not in his personal emotions, the emotions provoked by particular events in his life, that the poet is in any way remarkable or interesting. His particular emotions may be simple, or crude, or flat. The emotion in his poetry will be a very complex thing, but not with the complexity of the emotions of people who have very complex or unusual emotions in life. One error, in fact,

of eccentricity in poetry is to seek for new human emotions to express; and in this search for novelty in the wrong place it discovers the perverse. The business of the poet is not to find new emotions, but to use the ordinary ones and, in working them up into poetry, to express feelings which are not in actual emotions at all. And emotions which he has never experienced will serve his turn as well as those familiar to him. Consequently, we must believe that "emotion recollected in tranquility"[4] is an inexact formula. For it is neither emotion, nor recollection, nor, without distortion of meaning, tranquility. It is a concentration, and a new thing resulting from the concentration, of a very great number of experiences which to the practical and active person would not seem to be experiences at all; it is a concentration which does not happen consciously or of deliberation. These experiences are not "recollected," and they finally unite in an atmosphere which is "tranquil" only in that it is a passive attending upon the event. Of course this is not quite the whole story. There is a great deal, in the writing of poetry, which must be conscious and deliberate. In fact, the bad poet is usually unconscious where he ought to be conscious, and conscious where he ought to be unconscious. Both errors tend to make him "personal." Poetry is not a turning loose of emotion, but an escape from emotion; it is not the expression of personality, but an escape from personality. But, of course, only those who have personality and emotions know what it means to want to escape from these things.

### III

ὁ δὲ νοῦς ἴσως θειότερόν τι καὶ ἀπαθές ἐστιν.[5]

This essay proposes to halt at the frontier of metaphysics or mysticism, and confine itself to such practical conclusions as can be applied by the responsible person interested in poetry. To divert interest from the poet to the poetry is a

[3]Cyril Tourneur, *The Revenger's Tragedy,* III.iv. [Ed.]

[4]Eliot is quoting Wordsworth's Preface to *Lyrical Ballads;* see p. 295. [Ed.]

[5]"The mind may be too divine and therefore unimpassioned." Heracleitus. [Ed.]

laudable aim: for it would conduce to a juster estimation of actual poetry, good and bad. There are many people who appreciate the expression of sincere emotion in verse, and there is a smaller number of people who can appreciate technical excellence. But very few know when there is an expression of *significant* emotion, emotion which has its life in the poem and not in the history of the poet. The emotion of art is impersonal. And the poet cannot reach his impersonality without surrendering himself wholly to the work to be done. And he is not likely to know what is to be done unless he lives in what is not merely the present, but the present moment of the past, unless he is conscious; not of what is dead, but of what is already living.

# Marcel Proust
## 1871–1922

The author of *À la recherche du temps perdu* was born in Auteuil, a suburb of Paris, the eldest son of Adrien Proust, a noted surgeon, and Jeanne Weil, who came from a wealthy Jewish family. Despite debilitating attacks of asthma from the age of ten, Proust had a normal upper middle-class youth, including a stint of military service. He was educated at the Lycée Condorcet and the École des Sciences Politiques, where he took degrees in law and in literature and came under the influence of his cousin, the philosopher Henri Bergson. During the nineties, Proust began a rapid ascent in the realms of society and literature. He attended fashionable soirées given by the mothers of his school friends and cultivated acquaintances among the nobility until he became a habitué of the most exclusive drawing rooms in Paris. At the same time, in his early twenties, he began to publish short stories in little magazines, which were collected in *Les Plaisirs et les jours* (1896), with a laudatory preface by the leading man of letters of the day, Anatole France. His next work was an autobiographical novel, *Jean Santeuil,* which grew to nearly a thousand pages of manuscript between 1896 and 1900, when he abandoned it. Like many of Proust's youthful efforts, it functioned as a sort of draft version of *À la recherche*; it was ultimately published in 1952.

In the late 1890s France was split from top to bottom by the Dreyfus affair — a lengthy controversy that began when a Jewish army captain was framed as a German spy, and which ultimately compromised the moral integrity of the army, the courts, and the entire French government. Since most of the nobility was anti-Dreyfusard, Proust risked his hard-won social position by becoming involved on the side of Dreyfus, circulating petitions and assisting Dreyfus's lawyer Labori. Proust was not ostracized, and his partial withdrawal from society around the turn of the century was the result of growing ill-health, a compound of asthma and nerves aggravated by serious chronic diseases of his lungs and kidneys (he was that strange contradiction, the hypochondriac who is really very ill). By 1902, Proust was bedridden a good deal of the time with his various complaints, and he eventually evolved the legendary routine of remaining immured all day in his cork-lined room, emerging only in the late evening when the streets of Paris were sufficiently cool, dim, and dark.

In the early years of the century, when the deaths of his parents had left him financially independent, Proust discovered and translated into French the works of the English art critic and poet John Ruskin. Ruskin became the inspiration for Proust's aesthetic revolt against the established tastemakers of French society, especially the Goncourt brothers and Sainte-Beuve, whose ideas Proust attacked in a long, tendentious work, *Contre Sainte-Beuve* (1905, published in 1954). (Sainte-Beuve's essay "What Is a Classic?" appears in Ch. 8.)

Around 1907, Proust began work on the novel that was to occupy him full time for the rest of his life: *À la recherche du temps perdu*. This retrospective novel of over a million words, published in twelve volumes, recounts the psychologically complex process of how it came to be written. The story begins in the narrator Marcel's childhood on the evening his mother, trying to foster his independence, declines to come up and give him his customary good-night kiss — which is also the evening of a visit from Charles Swann, a socialite and dilettante whose fate is interlocked with that of the narrator. From this point, aided by the sensation of eating a madeleine — a small, shell-shaped cake soaked in tea, which unlocks the memories of his past — the narrator proceeds to recall and recount the yearnings and ambitions of his youth: how he longed to meet the beautiful young ladies at a seaside resort, to be accepted by the noble family of Guermantes, to see the world of art, to visit Venice, to become a writer.

By the end of the novel, the narrator has realized all his desires except the last, and all have turned to ashes in his mouth. His social ambitions have been corroded by a sense of the emptiness and sterility of fashionable life; the world of art seems corrupt and apish; and his youthful love for Albertine has been destroyed by possessiveness, suspicion, and jealousy. Physically ill and drained of hope, the narrator spends the years of World War I in a sanatorium and emerges feeling that his life has been wasted, his Time Lost, and the past too painful to recollect.

Finally, the narrator is invited to an afternoon reception given by the Princesse de Guermantes and attends out of nostalgic respect for the name. At the party he finds out that the flux of time has brought with it strange things: The princesse with the noble name is actually Madame de Verdurin, whom he knew long before as a rather vulgar patroness of the arts. But a series of tiny incidents at the party also revive long-repressed memories with shocking vividness and intensity, and as the narrator reflects on the meaning of memory, the nature of sensations, the human personality, and time itself, he understands that he has regained his lost life, and, what is more important, his lost vocation as a writer. He now knows that he must work — quickly against his approaching death — to record his life's experiences so that others can experience his universe with the purity and intensity that have just made it his own.

The first part of this story, *Du côté de chez Swann* (*Swann's Way*), was published by Bernard Grasset in 1913 at Proust's expense and was well received. Although more manuscript was available, further publication was delayed for some time by Proust's final personal loss: His secretary, Alfred Agnostelli, with whom he had been in love, fled his employment and, while Proust sought in vain for him, was killed in an accident. Proust recast his plans for the movement of his novel to include a heterosexual version of this event. The second volume, *À l'ombre des jeunes filles en fleurs* (*Within a Budding Grove*) eventually appeared in 1919 and won the Prix Goncourt. But from then on, Proust, like his narrator, was racing against time. The first part of *Le Côté de Guermantes* came out in 1920, the second the following year. The fourth book, *Sodome et Gomorrhe* (*Cities of the Plain*) was published in two parts in 1921 and 1922. In November of 1922, Proust died of pneumonia. His last three books were still in a partially revised manuscript and appeared posthumously: *La Prisonnière* (*The Captive*) in 1923, *La Fugitive* (*The Fugitive*) in 1925, and *Le Temps retrouvé* (*Time Regained*) in 1927.

The preceding summary of *À la recherche du temps perdu* is intended to illuminate the passages that follow, which are from the climactic revelatory section of *Le Temps retrouvé*. But one also needs to understand Proust's aesthetic in terms of its sources and antecedents — particularly his debt to Ruskin and his reaction against Sainte-Beuve. In Sainte-Beuve, Proust found a particularly vulgarized version of the romantic idea of artistic self-expression; and he was outraged at the notion that the artist expresses in his art the self that "we manifest in our habits, our social life, our vices." The world the artist creates is private and special, but the self that creates that world is also an ideal self, equally private and special, and knowable only through the experience of art, not through the gossip of the artist's valet. From Ruskin, Proust took his admiration of genuine realism — the artist's obligation to be faithful to the world of his experience and to convey its subjective qualities, while clearly maintaining the distinction between the artist's private inner world and the outer public world.

But if Proust absorbed from Ruskin a distrust of romantic subjectivism, the aesthetic Proust develops here goes far beyond Ruskin's. For Proust the function of art is less to make us see reality as it is than to see ourselves as we are. "Realist art" is false not because it falsifies reality but because it shows us the world as it already appears to our habitual selves. The audience recognizes what they have already seen but are not forced to see the world, or themselves, in a different way. Authentic art functions differently in that its inner reality — produced by the subjectivity of the artist — opens to the audience their own inner worlds, which lie closed to consciousness most of the time. And in the contrast between the sense of our own inner life and that of the artist who has made us aware of it lies the means of escape from the prison of the self, which is what we all seek through art:

> Real life, life at last laid bare and illuminated — the only life in consequence which can be said to be really lived — is literature, and life thus defined is in a sense all the time immanent in ordinary men no less than in the artist. But most men do not see it because they do not seek to shed light on it. . . . But art, if it means awareness of our own life, means also awareness of the lives of other people. . . . Through art alone are we able to emerge from ourselves, to know what another person sees of a universe which is not the same as our own and of which, without art, the landscapes would remain as unknown to us as those that may exist in the moon.

### Selected Bibliography

Blumenthal, Gerda R. *Thresholds: A Study of Proust*. Birmingham, Ala.: Summa Press, 1984.

Cocking, J. M. *Proust: Collected Essays on the Writer and His Art*. Cambridge and New York: Cambridge University Press, 1982.

De Lattre, Alain. *La Doctrine de la réalité chez Proust*. Paris: J. Corti, 1978.

Ellison, David R. *The Reading of Proust*. Baltimore: Johns Hopkins University Press, 1984.

Henry, Anne. *Marcel Proust: Theories pour une ésthetique*. Paris: Klincksieck, 1981.

Hughes, Edward J. *Marcel Proust: A Study in the Quality of Awareness*. New York: Cambridge University Press, 1983.

Poulet, George. *Proustian Space*. Baltimore: Johns Hopkins University Press, 1977.

Stackelberg, Jurgen von. *Drei Dichter als Kritiker: Andre Gide, Marcel Proust, Paul Valéry.* Göttingen: Vandenhoeck and Ruprecht, 1965.

# The Meditation on Time and Memory from *Time Regained*

Already at Combray I used to fix before my mind for its attention some image which had compelled me to look at it, a cloud, a triangle, a church spire, a flower, a stone, because I had the feeling that perhaps beneath these signs there lay something of a quite different kind which I must try to discover, some thought which they translated after the fashion of those hieroglyphic characters which at first one might suppose to represent only material objects. No doubt the process of decipherment was difficult, but only by accomplishing it could one arrive at whatever truth there was to read. For the truths which the intellect apprehends directly in the world of full and unimpeded light have something less profound, less necessary than those which life communicates to us against our will in an impression which is material because it enters us through the senses but yet has a spiritual meaning which it is possible for us to extract. In fact, both in the one case and in the other, whether I was concerned with impressions like the one which I had received from the sight of the steeples of Martinville or with reminiscences like that of the unevenness of the two steps or the taste of the madeleine[1] the task was to interpret the given sensations as signs of so many laws and ideas, by trying to think — that is to say, to draw forth from the shadow — what I had merely felt, by trying to convert it into its spiritual equivalent.

Translated by Terence Kilmartin.

[1]Like the spires of Martinville and the feel of the uneven steps, the taste of the madeleine is the physical key that opens to the narrator the memories of his childhood. [Ed.]

And this method, which seemed to me the sole method, what was it but the creation of a work of art? Already the consequences came flooding into my mind: first, whether I considered reminiscences of the kind evoked by the noise of the spoon or the taste of the madeleine, or those truths written with the aid of shapes for whose meaning I searched in my brain, where — church steeples or wild grass growing in a wall — they composed a magical scrawl, complex and elaborate, their essential character was that I was not free to choose them, that such as they were they were given to me. And I realized that this must be the mark of their authenticity. I had not gone in search of the two uneven paving-stones of the courtyard upon which I had stumbled. But it was precisely the fortuitous and inevitable fashion in which this and the other sensations had been encountered that proved the trueness of the past which they brought back to life, of the images which they released, since we feel, with these sensations, the effort that they make to climb back towards the light, feel in ourselves the joy of rediscovering what is real. And here too was the proof of the trueness of the whole picture formed out of those contemporaneous impressions which the first sensation brings back in its train, with those unerring proportions of light and shade, emphasis and omission, memory and forgetfulness to which conscious recollection and conscious observation will never know how to attain.

As for the inner book of unknown symbols (symbols carved in relief they might have been, which my attention, as it explored my unconscious, groped for and stumbled against and followed the contours of, like a diver exploring the ocean-bed), if I tried to read them no one could help me with any rules, for to read them was an act of creation in which no one can do our work for us or even collaborate with us. How many for this reason turn aside from writing! What tasks do men not take upon themselves in order to evade this task! Every public event, be it the Dreyfus case,[2] be it the war, furnishes the writer with a fresh excuse for not attempting to decipher this book: he wants to ensure the triumph of justice, he wants to restore the moral unity of the nation, he has no time to think of literature. But these are mere excuses, the truth being that he has not or no longer has genius, that is to say instinct. For instinct dictates our duty and the intellect supplies us with pretexts for evading it. But excuses have no place in art and intentions count for nothing: at every moment the artist has to listen to his instinct, and it is this that makes art the most real of all things, the most austere school of life, the true last judgment. This book, more laborious to decipher than any other, is also the only one which has been dictated to us by reality, the only one of which the "impression" has been printed in us by reality itself. When an idea — an idea of any kind — is left in us by life, its material pattern, the outline of the impression that it made upon us, remains behind as the token of its necessary truth. The ideas formed by the pure intelligence have no more than a logical, a possible truth, they are arbitrarily chosen. The book whose hieroglyphs are patterns not traced by us is the only book that really belongs to us. Not that the ideas which we form for ourselves cannot be correct in logic; that they may well be, but we cannot know whether they are true. Only the impression, however trivial its material may seem to be, however faint its traces, is a criterion of truth and deserves for that reason to be apprehended by the mind, for the mind, if it succeeds in extracting this truth, can by the

impression and by nothing else be brought to a state of greater perfection and given a pure joy. The impression is for the writer what experiment is for the scientist, with the difference that in the scientist the work of the intelligence precedes the experiment and in the writer it comes after the impression. What we have not had to decipher, to elucidate by our own efforts, what was clear before we looked at it, is not ours. From ourselves comes only that which we drag forth from the obscurity which lies within us, that which to others is unknown. . . .

I had arrived then at the conclusion that in fashioning a work of art we are by no means free, that we do not choose how we shall make it but that it pre-exists us and therefore we are obliged, since it is both necessary and hidden, to do what we should have to do if it were a law of nature, that is to say to discover it. But this discovery which art obliges us to make, is it not, I thought, really the discovery of what, though it ought to be more precious to us than anything in the world, yet remains ordinarily for ever unknown to us, the discovery of our true life, of reality as we have felt it to be, which differs so greatly from what we think it is that when a chance happening brings us an authentic memory of it we are filled with an immense happiness? In this conclusion I was confirmed by the thought of the falseness of so-called realist art, which would not be so untruthful if we had not in life acquired the habit of giving to what we feel a form of expression which differs so much from, and which we nevertheless after a little time take to be, reality itself. I began to perceive that I should not have to trouble myself with the various literary theories which had at moments perplexed me — notably those which practitioners of criticism had developed at the time of the Dreyfus case and had taken up again during the war, according to which "the artist must be made to leave his ivory tower" and the themes chosen by the writer ought to be not frivolous or sentimental but rather such things as great working-class movements or — in default of crowds — at least no longer as in the past unimportant men of leisure ("I must confess that the depiction of

[2]The miscarriage of justice based on forged evidence that sent Alfred Dreyfus to Devil's Island; the controversy over Dreyfus split French society. The "war" is World War I. [Ed.]

these useless characters rather bores me," Bloch[3] had been fond of saying), but noble intellectuals or men of heroic stature. In any case, quite apart from what I might think of the logical propositions which they contained, these theories seemed to me to indicate very clearly the inferiority of those who upheld them — my reaction was that of the truly well-brought-up child who, lunching in a strange house and hearing his hosts say: "We are frank, we don't hide our light under a bushel here," feels that the remark indicates a moral quality inferior to right conduct pure and simple, which says nothing. Authentic art has no use for proclamations of this kind, it accomplishes its work in silence. Moreover, those who theorized in this way used hackneyed phrases which had a curious resemblance to those of the idiots whom they denounced. And it is perhaps as much by the quality of his language as by the species of aesthetic theory which he advances that one may judge of the level to which a writer has attained in the moral and intellectual part of his work. Quality of language, however, is something the critical theorists think that they can do without, and those who admire them are easily persuaded that it is no proof of intellectual merit, for this is a thing which they cannot infer from the beauty of an image but can recognize only when they see it directly expressed. Hence the temptation for the writer to write intellectual works — a gross impropriety. A work in which there are theories is like an object which still has its price-tag on it. (And as to the choice of theme, a frivolous theme will serve as well as a serious one for a study of the laws of character, in the same way that a prosecutor can study the laws of anatomy as well in the body of an imbecile as in that of a man of talent, since the great moral laws, like the laws of the circulation of the blood or of renal elimination, vary scarcely at all with the intellectual merit of individuals.) A writer reasons, that is to say he goes astray, only when he has not the strength to force himself to make an impression pass through all the successive states which will culminate in its fixation, its

expression. The reality that he has to express resides, as I now began to understand, not in the superficial appearance of his subject but at a depth at which that appearance matters little; this truth had been symbolised for me by that clink of a spoon against a plate, that starched stiffness of a napkin, which had been of more value to me for my spiritual renewal than innumerable conversations of a humanitarian or patriotic or internationalist or metaphysical kind. "Enough of style," had been the cry, "enough of literature, let us have life!" And one may well imagine how since the beginning of the war even the simple theories of M. de Norpois, his denunciations of the "flute-players," had enjoyed a second vogue. For plenty of people who lack the artistic sense, who lack, that is to say, the faculty of submitting to the reality within themselves, may yet possess the ability to expatiate upon the theory of art until the crack of doom. And if they happen to be diplomats or financiers to boot, involved in the "realities" of the present age, they are likely to believe that literature is an intellectual game destined in the future to be progressively eliminated. (Some critics now liked to regard the novel as a sort of procession of things upon the screen of a cinematograph. This comparison was absurd. Nothing is further from what we have really perceived than the vision that the cinematograph presents.)

The idea of a popular art, like that of a patriotic art, if not actually dangerous seemed to me ridiculous. If the intention was to make art accessible to the people by sacrificing refinements of form, on the ground that they are "all right for the idle rich" but not for anybody else, I had seen enough of fashionable society to know that it is there that one finds real illiteracy and not, let us say, among electricians. In fact, an art that was "popular" so far as form was concerned would have been better suited to the members of the Jockey Club[4] than to those of the General Confederation of Labor — and as for subject, the working classes are as bored by novels of popular life as children are by the books which

<hr>

[3]One of the narrator's friends, an artist. [Ed.]

[4]Aristocratic men's club. [Ed.]

are written specially for them. When one reads, one likes to be transported into a new world, and working men have as much curiosity about princes as princes about working men. At the beginning of the war M. Barrès[5] had said that the artist (he happened to be talking about Titian) must first and foremost serve the glory of his country. But this he can do only by being an artist, which means only on condition that, while in his own sphere he is studying laws, conducting experiments, making discoveries which are as delicate as those of science, he shall think of nothing — not even his country — but the truth which is before him. Let us not imitate the revolutionaries who out of "civic sense" despised, if they did not destroy, the works of Watteau and La Tour, painters who have brought more honor upon France than all those of the Revolution. Anatomy is not perhaps the occupation that a kind-hearted man would choose, if he or any artist had the possibility of choice, and certainly it was not the kindness of a virtuous heart (though he was a truly kind man) that made Choderlos de Laclos write *Les Liaisons dangereuses,* nor was it any affection for the lower or upper bourgeoisie that made Flaubert choose the themes of *Madame Bovary* and *L'Éducation sentimentale* — but this is no valid criticism of the work of these writers.

Some people were also saying that the art of an age of haste would be brief, just as many people before the war had predicted that it would be short. The railway, according to this mode of thinking, was destined to kill contemplation and there was no sense in regretting the age of the diligence. But in fact the car has taken over its function and once more deposits tourists outside forgotten churches. . . .

An image presented to us by life brings with it, in a single moment, sensations which are in fact multiple and heterogeneous. The sight, for instance, of the binding of a book once read may weave into the characters of its title the moonlight of a distant summer night. The taste of our breakfast coffee brings with it that vague hope

of fine weather which so often long ago, as with the day still intact and full before us, we were drinking it out of a bowl of white porcelain, creamy and fluted and itself looking almost like vitrified milk, suddenly smiled upon us in the pale uncertainty of the dawn. An hour is not merely an hour, it is a vase full of scents and sounds and projects and climates, and what we call reality is a certain connection between these immediate sensations and the memories which envelop us simultaneously with them — a connection that is suppressed in a simple cinematographic vision, which just because it professes to confine itself to the truth in fact departs widely from it — a unique connection which the writer has to rediscover in order to link for ever in his phrase the two sets of phenomena which reality joins together. He can describe a scene by describing one after another the innumerable objects which at a given moment were present at a particular place, but truth will be attained by him only when he takes two different objects, states the connection between them — a connection analogous in the world of art to the unique connection which in the world of science is provided by the law of causality — and encloses them in the necessary links of a well-wrought style; truth — and life too — can be attained by us only when, by comparing a quality common to two sensations, we succeed in extracting their common essence and in reuniting them to each other, liberated from the contingencies of time, within a metaphor. Had not nature herself — if one considered the matter from this point of view — placed me on the path of art, was she not herself a beginning of art, she who, often, had allowed me to become aware of the beauty of one thing only in another thing, of the beauty, for instance, of noon at Combray in the sound of its bells, of that of the mornings at Doncières in the hiccups of our central heating? The link may be uninteresting, the objects trivial, the style bad, but unless this process has taken place the description is worthless.

But my train of thought led me yet further. If reality were indeed a sort of waste product of experience, more or less identical for each one of us, since when we speak of bad weather, a war, a taxi rank, a brightly lit restaurant, a garden

[5]Maurice Barrès, French writer and politician (1876–1923). [Ed.]

full of flowers, everybody knows what we mean, if reality were no more than this, no doubt a sort of cinematograph film of these things would be sufficient and the "style," the "literature" that departed from the simple data that they provide would be superfluous and artificial. But was it true that reality was no more than this? If I tried to understand what actually happens at the moment when a thing makes some particular impression upon one — on the day, for instance, when as I crossed the bridge over the Vivonne the shadow of a cloud upon the water had made me cry: "Gosh!" and jump for joy; or the occasion when, hearing a phrase of Bergotte's,[6] all that I had disengaged from my impression was the not specially relevant remark: "How splendid!"; or the words I had once heard Bloch use in exasperation at some piece of bad behavior, words quite inappropriate to a very commonplace incident: "I must say that that sort of conduct seems to me absolutely fffantastic!"; or that evening when, flattered at the politeness which the Guermantes[7] had shown to me as their guest and also a little intoxicated by the wines which I had drunk in their house, I could not help saying to myself half aloud as I came away alone: "They really are delightful people and I should be happy to see them every day of my life" — I realized that the words in each case were a long way removed from the impressions that I or Bloch had in fact received. So that the essential, the only true book, though in the ordinary sense of the word it does not have to be "invented" by a great writer — for it exists already in each one of us — has to be translated by him. The function and the task of a writer are those of a translator.

And if in some cases — where we are dealing, for instance, with the inaccurate language of our own vanity — the rectification of an oblique interior discourse (which deviates gradually more and more widely from the first and central impression) until it merges with the straight line which the impression ought to have produced is a laborious undertaking which our idleness would prefer to shirk, there are other circumstances —

for example, where love is involved — in which this same process is actually painful. Here all our feigned indifferences, all our indignation at the lies of whoever it is whom we love (lies which are so natural and so like those that we perpetrate ourselves), in a word all that we have not ceased, whenever we are unhappy or betrayed, not only to say to the loved one but, while we are waiting for a meeting with her, to repeat endlessly to ourselves, sometimes aloud in the silence of our room, which we disturb with remarks like: "No, really, this sort of behavior is intolerable," and: "I have consented to see you once more, for the last time, and I don't deny that it hurts me," all this can only be brought back into conformity with the felt truth from which it has so widely diverged by the abolition of all that we have set most store by, all that in our solitude, in our feverish projects of letters and schemes, has been the substance of our passionate dialogue with ourselves.

Even where the joys of art are concerned, although we seek and value them for the sake of the impression that they give us, we contrive as quickly as possible to set aside, as being inexpressible, precisely that element in them which is the impression that we sought, and we concentrate instead upon that other ingredient in aesthetic emotion which allows us to savor its pleasure without penetrating its essence and lets us suppose that we are sharing it with other art-lovers, with whom we find it possible to converse just because, the personal root of our own impression having been suppressed, we are discussing with them a thing which is the same for them and for us. Even in those moments when we are the most disinterested spectators of nature, or of society or of love or of art itself, since every impression is double and the one half which is sheathed in the object is prolonged in ourselves by another half which we alone can know, we speedily find means to neglect this second half, which is the one on which we ought to concentrate, and to pay attention only to the first half which, as it is external and therefore cannot be intimately explored, will occasion us no fatigue. To try to perceive the little furrow which the sight of a hawthorn bush or of a church has traced in us is a task that we find too difficult.

[6]A writer acquaintance of the narrator. [Ed.]

[7]The family that, for the narrator, serves as the quintessence of the French aristocracy. [Ed.]

But we play a symphony over and over again, we go back repeatedly to see a church until — in that flight to get away from our own life (which we have not the courage to look at) which goes by the name of erudition — we know them, the symphony and the church, as well as and in the same fashion as the most knowledgeable connoisseur of music or archaeology. And how many art-lovers stop there, without extracting anything from their impression, so that they grow old useless and unsatisfied, like life-long bachelors! They suffer, but their sufferings, like the sufferings of virgins and of lazy people, are of a kind that fecundity or work would cure. They get more excited about works of art than real artists, because for them their excitement is not the object of a laborious and inward-directed study but a force which bursts outwards, which heats their conversations and empurples their cheeks; at concerts they will shout "Bravo, bravo" till they are hoarse at the end of a work they admire and imagine as they do so that they are discharging a duty. But demonstrations of this kind do not oblige them to clarify the nature of their admiration and of this they remain in ignorance. Meanwhile, like a stream which can find no useful channel, their love of art flows over into even their calmest conversations, so that they make wild gestures and grimace and toss their heads whenever they mention the subject. "I was at a concert the other day. They played the first piece and I must say it left me cold. Then they started on the quartet. By Jove, what a difference!" (At this moment the face of the music-lover expresses a sudden anxiety, as if he were thinking: "Don't I see sparks? And I smell burning! Something's on fire.") "It's the most exasperating thing I've ever heard, damn it! It's not exactly a good composition, but it's stunning, it's something quite out of the ordinary." And yet, ludicrous though they may be, such people are not altogether to be despised. They are the first attempts of nature in her struggle to create the artist, experiments as misshapen, as unviable as those first animals that came before the species of to-day and were so constituted that they could not survive for long. And, with their sterile vellectities, the art-lovers are as touching to contemplate as those early machines which tried to leave the ground and could not, but which yet held within them, if not the secret, the still to be discovered means, at least the desire of flight. "You know, old boy," goes on the music-lover, as he takes you by the elbow, "this is the eighth time I've heard it, and I promise you it won't be the last." And indeed, since they fail to assimilate what is truly nourishing in art, they need artistic pleasures all the time, they are victims of a morbid hunger which is never satisfied. So they go to concert after concert to applaud the same work and think that they have a duty to put in an appearance whenever it is performed just as other people think they have a duty to attend a board meeting or a funeral. Then presently, whether it be in music or in literature or in painting, other works come along, works that may even be in the very opposite of the ones which they supersede. For the ability to launch ideas and systems — and still more of course the ability to assimilate them — has always been much commoner than genuine taste, even among those who themselves produce works of art, and with the multiplication of reviews and literary journals (and with them of factitious vocations as writer or artist) has become very much more widespread. Not so long ago, for instance, the best part of the younger generation, the most intelligent and the most disinterested of them, through a change of fashion admired nothing but works with a lofty moral and sociological, and even religious, significance. This they imagined to be the criterion of a work's value, renewing the old error of David and Chenavard and Brunetière[8] and all those who in the past thought like them. Bergotte, whose prettiest phrases had in fact demanded much deeper reflection on the part of the reader, was rated lower now than writers who seemed more profound simply because they wrote less well. The intricacy of his style was all right for fashionable people but not for anybody else, said democratic critics, paying to fashionable people a tribute which they did not deserve. The truth is that as soon as the reasoning

[8]Painters of the revolutionary era. [Ed.]

intelligence takes upon itself to judge works of art, nothing is any longer fixed or certain: you can prove anything you wish to prove. Whereas the reality of talent is something universal, whether it be a gift or an acquirement, and the first thing that a reader has to do is to find out whether this reality is present beneath a writer's superficial mannerism of thought and style, it is upon just these superficial mannerisms that criticism seizes when it sets out to classify authors. Because he has a peremptory tone, because he parades his contempt for the school that preceded him, criticism hails as a prophet a writer who in fact has no message that is new. And so frequent are these aberrations of criticism that a writer might almost with reason prefer to be judged by the general public (were not the public incapable even of understanding what an artist has attempted in a realm of discovery which is outside its experience). For there is a closer analogy between the instinctive life of the public and the talent of a great writer, which is simply an instinct religiously listened to in the midst of a silence imposed upon all other voices, an instinct made perfect and understood, than between this same talent and the superficial verbiage and changing criteria of the established judges of literature. From decade to decade their wordy battles are renewed, for it is not only social groups that are kaleidoscopic but ideas too about society and politics and religion; refracted through large bodies they can assume a momentary amplitude but their life-span is the brief one of ideas which owe their success to their novelty and gain the adherence only of such minds as are not particular about proof. So it is that parties and schools follow upon one another's heels, attaching to themselves always the same minds, those men of moderate intelligence who are an easy prey to the successive enthusiasms into which others more scrupulous and less easily satisfied in the matter of proof will decline to plunge. And unfortunately, just because those in the first category are no more than half-minds, they need to buttress themselves in action, with the result that, being more active than the better minds, they draw the crowd after them and create around them not only inflated reputations and victims of undeserved contempt but wars too, both civil and foreign, which a little self-examination of an old-fashioned Jansenist kind might well have prevented.

As for the enjoyment which is derived by a really discerning mind and a truly living heart from a thought beautifully expressed in the writings of a great writer, this is no doubt an entirely wholesome enjoyment, but, precious though the men may be who are truly capable of enjoying this pleasure — and how many of them are there in a generation? — they are nevertheless in the very process reduced to being no more than the full consciousness of another. If, for instance, a man of this type has done everything in his power to make himself loved by a woman who could only have made him unhappy, but has not even succeeded, in spite of efforts redoubled over the years, in persuading her to meet him in private, instead of seeking to express his sufferings and the danger from which he has escaped, he reads over and over again, appending to it "a million words" and the most moving memories of his own life, this observation of La Bruyère: "Men often want to love where they cannot hope to succeed; they seek their own undoing without being able to compass it, and, if I may put it thus, they are forced against their will to remain free." Whether or not this is the meaning that the aphorism had for the man who wrote it (to give it this meaning, which would make it finer, he should have said "to be loved" instead of "to love"), there is no doubt that, with this meaning, the sensitive lover of literature reanimates it and swells it with meaning until it is ready to burst, he cannot repeat it to himself without overflowing with joy, so true and beautiful does he find it — but in spite of all this he has added to it nothing, it remains merely an observation of La Bruyère.

How could the literature of description possibly have any value, when it is only beneath the surface of the little things which such a literature describes that reality has its hidden existence (grandeur, for example, in the distant sound of an aeroplane or the outline of the steeple of Saint-Hilaire, the past in the taste of a madeleine, and so on) and when the things in themselves are without significance until it has been extracted from them? Gradually, thanks to its preservation by our memory, the chain of all those inaccurate expressions in which there survives nothing of what we have really experienced comes to constitute for us our thought, our life, our "reality," and this lie is all that can be reproduced by the art that styles itself "true to life," an art that is as simple as life, without beauty, a mere vain and tedious duplication of what our eyes see and our intellect records, so vain and so tedious that one wonders where the writer who devotes himself to it can have found the joyous and impulsive spark that was capable of setting him in motion and making him advance in his task. The greatness, on the other hand, of true art, of the art which M. de Norpois would have called a dilettante's pastime, lay, I had come to see, elsewhere: we have to rediscover, to reapprehend, to make ourselves fully aware of that reality, remote from our daily preoccupations, from which we separate ourselves by an ever greater gulf as the conventional knowledge which we substitute for it grows thicker and more impermeable, that reality which it is very easy for us to die without ever having known and which is, quite simply, our life. Real life, life at last laid bare and illuminated — the only life in consequence which can be said to be really lived — is literature, and life thus defined is in a sense all the time immanent in ordinary men no less than in the artist. But most men do not see it because they do not seek to shed light upon it. And therefore their past is like a photographic dark-room encumbered with innumerable negatives which remain useless because the intellect has not developed them. But art, if it means awareness of our own life, means also awareness of the lives of other people — for style for the writer, no less than color for the painter, is a question not of technique but of vision: it is the revelation, which by direct and conscious methods would be impossible, of the qualitative difference, the uniqueness of the fashion in which the world appears to each one of us, a difference which, if there were no art, would remain for ever the secret of every individual. Through art alone are we able to emerge from ourselves, to know what another person sees of a universe which is not the same as our own and of which, without art, the landscapes would remain as unknown to us as those that may exist in the moon. Thanks to art, instead of seeing one world only, our own, we see that world multiply itself and we have at our disposal as many worlds as there are original artists, worlds more different one from the other than those which revolve in infinite space, worlds which, centuries after the extinction of the fire from which their light first emanated, whether it is called Rembrandt or Vermeer, send us still each one its special radiance.

This work of the artist, this struggle to discern beneath matter, beneath experience, beneath words, something that is different from them, is a process exactly the reverse of that which, in those everyday lives which we live with our gaze averted from ourself, is at every moment being accomplished by vanity and passion and the intellect, and habit too, when they smother our true impressions, so as entirely to conceal them from us, beneath a whole heap of verbal concepts and practical goals which we falsely call life. In short, this art which is so complicated is in fact the only living art. It alone expresses for others and renders visible to ourselves that life of ours which cannot effectually observe itself and of which the observable manifestations need to be translated and, often, to be read backwards and laboriously deciphered. Our vanity, our passions, our spirit of imitation, our abstract intelligence, our habits have long been at work, and it is the task of art to undo this work of theirs, making us travel back in the direction from which we have come to the depths where what has really existed lies unknown within us. And surely this was a most tempting prospect, this task of recreating one's true life, of rejuvenating one's impressions. But it required courage of many kinds, including the courage of one's emotions. For above all it meant the abrogation of one's dearest illusions, it meant giving up one's belief in the objectivity of what one had oneself elaborated, so that now, instead of soothing oneself for the hundredth time with the words: "She was very sweet," one would have to transpose the phrase so that it read: "I experienced pleasure when I kissed her." Certainly, what I had felt in my hours of love is what all men feel. One feels, yes, but what one feels is like a negative which shows only blackness until one has placed it near a special lamp and which must also be looked at in reverse. So with one's feelings: until one has brought them within range of the intellect one does not know what they represent. Then only, when the intellect has shed light upon them, has intellectualized them, does one distinguish, and with what difficulty, the lineaments of what one felt.

# John Dewey

## 1859–1952

John Dewey was born of middle-class parents in Burlington, Vermont; his father was a grocer. Until he reached college, Dewey was profoundly bored by the mechanical, rote learning imposed by his schoolmasters, a fact which may have influenced his philosophy of education. It took Dewey some time to find his niche, partly because nineteenth-century America did not keep abreast of European philosophical trends. His work at the tiny University of Vermont emphasized the Scottish Enlightenment of a century before, and he did not read the German idealists like Hegel until, after years of teaching school, he began graduate training at the then-new Johns Hopkins University. After receiving his doctorate in 1884 with a dissertation on the psychology of Kant, Dewey was hired as an instructor by the University of Michigan. At an Ann Arbor boarding house he met Alice Chipman, whom he married two years later. As Dewey's daughter puts it, "she was undoubtedly largely responsible for the early widening of Dewey's philosophical interests from the . . . classical to the field of contemporary life." In 1894, Dewey went on from Michigan to the just-founded University of Chicago, where he headed the Department of Philosophy, Psychology, and Education, and where he established the Laboratory School for the implementation of his educational philosophy. Around 1904, however, opposition to Dewey's ideas and methods crystallized around the appointment of his wife as principal of the school, and the Deweys left for Columbia University, where he taught for the rest of his long life.

Dewey stands in the mainstream of an American school of philosophy that includes his forebears Charles Sanders Peirce and William James (the elder brother of Henry James). The central contribution of American philosophy involves a positivistic and pragmatic conception of knowledge. Whereas the idealist philosophers (such as Kant and Hegel) thought that truth was judged purely by the internal coherence of the philosophical system and that the system tolerated an elaborate metaphysical structure of a priori categories from which the phenomenal world would have to be deduced, the Americans substituted for metaphysics an experimental notion of truth, inductive rather than deductive in character, with verifiability as the chief criterion. For American philosophers the self, moved by inner needs, interacts with the world and learns the truth through experience. Within this school, Dewey is distinguished as a *naturalist*. Rejecting Peirce's belief in innate ideas and James's mysticism, he stood for a commonsensical rationalism in which our sense of self emerges from its encounters with experience, just as, on the other side, our sense of the world emerges from that same encounter. If these ideas now seem tame, it is partly because, owing to Dewey's pervasive influence, they have become part of America's cultural heritage.

But Dewey's main influence upon American life was in education. He rejected the belief then common that the developing child was a trainable animal who should either be coaxed by pleasures or coerced by discipline to learn a body of facts. In the first place, Dewey held that a steady diet of facts — such as that prescribed by headmaster Gradgrind in Dickens's *Hard Times* — does not make for an educated citizen. In the second, Dewey, though an empiricist, was no behaviorist: For him children were psychologically more complex than trainable animals, and the best way to inspire learning was not by external conditioning but rather by stimulating the child's interests.

This belief followed from Dewey's theory of knowledge, which he regarded not as something above and beyond man but what man acquires to satisfy his pragmatic needs and interests. Because interests were the key, Dewey also rejected rote memorization, since he felt that what is learned without interest or a sense of utility is soon forgotten. Instead, he suggested that teaching should capitalize on a child's present interests to lead the child to finer and higher interests, and that learning should emphasize creativity and play. Dewey's writings have provided the ideals that have defined the theory, if not necessarily the practice, of American education — and indeed education throughout the Western world.

Dewey's aesthetics was a late development — *Art as Experience* dates from 1934, when the philosopher was in his seventies — but the ideas seem to follow directly from Dewey's notion that knowledge comes out of experience, especially the experience of the interaction of the self with the environment.

Dewey differentiated between *experience,* which is a ceaseless flowing out from the past into the future, and *an* experience, which has a satisfying emotional character because of its movement toward a fulfillment, an end that is "a consummation and not a cessation." Aesthetic experience is of the latter sort. All through our everyday lives we have sensations and feelings, but in art these feelings and sensations are channeled and clarified through a conscious and deliberate development, so that they become, for the audience as well as the maker, *an* experience.

For both Dewey and his contemporary, Benedetto Croce, art is a form of expression, but Croce and Dewey differ enormously in how the expression is arrived at. Croce, an idealist, stresses the mental side of the equation, the inchoate feelings and thoughts that are bound up as lyrical intuition and given mental expression. The third term, communication, is distinctly inferior, and Croce does not concern himself with the technical question of how the artist handles the medium of his or her art. For Dewey, the process of interaction of the artist with the medium is crucial. The thing the artist wishes to express is not full-blown in his mind but an inchoate idea. The expression cannot take shape immediately but emerges through a struggle with the medium, which resists the artist's attempts to shape it, and through its resistance, alters the artist's very conception in the process. Eventually, as Dewey says, "the real work of art is the building up of an integral experience out of the interaction of organic and environmental conditions and energies."

From the spectator's point of view, art has somewhat the same character. The audience does not, of course, replay the struggle of the artist with his environment, for they never (in the case of the sculptor, for example) experience the raw block of stone with which the artist interacted. But the audience too has an interior and an exterior environment into which they must attempt to integrate the meaning of the work of art.

It is not entirely clear what a Deweyan criticism would be like, but passages in *Art as Experience* suggest Dewey's hostility to both "judicial" and "impressionistic" criticism, to the former because no one can judge the value an experience can have for another and to the latter because it trivializes the genuine struggle of artists with their craft. Though Dewey never clearly defines the sort of criticism he would favor, it might be inferred that a critic needs to understand the struggle of the artist with his medium by examining drafts and sketches to get a sense of how a particular artist thought and worked. It is also possible that, on the audience's side, Dewey might have favored some sort of phenomenological criticism — an attempt on the part of the reader to clarify how a given text coheres as an integral experience and the order and progress by which its chaos of impressions is clarified and deepened into meaning.

## Selected Bibliography

Ballard, Edward G. "An Estimate of Dewey's *Art as Experience*." *Tulane Studies in Philosophy* 4 (1955): 5–18.

Edman, Irwin. "Dewey and Art." In *John Dewey: Philosopher of Science and Freedom,* ed. Sidney J. Hook. New York: Dial Press, 1950.

Hill, Knox. "Philosophic Method and Theory of Art in Croce and Dewey." Master's thesis, University of Chicago, 1956.

Hook, Sidney. *John Dewey: An Intellectual Portrait*. Westport, Conn.: Greenwood Press, 1976.

Melvin, Georgiana. "The Social Philosophy Underlying Dewey's Theory of Art." *Mills College Faculty Studies* 1 (1937): 124–36.

Tamme, Anne Mary. *A Critique of John Dewey's Theory of Fine Art*. Washington: Catholic University of America Press, 1956.

Zeltner, Philip M. *John Dewey's Aesthetic Philosophy*. Amsterdam: Gruner, 1975.

# The Act of Expression

Every experience, of slight or tremendous import, begins with an impulsion, rather *as* an impulsion. I say "impulsion" rather than "impulse." An impulse is specialized and particular; it is, even when instinctive, simply a part of the mechanism involved in a more complete adaptation with the environment. "Impulsion" designates a movement outward and forward of the whole organism to which special impulses are auxiliary.

It is the craving of the living creature for food as distinct from the reactions of tongue and lips that are involved in swallowing; the turning toward light of the body as a whole, like the heliotropism of plants, as distinct from the following of a particular light by the eyes.

Because it is the movement of the organism in its entirety, impulsion is the initial stage of any complete experience. Observation of children discovers many specialized reactions. But they are not, therefore, inceptive of complete experiences. They enter into the latter only as they are woven as strands into an activity that calls the whole self into play. Overlooking these generalized activities and paying attention only to the differentiations, the divisions of labor, which render them more efficient, are pretty much the source and cause of all further errors in the interpretation of experience.

Impulsions are the beginnings of complete experience because they proceed from need; from a hunger and demand that belongs to the organism as a whole and that can be supplied only by instituting definite relations (active relations, interactions) with the environment. The epidermis is only in the most superficial way an indication of where an organism ends and its environment begins. There are things inside the body that are foreign to it, and there are things outside of it that belong to it *de jure*, if not *de facto;*[1] that must, that is, be taken possession of if life is to continue. On the lower scale, air and food materials are such things; on the higher, tools, whether the pen of the writer or the anvil of the blacksmith, utensils and furnishings, property, friends and institutions — all the supports and sustenances without which a civilized life cannot be. The need that is manifest in the urgent impulsions that demand completion through what the environment — and it alone — can supply, is a dynamic acknowledgment of this dependence of the self for wholeness upon its surroundings.

It is the fate of a living creature, however, that it cannot secure what belongs to it without an adventure in a world that as a whole it does not own and to which it has no native title. Whenever the organic impulse exceeds the limit of the body, it finds itself in a strange world and commits in some measure the fortune of the self to external circumstance. It cannot pick just what it wants and automatically leave the indifferent and adverse out of account. If, and as far as, the organism continues to develop, it is helped on as a favoring wind helps the runner. But the impulsion also meets many things on its outbound

[1]By law, if not in actuality. [Ed.]

course that deflect and oppose it. In the process of converting these obstacles and neutral conditions into favoring agencies, the live creature becomes aware of the intent implicit in its impulsion. The self, whether it succeed or fail, does not merely restore itself to its former state. Blind surge has been changed into a purpose; instinctive tendencies are transformed into contrived undertakings. The attitudes of the self are informed with meaning.

An environment that was always and everywhere congenial to the straightaway execution of our impulsions would set a term to growth as surely as one always hostile would irritate and destroy. Impulsion forever boosted on its forward way would run its course thoughtless, and dead to emotion. For it would not have to give an account of itself in terms of the things it encounters, and hence they would not become significant objects. The only way it can become aware of its nature and its goal is by obstacles surmounted and means employed; means which are only means from the very beginning are too much one with an impulsion, on a way smoothed and oiled in advance, to permit of consciousness of them. Nor without resistance from surroundings would the self become aware of itself; it would have neither feeling nor interest, neither fear nor hope, neither disappointment nor elation. Mere opposition that completely thwarts, creates irritation and rage. But resistance that calls out thought generates curiosity and solicitous care, and, when it is overcome and utilized, eventuates in elation.

That which merely discourages a child and one who lacks a matured background of relevant experiences is an incitement to intelligence to plan and convert emotion into interest, on the part of those who have previously had experiences of situations sufficiently akin to be drawn upon. Impulsion from need starts an experience that does not know where it is going; resistance and check bring about the conversion of direct forward action into re-flection; what is turned back upon is the relation of hindering conditions to what the self possesses as working capital in virtue of prior experiences. As the energies thus involved reenforce the original impulsion, this operates more circumspectly with insight into end and method. Such is the outline of every experience that is clothed with meaning.

That tension calls out energy and that total lack of opposition does not favor normal development are familiar facts. In a general way, we all recognize that a balance between furthering and retarding conditions is the desirable state of affairs — provided that the adverse conditions bear intrinsic relation to what they obstruct instead of being arbitrary and extraneous. Yet what is evoked is not just quantitative, or just more energy, but is qualitative, a transformation of energy into thoughtful action, through assimilation of meanings from the background of past experiences. The junction of the new and old is not a mere composition of forces, but is a re-creation in which the present impulse gets form and solidity while the old, the "stored," material is literally revived, given new life and soul through having to meet a new situation.

It is this double change which converts an activity into an act of expression. Things in the environment that would otherwise be mere smooth channels or else blind obstructions become means, media. At the same time, things retained from past experience that would grow stale from routine or inert from lack of use, become coefficients in new adventures and put on a raiment of fresh meaning. Here are all the elements needed to define expression. The definition will gain force if the traits mentioned are made explicit by contrast with alternative situations. Not all outgoing activity is of the nature of expression. At one extreme, there are storms of passion that break through barriers and that sweep away whatever intervenes between a person and something he would destroy. There is activity, but not, from the standpoint of the one acting, expression. An onlooker may say "What a magnificent expression of rage!" But the enraged being is only raging, quite a different matter from *expressing* rage. Or, again, some spectator may say "How that man is expressing his own dominant character in what he is doing or saying." But the last thing the man in question is thinking of is to express his character; he is only giving way to a fit of passion. Again the

cry or smile of an infant may be expressive to mother or nurse and yet not be an act of expression of the baby. To the onlooker it is an expression because it tells something about the state of the child. But the child is only engaged in doing something directly, no more expressive from his standpoint than is breathing or sneezing — activities that are also expressive to the observer of the infant's condition.

Generalization of such instances will protect us from the error — which has fortunately invaded esthetic theory — of supposing that the mere giving way to an impulsion, native or habitual, constitutes expression. Such an act is expressive not in itself but only in reflective interpretation on the part of some observer — as the nurse may interpret a sneeze as the sign of an impending cold. As far as the act itself is concerned, it is, if purely impulsive, just a boiling over. While there is no expression, unless there is urge from within outwards, the welling up must be clarified and ordered by taking into itself the values of prior experiences before it can be an act of expression. And these values are not called into play save through objects of the environment that offer resistance to the direct discharge of emotion and impulse. Emotional discharge is a necessary but not a sufficient condition of expression.

There is no expression without excitement, without turmoil. Yet an inner agitation that is discharged at once in a laugh or cry, passes away with its utterance. To discharge is to get rid of, to dismiss; to express is to stay by, to carry forward in development, to work out to completion. A gush of tears may bring relief, a spasm of destruction may give outlet to inward rage. But where there is no administration of objective conditions, no shaping of materials in the interest of embodying the excitement, there is no expression. What is sometimes called an act of self-expression might better be termed one of self-exposure; it discloses character — or lack of character — to others. In itself, it is only a spewing forth.

The transition from an act that is expressive from the standpoint of an outside observer to one intrinsically expressive is readily illustrated by a simple case. At first a baby weeps, just as it turns its head to follow light; there is an inner urge but nothing to express. As the infant matures, he learns that particular acts effect different consequences, that, for example, he gets attention if he cries, and that smiling induces another definite response from those about him. He thus begins to be aware of the *meaning* of what he does. As he grasps the meaning of an act at first performed from sheer internal pressure, he becomes capable of acts of true expression. The transformation of sounds, babblings, lalling, and so forth, into language is a perfect illustration of the way in which acts of expression are brought into existence and also of the difference between them and mere acts of discharge.

There is suggested, if not exactly exemplified, in such cases the connection of expression with art. The child who has learned the effect his once spontaneous act has upon those around him performs "on purpose" an act that was blind. He begins to manage and order his activities in reference to their consequences. The consequences undergone because of doing are incorporated as the meaning of subsequent doings because the relation between doing and undergoing is perceived. The child may now cry for a purpose, because he wants attention or relief. He may begin to bestow his smiles as inducements or as favors. There is now art in incipiency. An activity that was "natural" — spontaneous and unintended — is transformed because it is undertaken as a means to a consciously entertained consequence. Such transformation marks every deed of art. The result of the transformation may be artful rather than esthetic. The fawning smile and conventional smirk of greeting are artifices. But the genuinely gracious act of welcome contains also a change of an attitude that was once a blind and "natural" manifestation of impulsion into an act of art, something performed in view of its place or relation in the processes of intimate human intercourse.

The difference between the artificial, the artful, and the artistic lies on the surface. In the former there is a split between what is overtly done and what is intended. The appearance is one of cordiality; the intent is that of gaining favor. Wherever this split between what is done and its purpose exists, there is insincerity, a trick, a simulation of an act that intrinsically has another effect. When the natural and the cultivated blend in one, acts of social intercourse are works of art. The animating impulsion of genial friendship and the deed performed completely coincide without intrusion of ulterior purpose. Awkwardness may prevent adequacy of expression. But the skillful counterfeit, however skilled, goes *through* the form of expression; it does not have the form of friendship and abide in it. The substance of friendship is untouched.

An act of discharge or mere exhibition lacks a medium. Instinctive crying and smiling no more require a medium than do sneezing and winking. They occur through some channel, but the means of outlet are not used as immanent means of an end. The act that *expresses* welcome uses the smile, the outreached hand, the lighting up of the face as media, not consciously but because they have become organic means of communicating delight upon meeting a valued friend. Acts that were primitively spontaneous are converted into means that make human intercourse more rich and gracious — just as a painter converts pigment into means of expressing an imaginative experience. Dance and sport are activities in which acts once performed spontaneously in separation are assembled and converted from raw, crude material into works of expressive art. Only where material is employed as media is there expression and art. Savage taboos that look to the outsider like mere prohibitions and inhibitions externally imposed may be to those who experience them media of expressing social status, dignity, and honor. Everything depends upon the way in which material is used when it operates as medium.

The connection between a medium and the act of expression is intrinsic. An act of expression always employs natural material, though it may be natural in the sense of habitual as well as in that of primitive or native. It becomes a medium when it is employed in view of its place and rôle, in its relations, an inclusive situation — as tones become music when ordered in a melody. The same tones might be uttered in connection with an attitude of joy, surprise, or sadness, and be natural outlets of particular feelings. They are *expressive* of one of these emotions when other tones are the medium in which one of them occurs.

Etymologically, an act of expression is a squeezing out, a pressing forth. Juice is expressed when grapes are crushed in the wine press; to use a more prosaic comparison, lard and oil are rendered when certain fats are subjected to heat and pressure. Nothing is pressed forth except from original raw or natural material. But it is equally true that the mere issuing forth or discharge of raw material is not expression. Through interaction with something external to it, the wine press, or the treading foot of man, juice results. Skin and seeds are separated and retained; only when the apparatus is defective are they discharged. Even in the most mechanical modes of expression there is interaction and a consequent transformation of the primitive material which stands as raw material for a product of art, in relation to what is actually pressed out. It takes the wine press as well as grapes to express juice, and it takes environing and resisting objects as well as internal emotion and impulsion to constitute an *expression* of emotion.

Speaking of the production of poetry, Samuel Alexander[2] remarked that "the artist's work proceeds not from a finished imaginative experience to which the work of art corresponds, but from passionate excitement about the subject matter. . . . The poet's poem is wrung from him by the subject which excites him." The passage is a text upon which we may hang four comments. One of these comments may pass for the present as a reënforcement of a point made in previous chapters. The real work of art is the building up of an integral experience out of the interaction of organic and environmental conditions and energies. Nearer to our present theme is the second point: The thing expressed is wrung from the producer by the pressure exercised by objective things upon the natural impulses and tendencies — so far is expression from being the direct and immaculate issue of the latter. The third point

[2]Samuel Alexander (1859–1938), Australian-born metaphysician and aesthetician. [Ed.]

follows. The act of expression that constitutes a work of art is a construction in time, not an instantaneous emission. And this statement signifies a great deal more than that it takes time for the painter to transfer his imaginative conception to canvas and for the sculptor to complete his chipping of marble. It means that the expression of the self in and through a medium, constituting the work of art, is *itself* a prolonged interaction of something issuing from the self with objective conditions, a process in which both of them acquire a form and order they did not at first possess. Even the Almighty took seven days to create the heaven and the earth, and, if the record were complete, we should also learn that it was only at the end of that period that He was aware of just what He set out to do with the raw material of chaos that confronted Him. Only an emasculated subjective metaphysics has transformed the eloquent myth of Genesis into the conception of a Creator creating without any unformed matter to work upon.

The final comment is that when excitement about subject matter goes deep, it stirs up a store of attitudes and meanings derived from prior experience. As they are aroused into activity they become conscious thoughts and emotions, emotionalized images. To be set on fire by a thought or scene is to be inspired. What is kindled must either burn itself out, turning to ashes, or must press itself out in material that changes the latter from crude metal into a refined product. Many a person is unhappy, tortured within, because he has at command no art of expressive action. What under happier conditions might be used to convert objective material into material of an intense and clear experience, seethes within in unruly turmoil which finally dies down after, perhaps, a painful inner disruption.

Materials undergoing combustion because of intimate contacts and mutually exercised resistances constitute inspiration. On the side of the self, elements that issue from prior experience are stirred into action in fresh desires, impulsions and images. These proceed from the subconscious, not cold or in shapes that are identified with particulars of the past, not in chunks and lumps, but fused in the fire of internal commotion. They do not seem to come from the self, because they issue from a self not consciously known. Hence, by a just myth, the inspiration is attributed to a god, or to the muse. The inspiration, however, is initial. In itself, at the outset, it is still inchoate. Inflamed inner material must find objective fuel upon which to feed. Through the interaction of the fuel with material already afire the refined and formed product comes into existence. The act of expression is not something which supervenes upon an inspiration already complete. It is the carrying forward to completion of an inspiration by means of the objective material of perception and imagery.[3]

An impulse cannot lead to expression save when it is thrown into commotion, turmoil. Unless there is com-pression nothing is ex-pressed. The turmoil marks the place where inner impulse and contact with environment, in fact or in idea, meet and create a ferment. The war dance and the harvest dance of the savage do not issue from within except there be an impending hostile raid or crops that are to be gathered. To generate the indispensable excitement there must be something at stake, something momentous and uncertain — like the outcome of a battle or the prospects of a harvest. A sure thing does not arouse us emotionally. Hence it is not mere excitement that is expressed but excitement-about-something; hence, also, it is that even mere excitement, short of complete panic, will utilize channels of action that have been worn by prior activities that dealt with objects. Thus, like the movements of an actor who goes through his part automatically, it simulates expression. Even an undefined uneasiness seeks outlet in song or pantomime, striving to become articulate.

Erroneous views of the nature of the act of

[3] In his interesting "The Theory of Poetry," Mr. Lascelles Abercrombie wavers between two views of inspiration. One of them takes what seems to me the correct interpretation. In the poem, an inspiration "completely and exquisitely defines itself." At other times, he says the inspiration *is* the poem; "something self-contained and self-sufficient, a complete and entire whole." He says that "each inspiration is something which did not and could not originally exist as words." Doubtless such is the case; not even a trigonometric function exists merely as words. But if it is already self-sufficient and self-contained, why does it seek and find words as a medium of expression? [Au.]

expression almost all have their source in the notion that an emotion is complete in itself within, only when uttered having impact upon external material. But, in fact, an emotion is *to* or *from* or *about* something objective, whether in fact or in idea. An emotion is implicated in a situation, the issue of which is in suspense and in which the self that is moved in the emotion is vitally concerned. Situations are depressing, threatening, intolerable, triumphant. Joy in the victory won by a group with which a person is identified is not something internally complete, nor is sorrow upon the death of a friend anything that can be understood save as an interpenetration of self with objective conditions.

This latter fact is especially important in connection with the individualization of works of art. The notion that expression is a direct emission of an emotion complete in itself entails logically that individualization is specious and external. For, according to it, fear is fear, elation is elation, love is love, each being generic, and internally differentiated only by differences of intensity. Were this idea correct, works of art would necessarily fall within certain types. This view has infected criticism but not so as to assist understanding of concrete works of art. Save nominally, there is no such thing as *the* emotion of fear, hate, love. The unique, unduplicated character of experienced events and situations impregnates the emotion that is evoked. Were it the function of speech to reproduce that to which it refers, we could never speak of fear, but only of fear-of-this-particular-oncoming-automobile, with all its specifications of time and place, or fear-under-specified-circumstances-of-drawing-a-wrong-conclusion from just-such-and-such-data. A lifetime would be too short to reproduce in words a single emotion. In reality, however, poet and novelist have an immense advantage over even an expert psychologist in dealing with an emotion. For the former build up a concrete situation and permit *it* to evoke emotional response. Instead of a description of an emotion in intellectual and symbolic terms, the artist "does the deed that breeds" the emotion.

That art is selective is a fact universally recognized. It is so because of the role of emotion in the act of expression. Any predominant mood automatically excludes all that is uncongenial with it. An emotion is more effective than any deliberate challenging sentinel could be. It reaches out tentacles for that which is cognate, for things which feed it and carry it to completion. Only when emotion dies or is broken to dispersed fragments, can material to which it is alien enter consciousness. The selective operation of materials so powerfully exercised by a developing emotion in a series of continued acts extracts matter from a multitude of objects, numerically and spatially separated, and condenses what is abstracted in an object that is an epitome of the values belonging to them all. This function creates the "universality" of a work of art.

If one examines into the reason why certain works of art offend us, one is likely to find that the cause is that there is no personally felt emotion guiding the selecting and assembling of the materials presented. We derive the impression that the artist, say the author of a novel, is trying to regulate by conscious intent the nature of the emotion aroused. We are irritated by a feeling that he is manipulating materials to secure an effect decided upon in advance. The facets of the work, the variety so indispensable to it, are held together by some external force. The movement of the parts and the conclusion disclose no logical necessity. The author, not the subject matter, is the arbiter.

In reading a novel, even one written by an expert craftsman, one may get a feeling early in the story that hero or heroine is doomed, doomed not by anything inherent in situations and character but by the intent of the author who makes the character a puppet to set forth his own cherished idea. The painful feeling that results is resented not because it is painful but because it is foisted upon us by something that we feel comes from outside the movement of the subject matter. A work may be much more tragic and yet leave us with an emotion of fulfillment instead of irritation. We are reconciled to the conclusion because we feel it is inherent in the movement of the subject matter portrayed. The incident is tragic but the world in which such fateful things happen is not an arbitrary and imposed world. The emotion of the author and that aroused in us are occasioned by scenes in that world and they blend with subject matter. It is for similar reasons that we are repelled by the intrusion of a moral design in literature while we estheically accept any amount of moral content if it is held together by a sincere emotion that controls the material. A white flame of pity or indignation may find material that feeds it and it may fuse everything assembled into a vital whole.

Just because emotion is essential to that act of expression which produces a work of art, it is easy for inaccurate analysis to misconceive its mode of operation and conclude that the work of art has emotion for its significant content. One may cry out with joy or even weep upon seeing a friend from whom one has been long separated. The outcome is not an expressive object — save to the onlooker. But if the emotion leads one to gather material that is affiliated to the mood which is aroused, a poem may result. In the direct outburst, an objective situation is the stimulus, the cause, of the emotion. In the poem, objective material becomes the content and matter of the emotion, not just its evocative occasion.

In the development of an expressive act, the emotion operates like a magnet drawing to itself appropriate material: appropriate because it has an experienced emotional affinity for the state of mind already moving. Selection and organization of material are at once a function and a test of the quality of the emotion experienced. In seeing a drama, beholding a picture, or reading a novel, we may feel that the parts do not hang together. Either the maker had no experience that was emotionally toned, or, although having at the outset a felt emotion, it was not sustained, and a succession of unrelated emotions dictated the work. In the latter case, attention wavered and shifted, and an assemblage of incongruous parts ensued. The sensitive observer or reader is aware of junctions and seams, of holes arbitrarily filled in. Yes, emotion must operate. But it works to effect continuity of movement, singleness of effect amid variety. It is selective of material and directive of its order and arrangement. But it is not *what* is expressed. Without emotion, there may be craftsmanship, but not art; it may be present and be intense, but if it is directly manifested the result is also not art.

There are other works that are overloaded with emotion. On the theory that manifestation of an emotion is its expression, there could be no overloading; the more intense the emotion, the more effective the "expression." In fact, a person overwhelmed by an emotion is thereby incapacitated for expressing it. There is at least that element of truth in Wordsworth's formula of "emotion recollected in tranquillity."[4] There is, when one is mastered by an emotion, too much undergoing (in the language by which having an experience has been described) and too little active response to permit a balanced relationship to be struck. There is too much "nature" to allow of the development of art. Many of the paintings of Van Gogh, for example, have an intensity that arouses an answering chord. But with the intensity, there is an explosiveness due to absence of assertion of control. In extreme cases of emotion, it works to disorder instead of ordering material. Insufficient emotion shows itself in a coldly "correct" product. Excessive emotion obstructs the necessary elaboration and definition of parts.

The determination of the *mot juste*, of the right incident in the right place, of exquisiteness of proportion, of the precise tone, hue, and shade that helps unify the whole while it defines a part, is accomplished by emotion. Not every emotion, however, can do this work, but only one informed by material that is grasped and gathered. Emotion is informed and carried forward when it is spent indirectly in search for material and in giving it order, not when it is directly expended.

Works of art often present to us an air of spontaneity, a lyric quality, as if they were the unpremeditated song of a bird. But man, whether fortunately or unfortunately, is not a bird. His most spontaneous outbursts, if expressive, are not overflows of momentary internal pressures. The spontaneous in art is complete absorption in subject matter that is fresh, the freshness of which holds and sustains emotion. Staleness of matter and obtrusion of calculation are the two enemies of spontaneity of expression. Reflection, even long and arduous reflection, may have been

[4]Preface to *Lyrical Ballads*; see p. 295. [Ed.]

concerned in the generation of material. But an expression will, nevertheless, manifest spontaneity if that matter has been vitally taken up into a present experience. The inevitable self-movement of a poem or drama is compatible with any amount of prior labor provided the results of that labor emerge in complete fusion with an emotion that is fresh. Keats speaks poetically of the way in which artistic expression is reached when he tells of the "innumerable compositions and decompositions which take place between the intellect and its thousand materials before it arrives at that trembling, delicate and snail-horn perception of beauty."

Each of us assimilates into himself something of the values and meanings contained in past experiences. But we do so in differing degrees and at differing levels of selfhood. Some things sink deep, others stay on the surface and are easily displaced. The old poets traditionally invoked the muse of Memory as something wholly outside themselves — outside their present conscious selves. The invocation is a tribute to the power of what is most deep-lying and therefore the furthest below consciousness, in determination of the present self and of what it has to say. It is not true that we "forget" or drop into unconsciousness only alien and disagreeable things. It is even more true that the things which we have most completely made a part of ourselves, that we have assimilated to compose our personality and not merely retained as incidents, cease to have a separate conscious existence. Some occasion, be it what it may, stirs the personality that has been thus formed. Then comes the need for expression. What is expressed will be neither the past events that have exercised their shaping influence nor yet the literal existing occasion. It will be, in the degree of its spontaneity, an intimate union of the features of present existence with the values that past experience have incorporated in personality. Immediacy and individuality, the traits that mark concrete existence, come from the present occasion; meaning, substance, content, from what is embedded in the self from the past.

I do not think that the dancing and singing of even little children can be explained wholly on the basis of unlearned and unformed responses to then existing objective occasions. Clearly there must be something in the present to evoke happiness. But the act is expressive only as there is in it a unison of something stored from past experience, something therefore generalized, with present conditions. In the case of the expressions of happy children the marriage of past values and present incidents takes place easily; there are few obstructions to be overcome, few wounds to heal, few conflicts to resolve. With maturer persons, the reverse is the case. Accordingly the achievement of complete unison is rare; but when it occurs it is so on a deeper level and with a fuller content of meaning. And then, even though after long incubation and after precedent pangs of labor, the final expression may issue with the spontaneity of the cadenced speech or rhythmic movement of happy childhood.

In one of his letters to his brother Van Gogh says that "emotions are sometimes so strong that one works without knowing that one works, and the strokes come with a sequence and coherence like that of words in a speech or letter." Such fullness of emotion and spontaneity of utterance come, however, only to those who have steeped themselves in experiences of objective situations; to those who have long been absorbed in observation of related material and whose imaginations have long been occupied with reconstructing what they see and hear. Otherwise the state is more like one of frenzy in which the sense of orderly production is subjective and hallucinatory. Even the volcano's outburst presupposes a long period of prior compression, and, if the eruption sends forth molten lava and not merely separate rocks and ashes, it implies a transformation of original raw materials. "Spontaneity" is the result of long periods of activity, or else it is so empty as not to be an act of expression.

What William James wrote about religious experience might well have been written about the antecedents of acts of expression. "A man's conscious wit and will are aiming at something only dimly and inaccurately imagined. Yet all the while the forces of mere organic ripening within him are going on to their own prefigured result, and his conscious strainings are letting loose subconscious allies behind the scenes which in their way work toward rearrangement, and the rearrangement toward which all these deeper forces tend is pretty surely definite, and definitely different from what he consciously conceives and determines. It may consequently be actually interfered with (jammed as it were) by his voluntary efforts slanting toward the true direction." Hence, as he adds, "When the new center of energy has been subconsciously incubated so long as to be just ready to burst into flower, 'hands off' is the only word for us; it must burst forth unaided."

It would be difficult to find or give a better description of the nature of spontaneous expression. Pressure precedes the gushing forth of juice from the wine press. New ideas come leisurely yet promptly to consciousness only when work has previously been done in forming the right doors by which they may gain entrance. Subconscious maturation precedes creative production in every line of human endeavor. The direct effort of "wit and will" of itself never gave birth to anything that is not mechanical; their function is necessary, but it is to let loose allies that exist outside their scope. At different times we brood over different things; we entertain purposes that, as far as consciousness is concerned, are independent, being each appropriate to its own occasion; we perform different acts, each with its own particular result. Yet as they all proceed from one living creature they are somehow bound together below the level of intention. They work together, and finally something is born almost in spite of conscious personality, and certainly not because of its deliberate will. When patience has done its perfect work, the man is taken possession of by the appropriate muse and speaks and sings as some god dictates.

Persons who are conventionally set off from artists, "thinkers," scientists, do not operate by conscious wit and will to anything like the extent popularly supposed. They, too, press forward toward some end dimly and imprecisely prefigured, groping their way as they are lured on by the identity of an aura in which their observations and reflections swim. Only the psychology that has separated things which in reality belong together holds that scientists and philosophers think while poets and painters follow their feelings. In both, and to the same extent in the degree in which they are of comparable rank, there is emotionalized thinking, and there are feelings whose substance consists of appreciated meanings or ideas. As I have already said, the only significant distinction concerns the kind of material to which emotionalized imagination adheres. Those who are called artists have for their subject-matter the qualities of things of direct experience; "intellectual" inquirers deal with these qualities at one remove, through the medium of symbols that stand for qualities but are not significant in their immediate presence. The ultimate difference is enormous as far as the technique of thought and emotion are concerned. But there is no difference as far as dependence on emotionalized ideas and subconscious maturing are concerned. Thinking directly in terms of colors, tones, images, is a different operation technically from thinking in words. But only superstition will hold that, because the meaning of paintings and symphonies cannot be translated into words, or that of poetry into prose, therefore thought is monopolized by the latter. If all meanings could be adequately expressed by words, the arts of painting and music would not exist. There are values and meanings that can be expressed only by immediately visible and audible qualities, and to ask what they mean in the sense of something that can be put into words is to deny their distinctive existence.

Different persons differ in the relative amount of participation of conscious wit and will which go into their acts of expression. Edgar Allan Poe left an account of the process of expression as it is engaged in by those of the more deliberate cast of mind. He is telling about what went on when he wrote "The Raven," and says: "The public is rarely permitted to take a peep behind the scenes at the vacillating crudities, of the true purpose seized at the last moment, at the wheels and pinions, the tackle for scene shifting, the step ladders and demon traps, the red paint and black patches, which, in ninety-nine cases out of a hundred, constitute the properties of the literary *histrio*."[5]

It is not necessary to take the numerical ration

stated by Poe too seriously. But the substance of what he says is a picturesque presentation of a sober fact. The primitive and raw material of experience needs to be reworked in order to secure artistic expression. Oftentimes, this need is greater in cases of "inspiration" than in other cases. In this process the emotion called out by the original material is modified as it comes to be attached to the new material. This fact gives us the clue to the nature of esthetic emotion.

With respect to the physical materials that enter into the formation of a work of art, every one knows that they must undergo change. Marble must be chipped; pigments must be laid on canvas; words must be put together. It is not so generally recognized that a similar transformation takes place on the side of "inner" materials, images, observations, memories and emotions. They are also progressively re-formed; they, too, must be administered. This modification is the building up of a truly expressive act. The impulsion that seethes as a commotion demanding utterance must undergo as much and as careful management in order to receive eloquent manifestation as marble or pigment, as colors and sounds. Nor are there in fact two operations, one performed upon the outer material and the other upon the inner and mental stuff.

The work is artistic in the degree in which the two functions of transformation are effected by a single operation. As the painter places pigment upon the canvas, or imagines it placed there, his ideas and feeling are also ordered. As the writer composes in his medium of words what he wants to say, his idea takes on for himself perceptible form.

The sculptor conceives his statue, not just in mental terms but in those of clay, marble or bronze. Whether a musician, painter, or architect works out his original emotional idea in terms of auditory or visual imagery or in the actual medium as he works is of relatively minor importance. For the imagery is of the objective medium undergoing development. The physical media may be ordered in imagination or in concrete material. In any case, the physical process develops imagination, while imagination is conceived in terms of concrete material. Only by progressive organization of "inner" and "outer"

[5]"The Philosophy of Composition"; see p. 372. [Ed.]

material in organic connection with each other can anything be produced that is not a learned document or an illustration of something familiar.

Suddenness of emergence belongs to appearance of material above the threshold of consciousness, not to the process of its generation. Could we trace any such manifestation to its roots and follow it through its history, we should find at the beginning an emotion comparatively gross and undefined. We should find that it assumed definite shape only as it worked itself through a series of changes in imagined material. What most of us lack in order to be artists is not the inceptive emotion, nor yet merely technical skill in execution. It is capacity to work a vague idea and emotion over into terms of some definite medium. Were expression but a kind of decalcomania,[6] or a conjuring of a rabbit out of the place where it lies hid, artistic expression would be a comparatively simple matter. But between conception and bringing to birth there lies a long period of gestation. During this period the inner material of emotion and idea is as much transformed through acting and being acted upon by objective material as the latter undergoes modification when it becomes a medium of expression.

It is precisely this transformation that changes the character of the original emotion, altering its quality so that it becomes distinctively esthetic in nature. In formal definition, emotion is esthetic when it adheres to an object formed by an expressive act, in the sense in which the act of expression has been defined.

In its beginning an emotion flies straight to its object. Love tends to cherish the loved object as hate tends to destroy the thing hated. Either emotion may be turned aside from its direct end. The emotion of love may seek and find material that is other than the directly loved one, but that is congenial and cognate through the emotion that draws things into affinity. This other material may be anything as long as it feeds the emotion. Consult the poets, and we find that love finds its

expression in rushing torrents, still pools, in the suspense that awaits a storm, a bird poised in flight, a remote star or the fickle moon. Nor is this material metaphorical in character, if by "metaphor" is understood the result of any act of conscious comparison. Deliberate metaphor in poetry is the recourse of mind when emotion does not saturate material. Verbal expression may take the form of metaphor, but behind the words lies an act of emotional identification, not an intellectual comparison.

In all such cases, some object emotionally akin to the direct object of emotion takes the place of the latter. It acts in place of a direct caress, of hesitating approach, of trying to carry by storm. There is truth in Hulme's statement that "beauty is the marking time, the stationary vibration, the feigned ecstasy, of an arrested impulse unable to reach its natural end."[7] If there is anything wrong with the statement, it is the veiled intimation that the impulsion *ought* to have reached "its natural end." If the emotion of love between the sexes had not been celebrated by means of diversion into material emotionally cognate but practically irrelevant to its direct object and end, there is every reason to suppose it would still remain on the animal plane. The impulse arrested in its direct movement toward its physiologically normal end is not, in the case of poetry, arrested in an absolute sense. It is turned into indirect channels where it finds other material than that which is "naturally" appropriate to it, and as it fuses with this material it takes on new color and has new consequences. This is what happens when any natural impulse is idealized or spiritualized. That which elevates the embrace of lovers above the animal plane is just the fact that when it occurs it has taken into itself, as its own meaning, the consequences of these indirect excursions that are imagination in action.

Expression is the clarification of turbid emotion; our appetites know themselves when they are reflected in the mirror of art, and as they know themselves they are transfigured. Emotion that is distinctively esthetic then occurs. It is not a form of sentiment that exists independently

---

[6]Now abbreviated "decal." Dewey intends the more general sense — transfer of a design from one medium to another. [Ed.]

[7]*Speculations*, p. 266. [Au.]

from the outset. It is an emotion induced by material that is expressive, and because it is evoked by and attached to this material it consists of natural emotions that have been transformed. Natural objects, landscapes, for example, induce it. But they do so only because when they are matter of an experience they, too, have undergone a change similar to that which the painter or poet effects in converting the immediate scene into the matter of an act that expresses the value of what is seen.

An irritated person is moved to do something. He cannot suppress his irritation by any direct act of will; at most he can only drive it by this attempt into a subterranean channel where it will work the more insidiously and destructively. He must act to get rid of it. But he can act in different ways, one direct, the other indirect, in manifestations of his state. He cannot suppress it any more than he can destroy the action of electricity by a fiat of will. But he can harness one or the other to the accomplishment of new ends that will do away with the destructive force of the natural agency. The irritable person does not have to take it out on neighbors or members of his family to get relief. He may remember that a certain amount of regulated physical activity is good medicine. He sets to work tidying his room, straightening pictures that are askew, sorting papers, clearing out drawers, putting things in order generally. He *uses* his emotion, switching it into indirect channels prepared by prior occupations and interests. But since there is something in the utilization of these channels that is emotionally akin to the means by which his irritation would find direct discharge, as he puts objects in order his emotion is ordered.

This transformation is of the very essence of the change that takes place in any and every natural or original emotional impulse when it takes the indirect road of expression instead of the direct road of discharge. Irritation may be let go like an arrow directed at a target and produce some change in the outer world. But having an outer effect is something very different from ordered use of objective conditions in order to give objective fulfillment to the emotion. The latter alone is expression and the emotion that attaches itself to, or is interpenetrated by, the resulting object is esthetic. If the person in question puts his room to rights as a matter of routine he is anesthetic. But if his original emotion of impatient irritation has been ordered and tranquillized by what he has done, the orderly room reflects back to him the change that has taken place in himself. He feels not that he has accomplished a needed chore but has done something emotionally fulfilling. His emotion as thus "objectified" is esthetic.

Esthetic emotion is thus something distinctive and yet not cut off by a chasm from other and natural emotional experiences, as some theorists in contending for its existence have made it to be. One familiar with recent literature on esthetics will be aware of a tendency to go to one extreme or the other. On one hand, it is assumed that there is in existence, at least in some gifted persons, an emotion that is aboriginally esthetic, and that artistic production and appreciation are the manifestations of this emotion. Such a conception is the inevitable logical counterpart of all attitudes that make art something esoteric and that relegate fine art to a realm separated by a gulf from everyday experiences. On the other hand, a reaction wholesome in intent against this view goes to the extreme of holding that there is no such thing as distinctively esthetic emotion. The emotion of affection that operates not through an overt act of caress but by searching out the observation or image of a soaring bird, the emotion of irritating energy that does not destroy or injure but that puts objects in satisfying order, is not numerically identical with its original and natural estate. Yet it stands in genetic continuity with it. The emotion that was finally wrought out by Tennyson in the composition of "In Memoriam" was not identical with the emotion of grief that manifests itself in weeping and a downcast frame: the first is an act of expression, the second of discharge. Yet the continuity of the two emotions, the fact that the esthetic emotion is native emotion transformed through the objective material to which it has committed its development and consummation, is evident.

Samuel Johnson with the Philistine's sturdy preference for reproduction of the familiar, criticized Milton's "Lycidas" in the following way: "It is not to be considered as the effusion of real passion, for passion runs not after remote allusions and obscure opinions. Passion plucks not berries from the myrtle and ivy, nor calls upon Arethusa and Mincius, nor tells of rough satyrs and fauns with cloven heel. Where there is leisure for fiction there is little grief."[8] Of course the underlying principle of Johnson's criticism would prevent the appearance of any work of art. It would, in strict logic, confine the "expression" of grief to weeping and tearing the hair. Thus, while the particular subject matter of Milton's poem would not be used today in an elegy, it, and any other work of art, is bound to deal with the remote in one of its aspects — namely, that remote from immediate effusion of emotion and from material that is worn out. Grief that has matured beyond the need of weeping and wailing for relief will resort to something of the sort that Johnson calls fiction — that is, imaginative material, although it be different matter from literature, classic and ancient myth. In all primitive peoples wailing soon assumes a ceremonial form that is "remote" from its native manifestation.

In other words, art is not nature, but is nature transformed by entering into new relationships where it evokes a new emotional response. Many actors remain outside the particular emotion they portray. This fact is known as Diderot's paradox since he first developed the theme. In fact, it is paradox only from the standpoint implied in the quotation from Samuel Johnson. More recent inquiries have shown, indeed, that there are two types of actors. There are those who report that they are at their best when they "lose" themselves emotionally in their rôles. Yet this fact is no exception to the principle that has been stated. For, after all, it is a rôle, a "part" with which actors identify themselves. As a part, it is conceived and treated as part of a whole; if there is art in acting, the rôle is subordinated so as to occupy the position of a part in the whole. It is thereby qualified by esthetic form. Even those who feel most poignantly the emotions of the character represented do not lose consciousness

that they are on a stage where there are other actors taking part; that they are before an audience, and that they must, therefore, coöperate with other players in creating a certain effect. These facts demand and signify a definite transformation of the primitive emotion. Portrayal of intoxication is a common device of the comic stage. But a man actually drunken would have to use art to conceal his condition if he is not to disgust his audience, or at least to excite a laughter that differs radically from that excited by intoxication when acted. The difference between the two types of actors is not a difference between expression of an emotion controlled by the relations of the situation into which it enters and a manifestation of raw emotion. It is a difference in methods of bringing about the desired effect, a difference doubtless connected with personal temperament.

Finally, what has been said locates, even if it does not solve, the vexed problem of the relation of esthetic or fine art to other modes of production also called art. The difference that exists in fact cannot be leveled, as we have already seen, by defining both in terms of technique and skill. But neither can it be erected into a barrier that is insuperable by referring the creation of fine art to an impulse that is unique, separated from impulsions which work in modes of expression not usually brought under the caption of fine art. Conduct can be sublime and manners gracious. If impulsion toward organization of material so as to present the latter in a form directly fulfilling in experience had no existence outside the arts of painting, poetry, music, and sculpture, it would not exist anywhere; there would be no fine art.

The problem of conferring esthetic quality upon all modes of production is a serious problem. But it is a human problem for human solution; not a problem incapable of solution because it is set by some unpassable gulf in human nature or in the nature of things. In an imperfect society — and no society will ever be perfect — fine art will be to some extent an escape from, or an adventitious decoration of, the main activities of living. But in a better-ordered society than that in which we live, an infinitely greater happiness than is now the case would attend all

[8] "Life of Milton." [Ed.]

modes of production. We live in a world in which there is an immense amount of organization, but it is an external organization, not one of the ordering of a growing experience, one that involves, moreover, the whole of the live creature, toward a fulfilling conclusion. Works of art that are not remote from common life, that are widely enjoyed in a community, are signs of a unified collective life. But they are also marvelous aids in the creation of such a life. The remaking of the material of experience in the act of expression is not an isolated event confined to the artist and to a person here and there who happens to enjoy the work. In the degree in which art exercises its office, it is also a remaking of the experience of the community in the direction of greater order and unity.

# Kenneth Burke

b. 1897

Kenneth Duva Burke was born on May 5, 1897, in Pittsburgh, where he was educated through high school. He attended college at Ohio State University in Columbus and Columbia University in New York but did not take a degree; this has been amply made up by the number of universities — over a dozen at last count — that have awarded him honorary doctorates. Burke worked as a researcher for the Laura Spelman Rockefeller Foundation, as the music critic for *The Dial* and *The Nation*, and as an editor for government publications, but his chief occupation during his long life has been that of itinerant scholar and critic. Burke has taken literally dozens of academic appointments at prestigious institutions but most of them, except for an eighteen-year appointment at Bennington College from 1943 to 1961, itself broken by visiting appointments elsewhere, have only been for a year or two. In addition to writing dozens of critical and philosophical books, Burke has been a poet since his eighteenth year, and his first publication (*The White Oxen,* 1924) was a collection of short stories. Burke, who now lives in Andover, New Jersey, has been married twice, to two sisters, and had three daughters by the first marriage and two sons by the second.

Burke, a quirky and individualistic thinker, has often and for understandable reasons been mischaracterized as a New Critic strongly influenced by Marx and Freud. Of the same generation as Brooks and Wimsatt, Burke was interested, like the New Critics, in the poem as a verbal creation, or as he put it himself, "a dance of attitudes"; and like most twentieth-century thinkers from Lionel Trilling to William Empson, he was also interested in the two most revolutionary thinkers of the later Victorian era. Nevertheless, Burke is more a philosopher than a literary critic as such, and his ideas, although primarily applied to literature and to prose texts, range far beyond our purposes here: his vision of language and literature as forms of symbolic action.

Perhaps we should begin at a very general level, with Burke's famous definition of Man. Burke conceived of man not as *homo sapiens* but as *homo symbolicus*, the only being capable of using (and therefore misusing) symbols. Man is therefore also the "inventor of the negative," since negation is a product only of symbol systems: Nature may not abhor a vacuum, but only language can explore the absence of something in a world that knows only presence. Man is also "separated from his natural condition by instruments of his own making," so conditioned by language and the social aspects of life that are created within and through language that even his physiology has changed from that of the arboreal apes from which he descended. Man is also "goaded by the spirit of hierarchy," a characteristically less pleasant way of saying "moved by a sense of order."

Finally, Burke likes to say that man is "rotten with perfection," in that our sense of order leads us to carry out our ideas to the nth degree, regardless of the consequences. One obvious instance is Hitler's idea of racial purity. Carried out to perfection, and with full negativity, using the power that rigidly enforced hierarchies give to a leader, the symbolic enactment leads to the horrors of the Holocaust. Although Burke's theory suggests that humanity has a drive to "perfect" such ideas in such a way, a utopian strain in Burke hopes that the strife between contrary symbol-systems (like capitalism and communism) can be indefinitely confined, with all our help, to symbolic battles, rather than exploding in that final negativity, nuclear annihilation.

The idea of conflict confined to a symbolic agon, a struggle of words, brings us back to Burke and literature. Saying something is another way of doing something. Essentially, Burke assumes that human beings write literature, just as they do everything else, in an effort to achieve some personal goal. Writing is itself a drama. Authors are *agents* who *act* within a certain *scene* (their environment) by means of a certain *agency* (writing) to achieve a *purpose*. These five terms — agent, act, scene, agency, and purpose — make up the Burkean *pentad*; their "ratios," or the relationships between the terms, are crucial to his criticism. Authors do not merely write as an end in itself, nor do they write for secular reasons — to make money or achieve fame. Rather, they select their particular subjects, topics, conflicts, for reasons that go beyond the secular, usually the purgation of their own sense of sinfulness, which leads to a sense of redemption within their lives. As Burke says in "Literature as Equipment for Living," there is no room for such a thing as "pure literature" of the sort the New Critics wished to analyze. Works of art are "equipment for living," "strategies for selecting enemies and allies, for socializing losses, for warding off evil eye, for purification, propitiation, and desanctification, consolation and vengeance, admonition and exhortation, implicit commands or instructions of one sort or another."

As an example of how the poet may socialize a loss or give himself symbolic instructions, we could take Burke's analysis of Milton's "Lycidas" in *Attitudes toward History* (1937). While a New Critic like John Crowe Ransom considered "Lycidas" "a poem nearly anonymous" in its exquisite variants on the general themes of the pastoral elegy, Burke boldly commits the intentional fallacy, even takes the poem, with its evocation of the death and resurrection of a poet, as a personal prophecy. After writing "Lycidas," Burke claims,

> Milton travelled in 1638 and 1639. And for the next twenty years thereafter, with the exception of an occasional sonnet, he devoted all his energies to his polemic prose. These dates, coupled with the contents of the poem, would justify us in contending that "Lycidas" was the symbolic dying of his poetic self. . . . In "Lycidas" he testifies that he is holding his dead self in abeyance, and that it will rise again. . . . So the poet remained, for all his dying; and at the Restoration, after the political interregnum of Cromwell, he would be reborn. "Paradise Lost" is the fulfillment of his contract.

Similarly, "The Rime of the Ancient Mariner" represents Coleridge's symbolic way of purging the guilt arising out of his failed marriage and his drug addiction, and of achieving an equally symbolic redemption. For Burke, the slain albatross can be equated with Sarah Coleridge, since they are "in the same equational cluster" — connected by similar imagery in "Mariner" and "The Aeolian Harp." Similarly, the watersnakes whom the mariner blesses as a part of nature connect with his drug addiction, which is referred to in a letter as "a scourge of ever restless, ever coiling and uncoiling serpents," while Coleridge feels "driven on from behind" — as the Mariner's ship is driven. In effect, Coleridge uses the poem to symbolically "bless" his drug addiction and "curse" his marriage — the scene of the poem itself involves a detained wedding-guest who misses the ceremony, and the poem ends by denigrating marriage in favor of the brotherhood of Nature and of humanity ("to walk together to the kirk, With a goodly company").

Not only may authors have their purgative/redemptive purposes, their societies also have them (and, we might add, the "affective" fallacy means as little to Burke as the "intentional" fallacy does). Burke's analysis of Shakespeare's *Coriolanus* in *Language as Symbolic Action* (1966) presents the hero of that play as the apotheosis of the aristocracy, with all the virtues and vices of the highborn — courage, pride, stoical fortitude, snobbery, family feeling — taken to the last extreme, "rotten with perfection," as Burke liked to put it. According to Burke, the action of the tragedy shapes everything toward the sacrifice of Coriolanus as a scapegoat — a symbolic destruction of the ultimate patrician enacted at a time when the strife between patrician and plebeian in English society was already becoming virulent, although it would not erupt into civil war for another three decades. The death of Coriolanus causes the reunification of Rome and symbolically allows the English Cavaliers and Roundheads, enemies-to-be, to join in unity in a purgative/redemptive experience.

Here and in the Milton example, Burke is characteristically cavalier in his use of the facts and delights in prophecy after-the-fact. One could pedantically object that Milton in 1637 could not have foreseen Cromwell and his secretaryship, that Coleridge was not fully addicted to laudanum at the time he wrote "The Ancient Mariner," that Shakespeare in 1609 could not have foreseen the Civil War. But the sort of conflict Burke is talking about always runs behind and above such facts: If Milton could not have predicted Cromwell, he certainly saw the conflict within himself between poetry and politics, and if Shakespeare could not have predicted the civil war that broke out twenty-five years after his death, he certainly understood the clash between classes within his own society. The same is true of Coleridge; even if one is not willing to claim (as Burke once did) that the poet was an *incipient* addict in 1796, there was surely a deep-seated and long-standing conflict in Coleridge between affections licensed by society (symbolized by the wedding in the poem) and affections that transcend and defy the social (like the Mariner's demonic bond with the watersnakes).

Burke's method of analyzing literature turns primarily on reducing the text to its scene of conflict, then viewing that conflict as symbolic of other conflicts within other scenes — within the poet's self, family, or society, including his or her relation with intellectual forebears or poetic rivals. The "scene" for which the poem is a grand metaphor can be psychological, economic, political, sociological, even theological. And as the example of Coleridge shows, Burke is willing to read other poems or letters onto the text under analysis. Everything is relevant.

If this allegorizing and psychologizing is utterly foreign to the formalist movements against which Burke defined his own poetics, he nevertheless resembles the New Critics in his concern for symbol, language, and imagery. The notion that themes essentially reside in clusters of images, that the associations of primary terms determine their psychic meaning, is close to the New Critical method. Nevertheless, the freewheeling Burke went considerably further than the New Critics were ever comfortable with in his "joycings" — puns, usually scatological, that reduce the high-flown meaning of a passage to a physiological level. Burke's analysis of Keats's "Ode on a Grecian Urn" in *A Grammar of Motives* (1945), reprinted here, is relatively decorous, but in the later *A Rhetoric of Motives* (1950), the "urn" is joyced to "urine," while the final sentiment, "Beauty is truth, truth beauty," is joyced to "Body is turd, turd body." Burke is not being childishly dirty-minded here. His point is that, in any poem so concerned with transcendence, the poet tends to repress the earthly and bodily functions that are being transcended; but what is repressed returns in language that, in distorted form, conveys what the poet has been avoiding talking about. In Burke conflict is unavoidable and language always takes over — that much is certain.

## Selected Bibliography

Frank, Armin Paul. *Kenneth Burke*. New York: Twayne, 1969.
Heath, Robert L. "Kenneth Burke's Break with Formalism." *Quarterly Journal of Speech* 70 (1984): 132–43.
———. *Realism and Relativism: A Perspective on Kenneth Burke*. Macon, Ga.: Mercer University Press, 1986.
Rueckert, William H. *Kenneth Burke and the Drama of Human Relations*. 2nd ed. Berkeley: University of California Press, 1982.
———. *The Rhetoric of Rebirth: A Study of the Literary Theory and Critical Practice of Kenneth Burke*. Ann Arbor: University Microfilms, 1957.
Southwell, Samuel B. *Kenneth Burke and Martin Heidegger, with a Note Against Deconstruction*. Gainesville: University Presses of Florida, 1987.
White, Hayden, and Margaret Brose, eds. *Representing Kenneth Burke*. Baltimore: Johns Hopkins University Press, 1982.

# Symbolic Action in a Poem by Keats

We are here set to analyze the "Ode on a Grecian Urn" as a viaticum that leads, by a series of transformations, into the oracle, "Beauty is truth, truth beauty." We shall analyze the Ode "dramatistically," in terms of symbolic action.

To consider language as a means of *informa-*

*tion* or *knowledge* is to consider it epistemologically, semantically, in terms of "science." To consider it as a mode of *action* is to consider it in terms of "poetry." For a poem is an act, the symbolic act of the poet who made it — an act of such a nature that, in surviving as a structure or object, it enables us as readers to re-enact it.

"Truth" being the essential word of knowledge (science) and "beauty" being the essential word of art or poetry, we might substitute accordingly. The oracle would then assert, "Poetry is science, science poetry." It would be particularly exhilarating to proclaim them one if there were a strong suspicion that they were at odds (as the assertion that "God's in his heaven, all's right with the world" is really a *counter*-assertion to doubts about God's existence and suspicions that much is wrong). It was the dialectical opposition between the "aesthetic" and the "practical," with "poetry" on one side and utility (business and applied science) on the other that was being ecstatically denied. The *relief* in this denial was grounded in the romantic philosophy itself, a philosophy which gave strong recognition to precisely the *contrast* between "beauty" and "truth."

Perhaps we might put it this way: If the oracle were to have been uttered in the first stanza of the poem rather than the last, its phrasing proper to that place would have been: "Beauty is *not* truth, truth *not* beauty." The five stanzas of successive transformation were necessary for the romantic philosophy of a romantic poet to transcend itself (raising its romanticism to a new order, or new dimension). An abolishing of romanticism through romanticism! (To transcend romanticism through romanticism is, when all is over, to restore in one way what is removed in another.)

But to the poem, step by step through the five stanzas.

As a "way in," we begin with the sweeping periodic sentence that, before the stanza is over, has swiftly but imperceptibly been transmuted in quality from the periodic to the breathless, a cross between interrogation and exclamation:

Thou still unravish'd bride of quietness,
  Thou foster-child of silence and slow time,
Sylvan historian, who canst thus express
  A flowery tale more sweetly than our rhyme:
What leaf-fring'd legend haunts about thy shape
  Of deities or mortals, or of both,
    In Tempe or the dales of Arcady?
What men or gods are these?    What maidens loth?
  What mad pursuit?    What struggle to escape?
    What pipes and timbrels?    What wild ecstasy?

Even the last quick outcries retain somewhat the quality of the periodic structure with which the stanza began. The final line introduces the subject of "pipes and timbrels," which is developed and then surpassed in Stanza II:

Heard melodies are sweet, but those unheard
  Are sweeter; therefore, ye soft pipes, play on;
Not to the sensual ear, but, more endear'd,
  Pipe to the spirit ditties of no tone:
Fair youth, beneath the trees, thou canst not leave
  Thy song, nor ever can those trees be bare;
    Bold Lover, never, never canst thou kiss,
Though winning near the goal — yet, do not grieve;
  She cannot fade, though thou hast not thy bliss,
    Forever wilt thou love, and she be fair!

If we had only the first stanza of this Ode, and were speculating upon it from the standpoint of motivation, we could detect there tentative indications of two motivational levels. For the lines express a doubt whether the figures on the urn are "deities or mortals" — and the motives of gods are of a different order from the motives of men. This bare hint of such a possibility emerges with something of certainty in the second stanza's development of the "pipes and timbrels" theme. For we explicitly consider a contrast between body and mind (in the contrast between "heard melodies," addressed "to the sensual ear," and "ditties of no tone," addressed "to the spirit").

Also, of course, the notion of inaudible sound brings us into the region of the mystic oxymoron (the term in rhetoric for "the figure in which an epithet of a contrary significance is added to a word: e.g., *cruel kindness; laborious idleness*"). And it clearly suggests a concern with the level of motives-behind-motives, as with the paradox of the prime mover that is itself at rest, being the unmoved ground of all motion and action. Here the poet whose sounds are the richest in our language is mediating upon *absolute* sound, the *essence* of sound, which would be soundless as the prime mover is motionless, or as the "principle" of sweetness would not be sweet, having transcended sweetness, or as the sub-atomic particles of the sun are each, in their isolate purity, said to be devoid of temperature.

Contrast Keats's unheard melodies with those of Shelley:

> Music, when soft voices die,
> Vibrates in the memory —
> Odours, when sweet violets sicken,
> Live within the sense they quicken.
>
> Rose leaves, when the rose is dead,
> Are heaped for the beloved's bed;
> And so thy thoughts, when thou art gone,
> Love itself shall slumber on.[1]

Here the futuristic Shelley is anticipating retrospection; he is looking forward to looking back. The form of thought is naturalistic and temporalistic in terms of *past* and *future*. But the form of thought in Keats is mystical, in terms of an *eternal present*. The Ode is striving to move beyond the region of becoming into the realm of *being*. (This is another way of saying that we are here concerned with two levels of motivation.)

In the last four lines of the second stanza, the state of immediacy is conveyed by a development peculiarly Keatsian. I refer not simply to translation into terms of the erotic, but rather to a quality of *suspension* in the erotic imagery, defining an eternal prolongation of the state just prior to fulfilment — not exactly arrested ecstasy, but rather an arrested pre-ecstasy.[2]

Suppose that we had but this one poem by Keats, and knew nothing of its author or its period, so that we could treat it only in itself, as a series of internal transformations to be studied in their development from a certain point, and without reference to any motives outside the Ode. Under such conditions, I think, we should require no further observations to characterize (from the standpoint of symbolic action) the main argument in the second stanza. We might go on to make an infinity of observations about the details of the stanza; but as regards major deployments we should deem it enough to note that the theme of "pipes and timbrels" is developed by the use of mystic oxymoron, and then surpassed (or given a development-atop-the-development) by the stressing of erotic imagery (that had been ambiguously adumbrated in the references to "maidens loth" and "mad pursuit" of Stanza I). And we could note the quality of *incipience* in this imagery, its state of arrest not at fulfilment, but at the point just prior to fulfilment.

Add, now, our knowledge of the poem's place as an enactment in a particular cultural scene, and we likewise note in this second stanza a variant of the identification between death and sexual love that was so typical of nineteenth-century romanticism and was to attain its musical monument in the Wagnerian *Liebestod*.[3] On a purely dialectical basis, to die in love would be to be born to love (the lovers dying as individual identities that they might be transformed into a common identity). Adding historical factors, one can note the part that capitalist individualism plays in sharpening this consummation (since a property structure that heightens the sense of individual identity would thus make it more imperiously a "death" for the individual to take on the new identity made by a union of two). We can thus see why the love-death equation would be particularly representative of a romanticism that was the reflex of business.

Fortunately, the relation between private property and the love-death equation is attested on unimpeachable authority, concerning the effect of consumption and consummation in a "mutual flame":

---

[1]Shelley's poem is titled "To ——— " in the *Posthumous Poems* of 1824. [Ed.]

[2]Mr. G. Wilson Knight, in *The Starlit Dome*, refers to "that recurring tendency in Keats to image a posed form, a stillness suggesting motion, what might be called a 'tiptoe' effect." [Au.]

[3]Love-death; the denouement of Wagner's *Tristan und Isolde* in which the lovers find their apotheosis in death. [Ed.]

So between them love did shine,
That the turtle saw his right
Flaming in the phoenix' sight;
Either was the other's mine.

Property was thus appall'd,
That the self was not the same;
Single nature's double name
Neither two nor one was called.[4]

The addition of fire to the equation, with its pun on sexual burning, moves us from purely dialectical considerations into psychological ones. In the lines of Shakespeare, fire is the third term, the ground term for the other two (the synthesis that ends the lovers' roles as thesis and antithesis). Less obviously, the same movement from the purely dialectical to the psychological is implicit in any imagery of a *dying* or a *falling* in common, which when woven with sexual imagery signalizes a "transcendent" sexual consummation. The figure appears in a lover's compliment when Keats writes to Fanny Brawne, thus:

> I never knew before, what such a love as you have made me feel, was; I did not believe in it; my Fancy was afraid of it lest it should burn me up. But if you will fully love me, though there may be some fire, 'twill not be more than we can bear when moistened and bedewed with pleasures.

Our primary concern is to follow the transformations of the poem itself. But to understand its full nature as a symbolic act, we should use whatever knowledge is available. In the case of Keats, not only do we know the place of this poem in his work and its time, but also we have material to guide our speculations as regards correlations between poem and poet. I grant that such speculations interfere with the symmetry of criticism as a game. (Criticism as a game is best to watch, I guess, when one confines himself to the single unit, and reports on its movements like a radio commentator broadcasting the blow-by-blow description of a prizefight.) But linguistic analysis has opened up new possibilities in the correlating of producer and product — and these concerns have such important bearing upon matters of culture and conduct in general that no

sheer conventions or ideals of criticism should be allowed to interfere with their development.

From what we know of Keats's illness, with the peculiar inclination to erotic imaginings that accompany its fever (as with the writings of D. H. Lawrence) we can glimpse a particular bodily motive expanding and intensifying the lyric state in Keats's case. Whatever the intense *activity* of his thoughts, there was the material *pathos* of his physical condition. Whatever transformations of mind or body he experienced, his illness was there as a kind of constitutional substrate, whereby all aspects of the illness would be imbued with their derivation from a common ground (the phthisic fever thus being at one with the phthisic chill, for whatever the clear contrast between fever and chill, they are but modes of the same illness, the common underlying substance).

The correlation between the state of agitation in the poems and the physical condition of the poet is made quite clear in the poignant letters Keats wrote during his last illness. In 1819 he complains that he is "scarcely content to write the best verses for the fever they leave behind." And he continues: "I want to compose without this fever." But a few months later he confesses, "I am recommended not even to read poetry, much less write it." Or: "I must say that for 6 Months before I was taken ill I had not passed a tranquil day. Either that gloom overspre[a]d me or I was suffering under some passionate feeling, or if I turn'd to versify that exacerbated the poison of either sensation." Keats was "like a sick eagle looking at the sky," as he wrote of his mortality in a kindred poem, "On Seeing the Elgin Marbles."

But though the poet's body was a *patient,* the poet's mind was an *agent.* Thus, as a practitioner of poetry, he could *use* his fever, even perhaps encouraging, though not deliberately, esthetic habits that, in making for the perfection of his lines, would exact payment in the ravages of his body (somewhat as Hart Crane could write poetry only by modes of living that made for the cessation of his poetry and so led to his dissolution).

Speaking of agents, patients, and action here, we might pause to glance back over the centuries thus: in the Aristotelian grammar of motives,

---

[4]Shakespeare, "The Phoenix and the Turtle." [Ed.]

action has its reciprocal in passion, hence *passion* is the property of a *patient*. But by the Christian paradox (which made the martyr's action identical with his passion, as the accounts of the martyrs were called both Acts and Passionals), *patience* is the property of a moral *agent*. And this Christian view, as secularized in the philosophy of romanticism, with its stress upon creativeness, leads us to the possibility of a bodily suffering redeemed by a poetic act.

In the third stanza, the central stanza of the Ode (hence properly the fulcrum of its swing) we see the two motives, the action and the passion, in the process of being separated. The possibility raised in the first stanza (which was dubious whether the level of motives was to be human or divine), and developed in the second stanza (which contrasts the "sensual" and the "spirit"), becomes definitive in Stanza III:

> Ah, happy, happy boughs! that cannot shed
> Your leaves, nor ever bid the Spring adieu;
> And, happy melodist, unwearied,
> For ever piping songs for ever new;
> More happy love! more happy, happy love!
> For ever warm and still to be enjoy'd,
> For ever panting, and for ever young;
> All breathing human passion far above,
> That leaves a heart high-sorrowful and cloy'd,
> A burning forehead, and a parching tongue.

The poem as a whole makes permanent, or fixes in a state of arrest, a peculiar agitation. But within this fixity, by the nature of poetry as a progressive medium, there must be development. Hence, the agitation that is maintained throughout (as a mood absolutized so that it fills the entire universe of discourse) will at the same time undergo internal transformations. In the third stanza, these are manifested as a clear division into two distinct and contrasted realms. There is a transcendental fever, which is felicitous, divinely above "all breathing human passion." And this "leaves" the other level, the level of earthly fever, "a burning forehead and a parching tongue." From the bodily fever, which is a passion, and malign, there has split off a spiritual activity, a wholly benign aspect of the total agitation.

Clearly, a movement has been finished. The poem must, if it is well-formed, take a new direction, growing out of and surpassing the curve that has by now been clearly established by the successive stages from "Is there the possibility of two motivational levels?" through "there are two motivational levels" to "the 'active' motivational level 'leaves' the 'passive' level."

Prophesying, with the inestimable advantage that goes with having looked ahead, what should we expect the new direction to be? First, let us survey the situation. Originally, before the two strands of the fever had been definitely drawn apart, the bodily passion could serve as the scene or ground of the spiritual action. But at the end of the third stanza, we abandon the level of bodily passion. The action is "far above" the passion, it "leaves" the fever. What then would this transcendent act require, to complete it?

It would require a scene of the same quality as itself. An act and a scene belong together. The nature of the one must be a fit with the nature of the other. (I like to call this the "scene-act ratio," or "dramatic ratio.") Hence, the act having now transcended its bodily setting, it will require, as its new setting, a transcendent scene. Hence, prophesying *post eventum,* we should ask that, in Stanza IV, the poem *embody* the transcendental act by endowing it with an appropriate scene.

The scene-act ratio involves a law of dramatic consistency whereby the quality of the act shares the quality of the scene in which it is enacted (the synecdochic relation of container and thing contained). Its grandest variant was in supernatural cosmogonies wherein mankind took on the attributes of gods by acting in cosmic scenes that were themselves imbued with the presence of godhead.[5]

Or we may discern the logic of the scene-act ratio behind the old controversy as to whether "God willed the good because it is good," or "the

---

[5] In an article by Leo Spitzer, "*Milieu and Ambiance*: An Essay in Historical Semantics," (September and December 1942 numbers of *Philosophy and Phenomenological Research*), one will find a wealth of material that can be read as illustrative of "dramatic ratio." [Au.]

good is good because God willed it." This strictly theological controversy had political implications. But our primary concern here is with the *dramatistic* aspects of this controversy. For you will note that the whole issue centers in the problem of the *grounds* of God's creative act.

Since, from the purely dramatic point of view, every act requires a scene in which it takes place, we may note that one of the doctrines (that "God willed the good because it is good") is more symmetrical than the other. For by it, God's initial act of creation is itself given a ground, or scene (the objective existence of goodness, which was so real that God himself did not simply make it up, but acted in conformity with its nature when willing it to be the law of his creation). In the scholastic formulas taken over from Aristotle, God was defined as "pure act" (though this pure act was in turn the ultimate ground or *scene* of human acting and willing). And from the standpoint of purely dramatic symmetry, it would be desirable to have some kind of "scene" even for God. This requirement is met, we are suggesting, in the doctrine that "God willed the good *because* it is good." For this word, "because," in assigning a reason for God's willing, gives us in principle a kind of scene, as we may discern in the pun of our word, "ground," itself, which indeterminately applies to either "place" or "cause."

If even theology thus responded to the pressure for dramatic symmetry by endowing God, as the transcendent act, with a transcendent scene of like quality, we should certainly expect to find analogous tactics in this Ode. For as we have noted that the romantic passion is the secular equivalent of the Christian passion, so we may recall Coleridge's notion that poetic action itself is a "dim analogue of Creation."[6] Keats in his way confronting the same dramatistic requirement that the theologians confronted in theirs, when he has arrived at his transcendent act at the end of Stanza III (that is, when the benign fever has split away from the malign bodily counterpart, as a divorcing of spiritual action from sensual passion), he is ready in the next stanza for the imagining of a scene that would correspond

in quality to the quality of the action as so transformed. His fourth stanza will concretize, or "materialize," the act, by dwelling upon its appropriate ground.

Who are these coming to the sacrifice?
    To what green altar, O mysterious priest,
Lead'st thou that heifer lowing at the skies,
    And all her silken flanks with garlands drest?
What little town, by river or sea shore,
    Or mountain built with peaceful citadel,
        Is emptied of this folk, this pious morn?
And, little town, thy streets for evermore
    Will silent be; and not a soul to tell
        Why thou art desolate, can e'er return.

It is a vision, as you prefer, of "death" or of "immortality." "Immortality," we might say, is the "good" word for "death," and must necessarily be conceived in terms of death (the necessity that Donne touches upon when he writes, ". . . but thinke that I / Am, by being dead, immortall"). This is why, when discussing the second stanza, I felt justified in speaking of the variations of the love-death equation, though the poem spoke not of love and *death,* but of love *for ever.* We have a deathy-deathless scene as the corresponding ground of our transcendent act. The Urn itself, as with the scene upon it, is not merely an immortal act in our present mortal scene; it was originally an immortal act in a mortal scene quite different. The imagery, of sacrifice, piety, silence, desolation, is that of communication with the immortal or the dead.[7]

---

[7]In imagery there is no negation, or disjunction. Logically, we can say, "this *or* that," "this, *not* that." In imagery we can but say "this *and* that," "this *with* that," "this-that," etc. Thus, imagistically considered, a commandment cannot be simply a proscription, but is also latently a provocation (a state of affairs that figures in the kind of stylistic scrupulosity and/or curiosity to which Gide's heroes have been particularly sensitive, as "thou shalt not . . ." becomes imaginatively transformed into "what would happen if . . ."). In the light of what we have said about the deathiness of immortality, and the relation between the erotic and the thought of a "dying," perhaps we might be justified in reading the last line of the great "Bright Star!" sonnet as naming states not simply alternative but also synonymous:

And so live ever — or else swoon to death.

This use of the love-death equation is as startlingly paralleled

---

[6]Coleridge goes even further in *Biographia Literaria,* chapter 13; see p. 301. [Ed.]

Incidentally, we might note that the return to the use of rhetorical questions in the fourth stanza serves well, on a purely technical level, to keep our contact with the mood of the opening stanza, a music that now but vibrates in the memory. Indeed, one even gets the impression that the form of the rhetorical question had never been abandoned; that the poet's questings had been couched as questions throughout. This is tonal felicity at its best, and something much like unheard tonal felicity. For the actual persistence of the rhetorical questions through these stanzas would have been wearisome, whereas their return now gives us an inaudible variation, by making us feel that the exclamations in the second and third stanzas had been questions, as the questions in the first stanza had been exclamations.

But though a lyric greatly profits by so strong a sense of continuousness, or perpetuity, I am trying to stress the fact that in the fourth stanza we *come upon* something. Indeed, this fourth stanza is related to the three foregoing stanzas quite as the sestet is related to the octave in Keats's sonnet, "On First Looking into Chapman's Homer":

> Much have I travell'd in the realms of gold,
>     And many goodly states and kingdoms seen;
>     Round many western islands have I been
> Which bards in fealty to Apollo hold.
> Oft of one wide expanse had I been told
>     That deep-brow'd Homer ruled as his demesne;
>     Yet did I never breathe its pure serene
> Till I heard Chapman speak out loud and bold;
> Then felt I like some watcher of the skies
>     When a new planet swims into his ken;
> Or like stout Cortez when with eagle eyes
>     He stared at the Pacific — and all his men
> Look'd at each other with a wild surmise —
>     Silent, upon a peak in Darien.

I am suggesting that, just as the sestet in this sonnet, *comes upon a scene,* so it is with the fourth stanza of the Ode. In both likewise we end on the theme of silence; and is not the Ode's

---

in a letter to Fanny Brawne:

I have two luxuries to brood over in my walks, your loveliness and the hour of my death. O that I could take possession of them both in the same moment. [Au.]

reference to the thing that "not a soul can tell" quite the same in quality as the sonnet's reference to a "wild surmise"?

Thus, with the Urn as viaticum (or rather, with the *poem* as viaticum, and *in the name* of the Urn), having symbolically enacted a kind of act that transcends our mortality, we round out the process by coming to dwell upon the transcendental ground of this act. The dead world of ancient Greece, as immortalized on an Urn surviving from that period, is the vessel of this deathy-deathless ambiguity. And we have gone dialectically from the "human" to the "divine" and thence to the "ground of the divine" (here tracing in poetic imagery the kind of "dramatistic" course we have considered, on the purely conceptual plane, in the theological speculations about the "grounds" for God's creative act). Necessarily, there must be certain inadequacies in the conception of this ground, precisely because of the fact that immortality can only be conceived in terms of death. Hence the reference to the "desolate" in a scene otherwise possessing the benignity of the eternal.

The imagery of pious sacrifice, besides its fitness for such thoughts of departure as when the spiritual act splits from the sensual pathos, suggests also a bond of communication between the levels (because of its immortal character in a mortal scene). And finally, the poem, in the name of the Urn, or under the aegis of the Urn, is such a bond. For we readers, by re-enacting it in the reading, use it as a viaticum to transport us into the quality of the scene which it depicts on its face (the scene containing as a fixity what the poem as act extends into a process). The scene *on* the Urn is really the scene *behind* the Urn; the Urn is literally the ground of this scene, but transcendentally the scene is the ground of the Urn. The Urn contains the scene out of which it arose.

We turn now to the closing stanza:

> O Attic shape! Fair attitude! with brede
>     Of marble men, and maidens overwrought,
> With forest branches and the trodden weed;
>     Thou, silent form, dost tease us out of thought
> As doth eternity: Cold Pastoral!
>     When old age shall this generation waste,
>     Thou shalt remain, in midst of other woe

Than ours, a friend to man, to whom thou say'st,
"Beauty is truth, truth beauty," — that is all
  Ye know on earth, and all ye need to know.

In the third stanza we were at a moment of heat, emphatically sharing an imagery of loves "panting" and "for ever warm" that was, in the transcendental order, companionate to "a burning forehead, and a parching tongue" in the order of the passions. But in the last stanza, as signalized in the marmorean utterance, "Cold Pastoral!" we have gone from transcendental fever to transcendental chill. Perhaps, were we to complete our exegesis, we should need reference to some physical step from phthisic chill, that we might detect here a final correlation between bodily passion and mental action. In any event we may note that, the mental action having departed from the bodily passion, the change from fever to chill is not a sufferance. For, as only the *benign* aspects of the fever had been left after the split, so it is a wholly benign chill on which the poem ends.[8]

I wonder whether anyone can read the reference to "brede of marble men and maidens overwrought" without thinking of "breed" for "brede" and "excited" for "overwrought." (Both expressions would thus merge notions of sexuality and craftsmanship, the erotic and the poetic.) As for the designating of the Urn as an "Attitude," it fits in admirably with our stress upon symbolic action. For an attitude is an arrested, or incipient *act* — not just an *object,* or *thing.*

Yeats, in *A Vision,* speaks of "the diagrams in Law's *Boehme,* where one lifts a paper to discover both the human entrails and the starry heavens." This equating of the deeply without and the deeply within (as also with Kant's famous remark) might well be remembered when we think of the sky that the "watcher" saw in

Keats's sonnet. It is an internal sky, attained through meditations induced by the reading of a book. And so the oracle, whereby truth and beauty are proclaimed as one, would seem to derive from a profound inwardness.

Otherwise, without these introductory mysteries, "truth" and "beauty" were at odds. For whereas "beauty" had its fulfillment in romantic poetry, "truth" was coming to have its fulfillment in science, technological accuracy, accountancy, statistics, actuarial tables, and the like. Hence, without benefit of the rites which one enacts in a sympathetic reading of the Ode (rites that remove the discussion to a different level), the enjoyment of "beauty" would involve an esthetic kind of awareness radically in conflict with the kind of awareness deriving from the practical "truth." And as regards the tactics of the poem, this conflict would seem to be solved by "estheticizing" the true rather than by "verifying" the beautiful.

Earlier in our essay, we suggested reading "poetry" for "beauty" and "science" for "truth," with the oracle deriving its *liberating* quality from the fact that it is uttered at a time when the poem has taken us to a level where earthly contradictions do not operate. But we might also, in purely conceptual terms, attain a level where "poetry" and "science" cease to be at odds; namely: by translating the two terms into the "grammar" that lies behind them. That is: we could generalize the term "poetry" by widening it to the point where we could substitute for it the term "act." And we could widen "science" to the point where we could substitute "scene." Thus we have:

"beauty" equals "poetry" equals "act"
"truth"   equals "science" equals "scene"

We would equate "beauty" with "act," because it is not merely a decorative thing, but an assertion, an affirmative, a creation, hence in the fullest sense an act. And we would equate "truth" or "science" with the "scenic" because science is a knowledge of *what is* — and *all that is* comprises the over-all universal *scene.* Our corresponding transcendence, then, got by "translation" into purely grammatical terms, would be: "Act is scene, scene act." We have got to this

---

[8]In a letter to Fanny Brawne, Keats touches upon the fever-chill contrast in a passage that also touches upon the love-death equation, though here the chill figures in an untransfigured state:

I fear that I am too prudent for a dying kind of Lover. Yet, there is a great difference between going off in warm blood like Romeo; and making one's exit like a frog in a frost. [Au.]

point by a kind of purely conceptual transformation that would correspond, I think, to the transformations of imagery leading to the oracle in the Ode.

"Act is scene, scene act." Unfortunately, I must break the symmetry a little. For poetry, as conceived in idealism (romanticism) could not quite be equated with *act,* but rather with *attitude.* For idealistic philosophies, with their stress upon the subjective, place primary stress upon the *agent* (the individual, ego, the will, etc.). It was medieval scholasticism that placed primary stress upon the *act.* And in the Ode the Urn (which is the vessel or representative of poetry) is called an "attitude," which is not outright an act, but an incipient or arrested act, a *state of mind,* the property of an *agent.* Keats, is calling the Urn an attitude, is *personifying* it. Or we might use the italicizing resources of dialectic by saying that for Keats, beauty (poetry) was not so much "the *act* of an agent" as it was "the act of an *agent.*"

Perhaps we can re-enforce this interpretation by examining kindred strategies in Yeats, whose poetry similarly derives from idealistic, romantic sources. Indeed, as we have noted elsewhere,[9] Yeats's vision of immortality in his Byzantium poems but carries one step further the Keatsian identification with the Grecian Urn:

Once out of nature I shall never take
My bodily form from any natural thing,
But such a form as Grecian goldsmiths make
Of hammered gold and gold enamelling . . .

Here certainly the poet envisions immortality as "esthetically" as Keats. For he will have immortality as a golden bird, a fabricated thing, a work of Grecian goldsmiths. Here we go in the same direction as the "overwrought" Urn, but farther along in that direction.

The ending of Yeats's poem, "Among School Children," helps us to make still clearer the idealistic stress upon agent:

Labour is blossoming or dancing where
The body is not bruised to pleasure soul,

[9] "On Motivation in Yeats" (*The Southern Review,* Winter 1942). [Au.]

Nor beauty torn out of its own despair,
Nor blear-eyed wisdom out of midnight oil.
O chestnut tree, great rooted blossomer,
Are you the leaf, the blossom or the bole?
O body swayed to music, O brightening glance,
How can we know the dancer from the dance?

Here the chestnut tree (as personified agent) is the ground of unity or continuity for all its scenic manifestations; and with the agent (dancer) is merged the act (dance). True, we seem to have here a commingling of act, scene, and agent, all three. Yet it is the *agent* that is "foremost among the equals." Both Yeats and Keats, of course, were much more "dramatistic" in their thinking than romantic poets generally, who usually center their efforts upon the translation of *scene* into terms of *agent* (as the materialistic science that was the dialectical counterpart of romantic idealism preferred conversely to translate *agent* into terms of *scene,* or in other words, to treat "consciousness" in terms of "matter," the "mental" in terms of the "physical," "people" in terms of "environment").

To review briefly: The poem begins with an ambiguous fever which in the course of the further development is "separated out," splitting into a bodily fever and a spiritual counterpart. The bodily passion is the malign aspect of the fever, the mental action its benign aspect. In the course of the development, the malign passion is transcended and the benign active partner, the intellectual exhilaration, takes over. At the beginning, where the two aspects were ambiguously one, the bodily passion would be the "scene" of the mental action (the "objective symptoms" of the body would be paralleled by the "subjective symptoms" of the mind, the bodily state thus being the other or ground of the mental state). But as the two become separated out, the mental action transcends the bodily passion. It becomes an act in its own right, making discoveries and assertions not grounded in the bodily passion. And this quality of action, in transcending the merely physical symptoms of the fever, would thus require a different ground or scene, one more suited in quality to the quality of the transcendent act.

The transcendent act is concretized, or "materialized," in the vision of the "immortal" scene, the reference in Stanza IV to the original scene of the Urn, the "heavenly" scene of the dead, or immortal, Greece (the scene in which the Urn was originally enacted and which is also fixed on its face). To indicate the internality of this vision, we referred to a passage in Yeats relating the "depths" of the sky without to the depths of the mind within; and we showed a similar pattern in Keats's account of the vision that followed his reading of Chapman's Homer. We suggested that the poet is here coming upon a new internal sky, through identification with the Urn as act, the same sky that he came upon through identification with the enactments of Chapman's translation.

This transcendent scene is the level at which the earthly laws of contradiction no longer prevail. Hence, in the terms of this scene, he can proclaim the unity of truth and beauty (of science and art), a proclamation which he needs to make precisely because here was the basic split responsible for the romantic agitation (in both poetic and philosophic idealism). That is, it was gratifying to have the oracle proclaim the unity

of poetry and science because the values of technology and business were causing them to be at odds. And from the perspective of a "higher level" (the perspective of a dead or immortal scene transcending the world of temporal contradictions) the split could be proclaimed once more a unity.

At this point, at this stage of exaltation, the fever has been replaced by chill. But the bodily passion has completely dropped out of account. All is now mental action. Hence, the chill (as in the ecstatic exclamation, "Cold Pastoral!") is proclaimed only in its benign aspect.

We may contrast this discussion with explanations such as a materialist of the Kretschmer school might offer. I refer to accounts of motivation that might treat disease as cause and poem as effect. In such accounts, the disease would not be "passive," but wholly active; and what we have called the mental action would be wholly passive, hardly more than an epiphenomenon, a mere symptom of the disease quite as are the fever and the chill themselves. Such accounts would give us no conception of the essential matter here, the intense linguistic activity.

# Literature as Equipment for Living

Here I shall put down, as briefly as possible, a statement in behalf of what might be catalogued, with a fair degree of accuracy, as a *sociological* criticism of literature. Sociological criticism in itself is certainly not new. I shall here try to suggest what partially new elements or emphasis I think should be added to this old approach. And to make the "way in" as easy as possible, I shall begin with a discussion of proverbs.

**I**

Examine random specimens in *The Oxford Dictionary of English Proverbs*. You will note, I think, that there is no "pure" literature here.

Everything is "medicine." Proverbs are designed for consolation or vengeance, for admonition or exhortation, for foretelling.

Or they name typical, recurrent situations. That is, people find a certain social relationship recurring so frequently that they must "have a word for it." The Eskimos have special names for many different kinds of snow (fifteen, if I remember rightly) because variations in the quality of snow greatly affect their living. Hence, they must "size up" snow much more accurately than we do. And the same is true of social phenomena. Social structures give rise to "type" situations, subtle subdivisions of the relationships involved in competitive and coöperative acts.

Many proverbs seek to chart, in more or less homey and picturesque ways, these "type" situations. I submit that such naming is done, not for the sheer glory of the thing, but because of its bearing upon human welfare. A different name for snow implies a different kind of hunt. Some names for snow imply that one should not hunt at all. And similarly, the names for typical, recurrent social situations are not developed out of "disinterested curiosity," but because the names imply a command (what to expect, what to look out for).

To illustrate with a few representative examples:

Proverbs designed for consolation: "The sun does not shine on both sides of the hedge at once." "Think of ease, but work on." "Little troubles the eye, but far less the soul." "The worst luck now, the better another time." "The wind in one's face makes one wise." "He that hath lands hath quarrels." "He knows how to carry the dead cock home." "He is not poor that hath little, but he that desireth much."

For vengeance: "At length the fox is brought to the furrier." "Shod in the cradle, barefoot in the stubble." "Sue a beggar and get a louse." "The higher the ape goes, the more he shows his tail." "The moon does not heed the barking of dogs." "He measures another's corn by his own bushel." "He shuns the man who knows him well." "Fools tie knots and wise men loose them."

Proverbs that have to do with foretelling (the most obvious are those to do with the weather): "Sow peas and beans in the wane of the moon, Who soweth them sooner, he soweth too soon." "When the wind's in the north, the skilful fisher goes not forth." "When the sloe tree is as white as a sheet, sow your barley whether it be dry or wet." "When the sun sets bright and clear, An easterly wind you need not fear. When the sun sets in a bank, A westerly wind we shall not want."

In short: "Keep your weather eye open": be realistic about sizing up today's weather, because your accuracy has bearing upon tomorrow's weather. And forecast not only the meteorological weather, but also the social weather: "When the moon's in the full, then wit's in the wane."

"Straws show which way the wind blows." "When the fish is caught, the net is laid aside." "Remove an old tree, and it will wither to death." "The wolf may lose his teeth, but never his nature." "He that bites on every weed must needs light on poison." "Whether the pitcher strikes the stone, or the stone the pitcher, it is bad for the pitcher." "Eagles catch no flies." "The more laws, the more offenders."

In this foretelling category we might also include the recipes for wise living, sometimes moral, sometimes technical: "First thrive, and then wive." "Think with the wise but talk with the vulgar." "When the fox preacheth, then beware your geese." "Venture a small fish to catch a great one." "Respect a man, he will do the more."

In the class of "typical, recurrent situations" we might put such proverbs and proverbial expressions as: "Sweet appears sour when we pay." "The treason is loved but the traitor is hated." "The wine in the bottle does not quench thirst." "The sun is never the worse for shining on a dunghill." "The lion kicked by an ass." "The lion's share." "To catch one napping." "To smell a rat." "To cool one's heels."

By all means, I do not wish to suggest that this is the only way in which the proverbs could be classified. For instance, I have listed in the "foretelling" group the proverb, "When the fox preacheth, then beware your geese." But it could obviously be "taken over" for vindictive purposes. Or consider a proverb like, "Virtue flies from the heart of a mercenary man." A poor man might obviously use it either to console himself for being poor (the implication being, "Because I am poor in money I am rich in virtue") or to strike at another (the implication being, "When he got money, what else could you expect of him but deterioration?"). In fact, we could even say that such symbolic vengeance would itself be an aspect of solace. And a proverb like "The sun is never the worse for shining on a dunghill" (which I have listed under "typical recurrent situations") might as well be put in the vindictive category.

The point of issue is not to find categories that "place" the proverbs once and for all. What I want is categories that suggest their active nature. Here is no "realism for its own sake." Here is realism for promise, admonition, solace, vengeance, foretelling, instruction, charting, all for the direct bearing that such acts have upon matters of welfare.

**2**

Step two: Why not extend such analysis of proverbs to encompass the whole field of literature? Could the most complex and sophisticated works of art legitimately be considered somewhat as "proverbs writ large"? Such leads, if held admissible, should help us to discover important facts about literary organization (thus satisfying the requirements of technical criticism). And the kind of observation from this perspective should apply beyond literature to life in general (thus helping to take literature out of its separate bin and give it a place in a general "sociological" picture).

The point of view might be phrased in this way: Proverbs are *strategies* for dealing with *situations*. In so far as situations are typical and recurrent in a given social structure, people develop names for them and strategies for handling them. Another name for strategies might be *attitudes*.

People have often commented on the fact that there are *contrary* proverbs. But I believe that the above approach to proverbs suggests a necessary modification of that comment. The apparent contradictions depend upon differences in *attitude*, involving a correspondingly different choice of *strategy*. Consider, for instance, the *apparently* opposite pair: "Repentance comes too late" and "Never too late to mend." The first is admonitory. It says in effect: "You'd better look out, or you'll get yourself too far into this business." The second is consolatory, saying in effect: "Buck up, old man, you can still pull out of this."

Some critics have quarreled with me about my selection of the word "strategy" as the name for this process. I have asked them to suggest an alternative term, so far without profit. The only one I can think of is "method." But if "strategy" errs in suggesting to some people an overly *conscious* procedure, "method" errs in suggesting an

overly *"methodical"* one. Anyhow, let's look at the documents:

*Concise Oxford Dictionary:* "Strategy: Movement of an army or armies in a campaign, art of so moving or disposing troops or ships as to impose upon the enemy the place and time and conditions for fighting preferred by oneself" (from a Greek word that refers to the leading of an army).

*New English Dictionary:* "Strategy: The art of projecting and directing the larger military movements and operations of a campaign."

André Cheron, *Traité Complet d'Echecs: "On entend par stratégie les manoeuvres qui ont pour but la sortie et le bon arrangement des pièces."*[1]

Looking at these definitions, I gain courage. For surely, the most highly alembicated and sophisticated work of art, arising in complex civilizations, could be considered as designed to organize and command the army of one's thoughts and images, and to so organize them that one "imposes upon the enemy the time and place and conditions for fighting preferred by oneself." One seeks to "direct the larger movements and operations" in one's campaign of living. One "maneuvers," and the maneuvering is an "art."

Are not the final results one's "strategy"? One tries, as far as possible, to develop a strategy whereby one "can't lose." One tries to change the rules of the game until they fit his own necessities. Does the artist encounter disaster? He will "make capital" of it. If one is a victim of competition, for instance, if one is elbowed out, if one is willy-nilly more jockeyed against than jockeying, one can by the solace and vengeance of art convert this very "liability" into an "asset." One tries to fight on his own terms, developing a strategy for imposing the proper "time, place, and conditions."

But one must also, to develop a full strategy, be *realistic*. One must *size things up* properly. One cannot accurately know how things *will be*, what is promising and what is menacing, unless he accurately knows how things *are*. So the wise strategist will not be content with strategies of merely a self-gratifying sort. He will "keep his

---

[1]*Complete Treatise on Chess:* "Strategy signifies the maneuvers whose goal is attack and correct position." [Ed.]

weather eye open." He will not too eagerly "read into" a scene an attitude that is irrelevant to it. He won't sit on the side of an active volcano and "see" it as a dormant plain.

Often, alas, he will. The great allurement in our present popular "inspirational literature," for instance, may be largely of this sort. It is a strategy for easy consolation. It "fills a need," since there is always a need for easy consolation — and in an era of confusion like our own the need is especially keen. So people are only too willing to "meet a man halfway" who will *play down* the realistic naming of our situation and *play up* such strategies as make solace cheap. However, I should propose a reservation here. We usually take it for granted that people who consume our current output of books on "How to Buy Friends and Bamboozle Oneself and Other People"[2] are reading as *students* who will attempt applying the recipes given. Nothing of the sort. *The reading of a book on the attaining of success is in itself the symbolic attaining of that success.* It is *while they read* that these readers are "succeeding." I'll wager that, in by far the great majority of cases, such readers make no serious attempt to apply the book's recipes. The lure of the book resides in the fact that the reader, while reading it, is then living in the aura of success. What he wants is *easy* success; and he gets it in symbolic form by the mere reading itself. To attempt applying such stuff in real life would be very difficult, full of many disillusioning problems.

Sometimes a different strategy may arise. The author may remain realistic, avoiding too easy a form of solace — yet he may get as far off the track in his own way. Forgetting that realism is an aspect for foretelling, he may take it as an end in itself. He is tempted to do this by two factors: (1) an *ill-digested* philosophy of science, leading him mistakenly to assume that "relentless" naturalistic "truthfulness" is a proper end in itself, and (2) a merely *competitive* desire to outstrip other writers by being "more realistic" than they. Works thus made "efficient" by tests

of competition internal to the book trade are a kind of academicism not so named (the writer usually thinks of it as the *opposite* of academicism). Realism thus stepped up competitively might be distinguished from the proper sort by the name of "naturalism." As a way of "sizing things up," the naturalistic tradition tends to become as inaccurate as the "inspirational" strategy, though at the opposite extreme.

Anyhow, the main point is this: A work like *Madame Bovary* (or its homely American translation, *Babbitt*) is the strategic naming of a situation. It singles out a pattern of experience that is sufficiently representative of our social structure, that recurs sufficiently often *mutatis mutandis,* for people to "need a word for it" and to adopt an attitude towards it. Each work of art is the addition of a word to an informal dictionary (or, in the case of purely derivative artists, the addition of a subsidiary meaning to a word already given by some originating artist). As for *Madame Bovary,* the French critic Jules de Gaultier proposed to add it to our *formal* dictionary by coining the word "Bovarysme" and writing a whole book to say what he meant by it.

Mencken's book on *The American Language,* I hate to say, is splendid. I console myself with the reminder that Mencken didn't write it. Many millions of people wrote it, and Mencken was merely the amanuensis who took it down from their dictation. He found a true "vehicle" (that is, a book that could be greater than the author who wrote it). He gets the royalties, but the job was done by a collectivity. As you read that book, you see a people who were up against a new set of typical recurrent situations, situations typical of their business, their politics, their criminal organizations, their sports. Either there were no words for these in standard English, or people didn't know them, or they didn't "sound right." So a new vocabulary arose, to "give us a word for it." I see no reason for believing that Americans are unusually fertile in word-coinage. American slang was not developed out of some exceptional gift. It was developed out of the fact that new typical situations had arisen and people needed names for them. They had to "size things up." They had to console and strike, to promise and admonish. They had to describe for purposes

---

[2]Burke is parodying Dale Carnegie's *How to Make Friends and Influence People* in particular, but the genre of the self-help book continues to thrive today. [Ed.]

of forecasting. And "slang" was the result. It is, by this analysis, simply *proverbs not so named,* a kind of "folk criticism."

## 3

With what, then, would "sociological criticism" along these lines be concerned? It would seek to codify the various strategies which artists have developed with relation to the naming of situations. In a sense, much of it would even be "timeless," for many of the "typical, recurrent situations" are not peculiar to our own civilization at all. The situations and strategies framed in Aesop's Fables, for instance, apply to human relations now just as fully as they applied in ancient Greece. They are, like philosophy, sufficiently "generalized" to extend far beyond the particular combination of events named by them in any one instance. They name an "essence." Or, we could say that they are on a "high level of abstraction." One doesn't usually think of them as "abstract," since they are usually so concrete in their stylistic expression. But they invariably aim to discern the "general behind the particular" (which would suggest that they are good Goethe).

The attempt to treat literature from the standpoint of situations and strategies suggests a variant of Spengler's notion of the "contemporaneous." By "contemporaneity" he meant corresponding stages of different cultures. For instance, if modern New York is much like decadent Rome, then we are "contemporaneous" with decadent Rome, or with some corresponding decadent city among the Mayas, etc. It is in this sense that situations are "timeless," "non-historical," "contemporaneous." A given human relationship may be at one time named in terms of foxes and lions, if there are foxes and lions about; or it may now be named in terms of salesmanship, advertising, the tactics of politicians, etc. But beneath the change in particulars, we may often discern the naming of the one situation.

So sociological criticism, as here understood, would seek to assemble and codify this lore. It might occasionally lead us to outrage good taste, as we sometimes found exemplified in some great sermon or tragedy or abstruse work of philosophy the same strategy as we found exemplified in a dirty joke. At this point, we'd put the sermon and the dirty joke together, thus "grouping by situation" and showing the range of possible particularizations. In his exceptionally discerning essay, "A Critic's Job of Work," R. P. Blackmur says, "I think on the whole his (Burke's) method could be applied with equal fruitfulness to Shakespeare, Dashiell Hammett, or Marie Corelli."[3] When I got through wincing, I had to admit that Blackmur was right. This article is an attempt to say for the method what can be said. As a matter of fact, I'll go a step further and maintain: You can't properly put Marie Corelli and Shakespeare apart until you have first put them together. First genus, then differentia. The strategy in common is the genus. The *range* or *scale* or *spectrum* of particularizations is the differentia.

Anyhow, that's what I'm driving at. And that's why reviewers sometime find in my work "intuitive" leaps that are dubious as "science." They are not "leaps" at all. They are classifications, groupings, made on the basis of some strategic element common to the items grouped. They are neither more nor less "intuitive" than *any* grouping or classification of social events. Apples can be grouped with bananas as fruits, and they can be grouped with tennis balls as round. I am simply proposing, in the social sphere, a method of classification with reference to *strategies*.

The method has these things to be said in its favor: It gives definite insight into the organization of literary works; and it automatically breaks down the barriers erected about literature as a specialized pursuit. People can classify novels by reference to three kinds, eight kinds, seventeen kinds. It doesn't matter. Students patiently copy down the professor's classification and pass examinations on it, because the range of possible academic classifications is endless. Sociological classification, as herein suggested, would derive its relevance from the fact that it should apply both to works of art and to social situations outside of art.

[3]Richard P. Blackmur, "A Critic's Job of Work" (1935), published in *Language as Gesture* (1952). [Ed.]

It would, I admit, violate current pieties, break down current categories, and thereby "outrage good taste." But "good taste" has become *inert*. The classifications I am proposing would be *active*. I think that what we need is active categories.

These categories will lie on the bias across the categories of modern specialization. The new alignment will outrage in particular those persons who take the division of faculties in our universities to be an exact replica of the way in which God himself divided up the universe. We have had the Philosophy of Being; and we have had the Philosophy of Becoming. In typical contemporary specialization, we have been getting the Philosophy of the Bin. Each of these mental localities has had its own peculiar way of life, its own values, even its own special idiom for seeing, thinking, and "proving." Among other things, a sociological approach should attempt to provide a reintegrative point of view, a broader empire of investigation encompassing the lot.

What would such sociological categories be like? They would consider works of art, I think, as strategies for selecting enemies and allies, for socializing losses, for warding off evil eye, for purification, propitiation, and desanctification, consolation and vengeance, admonition and exhortation, implicit commands or instructions of one sort or another. Art forms like "tragedy" or "comedy" or "satire" would be treated as *equipments for living,* that size up situations in various ways and in keeping with correspondingly various attitudes. The typical ingredients of such forms would be sought. Their relation to typical situations would be stressed. Their comparative values would be considered, with the intention of formulating a "strategy of strategies," the "over-all" strategy obtained by inspection of the lot.

# Lionel Trilling

## 1905–1975

Lionel Trilling was born in New York City, the son of David Trilling, a Jewish immigrant from Bialystok, Poland, who became a furrier and custom tailor, and Fannie Cohen Trilling, who grew up in London's East End and who imparted to her son a lifelong Anglophilia. Though a descendant of the Bialystoker Rabbi, Trilling was always ambivalent about his ethnic status: He identified himself as a Jew and wrote for periodicals like *Menorah Journal* and *Commentary*, but rather than priding himself on his roots, as did fellow New York intellectuals like Alfred Kazin, he aspired to assimilation within American culture. Trilling was educated at Columbia University, receiving his B.A. and M.A. degrees in 1925 and 1926. He went to the Midwest to teach for a year or so, then returned to Columbia for his doctorate, which was awarded in 1938; his dissertation on Matthew Arnold was published in 1939. The same year, at the insistence of Columbia president Nicholas Murray Butler, he was appointed assistant professor of English, the first Jew to hold faculty rank in that department. Trilling rose through the ranks quickly, reaching full professor in 1948 and a named chair in 1965. He retired from teaching in 1974 but continued part-time until just before his death the next year.

It was prophetic for Trilling's later career that his book on Arnold was an evaluation and an appreciation rather than a contribution to scholarship. Trilling continued to publish widely but substituted evaluative cultural criticism and belletristic writing (including a book of short stories and a novel, *The Middle of the Journey*) for the scholarly work most professors of English pursued. In his teaching he preferred undergraduates still learning the traditions of Western civilization to graduate students aspiring to standards of professional training in scholarship.

In his criticism, Trilling is allied with the cultural criticism of the group of radical New York intellectuals that included Edmund Wilson, Philip Rahv, Delmore Schwartz, Alfred Kazin, and Irving Howe, discussed later in this collection as American Marxists. But although Trilling was strongly influenced by Marx's examination of society, it would be going too far to label him a Marxist, even of the most fellow-traveler sort. While his criticism is neither formalistic nor New Critical but rather social and political, there is little sense of economic determinism or ideology, and he is clearly disillusioned with socialism, Stalin, Soviet Russia, and all the other panaceas of the 1930s. His political philosophy is that of liberalism as it would have been defined around 1950, when *The Liberal Imagination* appeared: greater equality of opportunity for minority groups and an end to intolerance; greater compassion for the poor, leading to a welfare state; greater internationalism of spirit, leading to an end to the cold war between West and East. But his political purpose in writing and in explicating the major texts of literature was precisely to prevent the oversimplification of liberal ideology. Trilling feared that the "ideas that can survive" the political process of organization, delegation, and bureaucracy "incline to be ideas of a certain . . . simplicity: they give up something of their largeness and modulation and complexity in order to survive." For Trilling, as for Arnold, literature was the "criticism of life." It was through literature — regardless of the political philosophy of the writer — that the ideas of the liberal persuasion were to be criticized, brought back to their "essential imagination of variousness and possibility, which implies the awareness of complexity and difficulty."[1]

Trilling was not a literary theorist but a critic, and deriving a literary theory from his work requires massive generalization. Much of Trilling's work took the form of essays devoted to the explication of particular texts: *The Liberal Imagination* is not a treatise but a collection of pieces, most originally published elsewhere, on Theodore Dreiser, Sherwood Anderson, Henry James, Freud, Rudyard Kipling, Tacitus, Twain, and others, as varied a group as one might wish. The essay reprinted here is perhaps the most theoretical piece Trilling ever wrote. It contemplates the central problem of the Arnoldian tradition to which he had attached himself, the relation between ideas and literature, the sense in which literature manifests ideas. The question is an old one — going back, like so many, to Plato — but it had been given renewed currency by the New Critics, then just beginning to attain hegemony, who asserted that poems do not "mean, but be," and that poetry makes not statements but pseudostatements.[2] The first half of Trilling's essay is a theoretical attack on T. S. Eliot's denigration of intellection, ideology, and personality in poetry, and on the charter of the New Critics as inscribed by René Wellek and Austin Warren's *Theory of Literature* (1949). Trilling was in fact willing to concede that "there is a large body of literature to which ideas, with their tendency to refer to action and effectiveness, are alien and inappropriate. But also much of literature wishes to give the sensations and to win the responses that are given and won by ideas, and it makes use of ideas to gain its effects, considering ideas — like people, sentiments, things and scenes — to be indispensable elements of human life." Trilling's response here would not have impressed the New Critics, who did not deny that literature could be thought of as referential. They had merely suggested that viewing literature as ideology denied to it its peculiarly literary qualities. But Trilling's point — that concentration on the aesthetic robs literature of its life within the world — is equally irrefutable.

The second half of the essay is less purely theoretical in scope; it concerns the relation between ideas and American literature, and the question of how intellectual power operates in the best American writers of the generation before World War II. Here Trilling argues that "in any extended work of literature, the aesthetic effect . . . depends in large degree upon intellectual power, upon the amount and recalcitrance of the material the mind works on, and upon the mind's success in mastering the large material." Mastery is not a function of ideology. In fact, Trilling seems to regard ideology as the enemy of literature in the sense that ideology generally remains unassimilated, a messianic or pessimistic prophecy

---

[1]Lionel Trilling, Introduction to *The Liberal Imagination* (New York: Macmillan, 1948), pp. xiv–xv.

[2]See the introduction to Formalism, Ch. 3 in Part II.

within what should be a coherent work of imagination. In exemplifying this point, Trilling contrasts Thomas Wolfe, John Dos Passos, and Eugene O'Neill — whom he sees as essentially passive intellectually, or ridden by their precommitments — with William Faulkner and Ernest Hemingway, who, he contends, have mastered their material without undue dependence on the pieties of religion or secular philosophy.

Trilling's ultimate problem, of course, is that the literature he respects most, that of the European moderns, was written by men whom he took to be "indifferent to, or even hostile to, the tradition of democratic liberalism as we know it. Yeats and Eliot, Proust and Joyce, Lawrence and Gide — these men do not seem to confirm us in the social and political ideals which we hold." Whatever we may think of these particular examples — and neither Proust nor Joyce took the reactionary side within their own societies — Trilling is faced with a very real problem for a liberal: the greatest writers are so often of a conservative bent. The tradition of "Tory wits" runs nearly unbroken from the late seventeenth century to the present. For Trilling, the remedy is the liberal imagination itself — if liberalism will use its imagination. A liberalism that produces "pellets of intellection or crystallizations of thought, precise and completed," will produce no literature worthy of the name; only if liberals think of ideas as "living things, inescapably connected with our wills and desires" will an "active literature" be realized from within this political framework, and the implicit conflict between liberal sentiments and reactionary wit be reconciled.

### Selected Bibliography

Abel, Lionel. "Lionel Trilling and His Critics." *Commentary* 82 (1986): 56–63.

Boyers, Robert. *Lionel Trilling: Negative Capability and the Wisdom of Avoidance*. Columbia: University of Missouri Press, 1977.

Chace, William M. *Lionel Trilling: Criticism and Politics*. Stanford: Stanford University Press, 1980.

Dickstein, Morris. "Lionel Trilling and the Liberal Imagination." *Sewanee Review* 94 (1986): 323–34.

Krupnick, Mark. *Lionel Trilling and the Fate of Cultural Criticism*. Evanston, Ill.: Northwestern University Press, 1986.

Shoben, Edward Joseph. *Lionel Trilling*. New York: Ungar, 1981.

# The Meaning of a Literary Idea

*. . . Though no great minist'ring reason sorts
Out the dark mysteries of human souls
To clear conceiving: yet there ever rolls
A vast idea before me, and I glean
Therefrom my liberty . . .*

KEATS, "Sleep and Poetry"

## I

The question of the relation which should properly obtain between what we call creative literature and what we call ideas is a matter of insistent importance for modern criticism. It did not always make difficulties for the critic, and that it now makes so many is a fact which tells us much about our present relation to literature.

Ever since men began to think about poetry, they have conceived that there is a difference between the poet and the philosopher, a difference in method and in intention and in result. These differences I have no wish to deny. But a solidly established difference inevitably draws the fire of our question; it tempts us to inquire whether it is really essential or whether it is quite so settled and extreme as at first it seems. To this temptation I yield perhaps too easily, and very possibly as the result of an impercipience on my part — it may be that I see the difference with insufficient sharpness because I do not have a proper notion either of the matter of poetry or of the matter of philosophy. But whatever the reason, when I consider the respective products of the poetic and of the philosophic mind, although I see that they are by no means the same and although I can conceive that different processes, even different mental faculties, were at work to make them and to make them different, I cannot resist the impulse to put stress on their similarity and on their easy assimilation to each other.

Let me suggest some of the ways in which literature, by its very nature, is involved with ideas. I can be quite brief because what I say will not be new to you.

The most elementary thing to observe is that literature is of its nature involved with ideas because it deals with man in society, which is to say that it deals with formulations, valuations, and decisions, some of them implicit, others explicit. Every sentient organism *acts* on the principle that pleasure is to be preferred to pain, but man is the sole creature who formulates or exemplifies this as an idea and causes it to lead to other ideas. His consciousness of self abstracts this principle of action from his behavior and makes it the beginning of a process of intellection or a matter for tears and laughter. And this is but one of the innumerable assumptions or ideas that are the very stuff of literature.

This is self-evident and no one ever thinks of denying it. All that is ever denied is that literature is within its proper function in bringing these ideas to explicit consciousness, or ever gains by doing so. Thus, one of the matters of assumption in any society is the worth of men as compared with the worth of women; upon just such an assumption, more or less settled, much of the action of the *Oresteia* is based, and we don't in the least question the propriety of this — or not until it becomes the subject of open debate between Apollo and Athene, who, on the basis of an elaborate biological speculation, try to decide which is the less culpable, to kill your father or to kill your mother. At this point we, in our modern way, feel that in permitting the debate Aeschylus has made a great and rather silly mistake, that he has for the moment ceased to be *literary*. Yet what drama does not consist of the opposition of formulable ideas, what drama, indeed, is not likely to break into the explicit exposition and debate of these ideas?

This, as I say, is elementary. And scarcely less elementary is the observation that whenever we put two emotions into juxtaposition we have what we can properly call an idea. When Keats brings together, as he so often does, his emotions about love and his emotions about death, we have a very powerful idea and the source of consequent ideas. The force of such an idea depends upon the force of the two emotions which are brought to confront each other, and also, of course, upon the way the confrontation is contrived.

Then it can be said that the very form of a literary work, considered apart from its content, so far as that is possible, is in itself an idea. Whether we deal with syllogisms or poems, we deal with dialectic — with, that is, a developing series of statements. Or if the word "statements" seems to pre-judge the question so far as literature is concerned, let us say merely that we deal with a developing series — the important word is "developing." We judge the value of the development by judging the interest of its several stages and the propriety and the relevance of their connection among themselves. We make the judgment in terms of the implied purpose of the developing series.

Dialectic, in this sense, is just another word for form, and has for its purpose, in philosophy or in art, the leading of the mind to some conclusion. Greek drama, for example, is an arrangement of moral and emotional elements in such a way as to conduct the mind — "inevitably," as we like to say — to a certain affective condition. This condition is a quality of personal being which may be judged by the action it can be thought ultimately to lead to.

We take Aristotle to be a better critic of the drama than Plato because we perceive that Aristotle understood and Plato did not understand that the form of the drama was of itself an idea which controlled and brought to a particular issue the subordinate ideas it contained. The form of the drama *is* its idea, and its idea *is* its form. And form in those arts which we call abstract is no less an idea than is form in the representational arts. Governments nowadays are very simple and accurate in their perception of this — much more simple and accurate than are academic critics and aestheticians — and they are as quick to deal with the arts of "pure" form as they are to deal with ideas stated in discourse: it is as if totalitarian governments kept in mind what the rest of us tend to forget, that "idea" in one of its early significations exactly means form and was so used by many philosophers.

It is helpful to have this meaning before us when we come to consider that particular connection between literature and ideas which presents us with the greatest difficulty, the connection that involves highly elaborated ideas, or ideas as we have them in highly elaborated systems such as philosophy, or theology, or science. The modern feeling about this relationship is defined by two texts, both provided by T. S. Eliot. In his essay on Shakespeare Mr. Eliot says, "I can see no reason for believing that either Dante or Shakespeare did any thinking on his own. The people who think that Shakespeare thought are always people who are not engaged in writing poetry, but who are engaged in thinking, and we all like to think that great men were like ourselves."[1] And in his essay on Henry James Mr. Eliot makes the well-known remark that James had a mind so fine that no idea could violate it.

In both statements, as I believe, Mr. Eliot

permits his impulse to spirited phrase to run away with him, yielding too much to what he conceives to be the didactic necessities of the moment, for he has it in mind to offer resistance to the nineteenth-century way of looking at poetry as a heuristic medium, as a communication of knowledge. This is a view which is well exemplified in a sentence of Carlyle's: "If called to define Shakespeare's faculty, I should say superiority of Intellect, and think I had included all in that." As between the two statements about Shakespeare's mental processes, I give my suffrage to Carlyle's as representing a more intelligible and a more available notion of intellect than Mr. Eliot's, but I think I understand what Mr. Eliot is trying to do with his — he is trying to rescue poetry from the kind of misinterpretation of Carlyle's view which was once more common than it is now; he is trying to save for poetry what is peculiar to it, and for systematic thought what is peculiar to it.

As for Mr. Eliot's statement about James and ideas, it is useful to us because it gives us a clue to what might be called the sociology of our question. "Henry James had a mind so fine that no idea could violate it." In the context "violate" is a strong word, yet we can grant that the mind of the poet is a sort of Clarissa Harlowe and that an idea is a sort of Colonel Lovelace, for it is a truism of contemporary thought that the whole nature of man stands in danger of being brutalized by the intellect, or at least by some one of its apparently accredited surrogates. A specter haunts our culture — it is that people will eventually be unable to say, "They fell in love and married," let alone understand the language of *Romeo and Juliet,* but will as a matter of course say, "Their libidinal impulses being reciprocal, they activated their individual erotic drives and integrated them within the same frame of reference."

Now this is not the language of abstract thought or of any kind of thought. It is the language of non-thought. But it is the language which is developing from the peculiar status which we in our culture have given to abstract thought. There can be no doubt whatever that it constitutes a threat to the emotions and thus to life itself.

[1]T. S. Eliot, "Shakespeare and the Stoicism of Seneca," *Selected Essays, 1917–32.* [Ed.]

The specter of what this sort of language suggests has haunted us since the end of the eighteenth century. When he speaks of the mind being violated by an idea, Mr. Eliot, like the Romantics, is simply voicing his horror at the prospect of life being intellectualized out of all spontaneity and reality.

We are the people of the idea, and we rightly fear that the intellect will dry up the blood in our veins and wholly check the emotional and creative part of the mind. And although I said that the fear of the total sovereignty of the abstract intellect began in the Romantic period, we are of course touching here upon Pascal's opposition between two faculties of the mind, of which *l'esprit de finesse* has its heuristic powers no less the *l'esprit de géométrie,*[2] powers of discovery and knowledge which have a particular value for the establishment of man in society and the universe.

But to call ourselves the people of the idea is to flatter ourselves. We are rather the people of ideology, which is a very different thing. Ideology is not the product of thought; it is the habit or the ritual of showing respect for certain formulas to which, for various reasons having to do with emotional safety, we have very strong ties of whose meaning and consequences in actuality we have no clear understanding. The nature of ideology may in part be understood from its tendency to develop the sort of language I parodied, and scarcely parodied, a moment ago.

It is therefore no wonder that any critical theory that conceives itself to be at the service of the emotions, and of life itself, should turn a very strict and jealous gaze upon an intimate relationship between literature and ideas, for in our culture ideas tend to deteriorate into ideology. And indeed it is scarcely surprising that criticism, in its zeal to protect literature and life from the tyranny of the rational intellect, should misinterpret the relationship. Mr. Eliot, if we take him literally, does indeed misinterpret the relationship when he conceives of "thinking" in such a way that it must be denied to Shakespeare and Dante. It must puzzle us to know what thinking is if Shakespeare and Dante did not do it.

And it puzzles us to know what René Wellek and Austin Warren mean when in their admirable *Theory of Literature* they say that literature can make use of ideas only when ideas "cease to be ideas in the ordinary sense of concepts and become symbols, or even myths." I am not sure that the ordinary sense of *ideas* actually is *concepts,* or at any rate concepts of such abstractness that they do not arouse in us feelings and attitudes. And I take it that when we speak of the relationship of literature and ideas, the ideas we refer to are not those of mathematics or of symbolic logic, but only such ideas as can arouse and traditionally have aroused the feelings — the ideas, for example, of men's relation to one another and to the world. A poet's simple statement of a psychological fact recalls us to a proper simplicity about the nature of ideas. "Our continued influxes of feeling," said Wordsworth, "are modified and directed by our thoughts, which are indeed the representatives of all our past feelings."[3] The interflow between emotion and idea is a psychological fact which we do well to keep clearly in mind, together with the part that is played by desire, will, and imagination in philosophy as well as in literature. Mr. Eliot, and Mr. Wellek and Mr. Warren — and in general those critics who are zealous in the defense of the autonomy of poetry — prefer to forget the ground which is common to both emotion and thought; they presume ideas to be only the product of formal systems of philosophy, not remembering, at least on the occasion of their argument, that poets too have their effect in the world of thought. *L'esprit de finesse* is certainly not to be confused with *l'esprit de géométrie,* but neither — which is precisely the point of Pascal's having distinguished and named the two different qualities of mind — is it to be denied its powers of comprehension and formulation.

Mr. Wellek and Mr. Warren tell us that "the artist will be hampered by too much ideology[4] if it remains unassimilated." We note the tautology

---

[2]Spirit of delicacy; spirit of geometry. [Ed.]

[3]Preface to *Lyrical Ballads;* see p. 287. [Ed.]
[4]The word is used by Mr. Wellek and Mr. Warren, not in the pejorative sense in which I have earlier used it, but to mean simply a body of ideas. [Au.]

of the statement — for what else is "too much" ideology except ideology that *is* unassimilated? — not because we wish to take a disputatious advantage over authors to whom we have reason to be grateful, but because the tautology suggests the uneasiness of the position it defends. We are speaking of art, which is an activity which defines itself exactly by its powers of assimilation and of which the essence is the just amount of any of its qualities or elements; of course too much or unassimilated ideology will "hamper" the artist, but so will too much of anything, so will too much metaphor: Coleridge tells us that in a long poem there can be too much *poetry*.[5] The theoretical question is simply being begged, out of an undue anxiety over the "purity" of literature, over its perfect literariness.

The authors of *Theory of Literature* are certainly right to question the "intellectualist misunderstanding of art" and the "confusions of the functions of art and philosophy" and to look for the flaws in the scholarly procedures which organize works of art according to their ideas and their affinities with philosophical systems. Yet on their own showing there has always been a conscious commerce between the poet and the philosopher, and not every poet has been violated by the ideas that have attracted him. The sexual metaphor is forced upon us, not only explicitly by Mr. Eliot but also implicitly by Mr. Wellek and Mr. Warren, who seem to think of ideas as masculine and gross and of art as feminine and pure, and who permit a union of the two sexes only when ideas give up their masculine, effective nature and "cease to be ideas in the ordinary sense and become symbols, or even myths." We naturally ask: symbols of what, myths about what? No anxious exercise of aesthetic theory can make the ideas of, say, Blake and Lawrence other than what they are intended to be — ideas relating to action and to moral judgment.

This anxiety lest the work of art be other than totally self-contained, this fear lest the reader make reference to something beyond the work itself, has its origin, as I have previously suggested, in the reaction from the earlier impulse

— it goes far back beyond the nineteenth century — to show that art is justified in comparison with the effective activity of the systematic disciplines. It arises too from the strong contemporary wish to establish, in a world of unremitting action and effectiveness, the legitimacy of contemplation, which it is now no longer convenient to associate with the exercises of religion but which may be associated with the experiences of art. We will all do well to advance the cause of contemplation, to insist on the right to a haven from perpetual action and effectiveness. But we must not enforce our insistence by dealing with art as if it were a unitary thing, and by making reference only to its "purely" aesthetic element, requiring that every work of art serve our contemplation by being wholly self-contained and without relation to action. No doubt there is a large body of literature to which ideas, with their tendency to refer to action and effectiveness, are alien and inappropriate. But also much of literature wishes to give the sensations and to win the responses that are given and won by ideas, and it makes use of ideas to gain its effects, considering ideas — like people, sentiments, things, and scenes — to be indispensable elements of human life. Nor is the intention of this part of literature always an aesthetic one in the strict sense that Mr. Wellek and Mr. Warren have in mind; there is abundant evidence that the aesthetic upon which the critic sets primary store is to the poet himself frequently of only secondary importance.

We can grant that the province of poetry is one thing and the province of intellection another. But keeping the difference well in mind, we must yet see that systems of ideas have a particular quality which is much coveted as their chief effect — let us even say as their chief aesthetic effect — by at least certain kinds of literary works. Say what we will as critics and teachers trying to defend the province of art from the dogged tendency of our time to ideologize all things into grayness, say what we will about the "purely" literary, the purely aesthetic values, we as readers know that we demand of our literature some of the virtues which define a successful work of systematic thought. We want it to have — at least when it is appropriate for it to have, which is by no means infrequently —

---

[5]Actually, he says that "a poem of any length neither can be, nor ought to be, all poetry." See *Biographia Literaria*, Ch. 14; p. 309 in this collection. [Ed.]

the authority, the cogency, the completeness, the brilliance, the *hardness* of systematic thought.[6]

Of late years criticism has been much concerned to insist on the indirection and the symbolism of the language of poetry. I do not doubt that the language of poetry is very largely that of indirection and symbolism. But it is not only that. Poetry is closer to rhetoric than we today are willing to admit; syntax plays a greater part in it than our current theory grants, and syntax connects poetry with rational thought, for, as Hegel says, "grammar, in its extended and consistent form" — by which he means syntax — "is the work of thought, which makes its categories distinctly visible therein." And those poets of our time who make the greatest impress upon us are those who are most aware of rhetoric, which is to say, of the intellectual content of their work. Nor is the intellectual content of their work simply the inevitable effect produced by good intelligence turned to poetry; many of these poets — Yeats and Eliot himself come most immediately to mind — have been at great pains to develop consistent intellectual positions along with, and consonant with, their work in poetry.

The aesthetic effect of intellectual cogency, I am convinced, is not to be slighted. Let me give an example for what it is worth. Of recent weeks my mind has been much engaged by two statements, disparate in length and in genre, although as it happens they have related themes. One is a couplet of Yeats:

We had fed the heart on fantasies,
The heart's grown brutal from the fare.

I am hard put to account for the force of the statement. It certainly does not lie in any meta-

[6]Mr. Wellek and Mr. Warren say something of the same sort, but only, as it were, in a concessive way: "Philosophy, ideological content, in its proper context, seems to enhance artistic value because it corroborates several important artistic values: those of complexity and coherence. . . . But it need not be so. The artist will be hampered by too much ideology if it remains unassimilated" (p. 122). Earlier (p. 27) they say: "Serious art implies a view of life which can be stated in philosophical terms, even in terms of systems. Between artistic coherence . . . and philosophic coherence there is some kind of correlation." They then hasten to distinguish between emotion and thinking, sensibility and intellection, etc., and to tell us that art is more complex than "propaganda." [Au.]

phor, for only the dimmest sort of metaphor is to be detected. Nor does it lie in any special power of the verse. The statement has for me the pleasure of relevance and cogency, in part conveyed to me by the content, in part by the rhetoric. The other statement is Freud's short book, his last, *An Outline of Psychoanalysis*, which gives me a pleasure which is no doubt different from that given by Yeats's couplet, but which is also similar; it is the pleasure of listening to a strong, decisive, self-limiting voice uttering statements to which I can give assent. The pleasure I have in responding to Freud I find very difficult to distinguish from the pleasure which is involved in responding to a satisfactory work of art.

Intellectual assent in literature is not quite the same thing as agreement. We can take pleasure in literature where we do not agree, responding to the power or grace of a mind without admitting the rightness of its intention or conclusion — we can take our pleasure from an intellect's *cogency*, without making a final judgment on the correctness or adaptability of what it says.

## II

And now I leave these general theoretical matters for a more particular concern — the relation of contemporary American literature to ideas. In order to come at this as directly as possible we might compare modern American prose literature — for American poetry is a different thing — with modern European literature. European literature of, say, the last thirty or forty years seems to me to be, in the sense in which I shall use the word, essentially an active literature. It does not, at its best, consent to be merely comprehended. It refuses to be understood as a "symptom" of its society, although of course it may be that, among other things. It does not submit to being taped. We as scholars and critics try to discover the source of its effective energy and of course we succeed in some degree. But inevitably we become aware that it happily exists beyond our powers of explanation, although not, certainly, beyond our powers of response. Proust, Joyce, Lawrence, Kafka, Yeats, and Eliot himself do not allow us to finish with them; and the refusal is repeated by a great many European writers less large than these. With exceptions that I shall note, the same thing cannot be said of modern American literature. American literature seems to me essentially passive: our minds tend always to be made up about this or that American author, and we incline to speak of him, not merely incidentally but conclusively, in terms of his moment in history, of the conditions of the culture that "produced" him. Thus American literature as an academic subject is not so much a *subject* as an *object* of study: it does not, as a literature should, put the scrutinizer of it under scrutiny but, instead, leaves its students with a too comfortable sense of complete comprehension.

When we try to discover the root of this difference between European and American literature, we are led to the conclusion that it is the difference between the number and weight or force of the ideas which the two literatures embody or suggest. I do not mean that European literature makes use of, as American literature does not, the ideas of philosophy or theology or science. Kafka does not exemplify Kierkegaard, Proust does not dramatize Bergson. One way of putting the relationship of this literature to ideas is to say that the literature of contemporary Europe is in competition with philosophy, theology, and science, that it seeks to match them in comprehensiveness and power and seriousness.

This is not to say that the best of contemporary European literature makes upon us the effect of a rational system of thought. Quite the contrary, indeed; it is precisely its artistic power that we respond to, which I take in part to be its power of absorbing and disturbing us in secret ways. But this power it surely derives from its commerce, according to its own rules, with systematic ideas.

For in the great issues with which the mind has traditionally been concerned there is, I would submit, something *primitive* which is of the highest value to the literary artist. I know that it must seem a strange thing to say, for we are in the habit of thinking of systematic ideas as being of the very essence of the not-primitive, of the highly developed. No doubt they are: but they are at the same time the means by which a complex civilization keeps the primitive in mind and refers to it. Whence and whither, birth and death,

fate, free will, and immortality — these are never far from systematic thought; and Freud's belief that the child's first inquiry — beyond which, really, the adult does not go in kind — is in effect a sexual one seems to me to have an empirical support from literature. The ultimate questions of conscious and rational thought about the nature of man and his destiny match easily in the literary mind with the dark *un*conscious and with the most primitive human relationships. Love, parenthood, incest, patricide: these are what the great ideas suggest to literature, these are the means by which they express themselves. I need but mention three great works of different ages to suggest how true this is: *Oedipus, Hamlet, The Brothers Karamazov.*

Ideas, if they are large enough and of a certain kind, are not only not hostile to the creative process, as some think, but are virtually inevitable to it. Intellectual power and emotional power go together. And if we can say, as I think we can, that contemporary American prose literature in general lacks emotional power, it is possible to explain the deficiency by reference to the intellectual weakness of American prose literature.

The situation in verse is different. Perhaps this is to be accounted for by the fact that the best of our poets are, as good poets usually are, scholars of their tradition. There is present to their minds the degree of intellectual power which poetry is traditionally expected to exert. Questions of form and questions of language seem of themselves to demand, or to create, an adequate subject matter; and a highly developed aesthetic implies a matter strong enough to support its energy. We have not a few poets who are subjects and not objects, who are active and not passive. One does not finish quickly, if at all, with the best work of, say, Cummings, Stevens, and Marianne Moore. This work is not exempt from our judgment, even from adverse judgment, but it is able to stay with a mature reader as a continuing element of his spiritual life. Of how many writers of prose fiction can we say anything like the same thing?

The topic which was originally proposed to me for this occasion and which I have taken the liberty of generalizing was the debt of four American writers to Freud and Spengler. The four writers were O'Neill, Dos Passos, Wolfe, and Faulkner. Of the first three how many can be continuing effective elements of our mental lives? I hope I shall never read Mr. Dos Passos without interest nor ever lose the warm though qualified respect that I feel for his work. But it is impossible for me to feel of this work that it is autonomous, that it goes on existing beyond our powers of explanation. As for Eugene O'Neill and Thomas Wolfe, I can respect the earnestness of their dedication, but I cannot think of having a living, reciprocal relation with what they have written. And I believe that is because these men, without intellectual capital of their own, don't owe a sufficient debt of ideas to anyone. Spengler is certainly not a great mind; at best he is but a considerable dramatist of the idea of world history and of, as it were, the natural history of cultures; and we can find him useful as a critic who summarizes the adverse views of our urban, naturalistic culture which many have held. Freud is a very great mind indeed. Without stopping to specify what actual influence of ideas was exerted by Spengler and Freud on O'Neill, Dos Passos, or Wolfe, or even to consider whether there was any influence at all, we can fairly assume that all are in something of the same ambiance. But if, in that ambiance, we want the sense of the actuality of doom — actuality being one of the qualities we expect of literature — surely we do better to seek it in Spengler himself than in any of the three literary artists, just as, if we want the sense of the human mystery, of tragedy truly conceived in the great terms of free will, necessity, and hope, surely we do far better to seek it directly in Freud himself than in these three literary men.

In any extended work of literature, the aesthetic effect, as I have said, depends in large degree upon intellectual power, upon the amount and recalcitrance of the material the mind works on, and upon the mind's success in mastering the large material. And it is exactly the lack of intellectual power that makes our three writers, after our first response of interest, so inadequate aesthetically. We have only to compare, say, Dos Passos's *USA* to a work of similar kind and intention, Flaubert's *L'Education Sentimentale,* to see that in Dos Passos's novel the matter encom-

passed is both less in amount and less in resistance than in Flaubert's; the energy of the encompassing mind is also less. Or we consider O'Neill's crude, dull notion of the unconscious and his merely elementary grasp of Freud's ideas about sex and we recognize the lamentable signs of a general inadequacy of mind. Or we ask what it is about Thomas Wolfe that always makes us uncomfortable with his talent, so that even his admirers deal with him not as a subject but as an object — an object which must be explained and accounted for — and we are forced to answer that it is the disproportion between the energy of his utterance and his power of mind. It is customary to say of Thomas Wolfe that he is an emotional writer. Perhaps: although it is probably not the most accurate way to describe a writer who could deal with but one single emotion; and we feel that it is a function of his unrelenting, tortured egoism that he could not submit his mind to the ideas that might have brought the variety and interest of order to the single, dull chaos of his powerful self-regard, for it is true that the intellect makes many emotions out of the primary egoistic one.

At this point it may be well to recall what our subject is. It is not merely the part that is played in literature by those ideas which may be derived from the study of systematic, theoretical works; it is the part that is played in literature by ideas in general. To be sure, the extreme and most difficult instance of the general relation of literature to ideas is the relation of literature to highly developed and formulated ideas; and because this is indeed so difficult a matter, and one so often misconceived, I have put a special emphasis upon it. But we do not present our subject adequately — we do not, indeed, represent the mind adequately — if we think of ideas only as being highly formulated. It will bring us back to the proper generality of our subject if I say that the two contemporary writers who hold out to me the possibility of a living reciprocal relationship with their work are Ernest Hemingway and William Faulkner — it will bring us back the more dramatically because Hemingway and Faulkner have insisted on their indifference to the conscious intellectual tradition of our time and have acquired the reputation of achieving their effects by means that have the least possible connection with any sort of intellectuality or even with intelligence.

In trying to explain a certain commendable quality which is to be found in the work of Hemingway and Faulkner — and a certain quality only, not a total and unquestionable literary virtue — we are not called upon by our subject to show that particular recognizable ideas of a certain force or weight are "used" in the work. Nor are we called upon to show that new ideas of a certain force and weight are "produced" by the work. All that we need to do is account for a certain aesthetic effect as being in some important part achieved by a mental process which is not different from the process by which discursive ideas are conceived, and which is to be judged by some of the criteria by which an idea is judged.

The aesthetic effect which I have in mind can be suggested by a word that I have used before — activity. We feel that Hemingway and Faulkner are intensely at work upon the recalcitrant stuff of life; when they are at their best they give us the sense that the amount and intensity of their activity are in a satisfying proportion to the recalcitrance of the material. And our pleasure in their activity is made the more secure because we have the distinct impression that the two novelists are not under any illusion that they have conquered the material upon which they direct their activity. The opposite is true of Dos Passos, O'Neill, and Wolfe; at each point of conclusion in their work we feel that *they* feel that they have said the last word, and we feel this even when they represent themselves, as O'Neill and Wolfe so often do, as puzzled and baffled by life. But of Hemingway and Faulkner we seldom have the sense that they have deceived themselves, that they have misrepresented to themselves the nature and the difficulty of the matter they work on. And we go on to make another intellectual judgment: we say that the matter they present, together with the degree of difficulty which they assume it to have, seems to be very cogent. This, we say, is to the point; this really has something to do with life as we live it; we cannot ignore it.

There is a traditional and aggressive rationalism that can understand thought only in its conscious, developed form and believes that the phrase "unconscious mind" is a meaningless contradiction in terms. Such a view, wrong as I think it is, has at least the usefulness of warning us that we must not call by the name of thought or idea all responses of the human organism whatever. But the extreme rationalist position ignores the simple fact that the life of reason, at least in its most extensive part, begins in the emotions. What comes into being when two contradictory emotions are made to confront each other and are required to have a relationship with each other is, as I have said, quite properly called an idea. Ideas may also be said to be generated in the opposition of ideals, and in the felt awareness of the impact of new circumstances upon old forms of feeling and estimation, in the response to the conflict between new exigencies and old pieties. And it can be said that a work will have what I have been calling cogency in the degree that the confronting emotions go deep, or in the degree that the old pieties are firmly held and the new exigencies strongly apprehended. In Hemingway's stories[7] a strongly charged piety toward the ideals and attachments of boyhood and the lusts of maturity is in conflict not only with the imagination of death but also with that imagination as it is peculiarly modified by the dark negation of the modern world. Faulkner as a Southerner of today, a man deeply implicated in the pieties of his tradition, is of course at the very heart of an exigent historical event which thrusts upon him the awareness of the inadequacy and wrongness of the very tradition he loves. In the work of both men the cogency is a function not of their conscious but of their unconscious minds. We can, if we admire Tolstoy and Dostoevsky, regret the deficiency of consciousness, blaming it for the inadequacy in both our American writers of the talent for generalization.[8] Yet it is to be remarked that the unconscious minds

[7]It is in the stories rather than in the novels that Hemingway is characteristic and at his best. [Au.]

[8]Although there is more impulse to generalization than is usually supposed. This is especially true of Faulkner, who has never subscribed to the contemporary belief that only concrete words have power and that only the representation of things and actions is dramatic. [Au.]

of both men have wisdom and humility about themselves. They seldom make the attempt at formulated solutions, they rest content with the "negative capability." And this negative capability, this willingness to remain in uncertainties, mysteries, and doubts, is not, as one tendency of modern feeling would suppose, an abdication of intellectual activity. Quite to the contrary, it is precisely an aspect of their intelligence, of their seeing the full force and complexity of their subject matter. And this we can understand the better when we observe how the unconscious minds of Dos Passos, O'Neill, and Wolfe do not possess humility and wisdom; nor are they fully active, as the intellectual histories of all three men show. A passivity on the part of Dos Passos before the idea of the total corruption of American civilization has issued in his later denial of the possibility of economic and social reform and in his virtually unqualified acceptance of the American status quo. A passivity on the part of O'Neill before the clichés of economic and metaphysical materialism issued in his later simplistic Catholicism. The passivity of Thomas Wolfe before all his experience led him to that characteristic *malice* toward the objects or partners of his experience which no admirer of his ever takes account of, and eventually to that simple affirmation, recorded in *You Can't Go Home Again,* that literature must become the agent of the immediate solution of all social problems and undertake the prompt eradication of human pain; and because his closest friend did not agree that this was a possible thing for literature to do, Wolfe terminated the friendship. These are men of whom it is proper to speak of their having been violated by ideas; but we must observe that it was an excess of intellectual passivity that invited the violence.

In speaking of Hemingway and Faulkner I have used the word "piety." It is a word that I have chosen with some care and despite the pejorative meanings that nowadays adhere to it, for I wished to avoid the word "religion," and piety is not religion, yet I wished too to have religion come to mind as it inevitably must when piety is mentioned. Carlyle says of Shakespeare that he was the product of medieval Catholicism, and implies that Catholicism *at the distance at which*

*Shakespeare stood from it* had much to do with the power of Shakespeare's intellect. Allen Tate has developed in a more particular way an idea that has much in common with what Carlyle here implies. Loosely put, the idea is that religion in its decline leaves a detritus of pieties, of strong assumptions, which afford a particularly fortunate condition for certain kinds of literature; these pieties carry a strong charge of intellect, or perhaps it would be more accurate to say that they tend to stimulate the mind in a powerful way.

Religious emotions are singularly absent from Shakespeare and it does not seem possible to say of him that he was a religious man. Nor does it seem possible to say of the men of the great period of American literature in the nineteenth century that they were religious men. Hawthorne and Melville, for example, lived at a time when religion was in decline and they were not drawn to support it. But from religion they inherited a body of pieties, a body of issues, if you will, which engaged their hearts and their minds to the very bottom. Henry James was not a religious man and there is not the least point in the world in trying to make him out one. But you need not accept all the implications of Quentin Anderson's thesis that James allegorized his father's religious system to see that Mr. Anderson is right when he says that James was dealing, in his own way, with the questions that his father's system propounded.[9] This will indicate something of why James so catches our imagination today, and why we turn so eagerly again to Hawthorne and Melville.

The piety which descends from religion is not the only possible piety, as the case of Faulkner reminds us, and perhaps also the case of Hemingway. But we naturally mention first that piety which does descend from religion because it is most likely to have in it the quality of transcendence which, whether we admit it or no, we expect literature at its best to have.

The subject is extremely delicate and complex and I do no more than state it barely and crudely. But no matter how I state it, I am sure that you

[9]Cf. Quentin Anderson, *The American Henry James* (1957). [Ed.]

will see that what I am talking about leads us to the crucial issue of our literary culture.

I know that I will not be wrong if I assume that most of us here are in our social and political beliefs consciously liberal and democratic. And I know that I will not be wrong if I say that most of us, and in the degree of our commitment to literature and our familiarity with it, find that the contemporary authors we most wish to read and most wish to admire for their literary qualities demand of us a great agility and ingenuity in coping with their antagonism to our social and political ideals. For it is in general true that the modern European literature to which we can have an active, reciprocal relationship, which is the right relationship to have, has been written by men who are indifferent to, or even hostile to, the tradition of democratic liberalism as we know it. Yeats and Eliot, Proust and Joyce, Lawrence and Gide — these men do not seem to confirm us in the social and political ideals which we hold.

If we now turn and consider the contemporary literature of America, we see that whatever we can describe it as patently liberal and democratic, we must say that it is not of lasting interest. I do not say that the work which is written to conform to the liberal democratic tradition is of no value but only that we do not incline to return to it, we do not establish it in our minds and affections. Very likely we learn from it as citizens; and as citizen-scholars and citizen-critics we understand and explain it. But we do not live in an active reciprocal relation with it. The sense of largeness, of cogency, of the transcendence which largeness and cogency can give, the sense of being reached in our secret and primitive minds — this we virtually never get from the writers of the liberal democratic tradition at the present time.

And since liberal democracy inevitably generates a body of ideas, it must necessarily occur to us to ask why it is that these particular ideas have not infused with force and cogency the literature that embodies them. This question is the most important, the most fully challenging question in culture that at this moment we can ask.

The answer to it cannot of course even be begun here, and I shall be more than content if now it is merely accepted as a legitimate question. But there are one or two things that may be said about the answer, about the direction we must take to reach it in its proper form. We will not find it if we come to facile conclusions about the absence from our culture of the impressive ideas of traditional religion. I have myself referred to the historical fact that religion has been an effective means of transmitting or of generating ideas of a sort which I feel are necessary for the literary qualities we want, and to some this will no doubt mean that I believe religion to be a necessary condition of great literature. I do not believe that; and what is more, I consider it from many points of view an impropriety to try to guarantee literature by religious belief.

Nor will we find our answer if we look for it in the weakness of the liberal democratic ideas in themselves. It is by no means true that the inadequacy of the literature that connects itself with a body of ideas is the sign of the inadequacy of those ideas, although it is no doubt true that some ideas have less affinity with literature than others.

Our answer, I believe, will rather be found in a cultural fact — in the kind of relationship which we, or the writers who represent us, maintain toward the ideas we claim as ours, and in our habit of conceiving the nature of ideas in general. If we find that it is true of ourselves that we conceive ideas to be pellets of intellection or crystallizations of thought, precise and completed, and defined by their coherence and their procedural recommendations, then we shall have accounted for the kind of prose literature we have. And if we find that we do indeed have this habit, and if we continue in it, we can predict that our literature will continue much as it is. But if we are drawn to revise our habit of conceiving ideas in this way and learn instead to think of ideas as living things, inescapably connected with our wills and desires, as susceptible of growth and development by their very nature, as showing their life by their tendency to change, as being liable, by this very tendency, to deteriorate and become corrupt and to work harm, then we shall stand in a relation to ideas which makes an active literature possible.

# Susanne K. Langer
## 1895–1985

One of the twentieth century's most important aestheticians was born Susanne Katherine Knauth on December 20, 1895, in New York City, the daughter of Antonio Knauth, a lawyer, and Else Uhlich. She was educated at Radcliffe College, where she received her bachelor's, master's, and doctoral degrees in 1920, 1924, and 1926, respectively. She married William L. Langer in 1921, by whom she had two sons; the Langers were divorced in 1942. Susanne Langer taught at Radcliffe from 1927 to 1942; thereafter she spent five years as professor of philosophy at Columbia University. She ended her career at Connecticut College in New London, where she was professor until her retirement in 1961 and a research fellow until her death at the age of eighty-nine.

Langer does not begin as Kant or Croce did, with the idea of the aesthetic: Like Aristotle, she believes in the *arts* rather than in *art* per se, though in the long run she accepts the idea that the genres of art share common factors:

> It has lately become acceptable again to assert that all the arts are really just one "Art" with a capital *A*. . . . My approach to the problem of interrelations among the arts has been the precise opposite: taking each art as autonomous, and asking about each in turn what it creates, what are the principles of creation in this art, what its scope and possible materials. Such a treatment shows up the difference among the several great genera of art — plastic, balletic, poetic. Pursuing these differences, rather than vehemently denying their importance, one finds that they go deeper than one would expect. Each genus, for instance, creates a different kind of experience altogether. . . . The plastic arts create a purely visual space, music a purely audible time, dance a realm of interacting powers, etc. . . . But if you trace the difference among the arts as far and as minutely as possible, there comes a point beyond which no more distinctions can be made. It is the point where the deeper structural devices — ambivalent images, intersecting forces, great rhythms . . . variations, congruences . . . all the organizing devices — reveal the principles of dynamic form that we learn from nature as spontaneously as we learn language from our elders.[1]

Langer's basic aesthetic principle is "expressive form": "A work of art is an expressive form created for our perception through sense or imagination, and what it expresses is human feeling . . . in the broadest sense, meaning *everything that can be felt,* from physical sensation . . . to the most complex emotions . . . of a conscious human life."[2] The use of the term *expression* might seem to link Langer with Croce, but for the postromantic Croce, expression is only the externalization of *intuition,* a form of knowing that occurs in the mind of the artist. Langer is more interested in the product than in the process; for her, the expressiveness of art is something characteristic of the object of art as a symbolic form rather than something defined by the activity of the artist. And the idea that art is self-

---

[1]Susanne K. Langer, *Problems of Art* (London: Routledge and Kegan Paul, 1957), pp. 76–79.
[2]Langer, p. 15.

expression is not one Langer favors: A crying baby is expressing itself, but its activity has nothing to do with creating a work of art.

The crucial, unmentioned element in Langer's definition is that art is symbolic, but symbolic in a special sense. In the first place, art is not generally dependent upon the language sign or, to put it more precisely, the discursive symbol. The symbols of art are *presentational*. (Even poetry, though using language as its medium, is not, as we shall see, discursive.) Furthermore, like Charles Sanders Peirce, Langer distinguishes between the sign that is an index or token of a property (the way smoke betokens fire or shaking hands are symptomatic of a bad night's sleep) and the symbol that externalizes and articulates emotion, which "presents feeling for our contemplation." There must be a conscious sense that an audience is perceiving the symbol and responding with the appropriate human feeling. This is somewhat similar to Eliot's idea of the "objective correlative," the poetic symbol that "serves as the formula for" some particular emotion or feeling.

The other important aspect of the definition is that the work of art is a *creation*. Like Aristotle, Langer sees the artist, whether poet, painter, composer, or choreographer, as a maker. But an artist's way of making is different from that of an artisan. Langer's point here is that what the artisan makes is *real* — a cobbler makes a pair of shoes — while what the artist creates has only a *virtual* existence. A picture "is made by deploying pigments on a piece of canvas, but the picture is not a pigment-and-canvas structure" the way a shoe is a structure of leather; "the picture that emerges from the canvas is a structure of space, and the space itself is an emergent whole of shapes, visible colored volumes. Neither the space nor the things in it were in the room before."[3] What the painter creates is an apparition. In the same way, the musician creates an audible apparition, an expressive form operating in virtual time, and so, each in their own ways, do the dancer and the poet. (The attempt to apply the concept of the virtual in architecture, however, creates some difficulties.)

Langer's aesthetics has been more influential in the fields of the plastic arts and music, which she has more persistently addressed, than in literature, but the essay on "Poetic Creation" reprinted here is typical of her penetrating but unabstruse approach to literature. Langer's primary aim is to clear up the confusion about the use of language in poetry, which surfaces most obviously in romantic criticism such as Coleridge's but which generated new controversies a century later, when analytical philosophy — the product of Ludwig Wittgenstein, Gottlob Frege, Bertrand Russell, and Alfred North Whitehead — became the most important branch in the Anglo-American tradition. Langer addresses herself primarily to Russell's attempt to solve the problem of the referentiality of poetry — the question of whether it is true or false that King Lear has three living daughters. It is difficult to say that the statement is either true or false, since the character Lear (not any historical Lear that may underlie the character) has existence only in a play by Shakespeare, and the daughters live and die only within the play. The usual criteria

---

[3]Langer, p. 28.

for checking the truth or falsehood of statements seem not to apply in this case; Russell's solution was to call propositions such as "Lear has three living daughters" pseudostatements. The notion that poetry includes not statements but pseudostatements, typical of an emotive rather than a referential use of language, was taken up later by I. A. Richards and the New Critics.

For Langer, the distinction between "emotive" and "referential" is beside the point and evades the genuine issue; the real distinction is that poetry does not make use of *discursive* symbols but of *presentational* symbols, which have an entirely different function. Using her general aesthetic principles, Langer cuts through these paradoxes, which to her seem nonissues, for the poet is not primarily a user of language but a creator, one who makes a virtual world out of the poetic image, "an *appearance* of events, persons, emotional reactions, experiences, conditions of life . . . . What is created is a composed and shaped apparition of a new human experience."[4]

The distinction between discursive and presentational symbolism is made clear in Langer's discussion of how language works in John Keats and Algernon Swinburne. She notes that in Keats's sonnet, "When I have Fears," the emotion peaks at the lines,

> When I behold, upon the night's starr'd face,
> Huge cloudy symbols of a high romance,
> And think that I may never live to trace
> Their shadows, with the magic hand of chance.

As a virtual image, it makes us aware of "knowledge and mystery, vastness and transience" concentrated into a very few words. Yet the virtual image is not *visual*: We are not aware of clouds casting shadows — in fact clouds on a starry night do not cast shadows whose outlines can be traced. As a discursive symbol, in other words, the lines are paradoxical or senseless — which is a sign that that is not how we are reading them. For Langer, the "factual distortion" that keeps the image emotive rather than visual is like "spatial distortion in paintings," which expresses feelings rather than physical relationships.

Similarly, in the case of Swinburne, Langer also finds artistic virtue in what would be a discursive fault: If the images in *Atalanta in Calydon* come at us too swiftly to be resolved, decomposed, experienced as visual imagery, it only proves that visual imagery was not what Swinburne was aiming for, but rather "a dynamic [image] — a vision of the emotional drive sometimes called 'Spring Fever.' . . . Swinburne's intent . . . is to crowd and pile impressions so they blur each other, and to drive ideas with ideas . . . . The result is an unearthly excitement, not distilled from the poetic image of spring, but absorbing all the images into itself."

In effect, factuality as an issue drops out of poetry in that facts take shape only within the virtual world of the poetic creation. And referentiality — to return to Russell's problem — can refer only to that virtual world. Shakespeare's Richard III murdered the princes in the tower, no matter what the actual King Richard did.

[4]Langer, p. 148.

"The relation of poetry to the world of facts is the same as that of painting to the world of objects." And just as painters distort objects and space for the sake of an expressive effect, so the poet's commitment is primarily to the creation of his virtual world, not to the reproduction of the actual one.

### Selected Bibliography

Barry, Jackson G. "Form or Formula: Comic Structure in Northrop Frye and Susanne Langer." *Education Theatre Journal* 16 (1964): 333–40.

Blum, Fred. *Susanne Langer's Music Aesthetics.* Iowa City: State University of Iowa Press, 1959.

Ghosh, Ranjan K. *Aesthetic Theory and Art: A Study in Susanne K. Langer.* Delhi: Ajanta Publications, 1979.

Hagberg, Garry. "Art and the Unsayable: Langer's Tractarian Aesthetics." *British Journal of Aesthetics* 24 (1984): 325–40.

Innis, Robert E. "Art, Symbol and Consciousness." *International Philosophy Quarterly* 17 (1977): 455–76.

Keel, John. "Langer and the Principles of Art." *Etc* 43 (1986): 297–302.

Lang, Berel. "Langer's Arabesque and the Collapse of the Symbol." *Review of Metaphysics* 16 (1962): 349–65.

Rod, David K. "Kenneth Burke and Susanne Langer on Drama and Its Audience." *Quarterly Journal of Speech* 72 (1986): 306–17.

# Poetic Creation

Poetry is universally regarded as one of the "fine arts," like music, painting, sculpture, architecture, and dance. It is an art of words. On that proposition I think all authorities agree.

In a sense, of course, all speech is an "art of words"; "art" in the sense in which we sometimes say of anything difficult that "it's an art," or even "it's a fine art." But that is not what people mean when they class poetry among the fine arts. They mean expressly to set the poetic use of language apart from its use in ordinary discourse; and in this attempt they often get deeper and deeper into the toils of semantics, psychology, and aesthetics. Fact and feeling, seeing and saying get mixed up in every conceivable combination, and yet no *principium divisionis*[1] emerges to distin-

guish the poetic function of words from any or all the rest. To find the source of this failure and a way of deciding between poetry and other products of language is my purpose tonight.

Ever since Locke, and to some extent Bacon and Hobbes before him, distinguished the strictly conceptual use of language in mathematics, logic, and physics from its emotional use in religious or political harangue, and noted the mixture of both functions in ordinary social intercourse, language has been regarded under these two aspects. Books have been written, courses given, and institutes founded on the fundamental distinction between the informative and the evocative use of words. The former is regarded as the proper, literal use that results in meaningful statements, or genuine propositions; the latter as self-expressive, communicating the speaker's feelings to other people who react either sym-

[1]Principle of classification. [Ed.]

pathetically or antipathetically. We are told that such utterances, though they sound like statements, really assert nothing; but these pseudo-propositions which have no scientific meaning are said to be, nevertheless, highly important instruments of social control.

This doctrine, which Bertrand Russell expounded some forty years ago, is still in vogue. In the simplified form to which popular presentation has reduced it, it is obvious enough to command general assent, and it contains enough truth to throw light on some rather bizarre phenomena, such as the ardor of other people's patently false beliefs, the effectiveness of sheer oratory in politics and in advertising, the strange social fact that people manage to talk together quite happily in sentences that cannot bear even the slightest degree of logical analysis. It is, indeed, a theory that lends itself admirably to popularization, and has become the main stock in trade of amateur philosophers today.

But its wide acceptance is bought at a price. When professional semanticists concentrate their efforts on finding ever simpler and more graphic ways of presenting and defending a theory, they stop working on the theory itself. They tend to ignore its difficulties beyond those which a general public would perceive and question. The danger of simplification is that it shelves the more abstruse problems and creates the appearance that they could easily be resolved if one wanted to expand one's exposition. The theory of the emotive use of language, for instance, employs the concept of self-expression, i.e., completion of the motor arc by speech, the concept of suggestion, or natural effect of self-expressive behavior, and the concept of communication, or deliberate imparting of value judgments leading to explicit agreement or disagreement. Self-expression, suggestion, and communication of value judgments are all "emotive uses of language," but each in a different way; and the interesting question of their involvements with each other are obscured by lumping all these uses together in simple contrast to the scientific use, the literal statement of facts (or supposed facts). Even if a speaker or writer says "Of course, this is a simplification," he is likely to stick to the simplified

version of semantic problems himself, and take for granted that other possible uses of language are subsidiary to one or the other of his two kinds.

An important illustration of this danger is the effect which the popularized simplified semantic doctrine has had on the philosophical treatment of poetry even by our leading scholars. Since language is used in poetry, but literal scientific statement is clearly not its intended use, it is uncritically assumed that the poet must be making the other use of his words, namely the evocative. He must be registering his emotional reactions to the subject of his poem, trying to make us have similar reactions, and/or pronouncing value judgments in non-literal pseudo-propositions. So we read, in current poetics and criticism, that the poet takes us into his confidence, that he tells us things between the lines, enlists our sympathy for his feelings, and imparts his ultimate religious, moral, and metaphysical judgments "through the language of the heart," that is to say, through the evocative use of words.

In reading such semantical studies of poetry one may be left wondering why poetic language is so often referred to as "creative," and its product as "poetic creation." What is created? If the reader's feelings are stirred up, and he is led to take various attitudes toward life, what is created, in a strict sense? The feelings? They are only stimulated, as they are by ordinary social communication. The facts of life? They are talked about, not made; they were there before. To call such suggestion and commentary "creation" sounds a bit pretentious, like referring to all works of art as "masterpieces."

Before we try to answer the major question I have just put before you — "What is created in poetry?" — it might be helpful to consider the nature of artistic creation in general, in other arts.

In a painting, the essential creation is the appearance of a space, which is not the space wherein the picture hangs and the spectator stands. The wall that supports the painting is not *in* the painting; it is not part of the picture space. The spectator is not in the picture space. That space which is the painter's creation is really new. The paints and the canvas, the materials of his work, were in the studio before, and have simply been moved about by his efforts. But the space we see as a result of that new development was not there before. It is a created apparition.

All created factors in a work of art are *elements* of it. Its elements are what we discover when, casually or carefully, we analyze it. Background and foreground, high lights, empty air, motion, accent, intensity of color, depth of darkness, objects in relation to each other — all these are elements. Canvas and paints, the actual light that falls on the picture, are materials. They are used, not created.

Music, like painting, is a purely created form not of space, but of time; its materials are tones of varying pitch, loudness, and quality, but its elements are tonal forms, moving, mingling, resolving, having direction and energy, violently active or abating toward complete rest. Its time, as well as all the great and small tonal forms (melodies, progressions) that make it up, are appearances made of sound; music is time made audible and articulated as a perceptible, dynamic form. Every art, indeed, creates a special sort of appearance, in terms of which all its works are made.

So much, then, for the meaning of "creation" in art generally. Now let us return to the question of poetry. What does a poet create? Poetry is made of words; but words are the poet's heritage, and not something he creates. They are materials which he uses. The poem, the work of art, somehow results from the way he uses them.

He seems to use them much as we would in writing a letter or speaking, to make statements, ask questions, or register his reactions to things by exclaiming over them. A poem is usually in the form of a discourse about something, just like a conversation or a report, and exhibits all the familiar structures we call "sentences" of various kinds. So, first of all, the poet seems to be *saying things.*

Now, it is universally recognized, I think, that *what the poet says* could also be said in somewhat different words — that is, that his statements could be quite faithfully repeated in paraphrase — but that the poetic composition would almost certainly be lost in such a retelling. A person making a poem evidently uses words not only to say things, but to say them in certain ways. And speculation has run high, for decades if not centuries, as to the parts played by the sound and sense of the words, the images they convey, the feelings they evoke. Meter and rhyme are certainly products of their sound, that have functioned traditionally in poetry. Imagery is a natural by-product of their sense. The total result is much more than a literal statement; it is a statement that makes the stated fact appear in a special light.

Everyone knows that the way an idea is expressed may serve to recommend it to people or to make it seem horrible. The selfsame fact wears two very different faces in the American and the Soviet press, respectively. It all depends on the way it is put. This obvious power of words to give the content of discourse almost any desired appearance is exploited today both by political and commercial interests; it is tne essence of propaganda and of advertising; both build on the fact that people will respond to a statement with enthusiasm, anger, indifference, or other emotion, according to the way it is worded.

In view of our preoccupation, in the present phase of history, with such emotional responses, it is perhaps inevitable that literary theorists should regard poetry, too, as an appeal to the reader's emotions, to enlist his sympathy for the poet's feeling about the world, the emptiness of life, the ugliness of war, the absurdity of everything, or whatever the poem presents. Poetry is quite generally regarded as a communication, not of facts, but of the values the poet puts upon facts which, simply as facts, are probably as well known to us as to him: the facts of living and dying, loving and loathing, playing the hypocrite, soldiering, worshipping, having children. The facts he mentions constitute *what he says;* the values are given to them by *the way he says it.* His aim, so we are told, is to make us share his particular way of experiencing these familiar events and conditions of the world.

If, now, we ask again my persistent question: what does a poet create? the critics to whom I refer can readily answer: the *appearance* that is given to the subject matter by his words. And in this I agree with them. What any artist — poet, painter, dancer, musician or what not — creates, is always an appearance. The appearance created in poetry is effected by the way words are handled. But beyond this I cannot go with them, namely, to the conclusion that the poet, like the orator or advertiser, is lending that created appearance to things in the actual world, about which he is talking to us. The entire problem of how and what a poet communicates to his reader seems to me a specious one, arising from the commonsense assumptions that if he writes declarative sentences he must be making statements, and *pari passu,* if he writes interrogative ones he must be asking questions, and if we are his readers he must be addressing them to us. These assumptions, though made by common sense, are wrong, and prevent us from treating poetry in the same way as all the other arts.

Under the aegis of scientific method, social science, and popular semantics, we have missed a trick, I think, in the philosophy of language. Most of our interest in language has been prompted by needs and problems of communication. Consequently communication by words has been the key concept of our studies of language; in fact, some semanticists regard language as originally and properly a signaling device, elaborated to an amazing degree — even to the point where the code suffers confusions, because its signs figure in too many connections at once and become overcharged with meanings, so that failure of communication or mixed deliveries result. That accounts, they believe, for the fact that most of the time language does not look like the conventional set of signals it is supposed to be.

The use of language for poetic creation has received no more than honorable mention in our schools; usually it is simply lumped with one or all of the familiar emotive functions. The reason is, I think, that we are so dominated by interest in communication, and the poetic use of words is not essentially communicative. Language is the material of poetry, but what is done with this material is not what we do with language in actual life; for *poetry is not a kind of discourse at all.* What the poet creates out of words is an *appearance* of events, persons, emotional reactions, experiences, places, conditions of life; these created things are the elements of poetry; they constitute what Cecil Day Lewis has called "the poetic image." A poem is, in precisely his sense, an image. This image is not necessarily visual; since the word "image" has an almost irresistible connotation of visualness, I prefer to call the poetic image a *semblance.* The created poetic semblance need not be a semblance of corresponding actual things, facts, persons, or experiences. It is quite normally a pure appearance, a sheer figment; it is essentially a virtual object; and such a virtual object is a work of art. It is entirely created. Its material is language, its motif, or model, usually discursive speech, but what is created is not actual discourse — what is created is a composed and shaped apparition of a new human experience.

The composed apparition has as definite a structure as a musical composition, a piece of sculpture, an architectural work, or a painting. It is not a report or comment, but a constructed form; if it is a good poetic work it is an *expressive form* in the same way that a work of plastic art is an expressive form — by virtue of the tensions and resolutions, balances and asymmetries among its own elements, which beget the illusion of organic nature that artists call "living form."

The general problem of expressive form, which I believe is the central problem of aesthetics, is not our subject today; but we cannot evade it entirely, since we are dealing with one of its special cases, the creation of a sheer appearance, or virtual event, by means of words. This is a use of words quite distinct from their usually recognized uses; it may be called the *formulative* function of language, which has its own primitive and advanced, unconscious and conscious levels. It is normally coincident with the communicative functions, but largely independent of them; and while its most spectacular exhibition is in poetry, it is profoundly, though not obviously, operative in our whole language-bound mental life. In autistic speech it is the paramount purpose. Communication is less likely to stimulate it than to set its limits, and hold spontaneous ways of shaping experience to something like a standard pattern. In this way, it is the communicative office of language that makes the actual world's appearance public, and reasonably fixed. The formulative power of words is the source and support of our imagination; before there can be more than animal communication, there has to be envisagement, and a means of developing perception in keeping with conception. Beings who have speech almost certainly have quite a different sort of direct experience of the world from creatures that use only self-expressive or directive signs.

The greatness of the gulf between speechless and speech-molded life has been contemplated and stressed particularly by the philosophers who trace their intellectual descent from Kant, and accept, howbeit with various reservations, the Hegelian concept of *"Geist"* — that is, the concept of the human mind as a creative entity not belonging to physical nature but to a different order of reality. Their metaphysical assumptions, however, are not necessary to every theory of mind that would recognize the role of conception in perception, memory, and feeling, and the role of language in conception. There are historical and psychological reasons why all nonidealistic philosophers have either missed or deliberately slighted the problem of verbal imagination, even to the point of side-stepping the whole phenomenon. But the involvements of language with all the rest of human mentality are really as amenable to naturalistic treatment as to an idealistic approach.

For the philosophical understanding of poetry and its relation to art in general, the current positivistic credo of "general semantics" is simply inadequate; a more intimate study of the functions of language is required than their customary divisions into propositional uses (subdivided into various modes) and emotional uses (with subdivisions casually suggested). The greatest work to date that has been done on the subject has come from another quarter, and may be found in Ernst Cassirer's *Philosophy of Symbolic Forms;* but there are scattered, more recent sources, chiefly in the fields of anthropology, linguistics, and poetics, for instance Whorf's[2] studies of the

---

[2]Benjamin Lee Whorf (1897–1941), American linguist. The "Whorf hypothesis" states that thought is conditioned by the grammatical categories of language. In its stronger forms, the hypothesis claims that we can only think the thoughts our language lets us think, and that translation of concepts across languages is not always possible. [Ed.]

Hopi language, from which only the most superficial and obvious conclusions have yet been drawn.

More promising, however, than the semantical approach to poetry is the approach from poetry to semantics. Poetry exhibits, like nothing else in the world, the formulative use of language; it is the paradigm of creative speech. For the poetic use of language is essentially formulative. Poetry is not a beautified discourse, a particularly effective way of telling things, although poetic structures may occur in discourse with truly artistic effect. Poetry as such is not discourse at all, it is the creation of a perceptible human experience which, from the standpoint of science and practical life, is illusory. It may create an apparition reminiscent of actual events and places, like a historical or locally oriented novel, or it may be a free invention of places, events, actions, and persons; but such different compositions are not different kinds of art. All poetry is pure poetry, though it be only more or less successful; it is primarily and not incidentally creative. In poetic composition one may see the formulative use of language deliberately and consciously pursued and the result spectacularly isolated. We are far more likely to learn the poetical function of words by studying poetry, and recognize it subsequently in more obscure contexts, such as dream psychology or history of language, than we are to find it in those contexts first and build a theory that can be made to fit poetry too.

The assumption that the poetic use of language is essentially formulative, and per se not communicative, has some interesting consequences. The most important is that, if propositions are not poetic elements, but materials out of which the elements of a poem are fashioned, then poetry may be regarded and treated as an art in exactly the same way as painting or music: as the creation of a self-contained, pure appearance, a perceptible expressive form. Such a conception of poetry frees us from the embarrassment of having to consider under different rubrics what, on the one hand, the poet is saying — that is, the sense and truth-value of his statements — and on the other hand the skill with which he says it; and of always having to strike a nice balance between those two interests. Poetic statements are no more actual statements than the peaches visible in a still life are actual dessert. The real question is what the poet *makes,* and that, of course, depends on how he goes about it. The task of poetic criticism, then, is not to learn from any and all available records what was the poet's philosophy, morality, life history, or psychosis, and to find the revelation of his own experiences in his words; it is to evaluate his fiction, the appearance of thought and feeling or outward events that he creates.

A poem that rises to great heights does so by virtue of the way it is built up — built out of words, but not therefore just a pattern of words. Consider Keats's sonnet, "When I have fears that I may cease to be"; it certainly reaches a poetic peak in the lines:

When I behold, upon the night's starr'd face,
Huge cloudy symbols of a high romance,
And think that I may never live to trace
Their shadows, with the magic hand of chance.

This rise, however, is not due to any burst of self-expression, nor reference to persons or events in Keats's life; it is due to a sudden concentrated appearance of knowledge and mystery, vastness and transience, effected by rather few words, sonorous and rhythmically slow. There is not even a visual image; for the clouds cannot be taken as clouds casting shadows. They are his immaterial visions and their images. Clouds against the night sky cast no outlined shadows; the figure is not a simple metaphor — it is poetically natural but not borrowed from nature. It contains a factual distortion, much like spatial distortion in paintings. What it creates is a moment of intense awareness of many feelings, paradoxical yet confluent. That moment would be great and important to the reader even if he did not know that Keats actually died young and was probably aware of his short lease of life. It is not by sympathy with Keats that one is moved, but by the poetic composition, which would be exactly as moving if it were anonymous.

To read poetry as a psychological document, in a context of the author's life, putting in further meanings and personal allusions from circumstantial knowledge, is to do violence to the poem. That is forcibly making statements out of its

lines, and expanding their meaning far beyond anything that serves the poetic figment. The result is sometimes fatal to the poem, making it sound false or silly, as *Ash Wednesday* did to Edmund Wilson, when he wrote: "I am made a little tired at hearing Eliot, only in his early forties, present himself as an 'agéd eagle' who asks why he should make the effort to stretch his wings."

The reaction shows, I think, the banefulness of the common assumption that a poem becomes more significant to the reader if he can read it in a context of the author's reconstructed life, and picture to himself the conditions under which the poem was written. All such supplements are really destructive of a composition. They have no creative function whatever, and clutter the work with inorganic added stuff. Where a reference to some place or person serves an artistic purpose the poet is, after all, free to put it in, perhaps in the title, perhaps directly in the work: "Composed on Westminister Bridge," or:

When it's yesterday in Oregon it's one A.M. in
   Maine,

or:

Mock on, mock on, Rousseau, Voltaire!

Many a time, however, names do not really relate to a poem to an actual setting. The use of specific names is often just as effective where these denote nothing known to the reader — like the place names in our translations of Chinese poetry — as where they refer to known places and persons, like Grantchester, Dublin, Bonaparte, Dante. That depends on the use the poet makes of them. Often his main intent is simply to create the semblance of individual reference, so he chooses proper names primarily for their sound and only in a general way for their connotation; or his first consideration may be to make the reference specific but strange, so he tosses unfamiliar words about, just making sure they will be taken as proper names:

Where the ninth wave flows in Perython,
Is the grave of Glwalchmai, the peerless one;
In Llanbadarn lies Clydno's son.

There would be nothing added to our perception and understanding of that poem by identifying the Welsh heroes and places whose names are woven into it, and uncovering their biographies. All they need to do for us is to sound Welsh and fill a cherished land with historic graves. For the Wales in the poem is a creation, constituted exactly as the poet presents it, and having no political, economic, or other aspects, to tie it up with British elections or American tourist agencies.

Some odd revaluations of poetic work may result if one shifts from the traditional question: "What is the poet telling us, and how does he communicate his experiences?" — to: "What has the poet created, and how did he do it?" Many strange turns, that serve neither to communicate ideas nor to express sentiments about the world or anything in it, are suddenly seen in an important role: they are constructing the "poetic image" itself, the poem as a virtual experience, which is neither the poet's nor ours, but exists for his and our imaginative perception. Consider, for instance, a poem we probably all have read, in school or in one of the famous anthologies — Browning's little song from *Pippa Passes:*

The year's at the spring
And day's at the morn;
Morning's at seven;
The hill-side's dew-pearl'd;
The lark's on the wing;
The snail's on the thorn;
God's in His heaven —
All's right with the world!

My English teacher in High School praised that poem as a fine expression of Browning's optimism. I thought his view of the world was very silly, for a man with a big beard. Oh, but Browning believed in progress, and he believed in God, and the key line to the whole poem was "God's in His heaven"!

Teacher explained that the song occurred in a play about two people who had lost all faith, and at the crucial moment heard Pippa's song outside the window, reassuring them. I thought it might take a little more than a young thing's opinion to reassure them. Pippa's view of life seemed

even less important than Browning's. And even if that utterance made sense in a play, why was the poem in the Oxford Book and everywhere else? I hated it.

Many years later I read it in its context, in the dramatic poem, *Pippa Passes.* It comes like a sudden distant call. It turns the action. And the key line *is,* "God's in His heaven"! Then I looked at it poetically, to see what made it *feel* the way it did.

An odd structure: each short line a complete statement, and in the first three lines the same colloquial turn of phrase, shifted from one colorless assertion to another until, in the third occurrence, it sounds artificial; then, the first image. The pattern of the verses is insistently schematic: three lines saying something is "at" something, then a statement of condition; three more lines saying something is "on" or "in" something, and another statement of condition, this time entirely general, universal. What does it sound like? — A roll call for "all aboard." This man is here, that man is there — one at this, one at that — the side is clear; each on his post, *the captain up there in his place —* she's trim!

It is this structure of the roll call, taken from its normal maritime setting and transposed to the countryside, the loud masculine "aye-aye, sir!" transmuted into a girl's song, the fierce sea images into gentle dewy slopes, that makes the perfect abstraction of feeling — the readiness, the eagerness of a launching. Not a mention, not a metaphor of the ship appears; only the same sense of beginning, launching the young day.

The little poem can bear quite persistent study. Every symbol is right, every bone of its structure covered. That is composition. And in this composition the final idea that is stated loses its philosophical weight: the whole image is only of the day. There is no optimistic belief expressed at all.

If we look at poetry as a created form, we find in every successful poem some unfamiliar devices, and have to beware of looking for the traditional ones before we are quite sure of what is in the works. An eminent critic has taken Swinburne to task for failing to develop his images even to the point of letting the reader grasp them before they pass. The poem that elicited this censure was the first chorus from *Atalanta in Calydon*. All its rich imagery, the critic claimed, is lost because the liquid flow of the words fairly drives one to read fast, and causes each image to pass before it is really formed, and to be crowded out by another that meets the same fate. And surely he is right; the lines fairly race, if you speak them in the most natural, unrhetorical way:

> When the hounds of springs are on winter's traces,
> The mother of months in meadow or plain
> Fills the shadows and windy places
> With lisp of leaves and ripple of rain;
> And the brown bright nightingale amorous
> Is half assuaged for Itylus,
> For the Thracian ships and the foreign faces,
> The tongueless vigil, and all the pain.
>
> Come, with bows bent and with emptying of quivers,
> Maiden most perfect, lady of light,
> With a noise of winds and many rivers,
> With a clamor of waters, and with might;
> Bind on thy sandals, O thou most fleet,
> Over the splendor and speed of thy feet;
> For the faint east quickens, the wan west shivers,
> Round the feet of the day and the feet of the night.
>
> Where shall we find her, how shall we sing to her,
> Fold our hands round her knees, and cling?
> O that man's heart were as fire and could spring to her,
> Fire, or the strength of the streams that spring!
> For the stars and the winds are unto her
> As raiment, as songs of the harp-player;
> For the risen stars and the fallen cling to her,
> And the southwest-wind and the west-wind sing.
>
> For winter's rains and ruins are over,
> And all the season of snows and sins;
> The day's dividing lover and lover,
> The light that loses, the night that wins;
> And time remembered is grief forgotten,
> And frosts are slain and flowers begotten,
> And in green underwood and cover
> Blossom by blossom, the spring begins.

If it was the poet's intention to describe the events in nature that constitute the coming of spring, make us realize them in imagination and share his way of seeing each one, then certainly they pass too swiftly, and never develop as sensuous experiences. But is a picture of spring the essential creation, the expressive form itself, or do his references to grass and flowers and rain and birdsong serve a different semblance? What is the motif?

The poem does not create a sensuous image, but a dynamic one — a vision of the emotional drive sometimes called "Spring Fever." That drive is from within; what elicits it is the totality of things, their separate qualities are irrelevant. Swinburne's intent, therefore, is to crowd and pile impressions so they blur each other, and to drive ideas with ideas, each emotionally toned, even quite highly strung, but none a fixed object of any emotion. The result is an unearthly excitement, not distilled from the poetic image of spring, but absorbing all the images into itself.

Statement, allusion, imagery, grammatical form, word rhythm, and any other elements in a poem all have essentially and purely creative functions. Even obscurity, which always goads critics into paraphrasing the problematical lines, is a poetic element; sometimes the reader is not supposed to find a line clear, any more than he is supposed to see an outline of the forms of chiaroscuro painting. Something is created by the difficulty of diction, the sense of incomprehensibility. Sometimes coherence of ideas is not needed; then it is left out. There is coherence of another sort, as in de la Mare's *Peacock Pie* — coherence of form or mood. Confession of feeling or opinion, made in the first person, is no more discourse than a self-portrait is the painter. Real confession would belong to another order. Poetry generates its own entire world, as painting generates its entire continuum of space. The relation of poetry to the world of facts is the same as that of painting to the world of objects: actual events, if they enter its orbit at all, are *motifs* of poetry, as actual objects are motifs of painting. No matter how faithful the image, it is a pure image, unmixed with bits of actuality. It is a created appearance, an expressive form, and there is properly nothing in it that does not enhance its symbolic expression of vitality, emotion, and consciousness. Poetry, like all art, is abstract and meaningful; it is organic and rhythmic, like music, and imaginal, like painting. It springs from the power of language to formulate the appearance of reality, a power fundamentally different from the communicative function, however involved with it in the evolution of speech. The pure product of the formulative use of language is verbal creation, composition, art; not statement, but *poesis*.

# Susan Sontag

b. 1933

Susan Sontag was born in New York City but raised in Tucson, Arizona, and in Los Angeles. She began her college work at the University of California, Berkeley, but transferred to the University of Chicago, where she received her B.A. in philosophy in 1951, at the age of eighteen. She did graduate work in English and philosophy at Harvard, where she received her M.A., and further graduate study at Oxford and the Sorbonne. Sontag has taught at Harvard, the University of Connecticut, Rutgers, and Columbia, but has supported herself mainly through her books and periodical essays.

Though she resists being classified "primarily as an essayist," Sontag is usually regarded nevertheless as a literary and cultural critic, her two novels, shorter fiction, and screenplays notwithstanding. Like Lionel Trilling, Sontag seems to function as a cultural barometer. Her fiction, like his, seems to be generated by her cultural observations and critical ideas. But where Trilling was primarily concerned with demonstrating the continuity of the present with the past, Sontag — operating in the sixties and seventies, rather than the forties and fifties — has always appeared less concerned with the traditions than with the discontinuities of contemporary life.

One of Sontag's major roles, at the outset of her career at least, was as a conduit between America and Europe of avant-garde ideas and personalities. Theorists like Walter Benjamin and Roland Barthes, now canonical, were almost unknown in the United States when they were recommended by Sontag in 1964 as writers who "reveal the sensuous surface of art without mucking about in it" in Section 8 of "Against Interpretation." In other essays in the early 1960s, she called attention on this side of the Atlantic to writers like Nathalie Sarraute, Antonin Artaud, and Alain Robbe-Grillet.

But Sontag is not a typical literary critic. She does not wish to analyze and interpret a series of standard texts so much as to discuss the conditions for their appearance, and the cultural assumptions that underlie their production and their reception. The subjects that have most appealed to her are the marginal areas of art, which sketch in the boundaries of a culture and its perceptions: the "camp" sensibility, the pornographic imagination, photography as an art form. Despite the variety of topics, Sontag's work, according to Susan Jeffords, "is of a piece. . . . No matter what form they take, Sontag asks the same questions — about the construction and resolution of identity, about manipulation and violence as a basis for social and aesthetic encounters, about the structure and function of cultural interpretation, about the inspiration of those outside accepted social boundaries — hoping that new answers will appear as a byproduct of new form. It is paradigmatic of Sontag's position as a modernist that they do not." Although she is not a reader-response critic in any of the usual senses of the term (see the introduction to Reader-Response Criticism, Ch. 7 in Part II), Sontag is most strongly engaged by the question of how readers process texts, and by the cultural uses to which literature is put. This is the central concern in "Against Interpretation."

The core of the essay is the three short sentences in Section 5: "Real art has the capacity to make us nervous. By reducing the work of art to its content and then interpreting *that,* one tames the work of art. Interpretation makes art manageable, comfortable." Interpretation, for Sontag, is a vicious and cowardly form of translation, in which the work of art is stripped of its sensuous life and reduced to a bare statement, which is then processed through the categories of the various schools of criticism (Marxist, Freudian, Christian) into a message that is inevitably familiar, indeed always already known. Appreciative and analytical criticism — not the nasty judgmental kind — has thus become the most deadly enemy of art.

The reaction to "Against Interpretation" was predictably fierce, and not merely from the Freudians and Marxists whose oxen were explicitly gored. Representatives of the New Criticism, then enjoying its hegemony, objected that they had been making Sontag's point for her all along (in such essays as Cleanth Brooks's "The Heresy of Paraphrase"). In fact, Sontag's strictures would apply equally against the New Critics, who, while granting lip service to the primacy of form, had always treated poetry as a general statement (or pseudostatement) about the world, albeit an especially complex sort of statement, riffed by paradox, irony, ambiguity, and other tropes. In New Critical terminology, theme is a part of form — and thus Sontag's dichotomy of "form" and "content" might mislead one to think she favored that school of exegesis. In fact, for Sontag any *translation* of the text into other terms is a betrayal of that text, and the *thematization* of any text always reduces it to a subartistic level.

Since "Against Interpretation" was published, there have been at least a few faltering steps toward exploring the "erotics of art" Sontag mentions. In particular, some of the newer versions of Freudian criticism (like that of Peter Brooks) have dropped the old dichotomy between latent and manifest content and attempted to discuss the form of the text as something other than a nicely wrapped container for fantasy and defense. Some of the new Marxist critics have moved beyond the representative quality and the political tendency of the text. Nevertheless, since translation and thematization have always been the mainstay of academic criticism, Sontag could be certain to find, in the pages of almost every scholarly journal today, specimens of the same destructive, spiritually impoverished interpretation she rejects.

## Selected Bibliography

Brooks, Peter. "Death of/as Metaphor." *Partisan Review* 46 (1979): 438–44.

Jeffords, Susan. "Susan Sontag." *Modern American Critics Since 1955,* ed. Gregory Jay. Detroit: Bruccoli-Clark-Layman, 1988.

Phillips, William. "Radical Styles." *Partisan Review* 36 (1969): 388–400.

Roudiez, Leon S. "Susan Sontag: Against the Ideological Grain." *World Literature Today* 57 (Spring 1983): 219–23.

Rubin, Louis D., Jr. "Susan Sontag and the Camp Followers." *Sewanee Review* 82 (Summer 1974): 503–10.

Shaw, Peter. "Two Afterthoughts on Susan Sontag." *Encounter* 58/59 (June/July 1982): 38–40.

# Against Interpretation

*Content is a glimpse of something, an encounter like a flash. It's very tiny — very tiny, content.*

— WILLEM DE KOONING, in an interview

*It is only shallow people who do not judge by appearances. The mystery of the world is the visible, not the invisible.*

— OSCAR WILDE, in a letter

## I

The earliest *experience* of art must have been that it was incantatory, magical; art was an instrument of ritual. (Cf. the paintings in the caves at Lascaux, Altamira, Niaux, La Pasiega, etc.) The earliest *theory* of art, that of the Greek philosophers, proposed that art was mimesis, imitation of reality.

It is at this point that the peculiar question of the *value* of art arose. For the mimetic theory, by its very terms, challenges art to justify itself.

Plato, who proposed the theory, seems to have done so in order to rule that the value of art is dubious. Since he considered ordinary material things as themselves mimetic objects, imitations of transcendent forms or structures, even the best painting of a bed would be only an "imitation of an imitation." For Plato, art is neither particularly useful (the painting of a bed is no good to sleep on), nor, in the strict sense, true. And Aristotle's arguments in defense of art do not really challenge Plato's view that all art is an elaborate *trompe l'oeil*,[1] and therefore a lie. But he does dispute Plato's idea that art is useless. Lie or no, art has a certain value according to Aristotle because it is a form of therapy. Art is useful, after all, Aristotle counters, medicinally useful in that it arouses and purges dangerous emotions.[2]

In Plato and Aristotle, the mimetic theory of art goes hand in hand with the assumption that art is always figurative. But advocates of the mimetic theory need not close their eyes to decorative and abstract art. The fallacy that art is necessarily a "realism" can be modified or scrapped without ever moving outside the problems delimited by the mimetic theory.

The fact is, all Western consciousness of and reflection upon art have remained within the confines staked out by the Greek theory of art as mimesis or representation. It is through this theory that art as such — above and beyond given works of art — becomes problematic, in need of defense. And it is the defense of art which gives birth to the odd vision by which something we have learned to call "form" is separated off from something we have learned to call "content," and to the well-intentioned move which makes content essential and form accessory.

Even in modern times, when most artists and critics have discarded the theory of art as representation of an outer reality in favor of the theory of art as subjective expression, the main feature of the mimetic theory persists. Whether we conceive of the work of art on the model of a picture (art as a picture of reality) or on the model of a statement (art as the statement of the artist), content still comes first. The content may have changed. It may now be less figurative, less lucidly realistic. But it is still assumed that a work of art *is* its content. Or, as it's usually put today,

---

[1] Deception of the eye. [Ed.]

[2] Sontag conflates Aristotle's *Poetics* with the reference to *katharsis* in the *Politics*, quoted in the introduction to Aristotle; see p. 41. [Ed.]

that a work of art by definition says something. ("What X is saying is . . . ," "What X is trying to say is . . . ," "What X said is . . ." etc., etc.)

## 2

None of us can ever retrieve that innocence before all theory when art knew no need to justify itself, when one did not ask of a work of art what it *said* because one knew (or thought one knew) what it *did*. From now to the end of consciousness, we are stuck with the task of defending art. We can only quarrel with one or another means of defense. Indeed, we have an obligation to overthrow any means of defending and justifying art which becomes particularly obtuse or onerous or insensitive to contemporary needs and practice.

This is the case, today, with the very idea of content itself. Whatever it may have been in the past, the idea of content is today mainly a hindrance, a nuisance, a subtle or not so subtle philistinism.

Though the actual developments in many arts may seem to be leading us away from the idea that a work of art is primarily its content, the idea still exerts an extraordinary hegemony. I want to suggest that this is because the idea is now perpetuated in the guise of a certain way of encountering works of art thoroughly ingrained among most people who take any of the arts seriously. What the overemphasis on the idea of content entails is the perennial, never consummated project of *interpretation*. And, conversely, it is the habit of approaching works of art in order to *interpret* them that sustains the fancy that there really is such a thing as the content of a work of art.

## 3

Of course, I don't mean interpretation in the broadest sense, the sense in which Nietzsche (rightly) says, "There are no facts, only interpretations." By interpretation, I mean here a conscious act of the mind which illustrates a certain code, certain "rules" of interpretation.

Directed to art, interpretation means plucking a set of elements (the X, the Y, the Z, and so forth) from the whole work. The task of inter-

pretation is virtually one of translation. The interpreter says, Look, don't you see that X is really — or, really means — A? That Y is really B? That Z is really C?

What situation could prompt this curious project for transforming a text? History gives us the materials for an answer. Interpretation first appears in the culture of late classical antiquity, when the power and credibility of myth had been broken by the "realistic" view of the world introduced by scientific enlightenment. Once the question that haunts post-mythic consciousness — that of the *seemliness* of religious symbols — had been asked, the ancient texts were, in their pristine form, no longer acceptable. Then interpretation was summoned, to reconcile the ancient texts to "modern" demands. Thus, the Stoics, to accord with their view that the gods had to be moral, allegorized away the rude features of Zeus and his boisterous clan in Homer's epics. What Homer really designated by the adultery of Zeus with Leto, they explained, was the union between power and wisdom. In the same vein, Philo of Alexandria interpreted the literal historical narratives of the Hebrew Bible as spiritual paradigms. The story of the exodus from Egypt, the wandering in the desert for forty years, and the entry into the promised land, said Philo, was really an allegory of the individual soul's emancipation, tribulations, and final deliverance.[3] Interpretation thus presupposes a discrepancy between the clear meaning of the text and the demands of (later) readers. It seeks to resolve that discrepancy. The situation is that for some reason a text has become unacceptable; yet it cannot be discarded. Interpretation is a radical strategy for conserving an old text, which is thought too precious to repudiate, by revamping it. The interpreter, without actually erasing or rewriting the text, *is* altering it. But he can't admit to doing this. He claims to be only making it intelligible, by disclosing its true meaning. However far the interpreters alter the text (another notorious example is the Rabbinic and Christian "spiritual" interpretations of the clearly erotic Song of Songs), they must claim to be reading off a sense that is already there.

[3]Dante's redaction of Philo's system appears in his letter to Can Grande della Scala, p. 119. [Ed.]

Interpretation in our own time, however, is even more complex. For the contemporary zeal for the project of interpretation is often prompted not by piety toward the troublesome text (which may conceal an aggression), but by an open aggressiveness, an overt contempt for appearances. The old style of interpretation was insistent, but respectful; it erected another meaning on top of the literal one. The modern style of interpretation excavates, and as it excavates, destroys; it digs "behind" the text, to find a sub-text which is the true one. The most celebrated and influential modern doctrines, those of Marx and Freud, actually amount to elaborate systems of hermeneutics, aggressive and impious theories of interpretation. All observable phenomena are bracketed, in Freud's phrase, as *manifest content*. This manifest content must be probed and pushed aside to find the true meaning — the *latent content* — beneath.[4] For Marx, social events like revolutions and wars; for Freud, the events of individual lives (like neurotic symptoms and slips of the tongue) as well as texts (like a dream or a work of art) — all are treated as occasions for interpretation. According to Marx and Freud, these events only *seem* to be intelligible. Actually, they have no meaning without interpretation. To understand *is* to interpret. And to interpret is to restate the phenomenon, in effect to find an equivalent for it.

Thus, interpretation is not (as most people assume) an absolute value, a gesture of mind situated in some timeless realm of capabilities. Interpretation must itself be evaluated, within a historical view of human consciousness. In some cultural contexts, interpretation is a liberating act. It is a means of revising, of transvaluing, of escaping the dead past. In other cultural contexts, it is reactionary, impertinent, cowardly, stifling.

**4**

Today is such a time, when the project of interpretation is largely reactionary, stifling. Like the fumes of the automobile and of heavy industry which befoul the urban atmosphere, the effusion of interpretations of art today poisons our sensi-

[4]See the introduction to Psychological Criticism, Ch. 2 in Part II. [Ed.]

bilities. In a culture whose already classical dilemma is the hypertrophy of the intellect at the expense of energy and sensual capability, interpretation is the revenge of the intellect upon art.

Even more. It is the revenge of the intellect upon the world. To interpret is to impoverish, to deplete the world — in order to set up a shadow world of "meanings." It is to turn *the* world into *this* world ("This world"! As if there were any other.)

The world, our world, is depleted, impoverished enough. Away with all duplicates of it, until we again experience more immediately what we have.

**5**

In most modern instances, interpretation amounts to the philistine refusal to leave the work of art alone. Real art has the capacity to make us nervous. By reducing the work of art to its content and then interpreting *that*, one tames the work of art. Interpretation makes art manageable, conformable.

This philistinism of interpretation is more rife in literature than in any other art. For decades now, literary critics have understood it to be their task to translate the elements of the poem or play or novel or story into something else. Sometimes a writer will be so uneasy before the naked power of his art that he will install within the work itself — albeit with a little shyness, a touch of the good taste of irony — the clear and explicit interpretation of it. Thomas Mann is an example of such an overcooperative author. In the case of more stubborn authors, the critic is only too happy to perform the job.

The work of Kafka, for example, has been subjected to a mass ravishment by no less than three armies of interpreters. Those who read Kafka as a social allegory see case studies of the frustrations and insanity of modern bureaucracy and its ultimate issuance in the totalitarian state. Those who read Kafka as a psychoanalytic allegory see desperate revelations of Kafka's fear of his father, his castration anxieties, his sense of his own impotence, his thralldom to his dreams. Those who read Kafka as a religious allegory explain that K. in *The Castle* is trying to gain access to heaven, that Joseph K. in *The Trial* is being judged by the inexorable and mysterious justice of God. . . . Another *oeuvre* that has attracted interpreters like leeches is that of Samuel Beckett. Beckett's delicate dramas of the withdrawn consciousness — pared down to essentials, cut off, often represented as physically immobilized — are read as a statement about modern man's alienation from meaning or from God, or as an allegory of psychopathology.

Proust, Joyce, Faulkner, Rilke, Lawrence, Gide . . . one could go on citing author after author; the list is endless of those around whom thick encrustations of interpretation have taken hold. But it should be noted that interpretation is not simply the compliment that mediocrity pays to genius. It is, indeed, *the* modern way of understanding something, and is applied to works of every quality. Thus, in the notes that Elia Kazan published on his production of *A Streetcar Named Desire,* it becomes clear that, in order to direct the play, Kazan had to discover that Stanley Kowalski represented the sensual and vengeful barbarism that was engulfing our culture, while Blanche Du Bois was Western civilization, poetry, delicate apparel, dim lighting, refined feelings and all, though a little the worse for wear to be sure. Tennessee Williams's forceful psychological melodrama now became intelligible: it was *about* something, about the decline of Western civilization. Apparently, were it to go on being a play about a handsome brute named Stanley Kowalski and a faded mangy belle named Blanche Du Bois, it would not be manageable.

## 6

It doesn't matter whether artists intend, or don't intend, for their works to be interpreted. Perhaps Tennessee Williams thinks *Streetcar* is about what Kazan thinks it to be about. It may be that Cocteau in *The Blood of a Poet* and in *Orpheus* wanted the elaborate readings which have been given these films, in terms of Freudian symbolism and social critique. But the merit of these works certainly lies elsewhere than in their "meanings." Indeed, it is precisely to the extent that Williams's plays and Cocteau's films do sug-

gest these portentous meanings that they are defective, false, contrived, lacking in conviction.

From interviews, it appears that Resnais and Robbe-Grillet consciously designed *Last Year at Marienbad* to accommodate a multiplicity of equally plausible interpretations. But the temptation to interpret *Marienbad* should be resisted. What matters in *Marienbad* is the pure, untranslatable, sensuous immediacy of some of its images, and its rigorous if narrow solutions to certain problems of cinematic form.

Again, Ingmar Bergman may have meant the tank rumbling down the empty night street in *The Silence* as a phallic symbol. But if he did, it was a foolish thought. ("Never trust the teller, trust the tale," said Lawrence.) Taken as a brute object, as an immediate sensory equivalent for the mysterious abrupt armored happenings going on inside the hotel, that sequence with the tank is the most striking moment in the film. Those who reach for a Freudian interpretation of the tank are only expressing their lack of response to what is there on the screen.

It is always the case that interpretation of this type indicates a dissatisfaction (conscious or unconscious) with the work, a wish to replace it by something else.

Interpretation, based on the highly dubious theory that a work of art is composed of items of content, violates art. It makes art into an article for use, for arrangement into a mental scheme of categories.

## 7

Interpretation does not, of course, always prevail. In fact, a great deal of today's art may be understood as motivated by a flight from interpretation. To avoid interpretation, art may become parody. Or it may become abstract. Or it may become ("merely") decorative. Or it may become non-art.

The flight from interpretation seems particularly a feature of modern painting. Abstract painting is the attempt to have, in the ordinary sense, no content; since there is no content, there can be no interpretation. Pop Art works by the opposite means to the same result; using a content so blatant, so "what it is," it, too, ends by being uninterpretable.

A great deal of modern poetry as well, starting from the great experiments of French poetry (including the movement that is misleadingly called Symbolism) to put silence into poems and to reinstate the *magic* of the word, has escaped from the rough grip of interpretation. The most recent revolution in contemporary taste in poetry — the revolution that has deposed Eliot and elevated Pound — represents a turning away from content in poetry in the old sense, an impatience with what made modern poetry prey to the zeal of interpreters.

I am speaking mainly of the situation in America, of course. Interpretation runs rampant here in those arts with a feeble and negligible avant-garde: fiction and the drama. Most American novelists and playwrights are really either journalists or gentlemen sociologists and psychologists. They are writing the literary equivalent of program music. And so rudimentary, uninspired, and stagnant has been the sense of what might be done with *form* in fiction and drama that even when the content isn't simply information, news, it is still peculiarly visible, handier, more exposed. To the extent that novels and plays (in America), unlike poetry and painting and music, don't reflect any interesting concern with changes in their form, these arts remain prone to assault by interpretation.

But programmatic avant-gardism — which has meant, mostly, experiments with form at the expense of content — is not the only defense against the infestation of art by interpretations. At least, I hope not. For this would be to commit art to being perpetually on the run. (It also perpetuates the very distinction between form and content which is, ultimately, an illusion.) Ideally, it is possible to elude the interpreters in another way, by making works of art whose surface is so unified and clean, whose momentum is so rapid, whose address is so direct that the work can be . . . just what it is. Is this possible now? It does happen in films, I believe. This is why cinema is the most alive, the most exciting, the most important of all art forms right now. Perhaps the way one tells how alive a particular art form is, is by the latitude it gives for making

mistakes in it, and still being good. For example, a few of the films of Bergman — though crammed with lame messages about the modern spirit, thereby inviting interpretations — still triumph over the pretentious intentions of their director. In *Winter Light* and *The Silence,* the beauty and visual sophistication of the images subvert before our eyes the callow pseudo-intellectuality of the story and some of the dialogue. (The most remarkable instance of this sort of discrepancy is the work of D. W. Griffith.) In good films, there is always a directness that entirely frees us from the itch to interpret. Many old Hollywood films, like those of Cukor, Walsh, Hawks, and countless other directors, have this liberating anti-symbolic quality, no less than the best work of the new European directors, like Truffaut's *Shoot the Piano Player* and *Jules and Jim,* Godard's *Breathless* and *Vivre Sa Vie,* Antonioni's *L'Avventura,* and Olmi's *The Fiancés.*

The fact that films have not been overrun by interpreters is in part due simply to the newness of cinema as an art. It also owes to the happy accident that films for such a long time were just movies; in other words, that they were understood to be part of mass, as opposed to high, culture, and were left alone by most people with minds. Then, too, there is always something other than content in the cinema to grab hold of, for those who want to analyze. For the cinema, unlike the novel, possesses a vocabulary of forms — the explicit, complex, and discussable technology of camera movements, cutting, and composition of the frame that goes into the making of a film.

## 8

What kind of criticism, of commentary on the arts, is desirable today? For I am not saying that works of art are ineffable, that they cannot be described or paraphrased. They can be. The question is how. What would criticism look like that would serve the work of art, not usurp its place?

What is needed, first, is more attention to form in art. If excessive stress on *content* provokes the arrogance of interpretation, more extended and more thorough descriptions of *form* would silence. What is needed is a vocabulary — a descriptive, rather than prescriptive, vocabulary — for forms.[5] The best criticism, and it is uncommon, is of this sort that dissolves considerations of content into those of form. On film, drama, and painting respectively, I can think of Erwin Panofsky's essay, "Style and Medium in the Motion Pictures," Northrop Frye's essay "A Conspectus of Dramatic Genres," Pierre Francastel's essay "The Destruction of a Plastic Space." Roland Barthes's book *On Racine* and his two essays on Robbe-Grillet are examples of formal analysis applied to the work of a single author. (The best essays in Erich Auerbach's *Mimesis*, like "The Scar of Odysseus," are also of this type.) An example of formal analysis applied simultaneously to genre and author is Walter Benjamin's essay, "The Story Teller: Reflections on the Works of Nicolai Leskov."

Equally valuable would be acts of criticism which would supply a really accurate, sharp, loving description of the appearance of a work of art. This seems even harder to do than formal analysis. Some of Manny Farber's film criticism, Dorothy Van Ghent's essay "The Dickens World: A View from Todgers'," Randall Jarrell's essay on Walt Whitman are among the rare examples of what I mean. These are essays which reveal the sensuous surface of art without mucking about in it.

**9**

*Transparence* is the highest, most liberating value in art — and in criticism — today. Transparence means experiencing the luminousness of the thing in itself, of things being what they are. This is the greatness of, for example, the films

of Bresson and Ozu and Renoir's *The Rules of the Game*.

Once upon a time (say, for Dante), it must have been a revolutionary and creative move to design works of art so that they might be experienced on several levels. Now it is not. It reinforces the principle of redundancy that is the principal affliction of modern life.

Once upon a time (a time when high art was scarce), it must have been a revolutionary and creative move to interpret works of art. Now it is not. What we decidedly do not need now is further to assimilate Art into Thought, or (worse yet) Art into Culture.

Interpretation takes the sensory experience of the work of art for granted, and proceeds from there. This cannot be taken for granted, now. Think of the sheer multiplication of works of art available to every one of us, superadded to the conflicting tastes and odors and sights of the urban environment that bombard our senses. Ours is a culture based on excess, on overproduction; the result is a steady loss of sharpness in our sensory experience. All the conditions of modern life — its material plenitude, its sheer crowdedness — conjoin to dull our sensory faculties. And it is in the light of the condition of our senses, our capacities (rather than those of another age), that the task of the critic must be assessed.

What is important now is to recover our senses. We must learn to *see* more, to *hear* more, to *feel* more.

Our task is not to find the maximum amount of content in a work of art, much less to squeeze more content out of the work than is already there. Our task is to cut back content so that we can see the thing at all.

The aim of all commentary on art now should be to make works of art — and, by analogy, our own experience — more, rather than less, real to us. The function of criticism should be to show *how it is what it is*, even *that it is what it is*, rather than to show *what it means*.

**10**

In place of a hermeneutics we need an erotics of art.

[5]One of the difficulties is that our idea of form is spatial (the Greek metaphors for form are all derived from notions of space). This is why we have a more ready vocabulary of forms for the spatial than for the temporal arts. The exception among the temporal arts, of course, is the drama; perhaps this is because the drama is a narrative (i.e., temporal) form that extends itself visually and pictorially, upon a stage. . . . What we don't have yet is a poetics of the novel, any clear notion of the forms of narration. Perhaps film criticism will be the occasion of a breakthrough here, since films are primarily a visual form, yet they are also a subdivision of literature. [Au.]

# CONTEMPORARY TRENDS
# IN LITERARY CRITICISM

Part Two

CONTEMPORARY TRENDS
IN LITERARY CRITICISM

# *I*

# MARXIST CRITICISM

*The experience of mankind on the earth is always changing as man develops and has to deal with new combinations of elements; and the writer who is to be anything more than an echo of his predecessors must always . . . master a new set of phenomena which has never yet been mastered.* — EDMUND WILSON

*It is the view of the world, the ideology or* weltanschauung *underlying a writer's work, that counts. And it is the writer's attempt to reproduce this view of the world which constitutes his "intention" and is the formative principle underlying the style of a given piece of writing.* — GEORG LUKÁCS

*The socialist critic does not see literature in terms of ideology and class-struggle because they happen to be his or her political interests, arbitrarily projected onto literary works. . . . Such matters are the very stuff of history, and in so far as literature is a historical phenomenon, they are the very stuff of literature too.* — TERRY EAGLETON

*Always historicize!* — FREDRIC JAMESON

Any linkage between the controversial figure of Karl Marx and the decorous subject of historical criticism and literary history may initially seem paradoxical. Perhaps it is best to begin the discussion with how they can be separated. Clearly literary history and criticism taking history as its intellectual base long predated the works of Marx. In his *Lives of the Poets* and the Preface to *Shakespeare,* Samuel Johnson treats the major English authors of the preceding century as men who must be judged, where morals are not concerned, by the standards of their own day rather than by those of his. A crude version of historical determinism enters the tradition of English studies well before Marx in Hippolyte Taine's *Histoire de la littérature anglaise* (1863), whose guiding precept was that literary works were essentially determined by the author's ancestry, environment, and times — his *race, milieu,* and *moment.* Aside from a few notable exceptions, like Christopher Hill's *Milton and the English Revolution* (1978), most important works of historical scholarship from that day to this have proceeded in deliberate disregard of Marx and his notions of the relations of history and culture. It would be absurd to label a politically conservative scholar like Kathleen Williams, author of *Jonathan Swift and the Age of Compromise* (1958), as a covert Marxist.

But if one can be a historical critic without being a Marxist, one cannot think deeply about the relation between literature and history without having to examine one's own ideas in relation to the Marxist tradition. Such a practice would benefit even those critics who would otherwise prefer to remain innocent of theory. It might have saved Williams, for example, from the error of assuming that, because Swift lived in an age of compromise, he must have been in agreement with that age rather than (as was equally plausible) in rebellion against it.


## MARX

Marx is usually classified as a "dialectical materialist." Like his great teacher Hegel, Marx believed that historical transformations occur through a *dialectic* of thesis, antithesis, and synthesis, whereby each historical force calls into being its Other so that the two opposites negate each other and ultimately give rise to a third force, which transcends this opposition (see the introduction to Hegel in Part I). But while Hegel was an idealist who believed in spiritual forces that bend and transform the material world, Marx was a materialist who contended that "it is not the consciousness of men that determines their being, but, on the contrary, their social being that determines their consciousness."

For Marx, the ultimate moving force of human history is economics, or perhaps one should use the older and broader term "political economy," since in Marxist thought the engine of change is a fusion of political and social as well as economic issues. Each society lives by certain "forces of production" — the methods and techniques by which it produces food, clothing, shelter, and the other necessities of life — and by the "social relations of production" these methods create. In an economy based on sheep-raising, for example, the shepherds work alone and relate primarily to the flock owner, while an economy based on manufacturing demands a division of labor, which in turn requires elaborate patterns of cooperation among workers and a hierarchy of managers. These modes of production and their accompanying social relations are the foundation (*Grundlage*) of a culture.

Marx posited that major historical changes came about not because of spiritual contradictions, as Hegel had thought, but because of economic ones. (It is in this sense that, as the cliché puts it, Marx stood Hegel on his head.) Feudalism, for example, was a relatively stable system as long as it was based on local agriculture; but as trade began to generate wealth, feudal rulers became rich and powerful by taxing it and secured their power by giving their towns and traders maximum freedom of action. By so doing, they created two rival centers of power, the feudal countryside and the bourgeois city. In the city, the merchants and manufacturers formed cooperative social relationships with one another and recognized their mutual class interests, which were not always in harmony with those of the agricultural feudatories. It was inevitable that the tightly organized city would gain ascendancy over the feudal lords, who were unaccustomed to cooperation. Conflict between feudal lords and the middle classes broke out most violently in bourgeois revolutions, like the English civil war in the 1640s, and the French Revolution of the 1790s. Marx devoted most of his efforts, of course, to demonstrating the internal contradictions of capitalism and to predicting the course of the proletarian revolution that would displace it.

If the material foundation of a culture is economics, the spiritual superstructure (*Überbau*) finds expression in the culture's *ideology*. Ideology — the culture's collective consciousness of its own being — comprises all its elaborate codes of law, politics, religion, art, and philosophy. By and large, the ideology of a society is consistent with and supportive of its dominant material basis. One would expect, for example, that a society whose economy is based on herds of livestock (like that of the Old Testament Hebrews) would erect a paternalistic monarchy and believe in a fatherly God. But the implicit contradictions within the economic base will somehow also find expression within the ideological superstructure. (For example, the aspiration of the capitalist classes to equality with the great lords emerges in literature as early as Chaucer in the sentiment that merchants too may possess "gentilesse.")[1]

Art and literature are therefore dependent features of the dominant ideology of the times. In part, this is true for obvious economic reasons: Making art is a way of earning a living and those who create art must flatter, or at least not affront, those in a position to pay for it. Note, for example, the aristocratic bias of Shakespeare's plays or the fact that genre painting arose in seventeenth-century Dutch society, which was dominated by merchants. But aside from this issue, there is Marx's more general assumption that individuals can only think the thoughts that are thinkable in their society. If Shakespeare regarded Jack Cade (in *2 Henry VI*) or the plebeian rebels (in *Coriolanus*) as bringers of chaos, chances are no one

---

[1]The Marxist term "ideology" is an essentially contested concept; the notion of ideology presented here is one of several currently used in Marxist circles, but there are many others, often in direct contradiction to it. Here it is used in the sense employed in the famous passage in *Critique of Political Economy*: "The distinction should always be made between the material transformation of the economic conditions of production . . . and the legal, political, religious, aesthetic or philosophic — in short, ideological — forms in which men become conscious of this conflict and fight it out" (see p. 569). If here "ideology" means any representation of consciousness, the most common use of "ideology" in Marx and Engels is the pejorative one of "false consciousness," a set of illusions fostered by the dominant class in order to assure social stability — and its own continued dominance (Letter to Mehring, 1893). Ideology in this sense is expected to wither away and vanish in the Marxist utopia of the dictatorship of the proletariat. Louis Althusser's dictum, "Ideology has no history," seems to contradict this view, since it implies that ideology will retain a function forever — and thus even in a worker's state. But Althusser's definition of ideology ("the 'lived' relation between men and their world, or a reflected form of this unconscious relation") is closer to the unpejorative usage of Marx in the *Critique of Political Economy*. See Raymond Williams, *Keywords: A Vocabulary of Culture and Society* (London: Oxford University Press, 1976), pp. 126–30; and Louis Althusser, *For Marx* (New York: Pantheon, 1969), p. 252.

Another worrisome ambiguity lurking in the term "ideology" arises from the relative concreteness with which it is represented in the consciousness. While most Marxist thinkers view "ideology" as something explicit and official, like a body of laws, a political doctrine, or a philosophy, other Marxists (or the same ones in other circumstances) use the term to denote something more vague and implicit, even unconscious: a way of understanding, a world-view.

else in Shakespeare's still-feudal society could imagine how a democratic commonwealth might function. On the other hand, in artistic matters at least, individuals can continue to think thoughts that their society no longer considers thinkable. Why the art of the distant past, which is based on social and political relationships that have long been superseded, should still have such an intense effect upon later audiences, is a question that has long troubled Marx and his followers.

This rather straightforward portrait of Marx as dialectical materialist, socialist revolutionary, and disciple of Hegel, has, since the late 1960s, become clouded by controversy. Marx's writing career spanned nearly forty-five years, and his thought developed and changed as he matured. While most of the Marxist literary critics before World War II assumed the essential continuity between the young and the mature Marx, a more recent school of structural Marxism has posited a split between the humanistic and Hegelian writings prior to 1845 and the more "scientific" writings after 1857 (the intervening writings being seen as transitional).

Generally, Marxist criticism tends to claim that the text is determined by historical conditions and that historical change is driven ultimately by social and economic factors. Beyond these common assumptions, Marxist criticism has taken a dizzying variety of forms, depending on how the text is defined in relation to material reality and to ideology. Wide discrepancies were inevitable, in part because Marxism is primarily a political and economic philosophy, not a guide to the explication of literary texts. Indeed, the few comments Marx addressed to questions of art left most of the important questions of method open. Differences also arise because Marxism is not only a philosophy but a movement with a conflicted history of its own, where ideas (including those about art) have had fateful political consequences.[2] As a result, there are many Marxist critics but no single Marxist school of criticism in any usual sense, and it is possible to include here only a few of the most important representatives of the tradition Marx began.

## THE AMERICAN LIBERALS

Largely because of the long-standing terror of Soviet Russia, there has been no strong American tradition of socialism since the Bolshevik revolution, and only the briefest of periods — in the mid-1930s — when the Communist party attracted any share of intellectuals. To the extent that American criticism was touched directly by this movement (as in the writings of Granville Hicks) it was of a form usually termed (not without reason) "vulgar Marxism," which featured the adulation of the proletariat: works written by proletarians themselves and works celebrating proletarian characters, denouncing capitalism, and forecasting the revolution. Leon Trotsky had himself written with contempt (in *Literature and Revolution*, 1923) of such efforts to force literature to serve politics directly. Yet Raymond Williams

---

[2]And aesthetic ideas are often "coded" political statements. For example, Georg Lukács's attack on naturalism has been interpreted as a covert attack on Soviet Realist Art, and therefore on its political sponsor, Josef Stalin.

has conceded that, although such a position is "crude and reductionist . . . no Marxist . . . can wholly give it up without abandoning the Marxist tradition."[3]

"Vulgar Marxism" as such did not become an important American tradition, but a group of New York intellectuals, associated with the left magazine *Partisan Review,* had flirted with Communism during the Spanish Civil War and had become disillusioned with Stalinist Russia but not with the utopian ideals that Marxism represented. The most broadly learned among them was Edmund Wilson, whose journalistic essays and books introduced European writers and ideas to what even in the 1930s and 1940s was a largely provincial America. Their leading literary critic, Lionel Trilling, was instrumental in turning the college of Columbia University into a training camp for ideas on culture and society. Important followers and contemporaries included Philip Rahv, Alfred Kazin, and Irving Howe. Neither Wilson nor Trilling should be credited with fashioning a significant critical methodology or a doctrinally pure way of reading Marx. Indeed, it may be going too far to call them Marxists, since both were influenced almost as heavily by Freud, and they avoided using most conventional Marxist terminology. They wrote, instead, in an Arnoldian tradition of cultural commentary, committed to literature as an expression of culture, and concerned primarily with expressing in their writings both the tension within their own responses to literature and the broadest and most complex views of life.

## REFLECTION THEORIES: TROTSKY AND LUKÁCS

At least two major theories derive from the notion that literature consists of an imitation of social reality. The first, which can be traced to Marx but is best expressed by Leon Trotsky, Georgii Plekhanov, and the writers of the Second International, equates mimesis with a pure "slice of life" and considers it unimportant that writers take a radical stance toward the reality they portray. The royalist reactionary Balzac is thus a more valuable writer in his accurate portraits of society than a less perceptive writer of doctrinally correct (i.e., socialist) tendencies.

A second, more complex version of reflection theory is found in the criticism of Georg Lukács. Lukács held that writers must do more than reflect the mere surface features of their society: They must also portray the various forces acting on that society that eventuate in social change. Lukács despised the naturalists (like Émile Zola and Theodore Dreiser) who were satisfied to present characters typical of the social order. In "The Ideology of Modernism" (1956), Lukács pours equal scorn on the modernists' exaltation of the subjective and the psychological at the expense of any portrayal of the dynamic movements underlying social change. To either naturalism or modernism, Lukács prefers the realism — less sophisticated though it be — of Walter Scott. Scott's Edward Waverley is not the typical English gentleman of his time, nor is he invested with much psychological depth; nevertheless, in Waverley, whose relationships and loyalties position him

[3] Raymond Williams, "Marxism, Structuralism, and Literary Analysis" in *New Left Review* 129 (Sept.–Oct., 1981): 51–66.

between the mercantile English and the still feudal Highland Scots on the eve of the 1745 rebellion, Scott has created a character who embodies the social and political conflicts of his epoch.

## FORMS OF MEDIATION THEORY: BENJAMIN AND ADORNO

Just as there have been various forms of Marxian "reflection" so have there also been different versions of the principle of "mediation" — the notion that ideology establishes relationships between the two levels of Marxist dialectic, between the base and the superstructure, between the relations of production and the work of art. These versions arose in part because of the aesthetic inadequacy of the concept of reflection. "Reflection" was a useful term for discussing the novel, but most other modes of literature and art could not incorporate, as a novel could, a view of an entire society. At times the term "mediation" has been used merely to denote the more subtle versions of mimesis — like that of Lukács[4] — but it more properly describes theories like Walter Benjamin's notion of correspondences.

One would not say that, for example, the poetry of Baudelaire reflects his society, in the sense that it depicts an image of it. But as Benjamin noted, industrialization had produced changes in the city and its crowds that resulted in a new version of both the individual and the individual's attitude toward himself, which connected with aspects of Baudelaire's poetry. Benjamin describes Baudelaire's notion of the *correspondance* as "an experience which seeks to establish itself in crisis-proof form." It is the artist's reaction to the impermanence of postindustrial urban life, typified in the shock and abrasion of the crowded streets. Benjamin viewed Baudelaire as nostalgic about the decline of that mystical quality of art Benjamin called "aura" — that spiritual quality, a relic of the human attachment to ritual and magic, which gives a work of art an almost animate sensibility: "To perceive the aura of an object means to invest it with the ability to look at us in return."

In "The Work of Art in the Age of Mechanical Reproduction," (1936), Benjamin examines the central fact of industrialism's relation to art in the twentieth century: that, for the first time, a painting or sculpture can be infinitely replicated. On the one hand there is the genuine possibility of art for the masses, not simply because anyone can possess a copy of Botticelli's *Birth of Venus* but also because of the evolution of film, a medium intended for mass audiences. On the other hand, the mystical aura, the cult value of the art object, is simultaneously beginning to disappear. As a socialist, Benjamin ought to be applauding this trend, but the essay is caught up in emotional ambiguity because of his own nostalgia for the cult of memory. Although the preface bravely declares that his theses "brush aside a number of outmoded concepts, such as creativity and genius, eternal value and mystery," the tone of the later sections seems at odds with this intent. When Benjamin contrasts the stage actor, engaged both in acting as an art and in a

[4]For example, see Williams, p. 57.

particular role, with the alienated film actor, who is at best an "exile" and at worst a "stage prop," or when he notes that aura survives in film in the obscene adulation paid to film stars, or when he observes that film is the art uniquely suited to the "distracted" and "absent-minded" spectator, a reader may infer that the proletarianization of art progressively dehumanizes both participants and spectators. Reading Benjamin, one may feel trapped within his ironies, but perhaps Benjamin was trapped in them himself. Although he knew well that socialism meant industrialization, mechanical reproduction, and the death of the cult value of art, he nevertheless felt intensely the loss of that value.

Benjamin was willing to allow for Baudelairean correspondences, for the mediation of ideology, at the level of content. Other members of the so-called Frankfurt school, like Theodor W. Adorno, were not so willing. For Adorno, the Frankfurt school's principal aesthetician, the relationship between art and society operated on the formal level and could easily be located even in nonreferential art such as music. Thus, in *Philosophy of Modern Music,* (1949), Adorno suggested that the rootless chaos and tragic ambiguity of Arnold Schoenberg's musical harmonies, together with his drive to mechanize and systematize composition, served as a correspondence with the dominant ideology of the early twentieth century. (Adorno judged Schoenberg to be a more authentic artist than Igor Stravinsky, whose shifting formal allegiances — from neoclassicism to primitivism — were either ideologically reactionary or attempts to evade history altogether.)

As one might expect, Adorno took the opposite position from Lukács on the issue of modernism in literature and defended the bleak vision of novelists like Kafka. While Adorno agrees with Lukács that modern fiction is morbidly subjective and obsessed with the torture of the individual consciousness, he claimed that the modern novel took "a critical posture towards social reality by means of its style . . . not by its 'content' or view of the world."[5] In a sense, modernist fiction exemplifies "negative dialectic" — Adorno's term for criticism that operates without reproducing the conceptual features of what it criticizes — a necessary feature in capitalist society, where, according to Adorno, concepts distort and mask social realities.

## GENETIC STRUCTURALISM:
## LUCIEN GOLDMANN AND RAYMOND WILLIAMS

Between the mediation theories of the Frankfurt school and the structural Marxism of the Althusserians, there are transitional modes of Marxist criticism. One of the most important was that practiced by Lucien Goldmann, who called himself a "genetic" structuralist because the structures he was concerned about were derived from the work's genesis in the ideology of its times. Like Adorno, Goldmann felt that the correspondences between a work and an age would be correspondences of form rather than content. But unlike most Marxist critics, who would claim that

[5]Gillian Rose, *The "Melancholy Science": An Introduction to the Thought of Theodor W. Adorno* (London: Macmillan, 1978), p. 124

the ideology of an age is invariably present in all of its products, Goldmann felt that only the greatest works of an age contain its deepest consciousness.

Goldmann's analysis of seventeenth-century France in *The Hidden God* (1955) presents *homologies* — analogies of function rather than content — between literary and ideological structures, which during that period take the form of tragic dilemmas. The seventeenth-century Jansenists were torn between obedience to a silent God and participation in the new rationalism; the "nobility of the robe" (the gentry deriving from the legal profession) were torn between the authority of the king and the new spirit of commercial enterprise. Similarly, in the plays of Racine, who was both a Jansenist and a scion of the *noblesse de robe*, the protagonists (such as Hippolytus and Andromache) must choose between service to a hidden God and the pleasures and duties of the world — and are damned no matter which they choose.

The most distinguished English practitioner of genetic structuralism was probably Raymond Williams. The son of working-class parents from the border country of Wales, Williams brought to his readings of literature a proletarian background highly unusual in a Marxist critic, few of whom have had any close acquaintance with hard manual labor. Instead of Benjamin's more abstract and aestheticized term "correspondences," Williams spoke of the "complex forms of feeling" within which literature and ideology find common ground. In "The Green Language," a chapter from Williams's *The Country and the City* (1973), his thought about the industrial revolution is filtered through his personal sense of what alienation from the countryside might have meant to the poets of the generation of Wordsworth and John Clare. As with Goldmann, the structures of feeling Williams found in poetry exhibit homologies with elements in the nonaesthetic segments of the superstructure or the relations of production in the base.

In fact, Williams talks of seeking "structures of feeling" in art instead of "ideology" as such; the novel phrase differentiates the concrete, lived experience represented in art ("social experiences *in solution*" as he calls it) from the "precipitated" manner in which social relationships are likely to be characterized in an expository text, a treatise, or a newspaper article.

It would be misleading to characterize Williams as merely a follower of Goldmann, however. Williams was a rather protean social and historical critic whose work shifted rapidly through a number of phases. He began his career rejecting the revolutionary doctrines of Marxism, particularly its concept of the masses, and went through a left-Leavisite phase of cultural criticism that kept what Williams himself termed "a certain conscious distance" from Marxism. After *Culture and Society* (1958), however, Williams converged with Marxist thought. Following his "genetic structuralist" phase, Williams became what he called a "cultural materialist," influenced primarily by the Italian Marxist Antonio Gramsci and his concept of *hegemony.*

To Gramsci, power is expressed partly through the direct means of control (*dominio:* rule) and partly through something at once less formal and conscious and yet more total (*egemonia:* hegemony). As Williams says,

Hegemony is . . . a lived system of meanings and values — constitutive and constituting — which, since they are experienced as practices, appear as reciprocally confirming. It thus constitutes a sense of reality for most people in the society . . . beyond which it is very difficult for most members of the society to move. . . . It is . . . in the strongest sense a "culture" but a culture which has also to be seen as the lived dominance and subordination of particular classes.[6]

Williams finds this conception attractive because it allows for the notion of *alternative* hegemonies centered in the working class and for revolutionary activity in the shape of cultural rather than political action. The implication is that hegemonies may be relatively successful, but they are never complete. Instead of a single ruling class, there are interpenetrating hegemonic groups; and instead of a single catastrophic revolution, there are dominant, emergent, and residual elements of culture belonging to classes whose power has peaked or is increasing or declining. This concept of hegemony modifies the rigid base/superstructure formula of Marxist thought, a modification Williams had already sought in the homologies of Goldmann. In general, Williams seems to have sought a more fluid and responsive Marxism — also an aim of Louis Althusser.

## LOUIS ALTHUSSER AND STRUCTURAL MARXISM

The newest development of Marxist thought — post-Althusserian Marxism — originates in the structural thought of the mature Marx as interpreted by Louis Althusser and in the theories of the signifier developed by Jacques Lacan (see Ch. 2), which were later to influence Jacques Derrida (Ch. 5). In *Reading Capital*, Althusser questions the traditional portrait of Marx as a Hegelian humanist; for Althusser there were two Marxes, a young Marx (up to the year 1845), whose ideas roughly corresponded with the usual view of dialectical materialism, and a mature Marx (from 1857 onwards), whose way of thinking was radically different. For Althusser, the older Marx, author of *Capital*, had evolved a form of dialectic that was different from Hegel's — not just an inversion of it — and no longer held to the simple deterministic relation of base and superstructure. Economics is determinative but only *"in the last instance"*.[7] But Althusser's most important shift is in his vision of history. Earlier writers on Marx had assumed that history is a real force, concrete, univocal, and ineluctible. In Althusser's reading of Marx, history has become a myth, or perhaps more properly, a text, in that it is a symbolic structure, produced by discourse. We cannot evade history any more than we can think without our faculty for symbolization, but neither can we view history from outside that subjective faculty.

In Althusser's interpretation, Marx becomes a canny reader of his own chosen texts, those of his predecessors, the classical economists; in quoting Marx, Al-

[6]Raymond Williams, *Marxism and Literature* (Oxford: Oxford University Press, 1977), p. 110.
[7]Louis Althusser, "Contradiction and Overdetermination," in *For Marx,* Trans. Ben Brewster (New York: Pantheon, 1969), pp. 84–114.

thusser presents him as aware of their oversights, their subtle shifts in point of view. Althusser's point is that these writers' areas of blindness are as significant as their areas of insight, for the gaps and incoherencies that a critical reading of the texts reveals are the signs of what the writers are unconsciously *hiding from themselves*. This is not the personal, Freudian repression of individuals, but a gap left by what the ideology of their age is unable to talk about.

Pierre Macherey's *A Theory of Literary Production* (1966) presents a literary-critical version of these ideas. In "Jules Verne: The Faulty Narrative," Macherey shows how Verne's plans for his novels went awry. *The Mysterious Island*, for example, originated in Verne's wish to rewrite *Robinson Crusoe* more rigorously. Unlike Defoe, who had provided Crusoe with a shipload of modern equipment and tools, Verne would demonstrate how castaways with a knowledge of science manage to recreate modern technology out of nothing on an empty island. The novel begins thus, but halfway along Verne reveals that the castaways are not alone on the island; he introduces Captain Nemo and his crew, who give the castaways a crate of tools. Most readers would interpret this as a mere lapse on Verne's part, a melodramatic corruption of his plan. For Macherey, there are no mistakes, and Verne's introduction of Nemo betokens his attempt to *evade* what he knows: That science cannot be pure knowledge, as he would wish, but relies on the technological capacity of a capitalistic society to bring it into being. Furthermore, Verne's book implicitly acknowledges that there are no empty lands, only those whose aborigines are rendered invisible by imperialist ideology, just as technology cannot arise purely from scientific knowledge but must in fact emerge from a technological social organization. Macherey argues that the rifts in Verne's plot are there because of preexisting rifts in the ideology of bourgeois capitalism and that the novel itself, as an aesthetic practice whose raw materials are ideology, tends to widen these rifts as it foregrounds them, making them visible to the reader.

By reifying the flat notions of ideology in the roundness of a narrative, the artist unwittingly exposes their incoherencies to the view of a critical reader. This version of Marxism is practiced by Raymond Williams's disciple, Terry Eagleton, and by Althusser's most important American disciple, Fredric Jameson. Jameson's highly acclaimed *The Political Unconscious* (1979) presents a theory of interpretation in which Althusser's politics and Lacan's theory of the unconscious intersect. Jameson's chapter on Conrad, part of which appears in this collection, suggests how much of Conrad's vision of the contradictions of late nineteenth-century imperialism and capitalism is contained with the "gaps" of *Lord Jim*, a tale ostensibly about courage and cowardice.

With the structural Marxism of Macherey, Eagleton, and especially Fredric Jameson, Marxist criticism has come a long way from its origins and reached a high level of textual sophistication. Indeed, in rejecting the young for the mature Marx, the Althusserians have discredited what many had supposed the central principle of Marxism, the causal primacy of economic and social factors. Culture and ideology are seen as "relatively autonomous" levels of production, equivalent in principle to economics, rather than as determinate effects of economic change.

Only time will tell whether this shift will give Marxist criticism greater flexibility of scope or deprive it of its coherence as a mode of explanation.

Jameson's criticism is distant from the origins of Marxism in another sense. As Terry Eagleton asked in *New Left Review:* "The question irresistibly raised for the Marxist reader of Jameson is simply this: how is a Marxist-structuralist critique of a minor novel of Balzac to help shake the foundations of capitalism?"[8] For the past fifty years, Marxist critics have attacked each other for "vulgar Marxism," a label progressively applied to Christopher Caudwell and Granville Hicks, to Georg Lukács and Lucien Goldmann. Jameson's Marxism, despite its emotional attachment to the utopian, seems to have given up on the proletariat, the class struggle, and most of the economic and political ideas of Marx. Perhaps here, at last, is a Marxism that (as Raymond Williams might have said) is simply not vulgar enough.

## Selected Bibliography

Adorno, Theodor. *Prisms: Cultural Criticism and Society.* 1955; London: Neville Spearman, 1967.

———. *Minima Moralia.* 1951; London: New Left Books, 1974.

Althusser, Louis. *For Marx.* New York: Pantheon, 1969.

———. *Lenin and Philosophy and Other Essays.* London: New Left Books, 1971.

Althusser, Louis, and Etienne Balibar. *Reading Capital.* New York: Pantheon, 1970.

Benjamin, Walter. *Illuminations.* New York: Harcourt Brace & World, 1968.

———. *Charles Baudelaire: A Lyric Poet in the Era of High Capitalism.* London: New Left Books, 1973.

———. *Reflections: Essays, Aphorisms, Autobiographical Writings.* Ed. Peter Demetz. New York: Harcourt Brace Jovanovich, 1978.

Bennett, Tony. *Formalism and Marxism.* London: Methuen, 1979.

Caudwell, Christopher. *Illusion and Reality: A Study of the Sources of Poetry.* New York: International Publishers, 1963.

Coward, Rosemary, and John Ellis. *Language and Materialism: Developments in Semiology and the Theory of the Subject.* London: Routledge and Kegan Paul, 1977.

Demetz, Peter. *Marx, Engels and the Poets: Origins of Marxist Literary Criticism.* Chicago: University of Chicago Press, 1967.

Dowling, William. *Jameson, Althusser, Marx: An Introduction to The Political Unconscious.* Ithaca: Cornell University Press, 1984.

Eagleton, Terry. *Criticism and Ideology: A Study in Marxist Literary Theory.* London: New Left Books, 1976.

———. *Marxism and Literary Criticism.* Berkeley: University of California Press, 1976.

Fekete, John. *The Critical Twilight.* Boston: Routledge and Kegan Paul, 1976.

Foley, Barbara. *Telling the Truth: The Theory and Practice of Documentary Fiction.* Ithaca: Cornell University Press, 1986.

Frow, John. *Marxism and Literary History.* Ithaca: Cornell University Press, 1986.

[8]Terry Eagleton, "The Idealism of American Criticism," *New Left Review* 127 (May-June 1981): 65.

Goldmann, Lucien. *The Hidden God: A Study of the Tragic Vision in the Pensées of Pascal and the Tragedies of Racine.* 1955; London: Routledge and Kegan Paul, 1964.

———. "Marxist Criticism." In *The Philosophy of the Enlightenment.* Cambridge: MIT Press, 1973, pp. 86–97.

Gramsci, Antonio. *The Modern Prince and Other Writings.* London: Lawrence and Wishart, 1957.

———. *Selections from the Prison Notebooks.* London: Lawrence and Wishart, 1971.

Hicks, Granville. *The Great Tradition: An Interpretation of American Literature Since the Civil War.* 1933; Chicago: Quadrangle Books, 1969.

Hohendahl, Peter Uwe. "Prolegomena to a History of Literary Criticism," *New German Critique* 11 (1977): pp. 151–63.

Jameson, Fredric. *Marxism and Form: Twentieth Century Dialectical Theories of Literature.* Princeton: Princeton University Press, 1971.

———. *The Prison-House of Language: A Critical Account of Structuralism and Russian Formalism.* Princeton: Princeton University Press, 1972.

———. *The Political Unconscious: Studies in the Ideology of Form.* Ithaca: Cornell University Press, 1979.

Kettle, Arnold. *Introduction to the English Novel.* 2 vols. 1951; New York: Harper and Row, 1960.

Lifshitz, Mikail. *The Philosophy of Art of Karl Marx.* 1933; London: Pluto Press, 1973.

Lukács, Georg. *Realism in Our Time: Literature and the Class Struggle.* 1957; New York: Harper and Row, 1964.

———. *The Historical Novel.* London: Merlin Press, 1962.

———. *The Theory of the Novel: A Historico-Philosophical Essay on the Forms of Great Epic Literature.* 1920; London, Merlin Press, 1971.

Macherey, Pierre. *A Theory of Literary Production.* 1966; Boston: Routledge and Kegan Paul, 1978.

Marcuse, Herbert. *The Aesthetic Dimension: Toward a Critique of Marxist Aesthetics.* Boston: Beacon Press, 1978.

Marx, Karl, and Friedrich Engels. *Marx and Engels on Literature and Art.* St. Louis: Telos Press, 1973.

Morris, William. *On Art and Socialism.* London: Lehmann, 1947.

Ohmann, Richard. *English in America: A Radical View of the Profession.* New York: Oxford University Press, 1976.

Orwell, George. *Critical Essays.* London: Secker and Warberg, 1946.

Robinson, Lillian S. *Sex, Class, and Culture.* Bloomington: Indiana University Press, 1978.

Rose, Gillian. *The "Melancholy Science": An Introduction to the Thought of Theodor W. Adorno.* London: Macmillan, 1978.

Sartre, Jean-Paul. *What Is Literature?* New York: Harper and Row, 1965.

———. *Between Existentialism and Marxism.* New York: Pantheon, 1974.

Smith, Steven B. *Reading Althusser.* Ithaca: Cornell University Press, 1984.

Trotsky, Leon. *Literature and Revolution.* 1924; Ann Arbor: University of Michigan Press, 1960.

Weimann, Robert. *Structure and Society in Literary History.* Charlottesville: University Press of Virginia, 1976.

Williams, Raymond. *Culture and Society, 1780–1950.* London: Chatto and Windus, 1958.

———. *The Country and the City.* New York: Oxford University Press, 1973.

———. *Marxism and Literature.* New York: Oxford University Press, 1977.

Wilson, Edmund. *Axel's Castle.* 1931; New York: Scribner's, 1961.

———. *The Triple Thinkers.* 1938; New York: Oxford University Press, 1948.

# Karl Marx

## 1818–1883

*Karl Marx, the chief philosopher and theorist of modern socialism, was born into a comfortable middle-class home in Trier, Germany. The son of a lawyer who converted from Judaism to Lutheranism, Marx studied law at Bonn and Berlin before turning to philosophy and taking his Ph.D. at Jena in 1841. He became editor of the* Rheinische Zeitung *in 1842, but his calls for radical reform led to its suppression in 1843. That same year he emigrated to Paris, where he began his lifelong partnership with Friedrich Engels, committed himself to socialism, and commenced his study of the works of the classical economists. Within a year he was expelled from France for his radical views and settled for the next three years in Brussels. His evolving theories, although written down in 1846, were only published in 1932 as* The German Ideology *(see excerpted here). In 1847 he joined the Communist League and with Engels wrote* The Communist Manifesto, *which was published in 1848 just before revolution swept the continent. Exiled from most European centers, Marx in 1849 settled permanently in London to a life of poverty, chronic illness, and arduous, unflagging devotion to the cause of world communism.* A Contribution to the Critique of Political Economy *(excerpted here) was published in 1859, and the next twelve years saw the founding of the First International Working Men's Council (1864), the publication of the first volume of his monumental* Capital *(1867), and* The Civil War in France *(1871), an analysis of the brutally surpressed Paris Commune of 1871. Marx's last years, clouded by ill-health and by the deaths of his eldest daughter and wife, were less precarious financially owing to the pension that Engels settled on him in 1869.*

# Consciousness Derived from Material Conditions
## from *The German Ideology*

The premises from which we begin are not arbitrary ones, not dogmas, but real premises from which abstraction can only be made in the imagination. They are the real individuals, their activity, and the material conditions under which they live, both those which they find already existing and those produced by their activity. These premises can thus be verified in a purely empirical way.

The first premise of all human history is, of course, the existence of living human individuals. Thus the first fact to be established is the physical organization of these individuals and

Translated by R. Pascal.

their consequent relation to the rest of nature. Of course, we cannot here go either into the actual physical nature of man, or into the natural conditions in which man finds himself — geological, orohydrographical, climatic, and so on. The writing of history must always set out from these natural bases and their modification in the course of history through the action of man.

Men can be distinguished from animals by consciousness, by religion, or anything else you like. They themselves begin to distinguish themselves from animals as soon as they begin to *produce* their means of subsistence, a step which is conditioned by their physical organization. By producing their means of subsistence men are indirectly producing their actual material life.

The way in which men produce their means of subsistence depends first of all on the nature of the actual means they find in existence and have to reproduce. This mode of production must not be considered simply as being the reproduction of the physical existence of the individuals. Rather it is a definite form of activity of these individuals, a definite form of expressing their life, a definite *mode of life* on their part. As individuals express their life, so they are. What they are, therefore, coincides with their production, both with *what* they produce and with *how* they produce. The nature of individuals thus depends on the material conditions determining their production.

This production only makes its appearance with the increase of population. In its turn this presupposes the intercourse of individuals with one another. The form of this intercourse is again determined by production.

The relations of different nations among themselves depend upon the extent to which each has developed its productive forces, the division of labor, and internal intercourse.[1] This statement is generally recognized. But not only the relation of one nation to others, but also the whole internal structure of the nation itself depends on the stage of development reached by its production and its internal and external intercourse. How far the productive forces of a nation are developed is shown most manifestly by the degree to which the division of labor has been carried. Each new productive force, insofar as it is not merely a quantitative extension of productive forces already known, (for instance, the bringing into cultivation of fresh land), brings about a further development of the division of labor.

The division of labor inside a nation leads at first to the separation of industrial and commercial from agricultural labor, and hence to the separation of town and country and a clash of interests between them. Its further development leads to the separation of commercial from industrial labor. At the same time through the division of labor there develop further, inside these various branches, various divisions among the individuals cooperating in definite kinds of labor. The relative position of these individual groups is determined by the methods employed in agriculture, industry, and commerce (patriarchalism, slavery, estates, classes). These same conditions are to be seen (given a more developed intercourse) in the relations of different nations to one another.

The various stages of development in the division of labor are just so many different forms of ownership; i.e., the existing stage in the division of labor determines also the relations of individuals to one another with reference to the material, instrument, and product of labor.

The first form of ownership is tribal ownership. It corresponds to the undeveloped stage of production, at which a people lives by hunting and fishing, by the rearing of beasts or, in the highest stage, agriculture. In the latter case it presupposes a great mass of uncultivated stretches of land. The division of labor is at this stage still very elementary and is confined to a further extension of the natural division of labor imposed by the family. The social structure is therefore limited to an extension of the family; patriarchal family chieftains; below them the members of the tribe; finally slaves. The slavery latent in the family only develops gradually with the increase of population, the growth of wants, and with the extension of external relations, of war or of trade.

The second form is the ancient communal and State ownership which proceeds especially from the union of several tribes into a city by agreement or by conquest, and which is still accompanied by slavery. Beside communal ownership we already find movable, and later also immovable, private property developing, but as an abnormal form subordinate to communal ownership. It is only as a community that the citizens hold power over their laboring slaves, and on this account alone, therefore, they are bound to the form of communal ownership. It is the communal private property which compels the active citizens to remain in this natural form of association over against their slaves. For this reason the whole structure of society based on this communal ownership, and with it the power of the people, decays in the same measure as immov-

[1]Markets within the economy of the nation. [Ed.]

able private property evolves. The division of labor is already more developed. We already find the antagonism of town and country; later the antagonism between those states which represent town interests and those which represent country, and inside the towns themselves the antagonism between industry and maritime commerce. The class relation between citizens and slaves is now completely developed.

This whole interpretation of history appears to be contradicted by the fact of conquest. Up till now violence, war, pillage, rape, and slaughter, etc. have been accepted as the driving force of history. Here we must limit ourselves to the chief points and take therefore only a striking example — the destruction of an old civilization by a barbarous people and the resulting formation of an entirely new organization of society. (Rome and the barbarians; Feudalism and Gaul; the Byzantine Empire and the Turks.) With the conquering barbarian people war itself is still, as hinted above, a regular form of intercourse, which is the more eagerly exploited as the population increases, involving the necessity of new means of production to supersede the traditional and, for it, the only possible, crude mode of production. In Italy it was, however, otherwise. The concentration of landed property (caused not only by buying-up and indebtedness but also by inheritance, since loose living being rife and marriage rare, the old families died out and their possessions fell into the hands of a few) and its conversion into grazing-land (caused not only by economic forces still operative today but by the importation of plundered and tribute-corn and the resultant lack of demand for Italian corn) brought about the almost total disappearance of the free population. The very slaves died out again and again, and had constantly to be replaced by new ones. Slavery remained the basis of the whole productive system. The plebeians, mid-way between freemen and slaves, never succeeded in becoming more than a proletarian rabble. Rome indeed never became more than a city; its connection with the provinces was almost exclusively political and could therefore easily be broken again by political events.

With the development of private property, we find here for the first time the same conditions which we shall find again, only on a more extensive scale, with modern private property. On the one hand the concentration of private property, which began very early in Rome (as the Licinian agrarian law[2] proves), and proceeded very rapidly from the time of the civil wars and especially under the Emperors; on the other hand, coupled with this, the transformation of the plebeian small peasantry into a proletariat, which, however, owing to its intermediate position between propertied citizens and slaves, never achieved an independent development.

The third form of ownership is feudal or estate-property. If antiquity started out from the town and its little territory, the Middle Ages started out from the country. This different starting-point was determined by the sparseness of the population at that time, which was scattered over a large area and which received no large increase from the conquerors. In contrast to Greece and Rome, feudal development therefore extends over a much wider field, prepared by the Roman conquests and the spread of agriculture at first associated with it. The last centuries of the declining Roman Empire and its conquest by the barbarians destroyed a number of productive forces; agriculture had declined, industry had decayed for want of a market, trade had died out or been violently suspended, the rural and urban population had decreased. From these conditions and the mode of organizations of the conquest determined by them, feudal property developed under the influence of the Germanic military constitution. Like tribal and communal ownership, it is based again on a community; but the directly producing class standing over against it is not, as in the case of the ancient community, the slaves, but the enserfed small peasantry. As soon as feudalism is fully developed, there also arises antagonism to the towns. The hierarchical system of land ownership, and the armed bodies of retainers associated with it, gave the nobility power over the serfs. This feudal organization was, just as much as the ancient communal ownership, an association against a subjected producing class;

[2] A law dating to the early days of the Republic that prevented the dispersal of estates by providing that the eldest son inherited the landed property. [Ed.]

but the form of association and the relation to the direct producers were different because of the different conditions of production.

This feudal organization of land-ownership had its counterpart in the towns in the shape of corporative property, the feudal organization of trades. Here property consisted chiefly in the labor of each individual person. The necessity for association against the organized robber-nobility, the need for communal covered markets in an age when the industrialist was at the same time a merchant, the growing competition of the escaped serfs swarming into the rising towns, the feudal structure of the whole country: these combined to bring about the guilds. Further, the gradually accumulated capital of individual craftsmen and their stable numbers, as against the growing population, evolved the relation of journeyman and apprentice, which brought into being in the towns a hierarchy similar to that in the country.

Thus the chief form of property during the feudal epoch consisted on the one hand of landed property with serf-labor chained to it, and on the other of individual labor with small capital commanding the labor of journeymen. The organization of both was determined by the restricted conditions of production — the small-scale and primitive cultivation of the land, and the craft type of industry. There was little division of labor in the heyday of feudalism. Each land bore in itself the conflict of town and country and the division into estates was certainly strongly marked; but apart from the differentiation of princes, nobility, clergy, and peasants in the country, and masters, journeymen, apprentices, and soon also the rabble of casual laborers in the towns, no division of importance took place. In agriculture it was rendered difficult by the strip-system, beside which the cottage industry of the peasants themselves emerged as another factor. In industry there was no division of labor at all in the individual trades themselves, and very little between them. The separation of industry and commerce was found already in existence in older towns; in the newer it only developed later, when the towns entered into mutual relations.

The grouping of larger territories into feudal kingdoms was a necessity for the landed nobility as for the towns. The organization of the ruling class, the nobility, had, therefore, everywhere a monarch at its head.

The fact is, therefore, that definite individuals who are productively active in a definite way enter into these definite social and political relations. Empirical observation must in each separate instance bring out empirically, and without any mystification and speculation, the connection of the social and political structure with production. The social structure and the State are continually evolving out of the life-process of definite individuals, but of individuals, not as they may appear in their own or other people's imagination, but as they really are; i.e., as they are effective, produce materially, and are active under definite material limits, presuppositions, and conditions independent of their will.

The production of ideas, of conceptions, of consciousness, is at first directly interwoven with the material activity and the material intercourse of men, the language of real life. Conceiving, thinking, the mental intercourse of men, appear at this stage as the direct efflux of their material behavior. The same applies to mental production as expressed in the language of the politics, laws, morality, religion, metaphysics of a people. Men are the producers of their conceptions, ideas, etc. — real, active men, as they are conditioned by a definite development of their productive forces and of the intercourse corresponding to these, up to its furthest forms. Consciousness can never be anything else than conscious existence, and the existence of men is their actual life-process. If in all ideology men and their circumstances appear upside down as in a *camera obscura,*[3] this phenomenon arises just as much from their historical life-process as the inversion of objects on the retina does from their physical life-process.

In direct contrast to German philosophy which descends from heaven to earth, here we ascend from earth to heaven. That is to say, we do not set out from what men say, imagine, conceive, nor from men as narrated, thought of, imagined, conceived, in order to arrive at men in the flesh. We set out from real, active men, and on the basis of their real life-process we demonstrate

[3]Marx refers to the fact that the lens of a camera inverts the image while projecting it onto the plate or film. [Ed.]

the development of the ideological reflexes and echoes of this life-process. The phantoms formed in the human brain are also, necessarily, sublimates of their material life-process, which is empirically verifiable and bound to material premises. Morality, religion, metaphysics, all the rest of ideology and their corresponding forms of consciousness, thus no longer retain the semblance of independence. They have no history, no development; but men, developing their material production and their material intercourse, alter, along with this their real existence, their thinking and the products of their thinking. Life is not determined by consciousness, but consciousness by life. In the first method of approach the starting point is consciousness taken as the living individual; in the second it is the real living individuals themselves, as they are in actual life, and consciousness is considered solely as *their* consciousness.

This method of approach is not devoid of premises. It starts out from the real premises and does not abandon them for a moment. Its premises are men, not in any fantastic isolation or abstract definition, but in their actual, empirically perceptible process of development under definite conditions. As soon as this active life-process is described, history ceases to be a collection of dead facts as it is with the empiricists (themselves still abstract), or an imagined activity of imagined subjects, as with the idealists.

# On Greek Art in Its Time
# from *Contribution to a Critique*
# *of Political Economy*

## THE MODE OF PRODUCTION OF MATERIAL LIFE DETERMINES THE SOCIAL, POLITICAL, AND INTELLECTUAL PROCESSES OF LIFE

In the social production which men carry on they enter into definite relations that are indispensable and independent of their will; these relations of production correspond to a definite stage of development of their material forces of production. The sum total of these relations of production constitutes the economic structure of society — the real foundation, on which rises a legal and political superstructure and to which correspond definite forms of social consciousness. The mode of production in material life determines the social, political, and intellectual life processes in general. It is not the consciousness of men that determines their being, but, on the contrary, their social being that determines their consciousness. At a certain stage of their development, the material forces of production in society come in conflict with the existing relations of production or — what is but a legal expression for the same thing — with the property relations within which they have been at work before. From forms of development of the forces of production these relations turn into their fetters. Then begins an epoch of social revolution. With the change of the economic foundation the entire immense superstructure is more or less rapidly transformed. In considering such transformations a distinction should always be made between the material transformation of the economic conditions of production which can be determined with the precision of natural science, and the legal, political, religious, aesthetic, or philosophic — in short, ideological — forms in which men become conscious of this conflict and fight it out. Just as our opinion of an individual is not based on what he thinks of himself, so can we not judge of such a period of transformation by its own consciousness, on the contrary this consciousness must be explained rather from the contradictions of material life, from the existing conflict between the

Translated by Nahum Isaac Stone.

social forces of production and the relations of production. No social order ever disappears before all the productive forces for which there is room in it have been developed; and new higher relations of production never appear before the material conditions of their existence have matured in the womb of the old society itself. Therefore, mankind always sets itself only such tasks as it can solve; since, looking at the matter more closely, we will always find that the task itself arises only when the material conditions necessary for its solution already exist or are at least in the process of formation. In broad outlines we can designate the Asiatic, the ancient, the feudal, and the modern bourgeois modes of production as so many epochs in the progress of the economic formation of society. The bourgeois relations of production are the last antagonistic form of the social process of production — antagonistic not in the sense of individual antagonism, but of one arising from the social conditions of life of the individuals; at the same time the productive forces developing in the womb of bourgeois society create the material conditions for the solution of that antagonism. This social formation constitutes, therefore, the closing chapter of the prehistoric stage of human society.

It is well known that certain periods of highest development of art stand in no direct connection with the general development of society, nor with the material basis and the skeleton structure of its organization. Witness the example of the Greeks as compared with the modern nations or even Shakespeare. As regards certain forms of art, as e.g., the epos, it is admitted that they can never be produced in the world-epoch making form as soon as art as such comes into existence; in other words, that in the domain of art certain important forms of it are possible only at a low stage of its development. If that be true of the mutual relations of different forms of art within the domain of art itself, it is far less surprising that the same is true of the relation of art as a whole to the general development of society. The difficulty lies only in the general formulation of these contradictions. No sooner are they specified than they are explained. Let us take for instance the relation of Greek art and of that of Shake-speare's time to our own. It is a well-known fact that Greek mythology was not only the arsenal of Greek art, but also the very ground from which it had sprung. Is the view of nature and of social relations which shaped Greek imagination and Greek [art] possible in the age of automatic machinery, and railways, and locomotives, and electric telegraphs? Where does Vulcan come in as against Roberts & Co.; Jupiter, as against the lightning rod; and Hermes, as against the Credit Mobilier?[1] All mythology masters and dominates and shapes the forces of nature in and through the imagination; hence it disappears as soon as man gains mastery over the forces of nature. What becomes of the Goddess Fame side by side with Printing House Square?[2] Greek art presupposes the existence of Greek mythology; i.e., that nature and even the form of society are wrought up in popular fancy in an unconsciously artistic fashion. That is its material. Not, however, any mythology taken at random, nor any accidental unconsciously artistic elaboration of nature (including under the latter all objects, hence [also] society). Egyptian mythology could never be the soil or womb which would give birth to Greek art. But in any event [there had to be] *a* mythology. In no event [could Greek art originate] in a society which excludes any mythological explanation of nature, any mythological attitude towards it and which requires from the artist an imagination free from mythology.

Looking at it from another side: is Achilles possible side by side with powder and lead? Or is the *Iliad* at all compatible with the printing press and steam press? Does not singing and reciting and the muses necessarily go out of existence with the appearance of the printer's bar, and do not, therefore, disappear the prerequisites of epic poetry?

But the difficulty is not in grasping the idea that Greek art and epos are bound up with certain

[1]Marx wittily compares ancient and modern institutions; Vulcan was the god of manufactures, while Roberts & Co. was a munitions maker; Jupiter controlled the lightning as now the lightning rod does; Hermes was the god of thieves, while the Credit Mobilier was a large financial institution. [Ed.]

[2]Where the London *Times* was printed. [Ed.]

forms of social development. It rather lies in understanding why they still constitute with us a source of aesthetic enjoyment and in certain respects prevail as the standard and model beyond attainment.

A man can not become a child again unless he becomes childish. But does he not enjoy the artless ways of the child and must he not strive to reproduce its truth on a higher plane? Is not the character of every epoch revived perfectly true to nature in child nature? Why should the social childhood of mankind, where it had obtained its most beautiful development, not exert an eternal charm as an age that will never return? There are ill-bred children and precocious children. Many of the ancient nations belong to the latter class. The Greeks were normal children. The charm their art has for us does not conflict with the primitive character of the social order from which it had sprung. It is rather the product of the latter, and is rather due to the fact that the unripe social conditions under which the art arose and under which alone it could appear can never return.

# Walter Benjamin
## 1892–1940

*It is said that Walter Benjamin, one of the most influential cultural theorists in the Marxist tradition, did not look into Marx's writings until the final decade of his tragically abbreviated life. Benjamin was born in Berlin to a wealthy Jewish family. His studies at Freiburg, Munich, Berlin, and Bern resulted in a doctorate in 1919, but his dissertation on German tragic drama — a brilliant but unorthodox performance completed when he was thirty-three — was rejected by the University of Frankfurt. With a university career closed to him, Benjamin appears to have turned to journalism. From 1925 to 1933 Benjamin made his living mainly with his pen and became friendly with a number of left-wing intellectuals, including Bertolt Brecht. His visit to Moscow in the winter of 1926–27 affirmed his sympathy with the Soviet state, although he never joined the Communist party. When the Nazi seizure of power drove him from Berlin — he emigrated to Paris in 1933 — commissions from the Frankfurt Institute for Social Research enabled him to eke out a living. During these years of exile, he wrote some of his most admired work, including "The Work of Art in the Age of Mechanical Reproduction" (1936). In 1940, Benjamin committed suicide in Port Bou, Spain, in the mistaken belief that his plan to emigrate to America had been thwarted and that he would have to return to Nazi-occupied France. The translation of "The Work of Art in the Age of Mechanical Reproduction" is from the collection* Illuminations *(1969).*

# The Work of Art in the Age of Mechanical Reproduction

*Our fine arts were developed, their types and uses were established, in times very different from the present, by men whose power of action upon things*

Translated by Harry Zohn.

*was insignificant in comparison with ours. But the amazing growth of our techniques, the adaptability and precision they have attained, the ideas and habits they are creating, make it a certainty that profound changes are impending in the ancient craft of the Beautiful. In all the arts there is a physical component which can no longer be considered or treated as it used to be, which cannot remain unaffected by our modern knowledge and power. For the last twenty years neither matter nor space nor time has been what it was from time immemorial. We must expect great innovations to transform the entire technique of the arts, thereby affecting artistic invention itself and perhaps even bringing about an amazing change in our very notion of art.[1]*

— PAUL VALÉRY, *Pièces sur l'art,*
"La Conquète de l'ubiquité," Paris

## PREFACE

When Marx undertook his critique of the capitalistic mode of production, this mode was in its infancy. Marx directed his efforts in such a way as to give them prognostic value. He went back to the basic conditions underlying capitalistic production and through his presentation showed what could be expected of capitalism in the future. The result was that one could expect it not only to exploit the proletariat with increasing intensity, but ultimately to create conditions which would make it possible to abolish capitalism itself.

The transformation of the superstructure, which takes place far more slowly than that of the substructure, has taken more than half a century to manifest in all areas of culture the change in the conditions of production. Only today can it be indicated what form this has taken. Certain prognostic requirements should be met by these statements. However, theses about the art of the proletariat after its assumption of power or about the art of a classless society would have less bearing on these demands than theses about the developmental tendencies of art under present conditions of production. Their dialectic is no less noticeable in the superstructure than in the economy. It would therefore be wrong to underestimate the value of such theses as a weapon. They brush aside a number of outmoded concepts, such as creativity and genius, eternal value and mystery — concepts whose uncontrolled

(and at present almost uncontrollable) application would lead to a processing of data in the Fascist sense. The concepts which are introduced into the theory of art in what follows differ from the more familiar terms in that they are completely useless for the purposes of Fascism. They are, on the other hand, useful for the formulation of revolutionary demands in the politics of art.

## I

In principle a work of art has always been reproducible. Manmade artifacts could always be imitated by men. Replicas were made by pupils in practice of their craft, by masters for diffusing their works, and, finally, by third parties in the pursuit of gain. Mechanical reproduction of a work of art, however, represents something new. Historically, it advanced intermittently and in leaps at long intervals, but with accelerated intensity. The Greeks knew only two procedures of technically reproducing works of art: founding and stamping. Bronzes, terra cottas, and coins were the only art works which they could produce in quantity. All others were unique and could not be mechanically reproduced. With the woodcut, graphic art became mechanically reproducible for the first time, long before script became reproducible by print. The enormous changes which printing, the mechanical reproduction of writing, has brought about in literature are a familiar story. However, within the phenomenon which we are here examining from the perspective of world history, print is merely a special, though particularly important, case. During the Middle Ages engraving and etching were added to the woodcut; at the beginning of the nineteenth century lithography made its appearance.

With lithography the technique of reproduction reached an essentially new stage. This much more direct process was distinguished by the tracing of the design of a stone rather than its incision on a block of wood or its etching on a copperplate and permitted graphic art for the first time to put its products on the market, not only in large numbers as hitherto, but also in daily changing forms. Lithography enabled graphic art to illustrate everyday life, and it began to keep

---

[1]Quoted from Paul Valéry, "The Conquest of Ubiquity," *Aesthetics,* trans. Ralph Manheim (New York: Pantheon Books, Bollingen Series, 1964) p. 225. [Tr.]

pace with printing. But only a few decades after its invention, lithography was surpassed by photography. For the first time in the process of pictorial reproduction, photography freed the hand of the most important artistic functions which henceforth devolved only upon the eye looking into a lens. Since the eye perceives more swiftly than the hand can draw, the process of pictorial reproduction was accelerated so enormously that it could keep pace with speech. A film operator shooting a scene in the studio captures the images at the speed of an actor's speech. Just as lithography virtually implied the illustrated newspaper, so did photography foreshadow the sound film. The technical reproduction of sound was tackled at the end of the last century. These convergent endeavors made predictable a situation which Paul Valéry pointed up in this sentence: "Just as water, gas, and electricity are brought into our houses from far off to satisfy our needs in response to a minimal effort, so we shall be supplied with visual or auditory images, which will appear and disappear at a simple movement of the hand, hardly more than a sign." Around 1900 technical reproduction had reached a standard that not only permitted it to reproduce all transmitted works of art and thus to cause the most profound change in their impact upon the public; it also had captured a place of its own among the artistic processes. For the study of this standard nothing is more revealing than the nature of the repercussions that these two different manifestations — the reproduction of works of art and the art of the film — have had on art in its traditional form.

## II

Even the most perfect reproduction of a work of art is lacking in one element: its presence in time and space, its unique existence at the place where it happens to be. This unique existence of the work of art determined the history to which it was subject throughout the time of its existence. This includes the changes which it may have suffered in physical condition over the years as well as the various changes in its ownership.[2]

²Of course, the history of a work of art encompasses

The traces of the first can be revealed only by chemical or physical analyses which it is impossible to perform on a reproduction; changes of ownership are subject to a tradition which must be traced from the situation of the original.

The presence of the original is the prerequisite of the concept of authenticity. Chemical analyses of the patina of a bronze can help to establish this, as does the proof that a given manuscript of the Middle Ages stems from an archive of the fifteenth century. The whole sphere of authenticity is outside technical — and, of course, not only technical — reproducibility.[3] Confronted with its manual reproduction, which was usually branded as a forgery, the original preserved all its authority; not so *vis à vis* technical reproduction. The reason is twofold. First, process reproduction is more independent of the original than manual reproduction. For example, in photography, process reproduction can bring out those aspects of the original that are unattainable to the naked eye yet accessible to the lens, which is adjustable and chooses its angle at will. And photographic reproduction, with the aid of certain processes, such as enlargement or slow motion, can capture images which escape natural vision. Secondly, technical reproduction can put the copy of the original into situations which would be out of reach for the original itself. Above all, it enables the original to meet the beholder halfway, be it in the form of a photograph or a phonograph record. The cathedral leaves its locale to be received in the studio of a lover of art; the choral production, performed in

more than this. The history of the Mona Lisa, for instance, encompasses the kind and number of its copies made in the seventeenth, eighteenth, and nineteenth centuries. [Au.]

³Precisely because authenticity is not reproducible, the intensive penetration of certain (mechanical) processes of reproduction was instrumental in differentiating and grading authenticity. To develop such differentiations was an important function of the trade in works of art. The invention of the woodcut may be said to have struck at the root of the quality of authenticity even before its late flowering. To be sure, at the time of its origin a medieval picture of the Madonna could not yet be said to be "authentic." It became "authentic" only during the succeeding centuries and perhaps most strikingly so during the last one. [Au.]

an auditorium or in the open air, resounds in the drawing room.

The situations into which the product of mechanical reproduction can be brought may not touch the actual work of art, yet the quality of its presence is always depreciated. This holds not only for the art work but also, for instance, for a landscape which passes in review before the spectator in a movie. In the case of the art object, a most sensitive nucleus — namely, its authenticity — is interfered with whereas no natural object is vulnerable on that score. The authenticity of a thing is the essence of all that is transmissible from its beginning, ranging from its substantive duration to its testimony to the history which it has experienced. Since the historical testimony rests on the authenticity, the former too, is jeopardized by reproduction when substantive duration ceases to matter. And what is really jeopardized when the historical testimony is affected is the authority of the object.[4]

One might subsume the eliminated element in the term "aura" and go on to say: that which withers in the age of mechanical reproduction is the aura of the work of art. This is a symptomatic process whose significance points beyond the realm of art. One might generalize by saying: the technique of reproduction detaches the reproduced object from the domain of tradition. By making many reproductions it substitutes a plurality of copies for a unique existence. And in permitting the reproduction to meet the beholder or listener in his own particular situation, it reactivates the object reproduced. These two processes lead to a tremendous shattering of tradition which is the obverse of the contemporary crisis and renewal of mankind. Both processes are intimately connected with the contemporary mass movements. Their most powerful agent is the film. Its social significance, particularly in its most positive form, is inconceivable without its destructive, cathartic aspect, that is, the liquidation of the traditional value of the cultural heritage. This phenomenon is most palpable in the great historical films. It extends to ever new positions. In 1927 Abel Gance exclaimed enthusiastically: "Shakespeare, Rembrandt, Beethoven will make films . . . all legends, all mythologies and all myths, all founders of religion, and the very religions . . . await their exposed resurrection, and the heroes crowd each other at the gate."[5] Presumably without intending it, he issued an invitation to a far-reaching liquidation.

## III

During long periods of history, the mode of human sense perception changes with humanity's entire mode of existence. The manner in which human sense perception is organized, the medium in which it is accomplished, is determined not only by nature but by historical circumstances as well. The fifth century, with its great shifts of population, saw the birth of the late Roman art industry and the Vienna Genesis, and there developed not only an art different from that of antiquity but also a new kind of perception. The scholars of the Viennese school, Riegl and Wickhoff, who resisted the weight of classical tradition under which these later art forms had been buried, were the first to draw conclusions from them concerning the organization of perception at the time. However far-reaching their insight, these scholars limited themselves to showing the significant, formal hallmark which characterized perception in late Roman times. They did not attempt — and, perhaps, saw no way — to show the social transformations expressed by these changes of perception. The conditions for an analogous insight are more favorable in the present. And if changes in the medium of contemporary perception can be comprehended as decay of the aura, it is possible to show its social causes.

The concept of aura which was proposed above with reference to historical objects may usefully be illustrated with reference to the aura

[4]The poorest provincial staging of *Faust* is superior to a Faust film in that, ideally, it competes with the first performance at Weimar. Before the screen it is unprofitable to remember traditional contents which might come to mind before the stage — for instance, that Goethe's friend Johann Heinrich Merck is hidden in Mephisto, and the like. [Au.]

[5]Abel Gance, "Le Temps de l'image est venu," *L'Art Cinématographique* 2 (Paris, 1927): 94–95. [Tr.] Gance was the director of the epic film *Napoleon* (1927). [Ed.]

of natural ones. We define the aura of the latter as the unique phenomenon of a distance, however close it may be. If, while resting on a summer afternoon, you follow with your eyes a mountain range on the horizon or a branch which casts its shadows over you, you experience the aura of those mountains, of that branch. This image makes it easy to comprehend the social bases of the contemporary decay of the aura. It rests on two circumstances, both of which are related to the increasing significance of the masses in contemporary life. Namely, the desire of contemporary masses to bring things "closer" spatially and humanly, which is just as ardent as their bent toward overcoming the uniqueness of every reality by accepting its reproduction.[6] Every day the urge grows stronger to get hold of an object at very close range by way of its likeness, its reproduction. Unmistakably, reproduction as offered by picture magazines and newsreels differs from the image seen by the unarmed eye. Uniqueness and permanence are as closely linked in the latter as are transitoriness and reproducibility in the former. To pry an object from its shell, to destroy its aura, is the mark of a perception whose "sense of the universal equality of things" has increased to such a degree that it extracts it even from a unique object by means of reproduction. Thus is manifested in the field of perception what in the theoretical sphere is noticeable in the increasing importance of statistics. The adjustment of reality to the masses and of the masses to reality is a process of unlimited scope, as much for thinking as for perception.

## IV

The uniqueness of a work of art is inseparable from its being imbedded in the fabric of tradition. This tradition itself is thoroughly alive and extremely changeable. An ancient statue of Venus,

for example, stood in a different traditional context with the Greeks, who made it an object of veneration, than with the clerics of the Middle Ages, who viewed it as an ominous idol. Both of them, however, were equally confronted with its uniqueness, that is, its aura. Originally the contextual integration of art in tradition found its expression in the cult. We know that the earliest art works originated in the service of a ritual — first the magical, then the religious kind. It is significant that the existence of the work of art with reference to its aura is never entirely separated from its ritual function.[7] In other words, the unique value of the "authentic" work of art has its basis in ritual, the location of its original use value. This ritualistic basis, however remote, is still recognizable as secularized ritual even in the most profane forms of the cult of beauty.[8] The secular cult of beauty, developed during the Renaissance and prevailing for three centuries, clearly showed that ritualistic basis in its decline and the first deep crisis which befell it. With the advent of the first truly revolutionary means of reproduction, photography, simultaneously with the rise of socialism, art sensed the approaching crisis which has become evident a century later. At the time, art reacted with the doctrine of *l'art*

[7]The definition of the aura as a "unique phenomenon of a distance however close it may be." represents nothing but the formulation of the cult value of the work of art in categories of space and time perception. Distance is the opposite of closeness. The essentially distant object is the unapproachable one. Unapproachability is indeed a major quality of the cult image. True to its nature, it remains "distant, however close it may be." The closeness which one may gain from its subject matter does not impair the distance which it retains in its appearance. [Au.]

[8]To the extent to which the cult value of the painting is secularized, the ideas of its fundamental uniqueness lose distinctness. In the imagination of the beholder the uniqueness of the phenomena which hold sway in the cult image is more and more displaced by the empirical uniqueness of the creator or of his creative achievement. To be sure, never completely so; the concept of authenticity always transcends mere genuineness. (This is particularly apparent in the collector who always retains some traces of the fetishist and who, by owning the work of art, shares in its ritual power.) Nevertheless, the function of the concept of authenticity remains determinate in the evaluation of art; with the secularization of art, authenticity displaces the cult value of the work. [Au.]

[6]To satisfy the human interest of the masses may mean to have one's social function removed from the field of vision. Nothing guarantees that a portraitist of today, when painting a famous surgeon at the breakfast table in the midst of his family, depicts his social function more precisely than a painter of the seventeenth century who portrayed his medical doctors as representing this profession, like Rembrandt in his *Anatomy Lesson*. [Au.]

*pour l'art,*[9] that is, with a theology of art. This gave rise to what might be called a negative theology in the form of the idea of "pure" art, which not only denied any social function of art but also any categorizing by subject matter. (In poetry, Mallarmé was the first to take this position.)

An analysis of art in the age of mechanical reproduction must do justice to these relationships, for they lead us to an all-important insight: for the first time in world history, mechanical reproduction emancipates the work of art from its parasitical dependence on ritual. To an ever greater degree the work of art reproduced becomes the work of art designed for reproducibility.[10] From a photographic negative, for example, one can make any number of prints; to ask for the "authentic" print makes no sense. But the instant the criterion of authenticity ceases to be applicable to artistic production, the total function of art is reversed. Instead of being based on ritual, it begins to be based on another practice — politics.

[9]Art for art's sake. [Ed.]

[10]In the case of films, mechanical reproduction is not, as with literature and painting, an external condition for mass distribution. Mechanical reproduction is inherent in the very technique of film production. This technique not only permits in the most direct way but virtually causes mass distribution. It enforces distribution because the production of a film is so expensive that an individual who, for instance, might afford to buy a painting no longer can afford to buy a film. In 1927 it was calculated that a major film, in order to pay its way, had to reach an audience of nine million. With the sound film, to be sure, a setback in its international distribution occurred at first: audiences became limited by language barriers. This coincided with the Fascist emphasis on national interests. It is more important to focus on this connection with Fascism than on this setback, which was soon minimized by synchronization. The simultaneity of both phenomena is attributable to the depression. The same disturbances which, on a larger scale, led to an attempt to maintain the existing property structure by sheer force led the endangered film capital to speed up the development of the sound film. The introduction of the sound film brought about a temporary relief, not only because it again brought the masses into the theaters but also because it merged new capital from the electrical industry with that of the film industry. Thus, viewed from the outside, the sound film promoted national interests, but seen from the inside it helped to internationalize film production even more than previously. [Au.]

## V

Works of art are received and valued on different planes. Two polar types stand out: with one, the accent is on the cult value; with the other, on the exhibition value of the work.[11] Artistic produc-

[11]This polarity cannot come into its own in the aesthetics of Idealism. Its idea of beauty comprises these polar opposites without differentiating between them and consequently excluded their polarity. Yet in Hegel this polarity announces itself as clearly as possible within the limits of Idealism. We quote from his *Philosophy of History*:

> Images were known of old. Piety at an early time required them for worship, but it could do without *beautiful* images. These might even be disturbing. In every beautiful painting there is also something nonspiritual, merely external, but its spirit speaks to man through its beauty. Worshipping, conversely, is concerned with the work as an object, for it is but a spiritless stupor of the soul. . . . Fine art has arisen . . . in the church . . . , although it has already gone beyond its principle as art.

Likewise, the following passage from *The Philosophy of Fine Art* indicates that Hegel sensed a problem here.

> We are beyond the stage of reverence for works of art as divine and objects deserving our worship. The impression they produce is one of a more reflective kind, and the emotions they arouse require a higher test. . . . — G. W. F. Hegel, *The Philosophy of Fine Arts,* trans., with notes, by F. P. B. Osmaston, vol. I (London, 1920), p. 12.

The transition from the first kind of artistic reception to the second characterizes the history of artistic reception in general. Apart from that, a certain oscillation between these two polar modes of reception can be demonstrated for each work of art. Take the Sistine Madonna. Since Hubert Grimme's research it has been known that the Madonna originally was painted for the purpose of exhibition. Grimme's research was inspired by the question: What is the purpose of the molding in the foreground of the painting which the two cupids lean upon? How, Grimme asked further, did Raphael come to furnish the sky with two draperies? Research proved that the Madonna had been commissioned for the public lying-in-state of Pope Sixtus. The Popes lay in state in a certain side chapel of St. Peter's. On that occasion Raphael's picture had been fastened in a nichelike background of the chapel, supported by the coffin. In this picture Raphael portrays the Madonna approaching the papal coffin in clouds from the background of the niche, which was demarcated by green drapes. At the obsequies of Sixtus a preeminent exhibition value of Raphael's picture was taken advantage of. Some time later it was placed on the high altar in the church of the Black Friars at Piacenza. The reason for this exile is to be found in the Roman rites which forbid the use of paintings exhibited at obsequies as cult objects on the high altar. This regulation devalued Raphael's picture to some

*more can see, charged purpose*

tion begins with ceremonial objects destined to serve in a cult. One may assume that what mattered was their existence, not their being on view. The elk portrayed by the man of the Stone Age on the walls of his cave was an instrument of magic. He did expose it to his fellow men, but in the main it was meant for the spirits. Today the cult value would seem to demand that the work of art remain hidden. Certain statues of gods are accessible only to the priest in the cella;[12] certain Madonnas remain covered nearly all year round; certain sculptures on medieval cathedrals are invisible to the spectator on ground level. With the emancipation of the various art practices from ritual go increasing opportunities for the exhibition of their products. It is easier to exhibit a portrait bust that can be sent here and there than to exhibit the statue of divinity that has its fixed place in the interior of a temple. The same holds for the painting as against the mosaic or fresco that preceded it. And even though the public presentability of a mass originally may have been just as great as that of a symphony, the latter originated at the moment when its public presentability promised to surpass that of the mass.

With the different methods of technical reproduction of a work of art, its fitness for exhibition increased to such an extent that the quantitative shift between its two poles turned into a qualitative transformation of its nature. This is comparable to the situation of the work of art in prehistoric times when, by the absolute emphasis on its cult value, it was, first and foremost, an instrument of magic. Only later did it come to be recognized as a work of art. In the same way today, by the absolute emphasis on its exhibition value the work of art becomes a creation with entirely new functions, among which the one we are conscious of, the artistic function, later may

be recognized as incidental.[13] This much is certain: today photography and the film are the most serviceable exemplifications of this new function.

## VI

In photography, exhibition value begins to displace cult value all along the line. But cult value does not give way without resistance. It retires into an ultimate retrenchment: the human countenance. It is no accident that the portrait was the focal point of early photography. The cult of remembrance of loved ones, absent or dead, offers a last refuge for the cult value of the picture. For the last time the aura emanates from the early photographs in the fleeting expression of a human face. This is what constitutes their melancholy, incomparable beauty. But as man withdraws from the photographic image, the exhibition value for the first time shows its superiority to the ritual value. To have pinpointed this new stage constitutes the incomparable significance of Atget,[14] who, around 1900, took photographs of deserted Paris streets. It has quite justly been said of him that he photographed them like scenes of crime. The scene of a crime, too, is deserted; it is photographed for the purpose of establishing evidence. With Atget, photographs become standard evidence for historical occurrences, and acquire a hidden political significance. They demand a specific kind of approach; free-floating contemplation is not appropriate to them. They stir the viewer; he feels challenged

[13]Bertolt Brecht, on a different level, engaged in analogous reflections: "If the concept of 'work of art' can no longer be applied to the thing that emerges once the work is transformed into a commodity, we have to eliminate this concept with cautious care but without fear, lest we liquidate the function of the very thing as well. For it has to go through this phase without mental reservation, and not as noncommittal deviation from the straight path; rather, what happens here with the work of art will change it fundamentally and erase its past to such an extent that should the old concept be taken up again — and it will, why not? — it will no longer stir any memory of the thing it once designated." [Au.]

[14]Jean-Eugène-August Atget (1857–1927), Parisian photographer. [Ed.]

degree. In order to obtain an adequate price nevertheless, the Papal See resolved to add to the bargain the tacit toleration of the picture above the high altar. To avoid attention the picture was given to the monks of the far-off provincial town. [Au.]

[12]Cell (prison or monastic). [Ed.]

by them in a new way. At the same time picture magazines begin to put up signposts for him, right ones or wrong ones, no matter. For the first time, captions have become obligatory. And it is clear that they have an altogether different character than the title of a painting. The directives which the captions give to those looking at pictures in illustrated magazines soon become even more explicit and more imperative in the film where the meaning of each single picture appears to be prescribed by the sequence of all preceding ones.

## VII

The nineteenth-century dispute as to the artistic value of painting versus photography today seems devious and confused. This does not diminish its importance, however; if anything, it underlines it. The dispute was, in fact, the symptom of a historical transformation the universal impact of which was not realized by either of the rivals. When the age of mechanical reproduction separated art from its basis in cult, the semblance of its autonomy disappeared forever. The resulting change in the function of art transcended the perspective of the century; for a long time it even escaped that of the twentieth century, which experienced the development of the film.

Earlier much futile thought had been devoted to the question of whether photography is an art. The primary question — whether the very invention of photography had not transformed the entire nature of art — was not raised. Soon the film theoreticians asked the same ill-considered question with regard to the film. But the difficulties which photography caused traditional aesthetics were mere child's play as compared to those raised by the film. Whence the insensitive and forced character of early theories of the film. Abel Gance, for instance, compares the film with hieroglyphs: "Here, by a remarkable regression, we have come back to the level of expression of the Egyptians. . . . Pictorial language has not yet matured because our eyes have not yet adjusted to it. There is as yet insufficient respect for, insufficient cult of, what it expresses."[15] Or, in the words of Séverin-Mars: "What art has been granted a dream more poetical and more real at the same time! Approached in this fashion the film might represent an incomparable means of expression. Only the most high-minded persons, in the most perfect and mysterious moments of their lives, should be allowed to enter its ambience."[16] Alexandre Arnoux concludes his fantasy about the silent film with the question: "Do not all the bold descriptions we have given amount to the definition of prayer?"[17] It is instructive to note how their desire to class the film among the "arts" forces these theoreticians to read ritual elements into it — with a striking lack of discretion. Yet when these speculations were published, films like *L'Opinion publique* and *The Gold Rush* had already appeared. This, however, did not keep Abel Gance from adducing hieroglyphs for purposes of comparison, nor Séverin-Mars from speaking of the film as one might speak of paintings by Fra Angelico. Characteristically, even today ultrareactionary authors give the film a similar contextual significance — if not an outright sacred one, then at least a supernatural one. Commenting on Max Reinhardt's film version of *A Midsummer Night's Dream*, Werfel states that undoubtedly it was the sterile copying of the exterior world with its streets, interiors, railroad stations, restaurants, motorcars, and beaches which until now had obstructed the elevation of the film to the realm of art. "The film has not yet realized its true meaning, its real possibilities . . . these consist in its unique faculty to express by natural means and with incomparable persuasiveness all that is fairylike, marvelous, supernatural."[18]

## VIII

The artistic performance of a stage actor is definitely presented to the public by the actor in person; that of the screen actor, however, is presented by a camera, with a twofold consequence.

[15]Abel Gance, pp. 100–101. [Tr.]

[16]Séverin-Mars, quoted by Abel Gance, p. 100 [Tr.]
[17]Alexandre Arnoux, *Cinéma pris* (1929), p. 28. [Tr.]
[18]Franz Werfel, "Einsommersnachtstraum, Ein Film von Shakespeare und Reinhardt," *Neues Wiener Journal*, cited in *Lu* (November 1935). [Tr.]

The camera that presents the performance of the film actor to the public need not respect the performance as an integral whole. Guided by the cameraman, the camera continually changes its position with respect to the performance. The sequence of positional views which the editor composes from the material supplied him constitutes the completed film. It comprises certain factors of movement which are in reality those of the camera, not to mention special camera angles, close-ups, etc. Hence, the performance of the actor is subjected to a series of optical tests. This is the first consequence of the fact that the actor's performance is presented by means of a camera. Also, the film actor lacks the opportunity of the stage actor to adjust to the audience during his performance, since he does not present his performance to the audience in person. This permits the audience to take the position of a critic, without experiencing any personal contact with the actor. The audience's identification with the actor is really an identification with the camera. Consequently the audience takes the position of the camera; its approach is that of testing.[19] This is not the approach to which cult values may be exposed.

## IX

For the film, what matters primarily is that the actor represents himself to the public before the camera, rather than representing someone else. One of the first to sense the actor's metamorphosis by this form of testing was Pirandello. Though his remarks on the subject in his novel

[19]"The film . . . provides — or could provide — useful insight into the details of human actions. . . . Character is never used as a source of motivation; the inner life of the persons never supplies the principal cause of the plot and seldom is its main result." (Bertolt Brecht, "Der Dreigroschenprozess," *Versuche*, p. 268.) The expansion of the field of the testable which mechanical equipment brings about for the actor corresponds to the extraordinary expansion of the field of the testable brought about for the individual through economic conditions. Thus, vocational aptitude tests become constantly more important. What matters in these tests are segmental performances of the individual. The film shot and the vocational aptitude test are taken before a committee of experts. The camera director in the studio occupies a place identical with that of the examiner during aptitude tests. [Au.]

*Si Gira* were limited to the negative aspects of the question and to the silent film only, this hardly impairs their validity. For in this respect, the sound film did not change anything essential. What matters is that the part is acted not for an audience but for a mechanical contrivance — in the case of the sound film, for two of them. "The film actor," wrote Pirandello, "feels as if in exile — exiled not only from the stage but also from himself. With a vague sense of discomfort he feels inexplicable emptiness: his body loses its corporeality, it evaporates, it is deprived of reality, life, voice, and the noises caused by his moving about, in order to be changed into a mute image, flickering an instant on the screen, then vanishing into silence. . . . The projector will play with his shadow before the public, and he himself must be content to play before the camera."[20] This situation might also be characterized as follows: for the first time — and this is the effect of the film — man has to operate with his whole living person, yet forgoing its aura. For aura is tied to his presence; there can be no replica of it. The aura which, on the stage, emanates from Macbeth, cannot be separated for the spectators from that of the actor. However, the singularity of the shot in the studio is that the camera is substituted for the public. Consequently, the aura that envelops the actor vanishes, and with it the aura of the figure he portrays.

It is not surprising that it should be a dramatist such as Pirandello who, in characterizing the film, inadvertently touches on the very crisis in which we see the theater. Any thorough study proves that there is indeed no greater contrast than that of the stage play to a work of art that is completely subject to or, like the film, founded in, mechanical reproduction. Experts have long recognized that in the film "the greatest effects are almost always obtained by 'acting' as little as possible. . . ." In 1932 Rudolf Arnheim saw "the latest trend . . . in treating the actor as a stage prop chosen for its characteristics and . . .

[20]Luigi Pirandello, *Si Gira*, quoted by Léon Pierre-Quint, "Signification du cinéma," *L'Art cinématographique*, pp. 14–15. [Tr.]

*reshoot, different times*

inserted at the proper place."[21] With this idea something else is closely connected. The stage actor identifies himself with the character of his role. The film actor very often is denied this opportunity. His creation is by no means all of a piece; it is composed of many separate performances. Besides certain fortuitous considerations, such as cost of studio, availability of fellow players, décor, etc., there are elementary necessities of equipment that split the actor's work into a series of mountable episodes. In particular, lighting and its installation require the presentation of an event that, on the screen, unfolds as a rapid and unified scene, in a sequence of separate shootings which may take hours at the studio; not to mention more obvious montage. Thus a jump from the window can be shot in the studio as a jump from a scaffold, and the ensuing flight, if need be, can be shot weeks later when outdoor scenes are taken. Far more paradoxical cases can easily be construed. Let us assume that an actor is supposed to be startled by a knock at the door. If his reaction is not satisfactory, the director can resort to an expedient: when the actor happens to be at the studio again he has a shot fired behind him without his being forewarned of it. The frightened reaction can be shot now and be cut into the screen version. Nothing more strikingly shows that art has left the realm of the "beautiful semblance" which, so far, had been taken to be the only sphere where art could thrive.

## X

The feeling of strangeness that overcomes the actor before the camera, as Pirandello describes it, is basically of the same kind as the estrangement felt before one's own image in the mirror. But now the reflected image has become separable, transportable. And where is it transported? Before the public.[22] Never for a moment does the screen actor cease to be conscious of this fact. While facing the camera he knows that ultimately he will face the public, the consumers who constitute the market. This market, where he offers not only his labor but also his whole self, his heart and soul, is beyond his reach. During the shooting he has as little contact with it as any article made in a factory. This may contribute to that oppression, that new anxiety which, according to Pirandello, grips the actor before the camera. The film responds to the

[21]Rudolf Arnheim, *Film als Kunst* (Berlin, 1932), pp. 176 f. In this context certain seemingly unimportant details in which the film director deviates from stage practices gain in interest. Such is the attempt to let the actor play without makeup, as made among others by Dreyer in his *Jeanne d'Arc*. Dreyer spent months seeking the forty actors who constitute the Inquisitors' tribunal. The search for these actors resembled that for stage properties that are hard to come by. Dreyer made every effort to avoid resemblances of age, build, and physiognomy. If the actor thus becomes a stage property, this latter, on the other hand, frequently functions as actor. At least it is not unusual for the film to assign a role to the stage property. Instead of choosing at random from a great wealth of examples, let us concentrate on a particularly convincing one. A clock that is working will always be a disturbance on the stage. There it cannot be permitted its function of measuring time. Even in a naturalistic play, astronomical time would clash with theatrical time. Under these circumstances it is highly revealing that the film can, whenever appropriate, use time as measured by a clock. From this more than from many other touches it may clearly be recognized that under certain circumstances each and every prop in a film may assume important functions. From here it is but one step to Pudovkin's statement that "the playing of an actor which is connected with an object and is built around it . . . is always one of the strongest methods of cinematic construction." (W. Pudovkin, *Filmregie und Filmmanuskript* [Berlin, 1928], p. 126.) The film is the first art form capable of demonstrating how matter plays tricks on man. Hence, films can be an excellent means of materialistic representation. [Au.]

[22]The change noted here in the method of exhibition caused by mechanical reproduction applies to politics as well. The present crisis of the bourgeois democracies comprises a crisis of the conditions which determine the public presentation of the rulers. Democracies exhibit a member of government directly and personally before the nation's representatives. Parliament is his public. Since the innovations of camera and recording equipment make it possible for the orator to become audible and visible to an unlimited number of persons, the presentation of the man of politics before camera and recording equipment becomes paramount. Parliaments, as much as theaters, are deserted. Radio and film not only affect the function of the professional actor but likewise the function of those who also exhibit themselves before this mechanical equipment, those who govern. Though their tasks may be different, the change affects equally the actor and the ruler. The trend is toward establishing controllable and transferrable skills under certain social conditions. This results in a new selection, a selection before the equipment from which the star and the dictator emerge victorious. [Au.]

shriveling of the aura with an artificial build-up of the "personality" outside the studio. The cult of the movie star, fostered by the money of the film industry, preserves not the unique aura of the person but the "spell of the personality," the phony spell of a commodity. So long as the movie-makers' capital sets the fashion, as a rule no other revolutionary merit can be accredited to today's film than the promotion of a revolutionary criticism of traditional concepts of art. We do not deny that in some cases today's films can also promote revolutionary criticism of social conditions, even of the distribution of property. However, our present study is no more specifically concerned with this than is the film production of Western Europe.

It is inherent in the technique of the film as well as that of sports that everybody who witnesses its accomplishments is somewhat of an expert. This is obvious to anyone listening to a group of newspaper boys leaning on their bicycles and discussing the outcome of a bicycle race. It is not for nothing that newspaper publishers arrange races for their delivery boys. These arouse great interest among the participants, for the victor has an opportunity to rise from delivery boy to professional racer. Similarly, the newsreel offers everyone the opportunity to rise from passer-by to movie extra. In this way any man might even find himself part of a work of art, as witness Vertoff's *Three Songs About Lenin* or Ivens's *Borinage*. Any man today can lay claim to being filmed. This claim can best be elucidated by a comparative look at the historical situation of contemporary literature.

For centuries a small number of writers were confronted by many thousands of readers. This changed toward the end of the last century. With the increasing extension of the press, which kept placing new political, religious, scientific, professional, and local organs before the readers, an increasing number of readers became writers — at first, occasional ones. It began with the daily press opening to its readers space for "letters to the editor." And today there is hardly a gainfully employed European who could not, in principle, find an opportunity to publish somewhere or other comments on his work, grievances, documentary reports, or that sort of thing.

Thus, the distinction between author and public is about to lose its basic character. The difference becomes merely functional; it may vary from case to case. At any moment the reader is ready to turn into a writer. As expert, which he had to become willy-nilly in an extremely specialized work process, even if only in some minor respect, the reader gains access to authorship. In the Soviet Union work itself is given a voice. To present it verbally is part of a man's ability to perform the work. Literary license is now founded on polytechnic rather than specialized training and thus becomes common property.[23]

[23]The privileged character of the respective techniques is lost. Aldous Huxley writes:

> Advances in technology have led . . . to vulgarity. . . . Process reproduction and the rotary press have made possible the indefinite multiplication of writing and pictures. Universal education and relatively high wages have created an enormous public who know how to read and can afford to buy reading and pictorial matter. A great industry has been called into existence in order to supply these commodities. Now, artistic talent is a very rare phenomenon; whence it follows . . . that, at every epoch and in all countries, most art has been bad. But the proportion of trash in the total artistic output is greater now than at any other period. That it must be so is a matter of simple arithmetic. The population of Western Europe has a little more than doubled during the last century. But the amount of reading — and seeing — matter has increased, I should imagine, at least twenty and possibly fifty or even a hundred times. If there were n men of talent in a population of x millions, there will presumably be 2n men of talent among 2x millions. The situation may be summed up thus. For every page of print and pictures published a century ago, twenty or perhaps even a hundred pages are published today. But for every man of talent then living, there are now only two men of talent. It may be of course that, thanks to universal education, many potential talents which in the past would have been stillborn are now enabled to realize themselves. Let us assume, then, that there are now three or even four men of talent to every one of earlier times. It still remains true to say that the consumption of reading — and seeing — matter has far outstripped the natural production of gifted writers and draughtsmen. It is the same with hearing-matter. Prosperity, the gramophone and the radio have created an audience of hearers who consume an amount of hearing-matter that has increased out of all proportion to the increase of population and the consequent natural increase of talented musicians. It follows from all this that in all the arts the output of trash is both absolutely and relatively greater than it was in the past; and that it must remain greater for just so long as the world continues to consume the present inordinate quantities of reading-matter,

All this can easily be applied to the film, where transitions that in literature took centuries have come about in a decade. In cinematic practice, particularly in Russia, this changeover has partially become established reality. Some of the players whom we meet in Russian films are not actors in our sense but people who portray *themselves* — and primarily in their own work process. In Western Europe the capitalistic exploitation of the film denies consideration to modern man's legitimate claim to being reproduced. Under these circumstances the film industry is trying hard to spur the interest of the masses through illusion-promoting spectacles and dubious speculations.

## XI

The shooting of a film, especially of a sound film, affords a spectacle unimaginable anywhere at any time before this. It presents as process in which it is impossible to assign to a spectator a viewpoint which would exclude from the actual scene such extraneous accessories as camera equipment, lighting machinery, staff assistants, etc. — unless his eye were on a line parallel with the lens. This circumstance, more than any other, renders superficial and insignificant any possible similarity between a scene in the studio and one on the stage. In the theater one is well aware of the place from which the play cannot immediately be detected as illusionary. There is no such place for the movie scene that is being shot. Its illusionary nature is that of the second degree, the result of cutting. That is to say, in the studio the mechanical equipment has penetrated so deeply into reality that its pure aspect freed from the foreign substance of equipment is the result of a special procedure, namely, the shooting by the specially adjusted camera and the mounting of the shot together with other similar ones. The equipment-free aspect of reality here has become

the height of artifice; the sight of immediate reality has become an orchid in the land of technology.

Even more revealing is the comparison of these circumstances, which differ so much from those of the theater, with the situation in painting. Here the question is: How does the cameraman compare with the painter? To answer this we take recourse to an analogy with a surgical operation. The surgeon represents the polar opposite of the magician. The magician heals a sick person by the laying on of hands; the surgeon cuts into the patient's body. The magician maintains the natural distance between the patient and himself; though he reduces it very slightly by the laying on of hands, he greatly increases it by virtue of his authority. The surgeon does exactly the reverse; he greatly diminishes the distance between himself and the patient by penetrating into the patient's body, and increases it but little by the caution with which his hand moves among the organs. In short, in contrast to the magician — who is still hidden in the medical practitioner — the surgeon at the decisive moment abstains from facing the patient man to man; rather, it is through the operation that he penetrates into him.

Magician and surgeon compare to painter and cameraman. The painter maintains in his work a natural distance from reality, the cameraman penetrates deeply into its web.[24] There is a tremendous difference between the pictures they obtain. That of the painter is a total one, that of the cameraman consists of multiple fragments which are assembled under a new law. Thus, for contemporary man the representation of reality by

[24]The boldness of the cameraman is indeed comparable to that of the surgeon. Luc Durtain lists among specific technical sleights of hand those "which are required in surgery in the case of certain difficult operations. I choose as an example a case from oto-rhino-laryngology; . . . the so-called endonasal perspective procedure; or I refer to the acrobatic tricks of larynx surgery which have to be performed following the reversed picture in the laryngoscope. I might also speak of ear surgery which suggests the precision work of watchmakers. What range of the most subtle muscular acrobatics is required from the man who wants to repair or save the human body! We have only to think of the couching of a cataract where there is virtually a debate of steel with nearly fluid tissue, or of the major abdominal operations (laparotomy)." — Luc Durtain. [Au.]

seeing-matter, and hearing-matter. — Aldous Huxley, *Beyond the Mexique Bay. A Traveller's Journal* (London, 1949), pp. 274 ff. First published in 1934.

This mode of observation is obviously not progressive. [Au.]

the film is incomparably more significant than that of the painter, since it offers, precisely because of the thoroughgoing permeation of reality with mechanical equipment, as aspect of reality which is free of all equipment. And that is what one is entitled to ask from a work of art.

## XII

Mechanical reproduction of art changes the reaction of the masses toward art. The reactionary attitude toward a Picasso painting changes into the progressive reaction toward a Chaplin movie. The progressive reaction is characterized by the direct, intimate fusion of visual and emotional enjoyment with the orientation of the expert. Such fusion is of great social significance. The greater the decrease in the social significance of an art form, the sharper the distinction between criticism and enjoyment by the public. The conventional is uncritically enjoyed, and the truly new is criticized with aversion. With regard to the screen, the critical and the receptive attitudes of the public coincide. The decisive reason for this is that individual reactions are predetermined by the mass audience response they are about to produce, and this is nowhere more pronounced than in the film. The moment these responses become manifest they control each other. Again, the comparison with painting is fruitful. A painting has always had an excellent chance to be viewed by one person or by a few. The simultaneous contemplation of paintings by a large public, such as developed in the nineteenth century, is an early symptom of the crisis of painting, a crisis which was by no means occasioned exclusively by photography but rather in a relatively independent manner by the appeal of art works to the masses.

Painting simply is in no position to present an object for simultaneous collective experience, as it was possible for architecture at all times, for the epic poem in the past, and for the movie today. Although this circumstance in itself should not lead one to conclusions about the social role of painting, it does constitute a serious threat as soon as painting, under special conditions and, as it were, against its nature, is confronted directly by the masses. In the churches and monasteries of the Middle Ages and at the princely courts up to the end of the eighteenth century, a collective reception of paintings did not occur simultaneously, but by graduated and hierarchized mediation. The change that has come about is an expression of the particular conflict in which painting was implicated by the mechanical reproducibility of paintings. Although paintings began to be publicly exhibited in galleries and salons, there was no way for the masses to organize and control themselves in their reception.[25] Thus the same public which responds in a progressive manner toward a grotesque film is bound to respond in a reactionary manner to surrealism.

## XIII

The characteristics of the film lie not only in the manner in which man presents himself to mechanical equipment but also in the manner in which, by means of this apparatus, man can represent his environment. A glance at occupational psychology illustrates the testing capacity of the equipment. Psychoanalysis illustrates it in a different perspective. The film has enriched our field of perception with methods which can be illustrated by those of Freudian theory. Fifty years ago, a slip of the tongue passed more or less unnoticed. Only exceptionally may such a slip have revealed dimensions of depth in a conversation which had seemed to be taking its course on the surface. Since the *Psychopathology of Everyday Life* things have changed. This book isolated and made analyzable things which had heretofore floated along unnoticed in the broad stream of perception. For the entire spectrum of optical, and now also acoustical, perception the film has brought about a similar deepening of apperception. It is only an obverse of this fact that behavior items shown in a movie can be

[25]This mode of observation may seem crude, but as the great theoretician Leonardo has shown, crude modes of observation may at times be usefully adduced. Leonardo compares painting and music as follows: "Painting is superior to music because, unlike unfortunate music, it does not have to die as soon as it is born. . . . Music which is consumed in the very act of its birth is inferior to painting which the use of varnish has rendered eternal." (Trattato I, 29.) [Au.]

analyzed much more precisely and from more points of view than those presented on paintings or on the stage. As compared with painting, filmed behavior lends itself more readily to analysis because of its incomparably more precise statements of the situation. In comparison with the stage scene, the filmed behavior item lends itself more readily to analysis because it can be isolated more easily. This circumstance derives its chief importance from its tendency to promote the mutual penetration of art and science. Actually, of a screened behavior item which is neatly brought out in a certain situation, like a muscle of a body, it is difficult to say which is more fascinating, its artistic value or its value for science. To demonstrate the identity of the artistic and scientific uses of photography which heretofore usually were separated will be one of the revolutionary functions of the film.[26]

By close-ups of the things around us, by focusing on hidden details of familiar objects, by exploring commonplace milieus under the ingenious guidance of the camera, the film, on the one hand, extends our comprehension of the necessities which rule our lives; on the other hand, it manages to assure us of an immense and unexpected field of action. Our taverns and our metropolitan streets, our offices and furnished rooms, our railroad stations and our factories appeared to have us locked up hopelessly. Then came the film and burst this prison-world asunder by the dynamite of the tenth of a second, so that now, in the midst of its far-flung ruins and debris, we calmly and adventurously go traveling. With the close-up, space expands; with slow motion, movement is extended. The enlargement of a

snapshot does not simply render more precise what in any case was visible, though unclear: it reveals entirely new structural formations of the subject. So, too, slow motion not only presents familiar qualities of movement but reveals in them entirely unknown ones "which, far from looking like retarded rapid movements, give the effect of singularly gliding, floating, supernatural motions."[27] Evidently a different nature opens itself to the camera than opens to the naked eye — if only because an unconsciously penetrated space is substituted for a space consciously explored by man. Even if one has a general knowledge of the way people walk, one knows nothing of a person's posture during the fractional second of a stride. The act of reaching for a lighter or a spoon is familiar routine, yet we hardly know what really goes on between hand and metal, not to mention how this fluctuates with our moods. Here the camera intervenes with the resources of its lowerings and liftings, its interruptions and isolations, its extensions and accelerations, its enlargements and reductions. The camera introduces us to unconscious optics as does psychoanalysis to unconscious impulses.

## XIV

One of the foremost tasks of art has always been the creation of a demand which could be fully satisfied only later.[28] The history of every art

[26]Renaissance painting offers a revealing analogy to this situation. The incomparable development of this art and its significance rested not least on the integration of a number of new sciences, or at least of new scientific data. Renaissance painting made use of anatomy and perspective, of mathematics, meteorology, and chromatology. Valéry writes: "What could be further from us than the strange claim of a Leonardo to whom painting was a supreme goal and the ultimate demonstration of knowledge? Leonardo was convinced that painting demanded universal knowledge, and he did not even shrink from a theoretical analysis which to us is stunning because of its very depth and precision. . . ." — Paul Valéry, "Autour de Corot," *Pièces sur l'art* (Paris), p. 191. [Au.]

[27]Rudolf Arnheim, p. 138. [Tr.]
[28]"The work of art," says André Breton, "is valuable only insofar as it is vibrated by the reflexes of the future." Indeed, every developed art form intersects three lines of development. Technology works toward a certain form of art. Before the advent of the film there were photo booklets with pictures which flitted by the onlooker upon pressure of the thumb, thus portraying a boxing bout or a tennis match. Then there were the slot machines in bazaars; their picture sequences were produced by the turning of a crank.

Secondly, the traditional art forms in certain phases of their development strenuously work toward effects which later are effortlessly attained by the new ones. Before the rise of the movie the Dadaists' performances tried to create an audience reaction which Chaplin later evoked in a more natural way.

Thirdly, unspectacular social changes often promote a change in receptivity which will benefit the new art form. Before the movie had begun to create its public, pictures that were no longer immobile captivated an assembled audience

form shows critical epochs in which a certain art form aspires to effects which could be fully obtained only with a changed technical standard, that is to say, in a new art form. The extravagances and crudities of art which thus appear, particularly in the so-called decadent epochs, actually arise from the nucleus of its richest historical energies. In recent years, such barbarisms were abundant in Dadaism.[29] It is only now that its impulse becomes discernible: Dadaism attempted to create by pictorial — and literary — means the effects which the public today seeks in the film.

Every fundamentally new, pioneering creation of demands will carry beyond its goal. Dadaism did so to the extent that it sacrificed the market values which are so characteristic of the film in favor of higher ambitions — though of course it was not conscious of such intentions as here described. The Dadaists attached much less importance to the sales value of their work than to its uselessness for contemplative immersion. The studied degradation of their material was not the least of their means to achieve this uselessness. Their poems are "word salad" containing obscenities and every imaginable waste product of language. The same is true of their paintings, on which they mounted buttons and tickets. What they intended and achieved was a relentless destruction of the aura of their creations, which they branded as reproductions with the very means of production. Before a painting of Arp's or a poem by August Stramm it is impossible to take time for contemplation and evaluation as one would before a canvas of Derain's or a poem by Rilke. In the decline of middle-class society, contemplation became a school for asocial behavior; it was countered by distraction as a variant of social conduct.[30] Dadaistic activities actually assured a rather vehement distraction by making works of art the center of scandal. One requirement was foremost: to outrage the public.

From an alluring appearance or persuasive structure of sound the work of art of the Dadaists became an instrument of ballistics. It hit the spectator like a bullet, it happened to him, thus acquiring a tactile quality. It promoted a demand for the film, the distracting element of which is also primarily tactile, being based on changes of place and focus which periodically assail the spectator. Let us compare the screen on which a film unfolds with the canvas of a painting. The painting invites the spectator to contemplation; before it the spectator can abandon himself to his associations. Before the movie frame he cannot do so. No sooner has his eye grasped a scene than it is already changed. It cannot be arrested. Duhamel, who detests the film and knows nothing of its significance, though something of its structure, notes this circumstance as follows: "I can no longer think what I want to think. My thoughts have been replaced by moving images."[31] The spectator's process of association in view of these images is indeed interrupted by their constant, sudden change. This constitutes the shock effect of the film, which, like all shocks, should be cushioned by heightened pres-

---

in the so-called *Kaiserpanorama*. Here the public assembled before a screen into which stereoscopes were mounted, one to each beholder. By a mechanical process individual pictures appeared briefly before the stereoscopes, then made way for others. Edison still had to use similar devices in presenting the first movie strip before the film screen and projection were known. This strip was presented to a small public which stared into the apparatus in which the succession of pictures was reeling off. Incidentally, the institution of the *Kaiserpanorama* shows very clearly a dialectic of the development. Shortly before the movie turned the reception of pictures into a collective one, the individual viewing of pictures in these swiftly outmoded establishments came into play once more with an intensity comparable to that of the ancient priest beholding the statue of a divinity in the cella. [Au.]

[29] Movement in the 1920s in both poetry and graphic art characterized by a parodistic treatment of mechanized society and an outrageous assault on the viewer. Major works of Dada include the Bunuel-Dali film *Un Chien Andalou* and Alfred Jarry's play *Ubu roi*; its principal theorist was André Breton. [Ed.]

[30] The theological archetype of this contemplation is the awareness of being alone with one's God. Such awareness, in the heyday of the bourgeoisie, went to strengthen the freedom to shake off clerical tutelage. During the decline of the bourgeoisie this awareness had to take into account the hidden tendency to withdraw from public affairs those forces which the individual draws upon in his communion with God. [Au.]

[31] Georges Duhamel, *Scènes de la vie future* (Paris, 1930), p. 52. [Tr.]

ence of mind.[32] By means of its technical structure, the film has taken the physical shock effect out of the wrappers in which Dadaism had, as it were, kept it inside the moral shock effect.[33]

## XV

The mass is a matrix from which all traditional behavior toward works of art issues today in a new form. Quantity has been transmuted into quality. The greatly increased mass of participants has produced a change in the mode of participation. The fact that the new mode of participation first appeared in a disreputable form must not confuse the spectator. Yet some people have launched spirited attacks against precisely this superficial aspect. Among these, Duhamel has expressed himself in the most radical manner. What he objects to most is the kind of participation which the movie elicits from the masses. Duhamel calls the movie "a pastime for helots,[34] a diversion for uneducated, wretched, worn-out creatures who are consumed by their worries . . . , a spectacle which requires no concentration and presupposes no intelligence . . . , which kindles no light in the heart and awakens no hope other than the ridiculous one of someday becoming a 'star' in Los Angeles."[35] Clearly, this is at bottom the same ancient lament that the masses

---

[32]The film is the art form that is in keeping with the increased threat to his life which modern man has to face. Man's need to expose himself to shock effects is his adjustment to the dangers threatening him. The film corresponds to profound changes in the apperceptive apparatus — changes that are experienced on an individual scale by the man in the street in big-city traffic, on a historical scale by every present-day citizen. [Au.]

[33]As for Dadaism, insights important for Cubism and Futurism are to be gained from the movie. Both appear as deficient attempts of art to accommodate the pervasion of reality by the apparatus. In contrast to the film, these schools did not try to use the apparatus as such for the artistic presentation of reality, but aimed at some sort of alloy in the joint presentation of reality and apparatus. In Cubism, the premonition that this apparatus will be structurally based on optics plays a dominant part; in Futurism, it is the premonition of the effects of this apparatus which are brought out by the rapid sequence of the film strip. [Au.]

[34]Slaves. [Ed.]

[35]Duhamel, p. 58. [Tr.]

seek distraction whereas art demands concentration from the spectator. That is a commonplace. The question remains whether it provides a platform for the analysis of the film. A closer look is needed here. Distraction and concentration form polar opposites which may be stated as follows: A man who concentrates before a work of art is absorbed by it. He enters into this work of art the way legend tells of the Chinese painter when he viewed his finished painting. In contrast, the distracted mass absorbs the work of art. This is most obvious with regard to buildings. Architecture has always represented the prototype of a work of art the reception of which is consummated by a collectivity in a state of distraction. The laws of its reception are most instructive.

Buildings have been man's companions since primeval times. Many art forms have developed and perished. Tragedy begins with the Greeks, is extinguished with them, and after centuries its "rules" only are revived. The epic poem, which had its origin in the youth of nations, expires in Europe at the end of the Renaissance. Panel painting is a creation of the Middle Ages, and nothing guarantees its uninterrupted existence. But the human need for shelter is lasting. Architecture has never been idle. Its history is more ancient than that of any other art, and its claim to being a living force has significance in every attempt to comprehend the relationship of the masses to art. Buildings are appropriated in a twofold manner: by use and by perception — or rather, by touch and sight. Such appropriation cannot be understood in terms of the attentive concentration of a tourist before a famous building. On the tactile side there is no counterpart to contemplation on the optical side. Tactile appropriation is accomplished not so much by attention as by habit. As regards architecture, habit determines to a large extent even optical reception. The latter, too, occurs much less through rapt attention than by noticing the object in incidental fashion. This mode of appropriation, developed with reference to architecture, in certain circumstances acquires canonical value. For the tasks which face the human apparatus of perception at the turning points of history cannot be solved by optical means, that is, by contemplation, alone. They are mastered gradually by habit, under the guidance of tactile appropriation.

The distracted person, too, can form habits. More, the ability to master certain tasks in a state of distraction proves that their solution has become a matter of habit. Distraction as provided by art presents a covert control of the extent to which new tasks have become soluble by apperception. Since, moreover, individuals are tempted to avoid such tasks, art will tackle the most difficult and most important ones where it is able to mobilize the masses. Today it does so in the film. Reception in a state of distraction, which is increasing noticeably in all fields of art and is symptomatic of profound changes in apperception, finds in the film its true means of exercise. The film with its shock effect meets this mode of reception halfway. The film makes the cult value recede into the background not only by putting the public in the position of the critic, but also by the fact that at the movies this position requires no attention. The public is an examiner, but an absent-minded one.

## EPILOGUE

The growing proletarianization of modern man and the increasing formation of masses are two aspects of the same process. Fascism attempts to organize the newly created proletarian masses without affecting the property structure which the masses strive to eliminate. Fascism sees its salvation in giving these masses not their right, but instead a chance to express themselves.[36] The

masses have a right to change property relations; Fascism seeks to give them an expression while preserving property. The logical result of Fascism is the introduction of aesthetics into political life. The violation of the masses, whom Fascism, with its *Führer* cult, forces to their knees, has its counterpart in the violation of an apparatus which is pressed into the production of ritual values.

All efforts to render politics aesthetic culminate in one thing: war. War and war only can set a goal for mass movements on the largest scale while respecting the traditional property system. This is the political formula for the situation. The technological formula may be stated as follows: Only war makes it possible to mobilize all of today's technical resources while maintaining the property system. It goes without saying that the Fascist apotheosis of war does not employ such arguments. Still, Marinetti[37] says in his manifesto on the Ethiopian colonial war: "For twenty-seven years we Futurists have rebelled against the branding of war as antiaesthetic. . . . Accordingly we state: . . . War is beautiful because it establishes man's dominion over the subjugated machinery by means of gas masks, terrifying megaphones, flame throwers, and small tanks. War is beautiful because it initiates the dreamt-of metalization of the human body. War is beautiful because it enriches a flowering meadow with the fiery orchids of machine guns. War is beautiful because it combines the gunfire, the cannonades, the cease-fire, the scents, and the stench of putrefaction into a symphony. War is beautiful because it creates new architecture, like that of the big tanks, the geometrical formation flights, the smoke spirals from burning villages, and many others. . . . Poets and artists of Futurism! . . . remember these principles of an aesthetics of war so that your struggle for a

---

[36]One technical feature is significant here, especially with regard to newsreels, the propagandist importance of which can hardly be overestimated. Mass reproduction is aided especially by the reproduction of masses. In big parades and monster rallies, in sports events, and in war, all of which nowadays are captured by camera and sound recording, the masses are brought face to face with themselves. This process, whose significance need not be stressed, is intimately connected with the development of the techniques of reproduction and photography. Mass movements are usually discerned more clearly by a camera than by the naked eye. A bird's-eye view best captures gatherings of hundreds of thousands. And even though such a view may be as accessible to the human eye as it is to the camera, the image received

by the eye cannot be enlarged the way a negative is enlarged. This means that mass movements, including war, constitute a form of human behavior which particularly favors mechanical equipment. [Au.]

[37]Italian-French futurist writer and enthusiastic backer of Mussolini (1876–1944), author of *Guerra sola igiene del mundo* (*War — Sole Hygiene of the World*, 1915). [Ed.]

new literature and a new graphic art . . . may be illumined by them!"

This manifesto has the virtue of clarity. Its formulations deserve to be accepted by dialecticians. To the latter, the aesthetics of today's war appears as follows: If the natural utilization of productive forces is impeded by the property system, the increase in technical devices, in speed, and in the sources of energy will press for an unnatural utilization, and this is found in war. The destructiveness of war furnishes proof that society has not been mature enough to incorporate technology as its organ, that technology has not been sufficiently developed to cope with the elemental forces of society. The horrible features of imperialistic warfare are attributable to the discrepancy between the tremendous means of production and their inadequate utilization in the process of production — in other words, to unemployment and the lack of markets. Imperialistic war is a rebellion of technology which collects, in the form of "human material," the claims

to which society has denied its natural material. Instead of draining rivers, society directs a human stream into a bed of trenches; instead of dropping seeds from airplanes, it drops incendiary bombs over cities; and through gas warfare the aura is abolished in a new way.

*"Fiat ars — pereat mundus,"*[38] says Fascism, and, as Marinetti admits, expects war to supply the artistic gratification of a sense perception that has been changed by technology. This is evidently the consummation of *"l'art pour l'art."* Mankind, which in Homer's time was an object of contemplation for the Olympian gods, now is one for itself. Its self-alienation has reached such a degree that it can experience its own destruction as an aesthetic pleasure of the first order. This is the situation of politics which Fascism is rendering aesthetic. Communism responds by politicizing art.

[38]Let art exist, let the world perish. [Ed.]

# Edmund Wilson
## 1895–1972

*In a career spanning over forty years, Edmund Wilson came to be widely recognized as the leading man of letters in the United States. Raised in genteel circumstances in Red Bank, New Jersey, Wilson attended Princeton University and served in the U.S. Army in France in World War I. He became the literary editor of* The New Republic *in 1926, and the appearance of* Axel's Castle *in 1931 established his reputation as a proponent of the modernist tradition. In 1938, the first year of his stormy marriage to the novelist and critic Mary McCarthy, he published the first edition of* The Triple Thinkers. *The revised edition (1948) would contain "The Historical Interpretation of Literature," originally delivered as a university lecture in 1941. An international traveler and no less intellectually peripatetic, he assimilated Marxist (*To the Finland Station, *1940) and Freudian (*The Wound and the Bow, *1941) ideas, edited F. Scott Fitzgerald's unfinished* The Last Tycoon, *and learned Hebrew in order to write a study of the Dead Sea Scrolls (1955). His complex "Civil War book,"* Patriotic Gore *(1962) is generally considered a classic; less well known are* A Piece of My Mind: Reflections at Sixty *(1956) and* The Fruits of the MLA *(1968), which testify to his often acerbic disposition in the traditional role of culture critic.*

# The Historical Interpretation of Literature

I want to talk about the historical interpretation of literature — that is, about the interpretation of literature in its social, economic, and political aspects.

To begin with, it will be worthwhile to say something about the kind of criticism which seems to be furthest removed from this. There is a kind of comparative criticism which tends to be nonhistorical. The essays of T. S. Eliot, which have had such an immense influence in our time, are, for example, fundamentally nonhistorical. Eliot sees, or tries to see, the whole of literature, so far as he is acquainted with it, spread out before him under the aspect of eternity. He then compares the work of different periods and countries, and tries to draw from it general conclusions about what literature ought to be. He understands, of course, that our point of view in connection with literature changes, and he has what seems to me a very sound conception of the whole body of writing of the past as something to which new works are continually being added, and which is not thereby merely increased in bulk but modified as a whole — so that Sophocles is no longer precisely what he was for Aristotle, or Shakespeare what he was for Ben Jonson or for Dryden or for Dr. Johnson, on account of all the later literature that has intervened between them and us. Yet at every point of this continual accretion, the whole field may be surveyed, as it were, spread out before the critic.[1] The critic tries to see it as God might; he calls the books to a Day of Judgment. And, looking at things in this way, he may arrive at interesting and valuable conclusions which could hardly be reached by approaching them in any other way. Eliot was able to see, for example — what I believe had never been noticed before — that the French Symbolist poetry of the nineteenth century had certain fundamental resemblances to the English poetry of the age of Donne. Another kind of critic would draw certain historical conclusions from these purely esthetic findings, as the Russian D. S. Mirsky[2] did; but Eliot does not draw them.

Another example of this kind of nonhistorical criticism, in a somewhat different way and on a somewhat different plane, is the work of the late George Saintsbury. Saintsbury was a connoisseur of wines; he wrote an entertaining book on the subject.[3] And his attitude toward literature, too, was that of the connoisseur. He tastes the authors and tells you about the vintages; he distinguishes the qualities of the various wines. His palate was as fine as could be, and he possessed the great qualification that he knew how to take each book on its own terms without expecting it to be some other book and was thus in a position to appreciate a great variety of kinds of writing. He was a man of strong social prejudices and peculiarly intransigent political views, but, so far as it is humanly possible, he kept them out of his literary criticism. The result is one of the most agreeable and most comprehensive commentaries on literature that have ever been written in English. Most scholars who have read as much as Saintsbury do not have Saintsbury's discriminating taste. Here is a critic who has covered the whole ground like any academic historian, yet whose account of it is not merely a chronology but a record of fastidious enjoyment. Since enjoyment is the only thing he is looking for, he does not need to know the causes of things, and the historical background of literature does not interest him very much.

[1] See Eliot, "Tradition and the Individual Talent," pp. 467–68. [Ed.]

[2] Prince Dmitri Svyatopolk Mirsky, Russian literary historian (1890–?). [Ed.]

[3] *Notes on a Cellarbook* (1920), by George Saintsbury, English literary historian, professor at Edinburgh University (1845–1933). [Ed.]

There is, however, another tradition of criticism which dates from the beginning of the eighteenth century. In the year 1725, the Neapolitan philosopher Vico published *La Scienza Nuova,* a revolutionary work on the philosophy of history, in which he asserted for the first time that the social world was certainly the work of man, and attempted what is, so far as I know, the first social interpretation of a work of literature. This is what Vico says about Homer: "Homer composed the *Iliad* when Greece was young and consequently burning with sublime passions such as pride, anger, and vengeance — passions which cannot allow dissimulation and which consort with generosity; so that she then admired Achilles, the hero of force. But, grown old, he composed the *Odyssey,* at a time when the passions of Greece were already somewhat cooled by reflection, which is the mother of prudence — so that she now admired Ulysses, the hero of wisdom. Thus also, in Homer's youth, the Greek people liked cruelty, vituperation, savagery, fierceness, ferocity; whereas, when Homer was old, they were already enjoying the luxuries of Alcinoüs, the delights of Calypso, the pleasures of Circe, the songs of the sirens and the pastimes of the suitors, who went no further in aggression and combat than laying siege to the chaste Penelope — all of which practices would appear incompatible with the spirit of the earlier time. The divine Plato is so struck by this difficulty that, in order to solve it, he tells us that Homer had foreseen in inspired vision these dissolute, sickly and disgusting customs. But in this way he makes Homer out to have been but a foolish instructor for Greek civilization, since, however much he may condemn them, he is displaying for imitation these corrupt and decadent habits which were not to be adopted till long after the foundation of the nations of Greece, and accelerating the natural course which human events would take by spurring the Greeks on to corruption. Thus it is plain that the Homer of the *Iliad* must have preceded by many years the Homer who wrote the *Odyssey*; and it is plain that the former must belong to the northeastern part of Greece, since he celebrates the Trojan War, which took place in his part of the country, whereas the latter belongs to the southeastern part, since he celebrates Ulysses, who reigned there."

You see that Vico has here explained Homer in terms both of historical period and of geographical origin. The idea that human arts and institutions were to be studied and elucidated as the products of the geographical and climatic conditions in which the people who created them lived, and of the phase of their social development through which they were passing at the moment, made great progress during the eighteenth century. There are traces of it even in Dr. Johnson, that most orthodox and classical of critics — as, for example, when he accounts for certain characteristics of Shakespeare by the relative barbarity of the age in which he lived, pointing out, just as Vico had done, that "nations, like individuals, have their infancy."[4] And by the eighties of the eighteenth century Herder, in his *Ideas on the Philosophy of History,* was writing of poetry that it was a kind of "Proteus among the people, which is always changing its form in response to the languages, manners, and habits, to the temperaments and climates, nay even to the accents of different nations." He said — what could still seem startling even so late as that — that "language was not a divine communication, but something men had produced themselves."[5] In the lectures on the philosophy of history that Hegel delivered in Berlin in 1822–23, he discussed the national literatures as expressions of the societies which had produced them — societies which he conceived as great organisms continually transforming themselves under the influence of a succession of dominant ideas.

In the field of literary criticism, this historical point of view came to its first complete flower in the work of the French critic Taine, in the middle of the nineteenth century. The whole school of historian-critics to which Taine belonged — Michelet, Renan, Sainte-Beuve — had been occupied in interpreting books in terms of their historical origins. But Taine was the first of

[4] See Johnson, "Preface to Shakespeare," p. 229. [Ed.]
[5] Johann Gottfried von Herder (1744–1803), German aesthetician and philosopher; his *Ideas on the Philosophy of History of Humanity* came out 1784–91. [Ed.]

these to attempt to apply such principles systematically and on a large scale in a work devoted exclusively to literature. In the Introduction to his *History of English Literature,* published in 1853, he made his famous pronouncement that works of literature were to be understood as the upshot of three interfusing factors: *the moment, the race and the milieu.* Taine thought he was a scientist and a mechanist, who was examining works of literature from the same point of view as the chemist's in experimenting with chemical compounds. But the difference between the critic and the chemist is that the critic cannot first combine his elements and then watch to see what they will do: he can only examine phenomena which have already taken place. The procedure that Taine actually follows is to pretend to set the stage for the experiment by describing the moment, the race and the milieu, and then to say: "Such a situation demands such and such a kind of writer." He now goes on to describe the kind of writer that the situation demands, and the reader finds himself at the end confronted with Shakespeare or Milton or Byron or whoever the great figure is — who turns out to prove the accuracy of Taine's prognosis by precisely living up to this description.

There was thus a certain element of imposture in Taine; but it was the rabbits he pulled out that saved him. If he had really been the mechanist that he thought he was, his work on literature would have had little value. The truth was that Taine loved literature for its own sake — he was at his best himself a brilliant artist — and he had very strong moral convictions which give his writing emotional power. His mind, to be sure, was an analytic one, and his analysis, though terribly oversimplified, does have an explanatory value. Yet his work was what we call creative. Whatever he may say about chemical experiments, it is evident when he writes of a great writer that the moment, the race and the milieu have combined, like the three sounds of the chord in Browning's poem about Abt Vogler, to produce not a fourth sound but a star.

To Taine's set of elements was added, dating from the middle of the century, a new element, the economic, which was introduced into the discussion of historical phenomena mainly by Marx and Engels. The non-Marxist critics themselves were at the time already taking into account the influence of the social classes. In his chapters on the Norman conquest of England, Taine shows that the difference between the literatures produced respectively by the Normans and by the Saxons was partly the difference between a ruling class, on the one hand, and a vanquished and repressed class, on the other. And Michelet, in his volume on the Regency, which was finished the same year that the *History of English Literature* appeared, studies the *Manon Lescaut* of the Abbé Prévost as a document representing the point of view of the small gentry before the French Revolution. But Marx and Engels derived the social classes from the way that people made or got their livings — from what they called the *methods of production;* and they tended to regard these economic processes as fundamental to civilization.

The Dialectical Materialism of Marx and Engels was not really so materialistic as it sounds. There was in it a large element of the Hegelian idealism that Marx and Engels thought they had got rid of. At no time did these two famous materialists take so mechanistic a view of things as Taine began by professing; and their theory of the relation of works of literature to what they called the *economic base* was a good deal less simple than Taine's theory of the moment, the race and the milieu. They thought that art, politics, religion, philosophy and literature belonged to what they called the *superstructure* of human activity; but they saw that the practitioners of these various professions tended also to constitute social groups, and that they were always pulling away from the kind of solidarity based on economic classes in order to establish a professional solidarity of their own. Furthermore, the activities of the superstructure could influence one another, and they could influence the economic base. It may be said of Marx and Engels in general that, contrary to the popular impression, they were tentative, confused and modest when it came down to philosophical first principles, where a materialist like Taine was cocksure. Marx once made an attempt to explain why the poems of Homer were so good when the society that produced them was from his point of view — that is, from the point of view of its industrial development — so primitive; and this gave him a good deal of trouble.[6] If we compare his discussion of this problem with Vico's discussion of Homer, we see that the explanation of literature in terms of a philosophy of social history is becoming, instead of simpler and easier, more difficult and more complex.

Marx and Engels were deeply imbued, moreover, with the German admiration for literature, which they had learned from the age of Goethe. It would never have occurred to either of them that *der Dichter*[7] was not one of the noblest and most beneficent of humankind. When Engels writes about Goethe, he presents him as a man equipped for "practical life," whose career was frustrated by the "misery" of the historical situation in Germany in his time, and reproaches him for allowing himself to lapse into the "cautious, smug, and narrow" philistinism of the class from which he came; but Engels regrets this, because it interfered with the development of the "mocking, defiant, world-despising genius," "der geniale Dichter," "der gewaltige Poet,"[8] of whom Engels would not even, he says, have asked that he should have been a political liberal if Goethe had not sacrificed to his bourgeois shrinkings his truer esthetic sense. And the great critics who were trained on Marx — Franz Mehring[9] and Bernard Shaw — had all this reverence for the priesthood of literature. Shaw deplores the absence of political philosophy and what he regards as the middle-class snobbery in Shakespeare; but he celebrates Shakespeare's poetry and his dramatic imagination almost as enthusiastically as Swinburne does, describing even those potboiling comedies, *Twelfth Night* and *As You Like It* — the themes of which seem to him most trashy — as "the Crown Jewels of English dramatic poetry." Such a critic may do more for a writer

by showing him as a real man dealing with a real world at a definite moment of time than the impressionist critic of Swinburne's type who flourished in the same period of the late nineteenth century. The purely impressionist critic approaches the whole of literature as an exhibit of belletristic jewels, and he can only write a rhapsodic catalogue. But when Shaw turned his spotlight on Shakespeare as a figure in the Shavian drama of history, he invested him with a new interest as no other English critic had done.

The insistence that the man of letters should play a political role, the disparagement of works of art in comparison with political action, were thus originally no part of Marxism. They only became associated with it later. This happened by way of Russia, and it was due to special tendencies in that country that date from long before the Revolution or the promulgation of Marxism itself. In Russia there have been very good reasons why the political implications of literature should particularly occupy the critics. The art of Pushkin itself, with its marvelous power of implication, had certainly been partly created by the censorship of Nicholas I, and Pushkin set the tradition for most of the great Russian writers that followed him. Every play, every poem, every story, must be a parable of which the moral is *implied*. If it were stated, the censor would suppress the book as he tried to do with Pushkin's *Bronze Horseman*, where it was merely a question of the packed implications protruding a little too plainly. Right down through the writings of Chekhov and up almost to the Revolution, the imaginative literature of Russia presents the peculiar paradox of an art that is technically objective and yet charged with social messages. In Russia under the Tsar, it was inevitable that social criticism should lead to political conclusions, because the most urgent need from the point of view of any kind of improvement was to get rid of the tsarist regime. Even the neo-Christian moralist Tolstoy, who pretended to be non-political, was to exert a subversive influence, because his independent preaching was bound to embroil him with the Church, and the Church was an integral part of the tsardom. Tolstoy's pamphlet called *What Is*

[6]See Marx, "Critique of Political Economy," p. 570. [Ed.]

[7]The literary writer. [Ed.]

[8]"The genial author, the powerful poet." [Ed.]

[9]Franz Mehring, (1846–1919), social-democratic journalist, biographer of Marx, ally of Rosa Luxemburg and the Spartacists. [Ed.]

*Art?*, in which he throws overboard Shakespeare and a large part of modern literature, including his own novels, in the interest of his intransigent morality, is the example which is most familiar to us of the moralizing Russian criticism;[10] but it was only the most sensational expression of a kind of approach which had been prevalent since Belinsky and Chernyshevsky in the early part of the century. The critics, who were usually journalists writing in exile or in a contraband press, were always tending to demand of the imaginative writers that they should dramatize bolder morals.

Even after the Revolution had destroyed the tsarist government, this state of things did not change. The old habits of censorship persisted in the new socialist society of the Soviets, which was necessarily made up of people who had been stamped by the die of the despotism. We meet here the peculiar phenomenon of a series of literary groups that attempt, one after the other, to obtain official recognition or to make themselves sufficiently powerful to establish themselves as arbiters of literature. Lenin and Trotsky and Lunacharsky had the sense to oppose these attempts: the comrade-dictators of Proletcult or Lev or Rapp[11] would certainly have been just as bad as the Count Benckendorff who made Pushkin miserable, and when the Stalin bureaucracy, after the death of Gorky, got control of this department as of everything else, they instituted a system of repression that made Benckendorff and Nicholas I look like Lorenzo de' Medici. In the meantime, Trotsky, who was the Commissar of War but himself a great political writer with an interest in belles-lettres, attempted, in 1924, apropos of one of these movements, to clarify the situation. He wrote a brilliant and valuable book called *Literature and Revolution*, in which he explained the aims of the government, analyzed the work of the Russian writers, and praised or rebuked the latter as they seemed to him in harmony or at odds with the former. Trotsky is intelligent, sympathetic; it is evident that he is really fond of literature and that he knows that a work of art does not fulfill its function in terms of the formulas of party propaganda. But Mayakovsky, the Soviet poet, whom Trotsky had praised with reservations, expressed himself in a famous joke when he was asked what he thought of Trotsky's book — a pun which implied that a Commissar turned critic was inevitably a Commissar still;[12] and what a foreigner cannot accept in Trotsky is his assumption that it is the duty of the government to take a hand in the direction of literature.

This point of view, indigenous to Russia, has been imported to other countries through the permeation of Communist influence. The Communist press and its literary followers have reflected the control of the Kremlin in all the phases through which it has passed, down to the wholesale imprisonment of Soviet writers which has been taking place since 1935. But it has never been a part of the American system that our Republican or Democratic administration should lay down a political line for the guidance of the national literature. A recent gesture in this direction on the part of Archibald MacLeish, who seems a little carried away by his position as Librarian of Congress, was anything but cordially received by serious American writers. So long as the United States remains happily a nontotalitarian country, we can very well do without this aspect of the historical criticism of literature.

Another element of a different order has, however, since Marx's time been added to the historical study of the origins of works of literature. I mean the psychoanalysis of Freud. This appears as an extension of something which had already got well started before, which had figured even in Johnson's *Lives of the Poets* and of which the great exponent had been Sainte-Beuve: the interpretation of works of literature in the light of the personalities behind them. But the Freudians made this interpretation more exact and more systematic. The great example of the psychoanalysis of an artist is Freud's own essay on

---

[10]See Tolstoy, "What is Art?" p. 437. [Ed.]

[11]RAPP was the Russian union of writers after the Bolshevik revolution; following the death of Lenin it became an instrument of oppression. [Ed.]

[12]Первый блин лег наркомом, The first pancake lies like a narkom (people's commissar) — a parody of the Russian saying, Первый блин лег комом, The first pancake lies like a lump. [Au.]

Leonardo da Vinci; but this has little critical interest: it is an attempt to construct a case history. One of the best examples I know of the application of Freudian analysis to literature is in Van Wyck Brooks's book, *The Ordeal of Mark Twain,* in which Mr. Brooks uses an incident of Mark Twain's boyhood as a key to his whole career. Mr. Brooks has since repudiated the method he resorted to here, on the ground that no one but an analyst can ever know enough about a writer to make a valid psychoanalytic diagnosis. This is true, and it is true of the method that it has led to bad results where the critic has built a Freudian mechanism out of very slender evidence, and then given us what is really merely a romance exploiting the supposed working of this mechanism, in place of an actual study that sticks close to the facts and the documents of the writer's life and work. But I believe that Van Wyck Brooks really had hold of something important when he fixed upon that childhood incident of which Mark Twain gave so vivid an account to his biographer — that scene at the deathbed of his father when his mother had made him promise that he would not break her heart. If it was not one of those crucial happenings that are supposed to determine the complexes of Freud, it has certainly a typical significance in relation to Mark Twain's whole psychology. The stories that people tell about their childhood are likely to be profoundly symbolic even when they have been partly or wholly made up in the light of later experience. And the attitudes, the compulsions, the emotional "patterns" that recur in the work of a writer are of great interest to the historical critic.

These attitudes and patterns are embedded in the community and the historical moment, and they may indicate its ideals and its diseases as the cell shows the condition of the tissue. The recent scientific experimentation in the combining of Freudian with Marxist method, and of psychoanalysis with anthropology, has had its parallel development in criticism. And there is thus another element added to our equipment for analyzing literary works, and the problem grows still more complex.

The analyst, however, is of course not concerned with the comparative values of his patients any more than the surgeon is. He cannot tell you why the neurotic Dostoevsky produces work of immense value to his fellows while another man with the same neurotic pattern would become a public menace. Freud himself emphatically states in his study of Leonardo that his method can make no attempt to account for Leonardo's genius. The problems of comparative artistic value still remain after we have given attention to the Freudian psychological factor just as they do after we have given attention to the Marxist economic factor and to the racial and geographical factors. No matter how thoroughly and searchingly we may have scrutinized works of literature from the historical and biographical points of view, we must be ready to attempt to estimate, in some such way as Saintsbury and Eliot do, the relative degrees of success attained by the products of the various periods and the various personalities. We must be able to tell good from bad, the first-rate from the second-rate. We shall not otherwise write literary criticism at all, but merely social or political history as reflected in literary texts, or psychological case histories from past eras, or, to take the historical point of view in its simplest and most academic form, merely chronologies of books that have been published.

And now how, in these matters of literary art, do we tell the good art from the bad? Norman Kemp Smith, the Kantian philosopher, whose courses I was fortunate enough to take at Princeton twenty-five years ago, used to tell us that this recognition was based primarily on an emotional reaction.[13] For purposes of practical criticism this is a safe assumption on which to proceed. It is possible to discriminate in a variety of ways the elements that in any given department go to make a successful work of literature. Different schools have at different times demanded different things of literature: *unity, symmetry, universality, originality, vision, inspiration, strangeness, suggestiveness, improving morality, socialist realism,*

---

[13]See Kant, *Critique of Judgment,* p. 248. [Ed.]

etc. But you could have any set of these qualities that any school of writing has called for and still not have a good play, a good novel, a good poem, a good history. If you identify the essence of good literature with any one of these elements or with any combination of them, you simply shift the emotional reaction to the recognition of the element or elements. Or if you add to your other demands the demand that the writer must have *talent,* you simply shift this recognition to the talent. Once people find some grounds of agreement in the coincidence of their emotional reactions to books, they may be able to discuss these elements profitably; but if they do not have this basic agreement, the discussion will make no sense.

But how, you may ask, can we identify this élite who know what they are talking about? Well, it can only be said of them that they are self-appointed and self-perpetuating, and that they will compel you to accept their authority. Impostors may try to put themselves over, but these quacks will not last. The implied position of the people who know about literature (as is also the case in every other art) is simply that they know what they know, and that they are determined to impose their opinions by main force of eloquence or assertion on the people who do not know. This is not a question, of course, of professional workers in literature — such as editors, professors and critics, who very often have no real understanding of the products with which they deal — but of readers of all kinds in all walks of life. There are moments when a first-rate writer, unrecognized or out of fashion with the official chalkers-up for the market, may find his support in the demand for his work of an appreciative cultivated public.

But what is the cause of this emotional reaction which is the critic's divining rod? This question has long been a subject of study by the branch of philosophy called esthetics, and it has recently been made a subject of scientific experimentation. Both these lines of inquiry are likely to be prejudiced in the eyes of the literary critic by the fact that the inquiries are sometimes conducted by persons who are obviously deficient in literary feeling or taste. Yet one should

not deny the possibility that something of value might result from the speculations and explorations of men of acute minds who take as their primary data the esthetic emotions of other men.

Almost everybody interested in literature has tried to explain to himself the nature of these emotions that register our approval of artistic works; and I of course have my own explanation.

In my view, all our intellectual activity, in whatever field it takes place, is an attempt to give a meaning to our experience — that is, to make life more practicable; for by understanding things we make it easier to survive and get around them. The mathematician Euclid, working in a convention of abstractions, shows us relations between the distances of our unwieldy and cluttered-up environment upon which we are able to count. A drama of Sophocles also indicates relations between the various human impulses, which appear so confused and dangerous, and it brings out a certain justice of Fate — that is to say, of the way in which the interaction of these impulses is seen in the long run to work out — upon which we can also depend. The kinship, from this point of view, of the purposes of science and art appears very clearly in the case of the Greeks, because not only do both Euclid and Sophocles satisfy us by making patterns, but they make much the same kind of patterns. Euclid's *Elements* takes simple theorems and by a series of logical operations builds them up to a climax in the square on the hypotenuse. A typical drama of Sophocles develops in a similar way.

Some writers (as well as some scientists) have a different kind of explicit message beyond the reassurance implicit in the mere feat of understanding life or of molding the harmony of artistic form. Not content with such an achievement as that of Sophocles — who has one of his choruses tell us that it is better not to born,[14] but who, by representing life as noble and based on law, makes its tragedy easier to bear — such writers attempt, like Plato, to think out and recommend a procedure for turning it into something better. But other departments of literature

[14]In *Oedipus at Colonus.* [Ed.]

— lyric poetry such as Sappho's, for example — have *less* philosophical content than Sophocles. A lyric gives us nothing but a pattern imposed on the expression of a feeling; but this pattern of metrical quantities and of consonants and vowels that balance has the effect of reducing the feeling, however unruly or painful it may seem when we experience it in the course of our lives, to something orderly, symmetrical, and pleasing; and it also relates this feeling to the more impressive scheme, works it into the larger texture, of the body of poetic art. The discord has been resolved, the anomaly subjected to discipline. And this control of his emotion by the poet has the effect at second-hand of making it easier for the reader to manage his own emotions. (Why certain sounds and rhythms gratify us more than others, and how they are connected with the themes and ideas that they are chosen as appropriate for conveying, are questions that may be passed on to the scientist.)

And this brings us back again to the historical point of view. The experience of mankind on the earth is always changing as man develops and has to deal with new combinations of elements; and the writer who is to be anything more than an echo of his predecessors must always find expression for something which has never yet been expressed, must master a new set of phenomena which has never yet been mastered. With each such victory of the human intellect, whether in history, in philosophy or in poetry, we experience a deep satisfaction: we have been cured of some ache of disorder, relieved of some oppressive burden of uncomprehended events.

This relief that brings the sense of power, and, with the sense of power, joy, is the positive emotion which tells us that we have encountered a first-rate piece of literature. But stay! you may at this point warn: are not people often solaced and exhilarated by literature of the trashiest kind? They are: crude and limited people do certainly feel some such emotion in connection with work that is limited and crude. The man who is more highly organized and has a wider intellectual range will feel it in connection with work that is finer and more complex. The difference between the emotion of the more highly organized man and the emotion of the less highly organized one is a matter of mere gradation. You sometimes discover books — the novels of John Steinbeck, for example — that seem to mark precisely the borderline between work that is definitely superior and work that is definitely bad. When I was speaking a little while back of the genuine connoisseurs who establish the standards of taste, I meant, of course, the people who can distinguish Grade A and who prefer it to the other grades.

# Georg Lukács
## 1885–1971

*The most influential Marxist aesthetician of the first half of this century, Georg Lukács was the son of a wealthy Hungarian family. Lukács wrote several essays on aesthetic and literary theory (including* Soul and Form *[1910],* Aesthetic Culture *[1913], and his influential* Theory of the Novel *[written 1916, published 1920]) in a Hegelian phase before joining the Hungarian Communist party in 1918. In 1919 he began a stint as commissar for culture and education in the regime of Bela Kun, an appointment that ended with the fall of Kun. Lukács left Hungary and settled in Vienna, where he produced* History and Class Consciousness *(1923), his most influential work of political theory. Driven by waves of political controversy, Lukács spent 1929–31 in Moscow, then moved to Berlin. When the Nazis came to power in 1933, he returned to Moscow, taking a post at the Soviet Academy of Sciences (1933–44). He managed, as a great many Central European intellectuals did not, to survive the Stalinist purges of 1937–38; it was in this dark time that he wrote* The Historical Novel *(published in English in 1962). Lukács was not to return to Hungary until the more receptive political climate of 1945, when he was made a parliamentary minister and professor of aesthetics* and cultural philosophy at the University of Budapest. In 1956, the year he wrote "The Ideology of Modernism," Lukács was again unseated by a political uprising and deported to Rumania, but he was allowed to return the following year. His late works include a two-volume treatise on Marxist aesthetics (1962) and a work on social ontology (1973).

# The Ideology of Modernism

It is in no way surprising that the most influential contemporary school of writing should still be committed to the dogmas of "modernist" antirealism. It is here that we must begin our investigation if we are to chart the possibilities of a bourgeois realism. We must compare the two main trends in contemporary bourgeois literature, and look at the answers they give to the major ideological and artistic questions of our time.

We shall concentrate on the underlying ideological basis of these trends (ideological in the above-defined, not in the strictly philosophical, sense). What must be avoided at all costs is the approach generally adopted by bourgeois-modernist critics themselves: that exaggerated concern with formal criteria, with questions of style and literary technique. This approach may appear to distinguish sharply between "modern" and "traditional" writing (i.e., contemporary writers who adhere to the styles of the last century). In fact, it fails to locate the decisive formal problems and turns a blind eye to their inherent dialectic. We are presented with a false polarization which, by exaggerating the importance of stylistic differences, conceals the opposing principles actually underlying and determining contrasting styles.

To take an example: the *monologue intérieur*. Compare, for instance, Bloom's monologue in the lavatory or Molly's monologue in bed, at the beginning and at the end of *Ulysses*, with Goethe's early-morning monologue as conceived by Thomas Mann in his *Lotte in Weimar*. Plainly, the same stylistic technique is being employed. And certain of Thomas Mann's remarks about Joyce and his methods would appear to confirm this.

Translated by John and Necke Mander.

Yet it is not easy to think of any two novels more basically dissimilar than *Ulysses* and *Lotte in Weimar*. This is true even of the superficially rather similar scenes I have indicated. I am not referring to the — to my mind — striking difference in intellectual quality. I refer to the fact that with Joyce the stream-of-consciousness technique is no mere stylistic device; it is itself the formative principle governing the narrative pattern and the presentation of character. Technique here is something absolute; it is part and parcel of the aesthetic ambition informing *Ulysses*. With Thomas Mann, on the other hand, the *monologue intérieur* is simply a technical device, allowing the author to explore aspects of Goethe's world which would not have been otherwise available. Goethe's experience is not presented as confined to momentary sense-impressions. The artist reaches down to the core of Goethe's personality, to the complexity of his relations with his own past, present, and even future experience. The stream of association is only apparently free. The monologue is composed with the utmost artistic rigor: it is a carefully plotted sequence gradually piercing to the core of Goethe's personality. Every person or event, emerging momentarily from the stream and vanishing again, is given a specific weight, a definite position, in the pattern of the whole. However unconventional the presentation, the compositional principle is that of the traditional epic; in the way the pace is controlled, and the transitions and climaxes are organized, the ancient rules of epic narration are faithfully observed.

It would be absurd, in view of Joyce's artistic ambitions and his manifest abilities, to qualify the exaggerated attention he gives to the detailed recording of sense-data, and his comparative neglect of ideas and emotions, as artistic failure. All this was in conformity with Joyce's artistic intentions; and, by use of such techniques, he may be said to have achieved them satisfactorily. But between Joyce's intentions and those of Thomas Mann there is a total opposition. The perpetually oscillating patterns of sense- and memory-data, their powerfully charged — but aimless and directionless — fields of force, give rise to an epic structure which is *static,* reflecting a belief in the basically static character of events.

These opposed views of the world — dynamic and developmental on the one hand, static and sensational on the other — are of crucial importance in examining the two schools of literature I have mentioned. I shall return to the opposition later. Here, I want only to point out that an exclusive emphasis on formal matters can lead to serious misunderstanding of the character of an artist's work.

What determines the style of a given work of art? How does the intention determine the form? (We are concerned here, of course, with the intention realized in the work; it need not coincide with the writer's conscious intention.) The distinctions that concern us are not those between stylistic "techniques" in the formalistic sense. It is the view of the world, the ideology or *weltanschauung*[1] underlying a writer's work, that counts. And it is the writer's attempt to reproduce this view of the world which constitutes his "intention" and is the formative principle underlying the style of a given piece of writing. Looked at in this way, style ceases to be a formalistic category. Rather, it is rooted in content; it is the specific form of a specific content.

Content determines form. But there is no content of which Man himself is not the focal point. However various the *données*[2] of literature (a particular experience, a didactic purpose), the basic question is, and will remain: what is Man?

Here is a point of division: if we put the question in abstract, philosophical terms, leaving aside all formal considerations, we arrive — for

the realist school — at the traditional Aristotelian dictum (which was also reached by other than purely aesthetic considerations): Man is *zoon politikon,* a social animal. The Aristotelian dictum is applicable to all great realistic literature. Achilles and Werther, Oedipus and Tom Jones, Antigone, and Anna Karenina: their individual existence — their *Sein an sich,*[3] in the Hegelian terminology; their "ontological being," as a more fashionable terminology has it — cannot be distinguished from their social and historical environment. Their human significance, their specific individuality cannot be separated from the context in which they were created.

The ontological view governing the image of man in the work of leading modernist writers is the exact opposite of this. Man, for these writers, is by nature solitary, asocial, unable to enter into relationships with other human beings. Thomas Wolfe once wrote: "My view of the world is based on the firm conviction that solitariness is by no means a rare condition, something peculiar to myself or to a few specially solitary human beings, but the inescapable, central fact of human existence." Man, thus imagined, may establish contact with other individuals, but only in a superficial, accidental manner; only, ontologically speaking, by retrospective reflection. For "the others," too, are basically solitary, beyond significant human relationship.

This basic solitariness of man must not be confused with that individual solitariness to be found in the literature of traditional realism. In the latter case, we are dealing with a particular situation in which a human being may be placed, due either to his character or to the circumstances of his life. Solitariness may be objectively conditioned, as with Sophocles' Philoctetes, put ashore on the bleak island of Lemnos. Or it may be subjective, the product of inner necessity, as with Tolstoy's Ivan Ilyitsch or Flaubert's Frédéric Moreau in the *Education Sentimentale.* But it is always merely a fragment, a phase, a climax, or anticlimax, in the life of the community as a whole. The fate of such individuals is character-

[1]World-picture. [Ed.]
[2]What is given: the subject matter chosen by the author. [Ed.]

[3]Being in itself. [Ed.]

istic of certain human types in specific social or historical circumstances. Beside and beyond their solitariness, the common life, the strife and togetherness of other human beings, goes on as before. In a word, their solitariness is a specific social fate, not a universal *condition humaine*.

The latter, of course, is characteristic of the theory and practice of modernism. I would like, in the present study, to spare the reader tedious excursions into philosophy. But I cannot refrain from drawing the reader's attention to Heidegger's description of human existence as a "thrownness-into-being" (*Geworfenheit ins Dasein*). A more graphic evocation of the ontological solitariness of the individual would be hard to imagine. Man is "thrown-into-being." This implies, not merely that man is constitutionally unable to establish relationships with things or persons outside himself; but also that it is impossible to determine theoretically the origin and goal of human existence.

Man, thus conceived, is an ahistorical being. (The fact that Heidegger does admit a form of "authentic" historicity in his system is not really relevant. I have shown elsewhere that Heidegger tends to belittle historicity as "vulgar"; and his "authentic" historicity is not distinguishable from ahistoricity). This negation of history takes two different forms in modernist literature. First, the hero is strictly confined within the limits of his own experience. There is not for him — and apparently not for his creator — any preexistent reality beyond his own self, acting upon him or being acted upon by him. Secondly, the hero himself is without personal history. He is "thrown-into-the-world": meaninglessly, unfathomably. He does not develop through contact with the world; he neither forms nor is formed by it. The only "development" in this literature is the gradual revelation of the human condition. Man is now what he has always been and always will be. The narrator, the examining subject, is in motion; the examined reality is static.

Of course, dogmas of this kind are only really viable in philosophical abstraction, and then only with a measure of sophistry. A gifted writer, however extreme his theoretical modernism, will in practice have to compromise with the demands of historicity and of social environment. Joyce uses Dublin, Kafka and Musil the Hapsburg Monarchy, as the locus of their masterpieces.[4] But the locus they lovingly depict is little more than a backcloth; it is not basic to their artistic intention.

This view of human existence has specific literary consequences. Particularly in one category, of primary theoretical and practical importance, to which we must now give our attention: that of *potentiality*. Philosophy distinguishes between *abstract* and *concrete* (in Hegel, "real") *potentiality*. These two categories, their interrelation and opposition, are rooted in life itself. *Potentiality* — seen abstractly or subjectively — is richer than actual life. Innumerable possibilities for man's development are imaginable, only a small percentage of which will be realized. Modern subjectivism, taking these imagined possibilities for actual complexity of life, oscillates between melancholy and fascination. When the world declines to realize these possibilities, this melancholy becomes tinged with contempt. Hofmannsthal's Sobeide expressed the reaction of the generation first exposed to this experience:

> The burden of those endlessly pored-over
> And now forever perished possibilities . . .[5]

How far were those possibilities even concrete or "real"? Plainly, they existed only in the imagination of the subject, as dreams or daydreams. Faulkner, in whose work this subjective potentiality plays an important part, was evidently aware that reality must thereby be subjectivized and made to appear arbitrary. Consider this comment of his: "They were all talking simultaneously, getting flushed and excited, quarrelling, making the unreal into a possibility, then into a probability, then into an irrefutable fact, as human beings do when they put their wishes into words." The possibilities in a man's mind, the particular pattern, intensity and suggestiveness they assume, will of course be characteristic of

---

[4] *Ulysses, The Castle,* and *The Man without Qualities,* respectively. [Ed.]

[5] *Die Hochzeit von Sobeide* (1899), a drama by Hugo von Hofmannsthal (1874–1929). [Ed.]

that individual. In practice, their number will border on the infinite, even with the most unimaginative individual. It is thus a hopeless undertaking to define the contours of individuality, let alone to come to grips with a man's actual fate, by means of potentiality. The *abstract* character of potentiality is clear from the fact that it cannot determine development — subjective mental states, however permanent or profound, cannot here be decisive. Rather, the development of personality is determined by inherited gifts and qualities; by the factors, external or internal, which further or inhibit their growth.

But in life potentiality can, of course, become reality. Situations arise in which a man is confronted with a choice; and in the act of choice a man's character may reveal itself in a light that surprises even himself. In literature — and particularly in dramatic literature — the denouement often consists in the realization of just such a potentiality, which circumstances have kept from coming to the fore. These potentialities are, then, "real" or concrete potentialities. The fate of the character depends upon the potentiality in question, even if it should condemn him to a tragic end. In advance, while still a subjective potentiality in the character's mind, there is no way of distinguishing it from the innumerable abstract potentialities in his mind. It may even be buried away so completely that, before the moment of decision, it has never entered his mind even as an abstract potentiality. The subject, after taking his decision, may be unconscious of his own motives. Thus Richard Dudgeon, Shaw's Devil's Disciple, having sacrificed himself as Pastor Anderson, confesses: "I have often asked myself for the motive, but I find no good reason to explain why I acted as I did."

Yet it is a decision which has altered the direction of his life. Of course, this is an extreme case. But the qualitative leap of the denouement, cancelling and at the same time renewing the continuity of individual consciousness, can never be predicted. The concrete potentiality cannot be isolated from the myriad abstract potentialities. Only actual decision reveals the distinction.

The literature of realism, aiming at a truthful reflection of reality, must demonstrate both the concrete and abstract potentialities of human beings in extreme situations of this kind. A character's concrete potentiality once revealed, his abstract potentialities will appear essentially inauthentic. Moravia, for instance, in his novel *The Indifferent Ones,* describes the young son of a decadent bourgeois family, Michel, who makes up his mind to kill his sister's seducer. While Michel, having made his decision, is planning the murder, a large number of abstract — but highly suggestive — possibilities are laid before us. Unfortunately for Michel the murder is actually carried out; and, from the sordid details of the action, Michel's character emerges as what it is — representative of that background from which, in subjective fantasy, he had imagined he could escape.

Abstract potentiality belongs wholly to the realm of subjectivity; whereas concrete potentiality is concerned with the dialectic between the individual's subjectivity and objective reality. The literary presentation of the latter thus implies a description of actual persons inhabiting a palpable, identifiable world. Only in the interaction of character and environment can the concrete potentiality of a particular individual be singled out from the "bad infinity" of purely abstract potentialities, and emerge as the determining potentiality of just this individual at just this phase of his development. This principle alone enables the artist to distinguish concrete potentiality from a myriad abstractions.

But the ontology on which the image of man in modernist literature is based invalidates this principle. If the "human condition" — man as a solitary being, incapable of meaningful relationships — is identified with reality itself, the distinction between abstract and concrete potentiality becomes null and void. The categories tend to merge. Thus Cesare Pavese notes with John Dos Passos, and his German contemporary, Alfred Döblin, a sharp oscillation between "superficial *verisme*"[6] and "abstract Expressionist schematism." Criticizing Dos Passos, Pavese writes that fictional characters "ought to be cre-

---

[6] A crudely realistic style akin to newspaper reportage. [Ed.]

ated by deliberate selection and description of individual features" — implying that Dos Passos's characterizations are transferable from one individual to another. He describes the artistic consequences: by exalting man's subjectivity, at the expense of the objective reality of his environment, man's subjectivity itself is impoverished.

The problem, once again, is ideological. This is not to say that the ideology underlying modernist writings is identical in all cases. On the contrary: the ideology exists in extremely various, even contradictory forms. The rejection of narrative objectivity, the surrender to subjectivity, may take the form of Joyce's stream of consciousness, or of Musil's "active passivity," his "existence without quality," or of Gide's "*action gratuite*,"[7] where abstract potentiality achieves pseudo-realization. As individual character manifests itself in life's moments of decision, so too in literature. If the distinction between abstract and concrete potentiality vanishes, if man's inwardness is identified with an abstract subjectivity, human personality must necessarily disintegrate.

T. S. Eliot described this phenomenon, this mode of portraying human personality, as

Shape without form, shade without colour,
Paralysed force, gesture without motion.[8]

The disintegration of personality is matched by a disintegration of the outer world. In one sense, this is simply a further consequence of our argument. For the identification of abstract and concrete human potentiality rests on the assumption that the objective world is inherently inexplicable. Certain leading modernist writers, attempting a theoretical apology, have admitted this quite frankly. Often this theoretical impossibility of understanding reality is the point of departure, rather than the exaltation of subjectivity. But in any case the connection between the two is plain. The German poet Gottfried Benn, for instance, informs us that "there is no outer reality, there is only human consciousness, constantly building, modifying, rebuilding new worlds out of its own creativity." Musil, as always, gives a moral twist to this line of thought. Ulrich, the hero of his *The Man without Qualities,* when asked what he would do if he were in God's place, replies: "I should be compelled to abolish reality." Subjective existence "without qualities" is the complement of the negation of outward reality.

The negation of outward reality is not always demanded with such theoretical rigor. But it is present in almost all modernist literature. In conversation, Musil once gave as the period of his great novel, "between 1912 and 1914." But he was quick to modify this statement by adding: "I have not, I must insist, written a historical novel. I am not concerned with actual events. . . . Events, anyhow, are interchangeable. I am interested in what is typical, in what one might call the ghostly aspect of reality." The word "ghostly" is interesting. It points to a major tendency in modernist literature: the attenuation of actuality. In Kafka, the descriptive detail is of an extraordinary immediacy and authenticity. But Kafka's artistic ingenuity is really directed towards substituting his *angst*-ridden vision of the world for objective reality. The realistic detail is the expression of a ghostly un-reality, of a nightmare world, whose function is to evoke *angst*. The same phenomenon can be seen in writers who attempt to combine Kafka's techniques with a critique of society — like the German writer, Wolfgang Koeppen, in his satirical novel about Bonn, *Das Treibhaus*. A similar attenuation of reality underlies Joyce's stream of consciousness. It is, of course, intensified where the stream of consciousness is itself the medium through which reality is presented. And it is carried *ad absurdum* where the stream of consciousness is that of an abnormal subject or of an idiot — consider the first part of Faulkner's *Sound and Fury* or, a still more extreme case, Beckett's *Molloy*.

Attenuation of reality and dissolution of personality are thus interdependent: the stronger the one, the stronger the other. Underlying both is the lack of a consistent view of human nature.

7"Gratuitous act": a crime committed to prove one's freedom. [Ed.]
8"The Hollow Men" (1925). [Ed.]

Man is reduced to a sequence of unrelated experiential fragments; he is as inexplicable to others as to himself. In Eliot's *Cocktail Party* the psychiatrist, who voices the opinions of the author, describes the phenomenon:

Ah, but we die to each other daily
What we know of other people
Is only our memory of the moments
During which we knew them. And they have
    changed since then.
To pretend that they and we are the same
Is a useful and convenient social convention
Which must sometimes be broken. We must also
    remember
That at every meeting we are meeting a stranger.

The dissolution of personality, originally the unconscious product of the identification of concrete and abstract potentiality, is elevated to a deliberate principle in the light of consciousness. It is no accident that Gottfried Benn called one of his theoretical tracts "*Doppelleben.*"[9] For Benn, this dissolution of personality took the form of a schizophrenic dichotomy. According to him, there was in man's personality no coherent pattern of motivation or behavior. Man's animal nature is opposed to his denatured, sublimated thought processes. The unity of thought and action is "backwoods philosophy"; thought and being are "quite separate entities." Man must be either a moral or a thinking being — he cannot be both at once.

These are not, I think, purely private, eccentric speculations. Of course, they are derived from Benn's specific experience. But there is an inner connection between these ideas and a certain tradition of bourgeois thought. It is more than a hundred years since Kierkegaard first attacked the Hegelian view that the inner and outer world form an objective dialectical unity, that they are indissolubly married in spite of their apparent opposition. Kierkegaard denied any such unity. According to Kierkegaard, the individual exists within an opaque, impenetrable "incognito."

This philosophy attained remarkable popularity after the Second World War — proof that even the most abstruse theories may reflect social reality. Men like Martin Heidegger, Ernst Jünger, the lawyer Carl Schmitt, Gottfried Benn and others passionately embraced this doctrine of the eternal incognito which implies that a man's external deeds are no guide to his motives. In this case, the deeds obscured behind the mysterious incognito were, needless to say, these intellectuals' participation in Nazism: Heidegger, as Rector of Freiburg University, had glorified Hitler's seizure of power at his Inauguration; Carl Schmitt had put his great legal gifts at Hitler's disposal. The facts were too well known to be simply denied. But, if this impenetrable incognito were the true "*condition humaine,*"[10] might not — concealed within their incognito — Heidegger or Schmitt have been secret opponents of Hitler all the time, only supporting him in the world of appearances? Ernst von Salomon's cynical frankness about his opportunism in *The Questionnaire* (keeping his reservations to himself or declaring them only in the presence of intimate friends) may be read as an ironic commentary on this ideology of the incognito as we find it, say, in the writings of Ernst Jünger.

This digression may serve to show, taking an extreme example, what the social implications of such an ontology may be. In the literary field, this particular ideology was of cardinal importance; by destroying the complex tissue of man's relations with his environment, it furthered the dissolution of personality. For it is just the opposition between a man and his environment that determines the development of his personality. There is no great hero of fiction — from Homer's Achilles to Mann's Adrian Leverkühn or Sholochov's Grigory Melyekov[11] — whose personality is not the product of such an opposition. I have shown how disastrous the denial of the distinction between abstract and concrete potentiality must be for the presentation of character. The destruction of the complex tissue of man's interaction with his environment likewise saps the

---

[9]Double life. [Ed.]

[10]Human condition. Lukács's use of the French alludes to the Marxist novel about opposition to Fascism, *La condition humaine* (*Man's Fate*) by André Malraux. [Ed.]

[11]Heroes of the *Iliad*, *Doctor Faustus*, and *Quiet Flows the Don*. [Ed.]

vitality of this opposition. Certainly, some writers who adhere to this ideology have attempted, not unsuccessfully, to portray this opposition in concrete terms. But the underlying ideology deprives these contradictions of their dynamic, developmental significance. The contradictions coexist, unresolved, contributing to the further dissolution of the personality in question.

It is to the credit of Robert Musil that he was quite conscious of the implications of his method. Of his hero Ulrich he remarked: "One is faced with a simple choice: either one must run with the pack (when in Rome, do as the Romans do); or one becomes a neurotic." Musil here introduces the problem, central to all modernist literature, of the significance of psychopathology.

This problem was first widely discussed in the Naturalist period. More than fifty years ago, that doyen of Berlin dramatic critics, Alfred Kerr, was writing: "Morbidity is the legitimate poetry of Naturalism. For what is poetic in everyday life? Neurotic aberration, escape from life's dreary routine. Only in this way can a character be translated to a rarer clime and yet retain an air of reality." Interesting, here, is the notion that the poetic necessity of the pathological derives from the prosaic quality of life under capitalism. I would maintain — we shall return to this point — that in modern writing there is a continuity from Naturalism to the Modernism of our day — a continuity restricted, admittedly, to underlying ideological principles. What at first was no more than dim anticipation of approaching catastrophe developed, after 1914, into an all-pervading obsession. And I would suggest that the ever-increasing part played by psychopathology was one of the main features of the continuity. At each period — depending on the prevailing social and historical conditions — psychopathology was given a new emphasis, a different significance and artistic function. Kerr's description suggests that in naturalism the interest in psychopathology sprang from an aesthetic need; it was an attempt to escape from the dreariness of life under capitalism. The quotation from Musil shows that some years later the opposition acquired a moral slant. The obsession with morbidity had ceased to have a merely decorative function, bringing color into the greyness of reality, and become a moral protest against capitalism.

With Musil — and with many other modernist writers — psychopathology became the goal, the *terminus ad quem*,[12] of their artistic intention. But there is a double difficulty inherent in their intention, which follows from its underlying ideology. There is, first, a lack of definition. The protest expressed by this flight into psychopathology is an abstract gesture; its rejection of reality is wholesale and summary, containing no concrete criticism. It is a gesture, moreover, that is destined to lead nowhere; it is an escape into nothingness. Thus the propagators of this ideology are mistaken in thinking that such a protest could ever be fruitful in literature. In any protest against particular social conditions, these conditions themselves must have the central place. The bourgeois protest against feudal society, the proletarian against bourgeois society, made their point of departure a criticism of the old order. In both cases the protest — reaching out beyond the point of departure — was based on a concrete *terminus ad quem*: the establishment of a new order. However indefinite the structure and content of this new order, the will towards its more exact definition was not lacking.

How different the protest of writers like Musil! The *terminus a quo*[13] (the corrupt society of our time) is inevitably the main source of energy, since the *terminus ad quem* (the escape into psychopathology) is a mere abstraction. The rejection of modern reality is purely subjective. Considered in terms of man's relation with his environment, it lacks both content and direction. And this lack is exaggerated still further by the character of the *terminus ad quem*. For the protest is an empty gesture, expressing nausea, or discomfort, or longing. Its content — or rather lack of content — derives from the fact that such a view of life cannot impact a sense of direction. These writers are not wholly wrong in believing that psychopathology is their surest refuge; it is the ideological complement of their historical position.

This obsession with the pathological is not

[12]End point. [Ed.]
[13]Starting point. [Ed.]

only to be found in literature. Freudian psycho-analysis is its most obvious expression. The treatment of the subject is only superficially different from that in modern literature. As everybody knows, Freud's starting point was "everyday life." In order to explain "slips" and daydreams, however, he had to have recourse to psychopathology. In his lectures, speaking of resistance and repression, he says: "Our interest in the general psychology of symptom-formation increases as we understand to what extent the study of pathological conditions can shed light on the workings of the normal mind." Freud believed he had found the key to the understanding of the normal personality in the psychology of the abnormal. This belief is still more evident in the typology of Kretschmer, which also assumes that psychological abnormalities can explain normal psychology. It is only when we compare Freud's psychology with that of Pavlov, who takes the Hippocratic view that mental abnormality is a deviation from a norm, that we see it in its true light.

Clearly, this is not strictly a scientific or literary-critical problem. It is an ideological problem, deriving from the ontological dogma of the solitariness of man. The literature of realism, based on the Aristotelean concept of man as *zoon politikon*,[14] is entitled to develop a new typology for each new phase in the evolution of a society. It displays the contradictions within society and within the individual in the context of a dialectical unity. Here, individuals embodying violent and extraordinary passions are still within the range of a socially normal typology (Shakespeare, Balzac, Stendhal). For, in this literature, the average man is simply a dimmer reflection of the contradictions always existing in man and society; eccentricity is a socially-conditioned distortion. Obviously, the passions of the great heroes must not be confused with "eccentricity" in the colloquial sense: Christian Buddenbrook is an "eccentric"; Adrian Leverkühn is not.

The ontology of *Geworfenheit* makes a true typology impossible; it is replaced by an abstract polarity of the eccentric and the socially average.

We have seen why this polarity — which in traditional realism serves to increase our understanding of social normality — leads in modernism to a fascination with morbid eccentricity. Eccentricity becomes the necessary complement of the average; and this polarity is held to exhaust human potentiality. The implications of this ideology are shown in another remark of Musil's: "If humanity dreamt collectively, it would dream Moosbrugger." Moosbrugger, you will remember, was a mentally retarded sexual pervert with homicidal tendencies.

What served, with Musil, as the ideological basis of a new typology — escape into neurosis as a protest against the evils of society — becomes with other modernist writers an immutable *condition humaine*. Musil's statement loses its conditional "if" and becomes a simple description of reality. Lack of objectivity in the description of the outer world finds its complement in the reduction of reality to a nightmare. Beckett's *Molloy* is perhaps the *ne plus ultra*[15] of this development, although Joyce's vision of reality as an incoherent stream of consciousness had already assumed in Faulkner a nightmare quality. In Beckett's novel we have the same vision twice over. He presents us with an image of the utmost human degradation — an idiot's vegetative existence. Then, as help is imminent from a mysterious unspecified source, the rescuer himself sinks into idiocy. The story is told through the parallel streams of consciousness of the idiot and of his rescuer.

Along with the adoption of perversity and idiocy as types of the *condition humaine,* we find what amounts to frank glorification. Take Montherlant's *Pasiphae,* where sexual perversity — the heroine's infatuation with a bull — is presented as a triumphant return to nature, as the liberation of impulse from the slavery of convention. The chorus — i.e., the author — puts the following question (which, though rhetorical, clearly expects an affirmative reply): "Si l'absence de pensée et l'absence de morale ne contribuent pas beaucoup à la dignité des bêtes, des plantes et des eaux . . . ?"[16] Montherlant ex-

---

[14]Political animal. [Ed.]

[15]Ultimate point. [Ed.]

[16]"If the absence of thought and the absence of morality

presses as plainly as Musil, though with different moral and emotional emphasis, the hidden — one might say repressed — social character of the protest underlying this obsession with psychopathology, its perverted Rousseauism,[17] its anarchism. There are many illustrations of this in modernist writing. A poem of Benn's will serve to make the point:

O that we were our primal ancestors,
Small lumps of plasma in hot, sultry swamps;
Life, death, conception, parturition
Emerging from those juices soundlessly.

A frond of seaweed or a dune of sand,
Formed by the wind and heavy at the base;
A dragonfly or gull's wing — already, these
Would signify excessive suffering.

This is not overtly perverse in the manner of Beckett or Montherlant. Yet, in his primitivism, Benn is at one with them. The opposition of man as animal to man as social being (for instance, Heidegger's devaluation of the social as "*das Man*,"[18] Klages's assertion of the incompatibility of *Geist* and *Seele*,[19] or Rosenberg's racial mythology)[20] leads straight to a glorification of the abnormal and to an undisguised antihumanism.

A typology limited in this way to the *homme moyen sensuel* and the idiot also opens the door to "experimental" stylistic distortion. Distortion becomes as inseparable a part of the portrayal of reality as the recourse to the pathological. But literature must have a concept of the normal if it is to "place" distortion correctly; that is to say, to see it *as* distortion. With such a typology this placing is impossible, since the normal is no longer a proper object of literary interest. Life under capitalism is, often rightly, presented as a distortion (a petrification or paralysis) of the human substance. But to present psychopathology

as a way of escape from this distortion is itself a distortion. We are invited to measure one type of distortion against another and arrive, necessarily, at universal distortion. There is no principle to set against the general pattern, no standard by which the petty-bourgeois and the pathological can be seen in their social context. And these tendencies, far from being relativized with time, become ever more absolute. Distortion becomes the normal condition of human existence; the proper study, the formative principle, of art and literature.

I have demonstrated some of the literary implications of this ideology. Let us now pursue the argument further. It is clear, I think, that modernism must deprive literature of a sense of *perspective*. This would not be surprising; rigorous modernists such as Kafka, Benn, and Musil have always indignantly refused to provide their readers with any such thing. I will return to the ideological implications of the idea of perspective later. Let me say here that, in any work of art, perspective is of overriding importance. It determines the course and content; it draws together the threads of the narration; it enables the artist to choose between the important and the superficial, the crucial and the episodic. The direction in which characters develop is determined by perspective, only those features being described which are material to their development. The more lucid the perspective — as in Molière or the Greeks — the more economical and striking the selection.

Modernism drops this selective principle. It asserts that it can dispense with it, or can replace it with its dogma of the *condition humaine*. A naturalistic style is bound to be the result. This state of affairs — which to my mind characterizes all modernist art of the past fifty years — is disguised by critics who systematically glorify the modernist movement. By concentrating on formal criteria, by isolating technique from content and exaggerating its importance, these critics refrain from judgment on the social or artistic significance of subject matter. They are unable, in consequence, to make the aesthetic distinction between *realism* and *naturalism*. This distinction depends on the presence or absence in a work of art of "hierarchy of significance" in the situations

---

do not contribute a good deal to the dignity of animals, plants, and bodies of water. . . ." [Ed.]

[17]Here, adulation of the primitive as noble. [Ed.]

[18]An untranslatable phrase signifying vague personhood. The German word *man* is the indefinite pronoun equivalent to the English "one." [Ed.]

[19]Spirit and soul. [Ed.]

[20]Alfred Rosenberg (1893–1946), a Nazi ideologist of anti-Semitism, author of *The Myth of the Twentieth Century* (1934). [Ed.]

and characters presented. Compared with this, formal categories are of secondary importance. That is why it is possible to speak of the basically *naturalistic* character of modernist literature — and to see here the literary expression of an ideological continuity. This is not to deny that variations in style reflect changes in society. But the particular form this principle of naturalistic arbitrariness, this lack of hierarchic structure, may take is not decisive. We encounter it in the all-determining "social conditions" of Naturalism, in Symbolism's impressionist methods and its cultivation of the exotic, in the fragmentation of objective reality in Futurism and Constructivism and the German *Neue Sachlichkeit,*[21] or, again, in Surrealism's stream of consciousness.

These schools have in common a basically static approach to reality. This is closely related to their lack of perspective. Characteristically, Gottfried Benn actually incorporated this in his artistic program. One of his volumes bears the title, *Static Poems*. The denial of history, of development, and thus of perspective, becomes the mark of true insight into the nature of reality.

> The wise man is ignorant
> of change and development
> his children and children's children
> are no part of his world.

The rejection of any concept of the future is for Benn the criterion of wisdom. But even those modernist writers who are less extreme in their rejection of history tend to present social and historical phenomena as static. It is, then, of small importance whether this condition is "eternal," or only a transitional stage punctuated by sudden catastrophes (even in early Naturalism the static presentation was often broken up by these catastrophes, without altering its basic character). Musil, for instance, writes in his essay, *The Writer in our Age*: "One knows just as little about the present. Partly, this is because we are, as always, too close to the present. But it is also because the present into which we were plunged some two decades ago is of a particularly all-embracing and inescapable character." Whether or not Musil knew of Heidegger's philosophy,

the idea of *Geworfenheit* is clearly at work here. And the following reveals plainly how, for Musil, this static state was upset by the catastrophe of 1914: "All of a sudden, the world was full of violence. . . . In European civilization, there was a sudden rift. . . . " In short: thus static apprehension of reality in modernist literature is no passing fashion; it is rooted in the ideology of modernism.

To establish the basic distinction between modernism and that realism which, from Homer to Thomas Mann and Gorky, has assumed change and development to be the proper subject of literature, we must go deeper into the underlying ideological problem. In *The House of the Dead* Dostoevsky gave an interesting account of the convict's attitude to work. He described how the prisoners, in spite of brutal discipline, loafed about, working badly or merely going through the motions of work until a new overseer arrived and allotted them a new project, after which they were allowed to go home. "The work was hard," Dostoevsky continues, "but, Christ, with what energy they threw themselves into it! Gone was all their former indolence and pretended incompetence." Later in the book Dostoevsky sums up his experiences: "If a man loses hope and has no aim in view, sheer boredom can turn him into a beast. . . . " I have said that the problem of perspective in literature is directly related to the principle of selection. Let me go further: underlying the problem is a profound ethical complex, reflected in the composition of the work itself. Every human action is based on a presupposition of its inherent meaningfulness, at least to the subject. Absence of meaning makes a mockery of action and reduces art to naturalistic description.

Clearly, there can be no literature without at least the appearance of change or development. This conclusion should not be interpreted in a narrowly metaphysical sense. We have already diagnosed the obsession with psychopathology in modernist literature as a desire to escape from the reality of capitalism. But this implies the absolute primacy of the *terminus a quo,* the condition from which it is desired to escape. Any movement towards a *terminus ad quem* is condemned to impotence. As the ideology of most

[21]New objectivity or impersonality. [Ed.]

modernist writers asserts the unalterability of outward reality (even if this is reduced to a mere state of consciousness) human activity is, *a priori,* rendered impotent and robbed of meaning.

The apprehension of reality to which this leads is most consistently and convincingly realized in the work of Kafka. Kafka remarks of Josef K., as he is being led to execution: "He thought of flies, their tiny limbs breaking as they struggle away from the fly-paper." This mood of total impotence, of paralysis in the face of the unintelligible power of circumstances, informs all his work. Though the action of *The Castle* takes a different, even an opposite, direction to that of *The Trial,* this view of the world, from the perspective of a trapped and struggling fly, is all-pervasive. This experience, this vision of a world dominated by *angst* and of man at the mercy of incomprehensible terrors, makes Kafka's work the very type of modernist art. Techniques, elsewhere of merely formal significance, are used here to evoke a primitive awe in the presence of an utterly strange and hostile reality. Kafka's *angst* is the experience *par excellence* of modernism.

Two instances from musical criticism — which can afford to be both franker and more theoretical than literary criticism — show that it is indeed a universal experience with which we are dealing. The composer, Hanns Eisler, says of Schönberg: "Long before the invention of the bomber, he expressed what people were to feel in the air raid shelters." Even more characteristic — though seen from a modernist point of view — is Theodor W. Adorno's analysis (in *The Aging of Modern Music*) of symptoms of decadence in modernist music: "The sounds are still the same. But the experience of *angst,* which made their originals great, has vanished." Modernist music, he continues, has lost touch with the truth that was its *raison d'être.* Composers are no longer equal to the emotional presuppositions of their modernism. And that is why modernist music has failed. The diminution of the original *angst*-obsessed vision of life (whether due, as Adorno thinks, to inability to respond to the magnitude of the horror or, as I believe, to the fact that this obsession with *angst* among bourgeois

intellectuals has already begun to recede) has brought about a loss of substance in modern music, and destroyed its authenticity as a modernist art form.

This is a shrewd analysis of the paradoxical situation of the modernist artist, particularly where he is trying to express deep and genuine experience. The deeper the experience, the greater the damage to the artistic whole. But this tendency towards disintegration, this loss of artistic unity, cannot be written off as a mere fashion, the product of experimental gimmicks. Modern philosophy, after all, encountered these problems long before modern literature, painting or music. A case in point is the problem of *time.* Subjective Idealism had already separated time, abstractly conceived, from historical change and particularity of place. As if this separation were insufficient for the new age of imperialism, Bergson widened it further. Experienced time, subjective time, now became identical with real time; the rift between this time and that of the objective world was complete. Bergson and other philosophers, who took up and varied this theme claimed that their concept of time alone afforded insight into authentic, i.e., subjective, reality. The same tendency soon made its appearance in literature.

The German left-wing critic and essayist of the twenties, Walter Benjamin, has well described Proust's vision and the techniques he uses to present it in his great novel: "We all know that Proust does not describe a man's life as it actually happens, but as it is remembered by a man who has lived through it. Yet this puts it far too crudely. For it is not actual experience that is important, but the texture of reminiscence, the Penelope's tapestry of a man's memory." The connection with Bergson's theories of time is obvious. But whereas with Bergson, in the abstraction of philosophy, the unity of perception is preserved, Benjamin shows that with Proust, as a result of the radical disintegration of the time sequence, objectivity is eliminated: "A lived event is finite, concluded at least on the level of experience. But a remembered event is infinite, a possible key to everything that preceded it and to everything that will follow it."

It is the distinction between a philosophical

and an artistic vision of the world. However hard philosophy, under the influence of Idealism, tries to liberate the concepts of space and time from temporal and spatial particularity, literature continues to assume their unity. The fact that, nevertheless, the concept of subjective time cropped up in literature only shows how deeply subjectivism is rooted in the experience of the modern bourgeois intellectual. The individual, retreating into himself in despair at the cruelty of the age, may experience an intoxicated fascination with his forlorn condition. But then a new horror breaks through. If reality cannot be understood (or no effort is made to understand it), then the individual's subjectivity — alone in the universe, reflecting only itself — takes on an equally incomprehensible and horrific character. Hugo von Hofmannsthal was to experience this condition very early in his poetic career:

It is a thing that no man cares to think on,
And far too terrible for mere complaint,
That all things slip from us and pass away,

And that my ego, bound by no outward force —
Once a small child's before it became mine —
Should now be strange to me, like a strange dog.

By separating time from the outer world of objective reality, the inner world of the subject is transformed into a sinister, inexplicable flux and acquires — paradoxically, as it may seem — a static character.

On literature this tendency towards disintegration, of course, will have an even greater impact than on philosophy. When time is isolated in this way, the artist's world disintegrates into a multiplicity of partial worlds. The static view of the world, now combined with diminished objectivity, here rules unchallenged. The world of man — the only subject matter of literature — is shattered if a single component is removed. I have shown the consequences of isolating time and reducing it to a subjective category. But time is by no means the only component whose removal can lead to such disintegration. Here, again, Hofmannsthal anticipated later developments. His imaginary "Lord Chandos" reflects: "I have lost the ability to concentrate my thoughts or set them out coherently." The result is a condition of apathy, punctuated by manic fits. The

development towards a definitely pathological protest is here anticipated — admittedly in glamorous, romantic guise. But it is the same disintegration that is at work.

Previous realistic literature, however violent its criticism of reality, had always assumed the unity of the world it described and seen it as a living whole inseparable from man himself. But the major realists of our time deliberately introduce elements of disintegration into their work — for instance, the subjectivizing of time — and use them to portray the contemporary world more exactly. In this way, the once natural unity becomes a conscious, constructed unity (I have shown elsewhere that the device of the two temporal planes in Thomas Mann's *Doctor Faustus* serves to emphasize its historicity). But in modernist literature the disintegration of the world of man — and consequently the disintegration of personality — coincides with the ideological intention. Thus *angst,* this basic modern experience, this by-product of *Geworfenheit,* has its emotional origin in the experience of a disintegrating society. But it attains its effects by evoking the disintegration of the world of man.

To complete our examination of modernist literature, we must consider for a moment the question of allegory. Allegory is that aesthetic genre which lends itself *par excellence* to a description of man's alienation from objective reality. Allegory is a problematic genre because it rejects that assumption of an immanent meaning to human existence which — however unconscious, however combined with religious concepts of transcendence — is the basis of traditional art. Thus in medieval art we observe a new secularity (in spite of the continued use of religious subjects) triumphing more and more, from the time of Giotto, over the allegorizing of an earlier period.

Certain reservations should be made at this point. First, we must distinguish between literature and the visual arts. In the latter, the limitations of allegory can be the more easily overcome in that transcendental, allegorical subjects can be clothed in an aesthetic immanence (even if of a merely decorative kind) and the rift in reality in some sense be eliminated — we have only to think of Byzantine mosaic art. This decorative element has no real equivalent in literature; it exists only in a figurative sense, and then only as a secondary component. Allegorical art of the quality of Byzantine mosaic is only rarely possible in literature. Secondly, we must bear in mind in examining allegory — and this is of great importance for our argument — a historical distinction: does the concept of transcendence in question contain within itself tendencies towards immanence (as in Byzantine art or Giotto), or is it the product precisely of a rejection of these tendencies?

Allegory, in modernist literature, is clearly of the latter kind. Transcendence implies here, more or less consciously, the negation of any meaning immanent in the world or the life of man. We have already examined the underlying ideological basis of this view and its stylistic consequences. To conclude our analysis, and to establish the allegorical character of modernist literature, I must refer again to the work of one of the finest theoreticians of modernism — to Walter Benjamin. Benjamin's examination of allegory was a product of his researches into German Baroque drama. Benjamin made his analysis of these relatively minor plays the occasion for a general discussion of the aethetics of allegory. He was asking, in effect, why it is that transcendence, which is the essence of allegory, cannot but destroy aesthetics itself.

Benjamin gives a very contemporary definition of allegory. He does not labor the analogies between modern art and the Baroque (such analogies are tenuous at best, and were much overdone by the fashionable criticism of the time). Rather, he uses the Baroque drama to criticize modernism, imputing the characteristics of the latter to the former. In do doing, Benjamin became the first critic to attempt a philosophical analysis of the aesthetic paradox underlying modernist art. He writes:

> In Allegory, the *facies hippocratica* of history looks to the observer like a petrified primeval landscape. History, all the suffering and failure it contains, finds expression in the human face — or, rather, in the human skull. No sense of freedom, no classical proportion, no human emotion lives in its features — not only human existence in general, but the fate of every individual human being is symbolized in this most palpable token of mortality. This is the core of the allegorical vision, of the Baroque idea of history as the passion of the world; History is significant only in the stations of its corruption. Significance is a function of mortality — because it is death that marks the passage from corruptibility to meaningfulness.

Benjamin returns again and again to this link between allegory and the annihilation of history:

> In the light of this vision history appears, not as the gradual realization of the eternal, but as a process of inevitable decay. Allegory thus goes beyond beauty. What ruins are in the physical world, allegories are in the world of the mind.

Benjamin points here to the aesthetic consequences of modernism — though projected into the Baroque drama — more shrewdly and consistently than any of his contemporaries. He sees that the notion of objective time is essential to any understanding of history, and that the notion of subjective time is a product of a period of decline. "A thorough knowledge of the problematic nature of art" thus becomes for him — correctly, from his point of view — one of the hallmarks of allegory in Baroque drama. It is problematic, on the one hand, because it is an art intent on expressing absolute transcendence that fails to do so because of the means at its disposal. It is also problematic because it is an art reflecting the corruption of the world and bringing about its own dissolution in the process. Benjamin discovers "an immense, anti-aesthetic subjectivity" in Baroque literature, associated with "a theologically-determined subjectivity." (We shall presently show — a point I have discussed elsewhere in relation to Heidegger's philosophy — how in literature a "religious atheism" of this kind can acquire a theological character.) Romantic — and, on a higher plane, Baroque — writers were well aware of this problem, and gave their understanding, not only theoretical, but artistic — that is to say allegorical — expression. "The image," Benjamin remarks, "becomes a rune in the sphere of allegorical intuition. When touched by the light of theology, its symbolic beauty is gone. The false appearance of totality vanishes. The image dies; the parable no longer holds true; the world it once contained disappears."

The consequences for art are far-reaching, and Benjamin does not hesitate to point them out: "Every person, every object, every relationship can stand for something else. This transferability constitutes a devastating, though just, judgment on the profane world — which is thereby branded as a world where such things are of small importance." Benjamin knows, of course, that although details are "transferable," and thus insignificant, they are not banished from art altogether. On the contrary. Precisely in modern art, with which he is ultimately concerned, descriptive detail is often of an extraordinary sensuous, suggestive power — we think again of Kafka. But this, as we showed in the case of Musil (a writer who does not consciously aim at allegory) does not prevent the materiality of the world from undergoing permanent alteration, from becoming transferable and arbitrary. Just this, modernist writers maintain, is typical of their own apprehension of reality. Yet presented in this way, the world becomes, as Benjamin puts it, "exalted and depreciated at the same time." For the conviction that phenomena are *not* ultimately transferable is rooted in a belief in the world's rationality and in man's ability to penetrate its secrets. In realistic literature each descriptive detail is both *individual* and *typical*. Modern allegory, and modernist ideology, however, deny the *typical*. By destroying the coherence of the world, they reduce detail to the level of mere particularity (once again, the connection between modernism and naturalism is plain). Detail, in its allegorical transferability, though brought into a direct, if paradoxical connection with transcendence, becomes an abstract function of the transcendence to which it points. Modernist literature thus replaces concrete typicality with abstract particularity.

We are here applying Benjamin's paradox directly to aesthetics and criticism, and particularly to the aesthetics of modernism. And, though we have reversed his scale of values, we have not deviated from the course of his argument. Elsewhere, he speaks out even more plainly — as though the Baroque mask had fallen, revealing the modernist skull underneath:

Allegory is left empty-handed. The forces of evil, lurking in its depths, owe their very existence to allegory. Evil is, precisely, the non-existence of that which allegory purports to represent.

The paradox Benjamin arrives at — his investigation of the aesthetics of Baroque tragedy has culminated in a negation of aesthetics — sheds a good deal of light on modernist literature, and particularly on Kafka. In interpreting his writings allegorically I am not, of course, following Max Brod, who finds a specifically religious allegory in Kafka's works. Kafka refuted any such interpretation in a remark he is said to have made to Brod himself: "We are nihilistic figments, all of us; suicidal notions forming in God's mind." Kafka rejected, too, the gnostic concept of God as an evil demiurge: "The world is a cruel whim of God, an evil day's work." When Brod attempted to give this an optimistic slant, Kafka shrugged off the attempt ironically: "Oh, hope enough, hope without end — but not, alas, for us." These remarks, quoted by Benjamin in his brilliant essay on Kafka, point to the general spiritual climate of his work: "His profoundest experience is of the hopelessness, the utter meaninglessness of man's world, and particularly that of present day bourgeois man." Kafka, whether he says so openly or not, is an atheist. An atheist, though, of that modern species who regard God's removal from the scene not as a liberation — as did Epicurus and the Encyclopedists — but as a token of the "God-forsakenness" of the world, its utter desolation of futility. Jacobsen's *Niels Lyhne* was the first novel to describe this state of mind of the atheistic bourgeois intelligentsia. Modern religious atheism is characterized, on the one hand, by the fact that unbelief has lost its revolutionary *élan* — the empty heavens are the projection of a world beyond hope of redemption. On the other hand, religious atheism shows that the desire for salvation lives on with undiminished force in a world without God, worshipping the voice created by God's absence.

The supreme judges in *The Trial*, the castle administration in *The Castle*, represent transcendence in Kafka's allegories: the transcendence of Nothingness. Everything points to them, and they could give meaning to everything. Everybody believes in their existence and omnipotence; but nobody knows them, nobody knows how they can be reached. If there is a God here, it can only be the God of religious atheism: *atheos absconditus*.[22] We become acquainted with a repellent host of subordinate authorities; brutal, corrupt, pedantic — and, at the same time, unreliable and irresponsible. It is a portrait of the bourgeois society Kafka knew, with a dash of Prague local coloring. But it is also allegorical in that the doings of this bureaucracy and of those dependent on it, its impotent victims, are not concrete and realistic, but a reflection of that Nothingness which governs existence. The hidden, nonexistent God of Kafka's world derives his spectral character from the fact that his own non-existence is the ground of all existence; and the portrayed reality, uncannily accurate as it is, is spectral in the shadow of that dependence. The only purpose of transcendence — the intangible *nichtendes Nichts*[23] — is to reveal the *facies hippocratica*[24] of the world.

That abstract particularity which we saw to be the aesthetic consequence of allegory reaches its high mark in Kafka. He is a marvelous observer; the spectral character of reality affects him so deeply that the simplest episodes have an oppressive, nightmarish immediacy. As an artist, he is not content to evoke the surface of life. He is aware that individual detail must point to general significance. But how does he go about the business of abstraction? He has emptied everyday life of meaning by using the allegorical method; he has allowed detail to be annihilated by his transcendental Nothingness. This allegorical

transcendence bars Kafka's way to realism, prevents him from investing observed detail with typical significance. Kafka is not able, in spite of his extraordinary evocative power, in spite of his unique sensibility, to achieve that fusion of the particular and the general which is the essence of realistic art. His aim is to raise the individual detail in its immediate particularity (without generalizing its content) to the level of abstraction. Kafka's method is typical, here, of modernism's allegorical approach. Specific subject matter and stylistic variation do not matter; what matters is the basic ideological determination of form and content. The particularity we find in Beckett and Joyce, in Musil and Benn, various as the treatment of it may be, is essentially of the same kind.

If we combine what we have up to now discussed separately we arrive at a consistent pattern. We see that modernism leads not only to the destruction of traditional literary forms; it leads to the destruction of literature as such. And this is true not only of Joyce, or of the literature of Expressionism and Surrealism. It was not André Gide's ambition, for instance, to bring about a revolution in literary style; it was his philosophy that compelled him to abandon conventional forms. He planned his *Faux-Monnayeurs*[25] as a novel. But its structure suffered from a characteristically modernist schizophrenia: it was supposed to be written by the man who was also the hero of the novel. And, in practice, Gide was forced to admit that no novel, no work of literature could be constructed in that way. We have here a practical demonstration that — as Benjamin showed in another context — modernism means not the enrichment, but the negation of art.

[22]The departed no-God. [Ed.]
[23]Annihilating nothingness. [Ed.]
[24]Hippocratic (i.e., medical) aspect. [Ed.]

[25]André Gide, *The Counterfeiters* (1949). [Ed.]

# Raymond Williams

## 1921–1988

*Born to working-class parents in a Welsh border village, Raymond Williams was that rare creature, a Marxist intellectual with genuine proletarian roots. After serving in the British army from 1941 until the close of the war, Williams earned his M.A. from Trinity College, Cambridge, in 1946, and then attended Oxford, where he worked his way up the ladder of appointments. A professor of drama at Jesus College, Cambridge, until 1983, he was considered by many to be the preeminent Marxist literary critic and theorist of postwar Britain. In addition to his landmark study* Culture and Society, 1780–1950 (1958) *and his masterpiece* The Country and the City (1973), *Williams wrote more than a dozen other books, including* The Long Revolution (1961), Drama from Ibsen to Brecht (1969), The English Novel from Dickens to Lawrence (1970), Keywords (1976), Marxism and Literature (1977), The Sociology of Culture (1982), *and* Writing in Society (1983).

# The Green Language

There is the separation of possession: the control of a land and its prospects. But there is also a separation of spirit: a recognition of forces of which we are part but which we may always forget, and which we must learn from, not seek to control. In these two kinds of separation the idea of Nature was held and transformed.

> "Why," asked Addison, "may not a whole Estate be thrown into a kind of garden by frequent Plantations. A man might make a pretty Landskip of his own Possessions."

Wordsworth, almost a century later, took as the centre of his world not a possessive man but a wondering child:

> Frail creature as he is, helpless as frail,
> An inmate of this active universe:
> For feeling has to him imparted power
> That through the growing faculties of sense
> Doth like an agent of the one great Mind
> Create, creator and receiver both,
> Working but in alliance with the works
> Which it beholds.

Two principles of Nature can then be seen simultaneously. There is nature as a principle of order, of which the ordering mind is part, and which human activity, by regulating principles, may then rearrange and control. But there is also nature as a principle of creation, of which the creative mind is part, and from which we may learn the truths of our own sympathetic nature.

This active sympathy is the real change of mind, the new consciousness if only in a minor-

ity, in the very period in which the willed transformation of nature, not only of land and water but of its raw materials and its essential elements, was to enter a new phase, in the processes we now call industrial. The agrarian confidence of the eighteenth century had been counterpointed, throughout, by feelings of loss and melancholy and regret: from the ambivalence of Thomson to the despair of Goldsmith. Now, with Wordsworth, an alternative principle was to be powerfully asserted: a confidence in nature, in its own workings, which at least at the beginning was also a broader, a more humane confidence in men.

This movement is not, at first sight, very easy to distinguish from what, in the second half of the eighteenth century, is an evident alteration of taste. It is significant and understandable that in the course of a century of reclamation, drainage, and clearing there should have developed, as a by-product, a feeling for unaltered nature, for wild land: the feeling that was known at the time as "picturesque." It is well known how dramatically the view of the Alps altered, from Evelyn's "strange, horrid and fearful crags and tracts," in the mid-1640s, or Dennis's "Ruins upon Ruins, in monstrous Heaps, and Heaven and Earth confounded" in 1688, to the characteristic awed praise of mid- and later eighteenth-century and nineteenth- and twentieth-century travellers:

> Not a precipice, not a torrent, not a cliff but is pregnant with religion and poetry.
>
> (Gray, 1739)

Motionless torrents! silent cataracts!
Who made you glorious as the Gates of Heaven
Beneath the keen full moon?

(Coleridge, 1802)

In the course of the change, comparable districts in Britain — the Lake District, from the 1760s under the influence of Dalton and Brown; the Wye Valley and South Wales, the Scottish Highlands, North Wales, the New Forest, from the 1780s, under the direct influence of William Gilpin — became places of fashionable visiting and even of pilgrimage. Johnson's attitude to the Highlands —

the appearance is that of matter, incapable of form or usefulness, dismissed by nature from her care and left in its original elemental state

— seemed left far behind. That Nature was an improver; the new Nature is an original. But we are bound to remember that most, though not all, of these tours to wild places were undertaken by people who were able to travel because "nature" had not left their own lands in an "original elemental state." The picturesque journeys — and the topographical poems, journals, paintings, and engravings which promoted and commemorated them — came from the profits of an improving agriculture and from trade. It is not, at this level, an alteration of sensibility; it is strictly an addition of taste. Like the landscaped parks, where every device was employed to produce a natural effect, the wild regions of mountain and forest were for the most part objects of conspicuous aesthetic consumption: to have been to the named places, to exchange and compare the travelling and gazing experiences, was a form of fashionable society. That in the course of the journeys some other experiences came we know well enough from Wordsworth and others; but it is Wordsworth who makes what for him is the vital distinction:

even in pleasure pleased
Unworthily, disliking here, and there
Liking, by rules of mimic art transferred
To things above all art; but more — for this,
Although a strong infection of the age,
Was never much my habit — giving way
To a comparison of scene with scene,
Bent overmuch on superficial things,

Pampering myself with meagre novelties
Of colour and proportion: to the moods
Of time or season, to the moral power,
The affections and the spirit of the place
Insensible.

The conventional "awe" of wild places, that Johnson in the Highlands had described as

terror without danger . . . one of the sports of fancy, a voluntary agitation of the mind, that is permitted no longer than it pleases

is something that Wordsworth had known, when he

sought *that* beauty, which, as Milton sings,
Hath terror in it.

But he had learned a more general perception:

When every day brought with it some new sense
Of exquisite regard for common things.
And all the earth was budding with these gifts
Of more refined humanity . . .
. . . a spirit, there for me enshrined
To penetrate the lofty and the low.

It is a complicated movement, including many feelings which were already familiar, but now united, even forced, into a principle of human respect and human community.

It is right to stress some continuity from Thomson and the eighteenth-century tradition. There is the use of the country, of "nature," as a retreat and solace from human society and ordinary human consciousness:

I well remember that those very plumes,
Those weeds, and the high spear-grass on that wall,
By mist and silent rain-drops silvered o'er,
As once I passed, into my heart conveyed
So still an image of tranquillity,
So calm and still, and looked so beautiful
Amid the uneasy thoughts which filled my mind,
That what we feel of sorrow and despair
From ruin and from change, and all the grief
That passing shows of Being leave behind,
Appeared an idle dream.

Characteristically, in this, it is the lonely observer who "passes," and what he sees is a "still life": an image against stress and change.

There is also continuity in a different dimension: the recognition, even the idealisation, of "humble" characters, in sympathy, in charity, and in community. *Michael* is subtitled "a pastoral poem," and it is so in the developed sense of the description of a rural independence — the shepherd and his family who are

> as a proverb in the vale
> For endless industry

— and its dissolution by misfortune, lack of capital, and final sale:

> The Cottage which was nam'd the Evening Star
> Is gone, the ploughshare has been through the ground
> On which it stood; final changes have been wrought
> In all the neighbourhood. . . .

It is significant that Wordsworth links the "gentle agency" of Nature with the fellow-feeling which binds him to such men as Michael: the link we observed in Thomson. Wordsworth often came closer to the actual men, but he saw them also as receding, moving away into a past which only a few surviving signs, and the spirit of poetry, could recall. In this sense the melancholy of loss and dissolution, which had been so marked in late eighteenth-century country writing, is continued in familiar terms.

But there is also an important development in Wordsworth: a new emphasis, corresponding to just this view of history, on the dispossessed, the lonely wanderer, the vagrant. It is here that the social observation is linked to the perceptions of the lonely observer, who is also the poet. The old Cumberland beggar, in the poem of that title, is a later version of the old man whom Crabbe[1] had observed, but the change of viewpoint is remarkable. He is not now evidence of the lack of community — of the village as a life of pain. On the contrary, more truly separated from its life in any direct way, he concentrates in himself, in his actual vagrancy, the community and charity which are the promptings of nature. It is in giving to him that fellow-feeling is kept alive. It is "Nature's law" that none should exist divorced from:

---

[1]George Crabbe's pastoral satire, *The Village* (1783) was a response to Goldsmith's "Deserted Village," which Crabbe thought too gentle. [Ed.]

> a spirit and pulse of good,
> A life and soul to every mode of being
> Inseparably link'd

The beggar is the agent of this underlying, almost lost community:

> And while, in that vast solitude to which
> The tide of things has led him, he appears
> To breathe and live but for himself alone,
> Unblam'd, uninjur'd, let him bear about
> The good which the benignant law of heaven
> Has hung around him, and, while life is his,
> Still let him prompt the unletter'd Villagers
> To tender offices and pensive thoughts.

The spirit of community, that is to say, has been dispossessed and isolated to a wandering, challenging if passive, embodiment in the beggar. It is no longer from the practice of community, or from the spirit of protest at its inadequacy, but from

> this solitary being,
> This helpless wanderer

that the instinct of fellow-feeling is derived. Thus an essential isolation and silence and loneliness have become the only carriers of nature and community against the rigours, the cold abstinence, the selfish ease of ordinary society.

It is a complex structure of feeling, but in its achievement a decisive phase of what must still be called country writing has been inaugurated. There is still the strong sense of observed nature as:

> a pastoral Tract,
> Like one of these, where Fancy might run wild,
> Though under skies less generous and serene;
> Yet there, as for herself, had Nature fram'd
> A pleasure-ground.

But the decisive development is towards that landscape in which:

> The elements and seasons in their change
> Do find their dearest fellow-labourer there,
> The heart of man, a district on all sides
> The fragrance breathing of humanity,
> Man free, man working for himself, with choice
> Of time, and place, and object.

These are the phrases of an actual rural independence, of the kind which has been directly observed in Cumberland, and then seen as threatened by change. But under the new stress there is a simultaneous affirmation and abstraction of "Man," of "Humanity":

> A solitary object and sublime
> Above all height . . .
>        . . . Thus was Man
> Ennobled outwardly before mine eyes . . .
>     . . . Remov'd, and at a distance that was fit.

The figure thus seen is at first the shepherd, moving and working in the mountains, but is then the idea of human nature —

>     the impersonated thought,
> The idea or abstraction of the Kind

— which sustains the poet against "the deformities of crowded life" and the distorted images of men in a pressing society. The labourer now merged with his landscape, a figure within the general figure of nature, is seen from a distance, in which the affirmation of Nature is intended as the essential affirmation of Man. It is in this spirit, at once separated and affirming a submerged general connection —

>     Sea, hill and wood,
> This populous village! Sea and hill and wood
> With all the numberless goings on of life
> Inaudible as dreams

— that a new emphasis is placed on the act of poetry itself, the act of creation; as Wordsworth described it so often, or as Coleridge put it, from the disturbance within the apparent calm:

> And would we aught behold, of higher worth,
> Than that inanimate cold world allowed
> To the poor loveless ever-anxious crowd,
> Ah! from the soul itself must issue forth
> A light, a glory, a fair luminous cloud
> Enveloping the earth.

It is not now the will that is to transform nature; it is the lonely creative imagination; the man driven back from the cold world and in his own natural perception and language seeking to find and recreate man.

This is the "green language" of the new poetry. The phrase is actually used by John Clare, in a poem called, significantly, *Pastoral Poesy*:

> A language that is ever green
> That feelings unto all impart,
> As hawthorn blossoms, soon as seen,
> Give May to every heart.

The conjunction is present also in Wordsworth's famous *Lines Written a Few Miles above Tintern Abbey*:

>     Therefore am I still
> A lover of the meadows and the woods,
> And mountains; and of all that we behold
> From this green earth; of all the mighty world
> Of eye and ear, both what they half create
> And what perceive; well pleased to recognize
> In nature and the language of the sense,
> The anchor of my purest thoughts, the nurse,
> The guide, the guardian of my heart, and soul
> Of all my moral being.

This is, in a new sense, the "green pastoral landscape":

> Here, if need be, struggling with storms, and there
> Strewing in peace life's humblest ground with herbs
> At every season green, sweet at all hours.

This is the philosophical conclusion; the climax, in *The Prelude,* of the formation of "a Poet's mind." But it was a new kind of poet, as it was a new kind of nature, that was now being formed.

John Clare, as a young labourer, had been excited beyond his capacity of explanation by some lines from Thomson's *Spring*:

> Come gentle Spring, ethereal mildness come,
> And from the bosom of yon dripping cloud,
> While music wakes around, veil'd in a shower
> Of shadowing roses, on our plains descend.

This can be read now as a theatrical invocation: a symbolic abstraction of the exalted movement of the seasons. But we can follow both a continuity and a transformation if we read, with it, some of Clare's developed verse:

> From dark green dumps among the dripping grain
> The lark with sudden impulse starts and sings
> And mid the smoking rain
> Quivers her russet wings.

The personified season has become the directly seen lark, but the movement is the same: the investment of nature with a quality of creation that is now, in its new form, internal; so that the more closely the object is described, the more directly, in a newly working language and rhythm, a feeling of the observer's life is seen and known, and the bird *is* the feeling, in the created poem.

Closer description of nature — of birds, trees, effects of weather and of light — is a very marked element in this new writing. Any anthology of natural descriptions would draw very heavily on verse and prose written since 1780. It is often a prolonged, rapt, exceptional description: an intricate working of particularity, as opposed to the more characteristic attribution of single identifying qualities in most earlier writing. This is clearly in part related to more intense observation, but we have only to compare it with the writing of men who were only (though remarkably) intent observers to realise what else is happening. Thus it would be easy to establish some kind of correlation between, say, Wordsworth and Clare on the one hand, and Gilbert White of Selborne[2] on the other; an intense devotion to watching and describing nature is evident in all three men. Yet we have only to remember Gilbert White to see the essential differences:

The ousel is larger than a blackbird, and feeds on haws . . .

That close observation and description is of a separated object, another creature. It is at the opposite pole from the human separation of Wordsworth and Clare: a separation that is mediated by a projection of personal feeling into a subjectively particularised and objectively generalised Nature.

This movement is well known, as a fact of literary history. But Clare is in every way a deeply significant figure, for in him there is not only the literary change but directly, in his person and his history, the inwardness of the social transformation.

He was in no way the first of the labourer poets. Stephen Duck, as we saw, had written one

fine poem before the court and the church and neoclassicism patronised and emasculated him. He had been followed by others, under a similar patronage: James Woodhouse the cobbler, who helped Shenstone lay out The Leasowes; Robert Dodsley the weaver; Robert Tatersal the bricklayer; Mary Collier the washer-woman; William Falconer the sailor; Ann Yearsley the milk-seller, who was encouraged to publish as Lactilla:

No vallies blow, no waving grain uprears
Its tender stalk to cheer my coming hour.

Robert Bloomfield ran away, at fourteen, from his work as a farmboy and became a cobbler in London, and in 1800 published *The Farmer's Boy,* with considerable effect, not excluding a description of him as "our own more chaste Theocritus."[3] *The Farmer's Boy* is an honest imitation of Thomson's *Seasons.* Bloomfield was, he said, "determined that what I said on Farming should be EXPERIMENTALLY true" but though his details have this accuracy of experience they are enclosed within a kind of external pointing and explanation, as in the general figure of Giles who has been projected from his own more immediate memories:

Who could resist the call? that Giles had done
Nor heard the birds, nor seen the rising sun,
Had not Benevolence, with cheering ray,
And Greatness stooped, indulgent to display
Praise which does surely not to Giles belong
But to the objects that inspired his song.

The creeping humility is an acquired taste. If it now provokes either anger or contempt we must not make the mistake of attacking Bloomfield but the men, the class, who reduced him and many thousands of others to this anxious obeisance. In a nonpoetical manner he had his own very different feelings, as when he attacked a remark of Windham's:

the *common people* of his native country, are a rough set no doubt, but I dislike the doctrine of keeping them in their dirt, for though it holds good as to the preservation of potatoes, it would be no grateful reflection to good minds to know that a man's natural abilities had been smother'd for want

---

[2]Gilbert White, English clergyman (1720–93), wrote *The Natural History and Antiquities of Selborne* (1789), one of the first major English works of natural history. [Ed.]

[3]Greek pastoral poet. [Ed.]

of beeing able to read and write. How can we consistently praise the inestimable blessing of letters and not wish to extend it.

The smothering, indeed, was all too general and conscious.

> To make the Society Happy and People Easy under the meanest Circumstances, it is requisite that great numbers of them should be Ignorant as well as Poor,

as Mandeville had expressed it, in a dominant attitude that lasted well into the nineteenth century. The taking-up for patronage may seem to contradict the smothering, but it was only another form of it. What was imposed on the labourer-poets was a definition of learning and cultivation, and more critically a definition of poetry, which, as it happened, was as mediocre as it was arrogant. Bloomfield could hardly get at his real experience because an external attitude had been consciously interposed —

> Live, trifling incidents, and grace my song,
> That to the humblest menial belong

— and even at his best he is constrained within a verse convention that is syntactically that of an observer rather than a participant: the third-person abstraction and personification of other men who labour; the ratification by literary allusion; the required periphrastic gesture:

> Dried fuel hoarded is his richest store
> And circling smoke obscures his little door:
> Whence creeping forth, to duty's call he yields,
> And strolls the Crusoe of his lonely fields.
> On whitethorns towering, and the leafless rose
> A frost-nipped feast in bright vermilion glows;
> Where clust'ring sloes in glossy order rise,
> He crops the loaded branch — a cumbrous prize.

Moreover, the possibilities of development were conditioned by the fact of patronage; the extravagant praise was so regularly followed by neglect, at a time when a decent independence was no easier in literature than on the land itself. Bloomfield turned to *Rural Tales,* in the simpler style of the ballads, and Clare thought his *Richard and Kate* made him "the first of Rural Bards in this country." Also, for money, he turned to topographical tourist poems: as it happens going

to my own native country, looking at mountains I have known all my life. What he makes of that landscape, in formal description, is not important; it is a catalogue of picturesque epithets. But he could say, with more feeling:

> Must scenes like these expand,
> Scenes so magnificently grand,
> And millions breathe, and pass away
> Unblessed, throughout their little day,
> With one short glimpse? By place confined,
> Shall many an anxious ardent mind,
> Sworn to the Muses, cower its pride,
> Doomed but to sing with pinions tied?

It is his own observation of a real experience, and it is not surprising that he moves at once to a contrast with Burns, in a different culture. It is as he touches his own limitations, in a whole social experience, that the strength he had tamed shows through.

John Clare's life must be seen in the same context. It is more tragic but also more urgent: more tragic because more urgent. We can properly see it, up to a certain point, in the context of rural change: the familiar association of Clare with the loss by enclosures. But to see it fully we shall have to go beyond this, to the experience and the poetic development which he shared with Wordsworth, in a much wider social change.

We can of course find in Clare, in an explicit way, strongly felt responses to the visible aspects of recent rural change. For example in the "May" of the *Shepherd's Calendar*:

> Old may day where's thy glorys gone
> All fled and left thee every one
> Thou comst to thy old haunts and homes
> Unnoticed as a stranger comes . . .
> . . . While the new thing that took thy place
> Wears faded smiles upon its face
> And where enclosure has its birth
> It spreads a mildew oer her mirth.

In "October" the surviving gipsies are observed:

> On commons where no farmers claims appear
> Nor tyrant justice rides to interfere.

Or again, in more conscious argument, in *The Village Minstrel:*

There once were lanes in nature's freedom dropt,
There once were paths that every valley wound —
Inclosure came, and every path was stopt;
Each tyrant fix'd his sign where paths were found,
To hint a trespass now who cross'd the ground:
Justice is made to speak as they command;
The high road now must be each stinted bound:
— Inclosure, thou'rt a curse upon the land,
And tasteless was the wretch who thy existence
    plann'd. . . .
O England! boasted land of liberty,
With strangers still thou mayst thy title own,
But thy poor slaves the alteration see,
With many a loss to them the truth is known:
Like emigrating bird thy freedom's flown,
While mongrel clowns, low as their rooting plough,
Disdain thy laws to put in force their own;
And every village owns its tyrants now,
And parish-slaves must live as parish kings allow

. . . Ye fields, ye scenes so dear to Lubin's eye,
Ye meadow-blooms, ye pasture-flowers, farewell!
Ye banish'd trees, ye make me deeply sigh,
Inclosure came, and all your glories fell.

There is an interesting edge of anger in the description of the enclosing gentry as "mongrel clowns," but also, of course, a familiar displacement: the ancient liberty of England is being suppressed, not by the visible and active landowners, but by "low" and, as it would seem, alien "tyrants." It is how Goldsmith had seen an earlier phase of the change; rural England then was

> a picture of Italy just before its conquest by Theodoric the Ostrogoth.

In the actual scale of the regulated conquest of land which enclosure, among other procedures, represented, this persistent image of invading barbarians is understandable. But the harder fact, that these barbarians were well-born Englishmen, is characteristically displaced. And then it is very much to the point that the first general word chosen to describe the instigators of the "curse" of enclosure is "tasteless." This connects with that structure of feeling which was beginning to form, from Goldsmith to the poets of the Romantic movement, and which is particularly visible in Clare: the loss of the "old country" is a loss of poetry; the cultivation of natural feeling is dispossessed by the consequences of improved

cultivation of the land; wealth is not only hard and cruel but tasteless.

Clare was very young when he wrote, in *Helpstone*, a familiar rural elegy and retrospect. Its terms are especially interesting, since it is "industry" (in its earlier meaning of work) which belongs to the old world, and "wealth" to the new:

Sweet rest and peace! ye dear, departed charms,
Which industry once cherishe'd in her arms;
When ease and plenty, known but now to few,
Were known to all, and labour had its due.

We need not ask when, for the point of the memory is the contrast:

Accursed Wealth! o'er-bounding human laws,
Of every evil thou remains't the cause:
Victims of want, those wretches such as me,
Too truly lay their wretchedness to thee:
Thou art the bar that keeps from being fed,
And thine our loss of labour and of bread.

As a way of seeing the dispossession of labour by capital, this is exact. But it is set in a structure of feeling in which what wealth is most visibly destroying is "Nature": that complex of the land as it was, in the past and in childhood, which both ageing and alteration destroy. There are the scenes of what is really an older agriculture —

Thou far fled pasture, long evanish'd scene!
Where nature's freedom spread the flow'ry
    green . . .
. . . Where lowing oxen roam'd to feed at large,
And bleeting there the Shepherd's woolly
    charge. . . .

— alongside the more primitive land which is being directly altered: the brooks diverted, the willows felled, in drainage and clearance.

Over a century and a half I can recognise what Clare is describing: particular trees, and a particular brook, by which I played as a child, have gone in just this way, in the last few years, in an improved use of marginal land. And then what one has to consider is the extension of this observation — one kind of loss against one kind of gain — into a loss of "Nature." It is not only the loss of what can be called — sometimes justly, sometimes affectedly — a piece of "unspoiled" country. It is also, for any particular man, the loss of a specifically human and historical landscape, in which the source of feeling is not really that it is "natural" but that it is "native":

Dear native spot! which length of time endears . . .
Nay e'en a post, old standard, or a stone
Moss'd o'er by age, and branded as her own
Would in my mind a strong attachment gain,
A fond desire that they might there remain;
And all old favourites, fond taste approves,
Griev'd me at heart to witness their removes.

And then what is most urgently being mourned — the "old favourites" approved by "fond taste" — is a loss of childhood through a loss of its immediate landscape:

But now, alas! those scenes exist no more;
The pride of life with thee, like mine, is o'er.

It is wholly understandable that this was written at the age of sixteen. A way of seeing has been connected with a lost phase of living, and the association of happiness with childhood has been developed into a whole convention, in which not only innocence and security but peace and plenty have been imprinted, indelibly, first on a particular landscape, and then, in a powerful extension, on a particular period of the rural past, which is now connected with a lost identity, lost relations and lost certainties, in the memory of what is called, against a present consciousness, Nature. The first feeling is so urgent that it inevitably connects widely with other experience:

His native scenes! O sweet endearing sound!
Sure never beats a heart, howe'er forlorn,
But the warm'd breast has soft emotions found
To cherish the dear spot where he was born:
E'en the poor hedger, in the early morn
Chopping the pattering bushes hung with dew,
Scarce lays his mitten on a branching thorn,
But painful memory's banish'd thoughts in view
Remind him, when 'twas young, what happy days
    he knew.

And the transition is then almost unnoticed, as in *Joys of Childhood*:

Dull is that memory, vacant is that mind,
Where no sweet vision of the past appears.

Living in this connecting feeling, Clare recognised, even while he created, the conversion of particular memories into the generalising "sweet vision of the past." His most crucial recognition, relating quite centrally to the tradition we have been examining, comes in another verse of the same poem:

Fancy spreads Edens wheresoe'er they be;
The world breaks on them like an opening flower,
Green joys and cloudless skies are all they see;
The hour of childhood is a rose's hour. . . .

The natural images of this Eden of childhood seem to compel a particular connection, at the very moment of their widest generality. Nature, the past and childhood are temporarily but powerfully fused:

In nature's quiet sleep as on a mother's breast.

The plough that disturbs this nature connects with the hardest emotions of maturity: dispossession, the ache of labour, the coldness of the available world: a complex of feeling and imagery in the experience of this man and of everyone; of each personal generation and of this generation in history. But what is then achieved, against this experience of pain, is a way of feeling which is also a way of writing:

A language that is ever green

— the language of what Clare now recreates as "pastoral poesy," in the title of the poem from which the line comes. This is a radical development of language and of the idea of literature; its strength in its connecting feelings of human warmth and community, in a time of real dispossession, eviction and social division; its paradoxical weakness in the making of this connection through withdrawal into "nature," into the "Eden" of the heart, and into a lonely, resigned and contemplative love of men:

Unruffled quietness hath made
A peace in every place,
And woods are resting in their shade
Of social loneliness.

It is wholly understandable, this development of responses to a disturbing history and an altering landscape: the real scenes of both at once dissolved and recreated in images which carry the meanings and yet compose a way of seeing that suppresses them. As so often in romantic poetry, it is the survival of human feeling in a factual dispossession:

> While threshing in the dusty barn
> Or squashing in the ditch to earn
> A pittance that would scarce allow
> One joy to smooth my sweating brow
> Where drop by drop would chase and fall
> Thy presence triumphed over all.

The presence is poetry, speaking to and for the humanity of the hedger, the thresher, the man actually altering the landscape in the service and for the gain of others; but distorted by its very loneliness into an opposition to that noise of the world, the noise of actual exploitation and, ironically, of direct response to it:

> Bred in a village full of strife and noise,
> Old senseless gossips, and blackguarding boys,
> Ploughmen and threshers, whose discourses led
> To nothing more than labour's rude employs,
> 'Bout work being slack, and rise and fall of bread
> And who were like to die, and who were like to wed.

It is from this actual village, where a community lives under pressure, that the poet withdraws to the quiet of nature, where he can speak for his own and others' humanity, through remembered ballads and contemplated scenes; a speaking silence from which he is torn, bitterly and desperately, to put what he has written back into the noise of the market: profit, malice, envy; a fashionable contempt for his simplicity; and then again, but now virtually breaking the mind, into the speaking silence of the neglected poet, the man alone with nature and with poverty, recreating a world in his green language:

> I am, but what I am
> Who cares or knows?

It was as far as the mind could go, within that structure. Any new direction required an alteration of structure and of essential convention. Clare marks the end of pastoral poetry, in the very shock of its collision with actual country experience. He could not accept Lamb's characteristic advice, which had tamed so many: "transplant Arcadia to Helpstone. The true rustic style, the Arcadian[4] English, I think is to be found in Shenstone." He is, rather, the culmination, in broken genius, of the movement which we can trace from a century before him: the separation of Nature from the facts of the labour that is creating it, and then the breaking of Nature, in altered and now intolerable relations between men. What we find in Clare is not Jonson's idealisation of a landscape yielding of itself, nor Thomson's idealisation of a productive order that is scattering and guarding plenty. There was a conscious reaction to this, in Goldsmith, in Langhorne, and in Crabbe. But there was also an unconscious reaction, to a country from which any acceptable social order had been decisively removed. Clare goes beyond the external observation of the poems of protest and of melancholy retrospect. What happens in him is that the loss is internal. It is to survive at all, as a thinking and feeling man, that he needs the green language of the new Nature.

[4]The ideal pastoral landscape. [Ed.]

# Fredric Jameson
b. 1934

*It has been said, not without reason, that Ohio-born Fredric R. Jameson, purveyor of a singularly rigorous, sophisticated, and comprehensive version of Marxian theory, is the foremost Marxist literary critic in North America today. Educated at Haverford College and Yale University (Ph.D., 1960), he has taught at Harvard University, the University of California at San Diego, Yale University, the University of California at Santa Cruz, Duke University, and at universities outside the United States. He has been awarded numerous grants and fellowships (including two Guggen-*

heims), *is an editor of* Social Text *and* The Minnesota Review, *and is a cofounder of the Marxist Literary Group. His books include studies of Sartre (1961) and Wyndham Lewis (1979); his major works are* Marxism and Form: Twentieth-Century Dialectical Theories of Literature (1971); The Prison-House of Language: A Critical Account of Russian Formalism and Structuralism *(1972); and* The Political Unconscious: Narrative as a Socially Symbolic Act *(1981), from which this selection on Conrad's* Lord Jim *is taken.*

# Romance and Reification: Lord Jim
# from *The Political Unconscious*

## IV

We . . . must now reconstruct the other slope of *Lord Jim,* the dimension (incommensurable with the molecular one of sentence production) of narrative proper, with its basic categories, the place of all those unavoidable false problems which are named character, event, plot, narrative meaning, and the like. Having, to use Hjelmslev's distinction,[1] examined the content of form — Conrad's style as a symbolic act and as ideology — we must now turn to the form of content.

First impressions, however, raise interpretive temptations: in particular the idea, encouraged by the text itself, that the novel is fundamentally "about" the problem of heroism, and indeed, even before we get as far as that, that the novel "has" a hero and is "about" Jim himself. These temptations our earlier chapter on the ideological nature of the category of a narrative "character" has perhaps supplied us with the means to withstand. Indeed, we there wondered whether it would not be desirable to consider the possibility that the literary "character" is no more substantive than the Lacanian ego,[2] and that it is to be seen rather as an "effect of system" than as a full representational identity in its own right. The idea was to explore the systems, the network of preconscious *pensée sauvage,*[3] in terms of which

a given "character" had meaning, whether that meaning took on the form of an antinomy, as will be found to be the case here in Conrad, or on the other hand was the bearer, as in Balzac, of a more stable quasi-allegorical content: the hypothesis of a character system presupposes another one, namely that the subject, in the immediacy of his or her consciousness, has no meaning, but that when a given subject is endowed with meaning (as, for example, when it becomes a representation for another subject or when another subject becomes part of the cast of characters of our own private fantasies), then that particular meaning can be traced back to the system that generates it, and of which we have taken Greimas's semantic or semiotic rectangle[4] as one of the most useful emblems.

In the present instance, it is certain that to dissolve the verisimilitude of the character of Jim into the mere effect or pole of some larger signifying system would at once discredit and dispatch into critical dilettantism the whole thematics of heroism and individual guilt and expiation about which we have already complained. On the other hand, it would seem that a book so

---

[1]Louis Hjelmslev, *Prolegomena to a Theory of Language,* trans. F. J. Whitfield (Madison: University of Wisconsin Press, 1961), ch. 13.

[2]See the introduction to Psychological Criticism, p. 637. [Ed.]

[3]Savage mind; in the work of Claude Lévi-Strauss, not the mentality of primitive peoples, but the primitive part of human mentality, which thinks through the use of myth. [Ed.]

[4]Jameson alludes to the "elementary structure of signification" in Algirdas Julien Greimas's *Du sens* (1970), in which a term is defined in relation to three others: its opposite, its contrary, and its contrapositive (good:evil::nongood:nonevil); Greimas also suggests that texts too can be thematized in terms of two pairs of contrary terms whose articulations set up four spaces. [Ed.]

completely organized around the investigation of a single individual destiny, a single unique yet also more largely consequent and socially significant life experience ("he was one of us"), risks being shattered by such a refusal to take it on its own organizational terms.

How does one go about rewriting and rereading this narrative in such a way that "Jim" comes to be the name for an empty slot in a system which then, far more than the "lifelike" character, proves to have been the absent center of the narrative? Such a process can often conveniently begin in typology, provided it gets out of it at the appropriate moment. The reiterated but enigmatic "one of us" suggests that the binary terms of Jim's system are probably not to be sought for in the direction of Marlow and his listeners, but rather elsewhere: for example, in Jim's own reflections on types of people and types of vocation during his enforced idleness in port after his accident:

> While waiting, he associated naturally with the men of his calling in the port. These were of two kinds. Some, very few and seen there but seldom, led mysterious lives, had preserved an undefaced energy with the temper of buccaneers and the eyes of dreamers. They appeared to live in a crazy maze of plans, hopes, dangers, enterprises, ahead of civilization, in the dark places of the sea; and their death was the only event of their fantastic existence that seemed to have a reasonable certitude of achievement. The majority were men who, like himself, thrown there by some accident, had remained as officers of country ships. They had now a horror of the home service, with its harder conditions, severer view of duty, and the hazard of stormy oceans. They were attuned to the eternal peace of Eastern sky and sea. They loved short passages, good deck-chairs, large native crews, and the distinction of being white. . . . In all they said — in their actions, in their looks, in their persons — could be detected the soft spot, the place of decay, the determination to lounge safely through existence. [8–9]

That Jim must initially test himself against these two categories, that neither is adequate to house him, suggests that the character system, if one is at work here, is far from complete and lacks certain key features or semes. Jim is presumably not one of the deck-chair captains, who from another point of view, are the nonnarrative terms,

the "characters" who have no story and no destiny; but though he may well, like the first group, have the eyes of a dreamer, the characterization of these Europeans is still, at least at this stage, too comic-satiric to suit him either, and ultimately finds a first generic fulfillment in the episode of the guano empire ("all at once, on the blank page, under the very point of the pen, the two figures of Chester and his antique partner, very distinct and complete, would dodge into view with stride and gestures, as if reproduced in the field of some optical toy. I would watch them for a while. No! They were too phantasmal and extravagant to enter into anyone's fate": p. 106): such dreamers will, however, return in a more baleful guise in the second half of the novel.

But in half a paragraph, Jim has a new berth (chief mate on the *Patna)* and in another half a page, in its passengers-to-be, confronts a new type of human being and a new category of human existence:

> They streamed aboard over three gangways, they streamed in urged by faith and the hope of paradise, they streamed in with a continuous tramp and shuffle of bare feet, without a word, a murmur, or a look back; and when clear of confining rails spread on all sides over the deck, flowed forward and aft, overflowed down the yawning hatchways, filled the inner recesses of the ship — like water filling a cistern, like water flowing into crevices and crannies, like water rising silently even with the rim. Eight hundred men and women with faith and hopes, with affections and memories, they had collected there, coming from north and south and from the outskirts of the East, after treading the jungle paths, descending the rivers, coasting in praus along the shallows, crossing in small canoes from island to island, passing through suffering, meeting strange sights, beset by strange fears, upheld by one desire. They came from solitary huts in the wilderness, from populous campongs, from villages by the sea. At the call of an idea they had left their forests, their clearings, the protection of their rulers, their prosperity, their poverty, the surroundings of their youth, and the graves of their fathers. . . .
> "Look at dese cattle," said the German skipper to his new chief mate. [9–10]

The crude irony underscores the most obvious feature that distinguishes the pilgrims from the

Europeans anatomized on the preceding page: their lack of "individualism." Yet even on this most superficial level, the initial stirrings of a differential system are at work; we return from these anonymous masses to the equally faceless "deck-chair captains" of the previous page, themselves each utterly lacking in individuality, yet living their indistinction one by one, in the isolation of their bourgeois comfort, rather than, as here, collectively.

Meanwhile, telltale expressions like "the call of an idea" not only warn of semic echoes with the other category of European seamen, those of the mysterious lives and "the eyes of dreamers," but also suggest that from our now distant vantage point in late twentieth-century consumer society we need a semantic reconstruction of these terms themselves — terms such as "idea," and later, in *Nostromo*, "sentimentalism" — which are too charged not to carry with them a whole historical ideology that must be drawn, massy and dripping, up into the light before the text can be considered to have been read. Conrad's discourse — an overlay of psychoanalytically charged terms and ideological, public slogans — must be regarded as a foreign language that we have to learn in the absence of any dictionary or grammar, ourselves reconstructing its syntax and assembling hypotheses about the meanings of this or that item of vocabulary for which we ourselves have no contemporary equivalent.

Before trying to reconstruct the semantics of this key passage, however, we must also argue something else: namely that what is merely a narrative device or pretext (Jim's crisis requires him to have put lives in danger, but it can scarcely matter which ones; these Mecca-bound pilgrims might just as easily have been replaced by Indian emigrants to South Africa, say, or by a group of families of overseas Chinese) has a substantive meaning in its own right, which is constitutive for the text. This is, it seems to me, the kind of situation in which the Althusserian notion of "overdetermination"[5] is useful: we can-

not argue the importance of this particular evocation of the pilgrims from its necessity in the mechanism of the plot, yet we can propose a secondary line of determination such that, even as narrative pretext, this content imposes itself and becomes unavoidable. Its necessity is, in other words, not to be found on the level of narrative construction, but outside, in the objective logic of the content, in the unavailability of any other "illustration" to fill this particular empty slot. So it is significant that from our enumeration of other possibilities, passengers of European stock were excluded (for one thing, the Europeans would not have remained calm while the officers abandoned ship); the other Asian possibilities are also inappropriate, since both would represent commerce and business motives rather than the religious pilgrimage here described, and itself reinforced (or once again, "overdetermined," if you like) by the attitude of the non-pilgrim Malay pilots, who keep their stations and continue to guide the abandoned ship for no reason other than sheer *faith* ("It never came into his mind then that the white men were about to leave the ship through fear of death. He did not believe it now. There might have been secret reasons": p. 61).[6] Here too, in this secondary loop of the plot, equally necessary for the construction of Jim's central ordeal — but was it not Valéry who observed that what is merely neces-

---

[5]Unlike older versions of Marxism, in which everything was determined by economics, aesthetic, social, and political practices are for Althusser relatively autonomous; hence a state of affairs can be multiply caused or "overdetermined." [Ed.]

[6]Obviously, the thematic selection of Islam is no historical accident; it is ironic that this mirage of plenitude attributed to the historical and cultural Other should also be the instrument—"Orientalism"—by which that same Other is systematically marginalized (see Edward W. Said, *Orientalism* [New York: Pantheon, 1978]). It is noteworthy that the passage in question already exists virtually word-for-word in the oldest sketch Conrad wrote of his novel-to-be; see "Tuan Jim," in Conrad, *Lord Jim*, ed. Thomas Moser (New York: Norton, 1968), pp. 283–91. This reading of the semantic content of one of the two "communities" who meet on the *Patna* (the other, dominant one is that of the British imperial bureaucracy, as we shall see in a moment) does not exclude the investment of other types of content in what is essentially an allegorical scheme: in particular, Gustav Morf's identification of the *Patna* with Poland, and his interpretation of Jim's guilt as a figure for Conrad's own obscure sense of having abandoned family, language, and nation, surely constitute one of the more dramatic interpretive gestures in recent criticism (Gustav Morf, *The Polish Heritage of Joseph Conrad* [London: Sampson Low, Marston, 1930], pp. 149–66). [Au.]

sary in art is the place of the flaw and the soft pocket of bad writing? — the apparently secondary content of blind faith comes as a "motivation of the device" and a reappropriation of the plot mechanism in the service of some quite different thematic and semantic system.

So at length we find ourselves interrogating, as though it were the fundamental concern of this sea story and adventure tale, the clearly secondary and marginal phenomenon of religion and religious belief. We do not generally associate Conrad with the nineteenth-century ideologeme[7] of aesthetic religion. The key moments in its development might be quickly sketched in as those of Chateaubriand, its inventor, in *Le Génie du christianisme* (1802), Flaubert's archeological passion for dead religions, his appropriation of that whole ideology of perception, sense-data, and hallucination mentioned above for the evocation of religious visions, as in *La Tentation de Saint Antoine* (1874) or *Trois Contes* (1877) — not to speak of the contemporaneous fascination with belief of the positivists, most notably Renan — and finally such late variants as Malraux's books on painting and sculpture after World War II, books in which the retreat from Marxism to a Gaullist nationalism seems to impose an intellectual detour through a meditation on all the dead religions, all the divers embodiments of the Absolute, in the human past. Into this genealogy of an ideological fascination now relatively foreign to us (and it should be noted that the religious revival of the late nineteenth century and, in particular, phenomena like neo-Catholicism are quite different from this aestheticizing contemplation of religion from without), we must assuredly insert its most intellectually illustrious and productive monument: the studies undertaken by Conrad's virtual contemporary, Max Weber, of the dynamics and function of religion, not only in *The Protestant Ethic,* but above all in the elaborate, posthumously published *Sociology of Religion.* Indeed, Weber's wry characterization of himself as "religiously unmusical" may serve as the motto for the curious intellectual stance of all of these nonbelievers, who combine

the allure of a religiously fellow-traveling agnosticism with the secret longings of the impotent matters of belief. In the British tradition, the institutional position of Anglicanism and the historical shock of Darwinism's implicit challenge to it lend the thematics of religious belief a somewhat different symbolic and political meaning than they held in the floodtide of bourgeois city life on the continent; still, Conrad was not really British, and it may be a useful estrangement to place him for a moment in a different context than those (English intellectuals of the Ford/Garnett type,[8] a romantic Polish intelligentsia, the world of the merchant marine) in which he is normally grasped.

The name of Weber makes it clear that we cannot begin to sense the real ideological function of religious aestheticism unless we place it within that larger intellectual and ideological preoccupation which is the study and interrogation of value, and which, even more than with Weber, is associated with the name of the latter's master, Nietzsche.[9] From this standpoint, Nietzsche's "transvaluation of all values" and Weber's misnamed and misunderstood ideal of a "value-free science" must both be seen as attempts to project an intellectual space from which one can study inner-worldly value as such, the whole chaotic variety of reasons and motives the citizens of a secular society have for pursuing the activities they set themselves. These ideals are implicit or explicit attempts to parry the powerful Marxian position, which sees intellectual activity as being historically situated and class-based: the Marxian objection makes it clear that the vocation to study value cannot simply embody one more inner-worldly value (the passion for knowledge? the pursuit of sheer disinterested science?) without at once itself becoming ideological, or, in the Nietzschean formula, one more embodiment of the will to power. Framed in

[7]Basic element of ideology; the term is from Julia Kristeva. [Ed.]

[8]Ford Madox Ford (1873–1939), author of *The Good Soldier* (1920) and the tetralogy of World War I novels collectively called *Parade's End* (1923–28); and critic Edward William Garnett (1868–1937) were friends and collaborators of Conrad's. [Ed.]

[9]See Eugène Fleischmann, "De Nietzsche à Weber," *Archives europénnes de sociologie*, 5 (1964), 190–238. [Au.]

these terms, then, the problem (it will later, with Max Scheler and Karl Mannheim, flatten itself out into that "subdiscipline" conventionally labeled the "sociology of knowledge") is insoluble; but what is interesting about it for us are its preconditions, namely, the objective historical developments without which such a "problem" could never have been articulated in the first place.

These are clearly, first and foremost, the secularization of life under capitalism and the breaking up (or, in the current euphemism, the "modernization") of the older tradition-oriented systems of castes and inherited professions, as the combined result of the French Revolution and the spread of the market system. Now indeed, for the first time in any general and irreversible way, the realm of values becomes problematical, with the result that it can, for the first time, be isolated as a realm in itself and contemplated as a separate object of study. To say that value becomes a semiautonomous object is to observe the way in which, in the new middle-class culture, for the first time people (but mainly men) must weigh the various activities against each other and choose their professions. What we call private life or the new subjectivity of individualism is objectively simply this distance which permits them to hold their professional activities at arm's length; hence the originality, in the realm of the novel, of the "Quel métier prendre?"[10] of a Stendhal, whose works explore, as it were, the atomic weights of the various professions and political regimes as alternate life forms.

In Weber's scheme of things, all social institutions describe a fatal trajectory from the traditional to the rationalized, passing through a crucial transitional stage which is the moment — the vanishing mediation — of so-called charisma. The activities of older societies are for the most part inherited (the blacksmith's father and grandfather were blacksmiths), and the question about value — about the reason for pursuing this or that life task, in this or that fashion — is short-circuited by the classic reply of all traditional societies: Because it was always done that way, because that is the way we have always lived. The problem of value cannot therefore arise in this environment; or, to put it another way, in the world of the traditional village, or even of tribal culture, each activity is symbolically unique, so that the level of abstraction upon which they could be compared with one another is never attained: there is no least-common-denominator available to compare iron-welding or the preparation of curare with basket-weaving or the making of bread or pots. To use the Marxian terminology, in such societies we can only contemplate an incomparable variety of qualitatively different forms of concrete work or productive activity, because the common denominator of all of these forms of activity — equivalent labor-power — has not yet been made visible by the objective process of abstraction at work within society.

For Weber, the charismatic moment amounts to a kind of myth of meaning, a myth of the value of this or that activity, which is briefly sustained by the personal power and authority of the charismatic figure, generally a prophet. But this moment tends to give way at once to a system in which all activities are ruthlessly rationalized and restructured in forms we have already described. The moment of rationalization, then, is Weber's equivalent of Marx's notion of the universalization of equivalent labor-power, or the commodification of all labor; yet if we see the latter subterranean infrastructural process as the objective precondition for the former developments in the relations of production and throughout the superstructure there need be no particular inconsistency between the two accounts.

What we are here concerned to stress is the paradox of the very notion of value itself, which becomes visible as abstraction and as a strange afterimage on the retina, only at the moment in which it has ceased to exist as such. The characteristic form of rationalization is indeed the reorganization of operations in terms of the binary system of means and ends; indeed, the means/ends opposition, although it seems to retain the term and to make a specific place for value, has the objective result of abolishing value

[10]"Which career to follow?" [Ed.]

as such, bracketing the "end" or drawing it back into the system of pure means in such a way that the end is merely the empty aim of realizing these particular means. This secret one-dimensionality of the apparent means/ends opposition is usefully brought out by the Frankfurt School's alternate formulation, namely the concept of instrumentalization,[11] which makes it clear that rationalization involves the transformation of everything into sheer means (hence the traditional formula of a Marxist humanism, that capitalism is a wholly rationalized and indeed rational system of means in the service of irrational ends).[12]

Thus, the study of value, the very idea of value, comes into being at the moment of its own disappearance and of the virtual obliteration of all value by a universal process of instrumentalization: which is to say that — as again in the emblematic case of Nietzsche — the study of value is at one with nihilism, or the experience of its absence. What is paradoxical about such an experience is obviously that it is contemporaneous with one of the most active periods in human history, with all the mechanical animation of late Victorian city life, with all the smoke and conveyance inherent in new living conditions and in the rapid development of business and industry, with the experimental triumphs of positivistic science and its conquest of the university system, with all the bustling parliamentary and bureaucratic activity of the new middle-class regimes, the spread of the press, the diffusion of literacy and the rise of mass culture, the ready accessibility of the newly mass-produced commodities of an increasingly consumer-oriented civilization. We must ponder the anomaly that it is only in the most completely humanized environment, the one most fully and obviously the end product of human labor, production, and transformation, that life becomes meaningless, and that existential despair first appears as such in direct proportion to the elimination of nature, the non- or antihuman, to the increasing rollback of everything that threatens human life and the prospect of a well-nigh limitless control over the external universe. The most interesting artists and thinkers of such a period are those who cling to the experience of meaninglessness itself as to some ultimate reality, some ultimate bedrock of existence of which they do not wish to be cheated by illusions or "philosophies of as-if": "Lieber will noch der Mensch *das Nichts* wollen," cried Nietzsche, "als *nicht* wollen."[13] Rather nihilism than ennui, rather an orchestral pessimism and a metaphysical vision of cosmic entropy than too stark and unpleasant a sense of the systematic exclusion of "value" by the new logic of capitalist social organization.

These are clearly the absolutes with which Conrad's own private pessimism has its "family resemblance" (although in the next section we will find it necessary to distinguish proto-existentialism as a metaphysic — pessimism, nihilism, the meaninglessness of existence, the absurd — from the rigorous analytic dissolution of acts and events by existentialism as a technical philosophy). It is also the perspective in which to grasp the ideological meaning of aesthetic religion: the melancholy of disbelief, the nostalgia of the nineteenth-century intellectual for the "wholeness" of a faith that is no longer possible,

[11]See in particular Max Horkheimer, *Eclipse of Reason* (New York: Seabury, 1947), chap. I ("Means and Ends"), pp. 3–57; as well as Horkheimer and Adorno, *Dialectic of Enlightenment*, and the prolongation of these themes in the critique of positivism by Adorno, Habermas, and others (see *The Positivist Dispute in German Sociology*, trans. G. Adey and D. Frisby [New York: Harper & Row, 1976]). [Au.]

[12]This description can be tested against that older and more elaborate anatomy of praxis furnished by the Aristotelian system of the four causes (material, effective, formal, and final), which clearly still maintains the place of concrete value. But the Aristotelian system is itself a transitional concept which reflects a transitional moment in the development of modern production, and this not merely because, as has often been pointed out, it essentially theorizes an artisanal or handicraft culture, but also because it systematically excludes whole areas of activity (in particular, agricultural production and warfare) from the concept of work it is meant to govern. Like so much in classical Greek culture, therefore, it cannot represent a positive solution or embody a concrete social or political or economic ideal for us. Still, it has the keenest diagnostic value, as a standard against which to measure the appalling rate and degree of dehumanization in modern society. See Jean-Pierre Vernant, "Travail et nature dans la Grèce ancienne," and "Aspects psychologiques du travail," in *Mythe et pensée chez les grecs* (Paris: Maspéro, 1965). [Au.]

[13]"People would rather will Nothingness than not will at all." [Ed.]

is itself a kind of ideological fable designed to transform into a matter of individual existence what is in reality a relationship between collective systems and social forms. Religion has the symbolic value of wholeness, no doubt: but it is the wholeness of the older organic society or *Gesellschaft*[14] that it conveys, and not that — in any case surely a mirage — of some fully unified monad. Religion, to the henceforth "religiously unmusical" subjects of the market system, is the unity of older social life perceived from the outside: hence its structural affinity with the image as such and hallucination. Religion is the superstructural projection of a mode of production, the latter's only surviving trace in the form of linguistic and visual artifacts, thought systems, myths and narratives, which look as though they had something to do with the forms in which our own consciousness is at home, and yet which remain rigorously closed to it. Because we can no longer think the figures of the sacred from within, we transform their external forms into aesthetic objects, but also monuments, pyramids, altars, presumed to have an inside, yet housing powers that will forever remain a mystery to us.[15]

So religion, in this particular sense, takes its place in that complex of ideological themes and terms with which the nineteenth century sought to explore the new world of universal instrumentalization and to express its bewilderment at what that world excluded as much as at what it contained: other motifs, some of which appear in the evocation of the pilgrims quoted above, are the "idea" or the "ideal" (generally art or love) as that which allows one to transcend the intolerable double bind of means and ends; the somewhat lower but also more overtly social concept of the "philanthropic," as we observed it at work in the previous chapter — a conception of a form of social action which would not be that of mere "interest," or would, in other words, transcend the antivalue of the purely instrumental; Conrad's

term "sentimentalism," finally, which comes to designate activities that cannot be reduced to interested motives and must therefore be credited to the account of some unbusinesslike and whimsically nonserious caprice (the Gidean *acte gratuit*[16] will be a final, more heroic avatar of this still fairly leisure-class attribute).

Now we may reinvest the language of *Lord Jim* with something like its original ideological and semantic content, and make an effort to disengage the "system" that generates the typology of characters we have begun to articulate, and beyond that, assigns the narrative its ultimate terminus and dynamics. I believe that this system may best be grasped in terms of the major themes of the dilemma just outlined, and in particular of the opposition between activity and value. It is an opposition not unlike that which underlies Lukács's *Theory of the Novel,* where it takes the form of a dissociation between *Leben,* life, sheer contingent, inner-worldly experience, and *Wesen,* essence, meaning, immanent wholeness.[17] The inner dynamism of such oppositions springs from their incommensurability, their eccentricity as a weighing of two incomparable phenomena: on the one hand, genuine degraded but existent inner-worldly experience, and on the other, sheer ideal, nostalgia, an imagined wholeness that is part of the existent real only insofar as it is dreamed there and projected by this particular real world, but has no other substance. In Conrad, however, as we have seen, owing to the coexistence of capitalism and precapitalist social forms on the imperialist periphery, the term value is still able to have genuine social and historical substance; it marks communities and ways of life which still, for another moment yet, exist, and have not been reduced to the icons and melancholy images of the mainstream of religious aestheticism.

The point about this binary opposition, however, is not its logical accuracy as a thought concerned to compare only comparable entities and oppose only terms of the appropriate category, but, on the contrary, its existence as a

[14]Society. [Ed.]
[15]This dialectic of inside and outside—Rabelais's Silenus box—is principally, as we have suggested in earlier chapters, what is stigmatized in the now canonical attacks on interpretation and on the hermeneutic model (as, e.g., in Derrida, *Of Grammatology,* pp. 30–65). [Au.]

[16]Gratuitous act: a crime committed to prove one's freedom. [Ed.]
[17]Lukács, *Theory of the Novel,* esp. pp. 40–55. [Au.]

symptom; the opposition between activity and value is not so much a logical contradiction, as rather an antinomy for the mind, a dilemma, an aporia, which itself expresses — in the form of an ideological closure — a concrete social contradiction.[18] Its existence as skewed thought, then, as a double bind and a conceptual scandal, is what accounts for the restless life of the system, its desperate attempts to square its own circles and to produce new terms out of itself which ultimately "solve" the dilemma at hand. Thus, in an initial move which Greimas's semantic rectangle allows us to register, each term generates its logical negation or "contradictory"; the nucleus of our ideological system thus contains the four terms of activity and value, and not-activity and not-value, articulated as in the diagram.

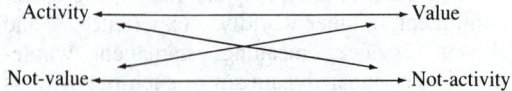

So far, clearly, these are semes or conceptual features, and not in any sense the slots of narrative characters or indeed other narrative categories. The place of characters and of a character system is opened up only at the point at which the mind seeks further release from its ideological closure by projecting combinations of these various semes: to work through the various possible combinations is then concretely to imagine the life forms, or the characterological types, that can embody and manifest such contradictions, which otherwise remain abstract and repressed. Thus, to follow our rectangle around clockwise beginning on the righthand side, it does not seem particularly farfetched to suggest that the synthesis of value and not-activity can be embodied only by the pilgrims, who are a breathing and living presence which does not exteriorize itself in any particular activity, in acts, struggles,

"goal-oriented behavior": even the pilgrimage is simply the emanation of their being, as of an element, water draining the great watertables of Malaysia, "rising silently even with the rim."

Moving to the lower horizontal opposition, between not-activity and not-value — a synthesis suggestively designated as the neutral term in Greimas's version of this model — we see that the very terms of the judgment are virtually explicit in Conrad's contemptuous account of the "deck-chair sailors" who have no ideal but that of their own comfort, and whose energies, insofar as they have any, are wholly dedicated to avoiding activity as much as possible. These are indeed the "neuters" of Conrad's universe, the faceless anonymity against which passions become identifiable in all their own specificity.

As for the next possible synthesis, which would unite activity with not-value, the evocation of Nietzsche has perhaps made it more familiar to us than Conrad's text, at this stage in our reading of it, would authorize: "There are people who would rather will *nothingness* than want nothing at all." What is meant here is clearly not the merely eccentric figures of South Sea port "originals" (of which Jim himself for a moment becomes one), so much as nihilism itself, that formidable combination of energy and, more than utter lack of scruple, a passion for nothingness. To test our hypothesis would be to expect the text at length to generate such a figure, which, indeed, it does in Jim's Nemesis, the character of Gentleman Brown (about whom we will have more to say in a later section).

Finally, we come to what Greimas calls the "complex term," the ideal synthesis of the two major terms of the contradiction and thus the latter's unimaginable and impossible resolution and *Aufhebung;*[19] the union of activity and value, of the energies of Western capitalism and the organic immanence of the religion of precapitalist societies, can only block out the place of Jim himself. But not the existential Jim, the antihero, of the first part of the novel: rather, the ideal Jim, the "Lord Jim" of the second half, the wish-

[18]See Chap. 1, pp. 46–49 and 82–83, and Chap. 3, pp. 166–68. [Au.] Jameson's note refers the reader to prior passages in *The Political Unconscious* which discuss the contradictions within ideology posited by Althusserian Marxism. [Ed.]

[19]Transcendence. The Hegelian term implies that what is transcended is both cancelled out and lifted up to a higher level of existence. [Ed.]

fulfilling romance, which is marked as a degraded narrative precisely by its claim to have "resolved" the contradiction and generated the impossible hero, who, remaining problematical in the *Patna* section of the book as the Lukács of *The Theory of the Novel* told us the hero of a genuine novel must do, now solicits that lowering of our reality principle necessary to accredit this final burst of legend.[20]

The completed character system may therefore be schematically presented as in Figure 1. Such a schema not only articulates the generation of the characters, insofar as it represents a contradiction to be "solved," or an antinomy to be effaced or overcome; it also suggests the ideological service which the production of this narrative is ultimately intended to perform — in other words, the resolution of this particular determinate contradiction — or, more precisely, following Lévi-Strauss's seminal characterization of mythic narrative, the imaginary resolution of this particular determinate real contradiction.[21] Such models — sometimes loosely formulated in terms of analogies with the "deep structures" and surface manifestations of linguistics — find their proper use in the staging of the fundamental problems of the narrative text — the antinomies or ideological closure it is called upon to imagine away — and in the evaluation of the narrative solution, or sequence of provisional solutions, invoked for this purpose. They are, however, less able to bridge the gap between an ideological deep structure and the sentence-by-sentence life of the narrative text, as a perpetual generation and dissolution of events, a process for which we must now propose a rather different kind of lens.

## V

*Lord Jim* is, however, a privileged text in this respect — a kind of reflexive or meta-text — in that its narrative construes the "event" as the analysis and dissolution of events in some more common everyday naive sense. The "event" in

[20]There has been considerable debate as to the "meaning" of the ending of *Lord Jim,* and in particular as to whether Jim can be said, by his death, to have "redeemed" himself; the exalted tone of the ending suggests a positive response which a sober reading of the narrative makes it rather difficult to accept. Surely this "undecidability" of the ending confirms the present analysis, and offers a virtual textbook illustration of an "imaginary resolution of a real contradiction," it being understood that an imaginary resolution is no resolution at all. All of Conrad's artfulness is in this concluding section mustered for a kind of prestidigitation designed to prevent the embarrassing question from being posed in the first place. [Au.]

[21]See Lévi-Strauss, "The Structural Study of Myth," in Ch. 4. [Ed.]

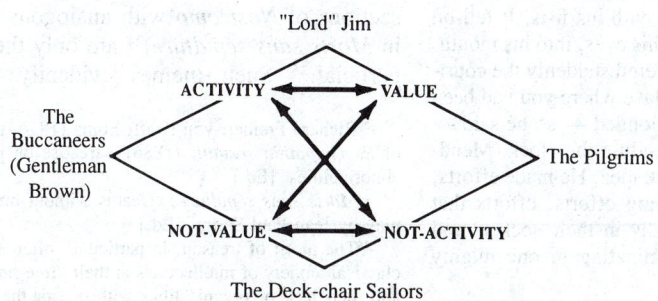

Figure 1

*Lord Jim* is the analysis and dissolution of the event. The originality of the text goes well beyond the conventional redoubling of plot and fable (Aristotle), *discours* and *histoire* (Benveniste), the conventional distinction between the exposition and "rendering" of narrative events and those events as sheer data, raw material, anecdotal precondition.[22] Certainly, the slow unfolding of the "real story" of the *Patna* has all the excitement of a detective story and not a little of that form's peculiarly specialized and redoubled structure: but we have understood very little about this narrative unless we have come to realize that even that "real story" itself is for Conrad hollow and empty, and that there is a void at the heart of events and acts in this work which goes well beyond simple anecdotal mystification.

Consider for instance the following moment of crisis in the Patusan narrative: on arrival, Jim finds himself virtually but unofficially emprisoned by an old adversary of Stein and his allies. He passes his time in a closed courtyard, amusing himself by repairing the Rajah's broken clock. Suddenly, in panic, for the first time conceiving his plight and imminent danger, he climbs the stockade and makes his way across the mud flats to freedom. What interests us is the inner structure of this event, which is indubitably an act on Jim's part:

> The higher firm ground was about six feet in front of him. . . . He reached and grabbed desperately with his hands, and only succeeded in gathering a horrible cold shiny heap of slime against his breast — up to his very chin. It seemed to him he was burying himself alive, and then he struck out madly, scattering the mud with his fists. It fell on his head, on his face, over his eyes, into his mouth. He told me that he remembered suddenly the courtyard, as you remember a place where you had been very happy years ago. He longed — so he said — to be back there again, mending the clock. Mending the clock — that was the idea. He made efforts, tremendous sobbing, gasping efforts, efforts that seemed to burst his eyeballs in their sockets and make him blind, and culminating in one mighty

supreme effort in the darkness to crack the earth asunder, to throw it off his limbs — and he felt himself creeping feebly up the bank. He lay full length on the firm ground and saw the light, the sky. Then as a sort of happy thought the notion came to him that he would go to sleep. He will have it that he *did* actually go to sleep; that he slept — perhaps for a minute, perhaps for twenty seconds, or only for one second, but he recollects distinctly the violent convulsive start of awakening. [155–56] [At which point, then, Jim leaps to his feet again and continues his escape, racing through the village to safety.]

Now a passage of this kind can be taken, as its contemporaries surely would have taken it, as a psychological curiosity; we can almost hear them admiring this knowledge of the "human heart," this exploration of the intricacies of human reactions. We have already mentioned the "psychological" framework which limits Jamesian point of view. Now we must go even further and grasp "psychology" as a particular episteme that includes within itself, alongside the appropriate blueprints of normal mental machinery, a fascination with the data of the abnormal and psychopathological as well, one that envelops Dostoyevsky and Krafft-Ebing,[23] and for which this particular "notation" of Conrad — extreme stress under crisis coupled with sleepiness — becomes an "insight" and a valuable note for the file.

But such a passage can also be read quite differently, and this is the moment to register the peculiar affinities of Conrad's work with certain of the themes of Sartrean existentialism, of which the obsession with treason and betrayal and the fascination with torture (compare the Monygham sections of *Nostromo* with analogous sequences in *Morts sans sépulture*)[24] are only the most superficial.[25] Such themes evidently find their

---

[22]Jameson's distinction — not explicitly found in Aristotle — is between what is usually called story and discourse, *fabula* and *sjuzet* in the work of the Russian Formalists. See the introduction to Formalism, Ch. 4. [Ed.]

[23]Richard Freiherr von Krafft-Ebing (1840–1902), author of *Psychopathia sexualis* (1886) a treatise on psychosexual abnormalities. [Ed.]

[24]*Morts sans sépultures* (Deaths without burials, 1946), play by Jean-Paul Sartre. [Ed.]

[25]The motif of treason, in particular, often expresses the classical anxiety of intellectuals at their "free-floating" status and their lack of organic links with one or the other of the fundamental social classes: this reflexive meaning is explicit in Sartre, but implicit only in writers like Conrad or Borges (on the meaning of treason in this last, see Jean Franco, "Borges," *Social Text,* no. 4 [Fall, 1980]). [Au.]

source in the common patrimony of Nietzschean nihilism and may in both cases be seen as a rather more consequent effort to imagine what kind of things are really possible if God is dead. The structural affinities between these two otherwise very different bodies of work must be ultimately sought in the nature of the concrete social situation they address. The juxtaposition of Conrad's work with existentialism, however, needs a further initial clarification: I have indeed already implied the need to distinguish between a properly existential "metaphysic" — in other words, a set of propositions about the "meaning of life," even where the latter is declared in fact to be "the absurd" — and that more properly existential analytic, found principally in Heidegger and Sartre, which, an offshoot and a development of certain phenomenological explorations, lays out a whole anatomy of lived time, action, choice, emotion, and the like. The former, the metaphysic, is an ideology; the latter can be used ideologically, but is not necessarily in itself ideological. The distinction is one between showing that there is never any irreducible temporal present or presence at the heart of a project, and concluding, from the demonstration that action is itself hollow and unreal. Both "existentialisms" are present in Conrad's work; but it is the latter, the existential analytic, that we will be concerned with in the present section.

It should be clear that I am neither suggesting an influence of Conrad on Sartre, nor, inversely, making a case for Conrad as Sartre's precursor in this or that area. What we can argue at most is that there are objective preconditions for working out a particular thought system or thematics, and that the superficial similarity of two quite different works from different moments and spaces of the recent European past ought to direct our attention first to the similarity of the social situations and historical conditions in which, as symbolic gestures, they are meaningful. We ought therefore to make a first step by trying to understand the historical conditions of possibility of the existential analytic — a project that, whatever it tells us about Conrad, would be the start of a more concrete historical regrounding of Sartre's work than has been done so far (see Lukács's book on existentialism, with its clumsy

mediations, for an object lesson in how not to do this particular job).[26] But the methodological resistance to a symptomal or sociological regrounding of technical philosophy is far greater than to similar operations in the areas of culture and ideology; that technical philosophy has historical preconditions is a view of the history of philosophy which has never adequately been worked out, indeed which the cruder Marxian efforts (like that of Lukács just mentioned) have tended to discredit.

Yet it seems clear that we are already in a position to construct a historical and social subtext able to naturalize or make more plausible the otherwise peculiar experience of moments of action like Jim's escape from the courtyard, in which the act itself suddenly yawns and discloses at its heart a void which is at one with the temporary extinction of the subject. (Compare, in *Nostromo*, Mrs. Gould's brief loss of consciousness in the proposal scene, and Decoud's unconsciousness after writing the letter: "he swayed over the table as if struck by a bullet" — p. 210; not to speak of his suicide: "the stiffness of the fingers relaxes, and the lover of Antonia Avellanos rolled overboard without having heard the cord of silence snap in the solitude of the Placid Gulf, whose glittering surface remained untroubled by the fall of his body" — p. 411.)

What we are witnessing in such passages is essentially the emergence of the once hegemonic but now antiquated modernist experience of temporality: to interrogate the objective conditions of possibility of representations like these is to ask what the social and historical preconditions are for an experience of time "as a still cord stretched to the breaking point," an experience in which "natural" or *naturwüchsige*[27] temporality, at first bracketed as a purely formal "unity of apperception" (Kant), then as though by way of some inexplicable muscular relaxation in the prospective and retrospective projections that bind future and past to this present of time, is suddenly seen to shatter like glass into random instants. To construct the subtext of that technical

[26]Georg Lukács, *Existentialisme ou marxisme* (Paris: Nagel, 1948). [Au.]
[27]Naturalistic. [Ed.]

Sartrean and Heideggerian interrogation of time (the former essentially considering its active form in the project and the choice, the latter its passive dimension as the suffering of mortal finitude), we must identify and reestablish the mediation of a concrete experience of temporal activity which — the specific precondition required for the development of this or that technical philosophical investigation — may then itself be studied as a social and historical phenomenon in its own right. The point is thus less the "truth" of the philosophical description — our condemnation to be free, the discontinuity of time, ultimately even, if one likes, the absurdity of natural or organic life and of being itself — which every modern individual is surely prepared to accept as such: it is rather the situation which suddenly allows the veil to be ripped away from this intolerable ontological bedrock, and imposes it on consciousness as the ultimate lucidity ("I want to see how much I can bear," Weber wrote of a similarly unpleasant vocation for truth). As for the relationship of Marxism to such descriptions, it would surely be preferable not to substitute edifying sermons for them: that life is meaningless is not a proposition that need be inconsistent with Marxism, whose affirmation is the quite different one that History is meaningful, however absurd organic life may happen to be. The real issue is not the propositions of existentialism, but rather their charge of affect: in future societies people will still grow old and die, but the Pascalian wager of Marxism[28] lies elsewhere, namely in the idea that death in a fragmented and individualized society is far more frightening and anxiety-laden than in a genuine community, in which dying is something that happens to the group more intensely than it happens to the individual subject. The hypothesis is that time will be no less structurally empty, or to use a current version, presence will be no less of a structural and ontological illusion, in a future communal social life, but rather that this particular "fundamental revelation of the nothingness of existence" will have lost its sharpness and pain and be of less consequence.

At any rate, this abstract structure of temporality clearly cannot emerge until the older traditional activities, projects, rituals through which time was experienced, and from which it was indistinguishable, have broken down. We are discussing a process of abstraction whereby, among many other things, a supreme abstract form slowly appears which is called that of Time itself, and which then holds out the mirage of some pure and immediate experience of itself. But as Kant showed (and in a different sense Hume before him), such temporality is not an object of experience but only a pure form,[29] so that the failure to replace its nature as an abstraction — the reality of Bergson's physical or clock time — with some plenitude of experience — the mirage of Bergson's full or lived time — is scarcely surprising, even though it may have disastrous consequences for the individual subject.[30]

My argument is, then, that the questions raised in Jim's apparent quest for self-knowledge — whether he was a coward and why, and the related Sartrean problem of whether cowardice is thus something that characterizes his very being, or whether it would be possible in some analogous situation, to choose otherwise — these ethical questions which turn around the nature of freedom are in fact (as in *Being and Nothingness*) something like a structural pretext for the quite different examination of what an act and what a temporal instant really are: when does the act happen, how much preparation is necessary, how far do you have to go in it before it suddenly "takes" and becomes irrevocable, is it then infinitely divisible like the sprint-lengths of the hare, or of Zeno's arrow, and if not, then (the other

[28]Pascal's wager (from the *Pensées*) posits that every individual is forced to bet with his beliefs and behavior on the existence of God, an afterlife, a heaven. Even if the odds on heaven are slim, the payoff — eternal life — is infinite, and infinity multiplied by any quantity greater than zero is infinite. And whatever the rewards of atheism and immorality, they must be finite. Comparing the two payoffs, the rational bettor would wager on heaven. For Jameson, the Marxist promise of utopia and community — if Marx is right and history is meaningful — functions as the promised heavenly afterlife in an analogous wager. [Ed.]

[29]See the introduction to Coleridge, pp. 299–300. [Ed.]
[30]Henri Bergson's views on time are in part expressed in Marcel's meditation on memory; see Proust, p. 478. [Ed.]

face of Zeno's paradox)[31] how could that single hard ultimate indivisible atom which is the instant of action ever come into being in the first place?

It has not been sufficiently observed that the very situation which will become symbolically invested and privileged for Jim — jumping into a lifeboat, fleeing the doomed *Patna* — is one to which, in its empty form, he has already been sensitized. The episode is not, therefore, an example of a moral illustration, that "simple form" or molecular genre which Jolles calls the *casum,*[32] a vehicle for the debate and exercise of all of those ethical questions which we have here regarded as diversionary rather than irrelevant. Jim's trauma is, on the contrary, quite literally that and is constructed on the basis of an initial *repetition*. There was indeed an earlier scene that contained the elements of this one: lifeboat, people in distress, hesitation at the abyss of the instant and on the brink of the leap to freedom. The point is that in that earlier scene Jim *failed* to jump:

> Jim felt his shoulder gripped firmly. "Too late, youngster." The captain of the ship laid a restraining hand on that boy, who seemed on the point of leaping overboard, and Jim looked up with the pain of conscious defeat in his eyes. The captain smiled sympathetically. "Better luck next time. This will teach you to be smart."[6]

So the cutter returns without Jim with its rescued survivors, and an alter ego wins the glory and the satisfaction of celebrating his own heroism ("Jim thought it a pitiful display of vanity"). No wonder, then, that at the climactic moment of decision in the *Patna* crisis — the cutter dancing ready below, people in imminent danger, Jim poised "as if I had been on the top of a tower" (68) — "instinctively" Jim corrects his earlier mistake and this time "does the right thing." The longing for the second chance, for the return of

a situation in which you can prove yourself, this time triumphantly, is, when it declares itself in Jim's agony after the *Patna* episode and his trial, merely the repetition of a repetition: the real second chance, in the event the only one, is the *Patna* crisis itself, in which Jim is now given the unexpected opportunity to complete his long-suspended act, and to land in the cutter over which he was poised so many years before.

It is of course now exactly the wrong decision; my point is, however, that this "irony," if we must call it that, is incommensurable either with the various "stable ironies" of satire and comedy, or with those other more disturbingly "unstable" ones of Jamesian or Flaubertian point of view.[33] If irony is the right word, then we must distinguish between those ironies, which remain locked in the categories of the individual subject (either more objective ethical judgments, or more solipsistic "psychological" experiences within the monad) and this one, which is transindividual and more properly historical in character, but by some ideological misunderstanding projected back onto individual experience. This kind of irony is that of the "lessons of history," from which one is said to learn, for example, that they teach no lessons; it is the irony of reequipping oneself better to wage the previous war, for which one was so grievously unprepared, with the result that one is equally unprepared, but in a new way, to fight the following one. Such irony is, if you like, a negative version of the Hegelian "ruse of reason," and one which in this form is relatively cyclical and has no content (the latter would begin to emerge only when in a determinate historical situation we ask why the French general staff learned the lessons of 1870 so well that they had to unlearn them in 1914, and so on). The value of *Nostromo,* however, will lie for us in its attempt to pose this question all over again, yet this time with concrete content, a remarkable and form-transfiguring effort at lifting this entire problematic of the empty act up to the level of collective experience. For, as we shall see shortly, *Nostromo* is, like *Lord Jim,* the interrogation of a hole in time, an act whose in-

---

[31]Zeno's paradox turns on the infinite divisibility of time and distance. For an arrow to reach its target it must first travel halfway, then half of the other half, then an eighth, then a sixteenth, and so forth: By halving the distance continually it will never reach the target. [Ed.]

[32]André Jolles, *Einfache Formen* (Halle: Niemeyer, 1929), pp. 171–199. [Au.]

[33]The distinction is Wayne Booth's, in *The Rhetoric of Irony* (Chicago: University of Chicago Press, 1974). [Au.]

nermost instant falls away — proving thus at once irrevocable and impossible, a source of scandal and an aporia for contemplation. But the contemplation of *Nostromo* is a meditation on History.

That of *Lord Jim* remains stubbornly deflected onto the problematic of the individual act, and puts over and over again to itself questions that cannot be answered. The analytical interrogation of Jim's climactic moment indeed shows that nothing was there: "'I had jumped . . .' he checked himself, averted his gaze. . . . 'It seems,' he added" (68). There is no present tense of the act, we are forever always before or after it, in past or future tenses, at the stage of the project or those of the consequences. The existential investigation has been rigorously prosecuted, but ends up in neither truth nor metaphysics, but in philosophical paradox.

At least for Jim himself. For however impossible the problem of the act may be at the level of the individual subject, it is evident that the social at once washes back across it, to transform it utterly. Here the focus on the existential problematic alters, or rather it becomes clear that there were always two problematics: the technical philosophical one, what we have called the existential analytic — Roquentin's "discovery" of being in *La Nausée,* with all the unavoidable results for himself as an individual subject — and that quite different matter which is the relationship of the social institution — the bourgeoisie of Bouville — and its structures of legitimation to this shattering discovery, and to the scandal of the asocial individual. Conrad pretends to tell us the story of an individual's struggle with his own fear and courage; but he knows very well that the real issues are elsewhere, in the social example Jim cannot but set, and the demoralizing effect of Jim's discovery of Sartrean freedom on the ideological myths that allow a governing class to function and to assert its unity and legitimacy: thus Brierly, Jim's judge, whose own suicide thereby becomes a social gesture and a class abdication rather than that existential discovery of nothingness that it has so often been interpreted to be:

"We aren't an organized body of men, and the only thing that holds us together is just the name for that kind of decency. Such an affair destroys one's confidence. A man may go pretty near through his whole sea-life without any call to show a stiff upper lip. But when the call comes. . . ." [42].

Nor is Marlow's reading any different, when at the inconspicuous turn of some elaborate sentence he blurts out his astonishment at his own interest in "an occurrence which, after all, concerned me no more than as a member of an obscure body of men held together by a community of inglorious toil and by fidelity to a certain standard of conduct" (31). But the body of men thus held together in the ideological cohesion of class values which cannot without peril be called into question is not merely the confraternity of the sea; it is the ruling class of the British Empire, the heroic bureaucracy of imperial capitalism which takes that lesser, but sometimes even more heroic, bureaucracy of the officers of the merchant fleet as a figure for itself.[34] Here, more even than in the practice of a Flaubertian verbal aesthetic, Conrad's work finally becomes contiguous to the elaborate presentation and self-questioning of the British aristocratic bureaucracy in Ford's *Parade's End,* and uses much the same anecdotal form of social *scandal* to deconceal social institutions otherwise imperceptible to the naked eye. In both works, therefore, the existential "extreme situation" (the *Patna*'s bulkhead, World War I) is less a laboratory experiment designed to expose the inner articulation of the act and of the instant than the pre-

[34]"Jim has been taught a code, a set of laws about sailing, and these are not only technical but in their essence moral — definitions of responsibility and of duty which are at once specific practical rules and general social laws. He is part of a hierarchy — the officers of the ship — in which those laws are manifest or are supposed to be manifest. His moral conflict is not the product of isolation, of the lack of a society and of shared beliefs. It is that earlier kind of conflict, historically earlier, in which a man's strength is tested under pressure; in which others break the agreed rules and he goes along with this to his subsequent shame; in which, that is to say, what is really being looked at is *conduct,* within an agreed scheme of values. The ship in Conrad has this special quality, which was no longer ordinarily available to most novelists. It is a knowable community of a transparent kind" (Williams, *The English Novel,* p. 141). [Au.]

condition for the revelation of the texture of ideology.

## VI

But if this is what *Lord Jim* is really all about, then it only remains to ask why nobody thinks so, least of all Conrad himself; it remains to raise the last but exceedingly troublesome formality of the reality of the appearance, the structural origins of a misreading which is at once error and objective reality. Our reading of this novel has been based on — and has perhaps tended to confirm — a model of modernism according to which the latter is grasped as canceled realism, as a negation of "realistic content" which, like a Hegelian *Aufhebung,* continues to bear that content, crossed out and lifted up all at once, within itself. In short, it is evidently wrong to imagine, as Lukács sometimes seems to do, that modernism is some mere ideological distraction, a way of systematically displacing the reader's attention from history and society to pure form, metaphysics, and experiences of the individual monad; it is all those things, but they are not so easy to achieve as one might think. The modernist project is more adequately understood as the intent, following Norman Holland's convenient expression,[35] to "manage" historical and social, deeply political impulses, that is to say, to defuse them, to prepare substitute gratifications for them, and the like. But we must add that such impulses cannot be managed until they are aroused; this is the delicate part of the modernist project, the place at which it must be realistic in order in another moment to recontain that realism which it has awakened.

The burden of our reading of *Lord Jim* has been to restore the whole socially concrete subtext of late nineteenth-century rationalization and reification of which this novel is so powerfully, and on so many different formal levels, the expression and the Utopian compensation alike. Now we must turn to the mechanisms that ensure a structural displacement of such content, and

[35]Norman Holland, *The Dynamics of Literary Response* (New York: Oxford University Press, 1968), pp. 289–301. [Au.]

that provide for a built-in substitute interpretive system whereby readers may, if they so desire — and we do all so desire, to avoid knowing about history! — rewrite the text in more inoffensive ways. The two strategies of containment which are constructed for this purpose are clearly both on some level ideologies, and they might well be examined as such. In the present instance, however, they are narrative projections of ideology, narrative strategies that have as their common aim the rewriting of a narrative whose dynamics might otherwise elude categories of the ethical and of the individual subject. Yet, as we have seen, the contents of *Lord Jim* are themselves heterogeneous, and are drawn from the seemingly unrelated dimensions of the microscopic (reified time, desacralized action) and the macroscopic (history and praxis). It is therefore appropriate that not one, but two distinct strategies of containment should be evolved in order to manage these two distinct sources of scandal and of ideological challenge.

The two strategies in question will therefore take forms we will characterize as metaphysical and melodramatic respectively; they aim to recontain the content of the events of Jim's narrative by locating "responsible parties" and assigning guilt. We have indeed already discussed the first of these strategies, the metaphysical, which projects a proto-existential metaphysic by singling out Nature, and in particular the sea — what crushes human life — as that ultimate villain against whom Jim must do anthropomorphic battle to prove himself. Nature in this personalized sense is fundamental if Jim's quest is to remain a matter of courage and fear, rather than that quite different thing we have shown it to be in the preceding section. This is not to say that people do not drown or that the sea is not frightening, but rather that any genuine existentialism would have to unravel itself and if nature is genuinely meaningless, would, in order to be consequent with itself, have painstakingly to undo all those anthropomorphic impressions of some "true horror behind the appalling face of things," "something invisible, a directing spirit of perdition that dwelt within, like a malevolent soul in a detestable body" (19).

But Jim is not destroyed at sea, and to prove

oneself in this sense always seems to require a human adversary (see the analogous displacements back from nature to human agency in *The End of the Tether* and *Typhoon*). Thus, if the second part of the novel is to retrieve or ideologically to "resolve" what the first part so implacably laid out in the form of a dilemma, we must have recourse to the rather different strategy of melodrama, where the malevolent agency of Nature is replaced by that of man, in the person of Gentleman Brown.

The problem is the "motivation" of this device: how to imagine and to cause readers to accredit a motive for this remorseless pursuit of Jim at the very moment of his triumph? But . . . such a motivation is available everywhere in late nineteenth-century ideology, devised initially as a psychological explanation of the revolt of mobs, but also for the revolutionary vocation of disaffected intellectuals, and then more largely applied to the presentation of daily life generally, and to the discrediting of the political impulse in particular: this is, of course, the concept of *ressentiment*,[36] of which Conrad is by way of being the epic poet. There is not a single work of his (although here too *Nostromo* is uniquely privileged and almost an exception) in which the typical, gratuitously malevolent bearer of this diseased passion does not lie in wait for the innocent and unsuspecting.[37] Indeed, the great political novels, *Under Western Eyes* and *The Secret Agent* — as powerful counterrevolutionary tracts in their own ways as the masterpieces of Dostoyevsky or Orwell — emit the message of *ressentiment* (and its role as the true source of all revolutionary vocation) so obsessively that they betray their own inner dynamic: the concept of

*ressentiment* being, as I have observed earlier, itself the product of the feeling in question.

This is not to say that Gentleman Brown is not a powerful figure, although even his single-minded nihilistic power depends on a rather complicated character system, whereby it is the lesser *homme de ressentiment,* Cornelius, who draws off everything that is grotesque about this passion to himself, thus leaving a purer vision of evil and energy for Jim's worthier and more absolute adversary:

> The others were merely vulgar and greedy brutes, but he seemed moved by some complex intention. He would rob a man as if only to demonstrate his poor opinion of the creature. [214–15] There was in the broken, violent speech of that man, unveiling before me his thoughts with the very hand of Death upon his throat, an undisguised ruthlessness of purpose, a strange vengeful attitude towards his own past, and a blind belief in the righteousness of his will against all mankind, something of that feeling which could induce the leader of a horde of wandering cut-throats to call himself proudly the Scourge of God. [225] I had to bear the sunken glare of his fierce crow-footed eyes, . . . reflecting how much certain forms of evil are akin to madness, derived from intense egoism, inflamed by resistance, tearing the soul to pieces, and giving factitious vigor to the body. [209]

In such powerful rhetoric, we can sense something of the violent displacement that must be done to narrative and to its *actants*[38] to produce what we may call the effect of melodrama, and to conjure up the mythic feeling of the villain — so archaic and historically ugly a feeling, which has its genealogy deep in immemorial lynchings and pogroms, in the expulsion of the scapegoat and the ritual curse. It is mind-cleansing to juxtapose with this self-perpetuating vision of evil the great Brechtian lines on the mask of the Japanese demon, with its swollen veins and hideous grimace

>   all betokening
> What an exhausting effort it takes
> To be evil.

[36]Rancor; in Nietzsche's *Genealogy of Morals*, this term denotes the feeling provoked in slavish weaklings by persons of strength and nobility. [Ed.]

[37]I must therefore feel that Fleischman's assertion — "in the entire body of Conrad's work, in fact, the only examples of radical evil are Gentleman Brown in *Lord Jim* and the weird trio of *Victory*" (*Conrad's Politics,* p. 28) — is singularly inexact. On the other hand, it is clear that to recognize the obsessive motif of *ressentiment* would unavoidably place the ideology of "organicism" that accompanies it in a new and less favorable light. [Au.]

[38]Agents. [Ed.]

# 2

# PSYCHOLOGICAL CRITICISM

*A piece of creative writing, like a daydream, is a continuation of, and a substitute for, what was once the play of childhood.* — SIGMUND FREUD

*The impact of an archetype, whether it takes the form of immediate experience or is expressed through the spoken word, stirs us because it summons up a voice that is stronger than our own. Whoever speaks in primordial images, speaks with a thousand voices; he enthralls and overpowers, while at the same time he lifts the idea he is seeking to express out of the occasional and the transitory into the real of the ever-enduring.*

— CARL GUSTAV JUNG

*The unconscious has the structure of a language.*       — JACQUES LACAN

Because Sigmund Freud once acknowledged that most of his discoveries about the unconscious mind had been anticipated by the poets and artists of the past, it should not be surprising that the light of depth psychology has long been trained upon literature in an effort to explain its origins, character, and effects. This section contains reflections on literature not only by Freud and his followers but by his student and opponent, Carl Gustav Jung, who set up the most important alternative form of depth psychology, and by Jacques Lacan, the French analyst whose recasting of Freudian doctrines in a new semiotic form has done much to revitalize the thinking about language and the mind. It also contains essays on critical theory by Harold Bloom and Northrop Frye, two literary scholars for whom Freud's and Jung's ideas have served not as doctrines but as enabling metaphors for building theories of literature.

Freud's ideas originated not in the ivory tower of theory but in his Vienna consulting room, where he practiced as a neurologist specializing in the treatment of hysteria. Only after experimenting with various physical cures, Freud came to believe that many of his patients' symptoms were caused by something less tangible. At first he hypothesized that hysteria was always a delayed psychosomatic reaction to a real trauma, like childhood rape or incest; eventually, however, he concluded that the cause was the patient's own incestuous desires, desires so unacceptable that they could not be admitted to consciousness but were instead repressed and held in the unconscious, emerging as symptoms in later life.

In Freud's original scheme, the unconscious was a part of a system consisting of the conscious mind; the preconscious mind, which included anything on which attention is not currently focused, including forgotten memories and thoughts that could with effort be brought back up into consciousness; and the unconscious itself, whose workings were not directly available to consciousness. The evidence for the existence of the unconscious as well as the sense of its contents, comes from dreams and fantasies and from *parapraxes* or meaningful mistakes — slips of the tongue, pen, or memory — that also reveal repressed desires and fears. In the original formulation, the unconscious was a realm of energies, generated by the instincts or drives, focusing and binding onto objects (*cathexis*), and being diverted from their goals. Two major drives function in the unconscious: the sexual drive (*libido*), which aims at pleasure, and the aggressive drive, which aims at destruction. These drives are generally fused, and often the term "libido" is used for both.

In the course of infancy and childhood, the libido is focused on different parts of the body (*erogenous zones*), starting with the mouth in early infancy and shifting to include the anus around the second year and the genitals in the third year. These are the oral, anal, and phallic phases of what is termed *infantile sexuality,* and whether or not it feels appropriate to use the term "sexual" for the pleasure infants get from sucking on their thumbs (or adults from smoking), it is clearly a drive, and one that has to do with pleasure rather than with nourishment or any other obviously physiological mechanism.

As Freud elaborated his notion of a mind within the mind, the unconscious was transformed from a simple, dark cave of repression into a complex transactional world. In his later, "topographical" formulation of the unconscious (1923), Freud theorized a polity inhabited in earliest infancy only by the *id* (the location of the drives). As the infant becomes socialized, however, the direct satisfaction of the drives is no longer possible. Most of us gradually learn to eat and eliminate wastes at socially appropriate times and to refrain from grabbing the man or woman we want and forcibly eliminating our rivals. Thus the unconscious develops as the battleground between the pleasure principle — the desire to gratify impulses immediately — and the reality principle, which controls these impulses for the sake of higher social values.

Part of this learning takes the form of the suppression or redirection of our unconscious drives: The libido is opposed by alternative energies or shifted to a more appropriate object or aim or occasion. These shiftings of the libido are called *defenses,* and their operation is the function of a differentiated part of the unconscious, the *ego.* One of the major defenses against the power of the drives is *repression,* which Freud discovered in his patients, but there are many others as well. Among those most often occurring in literature are *projection* (ascribing an impulse of one's own to someone else) and *symbolization* (shifting the object of a drive to something else that can stand as a metaphorical or metonymic substitute for it).

Freud used the term "primary process" to refer to the direct work of libido-energy within the unconscious — primary because it is how psychic energy functions before the development of the ego. It is characterized by the instantaneous gratification of impulses or their rapid rechanneling into other, similar activities. The person who cannot express anger at work but shouts at his or her spouse at home is engaging in "primary process thinking." The term "secondary process" denotes the working of the mature ego, which might channel the energy of inex-pressable anger at the boss into doing a better job at work — or finding a more satisfying career.

The third part of the unconscious is called the *superego*, which begins to form during childhood as a result of the Oedipus complex, one of the most powerfully determinative elements in the growth of the child. The Oedipus complex begins in a late phase of infantile sexuality, between the child's third and sixth year, and it takes a different form in males than it does in females. Boys and girls together begin life relating more powerfully to the mother than to the father, and both sexes wish to possess the mother exclusively. They also begin to sense that their claim to exclusive attention is thwarted by the mother's attention to the father, and, already in the phallic stage in which the genitals have become an erogenous zone, they connect that attention to the sexual activities that mother and father participate in and from which they are excluded. The result is a murderous rage against the father (and any other siblings who may be potential competitors) and a desire to possess the mother. (There is also a rage against the mother for permitting the primacy of the father.) Many things keep this rage from being acted out, including feelings of love for the father, dependency on him, and fear of loss of approval or retaliation for aggressive behavior.

Where the Oedipus complex differs in boys and girls is in the functioning of the related *castration complex*. Boys know from observing their own bodies and those of their fathers that they have a penis but that some people (including their mother) do not. Freud theorized that during the Oedipal rivalry, boys fantasize that punishment for their rage will take the form of the loss of the penis. Fear of this leads the boy to repress his rage and desire. In a successful Oedipal outcome, the boy learns to identify with the father in the hope of someday possessing a woman like his mother. In girls, the castration complex does not take the form of *anxiety*, because their lack of a penis suggests that the dreaded castration has already occurred, as it has to the desired mother as well. The result is a frustrated rage in which the girl shifts her sexual desire from the mother to the father (who possesses the penis she wants), and then, when her sexual advances to the father are opposed, begins to identify with the mother in order eventually to possess another man like the father.

The process, as Freud theorized it, is like so many love affairs, long and painful; it involves not only frustration and repression of desires but the turning of desire against itself in the form of self-criticism, self-punishment, and even self-hatred.

The conflict generates the moralist of the unconscious, the superego, which is itself divided into the ego-ideal, the repository of images of perfection against which the child (and later the adult) will unhappily compare him- or herself, and the conscience, where approval and disapproval of one's actions are registered. It must be remembered, of course, that Freud's conscience is part of the unconscious, and its work of judgment and self-punishment takes the form of irrational feelings of guilt and unworthiness, and neurotic behavior against which the ego must make defenses as surely as it does against the id.

The final topographical configuration of the unconscious as id, superego, and ego may seem rather like Plato's tripartite soul, mythologized in the *Phaedrus* as Evil Horse, Good Horse, and Charioteer, which may reflect Plato's intuitive sense of the unconscious as well as Freud's own classical education.

Freud analyzed a number of literary texts for their psychological content (including E. T. A. Hoffmann's *The Sandman* and Shakespeare's *King Lear*), but his most important general discussion of art is "Creative Writers and Daydreaming" (reprinted in this chapter). In this brief essay, Freud draws an analogy between nocturnal dreams and daytime fantasies, which are disguised versions of repressed wishes — the pleasure principle at play — and the conscious constructions of literary artists.

Freud does not explain his method of dream-analysis fully here (that method had been contained in his earlier treatise, *The Interpretation of Dreams* [1900]), but the key to his explication is that the dream is a disguised wish. This wish is the *latent content* of the dream. But the dream as it appears to the dreamer and is reported to the analyst consists of what Freud termed *manifest content* — it is a story that has, in effect, been censored by the defenses of the ego. One could say that latent content is to manifest content as primary process is to secondary process. The analysis of a dream involves peeling back the ego-defenses that have distorted the wish to reveal the working of the primary process beneath.

Like nocturnal dreams, literature contains a latent and a manifest content. The primary process that lurks behind popular novels (from *The Godfather* to *Love's Tender Fury*) obviously embodies the ambitious and erotic wishes to dominate others and to possess loved objects, wishes that formed during the Oedipal phase. But the difference between popular fiction and literature is not in the latent content but in the way the defenses are marshalled. Freud suggests that "better" fiction contains the same Oedipal fantasies but expressed in a form that is more carefully and elaborately defended. Because the form is less raw, it is therefore more acceptable to us as readers.

While Freud was once criticized for implying that the artist is sick, creating out of personal neurotic needs, this objection no longer seems sound. It is widely accepted that nearly all of us are at least slightly neurotic and that the artist's need to create comes not from lunacy but merely from a greater sensitivity to the lacks and dissatisfactions that plague us all. The primary objection to Freudian criticism is its insensitivity to aesthetic quality: Form enters the work of art merely as a sugar-coating that allows one to swallow down the dose of fantasy. Later analytic critics have tried to deal with this issue, although the function of artistic form remains one of the vexing questions within the analytic approach to literature.

## STYLES OF FREUDIAN CRITICISM

Traditionally, there have been three stages at which psychoanalysis may enter the study of the literary work: We can examine the mind of the author, the minds of the author's characters, and our own minds as we read the text. Though Freud concludes his essay with the suggestion that artistic works allow the audience to revel in their own forbidden fantasies, his focus is primarily on the text as the fantasy-construct of the artist. And there is a long tradition of Freudian criticism that seeks in the text for the buried motives and hidden neurotic conflicts that generated the writer's art. One widely admired study of this sort is Frederick C. Crews's *The Sins of the Fathers: Hawthorne's Psychological Themes* (1966), which examines the tales of the 1840s for the different ways in which they embody the unresolved Oedipus complex suggested by what we know of Hawthorne's youth and manhood. Hawthorne provided a great deal of material for such a study in his private diaries, and biographers began their work soon after his death. The hazards of doing psychoanalytic criticism in this mode are inversely proportional to the amount of material available on the author's life and private thoughts. It is never completely safe to guess at the psychic significance of a work of art, even that of a candid living author, and for some major writers (like Chaucer and Shakespeare), we have only the most minimal sense of what their private lives may have been like, so that psychoanalytic criticism in this mode must be mere speculation.

After the author, we can analyze the characters. This has also been a popular mode of criticism, beginning with *Hamlet and Oedipus* by Freud's disciple and biographer, Ernest Jones, who interpreted Hamlet's problematic hesitation to slay Claudius as stemming from an identification with his uncle, since Hamlet, too, wished to kill the elder Hamlet and marry Gertrude. It is tempting to analyze characters whom we see rendered with telling truth both internally and externally, but, in fact, the hazards of speculation about characters are even greater than about authors. Although Hamlet's actions and language reveal a great deal about him, all we will ever know is contained in the four thousand lines of Shakespeare's play.

Another problem stems from the fact that characters are both more and less than real persons. While some aspects of characters have a *mimetic* function (the representation of human action and motivation), others have primarily *textual* functions (the revelation — or concealment — of information to an audience), which has no precise parallel in life.[1] The contradictions in Hamlet's character may result from the psychic complexities Shakespeare imagined, but they also result from the fact that Hamlet is an agent in a tragic drama with a highly developed system of conventions. An additional problem of psychoanalytic interpretation is

[1]One should remember that though literary characters are not the same as real persons, real persons in the masks they present to the world often resemble literary characters.

whether a character's degree of self-awareness is to be seen as a psychological fact or an unintended consequence of the character's textual function. One might raise this question about James Bryan's discussion of J. D. Salinger's *The Catcher in the Rye* (1974), in which Holden Caulfield's maladjustment is ascribed to his repressed incestuous desires for his prepubescent sister Phoebe. The material on which Bryan bases his interpretation comes directly from Holden, whose only mildly embarrassed awareness of his sister's sexiness argues against rather than for Bryan's diagnosis of neurotic repression.[2]

It is tempting to seek in psychoanalysis the secret of a text, but it can be more illuminating to reverse the explanation and to look to literature, as Freud himself did, for clarifications of psychology. Such an approach is exemplified in Samuel Alexander's discussion (1939) of the *Henry IV* plays, which claims that they portray the growth of the ego (Prince Hal), resisting the id's blandishments of immediate gratification (Falstaff), rejecting also the superego's repression (the Chief Justice), mastering phallic desire (Hotspur), and reconciling his rivalry with the father (King Henry) before assuming the crown of adulthood.

Since authors may not provide much material for the would-be analyst and, since characters are not real persons, it would seem that the safest form of psychoanalytic criticism is the analysis of the audience. The readers' gaze into their own unconscious responses to literature is limited only by their insight into their own psychic processes. In the hands of Norman Holland and David Bleich (both in Ch. 7) this has produced a reader-response mode of analytic criticism. The questions that tend to be raised about methods like those of Holland and Bleich have less to do with the tact and accuracy of their findings than with their subjectivity. If readers find anal imagery in a poem, are they revealing its author's fixations or only their own? Two possible answers result, depending on whether the analytic critic believes in the objective existence of a "text" to be analyzed. Those who do believe, like David Bleich or Norman Holland in his early phase, have replied that in the first place, *all* criticism is necessarily subjective, and the personal character of analytic criticism is only more honestly and explicitly so; and that in the second place, idiosyncratic readings can be identified and corrected by the usual forms of reality-testing, through self-examination and self-analysis and through exposure to debate with others. Those who do not, like Holland in his later phase (*5 Readers Reading* [1975] and thereafter), would reply that the question, in the form in which it was posed, is meaningless. The poem has no meaning before it is read, and there can be no distinction between what is "in" the poem and what is "in" the reader.

Author, character, and audience usually exhaust the spectrum of Freudian criticism. A fourth alternative has been proposed by Peter Brooks in *Reading for the Plot* (1984). In its central chapter, "Freud's Masterplot," Brooks discusses *Beyond the Pleasure Principle* (1920), that ambiguous late treatise in which Freud examines the *repetition-compulsion,* a neurotic form of behavior that substitutes repetition

---

[2]James Bryan, "The Psychological Structure of *The Catcher in the Rye*," *PMLA* 89 (1974): 1065–74.

for remembrance when a memory is too distressing for repression to be overcome. Freud finds that he cannot account for the excruciating manifestations of the repetition-compulsion on the basis of the pleasure principle. He is forced to theorize that it the product of a death-drive, which balances the life-drive of libido. For Brooks, the repetition-compulsion is the central motif of literature. Repetition not only sets the conditions of narrative (one thinks of fairy tales, in which the same situation recurs three times), but it is also basic, through rhyme, refrains, and thematic devices, to poetry. Brooks reads *Beyond the Pleasure Principle* "as a text about textuality" in which "plot mediates meanings within the contradictory human world of the eternal and the mortal. Freud's masterplot speaks of the temporality of desire, and speaks to our very desire for fictional plots."

A more metaphorical variety of Freudian criticism is that of Harold Bloom, who begins with the notion that literary influence is analogous to paternity. Weak poets may merely copy their forebears, but for strong poets of the postromantic era, Bloom expects an Oedipal rivalry between the younger "ephebe" and the earlier strong poet he has chosen as his artistic "father." The "son" needs metaphorically to kill or castrate the "father" to make room for his own adult life, and he does so by creatively *misreading* his predecessor in ways that necessitate his own corrective labors. Bloom's theory is not simple, and he posits a vast repertoire of ways in which the younger "ephebe" can perform this liberating act of misprision. Bloom's work has not only proved influential in itself, it has also inspired imitation and challenge. In *The Madwoman in the Attic* (1979), Sandra Gilbert and Susan Gubar have appropriated Bloom's method for their feminist purposes. In effect, they discuss how Bloom's question must be adapted when talking of *women* writers and the Fathers who would seem to exclude them from the succession by reason of their sex, and the special anxiety of authorship women suffer, which can be overcome, at least in part, by participation in the powerful sisterhood of the female literary tradition. (See Chapter 6.)

## JUNG

In an Oedipal fashion that Harold Bloom would doubtless have admired, Freud was the object of a rebellion by his most famous pupil, the Swiss physician Carl Gustav Jung. Jung took from Freud the notion of a structured unconscious mind, but after this the differences between them are profound. In Jung, the unconscious of Freud's writings is termed the "personal unconscious"; it is but a "thin layer" under the conscious mind, relatively accessible by tricks of free association and parapraxis, and therefore not of supreme significance. More important is the "collective unconscious," or racial memory, through which the spirit of the whole human species manifests itself. This deeper layer of the unconscious is not accessible through the techniques of analysis; we understand its existence through our profound response to universal symbols.

Jung developed the idea of a racial memory through his study of anthropology and comparative mythology, sciences that were beginning to show interesting results by the first decade of the century. Studies like James Frazer's *The Golden Bough* (1890) revealed striking similarities between the myths and rituals of primitive peoples around the globe, peoples who seemed to be too distant to have influenced each other directly. Jung's hypothesis was that direct influence was unnecessary; that the similar mythologies were merely differing manifestations of structures deep in the human unconscious. These structures Jung termed "archetypes"; they manifest themselves not only in myth and in dreams but in the finished art of cultures like our own in the form of symbols.

The symbols take the shape of various aspects of the Self. On the surface of the Self is the *Mask,* the face we show to the outside world. Beneath this is the *Shadow,* a demonic image of evil that represents the side of the Self that we reject. Beneath this is the *Anima,* the feminine side of the male Self, and the *Animus,* the correspondingly masculine side of the female Self. (The Animus, for males, becomes an image of the Father.) For men, the Anima, the Great Mother, is characteristically split in the shadow of the Shadow into the nurturing Mother, the tempting Whore, and the destroying Crone. Women, in turn, split the Animus into a Protector, a Lover, and a Destroying Angel. Finally there is the image of the *Spirit*, symbolized by a wise old man or woman. The four principal archetypes — Shadow, Anima, Animus, and Spirit — make up what Jung called the *Syzygy:* a quaternion symbolizing wholeness, the quality of which people are usually in search. The search itself often culminates in another archetype, the *Night-Sea-Journey*, a voyage from life through death to a new rebirth.

In Jungian analysis, the patient recapitulates his life and looks for the ways in which these symbols have been embodied within its texture. Similarly, Jungian criticism is generally involved with a search for the embodiment of these symbols within particular works of art. The pleasures of Jungian criticism often come in noting the parallels between one work and another; how, for example, Cora and Alice in *The Last of the Mohicans,* Rebecca and Rowena in *Ivanhoe,* Becky Sharp and Amelia Sedley in *Vanity Fair,* and Eustacia and Thomasin in *The Return of the Native* all seem to be variations on the Dark Lady and the White Lady — split versions of the Anima. On the other hand, since all powerful literature embodies these archetypes, Jungian criticism can become a relatively monotonous and predictable approach, harping invariably on the same chord, finding the basic motifs of the Quest, the Shadow, and the Night-Sea-Journey in every text.

In a sense, Northrop Frye's criticism has had the same almost metaphoric relation to Jungian psychology as Harold Bloom's later ideas have had to the Freudian scheme. Frye feels (as does Bloom) that literature gets made out of other literature. But instead of the personal agon of poetic fathers and sons, Frye's notion of rewriting has the impersonality of Jung's collective unconscious: Each generation rewrites the stories of the past in ways that make sense for it, recycling a vast tradition over the ages. The great myths of the gods, created in the vast dream of mankind in an almost prehistoric past, are converted into legends of semidivine heroes, then into stories of people very much like ourselves.

Frye's "The Archetypes of Literature" (1951) promises in effect to go beyond the Jungian criticism of precursors such as Maud Bodkin by presenting, not just fragmentary insights, but the "ground plan of a systematic and comprehensive development of criticism"; what he eventually delivered was an encyclopaedic, and highly influential study, *Anatomy of Criticism* (1957). Here the schema of archetypal criticism is elaborated much further into an exhaustive mapping of the possibilities of literary form and content.

Frye begins with a theory of *modes* describing five levels of narrative (myth, legend, high mimetic, low mimetic, and ironic), which correspond to the stature and degree of freedom of action of the protagonist. For example, the tragic myth of the dying god of nature might descend to a legend in Malory's *Morte d'Arthur,* a high mimetic epic in Tennyson's *Idylls of the King,* a low mimetic novel in T. H. White's *The Once and Future King,* and an ironic parody in the film *Monty Python and the Holy Grail.*

A second theory of *symbols* differentiates five methods of symbolic interpretation, not unlike Dante's theory of polysemy: (1) In the *literal* approach to the symbol, the very shape of the signifier becomes important; (2) in the *descriptive* phase, the signifier is related to its signified — its usual meaning; (3) in the *formal* phase, the signifier is related to other similar signifiers in patterns of imagery; (4) in the *archetypal* phase, the signifier is related to its ritual significance; (5) in the *anagogic* phase, the signifier becomes a monad, a symbolic universe in itself, a function of the total dream of mankind.

Third, the theory of *mythos* elaborates the relationships between comedy, romance, tragedy, and irony discussed in "The Archetypes" as twenty-four variants on the monomyth of the quest. And finally, the theory of *genres* creates a schema for locating the various forms of presentation — lyric, drama, epos, and fiction; and within fiction to forms of novel, romance, confession, and anatomy. The result is a multidimensional space in which one may locate the position of any work of literature and its relationship to any other.

Frye's *Anatomy of Criticism* comes close to fleshing out T. S. Eliot's remark that "the works of literature form an ideal order among themselves." In this direction, Frye seems to reach out toward the Structuralists, then just beginning work on the Continent. In the other direction, he harks back to Jung, though he is careful to disclaim any belief in a collective unconscious or racial memory, or the dependence of his literary theories upon any such belief. Indeed, Frye reads Jung only as one who has provided "a grammar of literary symbolism," as a textual critic rather than as a psychologist.

## LACAN

The revisions to Freudian theory of Jacques Lacan, the French psychoanalyst whose thought has had such a broad influence on literary theory since the 1960s through seminars attended by Parisian intellectuals — including Louis Althusser, Michel Foucault, Paul Ricoeur, Roland Barthes, and Julia Kristeva — can only be discussed briefly. His ideas are unfamiliar to many practicing American psychoanalysts, perhaps because Lacan largely jettisoned the therapeutic model of psycho-analysis leading to the cure of symptoms, considering it a branch more of philosophy than of medicine. Of course, while Lacan deviated from the mainstream of psychoanalytic thought and was expelled from the International Psychoanalytic Association, he believed himself to be returning to Freud rather than departing from him.

Where Freud views the mechanisms of the unconscious as generated by libido (sexual energy) in a transactional system resembling that of thermodynamics, Lacan centers the theory of the unconscious on the sense within us of something *absent*.[3] The sense of absence can take the form of mere lack (*manque*) or need (*besoin*), which force the psyche to make demands, or it can take the higher form of desire (*désir*). It is in the true desire — for an object that is itself conscious and can desire us in return — that the higher forms of self-consciousness arise. (This dialectic of desire Lacan took not from Freud but from Hegel's *Phenomenology of Spirit*.) Lacan's term for the universal symbol, or signifier of desire is the *Phallus*. It is important not to confuse the Phallus in this sense with the male sexual organ, the penis. *Both* sexes experience the absence of and desire for the Phallus — which may be one reason Lacan's restructuring of Freud has appealed to feminists like Hélène Cixous and Luce Irigaray.

This revision of Freud shifts the description of mental processes from a purely biological model to a semiotic one. Freud, for instance, discusses the first phase of childhood as the oral phase, in which the child's pleasure comes largely from suckling; the anal phase follows, when the child learns to control and to enjoy controlling the elimination of feces. In Lacan, the analogue of the oral phase is the Mirror-Stage, from six to eighteen months, in which the child's image of its bodily self changes from mere formlessness and fragmentation to a jubilant iden-tification with the unified shape it can see in the mirror. During this development, the child experiences itself as "le Désir de la Mère," the desire of the mother in both senses. The baby not only knows it needs its mother but also feels itself to be what completes and fulfills the mother (the Phallus). Within this phase of development there is no unconscious, because there is nothing to repress and no way to repress it. From this phase Lacan derives the psychic field of the Imaginary, which continues into adult life, where the sense of reality is grasped purely as images and fantasies of the fulfillment of desire.

Repression and the unconscious arrive together with the insertion of the child into language, around eighteen months, when Freud's anal stage begins. As the child learns the names of things, its desires are no longer met automatically; the child finds that it must ask for what it wants and that it can no longer ask for things that do not have names. As the child learns to ask for a signified by pronouncing a signifier, it learns that one thing can symbolize another. As Muller and Richardson have put it, "from this point on the child's desire, like an endless

---

[3]Like the poststructuralist Jacques Derrida and the Marxist Louis Althusser, whom he influenced, Lacan subscribes to a metaphysic based on *absence* rather than one based on *presence*. See p. 561 and p. 959.

quest for a lost paradise, must be channelled like an underground river through the subterranean passageways of the symbolic order, which make it possible that things be present in their absence in some ways through words."[4] Now desires can be repressed, and the child can ask for something that metaphorically or metonymically replaces the desired object. Lacan punningly called this stage of development "le Nom-du-Père": "the Name-of-the-Father," which, in French, is pronounced like "the no-of-the-Father"; for language is only the first of the negations and subjections to law that will now begin to affect the child. The child has entered what Lacan calls the field of the Symbolic.

A third Lacanian field, less discussed in his writings than the others, is that of the Real. By this Lacan seems to mean those incomprehensible aspects of experience that exist beyond the grasp of images and symbols through which we think and constitute our reality. The Real functions rather like the noumena in Kant (p. 300). Lacan recognizes that adult humans are always inscribed within language, but he does not suggest that language must thereby constitute the ultimate reality.

Since in Lacan's dialectic of desire one object may symbolize another, which is a substitute for still another, Lacan has said that "the unconscious is structured like a language." Lacan derives his ideas of language and the unconscious not from Freud but from one of the fathers of semiotics, Ferdinand de Saussure, as he was interpreted by the structuralist anthropologist Claude Lévi-Strauss. Lévi-Strauss considered the unconscious not as "the repository of a unique history which makes each of us an irreplacible being" but rather as "reducible to a function — the symbolic function," which in turn was merely "the aggregate of the laws" of language.[5]

The primary laws of language in structural linguistics are those of the selection and combination of primary basic elements.[6] Metaphor is a mode of symbolization in which one thing is signified by another that is like it, that is part of the same paradigmatic class. And Lacan saw metaphor as equivalent to the Freudian defense of condensation (in which one symbol becomes the substitute for a whole series of associations). Metonymy is a mode of symbolization in which one thing is signified by another that is associated with it but not of the same class — a syntagmatic relationship — which Lacan regarded as equivalent to Freudian displacement. Because most of the Freudian defenses could be read as versions either of condensation or displacement, it appears that unconscious psychic mechanisms operate like linguistic tropes. On the other hand, we should not look within Lacan's linguistic psychology for anything like the hierarchical structure imposed on the elements of language by a syntax.[7]

[4]John P. Muller and William J. Richardson, *Lacan and Language: A Reader's Guide to Écrits* (New York: International Universities Press, 1982), p. 23.

[5]Claude Lévi-Strauss, "The Effectiveness of Symbols," *Structural Anthropology* (New York: Anchor Books, 1967), p. 198.

[6]Technically these are called paradigmatic and syntagmatic relationships and are discussed at greater length in the introduction to Chapter 4, Structuralism and Semiotics.

[7]This gap may betoken a blind spot in Lacan's use of linguistics. Much of the French theory that is ultimately based on Saussure (Lacan, Derrida, Althusser), seems trapped in the limitations of structural

If the unconscious is like a language, it is one characterized as a foreign tongue: "the discourse of the Other." What Lacan means by this is not clear or simple. Since in Lacan's thought the original Other is the father, the unconscious is Other in its origins — in the *Nom-du-Père*. But the unconscious is also the residence of alterity and alienation within ourselves, the Other to whom we must speak and whom we hear speaking in our internal dialogue. In treating the unconscious as a language rather than a polity, Lacan eliminates the notion of the ego as a homunculus inside ourselves, constantly defending itself against the depredations of the id. What he leaves in its place is far less solid and reified. The ego is an Imaginary construct, a false image of identity and wholeness; but the ego is less important to Lacan than the subject, and the subject is simply the fluid position from which the signification of desire takes place. The subject is not entirely effaced, but it is decentered from a privileged spot to that of a function of language.

Like Freud, Lacan approached literature primarily as material that, properly interpreted, illustrated the major concepts of his psychology. The major texts include Lacan's seminars on "Desire and the Interpretation of Desire in *Hamlet*";[8] and the somewhat more accessible "Seminar on 'The Purloined Letter'"[9] reprinted in this chapter. This essay takes off from a strictly Freudian account of Poe's "The Purloined Letter" by the analyst Marie Bonaparte, who, noting the resemblances between the detective Dupin and his quarry, the Minister D., suggested that the latter was a father figure and analyzed the story as an Oedipal triangle in which Dupin succeeds in destroying the father/minister for the sake of the mother/queen. Lacan finds that the resemblances and repetitions, once he starts to look, go much further than this, and involve the author — and the reader — in the Lacanian dialectic of desire.

Lacan's indirect influence on criticism has been considerable, primarily because his psychology has affected the philosophy and literary theory of the many French intellectuals who attended his seminars (and at a further remove, British and American scholars influenced by the French, as Fredric Jameson has been influenced by Althusser). But a strain of direct Lacanian criticism has also begun to appear in the past decade, in separate essays and in collections such as those edited by Shoshana Felman (1981) and Robert Con Davis (1983). Many of these works have taken the form of interpenetrative readings of Lacan and a literary text, which inevitably find the basic themes of Lacan's psychology within the text. Perhaps this is a workable compromise while Lacan's ideas are still relatively unfamiliar, but one suspects that, like Lacanian analysis itself, Lacanian criticism will be

---

linguistics, a rigid schema of polarized differences that was better able to explain the phonology and morphology of words than the hierarchical reorderings of grammar. If Lacan regretted that Freud's conception of language had been impoverished by the state of linguistics in his time, we may regret that Lacan was not exposed to the revolution in syntactic theory that began with Zellig Harris and Noam Chomsky.

[8]Published 1977 in *Yale French Studies* 55/56, and reprinted in Shoshana Felman's *Literature and Psychoanalysis: The Question of Reading: Otherwise* (Baltimore: Johns Hopkins University Press, 1981).

[9]Published in the French edition of *Écrits* and translated by Jeffrey Mehlman in *Yale French Studies* 47/48 (1966).

centered intensively on the Word and the chains of association that are developed within the text.

## Selected Bibliography

Alexander, Samuel. *Philosophic and Literary Pieces*. London: Macmillan, 1939.

Bleich, David. *Readings and Feelings: An Introduction to Subjective Criticism*. Urbana, Ill.: National Council of Teachers of English, 1975.

———. *Subjective Criticism*. Baltimore: Johns Hopkins University Press, 1978.

Bloom, Harold. *The Anxiety of Influence*. New York: Oxford University Press, 1975.

———. *A Map of Misreading*. Oxford and New York: Oxford University Press, 1980.

———. *Agon: Toward a Theory of Revisionism*. Oxford and New York: Oxford University Press, 1982.

Bodkin, Maud. *Archetypal Patterns in Poetry*. London: Oxford University Press, 1934.

Bonaparte, Marie. *The Life and Works of Edgar Allan Poe*. 1933; London: Imago, 1949.

Brenner, Charles. *An Elementary Textbook Of Psychoanalysis*. New York: Anchor Books, 1974.

Brooks, Peter. *Reading for the Plot*. New York: Knopf, 1984.

Clément, Catherine. *The Lives and Legends of Jacques Lacan*. New York: Columbia University Press, 1983.

Crews, Frederick. *The Sins of the Fathers: Hawthorne's Psychological Themes*. New York: Oxford University Press, 1966.

———. *Out of My System: Psychology, Ideology and Critical Method*. New York: Oxford University Press, 1976.

Davis, Robert Con, ed. *Lacan and Narration: The Psychoanalytic Difference in Narrative Theory*. Baltimore: Johns Hopkins University Press, 1983.

Deleuze, Gilles, and Félix Guattari. *Anti-Oedipus: Capitalism and Schizophrenia*. 1972; New York: Viking Press, 1977.

Derrida, Jacques. "The Purveyor of Truth." *Yale French Studies* 52 (1975): 31–113.

Felman, Shoshana, ed. *Literature and Psychoanalysis: The Question of Reading: Otherwise*. Baltimore, Johns Hopkins University Press, 1981.

———. "Turning the Screw of Interpretation." *Yale French Studies* 55/56 (1977): 94–207.

———. "Rereading Femininity." *Yale French Studies* 62 (1981): 19–44.

Freud, Anna. *The Ego and the Mechanisms of Defense*. 1936; New York: International Universities Press, 1966.

Freud, Sigmund. *The Standard Edition of the Complete Psychological Works*. 24 vols. 1940–68; London: Hogarth Press and the Institute of Psychoanalysis, 1953.

Frye, Northrop. *Anatomy of Criticism: Four Essays*. Princeton: Princeton University Press, 1957.

Gallop, Jane. *The Daughter's Seduction: Feminism and Psychoanalysis*. Ithaca: Cornell University Press, 1982.

———. *Reading Lacan*. Ithaca: Cornell University Press, 1984.

Gilbert, Sandra, and Susan Gubar. *The Madwoman in the Attic*. New Haven: Yale University Press, 1979.

Gilman, Sander L., ed. *Introducing Psychoanalytic Theory*. New York: Brunner/Mazel, 1982.

Hartman, Geoffrey H., ed. *Psychoanalysis and the Question of the Text: Selected Papers from the English Institute*. Baltimore: Johns Hopkins University Press, 1979.

Hertz, Neil. "Freud and the Sandman." In *Textual Strategies: Perspectives in Post-Structural Criticism,* ed. Josué V. Harari. Ithaca: Cornell University Press, 1979.

Holland, Norman N. *The Dynamics of Literary Response.* New York: Oxford University Press, 1968.

———. *Poems in Persons.* New York: Norton, 1975.

———. *5 Readers Reading.* New Haven: Yale University Press, 1975.

Johnson, Barbara. "The Frame of Reference: Poe, Lacan, Derrida." *Yale French Studies* 55/56 (1977): 457–505.

Jones, Ernest. *Hamlet and Oedipus.* New York: Doubleday, 1949.

Jung, Carl Gustav. *Complete Works.* 17 vols. Ed. Herbert Read, Michael Fordham, and Gerhard Adler. New York: Pantheon, 1953–.

Kris, Ernest. *Psychoanalytic Explorations in Art.* 1952; New York: Schocken Books, 1964.

Kristeva, Julia. *Desire in Language.* New York: Columbia University Press, 1980.

Kurzweil, Edith, and William Phillips, eds. *Literature and Psychoanalysis.* New York: Columbia University Press, 1983.

Lacan, Jacques. "The Seminar on 'The Purloined Letter.'" *Yale French Studies* 48 (1972): 39–72.

———. *Écrits: A Selection.* New York: Norton, 1977.

Laplanche, Jean, and Jean-Baptiste Pontalis. *The Language of Psychoanalysis.* London: Hogarth Press, 1973.

Lawrence, D. H. *Studies in Classical American Literature.* New York: Penguin, 1977.

Lesser, Simon O. *Fiction and the Unconscious.* Chicago: University of Chicago Press, 1957.

Muller, John P., and William J. Richardson. *Lacan and Language: A Reader's Guide to Écrits.* New York: International Universities Press, 1982.

Skura, Meredith Anne. *The Literary Use of the Psychoanalytic Process.* New Haven: Yale University Press, 1981.

Trilling, Lionel. "Art and Neurosis" and "Freud and Literature." *The Liberal Imagination.* New York: Doubleday, 1947.

Turkle, Sherry. *Psychoanalytic Politics: Freud's French Revolution.* New York: Basic Books, 1978.

Wilden, Anthony. *The Language of the Self: the Function of Language in Psychoanalysis.* New York: Dell, 1968.

Wright, Elizabeth. *Psychoanalytic Criticism: Theory in Practice.* New York and London: Methuen, 1984.

# Sigmund Freud

1856–1939

*Sigmund Freud, the patriarch of psychoanalysis, was born in Moravia (now Czechoslovakia) but lived most of his assiduous life in Vienna, where he received his medical degree from the university in 1881. He studied under Charcot in Paris, and then with Josef Breuer in Vienna, where their collaborative investigations of the treatment of hysterical patients, while not well received by the rest of the profession, did lead Freud to devise his famed analytical technique based on free association. Freud's epochal* The Interpretation of Dreams *(1899; dated 1900) and other ground-*

*breaking studies met with much skeptical antagonism; nevertheless, by 1910 his fame had spread throughout Europe and reached America. A group calling itself The International Psycho-Analytical Association gathered round him, but by 1913 — the year Freud published Totem and Taboo — two of its most impressive members, Carl Jung and Alfred Adler, had resigned and formed their own schools in protest against Freud's insistence on the primacy of infant sexuality. During and after the First World War, despite hardships that included an agonizing jaw cancer, Freud continued to publish important work, notably Beyond the Pleasure Principle (1920) and The Ego and the Id (1923). His last year was spent in London, where he fled in 1938 after the Nazi invasion of Austria. "Creative Writers and Daydreaming," delivered as a lecture in 1907, was published the following year.*

# Creative Writers and Daydreaming

We laymen have always been intensely curious to know — like the cardinal who put a similar question to Ariosto[1] — from what sources that strange being, the creative writer, draws his material, and how he manages to make such an impression on us with it and to arouse in us emotions of which, perhaps, we had not even thought ourselves capable. Our interest is only heightened the more by the fact that, if we ask him, the writer himself gives us no explanation, or none that is satisfactory; and it is not at all weakened by our knowledge that not even the clearest insight into the determinants of his choice of material and into the nature of the art of creating imaginative form will ever help to make creative writers of *us*.

If we could at least discover in ourselves or in people like ourselves an activity which was in some way akin to creative writing! An examination of it would then give us a hope of obtaining the beginnings of an explanation of the creative work of writers. And, indeed, there is some prospect of this being possible. After all, creative writers themselves like to lessen the distance between their kind and the common run of humanity; they so often assure us that every man is a poet at heart and that the last poet will not perish till the last man does.

Should we not look for the first traces of imaginative activity as early as in childhood? The child's best-loved and most intense occupation is with his play or games. Might we not say that every child at play behaves like a creative writer, in that he creates a world of his own, or, rather, rearranges the things of his world in a new way which pleases him? It would be wrong to think he does not take that world seriously; on the contrary, he takes his play very seriously and he expends large amounts of emotion on it. The opposite of play is not what is serious but what is real. In spite of all the emotion with which he cathects[2] his world of play, the child distinguishes it quite well from reality; and he likes to link his imagined objects and situations to the tangible and visible things of the real world. This linking is all that differentiates the child's "play" from "fantasying."

The creative writer does the same as the child at play. He creates a world of fantasy which he takes very seriously — that is, which he invests with large amounts of emotion — while separating it sharply from reality. Language has preserved this relationship between children's play and poetic creation. It gives the name of *Spiel* ["play"] to those forms of imaginative writing which require to be linked to tangible objects and which are capable of representation. It speaks of

Translated by I. F. Grant-Duff.

[1]Ariosto dedicated the *Orlando Furioso* to Cardinal Ippolito d'Este, who said in response, "Where did you find so many stories?" [Au.]

[2]Cathexis is the investment of *libido* energy in an activity. [Ed.]

a *Lustspiel* or *Trauerspiel* ["comedy" or "tragedy"] and describes those who carry out the representation as *Schauspieler* ["players"]. The unreality of the writer's imaginative world, however, has very important consequences for the technique of his art; for many things which, if they were real, could give no enjoyment, can do so in the play of fantasy, and many excitements which, in themselves, are actually distressing, can become a source of pleasure for the hearers and spectators at the performance of a writer's work.

There is another consideration for the sake of which we will dwell a moment longer on this contrast between reality and play. When the child has grown up and has ceased to play, and after he has been laboring for decades to envisage the realities of life with proper seriousness, he may one day find himself in a mental situation which once more undoes the contrast between play and reality. As an adult he can look back on the intense seriousness with which he once carried on his games in childhood, and, by equating his ostensibly serious occupations of today with his childhood games, he can throw off the too heavy burden imposed on him by life and win the high yield of pleasure afforded by *humor*.

As people grow up, then, they cease to play, and they seem to give up the yield of pleasure which they gained from playing. But whoever understands the human mind knows that hardly anything is harder for a man than to give up a pleasure which he has once experienced. Actually, we can never give anything up; we only exchange one thing for another. What appears to be a renunciation is really the formation of a substitute or surrogate. In the same way, the growing child, when he stops playing, gives up nothing but the link with real objects; instead of *playing*, he now *fantasies*. He builds castles in the air and creates what are called *daydreams*. I believe that most people construct fantasies at times in their lives. This is a fact which has long been overlooked and whose importance has therefore not been sufficiently appreciated.

People's fantasies are less easy to observe than the play of children. The child, it is true, plays by himself or forms a closed psychical system with other children for the purposes of a game; but even though he may not play his game in front of the grown-ups, he does not, on the other hand, conceal it from them. The adult, on the contrary, is ashamed of his fantasies and hides them from other people. He cherishes his fantasies as his most intimate possessions, and as a rule he would rather confess his misdeeds then tell anyone his fantasies. It may come about that for that reason he believes he is the only person who invents such fantasies and has no idea that creations of this kind are widespread among other people. This difference in the behavior of a person who plays and a person who fantasies is accounted for by the motives of these two activities, which are nevertheless adjuncts to each other.

A child's play is determined by wishes: in point of fact by a single wish — one that helps in his upbringing — the wish to be big and grown up. He is always playing at being "grown up," and in his games he imitates what he knows about the lives of his elders. He has no reason to conceal this wish. With the adult, the case is different. On the one hand, he knows that he is expected not to go on playing or fantasying any longer, but to act in the real world; on the other hand, some of the wishes which give rise to his fantasies are of a kind which it is essential to conceal. Thus he is ashamed of his fantasies as being childish and as being unpermissible.

But, you will ask, if people make such a mystery of their fantasying, how is it that we know such a lot about it? Well, there is a class of human beings upon whom, not a god, indeed, but a stern goddess — Necessity — has allotted the task of telling what they suffer and what things give them happiness. These are the victims of nervous illness, who are obliged to tell their fantasies, among other things, to the doctor by whom they expect to be cured by mental treatment. This is our best source of knowledge, and we have since found good reason to suppose that our patients tell us nothing that we might not also hear from healthy people.

Let us make ourselves acquainted with a few of the characteristics of fantasying. We may lay it down that a happy person never fantasies, only an unsatisfied one. The motive forces of fantasies are unsatisfied wishes, and every single fantasy is the fulfillment of a wish, a correction of un-satisfying reality. These motivating wishes vary according to the sex, character, and circum-stances of the person who is having the fantasy; but they fall naturally into two main groups. They are either ambitious wishes, which serve to elevate the subject's personality; or they are erotic ones. In young women the erotic wishes predominate almost exclusively, for their ambi-tion is as a rule absorbed by erotic trends. In young men egoistic and ambitious wishes come to the fore clearly enough alongside of erotic ones. But we will not lay stress on the opposition between the two trends; we would rather empha-size the fact that they are often united. Just as, in many altarpieces, the portrait of the donor is to be seen in a corner of the picture, so, in the majority of ambitious fantasies, we can discover in some corner or other the lady for whom the creator of the fantasy performs all his heroic deeds and at whose feet all his triumphs are laid. Here, as you see, there are strong enough mo-tives for concealment; the well-brought-up young woman is only allowed a minimum of erotic desire, and the young man has to learn to sup-press the excess of self-regard which he brings with him from the spoilt days of his childhood, so that he may find his place in a society which is full of other individuals making equally strong demands.

We must not suppose that the products of this imaginative activity — the various fantasies, cas-tles in the air and daydreams — are stereotyped or unalterable. On the contrary, they fit them-selves into the subject's shifting impressions of life, change with every change in his situation, and receive from every fresh active impression what might be called a "date-mark." The relation of a fantasy to time is in general very important. We may say that it hovers, as it were, between three times — the three moments of time which our ideation involves. Mental work is linked to some current impression, some provoking occa-sion in the present which has been able to arouse one of the subject's major wishes. From there it harks back to a memory of an earlier experience (usually an infantile one) in which this wish was fulfilled; and it now creates a situation relating to the future which represents a fulfillment of the wish. What it thus creates is a daydream or fan-tasy, which carries about it traces of its origin from the occasion which provoked it and from the memory. Thus past, present, and future are strung together, as it were, on the thread of the wish that runs through them.

A very ordinary example may serve to make what I have said clear. Let us take the case of a poor orphan boy to whom you have given the address of some employer where he may perhaps find a job. On his way there he may indulge in a daydream appropriate to the situation from which it arises. The content of his fantasy will perhaps be something like this. He is given a job, finds favor with his new employer, makes himself indispensable in the business, is taken into his employer's family, marries the charming young daughter of the house, and then himself becomes a director of the business, first as his employer's partner and then as his successor. In this fantasy, the dreamer has regained what he possessed in his happy childhood — the protect-ing house, the loving parents, and the first objects of his affectionate feelings. You will see from this example the way in which the wish makes use of an occasion in the present to construct, on the pattern of the past, a picture of the future.

There is a great deal more that could be said about fantasies; but I will only allude as briefly as possible to certain points. If fantasies become overluxuriant and overpowerful, the conditions are laid for an onset of neurosis or psychosis. Fantasies, moreover, are the immediate mental precursors of the distressing symptoms com-plained of by our patients. Here a broad bypath branches off into pathology.

I cannot pass over the relation of fantasies to dreams. Our dreams at night are nothing else than fantasies like these, as we can demonstrate from the interpretation of dreams. Language, in its unrivaled wisdom, long ago decided the ques-tion of the essential nature of dreams by giving the name of *daydreams* to the airy creations of fantasy. If the meaning of our dreams usually remains obscure to us in spite of this pointer, it is because of the circumstance that at night there also arise in us wishes of which we are ashamed; these we must conceal from ourselves, and they have consequently been repressed, pushed into the unconscious. Repressed wishes of this sort and their derivatives are only allowed to come to expression in a very distorted form. When scientific work had succeeded in elucidating this factor of *dream distortion,* it was no longer difficult to recognize that night dreams are wish-fulfillments in just the same way as daydreams — the fantasies which we all know so well.

So much for fantasies. And now for the creative writer. May we really attempt to compare the imaginative writer with the "dreamer in broad daylight," and his creations with daydreams? Here we must begin by making an initial distinction. We must separate writers who, like the ancient authors of epics and tragedies, take over their material ready-made, from writers who seem to originate their own material. We will keep to the latter kind, and, for the purposes of our comparison, we will choose not the writers most highly esteemed by the critics, but the less pretentious authors of novels, romances, and short stories, who nevertheless have the widest and most eager circle of readers of both sexes. One feature above all cannot fail to strike us about the creations of these story-writers: each of them has a hero who is the center of interest, for whom the writer tries to win our sympathy by every possible means and whom he seems to place under the protection of a special providence. If, at the end of one chapter of my story, I leave the hero unconscious and bleeding from severe wounds, I am sure to find him at the beginning of the next being carefully nursed and on the way to recovery; and if the first volume closes with the ship he is in going down in a storm at sea, I am certain, at the opening of the second volume, to read of his miraculous rescue — a rescue without which the story could not proceed. The feeling of security with which I follow the hero through his perilous adventures is the same as the feeling with which a hero in real life throws himself into the water to save a drowning man or exposes himself to the enemy's fire in order to storm a battery. It is the true heroic feeling, which one of our best writers has expressed in an inimitable phrase: "Nothing can happen to *me*!" It seems to me, however, that through this revealing characteristic of invulnerability we can immediately recognize His Maj-

esty the Ego, the hero alike of every daydream and of every story.

Other typical features of these egocentric stories point to the same kinship. The fact that all the women in the novel invariably fall in love with the hero can hardly be looked on as a portrayal of reality, but it is easily understood as a necessary constituent of a daydream. The same is true of the fact that the other characters in the story are sharply divided into good and bad, in defiance of the variety of human characters that are to be observed in real life. The "good" ones are the helpers, while the "bad" ones are the enemies and rivals, of the ego which has become the hero of the story.

We are perfectly aware that very many imaginative writings are far removed from the model of the naive daydream; and yet I cannot suppress the suspicion that even the most extreme deviations from that model could be linked with it through an uninterrupted series of transitional cases. It has struck me that in many of what are known as "psychological" novels only one person — once again the hero — is described from within. The author sits inside his mind, as it were, and looks at the other characters from outside. The psychological novel in general no doubt owes its special nature to the inclination of the modern writer to split up his ego, by self-observation, into many part-egos, and, in consequence, to personify the conflicting currents of his own mental life in several heroes. Certain novels, which might be described as "eccentric," seem to stand in quite special contrast to the types of the daydream. In these, the person who is introduced as the hero plays only a very small active part; he sees the actions and sufferings of other people pass before him like a spectator. Many of Zola's later works belong to this category. But I must point out that the psychological analysis of individuals who are not creative writers, and who diverge in some respects from the so-called norm, has shown us analogous variations of the daydream, in which the ego contents itself with the role of spectator.

If our comparison of the imaginative writer with the daydreamer, and of poetical creation with the daydream, is to be of any value, it must, above all, show itself in some way or other fruitful. Let us, for instance, try to apply to these authors' works the thesis we laid down earlier concerning the relation between fantasy and the three periods of time and the wish which runs through them; and, with its help, let us try to study the connections that exist between the life of the writer and his works. No one has known, as a rule, what expectations to frame in approaching this problem; and often the connection has been thought of in much too simple terms. In the light of the insight we have gained from fantasies, we ought to expect the following state of affairs. A strong experience in the present awakens in the creative writer a memory of an earlier experience (usually belonging to his childhood) from which there now proceeds a wish which finds its fulfillment in the creative work. The work itself exhibits elements of the recent provoking occasion as well as of the old memory.

Do not be alarmed at the complexity of this formula. I suspect that in fact it will prove to be too exiguous a pattern. Nevertheless, it may contain a first approach to the true state of affairs; and, from some experiments I have made, I am inclined to think that this way of looking at creative writings may turn out not unfruitful. You will not forget that the stress it lays on childhood memories in the writer's life — a stress which may perhaps seem puzzling — is ultimately derived from the assumption that a piece of creative writing, like a daydream, is a continuation of, and a substitute for, what was once the play of childhood.

We must not neglect, however, to go back to the kind of imaginative works which we have to recognize, not as original creations, but as the refashioning of ready-made and familiar material. Even here, the writer keeps a certain amount of independence, which can express itself in the choice of material and in changes in it which are often quite extensive. Insofar as the material is already at hand, however, it is derived from the popular treasure-house of myths, legends, and fairy tales. The study of constructions of folk psychology such as these is far from being complete, but it is extremely probable that myths, for instance, are distorted vestiges of the wishful fantasies of whole nations, the *secular dreams* of youthful humanity.

You will say that, although I have put the creative writer first in the title of my paper, I have told you far less about him than about fantasies. I am aware of that, and I must try to excuse it by pointing to the present state of our knowledge. All I have been able to do is to throw out some encouragements and suggestions which, starting from the study of fantasies, lead on to the problem of the writer's choice of his literary material. As for the other problem — by what means the creative writer achieves the emotional effects in us that are aroused by his creations — we have as yet not touched on it at all. But I should like at least to point out to you the path that leads from our discussion of fantasies to the problems of poetical effects.

You will remember how I have said that the daydreamer carefully conceals his fantasies from other people because he feels he has reasons for being ashamed of them. I should now add that even if he were to communicate them to us he could give us no pleasure by his disclosures. Such fantasies, when we learn them, repel us or at least leave us cold. But when a creative writer presents his plays to us or tells us what we are inclined to take to be his personal daydreams, we experience a great pleasure, and one which probably arises from the confluence of many sources. How the writer accomplishes this is his innermost secret; the essential *ars poetica*[3] lies in the technique of overcoming the feeling of repulsion in us which is undoubtedly connected with the barriers that rise between each single ego and the others. We can guess two of the methods used by this technique. The writer softens the character of his egoistic daydreams by altering and disguising it, and he bribes us by the purely formal — that is, aesthetic — yield of pleasure which he offers us in the presentation of his fantasies. We give the name of an *incentive bonus,* or a *forepleasure,* to a yield of pleasure such as this, which is offered to us so as to make possible the release of still greater pleasure arising from deeper psychical sources. In my opinion, all the aesthetic pleasure which a creative writer affords us has the character of a fore-

[3]Art of poetry. [Ed.]

pleasure of this kind, and our actual enjoyment of an imaginative work proceeds from a liberation of tensions in our minds. It may even be that not a little of this effect is due to the writer's enabling us thenceforward to enjoy our own day-

dreams without self-reproach or shame. This brings us to the threshold of new, interesting, and complicated inquiries; but also, at least for the moment, to the end of our discussion.

# Carl Gustav Jung
## 1875–1961

*Carl Gustav Jung, the founder of analytic psychology, was born in Switzerland. The son of a philologist and pastor, from a clan of many clergymen, Jung turned his back on the ministry to pursue philosophical and medical interests. He studied at Basel (1895–1900) and Zürich, where he earned his M.D. in 1902 after working under Eugen Bleuler at the Burghölzli Psychiatric Clinic. In 1907 he met Freud; their close collaboration ended in 1912, a year after Jung became president of The International Psycho-Analytical Association, when Jung published the clearly un-Freudian* The Psychology of the Unconscious. *Jung came to believe that the essential lifelong task of the person is to achieve individuation, a harmonious wholeness of conscious and unconscious. In 1933 he became professor of psychology at the Federal Polytechnical University in Zürich, and in 1943 professor of medical psychology at the University of Basel. Immensely prolific, Jung revised and reissued much of his work. His important books include* The Psychology of Dementia *(1906),* Psychological Types *(1921) and* Psychology and Alchemy *(1944). "On the Relation of Analytical Psychology to Poetry" was delivered to a German learned society as a lecture in 1922 and published later that year. "The Principal Archetypes" is from* Aion: Researches into the Phenomenology of Self *(1951), a late work that tidily summarizes many of Jung's key ideas.*

# On the Relation of Analytical Psychology to Poetry

In spite of its difficulty, the task of discussing the relation of analytical psychology to poetry affords me a welcome opportunity to define my views on the much debated question of the relations between psychology and art in general. Although the two things cannot be compared, the close connections which undoubtedly exist between them call for investigation. These connections arise from the fact that the practice of art is a psychological activity and, as such, can be approached from a psychological angle. Considered in this light, art, like any other human activity deriving from psychic motives, is a proper subject for psychology. This statement, however, involves a very definite limitation of the psychological viewpoint when we come to apply it in practice. Only that aspect of art which consists in the process of artistic creation can be a subject for psychological study, but not that which constitutes its essential nature. The question of what art is in itself can never be answered by the psychologist, but must be approached from the side of aesthetics.

A similar distinction must be made in the

Translated by R. F. C. Hull.

realm of religion. A psychological approach is permissible only in regard to the emotions and symbols which constitute the phenomenology of religion, but which do not touch upon its essential nature. If the essence of religion and art could be explained, then both of them would become mere subdivisions of psychology. This is not to say that such violations of their nature have not been attempted. But those who are guilty of them obviously forget that a similar fate might easily befall psychology, since its intrinsic value and specific quality would be destroyed if it were regarded as a mere activity of the brain, and were relegated along with the endocrine functions to a subdivision of physiology. This too, as we know, has been attempted.

Art by its very nature is not science, and science by its very nature is not art; both these spheres of the mind have something in reserve that is peculiar to them and can be explained only in its own terms. Hence when we speak of the relation of psychology to art, we shall treat only of that aspect of art which can be submitted to psychological scrutiny without violating its nature. Whatever the psychologist has to say about art will be confined to the process of artistic creation and has nothing to do with its innermost essence. He can no more explain this than the intellect can describe or even understand the nature of feeling. Indeed, art and science would not exist as separate entities at all if the fundamental difference between them had not long since forced itself on the mind. The fact that artistic, scientific, and religious propensities still slumber peacefully together in the small child, or that with primitives the beginnings of art, science, and religion coalesce in the undifferentiated chaos of the magical mentality, or that no trace of "mind" can be found in the natural instincts of animals — all this does nothing to prove the existence of a unifying principle which alone would justify a reduction of the one to the other. For if we go so far back into the history of the mind that the distinctions between its various fields of activity become altogether invisible, we do not reach an underlying principle of their unity, but merely an earlier, undifferentiated state in which no separate activities yet exist. But the elementary state is not an explanatory principle that would allow us to draw conclusions as to the nature of later, more highly developed states, even though they must necessarily derive from it. A scientific attitude will always tend to overlook the peculiar nature of these more differentiated states in favor of their causal derivation, and will endeavor to subordinate them to a general but more elementary principle.

These theoretical reflections seem to me very much in place today, when we so often find that works of art, and particularly poetry, are interpreted precisely in this manner, by reducing them to more elementary states. Though the material he works with and its individual treatment can easily be traced back to the poet's personal relations with his parents, this does not enable us to understand his poetry. The same reduction can be made in all sorts of other fields, and not least in the case of pathological disturbances. Neuroses and psychoses are likewise reducible to infantile relations with the parents, and so are a man's good and bad habits, his beliefs, peculiarities, passions, interests, and so forth. It can hardly be supposed that all these very different things must have exactly the same explanation, for otherwise we would be driven to the conclusion that they actually are the same thing. If a work of art is explained in the same way as a neurosis, then either the work of art is a neurosis or a neurosis is a work of art. This explanation is all very well as a play on words, but sound common sense rebels against putting a work of art on the same level as a neurosis. An analyst might, in an extreme case, view a neurosis as a work of art through the lens of his professional bias, but it would never occur to an intelligent layman to mistake a pathological phenomenon for art, in spite of the undeniable fact that a work of art arises from much the same psychological conditions as a neurosis. This is only natural, because certain of these conditions are present in every individual and, owing to the relative constancy of the human environment, are constantly the same, whether in the case of a nervous intellectual, a poet, or a normal human being. All have had parents, all have a father- or a mother-complex, all know about sex and therefore have certain common and typical human difficulties. One poet may be influenced more by his relation to his father, another by the tie to his mother, while a third shows unmistakable traces of sexual repression in his poetry. Since all this can be said equally well not only of every neurotic but of every normal human being, nothing specific is gained for the judgment of a work of art. At most our knowledge of its psychological antecedents will have been broadened and deepened.

The school of medical psychology inaugurated by Freud has undoubtedly encouraged the literary historian to bring certain peculiarities of a work of art into relation with the intimate, personal life of the poet. But this is nothing new in principle, for it has long been known that the scientific treatment of art will reveal the personal threads that the artist, intentionally or unintentionally, has woven into his work. The Freudian approach may, however, make possible a more exhaustive demonstration of the influences that reach back into earliest childhood and play their part in artistic creation. To this extent the psychoanalysis of art differs in no essential from the subtle psychological nuances of a penetrating literary analysis. The difference is at most a question of degree, though we may occasionally be surprised by indiscreet references to things which a rather more delicate touch might have passed over if only for reasons of tact. This lack of delicacy seems to be a professional peculiarity of the medical psychologist, and the temptation to draw daring conclusions easily leads to flagrant abuses. A slight whiff of scandal often lends spice to a biography, but a little more becomes a nasty inquisitiveness — bad taste masquerading as science. Our interest is insidiously deflected from the work of art and gets lost in the labyrinth of psychic determinants, the poet becomes a clinical case and, very likely, yet another addition to the curiosa of *psychopathia sexualis.*[1] But this means that the psychoanalysis of art has turned aside from its proper objective and strayed into a province that is as broad as mankind, that is not in the least specific to the artist and has even less relevance to his art.

This kind of analysis brings the work of art into the sphere of general human psychology,

where many other things besides art have their origin. To explain art in these terms is just as great a platitude as the statement that "every artist is a narcissist." Every man who pursues his own goal is a "narcissist" — though one wonders how permissible it is to give such wide currency to a term specifically coined for the pathology of neurosis. The statement therefore amounts to nothing; it merely elicits the faint surprise of a bon mot. Since this kind of analysis is in no way concerned with the work of art itself, but strives like a mole to bury itself in the dirt as speedily as possible, it always ends up in the common earth that unites all mankind. Hence its explanations have the same tedious monotony as the recitals which one daily hears in the consulting room.

The reductive method of Freud is a purely medical one, and the treatment is directed at a pathological or otherwise unsuitable formation which has taken the place of the normal functioning. It must therefore be broken down, and the way cleared for healthy adaptation. In this case, reduction to the common human foundation is altogether appropriate. But when applied to a work of art it leads to the results I have described. It strips the work of art of its shimmering robes and exposes the nakedness and drabness of *Homo sapiens,* to which species the poet and artist also belong. The golden gleam of artistic creation — the original object of discussion — is extinguished as soon as we apply to it the same corrosive method which we use in analyzing the fantasies of hysteria. The results are no doubt very interesting and may perhaps have the same kind of scientific value as, for instance, a postmortem examination of the brain of Nietzsche, which might conceivably show us the particular atypical form of paralysis from which he died. But what would this have to do with *Zarathustra?* Whatever its subterranean background may have been, is it not a whole world in itself, beyond the human, all-too-human imperfections, beyond the world of migraine and cerebral atrophy?

I have spoken of Freud's reductive method but have not stated in what that method consists. It is essentially a medical technique for investigating morbid psychic phenomena, and it is

[1]Sexual psychopathology. [Ed.]

solely concerned with the ways and means of getting round or peering through the foreground of consciousness in order to reach the psychic background, or the unconscious. It is based on the assumption that the neurotic patient represses certain psychic contents because they are morally incompatible with his conscious values. It follows that the repressed contents must have correspondingly negative traits — infantile-sexual, obscene, or even criminal — which make them unacceptable to consciousness. Since no man is perfect, everyone must possess such a background whether he admits it or not. Hence it can always be exposed if only one uses the technique of interpretation worked out by Freud.

In the short space of a lecture I cannot, of course, enter into the details of the technique. A few hints must suffice. The unconscious background does not remain inactive, but betrays itself by its characteristic effects on the contents of consciousness. For example, it produces fantasies of a peculiar nature, which can easily be interpreted as sexual images. Or it produces characteristic disturbances of the conscious processes, which again can be reduced to repressed contents. A very important source for knowledge of the unconscious contents is provided by dreams, since these are direct products of the activity of the unconscious. The essential thing in Freud's reductive method is to collect all the clues pointing to the unconscious background, and then, through the analysis and interpretation of this material, to reconstruct the elementary instinctual processes. Those conscious contents which give us a clue to the unconscious background are incorrectly called *symbols* by Freud. They are not true symbols, however, since according to his theory they have merely the role of *signs* or *symptoms* of the subliminal processes. The true symbol differs essentially from this, and should be understood as an expression of an intuitive idea that cannot yet be formulated in any other or better way. When Plato, for instance, puts the whole problem of the theory of knowledge in his parable of the cave,[2] or when Christ expresses the idea of the Kingdom of Heaven in

parables, these are genuine and true symbols, that is, attempts to express something for which no verbal concept yet exists. If we were to interpret Plato's metaphor in Freudian terms we would naturally arrive at the uterus, and would have proved that even a mind like Plato's was still stuck on a primitive level of infantile sexuality. But we would have completely overlooked what Plato actually created out of the primitive determinants of his philosophical ideas; we would have missed the essential point and merely discovered that he had infantile-sexual fantasies like any other mortal. Such a discovery could be of value only for a man who regarded Plato as superhuman, and who can now state with satisfaction that Plato too was an ordinary human being. But who would want to regard Plato as a god? Surely only one who is dominated by infantile fantasies and therefore possesses a neurotic mentality. For him the reduction to common human truths is salutary on medical grounds, but this would have nothing whatever to do with the meaning of Plato's parable.

I have purposely dwelt on the application of medical psychoanalysis to works of art because I want to emphasize that the psychoanalytic method is at the same time an essential part of the Freudian doctrine. Freud himself by his rigid dogmatism has ensured that the method and the doctrine — in themselves two very different things — are regarded by the public as identical. Yet the method may be employed with beneficial results in medical cases without at the same time exalting it into a doctrine. And against this doctrine we are bound to raise vigorous objections. The assumptions it rests on are quite arbitrary. For example, neuroses are by no means exclusively caused by sexual repression, and the same holds true for psychoses. There is no foundation for saying that dreams merely contain repressed wishes whose moral incompatibility requires them to be disguised by a hypothetical dream-censor. The Freudian technique of interpretation, so far as it remains under the influence of its own one-sided and therefore erroneous hypotheses, displays a quite obvious bias.

In order to do justice to a work of art, analytical psychology must rid itself entirely of medical prejudice; for a work of art is not a disease,

[2]In Plato, *Republic*, Book 7. [Ed.]

and consequently requires a different approach from the medical one. A doctor naturally has to seek out the causes of a disease in order to pull it up by the roots, but just as naturally the psychologist must adopt exactly the opposite attitude towards a work of art. Instead of investigating its typically human determinants, he will inquire first of all into its meaning, and will concern himself with its determinants only insofar as they enable him to understand it more fully. Personal causes have as much or as little to do with a work of art as the soil with the plant that springs from it. We can certainly learn to understand some of the plant's peculiarities by getting to know its habitat, and for the botanist this is an important part of his equipment. But nobody will maintain that everything essential has then been discovered about the plant itself. The personal orientation which the doctor needs when confronted with the question of etiology in medicine is quite out of place in dealing with a work of art, just because a work of art is not a human being, but is something suprapersonal. It is a thing and not a personality; hence it cannot be judged by personal criteria. Indeed, the special significance of a true work of art resides in the fact that it has escaped from the limitations of the personal and has soared beyond the personal concerns of its creator.

I must confess from my own experience that it is not at all easy for a doctor to lay aside his professional bias when considering a work of art and look at it with a mind cleared of the current biological causality. But I have come to learn that although a psychology with a purely biological orientation can explain a good deal about man in general, it cannot be applied to a work of art and still less to man as creator. A purely causalistic psychology is only able to reduce every human individual to a member of the species *Homo sapiens,* since its range is limited to what is transmitted by heredity or derived from other sources. But a work of art is not transmitted or derived — it is a creative reorganization of those very conditions to which a causalistic psychology must always reduce it. The plant is not a mere product of the soil; it is a living, self-contained process which in essence has nothing to do with the character of the soil. In the same way, the meaning and individual quality of a work of art inhere within it and not in its extrinsic determinants. One might almost describe it as a living being that uses man only as a nutrient medium, employing his capacities according to its own laws and shaping itself to the fulfillment of its own creative purpose.

But here I am anticipating somewhat, for I have in mind a particular type of art which I still have to introduce. Not every work of art originates in the way I have just described. There are literary works, prose as well as poetry, that spring wholly from the author's intention to produce a particular result. He submits his material to a definite treatment with a definite aim in view; he adds to it and subtracts from it, emphasizing one effect, toning down another, laying on a touch of color here, another there, all the time carefully considering the overall result and paying strict attention to the laws of form and style. He exercises the keenest judgment and chooses his words with complete freedom. His material is entirely subordinated to his artistic purpose; he wants to express this and nothing else. He is wholly at one with the creative process, no matter whether he has deliberately made himself its spearhead, as it were, or whether it has made him its instrument so completely that he has lost all consciousness of this fact. In either case, the artist is so identified with his work that his intentions and his faculties are indistinguishable from the act of creation itself. There is no need, I think, to give examples of this from the history of literature or from the testimony of the artists themselves.

Nor need I cite examples of the other class of works which flow more or less complete and perfect from the author's pen. They come as it were fully arrayed into the world, as Pallas Athene sprang from the head of Zeus. These works positively force themselves upon the author; his hand is seized, his pen writes things that his mind contemplates with amazement. The work brings with it its own form; anything he wants to add is rejected, and what he himself would like to reject is thrust back at him. While his conscious mind stands amazed and empty before this phenomenon, he is overwhelmed by a flood of thoughts and images which he never intended to create and which his own will could never have brought into being. Yet in spite of himself he is forced to admit that it is his own self speaking, his own inner nature revealing itself and uttering things which he would never have entrusted to his tongue. He can only obey the apparently alien impulse within him and follow where it leads, sensing that his work is greater than himself, and wields a power which is not his and which he cannot command. Here the artist is not identical with the process of creation; he is aware that he is subordinate to his work or stands outside it, as though he were a second person; or as though a person other than himself had fallen within the magic circle of an alien will.

So when we discuss the psychology of art, we must bear in mind these two entirely different modes of creation, for much that is of the greatest importance in judging a work of art depends on this distinction. It is one that had been sensed earlier by Schiller, who as we know attempted to classify it in his concept of the *sentimental* and the *naive*.[3] The psychologist would call "sentimental" art *introverted* and the "naive" kind *extraverted*. The introverted attitude is characterized by the subject's assertion of his conscious intentions and aims against the demands of the object, whereas the extraverted attitude is characterized by the subject's subordination to the demands which the object makes upon him. In my view, Schiller's plays and most of his poems give one a good idea of the introverted attitude: the material is mastered by the conscious intentions of the poet. The extraverted attitude is illustrated by the second part of *Faust:* here the material is distinguished by its refractoriness. A still more striking example is Nietzsche's *Zarathustra,* where the author himself observed how "one became two."

From what I have said, it will be apparent that a shift of psychological standpoint has taken place as soon as one speaks not of the poet as a person but of the creative process that moves him. When the focus of interest shifts to the latter, the poet comes into the picture only as a reacting subject. This is immediately evident in

[3]See Schiller, "On Naive and Sentimental Poetry," p. 274. [Ed.]

our second category of works, where the consciousness of the poet is not identical with the creative process. But in works of the first category the opposite appears to hold true. Here the poet appears to be the creative process itself, and to create of his own free will without the slightest feeling of compulsion. He may even be fully convinced of his freedom of action and refuse to admit that his work could be anything else than the expression of his will and ability.

Here we are faced with a question which we cannot answer from the testimony of the poets themselves. It is really a scientific problem that psychology alone can solve. As I hinted earlier, it might well be that the poet, while apparently creating out of himself and producing what he consciously intends, is nevertheless so carried away by the creative impulse that he is no longer aware of an "alien" will, just as the other type of poet is no longer aware of his own will speaking to him in the apparently "alien" inspiration, although this is manifestly the voice of his own self. The poet's conviction that he is creating in absolute freedom would then be an illusion: he fancies he is swimming, but in reality an unseen current sweeps him along.

This is not by any means an academic question, but is supported by the evidence of analytical psychology. Researches have shown that there are all sorts of ways in which the conscious mind is not only influenced by the unconscious but actually guided by it. Yet is there any evidence for the supposition that a poet, despite his self-awareness, may be taken captive by his work? The proof may be of two kinds, direct or indirect. Direct proof would be afforded by a poet who thinks he knows what he is saying but actually says more than he is aware of. Such cases are not uncommon. Indirect proof would be found in cases where behind the apparent free will of the poet there stands a higher imperative that renews its peremptory demands as soon as the poet voluntarily gives up his creative activity, or that produces psychic complications whenever his work has to be broken off against his will.

Analysis of artists consistently shows not only the strength of the creative impulse arising from the unconscious, but also its capricious and willful character. The biographies of great artists make it abundantly clear that the creative urge is often so imperious that it battens on their humanity and yokes everything to the service of the work, even at the cost of health and ordinary human happiness. The unborn work in the psyche of the artist is a force of nature that achieves its end either with tyrannical might or with the subtle cunning of nature herself, quite regardless of the personal fate of the man who is its vehicle. The creative urge lives and grows in him like a tree in the earth from which it draws its nourishment. We would do well, therefore, to think of the creative process as a living thing implanted in the human psyche. In the language of analytical psychology this living thing is an *autonomous complex*. It is a split-off portion of the psyche, which leads a life of its own outside the hierarchy of consciousness. Depending on its energy charge, it may appear either as a mere disturbance of conscious activities or as a supraordinate authority which can harness the ego to its purpose. Accordingly, the poet who identifies with the creative process would be one who acquiesces from the start when the unconscious imperative begins to function. But the other poet, who feels the creative force as something alien, is one who for various reasons cannot acquiesce and is thus caught unawares.

It might be expected that this difference in its origins would be perceptible in a work of art. For in the one case it is a conscious product shaped and designed to have the effect intended. But in the other we are dealing with an event originating in unconscious nature; with something that achieves its aim without the assistance of human consciousness, and often defies it by willfully insisting on its own form and effect. We would therefore expect that works belonging to the first class would nowhere overstep the limits of comprehension, that their effect would be bounded by the author's intention and would not extend beyond it. But with works of the other class we would have to be prepared for something suprapersonal that transcends our understanding to the same degree that the author's consciousness was in abeyance during the process of creation. We would expect a strangeness of form and content, thoughts that can only be apprehended intuitively, a language pregnant

with meanings, and images that are true symbols because they are the best possible expressions for something unknown — bridges thrown out towards an unseen shore.

These criteria are, by and large, corroborated in practice. Whenever we are confronted with a work that was consciously planned and with material that was consciously selected, we find that it agrees with the first class of qualities, and in the other case with the second. The example we gave of Schiller's plays, on the one hand, and *Faust II* on the other, or better still *Zarathustra,* is an illustration of this. But I would not undertake to place the work of an unknown poet in either of these categories without first having examined rather closely his personal relations with his work. It is not enough to know whether the poet belongs to the introverted or to the extraverted type, since it is possible for either type to work with an introverted attitude at one time, and an extraverted attitude at another. This is particularly noticeable in the difference between Schiller's plays and his philosophical writings, between Goethe's perfectly formed poems and the obvious struggle with his material in *Faust II,* and between Nietzsche's well-turned aphorisms and the rushing torrent of *Zarathustra.* The same poet can adopt different attitudes to his work at different times, and on this depends the standard we have to apply.

The question, as we now see, is exceedingly complicated, and the complication grows even worse when we consider the case of the poet who identifies with the creative process. For should it turn out that the apparently conscious and purposeful manner of composition is a subjective illusion of the poet, then his work would possess symbolic qualities that are outside the range of his consciousness. They would only be more difficult to detect, because the reader as well would be unable to get beyond the bounds of the poet's consciousness which are fixed by the spirit of the time. There is no Archimedean point outside his world by which he could lift his time-bound consciousness off its hinges and recognize the symbols hidden in the poet's work. For a symbol is the intimation of a meaning beyond the level of our present powers of comprehension.

I raise this question only because I do not want my typological classification to limit the possible significance of works of art which apparently mean no more than what they say. But we have often found that a poet who has gone out of fashion is suddenly rediscovered. This happens when our conscious development has reached a higher level from which the poet can tell us something new. It was always present in his work but was hidden in a symbol, and only a renewal of the spirit of the time permits us to read its meaning. It needed to be looked at with fresher eyes, for the old ones see in it only what they were accustomed to see. Experiences of this kind should make us cautious, as they bear out my earlier argument. But works that are openly symbolic do not require this subtle approach; their pregnant language cries out at us that they mean more than they say. We can put our finger on the symbol at once, even though we may not be able to unriddle its meaning to our entire satisfaction. A symbol remains a perpetual challenge to our thoughts and feelings. That probably explains why a symbolic work is so stimulating, why it grips us so intensely, but also why it seldom affords us a purely aesthetic enjoyment. A work that is manifestly not symbolic appeals much more to our aesthetic sensibility because it is complete in itself and fulfills its purpose.

What then, you may ask, can analytical psychology contribute to our fundamental problem, which is the mystery of artistic creation? All that we have said so far has to do only with the psychological phenomenology of art. Since nobody can penetrate to the heart of nature, you will not expect psychology to do the impossible and offer a valid explanation of the secret of creativity. Like every other science, psychology has only a modest contribution to make towards a deeper understanding of the phenomena of life, and is no nearer than its sister sciences to absolute knowledge.

We have talked so much about the meaning of works of art that one can hardly suppress a doubt as to whether art really "means" anything at all. Perhaps art has no "meaning," at least not as we understand meaning. Perhaps it is like nature, which simply *is* and "means" nothing beyond that. Is "meaning" necessarily more than mere interpretation — an interpretation secreted into something by an intellect hungry for meaning? Art, it has been said, is beauty, and "a thing of beauty is a joy forever."[4] It needs no meaning, for meaning has nothing to do with art. Within the sphere of art, I must accept the truth of this statement. But when I speak of the relation of psychology to art we are outside its sphere, and it is impossible for us not to speculate. We must interpret, we must find meanings in things, otherwise we would be quite unable to think about them. We have to break down life and events, which are self-contained processes, into meanings, images, concepts, well knowing that in doing so we are getting further away from the living mystery. As long as we ourselves are caught up in the process of creation, we neither see nor understand; indeed we ought not to understand, for nothing is more injurious to immediate experience than cognition. But for the purpose of cognitive understanding we must detach ourselves from the creative process and look at it from the outside; only then does it become an image that expresses what we are bound to call "meaning." What was a mere phenomenon before becomes something that in association with other phenomena has meaning, that has a definite role to play, serves certain ends, and exerts meaningful effects. And when we have seen all this we get the feeling of having understood and explained something. In this way we meet the demands of science.

When, a little earlier, we spoke of a work of art as a tree growing out of the nourishing soil, we might equally well have compared it to a child growing in the womb. But as all comparisons are lame, let us stick to the more precise terminology of science. You will remember that I described the nascent work in the psyche of the artist as an autonomous complex. By this we mean a psychic formation that remains subliminal until its energy-charge is sufficient to carry it over the threshold into consciousness. Its association with consciousness does not mean that it is assimilated, only that it is perceived; but it is not subject to conscious control, and can be

4Keats, "Endymion," I. [Ed.]

neither inhibited nor voluntarily reproduced. Therein lies the autonomy of the complex: it appears and disappears in accordance with its own inherent tendencies, independently of the conscious will. The creative complex shares this peculiarity with every other autonomous complex. In this respect it offers an analogy with pathological processes, since these too are characterized by the presence of autonomous complexes, particularly in the case of mental disturbances. The divine frenzy of the artist comes perilously close to a pathological state, though the two things are not identical. The *tertium comparationis*[5] is the autonomous complex. But the presence of autonomous complexes is not in itself pathological, since normal people, too, fall temporarily or permanently under their domination. This fact is simply one of the normal peculiarities of the psyche, and for a man to be unaware of the existence of an autonomous complex merely betrays a high degree of unconsciousness. Every typical attitude that is to some extent differentiated shows a tendency to become an autonomous complex, and in most cases it actually does. Again, every instinct has more or less the character of an autonomous complex. In itself, therefore, an autonomous complex has nothing morbid about it; only when its manifestations are frequent and disturbing is it a symptom of illness.

How does an autonomous complex arise? For reasons which we cannot go into here, a hitherto unconscious portion of the psyche is thrown into activity, and gains ground by activating the adjacent areas of association. The energy needed for this is naturally drawn from consciousness — unless the latter happens to identify with the complex. But where this does not occur, the drain of energy produces what Janet calls an *abaissement du niveau mental*.[6] The intensity of conscious interests and activities gradually diminishes, leading either to apathy — a condition very common with artists — or to a regressive development of the conscious functions, that is,

they revert to an infantile and archaic level and undergo something like a degeneration. The "inferior parts of the functions," as Janet calls them, push to the fore; the instinctual side of the personality prevails over the ethical, the infantile over the mature, and the unadapted over the adapted. This too is something we see in the lives of many artists. The autonomous complex thus develops by using the energy that has been withdrawn from the conscious control of the personality.

But in what does an autonomous *creative* complex consist? Of this we can know next to nothing so long as the artist's work affords us no insight into its foundations. The work presents us with a finished picture, and this picture is amenable to analysis only to the extent that we can recognize it as a symbol. But if we are unable to discover any symbolic value in it, we have merely established that, so far as we are concerned, it means no more than what it says, or to put it another way, that it *is* no more than what it *seems* to be. I used the word *seems* because our own bias may prevent a deeper appreciation of it. At any rate we can find no incentive and no starting point for an analysis. But in the case of a symbolic work we should remember the dictum of Gerhard Hauptmann: "Poetry evokes out of words the resonance of the primordial word." The question we should ask, therefore, is: what primordial image lies behind the imagery of art?

This question needs a little elucidation. I am assuming that the work of art we propose to analyze, as well as being symbolic, has its source not in the *personal unconscious* of the poet, but in a sphere of unconscious mythology whose primordial images are the common heritage of mankind. I have called this sphere the *collective unconscious,* to distinguish it from the personal unconscious. The latter I regard as the sum total of all those psychic processes and contents which are capable of becoming conscious and often do, but are then suppressed because of their incompatibility and kept subliminal. Art receives tributaries from this sphere too, but muddy ones; and their predominance, far from making a work of art a symbol, merely turns it into a symptom.

[5]Third element; the "middle term" or common factor between two disparate things. [Ed.]

[6]Lowering of mental level. [Ed.]

We can leave this kind of art without injury and without regret to the purgative methods employed by Freud.

In contrast to the personal unconscious, which is a relatively thin layer immediately below the threshold of consciousness, the collective unconscious shows no tendency to become conscious under normal conditions, nor can it be brought back to recollection by any analytical technique, since it was never repressed or forgotten. The collective unconscious is not to be thought of as a self-subsistent entity; it is no more than a potentiality handed down to us from primordial times in the specific form of mnemonic images or inherited in the anatomical structure of the brain. There are no inborn ideas, but there are inborn possibilities of ideas that set bounds to even the boldest fantasy and keep our fantasy activity within certain categories: a priori ideas, as it were, the existence of which cannot be ascertained except from their effects. They appear only in the shaped material of art as the regulative principles that shape it; that is to say, only by inferences drawn from the finished work can we reconstruct the age-old original of the primordial image.

The primordial image, or archetype, is a figure — be it a demon, a human being, or a process — that constantly recurs in the course of history and appears wherever creative fantasy is freely expressed. Essentially, therefore, it is a mythological figure. When we examine these images more closely, we find that they give form to countless typical experiences of our ancestors. They are, so to speak, the psychic residua of innumerable experiences of the same type. They present a picture of psychic life in the average, divided up and projected into the manifold figures of the mythological pantheon. But the mythological figures are themselves products of creative fantasy and still have to be translated into conceptual language. Only the beginnings of such a language exist, but once the necessary concepts are created they could give us an abstract, scientific understanding of the unconscious processes that lie at the roots of the primordial images. In each of these images there is a little piece of human psychology and human

fate, a remnant of the joys and sorrows that have been repeated countless times in our ancestral history, and on the average follow ever the same course. It is like a deeply graven river-bed in the psyche, in which waters of life, instead of flowing along as before in a broad but shallow stream, suddenly swell into a mighty river. This happens whenever that particular set of circumstances is encountered which over long periods of time has helped to lay down the primordial image.

The moment when this mythological situation reappears is always characterized by a peculiar emotional intensity; it is as though chords in us were struck that had never resounded before, or as though forces whose existence we never suspected were unloosed. What makes the struggle for adaptation so laborious is the fact that we have constantly to be dealing with individual and atypical situations. So it is not surprising that when an archetypal situation occurs we suddenly feel an extraordinary sense of release, as though transported, or caught up by an overwhelming power. At such moments we are no longer individuals, but the race; the voice of all mankind resounds in us. The individual man cannot use his powers to the full unless he is aided by one of those collective representations we call ideals, which releases all the hidden forces of instinct that are inaccessible to his conscious will. The most effective ideals are always fairly obvious variants of an archetype, as is evident from the fact that they lend themselves to allegory. The ideal of the "mother country," for instance, is an obvious allegory of the mother, as is the "fatherland" of the father. Its power to stir us does not derive from the allegory, but from the symbolical value of our native land. The archetype here is the *participation mystique* of primitive man with the soil on which he dwells, and which contains the spirits of his ancestors.

The impact of an archetype, whether it takes the form of immediate experience or is expressed through the spoken word, stirs us because it summons up a voice that is stronger than our own. Whoever speaks in primordial images speaks with a thousand voices; he enthralls and overpowers, while at the same time he lifts the idea he is seeking to express out of the occasional and the transitory into the realm of the ever-enduring. He transmutes our personal destiny into the destiny of mankind, and evokes in us all those beneficent forces that ever and anon have enabled humanity to find a refuge from every peril and to outlive the longest night.

That is the secret of great art, and of its effect upon us. The creative process, so far as we are able to follow it at all, consists in the unconscious activation of an archetypal image, and in elaborating and shaping this image into the finished work. By giving it shape, the artist translates it into the language of the present, and so makes it possible for us to find our way back to the deepest springs of life. Therein lies the social significance of art: it is constantly at work educating the spirit of the age, conjuring up the forms in which the age is most lacking. The unsatisfied yearning of the artist reaches back to the primordial image in the unconscious which is best fitted to compensate the inadequacy and one-sidedness of the present. The artist seizes on this image, and in raising it from deepest unconsciousness he brings it into relation with conscious values, thereby transforming it until it can be accepted by the minds of his contemporaries according to their powers.

People and times, like individuals, have their own characteristic tendencies and attitudes. The very word *attitude* betrays the necessary bias that every marked tendency entails. Direction implies exclusion, and exclusion means that very many psychic elements that could play their part in life are denied the right to exist because they are incompatible with the general attitude. The normal man can follow the general trend without injury to himself; but the man who takes to the back streets and alleys because he cannot endure the broad highway will be the first to discover the psychic elements that are waiting to play their part in the life of the collective. Here the artist's relative lack of adaptation turns out to his advantage; it enables him to follow his own yearnings far from the beaten path, and to discover what it is that would meet the unconscious needs of his age. Thus, just as the onesidedness of the individual's conscious attitude is corrected by reactions from the unconscious, so art represents a process of self-regulation in the life of nations and epochs.

I am aware that in this lecture I have only been able to sketch out my views in the barest outline. But I hope that what I have been obliged to omit, that is to say their practical application to poetic works of art, has been furnished by your own thoughts, thus giving flesh and blood to my abstract intellectual frame.

# The Principal Archetypes

## THE EGO

Investigation of the psychology of the unconscious confronted me with facts which required the formulation of new concepts. One of these concepts is the *self*. The entity so denoted is not meant to take the place of the one that has always been known as the *ego*, but includes it in a supraordinate concept. We understand the ego as the complex factor to which all conscious contents are related. It forms, as it were, the center of the field of consciousness; and, insofar as this comprises the empirical personality, the ego is

Translated by R. F. C. Hull.

the subject of all personal acts of consciousness. The relation of a psychic content to the ego forms the criterion of its consciousness, for no content can be conscious unless it is represented to a subject.

With this definition we have described and delimited the *scope* of the subject. Theoretically, no limits can be set to the field of consciousness, since it is capable of indefinite extension. Empirically, however, it always finds its limit when it comes up against the *unknown*. This consists of everything we do not know, which, therefore, is not related to the ego as the center of the field of consciousness. The unknown falls into two groups of objects: those which are outside and can be experienced by the senses, and those which are inside and are experienced immediately. The first group comprises the unknown in the outer world; the second the unknown in the inner world. We call this latter territory the *unconscious*.

The ego, as a specific content of consciousness, is not a simple or elementary factor but a complex one which, as such, cannot be described exhaustively. Experience shows that it rests on two seemingly different bases: the *somatic* and the *psychic*. The somatic basis is inferred from the totality of endosomatic perceptions, which for their part are already of a psychic nature and are associated with the ego, and are therefore conscious. They are produced by endosomatic stimuli, only some of which cross the threshold of consciousness. A considerable proportion of these stimuli occur unconsciously, that is, subliminally. The fact that they are subliminal does not necessarily mean that their status is merely physiological, any more than this would be true of a psychic content. Sometimes they are capable of crossing the threshold, that is, of becoming perceptions. But there is no doubt that a large proportion of these endosomatic stimuli are simply incapable of consciousness and are so elementary that there is no reason to assign them a psychic nature — unless of course one favors the philosophical view that all life-processes are psychic anyway. The chief objection to this hardly demonstrable hypothesis is that it enlarges the concept of the psyche beyond all bounds and interprets the life-process in a way not absolutely warranted by the facts. Concepts that are too broad usually prove to be unsuitable instruments because they are too vague and nebulous. I have therefore suggested that the term "psychic" be used only where there is evidence of a will capable of modifying reflex or instinctual processes. Here I must refer the reader to my paper "On the Nature of the Psyche," where I have discussed this definition of the "psychic" at somewhat greater length.

The somatic basis of the ego consists, then, of conscious and unconscious factors. The same is true of the psychic basis: on the one hand the ego rests on the *total field of consciousness*, and on the other, on the *sum total of unconscious contents*. These fall into three groups: first, temporarily subliminal contents that can be reproduced voluntarily (memory); second, unconscious contents that cannot be reproduced voluntarily; third, contents that are not capable of becoming conscious at all. Group two can be inferred from the spontaneous irruption of subliminal contents into consciousness. Group three is hypothetical; it is a logical inference from the facts underlying group two. It contains contents which have *not yet* irrupted into consciousness, or which never will.

When I said that the ego "rests" on the total field of consciousness I do not mean that it *consists* of this. Were that so, it would be indistinguishable from the field of consciousness as a whole. The ego is only the latter's point of reference, grounded on and limited by the somatic factor described above.

Although its bases are in themselves relatively unknown and unconscious, the ego is a conscious factor par excellence. It is even acquired, empirically speaking, during the individual's lifetime. It seems to arise in the first place from the collision between the somatic factor and the environment, and, once established as a subject, it goes on developing from further collisions with the outer world and the inner.

Despite the unlimited extent of its bases, the ego is never more and never less than consciousness as a whole. As a conscious factor the ego could, theoretically at least, be described completely. But this would never amount to more than a picture of the *conscious personality;* all those features which are unknown or unconscious to the subject would be missing. A total picture would have to include these. But a total description of the personality is, even in theory, absolutely impossible, because the unconscious portion of it cannot be grasped cognitively. This unconscious portion, as experience has abundantly shown, is by no means unimportant. On the contrary, the most decisive qualities in a person are often unconscious and can be perceived only by others, or have to be laboriously discovered with outside help.

Clearly, then, the *personality as a total phenomenon* does not coincide with the ego, that is, with the conscious personality, but forms an entity that has to be distinguished from the ego. Naturally the need to do this is incumbent only on a psychology that reckons with the fact of the unconscious, but for such a psychology the distinction is of paramount importance. Even for jurisprudence it should be of some importance whether certain psychic facts are conscious or not — for instance, in adjudging the question of responsibility.

I have suggested calling the total personality which, though present, cannot be fully known, the *self*. The ego is, by definition, subordinate to the self and is related to it like a part to the whole. Inside the field of consciousness it has, as we say, free will. By this I do not mean anything philosophical, only the well-known psychological fact of "free choice," or rather the subjective feeling of freedom. But, just as our free will clashes with necessity in the outside world, so also it finds its limits outside the field of consciousness in the subjective inner world, where it comes into conflict with the facts of the self. And just as circumstances or outside events "happen" to us and limit our freedom, so the self acts upon the ego like an *objective occurrence* which free will can do very little to alter. It is, indeed, well known that the ego not only can do nothing against the self, but is sometimes actually assimilated by unconscious components of the personality that are in the process of development and is greatly altered by them.

It is, in the nature of the case, impossible to give any general description of the ego except a formal one. Any other mode of observation would have to take account of the *individuality* which attaches to the ego as one of its main characteristics. Although the numerous elements composing this complex factor are, in themselves, everywhere the same, they are infinitely varied as regards clarity, emotional coloring, and scope. The result of their combination — the ego — is therefore, so far as one can judge, individual and unique, and retains its identity up to a certain point. Its stability is relative, because far-reaching changes of personality can sometimes occur. Alterations of this kind need not always be pathological; they can also be developmental and hence fall within the scope of the normal.

Since it is the point of reference for the field of consciousness, the ego is the subject of all successful attempts at adaptation so far as these are achieved by the will. The ego therefore has a significant part to play in the psychic economy. Its position there is so important that there are good grounds for the prejudice that the ego is the centre of the personality, and that the field of consciousness is the psyche *per se*. If we discount certain suggestive ideas in Leibniz, Kant, Schelling, and Schopenhauer, and the philosophical excursions of Carus and von Hartmann, it is only since the end of the nineteenth century that modern psychology, with its inductive methods, has discovered the foundations of consciousness and proved empirically the existence of a psyche outside consciousness. With this discovery the position of the ego, till then absolute, became relativized; that is to say, though it retains its quality as the centre of the field of consciousness, it is questionable whether it is the center of the personality. It is part of the personality but not the whole of it. As I have said, it is simply impossible to estimate how large or how small its share is; how free or how dependent it is on the qualities of this "extra-conscious" psyche. We can only say that its freedom is limited and its dependence proved in ways that are often decisive. In my experience one would do well not to underestimate its dependence on the unconscious. Naturally there is no need to say this to persons who already overestimate the latter's importance. Some criterion for the right measure is afforded by the psychic consequences of a wrong estimate, a point to which we shall return later on.

We have seen that, from the standpoint of the psychology of consciousness, the unconscious can be divided into three groups of contents. But from the standpoint of the psychology of the personality a twofold division ensues: an "extra-conscious" psyche whose contents are *personal*, and an "extra-conscious" psyche whose contents are *impersonal* and *collective*. The first group comprises contents which are integral components of the individual personality and could therefore just as well be conscious; the second group forms, as it were, an omnipresent, unchanging, and everywhere identical *quality or substrate of the psyche per se*. This is, of course, no more than a hypothesis. But we are driven to it by the peculiar nature of the empirical material, not to mention the high probability that the general similarity of psychic processes in all individuals must be based on an equally general and impersonal principle that conforms to law, just as the instinct manifesting itself in the individual is only the partial manifestation of an instinctual substrate common to all men.

## THE SHADOW

Whereas the contents of the personal unconscious are acquired during the individual's lifetime, the contents of the collective unconscious are invariably archetypes that were present from the beginning. Their relation to the instincts has been discussed elsewhere.[1] The archetypes most clearly characterized from the empirical point of view are those which have the most frequent and the most disturbing influence on the ego. These are the *shadow,* the *anima,* and the *animus.*[2] The most accessible of these, and the easiest to experience, is the shadow, for its nature can in large measure be inferred from the contents of the personal unconscious. The only exceptions to this rule are those rather rare cases where the positive qualities of the personality are repressed, and the ego in consequence plays an essentially negative or unfavorable role.

The shadow is a moral problem that challenges the whole ego-personality, for no one can become conscious of the shadow without considerable moral effort. To become conscious of it involves recognizing the dark aspects of the personality as present and real. This act is the essential condition for any kind of self-knowledge, and it therefore, as a rule, meets with considerable resistance. Indeed, self-knowledge as a psy-

chotherapeutic measure frequently requires much painstaking work extending over a long period.

Closer examination of the dark characteristics — that is, the inferiorities constituting the shadow — reveals that they have an *emotional* nature, a kind of autonomy, and accordingly an obsessive or, better, possessive quality. Emotion, incidentally, is not an activity of the individual but something that happens to him. Affects occur usually where adaptation is weakest, and at the same time they reveal the reason for its weakness, namely a certain degree of inferiority and the existence of a lower level of personality. On this lower level with its uncontrolled or scarcely controlled emotions one behaves more or less like a primitive, who is not only the passive victim of his affects but also singularly incapable of moral judgment.

Although, with insight and good will, the shadow can to some extent be assimilated into the conscious personality, experience shows that there are certain features which offer the most obstinate resistance to moral control and prove almost impossible to influence. These resistances are usually bound up with *projections,* which are not recognized as such, and their recognition is a moral achievement beyond the ordinary. While some traits peculiar to the shadow can be recognized without too much difficulty as one's own personal qualities, in this case both insight and good will are unavailing because the cause of the emotion appears to lie, beyond all possibility of doubt, in the *other person.* No matter how obvious it may be to the neutral observer that it is a matter of projections, there is little hope that the subject will perceive this himself. He must be convinced that he throws a very long shadow before he is willing to withdraw his emotionally-toned projections from their object.

Let us suppose that a certain individual shows no inclination whatever to recognize his projections. The projection-making factor then has a free hand and can realize its object — if it has one — or bring about some other situation characteristic of its power. As we know, it is not the conscious subject but the unconscious which does the projecting. Hence one meets with projections, one does not make them. The effect of projection is to isolate the subject from his en-

[1] "Instinct and the Unconscious" and "On the Nature of the Psyche," pars. 397ff. [Au.]

[2] The contents of this and the following chapter are taken from a lecture delivered to the Swiss Society for Practical Psychology, in Zurich, 1948. The material was first published in the *Wiener Zeitschrift für Nervenheilkunde und deren Grenzgebiete* I (1948): 4. [Au.]

vironment, since instead of a real relation to it there is now only an illusory one. Projections change the world into the replica of one's own unknown face. In the last analysis, therefore, they lead to an autoerotic or autistic condition in which one dreams a world whose reality remains forever unattainable. The resultant *sentiment d'incomplétude*[3] and the still worse feeling of sterility are in their turn explained by projection as the malevolence of the environment, and by means of this vicious circle the isolation is intensified. The more projections are thrust in between the subject and the environment, the harder it is for the ego to see through its illusions. A forty-five-year-old patient who had suffered from a compulsion neurosis since he was twenty and had become completely cut off from the world once said to me: "But I can never admit to myself that I've wasted the best twenty-five years of my life!"

It is often tragic to see how blatantly a man bungles his own life and the lives of others yet remains totally incapable of seeing how much the whole tragedy originates in himself, and how he continually feeds it and keeps it going. Not *consciously,* of course — for consciously he is engaged in bewailing and cursing a faithless world that recedes further and further into the distance. Rather, it is an unconscious factor which spins the illusions that veil his world. And what is being spun is a cocoon, which in the end will completely envelop him.

One might assume that projections like these, which are so very difficult if not impossible to dissolve, would belong to the realm of the shadow — that is, to the negative side of the personality. This assumption becomes untenable after a certain point, because the symbols that then appear no longer refer to the same but to the opposite sex, in a man's case to a woman and vice versa. The source of projections is no longer the shadow — which is always of the same sex as the subject — but a contrasexual figure. Here we meet the animus of a woman and the anima of a man, two corresponding archetypes whose autonomy and unconsciousness

explain the stubbornness of their projections. Though the shadow is a motif as well known to mythology as anima and animus, it represents first and foremost the personal unconscious, and its content can therefore be made conscious without too much difficulty. In this it differs from anima and animus, for whereas the shadow can be seen through and recognized fairly easily, the anima and animus are much further away from consciousness and in normal circumstances are seldom if ever realized. With a little self-criticism one can see through the shadow — so far as its nature is personal. But when it appears as an archetype, one encounters the same difficulties as with anima and animus. In other words, it is quite within the bounds of possibility for a man to recognize the relative evil of his nature, but it is a rare and shattering experience for him to gaze into the face of absolute evil.

## THE SYZYGY: ANIMA AND ANIMUS

What, then, is this projection-making factor? The East calls it the "Spinning Woman"[4] — Maya, who creates illusion by her dancing. Had we not long since known it from the symbolism of dreams, this hint from the Orient would put us on the right track: the enveloping, embracing, and devouring element points unmistakably to the mother,[5] that is, to the son's relation to the real mother, to her imago, and to the woman who is to become a mother for him. His Eros is passive like a child's; he hopes to be caught, sucked in, enveloped, and devoured. He seeks, as it were, the protecting, nourishing, charmed circle of the mother, the condition of the infant released from every care, in which the outside world bends over him and even forces happiness upon him. No wonder the real world vanishes from sight!

If this situation is dramatized, as the uncon-

---

[3]Feeling of incompleteness. [Ed.]

[4]Erwin Rousselle, "Seelische Führung im lebenden Taoismus," Pl. I, pp. 150, 170. Rousselle calls the spinning woman the "animal soul." There is a saying that runs, "The spinner sets in motion." I have defined the anima as a personification of the unconscious. [Au.]

[5]Here and in what follows, the word "mother" is not meant in the literal sense but as a symbol of everything that functions as a mother. [Au.]

scious usually dramatizes it, then there appears before you on the psychological stage a man living regressively, seeking his childhood and his mother, fleeing from a cold cruel world which denies him understanding. Often a mother appears beside him who apparently shows not the slightest concern that her little son should become a man, but who, with tireless and self-immolating effort, neglects nothing that might hinder him from growing up and marrying. You behold the secret conspiracy between mother and son, and how each helps the other to betray life.

Where does the guilt lie? With the mother, or with the son? Probably with both. The unsatisfied longing of the son for life and the world ought to be taken seriously. There is in him a desire to touch reality, to embrace the earth and fructify the field of the world. But he makes no more than a series of fitful starts, for his initiative as well as his staying power are crippled by the secret memory that the world and happiness may be had as a gift — from the mother. The fragment of world which he, like every man, must encounter again and again is never quite the right one, since it does not fall into his lap, does not meet him half way, but remains resistant, has to be conquered, and submits only to force. It makes demands on the masculinity of a man, on his ardor, above all on his courage and resolution when it comes to throwing his whole being into the scales. For this he would need a faithless Eros, one capable of forgetting his mother and undergoing the pain of relinquishing the first love of his life. The mother, foreseeing this danger, has carefully inculcated into him the virtues of faithfulness, devotion, loyalty, so as to protect him from the moral disruption which is the risk of every life adventure. He has learnt these lessons only too well, and remains true to his mother. This naturally causes her the deepest anxiety (when, to her greater glory, he turns out to be a homosexual, for example) and at the same time affords her an unconscious satisfaction that is positively mythological. For, in the relationship now reigning between them, there is consummated the immemorial and most sacred archetype of the marriage of mother and son. What, after all, has commonplace reality to offer, with its registry offices, pay envelopes, and monthly rent, that could outweigh the mystic awe of the *hieros gamos?*[6] Or the star-crowned woman whom the dragon pursues, or the pious obscurities veiling the marriage of the Lamb?

This myth, better than any other, illustrates the nature of the collective unconscious. At this level the mother is both old and young, Demeter and Persephone, and the son is spouse and sleeping suckling rolled into one. The imperfections of real life, with its laborious adaptations and manifold disappointments, naturally cannot compete with such a state of indescribable fulfilment.

In the case of the son, the projection-making factor is identical with the mother-imago, and this is consequently taken to be the real mother. The projection can only be dissolved when the son sees that in the realm of his psyche there is an imago not only of the mother but of the daughter, the sister, the beloved, the heavenly goddess, and the chthonic Baubo.[7] Every mother and every beloved is forced to become the carrier and embodiment of this omnipresent and ageless image, which corresponds to the deepest reality in a man. It belongs to him, this perilous image of Woman; she stands for the loyalty which in the interests of life he must sometimes forgo; she is the much needed compensation for the risks, struggles, sacrifices that all end in disappointment; she is the solace for all the bitterness of life. And, at the same time, she is the great illusionist, the seductress, who draws him into life with her Maya — and not only into life's reasonable and useful aspects, but into its frightful paradoxes and ambivalences where good and evil, success and ruin, hope and despair, counterbalance one another. Because she is his greatest danger she demands from a man his greatest, and if he has it in him she will receive it.

This image is "My Lady Soul," as Spitteler called her. I have suggested instead the term "anima," as indicating something specific, for which the expression "soul" is too general and too vague. The empirical reality summed up under the concept of the anima forms an extremely

---

[6]Priestess. Jung's allusions are to the book of Revelation. [Ed.]

[7]The earth mother, symbol of the grave to which man goes. [Ed.]

dramatic content of the unconscious. It is possible to describe this content in rational, scientific language, but in this way one entirely fails to express its living character. Therefore, in describing the living processes of the psyche, I deliberately and consciously give preference to a dramatic, mythological way of thinking and speaking, because this is not only more expressive but also more exact than an abstract scientific terminology, which is wont to toy with the notion that its theoretic formulations may one fine day be resolved into algebraic equations.

The projection-making factor is the anima, or rather the unconscious as represented by the anima. Whenever she appears, in dreams, visions, and fantasies, she takes on personified form, thus demonstrating that the factor she embodies possesses all the outstanding characteristics of a feminine being. She is not an invention of the conscious, but a spontaneous product of the unconscious. Nor is she a substitute figure for the mother. On the contrary, there is every likelihood that the numinous qualities which make the mother-imago so dangerously powerful derive from the collective archetype of the anima, which is incarnated anew in every male child.

Since the anima is an archetype that is found in men, it is reasonable to suppose that an equivalent archetype must be present in women; for just as the man is compensated by a feminine element, so woman is compensated by a masculine one. I do not, however, wish this argument to give the impression that these compensatory relationships were arrived at by deduction. On the contrary, long and varied experience was needed in order to grasp the nature of anima and animus empirically. Whatever we have to say about these archetypes, therefore, is either directly verifiable or at least rendered probable by the facts. At the same time, I am fully aware that we are discussing pioneer work which by its very nature can only be provisional.

Just as the mother seems to be the first carrier of the projection-making factor for the son, so is the father for the daughter. Practical experience of these relationships is made up of many individual cases presenting all kinds of variations on the same basic theme. A concise description of them can, therefore, be no more than schematic.

Woman is compensated by a masculine element and therefore her unconscious has, so to speak, a masculine imprint. This results in a considerable psychological difference between men and women, and accordingly I have called the projection-making factor in women the animus, which means mind or spirit. The animus corresponds to the paternal Logos[8] just as the anima corresponds to the maternal Eros.[9] But I do not wish or intend to give these two intuitive concepts too specific a definition. I use Eros and Logos merely as conceptual aids to describe the fact that woman's consciousness is characterized more by the connective quality of Eros than by the discrimination and cognition associated with Logos. In men, Eros, the function of relationship, is usually less developed than Logos. In women, on the other hand, Eros is an expression of their true nature, while their Logos is often only a regrettable accident. It gives rise to misunderstandings and annoying interpretations in the family circle and among friends. This is because it consists of *opinions* instead of reflections, and by opinions I mean *a priori* assumptions that lay claim to absolute truth. Such assumptions, as everyone knows, can be extremely irritating. As the animus is partial to argument, he can best be seen at work in disputes where both parties know they are right. Men can argue in a very womanish way, too, when they are anima-possessed and have thus been transformed into the animus of their own anima. With them the question becomes one of personal vanity and touchiness (as if they were females); with women it is a question of *power,* whether of truth or justice or some other "ism" — for the dressmaker and hairdresser have already taken care of their vanity. The "Father" (i.e., the sum of conventional opinions) always plays a great role in female argumentation. No matter how friendly and obliging a woman's Eros may be, no logic on earth can shake her if she is ridden by the animus. Often the man has the feeling — and he is not altogether wrong — that only seduction or a beating or rape would have the necessary power of persuasion. He is unaware that this highly

[8]Reason. [Ed.]
[9]Love, desire. [Ed.]

dramatic situation would instantly come to a banal and unexciting end if he were to quit the field and let a second woman carry on the battle (his wife, for instance, if she herself is not the fiery war horse). This sound idea seldom or never occurs to him, because no man can converse with an animus for five minutes without becoming the victim of his own anima. Anyone who still had enough sense of humor to listen objectively to the ensuing dialogue would be staggered by the vast number of commonplaces, misapplied truisms, clichés from newspapers and novels, shop-soiled platitudes of every description interspersed with vulgar abuse and brain-splitting lack of logic. It is a dialogue which, irrespective of its participants, is repeated millions and millions of times in all the languages of the world and always remains essentially the same.

This singular fact is due to the following circumstance: when animus and anima meet, the animus draws his sword of power and the anima ejects her poison of illusion and seduction. The outcome need not always be negative, since the two are equally likely to fall in love (a special instance of love at first sight). The language of love is of astonishing uniformity, using the well-worn formulas with the utmost devotion and fidelity, so that once again the two partners find themselves in a banal collective situation. Yet they live in the illusion that they are related to one another in the most individual way.

In both its positive and its negative aspects the anima/animus relationship is always full of "animosity," i.e., it is emotional, and hence collective. Affects lower the level of the relationship and bring it closer to the common instinctual basis, which no longer has anything individual about it. Very often the relationship runs its course heedless of its human performers, who afterwards do not know what happened to them.

Whereas the cloud of "animosity" surrounding the man is composed chiefly of sentimentality and resentment, in woman it expresses itself in the form of opinionated views, interpretations, insinuations, and misconstructions, which all have the purpose (sometimes attained) of severing the relation between two human beings. The woman, like the man, becomes wrapped in a veil of illusions by her demon-familiar, and, as the daughter who alone understands her father (that is, is eternally right in everything), she is translated to the land of sheep, where she is put to graze by the shepherd of her soul, the animus.

Like the anima, the animus too has a positive aspect. Through the figure of the father he expresses not only conventional opinion but — equally — what we call "spirit," philosophical or religious ideas in particular, or rather the attitude resulting from them. Thus the animus is a psychopomp, a mediator between the conscious and the unconscious and a personification of the latter. Just as the anima becomes, through integration, the Eros of consciousness, so the animus becomes a Logos; and in the same way that the anima gives relationship and relatedness to a man's consciousness, the animus gives to woman's consciousness a capacity for reflection, deliberation, and self-knowledge.

The effect of anima and animus on the ego is in principle the same. This effect is extremely difficult to eliminate because, in the first place, it is uncommonly strong and immediately fills the ego-personality with an unshakable feeling of rightness and righteousness. In the second place, the cause of the effect is projected and appears to lie in objects and objective situations. Both these characteristics can, I believe, be traced back to the peculiarities of the archetype. For the archetype, of course, exists *a priori*. This may possibly explain the often totally irrational yet undisputed and indisputable existence of certain moods and opinions. Perhaps these are so notoriously difficult to influence because of the powerfully suggestive effect emanating from the archetype. Consciousness is fascinated by it, held captive, as if hypnotized. Very often the ego experiences a vague feeling of moral defeat and then behaves all the more defensively, defiantly, and self-righteously, thus setting up a vicious circle which only increases its feeling of inferiority. The bottom is then knocked out of the human relationship, for, like megalomania, a feeling of inferiority makes mutual recognition impossible, and without this there is no relationship.

As I said, it is easier to gain insight into the shadow than into the anima or animus. With the shadow, we have the advantage of being prepared in some sort by our education, which has always endeavored to convince people that they are not one-hundred-per-cent pure gold. So everyone immediately understands what is meant by "shadow," "inferior personality," etc. And if he has forgotten, his memory can easily be refreshed by a Sunday sermon, his wife, or the tax collector. With the anima and animus, however, things are by no means so simple. Firstly, there is no moral education in this respect, and secondly, most people are content to be self-righteous and prefer mutual vilification (if nothing worse!) to the recognition of their projections. Indeed, it seems a very natural state of affairs for men to have irrational moods and women irrational opinions. Presumably this situation is grounded on instinct and must remain as it is to ensure that the Empedoclean game of the hate and love of the elements shall continue for all eternity. Nature is conservative and does not easily allow her courses to be altered; she defends in the most stubborn way the inviolability of the preserves where anima and animus roam. Hence it is much more difficult to become conscious of one's anima/animus projections than to acknowledge one's shadow side. One has, of course, to overcome certain moral obstacles, such as vanity, ambition, conceit, resentment, etc., but in the case of projections all sorts of purely intellectual difficulties are added, quite apart from the contents of the projection which one simply doesn't know how to cope with. And on top of all this there arises a profound doubt as to whether one is not meddling too much with nature's business by prodding into consciousness things which it would have been better to leave asleep.

Although there are, in my experience, a fair number of people who can understand without special intellectual or moral difficulties what is meant by anima and animus, one finds very many more who have the greatest trouble in visualizing these empirical concepts as anything concrete. This shows that they fall a little outside the usual range of experience. They are unpopular precisely because they seem unfamiliar. The consequence is that they mobilize prejudice and become taboo like everything else that is unexpected.

So if we set it up as a kind of requirement that projections should be dissolved, because it is wholesomer that way and in every respect more advantageous, we are entering upon new ground. Up till now everybody has been convinced that the idea "my father," "my mother," etc., is nothing but a faithful reflection of the real parent, corresponding in every detail to the original, so that when someone says "my father" he means no more and no less than what his father is in reality. This is actually what he supposes he does mean, but a supposition of identity by no means brings that identity about. This is where the fallacy of the *enkekalymmenos* ('the veiled one') comes in.[10] If one includes in the psychological equation X's picture of his father, which he takes for the real father, the equation will not work out, because the unknown quantity he has introduced does not tally with reality. X has overlooked the fact that his idea of a person consists, in the first place, of the possibly very incomplete picture he has received of the real person and, in the second place, of the subjective modifications he has imposed upon this picture. X's idea of his father is a complex quantity for which the real father is only in part responsible, an indefinitely larger share falling to the son. So true is this that every time he criticizes or praises his father he is unconsciously hitting back at himself, thereby bringing about those psychic consequences that overtake people who habitually disparage or overpraise themselves. If, however, X carefully compares his reactions with reality, he stands a chance of noticing that he has miscalculated somewhere by not realizing long ago from his father's behavior that the picture he has of him is a false one. But as a rule X is convinced that he is right, and if anybody is wrong it must be the other fellow. Should X have a poorly developed Eros, he will be either indifferent to the inadequate relationship he has with his father or else annoyed by the inconsistency and general incomprehensibility of a father whose behavior never really corresponds to the

[10]The fallacy, which stems from Eubulides the Megarian, runs: "Can you recognize your father?" Yes. "Can you recognize this veiled one?" No. "This veiled one is your father. Hence you can recognize your father and not recognize him." [Au.]

picture X has of him. Therefore X thinks he has every right to feel hurt, misunderstood, and even betrayed.

One can imagine how desirable it would be in such cases to dissolve the projection. And there are always optimists who believe that the golden age can be ushered in simply by telling people the right way to go. But just let them try to explain to these people that they are acting like a dog chasing its own tail. To make a person see the shortcomings of his attitude considerably more than mere "telling" is needed, for more is involved than ordinary common sense can allow. What one is up against here is the kind of fateful misunderstanding which, under ordinary conditions, remains forever inaccessible to insight. It is rather like expecting the average respectable citizen to recognize himself as a criminal.

I mention all this just to illustrate the order of magnitude to which the anima/animus projections belong, and the moral and intellectual exertions that are needed to dissolve them. Not all the contents of the anima and animus are projected, however. Many of them appear spontaneously in dreams and so on, and many more can be made conscious through active imagination. In this way we find that thoughts, feelings, and affects are alive in us which we would never have believed possible. Naturally, possibilities of this sort seem utterly fantastic to anyone who has not experienced them himself, for a normal person "knows what he thinks." Such a childish attitude on the part of the "normal person" is simply the rule, so that no one without experience in this field can be expected to understand the real nature of anima and animus. With these reflections one gets into an entirely new world of psychological experience, provided of course that one succeeds in realizing it in practice. Those who do succeed can hardly fail to be impressed by all that the ego does not know and never has known. This increase in self-knowledge is still very rare nowadays and is usually paid for in advance with a neurosis, if not with something worse.

The autonomy of the collective unconscious expresses itself in the figures of anima and animus. They personify those of its contents which, when withdrawn from projection, can be inte-grated into consciousness. To this extent, both figures represent *functions* which filter the contents of the collective unconscious through to the conscious mind. They appear or behave as such, however, only so long as the tendencies of the conscious and unconscious do not diverge too greatly. Should any tension arise, these functions, harmless till then, confront the conscious mind in personified form and behave rather like systems split off from the personality, or like part souls. This comparison is inadequate in so far as nothing previously belonging to the ego-personality has split off from it; on the contrary, the two figures represent a disturbing accretion. The reason for their behaving in this way is that though the *contents* of anima and animus can be integrated they themselves cannot, since they are archetypes. As such they are the foundation stones of the psychic structure, which in its totality exceeds the limits of consciousness and therefore can never become the object of direct cognition. Though the effects of anima and animus can be made conscious, they themselves are factors transcending consciousness and beyond the reach of perception and volition. Hence they remain autonomous despite the integration of their contents, and for this reason they should be borne constantly in mind. This is extremely important from the therapeutic standpoint, because constant observation pays the unconscious a tribute that more or less guarantees its co-operation. The unconscious as we know can never be "done with" once and for all. It is, in fact, one of the most important tasks of psychic hygiene to pay continual attention to the symptomatology of unconscious contents and processes, for the good reason that the conscious mind is always in danger of becoming one-sided, of keeping to well-worn paths and getting stuck in blind alleys. The complementary and compensating function of the unconscious ensures that these dangers, which are especially great in neurosis, can in some measure be avoided. It is only under ideal conditions, when life is still simple and unconscious enough to follow the serpentine path of instinct without hesitation or misgiving, that the compensation works with entire success. The more civilized, the more unconscious and complicated a man is, the less he is able to follow his instincts. His complicated living conditions and the influence of his environment are so strong that they drown the quiet voice of nature. Opinions, beliefs, theories, and collective tendencies appear in its stead and back up all the aberrations of the conscious mind. Deliberate attention should then be given to the unconscious so that the compensation can set to work. Hence it is especially important to picture the archetypes of the unconscious not as a rushing phantasmagoria of fugitive images but as constant, autonomous factors, which indeed they are.

Both these archetypes, as practical experience shows, possess a fatality that can on occasion produce tragic results. They are quite literally the father and mother of all the disastrous entanglements of fate and have long been recognized as such by the whole world. Together they form a divine pair,[11] one of whom, in accordance with his Logos nature, is characterized by *pneuma* and *nous*,[12] rather like Hermes with his ever-shifting hues, while the other, in accordance with her Eros nature, wears the features of Aphrodite, Helen (Selene), Persephone, and Hecate. Both of them are unconscious powers, "gods" in fact, as the ancient world quite rightly conceived them to be. To call them by this name is to give them that central position in the scale of psychological values which has always been theirs whether consciously acknowledged or not; for their power grows in proportion to the degree that they remain unconscious. Those who do not see them are in their hands, just as a typhus epidemic flourishes best when its source is undiscovered. Even in Christianity the divine syzygy has not become obsolete, but occupies the highest place as Christ and his bride the Church.[13] Parallels

like these prove extremely helpful in our attempts to find the right criterion for gauging the significance of these two archetypes. What we can discover about them from the conscious side is so slight as to be almost imperceptible. It is only when we throw light into the dark depths of the psyche and explore the strange and tortuous paths of human fate that it gradually becomes clear to us how immense is the influence wielded by these two factors that complement our conscious life.

Recapitulating, I should like to emphasize that the integration of the shadow, or the realization of the personal unconscious, marks the first stage in the analytic process, and that without it a recognition of anima and animus is impossible. The shadow can be realized only through a relation to a partner, and anima and animus only through a relation to a partner of the opposite sex, because only in such a relation do their projections become operative. The recognition of the anima gives rise, in a man, to a triad, one third of which is transcendent: the masculine subject, the opposing feminine subject, and the transcendent anima. With a woman the situation is reversed. The missing fourth element that would make the triad a quaternity is, in a man, the archetype of the Wise Old Man, which I have not discussed here, and in a woman the Chthonic Mother. These four constitute a half immanent and half transcendent quaternity, an archetype which I have called the *marriage quaternio*.[14] The marriage quaternio provides a schema not only for the self but also for the structure of primitive society with its cross-cousin marriage, marriage classes, and division of settlements into quarters. The self, on the other hand, is a God-image, or at least cannot be distinguished from one. Of this the early Christian spirit was not ignorant, otherwise Clement of Alexandria could never have said that he who knows himself knows God.

---

[11]Naturally this is not meant as a psychological definition, let alone a metaphysical one. As I pointed out in "The Relations between the Ego and the Unconscious" (pars. 296ff.), the syzygy consists of three elements: the femininity pertaining to the man and the masculinity pertaining to the woman; the experience which man has of woman and vice versa; and, finally, the masculine and feminine archetypal image. The first element can be integrated into the personality by the process of conscious realization, but the last one cannot. [Au.]

[12]Spirit and mind. [Ed.]

[13]"For the Scripture says, God made man male and female; the male is Christ, the female is the Church." —

---

Second Epistle of Clement to the Corinthians, xiv, 2 (trans. by Lake, I, p. 151). In pictorial representations, Mary often takes the place of the Church. [Au.]

[14]"The Psychology of the Transference," pars. 425ff. [Au.]

# Northrop Frye

## 1912–1991

*In his native Canada, Northrop Frye's intellectual stature has made him something of a national oracle and celebrity. In the world of literary theory and criticism, he is also a formidable and revered figure. Frye was born in Quebec, received his B.A. from the University of Toronto (1933), studied theology there at Emmanuel College, and was ordained a minister (1936). He received an M.A. from Merton College, Oxford (1940). In 1948 he became a professor of English at Victoria College, Toronto; in 1959 principal of the college; and in 1967 university professor at the University of Toronto. He has written more than forty books, including* Fearful Symmetry *(1947),* Fables of Identity *(1963),* The Modern Century *(1967),* The Stubborn Structure *(1970),* The Critical Path *(1971),* The Secular Scripture *(1976), and* The Great Code *(1982). His most celebrated work is* Anatomy of Criticism *(1957). "The Archetypes of Literature," first published in the* Kenyon Review *8 (1951) and later reprinted in* Fables of Identity, *is, in Frye's words, "to some extent a summarized statement of the critical program" later expanded in* Anatomy of Criticism.*

# The Archetypes of Literature

## I

Every organized body of knowledge can be learned progressively; and experience shows that there is also something progressive about the learning of literature. Our opening sentence has already got us into a semantic difficulty. Physics is an organized body of knowledge about nature, and a student of it says that he is learning physics, not that he is learning nature. Art, like nature, is the subject of a systematic study, and has to be distinguished from the study itself, which is criticism. It is therefore impossible to "learn literature": one learns about it in a certain way, but what one learns, transitively, is the criticism of literature. Similarly, the difficulty often felt in "teaching literature" arises from the fact that it cannot be done: the criticism of literature is all that can be directly taught. So while no one expects literature itself to behave like a science, there is surely no reason why criticism, as a systematic and organized study, should not be, at least partly, a science. Not a "pure" or "exact" science, perhaps, but these phrases form part of a nineteenth-century cosmology which is no longer with us. Criticism deals with the arts and

may well be something of an art itself, but it does not follow that it must be unsystematic. If it is to be related to the sciences too, it does not follow that it must be deprived of the graces of culture.

Certainly criticism as we find it in learned journals and scholarly monographs has every characteristic of a science. Evidence is examined scientifically; previous authorities are used scientifically; fields are investigated scientifically; texts are edited scientifically. Prosody is scientific in structure; so is phonetics; so is philology. And yet in studying this kind of critical science the student becomes aware of a centrifugal movement carrying him away from literature. He finds that literature is the central division of the "humanities," flanked on one side by history and on the other by philosophy. Criticism so far ranks only as a subdivision of literature; and hence, for the systematic mental organization of the subject, the student has to turn to the conceptual framework of the historian for events, and to that of the philosopher for ideas. Even the more centrally placed critical sciences, such as textual editing, seem to be part of a "background" that recedes into history or some other nonliterary field. The thought suggests itself that the ancillary critical disciplines may be related to a central expanding pattern of systematic comprehension which has not yet been established, but which, if it were established, would prevent them from being centrifugal. If such a pattern exists, then criticism would be to art what philosophy is to wisdom and history to action.

Most of the central area of criticism is at present, and doubtless always will be, the area of commentary. But the commentators have little sense, unlike the researchers, of being contained within some sort of scientific discipline: they are chiefly engaged, in the words of the gospel hymn, in brightening the corner where they are. If we attempt to get a more comprehensive idea of what criticism is about, we find ourselves wandering over quaking bogs of generalities, judicious pronouncements of value, reflective comments, perorations to works of research, and other consequences of taking the large view. But this part of the critical field is so full of pseudo-propositions, sonorous nonsense that contains no truth and no falsehood, that it obviously exists only because criticism, like nature, prefers a waste space to an empty one.

The term "pseudo-proposition" may imply some sort of logical positivist attitude on my own part.[1] But I would not confuse the significant proposition with the factual one; nor should I consider it advisable to muddle the study of literature with a schizophrenic dichotomy between subjective-emotional and objective-descriptive aspects of meaning, considering that in order to produce any literary meaning at all one has to ignore this dichotomy. I say only that the principles by which one can distinguish a significant from a meaningless statement in criticism are not clearly defined. Our first step, therefore, is to recognize and get rid of meaningless criticism: that is, talking about literature in a way that cannot help to build up a systematic structure of knowledge. Casual value-judgments belong not to criticism but to the history of taste, and reflect, at best, only the social and psychological compulsions which prompted their utterance. All judgments in which the values are not based on literary experience but are sentimental or derived from religious or political prejudice may be regarded as casual. Sentimental judgments are usually based either on nonexistent categories or antitheses ("Shakespeare studied life, Milton books") or on a visceral reaction to the writer's personality. The literary chitchat which makes the reputations of poets boom and crash in an imaginary stock exchange[2] is pseudo-criticism. That wealthy investor Mr. Eliot, after dumping Milton on the market, is now buying him again; Donne has probably reached his peak and will begin to taper off; Tennyson may be in for a slight flutter but the Shelley stocks are still bearish. This sort of thing cannot be part of any systematic study, for a systematic study can only progress: whatever dithers or vacillates or reacts is merely leisure-class conversation.

We next meet a more serious group of critics who say: the foreground of criticism is the impact of literature on the reader. Let us, then, keep the study of literature centripetal, and base the learning process on a structural analysis of the literary work itself. The texture of any great work of art is complex and ambiguous, and in unravelling the complexities we may take in as much history and philosophy as we please, if the subject of our study remains at the center. If it does not, we may find that in our anxiety to write about literature we have forgotten how to read it.

The only weakness in this approach is that it is conceived primarily as the antithesis of centrifugal or "background" criticism, and so lands us in a somewhat unreal dilemma, like the conflict of internal and external relations in philosophy. Antitheses are usually resolved, not by picking one side and refuting the other, or by making eclectic choices between them, but by trying to get past the antithetical way of stating the problem. It is right that the first effort of critical apprehension should take the form of a rhetorical or structural analysis of a work of art. But a purely structural approach has the same

[1]Logical positivists, like Ludwig Wittgenstein in the *Tractatus* (1922), believe that many "philosophical" questions are actually meaningless. [Ed.]

[2]Shocking as the admission may be, I was not aware when I wrote this that the same figure had appeared in Mr. Eliot's own essay, "What Is Minor Poetry?" [Au.]

limitation in criticism that it has in biology. In itself it is simply a discrete series of analyses based on the mere existence of the literary structure, without developing any explanation of how the structure came to be what it was and what its nearest relatives are. Structural analysis brings rhetoric back to criticism, but we need a new poetics as well, and the attempt to construct a new poetics out of rhetoric alone can hardly avoid a mere complication of rhetorical terms into a sterile jargon. I suggest that what is at present missing from literary criticism is a co-ordinating principle, a central hypothesis which, like the theory of evolution in biology, will see the phenomena it deals with as parts of a whole. Such a principle, though it would retain the centripetal perspective of structural analysis, would try to give the same perspective to other kinds of criticism too.

The first postulate of this hypothesis is the same as that of any science: the assumption of total coherence. The assumption refers to the science, not to what it deals with. A belief in an order of nature is an inference from the intelligibility of the natural sciences; and if the natural sciences ever completely demonstrated the order of nature they would presumably exhaust their subject. Criticism, as a science, is totally intelligible; literature, as the subject of a science, is, so far as we know, an inexhaustible source of new critical discoveries, and would be even if new works of literature ceased to be written. If so, then the search for a limiting principle in literature in order to discourage the development of criticism is mistaken. The assertion that the critic should not look for more in a poem than the poet may safely be assumed to have been conscious of putting there is a common form of what may be called the fallacy of premature teleology. It corresponds to the assertion that a natural phenomenon is as it is because Providence in its inscrutable wisdom made it so.

Simple as the assumption appears, it takes a long time for a science to discover that it is in fact a totally intelligible body of knowledge. Until it makes this discovery it has not been born as an individual science, but remains an embryo within the body of some other subject. The birth of physics from "natural philosophy" and of sociology from "moral philosophy" will illustrate the process. It is also very approximately true that the modern sciences have developed in the order of their closeness to mathematics. Thus physics and astronomy assumed their modern form in the Renaissance, chemistry in the eighteenth century, biology in the nineteenth and the social sciences in the twentieth. If systematic criticism, then, is developing only in our day, the fact is at least not an anachronism.

We are now looking for classifying principles lying in an area between two points that we have fixed. The first of these is the preliminary effort of criticism, the structural analysis of the work of art. The second is the assumption that there is such a subject as criticism, and that it makes, or could make, complete sense. We may next proceed inductively from structural analysis, associating the data we collect and trying to see larger patterns in them. Or we may proceed deductively, with the consequences that follow from postulating the unity of criticism. It is clear, of course, that neither procedure will work indefinitely without correction from the other. Pure induction will get us lost in haphazard guessing; pure deduction will lead to inflexible and oversimplified pigeonholing. Let us now attempt a few tentative steps in each direction, beginning with the inductive one.

## II

The unity of a work of art, the basis of structural analysis, has not been produced solely by the unconditioned will of the artist, for the artist is only its efficient cause:[3] it has form, and consequently a formal cause. The fact that revision is possible, that the poet makes changes not because he likes them better but because they are better, means that poems, like poets, are born and not made. The poet's task is to deliver the

[3]Here and later in this essay, Frye uses the Aristotelian terminology of the four causes (formal, material, efficient, and final) for the analysis of a manufactured object, but his use of the terminology is quite different from Aristotle's. For Aristotle, the material cause of a poem is language; for Frye, it is "the social conditions and cultural demands which produced it." [Ed.]

poem in as uninjured a state as possible, and if the poem is alive, it is equally anxious to be rid of him, and screams to be cut loose from his private memories and associations, his desire for self-expression, and all the other navel-strings and feeding tubes of his ego. The critic takes over where the poet leaves off, and criticism can hardly do without a kind of literary psychology connecting the poet with the poem. Part of this may be a psychological study of the poet, though this is useful chiefly in analyzing the failures in his expression, the things in him which are still attached to his work. More important is the fact that every poet has his private mythology, his own spectroscopic band or peculiar formation of symbols, of much of which he is quite unconscious. In works with characters of their own, such as dramas and novels, the same psychological analysis may be extended to the interplay of characters, though of course, literary psychology would analyze the behavior of such characters only in relation to literary convention.

There is still before us the problem of the formal cause of the poem, a problem deeply involved with the question of genres. We cannot say much about genres, for criticism does not know much about them. A good many critical efforts to grapple with such words as "novel" or "epic" are chiefly interesting as examples of the psychology of rumor. Two conceptions of the genre, however, are obviously fallacious, and as they are opposite extremes, the truth must lie somewhere between them. One is the pseudo-Platonic conception of genres as existing prior to and independently of creation, which confuses them with mere conventions of form like the sonnet. The other is that pseudobiological conception of them as evolving species which turns up in so many surveys of the "development" of this or that form.

We next inquire for the origin of the genre, and turn first of all to the social conditions and cultural demands which produced it — in other words to the material cause of the work of art. This leads us into literary history, which differs from ordinary history in that its containing categories, "Gothic," "Baroque," "Romantic," and the like are cultural categories, of little use to the ordinary historian. Most literary history does

not get as far as these categories, but even so we know more about it than about most kinds of critical scholarship. The historian treats literature and philosophy historically; the philosopher treats history and literature philosophically; and the so-called history of ideas approach marks the beginning of an attempt to treat history and philosophy from the point of view of an autonomous criticism.

But still we feel that there is something missing. We say that every poet has his own peculiar formation of images. But when so many poets use so many of the same images, surely there are much bigger critical problems involved than biographical ones. As Mr. Auden's brilliant essay *The Enchafèd Flood* shows, an important symbol like the sea cannot remain within the poetry of Shelley or Keats or Coleridge: it is bound to expand over many poets into an archetypal symbol of literature. And if the genre has a historical origin, why does the genre of drama emerge from medieval religion in a way so strikingly similar to the way it emerged from Greek religion centuries before? This is a problem of structure rather than origin, and suggests that there may be archetypes of genres as well as of images.

It is clear that criticism cannot be systematic unless there is a quality in literature which enables it to be so, an order of words corresponding to the order of nature in the natural sciences. An archetype should be not only a unifying category of criticism, but itself a part of a total form, and it leads us at once to the question of what sort of total form criticism can see in literature. Our survey of critical techniques has taken us as far as literary history. Total literary history moves from the primitive to the sophisticated, and here we glimpse the possibility of seeing literature as a complication of a relatively restricted and simple group of formulas that can be studied in primitive culture. If so, then the search for archetypes is a kind of literary anthropology, concerned with the way that literature is informed by preliterary categories such as ritual, myth and folk tale. We next realize that the relation between these categories and literature is by no means purely one of descent, as we find them reappearing in the greatest classics — in fact there seems to be a general tendency on the part of great classics to revert to them. This coincides with a feeling that we have all had: that the study of mediocre works of art, however energetic, obstinately remains a random and peripheral form of critical experience, whereas the profound masterpiece seems to draw us to a point at which we can see an enormous number of converging patterns of significance. Here we begin to wonder if we cannot see literature, not only as complicating itself in time, but as spread out in conceptual space from some unseen center.

This inductive movement towards the archetype is a process of backing up, as it were, from structural analysis, as we back up from a painting if we want to see composition instead of brushwork. In the foreground of the grave-digger scene in *Hamlet,* for instance, is an intricate verbal texture, ranging from the puns of the first clown to the *danse macabre*[4] of the Yorick soliloquy, which we study in the printed text. One step back, and we are in the Wilson Knight and Spurgeon group of critics, listening to the steady rain of images of corruption and decay.[5] Here too, as the sense of the place of this scene in the whole play begins to dawn on us, we are in the network of psychological relationships which were the main interest of Bradley.[6] But after all, we say, we are forgetting the genre: *Hamlet* is a play, and an Elizabethan play. So we take another step back into the Stoll and Shaw group and see the scene conventionally as part of its dramatic context.[7] One step more, and we can begin to glimpse the archetype of the scene, as the hero's *Liebestod*[8] and first unequivocal declaration of his love, his struggle with Laertes and the sealing

of his own fate, and the sudden sobering of his mood that marks the transition to the final scene, all take shape around a leap into and return from the grave that has so weirdly yawned open on the stage.

At each stage of understanding this scene we are dependent on a certain kind of scholarly organization. We need first an editor to clean up the text for us, then the rhetorician and philologist, then the literary psychologist. We cannot study the genre without the help of the literary social historian, the literary philosopher and the student of the "history of ideas," and for the archetype we need a literary anthropologist. But now that we have got our central pattern of criticism established, all these interests are seen as converging on literary criticism instead of receding from it into psychology and history and the rest. In particular, the literary anthropologist who chases the source of the Hamlet legend from the pre-Shakespeare play[9] to Saxo, and from Saxo to nature-myths, is not running away from Shakespeare: he is drawing closer to the archetypal form which Shakespeare recreated. A minor result of our new perspective is that contradictions among critics, and assertions that this and not that critical approach is the right one, show a remarkable tendency to dissolve into unreality. Let us now see what we can get from the deductive end.

## III

Some arts move in time, like music; others are presented in space, like painting. In both cases the organizing principle is recurrence, which is called rhythm when it is temporal and pattern when it is spatial. Thus we speak of the rhythm of music and the pattern of painting; but later, to show off our sophistication, we may begin to speak of the rhythm of painting and the pattern of music. In other words, all arts may be conceived both temporally and spatially. The score of a musical composition may be studied all at once; a picture may be seen as the track of an intricate dance of the eye. Literature seems to be

[4] Dance of the dead. [Ed.]

[5] Caroline Spurgeon and G. Wilson Knight, whose Shakespearean criticism involves the sorting of images into significant clusters. [Ed.]

[6] A. C. Bradley, in *Shakespearean Tragedy* (1904), discussed the relation of character and plot with great depth and subtlety. [Ed.]

[7] Elmer Edgar Stoll (1874–1959) was a historical critic of Shakespeare, author of *Shakespeare Studies* (1927) and *Art and Artifice in Shakespeare,* among many others. George Bernard Shaw, the playwright (1856–1950) wrote outrageous Shakespeare criticism, which has been collected by Edwin Wilson in *Shaw on Shakespeare* (1961). [Ed.]

[8] Love-death. [Ed.]

[9] The putative ur-*Hamlet* from which Shakespeare drew his plot. [Ed.]

intermediate between music and painting: its words form rhythms which approach a musical sequence of sounds at one of its boundaries, and form patterns which approach the hieroglyphic or pictorial image at the other. The attempts to get as near to these boundaries as possible form the main body of what is called experimental writing. We may call the rhythm of literature the narrative, and the pattern, the simultaneous mental grasp of the verbal structure, the meaning or significance. We hear or listen to a narrative, but when we grasp a writer's total pattern we "see" what he means.

The criticism of literature is much more hampered by the representational fallacy than even the criticism of painting. That is why we are apt to think of narrative as a sequential representation of events in an outside "life," and of meaning as a reflection of some external "idea." Properly used as critical terms, an author's narrative is his linear movement; his meaning is the integrity of his completed form. Similarly an image is not merely a verbal replica of an external object, but any unit of a verbal structure seen as part of a total pattern or rhythm. Even the letters an author spells his words with form part of his imagery, though only in special cases (such as alliteration) would they call for critical notice. Narrative and meaning thus become respectively, to borrow musical terms, the melodic and harmonic contexts of the imagery.

Rhythm, or recurrent movement, is deeply founded on the natural cycle, and everything in nature that we think of as having some analogy with works of art, like the flower or the bird's song, grows out of a profound synchronization between an organism and the rhythms of its environment, especially that of the solar year. With animals some expressions of synchronization, like the mating dances of birds, could almost be called rituals. But in human life a ritual seems to be something of a voluntary effort (hence the magical element in it) to recapture a lost rapport with the natural cycle. A farmer must harvest his crop at a certain time of year, but because this is involuntary, harvesting itself is not precisely a ritual. It is the deliberate expression of a will to synchronize human and natural energies at that time which produces the harvest songs, harvest sacrifices and harvest folk customs that we call rituals. In ritual, then, we may find the origin of narrative, a ritual being a temporal sequence of acts in which the conscious meaning or significance is latent: it can be seen by an observer, but is largely concealed from the participators themselves. The pull of ritual is toward pure narrative, which, if there could be such a thing, would be automatic and unconscious repetition. We should notice too the regular tendency of ritual to become encyclopedic. All the important recurrences in nature, the day, the phases of the moon, the seasons and solstices of the year, the crises of existence from birth to death, get rituals attached to them, and most of the higher religions are equipped with a definitive total body of rituals suggestive, if we may put it so, of the entire range of potentially significant actions in human life.

Patterns of imagery, on the other hand, or fragments of significance, are oracular in origin, and derive from the epiphanic moment, the flash of instantaneous comprehension with no direct reference to time, the importance of which is indicated by Cassirer in *Myth and Language*.[10] By the time we get them, in the form of proverbs, riddles, commandments, and etiological folk tales, there is already a considerable element of narrative in them. They too are encyclopedic in tendency, building up a total structure of significance, or doctrine, from random and empiric fragments. And just as pure narrative would be an unconscious act, so pure significance would be an incommunicable state of consciousness, for communication begins by constructing narrative.

The myth is the central informing power that gives archetypal significance to the ritual and archetypal narrative to the oracle. Hence the myth *is* the archetype, though it might be convenient to say myth only when referring to narrative, and archetype when speaking of significance. In the solar cycle of the day, the seasonal cycle of the year, and the organic cycle of human life, there is a single pattern of significance, out of which myth constructs a central narrative around a figure who is partly the sun, partly

[10]Ernst Cassirer, neo-Kantian philosopher (1874–1945): *Myth and Language* (1925). [Ed.]

vegetative fertility and partly a god or archetypal human being. The crucial importance of this myth has been forced on literary critics by Jung and Frazer[11] in particular, but the several books now available on it are not always systematic in their approach, for which reason I supply the following table of its phases:

1. The dawn, spring, and birth phase. Myths of the birth of the hero, of revival and resurrection, of creation and (because the four phases are a cycle) of the defeat of the powers of darkness, winter and death. Subordinate characters: the father and the mother. The archetype of romance and of most dithyrambic and rhapsodic poetry.[12]

2. The zenith, summer, and marriage or triumph phase. Myths of apotheosis, of the sacred marriage, and of entering into Paradise. Subordinate characters: the companion and the bride. The archetype of comedy, pastoral, and idyll.

3. The sunset, autumn, and death phase. Myths of fall, of the dying god, of violent death and sacrifice and of the isolation of the hero. Subordinate characters: the traitor and the siren. The archetype of tragedy and elegy.

4. The darkness, winter, and dissolution phase. Myths of the triumph of these powers; myths of floods and the return of chaos, of the defeat of the hero, and Götterdämmerung[13] myths. Subordinate characters: the ogre and the witch. The archetype of satire (see, for instance, the conclusion of *The Dunciad*).

The quest of the hero also tends to assimilate the oracular and random verbal structures, as we can see when we watch the chaos of local legends that results from prophetic epiphanies consolidating into a narrative mythology of departmental gods. In most of the higher religions this in turn has become the same central quest-myth that emerges from ritual, as the Messiah myth became the narrative structure of the oracles of Judaism. A local flood may beget a folk tale by accident, but a comparison of flood stories will show how quickly such tales become examples of the myth of dissolution. Finally, the tendency of both ritual and epiphany to become encyclopedic is realized in the definitive body of myth which constitutes the sacred scriptures of religions. These sacred scriptures are consequently the first documents that the literary critic has to study to gain a comprehensive view of his subject. After he has understood their structure, then he can descend from archetypes to genres, and see how the drama emerges from the ritual side of myth and lyric from the epiphanic or fragmented side, while the epic carries on the central encyclopedic structure.

Some words of caution and encouragement are necessary before literary criticism has clearly staked out its boundaries in these fields. It is part of the critic's business to show how all literary genres are derived from the quest-myth, but the derivation is a logical one within the science of criticism: the quest-myth will constitute the first chapter of whatever future handbooks of criticism may be written that will be based on enough organized critical knowledge to call themselves "introductions" or "outlines" and still be able to live up to their titles. It is only when we try to expound the derivation chronologically that we find ourselves writing pseudo-prehistorical fictions and theories of mythological contract. Again, because psychology and anthropology are more highly developed sciences, the critic who deals with this kind of material is bound to appear, for some time, a dilettante of those subjects. These two phases of criticism are largely undeveloped in comparison with literary history and rhetoric, the reason being the later development of the sciences they are related to. But the fascination which *The Golden Bough* and Jung's book on libido symbols have for literary critics is not based on dilettantism, but on the fact that these books are primarily studies in literary criticism, and very important ones.

In any case the critic who is studying the principles of literary form has a quite different interest from the psychologist's concern with

---

[11]Sir James Frazer, anthropologist, whose classic work, *The Golden Bough* (1890; 12-volume edition 1907–15), studied primitive myth in various cultures to argue the evolution of human thought from magic to religion and then to science. [Ed.]

[12]In *Anatomy of Criticism* (1957), Frye shifted romance to the summer season and comedy from summer to spring. [Ed.]

[13]Twilight of the gods. [Ed.]

states of mind or the anthropologist's with social institutions. For instance: the mental response to narrative is mainly passive; to significance mainly active. From this fact Ruth Benedict's *Patterns of Culture* develops a distinction between "Apollonian" cultures based on obedience to ritual and "Dionysiac" ones based on a tense exposure of the prophetic mind to epiphany. The critic would tend rather to note how popular literature which appeals to the inertia of the untrained mind puts a heavy emphasis on narrative values, whereas a sophisticated attempt to disrupt the connection between the poet and his environment produces the Rimbaud type of *illumination,* Joyce's solitary epiphanies, and Baudelaire's conception of nature as a source of oracles. Also how literature, as it develops from the primitive to the self-conscious, shows a gradual shift of the poet's attention from narrative to significant values, this shift of attention being the basis of Schiller's distinction between naive and sentimental poetry.[14]

The relation of criticism to religion, when they deal with the same documents, is more complicated. In criticism, as in history, the divine is always treated as a human artifact. God for the critic, whether he finds him in *Paradise Lost* or the Bible, is a character in a human story; and for the critic all epiphanies are explained, not in terms of the riddle of a possessing god or devil, but as mental phenomena closely associated in their origin with dreams. This once established, it is then necessary to say that nothing in criticism or art compels the critic to take the attitude of ordinary waking consciousness towards the dream or the god. Art deals not with the real but with the conceivable; and criticism, though it will eventually have to have some theory of conceivability, can never be justified in trying to develop, much less assume, any theory of actuality. It is necessary to understand this before our next and final point can be made.

We have identified the central myth of literature, in its narrative aspect, with the quest-myth. Now if we wish to see this central myth as a pattern of meaning also, we have to start with

the workings of the subconscious where the epiphany originates, in other words in the dream. The human cycle of waking and dreaming corresponds closely to the natural cycle of light and darkness, and it is perhaps in this correspondence that all imaginative life begins. The correspondence is largely an antithesis: it is in daylight that man is really in the power of darkness, a prey to frustration and weakness; it is in the darkness of nature that the "libido" or conquering heroic self awakes. Hence art, which Plato called a dream for awakened minds, seems to have as its final cause the resolution of the antithesis, the mingling of the sun and the hero, the realizing of a world in which the inner desire and the outward circumstance coincide. This is the same goal, of course, that the attempt to combine human and natural power in ritual has. The social function of the arts, therefore, seems to be closely connected with visualizing the goal of work in human life. So in terms of significance, the central myth of art must be the vision of the end of social effort, the innocent world of fulfilled desires, the free human society. Once this is understood, the integral place of criticism among the other social sciences, in interpreting and systematizing the vision of the artist, will be easier to see. It is at this point that we can see how religious conceptions of the final cause of human effort are as relevant as any others to criticism.

The importance of the god or hero in the myth lies in the fact that such characters, who are conceived in human likeness and yet have more power over nature, gradually build up the vision of an omnipotent personal community beyond an indifferent nature. It is this community which the hero regularly enters in his apotheosis. The world of this apotheosis thus begins to pull away from the rotary cycle of the quest in which all triumph is temporary. Hence if we look at the quest-myth as a pattern of imagery, we see the hero's quest first of all in terms of its fulfillment. This gives us our central pattern of archetypal images, the vision of innocence which sees the world in terms of total human intelligibility. It corresponds to, and is usually found in the form of, the vision of the unfallen world or heaven in religion. We may call it the comic vision of life, in contrast

---

[14]See Schiller, p. 274. [Ed.]

to the tragic vision, which sees the quest only in the form of its ordained cycle.

We conclude with a second table of contents, in which we shall attempt to set forth the central pattern of the comic and tragic visions. One essential principle of archetypal criticism is that the individual and the universal forms of an image are identical, the reasons being too complicated for us just now. We proceed according to the general plan of the game of Twenty Questions, or, if we prefer, of the Great Chain of Being:

1. In the comic vision the *human* world is a community, or a hero who represents the wish-fulfillment of the reader. The archetype of images of symposium, communion, order, friendship, and love. In the tragic vision the human world is a tyranny or anarchy, or an individual or isolated man, the leader with his back to his followers, the bullying giant of romance, the deserted or betrayed hero. Marriage or some equivalent consummation belongs to the comic vision; the harlot, witch, and other varieties of Jung's "terrible mother"[15] belongs to the tragic one. All divine, heroic, angelic, or other superhuman communities follow the human pattern.

2. In the comic vision the *animal* world is a community of domesticated animals, usually a flock of sheep, or a lamb, or one of the gentler birds, usually a dove. The archetype of pastoral images. In the tragic vision the animal world is seen in terms of beasts and birds of prey, wolves, vultures, serpents, dragons, and the like.

3. In the comic vision the *vegetable* world is a garden, grove or park, or a tree of life, or a rose or lotus. The archetype of Arcadian images, such as that of Marvell's green world or of Shakespeare's forest comedies. In the tragic vision it is a sinister forest like the one in *Comus* or at the opening of the *Inferno,* or a heath or wilderness, or a tree of death.

4. In the comic vision the *mineral* world is a city, or one building or temple, or one stone, normally a glowing precious stone — in fact, the whole comic series, especially the tree, can be conceived as luminous or fiery. The archetype of geometrical images: the "starlit dome"[16] belongs here. In the tragic vision the mineral world is seen in terms of deserts, rocks and ruins, or of sinister geometrical images like the cross.

5. In the comic vision the *unformed* world is a river, traditionally fourfold, which influenced the Renaissance image of the temperate body with its four humors.[17] In the tragic vision this world usually becomes the sea, as the narrative myth of dissolution is so often a flood myth. The combination of the sea and beast images gives us the leviathan and similar water-monsters.

Obvious as this table looks, a great variety of poetic images and forms will be found to fit it. Yeats's "Sailing to Byzantium," to take a famous example of the comic vision at random, has the city, the tree, the bird, the community of sages, the geometrical gyre and the detachment from the cyclic world. It is, of course, only the general comic or tragic context that determines the interpretation of any symbol: this is obvious with relatively neutral archetypes like the island, which may be Prospero's island or Circe's.[18]

Our tables are, of course, not only elementary but grossly oversimplified, just as our inductive approach to the archetype was a mere hunch. The important point is not the deficiencies of either procedure, taken by itself, but the fact that, somewhere and somehow, the two are clearly going to meet in the middle. And if they do meet, the ground plan of a systematic and comprehensive development of criticism has been established.

---

[15]The negative projection of the *anima.* See Jung, p. 671. [Ed.]

[16]Yeats's image of inanimate perfection in "Byzantium." [Ed.]

[17]The four humors were blood, bile, choler, and phlegm. Frye's notion of a fourfold balance is similar to Jung's quaternion, p. 676. [Ed.]

[18]In Shakespeare's *The Tempest* and Homer's *Odyssey,* respectively. [Ed.]

# Jacques Lacan

1901–1981

*Probably the most controversial figure in French psychiatry, Jacques Marie Émile Lacan dedicated himself to getting strictly back to Freud by way of structural linguistics. An admirer of the surrealists, Lacan published his doctoral thesis on paranoid psychosis (1932). Expelled in 1953 from the International Psychoanalytic Association for unorthodox analytical practices, Lacan with Daniel Lagache, another analyst, created the Société Française de Psychoanalyse. As his theoretical positions continued to develop, Lacan and his followers went on to found the École Freudienne in Paris in 1964. The publication of his* Écrits *(1966) gained Lacan international attention. Leading intellectuals flocked to his seminars, and he exercised a cryptic but powerful influence on the French cultural scene of the 1970s. Concerned that the École was losing its integrity, Lacan unilaterally dissolved it in 1980. His intention to begin a new one was unfulfilled at the time of his death from cancer the next year. Editions of Lacan available in English include selections from* Écrits *(1977);* The Language of the Self *(1968, translated and with a commentary by Anthony Wilden);* The Four Fundamental Concepts of Psychoanalysis *(1977); and* Feminine Sexuality *(1982). "Seminar on 'The Purloined Letter'" is from* Yale French Studies *48 (1972); most of the notes are the translator's.*

## Seminar on "The Purloined Letter"

### TRANSLATOR'S INTRODUCTION

If "psychoanalytic criticism" is an effort to bring analytic categories to bear in the solution of critical problems, Lacan's text is certainly not an example of that discipline. One has the feeling that, on the contrary, in the confrontation between analysis and literature, the former's role for Lacan is not to solve but to open up a new kind of textual problem. The Poe text, then, is in many ways a pretext, an exemplary occasion for Lacan to complicate the question of *Beyond the Pleasure Principle*.[1] It is indeed a "purloined letter."

The crux of the problem is in the ambiguity of the term *letter* in Lacan's analysis. It may mean either typographical character or epistle. Why?

1. As typographical character, the letter is a unit of signification without any meaning in itself. In this it resembles the "memory trace,"

which for Freud is never the image of an event, but a term which takes on meaning only through its differential opposition to other traces. It is a particular arrangement of "frayings." . . . The striking image of this situation in the tale is that we never know the *contents* of the crucial letter. Here then is a psychoanalysis indifferent to deep meanings, concerned more with a latent organization of the manifest than a latent meaning beneath it. In its refusal to accord any "positive" status to linguistic phenomena, this might be viewed as Lacan's Saussurean side (see text note 33).

2. As epistle, the letter allows Lacan to play on the intersubjective relations which expropriate the individual. ("To whom does a letter belong?") It is Lévi-Strauss (and Mauss) who are no doubt at the source of this effort to think of the Oedipus complex in terms of a structure of *exchange* crucial to the "fixation" of unconscious "memory traces."[2]

---

Translated by Jeffrey Mehlman.
[1] By Sigmund Freud (1922). [Ed.]

[2] See Lévi-Strauss, "The Structural Study of Myth," in Ch. 4. Marcel Mauss (1872–1950) was the French social anthropologist who wrote *The Gift* (1925). [Ed.]

These losses — of the plenitude of meaning and the security of (self-) possession — are thus the principal modes of the Lacanian *askesis*[3] in this parable of analysis. To which we may add a third: that of meta-language. By which we mean (a) that the Prefect is already repeating the "events" he recounts at the moment he pretends to view them objectively; (b) even Dupin (as analyst) is trapped in the fantasmatic circuit (repetitive structure, mobile scenario . . .) at the moment of his rage against the Minister. The difference between the Prefect (trapped in the transference) and Dupin (counteracting the countertransference) is that the latter is intermittently aware of his loss.

In translating the text, we found that a large measure of its difficulty was a function of Lacan's idiosyncratic use of prepositions. As a result, the reader has to play with various possibilities of subordination in a number of sentences in order to determine the "proper" one(s). For better or worse, in English we have (necessarily) chosen to normalize the use of prepositions. We have thus occasionally been obliged to chart a course through Lacan's labyrinth rather than reproduce that labyrinth whole. There has no doubt been a concomitant loss (in syntactical richness) and gain (in clarity).

The notes we have added to the text (signed — J.M.) are, on the whole, explanations of allusions or clarifications of particularly oblique points.

This text was originally written in 1956 and — along with an introductory postface — is the opening text of the *Écrits*.

— J.M.

*Und wenn es uns glückt,*
*Und wenn es sich schickt,*
*So sind es Gedanken.*[4]

Our inquiry has led us to the point of recognizing that the repetition automatism (*Wiederholungszwang*) finds its basis in what we have called the *insistence* of the signifying chain.[5] We have elaborated that notion itself as a correlate of the *ex-sistence* (or eccentric place) in which we must necessarily locate the subject of the unconscious if we are to take Freud's discovery seriously.[6] As is known, it is in the realm of experience inaugurated by psychoanalysis that we may grasp along what imaginary lines the human organism, in the most intimate recesses of its being, manifests its capture in a *symbolic* dimension.[7]

The lesson of this seminar is intended to maintain that these imaginary incidences, far from representing the essence of our experience, reveal only what in it remains inconsistent unless they are related to the symbolic chain which binds and orients them.

We realize, of course, the importance of these imaginary impregnations (*Prägung*) in those partializations of the symbolic alternative which give the symbolic chain its appearance. But we maintain that it is the specific law of that chain which governs those psychoanalytic effects that are decisive for the subject: such as foreclosure (*Verwerfung*), repression (*Verdrängung*), denial (*Verneinung*) itself — specifying with appropriate emphasis that these effects follow so faithfully the displacement (*Entstellung*) of the signifier that imaginary factors, despite their inertia, figure only as shadows and reflections in the process.[8]

But this emphasis would be lavished in vain

---

[3] Self-purgation. [Ed.]

[4] The three lines of poetry can be translated "And if we succeed, and if it is proper, then there are thoughts." But Lacan presents the lines as a series of puns on the German word *es* which means both "it" and the Freudian Id (*das Es*). The lines can therefore mean "And if Id makes us happy, and if Id sends itself, then there are thoughts." [Ed.]

[5] The translation of repetition *automatism* — rather than *compulsion* — is indicative of Lacan's speculative effort to reinterpret Freudian "overdetermination" in terms of the laws of probability. (Chance is *automaton*, a "cause not revealed to human thought," in Aristotle's *Physics*.) Whence the importance assumed by the Minister's passion for gambling later in Lacan's analysis. Cf. *Écrits*, pp. 41–61. — J.M.

[6] Cf. Heidegger, *Vom Wesen der Wahrheit*. Freedom, in this essay, is perceived as an "ex-posure." *Dasein* ex-sists, stands out "into the disclosure of what is." It is *Dasein*'s "ex-sistent in-sistence" which preserves the disclosure of beings. — J.M.

[7] For the meanings Lacan attributes to the terms *imaginary* and *symbolic*, see J. Laplanche and J. B. Pontalis, *The Language of Psychoanalysis*, translated by Donald Nicolson-Smith (London: Hogarth Press, 1973). — J.M.

[8] For the notion of *foreclosure*, the defense mechanism specific to psychosis, see Laplanche and Pontalis. — J.M.

if it served, in your opinion, only to abstract a general type from phenomena whose particularity in our work would remain the essential thing for you and whose original arrangement could be broken up only artificially.

Which is why we have decided to illustrate for you today the truth which may be drawn from that moment in Freud's thought under study — namely, that it is the symbolic order which is constitutive for the subject — by demonstrating in a story the decisive orientation which the subject receives from the itinerary of a signifier.[9]

It is that truth, let us note, which makes the very existence of fiction possible. And in that case, a fable is as appropriate as any other narrative for bringing it to light — at the risk of having the fable's coherence put to the test in the process. Aside from that reservation, a fictive tale even has the advantage of manifesting symbolic necessity more purely to the extent that we may believe its conception arbitrary.

Which is why, without seeking any further, we have chosen our example from the very story in which the dialectic of the game of even or odd — from whose study we have but recently profited — occurs.[10] It is, no doubt, no accident that this tale revealed itself propitious to pursuing a course of inquiry which had already found support in it.

As you know, we are talking about the tale which Baudelaire translated under the title *La lettre volée*. At first reading, we may distinguish a drama, its narration, and the conditions of that narration.

We see quickly enough, moreover, that these components are necessary and that they could not have escaped the intentions of whoever composed them.

The narration, in fact, doubles the drama with

a commentary without which no *mise en scène* would be possible. Let us say that the action would remain, properly speaking, invisible from the pit — aside from the fact that the dialogue would be expressly and by dramatic necessity devoid of whatever meaning it might have for an audience: in other words, nothing of the drama could be grasped, neither seen nor heard, without, dare we say, the twilighting which the narration, in each scene, casts on the point of view that one of the actors had while performing it.

There are two scenes, the first of which we shall straightway designate the primal scene,[11] and by no means inadvertently, since the second may be considered its repetition in the very sense we are considering today.

The primal scene is thus performed, we are told, in the royal boudoir, so that we suspect that the person of the highest rank, called the "exalted personage," who is alone there when she receives a letter, is the Queen. This feeling is confirmed by the embarrassment into which she is plunged by the entry of the other exalted personage, of whom we have already been told prior to this account that the knowledge he might have of the letter in question would jeopardize for the lady nothing less than her honor and safety. Any doubt that he is, in fact, the King is promptly dissipated in the course of the scene which begins with the entry of the Minister D———. At that moment, in fact, the Queen can do no better than to play on the King's inattentiveness by leaving the letter on the table "face down, address uppermost." It does not, however, escape the Minister's lynx eye, nor does he fail to notice the Queen's distress and thus to fathom her secret. From then on everything transpires like clockwork. After dealing in his customary manner with the business of the day, the Minister draws from his pocket a letter similar in appearance to the one in his view, and, having pretended to read it, he places it next to the other. A bit more conversation to amuse the royal company, whereupon, without flinching once, he seizes the embarrassing letter, making off with it, as the Queen, on

---

[9]For the notion of the signifier (and its relation to the Freudian "memory trace,") see Jeffrey Mehlman, "The Floating Signifier from Lévi-Strauss to Lacan," *Yale French Studies* 48 (1972): 10–37. — J.M.

[10]Lacan's analysis of the guessing game in Poe's tale entails demonstrating the insufficiency of an *imaginary* identification with the opponent as opposed to the *symbolic* process of an identification with his "reasoning." See *Écrits*, p. 59. — J.M.

[11]Lacan puns on the Freudian term for the traumatic event in which the child witnesses his parents copulating. [Ed.]

whom none of his maneuver has been lost, remains unable to intervene for fear of attracting the attention of her royal spouse, close at her side at that very moment.

Everything might then have transpired unseen by a hypothetical spectator of an operation in which nobody falters, and whose *quotient* is that the Minister has filched from the Queen her letter and that — an even more important result than the first — the Queen knows that he now has it, and by no means innocently.

A *remainder* that no analyst will neglect, trained as he is to retain whatever is significant, without always knowing what to do with it: the letter, abandoned by the Minister, and which the Queen's hand is now free to roll into a ball.

Second scene: in the Minister's office. It is in his hotel, and we know — from the account the Prefect of police has given Dupin, whose specific genius for solving enigmas Poe introduces here for the second time — that the police, returning there as soon as the Minister's habitual, nightly absences allow them to, have searched the hotel and its surroundings from top to bottom for the last eighteen months. In vain, although everyone can deduce from the situation that the Minister keeps the letter within reach.

Dupin calls on the Minister. The latter receives him with studied nonchalance, affecting in his conversation romantic ennui. Meanwhile, Dupin, whom this pretense does not deceive, his eyes protected by green glasses, proceeds to inspect the premises. When his glance catches a rather crumpled piece of paper — apparently thrust carelessly in a division of an ugly pasteboard card rack, hanging gaudily from the middle of the mantelpiece — he already knows that he's found what he's looking for. His conviction is reenforced by the very details which seem to contradict the description he has of the stolen letter, with the exception of the format, which remains the same.

Whereupon he has but to withdraw, after "forgetting" his snuff box on the table, in order to return the following day to reclaim it — armed with a facsimile of the letter in its present state. As an incident in the street, prepared for the proper moment, draws the Minister to the window, Dupin in turn seizes the opportunity to snatch the letter while substituting the imitation, and has only to maintain the appearances of a normal exit.

Here, as well, all has transpired, if not without noise, at least without commotion. The quotient of the operation is that the Minister no longer has the letter, but, far from suspecting that Dupin is the culprit who has ravished it from him, knows nothing of it. Moreover, what he is left with is far from insignificant for what follows. We shall return to what brought Dupin to inscribe a message on his counterfeit letter. Whatever the case, the Minister, when he tries to make use of it, will be able to read these words, written so that he may recognize Dupin's hand: "Un dessein si funeste / S'il n'est digne d'Atrée est digne de Thyeste," whose source, Dupin tells us, is Crébillon's *Atrée*.[12]

Need we emphasize the similarity of these two sequences? Yes, for the resemblance we have in mind is not a simple collection of traits chosen only in order to delete their difference. And it would not be enough to retain those common traits at the expense of the others for the slightest truth to result. It is rather the intersubjectivity in which the two actions are motivated that we wish to bring into relief, as well as the three terms through which it structures them.[13]

The special status of these terms results from their corresponding simultaneously to the three logical moments through which the decision is precipitated and the three places it assigns to the subjects among whom it constitutes a choice.

That decision is reached in a glance's time.[14] For the maneuvers which follow, however

---

[12]"So infamous a scheme, / If not worthy of Atreus, is worthy of Thyestes." The lines from Atreus's monologue in act 5, scene 5 of Crébillon's play refer to his plan to avenge himself by serving his brother the blood of the latter's own son to drink. — J.M.

[13]This intersubjective setting which coordinates three terms is plainly the oedipal situation. The illusory security of the initial *dyad* (King and Queen in the first sequence) will be shattered by the introduction of a *third* term. — J.M.

[14]The necessary reference here may be found in "Le Temps logique et l'Assertion de la certitude anticipée," *Écrits*, p. 197. [Au.]

stealthily they prolong it, add nothing to that glance, nor does the deferring of the deed in the second scene break the unity of that moment.

This glance presupposes two others, which it embraces in its vision of the breach left in their fallacious complementarity, anticipating in it the occasion for larceny afforded by that exposure. Thus, three moments, structuring three glances, borne by three subjects, incarnated each time by different characters.

The first is a glance that sees nothing: the King and the police.

The second, a glance which sees that the first sees nothing and deludes itself as to the secrecy of what it hides: the Queen, then the Minister.

The third sees that the first two glances leave what should be hidden exposed to whomever would seize it: the Minister and finally Dupin.

In order to grasp in its unity the intersubjective complex thus described, we would willingly seek a model in the technique legendarily attributed to the ostrich attempting to shield itself from danger; for that technique might ultimately be qualified as political, divided as it here is among three partners: the second believing itself invisible because the first has its head stuck in the ground and all the while letting the third calmly pluck its rear; we need only enrich its proverbial denomination by a letter, producing *la politique de l'autruiche,* for the ostrich itself to take on forever a new meaning.[15]

Given the intersubjective modulus of the repetitive action, it remains to recognize in it a *repetition automatism* in the sense that interests us in Freud's text.

The plurality of subjects, of course, can be no objection for those who are long accustomed to the perspectives summarized by our formula: *the unconscious is the discourse of the Other.*[16] And we will not recall now what the notion of

the *immixture of subjects,* recently introduced in our reanalysis of the dream of Irma's injection, adds to the discussion.

What interests us today is the manner in which the subjects relay each other in their displacement during the intersubjective repetition.

We shall see that their displacement is determined by the place which a pure signifier — the purloined letter — comes to occupy in their trio. And that is what will confirm for us its status as repetition automatism.

It does not, however, seem excessive, before pursuing this line of inquiry, to ask whether the thrust of the tale and the interest we bring to it — to the extent that they coincide — do not lie elsewhere.

May we view as simply a rationalization (in our gruff jargon) the fact that the story is told to us as a police mystery?

In truth, we should be right in judging that fact highly dubious as soon as we note that everything which warrants such mystery concerning a crime or offense — its nature and motives, instruments, and execution; the procedure used to discover the author, and the means employed to convict him — is carefully eliminated here at the start of each episode.

The act of deceit is, in fact, from the beginning as clearly known as the intrigues of the culprit and their effects on his victim. The problem, as exposed to us, is limited to the search for and restitution of the object of that deceit, and it seems rather intentional that the solution is already obtained when it is explained to us. Is *that* how we are kept in suspense? Whatever credit we may accord to conventions of a genre for provoking a specific interest in the reader, we should not forget that "the Dupin tale," this the second to appear, is a prototype, and that even if the genre were established in the first, it is still a little early for the author to play on a convention.[17]

It would, however, be equally excessive to reduce the whole thing to a fable whose moral would be that in order to shield from inquisitive

---

[15]*La politique de l'autruiche* condenses ostrich (*autruche*), other people (*autrui*), and (the politics of) Austria (*Autriche*). — J.M.

[16]Such would be the crux of the Oedipus complex: the assumption of a desire which is originally another's, and which, in its displacements, is perpetually other than "itself." — J.M.

[17]The first "Dupin tale" was "The Murders in the Rue Morgue." — J.M.

eyes one of those correspondences whose secrecy is sometimes necessary to conjugal peace, it suffices to leave the crucial letters lying about on one's table, even though the meaningful side be turned face down. For that would be a hoax which, for our part, we would never recommend anyone try, lest he be gravely disappointed in his hopes.

Might there then be no mystery other than, concerning the Prefect, an incompetence issuing in failure — were it not perhaps, concerning Dupin, a certain dissonance we hesitate to acknowledge between, on the one hand, the admittedly penetrating, though, in their generality, not always quite relevant remarks with which he introduces us to his method and, on the other, the manner in which he, in fact, intervenes?

Were we to pursue this sense of mystification a bit further we might soon begin to wonder whether, from that initial scene which only the rank of the protagonists saves from vaudeville, to the fall into ridicule which seems to await the Minister at the end, it is not this impression that everyone is being duped which makes for our pleasure.

And we would be all the more inclined to think so in that we would recognize in that surmise, along with those of you who read us, the definition we once gave in passing of the modern hero, "whom ludicrous exploits exalt in circumstances of utter confusion."[18]

But are we ourselves not taken in by the imposing presence of the amateur detective, prototype of a latter-day swashbuckler, as yet safe from the insipidity of our contemporary *superman*?

A trick . . . sufficient for us to discern in this tale, on the contrary, so perfect a verisimilitude that it may be said that truth here reveals its fictive arrangement.

For such indeed is the direction in which the principles of that verisimilitude lead us. Entering into its strategy, we indeed perceive a new drama we may call complementary to the first, insofar

as the latter was what is termed a play without words whereas the interest of the second plays on the properties of speech.[19]

If it is indeed clear that each of the two scenes of the real drama is narrated in the course of a different dialogue, it is only through access to those notions set forth in our teaching that one may recognize that it is not thus simply to augment the charm of the exposition, but that the dialogues themselves, in the opposite use they make of the powers of speech, take on a tension which makes of them a different drama, one which our vocabulary will distinguish from the first as persisting in the symbolic order.

The first dialogue — between the Prefect of police and Dupin — is played as between a deaf man and one who hears. That is, it presents the real complexity of what is ordinarily simplified, with the most confused results, in the notion of communication.

This example demonstrates indeed how an act of communication may give the impression at which theorists too often stop: of allowing in its transmission but a single meaning, as though the highly significant commentary into which he who understands integrates it, could, because unperceived by him who does not understand, be considered null.

It remains that if only the dialogue's meaning as a report is retained, its verisimilitude may appear to depend on a guarantee of exactitude. But here dialogue may be more fertile than seems, if we demonstrate its tactics, as shall be seen by focusing on the recounting of our first scene.

For the double and even triple subjective filter through which that scene comes to us: a narration by Dupin's friend and associate (henceforth to be called the general narrator of the story) — of the account by which the Prefect reveals to Dupin — the report the Queen gave him of it, is not merely the consequence of a fortuitous arrangement.

If indeed the extremity to which the original

<hr />

[18]Cf. "Fonction et champ de la parole et du langage" in *Écrits*. Translated by A. Wilden, *The Language of the Self* (Baltimore, 1968). [Au.]

[19]The complete understanding of what follows presupposes a rereading of the short and easily available text of "The Purloined Letter." [Au.]

narrator is reduced precludes her altering any of the events, it would be wrong to believe that the Prefect is empowered to lend her his voice in this case only by that lack of imagination on which he has, dare we say, the patent.

The fact that the message is thus retransmitted assures us of what may by no means be taken for granted: that it belongs to the dimension of language.

Those who are here know our remarks on the subject, specifically those illustrated by the counter case of the so-called language of bees, in which a linguist[20] can see only a simple signaling of the location of objects, in other words, only an imaginary function more differentiated than others.

We emphasize that such a form of communication is not absent in man, however evanescent a naturally given object may be for him, split as it is in its submission to symbols.

Something equivalent may no doubt be grasped in the communion established between two persons in their hatred of a common object, except that the meeting is possible only over a single object, defined by those traits in the individual each of the two resist.

But such communication is not transmissible in symbolic form. It may be maintained only in the relation with the object. In such a manner it may bring together an indefinite number of subjects in a common "ideal": the communication of one subject with another within the crowd thus constituted will nonetheless remain irreducibly mediated by an ineffable relation.[21]

This digression is not only a recollection of principles distantly addressed to those who impute to us a neglect of nonverbal communication: in determining the scope of what speech repeats, it prepares the question of what symptoms repeat.

Thus, the indirect telling sifts out the linguistic dimension, and the general narrator, by duplicating it, "hypothetically" adds nothing to it.

But its role in the second dialogue is entirely different.

For the latter will be opposed to the first like those poles we have distinguished elsewhere in language and which are opposed like word to speech.

Which is to say that a transition is made here from the domain of exactitude to the register of truth. Now that register, we dare think we needn't come back to this, is situated entirely elsewhere, strictly speaking at the very foundation of intersubjectivity. It is located there where the subject can grasp nothing but the very subjectivity which constitutes an Other as absolute. We shall be satisfied here to indicate its place by evoking the dialogue which seems to us to merit its attribution as a Jewish joke by that state of privation through which the relation of signifier to speech appears in the entreaty which brings the dialogue to a close: "Why are you lying to me?" one character shouts breathlessly. "Yes, why do you lie to me saying you're going to Cracow so I should believe you're going to Lemberg, when in reality you *are* going to Cracow?"[22]

We might be prompted to ask a similar question by the torrent of logical impasses, eristic[23] enigmas, paradoxes, and even jests presented to us as an introduction to Dupin's method if the fact that they were confided to us by a would-be disciple did not endow them with a new dimension through that act of delegation. Such is the unmistakable magic of legacies: the witness's fidelity is the cowl which blinds and lays to rest all criticism of his testimony.

What could be more convincing, moreover,

---

[20]Cf. Emile Benveniste, "Communication animale et langage humain," *Diogène*, no. 1, and our address in Rome, *Écrits*, p. 178. [Au.]

[21]For the notion of *ego ideal*, see Freud, *Group Psychology and the Analysis of the Ego*. — J.M.

[22]Freud comments on this joke in *Jokes and Their Relation to the Unconscious*, New York, 1960, p. 115: "But the more serious substance of the joke is what determines the truth. . . . Is it the truth if we describe things as they are without troubling to consider how our hearer will understand what we say? . . . I think that jokes of that kind are sufficiently different from the rest to be given a special position: What they are attacking is not a person or an institution but the certainty of our knowledge itself, one of our speculative possessions." Lacan's text may be regarded as a commentary on Freud's statement, an examination of the corrosive effect of the demands of an intersubjective communicative situation on any naive notion of "truth." — J.M.

[23]Argumentative. [Ed.]

than the gesture of laying one's cards face up on the table? So much so that we are momentarily persuaded that the magician has, in fact, demonstrated, as he promised, how his trick was performed, whereas he has only renewed it in still purer form, at which point we fathom the measure of the supremacy of the signifier in the subject.

Such is Dupin's maneuver when he starts with the story of the child prodigy who takes in all his friends at the game of even and odd with his trick of identifying with the opponent, concerning which we have nevertheless shown that it cannot reach the first level of theoretical elaboration, namely, intersubjective alternation, without immediately stumbling on the buttress of its recurrence.[24]

We are all the same treated — so much smoke in our eyes — to the names of La Rochefoucauld, La Bruyère, Machiavelli and Campanella, whose renown, by this time, would seem but futile when confronted with the child's prowess.

Followed by Chamfort, whose maxim that "it is a safe wager that every public idea, every accepted convention is foolish, since it suits the greatest number," will no doubt satisfy all who think they escape its law, that is, precisely, the greatest number. That Dupin accuses the French of deception for applying the word *analysis* to algebra will hardly threaten our pride since, moreover, the freeing of that term for other uses ought by no means to provoke a psychoanalyst to intervene and claim his rights. And there he goes making philological remarks which should positively delight any lovers of Latin: when he recalls without deigning to say any more that "*ambitus* doesn't mean ambition, *religio*, religion, *homines honesti*, honest men,"[25] who among you would not take pleasure in remem-

bering . . . what those words mean to anyone familiar with Cicero and Lucretius. No doubt Poe is having a good time. . . .

But a suspicion occurs to us: might not this parade of erudition be destined to reveal to us the key words of our drama? Is not the magician repeating his trick before our eyes, without deceiving us this time about divulging his secret, but pressing his wager to the point of really explaining it to us without us seeing a thing. *That* would be the summit of the illusionist's art: through one of his fictive creations to *truly delude us.*

And is it not such effects which justify our referring, without malice, to a number of imaginary heroes as real characters?

As well, when we are open to hearing the way in which Martin Heidegger discloses to us in the word *aletheia* the play of truth,[26] we rediscover a secret to which truth has always initiated her lovers and through which they learn that it is in hiding that she offers herself to them *most truly*.

Thus, even if Dupin's comments did not defy us so blatantly to believe in them, we should still have to make that attempt against the opposite temptation.

Let us track down [*dépistons*] his footprints there where they elude [*dépiste*] us.[27] And first of all in the criticism by which he explains the Prefect's lack of success. We already saw it surface in those furtive gibes the Prefect, in the first conversation, failed to heed, seeing in them only a pretext for hilarity. That it is, as Dupin insinuates, because a problem is too simple, indeed too evident, that it may appear obscure, will never have any more bearing for him than a vigorous rub of the rib cage.

---

[24]Cf. *Écrits*, p. 58. "But what will happen at the following step [of the game] when the opponent, realizing that I am sufficiently clever to follow him in his move, will show his own cleverness by realizing that it is by playing the fool that he has the best chance to deceive me? From then on my reasoning is invalidated, since it can only be repeated in an indefinite oscillation. . . ." [Au.]

[25]*Ambitus* can mean a revolution or circuit, *religio* scrupulousness or anxiety, and *honesti homines* respectable, or even noble persons. See p. 697. [Ed.]

[26]The Greek word *aletheia* ("truth") comes from the negation *a* and *lethe*, forgetfulness. Heidegger's comments are in the Introduction to *Being and Time*. [Ed.]

[27]We should like to present again to M. Benveniste the question of the antithetical sense of (primal or other) words after the magisterial rectification he brought to the erroneous philological path on which Freud engaged it (cf. *La Psychoanalyse*, vol. 1, pp. 5–16). For we think that the problem remains intact once the instance of the signifier has been evolved. Bloch and Von Wartburg date at 1875 the first appearance of the meaning of the verb *dépister* in the second use we make of it in our sentence. [Au.]

Everything is arranged to induce in us a sense of the character's imbecility. Which is powerfully articulated by the fact that he and his confederates never conceive of anything beyond what an ordinary rogue might imagine for hiding an object — that is, precisely the all-too-well-known series of extraordinary hiding places, which are promptly catalogued for us, from hidden desk drawers to removable table tops, from the detachable cushions of chairs to their hollowed-out legs, from the reverse side of mirrors to the "thickness" of book bindings.

After which, a moment of derision at the Prefect's error in deducing that because the Minister is a poet, he is not far from being mad, an error, it is argued, which would consist, but this is hardly negligible, simply in a false distribution of the middle term, since it is far from following from the fact that all madmen are poets.

Yes, indeed. But we ourselves are left in the dark as to the poet's superiority in the art of concealment — even if he be a mathematician to boot — since our pursuit is suddenly thwarted, dragged as we are into a thicket of bad arguments directed against the reasoning of mathematicians, who never, so far as I know, showed such devotion to their formulae as to identify them with reason itself. At least, let us testify that unlike what seems to be Poe's experience, it occasionally befalls us — with our friend Riguet, whose presence here is a guarantee that our incursions into combinatory analysis are not leading us astray — to hazard such serious deviations (virtual blasphemies, according to Poe) as to cast into doubt that "$x^2$ plus px is perhaps not absolutely equal to q," without ever — here we give the lie to Poe — having had to fend off any unexpected attack.

Is not so much intelligence being exercised, then, simply to divert our own from what had been indicated earlier as given, namely, that the police have looked *everywhere:* which we were to understand — vis-à-vis the area in which the police, not without reason, assumed the letter might be found — in terms of a (no doubt theoretical) exhaustion of space, but concerning which the tale's piquancy depends on our accepting it literally: the division of the entire volume into numbered "compartments," which was the principle governing the operation, being presented to us as so precise that "the fiftieth part of a line," it is said, could not escape the probing of the investigators. Have we not, then, the right to ask how it happened that the letter was not found *anywhere,* or rather to observe that all we have been told of a more far-ranging conception of concealment does not explain, in all rigor, that the letter escaped detection, since the area combed did, in fact, contain it, as Dupin's discovery eventually proves?

Must a letter, then, of all objects, be endowed with the property of *nullibiety:* to use a term which the thesaurus known as *Roget* picks up from the semiotic utopia of Bishop Wilkins?[28]

It is evident ("a little *too* self-evident")[29] that between *letter* and *place* exist relations for which no French word has quite the extension of the English adjective: *odd. Bizarre,* by which Baudelaire regularly translates it, is only approximate. Let us say that these relations are . . . *singuliers,* for they are the very ones maintained with place by the *signifier.*

You realize, of course, that our intention is not to turn them into "subtle" relations, nor is our aim to confuse letter with spirit, even if we receive the former by pneumatic dispatch, and that we readily admit that one kills whereas the other quickens, insofar as the signifier — you perhaps begin to understand — materializes the agency of death.[30] But if it is first of all on the materiality of the signifier that we have insisted, that materiality is *odd* [*singulière*] in many ways, the first of which is not to admit partition. Cut a letter in small pieces, and it remains the letter it

---

[28]The very one to which Jorge Luis Borges, in works which harmonize so well with the phylum of our subject, has accorded an importance which others have reduced to its proper proportions. Cf. *Les Temps modernes,* June–July 1955, pp. 2135–36 and October 1955, pp. 574–575. [Au.]

[29]Underlined by the author [Poe]. [Au.]

[30]The reference is to the "death instinct," whose "death," we should note, lies entirely in its diacritical opposition to the "life" of a naive vitalism or naturalism. As such, it may be compared with the logical moment in Lévi-Strauss's thought whereby "nature" exceeds, supplements, and symbolizes itself: the prohibition of incest. — J.M.

is — and this in a completely different sense than *Gestalttheorie*[31] would account for with the dormant vitalism informing its notion of the whole.[32]

Language delivers its judgment to whoever knows how to hear it, through the usage of the article as partitive particle. It is there that spirit — if spirit be living meaning — appears, no less oddly, as more available for quantification than its letter. To begin with meaning itself, which bears our saying: a speech rich with meaning ["plein *de* signification"], just as we recognize a measure of intention ["*de* l'intention"] in an act, or deplore that there is no more love ["plus *d'*-amour"]; or store up hatred ["*de la* haine"] and expend devotion ["*du* dévouement"], and so much infatuation ["tant *d'*infatuation"] is easily reconciled to the fact that there will always be ass ["*de la* cuisse"] for sale and brawling ["*du* rififi"] among men.

But as for the letter — be it taken as typographical character, epistle, or what makes a man of letters — we will say that what is said is to be understood *to the letter* [à la lettre], that *a letter* [une lettre] awaits you at the post office, or even that you are acquainted with *letters* [que vous avez des lettres] — never that there is *letter* [de la lettre] anywhere, whatever the context, even to designate overdue mail.

For the signifier is a unit in its very uniqueness, being by nature symbol only of an absence. Which is why we cannot say of the purloined letter that, like other objects, it must be *or* not be in a particular place but that unlike them it will be *and* not be where it is, wherever it goes.[33]

Let us, in fact, look more closely at what

happens to the police. We are spared nothing concerning the procedures used in searching the area submitted to their investigation: from the division of that space into compartments from which the slightest bulk could not escape detection, to needles probing upholstery, and, in the impossibility of sounding wood with a tap, to a microscope exposing the waste of any drilling at the surface of its hollow, indeed the infinitesimal gaping of the slightest abyss. As the network tightens to the point that, not satisfied with shaking the pages of books, the police take to counting them, do we not see space itself shed its leaves like a letter?

But the detectives have so immutable a notion of the real that they fail to notice that their search tends to transform it into its object. A trait by which they would be able to distinguish that object from all others.

This would, no doubt, be too much to ask them, not because of their lack of insight but rather because of ours. For their imbecility is neither of the individual nor the corporative variety; its source is subjective. It is the realist's imbecility, which does not pause to observe that nothing, however deep in the bowels of the earth a hand may seek to ensconce it, will ever be hidden there, since another hand can always retrieve it, and that what is hidden is never but what is *missing from its place,* as the call slip puts it when speaking of a volume lost in a library. And even if the book be on an adjacent shelf or in the next slot, it would be hidden there, however visibly it may appear. For it can *literally* be said that something is missing from its place only of what can change it: the symbolic. For the real, whatever upheaval we subject it to, is always in its place; it carries it glued to its heel, ignorant of what might exile it from it.

And, to return to our cops, who took the letter from the place where it was hidden, how could they have seized the letter? In what they turned between their fingers what did they hold but what *did not answer* to their description? "A letter, a litter": in Joyce's circle, they played on the homophony of the two words in English.[34] Nor does

[31]Psychological theory that understanding is holistic rather than built up from elements. [Ed.]

[32]This is so true that philosophers, in those hackneyed examples with which they argue on the basis of the single and the multiple, will not use to the same purpose a simple sheet of white paper ripped in the middle and a broken circle, indeed a shattered vase, not to mention a cut worm. [Au.]

[33]Cf. Saussure, *Cours de linguistique générale*, Paris, 1969, p. 166: "The preceding amounts to saying that *in language there are only differences*. Even more: a difference presupposes in general positive terms between which it is established, but in language there are only differences *without positive terms*." — J.M.

[34]Cf. *Our Exagmination Round his Factification for In-*

the seeming bit of refuse the police are now handling reveal its other nature for being but half torn. A different seal on a stamp of another color, the mark of a different handwriting in the superscription are here the most inviolable modes of concealment. And if they stop at the reverse side of the letter, on which, as is known, the recipient's address was written in that period, it is because the letter has for them no other side but its reverse.

What indeed might they find on its obverse? Its message, as is often said to our cybernetic joy? . . . But does it not occur to us that this message has already reached its recipient and has even been left with her, since the insignificant scrap of paper now represents it no less well than the original note?

If we could admit that a letter has completed its destiny after fulfilling its function, the ceremony of returning letters would be a less common close to the extinction of the fires of love's feasts. The signifier is not functional. And the mobilization of the elegant society whose frolics we are following would as well have no meaning if the letter itself were content with having one. For it would hardly be an adequate means of keeping it secret to inform a squad of cops of its existence.

We might even admit that the letter has an entirely different (if no more urgent) meaning for the Queen than the one understood by the Minister. The sequence of events would not be noticably affected, not even if it were strictly incomprehensible to an uninformed reader.

For it is certainly not so for everybody, since, as the Prefect pompously assures us, to everyone's derision, "the disclosure of the document to a third person, who shall be nameless" (that name which leaps to the eye like the pig's tail twixt the teeth of old Ubu[35]) "would bring in question the honor of a personage of most exalted station; and this fact gives the holder of the document an ascendancy over the illustrious personage whose honor and peace are so jeopardized."

In that case, it is not only the meaning but the text of the message which it would be dangerous to place in circulation, and all the more so to the extent that it might appear harmless, since the risks of an indiscretion unintentionally committed by one of the letter's holders would thus be increased.

Nothing, then, can redeem the police's position, and nothing would be changed by improving their "culture." *Scripta manent:* in vain would they learn from a deluxe-edition humanism the proverbial lesson which *verba volant*[36] concludes. May it but please heaven that writings remain, as is rather the case with spoken words: for the indelible debt of the latter impregnates our acts with its transferences.

Writings scatter to the winds blank checks in an insane charge.[37] And were they not such flying leaves, there would be no purloined letters.[38]

But what of it? For a purloined letter to exist, we may ask, to whom does a letter belong? We stressed a moment ago the oddity implicit in returning a letter to him who had but recently given wing to its burning pledge. And we generally deem unbecoming such premature publications as the one by which the Chevalier d'Eon[39] put several of his correspondents in a rather pitiful position.

Might a letter on which the sender retains

---

*camination of Work in Progress,* Shakespeare & Co., 12 rue de l'Odéon, Paris, 1929. [Au.] Lacan gives the working title, in 1929, of Joyce's *Finnegans Wake* (1939). [Ed.]

[35]Refers to the hero of Alfred Jarry's absurdist farce *Ubu Roi* (1896). [Ed.]

[36]*Verba volant, scripta manent:* Latin proverb: what is spoken flies away, what is written remains. [Ed.]

[37]The original sentence presents an exemplary difficulty in translation: "Les écrits emportent au vent les traites en blanc d'une cavalerie folle." The blank (bank) drafts (or transfers) are not delivered to their rightful recipients (the sense of *de cavalerie, de complaisance*). That is, in analysis, one finds absurd symbolic debts being paid to the "wrong" persons. At the same time, the mad, driven quality of the payment is latent in *traite,* which might also refer to the day's trip of an insane cavalry. In our translation, we have displaced the "switch-word" — joining the financial and equestrian series — from *traite* to *charge.* — J.M.

[38]*Flying leaves* (also fly-sheets) and *purloined letters* — *feuilles volantes* and *lettres volées* — employ different meanings of the same word in French. — J.M.

[39]Charles-Geneviève-Louis-Auguste-André-Timothée, Chevalier d'Eon de Beaumont (1728–1810), diplomat and secret agent, who dressed as a woman but was found at his autopsy to have been a man. [Ed.]

certain rights, then, not quite belong to the person to whom it is addressed? Or might it be that the latter was never the real receiver?

Let's take a look: we shall find illumination in what at first seems to obscure matters: the fact that the tale leaves us in virtually total ignorance of the sender, no less than of the contents, of the letter. We are told only that the Minister immediately recognized the handwriting of the address and only incidentally, in a discussion of the Minister's camouflage, is it said that the original seal bore the ducal arms of the S——— family. As for the letter's bearing, we know only the dangers it entails should it come into the hands of a specific third party and that its possession has allowed the Minister to "wield, to a very dangerous extent, for political purposes," the power it assures him over the interested party. But all this tells us nothing of the message it conveys.

Love letter or conspiratorial letter, letter of betrayal or letter of mission, letter of summons or letter of distress, we are assured of but one thing: the Queen must not bring it to the knowledge of her lord and master.

Now these terms, far from bearing the nuance of discredit they have in bourgeois comedy, take on a certain prominence through allusion to her sovereign, to whom she is bound by pledge of faith, and doubly so, since her role as spouse does not relieve her of her duties as subject, but rather elevates her to the guardianship of what royalty according to law incarnates of power — and which is called legitimacy.

From then on, to whatever vicissitudes the Queen may choose to subject the letter, it remains that the letter is the symbol of a pact, and that, even should the recipient not assume the pact, the existence of the letter situates her in a symbolic chain foreign to the one which constitutes her faith. This incompatibility is proven by the fact that the possession of the letter is impossible to bring forward publicly as legitimate, and that in order to have that possession respected, the Queen can invoke but her right to privacy, whose privilege is based on the honor that possession violates.

For she who incarnates the figure of grace and sovereignty cannot welcome even a private communication without power being concerned, and she cannot avail herself of secrecy in relation to the sovereign without becoming clandestine.

From then on, the responsibility of the author of the letter takes second place to that of its holder: for the offense to majesty is compounded by *high treason*.

We say the *holder* and not the *possessor*. For it becomes clear that the addressee's proprietorship of the letter may be no less debatable than that of anyone else into whose hands it comes, for nothing concerning the existence of the letter can return to good order without the person whose prerogatives it infringes upon having to pronounce judgment on it.

All of this, however, does not imply that because the letter's secrecy is indefensible, the betrayal of that secret would in any sense be honorable. The *honesti homines,* decent people, will not get off so easily. There is more than one *religio,* and it is not slated for tomorrow that sacred ties shall cease to rend us in two. As for *ambitus:* a detour, we see, is not always inspired by ambition. For if we are taking one here, by no means is it stolen (the word is apt), since, to lay our cards on the table, we have borrowed Baudelaire's title in order to stress not, as is incorrectly claimed, the conventional nature of the signifier, but rather its priority in relation to the signified.[40] It remains, nevertheless, that Baudelaire, despite his devotion, betrayed Poe by translating as "la lettre volée" (the stolen letter) his title, the purloined letter, a title containing a word rare enough for us to find it easier to define its etymology than its usage.

*To purloin,* says the Oxford dictionary, is an Anglo-French word, that is, composed of the prefix *pur-,* found in *purpose, purchase, purport,* and of the Old French word *loing, loigner, longé.* We recognize in the first element the Latin *pro-,* as opposed to *ante-,* insofar as it presupposes a rear in front of which it is borne, possibly as its warrant, indeed even as its pledge (whereas *ante-* goes forth to confront what it encounters). As for the second, an old French word *loigner,* a verb attributing place *au loing* (or, still in use, *longé*),

---

[40]See the discussion of Lévi-Strauss's statement — "the signifier precedes and determines the signified" — in my essay cited in note 9. — J.M.

it does not mean *au loin* (far off) but *au long de* (alongside); it is a question then of *putting aside,* or, to invoke a familiar expression which plays on the two meanings, *mettre à gauche* (to put to the left; to put amiss).

Thus, we are confirmed in our detour by the very object which draws us on into it: for we are quite simply dealing with a letter which has been diverted from its path; one whose course has been *prolonged* (etymologically, the word of the title), or, to revert to the language of the post office, a *letter in sufferance.*[41]

Here, then, *simple and odd,* as we are told on the very first page, reduced to its simplest expression, is the singularity of the letter, which as the title indicates, is the *true subject* of the tale: since it can be diverted, it must have a course *which is proper to it,* the trait by which its incidence as signifier is affirmed. For we have learned to conceive of the signifier as sustaining itself only in a displacement comparable to that found in electric news strips or in the rotating memories of our machines-that-think-like men, this because of the alternating operation which is its principle, requiring it to leave its place, even though it returns to it by a circular path.[42]

This is indeed what happens in the repetition automatism. What Freud teaches us in the text we are commenting on is that the subject must pass through the channels of the symbolic, but what is illustrated here is more gripping still: it is not only the subject, but the subjects, grasped in their intersubjectivity, who line up, in other words, our ostriches, to whom we here return, and who, more docile than sheep, model their very being on the moment of the signifying chain which traverses them.

If what Freud discovered and rediscovers with a perpetually increasing sense of shock has a meaning, it is that the displacement of the signifier determines the subjects in their acts, in their destiny, in their refusals, in their blindnesses, in their end and in their fate, their innate gifts and social acquisitions notwithstanding, without regard for character or sex, and that, willingly or not, everything that might be considered the stuff of psychology, kit and caboodle, will follow the path of the signifier.

Here we are, in fact, yet again at the crossroads at which we had left our drama and its round with the question of the way in which the subjects replace each other in it. Our fable is so constructed as to show that it is the letter and its diversion which governs their entries and roles. If *it* be "in sufferance," *they* shall endure the pain. Should they pass beneath its shadow, they become its reflection. Falling in possession of the letter — admirable ambiguity of language — its meaning possesses them.

So we are shown by the hero of the drama in the repetition of the very situation which his daring brought to a head, a first time, to his triumph. If he now succumbs to it, it is because he has shifted to the second position in the triad in which he was initially third, as well as the thief — and this by virtue of the object of his theft.

For if it is, now as before, a question of protecting the letter from inquisitive eyes, he can do nothing but employ the same technique he himself has already foiled: leave it in the open. And we may properly doubt that he knows what he is thus doing, when we see him immediately captivated by a dual relationship in which we find all the traits of a mimetic lure or of an animal feigning death, and, trapped in the typically imaginary situation of seeing that he is not seen, misconstrue the real situation in which he is seen not seeing.[43]

And what does he fail to see? Precisely the symbolic situation which he himself was so well able to see and in which he is now seen seeing himself not being seen.

The Minister acts as a man who realizes that the police's search is his own defense, since we are told he allows them total access by his ab-

---

[41]We revive this archaism (for the French: *lettre en souffrance*). The sense is a letter held up in the course of delivery. In French, of course, *en souffrance* means in a state of suffering as well. — J.M.

[42]See *Écrits,* p. 59: " . . . it is not unthinkable that a modern computer, by discovering the sentence which modulates without his knowing it and over a long period of time the choices of a subject, would win beyond any normal proportion at the game of even and odd. . . ." [Au.]

[43]See the Laplanche and Pontalis entry on the *imaginary.* — J.M.

sences: he nonetheless fails to recognize that outside of that search he is no longer defended.

This is the very *autruicherie* whose artisan he was, if we may allow our monster to proliferate, but it cannot be by sheer stupidity that he now comes to be its dupe.[44]

For in playing the part of the one who hides, he is obliged to don the role of the Queen, and even the attributes of femininity and shadow, so propitious to the act of concealing.

Not that we are reducing the hoary couple of *Yin* and *Yang*[45] to the elementary opposition of dark and light. For its precise use involves what is blinding in a flash of light, no less than the shimmering shadows exploit in order not to lose their prey.

Here sign and being, marvelously asunder, reveal which is victorious when they come into conflict. A man man enough to defy to the point of scorn a lady's fearsome ire undergoes to the point of metamorphosis the curse of the sign he has dispossessed her of.

For this sign is indeed that of woman, insofar as she invests her very being therein, founding it outside the law, which subsumes her nevertheless, originarily, in a position of signifier, nay, of fetish.[46] In order to be worthy of the power of that sign, she has but to remain immobile in its shadow, thus finding, moreover, like the Queen, that simulation of mastery in inactivity that the Minister's "lynx eye" alone was able to penetrate.

This stolen sign — here, then, is man in its possession: sinister in that such possession may be sustained only through the honor it defies, cursed in calling him who sustains it to punishment or crime, each of which shatters his vassalage to the Law.

There must be in this sign a singular *noli me tangere*[47] for its possession, like the Socratic stingray, to benumb its man to the point of making him fall into what appears clearly in his case to be a state of idleness.[48]

For in noting, as the narrator does as early as the first dialogue, that with the letter's use its power disappears, we perceive that this remark, strictly speaking, concerns precisely its use for ends of power — and at the same time that such a use is obligatory for the Minister.

To be unable to rid himself of it, the Minister indeed must not know what else to do with the letter. For that use places him in so total a dependence on the letter as such that in the long run it no longer involves the letter at all.

We mean that for that use truly to involve the letter, the Minister, who, after all, would be so authorized by his service to his master the King, might present to the Queen respectful admonitions, even were he to assure their sequel by appropriate precautions — or initiate an action against the author of the letter, concerning whom, the fact that he remains outside the story's focus reveals the extent to which it is not guilt and blame which are in question here but rather that sign of contradiction and scandal constituted by the letter, in the sense in which the Gospel says that it must come regardless of the anguish of whomever serves as its bearer — or even submit the letter as evidence to a qualified third person, to find out if he will have it issue in a Star Chamber for the Queen or the Minister's disgrace.

We will not know why the Minister does not resort to any of these uses, and it is fitting that we don't, since the effect of this non-use alone

---

[44]*Autruicherie* condenses, in addition to the previous terms, deception (*tricherie*). Do we not find in Lacan's proliferating "monster" something of the *proton pseudos,* the "first lie" of Freud's 1895 *Project:* the persistent illusion which seems to structure the mental life of the patient? — J.M.

[45]Feminine and masculine principles, respectively. [Ed.]

[46]The fetish, as replacement for the missing maternal phallus, at once masks and reveals the scandal of sexual difference. As such it is the analytic object par excellence. The female temptation to exhibitionism, understood as a desire to *be* the (maternal) phallus, is thus tantamount to being a fetish. — J.M.

[47]"Do not touch me!" (the risen Christ's words to Mary Magdalen). [Ed.]

[48]See Plato's *Meno:* "Socrates, . . . at this moment I feel you are exercising magic and witchcraft upon me and positively laying me under your spell until I am just a mass of helplessness. If I may be flippant, I think that not only in outward appearance but in other respects as well you are like the flat stingray that one meets in the sea. Whenever anyone comes in contact with it, it numbs him, and that is the sort of thing you are doing to me now . . ." — J.M.

concerns us; it suffices for us to know that the way in which the letter was acquired would pose no obstacle to any of them.

For it is clear that if the use of the letter, independent of its meaning, is obligatory for the Minister, its use for ends of power can only be potential, since it cannot become actual without vanishing in the process — but in that case the letter exists as a means of power only through the final assignations of the pure signifier, namely, by prolonging its diversion, making it reach whomever it may concern through a supplementary transfer, that is, by an additional act of treason whose effects the letter's gravity makes it difficult to predict — or indeed by destroying the letter, the only sure means, as Dupin divulges at the start, of being rid of what is destined by nature to signify the annulment of what it signifies.

The ascendancy which the Minister derives from the situation is thus not a function of the letter, but, whether he knows it or not, of the role it constitutes for him. And the Prefect's remarks indeed present him as someone "who dares all things," which is commented upon significantly: "those unbecoming as well as those becoming a man," words whose pungency escapes Baudelaire when he translates "ce qui est indigne d'un homme aussi bien que ce qui est digne de lui" (those unbecoming a man as well as those becoming him). For in its original form, the appraisal is far more appropriate to what might concern a woman.

This allows us to see the imaginary import of the character, that is, the narcissistic relation in which the Minister is engaged, this time, no doubt, without knowing it. It is indicated as well, as early as the second page of the English text, by one of the narrator's remarks, whose form is worth savoring: the Minister's ascendancy, we are told, "would depend upon the robber's knowledge of the loser's knowledge of the robber," words whose importance the author underscores by having Dupin repeat them literally after the narration of the scene of the theft of the letter. Here again we may say that Baudelaire is imprecise in his language in having one ask, the other confirm, in these words: "Le voleur sait-il? . . . ." (Does the robber know?), then: "Le voleur sait

. . . ." (the robber knows). What? "que la personne volée connaît son voleur" (that the loser knows his robber).

For what matters to the robber is not only that the said person knows who robbed her, but rather with what kind of a robber she is dealing; for she believes him capable of anything, which should be understood as her having conferred upon him the position that no one is, in fact, capable of assuming, since it is imaginary, that of absolute master.

In truth, it is a position of absolute weakness, but not for the person of whom we are expected to believe so. The proof is not only that the Queen dares to call the police. For she is only conforming to her displacement to the next slot in the arrangement of the initial triad in trusting to the very blindness required to occupy that place: "No more sagacious agent could, I suppose," Dupin notes ironically, "be desired or even imagined." No, if she has taken that step, it is less out of being "driven to despair," as we are told, than in assuming the charge of an impatience best imputed to a specular mirage.

For the Minister is kept quite busy confining himself to the idleness which is presently his lot. The Minister, in point of fact, is not *altogether* mad.[49] That's a remark made by the Prefect, whose every word is gold: it is true that the gold of his words flows only for Dupin and will continue to flow to the amount of the fifty thousand francs worth it will cost him by the metal standard of the day, though not without leaving him a margin of profit. The Minister, then, is not *altogether* mad in his insane stagnation, and that is why he will behave according to the mode of neurosis. Like the man who withdrew to an island to forget, what? he forgot — so the Minister, through not making use of the letter, comes to forget it, as is expressed by the persistence of his conduct. But the letter, no more than the neurotic's unconscious, does not forget him. It forgets him so little that it transforms him more and more in the image of her who offered it to

[49]Baudelaire translates Poe's "*altogether* a fool" as "*absolument* fou." In opting for Baudelaire, Lacan is enabled to allude to the realm of psychosis. — J.M.

his capture, so that he now will surrender it, following her example, to a similar capture.

The features of that transformation are noted, and in a form so characteristic in their apparent gratuitousness that they might validly be compared to the return of the repressed.

Thus, we first learn that the Minister in turn has *turned the letter over,* not, of course, as in the Queen's hasty gesture, but, more assiduously, as one turns a garment inside out. So he must proceed, according to the methods of the day for folding and sealing a letter, in order to free the virgin space on which to inscribe a new address.[50]

That address becomes his own. Whether it be in his hand or another, it will appear in an extremely delicate feminine script, and, the seal changing from the red of passion to the black of its mirrors, he will imprint his stamp upon it. This oddity of a letter marked with the recipient's stamp is all the more striking in its conception, since, though forcefully articulated in the text, it is not even mentioned by Dupin in the discussion he devotes to the identification of the letter.

Whether that omission be intentional or involuntary, it will surprise in the economy of a work whose meticulous rigor is evident. But in either case it is significant that the letter which the Minister, in point of fact, addresses to himself is a letter from a woman, as though this were a phase he had to pass through out of a natural affinity of the signifier.

Thus, the aura of apathy, verging at times on an affectation of effeminacy; the display of an ennui bordering on disgust in his conversation; the mood the author of the philosophy of furniture[51] can elicit from virtually impalpable

details (like that of the musical instrument on the table), everything seems intended for a character, all of whose utterances have revealed the most virile traits, to exude the oddest *odor di femmina*[52] when he appears.

Dupin does not fail to stress that this is an artifice, describing behind the bogus finery the vigilance of a beast of prey ready to spring. But that this is the very effect of the unconscious in the precise sense that we teach that the unconscious means that man is inhabited by the signifier: could we find a more beautiful image of it than the one Poe himself forges to help us appreciate Dupin's exploit? For with this aim in mind, he refers to those toponymical inscriptions which a geographical map, lest it remain mute, superimposes on its design, and which may become the object of a guessing game: who can find the name chosen by a partner? — noting immediately that the name most likely to foil a beginner will be one which, in large letters spaced out widely across the map, discloses, often without an eye pausing to notice it, the name of an entire country. . . .

Just so does the purloined letter, like an immense female body, stretch out across the Minister's office when Dupin enters. But just so does he already expect to find it, and has only, with his eyes veiled by green lenses, to undress that huge body.

And that is why, without needing any more than being able to listen in at the door of Professor Freud, he will go straight to the spot in which lies and lives what that body is designed to hide, in a gorgeous center caught in a glimpse, nay, to the very place seducers name Sant' Angelo's Castle in their innocent illusion of controlling the City from within it. Look! between the cheeks of the fireplace, there's the object already in reach of a hand the ravisher has but to extend . . . The question of deciding whether he seizes it above the mantelpiece, as Baudelaire translates, or beneath it, as in the original text, may be abandoned without harm to the inferences of those whose profession is grilling.[53]

---

[50]We felt obliged to demonstrate the procedure to an audience with a letter from the period concerning M. de Chateaubriand and his search for a secretary. We are amused to find that M. de Chateaubriand completed the first version of his recently restored memoirs in the very month of November 1841 in which the purloined letter appeared in *Chamber's Journal.* Might M. de Chateaubriand's devotion to the power he decries and the honor which that devotion bespeaks in him (*the gift* had not yet been invented), place him in the category to which we will later see the Minister assigned: among men of genius with or without principles? [Au.]

[51]Poe is the author of an essay with this title. [Au.]

[52]Fragrance of a woman. [Ed.]

[53]And even to the cook herself. [Au.]
The paragraph might be read as follows: analysis, in its

Were the effectiveness of symbols[54] to cease there, would it mean that the symbolic debt would as well be extinguished? Even if we could believe so, we would be advised of the contrary by two episodes which we may all the less dismiss as secondary in that they seem, at first sight, to clash with the rest of the work.

First of all, there's the business of Dupin's remuneration, which, far from being a closing pirouette, has been present from the beginning in the rather unself-conscious question he asks the Prefect about the amount of the reward promised him and whose enormousness the Prefect, however reticent he may be about the precise figure, does not dream of hiding from him, even returning later on to refer to its increase.

The fact that Dupin had been previously presented to us as a virtual pauper in his ethereal shelter ought rather to lead us to reflect on the deal he makes out of delivering the letter, promptly assured as it is by the checkbook he produces. We do not regard it as negligible that the unequivocal hint through which he introduces the matter is a "story attributed to the character, as famous as it was excentric," Baudelaire tells us, of an English doctor named Abernethy, in which a rich miser, hoping to sponge upon him for a medical opinion, is sharply told not to take medicine, but to take advice.

Do we not, in fact, feel concerned with good reason when for Dupin what is perhaps at stake is his withdrawal from the symbolic circuit of the letter — we who become the emissaries of all the purloined letters which at least for a time remain in sufferance with us in the transference? And is it not the responsibility their transference entails which we neutralize by equating it with

the signifier most destructive of all signification, namely, money?

But that's not all. The profit Dupin so nimbly extracts from his exploit, if its purpose is to allow him to withdraw his stakes from the game, makes all the more paradoxical, even shocking, the partisan attack, the underhanded blow, he suddenly permits himself to launch against the Minister, whose insolent prestige, after all, would seem to have been sufficiently deflated by the trick Dupin has just played on him.

We have already quoted the atrocious lines Dupin claims he could not help dedicating, in his counterfeit letter, to the moment in which the Minister, enraged by the inevitable defiance of the Queen, will think he is demolishing her and will plunge into the abyss: *facilis descensus Averni,*[55] he waxes sententious, adding that the Minister cannot fail to recognize his handwriting, all of which, since depriving of any danger a merciless act of infamy, would seem, concerning a figure who is not without merit, a triumph without glory, and the rancor he invokes, stemming from an evil turn done him at Vienna (at the Congress?) only adds an additional bit of blackness to the whole.[56]

Let us consider, however, more closely this explosion of feeling, and more specifically the moment it occurs in a sequence of acts whose success depends on so cool a head.

It comes just after the moment in which the decisive act of identifying the letter having been accomplished, it may be said that Dupin already *has* the letter as much as if he had seized it, without, however, as yet being in a position to rid himself of it.

He is thus, in fact, fully participant in the intersubjective triad, and, as such, in the median position previously occupied by the Queen and the Minister. Will he, in showing himself to be above it, reveal to us at the same time the author's intentions?

If he has succeeded in returning the letter to

---

violation of the imaginary integrity of the ego, finds its fantasmatic equivalent in rape. . . . But whether that "rape" takes place from in front or from behind (above or below the mantelpiece) is, in fact, a question of interest for policemen and not analysts. Implicit in the statement is an attack on those who have become wed to the ideology of "maturational development" (libidinal stages et al.) in Freud (i.e., the ego psychologists). — J.M.

[54]The allusion is to Lévi-Strauss's article of the same title ("L'efficacité symbolique") in *L'Anthropologie structurale.* — J.M.

[55]"Facilis descensus Averno": the descent to Hades is easy. [Ed.]

[56]Cf. Corneille, *Le Cid* (II,2): "A vaincre sans péril, on triomphe sans gloire." (To vanquish without danger is to triumph without glory). — J.M.

its proper course, it remains for him to make it arrive at its address. And that address is in the place previously occupied by the King, since it is there that it would reenter the order of the Law.

As we have seen, neither the King nor the Police who replaced him in that position were able to read the letter because that *place entailed blindness*.

*Rex et augur*,[57] the legendary, archaic quality of the words seems to resound only to impress us with the absurdity of applying them to a man. And the figures of history, for some time now, hardly encourage us to do so. It is not natural for man to bear alone the weight of the highest of signifiers. And the place he occupies as soon as he dons it may be equally apt to become the symbol of the most outrageous imbecility.[58]

Let us say that the King here is invested with the equivocation natural to the sacred, with the imbecility which prizes none other than the Subject.[59]

That is what will give their meaning to the characters who will follow him in his place. Not that the police should be regarded as constitutionally illiterate, and we know the role of pikes planted on the *campus* in the birth of the state. But the police who exercise their functions here are plainly marked by the forms of liberalism, that is, by those imposed on them by masters on the whole indifferent to eliminating their indiscreet tendencies, which is why on occasion words are not minced as to what is expected of them: "*Sutor ne ultra crepidam*, just take care of your crooks.[60] We'll even give you scientific

means to do it with. That will help you not to think of truths you'd be better off leaving in the dark."[61]

We know that the relief which results from such prudent principles shall have lasted in history but a morning's time, that already the march of destiny is everywhere bringing back — a sequel to a just aspiration to freedom's reign — an interest in those who trouble it with their crimes, which occasionally goes so far as to forge its proofs. It may even be observed that this practice, which was always well received to the extent that it was exercised only in favor of the greatest number, comes to be authenticated in public confessions of forgery by the very ones who might very well object to it: the most recent manifestation of the preeminence of the signifier over the subject.

It remains nevertheless that a police record has always been the object of a certain reserve, of which we have difficulty understanding that it amply transcends the guild of historians.

It is by dint of this vanishing credit that Dupin's intended delivery of the letter to the Prefect of police will diminish its import. What now remains of the signifier when, already relieved of its message for the Queen, it is now invalidated in its text as soon as it leaves the Minister's hands?

It remains for it now only to answer that very question, of what remains of a signifier when it has no more signification. But this is the same question asked of it by the person Dupin now finds in the spot marked by blindness.

For that is indeed the question which has led the Minister there, if he be the gambler we are told and which his act sufficiently indicates. For the gambler's passion is nothing but that question asked of the signifier, figured by the *automaton* of chance.

"What are you, figure of the die I turn over in your encounter (*tychē*) with my fortune?[62]

[57]King and prophet. [Ed.]
[58]We recall the witty couplet attributed before his fall to the most recent in date to have rallied Candide's meeting in Venice:

Il n'est plus aujourd'hui que cinq rois sur la terre,
Les quatre rois des cartes et le roi d'Angleterre.

(There are only five kings left on earth: four kings of cards and the king of England.) [Au.]
[59]For the antithesis of the "sacred," see Freud's "The Antithetical Sense of Primal Words." The idiom *tenir à* in this sentence means both to prize and to be a function of. The two senses — King and/as Subject — are implicit in Freud's frequent allusions to "His Majesty the Ego." — J.M.
[60]From Pliny, 35, 10, 35: "Cobbler, stick to your last." [Ed.]

[61]This proposal was openly presented by a noble lord speaking to the Upper Chamber in which his dignity earned him a place. [Au.]
[62]We note the fundamental opposition Aristotle makes between the two terms recalled here in the conceptual analysis of chance he gives in his *Physics*. Many discussions would be illuminated by a knowledge of it. [Au.]

Nothing, if not that presence of death which makes of human life a reprieve obtained from morning to morning in the name of meanings whose sign is your crook. Thus did Scheherazade for a thousand and one nights, and thus have I done for eighteen months, suffering the ascendancy of this sign at the cost of a dizzying series of fraudulent turns at the game of even or odd."

So it is that Dupin, *from the place he now occupies,* cannot help feeling a rage of manifestly feminine nature against him who poses such a question. The prestigious image in which the poet's inventiveness and the mathematician's rigor joined up with the serenity of the dandy and the elegance of the cheat suddenly becomes, for the very person who invited us to savor it, the true *monstrum horrendum,*[63] for such are his words, "an unprincipled man of genius."

It is here that the origin of that horror betrays itself, and he who experiences it has no need to declare himself (in a most unexpected manner) "a partisan of the lady" in order to reveal it to us: it is known that ladies detest calling principles into question, for their charms owe much to the mystery of the signifier.

Which is why Dupin will at last turn toward us the medusoid face of the signifier nothing but whose obverse anyone except the Queen has been able to read. The commonplace of the quotation is fitting for the oracle that face bears in its grimace, as is also its source in tragedy: "Un destin si funeste, / S'il n'est digne d'Atrée, est digne de Thyeste."[64]

So runs the signifier's answer, above and beyond all significations: "You think you act when I stir you at the mercy of the bonds through which I knot your desires. Thus do they grow in force and multiply in objects, bringing you back to the fragmentation of your shattered childhood. So be it: such will be your feast until the return of the stone guest I shall be for you since you call me forth."

Or, to return to a more moderate tone, let us say, as in the quip with which — along with some of you who had followed us to the Zurich Congress last year — we rendered homage to the local password, the signifier's answer to whomever interrogates it is "Eat your Dasein."[65]

Is that, then, what awaits the Minister at a rendezvous with destiny? Dupin assures us of it, but we have already learned not to be too credulous of his diversions.

No doubt the brazen creature is here reduced to the state of blindness which is man's in relation to the letters on the wall that dictate his destiny. But what effect, in calling him to confront them, may we expect from the sole provocations of the Queen, on a man like him? Love or hatred. The former is blind and will make him lay down his arms. The latter is lucid but will awaken his suspicions. But if he is truly the gambler we are told he is, he will consult his cards a final time before laying them down and, upon reading his hand, will leave the table in time to avoid disgrace.[66]

Is that all, and shall we believe we have deciphered Dupin's real strategy above and beyond the imaginary tricks with which he was obliged to deceive us? No doubt, yes, for if "any point requiring reflection," as Dupin states at the start, is "examined to best purpose in the dark," we may now easily read its solution in broad daylight. It was already implicit and easy to derive from the title of our tale, according to the very formula we have long submitted to your discretion, in which the sender, we tell you, receives from the receiver his own message in reverse form. Thus, it is that what the "purloined letter," nay, the "letter in sufferance" means is that a letter always arrives at its destination.

[63]Horrid monster. [Ed.]

[64]Lacan misquotes Crébillon (as well as Poe and Baudelaire) here by writing *destin* (destiny) instead of *dessein* (scheme). As a result, he is free to pursue his remarkable development on the tragic Don Juan ("multiply in objects . . . stone guest"). — J.M.

[65]"Dasein" is Heidegger's term, usually translated "Being-in-the-world." [Ed.]

[66]Thus, nothing shall (have) happen(ed) — the final turn in Lacan's theater of lack. Yet within the simplicity of that empty present the most violent of (pre-)oedipal dramas — Atreus, Thyestes — shall silently have played itself out. — J.M.

# Harold Bloom

b. 1930

*Harold Bloom's theories of poetic misprision and anxiety have changed how critics think about literary tradition. Bloom was born in New York City, took his B.A. at Cornell, and received his Ph.D. from Yale in 1955. He has been a member of the Yale faculty since then and is at present Sterling Professor of the Humanities. Bloom's brilliance is fabled; he possesses an eidetic memory and is said to have read English before he spoke it. In 1985 he received one of the so-called genius awards from the MacArthur Foundation. His studies of romantic poets include* Shelley's Mythmaking *(1959),* The Visionary Company: A Reading of English Romantic Poetry *(1961),* Blake's Apocalypse: A Study in Poetic Argument *(1963), and* The Ringers in the Tower: Studies in Romantic Tradition *(1971). His theories about creative misreading in the poetic tradition are unfolded — recursively — through several books, including* The Anxiety of Influence: A Theory of Poetry *(1973) excerpted here,* A Map of Misreading *(1975),* Kabbalah and Criticism *(1975),* Poetry and Repression: Revisionism from Blake to Stevens *(1976), and* Agon: Towards a Theory of Revisionism *(1982). He is currently engaged in the Johnsonian labor of editing and writing introductions to more than four hundred volumes of the Chelsea House critical series.*

# A Meditation upon Priority

This short book offers a theory of poetry by way of a description of poetic influence, or the story of intrapoetic relationships. One aim of this theory is corrective: to deidealize our accepted accounts of how one poet helps to form another. Another aim, also corrective, is to try to provide a poetics that will foster a more adequate practical criticism.

Poetic history, in this book's argument, is held to be indistinguishable from poetic influence, since strong poets make that history by misreading one another, so as to clear imaginative space for themselves.

My concern is only with strong poets, major figures with the persistence to wrestle with their strong precursors, even to the death. Weaker talents idealize; figures of capable imagination appropriate for themselves. But nothing is got for nothing, and self-appropriation involves the immense anxieties of indebtedness, for what strong maker desires the realization that he has failed to create himself? Oscar Wilde, who knew he had failed as a poet because he lacked strength to overcome his anxiety of influence, knew also the darker truths concerning influence. *The Ballad of Reading Gaol* becomes an embarrassment to read, directly one recognizes that every lustre it exhibits is reflected from *The Rime of the Ancient Mariner*; and Wilde's lyrics anthologize the whole of English High Romanticism. Knowing this, and armed with his customary intelligence, Wilde bitterly remarks in *The Portrait of Mr. W. H.* that: "Influence is simply a transference of personality, a mode of giving away what is most precious to one's self, and its exercise produces a sense, and, it may be, a reality of loss. Every disciple takes away something from his master." This is the anxiety of influencing, yet no reversal in this area is a true reversal. Two years later, Wilde refined this bitterness in one of Lord Henry Wotton's elegant observations in *The Picture of Dorian Gray*, where he tells Dorian that all influence is immoral:

> Because to influence a person is to give him one's own soul. He does not think his natural thoughts, or burn with his natural passions. His

virtues are not real to him. His sins, if there are such things as sins, are borrowed. He becomes an echo of someone else's music, an actor of a part that has not been written for him.

To apply Lord Henry's insight to Wilde, we need only read Wilde's review of Pater's *Appreciations,* with its splendidly self-deceptive closing observation that Pater "has escaped disciples." Every major aesthetic consciousness seems peculiarly more gifted at denying obligation as the hungry generations go on treading one another down. Stevens, a stronger heir of Pater than even Wilde was, is revealingly vehement in his letters:

> While, of course, I come down from the past, the past is my own and not something marked Coleridge, Wordsworth, etc. I know of no one who has been particularly important to me. My reality-imagination complex is entirely my own even though I see it in others.

He might have said: "particularly because I see it in others," but poetic influence was hardly a subject where Stevens's insights could center. Towards the end, his denials became rather violent, and oddly humored. Writing to the poet Richard Eberhart, he extends a sympathy all the stronger for being self-sympathy:

> I sympathize with your denial of any influence on my part. This sort of thing always jars me because, in my own case, I am not conscious of having been influenced by anybody and have purposely held off from reading highly mannered people like Eliot and Pound so that I should not absorb anything, even unconsciously. But there is a kind of critic who spends his time dissecting what he reads for echoes, imitations, influences, as if no one was ever simply himself but is always compounded of a lot of other people. As for W. Blake, I think that this means Wilhelm Blake.

This view, that poetic influence scarcely exists, except in furiously active pedants, is itself an illustration of one way in which poetic influence is a variety of melancholy or an anxiety-principle. Stevens was, as he insisted, a highly individual poet, as much an American original as Whitman or Dickinson, or his own contemporaries: Pound, Williams, Moore. But poetic influence need not make poets less original; as often it makes them more original, though not therefore necessarily better. The profundities of poetic influence cannot be reduced to source-study, to the history of ideas, to the patterning of images. Poetic influence, or as I shall more frequently term it, poetic misprision, is necessarily the study of the life-cycle of the poet-as-poet. When such study considers the context in which that life-cycle is enacted, it will be compelled to examine simultaneously the relations between poets as cases akin to what Freud called the family romance, and as chapters in the history of modern revisionism, "modern" meaning here post-Enlightenment. The modern poet, as W. J. Bate shows in *The Burden of the Past and the English Poet,* is the inheritor of a melancholy engendered in the mind of the Enlightenment by its skepticism of its own double heritage of imaginative wealth, from the ancients and from the Renaissance masters. In this book I largely neglect the area Bate has explored with great skill, in order to center upon intrapoetic relationships as parallels of family romance. Though I employ these parallels, I do so as a deliberate revisionist of some of the Freudian emphases.

Nietzsche and Freud are, so far as I can tell, the prime influences upon the theory of influence presented in this book. Nietzsche is the prophet of the antithetical, and his *Genealogy of Morals* is the profoundest study available to me of the revisionary and ascetic strains in the aesthetic temperament. Freud's investigations of the mechanisms of defense and their ambivalent functionings provide the clearest analogues I have found for the revisionary ratios that govern intrapoetic relations. Yet, the theory of influence expounded here is un-Nietzschean in its deliberate literalism, and in its Viconian insistence that priority in divination is crucial for every strong poet, lest he dwindle merely into a late-comer. My theory rejects also the qualified Freudian optimism that happy substitution is possible, that a second chance can save us from the repetitive quest for our earliest attachments. Poets as poets cannot accept substitutions, and fight to the end to have their initial chance alone.

Both Nietzsche and Freud underestimated poets and poetry, yet each yielded more power to phantasmagoria than it truly possesses. They too, despite their moral realism, overidealized the imagination. Nietzsche's disciple, Yeats, and Freud's disciple, Otto Rank, show a greater awareness of the artist's fight against art, and of the relation of this struggle to the artist's antithetical battle against nature.

Freud recognized sublimation as the highest human achievement, a recognition that allies him to Plato and to the entire moral traditions of both Judaism and Christianity. If Wordsworth's *Ode: Intimations of Immortality from Recollections of Early Childhood* possessed only the wisdom found also in Freud, then we could cease calling it "the Great Ode." Wordsworth too saw repetition or second chance as essential for development, and his ode admits that we can redirect our needs by substitution or sublimation. But the ode plangently also awakens into failure, and into the creative mind's protest against time's tyranny. A Wordsworthian critic, even one as loyal to Wordsworth as Geoffrey Hartman, can insist upon clearly distinguishing between *priority*, as a concept from the natural order, and *authority*, from the spiritual order, but Wordsworth's ode declines to make this distinction. "By seeking to overcome priority," Hartman wisely says, "art fights nature on nature's own ground, and is bound to lose." The argument of this book is that strong poets are condemned to just this unwisdom; Wordsworth's Great Ode fights nature on nature's own ground, and suffers a great defeat, even as it retains its greater dream. That dream, in Wordsworth's ode, is shadowed by the anxiety of influence, due to the greatness of the precursor-poem, Milton's *Lycidas,* where the human refusal wholly to sublimate is even more rugged, despite the ostensible yielding to Christian teachings of sublimation.

For every poet begins (however "unconsciously") by rebelling more strongly against the consciousness of death's necessity than all other men and women do. The young citizen of poetry, or ephebe as Athens would have called him, is already the antinatural or antithetical man, and from his start as a poet he quests for an impossible object, as his precursor quested before him.

That this quest encompasses necessarily the diminishment of poetry seems to me an inevitable realization, one that accurate literary history must sustain. The great poets of the English Renaissance are not matched by their Enlightened descendants, and the whole tradition of the post-Enlightenment, which is Romanticism, shows a further decline in its Modernist and post-Modernist heirs. The death of poetry will not be hastened by any reader's broodings, yet it seems just to assume that poetry in our tradition, when it dies, will be self-slain, murdered by its own past strength. An implied anguish throughout this book is that Romanticism, for all its glories, may have been a vast visionary tragedy, the self-baffled enterprise not of Prometheus but of blinded Oedipus, who did not know that the Sphinx was his Muse.

Oedipus, blind, was on the path to oracular godhood, and the strong poets have followed him by transforming their blindness towards their precursors into the revisionary insights of their own work. The six revisionary movements that I will trace in the strong poet's life-cycle could as well be more, and could take quite different names than those I have employed. I have kept them to six, because these seem to be minimal and essential to my understanding of how one poet deviates from another. The names, though arbitrary, carry on from various traditions that have been central in Western imaginative life, and I hope can be useful.

The greatest poet in our language is excluded from the argument of this book for several reasons. One is necessarily historical; Shakespeare belongs to the giant age before the flood, before the anxiety of influence became central to poetic consciousness. Another has to do with the contrast between dramatic and lyric form. As poetry has become more subjective, the shadow cast by the precursors has become more dominant. The main cause, though, is that Shakespeare's prime precursor was Marlowe, a poet very much smaller than his inheritor. Milton, with all his strength, yet had to struggle, subtly and crucially, with a major precursor in Spenser, and this struggle both formed and malformed Milton. Coleridge, ephebe of Milton and later of Wordsworth, would have been glad to find his Marlowe in

Cowper (or in the much weaker Bowles), but influence cannot be willed. Shakespeare is the largest instance in the language of a phenomenon that stands outside the concern of this book: the absolute absorption of the precursor. Battle between strong equals, father and son as mighty opposites, Laius and Oedipus at the crossroads; only this is my subject here, though some of the fathers, as will be seen, are composite figures. That even the strongest poets are subject to influences not poetical is obvious even to me, but again my concern is only with *the poet in a poet,* or the aboriginal poetic self.

A change like the one I propose in our ideas of influence should help us read more accurately any group of past poets who were contemporary with one another. To give one example, as misinterpreters of Keats, *in their poems,* the Victorian disciples of Keats most notably include Tennyson, Arnold, Hopkins, and Rossetti. That Tennyson triumphed in his long, hidden contest with Keats, no one can assert absolutely, but his clear superiority over Arnold, Hopkins, and Rossetti is due to his relative victory or at least holding of his own in contrast to their partial defeats. Arnold's elegiac poetry uneasily blends Keatsian style with anti-Romantic sentiment, while Hopkins's strained intensities and convolutions of diction and Rossetti's densely inlaid art are also at variance with the burdens they seek to alleviate in their own poetic selves. Similarly, in our time we need to look again at Pound's unending match with Browning, as at Stevens's long and largely hidden civil war with the major poets of English and American Romanticism — Wordsworth, Keats, Shelley, Emerson, and Whitman. As with the Victorian Keatsians, these are instances among many, if a more accurate story is to be told about poetic history.

This book's main purpose is necessarily to present one reader's critical vision, in the context both of the criticism and poetry of his own generation, where their current crises most touch him, and in the context of his own anxieties of influence. In the contemporary poems that most move me, like the *Corsons Inlet* and *Saliences* of A. R. Ammons and the *Fragment* and *Soonest*

*Mended* of John Ashbery, I can recognize a strength that battles against the death of poetry, yet also the exhaustions of being a latecomer. Similarly, in the contemporary criticism that clarifies for me my own evasions, in books like *Allegory* by Angus Fletcher, *Beyond Formalism* by Geoffrey Hartman, and *Blindness and Insight* by Paul de Man, I am made aware of the mind's effort to overcome the impasse of Formalist criticism, the barren moralizing that Archetypal criticism has come to be, and the antihumanistic plain dreariness of all those developments in European criticism that have yet to demonstrate that they can aid in reading any one poem by any poet whatsoever. My Interchapter, proposing a more antithetical practical criticism than any we now have, is my response in this area of the contemporary.

A theory of poetry that presents itself as a severe poem, reliant upon aphorism, apothegm, and a quite personal (though thoroughly traditional) mythic pattern, still may be judged, and may ask to be judged, as argument. Everything that makes up this book — parables, definitions, the working-through of the revisionary ratios as mechanisms of defense — intends to be part of a unified meditation on the melancholy of the creative mind's desperate insistence upon priority. Vico,[1] who read all creation as a severe poem, understood that priority in the natural order and authority in the spiritual order had been one and had to remain one, *for poets,* because only this harshness constituted Poetic Wisdom. Vico reduced both natural priority and spiritual authority to property, a Hermetic reduction that I recognize as the *Ananke,* the dreadful necessity still governing the Western imagination.

Valentinus,[2] second-century Gnostic speculator, came out of Alexandria to teach the Pleroma, the Fullness of thirty Aeons, manifold of Divinity: "It was a great marvel that they were in the Father without knowing Him." To search for

[1]Giambattista Vico (1668–1744), author of the *Scienza Nuova* (1725). [Ed.]

[2]Second-century Egyptian religious philosopher, founder of the Roman and Alexandrian Gnostics, author of *The Gospel of Truth*. [Ed.]

where you already are is the most benighted of quests, and the most fated. Each strong poet's Muse, his Sophia, leaps as far out and down as can be, in a solipsistic passion of quest. Valentinus posited a Limit, at which quest ends, but no quest ends, if its context is Unconditioned Mind, the cosmos of the greatest post-Miltonic poets. The Sophia of Valentinus recovered, wed again within the Pleroma, and only her Passion or Dark Intention was separated out into our world, beyond the Limit. Into this Passion, the Dark Intention that Valentinus called "strengthless and female fruit," the ephebe must fall. If he emerges from it, however crippled and blinded, he will be among the strong poets.

## SYNOPSIS: SIX REVISIONARY RATIOS

1. *Clinamen,* which is poetic misreading or misprision proper; I take the word from Lucretius,[3] where it means a "swerve" of the atoms so as to make change possible in the universe. A poet swerves away from his precursor, by so reading his precursor's poem as to execute a *clinamen* in relation to it. This appears as a corrective movement in his own poem, which implies that the precursor poem went accurately up to a certain point, but then should have swerved, precisely in the direction that the new poem moves.

2. *Tessera,* which is completion and antithesis; I take the word not from mosaic-making, where it is still used, but from the ancient mystery cults, where it meant a token of recognition, the fragment say of a small pot which with the other fragments would reconstitute the vessel. A poet antithetically "completes" his precursor, by so reading the parent-poem as to retain its terms but to mean them in another sense, as though the precursor had failed to go far enough.

3. *Kenosis,* which is a breaking-device similar to the defense mechanisms our psyches employ against repetition compulsions; *kenosis* then is a movement towards discontinuity with the precursor. I take the word from St. Paul, where

it means the humbling or emptying-out of Jesus by himself, when he accepts reduction from divine to human status. The later poet, apparently emptying himself of his own afflatus, his imaginative godhood, seems to humble himself as though he were ceasing to be a poet, but this ebbing is so performed in relation to a precursor's poem-of-ebbing that the precursor is emptied out also, and so the later poem of deflation is not as absolute as it seems.

4. *Daemonization,* or a movement towards a personalized Counter-Sublime, in reaction to the precursor's Sublime; I take the term from general Neo-Platonic usage, where an intermediary being, neither divine nor human, enters into the adept to aid him. The later poet opens himself to what he believes to be a power in the parent-poem that does not belong to the parent proper, but to a range of being just beyond that precursor. He does this, in his poem, by so stationing its relation to the parent-poem as to generalize away the uniqueness of the earlier work.

5. *Askesis,* or a movement of self-purgation which intends the attainment of a state of solitude; I take the term, general as it is, particularly from the practice of pre-Socratic shamans like Empedocles. The later poet does not, as in *kenosis,* undergo a revisionary movement of emptying, but of curtailing; he yields up part of his own human and imaginative endowment, so as to separate himself from others, including the precursor, and he does this in his poem by so stationing it in regard to the parent-poem as to make that poem undergo an *askesis* too; the precursor's endowment is also truncated.

6. *Apophrades,* or the return of the dead; I take the word from the Athenian dismal or unlucky days upon which the dead returned to reinhabit the houses in which they had lived. The later poet, in his own final phase, already burdened by an imaginative solitude that is almost a solipsism, holds his own poem so open again to the precursor's work that at first we might believe the wheel has come full circle, and that we are back in the later poet's flooded apprenticeship, before his strength began to assert itself in the revisionary ratios. But the poem is now *held* open to the precursor, where once it *was*

[3] In his cosmogony, *De rerum natura.* [Ed.]

open, and the uncanny effect is that the new poem's achievement makes it seem to us, not as though the precursor were writing it, but as though the later poet himself had written the precursor's characteristic work.

# Peter Brooks

b. 1938

*Peter Preston Brooks was born in New York City and received his A.B. (1959) and Ph.D. (1965) from Harvard University. Since 1965 he has been a professor of French and comparative literature at Yale. Brooks was a Guggenheim fellow in 1973–74 and became Chester D. Tripp Professor of Humanities at Yale in 1980. His publications include* The Novel of Worldliness *(1969),* The Child's Part *(1972), and* The Melodramatic Imagination *(1976); he has coedited* Man and His Fictions *(1973) and a collection of critical essays on Jean Genet (1978). "Freud's Masterplot: Questions of Narrative" is from* Yale French Studies *55/56 (1977), an issue which has been called a "classic manifesto" of the relationship between literature and modern French psychoanalysis. "Freud's Masterplot" was later revised and became a chapter in Brooks's* Reading for the Plot: Design and Intention in Narrative *(1984).*

# Freud's Masterplot

*As if they would confine th' Interminable,*
*And tie him to his own prescript.*

In one of his best essays in "narratology," where he is working toward a greater formalization of principles advanced by Vladimir Propp and Viktor Shklovsky,[1] Tzvetan Todorov elaborates a model of narrative transformation whereby narrative plot (*le récit*) is constituted in the tension of two formal categories, difference and resemblance.[2] Transformation — a change

in a predicate term common to beginning and end — represents a synthesis of difference and resemblance; it is, we might say, the same-but-different. Now "the same-but-different" is a common (and if inadequate, not altogether false) definition of metaphor. If Aristotle affirmed that the master of metaphor must have an eye for resemblances,[3] modern treatments of the subject have affirmed equally the importance of difference included within the operation of resemblance, the chief value of the metaphor residing in its "tension." Narrative operates as metaphor in its affirmation of resemblance, in that it brings into relation different actions, combines them through perceived similarities (Todorov's common predicate term), appropriates them to a common plot,

---

I wish at the outset of this essay to express my debt to two colleagues whose thinking has helped to clarify my own: Andrea Bertolini and David A. Miller. It is to the latter that I owe the term "the narratable." [Au.]

[1]See the introduction to Formalism, Propp, and Shklovsky in Ch. 3; pp. 721, 756, and 737. [Ed.]

[2]Tzvetan Todorov, "Les Transformations narratives," in *Poétique de la prose* (Paris: Seuil, 1971), p. 240. Todorov's terms *récit* and *histoire* correspond to the Russian Formalist distinction between *sjužet* and *fabula*. In English, we might

use with the same sense of distinctions: narrative *plot* and *story*. [Au.]

[3]See Aristotle, *Poetics*, p. 58. [Ed.]

---

which implies the rejection of merely contingent (or unassimilable) incident or action. The plotting of meaning cannot do without metaphor, for meaning in plot is the structure of action in closed and legible wholes. Metaphor is in this sense totalizing. Yet it is equally apparent that the key figure of narrative must in some sense be not metaphor but metonymy: the figure of contiguity and combination, the figure of syntagmatic relations.[4] The description of narrative needs metonymy as the figure of movement, of linkage in the signifying chain, of the slippage of the signified under the signifier. That Jacques Lacan has equated metonomy and desire[5] is of the utmost pertinence, since desire must be considered the very motor of narrative, its dynamic principle.

The problem with "the same-but-different" as a definition of narrative would be the implication of simultaneity and stasis in the formulation. The postulation of a static model indeed is the central deficiency of most formalist and structuralist work on narrative, which has sought to make manifest the structures of narrative in spatial and atemporal terms, as versions of Lévi-Strauss's "atemporal matrix structure."[6] Todorov is an exception in that, faithful to Propp, he recognizes the need to consider sequence and succession as well as the paradigmatic matrix. He supplements his definition with the remark: "Rather than a 'coin with two faces,' [transformation] is an operation in two directions: it affirms at once resemblance and difference; it puts time into motion and suspends it, in a single movement; it allows discourse to acquire a meaning without this meaning becoming pure information; in a word, it makes narrative possible and reveals its very definition."[7] The image of a double operation upon time has the value of returning us to the evident but frequently eluded fact that narrative meanings are developed in time, that any narrative partakes more or less of what Proust called "un jeu formidable . . . avec le Temps," and that this game of time is not merely in the world of reference (or in the *fabula*) but as well in the narrative, in the *sjužet*, be it only that the meanings developed by narrative *take time:* the time of reading.[8] If at the end of a narrative we can suspend time in a moment where past and present hold together in a metaphor which may be the very recognition which, said Aristotle, every good plot should bring,[9] that moment does not abolish the movement, the slidings, the errors and partial recognitions of the middle. As Roland Barthes points out, in what so far must be counted our most satisfactory dynamic analysis of plot, the proairetic and hermeneutic codes — code of actions, code of enigmas and answers — are irreversible: their interpretation is determined linearly, in sequence, in one direction.[10]

Ultimately — Barthes writes elsewhere — the passion that animates us as readers of narrative is the passion for (of) meaning.[11] Since for Barthes meaning (in the "classical" or "readable" text) resides in full predication, completion of the codes in a "plenitude" of signification, this passion appears to be finally a desire for the end. It is at the end — for Barthes as for Aristotle —

[4]See Roman Jakobson, "Two Types of Language and Two Types of Aphasic Disturbances," in Jakobson and Halle, *Fundamentals of Language* (The Hague: Mouton, 1956). Todorov in a later article adds to "transformation" the term "succession," and sees the pair as definitional of narrative. He discusses the possible equation of these terms with Jakobson's "metaphor" and "metonymy," to conclude that "the connection is possible but does not seem necessary." (Todorov, "The Two Principles of Narrative," *Diacritics*, Fall, 1971, p. 42.) But there seem to be good reasons to maintain Jakobson's terms as "master tropes" referring to two aspects of virtually any text. [Au.]

[5]See Jacques Lacan, "The Mirror Stage," in *Écrits: A Selection* (1977). [Ed.]

[6]See Claude Lévi-Strauss, "La Structure et la forme," *Cahiers de l'Institut de science économique appliquée*, 99, série M, no. 7 (1960), p. 29.This term is cited with approval by A. J. Greimas in *Sémantique structurale* (Paris: Larousse, 1966) and Roland Barthes, in "Introduction à l'analyse structurale des récits," *Communications* 8 (1966). [Au.]

[7]Todorov, "Les Transformations narratives," *Poétique de la prose*, p. 240. Translations from the French, here and elsewhere, are my own. [Au.]

[8]Proust's phrase is cited by Gérard Genette in "Discours du récit," *Figures III* (Paris: Seuil, 1972), p. 182. Whereas Barthes maintains in "Introduction à l'analyse structurale des récits" that time belongs only to the referent of narrative, Genette gives attention to the time of reading and its necessary linearity. See pp. 77–78. [Au.]

[9]See Aristotle, *Poetics*, p. 53. [Ed.]

[10]See Roland Barthes, *S/Z* (Paris: Seuil, 1970), p. 37. [Au.]

[11]"Introduction à l'analyse structurale des récits," p. 27. [Au.]

that recognition brings its illumination, which then can shed retrospective light. The function of the end, whether considered syntactically (as in Todorov and Barthes) or ethically (as in Aristotle) or as formal or cosmological closure (as in Barbara H. Smith or Frank Kermode)[12] continues to fascinate and to baffle. One of the strongest statements of its determinative position in narrative plots comes in a passage from Sartre's *La Nausée* which bears quotation once again. Roquentin is reflecting on the meaning of "adventure" and the difference between living and narrating. When you narrate, you appear to start with a beginning. You say, "It was a fine autumn evening in 1922. I was a notary's clerk in Marommes." But, says Roquentin:

> In reality you have started at the end. It was there, invisible and present, it is what gives these few words the pomp and value of a beginning. "I was out walking, I had left the town without realizing it, I was thinking about my money troubles." This sentence, taken simply for what it is, means that the man was absorbed, morose, a hundred miles from an adventure, exactly in a mood to let things happen without noticing them. But the end is there, transforming everything. For us, the man is already the hero of the story. His moroseness, his money troubles are much more precious than ours, they are all gilded by the light of future passions. And the story goes on in the reverse: instants have stopped piling themselves up in a haphazard way one on another, they are caught up by the end of the story which draws them and each one in its turn draws the instant preceding it: "It was night, the street was deserted." The sentence is thrown out negligently, it seems superfluous; but we don't let ourselves be duped, we put it aside: this is a piece of information whose value we will understand later on. And we feel that the hero has lived all the details of this night as annunciations, as promises, or even that he has lived only those that were promises, blind and deaf to all that did not herald adventure. We forget that the future wasn't yet there; the man was walking in a night without premonitions, which offered him in disorderly fashion its monotonous riches, and he did not choose.[13]

The beginning in fact presupposes the end. The very possibility of meaning plotted through time depends on the anticipated structuring force of the ending: the interminable would be the meaningless. We read the incidents of narration as "promises and annunciations" of final coherence: the metaphor reached through the chain of metonymies. As Roquentin further suggests, we read only those incidents and signs which can be construed as promise and annunciation, enchained toward a construction of significance — those signs which, as in the detective story, appear to be *clues* to the underlying intentionality of event.

The sense of beginning, then, is determined by the sense of an ending. And if we inquire further into the nature of the ending, we no doubt find that it eventually has to do with the human end, with death. In *Les Mots*, Sartre pushes further his reflection on ends. He describes how in order to escape contingency and the sense of being unjustified he had to imagine himself as one of the children in *L'Enfance des hommes illustrés*, determined, as promise and annunciation, by what he would become for posterity. He began to live his life retrospectively, in terms of the death that alone would confer meaning and necessity on existence. As he succinctly puts it, "I became my own obituary."[14] All narration is obituary in that life acquires definable meaning only at, and through, death. In an independent but convergent argument, Walter Benjamin has claimed that life assumes transmissible form only at the moment of death. For Benjamin, this death is the very "authority" of narrative: we seek in fictions the knowledge of death, which in our own lives is denied to us. Death — which may be figural but in the classic instances of the genre is so often literal — quickens meaning: it is the "flame," says Benjamin, at which we warm our "shivering" lives.[15]

---

[12]Barbara Herrnstein Smith's *Poetic Closure* (1968) analyzed "formal closure"; Frank Kermode's *The Sense of an Ending* (1967) invoked the concept of cosmological closure. [Ed.]

[13]Jean-Paul Sartre, *La Nausée* (Paris: Livre de Poche, 1957), pp. 62–63. [Au.]

[14]Sartre, *Les Mots* (Paris: Gallimard, 1968), p. 171. [Au.]

[15]Walter Benjamin, "The Storyteller," in *Illuminations*, translated by Harry Zohn (New York: Schocken Books, 1969), p. 101. [Au.]

We need to know more about this deathlike ending which is nonetheless animating of meaning in relation to initiatory desire, and about how the interrelationship of the two determines, shapes, necessitates the middle — Barthes's "dilatory space" of retard, postponement — and the kinds of vacillation between illumination and blindness that we find there. If the end is recognition which retrospectively illuminates beginning and middle, it is not the exclusive truth of the text, which must include the processes along the way — the processes of "transformation" — in their metonymical complexity. If beginning is desire, and is ultimately desire for the end, between lies a process we feel to be necessary (plots, Aristotle tells us, must be of "a certain length")[16] but whose relation to originating desire and to end remains problematic. It is here that Freud's most ambitious investigation of ends in relation to beginnings may be of help — and may suggest a contribution to a properly dynamic model of plot.

We undertake, then, to read *Beyond the Pleasure Principle* as an essay about the dynamic interrelationship of ends and beginnings, and the kind of processes that constitute the middle. The enterprise may find a general sort of legitimation in the fact that *Beyond the Pleasure Principle* is in some sense Freud's own masterplot, the text in which he most fully lays out a total scheme of how life proceeds from beginning to end, and how each individual life in its own way repeats the masterplot. Of Freud's various intentions in this text, the boldest — and most mysterious — may be to provide a theory of comprehension of the dynamic of the life-span, its necessary duration and its necessary end, hence, implicitly, a theory of the very narratability of life. In his pursuit of his "beyond," Freud is forced to follow the implications of argument — "to throw oneself into a line of thought and follow it wherever it leads," as he says late in the essay — to ends that he had not originally or consciously conceived.[17] *Beyond the Pleasure Principle* shows the very plotting of a masterplot made necessary by the structural demands of Freud's thought, and it is in this sense that we shall attempt to read it as a model for narrative plot.

Narrative always makes the implicit claim to be in a state of repetition, as a going over again of a ground already covered: a *sjužet* repeating the *fabula*, as the detective retraces the tracks of the criminal.[18] This claim to an act of repetition — "I sing," "I tell" — appears to be initiatory of narrative. It is equally initiatory of *Beyond the Pleasure Principle;* it is the first problem and clue that Freud confronts. Evidence of a "beyond" that does not fit neatly into the functioning of the pleasure principle comes first in the dreams of patients suffering from war neuroses, or from the traumatic neuroses of peace: dreams which return to the moment of trauma, to relive its pain in apparent contradiction of the wish-fulfillment theory of dreams. This "dark and dismal" example is superseded by an example from "normal" life, and we have the celebrated moment of child's play: the toy thrown away, the reel on the string thrown out of the crib and pulled back, to the alternate exclamation of *fort* and *da*.[19] When he has established the equivalence between making the toy disappear and the child's mother's disappearance, Freud is faced with a set of possible interpretations. Why does the child repeat an unpleasurable experience? It may be answered that by staging his mother's disappearance and return, the child is compensating for his instinctual renunciation. Yet the child has also staged disappearance alone, without reappearance, as a game. This may make one want to argue that the essential experience involved is the movement from a passive to an active role in regard to his mother's disappearance, claiming mastery in a situation which he has been compelled to submit to.

---

[16]See Aristotle, *Poetics,* p. 48. [Ed.]

[17]Sigmund Freud, "Beyond the Pleasure Principle" (1920), in *The Standard Edition of the Complete Psychological Works of Sigmund Freud,* ed. James Strachey (London:

Hogarth Press, 1955), 18, 59. Subsequent page references will be given between parentheses in the text. [Au.]

[18]J. Hillis Miller, in "Ariadne's Web" (unpublished manuscript), notes that the term *diegesis* suggests that narrative is a retracing of a journey already made. On the detective story, see Tzvetan Todorov, "Typologie du roman policier," *Poétique de la prose,* pp. 58–59. [Au.]

[19]"Gone" and "here." [Ed.]

Repetition as the movement from passivity to mastery reminds us of "The Theme of the Three Caskets," where Freud, considering Bassanio's choice of the lead casket in *The Merchant of Venice* — the correct choice in the suit of Portia — decides that the choice of the right maiden in man's literary play is also the choice of death; by this choice, he asserts an active mastery of what he must in fact endure. "Choice stands in the place of necessity, of destiny. In this way man overcomes death, which he has recognized intellectually."[20] If repetition is mastery, movement from the passive to the active; and if mastery is an assertion of control over what man must in fact submit to — choice, we might say, of an imposed end — we have already a suggestive comment on the grammar of plot, where repetition, taking us back again over the same ground, could have to do with the choice of ends.

But other possibilities suggest themselves to Freud at this point. The repetition of unpleasant experience — the mother's disappearance — might be explained by the motive of revenge, which would yield its own pleasure. The uncertainty which Freud faces here is whether repetition can be considered a primary event, independent of the pleasure principle, or whether there is always some direct yield of pleasure of another sort involved. The pursuit of this doubt takes Freud into the analytic experience, to his discovery of patients' need to repeat, rather than simply remember, repressed material: the need to reproduce and to "work through" painful material from the past as if it were present. The analyst can detect a "compulsion to repeat," ascribed to the unconscious repressed, particularly discernible in the transference, where it can take "ingenious" forms. The compulsion to repeat gives patients a sense of being fatefully subject to a "perpetual recurrence of the same thing"; it suggests to them pursuit by a daemonic power. We know also, from Freud's essay on "The Uncanny," that this feeling of the daemonic, arising from involuntary repetition, is a particular attribute of the literature of the uncanny.[21]

Thus in analytic work (as also in literary texts) there is slim but real evidence of a compulsion to repeat which can override the pleasure principle, and which seems "more primitive, more elementary, more instinctual than the pleasure principle which it overrides" (23). We might note at this point that the transference itself is a metaphor, a substitutive relationship for the patient's infantile experiences, and thus approximates the status of a text. Now repetition is so basic to our experience of literary texts that one is simultaneously tempted to say all and to say nothing on the subject. To state the matter baldly: rhyme, alliteration, assonance, meter, refrain, all the mnemonic elements of fictions and indeed most of its tropes are in some manner repetitions which take us back in the text, which allow the ear, the eye, the mind to make connections between different textual moments, to see past and present as related and as establishing a future which will be noticeable as some variation in the pattern. Todorov's "same but different" depends on repetition. If we think of the trebling characteristic of the folk tale, and of all formulaic literature, we may consider that the repetition by three constitutes the minimal repetition to the perception of series, which would make it the minimal intentional structure of action, the minimum plot. Narrative must ever present itself as a repetition of events that have already happened, and within this postulate of a generalized repetition it must make use of specific, perceptible repetitions in order to create plot, that is, to show us a significant interconnection of events. Event gains meaning by repeating (with variation) other events. Repetition is a *return* in the text, a doubling back. We cannot say whether this return is a return *to* or a return *of*: for instance, a return to origins or a return of the repressed. Repetition through this ambiguity appears to suspend temporal process, or rather, to subject it to an indeterminate shuttling or oscillation which binds different moments together as a middle which might turn forward or back. This inescapable middle is suggestive of the daemonic. The relation of narrative plot to story may indeed appear to partake of the daemonic, as a kind of tantalizing play with the primitive and the instinctual, the magic and the curse of reproduction or "representation." But in order to know more precisely the opera-

[20]Freud, "The Theme of the Three Caskets" (1913), *Standard Edition*, 12, 299. [Au.]

[21]See Freud, "The Uncanny" (*Das Unheimliche*) (1919), in *Standard Edition*, 17, 219–52. [Au.]

tions of repetition, we need to read further in Freud's text.

"What follows is speculation" (24). With this gesture, Freud, in the manner of Rousseau's dismissal of the facts in the *Discourse on the Origins of Inequality,* begins the fourth chapter and his sketch of the economic and energetic model of the mental apparatus: the system Pcpt-Cs and Ucs,[22] the role of the outer layer as shield against excitations, and the definition of trauma as the breaching of the shield, producing a flood of stimuli which knocks the pleasure principle out of operation. Given this situation, the repetition of traumatic experiences in the dreams of neurotics can be seen to have the function of seeking retrospectively to master the flood of stimuli, to perform a mastery or binding of mobile energy through developing the anxiety whose omission was the cause of the traumatic neurosis. Thus the repetition compulsion is carrying out a task that must be accomplished *before* the dominance of the pleasure principle can begin. Repetition is hence a primary event, independent of the pleasure principle and more primitive. Freud now moves into an exploration of the theory of the instincts.[23] The instinctual is the realm of freely mobile, "unbound" energy: the "primary process," where energy seeks immediate discharge, where no postponement of gratification is tolerated. It appears that it must be "the task of the higher strata of the mental apparatus to bind the instinctual excitation reaching the primary process" before the pleasure principle can assert its dominance over the psychic economy (34–35). We may say that at this point in the essay we have moved from a postulate of repetition as the assertion of mastery (as in the passage from passivity to activity in the child's game) to a conception whereby repetition works as a process of *binding* toward the creation of an energetic constant-state situation which will permit the emer-

gence of mastery, and the possibility of postponement.

That Freud at this point evokes once again the daemonic and the uncanny nature of repetition, and refers us not only to children's play but as well to their demand for exact repetition in storytelling, points our way back to literature. Repetition in all its literary manifestations may in fact work as a "binding," a binding of textual energies that allows them to be mastered by putting them into serviceable form within the energetic economy of the narrative. Serviceable form must in this case mean perceptible form: repetition, repeat, recall, symmetry, all these journeys back in the text, returns to and returns of, that allow us to bind one textual moment to another in terms of similarity or substitution rather than mere contiguity. Textual energy, all that is aroused into expectancy and possibility in a text — the term will need more definition, but corresponds well enough to our experience of reading — can become usable by plot only when it has been bound or formalized. It cannot otherwise be plotted in a course to significant discharge, which is what the pleasure principle is charged with doing. To speak of "binding" in a literary text is thus to speak of any of the formalizations (which, like binding, may be painful, retarding) that force us to recognize sameness within difference, or the very emergence of a *sjužet* from the material of *fabula.*

We need at present to follow Freud into his closer inquiry concerning the relation between the compulsion to repeat and the instinctual. The answer lies in "a universal attribute of instincts and perhaps of organic life in general," that "*an instinct is an urge inherent in organic life to restore an earlier state of things*" (36). Instincts, which we tend to think of as a drive toward change, may rather be an expression of "the conservative nature of living things." The organism has no wish to change; if its conditions remained the same, it would constantly repeat the very same course of life. Modifications are the effect of external stimuli, and these modifications are in turn stored up for further repetition, so that, while the instincts may give the appearance of tending toward change, they "are merely seeking to reach an ancient goal by paths alike old and new" (38). Hence Freud is able to proffer, with

[22]Standard abbreviations for "perceptual-conscious" and "unconscious." [Ed.]

[23]I shall use the term "instinct" since it is the translation of *Trieb* given throughout the Standard Edition. But we should realize that "instinct" is inadequate and somewhat misleading, since it loses the sense of "drive" associated with the word *Trieb.* The currently accepted French translation, *pulsion,* is more to our purposes: the model that interests me here might indeed be called "pulsional." [Au.]

a certain bravado, the formulation: "*the aim of all life is death*." We are given an evolutionary image of the organism in which the tension created by external influences has forced living substance to "diverge ever more widely from its original course of life and to make ever more complicated *détours* before reaching its aim of death" (38–49). In this view, the self-preservative instincts function to assure that the organism shall follow its own path to death, to ward off any ways of returning to the inorganic which are not immanent to the organism itself. In other words, "the organism wishes to die only in its own fashion." It must struggle against events (dangers) which would help it to achieve its goal too rapidly — by a kind of short-circuit.

We are here somewhere near the heart of Freud's masterplot for organic life, and it generates a certain analytic force in its superimposition on fictional plots. What operates in the text through repetition is the death instinct, the drive toward the end. Beyond and under the domination of the pleasure principle is this baseline of plot, its basic "pulsation," sensible or audible through the repetitions which take us back in the text. Repetition can take us both backwards and forwards because these terms have become reversible: the end is a time before the beginning. Between these two moments of quiescence, plot itself stands as a kind of divergence or deviance, a postponement in the discharge which leads back to the inanimate. For plot starts (must give the illusion of starting) from that moment at which story, or "life," is stimulated from quiescence into a state of narratability, into a tension, a kind of irritation, which demands narration. Any reflection on novelistic beginnings shows the beginning as an awakening, an arousal, the birth of an appetency, ambition, desire or intention.[24] To say this is of course to say — perhaps more pertinently — that beginnings are the arousal of an intention in reading, stimulation into a tension. (The specifically erotic nature of

the tension of writing and its rehearsal in reading could be demonstrated through a number of exemplary texts, notably Rousseau's account, in *The Confessions,* of how his novel *La Nouvelle Héloïse* was born of a masturbatory reverie and its necessary fictions, or the very similar opening of Jean Genet's *Notre-Dame des fleurs;* but of course the sublimated forms of the tension are just as pertinent.) The ensuing narrative — the Aristotelean "middle" — is maintained in a state of tension, as a prolonged deviance from the quiescence of the "normal" — which is to say, the unnarratable — until it reaches the terminal quiescence of the end. The development of a narrative shows that the tension is maintained as an ever more complicted postponement or *détour* leading back to the goal of quiescence. As Sartre and Benjamin compellingly argued, the narrative must tend toward its end, seek illumination in its own death. Yet this must be the right death, the correct end. The complication of the *détour* is related to the danger of short-circuit: the danger of reaching the end too quickly, of achieving the improper death. The improper end indeed lurks throughout narrative, frequently as the wrong choice: choice of the wrong casket, misapprehension of the magical agent, false erotic object-choice. The development of the subplot in the classical novel usually suggests (as William Empson has intimated) a different solution to the problems worked through by the main plot, and often illustrates the danger of short-circuit.[25] The subplot stands as one means of warding off the danger of short-circuit, assuring that the main plot will continue through to the right end. The desire of the text (the desire of reading) is hence desire for the end, but desire for the end reached only through the at least minimally complicated *détour,* the intentional deviance, in tension, which is the plot of narrative.

Deviance, *détour,* an intention which is irritation: these are characteristics of the narratable, of "life" as it is the material of narrative, of *fabula* become *sjužet*. Plot is a kind of arabesque or squiggle toward the end. It is like Corporal

---

[24]On the beginning as intention, see Edward Said, *Beginnings: Intention and Method* (New York: Basic Books, 1975). It occurs to me that the exemplary narrative beginning might be that of Kafka's *Metamorphosis:* waking up to find oneself transformed into a monstrous vermin. [Au.]

[25]See William Empson, "Double Plots," in *Some Versions of Pastoral* (New York: New Directions, 1960), pp. 25–84. [Au.]

Trim's arabesque with his stick, in *Tristram Shandy,* retraced by Balzac at the start of *La Peau de chagrin* to indicate the arbitrary, transgressive, gratuitous line of narrative, its deviance from the straight line, the shortest distance between beginning and end — which would be the collapse of one into the other, of life into immediate death. Freud's text will in a moment take us closer to understanding of the formal organization of this deviance toward the end. But it also at this point offers further suggestions about the beginning. For when he has identified both the death instincts and the life (sexual) instincts as conservative, tending toward the restoration of an earlier state of things, Freud feels obliged to deconstruct the will to believe in a human drive toward perfection, an impulsion forward and upward: a force which — he here quotes *Faust* as the classic text of man's forward striving — *"ungebändigt immer vorwärts dringt."*[26] The illusion of the striving toward perfection is to be explained by instinctual repression and the persisting tension of the repressed instinct, and the resulting difference between the pleasure of satisfaction *demanded* and that which is *achieved,* a difference which "provides the driving factor which will permit of no halting at any position attained" (36). This process of subtraction reappears in modified form in the work of Lacan, where it is the difference between *need* (the infant's need for the breast) and *demand* (which is always demand for recognition) that gives as its result *desire,* which is precisely the driving power, of plot certainly, since desire for Lacan is a metonymy, the forward movement of the signifying chain. If Roman Jakobson is able, in his celebrated essay, to associate the metonymic pole with prose fiction (particularly the nineteenth-century novel) — as the metaphoric pole is associated with lyric poetry — it would seem to be because the meanings peculiar to narrative inhere (or, as Lacan would say, "insist") in the metonymic chain, in the drive of desire toward meaning in time.[27]

The next-to-last chapter of *Beyond the Pleasure Principle* cannot here be rehearsed in detail. In brief, it leads Freud twice into the findings of biology, first on the track of the origins of death, to find out whether it is a necessary or merely a contingent alternative to interminability, then in pursuit of the origins of sexuality, to see whether it satisfies the description of the instinctual as conservative. Biology can offer no sure answer to either investigation, but it offers at least metaphorical confirmation of the necessary dualism of Freud's thought, and encouragement to reformulate his earlier opposition of ego instincts to sexual instincts as one between life instincts and death instincts, a shift in the grouping of oppositional forces which then allows him to reformulate the libidinal instincts themselves as the Eros "of the poets and philosophers" which holds all living things together, and which seeks to combine things in ever greater living wholes. Desire would then seem to be totalizing in intent, a process tending toward combination in new unities: metonymy in the search to become metaphor. But for the symmetry of Freud's opposition to be complete, he needs to be able to ascribe to Eros, as to the death instinct, the characteristic of a need to restore an earlier state of things. Since biology will not answer, Freud, in a remarkable gesture, turns toward myth, to come up with Plato's Androgyne, which precisely ascribes Eros to a search to recover a lost primal unity which was split asunder.[28] Freud's apologetic tone in this last twist to his argument is partly disingenuous, for we detect a contentment to have formulated the forces of the human masterplot as "philosopher and poet." The apology is coupled with a reflection that much of the obscurity of the processes Freud has been considering "is merely due to our being obliged to operate with the scientific terms, that is to say with the figurative language, peculiar to psychology" (60). *Beyond the Pleasure Principle,* we are to understand, is not merely metapsy-

---

[26]"Unhampered always moves forwards." [Ed.]

[27]See Jakobson, "Two Types of Language . . .". See, in Lacan's work, especially "Le Stade du miroir" and "L'Instance de la lettre dans l'inconscient," in *Écrits* (Paris: Seuil, 1966). [Au.]

[28]In the *Symposium,* Aristophanes explains the nature of love in the form of a fable. Humanity was originally designed to be androgynous, but a mischievous demiurge split the double-sexed creature in half. The result is that we are all incomplete, seeking in Eros for our missing halves. [Ed.]

chology, it is also mythopoesis, necessarily resembling "an equation with two unknown quantities" (57), or, we might say, a formal dynamic the terms of which are not substantial but purely relational. We perceive that *Beyond the Pleasure Principle* is itself a plot which has formulated that dynamic necessary to its own *détour.*

The last chapter of Freud's text recapitulates, but not without difference. He returns to the problem of the relationship between the instinctual processes of repetition and the dominance of the pleasure principle. One of the earliest and most important functions of the mental apparatus is to bind the instinctual impulses which impinge upon it, to convert freely mobile energy into a quiescent cathexis. This is a preparatory act on behalf of the pleasure principle, which permits its dominance. Sharpening his distinction between a *function* and a *tendency,* Freud argues that the pleasure principle is a "tendency operating in the service of a function whose business it is to free mental apparatus from excitation or to keep the amount of excitation in it constant or to keep it as low as possible" (62). This function is concerned "with the most universal endeavour of all living substance — namely to return to the quiescence of the inorganic world." Hence one can consider "binding" to be a preliminary function which prepares the excitation for its final elimination in the pleasure of discharge. In this manner, we could say that the repetition compulsion and the death instinct serve the pleasure principle; in a larger sense, the pleasure principle, keeping watch on the invasion of stimuli from without and especially from within, seeking their discharge, serves the death instinct, making sure that the organism is permitted to return to quiescence. The whole evolution of the mental apparatus appears as a taming of the instincts so that the pleasure principle — itself tamed, displaced — can appear to dominate in the complicated *détour* called life which leads back to death. In fact, Freud seems here at the very end to imply that the two antagonistic instincts serve one another in a dynamic interaction which is a perfect and self-regulatory economy which makes both end and *détour* perfectly necessary and interdependent. The organism must live in order to die in the proper manner, to die the right

death. We must have the arabesque of plot in order to reach the end. We must have metonymy in order to reach metaphor.

We emerge from reading *Beyond the Pleasure Principle* with a dynamic model which effectively structures ends (death, quiescence, non-narratability) against beginnings (Eros, stimulation into tension, the desire of narrative) in a manner that necessitates the middle as *détour,* as struggle toward the end under the compulsion of imposed delay, as arabesque in the dilatory space of the text. We detect some illumination of the necessary distance between beginning and end, the drives which connect them but which prevent the one collapsing back into the other: the way in which metonymy and metaphor serve one another, the necessary temporality of the same-but-different which to Todorov constitutes the narrative transformation. The model suggests further that along the way of the path from beginning to end — in the middle — we have repetitions serving to bind the energy of the text in order to make its final discharge more effective. In fictional plots, these bindings are a system of repetitions which are returns to and returns of, confounding the movement forward to the end with a movement back to origins, reversing meaning within forward-moving time, serving to formalize the system of textual energies, offering the possibility (or the illusion) of "meaning" wrested from "life."

As a dynamic-energetic model of narrative plot, then, *Beyond the Pleasure Principle* gives an image of how "life," or the *fabula,* is stimulated into the condition of narrative, becomes *sjužet:* enters into a state of deviance and *détour* (ambition, quest, the pose of a mask) in which it is maintained for a certain time, through an at least minimally complex extravagance, before returning to the quiescence of the non-narratable. The energy generated by deviance, extravagance, excess — an energy which belongs to the textual hero's career and to the readers' expectation, his desire of and for the text — maintains the plot in its movement through the vacillating play of the middle, where repetition as binding works toward the generation of significance, toward recognition and the retrospective illumination which will allow us to grasp the text as total

metaphor, but not therefore to discount the metonymies that have led to it. The desire of the
text is ultimately the desire for the end, for that
recognition which is the moment of the death of
the reader in the text. Yet recognition cannot
abolish textuality, does not annul the middle
which, in its oscillation between blindness and
recognition, between origin and endings, is the
truth of the narrative text.

It is characteristic of textual energy in narrative that it should always be on the verge of
premature discharge, of short-circuit. The reader
experiences the fear — and excitation — of the
improper end, which is symmetrical to — but far
more immediate and present than — the fear of
endlessness. The possibility of short-circuit can
of course be represented in all manner of threats
to the protagonist or to any of the functional
logics which demand completion; it most commonly takes the form of temptation to the mistaken erotic object choice, who may be of the
"Belle Dame sans merci" variety, or may be the
too-perfect and hence annihilatory bride.
Throughout the Romantic tradition, it is perhaps
most notably the image of incest (of the fraternal-
sororal variety) which hovers as the sign of a
passion interdicted because its fulfillment would
be too perfect, a discharge indistinguishable from
death, the very cessation of narrative movement.
Narrative is in a state of temptation to oversame-
ness, and where we have no literal threat of incest
(as in Chateaubriand, or Faulkner), lovers choose
to turn the beloved into a soul-sister so that possession will be either impossible or mortal:
Werther and Lotte, for instance, or, at the inception of the tradition, Rousseau's *La Nouvelle
Héloïse,* where Saint-Preux's letter to Julie following their night of love begins: "Mourons, ô
ma douce amie." Incest is only the exemplary
version of a temptation of short-circuit from
which the protagonist and the text must be led
away, into *détour,* into the cure which prolongs
narrative.

It may finally be in the logic of our argument
that repetition speaks in the text of a return which
ultimately subverts the very notion of beginning
and end, suggesting that the idea of beginning
presupposes the end, that the end is a time before
the beginning, and hence that the interminable

never can be finally bound in a plot. Analysis,
Freud would eventually discover, is inherently
interminable, since the dynamics of resistance
and the transference can always generate new
beginnings in relation to any possible end.[29] It is
the role of fictional plots to impose an end which
yet suggests a return, a new beginning: a rereading. A narrative, that is, wants at its end to refer
us back to its middle, to the web of the text: to
recapture us in its doomed energies.

One ought at this point to make a new beginning, and to sketch the possible operation of the
model in the study of the plot of a fiction. One
could, for instance, take Dickens's *Great Expectations.* One would have to show how the energy
released in the text by its liminary "primal scene"
— Pip's terrifying meeting with Magwitch in the
graveyard — is subsequently bound in a number
of desired but unsatisfactory ways (including
Pip's "being bound" as apprentice, the "dream"
plot of Satis House, the apparent intent of the
"expectations"), and simultaneously in censored
but ultimately more satisfying ways (through all
the returns of the repressed identification of Pip
and his convict). The most salient device of this
novel's "middle" is literally the journey back —
from London to Pip's home town — a repeated
return to apparent origins which is also a return
of the repressed, of what Pip calls "that old spell
of my childhood." It would be interesting to
demonstrate that each of Pip's choices in the
novel, while consciously life-furthering, forward
oriented, in fact leads back, to the insoluble question of origins, to the palindrome of his name,
so that the end of the narrative — its "discharge"
— appears as the image of a "life" cured of
"plot," as celibate clerk for Clarrikers.

Pip's story, while ostensibly the search for
progress, ascension, and metamorphosis, may
after all be the narrative of an attempted home-
coming: of the effort to reach an assertion of
origin through ending, to find the same in the
different, the time before in the time after. Most
of the great nineteenth-century novels tell this
same tale. Georg Lukács has called the novel
"the literary form of the transcendent homeless-

[29]See Freud, "Analysis Terminable and Interminable"
(1937), in *Standard Edition,* 23, 216–53. [Au.]

ness of the idea," and argued that it is in the discrepancy between idea and the organic that time, the process of duration, becomes constitutive of the novel as of no other genre:

> Only in the novel, whose very matter is seeking and failing to find the essence, is time posited together with the form: time is the resistance of the organic — which possesses a mere semblance of life — to the present meaning, the will of life to remain within its own completely enclosed immanence. . . . In the novel, meaning is separated from life, and hence the essential from the temporal; we might almost say that the entire inner action of the novel is nothing but a struggle against the power of time.[30]

The understanding of time, says Lukács, the transformation of the struggle against time into a process full of interest, is the work of memory — or more precisely, we could say with Freud, of "remembering, repeating, working through." Repetition, remembering, reenactment are the ways in which we replay time, so that it may not be lost. We are thus always trying to work back through time to that transcendent home, knowing of course that we cannot. All we can do is subvert or, perhaps better, pervert time: which is what narrative does.[31]

To forgo any true demonstration on a novel, and to bring a semblance of conclusion, we may return to the assertion, by Barthes and Todorov, that narrative is essentially the articulation of a set of verbs. These verbs are no doubt ultimately all versions of desire. Desire is the wish for the end, for fulfillment, but fulfillment delayed so that we can understand it in relation to origin, and to desire itself. The story of Scheherezade is doubtless the story of stories. This suggests that the tale as read is inhabited by the reader's desire, and that further analysis should be directed to that desire, not (in the manner of Norman Holland) his individual desire and its origins in his own personality,[32] but his transindividual and intertextually determined desire as a reader. Because it concerns ends in relation to beginnings and the forces that animate the middle in between, Freud's model is suggestive of what a reader engages when he responds to plot. It images that engagement as essentially dynamic, an interaction with a system of energy which the reader activates. This in turn suggests why we can read *Beyond the Pleasure Principle* as a text concerning textuality, and conceive that there can be psychoanalytic criticism of the text itself that does not become — as has usually been the case — a study of the psychogenesis of the text (the author's unconscious), the dynamics of literary response (the reader's unconscious), or the occult motivations of the characters (postulating an "unconscious" for them). It is rather the superimposition of the model of the functioning of the mental apparatus on the functioning of the text that offers the possibility of a psychoanalytic criticism. And here the superimposition of Freud's psychic masterplot on the plots of fiction seems a valid and useful maneuver. Plot mediates meanings with the contradictory human world of the eternal and the mortal. Freud's masterplot speaks of the temporality of desire, and speaks to our very desire for fictional plots.

[30]Georg Lukács, *The Theory of the Novel*, trans. Anna Bostock (Cambridge, Mass.: MIT Press, 1971), p. 122. [Au.]

[31]Genette discusses Proust's "perversion" of time in "Discours du récit," p. 182. "Remembering, Repeating, and Working Through" (*Erinnern, Wiederholen und Durcharbeiten*) (1914) is the subject of one of Freud's papers on technique. See *Standard Edition*, 12, 145–56. [Au.]

[32]See Holland, Introduction to *5 Readers Reading*, in Ch. 7. [Ed.]

# 3

# FORMALISM

*Habitualization devours works, clothes, furniture, one's wife, and the fear of war. . . . And art exists that one may recover the sensation of life; it exists to make one feel things, to make the stone* stony. *The purpose of art is to impart the sensation of things as they are perceived and not as they are known.* — VICTOR SHKLOVSKY

*Finding its proper symbol, defined and refined by the participating metaphors, the theme becomes a part of the reality in which we live — an insight, rooted and growing out of concrete experience, manysided, three-dimensional.* — CLEANTH BROOKS

*The laws underlying the operations by which the mind translates the world of which it is a part into the many worlds of its own creation must be simple, definite and regular, else we could not have common intuitive access to those worlds as, despite interpretive confusion, we know we do.* — RALPH RADER

The three movements discussed here cover a vast amount of geographical ground (centered in Moscow, in London and Nashville, and in Chicago), and they have flourished over a long stretch of the present century, from just after the First World War to the present day. Whether the theoretical territories inhabited by the formalists are seen as vast or confined depends on whether one looks at the positive ideas they have espoused or at their oppositions. All three versions of formalism proposed an "intrinsic" criticism that defined and addressed the specifically literary qualities in the text, and all three began in reaction to various forms of "extrinsic" criticism that viewed the text as either the product of social and historical forces or a document making an ethical statement. But no two of the three agreed on precisely what made a text "literary," what qualities of form, language, or content differentiated it from nonliterary discourse, or what the significance of literature was for humanity. There are major discrepancies among these three movements, as one might expect, but the divergences *within* each movement are almost as striking.

## RUSSIAN FORMALISM

Of the three movements, Russian formalism had the briefest flowering. It originated in Moscow in 1915 with a group of linguists and stylisticians known as OPOYAZ (Society for the Study of Poetic Language), grew for about a decade in postrevolutionary Russia, and as a movement was finally eliminated for political reasons by Joseph Stalin and his henchman Andrey Zhdanov around 1930. Most of its members either formally recanted (as did Victor Shklovsky) or emigrated (like Roman Jakobson). Their publications, suppressed in the USSR, were lost to the West until Victor Erlich's pioneering study *Russian Formalism: History — Doctrine* (1955) and Tzvetan Todorov's 1965 translation of the formalists into French. Nevertheless, the ultimate influence of the formalists was considerable. Roman Jakobson carried their ideas west, first to the Prague Linguistic Circle (which included Jan Mukařovský), and then to Paris, where he and Claude Lévi-Strauss helped create the structuralist movement that flourished from the early 1960s.

The origins of Russian formalism and the New Criticism show some interesting parallels, largely because the two movements developed in opposition to the same two main-stream forms of contemporary criticism. On the one hand they rejected the historicism of academic criticism, which was seen as a tedious investigation of the circumstances of poetic creation pursued in the absence of any coherent notion of poetics itself. On the other, they despised the liberal "social criticism" of reformers who wished to use literature as a means of cultural progress. What the moralist Paul Elmer More was to the New Critics, nineteenth-century socialist critics like Vissarion Belinsky, Nikolay Chernyshevsky, and Nikolay Dobrolyubov were to the Russian formalists.

Serious divergences occurred, however. The New Critics were essentially allied with the imagist poets (including T. E. Hulme, T. S. Eliot, and Ezra Pound), who viewed poetry as a means of communicating, through image and symbol, what could not be said in prose. The poetics of the New Critics centered in semantics, and set the critic the task of decoding the text by explicating its tropes. The systems of individual New Critics largely differed over which of the principal figures of speech or thought — such as metaphor, irony, and ambiguity — was chosen as the master trope.

The Russian formalists began by refining but ultimately rejecting the work of a nineteenth-century philologist who might be seen as a prototype New Critic. Alexander Potebnya viewed imagery as the master trope distinguishing poetry from prose, which he regarded as two distinct ways of knowing the world. This theory was embraced by the symbolist poets (like Andrei Bely and Dmitri Merezhkovsky), who looked to art to produce a mystical form of knowledge. Potebnya was as much an exemplar as he was an opponent of the formalists; he had been concerned about the line dividing the literary from the nonliterary (an issue about which the social critics cared little), and he had defined literariness as a function of language, a point of view the formalists were also to embrace.

Potebnya is chiefly known today, however, through the attack on his ideas in Victor Shklovsky's manifesto of formalism, "Art as Technique," which takes issue with the narrowness of Potebnya's conception of art in elevating metaphor and symbolism, imagery, or any single trope to master status. From Shklovsky's perspective, the central difficulty with Potebnya's conception of poetry was its obsession with semantics, with the notion that the things poetry had to express were mystically different from those of prose. For Shklovsky, the chief function of art is not to lead us to a knowledge above and beyond the world but to restore our capacity to see a world to which use and habit have blinded us. "As perception becomes habitual, it becomes automatic," says Shklovsky, "and art exists that one may recover the sensation of life . . . of things as they are perceived and not as they are known." By its use of unaccustomed language, art makes the world strange again, so that we can see it with the freshness of a child. *Ostranenie* (defamiliarization), the concept at the center of Shklovsky's poetics, is an inversion of Samuel Johnson's notion that art "approximates the remote and familiarizes the wonderful."

The concept of defamiliarization is central to the formalist project, but the term can be used in different ways at different levels of approach to the literary object. At the most basic level of discourse, the formalists analyzed sentences taken from literary texts to see how they estranged reality as a purely aesthetic end in itself. But at the higher level where discourse becomes social, the formalists saw texts' representations of reality as a technique for defamiliarizing the social ideas of the dominant culture, and thus for challenging our automatic acceptance of these ideas. They would say, for example, that an apparently naive and incoherent narrative voice (like that of Gogol's *The Nose*) functions so as to expose the cruelty and hypocrisy of the social ideas of the time.

At a still higher and more abstract level, the formalists, as Tony Bennett has put it, "were concerned with the formal mechanisms whereby literary works tended to reveal or make strange the systems of coherence imposed on reality by the codes and conventions of other, usually earlier literary forms."[1] For example, Shklovsky's essay on *Tristram Shandy* (1921) distinguishes between *fabula* (or story), that is, the temporal-causal sequence of narrated events that comprise the raw materials of the work, and *sjuzet* (or plot), the way in which these raw materials are formally manipulated, in order to argue that *Tristram Shandy*, as Bennett puts it, "is told in such a way as to limit and reveal the narrative conventions of the time. . . ."

The distinction between *fabula* and *sjuzet* owes a great deal to another nineteenth-century forebear of the Formalists, the academic literary historian Alexander Veselovsky. Around 1906, Veselovsky evolved a poetics of "motifs," in which the literary work is dissected into its smallest irreducible components, and plot is seen as a complex cluster of story-motifs, ordered, altered, and rearranged by art; Veselovsky thought that shifting motifs correlated with changes in cultural attitudes. The Formalists predictably disagreed with his version of historical determinism but adopted Veselovsky's techniques of thematic analysis, as exemplified by Boris Tomashevsky's "Thematics" (1925) and Vladimir Propp's *The Morphology of the Folk-Tale* (1928).

[1]Tony Bennett, *Formalism and Marxism* (London: Methuen, 1979), p. 23.

In effect, the formalists viewed literature as a mode of construction. Poetry was defined by its use of poetic language, fiction as the craft of manipulating story materials by narrative technique. What was not a matter of construction, such as the origins and the cultural meaning of a literary work, were not specifically literary, and were therefore dismissed as not a true part of poetics. The difficulty with such a view, as one historian of formalism has suggested, is that "it does not permit us to evaluate" individual texts. "But the *Opoyaz* members never introduced the problems of evaluation into their system."[2]

If Shklovsky established the principal issues governing the literary qualities of texts, Roman Jakobson most succinctly defined the poetic in what would today be called semiotic fashion: as a special use of language. Poetry was "an utterance oriented toward the mode of expression"; in poetry "a word is perceived as a word and not merely as a proxy for the denoted object or an outburst of emotion. . . . Words and their arrangement . . . their outward and inward form acquire weight and value of their own."[3]

At the outset, the Russian formalists talked as though it were the emotive quality of poetry that differentiated it from common language, but a *semantic* feature of that sort was bound to seem unsatisfactory in the long run; obviously some expressions of feeling are poetic and some are not, while a great deal of what is clearly poetry is not primarily emotional expression. Besides, emotion was a sort of content, and with such a discriminant, the Formalists would have been entrapped in the notion of an external form enclosing a crude content. Jakobson's idea made it possible to drop entirely the notion of a separable content and to view poetic form as that which integrates the raw material of language into a shaped structure. Jackobson's sense of form as a dynamic shaping process thus resembles the Aristotelian *eidos*; as we shall see, it has more in common with the Chicago neo-Aristotelians' notions of form than that of the New Critics.

## BAKHTIN

Mikhail Mikhailovich Bakhtin could be equally well labeled a Marxist as a formalist; his work is so individual that it is hard to categorize and so important that Marxists and formalists alike lay claim to him. Part of the difficulty in categorization stems from the still-disputed question of Bakhtin's contribution to three books published in the late 1920s. These books, attacks on Freudianism, on structural linguistics, and on Russian formalism itself, were published under the names of Bakhtin's friends Pavel Medvedev and V. N. Vološinov. The most recent evidence suggests, however, that the more orthodox Marxist texts of the Bakhtin circle owe their slant to their titular authors and that Bakhtin can be seen as a highly individualistic theorist concerned with problems similar to the ones that engrossed Shklovsky and other formalists, such as Yuri Tynyanov.

[2]Krystyna Pomorska, "Russian Formalism in Retrospect," in *Readings in Russian Poetics*, ed. Ladislaw Matejka and Krystyna Pomorska (Cambridge: MIT Press, 1971), p. 275.

[3]Victor Erlich, *Russian Formalism: History — Doctrine* (The Hague: Mouton, 1963), p. 183.

At the center of Bakhtin's ideas is the principle usually translated as *hetero-glossia* (in the original Russian: *raznorečie*, literally "the word of another"). This is the notion that the meaning of language is socially determined, that utterances reflect social values and depend for their meaning on their relation to other utterances. The idea is a familiar one in the purely linguistic context of speech-act theory: An imperative sentence can be an order, a command, a request, a plea, or a prayer, depending on who is talking to whom. We could say that Bakhtin — who was working on these ideas many years before the speech-act theorists Austin and Searle — essentially directs our attention to the *pragmatics* of literary discourse. He differentiates sharply between *dialogical* discourse, which explicitly or tacitly acknowledges the language of the Other, the controlling presence of a social context; and *monological* discourse, which tries to have its say in a vacuum. What many English and American critics find worth emulating in Bakhtin's criticism is the extraordinary sensitivity with which he succeeds in locating the various nuances — the responses to internal and external pressures — that go into the creation of dialogical fictional discourse.

But Bakhtin does not merely analyze literary pragmatics neutrally; he loathes single-voiced authoritative discourse, the unquestionable word that comes from above to dictate meaning. For Bakhtin, monologism denies the existence and validity of the Other, the auditor to whom one speaks without needing to listen. Instead, Bakhtin valorizes dialogism and the types of discourse he calls *double-voiced (dvugolosnoë slovo)*, in which a single sentence will bring into dialogue two or more different languages. These shifting planes of intention permit an exhilaratingly chaotic freedom of expression. Bakhtin particularly loves parody, which mediates comically between an audience and a previous discourse.

Thus, purity and clarity of speech, with clear levels of discourse of the sort Aristotle and Horace recommended, earn no points from Bakhtin. They suggest to him a closed and stratified society without freedom of thought, devoted to "terror, dogmatism, reverence, and piety." What he values instead is the Rabelaisian carnivalization of literature: the sociolinguistic fun fair where, as in the medieval festival of Carnival, rulers and ruled mix on equal terms in a parodic rout devoted to "ambivalent laughter, blasphemy, the profanation of everything sacred, full of debasing and obscenities, familiar contact with everyone and everything."

Bakhtin consequently prefers the novel — in which dialogism is possible — over poetry, which is typically single-voiced.[4] And within the novel he contrasts the single-voiced Tolstoy, whose multifarious characters nonetheless always express the author's dogmas, with the double-voiced Dostoevsky, whose characters engage in genuine dialogue. The distinction has nothing to do with the use of conversational dialogue as such. Dialogue appears for Bakhtin even in the narrator's discourse and in characters' solo speeches (like that of the Underground Man) so long as the speaker's language bears perceptibly the imprint, the pressure of the Other, inside or outside the novel, to whom it is addressed. Bakhtin's ideas widen

---

[4]Technically this is not a question of genre: There can be "novelized" forms within any genre. But the novel lends itself to heteroglossia more than poetry as such does.

out much further — his dialogism is the basis of a genre-criticism, which in turn is the basis for an innovative approach to the history of literature — but his notion of the languages competing within an individual's speech, the way one's discourse is at the same time the discourse of an Other, lies at the heart of his critical system.

## THE NEW CRITICISM

Bakhtin and the Russian formalists were Underground Men, whose ideas were absent from the critical dialogue of the West until the 1960s. The New Criticism, to the contrary, is one of the more conspicuous success stories of the century, and if the movement is centered somewhat less coherently than the others, that may have been one of the principal reasons for its popularity, since the New Criticism is associated less with a body of theoretical doctrine about the nature of language and poetry than with a method of critical exegesis and explication.

The name "New Criticism" seems to have been bestowed by John Crowe Ransom in a 1941 book of that title, which examines the work of I. A. Richards and William Empson, T. S. Eliot, Yvor Winters, and the philosopher Charles W. Morris. The most important New Critics include this group, Ransom himself, and his fellow Southern "fugitive" writers Allen Tate, Cleanth Brooks, and Robert Penn Warren. Other important theorists associated with the movement include René Wellek, R. P. Blackmur, Robert B. Heilman, Austin Warren, and Murray Krieger. After this point it is hard to tell where to stop, since by the 1950s the New Critical method of poetic explication had come to dominate the teaching of literature in England and America, and most working literary critics had been touched by it in one way or another. One should look to I. A. Richards and T. S. Eliot as the primary founders of this method, the former through his philosophical theories and the latter through his critical practice and tastes.

Like the Russian formalists, Richards was mainly concerned with what differentiated poetry from common language. For him the issue was principally referentiality. Richards held that in common language we make statements that refer to matters of fact, whereas in poetry we make pseudostatements that may appear to be referential but in fact are not. Statements made in poetry cannot be verified; their function is affective rather than cognitive. A poem arouses and allays feelings through the dance of conflicting attitudes stimulated by its complex language. Such an aesthetic moment shakes up the reader's established responses to real life by stimulating the reader's experience of a sense of harmony established among opposing impulses. The form of the poem consists of these stimuli and responses within an ideal reader. (Richards's notion of poetry is at bottom a more behavioristic version of Coleridge, who held that the imagination operates by reconciling opposing qualities into an ideal unity of form.) Richards was primarily a theorist; the critical practice inherent in his ideas was taken over by his student, William Empson. Empson's *Seven Types of Ambiguity* was an attempt to establish the ways in which texts create, through ambiguity, a multiplicity of meanings, which stimulate the reader to see their harmonious reconciliation.

Two decades later, the most rigorous of the American New Critics, including Ransom and Wimsatt, would reject this reader-oriented formulation: The "affective fallacy" would insist that the form of a poem is not to be identified with the psychological process undergone by its audience. (Since this process is likely to differ in various readers, it would leave the form at best indeterminate and at worst under the control of the audience.) But purged of its affective slant, Richards's view of form as an interplay of feelings and attitudes, like the interwoven themes of music, was to prove persuasive and fertile.

T. S. Eliot was also to lend ideas to the New Criticism. In "Tradition and the Individual Talent" Eliot spoke of literature as an "ideal order," a tradition which exists not successively in history but is somehow present simultaneously as it exerts influence upon the newly created work. (See Eliot's essay in Part I.) This viewpoint had justified the breach between the New Criticism and the historical scholarship that had dominated the academy. In "Hamlet and His Problems," Eliot also presented the "objective correlative," the idea of one-to-one correspondence between the images in a poem and the feelings for which the image is supposed to be the formula. Given this correspondence, poetry could have emotive significance, but its themes could be discussed *objectively* in a more concrete explication of the poem's emotional content. Although these were influential ideas, Eliot was perhaps even more influential in his tastes, which valorized the poets and playwrights of the English Renaissance over the Augustans, romantics, and Victorians who had dominated the canon, and in his critical practice, which lucidly explicated the poetry of Donne and the plays of Middleton as though they were his contemporaries.

Despite the efforts of René Wellek to give the New Criticism a pedigree in Kantian aesthetics, its development from the late 1930s on was primarily as a critical practice rather than a set of theoretical doctrines. The general theory was simply that literature was a special kind of language and that practical criticism reflects and is constrained by that principle. The most influential ideological statements tended to explain what criticism should not do, rather than what it should. Pride of place should be given to a pair of papers by William K. Wimsatt and Monroe Beardsley defending new critical practice against a series of "fallacies": One was "The Affective Fallacy" (1949), which rejected the notion that the poem could be defined in terms of the internal experiences of actual readers (although the New Critics, without precisely admitting to it, tended to analyze poetry in terms of the response of *ideal* readers).

Even more influential was "The Intentional Fallacy" (1946; included in Chapter 9), which, consistent with Eliot's assertion of the impersonality of poetry in "Tradition and the Individual Talent," attacked the notion of the work of art as the essentially private product of the internal experience of a particular individual. The poem is defined as a public text, and its meaning by what the public norms of language allow it to mean. The text's aesthetic success or failure must be judged in those terms alone. Within its original context, the intentional fallacy was a convincing refutation of Crocean idealism, which would have located the aesthetic object in the author's lyrical intuition, and of the old historicism, which referred the meaning of the text to the circumstances of its genesis and its historical context. The intent of the intentional fallacy was to liberate the reader: Thereafter, the only apparatus one needed to read Chaucer and Shakespeare was a good text and a historical dictionary. But the ultimate effect of anti-intentionalism was to foster the irresponsible interpretation of texts, a search for originality of reading without regard to the creator's probable purposes.[5]

There were other fallacies and heresies: the *fallacy of imitative form* attempted to cut the text off from the world it supposedly represented in order to purify the New Criticism of the mimetic principle, as it had already been purified of the expressive and affective ones. The *fallacy of neoclassic species* was aimed at R. S. Crane and the Chicago critics, whose formal theories located the text within an open system of genres. The *biographical heresy* was aimed at those who would identify the speaker of the poem with its author. In general, these treatises aimed to isolate the text as a "verbal icon" (to use Wimsatt's phrase) whose form was to be found entirely within itself.

As various historians of critical theory have pointed out, the creators of this version of formalism may have had ulterior reasons for purifying the text. Many of the American New Critics were from the South, a depressed region that during and after World War II had been undergoing a social and economic revolution, which had displaced traditional values and culture. As the Marxist Terry Eagleton puts it, the New Criticism "was the ideology of an uprooted, defensive intelligentsia who reinvented in literature what they could not find in reality. Poetry was the new religion, a nostalgic haven from the alienations of industrial capitalism."[6] Poetry was not only viewed as a force opposing the crassness and secularization of modern life, but as the location of the spiritual values these critics held dear. As Cleanth Brooks once confessed, "it is no accident that so many of the [New Critics] have gone on, either to avow an orthodox religious position or else to affirm the possibility and necessity for metaphysics as a science."[7] Brooks's associates at the *Kenyon Review*, including critics like John Crowe Ransom and Allen Tate, felt that "the whole effort of the literary imagination is toward a kind of incarnation of reality in language."[8]

We can see this quasi-religious impulse in the theories of John Crowe Ransom, who sought in poetry something larger than aesthetic form, something that in *The World's Body* (1941) he had called "ontological": a capturing of the *body* of experience. And in criticism he was seeking a way of helping the reader recapture that essence:

---

[5]See Ch. 9 on Authorial Intention.

[6]Terry Eagleton, *Literary Criticism: An Introduction* (Minneapolis: University of Minnesota Press, 1983), p. 47.

[7]"Metaphor and the Function of Criticism," in *Spiritual Problems in Contemporary Literature*, ed. S. R. Hooper (New York: Harper Torchbooks, 1957), p. 134.

[8]Allen Tate, quoted in Michael Millgate, "An Interview with Allen Tate," *Shenandoah* 12 (1961): 31.

The poet perpetuates in his poem an order of existence which in actual life is constantly crumbling beneath his touch. . . . For each poem even, ideally, there is distinguishable a logical object or universal, but at the same time a tissue of irrelevance from which it does not really emerge. The critic has to take the poem apart, or analyze it, for the sake of uncovering these features. With all the finesse possible, it is rude and patchy business. . . . But without it there could hardly be much understanding of the value of poetry, or of the natural history behind any adult poem.

For Ransom, poetry is defined by the interplay between structure and texture. Like prose, poetry has a determinate meaning (or logical structure), but in the case of poetry the determinate meaning is deformed by (among other things) the pressure of versification. The necessity of finding rhymes and rhythmic form results in an admixture of what he calls "indeterminate meaning," which may be a mere dross of verbiage that testifies to the human process of creation or may include wonderful, shockingly brilliant novelties that contribute to poetic texture.

Although there was considerable agreement on the principles of art and on the technique of literary explication that was the critic's "job of work," each New Critic developed a slightly different terminology for discussing the issues. For Cleanth Brooks, the terms equivalent to Ransom's structure and texture would be the "paraphrasable content" of a poem (which he equates with its "rational or logical structure") and its "essential structure." In "The Heresy of Paraphrase" (1947) (another heresy!), Brooks insists that the poem not only cannot be equated with its paraphrasable content, but that the content should not be seen as an inner core wrapped about in an exterior form consisting of metrical language. Harking back to Richards, in *The Well Wrought Urn* (1947) Brooks instead defines the "essential structure" of the poem as being like that of

architecture or painting: it is a pattern of resolved stresses. Or, to move closer still . . . the structure of a poem resembles that of a ballet or musical composition. It is a pattern of resolutions and balances and harmonizations developed through a temporal scheme.

The thematic criticism of the New Critics tended to operate by finding within the texture of the poem oppositions and conflicts that were resolved into a harmonious balance. The principal mediator of this resolution was poetic language, specifically the capacity of language to carry multiple meanings that could disclose hidden conflicts and tensions at the outset of the poem and converge into a harmonious balance at the end. For I. A. Richards's pupil William Empson, the proper term for this polysemic capacity of language was *ambiguity*, of which he distinguished and elaboratedly discussed seven distinct types. The American New Critics preferred to locate individual master tropes (or figures of speech) that would serve as the center for their discourse. For Cleanth Brooks, the master tropes were *paradox* and *irony*, the latter defined not in its strict sense — saying the opposite of what is intended — but very broadly, as occurring whenever a statement is undercut or qualified by its context. Similarly, for Allen Tate the chief issue in poetry was the "*tension* between two opposing forces." Although the criticism of Robert Penn Warren flirted with irony, his usual master trope, like that of R. P. Blackmur, was the literary *symbol*. For Robert B. Heilman, the principal issue was the *image*, and it was through the conflict of opposing clusters of images that eventual resolution was achieved. For Murray Krieger, as for the Russian formalists, the master trope was *metaphor*. These divergences were more apparent than real, for each of these literary figures of speech and of thought was in practice broadened from its usual definition to potentially include all the others as well.

What may seem strange, especially given the contrary example of the Russian formalists, is that despite the New Critical emphasis on poetic language, none of the major theorists had any interest in contemporary discoveries in linguistics and semiotics; in fact they disdained "professionalism" in the study of language. This disdain may have been held over from the amateur's stance that the New Critics cultivated, a stance opposed to the professionalism of historical scholarship, against which the movement had originally defined itself.

As we have noted, the dominance of the New Critical thematic explication was nearly absolute through the 1960s. Even today the critical practice of most American teachers of literature owes a great deal to Cleanth Brooks and William Empson. But as a theory, the New Criticism has few current defenders, and its vitality has suffered more than one might gather by counting its remaining devotees. This withering was perhaps inevitable: In an age of theory like that of the past few decades, a critical mode centered in interpretive practice was an easy target. Nevertheless, while the New Criticism has been supplanted by a variety of other interpretive modes, these modes have been forced to define themselves against a dominant New Critical tradition, and in this negative sense the New Criticism still lives.

Its more important surviving legacy is the cult of the interpretation and reinterpretation of texts that makes up so much of the critic's professional life. John Crowe Ransom had begun by noting that for the poem to capture the world's body, the critic must recapture it for the common reader. The New Criticism redefined the professoriate as the priesthood of twentieth-century humanism making the verbal icon accessible to the laity. The critic's proper job of work was the decoding of a text whose surface meaning, however evident to the average reader, is seen as insufficient. The journals and little magazines accordingly filled with interpretations, but eventually the very success of the New Critical methods bred failure. By the 1960s it had spawned an insistent hunger for reinterpretation of canonical texts (or at least for the books and articles upon which professional academic success depends). And eventually the New Criticism, within its formal strictures of fallacies and heresies, could provide for this demand only by more farfetched decodings. But if New Critical theory has been jettisoned in favor of readings based on Marxist, feminist, or deconstructionist literary theories, the view of literature as a mystery to which the critic alone has the key survives. The profession has not so readily relinquished the verbal icon.

## NEO-ARISTOTELIANISM

Just as the New Criticism arose out of the New South, neo-Aristotelianism grew out of the innovative Hutchins curriculum at the University of Chicago, which replaced the traditional lecture system with a program of the close study of the

"Great Books of the Western Tradition." Moved by the general intellectual ferment of the time and galvanized by the philosophical semantics of Richard McKeon, the historical scholar R. S. Crane came out in 1935 against teaching literature to undergraduates through its purely historical origins and in favor of a new approach using textual explication and aesthetics.[9] As chairman of the English department, Crane was able to hire over the next decade a number of humanists who assisted him in developing a critical theory and practice that has become known as neo-Aristotelianism or Chicago criticism; this group included Elder Olson, Norman Maclean, and W. R. Keast, in addition to McKeon and Crane himself.

Though Crane had placed himself on the side of the New Critics on the issue of history vs. criticism, he and his group were scornful of New Critical theories of literature, which they considered reductive, simplistic, and a serious distortion of the nature of literature and language. As a result, the 1940s and 1950s saw an acrimonious debate in the pages of scholarly journals and little magazines, intemperate on both sides, between Crane's group and such New Critics as Brooks, Wimsatt, Warren, and Heilman. By 1960, when the dust had settled, the New Critics held the field, primarily because their critical methods, propagated in successful textbooks like *Understanding Poetry* (1938), had revolutionized undergraduate and even secondary-school training in literature across America. The textual explications of the Chicago school, in contrast, were confined primarily to scholarly books and learned journals. And the neo-Aristotelian method of analyzing literature was a more complex approach, which did not lend itself to popularization. On the other hand, the New Criticism succeeded at the cost of ideological stagnation, while neo-Aristotelianism developed a second generation of critics (including Wayne C. Booth, Sheldon Sacks, Ralph Rader, Robert Marsh, Norman Friedman, Mary Doyle Springer, and Austin Wright) and a third generation (including Don Bialostosky, Walter Davis, Barbara Foley, Elizabeth Langland, James Phelan, Peter Rabinowitz, and Adena Rosmarin), all of whom have endeavored to revise, extend, and adapt Crane's ideas to new projects.

Aristotle's concept of *mimesis*, or imitation, is not central to Chicago criticism. The crucial Aristotelian concepts are from the *Metaphysics* rather than the *Poetics*; they include the *eidos*, or "shaping form," and the *synolon*, or "concrete whole" of formed matter, found in nature or manufactured by art. The *synolon* is analyzed in terms of its formal, material, efficient, and final causes. Poetic works of art are *synola* in which plot, character, and thought (the formal cause) give shape to language (the material cause) using various techniques or devices of disclosure (the efficient cause) to create an object with the power to affect a reader in various ways (the final cause).

The "concrete whole" is matter shaped by form to be "inherently meaningful and beautiful."[10] The work's power comes from the inferred sense of the whole, not from the parts; in fact our sense of the whole *as a pattern* is what governs the

---

[9]R. S. Crane, "History versus Criticism in the Study of Literature" (1935), reprinted in *The Idea of the Humanities* (Chicago: University of Chicago Press, 1967), vol. 2, pp. 3–24.

[10]Ralph Rader, "Defoe, Richardson, Joyce, and the Concept of Form in Fiction," in this chapter, p. 828.

perceived meaning of the parts. Language, however crucial to our perception of the form, does not define poetic form as it did for the New Critics: it is only a means — and not even the most important one — to an end. Not even plot, which was so crucial for Crane's notions of form, is wholly decisive. Although our sense of the whole takes shape through our experience of the parts, we revise our sense of the parts through our growing sense of the whole to which they contribute. And while the powers of some literary works may require temporary or permanent ambiguities, many merely *potential* ambiguities within a text are cleared up by this shaping process.

R. S. Crane viewed Aristotle primarily as the founder of a positivistic and "differential" method (one opposed to Plato's idealistic and synthesizing method). In tragedy the final cause, the *dynamis*, is the catharsis of pity and fear, and Aristotle judges various Attic tragedies by how well their various elements are designed, the ultimate criterion being their capacity to effect the tragic *dynamis*. Crane wanted to extend the systematic approach of the *Poetics* to other genres with different powers, which different structures of plot, character, thought, language, and technique were designed to serve.

In practice, Crane's genres were based primarily upon the formal and the final causes, and the efficient and material causes were unofficially relegated to relatively subordinate roles. And despite claims of empiricism, his literary classes are those of a proto-structuralist and derive from a large number of structural predicates, many of which Crane outlines in "The Concept of Plot and the Plot of *Tom Jones*" (1952). For example, the protagonist may be of either better, worse or the same moral quality as the reader, and this moral nature may be either static or capable of moving from one to another of these levels; the protagonist's fate may be either fortunate or unfortunate, in greater or less degree, in the short run or the long run; the protagonist may be responsible for this fate, or it may be the result of chance, fate, fortune, providence, or historical necessity; the plot as a whole may turn on a change in the protagonist's circumstances, moral character, or way of thinking; the text as a whole may be an imitation of human action (mimetic) or of an argument (didactic); and so on. The interplay of these predicates would generate hundreds, perhaps thousands of distinct genres.

While other genre critics (like Northrop Frye) felt the need to map literature as a field, for the Chicago critics, genres had a different purpose. They functioned as multiple models to which the critic might look in creating strong hypotheses about the specific texts under analysis, hypotheses leading to predictions that might (like scientific hypotheses) be verified or falsified by the text itself or by features of its creation or reception. The openness and pluralism of the genre system served to make it less likely that the critic would have to distort the text to make it fit a single procrustean model. The aim was a method similar to that of science, where conjectures are tested and refuted, and false leads eliminated, until the best explanation is found. Indeed, the critical aims of the Chicago school included the attainment of power through the successful search for objective truth. They were displaced scientists, unlike most of the New Critics, whose motivations, by their own accounts, were more like those of disappointed priests seeking in literature for a new Word to replace the one the world had lost.

Crane's genres are ideal forms, and his theory succeeded best with masterpieces like *Macbeth* and *Tom Jones*, in which a complex plot and a great variety of characters have been marshalled to the service of a single end. His approach was less effective with mixed forms like *The Vicar of Wakefield* or *Moby-Dick*, or with partial failures like Fielding's *Amelia*, in which the author failed at integrating didactic materials into a mimetic plot, and extraformal intentions were realized at the expense of the reader's emotional affect. The second generation of neo-Aristotelians, especially Wayne Booth and Ralph Rader, were to explore more adequately how architectonic notions of form could be reconciled with the multifarious intentions of authors and with the institutional shapes that culture bequeaths to literature.

Another difference between the first generation of Chicago critics and their successors is in their attitude toward literary autonomy. Despite Crane's attacks on the New Critics, he accepted the autonomy of the literary text:

> What is held constant is the whole complex of accidental causes of variation in poetry that depend on the talents, characters, educations, and intentions of individual authors, the opinions and tastes of the audiences they address, the state of the language in their time, and all the other external factors which affect their choice of materials and conventions in particular works. The provisional exclusion of these is necessary if the analysis is to be concentrated upon the internal causes which account for the peculiar construction and effect of any poem qua artistic whole.[11]

The exclusion of the extrinsic is a tactical gesture more than a statement of the *nature* of literature, but it may nevertheless have seriously distorted Crane's readings of poetry. In particular, the notion of autonomy long blinded the Chicago critics to fundamental differences between many forms of lyric poetry and other literary modes such as drama and fiction. With the author excluded, the lyric "I" had to be viewed as an externalized speaker, the principal character in a tiny agon that could be analyzed according to the same terms Crane had used for prose fiction and theatrical drama. This externalized speaker is seen as either "moved in a certain way by his situation" or "acting in a certain manner in relation to it" or as "deliberating morally in a certain frame of mind." Thus, lyric poems, like plays and novels, have something analogous to a plot, in fact have plots of thought, action, or character.

This sort of analysis works best in poems in which the "I" is indeed a dramatic character, felt as Other to the poet, as in Browning's "My Last Duchess." But as Ralph Rader has pointed out, in the majority of poems in the Western tradition the poet is immanent within the poem; that is, as a condition of reading them, a reader recognizes the speaker's voice as a projection, displaced or immediate, of the poet's. It is not a mere "accidental cause of variation" but integral to the nature of

---

[11]R. S. Crane, Introduction to *Critics and Criticism: Ancient and Modern* (Chicago: University of Chicago Press, 1952), p. 20.

lyric poetry that readers for the last two hundred years have viewed the words of "Elegy in a Country Churchyard" as the expression of one Thomas Gray rather than of a nameless, fully externalized "virtuous, sensitive, and ambitious young man of humble birth," as Crane was forced to see him.[12] And as Rader was to show in "Defoe, Richardson, Joyce, and the Concept of Form in the Novel" (1973; in this chapter), the author may be immanently present within the form of the text in fiction as well as in poetry. From the other side, the rhetorical criticism of Wayne C. Booth was to show that the reader was also immanently present within the form of the text, and how one is as manipulated by the subtle and indirect techniques of modern fiction as by the direct appeals of eighteenth-century narrative.

The most abstract feature of the Chicago critics' contribution to literary theory, and perhaps its least controversial, is their commitment to pluralism. Crane's version of pluralism begins with the premise that criticism is not a field like biochemistry, which slowly advances along a single front according to a common set of factual and methodological assumptions — what the philosopher of science Thomas Kuhn was later to call a paradigm. Criticism is instead "a collection of distinct and more or less incommensurable 'frameworks' or 'languages'" differing widely in "matters of assumed principle, definition and method."[13] Each of these "languages" has its own intrinsic powers and limitations, and certain areas of insight — questions it can pose and answer — while remaining blind to other, equally significant issues. Each separate mode of criticism should therefore be considered an instrument, a tool useful for one or more specific purposes but ill-adapted to a great many others. For all his investment in neo-Aristotelianism, Crane felt that there were questions it could not answer: "It is a method not at all suited, as is criticism in the grand line of Longinus, Coleridge, and Matthew Arnold, to the definition and appreciation of those general qualities of writing — mirroring the souls of writers — for the sake of which most of us read or at any rate to what we have read. It is a method that necessarily abstracts from history. . . . It is a method, above all, that completely fails, because of its essentially differentiating character, to give us insights into the larger moral and political values of literature or into any of the other organic relations with human nature and human experience in which literature is involved."[14]

Crane embraced pluralism as a way of coping with the diversity of critical languages that had begun, even by midcentury, to generate terminological squabbles and to make it difficult for literary scholars to understand one another. Later

[12]The New Critics had also banished authorial intention and spoke of an autonomous speaker within the poem, but for their mode of thematic analysis it made little practical difference whether the thematic focus was ascribed to the author or his creation. Given Crane's emphasis on character and action, the separation of speaker/actor from poet seemed considerably more artificial. In fact, there is no reason within Crane's system to insist upon such a rigid textual autonomy, and the poet/character relation in all its variations can be compassed under the aegis of Aristotle's efficient cause.

[13]R. S. Crane, *The Languages of Criticism and the Structure of Poetry* (Toronto: University of Toronto Press, 1953), p. 13.

[14]Crane, p. 192.

Chicago critics have advanced his commitment to pluralism. In *The Act of Interpretation* (1978), Walter Davis has suggested that critics are obliged to examine the available repertoire for the methodology that does the best justice to the particular text. Wayne C. Booth's *Critical Understanding* (1979) attempted to explore versions of pluralism other than Crane's as a way of leading fellow critics to a deeper understanding of one another's work and to an exchange of ideas in an ongoing, potentially progressive dialogue rather than a debate in Babel.

## Selected Bibliography

Bakhtin, Mikhail. *Rabelais and His World*. Cambridge: MIT Press, 1968.
———. *The Dialogic Imagination: Four Essays*. Austin: University of Texas Press, 1981.
———. *Problems of Dostoevsky's Poetics*. Minneapolis: University of Minnesota Press, 1984.
———. *Speech Genres, and Other Essays*. Austin: University of Texas Press, 1987.
Bann, Stephen, and John E. Bowlt, eds. *Russian Formalism: A Collection of Articles and Texts in Translation*. New York: Barnes and Noble, 1973.
Bennett, Tony. *Formalism and Marxism*. London: Methuen, 1979.
Blackmur, R. P. *Language as Gesture*. New York: Harcourt, Brace and World, 1952.
———. *The Lion and the Honeycomb*. New York: Harcourt, Brace and World, 1955.
———. *New Criticism in the United States*. Tokyo: Kenkyusha, 1959.
Booth, Wayne C. *The Rhetoric of Fiction*. Chicago: University of Chicago Press, 1961; 2nd edition, 1983.
———. *A Rhetoric of Irony*. Chicago: University of Chicago Press, 1974.
———. *Critical Understanding: The Powers and Limits of Pluralism*. Chicago: University of Chicago Press, 1979.
Brooks, Cleanth, and Robert Penn Warren. *Understanding Poetry*. New York: Henry Holt, 1938.
———. *Modern Poetry and the Tradition*. Chapel Hill: University of North Carolina Press, 1939.
———. *The Well Wrought Urn: Studies in the Structure of Poetry*. New York: Reynal and Hitchcock, 1947.
Clark, Katerina, and Michael Holquist. *Mikhail Bakhtin*. Cambridge: Belknap Press of Harvard University Press, 1984.
Crane, Ronald Salmon. *Critics and Criticism: Ancient and Modern*. Chicago: University of Chicago Press, 1952.
———. *The Languages of Criticism and the Structure of Poetry*. Toronto: University of Toronto Press, 1953.
———. *The Idea of the Humanities, and Other Essays*. 2 vols. Chicago: University of Chicago Press, 1967.
Davis, Walter A. *The Act of Interpretation: A Critique of Literary Reason*. Chicago: University of Chicago Press, 1978.
Eikhenbaum, Boris Mikhailovich. *O. Henry and the Theory of the Short Story*. Ann Arbor: Dept. of Slavic Languages and Literatures of the University of Michigan, 1968.
———. *Lermontov: A Study in Literary-Historical Evaluation*. Ann Arbor: Ardis, 1981.
Eliot, Thomas Stearns. *The Sacred Wood: Essays on Poetry and Criticism*. London: Methuen, 1920.
———. *For Lancelot Andrewes*. London: Faber and Gwyer, 1928.

————. *The Use of Poetry and the Use of Criticism*. London: Faber and Faber, 1933.

Empson, William. *Seven Types of Ambiguity*. London: Chatto & Windus, 1930.

Erlich, Victor. *Russian Formalism: History — Doctrine*. The Hague: Mouton, 1955.

Foley, Barbara. *Telling the Truth: The Theory and Practice of Documentary Fiction*. Ithaca: Cornell University Press, 1986.

Friedman, Norman. *Form and Meaning in Fiction*. Athens: University of Georgia Press, 1975.

Jakobson, Roman. *Selected Writings*. 7 vols. The Hague: Mouton, 1962–.

————. *The Framework of Language*. Ann Arbor: Graduate School of the University of Michigan. 1980.

Krieger, Murray. *The New Apologists for Poetry*. Minneapolis: University of Minnesota Press, 1956.

Langland, Elizabeth. *Society in the Novel*. Chapel Hill: University of North Carolina Press, 1984.

Lemon, Lee T., and Marion J. Reis, eds. *Russian Formalist Criticism: Four Essays*. Lincoln: University of Nebraska Press, 1965.

Matejka, Ladislav, and Krystyna Pomorska, eds. *Readings in Russian Poetics*. Cambridge: MIT Press, 1971.

Medvedev, P. N. *The Formal Method in Literary Scholarship*. Baltimore, 1978.

Morson, Gary Saul. *Bakhtin: Essays and Dialogues on His Work*. Chicago: University of Chicago Press, 1986.

Olson, Elder. *The Poetry of Dylan Thomas*. Chicago: University of Chicago Press, 1954.

————. *Tragedy and the Theory of Drama*. Chicago: University of Chicago Press, 1962.

————. *The Theory of Comedy*. Bloomington: Indiana University Press, 1975.

————. *On Value Judgments in the Arts*. Chicago: University of Chicago Press, 1976.

Phelan, James. *Worlds from Words: A Theory of Language in Fiction*. Chicago: University of Chicago Press, 1981.

Propp, Vladimir. *Theory and History of Folklore*. Minneapolis: University of Minnesota Press, 1984.

Rader, Ralph. "Defoe, Richardson, Joyce, and the Concept of Form in the Novel." In *Autobiography, Biography and the Novel*. Los Angeles: William Andrews Clark Memorial Library, 1973.

————. "Fact, Theory and Literary Explanation." *Critical Inquiry* 1 (1974): 245–72.

————. "The Concept of Genre and Eighteenth-Century Studies." In *New Approaches to Eighteenth Century Literature: Selected Papers from the English Institute*; ed. Philip Harth. New York: Columbia University Press, 1974.

————. "The Dramatic Monologue and Related Lyric Forms." *Critical Inquiry* 3 (1976); 131–51.

————. "The Literary-Theoretical Contribution of Sheldon Sacks." *Critical Inquiry* 6 (1979); 183–92.

Ransom, John Crowe. *The World's Body*. New York: Scribner's, 1938.

————. *The New Criticism*. Norfolk, Conn.: New Directions, 1941.

————. *Poems and Essays*. New York: Vintage, 1955.

Richter, David H. *Fable's End: Completeness and Closure in Rhetorical Fiction*. Chicago: University of Chicago Press, 1974.

————. "The Second Flight of the Phoenix: Neo-Aristotelianism Since Crane." *The Eighteenth Century: Theory and Interpretation* 23 (1982): 27–48.

Rosmarin, Adena. *The Power of Genre*. Minneapolis: University of Minnesota Press, 1985.

Sacks, Sheldon. *Fiction and the Shape of Belief*. Berkeley: University of California Press, 1964.

———. "Golden Birds and Dying Generations." *Comparative Literature Studies* 6 (1969): 274–91.

———. "*Clarissa* and the Tragic Traditions." In *Studies in Eighteenth-Century Culture*, ed. Harold E. Pagliaro, 195–221. Cleveland: Case Western Reserve University Press, 1972.

Shklovsky, Victor Borisovich. *Works*. Moscow: Khudozh' Lit'ra, 1973–4.

Springer, Mary Doyle. *Forms of the Modern Novella*. Chicago: University of Chicago Press, 1976.

Steiner, Peter. *Russian Formalism: A Meta-Poetics*. Ithaca: Cornell University Press, 1984.

Tate, Allen. *Reactionary Essays on Poetry and Ideas*. New York: Scribner's, 1936.

———. *Reason in Madness: Critical Essays*. New York: G. P. Putnam, 1941.

Thompson, Ewa Majewska. *Russian Formalism and Anglo-American New Criticism: A Comparative Study*. Hawthorne, N.Y.: Mouton, 1971.

Tynyanov, Yuri. *The Problem of Verse Language*. Ann Arbor: Ardis, 1981.

Todorov, Tzvetan. *Mikhail Bakhtin: The Dialogical Principle*. Minneapolis: University of Minnesota Press, 1985.

Vygotsky, L. S. *Mind in Society: The Development of Higher Psychological Processes*. Cambridge: Harvard University Press, 1978.

Warren, Austin. *Rage for Order: Essays in Criticism*. Ann Arbor: University of Michigan Press, 1948.

Wellek, René, and Austin Warren. *Theory of Literature*. New York: Harcourt, Brace and World, 1949.

———. *A History of Modern Criticism 1759–1950*. 6 vols. New Haven: Yale University Press, 1955–87.

———. *Concepts of Criticism*. New Haven: Yale University Press, 1963.

Wimsatt, William K. *The Verbal Icon: Studies in the Meaning of Poetry*. Lexington: University Press of Kentucky, 1954.

———. *Hateful Contraries: Studies in Literature and Criticism*. Lexington: University Press of Kentucky, 1965.

———, and Cleanth Brooks. *Literary Criticism: A Short History*. New York: Alfred A. Knopf, 1957.

# Victor Shklovsky

## 1893–1984

*The versatile Russian man of letters Victor Shklovsky was born the son of a teacher in Petersburg and studied at the university there. An outspoken founding member of the Russian literary society OPOYAZ, Shklovsky wrote one of the central theoretical statements of the formalist school ("Art as Technique," 1917) and his ideas were singled out for special denunciation by Leon Trotsky. Problems with the Bolsheviks prompted his emigration in 1921, but he returned two years later. Within a few years, after the publication of* The Theory of Prose *(1925) he backed away from the politically risky business of theorizing and took up other pursuits, particularly film criticism, screenwriting, and historical fiction. He wrote books on Tolstoy (1928), Mayakovsky (1940), and Dostoevsky (1957), and is also remembered for his autobiographical account of the revolutionary years, A Sentimental Journal: Memoirs 1917–1922 (1923). Ultimately, Shklovsky came to be considered an honored member of the Soviet literary establishment.*

# Art as Technique

"Art is thinking in images." This maxim, which even high school students parrot, is nevertheless the starting point for the erudite philologist who is beginning to put together some kind of systematic literary theory. The idea, originated in part by Potebnya, has spread. "Without imagery there is no art, and in particular no poetry," Potebnya writes.[1] And elsewhere, "Poetry, as well as prose, is first and foremost a special way of thinking and knowing."[2]

Poetry is a special way of thinking; it is, precisely, a way of thinking in images, a way which permits what is generally called "economy of mental effort," a way which makes for "a sensation of the relative ease of the process." Aesthetic feeling is the reaction to this economy. This is how the academician Ovsyaniko-Kulikovsky,[3] who undoubtedly read the works of Potebnya attentively, almost certainly understood and faithfully summarized the ideas of his teacher. Potebnya and his numerous disciples consider poetry a special kind of thinking — thinking by means of images; they feel that the purpose of imagery is to help channel various objects and activities into groups and to clarify the unknown by means of the known. Or, as Potebnya wrote:

The relationship of the image to what is being

clarified is that: (a) the image is the fixed predicate of that which undergoes change — the unchanging means of attracting what is perceived as changeable. . . . (b) the image is far clearer and simpler than what it clarifies.[4]

In other words:

Since the purpose of imagery is to remind us, by approximation, of those meanings for which the image stands, and since, apart from this, imagery is unnecessary for thought, we must be more familiar with the image than with what it clarifies.[5]

It would be instructive to try to apply this principle to Tyutchev's comparison of summer lightning to deaf and dumb demons or to Gogol's comparison of the sky to the garment of God.[6]

"Without imagery there is no art" — "Art is thinking in images." These maxims have led to far-fetched interpretations of individual works of art. Attempts have been made to evaluate even music, architecture, and lyric poetry as imagistic thought. After a quarter of a century of such attempts Ovsyaniko-Kulikovsky finally had to assign lyric poetry, architecture, and music to a special category of imageless art and to define them as lyric arts appealing directly to the emotions. And thus he admitted an enormous area of art which is not a mode of thought. A part of this area, lyric poetry (narrowly considered), is

---

Translated by Lee T. Lemon and Marion Reis.

[1] Alexander Potebnya, *Iz zapisok po teorii slovesnosti* [*Notes on the Theory of Language*] (Kharkov, 1905), p. 83. [Au.]

[2] *Ibid.*, p. 97. [Au.]

[3] Dmitry Ovsyaniko-Kulikovsky (1835–1920), a leading Russian scholar, was an early contributor to Marxist periodicals and a literary conservative, antagonistic towards the deliberately meaningless poems of the Futurists. [Tr.]

[4] Potebnya, *Iz zapisok po teorii slovesnosti*, p. 314. [Au.]

[5] *Ibid.*, p. 291. [Au.]

[6] Fyodor Tyutchev (1803–1873), a poet, and Nicholas Gogol (1809–1852), a master of prose fiction and satire, are mentioned here because their bold use of imagery cannot be accounted for by Potebnya's theory. Shklovsky is arguing that writers frequently gain their effects by comparing the commonplace to the exceptional rather than vice versa. [Tr.]

quite like the visual arts; it is also verbal. But, much more important, visual art passes quite imperceptibly into nonvisual art; yet our perceptions of both are similar.

Nevertheless, the definition "Art is thinking in images," which means (I omit the usual middle terms of the argument) that art is the making of symbols, has survived the downfall of the theory which supported it. It survives chiefly in the wake of Symbolism, especially among the theorists of the Symbolist movement.

Many still believe, then, that thinking in images — thinking, in specific scenes of "roads and landscape" and "furrows and boundaries"[7] — is the chief characteristic of poetry. Consequently, they should have expected the history of "imagistic art," as they call it, to consist of a history of changes in imagery. But we find that images change little; from century to century, from nation to nation, from poet to poet, they flow on without changing. Images belong to no one: they are "the Lord's." The more you understand an age, the more convinced you become that the images a given poet used and which you thought his own were taken almost unchanged from another poet. The works of poets are classified or grouped according to the new techniques that poets discover and share, and according to their arrangement and development of the resources of language; poets are much more concerned with arranging images than with creating them. Images are given to poets; the ability to remember them is far more important than the ability to create them.

Imagistic thought does not, in any case, include all the aspects of art nor even all the aspects of verbal art. A change in imagery is not essential to the development of poetry. We know that frequently an expression is thought to be poetic, to be created for aesthetic pleasure, although actually it was created without such intent — e.g., Annensky's opinion that the Slavic languages are especially poetic and Andrey Bely's ecstasy over the technique of placing adjectives after nouns, a technique used by eighteenth-century Russian

poets. Bely joyfully accepts the technique as something artistic, or more exactly, as intended, if we consider intention as art. Actually, this reversal of the usual adjective-noun order is a peculiarity of the language (which had been influenced by Church Slavonic). Thus a work may be (1) intended as prosaic and accepted as poetic, or (2) intended as poetic and accepted as prosaic. This suggests that the artistry attributed to a given work results from the way we perceive it. By "works of art," in the narrow sense, we mean works created by special techniques designed to make the works as obviously artistic as possible.

Potebnya's conclusion, which can be formulated "poetry equals imagery," gave rise to the whole theory that "imagery equals symbolism," that the image may serve as the invariable predicate of various subjects. (This conclusion, because it expressed ideas similar to the theories of the Symbolists, intrigued some of their leading representatives — Andrey Bely, Merezhkovsky and his "eternal companions" and, in fact, formed the basis of the theory of Symbolism.) The conclusion stems partly from the fact that Potebnya did not distinguish between the language of poetry and the language of prose. Consequently, he ignored the fact that there are two aspects of imagery: imagery as a practical means of thinking, as a means of placing objects within categories; and imagery as poetic, as a means of reinforcing an impression. I shall clarify with an example. I want to attract the attention of a young child who is eating bread and butter and getting the butter on her fingers. I call, "Hey, butterfingers!" This is a figure of speech, a clearly prosaic trope. Now a different example. The child is playing with my glasses and drops them. I call, "Hey, butterfingers!"[8] This figure of speech is a poetic trope. (In the first example, "butterfingers" is metonymic; in the second, metaphoric — but this is not what I want to stress.)

Poetic imagery is a means of creating the strongest possible impression. As a method it is, depending upon its purpose, neither more nor less effective than other poetic techniques; it is neither more nor less effective than ordinary or

[7]This is an allusion to Vyacheslav Ivanov's *Borozdy i mezhi* [*Furrows and Boundaries*] (Moscow, 1916), a major statement of Symbolist theory. [Tr.]

[8]The Russian text involves a play on the word for "hat," colloquial for "clod," "duffer," etc. [Tr.]

negative parallelism, comparison, repetition, balanced structure, hyperbole, the commonly accepted rhetorical figures, and all those methods which emphasize the emotional effect of an expression (including words or even articulated sounds.)[9] But poetic imagery only externally resembles either the stock imagery of fables and ballads or thinking in images — e.g., the example in Ovsyaniko-Kulikovsky's *Language and Art* in which a little girl calls a ball a little watermelon. Poetic imagery is but one of the devices of poetic language. Prose imagery is a means of abstraction: a little watermelon instead of a lampshade, or a little watermelon instead of a head, is only the abstraction of one of the object's characteristics, that of roundness. It is no different from saying that the head and the melon are both round. This is what is meant, but it has nothing to do with poetry.

The law of the economy of creative effort is also generally accepted. [Herbert] Spencer wrote:

> On seeking for some clue to the law underlying these current maxims, we may see shadowed forth in many of them, the importance of economizing the reader's or the hearer's attention. To so present ideas that they may be apprehended with the least possible mental effort, is the desideratum towards which most of the rules above quoted point. . . . Hence, carrying out the metaphor that language is the vehicle of thought, there seems reason to think that in all cases the friction and inertia of the vehicle deduct from its efficiency; and that in composition, the chief, if not the sole thing to be done, is to reduce this friction and inertia to the smallest possible amount.[10]

And R[ichard] Avenarius:

> If a soul possess inexhaustible strength, then, of course, it would be indifferent to how much might

be spent from this inexhaustible source; only the necessarily expended time would be important. But since its forces are limited, one is led to expect that the soul hastens to carry out the apperceptive process as expediently as possible — that is, with comparatively the least expenditure of energy, and, hence, with comparatively the best result.

Petrazhitsky, with only one reference to the general law of mental effort, rejects [William] James's theory of the physical basis of emotion, a theory which contradicts his own. Even Alexander Veselovsky acknowledged the principle of the economy of creative effort, a theory especially appealing in the study of rhythm, and agreed with Spencer: "A satisfactory style is precisely that style which delivers the greatest amount of thought in the fewest words." And Andrey Bely, despite the fact that in his better pages he gave numerous examples of "roughened" rhythm[11] and (particularly in the examples from Baratynsky) showed the difficulties inherent in poetic epithets, also thought it necessary to speak of the law of the economy of creative effort in his book[12] — a heroic effort to create a theory of art based on unverified facts from antiquated sources, on his vast knowledge of the techniques of poetic creativity, and on Krayevich's high school physics text.

These ideas about the economy of energy, as well as about the law and aim of creativity, are perhaps true in their application to "practical" language; they were, however, extended to poetic language. Hence they do not distinguish properly between the laws of practical language and the laws of poetic language. The fact that Japanese poetry has sounds not found in conversational Japanese was hardly the first factual indication of the differences between poetic and everyday language. Leo Jakubinsky has observed that the law of the dissimilation of liquid sounds does not apply to poetic language.[13] This suggested to him

---

[9]Shklovsky is here doing two things of major theoretical importance: (1) he argues that different techniques serve a single function, and that (2) no single technique is all-important. The second permits the formalists to be concerned with any and all literary devices; the first permits them to discuss the devices from a single consistent theoretical position. [Tr.]

[10]Herbert Spencer, *The Philosophy of Style* (Humboldt Library, vol. 34 New York, 1882), pp. 2–3. [Au.] Shklovsky's quoted reference, in Russian, preserves the idea of the original but shortens it. [Tr.]

[11]The Russian *zatrudyonny* means "made difficult." The suggestion is that poems with "easy" or smooth rhythms slip by unnoticed; poems that are difficult or "roughened" force the reader to attend to them. [Tr.]

[12]*Simvolizm*, probably. [Tr.]

[13]Leo Jakubinsky, "O zvukakh poeticheskovo yazyka" ["On the Sounds of Poetic Language"], *Sborniki* I (1916): 38. [Au.]

that poetic language tolerated the admission of hard-to-pronounce conglomerations of similar sounds. In his article, one of the first examples of scientific criticism, he indicates inductively, the contrast (I shall say more about this point later) between the laws of poetic language and the laws of practical language.[14]

We must, then, speak about the laws of expenditure and economy in poetic language not on the basis of an analogy with prose, but on the basis of the laws of poetic language.

If we start to examine the general laws of perception, we see that as perception becomes habitual, it becomes automatic. Thus, for example, all of our habits retreat into the area of the unconsciously automatic; if one remembers the sensations of holding a pen or of speaking in a foreign language for the first time and compares that with his feeling at performing the action for the ten thousandth time, he will agree with us. Such habituation explains the principles by which, in ordinary speech, we leave phrases unfinished and words half expressed. In this process, ideally realized in algebra, things are replaced by symbols. Complete words are not expressed in rapid speech; their initial sounds are barely perceived. Alexander Pogodin offers the example of a boy considering the sentence "The Swiss mountains are beautiful" in the form of a series of letters: *T, S, m, a, b.*[15]

This characteristic of thought not only suggests the method of algebra, but even prompts the choice of symbols (letters, especially initial letters). By this "algebraic" method of thought we apprehend objects only as shapes with imprecise extensions; we do not see them in their entirety but rather recognize them by their main characteristics. We see the object as though it were enveloped in a sack. We know what it is by its configuration, but we see only its silhouette. The object, perceived thus in the manner of prose perception, fades and does not leave even a first impression; ultimately even the essence of what it was is forgotten. Such perception explains why we fail to hear the prose word in its entirety (see Leo Jakubinsky's article[16]) and, hence, why (along with other slips of the tongue) we fail to pronounce it. The process of "algebrization," the over-automatization of an object, permits the greatest economy of perceptive effort. Either objects are assigned only one proper feature — a number, for example — or else they function as though by formula and do not even appear in cognition:

> I was cleaning a room and, meandering about, approached the divan and couldn't remember whether or not I had dusted it. Since these movements are habitual and unconscious, I could not remember and felt that it was impossible to remember — so that if I had dusted it and forgot — that is, had acted unconsciously, then it was the same as if I had not. If some conscious person had been watching, then the fact could be established. If, however, no one was looking, or looking on unconsciously, if the whole complex lives of many people go on unconsciously, then such lives are as if they had never been.[17]

And so life is reckoned as nothing. Habitualization devours works, clothes, furniture, one's wife, and the fear of war. "If the whole complex lives of many people go on unconsciously, then such lives are as if they had never been." And art exists that one may recover the sensation of life; it exists to make one feel things, to make the stone *stony*. The purpose of art is to impart the sensation of things as they are perceived and not as they are known. The technique of art is to make objects "unfamiliar," to make forms difficult, to increase the difficulty and length of perception because the process of perception is an aesthetic end in itself and must be prolonged. *Art is a way of experiencing the artfulness of an object; the object is not important.*

The range of poetic (artistic) work extends from the sensory to the cognitive, from poetry

---

[14]Leo Jakubinsky, "Skopleniye odinakovykh plavnykh v prakticheskom i poeticheskom yazykakh" ["The Accumulation of Identical Liquids in Practical and Poetic Language"], *Sborniki* II (1917): 13–21. [Au.]

[15]Alexander Pogodin, *Yazyk, kak tvorchestvo* [*Language as Art*] (Kharkov, 1913), p. 42. [Au.] The original sentence was in French, *"Les montaignes de la Suisse sont belles,"* with the appropriate initials. [Tr.]

[16]Jakubinsky, *Sborniki* I (1916). [Au.]

[17]Leo Tolstoy's *Diary*, entry dated February 29, 1897. [Au.] The date is transcribed incorrectly; it should read March 1, 1897. [Tr.]

to prose, from the concrete to the abstract: from Cervantes's Don Quixote — scholastic and poor nobleman, half consciously bearing his humiliation in the court of the duke — to the broad but empty Don Quixote of Turgenev; from Charlemagne to the name "king" [in Russian "Charles" and "king" obviously derive from the same root, korol]. The meaning of a work broadens to the extent that artfulness and artistry diminish; thus a fable symbolizes more than a poem, and a proverb more than a fable. Consequently, the least self-contradictory part of Potebnya's theory is his treatment of the fable, which, from his point of view, he investigated thoroughly. But since his theory did not provide for "expressive" works of art, he could not finish his book. As we know, Notes on the Theory of Literature was published in 1905, thirteen years after Potebnya's death. Potebnya himself completed only the section on the fable.[18]

After we see an object several times, we begin to recognize it. The object is in front of us and we know about it, but we do not see it[19] — hence we cannot say anything significant about it. Art removes objects from the automatism of perception in several ways. Here I want to illustrate a way used repeatedly by Leo Tolstoy, that writer who, for Merezhkovsky at least, seems to present things as if he himself saw them, saw them in their entirety, and did not alter them.

Tolstoy makes the familiar seem strange by not naming the familiar object. He describes an object as if he were seeing it for the first time, an event as if it were happening for the first time. In describing something he avoids the accepted names of its parts and instead names corresponding parts of other objects. For example, in "Shame" Tolstoy "defamiliarizes" the idea of flogging in this way: "to strip people who have broken the law, to hurl them to the floor, and to rap on their bottoms with switches," and, after a few lines, "to lash about on the naked buttocks." Then he remarks:

Just why precisely this stupid, savage means of causing pain and not any other — why not prick the shoulders or any part of the body with needles, squeeze the hands or the feet in a vise, or anything like that?

I apologize for this harsh example, but it is typical of Tolstoy's way of pricking the conscience. The familiar act of flogging is made unfamiliar both by the description and by the proposal to change its form without changing its nature. Tolstoy uses this technique of "defamiliarization" constantly. The narrator of "Kholstomer," for example, is a horse, and it is the horse's point of view (rather than a person's) that makes the content of the story seem unfamiliar. Here is how the horse regards the institution of private property:

I understood well what they said about whipping and Christianity. But then I was absolutely in the dark. What's the meaning of "his own," "his colt"? From these phrases I saw that people thought there was some sort of connection between me and the stable. At the time I simply could not understand the connection. Only much later, when they separated me from the other horses, did I begin to understand. But even then I simply could not see what it meant when they called me "man's property." The words "my horse" referred to me, a living horse, and seemed as strange to me as the words "my land," "my air," "my water."

But the words made a strong impression on me. I thought about them constantly, and only after the most diverse experiences with people did I understand, finally, what they meant. They meant this: In life people are guided by words, not by deeds. It's not so much that they love the possibility of doing or not doing something as it is the possibility of speaking with words, agreed on among themselves, about various topics. Such are the words "my" and "mine," which they apply to different things, creatures, objects, and even to land, people, and horses. They agree that only one may say "mine" about this, that, or the other thing. And the one who says "mine" about the greatest number of things is, according to the game which they've agreed to among themselves, the one they consider the most happy. I don't know the point of all this, but it's true. For a long time I tried to explain it to myself in terms of some kind of real gain, but I had to reject that explanation because it was wrong.

Many of those, for instance, who called me their

[18]Alexander Potebnya, Iz lektsy po teorii slovesnosti [Lectures on the Theory of Language] (Kharkov, 1914). [Au.]

[19]Victor Shklovsky, Voskresheniye slova [The Resurrection of the Word] (Petersburg, 1914). [Au.]

own never rode on me — although others did. And so with those who fed me. Then again, the coachman, the veterinarians, and the outsiders in general treated me kindly, yet those who called me their own did not. In due time, having widened the scope of my observations, I satisfied myself that the notion "my," not only in relation to us horses, has no other basis that a narrow human instinct which is called a sense of or right to private property. A man says "this house is mine" and never lives in it; he only worries about its construction and upkeep. A merchant says "my shop," "my dry goods shop," for instance, and does not even wear clothes made from the better cloth he keeps in his own shop.

There are people who call a tract of land their own, but they never set eyes on it and never take a stroll on it. There are people who call others their own, yet never see them. And the whole relationship between them is that the so-called "owners" treat the others unjustly.

There are people who call women their own, or their "wives," but their women live with other men. And people strive not for the good in life, but for goods they can call their own.

I am now convinced that this is the essential difference between people and ourselves. And therefore, not even considering the other ways in which we are superior, but considering just this one virtue, we can bravely claim to stand higher than men on the ladder of living creatures. The actions of men, at least those with whom I have had dealings, are guided by *words* — ours, by deeds.

The horse is killed before the end of the story, but the manner of the narrative, its technique, does not change:

Much later they put Serpukhovsky's body, which had experienced the world, which had eaten and drunk, into the ground. They could profitably send neither his hide, nor his flesh, nor his bones anywhere.

But since his dead body, which had gone about in the world for twenty years, was a great burden to everyone, its burial was only a superfluous embarrassment for the people. For a long time no one had needed him; for a long time he had been a burden on all. But nevertheless, the dead who buried the dead found it necessary to dress this bloated body, which immediately began to rot, in a good uniform and good boots; to lay it in a good new coffin with new tassels at the four corners, then to place this new coffin in another of lead and ship it to Moscow; there to exhume ancient bones and at just that spot, to hide this putrefying body, swarming with maggots, in its new uniform and clean boots, and to cover it over completely with dirt.

Thus we see that at the end of the story Tolstoy continues to use the technique even though the motivation for it [the reason for its use] is gone.

In *War and Peace* Tolstoy uses the same technique in describing whole battles as if battles were something new. These descriptions are too long to quote; it would be necessary to extract a considerable part of the four-volume novel. But Tolstoy uses the same method in describing the drawing room and the theater:

The middle of the stage consisted of flat boards; by the sides stood painted pictures representing trees, and at the back a linen cloth was stretched down to the floor boards. Maidens in red bodices and white skirts sat on the middle of the stage. One, very fat, in a white silk dress, sat apart on a narrow bench to which a green pasteboard box was glued from behind. They were all singing something. When they had finished, the maiden in white approached the prompter's box. A man in silk with tight-fitting pants on his fat legs approached her with a plume and began to sing and spread his arms in dismay. The man in the tight pants finished his song alone; then the girl sang. After that both remained silent as the music resounded; and the man, obviously waiting to begin singing his part with her again, began to run his fingers over the hand of the girl in the white dress. They finished their song together, and everyone in the theater began to clap and shout. But the men and women on stage, who represented lovers, start to bow, smiling and raising their hands.

In the second act there were pictures representing monuments and openings in the linen cloth representing the moonlight, and they raised lamp shades on a frame. As the musicians started to play the bass horn and counter-bass, a large number of people in black mantles poured onto the stage from right and left. The people, with something like daggers in their hands, started to wave their arms. Then still more people came running out and began to drag away the maiden who had been wearing a white dress but who now wore one of sky blue. They did not drag her off immediately, but sang with her for a long time before dragging her away. Three times they struck on something metallic behind the side scenes, and everyone got down on his knees and began to chant a prayer. Several times all of this activity was interrupted by enthusiastic shouts from the spectators.

The third act is described:

> . . . But suddenly a storm blew up. Chromatic scales and chords of diminished sevenths were heard in the orchestra. Everyone ran about and again they dragged one of the bystanders behind the scenes as the curtain fell.

In the fourth act, "There was some sort of devil who sang, waving his hands, until the boards were moved out from under him and he dropped down."[20]

In *Resurrection* Tolstoy describes the city and the court in the same way; he uses a similar technique in "Kreutzer Sonata" when he describes marriage — "Why, if people have an affinity of souls, must they sleep together?" But he did not defamiliarize only those things he sneered at:

> Pierre stood up from his new comrades and made his way between the campfires to the other side of the road where, it seemed, the captive soldiers were held. He wanted to talk with them. The French sentry stopped him on the road and ordered him to return. Pierre did so, but not to the campfire, not to his comrades, but to an abandoned, unharnessed carriage. On the ground, near the wheel of the carriage, he sat cross-legged in the Turkish fashion, and lowered his head. He sat motionless for a long time, thinking. More than an hour passed. No one disturbed him. Suddenly he burst out laughing with his robust, good natured laugh — so loudly that the men near him looked around, surprised at his conspicuously strange laughter.
>
> "Ha, ha, ha," laughed Pierre. And he began to talk to himself. "The soldier didn't allow me to pass. They caught me, barred me. Me — me — my immortal soul. Ha, ha, ha," he laughed with tears starting in his eyes.
>
> Pierre glanced at the sky, into the depths of the departing, playing stars. "And all this is mine, all this is in me, and all this is I," thought Pierre. "And all this they caught and put in a planked

enclosure." He smiled and went off to his comrades to lie down to sleep.[21]

Anyone who knows Tolstoy can find several hundred such passages in his work. His method of seeing things out of their normal context is also apparent in his last works. Tolstoy described the dogmas and rituals he attacked as if they were unfamiliar, substituting everyday meanings for the customarily religious meanings of the words common in church ritual. Many persons were painfully wounded; they considered it blasphemy to present as strange and monstrous what they accepted as sacred. Their reaction was due chiefly to the technique through which Tolstoy perceived and reported his environment. And after turning to what he had long avoided, Tolstoy found that his perceptions had unsettled his faith.

The technique of defamiliarization is not Tolstoy's alone. I cited Tolstoy because his work is generally known.

Now, having explained the nature of this technique, let us try to determine the approximate limits of its application. I personally feel that defamiliarization is found almost everywhere form is found. In other words, the difference between Potebnya's point of view and ours is this: An image is not a permanent referent for those mutable complexities of life which are revealed through it; its purpose is not to make us perceive meaning, but to create a special perception of the object — *it creates a "vision" of the object instead of serving as a means for knowing it.*

The purpose of imagery in erotic art can be studied even more accurately; an erotic object is usually presented as if it were seen for the first time. Gogol, in "Christmas Eve," provides the following example:

> Here he approached her more closely, coughed, smiled at her, touched her plump, bare arm with his fingers, and expressed himself in a way that showed both his cunning and his conceit.
>
> "And what is this you have, magnificent So-

---

[20]The Tolstoy and Gogol translations are ours. The passage occurs in Vol. II, Part 8, Chap. 9 of the edition of *War and Peace* published in Boston by the Dana Estes Co. in 1904–1912. [Tr.]

[21]Leo Tolstoy, *War and Peace*, IV, Part 13. Chap. 14. [Tr.]

lokha?" and having said this, he jumped back a little.

"What? An arm, Osip Nikiforovich!" she answered.

"Hmm, an arm! *He, he, he!*" said the secretary cordially, satisfied with his beginning. He wandered about the room.

"And what is this you have, dearest Solokha?" he said in the same way, having approached her again and grasped her lightly by the neck, and in the very same way he jumped back.

"As if you don't see, Osip Nikiforovich!" answered Solokha, "a neck, and on my neck a necklace."

"Hmm! On the neck a necklace! *He, he, he!*" and the secretary again wandered about the room, rubbing his hands.

"And what is this you have, incomparable Solokha?" . . . It is not known to what the secretary would stretch his longer fingers now.

And Knut Hamsun has the following in *Hunger*: "Two white prodigies appeared from beneath her blouse."

Erotic subjects may also be presented figuratively with the obvious purpose of leading us away from their "recognition." Hence sexual organs are referred to in terms of lock and key,[22] or quilting tools,[23] or bow and arrow, or rings and marlinspikes, as in the legend of Stavyor, in which a married man does not recognize his wife, who is disguised as a warrior. She proposes a riddle:

"Remember, Stavyor, do you recall
How we little ones walked to and fro in the street?
You and I together sometimes played with a mar-
    linspike —
You had a silver marlinspike,
But I had a gilded ring?
I found myself at it just now and then,
But you fell in with it ever and always."
Says Stavyor, son of Godinovich,
"What! I didn't play with you at marlinspikes!"
Then Vasilisa Mikulichna: "So he says.
Do you remember, Stavyor, do you recall,
Now must you know, you and I together learned
    to read and write;

Mine was an ink-well of silver,
And yours a pen of gold?
But I just moistened it a little now and then,
And I just moistened it ever and always."[24]

In a different version of the legend we find a key to the riddle:

Here the formidable envoy Vasilyushka
Raised her skirts to the very navel,
And then the young Stavyor, son of Godinovich,
Recognized her gilded ring. . . .[25]

But defamiliarization is not only a technique of the erotic riddle — a technique of euphemism — it is also the basis and point of all riddles. Every riddle pretends to show its subject either by words which specify or describe it but which, during the telling, do not seem applicable (the type: "black and white and 'red' — read — all over") or by means of odd but imitative sounds ("'Twas brillig, and the slithy toves / Did gyre and gimble in the wabe").[26]

Even erotic images not intended as riddles are defamiliarized ("boobies," "tarts," "piece," etc.). In popular imagery there is generally something equivalent to "trampling the grass" and "breaking the guelder-rose." The technique of defamiliarization is absolutely clear in the widespread image — a motif of erotic affectation — in which a bear and other wild beasts (or a devil, with a different reason for nonrecognition) do not recognize a man.[27]

[22][Dimitry] Savodnikov, *Zagadki russkovo naroda* [*Riddles of the Russian People*] (St. Petersburg, 1901), Nos. 102–107. [Au.]

[23]*Ibid.*, Nos. 588–591. [Au.]

[24]A. E. Gruzinsky, ed., *Pesni, sobrannye P[avel] N. Rybnikovym* [*Songs Collected by P. N. Rybnikov*] (Moscow, 1909–1910), No. 30. [Au.]

[25]*Ibid.*, No. 171.

[26]We have supplied familiar English examples in place of Shklovsky's word-play. Shklovsky is saying that we create words with no referents or with ambiguous referents in order to force attention to the objects represented by the similar-sounding words. By making the reader go through the extra step of interpreting the nonsense word, the writer prevents an automatic response. A toad is a toad, but "tove" forces one to pause and think about the beast. [Tr.]

[27]E. R. Romanov, "Besstrashny barin" *Velikorusskiye skazki* (Zapiski Imperskovo Russkovo Geograficheskovo Obschestva, XLII, No. 52). Belorussky sbornik, "Spravyadlivy soldat" ["The Intrepid Gentleman," *Great Russian Tales* (Notes of the Imperial Russian Geographical Society, XLII, No. 52). White Russian Anthology, "The Upright Soldier" (1886–1912).] [Au.]

The lack of recognition in the following tale is quite typical:

A peasant was plowing a field with a piebald mare. A bear approached him and asked, "Uncle, what's made this mare piebald for you?"

"I did the piebalding myself."

"But how?"

"Let me, and I'll do the same for you."

The bear agreed. The peasant tied his feet together with a rope, took the ploughshare from the two-wheeled plough, heated it on the fire, and applied it to his flanks. He made the bear piebald by scorching his fur down to the hide with the hot ploughshare. The man untied the bear, which went off and lay down under a tree.

A magpie flew at the peasant to pick at the meat on his shirt. He caught her and broke one of her legs. The magpie flew off to perch in the same tree under which the bear was lying. Then, after the magpie, a horsefly landed on the mare, sat down, and began to bite. The peasant caught the fly, took a stick, shoved it up its rear, and let it go. The fly went to the tree where the bear and the magpie were. There all three sat.

The peasant's wife came to bring his dinner to the field. The man and his wife finished their dinner in the fresh air, and he began to wrestle with her on the ground.

The bear saw this and said to the magpie and the fly, "Holy priests! The peasant wants to piebald someone again."

The magpie said, "No, he wants to break someone's legs."

The fly said, "No, he wants to shove a stick up someone's rump."[28]

The similarity of technique here and in Tolstoy's "Kholstomer," is, I think, obvious.

Quite often in literature the sexual act itself is defamiliarized; for example, the *Decameron* refers to "scraping out a barrel," "catching nightingales," "gay wool-beating work," (the last is not developed in the plot). Defamiliarization is often used in describing the sexual organs.

A whole series of plots is based on such a lack of recognition; for example, in Afanasyev's *Intimate Tales* the entire story of "The Shy Mistress" is based on the fact that an object is not called by its proper name — or, in other words, on a game of nonrecognition. So too in Onchukov's "Spotted Petticoats," tale no. 525, and also in "The Bear and the Hare" from *Intimate Tales*, in which the bear and the hare make a "wound."

Such constructions as "the pestle and the mortar," or "Old Nick and the infernal regions" (*Decameron*), are also examples of the technique of defamiliarization. And in my article on plot construction I write about defamiliarization in psychological parallelism. Here, then, I repeat that the perception of disharmony in a harmonious context is important in parallelism. The purpose of parallelism, like the general purpose of imagery, is to transfer the usual perception of an object into the sphere of a new perception — that is, to make a unique semantic modification.

In studying poetic speech in its phonetic and lexical structure as well as in its characteristic distribution of words and in the characteristic thought structures compounded from the words, we find everywhere the artistic trademark — that is, we find material obviously created to remove the automatism of perception; the author's purpose is to create the vision which results from that deautomatized perception. A work is created "artistically" so that its perception is impeded and the greatest possible effect is produced through the slowness of the perception. As a result of this lingering, the object is perceived not in its extension in space, but, so to speak, in its continuity. Thus "poetic language" gives satisfaction. According to Aristotle, poetic language must appear strange and wonderful; and, in fact, it is often actually foreign: the Sumerian used by the Assyrians, the Latin of Europe during the Middle Ages, the Arabisms of the Persians, the Old Bulgarian of Russian literature, or the elevated, almost literary language of folk songs. The common archaisms of poetic language, the intricacy of the sweet new style [*dolce stil nuovo*],[29] the obscure style of the language of Arnaut Daniel with the "roughened" [*harte*] forms *which make pronunciation difficult* — these are used in much the same way. Leo Jakubinsky has demonstrated the principle of pho-

[28]D[mitry] S. Zelenin, *Velikorusskiye skazki Permskoy gubernii* [*Great Russian Tales of the Permian Province* (St. Petersburg, 1913)], No. 70. [Au.]

[29]Dante, *Purgatorio*, 24:56. Dante refers to the new lyric style of his contemporaries. [Tr.]

netic "roughening" of poetic language in the particular case of the repetition of identical sounds. The language of poetry is, then, a difficult, roughened, impeded language. In a few special instances the language of poetry approximates the language of prose, but this does not violate the principle of "roughened" form.

Her sister was called Tatyana.
For the first time we shall
Wilfully brighten the delicate
Pages of a novel with such a name.[30]

wrote Pushkin. The usual poetic language of Pushkin's contemporaries was the elegant style of Derzhavin; but Pushkin's style, because it seemed trivial then, was unexpectedly difficult for them. We should remember the consternation of Pushkin's contemporaries over the vulgarity of his expressions. He used the popular language as a special device for prolonging attention, just as his contemporaries generally used Russian words in their usually French speech (see Tolstoy's examples in *War and Peace*).

Just now a still more characteristic phenomenon is under way. Russian literary language, which was originally foreign to Russia, has so permeated the language of the people that it has blended with their conversation. On the other hand, literature has now begun to show a tendency towards the use of dialects (Remizov, Klyuyev, Essenin, and others,[31] so unequal in talent and so alike in language, are intentionally provincial) and of barbarisms (which gave rise to the Severyanin group[32]). And currently Maxim Gorky is changing his diction from the old literary language to the new literary colloquialism of Leskov.[33] Ordinary speech and literary language have thereby changed places (see the work of Vyacheslav Ivanov and many others). And finally, a strong tendency, led by Khlebnikov, to create a new and properly poetic language has emerged. In the light of these developments we can define poetry as *attenuated, tortuous* speech. Poetic speech is *formed speech*. Prose is ordinary speech — economical, easy, proper, the goddess of prose [*dea prosae*] is a goddess of the accurate, facile type, of the "direct" expression of a child. I shall discuss roughened form and retardation as the general *law* of art at greater length in an article on plot construction.[34]

Nevertheless, the position of those who urge the idea of economy of artistic energy as something which exists in and even distinguishes poetic language seems, at first glance, tenable for the problem of rhythm. Spencer's description of rhythm would seem to be absolutely incontestable:

Just as the body in receiving a series of varying concussions, must keep the muscles ready to meet the most violent of them, as not knowing when such may come: so, the mind in receiving unarranged articulations, must keep its perspectives active enough to recognize the least easily caught sounds. And as, if the concussions recur in definite order, the body may husband its forces by adjusting the resistance needful for each concussion; so, if the syllables be rhythmically arranged, the mind may economize its energies by anticipating the attention required for each syllable.[35]

This apparently conclusive observation suffers from the common fallacy, the confusion of the laws of poetic and prosaic language. In *The Philosophy of Style* Spencer failed utterly to distinguish between them. But rhythm may have two functions. The rhythm of prose, or of a work song like "Dubinushka," permits the members of the work crew to do their necessary "groaning together" and also eases the work by making it automatic. And, in fact, it is easier to march with music than without it, and to march during an animated conversation is even easier, for the walking is done unconsciously. Thus the rhythm

---

[30]Alexander Pushkin, *Eugene Onegin*, I.ii.24. [Ed.]

[31]Alexy Remizov (1877–1957) is best known as a novelist and satirist; Nicholas Klyuyev (1885–1937) and Sergey Essenin (1895–1925) were "peasant poets." All three were noted for their faithful reproduction of Russian dialects and colloquial language. [Tr.]

[32]A group noted for its opulent and sensuous verse style. [Tr.]

[33]Nicholas Leskov (1831–1895), novelist and short story writer, helped popularize the *skaz*, or yarn, and hence, because of the part dialect peculiarities play in the *skaz*, also altered Russian literary language. [Tr.]

[34]Shklovsky is probably referring to his *Razvyortyvaniye syuzheta* [*Plot Development*] (Petrograd, 1291). [Tr.]

[35]Spencer, p. 169. Again the Russian text is shortened from Spencer's original. [Tr.]

of prose is an important automatizing element; the rhythm of poetry is not. There is "order" in art, yet not a single column of a Greek temple stands exactly in its proper order; poetic rhythm is similarly disordered rhythm. Attempts to systematize the irregularities have been made, and such attempts are part of the current problem in the theory of rhythm. It is obvious that the systematization will not work, for in reality the problem is not one of complicating the rhythm but of disordering the rhythm — a disordering which cannot be predicted. Should the disordering of rhythm become a convention, it would be ineffective as a device for the roughening of language. But I will not discuss rhythm in more detail since I intend to write a book about it.[36]

[36]We have been unable to discover the book Shklovsky promised. [Tr.]

# Yuri Tynyanov
## 1894–1943

*The Russian scholar, novelist, and literary critic Yuri Tynyanov was born in the town of Rezhitsa in the province of Vitebsk. Like Victor Shklovsky, a fellow member of the Society for the Study of Poetic Language (OPOYAZ), Tynyanov studied at the University of Petersburg, and like Shklovsky he eventually moved away from theorizing in the wake of official disapproval of formalist ideas. From 1921 to 1930 he was a lecturer in Russian poetry at the Petrograd State Institute of Art History. His early works, notably on Pushkin (1926) and Dostoevsky and Gogol (1921), are considered to be remarkable both for their dexterous scholarship and for the boldness of their interpretations. An important theoretical statement, "On Literary Evolution," appeared in 1927, but because Soviet hostility to formalism was on the rise, Tynyanov prudently turned mainly to writing historical fiction. Illness and premature death prevented him from finishing the huge novel about Pushkin he began writing in 1936.*

# On Literary Evolution

## I

Within the cultural disciplines literary history still retains the status of a colonial territory. On the one hand, individualistic psychologism dominates it to a significant extent, particularly in the West, unjustifiably replacing the problem of literature with the question of the author's psychology, while the problem of literary evolution becomes the problem of the genesis of literary phenomena. On the other hand, a simplified causal approach to a literary order leads to a sharp break between the literary order itself and the point of observation, which always turns out to be the major but also the most remote social orders. The organization of a closed literary order and the examination of the evolution within it sometimes collides with the neighboring cultural, behavioral, and social orders in the broad sense. Thus such an effort is doomed to incompleteness. The theory of value in literary investigation has brought about the danger of studying major but isolated works and has changed the history of literature into a *history of generals*. The blind rejection of a history of generals has in turn caused an interest in the study of mass literature,

Translated by C. A. Luplow.

but no clear theoretical awareness of how to study it or what the nature of its significance is.

Finally, the relationship between the history of literature and living contemporary literatures — a relationship useful and very necessary to science — is not always necessary and useful to the development of literature. The representatives of literature are ready to view the history of literature as the codification of certain traditional norms and laws and to confuse the historical character of a literary phenomenon with "historicism." As a result of this conflict, there has arisen an attempt to study isolated works and the laws of their construction on an extrahistorical plane, resulting in the abolition of the history of literature.

## 2

In order to become finally a science, the history of literature must claim reliability. All of its terminology, and first of all the very term, "the history of literature," must be reconsidered. The term proves to be extremely broad, covering both the material history of belles lettres, the history of verbal art, and the history of writing in general. It is also pretentious, since "the history of literature" considers itself a priori a discipline ready to enter into "the history of culture" as a system equipped with a scientific methodology. As yet it has no right to such a claim.

Meanwhile, the historical investigations of literature fall into at least two main types, depending on the points of observation: the investigation of the genesis of literary phenomena, and the investigation of the evolution of a literary order, that is, of literary changeability.

The point of view determines not only the significance but also the nature of the phenomenon being studied. In the investigation of literary evolution, the moment of genesis has its own significance and character, which are obviously not the same as in the investigation of the genesis per se.

Furthermore, the study of literary evolution or changeability must reject the theories of naive evaluation, which result from the confusion of points of observation, in which evaluation is carried over from one epoch or system into another.

At the same time, evaluation itself must be freed from its subjective coloring, and the "value" of a given literary phenomenon must be considered as having an "evolutionary significance and character."

The same must also apply to such concepts as "epigonism," "dilettantism," or "mass literature," which are for now evaluative concepts.[1]

Tradition, the basic concept of the established history of literature, has proved to be an unjustifiable abstraction of one or more of the literary elements of a given system within which they occupy the same plane and play the same role. They are equated with the like elements of another system in which they are on a different plane, thus they are brought into a seemingly unified, fictitiously integrated system.

The main concept for literary evolution is the *mutation* of systems, and thus the problem of "traditions" is transferred onto another plane.

## 3

Before this basic problem can be analyzed, it must be agreed that a literary work is a system, as is literature itself. Only after this basic agree-

[1]One need only examine the mass literature of the 1820s and 1830s to be convinced of their colossal evolutionary difference. In the 1830s, years of the automatization of preceding traditions, years of work on dusty literary material, "dilettantism" suddenly received a tremendous evolutionary significance. It is from dilettantism, from the atmosphere of "verse notes written on the margins of books," that a new phenomenon emerged — Tyutchev, who transformed poetic language and genres by his intimate intonations. The relationship of social conventions to literature, which seems to be its degeneration from an evaluative point of view, transforms the literary system. In the 1820s, the years of the "masters" and the creation of new poetic genres, dilettantism and mass literature were called "graphomania." The poets, who from the point of view of evolutionary significance were the leading figures of the 1830s, appeared to be determined as the "dilettantes" (Tyutchev, Polezhaev) or the "epigones" and "pupils" (Lermontov) in their struggle with the preceding norms. In the period of the 1820s, however, even the secondary poets appeared like leading masters; note, for example, the universality and grandioseness of the genres used by such mass poets as Olin. It is clear that the evolutionary significance of such phenomena as dilettantism or epigonism is different from period to period. Supercilious, evaluative treatment of these phenomena is the heritage of the old history of literature. [Au.]

ment has been established is it possible to create a literary science which does not superficially examine diverse phenomena but studies them closely. In this way the problem of the role of contiguous systems in literary evolution is actually posited instead of being rejected.

The analysis of the separate elements of a work, such as the composition, style, rhythm, and syntax in prose, and the rhythm and semantics in poetry, provides sufficient evidence that these elements, within certain limits, can be abstracted as a *working hypothesis*, although they are interrelated and interacting. The study of rhythm in poetry and prose was bound to show that the role of a given element is different in different systems.

The interrelationship of each element with every other in a literary work and with the whole literary system as well may be called the constructional *function* of the given element.

On close examination, such a function proves to be a complex concept. An element is on the one hand interrelated with similar elements in other works in other systems, and on the other hand it is interrelated with different elements within the same work. The former may be termed the *auto-function* and the latter, the *syn-function*.

Thus, for example, the lexicon of a given work is interrelated with both the whole literary lexicon and the general lexicon of the language, as well as with other elements of that given work. These two components or functions operate simultaneously but are not of equal relevance.

The function of archaisms, for example, depends wholly on the system within which they are used. In Lomonosov's system, in which lexical coloring plays a dominant role, such archaisms function as "elevated" word usage. They are used for their lexical association with Church Slavic. In Tyutchev's work archaisms have a different function. In some instances they are abstract, as in the pair: *fontan-vodomet* [fountain-spout]. An interesting example is the usage of archaisms in an ironical function: "*Pušek grom i musikija*" [Thunder of guns and musicke] is used by a poet who otherwise employs a word such as *musikijskij* [musicall] in a completely different function. The auto-function, although it is not decisive, makes the existence of the syn-function

possible and at the same time conditions it. Thus up to the time of Tyutchev, in the eighteenth and nineteenth centuries, there existed an extensive parodic literature in which archaisms had a parodic function. But the semantic and intonational system of the given work finally determines the function of a given expression, in this case determining the word usage to be "ironic" rather than "elevated."

It is incorrect to isolate the elements from one system outside their constructional function and to correlate them with other systems.

## 4

Is the so-called "immanent" study of a work as a system possible without comparing it with the general literary system? Such an isolated study of a literary work is equivalent to abstracting isolated elements and examining them outside their work. Such abstracting is continuously applied to contemporary works and may be successful in literary criticism, since the interrelationship of a contemporary work with contemporary literature is in advance an established, although concealed, fact. (The interrelationship of a work with other works by the same author, its relationship to genre, and so on, belong here.)

Even in contemporary literature, however, isolated study is impossible. The very existence of a fact *as literary* depends on its differential quality, that is, on its interrelationship with both literary and extraliterary orders. Thus, its existence depends on its function. What in one epoch would be a literary fact would in another be a common matter of social communication, and vice versa, depending on the whole literary system in which the given fact appears.

Thus the friendly letter of Derzhavin is a social fact. The friendly letter of the Karamzhin and Pushkin epoch is a literary fact. Thus one has the literariness of memories and diaries in one system and their extraliterariness in another.

We cannot be certain of the structure of a work if it is studied in isolation.

Finally, the auto-function, that is, the interrelationship of an element with similar elements in other systems, conditions the syn-function, that is, the constructional function of the element.

Thus, whether or not an element is "effaced" is important. But what is the effacement of a line, meter, plot structure, and so on? What, in other words, is the "automatization" of one or another element?

The following is an example from linguistics. When the referential meaning of a word is effaced, that word becomes the expression of a relationship, a connection, and thus it becomes an auxiliary word. In other words, its function changes. The same is true of the "automatization" of a literary element. It does not disappear. Its function simply changes, and it becomes auxiliary. If the meter of a poem is "effaced," then the other signs of verse and the other elements of the work become more important in its place, and the meter takes on other functions.

Thus the short feuilleton[2] verse of the newspaper uses mainly effaced, banal meters which have long been rejected by poetry. No one would read it as a "poem" related to "poetry." Here the effaced meter is a means of attaching feuilleton material from everyday life to literature. Meter thus has an auxiliary function, which is completely different from its function in a poetic work. This also applies to parody in the verse feuilleton. Parody is viable only in so far as what is being parodied is still alive. What literary significance can the thousandth parody of Lermontov's "When the gold cornfield sways . . ." or Pushkin's "The Prophet" have today? The verse feuilleton, however, uses such parody constantly. Here again we have the same phenomenon: the function of parody has become auxiliary, as it serves to apply extraliterary facts to literature.

In a work in which the so-called plot is effaced, the story carries out different functions than in a work in which it is not effaced. The story might be used merely to motivate style or as a strategy for developing the material. Crudely speaking, from our vantage point in a particular literary system, we would be inclined to reduce nature descriptions in old novels to an auxiliary role, to the role of making transitions or retardation; therefore we would almost ignore them, although from the vantage point of a different literary system we would be forced to consider nature descriptions as the main, dominant element. In other words, there are situations in which the story simply provides the motivation for the treatment of "static descriptions."

## 5

The more difficult and less studied question of literary genres can be resolved in the same way. The novel, which seems to be an integral genre that has developed in and of itself over the centuries, turns out to be not an integral whole but a variable. Its material changes from one literary system to another, as does its method of introducing extraliterary language materials into literature. Even the features of the genre evolve. The genres of the "short story" and the "novella" were defined by different features in the system of the twenties to forties than they are in our time, as is obvious from their very names. We tend to name genres according to secondary features or, crudely speaking, by size. For us the labels, short story, novella, and novel, are adequate only to define the quantity of printed pages. This proves not so much the "automatization" of genres in our literary system as the fact that we define genres by other features. The size of a thing, the quantity of verbal material, is not an indifferent feature; we cannot, however, define the genre of a work if it is isolated from the system. For example, what was called an ode in the 1820s or by Fet was so labeled on the basis of features different from those used to define an ode in Lomonosov's time.

Consequently, we may conclude that the study of isolated genres outside the features characteristic of the genre system with which they are related is impossible. The historical novel of Tolstoy is not related to the historical novel of Zagoskin, but to the prose of his contemporaries.

## 6

Strictly speaking, one cannot study literary phenomena outside of their interrelationships. Such, for example, is the problem of prose and poetry.

---

[2]Popular or kitsch art; literally a "notebook." [Ed.]

We tacitly consider metrical prose to be prose, and nonmetrical free verse to be poetry, without considering the fact that in another literary system we would thus be placed in a difficult position. The point is that prose and poetry are interrelated and that there is a mutually shared function of prose and poetry. (Note the interrelationship of prose and poetry in their respective development, as established by Boris Eichenbaum.)

The function of poetry in a particular literary system was fulfilled by the formal element of meter; but prose displays differentiation and develops, and so does poetry. The differentiation of one interrelated type leads to, or better, is connected with, the differentiation of another interrelated type. Thus metrical prose arises, as in the works of Andrei Bely. This is connected with the transfer of the verse function in poetry from meter onto other features which are in part secondary and resultant. Such features may be rhythm, used as the feature of verse units, a particular syntax or particular lexicon, and so on. The function of prose with regard to verse remains, but the formal elements fulfilling this function are different. In the course of centuries the further evolution of forms may consolidate the function of verse with regard to prose, transfer it onto a whole series of other features, or it may infringe upon it and make it unessential. And just as in contemporary literature the interrelationship of genres is hardly essential and is established according to secondary signs, so a period may come in which it will be unessential whether a work is written in prose or poetry.

### 7

The evolutionary relationship of function and formal elements is a completely uninvestigated problem. An example is given above of how the evolution of forms results in a change of function. There are also many examples of how a form with an undetermined function creates or defines a new one, and there are also others in which a function seeks its own form. I will give an example in which both occurred together.

In the archaist trend of the 1820s the function of the combined elevated and folk verse epos arises. *The interrelationship of literature with the social order led to the large verse form.* But there were no formal elements, and the demands of the social system turned out to be unequal to the demands of literature. Then the search for formal elements began. In 1824 Katenin advocated the octave[3] as the formal element of the poetic epopea.[4] The passionate quarrels concerning the seemingly innocent octave were appropriate to the tragic "orphanhood" of function without form. The epos of the archaists failed. Six years later Shevyrev and Pushkin used the form in a different function: to break with the whole iambic tetrameter epos and create a new, "debased" (as opposed to "elevated"), prosaicized epos, such as Pushkin's *Little House in Kolomna*.

The relationship between form and function is not accidental. The comparable combination of a particular lexicon with a particular meter by Katenin and then twenty or thirty years later by Nekrasov, who probably did not know about Katenin, was not accidental.

The variability of the functions of a given formal element, the rise of some new function of a formal element, and the attaching of a formal element to a function are all important problems of literary evolution; but there is no room to study or resolve these problems here. I would like to say only that the whole problem of literature as a system demands on further investigation.

### 8

The assumption that the interrelationship of literary phenomena occurs when a work enters into a synchronic literary system and there "acquires" a function is not entirely correct. The very concept of a continuously evolving synchronic system is contradictory. A literary system is first of all a *system of the functions of the literary order which are in continual interrelationship with other orders.* Systems change in their composi-

---

[3]*Ottava rima*, the stanza used by Byron in *Don Juan*. [Ed.]

[4]Narrative poetry. [Ed.]

tion, but the differentiation of human activities remains. The evolution of literature, as of other cultural systems, does not coincide either in tempo or in character with the systems with which it is interrelated. This is owing to the specificity of the material with which it is concerned. The evolution of the structural function occurs rapidly; the evolution of the literary function occurs over epochs; and the evolution of the functions of a whole literary system in relation to neighboring systems occurs over centuries.

## 9

Since a system is not an equal interaction of all elements but places a group of elements in the foreground — the "dominant" — and thus involves the deformation of the remaining elements, a work enters into literature and takes on its own literary function through this dominant. Thus we correlate poems with the verse category, not with the prose category, not on the basis of all their characteristics, but only of some of them. The same is true concerning genres. We relate a novel to "the novel" on the basis of its size and the nature of its plot development, while at one time it was distinguished by the presence of a love intrigue.

Another interesting fact from an evolutionary point of view is the following. A work is correlated with a particular literary system depending on its deviation, its "difference" as compared with the literary system with which it is confronted. Thus, for example, the unusually sharp argument among the critics of the 1820s over the genre of the Pushkin narrative poem arose because the Pushkin genre was a combined, mixed, new genre without a ready-made "name." The sharper the divergence or differentiation from a particular literary system, the more that system from which the derivation occurs is accentuated. Thus, free verse emphasized the verse principle of *nonmetrical* features, while Sterne's novel emphasized the compositional principle of *nonplot* features (Shklovsky). The following is an analogy from linguistics: "The variability of the word

stem makes it the center of maximum expressiveness and thus extricates it from the net of prefixes which do not change" (Vendryes).

## 10

What constitutes the interrelationship of literature with neighboring orders? What, moreover, are these neighboring orders? The answer is obvious: social conventions.

Yet, in order to solve the problem of the interrelationship of literature with social conventions, the question must be posited: *how and by what means* are social conventions interrelated with literature? Social conventions are by nature many-sided and complex, and only the function of all their aspects is specific in it. Social conventions are correlated with literature first of all in its verbal aspect. This interrelationship is realized through language. That is, literature in relation to social conventions has a verbal function.

We use the term "orientation." It denotes approximately the "creative intention of the author." Yet it happens that "the intention may be good, but the fulfillment bad." Furthermore, the author's intention can only be a catalyst. In using a specific literary material, the author may yield to it, thus departing from his first intention. Thus Griboedov's *Wit Works Woe* was supposed to be "elevated" and even "grandiose," according to the author's terminology. But instead it turned out to be a political publicistic comedy of the archaist school. *Eugene Onegin* was first meant to be a "satiric narrative poem" in which the author would be "brimming over with bitterness." However, while working on the fourth chapter, Pushkin had already said, "Where is my satire? There's not a trace of it in *Eugene Onegin*."

The structural function, that is, the interrelationship of elements within a work, changes the "author's intention" into a catalyst, but does nothing more. "Creative freedom" thus becomes an optimistic slogan which does not correspond to reality, but yields instead to the slogan "creative necessity."

The literary function, that is, the interrelationship of a work with the literary order, completes the whole thing. If we eliminate the teleological, goal-oriented allusion, the "intention," from the word "orientation," what happens? The "orientation" of a literary work then proves to be its verbal function, its interrelationship with the social conventions.

The "orientation" of the Lomonosov ode, its verbal function, is oratorical. The word is oriented on *pronunciation*. And to carry further the associations with actual life, the orientation is on declamation in the large palace hall. By the time of Karamzin, the ode was literarily "worn out." The "orientation" had died out or narrowed down in significance and had been transferred onto other forms related to life. Congratulatory odes, as well as others, became "uniform verses," i.e., what are purely real-life phenomena. Ready-made literary genres did not exist. Everyday verbal communication took their place. The verbal function, or orientation, was seeking its forms and found them in the romance, the joking play with rhymes, *bouts rimés*,[5] charades, and so on. And here the moment of genesis, the presence of certain forms of everyday speech, received evolutionary significance. These speech phenomena were found in the salon of Karamzin's epoch. And the salon, a fact of everyday life, at this time became a literary fact. In this way the forms of social life acquired a literary function.

Similarly, the semantics of the intimate domestic circle always exists, but in particular periods it takes on a literary function. Such, too, is the application of *accidental results*. The rough drafts of Pushkin's verse programs and the drafts of his "scenarios" became his finished prose. This is possible only through the evolution of a whole system — through the evolution of its orientation.

An analogy from our own time of the struggle between two orientations is seen in the mass orientation of Mayakovsky's poetry ("the ode") in competition with the romance, chamber-style orientation of Esenin ("the elegy").

[5]Rhyming games. [Ed.]

## II

The verbal function must also be taken into consideration in dealing with the problem of the reverse expansion of literature into actual life. The *literary personality*, or the *author's personality*, or at various times the *hero*, becomes the verbal orientation of literature. And from there it enters into real life. Such are the lyric heroes of Byron in relationship to his "literary personality," i.e., to the personality which came to life for the readers of his poems and which was thus transferred into life. Such is the "literary personality" of Heine, which is far removed from the real biographical Heine. In given periods, biography becomes oral, apocryphal literature. This happens naturally, in connection with the speech orientation of a given system. Thus, one has Pushkin, Tolstoy, Blok, Mayakovsky, and Esenin as opposed to the absence of a literary personality in Leskov, Turgenev, Fet, Maykov, Gumilev, and others. This corresponds to the absence of a speech orientation on "the literary personality." Obviously, special real-life conditions are necessary for the expansion of literature into life.

## 12

Such is the immediate social function of literature. It can be established and investigated only through the study of closely related conditions, without the forcible incorporation of remote, though major, causal orders.

Finally, the concept of the "orientation" of a speech function is applicable to a literary order but not to an individual work. A separate work must be related to a literary order before one can talk about its orientation. The law of large numbers does not apply to small numbers. In establishing the distant causal orders for separate works and authors, we study not the evolution of literature but its modification, not how literature changes and evolves in correlation with other orders, but how neighboring orders deform it. This problem too is worth studying, but on a completely different plane.

The direct study of the author's psychology and the construction of a causal "bridge" from the author's environment, daily life, and class to his works is particularly fruitless. The erotic poetry of Batyushkov[6] resulted from his work on the poetic language — note his speech, "On the Influence of Light Poetry on Language" — and Vyazemsky[7] refused to seek its genesis in Batyushkov's psychology. The poet, Polonsky, who was never a theoretician but who as a poet and master of his craft understood this, wrote of Benediktov,

> It is very possible that the severity of nature, the forests, the fields . . . influenced the impressionable soul of the child and future poet, but how did they influence it? This is a difficult question, and no one will resolve it without straining the point. It is not nature, which is the same for everyone, that plays the major role here.

Sudden changes in artists which are unexplainable in terms of their personal changes are typical. Such are the sudden changes in Derzhavin and Nekrasov, in whose youth "elevated" poetry went side by side with "low" satiric poetry, but later under objective conditions were merged, thus creating new phenomena. Clearly, the problem here is not one of individual psychological conditions, but of objective, evolving functions of the literary order in relation to the adjacent social order.

## 13

It is therefore necessary to reexamine one of the most complex problems of literary evolution, the problem of "influence." There are deep psychological and personal influences which are not reflected on the literary level at all, as with Chadaev and Pushkin. There are influences which modify and deform literature without having any evolutionary significance, as with Mikhailovsky and Gleb Uspensky. Yet what is most striking of all is the fact that you can have an extrinsic indication of an influence where no such influence has occurred. I have already cited the examples of Katenin and Nekrasov. There are other examples as well. The South American tribes created the myth of Prometheus without the influence of classical mythology. These facts point to a convergence or coincidence. They have proved to be so significant that they completely obscure the psychological approach to the problem of influence and make chronology ("Who said it first?") unessential. "Influence" can occur at such a time and in such a direction as literary conditions permit. In the case of functional coincidence, whatever influences him provides the artist with elements which permit the development and strengthening of the function. If there is no such "influence," then an analogous function may result in analogous formal elements without any influence.

## 14

It is now time to pose the problem of the main term with which literary history operates, namely, "tradition." If we agree that evolution is the change in interrelationships between the elements of a system — between functions and formal elements — then evolution may be seen as the "mutations" of systems. These changes vary from epoch to epoch, occurring sometimes slowly, sometimes rapidly. They do not entail the sudden and complete renovation or the replacement of formal elements, but rather the *new function of these formal elements*. Thus the very comparison of certain literary phenomena must be made on the basis of functions, not only forms. Seemingly dissimilar phenomena of diverse functional systems may be similar in function, and vice versa. The problem is obscured here by the fact that each literary movement in a given period seeks its supporting point in the preceding systems. This is what may be called "traditionalism."

Thus, perhaps, the functions of Pushkin's prose are closer to the functions of Tolstoy's prose than the functions of Pushkin's verse are to those of his imitators in the 1830s or those of Maykov.

[6]Konstantin Nikolaievich Batyushkov (1787–1855), poet who imitated the erotic verse of Tibullus and other Latin poets. [Ed.]

[7]Pyotr Andreievich Vyazemsky (1792–1878), poet and critic of Pushkin's circle. [Ed.]

**15**

To summarize, the study of literary evolution is possible only in relation to literature as a system, interrelated with other systems and conditioned by them. Investigation must go from constructional function to literary function; from literary function to verbal function. It must clarify the problem of the evolutionary interaction of functions and forms. The study of evolution must move from the literary system to the nearest correlated systems, not the distant, even though major, systems. In this way the prime significance of major social factors is not at all discarded. Rather, it must be elucidated to its full extent through the problem of the evolution of literature. This is in contrast to the establishment of the direct "influence" of major social factors, which replaces the study of *evolution* of literature with the study of the *modification* of literary works — that is to say, of their deformation.

# Vladimir Propp
## 1895–1970

*Vladimir Yakovlevich Propp is the originator of folklore studies in the mode of historical and structural typology. Initially a philologist of Russian and German, Propp in 1918 took his degree at Petersburg, where he taught from the 1930s (when the institution had become known as Leningrad University) until his death. Propp's work, such as the groundbreaking* Morphology of the Folktale *(1928), was suppressed because of official suspicion of formalist influence, but Western intellectuals, notably Claude Lévi-Strauss (see Ch. 4) rescued him from obscurity in the 1960s. Among Propp's other studies are those on the origins of the tale of enchantment (1947), the Russian heroic saga (1958), and the poetics of peasant folk songs (1963). The translation of "Fairy Tale Transformations" is from* Readings in Russian Poetics *(1971).*

# *Fairy Tale Transformations*

**I**

The study of the fairy tale may be compared in many respects to that of organic formation in nature. Both the naturalist and the folklorist deal with species and varieties which are essentially the same. The Darwinian problem of the origin of species arises in folklore as well. The similarity of phenomena both in nature and in our field resists any direct explanation which would be both objective and convincing. It is a problem in its own right. Both fields allow two possible points of view: either the internal similarity of two externally dissimilar phenomena does not derive from a common genetic root — the theory of spontaneous generation — or else this morphological similarity does indeed result from a known genetic tie — the theory of differentiation owing to subsequent metamorphoses or transformations of varying cause and occurrence.

In order to resolve this problem, we need a clear understanding of what is meant by similarity in fairy tales. Similarity has so far been invariably defined in terms of a plot and its variants. We find such an approach acceptable only if based upon the idea of the spontaneous generation of species. Adherents to this method do not compare plots; they feel such comparison to be impossible or, at the very least, erroneous.[1]

Translated by C. H. Severens.

[1]Antti A. Aarne warns against such an "error" in his

Without our denying the value of studying individual plots and comparing them solely from the standpoint of their similarity, another method, another basis for comparison may be proposed. Fairy tales can be compared from the standpoint of their composition or structure; their similarity then appears in a new light.[2]

We observe that the actors in the fairy tale perform essentially the same actions as the tale progresses, no matter how different from one another in shape, size, sex, and occupation, in nomenclature and other static attributes. This determines the relationship of the constant factors to the variables. The functions of the actors are constant; everything else is a variable. For example:

1. The king sends Ivan[3] after the princess; Ivan departs.
2. The king sends Ivan after some marvel; Ivan departs.
3. The sister sends her brother for medicine; he departs.
4. The stepmother sends her stepdaughter for fire; she departs.
5. The smith sends his apprentice for a cow; he departs.

The dispatch and the departure on a quest are constants. The dispatching and departing actors, the motivations behind the dispatch, and so forth, are variables. In later stages of the quest, obstacles impede the hero's progress; they, too, are essentially the same, but differ in the form of imagery.

The functions of the actors may be singled out. Fairy tales exhibit thirty-one functions, not all of which may be found in any one fairy tale; however, the absence of certain functions does not interfere with the order of appearance of the others. Their aggregate constitutes one system, one composition. This system has proved to be extremely stable and widespread. The investigator, for example, can determine very accurately that both the ancient Egyptian fairy tale of the two brothers and the tale of the firebird, the tale of *Morozka*, the tale of the fisherman and the fish, as well as a number of myths follow the same general pattern. An analysis of the details bears this out. Thirty-one functions do not exhaust the system. Such a motif as "Baba-Jaga[4] gives Ivan a horse" contains four elements, of which only one represents a function, while the other three are of a static nature.

In all, the fairy tale knows about one hundred and fifty elements or constituents. Each of these elements can be labeled according to its bearing on the sequence of action. Thus, in the above example, Baba-Jaga is a donor, the word "gives" signals the moment of transmittal, Ivan is a recipient, and the horse is the gift. If the labels for all one hundred and fifty fairy tale elements are written down in the order dictated by the tales themselves, then, by definition, all fairy tales will fit such a table. Conversely, any tale which fits such a table is a fairy tale, and any tale which does not fit it belongs in another category. Every rubric is a constituent of the fairy tale, and reading the table vertically yields a series of basic forms and a series of derived forms.

It is precisely these constituents which are subject to comparison. This would correspond in zoology to a comparison of vertebra with vertebra, of tooth with tooth, etc. But there is a significant difference between organic formations and the fairy tale which makes our task easier. In the first instance, a change in a part or feature brings about a change in another feature, whereas each element of the fairy tale can change independently of the other elements. This has been noted by many investigators, although there have been so far no attempts to infer from it all the conclusions, methodological and otherwise.[5]

---

*Leitfaden der vergleichenden Märchenforschung* (Hamina, 1913). [Au.]

[2]See Propp's *Morphology of the Folktale* (Austin, 1968). [Tr.]

[3]Russian equivalent of "Jack," as the standard name for the hero of a folk-tale. [Ed.]

[4]In Slavic folktales, a man-eating witch who lives in a hut that stands on chicken legs. [Ed.]

[5]See F. Panzer, *Märchen, Sage und Dichtung* (Munich, 1905.) "Seine Komposition ist eine Mosaikarbeit, die das schildernde Bild aus deutlich abgegrenzten Steinchen gefügt hat. Und diese Steinchen bleiben umso leichter *auswechsel-bar*, die einzelnen Motive können umso leichter variieren, als auch nirgends für eine Verbindung in die Tiefe gesorgt

Thus, Kaarle Krohn, in agreeing with Spiess on the question of constituent interchangeability, still considers it necessary to study the fairy tale in terms of entire structures rather than in terms of constituents. In so doing, Krohn does not (in keeping with the Finnish school) supply much in the way of evidence to support his stand. We conclude from this that the elements of the fairy tale may be studied independently of the plot they constitute. Studying the rubrics vertically reveals norms and types of transformations. What holds true for an isolated element also holds true for entire structures. This is owing to the mechanical manner in which the constituents are joined.

### 2

The present work does not claim to exhaust the problem. We will only indicate here certain basic guideposts which might subsequently form the basis of a broader theoretical investigation.

Even in a brief presentation, however, it is necessary before examining the transformations themselves to establish the criteria which allow us to distinguish between basic and derived forms. The criteria may be expressed in two ways: in terms of general principles and in terms of special rules.

First, the general principles. In order to establish these principles, the fairy tale has to be approached from a standpoint of its environment, that is, the conditions under which it was created and exists. Life and, in the broad sense of the word, religion are the most important for us here. The causes of transformations frequently lie outside the fairy tale, and we will not grasp the

evolution of the tale unless we consider the environmental circumstances of the fairy tale.

The basic forms are those connected with the genesis of the fairy tale. Obviously, the tale is born out of life; however, the fairy tale reflects reality only weakly. Everything which derives from reality is of secondary formation. In order to determine the origins of the fairy tale, we must draw upon the broad cultural material of the past.

It turns out that the forms which, for one reason or another, are defined as basic are linked with religious concepts of the remote past. We can formulate the following premise: if the same form occurs both in a religious monument and in a fairy tale, the religious form is primary and the fairy tale form is secondary. This is particularly true of archaic religions. Any archaic religious phenomenon, dead today, is older than its artistic use in a current fairy tale. It is, of course, impossible to prove that here. Indeed, such a dependency in general cannot be *proved*; it can only be *shown* on the basis of a large range of material. Such is the first general principle, which is subject to further development. The second principle may be stated thus: if the same element has two variants, of which one derives from religious forms and the other from daily life, the religious formation is primary and the one drawn from life is secondary.

However, in applying these principles, we must observe reasonable caution. It would be an error to try to trace all basic forms back to religion and all derived ones to reality. To protect ourselves against such errors, we need to shed more light on the methods to be used in comparative studies of the fairy tale and religion and the fairy tale and life.

We can establish several types of relationships between the fairy tale and religion. The first is a direct genetic dependency, which in some cases is patently obvious, but which in other cases requires special historical research. Thus, if a serpent is encountered both in the fairy tale and in religion, it entered the fairy tale by way of religion, not the other way around.

However, the presence of such a link is not obligatory even in the case of very great similarity. Its presence is probable only when we have access to direct cult and *ritual* material. Such

---

ist." (His composition is a mosaic that has fashioned the descriptive image out of clearly delineated pieces. And these pieces are more readily *interchangeable*, the individual *motifs* can vary more easily, since at no time is there any provision made for an interconnection in depth.) This is clearly a denial of the theory of stable combinations or permanent ties. The same thought is expressed even more dramatically and in greater detail by K. Spiess in *Das deutsche Volksmärchen* (Leipzig, 1917). See also K. L. Krohn, *Die folkloristische Arbeitsmethode* (Oslo, 1926). [Au.]

ritual material must be distinguished from a combination of religious and *epic* material. In the first case, we can raise the question of a direct kinship along descending lines, analogous to the kinship line of fathers and children; in the second case we can speak only of parallel kinship or, to continue the analogy, the kinship of brothers. Thus the story of Samson and Delilah[6] cannot be considered the prototype of the fairy tale resembling their story: both the fairy tale and the Biblical text may well go back to a common source.

The primacy of cult material should likewise be asserted with a certain degree of caution. Nonetheless, there are instances when this primacy may be asserted with absolute confidence. True, evidence is frequently not found in the document itself but in the concepts which are reflected there and which underlie the fairy tale. But we are often able to form our judgment about the concepts only by means of the documents. For example, the Rig-Veda,[7] little studied by folklorists, belongs to such sources of the fairy tale. If it is true that the fairy tale knows approximately one hundred and fifty constituents, it is noteworthy that the Rig-Veda contains no fewer than sixty. True, their use is lyrical rather than epic, but it should not be forgotten that these are hymns of high priests, not of commoners. It is doubtless true that in the hands of the people (shepherds and peasants) this lyric took on features of the epic. If the hymn praises Indra as the serpent-slayer (in which case the details sometimes coincide perfectly with those of the fairy tale), the people were able in one form or another to *narrate* precisely how Indra killed the serpent.

Let us check this assertion with a more concrete example. We readily recognize Baba-Jaga and her hut in the following hymn:

Mistress of the wood, mistress of the wood, whither do you vanish? Why do you not ask of the village? Are you afraid then?

When the hue and cry of birds bursts forth, the mistress of the wood imagines herself a prince riding forth to the sound of cymbals.

Cattle seem to be grazing on the edge of the woods. Or is it a hut which stands darkly visible there? In the night is heard a squeaking and creaking as of a heavy cart. It is the mistress of the wood.

An unseen voice calls to the cattle. An ax rings out in the woods. A voice cries out sharply. So fancies the nocturnal guest of the mistress of the wood.

The mistress of the wood will do no harm unless alarmed. Feed on sweet fruits and peacefully sleep to full contentment.

Smelling of spices, fragrant, unsowing but ever having plenty, mother of the wild beasts, I praise the mistress of the wood.

We have certain fairy tale elements here: the hut in the woods, the reproach linked with inquiry (in the fairy tale it is normally couched in the form of direct address), a hospitable night's rest (she provides food, drink and shelter), a suggestion of the mistress of the wood's potential hostility, an indication that she is the mother of the wild beasts (in the fairy tale she calls them together); missing are the chicken legs of her hut as well as any indication of her external appearance, etc. One small detail presents a remarkable coincidence: wood is apparently being chopped for the person spending the night in the forest hut. In Afanas'ev (No. 99)[8] the father, after leaving his daughter in the hut, straps a boot last to the wheel of his cart. The last clacks loudly, and the girl says: *Se mij baten' ka drovcja rubae* [Me pa be a-choppin' wood].

Furthermore, all of these coincidences are not accidental, for they are not the only ones. These are only a few out of a great many precise parallels between the fairy tale and the Rig-Veda.

The parallel mentioned cannot, of course, be viewed as proof that our Baba-Jaga goes back to the Rig-Veda. One can only stress that on the whole the line proceeds from religion to the fairy

---

[6]Judges 13–16. [Ed.]

[7]Oldest of the collections of Sanskrit hymns and lore (ca. 1000 B.C.). [Ed.]

[8]All references to Afanas'ev have been adjusted to the 1957 edition of *Narodnye russkie skazki A. N. Afanas'eva* (Moscow, 1957). [Tr.] Alexander Nikolaievich Afanasyev (1826–71) was a historian who in 1860 wrote the first systematic study of Russian folktales. [Ed.]

tale, not conversely, and that it is essential here to initiate accurate comparative studies.

However, everything said here is true only if religion and the fairy tale lie at a great chronological distance from each other, if, for example, the religion under consideration has already died out, and its origin is obscured by the prehistoric past. It is quite a different matter when we compare a living religion and a living fairy tale belonging to one and the same people. The reverse situation may occur, a dependency which is impossible in the case of a dead religion and a modern fairy tale. Christian elements in the fairy tale (the apostles as helpers, the devil as spoiler) are *younger* than the fairy tale, not older, as in the preceding example. In point of fact, we really ought not to call this relationship the reverse of the one in the preceding case. The fairy tale derives from ancient religions, but modern religions do not derive from the fairy tale. Modern religion does not create the fairy tale but merely *changes* its material. Yet there are probably isolated examples of a truly reversed dependency, that is, instances in which the elements of religion are derived from the fairy tale. A very interesting example is in the Western Church's canonization of the miracle of St. George the Dragon Slayer. This miracle was canonized much later than was St. George himself, and it occurred despite the stubborn resistance of the Church.[9] Because the battle with the serpent is a part of many pagan religions, we have to assume that it derives precisely from them. In the thirteenth century, however, there was no longer a living trace of these religions, only the epic tradition of the people could play the role of transmitter. The popularity of St. George on the one hand and his fight with the dragon on the other caused his image to merge with that of the dragon fight; the Church was forced to acknowledge the completed fusion and to canonize it.

Finally, we may find not only direct genetic dependency of the fairy tale on religion, not only parallelism and reversed dependency, but also the complete absence of any link despite outward similarity. Identical concepts may arise independently of one another. Thus the magic steed is comparable with the holy steeds of the Teutons and with the fiery horse Agni in the Rig-Veda. The former have nothing in common with Sivka-Burka, while the latter coincides with him in all respects. The analogy may be applied only if it is more or less complete. Heteronymous phenomena, however similar, must be excluded from such comparisons.

Thus the study of *basic* forms necessitates a comparison of the fairy tale with various religions.

Conversely, the study of *derived* forms in the fairy tale shows how it is linked with reality. A number of transformations may be explained as the intrusions of reality into the fairy tale. This forces us to clarify the problem concerning the methods to be used in studying the fairy tale's relationship to life.

In contrast to other types of tales (the anecdote, the novella, the fable, and so on), the fairy tale shows a comparatively sparse sprinkling of elements from real life. The role of daily existence in creating the fairy tale is often overrated. We can resolve the problem of the fairy tale's relationship to life only if we remember that artistic realism and the presence of elements from real life are two different concepts which do not always overlap. Scholars often make the mistake of searching for facts from real life to support a realistic narrative.

Nikolai Lerner, for example, takes the following lines from Pushkin's "Bova":

> This is really a golden Council,
> No idle chatter here, but deep thought:
> A long while the noble lords all thought.
> Arzamor, old and experienced,
> All but opened his mouth (to give counsel,
> Perhaps, was the old greybeard's desire),
> His throat he loudly cleared, but thought better
> And in silence his tongue did bite
> [All the council members keep silent and begin to
>   drowse.]

and comments:

> In depicting the council of bearded senility we may presume the poem to be a satire on the governmental forms of old Muscovite Russia. . . . We note that the satire might have been directed not

---

[9] J. B. Aufhauser, *Das Drachenwunder des heiligen Georg* (Leipzig, 1911). [Au.]

only against Old Russia but against Pushkin's Russia as well. The entire assembly of snoring 'thinkers' could easily have been uncovered by the young genius in the society of his own day.

In actual fact, however, this is strictly a *fairy tale* motif. In Afanas'ev (for example, in No. 140) we find: "He asked once — the boyars were silent; a second time — they did not respond; a third time — not so much as half a word." We have here the customary scene in which the supplicant entreats aid, the entreaty usually occurring three times. It is first directed to the servants, then to the boyars (clerks, ministers), and third to the hero of the story. Each party in this triad may likewise be trebled in its own right. Thus we are not dealing with real life but with the amplification and specification (added names, etc.) of a folklore element. We would be making the same mistake if we were to consider the Homeric image of Penelope and the conduct of her suitors as corresponding to the facts of life in ancient Greece and to Greek connubial customs. Penelope's suitors are *false suitors*, a well-known device in epic poetry throughout the world. We should first isolate whatever is folkloric and only afterward raise the question as to the correspondence between specifically Homeric moments and factual life in ancient Greece.

Thus we see that the problem which deals with the fairy tale's relationship to real life is not a simple one. To draw conclusions about life directly from the fairy tale is inadmissible.

But, as we will see below, the role of real life in the *transformation* of the fairy tale is enormous. Life cannot destroy the overall structure of the fairy tale, but it does produce a wealth of younger material which replaces the old in a wide variety of ways.

3

The following are the principal and more precise criteria for distinguishing the basic form of a fairy tale element from a derived form:

1. A fantastical treatment of a constituent in the fairy tale is older than its rational treatment. Such a case is rather simple and does not require special development. If in one fairy tale Ivan

receives a magical gift from Baba-Jaga and in another from an old woman passing by, the former is older than the latter. This viewpoint is theoretically based on the link between the fairy tale and religion. Such a viewpoint, however, may turn out to be invalid with respect to other types of tales (fables, etc.) which on the whole may be older than the fairy tale. The realism of such tales dates from time immemorial and cannot be traced back to religious concepts.

2. Heroic treatment is older than humorous treatment. This is essentially a frequent variant of the preceding case. Thus the idea of entering into mortal combat with a dragon precedes that of beating it in a card game.

3. A form used logically is older than a form used nonsensically.[10]

4. An international form is older than national form.

Thus, if the dragon is encountered virtually the world over but is replaced in some fairy tales of the North by a bear or, in the South, by a lion, then the basic form is the dragon, while the lion and bear are derived forms.

Here we ought to say a few words concerning the methods of studying the fairy tale on an international scale. The material is so expansive that a single investigator cannot possibly study all the one hundred elements in the fairy tales of the entire world. He must first work through the fairy tales of one people, distinguishing between their basic and their derived forms. He must then repeat the same procedure for a second people, after which he may proceed to a comparative study.

In this connection, the thesis on international forms may be narrowed and stated thus: a broadly national form is older than a regional or provincial form. But, if we once start along this path, we cannot refute the following statement: a widespread form predates an isolated form. However, it is theoretically possible that a truly ancient form has survived only in isolated instances and that all other occurrences of it are younger.

---

[10]For other examples, see I. V. Karnauxova in *Krest'janskoe iskusstvo SSSR* [Peasant Art in the USSR] (Leningrad, 1927). [Au.]

Therefore great caution must be exercised when applying the quantitative principle (the use of statistics); moreover, *qualitative* considerations of the material under study must be brought into play. An example: in the fairy tale "Pretty Vasilisa" (No. 104 in Afanas'ev) the figure of Baba-Jaga is accompanied by the appearance of three mounted riders who symbolize morning, day, and night. The question spontaneously arises: is this not a fundamental feature peculiar to Baba-Jaga, one which has been lost in the other fairy tales? Yet, after a rigorous examination of special considerations (which do not warrant mention at this point), this opinion must be rejected.

**4**

By way of example we will go through all the possible changes of a single element — Baba-Jaga's hut. Morphologically, the hut represents the abode of the donor (that is, the actor who furnishes the hero with the magical tool). Consequently, we will direct attention not only to the hut but to the appearance of all the donor's abodes. We consider the basic Russian form of the abode to be the hut on chicken legs; it is in the forest, and it rotates. But since *one* element does not yield all the changes possible in a fairy tale, we will consider other examples as well.

1. *Reduction.* Instead of the full form, we may find the following types of changes:

i. The hut on chicken legs in the forest.
ii. The hut on chicken legs.
iii. The hut in the forest.
iv. The hut.
v. The pine forest (Afanas'ev No. 95).
vi. No mention of the abode.

Here the basic form is truncated. The chicken legs, the rotation, and the forest are omitted, and finally the very hut is dispensed with. Reduction may be termed an incomplete basic form. It is to be explained by a lapse of memory which in turn has more complex causes. Reduction points to the lack of agreement between the fairy tale and the whole tenor of the life surrounding it; reduction points to the low degree of relevance

of the fairy tale to a given environment, to a given epoch, or to the reciter of the fairy tale.

2. *Expansion.* We turn now to the opposite phenomenon, by which the basic form is extended and broadened by the addition of extra detail. Here is an expanded form: The hut on chicken legs in the forest rests on pancakes and is shingled with cookies.

More often than not, expansion is accompanied by reduction. Certain features are omitted, others are added. Expansion may be divided into categories according to origin (as is done below for substitutions). Some expanded forms derive from daily life, others represent an embellished detail from the fairy tale canon. This is illustrated by the preceding example. Examination reveals the donor to be a blend of hostile and hospitable qualities. Ivan is usually welcomed at the donor's abode. The forms this welcome may take are extremely varied. (She gave him food and drink. Ivan addresses the hut with the words: "We'd like to climb up and have a bite to eat." The hero sees in the hut a table laid, he samples all the food or eats his fill; he goes outside and slaughters some of the donor's cattle and chickens, etc.) This quality on the part of the donor is expressed by his very abode. In the German fairy tale *Hansel and Gretel*, this form is used somewhat differently, in conformance with the childlike nature of the story.

3. *Contamination.* In general, the fairy tale is in a state of decline today, and contamination is relatively frequent. Sometimes contaminated forms spread and take root. The idea that Baba-Jaga's hut turns continuously on its axis is an example of contamination. In the course of the action, the hut has a very specific purpose: it is a watchtower; the hero is tested to see whether or not he is worthy of receiving the magical tool. The hut greets Ivan with its closed side, and consequently it is sometimes called the "windowless, doorless hut." Its open side, that is, the side with the door, faces away from Ivan. It would appear that Ivan could very easily go around to the other side of the hut and enter through the door. But this Ivan cannot and in the fairy tale never does do. Instead, he utters the incantation: "Stand with your back to the forest and your front to me," or "Stand, as your mother stood

you," and so on. The result was usually: "The hut turned." This "turned" became "spins," and the expression, "When it has to, it turns this way and that" became simply, "It turns this way and that." The expression thus lost its sense but was not deprived of a certain characteristic vividness.

4. *Inversion.* Often the basic form is reversed. Female members of the cast are replaced by males, and vice versa. This procedure may involve the huts as well. Instead of a closed and inaccessible hut, we sometimes get a hut with a wide-open door.

5–6. *Intensification and Attenuation.* These types of transformation only apply to the *actions* of the cast. Identical actions may occur at various degrees of intensity. One example of intensification: the hero is exiled instead of merely being sent on a quest. Dispatch is one of the constant elements of the fairy tale; this element occurs in such a variety of forms that all degrees of dispatch intensity are demonstrable. The dispatch may be initiated in various ways. The hero is often asked to go and fetch some unusual thing. Sometimes the hero is given a task. ("Do me the service.") Often it is an order accompanied by threats, should he fail, and promises, should he succeed. Dispatch may also be a veiled form of exile: an evil sister sends her brother for the milk of a fierce animal in order to get rid of him; the master sends his helper to bring back a cow supposedly lost in the forest; a stepmother sends her stepdaughter to Baba-Jaga for fire. Finally, we have literal exile. These are the basic stages of dispatch, each of which allows a number of variations and transitional forms; they are especially important in examining fairy tales dealing with exiled characters. The order, accompanied by threats and promises, may be regarded as the basic form of dispatch. If the element of promise is omitted, such a reduction may be simultaneously considered an intensification — we are left with a dispatch *and* a threat. Omission of the threat will soften and weaken this form. Further attenuation consists in completely omitting the dispatch. As he prepares to leave, the son asks his parents for their blessing.

The six types of transformations discussed so far may be interpreted as very familiar *changes* in the basic form. There are, however, two other large groups of transformations: substitutions and assimilations. Both of them may be analyzed according to their origin.

7. *Internally Motivated Substitution.* Looking again at their donor's dwelling, we find the following forms:

i. A palace.
ii. A mountain alongside a fiery river.

These are not cases of either reduction or expansion, etc. They are not changes but substitutions. The indicated forms, however, are not drawn from without; they are drawn from the fairy tale's own reserves. A dislocation, a rearrangement of forms and material, has taken place. The palace (often of gold) is normally inhabited by a princess. Subsequently this dwelling is ascribed to the donor. Such dislocations in the fairy tale play a very important role. Each element has its own peculiar form. However, this form is not always exclusively bound to the given element. (The princess, for example, usually a sought member of the cast, may play the role of the donor, or that of the helper, etc.) One fairy tale image suppresses another; Baba-Jaga's daughter may appear as the princess. In the latter case, appropriately enough, Baba-Jaga does not live in her hut but in a palace, that is, the abode normally associated with a princess. Linked to this one are the palaces of copper, silver, and gold. The maidens living in such palaces are simultaneously donor and princess. The palaces possibly came about as the result of trebling the golden palace. Possibly they arose in complete independence, having, for example, no connection whatsoever with the idea of the Ages of Gold, Silver, and Iron, etc.

Similarly, the mountain alongside the fiery river is no other than the abode of the dragon, an abode which has been attributed to the donor.

These dislocations play an enormous role in creating transformations. The majority of all transformations are substitutions or dislocations generated from within the fairy tale.

8. *Externally Motivated Substitutions.* If we have the forms:

i. An inn.
ii. A two-storied house,

it is apparent that the fantastic hut has been replaced by forms of dwelling normal to real life. The majority of such substitutions may be explained very easily, but there are substitutions which require a special ethnographic exegesis. Elements from life are always immediately obvious, and, more often than not, scholars center their attention upon them.

9. *Confessional Substitutions*. Current religion is also capable of suppressing old forms, replacing them with new ones. Here we are involved with instances in which the devil functions as a winged messenger, or an angel is the donor of the magical tool, or an act of penance replaces the performance of a difficult task (the donor tests the hero). Certain legends are basically fairy tales in which all elements have undergone supporting substitutions. Every people has its own confessional substitutions. Christianity, Islam, and Buddhism are reflected in the fairy tales of the corresponding peoples.

10. *Substitution by Superstition*. Obviously, superstition and local beliefs may likewise suppress the original material of a fairy tale. However, we encounter this type of substitution much more rarely than we might expect at first glance (the errors of the mythological school). Pushkin was mistaken in saying that in the fairy tale:

Wonders abound, a wood-demon lurks,
Rusalka sits in the boughs.

If we encounter a wood-demon in the fairy tale, he almost always replaces Baba-Jaga. Water nymphs are met with but a single time in the entire Afanas'ev collection, and then only in an introductory flourish of dubious authenticity. In the collections by Onchukov, Zelinin, the Sokolovs, and others, there is not a single mention of Rusalka. The wood-demon only finds its way into the fairy tale because, as a creature of the forest, it resembles Baba-Jaga. The fairy tale accepts only those elements which can be readily accommodated in its construction.

11. *Archaic Substitutions*. We have already mentioned that the basic forms of the fairy tale go back to extinct religious concepts. Based on this fact, we can sometimes separate the basic forms from the derived ones. In certain unique instances, however, the basic form (more or less normal in the fairy tale epic) has been replaced by a form no less ancient which can likewise be traced back to a religious source, but whose occurrence is unique. For example, rather than the battle with the dragon in the fairy tale "The Witch and the Sun's Sister" (No. 93 in Afanas'ev), we have the following: the dragon's mate suggests to the prince, "Let Prince Ivan come with me to the scales and we'll see who outweighs whom." The scales toss Ivan sky-high. Here we have traces of psychostasia (the weighing of souls). Where this form — well known in ancient Egypt — came from and how it came to be preserved in the fairy tale are questions which need study.

It is not always easy to distinguish between an archaic substitution and a substitution imposed by superstition. Both have their roots (sometimes) in deep antiquity. But if some item in the fairy tale is also found in a living faith, the substitution may be considered as a relatively new one (the wood-demon). A pagan religion may have two offshoots: one in the fairy tale and the other in a faith or custom. They may well have confronted each other in the course of centuries, and the one may have suppressed the other. Conversely, if a fairy tale element is not attested to in a living faith (the scales), the substitution has its origin in deep antiquity and may be considered archaic.

12. *Literary Substitutions*. Literary material shows the same low degree of likelihood of being accepted by the fairy tale that current superstition does. The fairy tale possesses such resistance that other genres shatter against it; they do not readily blend. If clash takes place, the fairy tale wins. Of all the various literary genres, that of the fairy tale is the most likely to absorb elements from legend and epic. On rare occasions the novel provides a substitution; but even in such a case, it is only the chivalric romance which plays a certain role. The chivalric romance itself, however, is frequently a product of the fairy tale. The process occurs in stages: fairy tale→romance→fairy tale. Therefore, works such as "Eruslan Lazarevich" are among the "purest" of fairy tales in terms of construction, despite the bookish nature of individual ele-

ments. The *Schwank*, the novella, and other forms of popular prose are more flexible and more receptive to elements from other genres.

13. *Modification*. There are substitutions whose origin is not readily ascertainable. More often than not, these are imaginative substitutions which came into being through the teller's own resourcefulness. Such forms defy ethnographic or historical specification. We should note, however, that these substitutions play a greater role in animal tales and other types of tales than in fairy tales. (The bear is replaced by the wolf, one bird by another, etc.) Of course, they may occur in the fairy tale, too. Thus, as the winged messenger, we find an eagle, a falcon, a raven, geese, and others. As the sought-after marvel, we find a stag with antlers of gold, a steed with a mane of gold, a duck with feathers of gold, a pig with bristles of gold, and so on. Derived, secondary forms are generally those most likely to undergo modification. This may be shown by comparing a number of forms in which the sought wonder is simply a transformation of the sought princess with golden locks. If a comparison of the basic and the derived forms exhibits a certain descending line, a comparison of two derived forms reveals a certain parallelism. There are elements in the fairy tale having a particular variety of forms. One example is the "difficult task." If the task does not have a basic form, it makes little difference to the fairy tale, in terms of the unity of its construction, what kind of task is assigned. This phenomenon is even more apparent when we compare elements which have never belonged to a basic type of fairy tale. Motivation is one such element. But transformations sometimes create the need to motivate a certain act. As a result, we see a wide variety of motivations for one and the same act. Thus the hero's exile (exile is a secondary formation) is motivated by widely varied circumstances. On the other hand, the dragon's abduction of the maidens (a primary form) is hardly ever motivated externally but is motivated from within.

Certain features of the hut are also subject to modification. Instead of a hut on chicken legs, we encounter a hut on goat horns or on sheep legs.

14. *Substitutions of Unknown Origin*. We have been discussing substitutions from the point of view of their origin, but their origin is not always ascertainable; it does not always appear as a simple modification. Therefore we require a category for substitutions of unknown origin. For example, the little sister of the sun from the fairy tale "Little Sister" (Afanas'ev No. 93) plays the donor's role and may be considered a rudimentary form of the princess. She lives in the "solar rooms." We cannot know whether this reflects a sun cult, or the creative imagination of the narrator, or some suggestion by the collector asking the storyteller whether he knows any fairy tales dealing with a particular subject, or whether thus and so can be found; in such a case, the teller sometimes fabricates something to please the collector.

This places a limitation on substitutions. We could, of course, set up several more varieties which might be applied to a given isolated case. However, there is no need for that now. The substitutions specified here are meaningful throughout the entire breadth of fairy tale material; their application to isolated cases may be easily inferred and demonstrated by employing the transformational types cited.

Let us turn to another class of changes, that of assimilations. By assimilation we understand an incomplete suppression of one form by another, the two forms merging into a single form. Because assimilations follow the same classification scheme as the substitutions, they will be enumerated in brief.

15. *Internally Motivated Assimilations*. An example occurs in the forms:

i. A hut under a golden roof.
ii. A hut by a fiery river.

In a fairy tale we often meet with a palace under a golden roof. A hut plus a palace under a golden roof equals a hut under a golden roof. The same is true in the case of the hut by the fiery river.

The fairy tale "Fedor Vodovich and Ivan Vodovich" (Onchukov No. 4) provides a very interesting example. Two such very heterogeneous elements as the miraculous birth of the hero and his pursuit by the dragon's wives (sisters) have been drawn together by assimilation. The wives of the dragon, in pursuing the hero, usually turn into a well, a cloud, or a bed and situate themselves in Ivan's path. If he samples some fruit or takes a drink of water, etc., he is torn to pieces. For the miraculous birth, this motif is used in the following manner: the princess strolls about her father's courtyard, sees a well with a small cup, and by it a bed (the apple tree has been forgotten). She drinks a cupful and lies down on the bed to rest. From this she conceives and gives birth to two sons.

16. *Externally Motivated Assimilations.* Take the form:

i. A hut on the edge of the village.
ii. A cave in the woods.

Here we find that the imaginary hut has become a real hut and a real cave, but the solitude of its inhabitant has been preserved. Indeed, in the second instance, the forest element is also preserved. Fairy tale plus reality produces an assimilation which favors real life.

17. *Confessional Assimilations.* This process may be exemplified by the replacement of the dragon by the devil; however, the devil, like the dragon, dwells in a lake. The concept of evil beings of the deep does not necessarily have anything in common with the so-called lower mythology of the peasants; it is often explained as simply one type of transformation.

18. *Assimilation via Superstition.* This is a relatively rare phenomenon. The wood-demon living in a hut on chicken legs is an example.

19–20. *Literary and Archaic Assimilations.* These are encountered even more rarely. Assimilations with the folk epic and legend are of some importance in the Russian fairy tale. Here, however, we are more likely to find suppression rather than the assimilation of one form by another, while the components of the fairy tale are preserved as such. Archaic assimilations require a detailed examination of each occurrence. They do occur, but identifying them is possible only after highly specialized research.

Our survey of the transformation of types can end at this point. It is impossible to assert that absolutely all fairy tale forms will be accommodated by our classificatory scheme, but at any rate a significant number clearly are. It would have been possible to bring in still other types of transformations, such as specification and generalization. In the first case, general phenomena become particularized (instead of the thrice-tenth kingdom, we find the city Khvalinsk); in the latter case, the opposite occurs (the thrice-tenth kingdom becomes simply a "different, other" kingdom, etc.). But almost all types of specification may also be regarded as substitutions, and generalizations, as reductions. This is true, too, for rationalization (a winged steed becomes an earthbound horse) as well as for the conversion of the fairy tale into an anecdote, etc. A correct and consistent application of the types of transformation indicated will give a firmer foundation to the study of the fairy tale in the process of its development.

What is true for the individual elements of the fairy tale is also true for the fairy tale as a whole. If an extra element is added, we have amplification; in the reverse case, we have reduction, etc. Applying these methods to entire fairy tales is important for comparative studies on fairy tale plots.

One very important problem remains. If we write out all the occurrences (or at least a great many of them) of one element, not all the forms of one element can be traced back to some single basis. Let us suppose that we accept Baba-Jaga as the basic form of the donor. Such forms are a witch, Grannie-Behind-the-Door, Grandma-Widow, an old lady, an old man, a shepherd, a wood-demon, an angel, the devil, three maids, the king's daughter, etc. — all may be satisfactorily explained as substitutions and other transformations of Baba-Jaga. But then we encounter a "fingernail-sized peasant with an elbow-length beard." Such a form for the donor does not come from Baba-Jaga. If such a form does occur in a religion, we have a form which has been coordinated with Baba-Jaga; if not, we have a substitution of unknown origin. Each element may have several basic forms, although the number of such parallel, coordinated forms is usually insignificant.

**5**

Our outline would be incomplete if we did not show a model for applying our observations. We will use more palpable material to exhibit a series of transformations; let us take the forms:

The dragon abducts the king's daughter —
the dragon tortures the king's daughter —
the dragon demands the king's daughter.

From the point of view of the morphology of the fairy tale, we are dealing here with an element which we will call *basic harm*. Such harm usually serves as the start of the plot. In accordance with the principles proposed in this paper, we should compare not only abduction with abduction, etc., but also with all the various types of basic harm as one of the components of the fairy tale.

Caution demands that all three forms be regarded as coordinated forms, but it is possible to suggest that the first is still the basic form. In Egypt we find death conceived of as the abduction of the soul by a dragon. But this concept has been forgotten, whereas the idea that illness is a demon settled within the body lives on today. Finally, the dragon's demand for the princess as tribute reflects a shadowy archaism from real life. It is accompanied by the appearance of an army, which surrounds the city and threatens war. However, we cannot be certain. Be that as it may, all three forms are very old, and each allows a number of transformations.

Let us take the first form:

The dragon abducts the king's daughter.

The dragon is viewed as the embodiment of evil. Confessional influence turns the dragon into a devil:

Devils abduct the king's daughter.

The same influence affects the object of abduction:

The devil abducts the priest's daughter.

The dragon figure has already become foreign to the village. It has been replaced by a dangerous animal that is better known (externally motivated substitution), the animal acquiring fantastic attributes (modifications):

A bear with fur of iron carries off the king's children.

The villain merges with Baba-Jaga. One part of the fairy tale influences another part (internally motivated substitution). Baba-Jaga is the essence of the female sex, and, correspondingly, the person abducted is a male (inversion):

A witch abducts the son of an old couple.

In one of the forms constantly complicating the fairy tale, the hero's brothers carry out a secondary abduction of their brother's prize. The intent to do harm has now been transferred to the hero's kin. This is a canonical form of complicating the action:

His brothers abduct Ivan's bride.

The wicked brothers are replaced by other villainous relatives from reserve members of the fairy tale's cast (internally motivated substitution):

The king (Ivan's father-in-law) abducts Ivan's wife.

The princess herself may take over the same function, and the fairy tale may assume more amusing forms. Here the figure of the villain has been reduced:

The princess flees from her husband.

In all these cases, a human being was abducted, but, by way of example, the light of day may be abducted (an archaic substitution):

The dragon abducts the light of the kingdom.

The dragon is replaced by other monstrous animals (modification); the object of abduction merges with the imagined life of the court:

The mink-beast pilfers animals from the king's menagerie.

Talismans play a significant role in the fairy tale. They are often the only means by which Ivan can attain his goal. Hence it is understandable that they are often the object of abduction.

If the action is thus complicated in the middle of the fairy tale, such an abduction is even obligatory as far as fairy tale canon is concerned. This middle moment in the fairy tale may be transferred to the beginning (internally motivated substitution). The abductor of the talisman is often a cheat, or a landowner, and so on (externally motivated substitution):

A shrewd lad abducts Ivan's talisman.
A landowner abducts the peasant's talisman.

The firebird fairy tale represents a transitional stage leading to other forms; here the stolen apples of gold are not talismans (cf. orpine apples). We should add that the theft of the talisman is not possible as a complication at the fairy tale's midpoint unless the talisman has already been acquired. The talisman can be made off with at the beginning only if its possession is properly motivated, however briefly. It is for this reason that the stolen items which appear at the beginning of the tale are not often talismans. The firebird found its way from the middle section of the tale back to the beginning. The bird is one of the basic forms of transporting Ivan to the thrice-tenth kingdom. Golden feathers and similar features are usually attributed to the animal life of the fairy tale:

The firebird steals the king's apples.

In every case the abduction is preserved. The disappearance of a bride, a daughter, a wife, etc., is ascribed to a mythic substratum in the fairy tale. However, this explanation of such a disappearance is alien to modern peasant life, therefore an alien, imported mythology is replaced by sorcery. Disappearance is ascribed to magic spells cast by evil sorcerers and sorceresses. The nature of the villainous deed changes, but its result is still the same: a disappearance entailing a quest (substitution via superstition):

A sorcerer abducts the king's daughter,
Nursie bewitches Ivan's bride and forces her to flee.

Again we see the activity transferred to wicked relatives:

Sisters force the girl's groom to flee.

Turning to the transformations of our second base form (a dragon tortures the king's daughter), we encounter transformations on the same patterns:

The devil tortures the king's daughter, etc.

Here the torture assumes the nature of seizure and vampirism, which can be fully explained ethnographically. Instead of the dragon and the devil, we see again another of the fairy tale's evil beings:

Baba-Jaga tortures the mistress of the knights.

A third variation of the basic form poses the threat of forced marriage:

The dragon demands the king's daughter.

This reveals a number of transformations:

A water sprite demands the king's son, etc.

This same form, morphologically speaking, may lead to a declaration of war without any of the king's offspring being demanded (reduction); a transfer of similar forms to relatives produces:

The sister, a witch, seeks to devour the king's son (her brother).

This case (Afanas'ev No. 93) is of special interest. Here the prince's sister is called a dragoness. Thus we have a classical example of internal assimilation. It points up the need for caution in studying kinship ties in the fairy tale. The marriage of brother and sister and other forms are not necessarily remnants of an old custom; rather, they may be the results of certain transformations, as the above case clearly shows.

The objection may be raised against all of the preceding that anything at all could be fitted into a single phrase having but two components. This is far from true. How would the start of the plot of the fairy tale "Frost, Sun and Wind" and many others fit into such a form? Second, the observed phenomena represent the same constructional element with respect to the over-all composition. Although differently stated, they result in identical patterns in the progress of the plot's: a plea for help may be masked as a departure from home, as a meeting with a donor, etc. Not every fairy tale containing a theft produces this construction. If this construction does not follow, subsequent patterns, however similar, cannot be compared, for they are heteronymous. Otherwise, we have to admit that an element from the fairy tale has entered a construction foreign to the tale. Thus we return to the necessity of making juxtapositions on the basis of identical components and not external similarity.

# I. A. Richards
## 1893–1979

*A pioneering thinker whose ideas would shape the New Criticism, Ivor Armstrong Richards was born in Sandbach, Cheshire. Educated at Magdalen College, Cambridge University, Richards was a lecturer there in the new discipline of "English" and the moral sciences from 1922 to 1929, years in which he wrote three profoundly influential books:* The Meaning of Meaning: A Study of the Influence of Language Upon Thought and of the Science of Symbolism *(1923) with C. K. Ogden,* Principles of Literary Criticism *(1924), and* Practical Criticism *(1929). His studies in psychology and semantics contributed to his interest in the "close reading" of a text. During the 1930s, Richards devoted much of his time to developing C. K. Ogden's system of Basic English, a synthetic language of only 850 words that, it was hoped, would become the language of universal human intelligibility — a program he brought to China, where he lived and taught from 1929 to 1936. (Meanwhile, his student William Empson developed Richards's ideas on reading into one variant of the New Criticism.) In 1944 Richards became a professor of English at Harvard University and in 1963 emeritus professor. Among his other works are* Science and Poetry *(1926),* Coleridge on Imagination *(1934),* The Philosophy of Rhetoric *(1936),* Speculative Instruments *(1955), and* Poetries *(1974).*

# From *Principles of Literary Criticism*

## Chapter XXXIV
## The Two Uses of Language

*The intelligible forms of ancient poets
The fair humanities of old religion . . .
They live no longer in the faith of reason:
But still the heart doth need a language, still
Doth the old instinct bring back the old names.*
— COLERIDGE, *Piccolomini*

There are two totally distinct uses of language. But because the theory of language is the most neglected of all studies they are in fact hardly ever distinguished. Yet both for the theory of poetry and for the narrower aim of understanding much which is said about poetry a clear comprehension of the differences between these uses is indispensable. For this we must look somewhat closely at the mental processes which accompany them.

It is unfortunate but not surprising that most of the psychological terms which we naturally employ tend to blur the distinction. "Knowledge," "belief," "assertion," "thought," and "understanding," for example, as ordinarily used, are ambiguous in a fashion which disguises and obscures the point which must be brought out. They record distinctions which are oblique to the distinctions required, they are cross-cuts of analysis made in the wrong place and in the wrong direction, useful enough for some purposes no doubt, but for this present purpose very confusing. We shall do well to put them out of mind for a while if possible.

The chief departure made from current conceptions in the sketch of the mind given in Chapter XI lay in the substitution of the *causes*, the *characters*, and the *consequences* of a mental event, for its aspects as *thought, feeling*, and *will*. This treatment was introduced with a view to the analysis which now occupies us. Among the causes of most mental events, we urged, two sets may be distinguished. On the one hand there are the present stimuli reaching the mind through the sensory nerves, and, in cooperation with these, the effects of past stimuli associated with them. On the other hand is a set of quite different factors, the state of the organism, its needs, its readiness to respond to this or that kind of stimulus. The impulses which arise take their character and their course from the interaction of these two sets. We must keep them clearly distinguished.

The relative importance of the two sets of factors varies enormously. A sufficiently hungry man will eat almost anything which can be chewed or swallowed. The nature of the substance, within these limits, has very little effect upon his behaviour. A replete person, by contrast, will only eat such things as he expects will taste pleasant, or regards as possessing definite beneficial properties, for example, medicines. His behaviour, in other words, depends almost entirely upon the character of his optical or olfactory stimulation.

So far as an impulse owes its character to its stimulus (or to such effects of past accompanying or connected stimuli as are revived) so far is it a *reference*, to use the term which we introduced in Chapter XI, to stand for the property of mental events which we substitute for thought or cognition.[1] It is plain that the independent internal conditions of the organism usually intervene to distort reference in some degree. But very many of our needs can only be satisfied if the impulses are left undistorted. Bitter experience has taught

us to leave some of them alone, to let them reflect or correspond with external states of affairs as much as they can, undisturbed as far as possible by internal states of affairs, our needs and desires.

In all our behaviour can be distinguished stimuli we receive, and the ways in which we use them. What we receive may be any kind of stimulus, but only when the reaction we make to it tallies with its nature and varies with it in quasi-independence of the uses we make of it does reference occur.

Those to whom visual images are of service in considering complex matters may find it convenient at this point to imagine a circle or sphere constantly bombarded by minute particles (stimuli). Within the sphere may be pictured complex mechanisms continually changing for reasons having nothing to do with the external stimuli. These mechanisms by opening little gateways select which of the stimuli shall be allowed to come in and take effect. So far as the subsequent convulsions are due to the nature of the impacts and to lingering effects of impacts which have accompanied similar impacts in the past, the convulsions are referential. So far as they are due to the independent motions of the internal mechanisms themselves, reference fails. This diagrammatic image may possibly be of convenience to some. By those who distrust such things it may with advantage be disregarded. It is not introduced as a contribution to neurology, and is in no way a ground for the author's view.

The extent to which reference is interfered with by needs and desires is underestimated even by those who, not having yet forgotten the events of 1914–1918, are most sceptical as to the independence of opinions and desires.[2] Even the most ordinary and familiar objects are perceived as it pleases us to perceive them rather than as they are, whenever error does not directly deprive us of advantages. It is almost impossible for anyone to secure a correct impression of his own personal appearance or of the features of

[1] The reader who is a psychologist will notice many points in this statement at which elaboration and qualifications are required. For example, when we are "introspecting," factors normally belonging to the second set may enter the first. But he will be able, if he grasps the general theory, to supply these complications himself. I did not wish to burden the text with unnecessary intricacies. [Au.]

[2] Richards's implication is that the destruction of World War I would not have occurred if both sides had not distorted the likely outcome based on "needs and desires." [Ed.]

anyone in whom he is personally interested. Nor is it perhaps often desirable that he should.

For the demarcation of the fields where impulse should be as completely as possible dependent upon and correspondent with external situation, those in which reference should take prior place from those in which it may be subordinated to appetencies with advantage, is not a simple matter. On many views of the good and of what should be, themselves results of subordinating reference to emotional satisfactions, there could be no question. Truth, it would be said, has claims prior to all other considerations. Love not grounded upon knowledge would be described as worthless. We ought not to admire what is not beautiful and if our mistress be not really beautiful when impartially considered we ought, so the doctrine runs, to admire her, if at all, for other reasons. The chief points of interest about such views are the confusions which make them plausible. Beauty as an internal quality of things is usually involved, as well as Good the unanalysable Idea. Both are special twists given to some of our impulses by habits deriving ultimately from desires. They linger in our minds because to think of a thing as Good or Beautiful gives more *immediate* emotional satisfaction than to *refer* to it as satisfying our impulses in one special fashion (cf. Chapter VII) or another (cf. Chapter XXXII).

To think about Good or Beauty is not necessarily to refer to anything. For the term "thinking" covers mental operations in which the impulses are so completely governed by internal factors and so out of control of stimulus that no reference occurs. Most "thinking of" includes reference in some degree, of course, but not all, and similarly much reference would not commonly be described as thinking. When we drop something which is too hot to hold we would not usually be said to have done so through thinking. The two terms overlap, and their definitions, if there be a definition of "thinking" as commonly used, are of different types. This is why "Thought" was on an earlier page described as marking an oblique distinction.

To return, the claims of reference are by no means easy to adjust with other claims. An immense extension of our powers of referring has recently been made. With amazing swiftness Science has opened out field after field of possible reference. Science is simply the organisation of references with a view solely to the convenience and facilitation of reference. It has advanced mainly because other claims, typically the claims of our religious desires, have been set aside. For it is no accident that Science and Religion conflict. They are different principles upon which impulses may be organised, and the more closely they are examined the more inevitable is the incompatibility seen to be. Any so-called reconciliation which is ever effected will involve bestowing the name Religion upon something utterly different from any of the systematisations of impulses which it now denotes, for the reason that the belief elements present would have a different character.

Many attempts have been made to reduce Science to a position of subjection to some instinct or emotion or desire, to curiosity for example. A special passion for knowledge for its own sake has even been invented. But in fact all the passions and all the instincts, all human needs and desires may *on occasion* supply the motive force for Science. There is no human activity which may not on occasion require undistorted reference. The essential point, however, is that Science is autonomous. The impulses developed in it are modified only by one another, with a view to the greatest possible completeness and systematisation, and for the facilitation of further references. So far as other considerations distort them they are not yet Science or have fallen out of it.

To declare Science autonomous is very different from subordinating all our activities to it. It is merely to assert that so far as any body of references is undistorted it belongs to Science. It is not in the least to assert that no references may be distorted if advantage can thereby be gained. And just as there are innumerable human activities which require undistorted references if they are to be satisfied, so there are innumerable other human activities not less important which equally require distorted references or, more plainly, *fictions*.

The use of fictions, the imaginative use of them rather, is not a way of hoodwinking ourselves. It is not a process of pretending to our-selves that things are not as they are. It is per-fectly compatible with the fullest and grimmest recognition of the exact state of affairs on all occasions. It is no make-believe. But so awk-wardly have our references and our attitudes be-come entangled that such pathetic spectacles as Mr. Yeats trying desperately to believe in fairies or Mr. Lawrence impugning the validity of solar physics, are all too common. To be forced by desire into any unwarrantable belief is a calamity. The state which ensues is often extraordinarily damaging to the mind. But this common misuse of fictions should not blind us to their immense services provided we do not take them for what they are not, degrading the chief means by which our attitudes to actual life may be adjusted into the material of a long-drawn delirium.[3]

If we knew enough it might be possible that all necessary attitudes could be obtained through scientific references alone. Since we do not know very much yet, we can leave this very remote possibility, once recognised, alone.

Fictions whether aroused by statements or by analogous things in other arts may be used in many ways. They may be used, for example, to deceive. But this is not a characteristic use in poetry. The distinction which needs to be kept clear does not set up fictions in opposition to verifiable truths in the scientific sense. A state-ment may be used for the sake of the *reference*, true or false, which it causes. This is the *scientific* use of language. But it may also be used for the sake of the effects in emotion and attitude pro-duced by the reference it occasions. This is the *emotive* use of language. The distinction once clearly grasped is simple. We may either use words for the sake of the references they pro-mote, or we may use them for the sake of the attitudes and emotions which ensue. Many ar-rangements of words evoke attitudes without any

reference being required *en route*. They operate like musical phrases. But usually references are involved *as conditions* for, or *stages in*, the en-suing development of attitudes, yet it is still the attitudes not the references which are important. It matters not at all in such cases whether the references are true or false. Their sole function is to bring about and support the attitudes which are the further response. The questioning, veri-ficatory way of handling them is irrelevant, and in a competent reader it is not allowed to inter-fere. "Better a plausible impossibility than an improbable possibility" said Aristotle very wise-ly;[4] there is less danger of an inappropriate re-action.

The differences between the mental processes involved in the two cases are very great, though easily overlooked. Consider what failure for each use amounts to. For scientific language a differ-ence in the references is itself failure: the end has not been attained. But for emotive language the widest differences in reference are of no im-portance if the further effects in attitude and emo-tion are of the required kind.

Further, in the scientific use of language not only must the references be correct for success, but the connections and relations of references to one another must be of the kind which we call logical. They must not get in one another's way, and must be so organised as not to impede further reference. But for emotive purposes logical ar-rangement is not necessary. It may be and often is an obstacle. For what matters is that the series of attitudes due to the references should have their own proper organisation, their own emo-tional interconnection, and this often has no de-pendence upon the logical relations of such ref-erences as may be concerned in bringing the attitudes into being.

A few notes of the chief uses of the word "Truth" in Criticism may help to prevent mis-understanding:

1. The scientific sense that, namely, in which references, and derivatively statements symbol-ising references, are true, need not delay us. A reference is true when the things to which it

[3]Revelation Doctrines when once given a foothold tend to interfere everywhere. They serve as a kind of omnipotent major premise justifying any and every conclusion. A spec-imen: "Since the function of Art is to pierce through the Real World, then it follows that the artist cannot be too definite in his outlines, and that good drawing is the foundation of all good art." — Charles Gardner, *Vision and Vesture*, p. 54. [Au.]

[4]Aristotle, *Poetics*, Ch. 25, p. 62. [Ed.]

refs are actually together in the way in which it refers to them. Otherwise it is false. This sense is one very little involved by any of the arts. For the avoidance of confusions it would be well if the term "true" could be reserved for this use. In purely scientific discourse it could and should be, but such discourse is uncommon. In point of fact the emotive power which attaches to the word is far too great for it to be abandoned in general discussion; the temptation to a speaker who needs to stir certain emotions and evoke certain attitudes of approval and acceptance is overwhelming. No matter how various the senses in which it may be used, and even when it is being used in no sense whatever, its effects in promoting attitudes will still make it indispensable; people will still continue to use the word with the same promiscuity as ever.

2. The most usual other sense is that of acceptability. The "Truth" of *Robinson Crusoe* is the acceptability of things we are told, their acceptability in the interests of the effects of the narrative, not their correspondence with any actual facts involving Alexander Selkirk[5] or another. Similarly the falsity of happy endings to *Lear* or to *Don Quixote*, is their failure to be acceptable to those who have fully responded to the rest of the work. It is in this sense that "Truth" is equivalent to "internal necessity" or rightness. That is "true" or "internally necessary" which completes or accords with the rest of the experience, which cooperates to arouse our ordered response, whether the response of Beauty or another. "What the Imagination seizes as Beauty must be Truth," said Keats, using this sense of "Truth," though not without confusion.[6] Sometimes it is held that whatever is redundant or otiose, whatever is not required, although not obstructive or disruptive, is also false. "Surplusage!" said Pater, "the artist will dread that, as the runner on his muscles" himself perhaps in this instance sweating his sentence down too finely.[7] But this is to make excessive demands upon the artist. It is to apply the axe of retrenchment in the wrong place. Superabundance is a common characteristic of great art, much less dangerous than the preciousness that too contrived an economy tends to produce. The essential point is whether what is unnecessary interferes or not with the rest of the response. If it does not, the whole thing is all the better probably for the extra solidity which it thereby gains.

This internal acceptability or "convincingness" needs to be contrasted with other acceptabilities. Thomas Rymer, for example, refused to accept Iago for external reasons: "To entertain the audience with something new and surprising against common sense and nature, he would pass upon us a close, dissembling rascal, instead of an open-hearted, frank, plain-dealing Souldier, a character constantly born by them for some thousands of years in the World." "The truth is," he observes, "this author's head was full of villainous, unnatural images."[8]

He is remembering no doubt Aristotle's remark that "the artist must preserve the type and yet ennoble it," but interpreting it in his own way. For him the type is fixed simply by convention and his acceptances take no note of internal necessities but are governed merely by accordance with external canons. His is an extreme case, but to avoid his error in subtler matters is in fact sometimes the hardest part of the critic's undertaking. But whether our conception of the type is derived in some such absurd way, or taken, for example, as from a handbook of zoology, is of slight consequence. It is the taking of any *external* canon which is critically dangerous. When in the same connection Rymer objects that there never was a Moorish General in the service of the Venetian Republic, he is applying another external canon, that of historic fact. This mistake is less insidious, but Ruskin used to be particularly fond of the analogous mistake in connection with the "truth" of drawing.

3. Truth may be equivalent to Sincerity. This character of the artist's work we have already touched upon briefly in connection with Tolstoy's theory of communication (Chapter XXIII).[9] It may perhaps be most easily defined from the

[5]The original on whose real-life adventures Defoe based *Robinson Crusoe*. [Ed.]
[6]See Keats, Letter to Benjamin Bailey, p. 318. [Ed.]
[7]*Essay on Style*, p. 19. [Au.]

[8]*A Short View of Tragedy*. [Au.]
[9]See Tolstoy, *What Is Art?*, p. 434. [Ed.]

critic's point of view negatively, as the absence of any apparent attempt on the part of the artist to work effects upon the reader which do not work for himself. Too simple definitions must be avoided. It is well known that Burns in writing "*Ae fond kiss*" was only too anxious to escape *Nancy's* (Mrs. Maclehose's) attentions, and similar instances could be multiplied indefinitely. Absurdly naïve views upon the matter[10] exemplified by the opinion that Bottomley must have believed himself to be inspired or he would not have moved his audiences, are far too common. At the level at which Bottomley harangued any kind of exaltation in the orator, whether due to pride or to champagne, would make his stuff effective. But at Burns's level a very different situation arises. Here his probity and sincerity *as an artist* are involved; external circumstances are irrelevant, but there is perhaps internal evidence in the poem of a flaw in its creating impulse. Compare as a closely similar poem in which there is no flaw, Byron's "*When we two parted.*"

## Chapter XXXV
## Poetry and Beliefs

*What I see very well is the wide-spread, infinite harm of putting fancy for knowledge (to speak like Socrates), or rather of living by choice in a twilight of the mind where fancy and knowledge are indiscernible.*    — *Euripides the Rationalist*

It is evident that the bulk of poetry consists of statements which only the very foolish would think of attempting to verify. They are not the kind of things which can be verified. If we recall what was said in Chapter XVI as to the natural generality or vagueness of reference we shall see another reason why references as they occur in poetry are rarely susceptible of scientific truth or falsity. Only references which are brought into certain highly complex and very special combinations, so as to correspond to the ways in which things actually hang together, can be either true

---

[10]Cf. A. Clutton-Brock, *The Times*, 11 July 1922, p. 13. [Au.] Horatio Bottomley was a demagogic politician. [Ed.]

or false, and most references in poetry are not knit together in this way.

But even when they are, on examination, frankly false, this is no defect. Unless, indeed, the obviousness of the falsity forces the reader to reactions which are incongruent or disturbing to the poem. And equally, a point more often misunderstood, their truth, when they are true, is no merit.[11] The people who say "How True!" at intervals while reading Shakespeare are misusing his work, and, comparatively speaking, wasting their time. For all that matters in either case is acceptance, that is to say, the initiation and development of the further response.

Poetry affords the clearest examples of this subordination of reference to attitude. It is the supreme form of *emotive* language. But there can be no doubt that originally all language was emotive; its scientific use is a later development, and most language is still emotive. Yet the late development has come to seem the natural and the normal use, largely because the only people who have reflected upon language were at the moment of reflection using it scientifically.

The emotions and attitudes resulting from a statement used emotively need not be directed towards anything to which the statement refers. This is clearly evident in dramatic poetry, but much more poetry than is usually supposed is dramatic in structure. As a rule a statement in poetry arouses attitudes much more wide and general in direction than the references of the statement. Neglect of this fact makes most verbal analysis of poetry irrelevant. And the same is true of those critical but emotive utterances about poetry which gave rise to this discussion. No one, it is plain, can read poetry successfully with-

---

[11]No merit, that is, *in this connection*. There may be some exceptions to this, cases in which the explicit recognition of the truth of a statement as opposed to the simple acceptance of it, is *necessary* to the full development of the further response. But I believe that such cases will on careful examination be found to be very rare with competent readers. Individual differences, corresponding to the different degrees to which individuals have their belief feelings, their references, and their attitudes entangled, are to be expected. There are, of course, an immense number of scientific beliefs present among the conditions of every attitude. But since acceptances would do equally well in their place they are not *necessary* to it. [Au.]

out, consciously or unconsciously, observing the distinction between the two uses of words. That does not need to be insisted upon. But further no one can understand such utterances about poetry as that quoted from Dr. Mackail in our third chapter, or Dr. Bradley's cry that "Poetry is a spirit," or Shelley's that "A poem is the very image of life expressed in its eternal truth,"[12] or the passages quoted above from Coleridge, without distinguishing the making of a statement from the incitement or expression of an attitude. But too much inferior poetry has been poured out as criticism, too much sack and too little bread; confusion between the two activities, on the part of writers and readers alike, is what is primarily responsible for the backwardness of critical studies. What other stultifications of human endeavour it is also responsible for we need not linger here to point out. The separation of prose from poetry, if we may so paraphrase the distinction, is no mere academic activity. There is hardly a problem outside mathematics which is not complicated by its neglect, and hardly any emotional response which is not crippled by irrelevant intrusions. No revolution in human affairs would be greater than that which a wide-spread observance of this distinction would bring about.

One perversion in especial needs to be noticed. It is constantly present in critical discussion, and is in fact responsible for Revelation Doctrines. Many attitudes, which arise without dependence upon any reference, merely by the interplay and resolution of impulses otherwise awakened, can be momentarily encouraged by suitable beliefs held as scientific beliefs are held. So far as this encouragement is concerned, the truth or falsity of these beliefs does not matter, the immediate effect is the same in either case. When the attitude is important, the temptation to base it upon some reference which is treated as established scientific truths are treated is very great, and the poet thus easily comes to invite the destruction of his work; Wordsworth puts forward his Pantheism, and other people doctrines of Inspiration, Idealism, and Revelation.

The effect is twofold; an appearance of se-

curity and stability is given to the attitude, which thus seems to be justified; and at the same time it is no longer so necessary to sustain this attitude by the more difficult means peculiar to the arts, or to pay full attention to form. The reader can be relied upon to do more than his share. That neither effect is desirable is easily seen. The attitude for the sake of which the belief is introduced is thereby made not more but less stable. Remove the belief, once it has affected the attitude; the attitude collapses. It may later be restored by more appropriate means, but that is another matter. And all such beliefs are very likely to be removed; their logical connections with other beliefs scientifically entertained are, to say the least, shaky. In the second place these attitudes, produced not by the appropriate means but, as it were by a short cut, through beliefs, are rarely so healthy, so vigorous and full of life as the others. Unlike attitudes normally produced they usually require an increased stimulus every time that they are reinstated. The belief has to grow more and more fervent, more and more convinced, in order to produce the same attitude. The believer has to pass from one paroxysm of conviction to another, enduring each time a greater strain.

This substitution of an intellectual formula for the poem or work of art is of course most easily observed in the case of religion, where the temptation is greatest. In place of an experience, which is a direct response to a certain selection of the possibilities of stimulation, we have a highly indirect response, made, not to the actual influences of the world upon us, but to a special kind of belief as to some particular state of affairs.[13] There is a suppressed conditional clause implicit in all poetry. If things were such and such then . . . and so the response develops. The amplitude and fineness of the response, its sanc-

[13]In view of a possible misunderstanding at this point, compare Chapter X, especially the final paragraph. If a belief in Retributive Justice, for example, is fatal to *Prometheus Unbound*, so in another way is the belief that the Millennium is at hand. To steer an unperplexed path between these opposite dangers is extremely difficult. The distinctions required are perhaps better left to the reader's reflection than laboured further in the faulty terminology which alone at present is available. [Au.]

[12]See Shelley, "A Defence of Poetry," p. 323. [Ed.]

tion and authority, in other words, depend upon this freedom from actual assertion in all cases in which the belief is questionable on any ground whatsoever. For any such assertion involves suppressions, of indefinite extent, which may be fatal to the wholeness, the *integrity* of the experience. And the assertion is almost always unnecessary; if we look closely we find that the greatest poets, as poets, though frequently not as critics, refrain from assertion. But it is easy, by what seems only a slight change of approach, to make the initial step an act of faith, and to make the whole response dependent upon a belief as to a matter of fact. Even when the belief is true, the damage done to the whole experience may be great, in the case of a person whose reasons for this belief are inadequate, for example, and the increased temporary vivacity which is the cause of perversion is no sufficient compensation. As a convenient example it may be permissible to refer to the Poet Laureate's anthology, *The Spirit of Man*, and I have the less hesitation since the passages there gathered together are chosen with such unerring taste and discrimination. But to turn them into a statement of a philosophy is very noticeably to degrade them and to restrict and diminish their value. The use of verse quotations as chapter headings is open to the same objection. The experiences which ensue may seem very similar to the experiences of free reading; they feel similar; but all the signs which can be most trusted, after-effects for example, show them to be different. The vast differences in the means by which they are brought about is also good ground for supposing them to be dissimilar, but this difference is obscured through the ambiguities of the term "belief."

There are few terms which are more troublesome in psychology than belief, formidable though this charge may seem. The sense in which we believe a scientific proposition is not the sense in which we believe emotive utterances, whether they are political "We will not sheathe the sword," or critical "The progress of poetry is immortal," or poetic. Both senses of belief are complicated and difficult to define. Yet we commonly appear to assume that they are the same or that they differ only in the kind and degree of evidence available. Scientific belief we may perhaps define as readiness to act as though the reference symbolised by the proposition which is believed were true. Readiness to act in *all* circumstances and in *all* connections into which it can enter. This rough definition would, of course, need elaborating to be complete, but for our present purposes it may suffice. The other element usually included in a definition of belief, namely a feeling or emotion of acceptance, the "This is sooth, accept it!" feeling, is often absent in scientific belief and is not essential.

Emotive belief is very different. Readiness to act as though some references were true is often involved, but the connections and circumstances in which this readiness remains are narrowly restricted. Similarly the extent of the action is ordinarily limited. Consider the acceptances involved in the understanding of a play, for example. They form a system any element of which is believed while the rest are believed and so long as the acceptance of the whole growing system leads to successful response. Some, however, are of the form "Given this then that would follow," general beliefs, that is to say, of the kind which led Aristotle, in the passage quoted above, to describe Poetry as a more philosophical thing than history because chiefly conversant of universal truth.[14] But if we look closely into most instances of such beliefs we see that they are entertained only in the special circumstances of the poetic experience. They are held as conditions for further effects, our attitudes and emotional responses, and not as we hold beliefs in laws of nature, which we expect fo find verified on all occasions. If dramatic necessities were actually scientific laws we should know much more psychology than any reasonable person pretends that we do. That these beliefs as to "how any person of a certain character would speak or act, probably or necessarily," upon which so much drama seems to depend, are not scientific, but are held only for the sake of their dramatic effect, is shown clearly by the ease with which we abandon them if the advantage lies the other way. The medical impossibility of Desdemona's last speech is perhaps as good an example as any.

[14]See Aristotle, *Poetics*, Ch. 9, p. 48. [Ed.]

The bulk of the beliefs involved in the arts are of this kind, provisional acceptances, holding only in special circumstances (in the state of mind which is the poem or work of art) acceptances made for the sake of the "imaginative experience" which they make possible. The difference between these emotive beliefs and scientific beliefs is not one of degree but of kind. As feelings they are very similar, but as attitudes their difference in structure has widespread consequences.

There remains to be discussed another set of emotive effects which may also be called beliefs. Instead of occurring part way in, or at the beginning of a response, they come as a rule at the end, and thus are less likely to be confused with scientific beliefs. Very often the whole state of mind in which we are left by a poem, or by music, or, more rarely perhaps, by other forms of art, is of a kind which it is natural to describe as a belief. When all provisional acceptances have lapsed, when the single references and their connections which may have led up to the final response are forgotten, we may still have an attitude and an emotion which has to introspection all the characters of a belief. This belief, which is a consequence not a cause of the experience, is the chief source of the confusion upon which Revelation Doctrines depend.

If we ask what in such cases it is which is believed, we are likely to receive, and to offer, answers both varied and vague. For strong belief-feelings, as is well known and as is shown by certain doses of alcohol or hashish, and preeminently of nitrous oxide, will readily attach themselves to almost any reference, distorting it to suit their purpose. Few people without experience of the nitrous-oxide revelation have any conception of their capacity for believing or of the extent to which belief-feelings and attitudes are parasitic. Thus when, through reading *Adonais*, for example, we are left in a strong emotional attitude which feels like belief, it is only too easy to think that we are believing in immortality or survival, or in something else capable of statement, and fatally easy also to attribute the value of the poem to the alleged effect, or conversely to regret that it should depend upon such a scientifically doubtful conclusion. Scien-

tific beliefs, as opposed to these emotive beliefs, are beliefs "*that* so and so." They can be stated with greater or less precision, as the case may be, but always in some form. It is for some people difficult to admit beliefs which are objectless, which are not about anything or in anything; beliefs which cannot be stated. Yet most of the beliefs of children and primitive peoples, and of the unscientific generally seem to be of this kind. Their parasitic nature helps to confuse the issue. What we have to distinguish are beliefs which are grounded in fact, i.e., are due to reference, and beliefs which are due to other causes, and merely attach themselves to such references as will support them.

That an objectless belief is a ridiculous or an incomplete thing is a prejudice deriving only from confusion. Such beliefs have, of course, no place in science, but in themselves they are often of the utmost value. Provided always that they do not furnish themselves with illicit objects. It is the objectless belief which is masquerading as a belief in this or that, which is ridiculous; more often than not it is also a serious nuisance. When they are kept from tampering with the development of reference such emotional attitudes may be, as revelation doctrines in such strange forms maintain, among the most important and valuable effects which the arts can produce.

It is often held that recent generations suffer more from nervous strain than some at least of their predecessors, and many reasons for this have been suggested. Certainly the types of nervous disease most prevalent seem to have changed. An explanation not sufficiently noticed perhaps is the break-down of traditional accounts of the universe, and the strain imposed by the vain attempt to orient the mind by belief of the scientific kind alone. In the prescientific era, the devout adherent to the Catholic account of the world, for example, found a sufficient basis for nearly all his main attitudes in what he took to be scientific truth. It would be fairer to say that the difference between ascertained fact and acceptable fiction did not obtrude itself for him. Today this is changed, and if he believes such an account, he does not do so, if intelligent, without considerable difficulty or without a fairly persistent strain. The complete sceptic, of course, is a new phenomenon, dissenters in the past having commonly disbelieved only because they held a different belief of the same kind. These topics have, it is true, been touched upon by psychoanalysts, but not with a very clear understanding of the situation. The Vienna School would merely have us away with antiquated lumber; the Zurich School would hand us a new outfit of superstitions.[15] Actually what is needed is a habit of mind which allows both reference and the development of attitudes their proper independence. This habit of mind is not to be attained at once, or for most people with ease. We try desperately to support our attitudes with beliefs as to facts, verified or accepted as scientifically established, and by so doing we weaken our own emotional backbone. For the justification of any attitude *per se* is its success for the needs of the being. It is not justified by the soundness of the views which may seem to be, and in pathological cases are, its ground and causes. The source of our attitudes should be in experience itself; compare Whitman's praise of the cow which does not worry about its soul. Opinion as to matters of fact, knowledge, belief, are not necessarily involved in any of our attitudes to the world in general, or to particular phases of it. If we bring them in, if, by a psychological perversion only too easy to fall into, we make them the basis of our adjustment, we run extreme risks of later disorganisation elsewhere.

Many people find great difficulty in accepting or even in understanding this position. They are so accustomed to regarding "recognised facts" as the natural basis of attitudes, that they cannot conceive how anyone can be otherwise organised. The hard-headed positivist and the convinced adherent of a religion from opposite sides encounter the same difficulty. The first at the best suffers from an insufficient material for the development of his attitudes; the second from intellectual bondage and unconscious insincerity. The one starves himself; the other is like the little pig in the fable who chose to have his house built of cabbages and ate it, and so the grim wolf with privy paw devoured him. For clear and impartial

---

[15]The psychoanalytic schools of Sigmund Freud and Carl Jung, respectively. [Ed.]

awareness of the nature of the world in which we live and the development of attitudes which will enable us to live in it finely are both necessities, and neither can be subordinated to the other. They are almost independent, such connections as exist in well-organised individuals being adventitious. Those who find this a hard saying may be invited to consider the effect upon them of those works of art which most unmistakably attune them to existence. The central experience of Tragedy and its chief value is an attitude indispensable for a fully developed life. But in the reading of *King Lear* what facts verifiable by science, or accepted and believed in as we accept and believe in ascertained facts, are relevant? None whatever. Still more clearly in the experiences of some music, of some architecture and of some abstract design, attitudes are evoked and developed which are unquestionably independent of all beliefs as to fact, and these are exceptional only in being protected by accident from the most insidious perversion to which the mind is liable. For the intermingling of knowledge and belief is indeed a perversion, through which both activities suffer degradation.

These objectless beliefs, which though merely attitudes seem to be knowledge, are not difficult to explain. Some system of impulses not ordinarily in adjustment within itself or adjusted to the world finds something which orders it or gives it fit exercise. Then follows the peculiar sense of ease, of restfulness, of free, unimpeded activity, and the feeling of acceptance, of something more positive than acquiescence. This feeling is the reason why such states may be called beliefs. They share this feeling with, for example, the state which follows the conclusive answering of a question. Most attitude-adjustments which are successful possess it in some degree, but those which are very regular and familiar, such as sitting down to meat or stretching out in bed, naturally tend to lose it. But when the required attitude has been long needed, where its coming is unforeseen and the manner in which it is brought about complicated and inexplicable, where we know no more than that formerly we were unready and that now we are ready for life in some particular phase, the feeling which results may be intense. Such are the occasions upon which the arts seem to lift away the burden of existence, and we seem ourselves to be looking into the heart of things. To be seeing whatever it is as it really is, to be cleared in vision and to be recipients of a revelation.

We have considered already the detail of these states of consciousness and their conjectural impulse basis. We can now take this feeling of a revealed significance, this attitude of readiness, acceptance and understanding, which has led to so many Revelation Doctrines, not as actually implying knowledge, but for what it is — the conscious accompaniment of our successful adjustment to life. But it is, we must admit, no certain sign by itself that our adjustment is adequate or admirable. Even the most firm adherents to Revelation Doctrines admit that there are bogus revelations, and on our account it is equally important to distinguish between "feelings of significance" which indicate that all is well and those which do not. In a sense all indicate that *something* is going well, otherwise there would be no acceptance, no belief but rejection. The real question is "What is it?" Thus after the queer reshuffling of inhibitions and releases which follows the taking of a dose of alcohol, for example, the sense of revelation is apt to occur with unusual authority. Doubtless this feeling of significance is a sign that as the organism is for the moment, its affairs are for the moment thriving. But when the momentary special condition of the system has given place to the more usual, more stable and more generally advantageous adjustment, the authority of the vision falls away from it; we find that what we were doing is by no means so wonderful or so desirable as we thought and that our belief was nonsensical. So it is less noticeably with many moments in which the world seems to be showing its real face to us.

The chief difficulty of all Revelation Doctrines has always been to discover what it is which is revealed. If these states of mind are knowledge it should be possible to state what it is that they know. It is often easy enough to find something which we can suppose to be what we know. Belief feelings, we have seen, are *parasitic*, and will attach themselves to all kinds of hosts. In literature it is especially easy to find hosts. But in music, in the nonrepresentive arts

of design, in architecture or ceramics, for example, the task of finding something to believe, or to believe in, is not so easy. Yet the "feeling of significance" is as common[16] in these other arts as in literature. Denial of this is usually proof only of an interest limited to literature.

This difficulty has usually been met by asserting that the alleged knowledge given in the revelation is nonintellectual. It refuses to be rationalised, it is said. Well and good; but if so why call it knowledge? Either it is capable of corroborating or of conflicting with the other things we usually call knowledge, such as the laws of thermodynamics, capable of being stated and brought into connection with what else we know; or it is not knowledge, not capable of being stated. We cannot have it both ways, and no sneers at the limitations of logic, the commonest of the resources of the confused, amend the dilemma. In fact it resembles knowledge only in being an attitude and a feeling very similar to some attitudes and feelings which may and often do accompany knowledge. But "Knowledge" is an immensely potent emotive word engendering reverence towards any state of mind to which it is applied. And these "feelings of significance" are those among our states of mind which most deserve to be revered. That they should be so obstinately described as knowledge even by those who most carefully remove from them all the characteristics of knowledge is not surprising.

Traditionally what is said to be known thus mystically through the arts is Beauty, a remote and divine entity not otherwise to be apprehended, one of the Eternal Absolute Values. And this is doubtless emotively a way of talking which is effective for a while. When its power abates, as the power of such utterances will, there

---

[16]Cf. Gurney, *The Power of Sound*, p. 126. "A splendid melodic phrase seems continually not like an object of sense, but like an *affirmation*; not so much prompting admiring ejaculation as compelling passionate assent." His explanation, through association with speech, seems to me inadequate. He adds that the use of terms such as "*expressiveness* and *significance*, as opposed to meaninglessness and triviality, may be allowed, without the implication of any reference to transcendental views which one may fail to understand, or theories of interpretation which one may entirely repudiate." [Au.]

are several developments which may easily be used to revive it. "Beauty is eternal, and we may say that it is already manifest as a heavenly thing — the beauty of Nature is indeed an earnest to us of the ultimate goodness which lies behind the apparent cruelty and moral confusion of organic life. . . . Yet we feel that these three are ultimately one, and human speech bears constant witness to the universal conviction that Goodness is beautiful, that Beauty is good, that Truth is Beauty. We can hardly avoid the use of the word 'trinity,' and if we are theists at all we cannot but say that they are one, because they are the manifestation of one God. If we are not theists there is no explanation."[17]

Human speech is indeed the witness, and to what else does it not witness? It would be strange if in a matter of such moment as this the greatest of all emotive words did not come into play. "In religion we believe that God is Beauty and Life, that God is Truth and Light, that God is Good-ness and Love, and that because he is all these they are all one, and the Trinity in Unity and Unity in Trinity is to be worshipped."[18] No one who can interpret emotive language, who can avoid the temptation to illicit belief so constantly presented by it need find such utterances "meaningless." But the wrong approach is easy and far too often pressingly invited by the speakers, labouring themselves under misconceptions. To excite a serious and reverent attitude is one thing. To set forth an explanation is another. To confuse the two and mistake the incitement of an attitude for a statement of fact is a practice which should be discouraged. For intellectual dishonesty is an evil which is the more dangerous the more it is hedged about with emotional sanctities. And after all there *is* another explanation, which would long ago have been quietly established to the world's great good had men been less ready to sacrifice the integrity of their thought and feeling for the sake of a local and limited advantage.

[17]Percy Dearmer, *The Necessity of Art*, p. 180. [Au.]

[18]A. W. Pollard, *ibidem*, p. 135. [Au.]

# Mikhail Bakhtin

## 1895–1975

*Nearly lost to the world because of Soviet political turbulence in the first half of the century, the literary and aesthetic theories of the Russian polymath Mikhail Mikhailovich Bakhtin have, in the past two decades, exerted a spellbinding and fertile power over critical imaginations in North America and Europe. Born in Orel, Russia (now USSR), Bakhtin attended the universities in Odessa and Petersburg. In 1920 he moved to the cultural center Vitebsk, and in 1924 to Leningrad, where he worked at the Historical Institute. Bakhtin's magisterial* Problems of Dostoevsky's Poetics *appeared in 1929, but its impact was stifled when a Stalinist purge sent its author into exile. During the next six precarious years, Bakhtin wrote the seminal essay* Discourse in the Novel *and a study of the German* Bildungsroman *that was thought lost when it disappeared from a publishing house during the German invasion; fragments of it have since been recovered and are being translated. On his return from exile in 1936, Bakhtin was offered a position at the Mordovian Teachers' College (later a university), where he taught until his retirement in 1961. In 1940, Bakhtin submitted a dissertation on Rabelais, but was unable to defend it until after the war; in 1949 when he was able to defend it, the dissertation's very originality worked against its acceptance. Its eventual publication in 1965 (as* Rabelais and His World*) lifted Bakhtin's ideas from obscurity and made them available to the international scholarly community. Bakhtin's thought also clearly informs the studies of Marxist linguistic philosophy (1929–30) and Freudianism (1927) by V. N. Voloshinov, and a tract* *on formalist literary scholarship (1928) by P. N. Medvedev. The first selection reprinted here is from* Discourse in the Novel, *one of four Bakhtin essays in* The Dialogic Imagination *(1981); the second is from* Problems of Dostoevsky's Poetics.

# From *Discourse in the Novel*

## The Topic of the Speaking Person

Before, then, taking up the issue of the artistic representation of another's speech conceived as the image of a language, we should say something about the importance in extra-artistic areas of life and ideology of the topic of the speaking person and his discourse. While in the many forms available for transmitting another's speech outside the novel there is no defining concern for the images of a language, such forms are used in the novel for self-enrichment — but not before they are first transformed and subjected within it to the new holistic unity of the novel itself (and, conversely, novels have a powerful influence on the extra-artistic perception and transmission of another's discourse).

The topic of a speaking person has enormous importance in everyday life. In real life we hear speech about speakers and their discourse at every step. We can go so far as to say that in real life people talk most of all about what others talk about — they transmit, recall, weigh and pass judgment on other people's words, opinions, assertions, information; people are upset by others' words, or agree with them, contest them, refer to them and so forth. Were we to eavesdrop on snatches of raw dialogue in the street, in a crowd, in lines, in a foyer and so forth, we would hear how often the words "he says," "people say," "he said . . . " are repeated, and in the conversational hurly-burly of people in a crowd, everything often fuses into one big "he says . . . you say . . . I say. . . . " Reflect how enormous is the weight of "everyone says" and "it is said" in public opinion, public rumor, gossip, slander and so forth. One must also consider the psychological importance in our lives of what

others say about us, and the importance, for us, of understanding and interpreting these words of others ("living hermeneutics").

The importance of this motif is in no way diminished in the higher and better-organized areas of everyday communication. Every conversation is full of transmissions and interpretations of other people's words. At every step one meets a "quotation" or a "reference" to something that a particular person said, a reference to "people say" or "everyone says," to the words of the person one is talking with, or to one's own previous words, to a newspaper, an official decree, a document, a book and so forth. The majority of our information and opinions is usually not communicated in direct form as our own, but with reference to some indefinite and general source: "I heard," "It's generally held that . . . ," "It is thought that . . ." and so forth. Take one of the most widespread occurrences in our everyday life, conversations about some official meeting: they are all constructed on the transmission, interpretation and evaluation of various kinds of verbal performance, resolutions, the rejected and accepted corrections that are made to them and so forth. Thus talk goes on about speaking people and their words everywhere — this motif returns again and again; it either accompanies the development of the other topics in everyday life, or directly governs speech as its leading theme.

Further examples of the significance of the topic of the speaking person in everyday life would be superfluous. We need only keep our ears open to the speech sounding everywhere around us to reach such a conclusion: in the everyday speech of any person living in society, no less than half (on the average) of all the words uttered by him will be someone else's words (consciously someone else's), transmitted with

Translated by Caryl Emerson and Michael Holquist.

varying degrees of precision and impartiality (or more precisely, partiality).

It goes without saying that not all transmitted words belonging to someone else lend themselves, when fixed in writing, to enclosure in quotation marks. That degree of otherness and purity in another's word that in written speech would require quotation marks (as per the intention of the speaker himself, how he himself determines this degree of otherness) is required much less frequently in everyday speech.

Furthermore, syntactic means for formulating the transmitted speech of another are far from exhausted by the grammatical paradigms of direct and indirect discourse: the means for its incorporation, for its formulation and for indicating different degrees of shading are highly varied. This must be kept in mind if we are to make good our claim that of all words uttered in everyday life, no less than half belong to someone else.

The speaking person and his discourse are not, in everyday speech, subjects for artistic representation, but rather they are topics in the engaged transmission of practical information. For this reason everyday speech is not concerned with forms of representation, but only with means of *transmission*. These means, conceived both as a way to formulate verbally and stylistically another's speech and as a way to provide an interpretive frame, a tool for reconceptualization and re-accenting — from direct verbatim quotation in a verbal transmission to malicious and deliberately parodic distortion of another's word, slander — are highly varied.[1]

The following must be kept in mind: that the speech of another, once enclosed in a context, is — no matter how accurately transmitted — always subject to certain semantic changes. The context embracing another's word is responsible for its dialogizing background, whose influence can be very great. Given the appropriate methods for framing, one may bring about fundamental changes even in another's utterance accurately

quoted. Any sly and ill-disposed polemicist knows very well which dialogizing backdrop he should bring to bear on the accurately quoted words of his opponent, in order to distort their sense. By manipulating the effects of context, it is very easy to emphasize the brute materiality of another's words, and to stimulate dialogic reactions associated with such "brute materiality"; thus it is, for instance, very easy to make even the most serious utterance comical. Another's discourse, when introduced into a speech context, enters the speech that frames it not in a mechanical bond but in a chemical union (on the semantic and emotionally expressive level); the degree of dialogized influence, one on the other, can be enormous. For this reason we cannot, when studying the various forms for transmitting another's speech, treat any of these forms in isolation from the means for its contextualized (dialogizing) framing — the one is indissolubly linked with the other. The formulation of another's speech as well as its framing (and the context can begin preparing for the introduction of another's speech far back in the text) both express the unitary act of dialogic interaction with that speech, a relation determining the entire nature of its transmission and all the changes in meaning and accent that take place in it during transmission.

The speaking person and his discourse in everyday speech, we have said, serves as a *subject* for the engaged, practical transmission of information, and not as a *means* of representation. As a matter of fact, all everyday forms for transmitting another's discourse, as well as the changes in discourse connected with those forms — from subtle nuances in meaning and emphasis to gross externalized distortions of the verbal composition — are defined by this practical engagement. But this emphasis on engaged discourse does not exclude certain aspects of representability. In order to assess and divine the real meaning of others' words in everyday life, the following are surely of decisive significance: *who* precisely is speaking, and under *what* concrete circumstances? When we attempt to understand and make assessments in everyday life, we do not separate discourse from the personality speaking it (as we can in the ideological realm),

[1]There are different ways to falsify someone else's words while taking them to their furthest extreme, to reveal their *potential* content. Rhetoric, the art of argument, and "heuristics" explore this area somewhat. [Au.]

because the personality is so materially present to us. And the entire speaking situation is very important: who is present during it, with what expression or mimicry is it uttered, with what shades of intonation? During everyday verbal transmission of another's words, the entire complex of discourse as well as the personality of the speaker may be expressed and even played with (in the form of anything from an exact replication to a parodic ridiculing and exaggeration of gestures and intonations). This representation is always subordinated to the tasks of practical, engaged transmission and is wholly determined by these tasks. This of course does not involve the artistic image of a speaking person and the artistic image of his discourse, and even less the image of a language. Nevertheless, everyday episodes involving the same person, when they become linked, already entail prose devices for the double-voiced and even double-languaged representation of another's words.

These conversations about speaking persons and others' words in everyday life do not go beyond the boundaries of the superficial aspects of discourse, the weight it carries in a specific situation; the deeper semantic and emotionally expressive levels of discourse do not enter the game. The topic of a speaking person takes on quite another significance in the ordinary ideological workings of our consciousness, in the process of assimilating our consciousness to the ideological world. The ideological becoming of a human being, in this view, is the process of selectively assimilating the words of others.

When verbal disciplines are taught in school, two basic modes are recognized for the appropriation and transmission — simultaneously — of another's words (a text, a rule, a model): "reciting by heart" and "retelling in one's own words." The latter mode poses on a small scale the task implicit in all prose stylistics: retelling a text in one's own words is to a certain extent a double-voiced narration of another's words, for indeed "one's own words" must not completely dilute the quality that makes another's words unique; a retelling in one's own words should have a mixed character, able when necessary to reproduce the style and expressions of the transmitted text. It is this second mode used in schools for transmitting another's discourse, "retelling in one's own words," that includes within it an entire series of forms for the appropriation while transmitting of another's words, depending upon the character of the text being appropriated and the pedagogical environment in which it is understood and evaluated.

The tendency to assimilate others' discourse takes on an even deeper and more basic significance in an individual's ideological becoming, in the most fundamental sense. Another's discourse performs here no longer as information, directions, rules, models and so forth — but strives rather to determine the very bases of our ideological interrelations with the world, the very basis of our behavior; it performs here as *authoritative discourse*, and an *internally persuasive discourse*.

Both the authority of discourse and its internal persuasiveness may be united in a single word — one that is *simultaneously* authoritative and internally persuasive — despite the profound differences between these two categories of alien discourse. But such unity is rarely a given — it happens more frequently that an individual's becoming, an ideological process, is characterized precisely by a sharp gap between these two categories: in one, the authoritative word (religious, political, moral; the word of a father, of adults and of teachers, etc.) that does not know internal persuasiveness, in the other internally persuasive word that is denied all privilege, backed up by no authority at all, and is frequently not even acknowledged in society (not by public opinion, nor by scholarly norms, nor by criticism), not even in the legal code. The struggle and dialogic interrelationship of these categories of ideological discourse are what usually determine the history of an individual ideological consciousness.

The authoritative word demands that we acknowledge it, that we make it our own; it binds us, quite independent of any power it might have to persuade us internally; we encounter it with its authority already fused to it. The authoritative word is located in a distanced zone, organically connected with a past that is felt to be hierarchically higher. It is, so to speak, the word of the fathers. Its authority was already *acknowledged* in the past. It is a *prior* discourse. It is therefore not a question of choosing it from among other possible discourses that are its equal. It is given (it sounds) in lofty spheres, not those of familiar contact. Its language is a special (as it were, hieratic) language. It can be profaned. It is akin to taboo, i.e., a name that must not be taken in vain.

We cannot embark here on a survey of the many and varied types of authoritative discourse (for example, the authority of religious dogma, or of acknowledged scientific truth or of a currently fashionable book), nor can we survey different degrees of authoritativeness. For our purposes only formal features for the transmission and representation of authoritative discourse are important, those common to all types and degrees of such discourse.

The degree to which a word may be conjoined with authority — whether the authority is recognized by us or not — is what determines its specific demarcation and individuation in discourse; it requires a *distance* vis-à-vis itself (this distance may be valorized as positive or as negative, just as our attitude toward it may be sympathetic or hostile). Authoritative discourse may organize around itself great masses of other types of discourses (which interpret it, praise it, apply it in various ways), but the authoritative discourse itself does not merge with these (by means of, say, gradual transitions); it remains sharply demarcated, compact and inert: it demands, so to speak, not only quotation marks but a demarcation even more magisterial, a special script, for instance.[2] It is considerably more difficult to incorporate semantic changes into such a discourse, even with the help of a framing context: its semantic structure is static and dead, for it is fully complete, it has but a single meaning, the letter is fully sufficient to the sense and calcifies it.

It is not a free appropriation and assimilation of the word itself that authoritative discourse seeks to elicit from us; rather, it demands our unconditional allegiance. Therefore authoritative

discourse permits no play with the context framing it, no play with its borders, no gradual and flexible transitions, no spontaneously creative stylizing variants on it. It enters our verbal consciousness as a compact and indivisible mass; one must either totally affirm it, or totally reject it. It is indissolubly fused with its authority — with political power, an institution, a person — and it stands and falls together with that authority. One cannot divide it up — agree with one part, accept but not completely another part, reject utterly a third part. Therefore the distance we ourselves observe vis-à-vis this authoritative discourse remains unchanged in all its projections: a playing with distances, with fusion and dissolution, with approach and retreat, is not here possible.

All these functions determine the uniqueness of authoritative discourse, both as a concrete means for formulating itself during transmission and as its distinctive means for being framed by contexts. The zone of the framing context must likewise be distanced — no familiar contact is possible here either. The one perceiving and understanding this discourse is a distant descendent; there can be no arguing with him.

These factors also determine the potential role of authoritative discourse in prose. Authoritative discourse can not be represented — it is only transmitted. Its inertia, its semantic finiteness and calcification, the degree to which it is hard-edged, a thing in its own right, the impermissibility of any free stylistic development in relation to it — all this renders the artistic representation of authoritative discourse impossible. Its role in the novel is insignificant. It is by its very nature incapable of being double-voiced; it cannot enter into hybrid constructions. If completely deprived of its authority it becomes simply an object, a *relic*, a *thing*. It enters the artistic context as an alien body, there is no space around it to play in, no contradictory emotions — it is not surrounded by an agitated and cacophonous dialogic life, and the context around it dies, words dry up. For this reason images of official-authoritative truth, images of virtue (of any sort: monastic, spiritual, bureaucratic, moral, etc.) have never been successful in the novel. It suffices to mention the hopeless attempts of Gogol and Dos-

[2]Often the authoritative word is in fact a word spoken by another in a foreign language (cf. for example the phenomenon of foreign-language religious texts in most cultures). [Au.]

toevsky in this regard.[3] For this reason the authoritative text always remains, in the novel, a dead quotation, something that falls out of the artistic context (for example, the evangelical texts in Tolstoy at the end of *Resurrection*).[4]

Authoritative discourses may embody various contents: authority as such, or the authoritativeness of tradition, of generally acknowledged truths, of the official line and other similar authorities. These discourses may have a variety of zones (determined by the degree to which they are distanced from the zone of contact) with a variety of relations to the presumed listener or interpreter (the apperceptive background presumed by the discourse, the degree of reciprocation between the two and so forth).

In the history of literary language, there is a struggle constantly being waged to overcome the official line with its tendency to distance itself from the zone of contact, a struggle against various kinds and degrees of authority. In this process discourse gets drawn into the contact zone, which results in semantic and emotionally expressive (intonational) changes: there is a weakening and degradation of the capacity to generate metaphors, and discourse becomes more reified, more concrete, more filled with everyday elements and so forth. All of this has been studied by psychology, but not from the point of view of its verbal formulation in possible inner monologues of developing human beings, the monologue that lasts a whole life. What confronts us is the complex problem presented by forms capable of expressing such a (dialogized) monologue.

When someone else's ideological discourse is internally persuasive for us and acknowledged by us, entirely different possibilities open up. Such discourse is of decisive significance in the evolution of an individual consciousness: consciousness awakens to independent ideological life precisely in a world of alien discourses surrounding it, and from which it cannot initially separate itself; the process of distinguishing between one's own and another's discourse, between one's own and another's thought, is activated rather late in development. When thought begins to work in an independent, experimenting and discriminating way, what first occurs is a separation between internally persuasive discourse and authoritarian enforced discourse, along with a rejection of those congeries of discourses that do not matter to us, that do not touch us.

Internally persuasive discourse — as opposed to one that is externally authoritative — is, as it is affirmed through assimilation, tightly interwoven with "one's own word."[5] In the everyday rounds of our consciousness, the internally persuasive word is half ours and half someone else's. Its creativity and productiveness consist precisely in the fact that such a word awakens new and independent words, that it organizes masses of our words from within, and that it does not remain in an isolated and static condition. It is not so much interpreted by us as it is further, that is, freely, developed, applied to new material, new conditions; it enters into interanimating relationships with new contexts. More than that, it enters into an intense interaction, a *struggle* with other internally persuasive discourses. Our ideological development is just such an intense struggle within us for hegemony among various available verbal and ideological points of view, approaches, directions and values. The semantic structure of an internally persuasive discourse is *not finite*, it is *open*; in each of the new contexts that dialogize it, this discourse is able to reveal ever newer *ways to mean*.

The internally persuasive word is either a contemporary word, born in a zone of contact with unresolved contemporaneity, or else it is a word that has been reclaimed for contemporaneity; such a word relates to its descendents as well as to its contemporaries as if *both* were contempor-

---

[3]Bakhtin refers to Gogol's and Dostoevsky's failed attempts to represent the ideal of holiness they believed in — such as Father Zossima in the latter's *Brothers Karamazov*. [Ed.]

[4]When analyzing a concrete example of authoritative discourse in a novel, it is necessary to keep in mind the fact that purely authoritative discourse may, in another epoch, be internally persuasive; this is especially true where ethics are concerned. [Au.]

[5]One's own discourse is gradually and slowly wrought out of others' words that have been acknowledged and assimilated, and the boundaries between the two are at first scarcely perceptible. [Au.]

aries; what is constitutive for it is a special conception of listeners, readers, perceivers. Every discourse presupposes a special conception of the listener, of his apperceptive background and the degree of his responsiveness; it presupposes a specific distance. All this is very important for coming to grips with the historical life of discourse. Ignoring such aspects and nuances leads to a reification of the word (and to a muffling of the dialogism native to it).

All of the above determine the methods for formulating internally persuasive discourse during its transmission, as well as methods for framing it in contexts. Such methods provide maximal interaction between another's word and its context, for the dialogizing influence they have on each other, for the free and creative development of another's word, for a gradation of transitions. They serve to govern the play of boundaries, the distance between that point where the context begins to prepare for the introduction of another's word and the point where the word is actually introduced (its "theme" may sound in the text long before the appearance of the actual word). These methods account for other peculiarities as well, which also express the essence of the internally persuasive word, such as that word's semantic openness to us, its capacity for further creative life in the context of our ideological consciousness, its unfinishedness and the inexhaustibility of our further dialogic interaction with it. We have not yet learned from it all it might tell us; we can take it into new contexts, attach it to new material, put it in a new situation in order to wrest new answers from it, new insights into its meaning, and even wrest from it new words of its *own* (since another's discourse, if productive, gives birth to a new word from us in response).

The means for formulating and framing internally persuasive discourse may be supple and dynamic to such an extent that this discourse may literally be *omnipresent* in the context, imparting to everything its own specific tones and from time to time breaking through to become a completely materialized thing, as another's word fully set off and demarcated (as happens in character zones). Such variants on the theme of another's discourse are widespread in all areas of

creative ideological activity, and even in the narrowly scientific disciplines. Of such a sort is any gifted, creative exposition defining alien world views: such an exposition is always a free stylistic variation on another's discourse; it expounds another's thought in the style of that thought even while applying it to new material, to another way of posing the problem; it conducts experiments and gets solutions in the language of another's discourse.

In other less obvious instances we notice analogous phenomena. We have in mind first of all those instances of powerful influence exercised by another's discourse on a given author. When such influences are laid bare, the half-concealed life lived by another's discourse is revealed within the new context of the given author. When such an influence is deep and productive, there is no external imitation, no simple act of reproduction, but rather a further creative development of another's (more precisely, half-other) discourse in a new context and under new conditions.

In all these instances the important thing is not only forms for transmitting another's discourse, but the fact that in such forms there can always be found the embryonic beginnings of what is required for an artistic representation of another's discourse. A few changes in orientation and the internally persuasive word easily becomes an object of representation. For certain kinds of internally persuasive discourse can be fundamentally and organically fused with the image of a speaking person: ethical (discourse fused with the image of, let us say, a preacher), philosophical (discourse fused with the image of a wise man), sociopolitical (discourse fused with an image of a Leader). While creatively stylizing upon and experimenting with another's discourse, we attempt to guess, to imagine, how a person with authority might conduct himself in the given circumstances, the light he would cast on them with his discourse. In such experimental guesswork the image of the speaking person and his discourse become the object of creative, artistic imagination.[6]

[6]In Plato, Socrates serves as just such an artistic image

This process — experimenting by turning persuasive discourse into speaking persons — becomes especially important in those cases where a struggle against such images has already begun, where someone is striving to liberate himself from the influence of such an image and its discourse by means of objectification, or is striving to expose the limitations of both image and discourse. The importance of struggling with another's discourse, its influence in the history of an individual's coming to ideological consciousness, is enormous. One's own discourse and one's own voice, although born of another or dynamically stimulated by another, will sooner or later begin to liberate themselves from the authority of the other's discourse. This process is made more complex by the fact that a variety of alien voices enter into the struggle for influence within an individual's consciousness (just as they struggle with one another in surrounding social reality). All this creates fertile soil for experimentally objectifying another's discourse. A conversation with an internally persuasive word that one has begun to resist may continue, but it takes on another character: it is questioned, it is put in a new situation in order to expose its weak sides, to get a feel for its boundaries, to experience it physically as an object. For this reason stylizing discourse by attributing it to a person often becomes parodic, although not crudely parodic — since another's word, having been at an earlier stage internally persuasive, mounts a resistance to this process and frequently begins to sound with no parodic overtones at all. Novelistic images, profoundly double-voiced and double-languaged, are born in such a soil, seek to objectivize the struggle with all types of internally persuasive alien discourse that had at one time held sway over the author (of such a type, for instance, is Pushkin's Onegin or Lermontov's Pechorin).[7] At the heart of the *Prüfungsroman*[8] is the same kind of subjective struggle with internally persuasive, alien discourse, and just such a liberation from this discourse by turning it into an object. Another illustration of what we mean here is provided by the *Bildungsroman*,[9] but in such novels the maturation — a selecting, ideological process — is developed as a theme within the novel, whereas in the *Prüfungsroman* the subjectivity of the author himself remains outside the work.

The works of Dostoevsky, in such a view, can be seen to occupy an extraordinary and unique place. The acute and intense interaction of another's word is present in his novels in two ways. In the first place in his characters' language there is a profound and unresolved conflict with another's word on the level of lived experience ("another's word about me"), on the level of ethical life (another's judgment, recognition or nonrecognition by another) and finally on the level of ideology (the world views of characters understood as unresolved and unresolvable dialogue). What Dostoevsky's characters *say* constitutes an arena of never-ending struggle with others' words, in all realms of life and creative ideological activity. For this reason these utterances may serve as excellent models of the most varied forms for transmitting and framing another's discourse. In the second place, the works (the novels) in their entirety, taken as utterances of their *author*, are the same never-ending, internally unresolved dialogues among characters (seen as embodied points of view) and between the author himself and his characters; the characters' discourse is never entirely subsumed and remains free and open (as does the discourse of the author himself). In Dostoevsky's novels, the life experience of the characters and their discourse may be resolved as far as plot is concerned, but internally they remain incomplete and unresolved.[10]

The enormous significance of the motif of the

<hr/>

of the wise man and teacher, an image employed for the purposes of experiment. [Au.]

[7]The antiheroes, respectively, of *Eugene Onegin* and *A Hero for Our Time*. [Ed.]

[8]Novel of testing. [Ed.]

[9]Novel of education. [Ed.]

[10]Cf. our book *Problems of Dostoevsky's Art* [*Problemy tvorčestva Dostoevskogo*], Leningrad, 1929 (in its second and third editions, *Problems of Dostoevsky's Poetics* [*Problemy poetiki Dostoevskogo*], Moscow, 1963, Moscow, 1972). This book contains stylistic analyses of characters' utterances, revealing various forms of transmission and contextual framing. [Au.]

speaking person is obvious in the realm of ethical and legal thought and discourse. The speaking person and his discourse is, in these areas, the major topic of thought and speech. All fundamental categories of ethical and legal inquiry and evaluation refer to speaking persons precisely as such: conscience (the "voice of conscience," the "inner word"), repentance (a free admission, a statement of wrongdoing by the person himself), truth and falsehood, being liable and not liable, the right to vote [*pravo golosa*] and so on. An independent, responsible and active discourse is *the* fundamental indicator of an ethical, legal and political human being. Challenges to this discourse, provocations of it, interpretations and assessments of it, the establishing of boundaries and forms for its activity (civil and political rights), the juxtaposing of various wills and discourses and so on — all these acts carry enormous weight in the realms of ethics and the law. It is enough to point out the role played in narrowly judicial spheres by formulation, analysis and interpretation of testimony, declarations, contracts, various documents and other forms of others' utterances; finally, of course, there is legal hermeneutics.

All this calls for further study. Juridical (and ethical) techniques have been developed for dealing with the discourse of another [after it has been uttered], for establishing authenticity, for determining degrees of veracity and so forth (for example, the process of notarizing and other such techniques). But problems connected with the methods used for formulating such kinds of discourse — compositional, stylistic, semantic and other — have not as yet been properly posed.

The problem of *confession* in cases being investigated for trial (what has made it necessary and what provokes it) has so far been interpreted only at the level of laws, ethics and psychology. Dostoevsky provides a rich body of material for posing this problem at the level of a philosophy of language (of discourse): the problem of a thought, a desire, a motivation that is authentic — as in the case of Ivan Karamazov, for instance — and how these problems are exposed in words; the role of the other in formulating discourse, problems surrounding an inquest and so forth.

The speaking person and his discourse, as subject of thought and speech, is of course treated in the ethical and legal realms only insofar as it contributes to the specific interests of these disciplines. All methods for transmitting, formulating and framing another's discourse are made subordinate to such special interests and orientations. However, even there elements of an artistic representation of another's word are possible, especially in the ethical realm: for example, a representation of the struggle waged by the voice of conscience with other voices that sound in a man, the internal dialogism leading to repentance and so forth. Artistic prose, the novelistic element present in ethical tracts, especially in confessions, may be quite significant — for example, in Epictetus, Marcus Aurelius, Augustine and Petrarch we can detect the embryonic beginnings of the *Prüfungs-* and *Bildungsroman*.

Our motif carries even greater weight in the realm of religious thought and discourse (mythological, mystical and magical). The primary subject of this discourse is a being who speaks: a deity, a demon, a soothsayer, a prophet. Mythological thought does not, in general, acknowledge anything not alive or not responsive. Divining the will of a deity, of a demon (good or bad), interpreting signs of wrath or beneficence, tokens, indications and finally the transmission and interpretation of words directly spoken by a deity (revelation), or by his prophets, saints, soothsayers — all in all, the transmission and interpretation of the divinely inspired (as opposed to the profane) word are acts of religious thought and discourse having the greatest importance. All religious systems, even primitive ones, possess an enormous, highly specialized methodological apparatus (hermeneutics) for transmitting and interpreting various kinds of holy word.

The situation is somewhat different in the case of scientific thought. Here, the significance of discourse as such is comparatively weak. Mathematical and natural sciences do not acknowledge discourse as a subject in its own right. In scientific activity one must, of course, deal with another's discourse — the words of predecessors, the judgments of critics, majority opinion and so forth; one must deal with various forms for transmitting and interpreting another's word — struggle with an authoritative discourse, overcoming influences, polemics, references, quotations and so forth — but all this remains a mere operational necessity and does not affect the subject matter itself of the science, into whose composition the speaker and his discourse do not, of course, enter. The entire methodological apparatus of the mathematical and natural sciences is directed toward mastery over *mute objects, brute things,* that do not reveal themselves in words, that do not *comment on themselves.* Acquiring knowledge here is not connected with receiving and interpreting words or signs from the object itself under consideration.

In the humanities — as distinct from the natural and mathematical sciences — there arises the specific task of establishing, transmitting and interpreting the words of others (for example, the problem of sources in the methodology of the historical disciplines). And of course in the philological disciplines, the speaking person and his discourse is the fundamental object of investigation.

Philology has specific aims and approaches to its subject (the speaker and his discourse) that determine the ways it transmits and represents others' words (for example, discourse as an object of study in the history of language). However, within the limits of the humanities (and even of philology in the narrow sense) there is possible a twofold approach to another's word when it is treated as something we seek to understand.

The word can be perceived purely as an object (something that is, in its essence, a thing). It is perceived as such in the majority of the linguistic disciplines. In such a word-object even meaning becomes a thing: there can be no dialogic approach to such a word of the kind immanent to any deep and actual understanding. Understanding, so conceived, is inevitably abstract: it is completely separated from the living, ideological power of the word to mean — from its truth or falsity, its significance or insignificance, beauty or ugliness. Such a reified word-thing cannot be understood by attempts to penetrate its meaning dialogically: there can be no conversing with such a word.

In philology, however, a dialogic penetration into the word is obligatory (for indeed without it no sort of understanding is possible): dialogizing it opens up fresh aspects in the word (semantic aspects, in the broadest sense), which, since they were revealed by dialogic means, become more immediate to perception. Every step forward in our knowledge of the word is preceded by a "stage of genius" — *a sharpened dialogic relationship to the word* — that in turn uncovers fresh aspects within the word.

Precisely such an approach is needed, more concrete and that does not deflect discourse from its actual power to mean in real ideological life, an approach where objectivity of understanding is linked with dialogic vigor and a deeper penetration into discourse itself. No other approach is in fact possible in the area of poetics, or the history of literature (and in the history of ideologies in general) or to a considerable extent even in the philosophy of discourse: even the driest and flattest positivism in these disciplines cannot treat the word neutrally, as if it were a thing, but is obliged to initiate talk not only about words but in words, in order to penetrate their ideological meanings — which can only be grasped dialogically, and which include evaluation and response. The forms in which a dialogic understanding is transmitted and interpreted may, if the understanding is deep and vigorous, even come to have significant parallels with the double-voiced representations of another's discourse that we find in prose art. It should be noted that the novel always includes in itself the activity of coming to know another's word, a coming to knowledge whose process is represented in the novel.

Finally, a few words about the importance of our theme in the rhetorical genres. The speaker and his discourse is, indisputably, one of the most important subjects of rhetorical speech (and all other themes are inevitably implicated in the topic of discourse). In the rhetoric of the courts, for example, rhetorical discourse accuses or defends the subject of a trial, who is, of course, a speaker, and in so doing relies on his words, interprets them, polemicizes with them, creatively erecting *potential* discourses for the accused or for the defense (just such free creation of likely, but never actually uttered, words, sometimes whole speeches — "as he must have said" or "as he might have said" — was a device very widespread in ancient rhetoric); rhetorical discourse tries to outwit possible retorts to itself, it passes on and compiles the words of witnesses and so forth. In political rhetoric, for example, discourse can support some candidacy, represent the personality of a candidate, present and defend his point of view, his verbal statements, or in other cases protest against some decree, law, order, announcement, occasion — that is, protest against the specific verbal utterances toward which it is dialogically aimed.

Publicistic discourse also deals with the word itself and with the individual as its agent: it criticizes a speech, an article, a point of view; it polemicizes, exposes, ridicules and so forth. When it analyzes an act it uncovers its verbal motifs, the point of view in which it is grounded, it formulates such acts in words, providing them the appropriate emphases — ironic, indignant and so on. This does not mean, of course, that the rhetoric behind the word forgets that there are deeds, acts, a reality outside words. But such rhetoric has always to do with social man, whose most fundamental gestures are made meaningful ideologically through the word, or directly embodied in words.

The importance of another's speech as a subject in rhetoric is so great that the word frequently begins to cover over and substitute itself for reality; when this happens the word itself is diminished and becomes shallow. Rhetoric is often limited to purely verbal victories over the word; when this happens, rhetoric degenerates into a formalistic verbal play. But, we repeat, when discourse is torn from reality, it is fatal for the word itself as well: words grow sickly, lose semantic depth and flexibility, the capacity to expand and renew their meanings in new living contexts — they essentially die as discourse, for the signifying word lives beyond itself, that is, it lives by means of directing its purposiveness outward. The exclusive concentration on another's discourse as a subject does not, however, *in itself* inevitably indicate such a rupture between discourse and reality.

Rhetorical genres possess the most varied forms for transmitting another's speech, and for the most part these are intensely dialogized forms. Rhetoric relies heavily on the vivid reaccentuating of the words it transmits (often to the point of distorting them completely) that is accomplished by the appropriate framing context. Rhetorical genres provide rich material for studying a variety of forms for transmitting another's speech, the most varied means for formulating and framing such speech. Using rhetoric, even a representation of a speaker and his discourse of the sort one finds in prose art is possible — but the rhetorical double-voicedness of such images is usually not very deep: its roots do not extend to the dialogical essence of evolving language itself; it is not structured on authentic heteroglossia but on a mere diversity of voices; in most cases the double-voicedness of rhetoric is abstract and thus lends itself to formal, purely logical analysis of the ideas that are parceled out in voices, an analysis that then exhausts it. For this reason it is proper to speak of a distinctive *rhetorical* double-voicedness, or, put another way, to speak of the double-voiced rhetorical transmission of another's word (although it may involve some artistic aspects), in contrast to the double-voiced *representation* of another's word in the novel with its orientation toward the *image of a language*.

Such, then, is the importance of the speaker and his discourse as a topic in all areas of everyday, as well as verbal-ideological, life. It might be said, on the basis of our argument so far, that in the makeup of almost every utterance spoken by a social person — from a brief response in a casual dialogue to major verbal-ideological works (literary, scholarly and others) — a significant number of words can be identified that are implicitly or explicitly admitted as someone else's, and that are transmitted by a variety of different means. Within the arena of almost every utterance an intense interaction and struggle between one's own and another's word is being waged, a process in which they oppose or dialogically interanimate each other. The utterance so conceived is a considerably more complex and dynamic organism than it appears when construed simply as a thing that articulates the intention of the person uttering it, which is to see the utterance as a direct, single-voiced vehicle for expression.

That one of the main subjects of human speech is discourse itself has not up to now been sufficiently taken into consideration, nor has its crucial importance been appreciated. There has been no comprehensive philosophical grasp of all the ramifications of this fact. The specific nature of discourse as a topic of speech, one that requires the transmission and reprocessing of another's word, has not been understood: one may speak of another's discourse only with the help of that alien discourse itself, although in the process, it is true, the speaker introduces into the other's words his own intentions and highlights the context of those words in his own way. To speak of discourse as one might speak of any other subject, that is, thematically, without any dialogized transmission of it, is possible only when such discourse is utterly reified, a thing; it is possible, for example, to talk about the word in such a way in grammar, where it is precisely the dead, thing-like shell of the word that interests us.

# From *Problems of Dostoevsky's Poetics*

The classification offered [in Table 1] is of course somewhat abstract in character. A concrete discourse may belong simultaneously to different varieties and even types. Moreover, interrelationships with another person's discourse in a concrete living context are of a dynamic and not a static character: the interrelationship of voices in discourse may change drastically, unidirectional words may turn into vari-directional ones, internal dialogization may become stronger or weaker, a passive type may be activized, and so forth.

"Notes from Underground" is a confessional *Ich-Erzählung*. Originally the work was entitled "A Confession."[1] And it is in fact an authentic confession. Of course, "confession" is understood here not in the personal sense. The author's intention is refracted here, as in any *Ich-Erzählung*; this is not a personal document but a work of art.

In the confession of the Underground Man what strikes us first of all is its extreme and acute

Translated by Caryl Emerson.
[1] "Notes from Underground" was originally announced by Dostoevsky under this title in "Time." [Au.]

dialogization: there is literally not a single monologically firm, undissociated word. From the very first sentence the hero's speech has already begun to cringe and break under the influence of the anticipated words of another, with whom the hero, from the very first step, enters into the most intense internal polemic.

"I am a sick man . . . I am a spiteful man. I am an unpleasant man." Thus begins the confession. The ellipsis and the abrupt change of tone after it are significant. The hero began in a somewhat plaintive tone "I am a sick man," but was immediately enraged by that tone: it looked as if he were complaining and needed sympathy, as if he were seeking that sympathy in another person, as if he needed another person! And then there occurs an abrupt dialogic turnaround, one of those typical breaks in accent so characteristic of the whole style of the "Notes," as if the hero wants to say: You, perhaps, were led to believe from my first word that I am seeking your sympathy, so take this: I am a spiteful man. I am an unpleasant man!

Characteristic here is a gradual increase in negative tone (to spite the other) under the influence of the other's anticipated reaction. Such

**Table 1**

I. Direct, unmediated discourse directed exclusively toward its referential object, as an expression of the speaker's ultimate semantic authority

II. Objectified discourse (discourse of a represented person)

    1. With a predominance of sociotypical determining factors

    2. With a predominance of individually characteristic determining factors

    } Various degrees of objectification.

III. Discourse with an orientation toward someone else's discourse (double-voiced discourse)

    1. Unidirectional double-voiced discourse:
       a. Stylization;
       b. Narrator's narration;
       c. Unobjectified discourse of a character who carries out (in part) the author's intentions;
       d. *Ich-Erzählung*[2]

    } When objectification is reduced, these tend toward a fusion of voices, i.e., toward discourse of the first type.

    2. Vari-directional double-voiced discourse:
       a. Parody with all its nuances;
       b. Parodistic narration;
       c. Parodistic *Ich-Erzählung*;
       d. Discourse of a character who is parodically represented;
       e. Any transmission of someone else's words with a shift in accent

    } When objectification is reduced and the other's idea activated, these become internally dialogized and tend to disintegrate into two discourses (two voices) of the first type.

    3. The active type (reflected discourse of another)
       a. Hidden internal polemic;
       b. Polemically colored autobiography and confession;
       c. Any discourse with a sideward glance at someone else's word;
       d. A rejoinder of a dialogue;
       e. Hidden dialogue

    } The other discourse exerts influence from without; diverse forms of inter-relationship with another's discourse are possible here, as well as various degrees of deforming influence exerted by one discourse on the other.

---

breaks in accent always lead to an accumulation of ever-intensifying abusive words or words that are, in any case, unflattering to the other person, as in this example:

To live longer than forty years is bad manners; it is vulgar, immoral. Who does live beyond forty? Answer that, sincerely and honestly. I will tell you who: fools and worthless people do. I tell all old men that to their face, all those respectable old men, all those silver-haired and reverend old men! I tell the whole world that to its face. I have a right to say so, for I'll go on living to sixty myself. I'll live till seventy! Till eighty! Wait, let me catch my breath. [*SS* IV, 135; "Notes," Part One, 1]

In the opening words of the confession, this internal polemic with the other is concealed. But the other's words are present invisibly, determining the style of speech from within. Midway into the first paragraph, however, the polemic has

[2]First person narrative. [Ed.]

already broken out into the open: the anticipated response of the other takes root in the narration, although, to be sure, still in a weakened form. "No, I refuse to treat it out of spite. You probably will not understand that. Well, but *I* understand it."

At the end of the third paragraph there is already a very characteristic anticipation of the other's reaction:

Well, are you not imagining, gentlemen, that I am repenting for something now, that I am asking your forgiveness for something? I am sure you are imagining that. However, I assure you it does not matter to me if you are.

At the end of the next paragraph comes the above-quoted polemical attack against the "reverend old men." The following paragraph begins directly with the anticipation of a response to the preceding paragraph:

No doubt you think, gentlemen, that I want to amuse you. You are mistaken in that, too. I am not at all such a merry person as you imagine, or as you may imagine; however, if irritated by all this babble (and I can feel that you are irritated) you decide to ask me just who I am — then my answer is, I am a certain low-ranked civil servant.

The next paragraph again ends with an anticipated response:

. . . I'll bet you think I am writing all this to show off, to be witty at the expense of men of action; and what is more, that out of ill-bred showing-off, I am clanking a sword, like my officer.

Later on such endings to paragraphs become more rare, but it remains true that all basic semantic sections of the work become sharper and more shrill near the end, in open anticipation of someone else's response.

Thus the entire style of the "Notes" is subject to the most powerful and all-determining influence of other people's words, which either act on speech covertly from within as in the beginning of the work, or which, as the anticipated response of another person, take root in the very fabric of speech, as in those above-quoted ending passages. The work does not contain a single word gravitating exclusively toward itself and its referential object; that is, there is not a single monologic word. We shall see that this intense relationship to another's consciousness in the Underground Man is complicated by an equally intense relationship to his own self. But first we shall make a brief structural analysis of this act of anticipating another's response.

Such anticipation is marked by one peculiar structural trait: it tends toward a vicious circle. The tendency of these anticipations can be reduced to a necessity to retain for oneself the final word. This final word must express the hero's full independence from the views and words of the other person, his complete indifference to the other's opinion and the other's evaluation. What he fears most of all is that people might think he is repenting before someone, that he is asking someone's forgiveness, that he is reconciling himself to someone else's judgment or evaluation, that his self-affirmation is somehow in need of affirmation and recognition by another. And it is in this direction that he anticipates the other's response. But precisely in this act of anticipating the other's response and in responding to it he again demonstrates to the other (and to himself) his own dependence on this other. He *fears* that the other might think he *fears* that other's opinion. But through this fear he immediately demonstrates his own dependence on the other's consciousness, his own inability to be at peace with his own definition of self. With his refutation, he confirms precisely what he wishes to refute, and he knows it. Hence the inescapable circle in which the hero's self-consciousness and discourse are trapped: "Well, are you not imagining, gentlemen, that I am repenting for something now? . . . I am sure you are imagining that. However, I assure you it does not matter to me if you are. . . ."

During that night out on the town, the Underground Man, insulted by his companions, wants to show them that he pays them no attention:

I smiled contemptuously and walked up and down the other side of the room, opposite the sofa, along the wall, from the table to the stove and back again. I tried my very utmost to show them that I could do without them, and yet I purposely stomped with my boots, thumping with my heels. But it was all in vain. They paid no attention at all. [*SS* IV, 199; "Notes," Part Two, Ch. IV]

Meanwhile our underground hero recognizes all this perfectly well himself, and understands perfectly well the impossibility of escaping from that circle in which his attitude toward the other moves. Thanks to this attitude toward the other's consciousness, a peculiar *perpetuum mobile*[3] is achieved, made up of his internal polemic with another and with himself, an endless dialogue where one reply begets another, which begets a third, and so on to infinity, and all of this without any forward motion.

Here is an example of that inescapable *perpetuum mobile* of the dialogized self-consciousness:

You will say that it is vulgar and base to drag all this [the hero's dreaming — M. B.] into public after all the tears and raptures I have myself admitted. But why is it base? Can you imagine that I am ashamed of it all, and that it was stupider than anything in your life, gentlemen? And I can assure you that some of these fancies were by no means badly composed. Not everything took place on the shores of Lake Como. And yet you are right — it really is vulgar and base. And what is most base of all is that I have now started to justify myself to you. And even more base than that is my making this remark now. But that's enough, or, after all, there will be no end to it; each step will be more base than the last. [*SS* IV, 181; "Notes," Part Two, Ch. II]

Before us is an example of a vicious circle of dialogue which can neither be finished nor finalized. The formal significance of such inescapable dialogic oppositions in Dostoevsky's work is very great. But nowhere in his subsequent works does this opposition appear in such naked, abstractly precise, one could even say directly mathematical, form.[4]

As a result of the Underground Man's attitude toward the other's consciousness and its discourse — extraordinary dependence upon it and at the same time extreme hostility toward it and

nonacceptance of its judgments — his narration takes on one highly essential artistic characteristic. This is a deliberate clumsiness of style, albeit subject to a certain artistic logic. His discourse does not flaunt itself and cannot flaunt itself, for there is not one before whom it can flaunt. It does not, after, all, gravitate naively toward itself and its referential object. It is addressed to another person and to the speaker himself (in his internal dialogue with himself). And in both of these directions it wants least of all to flaunt itself and be "artistic" in the usual sense of the word. In its attitude toward the other person it strives to be deliberately inelegant, to "spite" him and his tastes in all respects. But this discourse takes the same position even in regard to the speaker himself, for one's attitude toward oneself is inseparably interwoven with one's attitude toward another. Thus discourse is pointedly cynical, calculatedly cynical, yet also anguished. It strives to play the holy fool, for holy-foolishness is indeed a sort of form, a sort of aestheticism — but, as it were, in reverse.

As a result, the prosaic triteness of the portrayal of his inner life is carried to extreme limits. In its material, in its theme, the first part of "Notes from Underground" is lyrical. From a formal point of view, this is the same prose lyric of spiritual and emotional quest, of spiritual unfulfillment that we find, for example, in Turgenev's "Phantoms" or "Enough,"[5] or in any lyrical page from a confessional *Ich-Erzählung* or a page from *Werther*. But this is a peculiar sort of lyric, analogous to the lyrical expression of a toothache.

This expression of a toothache, oriented in an internally polemical way toward the listener and toward the sufferer, is spoken by the Underground Hero himself, and he speaks of it, of course, not by chance. He suggests eavesdropping on the groans of an "educated man of the

---

[3]Perpetual motion. [Ed.]

[4]This can be explained by the generic similarities between "Notes from Underground" and Menippean satire. [Au.]

[5]"Phantoms," the least successful of Turgenev's several stories on the supernatural; "Enough" is one of Turgenev's periodic gestures of withdrawal, a sort of prose poem announcing to the public his disillusionment with life and art. Both pieces, and their author, are vigorously parodied by Dostoevsky in the character of Karmazinov in *The Possessed*. [Tr.]

nineteenth century" who suffers from a toothache, on the second or third day of his illness. He tries to expose the peculiar sensuality behind this whole cynical expression of pain, an expression intended for the "public":

> His moans become nasty, disgustingly spiteful, and go on for whole days and nights. And, after all, he himself knows that he does not benefit at all from his moans; he knows better than anyone that he is only lacerating and irritating himself and others in vain; he knows that even the audience for whom he is exerting himself and his whole family now listen to him with loathing, do not believe him for a second, and that deep down they understand that he could moan differently, more simply, without trills and flourishes, and that he is only indulging himself like that out of spite, out of malice. Well, sensuality exists precisely in all these consciousnesses and infamies. "It seems I am troubling you, I am lacerating your hearts, I am keeping everyone in the house awake. Well, stay awake then, you, too, feel every minute that I have a toothache. I am no longer the hero to you now that I tried to appear before, but simply a nasty person, a scoundrel. Well, let it be that way, then! I am very glad that you see through me. Is it nasty for you to hear my foul moans? Well, let it be nasty. Here I will let you have an even nastier flourish in a minute. . . ." [SS IV, 144; "Notes," Part One, Ch. IV]

Of course any implied comparison here between the structure of the Underground Man's confession and the expression of a toothache is on the level of parodic exaggeration, and in this sense is cynical. But the orientation of this expression of a toothache, with all its "trills and flourishes," nevertheless does, in its relation to the listener and to the speaker himself, reflect very accurately the orientation of discourse in a confession — although, we repeat, it reflects not objectively but in a taunting, parodically exaggerating style, just as *The Double* reflected the internal speech of Golyadkin.

The destruction of one's own image in another's eyes, the sullying of that image in another's eyes as an ultimate desperate effort to free oneself from the power of the other's consciousness and to break through to one's self for the self alone — this, in fact, is the orientation of the Underground Man's entire confession. For this reason he makes his discourse about himself deliberately ugly. He wants to kill in himself any desire to appear the hero in others' eyes (and in his own): "I am no longer the hero to you now that I tried to appear before, but simply a nasty person, a scoundrel. . . ."

To accomplish this he must banish from his discourse all epic and lyrical tones, all "heroizing" tones; he must make his discourse *cynically* objective. A soberly objective definition of himself, without exaggeration or mockery, is impossible for a hero from the underground, because such a soberly prosaic definition would presuppose a word without a sideward glance, a word without a loophole; neither the one nor the other exist on his verbal palette. True, he is continually trying to break through to such a word, to break through to spiritual sobriety, but for him the path lies through cynicism and holy-foolishness. He has neither freed himself from the power of the other's consciousness nor admitted its power over him,[6] he is for now merely struggling with it, polemicizing with it maliciously, not able to accept it but also not able to reject it. In this striving to trample down his own image and his own discourse as they exist in and for the other person, one can hear not only the desire for sober self-definition, but also a desire to annoy the other person; and this forces him to overdo his sobriety, mockingly exaggerating it to the point of cynicism and holy-foolishness: "Is it nasty for you to hear my foul moans? Well, let it be nasty. Here I will let you have an even nastier flourish in a minute. . . ."

But the underground hero's word about himself is not only a word with a sideward glance; it is also, as we have said, a word with a loophole. The influence of the loophole on the style of his confession is so great that his style cannot be understood without a consideration of its formal activity. The word with a loophole has enormous significance in Dostoevsky's works in general, especially in the later works. And here we pass on to another aspect of the structure of "Notes from Underground": the hero's attitude toward his own self, which throughout the course

---

[6]According to Dostoevsky, such an admittance would also serve to calm down the discourse and purify it. [Au.]

of the entire work is interwoven and combined with his dialogue with another.

What, then, is this loophole of consciousness and of the word?

A loophole is the retention for oneself of the possibility for altering the ultimate, final meaning of one's own words. If a word retains such a loophole this must inevitably be reflected in its structure. This potential other meaning, that is, the loophole left open, accompanies the word like a shadow. Judged by its meaning alone, the word with a loophole should be an ultimate word and does present itself as such, but in fact it is only the penultimate word and places after itself only a conditional, not a final, period.

For example, the confessional self-definition with a loophole (the most widespread form in Dostoevsky) is, judging by its meaning, an ultimate word about oneself, a final definition of oneself, but in fact it is forever taking into account internally the responsive, contrary evaluation of oneself made by another. The hero who repents and condemns himself actually wants only to provoke praise and acceptance by another. Condemning himself, he wants and demands that the other person dispute this self-definition, and he leaves himself a loophole in case the other person should suddenly in fact agree with him, with his self-condemnation, and not make use of his privilege as the other.

Here is how the hero from the underground tells of his "literary" dreams:

> I, for instance, was triumphant over everyone; everyone, of course, lay in the dust and was *forced* to recognize my superiority *spontaneously*, and I forgave them all. I, a famous poet, and a courtier, fell in love; I inherited countless millions and immediately devoted them to humanity, and *at the same time I confessed before all the people my shameful deeds, which, of course, were not merely shameful, but contained an enormous amount of "the sublime and the beautiful," something in the Manfred[7] style. Everyone would weep and kiss me (what idiots they would be if they did not)*, while I would go barefoot and hungry preaching new ideas and fighting a victorious Austerlitz against the reactionaries. [*SS* IV, 181; "Notes," Part Two, Ch. II]

Here he ironically relates dreams of heroic deeds with a loophole, dreams of confession with a loophole. He casts a parodic light on these dreams. But his very next words betray the fact that his repentant confession of his dreams has its own loophole, too, and that he himself is prepared to find in these dreams and in his very confessing of them something, if not in the Manfred style, then at least in the realm of "the sublime and the beautiful," if anyone should happen to agree with him that the dreams are indeed base and vulgar: "You will say that it is vulgar and base to drag all this into public after all the tears and raptures I have myself admitted. But why is it base? Can you imagine that I am ashamed of it all, and that it was stupider than anything in your life, gentlemen? And I can assure you that some of these fancies were by no means badly composed. . . ."

And this passage, already cited by us above, is caught up in the vicious circle of self-consciousness with a sideward glance.

The loophole creates a special type of fictive ultimate word about oneself with an unclosed tone to it, obtrusively peering into the other's eyes and demanding from the other a sincere refutation. We shall see that the word with a loophole achieves especially sharp expression in Ippolit's[8] confession, but it is to one degree or another inherent in all the confessional self-utterances of Dostoevsky's heroes.[9] The loophole makes all the heroes' self-definitions unstable, the word in them has no hard and fast meaning, and at any moment, like a chameleon, it is ready to change its tone and its ultimate meaning.

The loophole makes the hero ambiguous and elusive even for himself. In order to break through to his self the hero must travel a very long road. The loophole profoundly distorts his attitude toward himself. The hero does not know whose opinion, whose statement is ultimately the final judgment on him: is it his own repentant and censuring judgment, or on the contrary is it another person's opinion that he desires and has compelled into being, an opinion that accepts and vindicates him? The image of Nastasya Filip-

---

[7]Demonic hero of Byron's dramatic poem. [Ed.]

[8]In *The Idiot*. [Ed.]
[9]Exceptions will be pointed out below. [Au.]

povna,[10] for example, is built almost entirely on this motif alone. Considering herself guilty, a fallen woman, she simultaneously assumes that the other person, precisely as the other, is obliged to vindicate her and cannot consider her guilty. She genuinely quarrels with Myshkin, who vindicates her in everything, but she equally genuinely despises and rejects all those who agree with her self-condemnation and consider her a fallen woman. Ultimately Nastasya Filippovna does not know even her own final word on herself: does she really consider herself a fallen woman, or does she vindicate herself? Self-condemnation and self-vindication, divided between two voices — I condemn myself, another vindicates me — but anticipated by a single voice, create in that voice interruptions and an internal duality. An anticipated and obligatory vindication by the other merges with self-condemnation, and both tones begin to sound simultaneously in that voice, resulting in abrupt interruptions and sudden transitions. Such is the voice of Nastasya Filippovna, such is the style of her discourse. Her entire inner life (and, as we shall see, her outward life as well) is reduced to a search for herself and for her own undivided voice beneath the two voices that have made their home in her.

The Underground Man conducts the same sort of inescapable dialogue with himself that he conducts with the other person. He cannot merge completely with himself in a unified monologic voice simply by leaving the other's voice entirely outside himself (whatever that voice might be, without a loophole), for, as is the case with Golyadkin, his voice must also perform the function of surrogate for the other person. He cannot reach an agreement with himself, but neither can he stop talking with himself. The style of his discourse about himself is organically alien to the period, alien to finalization, both in its separate aspects and as a whole. This is the style of internally endless speech which can be mechanically cut off but cannot be organically completed.

But precisely for that reason is Dostoevsky able to conclude his work in a way so organic and appropriate for the hero; he concludes it on

[10]In *The Idiot*. [Ed.]

precisely that which would foreground the tendency toward eternal endlessness embedded in his hero's notes.

> But enough; I don't want to write more from "underground." . . .
> The "notes" of this paradoxalist do not end here, however. He could not resist and continued them. But it also seems to me that we may stop here. [*SS* IV, 224; "Notes," Part Two, Ch. X]

In conclusion we will comment upon two additional characteristics of the Underground Man. Not only his discourse but his face too has its sideward glance, its loophole, and all the phenomena resulting from these. It is as if interference, voices interrupting one another, penetrate his entire body, depriving him of self-sufficiency and unambiguousness. The Underground Man hates his own face, because in it he senses the power of another person over him, the power of that other's evaluations and opinions. He himself looks on his own face with another's eyes, with the eyes of the other. And this alien glance interruptedly merges with his own glance and creates in him a peculiar hatred toward his own face:

> For instance, I hated my face; I thought it disgusting, and even suspected that there was something base in its expression and therefore every time I turned up at the office I painfully tried to behave as independently as possible so that I might not be suspected of being base, and to give my face as noble an expression as possible. "Let my face even be ugly," I thought, "but let it be noble, expressive, and above all, extremely intelligent." But I was absolutely and painfully certain that my face could never express those perfections; but what was worst of all, I thought it positively stupid-looking. And I would have been quite satisfied if I could have looked intelligent. In fact, I would even have put up with looking base if, at the same time, my face could have been thought terribly intelligent. [*SS* IV, 168; "Notes," Part Two, Ch. I]

Just as he deliberately makes his discourse about himself unattractive, so is he made happy by the unattractiveness of his face:

> I happened to look at myself in the mirror. My harassed face struck me as extremely revolting, pale, spiteful, nasty, with disheveled hair. "No

matter, I am glad of it," I thought; "I am glad that I shall seem revolting to her; I like that." [*SS* IV, 206; "Notes," Part Two, Ch. V]

This polemic with the other on the subject of himself is complicated in "Notes from Underground" by his polemic with the other on the subject of the world and society. The underground hero, in contrast to Devushkin and Golyadkin,[11] is an ideologist.

In his ideological discourse we can easily uncover the same phenomena that are present in his discourse about himself. His discourse about the world is both overtly and covertly polemical; it polemicizes not only with other people, with other ideologies, but also with the very subject of its thinking — with the world and its order. And in this discourse on the world there are two voices, as it were, sounding for him, among which he cannot find himself and his own world, because even the world he defines with a loophole. Just as his body has become an "interrupted" thing in his own eyes, so is the world, nature, society perceived by him as "interrupted." In each of his thoughts about them there is a battle of voices, evaluations, points of view. In everything he senses above all *someone else's will* predetermining him. It is within the framework of this alien will that he perceives the world order, nature with its mechanical necessity, the social order. His own thought is developed and structured as *the thought of someone personally insulted by the world order*, personally humiliated by its blind necessity. This imparts a profoundly intimate and passionate character to his ideological discourse, and permits it to become tightly interwoven with his discourse about himself. It seems (and such indeed was Dostoevsky's intent) that we are dealing here with a single discourse, and only by arriving at himself will the hero arrive at his world. Discourse about the world, just like discourse about oneself, is profoundly dialogic: the hero casts an energetic reproach at the world order, even at the mechanical necessity of nature, as if he were talking not about the world but with the world. Of these peculiarities of ideological discourse we will speak below, when we take up the general issue of hero-ideologists and Ivan Karamazov in particular; in him these features are especially acute and clear-cut.

The discourse of the Underground Man is entirely a discourse-address. To speak, for him, means to address someone; to speak about himself means to address his own self with his own discourse; to speak about another person means to address that other person; to speak about the world means to address the world. But while speaking with himself, with another, with the world, he simultaneously addresses a third party as well: he squints his eyes to the side, toward the listener, the witness, the judge.[12] This simultaneous triple-directedness of his discourse and the fact that he does not acknowledge any object without addressing it is also responsible for the extraordinarily vivid, restless, agitated, and one might say, obtrusive nature of this discourse. It cannot be seen as a lyrical or epic discourse, calmly gravitating toward itself and its referential object; no, first and foremost one reacts to it, responds to it, is drawn into its game; it is capable of agitating and irritating, almost like the personal address of a living person. It destroys footlights, but not because of its concern for topical issues or for reasons that have any direct philosophical significance, but precisely because of that formal structure analyzed by us above.

The element of *address* is essential to every discourse in Dostoevsky, narrative discourse as well as the discourse of the hero. In Dostoevsky's world generally there is nothing merely thing-like, no mere matter, no object — there are only subjects. Therefore there is no word-judgment, no word about an object, no secondhand referential word — there is only the word as address, the word dialogically contacting another word, a word about a word addressed to a word.

[11]Makar Devushkin is the protagonist of Dostoevsky's first novel, *Poor Folk*; Golyadkin, of *The Double*. [Ed.]

[12]We recall the characterization that Dostoevsky himself gave to the hero's speech in "A Meek One": ". . . he either argues with himself or addresses some unseen listener, a judge as it were. However, it is always like that in real life." [Au.]

# Cleanth Brooks
## b. 1906

*To many minds, Cleanth Brooks is the archetypal New Critic, the man whose catch phrases, critical studies, and college textbooks epitomized New Critical ideas, practice, and pedagogy. Brooks was born in Kentucky, educated at Vanderbilt, Tulane, and Oxford (where he was a Rhodes scholar), and began his teaching career at Louisiana State University in 1932. From 1935 to 1942, Brooks and the poet Robert Penn Warren edited* The Southern Review, *which promulgated the New Critical program; the two later collaborated on* Understanding Poetry *(1938) and* Understanding Fiction *(1943), textbooks which further advanced the New Critical cause. The year 1947 saw the publication of Brooks's classic of criticism,* The Well Wrought Urn, *and the beginning of his career at Yale, where he became a professor emeritus of rhetoric thirteen years later. Brooks's other works include two studies of William Faulkner (1963 and 1978),* Modern Poetry and the Tradition *(1939),* Literary Criticism: A Short History *(1957) with W. K. Wimsatt, and* A Shaping Joy: Studies in the Writer's Craft *(1972). "Irony as a Principle of Structure," from* Literary Opinion in America *(1951), edited by M. D. Zabel, is a revision of an article that first appeared in the February 1948 issue of* College English.

# Irony as a Principle of Structure

One can sum up modern poetic technique by calling it the rediscovery of metaphor and the full commitment to metaphor. The poet can legitimately step out into the universal only by first going through the narrow door of the particular. The poet does not select an abstract theme and then embellish it with concrete details. On the contrary, he must establish the details, must abide by the details, and through his realization of the details attain to whatever general meaning he can attain. The meaning must issue from the particulars; it must not seem to be arbitrarily forced upon the particulars. Thus, our conventional habits of language have to be reversed when we come to deal with poetry. For here it is the tail that wags the dog. Better still, here it is the tail of the kite — the tail that makes the kite fly — the tail that renders the kite more than a frame of paper blown crazily down the wind.

The tail of the kite, it is true, seems to negate the kite's function: it weights down something made to rise; and in the same way, the concrete particulars with which the poet loads himself seem to deny the universal to which he aspires. The poet wants to "say" something. Why, then, doesn't he say it directly and forthrightly? Why is he willing to say it only through his metaphors? Through his metaphors, he risks saying it partially and obscurely, and risks not saying it at all. But the risk must be taken, for direct statement leads to abstraction and threatens to take us out of poetry altogether.

The commitment to metaphor thus implies, with respect to general theme, a principle of indirection. With respect to particular images and statements, it implies a principle of organic relationship. That is, the poem is not a collection of beautiful or "poetic" images. If there really existed objects which were somehow intrinsically "poetic," still the mere assemblage of these would not give us a poem. For in that case, one might arrange bouquets of these poetic images and thus create poems by formula. But the elements of a poem are related to each other, not as blossoms juxtaposed in a bouquet, but as the blossoms are related to the other parts of a growing plant. The beauty of the poem is the flowering of the whole plant, and needs the stalk, the leaf, and the hidden roots.

If this figure seems somewhat highflown, let us borrow an analogy from another art: the poem is like a little drama. The total effect proceeds from all the elements in the drama, and in a good poem, as in a good drama, there is no waste motion and there are no superfluous parts.

In coming to see that the parts of a poem are related to each other organically, and related to the total theme indirectly, we have come to see the importance of *context*. The memorable verses in poetry — even those which seem somehow intrinsically "poetic" — show on inspection that they derive their poetic quality from their relation to a particular context. We may, it is true, be tempted to say that Shakespeare's "Ripeness is all" is poetic because it is a sublime thought, or because it possesses simple eloquence; but that is to forget the context in which the passage appears. The proof that this is so becomes obvious when we contemplate such unpoetic lines as "vitality is all," "serenity is all," "maturity is all," — statements whose philosophical import in the abstract is about as defensible as that of "ripeness is all." Indeed, the commonplace word "never" repeated five times becomes one of the most poignant lines in *Lear*, but it becomes so because of the supporting context. Even the "meaning" of any particular item is modified by the context. For what is said is said in a particular situation and by a particular dramatic character.

The last instances adduced can be most properly regarded as instances of "loading" from the context. The context endows the particular word or image or statement with significance. Images so charged become symbols; statements so charged become dramatic utterances. But there is another way in which to look at the impact of the context upon the part. The part is modified by the pressure of the context.

Now the *obvious* warping of a statement by the context we characterize as "ironical." To take the simplest instance, we say "this is a fine state of affairs," and in certain contexts the statement means quite the opposite of what it purports to say literally. This is sarcasm, the most obvious kind of irony. Here a complete reversal of meaning is effected: effected by the context, and

pointed, probably, by the tone of voice. But the modification can be most important even though it falls far short of sarcastic reversal, and it need not be underlined by the tone of voice at all. The tone of irony can be effected by the skillful disposition of the context. Gray's *Elegy* will furnish an obvious example:

> Can storied urn or animated bust
> Back to its mansion call the fleeting breath?
> Can Honour's voice provoke the silent dust,
> Or Flatt'ry soothe the dull cold ear of death?

In its context, the question is obviously rhetorical. The answer has been implied in the characterization of the breath as fleeting and of the ear of death as dull and cold. The form is that of a question, but the manner in which the question has been asked shows that it is no true question at all.

These are obvious instances of irony, and even on this level, much more poetry is ironical than the reader may be disposed to think. Many of Hardy's poems and nearly all of Housman's, for example, reveal irony quite as definite and overt as this. Lest these examples, however, seem to specialize irony in the direction of the sardonic, the reader ought to be reminded that irony, even in its obvious and conventionally recognized forms, comprises a wide variety of modes: tragic irony, self-irony, playful, arch, mocking, or gentle irony, etc. The body of poetry which may be said to contain irony in the ordinary senses of the term stretches from *Lear*, on the one hand, to "Cupid and Campaspe Played," on the other.

What indeed would be a statement wholly devoid of an ironic potential — a statement that did not show any qualification of the context? One is forced to offer statements like "Two plus two equals four," or "The square on the hypotenuse of a right triangle is equal to the sum of the squares on the two sides." The meaning of these statements is unqualified by any context; if they are true, they are equally true in any possible context.[1] These statements are properly abstract,

[1]This is not to say, of course, that such statements are not related to a particular "universe of discourse." They are indeed, as are all statements of whatever kind. But I distinguish here between "context" and "universe of discourse."

and their terms are pure denotations. (If "two" or "four" actually happened to have connotations for the fancifully minded, the connotations would be quite irrelevant: they do not participate in the meaningful structure of the statement.)

But connotations are important in poetry and do enter significantly into the structure of meaning which is the poem. Moreover, I should claim also — as a corollary of the foregoing proposition — that poems never contain abstract statements. That is, any "statement" made in the poem bears the pressure of the context and has its meaning modified by the context. In other words, the statements made — including those which appear to be philosophical generalizations — are to be read as if they were speeches in a drama. Their relevance, their propriety, their rhetorical force, even their meaning, cannot be divorced from the context in which they are imbedded.

The principle I state may seem a very obvious one, but I think that it is nonetheless very important. It may throw some light upon the importance of the term *irony* in modern criticism. As one who has certainly tended to overuse the term *irony* and perhaps, on occasion, has abused the term, I am closely concerned here. But I want to make quite clear what that concern is: it is not to justify the term *irony* as such, but rather to indicate why modern critics are so often tempted to use it. We have doubtless stretched the term too much, but it has been almost the only term available by which to point to a general and important aspect of poetry.

Consider this example: The speaker in Matthew Arnold's "Dover Beach" states that the world, "which seems to lie before us like a land of dreams . . . hath really neither joy nor love nor light. . . ." For some readers the statement will seem an obvious truism. (The hero of a typical Hemingway short story or novel, for ex-

ample, will say this, though of course in a rather different idiom.) For other readers, however, the statement will seem false, or at least highly questionable. In any case, if we try to "prove" the proposition, we shall raise some very perplexing metaphysical questions, and in doing so, we shall certainly also move away from the problems of the poem and, finally, from a justification of the poem. For the lines are to be justified in the poem in terms of the context: the speaker is standing beside his loved one, looking out of the window on the calm sea, listening to the long withdrawing roar of the ebbing tide, and aware of the beautiful delusion of moonlight which "blanches" the whole scene. The "truth" of the statement, and of the poem itself, in which it is imbedded, will be validated, not by a majority report of the association of sociologists, or a committee of physical scientists, or of a congress of metaphysicians who are willing to stamp the statement as proved. How is the statement to be validated? We shall probably not be able to do better than to apply T. S. Eliot's test: does the statement seem to be that which the mind of the reader can accept as coherent, mature, and founded on the facts of experience? But when we raise such a question, we are driven to consider the poem as drama. We raise such further questions as these: Does the speaker seem carried away with his own emotions? Does he seem to oversimplify the situation? Or does he, on the other hand, seem to have won to a kind of detachment and objectivity? In other words, we are forced to raise the question as to whether the statement grows properly out of a context; whether it acknowledges the pressures of the context; whether it is "ironical" — or merely callow, glib, and sentimental.

I have suggested elsewhere that the poem which meets Eliot's test comes to the same thing as I. A. Richards's "poetry of synthesis" — that is, a poetry which does not leave out what is apparently hostile to its dominant tone, and which, because it is able to fuse the irrelevant and discordant, has come to terms with itself and is invulnerable to irony.[2] Irony, then, in this fur-

---

"Two plus two equals four" is not dependent on a special dramatic context in the way in which a "statement" made in a poem is. Compare "two plus two equals four" and the same "statement" as contained in Housman's poem:

— To think that two and two are four
  And neither five nor three
The heart of man has long been sore
  And long 'tis like to be.    [Au.]

[2]See I. A. Richards, *Principles of Literary Criticism*, p. 774ff. [Ed.]

ther sense, is not only an acknowledgment of the pressures of a context. Invulnerability to irony is the stability of a context in which the internal pressures balance and mutually support each other. The stability is like that of the arch: the very forces which are calculated to drag the stones to the ground actually provide the principle of support — a principle in which thrust and counterthrust become the means of stability.

In many poems the pressures of the context emerge in obvious ironies. Marvell's "To His Coy Mistress" or Raleigh's "Nymph's Reply" or even Gray's "Elegy" reveal themselves as ironical, even to readers who use irony strictly in the conventional sense.

But can other poems be subsumed under this general principle, and do they show a comparable basic structure? The test case would seem to be presented by the lyric, and particularly the simple lyric. Consider, for example, one of Shakespeare's songs:

> Who is Silvia: what is she
>    That all our swains commend her?
> Holy, fair, and wise is she;
>    The heavens such grace did lend her,
> That she might admired be.
>
> Is she kind as she is fair?
>    For beauty lives with kindness.
> Love doth to her eyes repair,
>    To help him of his blindness,
> And, being help'd, inhabits there.
>
> Then to Silvia let us sing,
>    That Silvia is excelling;
> She excels each mortal thing
>    Upon the dull earth dwelling:
> To her let us garlands bring.

On one level the song attempts to answer the question "Who is Silvia?" and the answer given makes her something of an angel and something of a goddess. She excels each mortal thing "Upon the dull earth dwelling." Silvia herself, of course, dwells upon that dull earth, though it is presumably her own brightness which makes it dull by comparison. (The dull earth, for example, yields bright garlands which the swains are bringing to her.) Why does she excel each mortal thing? Because of her virtues ("Holy, fair, and wise is she"), and these are a celestial gift. She is heaven's darling ("The heavens such grace did lend her").

Grace, I suppose, refers to grace of movement, and some readers will insist that we leave it at that. But since Silvia's other virtues include holiness and wisdom, and since her grace has been lent from above, I do not think that we can quite shut out the theological overtones. Shakespeare's audience would have found it even more difficult to do so. At any rate, it is interesting to see what happens if we are aware of these overtones. We get a delightful richness, and we also get something very close to irony.

The motive for the bestowal of grace — that she might admired be — is oddly untheological. But what follows is odder still, for the love that "doth to her eyes repair" is not, as we might expect, Christian "charity" but the little pagan god Cupid ("Love doth to her eyes repair, / To help him of his blindness.") But if Cupid lives in her eyes, then the second line of the stanza takes on another layer of meaning. "For beauty lives with kindness" becomes not merely a kind of charming platitude — actually often denied in human experience. (The Petrarchan lover, for example, as Shakespeare well knew, frequently found a beautiful and *cruel* mistress.) The second line, in this context, means also that the love god lives with the kind Silvia, and indeed has taken these eyes that sparkle with kindness for his own.

Is the mixture of pagan myth and Christian theology, then, an unthinking confusion into which the poet has blundered, or is it something wittily combined? It is certainly not a confusion, and if blundered into unconsciously, it is a happy mistake. But I do not mean to press the issue of the poet's self-consciousness (and with it, the implication of a kind of playful irony). Suffice it to say that the song is charming and delightful, and that the mingling of elements is proper to a poem which is a deft and light-fingered attempt to suggest the quality of divinity with which lovers perennially endow maidens who are finally mortal. The touch is light, there is a lyric grace, but the tone is complex, nonetheless.

I shall be prepared, however, to have this last example thrown out of court since Shakespeare, for all his universality, was a contemporary of the metaphysical poets, and may have incorporated more of their ironic complexity than is necessary or normal. One can draw more innocent and therefore more convincing examples from Wordsworth's Lucy poems.

> She dwelt among the untrodden ways
>   Beside the springs of Dove,
> A maid whom there were none to praise
>   And very few to love;
>
> A violet by a mossy stone
>   Half hidden from the eye!
> Fair as a star, when only one
>   Is shining in the sky.
>
> She lived unknown, and few could know
>   When Lucy ceased to be;
> But she is in her grave, and, oh,
>   The difference to me.

Which is Lucy really like — the violet or the star? The context in general seems to support the violet comparison. The violet, beautiful but almost unnoticed, already half hidden from the eye, is now, as the poem ends, completely hidden in its grave, with none but the poet to grieve for its loss. The star comparison may seem only vaguely relevant — a conventional and here a somewhat anomalous compliment. Actually, it is not difficult to justify the star comparison: to her lover's eyes, she is the solitary star. She has no rivals, nor would the idea of rivalry, in her unselfconscious simplicity, occur to her.

The violet and the star thus balance each other and between themselves define the situation: Lucy was, from the viewpoint of the great world, unnoticed, shy, modest, and half hidden from the eye, but from the standpoint of her lover, she is the single star, completely dominating that world, not arrogantly like the sun, but sweetly and modestly, like the star. The implicit contrast is that so often developed ironically by John Donne in his poems where the lovers, who amount to nothing in the eyes of the world, become, in their own eyes, each the other's world — as in "The Good-Morrow," where their love makes "one little room an everywhere," or as in "The Canonization," where the lovers drive into the mirrors of each other's eyes the "towns, countries, courts" — which make up the great world; and thus find that world in themselves. It is easy to imagine how Donne would have ex-

ploited the contrast between the violet and the star, accentuating it, developing the irony, showing how the violet was really like its antithesis, the star, etc.

Now one does not want to enter an Act of Uniformity against the poets. Wordsworth is entitled to his method of simple juxtaposition with no underscoring of the ironical contrast. But it is worth noting that the contrast with its ironic potential is there in his poem. It is there in nearly all of Wordsworth's successful lyrics. It is certainly to be found in "A slumber did my spirit seal."

> A slumber did my spirit seal;
>   I had no human fears:
> She seemed a thing that could not feel
>   The touch of earthly years.
>
> No motion has she now, no force;
>   She neither hears nor sees,
> Rolled round in earth's diurnal course,
>   With rocks, and stones, and trees.

The lover's insensitivity to the claims of mortality is interpreted as a lethargy of spirit — a strange slumber. Thus the "human fears" that he lacked are apparently the fears normal to human beings. But the phrase has a certain pliability. It could mean fears *for* the loved one as a mortal human being; and the lines that follow tend to warp the phrase in this direction: it does not occur to the lover that he needs to fear for one who cannot be touched by "earthly years." We need not argue that Wordsworth is consciously using a witty device, a purposed ambiguity; nor need we conclude that he is confused. It is enough to see that Wordsworth has developed, quite "normally," let us say, a context calculated to pull "human fears" in opposed directions, and that the slightest pressure of attention on the part of the reader precipitates an ironical effect.

As we move into the second stanza, the potential irony almost becomes overt. If the slumber has sealed the lover's spirit, a slumber, immersed in which he thought it impossible that his loved one could perish, so too a slumber has now definitely sealed *her* spirit: "No motion has she now, no force; / She neither hears nor sees." It is evident that it is her unnatural slumber that has waked him out of his. It is curious to speculate on what Donne or Marvell would have made of this.

Wordsworth, however, still does not choose to exploit the contrast as such. Instead, he attempts to suggest something of the lover's agonized shock at the loved one's present lack of motion — of his response to her utter and horrible inertness. And how shall he suggest this? He chooses to suggest it, not by saying that she lies as quiet as marble or as a lump of clay; on the contrary, he attempts to suggest it by imagining her in violent motion — violent, but imposed motion, the same motion indeed which the very stones share, whirled about as they are in earth's diurnal course. Why does the image convey so powerfully the sense of something inert and helpless? Part of the effect, of course, resides in the fact that a dead lifelessness is suggested more sharply by an object's being whirled about by something else than by an image of the object in repose. But there are other matters which are at work here: the sense of the girl's falling back into the clutter of things, companioned by things chained like a tree to one particular spot, or by things completely inanimate, like rocks and stones. Here, of course, the concluding figure leans upon the suggestion made in the first stanza, that the girl once seemed something not subject to earthly limitations at all. But surely, the image of the whirl itself is important in its suggestion of something meaningless — motion that mechanically repeats itself. And there is one further element: the girl, who to her lover seemed a thing that could not feel the touch of earthly years, is caught up helplessly into the empty whirl of the earth which measures and makes time. She is touched by and held by earthly time in its most powerful and horrible image. The last figure thus seems to me to summarize the poem — to offer to almost every facet of meaning suggested in the earlier lines a concurring and resolving image which meets and accepts and reduces each item to its place in the total unity.[3]

Wordsworth, as we have observed above, does not choose to point up specifically the ironical contrast between the speaker's former slumber and the loved one's present slumber. But there is one ironical contrast which he does stress: this is the contrast between the two senses in which the girl becomes insulated against the "touch of earthly years." In the first stanza, she "could not feel / The touch of earthly years" because she seemed divine and immortal. But in the second stanza, now in her grave, she still does not "feel the touch of earthly years," for, like the rocks and stones, she feels nothing at all. It is true that Wordsworth does not repeat the verb "feels"; instead he writes "She neither *hears* nor *sees*." But the contrast, though not commented upon directly by any device of verbal wit, is there nonetheless, and is bound to make itself felt in any sensitive reading of the poem. The statement of the first stanza has been literally realized in the second, but its meaning has been ironically reversed.

Ought we, then, to apply the term *ironical* to Wordsworth's poem? Not necessarily. I am trying to account for my temptation to call such a poem ironical — not to justify my yielding to the temptation — least of all to insist that others so transgress. Moreover, Wordsworth's poem seems to be admirable, and I entertain no notion that it might have been more admirable still had John Donne written it rather than William Wordsworth. I shall be content if I can make a much more modest point: namely, that since both Wordsworth and Donne are poets, their work has at basis a similar structure, and that the dynamic structure — the pattern of thrust and counterthrust — which we associate with Donne has its counterpart in Wordsworth. In the work of both men, the relation between part and part is organic, which means that each part modifies and is modified by the whole.

Yet to intimate that there are potential ironies in Wordsworth's lyric may seem to distort it. After all, is it not simple and spontaneous? With these terms we encounter two of the critical catchwords of the nineteenth century, even as *ironical* is in danger of becoming a catchword of our own period. Are the terms *simple* and *ironical* mutually exclusive? What after all do we mean by *simple* or by *spontaneous*? We may mean that the poem came to the poet easily and even spontaneously: very complex poems may

---

[3] Brooks's reading here is discussed in E. D. Hirsch, "Objective Interpretation," in Ch. 9. [Ed.]

— indeed have — come just this way. Or the poem may seem in its effect on the reader a simple and spontaneous utterance: some poems of great complexity possess this quality. What is likely to cause trouble here is the intrusion of a special theory of composition. It is fairly represented as an intrusion since a theory as to how a poem is written is being allowed to dictate to us how the poem is to be read. There is no harm in thinking of Wordsworth's poem as simple and spontaneous unless these terms deny complexities that actually exist in the poem, and unless they justify us in reading the poem with only half our minds. A slumber ought not to seal the *reader's* spirit as he reads this poem, or any other poem.

I have argued that irony, taken as the acknowledgment of the pressures of context, is to be found in poetry of every period and even in simple lyrical poetry. But in the poetry of our own time, this pressure reveals itself strikingly. A great deal of modern poetry does use irony as its special and perhaps its characteristic strategy. For this there are reasons, and compelling reasons. To cite only a few of these reasons: there is the breakdown of a common symbolism; there is the general scepticism as to universals; not least important, there is the depletion and corruption of the very language itself, by advertising and by the mass-produced arts of radio, the moving picture, and pulp fiction. The modern poet has the task of rehabilitating a tired and drained language so that it can convey meanings once more with force and with exactitude. This task of qualifying and modifying language is perennial; but it is imposed on the modern poet as a special burden. Those critics who attribute the use of ironic techniques to the poet's own bloodless sophistication and tired scepticism would be better advised to refer these vices to his potential readers, a public corrupted by Hollywood and the Book of the Month Club. For the modern poet is not addressing simple primitives but a public sophisticated by commercial art.

At any rate, to the honor of the modern poet be it said that he has frequently succeeded in using his ironic techniques to win through to clarity and passion. Randall Jarrell's "Eighth Air Force" represents a success of this sort.

If, in an odd angle of the hutment,
A puppy laps the water from a can
Of flowers, and the drunk sergeant shaving
Whistles *O Paradiso!* — shall I say that man
Is not as men have said: a wolf to man?

The other murderers troop in yawning;
Three of them play Pitch, one sleeps, and one
Lies counting missions, lies there sweating
Till even his heart beats: One; One; One.
*O murderers!* . . . Still, this is how it's done:

This is a war. . . . But since these play, before
   they die,
Like puppies with their puppy; since, a man,
I did as these have done, but did not die —
I will content the people as I can
And give up these to them: Behold the man!

I have suffered, in a dream, because of him,
Many things; for this last saviour, man,
I have lied as I lie now. But what is lying?
Men wash their hands, in blood, as best they can:
I find no fault in this just man.

There are no superfluous parts, no dead or empty details. The airmen in their hutment are casual enough and honest enough to be convincing. The raw building is domesticated: there are the flowers in water from which the mascot, a puppy, laps. There is the drunken sergeant, whistling an opera aria as he shaves. These "murderers," as the poet is casually to call the airmen in the next stanza, display a touching regard for the human values. How, then, can one say that man is a wolf to man, since these men "play before they die, like puppies with their puppy." But the casual presence of the puppy in the hutment allows us to take the stanza both ways, for the dog is a kind of tamed and domesticated wolf, and his presence may prove on the contrary that the hutment is the wolf den. After all, the timber wolf plays with its puppies.

The second stanza takes the theme to a perfectly explicit conclusion. If three of the men play pitch, and one is asleep, at least one man is awake and counts himself and his companions murderers. But his unvoiced cry "O murderers" is met, countered, and dismissed with the next two lines: ". . . Still this is how it's done: / This is a war. . . ."

The note of casuistry and cynical apology prepares for a brilliant and rich resolving image, the image of Pontius Pilate, which is announced specifically in the third stanza:

> I will content the people as I can
> And give up these to them: behold the man!

Yet if Pilate, as he is first presented, is a jesting Pilate, who asks "What is truth?" it is a bitter and grieving Pilate who concludes the poem. It is the integrity of Man himself that is at stake. Is man a cruel animal, a wolf, or is he the last savior, the Christ of our secular religion of humanity?

The Pontius Pilate metaphor, as the poet uses it, becomes a device for tremendous concentration. For the speaker (presumably the young airman who cried "O murderers") is himself the confessed murderer under judgment, and also the Pilate who judges, and, at least as a representative of man, the savior whom the mob would condemn. He is even Pilate's better nature, his wife, for the lines "I have suffered, in a dream, because of him, / Many things" is merely a rearrangement of *Matthew* 27:19, the speech of Pilate's wife to her husband. But this last item is more than a reminiscence of the scriptural scene. It reinforces the speaker's present dilemma. The modern has had high hopes for man; are the hopes merely a dream? Is man incorrigible, merely a cruel beast? The speaker's present torture springs from that hope and from his reluctance to dismiss it as an empty dream. This Pilate is even harder-pressed than was the Roman magistrate. For he must convince himself of this last savior's innocence. But he has lied for him before. He will lie for him now.

> Men wash their hands in blood, as best they can:
> I find no fault in this just man.

What is the meaning of "Men wash their hands in blood, as best they can"? It can mean: Since my own hands are bloody, I have no right to condemn the rest. It can mean: I know that man can love justice, even though his hands are bloody, for there is blood on mine. It can mean: Men are essentially decent: they try to keep their hands clean even if they have only blood in which to wash them.

None of these meanings cancels out the others. All are relevant, and each meaning contributes to the total meaning. Indeed, there is not a facet of significance which does not receive illumination from the figure.

Some of Jarrell's weaker poems seem weak to me because they lean too heavily upon this concept of the goodness of man. In some of them, his approach to the theme is too direct. But in this poem, the affirmation of man's essential justness by a Pilate who contents the people as he washes his hands in blood seems to me to supply every qualification that is required. The sense of self-guilt, the yearning to believe in man's justness, the knowledge of the difficulty of so believing — all work to render accurately and dramatically the total situation.

It is easy at this point to misapprehend the function of irony. We can say that Jarrell's irony pares his theme down to acceptable dimensions. The theme of man's goodness has here been so qualified that the poet himself does not really believe in it. But this is not what I am trying to say. We do not ask a poet to bring his poem into line with our personal beliefs — still less to flatter our personal beliefs. What we do ask is that the poem dramatize the situation so accurately, so honestly, with such fidelity to the total situation that it is no longer a question of our beliefs, but of our participation in the poetic experience. At his best, Jarrell manages to bring us, by an act of imagination, to the most penetrating insight. Participating in that insight, we doubtless become better citizens. (One of the "uses" of poetry, I should agree, is to make us better citizens.) But poetry is not the eloquent rendition of the citizen's creed. It is not even the accurate rendition of his creed. Poetry must carry us beyond the abstract creed into the very matrix out of which, and from which, our creeds are abstracted. That is what "The Eighth Air Force" does. That is what, I am convinced, all good poetry does.

For the theme in a genuine poem does not confront us as abstraction — that is, as one man's generalization from the relevant particulars. Finding its proper symbol, defined and refined by the participating metaphors, the theme becomes a part of the reality in which we live — an insight, rooted in and growing out of concrete experience, many-sided, three-dimensional. Even the resistance to generalization has its part in this process — even the drag of the particulars away from the universal — even the tension of opposing themes — play their parts. The kite properly loaded, tension maintained along the kite string, rises steadily *against* the thrust of the wind.

# R. S. Crane
## 1886–1967

*Ronald Salmon Crane was the leader and moving spirit of the Chicago School of neo-Aristotelian criticism, one of the two major formalist movements in America. Crane was born in Michigan, took his A.B. from the University of Michigan, Ann Arbor (1908) and his doctorate at the University of Pennsylvania (1911). In 1911 he started teaching at Northwestern University in Illinois, then moved on in 1924 to the University of Chicago, where he became full professor in 1925 and head of the English department in 1935. Crane's interest in literary theory and his notion that criticism, rather than historical scholarship, was the preferred mode of teaching literature, began in the 1930s during the implementation of the innovative Hutchins curriculum. Crane's publications are primarily academic articles dense with thought, rather than critical books; the best and farthest reaching of his articles were collected in two volumes as* The Idea of the Humanities and Other Essays Critical and Historical *(1967). His only theoretical treatise (from which this selection is taken) is* The Languages of Criticism and the Structure of Poetry *(1953).*

# Toward a More Adequate Criticism of Poetic Structure

## II

It is not a question of regarding the *Poetics*, in Mr. Blackmur's phrase, as a "sacred book"[1] and certainly not of looking upon ourselves, in any exclusive sense, as forming an "Aristotelian" or "Neo-Aristotelian" school. It would be a desirable thing, indeed, if we could do away with "schools" in criticism as they have been done away with in most of the disciplines in which learning as distinguished from doctrine has been advanced. But our loyalty at any rate should be to problems rather than to ancient masters; and if it happens that we have problems for which Aristotle can give us the means, or some of the means, of solution, we should be prepared to

benefit from his initiative in precisely the same way as many of our contemporaries have benefited from the more recent initiatives of Coleridge, Richards, Frazer, and Freud without necessarily becoming disciples of any of these men. And it is not difficult to see what there is in Aristotle, or what we can develop out of him, that is immediately pertinent to the problem of poetic structure in the particular form in which I have defined it at the beginning of this lecture.

I should put first in the list the conception of poetic works as "concrete wholes." Now anything is a concrete whole, as I have said before, the unity of which can be adequately stated only by saying that it "is such and such a form embodied in this or that matter, or such and such a matter with this or that form; so that its shape and structure must be included in our descrip-

¹*Hudson Review* 3 (1951): 297. [Au.]

tion" as well as that out of which it is constituted or made. And of the two natures which must join in any such whole, or in our account of it, "the formal nature is of greater importance than the material nature" inasmuch as the "form" of any individual object, such as a man or a couch, is the principle or cause "by reason of which the matter is some definite thing."[2] In spite of the now somewhat unfamiliar language in which the conception is stated in Aristotle, the underlying insight is one that we can easily translate into the terms of common experience. I take, for instance, a piece of modelling clay. There are many things which I cannot do with it — of which, as Aristotle would say, it cannot be the matter; but on the other hand the potentialities it does hold out, within these limits, are indefinite in number: I can make of it, if I wish, a geographical globe, with all its continents indicated, or the model of a house, or the bust of a sinister-looking man, and so on through a vast range of similar possibilities that is bounded only by my invention and skill. In any of these realizations the thing I make remains a thing of clay, having all the permanent characteristics of such a thing; but it remains this only in a partial sense; in itself, as a particular object to which we may respond practically or aesthetically, it is at the same time something else — a globe, a house, a sinister-looking man; and any description we may give of it, though it must obviously specify its clayness — that is, its material nature — would be of no use to anybody unless it also specified the definite kind of thing into which the clay has been shaped — that is, its formal nature. And the latter is clearly more important than the former since it is what accounts, in any particular case, for the clay being handled thus and not otherwise and for our response being of such and such a quality rather than any other.

It is not difficult to see how the conception fits the work of the poet or of any other writer. Here is a speech in a famous novel:

"Ah, my poor dear child, the truth is, that in London it is always a sickly season. Nobody is

healthy in London — nobody can be. It is a dreadful thing to have you forced to live there; so far off! and the air so bad!"

Taken in isolation, this may be described simply as an expression of regret that the person addressed has to live in London, based on the commonplace thought that the air of London, as compared with the air of the country, is far from healthy. The speech, we may say, is made out of this matter; but it is a matter, obviously, that permits of a variety of particular uses: it might be a speech in an idyll, or in a satire, or in a moral epistle in the manner of Cowper; and in each case its formal nature and hence our response would be different. It is actually, of course, a speech by Mr. Woodhouse in *Emma*; and when it is so read, in its position in the dialogue of Chapter 12 and in the light of what we have already seen of Emma's father, it assumes the nature of a characteristic comic act, wherein the most important thing is not the commonplace thought itself, but the excessive and inappropriate emotion, at the prospect of Isabella's coming departure for home, which this is made to express, and which is the formal principle shaping the matter of the speech into a definite, though not self-contained, artistic unit capable of directing our thoughts in a particular way.

Or here again is a whole poem, the material nature of which is comprised of the following sequence of happenings:

A young Italian duke, influenced by his idle companions, dismisses the wise counsellor his father had recommended to him, refuses the advice of his fiancée, and devotes himself to a life of private pleasure and neglect of public duty. A Turkish corsair takes advantage of this situation to storm the Duke's castle and to reduce him and all his court to slavery; and the Duke falls into despair when he learns that his fiancée is destined for the conqueror's harem. She, however, deceives the corsair into giving her a delay of three days and a chance to speak to her lover. She uses this time to rouse the Duke to repentance for his past errors and to work out with him a plan whereby he and his father's counsellor will attempt a rescue before the three days are up. The plan succeeds; the Duke

[2]*On the Parts of Animals* i.1.640$^b$25–29; *Metaphysics* vii.17.1041$^b$5–8. [Au.]

and his friends overcome the corsair's troops and make him prisoner. The Duke's false companions then demand that the Turk be executed; but the Duke, grateful for the lesson his captivity has taught him, responds by banishing them and allowing the corsair to depart unharmed; whereupon he marries his fiancée and resolves to rule more wisely in the future.

As an action this is clearly not without some form, being a coherent and complete chain of possible events, to which we are likely to respond by taking sides with the Duke and the girl against their captors. I am sure, however, that anyone who reads *The Duke of Benevento* for the first time after hearing my summary will think that I have given a very indefinite account of what happens in Sir John Henry Moore's poem and hence misled him completely as to the poem's distinctive nature and effect. He will probably be prepared to read a vaguely tragicomic romance or drama of a kind common enough in the 1770s; what he will actually find is a short piece of 204 lines beginning as follows:

I hate the prologue to a story
Worse than the tuning of a fiddle,
  Squeaking and dinning;
Hang order and connection,
I love to dash into the middle;
  Exclusive of the fame and glory,
There is a comfort on reflection
  To think you've done with the beginning.
And so at supper one fine night,
  Hearing a cry of Alla, Alla,
The Prince was damnably confounded,
  And in a fright,
But more so when he saw himself surrounded
By fifty Turks; and at their head the fierce Abdalla,
And then he look'd a little grave
To find himself become a slave, . . . .

And so on consistently to the end, in a rapidly narrated episode of which the formal nature is the kind of anti-romantic comedy clearly foreshadowed in these lines — a form that is only potentially in the story of the poem (since this could yield several other forms) and is created out of it, partly indeed by Moore's pre-Byronic language and manner of narration, but also, as a reading of the whole poem will show, by the notably unheroic qualities of character and

thought which he gives to his hero and heroine, with the result that we are unable to take their predicament any more tragically than they themselves do.

It can be seen from these illustrations how different is such a conception of the internal relations of form and matter in a "concrete whole" from the later and much commoner analytic in which form or art is set over against content or subject-matter in one or another of the many ways we have already illustrated. A poem, on the view of its structure suggested by Aristotle, is not a composite of *res* and *verba*[3] but a certain matter formed in a certain way or a certain form imposed upon or wrought out of a certain matter. The two are inseparable aspects of the same individual thing, though they are clearly distinct analytically as principles or causes, and though, of the two, the formal nature is necessarily the more important as long as our concern is with the poem as a concrete object. On the one hand, we do not cease to talk about the matter of a poem when we examine its formal structure, and, on the other hand, there is a sense in which nothing in a completed poem, or any distinguishable part thereof, is matter or content merely, in relation to which something else is form. In a well-made poem, everything is formed, and hence rendered poetic (whatever it may have been in itself), by virtue simply of being made to do something definite in the poem or to produce a definitely definable effect, however local, which the same materials of language, thought, character-traits, or actions would be incapable of in abstraction from the poem, or the context in the poem, in which they appear. We are not speaking poetically but only materially of anything in a poem, therefore, when we abstract it from its function or effect in the poem; we speak poetically, or formally, only when we add to a description of the thing in terms of its constituent elements (for example, the content of a metaphor or the events of a plot) an indication of the definite quality it possesses or of that in the poem for the sake of which it is there. In an absolute sense, then, nothing in a successful poem is non-

[3]Subject-matter and language. [Ed.]

formal or nonpoetic; but it is also true that structure of any kind necessarily implies a subordination of some parts to others; and in this relative sense we may intelligibly say of one formed element of a poem that it is material to something else in the same poem, the existence and specific effectiveness of which it makes possible. We may thus speak of the words of a poem as the material basis of the thought they express, although the words also have form as being ordered in sentences and rhythms; and similarly we may speak of thought as the matter of character, of character and thought in words as the matter of action or emotion, and so on up to but not including the overall form which synthesizes all these subordinate elements, formally effective in themselves, into a continuous poetic whole. Or we can reverse the order of consideration, and ask what matter of action, character, and thought a poem requires if its plot or lyric structure is to be formally of a certain kind, or what kind of character a speech ought to suggest if it is to serve adequately its function in a scene, or what selection and arrangement of words will render best or most economically a given state of mind.

Here then is an intelligible, universally applicable, and analytically powerful conception of the basic structural relations in poems which we can take over from Aristotle without committing ourselves to the total philosophy in which it was evolved. We can also take over, in the second place, the method of investigation and reasoning which he found appropriate to structures of this kind. The conception and the method, indeed, can hardly be divorced. For if we are to consider poetic works, in practical criticism, from the point of view of their concrete wholeness, then our central problem is to make their elements and subordinate structures causally intelligible in the light of their respective organizing forms. This can be done, however, only by means of general concepts embodying answers to two major questions relative to such kinds of poetry as we may be interested in: first, what different forms can go with what different matters, and, second, what parts, and what constructions of each of them, are necessary to the achievement of any given form. But these, it is obvious, are ques-

tions of fact, the answers to which can never be given by any "abstract" method but must depend upon inquiries of an *a posteriori* type which move inductively (in Aristotle's sense of induction) from particulars to the universals they embody and from ends or forms thus defined, by hypothetical necessity to the essential conditions of their realization in poetic matter. The method, of course, is not Aristotelian in any unique sense, but no one has shown as fully as he did how it may be applied to poetics or how completely it depends, in this application, upon an adequate knowledge of literary history.

The method is factual, but it is not indifferent to values; and the third thing we can learn from Aristotle is a manner of considering questions of better and worse in poetry which is likewise appropriate to the conception of poems as concrete wholes organized by formal principles. As things made by and for men, poems, as I have said before, can have a great variety of uses and be judged not improperly in terms of many different criteria, moral, political, intellectual, grammatical, rhetorical, historical. To judge them as poems, however, is to judge them in their distinctive aspects as wholes of certain kinds, in the light of the assumption that the poet's end — the end which makes him a poet — is simply the perfecting of the poem as a beautiful or intrinsically excellent thing. I do not mean by this that poems are ever perfected in an absolute sense. We need not quarrel with R. G. Collingwood when he remarks, in his *Autobiography*, that as a boy living in a household of artists he "learned to think of a picture not as a finished product exposed for the admiration of virtuosi, but as the visible record, lying about the house, of an attempt to solve a definite problem in painting, so far as the attempt has gone." "I learned," he adds, "what some critics and aestheticians never know to the end of their lives, that no 'work of art' is ever finished, so that in that sense of the phrase there is no such thing as a 'work of art' at all. Work ceases upon the picture or manuscript, not because it is finished, but because sending-in day is at hand, or because the printer is clamorous for copy, or because 'I am sick of working at this thing' or 'I can't see what more

I can do to it.'"[4] This is sound sense, which critics and aestheticians ought to learn if they do not know it; but it is clearly not incompatible with the assumption that what a poet seeks to do, as a poet, is to make as good a work poetically speaking as he can; and this goodness, we can surely agree with Aristotle, must always consist in a mean between doing too much and not doing enough in his invention and handling of all its parts. The criterion, again, is not an absolute one; the mean in art, as in morals, is a relative mean, which has to be determined in adjustment to the particular necessities and possibilities of the form the artist is trying to achieve. And just as the poet can know these only by trial and error plus reflection upon the general conditions of his art and on what other poets have been able to do, so the critic can know them, and the ends to which they are relative, only by similar *ex post facto* means. He must therefore leave to other critics with less strictly "poetic" preoccupations the task of formulating criteria for poetry on the basis of general "abstract" principles; his business is to take the point of view of the poet and his problems and to judge what he has done, as sympathetically as possible, in terms of what must and what might be done *given* the distinctive form, new or old, which the poet is trying to work out of his materials.[5] And here, once more, the procedure of Aristotle can be of use.

We can still profit, moreover, not merely from these general features of his approach — all of them relevant also to other than critical problems — but likewise from many of the more particular applications of his method in the *Poetics*, including, first of all, the fundamental distinction, on which the whole treatise is based, between poetry which is "imitation" and poetry which is not.[6] The former, for Aristotle, is poetry in the most distinctive sense, since its principles are not the principles of any other art; but to insist on this is not to question the possibility of discussing as "poetry" other kinds of works of which the materials and devices, though not the forms, are those of poems in the stricter meaning of the word; the difference is not one of relative dignity or value but purely of constructive principle, and hence of the kinds of hypotheses and terms that are required, respectively, for the analysis and judgment of works belonging to each. The distinction, as Aristotle understood it, has played no important part in the subsequent history of criticism. A class of "didactic" poems has, it is true, been more or less constantly recognized, but the differentiation between these and other poems has most often been made in terms of purpose, content, and technique rather than of matter and form, a "didactic" poem being distinguished sometimes as one in which the end of instruction is more prominent than that of delight, sometimes as one that uses or springs from or appeals to the reason rather than the imagination, sometimes as one that relies mainly on precepts instead of fictions and images or that uses direct rather than indirect means of expression. This breakdown of the original distinction was natural enough in the periods of criticism in which the ends of poetry were defined broadly as instruction and pleasure, and it is still natural in a period, such as our own, when the great preoccupation is with "meaning" and with poetry as a special kind of language for expressing special modes of signification. In both periods, although some classes of poems have been set apart as "didactic" in a peculiar and frequently pejorative sense, all poetry, or all poetry except that which can be described as "entertainment" merely, has tended to assume an essentially didactic character and function. The prevalence nowadays of "thematic analysis" as a method of discussion applicable to all poetic works that can be taken seriously at all is a clear sign of this, as is also the currency of "archetypal" analogies.[7] The result, however, has been to banish from

---

[4] *An Autobiography*, p. 2. [Au.]

[5] On the kind of criticism which refuses to grant to an artist the "subject" he has chosen, see the remarks of Henry James in his preface to *The Portrait of a Lady*. [Au.]

[6] See Aristotle, *Poetics*, in Part 1, p. 42, and the note that clarifies the accidental relation in Aristotle between imitation and poetry. [Ed.]

[7] Crane alludes to the New Criticism, such as that of Cleanth Brooks, p. 799, and to archetypal criticism, such as that of Northrop Frye, p. 677. [Ed.]

criticism, or to confuse beyond clear recognition, a distinction which has as much validity now as when it was first made and which has not been supplanted by any of the later distinctions, since these all rest on quite different bases of principle. The distinction is simply between works, on the one hand, in which the formal nature is constituted of some particular human activity or state of feeling qualified morally and emotionally in a certain way, the beautiful rendering of this in words being the sufficient end of the poet's effort, and works, on the other hand (like the *Divine Comedy, Absalom and Achitophel, Don Juan, 1984*, etc.), in which the material nature is "poetic" in the sense that it is made up of parts similar to those of imitative poems and the formal nature is constituted of some particular thesis, intellectual or practical, relative to some general human interest, the artful elaboration and enforcement of this by whatever means are available and appropriate being the sufficient end of the poet's effort. Great and serious works can be and have been written on either of these basic principles of construction, but the principles themselves, it must be evident, are sharply distinct, and the difference is bound to be reflected, in innumerable subtle as well as obvious ways, in everything that poets have to do or can do in the two major kinds. To continue to neglect the distinction, therefore, is merely to deprive ourselves unnecessarily of an analytical device — however hard to apply in particular cases — which can only serve, when intelligently used, to introduce greater exactness into our critical descriptions and greater fairness into our critical judgments.

Of the many other distinctions and concepts in the *Poetics* which are still valid and useful — at least for the kind of discussion of poetic structure we now have in mind — nearly all are limited, in their strict applicability, to imitative works. For any inquiry into such forms we cannot neglect, to begin with, the all-important distinctions of object, means, manner, and *dynamis*[8] upon which the definition of tragedy in Chapter

6 is based. They are, as I have tried to show in the second lecture, the essential and basic determinants of the structure of any species of imitative works when these are viewed as concrete wholes, for we can conceive adequately of such a whole only when we consider as precisely as possible what kind of human experience is being imitated, by the use of what possibilities of the poetic medium, through what mode of representation, and for the sake of evoking and resolving what particular sequence of expectations and emotions relative to the successive parts of the imitated object. It is always some definite combination of these four things that defines, for the imitative writer, the necessities and possibilities of any work he may have in hand; for what he must and can do at any point will differ widely according as he is imitating a character, a state of passion, or an action, and if an action (with character, thought, and passion inevitably involved), whether one of which the central figures are men and women morally better than we are, or like ourselves, or in some sense worse; and according as he is doing this in verse of a certain kind or in prose or in some joining of the two; and according as he is doing it in a narrative or a dramatic or a mixed manner; and according, finally, as he is shaping his incidents and characters and their thoughts and feelings, his language, and his technique of representation (whatever it may be) so as to give us, let us say, the peculiar kind of comic pleasure we get from *Tom Jones* or that we get from *The Alchemist* or, to add still another possible nuance of comic effect, from *Volpone*. These, then, are indispensable distinctions for the critic who wishes to grasp the principles of construction and the consequences thereof in any imitative work; and he will be sacrificing some of the precision of analysis possible to him if he fails to take them all into consideration as independent variables — if he talks, for instance, about the plot of a novel or the pattern of images in a lyric poem without specifying the emotional "working or power" which is its controlling form, or if, in dealing with any kind of imitative work, he neglects to distinguish clearly between the "things" being imitated, upon which the *dynamis* primarily de-

[8]Power: Aristotle's general term for the end or final cause of a poetic genre. [Ed.]

pends, and the expedients of representational manner by which the writer has sought to clarify or maximize their peculiar effect.[9]

There remains, lastly, the detailed analytic of imitative forms which is represented in the *Poetics* by the chapters on tragedy and epic. I need not repeat what I have said in the second lecture about Aristotle's distinctive conceptions — which have largely vanished from later criticism — of plot, character, thought, and diction — or about the relationships of causal subordination in which these "parts" are made to stand to one another in the tragic and epic structures, so that the last three (together with music and spectacle in tragedy), while being capable of form themselves, have the status of necessary material conditions of the plot, which, in the most specific sense of the synthesis of things done and said in a work as determined to a certain "working or power," is the principal part or controlling form of the whole. I have said why this analysis seems to me sound, given the assumptions on which it is based and its limited applicability to works of which the subjects are actions of the more or less extended sort Aristotle here had in mind. We can therefore still use it, and the many constituent definitions and distinctions it involves, in the criticism of the larger poetic forms; and we can profit particularly, I think, from the discussion of tragic plot-form in Chapter 13, not only because it gives us a clue to the structure of many later "tragic" works (this plot-form is clearly the formula, for example, of *Othello*, though not quite of *Macbeth*, and certainly not of *Richard III*) but also, and chiefly, because it suggests the four general questions we have to ask ourselves about any work having a plot as its principle of construction if we are to see clearly what problems its writer faced in composing it: as to precisely what the change is, from what it starts and

to what it moves; in what kind of man it takes place; by reason of what causes in the man's thoughts and actions or outside him; and with what succession of emotional effects in the representation.

## III

We should be merely "Aristotelians," however, rather than independent scholars were we to remain content with what we can thus extract from Aristotle for present-day critical use; and we should be able to deal only crudely and inadequately with a great many of the most interesting structural problems raised by modern works. We need therefore to push the Aristotelian type of theoretical analysis far beyond the point where Aristotle himself left off, and this in several different directions.

There are, to begin with, the many non-imitative species of poetry or imaginative literature with which the *Poetics* does not deal at all. A large number of these have been roughly distinguished in the nomenclature and theories of subsequent criticism under such heads as: philosophical poems, moral essays, epigrams, treatises in verse, occasional poems; Horatian satires, Juvenalian satires, Varronian or Menippean satires; allegories, apologues, fables, parables, exempla, thesis or propaganda dramas and novels. But though a vast deal of critical and historical discussion has been devoted to these forms, we have as yet only fragments and beginnings of a usable inductive analytic of their structural principles as distinguished from their material conventions.[10]

Again, there are all the shorter imitative forms, most of them later in origin or artistic development than Aristotle, which we commonly group together as lyric poems; much of the best criticism of these has been concerned either with their techniques and fixed conventional patterns or with a dialectical search for the qualities of subject-matter and expression which are thought to differentiate lyric poetry, as a homogeneous

[9]Cf. Olson, in Crane, *Critics and Criticism*, pp. 71 ff., 562–63. With the remarkable development, in modern literature, of elaborate representational means for making effective relatively simple or universalized plots, the problem of distinguishing the two is sometimes a delicate one; there has been a good deal of confusion, consequently, in some of the discussions of works like *Ulysses*, *A Passage to India*, and Hemingway's "The Killers." [Au.]

[10]Cf. Norman Maclean, in Crane, *Critics and Criticism*, pp. 408 ff. [Au.]

type, from other poetic kinds.[11] What we need to have, therefore, is a comprehensive study, free from "abstract" assumptions, of the existing species of such poems in terms both of the different "proper pleasures" achievable in them and of the widely variant material structures in which the pleasures may inhere. Lyrics, it is plain, do not have plots, but any successful lyric obviously has something analogous to a plot in the sense of a specific form which synthesizes into a definite emotional whole what is said or done in the poem and conditions the necessities and probabilities which the poet must embody somehow in his lines; and the nature of this formal principle — whether it is, for example, a man in an evolving state of passion interpreted for him by his thought (as in the "Ode to a Nightingale") or a man adjusting himself voluntarily to an emotionally significant discovery about his life (as in the "Ode on Intimations of Immortality") — has to be grasped with some precision if we are to be able to speak appropriately and adequately about the poem's construction in all its parts and the degree of its artistic success. And here too most of the necessary analytical work still remains to be done.

We are much better off, thanks to Aristotle, with respect to the full-length imitative forms of narrative and drama; but even in this field of theory there are many important outstanding questions. Except for one suggestive paragraph in Chapter 5 on the general nature of the ridiculous, the *Poetics* as we have it is silent on comedy; and although there is much to be learned from the innumerable later discussions, especially since the eighteenth century, the insights these make available still have to be translated out of the rhetorical and psychological languages in which they are, for the most part, embodied into the more consistently "poetic" language we are committed to using. That there are a good many distinguishable comic plot-forms, both in drama and in narrative, must be evident to every one; but as to what they are, and what different artistic necessities and possibilities each of them involves, we have as yet, I think, only rather vague general notions; and the problem has not been greatly advanced by the traditional classifications into comedy of intrigue, comedy of manners, comedy of character, and so on. The same thing is true of the many intermediate forms between comedy in the stricter sense and tragedy proper: of tragicomedy, for example, or the "serious" and "tender" comedy which emerged in the eighteenth century, or the kind of domestic novel which Jane Austen wrote in *Pride and Prejudice, Mansfield Park*, and *Persuasion*, or the adventure romance in its earlier as well as its contemporary forms, or even the detective novel, much as has been written about the "poetics" of that. Nor is tragedy itself in much better case. What the *Poetics* gives us is an analytic of only one among the many plot-forms which the critical opinion as well as the common sense of later times has thought proper to call "tragic"; and it is one of the unfortunate results of the respect which Aristotle has always commanded that critics have tended to blur the distinctive principles of construction and effect, or to impair the artistic integrity, of these "non-Aristotelian" tragic forms in their eagerness to bring them in some fashion under his definition. We need therefore a fresh attempt at analysis, by the same method but in more appropriate terms, for such plot-forms, among others, as are represented severally by *Richard III* and *The Duchess of Malfi*,[12] by *The Orphan*, by *The Brothers Karamazov*, and by *A Passage to India*.

It is not merely of the forms of drama and narrative, however, that we require a better theory but also of many of their characteristic structural devices. We still tend to think of plot in its material aspects in the limited terms in which it is treated in the *Poetics* on the basis of the somewhat elementary practice of the Greeks, with the result that when we have to deal with works that combine in various ways two or many lines of action or concern themselves primarily not with external actions but with changes in thought and

---

[11]Cf. Norman Maclean, *ibid.*, pp. 408 ff. [Au.]

[12]One of my former students, Mr. Richard Levin, is completing a study of the plot-forms of these and other similar works in Renaissance English drama. [Au.]

feeling or with the slow development or degeneration of moral character or with the fortunes of groups rather than of individuals, we often fall into the confusion which has led many modern critics to reject the concept of plot altogether. This is clearly no solution, but the remedy can be only a more comprehensive and discriminating induction of possible dramatic and narrative structures than Aristotle was able to provide. And there is also the complex question of how plots of whatever kind, or their equivalents in other forms, have to be or can be represented in the words — the question, in short, of imitative manner in a sense that goes beyond, while still depending upon, Aristotle's distinction of the three manners in his third chapter. Of all the topics I have mentioned, this is perhaps the one on which the largest body of precise and useful observation has been accumulated, by all those critics from the Renaissance to our day who have devoted themselves to the "techniques" first of the drama and epic and then of the novel, short-story, and lyric. Even here, however, much remains to be done; and one of the chief requisites, I think, is a clearer posing of the whole problem in such a way as to correlate the many devices of manner which these critics have discriminated, as well as others that have escaped them, with the distinguishable functions which manner has to serve with respect to form. I have touched upon some of these functions in the second lecture, and I will add only the suggestion that there are likely to be, in all richly developed imitative works, incidents, characters, speeches, and images which are not parts of the plot-form but must be viewed by the critic as elements of "thought" in a sense akin to but distinct from that intended by Aristotle in Chapters 6 and 19. We may treat as "thought" of this kind anything permitting of inference in a poetic work, over and above the direct working of the imitated object, that functions as a device, vis-à-vis the audience, for disclosing or hinting at relevant traits of character or situation, awakening or directing expectations, conditioning states of mind, emphasizing essential issues, suggesting in what light something is to be viewed, or, more broadly still, setting the action or some part of it in a larger context of ideas or analogies so that it may come to seem,

in its universal implications for human beings, not simply the particular and untypical action it might otherwise be taken to be. Every novelist or dramatist — or lyric poet, for that matter — who reflects on his own work will understand what this means; but the conception has still to become widely recognized among critics, or it surely would have been applied long since to such things as the apparently superfluous episodes and characters and the recurrent general words and patterns of images in Shakespeare — the dialectic of "Nature" in *King Lear*, for instance — concerning which most recent writers have thought it necessary to offer much more profound explanations.

It would be well, finally, if we could carry our method of inductive and causal analysis into some of the larger questions of theory — common to both imitative and non-imitative poetry — to which these writers and other contemporary critics have given special prominence: we could profit greatly, for example, from a re-examination, in our distinctive language, of poetic images, of the elements and functions of diction in poetry, of the various modes and uses of symbols, and of the structural characteristics of myths.

We need not wait, however, for the completion of these possible studies before beginning to use such theory of poetic forms as we now possess in the service of practical criticism. There is after all a close mutual interdependence, in the method we are considering, between theoretical analysis and the investigation of particular works; and as our attempts at application become more numerous and more varied in their objects, so will our grasp of the necessary general distinctions and principles tend to improve.

## IV

In these attempts, as should be clear from what I have said, we shall be making a pretty complete break with the tradition of practical criticism discussed in the last two lectures — a tradition in which it has always been necessary, before individual works of poetic art can be analysed or judged, to conceive of poetry as a homogeneous whole and to define its nature in some kind of dialectical relation to other modes of discourse and thought. We shall not need, for our purposes, to commit ourselves to any of the numerous and apparently inconsistent theories of poetry, tragedy, lyric, or the like, based on such a presupposition, which this tradition has developed. We shall not need to worry, as so many contemporaries have done, about how poetry differs from science or prose, or about what its mission is in the modern world. We shall not need to decide in advance of our studies of poems whether poetry in general is best defined as a kind of language or a kind of subject-matter; whether its end is pleasure or some species of knowledge or practical good; whether its proper domain includes all the kinds of imaginative writing or only some of these; whether it is most closely akin to rhetoric and dialectic or to ritual, myth, or dream; or whether it is or is not a separable element in prose fiction and drama. Nor shall we need to assume that all good poems have "themes" or that poetic expression is always indirect, metaphorical, and symbolic. Not merely would such speculative commitments be useless to us, given our empirical starting-point, but they would be fatal, in proportion as we allowed our analyses to be directed by them, to our very effort, since they would inevitably blind us to all those aspects of our problem which our particular doctrine of poetry failed to take into account.

I do not mean that we shall not have to make some assumptions of our own, but only that these need not and ought not to be particularized assumptions about the intrinsic nature and necessary structure of our objects considered as a unitary class of things. We shall have to assume that any poetic work, like any other production of human art, has, or rather is, a definite structure of some kind which is determined immediately by its writer's intuition of a form to be achieved in its materials by the right use of his medium, and, furthermore, that we can arrive at some understanding of what this form actually is and use our understanding as a principle in the analysis and criticism of the work. We shall have to come to some agreement, moreover, as to what we will mean by "poetic works"; but here again the fewer specifications we impose on ourselves in advance the better. It will be sufficient for all

our purposes if we begin, simply, by taking as "poems" or "works of literary art" all those kinds of productions which have been commonly called such at different times, but without any supposition that, because these have the same name, they are all "poems" or "works of literary art" in the same fundamental structural sense — that the art necessary to write *The Divine Comedy* or *The Faerie Queene* is the same art, when viewed in terms of its peculiar principles of form, as the art which enabled Shakespeare to write *King Lear* and *Othello*. And for such productions we shall need to assume, in addition, only one common characteristic: that they are all works which, in one degree or another, justify critical consideration primarily for their own sake, as artistic structures, rather than merely for the sake of the knowledge or wisdom they express or the practical utility we may derive from them, though either or both of these other values may be importantly involved in any particular case.

The problem of structure, for any individual work of this kind, is the problem — to give it its most general statement — of how the material nature of the work is related to its formal nature, when we understand by form that principle, or complex of principles, which gives to the subject-matter the power it has to affect our opinions and emotions in a certain definite way such as would not have been possible had the synthesizing principle been of a different kind. The question, as I have said, is primarily one of fact and cause; and it is answered, for a given work, when we have made as intelligible as we can the fashion in which its material elements of whatever kind — words, images, symbols, thoughts, character-traits, incidents, devices of representation — are made to function in relation to a formal whole which we can warrantably assert was the actual final cause of its composition. By "actual final cause" I mean simply a cause without the assumption of which, as somehow effective in the writing, the observable characteristics of the parts, their presence in the poem, their arrangement and proportioning, and their interconnections cannot be adequately understood. In discovering what this shaping principle is in any work we must make use of such evidence as there may be concerning the history of its conception and writing, including any statements the writer may have made about his intentions. Our task, however, is not to explain the writer's activity but the result thereof; our problem is not psychological but artistic; and hence the causes that centrally concern us are the internal causes of which the only sufficient evidence is the work itself as a completed product. What we want to know is not the actual process but the actual rationale of the poem's construction in terms of the poetic problems the writer faced and the reasons which determined his solutions. And in looking for these we shall assume that if the poem holds together as an intelligibly effective whole, in which a certain form is realized in a certain matter which never before had this form, the result can be understood fully only by supposing that such and such problems were involved and were solved by the writer in accordance with reasons which, in part at least, we can state; and this clearly does not commit us to holding that the problems and reasons we uncover in our analysis, as necessarily implied by the completed poem, must have presented themselves to the writer explicitly as such in a continuous movement of self-conscious deliberation; it will be sufficient if we can show that the poem could hardly have been written as it is or have the effect it does on our minds had the writer not done, somehow or at some time, what these particular problems and reasons dictate.

We can never, of course, know such things directly, but only by inference from the consequences of the conceived form, whether of the whole or of any of its parts, in the details of the completed work; and there can be no such inference except by way of hypotheses which both imply and are implied by the observable traits of the work. There are, however, hypotheses and hypotheses, and the character of those we shall have to make is determined by the nature of our problem. We propose to consider poems as unique existent things the structural principles of which are to be discovered, rather than as embodiments of general truths about the structure of poetry already adequately known. Hence our procedure must be the reverse of that procedure by way of preferred paradigms or models of structure which we have seen to be so character-

istic of contemporary practical criticism. Our task is not to show the reflection in poems of complex or "ironical" attitudes, interactions of prose and poetry or of logical structure and irrelevant texture, patterns of ritual drama, or basic mythical themes, on the assumption that if the poem is a good poem it will inevitably have whichever of these or other similarly derived general structures we happen to be interested in finding examples of; it is rather the task of making formal sense out of any poetic work before us on the assumption that it may in fact be a work for whose peculiar principles of structure there are nowhere any usable parallels either in literary theory or in our experience of other works. The hypotheses we have to make, therefore, will not be of the fixed and accredited kind which scientists employ only when their problem is not to find out something still unknown but to "demonstrate" a classic experiment to beginners, but rather of the tentative kind — to be modified or rejected altogether at the dictation of the facts — which are the proper means to any serious inductive inquiry. They will be particular working hypotheses for the investigation of the structures of individual poems, not general hypotheses about such things as poetry or "poetic drama" in which the specific nature of the individual structures to be examined is already assumed.

We must also distinguish between critical hypotheses in the strict sense and interpretative hypotheses concerning the details of literary works in their material aspects. It is not one of our presuppositions that "form" in poetry is "meaning"; we should hold, rather, that meaning is something involved in poems as a necessary, but not sufficient, condition of the existence in them of poetic form, and hence that the recovery of meaning is an essential prerequisite to the discovery of form though not in itself such a discovery. Before we can understand a poem as an artistic structure we must understand it as a grammatical structure made up of successive words, sentences, paragraphs, and speeches which give us both meanings in the ordinary sense of that term and signs from which we may infer what the speakers, whether characters or narrators, are like and what they are thinking, feeling, or doing. The great temptation for critics who are not trained and practising scholars is to take this understanding for granted or to think that it may easily be obtained at second hand by consulting the works of scholars. This is an illusion, just as it is an illusion in scholars to suppose that they can see, without training in criticism, all the problems which their distinctive methods are fitted to solve. The ideal would be that all critics should be scholars and all scholars critics; but, although there ought to be the closest correlation of the two functions in practice, they are nevertheless distinct in nature and in the kinds of hypotheses to which they lead. The hypotheses of interpretation are concerned with the meanings and implications in texts that result from their writers' expressive intentions in setting down particular sequences. Such meanings and implications, indeed, are forms, of which words and sentences are the matter; but they are forms of a kind that can appear in any sort of discourse, however unpoetic. They are to be interpreted by resolving the forms into the elements which poems share with the common speech or writing and the common thought and experience of the times when they were written; and this requires the use of techniques and principles quite different from any that poetic theory can afford: the techniques and principles of historical grammar, of the analysis and history of ideas, of the history of literary conventions, manners, and so on, and the still more general techniques and principles, seldom methodized, by which we construe characters and actions in everyday life.

The hypotheses of criticism, on the contrary, are concerned with the shaping principles, peculiar to the poetic arts, which account in any work for the power of its grammatical materials, in the particular ordering given to these, to move our opinions and feelings in such-and-such a way. They will be of two sorts according as the questions to which they are answers relate to the principles by which poetic works have been constructed as wholes of certain definite kinds or to the reasons which connect a particular part of a given work, directly or indirectly, with such a principle by way of the poetic problems it set for the writer at this point. And there can be no good practical criticism in this mode in which both

sorts are not present; for although the primary business of the critic is with the particulars of any work he studies down to its minuter details of diction and rhythm, he can never exhibit the artistic problems involved in these or find other than extra-poetic reasons for their solutions without the guidance of an explicit definition of the formal whole which they have made possible.

A single work will suffice to illustrate both kinds of critical hypotheses as well as the relation between them, and I will begin by considering what idea of the governing form of *Macbeth* appears to accord best with the facts of that play and the sequence of emotions it arouses in us. I need not say again why it seems to me futile to look for an adequate structural formula for *Macbeth* in any of the more "imaginative" directions commonly taken by recent criticism; I shall assume, therefore, without argument, that we have to do, not with a lyric "statement of evil" or an allegory of the workings of sin in the soul and the state or a metaphysical myth of destruction followed by recreation or a morality play with individualized characters rather than types, but simply with an imitative tragic drama based on historical materials. To call it an imitative tragic drama, however, does not carry us very far; it merely limits roughly the range of possible forms we have to consider. Among these are the contrasting plot-forms embodied respectively in *Othello* and in *Richard III*: the first a tragic plot-form in the classic sense of Aristotle's analysis in *Poetics* 13; the second a plot-form which Aristotle rejected as non-tragic but which appealed strongly to tragic poets in the Renaissance — a form of serious action designed to arouse moral indignation for the deliberately unjust and seemingly prospering acts of the protagonist and moral satisfaction at his subsequent ruin. The plot-form of *Macbeth* clearly involves elements which assimilate it now to the one and now to the other of both these kinds. The action of the play is twofold, and one of its aspects is the punitive action of Malcolm, Macduff, and their friends which in the end brings about the protagonist's downfall and death. The characters here are all good men, whom Macbeth has unforgivably wronged, and their cause is the unqualifiedly just cause of freeing Scotland from a bloody tyrant and restoring the rightful line of kings. All this is made clear in the representation not only directly through the speeches and acts of the avengers but indirectly by those wonderfully vivid devices of imagery and general thought in which modern critics have found the central value and meaning of the play as a whole; and our responses, when this part of the action is before us, are such as are clearly dictated by the immediate events and the poetic commentary: we desire, that is, the complete success of the counter-action and this as speedily as possible before Macbeth can commit further horrors. We desire this, however — and that is what at once takes the plot-form out of the merely retributive class — not only for the sake of humanity and Scotland but also for the sake of Macbeth himself. For what most sharply distinguishes our view of Macbeth from that of his victims and enemies is that, whereas they see him from the outside only, we see him also, throughout the other action of the play — the major action — from the inside, as he sees himself; and what we see thus is a moral spectacle the emotional quality of which, for the impartial observer, is not too far removed from the tragic *dynamis* specified in the *Poetics*. This is not to say that the main action of *Macbeth* is not significantly different, in several respects, from the kind of tragic action which Aristotle envisages. The change is not merely from good to bad fortune, but from a good state of character to a state in which the hero is almost, but not quite, transformed into a monster; and the tragic act which initiates the change, and still more the subsequent unjust acts which this entails, are acts done — unlike Othello's killing of Desdemona — in full knowledge of their moral character. We cannot, therefore, state the form of this action in strictly Aristotelian terms, but the form is none the less one that involves, like tragedy in Aristotle's sense, the arousal and catharsis of painful emotions for, and not merely with respect to, the protagonist — emotions for which the terms pity and fear are not entirely inapplicable.

Any adequate hypothesis about the structure of *Macbeth*, then, would have to take both of these sets of facts into account. For both of the views we are given of the hero are true: he is in fact, in terms of the nature and objective consequences of his deeds, what Macduff and Malcolm say he is throughout Acts IV and V, but he is also — and the form of the play is really the interaction of the two views in our opinions and emotions — what we ourselves see him to be as we witness the workings of his mind before the murder of Duncan, then after the murder, and finally when, at the end, all his illusions and hopes gone, he faces Macduff. He is one who commits monstrous deeds without becoming wholly a monster, since his knowledge of the right principle is never altogether obscured, though it is almost so in Act IV. We can understand such a person and hence feel fear and pity of a kind for him because he is only doing upon a grander scale and with deeper guilt and more terrifying consequences for himself and others what we can, without too much difficulty, imagine ourselves doing, however less extremely, in circumstances generally similar. For the essential story of *Macbeth* is that of a man, not naturally depraved, who has fallen under the compulsive power of an imagined better state for himself which he can attain only by acting contrary to his normal habits and feelings; who attains this state and then finds that he must continue to act thus, and even worse, in order to hold on to what he has got; who persists and becomes progressively hardened morally in the process; and who then, ultimately, when the once alluring good is about to be taken away from him, faces the loss in terms of what is left of his original character. It is something like this moral universal that underlies, I think, and gives emotional form to the main action of *Macbeth*. It is a form that turns upon the difference between what seemingly advantageous crime appears to be in advance to a basically good but incontinent man and what its moral consequences for such a man inevitably are; and the catharsis is effected not merely by the man's deserved overthrow but by his own inner suffering and by his discovery, before it is too late, of what he had not known before he began to act. If we are normal human beings we must abhor his crimes; yet we cannot completely abhor but must rather pity the man himself, and even when he seems most the monster (as Macbeth does in Act IV) we must still wish for such an outcome as will be best, under the circumstances, not merely for Scotland but for him.

But if this, or something close to it, is indeed the complex emotional structure intended in *Macbeth*, then we have a basis for defining with some precision the various problems of incident, character, thought, imagery, diction, and representation which confronted Shakespeare in writing the play, and hence a starting-point for discussing, in detail, the rationale of its parts.[13] Consider — to take only one instance — the final scene. In the light of the obvious consequences of the form I have attributed to the play as a whole, it is not difficult to state what the main problems at this point are. If the catharsis of the tragedy is to be complete, we must be made to feel both that Macbeth is being killed in a just cause and that his state of mind and the circumstances of his death are such as befit a man who, for all his crimes, has not altogether lost our pity and goodwill. We are of course prepared for this double response by all that has gone before, and, most immediately, in the earlier scenes of Act V, by the fresh glimpses we are given of the motivation of the avengers and by Macbeth's soliloquies. But it will clearly be better if the dual effect can be sustained until the very end; and this requires, on the one hand, that we should be vividly reminded once more of Macbeth's crimes and the justified hatred they have caused and of the prospect of a new and better time which his death holds out for Scotland, and, on the other hand, that we should be allowed to take satisfaction, at last, in the manner in which Macbeth himself behaves. The artistic triumph of the scene lies in the completeness with which both problems are solved: the first in the words and actions of Macduff, the speeches about young Siward, and Malcolm's closing address; the second by a variety of devices, both of invention and of representation, the appropriateness of

which to the needed effect can be seen if we ask what we would not want Macbeth to do at this moment. We want him to be killed, as I have said, for his sake no less than that of Scotland; but we would not want him either to seek out Macduff or to flee the encounter when it comes or to "play the Roman fool"; we would not want him to show no recognition of the wrongs he has done Macduff or, when his last trust in the witches has gone, to continue to show fear or to yield or to fight with savage animosity; and he is made to do none of these things, but rather the contraries of all of them, so that he acts in the end as the Macbeth whose praises we have heard in the second scene of the play. And I would suggest that the cathartic effect of these words and acts is reinforced indirectly, in the representation, by the analogy we can hardly help drawing between his conduct now and the earlier conduct of young Siward, for of Macbeth too it can be said that "he parted well and paid his score"; the implication of this analogy is surely one of the functions, though not the only one, which the lines about Siward are intended to serve.

Such are the kinds of hypotheses we shall need to make if we are to have critical knowledge of the shaping principles of poetic works or of the artistic reasons governing the character and interrelation of their parts. They are working suppositions which, as I have said, both imply and are implied by the particulars of the works for which they are constructed; and they can never be made well by any critic who is not naturally sensitive to such particulars and in the habit of observing them closely. These, however, though indispensable, are not sufficient conditions. It never happens in any inquiry into matters of fact that the particulars we observe determine their own meaning automatically; the concrete or the individual is never intelligible except through the general and the abstract; and if we are to allow the facts to speak for themselves, we must in some fashion supply them with a language in which to talk. Hypotheses, in short, are not made out of nothing, but presuppose on the part of the inquirer who forms them a systematic body of concepts relative to the subject-matter with which he is dealing. The critic who proposes to explore

---

[13]See, in addition to what follows, Wayne C. Booth, *Journal of General Education* 6 (1951): 21–25. For a somewhat similar discussion of an episode in *King Lear*, cf. Maclean, in *Critics and Criticism*, pp. 595–615. [Au.]

hypothetically the structures of individual poems is in the same predicament; he must bring to his task, inescapably, general ideas about poetic structure, or he can never construct a workable hypothesis about the structure of any poem.

Hence the crucial importance for the practical critic of poetic forms, in the sense we are now giving to this term, of the kind of analytic of poetry which was outlined earlier in this lecture. From the point of view of the criticism of individual poems, the concepts and distinctions involved in that analytic differ from those which most contemporary critics have been content to use: they supply, not a unified set of terms for constituting structural patterns in poems (like Mr. Heilman's formula for "poetic drama" or the theories that make all good poetry a species of "ironical" or "paradoxical" structure), but a great variety of terms designating distinct and alternative principles, devices, and functions in poetry from which the critic need select only such combinations as appear to be relevant to the poems he is examining. What he thus acquires are not hypotheses ready formed but elements out of which he may form such hypotheses as the facts of his poems seem to warrant — in short, knowledge of structural possibilities only, resting on inductive inquiry into the principles poets have actually used in building poems and hence expanding with the development and progressive differentiation of poetry itself, so that he brings to the discussion of individual poems merely conceptual materials for framing pertinent questions about them without any predetermination of the substance of his answers, much as a physician uses the alternatives given him by medical theory in diagnosing symptoms in one of his patients. In the other mode of criticism the relation of theory to a particular poem is the relation of a previously selected idea or pattern of structure to its embodiment or reflection in a given work; here the relation is one of many known possibilities of structural patterning in poetry to the actualization in the poem examined of some one or more of these.

A critic using the first type of theory might argue somewhat as follows, for example, about the structure of Gray's *Elegy*. We must assume, he might say, the language of poetry being what

it is, that the principle of structure in any good poem is a principle of balancing and harmonizing discrepant connotations, attitudes, and meanings; we must look therefore for a structure of this kind in Gray's poem or be content to relegate it to an inferior class of poetry; and our quest, indeed, is not in vain, for when we examine the text in the light of our general hypothesis of "ironical" structure, we quickly find that all the details of the *Elegy* can be subsumed under the theme of a continuous contrast of two modes of burial — in the church itself and in the churchyard — in which, as in all good poetry, opposing meanings are finally resolved.[14] A critic, however, whose theory was of the second type, would proceed in an altogether different way. He would have no favourite hypothesis of structure as such, but would know merely that among short poems which, like the *Elegy*, evoke in us serious emotions, the shaping principle may be of several essentially distinct types, each of them generating distinct artistic problems for the poet; and he would use this knowledge as a basis for asking himself some such questions as these: Is what happens in the *Elegy* best explained by supposing, as the other critic has clearly done, that the poem is intended to be read as an emotionalized argument in verse (whether about modes of burial or something else), the personal qualities of the speaker and the setting of his meditation being simply devices for enforcing the unifying dialectic? Or is the poem better read — better, that is, with respect to the actual shaping principle of its construction — as an imitative lyric? And if it is this latter kind of structure, is the form one in which the speaker is conceived as being merely moved in a certain way by his situation (as in Gray's "Ode on a Distant Prospect of Eton College"), or as acting in a certain manner in relation to it (as in Marvell's "To His Coy Mistress"), or as deliberating morally in a certain state of mind on what is for him a serious issue in life? Weighing these possibilities (which give us perhaps the major forms which short serious imitative poems can have), our second critic would probably conclude that it is the last possibility which best

[14]Cleanth Brooks, *The Well Wrought Urn*, pp. 96–113. [Au.]

explains both the constructed matter and the arrangement of the *Elegy* and the peculiar quality of the emotions which Gray's words and rhythms arouse in us. He might then describe the *Elegy* as an imitative lyric of moral choice rather than of action or of mood, representing a situation in which a virtuous, sensitive, and ambitious young man of undistinguished birth confronts the possibility of his death while still to "Fortune and to Fame unknown," and eventually, after much disturbance of mind (hinted at in the Swain's description of him), reconciles himself to his probable fate by reflecting that none of the rewards of successful ambition can "sooth the dull cold ear of Death," which comes as inevitably to the great as to the obscure; that a life passed "far from the madding crowd's ignoble strife," though circumscribing the exercise of virtue and talent, may yet be a means of preserving innocence; and that he can at any rate look forward to — what all men desire as a minimum — living on in the memory of at least one friend, while his merits and frailties alike repose "in trembling hope" on the bosom of his Father and his God. Something like this, I think (pedantic as any brief statement of it must sound), is the answer our second critic would give; but the point is that in arriving at it he would be using his theory of possible principles of structure in short poems simply to furnish him with the distinctions he needs if he is not to substitute a structure of his own for the structure Gray achieved.

The more extensive and discriminating such general knowledge, therefore, the better the critic's hypotheses are likely to be. But it is also the nature of this kind of theoretical knowledge to be always inadequate, though in varying degrees, to the particulars we use it to illuminate. We can never know in advance all the possibilities, and we can never, consequently, form a hypothesis about a work of any artistic complexity or even about many simpler works without making a shorter or longer inductive leap from the words and sentences before us to the peculiar combination of universals which define their poetic form. And that is why, in this mode of criticism, we can make no separation except analytically between theory and application, the latter being possible only if the former already exists at least

up to a certain point and the former being constantly refined and enlarged as we proceed with the latter.

Application, however, is our main problem here, and its success depends upon the extent to which the universal terms of our hypotheses and the perceived and felt particulars of the texts for which they are constructed can be made to fit together. The general conditions are two: first, our ability to keep our explanatory formulae fluid and to submit them to constant revisions in principle or in detail before we transform them into conclusions; and, second, our willingness to use systematically what has been called "the method of multiple working hypotheses."[15] We have to remember, that is, that the value of a hypothesis is always relative, not merely to the facts it is intended to explain, but to all the other variant hypotheses which the same facts might suggest if only we gave them a chance; that the best hypothesis is simply the best among several possible hypotheses, relevant to the same work or problem, with which we have actually compared it; and that unless we make such comparisons a regular part of our procedure, we always court the danger of missing either slightly or altogether what our author was really attempting to do.

There are also, in addition to these very general rules, several more particular criteria. Our aim is an explanation and judgment of poetic works in terms of their structural causes; hence, in the first place, the necessity of so framing our hypotheses that they are not descriptive formulae merely but clearly imply practical artistic consequences, in what the writers must or cannot or might well do in the act of writing, for the details of the works they are being used to explain; that is the character, for example, of Aristotle's definition of tragic plot-form in *Poetics* 13, and I have tried to impart a similar character to the statements above about *Macbeth*. The ideal is to have a central principle of explanation that will

[15]By T. C. Chamberlin, in a paper with this title, first published in *Science*, Old Series, 15 (1890): 92–96; reprinted in the *Journal of Geology* 39 (1931): 155–65. The "method of multiple working hypotheses" is contrasted with "the method of the ruling theory" and "the method of the working hypothesis." [Au.]

enable us to see precisely the functional relations between all the particular problems a writer has attempted to solve and the form of his work as a whole, even though we may have to conclude, in some cases, that the relation is a very tenuous one. In the second place, our aim is an explanation and judgment in terms adapted as closely as possible to the peculiar structure and power of the work before us; hence the necessity of trying to go beyond formulae that imply the work as a whole or any of its parts only generically; as when, for instance, we neglect to distinguish between the different material structures possible in lyrics and treat a particular lyric without regard to such distinctions, or as when we discuss a work like Jane Austen's *Emma* merely as a comedy, failing to see how little this can tell us about its distinctive comic construction. In the third place, we aspire to completeness of explanation; and this means that in framing a hypothesis about any work we must consider everything in the text as significant evidence that involves in any way a free choice on the writer's part between possible alternative things to be done with his materials or ways of doing them at any point. The hypothesis must therefore be complex rather than simple; it must recognize that the same parts may have different functions, including that of mere adornment; and, above all, it cannot be arrived at by giving a privileged position, on *a priori* grounds, to a particular variety of signs of artistic intention, in a complex work, to the exclusion of other and often conflicting signs of the same thing. This last is conspicuously the error of those interpreters of *Macbeth* who have inferred the central form of that play chiefly from the thought and imagery that serve to emphasize the "unnatural" character of the hero's crimes and the inevitability of a just retribution, without attempting to correlate with this the many signs, both in the construction of the plot and in its extraordinarily artful representation, of the distinctive moral quality of Macbeth's actions when these are seen from the inside. There will always be incompleteness in any hypothesis, moreover, or in any criticism that follows its use, that leaves out of account, as one of the crucial facts, the peculiar sequence of emotions we feel when we read the work unbiased by critical doctrine; for,

as we have seen, the most important thing about any poetic production is the characteristic power it has to affect us in this definite way rather than that. Completeness, however, is impossible without coherence; hence our hypotheses, in the fourth place, must aim at a maximum of internal unity, on the assumption that, although many works are episodic and although many predominantly imitative works, for example, also have didactic or topical parts, this can best be seen if we begin by presuming that literary artists usually aim at creating wholes.

The only proof there can be of a hypothesis about any particular thing lies in its power of completeness and coherence of explanation within the limits of the data it makes significant — and this always relatively to the other hypotheses pertinent to the same data with which it has been compared. We must be guided, however, in choosing among alternative hypotheses, by a further criterion — the classic criterion of economy: that that hypothesis is the best, other things being equal, which requires the fewest supplementary hypotheses to make it work or which entails the least amount of explaining away; it is no recommendation, thus, for Mr. [L. C.] Knight's interpretation of *Macbeth* that he has to say of the emotion aroused in most readers as well as in [A. C.] Bradley by Macbeth's soliloquies in Act V, that this is mere conventional 'sympathy for the hero,' " which ought not to be allowed to distort that dialectical system of values in the play that is for him "the pattern of the whole."[16] And we must be careful, further, not to construe our "data" in too narrow a sense and so be satisfied with hypotheses that clearly conflict with facts external to the works we are considering but relevant nevertheless to their interpretation; I mean not only such particular evidences as we can often find of writers' intentions — for example, Coleridge's statements about the kind of poem he designed *The Rime of the Ancient Mariner* to be — but also such general probabilities with respect to the works of a given period or genre or with respect to poetic

[16]"How Many Children Had Lady Macbeth?" in *Explorations*, p. 36. [Ed.]

works of any kind or age as are supplied by either our historical knowledge or our common sense. It is not likely, for instance, that a Shakespearean tragedy intended for the popular stage should really have a kind of basic structure which practising playwrights of any time would find it difficult or impossible to make effective for their audiences. Nor is it ever a sensible thing in a critic to cultivate indifference to common opinion about the works he is discussing. The opinion may be wrong or, as often happens, it may need to be corrected and refined; but in such conflicts — at least when they involve the larger aspects and effects of works — the burden of proof is on him. For the secrets of art are not, like the secrets of nature, things lying deeply hid, inaccessible to the perception and understanding of all who have not mastered the special techniques their discovery requires. The critic does, indeed, need special techniques, but for the sake of building upon common sense apprehensions of his objects, not of supplanting these; and few things have done greater harm to the practice and repute of literary criticism in recent times than the assumption that its discoveries, like those of the physical sciences, must gain in importance and plausibility as they become more and more paradoxical in the ancient sense of that word: as if — to adapt a sharp saying of Professor Frank Knight about social studies — now that everybody is agreed that natural phenomena are not like works of art, the business of criticism must be to show that works of art are like natural phenomena.

It remains, finally, to consider the bearing of all this on judgments of poetic value. And the first thing to observe is that, if our hypothesis concerning the shaping principle of any work is adequate, it will give us a basis for saying with some precision (as my example of Act V of *Macbeth* will perhaps suggest) what are the necessities which such a form imposes on any artist whose aim is its successful realization in his materials. Some of them will be necessities common to all self-contained poetic works of no matter what kind, such as the necessity, if the parts are to cohere, of devices for effecting continuity from beginning through middle to end; others will be more and more specific necessities

determined by the nature of the form we assume to have been intended, such as the necessity, if a comic effect like that of *Tom Jones* is to be obtained, of keeping the ridiculous mistakes of the hero from obscuring the sympathetic traits that make us wish him ultimate good fortune. These will all be consequences inferable from our basic definition of the form, and our primary task will be to trace them, in detail, throughout the particulars of the work at all its levels from plot or lyric situation down to the imagery and words. A kind of judgment of value will thus emerge in the very process of our analysis: if the writer has indeed done, somehow, all the essential things he would need to do on the assumption that he is actually writing the kind of work we have defined, then to that extent the work is good, or at least not artistically bad; and we should have to use very little rhetoric in addition to make this clear. But this is only half of the problem, for it is true of most mediocre writers that they usually do, in some fashion, a great part or all of the things their particular forms require, but do little more besides. The crucial question, therefore, concerns not so much the necessities of the assumed form as its possibilities. What is it that the writer might have done, over and above the minimum requirements of this task, which he has not done, or what is it that we have not expected him to do which he has yet triumphantly accomplished? These are the things our analyses ought peculiarly to attend to if they are to be adequate to their objects.

The possible in this sense, as distinguished from the necessary, is that which tends to perfect — to warrant praise of a positive rather than a merely negative kind. We can know it in two ways: by having our minds stored with memories of what both the most and the least perfect of artists have done when confronted with similar problems of invention, representation, and writing; and by considering theoretically the conditions under which any particular effect aimed at in a given work might be better or worse achieved — by asking, for instance, what would in general make a predicament like that of Tom Jones on the discovery of his first affair with Molly seem most completely comic, and then discussing the episode, as it is actually developed by Fielding, in these terms. Both methods are comparative, but the comparisons, if they are not to result in unfair impositions on the writer whose work we are considering, must take account of the fact that the desirable or admirable in literature is never something absolute but is always relative, in any given part of a work, to the requirements of the overall form and to the function of the part as only one part along with many others: forgetting this, we should make the mistake of Mr. Joyce Cary's critic and demand neatness where clumsiness is what "belongs," vividness and particularity where faintness and generality are needed, doing more than is done when this would be doing too much.

The judgments of value we should thus be trying to make would for this reason always be judgments in kind, grounded on a prior definition of the writer's problems as problems peculiar, at least in their concrete determination, to the formal nature of the work he is writing. They would also be judgments in terms of intentions — what is it that the writer aimed to do here and how well has he succeeded in doing it? — but the intentions we should take as principles would not be those, except accidentally, which the writer had stated explicitly before or after writing or those which can be defined for the writer by saying that he must have intended to write this work because this is what he has written. The common objections to criticism based on "intention" in either of these senses are unanswerable. They do not hold, however, when we identify intention with the hypothesized form of a poetic work and then consider how fully what we know of the necessities and possibilities of this form are achieved in the work, on the assumption that, if the work shows any serious concern with art at all, the writer must have wished or been willing to be judged in this way. There is nothing unfair to the writer in such an approach, inasmuch as we are not engaged in a judicial process of bringing his work under a previously formulated general theory of literary value but in a free inquiry whose aim is simply the discovery of those values in his work — among them, we always hope, unprecedented values — which he has been able to put there. They will always be values incident to the relation between the form of the work and its matter at all of its structural levels; and it will be appropriate to interpret what we find in terms of a distinction between three classes of works considered from this point of view: works that are well conceived as wholes but contain few parts the formal excellence of which remains in our memory or invites us to another reading; works that are rich in local virtues but have only a loose or tenuous overall form; and works that satisfy Coleridge's criterion for a poem, that it aims at "the production of as much immediate pleasure in parts, as is compatible with the largest sum of pleasure in the whole."[17] These last are the few relatively perfect productions in the various literary kinds, and as between the other two we shall naturally prefer the second to the first.

## VI

When all this is said, however, it is still true that what I have been talking about in this lecture is only one out of many possible legitimate approaches to the question of poetic structure, not to speak of the innumerable other questions with which critics can profitably concern themselves. I should not want to leave the impression, therefore, that I think it the only mode of criticism seriously worth cultivation at the present time by either teachers of literature or critics, but simply that its development, along with the others, might have many fruitful consequences for our teaching and criticism generally. What distinguishes it from the other modes is its preoccupation with the immediate constructive problems of writers in the making of individual works and with the artistic reasoning necessarily involved in their successful solution; and its great claim to consideration is that it can deal with these matters more precisely and adequately, and with a more complete reliance on the canons of inductive inquiry, unhampered by doctrinal preconceptions, than any of the other existing critical languages. It can give us, consequently, a body of primary literary facts about literary

[17]*Coleridge's Shakespearean Criticism*, ed. T. M. Raysor (London, 1930), II, 66–67; cf. *Biographia literaria*, II, 9–10. [Au.]

works, in their aspect as concrete wholes, in the light of which we can judge the relevance and validity — or see the precise bearing — of such observations and statements of value as result from the application to the same works of other critical principles and procedures: if the structural principles of *Macbeth* or of Gray's *Elegy* are actually what we have taken them to be, then whatever else may be truly said about these same works, in answer to other questions or in the context of other ways of reasoning about them, must obviously be capable of being brought into harmony with this prior factual knowledge of the distinctive how and why of their construction. Here is something, therefore, which critics who prefer a more generalizing or a more speculative approach to literary works can hardly neglect if they wish to be responsible students of literature rather than merely rhetoricians bent on exploiting favorite theses at any cost. For though it is true enough, for example, that what writers do is conditioned by their personal lives and complexes, their social circumstances, and their literary traditions, there is always a risk that exclusive explanations of literary peculiarities in terms of such remoter causes will collapse and seem absurd as soon as we consider, for any work to which they have been applied, what are the immediate artistic exigencies which its writer faced because of his choice of form or manner in this particular work.[18] These exigencies can never be

safely disregarded so long as the genetic relation between art and its sources and materials in life remains the very indirect relation we know it is; and it is perhaps not the least of the utilities to be found in the criticism of forms that its cultivation, in a context of the many other kinds of critical inquiry, would help to keep critics of all schools constantly reminded of their existence and importance.

But the other kinds ought to be there. Of the truth about literature, no critical language can ever have a monopoly or even a distant approach to one; and there are obviously many things which the language I have been speaking of cannot do. It is a method not at all suited, as is criticism in the grand line of Longinus, Coleridge, and Matthew Arnold, to the definition and appreciation of those general qualities of writing — mirroring the souls of writers — for the sake of which most of us read or at any rate return to what we have read. It is a method that necessarily abstracts from history and hence requires to be supplemented by other very different procedures if we are to replace the works we study in the circumstances and temper of their times and see them as expressions and forces as well as objects of art. It is a method, above all, that completely fails, because of its essentially differentiating character, to give us insights into the larger moral and political values of literature or into any of the other organic relations with human nature and human experience in which literature is involved. And yet who will say that these are not as compelling considerations for criticism as anything comprised in the problem of poetic structure as we have been discussing it in these lectures? The moral is surely that we ought to have at our command, collectively at least, as many different critical methods as there are distinguishable major aspects in the construction, appreciation, and use of literary works. The multiplicity of critical languages is therefore something not to be de-

[18]An instance in point, verging on caricature of the fault I speak of in the text, is a recent discussion of the character of Jane Austen's Darcy. Why, the critic asks, "is he, among the major figures in *Pride and Prejudice*, the only one disturbingly derived and wooden?" And the answer, in terms of his psychoanalytical thesis, is given at once, without any consideration of the great difficulties that must have arisen, for the novelist, from the role which Darcy had to play in the first part of the plot and from the fact that the choice of point of view prevented even later any direct or sustained disclosure of his unspoken thought: "The reason seems to be the same as that which *compelled* Jane Austen to falsify her tone and commentary concerning Wickham's seductions and to supply Elinor and Marianne Dashwood with such nonentities for husbands. The socially unmanageable, the personally involving aspects of sex, Jane Austen *can* no longer treat with irony, nor *can* she as yet treat them straightforwardly. Darcy is the hero, he is the potential lover of a complex young woman much like the author herself; and as such Jane Austen *cannot* animate him with emotion, or with her char-

acteristic informing irony. She borrows him from a book; and, though she alters and illuminates everything else, she *can* do nothing more with him than fit him functionally into the plot." Marvin Mudrick, *Jane Austen: Irony as Defense and Discovery*, p. 117; italics mine. [Au.]

plored but rather rejoiced in, as making possible a fuller exploration of our subject in its total extent than we could otherwise attain; and for my part I have as fond a regard for Longinus and for the masters of historical criticism as I have for Aristotle, and as strong a conviction of their continuing utility. Nor will there ever cease to be employment for criticism of the less rigorous or more imaginative types — in directing attention to aspects of poems which only a new model or analogy can bring into view, in formulating and promoting new ideals of poetic excellence or new poetic styles, in suggesting to poets unrealized possibilities in subject-matter and language, in relating poetry, for readers, to large non-poetic human contexts of emotion and meaning, in keeping the life of poetry and of taste from declining into orthodoxy and routine.

The best hope for criticism in the future, indeed, lies in the perpetuation of this multiplicity; nothing could be more damaging than the practical success of any effort to define authoritatively the frontiers and problems of our subject or to assign to each of its variant languages a determinate place in a single hierarchy of critical modes. Better far than that the chaos of schools and splinter parties we have with us now! But there need be no such choice; for the great obstacle to advance in criticism is not the existence of independent groups of critics each pursuing separate interests, but the spirit of exclusive dogmatism which keeps them from learning what they might from one another; and for that the only effective remedy, I think, is to take to heart the two lessons which the persistence throughout history of many distinct critical languages ought to teach us. The first is the lesson of self-knowledge: we can attempt to become more clearly aware than we have usually been of just what it is that we ourselves are doing — and why — when we make critical statements of any kind, and at the same time try to extend that clarity, in as intellectually sympathetic a way as possible, to the statements of other critics, and especially to those that appear to be most inconsistent with our own. And it will be all the easier to attain this self-understanding, with its natural discouragements to doctrinal prejudice, if we also learn the second lesson, and come habitually to think of the various critical languages of the past and present, including our own, no longer as rival attempts to foreclose the "real" or "only profitable" truth about poetry, so that we have to choose among them as we choose among religious dogmas or political causes, but simply as tools of our trade — as so many distinct conceptual and logical means, each with its peculiar capacities and limitations, for solving truly the many distinct kinds of problems which poetry, in its magnificent variety of aspects, presents to our view.[19]

[19]I have discussed some of the practical consequences of this view in an essay, to be published soon, entitled, "Questions and Answers in the Teaching of Literature." [Au.] "Questions and Answers" is reprinted in Crane's *The Idea of the Humanities* (1967). [Ed.]

# Ralph Rader

b. 1930

*Born in Michigan, Ralph Wilson Rader received a B.S. degree from Purdue in 1952 and his doctorate in literature from Indiana University in 1958. Since 1956 Rader has taught English at the University of California at Berkeley, becoming a full professor in 1967 and chair of the department from 1976 to 1982. He was the recipient of a Guggenheim fellowship for 1972–73. Rader began his career in Victorian poetry and published a study of Tennyson's* Maud *(1963). His formalist ideas began to develop at Berkeley, owing partly to the influence of Sheldon Sacks, founder of* Critical Inquiry. *Rader's theoretical manifesto was published in that journal as "Fact, Theory, and Literary Explanation" (1974). Some of his subsequent essays have addressed the issue of genre in the eighteenth century and the relation between the poet and the speaker in lyric and dramatic poetry. Since 1973, when he published "Defoe, Richardson, Joyce, and the Concept of Form in the Novel," Rader has been working on a study of the history of the English novel using his notion of genres as emergent forms. The book has been appearing piecemeal in articles on Fielding, Burney, Austen, Dickens, Eliot, Trollope, Conrad, and Joyce.*

# Defoe, Richardson, Joyce, and the Concept of Form in the Novel

We experience literary works as inherently meaningful and beautiful. This not very challenging statement raises a troubling question: if literary works do in fact have an inherent structure of meaning and value which is the ground of our response to them, how is it possible for us to disagree and even flatly contradict one another as we do in our conceptions of what their meaning and value are? Let us put the question more usefully: what must the objective basis of our intuitive experience of literary works be like for us to misunderstand and disagree about them as we do?

A theory developed to answer this question would have to begin with the assumption that it is in fact just the intrinsic meaning and value of literary works which makes us respond to them as literature, and it would accordingly have to describe all such works as possessing forms which could present themselves to intuition as self-intelligible and self-justifying, that is, as forms the act of understanding which could be experienced as its own justification. The theory would have to elaborate a kind of grammar of the natural imagination which could spell out the general and particular ways in which works might differ from each other in their self-justifying intelligibility and do this clearly and distinctly enough so that we could understand how our ideas about our experience of them, singly and together, might have come to be confused and contradictory.

I want to develop an example of the kind of critical procedure such a theory might entail by posing and attempting to resolve some especially confusing problems raised by the contemporary

controversy concerning the form of *Moll Flanders* as related to the form of *Pamela* and the standard novel on the one hand, and to *Portrait of the Artist* and *Ulysses* on the other. My attempt will be to define all the particular forms involved in such a way as to offer a solution to the specific problems associated with each, but to do this as just indicated within a single controlling theoretical perspective which can be seen to relate them coherently to each other and to clarify our overall conception of the nature and history of the novel form.

I begin by pointing out that there are, generally speaking, two current views of *Moll Flanders*. On the one hand, the book is seen as a work which achieves that realism held to be characteristic of the novel form but which lacks plot and a coherent dimension of moral judgment; and, on the other, it is seen as an ironic masterpiece similar in structure and quality to twentieth-century forms.[1] Opposed as these views are, they nevertheless attempt to measure *Moll* in terms of the same general formal conception: the first sees it as an example of failure in a simple version of the realism-plot-judgment form, the second sees it as an example of success in what is in effect a complex version of the same form.

The ubiquity of something like the realism-plot-judgment concept in novel criticism suggests to me that there is indeed an intuitively recognized class of works to which it refers. But the very fact that *Moll* itself is ambiguously per-

---

[1] The controversy over *Moll* is brilliantly surveyed and summed up by Ian Watt in "The Recent Critical Fortunes of *Moll Flanders*," *ECS* I (1967): 109–26. [Au.]

ceived in relation to the class would seem to imply that *Moll* is not a member of it. We can of course say that *Moll* is a deficient member of the class, but if the basis of classification is an intuitive recognition that its members in fact share a common principle of self-justifying intelligibility, then this would mean that *Moll* was deficient in those very qualities which render the class as a whole meaningful and valuable to readers, and any such conclusion is adequately contradicted by the book's enduring popularity and interest. When we find two critics as careful but as divergent in their theoretical outlook as Ian Watt and Sheldon Sacks both declaring that, measured against their conceptions, *Moll Flanders* is an incomplete or incoherent member of a class of which *Pamela* is a complete and coherent member, and when we find that both believe their classification to be based on just those features of the class which render it inherently coherent and significant,[2] then I believe that the logic of the situation instructs us to tighten up our conceptions in a way that will at the same time more clearly define the common class and exclude *Moll Flanders* from membership in it. It would also instruct us then to develop a concept of another principle of form which would account for the independent intelligibility and significance of *Moll Flanders* and which would describe also the ambiguities which cause it to be confused in the first place with works written on principles different from its own.

I want now to develop some concepts of form that in my view satisfy these conditions. I will offer first a highly specific conception of the realism-plot-judgment form from which I will develop a concept of *Pamela*. I will call this conception and others to be developed later *models*, in order to emphasize their hypothetical character and their function as artificial similitudes of independently cognitive form. The model is a revision of the R. S. Crane–Sheldon Sacks concept of represented action designed to make it meet clearly the condition just mentioned, namely to define the principle of the realism-plot-judgment class and to exclude *Moll Flanders*.[3] I should say that the models are deductive models; that is, they are meant to define the most general differentiating principle of a work's form in such a way that its more particular aspect can be rigorously deduced from it.

The general action model, as I shall call it, is meant to indicate the form common to all those works that make up our idea of the standard novel and to permit a unique model to be drawn up within it for every particular standard novel. The cumbersome definition is necessary for explanatory adequacy. I shall simplify it for convenience after I give the full definition. Let us say then that the general action model specifies works of fiction designed to develop and maximize concern for a character (or characters) along a line of development in which the ground of concern

[2] See Ian P. Watt, *The Rise of the Novel* (Berkeley and Los Angeles: University of California Press, 1957), and Sheldon Sacks, *Fiction and the Shape of Belief* (Berkeley and Los Angeles: University of California Press, 1964). Watt conceives Defoe to have achieved the realism which is the "lowest common denominator of the novel genre as a whole" (p. 34) but not the "intrinsic coherence" of a plot in which character relationships are informed by a "controlling moral intention," a coherence characteristic of the mature novel as first achieved by Richardson (p. 131). Sacks says that *Moll Flanders*, though not like *Pamela* a "represented action" (a concept intuitively but not functionally identical with Watt's realism-plot-judgment formulation), is nevertheless formally incoherent in comparison with it (pp. 267–70). I should emphasize that though both critics perceive that Defoe's intention was not to create a form of the order of *Pamela* (see Watt, pp. 100ff, and my discussion in note 7 below), neither quite frees himself from the notion that *Moll* is an approximation to the form that Richardson was to achieve. [Au.]

[3] Sacks's reformulation of the neo-Aristotelian concept of an action as a "work organized so that it introduces characters, about whose fates we are made to care, in unstable relationships which are then further complicated until the complication is finally resolved by the removal of the represented instability" (*Fiction and the Shape of Belief*, p. 26) is descriptively more flexible than R. S. Crane's four-cause definition emphasizing the fate/desert relationship which constitutes the "working or power" of an action; see Crane's "The Concept of Plot and the Plot of *Tom Jones*," *Critics and Criticism*, ed. Crane (Chicago: University of Chicago Press, 1952), pp. 616–47. But though Sacks also employs the fate/desert contrast to make sub-classifications, his emphasis in the general concept on "unstable relationships" and indefinite "caring" makes the flexibility a potential liability, since it allows application of the concept to works like Defoe's and Joyce's to which, as I argue below, it does not apply. In my own development of the action concept, therefore, I emphasize even more than Crane the primacy of the fate/desert contrast as the formal basis of the whole. [Au.]

is a dynamically shifting contrast between the reader's sense of the immediate and ultimate fate of the character (or characters) as compared with his (or their) immediate and ultimate desert, and to resolve this concern by a surprising but probable extension of the means used to raise it, so as to give the reader the greatest satisfaction in the ultimate fate of the character (or characters). To put it more simply, the author pits our induced sense of what will happen to a character against our induced sense of what we want to happen to him, our hopes against our fears, in order to give the greatest pleasure appropriate to their resolution.

The action model describes a work which the reader at some level of consciousness must know from the outset is being shaped beneath its realistic surface to meet the created requirements of desire. It has therefore the character of an objective fantasy, not such a fantasy as makes a reader the passive victim of a process hidden from his consciousness, but a deliberate, determinate, conscious, controlled fantasy identical with the cognitive structure of the book. I emphasize that the description is not pejorative. If it suggests the simple wish-fulfillment of shallow novels, it also suggests the possibility in serious novels of cathartically working out the shape of desire against the resistance of our ideals on the one hand and the objective conditions of experience on the other.

A particular model of *Pamela* would specify that the reader is meant to feel for Pamela a serious fear, which can be defined by saying that her merit and fate develop along a line of branching alternatives, where one branch, always closed by circumstance or choice, leads to an ethically acceptable but materially undesirable safety, while the other leads overtly and immediately to greater danger but covertly and ultimately to the most desirable resolution of her difficulties.[4] "Overtly" here means that of which Pamela herself is aware, "covertly" means that of which only the reader is aware.

Notice that the model locates at once and insists upon the sources of the most common

critical complaints about *Pamela* — the quality that Ian Watt calls its "immitigable vulgarity of . . . moral texture"[5] and the ambiguity of Pamela's status as heroine-hypocrite. The model also clearly explicates the difficulties. It says that it was no part of Richardson's intention that Pamela should be judged as a hypocrite but that it was likely, given the form, that a reader might react to her as one. We can see this more clearly if we consider that the first-person report of the narrative was, on the one hand, necessary to bring the reader close to Pamela's own fears and uncertainty about the future and to provide that inner account of her motives essential to the reader's admiration of her, but that, on the other hand, the choice involved the necessity of creating through Pamela as narrator the covert sense of potential prosperity so necessary to the special fantasy pleasure objectified in the form but which, as a condition of that pleasure, must not be attributed to Pamela. She must remain immune to the pressure of those material desires which the reader is nonetheless solicited to indulge actively on her behalf. (The formal situation is neatly epitomized in Pamela's exclamatory description of one of the early rape attempts: "O dreadful!" she says, "out rushed my master in a rich silk and silver morning gown." The danger-in-reward notation of the emblems of Mr. B's wealth is not to be taken as specially characterizing Pamela's consciousness but as part of the objective content of the scene. (In a cinematic version the camera would show the richness of the morning gown, with Pamela the image of uncalculating terror; but since Pamela herself is Richardson's only available camera, the notation must be potentially ambiguous.) We conclude, then, as a solution to our critical difficulties, that Pamela may appear at times to be a hypocrite in accidental consequence of an inner necessity of the form, whereas the tawdry moral effect of the novel, such as it is, is clearly the intended consequence of the form.

I will now very briefly indicate how the matter of an action novel is generated from the necessities imposed by its inner core and at the same

---

[4]Cf. Sacks, *Fiction and the Shape of Belief*, p. 23. [Au.]

[5]Watt, *The Rise of the Novel*, p. 171. [Au.]

time illustrate the specific explanatory capacity of the abstract model by asking it to explain the traits and actions of two characters in the novel — Mrs. Jewkes and Mr. Williams — and in particular to explain why Mrs. Jewkes is sensual and repulsively fat and why Mr. Williams is a clergyman.

The model directs an answer somewhat as follows: Richardson's chief problem in the novel is the need his form imposes to make Mr. B. both a villain and a hero. B. must threaten Pamela and threaten her increasingly, else our sense of her danger and the merit which develops from her response to danger will not increase, as the form requires, along lines that make her ultimate reward possible; but the more directly and villainously he does threaten her, the less acceptable he will appear as an ultimate and satisfactory reward for her, something that the form requires also. Richardson's attempt to face and minimize this paradox is implicit in almost every aspect of the book, but let us consider the problem only as it relates to Jewkes and Williams.

First of all, B.'s abduction of Pamela to Lincolnshire in general allows Pamela's danger to increase in respect to B. but in such a way that B.'s direct culpability is minimized. Mrs. Jewkes becomes Pamela's direct oppressor, with ambiguous authority from B., while B. himself remains in the wings temporarily safe from blame but a real and increasing threat as, one by one, the possibilities of Pamela's escape are cut off. It was an ingenious solution to Richardson's problem except for one thing: B.'s physical absence removes the basis of the sexual fear which is a chief element in the reader's continuing concern for Pamela. And here we can see why Mrs. Jewkes is sensual and fat. Her repulsive fleshiness, especially as conjoined with her tendency to fondle Pamela, keeps the idea of B.'s sexual threat constantly before the reader's imagination, while Jewkes' often manifested physical strength makes her prospective cooperation with Mr. B. seem certain to result in successful rape. Yet upon reflection we see that Mrs. Jewkes is gross and repulsive very much in excess of B.'s actual threat, and we may be puzzled by this until the complex demands of the model force the recognition that she must not only condition our sense

of Pamela's immediate danger but contribute also to our sense of her ultimate fate. Then we see that she is designed to be so repulsive that B. will seem actually attractive in contrast; in comparison with her he is seen to stand well within the outer limits of sensual sinfulness.

Mr. Williams is the last of a series of secure but unsatisfactory escape routes that are opened and closed for Pamela in her Lincolnshire imprisonment, as she waits trembling for B.'s arrival. Respectable and well-intentioned, Williams in his admiration for Pamela and willingness to help and marry her increases our developing sense of Pamela's social worth and thus the probability of her eventual marriage to B. At the same time, Williams' strength and merit must be sharply limited. If he were stronger and more morally forceful than he is, the reader's sense of Pamela's isolated danger and resourcefulness would decrease and his feeling that Pamela could and should escape would increase. As it is, Pamela consistently appears to be morally and prudentially the superior of the bumbling, somewhat timorous Williams. Both her danger and her merit are heightened, as just remarked, but more importantly the reader is made to feel an active desire that Pamela *not* run away with Williams and marry him — the potentially safe out becomes unacceptable. The reader feels the clear superiority of B. as a potential husband for Pamela, and so the as yet remote happy ending is built up as desirable, probable, and deserved.

But why specifically is Williams a clergyman? We see, on the one hand, that he must be a virtuous gentleman genuinely concerned for Pamela or he cannot contribute adequately to our sense of her moral and social merit. However, a gentleman willing to help Pamela would almost by definition be able to thwart Mrs. Jewkes effectively and take Pamela away, something that Richardson cannot allow to happen. Williams must therefore be a dependent gentleman, a contradiction in terms which can only be resolved if he is a clergyman in the service of Mr. B. His clerical capacity also has a further rationale in Richardson's need to use him to give retrospective sanction to B.'s outré behavior.

With a little work we can get the model to

answer all sorts of interesting formal questions — Why should the good Mrs. Jervis at times be morally ambiguous? Why does the novel not end with the marriage? etc. — but perhaps enough has been said to establish tentatively the important general conclusion that in works of the action model kind the objective characters and events of the story are all at some level functions of the underlying fantasy structure. (I will only remark further that a slight change in the *Pamela* model — separating rather than joining merit and reward in the line of alternatives — produces a model that can be used to provide a precise account of *Clarissa* in its contrasting moral grandeur, one which enables us to see clearly how Richardson constructed *Clarissa* out of the same psychic materials as *Pamela* but with an intention now to separate in sharp moral austerity the moral and material goods which he had been accused in *Pamela* of joining with hypocritical ease.)[6]

Moving now to *Moll Flanders*, I will say at once that if we test any version of the general action model against *Moll*, the results are absolutely negative; the model rejects *Moll* and *Moll* rejects the model. Either Defoe was not writing a work on the action model as here specified, or else he was doing such an impossibly bad job of it that the result could not be called even a deficient example of the form.

I will not seek to demonstrate the point further, because it should become incontestable later. I proceed then to build a new model for *Moll* on a different principle of natural intelligibility and inherent significance.

Let us say what has often been said but never fully understood: *Moll Flanders* is an imitation of a real autobiography.[7] The implications of this

fact begin to be clear when we realize that *Moll* is an imitation of real autobiography in a sense totally different from that in which *Pamela* is an imitation of real letters, though the difference is not easily perceived by those who think of realism as involving a single kind of imaginative relationship to the natural world. The "real documents" of *Pamela* cannot, as our model tells us, be like natural letters at all in the sense that they must at every point tell us Richardson's "once upon a time" story clearly and powerfully while they only seem to tell Pamela's story to her parents. In fact, the dramatic vividness of the letters (and the events they relate) is not the result of their likeness to real letters (and real events) but of their unlikeness to them, though, of course, the minimal signs of likeness given are a necessary condition of the illusion. Everyone will agree that the letters are the author's device, but I will say further that every reader of the work intuitively knows they are, in the midst of and as a condition of the illusion. He knows just as he knows in "once upon a time," as a natural condition of the fantasy.

Now the primary formal fact about *Moll Flanders* is that its form does not within itself convey the information that *Moll* is not the real agent of the story. To the contrary, it may be said to be

---

[6] A specific *Clarissa* model would describe Clarissa's merit and fate as developing along a line of branching alternatives where one branch, always refused by Clarissa or closed by circumstance, is defined as ethically acceptable but not impeccable and apparently promises earthly felicity, while the other, always chosen by Clarissa, is defined as ethically impeccable and increasingly excludes the possibility of her earthly felicity. [Au.]

[7] Almost fifty years ago Arthur Secord strongly emphasized the fact that Defoe attempts to make his stories seem to be authentic history (*Studies in the Narrative Method of Defoe* [Urbana: University of Illinois Press, 1924], p. 232 and elsewhere), as had others still before him. In view of my comments above, I should call particular attention to the fact that Professor Watt presents a concept of *Moll Flanders* directly equivalent to the one I offer here when he says that Defoe's "basic literary purpose" in the novel is "to produce a convincing likeness to the autobiographical memoir of a real person" (*Rise of the Novel*, p. 100). Yet, despite the excellent analysis which Watt develops from the idea, he seems, in describing the novel finally as an "ironic object" lacking artistic design (pp. 130–131), to miss the full logic of this accurate formal concept. Our difficulty with the book is, as Watt says, largely owing to the fact that "our whole critical vocabulary for fiction is still confusing in itself" ("Recent Critical Fortunes," p. 125), and my own attempt is to make clear that the contradictions and incoherence in *Moll*, which Watt properly emphasizes in arguing against those who see it as a coherent fiction, are the result not of artistic failure but of the positive artistic requirements of Defoe's special pseudo-factual form and of the impossibility of resolving the imaginative contradictions which it necessarily involved. [Au.]

an obviously positive feature of the form to make Moll seem the real author of the story but not of the events of the story — to make the work seem, in a word, literally true. This formal argument is entirely confirmed by the external historical fact that many sophisticated readers have mistaken Defoe's unidentified fictions for fact, as Donald Stauffer in 1941 mistook *Robert Drury's Journal*,[8] whereas not even an unsophisticated reader could so mistake Richardson's fictions.

The point can be made more clear if we think of three figures: an angry man, a man acting the part of an angry man, and a man pretending to be angry. The first has the appearance he does because he is really angry: his outside expresses his inside. The second has an appearance quite different from his internal state, and the audience knows this, else it could not take pleasure in his performance, since it would not know that it was a performance. The third man — the pretender — has the appearance of the first — the angry man — and, as long as we do not see behind the appearance, we react to him so. When we do see behind the appearance, we understand that we have been deceived. Notice, for later use, that we cannot actively think of him as angry and know that we are deceived at the same time. Now *Pamela* is clearly analogous to the second instance — the actor — and *Moll* is clearly analogous to the third instance — the pretender.

If we take seriously the idea that an intention to make *Moll* seem like a real story is the whole principle of the book, then it follows directly that, as a matter of positive artistic principle, it would display neither of those features called plot and judgment, the desert/fate curve of the action model. To do so, we see, would have revealed at once the immanent presence of the real agent behind the apparent agent and destroyed the principle of the form. Simple and inevitable as this conclusion is, Defoe's critics have time and again noticed that Defoe was writing in imitation of real documents and gone on to say that he did

not know how to make plots or that he failed to judge his characters.[9] Part of the reason for this is the difficulty of seeing what the full positive principle of the form of *Moll Flanders* is.

We can begin to understand the principle if we think a bit about the form of true stories. We should note first that we react to true stories as true not primarily because we know them to be so in an objective, referential sense but because they require us to do so hypothetically in order to understand them. The true story invites us to believe it as an account of fact and makes sense only if we do think of it as referring beyond itself to what its author did not create; it presents itself as true — reality referring — and our assumption that it is true governs our entire imaginative participation in its meaning and value, so that if we do discover, for instance, that a fascinating true story is false, we do not think that we have been entertained with a good fiction, we think we have been told a lie. Both the intelligibility and the effect of the true story, then, depend on its factuality considered merely as form, quite independent of the actual connection with external reality which the form of course implies.

Now Defoe's aim was to simulate both the intelligibility and effect of a true story. But what kind of true story? A kind of story that I would call a naïve incoherent autobiography, a story really told by a real person like Moll. There are no well-known examples of the genre, because such works are by definition deficient in art. They depend for such interest as they have on the extraordinary, as does all factual literature, but in the special sense of the naturally improbable or bizarre. "Man bites dog" or "truth is stranger than fiction" hits it exactly.

*Moll Flanders* can be understood very well as an imitation of a work of this kind designed to maximize the effects possible to the form. When we sit down by woeful chance with the talkative lady on the bus, we can ordinarily expect to be bored, but occasionally it may turn out that she has led an interesting life — has been hostess of

---

[8]See Arthur W. Secord, *"Robert Drury's Journal" and Other Studies* (Urbana: University of Illinois Press, 1961), p. 1, and the references there to Stauffer's *The Art of Biography in Eighteenth-Century England* (Princeton University Press, 1941), pp. 136, 209–10, 524. [Au.]

[9]A striking example is Secord's following his remarks on Defoe's intention to imitate true history with the comment that Defoe was "deficient in the construction of plot" (*Narrative Method*, p. 234). [Au.]

a speakeasy, say, a carnival shill, and a pick-pocket — so that her wandering and formless tale, thanks not to her art but to her material, including her naïve self, turns out to be worthy of our interest.

The maker of the simulated naïve incoherent autobiography, however, would make very sure that his story was *not* boring, however wandering and apparently artless. How would an author proceed if he were going to write *Moll Flanders*? He would, first of all, need a good many extraordinary, even sensational incidents: a kidnapping by gypsies, for instance; a strange love triangle; a marriage based on mutual deception; an incident of clairvoyance; a case of accidental incest; a varied career in crime, replete with many small but interesting episodes; a capture and trial; a conversion in the face of execution; a reunion with a long-lost lover; and a happy establishment after all. Described and listed thus, the events clearly manifest Defoe's intention, as they do not in the story, where they are intermixed with many minor events, pieces of the unsensational ordinary made interesting by means which I shall discuss in a moment. In presenting both kinds of material, the author — Defoe — might well refine the crude procedures of earlier factual stories. In a work like Francis Kirkman's *The Counterfeit Lady*, for instance, the writer assumes the reader's belief in the actuality of the story and milks it for sensational effect,[10] but Defoe reverses this emphasis, using a constructed sense of unsensational reality to produce imaginative belief, which is itself the effect. He does this by systematically crossing the lines of expected effect. On the one hand, he makes the inherently sensational incidents seem real by submerging sensation in the sense of the normal and probable. When, for instance, Moll discovers that she is married to her brother, she does not tear out her eyes but keeps her uneasy peace for three years. On the other hand, he makes the minor incidents seem oddly real by pointing up the unexpected and improbable, after the "man bites

dog" principle. Thus Moll sleeps with her gentleman friend for months, but in complete innocence; a maid is offered a bribe of £100 — many times her annual wages — and for no specified reason refuses; Moll standing in the street is given a horse to hold, and, on impulse, just walks away with it. Thus, the usual is moved away from the expected toward the unusual, and the unusual is moved away from the expected toward the usual. Everything is countersensational. What is the reason for telling me these odd things? the reader asks himself. Because they happened, is the only answer; they would not be told thus, otherwise. But since they *did* happen, then, how curious! how full of the strangeness of life! And Defoe has his effect.

Since the detailed story is to be taken as true, all the events will have to be fitted into the range of one life and narrated autobiographically. This is the first rule of Defoe's pseudofactual stories, a rule which could have been used long ago to solve the problem of "The Apparition of Mrs. Veal," thought at first to be fiction and discovered to be fact. Since that story is narrated in the third-person, it was almost certain to be true (that is, genuinely factual) *a priori*. In *Moll*, the first-person report will have to be bland, unemotional, and matter of fact so as not to call attention to the unnatural succession of the natural extraordinary. For style, the tone of rambling speech will do — perfectly clear in its apparent naïve lack of clarity, a little repetitious, but, most of all, without apparent design.

So far as overall form goes, in a pseudo-natural story a pseudo-natural form will do, the apparent form of incoherent natural life. Life, someone has said, is just one damn thing after another, and the tortuous progress of Moll Flanders will violate no reader's sense of life (unless he were an analytical sort inclined to remember forgotten children and notice how conveniently husbands die when the run of incident needs freshening). Even then we might, as a last touch, give the life a little shape in its shapelessness, a semicoherent natural shape familiar from the popular literature of spiritual autobiography and therefore presumptively real; but we would have to be careful not to give the shape any determi-

[10]See *The Counterfeit Lady Unveiled and Other Criminal Fiction of Seventeenth-Century England*, ed. Spiro Peterson (Garden City, N.Y.: Anchor Books, 1961). [Au.]

nate homiletic or sentimental force, to avoid any sense of plottedness.[11] (The incident of conversion would serve furthermore as an effective bridge from one improbable incident — the last-minute deliverance from execution — to another, the transportation to New World safety. The last incident itself would do nicely to end, an undeserved good fate but not wholly good. Moll does not quite live happily ever after).

I have so far emphasized Moll as almost a device to hold the material events together, and this is quite proper, I think, for Defoe mainly wanted to maximize the episode-by-episode interest and believability of the story. In Defoe's weaker psuedofactual stories — *The King of the Pirates*, for instance — we can see clearly how secondary his interest in his protagonists actually is, but it is an obvious virtue in such stories to give the narrator himself or herself as much interest as the matter of the story will allow. Since she is so much engaged in questionable activities, it is easy to give Moll a great deal of psychological and moral interest and even to have her comment on her activities in a morally interesting way.[12] What must be avoided at all costs is a sense of full consistency either by psychological portraiture or implicit ethical judgment. Everything about Moll must be left ultimately a little skew and incoherent, as a real person seems when presenting himself naïvely. The image of himself which a natural person projects to others expresses his inner unity only tacitly; the self which expresses the image is not itself expressed. An artist attempting to simulate the image projected by another from within will not really be able to do so, since, if he achieves his purpose, the image will be informed by his explicit purposiveness and be, therefore, unlike the actual image; and if he leaves it unachieved, the partial incoherence will only superficially *seem* to replicate the tacit unity of the actual. The only solution is for the artist to project his own tacitness into the image, in which case the image becomes in its inner essence the image not of another but of himself. (I will return to this problem, with Joyce.) The point here is, though, not that Defoe tried and failed to make Moll coherent; he didn't really care if she was or not, only that the reader should interpret her incoherence as that puzzling surface complexity of the real which betokens its underlying unity.

And so we return to the paradox at the heart of *Moll Flanders*. Fictional artists are supposed to show and not tell, but Defoe "shows" most effectively not by showing but by not telling, as when we feel through Moll's glancing reference the horror of the pickpocket's lynching at the hands of the street mob. The reason for this is that the form of the book forces our imagination to construe its matter as real. A reader who in-

[11]G. A. Starr, *Defoe and Spiritual Autobiography* (Princeton: Princeton University Press, 1965), has clearly demonstrated the influence upon the book of the tradition of spiritual autobiography. My point is that Defoe is borrowing from the conventions of that tradition not, as Starr feels, to give his books a religious significance analogous to that of real spiritual autobiographies (which would make them a kind of didactic fiction) but simply to reinforce the sense that *Moll* and the other books are true, since they possess a shape which life was known to have in admittedly true stories. This would account for the fact, recognized by Starr, that the pattern of religious significance in the books is not made formally complete and emotionally effective, though from the formal point of view I am offering, it can be seen that the presence of the pattern effectively increases interest as well as verisimilitude. On this matter, see also Watt, "Recent Critical Fortunes," p. 119. [Au.]

[12]This aspect of *Moll Flanders* is treated very well by G. A. Starr in his *Defoe and Casuistry* (Princeton: Princeton University Press, 1971), though, as with his earlier study (see previous footnote), I believe his analysis needs to be qualified by the recognition that he imputes to a feature of the book derived from a nonfictional tradition a value which it possessed in that tradition but which in Defoe is subordinate to his intention to produce the illusion and interest of naïve autobiography. The "tension between sympathy and judg-

ment" (p. 165) which Starr finds characteristic of Defoe's fiction is not the result of Defoe's attempt to edify the reader and instruct him in the complexities of life but simply the result of his wish, partly with devices and material derived from the tradition of casuistry, to give maximum moral interest to his story while clearly avoiding anything that might look like authorial judgment. Hence the "tension" that Starr finds, the irony, uncertainty, or contradiction that others have found, in what is calculated ambiguity. (I should notice that Professor Starr's discussion of my views [pp. 108–9] refers to an earlier version of the first half of the present paper, read to the All-University Eighteenth-Century Conference held at UCLA in the fall of 1969.) [Au.]

spects his reaction to the story closely will discover that he gives Defoe the creative artist very little credit because he has in fact thought of the incidents as if they were not invented but merely reported.

But the hidden substance of the real to which we respond isn't there. When Moll tells us that she discovered the fact of her incest when her mother-in-law mother mentions her early name, and when later Moll tells us that she convinced her mother of the relationship "by such other tokens as she could not deny," we accept the complete vagueness as correlated with the truth of the facts alleged. It is told so because it was so, whereas in a fiction the causal line for such a coincidence would have to be fully established (cf. *Oedipus Rex* and *Tom Jones*). If our attention is then directed to Moll's earlier story that her first memory is of being left by gypsies at Colchester, we should infer — from a logical point of view, we cannot help but infer — that she can know nothing of her mother and so cannot recognize her by any tokens at all. But we are not able to infer this within our imaginative participation in the story, because to do so contradicts the assumption we have made in order to understand the story. If we infer the contradiction, the story disappears. My point here is difficult to grasp just because it forces us to turn in so sharply on our mental processes. We are likely to think that just because we know *Moll* to be made up, we are free to react to it as a fiction, especially since its deceit is not referential, not forgery; but we aren't. We aren't free, just as in our original analogy we aren't free to perceive the pretender as if he were acting. *Moll*, like the pretender, can be seen from only one perspective at a time. The pseudofactual story does not turn itself into a workable fiction because of our knowledge but remains a story which the imagination must construe as real and cannot therefore fully interpret. When we are most caught up in the intended effect of the work, we cannot be conscious within the illusion that it is a work of art; and when we are most fully aware of it as a work of art, we cannot within that consciousness feel the effect. The wholeness of the work can be understood but not experienced because it affirms an imaginative contradiction.

If this is an accurate description of the form,

it is possible to see where twentieth-century critical difficulties with the book come from. Knowing it to be a fiction in *fact*, critics try to understand it as if it were a fiction in *form*. Since a fiction is always created within the consciousness of an implied author, to use Wayne Booth's term, and since there are many obscure signs in *Moll* that someone other than Moll wrote it, critics then assume that Defoe is formally present in his fiction. But the *signs* are just that — inadvertent traces of his role that Defoe did not or could not avoid; they are not *signals*. All the signals in the book say that Moll wrote the book, that Defoe isn't there except as a kind of editor. But when the work is interpreted as fiction, when the signs are taken as signals, they are seen to have no clear or consistent meaning, and the critics are left to say, on the one hand, that Defoe is "failing" to judge his material or, on the other hand, that he is judging it in ironic detachment. As Ian Watt neatly puts it, there seem to be only two possibilities, neither completely satisfactory: one that *Moll Flanders* is a work of irony, the other that it is an ironic object.[13] But we need not choose between these alternatives. I am persuaded that anyone who examines his experience of the book closely from the perspective I have offered will come to see that it is neither a work of irony nor an ironic object but an ambiguous object in a sense that no work of any other well-known author is.

Understood in this way, *Moll Flanders* and Defoe's other stories of the pseudofactual type fit cleanly into literary history. We see why the standard novel is usually not thought of as springing from Defoe, and why it was Richardson, rather, who was perceived by contemporaries as founding a new way of writing. Defoe, whom studies have shown to have ancestors but no posterity, is the last and most perfect artist in a tradition of works designed to exploit the interest naturally attaching to true stories. Richardson, with an ample posterity but no real ancestors, begins a new line of action-model fictions. The twenty-year gap between their stories is the dead space between two traditions.

It remains to consider more fully the set of

[13]See *The Rise of the Novel*, p. 130, and "Recent Critical Fortunes," p. 124. [Au.]

formal problems related to the fact that *Moll* has been taken to be not only an imperfect *Pamela* but also a fully perfected work akin to those of such sophisticated twentieth-century writers as Joyce or Virginia Woolf. Since both Joyce and Woolf recognized a kinship with Defoe and admired him in preference to grander names in English fiction, one would expect any explicit model of their work to reveal the formal similarity to *Moll* upon which their admiration was intuitively based. But given the fact that Defoe has his historical place at the rude beginnings of the novel, Joyce and Woolf at its sophisticated end — that Defoe comes before Richardson, Joyce and Woolf after Flaubert and James — one would expect that model also to reveal a profound difference within the similarity which sets both off from the intervening action model or realism-plot-judgment novelists.

In order really to test any model of Joyce's work, however — leaving Virginia Woolf aside — it will be necessary not only to compare the model with *Moll Flanders* but also to apply it to an analysis of Joyce's forms themselves and the disagreements which have arisen about them. Why should irony be an apparently baffling problem in *Portrait* as in *Moll Flanders*, and how is the problem to be resolved? How are we to evaluate Stephen's aesthetic in *Portrait* and understand its function in the book? What is the rationale of the symbolism of *Portrait*, and what limits can be placed on arcane symbolical interpretation? How is the form of *Portrait* related to the form of *Ulysses*?

Although I want to confess at the outset that I am a Joycean amateur, ready to defer at all points to veterans of the labyrinth, I think that a consideration from a general formal point of view of the problems which have arisen in the interpretation of Joyce's work can be of help to insiders. Much of the difficulty, as with *Moll Flanders*, derives, it seems to me, from the critical mixing up of accurate intuitive perception and understanding of the work with confused general concepts of form, usually implicit and only half-recognized, which distort and confuse both intuition and the expression of intuition.

To begin, let me assert that the feature which Defoe's and Joyce's novels have in common, in contrast to the action-fantasy forms of the standard novel, is that both project images of the actual as opposed to the fictional; the effects of both novelists depend, in very different ways, upon the reader's imaginative sense that he is in contact with life as in nature it actually is, whereas in action novels the effect depends on the reader's tacit sense of the ways in which, despite his sense of realistic illusion, the story, shaped for effect, is in contrast with the natural shape of the actual. What Joyce — and Woolf — admired in Defoe was the sense of the actual, re-created undisturbed, for its own sake.

But between Defoe and Joyce there is a very great formal difference that we may begin to specify by saying that Defoe presents false natural facts as truth, whereas Joyce presents something like real natural facts as fiction. When I say that Defoe's images are false, I mean simply that the sense of inner coherence in *Moll*, of a mental-spiritual unity underlying the surface reality, is an illusion, not imagined by the author at all. But it is the inner mental-spiritual unity that is most real, most fully imagined in Joyce. In *Moll* the coherent substrate seems to be there but isn't, whereas in *Ulysses* it seems not to be there but is.

This maximum contrast within minimum similarity persists in other aspects of comparison, as with the effects which each author seeks. Defoe, we have seen, makes the extraordinary seem ordinary for the sake of the emotional effect inherent in formal belief in the coincidental and contingent, whereas Joyce in *Ulysses*, as Richard Ellmann has said, shows that "the ordinary is the extraordinary,"[14] revealing in an image of one time and place the universal inner beauty that is always and everywhere.

As a natural consequence of their intentions, the authors will be formally detached — "absent" — from both kinds of works, but Defoe will seem really absent, while Joyce's presence in detachment from the autonomous matter of his

[14]Richard Ellmann, *James Joyce* (New York: Oxford University Press, 1959), p. 3. My views of Joyce's forms have been much influenced by this book. I did not read Professor Ellmann's more recent *Ulysses on the Liffey* (New York: Oxford University Press, 1972), however, until after this essay was completed, and it seemed best not to attempt any revision in response to its complex revelations. [Au.]

books is a constant source of the reader's aesthetic delight. Our awareness of Defoe's presence in his works is contradictory and puzzling, and the more we become conscious of his role in them, the more their intended effect diminishes. Our awareness of Joyce within and behind his novels is magically, lucidly pervasive, and the more we become conscious of it, the more the effect proper to the work increases.

It would be a contradiction of both novelists' purposes to draw upon conventional fictional probability within their novels; both adhere rigorously to the probability of nature. Yet both do borrow literary forms (Joyce's symbolic frames; Defoe's patterns from spiritual autobiography). But Joyce uses the forms to emphasize the artificiality, the madeness of the work, while Defoe uses them to emphasize and make acceptable its apparent truthfulness, its unmadeness.

These reflections define the genuine but superficial similarity between Defoe's and Joyce's forms which sets them off together from the standard novel form, as well as the very great difference which, if generally recognized, would prevent the confusion which has arisen about Defoe because of his *ex post facto* relation to Joyce. These reflections also make it possible to see a clear developmental logic in the overall history of the novel, a glimpse of the kind of critical orientation that a full developmental history of literary forms would give us: Defoe's works appear clearly, as I said earlier, as the last and most perfect realization of the entertainment potential of the false true story, while Richardson's are seen as the first to exploit the possibility of building from the reader's sense of the actual a story which would define and satisfy the wishes of his inner nature. Joyce — and Woolf and Proust and others — would then appear as writers who, wearied with novels which used the inmost feelings to shape a sense of the world, decided to use their sense of the objective world to shape and realize their inmost feelings. In action-fantasy novels, to sum up the contrast, the world meets the terms of our wishes; in simular novels, as I would call those of Joyce, Woolf, and Proust — novels built as artificial simulations of the actual — our wishes are made to meet the terms of the world. This simple set of concepts —

pseudofactual, action-fantasy, simular — makes clear without distortion, I believe, the basic formal principles which lie beneath the large shifts in the history of the novel as well as the distinctive shape of the most characteristically modern novels.

I turn now to a more particular definition of Joyce's forms, in order to render more precisely than I have so far the peculiar way in which Joyce's fictions are related to the actual. The dependence of Joyce's novels upon his life has from the first been so unavoidably plain that critics have tended to lose sight of the fact that the obtrusive interconnection is deliberate and formal, an inherent aspect of the intelligibility and effect of the works. Commentators have felt free to use the life to comment on the work and *vice versa*, they have felt and responded to the force of the integral relationship; but partly because we live in a critical era when to commit the intentional and biographical fallacies is a hanging offense, partly because the fictions are in a very clear sense set apart from life, the commentators have often omitted to follow out the full logic of the relationship, thinking of it as only a specially intense instance of the kind of connection between life and art which obtains in any work rather than as the very principle of the form.

The fact is that *Portrait* and *Ulysses*, unlike *David Copperfield* or *Women in Love*, cannot be read without at least tacit awareness that they are versions of real life — every reader senses the quality deriving from the fact — and, as I have said, the full force and significance of the novels can be felt only when the relation between the author outside the work to the representation of his life inside the work is actively experienced. On the first point, for instance, Joyce's failure in *Portrait* to fill in the reader's knowledge of Dante or Mr. Casey or any minor character would be a *prima facie* sin in an action novel, but we believe in the characters entirely, not because we have been induced to imagine a nonexistent whole where we see a part, as in *Moll Flanders*, but because we feel their mysterious outwardness, their existence independent of perceiving Stephen and, I think every reader feels, independent of Joyce also. Whereas in a standard novel, as we have seen with *Pamela*, the reader understands at some level that all the characters have been invented for the sake of an effect, in reading *Portrait* we feel that all the characters derive from, though they are aesthetically independent of, a reality which the author did not invent. I reserve discussion of the second point — that awareness of the interdependence is necessary for the full effect.

The failure to absorb the full implications of the life/art interpretation as immanent formal principle lies behind the many disagreements concerning various aspects of *Portrait of the Artist* — its supposed irony, its symbolism, its aesthetic. In recent years, as more and more has become known about Joyce's early life, the more extreme ironic and symbolic interpretations have come to appear more striking than substantial, but many recent commentators still see considerable irony in the book, and even the most authoritative seem to insist that the aesthetic is to be seen as inherently pretentious and/or irrelevant.

Since the aesthetic does seem to be the element of the book least understood and since in my view it expresses the inner logic of the forms of *Portrait* and *Ulysses*, I shall begin with it and use it as the basis of my own model.

If we take seriously and literally Stephen's short statement of his artistic ambition — "to recreate life out of life"[15] — we notice that he is not mouthing second-hand aesthetic generalities but specifically describing the peculiar kind of art which I have been emphasizing Joyce's is — a re-creation of actual life as actual, or, as Stephen has it elsewhere, "life purified in and reprojected from the human imagination" (p. 215). Art does not involve the invention of fictional images which resemble life but the re-creation in perfected aesthetic objectivity of images taken *from* life. This doesn't mean that they are literal, remembered, always, but that they are built as perfected fictional correlatives of the significance of remembered experience and have therefore the objective character of the actual. They are not

real experience but the imaginative equivalent of real experience. Looking, then, at Stephen's conception of the lyric, epic, and drama, we see that it is peculiar indeed if taken as descriptive of literary works in general, since all three forms seem to involve the presence of the poet's own proper self and life. Reserving the epic for later treatment, we need only consider Stephen's idea of lyric as the form wherein "the artist presents his image in immediate relation to himself" (p. 214), that is to say, where the artist presents *himself* as an object of aesthetic intuition and as center of emotional gravity in relation to himself as perceiving artist. We can see that this precisely describes the imaginative form of *Portrait*, where, as Stanislaus Joyce says, we are always in the center of Stephen's brain,[16] conscious of the artist only implicitly as our transparent means of access to Stephen's conciousness, which we understand in its whatness from within, as he understands himself. The novel is so fixed in this mode that, for example, the long hellfire sermons spoken by the priest in the first person and presented by the author in the third, are automatically interpreted by the reader as representations *from within* of Stephen's consciousness.

Stephen says that the business of the artist is "to express, to press out again, from the gross earth or what it brings forth, from sound and shape and colour which are the prison gates of our soul, an image of the beauty we have come to understand" (p. 207). If we look back over the novel, we see that from the beginning it has shown us Stephen in continuous development of his capacity to do this — to press out images of what he comes to understand. It is sometimes said that we see Stephen developing patterns of sensory association or moving through a flux of impression. Such emphasis on Stephen's mental passivity is understandable enough in an age dominated till recently by a behavioristic as opposed to a cognitive psychology. But if we look closely at the book, particularly the first chapter on which such judgments are usually based, we will see that what is represented is Stephen's process of cognition. We do not hear his father

---

[15]*A Portrait of the Artist as a Young Man*, ed. Chester G. Anderson (New York: Viking Press, 1968), p. 172. Subsequent references are to this edition. [Au.]

[16]Stanislaus Joyce, *My Brother's Keeper*, ed. Richard Ellmann (New York: Viking Press, 1958), p. 18. [Au.]

telling him a story; we understand him understanding that his father told him that story; we do not share Stephen's passive experience on the first page and thereafter, but we understand Stephen's moments of actively understanding or seeking to understand his experience, his attempts to grasp and press objectively out its mystery.

We feel him sometimes reconstructing the pat answers given him by the grownups, sometimes merely being puzzled by the queerness of things ("Why did people do that with their two faces?"), but sometimes also coming upon talismanic intuitions of his own: "How could a woman be a tower of ivory or a house of gold?" he asks, and then later: "Eileen had long thin cool white hands too because she was a girl. They were like ivory; only soft. That was the meaning of *Tower of Ivory* but protestants could not understand it and made fun of it. . . . Her fair hair had streamed out behind her like gold in the sun. *Tower of Ivory. House of Gold.* By thinking of things you could understand them" (pp. 35, 42–43).

By thinking of things you could understand them. The whole book is given over to the representation of Stephen's turning passive impression to active aesthetic cognition, pressing out the meaning of things until at the end he is no longer puzzled but sees the world and himself in relation to it with clarity and cold detachment. Suddenly the narrative which has been the cognition of Stephen's developing cognitions turns from third person to first, as the author gives us an image of the object of his knowing becoming the potential agent of that knowing and the potential creator of the objectified act of understanding in which we have just participated; and we understand that we have seen not life, not autobiography, but life purified and recreated in its essential significance and liberated beauty. The image of the artist as object becomes the image of the artist as subject; the logic of the book as expressed in its aesthetic is made fully manifest.

It is difficult to see in what sense a work of this kind could be thought ironical, and I venture to assert, not without apprehension, that those who see it as ironical are mistaken. But the problem here, as with *Moll Flanders*, is not to deny the problem but to see how it arises.

Wayne Booth, noticing that critical opinion is about equally divided on the question of viewing Stephen positively or negatively, concludes that the controversy shows that Joyce in his indirection has not given us adequate means to judge Stephen accurately, and he cites in support of his argument an explicit judgment of Stephen from *Stephen Hero* which, he points out, could not possibly be inferred from the parallel passage in *Portrait*.[17] But this analysis tacitly assumes that *Portrait* is intended to be a form where judgment — specification of ethical sympathy as a measure of dramatic expectation — is formally appropriate, as in all action forms it is. Critics of prose fiction ordinarily mean by irony the implicitly established desert/fate judgment of actions, as in Austen, James, and Flaubert. But in *Portrait* there is no expectation at all, no desert, no ethical evaluation. We neither actively expect anything particular to happen nor think one outcome preferable to another. Indeed, we have no thought of outcome, of developing possibility. Our experience is simply the experience of knowing Stephen's knowing at particular moments as we move through the novel, and perceiving the inner inherent logic that connects them.

If there were formalized judgment of characters in the book, as, again, there must be in actions, we would be broken away, disjoined from Stephen's consciousness, whereas that we should move in vital empathy with it is the first formal necessity of the book. The artist's image of the artist must fill the reader's mind as it filled the artist's own. If there is room for irony, the effect of the work fails. We see Stephen always, or are meant to see him, without external sympathy or antipathy, as in the action model, but in his whatness, from within; when he is a child,

[17]See Wayne C. Booth, *The Rhetoric of Fiction* (Chicago: University of Chicago Press, 1961), pp. 323–36. In these pages Professor Booth brings the contradictions of critical commentary on *Portrait* most forcefully into view, but I would interpret much of what Booth says about the formal shortcomings of *Portrait* — and *Moll Flanders* (pp. 321–22) — as resulting from mistaken assumptions about the generic intentions of the two works. [Au.]

we understand him in limpid childishness; when he is a callow teen-ager, we feel what it is to be him in his callowness.[18]

If we look back to *Stephen Hero*, we can see that the frequent judgments of Stephen by the author do not contradict this view but, in fact, bear it out. The judgments are in effect apologies for Stephen, assertions which have their origin in the author's embarrassed awareness that he has not been able to project as objective the inward grounds which memory gives him for feeling with Stephen as he does. The result is the peculiar aesthetic deadness which every reader feels in *Stephen Hero*. In *Portrait*, by contrast, Joyce was finally able to create an image adequate to the inchoate impression of himself with which he had begun his original "Portrait of the Artist" sketch. What Joyce wishes the reader to understand about Stephen is simply there objectified upon the page, ready to draw the reader's mind into imaginative conflation with it.

All this — the contrast with what I have called the action model form, the absence of judgment — is clearly spelled out by Stuart Gilbert, certainly as prompted by Joyce, in a passage which, though it refers to *Ulysses*, clearly applies to *Portrait* as well: "In most novels the reader's interest is aroused and his attention held by the presentation of dramatic situations, of problems deriving from conduct or character and the reactions of the fictitious personages among themselves [cf. the action model]. The personages of *Ulysses* [and by implication of *Portrait*] are *not fictitious* and its true significance does not lie in problems of conduct or character. . . . All these people are as they must be; they act, we see, according to some *lex eterna*, an ineluctable condition of their very existence."[19] There is, in short, no judgment, only whatness. Characters can be perceived with informing clarity in their

uniqueness and limitation, if that is irony, but not with the kinetic reflex of ironic disapproval.

But why, then, should the question of irony arise? Primarily, I think, because Stephen has the traits of an actual person and is not shaped, as all action protagonists, even criminals, are (witness Raskolnikov and Macbeth) to be the reader's alter ego, so that, if one is not drawn fully into the experience of the work, there appear plenty of pegs to hang judgments on. When Wyndham Lewis pointed out long ago that the proud, priggish, selfish Stephen in fact had such negative qualities, critics were soon eager to show that Joyce knew this very well and, in fact, was ironically insisting on Stephen's deficiencies, and they quoted in support of this view Joyce's remark to Frank Budgen, that the portrait was of the artist as a *young* man. Joyce meant, not that he had presented a negative view of an immature, fictive Stephen, but simply that he had represented his earlier self as he was. He also said to Budgen in a remark less quoted: "Many writers have written about themselves. I wonder if any of them have been as candid as I have?"[20] And now that so many reminiscences by Joyce's youthful contemporaries have appeared, it is plain that the early Joyce was just what Stephen is — proud, selfish, priggish, and cruel, more so even than Stephen, whom Stanislaus considered an idealized portrait.[21]

[20]Both remarks are recorded in Budgen's *James Joyce and the Making of "Ulysses"* (Bloomington: Indiana University Press, 1960), pp. 51 and 60.

[21]Stanislaus, who described the Joyce of this period as characterized by a "proud, willful, vicious selfishness" (*The Dublin Diary of Stanislaus Joyce*, ed. George H. Healey [Ithaca: Cornell University Press, 1962], p. 14), remarked of Joyce's self-portrait in *Stephen Hero*: " 'Jim is thought to be very frank about himself but his style is such that it might be contended that he confesses in a foreign language — an easier confession than in the vulgar tongue' " (quoted from Stanislaus's ms. diary by Ellmann, *James Joyce*, p. 153). Joyce himself, in a letter to Nora dated September 10, 1904, speaks of his delight in proving that "I am really selfish, proud, cunning, and regardless of others," *Letters of James Joyce*, vols. II and III, ed. Richard Ellmann (New York: Viking Press, 1966), II, 52. As for the views of his contemporaries, the comments on his youthful character as "aloof, icy and imperturbable" (Eugene Sheehy) and the "condensed essence of studied, insolent, conceit" (A.E., via Joseph Hol-

[18]See Ellmann, *James Joyce*, p. 150. [Au.]

[19]*James Joyce's "Ulysses": A Study* (New York: Vintage Books, 1955), p. 8. Joyce's early hostility to the pleasing falsifications of the action form is clearly set forth by Stanislaus in *My Brother's Keeper*, p. 92. [Au.]

It will become increasingly clear, I think, that the passages in *Portrait* which have been deemed most ironic are those in which Joyce is not most detached from Stephen but where he is least detached. What we have in these passages is not lucid aesthetic knowledge of Stephen's limitation, as in the passages dealing with his religiosity, but what will seem to some readers, especially older ones, the author's too fervent participation in Stephen's self-exaltation. When *Portrait* is working properly, we are moved with the author at the luminous static *idea* — the intellectual perception — of the nature of Stephen's emotion, but as Stephen grows closer to the author, Joyce is sometimes stirred into a kinesis in which the reader may or may not be willing to participate. As for myself, I confess that I have little trouble participating. The more I become aware that the portrait is not of a fictive romantic aesthete, as some think, but of a particular artist overcome with his sense of a mission which is to involve the sacrifice of his entire practical life as a means toward the re-creation of life in art, the more I am inclined to forgive him his self-exaltation.[22] I find it hard to be ironically superior to the image of the mind of a genius who changed the course of a century's literature. From this point of view I find it especially hard to understand those who suspect that Stephen, with his scholastic aesthetic and swooning villanelle, is no artist at all. Surely our knowledge of Stephen involves the knowledge

that his mind could only have been re-created reflexively by the mind which created the book. Doubting that Stephen's is the mind of an artist is like doubting that water is wet.

These considerations lead naturally to the related problem of symbolism in *Portrait*. Here again, I believe, a generalized conception of a literary device as if it were constant in all modes has led to distorted perception and evaluation. If *Portrait* is indeed to be understood as simulating an actual artistic development implicitly the author's it would follow that any symbolic dimension of the book would be developed as an extension of this formality — that it would not violate the restriction of the book to essential actuality and would merely be a means of rendering explicit and perfecting the inner meaning of the represented experience.

These assumptions explain — and limit — the symbolism of *Portrait* quite well. Although critical discussions usually lump modern symbolism together as one kind of device, we can see from the model that neither Stephen nor the other characters of *Portrait* are symbolic as Yeats's Leda is symbolic, say, or Eliot's Prufrock. Stephen as Christ, as Satan, as Stephen martyr, as priest, as Daedalus-artificer, is not a symbol *of* anything; he does not embody a meaning which refers beyond himself; rather, the symbolic meanings are attributed by him with calculated artificiality to his sense of himself, his artistic mission and its peculiar requirements of rebellion, betrayal, exile, self-immolation, resurrection, and re-creation. The symbolism is one with the aesthetic program as sketched in the book and executed by Joyce — exile is ultimate detachment as preparatory to artistic return — and it insists upon the identity between author and subject. The meaning of the book is the literal reality of the peculiar artistic vocation, which just because it is literal and actual can be expressed under a contradictory and overlapping set of approximating ideas; Stephen can be simultaneously Satan-Christ-Martyr-Priest-Daedalus just because beneath these attributive labels lies his concrete individual natural self. The names serve to define and dignify the role he has discovered. His name, Stephen Daedalus, is an exception to the other symbolic meanings in that it is not invented by

loway) seem typical (quotations from material reprinted in *The Workshop of Daedalus: James Joyce and the Raw Materials for "A Portrait of the Artist as a Young Man,"* ed. Robert Scholes and Richard M. Kain [Evanston: Northwestern University Press, 1965], pp. 141 and 166). [Au.]

[22]Critics inclined to ironize Stephen might consider the implications of Stanislaus's description of young Joyce as "temperamentally capable of absolute devotion to a mission to which he felt called by the accident of having been born with talent, even if, as he foresaw from the beginning, that mission would make him an outcast. He understood better than those who were wont to quote the text how inexorably an inner necessity can turn son against father and against mother, too; and yet it was inspiring to live with one so young and purposeful. His faith in life sustained him with the joyous certainty that in spite of the squalor that surrounded him, life had some not ignoble meaning" (*My Brother's Keeper*, pp. 108–109). [Au.]

Stephen, but it is understood as the author's way of objectifying the fact that Stephen senses his artistic calling as coming from beyond the point where his conscious self is attached to the mystery of nature. The fact that Stephen inside and the author outside the novel cooperate in the construction of a single artificial symbolic matrix is to be understood as implying, like every other aspect of the book, their ultimate identity and their common sense of his mysterious mission.

This view also clarifies the somewhat puzzling symbolism of the other characters, Cranly as John the Baptist, in particular. Cranly does not seem in any way adapted to express any meaning at all except himself as a real, natural person; how can he be a symbol? That is the point; he isn't. We understand his symbolic role as attributed to him by Stephen in the process of constructing a sense of himself as artist-Christ; he is symbolic only to Stephen.

All this, you may be thinking, is tediously obvious, and I agree; yet if it is obvious and true, another fact becomes obvious also: the emptiness of the elaborate, allegorizing readings of *Portrait* so sanctified in the casebooks. These readings mistakenly attempt to extend the symbolic patterns invented by Stephen and make them inherent in the matter of the book, so that it becomes the vehicle of meanings of which Stephen is not and could not become aware and which cannot be understood as expressing any aspect of the actual natural reality which the book presents. I venture to guess that these meanings, so obscure in contrast to the others so artificially plain, are in fact not in the book and that they have been found there only through a false analogy with *Dubliners* and *Ulysses*, which require a symbolic backscreen in a way which *Portrait* does not.

I should like to conclude by saying something about the way in which the form of *Ulysses* can be related to *Portrait* and the *Portrait* aesthetic within the general theoretical perspective I have been developing. Since I have taken the aesthetic seriously in explicating *Portrait* and propose to take it seriously in commenting upon *Ulysses*, I may remark in passing that, despite the extensive disparagement which the aesthetic theory has suffered at the hands even of recent critics, there seems every external reason to suppose that

Joyce took it with complete seriousness. One notes, first of all, that he allowed, indeed must have prompted, Stuart Gilbert to say that Stephen's is the functioning aesthetic of *Ulysses*.[23] There is beyond this the well-documented but unappreciated fact that Joyce at the point in his life corresponding to that at which Stephen formulates his aesthetic could have offered nothing at all comparable. It was not until he was several years older than Stephen that Joyce achieved in all seriousness for himself the views set down in *Portrait* and very probably not until 1914 that he was able to give complete integrated expression to the theory — at the time, that is, when he was completing the final chapters of *Portrait* with the conception of *Ulysses* already in his head.[24] It is incredible that Joyce should be supposed to attribute his own mature theory to Stephen as a sign of Stephen's immaturity, as so many have supposed. The fact is that he was exaggerating Stephen's maturity — giving him the capacity to express objectively and explicitly what Joyce at the corresponding chronological point had been able to express only as a confused and nearly inchoate intuition in the original "Portrait of the Artist" sketch. (I may remark in passing that I suspect that almost all of the significances represented in *Portrait* as achieved in 1904 were probably not objectified in Joyce's understanding till as late as 1912 or thereafter.)[25] As for the

[23]*James Joyce's "Ulysses,"* pp. in., 9–10. [Au.]

[24]See *The Critical Writings of James Joyce*, ed. Ellsworth G. Mason and Richard Ellmann (New York: Viking Press, 1964), pp. 141–48. In *The Workshop of Daedalus* (cited above) Robert Scholes and Richard Kain, while bringing together materials which clearly show that the aesthetic was a slow and serious creation of the period of Joyce's life after that which he represents in *Portrait*, curiously deflect the force of this evidence in their comment (p. 111) that the "esthetic theory . . . is apparently a redaction of many episodes in his undergraduate career, deriving from papers delivered before the Literary and Historical Society and from his essay 'The Day of the Rabblement,'" with which works the substance of the aesthetic theory has little to do. [Au.]

[25]In Mary and Padraic Colum, *Our Friend James Joyce* (Garden City, N.Y.: Doubleday, 1958), pp. 101–4, Padraic Colum argues strongly for the effective identification of Joyce's final departure from Dublin in 1912, after the rejection of *Dubliners*, with the exile objectified in *Portrait*. The association of the end of *Portrait* with this period gains support from some of Joyce's contemporary letters, particu-

aesthetic, there seems ample support for applying it to *Ulysses*.

Given the aesthetic, we should understand Stephen quite literally when he goes forth at the end of *Portrait* to encounter "the reality of experience," and we may imagine Joyce, having finished *Portrait*, seeking again to "recreate life out of life," life as it actually is and is experienced, in space and time; but, this time, seeking not to re-create the inner coherence of his own artistic consciousness in immediate relationship to himself but to present a wider image of life in its surface incoherence in mediate relationship to himself and others, that is, with himself as artist posted imaginatively midway between his represented self as subject and others as subject. The image of Joyce as Stephen would reappear in this new work but would be understood now not from the inside out but from the outside in, not as if he were the artist's self but as if he were another person; and we notice that we understand Stephen's mental innerness in *Ulysses* not as we understand it in *Portrait*, as he understands it himself, but as we might understand another person from the outside if we suddenly became connected with his stream of thought, coherent to him but not immediately to us. This is why Stephen and the whole book, unlike the lucid *Portrait*, are nearly opaque at first reading. Another consequence of the outwardness of the representation is obvious but not often pointed out: the fact that Stephen in *Ulysses*, though we are often inside him, is imagined as a body external to us as he is not in *Portrait*, where we are inside his

body. When we think of Stephen in *Ulysses* we have the uncanny sense that we are looking with the author at himself as if he were outside himself.

But what of the "others" in the book? They are of two kinds: the real natural others, Stephen's father, family, and acquaintances, seen not peripherally, as in *Portrait* from within Stephen, but from the outside, as flashes of fragmentary, fully persuasive outward otherness; and the fabricated natural others, Bloom and Molly, known, from the outside in, in their moment-by-moment innerness, the reader equally aware of them in their seeming autonomy and of the fabulous artificer who made them.

The real natural others were no problem; Joyce could make their fragments out of memory, just as he could build out of memory and research the dimensions in real time and space to which they were attached. But to create the continuing coherence of a fictional other person conceived as actual was no easier for him than for Defoe. The coherence of *Portrait* had been possible only because the "fluid succession of presents"[26] that the work images could be built out of the genuine coherence of the remembered past; but the lifelong coherence of another person was out of the question. A day's worth would be enough, and even then there were problems. But building the external Bloom carefully on hints from real models, and Molly largely from his knowledge of Nora Barnacle — working in a microscopic way of which Defoe never dreamed — he achieved characters which have been praised, rightly, for their overwhelming actuality; and yet careful critics have pointed out that Bloom is not ultimately a totally persuasive Jew nor Molly a totally persuasive woman. These facts might seem to suggest that Joyce no more than Defoe was able ultimately to pass through the solipsistic barrier of the human mind into the innerness of another. But whereas Defoe tries to keep us from seeing that the problem is there, Joyce, we finally understand, is insisting upon it as an inherent aspect of his form. He is not presenting Bloom ulti-

---

larly from such a sentence as this to Nora: "I am one of the writers of this generation who are perhaps creating at last a conscience in the soul of this wretched race" (*Letters*, II, 311; August 22, 1912). Though Joyce had long before decided that he "could not enter the social order except as a vagabond," that he was a "voluntary exile" (*Letters*, II, 48 and 84), it seems likely that the whole period 1904–14 (or 1915) during which *Portrait* was achieved involved a gradual movement toward the objectification and expression of ideas and emotions which at the outset had been nearly inchoate; the meaning had been there to begin with but took a long while to press out. Whatever the precise state of chronological affairs, the evidence as a whole strongly emphasizes the closeness, not the distance, between Joyce and Stephen. [Au.]

[26]The phrase occurs in the original "Portrait of the Artist" sketch, reprinted in *The Workshop of Daedalus*, p. 60. [Au.]

mately as really an autonomous other, as Defoe does Moll.

Though Joyce does all he can to objectify Bloom's otherness, he is, in the last analysis, basing Bloom's tacit unity on his own. Just as Stephen is implicitly the real young Joyce imagined as another, so the inner Bloom is implicitly (and explicitly, when all the signs are read) an attempt to imagine a fictional other as himself in his maturity; so that we have the author, central in the epical event, first himself as another and then another as himself, just what the extended logic of Stephen's aesthetic demands. But what of Molly and the reality of her otherness? Joyce could not ultimately really understand Molly, as Nora insisted: "He knows nothing at all about women." But Joyce did his objectifying best and earned Jung's praise.[27] Nevertheless, Nora was right, and we must understand the passionate inner coherence of Molly's "dark rhapsody," as Professor Adams wonderfully calls it, to derive not from Joyce's fabricating detachment but from what Professor Adams again describes as "a head-long plunge into the pit of the [author's] self," into and through the "gaping, irrational void which is the condition of modern life."[28] Thus did Joyce crucify himself upon the paradox of otherness in a world where one knows fully only himself. The author who knows himself first in serene detachment from himself as Stephen, and then in projection from himself as Bloom, cuts loose from his psychic moorings and plunges at last into the utter earthly otherness of Molly, the self turning itself inside out, abandoning itself to and realizing itself within its polar opposite, "the flesh made word."[29]

All of this has been beautifully expressed by Professor Adams — not only the crucial matter

of Molly, but the inside-outside relation of Stephen, Bloom, and the author who is *"terminus ad quem"* of the whole,[30] as explicated in Stephen's Shakespeare theory which "enables us to see the book before us as a sufficient answer to the questions posed within it."[31] So fully and movingly, in fact, has Professor Adams described all this as indicating "the perfect coincidence of autobiographical with artistic unity"[32] that I hesitate, in my indebtedness, to question Professor Adams's feeling that in some respects *Ulysses* lacks consistent and non-contradictory form, as well as the negative view he takes of the aesthetic of *Portrait*.[33]

I hesitate because it is so much more than likely that I am belaboring the obvious by following out the merely schematic point that the work which Professor Adams describes is specifically if cryptically envisioned in the *Portrait* aesthetic and the more important point that formally *Ulysses* is precisely as a work must be which is built out of the actual in the way that *Ulysses* is. On the first point, I note that Stuart Gilbert, following out the continuous line of the triadic procession of forms outlined in *Portrait*, describes *Ulysses* as an "aesthetic image of the world" which is ultimately but "a sublimation of the [lyrical] *cri de coeur* in which the art of creation begins,"[34] which is to say in Stephen's terms that the book is just that plunge of the artist's actual self into fictive otherness that Professor Adams says it is. Further evidence that *Ulysses* is a deliberate carrying-out of the *Por-*

---

[27]Jung's comment and Nora's are given on p. 642 of Ellmann's *James Joyce*. [Au.]

[28]The first two quotations are taken from Robert Martin Adams, *Surface and Symbol: The Consistency of James Joyce's "Ulysses"* (New York: Oxford University Press, 1967), p. 255, and the third from Adams's *James Joyce: Common Sense and Beyond* (New York: Random House, 1966), p. 168. See also Adams's comments in the latter work, pp. 165–66. [Au.]

[29]This phrase from *Finnegans Wake* is applied to Molly by Ellmann, *James Joyce*, p. 388. [Au.]

[30]*Surface and Symbol*, p. 251. [Au.]

[31]*Common Sense and Beyond*, p. 147. [Au.]

[32]*Surface and Symbol*, p. 254. [Au.]

[33]For Professor Adams's comment on the aesthetic, see *Common Sense and Beyond*, pp. 106–07. The reservations Adams expresses about the structural consistency of *Ulysses*, especially in the concluding chapter of *Surface and Symbol*, puzzle me particularly, as I say, in that they occur in the context of what appears to me a beautiful description of the aesthetic coherence of the novel. I suspect that there may again be conceptual interference from standards derived from action novels, but anything approaching a truly valid response would require a more detailed consideration than I offer briefly below of the ways in which I conceive the symbolism of *Ulysses* to be related to what I have called its "simular" structure. [Au.]

[34]*James Joyce's "Ulysses,"* p. 21. [Au.]

*trait* aesthetic is to be seen in the fact that Stephen's ruminations in Scylla and Charybdis deliberately echo the aesthetic. Stephen thinks of a time "in the future, the sister of the past [when], I may see myself as I sit here now but by reflection from that which then I shall be,"[35] thus articulating the Joyce/Stephen/Bloom self-as-other, other-as-self relation implied by his concept of epic. The rationale of the aesthetic is specifically recapitulated twice again, once in theological transposition when the Holy Ghost is presented as "middler" posted "between himself and [the] others" of the Trinity (p. 197), once and climatically in the Shakespeare theory when Eglinton sums up the relation between Shakespeare and *Hamlet* by saying, "The truth is midway. . . . He is the ghost and the prince. He is all in all" and Stephen replies, "He is" (p. 212).

On the second point, concerning the seeming formal contradictions of *Ulysses*, it is to be remarked that the larger ones, at least, are the intended and inescapable consequences of its form and inseparable from the sources of its beauty. One may consider that Joyce's formal intention required Joyce, on the one hand, to present a Stephen whose nature was rooted in and inseparable from the reality of the world, which Joyce had not created but could only recreate, and, on the other hand, a fictive Bloom and Molly whose essence we have seen is that they derive their quality as images of the real not from actual counterparts but from Joyce's creative projection of himself. The minds and lives of these two figures, nevertheless, had to be placed within and connected with the frame of reality provided by the objective world as recreated in the book, so that they could be perceived and understood as if they were uninvented parts continuous with its total substance.[36] By its very nature, however, this hybrid procedure entailed contradiction and incompleteness, as the requirements of the fictive hemisphere were adjusted both to the fact of the actual and to the symbolic structure which at once controlled and expressed the nature and significance of the whole. Inherently and unavoidably, material consistency could not be achieved, so that the unavoidable incoherencies of the material surface are to be adjudged not so much aesthetic faults as markers on the outer boundaries of possible success. It is entirely of course that looking behind the organic surface one should perceive the seams of the artifice and the traces of the artificer; golden birds are made, not born. The wonder of the book lies just in the fact of its two-sided is-ness/madeness, a wonder epitomized for me in the thought of Simon and Dilly Daedalus in the work, the palpable images of the author's loved flesh and blood whom in the flesh he would never see again, being looked on with utter detachment under the aspect of eternity, and the thought, on the other hand, of the author's passionate entry into Molly, the woman who never was.

In all his complication Joyce, as he liked to say, was ultimately simple, and so it must be also with the human imagination in literature. The laws underlying the operations by which the mind translates the world of which it is a part into the many worlds of its own creation must be simple, definite, and regular, else we could not have common intuitive access to those worlds as, despite interpretative confusion, we know we do. But these worlds have become so many and the relationships among them and to the real world so complex that intuition is not able to prevent the confusion of concepts appropriate to one with concepts appropriate to another. The result is to make analysis itself often seem inherently futile and empty and to blur even more the wonderful reality of literary experience. Knowledge of the structure of imaginative experience is itself of intrinsic value, but we need to try to make that knowledge as specific and explicit as we can not only for its own sake but also and more importantly so that we may purify our concrete participation in that experience and render it more full and true.

[35]*Ulysses* (New York: Modern Library, 1961), p. 194. [Au.]

[36]Professor John Henry Raleigh has worked out in detail the chronology of the Blooms's fictional history as devised by Joyce and will present the results in a forthcoming book. [Au.]

# 4

# STRUCTURALISM
# AND SEMIOTICS

*[Poetic language] is not used in the services of communication but in order to place in the foreground the act of expression, the act of speech itself.* — JAN MUKAŘOVSKÝ

*Criticism . . . is the search for truth, not its revelation — the quest for the treasure rather than the treasure itself, for the treasure can only be absent.* — TZVETAN TODOROV

*What requires explanation is not the text itself so much as the possibility of reading and interpreting the text, the possibility of literary effects and literary communication.*
— JONATHAN CULLER

The special insight of the structuralist approach is that, though language may not be everything, practically everything we do that is specifically human is expressed in language. Most obviously we communicate with one another in hundreds of "natural" languages, whose conventions predate any human memory; and in recent decades we have become dependent upon computers, whose functioning is based on the creation of artificial languages for sorting and processing data, and for solving problems.

But most of the other activities of daily life, from the elegant to the homely, are equally dependent upon various codes. The performance of music requires a complex notation, as does the solution of mathematical problems. Our economic life rests upon the exchange of labor and goods for symbols, such as cash, checks, stock certificates, and various other documents that are more or less easily exchangeable for each other and for other people's labor and goods. The language of fashion is one we learn to speak with difficulty, and when we wonder if our tie is too loud or our dress too formal, we are considering whether our friends will be upset by the message our clothes convey. Social life depends on the meaningful gestures and signals of "body language" and revolves around the exchange of small, symbolic favors: drinks, parties, dinners. Family connections in patriarchal culture depend on the exchange — so momentous that it is difficult to think of it as symbolic — of a woman from one family group into another.

Merely noting that everything is language and cataloging the overwhelming variety of ways in which reality is structured in systems of signs and symbols does not get us very far. Structuralism required a method of analyzing systems of symbols, and this was provided by two developments. One was the theory of the nineteenth-century American philosopher Charles Sanders Peirce, which is termed *semiotics*. Peirce analyzed sign systems into three general types: (1) iconic signs, in which the signifier resembles the thing signified (such as the stick figures on washroom doors that signify "Men" or "Women"); (2) indexes, in which the signifier is a reliable indicator of the presence of the signified (like smoke and fire); and (3) true symbols, in which the signifier's relation to the thing signified is completely arbitrary and conventional (just as the sound /kat/ or the written word *cat* are conventional signs for the familiar feline).

The other development was the linguistic theory of Ferdinand de Saussure, who established that the special symbol systems of the natural languages are systems based on differences. In his lecture notes published posthumously as *Cours de linguistique générale* (1916), Saussure established the basic principles of structural linguistics and of structuralism more generally.[1] These principles rest on a number of technical distinctions:

1. *Langue* vs. *parole*. A language is a system of constitutive rules — that is, the rules *are* the language in the same way that the rules of chess constitute the game of chess. (If we break the rules of chess by, say, taking two moves at a time, there is no penalty as there is when we break traffic laws or other normative rules; we just aren't playing chess any longer.) But the system of the language (*langue*) appears only in the behavior of its individual speakers, who produce instances of speech (*parole*). Speakers may or may not be aware of the rules of the language, but they usually know whether an individual instance is correct or deviant. The activity of the linguist is to infer the rules of the *langue* from the evidence of *parole*. American linguist Noam Chomsky's distinction between *competence* (ideal language ability) and *performance* (individual activity) is similar to that of *langue* and *parole*.

2. *Synchronic* vs. *diachronic*. The system of a *langue* is complete at any one time, but languages, in their sound systems (phonology), their grammatical relationships (syntax), and their lexicons, change over time. In studying a language, one has to distinguish between a synchronic study, which attempts to display the *langue* at one particular time, and a *diachronic* investigation, which studies change.

3. *Paradigmata* and *syntagmata*. The two fundamental relationships of symbols are parataxis and syntax. An example of parataxis is the relationship of items in

[1]"Semiotics" and "structuralism" have been used here as though they were essentially similar terms, and certainly there was a great deal that connected the two movements. But semiotics takes off from Peirce — for whom language is one of numerous sign systems — and structuralism takes off from Saussure, for whom language was the sign system par excellence. As a result, semioticians discuss sign systems generically, while structuralists tend to use linguistic models exclusively — to speak of "the language of fashion" and so forth. A structuralist would compose a grammar of narrative, while a semiotician would analyze the multiple codes that relate expression to content, and so on.

the same category on a menu: In ordering soup, one may choose the beef consommé *or* the lobster bisque *or* the clam chowder. The items are similar enough to belong to one category (soups) yet different (in their ingredients). In a language, the consonants and vowels are paradigms on the phonological level, nouns and verbs are paradigms on the grammatical level, and so on.

Syntaxis is the relationship of items from different categories in a meaningful structure. Back in the restaurant, when we choose a soup, an appetizer, a main course, and a dessert, we try to select a combination that will "go together" pleasantly. Or we try to pick items of clothing that will harmonize in color, texture, and social tone when worn together. The rules of syntax in a natural language are far more complex than the rules for wearing clothes or for ordering in a restaurant; it takes several years of hard work, from the ages of two to four, to learn the most basic relationships. But when we have succeeded, we comprehend subtle differences in the syntax of sentences, even some that traditional grammar textbooks ignore.

In Noam Chomsky's famous pair of sentences, "John is eager to please" and "John is easy to please," for example, the sentences appear to differ merely in one lexical item: for the third word of each sentence, a different member of the paradigm class of adjectives has been selected. But any native speaker also intuitively knows that the sentences also differ in their syntax. "John" is implicitly the "subject" of *please* in the first sentence and the "object" of *please* in the second, despite the fact that the sentences are apparently cut to the same pattern, and that "John" is by traditional standards the subject of the copula "is" in both.

4. The basic units, or *emes*. To return to paradigm classes, the problem is one of identifying the basic categories in an unfamiliar language, where the categories may not be the same as in one's native tongue. Saussure's basic principle was that distinctions within categories depend on differences; the practical difficulty is figuring out which differences, of all those we can learn to distinguish, really make a difference — which is not a simple matter.

Take the sound system of English. The letter *t* stands for the sound /t/ — but at various positions in words /t/ is not a single sound but several different sounds. The first sound in the word *tip* is not the same as the last sound in the word *pit*. The first *t* is *aspirated* — pronounced with an explosion of air — while the second is not. To complicate things further, the *t* sound in *bottle* is not the same as either of the other two. But in English, these differences *do not* make a difference. If you pronounce *pit* with an aspirated *t,* you have still said *pit*; no one will mistake which word you have pronounced. Aspiration is a feature that does not make a basic difference in English (though it does in Hindi and in several other languages). But voicing does make a difference in English. Words like *tip* and *dip,* or *pit* or *bit,* differ according to whether the initial consonant is *voiced* (pronounced with the vocal cords vibrating) or *unvoiced*. The point is that /t/ in all its various pronunciations (allophones) is a single *phoneme* in English, a basic and minimal unit of the sound system. And the phoneme /t/ differs from the phoneme /d/

because of the feature of voicing, and from all the other phonemes of English because of various other sorts of differences.

If the basic minimal unit of a sound system is the phoneme, the basic minimal unit of grammar is the *morpheme*. One example of a morpheme in English is the plural, which is formed in a number of different ways, usually by adding /s/ or /z/ or /iz/ to the singular noun (as in bat/bats, pin/pins, church/churches, respectively), but sometimes by changing the vowel (mouse/mice), or in other irregular ways. Languages other than English often have similar grammatical categories, but even languages with a common origin employ important variations (verbs in French have many more tenses, nouns in French always show gender). Some languages have grammatical categories and relationships that are totally distinct from those found in European languages. In each case it is important to locate the individual units of meaning as they occur, as spaces within a system made up of *differences*.

The impact of Saussure's general principles for discussing the structure of a language was felt first in linguistics. For several decades after Saussure's death, linguists and anthropologists trained in linguistics traveled to remote corners of the world, recording and analyzing the principles of hundreds of natural languages. But soon after the development of structural linguistics, the basic principles began to be generalized to other sorts of codes and structures, which could be analyzed in analogous fashion in terms of the combinations and permutations of various "emes," or basic elements. The smallest units or building blocks of stories were termed "mythemes" by Claude Lévi-Strauss; Julia Kristeva has called the irreducible atoms of social thought "ideologemes."

As Roland Barthes said in "The Structuralist Activity" (1964), structuralism is not a set of beliefs, but two complementary practices: analysis and synthesis. The structuralist analyzes the products of human making into their smallest significant component parts, then tries to discover the principles of their articulation — how the parts fit together and function.[2] In this very broad sense, the first structuralist was Aristotle, and the *Poetics* the first work of structuralist literary criticism. It would not be odd to consider formalist critics like R. S. Crane and Northrop Frye as structuralists. But today, the term is usually restricted to those whose practice of analysis and synthesis is performed using the tools, techniques, and terminology of linguistics.

Perhaps the chief human vector for the spread of structuralism was Roman Jakobson, one of the great linguists of the century, who began as an ally of the Russian Formalists in the 1920s, migrated to Czechoslovakia, where he joined the Prague Linguistic Circle in the 1930s, and then traveled to New York, where he exerted a wide influence on numerous intellectuals, including the ethnologist Claude Lévi-Strauss. They collaborated on literary essays, including an essay on Baudelaire's sonnet, "The Cats" (reprinted in this chapter), but the most important product was Lévi-Strauss's integration of linguistics and myth in his book *Struc-*

---

[2]Roland Barthes, "The Structuralist Activity," in *Critical Essays,* trans. by Richard Howard (New York: Farrar, Straus and Giroux, 1972).

*tural Anthropology* (1958), which has changed the theory and practice of cultural studies around the world.

## BETWEEN FORMALISM AND STRUCTURALISM

The work of the Prague School links the Russian formalists (Ch. 3) and the structuralist movement, which was centered in Paris. The Prague School, begun in 1926 under the leadership of Vilem Mathesius, was programmatically devoted to the synchronic study of language — a revolutionary break with the traditional basis of historical philology. When Russian linguists like Nikolai Trubetzkoy and Roman Jakobson joined in the late 1920s, the group developed a functionalist linguistics based on the analysis of *contrastive structures,* minimal pairs separated by differences.

Jan Mukařovský's "Standard Language and Poetic Language" is a typical product of the Prague School. Mukařovský insists that the difference between poetry and other forms is linguistic, not thematic, and that the primary feature of poetry is deviance from standard language. We all speak of "poetic license," the freedom of the poet to dispense with the usual rules of language, but for Mukařovský this license is part of what *defines* the poetic text. In a sense, this goes back to Shklovsky and the Russian formalists, who had insisted that literature works by defamiliarizing common things, by talking about them in unusual language. But a further idea is involved — a theory about the various functions of language that derives from Jakobson's paper on "Linguistics and Poetics" (translated in 1960).

Jakobson had presented the following model of the act of communication: A *sender,* having made *contact* with a *receiver,* sends a *message* about some external *context* using a *code.* These six factors — sender, contact, receiver, message, context, and code — define the six functions of communication. Most normal communication is *referential:* It emphasizes the context, the content that is to be conveyed. The *emotive* function of communication emphasizes the sender, while the *conative* emphasizes the receiver. The *phatic* function is that of establishing contact, like saying "hello" when we pick up the telephone. The *metalinguistic* function is to investigate the code that sender and receiver are both using to clear up disagreements or ambiguities. Finally, there is the linguistic function that centers on the message qua message. This Jakobson defines as the *poetic* function.

Mukařovský's paper on poetic language explores how the poetic function can be exercised. To call attention to itself as pure message, the language of poetry must stand out from the standard language, which we automatically process as though it were the transparent medium of thought. To stand out, it must be deviant in some way, but it cannot be deviant in every way at once. There must be some dominant feature (phonology, the lexicon, syntax, semantics) on which the difference from the standard is centered. Mukařovský is able to show that various traditions in Czech poetry differ in these ways. (The reader may find it an interesting exercise to seek out equivalent examples in the English tradition.) Mukařovský proposes the theory that poetry that deviated from the standard in every respect would be reautomatized — that is, processed as the standard — by the reader. This is not completely convincing; it seems likelier that language which deviates from the standard too far and in too many respects at once would not be processible by the receiver at all. We should also be aware that "deviance" means something rather different in syntax than in the lexicon. In the former, the poet is breaking a constitutive rule of the *langue;* in the latter, the poet is simply using unusual, *statistically* deviant, words.

## MYTH AND LANGUAGE

Claude Lévi-Strauss began his career with a dissertation on *The Elementary Structures of Kinship* (1949), which was a synthesis of the available data on the rules by which a vast number of cultures regulated marriage and kinship ties. Lévi-Strauss's method was to use language-data to verify social rules (for example, if a culture has a word for "mother's brother" that is *also* its word for "father-in-law," this correspondence strongly suggests that a boy is supposed to marry his maternal cross-cousin). In the course of his research, Lévi-Strauss developed a general theory of the way in which the exchange and circulation of women between families is used to knit cultures together.

But in the course of that study he recognized that another aspect of culture is used for exchange and circulation: language. As Lévi-Strauss began to theorize about the homologies between languages and kinship systems, it occurred to him that cultures with complex kinship structures, which gave the individual a small number of marital choices, tended to speak languages with complex syntax and a small lexicon, while cultures (like our own) with simple kinship structures, which give the individual a vast number of marital choices, tended to speak languages with simple syntax and a large lexicon.[3] We can see here a key feature of Lévi-Strauss's method: to try to construct revealing analogies between very different aspects of life and society by seeing each as a structural system of symbols. While the surface structure of the symbols might be very different, the way in which they are combined (syntaxis) might point to a similar deep structure.

Given this interest, Lévi-Strauss was attracted to the study of the richest source of symbols in anthropology: mythology. His four volumes of *Mythologiques* (*The Raw and the Cooked* [1964]; *From Honey to Ashes* [1967]; *The Origin of Table Manners* [1968]; and *L'Homme Nu* [1971]) present an elaborate survey of world myths to illustrate his basic thesis about mythic thinking: That myths are the way the "savage mind" — not the minds of savages, but the untamed mind within all of us — gives order to the world.

"The Structural Study of Myth" (1955), reprinted in part here, presents Lévi-Strauss's method in its purest form, as a way of reconstructing the *langue* of myth by the analysis of a particular *parole*. His analysis of the Oedipus myth demonstrates how he breaks down the chronological structure of the story in order to

[3]Claude Lévi-Strauss, "Language and the Analysis of Social Laws," (1951) in *Structural Anthropology* (New York: Basic Books, 1963), pp. 62–63.

isolate the various elements (or *mythemes*) operating within the text. He next attempts to understand the relation between the mythemes as members of paradigm classes separated from one another by the way they embody concrete differences. He then finds a way of generalizing the concrete issues of the story as a system of abstract binary terms. Finally, he interprets the interaction of the mythemes as giving order and structure to a significant spiritual conflict. In the case of Oedipus, the myth mediates between conflicting theories: that humanity is born out of the earth (autochthonous) or of the sexual union between man and woman.[4] Lévi-Strauss's point is that as long as the spiritual conflict continues (and if it is a genuine conflict, it can never be fully resolved), the myth will continue to be told, elaborated, varied, and retold in other forms that — structurally, at least — address the same issue.

## STRUCTURALIST POETICS

One of the central texts of high structuralism in its most confident phase is the collaborative essay of Roman Jakobson and Lévi-Strauss on Baudelaire's sonnet, "The Cats." Their elaborate analysis of the geometrical symmetry of the grammatical structures within the sonnet shows the limits of what structuralism can do. But their conclusion — that the cats symbolize love cleansed of feminine impurity and knowledge cleansed of the sages' austerity — has despite the seemingly scientific method not won universal assent. As Michael Riffaterre has said, "the poem has been rebuilt by the two critics into a 'superpoem' inaccessible to the normal reader, and yet the structures described do not explain what establishes contact between poetry and reader. No grammatical analysis of a poem can give us more than the grammar of the poem."[5]

The difficulty is not with grammatical analysis as such (in fact, Riffaterre continues with his own grammatical analysis of "Les Chats"). Stylistics, the linguistic analysis of literary effects, is a venerable and useful tool of criticism, but most linguists would begin with an impression of the poem's effect and then seek something in the syntax that might have caused that effect.[6] The problem arises from the hypothesis that, by checking successively into every symmetry of every grammatical category, the critic will stumble onto the secret of the poem. As Jonathan Culler attempted to show in the first half of *Structuralist Poetics* (1975), this hypothesis simply doesn't work: Structural analysis is not an effective discovery procedure. Or rather, it is too effective. Culler demonstrates that the elaborate syntactic symmetries that Jakobson and Lévi-Strauss found in the four

[4]Two further examples of the interpretation of myth, dealing with relatively unfamiliar American Indian tales, have been omitted.

[5]Michael Riffaterre, "Describing Poetic Structures: Two Approaches to Baudelaire's *Les Chats*," in *Structuralism,* ed. Jacques Ehrmann (New York: Doubleday, 1970), pp. 201–202.

[6]As for example in David Richter, "Two Studies in Iconic Syntax: Alfred Lord Tennyson's 'Tears, Idle Tears' and William Carlos Williams's 'The Dance.'" *Language and Style* 18 (Spring 1985): 136–51.

strophes of "The Cats" can also be found in the first four prosy sentences of Jakobson's own "Postscriptum" to *Questions de poétique*.

As Culler suggests in the selection reprinted here, structuralist techniques would be more fruitfully applied to literature, not in the search for new interpretations of texts or as an algorithm for generating interpretations, but in investigating how literary interpretation takes place. The title of Culler's chapter, "Literary Competence," is derived from Noam Chomsky's notion of linguistic competence — the ability of native speakers to create and understand sentences they have never heard before. In effect, Culler argues, structuralists should return to Saussure's original goal of understanding the rules of literary *langue* rather than investigate individual performances.[7]

In a long and useful pair of chapters, Culler goes on to discuss the poetics of the lyric poem in terms of the conventions through which we interpret its form and meaning and the operations we perform on the text in order to "naturalize" its language. (In effect, he suggests that to read a poem we have to *undo* the poet's defamiliarization of the material.) After giving a reading of a minimalist one-line poem by Apollinaire, Culler presents the universal principles underlying his performance:

> Such an interpretation depends upon three general conventions — that a poem should be unified, that it should be thematically significant, and that this significance can take the form of reflection on poetry — and four general interpretive operations: that one should try to establish binary relations of opposition or equivalence, that one should look for and integrate puns and ambiguities, that items may be read as synecdoches (or metaphors, etc.) in order to attain the level of generality required, and that what a poem says can be related to the fact that it is a poem. (p. 177)

Culler's discussion of the poetics of fiction is less successful, partly because only a small fraction of novels depend for their effect, to the extent that modernist lyric poems do, upon peculiarities of language and thus upon the conventions and naturalization operations through which we read them. The lyric is typically a short and difficult utterance, but in scope it is often scarcely longer than a single speech by a character in a fictional work. The difficulty in analyzing fiction comes instead from the immense number of levels of plot, character, theme, and narrative structure that have to be integrated by the reader. Instead of presenting his own poetics of the novel, Culler presents elements from a variety of theories, including those of Northrop Frye, Tzvetan Todorov, and Roland Barthes.

---

[7]Culler's idea of literary competence is not precisely equivalent to Chomsky's notion of linguistic competence. Chomsky's notion of competence is constant throughout very different natural languages, and he has claimed that certain analytic and synthetic capacities are linguistic universals. Culler's notion of competence is restricted to a description of interpretive conventions in Western Europe and America during the late twentieth century. One of his notions, seemingly incontrovertible when the book appeared — that poems will be interpreted to maximize their unity — no longer seems so solid in the poststructuralist age.

# THE POETICS OF FICTION: ECO, TODOROV, GENETTE

When Culler wrote *Structuralist Poetics,* very little of the work of Umberto Eco had been translated from Italian; *The Role of the Reader* did not appear until 1979, although its constituent essays had been printed in various periodicals as early as 1962. Eco is surely one of the most important semioticians currently at work, though he has become famous more for his best-selling medieval detective story, *The Name of the Rose* (1983), than for his semiological theories. The essay reprinted here, "The Myth of Superman" from *The Role of the Reader,* is typical in its combination of wit and intellectual rigor and in its immense range of reference, from revered texts like *Oedipus Rex* and *Finnegans Wake* to ephemera like Superman comics, Nero Wolfe detective stories, and the "Doctor Kildare" television series. Eco's essay takes up only one very limited question within narrative poetics: the way narrative time needs to be handled in fiction that belongs to a series, which must therefore be designed to have an indefinite number of sequels. It has been included as an example of what can be done practically, using a structuralist poetics of narrative. But *The Role of the Reader* as a whole has a much broader program: to understand the levels of discourse that occur within narratives (Eco's complex diagram lists ten such levels) and the interactions among them that give rise to interpretation. The result will be to reveal how each text produces the exact sort of Model Reader it needs to bring out its qualities — how "closed" texts elicit passively credulous and "open" texts actively suspicious readings.[8]

Tzvetan Todorov's "The Structural Analysis of Literature," also an essay in practical criticism, takes up a more respectable subject than Superman comics: the tales of Henry James. Todorov's essay uses a model of the structural analysis of fiction to justify the hypothesis that "the Jamesian narrative is always based on *the quest for an absolute and absent cause*" (italics in original). Like Eco, Todorov is applying a broader theory, which he calls "the grammar of narrative." In this grammar, Todorov uses some of the traditional parts of speech as narratological categories: Narratives are an interaction between *proper names* (i.e., characters), *verbs* (actions), and *adjectives* (qualities); the *modal auxiliaries* give us the special moods and outcomes of the stories. Todorov often gets striking results with his method, as in the essay reprinted here, but the method itself is primarily a typology of characters and actions such as was previously explored by Russian formalists like Boris Tomashevsky and Vladimir Propp. (Todorov, it may be recalled, was the Bulgaria-born critic who translated the Russian formalists into French and popularized their work.)

Perhaps the most influential theorist of narrative is Gérard Genette, whose trilogy *Figures* contains a series of arrestingly original and interconnected essays on the art of both fiction and poetry. As the overall title of the three volumes suggests,

---

[8]These are not exhaustive categories. Eco finds a third sort of text, "an exclusive club whose chairman is probably *Tristam Shandy,*" which is neither open nor closed but operates as a trap. It lures the reader into "an excess of cooperation and then punishes him for having overdone it."

Genette's interest was in tropes, figures of speech; but he is far from being a naive grammarian, interested only in classifying and regulating the use of tropes. Figures of speech are important because they introduce into the usual system of signification a discontinuity requiring the reader's mediation. When we refer to "twenty sail of the line" instead of "twenty ships" we use the figure of *synecdoche* — the part for the whole. As we interpret the figure, we note the presence of one signifier (sail) and the absence of another (ship). Thus, the working of the figure depends on something it cannot contain: the reader's sense of the absent signifier. Or, as Genette put it, "A figure is a gap in relation to usage, but a gap that is nevertheless a part of usage: that is the paradox of rhetoric."

In "Frontiers of Narrative" Genette goes over some of the commonplace distinctions of narratology, such as the *diegetic* (narrative) versus the *mimetic* (dramatic), or narration and description, always with a view toward shaking up the conventional distinctions and making the reader see the issues anew. For instance, Genette examines the distinctions between narrative (which presumes the existence of a narrator, a speaker, and hence a point of view), and pure discourse (which has no speaker and seems to come from no subjective source). Stylisticians, like Émile Benveniste, had suggested that the distinction between narrative and discourse was essentially grammatical, that narrative could be defined in terms of certain words or usages — the first- and second-person pronouns, or adverbs like "here" or "then," which presuppose a spatial or temporal reference. Genette demonstrates to the contrary that the matter is far subtler and more complex and that apparently pure discourse often contains implicit appeals and judgments that make sense only in the context of a narrative. With both poetic figures and narrative techniques, Genette's version of the reader's necessary participation in the literary process links him, as it links the semiotician Umberto Eco, with the reader-response theorists in Chapter 7.

## THE PASSING OF STRUCTURALISM

Here we should conclude by considering the decline of structuralism as a movement. Structuralism had slowly grown in influence from just after World War II until the middle of the 1960s, spreading from the anthropological studies of Lévi-Strauss to affect the study of literature, philosophy, history, mathematics, politics, economics — all the human sciences. There was a palpable sense at the time that a new method for the synthesis of knowledge was at hand, a method more powerful than the synthesis provided by Platonic dialectic in the ancient world or by Thomistic logic in the Middle Ages. The notion, barely glimpsed, that by using the tools of semiotics and linguistics, structuralism might manage to reunite the branches of knowledge that post-Renaissance specialization had severed, gave its adherents a messianic sense of mission. But in the late 1960s, as radical politics came and went leaving disillusion in its wake, the confident, broadly humanistic, universalizing mission of structuralism floundered as well.

The primary problem was the irresponsible promises of a synthesis of all human knowledge, promises that were slow in bearing fruit. Many adherents expounded the principles of structuralism and made claims for what structuralism would surely do for the study of literature, but few produced concrete achievements that justified those claims. The claims may in fact have been implausible. One question we have already raised in the discussion of Baudelaire's "The Cats" is whether the enabling assumption of structuralism — that everything is a language — is adequate. As James Phelan has suggested, literature is a *second-order* sign system built upon the *first-order* sign system of language. In effect, structuralism stands or falls on its assumption that a second-order system must reproduce the categories and relations of the first-order system. But we have no evidence that this must be the case, and natural science suggests the contrary: Biology, built on biochemistry, does not imitate its organization nor does chemistry, built on molecular physics, reproduce its lower-order system.

Structuralism may also have lost momentum because it had shifted the focus of the study of literature from the exegesis of individual texts to the exploration of general conditions of the act of interpretation. Ironically, the poststructuralist method of deconstruction, despite its implicit attack on the traditional values and bases of humanistic study, proceeds according to the techniques of close reading in which literary critics throughout the English-speaking world had already been trained under the dominance of New Criticism. In some ways, therefore, it was easier for American academics to follow deconstructionists such as Jacques Derrida and Paul de Man than to carry on the quest of Jakobson, Todorov, and Genette.

But of course, in another sense, structuralism is not dead at all. Though it has had to relinquish its broadest assumptions together with its character as a world-historical movement, most of its original adherents — like Todorov and Eco, Genette and Riffaterre — have continued to pursue the study of systems of signs, and the results of their study have become, under the names semiotics, stylistics, and narratology, essential elements in the current battery of approaches to literature.

## Selected Bibliography

Bal, Mieke. *Narratology.* Paris: Klincksieck, 1977.
Barthes, Roland. *Writing Degree Zero.* 1953; New York: Beacon, 1970.
———. *Critical Essays.* 1964; Evanston: Northwestern University Press, 1970.
———. *Mythologies.* 1957; New York: Hill and Wang, 1972.
———. *S/Z.* 1970; New York: Hill and Wang, 1974.
———. *The Pleasure of the Text.* New York: Hill and Wang, 1975.
———. *Sade, Fourier, Loyola.* New York: Hill and Wang, 1976.
———. *Image, Music, Text.* New York: Hill and Wang, 1977.
———. *A Barthes Reader.* New York: Hill and Wang, 1982.
———. *The Responsibility of Forms: New Critical Essays on Music, Art and Representation.* New York: Hill and Wang, 1984.
———. *The Rustle of Language.* New York: Hill and Wang, 1986.
Benveniste, Émile. *Problems in General Linguistics.* Coral Gables, Fla.: University of Miami Press, 1971.

Boon, James A. *From Symbolism to Structuralism: Lévi-Strauss in a Literary Tradition*. Oxford: Blackwell, 1972.

Brooke-Rose, Christine. *A Grammar of Metaphor*. London: Secker and Warburg, 1958.

———. *A Structural Analysis of Pound's Usura Canto: Jakobson's Method Extended and Applied to Free Verse*. The Hague: Mouton, 1976.

———. *A Rhetoric of the Unreal: Studies in Narrative and Structure, Especially of the Fantastic*. New York: Cambridge University Press, 1981.

Cassirer, Ernst. "Structuralism in Modern Linguistics." *Word* 1 (1945): 99–120.

———. *Symbol, Myth and Culture*. New Haven: Yale University Press, 1979.

Chatman, Seymour, ed. *Essays on the Language of Literature*. Boston: Houghton Mifflin, 1967.

———. *Story and Discourse: Narrative Structure in Fiction and Film*. Ithaca: Cornell University Press, 1978.

Chomsky, Noam. *Syntactic Structures*. The Hague: Mouton, 1957.

———. *Aspects of the Theory of Syntax*. Cambridge: MIT Press, 1965.

Cohn, Dorrit. *Transparent Minds: Narrative Modes for Presenting Consciousness in Fiction*. Princeton: Princeton University Press, 1978.

Culler, Jonathan. *Structuralist Poetics*. Ithaca: Cornell University Press, 1975.

———. *Roland Barthes*. New York: Oxford University Press, 1984.

———. *Ferdinand de Saussure*. Ithaca: Cornell University Press, 1986.

Eco, Umberto. *A Theory of Semiotics*. Bloomington: Indiana University Press, 1975.

———. *The Role of the Reader: Explorations in the Semiotics of Texts*. Bloomington, Indiana University Press, 1979.

———. *Semiotics and the Philosophy of Language*. London: Macmillan, 1984.

Foucault, Michel. *The Order of Things: An Archaeology of the Human Sciences*. London: Tavistock, 1970.

———. *Language, Counter-Memory, Practice*. Ithaca: Cornell University Press, 1977.

Fowler, Roger. *Linguistics and the Novel*. London: Methuen, 1977.

Garvin, Paul. *A Prague School Reader on Esthetics, Literary Structure, and Style*. Washington, D.C.: Georgetown University Press, 1964.

Genette, Gérard. *Narrative Discourse: An Essay in Method*. Ithaca: Cornell University Press, 1980.

———. *Figures of Literary Discourse*. New York: Columbia University Press, 1982.

Greimas, A. J. *Structural Semantics: An Attempt at a Method*. Lincoln: University of Nebraska Press, 1984.

Guillèn, Claudio. *Literature as System*. Princeton: Princeton University Press, 1971.

Harari, Josué. *Structuralists and Structuralisms*. Ithaca: Diacritics, 1971.

Harris, Zellig. *Methods in Structural Linguistics*. Chicago: University of Chicago Press, 1951.

Hartman, Geoffrey H. *Beyond Formalism*. New Haven: Yale University Press, 1970.

Hawkes, Terence. *Structuralism and Semiotics*. Berkeley: University of California Press, 1977.

Hjelmslev, Louis. *Prolegomena to a Theory of Language*. Madison: University of Wisconsin Press, 1961.

Jakobson, Roman. *Selected Writings*. 7 vols. The Hague: Mouton, 1962–.

Jakobson, Roman, and Lawrence Jones. *Shakespeare's Verbal Art in "Th' Expense of Spirit."* The Hague: Mouton, 1970.

Jameson, Fredric. *The Prison House of Language: A Critical Account of Structuralism and Russian Formalism*. Princeton: Princeton University Press, 1971.

Lane, Michael, ed. *Structuralism: A Reader*. London: Cape, 1970.

Leach, Edmund. *Genesis as Myth and Other Essays*. London: Cape, 1969.

Lévi-Strauss, Claude. *Structural Anthropology*. 1958; New York: Basic Books, 1963.

———. *The Savage Mind*. Chicago: University of Chicago Press, 1966.

———. *The Raw and the Cooked*. 1964; New York: Harper and Row, 1969.

———. *From Honey to Ashes*. 1966; London: Cape, 1973.

Lotman, Yuri. *Analysis of the Poetic Text*. Ann Arbor: Ardis, 1976.

Lyons, John. *Structural Semantics*. Oxford: Blackwell, 1973.

Macksey, Richard, and Eugenio Donato, eds. *The Languages of Criticism and the Sciences of Man*. Baltimore: Johns Hopkins University Press, 1970.

Piaget, Jean. *Structuralism*. New York: Basic Books, 1970.

Prince, Gerald. "Introduction à l'étude du narrataire." *Poétique* 14 (1963): 178–96.

Propp, Vladimir. *The Morphology of the Folktale*. Bloomington: Indiana Research Center in Anthropology, 1958.

Ricoeur, Paul. *The Conflict of Interpretations: Essays in Hermeneutics*. Evanston: Northwestern University Press, 1974.

———. *The Rule of Metaphor*. Toronto: University of Toronto Press, 1977.

———. *Time and Narrative*. Chicago: University of Chicago Press, 1984.

Riffaterre, Michael. *Semiotics of Poetry*. Bloomington: Indiana University Press, 1978.

———. *Text Production*. New York: Columbia University Press, 1983.

Robey, David, ed. *Structuralism: An Introduction*. London: Oxford University Press, 1973.

Saussure, Ferdinand de. *Course in General Linguistics*. 1923; New York: Philosophical Library, 1959.

Scholes, Robert. "Toward a Semiotics of Literature." *Critical Inquiry* 4 (1977): 105–20.

Searle, John. *Speech Acts*. Cambridge: Cambridge University Press, 1969.

Sebeok, Thomas, ed. *Style in Language*. Cambridge: MIT Press, 1964.

———, ed. *Approaches to Semiotics*. The Hague: Mouton, 1964.

Segre, Cesare. *Semiotics and Literary Criticism*. The Hague: Mouton, 1975.

Starobinski, Jean. *Words upon Words: The Anagrams of Ferdinand de Saussure*. New Haven: Yale University Press, 1979.

Todorov, Tzvetan. *The Fantastic: A Structural Approach to a Literary Genre*. Ithaca: Cornell University Press, 1975.

———. *The Poetics of Prose*. Ithaca: Cornell University Press, 1977.

———. *Introduction to Poetics*. Minneapolis: University of Minnesota Press, 1981.

———. *Symbolism and Interpretation*. Ithaca: Cornell University Press, 1982.

———. *Theories of the Symbol*. Ithaca: Cornell University Press, 1982.

Ullmann, Stephen. *Language and Style*. Oxford: Blackwell, 1964.

Uspensky, Boris. *A Poetics of Composition*. Berkeley: University of California Press, 1973.

Vachek, Joseph. *The Linguistic School of Prague*. Bloomington: Indiana University Press, 1966.

# Jan Mukařovský

## 1891–1975

*The philosopher Jan Mukařovský, best known in America for his work with the Prague school of structural linguistics, was born in Písek, Czechoslovakia. For virtually all of his professional life he was affiliated with Charles University in Prague, where he was appointed lecturer in aesthetics in 1929 and full professor in 1938. Mukařovský was the director of the Institute for Czech Literature and the cofounder of the Czechoslovak Academy of Sciences (1951). His academic and civil honors were numerous, as were his publications, although relatively few of them have been translated into English. "Standard Language and Poetic Language" was first published in 1948 in the second edition of* Chapters on Czech Poetry; *this translation is from* A Prague School Reader on Esthetics, Literary Structure, and Style *(1964), edited by Paul L. Garvin. Samples of Mukařovský's work have been more recently collected and translated by John Burbank and Peter Steiner in* The Word in Verbal Art *(1977) and* Structure, Sign, and Function *(1978).*

# Standard Language and Poetic Language

The problem of the relationship between standard language and poetic language can be considered from two standpoints. The theorist of poetic language poses it somewhat as follows: is the poet bound by the norms of the standard? Or perhaps: how does this norm assert itself in poetry? The theorist of the standard language, on the other hand, wants to know above all to what extent a work of poetry can be used as data for ascertaining the norm of the standard. In other words, the theory of poetic language is primarily interested in the differences between the standard and poetic language, whereas the theory of the standard language is mainly interested in the similarities between them. It is clear that with a good procedure no conflict can arise between the two directions of research: there is only a difference in the point of view and in the illumination of the problem. Our study approaches the problem of the relationship between poetic language and the standard from the vantage point of poetic language. Our procedure will be to subdivide the general problem into a number of special problems.

Translated by Paul L. Garvin.

The first problem, by way of introduction, concerns the following: what is the *relationship* between the extension of *poetic language* and that of the *standard,* between the places of each in the total system of the whole of language? Is poetic language a special brand of the standard, or is it an independent formation? — Poetic language cannot be called a brand of the standard, if for no other reason that poetic language has at its disposal, from the standpoint of lexicon, syntax, etc., all the forms of the given language — often of different developmental phases thereof. There are works in which the lexical material is taken over completely from another form of language than the standard (thus, Villon's or Rictus's slang poetry in French literature). Different forms of the language may exist side by side in a work of poetry (for instance, in the dialogues of a novel dialect or slang, in the narrative passages the standard). Poetic language finally also has some of its own lexicon and phraseology as well as some grammatical forms, the so-called poetisms such as *zor* [gaze], *oř* [steed], *pláti* [be aflame], 3rd p. sg. *můž* [can; cf. English *-th*] (a rich selection of examples can be found in the ironic description of "moon language" in [Svatopluk] Čech's [1846–1908, a realist] *Výlet pana*

*Broučka do měsíce* [Mr. Brouček's Trip to the Moon]). Only some schools of poetry, of course, have a positive attitude towards poetisms (among them the Lumír Group including Svatopluk Čech), others reject them.

Poetic language is thus not a brand of the standard. This is not to deny the close connection between the two, which consists in the fact that, for poetry, the standard language is the background against which is reflected the esthetically intentional distortion of the linguistic components of the work, in other words, the intentional violation of the norm of the standard. Let us, for instance, visualize a work in which this distortion is carried out by the interpretation of dialect speech with the standard; it is clear, then, that it is not the standard which is perceived as a distortion of the dialect, but the dialect as a distortion of the standard, even when the dialect is quantitatively preponderant. The violation of the norm of the standard, its systematic violation, is what makes possible the poetic utilization of language; without this possibility there would be no poetry. The more the norm of the standard is stabilized in a given language, the more varied can be its violation, and therefore the more possibilities for poetry in that language. And on the other hand, the weaker the awareness of this norm, the fewer possibilities of violation, and hence the fewer possibilities for poetry. Thus, in the beginnings of Modern Czech poetry, when the awareness of the norm of the standard was weak, poetic neologisms with the purpose of violating the norm of the standard were little different from neologisms designed to gain general acceptance and become a part of the norm of the standard, so that they could be confused with them.

Such is the case of M. Z. Polák [1788–1856, an early romantic], whose neologisms are to this day considered poor neologisms of the standard.

A structural analysis of Polák's[1] poem would

show that [Josef] Jungmann [a leading figure of the Czech national renascence] was right [in evaluating Polák's poetry positively]. We are here citing the disagreement in the evaluation of Polák's neologisms merely as an illustration of the statement that, when the norm of the standard is weak — as was the case in the period of national renascence, it is difficult to differentiate the devices intended to shape this norm from those intended for its consistent and deliberate violation, and that a language with a weak norm of the standard therefore offers fewer devices to the poet.

This relationship between poetic language and the standard, one which we could call negative, also has its positive side which is, however, more important for the theory of the standard language than for poetic language and its theory. Many of the linguistic components of a work of poetry do not deviate from the norm of the standard because they constitute the background against which the distortion of the other components is reflected. The theoretician of the standard language can therefore include works of poetry in his data with the reservation that he will differentiate the distorted components from those that are not distorted. An assumption that all components have to agree with the norm of the standard would, of course, be erroneous.

The second special question which we shall attempt to answer concerns the different *function* of the two forms of language. This is the core of the problem. The function of poetic language consists in the maximum of foregrounding of the utterance. Foregrounding is the opposite of automatization, that is, the deautomatization of an act;[2] the more an act is automatized, the less it is consciously executed: the more it is foregrounded, the more completely conscious does it become. Objectively speaking: automatization schematizes an event; foregrounding means the violation of the scheme. The standard language in its purest form, as the language of science with formulation as its objective, avoids foregrounding [aktualisace]: thus, a new expression, foregrounded because of its newness, is imme-

---

[1]It is important to note that Polák himself in lexical notes to his poem clearly distinguishes little-known works (including obvious neologisms and new loans) from those which he used "for better poetic expression," that is, as is shown by the evidence, from poetic neologisms. [Au.]

[2]See Victor Shklovsky's treatment of the estrangement of language by art in "Art as Technique," in Ch. 3. [Ed.]

diately automatized in a scientific treatise by an exact definition of its meaning. Foregrounding is, of course, common in the standard language, for instance, in journalistic style, even more in essays. But here it is always subordinate to communication: its purpose is to attract the reader's (listener's) attention more closely to the subject matter expressed by the foregrounded means of expression. All that has been said there about foregrounding and automatization in the standard language has been treated in detail in Havránek's paper in this cycle; we are here concerned with poetic language. In poetic language foregrounding achieves maximum intensity to the extent of pushing communication into the background as the objective of expression and of being used for its own sake; it is not used in the services of communication, but in order to place in the foreground the act of expression, the act of speech itself. The question is then one of how this maximum of foregrounding is achieved in poetic language. The idea might arise that this is a quantitative effect, a matter of the foregrounding of the largest number of components, perhaps of all of them together. This would be a mistake, although only a theoretical one, since in practice such a complete foregrounding of all the components is impossible. The foregrounding of any one of the components is necessarily accompanied by the automatization of one or more of the other components; thus, for instance, the foregrounded intonation in [Jaroslav] Vrchlický [1853–1912, a poet of the Lumír Group, see above] and [Svatopluk] Čech has necessarily pushed to the lowest level of automatization the meaning of the word as a unit, because the foregrounding of its meaning would give the word phonetic independence as well and lead to a disturbance of the uninterrupted flow of the intonational (melodic) line; an example of the degree to which the semantic independence of the word in context also manifests itself as intonational independence can be found in [Karel] Toman's [1877–1946, a modern poet] verse. The foregrounding of intonation as an uninterrupted melodic line is thus linked to the semantic "emptiness" for which the Lumír Group has been criticized by the younger generation as being "verbalistic." — In addition to the practical impossibility of the foregrounding of all components, it can also be pointed out that the simultaneous foregrounding of all the components of a work of poetry is unthinkable. This is because the foregrounding of a component implies precisely its being placed in the foreground; the unit in the foreground, however, occupies this position by comparison with another unit or units that remain in the background. A simultaneous general foregrounding would thus bring all the components into the same plane and so become a new automatization.

The devices by which poetic language achieves its maximum of foregrounding must therefore be sought elsewhere than in the quantity of foregrounded components. They consist in the consistency and systematic character of foregrounding. The consistency manifests itself in the fact that the reshaping of the foregrounded component within a given work occurs in a stable direction; thus, the deautomatization of meanings in a certain work is consistently carried out by lexical selection (the mutual interlarding of contrasting areas of the lexicon), in another equally consistently by the uncommon semantic relationship of words close together in the context. Both procedures result in a foregrounding of meaning, but differently for each. The systematic foregrounding of components in a work of poetry consists in the gradation of the interrelationships of these components, that is, in their mutual subordination and superordination. The component highest in the hierarchy becomes the dominant. All other components, foregrounded or not, as well as their interrelationships, are evaluated from the standpoint of the dominant. The dominant is that component of the work which sets in motion, and gives direction to, the relationships of all other components. The material of a work of poetry is intertwined with the interrelationships of the components even if it is in a completely unforegrounded state. Thus, there is always present, in communicative speech as well, the potential relationship between intonation[3] and meaning, syntax, word order, or the relationship of the word as a meaningful unit

[3]Pronunciation: the phonetic component of language. [Ed.]

to the phonetic structure of the text, to the lexical selection found in the text, to other words as units of meaning in the context of the same sentence. It can be said that each linguistic component is linked directly or indirectly, by means of these multiple interrelationships, in some way to every other component. In communicative speech these relationships are for the most part merely potential, because attention is not called to their presence and to their mutual relationship. It is, however, enough to disturb the equilibrium of this system at some point and the entire network of relationships is slanted in a certain direction and follows it in its internal organization: tension arises in one portion of this network (by consistent unidirectional foregrounding), while the remaining portions of the network are relaxed (by automatization perceived as an intentionally arranged background). This internal organization of relationships will be different in terms of the point affected, that is, in terms of the dominant. More concretely: sometimes intonation will be governed by meaning (by various procedures), sometimes, on the other hand, the meaning structure will be determined by intonation; sometimes again, the relationship of a word to the lexicon may be foregrounded, then again its relationship to the phonetic structure of the text. Which of the possible relationships will be foregrounded, which will remain automatized, and what will be the direction of foregrounding — whether from component A to component B or vice versa, all this depends on the dominant.

The dominant thus creates the unity of the work of poetry. It is, of course, a unity of its own kind, the nature of which in esthetics is usually designated as "unity in variety," a dynamic unity in which we at the same time perceive harmony and disharmony, convergence and divergence. The convergence is given by the trend towards the dominant, the divergence by the resistance of the unmoving background of unforegrounded components against this trend. Components may appear unforegrounded from the standpoint of the standard language, or from the standpoint of the poetic canon, that is, the set of firm and stable norms into which the structure of a preceding school of poetry has dissolved by automatization, when it is no longer perceived

as an indivisible and undissociable whole. In other words, it is possible in some cases for a component which is foregrounded in terms of the norms of the standard, not to be foregrounded in a certain work because it is in accord with the automatized poetic canon. Every work of poetry is perceived against the background of a certain tradition, that is, of some automatized canon with regard to which it constitutes a distortion. The outward manifestation of this automatization is the ease with which creation is possible in terms of this canon, the proliferation of epigones, the liking for obsolescent poetry in circles not close to literature. Proof of the intensity with which a new trend in poetry is perceived as a distortion of the traditional canon is the negative attitude of conservative criticism which considers deliberate deviations from the canon errors against the very essence of poetry.

The background which we perceive behind the work of poetry as consisting of the unforegrounded components resisting foregrounding is thus dual: the norm of the standard language and the traditional esthetic canon. Both backgrounds are always potentially present, though one of them will predominate in the concrete case. In periods of powerful foregrounding of linguistic elements, the background of the norm of the standard predominates, while in periods of moderate foregrounding, that of the traditional canon. If the latter has strongly distorted the norm of the standard, then its moderate distortion may, in turn, constitute a renewal of the norm of the standard, and this precisely because of its moderation. The mutual relationships of the components of the work of poetry, both foregrounded and unforegrounded, constitute its *structure*, a dynamic structure including both convergence and divergence and one that constitutes an indissociable artistic whole, since each of its components has its value precisely in terms of its relation to the totality.

It is thus obvious that the possibility of distorting the norm of the standard, if we henceforth limit ourselves to this particular background of foregrounding, is indispensable to poetry. Without it, there would be no poetry. To criticize the deviations from the norm of the standard as faults, especially in a period which, like the present, tends towards a powerful foregrounding of linguistic components, means to reject poetry. It could be countered that in some works of poetry, or rather in some genres, only the "content" (subject matter) is foregrounded, so that the above remarks do not concern them. To this it must be noted that in a work of poetry of any genre there is no fixed border, nor, in a certain sense, any essential difference between the language and the subject matter. The subject matter of a work of poetry cannot be judged by its relationship to the extralinguistic reality entering into the work; it is rather a component of the semantic side of the work (we do not want to assert, of course, that its relationship to reality cannot become a factor of its structure, as for instance in realism). The proof of this statement could be given rather extensively; let us, however, limit ourselves to the most important point: the question of truthfulness does not apply in regard to the subject matter of a work of poetry, nor does it even make sense. Even if we posed the question and answered it positively or negatively as the case may be, the question has no bearing on the artistic value of the work; it can only serve to determine the extent to which the work has documentary value. If in some work of poetry there is emphasis on the question of truthfulness (as in [Vladislav] Vančura's [1891–1942, a modern author] short story *Dobrá míra* [The Good Measure]), this emphasis only serves the purpose of giving the subject matter a certain semantic coloration. The status of subject matter is entirely different in case of communicative speech. There, a certain relationship of the subject matter to reality is an important value, a necessary prerequisite. Thus, in the case of a newspaper report the question whether a certain event has occurred or not is obviously of basic significance.

The subject matter of a work of poetry is thus its largest semantic unit. In terms of being meaning, it has certain properties which are not directly based on the linguistic sign, but are linked to it insofar as the latter is a general semiological unit (especially its independence of any specific signs, or sets of signs, so that the same subject matter may without basic changes be rendered by different linguistic devices, or even transposed into a different set of signs altogether, as in the transposition of subject matter from one art form to another), but this difference in properties does not affect the semantic character of the subject matter. It thus holds, even for works and genres of poetry in which the subject matter is the dominant, that the latter is not the "equivalent" of a reality to be expressed by the work as effectively (for instance, as truthfully) as possible, but that it is a part of the structure, is governed by its laws, and is evaluated in terms of its relationship to it. If this is the case, then it holds for the novel as well as for the lyrical poem that to deny a work of poetry the right to violate the norm of the standard is equivalent to the negation of poetry. It cannot be said of the novel that here the linguistic elements are the esthetically indifferent expression of content, not even if they appear to be completely devoid of foregrounding: the structure is the total of all the components, and its dynamics arises precisely from the tension between the foregrounded and unforegrounded components. There are, incidentally, many novels and short stories in which the linguistic components are clearly foregrounded. Changes effected in the interest of correct language would thus, even in the case of prose, often interfere with the very essence of the work; this would, for instance, happen if the author or even translator decided, as was asked in *Naše Řeč,* to eliminate "superfluous" relative clauses.

There still remains the problem of *esthetic values* in language outside of the realm of poetry. A recent Czech opinion has it that "esthetic evaluation must be excluded from language, since there is no place where it can be applied. It is useful and necessary for judging style, but not language" (J. Haller, *Problém jazykové správnosti* [The Problem of Correct Language], Výroční zpráva č. st. ref reál. gymnasia v Ústí nad Labem za r. (1930–31, p. 23). I am leaving aside the criticism of the terminologically inaccurate opposition of style and language; but I do want to point out, in opposition to Haller's thesis, that esthetic valuation is a very important factor in the formation of the norm of the standard; on the one hand because the conscious refinement of the language cannot do without it, on the other hand because it sometimes, in part, determines the development of the norm of the standard.

Let us start with a general discussion of the field of esthetic phenomena. It is clear that this field by far exceeds the confines of the arts. Dessoir says about it: "The striving for beauty need not be limited in its manifestations to the specific forms of the arts. The esthetic needs are, on the contrary, so potent that they affect *almost all* acts of man."[4] If the area of esthetic phenomena is indeed so broad, it becomes obvious that esthetic valuation has its place beyond the confines of the arts; we can cite as examples the esthetic factors in sexual selection, fashion, the social amenities, the culinary arts, etc. There is, of course, a difference between esthetic valuation in the arts and outside of art. In the arts, esthetic valuation necessarily stands highest in the hierarchy of the values contained in the work, whereas outside of art its position vacillates and is usually subordinate. Furthermore, in the arts we evaluate each component in terms of the structure of the work in question, and the yardstick is in each individual case determined by the function of the component within the structure. Outside of art, the various components of the phenomenon to be evaluated are not integrated into an esthetic structure and the yardstick becomes the established norm that applies to the component in question, wherever the latter occurs. If, then, the area of esthetic valuation is so broad that it includes "almost all of the acts of man," it is indeed not very probable that language would be exempt from esthetic valuation; in other words, that its use would not be subject to the laws of taste. There is direct proof that esthetic valuation is one of the basic criteria of purism, and that even the development of the norm of the standard cannot be imagined without it.

Esthetic valuation clearly has its indispensable place in the refinement of language, and those purists who deny its validity are unconsciously passing judgment on their own practice. Without an esthetic point of view, no other form of the cultivation of good language is possible, even one much more efficient than purism. This does not mean that he who intends to cultivate good language has the right to judge language in line with his personal taste, as is done precisely by the purists. Such an intervention into the development of the standard language is efficient and purposeful only in periods when the conscious esthetic valuation of phenomena has become a social fact — as was the case in France in the 17th century. In other periods, including the present, the esthetic point of view has more of a regulatory function in the cultivation of good language: he who is active in the cultivation of good language must take care not to force upon the standard language, in the name of correct language, modes of expression that violate the esthetic canon (set of norms) given in the language implicitly, but objectively; intervention without heed to the esthetic norms hampers, rather than advances, the development of the language. The esthetic canon, which differs not only from language to language, but also for different developmental periods of the same language (not counting in this context other functional formations of which each has its own esthetic canon), must therefore be ascertained by scientific investigation and be described as accurately as possible. This is the reason for the considerable significance of the question of the manner in which esthetic valuation influences the development of the norm of the standard. Let us first consider the manner in which the lexicon of the standard language is increased and renewed. Words originating in slang, dialects, or foreign languages, are, as we know from our own experience, often taken over because of their novelty and uncommonness, that is, for purposes of foregrounding in which esthetic valuation always plays a significant part. Words of the poetic language, poetic neologisms, can also enter the standard by this route, although in these cases we can also be dealing with acceptance for reasons of communication (need for a new shade of meaning). The influence of poetic language on the standard is, however, not limited to the vocabulary: intonational and syntactic patterns (clichés) can, for instance, also be taken over — the latter only for esthetic reasons since there is hardly any communicative necessity for a change of the sentence and intonation structure current

[4]M. Dessoir, *Ästhetik und allgemeine Kunstwissenschaft*, Stuttgart, 1906, p. 112. [Au.]

until then. Very interesting in this respect is the observation by the poet J. Cocteau in his book *Le secret professionnel* (Paris, 1922, p. 36) that "Stéphane Mallarmé even now influences the style of the daily press without the journalists' being aware of it." By way of explanation it must be pointed out that Mallarmé has very violently distorted French syntax and word order which is incomparably more bound in French than in Czech, being a grammatical factor. In spite of this intensive distortion, or perhaps because of it, Mallarmé influenced the development of the structure of the sentence in the standard language.

The effect of esthetic valuation on the development of the norm of the standard is undeniable; this is why the problem deserves the attention of the theorists. So far, we have, for instance, hardly even any lexical studies of the acceptance of poetic neologisms in Czech and of the reasons for this acceptance; [Antonín] Frinta's article *Rukopisné podvrhy a naše spisovná řeč* [The Fake Manuscripts (Václav Hanka's forgeries of purportedly Old Czech poetry, 1813, 1817) and our Standard Language] (Naše Řeč, vol. II) has remained an isolated attempt. It is also necessary to investigate the nature and range of esthetic valuation in the standard language. Esthetic valuation is based here, as always when it is not based on an artistic structure, on certain generally valid norms. In art, including poetry, each component is evaluated in relation to the structure. The problem in evaluating is to determine how and to what extent a given component fulfills the function proper to it in the total structure; the yardstick is given by the context of a given structure and does not apply to any other context. The proof lies in the fact that a certain component may by itself be perceived as a negative value in terms of the pertinent esthetic norm, if its distortional character is very prominent, but may be evaluated positively in terms of a particular structure and as its essential component precisely because of this distortional character. There is no esthetic structure outside of poetry, none in the standard language (nor in language in general). There is, however, a certain set of esthetic norms, each of which applies independently to a certain component of language. This set, or

canon, is constant only for a certain period and for a certain linguistic milieu; thus, the esthetic canon of the standard is different from that of slang. We therefore need a description and characterization of the esthetic canon of the standard language of today and of the development of this canon in the past. It is, of course, clear to begin with that this development is not independent of the changing structures in the art of poetry. The discovery and investigation of the esthetic canon accepted for a certain standard language would not only have theoretical significance as a part of its history, but also, as has already been said, be of practical importance in its cultivation.

Let us now return to the main topic of our study and attempt to draw some conclusions from what was said above of the relationship between the standard and poetic language.

Poetic language is a different form of language with a different function from that of the standard. It is therefore equally unjustified to call all poets, without exception, creators of the standard language as it is to make them responsible for its present state. This is not to deny the possibility of utilizing poetry as data for the scientific description of the norm of the standard (cf. pp. 18–19), nor the fact that the development of the norm of the standard does not occur uninfluenced by poetry. The distortion of the norm of the standard is, however, of the very essence of poetry, and it is therefore improper to ask poetic language to abide by this norm. This was clearly formulated as early as 1913 by Ferdinand Brunot (L'autorité en matière de langage, *Die neueren Sprachen,* vol. XX): "Modern art, individualistic in essence, cannot always and everywhere be satisfied with the standard language alone. The laws governing the usual communication of thought must not, lest it be unbearable tyranny, be categorically imposed upon the poet who, beyond the bounds of the accepted forms of language, may find personalized forms of intuitive expression. It is up to him to use them in accord with his creative intuition and without other limits than those imposed by his own inspiration. Public opinion will give the final verdict." It is interesting to compare Brunot's statement to one of Haller's of 1931 (*Problém jazykové správnosti,* op. cit. 3): "Our writers and poets in their creative effort attempt to replace the thorough knowledge of the material of the language by some sort of imaginary ability of which they themselves are not too sincerely convinced. They lay claim to a right which can but be an unjust privilege. Such an ability, instinct, inspiration, or what have you, cannot exist in and of itself; just as the famous feel for the language, it can only be the final result of previous cognition, and without consciously leaning on the finished material of the language, it is no more certain than any other arbitrary act." If we compare Brunot's statement to Haller's, the basic difference is clear without further comment. Let us also mention Jungmann's critique of Polák's *Vznešenost přírody* [The Sublimity of Nature] cited elsewhere in this study (p. 125 [see above]); Jungmann has there quite accurately pointed out as a characteristic feature of poetic language its "uncommonness," that is, its distortedness. — In spite of all that has been said here, the condition of the norm of the standard language is not without its significance to poetry, since the norm of the standard is precisely the background against which the structure of the work of poetry is projected, and in regard to which it is perceived as a distortion; the structure of a work of poetry can change completely from its origin if it is, after a certain time, projected against the background of a norm of the standard which has since changed.

In addition to the relationship of the norm of the standard to poetry, there is also the opposite relationship, that of poetry to the norm of the standard. We have already spoken of the influence of poetic language on the development of the standard; some remarks remain to be added. First of all, it is worth mentioning that the poetic foregrounding of linguistic phenomena, since it is its own purpose, cannot have the purpose of creating new means of communication (as Vossler and his school think). If anything passes from poetic language into the standard, it becomes a loan in the same way as anything taken over by the standard from any other linguistic milieu; even the motivation of the borrowing may be the same: a loan from poetic language may likewise be taken over by the standard from any other linguistic milieu; even the motivation of the bor-

rowing may be the same: a loan from poetic language may likewise be taken over for extra-esthetic, that is, communicative reasons, and conversely the motivation for borrowings from other functional dialects, such as slang, may be esthetic. Borrowings from poetic language are beyond the scope of the poet's intent. Thus, poetic neologisms arise as intentionally esthetic new formations, and their basic features are unexpectedness, unusualness, and uniqueness. Neologisms created for communicative purposes, on the other hand, tend towards common derivation patterns and easy classifiability in a certain lexical category; these are the properties allowing for their general usability. If, however, *poetic* neologisms were formed in view of their general usability, their esthetic function would be endangered thereby; they are, therefore, formed in an unusual manner, with considerable violence to the language, as regards both form and meaning.

The relationship between poetic language and the standard, their mutual approximation or increasing distance, changes from period to period. But even within the same period, and with the same norm of the standard, this relationship need not be the same for all poets. There are, generally speaking, three possibilities: the writer, say a novelist, may either not distort the linguistic components of his work at all (but this nondistortion is, as was shown above, in itself a fact of the total structure of his work), or he may distort it, but subordinate the linguistic distortion to the subject matter by giving substandard color to his lexicon in order to characterize personages and situations, for instance; or finally, he may distort the linguistic components in and of themselves by either subordinating the subject matter to the linguistic deformation, or emphasizing the contrast between the subject matter and its linguistic expression. An example of the first possibility might be [Jakub] Arbes [1840–1914, an early naturalist], of the second, some realistic novelists such as T. Nováková [1853–1912] or Z. Winter [1846–1912], of the third, [Vladislav] Vančura. It is obvious that as one goes from the first possibility to the third, the divergence between poetic language and the standard increases. This classification has of course been highly schematized for purposes of simplicity; the real situation is much more complex.

The problem of the relationship between the standard and poetic language does not, however, exhaust the significance of poetry as the art form which uses language as its material, for the standard language, or for the language of a nation in general. The very existence of poetry in a certain language has fundamental importance for this language. . . . By the very fact of foregrounding, poetry increases and refines the ability to handle language in general; it gives the language the ability to adjust more flexibly to new requirements and it gives it a richer differentiation of its means of expression. Foregrounding brings to the surface and before the eyes of the observer even such linguistic phenomena as remain quite covert in communicative speech, although they are important factors in language. Thus, for instance, Czech symbolism, especially O. Březina's [1868–1929] poetry, has brought to the fore of linguistic consciousness the essence of sentence meaning and the dynamic nature of sentence construction. From the standpoint of communicative speech, the meaning of a sentence appears as the total of the gradually accumulated meanings of the individual words, that is, without having independent existence. The real nature of the phenomenon is covered up by the automatization of the semantic design of the sentence. Words and sentences appear to follow each other with obvious necessity, as determined only by the nature of the message. Then there appears a work of poetry in which the relationship between the meanings of the individual words and the subject matter of the sentence has been foregrounded. The words here do not succeed each other naturally and inconspicuously, but within the sentence there occur semantic jumps, breaks, which are not conditioned by the requirements of communication, but given in the language itself. The device for achieving these sudden breaks is the constant intersection of the plane of basic meaning with the plane of figurative and metaphorical meaning; some words are for a certain part of the context to be understood in their figurative meaning, in other parts in their basic meaning, and such words, carrying a dual meaning, are precisely the points at which there are semantic breaks. There is also foregrounding of the relationship between the subject matter of the sentence and the words as well as of the semantic interrelationships of the words in the sentence. The subject matter of the sentence then appears as the center of attraction given from the beginning of the sentence, the effect of the subject matter on the words and of the words on the subject matter is revealed, and the determining force can be felt with which every word affects every other. The sentence comes alive before the eyes of the speech community: the structure is revealed as a concert of forces. (What was here formulated discursively, must of course be imagined as an unformulated intuitive cognition stored away for the future in the consciousness of the speech community.) Examples can be multiplied at will, but we shall cite no more. We wanted to give evidence for the statement that the main importance of poetry for language lies in the fact that it is an art.

# Claude Lévi-Strauss

b. 1908

*Claude Lévi-Strauss, one of the major figures of social anthropology and of twentieth-century intellectual life generally, was born in Brussels and took degrees in philosophy and law at the University of Paris (1927–32). From 1934 to 1937, Lévi-Strauss served as a professor of sociology at the University of São Paulo in Brazil; his research among the Brazilian Indians informs the heart of his intellectual autobiography,* Tristes Tropiques *(1955). From 1941 to 1945 he was a visiting professor at the New School for Social Research in New York, where he came in contact with the ideas of Roman Jakobson. Made director of studies at the École Practique des Haute Études of the University of Paris in 1950, he was appointed in 1959 to the chair of social anthropology at the Collège de France. Lévi-Strauss's works include* The Elementary Structures of Kinship *(1949),* Structural Anthropology *(1958),* The Savage Mind *(1962), and the four volumes of* Mythologiques *(1964–71; translations 1969 ff.) "The Structural Study of Myth" first appeared in* Journal of American Folklore *78 (1955); this version is from the 1963 translation of* Structural Anthropology.

# The Structural Study of Myth

*It would seem that mythological worlds have been built up only to be shattered again, and that new worlds were built from the fragments.*

— FRANZ BOAS[1]

Despite some recent attempts to renew them, it seems that during the past twenty years anthropology has increasingly turned from studies in the field of religion. At the same time, and precisely because the interest of professional anthropologists has withdrawn from primitive religion, all kinds of amateurs who claim to belong to other disciplines have seized this opportunity to move in, thereby turning into their private playground what we had left as a wasteland. The prospects for the scientific study of religion have thus been undermined in two ways.

The explanation for this situation lies to some extent in the fact that the anthropological study of religion was started by men like Tylor, Frazer, and Durkheim, who were psychologically oriented although not in a position to keep up with the progress of psychological research and theory. Their interpretations, therefore, soon became vitiated by the outmoded psychological approach which they used as their basis. Although they were undoubtedly right in giving their attention to intellectual processes, the way they handled these remained so crude that it discredited them altogether. This is much to be regretted, since, as Hocart so profoundly noted in his introduction to a posthumous book recently published,[2] psychological interpretations were withdrawn from the intellectual field only to be introduced again in the field of affectivity, thus adding to "the inherent defects of the psychological school . . . the mistake of deriving clear-cut ideas . . . from vague emotions." Instead of trying to enlarge the framework of our logic to include processes which, whatever their apparent differences, belong to the same kind of intellectual operation, a naïve attempt was made to reduce them to inarticulate emotional drives, which resulted only in hampering our studies.

Of all the chapters of religious anthropology probably none has tarried to the same extent as studies in the field of mythology. From a theoretical point of view the situation remains very much the same as it was fifty years ago, namely, chaotic. Myths are still widely interpreted in conflicting ways: as collective dreams, as the outcome of a kind of esthetic play, or as the basis of ritual. Mythological figures are considered as personified abstractions, divinized heroes, or fallen gods. Whatever the hypothesis, the choice amounts to reducing mythology either to idle play or to a crude kind of philosophic speculation.

In order to understand what a myth really is, must we choose between platitude and sophism? Some claim that human societies merely express, through their mythology, fundamental feelings common to the whole of mankind, such as love, hate, or revenge or that they try to provide some kind of explanations for phenomena which they cannot otherwise understand — astronomical,

Translated by Claire Jacobson and Brooke Grundfest Schoepf.

[1]In Boas's Introduction to James Teit, "Traditions of the Thompson River Indians of British Columbia," *Memoirs of the American Folklore Society,* VI (1898), p. 18. [Au.]

[2]A. M. Hocart, *Social Origins* (London: 1954), p. 7. [Au.]

meteorological, and the like. But why should these societies do it in such elaborate and devious ways, when all of them are also acquainted with empirical explanations? On the other hand, psychoanalysts and many anthropologists have shifted the problems away from the natural or cosmological toward the sociological and psychological fields. But then the interpretation becomes too easy: If a given mythology confers prominence on a certain figure, let us say an evil grandmother, it will be claimed that in such a society grandmothers are actually evil and that mythology reflects the social structure and the social relations; but should the actual data be conflicting, it would be as readily claimed that the purpose of mythology is to provide an outlet for repressed feelings. Whatever the situation, a clever dialectic will always find a way to pretend that a meaning has been found.

Mythology confronts the student with a situation which at first sight appears contradictory. On the one hand it would seem that in the course of a myth anything is likely to happen. There is no logic, no continuity. Any characteristic can be attributed to any subject; every conceivable relation can be found. With myth, everything becomes possible. But on the other hand, this apparent arbitrariness is belied by the astounding similarity between myths collected in widely different regions. Therefore the problem: If the content of a myth is contingent, how are we going to explain the fact that myths throughout the world are so similar?

It is precisely this awareness of a basic antinomy pertaining to the nature of myth that may lead us toward its solution. For the contradiction which we face is very similar to that which in earlier times brought considerable worry to the first philosophers concerned with linguistic problems; linguistics could only begin to evolve as a science after this contradiction had been overcome. Ancient philosophers reasoned about language the way we do about mythology. On the one hand, they did notice that in a given language certain sequences of sounds were associated with definite meanings, and they earnestly aimed at discovering a reason for the linkage between those *sounds* and that *meaning*. Their attempt, however, was thwarted from the very beginning

by the fact that the same sounds were equally present in other languages although the meaning they conveyed was entirely different. The contradiction was surmounted only by the discovery that it is the combination of sounds, not the sounds themselves, which provides the significant data.

It is easy to see, moreover, that some of the more recent interpretations of mythological thought originated from the same kind of misconception under which those early linguists were laboring. Let us consider, for instance, Jung's idea that a given mythological pattern — the so-called archetype — possesses a certain meaning. This is comparable to the long-supported error that a sound may possess a certain affinity with a meaning: for instance, the "liquid" semivowels with water, the open vowels with things that are big, large, loud, or heavy, etc., a theory which still has its supporters.[3] Whatever emendations the original formulation may now call for,[4] everybody will agree that the Saussurean principle of the *arbitrary character of linguistic signs* was a prerequisite for the accession of linguistics to the scientific level.

To invite the mythologist to compare his precarious situation with that of the linguist in the prescientific stage is not enough. As a matter of fact we may thus be led only from one difficulty to another. There is a very good reason why myth cannot simply be treated as language if its specific problems are to be solved; myth *is* language: to be known, myth has to be told; it is a part of human speech. In order to preserve its specificity we must be able to show that it is both the same thing as language, and also something different from it. Here, too, the past experience of linguists may help us. For language itself can be analyzed into things which are at the same time similar and yet different. This is precisely what is expressed in Saussure's distinction between *langue* and *parole,* one being the structural side

[3]See, for instance, Sir R. A. Paget, "The Origin of Language," *Journal of World History,* I, No. 2 (UNESCO, 1953). [Au.]

[4]See Émile Benveniste, "Nature du signe linguistique," *Acta Linguistica,* I, No. 1 (1939); and Chapter V in *Structural Anthropology.* [Au.]

of language, the other the statistical aspect of it, *langue* belonging to a reversible time, *parole* being nonreversible. If those two levels already exist in language, then a third one can conceivably be isolated.

We have distinguished *langue* and *parole* by the different time referents which they use. Keeping this in mind, we may notice that myth uses a third referent which combines the properties of the first two. On the one hand, a myth always refers to events alleged to have taken place long ago. But what gives the myth an operational value is that the specific pattern described is timeless; it explains the present and the past as well as the future. This can be made clear through a comparison between myth and what appears to have largely replaced it in modern societies, namely, politics. When the historian refers to the French Revolution, it is always as a sequence of past happenings, a nonreversible series of events the remote consequences of which may still be felt at present. But to the French politician, as well as to his followers, the French Revolution is both a sequence belonging to the past — as to the historian — and a timeless pattern which can be detected in the contemporary French social structure and which provides a clue for its interpretation, a lead from which to infer future developments. Michelet, for instance, was a politically minded historian. He describes the French Revolution thus: "That day . . . everything was possible. . . . Future became present . . . that is, no more time, a glimpse of eternity."[5] It is that double structure, altogether historical and ahistorical, which explains how myth, while pertaining to the realm of *parole* and calling for an explanation as such, as well as to that of *langue* in which it is expressed, can also be an absolute entity on a third level which, though it remains linguistic by nature, is nevertheless distinct from the other two.

A remark can be introduced at this point which will help to show the originality of myth in relation to other linguistic phenomena. Myth is the part of language where the formula *tra-*

*duttore, traditore*[6] reaches its lowest truth value. From that point of view it should be placed in the gamut of linguistic expressions at the end opposite to that of poetry, in spite of all the claims which have been made to prove the contrary. Poetry is a kind of speech which cannot be translated except at the cost of serious distortions; whereas the mythical value of the myth is preserved even through the worst translation. Whatever our ignorance of the language and the culture of the people where it originated, a myth is still felt as a myth by any reader anywhere in the world. Its substance does not lie in its style, its original music, or its syntax, but in the *story* which it tells. Myth is language, functioning on an especially high level where meaning succeeds practically at "taking off" from the linguistic ground on which it keeps on rolling.

To sum up the discussion at this point, we have so far made the following claims: (1) If there is a meaning to be found in mythology, it cannot reside in the isolated elements which enter into the composition of a myth, but only in the way those elements are combined. (2) Although myth belongs to the same category as language, being, as a matter of fact, only part of it, language in myth exhibits specific properties. (3) Those properties are only to be found *above* the ordinary linguistic level, that is, they exhibit more complex features than those which are to be found in any other kind of linguistic expression.

If the above three points are granted, at least as a working hypothesis, two consequences will follow: (1) Myth, like the rest of language, is made up of constituent units. (2) These constituent units presuppose the constituent units present in language when analyzed on other levels — namely, phonemes, morphemes, and sememes — but they, nevertheless, differ from the latter in the same way as the latter differ among themselves; they belong to a higher and more complex order. For this reason, we shall call them *gross constituent units*.

How shall we proceed in order to identify and isolate these gross constituent units or myth-

---

[5] Jules Michelet, *Histoire de la Révolution française*, IV, 1. I took this quotation from M. Merleau-Ponty, *Les Aventures de la dialectique* (Paris: 1955), p. 273. [Au.]

[6] To translate is to betray. [Ed.]

emes? We know that they cannot be found among phonemes, morphemes, or sememes, but only on a higher level; otherwise myth would become confused with any other kind of speech. Therefore, we should look for them on the sentence level. The only method we can suggest at this stage is to proceed tentatively, by trial and error, using as a check the principles which serve as a basis for any kind of structural analysis: economy of explanation; unity of solution; and ability to reconstruct the whole from a fragment, as well as later stages from previous ones.

The technique which has been applied so far by this writer consists in analyzing each myth individually, breaking down its story into the shortest possible sentences, and writing each sentence on an index card bearing a number corresponding to the unfolding of the story.

Practically each card will thus show that a certain function is, at a given time, linked to a given subject. Or, to put it otherwise, each gross constituent unit will consist of a *relation*.

However, the above definition remains highly unsatisfactory for two different reasons. First, it is well known to structural linguists that constituent units on all levels are made up of relations, and the true difference between our *gross* units and the others remains unexplained; second, we still find ourselves in the realm of a nonreversible time, since the numbers of the cards correspond to the unfolding of the narrative. Thus the specific character of mythological time, which as we have seen is both reversible and nonreversible, synchronic and diachronic, remains unaccounted for. From this springs a new hypothesis, which constitutes the very core of our argument: The true constituent units of a myth are not the isolated relations but *bundles of such relations,* and it is only as bundles that these relations can be put to use and combined so as to produce a meaning. Relations pertaining to the same bundle may appear diachronically at remote intervals, but when we have succeeded in grouping them together we have reorganized our myth according to a time referent of a new nature, corresponding to the prerequisite of the initial hypothesis, namely a two-dimensional time referent which is simultaneously diachronic and synchronic, and which accordingly integrates the characteristics of *langue* on the one hand, and those of *parole* on the other. To put it in even more linguistic terms, it is as though a phoneme were always made up of all its variants.

Two comparisons may help to explain what we have in mind.

Let us first suppose that archaeologists of the future coming from another planet would one day, when all human life had disappeared from the earth, excavate one of our libraries. Even if they were at first ignorant of our writing, they might succeed in deciphering it — an undertaking which would require, at some early stage, the discovery that the alphabet, as we are in the habit of printing it, should be read from left to right and from top to bottom. However, they would soon discover that a whole category of books did not fit the usual pattern — these would be the orchestra scores on the shelves of the music division. But after trying, without success, to decipher staffs one after the other, from the upper down to the lower, they would probably notice that the same patterns of notes recurred at intervals, either in full or in part, or that some patterns were strongly reminiscent of earlier ones. Hence the hypothesis: What if patterns showing affinity, instead of being considered in succession, were to be treated as one complex pattern and read as a whole? By getting at what we call *harmony,* they would then see that an orchestra score, to be meaningful, must be read diachronically along one axis — that is, page after page, and from left to right — and synchronically along the other axis, all the notes written vertically making up one gross constituent unit, that is, one bundle of relations.

The other comparison is somewhat different. Let us take an observer ignorant of our playing cards, sitting for a long time with a fortune-teller. He would know something of the visitors: sex, age, physical appearance, social situation, etc., in the same way as we know something of the different cultures whose myths we try to study. He would also listen to the séances and record them so as to be able to go over them and make comparisons — as we do when we listen to mythtelling and record it. Mathematicians to whom I have put the problem agree that if the man is bright and if the material available to him is sufficient, he may be able to reconstruct the nature of the deck of cards being used, that is, fifty-two or thirty-two cards according to the case, made up of four homologous sets consisting of the same units (the individual cards) with only one varying feature, the suit.

Now for a concrete example of the method we propose. We shall use the Oedipus myth, which is well known to everyone. I am well aware that the Oedipus myth has only reached us under late forms and through literary transmutations concerned more with esthetic and moral preoccupations than with religious or ritual ones, whatever these may have been. But we shall not interpret the Oedipus myth in literal terms, much less offer an explanation acceptable to the specialist. We simply wish to illustrate — and without reaching any conclusions with respect to it — a certain technique, whose use is probably not legitimate in this particular instance, owing to the problematic elements indicated above. The "demonstration" should therefore be conceived, not in terms of what the scientist means by this term, but at best in terms of what is meant by the street peddler, whose aim is not to achieve a concrete result, but to explain, as succinctly as possible, the functioning of the mechanical toy which he is trying to sell to the onlookers.

The myth will be treated as an orchestra score would be if it were unwittingly considered as a unilinear series; our task is to re-establish the correct arrangement. Say, for instance, we were confronted with a sequence of the type: 1,2,4,7,8,2,3,4,6,8,1,4,5,7,8,1,2,5,7,3,4,5,6,8 . . . , the assignment being to put all the 1's together, all the 2's, the 3's, etc.; the result is a chart:

| 1 | 2 |   | 4 |   |   | 7 | 8 |
|---|---|---|---|---|---|---|---|
|   | 2 | 3 | 4 |   | 6 |   | 8 |
| 1 |   |   | 4 | 5 |   | 7 | 8 |
| 1 | 2 |   |   | 5 |   | 7 |   |
|   |   | 3 | 4 | 5 | 6 |   | 8 |

We shall attempt to perform the same kind of operation on the Oedipus myth, trying out several arrangements of the mythemes until we find one which is in harmony with the principles enumerated above. Let us suppose, for the sake of argument, that the best arrangement is as shown in Table 1 (although it might certainly be improved with the help of a specialist in Greek mythology).

We thus find ourselves confronted with four vertical columns, each of which includes several relations belonging to the same bundle. Were we to *tell* the myth, we would disregard the columns and read the rows from left to right and from top to bottom. But if we want to *understand* the myth, then we will have to disregard one half of the diachronic dimension (top to bottom) and read from left to right, column after column, each one being considered as a unit.

All the relations belonging to the same column exhibit one common feature which it is our task to discover. For instance, all the events grouped in the first column on the left have something to do with blood relations which are overemphasized, that is, are more intimate than they should be. Let us say, then, that the first column has as its common feature the *overrating of blood relations*. It is obvious that the second column expresses the same thing, but inverted: *underrating of blood relations*. The third column refers to monsters being slain. As to the fourth, a few words of clarification are needed. The remarkable connotation of the surnames in Oedipus' father-line has often been noticed. However, linguists usually disregard it, since to them the only way to define the meaning of a term is to investigate all the contexts in which it appears, and personal names, precisely because they are used as such, are not accompanied by any context. With the method we propose to follow the objection disappears, since the myth itself provides its own context. The significance is no longer to be sought in the eventual meaning of each name, but in the fact that all the names have a common feature: All the hypothetical meanings (which may well remain hypothetical) refer to *difficulties in walking straight and standing upright*.

What then is the relationship between the two columns on the right? Column three refers to monsters. The dragon is a chthonian[7] being

---

[7]Living within or under the earth. [Ed.]

**Table I**

| | | | |
|---|---|---|---|
| Cadmos seeks his sister Europa, ravished by Zeus | | | |
| | | Cadmos kills the dragon | |
| | The Spartoi kill one another | | |
| | | | Labdacos (Laios' father) = *lame (?)* |
| | Oedipus kills his father, Laios | | Laios (Oedipus' father) = *left-sided (?)* |
| | | Oedipus kills the Sphinx | |
| | | | Oedipus = *swollen-foot (?)* |
| Oedipus marries his mother, Jocasta | | | |
| | Eteocles kills his brother, Polynices | | |
| Antigone buries her brother, Polynices, despite prohibition | | | |

which has to be killed in order that mankind be born from the Earth; the Sphinx is a monster unwilling to permit men to live. The last unit reproduces the first one, which has to do with the *autochthonous*[8] origin of mankind. Since the monsters are overcome by men, we may thus say that the common feature of the third column is *denial of the autochthonous origin of man.*[9]

[8]Born or sprung from the earth. Lévi-Strauss uses the term in a sense in opposition to "born from the sexual union of man and woman." [Ed.]

[9]We are not trying to become involved with specialists in an argument; this would be presumptuous and even meaningless on our part. Since the Oedipus myth is taken here merely as an example treated in arbitrary fashion, the chthonian nature ascribed to the Sphinx might seem surprising; we shall refer to the testimony of Marie Delcourt: "In the archaic legends, [she is] certainly born of the Earth itself" (*Oedipe ou la légende du conquérant* [Liège: 1944], p. 108). No

matter how remote from Delcourt's our method may be (and our conclusions would be, no doubt, if we were competent to deal with the problem in depth), it seems to us that she has convincingly established the nature of the Sphinx in the archaic tradition, namely, that of a female monster who attacks and rapes young men; in other words, the personification of a female being with an inversion of the sign. This explains why, in the handsome iconography compiled by Delcourt at the end of her work, men and women are always found in an inverted "sky/earth" relationship.

As we shall point out below, we selected the Oedipus myth as our first example because of the striking analogies that seem to exist between certain aspects of archaic Greek thought and that of the Pueblo Indians, from whom we have borrowed the examples that follow. In this respect it should be noted that the figure of the Sphinx, as reconstructed by Delcourt, coincides with two figures of North American mythology (who probably merge into one). We are referring, on the one hand, to "the old hag," a repulsive witch whose physical appearance presents a "problem" to the young hero. If he "solves" this problem — that is, if he responds to the advances of the abject creature — he will find in his bed, upon awakening, a beautiful young woman who will confer

This immediately helps us to understand the meaning of the fourth column. In mythology it is a universal characteristic of men born from the Earth that at the moment they emerge from the depth they either cannot walk or they walk clumsily. This is the case of the chthonian beings in the mythology of the Pueblo: Muyingwu, who leads the emergence, and the chthonian Shumaikoli are lame ("bleeding-foot," "sore-foot"). The same happens to the Koskimo of the Kwakiutl after they have been swallowed by the chthonian monster, Tsiakish: When they returned to the surface of the earth "they limped forward or tripped sideways." Thus the common feature of the fourth column is *the persistence of the autochthonous origin of man*. It follows that column four is to column three as column one is to column two. The inability to connect two kinds of relationships is overcome (or rather replaced) by the assertion that contradictory relationships are identical inasmuch as they are both self-contradictory in a similar way. Although this is still a provisional formulation of the structure of mythical thought, it is sufficient at this stage.

Turning back to the Oedipus myth, we may now see what it means. The myth has to do with the inability, for a culture which holds the belief that mankind is autochthonous (see, for instance, Pausanias, VIII, xxix, 4: plants provide a *model* for humans), to find a satisfactory transition between this theory and the knowledge that human beings are actually born from the union of man and woman. Although the problem obviously

cannot be solved, the Oedipus myth provides a kind of logical tool which relates the original problem — born from one or born from two? — to the derivative problem: born from different or born from same? By a correlation of this type, the overrating of blood relations is to the underrating of blood relations as the attempt to escape autochthony is to the impossibility to succeed in it. Although experience contradicts theory, social life validates cosmology by its similarity of structure. Hence cosmology is true.

Two remarks should be made at this stage.

In order to interpret the myth, we left aside a point which has worried the specialists until now, namely, that in the earlier (Homeric) versions of the Oedipus myth, some basic elements are lacking, such as Jocasta killing herself and Oedipus piercing his own eyes. These events do not alter the substance of the myth although they can easily be integrated, the first one as a new case of autodestruction (column three) and the second as another case of crippledness (column four). At the same time there is something significant in these additions, since the shift from foot to head is to be correlated with the shift from autochthonous origin to self-destruction.

Our method thus eliminates a problem which has, so far, been one of the main obstacles to the progress of mythological studies, namely, the quest for the *true* version, or the *earlier* one. On the contrary, we define the myth as consisting of all its versions; or to put it otherwise, a myth remains the same as long as it is felt as such. A striking example is offered by the fact that our interpretation may take into account the Freudian use of the Oedipus myth and is certainly applicable to it. Although the Freudian problem has ceased to be that of autochthony *versus* bisexual reproduction, it is still the problem of understanding how *one* can be born from *two:* How is it that we do not have only one procreator, but a mother plus a father? Therefore, not only Sophocles, but Freud himself, should be included among the recorded versions of the Oedipus myth on a par with earlier or seemingly more "authentic" versions.

An important consequence follows. If a myth is made up of all its variants, structural analysis should take all of them into account. After ana-

power upon him (this is also a Celtic theme). The Sphinx, on the other hand, recalls even more "the child-protruding woman" of the Hopi Indians, that is, a phallic mother par excellence. This young woman was abandoned by her group in the course of a difficult migration, just as she was about to give birth. Henceforth she wanders in the desert as the "Mother of Animals," which she withholds from hunters. He who meets her in her bloody clothes "is so frightened that he has an erection," of which she takes advantage to rape him, after which she rewards him with unfailing success in hunting. See H. R. Voth, "The Oraibi Summer Snake Ceremony," *Field Columbian Museum,* Publication No. 83, Anthropological Series, Vol. III, No. 4 (Chicago: 1903), pp. 352–53 and p. 353, *n* 1. [Au.]

lyzing all the known variants of the Theban version, we should thus treat the others in the same way: first, the tales about Labdacos' collateral line including Agave, Pentheus, and Jocasta herself; the Theban variant about Lycos with Amphion and Zetos as the city founders; more remote variants concerning Dionysus (Oedipus' matrilateral cousin); and Athenian legends where Cecrops takes the place of Cadmos, etc. For each of them a similar chart should be drawn and then compared and reorganized according to the findings: Cecrops killing the serpent with the parallel episode of Cadmos; abandonment of Dionysus with abandonment of Oedipus; "Swollen Foot" with Dionysus' *loxias*, that is, walking obliquely; Europa's quest with Antiope's; the founding of Thebes by the Spartoi or by the brothers Amphion and Zetos; Zeus kidnapping Europa and Antiope and the same with Semele; the Theban Oedipus and the Argian Perseus, etc. We shall then have several two-dimensional charts, each dealing with a variant, to be organized in a three-dimensional order, as shown in Figure 1, so that three different readings become possible: left to right, top to bottom, front to back (or vice versa). All of these charts cannot be expected to be identical; but experience shows that any difference to be observed may be correlated with other differences, so that a logical treatment of the whole will allow simplifications, the final outcome being the structural law of the myth.

At this point the objection may be raised that the task is impossible to perform, since we can only work with known versions. Is it not possible that a new version might alter the picture? This is true enough if only one or two versions are available, but the objection becomes theoretical as soon as a reasonably large number have been recorded. Let us make this point clear by a comparison. If the furniture of a room and its arrangement were known to us only through its reflection in two mirrors placed on opposite walls, we should theoretically dispose of an almost infinite number of mirror images which would provide us with a complete knowledge. However, should the two mirrors be obliquely set, the number of mirror images would become very small; nevertheless, four or five such images would very likely give us, if not complete information, at least a sufficient coverage so that we would feel sure that no large piece of furniture is missing in our description.

On the other hand, it cannot be too strongly emphasized that all available variants should be taken into account. If Freudian comments on the Oedipus complex are a part of the Oedipus myth, then questions such as whether Cushing's version of the Zuni origin myth should be retained or discarded become irrelevant. There is no single "true" version of which all the others are but copies or distortions. Every version belongs to the myth.

The reason for the discouraging results in works on general mythology can finally be understood. They stem from two causes. First, comparative mythologists have selected preferred versions instead of using them all. Second, we have seen that the structural analysis of *one* variant of *one* myth belonging to *one* tribe (in some cases, even *one* village) already requires two dimensions. When we use several variants of the same myth for the same tribe or village, the frame of reference becomes three-dimensional, and as soon as we try to enlarge the comparison, the number of dimensions required increases until it appears quite impossible to handle them intuitively. The confusions and platitudes which are the outcome of comparative mythology can be explained by the fact that multidimensional frames of reference are often ignored or are na-

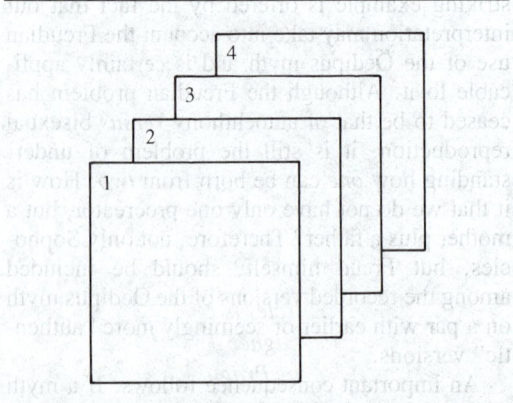

**Figure 1**

ively replaced by two- or three-dimensional ones. Indeed, progress in comparative mythology depends largely on the cooperation of mathematicians who would undertake to express in symbols multidimensional relations which cannot be handled otherwise.

Three final remarks may serve as conclusion.

First, the question has often been raised why myths, and more generally oral literature, are so much addicted to duplication, triplication, or quadruplication of the same sequence. If our hypotheses are accepted, the answer is obvious: The function of repetition is to render the structure of the myth apparent. For we have seen that the synchronic-diachronic structure of the myth permits us to organize it into diachronic sequences (the rows in our tables) which should be read synchronically (the columns). Thus, a myth exhibits a "slated" structure, which comes to the surface, so to speak, through the process of repetition.

However, the slates are not absolutely identical. And since the purpose of myth is to provide a logical model capable of overcoming a contradiction (an impossible achievement if, as it happens, the contradiction is real), a theoretically infinite number of slates will be generated, each one slightly different from the others. Thus, myth grows spiral-wise until the intellectual impulse which has produced it is exhausted. Its *growth* is a continuous process, whereas its *structure* remains discontinuous. If this is the case, we should assume that it closely corresponds, in the realm of the spoken word, to a crystal in the realm of physical matter. This analogy may help us to better understand the relationship of myth to both *langue* on the one hand and *parole* on the other. Myth is an intermediary entity between a statistical aggregate of molecules and the molecular structure itself.

Prevalent attempts to explain alleged differences between the so-called primitive mind and scientific thought have resorted to qualitative differences between the working processes of the mind in both cases, while assuming that the entities which they were studying remained very much the same. If our interpretation is correct, we are led toward a completely different view — namely, that the kind of logic in mythical thought is as rigorous as that of modern science, and that the difference lies, not in the quality of the intellectual process, but in the nature of the things to which it is applied. This is well in agreement with the situation known to prevail in the field of technology: What makes a steel ax superior to a stone ax is not that the first one is better made than the second. They are equally well made, but steel is quite different from stone. In the same way we may be able to show that the same logical processes operate in myth as in science, and that man has always been thinking equally well; the improvement lies, not in an alleged progress of man's mind, but in the discovery of new areas to which it may apply its unchanged and unchanging powers.

# Roman Jakobson and

1896–1982

# Claude Lévi-Strauss

b. 1908

*Roman Jakobson, the most eminent member of the Prague Linguistic Circle, is one of this century's foremost linguists. Jakobson became a professor of Russian at the Higher Dramatic School in Moscow, his birthplace, in 1920. In 1929, he and two other members of the Prague school announced a substantive break with the theories of Ferdinand de Saussure, perhaps the most potent influence on their own studies until then. In 1933 Jakobson began his association with Masarykova (later*

*Purkyně) University in Czechoslovakia, becoming professor of Russian philology in 1934 and of Czech medieval literature in 1936. The unsettled politics of the time precipitated his departure from the university; he sojourned briefly at the universities of Copenhagen, Oslo, and Uppsala before finding his way to New York City in 1941. From 1943 to 1947 he taught at Columbia University, and then moved on to Harvard University, where he was a professor of Slavic languages and literature and general linguistics until 1967. Jakobson has written a wealth of speech studies; he is the author, with Morris Halle and C. G. M. Fant, of* Preliminaries to Speech Analysis *(1952), and with Halle of* Fundamentals of Language *(1956). More recently he has written on Shakespeare (1970), Yeats (1977), and the grammatical structure of children's speech (1977). The explication of "Les Chats" first appeared in the French publication* L'Homme *in 1962.*

*For biographical information on Lévi-Strauss, see p. 868.*

# Charles Baudelaire's "Les Chats"

It may come as a surprise that an anthropological review should publish a study devoted to a nineteenth-century French poem; there is, however, a simple explanation. If a linguist and an ethnologist have seen fit to join forces in their efforts to try to understand what a Baudelaire sonnet is made of, it is because, independently, they have found themselves confronted with complementary problems. The linguist discerns structures in works of poetry which are strikingly analogous to those which the analysis of myths reveals to the ethnologist. For his part, the latter cannot fail to recognize that myths do not consist simply of arrangements of concepts but that they are also works of art which arouse in those who hear them (and in the ethnologist himself when he reads them in transcription) profound aesthetic emotions. Is it possible that the two problems are but one and the same?

Admittedly, the author of this preliminary note has at one time described the myth as being in opposition to the poetic work (see C. Lévi-Strauss, *Anthropologie structurale*, p. 232), but those who have reproached him for this have not taken into account the fact that the very notion of opposition implies that the two forms were originally conceived of as complementary terms, forming a part of the same classification. The

relationship outlined here does not in any way detract from the quality of discreteness which we first emphasized, that is, that each work of poetry, considered in isolation, contains within itself its own variables ranged on an axis which can be described as vertical, since it consists of superimposed levels: phonology, phonetics, syntax, prosody, semantics, etc.; whereas the myth can at the very most be interpreted only on the semantic level, the system of variables (always an indispensable part of structural analysis) being supplied by the multiplicity of versions of the same myth, that is to say a cross-section through a body of myths at the semantic level only. However, one should bear in mind that this distinction fulfils a particular practical need, in that it enables the structural analysis of myths to take place in the absence of a genuine linguistic basis. Only by pursuing both methods, even at the cost of imposing on oneself abrupt changes of viewpoint, can one begin to some extent to lay the first bet: that if either method can be selected according to circumstance, in the final analysis it is because they can be substituted one for the other, without necessarily being completely interchangeable.

C. L. S.

[1]Les amoureux fervents et les savants austères
[2]Aiment également, dans leur mûre saison,
[3]Les chats puissants et doux, orgueil de la maison,

Translated by Katie Furness-Lane; edited by Stephen Rudy.

⁴Qui comme eux sont frileux et comme eux sédentaires.

⁵Amis de la science et de la volupté,
⁶Ils cherchent le silence et l'horreur des ténèbres;
⁷L'Érèbe les eût pris pour ses coursiers funèbres,
⁸S'ils pouvaient au servage incliner leur fierté.

⁹Ils prennent en songeant les nobles attitudes
¹⁰Des grands sphinx allongés au fond des solitudes,
¹¹Qui semblent s'endormir dans un rêve sans fin;

¹²Leurs reins féconds sont pleins d'étincelles magiques,
¹³Et des parcelles d'or, ainsi qu'un sable fin,
¹⁴Étoilent vaguement leurs prunelles mystiques.¹

If one puts one's faith in the article "Le Chat Trott" by Champfleury, in which the above Baudelaire sonnet was first published (*Le Corsaire*, November 1847), it must already have been written by March 1840 and — contrary to the claims of various purists — the text in *Le Corsaire* and that in *Les Fleurs du Mal* correspond word for word.

The poet has arranged the rhymes according to the following scheme: aBBa CddCeeFgFg (uppercase letters being used to denote the lines ending in masculine rhymes and lowercase letters

---

¹Though without a working knowledge of French the reader will soon be lost in technicalities, one might glimpse the sense and tone of "The Cats" through this rather literal translation:

Fervent lovers and austere scholars
In their maturity love equally
Their sweet potent cats, pride of their house,
Who, like them, feel the cold and hate to move.

Friends to science and sensuality,
They seek the silence and horror of the shade;
Hell would have chosen them steeds of death,
Could they have bowed their pride to such service.

While dreaming, they take on the noble postures
Of great sphinxes, stretched out in the depth of solitude,
Who seem to sleep on in an endless dream.

Their fertile loins are full of magic sparks,
And flecks of gold, like grains of fine sand,
Gleam vaguely in the pupils of their mysterious eyes.

[Ed.]

---

for the lines ending in feminine rhymes). This pattern of rhymes is divided into three groups: two quatrains, and one sestet composed of two tercets, which do nevertheless form a whole because, as has been shown by Grammont, the use of rhymes in the sonnet is governed by "the same rules applied to all sestets."²

The rhyme-scheme of the sonnet in question is the product of three different rules:

1. Two couplets with alternating masculine and feminine rhymes cannot follow one another.
2. Where two contiguous lines each have a different rhyme, one of them must be feminine and the other masculine.
3. The final lines of contiguous verses must have alternating masculine and feminine rhymes: ⁴*sédentaires* — ⁸*fierté* — ¹⁴*mystiques*.

According to classical rules, so-called feminine rhymes should always end with an unstressed syllable, and masculine rhymes with a stressed syllable, but the distinction between the two types of rhyme does persist in current pronunciation where the lapsed "e" of the final syllable is omitted, the stressed final vowel being followed by a consonant in all feminine rhymes in the sonnet (*austères* — *sédentaires*, *ténèbres* — *funèbres*, *attitudes* — *solitudes*, *magiques* — *mystiques*), whereas all the masculine rhymes end with a vowel (*saison* — *maison*, *volupté* — *fierté*, *fin* — *fin*).

The close link between classification of rhyme and choice of grammatical category emphasizes the importance of the role of grammar in addition to the rhyme-scheme in the structure of this sonnet.

Every line ends with a noun, whether it be substantive (8) or adjectival (6). All the substantives are feminine. In the eight longer lines with a feminine rhyme, the final noun is plural, whether the ending is a stressed syllable in the traditional manner, or a post-vocal consonant as in present-day pronunciation; conversely the

---

²M. Grammont, *Petit traité de versification française* (Paris, 1908), p. 86. [Au.]

shorter lines with a masculine rhyme in all six cases end with a singular noun.

In the two quatrains, the masculine rhymes are constituted by substantives and the feminine rhymes by adjectives, with the exception of the key-word [6]*ténèbres* which rhymes with [7]*funèbres*. We shall return later to the whole question of the relationship between these two particular lines. As far as the tercets are concerned, the three lines of the first tercet all end with a substantive, and those of the second with an adjective. Thus the rhyme which links the two tercets — the only instance in this poem of a homonymous rhyme ([11]*sans fin* — [13]*sable fin*) — places a masculine adjective in opposition to a feminine substantive — and it is the only adjective, and the only example of the masculine gender, amongst the masculine rhymes in the sonnet.

The sonnet is made up of three compound sentences, indicated by full stops, i.e., each of the two quatrains, and the two tercets together. These three sentences form an arithmetical progression according to the number of independent clauses and the personal verb-forms in each one:

1. One single finite verb (*aiment*);
2. Two finite verbs (*cherchent, eût pris*);
3. Three finite verbs (*prennent, sont, étoilent*).

On the other hand, the subordinate clause in each of the three sentences has but one finite verb: 1. *qui . . . sont*; 2. *s'ils pouvaient*; 3. *qui semblent*.

The ternary division of the sonnet implies an antinomy between the two-rhyme verse units and the three-rhyme verse units. It is counterbalanced by a dichotomy which divides the piece into two pairs of verses, that is to say, one pair of quatrains and one pair of tercets. This binary principle, supported in turn by the grammatical structure of the text, also indicates a further antinomy between the first section of four rhymes and the second of three, and between the first two subdivisions or four-line verses and the last two three-line verses. It is on the tension between these two modes of arrangement and between their symmetric and dissymmetric elements that the composition of the whole piece is based.

There is a clearly visible syntactical parallel between the pair of quatrains on the one hand and the pair of tercets on the other. Both the first quatrain and the first tercet consist of two clauses, of which the second is relative, and introduced in both cases by the same pronoun, *qui*. This clause comprises the last line of its verse and is dependent on a masculine plural substantive, acting as complement in the main clause ([3]*Les chats*, [10]*Des . . . sphinx*). The second quatrain (and similarly the second tercet) contains two coordinate clauses, of which the second, compound in its turn, comprises the last two lines of the verse (7–8 and 13–14) and is composed of a subordinate clause linked to the main clause by a conjunction. In the quatrain that clause is conditional ([8]*S'ils pouvaient*) and in the tercet it is comparative ([13]*ainsi qu'un*). The first is consecutive, whereas the second is incomplete and parenthetical.

In the 1847 *Le Corsaire* text, the punctuation corresponds to this division. The first tercet ends with a full stop as does the first quatrain and the last two lines of the second tercet and of the second quatrain are preceded by a semicolon.

A semantic view of the grammatical subjects reinforces the parallel between the two quatrains on the one side and the two tercets on the other.

| I | Quatrains | II | Tercets |
|---|-----------|----|---------|
| 1. | First | 1. | First |
| 2. | Second | 2. | Second |

The subjects in the first quatrain and the first tercet are all animate objects, whilst one of the two subjects in the second quatrain and all in the second tercet are inanimate substantives: [7]*L'Érèbe*, [12]*Leurs reins*, [13]*des parcelles*, [13]*un sable*. In addition to these so-to-speak horizontal correlations, a correlation which could be described as vertical emerges, placing the group of two quatrains in opposition to the group of two tercets. Whilst all the direct objects in the two tercets are inanimate substantives ([9]*les nobles attitudes*, [14]*leurs prunelles*), the only direct object in the first quatrain is an animate substantive ([3]*Les chats*), and the objects in the second quatrain include, in addition to the inanimate substantives (⁶*le silence et l'horreur*), the pronoun *les* which refers to *les chats* in the preceding sentence. If we look at the relationship between subject and object, the sonnet presents two correlations which could be represented by diagonals. One descending diagonal links the outside verses (the first quatrain and the last tercet) and puts them in opposition to an ascending diagonal which links the two inside verses. In the outside verses subject and object form part of the same semantic category: animate in the first quatrain (*amoureux, savants — chats*) and inanimate in the second tercet (*reins, parcelles — prunelles*). Conversely, in the inside verses, object and subject are in opposing categories: in the first tercet the inanimate object is opposed to the animate subject (*ils* [=*chats*] — *attitudes*), whilst in the second quatrain the same link (*ils* [=*chats*] — *silence, horreur*) alternates with the link between animate object and inanimate subject (*Érèbe — les* [=*chats*]).

Thus each of the four verses retains its own individuality: the animate genre, which is common to both subject and object in the first quatrain, is peculiar to the subject only in the first tercet; in the second quatrain this genre characterizes either subject or object; and in the second tercet, neither one nor the other.

There are several striking relations in the grammatical structure both of the beginning and of the end of the sonnet. At the end, as at the beginning, but nowhere else, there are two subjects with only one predicate and only one direct object. Each of these subjects and objects is governed by a determinant (*Les amoureux fervents, les savants austères — Les chats puissants et doux; des parcelles d'or, un sable fin — leurs prunelles mystiques*), and the two predicates, the first and last in the sonnet, are the only ones accompanied by adverbs, both of them derived from adjectives and linked to one another by an assonant rhyme: ²*Aiment également —* ¹⁴*Étoilent vaguement.* The second and penultimate predicates are the only ones with a copula and an attributive predicate, the latter being emphasized in both cases by an internal rhyme: ⁴*Qui comme eux sont frileux;* ¹²*Leurs reins féconds sont pleins.* Generally speaking, only the two outside verses are rich in adjectives: nine in the quatrain

and five in the tercet; whilst the inside verses have only three adjectives in all (*funèbres, nobles, grands*).

As we have already noted, it is only at the beginning and at the end of the poem that the subjects are of the same genre as the objects: each one belongs to the animate in the first quatrain and to the inanimate in the second tercet. Animate beings, their functions and their activities, dominate the first verse. The first line contains nothing but adjectives. Of these, the two substantival forms which act as subjects — *Les amoureux* and *les savants* — have verbal roots; the test is inaugurated by "ceux qui aiment" and by "ceux qui savent." In the last line of the poem, this is reversed: the transitive verb *Étoilent,* which acts as predicate, is derived from a substantive. The latter is related to the series of inanimate and concrete appellatives which dominate this tercet and distinguish it from the three preceding verses. A clear homophony can be heard between this verb and the members of the series in question: /etẽsɛʃə/ – / e de parsɛʃə/ – /etwɑʃə. Finally, the subordinate clauses contained in the last lines of these two verses each include an adverbial infinitive, these two object-complements being the only two infinitives in the entire poem: ⁸*S'ils pouvaient . . . incliner;* ¹¹*Qui semblent s'endormir.*

It is apparent that neither the dichotomous partition of the sonnet, nor the division into three verses, leads to a balance of the isometric parts. But if one were to divide the fourteen lines into two equal parts, the seventh line would end the first half of the work, and the eighth would mark the beginning of the second. It is, therefore, significant that it is these two middle lines which most clearly distinguish themselves by their grammatical construction from the rest of the poem.

Thus, in more than one respect, the poem falls into three parts: in this case into a middle couplet and two isometric groups, that is to say, the six lincs which precede the couplet and the six which follow it. One has then a kind of distich inserted between two sestets.

All personal verb-forms and pronouns and all subjects of verbal clauses are plural throughout the sonnet, except in line seven. *L'Érèbe les eût pris pour ses coursiers funèbres,* which contains the only proper noun in the poem, and is the only instance of both the finite verb and its subject being in the singular. Furthermore, it is the only line in which the possessive pronoun (*ses*) refers back to the singular.

Only the third person is used in the sonnet. The only tense used is the present, except in lines 7 and 8, where the poet envisages an imaginary action (⁷*eût pris*) arising out of an unreal premiss (⁸*S'ils pouvaient*).

The sonnet shows a pronounced tendency to provide every verb and every substantive with a determinant. Each verbal form is accompanied by a governing term (substantive, pronoun, infinitive) or perhaps an attribute. All transitive verbs govern only substantives (²⁻³*Aiment . . . Les chats;* ⁶*cherchent le silence et l'horreur;* ⁹*prennent . . . les attitudes;* ¹⁴*Étoilent . . . leurs prunelles*). The pronoun which acts as the object in the seventh line is the only exception: *les eût pris.*

With the exception of adnominal complements, which are never accompanied by any determinant in the sonnet, the substantives (including the adjectival ones) are always governed by epithets (e.g., ³*chats puissants et doux*) or by complements (⁵*Amis de la science et de la volupté*); line seven again provides the only exception: *L'Érèbe les eût pris.*

All five epithets in the first quatrain (¹*fervents,* ¹*austères,* ²*mûre,* ³*puissants,* ³*doux*) and all six in the two tercets (⁹*nobles,* ¹⁰*grands,* ¹²*féconds,* ¹²*magiques,* ¹³*fin,* ¹⁴*mystiques*) are qualifying adjectives, whilst there are no other adjectives in the second quatrain other than the determinative epithet in the seventh line (*coursiers funèbres*).

It is also this line which reverses the animate/inanimate order governing the link between subject and object in the other lines of this quatrain, and which is, in fact, the only one in the sonnet to adopt this inanimate/animate order.

Several striking characteristics clearly distinguish line seven, and indeed the last two lines of the second quatrain, as unique. However, it must be noted that the tendency for the central couplet to stand out agrees with the idea of an asymmetric trichotomy, which puts the whole of the second quatrain in opposition to the first quatrain

on the one hand and in opposition to the final sestet on the other, thus creating a central verse discrete in several respects from the verses either side of it. We have already shown that only in the seventh line are subject and predicate in the singular, but this observation can be extended: only within the lines of the second quatrain do we find either subject or object in the singular and whereas in the seventh line the singularity of the subject (*L'Érèbe*) is contrasted with the plurality of the object (*les*), the neighboring lines reverse this relationship, having a plural subject and a singular object (⁶*Ils cherchent le silence et l'horreur;* ⁸*S'ils pouvaient . . . incliner leur fierté*).

In the remaining verses, both object and subject are plural (¹⁻³*Les amoureux . . . et les savants . . . Aiment . . . Les chats;* ⁹*Ils prennent . . . les . . . attitudes;* ¹³⁻¹⁴*Et des parcelles . . . Étoilent . . . leurs prunelles*). It is notable that in the second quatrain singularity of subject and object coincides with the inanimate and plurality with the animate. The importance of grammatical number to Baudelaire becomes particularly noticeable by virtue of the role it plays in opposition-relations in the rhymes of the poem.

It must be added that the rhymes in the second quatrain are distinguishable by their structure from all other rhymes in the work. The feminine rhyme *ténèbres — funèbres* in the second quatrain is the only one which confronts two different parts of speech. All other rhymes in the sonnet, except those in the quatrain in question, present one or more identical phonemes, either immediately preceding or some distance in front of the tonic syllable, usually reinforced by a supporting consonant: ¹*savants austères —* ⁴*sédentaires,* ²*mûre saison —* ³*maison,* ⁹*attitudes —* ¹⁰*solitudes,* ¹¹*un rêve sans fin —* ¹³*un sable fin,* ¹²*étincelles magiques —* ¹⁴*prunelles mystiques.* There is no correspondence between the syllables immediately preceding either of the two pairs of rhymes ⁵*volupté —* ⁸*fierté* and ⁶*ténèbres —* ⁷*funèbres.* However, the final words in the seventh and eighth lines are alliterative, *funèbres — fierté,* and the sixth and fifth lines are linked by the repetition of the final syllable of *volupté* in *ténèbres,* and by the internal rhyme ⁵*science —* ⁶*silence,* which reinforces the affinity between the two lines. Thus the lines themselves reveal a certain relaxation in the relationship between the two halves of the second quatrain.

The phonic texture of the sonnet is dominated by the role of the nasal vowel. These vowels, "as though veiled by nasality," as Grammont[3] appropriately puts it, occur very frequently in the first quatrain (9 nasals, from 2 to 3 per line) but most particularly in the final sestet (21 nasals with increasing frequency throughout the first tercet, $^9$3 — $^{10}$4 — $^{11}$6: '*Qui semblent s'endormir dans un rêve sans fin*' — and with a decreasing frequency throughout the second tercet $^{12}$5 — $^{13}$3 — $^{14}$1). In contrast, the second quatrain contains only three: one per line, excepting the seventh — the only line in the sonnet without a nasal vowel; this quatrain is also the only verse where the masculine rhyme does not contain a nasal vowel. On the other hand, in the second quatrain, the role of dominant phonic passes from the vowel-sounds to the consonant phonemes, in particular to the liquid consonants. The second quatrain is the one that reveals an excessive number of these liquid phonemes, twenty-three in all, as opposed to fifteen in the first quatrain, eleven in the first tercet and fourteen in the second. There are rather more /l/'s than /r/'s in the quatrains, but rather fewer in the tercets. The seventh line has only two /l/'s but five /r/'s, that is to say, more than any other line in the sonnet — *L'Érèbe les eût pris pour ses coursiers funèbres*. We should always remember that, according to Grammont, where one puts /l/ in opposition to /r/ it "gives the impression of a sound that is neither grating, rasping, nor rough but, on the contrary, that glides and flows, that is limpid."[4] The abruptness of /r/, and particularly of the French /r/, in relation to the glissando of the /l/ is clearly illustrated in the accoustical analysis of these phenomena in Mlle Durand's[5] recent study; the effacement of /r/ before /l/ eloquently evokes the transition of the empirical cat to its phantastical transfigurations.

[3]M. Grammont, *Traité de phonétique* (Paris, 1930), p. 384 (my translation). [Au.]

[4]Grammont, *Traité de phonétique*, p. 388. [Au.]

[5]M. Durand, "La Spécifité du phonème. Application au cas de R/L," *Journal de Psychologie*, LVII (1960), pp. 405–19. [Au.]

The first six lines of the sonnet are linked by a characteristic reiteration: a symmetric pair of coordinate phrases linked by the same conjunction *et*: $^1$*Les amoureux fervents et les savants austères;* $^3$*Les chats puissants et doux;* $^4$*Qui comme eux sont frileux et comme eux sédentaires;* $^5$*Amis de la science et de la volupté.* The binarism of the determinants thus forms a chiasmus with the binarism of the determined in the next line — $^6$*le silence et l'horreur des ténèbres* — thus completing the binary structure. This structure, common to almost all the lines of this "sestet," does not recur in the remainder of the poem. The juxtapositions without a conjunction are a variation on the same theme: $^2$*Aiment également dans leur mûre saison* (parallel circumstantial complements); $^3$*Les chats . . . orgueil . . .* (one noun in apposition to another).

These pairs of coordinate phrases and their rhymes (not only those which are exterior and underline the semantic links such as $^1$*austères* — $^4$*sédentaires,* $^2$*saison* — $^3$*maison,* but also and especially the interior ones) serve to draw the lines of this introduction closer together: $^1$*amoureux* — $^4$*comme eux* — $^4$*frileux* — $^4$*comme eux;* $^1$*fervents* — $^1$*savants* — $^2$*également* — $^2$*dans* — $^3$*puissants;* $^5$*science* — $^6$*silence.* Thus all the adjectives characterizing the persons in the first quatrain are rhyme-words, with the one exception $^3$*doux.* A double etymological figure of speech links the openings of three of the lines: $^1$*Les amoureux* — $^3$*Aiment* — $^5$*Amis,* in accordance with the unity of this crypto-stanza of six lines, which starts and ends with a couplet, each of whose first hemistiches rhyme: $^1$*fervents* — $^2$*également;* $^5$*science* — $^6$*silence.*

$^3$*Les chats,* who are the direct object of the clause comprising the first three lines of the sonnet, become the implied subject of the clauses in the following three lines ($^4$*Qui comme eux sont frileux;* $^6$*Ils cherchent le silence*), revealing the outline of a division of this quasi-sestet into two quasi-tercets. The central couplet recapitulates the metamorphosis of the cats from object (in this case understood) in the seventh line (*L'Érèbe les eût pris*) to subject, again understood, in the eighth line (*S'ils pouvaient*). Through this the eighth line is linked to the next sentence ($^9$*Ils prennent*). On the whole, the subordinate, consecutive clauses make a kind of transition between the subordinating clause and the sentence which follows it. Thus, the implied subject *chats* from the ninth and tenth lines gives rise to a reference to the metaphor *sphinx* in the relative clause in line eleven (*Qui semblent s'endormir dans un rêve sans fin*) and, as a result, forges a link between the tropes used as the grammatical subjects in the final tercet. The indefinite article, a complete stranger to the first ten lines with their fourteen definite articles, is the only one admitted in the last four lines of the sonnet. Thus, by virtue of the veiled references of the two relative clauses in the eleventh and the fourth lines, the four final lines tentatively disclose the outline of an imaginary quatrain which gives the appearance of corresponding to the real initial quatrain of the sonnet. Animate subjects are never expressed by substantives, but rather by adjectival substantives in the first line of the sonnet (*Les amoureux, les savants*) and by personal or relative pronouns in the final clauses. Human beings appear only in the first clause, in the form of a double subject supported by adjectival verb-substantives. *Les chats,* named in the title of the sonnet, appear by name only once in the body of the text, as the direct object in the first clause [1]*Les amoureux . . . et les savants . . .* [2]*Aiment . . .* [3]*Les chats.* Not only does the word *chats* not appear again in the course of the poem but even the shushing sound of the initial /ʃ/ only reappears in one word: [6]*il ʃɛrʃə*, the repetition of the sound representing the primary action of the feline species. This muted hissing associated with the name of the poem's subject is carefully avoided throughout the remainder of the work. In the third line, *les chats* become an understood subject, the last animate subject in the sonnet. The substantive *chats* in the role of subject, object and adnominal complement is replaced by anaphoric pronouns: [6, 8, 9]*ils,* [7]*les,* [8, 12, 14]*leur(s),* and it is only to *les chats* that the pronominal substantives *ils* and *les* refer. These accessory adverbal forms occur only in the two inside verses: in the second quatrain and in the first tercet. The autonomous form [4]*eux* (twice) occurring in the initial quatrain corresponds to them, and this form refers only to human beings in the sonnet, whilst the last tercet contains no pronominal substantive.

The two subjects of the opening clause of the sonnet have one single predicate and one single object: it is thus that [1]*Les amoureux fervents et les savants austères* finally [2]*dans leur mûre saison* identify themselves with an intermediary, an animal which embodies the paradoxical characteristics of two human but opposed conditions. The two human categories contrast with each other as sensual/intellectual and the cats act as the intermediary agents. From this point, the role of subject is implicitly assumed by the cats who are at the same time *amoureux . . . et . . . savants.*

We are given an objective representation of the personages: *les chats* in the two quatrains; whilst in the two tercets their transfiguration is presented. However, the second quatrain differs fundamentally from the first and, on the whole, from the remaining verses. The equivocal *ils cherchent le silence et l'horreur des ténèbres,* gives rise to the misapprehension provoked by the seventh line of the sonnet and denounced in the next line. The Delphic quality of this quatrain, particularly the ambiguity of its latter half, and more particularly of line seven, is accentuated by the peculiarities of its grammatical and phonic texture.

The semantic affinity between *L'Érèbe* ("shady region bordering on Hell," metonymic substitute for "the powers of darkness," and particularly for Erebus, "brother of Night") and the cats' predilection for *l'horreur des ténèbres,* supported by the phonic parallel between /tenɛbra/ and /erɛbə/, all but harnesses the cats, heroes of the poem, to the grisly task of *coursiers funèbres.* Does the line which implies that *L'Érèbe les eût pris pour ses coursiers funèbres* raise a question of frustrated desire or one of mistaken identity? The exact meaning of this passage, long questioned by the critics,[6] is still ambiguous.

Each of the quatrains and tercets tries to give the cats a new identity. The first quatrain associates them with two types of human condition, and, by virtue of their pride, they succeed in rejecting the new identity put forward in the second quatrain, which would associate them with an animal condition: that of chargers in a myth-

[6]Cf. "L'Intermédiaire des chercheurs et des curieux," LXVII, cols. 338 and 509. [Au.]

ological context. It is the only identification that is rejected in the course of the whole piece. The grammatical structure of this section, in clear contrast to that of the other verses, betrays its characteristic isolation: unreality of form, lack of qualifying epithets, a singular inanimate subject void of any determinant and governing a plural animate object.

The verses are linked by allusive oxymorons: [8]*S'ils POUVAIENT au servage incliner leur fierté* — but they *can*/not do so because they are truly [3]*PUISSANTS*. They cannot be passively *PRIS* to play an active role, which is demonstrated by the way in which they themselves actively [9]*PRENNENT* a passive role because they are obstinately *sédentaires*. *Leur fierté* predestines them for the [9]*nobles attitudes* [10]*Des grands sphinx*. The [10]*sphinx allongés* and the cats which mimic them [9]*en songeant* are linked by a paranomastic connection between the two participles — the only participal forms in the sonnet: /ãsɔ̃ʒe/ and /alɔ̃ʒe/. The cats seem to identify themselves with the sphinxes who in their turn [11]*semblent s'endormir*, but the illusory comparison to *les chats sédentaires* (and by implication to all who are [4]*comme eux*) and to the immobility of supernatural beings achieves the status of a metamorphosis. The cats and the human beings who are identified with them unite as mythical beasts with human heads and animal bodies. Thus the rejected identity is replaced with a new and equally mythological identity.

[9]*En songeant*, the cats come to be identified with the [10]*grands sphinx*, and a chain of word-plays linked to these key-words and combining nasal vowels with constrictive dentals and labials reinforces the metamorphosis. [9]*en songeant* /ãsɔ̃ . . . / — [10]*grands sphinx*/ . . . ãsfɛ . . . /—[10]*fond*/fõ/[11]*semblent*/sã. . . . /—[11]*s'endormir* /sã . . . . . / — [11]*dans un*/.ãzœ̃/ — [11]*sans fin* /sãfɛ̃/. The sharp nasal /ɛ̃/ and the other phonemes in the word [10]*sphinx*/sfɛ̃ks/ recur in the lasttercet: [12]*reins*/.ɛ̃/—[12]*pleins*/. .ɛ̃/—[12]*étincelles* / . . . ɛ̃s . . . / — [13]*ainsi* /ɛ̃s/ — [13]*qu'un sable* /kœ̃s . . . /.

We read in the first quatrain [3]*Les chats puissants et doux, orgueil de la maison*. Does it mean that the cats, proud of their home, are the embodiment of that pride, or that the house, proud of its feline inhabitants, tries, like Erebus, to domesticate them? Whichever it is, the [3]*maison* which circumscribes the cats in the first quatrain is transformed into a spacious desert, [10]*fond des solitudes*. And the fear of cold which is common to *les chats* [4]*frileux* and [1]*Les amoureux fervents* (note the word-play /fɛrvã/ — /frilø/) is dispelled by the appropriate climate of the *solitudes austères* (*austères* like the *savants*) of the torrid desert (torrid like the *amoureux fervents*) surrounding the sphinxes. On the temporal plain, the [2]*mûre saison*, rhyming with [3]*la maison* in the first quatrain and related to it by signification, has a clear counterpart in the first tercet: these two visibly parallel groups of words ([2]*dans leur mûre saison* and [11]*dans un rêve sans fin*), the one evoking numbered days and the other eternity. Constructions using *dans,* or any other adverbial preposition, do not occur elsewhere in the sonnet.

The miraculous quality of *les chats* pervades the two tercets. The metamorphosis unfolds right to the end of the sonnet. In the first tercet the image of the sphinxes lying stretched out in the desert already hovers between the creature and its effigy, and in the next tercet animate beings become effaced by material objects. Synecdoche substitutes for the cat-sphinxes various parts of the body: [12]*leurs reins,* [14]*leurs prunelles*. In the final tercet, the understood subject of the inside verses again becomes the complement: the cats first appear as an implicit complement of the subject — [12]*Leurs reins féconds sont pleins* — then, in the last clause of the poem, they are no more than an implicit complement to the object [14]*Étoilent vaguement leurs prunelles*. Thus the cats are linked to the object of the transitive verb in the last clause of the sonnet and to the subject in the penultimate, attributive clause, thereby making a double parallel on the one hand with *les chats* as the direct object of the first clause of the sonnet and on the other with *les chats* as the subject of the second clause, this being at the same attributive.

Whereas at the beginning of the sonnet both subject and object were animate, the two word-groups of the final clause are both inanimate. In principle, all the nouns in the final tercet are concrete and animate — [12]*reins,* [12]*étincelles,* [13]*parcelles,* [13]*or,* [13]*sable,* [14]*prunelles* — whilst in the inside stanzas all the inanimate appellatives, with the exception of the adnominal ones, are abstract nouns: [2]*saison,* [3]*orgueil,* [6]*horreur,* [8]*servage,* [8]*fierté,* [9]*attitudes,* [11]*rêve.* The inanimate feminine gender, common to the subject and object of the final clause — [13–16]*des parcelles d'or . . . Étoilent . . . Leurs prunelles* — counterbalances the subject and the object of the initial clause, both of which are animate and masculine: [1–3]*Les amoureux . . . et les savants . . . Aiment . . . Les chats.* [13]*Parcelles* is the only feminine subject in the sonnet, contrasting with the masculine [13]*sable fin* at the end of the same line, which is itself the only example of the masculine gender in a masculine rhyme.

In the last tercet, the final fragments of matter take it in turns to be object and subject. They are the incandescent fragments that a new image, the last one in the sonnet, identifies with the *sable fin* and transforms into stars.

The distinctive rhyme linking the two tercets is the only homonymous rhyme in the whole sonnet and the only masculine rhyme which juxtaposes different parts of speech. There is also a certain syntactical symmetry between the two rhyme-words, since they are the final words in subordinate clauses, one of which is finite and the other elliptical. The phonetic parallel, far from being confined to the last syllable of each line, closely links the whole of both lines: [11]sāblə sādərmir danzœ rɛvə sã fɛ̃/ — [13]parsɛlə dər ɛ̃si kœ̃ sablə fɛ̃/. It is not by chance that precisely the rhyme that links the two tercets evokes *un sable fin,* thus taking the desert motif up again, in the same position as *un rêve sans fin* of the *grands sphinx* appears in the first tercet.

[3]*La maison,* which circumscribes the cats in the first quatrain, disappears altogether in the first tercet, where desert solitude holds sway, a true home for the sphinx-cats who hold in the irises of their eyes the sands of the desert and the light of the stars. The epilogue again takes up the original theme of the *amoureux* and the *savants* united in *Les chats puissants et doux.* The first line of the second tercet seems to answer the first line of the second quatrain, the cats being [5]*Amis de la volupté;* [12]*Leurs reins féconds sont pleins.* One is tempted to believe that the poem is talking about creative force, but Baudelaire's work is all too open to ambiguous interpretation. Does it

refer to power in their actual loins, or electric sparks in the animal's fur? Whatever it may be, it is a *magic* power that is attributed to them. The second quatrain opens with two coordinate complements: [5]*Amis de la science et de la volupté;* and the final tercet refers back not just to [1]*Les amoureux fervents* but equally to [1]*les savants austères.*

In the last tercet, the rhyming suffixes accentuate the strong semantic link between [12]*les étinCELLES,* [13]*parCELLES* d'or and [14]*prunELLES* of the cat-sphinxes on the one hand, and on the other between the [12]*MagIQUES* sparks from the animal, its *MystIQUES prunelles,* illuminated by an internal light, open yet closed. This is the only rhyme in the sonnet which is stripped of its supporting consonant, as if to lay bare the balance of the morphemes, and the alliteration of the initial "m"s juxtaposes the two adjectives. [6]*L'horreur des ténèbres* is dissipated by this double luminescence, which is reflected on the phonic plane by the predominating phonemes of light timbre in the nasal vocalization of the final stanza (seven palatals and six gutturals), whereas in the preceding verses there have been a far greater number of gutturals (sixteen to none in the first quatrain, two to one in the second, ten to five in the first tercet).

Due to the preponderance of synecdoche at the end of the sonnet, where parts of the animal are substituted for the whole, and the animal itself is substituted for the universe of which it is a part, the images seem to take on an intentional obscurity by their imprecision. The definite article gives way to the indefinite article and the verbal metaphor selected by the poet — [14]*Étoilent vaguement* — brilliantly reflects the poesy of the epilogue. The conformity between the tercets and the corresponding quatrains (in horizontal parallel) is striking. The restrictions of space ([3]*maison*) and time ([2]*mûre saison*) imposed in the first quatrain are answered in the first tercet, by distancing, or by breaking down of barriers ([10]*fond des solitudes,* [11]*rêve sans fin*). Similarly, in the second tercet, the magic of the light irradiated by *Les chats* triumphs over [16]*l'horreur des ténèbres,* which nearly wrought such deception in the second quatrain.

Now, in drawing the parts of our analysis

together, we shall try to show how the different levels on which we touched blend, complement each other, or combine to give the poem the nature of an absolute object.

First of all, division of the text: several divisions can be clearly distinguished, as much from the grammatical point of view as from the semantic links between different parts of the poem.

As we have already pointed out, there is a primary division corresponding to the three parts which end with a full stop, that is to say, each of the two quatrains and the sum of the two tercets. The first quatrain presents, in the form of an objective and static picture, a factual situation, or one that purports to be so. The second quatrain attributes to the cats a purpose, interpreted by the powers of Erebus; and attributes to the powers of Erebus an intention towards the cats which the latter resist. Thus, in these two sections, the cats are seen from outside, firstly through the passivity with which lovers and savants are particularly associated, and secondly through the activity seen in and by the powers of Erebus. By contrast, in the last part this opposition is overcome by realizing in the cats an actively assumed passivity, no longer interpreted from the outside but from within.

A secondary division gives us the contrast of the sum of the two tercets with the sum of the two quatrains, at the same time revealing a close connection between the first quatrain and the first tercet, and between the second quatrain and the second tercet.

Thus:

1. The sum of the two quatrains contrasts with the sum of the tercets in the sense that the latter dispenses with the point of view of the observer (*amoureux, savants,* powers of Erebus) and places the cats outside all spatial and temporal limits.
2. The first quatrain introduces these spatio-temporal limits (*maison, saison*) and the first tercet abolishes them (*au fond des solitudes, rêve sans fin*).
3. The second quatrain defines the cats in terms of the shades wherein they dwell and the second tercet in terms of the light they irradiate (*étincelles, étoiles*).

Finally, a third division can be added to these two, by regrouping the text this time in a chiasmus with the initial quatrain and the final tercet on the one hand, and, on the other, the two inside verses: the second quatrain and the first tercet. In the first group, the independent clauses assign to the cats the function of complement, whereas from the outset the other two stanzas assign to the cats the function of subject. Thus, these phenomena of distribution have a semantic basis. The point of departure in the first quatrain is provided by the context: cats, savants and lovers in the same house. A double comparison arises out of this contiguity (*comme eux . . . comme eux*). Similarly, a contiguous relationship in the last tercet evolves towards a comparison. Whereas in the first quatrain a metonymic link between the feline and human inhabitants of the house forms the basis of their metaphorical relationship, in the final tercet the situation is, in a manner of speaking, interiorized: the link derives from synecdoche rather than from the metonymy itself. *Reins, prunelles,* the parts of the cat's body, provide a metaphorical evocation of the astral, cosmic cat, allied to the transition from precision to imprecision (*également — vaguement*). The analogy between the two inside verses rests on relations of equivalence, the one rejected in the second quatrain (cats and *coursiers funèbres*) and the other accepted in the first tercet (cats and sphinxes), which indicate in the first instance a refusal of location (of the cats in Erebus) and in the second the establishment of the cats *au fond des solitudes*. Here we have the reverse of the preceding situation; a transition is made from a relation of equivalence, reinforced by a comparison (in this case by metaphor) to a relation of contiguity (in this case by metonymy), whether negative or positive.

Up to this point, the poem has appeared to be composed of relations of equivalence, which fit into one another like boxes and which form as a whole an apparently closed system. There is, however, yet another way of looking at it, whereby the poem takes on the appearance of an open system in dynamic progression from start to finish.

In this first part of this study we elucidated a division of the poem into two sestets separated by a couplet whose structure was in marked contrast to the remainder. In the course of our recapitulation, we provisionally set this division to one side, because we felt that, unlike the others, it marks the stages of a progression from the real order (the first sestet) to the surreal (second sestet). This transition operates via the distich, whose combination of semantics and form carries the reader for a brief moment into a doubly unreal universe, since, whilst sharing the characteristic exteriority of the first sestet, it still introduces the mythological tone of the second sestet.

| I to 6 | 7 to 8 | 9 to I4 |
|--------|--------|---------|
| Extrinsic | | Intrinsic |
| Empirical | Mythological | |
| Real | Unreal | Surreal |

By this sudden oscillation both of tone and theme, the couplet fulfills a function which bears a strong resemblance to modulation in musical composition. The purpose of this modulation is to resolve the implicit or explicit conflict set up from the beginning of the poem between metaphor and metonymy. The solution accomplished in the final sestet is achieved by transferring this conflict to the very heart of the metonymy, whilst expressing it in a metaphorical form. In effect, each of the tercets advances an inverse image of the cat. In the first tercet, the cats traditionally enclosed in the house are so to speak extravasated from it in order to expand spatially and temporally in the infinite deserts and the dream without end. The movement is from inside to outside, from cats in seclusion to cats at liberty. The breaking down of barriers in the second tercet is expressed by the cats attaining cosmic proportions, i.e., they conceal in certain parts of their bodies (*reins and prunelles*) the sands of the desert and the stars of heaven. In both cases the transformation is effected by metaphor, but the two transformations are not exactly equivalent: the first is still concerned with the nature of

appearances (*prennent . . . les . . . attitudes . . . qui semblent s'endormir*) and of the dream (*en songeant . . . dans un rêve . . .* ), whilst the second really brings the whole thing to a conclusion by its affirmative nature (*sont pleins . . . Étoilent*). In the first, the cats close their eyes to sleep, in the second they keep them open.

However, these ample metaphors of the final sestet simply transpose on to a universal scale a conflict that was already implicitly formulated in the first line of the poem. Around the *amoureux* and the *savants* terms are assembled which unite them respectively in a contracted or a dilated relationship: the lover is joined to the woman as the *savant* is to the universe: two types of conjunction, the one close and the other distant.[7] A parallel relationship is evoked in the final transfigurations: dilation of the cats in time and space — confinement of time and place within the beings of the cats. Here again, just as we noted earlier, the symmetry between the two formulae is not complete. The latter contains within it a collection of all the conflicts: the *reins féconds* recall the *volupté* of the *amoureux*, as do the *prunelles,* the *science* of the *savants; magiques* refers to the active fervor of the one, *mystiques* to the contemplative attitude of the other.

Two final points:

The fact that all the grammatical subjects in the sonnet (with the exception of the proper noun *L'Érèbe*) are plural, and that all feminine rhymes are plural (including the substantive *solitudes*), is curiously illuminated (as indeed is much of the

[7]M. E. Benveniste, who would have liked to read this study in manuscript, has drawn our attention to the fact that between *les amoureux fervents* and *les savants austéres, la mûre saison* also plays the role of intermediary: it is in effect in *leur mûre saison* that they come together to identify equally with the cats. For, according to M. Benveniste, still to be *amoureux fervents* in *leur mûre saison* is to be outside the common run, just as *les savants austéres* are by their vocation. The opening situation in the sonnet is that of a life outside this world (nevertheless life in the underworld is rejected) and it develops, transferred to the cats, from frail seclusion to a vast star-spangled solitude where *science et volupté* are a dream without end.

In support of these comments, for which we thank the author, we would cite the theme from another poem in *Les Fleurs du Mal:* "Le savant amour . . . fruit d'automne aux saveurs souveraines" ("L'Amour du mensonge"). [Au.]

rest of the sonnet) in these quotations from *Foules:* "Multitude, solitude: terms which are equal and full of potential for the active and creative poet . . . The poet enjoys that incomparable privilege, that he can, at will, be both himself and someone else. What men call love is very small, very restrained and very weak compared with that ineffable orgy, that blessèd prostitution of the soul which gives itself in its entirety, its poetry and charity to the unexpected event or to the passing stranger."[8]

In the Baudelaire sonnet, the cats are initially described as *puissants et doux* and in the final line their *prunelles* are likened to the stars; Crépet and Blin[9] compare this to a line in Sainte-Beuve . . . "Astre puissant et doux" (1829); and point out the use of the same epithets in a poem by Brizeux (1832), in which women are thus apostrophized: "Êtres deux fois doués! Êtres puissants et doux!"

This would reaffirm, were there any need to do so, that for Baudelaire the image of the cat is closely linked to that of the woman, as is explicit in his two other poems on the same theme, i.e., the sonnet: "Viens, mon beau chat, sur mon coeur amoureux" (which contains the illuminating line: "Je vois ma femme en esprit . . ."); and the poem: "Dans ma cervelle se promène . . . Un beau chat, fort doux . . ." (which asks outright "est-il fée, est-il dieu?").

This motive of oscillation between male and female in "Les Chats" becomes evident in the intentional ambiguities *(Les amoureux . . . Aiment . . . Les chats puissants et doux . . . Leurs reins féconds . . .).* Michel Butor is justified in his claim that in Baudelaire "the two aspects of femininity and supervirility, far from being mutually exclusive are in fact bound together."[10] All beings in the sonnet are masculine but the cats and their alter ego, *les grands sphinx,*

are of an androgynous nature. This very ambiguity is emphasized throughout the sonnet by the paradoxical choice of feminine substantives for so-called masculine rhymes.[11] Through the mediation of the cats, woman is eliminated from the poem's initial galaxy of *amoureux* and *savants,* leaving face to face, if not totally enmeshed, "le poète des chats" freed from love "bien restreint" and the universe, unfettered by the savants' austerity.

[8]Ch. Baudelaire, (Œuvres, II (Bibliothéque de la Pléiade, Paris, 1961), p. 243. [Au.]

[9]Ch. Baudelaire, *Les Fleurs du Mal* (Édition Critique établie par J. Crépet et G. Blin, Paris, 1942), p. 413. [Au.]

[10]M. Butor, *Histoire extraordinaire, essai sur un rêve de Baudelaire* (Paris, 1961), p. 85. [Au.]

[11]In L. Rudrauf's article, *Rime et Sexe* (Tartu, 1936), the exposé of "A theory of the alternation of masculine and feminine rhymes in French poetry" is "followed by a controversy" with Maurice Grammont (p. 47). According to the latter, for alternation as established in the sixteenth century and depending on the presence or absence of an unstressed "e" at the end of the word, we have availed ourselves of the terms masculine and feminine because the unstressed "e" at the end of a word was, in the majority of cases, indicative of the feminine gender: *un petit chat, une petite chatte,* or rather one could say that the specific mark of the feminine as opposed to the masculine was that it always had an unstressed "e." However, Rudrauf expressed certain doubts: "But was it purely the grammatical consideration that directed the sixteenth-century poets in their laying down of the rules of alternation and in their choice of the epithets 'masculine' and 'feminine' to describe the two sorts of rhyme? Let us not forget that the Pléiade poets wrote their verses in song-form and that song accentuates, far more than the spoken word, the alternation of a strong (masculine) syllable and a weak (feminine) syllable. Consciously or unconsciously, the musical and sexual points of view must have played a role along with the grammatical analogy" (p. 49).

Given that this alternation of rhymes relying on the presence or absence of an unstressed "e" at the ends of lines has become unrealistic, Grammont envisages it giving way to an alternation of rhymes ending with either a consonant or a stressed vowel. Whilst fully prepared to recognize that vocalized endings are all masculine (p. 46), Rudrauf is at the same time tempted to set up a twenty-four-point scale for consonantal rhymes "ranging from the most brusque and masculine to the most suave and feminine" (p. 12). Muted occlusives are the extreme masculine pole (1°) and sonorous aspirants are the feminine pole (24°) of the scale in question.

*Notes:* If one applies this tentative classification to the consonantal rhymes in "Les Chats," one is conscious of a gradual movement towards the masculine pole, which finishes by attenuating the contrast between the two kinds of rhymes: [1]*austères*–[4]*sédentaires* (liquid: 19°); [6]*ténèbres*–[7]*funèbres* (sonorous and liquid occlusives: 15°); [9]*attitudes*–[10]*solitudes* (sonorous occlusive: 13°); [12]*magiques*–[14]*mystiques* (muted occlusive: 1°). [Au.]

# Gérard Genette

b. 1930

*Gérard Genette, one of the founders of the structuralist journal* Poétique *(1970), was born in Paris in 1930 and educated at the École Normale Supériéure, where he took his Agrégé de lettres classiques in 1954; he received his Docteur en lettres in 1972. After teaching for several years in provincial lycées, he was appointed to the Sorbonne in 1963 and taught there until 1967. Since 1967 Genette has been on the faculty at the École Practique des Hautes Études en sciences sociales in Paris, where he is one of the Directeurs d'études, combining this appointment with frequent visiting professorships at New York University. Genette's publications include the three volumes of essays published as* Figures *(1966, 1969, 1972); the long essay on Proust from* Figures III *was translated as* Narrative Discourse. *A selection of shorter essays, from which "Frontiers of Narrative" is taken, was translated as* Figures of Literary Discourse *in 1982. His other works include* Mimologiques *(1976),* Introduction à l'architexte *(1979), and* Seuils *(1987).*

# *Frontiers of Narrative*

If one agrees, following convention, to confine oneself to the domain of literary expression, one will define narrative without difficulty as the representation of an event or sequence of events, real or fictitious, by means of language and, more particularly, by means of written language. This positive (and current) definition has the merit of being simple and self-evident; its principal inconvenience may be precisely that it confines itself and confines us to self-evidence, that it conceals from us what specifically, in the very being of narrative, constitutes a problem and a difficulty, by effacing as it were the frontiers of its operation, the conditions of its existence. To define the narrative positively is to give credence, perhaps dangerously, to the idea of feeling that narrative *tells itself*, that nothing is more natural than to tell a story or to put together a set of actions in a myth, a tale, an epic, or a novel. The evolution of literature and of literary consciousness in the last half century will have had, among other fortunate consequences, that of

Translated by Alan Sheridan.

drawing our attention, on the contrary, to the singular, artificial, and problematic aspect of the narrative act. We must return once more to Valéry's amazement at a statement like "the marquise went out at five o'clock." We know how, in various and sometimes contradictory ways, modern literature has lived and illustrated this fruitful amazement, how it has striven and succeeded, in its very foundations, to be a questioning, a disturbance, a contestation of the notion of narrative. That falsely naive question "why narrative?" could at least encourage us to seek, or more simply to recognize, what might be called the negative limits of narrative, to consider the principal sets of oppositions through which narrative is defined, and constitutes itself over against the various forms of the non-narrative.

## DIEGESIS AND MIMESIS

The first opposition to occur to us is that indicated by Aristotle in a few brief sentences in the *Poetics*. For Aristotle, narrative (*diegesis*) is one of the two modes of poetic imitation (*mimesis*), the other being the direct representation of events by actors speaking and moving before the public.[1] It is here that the classic distinction between narrative poetry and dramatic poetry is established. This distinction was already suggested by Plato in the third book of the *Republic,* though with two differences: first, Socrates denied to narrative the quality (that is to say, for him, the defect) of imitation and, second, he took into account aspects of direct representation (dialogues) that can be included in a nondramatic poem like those of Homer. There are, therefore, at the origins of the classical tradition, two apparently contradictory divisions, in which narrative is opposed to imitation, either as its antithesis or as one of its modes.

For Plato, the domain of what he calls *lexis* (or way of saying, as opposed to *logos,* which designates what is said) is theoretically divided into imitation proper (*mimesis*) and simple narrative (*diegesis*). By simple narrative, Plato means whatever the poet relates "in his own person," without trying "to persuade us that the speaker is anyone but himself,"[2] as when Homer, in Book I of the *Iliad,* tells us of Chryses: "[He] had come to the Achaean ships to recover his captured daughter. He brought with him a generous ransom and carried the chaplet of the Archer God Apollo on a golden staff in his hand. He appealed to the whole Achaean army, and most of all to its two commanders, the sons of Atreus."[3] Imitation, on the other hand, begins with the next line, when Homer has Chryses himself say, or rather, according to Plato, when Homer speaks in the person of Chryses and "does his best to make us think that it is not Homer but an aging priest that is talking." This is the text of Chryses' speech: "My lords, and you Achaean men-at-arms; you hope to sack King Priam's city and get home in safety. May the gods that live on Olympus grant your wish — on this condition, that you show your reverence for the Archer-god Apollo Son of Zeus by accepting this ransom and releasing my daughter." Now, Plato adds, Homer could equally well have continued his narrative in a purely narrative form, *recounting* Chryses' words instead of quoting them, which, for the same passage, would have given, in indirect style and in prose: "The priest came and prayed that the gods would allow the Achaeans to capture Troy and return in safety, and begged the Achaeans to show their respect for the god by releasing his daughter in exchange for the ransom."[4] This theoretical division, which opposes, within poetic diction, the two pure, heterogeneous modes of narrative and imitation, brings with it and establishes a practical classification of the genres, which comprises the two pure modes (narrative, represented by the ancient dithyramb, and mimetic, represented by the theater), plus a mixed or, to be more precise, alternate mode, which is that of the epic, as we have just seen with the example from the *Iliad.*

At first sight Aristotle's classification is quite different, since it reduces all poetry to imitation, distinguishing only two imitative modes, the direct, which is the one Plato calls strict imitation, and the narrative, which he calls, as does Plato, *diegesis.* On the other hand, Aristotle seems to fully identify not only, like Plato, the dramatic genre with the imitative mode, but also, without taking into account in principle its mixed character, the epic genre with the pure narrative mode. This reduction may derive from the fact that Aristotle defines the imitative mode, more strictly than Plato, by the scenic conditions of dramatic representation. It might also be justified by the fact that the epic work, however important a part is played in it by dialogues or discourse in the direct style, and even if this part exceeds that of the narrative, remains essentially narrative, in that the dialogues are necessarily framed in it and induced by narrative parts that constitute, in the strict sense, the *basis* or, to put it another way, the web of its discourse. In any case, Aristotle recognizes Homer's superiority over all other epic poets in that he intervenes personally as little as possible in his poem, usually dramatizing his characters directly, in accor-

---

[1]Aristotle, *Poetics,* 1448a [Au.]; see p. 44. [Ed.]

[2]Plato, *Republic,* 393a; *Republic,* D. Lee, tr. 2d. rev. ed., (Harmondsworth: Penguin, 1974), p. 150 [Au.]

[3]Homer, *Iliad,* Book I, lines 12–16; *Iliad,* E. V. Rieu, tr. (Harmondsworth: Penguin, 1953), p. 23. [Au.]

[4]Plato, *Republic,* 393e; *Repub.,* p. 151. [Au.]

dance with the role of the poet, which is to imitate as much as possible.[5] This would suggest that he implicitly recognizes the imitative character of the Homeric dialogues and therefore the mixed character of epic diction, basically narrative, but dramatic in a wider sense.

The difference between Plato's and Aristotle's classifications amounts, then, to a simple variation of terms; these two classifications certainly agree on the main point, that is to say, the opposition between the dramatic and the narrative, the first being regarded by both philosophers as more fully imitative than the second: an agreement on facts that is in a sense brought out more by the disagreement on values, since Plato condemns poets as imitators, beginning with the dramatists, and not excepting Homer, who is regarded as still being too mimetic for a narrative poet, admitting into the City only some ideal poet whose austere diction would be as little mimetic as possible;[6] whereas Aristotle, symmetrically, places tragedy above epic, and praises in Homer whatever brings his writing closer to dramatic diction.[7] The two systems, then, are certainly identical, except for a reversal of values: for Plato as for Aristotle, narrative is the weakened, attenuated mode of literary representation — and it is difficult, at first sight, to see how one could come to a different conclusion.

However, we must introduce here an observation which does not seem to have concerned either Plato or Aristotle, and which will restore to the narrative all its value and all its importance. Direct imitation, as it functions on the stage, consists of gestures and speech. Insofar as it consists of gestures, it can obviously represent actions, but at this point it escapes from the linguistic plane, which is that in which the specific activity of the poet is practised. Insofar as it consists of words, discourse spoken by characters (and it goes without saying that in a narrative work the role of direct imitation is reduced to that), it is not strictly speaking representative, since it is confined to reproducing a real or fictitious discourse as such. It can be said that

verses 12 to 16 of the *Iliad,* quoted above, give us a verbal representation of Chryses' actions, but the same cannot be said of the next five lines; they do not *represent* Chryses' speech: if this is a speech, actually spoken, they *repeat* it, literally, and if it is fictitious speech, they *constitute* it, just as literally. In both cases, the work of representation is nil; in both cases, Homer's five lines are strictly identical with Chryses' speech: this is obviously not so in the case of the five narrative lines preceding it, which are in no way identical with Chryses' actions: "The word 'dog' does not bite," William James remarked. If we call poetic imitation the fact of representing by verbal means a nonverbal reality and, in exceptional circumstances, a verbal reality (as one calls pictorial imitation the fact of representing in pictorial means nonpictorial reality and, in exceptional circumstances, a pictorial reality), it must be admitted that imitation is to be found in the five narrative lines and not at all in the five dramatic lines, which consist simply in the interpolation, in the middle of a text representing events, of another text directly taken from those events: as if a seventeenth-century Dutch painter, anticipating certain modern methods, had placed in the middle of a still life, not the painting of an oyster shell, but a real oyster shell. I make this simplistic comparison in order to point out the profoundly heterogeneous character of a mode of expression to which we are so used that we do not perceive its most sudden changes of register. Plato's "mixed" narrative, that is to say, the most common and universal mode or relation, "imitates" alternately and in the same register ("without even seeing the difference," as Michaux would say), nonverbal material, which in fact it must represent as best it can, and verbal material that represents itself, and which it is usually content to quote. In the case of a strictly faithful historical account, the historian-narrator must certainly be aware of the change of manner when he passes from the narrative effort of relating completed actions to the mechanical transcription of spoken words, but in the case of a partially or totally fictitious narrative, fictional activity, which bears equally on the verbal and nonverbal contents, no doubt has the effect of concealing the difference that separates the two

[5]Aristotle, *Poetics*, 1460a [Au.]; see p. 61. [Ed.]
[6]See Plato, *Republic*, Book X, pp. 28–29. [Ed.]
[7]See Aristotle, *Poetics*, p. 61. [Ed.]

types of imitation, one of which involves, if I may so put it, direct contact, while the other introduces a rather more complex system of levels. Even if one admits (as is difficult enough) that imagining actions and imagining spoken words proceed from the same mental operation, "telling" these actions and telling these words constitute two very different verbal operations. Or rather, only the first constitutes a true operation, an act of *diction* in the Platonic sense, involving a series of transpositions and equivalences, and a series of inevitable choices between the elements of the *story* to be retained and the elements to be left out, between the various possible points of view, and so on — all of which are operations that are obviously absent when the poet or historian confines himself to transcribing a speech. One may certainly (indeed one must) challenge this distinction between the act of mental representation and the act of verbal representation, between the *logos* and the *lexis,* but it amounts to challenging the very theory of imitation, which conceives poetic fiction as a simulacrum of reality, as transcendent to the discourse that sustains it as the historical event is external to the discourse of the historian or the landscape represented to the picture that represents it: a theory that makes no distinction between fiction and representation, the object of fiction being reduced to a feigned reality that is simply awaiting representation. Now it appears that from this point of view the very notion of imitation on the level of the *lexis* is a pure mirage, which vanishes as one approaches it; the only thing that language can imitate perfectly is language, or, to be more precise, a discourse can imitate only itself. *Qua lexis,* direct imitation is simply a tautology.

So we are led to this unexpected conclusion, that the only mode that knows literature as representation is the narrative, the verbal equivalent of nonverbal events and also (as the example made up by Plato shows) of verbal events, unless it vanishes, as in the last case, before a direct quotation in which all representative function is abolished, rather as a speaker in a court of law may interrupt his speech to allow the court to scrutinize some exhibit. Literary representation, the *mimesis* of the ancients, is not, therefore,

narrative plus "speeches": it is narrative, and only narrative. Plato opposed *mimesis* to *diegesis* as a perfect imitation to an imperfect imitation; but (as Plato himself showed in the *Cratylus*) perfect imitation is no longer an imitation, it is the thing itself, and, in the end, the only imitation is an imperfect one. *Mimesis* is *diegesis.*

## NARRATION AND DESCRIPTION

But if literary representation defined in this way is identical with narrative (in the broad sense), it is not to be reduced to the purely narrative elements (in the narrow sense) of the narrative. We must now admit, within diegesis itself, a distinction that appears neither in Plato nor in Aristotle, and which will draw a new frontier within the domain of representation. Every narrative in fact comprises two kinds of representations, which however are closely intermingled and in variable proportions: on the one hand, those of actions and events, which constitute the narration in the strict sense and, on the other hand, those of objects or characters that are the result of what we now call *description*. The opposition between narration and description, which was so stressed by academic tradition, is one of the major features of our literary consciousness. Yet it is a relatively recent distinction, the birth and development of which in the theory and practice of literature should one day be studied. It does not seem, at first sight, that it enjoyed a very active existence before the nineteenth century, when the introduction of long descriptive passages in a typically narrative genre like the novel brought out the resources and the requirements of the method.[8]

This persistent confusion, or carelessness of distinction, which in Greek is shown very clearly by the use of the common term *diegesis,* derives perhaps above all from the very unequal literary status of the two types of representation. In principle, it is obviously possible to conceive of purely descriptive texts, the aim of which is to

[8]It is to be found however in Boileau on the subject of the epic: "Soyez vif et pressé dans vos narations;/Soyez riche et pompeux dans vos descriptions." (*Art Poétique*, III, 257–58). [Au.]

represent objects simply and solely in their spatial existence, outside any event and even outside any temporal dimension. It is even easier to conceive of a pure description of any narrative element than the reverse, for the most neutral designation of the elements and circumstances of a process can already be regarded as the beginnings of a description: a sentence like "The house is white, with a slate roof and green shutters," involves no element of narration, whereas a sentence like "The man went over to the table and picked up a knife," contains at least, apart from two verbs of action, three substantives which, however little qualified, can be regarded as descriptive by the very fact that they designate animate or inanimate beings; even a verb can be more or less descriptive, in the precision that it gives to the spectacle of the action (one has only to compare "grabbed a knife," for example, with "picked up a knife"), and consequently no verb is quite exempt from descriptive resonance. It may be said, then, that description is more indispensable than narration, since it is easier to describe without relating than it is to relate without describing (perhaps because objects can exist without movement, but not movement without objects). But this elementary situation already indicates, in fact, the nature of the relation that unites the two functions in the overwhelming majority of literary texts: description might be conceived independently of narration, but in fact it is never found in a so to speak free state; narration cannot exist without description, but this dependence does not prevent it from constantly playing the major role. Description is quite naturally *ancilla narrationis*,[9] the ever-necessary, ever-submissive, never-emancipated slave. There are narrative genres, such as the epic, the tale, the novella, the novel, in which description can occupy a very large place, even in terms of sheer quantity the larger place, without ceasing to be, by its very vocation, a mere auxiliary of the narrative. On the other hand, there are no descriptive genres, and one finds it difficult to imagine, outside the didactic domain (or semididactic fictions such as those of Jules Verne) a work in which narrative would serve as an auxiliary to description.

The study of the relations between the narrative and the descriptive amounts, then, in essence, to a consideration of the *diegetic functions* of description, that is to say, the role played by the descriptive passages or aspects in the general economy of narrative. Without attempting to go into the detail of such a study here, one could at least mention, in the "classical" literary tradition (from Homer to the end of the nineteenth century), two relatively distinct functions. The first is of what might be called a decorative kind. We know that traditional rhetoric places description, together with the other figures of style, among the ornaments of discourse: extended, detailed description appears here as a recreational pause in the narrative, carrying out a purely esthetic role, like that of sculpture in a classical building. The most famous example is perhaps the description of Achilles' shield in Book XVIII of the *Iliad*.[10] It is no doubt this decorative role that Boileau has in mind when he recommends richness and splendor in this kind of piece. The Baroque epic was noted for a sort of proliferation of the descriptive excursus, very marked for example in Saint-Amant's *Moyse sauvé*, which finally destroyed the balance of the narrative poem in its decline.

The second major function of description, and the most obvious in our own day because it was imposed, with Balzac, on the tradition of the novel, is both explanatory and symbolic: physical portraits, descriptions of dress and furniture tend, in Balzac and his realist successors, to reveal and at the same time to justify the psychology of the characters, of which they are at once the sign, the cause, and the effect. Description becomes here a major element in the exposition, which it was not in the classical period: one has only to think of the houses of Mlle Cormon in *La Vieille fille* or of Balthazar Claës in *La Recherche de l'absolu*. But all this is too well known to be labored here. I would just like to remark that, in

<hr>

[9]The servant of narration. [Ed.]

[10]At least as interpreted and imitated by the classical tradition. It should be noted however that description here tends to become animated and therefore to turn itself into narrative. [Au.]

substituting significant description for ornamental description, the evolution of narrative form has tended (at least until the early twentieth century) to reinforce the domination of the narrative element: without the slightest doubt description has lost in terms of autonomy what it has gained in dramatic importance. As for certain forms of the contemporary novel that appeared initially as attempts to free the descriptive mode from the tyranny of the narrative, it is by no means certain that the question should really be interpreted in this way: if one considers it from this point of view, the work of Robbe-Grillet appears rather perhaps as an effort to constitute a narrative (a *story*) almost exclusively by means of descriptions imperceptibly modified from one page to the next, which can be regarded both as a spectacular promotion of the descriptive function and as a striking confirmation of its irreducible narrative finality.

Lastly, it should be noted that all the differences which separate description and narration are differences of content, which, strictly speaking, have no semiological existence: narration is concerned with actions or events considered as pure processes, and by that very fact it stresses the temporal, dramatic aspect of the narrative; description, on the other hand, because it lingers on objects and beings considered in their simultaneity, and because it considers the processes themselves as spectacles, seems to suspend the course of time and to contribute to spreading the narrative in space. These two types of discourse may, then, appear to express two antithetical attitudes to the world and to existence, one more active, the other more contemplative, and therefore, following a traditional equivalence, more "poetic." But from the point of view of modes of representation, to recount an event and to describe an object are two similar operations, which bring into play the same resources of language. The most significant difference might be that narration restores, in the temporal succession of its discourse, the equally temporal succession of events, whereas description must modulate, in discursive succession, the representation of objects that are simultaneous and juxtaposed in space: narrative language, then, would appear to be distinguished by a sort of temporal coincidence with its object, of which descriptive language would, on the contrary, be irremediably deprived. But this opposition loses much of its force in written literature, where nothing prevents the reader from going back and considering the text, in its spatial simultaneity, as an *analogon* of the spectacle that it describes: Apollinaire's calligrams or the graphic dispositions of Mallarmé's *coup de dés* simply push to the limit the exploitation of certain resources latent in written expression. Furthermore, no narration, not even that of broadcast reporting, is strictly synchronic with the events that it relates, and the variety of the relations which can exist between the time of the story and that of the narrative have the effect of reducing the specificity of narrative representation. Aristotle already observed that one of the advantages of narrative over theatrical representation was that it could deal with several simultaneous actions;[11] but it has to deal with them successively, and from then on its situation, its resources, and its limits are similar to those of descriptive language.

It would appear then that description, as a mode of literary representation, does not distinguish itself sufficiently clearly from narration, either by the autonomy of its ends, or by the originality of its means, for it to be necessary to break the narrative-descriptive (chiefly narrative) unity that Plato and Aristotle have called narrative. If description marks one of the frontiers of narrative, it is certainly an internal frontier, and really a rather vague one: it will do no harm, therefore, if we embrace within the notion of narrative all forms of literary representation and consider description not as one of its modes (which would imply a specificity of language), but, more modestly, as one of its aspects — if, from a certain point of view, the most attractive.

## NARRATIVE AND DISCOURSE

Reading the *Republic* and the *Poetics*, it would seem that, from the outset, Plato and Aristotle implicitly reduce the field of literature to the particular domain of representative literature:

[11]Aristotle, *Poetics*, 1459b; see p. 60. [Ed.]

*poiesis* = *mimesis*. If one considers everything that is excluded from the poetic by this decision, we see the emergence of a last frontier of narrative that might be the most important and most significant. This frontier concerns nothing less than lyric, satirical, and didactic poetry: namely, to confine ourselves to a few of the names that would be known to a fifth- or fourth-century Greek, Pindar, Alcaeus, Sappho, Archilochos, and Hesiod. Thus, for Aristotle, Empedocles is not a poet, even though he uses the same meter as Homer: "Hence the proper term for the one is 'poet,' for the other 'science-writer' rather than 'poet.'"[12] But certainly Archilochos, Sappho, and Pindar cannot be called scientists: what all those excluded from the *Poetics* have in common is that their work does not consist in the imitation, by narrative or theatrical representation, of an action, real or pretended, external to the person and speech of the poet, but simply in a discourse spoken by him directly and in his own name. Pindar sings the merits of the winner at the Olympics, Archilochos inveighs against his political enemies, Hesiod gives advice to farmers, Empedocles or Parmenides expounds his theory of the universe: no representation, no fiction is involved here, simply speech that is invested directly in the discourse of the work. The same could be said of Latin elegiac poetry and of everything that makes use of eloquence, moral and philosophical reflection,[13] scientific or parascientific exposition, the essay, correspondence, the journal, etc. All this vast domain of direct expression, whatever the modes, peculiarities, forms, eludes the consideration of the *Poetics* in that it neglects the representative function of poetry. We have here a new division, of very wide scope, since it divides into two parts of roughly equal importance the whole of what we now call literature.

This division corresponds more or less to the distinction proposed by Émile Benveniste be-tween *narrative* (or *story*) and *discourse*,[14] except that Benveniste includes in the category of discourse everything that Aristotle called direct imitation, and which actually consists, at least as far as its verbal part is concerned, of discourse attributed by the poet or narrator to one of his characters. Benveniste shows that certain grammatical forms, like the pronoun "I" (and its implicit reference "you"), the pronominal (certain demonstratives), or adverbial indicators (like "here," "now," "yesterday," "today," "tomorrow," etc.) and — at least in French — certain tenses of the verb, like the present, the present anterior, or the future, are confined to discourse, whereas narrative in its strict form is marked by the exclusive use of the third person and such forms as the aorist (past definite) and the pluperfect. Whatever the details and variations from one idiom to another, all these differences amount clearly to an opposition between the objectivity of narrative and the subjectivity of discourse; but it should be pointed out that such objectivity and subjectivity are defined by criteria of a strictly linguistic order: "subjective" discourse is that in which, explicitly or not, the presence of (or reference to) *I* is marked, but this is not defined in any other way except as the person who is speaking this discourse, just as the present, which is the tense *par excellence* of the discursive mode, is not defined other than as the moment when the discourse is being spoken, its use marking "the coincidence of the event described with the instance of discourse that describes it."[15] Conversely, the objectivity of narrative is defined by the absence of any reference to the narrator: "As a matter of fact, there is then no longer even a narrator. The events are set forth chronologically, as they occur. No one speaks here; the events seem to narrate themselves."[16]

[12]Aristotle, *Poetics*, 1447b; see p. 42. [Ed.]

[13]Since it is the diction that counts here, and not what is said, we will exclude from this list, as does Aristotle (*Poetics* 1447b; *Poet.*, p. 17), Plato's Socratic dialogues, and all expositions in dramatic form, which belong to imitation in prose. [Au.]

[14]Émile Benveniste, "Les relations de temps dans le verbe français," *Problèmes de linguistique générale*, pp. 237–50; "The Correlations of Tense in the French Verb," *Problems in General Linguistics*, M. E. Meek, tr. (Coral Cables, Florida: University of Miami Press, 1971), pp. 205–15. [Au.]

[15]Émile Benveniste, "De la subjectivité dans le langage" in *Problèmes*, p. 262; "Subjectivity in Language" in *Problems*, p. 227. [Au.]

[16]Benveniste, "Les relations des temps," p. 241; *Problems*, p. 208. [Au.]

We have here, no doubt, a perfect description of what is, in its essence and in its radical opposition to any form of personal expression on the part of the speaker, narrative in the pure state, as it may be conceived ideally and as it may in fact be grasped in a few privileged examples, like those borrowed by Benveniste himself from the historian Glotz and from Balzac. Let us reproduce here the extract from the latter's *Gambara*, which we will have to consider with some attention:

> After a walk round the gallery, the young man looked in turn at the sky and at his watch, made a gesture of impatience, entered a tobacconist's, lit a cigar, placed himself in front of a mirror, and examined his clothes, which were somewhat richer than the laws of taste allow in France. He adjusted his collar and black velvet waistcoat over which was crossed several times one of those thick gold chains made in Genoa; then, after flinging his velvet-lined overcoat over his left shoulder, draping it elegantly, in a single movement, he resumed his walk without allowing himself to be distracted by the bourgeois glances cast in his direction. When the shops began to light up and the night seemed dark enough, he walked towards the Place du Palais-Royal like a man who was fearful of being recognized, for he skirted the square as far as the fountain, before reaching, under cover of the cabs, the end of the Rue Froidmanteau.

At this degree of purity, the diction proper to the narrative is in some sense the absolute transitivity of the text, the complete absence (if we ignore a few exceptions to which we will return shortly), not only of the narrator, but also of the narration itself, by the rigorous expunging of any reference to the instance of discourse that constitutes it. The text is there, before our eyes, without being proffered by anyone, and none (or almost none) of the information it contains needs, in order to be understood or appreciated, to be related to its source, judged by its distance from or its relation to the speaker or to the utterance. If we compare such a statement to a sentence like "I was waiting to write to you that I had definitely decided to stay. At last I have made up my mind: I shall spend the winter here,"[17]

[17]Senancour, *Obermann*, Lettre v. [Au.]

one appreciates to what extent the autonomy of narrative is opposed to the dependence of discourse, the essential determinations of which (who is "I," who is "you," what place is referred to by "here"?) can be deciphered only in relation to the situation in which it was produced. In discourse, someone speaks, and his situation in the very act of speaking is the focus of the most important significations; in narrative, as Benveniste forcefully puts it, *no one speaks*, in the sense that at no moment do we ask ourselves *who is speaking, where, when,* and so forth, in order to receive the full signification of the text.

But it should be added at once that these essences of narrative and discourse so defined are almost never to be found in their pure state in any text: there is almost always a certain proportion of narrative in discourse, a certain amount of discourse in narrative. In fact, the symmetry stops here, for it is as if both types of expression were very differently affected by the contamination: the insertion of narrative elements in the level of discourse is not enough to emancipate discourse, for they generally remain linked to the reference by the speaker, who remains implicitly present in the background, and who may intervene again at any moment without this return being experienced as an "intrusion." Thus, we read in Chateaubriand's *Mémoires d'outre-tombe* this apparently objective passage:

> When the sea was high and it was stormy, the waves, beating at the foot of the castle, along the great shore, spouted up as far as the great towers. Twenty feet above the base of one of these towers was a granite parapet, narrow and gleaming, sloping outwards, from which one communicated with the ravelin that defended the moat: we would seize the moment between two waves, and cross the perilous place before the flow broke again and covered the tower.[18]

But we know that the narrator, who has momentarily effaced himself during this passage, is not very far away, and we are neither surprised nor embarrassed when he speaks again, adding: "Not one of *us* refused the adventure, but *I* have

[18]F. R. de Chateaubriand, *Mémoires d'Outre-tombe,* Book I, ch. 5. [Au.]

seen children pale before attempting it." The narration had not really emerged from the order of discourse in the first person, which had absorbed it without effort or distortion, and without ceasing to be itself. On the contrary, any intervention of discursive elements within a narrative is felt as a relaxation of the rigor of the narrative part. The same goes for the brief reflection inserted by Balzac mentioned above: "his clothes, which were *somewhat richer than the laws of taste allow in France.*" The same can be said for the demonstrative expression "*one of those thick gold chains made at Genoa,*" which obviously contains the beginnings of a passage ("made" corresponds not to *which were made,* but *which are made*) and of a direct address to the reader, who is implicitly taken as a witness. Again, the same could be said of the adjective in "*bourgeois* glances" and of the adverb "*elegantly,*" which imply a judgment the source of which is here quite obviously the narrator; the relative expression "*like a man who was fearful,*" which Latin would mark with a subjunctive for the personal appraisal that it involves; and lastly of the conjunction "*for* he skirted," which introduces an explanation offered by the narrator. It is obvious that narrative does not integrate these discursive enclaves, rightly called by Georges Blin "authorial intrusions," as easily as discourse receives the narrative enclaves: narrative inserted into discourse is transformed into an element of discourse, discourse inserted into narrative remains discourse and forms a sort of cyst that is very easy to recognize and to locate. The purity of narrative, one might say, is more manifest than that of discourse.

Though the reason for this dissymmetry is very simple, it indicates for us a decisive character of narrative: in fact, discourse has no purity to preserve, for it is the broadest and most universal "natural" mode of language, welcoming by definition all other forms; narrative, on the other hand, is a particular mode, marked, defined by a number of exclusions and restrictive conditions (refusal of the present, the first person, and so forth). Discourse can "recount" without ceasing to be discourse, narrative cannot "discourse" without emerging from itself. Nor can it

abstain from it completely, however, without falling into aridity and poverty: this is why narrative exists nowhere, so to speak, in its strict form. The slightest general observation, the slightest adjective that is little more than descriptive, the most discreet comparison, the most modest "perhaps," the most inoffensive of logical articulations introduces into its web a type of speech that is alien to it, refractory as it were. In order to study the detail of these sometimes microscopic accidents, we would need innumerable, meticulous analyses of texts. One of the objects of this study would be to list and classify the means by which narrative literature (and in particular the novel) has tried to organize in an acceptable way, within its own *lexis,* the delicate relations maintained within it between the requirements of narrative and the needs of discourse.

We know in fact that the novel has never succeeded in resolving in a convincing and definitive way the problem posed by these relations. Sometimes, as was the case in the classical period, with a Cervantes, a Scarron, a Fielding, the author-narrator, happily assuming his own discourse, intervenes in the narrative with ironically labored indiscretion, addressing his reader in a familiar, conversational tone; sometimes, on the other hand, as we also see in the same period, he transfers all responsibility for the discourse to a principal character who will *speak,* that is to say, both recount events and comment on them in the first person: this is the case of the picaresque novels, from *Lazarillo de Tormes* to *Gil Blas,* and other fictively autobiographical works, such as *Manon Lescaut* and *La Vie de Marianne*; sometimes, again, being unable to make up his mind whether to speak in his own name or to entrust this task to a single character, he distributes discourse between the various actors, either in the form of letters, as was often the case in the eighteenth-century novel (*La Nouvelle Héloïse, Les Liaisons dangereuses*) or, in the more supple and subtle manner of a Joyce or a Faulkner, by letting his principal characters assume the narrative successively through their interior discourse. The only moment when the balance between narrative and discourse seems to have been assumed with a perfectly good conscience, without either scruple or ostentation, is obviously in the nineteenth century, the classical age of objective narration, from Balzac to Tolstoy; we see, on the contrary, how the modern period has stressed awareness of difficulty to the extent of making certain types of elocution almost physically impossible for the most lucid and rigorous of writers.

We know, for example, how the effort to bring narrative to its highest degree of purity led certain American writers, such as Hammett or Hemingway, to exclude any exposition of psychological motives, which are always difficult to carry off without recourse to general considerations of a discursive kind, qualifications implying a personal judgment on the part of the narrator, logical links, and the like, to the point of reducing fictional diction to that jerky succession of short sentences without articulations, which Sartre recognized in 1943 in Camus' *L'Étranger,* and which were to turn up again ten years later in Robbe-Grillet. What has often been interpreted as an application to literature of behaviorist theories may have been no more than the effect of a particularly acute sensitivity to certain incompatibilities of language. All the fluctuations of contemporary fictional writing could no doubt be analyzed from this point of view, and particularly the tendency today, perhaps the reverse of the earlier one, and quite overt in a Phillipe Sollers of a Jean Thibaudeau, for example, to absorb the narrative in the present discourse of the writer in the process of writing, in what Michel Foucault calls "discourse bound up with the act of writing, contemporary with its unfolding and enclosed within it."[19] It is as if literature had exhausted or overflowed the resources of its representative mode, and wanted to fold back into the indefinite murmur of its own discourse. Perhaps the novel, after poetry, is about to emerge definitively from the age of representation. Perhaps narrative, in the negative singularity that we have just attributed to it, is already for us, as art was for Hegel, *a thing of the past,* which we must hurry to consider as it retreats, before it has completely disappeared from our horizon.

[19]"L'Arrière-fable," *L'Arc* (1965), 29:6. [Au.]

# Tzvetan Todorov

b. 1939

*Like Gérard Genette, Tzvetan Todorov is known primarily for his applications of structural theories to literature. Todorov was born in Bulgaria, and received an M.A. from the University of Sofia and dual doctorates from the University of Paris. He is associated with the École Pratique des Hautes Études, and since 1968 has been on the staff of the Centre National de la Recherche Scientifique in Paris. Todorov translated the Russian formalists into French in 1965, and his theory of narrative shows the influence of Vladímir Propp — perhaps most markedly in his analysis of the grammar of Boccaccio's* Decameron *(1969). His other writings include* Literature and Signification *(1967);* The Fantastic: A Structuralist Approach to a Literary Genre *(1970);* Theories of the Symbol *(1973); and* The Conquest of America *(1982), as well as book-length studies of Mikhail Bakhtin (1984) and Jean-Jacques Rousseau (1985). The selection is taken from* Structuralism: An Introduction, *edited by David Robey; another version appeared as "The Secret of Narrative" in Todorov's* The Poetics of Prose *(1971), translated in 1977 by Richard Howard.*

# The Structural Analysis of Literature: The Tales of Henry James

In his famous story *The Figure in the Carpet* (1896),[1] James tells how a young critic who has just written an article on one of the authors, Hugh Vereker, he most admires, happens to meet him shortly afterwards. The author does not hide from him the fact that he is disappointed with the study dedicated to him. It is not that it lacks subtlety; but it fails to name the secret of his work, a secret which constitutes at the same time its motive principle and its general meaning.

> There's an idea in my work [Vereker explains] without which I wouldn't have given a straw for the whole job. It's the finest, fullest intention of the lot, and the application of it has been, I think, a triumph of patience, of ingenuity . . . It stretches, this little trick of mine, from book to book, and everything else, comparatively, plays over the surface of it. (pp. 281–82)

Pressed by his young interlocutor's question ("Can't you give a fellow a clue?") Vereker adds: "My whole lucid effort gives him the clue — every page and line and letter. The thing's as concrete there as a bird in a cage, a bait on a hook, a piece of cheese in a mouse-trap . . . It governs every line, it chooses every word, it dots every i, it places every comma" (pp. 283–84).

The young critic throws himself into a desperate search. Seeing Vereker again, he tries to obtain more precise information: "It was something, I guessed, in the primal plan, something like a complex figure in a Persian carpet. He highly approved of this image when I used it, and he used another himself. 'It's the very string, he said, that my pearls are strung on'" (p. 289).

In approaching Henry James's work, let us take up Vereker's challenge (Vereker said, after all: "So it's naturally the thing for the critic to look for. It strikes me . . . even as the thing for the critic to find" [p. 282]). Let us try to find the figure in Henry James's carpet, the primal plan on which everything else depends, as it appears in each one of his works.

The search for such an invariant factor can only be carried out, as the characters of *The Figure in the Carpet* well know, by superimposing the different works one on the other, like Galton's photographs,[2] reading them as if they were a series of transparencies. However, I have no desire to make the reader impatient, and shall reveal the secret immediately, even if I run the risk thereby of being less convincing. In this way the works I shall examine will, I hope, confirm my hypothesis, instead of leaving the reader the trouble of formulating it for himself.

James's tales are based on the quest for an absolute and absent cause. Let me explain one by one the terms of this formula. There exists a cause — to be understood in a very broad sense. It is often a character, but sometimes also an event or an object. Its effect is the tale, the story which we are told. The cause is absolute: everything in the story owes its presence, in the last analysis, to it. But it is absent and we set off in quest of it. And it is not only absent but for most of the time unknown as well; only its existence, not its nature, is suspected. There is a quest: that is, the story consists in the search for, the pursuit of this initial cause, this primary essence. The story stops if it is found. On the one hand then, there is an absence (of the cause, of the essence, of the truth) but this absence determines every-

Translated by David Robey.

[1] *The Complete Tales of Henry James*, ed. Leon Edel (Rupert Hart-Davis, London, 1962–64), ix. 273–315. Except where a contrary indication is given all references in the following pages to James's tales will be to this edition (to be given as *Tales*). [Tr.]

[2] Sir Francis Galton (1822–1911), explorer, anthropologist, founder of eugenics, also pioneered the development of composite photographs. [Ed.]

thing; on the other hand, there is a presence (of the quest) which is simply the pursuit of the absence. The secret of James's tales is, therefore, precisely this existence of an essential secret, of something which is not named, of an absent, overwhelming force which puts the whole present machinery of the narrative into motion. The movement of James's stories is a double and, in appearance, contradictory one (which allows him to start it ceaselessly over and over again): on the one hand he deploys all his strength to reach the hidden essence, to unveil the secret object; on the other, he constantly moves it further and further away. He protects it up to the end of the story, if not beyond. The absence of the cause (or of the truth) is present in the text; still more, it is its logical origin, its *raison d'être;* the cause is that which, by its absence, gives rise to the text. The essential element is absent; absence is an essential element.

Before illustrating the many variations of this "figure in the carpet," I must deal with a possible objection: that not all of James's works follow this same pattern. Even limiting ourselves to the tales alone, we find some which do not share this movement, though it is present in most of them. Two further explanations are therefore necessary. The first is that this "figure" is tied more especially to one period in James's life: it dominates his work almost exclusively from 1892 until at least 1903, when James was in his fifties. During these twelve years James wrote almost half his tales. Those written before this period can only be considered, in the light of this hypothesis, as work of a preparatory nature, brilliant, but not original, exercises, which fall within the framework of the lesson James learnt from Flaubert and Maupassant. The second explanation is of a theoretical, not a historical order: it may be supposed, it seems to me, that an author approaches this "figure in the carpet," which resumes and underlies the whole of his writing, more closely in some of his works than in others. And this explains the fact that, even after 1892, James continued to write tales that belong among his "realistic" exercises.

Let us begin with the most elementary case: that in which the story is formed around a char-

acter or a phenomenon surrounded by an aura of mystery which is lifted at the end. *Sir Dominick Ferrand* (1892)[3] can be taken as an example of this type. It is the story of a poor writer, Peter Baron, who lives in the same house as a musical widow, Mrs. Ryves. One day Baron buys an old desk; and, by the greatest of chances, he discovers it to have a double back and therefore a secret drawer. Baron is fascinated by this first mystery, and succeeds in penetrating it: he takes a few bundles of old letters out of the drawer. An unexpected visit from Mrs. Ryves — with whom he is secretly in love — interrupts his exploration; she has had an intuition that Peter is threatened by some danger, and, noticing the bundles of letters, begs him never to look at them. This sudden action creates two new mysteries: what is the content of the letters? how can Mrs. Ryves have had such an intuition? The first of these is resolved a few pages later: the letters contain compromising information about Sir Dominick Ferrand, a statesman who died several years beforehand. But the second mystery persists until the end of the novel, and its explanation is delayed by other repercussions. These concern Peter Baron's hesitation as to what to do with the letters. He is approached by the editor of a magazine, to whom he has revealed their existence, and who offers him a considerable sum for them. Each time he is tempted (he is extremely poor) to make the letters public, a new "intuition" of Mrs. Ryves's, with whom he is falling more and more in love, arrives to stop him. It is this second force that wins the day, and in the end, Peter burns the compromising letters. The final revelation follows: Mrs. Ryves confesses to him, in an outburst of sincerity, that she is the illegitimate daughter of Sir Dominick Ferrand, the child of the same liaison as the letters are about.

Behind this vaudevillelike plot — with characters turning out in the end to be close relatives of one another — one can discern the fundamental scheme of James's tales: the absolute and secret cause of all the events is an absent factor (Sir Dominick Ferrand) and a mystery (the relationship between him and Mrs. Ryves). The

[3]*Tales,* viii. 343–405. [Tr.]

whole of her strange behavior is founded (with hints of the supernatural) on this secret relationship, and her behavior, moreover, determines Baron's. The intermediary mysteries (what is in the desk? what are the letters about?) are other causes which, because they are unknown, provoke the presence of the tale. The appearance of the cause brings the tale to an end; once the mystery has been uncovered, there is nothing else to tell. The presence of the truth is possible, but it is incompatible with the tale.

*In the Cage* (1898)[4] is another step in the same direction. Ignorance, here, is not due to a secret which could be revealed at the end of the story, but to the imperfection of our means of knowledge; and the "truth" which is arrived at in the final pages is, in contrast with the certain and definitive truth of *Sir Dominick Ferrand,* nothing else but a lesser degree of ignorance. This lack of knowledge is caused by the profession of the principal character and by the centre of her interests: the young lady whose name we never learn is a telegraphist, and all her attention is directed towards two persons whom she only knows through their telegrams: Captain Everard and Lady Bradeen.

The young telegraphist possesses hardly any information concerning the lives of the two people that interest her. In fact she only has three telegrams, around which she builds up her hypotheses. The first is this: "Everard, Hôtel Brighton, Paris. Only understand and believe. 22nd to 26th, and certainly 8th and 9th. Perhaps others. Come. Mary" (p. 145). The second: "Miss Dolman, Parade Lodge, Parade Terrace, Dover. Let him instantly know right one, Hôtel de France, Ostend. Make it seven nine four nine six one. Wire me alternative Burfield's" (p. 181). And the last: "Absolutely necessary to see you. Take last train Victoria if you can catch it. If not, earliest morning, and answer me direct either way" (p. 219). On this meagre canvas the telegraphist embroiders a whole romance in her imagination. The absolute cause here is the life of Everard and Lady Bradeen; but the telegraphist knows nothing of it, shut up as she is in her cage

[4]*Tales,* x. 139–242. [Tr.]

at the post-and-telegraph-office. Her quest is thus all the longer, all the more difficult, and, at the same time, all the more exciting.

The only meeting that she has with Everard outside the post office — between the second and the third telegrams — sheds little light on his character. She can see what he looks like physically, observe his gestures, listen to his voice, but his "essence" remains as intangible as it was when they were separated by the glass cage, and possibly more so. The senses perceive only what is secondary — appearances. They cannot reach as far as the truth. The only revelation (but we dare not call it that) comes at the end, in a conversation between the telegraphist and her friend Mrs. Jordan. This lady's husband, Mr. Drake, has been engaged by Lady Bradeen; so Mrs. Jordan is able to help her friend, though only slightly, to understand what has happened to Lady Bradeen and Captain Everard. Her understanding is made particularly difficult, however, by the fact that she pretends to know much more than she actually does, so as not to be humiliated in front of her friend; her ambiguous replies prevent certain revelations from being made. "Why, don't you know the scandal?" Mrs. Jordan asks, to which her friend answers evasively: "Oh, there was nothing public." One must not, however, overestimate the extent of Mrs. Jordan's knowledge; in answer to her friend's further questions she explains:

"Why, he was *in* something."
Her comrade wondered. "In what?"
"I don't know. Something bad. As I tell you, something was found." (pp. 239–40)

There is no truth; there is no certainty. All we are left with at the end is this "something bad." Once the story is finished we cannot say we know who Captain Everard was; we are simply less ignorant than we were at the beginning. The essence has not made itself present.

When, in *The Figure in the Carpet,* the young critic was searching for Vereker's secret, he asked the following question: "'Is it something in the style or something in the thought? An element of form or an element of feeling?' He indulgently shook my hand again, and I felt my questions to be crude and my distinctions pitiful"

(p. 284). Vereker's condescension is understandable. Were we to be asked the same question about the figure in Henry James's carpet, we should have just as much difficulty in finding a reply. Every aspect of the story shares the same movement, as we shall try to prove.

Critics have frequently pointed out (as James himself did) a "technical" feature of these tales: every event is described from someone's point of view.[5] We learn the truth about Sir Dominick Ferrand not directly, but through the eyes of Peter Baron; in fact as readers we never see anything but Baron's consciousness. The same is true of *In the Cage:* the narrator never at any moment places before the eyes of the reader the experiences of Everard and Lady Bradeen, but only presents him with the telegraphist's picture of these experiences. An omniscient narrator could have named the essence, but the girl is not capable of doing so.

James cherished this indirect "vision" above everything else — "that magnificent and masterly indirectness,"[6] as he calls it in a letter — and carried the exploration of it to considerable lengths. He describes his work thus: "I must add indeed that, such as they were [the Moreens, characters in *The Pupil*], or as they may at present incoherently appear, I don't pretend really to have 'done' them; all I have given in 'The Pupil' is little Morgan's troubled vision of them as reflected in the vision, also troubled enough, of his devoted friend."[7] We do not see the Moreens directly, we see X's perception of the perception of Y, who sees them. An even more complex case appears at the end of *In the Cage:* we observe the telegraphist's perception of Mrs. Jordan's perception, and she in turn tells what she extracted from Mr. Drake who, in *his* turn, only knows Captain Everard and Lady Bradeen from a distance.

Speaking of himself in the third person, James continues: "Addicted to seeing through — one thing through another, accordingly, and still other things through that — he takes, too greedily perhaps, on any errand, as many things as possible by the way" (p. xviii). Or, as the narrator of *The Beldonald Holbein* says: "It is not my fault if I am so put together as often to find more life in situations obscure and subject to interpretation than in the gross rattle of the foreground."[8] It is not surprising, therefore, that we only see the "vision" of a character, and never, directly, the object of this "vision"; nor is it surprising to find in James's writings sentences like this: "He knew I really couldn't help him and that I knew he knew I couldn't."[9]

But this "technique," about which so much has been written, of "visions," or points of view, is no more a "technique" than, let us say, the themes of the text. We now see that James's indirect "vision" is a part of the same "figure in the carpet" as we discovered in our analysis of the plots of his stories. The fact that he never gives a clear and full representation of the object of perception, the cause of all the characters' efforts, is nothing but a translation into another form of the general theme of the tales: the quest for an absolute and absent cause. The "technical" elements of these works have the same significance, therefore, as the thematic, and these, in turn, are as "technical" (that is to say, organized) as the rest.

What is the origin of this idea of James's? In a sense all he has done is to erect his method as a narrator into a philosophical concept. There are, basically, two ways of depicting character. Here is an example of the first:

This dark-skinned, broad-shouldered priest, condemned hitherto to the austere chastity of the cloister, shivered and burned alternately at this night-scene of love and passion. The sight of this lovely, dishevelled girl in the arms of a young and ardent lover turned the blood in his veins to molten lead. He felt an extraordinary commotion within him; his eye penetrated with lascivious jealousy under

[5] I have here used the words "point of view," "perception," and "vision" (the last used by James himself) to translate the single French word *vision.* [Tr.]

[6] Letter to Mrs. Humphry Ward (July 1899), quoted from Edith Wharton, "The Man of Letters," in *Henry James, A Collection of Critical Essays,* ed. Leon Edel (Prentice-Hall, Englewood Cliffs, N.J., 1963), p. 34. [Au.]

[7] *The Novels and Tales of Henry James,* New York edition (Macmillan, London, 1909), vol. xi, pp. xvii–xviii. [Au.]

[8] *Tales,* xi. 295–96. [Au]

[9] From *Brooksmith, Tales,* viii. 23. [Au.]

all these unfastened clasps and laces (Victor Hugo, *Notre-Dame de Paris*).[10]

And here is an example of the second:

> She noted that his nails were longer than was the custom in Yonville. Looking after them was one of the clerk's principal occupations; and he kept a special knife for this purpose in his desk (Flaubert, *Madame Bovary*).[11]

In the first case the character's feelings are directly described (in our example the direct character of the narrative is attenuated by rhetorical figures). In the second, the essence is not named. On the one hand it is presented to us through someone's vision of it; on the other, the description of the features of a character's personality is replaced by that of an isolated habit — the famous "art of the detail," in which the part replaces the whole, following the well-known rhetorical figure of synecdoche.

For some time James followed in Flaubert's wake. When we spoke of his earlier "exercises" we were referring to those texts, precisely, in which he carries his use of synecdoche to perfection, and one can find examples of the same tendency right up to the end of his life. But in the stories with which we are concerned, James has gone one step further: he has become aware of Flaubert's sensationalism (or anti-essentialism), and instead of using it simply as a means, he makes it the constructive principle of his work. All that we can see is appearances, and their interpretation remains doubtful; only the quest for truth can be present; truth itself, although the cause of this movement, remains absent (as, for instance, in *In the Cage*).[12]

Let us now take another "technical" element: composition. What does the classic short story, for instance Boccaccio's, consist in? If we approach it at a fairly general level we could say

that, at its most simple, it tells of the passage from a state of equilibrium or disequilibrium to another such similar state.[13] In the *Decameron* it is often the conjugal ties of the two protagonists that constitute this initial equilibrium, which is then upset by the infidelity of the wife. A second state of disequilibrium appears at a second level at the end: the two lovers escape the punishment threatened by the deceived husband. At the same time a new equilibrium is introduced, since adultery acquires the status of a norm.

Keeping to the same level of generality we may observe a similar design in James's stories. Thus in *In the Cage* the stable situation of the telegraphist at the beginning is disturbed by the appearance of Captain Everard, and this disequilibrium reaches its climax during the meeting in the park. At the end of the story equilibrium is reestablished by the marriage of Everard and Lady Bradeen: the telegraphist abandons her dreams, leaves her job, and gets married herself shortly afterwards. The initial equilibrium is not identical to the final one: the first permits the telegraphist's dreams and hopes; the second does not.

But in making this summary of the plot of *In the Cage* we have only followed one of the lines of force of the narrative. The other involves the theme of apprenticeship; in contrast to the first, with its ebb-and-flow pattern, this one marks a gradation. At the beginning the telegraphist does not know anything about Captain Everard; at the end she reaches the peak of her knowledge about him. The first movement is a horizontal one, and is composed of the events which fill the telegraphist's life. The second suggests, rather, the image of a vertical spiral; it consists of successive glimpses (not, however, ordered in time) of the life and personality of Captian Everard. In the first the reader's interest is directed towards the future: what will come of the relationship between Everard and the girl? In the second it is turned towards the past: who is Everard, and what has happened to him?

The movement of the tale is the sum of these two lines of force; some events relate to the first,

---

[10]Tr. Andrew Lang (Heinemann, London, 1924), p. 298. [Tr.]

[11](Garnier, Paris, 1964), p. 88. [Au.]

[12]Flaubert himself wrote in a letter: "Have you ever believed in the existence of things? Is not everything illusion? There is no truth except in 'relations,' that is, in the way in which we perceive objects" (to Maupassant, 15 Aug. 1878). Tr. from G. Flaubert, *Correspondance*, viii (Conard, Paris, 1930), 135. [Au.]

[13]Cf. T. Todorov, *Grammaire du Décaméron* (Mouton, The Hague, 1969). [Tr.]

others to the second, and others still relate to both. Thus the girl's conversations with Mrs. Jordan do not advance the "horizontal" line at all, whilst her meetings with her future husband, Mr. Mudge, relate to this one alone. Evidently the search for knowledge takes precedence over the development of events, so that the "vertical" tendency is stronger than the "horizontal." Now this movement towards the comprehension of events, which replaces the movement of the events themselves, takes us back to the figure in the carpet: the presence of a quest, and the absence of its object. The "essence" of the events is not given to us straightaway; each fact, each phenomenon first appears surrounded by an aura of mystery; our interest, naturally, is directed towards "being," not towards "doing."

We now come finally to James's "style," which has always been described as excessively complex, obscure, unnecessarily difficult. In fact at this level too James surrounds the "truth," the event itself (which is frequently summed up in the main clause), with a number of subordinate clauses, each of which is simple in itself, but which produce, in their accumulation, an effect of complexity. However, these subordinate clauses are necessary because they illustrate the many intermediary stages which must be passed before one reaches the "kernel." Here is an example from the same story:

> There were times when all the wires in the country seemed to start from the little hole-and-corner where she plied for a livelihood, and where, in the shuffle of feet, the flutter of "forms," the straying of stamps and the ring of change over the counter, the people she had fallen into the habit of remembering and fitting together with others, and of having her theories and interpretations of, kept up before her their long procession and rotation (p. 153).

If we extract the principal proposition of this entangled sentence, we have: "There were times when . . . the people . . . kept up before her their long procession and rotation." But around this flat, banal "truth" James accumulates innumerable details and observations which are much more present than the principal proposition itself, the "kernel" which as an absolute cause has oc-

casioned this movement, but which none the less remains a quasi-absence. An American stylistician, R. Ohmann, has suggested that much of the complexity of James's style is due to this tendency to "self-embedding," the "embedded" elements having a much greater importance than the main part of the sentence.[14] We may go further and say that the complexity of James's style depends entirely on this constructive principle, and not at all on any referential, for instance psychological, complexity. The "style" and "sentiments," the "form" and the "content" all say the same thing. They all repeat the same figure in the carpet.

This variant of our general theme allows us to penetrate the secret: at the end of the story Peter Baron acquires the information, the search for which constituted its mainspring; equally, if absolutely necessary, the telegraphist could have found out the truth about Captain Everard. We are, then, in the domain of the *hidden*; but there are other instances in which the "absence" cannot be overcome by human means, instances where the absolute cause is a *ghost*. There is no risk of such a hero passing as it were unnoticed; the whole text organizes itself around the search for him.

We could go further and say that, if this ever-absent cause is to become present, it *has* to be a ghost. For, curiously enough, Henry James always speaks of ghosts as *presences*. Here are some sentences taken at random from various stories dealing with ghosts: "I felt his presence as a strong appeal, almost an oppression."[15] "A perfect presence . . . A splendid presence."[16] "The hideous plain presence . . ."[17] "He was absolutely, on this occasion, a living, detestable, dangerous presence."[18] ". . . The spot where he had turned cold with extinction of his last pulse of doubt as to there being in the place another presence than his own."[19] "The image of the

[14]R[ichard] Ohmann, "Generative Grammars and the Concept of Literary Style," *Word*, xx (1964), 436–37. [Au.]
[15]From *Sir Edmund Orme, Tales*, viii. 133–34. [Au.]
[16]Ibid., p. 135. [Au.]
[17]*The Turn of the Screw, Tales*, x. 115. [Au.]
[18]Ibid., p. 71. [Au.]
[19]*The Jolly Corner, Tales*, xii. 221. [Au.]

'presence', whatever it was, waiting there for him to go — this image had not yet been so concrete for his nerves as when he stopped short of the point at which certainty would have come to him."[20] "Wasn't he now in the *most* immediate presence of some inconceivable occult activity?"[21] "It gloomed, it loomed, it was something, it was somebody, the prodigy of a personal presence."[22] And finally, this lapidary and falsely tautological formula: "The presence before him was a presence."[23] The essence is never present except when it is a ghost, that is, when it is absence *par excellence*.

Any one of James's ghost stories can prove to us the intensity of this presence. *Sir Edmund Orme* (1891)[24] tells the story of a young man who suddenly sees, at the side of Charlotte Marden, the girl that he loves, a strange pale man who, curiously, passes unobserved by everyone except him. The first time this half-visible, half-invisible character sits down next to Charlotte in a church ("He was a pale young man in black, with the air of a gentleman" [p. 128]). He appears again a little later in a reception-room:

> He held himself with a kind of habitual majesty, as if he were different from us . . . He stood there without speaking — young, pale, handsome, clean-shaven, decorous, with extraordinary light blue eyes and something old-fashioned, like a portrait of years ago, in his head, his manner of wearing his hair. He was in complete mourning . . . and he carried his hat in his hand (pp. 133–34).

He joins the most intimate conversations between the young couple: "He stood there . . . looking at me with the expressionless attention which borrowed its sternness from his sombre distinction" (p. 139). The narrator concludes: "Of what transcendent essence he was composed I knew not; I have no theory about him (leaving that to others), any more than I have one about such or such another of my fellow-mortals whom I have elbowed in life. He was as positive, as

individual, as ultimate a fact as any of these" (p. 145).

This "presence" of the ghost, one can guess, determines the evolution of the relationship between the narrator and Charlotte and, more generally, the development of the story as a whole. Charlotte's mother also sees the ghost, and recognizes it; it is the ghost of a young man who loved her, who committed suicide because she rejected him. The ghost returns to make sure that such feminine coquetry will not play the same trick on the suitor of the daughter of the woman who caused his death. In the end Charlotte decides to marry the narrator, the mother dies, and the ghost of Sir Edmund Orme disappears.

The tale of the fantastic is a form which lends itself well to James's design. Unlike tales of the marvelous (such as those of the *Thousand and One Nights*), it is characterized not by the mere presence of supernatural beings or phenomena, but by the hesitation that governs the reader's perception of the events represented in it. Throughout the story the reader asks himself (and often, within the book, a character does too) whether the facts which are recounted are to be attributed to natural or to supernatural causes, whether it is a matter of illusion or reality. This hesitation derives from the fact that the extraordinary (and thus potentially supernatural) event occurs not in a marvelous world, but in a familiar, everyday context.[25] The tale of the fantastic is therefore the story of a perception, and we have already seen how such a construction can be directly fitted into James's "figure in the carpet."

A tale like *Sir Edmund Orme* conforms fairly to this general description of the fantastic genre. A good many of the occult presence's appearances cause the narrator to hesitate, and his hesitation is crystallized in sentences of the "either . . . or" type: "It was either all a mistake or Sir Edmund Orme had vanished" (p. 148). Or: "Was the sound I heard when Chartie shrieked — the other and still more tragic sound I mean — the despairing cry of the poor lady's deathshock or

---

[20]Ibid. [Au.]

[21]Ibid., p. 224. [Au.]

[22]Ibid. [Au.]

[23]Ibid., p. 226. [Au.]

[24]*Tales*, viii. 119–51. [Au.]

[25]See Tzvetan Todorov, *The Fantastic: A Structural Approach to a Literary Genre* (Cleveland: Case Western Reserve Press, 1973). [Ed.]

the articulate sob (it was like a waft from a great tempest), of the exorcised and pacified spirit?" (p. 151). And so on.

Henry James's text has other characteristics in common with the genre of the fantastic in general. There is, for instance, a tendency to allegory (which, however, never becomes very strong or it would destroy the fantastic element), so that one sometimes wonders whether his is not simply a morality tale. The narrator interprets the whole episode thus: "It was a case of retributive justice. The mother was to pay, in suffering, for the suffering she had inflicted, and as the disposition to jilt a lover might have been transmitted to the daughter, the daughter was to be watched, so that *she* might be made to suffer should she do an equal wrong" (p. 146).

Similarly the story follows the gradation of supernatural appearances common to the tale of the fantastic; the narrator is present within the work itself, thus making it easier to integrate the reader into the world of the story; the allusions to the supernatural scattered throughout the text prepare us for an acceptance of it. But apart from these features which link James's tale with the fantastic genre, there are others which distinguish it from it, and which help to define its specific character. We can see this best in another text, the longest of the tales and probably the most famous: *The Turn of the Screw* (1896).[26]

The ambiguity of this story is just as important as that of *Sir Edmund Orme*. The narrator is a young woman, the governess of two children on a country estate. At a certain moment she realizes that the house in which they live is haunted by two former servants, now dead, of depraved morals. These two apparitions are all the more formidable for having established some sort of contact with the children, though the children pretend not to know about it. The governess has no doubts whatever concerning their presence ("It was not, I am sure today as I was sure then, my mere infernal imagination . . . " [pp. 84–85]. Or again: "Even while she spoke the hideous plain presence stood undimmed and undaunted" [p. 115]). To support her conviction she finds perfectly rational arguments:

[26]*Tales*, x. 15–138. [Au.]

Late that night, while the house slept, we had another talk in my room; when she went all the way with me as to its being beyond doubt that I had seen exactly what I had seen. To hold her perfectly in the pinch of that, I found, I had only to ask her how, if I had "made it up," I came to be able to give, of each of the persons appearing to me, a picture disclosing, to the last detail, their special marks — a portrait on the exhibition of which she had instantly recognized and named them (p. 61).

The governess tries to exorcise the children: as a result one falls seriously ill, whilst only death can "purify" the other.

However, this same series of events could be presented in an entirely different manner, avoiding altogether the introduction of infernal forces into the story. For the governess's testimony is continually contradicted by that of the other characters ("What a dreadful turn, to be sure, Miss! Where on earth do you see anything?" the housekeeper exclaims [p. 115]; and on the same occasion one of the children, Flora, cries: "I don't know what you mean. I see nobody. I see nothing. I never *have*" [p. 116]). This contradiction reaches such a point that at the end the governess herself has a terrifying suspicion: "Within a minute there had come to me out of my very pity the appalling alarm of his being perhaps innocent. It was for the instant confounding and bottomless, for if he *were* innocent, what then on earth was *I*?" (p. 136).

It is not of course difficult to find realistic explanations for the governess's hallucinations. She is an excitable and hypersensitive person, and, on the other hand, dreaming up this danger is the only way of bringing the children's uncle, with whom she is secretly in love, to the estate. She herself feels the need to defend herself against a possible accusation of insanity: "She accepted without directly impugning my sanity the truth as I gave it to her," she says of the housekeeper (p. 48); and later: "I go on, I know, as if I were crazy; and it's a wonder I'm not" (p. 81). If we add to this the fact that the apparitions always occur at twilight or even during the night and that, on the other hand, certain of the children's reactions which might otherwise seem strange could easily be explained by the governess's own power of suggestion, the story would retain nothing of the supernatural, and we should simply be faced with the account of a neurosis.

This possibility of a double interpretation of the tale has given rise to interminable discussions among the critics: do the ghosts really exist in *The Turn of the Screw,* or do they not? Yet the answer is obvious: in preserving this ambiguity at the very heart of the story James has simply followed the rules of the genre. Not everything in this story, however, is conventional. Whereas the classic nineteenth-century tale of the fantastic has as its principal and explicit theme the hesitation of the protagonist, in James's work the representation of such hesitation is virtually eliminated, and only survives in the reader. The narrators of *Sir Edmund Orme* and of *The Turn of the Screw* are both convinced of the reality of their visions.

At the same time we find in this text those same features of James's narrative as we have already observed elsewhere. Not only is the whole story based on the two ghostly characters, Miss Jessel and Peter Quint, but, for the governess, the essential question is whether the children have perceived the ghosts as well. In the quest which forms the subject of the story perception and knowledge take the place of the object which is, or is to be, perceived. The governess is less terrified by the vision of Peter Quint than by the possibility that the children should also have seen him. Similarly in *Sir Edmund Orme* the mother of Charlotte Marden is less afraid of the sight of the ghost than she is that it should appear to her daughter.

The source of evil (and also of the action) in the story remains hidden: it is the vices of the two dead employees, unnamed vices which are transmitted to the children ("strange passages and perils, secret disorders, vices more than suspected" [pp. 52–53]). The acuteness of the danger is due precisely to the absence of any information about it: "What it was most impossible to get rid of was the cruel idea that, whatever I had seen, Miles and Flora saw *more* — things terrible and unguessable and that sprang from dreadful passages of intercourse in the past" (pp. 88–89).

To the question as to what really happened at Bly James answers in an oblique fashion: he casts doubt on the word *really,* and affirms the uncertainty of the experience in contrast to the stability — but also the absence — of the essence. One does not even have the right to say that the governess is such-and-such, or that Peter Quint is not. In this world the verb *to be* has lost one of its functions, that of affirming the existence or nonexistence of an object. None of our truths is better founded than that of the governess; it may be that the phantom existed, but little Miles paid with his life for the attempt to eliminate the uncertainty as to whether it did or not.[27]

The first variant of our figure in the carpet involved a natural and relative absence: the nature of the secret was such that it was not inconceivable that it should be penetrated. The second variant, on the other hand, described the absolute and supernatural absence of a ghost. A third variant presents us with an absence which is both absolute and natural: *death.*

We can observe this first of all in a tale which is very close to the "fantastic" variant: *The Friends of the Friends*[28] (1896). A man has seen the ghost of his mother at the moment of her death, and a woman has had the same experience with her father. Struck by this coincidence their common friends — the narrator in particular — try to organize a meeting between them. But all efforts fail to bring them together, each time, as it happens, for the most harmless of reasons. The woman dies, and the man (who is also engaged to the female narrator) claims to have met her on the day of her death. Was it a living being or a ghost that he met? No one will ever know the answer, and as a result of this meeting the engagement between the man and the narrator is broken off.

While both of them were alive, a meeting between them — their love — was impossible. Physical presence would have destroyed life. Not that they knew this in advance: they tried, though always in vain, to meet, but after a final effort, which fails because of the narrator's fear, the

[27]For a fuller treatment of James's ghost stories, see my essay "Les Fantômes de Henry James" in *Poétique de la prose,* pp. 186–96. [Au.]

[28]Originally entitled *The Way it Came.* In *Tales,* ix. 371–401. [Au.]

woman resigns herself to her fate: "I shall never, never see him" (p. 383). A few hours later she is dead, as if death were a necessary condition for their meeting to take place (just as they both met their parents as these were about to die). The moment that life (an insignificant presence) ends, there comes the triumph of that essential absence, death. If one believes the man, the woman visited him between ten and eleven in the evening, without saying a word; at midnight she was dead. The narrator has to decide whether this meeting "really" took place, or whether it is of the same nature as the meetings with the dying parents. She would like to opt for the first solution ("It is remarkable that for a moment, though only for a moment, I found relief in the more personal, as it were, but also the more natural of the two odd facts" [p. 388]); however, this relief does not last, for she realizes that this version of events is too easy, and fails to explain the change which has taken place in her friend.

One cannot speak of death *in itself*; one always dies for someone. "She's buried, but she's not dead. She's dead for the world — she's dead for me. But she's not dead for *you*," says the narrator (p. 397). And: "My unextinguished jealousy — that was the Medusa-mark. It hadn't died with her death, it had lividly survived, and it was fed by suspicions unspeakable" (p. 397). And she is right, for this meeting which had never taken place in life gives birth to an incredible love. All that we know about it is what the narrator herself believes, but she succeeds in convincing us: "How *can* you hide it when you're abjectly in love with her, when you're sick almost to death with the joy of what she gives you? . . . You love her as you've *never* loved, and, passion for passion, she gives it straight back!" (p. 400). Her fiancé does not dare deny this, and the engagement is broken off. The next stage is rapidly reached: since only death can provide the conditions for the man's love, he takes refuge in it himself.

When six years later, in solitude and silence, I heard of his death I hailed it as a direct contribution to my theory. It was sudden, it was never properly accounted for, it was surrounded by circumstances in which — for oh, I took them to pieces! — I distinctly read an intention, the mark of his own hidden hand. It was the result of a long necessity,

of an unquenchable desire. To say exactly what I mean, it was a response to an irresistible call (pp. 400–401).

Death makes a character become the absolute and absent cause of life. More still, death is the source of life, and love is born out of death instead of being interrupted by it. This romantic theme (that of Gautier's *Spirite*) reaches its fullest development in *Maud-Evelyn* (1900).[29] This tale tells the story of a young man, Marmaduke, who falls in love with Maud-Evelyn, a young girl who died fifteen years before he even learned of her existence. (One might note how often the title of a tale puts into relief the absent, essential character in it: *Sir Dominick Ferrand, Sir Edmund Orme, Maud-Evelyn*; and similarly in other stories like *Nona Vincent*.)

Marmaduke's love, and therefore the "reality" of Maud-Evelyn, goes through all the stages of a gradation. At the beginning Marmaduke merely admires the girl's parents, who behave as if she were not dead at all; then he begins to think as they do; finally, to use the words of his former friend Lavinia: "He thinks he knew her" (p. 61). A little later Lavinia declares: "He *was* in love with her" (p. 62). Next comes their "marriage," after which Maud-Evelyn "dies" ("He has lost his wife," Lavinia says [p. 70], in order to explain the fact that he is in mourning). Marmaduke dies in his turn, but Lavinia takes his belief over herself.

In James's usual manner the absent central character of the story, Maud-Evelyn, is viewed not directly, but through a series of multiple reflections. The story is told by a certain Lady Emma, who derives her impressions from her conversations with Lavinia, who in turn meets Marmaduke. He, moreover, only knows Maud-Evelyn's parents, the Dedricks, who evoke the memory of their dead daughter. Thus the "truth" is four times deformed. Besides, these "visions" are not identical, but constitute a gradation in themselves. For Lady Emma Marmaduke's behavior is mere folly ("Was he altogether silly or was he only altogether mercenary?" [p. 57]). She lives in a world in which the imaginary and the real form two distinct and separate blocks. La-

[29]*Tales*, xi. 43–75. [Au.]

vinia adheres to the same standards, but she is prepared to accept Marmaduke's act because she judges it to be beautiful: "It's self-deception, no doubt, but it comes from something that . . . is beautiful when one does hear of it" (p. 63). And later she says: "Of course it's only an idea, . . . but it seems to me a beautiful one" (p. 71). For Marmaduke himself death is not a step into nonbeing; on the contrary, death allowed him to have the most extraordinary of experiences ("The moral appeared to be that nothing in the way of human experience of the exquisite could again particularly matter" [p.65]). Finally the Dedricks take Maud-Evelyn's existence quite literally, communicating with her through mediums, etc. James has illustrated here, therefore, four possible attitudes towards the imaginary or, alternatively, towards the figurative sense of an expression: the realistic attitude of refusal and condemnation, the aestheticizing attitude of admiration mingled with incredulity, the poetic attitude which admits the coexistence of being and nonbeing, and finally the naïve attitude which interprets the figurative meaning literally.

We have seen that, in their composition, James's stories are turned towards the past: the quest for an essential and permanently evanescent secret implies that the tale should be an exploration of the past rather than a progression into the future. In *Maud-Evelyn* the past becomes a thematic element, and its glorification one of the principal subjects of the story. Maud-Evelyn's second life is the result of this exploration: "It's the gradual effect of brooding over the past; the past, that way, grows and grows" (p. 62). There are no limits to the enrichment which the past offers, which is why the parents of Maud-Evelyn act as they do. Marmaduke says: "You see, they couldn't do much, the old people — and they can do still less now — with the future; so they had to do what they could with the past" (p. 67). And he concludes: "The more we live in the past, the more things we find in it" (p. 70). To "limit" oneself to the past is to deny the originality of events, to consider that one lives in a world of memories. Following the chain of reactions to discover the initial motive, the absolute beginning, one comes up suddenly against death, the end *par excellence*. Death is the origin

and essence of life, the past is the future of the present, the answer precedes the question.

James wrote another story, a veritable requiem which undoubtedly merits first place among his explorations of the life of the dead: *The Altar of the Dead* (1896).[30] Nowhere else is the force of death, the presence of absence, so intensely affirmed. Stransom, the principal character of this tale, lives in the cult of the dead. All he knows is absence and he prefers it to everything else. His fiancée died before the first "bridal embrace" (p. 231); but Stransom's life has not suffered as a result, and he enjoys being "for ever widowed" (ibid.). His life was still "ruled by a pale ghost, it was still ordered by a sovereign presence" (ibid.); it is organized perfectly around its "central hollow" (p. 249).

One day he meets a friend, Paul Creston, widowed a few months beforehand. Suddenly he notices beside him another woman whom his friend introduces with some embarrassment as his new wife. This replacement of a sublime absence by a vulgar presence shocks Stransom deeply. "That new woman, that hired performer, Mrs. Creston? Mrs. Creston had been more living for him than any woman but one . . . . He felt quite determined, as he walked away, never in his life to go near her. She was perhaps a human being, but Creston oughtn't to have shown her without precautions, oughtn't indeed to have shown her at all" (p. 235). For him the new wife, the presence, is a forgery, a "wife for foreign service or purely external use" (p. 236); it is monstrous to have substituted her for the memory of the absent woman.

Little by little Stransom enlarges and elaborates his cult of the dead. He wants to perform "some material act" (p. 239), and decides to dedicate an altar to them. Each of his many dead friends ("He had perhaps not had more losses than most men, but he had counted his losses more" [p. 232]) is given a candle, and Stransom sinks into an attitude of admiring contemplation in front of them. Stransom's pleasure is even greater than he had expected, because he can thus reintegrate his past:

[30]*Tales,* ix. 231–71. [Au.]

Half the satisfaction of the spot for this mysterious and fitful worshipper was that he found the years of his life there, and the ties, the affections, the struggles, the submissions, the conquests, if there had been such, a record of that adventurous journey in which the beginnings and the endings of human relations are the lettered milestones (pp. 241–42).

Another reason is that death is a purification ("The fellow had only had to die for everything that was ugly in him to be washed out in a torrent" [p.260]), and that death renders possible, finally, the establishment of the harmony which is the end of life. The dead represented by the candles are infinitely close to him: "Various persons in whom his interest had not been intense drew closer to him by entering this company." And as a natural consequence "he almost caught himself wishing that certain of his friends would now die, that he might establish with them in this manner a connection more charming than, as it happened, it was possible to enjoy with them in life" (p. 242).

Only one further step remains to be taken, and Stransom is not held up by it: that of envisaging his own death. He has already begun to dream of this "rich future" (p. 265): "'The chapel will never be full till a candle is set up before which all the others will pale. It will be the tallest candle of all.' Her mild wonder rested on him. 'What candle do you mean?' 'I mean, dear lady, my own'" (p. 250).

Suddenly a false note enters into this praise of death. Stransom meets, in front of his altar, a lady in mourning who attracts him precisely on account of her devotion to the dead. But when this acquaintance becomes more intimate, he learns that the lady mourns for one person alone, Acton Hague, a formerly intimate friend of Stransom's with whom he had violently quarrelled, and the only dead friend for whom he has never lit a candle. The woman realizes this as well, and the charm of their relationship is broken. Death is present: "Acton Hague was between them, that was the essence of the matter; and he was never so much between them as when they were face to face" (p. 263). Thus the woman is forced to choose between Stransom and Hague (she prefers Hague), and Stransom to choose between the resentment he feels towards Hague and his affection for the woman (his resentment gets the upper hand). And so we have this moving dialogue: "'Will you give him his candle?' she asked . . . 'I can't do that!' he declared at last. 'Then good-bye'" (p. 258). It is death that determines the life of the living. At the same time the living do not cease to act upon the life of the dead (since interpenetration is possible in both directions). As soon as his friend abandons him, Stransom discovers that his affection for the dead disappears: "All the lights had gone out — all his Dead had died again" (p. 266).

One further step, therefore, remains to be taken. After falling seriously ill, Stransom returns to the church, having made up his mind to forgive Acton Hague. He finds his friend there, and a corresponding change has occurred in her as well: she is prepared to forget her one Dead, and to devote herself to the cult of *the* dead. Thus this cult reaches its ultimate sublimation: love, friendship, or resentment no longer govern it; death is glorified in its pure state, without any regard for those whom it has touched. Forgiveness has removed the final barrier on the road to death.

So Stransom can entrust his own life to his friend and die; he expires in her arms, whilst she feels a great dread seize hold of her heart.

We now come to the final variant of our "figure in the carpet": that in which the place occupied successively by the hidden, the ghost, and by death, is taken by the *work of art*. And if the short story tends in general, more than the novel, to become a theoretical statement, James's tales about art are veritable aesthetic treatises.

*The Real Thing* (1892)[31] is a fairly simple parable. The narrator, a painter, receives a visit one day from a couple who bear every sign of nobility. They ask if they might pose for any book-illustrations that he might be doing, since they are reduced to a state of extreme poverty. They are sure of fitting this role well, for the painter has to depict figures belonging precisely to the leisured classes to which they themselves previously belonged. "We thought," the husband

[31]*Tales*, viii. 229–58. [Au.]

says, "that if you ever have to do people like us, we might be something like it. *She*, particularly — for a lady in a book, you know" (p. 233).

The couple are indeed the "real thing," but this does not in any way facilitate the painter's task. On the contrary, his illustrations become worse and worse, until one day one of his friends points out to him that the fault is perhaps his models'. On the other hand his other models have nothing "real" about them, but they nonetheless inspire the most successful illustrations. One Miss Churm was "only a freckled cockney, but she could represent everything, from a fine lady to a shepherdess" (p. 239). A vagabond Italian named Oronte is also perfectly suited to illustrations of princes and gentlemen.

The absence of "real" qualities in Miss Churm and Oronte is precisely what gives them their essential value, so necessary to the work of art; whereas the presence of such qualities in the more distinguished models can only be superfluous. The painter explains this by his "innate preference for the represented subject over the real one: the defect of the real one was so apt to be a lack of representation. I liked things that appeared; then one was sure. Whether they *were* or not was a subordinate and always a profitless question" (p. 237). So it is that, at the end, we find the two uncultivated and low-born characters playing "noble" parts to perfection, while the "noble" models do the washing up, following the "perverse and cruel law in virtue of which the real thing could be so much less precious than the unreal" (p. 258).

Art therefore is not the reproduction of a given "reality," nor is it created through the imitation of such a reality. It demands quite different qualities; to be "real" can even, as in the present case, be harmful. In the realm of art there is nothing preliminary to the work, nothing which constitutes its origin. It is the work of art itself that is original; the secondary becomes primary. Hence the frequent comparisons in James's work that explain "nature" through "art," for instance:

> That was the way many things struck me at that time, in England — as reproductions of something that existed primarily in art or literature. It was not the picture, the poem, the fictive page, that seemed to me a copy; these things were the originals and

the life of happy and distinguished people was fashioned in their image.[32]

Several other stories, in particular *The Death of the Lion* (1894),[33] take up the problem of art and life, but from another point of view, that of the relationship between an author's life and his work. A writer becomes famous towards the end of his days; however, the public's interest in him relates not to his work but only to his life. Journalists ask him avidly for details of his personal existence, and his admirers prefer to see the man to reading his books. The ending of the story, at once sublime and grotesque, shows the profound indifference felt for the work by those very persons who, in admiring its author, claim to admire the work as well. This misapprehension has fatal consequences: not only can the writer no longer write after his "success," but at the end he is killed (literally) by his adorers.

"The artist's life's his work, and this is the place to observe him," says the narrator, a young writer himself (p. 91). Later he makes a similar point: "Let whoever would represent the interest in his presence . . . I should represent the interest in his work — in other words in his absence" (p. 95). These words merit reflection. Psychological criticism (which, after "realistic" criticism, is here brought into question) considers the work as a presence — although of little importance in itself — and the author as its absent and absolute cause. James reverses the relationship: the author's life is only an appearance, a contingency, an accident; it is an inessential presence. The work of art is the truth to be sought after, even if there is no hope of finding it. To understand a work better it is no use knowing its author; on the contrary, this course of action kills both the man (Paraday dies) and the work (the manuscript is lost).

The same problem lies at the heart of the story *The Private Life* (1892)[34] where the configuration of absence and presence is drawn in all its details. Of the two opposed characters in it Lord Mellifont is a man of the world; his existence is all

[32]From *The Author of "Beltraffio," Tales*, v. 307. [Au.]
[33]*Tales*, ix. 77–118. [Au.]
[34]*Tales*, viii. 189–227. [Au.]

presence, all inessential. He is the most agreeable of companions; his conversation is rich, relaxed, and instructive. But it would be vain to try and find anything deep or personal in him; he only exists as a function of others. He has a splendid presence, but it dissimulates nothing, so much so that no one ever succeeds in observing him alone. "He's there from the moment he knows somebody else," one of the characters says of him (p. 218); as soon as he is alone he ceases to be.

Beside him Clare Vawdrey exemplifies the other possible combination of presence and absence, a combination which is possible because of the fact that he is a writer and creates works of art. This great writer's presence is mediocre, null; his behavior does not correspond in any way at all to his work. For instance the narrator tells of being alone with him during a mountain storm:

> Clare Vawdrey was disappointing. I don't know exactly what I should have predicated of a great author exposed to the fury of the elements, I can't say what particular Manfred attitude I should have expected my companion to assume, but it seemed to me somehow that I shouldn't have looked to him to regale me in such a situation with stories (which I had already heard), about the celebrated Lady Ringrose (p. 225).

However, this Clare Vawdrey is not the "real" one; at the same time as the narrator is exchanging literary gossip with him, another Clare is sitting in front of his desk writing pages of magnificent prose. "The world was vulgar and stupid, and the real man would have been a fool to come out for it when he could gossip and dine by deputy" (ibid.).

The contrast is thus complete: Clare Vawdrey is double, and Lord Mellifont is not even single. "He [Lord Mellifont] was all public and had no corresponding private life, just as Clare Vawdrey was all private and had no corresponding public one" (p. 212). We have here, then, the two complementary aspects of a single movement: the presence is hollow (Lord Mellifont), and the absence is full (the work of art). In the paradigm in which we have inscribed it the work of art has a place all of its own; it is more essential than

the hidden, more accessible than the ghost, more material than death; it offers the only way of experiencing essence. The other Clare Vawdrey sitting in the darkness is hidden by the work itself; he is the text that writes itself, the absence that is more present than any other.

The perfect symmetry that forms the basis of this story is characteristic of Henry James's conception of the plot of his tales. They abound, generally, with coincidences and symmetries. One thinks, for instance, of Guy Walsingham, a woman with a male pseudonym, and Dora Forbes, a man with a female pseudonym, in *The Death of the Lion*; of the incredible coincidences by means of which the plot is resolved in *The Tone of Time* (where the two women loved the same man) or *The Altar of the Dead* (where the same dead figure determines the behavior of the two characters); of the resolution of *Sir Dominick Ferrand*, and so on. We know that for James the interest of the tale lies not in its "horizontal" movement, but in the "vertical" exploration of a single event, and this is what explains the conventional and entirely predictable side of his stories.

*The Birthplace* (1903)[35] takes up and develops the theme of *The Death of the Lion*, that of the relation between a work of literature and the life of its author. This story tells of the public cult of the nation's greatest poet, dead now for many centuries; and in particular of the experience of a couple, Mr. and Mrs. Gedge, the keepers of the museum in the poet's "birthplace." A true interest in the poet should involve reading and admiring his work; on the other hand in dedicating oneself to his cult, one substitutes an insignificant presence for the essential absence. "None of Them care tuppence about Him. The only thing They care about is this empty shell — or rather, for it isn't empty, the extraneous, preposterous stuffing of it" (p. 421).

After feeling so happy, originally, because of his admiration for the poet, at being appointed keeper of the museum, Morris Gedge comes to notice the contradiction which lies at the root of the situation. His public duties oblige him to

[35]*Tales,* xi. 403–65. [Au.]

affirm the poet's presence in the house, and its objects; but his love for the poet — and for truth — leads him to question this presence ("I'll be hanged if He's *here!*" [p. 436]). To begin with, almost nothing is known about the poet's life; even the most basic facts about it are surrounded with uncertainty. "Well, I grant you there was somebody," Gedge says, "but the details are naught. The links are missing. The evidence — in particular about that room upstairs, in itself our Casa Santa — is *nil.* It was so awfully long ago" (p. 430). We know neither whether he was actually born in this room, nor even whether he was born at all. So Gedge suggests "modalising" the speech which in their capacity as guides they deliver to the public. "Couldn't you adopt . . . a slightly more *discreet* method? What we can say is that things have been *said;* that's all *we* have to do with" (p. 429).

Yet even this attempt to replace the reality of *being* by that which is *said,* by the reality of speech, does not go far enough. One should not regret the lack of information concerning the poet's life; one should be glad at it. The essence of the poet is his work, not his house; it is preferable, therefore, that his house should bear no trace of him whatever. As the wife of a visitor remarks: "It's rather a pity, you know, that He *isn't* here. I mean as Goethe's at Weimar. For Goethe *is* at Weimar." To which her husband replies: "Yes my dear; that's Goethe's bad luck. There he sticks. *This* man isn't anywhere. I defy you to catch him" (p. 436).

One last stage remains to be passed, and Gedge does not hesitate: "Practically . . . there *is* no author; that is for us to deal with. There are all the immortal people — *in* the work; but there's nobody else" (p. 439). Not only is the author a product of the work; he is also a useless product. The illusion of *being* must be dispelled: "There *is* no such Person" (ibid.).

The plot of the story takes up this same idea (which up to now we only saw in Gedge's statements). At the beginning the keeper of the museum tried to tell the public the truth, but all this brought him was the threat of dismissal from his post. So Gedge chooses another way; instead of reducing his little speech to the bare minimum which the facts of the matter permit, he amplifies

it to the point of absurdity, inventing nonexistent but plausible details about the poet's life in his birthplace. "It was a way like another, at any rate, of reducing the place to the absurd" (p. 453); exaggeration has the same sense as efface-ment. But the two ways are distinguished by one important property: whilst the first was simply the statement of the truth, the second has for him all the advantages of art. Gedge's speech is ad-mirable; it is a work of art in itself. Nor is his reward late in coming; instead of being dis-missed, Gedge finds his salary doubled at the end of the story, because of everything he has done for the poet.

James's very last tales avoid so categorical a formulation of any opinion whatever. They re-main indecisive, ambiguous; the bold colors of earlier years are blurred by new nuances. *The Velvet Glove* (1909)[36] takes up the same problem of the relation beteen "art" and "life," but gives a much less clear answer. John Berridge is a successful writer; in a fashionable *salon* he meets two striking characters, the Lord and the Prin-cess, who, like Olympians descended on to the earth, incarnate everything he has always dreamt of. The Princess flirts a little with Berridge, and he is on the point of losing his head over her when he realizes that she wants only one thing of him, that he should write the preface of her latest novel.

At first sight this tale is a praise of "life" in contrast to writing. From the very beginning of the reception Berridge says to himself: "What was the pale page of fiction compared with the intimately personal adventure that, in almost any direction, he [the young Lord] would have been all so stupidly, all so gallantly, all so instinctively . . . ready for?" (p. 237). As for the Princess, he is struck by the

really "decadent" perversity, recalling that of the most irresponsibly insolent of the old Romans and Byzantines, that could lead a creature so formed for living and breathing her Romance, and so com-mitted, up to the eyes, to the constant fact of her personal immersion in it and genius for it, the dreadful amateurish dance of ungrammatically

[36]*Tales,* xii. 233–65. [Au.]

scribbling it, with editions and advertisements and reviews and royalties and every other futile item . . . ? (p. 252).

Imagining himself an Olympian as well, Berridge throws as far as possible from him everything to do with writing:

He would leave his own stuff snugly unread, to begin with; that would be a beautiful start for an Olympian career. He should have been as unable to write those works in short as to make anything else of them; and he should have had no more arithmetic for computing fingers than any perfect-headed marble Apollo mutilated at the wrists. He should have consented to know but the grand personal adventure on the grand personal basis: nothing short of this . . . would begin to be, on any side, Olympian enough (p. 245).

But the moral that Berridge draws is not necessarily the moral of the tale. For one thing, the attitude of this famous writer might usefully be placed side by side with that of the Princess: both of them want to become what they are not. Berridge writes good novels, but sees himself, in his imagination, as a "prepossessing young shepherd" (p. 247); the Princess lives the life of the Gods, and at the same time wants to be a successful novelist. As James puts it:

The mysterious values of other types kept looming larger before you than the doubtless often higher but comparatively familiar ones of your own, and if you had anything of the artist's real feeling for life the attraction and the amusement of possibilities so projected were worth more to you, in nineteen moods out of twenty, than the sufficiency, the serenity, the felicity, whatever it might be, of your stale personal certitudes (p. 236).

On the other hand, to describe the "life" which is thus affirmed in opposition to writing, Berridge (and James) have only one word: "romantic." The young Lord's rendez-vous must be "of a high romantic order" (p. 237), and he himself resembles "far-off romantic and 'plastic' figures" (p. 248); the adventures of the Princess would have to have the "absolute attraction of romance" (p. 245). Thinking that the Princess loves him, it is only in books that Berridge can find an image of his feeling: "It was ground he had ventured on, scenically, representationally, in the artistic

sphere, but without ever dreaming he should 'realize' it thus in the social" (p. 253). It is not "life" that is affirmed in opposition to the novel, but rather the role of a character in relation to that of an author.

Besides John Berridge has as little success in becoming a "prepossessing shepherd" as the Princess in becoming a popular novelist. Just as Clare Vawdrey, in *The Private Life,* could not be both a great writer and a brilliant man of the world at the same time, so here Berridge must return to the unromantic condition of a novelist, after a romantic gesture (he kisses the Princess), the purpose of which is precisely to prevent her from playing the part of a novelist. Art and life are incompatible; with serene bitterness Berridge exclaims at the end: "You *are* Romance . . . , so what more do you want?" (p. 263). James leaves it to the reader to decide for himself which of the two alternatives he prefers; and we begin to perceive a possible reversal of the "figure in the carpet."

The motive force of Henry James's stories, that which determines their structure, is the essential secret. Moreover this organizing principle becomes itself the explicit theme of at least two of them. These are, as it were, metaliterary stories, stories devoted to the constructive principle of the story.

The first of these — *The Figure in the Carpet* — was discussed at the beginning of this study. The secret whose existence Vereker revealed becomes a motive force in the narrator's life; then in those of his friend, George Corvick, and of his friend's fiancée and wife, Gwendolen Erme; and finally in that of Gwendolen's second husband, Drayton Deane. At one point Corvick claims to have discovered the secret, but dies shortly afterwards. Gwendolen learns the solution shortly before her husband's death, but does not tell it to anyone else, keeping it silent until her own death. Thus at the story's end we are as ignorant as we were at the beginning.

This lack of change is, however, only apparent, for between the beginning and the end is the tale, that is, the search for the secret. And now we know that Henry James's secret (and, no doubt, Vereker's as well) consists precisely in the existence of a secret as such, of an absolute and absent cause, and in the effort to discover this secret, to make the absence present. Vereker's secret was thus revealed to us, but in the only way possible: if it had been named, it would no longer have existed, and it is precisely its existence that constitutes the secret. The secret is by definition inviolable, because it consists in the very fact that it exists. The quest of the secret must never finish, because it is identical with the secret itself. Some critics have already interpreted *The Figure in the Carpet* in this sense; thus Blackmur spoke of the "exasperation of the mystery without the presence of mystery";[37] Blanchot refers to this "art which cannot be deciphered, but is itself the cipher of the indecipherable";[38] and, with a greater degree of precision, Philippe Sollers explains it thus: "The solution of the problem which is expounded to us is nothing other than the exposition of the problem itself."[39]

On a more serious note, the same answer is taken up once again, and this time with a greater degree of nuance, in *The Beast in the Jungle* (1903).[40] John Marcher believes that some unknown but essential event is going to occur in his life, and he organizes it entirely around this future moment. His friend May Bartram describes his feeling thus: "You said you had had from your earliest time, as the deepest thing within you, the sense of being kept for something rare and strange, possibly prodigious and terrible, that was sooner or later to happen to you, that you had in your bones the foreboding and the conviction of, and that would perhaps overwhelm you" (p. 359).

May Bartram decides to join with Marcher in his watching for this event. He is very appreciative of her solicitude, and does not fail to wonder sometimes if this strange thing is connected with her. Thus when she moves into a house nearer to him, it occurs to him that "perhaps the great thing he had so long felt as in the lap of

the gods was no more than this circumstance, which touched him so nearly, of her acquiring a house in London" (p. 366). Similarly, when she falls ill, he "caught himself — for he *had* so done — *really* wondering if the great accident would take form now as nothing more than his being condemned to see this charming woman, this admirable friend, pass away from him" (p. 378). As her death approaches, this fear becomes almost a conviction: "Her dying, her death, his consequent solitude — *that* was what he had figured as the beast in the jungle, that was what had been in the lap of the gods" (p. 388).

However, this supposition never becomes a complete certainty, and Marcher, whilst appreciating May Bartram's efforts to help him, still continues to pass his life in an endless state of waiting. Before dying May tells him that the Thing is no longer there to be waited for, but that it has already happened. Marcher has the same feeling, but tries in vain to understand what this Thing consists in. Finally one day in front of May's tomb the revelation comes: "All the while he had waited the wait was itself his portion" (p. 401). The secret is the existence of the secret itself. Horrified by this realization, Marcher throws himself sobbing on to the tomb, and the story finishes with this picture.

"It wouldn't have been failure to be bankrupt, dishonoured, pilloried, hanged; it was failure not to be anything" (p. 379). Marcher could have avoided this; it would have been enough to pay a different sort of attention to May's existence. She was not the hidden secret, as he had sometimes thought; but by loving her he would have been able to avoid the mortal despair with which he was seized at the sight of the truth. May had understood this: in loving him she had found the secret of her life; helping Marcher in his search was her "essential thing." She asked for nothing better than to be interested in him, and in the end she has her reward: "I'm more sure than ever my curiosity, as you call it, will be but too well repaid" (p. 371). Marcher does not know how right he is when he says, dismayed at the idea of her death, that her absence would be "the absence of everything" (p. 391). The search for the secret and for truth is never anything but a search, a search without any content whatever;

[37]R. P. Blackmur, "In the Country of the Blue," *The Kenyon Review*, v (1943), 609. [Au.]

[38]M. Blanchot, *Le Livre à venir* (Gallimard, Paris, 1959), p. 161. [Au.]

[39]P. Sollers, *Logiques* (Seuil, Paris, 1968), p. 121. [Au.]

[40]*Tales*, xi. 351–402. [Au.]

May Bartram's life, on the other hand, has as its content her love for Marcher. The figure which we have observed in the course of our examination of the stories reaches here its ultimate, supreme form, which is at the same time its dialectical negation.

If Henry James's secret, the figure in the carpet of his work, the string on which the pearls of the individual stories are strung, if this secret is precisely the existence of a secret, how is it that we can now name it, and make the absence present? Are we not thus betraying James's fundamental precept, which consists in this affirmation of the absence, of the impossibility of describing the truth by its name? But criticism too (including ours) has always obeyed the same law. It is the search for truth, not its revelation — the quest for the treasure rather than the treasure itself, for the treasure can only be absent. Thus, once we have finished this "reading" of James, we must begin to read him, and throw ourselves into the quest for the sense of his work, though knowing as we do that this sense is nothing other than the quest itself.

# Jonathan Culler

b. 1944

*To the extent that structuralism and poststructuralism have been well received in North America, much of the credit should be given to Jonathan Dwight Culler, whose lucid distillations of structuralist, semiotic, and deconstructivist theories have reached a wide audience. Culler was born in Cleveland, Ohio, but moved with his family to New Haven, Connecticut, in 1946, when his father, A. Dwight Culler, accepted a position as professor of Victorian literature at Yale. Culler received a B.A. in history and literature (1966) at Harvard and a Rhodes scholarship to St. John's College at Oxford (1966–69), where he took a B.Phil. in comparative literature (1968) and a D.Phil. in modern languages (1972). Culler was a fellow of Selwyn College, Cambridge (1969–74), and of Brasenose College, Oxford (1974–77), and since 1977 he has been a professor of English and comparative literature at Cornell University. His list of publications is extensive — his books include* Flaubert: The Uses of Uncertainty *(1974),* Saussure *(1976, 1977; revised 1986),* The Pursuit of Signs *(1981), and* On Deconstruction *(1983). "Literary Competence" is the sixth chapter of* Structuralist Poetics *(1975), a revised version of his doctoral thesis, which won the Modern Language Association's prestigious James Russell Lowell Award.*

## Literary Competence

> To understand a sentence means to understand a language. To understand a language means to be master of a technique.   — WITTGENSTEIN[1]

When a speaker of a language hears a phonetic sequence, he is able to give it meaning because

[1]Ludwig Wittgenstein, *Philosophical Investigations*. [Ed.]

he brings to the act of communication an amazing repertoire of conscious and unconscious knowledge. Mastery of the phonological, syntactic and semantic systems of his language enables him to convert the sounds into discrete units, to recognize words, and to assign a structural description and interpretation to the resulting sentence, even though it be quite new to him. Without this implicit knowledge, this internalized grammar, the sequence of sounds does not speak to him. We are nevertheless inclined to say that the phonological and grammatical structure and the meaning are *properties* of the utterance, and there is no harm in that way of speaking so long as we remember that they are properties of the utterance only with respect to a particular grammar. Another grammar would assign different properties to the sequence (according to the grammar of a different language, for example, it would be nonsense). To speak of the structure of a sentence is necessarily to imply an internalized grammar that gives it that structure.

We also tend to think of meaning and structure as properties of literary works, and from one point of view this is perfectly correct: when the sequence of words is treated *as a literary work* it has these properties. But that qualification suggests the relevance and importance of the linguistic analogy. The work has structure and meaning because it is read in a particular way, because these potential properties, latent in the object itself, are actualized by the theory of discourse applied in the act of reading. "How can one discover structure without the help of a methodological model?" asks Barthes (*Critique et vérité*, p. 19).[2] To read a text as literature is not to make one's mind a *tabula rasa*[3] and approach it without preconceptions; one must bring to it an implicit understanding of the operations of literary discourse which tells one what to look for.

Anyone lacking this knowledge, anyone wholly unacquainted with literature and unfamiliar with the conventions by which fictions are read, would, for example, be quite baffled if presented with a poem. His knowledge of the language would enable him to understand phrases and sentences, but he would not know, quite literally, what to *make* of this strange concatenation of phrases. He would be unable to read it *as* literature — as we say with emphasis to those who would use literary works for other purposes

— because he lacks the complex "literary competence" which enables others to proceed. He has not internalized the "grammar" of literature which would permit him to convert linguistic sequences into literary structures and meanings.

If the analogy seems less than exact it is because in the case of language it is much more obvious that understanding depends on mastery of a system. But the time and energy devoted to literary training in schools and universities indicate that the understanding of literature also depends on experience and mastery. Since literature is a second-order semiotic system which has language as its basis, a knowledge of language will take one a certain distance in one's encounter with literary texts, and it may be difficult to specify precisely where understanding comes to depend on one's supplementary knowledge of literature. But the difficulty of drawing a line does not obscure the palpable difference between understanding the language of a poem, in the sense that one could provide a rough translation into another language, and understanding the poem. If one knows French, one can translate Mallarmé's "Salut," but that translation is not a thematic synthesis — it is not what we would ordinarily call "understanding the poem" — and in order to identify various levels of coherence and set them in relation to one another under the synoptic heading or theme of the "literary quest" one must have considerable experience of the conventions for reading poetry.

The easiest way to grasp the importance of these conventions is to take a piece of journalistic prose or a sentence from a novel and set it down on the page as a poem. The properties assigned to the sentence by a grammar of English remain unchanged, and the different meanings which the text acquires cannot therefore be attributed to one's knowledge of the language but must be ascribed to the special conventions for reading poetry which lead one to look at the language in new ways, to make relevant properties of the language which were previously unexploited, to subject the text to a different series of interpretive operations. But one can also show the importance of these conventions by measuring the distance between the language of a poem and its critical

---

[2]See Roland Barthes, *Criticism and Truth* (London: Athlone, 1987). [Ed.]

[3]Blank slate. [Ed.]

interpretation — a distance bridged by the conventions of reading which comprise the institution of poetry.

Anyone who knows English understands the language of Blake's "Ah! Sun-flower":

Ah, Sun-flower, weary of time,
Who countest the steps of the Sun,
Seeking after that sweet golden clime
Where the traveller's journey is done:
Where the Youth pined away with desire,
And the pale Virgin shrouded in snow
Arise from their graves, and aspire
Where my Sun-flower wishes to go.

But there is some distance between an understanding of the language and the thematic statement with which a critic concludes his discussion of the poem: "Blake's dialectical thrust at asceticism is more than adroit. You do not surmount Nature by denying its prime claim of sexuality. Instead you fall utterly into the dull round of its cyclic aspirations."[4] How does one reach this reading? What are the operations which lead from the text to this representation of understanding? The primary convention is what might be called the rule of significance: read the poem as expressing a significant attitude to some problem concerning man and/or his relation to the universe. The sunflower is therefore given the value of an emblem and the metaphors of "counting" and "seeking" are taken not just as figurative indications of the flower's tendency to turn towards the sun but as metaphorical operators which make the sunflower an instance of the human aspirations compassed by these two lines. The conventions of metaphorical coherence — that one should attempt through semantic transformations to produce coherence on the levels of both tenor and vehicle — lead one to oppose time to eternity and to make "that sweet golden clime" both the sunset which marks the closure of the daily temporal cycle and the eternity of death when "the traveller's journey is done." The identification of sunset and death is further justified by the convention which allows one to

inscribe the poem in a poetic tradition. More important, however, is the convention of thematic unity, which forces one to give the youth and virgin of the second stanza a role which justifies choosing them as examples of aspiration; and since the semantic feature they share is a repression of sexuality, one must find a way of integrating that with the rest of the poem. The curious syntactic structure, with three clauses each depending on a "where," provides a way of doing this:

> The Youth and the Virgin have denied their sexuality to win the allegorical abode of the conventionally visualized heaven. Arriving there, they arise from their graves to be trapped in the same cruel cycle of longings; they are merely at the sunset and aspire to go where the Sun-flower seeks his rest, which is precisely where they already are.[5]

Such interpretations are not the result of subjective associations. They are public and can be discussed and justified with respect to the conventions of reading poetry — or, as English allows us to say, of *making* sense. Such conventions are the constituents of the institution of literature, and in this perspective one can see that it may well be misleading to speak of poems as harmonious totalities, autonomous natural organisms, complete in themselves and bearing a rich immanent meaning. The semiological approach suggests, rather, that the poem be thought of as an utterance that has meaning only with respect to a system of conventions which the reader has assimilated. If other conventions were operative its range of potential meanings would be different.

Literature, as Genette says, "like any other activity of the mind, is based on conventions of which, with some exceptions, it is not aware" (*Figures*, p. 258). One can think of these conventions not simply as the implicit knowledge of

[4]Harold Bloom, *The Visionary Company* (New York, 1961), p. 42 [Au.]

[5]Ibid. [Au.] The syntax of Blake's "Sun-flower" is even more curious than Culler and Bloom acknowledge; it is a sentence fragment consisting of a series of adjectival and adverbial clauses, all linked to the opening vocative, or to each other, but lacking any usual predicate. Like the sunflower itself, Blake's sentence yearns after completeness. [Ed.]

the reader but also as the implicit knowledge of authors. To write a poem or a novel is immediately to engage with a literary tradition or at the very least with a certain idea of the poem or the novel. The activity is made possible by the existence of genre, which the author can write against, certainly, whose conventions he may attempt to subvert, but which is none the less the context within which his activity takes place, as surely as the failure to keep a promise is made possible by the institution of promising. Choices between words, between sentences, between different modes of presentation, will be made on the basis of their effects; and the notion of effect presupposes modes of reading which are not random or haphazard. Even if the author does not think of readers, he is himself a reader of his own work and will not be satisfied with it unless he can read it as producing effects. One would find very strange the notion of a poet saying, "when I reflect on the sunflower I have a particular feeling, which I shall call '$p$' and which I think can be connected with another feeling which I shall call '$q$,'" and then writing "if $p$ then $q$" as a poem on the sunflower. This would not be a poem because even the poet himself cannot read the meanings in that series of signs. He can take them as referring to the feelings in question, but that is very much another matter. His text does not explore, evoke or even make use of the feelings, and he will be unable to read it as if it did. To experience any of the satisfactions of having written a poem he must create an order of words which he can read according to the conventions of poetry: he cannot simply assign meaning but must make possible, for himself and for others, the production of meaning.

"Every work," wrote Valéry, "is the work of many things besides an author"; and he proposed that literary history be replaced by a poetics which would study "the conditions of the existence and development of literature." Among all the arts, it is "the one in which convention plays the greatest role," and even those authors who may have thought their works due only to personal inspiration and the application of genius had developed, without suspecting it, a whole system of habits and notions which were the fruit of

their experience and indispensable to the process of production. However little they might have suspected all the definitions, all the conventions, the logic and the system of combinations that composition presupposes, however much they believed that they owed nothing but to the instant itself, their work necessarily called into play all these procedures and these inevitable operations of the mind.[6]

The conventions of poetry, the logic of symbols, the operations for the production of poetic effects, are not simply the property of readers but the basis of literary forms. However, for a variety of reasons it is easier to study them as the operations performed by readers than as the institutional context taken for granted by authors. The statements authors make about the process of composition are notoriously problematic, and there are few ways of determining what they are taking for granted. Whereas the meanings readers give to literary works and the effects they experience are much more open to observation. Hypotheses about the conventions and operations which produce these effects can therefore be tested not only by their ability to account for the effects in question but by their ability, when applied to other poems, to account for the effects experienced in those cases. Moreover, when one is investigating the process of reading one can make alterations in the language of a text so as to see how this changes literary effects, whereas that kind of experimentation is not possible if one is investigating the conventions assumed by authors, who are not available to give their reactions to the effects of proposed alterations in their texts. As the example of transformational grammar suggests, the best way of producing a formal representation of the implicit knowledge of both speakers and hearers is to present sentences to oneself or to colleagues and then to formulate rules which account for the hearer's judgments about meaning, well-formedness, deviance, constituent structure, and ambiguity.

To speak, therefore, as I shall do, of literary competence as a set of conventions for reading literary texts is in no way to imply that authors

[6]P. Valéry, Œuvres, II, pp. 629 and I, pp. 1439–41. [Au.]

are congenital idiots who simply produce strings of sentences, while all the truly creative work is done by readers who have artful ways of processing these sentences. Structuralist discussions may seem to promote such a view by their failure to isolate and praise an author's "conscious art," but the reason is simply that here, as in most other human activities of any complexity, the line between the conscious and the unconscious is highly variable, impossible to identify, and supremely uninteresting. *"When* do you know how to play chess? All the time? or just while you are making a move? And the *whole* of chess during each move?"[7] When driving a car is it consciously or unconsciously that you keep to the correct side of the road, change gears, apply the brakes, dip the headlights? To ask of what an author is conscious and of what unconscious is as fruitless as to ask which rules of English are consciously employed by speakers and which are followed unconsciously. Mastery may be largely unconscious or it may have reached a stage of highly self-conscious theoretical elaboration, but it is mastery in both cases. Nor does one in any way impugn the author's talent in speaking of his mastery as an ability to construct artefacts which prove extremely rich when subjected to the operations of reading.

The task of a structuralist poetics, as Barthes defines it, would be to make explicit the underlying system which makes literary effects possible. It would not be a "science of contents" which, in hermeneutic fashion, proposed interpretations for works,

> but a science of the conditions of content, that is to say of forms. What interests it will be the variations of meaning generated and, as it were, capable of being generated by works; it will not interpret symbols but describe their polyvalence. In short, its object will not be the full meanings of the work but on the contrary the empty meaning which supports them all. (*Critique et vérité*, p. 57)

In this sense structuralism effects an important reversal of perspective, granting precedence to the task of formulating a comprehensive theory of literary discourse and assigning a secondary

place to the interpretation of individual texts. Whatever the benefits of interpretation to those who engage in it, within the context of poetics it becomes an ancillary activity — a way of using literary works — as opposed to the study of literature itself as an institution. To say that is in no way to condemn interpretation, as the linguistic analogy should make perfectly evident. Most people are more interested in using language to communicate than in studying the complex linguistic system which underlies communication, and they need not feel that their interests are threatened by those who make the study of linguistic competence a coherent and autonomous discipline. Similarly, a structuralist poetics would claim that the study of literature involves only indirectly the critical act of placing a work in situation, reading it as a gesture of a particular kind, and thus giving it a meaning. The task is rather to construct a theory of literary discourse which would account for the possibilities of interpretation, the "empty meanings" which support a variety of full meanings but which do not permit the work to be given just any meaning.

This would not need to be said if interpretive criticism had not tried to persuade us that the study of literature means the elucidation of individual works. But in this cultural context it is important to reflect on what has been lost or obscured in the practice of an interpretive criticism which treats each work as an autonomous artefact, an organic whole whose parts all contribute to a complex thematic statement. The notion that the task of criticism is to reveal thematic unity is a post-Romantic concept, whose roots in the theory of organic form are, at the very least, ambiguous. The organic unity of a plant is not easily translated into thematic unity, and we are willing to admit that the botanical gaze be allowed to compare one plant with another, isolating similarities and differences, or to dwell on formal organization without immediately invoking some teleological purpose or thematic unity. Nor has discourse on literature always been so imperiously committed to interpretation. It used to be possible, in the days before the poem became pre-eminently the act of an individual and emotion recollected in tranquillity, to study its

[7]Wittgenstein, p. 59 [Au.]

interaction with norms of rhetoric and genre, the relation of its formal features to those of the tradition, without feeling immediately compelled to produce an interpretation which would demonstrate their thematic relevance. One did not need to move from poem to world but could explore it within the institution of literature, relating it to a tradition and identifying formal continuities and discontinuities. That this should have been possible may tell us something important about literature or at least lead us to reflect on the possibility of loosening interpretation's hold on critical discourse.

Such loosening is important because if the analyst aims at understanding how literature works he must, as Northrop Frye says, set about "formulating the broad laws of literary experience, and in short writing as though he believed that there is a totally intelligible structure of knowledge attainable about poetry, which is not poetry itself, or the experience of it, but poetics" (*Anatomy of Criticism,* p. 14).[8] Few have put the case for poetics more forcefully than Frye, but in his perspective, as this quotation shows, the relationship between poetry, the experience of poetry and poetics remains somewhat obscure, and that obscurity affects his later formulations. His discussions of modes, symbols, myths and genres lead to the production of taxonomies which capture something of the richness of literature, but the status of his taxonomic categories is curiously indeterminate. What is their relation to literary discourse and to the activity of reading? Are the four mythic categories of Spring, Summer, Autumn and Winter devices for classifying literary works or categories on which the experience of literature is based? As soon as one asks why these categories are to be preferred to those of other possible taxonomies it becomes evident that there must be something implicit in Frye's theoretical framework which needs to be made explicit.

The linguistic model provides a slight reorientation which makes apparent what is needed. Study of the linguistic system becomes theoretically coherent when we cease thinking that our goal is to specify the properties of objects in a corpus and concentrate instead on the task of formulating the internalized competence which enables objects to have the properties they do for those who have mastered the system. To discover and characterize structures one must analyse the system which assigns structural descriptions to the objects in question, and thus a literary taxonomy should be grounded on a theory of reading. The relevant categories are those which are required to account for the range of acceptable meanings which works can have for readers of literature.

The notion of literary competence or of a literary system is, of course, anathema to some critics, who see in it an attack on the spontaneous, creative and affective qualities of literature. Moreover, they might argue, the very concept of literary competence, which carries the presumption that we can distinguish between competent and incompetent readers, is objectionable for precisely those reasons which lead one to propose it: the postulation of a norm for "correct" reading. In other human activities where there are clear criteria for success and failure, such as playing chess or climbing mountains, we can speak of competence and incompetence, but the richness and power of literature depend, precisely, on the fact that it is not an activity of this kind and that appreciation is varied, personal, and not subject to the normative legislation of self-styled experts.

Such arguments, however, would seem to miss the point. None would deny that literary works, like most other objects of human attention, can be enjoyed for reasons that have little to do with understanding and mastery — that texts can be quite blatantly misunderstood and still be appreciated for a variety of personal reasons. But to reject the notion of misunderstanding as a legislative imposition is to leave unexplained the common experience of being shown where one went wrong, of grasping a mistake and seeing why it was a mistake. Though acquiescence may occasionally be disgruntled yielding to a higher authority, none would maintain that it was always thus; more often one feels that one has indeed been shown the way to a fuller understanding of literature and a better grasp of the

[8]For a similar statement, see Frye, p. 677. [Ed.]

procedures of reading. If the distinction between understanding and misunderstanding were irrelevant, if neither party to a discussion believed in the distinction, there would be little point to discussing and arguing about literary works and still less to writing about them.

Moreover, the claims of schools and universities to offer literary training cannot be lightly dismissed. To believe that the whole institution of literary education is but a gigantic confidence trick, would strain even a determined credulity, for it is, alas, only too clear that knowledge of a language and a certain experience of the world do not suffice to make someone a perceptive and competent reader. That achievement requires acquaintance with a range of literature and in many cases some form of guidance. The time and effort devoted to literary education by generations of students and teachers creates a strong presumption that there is something to be learned, and teachers do not hesitate to judge their pupil's progress towards a general literary competence. Most would claim, no doubt with good reason, that their examinations are designed not simply to determine whether their students have read various set works but to test their acquisition of an ability.

"Everyone who has seriously studied literature," Northrop Frye maintains, "knows that the mental process involved is as coherent and progressive as the study of science. A precisely similar training of the mind takes place, and a similar sense of the unity of the subject is built up" (*ibid.*, pp. 10–11). If that seems overstated it is no doubt because what is explicit in the teaching of science usually remains implicit in the teaching of literature. But it is clear that study of one poem or novel facilitates the study of the next: one gains not only points of comparison but a sense of how to read. One develops a set of questions which experience shows to be appropriate and productive and criteria for determining whether they are, in a given case, productive; one acquires a sense of the possibilities of literature and how these possibilities may be distinguished. We may speak, if we like, of extrapolating from one work to another, so long as we do not thereby obscure the fact that the process of extrapolation is precisely what requires

explanation. To account for extrapolation, to explain what are the formal questions and distinctions whose relevance the student learns, would be to formulate a theory of literary competence. If we are to make any sense at all of the process of literary education and of criticism itself we must, as Frye argues, assume the possibility of "a coherent and comprehensive theory of literature, logically and scientifically organized, some of which the student unconsciously learns as he goes on, but the main principles of which are as yet unknown to us" (p. 11).

It is easy to see why, from this perspective, linguistics offers an attractive methodological analogy: a grammar, as Chomsky says, "can be regarded as a theory of a language," and the theory of literature of which Frye speaks can be regarded as the "grammar" of literary competence which readers have assimilated but of which they may not be consciously aware. To make the implicit explicit is the task of both linguistics and poetics, and generative grammar has placed renewed emphasis on two fundamental requirements for theories of this kind: that they state their rules as formal operations (since what they are investigating is a kind of intelligence, they cannot take for granted intelligence used in applying rules but must make them as explicit as possible) and that they be testable (they must reproduce, as it were, attested facts about semiotic competence).

Can this step be taken in literary criticism? The major obstacle would seem to be that of determining what will count as evidence about literary competence. In linguistics it is not difficult to identify facts that an adequate grammar must account for: though one may need to speak of "degrees of grammaticalness" one can produce lists of sentences which are incontestably well formed and sentences which are unquestionably deviant. Moreover, we have a sufficiently strong intuitive sense of paraphrase relations to be able to say roughly what a sentence means for speakers of a language. In the study of literature, however, the situation is considerably more complex. Notions of "well-formed" or "intelligible" literary works are notoriously problematic, and it may be difficult to secure agreement about what should count as a proper "understanding" of a text. That critics should differ so widely in their interpretations might seem to undermine any notion of a general literary competence.

But in order to overcome this apparent obstacle we have only to ask what we want a theory of literature to account for. We cannot ask it to account for the "correct" meaning of a work since we manifestly do not believe that for each work there is a single correct reading. We cannot ask it to draw a clear line between the well-formed and the deviant work if we believe that no such line exists. Indeed, the striking facts that do require explanation are how it is that a work can have a variety of meanings but not just any meaning whatsoever or how it is that some works give an impression of strangeness, incoherence, incomprehensibility. The model does not imply that there must be unanimity on any particular count. It suggests only that we must designate a set of facts, of whatever kind, which seem to require explanation and then try to construct a model of literary competence which would account for them.

The facts can be of many kinds: that a given prose sentence has different meanings if set down as a poem, that readers are able to recognize the plot of a novel, that some symbolic interpretations of a poem are more plausible than others, that two characters in a novel contrast with one another, that *The Waste Land* or *Ulysses* once seemed strange and now seems intelligible. Poetics bears, as Barthes says, not so much on the work itself as on its intelligibility (*Critique et vérité*, p. 62) and therefore problematic cases — the work which some find intelligible and others incoherent, or the work which is read differently in two different periods — furnish the most decisive evidence about the system of operative conventions. Any work can be made intelligible if one invent appropriate conventions: the most obscure poem could be interpreted if there were a convention which permitted us to replace every lexical item by a word beginning with the same letter of the alphabet and chosen according to the ordinary demands of coherence. There are numerous other bizarre conventions which might be operative if the institution of literature were different, and hence the difficulty of interpreting some works provides evidence of the restricted

nature of the conventions actually in force in a culture. Moreover, if a difficult work later becomes intelligible it is because new ways of reading have been developed in order to meet what is the fundamental demand of the system: the demand for sense. A comparison of old and new readings will shed light on the change in the institution of literature.

As in linguistics, there is no automatic procedure for obtaining information about competence, but there is no dearth of facts to be explained.[9] To take surveys of the behaviour of readers would serve little purpose, since one is interested not in performance itself but in the tacit knowledge or competence which underlies it. Performance may not be a direct reflection of competence, for behaviour can be influenced by a host of irrelevant factors: I may not have been paying attention at a given moment, may have been led astray by purely personal associations, may have forgotten something important from an earlier part of the text, may have made what I would recognize as a mistake, if it were pointed out to me. One's concern is with the tacit knowledge that recognition of a mistake would show rather than with the mistake itself, and so even if one were to take surveys one would still have to judge whether particular reactions were in fact a direct reflection of competence. The question is not what actual readers happen to do but what an ideal reader must know implicitly in order to read and interpret works in ways which we consider acceptable, in accordance with the institution of literature.

The ideal reader is, of course, a theoretical construct, perhaps best thought of as a representation of the central notion of acceptability. Poetics, Barthes writes, "will describe the logic according to which meanings are engendered in ways that can be *accepted* by man's logic of symbols, just as the sentences of French are *accepted* by the linguistic intuitions of Frenchmen" (*Critique et vérité*, p. 63). Though there is no automatic procedure for determining what is acceptable, that does not matter, for one's proposals will be sufficiently tested by one's readers'

[9]See N[oam] Chomsky, *Aspects of the Theory of Syntax*, p. 19. [Au.]

acceptance or rejection of them. If readers do not accept the facts one sets out to explain as bearing any relation to their knowledge and experience of literature, then one's theory will be of little interest; and therefore the analyst must convince his readers that meanings or effects which he is attempting to account for are indeed appropriate ones. The meaning of a poem within the institution of literature is not, one might say, the immediate and spontaneous reaction of individual readers but the meanings which they are willing to accept as both plausible and justifiable when they are explained. "Ask yourself: How does one *lead* anyone to comprehension of a poem or of a theme? The answer to this tells us how meaning is to be explained here."[10] The paths by which the reader is led to comprehension are precisely those of the logic of literature: the effects must be related to the poem in such a way that the reader sees the connection to be just in terms of his own knowledge of literature.

One cannot therefore emphasize too strongly that every critic, whatever his persuasion, encounters the problems of literary competence as soon as he begins to speak or write about literary works, and that he takes for granted notions of acceptability and common ways of reading. The critic would not write unless he thought he had something new to say about a text, yet he assumes that his reading is not a random and idiosyncratic phenomenon. Unless he thinks that he is merely recounting to others the adventures of his own subjectivity, he claims that his interpretation is related to the text in ways which he presumes his readers will accept once those relations are pointed out: either they will accept his interpretation as an explicit version of what they intuitively felt or they will recognize from their own knowledge of literature the justice of the operations that lead the critic from text to interpretation. Indeed, the possibility of critical argument depends on shared notions of the acceptable and the unacceptable, a common ground which is nothing other than the procedures of reading. The critic must invariably make decisions about what can in fact be taken for granted,

what must be explicitly defended, and what constitutes an acceptable defence. He must show his readers that the effects he notices fall within the compass of an implicit logic which they are presumed to accept; and thus he deals in his own practice with the problems which a poetics would hope to make explicit.

William Empson's *Seven Types of Ambiguity* is a work from a nonstructuralist tradition which shows considerable awareness of the problems of literary competence and illustrates just how close one comes to a structuralist formulation if one begins to reflect on them. Even if Empson were content to present his work as a display of ingenuity in discovering ambiguities, his enterprise would still be governed by conceptions of plausibility. But of course he wants to make broader claims for his analysis and finds that to do so entails a position very like that recommended above:

> I have continually employed a method of analysis which jumps the gap between two ways of thinking; which produces a possible set of alternative meanings with some ingenuity, and then says it is grasped in the preconsciousness of the reader by a native effort of the mind. This must seem very dubious; but then the facts about the apprehension of poetry are in any case very extraordinary. Such an assumption is best judged by the way it works in detail. (p. 239)[11]

Poetry has complex effects which are extremely difficult to explain, and the analyst finds that his best strategy is to assume that the effects he sets out to account for have been conveyed to the reader and then to postulate certain general operations which might explain these effects and analogous effects in other poems. To those who protest against such assumptions one might reply, with Empson, that the test is whether one succeeds in accounting for effects which the reader accepts when they are pointed out to him. The assumption is in no way dangerous, for the analyst "must convince the reader that he knows what he is talking about" — make him see the appropriateness of the effects in question — and

[10]L[udwig] Wittgenstein, p. 144. [Au.]

[11]Culler's references are to the 1961 Penguin edition of *Seven Types of Ambiguity* (1930). [Ed.]

"must coax the reader into seeing that the cause he names does, in fact, produce the effect which is experienced; otherwise they will not seem to have anything to do with each other" (p. 249). If the reader is brought to accept both the effects in question and the explanation he will have helped to validate what is, in essence, a theory of reading. "I have claimed to show how a properly-qualified mind works when it reads the verses, how those properly-qualified minds have worked which have not at all understood their own working" (p. 248). Such claims about literary competence are not to be verified by surveys of readers' reactions to poems but by readers' assent to the effects which the analyst attempts to explain and the efficacy of his explanatory hypotheses in other cases.

It is Empson's self-awareness and outspokenness as much as his brilliance which make his work invaluable to students of poetics; he has little respect for the critical piety that meanings are always implicitly and objectively present in the language of the poem, and thus he can attend to the operations which produce meanings. Discussing the translation of a Chinese fragment,

Swiftly the years, beyond recall.
Solemn the stillness of this spring morning.

he notes that

these lines are what we should normally call poetry only by virtue of their compactness; two statements are made as if they were connected, and the reader is forced to consider their relations for himself. The reason why these facts should have been selected for a poem is left for him to invent; he will invent a variety of reasons and order them in his own mind. This, I think, is the essential fact about the poetical use of language. (p. 25)

This is indeed an essential fact, and one should hasten to point out what it implies: reading poetry is a rule-governed process of producing meanings; the poem offers a structure which must be filled up and one therefore attempts to invent something, guided by a series of formal rules derived from one's experience of reading poetry, which both make possible invention and impose limits on it. In this case the most obvious feature of literary competence is the intent at totality of the interpretive process: poems are supposed to cohere, and one must therefore discover a semantic level at which the two lines can be related to one another. An obvious point of contact is the contrast between "swiftly" and "stillness," and there is thus a primary condition on "invention": any interpretation should succeed in making thematic capital out of this opposition. Moreover, "years" in the first sentence and "this morning" in the second, both located in the dimension of time, provide another opposition and point of contact. The reader might hope to find an interpretation which relates these two pairs of contrasts. If this is indeed what happens it is no doubt because the experience of reading poetry leads to implicit recognition of the importance of binary oppositions as thematic devices: in interpreting a poem one looks for terms which can be placed on a semantic or thematic axis and opposed to one another.

The resulting structure or "empty meaning" suggests that the reader try to relate the opposition between "swiftly" and "stillness" to two ways of thinking about time and draw some kind of thematic conclusion from the tension between the two sentences. It seems eminently possible to produce in this way a reading which is "acceptable" in terms of poetic logic. On the one hand, taking a large panoramic view, we can think of the human life-span as a unit of time and of the years as passing swiftly; on the other, taking the moment of consciousness as the unit, we can think of the difficulty of experiencing time except discontinuously, of the stillness of a clock's hand when one looks at it. "Swiftly the years" implies a vantage point from which one can consider the passage of time, and the swiftness of passage is compensated for by what Empson calls "the answering stability of self-knowledge" implicit in this view of life (p. 24). "This morning" implies other mornings — a discontinuity of experience reflected in the ability to separate and name — and hence an instability which makes "stillness" the more valued. This process of binary structuring, then, can lead one to find tension within each of the lines as well as between the two lines. And since thematic contrasts should be related to opposed values we are led to think about the advantages and disadvantages of these two ways of conceiving of time. A variety of conclusions are of course possible. The claim is not that competent readers would agree on an interpretation but only that certain expectations about poetry and ways of reading guide the interpretive process and impose severe limitations on the set of acceptable or plausible readings.

Empson's example indicates that as soon as one reflects seriously on the status of critical argument and the relation of interpretation to text one approaches the problems which confront poetics, in that one must justify one's reading by locating it within the conventions of plausibility defined by a generalized knowledge of literature. From the point of view of poetics, what requires explanation is not the text itself so much as the possibility of reading and interpreting the text, the possibility of literary effects and literary communication. To account for the notions of acceptability and plausibility on which criticism relies is, as J.-C. Gardin emphasizes, the primary task of the systematic study of literature.

> This is in any case the only sort of objective that a "science" may set for itself, even if it be a science of literature: the regularities unveiled by natural phenomena correspond, in the literary field, to certain convergences of perception for members of a given culture.[12]

But one should stress that even if the analyst showed little explicit interest in notions of acceptability and merely set out to explain in a systematic way his own reading of literature, the results would be of considerable moment for poetics. If he began by noting his own interpretations and reactions to literary works and succeeded in formulating a set of explicit rules which accounted for the fact that he produced these interpretations and not others, one would then possess the basis of an account of literary competence. Adjustments could be made to include other readings which seemed acceptable and to exclude any readings which seemed wholly personal and idiosyncratic, but there is

[12]J.-C. Gardin. "Semantic Analysis Procedures in the Sciences of Man," *Social Science Information* 8 (1969): 33. [Ed.]

every reason to expect that other readers would be able to recognize substantial portions of their own tacit knowledge in his account. To be an experienced reader of literature is, after all, to have gained a sense of what can be done with literary works and thus to have assimilated a system which is largely interpersonal. There is little reason to worry initially about the validity of the facts which one sets out to explain; the only risk one runs is that of wasting one's time. The important thing is to start by isolating a set of facts and then to construct a model to account for them, and though structuralists have often failed to do this in their own practice, it is at least implicit in the linguistic model: "Linguistics can give literature the generative model which is the principle of all science, since it is a matter of making use of certain rules to explain particular results" (Barthes, *Critique et vérité*, p. 58).

Since poetics is essentially a theory of reading, critics of every persuasion who have tried to be explicit about what they are doing have made some contribution to it and indeed in many cases have more to offer than structuralists themselves. What structuralism does provide is a reversal of critical perspective and a theoretical framework within which the work of other critics can be organized and exploited. Granting precedence to the task of formulating a theory of literary competence and relegating critical interpretation to a secondary role, it leads one to reformulate as conventions of literature and operations of reading what others might think of facts about various literary texts. Rather than say, for example, that literary texts are fictional, we might cite this as a convention of literary interpretation and say that to read a text as literature is to read it as fiction. Such a reversal may, at first sight, seem trivial, but to restate propositions about poetic or novelistic discourse as procedures of reading is a crucial reorientation for a number of reasons, wherein lie the revitalizing powers of a structuralist poetics.

First of all, to stress literature's dependence on particular modes of reading is a firmer and more honest starting point than is customary in criticism. One need not struggle, as other theorists must, to find some objective property of language which distinguishes the literary from the non-literary but may simply start from the fact that we can read texts as literature and then inquire what operations that involves. The operations will, of course, be different for different genres, and here by the same model we can say that genres are not special varieties of language but sets of expectations which allow sentences of a language to become signs of different kinds in a second-order literary system. This same sentence can have a different meaning depending on the genre in which it appears. Nor is one upset, as a theorist working on the distinctive properties of literary language must be, by the fact that the boundaries between the literary and the non-literary or between one genre and another change from age to age. On the contrary, change in modes of reading offers some of the best evidence about the conventions operative in different periods.

Second, in attempting to make explicit what one does when reading or interpreting a poem one gains considerably in self-awareness and awareness of the nature of literature as an institution. As long as one assumes that what one does is natural it is difficult to gain any understanding of it and thus to define the differences between oneself and one's predecessors or successors. Reading is not an innocent activity. It is charged with artifice, and to refuse to study one's modes of reading is to neglect a principal source of information about literary activity. By seeing literature as something animated by special sets of conventions one can attain more easily a sense of its specificity, its peculiarity, its difference, shall we say, from other modes of discourse about the world. Those differences lie in the work of the literary sign: in the ways in which meaning is produced.

Third, a willingness to think of literature as an institution composed of a variety of interpretive operations makes one more open to the most challenging and innovatory texts, which are precisely those that are difficult to process according to received modes of understanding. An awareness of the assumptions on which one proceeds, an ability to make explicit what one is attempting to do, makes it easier to see where and how the text resists one's attempts to make sense of it

and how, by its refusal to comply with one's expectations, it leads to that questioning of the self and of ordinary social modes of understanding which has always been the result of the greatest literature. My readers, says the narrator at the end of *A la recherche du temps perdu,* will become "les propres lecteurs d'eux-mêmes"[13]: in my book they will read themselves and their own limits. How better to facilitate a reading of oneself than by trying to make explicit one's sense of the comprehensible and the incomprehensible, the significant and the insignificant, the ordered and the inchoate. By offering sequences and combinations which escape our accustomed grasp, by subjecting language to a dislocation which fragments the ordinary signs of our world, literature challenges the limits we set to the self as a device or order and allows us, painfully or joyfully, to accede to an expansion of self. But that requires, if it is to be fully accomplished, a measure of awareness of the interpretive models which inform one's culture. Structuralism, because of its interest in the adventures of the sign, has been exceedingly open to the revolutionary work, finding in its resistance to the operations of reading confirmation of the fact that literary effects depend on these conventions and that literary evolution proceeds by displacement of old conventions of reading and the development of new.

And so, finally, structuralism's reversal of perspective can lead to a mode of interpretation based on poetics itself, where the work is read against the conventions of discourse and where one's interpretation is an account of the ways in which the work complies with or undermines our procedures for making sense of things. Though it does not, of course, replace ordinary thematic interpretations, it does avoid premature foreclosure — the unseemly rush from word to world — and stays within the literary system for as long as possible. Insisting that literature is something other than a statement about the world, it establishes, finally, an analogy between the production or reading of signs in literature and in other areas of experience and studies the ways

[13]"Proper readers of themselves." See Proust, p. 482. [Ed.]

in which the former explores and dramatizes the limitations of the latter. In this kind of interpretation the meaning of the work is what it shows the reader, by the acrobatics in which it involves him, about the problems of his condition as *homo significans*, maker and reader of signs. The notion of literary competence thus comes to serve as the basis of a reflexive interpretation.

# Umberto Eco

b. 1932

*Although his surprise best-selling novel* The Name of the Rose *(1980; tr. 1983) made him internationally famous, Umberto Eco has long been recognized in other circles as the leading contemporary theorist of semiotics. Born in Alessandria, Italy, Eco was educated at the University of Turin (Ph.D. 1954) and has taught at the universities of Turin, Florence, Milan, and Bologna, where he has been professor of semiotics since 1975. Eco has also been a visiting professor at universities the world over — in the United States alone he has taught at New York University, Yale, Columbia, and Northwestern. The sheer number of Eco's publications is daunting; those books that deal with semiotics and are available in English include* A Theory of Semiotics *(1975),* The Role of the Reader: Explorations in the Semiotics of Texts *(1979),* Semiotics and the Philosophy of Language *(1984), and a more accessible volume of essays,* Travels in Hyperreality *(1986). "The Myth of Superman," from* The Role of the Reader, *was first published in English in a 1972 issue of* Diacritics.

## The Myth of Superman

The hero equipped with powers superior to those of the common man has been a constant of the popular imagination — from Hercules to Siegfried, from Roland to Pantagruel, all the way to Peter Pan. Often the hero's virtue is humanized, and his powers, rather than being supernatural, are the extreme realization of natural endowments such as astuteness, swiftness, fighting ability, or even the logical faculties and the pure spirit of observation found in Sherlock Holmes. In an industrial society, however, where man becomes a number in the realm of the organization which has usurped his decision-making role, he has no means of production and is thus deprived of his power to decide. Individual strength, if not exerted in sports activities, is left abased when confronted with the strength of ma-

chines which determine man's very movements. In such a society the positive hero must embody to an unthinkable degree the power demands that the average citizen nurtures but cannot satisfy.

Superman is not from Earth; he arrived here as a youth from the planet Krypton. Growing up on Earth, Superman finds he is gifted with superhuman powers. His strength is practically unlimited. He can fly through space at the speed of light, and, when he surpasses that speed, he breaks through the time barrier and can transfer himself to other epochs. With no more than the pressure of his hands, he can subject coal to the temperature required to change it into diamond; in a matter of seconds, at supersonic speed, he can fell an entire forest, make lumber from trees, and construct a ship or a town; he can bore through mountains, lift ocean liners, destroy or construct dams; his X-ray vision allows him to

Translated by Natalie Chilton.

see through any object to almost unlimited distances and to melt metal objects at a glance; his superhearing puts him in extremely advantageous situations permitting him to tune in on conversations however far away. He is kind, handsome, modest, and helpful; his life is dedicated to the battle against the forces of evil; and the police find him an untiring collaborator.

Nevertheless, the image of Superman is not entirely beyond the reach of the reader's self-identification. In fact, Superman lives among men disguised as the journalist Clark Kent; as such, he appears fearful, timid, not overintelligent, awkward, nearsighted, and submissive to his matriarchal colleague, Lois Lane, who, in turn, despises him, since she is madly in love with Superman. In terms of narrative, Superman's double identity has a function, since it permits the suspense characteristic of a detective story and great variation in the mode of narrating our hero's adventures, his ambiguities, his histrionics. But, from a mythopoeic point of view, the device is even subtle: in fact, Clark Kent personifies fairly typically the average reader who is harassed by complexes and despised by his fellow men; though an obvious process of self-identification, any accountant in any American city secretly feeds the hope that one day, from the slough of his actual personality, there can spring forth a superman who is capable of redeeming years of mediocre existence.

## THE STRUCTURE OF MYTH AND THE "CIVILIZATION" OF THE NOVEL

With the undeniable mythological connotation of our hero established, it is necessary to specify the narrative structure through which the myth is offered daily or weekly to the public. There is, in fact, a fundamental difference between the figure of Superman and the traditional heroic figures of classical and nordic mythology or the figures of Messianic religions.

The traditional figure of religion was a character of human or divine origin, whose image had immutable characteristics and an irreversible destiny. It was possible that a story, as well as a number of traits, backed up the character; but the story followed a line of development already established, and it filled in the character's features in a gradual, but definitive, manner.

In other words, a Greek statue could represent Hercules or a scene of Hercules' labors; in both cases, but more so in the latter, Hercules would be seen as someone who has a story, and this story would characterize his divine features. The story has taken place and can no longer be denied. Hercules has been made real through a development of temporal events. But once the development ended his image symbolized, along with the character, the story of his development, and it became the substance of the definitive record and judgments about him. Even the account greatly favored by antiquity was almost always the story of something which had already happened and of which the public was aware.

One could recount for the $n$th time the story of Roland the Paladin, but the public already knew what happened to the hero. New additions and romantic embellishments were not lacking, but neither would they have impaired the substance of the myth being narrated. A similar situation existed in the plastic arts and the paintings of Gothic cathedrals or of Counter-Reformation and Renaissance churches. What had already happened was often narrated in moving and dramatic ways.

The "civilization" of the modern novel offers a story in which the reader's main interest is transferred to the unpredictable nature of *what will happen* and, therefore, to the plot invention which now holds our attention. The event has not happened *before* the story; it happens *while* it is being told, and usually even the author does not know what will take place.

At the time of its origin, the *coup de théâtre*[1] where Oedipus finds himself guilty as a result of Tiresias' revelation "worked" for the public, not because it caught them unaware of the myth, but because the mechanism of the "plot," in accordance with Aristotelian rules, succeeded in making them once more co-participants through pity and terror. The reader is brought to identify both with the situation and with the character. In contrast, there is Julien Sorel shooting Madame de

---

[1] A sudden dramatic event that alters a situation, which Aristotle called a *peripeteia*. [Ed.]

Rênal, or Poe's detective discovering the party guilty of the double crime in Rue de la Morgue, or Javert paying his debt of gratitude to Jean Valjean,[2] where we are spectators to a *coup de théâtre* whose unpredictable nature is part of the invention and, as such, takes on aesthetic value. This phenomenon becomes important in direct proportion to the popularity of the novel, and the *feuilleton*,[3] for the masses — the adventures of Rocambole and of Arsène Lupin[4] — have, as craft, no other value than the ingenious invention of unexpected events.

This new dimension of the story sacrifices for the most part the mythic potential of the character. The mythic character embodies a law, or a universal demand, and therefore must be in part *predictable* and cannot hold surprises for us; the character of a novel wants, rather, to be a man like anyone else, and what could befall him is as unforeseeable as what may happen to us. Such a character will take on what we will call an "aesthetic universality," a capacity to serve as a reference point for behavior and feelings which belong to us all. He does not contain the universality of myth, nor does he become an archetype, the emblem of a supernatural reality. He is the result of a universal rendering of a particular and eternal event. The character of a novel is a "historic type." Therefore, to accommodate this character, the aesthetics of the novel must revive an old category particularly necessary when art abandons the territory of myth; this we may term the "typical."

The mythological character of comic strips finds himself in this singular situation: he must be an archetype, the totality of certain collective aspirations, and therefore he must necessarily become immobilized in an emblematic and fixed nature which renders him easily recognizable

(this is what happens to Superman); but, since he is marketed in the sphere of a "romantic" production for a public that consumes "romances," he must be subjected to a development which is typical, as we have seen, of novelistic characters.

## THE PLOT AND THE "CONSUMPTION" OF THE CHARACTER

A tragic plot, according to Aristotle, involves the character in a series of events, reversals, recognitions, pitiful and terrifying cases that culminate in a catastrophe;[5] a novelistic plot, let us add, develops these dramatic units in a continuous and narrated series which, in the popular novel, becomes an end in itself. They must proliferate as much as possible *ad infinitum*. The Three Musketeers, whose adventures continue in *Twenty Years Later* and conclude finally in *The Vicomte de Bragelonne* (but here intervene parasitic narrators who continue to tell us about the adventures of the Musketeers' sons, or the clash between d'Artagnan and Cyrano de Bergerac, and so on), is an example of narrative plot which multiplies like a tapeworm; the greater its capacity to sustain itself through an indefinite series of contrasts, oppositions, crises, and solutions, the more vital it seems.

Superman, by definition the character whom nothing can impede, finds himself in the worrisome narrative situation of being a hero without an adversary and therefore without the possibility of any development. A further difficulty arises because his public, for precise psychological reasons, cannot keep together the various moments of a narrative process over the space of several days. Each story concludes within the limits of a few pages; or, rather, every weekly edition is composed of two or three complete stories in which a particular narrative episode is presented, developed, and resolved. Aesthetically and commercially deprived of the possibility of narrative development, Superman gives serious problems to his scriptwriters. Little by little, varying formulae are offered to provoke and justify a con-

---

[2]Eco refers to Stendhal's *The Red and the Black,* Poe's "Murders in the Rue Morgue," and Hugo's *Les Misérables.* [Ed.]

[3]Light, serialized fiction, such as that contained in those parts of a French newspaper also devoted to reviews and entertaining articles. [Ed.]

[4]*Rocambole, or The Knaves of Hearts and the Companions of Crime:* a romance by Pierre Alexis, Vicomte de Ponson du Terrail (1829–71). *Arsène Lupin, Gentleman-burglar,* a romance by Maurice Leblanc (1864–1941). [Ed.]

[5]See Aristotle, *Poetics,* p. 46ff. [Ed.]

trast; Superman, for example, does have a weakness. He is rendered almost helpless by the radiation of kryptonite, a metal of meteoric origin, which his adversaries naturally procure at any cost in order to neutralize their avenger. But a creature gifted with superhuman intellectual and physical powers easily finds a means to get out of such scrapes, and that is what Superman does. Furthermore, one must consider that as a narrative theme the attempt to weaken him through the employment of kryptonite does not offer a broad range of solutions, and it must be used sparingly.

There is nothing left to do except to put Superman to the test of several obstacles which are intriguing because they are unforeseen but which are, however, surmountable by the hero. In that case two effects are obtained. First, the reader is struck by the strangeness of the obstacles — diabolically conceived inventions, curiously equipped apparitions from outer space, machines that can transmit one through time, teratological results of new experiments, the cunning of evil scientists to overwhelm Superman with kryptonite, the hero's struggles with creatures endowed with powers equal to his, such as Mxyzptlk, the gnome, who comes from the fifth dimension and who can be countered only if Superman manages to make him pronounce his own name backwards (Kltpzyxm), and so on. Second, thanks to the hero's unquestionable superiority, the crisis is rapidly resolved and the account is maintained within the bounds of the short story.

But this resolves nothing. In fact, the obstacle once conquered (and within the space allotted by commercial requirements), Superman has still *accomplished something*. Consequently, the character has made a gesture which is inscribed in his past and which weighs on his future. He has taken a step toward death, he has gotten older, if only by an hour; his storehouse of personal experiences has irreversibly enlarged. *To act,* then, for Superman, as for any other character (or for each of us), means to "consume" himself.

Now, Superman cannot "consume" himself, since a myth is "inconsumable." The hero of the classical myth became "inconsumable" precisely because he was already "consumed" in some exemplary action. Or else he had the possibility of a continuing rebirth or of symbolizing some vegetative cycle — or at least a certain circularity of events or even of life itself. But Superman is myth on condition of being a creature immersed in everyday life, in the present, apparently tied to our own conditions of life and death, even if endowed with superior faculties. An immortal Superman would no longer be a man, but a god, and the public's identification with his double identity would fall by the wayside.

Superman, then, must remain "inconsumable" and at the same time be "consumed" according to the ways of everyday life. He possesses the characteristics of timeless myth, but is accepted only because his activities take place in our human and everyday world of time. The narrative paradox that Superman's scriptwriters must resolve somehow, even without being aware of it, demands a paradoxical solution with regard to time.

## TEMPORALITY AND "CONSUMPTION"

The Aristotelian definition of time is "the amount of movement from before to after," and since antiquity time has implied the idea of *succession;* the Kantian analysis has established unequivocally that this idea must be associated with an idea of *causality:* "It is a necessary law of our sensibility and therefore a condition of all perception that preceding Time necessarily determines what follows."[6] This idea has been maintained even by relativistic physics, not in the study of the transcendental conditions of the perceptions, but in the definition of the nature of time in terms of cosmological objectivity, in such a way that time would appear as the *order of causal chains.* Reverting to these Einsteinian concepts, Reichenbach recently redefined the order of time as the order of causes, the order of open causal chains which we see verified in our universe, and the *direction* of time in terms of *growing entropy*[7] (taking up in terms even of information theory the thermodynamic concept

[6]*Critique of Pure Reason,* "Analytic of Principles," Ch. 2, sec. 3. [Au.]

[7]Disorder. [Ed.]

which had recurrently interested philosophers and which they adopted as their own in speaking of the irreversibility of time.[8]

*Before* causally determines *after,* and the series of these determinations cannot be traced back, at least in our universe (according to the epistemological model that explains the world in which we live), but is irreversible. That other cosmological models can foresee other solutions to this problem is well known; but, in the sphere of our daily understanding of events (and, consequently, in the structural sphere of a narrative character), this concept of time is what permits us to move around and to recognize events and their directions.

Expressing themselves in other words, but always on the basis of the order of *before* and *after* and of the causality of the before on the after (emphasizing variously the determination of the before on the after), existentialism and phenomenology have shifted the problem of time into the sphere of the structures of subjectivity, and discussions about action, possibility, plan, and liberty have been based on time. Time as a *structure of possibility* is, in fact, the problem of our moving toward a future, having behind us a past, whether this past is seen as a block with respect to our freedom to plan (planning which forces us to choose necessarily what we have already been) or is understood as a basis of future possibilities and therefore possibilities of conserving or changing what has been, within certain limits of freedom, yet always within the terms of positive processes.

Sartre says that "the past is the ever-growing totality of the in-itself which we are." When I want to tend toward a possible future, I must be and cannot not be this past. My possibilities of choosing or not choosing a future depend upon acts already accomplished, and they constitute the point of departure for my possible decisions. And as soon as I make another decision, it, in turn, belongs to the past and modifies what I am and offers another platform for successive projects. If it is meaningful to put the problem of

freedom and of the responsibility of our decisions in philosophical terms, the basis of the discussion and the point of departure for a phenomenology of these acts is always the structure of temporality.[9]

For Husserl, the "I" is free inasmuch as it is in the past. In effect, the past determines me and therefore also determines my future, but the future, in turn, "frees" the past. My temporality is my freedom, and on my freedom depends my "Being-having-been" which determines me. But, in its continuous synthesis with the future, the content of my "Being-having-been" depends on the future. Now, if the "I" is free because it is already determined together with the "I-that-should-be," there exists within this freedom (so encumbered by conditions, so burdened with what was and is hence irreversible) a "sorrowfulness" (*Schmerzhaftigkeit*) which is none other than "facticity." (Compare with Sartre: "I am my future in the continuous prospective of the possibility of not being it. In this is the suffering which we described before and which gives sense to my present; I am a being whose sense is always problematic.")[10] Each time I plan I notice the tragic nature of the condition in which I find myself, without being able to avoid it. Nevertheless, I plan to oppose the tragic elements with the possibility of something positive, which is a change from that which is and which I put into effect as I direct myself toward the future. Plan, freedom, and condition are articulated while I observe this connection of structures in my actions, according to a dimension of *responsibility*. This is what Husserl observes when he says that, in this "directed" being of the "I" toward possible scopes, an ideal "teleology" is established and that the future as possible "having" with respect to the original futurity in which I already always *am* is the universal prefiguration of the aim of life.

In other words, the subject situated in a temporal dimension is aware of the gravity and difficulty of his decisions, but at the same time he is aware that he must decide, that it is he who

[8]See in particular Hans Reichenbach, *The Direction of Time* (Berkeley and Los Angeles: University of California Press, 1956). [Au.]

[9]For the Sartrian discussion, see *Being and Nothingness,* Ch. 2. [Au.]
[10]Ibid. [Au.]

must decide, and that this process is linked to an indefinite series of necessary decision making that involves all other men.

## A PLOT WHICH DOES NOT "CONSUME" ITSELF

If contemporary discussions which involve man in meditation upon his destiny and his condition are based on this concept of time, the narrative structure of Superman certainly evades it in order to save the situation which we have already discussed. In Superman it is the concept of time that breaks down. The very structure of time falls apart, not in the time *about which,* but, rather, in the time *in which the story is told.*

In Superman stories the time that breaks down is the *time of the story,* that is, the notion of time which ties one episode to another. In the sphere of a story, Superman accomplishes a given job (he routs a band of gangsters); at this point the story ends. In the same comic book, or in the edition of the following week, a new story begins. If it took Superman up again at the point where he left off, he would have taken a step toward death. On the other hand, to begin a story without showing that another had preceded it would manage, momentarily, to remove Superman from the law that leads from life to death through time. In the end (Superman has been around since 1938), the public would realize the comicality of the situation — as happened in the case of Little Orphan Annie, who prolonged her disaster-ridden childhood for decades.

Superman's scriptwriters have devised a solution which is much shrewder and undoubtedly more original. The stories develop in a kind of oneiric climate — of which the reader is not aware at all — where what has happened before and what has happened after appear extremely hazy. The narrator picks up the strand of the event again and again, as if he had forgotten to say something and wanted to add details to what had already been said.

It occurs, then, that along with Superman stories, Superboy stories are told, that is, stories of Superman when he was a boy, or a tiny child under the name of Superbaby. At a certain point, Supergirl appears on the scene. She is Super-man's cousin, and she, too, escaped from the destruction of Krypton. All of the events concerning Superman are retold in one way or another in order to account for the presence of this new character (who has hitherto not been mentioned, because, it is explained, she has lived in disguise in a girls' school, awaiting puberty, at which time she could come out into the world; the narrator goes back in time to tell in how many and in which cases she, of whom nothing was said, participated during those many adventures where we saw Superman alone involved). One imagines, using the solution of travel through time, that Supergirl, Superman's contemporary, can encounter Superboy in the past and be his playmate; and even Superboy, having broken the time barrier by sheer accident, can encounter Superman, his own self of many years later.

But, since such a fact could comprise the character in a series of developments capable of influencing his future actions, the story ends here and insinuates that Superboy has dreamed, and one's approval of what has been said is deferred. Along these lines the most original solution is undoubtedly that of the *Imaginary Tales.* It happens, in fact, that the public will often request delightful new developments of the scriptwriters; for example, why doesn't Superman marry Lois Lane, the journalist, who has loved him for so long? If Superman married Lois Lane, it would of course be another step toward his death, as it would lay down another irreversible premise; nevertheless, it is necessary to find continually new narrative stimuli and to satisfy the "romantic" demands of the public. And so it is told "what would have happened *if* Superman had married Lois." The premise is developed in all of its dramatic implications, and at the end is the warning: Remember, this is an "imaginary" story which in truth has not taken place. (In this respect, note Roberto Giammanco's remarks about the consistently homosexual nature of characters like Superman or Batman — another variation of the theme of "superpowers." This aspect undoubtedly exists, particularly in Batman, and Giammanco offers reasons for it which we refer to later; but, in the specific case of Superman, it seems that we must speak not so much of homosexuality as of "parsifalism."[11] In Superman the element of masculine societies is nearly absent, though it is quite evident in characters like Batman and Robin, Green Arrow and his partner, and so on. Even if he often collaborates with the Legion of Super Heroes of the Future — youngsters gifted with extraordinary powers, usually ephebic but of both sexes — Superman does not neglect working with his cousin, Supergirl, as well, nor can one say that Lois Lane's advances, or those of Lana Lang, an old schoolmate and rival of Lois, are received by Superman with the disgust of a misogynist. He shows, instead, the bashful embarrassment of an average young man in a matriarchal society. On the other hand, the most perceptive philologists have not overlooked his unhappy love for Lori Lemaris, who, being a mermaid, could offer him only an underwater *ménage*[12] corresponding to a paradisiacal exile which Superman must refuse because of his sense of duty and the indispensable nature of his mission. What characterizes Superman is, instead, the platonic dimension of his affections, the implicit vow of chastity which depends less on his will than on the state of things, and the singularity of his situation. If we have to look for a structural reason for this narrative fact, we cannot but go back to our preceding observations: the "parsifalism" of Superman is one of the conditions that prevents his slowly "consuming" himself, and it protects him from the events, and therefore from the passing of time, connected with erotic ventures.)

The *Imaginary Tales* are numerous, and so are the *Untold Tales* or those stories that concern events already told but in which "something was left out," so they are told again from another point of view, and in the process lateral aspects come to the fore. In this massive bombardment of events which are no longer tied together by any strand of logic, whose interaction is ruled no longer by any necessity, the reader, without realizing it, of course, loses the notion of temporal progression. Superman happens to live in an imaginary universe in which, as opposed to ours, causal chains are not open (A provokes B, B provokes C, C provokes D, and so on, *ad infinitum*), but closed (A provokes B, B provokes C, C provokes D, and D provokes A), and it no longer makes sense to talk about temporal progression on the basis of which we usually describe the happenings of the macrocosm.

One could observe that, apart from the mythopoeic and commercial necessities which together force such a situation, a similar structural assessment of Superman stories reflects, even though at a low level, a series of diffuse persuasions in our culture about the problem of concepts of causality, temporality, and the irreversibility of events; and, in fact, a great deal of contemporary art, from Joyce to Robbe-Grillet, or a film such as *Last Year at Marienbad*, reflects paradoxical temporal situations, whose models, nevertheless, exist in the epistemological discussions of our times. But it is a fact that, in works such as *Finnegans Wake* or Robbe-Grillet's *In the Labyrinth*, the breakdown of familiar temporal relations happens in a conscious manner, on the part both of the writer and of the one who derives aesthetic satisfaction from the operation. The disintegration of temporality has the function both of quest and of denunciation and tends to furnish the reader with imaginative models capable of making him accept situations of the new science and of reconciling the activity of an imagination accustomed to old schemes with the activity of an intelligence which ventures to hypothesize or to describe universes that are not reducible to an image or a scheme. In consequence, these works (but here another problem opens up) carry out a mythopoeic function, offering the inhabitant of the contemporary world a kind of symbolic suggestion or allegorical diagram of that absolute which science has resolved, not so much in a metaphysical modality of the world, but in a possible way of establishing our relation with the world and, therefore, in a possible way of describing the world.

The adventures of Superman, however, do not have this critical intention, and the temporal paradox on which they are sustained should not be obvious to the reader (just as the authors themselves are probably unaware of it), since a con-

---

[11]In Wolfram von Eschenbach's medieval epic, *Parsifal*, the hero, of amazing powers, is a pure but utterly naive and foolish boy. [Ed.]

[12]Household. [Ed.]

fused notion of time is the only condition which makes the story credible. Superman comes off as a myth only if the reader loses control of the temporal relationships and renounces the need to reason on their basis, thereby giving himself up to the uncontrollable flux of the stories which are accessible to him and, at the same time, holding on to the illusion of a continuous present. Since the myth is not isolated exemplarily in a dimension of eternity, but, in order to be assimilated, must enter into the flux of the story in question, this same story is refuted as flux and seen instead as an immobile present.

In growing accustomed to the idea of events happening in an ever-continuing present, the reader loses track of the fact that they should develop according to the dictates of time. Losing consciousness of it, he forgets the problems which are at its base, that is, the existence of freedom, the possibility of planning, the necessity of carrying plans out, the sorrow that such planning entails, the responsibility that it implies, and, finally, the existence of an entire human community whose progressiveness is based on making plans.

## SUPERMAN AS A MODEL OF "HETERODIRECTION"

The proposed analysis would be greatly abstracted and could appear apocalyptic if the man who reads Superman, and for whom Superman is produced, were not the selfsame man with whom several sociological reports have dealt and who has been defined as "other directed man."

In advertising, as in propaganda, and in the area of human relations, the absence of the dimension of "planning" is essential to establishing a paternalistic pedagogy, which requires the hidden persuasion that the subject is not responsible for his past, nor master of his future, nor even subject to the laws of planning according to the three "ecstasies" of temporality (Heidegger). All of this would imply pain and labor, while society is capable of offering to the heterodirected man the results of projects already accomplished. Such are they as to respond to man's desires, which themselves have been introduced in man

in order to make him recognize that what he is offered is precisely what he would have planned.

The analysis of temporal structures in Superman has offered us the image of a *way of telling stories* which would seem to be fundamentally tied to pedagogic principles that govern that type of society. Is it possible to establish connections between the two phenomena affirming that Superman is no other than one of the pedagogic instruments of this society and that the destruction of time that it pursues is part of a plan to make obsolete the idea of planning and of personal responsibility?

## DEFENSE OF THE ITERATIVE SCHEME

A series of events repeated according to a set scheme (iteratively, in such a way that each event takes up again from a sort of virtual beginning, ignoring where the preceding event left off) is nothing new in popular narrative. In fact, this scheme constitutes one of its more characteristic forms.

The device of iteration is one on which certain escape mechanisms are founded, particularly the types realized in television commercials: one distractedly watches the playing out of a sketch, then focuses one's attention on the punch line that reappears at the end of the episode. It is precisely on this foreseen and awaited reappearance that our modest but irrefutable pleasure is based.

This attitude does not belong only to the television spectator. The reader of detective stories can easily make an honest self-analysis to establish the modalities that explain his "consuming" them. First, from the beginning the reading of a traditional detective story presumes the enjoyment of following a scheme: from the crime to the discovery and the resolution through a chain of deductions. The scheme is so important that the most famous authors have founded their fortune on its very immutability. Nor are we dealing only with a schematism in the order of a "plot," but with a fixed schematism involving the same sentiments and the same psychological attitudes: in Simenon's Maigret or in Agatha Christie's Poirot, there is a recurrent movement of compassion to which the detective is led by his discovery of the facts and which merges into an empathy with the motives of the guilty party, an act of *caritas* which is combined with, if not opposed to, the act of justice that unveils and condemns.

Furthermore, the writer of stories then introduces a continuous series of connotations (for example, the characteristics of the policeman and of his immediate "entourage") to such an extent that their reappearance in each story is an essential condition of its reading pleasure. And so we have the by now historical "tics" of Sherlock Holmes, the punctilious vanity of Hercule Poirot, the pipe and the familiar fixes of Maigret, on up to the daily idiosyncrasies of the most unabashed heroes of postwar detective stories, such as the cologne water and Player's #6 of Peter Cheyney's Slim Callaghan or the cognac with a glass of cold water of Brett Halliday's Michael Shayne. Vices, gestures, nervous tics permit us to find an old friend in the character portrayed, and they are the principal conditions which allow us to "enter into" the event. Proof of this is when our favorite author writes a story in which the usual character does not appear and we are not even aware that the fundamental scheme of the book is still like the others: we read the book with a certain detachment and are immediately prone to judge it a "minor" work, a momentary phenomenon, or an interlocutory remark.

All this becomes very clear if we take a famous character such as Nero Wolfe, immortalized by Rex Stout. For sheer preterition[13] and by way of caution, in the likelihood of one of our readers' being so "highbrow" as to have never encountered our character, let us briefly recall the elements which combine to form Nero Wolfe's "type" and his environment. Nero Wolfe, from Montenegro, a naturalized American from time immemorial, is outlandishly fat, so much so that his leather easy chair must be expressly designed for him. He is fearfully lazy. In fact, he never leaves the house and depends, for his investigations, on the open-minded Archie Goodwin, with whom he indulges in a continuous relationship of a sharp and tensely polemic

nature, tempered somewhat by their mutual sense of humor. Nero Wolfe is an absolute glutton, and his cook, Fritz, is the vestal virgin in the pantry, devoted to the unending care of this highly cultivated palate and equally greedy stomach; but along with the pleasures of the table, Wolfe cultivates an all-absorbing and exclusive passion for orchids; he has a priceless collection of them in the greenhouse on the top floor of the villa where he lives. Quite possessed by gluttony and flowers, assailed by a series of accessory tics (love of scholarly literature, systematic misogyny, insatiable thirst for money), Nero Wolfe conducts his investigations, masterpieces of psychological penetration, sitting in his office, carefully weighing the information with which the enterprising Archie furnishes him, studying the protagonists of each event who are obliged to visit him in his office, arguing with Inspector Cramer (attention: he always holds a methodically extinguished cigar in his mouth), quarreling with the odious Sergeant Purley Stebbins; and, finally, in a fixed setting from which he never veers, he summons the protagonists of the case to a meeting in his studio, usually in the evening. There, with skillful dialectical subterfuges, almost always before he himself knows the truth, he drives the guilty one into a public demonstration of hysteria and thus into giving himself away.

Those who know Rex Stout's stories know that these details hardly scratch the surface of the repertoire of *topoi,* of recurrent stock situations which animate these stories. The gamut is much more ample: Archie's almost canonic arrest under suspicion of reticence and false testimony; the legal diatribes about the conditions on which Wolfe will take on a client; the hiring of part-time agents like Saul Panzer or Orrie Cather; the painting in the studio behind which Wolfe or Archie can watch, through a peephole, the behavior and reactions of a subject put to the test in the office itself; the scenes with Wolfe and an insincere client — one could go on forever; we realize, at the end, that the list of these *topoi* is such that it could exhaust almost every possibility of the events permitted within the number of pages allowed to each story. Nevertheless, there are infinite variations of the theme; each crime has new psychological and economic motiva-

---

[13]There is a problem with the translation: preterition means an intentional act of omission. [Ed.]

tions, each time the author devises what appears as a new situation. We say "appear"; the fact is that the reader is never brought to verify the extent to which something new is told. The noteworthy moments are those when Wolfe repeats his usual gestures, when he goes up for the $n$th time to take care of his orchids while the case itself is reaching its dramatic climax, when Inspector Cramer threateningly enters with one foot between the door and the wall, pushing aside Goodwin and warning Wolfe with a shake of his finger that this time things will not go so smoothly. The attraction of the book, the sense of repose, of psychological extension which it is capable of conferring, lies in the fact that, plopped in an easy chair or in the seat of a train compartment, the reader continuously recovers, point by point, what he already knows, what he wants to know again: that is why he has purchased the book. He derives pleasure from the nonstory (if indeed a story is a development of events which should bring us from the point of departure to a point of arrival where we would never have dreamed of arriving); the distraction consists in the refutation of a development of events, in a withdrawal from the tension of past-present-future to the focus of an *instant,* which is loved because it is recurrent.

## THE ITERATIVE SCHEME AS A REDUNDANT MESSAGE

It is certain that mechanisms of this kind proliferate more widely in the popular narrative of today than in the eighteenth-century romantic *feuilleton,* where, as we have seen, the event was founded upon a *development* and where the character was required to "consume" himself through to death. Perhaps one of the first inexhaustible characters during the decline of the *feuilleton* and bridging the two centuries at the close of *la belle époque*[14] is Fantomas.[15] (Each episode of *Fantomas* closes with a kind of "unsuccessful catharsis"; Juve and Fandor finally come to get their

[14]The turn of the twentieth century. [Ed.]

[15]*Fantomas* (1911–13) was a serialized novel by Marcel Allain (1885–1969) and Pierre Souvestre (1874–1914) about an elusive criminal. [Ed.]

hands on the elusive one when he, with an unforeseeable move, foils the arrest. Another singular fact: Fantomas — responsible for blackmail and sensational kidnappings — at the beginning of each episode finds himself inexplicably poor and in need of money and, therefore, also of new "action." In this way the cycle can keep going.) With him the epoch ends. It remains to be asked if modern iterative mechanisms do not answer some profound need in contemporary man and, therefore, do not seem more justifiable and better motivated than we are inclined to admit at first glance.

If we examine the iterative scheme from a structural point of view, we realize that we are in the presence of a typical *high-redundance message.* A novel by Souvestre and Allain or by Rex Stout is a message which informs us very little and which, on the contrary, thanks to the use of redundant elements, keeps hammering away at the same meaning which we have peacefully acquired upon reading the first work of the series (in the case in point, the meaning is a certain mechanism of the action, due to the intervention of "topical" characters). The taste for the iterative scheme is presented then as a taste for redundance. The hunger for entertaining narrative based on these mechanisms is a *hunger for redundance.* From this viewpoint, the greater part of popular narrative is a narrative of redundance.

Paradoxically, the same detective story that one is tempted to ascribe to the products that satisfy the taste for the unforeseen or the sensational is, in fact, read for exactly the opposite reason, as an invitation to that which is taken for granted, familiar, expected. Not knowing who the guilty party is becomes an accessory element, almost a pretext; certainly, it is true that in the action detective story (where the iteration of the scheme triumphs as much as in the investigation detective story), the suspense surrounding the guilty one often does not even exist; it is not a matter of discovering who committed the crime, but, rather, of following certain "topical" gestures of "topical" characters whose stock behavior we already love. To explain this "hunger for redundance," extremely subtle hypotheses are not needed. The *feuilleton,* founded on the triumph of information, represented the preferred fare of a society that lived in the midst of messages loaded with redundance; the sense of tradition, the norms of associative living, moral principles, the valid rules of proper comportment in the environment of eighteenth-century bourgeois society, of the typical public which represented the consumers of the *feuilleton* — all this constituted a system of foreseeable communication that the social system provided for its members and which allowed life to flow smoothly without unexpected jolts and without upsets in its value system. In this sphere the "informative" shock of a short story by Poe or the *coup de théâtre* of Ponson du Terrail[16] acquired a precise meaning. In a contemporary industrial society, instead, the alternation of standards, the dissolution of tradition, social mobility, the fact that models and principles are "consumable" — everything can be summed up under the sign of a continuous load of information which proceeds by way of massive jolts, implying a continual reassessment of sensibilities, adaptation of psychological assumptions, and requalification of intelligence. Narrative of a redundant nature would appear in this panorama as an indulgent invitation to repose, the only occasion of true relaxation offered to the consumer. Conversely, "superior" art only proposes schemes in evolution, grammars which mutually eliminate each other, and codes of continuous alternations.

Is it not also natural that the cultured person who in moments of intellectual tension seeks a stimulus in an action painting or in a piece of serial music should in moments of relaxation and escape (healthy and indispensable) tend toward triumphant infantile laziness and turn to the consumer product for pacification in an orgy of redundance?

As soon as we consider the problem from this angle, we are tempted to show more indulgence toward escape entertainments (among which is included our myth of Superman), reproving ourselves for having exercised an acid moralism on what is innocuous and perhaps even beneficial.

The problem changes according to the degree to which pleasure in redundance breaks the convulsed rhythm of an intellectual existence based upon the reception of information and becomes the *norm* of every imaginative activity.

The problem is not to ask ourselves if different ideological contents conveyed by the same narrative scheme can elicit different effects. Rather, an iterative scheme becomes and remains that *only* to the extent that the scheme sustains and expresses a world; we realize this even more, once we understand how the world has the same configuration as the structure which expressed it. The case of Superman reconfirms this hypothesis. If we examine the ideological contents of Superman stories, we realize that, on the one hand, that content sustains itself and functions communicatively thanks to the narrative structure; on the other hand, the stories help define their expressive structure as the circular, static conveyance of a pedagogic message which is substantially immobilistic.

## CIVIC CONSCIOUSNESS AND POLITICAL CONSCIOUSNESS

Superman stories have a characteristic in common with a series of other adventures that hinge on heroes gifted with *superpowers*. In Superman the real elements blend into a more homogeneous totality, which justifies the fact that we have devoted special attention to him; and it is no accident that Superman is the most popular of the heroes we talk about: he not only represents the forerunner of the group (in 1938), but of all the characters he is still the one who is most carefully sketched, endowed with a recognizable personality, dug out of longstanding anecdote, and so he can be seen as the representative of all his similars. (In any case, the observation that follows can be applied to a whole series of superheroes, from Batman and Robin to Green Arrow, Flash, the Manhunter from Mars, Green Lantern, and Aquaman up to the more recent Fantastic Four, Devil, and Spider Man, where the literary "genre," however, has acquired a more sophisticated form of self-irony.)

Each of these heroes is gifted with such powers that he could actually take over the government, defeat the army, or alter the equilibrium of planetary politics. On the other hand, it is

---

[16]Author of romances like *Rocambole* in n. 4. [Ed.]

clear that each of these characters is profoundly kind, moral, faithful to human and natural laws, and therefore it is right (and it is nice) that he use his powers only to the end of good. In this sense the pedagogic message of these stories would be, at least on the plane of children's literature, highly acceptable, and the same episodes of violence with which the various stories are interspersed would appear directed toward this final indictment of evil and the triumph of honest people.

The ambiguity of the teaching appears when we ask ourselves, *What is Good?* It is enough to reexamine in depth the situation of Superman, who encompasses the others, at least in their fundamental structure.

Superman is practically omnipotent, as we have said, in his physical, mental, and technological capacities. His operative capacity extends to a cosmic scale. A being gifted with such capacities offered to the good of humanity (let us pose the problem with a maximum of candor and of responsibility, taking everything as probable) would have an enormous field of action in front of him. From a man who could produce work and wealth in astronomic dimensions in a few seconds, one could expect the most bewildering political, economic, and technological upheavals in the world. From the solution of hunger problems to the tilling of uninhabitable regions, from the destruction of inhuman systems (if we read Superman into the "spirit of Dallas," why does he not go to liberate six hundred million Chinese from the yoke of Mao?), Superman could exercise good on a cosmic level, or on a galactic level, and furnish us in the meantime with a definition that through fantastic amplification could clarify precise ethical lines everywhere.

Instead, Superman carries on his activity on the level of the small community where he lives (Smallville as a youth, Metropolis as an adult), and — as in the case of the medieval countryman who could have happened to visit the Sacred Land, but not the closed and separate community which flourished fifty kilometers from the center of his life — if he takes trips to other galaxies with ease, he practically ignores, not exactly the dimension of the "world," but that of the "United States" (only once, but in one of the *Imaginary*

*Tales,* he becomes president of the United States).

In the sphere of his own little town, evil, the only evil to combat, is incarnate in a species which adheres to the underworld, that of organized crime. He is busy by preference, not against blackmarket drugs, nor, obviously, against corrupt administrators or politicians, but against bank and mail-truck robbers. In other words, *the only visible form that evil assumes is an attempt on private property.* Outerspace evil is added spice; it is casual, and it always assumes unforeseeable and transitory forms; the underworld is an endemic evil, like some kind of impure stream that pervades the course of human history, clearly divided into zones of Manichaean incontrovertibility — where each authority is fundamentally pure and good and where each wicked man is rotten to the core without hope of redemption.

As others have said, in Superman we have a perfect example of civic consciousness, completely split from political consciousness. Superman's civic attitude is perfect, but it is exercised and structured in the sphere of a small, closed community (a "brother" of Superman — as a model of absolute fidelity to established values — might appear in someone such as the movie and television hero Dr. Kildare).

It is strange that Superman, devoting himself to good deeds, spends enormous amounts of energy organizing benefit performances in order to collect money for orphans and indigents. The paradoxical waste of means (the same energy could be employed to produce directly riches or to modify radically larger situations) never ceases to astound the reader who sees Superman forever employed in parochial performances. As evil assumes only the form of an offense to private property, *good is represented only as charity.* This simple equivalent is sufficient to characterize Superman's moral world. In fact, we realize that Superman is obliged to continue his activities in the sphere of small and infinitesimal modifications of the immediately visible for the same motives noted in regard to the static nature of his plots: each general modification would draw the world, and Superman with it, toward final consumption.

On the other hand, it would be inexact to say that Superman's judicious and measured virtue depends only on the structure of the plot, that is, on the need to forbid the release of excessive and irretrievable developments. The contrary is also true: the immobilizing metaphysics underlying this kind of conceptual plot is the direct, though not the desired, consequence of a total structural mechanism which seems to be the only one suited to communicate, through the themes discussed, a particular kind of teaching. The plot must be static and must evade any development, because Superman *must* make virtue consist of many little activities on a small scale, never achieving a total awareness. Conversely, virtue must be characterized in the accomplishment of only partial acts, so that the plot can remain static. Again, the discussion does not take on the features of the authors' preferences as much as their adaptation to a concept of "order" which pervades the cultural model in which the authors live and where they construct on a small scale "analogous" models which mirror the larger one.

# 5

# POSTSTRUCTURALISM

*The passage beyond philosophy does not consist in turning the page of philosophy (which usually comes down to philosophizing badly), but in continuing to read philosophers in a certain way.*

— JACQUES DERRIDA

*The author has disappeared; God and man died a common death.*

— MICHEL FOUCAULT

*The work is normally the object of consumption. . . . The Text . . . decants the work . . . from its consumption, and gathers it up as play, activity, production, practice. This means that the Text requires that one try to abolish . . . the distance between writing and reading.*

— ROLAND BARTHES

What does it mean to be *post*? The postmodern novel simultaneously uses the narrative techniques of modernist fiction yet rejects its enabling assumptions. The result, in writers like John Barth, Robert Coover, and Vladimir Nabokov, is a superrealist fiction, in which narrative technique becomes the self-conscious vehicle for exploring the limits and paradoxes of story-telling itself. But the ends writers like Joyce and Woolf tried to achieve — creating a fully subjective narrative that would be true to psychological reality, that would mimic adequately the perceived texture of life itself — either seem no longer within reach or not worth attempting. The postmodern novel announces itself as nothing more — or less — than a book.

Similarly, poststructuralism takes off from the stratagem of structuralism: the notion that everything is a text in some form or other. But the ultimate goal of the structuralists — discovering the rules by which signifiers encode the signified reality and thereby establishing a new synthesis of all the human sciences — is viewed by the new generation of poststructuralists as impossible because of the very nature of language and textuality itself. If structuralism is founded upon confidence in the stability of linguistic structures and their ability to mirror the movements of mind, poststructuralism is a radical critique of these notions of language and of any philosophy built upon them.

Like structuralism, poststructuralism is more easily characterized as an activity than as a philosophy: It is not a body of accepted doctrines — indeed, its central aim is to generate skepticism about most of the doctrines we unquestioningly accept. Although poststructuralism has by now become an international movement, its two central figures are French-speaking philosophers, Jacques Derrida and the late Michel Foucault, whose ideas need to be discussed in more than usual detail.

## DERRIDA AND DECONSTRUCTION

One of the difficulties in reading Derrida is that there is no central document, no single, classic essay, like Sidney's "Apology for Poetry" or Kant's *Critique of Judgment,* that contains and expresses a body of systematic thought. In this, he is like some earlier philosophers, such as Hegel and Nietzsche, for whom no selection can give a sense of the whole. But what is unique to Derrida is that, while his rhetoric circles around the same themes, his terminology changes from essay to essay. (Even his principal term, "deconstruction," is not fully stable. At one point, Derrida wanted to replace it with "de-sedimentation," though that word never quite caught on.) This fluidity is entirely by design. Given his program, Derrida has tried to resist anything that would lead to setting up deconstruction as a *system of thought.*

Although it is risky to state that Derrida has a central issue, we can begin with his notion that all thought is necessarily inscribed in language, and that language itself is fraught with intractable paradoxes. We can repress or ignore these paradoxes, but we cannot escape from them or solve them. This is the burden of Derrida's most difficult work, *Of Grammatology.*

Derrida's basic concern is with how Western philosophy has built its metaphysics on a pervasive but fragile base, one that privileges the activity of *speech* over that of *writing*. Speech is opposed to writing and held to be logically prior as well as chronologically older. The valorization of speech begins in Plato's *Phaedrus,* in which Socrates condemns writing as a bastardized form of communication, separated from the Father (the moment of origin). Writing can easily mislead because the speaker is no longer there to explain what he had in mind. Socrates prefers speech because the speaker seems so immediately present in the voice. Meaning enters into sound, and sound as a real presence enters the listener and becomes meaning once more.

Derrida traces this position from Plato down through the centuries to philosophers such as Edmund Husserl and Martin Heidegger. Here we can discuss one classic example, that of the founder of structuralism. Ferdinand de Saussure treats writing as a means of representing speech; it remains an external accessory, however, a supplement that need not be fully taken into account in any philosophy of language. In fact, Saussure feels that writing is in a sense dangerous because it "disguises" language and "usurps" the role of speech (writing corrupts speech at times, as when people mispronounce words because of the way they are spelled). For all these reasons, writing is a *dangerous* supplement, which threatens the integrity of speech. The notion of the "dangerous supplement" is important to Derrida, for the very idea of a supplement challenges and calls into question the dichotomies and hierarchies on which philosophies are built. Like the appendix to a book, a supplement is part of and not part of the text at the same time: It seems to be adding something to what is already complete in itself, and the addition is thus implicitly a correction, even in a sense a recantation.

In Derrida's analysis of the writings of Jean-Jacques Rousseau, for example, he calls attention to Rousseau's characterization of education as a supplement to nature. As a supplement, education adds to something that is already supposedly complete in itself; at the same time, if education adds to nature, then nature must be somehow incomplete — at least to the extent that one must be educated to know what is natural and what is not. Nature is the prior term, a presence that is there at the start. Yet the "supplement" of education reveals an inherent absence or lack within nature — and also an essential condition of its being.

At another point in the *Confessions,* Rousseau himself speaks of masturbation as a "dangerous supplement" to coital sexuality: a perverse addition that can substitute for and take the place of heterosexual intercourse. But paradoxically, the fact that masturbation can act as a supplement shows that it shares in the nature of sexuality. Furthermore, what characterizes masturbation — the focus on an imagined sexual object, the impossibility of genuinely possessing what one desires — also characterizes heterosexual intercourse. One could thus turn the dichotomy upside down and claim that heterosexual intercourse is a more generalized version of masturbation.

To generalize Derrida's method from the last example: a dominant entity is defined by a form of presence (heterosexual intercourse) next to its supplement (masturbation), which is defined by a corresponding absence as inferior and marginal. But the distinguishing qualities of the marginal entity are in fact the defining qualities of the dominant. The result is that the rigid hierarchy of the dichotomy dissolves: As we consider the matter, it is no longer clear which is dominant and which marginal.

To come back now to where we began, with Derrida's analysis of the dichotomy of speech and writing, we valorize speech over writing because there, signifier and signified, sound and meaning, seem to be given together, fused for the moment. Form and meaning are simultaneously present. Voice appears as the direct manifestation of thought. In contrast, written words lack this presence; they are physical marks a reader must interpret and animate to supply meanings that do not seem to be *given.*

But in fact, the kind of absence that distinguishes writing from speech is the very condition of the existence of signs in the first place. Language presupposes absence in the sense that it is an elaborate system of presences and absences that allows signifiers to operate. The letter or phoneme /t/ exists only as part of a system of differences that distinguish it from /d/ or /f/ or any of the other letters or phonemes. The phoneme /t/ differs from /d/ by the quality of voicing (vibration of the vocal cords), which is absent in the former and present in the latter. But /t/ is not a defective /d/; there is only a relational meaning here, not a real presence (see the introduction to Ch. 4, Structuralism and Semiotics).

Furthermore, for a form to be a sign, it must be iterable — repeatable. We learn the meaning of a sign by hearing the same sound in similar contexts. The difference between a sign and a mere noise is that one cannot repeat the latter (even if one clap of thunder were exactly like another, it would make no difference). In the case of a language-sign, one must be able to repeat it back, to quote it; but to quote a sign is to produce it as an example, to reproduce it in the absence of the original communicative intention. For a signifier to have value as a sign, therefore, it must be possible to counterfeit it, and when a sign is counterfeited or cited or produced as an example, it is without its original meaning. But this is *always* possible for *any* sign. Therefore the notion that a sign depends upon the presence conferred by voice cannot be maintained, and we cannot hold that speech is logically prior to writing. (Derrida is not denying, of course, that speech preceded writing historically.)

If speech is not prior to writing, then it does not make sense to treat writing as an auxiliary form of speech; indeed, Derrida suggests, we should treat speech as a form of writing — and refer both to an *arché-écriture* (from the Greek and French: "original-writing"). Rather than achieving meaning through the presence of voice, language strives toward meaning through the play of signifiers. This play occurs through the mechanism of what Derrida calls *différance* (a coinage that blends the French words for "difference" and "deferral"). A word, a letter, or a sound is known not through what it is but through its differences relative to other possibilities — the other possibilities that are not present but absent, existing only through the transient traces they leave on memory. Ultimate meaning, genuine presence, is always deferred — just as looking one word up in a dictionary leads to another and so on indefinitely. Between signifier and signified, therefore, there is not the rigid relation of container and contained. Rather, there is always "free-play" (*jeu*), which suggests that language can never be pinned down to meaning, that it is always already indeterminate.

It is hard to overestimate the furor Derrida's theory of language provoked. He was not merely saying, like the New Critic William Empson, that poetry depends on seven types of ambiguity. He was claiming in effect that everything in the human sciences — history, political philosophy, psychology, and so on — was a species of poetry, invariably based on a terminology that was necessarily as indeterminate as the language in which it was written. But the real target of his notion of language was the structuralist attempt to synthesize all humanistic knowledge by using the tools of linguistics, for if there was freeplay in the signifier-signified relationship, there was no guarantee of even making sense. In the 1920s, the German mathematician Kurt Gödel put an end to the massive Russell-Whitehead project for systematizing mathematics by proving conclusively that any mathematical system complicated enough to be useful had either to contain contradictions or to be incomplete. Derrida's "Grammatology" was in effect the Gödel's proof for the human sciences in the late 1960s. It split the structuralist community down the middle, and even twenty years later, the debate continues between those who accept and those who dispute the validity and the motivation of the deconstructive turn.

But there is more at stake than the apparently abstract question of whether or not there is freeplay between the signifier and the signified. For, in its most general sense, the activity of deconstruction involves the skeptical re-examination, not just of speech and writing, but of *all* the dialectical polarities that have formed the basis of Western culture, a re-examination searching for the point of privilege upon which standard hierarchies rest. We are used to arguing about various other presences and absences: art vs. genius, culture vs. nature, transcendence vs. immanence, soul vs. body, divine vs. human, human vs. animal, man vs. woman, being vs. becoming, and so on. In each case, the first term denotes the presence and the second the absence of something. Derrida uses the paradoxes involved in the logic of "supplements" in an effort to decenter the first term of each pair, to remove it from its privileged position relative to the second. Against the dominant metaphysics of presence, Derrida sets the countermetaphysics of absence. To the extent that these polarities are at the heart of Western culture, deconstruction attempts to expose the illusions upon which authority in Western culture is established. Where the conservative W. B. Yeats complained that "Things fall apart. The center cannot hold," the anarchistic Derrida calls into question the very concept of a center. This is the argument of Derrida's most famous single essay, "Structure, Sign, and Play in the Discourse of the Human Sciences," reprinted here.

Invited to a conference on structuralism in 1966, Derrida proceeded to question the "whole history of the concept of structure" as the activity of naming and renaming in a succession of metaphors the center of the totality of existence: "the history of metaphysics, like the history of the West, is the history of these metaphors." Derrida then proceeded to deconstruct the concept of the center, beginning with the geometrical paradox that the center *defines* the circle but is not part of the line that *is* the circle. This center is, in effect, a transcendental point of absolute presence. So long as we can believe in a transcendental signified — a point of absolute meaning outside and above the world of discourse that gives significance to the whole — the center holds. But once we cease to have God and have only god-terms, once we accept that everything is a text and falls within the framework of discourse, then the very notion of a center must be challenged. And that, says Derrida, is where we currently stand: after the critiques of metaphysics by Nietzsche and Heidegger, after the critique of consciousness by Freud, the fundamental notions of being, truth, and self cannot be naively "centered" as they have been by the major philosophers from Plato through Hegel.

This brings Derrida to structuralism and its attempts to find a center through the science of signs. Most of "Structure, Sign, and Play" is devoted to a deconstruction of the opposition between nature and culture in the work of the founder of structuralism, Claude Lévi-Strauss. One must work out for oneself the chain of paradoxes, one within another, that Derrida finds in Lévi-Strauss's project in *Mythologiques* — for instance, that it is an empirical study that nevertheless rejects the principle of empiricism.[1] Derrida concludes by exposing the ambivalence, the duality of Lévi-Strauss's attitudes. On the one hand, Lévi-Strauss accepts the

[1] See the introduction to Structuralism and Semiotics, Ch. 4.

presence of freeplay within the structure of myths and embraces the notion that mythography is itself a sort of mythical thinking; on the other hand, there is Lévi-Strauss's "ethic of presence, an ethic of nostalgia for origins, an ethic of archaic and natural innocence, of a purity of presence and self-presence in speech." Lévi-Strauss, and thus the structuralist activity in general, seems to be caught halfway between the old metaphysics, which "dreams of deciphering a truth or an origin," and the new revolutionary philosophy, like his own, that "tries to pass beyond man and humanism."

In his conclusion to "Structure, Sign, and Play," Derrida seems to be disclosing his attitudes toward the great precursors. In particular, he seems to be defining himself in opposition to Hegel and as a disciple of Nietzsche. Derrida always circumvents Hegel's historical, progressive uses of dialectic; his oppositions always stay open, undecidable, untranscended. And like Nietzsche's philosophy, Derrida's attitudes toward political and social issues seem to be based on aesthetics rather than ethics; he revels in the sense of intellectual crisis and welcomes the coming transvaluation of all values.[2]

But what is more significant, Derrida's ironic gibe at "the nostalgia for the origin" is a slap directed at the existentialist philosopher Martin Heidegger, who influenced him deeply and against whom he reacted equally intensely. Although Heidegger, like Derrida, was an opponent of metaphysics, he did not go far enough for his disciple. As Christopher Norris has put it, Derrida questioned "Heidegger's own metaphysical motives, his quest for a grounding philosophy which would point the way back toward primordial Being. This nostalgic attachment to a lost or forgotten origin is, according to Derrida, the hallmark of all metaphysics."[3] Metaphysics, the abstract bugbear of twentieth-century philosophers from Wittgenstein onward, is like the "tar-baby" of the Uncle Remus stories: In combatting it one inevitably gets involved in it. As Derrida states in "Structure, Sign, and Play," "*there is no sense* in doing without the concepts of metaphysics in order to attack metaphysics. We . . . cannot utter a single destructive proposition which has not already slipped into the form, the logic, and the implicit postulations of precisely what it seeks to contest." Derrida's strategy is to disrupt systematic thought, to wage a guerrilla campaign against it in constantly shifting terms, to stay on the margins of philosophy and avoid its central castle. "The passage beyond philosophy does not consist in turning the page of philosophy . . . but in continuing to read philosophers *in a certain way.*"

## BARTHES

As Derrida's message began its guerrilla war on the ends and assumptions of structuralism, a number of structuralism's leading figures became converts, including Roland Barthes, whose shifting aims and ideas are instructive. Barthes's interest, since his 1953 essay "Writing Degree Zero," has been in the immense

[2]See the headnotes to Hegel and to Nietzsche, p. 341 and p. 403.
[3]Christopher Norris, *The Deconstructive Turn* (London: Methuen, 1983), p. 24.

tacit knowledge the reader must possess, over and above the syntax and basic semantics of a given language, to understand and interpret cultural systems of symbols. Barthes worked in *mythologies* to demystify the complex languages spoken in wrestling matches, advertisements, and other maps of popular culture. The apex of this structuralist project appeared in the 1966 essay, "Introduction to the Structural Analysis of Narratives," a densely written attempt to do complete justice to the *langue* of fiction. Though he is normally a supple and witty stylist, Barthes's tone here was dry and abstract, as though he was somewhat daunted by the complex task of analyzing into their separate components the elements (the *emes*) in the interpretation of narrative, and he characterized his essay, which was based on the previous work of Vladimir Propp, Claude Bremond, A. J. Greimas, and Tzvetan Todorov, as a "tentative effort" rather than a triumphant success.

In *S/Z* (1970), Barthes simplified and reduced these multiple integrative dimensions into a skein of five *codes,* to which the individual bits of text (*lexies*) each make their contribution. Barthes distinguished a *hermeneutic* code of enigmas and their solutions; a *semic* code of characteristics that go into the description of characters and places; a *proairetic* code of actions; a *symbolic* code of themes; and a *referential* code comprising the historical and cultural allusions within the text. The elaborate result was a 220-page commentary on "Sarrasine" (a minor story by Balzac) that — since it remained on the levels of "functions" and "actions" and was incomplete even there — was clearly only a mere sketch toward a full interpretation. *S/Z* was simultaneously the masterpiece and the reductio ad absurdum of Barthes' holistic approach to fiction, because it made clear that any genuinely complete analysis of a fictional text would be so long and complex as to be nearly unreadable. It was widely admired but never imitated, even by Barthes himself.

By the next year, Barthes had produced "From Work to Text," an account of the difference in the way the object of literary study is perceived by formal and structural criticism on the one hand, and by poststructural criticism on the other. The essay is short, terse, informal, almost a set of jottings, but Barthes manages to characterize the stance of the deconstructive critic with lucidity and accuracy. Perhaps the most influential section of "From Work to Text" is the last, in which Barthes contrasts the emotional involvement of the reader before and after the deconstructive turn. The older, passive way of reading produced *plaisir* (pleasure), the consumer's enjoyment in being immersed in another's vision, actions, characters. The new way produces what Barthes terms *jouissance,* a nearly untranslatable word ("bliss" is the usual equivalent) that suggests both the joy and the sense of loss experienced in the sexual climax. Here and in later, more elaborate treatments of the phenomenology of reading, such as *The Pleasure of the Text,* Barthes's central contribution to Derrida's project was in clarifying its emotional as well as its intellectual appeal.

## DECONSTRUCTION AND CRITICISM

Like the structuralism it questions and attempts to supplant, deconstruction is not solely, or even primarily, a mode of literary criticism. As Derrida says in "Structure, Sign, and Play," he only wants "to read philosophers *in a certain way*." Indeed, deconstructionalists like Rodolphe Gasché have suggested that the application of Derrida's methods to literary texts in search of new interpretations is paradoxical, almost perverse, since Derrida's revolutionary contribution was to treat philosophical texts as if they were bound by the same sorts of linguistic ambiguity and fluidity that had long been thought to characterize literature. (In effect Derrida constitutes the ultimate vindication of poetry against Plato's attack. For Derrida it is the poets, celebrating the freeplay of the signifier, who have had the right notion of language, and the philosophers, aiming for precision of terminology, who have been pursuing a will o' the wisp.)

Nevertheless, Derrida has had more impact in departments of English and French than in philosophy, as deconstruction has been applied less to Ayer or Sartre than to Yeats and Proust. To a large extent, the deconstruction of literature was made possible by the previous triumph of the New Criticism, which treated poetry as an especially complex mode of discourse, essentially dependent on tropes like irony or ambiguity, that led to the evocation of a set of propositions or attitudes toward the real world. If the ultimate purpose of poetry was to say something — in however complicated a form — then, like traditional philosophy and the other humane sciences, it was a discourse that sought "a truth and an origin." As such, it could also read "*in a certain way*." Furthermore, scholars trained in the New Criticism could easily adapt their methods to deconstruction; if once they sought paradox and ambiguity in pursuit of the meaning of texts, they could now seek it in the pursuit of the posited void at the center of meaning. In effect, the move from New Criticism to deconstruction principally involved abandoning the search for the balance and resolution that critics like Cleanth Brooks had sought behind the paradoxes and ambiguities of the text.

In America in the 1970s, the prime locus for this new mode of reading was Yale University, which had also become a haven for many of the New Critics in their last years. Professors Harold Bloom, Geoffrey Hartman, and J. Hillis Miller of the Yale English department and the late Paul de Man of the department of French and Comparative Literature became known collectively as the "Gang of Four," in ironic token of the radicalism of their readings and their coherence as a group. With the death of de Man in 1983 and the departure of Miller for California a few years later, the group broke up, but not before it had succeeded in bringing deconstruction to America.

Actually, Bloom (see Ch. 2) was never really a philosophically orthodox deconstructionist, though his notion that all reading was in fact creative misreading was not inconsistent with the Derridean notion of freeplay. With respect to the other three, it seems clear that the intellectual center and prime mover was de Man, whose "Semiology and Rhetoric" is reprinted here.

This essay is not only a defense of deconstruction but a brief and telling demonstration of its powers applied to three short texts, ranging from a trivial joke from the television comedy "All in the Family" to a moving passage from Proust's *Remembrance of Things Past*. The central argument of de Man's essay — that meaning is not a dependable function of syntax — challenges a form of structuralism that had long ceased to be current, but de Man's conclusion — that one does not deconstruct *texts* so much as show the means by which they deconstruct *themselves* — is crucially important. Or to use a metaphor derived from Roland Barthes, the deconstructionist finds the thread dangling from the sweater, pulls on it, and watches as the fabric of the garment unravels into the pile of yarn from which it was made.

If every text can be said to contain its own deconstruction, de Man's essay supplies most of the methods employed in the deconstructive act. What we find most often is not an overt contradiction within a single level of the structure of the text — a paradox of the sort Cleanth Brooks would have appreciated — but a demonstration of the inconsistency between a text's grammar and its rhetoric, between its message and its activity, between what a text means and the way it goes about meaning it. Thus de Man shows how Proust's passage evoking the power of metaphor operates less in terms of metaphor (substitution) than in terms of metonymy (association). In *The Purveyor of Truth*, Derrida himself shows how Lacan's reading of "The Purloined Letter" (see Ch. 2) inevitably distorts that tale into an allegory of Lacanian analysis, a triad of *voices*. In so doing, it ignores the *literary* dimension of Poe's tale, "the game of doubles, the endless divisibility, the textual references from facsimile to facsimile, the framing of frames, the inter-minable supplementarity of quotation marks, the insertion of 'The Purloined Letter' in a purloined letter . . . , the text in a text."[4]

From the reader's point of view, the usual end product of deconstructive criticism is *aporia*: the intellectual vertigo caused by looking into an apparently endless hall of mirrors. This is an effect that, unfortunately, palls on repetition. Many critics, initially struck by the power of deconstructive criticism, find that, no matter how inventive the path, each venture leads to the same vista. One exception to this repetitive experience, perhaps, is Barbara Johnson's essay, "Melville's Fist: The Execution of *Billy Budd*," reprinted here. Although Johnson aptly and cleverly uses de Man's technique of presenting characters and passages as allegories for modes of reading, her essay moves beyond the standard abysses of textuality and restores Melville's novella to the political and ethical contexts in which some of its undecidabilities reside.

## FOUCAULT: TRUTH AND POWER

If Derrida's radical critique of the linguistic theories of structuralism led him into the labyrinth of textuality itself, Michel Foucault's equally radical abandonment of them led him instead in the early 1960s to the issues of power and history. It is hard to know what to call Foucault. He refused to be termed a philosopher, though philosophy was the subject of his baccalaureate, and for a time he held the chair in philosophy at the Collège de France. He was certainly not a literary critic,

---

[4]Derrida alters the persistent triads Lacan finds in "The Purloined Letter" to sets of twos and fours. The numerology is important to Derrida; three is the number of Hegel's transcendental dialectic, whereas with twos and fours the dialectical opposition is either untranscended or blown apart.

though he exerted an enormous and spreading influence on criticism in North America and in Europe.

Many of Foucault's major works are in the field of social history. *Folie et déraison: Histoire de la folie à l'âge classique* (1961)[5] purports to be a history of the forms of treatment for insanity since the Renaissance; *Surveiller et punir: Naissance de la prison* (1975)[6] deals with the treatment of crime and social delinquency in the same period; *Histoire de la sexualité,* a projected six-volume treatise left unfinished at his death in 1984, examines moral attitudes toward sexual desire beginning with the ancient Greeks.[7] In a sense, Foucault's work seems to run parallel with the French histories of *mentalités* like Philippe Ariès's histories of childhood and of death or Emmanuel LeRoi Ladurie's histories of deviant communities like the heretics of medieval Montaillou. Foucault is seldom viewed as the usual sort of historian, however, partly because of his notoriously cavalier use of documents and sources, which may be explained, if not entirely excused, by Foucault's belief that the exploration of the past is only a route to the understanding of the present.

Foucault was interested in moments of transition, in sudden, seemingly inexplicable changes in the way society deals with its internal problems, in the irrational, and in deviance of one form or another. For instance, in *Folie et déraison,* Foucault posits that, as the disease of leprosy declined at the end of the Middle Ages, society looked to the insane as a new deviant group to be persecuted and confined, the Other against which it would define itself. The thesis that runs through all of Foucault's historical works is that social crisis is resolved by a change, not only in the way institutions are organized, but in discourse, the way people talk and think. Each society develops what Foucault called an *epistemé*: a way of knowing things that is coextensive with the discourse it generates. Foucault was interested in history as it provides a sense of the transitions between *epistemés,* the sudden ruptures during which the old ways of thinking fail and people are forced to find a new mode of discourse. Ultimately, however, Foucault was not obsessed with the social crises of the past for their own sake but rather because of his own sense of a contemporary crisis.

At bottom, Foucault was a disciple of the later Nietzsche and saw the will-to-power as dominant over any search for truth — as defining, in fact, the meaning and location of truth. As he puts it in his essay "Truth and Power":

> Truth isn't outside power, or lacking in power: contrary to a myth whose history and functions would repay further study, truth isn't the reward of free spirits, the child of protracted solitude, nor the privilege of those who have succeeded in liberating themselves. Truth is a thing of this world: it is produced only by virtue of multiple forms of constraint. And it induces regular effects of power. Each society has its regime of truth,

---

[5]Translated in an abridged form as *Madness and Civilization: A History of Insanity in the Age of Reason* (New York: Pantheon, 1965).

[6]Translated as *Discipline and Punish: The Birth of the Prison* (New York: Pantheon, 1978).

[7]Volume 1 of *History of Sexuality* appeared in English translation in 1978, volume 2 in 1987.

its "general politics" of truth: that is, the types of discourse which it accepts and makes function as true; the mechanisms and instances which enable one to distinguish true and false statements, the means by which each is sanctioned; the techniques and procedures accorded value in the acquisition of truth, the status of those who are charged with saying what is true.[8]

Today, Foucault goes on, the general politics confers truth on the form of scientific discourse; statements are true if and only if they have been the object of well-financed studies, and capitalism not only creates the studies but devotes other massive institutions (education, the media, and so on) to the diffusion and consumption of this form of truth. But though this might be true today, Foucault, like Derrida, became convinced that Western civilization was moving toward a new moment of crisis, a change in the dominant *epistemé,* and his work is marked by an apocalyptic sense that it was in our interest — and our duty — to prepare the way for a new power and truth.

## FOUCAULT AND LITERATURE:
## SAID, KRISTEVA, AND THE NEW HISTORICISM

We can find some of these strains within Foucault's thought in his essay "What Is an Author?" included here. Foucault concentrates on the humanistic version of truth-power: authorship seem as a form of author-ity. Despite the apparent collapse of the Romantic conception of the author as incomprehensible genius and the advent of formalism and structuralism, which have successively substituted the central terms of *work* and of *écriture* (writing) for the romantic god-term of *author,* Foucault claims that authorship still retains its old power within advanced capitalism. While the author has been declared dead by some literary theorists, the author-function remains, "a certain functional principle by which, in our culture, one limits, excludes, and chooses; in short, by which one impedes the free circulation, the free manipulation, the free composition, decomposition, and recomposition of fiction. . . . The author is therefore the ideological figure by which one marks the manner in which we fear the proliferation of meaning." As long as literature belongs to the author, it cannot be truly ours. But Foucault looks forward to a moment of change in society when the "author-function will disappear." Foucault has no faith, however, that as author-ity fades, literature will belong to "us." He pessimistically foresees that it will instead be replaced by a new "system of constraint" yet to be understood or experienced. The old order changes, giving way to the new, but for Foucault, order is always a synonym for the prisons and asylums through which society controls thought. Only a total breakdown of society could liberate us from the order of discourse.

Foucault's influence on literary criticism has been profound but curiously indirect. Instead of disciples, like Derrida, he seems to have fellow-travelers, who

[8]Michel Foucault, "Truth and Power," in *The Foucault Reader,* ed. Paul Rabinow (New York: Pantheon Books, 1984), pp. 72–73.

have absorbed his ideas about power and discourse and strive to find their proper application to literature. Of these perhaps the best known is the Palestinian-born theorist Edward W. Said, whose book *Orientalism* (1978) attacked the discourse through which nineteenth-century European society simultaneously celebrated and denigrated the Arab and Asian worlds in order to justify its imperialism. Said's "The Text, the World, the Critic" might be seen as a rejection of the hermeticism of both structuralism and deconstruction, which, because they see nothing but the textuality of literature, lose touch with its being in the world. Basing his linguistic ideas on those of the Zahirites, medieval Arab theorists of grammar, Said presents a notion of language that combines pure signification (the signifier as token for the signified) with a play of correspondences and resemblances that move the word into a larger world. But Said is even more obviously indebted to Foucault's notions of society as the controller and manager of discourse, and of discourse as a mode of power and oppression. He sees the literary text as a "worldly" work operating within history and the critic as a politically engaged intellectual situated in the contemporary world. Faced with the structure of power, the critic too must choose sides, must minimally cease to pretend that the sort of discourse we choose has nothing to do with the kind of world we live in.

Another independent thinker whose work on literature seems to run parallel with the theories of Foucault is Julia Kristeva, the Bulgarian-born theorist whose 1969 doctoral dissertation, Σημειωτιχὴ was a critique of structuralism. Kristeva is an unabashed eclectic who has been influenced by most of the major modes of twentieth-century thought. With the semiotics of her structuralist training she combines the views of Althusser's Marxism, Lacan's psychology, Bakhtin's theories of carnivalization and dialogism, and contemporary French feminism. As the reader will see in "The Bounded Text," a section of Σημειωτιχὴ reprinted here, in every case she adopts these modes with a difference, adapting them to each other and to her own vision of the relation of power to discourse. "The Bounded Text" takes up the late medieval novel *Jehan de Saintré* as an *ideologème* — an example of contemporary productions of language and thought — and relates its peculiar semiotic practices, in particular its transitional uses of medieval symbolism, to the weakening of the bonds of feudal society and the approaching birth of the capitalism in the Renaissance.

Kristeva's presentation of literature as an act of discourse that is therefore, necessarily, a political act, shows some affinities to the work of what has come to be called the New Historicism. Exactly how one should define the New Historicism is a vexed question, however, made somewhat more difficult by the fact that the New Historicists themselves are primarily scholars and critics rather than theorists, who have generally been more interested in getting on with their practical projects than with defining themselves as a movement. On the one hand, there is an American group led by Stephen Greenblatt and Louis Montrose, and strongly influenced by Michel Foucault, that has revolutionized Renaissance studies over the past decade. Greenblatt and most of his group are not Marxists; nevertheless, they are connected methodologically with a group of British critics led by Jonathan

Dollimore who call themselves "cultural materialists" and whose version of historical criticism is allied with that of Raymond Williams (see Ch. 1).

On the other hand, there is a vast penumbra of critics who are more or less "new" and more or less "historicist" but who do not necessarily connect with Greenblatt or Dollimore or, indeed, with each other. The latter sort of New Historicism is a larger and less coherent enterprise than the former. As defined by Herbert Lindenberger, it seems to include a disparate array of thinkers, such as Thomas Kuhn, Walter Benjamin, Jerome McGann, Mikhail Bakhtin, and even a group of literary theorists (like Frank Lentricchia, Fredric Jameson, and other American structural Marxists) who have been outspoken in attacking Greenblatt and the central group.[9]

For Lindenberger, and even to an extent for Greenblatt, the primary novelty of the New Historicism is the view that history cannot be objectively true in the way Leopold von Ranke had supposed one hundred fifty years ago, when he proposed to write history *wie es eigentlich gewesen* — how things had really happened. If this is a novelty to some literary historians, however, it has been perfectly clear to philosophers of history for at least the fifty years since R. G. Collingwood.

Perhaps the genuine innovation Greenblatt has brought to literary history is implicit in the poststructuralist notion that history and literature are equally "texts." Part of his vision derives from Foucault and his conception of the *episteme* that runs through a culture during the stretches of time between crises. Part derives from the anthropological theories of Clifford Geertz, whose research into Western and Asian cultures has shown how dependent those cultures are on symbolic and ritual enactments. And surely the New Historicism derives some of its attitudes toward history from Hayden White's literary-critical approach to the historians of the nineteenth and early twentieth centuries, and his demonstration of how the rhetoric of these apparently objective thinkers rested on tropes — the figures of speech that underlie poetic discourse.

These influences have led to a blurring of the boundaries between historical and literary materials, so that we can now see that "literary" events like the publication of Sidney's *Arcadia* or the presentation of Shakespeare's *Henry VIII* were political acts, and conversely, that self-evidently political acts, such as the order and arrangement of Elizabeth's coronation, were composed with the same attention to symbol and effect as an epic poem. Social and athletic events like the Henrician and Elizabethan tournaments no longer appear quaint anachronisms but, instead, theatrical rituals that translate into political acts just as definitive of Tudor culture as the cockfight is of Balinese culture in the anthropological studies of Clifford Geertz.[10] In a sense, this revaluation might be seen as redressing a balance: The

---

[9]Herbert Lindenberger, "Toward a New History in Literary Study," *Profession 84* (1984): 16–23.

[10]All these ideas are traced by New Historicist Richard McCoy: on Sidney, see *Rebellion in Arcadia* (New Brunswick, N.J.: Rutgers University Press, 1979); on Shakespeare's *Henry VIII*, see *The Rites of Knighthood: The Literature and Politics of Elizabethan Chivalry* (forthcoming); on Elizabeth's coronation, see "'Thou Idol Ceremony': Elizabeth I, the *Henriad,* and the Rites of the English Monarchy," *Urban Life in the Renaissance,* ed. Ron Weissman and Susan Zimmerman (Cranbury, N.J.: Associated University Presses, 1988); on the Henrician and Elizabethan tournament, see "From

literature of other ages, such as the eighteenth century, has long been seen as deeply informed by factional politics, and it was time for the Elizabethans to lose their strange status as artistic icons and be read once more as belonging to the stream of history.

Michel Foucault and Jacques Derrida, the two most pervasive influences on poststructuralist thought, are extraordinarily different as theorists, both in the terminology they use and in the methods they employ. What links them as the central figures of poststructuralism is their common roots in European philosophy, especially their debt to the later thought of Friedrich Nietzsche and Martin Heidegger. They also share a common perception that opposes the central Western belief in the progressive continuity of history with the notion of fundamental discontinuity and crisis. Derrida seeks an end to the metaphysical nostalgia for origins and truth, and a new humanity that will be immune to this nostalgia. For his part, Foucault views truth as a function of power, and freedom as possible only with the collapse of all systems of authority, all order of discourse. As Tzvetan Todorov has pointed out, the swerve into poststructuralism was a turning against humanism, against the traditional values of Western civilization.[11]

To conservatives who believe in the order the West has inherited from the past, poststructural thought proposes only a horrible anarchy in its stead. On the other hand, for women and members of minority groups, the polarities underlying current Western thought, the present order of discourse, has meant subservience and marginality. To those who are sensitive to or immediately affected by these inconscient forms of injustice, poststructuralism's critique of these orderings and hierarchies has promised the possibility of change. As with structuralism, the question is whether poststructuralism will live up to its promises. Will the preoccupation with textuality, in the Derridean mode, lead to a new understanding of the basis of language in society and to a restructuring of our conception of society itself, or will it lead away from politics and history into a new and different solipsism? Will it lead to an expansion of literary study or merely a new excuse to celebrate the same canonical texts? Is the Foucauldian critique of the order of discourse an improvement on the Marxist critique of society or a distraction from it? These are some of the questions around which the evaluation of poststructural thought may eventually turn.

## Selected Bibliography

Abrams, M. H. "The Deconstructive Angel." *Critical Inquiry* 3 (1977), 425–38.
Arac, Jonathan, Wlad Godzich, and Wallace Martin, eds. *The Yale Critics: Deconstruction in America*. Minneapolis: University of Minnesota Press, 1983.

---

the Tower to the Tiltyard: Robert Dudley's Return to Glory," *Historical Journal* 27 (1984): 425–35 and "'A Dangerous Image': The Earl of Essex and Elizabethan Chivalry," *Journal of Medieval and Renaissance Studies* 13 (1983): 313–29.

[11]Tzvetan Todorov, "AntiHumanisms," *TLS*, October 5, 1985, p. 1041. Todorov's moralizing is underscored by recent revelations of Paul de Man's anti-Semitic collaborationist writings during the Nazi occupation of his native Belgium.

Barthes, Roland. *S/Z*. 1970; New York: Hill and Wang, 1974.

———. *The Pleasure of the Text*. New York: Hill and Wang, 1974.

Baudrillard, Jean. *Oublier Foucault*. Paris: Editions Galilee, 1977.

Bloom, Harold. *The Anxiety of Influence: A Theory of Poetry*. New York: Oxford University Press, 1973.

———. *A Map of Misreading*. New York: Oxford University Press, 1975.

———, et al. *Deconstruction and Criticism*. New York: Seabury, 1979.

———. *Agon: Towards a Theory of Revisionism*. New York: Oxford University Press, 1982.

Bové, Paul. *Deconstructive Poetics: Heidegger and Modern American Poetry*. New York: Columbia University Press, 1980.

Cain, William E. "Deconstruction in America: The Recent Literary Criticism of J. Hillis Miller." *College English* 41 (1979), 367–82.

Carroll, David. *The Subject in Question: The Languages of Theory and the Strategies of Fiction*. Chicago: University of Chicago Press, 1982.

Chase, Cynthia. "The Decomposition of the Elephants: Double-Reading *Daniel Deronda*." *PMLA* 93 (1978): 215–27.

Coward, Rosalind, and John Ellis. *Language and Materialism: Developments in Semiology and the Theory of the Subject*. London: Routledge and Kegan Paul, 1977.

Culler, Jonathan. *The Pursuit of Signs: Semiotics, Literature, Deconstruction*. Ithaca: Cornell University Press, 1981.

———. *On Deconstruction: Theory and Criticism after Structuralism*. Ithaca: Cornell University Press, 1982.

de Man, Paul. *Blindness and Insight*. New York: Oxford University Press, 1971.

———. *Allegories of Reading: Figural Language in Rousseau, Nietzsche, Rilke, and Proust*. New Haven: Yale University Press, 1979.

———. *The Rhetoric of Romanticism*. New York: Columbia University Press, 1984.

———. *The Resistance to Theory*. Minneapolis: University of Minnesota Press, 1986.

Derrida, Jacques. *Of Grammatology*. 1967; Baltimore: Johns Hopkins University Press, 1976.

———. *Writing and Difference*. 1967; Chicago: University of Chicago Press, 1978.

———. *Margins of Philosophy*. 1972; Chicago: University of Chicago Press, 1982.

———. *Positions*. Tran. Alan Bass. 1972; Chicago: University of Chicago Press, 1981.

———. *Dissemination*. 1972; Chicago: University of Chicago Press, 1982.

———. *Speech and Phenomena, and Other Essays on Husserl's Theory of Signs*. 1973; Evanston: Northwestern University Press, 1978.

———. *Glas*. 1974; Lincoln: University of Nebraska Press, 1986.

———. *The Post Card: From Socrates to Freud and Beyond*. 1980; Chicago: University of Chicago Press, 1987.

Dollimore, Jonathan. *Radical Tragedy: Religion, Ideology and Power in the Drama of Shakespeare and His Contemporaries*. Brighton, Eng.: Harvester Press, 1984.

Donoghue, Denis. *Ferocious Alphabets*. Boston: Little, Brown, 1981.

Dreyfus, Hubert L., and Paul Rabinow. *Michel Foucault: Beyond Structuralism and Hermeneutics*. 2nd ed.; Chicago: University of Chicago Press, 1983.

Foucault, Michel. *Madness and Civilization: A History of Insanity in the Age of Reason*. 1961; New York: Pantheon, 1973.

———. *The Birth of the Clinic: An Archaeology of Medical Perception*. 1963; New York: Pantheon, 1973.

————. *Death and the Labyrinth: The World of Raymond Roussel.* 1963; Garden City, N.Y.: Doubleday, 1986.

————. *The Order of Things: An Archaeology of the Human Sciences.* 1966; London: Tavistock, 1970.

————. *The Archeology of Knowledge.* 1969; New York: Pantheon, 1972.

————. *Discipline and Punish: The Birth of the Prison.* 1975; New York: Pantheon Books, 1977.

————. *Language, Counter-Memory, Practice.* Ithaca: Cornell University Press, 1977.

————. *The History of Sexuality.* 1976; New York: Pantheon Books, 1978, 1986.

————. *The Foucault Reader.* New York: Pantheon, 1984.

Gasché, Rodolphe. "The Scene of Writing: A Deferred Outset." *Glyph* 1 (1977): 150–71.

————. "Deconstruction as Criticism." *Glyph* 6 (1979): 177–216.

Geertz, Clifford. *The Interpretation of Cultures: Selected Essays.* New York: Basic Books, 1973.

Girard, René. *Deceit, Desire, and the Novel: The Self and Other in Literary Structure.* Baltimore: Johns Hopkins University Press, 1965.

————. *Violence and the Sacred.* Baltimore: Johns Hopkins University Press, 1977.

Goldberg, Jonathan. *James I and the Politics of Literature.* Baltimore: Johns Hopkins University Press, 1983.

Graff, Gerald. *Literature Against Itself: Literary Ideas in Modern Society.* Chicago: University of Chicago Press, 1979.

Greenblatt, Stephen. *Renaissance Self-Fashioning: From More to Shakespeare.* Chicago: University of Chicago Press, 1980.

————, ed. *The Power of Forms in the English Renaissance.* Norman: University of Oklahoma Press, 1982.

Harari, Josué, ed. *Textual Strategies: Perspectives in Post-Structuralist Criticism.* Ithaca: Cornell University Press, 1979.

Hartman, Geoffrey H. *The Fate of Reading and Other Essays.* Chicago: University of Chicago Press, 1975.

————. *Criticism in the Wilderness.* New Haven: Yale University Press, 1980.

————. *Saving the Text: Literature/Derrida/Philosophy.* Baltimore: Johns Hopkins University Press, 1981.

Hartman, Geoffrey H., and Sanford Budick, eds. *Midrash and Literature.* New Haven: Yale University Press, 1986.

Hartman, Geoffrey H., and Patricia Parker, eds. *Shakespeare and the Question of Theory.* New York: Methuen, 1985.

Heidegger, Martin. *Poetry, Language, and Thought.* New York: Harper and Row, 1971.

————. *On the Way to Language.* New York: Harper and Row, 1971.

————. *The End of Philosophy.* New York: Harper and Row, 1973.

————. *Nietzsche.* San Francisco: Harper and Row, 1979.

Horton, Susan. *Interpreting Interpreting: Interpreting Dickens' Dombey.* Baltimore: Johns Hopkins University Press, 1979.

Husserl, Edmund. *The Idea of Phenomenology.* The Hague: M. Nijhoff, 1964.

Jacobs, Carol. *The Dissimulating Harmony: The Image of Interpretation in Nietzsche, Rilke, Artaud, and Benjamin.* Baltimore: Johns Hopkins University Press, 1978.

Johnson, Barbara. *The Critical Difference: Essays in the Contemporary Rhetoric of Reading.* Baltimore: Johns Hopkins University Press, 1980.

————. *A World of Difference.* Baltimore: Johns Hopkins University Press, 1987.

Kofman, Sarah. *Nietzsche et la scène philosophique*. Paris Union generale d'editions, 1979.

———. *Lectures de Derrida*. Paris: Editions Galilee, 1984.

Kristeva, Julia. *Essays in Semiotics*. The Hague: Mouton, 1971.

———. *About Chinese Women*. London: Boyars, 1977.

———. *Desire in Language: A Semiotic Approach to Literature and Art*. New York: Columbia University Press, 1980.

———. *Powers of Horror: An Essay on Abjection*. New York: Columbia University Press, 1982.

———. *Revolution in Poetic Language*. New York: Columbia University Press, 1984.

Leitch, Vincent. *Deconstructive Criticism: An Advanced Introduction*. New York: Columbia University Press, 1983.

Lindenberger, Herbert. *Historical Drama: The Relation of Literature and Reality*. Chicago: University of Chicago Press, 1975.

———. "Toward a New History in Literary Study." *Profession 84* (1984): 16–23.

Lyotard, Jean-François. *The Post-Modern Condition: A Report on Knowledge*. 1979; Minneapolis: University of Minnesota Press, 1984.

Macksey, Richard, and Eugenio Donato, eds. *The Structuralist Controversy: The Languages of Criticism and the Sciences of Man*. Baltimore, Johns Hopkins University Press, 1970.

McDonald, Christie V. "Jacques Derrida's Reading of Rousseau." *The Eighteenth Century: Theory and Interpretation* 20 (1970): 82–95.

McGann, Jerome. *The Beauty of Inflections: Literary Investigations in Historical Method and Theory*. Oxford: Clarendon Press, 1985.

———, ed. *Historical Studies and Literary Criticism*. Madison: University of Wisconsin Press, 1985.

Miller, J. Hillis. "Ariadne's Thread: Repetition and the Narrative Line." *Critical Inquiry* 3 (1976): 57–78.

———. *Fiction and Repetition: Seven English Novels*. Cambridge: Harvard University Press, 1982.

———. *The Linguistic Moment: From Wordsworth to Stevens*. Princeton: Princeton University Press, 1985.

———. *The Ethics of Reading: Kant, de Man, Eliot, Trollope, James and Benjamin*. New York: Columbia University Press, 1987.

Montrose, Louis. *"Curious-knotted garden": The Form, Themes, and Contexts of Shakespeare's "Love's Labour's Lost."* Salzburg: Institut für Englische Sprache und Literatur, 1977.

Nietzsche, Friedrich. *Complete Works*. 18 vols. Ed. Oscar Levy. New York: Russell and Russell, 1964.

Norris, Christopher. *The Deconstructive Turn: Essays in the Rhetoric of Philosophy*. New York: Methuen, 1984.

———. *The Contest of Faculties: Philosophy and Theory after Deconstruction*. New York: Methuen, 1985.

Rorty, Richard. "Philosophy as a Kind of Writing: An Essay on Derrida." *New Literary History* 10 (1978): 1411–60.

Ryan, Michael. *Marxism and Deconstruction*. Baltimore: Johns Hopkins University Press, 1982.

Said, Edward W. *Beginnings: Intention and Method*. New York: Basic Books, 1975.

———. *The World, the Text, and the Critic*. Cambridge: Harvard University Press, 1983.

Searle, John. "Reiterating the Differences: A Reply to Derrida." *Glyph* 1 (1977): 198–208.

Smith, Barbara Herrnstein. *On the Margins of Discourse: The Relation of Literature to Language*. Chicago: University of Chicago Press, 1979.

Sprinker, Michael. "Textual Politics: Foucault and Derrida." *Boundary 2* 8 (1980): 75–98.

Tennenhouse, Leonard. *Power on Display: The Politics of Shakespeare's Genres*. New York: Methuen, 1986.

White, Hayden. *Metahistory: The Historical Imagination in Nineteenth-Century Europe*. Baltimore: Johns Hopkins University Press, 1974.

———. *Tropics of Discourse: Essays in Cultural Criticism*. Baltimore: Johns Hopkins University Press, 1978.

# Jacques Derrida

b. 1930

*The prime mover of poststructuralism, Jacques Derrida was born in Algiers and educated in France. Trained as a philosopher — early in his career he published a study of Edmund Husserl, the founder of phenomenology — Derrida teaches the history of philosophy at the École des Hautes Études en sciences sociales while maintaining a part-time residency at Yale University. Derrida's fame — or notoriety — in America can be traced to a talk he delivered at a structuralist conference at The Johns Hopkins University in 1966. "Structure, Sign, and Play in the Discourse of the Human Sciences" confounded the structuralist enterprise and many of its adherents and precipitated the rise of poststructuralist theories. Derrida's publications are steadily being translated into English; among them are* Speech and Phenomena *(1967),* Of Grammatology *(1967),* Writing and Difference *(1967),* Margins of Philosophy *(1972),* Positions *(1972),* Glas *(1974), and* The Post Card *(1980). This translation of "Structure, Sign, and Play in the Discourse of the Human Sciences" is from* The Structuralist Controversy *(1970), edited by Richard Macksey and Eugenio Donato; another version appears in* Writing and Difference *(1967; translated 1978 by Alan Bass). "The Purloined Letter" is excerpted from* The Purveyor of Truth, *a long essay from* Yale French Studies *52 (1975).*

## Structure, Sign, and Play in the Discourse of the Human Sciences

Perhaps something has occurred in the history of the concept of structure that could be called an "event," if this loaded word did not entail a meaning which it is precisely the function of structural — or structuralist — thought to reduce or to suspect. But let me use the term "event" anyway, employing it with caution and as if in quotation marks. In this sense, this event will have the exterior form of a *rupture* and a *redoubling*.

It would be easy enough to show that the concept of structure and even the word "structure" itself are as old as the *episteme*[1] — that is to say, as old as western science and western

Translated by Richard Macksey and Eugenio Donato.

[1]Knowledge. [Ed.]

philosophy — and that their roots thrust deep into the soil of ordinary language, into whose deepest recesses the *epistemé* plunges to gather them together once more, making them part of itself in a metaphorical displacement. Nevertheless, up until the event which I wish to mark out and define, structure — or rather the structurality of structure — although it has always been involved, has always been neutralized or reduced, and this by a process of giving it a center or referring it to a point of presence, a fixed origin. The function of this center was not only to orient, balance, and organize the structure — one cannot in fact conceive of an unorganized structure — but above all to make sure that the organizing principle of the structure would limit what we might call the *freeplay* of the structure. No doubt that by orienting and organizing the coherence of the system, the center of a structure permits the freeplay of its elements inside the total form. And even today the notion of a structure lacking any center represents the unthinkable itself.

Nevertheless, the center also closes off the freeplay it opens up and makes possible. *Qua* center, it is the point at which the substitution of contents, elements, or terms is no longer possible. At the center, the permutation or the transformation of elements (which may of course be structures enclosed within a structure) is forbidden. At least this permutation has always remained *interdicted*[2] (I use this word deliberately). Thus it has always been thought that the center, which is by definition unique, constituted that very thing within a structure which governs the structure, while escaping structurality. This is why classical thought concerning structure could say that the center is, paradoxically, *within* the structure and *outside* it. The center is at the center of the totality, and yet, since the center does not belong to the totality (is not part of the totality), the totality *has its center elsewhere*. The center is not the center. The concept of centered structure — although it represents coherence itself, the condition of the *epistemé* as philosophy or science — is contradictorily coherent. And, as always, coherence in contradiction expresses the force of a desire. The concept of centered structure is in fact the concept of a freeplay based on a fundamental ground, a freeplay which is constituted upon a fundamental immobility and a reassuring certitude, which is itself beyond the reach of the freeplay. With this certitude anxiety can be mastered, for anxiety is invariably the result of a certain mode of being implicated in the game, of being caught by the game, of being as it were from the very beginning at stake in the game.[3] From the basis of what we therefore call the center (and which, because it can be either inside or outside, is as readily called the origin as the end, as readily *arché* as *telos*),[4] the repetitions, the substitutions, the transformations, and the permutations are always *taken* from a history of meaning [*sens*] — that is, a history, period — whose origin may always be revealed or whose end may always be anticipated in the form of presence. This is why one could perhaps say that the movement of any archeology, like that of any eschatology,[5] is an accomplice of this reduction of the structurality of structure and always attempts to conceive of structure from the basis of a full presence which is out of play.

If this is so, the whole history of the concept of structure, before the rupture I spoke of, must be thought of as a series of substitutions of center for center, as a linked chain of determinations of the center. Successively, and in a regulated fashion, the center receives different forms or names. The history of metaphysics, like the history of the West, is the history of these metaphors and metonymies. Its matrix — if you will pardon me for demonstrating so little and for being so elliptical in order to bring me more quickly to my principal theme — is the determination of being as *presence* in all the senses of this word. It would be possible to show that all the names related to fundamentals, to principles, or to the center have always designated the constant of a

[3]". . . qui naît toujours d'une certaine manière d'être impliqué dans le jeu, d'être pris au jeu, d'être comme être d'entreé de jeu dans le jeu." [Tr.]

[4]Beginning as end. *Telos* means "end" in the sense of "purpose." [Ed.]

[5]Study of last things. [Ed.]

[2]*Interdite:* "forbidden," "disconcerted," "confounded," "speechless." [Tr.]

presence — *eidos, arché, telos, energeia, ousia* (essence, existence, substance, subject) *aletheia*,[6] transcendentality, consciousness, or conscience, God, man, and so forth.

The event I called a rupture, the disruption I alluded to at the beginning of this paper, would presumably have come about when the structurality of structure had to begin to be thought, that is to say, repeated, and this is why I said that this disruption was repetition in all of the senses of this word. From then on it became necessary to think the law which governed, as it were, the desire for the center in the constitution of structure and the process of signification prescribing its displacements and its substitutions for this law of the central presence — but a central presence which was never itself, which has always already been transported outside itself in its surrogate. The surrogate does not substitute itself for anything which has somehow pre-existed it. From then on it was probably necessary to begin to think that there was no center, that the center could not be thought in the form of a being-present, that the center had no natural locus, that it was not a fixed locus but a function, a sort of non-locus in which an infinite number of sign-substitutions came into play. This moment was that in which language invaded the universal problematic; that in which, in the absence of a center or origin, everything became discourse — provided we can agree on this word — that is to say, when everything became a system where the central signified, the original or transcendental signified, is never absolutely present outside a system of differences. The absence of the transcendental signified extends the domain and the interplay of signification *ad infinitum*.

Where and how does this decentering, this notion of the structurality of structure, occur? It would be somewhat naïve to refer to an event, a doctrine, or an author in order to designate this occurrence. It is no doubt part of the totality of an era, our own, but still it has already begun to proclaim itself and begun to *work*. Nevertheless, if I wished to give some sort of indication by choosing one or two "names," and by recalling those authors in whose discourses this occurrence has most nearly maintained its most radical formulation, I would probably cite the Nietzschean critique of metaphysics, the critique of the concepts of being and truth, for which were substituted the concepts of play, interpretation, and sign (sign without truth present); the Freudian critique of self-presence, that is, the critique of consciousness, of the subject, of self-identity and of self-proximity or self-possession; and, more radically, the Heideggerean destruction of metaphysics, of onto-theology, of the determination of being as presence. But all these destructive discourses and all their analogues are trapped in a sort of circle. This circle is unique. It describes the form of the relationship between the history of metaphysics and the destruction of the history of metaphysics. *There is no sense* in doing without the concepts of metaphysics in order to attack metaphysics. We have no language — no syntax and no lexicon — which is alien to this history; we cannot utter a single destructive proposition which has not already slipped into the form, the logic, and the implicit postulations of precisely what it seeks to contest. To pick out one example from many: the metaphysics of presence is attacked with the help of the concept of the *sign*. But from the moment anyone wishes this to show, as I suggested a moment ago, that there is no transcendental or privileged signified and that the domain or the interplay of signification has, henceforth, no limit, he ought to extend his refusal to the concept and to the word sign itself — which is precisely what cannot be done. For the signification "sign" has always been comprehended and determined, in its sense, as sign-of, signifier referring to a signified, signifier different from its signified. If one erases the radical difference between signifier and signified, it is the word signifier itself which ought to be abandoned as a metaphysical concept. When Lévi-Strauss says in the preface to *The Raw and the Cooked*[7] that he has "sought to transcend the opposition between the sensible and the intelligible by placing [himself] from the very beginning at the level of signs," the necessity, the

---

[6]The six preceding Greek terms mean, respectively: form, origin, purpose, energy, being, and truth. [Ed.]

[7]*Le cru et le cuit* (Paris: Plon, 1964). [Tr.]

force, and the legitimacy of his act cannot make us forget that the concept of the sign cannot in itself surpass or bypass this opposition between the sensible and the intelligible. The concept of the sign is determined by this opposition: through and throughout the totality of its history and by its system. But we cannot do without the concept of the sign, we cannot give up this metaphysical complicity without also giving up the critique we are directing against this complicity, without the risk of erasing difference [altogether] in the self-identity of a signified reducing into itself its signifier, or, what amounts to the same thing, simply expelling it outside itself. For there are two heterogenous ways of erasing the difference between the signifier and the signified: one, the classic way, consists in reducing or deriving the signifier, that is to say, ultimately in *submitting* the sign to thought; the other, the one we are using here against the first one, consists in putting into question the system in which the preceding reduction functioned: first and foremost, the opposition between the sensible and the intelligible. The *paradox* is that the metaphysical reduction of the sign needed the opposition it was reducing. The opposition is part of the system, along with the reduction. And what I am saying here about the sign can be extended to all the concepts and all the sentences of metaphysics, in particular to the discourse on "structure." But there are many ways of being caught in this circle. They are all more or less naïve, more or less empirical, more or less systematic, more or less close to the formulation or even to the formalization of this circle. It is these differences which explain the multiplicity of destructive discourses and the disagreement between those who make them. It was within concepts inherited from metaphysics that Nietzsche, Freud, and Heidegger worked, for example. Since these concepts are not elements or atoms and since they are taken from a syntax and a system, every particular borrowing drags along with it the whole of metaphysics. This is what allows these destroyers to destroy each other reciprocally — for example, Heidegger considering Nietzsche, with as much lucidity and rigor as bad faith and misconstruction, as the last metaphysician, the last "Platonist." One could do the same for Heidegger

himself, for Freud, or for a number of others. And today no exercise is more widespread.

What is the relevance of this formal schema when we turn to what are called the "human sciences"? One of them perhaps occupies a privileged place — ethnology.[8] One can in fact assume that ethnology could have been born as a science only at the moment when a de-centering had come about: at the moment when European culture — and, in consequence, the history of metaphysics and of its concepts — had been *dislocated,* driven from its locus, and forced to stop considering itself as the culture of reference. This moment is not first and foremost a moment of philosophical or scientific discourse, it is also a moment which is political, economic, technical, and so forth. One can say in total assurance that there is nothing fortuitous about the fact that the critique of ethnocentrism — the very condition of ethnology — should be systematically and historically contemporaneous with the destruction of the history of metaphysics. Both belong to a single and same era.

Ethnology — like any science — comes about within the element of discourse. And it is primarily a European science employing traditional concepts, however much it may struggle against them. Consequently, whether he wants to or not — and this does not depend on a decision on his part — the ethnologist accepts into his discourse the premises of ethnocentrism at the very moment when he is employed in denouncing them. This necessity is irreducible; it is not a historical contingency. We ought to consider very carefully all its implications. But if nobody can escape this necessity, and if no one is therefore responsible for giving in to it, however little, this does not mean that all the ways of giving in to it are of an equal pertinence. The quality and the fecundity of a discourse are perhaps measured by the critical rigor with which this relationship to the history of metaphysics and to inherited concepts is thought. Here it is a question of a critical relationship to the language of the human sciences and a question of a critical responsibility of the discourse. It is a question of putting ex-

[8]Cultural anthropology. [Ed.]

pressly and systematically the problem of the status of a discourse which borrows from a heritage the resources necessary for the deconstruction of that heritage itself. A problem of *economy* and *strategy*.

If I now go on to employ an examination of the texts of Lévi-Strauss as an example, it is not only because of the privilege accorded to ethnology among the human sciences, nor yet because the thought of Lévi-Strauss weighs heavily on the contemporary theoretical situation. It is above all because a certain choice has made itself evident in the work of Lévi-Strauss and because a certain doctrine has been elaborated there, and precisely in a *more or less explicit manner*, in relation to this critique of language and to this critical language in the human sciences.

In order to follow this movement in the text of Lévi-Strauss, let me choose as one guiding thread among others the opposition between nature and culture. In spite of all its rejuvenations and its disguises, this opposition is congenital to philosophy. It is even older than Plato. It is at least as old as the Sophists. Since the statement of the opposition — *physis/nomos, physis/techné*[9] — it has been passed on to us by a whole historical chain which opposes "nature" to the law, to education, to art, to technics — and also to liberty, to the arbitrary, to history, to society, to the mind, and so on. From the beginnings of his quest and from his first book, *The Elementary Structures of Kinship*,[10] Lévi-Strauss has felt at one and the same time the necessity of utilizing this opposition and the impossibility of making it acceptable. In the *Elementary Structures*, he begins from this axiom or definition: that belongs to nature which is *universal* and spontaneous, not depending on any particular culture or on any determinate norm. That belongs to culture, on the other hand, which depends on a system of *norms* regulating society and is therefore capable of *varying* from one social structure to another. These two definitions are of the traditional type. But, in the very first pages of the *Elementary Structures*, Lévi-Strauss, who has begun to give

these concepts an acceptable standing, encounters what he calls a *scandal,* that is to say, something which no longer tolerates the nature/culture opposition he has accepted and which seems to require *at one and the same time* the predicates of nature and those of culture. This scandal is the *incest-prohibition.* The incest-prohibition is universal; in this sense one could call it natural. But it is also a prohibition, a system of norms and interdicts; in this sense one could call it cultural.

> Let us assume therefore that everything universal in man derives from the order of nature and is characterized by spontaneity, that everything which is subject to a norm belongs to culture and presents the attributes of the relative and the particular. We then find ourselves confronted by a fact, or rather an ensemble of facts, which, in the light of the preceding definitions, is not far from appearing as a scandal: the prohibition of incest presents without the least equivocation, and indissolubly linked together, the two characteristics in which we recognized the contradictory attributes of two exclusive orders. The prohibition of incest constitutes a rule, but a rule, alone of all the social rules, which possesses at the same time a universal character (p. 9).

Obviously there is no scandal except in the *interior* of a system of concepts sanctioning the difference between nature and culture. In beginning his work with the *factum*[11] of the incest-prohibition, Lévi-Strauss thus puts himself in a position entailing that this difference, which has always been assumed to be self-evident, becomes obliterated or disputed. For, from the moment that the incest-prohibition can no longer be conceived within the nature/culture opposition, it can no longer be said that it is a scandalous fact, a nucleus of opacity within a network of transparent significations. The incest-prohibition is no longer a scandal one meets with or comes up against in the domain of traditional concepts; it is something which escapes these concepts and certainly precedes them — probably as the condition of their possibility. It could perhaps be said that the whole of philosophical conceptualization, systematically relating itself to the na-

[9]Nature vs. culture; nature vs. art. [Ed.]

[10]*Les structures élémentaires de la parenté* (Paris: Presses Universitaires de France, 1949). [Tr.]

[11]Given fact. [Ed.]

ture/culture opposition, is designed to leave in the domain of the unthinkable the very thing that makes this conceptualization possible: the origin of the prohibition of incest.

I have dealt too cursorily with this example, only one among so many others, but the example nevertheless reveals that language bears within itself the necessity of its own critique. This critique may be undertaken along two tracks, in two "manners." Once the limit of nature/culture opposition makes itself felt, one might want to question systematically and rigorously the history of these concepts. This is a first action. Such a systematic and historic questioning would be neither a philological nor a philosophical action in the classic sense of these words. Concerning oneself with the founding concepts of the whole history of philosophy, de-constituting them, is not to undertake the task of the philologist or of the classic historian of philosophy. In spite of appearances, it is probably the most daring way of making the beginnings of a step outside of philosophy. The step "outside philosophy" is much more difficult to conceive than is generally imagined by those who think they made it long ago with cavalier ease, and who are in general swallowed up in metaphysics by the whole body of the discourse that they claim to have disengaged from it.

In order to avoid the possibly sterilizing effect of the first way, the other choice — which I feel corresponds more nearly to the way chosen by Lévi-Strauss — consists in conserving in the field of empirical discovery all these old concepts, while at the same time exposing here and there their limits, treating them as tools which can still be of use. No longer is any truth-value attributed to them; there is a readiness to abandon them if necessary if other instruments should appear more useful. In the meantime, their relative efficacy is exploited, and they are employed to destroy the old machinery to which they belong and of which they themselves are pieces. Thus it is that the language of the human sciences criticizes *itself*. Lévi-Strauss thinks that in this way he can separate *method* from *truth,* the instruments of the method and the objective significations aimed at by it. One could almost say that this is the primary affirmation of Lévi-

Strauss; in any event, the first words of the *Elementary Structures* are: "One begins to understand that the distinction between state of nature and state of society (we would be more apt to say today: state of nature and state of culture), while lacking any acceptable historical signification, presents a value which fully justifies its use by modern sociology: its value as a methodological instrument."

Lévi-Strauss will always remain faithful to this double intention: to preserve as an instrument that whose truth-value he criticizes.

*On the one hand,* he will continue in effect to contest the value of the nature/culture opposition. More than thirteen years after the *Elementary Structures, The Savage Mind*[12] faithfully echoes the text I have just quoted: "The opposition between nature and culture which I have previously insisted on seems today to offer a value which is above all methodological." And this methodological value is not affected by its "ontological" non-value (as could be said, if this notion were not suspect here): "It would not be enough to have absorbed particular humanities into a general humanity; this first enterprise prepares the way for others . . . which belong to the natural and exact sciences: to reintegrate culture into nature, and finally, to reintegrate life into the totality of its physiochemical conditions" (p. 327).

*On the other hand,* still in *The Savage Mind,* he presents as what he calls *bricolage*[13] what might be called the discourse of this method. The *bricoleur,* says Lévi-Strauss, is someone who uses "the means at hand," that is, the instruments he finds at his disposition around him, those which are already there, which had not been especially conceived with an eye to the operation for which they are to be used and to which one tries by trial and error to adapt them, not hesitating to change them whenever it appears necessary, or to try several of them at once, even if their form and their origin are heterogenous — and so forth. There is therefore a critique of

---

[12]*La pensée sauvage* (Paris: Plon, 1962). [Tr.]

[13]A *bricoleur* is a jack-of-all-trades, someone who potters about with odds-and-ends, who puts things together out of bits and pieces. [Tr.]

language in the form of *bricolage,* and it has even been possible to say that *bricolage* is the critical language itself. I am thinking in particular of the article by G[érard] Genette, "Structuralisme et Critique littéraire," published in homage to Lévi-Strauss in a special issue of *L'Arc* (no. 26, 1965), where it is stated that the analysis of *bricolage* could "be applied almost word for word" to criticism, and especially to "literary criticism."[14]

If one calls *bricolage* the necessity of borrowing one's concept from the text of a heritage which is more or less coherent or ruined, it must be said that every discourse is *bricoleur.* The engineer, whom Lévi-Strauss opposes to the *bricoleur,* should be one to construct the totality of his language, syntax, and lexicon. In this sense the engineer is a myth. A subject who would supposedly be the absolute origin of his own discourse and would supposedly construct it "out of nothing," "out of whole cloth," would be the creator of the *verbe,* the *verbe* itself. The notion of the engineer who had supposedly broken with all forms of *bricolage* is therefore a theological idea; and since Lévi-Strauss tells us elsewhere that *bricolage* is mythopoetic, the odds are that the engineer is a myth produced by the *bricoleur.* From the moment that we cease to believe in such an engineer and in a discourse breaking with the received historical discourse, as soon as it is admitted that every finite discourse is bound by a certain *bricolage,* and that the engineer and the scientist are also species of *bricoleurs* then the very idea of *bricolage* is menaced and the difference in which it took on its meaning decomposes.

This brings out the second thread which might guide us in what is being unraveled here.

Lévi-Strauss describes *bricolage* not only as an intellectual activity but also as a mythopoetical activity. One reads in *The Savage Mind,* "Like *bricolage* on the technical level, mythical reflection can attain brilliant and unforeseen results on the intellectual level. Reciprocally, the mythopoetical character of *bricolage* has often been noted" (p. 26).

[14]Reprinted in: G. Genette, *Figures* (Paris: Editions du Seuil, 1966), p. 145. [Tr.]

But the remarkable endeavor of Lévi-Strauss is not simply to put forward, notably in the most recent of his investigations, a structural science or knowledge of myths and of mythological activity. His endeavor also appears — I would say almost from the first — in the status which he accords to his own discourse on myths, to what he calls his "mythologicals." It is here that his discourse on the myth reflects on itself and criticizes itself. And this moment, this critical period, is evidently of concern to all the languages which share the field of the human sciences. What does Lévi-Strauss say of his "mythologicals"? It is here that we rediscover the mythopoetical virtue (power) of *bricolage.* In effect, what appears most fascinating in this critical search for a new status of the discourse is the stated abandonment of all reference to a *center,* to a *subject,* to a privileged *reference,* to an origin, or to an absolute *arché.* The theme of this decentering could be followed throughout the "Overture" to his last book, *The Raw and the Cooked.* I shall simply remark on a few key points.

1. From the very start, Lévi-Strauss recognizes that the Bororo myth which he employs in the book as the "reference-myth" does not merit this name and this treatment. The name is specious and the use of the myth improper. This myth deserves no more than any other its referential privilege:

> In fact the Bororo myth which will from now on be designated by the name *reference-myth* is, as I shall try to show, nothing other than a more or less forced transformation of other myths originating either in the same society or in societies more or less far removed. It would therefore have been legitimate to choose as my point of departure any representative of the group whatsoever. From this point of view, the interest of the reference-myth does not depend on its typical character, but rather on its irregular position in the midst of a group (p. 10).

2. There is no unity or absolute source of the myth. The focus or the source of the myth are always shadows and virtualities which are elusive, unactualizable, and nonexistent in the first place. Everything begins with the structure, the

configuration, the relationship. The discourse on this acentric structure, the myth, that is, cannot itself have an absolute subject or an absolute center. In order not to short change the form and the movement of the myth, that violence which consists in centering a language which is describing an acentric structure must be avoided. In this context, therefore, it is necessary to forego scientific or philosophical discourse, to renounce the *epistemé* which absolutely requires, which is the absolute requirement that we go back to the source, to the center, to the founding basis, to the principle, and so on. In opposition to *epistémic* discourse, structural discourse on myths — *mythological* discourse — must itself be *mythomorphic*. It must have the form of that of which it speaks. This is what Lévi-Strauss says in *The Raw and the Cooked,* from which I would now like to quote a long and remarkable passage:

> In effect the study of myths poses a methodological problem by the fact that it cannot conform to the Cartesian principle of dividing the difficulty into as many parts as are necessary to resolve it. There exists no veritable end or term to mythical analysis, no secret unity which could be grasped at the end of the work of decomposition. The themes duplicate themselves to infinity. When we think we have disentangled them from each other and can hold them separate, it is only to realize that they are joining together again, in response to the attraction of unforeseen affinities. In consequence, the unity of the myth is only tendential and projective; it never reflects a state or a moment of the myth. An imaginary phenomenon implied by the endeavor to interpret, its role is to give a synthetic form to the myth and to impede its dissolution into the confusion of contraries. It could therefore be said that the science or knowledge of myths is an *anaclastic,* taking this ancient term in the widest sense authorized by its etymology, a science which admits into its definition the study of the reflected rays along with that of the broken ones. But, unlike philosophical reflection, which claims to go all the way back to its source, the reflections in question here concern rays without any other than a virtual focus. . . . In wanting to imitate the spontaneous movement of mythical thought, my enterprise, itself too brief and too long, has had to yield to its demands and respect its rhythm. Thus is this book, on myths itself and in its own way, a myth.

This statement is repeated a little farther on (p. 20): "Since myths themselves rest on second-order codes (the first-order codes being those in which language consists), this book thus offers the rough draft of a third-order code, destined to insure the reciprocal possibility of translation of several myths. This is why it would not be wrong to consider it a myth: the myth of mythology, as it were." It is by this absence of any real and fixed center of the mythical or mythological discourse that the musical model chosen by Lévi-Strauss for the composition of his book is apparently justified. The absence of a center is here the absence of a subject and the absence of an author: "The myth and the musical work thus appear as orchestra conductors whose listeners are the silent performers. If it be asked where the real focus of the work is to be found, it must be replied that its determination is impossible. Music and mythology bring man face to face with virtual objects whose shadow alone is actual. . . . Myths have no authors" (p. 25).

Thus it is at this point that ethnographic *bricolage* deliberately assumes its mythopoetic function. But by the same token, this function makes the philosophical or epistemological requirement of a center appear as mythological, that is to say, as a historical illusion.

Nevertheless, even if one yields to the necessity of what Lévi-Strauss has done, one cannot ignore its risks. If the mythological is mythomorphic, are all discourses on myths equivalent? Shall we have to abandon any epistemological requirement which permits us to distinguish between several qualities of discourse on the myth? A classic question, but inevitable. We cannot reply — and I do not believe Lévi-Strauss replies to it — as long as the problem of the relationships between the philosopheme or the theorem, on the one hand, and the mytheme or the mythopoem(e), on the other, has not been expressly posed. This is no small problem. For lack of expressly posing this problem, we condemn ourselves to transforming the claimed transgression of philosophy into an unperceived fault in the interior of the philosophical field. Empiricism would be the genus of which these faults would always be the species. Trans-philosophical concepts would be transformed into philosophical naïvetés. One could give many examples to demonstrate this risk: the concepts of sign, history, truth, and so forth. What I want to emphasize is simply that the passage beyond philosophy does not consist in turning the page of philosophy (which usually comes down to philosophizing badly), but in continuing to read philosophers *in a certain way*. The risk I am speaking of is always assumed by Lévi-Strauss and it is the very price of his endeavor. I have said that empiricism is the matrix of all the faults menacing a discourse which continues, as with Lévi-Strauss in particular, to elect to be scientific. If we wanted to pose the problem of empiricism and *bricolage* in depth, we would probably end up very quickly with a number of propositions absolutely contradictory in relation to the status of discourse in structural ethnography. On the one hand, structuralism justly claims to be the critique of empiricism.[15] But at the same time there is not a single book or study by Lévi-Strauss which does not offer itself as an empirical essay which can always be completed or invalidated by new information. The structural schemata are always proposed as hypotheses resulting from a finite quantity of information and which are subjected to the proof of experience. Numerous texts could be used to demonstrate this double postulation. Let us turn once again to the "Overture" of *The Raw and the Cooked,* where it seems clear that if this postulation is double, it is because it is a question here of a language on language:

> Critics who might take me to task for not having begun by making an exhaustive inventory of South American myths before analyzing them would be making a serious mistake about the nature and the role of these documents. The totality of the myths of a people is of the order of the discourse. Provided that this people does not become physically or morally extinct, this totality is never closed. Such a criticism would therefore be equivalent to reproaching a linguist with writing the grammar of a language without having recorded the totality of the words which have been uttered since that language came into existence and without knowing the verbal exchanges which will take place as long as the language continues to exist. Experience proves that an absurdly small number of sentences

[15]Because the aim of structuralism is to learn the constitutive rules of an activity, which are implicit in every instance of the activity, so that the massing of large quantities of data is unnecessary. [Ed.]

. . . allows the linguist to elaborate a grammar of the language he is studying. And even a partial grammar or an outline of a grammar represents valuable acquisitions in the case of unknown languages. Syntax does not wait until it has been possible to enumerate a theoretically unlimited series of events before becoming manifest, because syntax consists in the body of rules which presides over the generation of these events. And it is precisely a syntax of South American mythology that I wanted to outline. Should new texts appear to enrich the mythical discourse, then this will provide an opportunity to check or modify the way in which certain grammatical laws have been formulated, an opportunity to discard certain of them and an opportunity to discover new ones. But in no instance can the requirement of a total mythical discourse be raised as an objection. For we have just seen that such a requirement has no meaning (pp. 15–16).

Totalization is therefore defined at one time as *useless,* at another time as *impossible.* This is no doubt the result of the fact that there are two ways of conceiving the limit of totalization. And I assert once again that these two determinations coexist implicitly in the discourses of Lévi-Strauss. Totalization can be judged impossible in the classical style: one then refers to the empirical endeavor of a subject or of a finite discourse in a vain and breathless quest of an infinite richness which it can never master. There is too much, more than one can say. But nontotalization can also be determined in another way: not from the standpoint of the concept of finitude as assigning us to an empirical view, but from the standpoint of the concept of *freeplay*. If totalization no longer has any meaning, it is not because the infinity of a field cannot be covered by a finite glance or a finite discourse, but because the nature of the field — that is, language and a finite language — excludes totalization. This field is in fact that of *freeplay,* that is to say, a field of infinite substitutions in the closure of a finite ensemble. This field permits these infinite substitutions only because it is finite, that is to say, because instead of being an inexhaustible field, as in the classical hypothesis, instead of being too large, there is something missing from it: a center which arrests and founds the freeplay of substitutions. One could say — rigorously using that word whose scandalous signification is always obliterated in French — that this movement of the freeplay, permitted by the lack, the absence of a center or origin, is the movement of *supplementarity*. One cannot determine the center, the sign which *supplements*[16] it, which takes its place in its absence — because this sign adds itself, occurs in addition, over and above, comes as a *supplement*.[17] The movement of signification adds something, which results in the fact that there is always more, but this addition is a floating one because it comes to perform a vicarious function, to supplement a lack on the part of the signified. Although Lévi-Strauss in his use of the word supplementary never emphasizes as I am doing here the two directions of meaning which are so strangely compounded within it, it is not by chance that he uses this word twice in his "Introduction to the Work of Marcel Mauss,"[18] at the point where he is speaking of the "superabundance of signifier, in relation to the signifieds to which this superabundance can refer":

In his endeavor to understand the world, man therefore always has at his disposition a surplus of signification (which he portions out amongst things according to the laws of symbolic thought — which it is the task of ethnologists and linguists to study). This distribution of a *supplementary* allowance [*ration* supplémentaire] — if it is permissible to put it that way — is absolutely necessary in order that on the whole the available signifier and the signified it aims at may remain in the relationship of complementarity which is the very condition of the use of symbolic thought (p. xlix).

(It could no doubt be demonstrated that this *ration supplémentaire* of signification is the origin of the *ratio* itself.) The word reappears a little farther on, after Lévi-Strauss has mentioned "this

floating signifier, which is the servitude of all finite thought":

In other words — and taking as our guide Mauss's precept that all social phenomena can be assimilated to language — we see in *mana*, *Wakau*, *oranda* and other notions of the same type, the conscious expression of a semantic function, whose role it is to permit symbolic thought to operate in spite of the contradiction which is proper to it. In this way are explained the apparently insoluble antinomies attached to this notion. . . . At one and the same time force and action, quality and state, substantive and verb; abstract and concrete, omnipresent and localized — *mana* is in effect all these things. But is it not precisely because it is none of these things that *mana* is a simple form, or more exactly, a symbol in the pure state, and therefore capable of becoming charged with any sort of symbolic content whatever? In the system of symbols constituted by all cosmologies, *mana* would simply be a *valeur symbolique zéro*, that is to say, a sign marking the necessity of a symbolic content *supplementary* [my italics] to that with which the signified is already loaded, but which can take on any value required, provided only that this value still remains part of the available reserve and is not, as phonologists put it, a group-term.

Lévi-Strauss adds the note:

Linguists have already been led to formulate hypotheses of this type. For example: "A zero phoneme is opposed to all the other phonemes in French in that it entails no differential characters and no constant phonetic value. On the contrary, the proper function of the zero phoneme is to be opposed to phoneme absence." (R. Jakobson and J. Lutz, "Notes on the French Phonemic Pattern," *Word,* vol. 5, no. 2 [August, 1949], p. 155). Similarly, if we schematize the conception I am proposing here, it could almost be said that the function of notions like *mana* is to be opposed to the absence of signification, without entailing by itself any particular signification (p. 1 and note).

The *superabundance* of the signifier, its *supplementary* character, is thus the result of a finitude, that is to say, the result of a lack which must be *supplemented*.

It can now be understood why the concept of freeplay is important in Lévi-Strauss. His references to all sorts of games, notably to roulette, are very frequent, especially in his *Conversa-*

[16]The point being that the word, both in English and French, means "to supply a deficiency," on the one hand, and "to supply something additional," on the other. [Tr.] See the introduction to this chapter, pp. 943–44, on Derrida's antinomy of the supplement. [Ed.]

[17]". . . ce signe s'ajoute, vient en sus, en *supplément.*" [Tr.]

[18]"Introduction à l'oeuvre de Marcel Mauss," in: Marcel Mauss, *Sociologie et anthropologie* (Paris: Presses Universitaires de France, 1950). [Tr.] Marcel Mauss (1872–1950) was the French social anthropologist who wrote *The Gift* (1925). [Ed.]

*tions*,[19] in *Race and History*,[20] and in *The Savage Mind*. This reference to the game or free-play is always caught up in a tension.

It is in tension with history, first of all. This is a classical problem, objections to which are now well worn or used up. I shall simply indicate what seems to me the formality of the problem: by reducing history, Lévi-Strauss has treated as it deserves a concept which has always been in complicity with a teleological and eschatological metaphysics, in other words, paradoxically, in complicity with that philosophy of presence to which it was believed history could be opposed. The thematic of historicity, although it seems to be a somewhat late arrival in philosophy, has always been required by the determination of being as presence. With or without etymology, and in spite of the classic antagonism which opposes these significations throughout all of classical thought, it could be shown that the concept of *epistemé* has always called forth that of *historia*, if history is always the unity of a becoming, as tradition of truth or development of science or knowledge oriented toward the appropriation of truth in presence and self-presence, toward knowledge in consciousness-of-self.[21] History has always been conceived as the movement of a resumption of history, a diversion between two presences. But if it is legitimate to suspect this concept of history, there is a risk, if it is reduced without an express statement of the problem I am indicating here, of falling back into an anhistoricism of a classical type, that is to say, in a determinate moment of the history of metaphysics. Such is the algebraic formality of the problem as I see it. More concretely, in the work of Lévi-Strauss it must be recognized that the respect for structurality, for the internal originality of the structure, compels a neutralization of time and history. For example, the appearance of a new structure, of an original system, always

---

[19]Presumably: G. Charbonnier, *Entretiens avec Claude Lévi-Strauss* (Paris: Plon-Julliard, 1961). [Tr.]

[20]*Race and History* (Paris: UNESCO Publications, 1958). [Tr.]

[21]". . . l'unité d'un devenir, comme tradition de la vérité dans la présence et la présence à soi, vers le savoir dans la conscience de soi." [Tr.]

comes about — and this is the very condition of its structural specificity — by a rupture with its past, its origin, and its cause. One can therefore describe what is peculiar to the structural organization only by not taking into account, in the very moment of this description, its past conditions: by failing to pose the problem of the passage from one structure to another, by putting history into parentheses. In this "structuralist" moment, the concepts of chance and discontinuity are indispensable. And Lévi-Strauss does in fact often appeal to them as he does, for instance, for that structure of structures, language, of which he says in the "Introduction to the Work of Marcel Mauss" that it "could only have been born in one fell swoop":

> Whatever may have been the moment and the circumstances of its appearance in the scale of animal life, language could only have been born in one fell swoop. Things could not have set about signifying progressively. Following a transformation the study of which is not the concern of the social sciences, but rather of biology and psychology, a crossing over came about from a stage where nothing had a meaning to another where everything possessed it (p. xlvi).

This standpoint does not prevent Lévi-Strauss from recognizing the slowness, the process of maturing, the continuous toil of factual transformations, history (for example, in *Race and History*). But, in accordance with an act which was also Rousseau's and Husserl's, he must "brush aside all the facts" at the moment when he wishes to recapture the specificity of a structure. Like Rousseau, he must always conceive of the origin of a new structure on the model of catastrophe — an overturning of nature in nature, a natural interruption of the natural sequence, a brushing aside *of* nature.

Besides the tension of freeplay with history, there is also the tension of freeplay with presence. Freeplay is the disruption of presence. The presence of an element is always a signifying and substitutive reference inscribed in a system of differences and the movement of a chain. Freeplay is always an interplay of absence and presence, but if it is to be radically conceived, freeplay must be conceived of before the alternative of presence and absence; being must be conceived of as presence or absence beginning with the possibility of freeplay and not the other way around. If Lévi-Strauss, better than any other, has brought to light the freeplay of repetition and the repetition of freeplay, one no less perceives in his work a sort of ethic presence, an ethic of nostalgia for origins, an ethic of archaic and natural innocence, of a purity of presence and self-presence in speech[22] — an ethic, nostalgia, and even remorse which he often presents as the motivation of the ethnological project when he moves toward archaic societies — exemplary societies in his eyes. These texts are well known.

As a turning toward the presence, lost or impossible, of the absent origin, this structuralist thematic of broken immediateness is thus the sad, *negative,* nostalgic, guilty, Rousseauist facet of the thinking of freeplay of which the Nietzschean *affirmation* — the joyous affirmation of the freeplay of the world and without truth, without origin, offered to an active interpretation — would be the other side. *This affirmation then determines the non-center otherwise than as loss of the center.* And it plays the game without security. For there is a *sure* freeplay: that which is limited to the *substitution of given and existing, present,* pieces. In absolute chance, affirmation also surrenders itself to *genetic* indetermination, to the *seminal* adventure of the trace.[23]

There are thus two interpretations of interpretation, of structure, of sign, of freeplay. The one seeks to decipher, dreams of deciphering, a truth or an origin which is free from freeplay and from the order of the sign, and lives like an exile the necessity of interpretation. The other, which is no longer turned toward the origin, affirms freeplay and tries to pass beyond man and humanism, the name man being the name of that being who, throughout the history of metaphysics or of onto-theology — in other words, through the history of all of his history — has dreamed of full presence, the reassuring foundation, the origin and the end of the game. The second interpretation of interpretation, to which Nietzsche showed us the way, does not seek in ethnography, as Lévi-Strauss wished, the "inspiration of a new humanism" (again from the "Introduction to the Work of Marcel Mauss").

There are more than enough indications today to suggest we might perceive that these two interpretations of interpretation — which are absolutely irreconcilable even if we live them simultaneously and reconcile them in an obscure economy — together share the field which we call, in such a problematic fashion, the human sciences.

For my part, although these two interpretations must acknowledge and accentuate their difference and define their irreducibility, I do not believe that today there is any question of *choosing* — in the first place because here we are in a region (let's say, provisionally, a region of historicity) where the category of choice seems particularly trivial; and in the second, because we must first try to conceive of the common ground, and the *différence* of this irreducible difference.[24] Here there is a sort of question, call it

---

[22]". . . de la présence à soi dans la parole." [Tr.]

[23]"Tournée vers la présence, perdue ou impossible, de l'origine absente, cette thématique structuraliste de l'immédiateté rompue est donc la face triste, *négative,* nostalgique, coupable, rousseauiste, de la pensée du jeu dont *l'affirmation* nietzschéenne, l'affirmation joyeuse du jeu du monde et de l'innocence du devenir, l'affirmation d'un monde de signes sans faute, sans vérité, sans origine, offert à une interprétation active, serait l'autre face. *Cette affirmation détermine alors le non-centre autrement que comme perte du centre.* Et elle joue sans sécurité. Car il y a un jeu *sûr:* celui qui se limite à la *substitution de pièces données et existantes, présentes.* Dans le hasard absolu, l'affirmation se livre aussi à l'indétermination *génétique,* à l'aventure *séminale* de la trace." [Tr.] Derrida contrasts two methods of freeplay, Lévi-Strauss's and his own. The former is "sad" and "negative" in that it seeks a substitute for the absent center once provided by metaphysics; it is "nostalgic" for origins, "guilty" over European imperialism, "Rousseauist" in propounding a myth of the noble savage and privileging myth over rational thought. Its method of freeplay is "sure" in that its substitutions of one mytheme for another within the system of myths

create a closed system. On the contrary, Derrida's system of freeplay, like the philosophy of Nietzsche, is "joyful" in its affirmation of the power of the will to assign and alter all values. For Derrida, the lack of a center betokens freedom, not the loss of security. The Derridean is an adventurer who must abandon certainty for chance in following the "trace" — the chain of signifiers — wherever it leads. [Ed.]

[24]From *différer,* in the sense of "to postpone," "put off," "defer." Elsewhere Derrida uses the word as a synonym for the German *Aufschub:* "postponement," and relates it to the central Freudian concepts of *Verspätung, Nachträglichkeit,* and to the "*détours* to death" of *Beyond the Pleasure Prin-*

historical, of which we are only glimpsing today the *conception, the formation, the gestation, the labor*. I employ these words, I admit, with a glance toward the business of childbearing —

but also with a glance toward those who, in a company from which I do not exclude myself, turn their eyes away in the face of the as yet unnameable which is proclaiming itself and which can do so, as is necessary whenever a birth is in the offing, only under the species of the non-species, in the formless, mute, infant, and terrifying form of monstrosity.

---

*ciple* by Sigmund Freud (Standard Edition, ed. James Strachey, vol. XIX, London, 1961), Ch. V. [Tr.]

# "The Purloined Letter" from *The Purveyor of Truth*

. . . Let us return to the "Purloined Letter" to get a "glimpse" there of the disseminal structure, i.e., the no-possible-return of the letter, the other scene of its remnance [*restance*].

Because there is a narrator on the scene, the "general" scene is not limited to a narration, a "tale," or a "story." We have already recognized the effects of the indivisible framing, from frame to frame, *from within which* psychoanalytical interpretations (semantico-biographical or triado-formalist) drew their triangles.[1] By overlooking the narrator's position, the narrator's involvement in the content of what he seems to be recounting, one omits from the scene of writing anything going beyond the two triangular scenes.

And first of all (one omits that) in question is a scene of writing — its access or border undeterminable — whose boundaries are blurred [*abîmés*]. From the simulacrum of an overture, of the "first word," the narrator, as he narrates himself, advances a few statements which carry the unity of the "tale" into an endless drifting-off-course: a textual drifting not at all taken into account in the Seminar. But if one were to take it into account, one ought not to turn it into the "*real subject* of the tale." Who would not have done it!

---

Translated by Willis Domingo, James Hulbert, Moshe Ron, and Marie-Rose Logan.

[1]Derrida has already analyzed the psychological interpretations of Edgar Allan Poe's story "The Purloined Letter" by Marie Bonaparte ("semantico-biographical") and Jacques Lacan ("triado-formalist") (see Lacan's "Seminar on 'The Purloined Letter'" in Ch. 2). He notes that both interpretations neglect the framing of the tale by the nameless narrator. [Ed.]

1. Everything begins "in" a library: among books, writing, references. Hence nothing begins. Simply a drifting or a disorientation from which one never moves away.

2. There is explicit reference, moreover, to two other stories to which "this one" is grafted. The "analogy" between the three stories is the core of "The Purloined Letter." The independences of the tale, as presumed in the Seminar, is thus the effect of an ablation, even if it is considered in its totality, with its narrator and narration. This ablation is all the more faint as the "analogy" is recalled from the very first paragraph on. It is true that the word "analogy," or, more precisely, "coincidence," authorizes, invites the ablation, and thus functions as a trap. The work of the Seminar begins only after the arrival of the Prefect of the Parisian police. Before this, however, the title, the epigraph, the first paragraph provided something to read (in silence, the silence).

### The Purloined Letter

*Nil sapientiae odiosius acumine nimio.*

— SENECA

At Paris, just after dark one gusty evening in the autumn of 18— , I was enjoying the twofold luxury of meditation and a meerschaum, in company with my friend C. Auguste Dupin, in his little back library, or book-closet *au troisième, No. 33 Rue Dunôt, Faubourg St. Germain*. For one hour at least we had maintained a profound silence; while each, to any casual observer might have seemed intently and exclusively occupied with the curling eddies of smoke that oppressed the atmosphere of the chamber. For myself, however, I was mentally discussing certain topics which had formed matter for conversation between us at an earlier period of the evening; I mean the affair of the Rue Morgue and the mystery attending the murder of Marie Rogêt. I looked upon it, therefore, as something of a coincidence, when the door of our apartment was thrown open and admitted our old acquaintance, Monsieur G— , the Prefect of the Parisian police.

. . . We had been sitting in the dark, and Dupin now arose for the purpose of lighting a lamp, but sat down again, without doing so. . . .


Thus everything "begins" by obscuring this opening in "silence," the "smoke" and the "dark" of this library. The casual observer sees only the smoking meerschaum: in short, a literary setting, the ornamental frame of a story. On this border, negligible for the interpreter interested in the center of the painting and the interior of representation, it was already possible to read that the whole thing was a matter of writing, and of writing off its course, in a writing-space unboundedly open to grafting onto other writing, and that this matter of writing, the third of a series in which the "coincidence" between the first two is noticeable, breaks suddenly into the text with its first word "au troisième, No. 33. Rue Dunôt, Faubourg St. Germain": in French in the original.

Fortuitous remarks, eddies of smoke, contingencies of framing? The fact that they go beyond "the author's intention," about which the Seminar is tempted to turn to Dupin for information, the fact that they are even purely accidental "coincidence," chance events, can only render them of greater interest for the reading of a text that makes of chance as writing what we shall be careful not to call "the *real subject* of the tale."

Rather, its remarkable ellipsis. Indeed, if, as we are invited to do even in the internal boundary of the frame, we go back before "The Purloined Letter," the same remarkable elements persist: scene of writing, library, chance events, coincidences. At the beginning of "The Murders in the Rue Morgue," what could be called the meeting place between the narrator (narrating-narrated)

and Dupin is *already an obscure library,* the *coïncidence* (this is the word, rather than *analogie,* with which Baudelaire[2] translates "accident"[3] of the fact that they are "in search of the same very rare and very remarkable volume." And the relationship formed then in this meeting

[2]Charles Baudelaire translated "The Purloined Letter" into French. [Ed.]

[3]Before dropping them, as everyone does with prefaces, or holding them up as the properly instructive theoretical concept, the truth of the story, I should like to draw from them a few statements. These are not necessarily the best of them; one should also recall each word of the title, and again the epithet about Achilles' name when he hid among women. "The mental features discoursed of as the analytical, are, in themselves, but little susceptible of analysis. . . . The analyst [glories] in that moral activity which *disentangles.* He derives pleasure from even the most trivial occupations bringing his talents into play. He is fond of enigmas, of conundrums, of hieroglyphics. . . . Yet to calculate is not in itself to analyze. A chess-player, for example, does the one without effort at the other. . . . I will, therefore, take occasion to assert that the higher powers of the reflective intellect are more decidedly and more usefully tasked by the unostentatious game of draughts [*jeu de dames*] than by all the elaborate frivolity of chess. . . . To be less abstract — Let us suppose a game of draughts where the pieces are reduced to four kings [*quatre dames* (in the game of draughts, or checkers, the "kings," like the game itself, are called in French "ladies," *dames*)], and where, of course, no oversight is to be expected. It is obvious that here the victory can be decided (the players being at all equal) only by some *recherché* movement, the result of some strong assertion of the intellect. Deprived of ordinary resources, the analyst throws himself into the spirit of his opponent, identifies himself therewith, and not unfrequently sees thus, at a glance, the sole methods (sometimes indeed absurdly simple ones) by which he may seduce into error or hurry into miscalculation . . . But it is in matters beyond the limits of mere rule that the skill of the analyst is evinced . . . . Our player confines himself not at all; nor, because the game is the object, does he reject deductions from things external to the game." Etc. One must read the complete text, in both languages. I have taken some liberties [*Je me suis livré à quelque cuisine*] with Baudelaire's translation, which I do not always follow.

Méryon asked Baudelaire whether he believed "in the real existence of this Edgar Allan Poe"; Méryon attributed Poe's tales "to a group of highly skilled and most powerful men of letters, acutely aware of everything that was going on." The said group, then, does not specify whether the "things external to the game" border on a game recounted in the text or constituted by the text, nor whether *the game* that *is the object* is (in) the story or not. Nor whether the seduction seeks its prey among the characters or among the readers. The question of the narratee, and that of the receiver, which is not the same question. [Au.]

place will, to say the least, never allow the so-called general narrator the position of a neutral, transparent reporter who does not intervene in the transaction going on. For example — but this time the example, read from the frame, is not at the beginning of the text. The frame describing the "meeting" cuts across the narration, so to speak. The frame is preceded, before Dupin appears in the story, by a feint in the form of an abandoned preface, a false short-treatise on analysis. "I am not now writing a treatise, but simply prefacing a somewhat peculiar narrative by observations very much at random." Not a treatise, a preface (to be dropped, of course).[4] At the end of the preface, the narrator simulates the Seminar:

The narrative which follows will appear to the reader in the light of a commentary upon the propositions just advanced.

Residing in Paris during the spring and part of the summer of 18— , I there became acquainted with a Monsieur C. Auguste Dupin. This young gentleman was of an excellent — indeed of an illustrious family, but, by a variety of untoward events, had been reduced to such poverty that the energy of his character succumbed beneath it, and he ceased to bestir himself in the world, or to care for the retrieval of his fortunes. By courtesy of his creditors, there still remained in his possession a small remnant of his patrimony; and, upon the income arising from this, he managed, by means of a rigorous economy, to procure the necessaries of life, without troubling himself about its superfluities. Books, indeed, were his sole luxuries, and in Paris these are easily obtained.

With a remnant of his paternal inheritance,

---

[4] The Seminar completely disregards the very definite involvement of the narrator in the narrative. Ten years later, in an addition made in 1966, Lacan writes as follows:

"An effect [of the signifier] as obviously graspable here as in the fiction of the purloined letter.

Whose essence is that the letter has been able to carry its effects into the interior — to the actors in the tale, including the narrator — as well as to the exterior — to us readers and also to its author — without anyone ever having been concerned about what it meant. This is the usual outcome of everything that is written" (*Écrits*, pp. 56f.)

Thus while subscribing up to a certain point, we still must point out that the Seminar said nothing about the effects on the narrator, *neither in fact nor in principle*. The structure of the interpretation excluded it. And about the nature of these effects, about the structure of the involvement of the narrator, the note of repentance still says nothing, limiting itself to the frame constructed by the Seminar. The claim that in this matter everything has happened "without anyone ever having been concerned about what it [the letter] meant," is incorrect for several reasons:

1. Everyone, as the police Prefect reminds us, knows that the letter contains at least something that would "bring into question the honor of a personage of most exalted station" and her "peace": a sturdy semantic mooring rope.

2. This knowledge is repeated by the Seminar and bolsters it on two levels: (a) as for the minimal, active meaning of this letter, the Seminar reports and transcribes the information of the police Prefect: "But all this tells us nothing of the message it conveys."

Love letter or conspiratorial letter, letter of betrayal or letter of mission, letter of summons or letter of distress, we are assured of but one thing: the Queen must not bring it to the knowledge of her lord and master" (SPL, p. 57). This tells us the essentials of the message it conveys: the variations proposed on this subject are not indifferent, even if they seek to make us believe that they are. In all the imagined hypotheses, the message of the letter (not only the fact that it is sent) must imply the betrayal of a pact, of a "pledge of faith." It was not forbidden for any person to send any letter at all to the Queen, nor for her to receive letters. The Seminar contradicts itself when a few lines later it radicalizes the logic of the signifier and of its literal place while pretending to neutralize the "message," then arrests or anchors this logic in its meaning or its symbolic truth: "It remains that the letter is the symbol of a pact." Contrary to what the Seminar says (an appalling proposition by virtue of the blindness that it could induce, but indispensable for the demonstration), it is indeed necessary that everyone "be concerned about what it (the letter) meant." Ignorance or indifference about this remains minimal and concerns details. Everyone knows, everyone is concerned, the author of the Seminar first of all. And if it did not have a fully determined meaning, no one would care about having a different one palmed off on him, which is what happens to the Queen and then to the Minister. Everyone makes certain, from the Minister to Lacan, including Dupin, that it is the letter in question and that it does indeed say what it says: the betrayal of the pact, and what it says, "the symbol of the pact." Otherwise there would be no "abandoned" letter: abandoned either by the Minister first or by Dupin and finally by Lacan. They all make sure of the content of the letter, of the "right one," they all mime the police Prefect, who, taking the letter from Dupin's hands in exchange for remuneration, checks its content: "This functionary grasped it in a perfect agony of joy, opened it with a trembling hand, cast a rapid glance at its contents, and then scrambling and struggling to the door, rushed at length unceremoniously from the room. . . ." The exchange of the check and the letter takes place over an *escritoire* (in French in the original) in which Dupin had the document locked up. [Au.]

apparently surrendered without calculation to the debtor who knows how, by calculating ("rigorous economy"), to draw from it a *rente,* an income, the surplus-value of a capital that works all alone, Dupin allows himself one extra, one luxury, in which the initial remnant reappears, passing through the restricted economy like a one-way gift. This luxury ("his sole luxuries": this is the word which appears again in the second line of "The Purloined Letter," but this time in the singular: "the twofold luxury of meditation and a meerschaum") is writing: the books that will structure the locus of the meeting and the *mise en abîme*[5] of the whole so-called general narration. The locus of the meeting for the meeting between the narrator and Dupin is a result of the meeting of their interests in the same book, which they are never said to have found. This is literally the accident:

> Our first meeting was at an obscure library in the Rue Montmartre, where the accident of our both being in search of the same very rare and very remarkable volume, brought us into closer communion. We saw each other again and again. I was deeply interested in the little family history which he detailed to me with all that candor which a Frenchman indulges whenever mere self is the theme.

The narrator thus lets himself be narrated: that he is "deeply interested in [Dupin's] little family history," that particular one which leaves a remnant of income with which to purchase the luxury of books; then, as we shall see, that it is above all else Dupin's capacity for reading which astonishes the narrator, and that the society of such a man is therefore to him "a treasure beyond price." The narrator will thus purchase for himself Dupin's being-without-a-price, who purchases for himself writing's being-without-a-price, which is without-price in that very way. For the narrator, confiding openly in Dupin — or, as Baudelaire puts it, *se livrant* frankly to him, must pay for the privilege. He must rent the analyst's office — and furnish the economic equivalent of what is without-price. The analyst

— or rather the narrator's own financial situation, almost the same as Dupin's, merely "somewhat less embarrassed" — authorizes him to do so: "I was permitted to be at the expense of renting. . . ." The narrator is thus the first one to pay Dupin to assure himself the availability of the "letters." Let us then follow the movement of the chain. What the narrator is paying for is also the locus of the narration, the writing in which the entire story will be told and offered for interpretations. And if he pays to write or speak, he also makes Dupin speak, makes him give his letters back and gives him the last word, in the form of a confession. In the economics of this office [*cabinet*], since the narrator himself appears on the scene in a function that is indeed that of a "corporation" (*société anonyme*) of capital and desire, no neutralization is possible, no general point of view, no overhang, no "destruction" of meaning by money. Not only Dupin but also the narrator is a "recipient." As soon as he makes Dupin give up his letters — and not only to the Queen (the other Queen), the letter is divided, it is no longer atomic (atomism, Epicurean atomism, is also, as we know, one of Dupin's topics in "The Murders in the Rue Morgue") and thus loses any assurance of destination. The divisibility of the letter — this is why we insisted on this key or theoretical safety bolt [*verrou de sûreté théorique*] of the Seminar: the atomystique of the letter — is what puts in jeopardy and leads astray, with no guarantee of return, the remnant of anything whatever: a letter does *not always* arrive at its destination, and since this belongs to its structure, it can be said that it never really arrives there, that when it arrives, its possibly-not-arriving [*son pouvoir-ne-pas-arriver*], torments it with an internal divergence.

The divisibility of the letter is also the divisibility of the signifier to which it gives rise, and thus of the "subjects," "characters," or "positions" that are subject to them and that "represent" them. Before showing this in the text, let us recall a quotation:

> I was astonished, too, at the vast extent of his reading; and, above all, I felt my soul enkindled within me by the wild fervor, and the vivid freshness of his imagination. Seeking in Paris the objects I then sought, I felt that the society of such a man

---

[5]Free fall into an abyss; Derrida's metaphor for the aporia caused by the radical ambiguity of language. [Ed.]

would be to me a treasure beyond price; and this feeling I frankly confided to him. It was at length arranged that we should live together during my stay in the city; and as my worldly circumstances were somewhat less embarrassed than his own, I was permitted to be at the expense of renting, and furnishing, in a style which suited the rather fantastic gloom of our common temper, a time-eaten and grotesque mansion, long deserted through superstitions into which we did not inquire, and tottering to its fall in a retired and desolate portion of the Faubourg St. Germain.

Thus we have two (gloomy) fantastics, one of whom does not tell us who his "former associates" are, from whom he will now conceal the "secret" of the "locality." The entire space is now enclosed in the speculations of these two "madmen":

Had the routine of our life at this place been known to the world, we should have been regarded as madmen — although, perhaps, as madmen of a harmless nature. Our seclusion was perfect. We admitted no visitors. Indeed the locality of our retirement had been carefully kept a secret from my own former associates; and it had been many years since Dupin had ceased to know or be known in Paris. We existed within ourselves alone.

From this point on, the narrator lets himself narrate his progressive identification with Dupin. And in the first instance in "loving" the night, the "sable divinity" whose "presence" they "counterfeit" when she is not there:

It was a freak of fancy in my friend (for what else shall I call it?) to be enamored of the Night for her own sake; and into this *bizarrerie,* as into all his others, I quietly fell; giving myself up to his wild whims with a perfect *abandon.* The sable divinity would not herself dwell with us always; but we could counterfeit her presence.

Thus the narrator, already positionally double, *identifies* with Dupin, whose "particular analytical ability" he "cannot help remarking and admiring" and who gives him countless proofs of Dupin's "intimate knowledge" of the narrator's own "bosom" [*personne*]. But Dupin himself, at these very moments, appears double. And this time it is a "fantasy" [*une fantastique*] of the narrator which sees Dupin as double:

His manner at these moments was frigid and abstract his eyes were vacant in expression; while his voice, usually a rich tenor, rose into a treble which would have sounded petulantly but for the deliberateness and entire distinctness of the enunciation. Observing him in these moods, I often dwelt meditatively on the old philosophy of the Bi-Part Soul, and amused myself with the fancy of a double Dupin — the creative and the resolvent.

The fancy of an identification between two doubles themselves double, the powerful cathexis [*investissement*] of the binding relationship [*liaison*] that involves Dupin *outside* of the "intersubjective triads" of the "real drama" and involves the narrator *in* what he narrates, the circulation of wishes and capital, of signifiers and letters before and beyond the two "primal" and secondary "triangles," the chain-fission of positions, beginning with the position of Dupin, who, like *all* the characters, inside and outside the narrative, occupies *all* the places — all this makes triangular logic a very limited part of the drama [*une pièce très limitée dans la pièce*]. And if the dual relationship between the two doubles (which Lacan would reduce to the imaginary) includes all of the space referred to as "symbolic," surpasses it and stimulates it, engulfs it and breaks it down endlessly, then the opposition of the imaginary and the symbolic, and above all its implicit hierarchy, seems to be of very limited relevance: at least if it is measured within the scope of [*à la carrure de*] a scene of writing like this one.

We have seen that *all* the characters of "The Purloined Letter," particularly those of the "real drama," including Dupin, occupied successively and structurally *all* the positions, that of King / dead man / blind man (and that of the police Prefect at the same time), after that of the Queen, and then of the Minister. Each position identifies with the other and is fragmented, even that of the dead man and of a supplementary fourth. The distinction of the three glances proposed by the Seminar to determine the proper course of the circulation is thus compromised. And above all the opening (duplicitous and identificatory) turned aside, toward the narrator (narrating, narrated), makes one letter come back only to send another astray.

And the phenomena of the double, hence of the "Unheimlichkeit,"[6] belong not only to the trilogical "context" of "The Purloined Letter." The question is indeed asked, in a conversation between the narrator and Dupin, whether the Minister is himself or his brother ("There are two brothers," "both have attained reputation"; where? "in letters"). Dupin affirms that the Minister is both "poet and mathematician." The two brothers almost indistinguishable in him. Rivals within him, one playing and foiling [*jouant et déjouant*] the other. "'You are mistaken; I know him well; he is both [*il est les deux*]. As poet *and* mathematician, he would reason well; as mere mathematician, he could not have reasoned at all, and thus would have been at the mercy of the Prefect.'"

But at the Minister who "'is well acquainted with my MS.,'" Dupin strikes a blow signed brother or confrère, twin or younger or older brother (Atreus / Thyestes). This rival and duplicitous identification of the brothers, far from fitting into the symbolic space of the family triangle (the first, the second, or the one after), carries it off infinitely far away in a labyrinth of doubles without originals, of facsimile without an authentic, an indivisible letter, of casual counterfeits [*contrefaçons sans façon*], imprinting the purloined letter with an incorrigible indirection.

The text entitled "The Purloined Letter" imprints / is imprinted in these effects of indirection. I have only indicated the most conspicuous of these effects in order to begin to unlock their reading: the game of doubles, the endless divisibility, the textual references from facsimile to facsimile, the framing of frames, the interminable supplementarity of quotation marks, the insertion of "The Purloined Letter" in a purloined letter that begins with it, throughout the narratives of narrative of "The Murders in the Rue Morgue," the newspaper clippings of "The Mystery of Marie Rogêt" ("A Sequel to 'The Murders in the Rue Morgue'"). Above all else, the *mise en abîme* of the title: "The Purloined Letter" is the text, the text in a text (the purloined letter as a trilogy). The title is the title of the text, it names the text, it names itself and thus includes itself while pretending to name an object described in the text. "The Purloined Letter" functions as a text that escapes all assignable destination and produces, or rather induces by deducing itself, this inassignability at the exact moment in which it narrates the arrival of a letter. It pretends to mean [*vouloir-dire*] and to make one think that "a letter always arrives at its destination," authentic, intact, and undivided, at the moment and the place where the simulation, as writing *avant la lettre*,[7] leaves its path. In order to make another leap — to the side. At this very place, of course.

Who signs? Dupin wants to sign, no matter what. And indeed the narrator, after having made or let him speak, gives him the last word,[8] the last word of the last of the three stories. So it seems. This is not an attempt to put the narrator, in turn, much less the author, in the position of the analyst who knows how to keep silent. There may not be here, measured in terms of [*à la carrure de*] this scene of writing, a possible enclosure for an analytic situation. There may not even be a possible analyst, at least in the situation of psychoanalysis in X——. Only four kings, hence four queens, four police prefects, four

[6]Uncanniness. [Ed.]

[7]Before the letter. [Ed.]

[8]One can even consider that he is the only one who "speaks" in the story. His discourse dominates with loquacious, didactic braggadocio, truly magisterial, handing out directives, giving directions, righting wrongs, teaching everyone. He spends his own time and that of others making corrections and reminding them of the rules. He assumes his post and speaks up. Only the address matters, the right one, the authentic one. It devolves, according to the law, to the proper quarter. Thanks to the man of the law and the rector of the proper course. All of "The Purloined Letter" is written so that he finally brings it back through the proper course. And since he proves himself to be cleverer than the others, the letter plays one more trick on him just as he spots its locus and its true destination. The letter eludes and deceives him (literature on stage left [*côté cour*] just at the time when, speaking up, he hears that he deceives while explicating deception, just at the time when he returns the blow and the letter. He agrees to every demand without knowing it; he doubles, or rather replaces the Minister and the Police, and if there were only one dupe — hypothesis not taken up — he would be the most splendid one in the "story" [*de l' "histoire"*]. Yet — what about the lady [*quoi — de la belle*]. *Il l'adresse-la Reine-l'adresse-la-dupe*. [Au.]

ministers, four analysts Dupin, four narrators, four readers, four kings, etc., all more insightful and more foolish than the others, more powerful and more powerless.

Thus Dupin wants to sign, indeed, doubtless, the last word of the last message of the purloined letter. First by being unable to resist leaving his own mark — the seal, at least, with which he must be identified — on the facsimile that he leaves for the Minister. He fears the facsimile and, insisting on his utterly confraternal vengeance, he demands that the Minister know where it came from. Thus he limits the facsimile, the counterfeit exterior of the letter. The interior is authentic and properly identifiable. Indeed: at the moment when the madman ("'the pretended lunatic'" who is "'a man in my own pay'") distracts everyone with his "frantic behavior," what does Dupin do? He adds a note. He leaves the false letter, that is, the one that interests him, *the real one,* which is not a facsimile *except for the exterior.* If there were a man of truth, a lover of the authentic, in all this, Dupin would indeed be the model: "'In the meantime, I stepped to the card-rack, took the letter, put it in my pocket, and replaced it by a *fac-simile,* (so far as regards externals [*quant à l'extérieur*],) which I had carefully prepared at my lodgings; imitating the D—— cipher, very readily, by means of a seal formed of bread.'"

Thus D—— will have to decipher, on the inside, what the decipherer meant and whence and why he deciphered, with what end in mind, in the name of whom and what. The initial — the same, D, for the Minister and for Dupin — is a facsimile on the outside *but on the inside it is the thing itself.*

But what is this thing itself on the inside? This signature? This "last word" of a doubly confraternal war?

Again, a quotation by means of which the signer is dispossessed, whatever he may have: "I just copied into the middle of the blank sheet the words —

— Un dessein si funeste,
S'il n'est digne d'Atrée, est digne de Thyeste."

A play on quotation marks. In the French translation, there are no quotation marks, and the lines from Crébillon appear in small type. The sentence that follows ("Vous trouverez cela dans l'*Atrée* de Crébillon," "They are to be found in Crébillon's 'Atrée'") can be attributed equally well to the author of "The Purloined Letter," or the narrator, or the author of the letter left behind (Dupin). But the American edition at my disposal no longer leaves this doubt. It is, however, faulty in that it appears as follows, leaving interior quotation marks, suspended quotation marks called in French "*guillemets anglais.*"

". . . He is well acquainted with my MS., and I just copied into the middle of the blank sheet the words —

"' — Un dessein si funeste,
S'il n'est digne d'Atrée, est digne de Thyeste.

They are to be found in Crébillon's 'Atrée.'"

Thus it is clear that this final sentence is to be attributed to Dupin, Dupin saying to the Minister: I, the undersigned, Dupin, inform you of the fate of the letter, of what it means, of my purpose in stealing one from you in order to render it to its receiver, and why I am replacing it by this one, remember.

But, beyond the quotation marks that surround the entire story Dupin is obliged to quote this last word in quotation marks, to recount his signature: that is what I wrote to him and how I signed it. What is a signature within quotation marks? Then, within these quotation marks, the seal itself is a quotation within quotation marks. This remnant is still literature.

Two times out of three, the author of the Seminar[9] transforms the word "*dessein*" (design) into "*destin*" (destiny), thus perhaps rendering a meaning [*vouloir-dire*] to its destination: deliberately, probably — there is no reason to rule out design anywhere. (These last words are dedicated of their own accord to Father Peter Coppieters de Gibson, who did not overlook the matter: the alteration coming to steal a letter in order to achieve its destiny along the way.)

"Whatever the case, the Minister, when he tries to make use of it, will be able to read these words, written so that he may recognize Dupin's

[9]Lacan. [Ed.]

hand: . . . *Un dessein si funeste / S'il n'est digne d'Atrée est digne de Thyeste* whose source, Dupin tells us, is Crébillon's *Atrée*" (SPL, p. 43).

Then: "The commonplace of the quotation is fitting for the oracle that face bears in its grimace, as is also its source in tragedy: '. . . *Un destin si funeste, / S'il n'est digne d'Atrée, est digne de Thyeste*'" (SPL, p. 71).

And finally: ". . . and I add (p. 52) that there is no chance that the crowing with which this Lecoq would like to waken him ['*un destin si funeste*'] in the little love note [*poulet*] he leaves for him [*qu'il lui destine*] — that there is no chance that that crowing will reach his ears" ("Points" Introduction, p. 8).

# Michel Foucault

## 1926–1984

*Michel Foucault, a major intellectual presence in France since the 1960s, was renowned for his writings, which attempted to erase the traditional boundaries between the disciplines of science, history, philosophy, and sociology. Born in Poitiers, the son of a doctor, Foucault was trained as a philosopher, but his earliest work, such as* Madness and Civilization *(1961), dealt with history — specifically, the history of attitudes toward mental illness and its treatment. Foucault taught at the University of Clermont-Ferrand between 1960 and 1968, spent two years at the University of Paris-Vincennes, and in 1970 was elevated to a professorship at the Collège de France — the highest position in the French academic system. He was also a visiting professor at a host of universities worldwide. In addition to* Madness and Civilization, *other works that have been translated into English include* The Birth of the Clinic *(1963),* The Order of Things *(1966),* The Archaeology of Knowledge *(1969),* Discipline and Punish *(1975), the first volume of* The History of Sexuality *(1976), and* Power/Knowledge *(1980). "What Is an Author?" originally appeared in the* Bulletin de la Société française de Philosophie *in 1969.*

## *What Is an Author?*

The coming into being of the notion of "author" constitutes the privileged moment of *individualization* in the history of ideas, knowledge, literature, philosophy, and the sciences. Even today, when we reconstruct the history of a concept, literary genre, or school of philosophy, such categories seem relatively weak, secondary, and superimposed scansions in comparison with the solid and fundamental unit of the author and the work.

I shall not offer here a sociohistorical analysis of the author's persona. Certainly it would be

Translated by Josué Harari.

worth examining how the author became individualized in a culture like ours, what status he has been given, at what moment studies of authenticity and attribution began, in what kind of system of valorization the author was involved, at what point we began to recount the lives of authors rather than of heroes, and how this fundamental category of "the-man-and-his-work criticism" began. For the moment, however, I want to deal solely with the relationship between text and author and with the manner in which the text points to this "figure" that, at least in appearance, is outside it and antecedes it.

Beckett nicely formulates the theme with

which I would like to begin: "'What does it matter who is speaking,' someone said, 'what does it matter who is speaking.'" In this indifference appears one of the fundamental ethical principles of contemporary writing [*écriture*]. I say "ethical" because this indifference is not really a trait characterizing the manner in which one speaks and writes, but rather a kind of immanent rule, taken up over and over again, never fully applied, not designating writing as something completed, but dominating it as a practice. Since it is too familiar to require a lengthy analysis, this immanent rule can be adequately illustrated here by tracing two of its major themes.

First of all, we can say that today's writing has freed itself from the dimension of expression. Referring only to itself, but without being restricted to the confines of its interiority, writing is identified with its own unfolded exteriority. This means that it is an interplay of signs arranged less according to its signified content than according to the very nature of the signifier. Writing unfolds like a game [*jeu*] that invariably goes beyond its own rules and transgresses its limits. In writing, the point is not to manifest or exalt the act of writing, nor is it to pin a subject within language; it is rather a question of creating a space into which the writing subject constantly disappears.

The second theme, writing's relationship with death, is even more familiar. This link subverts an old tradition exemplified by the Greek epic, which was intended to perpetuate the immortality of the hero: if he was willing to die young, it was so that his life, consecrated and magnified by death, might pass into immortality; the narrative then redeemed this accepted death. In another way, the motivation, as well as the theme and the pretext of Arabian narratives — such as *The Thousand and One Nights* — was also the eluding of death: one spoke, telling stories into the early morning, in order to forestall death, to postpone the day of reckoning that would silence the narrator. Scheherazade's narrative is an effort, renewed each night, to keep death outside the circle of life.

Our culture has metamorphosed this idea of narrative, or writing, as something designed to ward off death. Writing has become linked to sacrifice, even to the sacrifice of life: it is now a voluntary effacement which does not need to be represented in books, since it is brought about in the writer's very existence. The work, which once had the duty of providing immortality, now possesses the right to kill, to be its author's murderer, as in the cases of Flaubert, Proust, and Kafka. That is not all, however: this relationship between writing and death is also manifested in the effacement of the writing subject's individual characteristics. Using all the contrivances that he sets up between himself and what he writes, the writing subject cancels out the signs of his particular individuality. As a result, the mark of the writer is reduced to nothing more than the singularity of his absence; he must assume the role of the dead man in the game of writing.

None of this is recent; criticism and philosophy took note of the disappearance — or death — of the author some time ago. But the consequences of their discovery of it have not been sufficiently examined, nor has its import been accurately measured. A certain number of notions that are intended to replace the privileged position of the author actually seem to preserve that privilege and suppress the real meaning of his disappearance. I shall examine two of these notions, both of great importance today.

The first is the idea of the work. It is a very familiar thesis that the task of criticism is not to bring out the work's relationships with the author, not to reconstruct through the text a thought or experience, but rather, to analyze the work through its structure, its architecture, its intrinsic form, and the play of its internal relationships. At this point, however, a problem arises: "What is a work? What is this curious unity which we designate as a work? Of what elements is it composed? Is it not what an author has written?" Difficulties appear immediately. If an individual were not an author, could we say that what he wrote, said, left behind in his papers, or what has been collected of his remarks, could be called a "work"? When Sade was not considered an author, what was the status of his papers? Were they simply rolls of paper onto which he ceaselessly uncoiled his fantasies during his imprisonment?

Even when an individual has been accepted

as an author, we must still ask whether everything that he wrote, said, or left behind is part of his work. The problem is both theoretical and technical. When undertaking the publication of Nietzsche's works, for example, where should one stop? Surely everything must be published, but what is "everything"? Everything that Nietzsche himself published, certainly. And what about the rough drafts for his works? Obviously. The plans for his aphorisms? Yes. The deleted passages and the notes at the bottom of the page? Yes. What if, within a workbook filled with aphorisms, one finds a reference, the notation of a meeting or of an address, or a laundry list: is it a work, or not? Why not? And so on, ad infinitum. How can one define a work amid the millions of traces left by someone after his death? A theory of the work does not exist, and the empirical task of those who naively undertake the editing of works often suffers in the absence of such a theory.

We could go even further: does *The Thousand and One Nights* constitute a work? What about Clement of Alexandria's *Miscellanies* or Diogenes Laertius' *Lives*? A multitude of questions arises with regard to this notion of the work. Consequently, it is not enough to declare that we should do without the writer (the author) and study the work in itself. The word "work" and the unity that it designates are probably as problematic as the status of the author's individuality.

Another notion which has hindered us from taking full measure of the author's disappearance, blurring and concealing the moment of this effacement and subtly preserving the author's existence, is the notion of writing [*écriture*]. When rigorously applied, this notion should allow us not only to circumvent references to the author, but also to situate his recent absence. The notion of writing, as currently employed, is concerned with neither the act of writing nor the indication — be it symptom or sign — of a meaning which someone might have wanted to express. We try, with great effort, to imagine the general condition of each text, the condition of both the space in which it is dispersed and the time in which it unfolds.

In current usage, however, the notion of writing seems to transpose the empirical characteristics of the author into a transcendental anonymity. We are content to efface the more visible marks of the author's empiricity by playing off, one against the other, two ways of characterizing writing, namely, the critical and the religious approaches. Giving writing a primal status seems to be a way of retranslating, in transcendental terms, both the theological affirmation of its sacred character and the critical affirmation of its creative character. To admit that writing is, because of the very history that it made possible, subject to the test of oblivion and repression, seems to represent, in transcendental terms, the religious principle of the hidden meaning (which requires interpretation) and the critical principle of implicit significations, silent determinations, and obscured contents (which gives rise to commentary). To imagine writing as absence seems to be a simple repetition, in transcendental terms, of both the religious principle of inalterable and yet never fulfilled tradition, and the aesthetic principle of the work's survival, its perpetuation beyond the author's death, and its enigmatic *excess* in relation to him.

This usage of the notion of writing runs the risk of maintaining the author's privileges under the protection of writing's a priori status: it keeps alive, in the grey light of neutralization, the interplay of those representations that formed a particular image of the author. The author's disappearance, which, since Mallarmé, has been a constantly recurring event, is subject to a series of transcendental barriers. There seems to be an important dividing line between those who believe that they can still locate today's discontinuities [*ruptures*] in the historico-transcendental tradition of the nineteenth century, and those who try to free themselves once and for all from that tradition.[1]

It is not enough, however, to repeat the empty affirmation that the author has disappeared. For the same reason, it is not enough to keep repeating (after Nietzsche) that God and man have

[1]For a discussion of the notions of discontinuity and historical tradition see Foucault's *Les Mots et les choses* (Paris: Gallimard, 1966), translated as *The Order of Things* (New York: Pantheon, 1971). [Tr.]

died a common death. Instead, we must locate the space left empty by the author's disappearance, follow the distribution of gaps and breaches, and watch for the openings that this disappearance uncovers.

First, we need to clarify briefly the problems arising from the use of the author's name. What is an author's name? How does it function? Far from offering a solution, I shall only indicate some of the difficulties that it presents.

The author's name is a proper name, and therefore it raises the problems common to all proper names. (Here I refer to Searle's analyses, among others.[2]) Obviously, one cannot turn a proper name into a pure and simple reference. It has other than indicative functions: more than an indication, a gesture, a finger pointed at someone, it is the equivalent of a description. When one says "Aristotle," one employs a word that is the equivalent of one, or a series of, definite descriptions, such as "the author of the *Analytics*," "the founder of ontology," and so forth. One cannot stop there, however, because a proper name does not have just one signification. When we discover that Rimbaud did not write *La Chasse spirituelle,* we cannot pretend that the meaning of this proper name, or that of the author, has been altered. The proper name and the author's name are situated between the two poles of description and designation: they must have a certain link with what they name, but one that is neither entirely in the mode of designation nor in that of description; it must be a *specific* link. However — and it is here that the particular difficulties of the author's name arise — the links between the proper name and the individual named and between the author's name and what it names are not isomorphic and do not function in the same way. There are several differences.

If, for example, Pierre Dupont does not have blue eyes, or was not born in Paris, or is not a doctor, the name Pierre Dupont will still always refer to the same person; such things do not modify the link of designation. The problems raised by the author's name are much more complex, however. If I discover that Shakespeare was not born in the house that we visit today, that is a modification which, obviously, will not alter the functioning of the author's name. But if we proved that Shakespeare did not write those sonnets which pass for his, that would constitute a significant change and affect the manner in which the author's name functions. If we proved that Shakespeare wrote Bacon's *Organon* by showing that the same author wrote both the works of Bacon and those of Shakespeare, that would be a third type of change which would entirely modify the functioning of the author's name. The author's name is not, therefore, just a proper name like the rest.

Many other facts point out the paradoxical singularity of the author's name. To say that Pierre Dupont does not exist is not at all the same as saying that Homer or Hermes Trismegistus did not exist. In the first case, it means that no one has the name Pierre Dupont; in the second, it means that several people were mixed together under one name, or that the true author had none of the traits traditionally ascribed to the personae of Homer or Hermes. To say that X's real name is actually Jacques Durand instead of Pierre Dupont is not the same as saying that Stendhal's name was Henri Beyle.[3] One could also question the meaning and functioning of propositions like "Bourbaki is so-and-so, so-and-so, etc."[4] and "Victor Eremita, Climacus, Anticlimacus, Frater Taciturnus, Constantine Constantius, all of these are Kierkegaard."

These differences may result from the fact that an author's name is not simply an element in a discourse (capable of being either subject or object, of being replaced by a pronoun, and the like); it performs a certain role with regard to narrative discourse, assuring a classificatory function. Such a name permits one to group together a certain number of texts, define them, differentiate them from and contrast them to others. In addition, it establishes a relationship among the texts. Hermes Trismegistus did not

[2]John Searle, *Speech Acts: An Essay in the Philosophy of Language* (Cambridge: Cambridge University Press, 1969), pp. 162–74. [Tr.]

[3]Marie-Henri Beyle wrote under the name of Stendhal. [Ed.]

[4]Bourbaki was the collective name of a group of French mathematicians. [Ed.]

exist, nor did Hippocrates — in the sense that Balzac existed — but the fact that several texts have been placed under the same name indicates that there has been established among them a relationship of homogeneity, filiation,[5] authentification of some texts by the use of others, reciprocal explication, or concomitant utilization. The author's name serves to characterize a certain mode of being of discourse: the fact that the discourse has an author's name, that one can say "this was written by so-and-so" or "so-and-so is its author," shows that this discourse is not ordinary everyday speech that merely comes and goes, not something that is immediately consumable. On the contrary, it is a speech that must be received in a certain mode and that, in a given culture, must receive a certain status.

It would seem that the author's name, unlike other proper names, does not pass from the interior of a discourse to the real and exterior individual who produced it; instead, the name seems always to be present, marking off the edges of the text, revealing, or at least characterizing, its mode of being. The author's name manifests the appearance of a certain discursive set and indicates the status of this discourse within a society and a culture. It has no legal status, nor is it located in the fiction of the work; rather, it is located in the break that founds a certain discursive construct and its very particular mode of being. As a result, we could say that in a civilization like our own there are a certain number of discourses that are endowed with the "author-function," while others are deprived of it. A private letter may well have a signer — it does not have an author; a contract may well have a guarantor — it does not have an author. An anonymous text posted on a wall probably has a writer — but not an author. The author-function is therefore characteristic of the mode of existence, circulation, and functioning of certain discourses within a society.

Let us analyze this "author-function" as we have just described it. In our culture, how does one characterize a discourse containing the author-function? In what way is this discourse different from other discourses? If we limit our remarks to the author of a book or a text, we can isolate four different characteristics.

First of all, discourses are objects of appropriation. The form of ownership from which they spring is of a rather particular type, one that has been codified for many years. We should note that, historically, this type of ownership has always been subsequent to what one might call penal appropriation. Texts, books, and discourses really began to have authors (other than mythical, "sacralized" and "sacralizing" figures) to the extent that authors became subject to punishment, that is, to the extent that discourses could be transgressive. In our culture (and doubtless in many others), discourse was not originally a product, a thing, a kind of goods; it was essentially an act — an act placed in the bipolar field of the sacred and the profane, the licit and the illicit, the religious and the blasphemous. Historically, it was a gesture fraught with risks before becoming goods caught up in a circuit of ownership.

Once a system of ownership for texts came into being, once strict rules concerning author's rights, author-publisher relations, rights of reproduction, and related matters were enacted — at the end of the eighteenth and the beginning of the nineteenth century — the possibility of transgression attached to the act of writing took on, more and more, the form of an imperative peculiar to literature. It is as if the author, beginning with the moment at which he was placed in the system of property that characterizes our society, compensated for the status that he thus acquired by rediscovering the old bipolar field of discourse, systematically practicing transgression and thereby restoring danger to a writing which was now guaranteed the benefits of ownership.

The author-function does not affect all discourses in a universal and constant way, however. This is its second characteristic. In our civilization, it has not always been the same types of texts which have required attribution to an author. There was a time when the texts that we today call "literary" (narratives, stories, epics, tragedies, comedies) were accepted, put into circulation, and valorized without any question

[5]Descent, derivation. [Ed.]

about the identity of their author; their anonymity caused no difficulties since their ancientness, whether real or imagined, was regarded as a sufficient guarantee of their status. On the other hand, those texts that we now would call scientific — those dealing with cosmology and the heavens, medicine and illnesses, natural sciences and geography — were accepted in the Middle Ages, and accepted as "true," only when marked with the name of their author. "Hippocrates said," "Pliny recounts," were not really formulas of an argument based on authority; they were the markers inserted in discourses that were supposed to be received as statements of demonstrated truth.

A reversal occurred in the seventeenth or eighteenth century. Scientific discourses began to be received for themselves, in the anonymity of an established or always redemonstrable truth; their membership in a systematic ensemble, and not the reference to the individual who produced them, stood as their guarantee. The author-function faded away, and the inventor's name served only to christen a theorem, proposition, particular effect, property, body, group of elements, or pathological syndrome. By the same token, literary discourses came to be accepted only when endowed with the author-function. We now ask of each poetic or fictional text: from where does it come, who wrote it, when, under what circumstances, or beginning with what design? The meaning ascribed to it and the status or value accorded it depend upon the manner in which we answer these questions. And if a text should be discovered in a state of anonymity — whether as a consequence of an accident or the author's explicit wish — the game becomes one of rediscovering the author. Since literary anonymity is not tolerable, we can accept it only in the guise of an enigma. As a result, the author-function today plays an important role in our view of literary works. (These are obviously generalizations that would have to be refined insofar as recent critical practice is concerned.)

The third characteristic of this author-function is that it does not develop spontaneously as the attribution of a discourse to an individual. It is, rather, the result of a complex operation which constructs a certain rational being that we call "author." Critics doubtless try to give this intelligible being a realistic status, by discerning, in the individual, a "deep" motive, a "creative" power, or a "design," the milieu in which writing originates. Nevertheless, these aspects of an individual which we designate as making him an author are only a projection, in more or less psychologizing terms, of the operations that we force texts to undergo, the connections that we make, the traits that we establish as pertinent, the continuities that we recognize, or the exclusions that we practice. All these operations vary according to periods and types of discourse. We do not construct a "philosophical author" as we do a "poet," just as, in the eighteenth century, one did not construct a novelist as we do today. Still, we can find through the ages certain constants in the rules of author-construction.

It seems, for example, that the manner in which literary criticism once defined the author — or rather constructed the figure of the author beginning with existing texts and discourses — is directly derived from the manner in which Christian tradition authenticated (or rejected) the texts at its disposal. In order to "rediscover" an author in a work, modern criticism uses methods similar to those that Christian exegesis employed when trying to prove the value of a text by its author's saintliness. In *De viris illustribus,* Saint Jerome explains that homonymy is not sufficient to identify legitimately authors of more than one work: different individuals could have had the same name, or one man could have, illegitimately, borrowed another's patronymic. The name as an individual trademark is not enough when one works within a textual tradition.

How then can one attribute several discourses to one and the same author? How can one use the author-function to determine if one is dealing with one or several individuals? Saint Jerome proposes four criteria: (1) if among several books attributed to an author one is inferior to the others, it must be withdrawn from the list of the author's works (the author is therefore defined as a constant level of value); (2) the same should be done if certain texts contradict the doctrine expounded in the author's other works (the author is thus defined as a field of conceptual or theoretical coherence); (3) one must also exclude works that are written in a different style, containing words and expressions not ordinarily found in the writer's production (the author is here conceived as a stylistic unity); (4) finally, passages quoting statements that were made, or mentioning events that occurred after the author's death must be regarded as interpolated texts (the author is here seen as a historical figure at the crossroads of a certain number of events).

Modern literary criticism, even when — as is now customary — it is not concerned with questions of authentication, still defines the author the same way: the author provides the basis for explaining not only the presence of certain events in a work, but also their transformations, distortions, and diverse modifications (through his biography, the determination of his individual perspective, the analysis of his social position, and the revelation of his basic design). The author is also the principle of a certain unity of writing — all differences having to be resolved, at least in part, by the principles of evolution, maturation, or influence. The author also serves to neutralize the contradictions that may emerge in a series of texts: there must be — at a certain level of his thought or desire, of his consciousness or unconscious — a point where contradictions are resolved, where incompatible elements are at last tied together or organized around a fundamental or originating contradiction. Finally, the author is a particular source of expression that, in more or less completed forms, is manifested equally well, and with similar validity, in works, sketches, letters, fragments, and so on. Clearly, Saint Jerome's four criteria of authenticity (criteria which seem totally insufficient for today's exegetes) do define the four modalities according to which modern criticism brings the author-function into play.

But the author-function is not a pure and simple reconstruction made secondhand from a text given as passive material. The text always contains a certain number of signs referring to the author. These signs, well known to grammarians, are personal pronouns, adverbs of time and place, and verb conjugation. Such elements do not play the same role in discourses provided with the author-function as in those lacking it. In the latter, such "shifters" refer to the real speaker and to the spatio-temporal coordinates of his discourse (although certain modifications can occur, as in the operation of relating discourses in the first person). In the former, however, their role is more complex and variable. Everyone knows that, in a novel narrated in the first person, neither the first person pronoun, nor the present indicative refer exactly either to the writer or to the moment in which he writes, but rather to an alter ego whose distance from the author varies, often changing in the course of the work. It would be just as wrong to equate the author with the real writer as to equate him with the fictitious speaker; the author-function is carried out and operates in the scission itself, in this division and this distance.

One might object that this is a characteristic peculiar to novelistic or poetic discourse, a "game" in which only "quasi-discourses" participate. In fact, however, all discourses endowed with the author-function do possess this plurality of self. The self that speaks in the preface to a treatise on mathematics — and that indicates the circumstances of the treatise's composition — is identical neither in its position nor in its functioning to the self that speaks in the course of a demonstration, and that appears in the form of "I conclude" or "I suppose." In the first case, the "I" refers to an individual without an equivalent who, in a determined place and time, completed a certain task; in the second, the "I" indicates an instance and a level of demonstration which any individual could perform provided that he accept the same system of symbols, play of axioms, and set of previous demonstrations. We could also, in the same treatise, locate a third self, one that speaks to tell the work's meaning, the obstacles encountered, the results obtained, and the remaining problems; this self is situated in the field of already existing or yet-to-appear mathematical discourses. The author-function is not assumed by the first of these selves at the expense of the other two, which would then be nothing more than a fictitious splitting in two of the first one. On the contrary, in these discourses the author-function operates so as to effect the dispersion of these three simultaneous selves.

No doubt analysis could discover still more characteristic traits of the author-function. I will limit myself to these four, however, because they seem both the most visible and the most important. They can be summarized as follows: (1) the author-function is linked to the juridical and institutional system that encompasses, determines, and articulates the universe of discourses; (2) it does not affect all discourses in the same way at all times and in all types of civilization; (3) it is not defined by the spontaneous attribution of a discourse to its producer, but rather by a series of specific and complex operations; (4) it does not refer purely and simply to a real individual, since it can give rise simultaneously to several selves, to several subjects — positions that can be occupied by different classes of individuals.

Up to this point I have unjustifiably limited my subject. Certainly the author-function in painting, music, and other arts should have been discussed, but even supposing that we remain within the world of discourse, as I want to do, I seem to have given the term "author" much too narrow a meaning. I have discussed the author only in the limited sense of a person to whom the production of a text, a book, or a work can be legitimately attributed. It is easy to see that in the sphere of discourse one can be the author of much more than a book — one can be the author of a theory, tradition, or discipline in which other books and authors will in their turn find a place. These authors are in a position which we shall call "transdiscursive." This is a recurring phenomenon — certainly as old as our civilization. Homer, Aristotle, and the Church Fathers, as well as the first mathematicians and the originators of the Hippocratic tradition, all played this role.

Furthermore, in the course of the nineteenth century, there appeared in Europe another, more uncommon, kind of author, whom one should confuse with neither the "great" literary authors, nor the authors of religious texts, nor the founders of science. In a somewhat arbitrary way we shall call those who belong in this last group "founders of discursivity." They are unique in that they are not just the authors of their own works. They have produced something else: the possibilities and the rules for the formation of other texts. In this sense, they are very different,

for example, from a novelist, who is, in fact, nothing more than the author of his own text. Freud is not just the author of *The Interpretation of Dreams* or *Jokes and Their Relation to the Unconscious*; Marx is not just the author of the *Communist Manifesto* or *Capital*: they both have established an endless possibility of discourse.

Obviously, it is easy to object. One might say that it is not true that the author of a novel is only the author of his own text; in a sense, he also, provided that he acquires some "importance," governs and commands more than that. To take a very simple example, one could say that Ann Radcliffe not only wrote *The Castles of Athlin and Dunbayne* and several other novels, but also made possible the appearance of the Gothic horror novel at the beginning of the nineteenth century; in that respect, her author-function exceeds her own work. But I think there is an answer to this objection. These founders of discursivity (I use Marx and Freud as examples, because I believe them to be both the first and the most important cases) make possible something altogether different from what a novelist makes possible. Ann Radcliffe's texts opened the way for a certain number of resemblances and analogies which have their model or principle in her work. The latter contains characteristic signs, figures, relationships, and structures which could be reused by others. In other words, to say that Ann Radcliffe founded the Gothic horror novel means that in the nineteenth-century Gothic novel one will find, as in Ann Radcliffe's works, the theme of the heroine caught in the trap of her own innocence, the hidden castle, the character of the black, cursed hero devoted to making the world expiate the evil done to him, and all the rest of it.

On the other hand, when I speak of Marx or Freud as founders of discursivity, I mean that they made possible not only a certain number of analogies, but also (and equally important) a certain number of differences. They have created a possibility for something other than their discourse, yet something belonging to what they founded. To say that Freud founded psychoanalysis does not (simply) mean that we find the concept of the libido or the technique of dream analysis in the works of Karl Abraham or

Melanie Klein; it means that Freud made possible a certain number of divergences — with respect to his own texts, concepts, and hypotheses — that all arise from the psychoanalytical discourse itself.

This would seem to present a new difficulty, however: is the above not true, after all, of any founder of a science, or of any author who has introduced some important transformation into a science? After all, Galileo made possible not only those discourses that repeated the laws that he had formulated, but also statements very different from what he himself had said. If Cuvier is the founder of biology or Saussure the founder of linguistics, it is not because they were imitated, nor because people have since taken up again the concept of organism or sign; it is because Cuvier made possible, to a certain extent, a theory of evolution diametrically opposed to his own fixism; it is because Saussure made possible a generative grammar radically different from his structural analyses. Superficially, then, the initiation of discursive practices appears similar to the founding of any scientific endeavor.

Still, there is a difference, and a notable one. In the case of a science, the act that founds it is on an equal footing with its future transformations; this act becomes in some respects part of the set of modifications that it makes possible. Of course, this belonging can take several forms. In the future development of a science, the founding act may appear as little more than a particular instance of a more general phenomenon which unveils itself in the process. It can also turn out to be marred by intuition and empirical bias; one must then reformulate it, making it the object of a certain number of supplementary theoretical operations which establish it more rigorously, etc. Finally, it can seem to be a hasty generalization which must be limited, and whose restricted domain of validity must be retraced. In other words, the founding act of a science can always be reintroduced within the machinery of those transformations that derive from it.

In contrast, the initiation of a discursive practice is heterogeneous to its subsequent transformations. To expand a type of discursivity, such as psychoanalysis as founded by Freud, is not to give it a formal generality that it would not have permitted at the outset, but rather to open it up to a certain number of possible applications. To limit psychoanalysis as a type of discursivity is, in reality, to try to isolate in the founding act an eventually restricted number of propositions or statements to which, alone, one grants a founding value, and in relation to which certain concepts or theories accepted by Freud might be considered as derived, secondary, and accessory. In addition, one does not declare certain propositions in the work of these founders to be false: instead, when trying to seize the act of founding, one sets aside those statements that are not pertinent, either because they are deemed inessential, or because they are considered "prehistoric" and derived from another type of discursivity. In other words, unlike the founding of a science, the initiation of a discursive practice does not participate in its later transformations.

As a result, one defines a proposition's theoretical validity in relation to the work of the founders — while, in the case of Galileo and Newton, it is in relation to what physics or cosmology *is* (in its intrinsic structure and "normativity") that one affirms the validity of any proposition that those men may have put forth. To phrase it very schematically: the work of initiators of discursivity is not situated in the space that science defines; rather, it is the science or the discursivity which refers back to their work as primary coordinates.

In this way we can understand the inevitable necessity, within these fields of discursivity, for a "return to the origin." This return, which is part of the discursive field itself, never stops modifying it. The return is not a historical supplement which would be added to the discursivity, or merely an ornament; on the contrary, it constitutes an effective and necessary task of transforming the discursive practice itself. Reexamination of Galileo's text may well change our knowledge of the history of mechanics, but it will never be able to change mechanics itself. On the other hand, re-examining Freud's texts modifies psychoanalysis itself just as a re-examination of Marx's would modify Marxism.[6]

[6]To define these returns more clearly, one must also emphasize that they tend to reinforce the enigmatic link between

What I have just outlined regarding the initiation of discursive practices is, of course, very schematic; this is true, in particular, of the opposition that I have tried to draw between discursive initiation and scientific founding. It is not always easy to distinguish between the two; moreover, nothing proves that they are two mutually exclusive procedures. I have attempted the distinction for only one reason: to show that the author-function, which is complex enough when one tries to situate it at the level of a book or a series of texts that carry a given signature, involves still more determining factors when one tries to analyze it in larger units, such as groups of works or entire disciplines.

To conclude, I would like to review the reasons why I attach a certain importance to what I have said.

First, there are theoretical reasons. On the one hand, an analysis in the direction that I have outlined might provide for an approach to a typology of discourse. It seems to me, at least at first glance, that such a typology cannot be constructed solely from the grammatical features, formal structures, and objects of discourse: more likely there exist properties or relationships peculiar to discourse (not reducible to the rules of grammar and logic), and one must use these to distinguish the major categories of discourse. The relationship (or nonrelationship) with an author, and the different forms this relationship takes, constitutes — in a quite visible manner — one of these discursive properties.

On the other hand, I believe that one could find here an introduction to the historical analysis of discourse. Perhaps it is time to study discourses not only in terms of their expressive value or formal transformations, but according to their modes of existence. The modes of circulation, valorization, attribution, and appropriation of discourses vary with each culture and are modified within each. The manner in which they are articulated according to social relationships can be more readily understood, I believe, in the activity of the author-function and in its modifications, than in the themes or concepts that discourses set in motion.

It would seem that one could also, beginning with analyses of this type, re-examine the privileges of the subject. I realize that in undertaking the internal and architectonic analysis of a work (be it a literary text, philosophical system, or scientific work), in setting aside biographical and psychological references, one has already called back into question the absolute character and founding role of the subject. Still, perhaps one must return to this question, not in order to re-establish the theme of an originating subject, but to grasp the subject's points of insertion, modes of functioning, and system of dependencies. Doing so means overturning the traditional problem, no longer raising the questions "How can a free subject penetrate the substance of things and give it meaning? How can it activate the rules of a language from within and thus give rise to the designs which are properly its own?" Instead, these questions will be raised: "How, under what conditions, and in what forms can something like a subject appear in the order of discourse? What place can it occupy in each type of discourse, what functions can it assume, and by obeying what rules?" In short, it is a matter of depriving the subject (or its substitute) of its role as originator, and of analyzing the subject as a variable and complex function of discourse.

Second, there are reasons dealing with the "ideological" status of the author. The question then becomes: How can one reduce the great peril, the great danger with which fiction threatens our world? The answer is: One can reduce it with the author. The author allows a limitation of the cancerous and dangerous proliferation of

an author and his works. A text has an inaugurative value precisely because it is the work of a particular author, and our returns are conditioned by this knowledge. As in the case of Galileo, there is no possibility that the rediscovery of an unknown text by Newton or Cantor will modify classical cosmology or set theory as we know them (at best, such an exhumation might modify our historical knowledge of their genesis). On the other hand, the discovery of a text like Freud's "Project for a Scientific Psychology" — insofar as it is a text by Freud — always threatens to modify not the historical knowledge of psychoanalysis, but its theoretical field, even if only by shifting the accentuation or the center of gravity. Through such returns, which are part of their make-up, these discursive practices maintain a relationship with regard to their "fundamental" and indirect author unlike that which an ordinary text entertains with its immediate author. [Tr.]

significations within a world where one is thrifty not only with one's resources and riches, but also with one's discourses and their significations. The author is the principle of thrift in the proliferation of meaning. As a result, we must entirely reverse the traditional idea of the author. We are accustomed, as we have seen earlier, to saying that the author is the genial creator of a work in which he deposits, with infinite wealth and generosity, an inexhaustible world of significations. We are used to thinking that the author is so different from all other men, and so transcendent with regard to all languages that, as soon as he speaks, meaning begins to proliferate, to proliferate indefinitely.

The truth is quite the contrary: the author is not an indefinite source of significations which fill a work; the author does not precede the works, he is a certain functional principle by which, in our culture, one limits, excludes, and chooses; in short, by which one impedes the free circulation, the free manipulation, the free composition, decomposition, and recomposition of fiction. In fact, if we are accustomed to presenting the author as a genius, as a perpetual surging of invention, it is because, in reality, we make him function in exactly the opposite fashion. One can say that the author is an ideological product, since we represent him as the opposite of his historically real function. (When a historically given function is represented in a figure that inverts it, one has an ideological production.) The author is therefore the ideological figure by which one marks the manner in which we fear the proliferation of meaning.

In saying this, I seem to call for a form of culture in which fiction would not be limited by the figure of the author. It would be pure romanticism, however, to imagine a culture in which the fictive would operate in an absolutely free

state, in which fiction would be put at the disposal of everyone and would develop without passing through something like a necessary or constraining figure. Although, since the eighteenth century, the author has played the role of the regulator of the fictive, a role quite characteristic of our era of industrial and bourgeois society, of individualism and private property, still, given the historical modifications that are taking place, it does not seem necessary that the author-function remain constant in form, complexity, and even in existence. I think that, as our society changes, at the very moment when it is in the process of changing, the author-function will disappear, and in such a manner that fiction and its polysemic texts will once again function according to another mode, but still with a system of constraint — one which will no longer be the author, but which will have to be determined or, perhaps, experienced.

All discourses, whatever their status, form, value, and whatever the treatment to which they will be subjected, would then develop in the anonymity of a murmur. We would no longer hear the questions that have been rehashed for so long: "Who really spoke? Is it really he and not someone else? With what authenticity or originality? And what part of his deepest self did he express in his discourse?" Instead, there would be other questions, like these: "What are the modes of existence of this discourse? Where has it been used, how can it circulate, and who can appropriate it for himself? What are the places in it where there is room for possible subjects? Who can assume these various subject-functions?" And behind all these questions, we would hear hardly anything but the stirring of an indifference: "What difference does it make who is speaking?"

# Julia Kristeva

b. 1941

*Born in Bulgaria, Julia Kristeva took a degree from the Literary Institute of Sofia before going to Paris in 1966 and submitting a* troisième cycle *doctoral thesis and then a thesis for the* Doctorat d'État. *A tenured professor at the University of Paris, she was an early contributor to the influential avant-garde journal* Tel Quel, *an officer of the International Association of Semiotics, and an editor of the review* Sémiotica. *She is also a "Lacanian" psychoanalyst, which is not to suggest that Kristeva is merely an epigone or follower of Jacques Lacan or of the other imposing figures she has studied under, such as Lucien Goldmann and Claude Lévi-Strauss. Rather, Kristeva has persistently contributed to the development of structuralist and poststructuralist thought, at once helping shape emerging ideas and incorporating them as they emerge into her own eclectic, ever-evolving body of thought. Her* Σημειωτιχὴ *(1969), for example, is a critique of structuralism that pointed in the direction of the notion of "semanalysis" — a semiotic/psychoanalytical approach to texts for which Kristeva is perhaps best known. Her other works include* The Text of the Novel *(1970),* About Chinese Women *(1974),* Revolution in Poetic Language *(1974), and* Powers of Horror: An Essay on Abjection *(1980). "The Bounded Text" is from a collection of Kristeva's essays,* Desire in Language: A Semiotic Approach to Literature and Art *(1980).*

# The Bounded Text

## THE UTTERANCE AS IDEOLOGEME

1. Rather than *a discourse,* contemporary semiotics takes as its object *several semiotic practices* which it considers as *translinguistic;* that is, they operate through and across language, while remaining irreducible to its categories as they are presently assigned.

In this perspective, the *text* is defined as a trans-linguistic apparatus that redistributes the order of language by relating communicative speech, which aims to inform directly, to different kinds of anterior or synchronic utterances. The text is therefore a *productivity,* and this means: first, that its relationship to the language in which it is situated is redistributive (destructive-constructive), and hence can be better approached through logical categories rather than linguistic ones; and second, that it is a permutation of texts, an intertextuality: in the space of a given text, several utterances, taken from other texts, intersect and neutralize one another.[1]

Translated by Leon S. Roudiez, Alice Jardine, and Thomas Gora.

[1]The idea of intertextuality here seems equivalent to Bakhtin's notion of the dialogical utterance. See Bakhtin, Ch. 3. [Ed.]

2. One of the problems for semiotics is to replace the former, rhetorical division of genres with a *typology of texts;* that is, to define the specificity of different textual arrangements by placing them within the general text (culture) of which they are part and which is in turn, part of them.[2] The ideologeme is the intersection of a given textual arrangement (a semiotic practice) with the utterances (sequences) that it either assimilates into its own space or to which it refers in the space of exterior texts (semiotic practices). The ideologeme is that intertextual function read as "materialized" at the different structural levels

[2]When considering semiotic practices in relation to the sign, one can distinguish three types: first, a *systematic* semiotic practice founded on the sign, therefore on meaning; conservative and limited, its elements are oriented toward denotata; it is logical, explicative, interchangeable, and not at all destined to transform the other (the addressee). Second, a *transformative* semiotic practice, in which the "signs" are released from denotata and oriented toward the other, whom they modify. Third, a paragrammatic semiotic practice, in which the sign is eliminated by the correlative paragrammatic sequence, which could be seen as a tetralemma — each sign has a denotatum; each sign does not have a denotatum; each sign has and does not have a denotatum; it is not true that each sign has and does not have a denotatum. See my "Pour une sémiologie des paragrammes," in Σημειωτιχὴ: *recherches pour une sémanalyse* (Paris: Seuil, 1969), pp. 196ff. [Au.]

of each text, and which stretches along the entire length of its trajectory, giving it its historical and social coordinates. This is not an interpretative step coming after analysis in order to explain "as ideological" what was first "perceived" as "linguistic." The concept of text as ideologeme determines the very procedure of a semiotics that, by studying the text as intertextuality, considers it as such within (the text of) society and history. The ideologeme of a text is the focus where knowing rationality grasps the transformation of *utterances* (to which the text is irreducible) into a totality (the text) as well as the insertions of this totality into the historical and social text.[3]

3. The *novel,* seen as a text, is a semiotic practice in which the synthesized patterns of several utterances can be read.

For me, the *utterance* specific to the novel is not a minimal sequence (a definitely set entity). It is an *operation,* a motion that links, and even more so, *constitutes* what might be called the *arguments* of the operation, which, in the study of a written text, are either words or word sequences (sentences, paragraphs) as sememes.[4] Instead of analyzing entities (sememes in themselves), I shall study the *function* that incorporates them within the text. That function, a dependent variable, is determined along with the independent variables it links together; more simply put, there is univocal correspondence between words or word sequences. It is therefore clear that what I am proposing is an analysis that, while dealing with linguistic units (words, sentences, paragraphs), is of a translinguistic order. Speaking metaphorically, linguistic units (and especially semantic units) will serve only as springboards in establishing different *kinds of novelistic utterances as functions*. By bracketing the question of semantic sequences, one can bring out the *logical practice* organizing them, thus proceeding at a *suprasegmental* level.[5]

Novelistic utterances, as they pertain to this suprasegmental level, are linked up within the totality of novelistic production. By studying them as such, I shall establish a typology of these utterances and then proceed to investigate, as a second step, their origins outside of the novel. Only in this way can the novel be defined in its unity and/or as ideologeme. To put it another way, the functions defined according to the extra-novelistic textual set (Te) take on value within the novelistic textual set (Tn). The ideologeme of the novel is precisely this *intertextual* function defined according to Te and having value within Tn.

Two kinds of analyses, sometimes difficult to distinguish from each other, make it possible to isolate the *ideologeme of the sign* in the novel: first, a suprasegmental analysis of utterances contained within the novel's framework will reveal it as a bounded text (with its initial programming, its arbitrary ending, its dyadic[6] figuration, its deviations and their concatenation); second, an *intertextual* analysis of these utterances will reveal the relationship between writing and speech in the text of the novel. I will show that the novel's textual order is based more on speech than on writing and then proceed to analyze the topology of this "phonetic order" (the arrangement of speech acts in relation to one another).

Since the novel is a text dependent on the ideologeme of the sign, let me first briefly describe the particularities of the sign as ideologeme.

[3]"Literary scholarship is one branch of the study of ideologies [which] . . . embraces all areas of man's ideological creativity." P. N. Medvedev and M. Bakhtin, *The Formal Method in Literary Scholarship: A Critical Introduction to Sociological Poetics,* Albert J. Wehrle, trans. (Baltimore: Johns Hopkins University Press, 1978), p. 3. I have borrowed the term "ideologeme" from this work. [Au.]

[4]I use the term "sememe" as it appears in the terminology of A. J. Greimas, who defines it as a combination of the semic nucleus and contextual semes. He considers it as belonging to the level of manifestation, as opposed to the level of immanence, which is that of the seme. See A. J. Greimas, *Sémantique Structurale* (Paris: Larousse, 1966), p. 42. [Au.]

[5]In structural linguistics, suprasegmentals are aspects of language whose variance depends on larger features of discourse than the most basic level of "emes." For example, the variety of pauses or the shifting of pitch in English are "phonological" features that are expressed in sound but are controlled by syntactic factors far above the level of the phoneme. By analogy, Kristeva is seeking the suprasegmental features that control discourse above the level of the ideologeme. [Ed.]

[6]Binary. [Ed.]

# FROM SYMBOL TO SIGN

1. The second half of the Middle Ages (thirteenth to fifteenth centuries) was a period of transition for European culture: thought based on the sign replaced that based on the symbol. A semiotics of the symbol characterized European society until around the thirteenth century, as clearly manifested in this period's literature and painting. It is, as such, a semiotic practice of cosmogony: these elements (symbols) refer back to one (or several) unrepresentable and unknowable universal transcendence(s); univocal connections link these transcendences to the units evoking them; the symbol does not "resemble" the object it symbolizes; the two spaces (symbolized-symbolizer) are separate and do not communicate.

The symbol assumes the symbolized (universals) as irreducible to the symbolizer (its markings). Mythical thought operates within the sphere of the symbol (as in the epic, folk tales, chansons de geste, et cetera) through symbolic units — *units of restriction* in relation to the symbolized universals ("heroism," "courage," "nobility," "virtue," "fear," "treason," etc.). The symbol's function, in its vertical dimension (universals — markings), is thus one of *restriction*. The symbol's function in its horizontal dimension (the articulation of signifying units among themselves) is one of escaping paradox; one could even say that the symbol is horizontally *antiparadoxical*: within its logic, two opposing units are exclusive.[7] The good and the bad are incompatible — as are the raw and the cooked, honey and ashes, et cetera.[8] The contradiction,

[7]Within Western scientific thinking, three fundamental currents break away from the symbol's domination, one after another, moving through the sign to the variable. These three are Platonism, conceptualism, and nominalism. See V. Willard Quine, "Reification of Universals," in *From a Logical Point of View* (Cambridge: Harvard University Press, 1953). I have borrowed from this study the differentiation between two meanings of signifying units: one within the space of the symbol, the other within that of the sign. [Au.]

[8]Kristeva alludes to binary polarities isolated as "mythologiques" by Claude Lévi-Strauss. See the introduction to Structuralism and Semiotics, Ch. 4. [Ed.]

once it appears, immediately demands resolution. It is thus concealed, "resolved," and therefore put aside.

The key to symbolic semiotic practice is given from the very beginning of symbolic discourse: the course of semiotic development is circular since the end is programmed, given in embryo, from the beginning (whose end *is* the beginning) because the symbol's function (its ideologeme) antedates the symbolic utterance itself. Thus are implied the general characteristics of a symbolic semiotic practice: the *quantitative limitation* of symbols, their *repetition, limitation,* and *general nature*.

2. From the thirteenth to the fifteenth century, the symbol was both challenged and weakened, but it did not completely disappear. Rather, during this period, its passage (its assimilation) into the sign was assured. The transcendental unity supporting the symbol — its otherworldly casing, its transmitting focus — was put into question. Thus, until the end of the fifteenth century, theatrical representations of Christ's life were based on both the canonical and apocryphal Gospels or the Golden legend (see the Mysteries dated c. 1400 published by Achille Jubinal in 1837 and based on the manuscript at the Library of Sainte-Geneviève). Beginning in the fifteenth century, the theater as well as art in general was invaded by scenes devoted to Christ's public life (as in the Cathedral of Evreux). The transcendental foundation evoked by the symbol seemed to capsize. This heralds a new signifying relation between two elements, both located on the side of the "real" and "concrete." In thirteenth-century art, for example, the prophets were contrasted with the apostles; whereas in the fifteenth century, the four great evangelists were no longer set against the four prophets, but against the four fathers of the Latin Church (Saint Augustine, Saint Jerome, Saint Ambrose, and Gregory the Great as on the altar of Notre Dame of Avioth). Great architectural and literary compositions were no longer possible: the miniature replaced the cathedral and the fifteenth century became the century of the miniaturists. The serenity of the symbol was replaced by the strained ambivalence of the *sign's* connection, which lays claim

to resemblance and identification of the elements it holds together, while first postulating their radical difference. Whence the obsessive insistence on the theme of *dialogue* between two *irreducible* but *similar* elements (dialogue — generator of the pathetic and psychological) in this transitional period. For example, the fourteenth and fifteenth centuries abound in dialogues between God and the human soul: the Dialogue of the Crucifix and Pilgrim, Dialogue of the Sinful Soul and Christ, et cetera. Through this movement, the Bible was moralized (see the famous moralized Bible of the Duke of Burgundy's library). It was even replaced by pastiches that bracketed and erased the transcendental basis of the symbol (the Bible of the Poor and the Mirror of Human Salvation).[9]

3. The sign that was outlined through these mutations retained the fundamental characteristic of the symbol: irreducibility of terms, that is, in the case of the sign, of the referent to the signified, of the signified to the signifier, and, in addition, all the "units" of the signifying structure itself. The ideologeme of the sign is therefore, in a general way, like the ideologeme of the symbol: the sign is dualist, hierarchical, and hierarchizing. A difference between the sign and the symbol can, however, be seen vertically as well as horizontally: within its vertical function, the sign refers back to entities both of lesser scope and more *concretized* than those of the symbol. They are *reified* universals become *objects* in the strongest sense of the word. Put into a relationship within the structure of sign, the entity (phenomenon) under consideration is, at the same time, transcendentalized and elevated to the level of theological unity. The semiotic practice of the sign thus assimilates the metaphysics of the symbol and projects it onto the "immediately perceptible." The "immediately perceptible," valorized in this way, is then transformed into an *objectivity* — the reigning law of discourse in the civilization of the sign.

Within their horizontal function, the units of the sign's semiotic practice are articulated as a *metonymical concatenation of deviations from the norm* signifying a *progressive creation of metaphors*. Oppositional terms, always exclusive, are caught within a network of multiple and always possible deviations (surprises in narrative structures), giving the illusion of an *open* structure, impossible to finish, with an *arbitrary* ending. In literary discourse the semiotic practice of the sign first clearly appeared, during the Renaissance, in the adventure novel, which is structured on what is unforeseeable and on *surprise* as reification (at the level of narrative structure) of the deviation from the norm specific to every practice of the sign. The itinerary of this concatenation of deviations is practically infinite, whence the impression of the work's *arbitrary* ending. This is, in fact, the *illusory* impression which defines all "literature" (all "art"), since such itinerary is programmed by the ideologeme constituting the sign. That is, it is programmed by a closed (finite), dyadic process, which, first, institutes the referent-signified-signifier hierarchy and secondly, interiorizes these oppositional dyads all the way to the very level of the articulation of terms, put together — like the symbol — as resolution of contradiction. In a semiotic practice based on the symbol, contradiction was resolved by *exclusive disjunction* (nonequivalence) — ≠ — or by nonconjunction — | — ; in a semiotic practice based on the sign, contradiction is resolved by nondisjunction — $\overline{V}$—.[10]

## THE IDEOLOGEME OF THE NOVEL: NOVELISTIC ENUNCIATION

Every literary work partaking of the semiotic practice of the sign (all "literature" before the epistemological break of the nineteenth/twentieth centuries) is therefore, as ideologeme, closed and terminated in its very beginnings. It is related to conceptualist (antiexperimental) thought in the same way as the symbolic is to Platonism.[11] The novel is one of the characteristic manifestations of this ambivalent ideologeme (closure, nondisjunction, linking of deviations) — the sign. Here I will examine this ideologeme in Antoine de La Sale's *Jehan de Saintré*.

[9]Emile Mâle, *L'Art religieux de la fin du Moyen Age en France* (Paris: A. Colin 1908). [Au.]

[10]In symbolic logic, the symbol for "nor." [Ed.]

[11]As a semiotic practice, the symbol was suited to the transcendental thought of Platonism. [Ed.]

Antoine de La Sale wrote *Jehan de Saintré* in 1456, after a long career as page, warrior, and tutor, for educational purposes and as a lament for a departure (for puzzling reasons, and after forty-eight years of service, he left the Kings of Anjou to become tutor of the Count of Saint Pol's three sons in 1448). *Jehan de Saintré* is the only novel to be found among La Sale's writings, which are otherwise presented as compilations of edifying narratives (*La Salle*, 1448–1451), as "scientific" tracts, or as accounts of his travels (*Lettres à Jacques de Luxembourg sur les tournois*, 1459; *Réconfort à Madame de Fresne*, 1457) — all of these being constructed as historical discourse or as heterogeneous mosaics of texts. Historians of French literature have neglected this particular work — perhaps the first writing in prose that could be called a novel (if one labels as such those works that depend on the ambiguous ideologeme of the sign). The few studies that have been devoted to it[12] concentrate on its references to the mores of the time, attempt to find the "key" to the characters by identifying them with personalities La Sale might have known, accuse the author of underestimating the historical events of his time (the Hundred Years War, et cetera) as well as of belonging — as a true reactionary — to a world of the past, and so on. Literary history, immersed in referential opacity, has not been able to bring to light the *transitory structure* of this text, which situates it at the threshold of the two eras[13] and shows, through La Sale's naive poetics, the articulation of this ideologeme of the sign, which continues

to dominate our intellectual horizon.[14] What is more, Antoine de La Sale's narrative confirms the narrative of his own writing: La Sale speaks but also, writing, enunciates *himself*. The story of Jehan de Saintré merges with the book's story and becomes, in a sense, its rhetorical representation, its other, its inner lining.

1. The text opens with an introduction that shapes (shows) the entire itinerary of the novel: La Sale *knows* what his text *is* ("three stories") and *for what* reason it exists (a message to Jehan d'Anjou). Having thus uttered his purpose and named its addressee, he marks out within twenty lines the *first loop*[15] that encloses the textual set and programs it as a means of exchange and, therefore, as sign: this is the loop *utterance* (exchange object)/*addressee* (the duke, or, simply, the reader). All that remains is to tell, that is, to fill in, to detail, what was already conceptualized, known, before any contact between pen and paper — "the story as word upon word it proceeds."

2. The *title* can now be presented: "And first, the story of the Lady of the Beautiful Cousins (of whom I have already spoken) and of Saintré," which requires a second loop — this one found at the thematic level of the message. La Sale gives a shortened version of Jehan de Saintré's life from beginning to end ("his passing away from this world," p. 2). We thus *already* know how the story will end: the end of the narrative

---

[12]The following are among the most important: F. Desonay, "Le Petit Jehan de Saintré," in *Revue du Seizième Siècle* (1927) 14:1–48 & 213–80; "Comment un écrivain se corrigeait au XVe siècle, " in *Revue Belge de Philologie et d'Histoire* (1927), 6:81–121; Y. Otaka, "Establissement du texte définitif du Petit Jehan de Saintré," in *Etudes de Langue et Littérature Françaises* (Tokyo, 1965), 6:15–28; W. S. Shepard, "The Syntax of Antoine de La Sale," in *PMLA* (1905), 20:435–501; W. P. Soderhjelm, *La Nouvelle française au XVe siècle* (Paris: H. Champion 1910); *Notes sur Antoine de La Sale et ses oeuvres* (Helsingfors: Ex officina typographica Societatis Litterariae fennicae, 1904). All my references are to the text edited by Jean Misrahi (Fordham University) and Charles A. Knudson (University of Illinois) and published by Droz (Geneva, 1965). [Au.]

[13]The Middle Ages and the Renaissance. [Ed.]

[14]Any contemporary novel that struggles with the problems of "realism" and "writing" is related to the structural ambivalence of *Jehan de Saintré*. Contemporary realist literature is situated at the other end of the history of the novel, at a point where it has been reinvented in order to proceed to a scriptural productivity that keeps close to narration without being repressed by it. It evokes the task of organizing disparate utterances that Antoine de La Sale had undertaken at the dawn of the novelistic journey. The relationship between the two is obvious and, as Louis Aragon admits, desired in the case of his own novel, *La Mise à mort* (1965), where the Author (Antoine) sets himself apart from the Actor (Alfred), going so far as to take the name Antoine de La Sale. [Au.]

[15]This term is used by Victor Shklovsky in the chapter of his book, *O teorii prozy* (Moscow 1929), that was translated into French as "La Construction de la nouvelle et du roman" in Tzvetan Todorov, ed., *Théorie de la littérature* (Paris: Seuil, 1965), p. 170. [Au.]

is given before the narrative itself even begins. All anecdotal interest is thus eliminated: the novel will play itself out by rebuilding the distance between life and death; it will be nothing other than an inscription of *deviations* (surprises) that do not destroy the certainty of the thematic loop (life-death) holding the set together. The text turns on a thematic axis: the interplay between two exclusive oppositions, whose names might change (vice-virtue, love-hate, praise-criticism; for example, the Apology of the widow in the Roman texts is directly followed by the misogynist remarks of Saint Jerome). But the semic axis of these oppositions remains the same (positive-negative); they will alternate according to a trajectory limited by nothing but the initially presupposed *excluded middle*; that is, the inevitable choice of one *or* the other term (with the "or" being exclusive).

Within the ideologeme of the novel (as with the ideologeme of the sign), the irreducibility of opposite terms is admitted only to the extent that the empty space of rupture separating them is provided with ambiguous semic combinations. The initially recognized opposition, setting up the novel's trajectory, is immediately repressed with a *before,* only to give way — within a *now* — to a network of paddings, to a concatenation of deviations oscillating between two opposite poles, and, in an attempt at synthesis, resolving within a figure of *dissimulation* or *mask.* Negation is thus repeated in the affirmation of duplicity. The exclusiveness of the two terms posited by the novel's thematic loop is replaced by a *doubtful positivity* in such a way that the *disjunction* which both opens and closes the novel is replaced by a *yes-no* structure (nondisjunction). This function does not bring about a parathetic[16] silence, but combines carnivalistic play[17] with its nondiscursive logic; all figures found in the novel (as heir to the carnival) that can be read in two ways are organized on the model of this function: ruses, treason, foreigners, andro-

gynes, utterances that can be doubly interpreted or have double destinations (at the level of the novelistic signified), blazonry, "cries" (at the level of the novelistic signifier), and so on. The trajectory of the novel would be impossible without this nondisjunctive function — *this double* — which programs it from its beginning. La Sale first introduces it through the Lady's doubly oriented utterance: as a message destined to the Lady's female companions and to the Court, this utterance connotes aggressivity towards Saintré; as a message destined to Saintré himself, it connotes a "tender" and "testing" love. The nondisjunctive function of the Lady's utterance is revealed in stages that are quite interesting to follow. At first, the message's duplicity is known only to the speaker herself (the Lady), to the author (subject of the novelistic utterance), and to the reader (addressee of the novelistic utterance). The Court (neutrality = objective opinion), as well as Saintré (passive object of the message), are dupes of the Lady's univocal aggressivity towards the page. In the second stage, the duplicity is displaced: Saintré becomes part of it and accepts it; but in the same gesture, he ceases to be the object of a message and becomes the subject of utterances for which he assumes authority. In a third stage, Saintré forgets the nondisjunction; he completely transforms into something positive what he knew to be *also* negative; he loses sight of the dissimulation and is taken in by the game of a univocal (and therefore erroneous) interpretation of a message that remains double. Saintré's defeat — and the end of the narrative — is due to this error of substituting an utterance accepted as disjunctive and univocal for the nondisjunctive function of an utterance.

Negation in the novel thus operates according to a double modality: *alethic* (the opposition of contraries is necessary, possible, contingent, or impossible) and *deontic* (the reunion of contraries is obligatory, permissible, indifferent, or forbidden). The novel becomes possible when the *alethic* modality of opposition joins with the *deontic* modality of reunion.[18] The novel covers the

---

16Beyond discourse. [Ed.]

17In Bakhtin, carnival is the period when all barriers between classes, genders, occupational groups — and all authoritative, single-voiced discourse — break down, and when discourse becomes infinitely dialogical. [Ed.]

18See Georg Henrik von Wright, *An Essay on Modal Logic* (Amsterdam: North-Holland, 1951). [Au.]

trajectory of deontic synthesis in order to condemn it and to affirm, in the alethic mode, the opposition of contraries. The double (dissimulation, mask), as fundamental figure of the carnival,[19] thus becomes the pivotal springboard for the deviations filling up the silence imposed by the disjunctive function of the novel's thematic-programmatic loop. In this way, the novel absorbs the duplicity (the dialogism) of the carnivalesque scene while submitting it to the univocity (monologism) of the symbolic disjunction guaranteed by a transcendence — the author — that subsumes the totality of the novelistic utterance.

3. It is, in fact, precisely at this point in the textual trajectory — that is, after the enunciation of the text's toponymical (message-addressee) and thematic (life-death) closure (loop) — that the word "*actor*" is inscribed. It reappears several times, introducing the *speech* of he who is writing the narrative as being the *utterance* of a character in this *drama* of which he is also the *author*. Playing upon a homophony (Latin: *actor-auctor*, French: *acteur-auteur*), La Sale touches upon the very point where the speech *act* (work) tilts towards discursive *effect* (product), and thus, upon the very constituting process of the "literary" object. For La Sale, the writer is both actor and author; that means that he conceived the text of the novel as both practice (actor) and product (author), process (actor) and effect (author), play (actor) and value (author); and yet, the already set notions of oeuvre (message) and owner (author) do not succeed in pushing the play that preceded them into oblivion.[20] Novelistic speech

is thus inserted into the novelistic utterance and accounted for as one of its elements. (I have examined elsewhere the topology of speech acts in the text of the novel.)[21] It unveils the writer as principal actor in the speech play that ensues and, at the same time, brings together two modes of the novelistic utterance, *narration* and *citation*, into the single speech of he who is both *subject* of the book (the author) and *object* of the spectacle (actor), since, within novelistic nondisjunction, the message is both discourse and representation. The author-actor's utterance unfolds, divides, and faces in two directions: first, towards a referential utterance, *narration* — the speech assumed by he who inscribes himself as actor-author; and second, toward textual premises, *citation* — speech attributed to an other and whose authority he who inscribes himself as actor-author acknowledges. These two orientations intertwine in such a way as to merge. For example, La Sale easily shifts from the story as "lived" by the Lady of the Beautiful Cousins (to which he is witness, i.e., witness to the narration) to the story of Aeneas and Dido as read (cited), and so on.

4. In conclusion, let me say that the modality of novelistic enunciation is *inferential*: it is a process within which the subject of the novelistic utterance affirms a sequence, as *conclusion of the inference*, based on other sequences (referential — hence narrative, or textual — hence citational), which are the *premises of the infer-*

---

[19]I am indebted to Mikhail Bakhtin for his notion of the double and ambiguity as the fundamental figure in the *novel* linking it to the oral carnivalesque tradition, to the mechanism of laughter and the mask, and to the structure of Menippean satire. See his *Problems of Dostoevsky's Poetics* (Ann Arbor: Ardis, 1973), *Rabelais and His World* (Cambridge: MIT Press, 1968), and my essay, "Word, Dialogue, and Novel," in this volume. [Au.]

[20]The notion of "author" appears in Romance poetry about the beginning of the twelfth century. At the time, a poet would publish his verse and entrust them to the memory of minstrels of whom he demanded accuracy. The smallest change was immediately noticed and criticized: "Jograr bradador" (Ramon Menendez-Pidal, *Poesia juglaresca y origines de las literaturas románicas* [Madrid: Instituto de Es-

tudios Políticos, 1957], p. 14, note 1). "'Erron o juglar!' exclamaba condenatorio el trovador gallego y con eso y con el cese del canto para la poesia docta, el juglar queda excluído de la vida literaria; queda como simple musico, y aun en este oficio acabe siendo sustituído par el ministril, tipo del musico ejecutante venido del extranjero y que en el paso del siglo XIV al XV, convive con el juglar" (*Ibid.*, p. 380). In this way, the passage from minstrel as Actor (a character in a dramatic production, an accuser — cf. in juridical Latin: *actor*, the accuser, the controller of the narrative) to minstrel as Author (founder, maker of a product, the one who makes, implements, organizes, generates, and creates an object of which he no longer is the producer but the salesman — cf. in juridical Latin: *auctor*, salesman). [Au.] See also Foucault, "What Is an Author?" p. 978. [Ed.]

[21]See my book *Le Texte du roman* (The Hague: Mouton, 1970), a semiotic approach to a transformational discursive structure. [Au.]

ence and, as such, considered to be true. The novelistic inference is exhausted through the naming process of the two premises and, particularly, through their concatenation, without leading to the syllogistic conclusion proper to logical inference. The function of the author-actor's enunciation therefore consists in binding his discourse to his readings, his speech act to that of others.

The words that mediate this inference are worth noting: "*it seems to me* at first view that she wished to imitate the widows of ancient times . . ." "if, *as* Vergil says . . ." "and *thereupon* Saint Jerome *says* . . ." and so on. These are empty words whose functions are both *junctive* and *translative*. As junctive, they tie together (totalize) two minimal utterances (narrative and citational) within the global, novelistic utterance. They are therefore internuclear. As translative, they transfer an utterance from one textual space (vocal discourse) into another (the book), changing its ideologeme. They are thus intranuclear (for example, the transposition of hawkers' cries and blazons into a written text).[22]

These inferential agents imply the juxtaposition of a *discourse* invested in a subject with another *utterance* different from the author's. They make possible the deviation of the novelistic utterance from its subject and its self-presence, that is, its displacement from a discursive (informational, communicative) level to a textual level (of productivity). Through this inferential gesture, the author refuses to be an objective "witness" — possessor of a truth he symbolizes by the word — in order to inscribe himself as reader or listener, structuring his text through and across a permutation of *other* utterances. He does not so much *speak* as *decipher*. The inferential agents allow him to bring a referential utterance (narration) back to textual premises (citations) and vice versa. They establish a similitude, a resemblance, an equalization of two different discourses. The ideologeme of the sign once again crops up here, at the level of the novelistic enunciation's inferential mode: it admits the existence

of an *other* (discourse) only to the extent that it makes it *its own*. This splitting of the mode of enunciation did not exist in the epic: in the chansons de geste, the speaker's utterance is univocal; it names a referent ("real" object or discourse); it is a signifier symbolizing transcendental objects (universals). Medieval literature, dominated by the symbol, is thus a "signifying," "phonetic" literature, supported by the monolithic presence of signified transcendence. The scene of the carnival introduces the split speech act: the *actor* and the *crowd* are each in turn simultaneously subject and addressee of discourse. The carnival is also the bridge between the two split occurrences as well as the place where each of the terms is acknowledged: the author (actor + spectator). It is this third mode that the novelistic inference adopts and effects within the author's utterance. As irreducible to any of the premises constituting the inference, the mode of novelistic enunciation is the invisible focus where the phonetic (referential utterance, narration) and written (textual premises, citation) intersect. It is the hollow, unrepresentable space signaled by "*as*," "*it seems to me*," "*says thereupon*," or other inferential agents that refer back, tie together, or bound. We thus uncover a third programmation of the novelistic text which brings it to a close before the beginning of the actual story: novelistic enunciation turns out to be a nonsyllogistic inference, a compromise between testimony and citation, between the voice and the book. The novel will be performed within this empty space, within this unrepresentable trajectory bringing together two types of utterances with their *different* and *irreducible* "subjects."

## THE NONDISJUNCTIVE FUNCTION OF THE NOVEL

1. The novelistic utterance conceives of the opposition of terms as a nonalternating and absolute opposition between two groupings that are competitive but never solidary, never complementary, and never reconcilable through indestructible rhythm. In order for this nonalternating disjunction to give rise to the discursive trajectory of the novel, it must be embodied within a

<hr>

[22]For these terms borrowed from structural syntax, see Léon Tesnière, *Esquisse d'une syntaxe structurale* (Paris: Klincksieck, 1953). [Au.]

negative function: nondisjunction. It is this non-disjunctive function that intervenes on a secondary level and instead of an *infinity complementary to bipartition* (which could have taken shape within another conception of negation one might term radical, and this presupposes that the opposition of terms is, *at the same time,* thought of as communion or symmetrical reunion) it introduces the figure of dissimulation, of ambivalence, of the *double.* The initial nonalternating opposition thus turns out to be a pseudo-opposition — and this at the time of its very inception, since it doesn't integrate its own opposition, namely, the solidarity of rivals. Life is opposed to death in an absolute way (as is love to hate, virtue to vice, good to bad, being to nothingness) without the opposition's complementary negation that would transform bipartition into rhythmic totality. The negation remains incomplete and unfinished unless it includes this doubly negative movement that reduces the *difference* between two terms to a radical *disjunction* with permutation of those terms; that is, to an empty space around which they move, dying out as entities and turning into an alternating rhythm. By positing two opposing terms without affirming their identity in the same gesture and simultaneously, such a negation splits the movement of *radical negation* into two phases: disjunction and nondisjunction.

2. This division introduces, first of all, *time*: temporality (history) is the *spacing* of this splitting negation, i.e, what is introduced between two isolated and nonalternating scansions (opposition-conciliation). In other cultures, it has been possible to develop an irrevocable negation that ties the two scansions into an equalization, thus avoiding the spacing of the negative process (duration) and substituting in its place an emptiness (space) that produces the permutation of contraries.

Rendering negation ambiguous brings about, in the same way, a finality, a theological principle (God, "meaning"). To the extent that disjunction is recognized as an initial phase, there imposes itself at a second stage a synthesis of the two into *one,* presented as a unification that "forgets" opposition in the same way that the opposition did not "assume" unification. If God appears at the second stage to mark the bounding of a semiotic practice organized according to nonalternating negation, it is obvious that this closure is already present at the first stage of the simple, absolute opposition (nonalternating opposition).

It is within this split negation that all *mimesis* is born. Nonalternating negation is the law of narrative: every narration is made up, nourished by time, finality, history, and God. Both epic and narrative prose take place within this spacing and move toward the theology produced by nonalternating negation. We would have to look to other civilizations to find a nonmimetic discourse — whether scientific or sacred, moral or ritual — constructed through a process of deletion by rhythmic sequences, enclosing antithetical semic couplings within an orchestrated movement.[23] The novel is no exception to that narrative law. It is a particular case within the plurality of narratives where the nondisjunctive function is concretized at all levels (thematic, syntagmatic, actants, et cetera) of the entire novelistic utterance. It is precisely the second stage of nonalternating negation — that is, nondisjunction — that determines the ideologeme of the novel.

3. Indeed, disjunction (the thematic loops: life-death, love-hate, fidelity-treason) frames the novel, as was found to be the case in the bounded structures programming the novel's beginning. But the novel is not possible unless the disjunction between two terms can be denied while all the time being there, confirmed, and approved. It is presented, now, as *double* rather than as *two irreducible elements.* The figures of traitor, scoffed-at sovereign, vanquished warrior, and unfaithful woman stem from this nondisjunctive function found at the novel's origin.

The epic, on the other hand, was organized according to the symbolic function of exclusive disjunction or nondisjunction. In the *Song of Roland* and the Round Table Cycles, hero and traitor, good and evil, duty and love, pursue one another in irreconcilable hostility from beginning to end, without any possibility of compromise. The "classical" epic, by obeying the law of non-

[23]Michel Granet, *La Pensée chinoise* (Paris: Albin Michel, 1968), Ch. 2, "Le Style," p. 50. (Originally published in 1934.) [Au.]

conjunction (symbolic), can therefore engender neither personalities nor psychologies.[24] Psychology will appear along with the nondisjunctive function of the sign, finding in its ambiguity a terrain conducive to its meanderings. It would be possible, however, to trace the appearance of the *double* as precursor to the conception of personality within the evolution of the epic. Near the end of the twelfth century — and especially in the thirteenth and fourteenth centuries — there spreads an ambiguous epic: emperors are ridiculed, religion and barons become grotesque, heroes are cowardly and suspect ("Charlemagne's Pilgrimage"); the king is worthless, virtue is no longer rewarded (the Garin de Monglan Cycle), and the traitor becomes a principal actant (the Doon de Mayence Cycle or the "Raoul de Cambrai" poem). Neither satirical, laudatory, stigmatizing, nor approving, this epic is witness to a dual semiotic practice, founded on the resemblance of contraries, feeding on miscellany and ambiguity.

4. The courtly literature of Southern France is of particular interest within this transition from symbol to sign. Recent studies have demonstrated the analogies between the cult of the Lady in these texts and those of ancient Chinese poetry.[25] There would be evidence showing influ-

ence of a hieroglyphic semiotic practice based on "conjunctive disjunction" (dialectical negation) upon a semiotic practice based on nondisjunctive opposition (Christianity, Europe). Such hieroglyphic semiotic practice is also and above all a conjunctive disjunction of the two sexes as irreducibly differentiated and, at the same time, alike. This explains why, over a long period, a major semiotic practice of Western society (courtly poetry) attributed to the *Other* (Woman) a *primary* structural role. In our civilization — caught in the passage from the symbol to the sign — a hymn to conjunctive disjunction was transformed into an apology for only *one* of the opposing terms: the Other (Woman), within which is projected and with which is *later* fused the Same (the Author, Man). At the same time there was produced an exclusion of the Other, inevitably presented as an exclusion of woman, as nonrecognition of sexual (and social) opposition. The rhythmic order of Oriental texts organizing the sexes (differences) within conjunctive disjunction (hierogamy)[26] is here replaced by a centered system (Other, Woman) whose center is there only so as to permit those making up the Same to identify with it. It is therefore a pseudocenter, a mystifying center, a blind spot whose value is invested in the Same giving the Other (the center) to itself in order to live as one, alone, and unique. Hence, the exclusive positivity of this blind center (Woman), stretching out to infinity (of "nobility" and "qualities of the heart"), erasing disjunction (sexual difference), and dis-

---

[24]In the epic, man's individuality is limited by his linear relationship to one of two categories: the good or the bad people, those with positive or negative attributes. Psychological states seem to be "free of personalities. Consequently, they are free to change with extraordinary rapidity and to attain unbelievable dimensions. Man may be transformed from good to bad, changes in his psychological state happening in a flash." D. S. Lichachov, *Chelovek v literature drevnej Rusi* [Man in the Literature of Old Russia] (Moscow-Leningrad, 1958), p. 81. [Au.]

[25]See Alois Richard Nykl, *Hispano-Arabic Poetry and Its Relations with the Old Provençal Troubadours* (Baltimore: J. H. Furst, 1946). This study demonstrates how, without mechanically "influencing" Provençal poetry, Arabic poetry *contributed* by contact with Provençal discourse to the formation and development of courtly lyricism in regards to both its content and types, as well as its rhythm, rhyme scheme, internal division, and so on. The Russian academician Nikolai Konrad has demonstrated that the Arab world was in contact, on the other side of Islam, with the Orient and China (in 751, on the banks of the river Talas, the army of the Halifat of Bagdad met the army of the T'ang Empire).

Two Chinese collections, "Yüeh-fu" and "Yü-t'ai hsin-yung," which date from the third and fourth centuries A.D., evoke the themes and organization of courtly Provençal poetry of the twelfth through the fifteenth centuries. Chinese songs, on the other hand, constitute a *distinct* series and stem from a different world of thought. Nonetheless, contact and contamination are a fact of those two cultures — the Arabic and the Chinese (Islamization of China, followed by infiltration of Chinese signifying structure [art and literature] into Arabic rhetoric and, consequently, into Mediterranean culture). See Nikolai Konrad, "Contemporary Problems in Comparative Literature," in *Izvestija Akademii nauk SSSR*, "Literature and Language" series (1959), 18:fasc. 4, p. 335. [Au.]

[26]Sacred marriage. [Ed.]

solving into a series of images (from the angel to the Virgin). The unfinished negative gesture is, therefore, *already* theological: it is stopped before having designated the *Other* (Woman) as being *at the same time* opposed and equal to the *Same* (Man, Author), before being denied through the correlation of contraries (the identity of Man and Woman *simultaneous* to their disjunction). It eventually identified with religious attitudes, and in its incompletion it evokes Platonism.

Scholars have interpreted the theologization of courtly literature as an attempt to save love poetry from the persecutions of the Inquisition;[27] or, on the contrary, as evidence of the infiltration in Southern French society of the Inquisition Tribunals' activity, or that of the Dominican and Franciscan orders, after the debacle of the Albigenses.[28] Whatever the empirical facts may be, the spiritualization of courtly literature was already a given within the structure of this semiotic practice characterized by pseudo-negation as well as nonrecognition of the conjunctive disjunction of semic terms. Within such an ideologeme, the idealization of woman (of the Other) signifies the refusal of a society to constitute itself through the recognition of the *differential* but *nonhierarchizing* status of opposed groups. It also signifies the structural necessity for this society to give itself a permutative center, an *Other* entity, which has no value except as an *object of exchange*[29] among members of the *Same*. Sociology has described how women came to occupy this permutational center (as object of exchange). This devalorizing valorization prepared the terrain for, and cannot be fundamentally distinguished from, the explicit devalorization of

women beginning with fourteenth-century bourgeois literature (in fabliaux, soties,[30] and farces).

5. Antoine de La Sale's novel, situated halfway between these two types of utterances, contains both: the Lady is a dual figure within the novel's structure. She is no longer only the deified mistress required by the code of courtly poetry, that is, the valorized term of a nondisjunctive connection. She is also disloyal, ungrateful, and infamous. In *Jehan de Saintré*, the two attributive terms are no longer semically opposed through nonconjunction as would be required in a semiotic practice dependent on the symbol (the courtly utterance); rather, they are nondisjunctive within a single ambivalent unity connoting the ideologeme of the sign. Neither deified nor ridiculed, neither mother nor mistress, neither enamored of Saintré nor faithful to the Abbot, the Lady becomes the nondisjunctive figure par excellence in which the novel is centered.

Saintré is also part of this nondisjunctive function: he is both child and warrior, page and hero, the Lady's fool and conqueror of soldiers, cared for and betrayed, lover of the Lady and loved either by the king or a comrade in arms — Boucicault (p. 141). Never masculine, child-lover for the Lady or comrade-friend sharing a bed with the king or Boucicault, Saintré is the accomplished androgyne; the sublimation of sex (without sexualization of the sublime). His homosexuality is merely the narrativization of the nondisjunctive function peculiar to the semiotic process of which he is a part. He is the pivot-mirror within which the other arguments of the novelistic function are projected in order to fuse with themselves: the Other is the Same for the Lady (the man is the child, and therefore the woman herself finds there her self-identity nondisjoined from the Other, while remaining opaque to the irreducible *difference* between the two). He is the *Same* who is also the *Other* for the king, the warriors, or Boucicault (as the man who is also the woman who possesses him). The Lady's nondisjunctive function, to which Saintré is assimilated, assures her a role as object of

---

[27]J. Coulet, *Le Troubadour Guilhem Montahagal* (Toulouse: *Bibliothèque Meridionale,* 1928), Series 12, IV. [Au.]

[28]Joseph Anglade, *Le Troubadour Guirault Riquier: Etude sur la décadence de l'ancienne poésie provençale* (Paris: U. de Paris, 1905). [Au.]

[29]Antoine François Campaux, "La Question des femmes au XVe siècle," in *Revue des Cours Littéraires de la France et de l'Etranger* (Paris: I. P., 1864), p. 458ff.; P. Gide, *Etude sur la condition privée de la femme dans le droit ancien et moderne* (Paris: Durand et Pédone-Lauriel, 1885), p. 381. [Au.]

[30]Fabliaux are comic bawdy tales; soties, satirical farces of the fourteenth and fifteenth centuries. [Ed.]

exchange in male society. Saintré's own nondisjunctive function assures him a role as object of exchange between the masculine and feminine of society; together, they tie up the elements of a cultural text into a stable system dominated by nondisjunction (the sign).

## THE AGREEMENT OF DEVIATIONS

1. The novel's nondisjunctive function is manifested, at the level of the concatenation of its constituent utterances, as an *agreement of deviations*: the two originally opposed arguments (forming the thematic loops life-death, good-evil, beginning-end, etc.) are connected and mediated by a series of utterances whose relation to the originally posited opposition is neither explicit nor logically necessary. They are concatenated without any major imperative putting an end to this juxtaposition. These utterances, as deviations in relation to the oppositional loop framing the novelistic utterance, are *laudatory descriptions* of either objects (clothes, gifts, and weapons) or events (the departures of troops, banquets, and combats); such are the descriptions of commerce, purchases, and apparel (pp. 51, 63, 71–72, 79) or of weapons (p. 50), etc. These kinds of utterances reappear with obligatory monotony and make of the text an aggregate of recurrences, a succession of closed, cyclical utterances, complete in themselves. Each one is centered in a certain *point,* which can connote space (the tradesman's shop, the Lady's chamber), time (the troops' departure, Saintré's return), the subject of enunciation, or all three at once. These descriptive utterances are minutely detailed and return periodically according to a *repetitive* rhythm placing its grid upon the novel's temporality. Indeed, La Sale does not describe events evolving over a period of time. Whenever an utterance assumed by an Actor (Author) intervenes to serve as a temporary connecting device, it is extremely laconic and does nothing more than link together *descriptions* that first place the reader before an army ready to depart, a shopkeeper's place, a costume or piece of jewelry and then proceed to praise these objects put together according to no causality whatsoever. The imbrications of these deviations are apt to open up — praises could be repeated indefinitely. They are, however, *terminated* (bounded and determined) by the fundamental function of the novelistic utterance: nondisjunction. Caught up within the novel's totality — that is, seen in reverse, from the end of the novel where exaltation has been transformed into its contrary (desolation) before ending in death — these laudatory descriptions become relativized, ambiguous, deceptive, and double: their univocity changes to duplicity.

2. Besides laudatory descriptions, another kind of deviation operating according to nondisjunction appears along the novel's trajectory: Latin *citations* and moral precepts. Examples include Thales of Miletus, Socrates, Timides, Pittacus of Misselene, the Gospels, Cato, Seneca, Saint Augustine, Epicurus, Saint Bernard, Saint Gregory, Saint Paul, Avicenna, etc.; in addition to acknowledged borrowings, a considerable number of plagiarisms have also been pointed out.

It is not difficult to find the extranovelistic sources of these two kinds of deviations: the laudative description and the citation.

The first comes from the fair, marketplace, or public square. It is the utterance of the merchant vaunting his wares or of the herald announcing combat. Phonetic speech, oral utterance, sound itself, become text: less than writing, the novel is thus the transcription of vocal communication. An arbitrary *signifier* (the word as phone) is transcribed onto paper and presented as adequate to its signified and referent. It represents a "reality" that is already there, preexistent to the signifier, duplicated so as to be integrated into the circuit of exchange; it is therefore reduced to a *representamen* (sign) that is manageable and can be circulated as an element assuring the cohesion of a communicative (commercial) structure endowed with *meaning* (value).

These laudatory utterances, known as *blazons,* were abundant in France during the fourteenth and fifteenth centuries. They come from a communicative discourse, shouted in public squares, and designed to give direct information to the crowd on wars (the number of soldiers, their direction, armaments, etc.), or on the marketplace (the quality and price of merchandise).[31] These solemn, tumultuous, or monumental enumerations belong to a culture that might be called phonetic. The culture of exchange, definitively imposed by the European Renaissance, is engendered through the *voice* and operates according to the structures of the discursive (verbal, phonetic) circuit, inevitably referring back to a reality with which it identified by duplicating it (by "signifying it"). "Phonetic" literature is characterized by this kind of laudatory and repetitive utterances-enumerations.[32]

The blazon later lost its univocity and became ambiguous; praise and blame at the same time. In the fifteenth century, the blazon was already the nondisjunctive figure par excellence.[33]

Antoine de La Sale's text captures the blazon just before this splitting into praise and/or blame. Blazons are recorded into the book as univocally laudatory. But they become ambiguous as soon as they are read from the point of view of the novelistic text's general function: the Lady's treachery skews the laudatory tone and shows its ambiguity. The blazon is transformed into blame and is thus inserted into the novel's nondisjunctive function as noted above: the function established according to the extratextual set (Te)

changes within the novelistic textual set (Tn) and in this way defines it as ideologeme.

This splitting of the utterance's univocity is a typically oral phenomenon which can be found within the entire discursive (phonetic) space of the Middle Ages and especially in the carnival scene. The splitting that makes up the very nature of the sign (object/sound, referent/signified/signifier) as well as the topology of the communicative circuit (subject-addressee, Same-pseudo Other), reaches the utterance's logical level (phonetic) and is presented as nondisjunctive.

3. The second kind of deviation — the citation — comes from a written text. Latin as well as *other* books (already read) penetrate the novel's text either as directly copied (citations) or as mnesic traces (memories). They are carried intact from their own space into the space of the novel being written; they are transcribed within quotation marks or are plagiarized.[34]

While emphasizing the phonetic and introducing into the cultural text the (bourgeois) space of the fair, marketplace, and street, the end of the Middle Ages was also characterized by a massive infiltration of the written text: the book ceased to be the privilege of nobles or scholars and was democratized.[35] As a result, phonetic culture

[31]Such are, for instance, the famous "Parisian hawkers' cries" — repetitive utterances and laudatory enumerations that fulfilled the purposes of advertisement in the society of the time. See Alfred Franklin, *Vie privée d'autrefois: I. L'Annonce et la réclame* (Paris: Plon-Nourrit, 1897–1902); and J. G. Kastner, *Les Voix de Paris: essai d'une histoire littéraire et musicale des cris populaires* (Paris: G. Brandus, 1857). [Au.]

[32]See *Le Mystère de Vieux Testament* (fifteenth century), in which the officers of Nebuchadnezzar's army enumerate forty-three kinds of weapons; and *Le Martyr de saint Canten* (late fifteenth century), in which the leader of the Roman troops enumerates forty-five weapons; and so on. [Au.]

[33]Thus, in Grimmelshausen's *Der Satyrische Pylgrad* (1666), there first appear twenty semantically positive utterances that are later restated as semantically pejorative and, finally, as double (neither positive nor pejorative). The blazon appears frequently in mysteries and satirical farces. See Anatole de Montaiglon, *Recueil de poesies françoises des XV et XVIe siècles* (Paris: P. Jannet-P. Daffis, 1865–1878), 1:11–16, and 3:15–18; and *Dits des pays*, 5:110–16. In the matter of blazons, see H. Gaidoz and P. Sebillot, *Blason populaire de la France* (Paris: L. Cerf, 1884) and G. D'Haucourt and G. Durivault, *Le Blason* (Paris: Presses Universitaires de France, 1960). [Au.]

[34]Concerning borrowings and plagiarisms by Antoine de La Sale, see M. Lecourt, "Antoine de La Sale et Simon de Hesdin," in *Mélanges offerts à M. Emile Châtelain* (Paris: H. Champion, 1910), pp. 341–50, and "Une Source d'Antoine de La Sale: Simon de Hesdin," in *Romania* (1955), 76:39–83 & 183–211. [Au.]

[35]Following a period when books were considered as sacred objects (sacred book = Latin book), the late Middle Ages went through a period when books were devalorized, and this was accompanied by texts being replaced with imagery. "Beginning with the middle of the twelfth century, the role and fate of books changed. As the place of production and exchange, the city had undergone the impact of books and stimulated their appearance. Deeds and words had an echo in them and were multiplied in a proliferating dialectic. The book as a product of prime necessity entered into the cycle of Medieval production. It became a profitable and marketable product; but it also became a protected product." Albert Flocon, *L'Univers des livres* (Paris: Hermann, 1961), p. 1. *Secular* books soon began to appear: the Roland cycle, courtly novels (the Novel of Alexander the Great, the Novel of Thebes), Breton novels (King Arthur, the Grail), the Romance of the Rose, troubadour and trouvere poems, the poetry of Rutebeuf, fabliaux, the Roman de Renart, miracle plays, liturgical drama, etc. An actual *trade* in manuscript

claimed to be a scriptural one. To the extent that every book in our civilization is a transcription of oral speech,[36] citation and plagiarism are as phonetic as the blazon even if their extrascriptural (verbal) source goes back to a few books before Antoine de La Sale's.

4. Nevertheless, the reference to a written text upsets the laws imposed on the text by oral transcription: enumeration, repetition, and therefore temporality (cf. *supra*). The introduction of writing has two major consequences.

First, the temporality of La Sale's text is less

a discursive temporality (the narrative sequences are not ordered according to the temporal laws of the verb phrase) than what we might call a *scriptural* temporality (the narrative sequences are oriented towards and rekindled by the very activity of writing). The succession of "events" (descriptive utterances or citations) obeys the motion of the hand working on the empty page — the very economy of inscription. La Sale often interrupts the *course* of discursive time to introduce the *present time* of his work on the text: "To return to my point," "to put it briefly," "as I will tell you," and "here I will stop speaking for a bit of Madame and her Ladies to return to little Saintré," etc. Such junctives signal a temporality other than that of the discursive (linear) chain: the *massive present* of inferential enunciation (of the scriptural work).

Second, the (phonetic) utterance having been transcribed onto paper and the foreign text (citation) having been copied down, both of them form a written text within which the very act of writing shifts to the background and appears, in its *totality,* as *secondary*: as a transcription-copy, as a sign, as a "letter," no longer in the sense of inscription but of exchange object ("which I send to you in the manner of a letter").

The novel is thus structured as dual space: it is both phonetic utterance and scriptural level, overwhelmingly dominated by discursive (phonetic) order.

## ARBITRARY COMPLETION AND STRUCTURAL FINITUDE

1. All ideological activity appears in the form of utterances compositionally *completed*. This completion is to be distinguished from the *structural finitude* to which only a few philosophical systems (Hegel) as well as religions have aspired. The structural finitude characterizes, as a fundamental trait, the object that our culture consumes as a finished product (effect, impression) while refusing to read the process of its productivity: "literature" — within which the novel occupies a privileged position. The notion of literature coincides with the notion of the novel, as much on account of chronological origins as of

---

books sprang up and saw considerable expansion in the fifteenth century in Paris, Bruges, Ghent, Antwerp, Augsburg, Cologne, Strasburg, Vienna. In markets and fairs, near the churches, paid copyists would spread out their offerings and hawk their wares. See Svend Dahl, *Histoire du livre de l'antiquité à nos jours* (Paris: Poinat, 1960). The cult of books extended into the court of the kings of Anjou (who were closely linked to the Italian Renaissance) where Antoine de La Sale worked. René of Anjou (1480) owned twenty-four Turkish and Arabic manuscripts, and in his chamber there hung "a large panel on which were written the ABC's with which one can write throughout all the Christian and Saracenic countries." [Au.]

[36]It seems natural for Western thought to consider any writing as *secondary*, as coming after vocalization. This devalorization of writing harkens back to Plato, as do many of our philosophical presuppositions: "There neither is nor ever will be a treatise of mine [on my teaching]. For it does not admit of exposition like other branches of knowledge; but after much converse about the matter itself and a life lived together, suddenly a light, as it were, is kindled in one soul by a flame that leaps to it from another, and thereafter sustains itself" (*The Platonic Epistles,* J. Harward, trans. [Cambridge: Cambridge University Press, 1932], 7:135). Such is the case unless writing happens to be assimilated to an authority figure or to an immutable truth, unless it manages "to write what is of great service to mankind and to bring the nature of things into the light for all to see" (*ibid.*). But idealist reasoning sceptically discovers that "further, on account of the weakness of language [ . . . ] no man of intelligence will venture to express his philosophical views in language, especially not a language that is unchangeable, which is true of that which is set down in written characters" (*ibid.,* pp. 136–37). Historians of writing generally agree with that thesis. See James G. Février, *Histoire de l'écriture* (Paris: Payot, 1948). On the other hand, some historians insist on writing's preeminence over spoken language. See Chang Chen-ming, *L'Ecriture chinoise et le geste humain* (Paris: P. Geuthner, 1937) and J. Van Ginneken, *La Reconstitution typologique des langages archaïques de l'humanité* (Amsterdam: Noord-Hollandsche uitgevers-maatschappij, 1939). [Au.]

structural bounding.[37] Explicit completion is often lacking, ambiguous, or assumed in the text of the novel. This incompletion nevertheless underlines the text's structural finitude. Every genre having its own particular structural finitude, I shall try to isolate that of *Jehan de Saintré*.

2. The initial programming of the book is already its structural finitude. Within the figures described above, the trajectories close upon themselves, return to their point of departure or are confirmed by a censoring element in such a way as to outline the limits of a closed discourse. The book's compositional completion nevertheless reworks the structural finitude. The novel ends with the utterance of the author who, after having brought the story of his character, Saintré, to the point of the Lady's punishment, interrupts the narrative to announce the end: "And here I shall begin the end of this story . . ." (p. 307).

The story can be considered finished as soon as there is completion of one of the loops (resolution of one of the oppositional dyads) the series of which was opened by the initial programming. This loop is the condemnation of the Lady, signifying a condemnation of ambiguity. The *narrative* stops there. I shall call this completion of the narrative by a concrete loop a reworking of the structural finitude.

But the structural finitude, once more manifested by a concretization of the text's fundamental figure (the oppositional dyad and its relation to nondisjunction) is not sufficient for the bounding of the author's discourse. Nothing in speech can put an end — except arbitrarily — to the infinite concatenation of loops. The real arresting act is performed by the appearance, within the novelistic utterance, of the very work that produces it, here, on the actual page. Speech ends when its subject dies and it is the act of writing (of work) that produces this murder.

A new rubric, the "*actor*," signals the second — the actual — reworking of the ending: "And here I shall give an ending to the book of the most valiant knight who . . ." (p. 308). A brief narrative of the narrative follows, terminating the

novel by bringing the utterance back to the act of writing ("Now, most high, and most powerful and most excellent prince and my most feared lord, if I have erred in any way either by *writing* too much or too little [. . .] I have made this book, said Saintré, which I send to you in the manner of a *letter*" — p. 309, emphasis mine) and by substituting the present of script for the past of speech ("And in conclusion, for the *present,* my most feared lord, I write you nothing else" [p. 309] — emphasis mine).

Within this dual surface of the text (story of Saintré — story of the writing process) — the scriptural activity having been narrated and the narrative having been often interrupted to allow the act of production to surface — (Saintré's) death as rhetorical image coincides with the stopping of discourse (erasure of the actor). Nevertheless — as another retraction of speech — this death, repeated by the text at the moment it becomes silent, cannot be spoken. It is asserted by a (tomblike) writing, which writing (as text of the novel) places in quotation marks. In addition — another retraction, this time of the place of *language* — this citation of the tombstone inscription is produced in a dead language (Latin). Set back in relation to French, the Latin reaches a standstill where it is no longer the narrative that is being completed (having been terminated in the preceding paragraph: "And here I shall begin the end of this story . . .") but rather the *discourse* and its product — "literature"/the "letter" ("And here I shall give an ending to the book . . .").

3. The narrative could again take up Saintré's adventures or spare us several of them. The fact remains nevertheless that it is bounded, born dead: what terminates it structurally are the bounded functions of the sign's ideologeme, which the narrative repeats with variation.[38] What bounds it compositionally and as cultural artifact is the expliciting of the narrative as a written text.

Thus, at the close of the Middle Ages and therefore before consolidation of "literary" ide-

---

[37]See Medvedev and Bakhtin, *The Formal Method in Literary Scholarship*. [Au.]

[38]Compare Kristeva's analysis of completeness and closure here with Eco's analysis of the same issue in recent popular literature in "The Myth of Superman," ch. 4. [Ed.]

ology and the society of which it is the super-structure, Antoine de La Sale doubly terminated his novel: as narrative (structurally) and as discourse (compositionally). This compositional closure, by its very naiveté, reveals a major fact later occulted by bourgeois literature.

The novel has a double semiotic status: it is a linguistic (narrative) *phenomenon* as well as a discursive *circuit* (letter, literature). The fact that it is a *narrative* is but one aspect — an anterior one — of this particularity: it is *"literature."* That is the difference characterizing the novel in relation to narrative: the novel is already "literature"; that is, as product of speech, a (discursive) object of exchange with an owner (author), value, and consumer (the public, addressee). The narrative's conclusion coincides with the conclusion of one loop's trajectory.[39] The novel's finitude, however, does not stop at this conclusion. An instance of speech, often in the form of an epilogue, occurs at the end to slow down the narration and to demonstrate that one is indeed dealing with a verbal construction under the control of a subject who speaks.[40] The narrative is presented as a story, the novel as a discourse (independent of the fact that the author — more or less consciously — recognizes it as such). In this, it constitutes a decisive stage in the development of the speaking subject's critical consciousness in relation to his speech.

To terminate the novel as *narrative* is a rhe-torical problem consisting of reworking the bounded ideologeme of the sign which opened it. To complete the novel as literary artifact (to understand it as discourse or sign) is a problem of social practice, of cultural text, and it consists in confronting speech (the product, the Work) with its own death — writing (textual productivity). It is here that there intervenes a third conception of the book as *work* and no longer as a phenomenon (narrative) or as literature (discourse). La Sale, of course, never reaches this stage. The succeeding social text eliminates all notions of production from its scene in order to substitute a product (effect, value): the reign of *literature* is the reign of *market value* occulting even what La Sale practiced in a confused way: the discursive origins of the literary event. We shall have to wait for a reevaluation of the bourgeois social text in order for a reevaluation of "literature" (of discourse) to take place through the advent of scriptural work within the text.[41]

4. In the meantime, this function of writing as work destroying literary representation (the literary artifact) remains latent, misunderstood, and unspoken, although often at work in the text and made evident when deciphered. For La Sale, as well as for any so-called "realist" writer, writing *is* speech as law (with no possible transgression).

Writing is revealed, for him who thinks of himself as "author," as a function that ossifies, petrifies, and blocks. For the *phonetic* consciousness — from the Renaissance to our time[42] — writing is an artificial limit, an arbitrary law, a subjective finitude. The intervention of writing in the text is often an excuse used by the author to justify the arbitrary ending of his narrative. Thus, La Sale inscribes himself as writing in order to justify the end of his writing: his narrative is a letter whose death coincides with the end of his pen work. Inversely, Saintré's death

[39] "'Short story' is a term referring exclusively to plot, one assuming a combination of two conditions: small size and the impact of plot on the ending" (B. M. Eikhenbaum, "O. Henry and the Theory of the Short Story," I. R. Titunik, trans., in *Readings in Russian Poetics: Formalist and Structuralist Views* [Ann Arbor: University of Michigan Press, 1978], pp. 231–32). [Au.]

[40] The poetry of troubadours, like popular tales, stories of voyages, and other kinds of narratives, often introduces at the end the speaker as a witness to or participant in the narrated "facts." Yet, in novelistic conclusions, the author speaks not as a witness to some "event" (as in folk tales), not to express his "feelings" or his "art" (as in troubadour poetry); rather, he speaks in order to assume ownership of the discourse that he appeared at first to have given to someone else (a character). He envisions himself as the actor of *speech* (and not of a sequence of events), and he follows through the loss of that speech (its death), after all interest in the narrated events has ended (the death of the main character, for instance). [Au.]

[41] An example of this would be Philippe Sollers's book, *The Park,* A. M. Sheridan-Smith, trans. (New York: Red Dust, 1969), which inscribes the production of its writing before the conceivable *effects* of an "oeuvre" as a phenomenon of (representative) discourse. [Au.]

[42] As to the impact of phonetism in Western culture, see Jacques Derrida, *Of Grammatology* (Baltimore: Johns Hopkins University Press, 1976). [Au.]

is not the narration of an adventure: La Sale, often verbose and repetitive, restricts himself, in announcing this major fact, to the transcription from a tomb in two languages — Latin and French.

There we have a paradoxical phenomenon that dominates, in different forms, the entire history of the novel: the devalorization of writing, its categorization as pejorative, paralyzing, and deadly. This phenomenon is on a par with its other aspect: valorization of the oeuvre, the Author, and the literary artifact (discourse). Writing itself appears only to bound the book, that is, discourse. What opens it is speech: "of which the first shall tell of the Lady of the Beautiful Cousins." The act of writing is the differential act par excellence, reserving for the text the status of *other,* irreducible to what is different from it; it is also the correlational act par excellence,

avoiding any bounding of sequences within a finite ideologeme, and opening them up to an infinite arrangement. Writing, however, has been suppressed, evoked only to oppose "objective reality" (utterance, phonetic discourse) to a "subjective artifice" (scriptural practice). The opposition phonetic/scriptural, utterance/text — at work within the bourgeois novel with devalorization of the second term (of the scriptural, textual) — misled the Russian Formalists. It permitted them to interpret the insertion of writing into narrative as proof of the text's "arbitrariness" or of the work's so-called "literariness." It is evident that the concepts of "arbitrariness" or "literariness" can only be accepted within an ideology of valorization of the oeuvre (as phonetic, discursive) to the detriment of writing (textual productivity); in other words, only within a bounded (cultural) text.

# Roland Barthes
1915–1980

*Before his untimely death in a traffic accident, the French critic and man of letters Roland Barthes was a prolific interpreter, disseminator, and reviser of most of the complex theoretical concepts that wound through his country's centers of learning from the 1950s on. Barthes's father, a naval officer, died in battle in the first year of his son's life. Barthes grew up in Bayonne, attended secondary school in Paris, and received degrees in classical letters (1939) and grammar and philosophy (1943) from the University of Paris. He taught French in Bucharest (1948–49) and Alexandria (1949–50). Although Barthes was director of the social sciences at the École Pratique des Hautes Études in Paris from 1960 to 1977, there is the sense that he was more comfortable intellectually on the margins of the academy, carrying on guerrilla conversation with it. (On Racine [1963], for example, caused a furor among institutional classicists because of its nontraditional approach to the canonical playwright.) Barthes was elected to the chair of literary semiology at the Collège de France in 1976 and acknowledged as the leading critic of his generation in 1978. Barthes's works, many of which have been translated since his death, include* Writing Degree Zero *(1953),* Mythologies *(1957),* Elements of Semiology *(1964),* Criticism and Truth *(1966),* S/Z *(1970),* Sade/Fourier/Loyola *(1971),* New Critical Essays *(1972),* The Pleasure of the Text *(1973),* A Lover's Discourse: Fragments *(1977),* The Grain of the Voice *(1981),* The Responsibilities of Forms *(1982), and* The Rustle of Language *(1984). "From Work to Text" is from* Image — Music — Text *(1977).*

# From Work to Text

It is a fact that over the last few years a certain change has taken place (or is taking place) in our conception of language and, consequently, of the literary work which owes at least its phenomenal existence to this same language. The change is clearly connected with the current development of (amongst other disciplines) linguistics, anthropology, Marxism and psychoanalysis (the term "connection" is used here in a deliberately neutral way: one does not decide a determination, be it multiple and dialectical). What is new and which affects the idea of the work comes not necessarily from the internal recasting of each of these disciplines, but rather from their encounter in relation to an object which traditionally is the province of none of them. It is indeed as though the *interdisciplinarity* which is today held up as a prime value in research cannot be accomplished by the simple confrontation of specialist branches of knowledge. Interdisciplinarity is not the calm of an easy security; it begins *effectively* (as opposed to the mere expression of a pious wish) when the solidarity of the old disciplines breaks down — perhaps even violently, via the jolts of fashion — in the interests of a new object and a new language neither of which has a place in the field of the sciences that were to be brought peacefully together, this unease in classification being precisely the point from which it is possible to diagnose a certain mutation. The mutation in which the idea of the work seems to be gripped must not, however, be over-estimated: it is more in the nature of an epistemological slide than of a real break. The break, as is frequently stressed, is seen to have taken place in the last century with the appearance of Marxism and Freudianism; since then there has been no further break, so that in a way it can be said that for the last hundred years we have been living in repetition. What History, our History, allows us today is merely to slide, to vary, to exceed, to repudiate. Just as Einsteinian science demands that *the relativity of the frames of reference* be included in

Translated by Richard Howard.

the object studied, so the combined action of Marxism, Freudianism and structuralism demands, in literature, the relativization of the relations of writer, reader and observer (critic). Over against the traditional notion of the *work,* for long — and still — conceived of in a, so to speak, Newtonian way, there is now the requirement of a new object, obtained by the sliding or overturning of former categories. That object is the *Text.* I know the word is fashionable (I am myself often led to use it) and therefore regarded by some with suspicion, but that is exactly why I should like to remind myself of the principal propositions at the intersection of which I see the Text as standing. The word "proposition" is to be understood more in a grammatical than in a logical sense: the following are not argumentations but enunciations, "touches," approaches that consent to remain metaphorical. Here then are these propositions; they concern method, genres, signs, plurality, filiation, reading and pleasure.

1. The Text is not to be thought of as an object that can be computed. It would be futile to try to separate out materially works from texts. In particular, the tendency must be avoided to say that the work is classic, the text avant-garde; it is not a question of drawing up a crude honours list in the name of modernity and declaring certain literary productions "in" and others "out" by virtue of their chronological situation: there may be "text" in a very ancient work, while many products of contemporary literature are in no way texts. The difference is this: the work is a fragment of substance, occupying a part of the space of books (in a library for example), the Text is a methodological field. The opposition may recall (without at all reproducing term for term) Lacan's distinction between "reality" and "the real": the one is displayed, the other demonstrated; likewise, the work can be seen (in bookshops, in catalogues, in exam syllabi), the text is a process of demonstration, speaks according to certain rules (or against certain rules); the work can be held in the hand, the text is held in lan-

guage, only exists in the movement of a discourse (or rather, it is Text for the very reason that it knows itself as text); the Text is not the decomposition of the work, it is the work that is the imaginary tail of the Text; or again, *the Text is experienced only in an activity of production*. It follows that the Text cannot stop (for example on a library shelf); its constitutive movement is that of cutting across (in particular, it can cut across the work, several works).

2. In the same way, the Text does not stop at (good) Literature; it cannot be contained in a hierarchy, even in a simple division of genres. What constitutes the Text is, on the contrary (or precisely), its subversive force in respect of the old classifications. How do you classify a writer like Georges Bataille? Novelist, poet, essayist, economist, philosopher, mystic? The answer is so difficult that the literary manuals generally prefer to forget about Bataille who, in fact, wrote texts, perhaps continuously one single text. If the Text poses problems of classification (which is furthermore one of its "social" functions), this is because it always involves a certain experience of limits (to take up an expression from Philippe Sollers). Thibaudet used already to talk — but in a very restricted sense — of limit-works (such as Chateaubriand's *Vie de Rancé,* which does indeed come through to us today as a "text"); the Text is that which goes to the limit of the rules of enunciation (rationality, readability, etc.). Nor is this a rhetorical idea, resorted to for some "heroic" effect: the Text tries to place itself very exactly *behind* the limit of the *doxa*[1] (is not general opinion — constitutive of our democratic societies and powerfully aided by mass communications — defined by its limits, the energy with which it excludes, its *censorship*?). Taking the word literally, it may be said that the Text is always *paradoxical*.

3. The Text can be approached, experienced, in reaction to the sign. The work closes on a signified. There are two modes of signification which can be attributed to this signified: either it is claimed to be evident and the work is then the object of a literal science, of philology, or else

it is considered to be secret, ultimate, something to be sought out, and the work then falls under the scope of a hermeneutics, of an interpretation (Marxist, psychoanalytic, thematic, etc.); in short, the work itself functions as a general sign and it is normal that it should represent an institutional category of the civilization of the Sign. The Text, on the contrary, practises the infinite deferment of the signified, is dilatory; its field is that of the signifier and the signifier must not be conceived of as "the first stage of meaning," its material vestibule, but, in complete opposition to this, as its *deferred action*. Similarly, the *infinity* of the signifier refers not to some idea of the ineffable (the unnameable signified) but to that of a *playing*; the generation of the perpetual signifier (after the fashion of a perpetual calendar) in the field of the text (better, of which the text is the field) is realized not according to an organic progress of maturation or a hermeneutic course of deepening investigation, but, rather, according to a serial movement of disconnections, overlappings, variations. The logic regulating the Text is not comprehensive (define "what the work means") but metonymic; the activity of associations, contiguities, carryings-over coincides with a liberation of symbolic energy (lacking it, man would die); the work — in the best of cases — is *moderately* symbolic (its symbolic runs out, comes to a halt); the Text is *radically* symbolic: *a work conceived, perceived and received in its integrally symbolic nature is a text*. Thus is the Text restored to language; like language, it is structured but off-centred, without closure (note, in reply to the contemptuous suspicion of the "fashionable" sometimes directed at structuralism, that the epistemological privilege currently accorded to language stems precisely from the discovery there of a paradoxical idea of structure: a system with neither close nor centre).

4. The Text is plural. Which is not simply to say that it has several meanings, but that it accomplishes the very plural of meaning: an *irreducible* (and not merely an acceptable) plural. The Text is not a co-existence of meanings but a passage, an overcrossing; thus it answers not to an interpretation, even a liberal one, but to an explosion, a dissemination. The plural of the

[1]Opinion. [Ed.]

Text depends, that is, not on the ambiguity of its contents but on what might be called the *stereographic plurality* of its weave of signifiers (etymologically, the text is a tissue, a woven fabric). The reader of the Text may be compared to someone at a loose end (someone slackened off from any imaginary); this passably empty subject strolls — it is what happened to the author of these lines, then it was that he had a vivid idea of the Text — on the side of a valley, a *oued*[2] flowing down below (*oued* is there to bear witness to a certain feeling of unfamiliarity); what he perceives is multiple, irreducible, coming from a disconnected, heterogeneous variety of substances and perspectives: lights, colours, vegetation, heat, air, slender explosions of noises, scant cries of birds, children's voices from over on the other side, passages, gestures, clothes of inhabitants near or far away. All these *incidents* are half-identifiable: they come from codes which are known but their combination is unique, founds the stroll in a difference repeatable only as difference. So the Text: it can be it only in its difference (which does not mean its individuality), its reading is semelfactive[3] (this rendering illusory any inductive-deductive science of texts — no "grammar" of the text) and nevertheless woven entirely with citations, references, echoes, cultural languages (what language is not?), antecedent or contemporary, which cut across it through and through in a vast stereophony. The intertextual in which every text is held, it itself being the text-between of another text, is not to be confused with some origin of the text: to try to find the "sources," the "influences" of a work, is to fall in with the myth of filiation; the citations which go to make up a text are anonymous, untraceable, and yet *already read*: they are quotations without inverted commas. The work has nothing disturbing for any monistic philosophy (we know that there are opposing examples of these); for such a philosophy, plural is the Evil. Against the work, therefore, the text could well take as its motto the words of the man possessed by demons (*Mark* 5:9):

"My name is Legion: for we are many." The plural of demoniacal texture which opposes text to work can bring with it fundamental changes in reading, and precisely in areas where monologism appears to be the Law: certain of the "texts" of Holy Scripture traditionally recuperated by theological monism (historical or anagogical) will perhaps offer themselves to a diffraction of meanings (finally, that is to say, to a materialist reading), while the Marxist interpretation of works, so far resolutely monistic, will be able to materialize itself more by pluralizing itself (if, however, the Marxist "institutions" allow it).

5. The work is caught up in a process of filiation.[4] Are postulated: a *determination* of the work by the world (by race, then by History), a *consecution* of works amongst themselves, and a *conformity* of the work to the author. The author is reputed the father and the owner of his work: literary science therefore teaches *respect* for the manuscript and the author's declared intentions, while society asserts the legality of the relation of author to work (the "*droit d'auteur*" or "copyright," in fact of recent date since it was only really legalized at the time of the French Revolution). As for the Text, it reads without the inscription of the Father. Here again, the metaphor of the Text separates from that of the work: the latter refers to the image of an *organism* which grows by vital expansion, by "development" (a word which is signficantly ambiguous, at once biological and rhetorical); the metaphor of the Text is that of the *network*; if the Text extends itself, it is as a result of a combinatory systematic (an image, moreover, close to current biological conceptions of the living being). Hence no vital "respect" is due to the Text: it can be *broken* (which is just what the Middle Ages did with two nevertheless authoritative texts — Holy Scripture and Aristotle); it can be read without the guarantee of its father, the restitution of the inter-text paradoxically abolishing any legacy. It is not that the Author may not "come back" in the Text, in his text, but he then does so as a "guest." If he is a novelist, he is

[2]A north African watercourse; a wadi. [Ed.]
[3]A nonce word made up from the Latin roots "semel" (half) and "factive" (creative). [Ed.]

[4]Descent, derivation. [Ed.]

inscribed in the novel like one of his characters, figured in the carpet; no longer privileged, paternal, aletheological,[5] his inscription is ludic.[6] He becomes, as it were, a paper-author: his life is no longer the origin of his fictions but a fiction contributing to his work; there is a reversion of the work on to the life (and no longer the contrary); it is the work of Proust, of Genet which allows their lives to be read as a text. The word "bio-graphy" re-acquires a strong, etymological sense, at the same time as the sincerity of the enunciation — veritable "cross" borne by literary morality — becomes a false problem: the *I* which writes the text, it too, is never more than a paper-*I*.

6. The work is normally the object of a consumption; no demagogy is intended here in referring to the so-called consumer culture but it has to be recognized that today it is the "quality" of the work (which supposes finally an appreciation of "taste") and not the operation of reading itself which can differentiate between books: structurally, there is no difference between "cultured" reading and casual reading in trains. The Text (if only by its frequent "unreadability") decants the work (the work permitting) from its consumption and gathers it up as play, activity, production, practice. This means that the Text requires that one try to abolish (or at the very least to diminish) the distance between writing and reading, in no way by intensifying the projection of the reader into the work but by joining them in a single signifying practice. The distance separating reading from writing is historical. In the times of the greatest social division (before the setting up of democratic cultures), reading and writing were equally privileges of class. Rhetoric, the great literary code of those times, taught one to *write* (even if what was then normally produced were speeches, not texts). Significantly, the coming of democracy reversed the word of command: what the (secondary) School prides itself on is teaching to *read* (well) and no longer to write (consciousness of the deficiency is becoming fashionable again today: the teacher

is called upon to teach pupils to "express themselves," which is a little like replacing a form of repression by a misconception). In fact, *reading,* in the sense of consuming, is far from *playing* with the text. "Playing" must be understood here in all its polysemy:[7] the text itself *plays* (like a door, like a machine with "play") and the reader plays twice over, playing the Text as one plays a game, looking for a practice which reproduces it, but, in order that that practice not be reduced to a passive, inner *mimesis* (the Text is precisely that which resists such a reduction), also playing the Text in the musical sense of the term. The history of music (as a practice, not as an "art") does indeed parallel that of the Text fairly closely: there was a period when practising amateurs were numerous (at least within the confines of a certain class) and "playing" and "listening" formed a scarcely differentiated activity; then two roles appeared in succession, first that of the performer, the interpreter to whom the bourgeois public (though still itself able to play a little — the whole history of the piano) delegated its playing, then that of the (passive) amateur, who listens to music without being able to play (the gramophone record takes the place of the piano). We know that today post-serial music has radically altered the role of the "interpreter," who is called on to be in some sort the co-author of the score, completing it rather than giving it "expression." The Text is very much a score of this new kind: it asks of the reader a practical collaboration. Which is an important change, for who executes the work? (Mallarmé posed the question, wanting the audience to *produce* the book). Nowadays only the critic executes the work (accepting the play on words). The reduction of reading to a consumption is clearly responsible for the "boredom" experienced by many in the face of the modern ('unreadable') text, the avant-garde film of painting: to be bored means that one cannot produce the text, open it out, *set it going*.

7. This leads us to pose (to propose) a final approach to the Text, that of pleasure. I do not know whether there has ever been a hedonistic

[5]A portmanteau word composed of *aletheia,* "truth," and *theological.* [Ed.]

[6]Playful. [Ed.]

[7]Multiplicity of meaning. [Ed.]

aesthetics (eudæmonist philosophies are themselves rare). Certainly there exists a pleasure of the work (of certain works); I can delight in reading and re-reading Proust, Flaubert, Balzac, even — why not? — Alexandre Dumas. But this pleasure, no matter how keen and even when free from all prejudice, remains in part (unless by some exceptional critical effort) a pleasure of consumption; for if I can read these authors, I also know that I cannot *re-write* them (that it is impossible today to write "like that") and this knowledge, depressing enough, suffices to cut me off from the production of these works, in the very moment their remoteness establishes my modernity (is not to be modern to know clearly what cannot be started over again?). As for the Text, it is bound to *jouissance*,[8] that is to a pleasure without separation. Order of the signifier, the Text participates in its own way in a social utopia; before History (supposing the latter does not opt for barbarism), the Text achieves,

[8]Joy, bliss. See the introduction to Poststructuralism, p. 948. [Ed.]

if not the transparence of social relations, that at least of language relations: the Text is that space where no language has a hold over any other, where languages circulate (keeping the circular sense of the term).

These few propositions, inevitably, do not constitute the articulations of a Theory of the Text and this is not simply the result of the failings of the person here presenting them (who in many respects has anyway done no more than pick up what is being developed round about him). It stems from the fact that a Theory of the Text cannot be satisfied by a metalinguistic exposition: the destruction of metalanguage, or at least (since it may be necessary provisionally to resort to metalanguage) its calling into doubt, is part of the theory itself: the discourse on the Text should itself be nothing other than text, research, textual activity, since the Text is that *social* space which leaves no language safe, outside, nor any subject of the enunciation in position as judge, master, analyst, confessor, decoder. The theory of the Text can coincide only with a practice of writing.

# Paul de Man
## 1919–1983

*At once the most suasive and reticent of deconstructive theorists, Paul de Man exerted a powerful influence on a generation of the most elite students of literature in the United States. Born in Antwerp to a prominent Belgian family, de Man studied science and philosophy at the University of Brussels from 1939 to 1942. In 1947 he moved to New York City and from 1949 to 1951 taught at Bard College. Starting in 1952 de Man attended Harvard University, earning a Ph.D. in comparative literature in 1960. From there he moved on to teach at Cornell (1960–67), Johns Hopkins (1967–70), and Yale (1970–83), where he taught until his death. For a theorist of his stature, de Man published little criticism, all of it in the form of essays:* Blindness and Insight: Essays in the Rhetoric of Contemporary Criticism *(1971; revised 1983);* Allegories of Reading: Figural Language in Rousseau, Nietzsche, Rilke, and Proust *(1979);* The Rhetoric of Romanticism *(1984);* The Resistance to Theory *(1986; edited by Wlad Godzich). Since his death, de Man's reputation has been tarnished by the revelation that during World War II, when he was a student at the University of Brussels, he wrote anti-Semitic articles for a publication that sympathized with the Nazi regime (these columns and reviews are collected in* Wartime Journalism: 1940–1942, 1988). *"Semiology and Rhetoric," originally published in* Diacritics *(1975), is reprinted from* Allegories of Reading.

# Semiology and Rhetoric

To judge from various recent publications, the spirit of the times is not blowing in the direction of formalist and intrinsic criticism. We may no longer be hearing very much about relevance, but we do continue to hear a great deal about reference, about the nonverbal "outside" to which language refers, by which it is conditioned, and upon which it acts. The stress falls not so much on the fictional status of literature — a property now perhaps somewhat too easily taken for granted — but on the interplay between these fictions and categories that are said to partake of reality, such as the self, man, society, "the artist, his culture, and the human community," as one critic puts it. Hence the emphasis on hybrid texts considered to be partly literary and partly referential, on popular fictions deliberately aimed toward social and psychological gratification, on literary autobiography as a key to the understanding of the self, and so on. We speak as if, with the problems of literary form resolved once and forever, and with techniques of structural analysis refined to near-perfection, we could now move "beyond formalism" toward the questions that really interest us and reap, at last, the fruits of the ascetic concentration on techniques that prepared us for this decisive step. With the internal law and order of literature well policed, we can now confidently devote ourselves to the foreign affairs, the external politics of literature. Not only do we feel able to do so, but we also think we owe it to ourselves to take this step: our moral conscience would not allow us to do otherwise. Behind the assurance that valid interpretation is possible, behind the recent interest in writing and reading as potentially effective public speech acts, stands a highly respectable moral imperative that strives to reconcile the internal, formal, private structures of literary language with their external, referential, and public effects.

I want, for the moment, to consider briefly this tendency in itself, as an undeniable and recurrent historical fact, without regard for its truth or falseness or for its value as desirable or pernicious. It is a fact that this sort of thing happens again and again in literary studies. On the one hand, literature cannot merely be received as a definite unit of referential meaning that can be decoded without leaving a residue. The code is unusually conspicuous, complex, and enigmatic; it attracts an inordinate amount of attention to itself, and this attention has to acquire the rigor of a method. The structural moment of concentration on the code for its own sake cannot be avoided, and literature necessarily breeds its own formalism. Technical innovations in the methodological study of literature only occur when this kind of attention predominates. It can legitimately be said, for example, that, from a technical point of view, very little has happened in American criticism since the innovative works of the New Criticism. There certainly have been numerous excellent books of criticism since, but in none of them have the techniques of description and interpretation evolved beyond the techniques of close reading established in the forties. Formalism, it seems, is an all-absorbing and tyrannical muse; the hope that one can be at the same time technically original and discursively eloquent is not borne out by the history of literary criticism.

On the other hand — and this is the real mystery — no literary formalism, no matter how accurate and enriching in its analytic powers, is ever allowed to come into being without seeming reductive. When form is considered to be the external trappings of literary meaning or content, it seems superficial and expendable. The development of intrinsic, formalist criticism in the twentieth century has changed this model: form is now a solipsistic category of self-reflection, and the referential meaning is said to be extrinsic. The polarities of inside and outside have been reversed, but they are still the same polarities that are at play: internal meaning has become outside reference, and the outer form has become the intrinsic structure. A new version of reductiveness at once follows this reversal: formalism nowadays is mostly described in an imagery of imprisonment and claustrophobia: the "prison house of language," "the impasse of formalist criticism," and the like. Like the grandmother in Proust's novel, ceaselessly driving the young Marcel out into the garden, away from the unhealthy inwardness of his closeted reading, critics cry out for the fresh air of referential meaning. Thus, with the structure of the code so opaque, but with the meaning so anxious to blot out the obstacle of form, it is no wonder that the reconciliation of form and meaning seems so attractive. The attraction of reconciliation is the elective breeding-ground of false models and metaphors; it accounts for the metaphorical model of literature as a kind of box that separates an inside from an outside, with the reader or critic as the person who opens the lid in order to release into the open what was secreted but inaccessible inside. It matters little whether we call the inside of the box the content or the form and the outside the meaning or the appearance. The recurrent debate opposing intrinsic to extrinsic criticism stands under the aegis of an inside/ outside metaphor that has never been seriously questioned.

Metaphors are much more tenacious than facts, and I certainly don't expect to dislodge this age-old model in one short expository essay. I merely wish to speculate on a different set of terms, perhaps less simple in their differential relationship than the strictly polar, binary opposition between inside and outside, and therefore less likely to enter into the easy play of chiasmic reversals. I derive these terms (which are as old as the hills) pragmatically from the observation of developments and debates in recent critical methodology.

One of the most controversial among these developments coincides with a new approach to poetics — or, as it is called in Germany, poetology — as a branch of general semiotics. In France, a semiology of literature was the outcome of the long-deferred but all the more explosive encounter of the nimble French literary mind with the category of form. Semiology, as opposed to semantics, is the science or study of signs as signifiers; it does not ask what words mean but how they mean. Unlike American New Criticism, which derived the internalization of

form from the practice of highly self-conscious modern writers, French semiology turned to linguistics for its model and adopted Saussure and Jakobson rather than Valéry or Proust for its masters.[1] By an awareness of the arbitrariness of the sign (Saussure) and of literature as an autotelic statement "focused on the way it is expressed" (Jakobson), the entire question of meaning can be bracketed, thus freeing critical discourse from the debilitating burden of paraphrase. The demystifying power of semiology, within the context of French historical and thematic criticism, has been considerable. It demonstrated that the perception of the literary dimensions of language is largely obscured if one submits uncritically to the authority of reference. It also revealed how tenaciously this authority continues to assert itself in a variety of disguises, ranging from the crudest ideology to the most refined forms of aesthetic and ethical judgment. It especially exploded the myth of semantic correspondence between sign and referent, the wishful hope of having it both ways, of being, to paraphrase Marx, a formalist critic in the morning and a communal moralist in the afternoon, of serving both the technique of form and the substance of meaning. The results, in the practice of French criticism, have been as fruitful as they are irreversible. Perhaps for the first time since the late eighteenth century, French critics can come at least somewhat closer to the kind of linguistic awareness that never ceased to be operative in French poets and novelists, that forced all of them, including Sainte-Beuve, to write their main works "contre Sainte-Beuve."[2] The distance was never so considerable in England and the United States, which does not mean, however, that we may be able, in this country, to dispense with a preventative semiological hygiene altogether.

One of the most striking characteristics of literary semiology as it is practiced today, in France and elsewhere, is the use of grammatical (especially syntactical) structures conjointly with

[1]See the introduction to Structuralism and Semiotics, Ch. 4. [Ed.]

[2]"Against Sainte-Beuve," the title of a book by Marcel Proust. [Ed.]

rhetorical structures, without apparent awareness of a possible discrepancy between them. In their literary analyses, Barthes, Genette, Todorov, Greimas, and their disciples all simplify and regress from Jakobson in letting grammar and rhetoric function in perfect continuity, and in passing from grammatical to rhetorical structures without difficulty or interruption. Indeed, as the study of grammatical structures is refined in contemporary theories of generative, transformational, and distributive grammar, the study of tropes and of figures (which is how the term rhetoric is used throughout this essay, not in the derived sense of comment, eloquence, or persuasion) becomes a mere extension of grammatical models, a particular subset of syntactical relations. In the recent *Dictionnaire encyclopédique des sciences du langage,* Ducrot and Todorov write: " . . . rhetoric has always been satisfied with a paradigmatic view over words (word substituting for each other), without questioning their syntagmatic relationship (the contiguity of words to each other). There ought to be another perspective, complementary to the first, in which metaphor, for example, would not be defined as a substitution but as a particular type of combination. Research inspired by linguistics or, more narrowly, by syntactical studies, has begun to reveal this possibility — but it remains to be explored."[3] Todorov, who calls one of his books a *Grammar of the Decameron,*[4] rightly thinks of his own work and that of his associates as first explorations in the elaboration of a systematic grammar of literary modes, genres, and also literary figures. Perhaps the most perceptive work to come out of this school, Genette's studies of figural modes, can be shown to be assimilations of rhetorical transformations or combinations to syntactical, grammatical patterns. Thus a recent study, now printed in *Figures III* and entitled "Métonymie chez Proust," shows the combined presence, in a wide and astute selection of passages, of paradigmatic, metaphorical figures with syntagmatic, metonymic structures.[5] The combination of both is treated descriptively and nondialectically without suggesting the possibility of logical tensions.

One can ask whether this reduction of figure to grammar is legitimate. The existence of grammatical structures within and beyond the unit of the sentence in literary texts is undeniable, and their description and classification are indispensable. The question remains if and how figures of rhetoric can be included in such a taxonomy. This question is at the core of the debate going on, in a wide variety of apparently unrelated forms, in contemporary poetics; but I do not plan to make clear the connection between this "real" problem and the countless pseudo-problems that agitate literary studies. This historical picture of contemporary criticism is too confused to make the mapping out of such a topography a useful exercise. Not only are these questions mixed in and mixed up within particular groups or local trends, but they are often co-present, without apparent contradiction, within the work of a single author.

Neither is the theory of the question suitable for quick expository treatment. To distinguish the epistemology of grammar from the epistemology of rhetoric is a redoubtable task. On an entirely naive level, we tend to conceive of grammatical systems as tending toward universality and as simply generative, that is, as capable of deriving an infinity of versions from a single model (that may govern transformations as well as derivations) without the intervention of another model that would upset the first. We therefore think of the relationship between grammar and logic, the passage from grammar to propositions, as being relatively unproblematic: no true propositions are conceivable in the absence of grammatical consistency or of controlled deviation from a system of consistency no matter how complex. Grammar and logic stand to each other in a dyadic relationship of unsubverted support. In a logic of acts rather than of statements, as in Austin's theory of speech acts,[6] which has had such a

---

[3]From the entry on rhetoric in Ducrot and Todorov, *Dictionnaire encyclopédique des sciences du langage* (Paris, Seuil, 1972), p. 352. [Au.]

[4]Tzvetan Todorov, *Grammaire du Décaméron* (The Hague: Mouton, 1969). [Ed.]

[5]Gérard Genette, *Figures III* (Paris: Seuil, 1972), pp. 41–63. [Au.]

[6]See J. L. Austin, *How to Do Things with Words.* [Ed.]

strong influence on recent American work in literary semiology, it is also possible to move between speech acts and grammar without difficulty. The performance of what are called illocutionary acts, such as ordering, questioning, denying, and assuming, within the language is congruent with the grammatical structures of syntax in the corresponding imperative, interrogative, negative, and optative sentences. "The rules of illocutionary acts," writes Richard Ohmann in a recent paper, "determine whether performance of a given act is well-executed, in just the same way as grammatical rules determine whether the product of a locutionary act — a sentence — is well formed. . . . But whereas the rules of grammar concern the relationships among sound, syntax, and meaning, the rules of illocutionary acts concern relationships among people."[7] And since rhetoric is then conceived exclusively as persuasion, as actual action upon others (and not as an intralinguistic figure or trope), the continuity between the illocutionary realm of grammar and the perlocutionary realm of rhetoric is self-evident. It becomes the basis for a new rhetoric that, exactly as is the case for Todorov and Genette, would also be a new grammar.

Without engaging the substance of the question, it can be pointed out, without having to go beyond recent and American examples, and without calling upon the strength of an age-old tradition, that the continuity here assumed between grammar and rhetoric is not borne out by theoretical and philosophical speculation. Kenneth Burke mentions *deflection* (which he compares structurally to Freudian displacement), defined as "any slight bias or even unintended error," as the rhetorical basis of language, and deflection is then conceived as a dialectical subversion of the consistent link between sign and meaning that operates within grammatical patterns;[8] hence Burke's well-known insistence on the distinction between grammar and rhetoric. Charles Sanders Peirce, who, with Nietzsche and Saussure, laid the philosophical foundation for modern semiology, stressed the distinction between grammar and rhetoric in his celebrated and so suggestively unfathomable definition of the sign. He insists, as is well known, on the necessary presence of a third element, called the interpretant, within any relationship that the sign entertains with its object. The sign must be interpreted if we are to understand the idea it is to convey, and this is so because the sign is not the thing but a meaning derived from the thing by a process — here called representation — that is not simply generative, that is, dependent on a univocal origin. The interpretation of the sign is not, for Peirce, a meaning but another sign; it is a reading, not a decodage, and this reading has, in its turn, to be interpreted into another sign, and so on, ad infinitum. Peirce calls this process by means of which "one sign gives birth to another" pure rhetoric, as distinguished from pure grammar, which postulates the possibility of unproblematic, dyadic meaning, and pure logic, which postulates the possibility of the universal truth of meanings. Only if the sign engendered meaning in the same way that the object engenders the sign — that is, by representation — would there be no need to distinguish between grammar and rhetoric.[9]

These remarks should indicate at least the existence and the difficulty of the question, a difficulty which puts its concise theoretical exposition beyond my powers. I must retreat therefore into a pragmatic discourse and try to illustrate the tension between grammar and rhetoric in a few specific textual examples. Let me begin by considering what is perhaps the most commonly known instance of an apparent symbiosis between a grammatical and a rhetorical structure,

[7]"Speech, Literature, and the Space in Between," *New Literary History* 4 (1971). [Au.]

[8]Kenneth Burke, "Rhetoric — Old and New," *Journal of General Education* 5 (1951), rpt. in *New Rhetorics*, ed. Martin Steinmann, Jr. (New York: Scribner, 1967), p. 75. [Au.]

[9]See Peirce, *Collected Papers*, ed. Charles Hartshorne and Paul Weiss (Cambridge, Mass.: Harvard University Press, 1960), II, 156–157: " . . . if a sunflower, in turning toward the sun, becomes by that very act fully capable, without further condition, of reproducing a sunflower which turns in precisely corresponding ways toward the sun, and of so doing with the same reproductive power, the sunflower would become a Representamen [and not a sign] of the sun." It seems, however, that thought-signs, or words, are in this respect precisely not heliotropic. [Au.]

the so-called rhetorical question, in which the figure is conveyed directly by means of a syntactical device. I take the first example from the subliterature of the mass media: asked by his wife whether he wants to have his bowling shoes laced over or laced under, Archie Bunker[10] answers with a question. He asks, "What's the difference?" Being a reader of sublime simplicity, his wife replies by patiently explaining the difference between lacing over and lacing under, whatever this may be, but provokes only ire. "What's the difference?" did not ask for difference but meant instead "I don't give a damn what the difference is." The same grammatical pattern engenders two meanings that are mutually exclusive: the literal meaning asks for the concept (difference) whose existence is denied by the figurative meaning. As long as we are talking about bowling shoes, the consequences are relatively trivial; Archie Bunker, who is a great believer in the authority of origins (as long, of course, as they are the right origins), muddles along in a world where literal and figurative meanings get in each other's way, though not without discomforts. But if a de-Bunker rather than a Bunker, a de-bunker of the *arché* (origin), an "Archie Debunker" such as Nietzsche or Jacques Derrida, asks the question "What is the Difference?" we cannot even tell from his grammar whether he "really" wants to know "what" difference is or is merely telling us that we should not even try to find out. Confronted with the question of the difference between grammar and rhetoric, grammar allows us to ask the question, but the sentence by means of which we ask it may deny the very possibility of asking. For what is the use of asking, I ask, when we cannot even authoritatively decide whether a question asks or doesn't ask?

The point is as follows. A perfectly clear syntactical paradigm (the question) engenders a sentence that has at least two meanings, one which asserts and the other which denies its own illocutionary mode. It is not that there are simply two meanings, one literal and the other figural, and that we have to decide which one of these

meanings is the right one in this particular situation. The confusion can only be cleared up by the intervention of an extratextual intention, such as Archie Bunker setting his wife straight; but the very anger he displays is indicative of more than impatience: it reveals his despair when confronted with a structure of linguistic meaning that he cannot control and that holds the discouraging prospect of an infinity of similar future confusions, all of them potentially catastrophic in their consequences. Nor is this intervention really a part of the minitext constituted by the figure, which holds our attention only as long as it remains suspended and unresolved. I follow the usage of common speech in calling this semiological enigma "rhetorical." The grammatical model of the question becomes rhetorical not when we have, on the one hand, a literal meaning and, on the other hand, a figural meaning, but when it is impossible to decide by grammatical or other linguistic devices which of the two meanings (that can be entirely contradictory) prevails. Rhetoric radically suspends logic and opens up vertiginous possibilities of referential aberration. And although it would perhaps be somewhat more remote from common usage, I would not hesitate to equate the rhetorical, figural potentiality of language with literature itself. I could point to a great number of antecedents to this equation of literature with figure; the most recent reference would be to Monroe Beardsley's insistence in his contribution to the essays in honor of William Wimsatt that literary language is characterized by being "distinctly above the norm in ratio of implicit (or, I would say rhetorical) to explicit meaning."[11]

Let me pursue the question of the rhetorical question through one more example. Yeats's "Among School Children" ends with the famous line: "How can we know the dancer from the dance?" Although there are some revealing inconsistencies within the commentaries, the line is usually interpreted as stating, with the increased emphasis of a rhetorical device, the po-

---

[10]Irascible protagonist of the 1970s television comedy series *All in the Family.* [Ed.]

[11]Frank Brady, John Palmer, and Martin Price, eds., *Literary Theory and Structure: Essays in Honor of William K. Wimsatt* (New Haven: Yale University Press, 1973), p. 37. [Au.]

tential unity between form and experience, between creator and creation. It could be said that it denies the discrepancy between the sign and the referent from which we started. Many elements in the imagery and the dramatic development of the poem strengthen this traditional reading; without having to look any further than the immediately preceding lines, one finds powerful consecrated images of the continuity from part to whole that makes synecdoche into the most seductive of metaphors: the organic beauty of the tree, stated in the parallel syntax of a similar rhetorical question, or the convergence, in the dance, of erotic desire with musical form:

> O chestnut tree, great-rooted blossomer,
> Are you the leaf, the blossom or the bole?
> O body swayed to music, O brightening glance,
> How can we know the dancer from the dance?

A more extended reading, always assuming that the final line is to be read as a rhetorical question, reveals that the thematic and rhetorical grammar of the poem yields a consistent reading that extends from the first line to the last and that can account for all the details in the text. It is equally possible, however, to read the last line literally rather than figuratively, as asking with some urgency the question asked at the beginning of this essay within the context of contemporary criticism: it is *not* that sign and referent are so exquisitely fitted to each other that all difference between them is at times blotted out; but, rather, since the two essentially different elements, sign and meaning, are so intricately intertwined in the imagined "presence" which the poem addresses, how can we possibly make the distinctions that would shelter us from the error of identifying what cannot be identified? The clumsiness of the paraphrase reveals that it is not necessarily the literal reading which is simpler than the figurative one, as was the case in my first example; here the figural reading, which assumes the question to be rhetorical, is perhaps naive, whereas the literal reading leads to greater complications of theme and statement. For it turns out that the entire scheme set up by the first reading can be undermined, or reconstructed, in the terms of the second, in which the final line is read literally as meaning that, since the dancer and the dance are

not the same, it might be useful, perhaps even desperately necessary — for the question can be given a ring of urgency: "Please tell me, how *can* I know the dancer from the dance?" — to tell them apart. But this will replace the reading of each symbolic detail by a divergent interpretation. The oneness of trunk, leaf, and blossom, for example, that would have appealed to Goethe, would find itself replaced by the much less reassuring Tree of Life from the Mabinogion[12] that appears in the poem "Vacillation," in which the fiery blossom and the earthly leaf are held together, as well as apart, by the crucified and castrated god Attis, of whose body it can hardly be said that it is "not bruised to pleasure soul." This hint should suffice to suggest that two entirely coherent but entirely incompatible readings can be made to hinge on one line whose grammatical structure is devoid of ambiguity but whose rhetorical mode turns the mood as well as the mode of the entire poem upside down. Neither can we say, as was already the case in the first example, that the poem simply has two meanings which exist side by side. The two readings have to engage each other in direct confrontation, for the one reading is precisely the error denounced by the other and has to be undone by it. Nor can we in any way make a valid decision as to which of the readings can be given priority over the other; neither can exist in the other's absence. There can be no dance without a dancer, no sign without a referent. On the other hand, the authority of the meaning engendered by the grammatical structure is fully obscured by the duplicity of a figure that cries out for the differentiation that it conceals.

Yeats's poem is not explicitly "about" rhetorical questions but about images or metaphors, and about the possibility of convergence between experiences of consciousness such as memory or emotions (what the poem calls passion, piety, and affection) and entities accessible to the senses, such as bodies, persons, or icons. We return to the inside/outside model from which we started and which the poem puts into question by means of a syntactical device (the question) made

12Welsh Arthurian epic. [Ed.]

to operate on a grammatical as well as on a rhetorical level. The couple grammar/rhetoric, certainly not a binary opposition since they in no way exclude each other, disrupts and confuses the neat antithesis of the inside/outside pattern. We can transfer this scheme to the act of reading and interpretation. By reading we get, as we say, inside a text that was first something alien to us and which we now make our own by an act of understanding. But this understanding becomes at once the representation of an extratextual meaning; in Austin's terms, the illocutionary speech act becomes a perlocutionary actual act; in Frege's terms, *Bedeutung* becomes *Sinn*.[13] Our recurrent question is whether this transformation is semantically controlled along grammatical or along rhetorical lines. Does the metaphor of reading really unite outer meaning and inner understanding, action and reflection, into one single totality? The assertion is powerfully and suggestively made in a passage from Proust that describes the experience of reading as such a union. It describes the young Marcel hiding in the closed space of his room in order to read. The example differs from the earlier ones in that we are not dealing with a grammatical structure which also functions rhetorically but have instead the representation, the dramatization, in terms of the experience of a subject, of a rhetorical structure — just as, in many other passages, Proust dramatizes tropes by means of landscapes or descriptions of objects. The figure here dramatized is that of metaphor, an inside/outside correspondence as represented by the act of reading. The reading scene is the culmination of a series of actions taking place in enclosed spaces and leading up to the "dark coolness" of Marcel's room.

I had stretched out on my bed, with a book, in my room which sheltered, tremblingly, its transparent and fragile coolness against the afternoon sun, behind the almost closed blinds through which a glimmer of daylight had nevertheless managed to push its yellow wings, remaining motionless between the wood and the glass, in a corner, poised like a butterfly. It was hardly light enough to read, and the sensation of the light's splendor was given to me only by the noise of Camus . . . hammering dusty crates; resounding in the sonorous atmosphere that is peculiar to hot weather, they seemed to spark off scarlet stars; and also by the flies executing their little concert, the chamber music of summer: evocative not in the manner of a human tune that, heard perchance during the summer, afterwards reminds you of it; it is connected to summer by a more necessary link: born from beautiful days, resurrecting only when they return, containing some of their essence, it does not only awaken their image in our memory; it guarantees their return, their actual, persistent, unmediated presence.

The dark coolness of my room related to the full sunlight of the street as the shadow relates to the ray of light, that is to say it was just as luminous and it gave my imagination the total spectacle of the summer, whereas my senses, if I had been on a walk, could only have enjoyed it by fragments; it matched my repose which (thanks to the adventures told by my book and stirring my tranquility) supported, like the quiet of a motionless hand in the middle of a running brook, the shock and the motion of a torrent of activity.[14]

From the beginning of the passage, inwardness is valorized positively as something desirable that has to protect itself against the intrusion of outside forces, but that nevertheless has to borrow, as it were, some of its constitutive properties from the outside. A chain of binary properties is set up and antithetically differentiated in terms of the inside/outside polarity: properties of coolness, darkness, repose, silence, imagination, and totality, associated with inwardness, contrast with the heat, the light, the activity, the sounds, the senses, and the fragmentation that govern the outside. By the act of reading, these static oppositions are put in motion, thus allowing for the play of substitutions by means of which the claim for totalization can be made. Thus, in a beautifully seductive effort of chiaroscuro,[15] mediated by the metaphor of light as a poised butterfly, the inner room is convincingly said to acquire the amount of light necessary to reading. In the wake of this light, warmth can also enter the

[13]Significance becomes meaning. For a discussion of these terms in Frege, see Hirsch, Ch. 9. [Ed.]

[14]*A la recherche du temps perdu* (Paris: Pléiade, 1954), I, 83. Translation by de Man. [Au.]

[15]Mixture of light and shadow. [Ed.]

room, incarnate in the auditive synaesthesia[16] of the various sounds. According to the narrator, these metaphorical substitutions and reversals render the presence of summer in the room more completely than the actual experience of summer in the outside world could have done. The text achieves this synthesis and comments on it in normative[17] terms, comparable to the manner in which treatises of practical rhetoric recommend the use of one figure in preference to another in a given situation: here it is the substitutive totalization by metaphor which is said to be more effective than the mere contiguity of metonymic association. As opposed to the random contingency of metonymy ("*par hasard*"),[18] the metaphor is linked to its proper meaning by, says Proust, the "necessary link" that leads to perfect synthesis. In the wake of this synthesis, the entire conceptual vocabulary of metaphysics enters the text: a terminology of generation, of transcendental necessity, of totality, of essence, of permanence, and of unmediated presence. The passage acts out and asserts the priority of metaphor over metonymy in terms of the categories of metaphysics and with reference to the act of reading.

The actual test of the truth of the assertion comes in the second paragraph when the absurd ratio set up at the beginning has to be verified by a further substitution. This time, what has to be exchanged are not only the properties of light and dark, warm and cool, fragment and totality (part and whole), but the properties of action and repose. The full seduction of the text can come into being only when the formal totalization of light and dark is completed by the transfer from rest to action that represents the extratextual, referential moment. The text asserts the transfer in the concluding sentence: "The dark coolness of my room . . . supported, like the quiet of a motionless hand in the middle of a running brook, the shock and the motion of a torrent of activity." The verb "to support" here carries the full weight of uniting rest and action (*repos et*

*activité*), fiction and reality, as firmly as the base supports the column. The transfer, as is so often the case in Proust, is carried out by the liquid element of the running brook. The natural, representational connotation of the passage is with coolness, so particularly attractive within the predominant summer-mood of the entire *Recherche*. But coolness, it will be remembered, is one of the characteristic properties of the "inside" world. It cannot therefore by itself transfer us into the opposite world of activity. The movement of the water evokes a freshness which in the binary logic of the passage is associated with the inward, imaginary world of reading and fiction. In order to accede to action, it would be necessary to capture one of the properties belonging to the opposite chain, such as warmth. The mere "cool" action of fiction cannot suffice: it is necessary to reconcile the cool immobility of the hand with the heat of action if the claim made by the sentence is to stand up as true. This transfer is carried out, within the same sentence, when it is said that repose supports "a torrent of activity." The expression "torrent d'activité" is not, or is no longer, a metaphor in French: it is a cliché, a dead or sleeping metaphor that has lost the suggestive, connotative values contained in the word "torrent." It simply means "a great deal of activity," the amount of activity that is likely to agitate one to the point of getting hot. Heat is thus surreptitiously smuggled into the passage from a cold source, closing the ring of antithetical properties and allowing for their exchange and substitution: from the moment tranquility can be active and warm without losing its coolness and its distinctive quality of repose, the fragmented experience of reality can become whole without losing its quality of being real.

The transfer is made to seem convincing and seductive by the double play of the cliché "torrent of activity." The proximate, contiguous image of the brook awakens, as it were, the sleeping beauty of the dozing metaphor which, in its common use, had become the metonymic association of two words united by sheer habit and no longer by the inner necessity, the "necessary link," of a transcendental signification. "Torrent" functions in a double semantic register: in its reawakened literal meaning it relays the attribute of coolness

---

[16]Sensual confusion, as when a sound strikes one as like a color. [Ed.]

[17]Evaluative. [Ed.]

[18]By chance. [Ed.]

that is actually part of the running water, whereas in its figural nonmeaning it designates the quantity of activity connotative of the contrary property of warmth.

The rhetorical structure of this sentence is therefore not simply metaphorical. It is at least doubly metonymic, first because the coupling of words in a cliché is governed not by the necessary link that reveals their potential identity but by the contingent habit of proximity; second, because the reawakening of the metaphorical term "torrent" is carried out by a statement that happens to be in the vicinity, but without there being any necessity for this proximity on the level of the referential meaning. The most striking thing is that this doubly metonymic structure is found in a text that also contains highly seductive and successful metaphors (as in the chiaroscuro effect of the beginning, or in the condensation of light in the butterfly image) and that explicitly asserts the superiority of metaphor over metonymy in terms of metaphysical categories.

That these metaphysical categories do not remain unaffected by such a reading would become clear from an inclusive reading of Proust's novel and would become even more explicit in a language-conscious philosopher such as Nietzsche who, as a philosopher, has to be concerned with the epistemological consequences of the kind of rhetorical seductions exemplified by the Proust passage. It can be shown that the systematic critique of the main categories of metaphysics undertaken by Nietzsche in his late work, the critique of the concepts of causality, of the subject, of identity, of referential and revealed truth, and others, occurs along the same pattern of deconstruction that is operative in Proust's text; and it can also be shown that this pattern exactly corresponds to Nietzsche's description, in texts that precede *The Will to Power* by more than fifteen years, of the structure of the main rhetorical tropes. The key to this critique of metaphysics, which is itself a recurrent gesture throughout the history of thought, is the rhetorical model of the trope or, if one prefers to call it that, literature. It turns out that in these innocent-looking didactic exercises we are in fact playing for very sizable stakes.

It is therefore all the more necessary to know

what is linguistically involved in a rhetorically conscious reading of the type here undertaken on a brief fragment from a novel and extended by Nietzsche to the entire text of post-Hellenic thought. Our first examples, which dealt with rhetorical questions, were rhetorizations of grammar, figures generated by syntactical paradigms, whereas the Proust example could be better described as a grammatization of rhetoric. The passage from a paradigmatic structure based on contingent association, such as metonymy, shows the mechanical, repetitive aspect of grammatical forms to be operative in a passage that seems at first sight to celebrate the self-willed and autonomous inventiveness of a subject. Figures are assumed to be inventions, the products of a highly particularized individual talent, whereas no one can claim credit for the programmed pattern of grammar. Yet our reading of the Proust passage shows that precisely when the highest claims are being made for the unifying power of metaphor, these very images rely in fact on the deceptive use of semi-automatic grammatical patterns. The deconstruction of metaphor and of all rhetorical patterns, such as mimesis, paronomasis,[19] or personification, that use resemblance as a way to disguise differences, takes us back to the impersonal precision of grammar and of a semiology derived from grammatical patterns. Such a deconstruction puts into question a whole series of concepts that underlie the value judgments of our critical discourse: the metaphors of primacy, of genetic history, and, most notably, of the autonomous power to will of the self.

There seems to be a difference, then, between what I called the rhetorization of grammar (as in the rhetorical question) and the grammatization of rhetoric, as in the deconstructive readings of the type sketched in the passage from Proust. The former ends up in indetermination, in a suspended uncertainty that was unable to choose between two modes of reading, whereas the latter seems to reach a truth, albeit by the negative road of exposing an error, a false pretense. After the deconstructive reading of the Proust passage we can no longer believe the assertion made in

---

[19]Paronomasia: plays on words, puns. [Ed.]

this passage about the intrinsic, metaphysical superiority of metaphor over metonymy. We seem to end up in a mood of negative assurance that is highly productive of critical discourse. The further text of Proust's novel, for example, responds perfectly to an extended application of this deconstructive pattern: not only can similar gestures be repeated throughout the novel, at all the crucial articulations or all passages where large aesthetic and metaphysical claims are being made (the scenes of involuntary memory, the workshop of Elstir, the septette of Vinteuil, the convergence of author and narrator at the end of the novel), but a vast thematic and semiotic network is revealed, a network that structures the entire narrative and that remains invisible to a reader caught in a naive metaphorical mystification. The whole of literature would respond in similar fashion, although the techniques and the patterns would have to vary considerably, of course, from author to author. But there is absolutely no reason why analyses of the kind here suggested for Proust would not be applicable, with proper modifications of technique, to Milton or to Dante or to Hölderlin. This will in fact be the task of literary criticism in the coming years.

It would seem that we are saying that criticism is the deconstruction of literature, the reduction to the rigors of grammar of rhetorical mystifications. And if we hold up Nietzsche as the philosopher of such a critical deconstruction, then the literary critic would become the philosopher's ally in his struggle with the poets. Criticism and literature would separate around the epistemological axis that distinguishes grammar from rhetoric. It is easy enough to see that this apparent glorification of the critic-philosopher in the name of truth is in fact a glorification of the poet as the primary source of this truth; if truth is the recognition of the systematic character of a certain kind of error, then it would be fully dependent on the prior existence of this error. Philosophers of science like Gaston Bachelard or Wittgenstein are notoriously dependent on the aberrations of the poets. We are back at our unanswered question: does the grammatization of rhetoric end up in the negative certainty, or does it, like the rhetorization of grammar, remain suspended in the ignorance of its own truth or falsehood?

Two concluding remarks should suffice to answer the question. First of all, it is not true that Proust's text can simply be reduced to the mystified assertion — the superiority of metaphor over metonymy — that our reading deconstructs. The reading is not "our" reading, since it uses only the linguistic elements provided by the text itself; the distinction between author and reader is one of the false distinctions that the deconstruction makes evident. The deconstruction is not something we have added to the text; it constituted the text in the first place. A literary text simultaneously asserts and denies the authority of its own rhetorical mode; and, by reading the text as we did, we were only trying to come closer to being as rigorous a reader as the author had to be in order to write the sentence in the first place. Poetic writing is the most advanced and refined mode of deconstruction; it may differ from critical or discursive writing in the economy of its articulation, but it is not different in kind.

But if we recognize the existence of the deconstructive moment as constitutive of all literary language, we have surreptitiously reintroduced the categories that this deconstruction was supposed to eliminate and that have merely been displaced. We have, for example, displaced the question of the self from the referent into the figure of the narrator, who then becomes the *signifié*[20] of the passage. It again becomes possible to ask such naive questions as what Proust's, or Marcel's, motives may have been in thus manipulating language: was he fooling himself, or was he represented as fooling himself and fooling us into believing that fiction and action are as easy to unite, by reading, as the passage asserts? The pathos of the entire section, which would have been more noticeable if the quotation had been a little more extended, the narrator's constant vacillation between guilt and well-being, invites such questions. They are absurd questions, of course, since the reconciliation of fact and fiction occurs itself as a mere assertion made in a text, and is thus productive of more text at the moment when it asserts its decision to escape from textual confinement. But even if we free ourselves of all false questions of intent and

[20]Signified; the thing represented by a sign. [Ed.]

rightfully reduce the narrator to the status of a mere grammatical pronoun, without which the deconstructive narrative could not come into being, this subject remains endowed with a function that is not grammatical but rhetorical, in that it gives voice, so to speak, to a grammatical syntagm.[21] The term "voice," even when we speak of the passive or interrogative voice, is, of course, a metaphor inferring by analogy the intent of the subject from the structure of the predicate. In the case of the deconstructive discourse that we call literary, or rhetorical, or poetic, this creates a distinctive complication illustrated by the Proust passage. The deconstructive reading revealed a first paradox: the passage valorizes metaphor as being the "right" literary figure, but then proceeds to constitute itself by means of the epistemologically incompatible figure of metonymy. The deconstructive critical discourse reveals the presence of this delusion and affirms it as the irreversible mode of its truth. It cannot pause there however. For if we then ask the obvious and simple next question, whether the rhetorical mode of the text in question is that of metaphor or metonymy, it is impossible to give an answer. Individual metaphors, such as the chiaroscuro effect or the butterfly, are shown to be subordinate figures in a general clause whose syntax is metonymic; from this point of view, it seems that the rhetoric is superseded by a grammar that deconstructs it. But this metonymic clause has as its subject a voice whose relationship to this clause is again metaphorical. The narrator who tells us about the impossibility of metaphor is himself, or itself, a metaphor, the metaphor of a grammatical syntagm whose meaning is the denial of metaphor stated, by antiphrasis, as its priority. And this subject-metaphor is, in its turn, open to the kind of deconstruction to the second degree, the rhetorical deconstruction of psycholinguistics, in which the more advanced investigations of literature are presently engaged, against considerable resistance.

We end up, therefore, in the case of the rhetorical grammatization of semiology, just as in the grammatical rhetorization of illocutionary phrases, in the same state of suspended ignorance. Any question about the rhetorical mode of a literary text is always a rhetorical question that does not even know whether it is really questioning. The resulting pathos is an anxiety (or bliss, depending on one's momentary mood or individual temperament) of ignorance, not an anxiety of reference — as becomes thematically clear in Proust's novel when reading is dramatized, in the relationship between Marcel and Albertine, not as an emotive reaction to what language does, but as an emotive reaction to the impossibility of knowing what it might be up to. Literature as well as criticism — the difference between them being delusive — is condemned (or privileged) to be forever the most rigorous and, consequently, the most unreliable language in terms of which man names and modifies himself.

[21]Linkage. [Ed.]

# Edward W. Said

## b. 1935

*Although his early writings tended to focus on the usefulness of Continental philosophy and interdisciplinary approaches to literary studies, Edward W. Said's work has increasingly come to deal with questions of the relation of literary criticism to politics. Said was born in Jerusalem, and attended Western schools in Jerusalem, Cairo, and Massachusetts; he went on to take his B.A. at Princeton University (1960) and his Ph.D. at Harvard (1964). Since 1963 he has been a professor of English and comparative literature at Columbia University and a visiting professor at Yale, Stanford, Harvard, and Johns Hopkins. Said's professional awards are legion, including a Gug-*

genheim fellowship (1972); his book Orientalism (1978) was a runner up for a National Book Award for criticism. His other work includes Joseph Conrad and the Fiction of Autobiography (1966); Beginnings: Intention and Method (1975); The Question of Palestine (1979); The World, the Text, the Critic (1983); and After the Last Sky: Palestinian Lives (1986). "The Text, the World, the Critic" is reprinted from Textual Strategies (1979), edited by Josué Harari.

# The Text, the World, the Critic

Since he deserted the concert stage during the 1960s, the Canadian pianist Glenn Gould has confined his work to records, television, and radio. There is some disagreement among critics as to whether Gould is always, or only sometimes, a convincing interpreter of one or another piano piece, but there is scarcely a doubt that each of his performances now is at least special. A few years ago, Gould issued a record of his performance of Beethoven's Fifth Symphony in the Liszt piano transcription. Quite aside from being a surprisingly eccentric choice of piece even for the arch-eccentric Gould, who had always been associated with classical music, this particular release had a number of other oddities about it. The piece was not only of the nineteenth century, but of its most discredited aspect, pianistically speaking: the aspect that did not content itself with transforming the concert experience into a feast for the virtuoso's exhibitionism, but also raided the literature of other instruments, making of their music a flamboyant occasion for the pianist's skill. Most transcriptions tend on the whole to sound thick and muddy, since frequently the piano is attempting to copy the sound texture of an orchestra or organ. Liszt's Fifth Symphony was less offensive than most transcriptions, mainly because it was brilliantly reduced for the piano, but even at its most clear the sound was an unusual one for Gould to be producing. His sound previously had been the clearest and most unadorned of all pianists', which was why he had the uncanny ability to turn Bach's counterpoint into an almost visual experience. The Liszt transcription, in short, was an entirely different idiom, yet Gould was very successful in it. He sounded as Lisztian now as he had sounded Bachian in the past.

Nor was this all. Accompanying the main disc was another one, a longish, informal interview of Gould by a record company executive. During the interview Gould told his interlocutor that one reason for his escape from "live" performance was the development of a bad habit in his pianism. On his tours of the Soviet Union, for example, he would notice that the large halls in which he was performing caused him perforce to distort the phrases in a Bach partita — here he demonstrated by playing the distorted phrases — so that he could more effectively "catch" and address his listeners in the eighth balcony. He then played the same phrases to illustrate how much more correctly, and less seductively, he was performing music now that no actual audience was present.

It may seem slightly heavy-handed to draw out some of the little ironies from this situation — transcription, interview, and illustrated performance styles all included. But doing so serves my main point about Gould and the Fifth Symphony: that any occasion involving the aesthetic document or experience on the one hand, and the critic's role and his "worldliness" on the other, cannot be a simple one. Indeed Gould's strategy is something of a parody of all the directions we might take in trying to get at what occurs between the world and the aesthetic object. Here is a pianist who once represented the ascetic performer in the service of the music, transformed now into unashamed virtuoso, whose principal aesthetic standard is supposed to be little higher than that of a musical whore. A man who left the recital stage because it had led him to solicit his audience's attention by altering his playing, now markets his record as a "first" and then adds to it, not more music, but the kind of bid for attention and immediacy offered by a personal interview. And finally all this is fixed on a mechanically replicable object, which controls the most obvious signs of immediacy (Gould's voice, the peacocklike style of the Liszt transcription, the brash informality of an interview packed along with a disembodied performance) beneath, or inside (or is it outside?) a dumb, anonymous, and disposable disc of black plastic.

If one thinks about Gould and his record, parallels will emerge out of the circumstances of written performance. First of all, there is the reproducible material existence of a text. Both a recording and a printed object are subject to similar legal, political, economic, and social constraints, insofar as their sustained production and distribution are concerned; why and how they are distributed are different matters that need not occupy us here. The main thing is that a written text of the sort we care about is originally the result of some immediate contact between author and medium. Thereafter it can be reproduced for the benefit of the world; however much the author demurs at the publicity he receives, once he lets the text go into more than one copy, his work is in the world.

Second, a written and a musical performance are both instances on some level at least of style, in the simplest and least honorific sense of that very complex phenomenon. Once again I must arbitrarily exclude all the more interesting complexities that go into making up the very question of style, in order to insist on style as, from the standpoint of producer and receiver, the recognizable, repeatable, preservable sign of an author who reckons with an audience. Even if the audience is as restricted as his self or as wide as the whole world, the author's style is partially a phenomenon of repetition and reception. But what makes style receivable as the signature of its author's manner is a collection of features variously called idiolect, voice, or more firmly, irreducible individuality. The paradox is that something as impersonal as a text, or a record, can nevertheless deliver an imprint or a trace of something as lively, immediate, and transitory as a "voice." Glenn Gould's interview simply makes brutally explicit the frequent need for recognition that a text carries even in its most pristine, enshrined form; a text needs to show how it bears a personality, for which a common analogy is a talking voice addressing someone. Considered as I have been considering it, style neutralizes, if it does not cancel, the worldlessness, the silent, seemingly uncircumstanced existence of a solitary text. It is not only that any text, if it is not immediately destroyed, is a network of often colliding forces, but also that a text in being a text is a being in the world; it addresses anyone who reads, just as Gould addresses everyone who hears throughout the very same record that is supposed to represent both his withdrawal from the world and his "new" silent style of playing without a live audience.

Of course, texts do not speak in the ordinary sense of the word. Yet any simple diametric opposition that is asserted between speech, on the one hand — or that aspect of speech described by Paul Ricoeur as the situation of discourse and the function of reference — and, on the other hand, the text as an *interception* or *suspension* of speech's worldliness is, I think, misleading and grossly simplified. Here is how Ricoeur puts this opposition, which he claims to be setting up only for the sake of analytic clarification:

In speech the function of reference is linked to the role of the situation of discourse within the exchange of language itself: in exchanging speech, the speakers are present to each other, but also to the circumstantial setting of discourse, not only the perceptual surroundings, but also the cultural background known by both speakers. It is in relation to this situation that discourse is fully meaningful: the reference to reality is in the last analysis reference to that reality which can be pointed out "around," so to speak, the instance of discourse itself. Language . . . and in general all the ostensive indicators of language serve to anchor discourse in the circumstantial reality which surrounds the instance of discourse. Thus, in living speech, the *ideal* meaning of what one says bends towards a *real* reference, namely to that "about which" one speaks. . . .

This is no longer the case when a text takes the place of speech. . . . A text . . . is not without reference; it will be precisely the task of reading, as interpretation, to actualize the reference. At least, in this suspension wherein reference is deferred, in the sense that it is postponed, a text is somehow "in the air" outside of the world or without a world; by means of this obliteration of all relation to the world, every text is free to enter into relation with all the other texts which come to take the place of the circumstantial reality shown by living speech.[1]

I cannot see that such an idealization of the difference between speech and writing is useful. Speech and circumstantial reality exist, according to Ricoeur, in a state of presence, in reality, in the world; writing, the text, exist in a state of suspension — that is, outside circumstantial reality — until they are "actualized" and made present by the reader-critic. There are so many things wrong with this set of ideas that I scarcely know where to begin my attack. Ricoeur makes it seem as if the text and circumstantial reality, or what I shall call worldliness, play a game of musical chairs with each other, one intercepting and replacing the other according to fairly crude signals. But, we might ask, where does this game take place? Certainly not in reality, but in the interpreter's head, a locale presumably without worldliness or circumstantiality. The critic-interpreter has his position reduced to that of a central stock-exchange on whose floor the transaction occurs by which the text is shown to be meaning X while saying Y. And what becomes of what Ricoeur calls "deferred reference" during the interpretation? Quite simply, on the basis of a model of direct exchange, it comes back, brought back whole and actual by the critic's reading.

I suppose the principal difficulty with Ricoeur's opposition is that he assumes, quite without sufficient argument, that circumstantial reality, worldliness as I shall call it, is symmetrically and exclusively the property of speech or the speech situation, or what the writer would have wanted *to say* had he been able to do so, had he not instead chosen to write. My contention is that worldliness does not come and go, nor is it here and there in the apologetic and soupy way we often say that something is "historical," a euphe-

mism in such cases for the impossibly vague notion that all things take place in history. Moreover a critic may often be, but is not merely, the alchemical translator of texts into circumstantial reality or worldliness; for he too is subject to and a producer of circumstances, and these are felt regardless of whatever objectivity his method possesses. Texts have ways of existing, both theoretical and practical, that even in their most rarefied form are always enmeshed in circumstance, time, place, and society — in short, they are in the world, and hence worldly.[2] The same is doubtless true of the critic, as reader and as writer. I shall not be hammering away at these points so much as, in the main part of this essay, trying to note them, to illustrate them as concretely as possible, given the very complex circumstances surrounding and involving all verbal activity.

If my use of Gould's recording of the Beethoven Fifth Symphony served any serious purpose, it provided an instance of a quasi-textual object whose ways of engaging the world are both numerous and complicated, more complicated than the demarcation drawn between text and speech by Ricoeur. These engagements are what I have been calling worldliness. But my principal concern here is not with an aesthetic object in general, but rather with the text in particular. Most critics will subscribe to the notion — a sloppy one, I think — that every literary text, for example, is in some way burdened with its occasion, with the brute empirical realities out of which it emerged. Pressed too far, such a notion earns the justified polemic of a stylistician like Michael Riffaterre, who in an essay entitled "The Self-sufficient Text" calls any reduction of a text to its circumstances a fallacy, biographical, genetic, psychological, or analogic.[3] Most critics would probably go along with Riffaterre in saying, yes, let us make sure that the text does not disappear under the weight of these fallacies, but, and here I speak mainly for myself, they are not entirely satisfied with the idea of a self-sufficient

[1]"What Is a Text? Explanation and Interpretation," in David Rasmussen, *Mythic-Symbolic Language and Philosophical Anthropology: A Constructive Interpretation of the Thought of Paul Ricoeur* (The Hague: Nijhoff, 1971), p. 138. [Au.]

[2]I have discussed this in chapter 4 of *Beginnings: Intention and Method* (New York: Basic Books, 1975). [Au.]

[3]"The Self-sufficient Text," *Diacritics* 3 (Fall 1973): 40. [Au.]

text. Is the alternative to the various fallacies *only* a quite hermetic textual cosmos, a cosmos whose significant dimension of meaning is, as Riffaterre says, a wholly inward one? Is there no way to deal with a text and its worldliness fairly? Is there no means of grappling with the problems of literary language except by cutting those off from the more plainly urgent ones of everyday worldly language?

I have found a way of starting to deal with these questions in an unexpected place, which is why I shall seem to be digressing now from the immediate subject at hand. Several years ago I had the leisure to explore the relatively untapped field of Arabic linguistic speculation. At the time I was very interested, as I still am, in speculation about language in Europe, that is, in that special combination of theoretical imagination and empirical observation characterizing romantic philology, the rise of linguistics in the early nineteenth century, and the whole rich phenomenon of what Foucault has called the discovery of language. I was staggered at my discovery that there had existed among Islamic linguists, during the eleventh century in Andalusia, a remarkably sophisticated and unexpectedly prophetic school of philosophic grammarians, whose polemics anticipated in an uncanny way twentieth-century debates between structuralists and generative grammarians, between descriptivists and behaviorists. Nor was this all. I discovered a small group of linguists whose energies were directed against tendencies among rival linguists to turn the question of meaning in language into esoteric and allegorical exercises. I am referring to three eleventh-century linguists and theoretical grammarians, Ibn Hazm, Ibn Ginni, and Ibn Mada al-Qurtobi, all of Cordova, all Zahirites, all antagonists of Batinism. Batinites — as their name implies — believed that meaning in language is concealed within the words; meaning is therefore available only as the result of what we would call an inward-tending exegesis. The Zahirites — their name derives from the word in Arabic for clear and apparent and phenomenal — argued for the surface meaning of words, a meaning anchored to a particular usage, circumstance, historical and religious anomaly.

Both groups trace their origins back to read-ings of the sacred text, the Koran, and how that unique event — for the Koran, unlike the Bible, is an event — is to be read, understood, transmitted, and taught by later generations of believers. The Cordovan Zahirites attacked the excesses of the Batinites, arguing that the very profession of grammar (in Arabic, *nahu*) was an invitation to spinning out private meanings in an otherwise divinely pronounced text. According to Ibn Mada, it was absurd even to associate grammar with a logic of understanding, since as a science grammar simply assumed, even created reasons and functions for language use that implied a hidden level beneath words, available only to private initiates.[4] Once you resort to such a level, anything more or less becomes permissible in the way of interpretation: there can be no strict meaning, no control over what words in fact say, no responsibility toward the words. The Zahirite effort was to restore and rationalize a system of reading a text in which attention was focused on the words themselves, not on hidden meanings they might contain. The Cordovan Zahirites in particular went very far in trying to provide a reading system placing the tightest possible control over the reader and his circumstances by means of a theory of the text.

I can not here go into this theory in detail. What I can do, however, is indicate how the controversy itself is endemic to a circumstantial, or if you like, a worldly notion of the sacred text, a notion that essentially puts a line of demarcation between Islamic ideas and the main Judeo-Christian textual traditions. There is a brilliant and concise account of this difference in Roger Arnaldez's book on Ibn Hazm, and I can do little better than paraphrase some of his observations. The Judeo-Christian text, at whose center is Revelation, cannot be reduced to a specific point of impact by which the Word of God entered the world; rather the Word enters human history, all along that history, continually, and therefore a very important place is given to what Arnaldez calls "human factors" in the reception,

[4]This is the main, polemical point in his tract *Ar-rad ala l nuhat*, ed. Shawki Daif (Cairo, 1947). The text dates from A.D. 1180. [Au.]

transmission, and understanding of such a text.[5] By contrast the Koran is the result of a unique event, the "descent" into worldliness of a text, whose language and form are thereafter to be viewed as stable, complete, unchanging; the language of the text is Arabic, therefore a greatly privileged language, and its vessel, the messenger Mohammed, similarly privileged. Such a text is an absolute and cannot be referred back to any particular interpreter or interpretation, although this is clearly what the Batinites tried to do (perhaps, it is suggested, under the influence of Judeo-Christian exegetical techniques). Arnaldez puts his description of the Koran in the following terms: the Koran speaks of historical events, yet is not itself historical. It repeats past events, which it condenses and particularizes, yet it is not itself an actually lived experience; it ruptures the human continuity of life; God does not enter temporality by a sustained and/or concerted act. The Koran evokes the memory of actions whose content repeats itself eternally in ways identical with itself, as warnings, orders, imperatives, punishments, rewards (p. 12). In short, the Zahirite position adopts a view of the Koran that is absolutely circumstantial and worldly, without at the same time making that worldliness *dominate* the actual sense of the text — this is the ultimate avoidance of vulgar determination in the Zahirite position.

Hence Ibn Hazm's linguistic theory is based upon an analysis of the *imperative* mode since, in its most radical and verbal form, the Koran, according to Ibn Hazm, is a text controlled by two paradigmatic imperatives, *iqra*: read, or recite, and *qul*: tell (p. 69). Since those imperatives obviously control the circumstantial, worldly, and historical appearance of the Koran (and its uniqueness as an event), and since they must also control uses (that is, readings) of the text thereafter, Ibn Hazm connects his analysis of the imperative mode with a juridical notion of *hadd,* a word meaning both a logico-grammatical defi-

nition and a limit. What transpires in the imperative mode, between the injunctions to read and write, is the delivery of an utterance (*khabar* in Arabic, translated by Arnaldez as *énoncé*), which is the verbal realization of a signifying intention, *niyah.* Now the signifying intention is synonymous not with a psychological intention, but exclusively with a verbal intention, itself something highly worldly — that is, it takes place exclusively in the world, it is occasional and circumstantial in both a very precise and wholly pertinent way. To signify is only to use language, and to use language is to do so according to certain rules, lexical and syntactic, by which language is in and of the world; by that the Zahirite means that language is regulated by real usage, and neither by abstract prescription nor by speculative freedom. Above all, language stands between man and a vast indefiniteness: if the world is a gigantic system of correspondences, then it is verbal form — language in actual grammatical use — that allows us to isolate from among these correspondences the denominated object. Thus, as Arnaldez puts it, fidelity to such true aspects of language is an *askesis* of the imagination (p. 77). A word has a strict meaning understood as an imperative, and with that meaning also a strictly ordained series of resemblances (correspondences) to other words and meanings, which play, strictly, around the first word. Thus figurative language (as it occurs even in the Koran), otherwise elusive and at the mercy of the virtuosic interpreter, is part of the actual, not virtual, structure of language, is a resource therefore of the collectivity of language users.

What Ibn Hazm does, Arnaldez reminds us, is to view language as possessing two seemingly antithetical characteristics: first, that of a divinely ordained institution, unchanging, immutable, logical, rational, intelligible; and second, that of an instrument existing as pure contingency, that is, as an institution signifying meanings anchored in specific utterances (p. 80). It is exactly because the Zahirite sees language in this double perspective that he rejects reading techniques that reduce words and their meanings back to radicals from which (in Arabic at least) they may be seen grammatically to derive. Each utterance is its own occasion and, as such, is firmly anchored

[5]*Grammaire et théologie chez Ibn Hazm de Cordoue* (Paris: J. Vrin, 1956), pp. 12 and passim. There is a clear, somewhat schematic account of Ibn Ginni, Ibn Mada, and others in Anis Fraiha, *Nathariyat fil Lugha* (Beirut: Al-Maktaba al Jamiya, 1973). [Au.]

in the worldly context in which it is applied. And because the Koran, which is the paradigmatic case of divine-and-human language, is a text that incorporates speaking and writing, reading and telling, Zahirite interpretation itself accepts as inevitable not the separation between speech and writing, nor the disjunction between a text and its circumstantiality, but rather their necessary interplay. It is this field of interaction that generates meaning, indeed that makes meaning (in the severe Zahirite sense of the word) at all possible.

I have summarized very quickly an enormously complex theory, in relation to which my own position is still that of an uncertain novice. I cannot claim any particular influence for such a theory, certainly not in Western European literature since the Renaissance, perhaps not even in Arabic literature since the Middle Ages. But what has struck me forcibly about this whole theory is that it represents a considerably articulated thesis for dealing with a text as significant form, in which — and I put this as carefully as I can — worldliness, circumstantiality, the text's status as an event having sensuous particularity as well as historical contingency, are incorporated in the text, are an infrangible part of its capacity for conveying and producing meaning. This means that a text has a specific situation, a situation that places restraints upon the interpreter and his interpretation not because the situation is hidden within the text as a mystery, but rather because the situation exists at the same level of more or less surface particularity as the textual object itself. There are many ways for conveying such a situation, and I shall consider some examples presently. But what I will be drawing attention to is an ambition on the part of a writer to deliver his text as an object whose interpretation — by virtue of the exactness of its situation in the world — *has already commenced* and is therefore already constrained in, and constraining, its interpretation. Such a text can thereafter be construed as needing at most complementary, as opposed to supplementary, reading.

My principal task now is to discuss ways by which texts impose constraints and limits upon their interpretation. Recent critical theory has placed undue emphasis upon the limitlessness of interpretation. Part of this emphasis has been due to a conception of the textual universe, having no connection with actuality. This is a view I oppose, not simply because texts are in the world, but also because as texts they *place* themselves — that is, one of their functions as texts is to place themselves — and they *are* themselves by acting, in the world. Moreover, their manner of doing this is to place restraints upon what can be done with (and to) them interpretively.

Modern literary history gives us a number of examples of writers whose text, as a text, incorporates quite explicitly the circumstances of its very concretely imagined, and even described, situation. One type of author — exemplified by Hopkins, Wilde, and Conrad — conceives his text as supported explicitly by a discursive situation involving speaker and audience; the designed interplay between speech and reception, between verbality and textuality *is* the text's situation, its placing of itself in the world.

The three authors I mentioned wrote their major works between 1875 and 1915. The subject matter of their writing varies so widely that similarities among the three have to be looked for elsewhere. Let me begin with a journal entry by Hopkins:

The winter was called severe. There were three spells of frost with skating, the third beginning on Feb. 9. No snow to speak of till that day. Some days before Feb. 7 I saw catkins hanging. On the 9th there was snow but not lying on the roads. On the grass it became a crust lifted on the heads of the blades. As we went down a field near Caesar's Camp I noticed it before me *squalentem,* coat below coat, sketched in intersecting edges bearing "idiom," all down the slope: — I have no other word yet for that which takes the eye or mind in a bold hand or effective sketching or in marked features or again in graphic writing, which not being beauty nor true inscape yet gives interest and makes ugliness even better than meaninglessness.[6]

Hopkins's earliest writing attempts in this manner to render scenes from nature as exactly as

[6]*The Journals and Papers of Gerard Manley Hopkins,* ed. Humphry House and Graham Storey (London: Oxford University Press, 1959), p. 195. [Au.]

possible. Yet he is never a passive transcriber since for him "this world then is word, expression, news of God."[7] Every phenomenon in nature, he wrote in the sonnet "As kingfishers catch fire," *tells* itself in the world as a sort of lexical unit:

Each mortal thing does one thing and the same:
Deals out that being indoors each one dwells;
Selves — goes itself; *myself* it speaks and spells,
Crying *What I do is me: for that I came.*[8]

So in the notebook entry Hopkins's observation of nature is dynamic. He sees in the frost an intention to speak or mean, its layered coats *taking* one's attention because of the idiom it bears toward meaning or expression. The writer is as much a respondent as he is a describer: similarly the reader is a full participant in the production of meaning, being obliged, as a mortal thing, to do — that is, to act — himself, to produce the sense that, even though ugly, is better than meaninglessness.

This dialectic of production is everywhere present in Hopkins's work. Writing is telling; nature is telling; reading is telling. He wrote to Robert Bridges on May 21, 1878 that in order to do a certain poem justice, "you must not slovenly read it with the eyes but with your ears, as if the paper were declaiming it at you. . . . Stress is the life of it."[9] Seven years later he specified more strictly that "poetry is the darling child of speech, of lips and spoken utterance: it must be spoken; *till it is spoken it is not performed*, it does not perform, it is not itself. Sprung rhythm gives back to poetry its true soul and self. As poetry is emphatically speech, speech purged of dross like gold in the furnace, so it must have emphatically the essential elements of speech."[10] So close is the identification in Hopkins's mind between world, word, and the utterance, the three coming alive together as a moment of performance, that there is no need of critical intervention. It is the written text that provides the immediate circumstantial reality for the poem's "play" (the word is Hopkins's). So far from being a document associated with other lifeless, worldless texts, Hopkins's own text was for him his child; when he destroyed his poems he spoke of the slaughter of the innocents, and everywhere in his career he speaks of writing as the exercise of his male gift. At the moment of great desolation in his career, in such a poem as "To R. B.," the urgency of his feeling of poetic aridity is expressed biologically throughout. When he comes to describe finally what it is he now writes he says:

O then if in my lagging lines you miss
The roll, the rise, the carol, the creation,
My winter world, that scarcely breathes that bliss
Now, yields, you, with some sighs, our explanation.[11]

Because his text has lost its ability to incorporate the stress of creation, and because it is no longer performance but what in another poem he calls "dead letters," he now can write only an explanation, which is lifeless speech "bending towards a real reference" (*pace* Ricoeur).

It was said of Wilde by one of his contemporaries that everything he spoke sounded as if it were enclosed in quotation marks. This is no less true of everything he wrote, for such was the consequence of having a pose, which Wilde defined as "a formal recognition of the importance of treating life from a definite reasoned standpoint."[12] Or as Algernon retorts to Jack's accusation that "you always want to argue about things" in *The Importance of Being Earnest*: "That's exactly what things were originally made for."[13] Always ready with a quotable comment, Wilde filled his manuscripts with epigrams on every conceivable subject. Everything he wrote was intended either for more comment or for quotation or, most important, for tracing back to

[7]Ibid., p. 129 [Au.]

[8]*The Poems of Gerard Manley Hopkins,* ed. W. H. Gardner and N. H. Mackenzie (London: Oxford University Press, 1967), p. 90. [Au.]

[9]*The Letters of Gerard Manley Hopkins to Robert Bridges,* ed. Claude Colleer Abbott (Oxford: Oxford University Press, 1955), pp. 51–52. [Au.]

[10]Quoted in Anthony Bisshof, S. J., "Hopkins' Letters to His Brother," *Times Literary Supplement,* December 8, 1972, p. 1511. [Au.]

[11]*Poems of Hopkins,* p. 108. [Au.]

[12]*The Artist as Critic: Critical Writings of Oscar Wilde,* ed. Richard Ellmann (New York: Vintage, 1970), p. 386. [Au.]

[13]*Complete Works of Oscar Wilde,* ed. J. B. Foreman (London: Collins, 1971), p. 335. [Au.]

him. There are obvious social reasons for some of this egoism, which Wilde made no attempt to conceal in his quip "To love oneself is the beginning of a life-long romance," but they do not exhaust the speech of Wilde's style. Having forsworn action, life, and nature for their incompleteness and diffusion, Wilde took as his province a theoretical, ideal world in which, as he told Alfred Douglas in *De Profundis*, conversation was the basis of all human relations.[14] Since conflict inhibited conversation as Wilde understood it from the Platonic dialogue, the mode of interchange was to be by epigram. This epigram is Wilde's radical of presentation: a compact utterance capable of the utmost range of subject matter, the greatest authority, and the least equivocation as to its author. When he invaded other forms of art Wilde converted them into longer epigrams. As he said of drama: "I took the drama, the most objective form known to art, and made it as personal a mode of expression as the lyric or the sonnet, at the same time that I widened its range and enriched its characterization" (p. 80). No wonder he could say: "I summed up all systems in a phrase, and all existence in an epigram" (p. 81).

*De Profundis* records the destruction of the utopia whose individualism and unselfish selfishness Wilde has adumbrated in *The Soul of Man under Socialism*. From a free world to a prison and a circle of suffering: how is the change accomplished? Wilde's conception of freedom was to be found in *The Importance of Being Earnest*, where conflicting characters turn out to be brothers after all just because they say they are. What is written down (for example, the army lists consulted by Jack) merely confirms what all along has been capriciously, but stylistically, said. This transformation, from opponent into brother, is what Wilde had in mind in connecting the intensification of personality with its multiplication. When the communication between men no longer possesses the freedom of conversation, when it is confined to the merely legal liability of print, which is now ingenuously quotable but, because it has been signed, is now criminally actionable, the utopia crumbles. As he reconsidered his life

in *De Profundis,* Wilde's imagination was transfixed by the effects of one text upon his life. But he uses it to show how in going from speech to print, which in a sense all of his other more fortunate texts had managed somehow to avoid by virtue of this epigrammatic individuality, he had been ruined. Wilde's lament in what follows is that a text has too much, not too little, circumstantial reality, and hence, the Wildean paradox, its vulnerability:

> You send me a very nice poem, of the undergraduate school of verse, for my approval: I reply by a letter of fantastic literary conceits. . . . Look at the history of that letter! It passes from you into the hands of a loathsome companion: from him to a gang of blackmailers: copies of it are sent about London to my friends, and to the manager of the theatre where my work is being performed: every construction but the right one is put on it: Society is thrilled with the absurd rumours that I have had to pay a huge sum of money for having written an infamous letter to you: this forms the basis of your father's worst attack: I produce the original letter myself in Court to show what it really is: it is denounced by your father's counsel as a revolting and insidious attempt to corrupt Innocence: ultimately it forms part of a criminal charge: the Crown takes it up: the Judge sums up on it with little learning and much morality: I go to prison for it at last. That is the result of writing you a charming letter (pp. 34–35).

In a world described by George Eliot as a "huge whispering gallery," the effects of writing can be grave indeed: "As the stone which has been kicked by generations of clowns may come by curious little links of effect under the eyes of a scholar, through whose labours it may at last fix the date of invasions and unlock religions, so a bit of ink and paper which has long been an innocent wrapping or stop-gap may at last be laid open under the one pair of eyes which have knowledge enough to turn it into the opening of a catastrophe."[15] If Dr. Casaubon's caution has a purpose, it is by rigid secrecy and an endlessly postponing scriptive will to forestall "the opening of a catastrophe." Yet he cannot succeed, since Eliot is at pains to show that even his tremen-

[14]*De Profundis* (New York: Vintage, 1964), p. 18. [Au.]

[15]*Middlemarch*, ed. Gordon S. Haight (Boston: Houghton Mifflin, 1956), p. 302. [Au.]

dously nursed *Key* is a text, and therefore in the world. Unlike Wilde's, Casaubon's disgrace is posthumous, but their textual implication takes place for the same reason, which is their commitment to what Eliot calls an "embroiled medium."

Last let me consider Conrad. Elsewhere I have described the extraordinary *presentational* mode of his narratives, how each of them, almost without exception, dramatizes, motivates, and circumstances the occasion of its telling, how all of Conrad's work is really made out of secondary, reported speech, and how the interplay between appeals to the eye and the ear is highly organized and subtle and constitutes that work's meaning.[16] The Conradian encounter is not simply between a man and his destiny embodied in a moment of extremity but, just as persistently, it is the encounter between speaker and hearer. Marlow is Conrad's chief invention for this encounter, Marlow with his haunting knowledge that a man such as Kurtz or Jim "existed for me, and after all it is only through me that he exists for you."[17] The chain of humanity — "we exist only in so far as we hang together" (p. 160) — is the transmission of actual speech, and existence, from one mouth, and then after that, from one eye, to another. Every text that Conrad wrote, whether formally, aesthetically, or thematically considered, presents itself as unfinished and still in the making. "And besides, the last word is not said — probably shall never be said. Are not our lives too short for that full utterance which through all our stammerings is of course our only and abiding intention?" (p. 161). Texts convey the stammerings, but that full utterance, the statement of wholly satisfactory presence, remains distant, attenuated somewhat by a grand gesture like Jim's self-sacrifice, which closes off a text circumstantially without in any way emptying it of its actual urgency. Quite the contrary.

This is a good time to remark that the Western novelistic tradition, from *Don Quixote* on, is full of examples of texts insisting not only upon their circumstantial reality but also upon their status as *already* fulfilling a function, a reference, or a meaning *in the world*. Cervantes and Cide Hamete come immediately to mind. More impressive is Richardson playing the role of mere editor for *Clarissa,* "simply" placing those letters in successive order after they have done what they have done, arranging to fill the text with printer's devices, reader's aids, analytical contents, retrospective meditations, commentary, so that a collection of letters grows to fill the world and occupy all space, to become a circumstance as large and as engrossing as the reader's understanding itself. Surely the novelistic imagination has always included this unwillingness to cede control over the text in the world, or to release it from the discursive and human obligations of all human presence; hence the desire, which is almost a principal action of many novels, to turn the text back, if not directly into speech, then at least into circumstantial, as opposed to meditative duration.

No novelist, however, can be quite as explicit about circumstances as Marx is in *The Eighteenth Brumaire of Louis Bonaparte*. To my mind no other work is as brilliant and as compelling in the exactness with which circumstances (the German word is *Umstände*) are shown to have made the nephew possible, not as an innovator, but as a farcical repetition of the uncle. What Marx attacks are the atextual theses (1) that history is made up of free events, and (2) that history is guided by superior individuals.[18] By inserting Louis Bonaparte in a whole intricate system of repetitions, by which first Hegel, then the ancient Romans, then the 1789 revolutionaries, then Napoleon I, then the bourgeois interpreters, then finally the fiascos of 1848–51 are all seen in a pseudoanalogical order of descending worth, increasing derivativeness, and deceptively harmless masquerading, Marx effectively circumstances, *textualizes,* the random appearance of a new Caesar. Here we have the case of a text itself providing a world historical situation with circumstances otherwise hidden in the deception

[16]See Edward W. Said, "Conrad: The Presentation of Narrative," *Novel,* 7 (Winter 1974), 116–132. [Au.]

[17]*Lord Jim* (Boston: Houghton Mifflin, 1958), p. 161. [Au.]

[18]Marx, *Der Achizehnte Brumaire des Louis Bonaparte* (1852; Berlin: Dietz Verlag, 1947), p. 8. [Au.]

of a *roi des drôles*. What is ironic — and to be sure in need of extensive analysis — is how a text, by being a text, by insisting upon and employing all the devices of textuality, preeminent among them *repetition,* historicizes and problematizes all the fugitive significance that has chosen Louis Bonaparte as its representative.

There is another aspect to what I have been saying about the novel generally, and about Hopkins, Wilde, and Conrad. In producing texts with either a firm claim on, or an explicit will to worldliness, these writers and genres have valorized speech, making it the tentacle by which an otherwise silent text ties itself into the world of discourse. By the valorization of speech I mean that the discursive, circumstantially dense interchange of speaker facing hearer is made to stand — sometimes misleadingly — for a democratic equality and copresence in actuality between speaker and hearer. Not only is the discursive relation far from equal in actuality (as I shall argue presently), but also the text's attempt to dissemble, by seeming to be open democratically to anyone who might read it, is an act of bad faith. (Incidentally, one of the strengths of Zahirite theory is that it dispels the illusion that a surface reading, which is the Zahirite ambition, is anything but difficult.) Texts of such a length as *Tom Jones* aim to occupy leisure time of a quality not available to just anyone. Moreover, all texts essentially displace, dislodge other texts or, more frequently, they take the place of something else. As Nietzsche had the perspicacity to see, texts are fundamentally facts of power, not of democratic exchange.[19] They compel attention away from the world even as their beginning intention as texts, coupled with the inherent authoritarianism of the authorial authority (the repetition in this phrase is a deliberate emphasis on some tautology within all texts, since all texts are in some way self-confirmatory), makes for sustained power.

Yet in the patrimony of texts there is a first text, a sacred prototype, a scripture, which the reader is always approaching through the text before him either as petitioning suppliant or as an initiate among many in a sacred chorus supporting the central patriarchal text. Northrop Frye's theory of literature makes it apparent that the displacing power in all texts derives finally from the displacing power of the Bible, whose centrality, potency, and dominating anteriority inform all Western literature.[20] The same is no less true, in the different modes I discussed earlier, of the Koran and its priority. Both in the Judeo-Christian and in the Islamic traditions these hierarchies repose upon a solidly divine, or quasi-divine, language, a language whose uniqueness is that it is theologically and humanly circumstantial.

It is too often forgotten that modern Western philology, which begins in the early nineteenth century, undertook to revise commonly accepted ideas about language and its divine origins. That revision tried first to determine which was the first language and then, failing to achieve that ambition, proceeded thereafter to reduce language to specific circumstances: language-groups, historical and racial theories, geographical and anthropological theses. A particularly interesting example of how such investigations went is Ernest Renan's career as a philologist: *that* was his real profession, and not that of the boring sage. His first serious work was his 1847 analysis of Semitic languages, revised and published in 1855 as the *Histoire générale et système comparé des langues sémitiques.* Without this study, the *Vie de Jésus* could not have been written. The accomplishment of the *Histoire générale* was scientifically to describe the *inferiority* of Semitic languages, principally Hebrew, Aramaic, and Arabic, the medium of three purportedly sacred, spoken (by God) texts, the Torah, the Koran, and later, the derivative Gospels. Thus in the *Vie de Jésus* Renan would be able to insinuate that the so-called sacred texts, delivered by Moses, Jesus, and Mohammed, could not have anything divine in them if the very medium of their supposed divinity, as well as the

---

[19]Nietzsche's analyses of texts in this light are to be found everywhere in his work, but especially in *The Genealogy of Morals* and *The Will to Power.* [Au.]

[20]See Frye, *Anatomy of Criticism* (1957) and "The Archetypes of Literature," p. 677. [Ed.]

body of their message to and in the world, was made up of such comparatively poor worldly stuff. Renan argued that even if these texts were prior to all others in the West, they held nonetheless only a primitive, not a theologically dominant, position.

Renan first reduced texts from objects of divine intervention in the world's business to objects of historical materiality; God as author-authority had little value after Renan's philological and textual revisionism. Yet in dispensing with divine authority, Renan put philological power in its place. What is born to replace divine authority is the textual authority of the philological critic who has the effective skill to separate Semitic, that is, Oriental, languages from the languages of Indo-European culture. Not only therefore did Renan kill off the extratextual validity of the great Semitic sacred texts, he confined them as objects of European study to a scholarly field thereafter to be known as Oriental, and ruled by the Orientalist.[21] The Orientalist is a Renan, or a Gobineau,[22] Renan's contemporary quoted here and there in the 1855 edition of the *Histoire générale et système comparé des langues sémitiques,* for whom the old hierarchy of sacred Semitic texts has been destroyed as if by an act of parricide; the passing of divine authority makes possible the appearance of European ethnocentrism, whereby the methods and the discourse of Western scholarship analyze and characterize as inferior non-European cultures so as to confine them to a position of subordination. Oriental texts come to inhabit a realm without development or power — it is a realm that corresponds exactly to the position of a colony for European texts and culture. All this takes place at the same time that the great European colonial empires in the East are emerging or, in some cases, flourishing.

I have introduced this brief account of the twin origin of the Higher Criticism and of Orientalism as a European scholarly discipline in order to be able to speak about the fallacy of imagining the life of texts as being pleasantly ideal and without force or conflict, and conversely, the fallacy of imagining the discursive relations in actual speech to be, as Ricoeur would have it, a relation of equal copresence between hearer and speaker.

Texts incorporate discourse, sometimes violently, in the ways I have been discussing. There are other ways, too. Michel Foucault's archeological analyses of what he calls systems of discourse are premised on the thesis, originally adumbrated by Marx and Engels in *The German Ideology,* that "in every society the production of discourse is at once controlled, selected, organized and redistributed according to a certain number of procedures, whose role is to avert its powers and dangers, to cope with chance events, to evade its ponderous, awesome materiality."[23] Discourse in this passage means what is written as well as what is spoken. Foucault's contention is that the fact of writing itself is a systematic conversion of the power relationship between the controller and the controlled into mere written words; the reason this happens is to let it seem that writing is only writing, whereas writing is one way of disguising the awesome materiality of so tightly controlled and managed a production. Foucault continues:

In a society such as our own we all know the rules of *exclusion.* The most obvious and familiar of these concerns what is *prohibited.* We know perfectly well that we are not free to say just anything. We have three types of prohibition, covering objects, ritual with its surrounding circumstances, the privileged or exclusive right to speak of a particular subject; these prohibitions interrelate, reinforce and complement each other, forming a complex web, continually subject to modification. I will note simply that the areas where this web is most tightly woven today, where the danger spots are most numerous, are those dealing with politics and sexuality. . . . In appearance, speech may well be of little account, but the prohibitions surrounding it soon reveal its links with desire and power . . . speech is no mere verbalization of conflicts and

---

[21]See in particular Renan, *Histoire générale et système comparé des langues sémitiques,* in *Oeuvres complètes,* Vol. 8, ed. Henriette Psichari (Paris: Calmann-Lévy, 1947–1961), pp. 147–157 and *passim.* [Au.]

[22]Racist philosopher of the mid-nineteenth century. [Ed.]

[23]Michel Foucault, "The Discourse on Language," in *The Archeology of Knowledge,* trans. A. M. Sheridan Smith (New York: Pantheon, 1972), p. 216. [Au.]

systems of domination, but that it is the very object of man's conflicts.

The discursive situation, despite Ricoeur's simplification of it, far from being a type of idyllic conversation between equals, is more usually of a kind typefied by the relation between colonizer and colonized, the oppressor and the oppressed. It is too little recalled that the great modernists (Proust and Joyce are instances) had an acute understanding of this fact; their representations of the discursive situation always show it in this power-political light. A formative moment in Stephen Dedalus's rebellious consciousness occurs as he converses with the English dean of studies:

> What is that beauty which the artist struggles to express from lumps of earth, said Stephen coldly.
> The little word seemed to have turned a rapier point of his sensitiveness against this courteous and vigilant foe. He felt with a smart of dejection that the man to whom he was speaking was a countryman of Ben Jonson. He thought: — The language in which we are speaking is his before it is mine. How different are the words *home, Christ, ale, master,* on his lips and on mine! I cannot speak or write these words without unrest of spirit. His language, so familiar and so foreign, will always be for me an acquired speech. I have not made or accepted its words. My voice holds them at bay. My soul frets in the shadow of his language.[24]

Joyce's oeuvre is a recapitulation of those political and racial separations, exclusions, prohibitions instituted ethnocentrically by the ascendant European culture throughout the nineteenth century. The situation of discourse, Stephen Dedalus knows, hardly puts equals across from each other. Rather, discourse places one interlocutor above another or, as Fanon brilliantly described it in *The Wretched of the Earth,* discourse reenacts the geography of the colonial city, "this world cut in two is inhabited by two different species . . . where the agents of government speak the language of pure force":

> The zone where the natives live is not complementary to the zone inhabited by the settlers. The two zones are opposed, but not in the service of a higher unity. Obedient to the rules of pure Aristotelian logic, they both follow the principle of reciprocal exclusivity. No conciliation is possible, for of the two terms, one is superfluous. The settlers' town is a strongly-built town, all made of stone and steel. It is a brightly-lit town; the streets are covered with asphalt and the garbage-cans swallow all the leavings, unseen, unknown, and hardly thought about. The settler's feet are never visible, except perhaps in the sea; but there you're never close enough to see them. His feet are protected by strong shoes although the streets of his town are clean and even, with no holes or stones. The settler's town is a well-fed town, an easygoing town; its belly is always full of good things. The settler's town is a town of white people, of foreigners.
> The town belonging to the colonized people, or at least the native town, the negro village, the medina, the reservation, is a place of ill fame, peopled by men of evil repute. They are born there, it matters little where or how; they die there, it matters not where, nor how. It is a world without spaciousness; men live there on top of each other, and their huts are built on top of the other. The native town is a hungry town, starved of bread, of meat, of shoes, of coal, of light. The native town is a crouching village, a town on its knees, a town wallowing in the mire. It is a town of niggers and dirty arabs. The look that the native turns on the settler's town is a look of lust, a look of envy; it expresses his dreams of possession — all manner of possession: to sit at the settler's table, to sleep in the settler's bed, with his wife if possible. The colonised man is an envious man. And this the settler knows very well; when their glances meet he ascertains bitterly, always on the defensive, "They want to take our place." It is true, for there is no native who does not dream at least once a day of setting himself up in the settler's place.[25]

No wonder that the Fanonist solution to such discourse is violence.

My choice of examples, extreme though most of them may have been, has done for me the job of rejecting simple oppositions between texts and the world, or between texts and speech. Too many exceptions, too many historical, ideological, and formal circumstances implicate the text in actuality, even if a text may also be considered

[24]Joyce, *A Portrait of the Artist as a Young Man* (New York: Viking, 1964), p. 189. [Au.]

[25]*The Wretched of the Earth,* trans. Constance Farrington (New York: Grove, 1966), pp. 31–32. [Au.]

a silent printed object with its own unheard melodies which play "not to the sensual ear, but, more endeared, / Pipe to the spirit ditties of no tone."[26] The play of forces by which a text is engendered and maintained as a fact not of mute ideality but of *production* completely dispels the symmetry of even heuristic oppositions. Moreover the textual utopia that T. S. Eliot and Northrop Frye envisioned each in his own way,[27] whose nightmarish converse is Borges's library, is at complete odds with the *eccentric,* dialectical intermingling of history with form in texts. My thesis is that any centrist, exclusivist conception of the text, or for that matter of the discursive situation as defined wrongly by Paul Ricoeur, ignores the ethnocentrism and the erratic will to power from which texts can spring.

But where in all this is the critic and *his* text?

Scholarship, commentary, exegesis, *explication de texte,* history of ideas, rhetorical or semiological analyses: all these are modes of pertinence, of attention, to the textual matter usually presented to the critic as already at hand. I shall concentrate now on the essay, the traditional form in which criticism has expressed itself. The central problematic of the essay as a form is its *place,* by which I mean a series of three different but connected ways the essay has of being the form the critic takes, and locates himself in, to do his work. Place therefore involves relations the critic fashions with the texts he addresses and the audience he addresses; it also involves the dynamic *taking place* of his own text as it produces itself.

The first mode of place is the essay's relation to the text it attempts to approach. How does it come to the text of its choice? How does it enter the text? What is the concluding definition of its relation to the text it has dealt with? The second mode of place is the essay's intention (and the intention, presumed or perhaps created by the essay, that its audience has) in attempting an approach. Is the critical essay an attempt *to identify* or *to identify with* the text of its choice? Does

it stand between the text and the reader, or to one side of one of them? How great, or how little, is the ironic disparity between its essential formal incompleteness, because it is *an essay,* and the formal completion of the text it treats? The third mode of place concerns the essay as a zone in which certain kinds of occurrences, events, happen as an aspect of the essay's production. What is the essay's consciousness of its marginality to the text it discusses? What is the method by which the essay permits history a role during the making of its own history, that is, as the essay moves from beginning to development to conclusion? What is the quality of the essay's speech, toward, away from, into the *actuality,* the arena of nontextual historical vitality and presence that is taking place simultaneously with the essay itself? Finally is the essay a text, an intervention between texts, an intensification of the notion of textuality, or a dispersion of language away from a contingent page to occasions, tendencies, currents, or movements in and for history?

Put as jaggedly and as abstractly as this, these questions are not immediately answerable. It is entirely possible that my scattering, grapeshot manner of formulating them prevents, rather than encourages, answers from appearing; also one is tempted perhaps to be impatient and say that these questions are fairly abtruse solipsisms that take the critic away from his real business, which is writing criticism *tout court.* Perhaps I would argue, however, that a juster response to these questions is a realization of how unfamiliar and how rare such questions are in the general discussion of contemporary criticism. It is not that the problems of criticism are undiscussed, but rather that criticism is considered essentially as defined once and for all by its secondariness, by its temporal misfortune of having come *after* the text (or texts) it is supposed to be treating. Just as it is all too often true that texts are thought of as monolithic objects of the past, to which criticism is a despondent appendage in the present, then the very conception of criticism symbolizes being outdated, being dated *from* the past rather than *by* the present. Everything I tried earlier to say about a text — its dialectic of engagement in time and the senses, the paradoxes in a text

[26]Keats, "Ode on a Grecian Urn." [Ed.]

[27]See Eliot, "Tradition and the Individual Talent," p. 466; Frye, *Anatomy of Criticism* (see p. 645); Jorge Luis Borges, "The Library of Babylon." [Ed.]

by which discourse is shown to be immutable and yet contingent, as fraught and politically intransigeant as the struggle between dominant and dominated — all this was an implicit rejection of the secondary after-role usually assigned to criticism. For if we assume instead that texts make up what Foucault calls archival facts, the archive being defined as the text's social discursive presence in the world, then criticism, too, is another aspect of that present. In other words, one should prefer to say that rather than being defined by the silent past, commanded by it to speak in the present, criticism, no less than any other text, is the present in the course of its articulation, struggles for definition, attempts at overcoming.

We must not forget that the critic does not, cannot speak without the mediation of writing, the ambivalent *pharmakon* so suggestively portrayed by Derrida as the constituted milieu where the oppositions are opposed: this is where the movement and the play occur that bring the oppositions into direct contact with each other, that overturn oppositions and transform one pole into another, soul and body, good and evil, inside and outside, memory and oblivion, speech and writing.[28] In particular the critic is committed to the essay, whose metaphysics were sketched by Lukács in the first chapter of his *Die Seele und die Formen*. There Lukács said that as a form the essays allows, and indeed is, the coincidence of inchoate soul with exigent material form.[29] Essays are concerned with the relations between things, with values and concepts, in fine, with significance (p. 12). Whereas poetry deals in images, the essay is the abandonment of images; this abandonment the essay ideally shares with Platonism and mysticism (p. 13). If, Lukács continues, the various forms of literature are compared with sunlight refracted in a prism, then the essay is ultraviolet light (p. 15). What the essay expresses is a yearning for conceptuality and intellectuality, as well as for great ultimate questions such as what is life or man and destiny

(p. 15). (Throughout his analysis Lukács refers to the Platonic Socrates as the typical essayistic figure, always talking of immediate mundane matters while at the same time through his life there sounds the purest, the most profound, and the most concealed yearning — *Die tiefste, die verborgenste Sehnsucht ertönt aus diesem Leben*.)[30]

Thus the essay's mode is ironic, which means, first, that the form is patently insufficient in its intellectuality with regard to living experience and, second, that the very form of the essay, its being an essay, is an ironic destiny with regard to the great questions of life (p. 16). Socrates' death perfectly symbolizes, in its arbitrariness and irrelevance to those questions he debates, the essayistic destiny, or rather the absence of real (that is, tragic) destiny in the essay; there is no internal conclusion for an essay, for only something outside it can interrupt or end it, as Socrates' death is decreed offstage and ends his life of questioning. Form fills the function in an essay that images do in poetry: form is the reality of the essay, and form gives the essayist a voice with which to ask questions of life, even if that form must always make use of art — a book, a painting, a piece of music — as the initial subject matter of its investigations (p. 17).

Lukács, in his analysis of the essay, a small part of which I have summarized only to indicate the kind of thought available to the critic about his extremely complex relations with the world and with his medium, holds in common with Wilde the view that criticism in general, and the essay in particular, is rarely what it seems, not least in its form. Criticism adopts the mode of commentary on and evaluation of art; yet in reality criticism matters more as a necessarily incomplete and preparatory *process toward* judgement and evaluation. What the critical essay does is *to begin* to create the values by which art is judged. I said earlier that a major inhibition on the critic is that his function as critic is often dated and circumscribed for him by the past, that is, by an already created work of art. Lukács acknowledges the inhibition, but he shows how

---

[28] Derrida, "La Pharmacie de Platon," in *La Dissémination* (Paris: Seuil, 1972), pp. 145 and *passim*. [Au.]

[29] *Die Seele und die Formen* (1911; reprinted Berlin: Luchterhand, 1971), p. 17. [Au.]

[30] "The deepest, the most hidden yearning sounds out of this life" (p. 25). [Ed.]

in fact the critic appropriates for himself the function of starting to make values, and therefore the work he is judging. Wilde said it more flamboyantly: criticism "treats the work of art as a starting point for a new creation."[31] Lukács put it more cautiously: "the essayist is a pure instance of the precursor" ([*Der Essayist*] *ist der reine Typus des Vorläufers*).[32]

I prefer the latter description, for as Lukács develops it the critic's position is vulnerable because he awaits and prepares for a great aesthetic revolution whose result, ironically enough, will render him marginal. Of course this idea, this consciousness of the possibility of the future, as well as the need in consciousness for a constant conversion of thought from static to dynamic, itself prefigures Lukács's later ideas about the role of the proletariat dynamic class consciousness which will bring about the overthrow of bourgeois reification.[33] What I wish to emphasize here in conclusion is not so much the critic's role in writing as dialectically creating the values by which art might be judged and understood, but the critic's role in creating the processes of the *present,* as process and inauguration, the actual conditions by means of which art and writing bear significance. By this I mean not only what R. P. Blackmur, following Hopkins, called the bringing of literature to performance, but more explicitly, the articulation of those voices dominated, displaced, or silenced by the textuality of texts. Texts are a system of forces institutionalized at some expense by the reigning culture, not an ideal cosmos of ideally equal poems. Looking at the Grecian urn, Keats *sees* graceful figures adorning its exterior, and also he actualizes in language (and perhaps nowhere else) the little town "emptied of this folk, this pious morn." The critic's attitude to some extent is restorative in a similar way; it should in addition and more often be frankly inventive, in the traditional rhetorical sense of *inventio* employed so fruitfully by Vico, finding and exposing things that otherwise lie hidden beneath piety, heedlessness, or routine. Most of all, I think, criticism is worldly and in the world so long as it opposes *monocentrism* in the narrowest as well as the widest sense of that too infrequently considered notion: for monocentrism is a concept I take in conjunction with ethnocentrism, the assumption that culture masks itself as the sovereignty of *this* one and *this* human, whereas culture is the process of domination and struggle always dissembling, always deceiving. Monocentrism is practiced when we mistake one idea as the only idea, instead of recognizing that an idea in history is always one among many. Monocentrism denies plurality, it totalizes structure, it sees profit where there is waste, it decrees the concentricity of Western culture instead of its eccentricity, it believes continuity to be given and will not try to understand, instead, how continuity as much as discontinuity is made.

My inclinations now are to say that worldliness — as expressed in such denials and affirmations as the ones I have examined — is enough for criticism: for if this worldliness prepares for a still more liberating one to come after it, then so much the better.

[31]*The Artist as Critic*, p. 367. [Au.]
[32]*Die Seele und die Formen*, p. 29. [Au.]
[33]See Lukács, *History and Class Consciousness: Studies in Marxist Dialectics,* trans. Rodney Livingstone (London: Merlin Press, 1971), pp. 178–209. [Au.]

# Barbara Johnson

b. 1947

*Barbara Ellen Johnson was born in Boston, Massachusetts. She took a B.A. at Oberlin in 1969 and a Ph.D. in French at Yale in 1977, where her mentor was Paul de Man. After receiving her doctorate, Johnson accepted a teaching position at Yale and was promoted in 1980 to associate professor of French and comparative literature. She is currently professor of French at Harvard*

University. *A Guggenheim recipient in 1985–86, her publications include "The Frame of Reference: Poe, Lacan, Derrida" (1978),* Défigurations de langage poétique *(1979),* The Critical Difference: Essays in the Contemporary Rhetoric of Reading *(1980), from which "Melville's Fist" is taken, and a translation of Derrida's* Dissemination *(1981). In her most recent work,* A World of Difference *(1987), Johnson adapts the Derridean logic of* différance *to social and gender issues.*

# Melville's Fist:
# The Execution of Billy Budd

## THE SENSE OF AN ENDING

*Truth uncompromisingly told will always have its ragged edges; hence the conclusion of such a narration is apt to be less finished than an architectural finial.*
　　　　　　　　　　　— MELVILLE, *Billy Budd*

The plot of Melville's *Billy Budd* is well known, and, like its title character, appears entirely straightforward and simple. It is a tale of three men in a boat: the innocent, ignorant foretopman, handsome Billy Budd; the devious, urbane master-at-arms, John Claggart; and the respectable, bookish commanding officer, Captain the Honorable Edward Fairfax ("Starry") Vere. Falsely accused by Claggart of plotting mutiny aboard the British man-of-war *Bellipotent,* Billy Budd, his speech impeded by a stutter, strikes his accuser dead in front of the captain, and is condemned, after a summary trial, to hang.

In spite of the apparent straightforwardness of the facts of the case, however, there exists in the critical literature on *Billy Budd* a notable range of disagreement over the ultimate meaning of the tale. For some, the story constitutes Melville's "testament of acceptance," his "everlasting yea," his "acceptance of tragedy," or at least his "recognition of necessity."[1] For others, Melville's

"final stage" is, on the contrary, "irony": *Billy Budd* is considered a "testament of resistance," "ironic social criticism," or the last vituperation in Melville's "quarrel with God."[2] More recently, critical attention has devoted itself to the ambiguity in the story, sometimes deploring it, sometimes revelling in it, and sometimes simply listing it.[3] The ambiguity is attributed to various causes: the unfinished state of the manuscript, Melville's change of heart toward Vere, Melville's unreconciled ambivalence toward authority or his guilt about paternity, the incompatibility between the "plot" and the "story."[4] But however great the disagreement over the meaning of this posthumous novel, all critics seem to agree in considering it Melville's "last word."

[1]E. L. Grant Watson, "Melville's Testament of Acceptance," *New England Quarterly* 6 (June 1933): 319–27; the expression appears in both John Freeman, *Herman Melville* (New York: Macmillan Co., 1926), p. 136, and Raymond M. Weaver, *The Shorter Novels of Herman Melville* (New York: Liveright, 1928), p. li; William E. Sedgwick, *Herman Melville: The Tragedy of Mind* (Cambridge: Harvard University Press, 1944), pp. 231–49; F. Barron Freeman, *Melville's "Billy Budd"* (Cambridge: Harvard University Press, 1948), pp. 115–24. [Au.]

[2]Joseph Schiffman, "Melville's Final Stage: Irony," *American Literature* 22, no. 2 (May 1950): 128–36; Philip Withim, "*Billy Budd:* Testament of Resistance," *Modern Language Quarterly* 20 (June 1959): 115–27; Karl E. Zink, "Herman Melville and the Forms — Irony and Social Criticism in *Billy Budd,*" *Accent* 12, no. 3 (Summer 1952): 131–39; Lawrance Thompson, *Melville's Quarrel with God* (Princeton: Princeton University Press, 1952). [Au.]

[3]Kenneth Ledbetter, "The Ambiguity of *Billy Budd,*" *Texas Studies in Literature and Language* 4, no. 1 (Spring 1962): 130–34; S. E. Hyman, quoted in R. H. Fogle, "*Billy Budd* — Acceptance or Irony," *Tulane Studies in English* 8 (1958): 107; Edward M. Cifelli, "*Billy Budd:* Boggy Ground to Build On," *Studies in Short Fiction* 13, no. 4 (Fall 1976): 463–69. [Au.]

[4]Lee T. Lemon, "*Billy Budd:* The Plot Against the Story," in *Studies in Short Fiction* 2, no. 1 (Fall 1964): 32–43. [Au.]

"With the mere fact of the long silence in our minds," writes John Middleton Murry, "we could not help regarding 'Billy Budd' as the last will and spiritual testament of a man of genius."[5]

To regard a story as its author's last will and testament is clearly to grant it a privileged, determining position in the body of that author's work. As its name implies, the "will" is taken to represent the author's final "intentions": in writing his will, the author is presumed to have summed up and evaluated his entire literary output, and directed it — as proof against "dissemination" — toward some determinable destination. The "ending" thus somehow acquires the metalinguistic authority to confer finality and intelligibility upon all that precedes it.

Now, since this sense of Melville's ending is so central to *Billy Budd* criticism, it might be useful to take a look at the nature of the ending of the story itself. Curiously enough, we find that *Billy Budd* ends not once, but no less than four times. As Melville himself describes it, the story continues far beyond its "proper" end: "How it fared with the Handsome Sailor during the year of the Great Mutiny has been faithfully given. But though *properly* the story ends with his life, something in the way of sequel will not be amiss"[6] (emphasis mine here and passim). This "sequel" consists of "three brief chapters": (1) the story of the death of Captain Vere after an encounter with the French ship, the *Athée*; (2) a transcription of the Budd-Claggart affair published in an "authorized" naval publication, in which the characters of the two men are reversed, with Budd represented as the depraved villain and Claggart as the heroic victim; and (3) a description of the posthumous mythification of Billy Budd by his fellow sailors and a transcription of the ballad written by one of them, which presents itself as a monologue spoken by Billy on the eve of his execution. Billy Budd's last

words, like Melville's own, are thus spoken posthumously — indeed the final line of the story is uttered from the bottom of the sea.

The question of the sense of Melville's ending is thus raised *in* the story as well as *by* the story. But far from tying up the loose ends of a confusing literary life, Melville's last words are an affirmation of the necessity of "ragged edges":

> The symmetry of form attainable in pure fiction cannot so readily be achieved in a narration essentially having less to do with fable than with fact. Truth uncompromisingly told will always have its ragged edges; hence the conclusion of such a narration is apt to be less finished than an architectural finial. (p. 405)

The story ends by fearlessly fraying its own symmetry, thrice transgressing its own "proper" end; there is something inherently improper about this testamentary disposition of Melville's literary property. Indeed, far from totalizing itself into intentional finality, the story in fact begins to repeat itself — retelling itself first in reverse, and then in verse. The ending not only lacks special authority, it problematizes the very *idea* of authority by placing its own reversal in the pages of an "authorized" naval chronicle. To end is to repeat, and to repeat is to be ungovernably open to revision, displacement, and reversal.[7] The sense of Melville's ending is to empty the ending of any privileged control over sense.

## THE PLOT AGAINST THE CHARACTERS

*For Tragedy is an imitation, not of men, but of action and of life, consists in action, and its end is a mode of action, not a quality. Now character determines men's qualities, but it is by their actions that they are happy or the reverse.*
— ARISTOTLE, *Poetics*

In beginning our study of *Billy Budd* with its ending, we, too, seem to have reversed the

---

[5]John Middleton Murry, "Herman Melville's Silence," *Times Literary Supplement*, 10 July 1924, p. 433. [Au.]

[6]Herman Melville, *Billy Budd*, in *Billy Budd, Sailor, and Other Stories*, ed. Harold Beaver (New York: Penguin Books, 1967), p. 405; emphasis mine. Unless otherwise indicated, all references to *Billy Budd* are to this edition, which reprints the Hayford and Sealts reading text. [Au.]

[7]It is interesting that reversibility seems to constitute not only *Billy Budd*'s ending but also its origin: the *Somers* mutiny case, which commentators have seen as a major source for the story, had been brought back to Melville's attention at the time he was writing *Billy Budd* by two opposing articles that reopened and retold the *Somers* case, forty-six years after the fact, in antithetical terms. [Au.]

"proper" order of things. Most studies of the story tend to begin, after a few general remarks about the nature of good and evil, with a delineation of the three main characters: Billy, Claggart, and Vere. As Charles Weir puts it, "The purely physical action of the story is clear enough, and about its significant details there is never any doubt. . . . It is, therefore, with some consideration of the characters of the three principal actors that any analysis must begin."[8] "Structurally," writes F. B. Freeman, "the three characters *are* the novel"[9] (emphasis in original).

Melville goes to great lengths to describe both the physical and the moral characteristics of his protagonists. Billy Budd, a twenty-one-year-old "novice in the complexities of factitious life," is remarkable for his "significant personal beauty," "reposeful good nature," "straightforward simplicity" and "unconventional rectitude." But Billy's intelligence ("such as it was," says Melville) is as primitive as his virtues are pristine. He is illiterate, he cannot understand ambiguity, and he stutters.

Claggart, on the other hand, is presented as the very image of urbane, intellectualized, articulate evil. Although "of no ill figure upon the whole" (p. 342), something in Claggart's pallid face consistently inspires uneasiness and mistrust. He is a man, writes Melville, "in whom was the mania of an evil nature, not engendered by vicious training or corrupting books or licentious living, but born with him and innate, in short, 'a depravity according to nature'" (p. 354). The mere sight of Billy Budd's rosy beauty and rollicking innocence does not fail to provoke in such a character "an antipathy spontaneous and profound" (p. 351).

The third man in the drama, who has inspired the greatest critical dissent, is presented in less vivid but curiously more contradictory terms. The *Bellipotent*'s captain is described as both unaffected and pedantic, dreamy and resolute, irascible and undemonstrative, "mindful of the welfare of his men, but never tolerating an infraction of discipline," "intrepid to the verge of temerity, though never injudiciously so" (p. 338). While Billy and Claggart are said to owe their characters to "nature," Captain Vere is shaped mainly by his fondness for books:

He loved books, never going to sea without a newly replenished library, compact but of the best. . . . With nothing of that literary taste which less heeds the thing conveyed than the vehicle, his bias was toward those books to which every serious mind of superior order occupying any active post of authority in the world naturally inclines: books treating of actual men and events no matter of what era — history, biography, and unconventional writers like Montaigne, who, free from cant and convention, honestly and in the spirit of common sense philosophize upon realities. (p. 340)

Vere, then, is an honest, serious reader, seemingly well suited for the role of judge and witness that in the course of the story he will come to play.

No consideration of the nature of character in *Billy Budd,* however, can fail to take into account the fact that the fate of each of the characters is the direct reverse of what one is led to expect from his "nature." Billy is sweet, innocent, and harmless, yet he kills. Claggart is evil, perverted, and mendacious, yet he dies a victim. Vere is sagacious and responsible, yet he allows a man whom he feels to be blameless to hang. It is this discrepancy between character and action that gives rise to the critical disagreement over the story: readers tend either to save the plot and condemn Billy ("acceptance," "tragedy," or "necessity"), or to save Billy and condemn the plot ("irony," "injustice," or "social criticism").

In an effort to make sense of this troubling incompatibility between character and plot, many readers are tempted to say of Billy and Claggart, as does William York Tindall, that "each is more important for what he is than what he does. . . . Good and bad, they occupy the region of good and evil."[10] This reading effectively preserves the allegorical values suggested by Melville's opening chapters, but it does so only by denying the

[8]Charles Weir, Jr., "Malice Reconciled," *Critics on Melville,* ed. Thomas Rountree. (Coral Gables, Fla.: University of Miami Press, 1972), p. 121. [Au.]

[9]Freeman, *Melville's "Billy Budd,"* p. 73. [Au.]

[10]William York Tindall, quoted in William T. Stafford, ed., *"Billy Budd" and the Critics* (Belmont, Calif.: Wadsworth, 1969), p. 188. [Au.]

importance of the plot. It ends where the plot begins: with the identification of the moral natures of the characters. One may therefore ask whether the allegorical interpretation (good vs. evil) depends as such on this sort of preference for being over doing, and if so, what effect the incompatibility between character and action may have on the allegorical functioning of *Billy Budd*.

Interestingly enough, Melville both invites an allegorical reading and subverts the very terms of its consistency when he writes of the murder: "Innocence and guilt personified in Claggart and Budd in effect changed places" (p. 380). Allowing for the existence of personification but reversing the relation between personifier and personified, positioning an opposition between good and evil only to make each term take on the properties of its opposite, Melville sets up his plot in the form of a chiasmus:

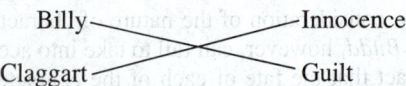

This story, which is often read as a retelling of the story of Christ, is thus literally a cruci-fiction — a fiction structured in the shape of a cross. At the moment of the reversal, an instant before his fist shoots out, Billy's face seems to mark out the point of crossing, bearing "an expression which was as a crucifixion to behold" (p. 376). Innocence and guilt, criminal and victim, change places through the mute expressiveness of Billy's inability to speak.

If *Billy Budd* is indeed an allegory, it is an allegory of the questioning of the traditional conditions of allegorical stability. The requirement of Melville's plot that the good act out the evil designs of the bad while the bad suffer the unwarranted fate of the good indicates that the real opposition with which Melville is preoccupied here is less the static opposition between evil and good than the dynamic opposition between a man's "nature" and his acts, or, in Tindall's terms, the relation between human "being" and human "doing."

Curiously enough, it is precisely this question of being versus doing that is brought up by the only sentence we ever see Claggart directly address to Billy Budd. When Billy accidentally spills his soup across the path of the master-at-arms, Claggart playfully replies, "Handsomely done, my lad! And handsome *is* as handsome *did* it, too!" (p. 350). The proverbial expression "handsome is as handsome does," from which this exclamation springs, posits the possibility of a continuous, predictable, transparent relationship between being and doing. It supposes that the inner goodness of Billy Budd is in harmonious accord with his fair appearance, that, as Melville writes of the stereotypical "Handsome Sailor" in the opening pages of the story, "the moral nature" is not "out of keeping with the physical make" (p. 322). But it is this very continuity between the physical and the moral, between appearance and action, or between being and doing, that Claggart questions in Billy Budd. He warns Captain Vere not to be taken in by Billy's physical beauty: "You have but noted his fair cheek. A mantrap may be under the ruddy-tipped daisies" (p. 372). Claggart indeed soon finds his suspicions confirmed with a vengeance: when he repeats his accusation in front of Billy, the master-at-arms is struck down dead. It would thus seem that to question the continuity between character and action cannot be done with impunity, that fundamental questions of life and death are always surreptitiously involved.

In an effort to examine what is at stake in Claggart's accusation, it might be helpful to view the opposition between Billy and Claggart as an opposition not between innocence and guilt but between two conceptions of language, or between two types of reading. Billy seemingly represents the perfectly *motivated* sign; that is, his inner self (the signified) is considered transparently readable from the beauty of his outer self (the signifier). His "straightforward simplicity" is the very opposite of the "moral obliquities" or "crookedness of heart" that characterize "citified" or rhetorically sophisticated man. "To deal in double meanings and insinuations of any sort," writes Melville, "was quite foreign to his nature" (p. 327). In accordance with his "nature," Billy reads everything at face value, never questioning the meaning of appearances. He is dumbfounded at the Dansker's suggestion, "incomprehensible to a novice," that Claggart's very pleasantness can be interpreted as its opposite, as a sign that he is "down on" Billy Budd. To Billy, "the occasional frank air and pleasant word *went for what they purported to be,* the young sailor never having heard as yet of the 'too fair-spoken man'" (pp. 365–66). As a reader, then, Billy is symbolically as well as factually illiterate. His literal-mindedness is represented by his illiteracy because, in assuming that language can be taken at face value, he excludes the very functioning of *difference* that makes the act of reading both indispensable and undecidable.

Claggart, on the other hand, is the image of difference and duplicity, both in his appearance and in his character. His face is not ugly, but it hints of something defective or abnormal. He has no vices, yet he incarnates evil. He is an intellectual, but uses reason as "an ambidexter implement for effecting the irrational" (p. 354). Billy inspires in him both "profound antipathy" and "soft yearning." In the incompatibility of his attributes, Claggart is thus a personification of ambiguity and ambivalence, of the distance between signifier and signified, of the separation between being and doing: "apprehending the good, but powerless to be it, a nature like Claggart's . . . . what recourse is left to it but to recoil upon itself" (p. 356). As a reader, Claggart has learned to "exercise a distrust keen in proportion to the fairness of the appearance" (p. 364). He is properly an ironic reader, who, assuming the sign to be arbitrary and unmotivated, reverses the value signs of appearances and takes a daisy for a mantrap and an unmotivated accidental spilling of soup for an intentional, sly escape of antipathy. Claggart meets his downfall, however, when he attempts to master the arbitrariness of the sign for his own ends by falsely (that is, arbitrarily) accusing Billy of harboring arbitrariness, of hiding a mutineer beneath the appearance of a baby.

Such a formulation of the Budd/Claggart relationship enables one to take a new look not only at the story itself but at the criticism as well. For this opposition between the literal reader (Billy) and the ironic reader (Claggart) is reenacted in the critical readings of *Billy Budd* in the opposition between the "acceptance" school and the "irony" school. Those who see the story as a "testament of acceptance" tend to take Billy's final benediction of Vere at face value; as Lewis Mumford puts it, "As Melville's own end approached, he cried out with Billy Budd: God Bless Captain Vere! In this final affirmation Herman Melville died."[11] In contrast, those who read the tale ironically tend to take Billy's sweet farewell as Melville's bitter curse. Joseph Schiffman writes, "At heart a kind man, Vere, strange to say, makes possible the depraved Claggart's wish — the destruction of Billy. 'God bless Captain Vere!' Is this not piercing irony? As innocent Billy utters these words, does not the reader gag?"[12] But since the acceptance/irony dichotomy is already contained within the story, since it is obviously one of the things the story is *about,* it is not enough to try to decide which of the readings is correct. What the reader of *Billy Budd* must do is to analyze what is at stake in the very opposition between literality and irony. This question, crucial for an understanding of *Billy Budd* not only as a literary but also as a critical phenomenon, will be taken up again in the final pages of the present chapter, but first let us examine further the linguistic implications of the murder itself.

## THE FIEND THAT LIES LIKE TRUTH

*Outwardly regarded, our craft is a lie; for all that is outwardly seen of it is the clean-swept deck, and oft-painted planks comprised above the water-line; whereas, the vast mass of our fabric, with all its store-rooms of secrets, forever slides along far under the surface.* — MELVILLE, *White-Jacket*

If Claggart's accusation that Billy is secretly plotting mutiny is essentially an affirmation of the possibility of a discontinuity between being and doing, of an arbitrary, nonmotivated relation between signifier and signified, then Billy's blow must be read as an attempt violently to deny that discontinuity or arbitrariness. The blow, as a denial, functions as a substitute for speech, as Billy explains during his trial: "I did not mean to kill

---

[11]Lewis Mumford, quoted in Stafford, *"Billy Budd" and the Critics,* p. 135. [Au.]

[12]Schiffman, "Melville's Final Stage," p. 133. [Au.]

him. Could I have used my tongue I would not have struck him. But he foully lied to my face and in presence of my captain, and I had to say something, and I could only say it with a blow" (p. 383). But in striking a blow in defense of the sign's motivation, Billy actually personifies the very *absence* of motivation: "I did not mean . . ." His blow is involuntary, accidental, properly unmotivated. He is a sign that does not mean to mean. Billy, who cannot understand ambiguity, who takes pleasant words at face value and then obliterates Claggart for suggesting that one could do otherwise, whose sudden blow is a violent denial of any discrepancy between his being and his doing, ends up radically illustrating the very discrepancy he denies.

The story thus takes place between the postulate of continuity between signifier and signified ("handsome is as handsome does") and the postulate of their discontinuity ("a mantrap may be under the ruddy-tipped daisies"). Claggart, whose accusations of incipient mutiny are apparently false and therefore illustrate the very double-facedness that they attribute to Billy, is negated for proclaiming the lie about Billy which Billy's act of negation paradoxically proves to be the truth.

This paradox can also be stated in another way, in terms of the opposition between the performative and the constative functions of language. Constative language is language used as an instrument of cognition — it describes, reports, speaks *about* something other than itself. Performative language is language that itself functions as an act, not as a report of one. Promising, betting, swearing, marrying, and declaring war, for example, are not descriptions of acts but acts in their own right. The proverb "handsome is as handsome does" can thus also be read as a statement of the compatibility between the constative (being) and the performative (doing) dimensions of language. But what Billy's act dramatizes is their radical *incompatibility* — Billy performs the truth of Claggart's report to Vere only by means of his absolute and blind denial of its cognitive validity. If Billy had understood the truth, he would not have performed it. Handsome cannot both be and do its own undoing.

The knowledge that being and doing are incompatible cannot know the ultimate performance of its own confirmation.

Melville's chiasmus thus creates a reversal not only of the places of guilt and innocence but also of the postulate of continuity and the postulate of discontinuity between doing and being, performance and cognition. When Billy's fist strikes Claggart's forehead, it is no longer possible for knowing and doing to meet. Melville's story does not report the occurrence of a particularly deadly performative utterance, the tale itself performs the radical incompatibility between knowledge and acts.

All this, we recall, is triggered by a stutter, a linguistic defect. No analysis of the story's dramatization of linguistic categories can be complete without careful attention to this glaring infelicity. Billy's "vocal defect" is presented and explained in the story in the following terms:

> There was just one thing amiss in him . . . an occasional liability to a vocal defect. Though in the hour of elemental uproar or peril he was everything that a sailor should be, yet under sudden provocation of strong heart-feeling his voice, otherwise singularly musical, as if expressive of the harmony within, was apt to develop an organic hesitancy, in fact more or less of a stutter or even worse. In this particular Billy was a striking instance that the arch interferer, the envious marplot of Eden, still has more or less to do with every human consignment to this planet of Earth. In every case, one way or another he is sure to slip in his little card, as much as to remind us — I too have a hand here. (pp. 331–32)

It is doubtless this satanic "hand" that shoots out when Billy's speech fails him. Billy is all too literally a *"striking* instance" of the workings of the "envious marplot."

Melville's choice of the word *marplot* to characterize the originator of Billy's stutter deserves special note. It seems logical to understand that the stutter "mars" the plot in that it triggers the reversal of roles between Billy and Claggart. Yet in another sense this reversal does not mar the plot, it constitutes it. Here, as in the story of Eden, what the envious marplot mars is not the plot, but the state of plotlessness that exists "in the beginning." What both the Book of Genesis and *Billy Budd* narrate is thus not the story of a fall, but a fall into story.

In this connection, it is relevant to recall that Claggart falsely accuses Billy of instigating a *plot,* of stirring up mutiny against the naval authorities. What Claggart is in a sense doing by positing this fictitious plot is trying desperately to scare up a plot for the story. And it is Billy's very act of denial of his involvement in any plot that finally brings him *into* the plot. Billy's involuntary blow is an act of mutiny not only against the authority of his naval superiors but also against the authority of his own conscious intentions. Perhaps it is not by chance that the word *plot* can mean both "intrigue" and "story." If all plots somehow tell the story of their own marring, then perhaps it could be said that all plots are plots against authority, that authority creates the scene of its own destruction, that all stories necessarily recount by their very existence the subversion of the father, of the gods, of consciousness, of order, of expectations, or of meaning.

But is Billy truly as "plotless" as he appears? Does his "simplicity" hide no division, no ambiguity? As many critics have remarked, Billy's character seems to result mainly from his exclusion of the negative. When informed that he is being arbitrarily impressed for service on a man-of-war, Billy "makes no demur" (p. 323). When invited to a clandestine meeting by a mysterious stranger, Billy acquiesces through his "incapacity of plumply saying *no*" (p. 359, emphasis in original). But it is interesting to note that although all the words used to describe him are negative in form: innocent, unconventional, illiterate, unsophisticated, unadulterate, etc. And although he denies any discrepancy between what is said and what is meant, he does not prove to be totally incapable of lying. When asked about the shady visit of the afterguardsman, he distorts his account in order to edit out anything that indicates any incompatibility with the absolute maintenance of authority. He neglects to report the questionable proposition even though "it was his duty as a loyal bluejacket" (p. 362) to do so. In thus shrinking from "the dirty work of a telltale"

(p. 362), Billy maintains his "plotlessness" not spontaneously but through a complex act of filtering. Far from being simply and naturally pure, he is obsessed with maintaining his own irreproachability in the eyes of authority. After witnessing a flogging, he is so horrified that he resolves "that never through remissness would he make himself liable to such a visitation or do or omit aught that might merit even verbal reproof" (p. 346). Billy does not simply exclude the negative; he represses it. His reaction to questionable behavior of any sort (such as that of Red Whiskers, the afterguardsman, Claggart) is to obliterate it. He retains his "*blank* ignorance" (p. 363) only by a vigorous act of erasing. As Melville says of Billy's reaction to Claggart's petty provocations, "the ineffectual speculations into which he was led were so disturbingly alien to him that *he did his best to smother them*" (p. 362).

> In his *disgustful recoil* from an overture which, though he but ill comprehended, he *instinctively knew* must involve evil of some sort, Billy Budd was like a young horse fresh from the pasture suddenly inhaling a vile whiff from some chemical factory, and by repeated snortings trying to *get it out* of his nostrils and lungs. This frame of mind *barred all desire* of holding further parley with the fellow, even were it but for the purpose of gaining some enlightenment as to his design in approaching him. (p. 361)

Billy maintains his purity only through constant, though unconscious, censorship. "Innocence," writes Melville, "was his blinder" (p. 366).

It is interesting to note that while the majority of readers see Billy as a personification of goodness and Claggart as a personification of evil, those who do not, tend to read from a psychoanalytical point of view. Much has been made of Claggart's latent homosexuality, which Melville clearly suggests. Claggart, like the hypothetical "X— ," "is a nut not to be cracked by the tap of a lady's fan" (p. 352). The "unobserved glance" he sometimes casts upon Billy contains "a touch of soft yearning, as if Claggart could even have loved Billy but for fate and ban" (p. 365). The spilling of the soup and Claggart's reaction to it are often read symbolically as a sexual exchange, the import of which, of course, is lost on Billy, who cannot read.

According to this perspective, Claggart's so-called evil is thus really a repressed form of love. But it is perhaps even more interesting to examine the way in which the psychoanalytical view treats Billy's so-called goodness as being in reality a repressed form of hate:

> The persistent feminine imagery . . . indicate[s] that Billy has identified himself with the mother at a pre-Oedipean level and has adopted the attitude of harmlessness and placation toward the father in order to avoid the hard struggle of the Oedipus conflict. . . . That all Billy's rage and hostility against the father are unconscious is symbolized by the fact that whenever aroused it cannot find expression in spoken language. . . . This is a mechanism for keeping himself from admitting his own guilt and his own destructiveness.[13]

> All of Billy's conscious acts are toward passivity. . . . In symbolic language, Billy Budd is seeking his own castration — seeking to yield up his vitality to an authoritative but kindly father, whom he finds in Captain Vere.[14]

> Quite often a patient begins to stutter when he is particularly eager to prove a point. Behind his apparent zeal he has concealed a hostile or sadistic tendency to destroy his opponent by means of words, and the stuttering is both a blocking of and a punishment for this tendency. Still more often stuttering is exacerbated by the presence of prominent or authoritative persons, that is, of paternal figures against whom the unconscious hostility is most intense.[15]

> Although Billy Budd, Sailor is placed in historical time . . . the warfare is not between nations for supremacy on the seas but between father and son in the eternal warfare to determine succession.[16]

> When Vere becomes the father, Claggart and Billy are no longer sailors but sons in rivalry for his

favor and blessing. Claggart manifestly is charging mutiny but latently is accusing the younger son or brother of plotting the father's overthrow. . . . When Billy strikes Claggart with a furious blow to the forehead, he puts out the "evil eye" of his enemy-rival, but at the same time the blow is displaced, since Billy is prohibited from striking the father. After Claggart is struck and lies on the deck "a dead snake," Vere covers his face in silent recognition of the displaced blow.[17]

> Billy's type of innocence is . . . *pseudoinnocence*. . . . Capitalizing on naiveté, it consists of a childhood that is never outgrown, a kind of fixation on the past. . . . When we face questions too big and too horrendous to contemplate . . . we tend to shrink into this kind of innocence and make a virtue of powerlessness, weakness, and helplessness. . . . It is this innocence that cannot come to terms with the destructiveness in one's self or others; and hence, as with Billy Budd, it actually becomes self-destructive.[18]

The psychoanalytical reading is thus a demystification of the notion of innocence portrayed in *Billy Budd*. In the psychoanalytical view, what underlies the metaphysical lament that in this world "goodness is impotent" is the idea that impotence is good, that harmlessness is innocent, that naiveté is lovable, that "giving no cause of offense to anybody" and resolving never "to do or omit aught that might merit . . . reproof" (p. 346) are the highest ideals in human conduct. While most readers react to Billy as do his fellow crew-members ("they all love him," [p. 325] ), the psychoanalysts share Claggart's distrust ("for all his youth and good looks, a deep one," [p. 371] ) and even disdain "to be nothing more than innocent!" [p. 356] ).

In this connection it is curious to note that while the psychoanalysts have implicitly chosen to adopt the attitude of Claggart, Melville, in the crucial confrontation scene, comes close to presenting Claggart as a psychoanalyst:

> With the measured step and calm collected air of an asylum physician approaching in the public hall

[13]Richard Chase, *Herman Melville: A Critical Study,* excerpted in Stafford, *"Billy Budd" and the Critics*, p. 174. [Au.]

[14]Ibid., p. 173. [Au.]

[15]Otto Fenichel, *The Psychoanalytic Theory of Neuroses*, quoted in ibid., p. 176. [Au.]

[16]Edwin Haviland Miller, *Melville* (New York: Persea Books, 1975), p. 358. [Au.]

[17]Ibid., p. 362. [Au.]

[18]Rollo May, *Power and Innocence* (New York: W. W. Norton, 1972), pp. 49–50. [Au.]

some patient beginning to show indications of a coming paroxysm, Claggart deliberately advanced within short range of Billy, and, mesmerically looking him in the eye, briefly recapitulated the accusation. (p. 375)

It is as though Claggart as analyst, in attempting to bring Billy's unconscious hostility to consciousness, unintentionally unleashes the destructive acting-out of transferential rage. The fatal blow, far from being an unmotivated accident, is the gigantic return of the power of negation that Billy has been repressing all his life. And in his blind destructiveness, Billy lashes out against the "father" as well as against the very process of analysis itself.

The difference between the psychoanalytical and the traditional "metaphysical" readings of *Billy Budd* lies mainly in the status accorded to the fatal blow. If Billy represents pure goodness, then his act is unintentional but symbolically righteous, since it results in the destruction of the "evil" Claggart. If Billy is a case of neurotic repression, then his act is determined by his unconscious desires, and reveals the destructiveness of the attempt to repress one's own destructiveness. In the first case, the murder is accidental; in the second, it is the fulfillment of a wish. Strangely enough, this question of accident versus motivation is brought up again at the end of the story, in the curious lack of spontaneous ejaculations in Billy's corpse. Whether the lack of spasm is as mechanical as its presence would have been, or whether it results from what the purser calls "will power" or "euthanasia," the incident stands as a negative analogue of the murder scene. In the former, it is the absence; in the latter, the presence, of physical violence that offers a challenge to interpretation. The burlesque discussion of the "prodigy of repose" by the purser and the surgeon, interrupting as it does the solemnity of Billy's "ascension," can have no other purpose than to dramatize the central importance for the story of the question of arbitrary accident versus determinable motivation. If the psychoanalytical and the metaphysical readings, however incompatible, are both equally supported by textual evidence, then perhaps Melville, rather than asking us to choose between

them, is presenting us with a context in which to examine what is at stake in the very oppositions betwen psychoanalysis and metaphysics, chance and determination, the willed and the accidental, the unconscious and the moral.

## THE DEADLY SPACE BETWEEN

*And thus do we of wisdom and of reach,*
*With windlasses and with assays of bias,*
*By indirections find directions out.* — Hamlet 2.1

While Billy stands as a performative riddle (are his actions motivated or accidental?), John Claggart is presented as an enigma for cognition, a man "who for reasons of his own was keeping *incog*" (p. 343). Repeatedly referred to as a "mystery," Claggart, it seems, is difficult, even perilous, to describe:

For the adequate comprehending of Claggart by a normal nature these hints are insufficient. To pass from a normal nature to him one must cross "the deadly space between." And this is best done by indirection. (p. 352)

Between Claggart and a "normal nature" there exists a gaping cognitive chasm. In a literal sense, this image of crossing a "deadly space" in order to reach Claggart can almost be seen as an ironic prefiguration of the murder. Billy does indeed "cross" the "space" between himself and Claggart by means of a "deadly" blow. The phrase "space between" recurs, in fact, just after the murder, to refer to the physical separation between the dead Claggart and the condemned Billy:

Aft, and on either side, was a small stateroom, the one now temporarily a jail and the other a deadhouse, and a yet smaller compartment, leaving a *space between* expanding forward. (p. 382)

It is by means of a deadly chiasmus that the spatial chasm is crossed.

But physical separation is obviously not the only kind of "deadly space" involved here. The expression "deadly space between" refers primarily to a gap in cognition, a boundary beyond which ordinary understanding does not normally go. This sort of space, which stands as a limit to comprehension, seems to be an inherent feature of the attempt to describe John Claggart. From the very beginning, Melville admits:

His portrait, I essay, but shall never hit it. (p. 342)

What Melville says he will *not* do here is precisely what Billy Budd *does* do: hit John Claggart. It would seem that speaking and killing are thus mutually exclusive; Billy Budd kills because he cannot speak, while Melville, through the very act of speaking, does not kill. Billy's fist crosses the "deadly space" directly; Melville's crossing, "done by indirection," leaves its target intact.

This state of affairs, reassuring as it sounds on a moral level, is rather unsettling, however, if one examines what it implies about Melville's writing. For how reliable can a description be if it does not hit its object? What do we come to know of John Claggart if what we learn is that his portrait is askew? If to describe perfectly, to refer adequately, would be to "hit" the referent and thus annihilate it; if to know completely would be to obliterate the very object known; if the perfect fulfillment of the constative, referential function of language would consist in the total obliteration of the object of that function; then language can retain its "innocence" only by giving up its referential validity. Melville can avoid murder only by grounding his discourse in ineradicable error. If to cross a space by indirection — that is, by rhetorical displacement — is to escape deadlines, that crossing can succeed only on the condition of radically losing its way.

It can thus be said that the "deadly space" that runs through *Billy Budd* is located between cognition and performance, knowing and doing, error and murder. But even this formulation is insufficient if it is taken to imply that doing is deadly while speaking is not, or that directness is murderous while avoidance is innocent. Melville does not simply recommend the replacement of doing by speaking or of direct by indirect language. He continues to treat obliquity and deviation as evils, and speaks of digression as a "literary sin":

In this matter of writing, resolve as one may to keep to the main road, some bypaths have an enticement not readily to be withstood. I am going to err into such a bypath. If the reader will keep me company I shall be glad. At the least, we can promise ourselves that pleasure which is wickedly said to be in sinning, for a literary sin the divergence will be. (p. 334)

Directness and indirectness are equally suspect and equally innocent. Further complications of the moral status of rhetoric will be examined later in this chapter, but first let us pursue the notion of the "deadly space."

If the space at work in *Billy Budd* cannot be located simply and unequivocally between language and action or between directness and indirection, where is it located and how does it function? Why is it the space itself that is called "deadly"? And how, more particularly, does Melville go about *not* hitting John Claggart?

Melville takes up the question of Claggart's "nature" many times. Each time, the description is proffered as a necessary key to the understanding of the story. And yet, each time, what we learn about the master-at-arms is that we cannot learn anything:

Nothing was known of his former life. (p. 343)

About as much was really known to the *Bellipotent's* tars of the master-of-arms' career before entering the service as an astronomer knows about a comet's travels prior to its first observable appearance in the sky. (p. 345)

What can more partake of the mysterious than an antipathy spontaneous and profound . . . ? (p. 351)

Dark sayings are these, some will say. But why? Is it because they somewhat savor of Holy Writ in its phrase "mystery of iniquity"? (p. 354)

And, after informing us that the crossing of the "deadly space" between Claggart and a "normal nature" is "best done by indirection," Melville's narrator takes himself at his word; he digresses into a long fictitious dialogue between himself as a youth and an older "honest scholar" concerning a mysterious Mr. "X— ," whose "labyrinth" cannot be penetrated by "knowledge of the world," a dialogue so full of periphrases that the youthful participant himself "did not quite see" its "drift" (p. 353). The very phrase "the deadly space between" is, according to editors Hayford and

Sealts, a quotation of unknown origin; the source of the expression used to designate what is not known is thus itself unknown. Even the seemingly satisfactory Platonic definition of Claggart's evil — "Natural Depravity: a depravity according to nature" — is in fact, as F. B. Freeman points out, nothing but a tautology. Syntactically, the definition fulfills its function, but it is empty of any cognitive information. The place of explanation and definition is repeatedly filled, but its content is always lacking. The progress of Melville's description describes an infinite regress of knowledge. The "deadly space" is situated not between Claggart and his fellow men, but within Melville's very attempts to account for him.

It would seem that rather than simply separating language from action, the space in question is also at work within language itself. In the tautology of Claggart's evil, it marks an empty articulation between the expression and its definition. Other linguistic spaces abound. What, indeed, is Billy's fateful stutter, if not a deadly gap in his ability to speak? The space opened up by the stutter is the pivot on which the entire story turns. And the last words of the dying Captain Vere, which stand in the place of ultimate commentary upon the drama, are simply "Billy Budd, Billy Budd," the empty repetition of a name. At all the crucial moments in the drama — in the origin of evil, in the trigger of the act, in the final assessment — the language of *Billy Budd* stutters. At those moments, the constative or referential content is eclipsed; language conveys only its own empty, mechanical functioning. But these very gaps in understanding are what Melville is asking us to understand.

The cognitive spaces marked out by these eclipses of meaning are important not because they mark the limits of interpretation but because they function as its cause. The gaps in understanding are never directly perceived as such by the characters in the novel; those gaps are themselves taken as interpretable signs and triggers for interpretation. The lack of knowledge of Claggart's past, for example, is seen as a sign that he has something to hide:

Nothing was known of his former life. . . . Among certain grizzled sea gossips of the gun decks and forecastle went a rumor perdue that the master-of-arms was a *chevalier* [emphasis in original] who had volunteered into the King's navy by way of compounding for some mysterious swindle whereof he had been arraigned at the King's Bench. *The fact that nobody could substantiate this report was, of course, nothing against its secret currency. . . .* Indeed a man of Claggart's accomplishments, without prior nautical experiences entering the navy at mature life, as he did, and necessarily allotted at the start to the lowest grade in it; a man too who never made allusion to his previous life ashore; these were circumstances which *in the dearth of exact knowledge* as to his true antecedents opened to the invidious *a vague field for unfavorable surmise.* (p. 343)

In other words, the absence of knowledge here leads to the propagation of tales. The absence of knowledge of Claggart's origins is not a simple, contingent, theoretically remediable lack of information; it is the very *origin* of his "evil nature." Interestingly, in Billy's case, an equal lack of knowledge leads some readers to see his origin as divine. Asked who his father is, Billy replies, "God knows." The divine and the satanic can thus be seen as metaphysical interpretations of discontinuities in knowledge. In *Billy Budd,* a stutter and a tautology serve to mark the spot from which evil springs.

Evil, then, is essentially the misreading of discontinuity through the attribution of meaning to a space or division in language. But the fact that stories of Claggart's evil arise out of a seemingly meaningless gap in knowledge is hardly a meaningless or innocent fact in itself, either in its cause or in its consequences. Claggart's function is that of a policeman "charged among other matters with the duty of preserving order on the populous lower gun decks" (p. 342). As Melville points out, "no man holding his office in a man-of-war can ever hope to be popular with the crew" (p. 345). The inevitable climate of resentment surrounding the master-at-arms might itself be sufficient to turn the hypothesis of depravity into a self-fulfilling prophecy. As Melville put it, "The point of the present story *turn[s] on the hidden nature* of the master-at-arms" (p. 354). The entire plot of *Billy Budd* could conceivably be seen as a consequence not of what Claggart does but of what he does not say.

It is thus by means of the misreading of gaps in knowledge and of discontinuities in action that the plot of *Billy Budd* takes shape. But because Melville describes both the spaces and the readings they engender, his concentration of the vagaries of interpretive error opens up within the text the possibility of substantiating quite a number of "inside narratives" different from the one with which we are explicitly presented. What Melville's tale tells is the snowballing of tale-telling. It is possible, indeed, to retell the story from a point of view that fully justifies Claggart's suspicions, merely by putting together a series of indications already available in the narrative.

1. As Billy is being taken from the merchant ship to the warship, he shouts in farewell, "And good-bye to you too, old *Rights-of-Man*" (emphasis in original). Ratcliffe, who later recounts the incident to Claggart (as is shown by the latter's referring to it in making his accusation to Vere), interprets this as "a sly slur at impressment in general, and that of himself in especial" (p. 327). The first information Claggart is likely to have gleaned on Billy Budd has thus passed through the filter of the lieutenant's interpretation that the handsome recruit's apparent gaiety conceals resentment.

2. When Billy resolves, after seeing the flogging of another novice, "never to merit reproof," his "punctiliousness in duty" (p. 346) is laughed at by his topmates. Billy tries desperately to make his actions coincide with his desire for perfect irreproachability, but he nevertheless finds himself "getting into petty trouble" (p. 346). Billy's "unconcealed anxiety" is considered "comical" by his fellows (p. 347). It is thus Billy's obsessive concern with his own perfection that starts a second snowball rolling, since Claggart undertakes a subtle campaign of petty persecutions "to try the temper of the man" (p. 358). The instrument used by Claggart to set "little traps for the worriment of the foretopman" is a corporal called "Squeak," who, "having naturally enough concluded that his master could have no love for the sailor, made it his business,

faithful understrapper that he was, to foment the ill blood by perverting to his chief certain innocent frolics of the good-natured foretopman, besides inventing for his mouth sundry contumelious epithets he claimed to have overheard him let fall" (p. 357). Again, Claggart perceives Billy only through the distortion of an unfavorable interpretation.

3. With this impression of Billy already in his mind, Claggart proceeds to take Billy's spilling of the soup across his path "not for the mere accident it assuredly was, but for the sly escape of a spontaneous feeling on Billy's part more or less answering to the antipathy on his own" (p. 356). If this is an overreading, it is important to note that the critical tendency to see sexual or religious symbolism in the soup scene operates on exactly the same assumption as that made by Claggart — what appears to be an accident is actually motivated and meaningful. Claggart's spontaneous interpretation, hidden behind his playful words ("Handsomely done"), is not only legitimate enough on its own terms, but receives unexpected confirmation in Billy's naive outburst: "There now, who says that Jemmy Legs is down on me?" This evidence of a preexisting context in which Claggart, referred to by his disrespectful nickname, has been discussed by Billy with others — apparently a number of others, although in fact it is only one person — provides all the support Claggart needs to substantiate his suspicions. And still, he is willing to try another test.

4. Claggart sends an afterguardsman to Billy at night with a proposition to join a mutinous conspiracy of impressed men. Although Billy rejects the invitation, he does not report it as loyalty demands. He is thus protecting the conspirators. Claggart's last test has been completed; Billy is a danger to the ship. In his function as chief of police, it is Claggart's duty to report the danger.

This "reversed" reading is no more — but certainly no less — legitimate than the ordinary "good versus evil" interpretation. But its very possibility — evoked not only by these behind-the-scenes hints and nuances but also by the "garbled" newspaper report — can be taken as a sign of the centrality of the question of reading posed not only *by* but also *in* the text of *Billy Budd*. Far from recounting an unequivocal "clash of opposites"[19] the confrontation between Billy and Claggart is built by a series of minute gradations and subtle insinuations. The opposites that clash here are not two *characters* but two *readings*.

## THREE READINGS OF READING

It is no doubt significant that the character around whom the greatest critical dissent has revolved is neither the good one nor the evil one but the one who is explicitly presented as a *reader,* Captain Vere. On some level, readers of *Billy Budd* have always testified to the fact that reading, as much as killing, is at the heart of Melville's story. But how is the act of reading being manifested? And what, precisely, are its relations with the deadliness of the spaces it attempts to comprehend?

As we have noted, critical readings of *Billy Budd* have generally divided themselves into two opposing groups, the "testament of acceptance" school on the one hand and the "testament of resistance" or "irony" school on the other. The first is characterized by its tendency to take at face value the narrator's professed admiration of Vere's sagacity and the final benediction of Vere uttered by Billy. The second group is characterized by its tendency to distance the reader's point of view from that of any of the characters, including the narrator, so that the injustice of Billy's execution becomes perceptible through a process of reversal of certain explicit pronouncements within the tale. This opposition between "acceptance" and "irony" quite strikingly mirrors, as we mentioned earlier, the opposition within the story between Billy's naiveté and Claggart's paranoia. We will therefore begin our analysis of Melville's study of the nature of reading with an examination of the way in which the act of reading is manifested in the confrontation between these two characters.

[19]John Middleton Murry, quoted in Stafford, *"Billy Budd" and the Critics,* p. 132. [Au.]

It seems evident that Billy's method consists of taking everything at face value, while Claggart's consists of seeing a mantrap under every daisy. Yet in practice, neither of these methods is rigorously upheld. The naive reader is not naive enough to forget to edit out information too troubling to report. The instability of the space between sign and referent, normally denied by the naive reader, is called upon as an instrument whenever that same instability threatens to disturb the content of meaning itself. Billy takes every sign as transparently readable as long as what he reads is consistent with transparent peace, order, and authority. When this is not so, his reading clouds accordingly. And Claggart, for whom every sign can be read as its opposite, neglects to doubt the transparency of any sign that tends to confirm his own doubts: "the master-of-arms *never suspected the veracity*" (p. 357) of Squeak's reports. The naive believer thus refuses to believe any evidence that subverts the transparency of his beliefs, while the ironic doubter forgets to suspect the reliability of anything confirming his own suspicions.

Naiveté and irony stand as symmetrical opposites blinded by their very incapacity to see anything but symmetry. Claggart, in his antipathy, "can really form no conception of an *unreciprocated* malice" (p. 358). And Billy, conscious of his own blamelessness, can see nothing but pleasantness in Claggart's pleasant words: "Had the foretopman been conscious of having done or said anything to provoke the ill-will of the official, it would have been different with him, and his sight might have been purged if not sharpened. As it was, innocence was his blinder" (p. 366). Each character sees the other only through the mirror of his own reflection. Claggart, looking at Billy, mistakes his own twisted face for the face of an enemy, while Billy, recognizing in Claggart the negativity he smothers in himself, strikes out.

The naive and the ironic readers are thus equally destructive, both of themselves and of each other. It is significant that both Billy and Claggart should die. Both readings do violence to the plays of ambiguity and belief by forcing upon the text the applicability of a universal and absolute law. The one, obsessively intent on preserving peace and eliminating equivocation, murders the text; the other, seeing nothing but universal war, becomes the spot on which aberrant premonitions of negativity become truth.

But what of the third reader in the drama, Captain Vere? What can be said of a reading whose task is precisely to read the *relation* between naiveté and paranoia, acceptance and irony, murder and error?

For many readers, the function of Captain Vere has been to provide "complexity" and "reality" in an otherwise "oversimplified" allegorical confrontation:

> Billy and Claggart, who represent almost pure good and pure evil, are too simple and too extreme to satisfy the demands of realism; for character demands admixture. Their all but allegorical blackness and whiteness, however, are functional in the service of Vere's problem, and Vere, goodness knows, is real enough.[20]

> *Billy Budd* seems different from much of the later work, less "mysterious," even didactic. . . . Its issues seem somewhat simplified, and, though the opposition of Christly Billy and Satanic Claggart is surely diagrammatic, it appears almost melodramatic in its reduction of values. Only Captain Vere seems to give the story complexity, his deliberations acting like a balance wheel in a watch, preventing a rapid, obvious resolution of the action. . . . It is Vere's decision, and the debatable rationale for it, which introduces the complexity of intimation, the ambiguity.[21]

As the locus of complexity, Captain Vere then becomes the "balance wheel" not only in the clash between good and evil but also in the clash between "accepting" and "ironic" interpretations of the story. Critical opinion has pronounced the captain "vicious" and "virtuous," "self-mythifying" and "self-sacrificing," "capable" and "cowardly," "responsible" and "criminal," "moral" and "perverted," "intellectual" and "stupid,"

"moderate" and "authoritarian."[22] But how does the same character provoke such diametrically opposed responses? Why is it the judge that is so passionately judged?

In order to analyze what is at stake in Melville's portrait of Vere, let us first examine the ways in which Vere's reading differs from those of Billy Budd and John Claggart:

1. While the naive/ironic dichotomy was based on a symmetry between *individuals,* Captain Vere's reading takes place within a social *structure:* the rigidly hierarchical structure of a British warship. While the naive reader (Billy) destroys the other in order to defend the self, and while the ironic reader (Claggart) destroys the self by projecting aggression onto the other, the third reader (Vere) subordinates both self and other, and ultimately sacrifices both self and other, for the preservation of a political order.

2. The apparent purpose of both Billy's and Claggart's readings was to determine character; to preserve innocence or to prove guilt. Vere, on the other hand, subordinates character to action, being to doing. "A martial court," he tells his officers, "must needs in the present case confine its attention to the *blow's consequence,* which consequence justly is to be deemed not otherwise than as the *striker's deed*" (p. 384).

3. In the opposition between the metaphysical and psychoanalytical readings of Billy's deed, the deciding question was whether the blow should be considered accidental or (unconsciously) motivated. But in Vere's courtroom reading, both these alternatives are irrelevant:

[20]Tindall, *"Billy Budd" and the Critics,* p. 187. [Au.]

[21]John Seelye, *Melville: The Ironic Diagram* (Evanston, Ill.: Northwestern University Press, 1970), p. 162. [Au.]

[22]Kingsley Widmer, *The Ways of Nihilism: A Study of Herman Melville's Short Novels* (Los Angeles: Ritchie, Ward, Press, for California State Colleges, 1970), p. 21; Hannah Arendt, *On Revolution* (New York: Viking Press, 1963), pp. 77–83; Widmer, *Nihilism,* p. 33; Milton Stern, *The Fine Hammered Steel of Herman Melville* (Urbana: University of Illinois Press, 1957), pp. 206–50; Weir, "Malice Reconciled," p. 121; Withim, *"Billy Budd,"* p. 126; Weir, "Malice Reconciled," p. 121; Thompson, *Melville's Quarrel,* p. 386; Weir, "Malice Reconciled," p. 124; Leonard Casper, "The Case against Captain Vere," *Perspective* 5, no. 3 (Summer 1952): p. 151; Weir, "Malice Reconciled," p. 121; Thompson, *Melville's Quarrel,* p. 386; James E. Miller, *"Billy Budd*: The Catastrophe of Innocence," *MLN* 73 (March, 1958): p. 174; Widmer, *Nihilism,* p. 29. [Au.]

"Budd's intent or non-intent is nothing to the purpose" (p. 389). What matters is not the cause but the consequences of the blow.

4. The naive or literal reader takes language at face value and treats signs as *motivated;* the ironic reader assumes that the relation between sign and meaning can be *arbitrary* and that appearances are made to be reversed. For Vere, the functions and meanings of signs are neither transparent nor reversible but fixed by socially determined *convention*. Vere's very character is determined not by a relation between his outward appearance and his inner being but by the "buttons" that signify his position in society. While both Billy and Claggart are said to owe their character to "nature," Vere sees his actions and being as meaningful only within the context of a contractual allegiance:

> Do these buttons that we wear attest that our allegiance is to Nature? No, to the King. Though the ocean, which is inviolate Nature primeval, though this be the element where we move and have our being as sailors, yet as the King's officers lies our duty in a sphere correspondingly natural? So little is that true, that in receiving our commissions we in the most important regards ceased to be natural free agents. When war is declared are we the commissioned fighters previously consulted? We fight at command. If our judgments approve the war, that is but coincidence. (p. 387)

Judgment is thus for Vere a function neither of individual conscience nor of absolute justice but of "the rigor of martial law" (p. 387) operating *through* him.

5. While Billy and Claggart read spontaneously and directly, Vere's reading often makes use of precedent (historical facts, childhood memories), allusions (to the Bible, to various ancient and modern authors), and analogies (Billy is like Adam, Claggart is like Ananias). Just as both Billy and Claggart have no known past, they read without memory; just as their lives end with their reading, they read without foresight. Vere, on the other hand, interrogates both past and future for interpretative guidance.

6. While Budd and Claggart thus oppose each other directly, without regard for circumstance or consequence, Vere reads solely in function of the attending historical situation; the Nore and Spithead mutinies have created an atmosphere "critical to naval authority" (p. 380), and, since an engagement with the enemy fleet is possible at any moment, the *Bellipotent* cannot afford internal unrest.

The fundamental factor that underlies the opposition between the metaphysical Budd/Claggart conflict on the one hand and the reading of Captain Vere on the other can be summed up in a single word: history. While the naive and the ironic readers attempt to impose upon language the functioning of an absolute, timeless, universal law (the sign as either motivated or arbitrary), the question of *martial* law arises within the story precisely to reveal the law as a historical phenomenon, to underscore the element of contextual mutability in the conditions of any act of reading. Arbitrariness and motivation, irony and literality, are parameters between which language constantly fluctuates, but only historical context determines which proportion of each is perceptible to each reader. Melville indeed shows history to be a story not only of events but also of fluctuations in the very functioning of irony and belief:

> The event *converted into irony for a time* those spirited strains of Dibdin. . . . (p. 333)

> Everything is *for a term venerated* in navies. (p. 408)

The opposing critical judgments of Vere's decision to hang Billy are divided, in the final analysis, according to the place they attribute to history in the process of justification. For the ironists, Vere is misusing history for his own self-preservation or for the preservation of a world safe for aristocracy. For those who accept Vere's verdict as tragic but necessary, it is Melville who has stacked the historical cards in Vere's favor. In both cases, the conception of history as an interpretive instrument remains the same: it is its *use* that is being judged. And the very direction of *Billy Budd* criticism itself, historically moving from acceptance to irony, is no doubt itself interpretable in the same historical terms.

Evidence can be found in the text for both pro-Vere and anti-Vere judgments:

Full of disquietude and misgivings, the surgeon left the cabin. Was Captain Vere suddenly affected in his mind? (p. 378)

Whether Captain Vere, as the surgeon professionally and privately surmised, was really the sudden victim of any degree of aberration, every one must determine for himself by such light as this narrative may afford. (pp. 379–80)

That the unhappy event which has been narrated could not have happened at a worse juncture was but too true. For it was close on the heel of the suppressed insurrections, an aftertime very critical to naval authority, demanding from every English sea commander two qualities not readily interfusable — prudence and rigor. (p. 380)

Small wonder then that the *Bellipotent's* captain . . . felt that circumspection not less than promptitude was necessary. . . . Here he may or may not have erred. (p. 380)

The effect of these explicit oscillations of judgment within the text is to underline the importance of the act of judging while rendering its outcome undecidable. Judgment, however difficult, is clearly the central preoccupation of Melville's text, whether it be the judgment pronounced *by* Vere or *upon* him.

There is still another reason for the uncertainty over Vere's final status, however: the unfinished state of the manuscript at Melville's death. According to editors Hayford and Sealts,[23] it is the "late pencil revisions" that cast the greatest doubt upon Vere; Melville was evidently still fine-tuning the text's attitude toward its third reader when he died. The ultimate irony in the tale is thus that our final judgment of the very reader who takes history into consideration is made problematic by the intervention of history; by the historical accident of the author's death. History here affects interpretation not only within the content of the narration but also within the very production of the narrative. And what remains suspended by this historical accident is nothing less than the exact signifying value of history. Clearly, the meaning of "history" as a feature

[23]See especially pp. 34–35, Editors' Introduction, *Billy Budd, Sailor* (Chicago: University of Chicago Press, 1962). [Au.]

distinguishing Vere's reading from those of Claggart and Budd can in no way be taken for granted.

## JUDGMENT AS POLITICAL PERFORMANCE

> *When a poet takes his seat on the tripod of the Muse, he cannot control his thoughts. . . . When he represents men with contrasting characters he is often obliged to contradict himself, and he doesn't know which of the opposing speeches contains the truth. But for the legislator, this is impossible: he must not let his laws say two different things on the same subject.*
> — PLATO, *The Laws*

In the final analysis, the question is not, What did Melville really think of Captain Vere? but rather, What is at stake in his way of presenting him? What can we learn from him about the act of judging? Melville seems to be presenting us less with an object for judgment than with an example of judgment. And the very vehemence with which the critics tend to praise or condemn the justice of Vere's decision indicates that it is judging, not murdering, that Melville is asking us to judge.

And yet Vere's judgment *is* an act of murder. Captain Vere is a reader who kills, not, like Billy, instead of speaking, but rather, precisely by means of speaking. While Billy kills through verbal impotence, Vere kills through the very potency and sophistication of rhetoric. Judging, in Vere's case, is nothing less than the wielding of the power of life and death through language. In thus occupying the point at which murder and language meet, Captain Vere positions himself astride the "deadly space between." While Billy's performative force occupies the vanishing point of utterance and cognition, and while the validity of Claggart's cognitive perception is realized only through the annihilation of the perceiver, Captain Vere's reading mobilizes both power and knowledge, performance and cognition, error and murder. Judgment is cognition functioning as an act. This combination of performance and cognition defines Vere's reading not merely as historical but as political. If politics is defined as the attempt to reconcile action with understanding, then Melville's story offers an exemplary context in which to analyze the interpretive and performative structures that make politics so problematic.

Melville's story amply demonstrates that the alliance between knowledge and action is by no means an easy one. Vere indeed has often been seen as the character in the tale who experiences the greatest suffering; his understanding of Billy's character and his military duty are totally at odds. On the one hand, cognitive exactitude requires that "history" be taken into consideration. Yet what constitutes "knowledge of history"? How are "circumstances" to be defined? What sort of causality does "precedent" imply? And what is to be done with overlapping but incompatible "contexts"? Before deciding upon innocence and guilt, Vere must define and limit the frame of reference within which his decision is to be possible. He does so by choosing the "legal" context over the "essential" context:

> In a *legal view* the apparent victim of the tragedy was he who had sought to victimize a man blameless; and the indisputable deed of the latter, *navally regarded,* constituted the most heinous of military crimes. Yet more. The *essential right and wrong* involved in the matter, the clearer that might be, so much the worse for the responsibility of a loyal sea commander, inasmuch as he was not authorized to determine the matter on that primitive basis. (p. 380)

Yet is precisely this determination of the proper frame of reference that dictates the outcome of the decision; once Vere has defined his context, he has also in fact reached his verdict. The very choice of the *conditions* of judgment itself constitutes a judgment. But what are the conditions of choosing the conditions of judgment?

The alternative, it seems, is between the "naval" and the "primitive," between "Nature" and "the King," between the martial court and what Vere calls the "Last Assizes" (p. 388). But the question arises of exactly what the concept "Nature" entails in such an opposition. In what way, and with what changes, would it have been possible for Vere's allegiance to be to "Nature"? How can a legal judgment exemplify "primitive" justice?

In spite of his allegiance to martial law and conventional authority, Vere clearly finds the "absolute" criteria equally applicable to Billy's deed, for he responds to each new development with the following exclamations:

> "It is the divine judgment on Ananias!" (p. 278)

> "Struck dead by an angel of God! Yet the angel must hang!" (p. 378)

> "Before a court less arbitrary and more merciful than a martial one, that plea would largely extenuate. At the Last Assizes it shall acquit." (p. 388)

> "Ay, there is a mystery; but, to use a scriptural phrase, it is a 'mystery of iniquity,' a matter for psychologic theologians to discuss." (p. 385)

This last expression, which refers to the source of Claggart's antipathy, has already been mentioned by Melville's narrator and dismissed as being "tinctured with the biblical element":

> If that lexicon which is based on Holy Writ were any longer popular, one might with less difficulty define and denominate certain phenomenal men. As it is, one must turn to some authority not liable to the charge of being tinctured with the biblical element. (p. 353)

Vere turns to the Bible to designate Claggart's "nature"; Melville turns to a Platonic tautology. But in both cases, the question arises, What does it mean to seal an explanation with a quotation? And what, in Vere's case, does it mean to refer a legal mystery to a religious text?

If Vere names the "absolute" — as opposed to the martial — by means of quotations and allusions, does this not suggest that the two alternative frames of reference within which judgment is possible are not nature and the king, but rather two types of textual authority: the Bible and the Mutiny Act? This is not to say that Vere is "innocently" choosing one text over another, but that the nature of "nature" in a legal context cannot be taken for granted. Even Thomas Paine, who is referred to by Melville in his function as proponent of "natural" human rights, cannot avoid grounding his concept of nature in biblical myth. In the very act of rejecting the authority of antiquity, he writes:

The fact is, that portions of antiquity, by proving every thing, establish nothing. It is authority against authority all the way, till we come to the divine origin of the rights of man, at the Creation. Here our inquiries find a resting-place, and our reason finds a home.[24]

The final frame of reference is neither the heart nor the gun, neither nature nor the king, but the authority of a sacred text. Authority seems to be nothing other than the vanishing-point of textuality. And nature is authority whose textual origins have been forgotten. Even behind the martial order of the world of the man-of-war, there lies a religious referent: the *Bellipotent*'s last battle is with a French ship called the *Athée*.

Judgment, then, would seem to ground itself in a suspension of the opposition between textuality and referentiality, just as politics can be seen as that which makes it impossible to draw the line between "language" and "life." Vere, indeed, is presented as a reader who does not recognize the "frontier" between "remote allusions" and current events:

> In illustrating of any point touching the stirring personages and events of the time he would be as apt to cite some historic character or incident of antiquity as he would be to cite from the moderns. He seemed unmindful of the circumstances that to his bluff company such remote allusions, however pertinent they might really be, were altogether alien to men whose reading was mainly confined to the journals. But considerateness in such matters is not easy to natures constituted like Captain Vere's. Their honesty prescribes to them directness, sometimes far-reaching like that of a migratory fowl that in its flight never heeds when it crosses a frontier. (p. 341)

Yet it is by inviting Billy Budd and John Claggart to "cross" the "frontier" between their proper territory and their superior's cabin, between the private and the political realms, that Vere unwittingly sets up the conditions for the narrative chiasmus he must judge.

As was noted earlier, Captain Vere's function, according to many critics, is to insert "ambiguity" into the story's "oversimplified" allegorical

opposition. Yet, at the same time, it is Captain Vere who inspires the most vehement critical oppositions. In other words, he seems to mobilize simultaneously the seemingly contradictory forces of ambiguity and polarity.

In his median position between the Budd/Claggart opposition and the acceptance/irony opposition, Captain Vere functions as a focus for the conversion of polarity into ambiguity and back again. Interestingly, he plays exactly the same role in the progress of the plot. It is Vere who brings together the "innocent" Billy and the "guilty" Claggart in order to test the validity of Claggart's accusations, but he does so in such a way as to effect not a clarification but a reversal of places between guilt and innocence. Vere's fatherly words to Billy trigger the ambiguous deed upon which Vere must pronounce a verdict of "condemn *or* let go." Just as Melville's readers, faced with the ambiguity they themselves recognize as being provided by Vere, are quick to pronounce the captain vicious *or* virtuous, evil *or* just; so, too, Vere, who clearly perceives the "mystery" in the "moral dilemma" confronting him, must nevertheless reduce the situation to a binary opposition.

It would seem, then, that the function of judgment is to convert an ambiguous situation into a decidable one. But it does so by converting a difference *within* (Billy as divided between conscious submissiveness and unconscious hostility, Vere as divided between understanding father and military authority) into a difference *between* (between Claggart and Billy, between Nature and the King, between authority and criminality). A difference *between* opposing forces presupposes that the entities in conflict be knowable. A difference *within* one of the entities in question is precisely what problematizes the very *idea* of an entity in the first place, rendering the "legal point of view" inapplicable. In studying the plays of both ambiguity and binarity, Melville's story situates *its* critical difference neither within nor between, but in the *relation between the two* as the fundamental question of all human politics. The political context in *Billy Budd* is such that on all levels the differences *within* (mutiny on the warship, the French revolution as a threat to "lasting institutions," Billy's unconscious hostil-

---

[24]Thomas Paine, *The Rights of Man* (Garden City: Anchor Press, 1973), p. 303. [Au.]

ity) are subordinated to differences *between* (the *Bellipotent* vs. the *Athée,* England vs. France, murderer vs. victim). This is why Melville's choice of historical setting is so significant; the war between France and England at the time of the French Revolution is as striking an example of the simultaneous functioning of differences within and between as is the confrontation between Billy and Claggart in relation to their own internal divisions. War, indeed, is the absolute transformation of all differences into binary differences.

It would seem, then, that the maintenance of political authority requires that the law function as a set of rules for the regular, predictable misreading of the "difference within" as a "difference between." Yet if, as our epigraph from Plato suggests, law is thus defined in terms of its repression of ambiguity, then it is itself an overwhelming example of an entity based on a "difference within." Like Billy, the law, in attempting to eliminate its own "deadly space," can only inscribe itself in a space of deadliness.

In seeking to regulate the violent effects of difference, the political work of cognition is thus an attempt to situate that which must be eliminated. Yet in the absence of the possibility of knowing the locus and origin of violence, cognition itself becomes an act of violence. In terms of pure understanding, the drawing of a line between opposing entities does violence to the irreducible ambiguities that subvert the very possibility of determining the limits of what an "entity" is:

> Who in the rainbow can draw the line where the violet tint ends and the orange tint begins? Distinctly we see the difference of the colors, but where exactly does the first blendingly enter into the other? So with sanity and insanity. In pronounced cases there is no question about them. But in some supposed cases, in various degrees supposedly less pronounced, to draw the exact line of demarcation few will undertake, though for a fee becoming considerate some professional experts will. There is nothing nameable but that some men will, or undertake to, do it for pay. (p. 379)

As an act, drawing a line is inexact and violent; and it also problematizes the very possibility of situating the "difference between" the judge and what is judged, between the interests of the "expert" and the truth of his expertise. What every act of judgment manifests is not the value of the object but the position of the judge within a structure of exchange. There is, in other words, no position from which to judge that would be outside the lines of force involved in the object judged.

But if judging is always a *partial* reading (in both senses of the word), is there a place for reading beyond politics? Are we, as Melville's readers, outside the arena in which power and fees are exchanged? If law is the forcible transformation of ambiguity into decidability, is it possible to read ambiguity *as such,* without that reading functioning as a political act?

Melville has something to say even about this. For there is a fourth reader in *Billy Budd,* one who "never interferes in aught and never gives advice" (p. 363): the old Dansker. A man of "few words, many wrinkles" and "the complexion of an antique parchment" (p. 347), the Dansker is the very picture of one who understands and emits ambiguous utterances. When asked by Billy for an explanation of his petty troubles, the Dansker says only, "Jemmy Legs [Claggart] is down on you" (p. 349). This interpretation, entirely accurate as a reading of Claggart's ambiguous behavior, is handed down to Billy without further explanation:

> Something less unpleasantly oracular he tried to extract; but the old sea Chiron, thinking perhaps that for the nonce he had sufficiently instructed his young Achilles, pursed his lips, gathered all his wrinkles together, and would commit himself to nothing further. (p. 349)

As a reader who understands ambiguity yet refuses to "commit himself," the Dansker thus dramatizes a reading that attempts to be as cognitively accurate and as performatively neutral as possible. Yet however neutral he tries to remain, the Dansker's reading does not take place outside the political realm; it is his very refusal to participate in it, whether by further instruction or by direct intervention, that leads to Billy's exclamation in the soup episode ("There now, who says Jemmy Legs is down on me?"). The transference of knowledge is no more innocent than the transference of power, for it is through the impossibility of finding a spot from which knowledge could be all-encompassing that the plays of political power proceed.

Just as the attempt to know without doing can itself function as a deed, the fact that judgment is always explicitly an act adds a further insoluble problem to its cognitive predicament. Since, as Vere points out, no judgment can take place in the "*Last* Assizes," no judge can ever pronounce a Last Judgment. In order to reach a verdict, Vere must determine the consequences not only of the fatal blow but also of his own verdict. Judgment is an act not only because it kills, but because it is in turn open to judgment:

> "Can we not convict and yet mitigate the penalty?" asked the sailing master. . . .
> "Gentlemen, were that clearly lawful for us under the circumstances, consider the consequences of such clemency. . . . To the people the foretopman's deed, however it be worded in the announcement, will be plain homicide committed in a flagrant act of mutiny. What penalty for that should follow, they know. But it does not follow. *Why?* They will ruminate. You know what sailors are. Will they not revert to the recent outbreak at the Nore?" (p. 389)

The danger is not only one of repeating the Nore mutiny, however. It is also one of forcing Billy, for all his innocence, to repeat his crime. Billy is a politically charged object from the moment he strikes his superior. He is no longer, and can never again be, plotless. If he were set free, he himself would be unable to explain why. As a focus for the questions and intrigues of the crew, he would be even less capable of defending himself than before, and would surely strike again. The political reading, as cognition, attempts to understand the past; as performance, it attempts to eliminate from the future any necessity for its own recurrence.

What this means is that every judge is in the impossible position of having to include the ef-fects of his own act of judging within the cognitive context of his decision. The question of the nature of the type of historical causality that would govern such effects can neither be decided nor ignored. Because of his official position, Vere cannot choose to read in such a way that his reading would not be an act of political authority. But Melville shows in *Billy Budd* that authority consists precisely in the impossibility of containing the effects of its own application.

As a political allegory, Melville's *Billy Budd* is thus much more than a study of good and evil, justice and injustice. It is a dramatization of the twisted relations between knowing and doing, speaking and killing, reading and judging, which make political understanding and action so problematic. In the subtle creation of Claggart's "evil" out of a series of spaces in knowledge, Melville shows that gaps in cognition, far from being mere absences, take on the performative power of true acts. The *force* of what is not known is all the more effective for not being perceived as such. The crew, which does not understand that it does not know, is no less performative a reader than the captain, who clearly perceives and represses the presence of "mystery." The legal order, which attempts to submit "brute force" to "forms, measured forms," can only eliminate violence by transforming violence into the final authority. And cognition, which perhaps begins as a power play against the play of power, can only increase, through its own elaboration, the range of what it tries to dominate. The "deadly space" or "difference" that runs through *Billy Budd* is not located between knowledge and action, performance and cognition. It is that which, within cognition, functions as an act; it is that which, within action, prevents us from ever knowing whether what we hit coincides with what we understand. And this is what makes the meaning of Melville's last work so *striking*.

# Stephen Greenblatt
b. 1943

*Renaissance scholar Stephen Jay Greenblatt is in the vanguard of academics responsible for the rise of New Historicist studies in the United States. Greenblatt was born in Cambridge, Massachusetts; he took a B.A. (1964), an M.Phil. (1968), and a Ph.D. (1969) in English at Yale, and an A.B. (1966) and M.A. (1968) at Pembroke College, Cambridge University. Since 1969 Greenblatt has taught at the University of California at Berkeley, becoming a full professor in 1980. Among Greenblatt's honors are a Fulbright scholarship (1964–66), a Guggenheim fellowship (1975), and a visiting professorship at the University of Peking (1982). His books include* Sir Walter Raleigh: The Renaissance Man and His Roles *(1973),* Allegory and Representation *(1979),* Renaissance Self-Fashioning: From More to Shakespeare *(1980),* Representing the English Renaissance *(1988), and* Shakespearean Negotiations: The Circulation of Social Energy in Renaissance England. *Greenblatt is also the editor of* Representations, *a Berkeley-based journal in which New Historicist articles regularly appear. The selections here are from a special issue of* Genre *(Spring/Summer 1982), titled* The Power of Forms in the English Renaissance. *In the Introduction, Greenblatt makes reference to some of the other essays in the volume but not to his own "King Lear and Harsnett's 'Devil-Fiction.'"*

# Introduction to *The Power of Forms in the English Renaissance*

"I am Richard II. Know ye not that?" exclaimed Queen Elizabeth on August 4, 1601, in the wake of the abortive Essex rising. On the day before the rising, someone had paid the Lord Chamberlain's Men forty shillings to revive their old play about the deposing and killing of Richard II. As far as we know, the play — almost certainly Shakespeare's — was performed only once at the Globe, but in Elizabeth's bitter recollection the performance has metastasized: "this tragedy was played 40tie times in open streets and houses."[1]

The Queen enjoyed and protected the theater; against moralists who charged that it was a corrupting and seditious force, she evidently sided with those who replied that it released social tensions, inculcated valuable moral lessons, and

occupied with harmless diversion those who might otherwise conspire against legitimate authority. But there were some in the Essex faction who saw in the theater the power to subvert, or rather the power to wrest legitimation from the established ruler and confer it on another. This power, notwithstanding royal protection, censorship, and the players' professions of unswerving loyalty, could be purchased for forty shillings.

The story of Richard II was obviously a highly charged one in a society where political discussion was conducted, as in parts of the world today, with Aesopian indirection. Clearly it is not the text alone — over which the censor had some control — that bears the full significance of Shakespeare's play, or of any version of the story. It is rather the story's full situation — the genre it is thought to embody, the circumstances of its performance, the imaginings of its audience — that governs its shifting meanings. "40tie times in open streets and houses": for the Queen the repeatability of the tragedy, and hence the

[1]Elizabeth was speaking to William Lambarde the antiquary; see the Arden edition of Shakespeare's *King Richard II*, ed. Peter Ure (Cambridge: Harvard University Press, (156), pp. lvii–lxii. [Au.]

numbers of people who have been exposed to its infection, is part of the danger, along with the fact (or rather her conviction) that the play had broken out of the boundaries of the playhouse, where such stories are clearly marked as powerful illusions, and moved into the more volatile zone — the zone she calls "open" — of the streets. In the streets the story begins to lose the conventional containment of the playhouse, where audiences are kept at a safe distance both from the action on stage and from the world beyond the walls. And in the wake of this subversive deregulation, the terms that mark the distinction between the lucid and the real become themselves problematic: are the "houses" to which Elizabeth refers public theaters or private dwellings where her enemies plot her overthrow? can "tragedy" be a strictly literary term when the Queen's own life is endangered by the play?[2]

Modern historical scholarship has assured Elizabeth that she had nothing to worry about: *Richard II* is not at all subversive but rather a hymn to Tudor order. The play, far from encouraging thoughts of rebellion, regards the deposition of the legitimate king as a "sacrilegious" act that drags the country down into "the abyss of chaos"; "that Shakespeare and his audience regarded Bolingbroke as a usurper," declares J. Dover Wilson, "is incontestable."[3] But in 1601 neither Queen Elizabeth nor the Earl of Essex were so sure: after all, someone on the eve of a rebellion thought the play sufficiently seditious to warrant squandering two pounds on the players, and the Queen understood the performance as a threat. Moreover, even before the Essex rising, the actual deposition scene (IV.i.154–318 in the Arden edition) was carefully omitted from

the first three quartos of Shakespeare's play and appears for the first time only after Elizabeth's death.

How can we account for the discrepancy between Dover Wilson's historical reconstruction and the anxious response of the figures whose history he purports to have accurately reconstructed? The answer lies at least in part in the difference between a conception of art that has no respect whatsoever for the integrity of the text ("I am Richard II. Know ye not that?") and one that hopes to find, through historical research, a stable core of meaning within the text, a core that united disparate and even contradictory parts into an organic whole. That whole may provide a perfectly orthodox celebration of legitimacy and order, as measured by homilies, royal pronouncements, and official propaganda, but the Queen is clearly responding to something else: to the presence of *any* representation of deposition, whether regarded as sacrilegious or not; to the choice of this particular story at this particular time; to the place of the performance; to her own identity as it is present in the public sphere and as it fuses with the figure of the murdered king. Dover Wilson is not a New Critic: he does not conceive of the text as an iconic object whose meaning is perfectly contained within its own formal structure. Yet for him historical research has the effect of conferring autonomy and fixity upon the text, and it is precisely this fixity that is denied by Elizabeth's response.

Dover Wilson's work is a distinguished example of the characteristic assumptions and methods of the mainstream literary history practiced in the first half of our century, and a further glance at these may help us to bring into focus the distinctive assumptions and methods exemplified in the essays collected in this volume. To be sure, these essays are quite diverse in their concerns and represent no single critical practice; a comparative glance, for example, at the brilliant pieces by Franco Moretti and John Traugott will suggest at once how various this work is. Yet diverse as they are, many of the present essays give voice, I think, to what we may call the new historicism, set apart from both the dominant historical scholarship of the past and the

[2]The ambiguity is intensified by the Queen's preceding comment, according to Lambarde: "*Her Majestie*. 'He that will forget God, will also forget his benefactors; this tragedy was played 40tie times in open streets and houses'" (Ure, p. lix). [Au.]

[3]John Dover Wilson, "The Political Background of Shakespeare's *Richard II* and *Henry IV*," *Shakespeare-Jahrbuch*, 75 (1939), 47. The condemnation of Bolingbroke is "evident," we are told, "from the whole tone and emphasis of *Richard II*" (p. 48). I am grateful to Patricia Allen for the reference to this essay. [Au.]

formalist criticism that partially displaced this scholarship in the decades after World War Two. The earlier historicism tends to be monological; that is, it is concerned with discovering a single political vision, usually identical to that said to be held by the entire literate class or indeed the entire population ("In the eyes of the later middle ages," writes Dover Wilson, Richard II "represented the type and exemplar of royal martyrdom" [p. 50]). This vision, most often presumed to be internally coherent and consistent, though occasionally analyzed as the fusion of two or more elements, has the status of an historical fact. It is not thought to be the product of the historian's interpretation, nor even of the particular interests of a given social group in conflict with other groups. Protected then from interpretation and conflict, this vision can serve as a stable point of reference, beyond contingency, to which literary interpretation can securely refer. Literature is conceived to mirror the period's beliefs, but to mirror them, as it were, from a safe distance.

The new historicism erodes the firm ground of both criticism and literature. It tends to ask questions about its own methodological assumptions and those of others: in the present case, for example, it might encourage us to examine the ideological situation not only of *Richard II* but of Dover Wilson on *Richard II*. The lecture from which I have quoted — "The Political Background of Shakespeare's *Richard II* and *Henry IV*" — was delivered before the German Shakespearean Society, at Weimar, in 1939. We might, in a full discussion of the critical issues at stake here, look closely at the relation between Dover Wilson's reading of *Richard II* — a reading that discovers Shakespeare's fears of chaos and his consequent support for legitimate if weak authority over the claims of ruthless usurpers — and the eerie occasion of his lecture ("these plays," he concludes, "should be of particular interest to German students at this moment of that everlasting adventure which we call history" [p. 51]).

Moreover, recent criticism has been less concerned to establish the organic unity of literary works and more open to such works as fields of force, places of dissension and shifting interests, occasions for the jostling of orthodox and subversive impulses. "The Elizabeth playhouse, playwright, and player," writes Louis Adrian Montrose in a brilliant recent essay, "exemplify the contradictions of Elizabethan society and make those contradictions their subject. If the world is a theatre and the theatre is an image of the world, then by reflecting upon its own artifice, the drama is holding the mirror up to nature."[4] As the problematizing of the mirror metaphor suggests, Renaissance literary works are no longer regarded either as a fixed set of texts that are set apart from all other forms of expression and that contain their own determinate meanings or as a stable set of reflections of historical facts that lie beyond them. The critical practice represented in [*The Power of Forms in the English Renaissance*] challenges the assumptions that guarantee a secure distinction between "literary foreground" and "political background" or, more generally, between artistic production and other kinds of social production. Such distinctions do in fact exist, but they are not intrinsic to the texts; rather they are made up and constantly redrawn by artists, audiences, and readers. These collective social constructions on the one hand define the range of aesthetic possibilities within a given representational mode and, on the other, link that mode to the complex network of institutions, practices, and beliefs that constitute the culture as a whole. In this light, the study of genre is an exploration of the poetics of culture.

---

[4]"The Purpose of Playing: Reflections on a Shakespearean Anthropology," *Helios*, n.s. 7 (1980), 57. [Au.]

# King Lear *and*
# *Harsnett's "Devil-Fiction"*

Modern critics tend to assume that Shake-spearean self-consciousness and irony lead to a radical transcendence of the network of social conditions, paradigms, and practices in the plays. I would argue, by contrast, that Renaissance theatrical representation itself is fully implicated in this network and that Shakespeare's self-consciousness is in significant ways bound up with the institutions and the symbology of power it anatomizes.

To grasp this we might consider *King Lear*. We happen to know one of the books that Shakespeare had been reading and seems indeed to have had open before him as he revised the old play of *King Leir*. The book, printed in 1603, is by Samuel Harsnett, then chaplain to the Bishop of London, and is entitled *A Declaration of Egregious Popish Impostures, to with-draw the harts of her Majesties Subjects from their allegeance, and from the truth of Christian Religion professed in England, under the pretense of casting out devils. Practised by Edmunds, alias Weston a Jesuit, and divers Romish Priests his wicked associates. Where-unto are annexed the Copies of the Confessions and Examinations of the parties themselves, which were pretended to be possessed, and dispossessed, taken upon oath before her Majesties Commissioners for Causes Ecclesiasticall.*[1] From this remarkable book — a scathing account of a series of spectacular exorcisms conducted between the spring of 1585 and the summer of 1586 principally in the house of a recusant gentleman, Sir George Peckham of Denham, Buckinghamshire — Shakespeare took

[1]On Harsnett, see D. P. Walker, *Unclean Spirits: Possession and Exorcism in France and England in the Late Sixteenth and Early Seventeenth Centuries* (Philadelphia: University of Pennsylvania Press, 1981), pp. 43–49; Keith Thomas, *Religion and the Decline of Magic* (London: Weidenfeld and Nicolson, 1971), pp. 477–92. On Harsnett and *Lear*, see Kenneth Muir, "Samuel Harsnett and *King Lear*," *RES*, New Series 2 (1951), 11–21; William Elton, *King Lear and the Gods* (San Marino, CA: Huntington Library, 1966). [Au.]

many small details, especially for the demonology Edgar exhibits in his disguise as the possessed Poor Tom. My interest here is not in these details which have been noted since the eighteenth century, but in the broader institutional implications of Harsnett's text and of the uses to which Shakespeare puts it.

The *Declaration* is a semi-official attack on exorcism as practised by Jesuits secretly residing in England (and under constant threat of capture and execution), but the charges are not limited to Catholicism, since Harsnett had earlier written against the Puritan exorcist John Darrell. Like other spokesmen for the Anglican establishment, Harsnett concedes that at some distant time exorcism was a legitimate practice (as, of course, it is in the Bible), but miracles have ceased and corporeal possession by demons is no longer possible. What has taken its place, he writes, is fraud, and, more precisely, theater: exorcisms are stage plays written by cunning clerical dramatists and performed by skilled actors. To be sure, not all the participants are professionals, but the priests, as Harsnett depicts them, run what is in effect an acting school. They begin by talking about the way successful exorcisms abroad had taken place and describe in lurid detail the precise symptoms of the possessed; then the young "schollers," as Harsnett calls those whom the priests have chosen to manipulate, "*frame* themselves jumpe and fit unto the Priests humors, to mop, mow, jest, raile, rave, roare, commend & discommend, and as the priest would have them, upon fitting occasions (according to the difference of times, places, and commers in) in all things to play the devils accordinglie" (p. 38).

Harsnett's *Declaration* then is a massive document of disenchantment; the solemn ceremony of exorcism is, as the attack on Darrell puts it, "now discovered to be but a pure play," and the reverence and fear that the performance inspires are nothing but "miserable shiftes to helpe [the exorcist] off the stage, that he might not be hissed at of all the world."[2] The Jesuits and their retinue are not a holy band driven by religious persecution to move from place to place but closely resemble "vagabond players, that coast from Towne to Towne with a trusse and a cast of fiddles, to carry in theyr consort, broken queanes, and *Ganimedes,* as well for their night pleasance, as their dayes pastime" (p. 149). The power this sleazy crew possesses is the power of the theater. If the end of a comedy, Harsnett notes, is applause for the author and actors, while the end of a tragedy is the "moving of affection, and passion in the spectators," our *"Daemonopoiia,* or devil-fiction, is *Tragico-commaedia,"* for it elicits both exclamations of admiration — *"O that all the Protestans* (sic) *in England did see the power of the Catholick Church"* — and tears (p. 50).

The spectators, of course, do not know that they are merely responding to an effective if tawdry play; they believe that they are celebrants at a moving and sanctified communal ritual. "The devil speaks treason . . . so aptly, distinctly, and elegantly on the stage, that it enchaunted the harts, and affections of the poore bewitched people, and chained them to the Pope" (p. 154); the lowest estimate of the conversions achieved "by this well acted tragedie" is five hundred, and Harsnett states that "devil-tragedians" themselves claim four to five thousand converts. To impress these large crowds, the exorcists, led by Father Edmunds, invoke the vast forces of heaven and hell, call forth by name whole legions of devils, and drive them from the bodies of the possessed by means of powerful amulets and charms. The performance is spectacular, with the writhing demoniac bound in a chair and tortured until the devils are compelled to depart. But the devils, says Harsnett, are tattered figures from the old Church plays, their names grotesque forgeries, and the hallowed vestments and holy objects contemptible stage properties. As for the possessed themselves, they are either histrionic scoundrels like Robert Maynie or servant girls like the sisters Sara and Friswood Williams, whose position of

social dependency made them susceptible to the powers of suggestion, intimidation, and torture.

Harsnett's detailed identification of exorcism as theater, a conception that is elaborated through almost three hundred pages, is more than a satirical analogy; it is a polemical institutional analysis whose purpose is not only to expose the fraudulence of exorcism but to link that practice to the pervasive theatricality of the Catholic Church (or, as Harsnett elsewhere terms it, "the Pope's playhouse").[3] Priests do not actually believe in their "charmes, and consecrate attire," but only "act, fashion, and play them" in order to gull the ignorant (p. 88); the Mass itself is nothing but "a pageant of moppes, mowes, elevations, crouches, and ridiculous gesticulations" (p. 158). Theatricality here is not so much the consequence of the Church's deviation from the truth as the very essence of that deviation and hence the explanatory key to the entire institution: Catholicism is a "Mimick superstition (it being the onely religion to catch fooles, children, and women, by reason it is naught else, save a conceited pageant of Puppits, and gaudes" (p. 20).

Now *King Lear* at once stages a version of these disenchanted perceptions — most notably in the representation of Edgar's histrionic and fraudulent demonic possession, complete with names drawn directly from the *Declaration* — and insinuates itself paradoxically into the place made vacant by Harsnett's attack: that is, where Harsnett had condemned exorcism as a stage play, Shakespeare's play is itself a secular version of the ritual of exorcism. What exactly is being exorcised? Harsnett would say, in effect, that the question is misguided: what matters is the theatrical experience, the power of the performance to persuade the audience that it has heard the voices of radical evil and witnessed the violent expulsion of the agents of Darkness.

The ritual in this staged form is acceptable because the institution it serves is not a theatrical church but a public, state-supervised theater, and the on-lookers are induced to pay homage (and the price of admission) not to a competing reli-

---

[2]Samuel Harsnett, *A Discovery of the Fraudulent Practices of John Darrel* (London, 1599), p. A3$^r$. [Au.]

[3]Harsnett, *Discovery,* p. A3$^r$. [Au.]

gious authority but to professional entertainers safely circumscribed by the wooden walls of the playhouse. Within these walls, the force of Shakespeare's theatrical improvisation is to appropriate the power of the traditional, quasi-magical practice and of the newer, rationalized analysis and then, with this convergent power, to raise questions about the production of the enabling distinctions between supernatural and secular evil, real and theatrical ritual, authority and madness, belief and illusion. Such disturbing questions are at once licensed and contained by the aesthetic, economic, and physical demarcation of playing companies in a play space. Hence the ideological and historical situation of *King Lear* produces the oscillation, the simultaneous affirmation and negation, the constant undermining of its own assertions and questioning of its own practices — in short, the supreme aesthetic self-consciousness — that lead us to celebrate its universality, its literariness, and its transcendence of all ideology.

# 6

# FEMINIST LITERARY CRITICISM

*When . . . one reads of a witch being ducked, of a woman possessed by devils, of a wise woman selling herbs, or even of a very remarkable man who had a mother, then I think we are on the track of a lost novelist, a suppressed poet, of some mute and inglorious Jane Austen, some Emily Brontë who dashed her brains out on the moor or mopped and mowed about the highways crazed with the torture that her gift had put her to.*

— VIRGINIA WOOLF

*For each [male writer], the ideal woman will be she who incarnates most exactly the Other capable of revealing him to himself.* — SIMONE DE BEAUVOIR

*The woman writer . . . has entered literary history as the enemy.* — NINA BAYM

*Not only have Black women writers been "disenfranchised" . . . by white women scholars on the "female tradition," but they have also been frequently excised from . . . the Afro-American literary tradition by Black scholars, most of whom are males.*

— DEBORAH E. MCDOWELL

What is feminist criticism — and what is it not? To begin with, feminist criticism does not include all literary criticism written by women, since not all women are feminists. Nor does it include all criticism written by feminists: Julia Kristeva and Barbara Johnson have both written eloquently on feminist subjects, but Kristeva's "The Bounded Text" and Johnson's "Melville's Fist" fall under the heading of poststructuralism rather than feminism (see Ch. 5). The characteristic common to the essays grouped together here — all of them, as it happens, by women, though this need not have been so — is their concern for the impact of gender upon writing and reading: how men write about women; how women read both men's and women's writing; how feminine language and creativity differ from masculine language and creativity.

Histories of feminist criticism, like those by Elaine Showalter, Kenneth Ruthven, and Toril Moi, usually present an evolutionary sequence. It begins with a critique of patriarchal culture; in the field of literary criticism this has taken the form of exposing the explicit and implicit prejudices in male writing about women. This phase would also include, as a corrective, a presentation of the very different ways in which women read male writers — and each other. The second phase might be characterized by what Showalter has termed "gynocritics": a concern about the place of female writers within a canon largely created by male publishers and academics and about the specifics of women's creativity and language. The third phase is a search for an *écriture féminine,* a feminine theory of the text, and for modes of textuality that are specifically gender-based.

While this description is a useful first approximation, it tidies up the messy facts of history. For one thing, if this were an evolutionary sequence, one might expect later entries to supersede the earlier ones. In fact, all these forms of criticism are alive, well, and progressing. The recent concern about textuality has not displaced any of the other questions, which feminist critics continue to ask and answer. For another, this sequence might look reasonable from the perspective of America or England, but a feminist in France would have experienced a different sequence. Finally, one might justly claim that the feminist issues of the seventies and eighties are scarcely new at all, since most of them were raised nearly sixty years ago by Virginia Woolf in her essay, *A Room of One's Own.*

## WOOLF

The most famous section of *A Room of One's Own* — a personal brief for women writers expanded from two lectures Woolf gave at Newnham and Girton colleges — is that which traces the tragically wasted career of "Shakespeare's sister," whose imaginative gifts could have found no outlet whatsoever in the society of the sixteenth century. This is, however, merely the opening for a historical sketch of actual women writers and the difficulties they experienced in their work, from Aphra Behn, the first female dramatist to make a living by her pen, through the noble bluestockings of the eighteenth century, to the four major novelists of the nineteenth: Jane Austen, Emily and Charlotte Brontë, and George Eliot. Overall, in her manifesto, written in 1929, ten years after women received the vote, and sixty-five years after the founding of Somerville, the first women's college at Oxford, Woolf remains painfully conscious of the disparities that still exist between women and men. But she is convinced that the rebirth of a female Shakespeare, one with the same "incandescent" spirit capable of unimpeded expression, is possible within the century — if the rest of her sisters work to prepare her way.

In the course of tracing that history, Woolf touches on a great many issues taken up by later feminists. Her ironic commentary, set in the British Museum, on the way women have traditionally been defined and analyzed as inferiors by men previews the issues raised by Simone de Beauvoir, Kate Millett and Mary Ellmann, and the images-of-women critics. In Woolf's analysis of the women novelists of the nineteenth century — of how the adoption of a masculine prose by Charlotte Brontë and George Eliot hampered their expressiveness, and of how Austen succeeded in devising a feminine prose that allowed her to say what she needed to —

she anticipates current research on women's language and *écriture féminine*. And in her emphatic endorsement of Coleridge's claim that a great mind is androgynous, she takes a stand on the most contested feminist question — whether there are distinct masculine and feminine modes of creativity. For this, Woolf would be attacked by critics like Showalter (who is committed to a feminine poetics) and by French feminists exploring a more polymorphous sexuality.

## WOMEN READING MEN READING WOMEN

Woolf's groundbreaking exploration of the major issues precipitated no immediate outpouring of feminist studies. Feminist criticism is a cultural outgrowth of the women's movement in general, and the 1930s and 1940s, owing to the Depression, the rise of fascism, and the Second World War, were not favorable times for feminist politics. After the war, however, feminist criticism revived and focused on the ways in which male authors present women — distorted by their own masculine prejudices and needs. The precursor text here is Simone de Beauvoir's *The Second Sex* (1949). Underlying this critique of patriarchy is the existentialist ethos de Beauvoir shared with Jean-Paul Sartre. The existentialist moral imperative is to accept the burdens of one's own freedom and to grant other human beings the dignity of personhood, rather than treating them like objects. As de Beauvoir analyzes it, French society — and Western society generally — is a patriarchy that consistently denies freedom and personhood to women. Women, for men, are the Other, not seen or observed as they are, but rather projected out of male needs and defined in subordinate relation to male norms. De Beauvoir analyzes sexism in most of its cultural forms; the selection included here (p. 1087) summarizes her analysis of five major writers whose different attitudes toward women nonetheless betray an essential likeness. Even the greatest poets and writers, and even those who were most favorably disposed toward women, like Stendhal, created Women either subtly or grossly as the Other they required.

Although *The Second Sex* was published in North America in 1953, de Beauvoir did not become an iconic figure here until the 1970s, when the American feminist movement began to gather steam. By that time, two other important American works, Mary Ellmann's *Thinking about Women* (1968) and Kate Millett's *Sexual Politics* (1970), had launched the feminist critique of male writing. Ellmann's *Thinking about Women* is an ironic work, concerned less about the way male writers talk about women than about the way male reviewers talk about women *writers*; the result is a "phallic criticism" that emphasizes the writers' figurative "bust, waist, and hip measurements" rather than their literary qualities. Kate Millett's book proclaimed the general thesis that, if the century from 1830–1930 had been one of sexual revolution, the succeeding three decades had been years of counterrevolution. In the earlier period, women gained the right to education, the right to work and the right to vote, and generally achieved the capacity for political existence independent of men; in the more recent period, ideologies from Freudian psychology to Marxism to fascism had conspired to keep women in their place. In literary terms, Millett's critique of the new patriarchy operates through readings of Henry Miller, Norman Mailer, and D. H. Lawrence. By the standards of today's feminist writers, Millett's readings of texts can often seem simplistic and reductive; her passages for analysis, however are aptly chosen for the polemical points she makes.

## WOMEN READING

In the 1960s Millett and Ellmann were primarily concerned with how men read women; in the 1970s women began to read men — and each other — in new and theoretically interesting ways. Perhaps the most sophisticated of the reader-response feminist critics is Annette Kolodny, whose "Some Notes on Defining a 'Feminist Literary Criticism'" (1975), explored problems of methodology, aiming to prove to prejudiced males that feminist questions required serious thought. Kolodny's position was empiricist. While women's experience in the past and present differed from men's, it would be unsafe to claim that women's literature was distinctive until this could be demonstrated directly. Kolodny appears to be skeptical about contemporary claims, like those of Showalter, for a distinctively female kind of writing. The case she makes out is that women read differently from men; they read both life and literature from the perspective of a disparate personal experience.[1] Kolodny's "A Map for Rereading" (1980) discusses two issues: how the differing interpretive modes of men and women appear *within* two stories (Charlotte Perkins Gilman's "The Yellow Wallpaper" and Susan Keating Glaspell's "A Jury of Her Peers"); and how the discrepancy between male and female ways of apprehending the world was mirrored in the fate of these two stories in the male-dominated literary marketplace.

Kolodny's theoretical perspective on the differences between male and female ways of reading the codes of literature and life is echoed in the practical criticism of Judith Fetterley. Fetterley's book, *The Resisting Reader* (1978), begins by dismantling the assumption that texts — in her case, the primary texts of American fiction — are written for a universal audience. In fact, Fetterley states, "to read the canon of what is currently considered classic American literature is perforce to identify as male. . . . It insists on its universality at the same time that it defines that universality in specifically male terms" (p. xii). Traditionally, women have allowed themselves to be "immasculated" — inscribed within masculinity — in reading these texts, but they do so at the heavy price of internalizing self-hatred or at least self-doubt. Today, that price is too high: "The first act of the feminist critic must be to become a resisting rather than an assenting reader, to begin the process of exorcising the male mind that has been implanted in us" (p. xxii). If

[1]"Some Notes on Defining a 'Feminist Literary Criticism,'" *Critical Inquiry* 2 (Fall 1975): 75–92. Kolodny has been more concerned than most feminist critics with finding a rhetoric to counter male opposition to feminism. In "Dancing through the Minefield" (*Feminist Studies* 6 [1980]: 1–25). Kolodny presents her feminist theses so "that current hostilities might be transformed into a true dialogue with our critics."

Kolodny and Fetterley present a theory of gender differences in reading, we can look to Elizabeth Flynn for pragmatic research on how actual men and women differ in their responses to fiction (see "Gender and Reading," reprinted and discussed in Chapter 7, Reader-Response Criticism).

## WOMEN TALKING

One of the more intriguing questions feminist criticism has broached is whether there is a special "women's language" that is different from that spoken by men. One would expect that inscription within patriarchy would have its effects on the way women speak, and this notion has been firmly endorsed by the pioneering studies of linguist Robin Lakoff in *Language and Woman's Place* (1975). Lakoff suggests that more is involved in "talking like a lady" than mere vocabulary (e.g., the use of adjectives like "adorable" or "divine" and of color-words like "mauve"; the avoidance of scatological terms). Lakoff considers some syntactic constructions as typically female, like the "tag-question," which seeks agreement rather than aggressively taking a stand (e.g., "Mozart is a wonderful composer, isn't he?"). She suggests that women's traditional powerlessness is reflected in their greater use of indirect utterances but that such usages also reinforce current sex roles.

While Lakoff was developing the concept of "genderlect" — dialectical differences owing to gender — she tended to believe that sexist usages were unalterably fixed in language. She doubted that it was possible to dislodge the generic use of "man" to include women or of "he" as the neutral pronoun; but she was equally uncertain that these forms were seriously sexist and was inclined to consider them innocuous asymmetries. But are they innocuous? In an empirical study (1980), Jeanette Silveira found that respondents often did not understand that females were included in the generic "man" or "he," and that this was true of female as well as male subjects.[2] On the issue of change, Lakoff's conservatism seemed justified at the time by the long and futile history — going back to 1850 — of attempts at pronoun reform (the use of constructed neuter pronouns like "thon" or "hiser"). But since 1975 an effective series of guidelines for using sex-neutral language has been adopted by most publishers. Not only has the generic masculine been dropped but also phrases suggesting that certain jobs are gender-oriented, either by direct implication ("fireman" or "policeman") or by marking the less-common gender (e.g., "lady lawyer" or "male nurse"). Another sexist practice noted by Lakoff, that of referring to a female author by both first and last names (Jane Austen, Emily Dickinson) but to a male author by last name alone (Dickens, Lawrence), seems to be passing. Similarly "Ms." as the marriage-neutral form of address for women has become common if not universal. In effect, Lakoff's work has dated because society has become sensitive to sexist language and has made some significant attempts at reform.

Lakoff's work has dated in another sense, too: Some of its assertions have been

[2]Jeanette Silveira, "Generic Masculine Words and Thinking," in *The Voices and Words of Women and Men,* ed. Cheris Kramarae, pp. 165–78. Oxford: Pergamon Press, 1980.

questioned by later empirical studies. For example, her claim that women use tag questions more often than men do was supported by two experiments and refuted by three others. It now appears that social setting may be more important than gender in determining whether speakers produce tag questions; even powerful males tend to use many tag questions when they are running meetings. In general, theories of "genderlect" are less popular than they were in the 1970s, as researchers recognize that the variations in speech patterns *within* each gender are greater than the differences *between* genders.

Feminist linguists have focused instead on sociolinguistic issues, such as the frequency with which women are addressed in familiar terms ("dear" or "honey") by people they do not know, the relative frequency with which women and men interrupt each other and allow themselves to be interrupted,[3] the large number of pejorative terms for women as opposed to those for men,[4] and the unexamined assumptions that women will take their father's name at birth and their husband's name upon marriage. (Feminist linguists sensitive to this issue have changed or reinvented their names: e.g., Cheris Kramarae previously published as Chris Kramer, Julia Penelope Stanley is now Julia Penelope.)

## WOMEN WRITING

Perhaps the least controversial aspect of recent feminist studies has been its attempt to locate and expand a female tradition of writing. Some authors (from Christine de Pisan to Kate Chopin) have been exhumed from near-oblivion and raised to the status of classics; others (like Anne Bradstreet and Mary Shelley), never really lost to sight, have been reinterpreted as central to the literary canon rather than as marginal, if well-known, figures. As in all efforts to expand the canon, more candidates will inevitably be proposed than will eventually find a place within. And if some writers now receiving general attention are those like Charlotte Perkins Gilman, who enrich and deepen feminists' sense of their own history, others, like Mary Shelley and Anna Laetitia Barbauld, espoused conservative attitudes toward "woman's place," which their present-day readers would be loath to adopt.

If the criterion is whether literature by women is taught in colleges and universities, the effort to expand the canon has been successful. But much of this success has occurred within special "women's studies" programs and in special courses within traditional programs, so that one may wonder whether women have truly been included within the traditional canon or whether a countercanon of literature by women has been advanced to parallel the former canon defined primarily by men. And feminist critics like Nina Baym have questioned whether the canon has been created in a gender-neutral fashion or whether the books have been cooked.

---

[3]Candice West and Don H. Zimmerman, "Small Insults: A Study of Interruptions in Cross-sex Conversations between Unacquainted Persons," in *Language, Gender, and Society*, ed. Barrie Thorne *et al.*, pp. 103–18 (Rowley, Mass.: Newbury House, 1983).

[4]Julia Penelope Stanley found 220 terms for a sexually promiscuous woman, only 22 for a man. See "Paradigmatic Woman: The Prostitute," in *Papers in Language Variation*, ed. David Shores (Birmingham: University of Alabama Press, 1977).

When literary theorists define the archetypal American novel in such a way as to privilege male experience, women writers are automatically relegated to the sidelines. This is the argument Baym advances in "Melodramas of Beset Manhood."

The question that remains is how to understand the body of literature by women, and whether it forms a tradition on its own that can be understood apart from the body of literature by men. Most critics are likely to identify three major texts of the second phase of feminist criticism, the analysis of women's writing, as Ellen Moers's *Literary Women* (1976), Elaine Showalter's *A Literature of Their Own* (1977), and Sandra Gilbert and Susan Gubar's *The Madwoman in the Attic* (1979). As Toril Moi's recent survey of feminist criticism puts it, "Taken together, these three books represent the coming-of-age of Anglo-American feminist criticism."[5]

Moers's *Literary Women* is subtitled "The Great Writers," as if to establish its relationship to F. R. Leavis's *The Great Tradition* (1948; see p. 1300), and there is indeed something Leavisite about its socially oriented survey of centuries of female creativity. Moers focuses on those aspects of women writers that derive from the central fact of their being women and ignores the rest as far as possible. Thus, Moers interprets Mary Shelley's *Frankenstein* as a myth of birth, in which the newborn is "at once monstrous agent of destruction and piteous victim of parental abandonment," a myth she sees as the product of Shelley's personal history — as an unwed mother at the time of its writing and as an infant whose birth occasioned her mother's death. Moers's method, if it can be called that, is impressionistic and biographical; in calling up her most admired heroine, George Sand, she asks the reader to picture "her typical country evening at Nohant. At the center sits Madame Sand with the needle work she loved in her hands, surrounded by a houseful of friends, children, lovers, guests, neighbors. Nohant was a messy household, full of laughter and games and theatricals and family arguments and good intellectual talk and tobacco smoke and music — just like yours and mine." Later critics were to avoid her chattiness and decry her insistence on biographical explanations, but feminist criticism was advanced by her wide-ranging discussion of the canon of women's literature and the central place of women's experience in forming that canon.

Elaine Showalter's book, *A Literature of Their Own*, has been more influential than Moers's. In addition to establishing a complex relationship to Woolf's *A Room of One's Own*, Showalter's title alludes ironically to J. S. Mill, who in *The Subjection of Women* stated that "if women lived in a different country from men and had never read any of their writings, they would have a literature of their own." As things stood, Mill thought, they did not: "[A] much longer time is necessary . . . before [women's literature] can emancipate itself from the influence of accepted models, and guide itself by its own impulses." Showalter would not claim that the body of texts produced by women has the coherent character of a national literature that can be studied entirely apart from the texts produced by men, and she suspects that the hypothesis of a distinctive "female imagination"

---

[5]Toril Moi, *Sexual/Textual Politics: Feminist Literary Theory* (New York: Methuen, 1985), p. 52.

will encourage the stereotyped images of women that feminists have been so eager to dispel. Nevertheless, Showalter claims that women, as a subculture within English society, have produced something definable as a "female literary tradition" in the English novel from the generation of the Brontës to the present.

Showalter's analysis of nineteenth-century English fiction by women presents an evolutionary theory of the development of women's writing, which she feels ran parallel to that by blacks, Jews, and other groups outside the white Christian male power elite:

> In looking at literary subcultures . . . we can see that they all go through three major phases. First, there is a prolonged phase of *imitation* of the prevailing modes of the dominant tradition, and *internalization* of its standards of art and its views on social roles. Second, there is a phase of *protest* against these standards and values, and *advocacy* of minority rights and values, including a demand for autonomy. Finally, there is a phase of *self-discovery,* a turning inward freed from some of the dependency of opposition, a search for identity. An appropriate terminology for women writers is to call these stages *Feminine, Feminist,* and *Female*. These are obviously not rigid categories. . . . The phases overlap. . . . One might . . . find all three phases in the career of a single novelist. Nonetheless, it seems useful to point to periods of crisis when a shift of literary values occurred. In this book I identify the Feminine phase as the period from the appearance of the male pseudonym in the 1840s to the death of George Eliot in 1880; the Feminist phase as 1880 to 1920, or the winning of the vote; and the Female phase as 1920 to the present, but entering a new stage of self-awareness about 1960.

Obviously in Showalter's program there is some danger of overestimating the extent to which the female tradition and the male tradition are separable and (as Kenneth Ruthven has put it) of feminist critics "repeating exactly the same mistake for which they take male critics to task, namely an exclusive preoccupation with the writings of one sex."[6] This is a problem, however, of which Showalter is well aware. What seems less guarded is her bias against that version of feminism represented by Virginia Woolf — a foremother whom she attacks with what may seem an Electra's fury. Showalter considers Woolf's idealization of androgyny a mere flight from any genuine femininity and terms her vision of womanhood "as deadly as it is disembodied." Showalter's arguments against an androgynous ideal seem *ad feminam* (so to speak), and she does not understand the appeal of androgyny even to women (like Mary Shelley) who loved men and were devoted to their children.

Whatever the controversies surrounding Showalter's attitudes toward nineteenth- and twentieth-century fiction by women, her methodology is simple and straight-forward. *The Madwoman in the Attic,* by Sandra Gilbert and Susan Gubar, brought to the female tradition some less traditional ways of reading, similar to those we associate with Yale (which eventually published their study). In particular, Gilbert and Gubar take off from the poetics of Harold Bloom's *Anxiety of Influence* (see Ch. 2). But where Bloom was concerned with the Oedipal relation between the

---

[6]K. K. Ruthven, *Feminist Literary Studies: An Introduction* (Cambridge: Cambridge University Press, 1984), p. 125.

"strong" poet and the forebear he has chosen as his ghostly "father," whose works he must misread to make room for his own, Gilbert and Gubar are concerned with the female half of the equation, with the woman writer who, defined always by men, is uncomfortable defining herself, who, lacking a pen/penis, is anxious about whether she can create at all. Whatever women's lesser disabilities today, women writers in the nineteenth century eventually "overcame their 'anxiety of authorship,' repudiated debilitating patriarchal prescriptions, and recovered or remembered the lost foremothers who could help them find their distinctive female power" (p. 59).

But within a patriarchy, women's writing cannot fully express itself; as a result, women writers (consciously or unconsciously) revised their own meanings to make them acceptable to their culture. "Women from Jane Austen and Mary Shelley to Emily Brontë and Emily Dickinson produced literary works . . . whose surface designs conceal or obscure deeper, less accessible (and less socially acceptable) levels of meaning" (p. 73). Women authors used a "cover story" — coded messages disguising their intent. They often created villainesses, in Gilbert and Gubar's readings of the novels, who speak powerfully for the values they were forced to repress. Under the surface, Bertha Mason Rochester, the titular Madwoman in the Attic, is the true heroine of *Jane Eyre*. Her frank impulsiveness and sensuality underlie what the reader values in Jane herself.

*The Madwoman in the Attic* gave an enormous new impetus to feminist criticism, yet there were skeptics, largely among Gilbert and Gubar's fellow feminists. In her review of *Madwoman* in *Signs,* Mary Jacobus attacked the book's "unstated complicity with the autobiographical 'phallacy,' whereby male critics hold that women's writing is somehow closer to their own experience than men's, that the female text *is* the author."[7] From her own poststructuralist perspective, Toril Moi has a rather different problem with *Madwoman,* in fact, a set of problems.[8] In the first place, Moi is unhappy with the implication of the "cover story," because the result is that everywhere in literature by women one can find nothing but overt or disguised versions of the author's "constant, never-changing *feminist rage.* This position . . . manages to transform *all* texts written by women into feminist texts." Moi also worries about the Gilbert and Gubar notion of patriarchy as a relentless and all-pervasive force, and wonders how, if this were so, women learned to write at all. Moi thinks that Gilbert and Gubar need to learn the Althusserian lesson: that patriarchal ideology is actually contradictory and fragmentary, rather than coherent and irresistible.

## THE FEMALE (AS) TEXT

The search for a new theoretical base for feminist criticism has largely been led by feminists in France, the place of origin of so much recent theory. The issues here are clarified — and complicated — by the distinction the English language makes between sex and gender: people are male or female by sex, masculine or

[7]*Signs* 6 (1981): 520.
[8]Moi, pp. 57–69.

feminine by gender. The former distinction is by and large absolute; the latter allows for admixtures of qualities, with androgyny as a central position between the extremes. In contrast, the French language conflates the distinctions: *Féminité* means "femaleness" as well as "femininity."

One of the most influential of the French theorists, Luce Irigaray, is a disciple of Lacan. Irigaray's difficult, learned, ironically allusive thesis, *Speculum of the Other Woman* (1974), undertakes a re-examination of Plato, Freud, and a dozen thinkers in between. Like de Beauvoir, Irigaray is outraged about the way women have been seen as an Other by men, spoken about and spoken for, but never allowed to speak themselves. Her critique of Freud is largely of his theories of sexual differences (like the notions of penis envy and the castration complex), theories that falter, as Irigaray sees the case, on Freud's failure to perceive that men and women actually *are* different, rather than more or less adequate versions of the same (male) norm. Quoting Freud against himself, Irigaray demonstrates the incoherence of his theories of femininity.

Despite Irigaray's training as a Lacanian psychoanalyst, her own version of femininity seems to have a biological basis that harks back to the source of the errors she exposes in Freud. In her most famous essay, "This Sex Which Is Not One," she characterizes both males and females as essentially like their primary genitalia: men, like the phallus, are single (-minded), hard, simple, direct; women, like the two lips of the vulva and their sensations, are multiple, diffuse, soft, indirect. Similarly, Irigaray's notion of women's writing takes off from this genital analogy of the labia, which always touch each other:

> This "style" or "writing" of women tends to put the torch to fetish words, proper terms, well-constructed forms. This "style" does not privilege sight; instead, it takes each figure back to its source, which is among other things *tactile*. It comes back in touch with itself in that origin without ever constituting in it, constituting itself in it, as some sort of unity. *Simultaneity* is its "proper" aspect — a proper(ty) that is never fixed in the possible identity-to-self of some form or other. It is always *fluid*, without neglecting the characteristics of fluids that are difficult to idealize: those rubbings between two infinitely near neighbors that create a dynamics. Its "style" resists and explodes every firmly established form, figure, idea, or concept. Which does not mean that it lacks style . . . but its "style" cannot be upheld as a thesis, cannot be the object of a position.[9]

Despite the abstract tenor of this characterization, the general traits Irigaray posits for women's discourse — inconsistency, fluidity, incoherence, tactility — are the very ones men have used to denigrate the female intellect. Irigaray's position seems a jumping-off point for a separatist feminism that renounces for women whatever has been tainted by masculinity — logic, coherence, power. But this position could potentially divide feminism as a movement. Those feminists who seek above all a sense of the differences between femininity and masculinity may find Irigaray a compelling theorist; those more concerned with pragmatic goals —

---

[9]Luce Irigaray, "The Power of Discourse," in *This Sex Which Is Not One* (Ithaca: Cornell University Press, 1985), p. 79.

who prefer to get their share of the things men have traditionally dominated — may find her quietism less useful.

Hélène Cixous is a more difficult writer than Irigaray, but the problems of reading her are somewhat different. Where Irigaray is learned, detached, abstract, and so ambiguously ironical that her meaning is often in danger of being misunderstood, Cixous speaks primarily through images and metaphors. The intense poetic quality of her prose is part of what has caused her essay "The Laugh of the Medusa" to become the central manifesto of French feminism. Cixous's difficulty is intentional and programmatic: feeling that the major modes of conceptual analysis themselves are anti-female, she writes in a way that resists dialectic. To show this, Cixous (following Derrida in *Of Grammatology*) sets up a series of binary oppositions (active/passive, sun/moon, culture/nature, day/night, father/mother, logos/pathos). Each pair can be analyzed as a hierarchy in which the former term represents the positive and masculine and the latter the negative and feminine principle. Nor can the terms live in harmony: Cixous suggests that, in each case, the masculine term is forced to "kill" the feminine one. This for her is the deadly "phallocentric" principle that she derives from Derrida's critique of logocentrism. Cixous rejects the idea of "feminine writing," as "a dangerous and stylish expression full of traps. . . . My work in fact aims at getting rid of words like 'feminine and masculine,' even 'man' and 'woman.' . . ."[10]

One might think Cixous, like Woolf, would be an exponent of androgyny; in fact Cixous attacks androgyny as an annulment of differences, and supports instead what she calls "the *other bisexuality*," which involves the "multiplication of the effects of the inscription of desire, over all parts of my body and the other body, indeed, this *other bisexuality* doesn't annul differences, but stirs them up, pursues them, increases them" ("The Laugh of the Medusa"). For Cixous, woman is bisexual; man, unwilling to give up the phallus, is monosexual. This is the point at which the binary polarities, having been kicked out the door, creep back in through the window, and they return upside down, with the female terms on top. At one point Cixous speaks "of a decipherable libidinal femininity which can be read in a writing produced by a male or a female." But as she later explains "libidinal femininity," she ends up attributing it almost exclusively to biological females. She finds its essential, moist, life-giving properties, for example, in the work of women writers like Clarice Lispector, while the work of a male writer like Maurice Blanchot is "a text that goes toward the drying up." (She finds a feminine sensibility in one male writer, Heinrich von Kleist, but that, as she says, is "highly exceptional.") Female sexuality is "giving," where the male is retentive, avaricious; female sexuality achieves full genitality, while male sexuality is fixated in oral dominance or anal "exchange."[11] Where Derrida presented the standard polarities of Western culture in order to dismantle and discredit dialectical thinking,

[10]Interview with Cixous in Verena Andermatt Conley, *Hélène Cixous: Writing the Feminine* (Lincoln and London: University of Nebraska Press, 1984), p. 129.

[11]Conley, 129–33.

it seems that Cixous has adopted Derridean terminology for a philosophically different program that simply inverts the standard pairings.

## ON THE MARGINS

Elaine Showalter's attempt to describe female writing as a variant of the experience of minority cultures searching for a place within the mainstream implicitly suggests that women's writing belongs to the White, Male, Protestant, and British or American traditions with one exception: that of gender. While this was true of the British writers Showalter discussed, obviously some women may be multiply marginalized, not only as women but as blacks, Chicanos, Asian-Americans, Caribbean Islanders, or as lesbians on the margin of the heterosexual majority.

The marginalization of the black female writer has become a significant issue as writers such as Phillis Wheatley and Zora Neale Hurston, Alice Walker and Toni Morrison, Gwendolyn Brooks and Nikki Giovanni are entering the canon, either in courses in American literature or through their success as popular best-sellers. In a number of ways, the issues of black feminist criticism overlap with white feminism. But black women have long been excluded from white feminist politics, and some of the central texts of women's studies ignore women who are not white. In her manifesto, "Toward a Black Feminist Criticism," Barbara Smith is outraged at this failure to recognize that "Black and female identity ever coexist, specifically in a group of Black women writers." Smith attacks as "barely disguised cultural imperialism" Showalter's proposal to build a feminist scholarship on the model of "black American novelists." Smith also notes that most studies of women writers written by white women tend to ignore blacks and other minorities — Moers's *Literary Women* "includes the names of four Black and one Puertorriqueña women in her seventy pages of bibliographical notes" — and that other feminist writers show a "suspiciously selective" ignorance of the existence of black women writers. The feminists are not the only target here, however, for Smith sees both black and white male scholars of black writing as even more distortive of the creative achievements of black women. The essay by Deborah McDowell, "New Directions for Black Feminist Criticism," while entirely sympathetic to the sense of marginality against which earlier black feminists reacted, seeks to escape the divisiveness of black vs. white, women vs. men, lesbian vs. heterosexual, that organizes Smith's manifesto. For McDowell black feminist criticism is less a cause than a task, for which one must go beyond politics and slogans. Whereas earlier black feminists had simply equated their race and sex with a special use of language, McDowell calls instead for concrete investigations into the content of black female poetics using contemporary methodologies. Like Kolodny, McDowell considers the walls of separation between male and female, black and white, at best a mixed blessing. She quotes the Nigerian playwright Wole Soyinka on the creative asphyxiation that accompanies too exclusive an attention to ideology, fearing that a separatist black feminist criticism could become a narrower and less vital enterprise than it has the potential to be.

Lesbian feminist literary criticism centers on a different sort of marginality. Just as black women writers and critics have felt excluded from white feminist studies, so lesbian writers and critics have been excluded by feminist attempts to seek a specifically heterosexual female identity. Bonnie Zimmerman points up the homophobia of both Moers's *Literary Women* and Patricia Meyer Spacks's *The Female Imagination*: "Spacks claims that Gertrude Stein, 'whose life lack[ed] real attachments' (a surprise to Alice B. Toklas) also 'denied whatever is special to women' (which lesbianism is not?)"[12] Lesbian feminist criticism confronts some of the same difficulties as heterosexual feminism, such as whether lesbian writing has a historical continuity apart from the writing of women and, indeed, of men, and whether it encounters unique difficulties of its own. For example, establishing the canon of lesbian writers involves first establishing writers' sexual orientation, which may be ambiguous or simply indecipherable owing to lack of evidence. Lesbian literature itself is difficult to define: Adrienne Rich defines lesbianism so inclusively as to embrace all female bonding and most female creativity, yet the lesbian canon might also be restricted to texts by exclusively homosexual women.

The expansion of the feminist dialogue to take into account various groups previously marginalized within the women's movement is only one version, perhaps, of the tendency of women's studies to expand its boundaries and to address areas traditionally dominated by men. It is impossible to do justice to the breadth of the movement here, but no study of feminist criticism can be complete without at least mentioning the connections between feminism and psychoanalysis (drawn by writers such as Juliet Richardson, Jane Gallop, and Mary Jacobus), between feminism and deconstruction (Peggy Kamuf and Nancy K. Miller), and between feminism and Marxism (Judith Lowder Newton and Lillian Robinson).

Like Marxism, feminism was a social and political movement long before it was a mode of literary criticism, but, also like Marxism, the cultural wing of the ideology has naturally attracted many of the brightest and most energetic minds. This poses a problem to the movement as a whole. Just as Terry Eagleton scoffed at the idea that Jameson's analyses of Balzac were going to shake the foundations of capitalism, so some feminists have wondered how analyzing Charlotte Brontë would alter the fact that women's pay is only sixty percent of men's.

It is obviously necessary for women to understand their past and the accomplishments that their forebears have achieved against heavy odds. But there is at least a slight edge of irony about the success of feminist criticism as an academic career choice. Lillian Robinson has been concerned that feminist critics be feminists first and critics second. "Some people are trying to make an honest woman out of the feminist critic, to claim that every 'worthwhile' department should stock one. I am not terribly interested in whether feminism becomes a respectable part of academic criticism. I am very much concerned that feminist critics become a useful part of the women's movement. . . . Marx's note about philosophers may apply

---

[12]Bonnie Zimmerman, "What Has Never Been: An Overview of Lesbian Feminist Literary Criticism," in *The New Feminist Criticism,* ed. Elaine Showalter (New York: Pantheon, 1985), p. 203.

to cultural critics as well: that up to now they have interpreted the world and the real point is to change it."[13]

## Selected Bibliography

Abel, Elizabeth, ed. *Writing and Sexual Difference*. Chicago: University of Chicago Press, 1982.

Baym, Nina. *Woman's Fiction: A Guide to Novels by and about Women in America*. Ithaca: Cornell University Press, 1978.

Beauvoir, Simone de. *Le deuxième sexe*. Paris: Gallimard, 1949. Trans. H. M. Parshley as *The Second Sex*. New York: Knopf, 1972.

Belsey, Catherine. *Critical Practice*. London: Methuen, 1980.

Brownstein, Rachel. *Becoming a Heroine: Reading about Women in Novels*. New York: Viking, 1982.

Chodorow, Nancy. *The Reproduction of Mothering: Psychoanalysis and the Sociology of Gender*. Berkeley: University of California Press, 1978.

Christian, Barbara. *Black Women Novelists: The Development of a Tradition*. Westport, Conn.: Greenwood Press, 1980.

Cixous, Hélène. "Le Rire de la Méduse." *L'Arc* 61 (1975): 39–54. Trans. Keith and Paula Cohen as "The Laugh of the Medusa," *Signs* 1 (1976): 875–99.

———. *La Jeune née* (with Catherine Clément). Paris: UGE Press, 1975.

Conley, Verena Andermatt. *Hélène Cixous: Writing the Feminine*. Lincoln: University of Nebraska Press, 1984.

Delany, Sheila. *Writing Women: Women Writers and Women in Literature, Medieval to Modern*. New York: Schocken, 1984.

Donovan, Josephine, ed. *Feminist Literary Criticism: Explorations in Theory*. Lexington: University Press of Kentucky, 1975.

Douglas, Ann. *The Feminization of American Culture*. New York: Knopf, 1978.

Ellmann, Mary. *Thinking about Women*. New York: Harcourt Brace Jovanovich, 1968.

Faderman, Lillian. *Surpassing the Love of Men: Romantic Friendship and Love Between Women from the Renaissance to the Present*. New York: William Morrow, 1981.

Felman, Shoshana. "Rereading Femininity." *Yale French Studies* 62 (1981): 19–44.

Fetterley, Judith. *The Resisting Reader: A Feminist Approach to American Fiction*. Bloomington: Indiana University Press, 1978.

Flynn, Elizabeth A., and Patrocinio P. Schweickart. *Gender and Reading: Essays on Readers, Texts and Contexts*. Baltimore: Johns Hopkins University Press, 1986.

Gallop, Jane. *The Daughter's Seduction: Feminism and Psychoanalysis*. Ithaca: Cornell University Press, 1982.

Gilbert, Sandra M., and Susan Gubar. *The Madwoman in the Attic: The Woman Writer and the Nineteenth-Century Literary Imagination*. New Haven: Yale University Press, 1979.

Greer, Germaine. *The Female Eunuch*. London: McGibbon and Kee, 1970.

Irigaray, Luce. *Speculum de l'autre femme*. Paris: Editions de Minuit, 1974. Trans. Gillian C. Gill as *Speculum of the Other Woman*. Ithaca: Cornell University Press, 1985.

[13]Lillian S. Robinson, *Sex, Class, and Culture* (Bloomington: Indiana University Press, 1978), pp. 19–20.

————. *Ce sexe qui n'en est pas un*. Paris: Editions de Minuit, 1977. Translated as *This Sex Which Is Not One*. Ithaca: Cornell University Press, 1985.

Jacobus, Mary. *Women's Writing and Writing about Women*. New York: Barnes and Noble, 1979.

Jehlen, Myra. "Archimedes and the Paradox of Feminist Criticism." *Signs* 6 (1981): 575–601.

Kahn, Coppélia, and Gayle Greene, eds. *Making a Difference: Feminist Literary Criticism*. New York: Methuen, 1985.

Kamuf, Peggy. "Replacing Feminist Criticism." *Diacritics* 12 (1982): 42–47.

Kennard, Jean. "Ourself Behind Ourself: A Theory for Lesbian Readers." *Signs* 9 (1984): 647–62.

Kolodny, Annette. "Some Notes on Defining a 'Feminist Literary Criticism.'" *Critical Inquiry* 2 (1975): 75–92.

————. "Dancing through the Minefield: Some Observations on the Theory, Practice and Politics of a Feminist Literary Criticism." *Feminist Studies* 6 (1981): 1–25.

————. *The Land Before Her: Fantasy and Experience of the American Frontiers, 1630–1860*. Chapel Hill: University of North Carolina Press, 1984.

Kramarae, Cheris. *Women and Men Speaking: Frameworks for Analysis*. Rowley, Mass.: Newbury House, 1981.

Kristeva, Julia. *About Chinese Women*. New York: Urizen Books, 1977.

————. "Women's Time." *Signs* 7 (1981): 13–35.

Lakoff, Robin. *Language and Women's Place*. New York: Harper and Row, 1975.

McConnell-Ginet, Sally, Ruth Borker, and Nelly Furman, eds. *Women and Language in Literature and Society*. New York: Praeger, 1980.

Marks, Elaine, and Isabelle de Courtivron, eds. *New French Feminisms: An Anthology*. Amherst: University of Massachusetts Press, 1980.

Martin, Wendy. *An American Triptych: Anne Bradstreet, Emily Dickinson, and Adrienne Rich*. Chapel Hill: University of North Carolina Press, 1984.

Miller, Nancy K. "The Text's Heroine: A Feminist Critic and Her Fictions." *Diacritics* 12 (1982): 48–53.

Millett, Kate. *Sexual Politics*. New York: Avon Books, 1970.

Mitchell, Juliet. *Psychoanalysis and Feminism*. New York: Pantheon, 1974.

Moers, Ellen. *Literary Women*. New York: Doubleday, 1976.

Moi, Toril. *Sexual/Textual Politics: Feminist Literary Theory*. New York: Methuen, 1985.

Newton, Judith Lowder. *Women, Power, and Subversion: Social Strategies in British Fiction, 1778–1860*. Athens: University of Georgia Press, 1981.

Poovey, Mary. *The Proper Lady and the Woman Writer: Ideology as Style in the Works of Mary Wollstonecraft, Mary Shelley, and Jane Austen*. Chicago: University of Chicago Press, 1984.

Rich, Adrienne. *On Lies, Secrets and Silence*. New York: Norton, 1979.

Robinson, Lillian. *Sex, Class and Culture*. Bloomington: Indiana University Press, 1978.

Ruthven, Kenneth K. *Feminist Literary Studies: An Introduction*. Cambridge: Cambridge University Press, 1984.

Showalter, Elaine. *A Literature of Their Own: British Women Novelists from Brontë to Lessing*. Princeton: Princeton University Press, 1977.

————, ed. *The New Feminist Criticism: Essays on Women, Literature, Theory*. New York: Pantheon, 1985.

Smith, Barbara. *Towards a Black Feminist Criticism*. New York: Out and Out Books, 1977.

Spacks, Patricia Meyer. *The Female Imagination*. New York: Knopf, 1975.

Spender, Dale. *Man Made Language*. London: Routledge and Kegan Paul, 1980.

Thorne, Barrie, Cheris Kramarae, and Nancy Henley, eds. *Language, Gender, and Society*. Rowley, Mass.: Newbury House, 1983.

Walker, Alice. *In Search of Our Mothers' Gardens*. New York: Harcourt Brace Jovanovich, 1983.

Washington, Mary Helen. *Midnight Birds: Stories of Contemporary Black Women Writers*. Garden City, N.Y.: Anchor Books, 1980.

Zimmerman, Bonnie. "What Has Never Been: An Overview of Lesbian Feminist Literary Criticism." *Feminist Studies* 7 (1981): 451–75.

# Virginia Woolf

1882–1941

*The novelist and critic Virginia Woolf, one of the founders of literary modernism in fiction, was born in London. The daughter of the Victorian intellectual Sir Leslie Stephen, Woolf educated herself thoroughly using the resources of her father's library and friends. On her father's death in 1904, she moved to Gordon Square in the Bloomsbury neighborhood that houses the University of London and the British Museum. There she and her sister Vanessa gathered around them that coterie of artists and intellectuals known as the "Bloomsbury Group." In 1912 she married the journalist and editor Leonard Woolf, and together in 1917 they founded the Hogarth Press, a small press distinguished for publishing not only her work but also the English translations of Sigmund Freud. Woolf's early* The Voyage Out *(1915) and* Night and Day *(1919) prepared the way for her more ambitious, experimental* Jacob's Room *(1922) and the novels for which she is most admired,* Mrs. Dalloway *(1925),* To the Lighthouse *(1927), and* The Waves *(1931). Her other novels include* Orlando *(1928),* The Years *(1937), and* Between the Acts *(1941). After completing the last, Woolf suffered a recurrence of the nervous disorder and depression that had plagued her since childhood and drowned herself in the River Ouse. The criticism for which Woolf is also renowned was collected during her life and after her death in the two volumes of* The Common Reader *(1925 and 1932), in* The Death of the Moth *(1942), and in* Granite and Rainbow *(1958). The selections below are from her long essay,* A Room of One's Own *(1929).*

## Shakespeare's Sister
## from *A Room of One's Own*

Let me imagine, since facts are so hard to come by, what would have happened had Shakespeare had a wonderfully gifted sister, called Judith, let us say. Shakespeare himself went, very probably — his mother was an heiress — to the grammar school, where he may have learnt Latin — Ovid, Virgil and Horace — and the elements of grammar and logic. He was, it is well known, a wild boy who poached rabbits, perhaps shot a deer, and had, rather sooner than he should have done, to marry a woman in the neighborhood, who bore him a child rather quicker than was right. That escapade sent him to seek his fortune in London. He had, it seemed, a taste for the theatre; he began by holding horses at the stage door. Very soon he got work in the theatre, became a successful actor, and lived at the hub of the universe, meeting everybody, knowing everybody, practising his art on the boards, exercising his wits in the streets, and even getting access to the palace of the queen. Meanwhile his extraordinarily gifted sister, let us suppose, remained at home. She was as adventurous, as imaginative, as agog to see the world as he was. But she was not sent to school. She had no chance of learning grammar and logic, let alone of reading Horace and Virgil. She picked up a book now and then, one of her brother's perhaps, and read a few pages. But then her parents came in and told her to mend the stockings or mind the stew and not moon about with books and papers. They would have spoken sharply but kindly, for they were substantial people who knew the conditions of life for a woman and loved their daughter — indeed, more likely than not she was the apple of her father's eye. Perhaps she scribbled some pages up in an apple loft on the sly, but was careful to hide them or set fire to them. Soon, however, before she was out of her teens, she was to be betrothed to the son of a neighbouring wool-stapler. She cried out that marriage was hateful to her, and for that she was severely beaten by her father. Then he ceased to scold her. He begged her instead not to hurt him, not to shame him in this matter of her marriage. He would give her a chain of beads or a fine petticoat, he said; and there were tears in his eyes. How could she disobey him? How could she break his heart? The force of her own gift alone drove her to it. She made up a small parcel of her belongings, let herself down by a rope one summer's night and took the road to London. She was not seventeen. The birds that sang in the hedge were not more musical than she was. She had the quickest fancy, a gift like her brother's, for the tune of words. Like him, she had a taste for the theatre. She stood at the stage door; she wanted to act, she said. Men laughed in her face. The manager — a fat, loose-lipped man — guffawed. He bellowed something about poodles dancing and women acting — no woman, he said, could possibly be an actress. He hinted — you can imagine what. She could get no training in her craft. Could she even seek her dinner in a tavern or roam the streets at midnight? Yet her genius was for fiction and lusted to feed abundantly upon the lives of men and women and the study of their ways. At last — for she was very young, oddly like Shakespeare the poet in her face, with the same grey eyes and rounded brows — at last Nick Greene the actor-manager took pity on her; she found herself with child by that gentleman and so — who shall measure the heat and violence of the poet's heart when caught and tangled in a woman's body? — killed herself one winter's night and lies buried at some cross-roads where the omnibuses now stop outside the Elephant and Castle.[1]

That, more or less, is how the story would run, I think, if a woman in Shakespeare's day had had Shakespeare's genius. But for my part, I agree with the deceased bishop, if such he was — it is unthinkable that any woman in Shakespeare's day should have had Shakespeare's genius. For genius like Shakespeare's is not born among labouring, uneducated, servile people. It was not born in England among the Saxons and the Britons. It is not born today among the working classes. How, then, could it have been born among women whose work began, according to Professor Trevelyan,[2] almost before they were out of the nursery, who were forced to it by their parents and held to it by all the power of law and custom? Yet genius of a sort must have existed among women as it must have existed among the working classes. Now and again an Emily Brontë or a Robert Burns blazes out and proves its presence. But certainly it never got itself on to paper. When, however, one reads of a witch being ducked, of a woman possessed by devils, of a wise woman selling herbs, or even of a very remarkable man who had a mother, then I think we are on the track of a lost novelist,

[1]Public square in London on the south bank of the Thames. [Ed.]

[2]George Macaulay Trevelyan (1876–1962), Regius professor of modern history at Cambridge, author of *England in the Age of Wycliffe* (1899) and *British History in the Nineteenth Century* (1922). [Ed.]

a suppressed poet, of some mute and inglorious Jane Austen, some Emily Brontë who dashed her brains out on the moor or mopped and mowed about the highways crazed with the torture that her gift had put her to. Indeed, I would venture to guess that Anon, who wrote so many poems without signing them, was often a woman. It was a woman Edward Fitzgerald, I think, suggested who made the ballads and the folk-songs, crooning them to her children, beguiling her spinning with them, or the length of the winter's night.

This may be true or it may be false — who can say? — but what is true in it, so it seemed to me, reviewing the story of Shakespeare's sister as I had made it, is that any woman born with a great gift in the sixteenth century would certainly have gone crazed, shot herself, or ended her days in some lonely cottage outside the village, half witch, half wizard, feared and mocked at. For it needs little skill in psychology to be sure that a highly gifted girl who had tried to use her gift for poetry would have been so thwarted and hindered by other people, so tortured and pulled asunder by her own contrary instincts, that she must have lost her health and sanity to a certainty. No girl could have walked to London and stood at a stage door and forced her way into the presence of actor-managers without doing herself a violence and suffering an anguish which may have been irrational — for chastity may be a fetish invented by certain societies for unknown reasons — but were none the less inevitable. Chastity had then, it has even now, a religious importance in a woman's life, and has so wrapped itself round with nerves and instincts that to cut it free and bring it to the light of day demands courage of the rarest. To have lived a free life in London in the sixteenth century would have meant for a woman who was poet and playwright a nervous stress and dilemma which might well have killed her. Had she survived, whatever she had written would have been twisted and deformed, issuing from a strained and morbid imagination. And undoubtedly, I thought, looking at the shelf where there are no plays by women, her work would have gone unsigned. That refuge she would have sought certainly. It was the relic of the sense of chastity that dictated anonymity to women even so late as the nineteenth century. Currer Bell, George Eliot, George Sand, all the victims of inner strife as their writings prove, sought ineffectively to veil themselves by using the name of a man. Thus they did homage to the convention, which if not implanted by the other sex was liberally encouraged by them (the chief glory of a woman is not to be talked of, said Pericles, himself a much-talked-of man), that publicity in women is detestable. Anonymity runs in their blood. The desire to be veiled still possesses them. They are not even now as concerned about the health of their fame as men are, and, speaking generally, will pass a tombstone or a signpost without feeling an irresistible desire to cut their names on it, as Alf, Bert or Chas. must do in obedience to their instinct, which murmurs if it sees a fine woman go by, or even a dog, Ce chien est à moi.[3] And, of course, it may not be a dog, I thought, remembering Parliament Square, the Sieges Allee[4] and other avenues; it may be a piece of land or a man with curly black hair. It is one of the great advantages of being a woman that one can pass even a very fine negress without wishing to make an Englishwoman of her.

That woman, then, who was born with a gift of poetry in the sixteenth century, was an unhappy woman, a woman at strife against herself. All the conditions of her life, all her own instincts, were hostile to the state of mind which is needed to set free whatever is in the brain. But what is the state of mind that is most propitious to the act of creation, I asked. Can one come by any notion of the state that furthers and makes possible that strange activity? Here I opened the volume containing the Tragedies of Shakespeare. What was Shakespeare's state of mind, for instance, when he wrote *Lear* and *Antony and Cleopatra*? It was certainly the state of mind most favourable to poetry that there has ever existed. But Shakespeare himself said nothing about it. We only know casually and by chance that he "never blotted a line." Nothing indeed was ever said by the artist himself about his state of mind until the eighteenth century perhaps. Rousseau perhaps began it. At any rate,

[3]The dog is mine. [Ed.]
[4]Broad avenue in Berlin. [Ed.]

by the nineteenth century self-consciousness had developed so far that it was the habit for men of letters to describe their minds in confessions and autobiographies. Their lives also were written, and their letters were printed after their deaths. Thus, though we do not know what Shakespeare went through when he wrote *Lear,* we do know what Carlyle went through when he wrote the *French Revolution;* what Flaubert went through when he wrote *Madame Bovary;* what Keats was going through when he tried to write poetry against the coming of death and the indifference of the world.

And one gathers from this enormous modern literature of confession and self-analysis that to write a work of genius is almost always a feat of prodigious difficulty. Everything is against the likelihood that it will come from the writer's mind whole and entire. Generally material circumstances are against it. Dogs will bark; people will interrupt; money must be made; health will break down. Further, accentuating all these difficulties and making them harder to bear is the world's notorious indifference. It does not ask people to write poems and novels and histories; it does not need them. It does not care whether Flaubert finds the right word or whether Carlyle scrupulously verifies this or that fact. Naturally, it will not pay for what it does not want. And so the writer, Keats, Flaubert, Carlyle, suffers, especially in the creative years of youth, every form of distraction and discouragement. A curse, a cry of agony, rises from those books of analysis and confession. "Mighty poets in their misery dead" — that is the burden of their song. If anything comes through in spite of all this, it is a miracle, and probably no book is born entire and uncrippled as it was conceived.

But for women, I thought, looking at the empty shelves, these difficulties were infinitely more formidable. In the first place, to have a room of her own, let alone a quiet room or a sound-proof room, was out of the question, unless her parents were exceptionally rich or very noble, even up to the beginning of the nineteenth century. Since her pin money, which depended on the good will of her father, was only enough to keep her clothed, she was debarred from such alleviations as came even to Keats or Tennyson or Carlyle, all poor men, from a walking tour, a little journey to France, from the separate lodging which, even if it were miserable enough, sheltered them from the claims and tyrannies of their families. Such material difficulties were formidable; but much worse were the immaterial. The indifference of the world which Keats and Flaubert and other men of genius have found so hard to bear was in her case not indifference but hostility. The world did not say to her as it said to them, Write if you choose; it makes no difference to me. The world said with a guffaw, Write? What's the good of your writing?

# Austen–Brontë–Eliot
# from *A Room of One's Own*

Here, then, one had reached the early nineteenth century. And here, for the first time, I found several shelves given up entirely to the works of women. But why, I could not help asking, as I ran my eyes over them, were they, with very few exceptions, all novels? The original impulse was to poetry. The "supreme head of song" was a poetess. Both in France and in England the women poets precede the women novelists. Moreover, I thought, looking at the four famous names, what had George Eliot in common with Emily Brontë? Did not Charlotte Brontë fail entirely to understand Jane Austen? Save for the possibly relevant fact that not one of them had a child, four more incongruous characters could not have met together in a room — so much so that it is tempting to invent a meeting and a dialogue between them. Yet by some strange force they were all compelled, when they wrote, to write novels. Had it something to do with being born of the middle class, I asked; and with the fact, which Miss Emily Davies[1] a little later was so strikingly to demonstrate, that the middle-class family in the early nineteenth century was possessed only of a single sitting-room between them? If a woman wrote, she would have to write in the common sitting-room. And, as Miss Nightingale was so vehemently to complain, — "women never have an half hour . . . that they can call their own" — she was always interrupted. Still it would be easier to write prose and fiction there than to write poetry or a play. Less concentration is required. Jane Austen wrote like that to the end of her days. "How she was able to effect all this," her nephew writes in his Memoir, "is surprising, for she had no separate study to repair to, and most of the work must have been done in the general sitting-room, subject to all kinds of casual interruptions. She was careful that her occupation should not be suspected by servants or visitors or any persons beyond her own family party."[2] Jane Austen hid her manuscripts or covered them with a piece of blotting-paper. Then, again, all the literary training that a woman had in the early nineteenth century was training in the observation of character, in the analysis of emotion. Her sensibility had been educated for centuries by the influences of the common sitting-room. People's feelings were impressed on her; personal relations were always before her eyes. Therefore, when the middle-class woman took to writing, she naturally wrote novels, even though, as seems evident enough, two of the four famous women here named were not by nature novelists. Emily Brontë should have written poetic plays; the overflow of George Eliot's capacious mind should have spread itself when the creative impulse was spent upon history or biography. They wrote novels, however; one may even go further, I said, taking *Pride and Prejudice* from the shelf, and say that they wrote good novels. Without boast-

ing or giving pain to the opposite sex, one may say that *Pride and Prejudice* is a good book. At any rate, one would not have been ashamed to have been caught in the act of writing *Pride and Prejudice*. Yet Jane Austen was glad that a hinge creaked, so that she might hide her manuscript before any one came in. To Jane Austen there was something discreditable in writing *Pride and Prejudice*. And, I wondered, would *Pride and Prejudice* have been a better novel if Jane Austen had not thought it necessary to hide her manuscript from visitors? I read a page or two to see; but I could not find any signs that her circumstances had harmed her work in the slightest. That, perhaps, was the chief miracle about it. Here was a woman about the year 1800 writing without hate, without bitterness, without fear, without protest, without preaching. That was how Shakespeare wrote, I thought, looking at *Antony and Cleopatra;* and when people compare Shakespeare and Jane Austen, they may mean that the minds of both had consumed all impediments; and for that reason we do not know Jane Austen and we do not know Shakespeare, and for that reason Jane Austen pervades every word that she wrote, and so does Shakespeare. If Jane Austen suffered in any way from her circumstances it was in the narrowness of life that was imposed upon her. It was impossible for a woman to go about alone. She never travelled; she never drove through London in an omnibus or had luncheon in a shop by herself. But perhaps it was the nature of Jane Austen not to want what she had not. Her gift and her circumstances matched each other completely. But I doubt whether that was true of Charlotte Brontë, I said, opening *Jane Eyre* and laying it beside *Pride and Prejudice.*

I opened it at chapter twelve and my eye was caught by the phrase, "Anybody may blame me who likes." What were they blaming Charlotte Brontë for, I wondered? And I read how Jane Eyre used to go up on the roof when Mrs. Fairfax was making jellies and looked over the fields at the distant view. And then she longed — and it was for this that they blamed her — that "then I longed for a power of vision which might overpass that limit; which might reach the busy world, towns, regions full of life I had heard of

[1]Sarah Emily Davies (1830–1921), British feminist responsible for the admission of women to University College, London (1870) and the foundation of Girton College, Cambridge (1873). [Ed.]

[2]*Memoir of Jane Austen*, by her nephew, James Edward Austen-Leigh. [Au.]

but never seen: that then I desired more of practical experience than I possessed; more of intercourse with my kind, of acquaintance with variety of character than was here within my reach. I valued what was good in Mrs. Fairfax, and what was good in Adèle; but I believed in the existence of other and more vivid kinds of goodness, and what I believed in I wished to behold.

"Who blames me? Many, no doubt, and I shall be called discontented. I could not help it: the restlessness was in my nature; it agitated me to pain sometimes. . . .

"It is vain to say human beings ought to be satisfied with tranquillity: they must have action; and they will make it if they cannot find it. Millions are condemned to a stiller doom than mine, and millions are in silent revolt against their lot. Nobody knows how many rebellions ferment in the masses of life which people earth. Women are supposed to be very calm generally: but women feel just as men feel; they need exercise for their faculties and a field for their efforts as much as their brothers do; they suffer from too rigid a restraint, too absolute a stagnation, precisely as men would suffer; and it is narrow-minded in their more privileged fellow-creatures to say that they ought to confine themselves to making puddings and knitting stockings, to playing on the piano and embroidering bags. It is thoughtless to condemn them, or laugh at them, if they seek to do more or learn more than custom has pronounced necessary for their sex.

"When thus alone I not unfrequently heard Grace Poole's laugh. . . ."

That is an awkward break, I thought. It is upsetting to come upon Grace Poole all of a sudden. The continuity is disturbed. One might say, I continued, laying the book down beside *Pride and Prejudice,* that the woman who wrote those pages had more genius in her than Jane Austen; but if one reads them over and marks that jerk in them, that indignation, one sees that she will never get her genius expressed whole and entire. Her books will be deformed and twisted. She will write in a rage where she should write calmly. She will write foolishly where she should write wisely. She will write of herself where she should write of her characters. She is at war with her lot. How could she help but die young, cramped and thwarted?

One could not but play for a moment with the thought of what might have happened if Charlotte Brontë had possessed say three hundred a year — but the foolish woman sold the copyright of her novels outright for fifteen hundred pounds; had somehow possessed more knowledge of the busy world, and towns and regions full of life; more practical experience, and intercourse with her kind and acquaintance with a variety of character. In those words she puts her finger exactly not only upon her own defects as a novelist but upon those of her sex at that time. She knew, no one better, how enormously her genius would have profited if it had not spent itself in solitary visions over distant fields; if experience and intercourse and travel had been granted her. But they were not granted; they were withheld; and we must accept the fact that all those good novels, *Villette, Emma, Wuthering Heights, Middlemarch,* were written by women without more experience of life than could enter the house of a respectable clergyman; written too in the common sitting-room of that respectable house and by women so poor that they could not afford to buy more than a few quires of paper at a time upon which to write *Wuthering Heights* or *Jane Eyre.* One of them, it is true, George Eliot, escaped after much tribulation, but only to a secluded villa in St. John's Wood. And there she settled down in the shadow of the world's disapproval. "I wish it to be understood," she wrote, "that I should never invite any one to come and see me who did not ask for the invitation"; for was she not living in sin with a married man and might not the sight of her damage the chastity of Mrs. Smith or whoever it might be that chanced to call? One must submit to the social convention, and be "cut off from what is called the world." At the same time, on the other side of Europe, there was a young man living freely with this gipsy or with that great lady; going to the wars; picking up unhindered and uncensored all that varied experience of human life which served him so splendidly later when he came to write his books. Had Tolstoy lived at the Priory in seclusion with a married lady "cut off from what is called the world," however edifying the moral lesson, he could scarcely, I thought, have written *War and Peace*.

But one could perhaps go a little deeper into the question of novel-writing and the effect of sex upon the novelist. If one shuts one's eyes and thinks of the novel as a whole, it would seem to be a creation owning a certain looking-glass likeness to life, though of course with simplifications and distortions innumerable. At any rate, it is a structure leaving a shape on the mind's eye, built now in squares, now pagoda shaped, now throwing out wings and arcades, now solidly compact and domed like the Cathedral of Saint Sofia at Constantinople. This shape, I thought, thinking back over certain famous novels, starts in one the kind of emotion that is appropriate to it. But that emotion at once blends itself with others, for the "shape" is not made by the relation of stone to stone, but by the relation of human being to human being. Thus a novel starts in us all sorts of antagonistic and opposed emotions. Life conflicts with something that is not life. Hence the difficulty of coming to any agreement about novels, and the immense sway that our private prejudices have upon us. On the one hand, we feel You — John the hero — must live, or I shall be in the depths of despair. On the other, we feel, Alas, John, you must die, because the shape of the book requires it. Life conflicts with something that is not life. Then since life it is in part, we judge it as life. James is the sort of man I most detest, one says. Or, This is a farrago of absurdity. I could never feel anything of the sort myself. The whole structure, it is obvious, thinking back on any famous novel, is one of infinite complexity, because it is thus made up of so many different judgments, of so many different kinds of emotion. The wonder is that any book so composed holds together for more than a year or two, or can possibly mean to the English reader what it means for the Russian or the Chinese. But they do hold together occasionally very remarkably. And what holds them together in these rare instances of survival (I was thinking of *War and Peace*) is something that one calls integrity, though it has nothing to do with paying one's bills or behaving honourably in an emergency. What one means by integrity, in the case of the novelist, is the conviction

that he gives one that this is the truth. Yes, one feels, I should never have thought that this could be so; I have never known people behaving like that. But you have convinced me that so it is, so it happens. One holds every phrase, every scene to the light as one reads — for Nature seems, very oddly, to have provided us with an inner light by which to judge of the novelist's integrity or disintegrity. Or perhaps it is rather that Nature, in her most irrational mood, has traced in invisible ink on the walls of the mind a premonition which these great artists confirm; a sketch which only needs to be held to the fire of genius to become visible. When one so exposes it and sees it come to life one exclaims in rapture, But this is what I have always felt and known and desired! And one boils over with excitement, and, shutting the book even with a kind of reverence as if it were something very precious, a stand-by to return to as long as one lives, one puts it back on the shelf, I said, taking *War and Peace* and putting it back in its place. If, on the other hand, these poor sentences that one takes and tests rouse first a quick and eager response with their bright colouring and their dashing gestures but there they stop: something seems to check them in their development: or if they bring to light only a faint scribble in that corner and a blot over there, and nothing appears whole and entire, then one heaves a sigh of disappointment and says, Another failure. This novel has come to grief somewhere.

And for the most part, of course, novels do come to grief somewhere. The imagination falters under the enormous strain. The insight is confused; it can no longer distinguish between the true and the false; it has no longer the strength to go on with the vast labour that calls at every moment for the use of so many different faculties. But how would all this be affected by the sex of the novelist, I wondered, looking at *Jane Eyre* and the others. Would the fact of her sex in any way interfere with the integrity of a woman novelist — that integrity which I take to be the backbone of the writer? Now, in the passages I have quoted from *Jane Eyre,* it is clear that anger was tampering with the integrity of Charlotte Brontë the novelist. She left her story, to which her entire devotion was due, to attend to some personal grievance. She remembered that she had been starved of her proper due of experience — she had been made to stagnate in a parsonage mending stockings when she wanted to wander free over the world. Her imagination swerved from indignation and we feel it swerve. But there were many more influences than anger tugging at her imagination and deflecting it from its path. Ignorance, for instance. The portrait of Rochester is drawn in the dark. We feel the influence of fear in it; just as we constantly feel an acidity which is the result of oppression, a buried suffering smouldering beneath her passion, a rancour which contracts those books, splendid as they are, with a spasm of pain.

And since a novel has this correspondence to real life, its values are to some extent those of real life. But it is obvious that the values of women differ very often from the values which have been made by the other sex; naturally, this is so. Yet it is the masculine values that prevail. Speaking crudely, football and sport are "important"; the worship of fashion, the buying of clothes "trivial." And these values are inevitably transferred from life to fiction. This is an important book, the critic assumes, because it deals with war. This is an insignificant book because it deals with the feelings of women in a drawing-room. A scene in a battlefield is more important than a scene in a shop — everywhere and much more subtly the difference of value persists. The whole structure, therefore, of the early nineteenth-century novel was raised, if one was a woman, by a mind which was slightly pulled from the straight, and made to alter its clear vision in deference to external authority. One has only to skim those old forgotten novels and listen to the tone of voice in which they were written to divine that the writer was meeting criticism; she was saying this by way of aggression, or that by way of conciliation. She was admitting that she was "only a woman," or protesting that she was "as good as a man." She met that criticism as her temperament dictated, with docility and diffidence, or with anger and emphasis. It does not matter which it was; she was thinking of something other than the thing itself. Down comes her book upon our heads. There was a flaw in the centre of it. And I thought of all the women's novels that lie scattered, like small pock-marked apples in an orchard, about the secondhand book shops of London. It was the flaw in the centre that had rotted them. She had altered her values in deference to the opinion of others.

But how impossible it must have been for them not to budge either to the right or to the left. What genius, what integrity it must have required in face of all that criticism, in the midst of that purely patriarchal society, to hold fast to the thing as they saw it without shrinking. Only Jane Austen did it and Emily Brontë. It is another feather, perhaps the finest, in their caps. They wrote as women write, not as men write. Of all the thousand women who wrote novels then, they alone entirely ignored the perpetual admonitions of the eternal pedagogue — write this, think that. They alone were deaf to that persistent voice, now grumbling, now patronising, now domineering, now grieved, now shocked, now angry, now avuncular, that voice which cannot let women alone, but must be at them, like some too conscientious governess, adjuring them, like Sir Egerton Brydges, to be refined; dragging even into the criticism of poetry criticism of sex;[3] admonishing them, if they would be good and win, as I suppose, some shiny prize, to keep within certain limits which the gentleman in question thinks suitable: ". . . female novelists should only aspire to excellence by courageously acknowledging the limitations of their sex."[4] That puts the matter in a nutshell, and when I tell you, rather to your surprise, that this sentence was written not in August 1828 but in August 1928, you will agree, I think, that however delightful it is to us now, it represents a vast body of opinion — I am not going to stir those old pools, I take only what chance has floated to my feet — that was far more vigorous and far more

[3]"[She] has a metaphysical purpose, and that is a dangerous obsession, especially with a woman, for women rarely possess men's healthy love of rhetoric. It is a strange lack in the sex which is in other things more primitive and more materialistic." — *New Criterion*, June 1928. [Au.]

[4]"If, like the reporter, you believe that female novelists should only aspire to excellence by courageously acknowledging the limitations of their sex (Jane Austen [has] demonstrated how gracefully this gesture can be accomplished). . . ." — *Life and Letters*, August 1928. [Au.]

vocal a century ago. It would have needed a very stalwart young woman in 1828 to disregard all those snubs and chidings and promises of prizes. One must have been something of a firebrand to say to oneself, Oh, but they can't buy literature too. Literature is open to everybody. I refuse to allow you, Beadle though you are, to turn me off the grass. Lock up your libraries if you like; but there is no gate, no lock, no bolt that you can set upon the freedom of my mind.

But whatever effect discouragement and criticism had upon their writing — and I believe that they had a very great effect — that was unimportant compared with the other difficulty which faced them (I was still considering those early nineteenth-century novelists) when they came to set their thoughts on paper — that is that they had no tradition behind them, or one so short and partial that it was of little help. For we think back through our mothers if we are women.[5] It is useless to go to the great men writers for help, however much one may go to them for pleasure. Lamb, Browne, Thackeray, Newman, Sterne, Dickens, De Quincey — whoever it may be — never helped a woman yet, though she may have learnt a few tricks of them and adapted them to her use. The weight, the pace, the stride of a man's mind are too unlike her own for her to lift anything substantial from him successfully. The ape is too distant to be sedulous. Perhaps the first thing she would find, setting pen to paper, was that there was no common sentence ready for her use. All the great novelists like Thackeray and Dickens and Balzac have written a natural prose, swift but not slovenly, expressive but not precious, taking their own tint without ceasing to be common property. They have based it on the sentence that was current at the time. The sentence that was current at the beginning of the nineteenth century ran something like this perhaps: "The grandeur of their works was an argument with them, not to

[5]See Gilbert and Gubar, p. 1119. [Ed.]

stop short, but to proceed. They could have no higher excitement or satisfaction than in the exercise of their art and endless generations of truth and beauty. Success prompts to exertion; and habit facilitates success." That is a man's sentence; behind it one can see Johnson, Gibbon and the rest. It was a sentence that was unsuited for a woman's use. Charlotte Brontë, with all her splendid gift for prose, stumbled and fell with that clumsy weapon in her hands. George Eliot committed atrocities with it that beggar description. Jane Austen looked at it and laughed at it and devised a perfectly natural, shapely sentence proper for her own use and never departed from it. Thus, with less genius for writing than Charlotte Brontë, she got infinitely more said. Indeed, since freedom and fullness of expression are of the essence of the art, such a lack of tradition, such a scarcity and inadequacy of tools, must have told enormously upon the writing of women. Moreover, a book is not made of sentences laid end to end, but of sentences built, if an image helps, into arcades or domes. And this shape too has been made by men out of their own needs for their own uses. There is no reason to think that the form of the epic or of the poetic play suits a woman any more than the sentence suits her. But all the older forms of literature were hardened and set by the time she became a writer. The novel alone was young enough to be soft in her hands — another reason, perhaps, why she wrote novels. Yet who shall say that even now "the novel" (I give it inverted commas to mark my sense of the words' inadequacy), who shall say that even this most pliable of all forms is rightly shaped for her use? No doubt we shall find her knocking that into shape for herself when she has the free use of her limbs; and providing some new vehicle, not necessarily in verse, for the poetry in her. For it is the poetry that is still denied outlet. And I went on to ponder how a woman nowadays would write a poetic tragedy in five acts — would she use verse — would she not use prose rather?

# Simone de Beauvoir

## 1908–1986

*Born and raised in a middle-class Parisian household that discouraged her interest in philosophy, Simone de Beauvoir went on to obtain a prestigious* agrégation *in 1929 at the University of Paris and to write what is surely the most influential feminist treatise of all time,* The Second Sex. *While preparing for her degree, de Beauvoir met Jean-Paul Sartre, who became her companion in a lifelong nonmarital union. In 1945 the two of them founded the important intellectual journal* Les Temps modernes, *which she continued to review and edit after Sartre's death in 1980. Starting her career as a teacher, de Beauvoir lost her position during the war, in the same year that her first novel,* L'Invitée (1943), *was published.* The Second Sex (1949) *caused a scandal, but de Beauvoir's novel* The Mandarins (1954), *which depicted the intellectual circles she moved in, won the favor of the literary establishment and was awarded the Prix Goncourt. In addition to her left-wing political and polemical writings, de Beauvoir is famed for her autobiographical works, which include* Memoirs of a Dutiful Daughter (1958); A Very Easy Death (1964), *an account of her mother's last illness; and* La Cérémonie des adieux (1982), *an unflinching look at her last years with Sartre. The excerpt below is from the H. M. Parshley translation of* The Second Sex (1953).

# Myths: Of Women in Five Authors

It is to be seen from these examples that each separate writer reflects the great collective myths: we have seen woman as *flesh;* the flesh of the male is produced in the mother's body and re-created in the embraces of the woman in love. Thus woman is related to *nature,* she incarnates it: vale of blood, open rose, siren, the curve of a hill, she represents to man the fertile soil, the sap, the material beauty and the soul of the world. She can hold the keys to *poetry;* she can be *mediatrix* between this world and the beyond: grace or oracle, star or sorceress, she opens the door to the supernatural, the surreal. She is doomed to *immanence;* and through her passivity she bestows peace and harmony — but if she declines this role, she is seen forthwith as a praying mantis, an ogress. In any case she appears as the *privileged Other,* through whom the subject fulfills himself: one of the measures of man, his counterbalance, his salvation, his adventure, his happiness.

But these myths are very differently orchestrated by our authors. The *Other* is particularly defined according to the particular manner in which the *One* chooses to set himself up. Every man asserts his freedom and transcendence — but they do not all give these words the same sense. For Montherlant[1] transcendence is a situation: he is the transcendent, he soars in the sky of heroes; woman crouches on earth, beneath his feet; it amuses him to measure the distance that separates him from her; from time to time he raises her up to him, takes her, and then throws her back; never does he lower himself down to her realm of slimy shadows. Lawrence places transcendence in the phallus; the phallus is life and power only by grace of woman; immanence is therefore good and necessary; the false hero who pretends to be above setting foot on earth, far from being a demigod, fails to attain man's estate. Woman is not to be scorned, she is deep richness, a warm spring; but she should give up

Translated by H. M. Parshley.

[1]Henry de Montherlant (1896–1972), antifeminist author of *Les Jeune filles* (1936), *Pitié pour les femmes* (1936), *Le Démon du bien* (1937), and *Les Lepreuses* (1939). [Ed.]

all personal transcendence and confine herself to furthering that of her male. Claudel[2] asks her for the same devotion: for him, too, woman should maintain life while man extends its range through his activities; but for the Catholic all earthly affairs are immersed in vain immanence: the only transcendent is God; in the eyes of God the man in action and the woman who serves him are exactly equal; it is for each to surpass his or her earthly state: salvation is in all cases an autonomous enterprise. For Breton[3] the rank of the sexes is reversed; action and conscious thought, in which the male finds his transcendence, seem to Breton to constitute a silly mystification that gives rise to war, stupidity, bureaucracy, the negation of anything human; it is immanence, the pure, dark presence of the real, which is truth; true transcendence would be accomplished by a return to immanence. His attitude is the exact opposite of Montherlant's: the latter likes war because in war one gets rid of women; Breton venerates woman because she brings peace. Montherlant confuses mind and subjectivity — he refuses to accept the given universe; Breton thinks that mind is objectively present at the heart of the world; woman endangers Montherlant because she breaks his solitude; she is revelation for Breton because she tears him out of his subjectivity. As for Stendhal,[4] we have seen that for him woman hardly has a mystical value: he regards her as being, like man, a transcendent; for this humanist, free beings of both sexes fulfill themselves in their reciprocal relations; and for him it is enough if the *Other* be simply an other so that life may have what he calls "a pungent saltiness." He is not seeking a "stellar equilibrium," he is not fed on the bread of disgust; he is not looking for a miracle; he does not wish to be concerned with the cosmos or with poetry, but with free human beings.

More, Stendhal feels that he is himself a clear, free being. The others — and this is a most important point — pose as transcendents but feel themselves prisoners of a dark presence in their own hearts: they project this "unbreakable core of night" upon woman. Montherlant has an Adlerian complex, giving rise to his thick-witted bad faith: it is this tangle of pretensions and fears that he incarnates in woman; his disgust for her is what he dreads feeling for himself. He would trample underfoot, in woman, the always possible proof of his own insufficiency; he appeals to scorn to save him; and woman is the trench into which he throws all the monsters that haunt him. The life of Lawrence[5] shows us that he suffered from an analogous though more purely sexual complex: in his works woman serves as a compensation myth, exalting a virility that the writer was none too sure of; when he describes Kate at Don Cipriano's feet, he feels as if he had won a male triumph over his wife, Frieda; nor does he permit his companion to raise any questions: if she were to oppose his aims he would doubtless lose confidence in them; her role is to reassure him. He asks of her peace, repose, faith, as Montherlant asks for certainty regarding his superiority: they demand what is missing in them. Claudel's lack is not that of self-confidence: if he is timid it is only in secret with God. Nor is there any trace of the battle of the sexes in his work. Man boldly assumes woman's weight; she is a possibility for temptation or for salvation. It would seem that for Breton man is true only through the mystery that is within him; it pleases him for Nadja to see that star toward which he moves and which is like "the heart of a heartless flower." In his dreams, his presentiments, the spontaneous flow of his stream of consciousness — in such activities, which escape the control of the will and the reason, he recognizes his true self; woman is the visible image of that veiled presence which is infinitely more essential than his conscious personality.

[2]Paul Claudel (1868–1955), poet and playwright, author of *L'Annonce faite à Marie* (1912) and *Le Soulier de satin* (1937), which contains the salvation of Rodrigue by Prouhèze that Beauvoir refers to later. [Ed.]

[3]André Breton (1896–1966), surrealist poet and novelist, author of *Nadja* (1928) and *L'Amour fou* (1937). [Ed.]

[4]Marie-Henri Beyle (1783–1842), psychological novelist who wrote as Stendhal; his works include *Le Rouge et le noir* (1830) and *La Chartreuse de Parme* (1839). [Ed.]

[5]D. H. Lawrence (1885–1930), author of *Sons and Lovers* (1913) and *Women in Love* (1920); Beauvoir's later discussion of "Kate" and "Don Cipriano" refers to his novel, *The Plumed Serpent* (1926). [Ed.]

Stendhal is in tranquil agreement with himself; but he needs woman as she needs him in order to gather his diffuse existence into the unity of a single design and destiny: it is as though man reaches manhood for another; but still he needs to have the lending of the other's consciousness. Other males are too indifferent toward their fellows; only the loving woman opens her heart to her lover and shelters him there, wholly. Except for Claudel, who finds in God his preferred witness, all the writers we have considered expect that woman will cherish in them what Malraux[6] calls "this incomparable monster" known to themselves only. In cooperation or contest men face each other as generalized types. Montherlant is for his fellows a writer, Lawrence a doctrinaire, Breton a school principal, Stendhal a diplomat or man of wit; it is woman who reveals in one a magnificent and cruel prince, in another a disquieting faun, in this one a god or a sun or a being "black and cold as a man struck by lightning at the feet of the Sphinx,"[7] in the last a seducer, a charmer, a lover.

For each of them the ideal woman will be she who incarnates most exactly the *Other* capable of revealing him to himself. Montherlant, the solar spirit, seeks pure animality in her; Lawrence, the phallicist, asks her to sum up the feminine sex in general; Claudel defines her as a soul-sister; Breton cherishes Mélusine, rooted in nature, pinning his hope on the woman-child; Stendhal wants his mistress intelligent, cultivated, free in spirit and behavior: an equal. But the sole earthly destiny reserved for the equal, the woman-child, the soul-sister, the woman-sex, the woman-animal is always man! Whatever ego may seek himself through her, he can find himself only if she is willing to act as his crucible. She is required in every case to forget self and to love. Montherlant consents to have pity upon the woman who allows him to measure his virile potency; Lawrence addresses a burning hymn to

the woman who gives up being herself for his sake; Claudel exalts the handmaid, the female servant, the devotee who submits to God in submitting to the male; Breton is in hopes of human salvation from woman because she is capable of total love for her child or her lover; and even in Stendhal the heroines are more moving than the masculine heroes because they give themselves to their passion with a more distraught violence; they help man fulfill his destiny, as Prouhèze contributes to the salvation of Rodrigue; in Stendhal's novels it often happens that they save their lovers from ruin, prison, or death. Feminine devotion is demanded as a duty by Montherlant and Lawrence; less arrogant, Claudel, Breton, and Stendhal admire it as a generous free choice; they wish for it without claiming to deserve it; but — except for the astounding Lamiel — all their works show that they expect from woman that altruism which Comte[8] admired in her and imposed upon her, and which according to him constituted a mark at once of flagrant inferiority and of an equivocal superiority.

We could multiply examples, but they would invariably lead us to the same conclusions. When he describes woman, each writer discloses his general ethics and the special idea he has of himself; and in her he often betrays also the gap between his world view and his egotistical dreams. The absence or insignificance of the feminine element throughout the work of an author is in its own way symptomatic; but that element is extremely important when it sums up in its totality all the aspects of the Other, as happens with Lawrence. It remains important when woman is viewed simply as an other but the writer is interested in the individual adventure of her life, as with Stendhal; it loses importance in an epoch such as ours when personal problems of the individual are of secondary interest. Woman, however, as the other still plays a role to the extent that, if only to transcend himself, each man still needs to learn more fully what he is.

[6]André Malraux (1901–76), novelist and political figure; his works include *La condition humaine* (1933) and *Les voix du silence* (1951). [Ed.]

[7]Breton's *Nadja*. [Au.]

[8]August Comte (1798–1857), French philosopher and sociologist, author of *Système de politique positive* (1851–54). [Ed.]

# Hélène Cixous

b. 1937

*Hélène Cixous, one of the most versatile and radical voices in contemporary French feminism, was born in Oran, Algeria. A brilliant student, she received her* agrégation *in English in 1959 and her* Docteur en lettres *in 1968, the year that also saw her participation in the May student uprisings. Cixous taught at the University of Bordeaux (1962), the Sorbonne (1965–67), Nanterre (1967), and the University of Paris VIII-Vincennes (now at Saint-Denis), where she is a professor of English literature. In 1970 with Gérard Genette and Tzvetan Todorov she founded the structuralist journal* Poétique, *and in 1974 established a center for women's studies at the University of Paris VIII. The work of Shakespeare and James Joyce (about whom she wrote her doctoral thesis), Heinrich von Kleist and Franz Kafka, Arthur Rimbaud and the Brazilian writer Clarice Lispector, Jacques Derrida and Jacques Lacan has been particularly important to her. Cixous has written short stories (*Le Prénom de Dieu, *1966), novels (*Dédans, *1969, which won the Prix Médicis), and a great deal of literary and cultural criticism. Some of her other writings are* Portrait of Dora *(1976),* The Newly Born Woman *(1975; with Catherine Clément), and* La Venue à l'écriture *(1977; with Annie LeClerc and Madeleine Gagnon). "The Laugh of the Medusa," first published in* L'Arc *in 1975, was translated for the first volume of the feminist journal* Signs *(1976).*

## The Laugh of the Medusa

I shall speak about women's writing: about *what it will do*. Woman must write her self: must write about women and bring women to writing, from which they have been driven away as violently as from their bodies — for the same reasons, by the same law, with the same fatal goal. Woman must put herself into the text — as into the world and into history — by her own movement.

The future must no longer be determined by the past. I do not deny that the effects of the past are still with us. But I refuse to strengthen them by repeating them, to confer upon them an irremovability the equivalent of destiny, to confuse the biological and the cultural. Anticipation is imperative.

Since these reflections are taking shape in an area just on the point of being discovered, they necessarily bear the mark of our time — a time during which the new breaks away from the old,

Translated by Keith Cohen and Paula Cohen.

and, more precisely, the (feminine) new from the old (*la nouvelle de l'ancien*). Thus, as there are no grounds for establishing a discourse, but rather an arid millennial ground to break, what I say has at least two sides and two aims: to break up, to destroy; and to foresee the unforeseeable, to project.

I write this as a woman, toward women. When I say "woman," I'm speaking of woman in her inevitable struggle against conventional man; and of a universal woman subject who must bring women to their senses and to their meaning in history. But first it must be said that in spite of the enormity of the repression that has kept them in the "dark" — that dark which people have been trying to make them accept as their attribute — there is, at this time, no general woman, no one typical woman. What they have *in common* I will say. But what strikes me is the infinite richness of their individual constitutions: you can't talk about *a* female sexuality, uniform, homogeneous, classifiable into codes — any more than you can talk about one unconscious resembling another. Women's imaginary[1] is inexhaustible, like music, painting, writing: their stream of phantasms is incredible.

I have been amazed more than once by a description a woman gave me of a world all her own which she had been secretly haunting since early childhood. A world of searching, the elaboration of a knowledge, on the basis of a systematic experimentation with the bodily functions, a passionate and precise interrogation of her erotogeneity. This practice, extraordinarily rich and inventive, in particular as concerns masturbation, is prolonged or accompanied by a production of forms, a veritable aesthetic activity, each stage of rapture inscribing a resonant vision, a composition, something beautiful. Beauty will no longer be forbidden.

I wished that that woman would write and proclaim this unique empire so that other women, other unacknowledged sovereigns, might exclaim: I, too, overflow; my desires have invented new desires, my body knows unheard-of songs. Time and again, I, too, have felt so full of luminous torrents that I could burst — burst with forms much more beautiful than those which are put up in frames and sold for a stinking fortune. And I, too, said nothing, showed nothing; I didn't open my mouth, I didn't repaint my half of the world. I was ashamed. I was afraid, and I swallowed my shame and my fear. I said to myself: You are mad! What's the meaning of these waves, these floods, these outbursts? Where is the ebullient, infinite woman who, immersed as she was in her naiveté, kept in the dark about herself, led into self-disdain by the great arm of parental-conjugal phallocentrism, hasn't been ashamed of her strength? Who, surprised and horrified by the fantastic tumult of her drives (for she was made to believe that a well-adjusted normal woman has a . . . divine composure), hasn't accused herself of being a monster? Who, feeling a funny desire stirring inside her (to sing, to write, to dare to speak, in short, to bring out something new), hasn't thought she was sick? Well, her shameful sickness is that she resists death, that she makes trouble.

And why don't you write? Write! Writing is for you, you are for you; your body is yours, take it. I know why you haven't written. (And why I didn't write before the age of twenty-seven.) Because writing is at once too high, too great for you, it's reserved for the great — that is, for "great men"; and it's "silly." Besides, you've written a little, but in secret. And it wasn't good, because it was in secret, and because you punished yourself for writing, because you didn't go all the way; or because you wrote, irresistibly, as when we would masturbate in secret, not to go further, but to attenuate the tension a bit, just enough to take the edge off. And then as soon as we come, we go and make ourselves feel guilty — so as to be forgiven; or to forget, to bury it until the next time.

Write, let no one hold you back, let nothing stop you: not man; not the imbecilic capitalist machinery, in which publishing houses are the crafty, obsequious relayers of imperatives handed down by an economy that works against us and off our backs; and not *yourself*. Smug-faced readers, managing editors, and big bosses don't like the true texts of women — female-sexed texts. That kind scares them.

I write woman: woman must write woman. And man, man. So only an oblique consideration will be found here of man; it's up to him to say where his masculinity and femininity are at: this will concern us once men have opened their eyes and seen themselves clearly.[2]

---

[1]The imaginary is a "field" in the psychology of Jacques Lacan. Cixous refers later to the other Lacanian field, the symbolic, and to Lack (*manque*), the sense of absence that is the basis of unconscious desire. See the introduction to Psychological Criticism, Ch. 2. [Ed.]

[2]Men still have everything to say about their sexuality, and everything to write. For what they have said so far, for the most part, stems from the opposition activity/passivity, from the power relation between a fantasized obligatory virility meant to invade, to colonize, and the consequential phantasm of woman as a "dark continent" to penetrate and to "pacify." (We know what "pacify" means in terms of scotomizing the other and misrecognizing the self.) Conquering her, they've made haste to depart from her borders, to get out of sight, out of body. The way man has of getting out of himself and into her whom he takes not for the other but for his own, deprives him, he knows, of his own bodily territory. One can understand how man, confusing himself with his penis and rushing in for the attack, might feel

Now women return from afar, from always: from "without," from the heath where witches are kept alive; from below, from beyond "culture"; from their childhood which men have been trying desperately to make them forget, condemning it to "eternal rest." The little girls and their "ill-mannered" bodies immured, well-preserved, intact unto themselves, in the mirror. Frigidified. But are they ever seething underneath! What an effort it takes — there's no end to it — for the sex cops to bar their threatening return. Such a display of forces on both sides that the struggle has for centuries been immobilized in the trembling equilibrium of a deadlock.

Here they are, returning, arriving over and again, because the unconscious is impregnable. They have wandered around in circles, confined to the narrow room in which they've been given a deadly brainwashing. You can incarcerate them, slow them down, get away with the old Apartheid routine, but for a time only. As soon as they begin to speak, at the same time as they're taught their name, they can be taught that their territory is black: because you are Africa, you are black. Your continent is dark. Dark is dangerous. You can't see anything in the dark, you're afraid. Don't move, you might fall. Most of all, don't go into the forest. And so we have internalized this horror of the dark.

Men have committed the greatest crime against women. Insidiously, violently, they have led them to hate women, to be their own enemies, to mobilize their immense strength against themselves, to be the executants of their virile needs. They have made for women an antinarcissism! A narcissism which loves itself only to be loved for what women haven't got! They have constructed the infamous logic of antilove.

We the precocious, we the repressed of culture, our lovely mouths gagged with pollen, our wind knocked out of us, we the labyrinths, the ladders, the trampled spaces, the bevies — we are black and we are beautiful.

We're stormy, and that which is ours breaks

loose from us without our fearing any debilitation. Our glances, our smiles, are spent; laughs exude from all our mouths; our blood flows and we extend ourselves without ever reaching an end; we never hold back our thoughts, our signs, our writing; and we're not afraid of lacking.

What happiness for us who are omitted, brushed aside at the scene of inheritances; we inspire ourselves and we expire without running out of breath, we are everywhere!

From now on, who, if we say so, can say no to us? We've come back from always.

It is time to liberate the New Woman from the Old by coming to know her — by loving her for getting by, for getting beyond the Old without delay, by going out ahead of what the New Woman will be, as an arrow quits the bow with a movement that gathers and separates the vibrations musically, in order to be more than her self.

I say that we must, for, with a few rare exceptions, there has not yet been any writing that inscribes femininity; exceptions so rare, in fact, that, after plowing through literature across languages, cultures, and ages,[3] one can only be startled at this vain scouting mission. It is well known that the number of women writers (while having increased very slightly from the nineteenth century on) has always been ridiculously small. This is a useless and deceptive fact unless from their species of female writers we do not first deduct the immense majority whose workmanship is in no way different from male writing, and which either obscures women or reproduces the classic representations of women (as sensitive — intuitive — dreamy, etc.).[4]

Let me insert here a parenthetical remark. I mean it when I speak of male writing. I maintain

[3] I am speaking here only of the place "reserved" for women by the Western world. [Au.]

[4] Which works, then, might be called feminine? I'll just point out some examples: one would have to give them full readings to bring out what is pervasively feminine in their significance. Which I shall do elsewhere. In France (have you noted our infinite poverty in this field? — the Anglo-Saxon countries have shown resources of distinctly greater consequence), leafing through what's come out of the twentieth century — and it's not much — the only inscriptions of femininity that I have seen were by Colette, Marguerite Duras, . . . and Jean Genêt. [Au.]

resentment and fear of being "taken" by the woman, of being lost in her, absorbed, or alone. [Au.]

unequivocally that there is such a thing as *marked* writing; that, until now, far more extensively and repressively than is ever suspected or admitted, writing has been run by a libidinal and cultural — hence political, typically masculine — economy; that this is a locus where the repression of women has been perpetuated, over and over, more or less consciously, and in a manner that's frightening since it's often hidden or adorned with the mystifying charms of fiction; that this locus has grossly exaggerated all the signs of sexual opposition (and not sexual difference), where woman has never *her* turn to speak — this being all the more serious and unpardonable in that writing is precisely *the very possibility of change,* the space that can serve as a springboard for subversive thought, the precursory movement of a transformation of social and cultural structures.

Nearly the entire history of writing is confounded with the history of reason, of which it is at once the effect, the support, and one of the privileged alibis. It has been one with the phallocentric tradition. It is indeed that same self-admiring, self-stimulating, self-congratulatory phallocentrism.

With some exceptions, for there have been failures — and if it weren't for them, I wouldn't be writing (I-woman, escapee) — in that enormous machine that has been operating and turning out its "truth" for centuries. There have been poets who would go to any lengths to slip something by at odds with tradition — men capable of loving love and hence capable of loving others and of wanting them, of imagining the woman who would hold out against oppression and constitute herself as a superb, equal, hence "impossible" subject, untenable in a real social framework. Such a woman the poet could desire only by breaking the codes that negate her. Her appearance would necessarily bring on, if not revolution — for the bastion was supposed to be immutable — at least harrowing explosions. At times it is in the fissure caused by an earthquake, through that radical mutation of things brought on by a material upheaval when every structure is for a moment thrown off balance and an ephemeral wildness sweeps order away, that the

poet slips something by, for a brief span, of woman. Thus did Kleist expend himself in his yearning for the existence of sister-lovers, maternal daughters, mother-sisters, who never hung their heads in shame. Once the palace of magistrates is restored, it's time to pay: immediate bloody death to the uncontrollable elements.

But only the poets — not the novelists, allies of representationalism. Because poetry involves gaining strength through the unconscious and because the unconscious, that other limitless country, is the place where the repressed manage to survive: women, or as Hoffmann would say, fairies.

She must write her self, because this is the invention of a *new insurgent* writing which, when the moment of her liberation has come, will allow her to carry out the indispensable ruptures and transformations in her history, first at two levels that cannot be separated.

1. Individually. By writing her self, woman will return to the body which has been more than confiscated from her, which has been turned into the uncanny stranger on display — the ailing or dead figure, which so often turns out to be the nasty companion, the cause and location of inhibitions. Censor the body and you censor breath and speech at the same time.

Write your self. Your body must be heard. Only then will the immense resources of the unconscious spring forth. Our naphtha will spread, throughout the world, without dollars — black or gold — nonassessed values that will change the rules of the old game.

To write. An act which will not only "realize" the decensored relation of woman to her sexuality, to her womanly being, giving her access to her native strength; it will give her back her goods, her pleasures, her organs, her immense bodily territories which have been kept under seal; it will tear her away from the superegoized structure in which she has always occupied the place reserved for the guilty (guilty of everything, guilty at every turn: for having desires, for not having any; for being frigid, for being "too hot"; for not being both at once; for being too motherly and not enough; for having children and for not having any; for nursing and for not nursing . . .) — tear her away by means of this research, this job of analysis and illumination, this emancipation of the marvelous text of her self that she must urgently learn to speak. A woman without a body, dumb, blind, can't possibly be a good fighter. She is reduced to being the servant of the militant male, his shadow. We must kill the false woman who is preventing the live one from breathing. Inscribe the breath of the whole woman.

2. An act that will also be marked by woman's *seizing* the occasion to *speak,* hence her shattering entry into history, which has always been based *on her suppression.* To write and thus to forge for herself the antilogos weapon. To become *at will* the taker and initiator, for her own right, in every symbolic system, in every political process.

It is time for women to start scoring their feats in written and oral language.

Every woman has known the torment of getting up to speak. Her heart racing, at times entirely lost for words, ground and language slipping away — that's how daring a feat, how great a transgression it is for a woman to speak — even just open her mouth — in public. A double distress, for even if she transgresses, her words fall almost always upon the deaf male ear, which hears in language only that which speaks in the masculine.

It is by writing, from and toward women, and by taking up the challenge of speech which has been governed by the phallus, that women will confirm women in a place other than that which is reserved in and by the symbolic, that is, in a place other than silence. Women should break out of the snare of silence. They shouldn't be conned into accepting a domain which is the margin or the harem.

Listen to a woman speak at a public gathering (if she hasn't painfully lost her wind). She doesn't "speak," she throws her trembling body forward; she lets go of herself, she flies; all of her passes into her voice, and it's with her body that she vitally supports the "logic" of her speech. Her flesh speaks true. She lays herself bare. In fact, she physically materializes what she's thinking; she signifies it with her body. In

a certain way she *inscribes* what she's saying, because she doesn't deny her drives the intractable and impassioned part they have in speaking. Her speech, even when "theoretical" or political, is never simple or linear or "objectified," generalized: she draws her story into history.

There is not that scission, that division made by the common man between the logic of oral speech and the logic of the text, bound as he is by his antiquated relation — servile, calculating — to mastery. From which proceeds the niggardly lip service which engages only the tiniest part of the body, plus the mask.

In women's speech, as in their writing, that element which never stops resonating, which, once we've been permeated by it, profoundly and imperceptibly touched by it, retains the power of moving us — that element is the song: first music from the first voice of love which is alive in every woman. Why this privileged relationship with the voice? Because no woman stockpiles as many defenses for countering the drives as does a man. You don't build walls around yourself, you don't forego pleasure as "wisely" as he. Even if phallic mystification has generally contaminated good relationships, a woman is never far from "mother" (I mean outside her role functions: the "mother" as nonname and as source of goods). There is always within her at least a little of that good mother's milk. She writes in white ink.

*Woman for women.* — There always remains in woman that force which produces/is produced by the other — in particular, the other woman. *In* her, matrix, cradler; herself giver as her mother and child; she is her own sister-daughter. You might object, "What about she who is the hysterical offspring of a bad mother?" Everything will be changed once woman gives woman to the other woman. There is hidden and always ready in woman the source; the locus for the other. The mother, too, is a metaphor. It is necessary and sufficient that the best of herself be given to woman by another woman for her to be able to love herself and return in love the body that was "born" to her. Touch me, caress me, you the living no-name, give me my self as myself. The relation to the "mother," in terms of intense pleasure and violence, is curtailed no more than the relation to childhood (the child that she was, that she is, that she makes, remakes, undoes, there at the point where, the same, she others herself). Text: my body — shot through with streams of song; I don't mean the overbearing, clutchy "mother" but, rather, what touches you, the equivoice that affects you, fills your breast with an urge to come to language and launches your force; the rhythm that laughs you; the intimate recipient who makes all metaphors possible and desirable; body (body? bodies?), no more describable than god, the soul, or the Other; that part of you that leaves a space between yourself and urges you to inscribe in language your woman's style. In women there is always more or less of the mother who makes everything all right, who nourishes, and who stands up against separation; a force that will not be cut off but will knock the wind out of the codes. We will rethink womankind beginning with every form and every period of her body. The Americans remind us, "We are all Lesbians"; that is, don't denigrate woman, don't make of her what men have made of you.

Because the "economy" of her drives is prodigious, she cannot fail, in seizing the occasion to speak, to transform directly and indirectly *all* systems of exchange based on masculine thrift. Her libido will produce far more radical effects of political and social change than some might like to think.

Because she arrives, vibrant, over and again, we are at the beginning of a new history, or rather of a process of becoming in which several histories intersect with one another. As subject for history, woman always occurs simultaneously in several places. Woman un-thinks[5] the unifying, regulating history that homogenizes and channels forces, herding contradictions into a single battlefield. In woman, personal history blends together with the history of all women, as well as national and world history. As a militant, she is an integral part of all liberations. She must be farsighted, not limited to a blow-by-blow interaction. She foresees that her liberation will do more than modify power relations or toss the ball

over to the other camp; she will bring about a mutation in human relations, in thought, in all praxis: hers is not simply a class struggle, which she carries forward into a much vaster movement. Not that in order to be a woman-in-struggle(s) you have to leave the class struggle or repudiate it; but you have to split it open, spread it out, push it forward, fill it with the fundamental struggle so as to prevent the class struggle, or any other struggle for the liberation of a class or people, from operating as a form of repression, pretext for postponing the inevitable, the staggering alteration in power relations and in the production of individualities. This alteration is already upon us — in the United States, for example, where millions of night crawlers are in the process of undermining the family and disintegrating the whole of American sociality.

The new history is coming; it's not a dream, though it does extend beyond men's imagination, and for good reason. It's going to deprive them of their conceptual orthopedics, beginning with the destruction of their enticement machine.

It is impossible to *define* a feminine practice of writing, and this is an impossibility that will remain, for this practice can never be theorized, enclosed, coded — which doesn't mean that it doesn't exist. But it will always surpass the discourse that regulates the phallocentric system; it does and will take place in areas other than those subordinated to philosophico-theoretical domination. It will be conceived of only by subjects who are breakers of automatisms, by peripheral figures that no authority can ever subjugate.

Hence the necessity to affirm the flourishes of this writing, to give form to its movement, its near and distant byways. Bear in mind to begin with (1) that sexual opposition, which has always worked for man's profit to the point of reducing writing, too, to his laws, is only a historico-cultural limit. There is, there will be more and more rapidly pervasive now, a fiction that produces irreducible effects of femininity. (2) That it is through ignorance that most readers, critics, and writers of both sexes hesitate to admit or deny outright the possibility or the pertinence of a distinction between feminine and masculine writing. It will usually be said, thus disposing of

[5]"*Dé-pense*," a neologism formed on the verb *penser*, hence "unthinks," but also "spends" (from *dépenser*). [Tr.]

sexual difference: either that all writing, to the extent that it materializes, is feminine; or, inversely — but it comes to the same thing — that the act of writing is equivalent to masculine masturbation (and so the woman who writes cuts herself out a paper penis); or that writing is bisexual, hence neuter, which again does away with differentiation. To admit that writing is precisely working (in) the in-between, inspecting the process of the same and of the other without which nothing can live, undoing the work of death — to admit this is first to want the two, as well as both, the ensemble of the one and the other, not fixed in sequences of struggle and expulsion or some other form of death but infinitely dynamized by an incessant process of exchange from one subject to another. A process of different subjects knowing one another and beginning one another anew only from the living boundaries of the other: a multiple and inexhaustible course with millions of encounters and transformations of the same into the other and into the in-between, from which woman takes her forms (and man, in his turn; but that's his other history).

In saying "bisexual, hence neuter," I am referring to the classic conception of bisexuality, which, squashed under the emblem of castration fear and along with the fantasy of a "total" being (though composed of two halves), would do away with the difference experienced as an operation incurring loss, as the mark of dreaded sectility.

To this self-effacing, merger-type bisexuality, which would conjure away castration (the writer who puts up his sign: "bisexual written here, come and see," when the odds are good that it's neither one nor the other), I oppose the *other bisexuality* on which every subject not enclosed in the false theater of phallocentric representationalism has founded his/her erotic universe. Bisexuality: that is, each one's location in self (*repérage en soi*) of the presence — variously manifest and insistent according to each person, male or female — of both sexes, nonexclusion either of the difference or of one sex, and, from this "self-permission," multiplication of the effects of the inscription of desire, over all parts of my body and the other body.

Now it happens that at present, for historico-cultural reasons, it is women who are opening up to and benefiting from this vatic bisexuality which doesn't annul differences but stirs them up, pursues them, increases their number. In a certain way, "woman is bisexual"; man — it's a secret to no one — being poised to keep glorious phallic monosexuality in view. By virtue of affirming the primacy of the phallus and of bringing it into play, phallocratic ideology has claimed more than one victim. As a woman, I've been clouded over by the great shadow of the scepter and been told: idolize it, that which you cannot brandish. But at the same time, man has been handed that grotesque and scarcely enviable destiny (just imagine) of being reduced to a single idol with clay balls. And consumed, as Freud and his followers note, by a fear of being a woman! For, if psychoanalysis was constituted from woman, to repress femininity (and not so successful a repression at that — men have made it clear), its account of masculine sexuality is now hardly refutable; as with all the "human" sciences, it reproduces the masculine view, of which it is one of the effects.

Here we encounter the inevitable man-with-rock, standing erect in his old Freudian realm, in the way that, to take the figure back to the point where linguistics is conceptualizing it "anew," Lacan preserves it in the sanctuary of the phallos (ϕ) "sheltered" from *castration's lack*! Their "symbolic" exists, it holds power — we, the sowers of disorder, know it only too well. But we are in no way obliged to deposit our lives in their banks of lack, to consider the constitution of the subject in terms of a drama manglingly restaged, to reinstate again and again the religion of the father. Because we don't want that. We don't fawn around the supreme hole. We have no womanly reason to pledge allegiance to the negative. The feminine (as the poets suspected) affirms: ". . . And yes," says Molly, carrying *Ulysses* off beyond any book and toward the new writing; "I said yes, I will Yes."

*The Dark Continent is neither dark nor unexplorable.* — It is still unexplored only because we've been made to believe that it was too dark to be explorable. And because they want to make us believe that what interests us is the white continent, with its monuments to Lack. And we believed. They riveted us between two horrifying myths: between the Medusa and the abyss. That would be enough to set half the world laughing, except that it's still going on. For the phallologocentric sublation[6] is with us, and it's militant, regenerating the old patterns, anchored in the dogma of castration. They haven't changed a thing: they've theorized their desire for reality! Let the priests tremble, we're going to show them our sexts!

Too bad for them if they fall apart upon discovering that women aren't men, or that the mother doesn't have one. But isn't this fear convenient for them? Wouldn't the worst be, isn't the worst, in truth, that women aren't castrated, that they have only to stop listening to the Sirens (for the Sirens were men) for history to change its meaning? You only have to look at the Medusa straight on to see her. And she's not deadly. She's beautiful and she's laughing.

Men say that there are two unrepresentable things: death and the feminine sex. That's because they need femininity to be associated with death; it's the jitters that gives them a hard-on! for themselves! They need to be afraid of us. Look at the trembling Perseuses moving backward toward us, clad in apotropes.[7] What lovely backs! Not another minute to lose. Let's get out of here.

Let's hurry: the continent is not impenetrably dark. I've been there often. I was overjoyed one day to run into Jean Genêt. It was in *Pompes funèbres*.[8] He had come there led by his Jean. There are some men (all too few) who aren't afraid of femininity.

Almost everything is yet to be written by women about femininity: about their sexuality, that is, its infinite and mobile complexity, about their eroticization, sudden turn-ons of a certain miniscule-immense area of their bodies; not about destiny, but about the adventure of such

and such a drive, about trips, crossings, trudges, abrupt and gradual awakenings, discoveries of a zone at one time timorous and soon to be forthright. A woman's body, with its thousand and one thresholds of ardor — once, by smashing yokes and censors, she lets it articulate the profusion of meanings that run through it in every direction — will make the old single-grooved mother tongue reverberate with more than one language.

We've been turned away from our bodies, shamefully taught to ignore them, to strike them with that stupid sexual modesty; we've been made victims of the old fool's game: each one will love the other sex. I'll give you your body and you'll give me mine. But who are the men who give women the body that women blindly yield to them? Why so few texts? Because so few women have as yet won back their body. Women must write through their bodies, they must invent the impregnable language that will wreck partitions, classes, and rhetorics, regulations and codes, they must submerge, cut through, get beyond the ultimate reserve-discourse, including the one that laughs at the very idea of pronouncing the word "silence," the one that, aiming for the impossible, stops short before the word "impossible" and writes it as "the end."

Such is the strength of women that, sweeping away syntax, breaking that famous thread (just a tiny little thread, they say) which acts for men as a surrogate umbilical cord, assuring them — otherwise they couldn't come — that the old lady is always right behind them, watching them make phallus, women will go right up to the impossible.

When the "repressed" of their culture and their society returns, it's an explosive, *utterly* destructive, staggering return, with a force never yet unleashed and equal to the most forbidding of suppressions. For when the Phallic period comes to an end, women will have been either annihilated or borne up to the highest and most violent incandescence. Muffled throughout their history, they have lived in dreams, in bodies (though muted), in silences, in aphonic revolts.

And with such force in their fragility; a fra-

---

[6]Standard English term for the Hegelian *Aufhebung,* the French *la relève.* [Tr.]

[7]A coinage from two Greek roots meaning "to turn away." [Ed.]

[8]Jean Genêt, *Pompes funèbres* (Paris, 1948), p. 185. [Au.]

gility, a vulnerability, equal to their incomparable intensity. Fortunately, they haven't sublimated; they've saved their skin, their energy. They haven't worked at liquidating the impasse of lives without futures. They have furiously inhabited these sumptuous bodies: admirable hysterics who made Freud succumb to many voluptuous moments impossible to confess, bombarding his Mosaic statue with their carnal and passionate body words, haunting him with their unaudible and thundering denunciations, dazzling, more than naked underneath the seven veils of modesty. Those who, with a single word of the body, have inscribed the vertiginous immensity of a history which is sprung like an arrow from the whole history of men and from biblico-capitalist society, are the women, the supplicants of yesterday, who come as forebears of the new women, after whom no intersubjective relation will ever be the same. You, Dora,[9] you the indomitable, the poetic body, you are the true "mistress" of the Signifier. Before long your efficacy will be seen at work when your speech is no longer suppressed, its point turned in against your breast, but written out over against the other.

*In body.* — More so than men who are coaxed toward social success, toward sublimation, women are body. More body, hence more writing. For a long time it has been in body that women have responded to persecution, to the familial-conjugal enterprise of domestication, to the repeated attempts at castrating them. Those who have turned their tongues 10,000 times seven times before not speaking are either dead from it or more familiar with their tongues and their mouths than anyone else. Now, I-woman am going to blow up the Law: an explosion henceforth possible and ineluctable; let it be done, right now, *in* language.

Let us not be trapped by an analysis still encumbered with the old automatisms. It's not to be feared that language conceals an invincible adversary, because it's the language of men and their grammar. We mustn't leave them a single place that's any more theirs alone than we are.

If woman has always functioned "within" the discourse of man, a signifier that has always referred back to the opposite signifier which annihilates its specific energy and diminishes or stifles its very different sounds, it is time for her to dislocate this "within," to explode it, turn it around, and seize it; to make it hers, containing it, taking it in her own mouth, biting that tongue with her very own teeth to invent for herself a language to get inside of. And you'll see with what ease she will spring forth from that "within" — the "within" where once she so drowsily crouched — to overflow at the lips she will cover the foam.

Nor is the point to appropriate their instruments, their concepts, their places, or to begrudge them their position of mastery. Just because there's a risk of identification doesn't mean that we'll succumb. Let's leave it to the worriers, to masculine anxiety and its obsession with how to dominate the way things work — knowing "how it works" in order to "make it work." For us the point is not to take possession in order to internalize or manipulate, but rather to dash through and to "fly."[10]

Flying is woman's gesture — flying in language and making it fly. We have all learned the art of flying and its numerous techniques; for centuries we've been able to possess anything only by flying; we've lived in flight, stealing away, finding, when desired, narrow passageways, hidden crossovers. It's no accident that *voler* has a double meaning, that it plays on each of them and thus throws off the agents of sense. It's no accident: women take after birds and robbers just as robbers take after women and birds. They (*illes*)[11] go by, fly the coop, take pleasure in jumbling the order of space, in disorienting it, in changing around the furniture, dislocating things and values, breaking them all up, emptying structures, and turning propriety upside down.

[9]The female subject of Freud's first case study in hysteria. [Ed.]

[10]Also, "to steal." Both meanings of the verb *voler* are played on, as the text itself explains in the following paragraph. [Tr.]

[11]*Illes* is a fusion of the masculine pronoun *ils*, which refers back to birds and robbers, with the feminine pronoun *elles*, which refers to women. [Tr.]

What woman hasn't flown/stolen? Who hasn't felt, dreamt, performed the gesture that jams sociality? Who hasn't crumbled, held up to ridicule, the bar of separation? Who hasn't inscribed with her body the differential, punctured the system of couples and opposition? Who, by some act of transgression, hasn't overthrown successiveness, connection, the wall of circumfusion?

A feminine text cannot fail to be more than subversive. It is volcanic; as it is written it brings about an upheaval of the old property crust, carrier of masculine investments; there's no other way. There's no room for her if she's not a he. If she's a her-she, it's in order to smash everything, to shatter the framework of institutions, to blow up the law, to break up the "truth" with laughter.

For once she blazes *her* trail in the symbolic, she cannot fail to make of it the chaosmos of the "personal" — in her pronouns, her nouns, and her clique of referents. And for good reason. There will have been the long history of gynocide. This is known by the colonized peoples of yesterday, the workers, the nations, the species off whose backs the history of men has made its gold; those who have known the ignominy of persecution derive from it an obstinate future desire for grandeur; those who are locked up know better than their jailers the taste of free air. Thanks to their history, women today know (how to do and want) what men will be able to conceive of only much later. I say woman overturns the "personal," for if, by means of laws, lies, blackmail, and marriage, her right to herself has been extorted at the same time as her name, she has been able, through the very movement of mortal alienation, to see more closely the inanity of "propriety," the reductive stinginess of the masculine-conjugal subjective economy, which she doubly resists. On the one hand she has constituted herself necessarily as that "person" capable of losing a part of herself without losing her integrity. But secretly, silently, deep down inside, she grows and multiplies, for, on the other hand, she knows far more about living and about the relation between the economy of the drives and the management of the ego than any man. Unlike man, who holds so dearly to his title and his titles, his pouches of value, his cap, crown,

and everything connected with his head, woman couldn't care less about the fear of decapitation (or castration), adventuring, without the masculine temerity, into anonymity, which she can merge with without annihilating herself: because she's a giver.

I shall have a great deal to say about the whole deceptive problematic of the gift. Woman is obviously not that woman Nietzsche dreamed of who gives only in order to.[12] Who could ever think of the gift as a gift-that-takes? Who else but man, precisely the one who would like to take everything?

If there is a "propriety of woman," it is paradoxically her capacity to depropriate unselfishly: body without end, without appendage, without principal "parts." If she is a whole, it's a whole composed of parts that are wholes, not simple partial objects but a moving, limitlessly changing ensemble, a cosmos tirelessly traversed by Eros, an immense astral space not organized around any one sun that's any more of a star than the others.

This doesn't mean that she's an undifferentiated magma, but that she doesn't lord it over her body or her desire. Though masculine sexuality gravitates around the penis, engendering that centralized body (in political anatomy) under the dictatorship of its parts, woman does not bring about the same regionalization which serves the couple head/genitals and which is inscribed only within boundaries. Her libido is cosmic, just as her unconscious is worldwide. Her writing can only keep going, without ever inscribing or discerning contours, daring to make these vertiginous crossings of the other(s) ephemeral and passionate sojourns in him, her, them, whom she inhabits long enough to look at from the point closest to their unconscious from the moment they awaken, to love them at the point closest to their drives; and then further, impreg-

[12]Reread Derrida's text, "Le Style de la femme," in *Nietzsche aujourd'hui* (Paris: Union Générale d'Editions, Coll. 10/18), where the philosopher can be seen operating an *Aufhebung* of all philosophy in its systematic reducing of woman to the place of seduction: she appears as the one who is taken for; the bait in person, all veils unfurled, the one who doesn't give but who gives only in order to (take). [Au.]

nated through and through with these brief, identificatory embraces, she goes and passes into infinity. She alone dares and wishes to know from within, where she, the outcast, has never ceased to hear the resonance of fore-language. She lets the other language speak — the language of 1,000 tongues which knows neither enclosure nor death. To life she refuses nothing. Her language does not contain, it carries; it does not hold back, it makes possible. When id is ambiguously uttered — the wonder of being several — she doesn't defend herself against these unknown women whom she's surprised at becoming, but derives pleasure from this gift of alterability. I am spacious, singing flesh, on which is grafted no one knows which I, more or less human, but alive because of transformation.

Write! and your self-seeking text will know itself better than flesh and blood, rising, insurrectionary dough kneading itself, with sonorous, perfumed ingredients, a lively combination of flying colors, leaves, and rivers plunging into the sea we feed. "Ah, there's her sea," he will say as he holds out to me a basin full of water from the little phallic mother from whom he's inseparable. But look, our seas are what we make of them, full of fish or not, opaque or transparent, red or black, high or smooth, narrow or bankless; and we are ourselves sea, sand, coral, seaweed, beaches, tides, swimmers, children, waves. . . . More or less wavily sea, earth, sky — what matter would rebuff us? We know how to speak them all.

Heterogeneous, yes. For her joyous benefit she is erogenous; she is the erotogeneity of the heterogeneous: airborne swimmer, in flight, she does not cling to herself; she is dispersible, prodigious, stunning, desirous and capable of others, of the other woman that she will be, of the other woman she isn't, of him, of you.

Woman be unafraid of any other place, of any same, or any other. My eyes, my tongue, my ears, my nose, my skin, my mouth, my body-for-(the)-other — not that I long for it in order to fill up a hole, to provide against some defect of mine, or because, as fate would have it, I'm spurred on by feminine "jealousy"; not because I've been dragged into the whole chain of substitutions that brings that which is substituted back to its ultimate object. That sort of thing you would expect to come straight out of "Tom Thumb," out of the *Penisneid* whispered to us by old grandmother ogresses, servants to their father-sons. If they believe, in order to muster up some self-importance, if they really need to believe that we're dying of desire, that we are this hole fringed with desire for their penis — that's their immemorial business. Undeniably (we verify it at our own expense — but also to our amusement), it's their business to let us know they're getting a hard-on, so that we'll assure them (we the maternal mistresses of their little pocket signifier) that they still can, that it's still there — that men structure themselves only by being fitted with a feather. In the child it's not the penis that the woman desires, it's not that famous bit of skin around which every man gravitates. Pregnancy cannot be traced back, except within the historical limits of the ancients, to some form of fate, to those mechanical substitutions brought about by the unconscious of some eternal "jealous woman"; not to penis envies; and not to narcissism or to some sort of homosexuality linked to the everpresent mother! Begetting a child doesn't mean that the woman or the man must fall ineluctably into patterns or must recharge the circuit of reproduction. If there's a risk there's not an inevitable trap: may women be spared the pressure, under the guise of consciousness-raising, of a supplement of interdictions. Either you want a kid or you don't — *that's your business*. Let nobody threaten you; in satisfying your desire, let not the fear of becoming the accomplice to a sociality succeed the old-time fear of being "taken." And man, are you still going to bank on everyone's blindness and passivity, afraid lest the child make a father and, consequently, that in having a kid the woman land herself more than one bad deal by engendering all at once child — mother — father — family? No; it's up to you to break the old circuits. It will be up to man and woman to render obsolete the former relationship and all its consequences, to consider the launching of a brand-new subject, alive, with defamilialization. Let us demater-paternalize rather than deny woman, in an effort to avoid the co-optation of procreation, a thrilling era of the body. Let us defetishize. Let's get away from the dialectic which has it that the only good father is a dead one, or that the child is the death of his parents. The child is the other, but the other without violence, bypassing loss, struggle. We're fed up with the reuniting of bonds forever to be severed, with the litany of castration that's handed down and genealogized. We won't advance backward anymore; we're not going to repress something so simple as the desire for life. Oral drive, anal drive, vocal drive — all these drives are our strengths, and among them is the gestation drive — just like the desire to write: a desire to live self from within, a desire for the swollen belly, for language, for blood. We are not going to refuse, if it should happen to strike our fancy, the unsurpassed pleasures of pregnancy which have actually been always exaggerated or conjured away — or cursed — in the classic texts. For if there's one thing that's been repressed here's just the place to find it: in the taboo of the pregnant woman. This says a lot about the power she seems invested with at the time, because it has always been suspected, that, when pregnant, the woman not only doubles her market value, but — what's more important — takes on intrinsic value as a woman in her own eyes and, undeniably, acquires body and sex.

There are thousands of ways of living one's pregnancy; to have or not to have with that still invisible other a relationship of another intensity. And if you don't have that particular yearning, it doesn't mean that you're in any way lacking. Each body distributes in its own special way, without model or norm, the nonfinite and changing totality of its desires. Decide for yourself on your position in the arena of contradictions, where pleasure and reality embrace. Bring the other to life. Women know how to live detachment; giving birth is neither losing nor increasing. It's adding to life an other. Am I dreaming? Am I mis-recognizing? You, the defenders of "theory," the sacrosanct yes-men of Concept, enthroners of the phallus (but not of the penis):

Once more you'll say that all this smacks of "idealism," or what's worse, you'll splutter that I'm a "mystic."

And what about the libido? Haven't I read the "Signification of the Phallus"? And what about separation, what about that bit of self for which, to be born, you undergo an ablation — an abla-

tion, so they say, to be forever commemorated by your desire?

Besides, isn't it evident that the penis gets around in my texts, that I give it a place and appeal? Of course I do. I want all. I want all of me with all of him. Why should I deprive myself of a part of us? I want all of us. Woman of course has a desire for a "loving desire" and not a jealous one. But not because she is gelded; not because she's deprived and needs to be filled out, like some wounded person who wants to console herself or seek vengeance: I don't want a penis to decorate my body with. But I do desire the other for the other, whole and entire, male or female; because living means wanting everything that is, everything that lives, and wanting it alive. Castration? Let others toy with it. What's a desire originating from a lack? A pretty meager desire.

The woman who still allows herself to be threatened by the big dick, who's still impressed by the commotion of the phallic stance, who still leads a loyal master to the beat of the drum: that's the woman of yesterday. They still exist, easy and numerous victims of the oldest of farces: either they're cast in the original silent version in which, as titanesses lying under the mountains they make with their quivering, they never see erected that theoretic monument to the golden phallus looming, in the old manner, over their bodies. Or, coming today out of their *infans*[13] period and into the second, "enlightened" version of their virtuous debasement, they see themselves suddenly assaulted by the builders of the analytic empire and, as soon as they've begun to formulate the new desire, naked, nameless, so happy at making an appearance, they're taken in their bath by the new old men, and then, whoops! Luring them with flashy signifiers, the demon of interpretation — oblique, decked out in modernity — sells them the same old handcuffs, baubles, and chains. Which castration do you prefer? Whose degrading do you like better, the father's or the mother's? Oh, what pwetty eyes, you pwetty little girl. Here, buy my glasses and you'll see the Truth-Me-Myself tell you everything you should know. Put them on your nose and take a fetishist's look (you are me, the

[13]Mute. [Ed.]

other analyst — that's what I'm telling you) at your body and the body of the other. You see? No? Wait, you'll have everything explained to you, and you'll know at last which sort of neurosis you're related to. Hold still, we're going to do your portrait, so that you can begin looking like it right away.

Yes, the naives to the first and second degree are still legion. If the New Women, arriving now, dare to create outside the theoretical, they're called in by the cops of the signifier, fingerprinted, remonstrated, and brought into the line of order that they are supposed to know; assigned by force of trickery to a precise place in the chain that's always formed for the benefit of a privileged signifier. We are pieced back to the string which leads back, if not to the Name-of-the-Father, then, for a new twist, to the place of the phallic-mother.

Beware, my friend, of the signifier that would take you back to the authority of a signified! Beware of diagnoses that would reduce your generative powers. "Common" nouns are also proper nouns that disparage your singularity by classifying it into species. Break out of the circles; don't remain within the psychoanalytic closure. Take a look around, then cut through!

And if we are legion, it's because the war of liberation has only made as yet a tiny breakthrough. But women are thronging to it. I've seen them, those who will be neither dupe nor domestic, those who will not fear the risk of being a woman; will not fear any risk, any desire, any space still explored in themselves, among themselves and others or anywhere else. They do not fetishize, they do not deny, they do not hate. They observe, they approach, they try to see the other woman, the child, the lover — not to strengthen their own narcissism or verify the solidity or weakness of the master, but to make love better, to invent.

*Other love.* — In the beginning are our differences. The new love dares for the other, wants the other, makes dizzying, precipitous flights between knowledge and invention. The woman arriving over and over again does not stand still; she's everywhere, she exchanges, she is the desire-that-gives. (Not enclosed in the paradox of the gift that takes nor under the illusion of unitary fusion. We're past that.) She comes in, comes-in-between herself me and you, between the other me where one is always infinitely more than one and more than me, without the fear of ever reaching a limit; she thrills in our becoming. And we'll keep on becoming! She cuts through defensive loves, motherages, and devourations: beyond selfish narcissism, in the moving, open, transitional space, she runs her risks. Beyond the struggle-to-the-death that's been removed to the bed, beyond the love-battle that claims to represent exchange, she scorns at an Eros dynamic that would be fed by hatred. Hatred: a heritage, again, a remainder, a duping subservience to the phallus. To love, to watch-think-seek the other in the other, to despecularize, to unhoard. Does this seem difficult? It's not impossible, and this is what nourishes life — a love that has no commerce with the apprehensive desire that provides against the lack and stultifies the strange; a love that rejoices in the exchange that multiplies. Wherever history still unfolds as the history of death, she does not tread. Opposition, hierarchizing exchange, the struggle for mastery which can end only in at least one death (one master — one slave, or two nonmasters ≠ two dead) — all that comes from a period in time governed by phallocentric values. The fact that this period extends into the present doesn't prevent woman from starting the history of life somewhere else. Elsewhere, she gives. She doesn't "know" what she's giving, she doesn't measure it; she gives, though, neither a counterfeit impression nor something she hasn't got. She gives more, with no assurance that she'll get back even some unexpected profit from what she puts out. She gives that there may be life, thought, transformation. This is an "economy" that can no longer be put in economic terms. Wherever she loves, all the old concepts of management are left behind. At the end of a more or less conscious computation, she finds not her sum but her differences. I am for you what you want me to be at the moment you look at me in a way you've never seen me before: at every instant. When I write, it's everything that we don't know we can be that is written out of me, without exclusions, without stipulation, and everything we will be calls us to the unflagging, intoxicating, unappeasable search for love. In one another we will never be lacking.

# Elaine Showalter

b. 1941

*A founder of feminist criticism in the United States, Elaine Showalter remains one of its most creative and influential proponents. Showalter developed the concept and practice of gynocriticism. Showalter was born Elaine Cottler in Cambridge, Massachusetts. Against the wishes of her parents, she pursued an intellectual career, taking degrees in English at Bryn Mawr College (B.A., 1962), at Brandeis University (M.A., 1964), and at the University of California-Davis (Ph.D., 1970). She has taught at Davis, at the University of Delaware, and at the Douglass College of Rutgers University, and she is now a professor of English at Princeton University. Her academic honors include a Guggenheim fellowship (1977–78) and a Rockefeller Humanities fellowship (1981–82). Author of the pioneering* A Literature of Their Own: British Women Novelists from Brontë to Lessing *(1977; the first chapter is reprinted here), Showalter has more recently published* The Female Malady: Women, Madness, and English Culture (1830–1980) *(1986). She has also published dozens of articles and essays on feminist topics and has edited* Women's Liberation and Literature *(1971), the first textbook on women in literature;* These Modern Women: Autobiographies of American Women in the 1920s *(1978); and* The New Feminist Criticism *(1985).*

## The Female Tradition

*The advent of female literature promises woman's view of life, woman's experience: in other words, a new element. Make what distinctions you please in the social world, it still remains true that men and women have different organizations, consequently different experiences. . . . But hitherto . . . the literature of women has fallen short of its functions owing to a very natural and a very explicable weakness — it has been too much a literature of imitation. To write as men write is the aim and besetting sin of women; to write as women is the real task they have to perform.*

—G. H. Lewes, *"The Lady Novelists,"* 1852

English women writers have never suffered from the lack of a reading audience, nor have they wanted for attention from scholars and critics. Yet we have never been sure what unites them as women, or, indeed, whether they share a common heritage connected to their womanhood at all. Writing about female creativity in *The Subjection of Women* (1869), John Stuart Mill argued that women would have a hard struggle to overcome the influence of male literary tradition, and to create an original, primary, and independent art. "If women lived in a different country from men," Mill thought, "and had never read any of their writings, they would have a literature of their own." Instead, he reasoned, they would always be imitators and never innovators. Paradoxically, Mill would never have raised this point had women not already claimed a very important literary place. To many of his contemporaries (and to many of ours), it seemed that the nineteenth century was the Age of the Female Novelist. With such stellar examples as Jane Austen, Charlotte Brontë, and George Eliot, the question of women's aptitude for fiction, at any rate, had been answered. But a larger question was whether women, excluded by custom and education from achieving distinction in poetry, history, or drama, had, in defining their literary culture in the novel, simply appropriated another masculine genre. Both George Henry Lewes and Mill, spokesmen for women's rights and Victorian liberalism in general, felt that, like the Romans in the shadow of Greece, women were overshadowed by male cultural imperialism: "If women's literature is destined to have a different collective character from that of men," wrote Mill, "much longer time is necessary than has yet elapsed before it can emancipate itself from the influence of accepted models, and guide itself by its own impulses."[1]

There is clearly a difference between books that happen to have been written by women, and a "female literature," as Lewes tried to define it, which purposefully and collectively concerns itself with the articulation of women's experience, and which guides itself "by its own impulses" to autonomous self-expression. As novelists, women have always been self-conscious, but only rarely self-defining. While they have been deeply and perennially aware of their individual identities and experiences, women writers have very infrequently considered whether these experiences might transcend the personal and local, assume a collective form in art, and reveal a history. During the intensely feminist period from 1880 to 1910, both British and American women writers explored the theme of an Amazon utopia, a country entirely populated by women and completely isolated from the male world. Yet even in these fantasies of autonomous female communities, there is no theory of female art. Feminist utopias were not visions of primary womanhood, free to define its own nature and culture, but flights from the male world to a culture defined in opposition to the male tradition. Typically the feminist utopias are pastoral sanctuaries, where a population of prelapsarian Eves cultivate their organic gardens, cure water pollution, and run exemplary child care centers, but do not write books.

In contradiction to Mill, and in the absence, until very recently, of any feminist literary manifestoes, many readers of the novel over the past two centuries have nonetheless had the indistinct but persistent impression of a unifying voice in women's literature. In *The History of the English Novel*, Ernest Baker devotes a separate chapter to the women novelists, commenting that "the woman of letters has peculiarities that mark her off from the other sex as distinctly as peculiarities of race or of ancestral traditions. Whatever variety of talent, outlook or personal disposition

may be discernible among any dozen women writers taken at random, it will be matched and probably outweighed by resemblances distinctively feminine."[2] Baker wisely does not attempt to present a taxonomy of these feminine "peculiarities"; most critics who have attempted to do so have quickly found themselves expressing their own cultural biases rather than explicating sexual structures. In 1852, Lewes thought he could identify the feminine literary traits as Sentiment and Observation; in 1904, William L. Courtney found that "the female author is at once self-conscious and didactic"; in 1965, Bernard Bergonzi explained that "women novelists . . . like to keep their focus narrow."[3] Women reading each other's books have also had difficulties in explaining their potential for what George Eliot called a "precious speciality, lying quite apart from masculine aptitudes and experience." Eliot herself tried to locate the female speciality in the maternal affections.[4]

Statements about the personal and psychological qualities of the woman novelist have also flourished, and have been equally impressionistic and unreliable. The "lady novelist" is a composite of many stereotypes: to J. M. Ludlow, she is a creature with ink halfway up her fingers, dirty shawls, and frowsy hair; and to W. S. Gilbert, a "singular anomaly" who never would be missed.[5]

[2] "Some Women Novelists," *History of the English Novel*, X, London, 1939, p. 194. [Au.]

[3] G. H. Lewes, "The Lady Novelists," *Westminster Review*, n.s. II (1852): 137; W. L. Courtney, *The Feminine Note in Fiction*, London, 1904, p. xiii; Bernard Bergonzi, *New York Review of Books*, June 3, 1965. In a review of Beryl Bainbridge's *The Bottle Factory Outing*, Anatole Broyard comments "that quite a few extremely attractive women write rather despairing books" (*New York Times*, May 26, 1975, p. 13). [Au.]

[4] "Silly Novels by Lady Novelists," *Westminster Review* LXVI (1856); reprinted in *Essays of George Eliot*, ed. Thomas Pinney, New York, 1963, p. 324. [Au.]

[5] "Ruth," *North British Review* XIX (1853): 90–91; and "Ko-Ko's Song" in *The Mikado*. The stereotype of the woman novelist that emerges in the early nineteenth century conflates the popular images of the old maid and the bluestocking; see Vineta Colby, *Yesterday's Woman: Domestic Realism in the English Novel*, Princeton, 1974, pp. 115–116, and Katharine M. Rogers, *The Troublesome Helpmate: A History of Misogyny in Literature*, Seattle, 1966, pp. 201–207. [Au.]

[1] "The Subjection of Women," in John Stuart Mill and Harriet Taylor Mill, *Essays on Sex Equality*, ed. Alice S. Rossi, Chicago, 1970, ch. III, p. 207. [Au.]

To critics of the twentieth century, she is childless and, by implication, neurotic: "We remind ourselves," writes Carolyn Heilbrun, "that of the great women writers, most have been unmarried, and those who have written in the state of wedlock have done so in peaceful kingdoms guarded by devoted husbands. Few have had children."[6] Nancy Milford asks whether there were any women "who married in their youth and bore children and continued to write . . . think of the women who have written: the unmarried, the married and childless, the very few with a single child and that one observed as if it were a rock to be stubbed against."[7]

There are many reasons why discussion of women writers has been so inaccurate, fragmented, and partisan. First, women's literary history has suffered from an extreme form of what John Gross calls "residual Great Traditionalism,"[8] which has reduced and condensed the extraordinary range and diversity of English women novelists to a tiny band of the "great," and derived all theories from them. In practice, the concept of greatness for women novelists often turns out to mean four or five writers — Jane Austen, the Brontës, George Eliot, and Virginia Woolf — and even theoretical studies of "the woman novelist" turn out to be endless recyclings and recombinations of insights about "indispensable Jane and George."[9] Criticism of women novelists, while focusing on these happy few, has ignored those who are not "great," and left them out of anthologies, histories, textbooks, and theories. Having lost sight of the minor novelists, who were the links in the chain that bound one generation to the next, we have not had a very clear understanding of the continuities in women's writing, nor any reliable information about the relationships between the writers' lives and

the changes in the legal, economic, and social status of women.

Second, it has been difficult for critics to consider women novelists and women's literature theoretically because of their tendency to project and expand their own culture-bound stereotypes of femininity, and to see in women's writing an eternal opposition of biological and aesthetic creativity. The Victorians expected women's novels to reflect the feminine values they exalted, although obviously the woman novelist herself had outgrown the constraining feminine role. "Come what will," Charlotte Brontë wrote to Lewes, "I cannot, when I write, think always of myself and what is elegant and charming in femininity; it is not on these terms, or with such ideas, that I ever took pen in hand."[10] Even if we ignore the excesses of what Mary Ellmann calls "phallic criticism" and what Cynthia Ozick calls the "ovarian theory of literature," much contemporary criticism of women writers is still prescriptive and circumscribed.[11] Given the difficulties of steering a precarious course between the Scylla of insufficient information and the Charybdis of abundant prejudice, it is not surprising that formalist-structuralist critics have evaded the issue of sexual identity entirely, or dismissed it as irrelevant and subjective. Finding it difficult to think intelligently about women writers, academic criticism has often overcompensated by desexing them.

Yet since the 1960s, and especially since the reemergence of a Women's Liberation Movement in England and in America around 1968, there has been renewed enthusiasm for the idea that "a special female self-awareness emerges through literature in every period."[12] The interest in establishing a more reliable critical vocabulary and a more accurate and systematic literary history for women writers is part of a larger interdisciplinary effort by psychologists, sociologists,

---

[6]Introduction to May Sarton, *Mrs. Stevens Hears the Mermaids Singing*, New York, 1974, p. xvi. [Au.]

[7]"This Woman's Movement" in *Adrienne Rich's Poetry*, ed. Barbara Charlesworth Gelpi and Albert Gelpi, New York, 1975, p. 189. [Au.]

[8]*The Rise and Fall of the Man of Letters*, London, 1969, p. 304. [Au.]

[9]Cynthia Ozick, "Women and Creativity," in *Woman in Sexist Society*, ed. Vivian Gornick and Barbara K. Moran, New York, 1971, p. 436. [Au.]

[10]Letter of November 1849, in Clement Shorter, *The Brontës: Life and Letters*, II, London, 1908, p. 80. [Au.]

[11]Mary Ellmann, *Thinking about Women*, New York, 1968, pp. 28–54; and Ozick, "Women and Creativity," p. 436. [Au.]

[12]Patricia Meyer Spacks, *The Female Imagination*, New York, 1975, p. 3. [Au.]

social historians, and art historians to reconstruct the political, social, and cultural experience of women.

Scholarship generated by the contemporary feminist movement has increased our sensitivity to the problems of sexual bias or projection in literary history, and has also begun to provide us with the information we need to understand the evolution of a female literary tradition. One of the most significant contributions has been the unearthing and reinterpretation of "lost" works by women writers, and the documentation of their lives and careers.

In the past, investigations have been distorted by the emphasis on an elite group, not only because it has excluded from our attention great stretches of literary activity between, for example, George Eliot and Virginia Woolf, but also because it has rendered invisible the daily lives, the physical experiences, the personal strategies and conflicts of ordinary women. If we want to define the ways in which "female self-awareness" has expressed itself in the English novel, we need to see the woman novelist against the backdrop of the women of her time, as well as in relation to other writers in history. Virginia Woolf recognized that need:

The extraordinary woman depends on the ordinary woman. It is only when we know what were the conditions of the average woman's life — the number of her children, whether she had money of her own, if she had a room to herself, whether she had help in bringing up her family, if she had servants, whether part of the housework was her task — it is only when we can measure the way of life and the experience of life made possible to the ordinary woman that we can account for the success or failure of the extraordinary woman as writer.[13]

As scholars have been persuaded that women's experience is important, they have begun to see it for the first time. With a new perceptual framework, material hitherto assumed to be nonexistent has suddenly leaped into focus. Interdisciplinary studies of Victorian women have opened up new areas of investigation in medi-

cine, psychology, economics, political science, labor history, and art.[14] Questions of the "female imagination" have taken on intellectual weight in the contexts of theories of Karen Horney about feminine psychology, Erik Erikson about womanhood and the inner space, and R. D. Laing about the divided self. Investigation of female iconography and imagery has been stimulated by the work of art historians like Linda Nochlin, Lise Vogel, and Helene Roberts.[15]

As the works of dozens of women writers have been rescued from what E. P. Thompson calls "the enormous condescension of posterity,"[16] and considered in relation to each other, the lost continent of the female tradition has risen like Atlantis from the sea of English literature. It is now becoming clear that, contrary to Mill's theory, women have had a literature of their own all along. The woman novelist, according to Vineta Colby, was "really neither single nor anomalous," but she was also more than a "register and a spokesman for her age."[17] She was part of a tradition that had its origins before her age, and has carried on through our own.

Many literary historians have begun to reinterpret and revise the study of women writers. Ellen Moers sees women's literature as an international movement, "apart from, but hardly subordinate to the mainstream: an undercurrent, rapid and powerful. This 'movement' began in the late eighteenth century, was multinational, and produced some of the greatest literary works

[13]"Women and Fiction," *Collected Essays*, London, 1967, p. 142. [Au.]

[14]See, for example, Sheila Rowbotham, *Hidden from History*, London, 1973; Martha Vicinus, ed., *Suffer and Be Still: Women in the Victorian Age*, Bloomington, Indiana, 1972; Mary S. Hartman and Lois N. Banner, eds., *Clio's Consciousness Raised: New Perspectives on the History of Women*, New York, 1974, and Françoise Basch, *Relative Creatures: Victorian Women in Society and the Novel*, New York, 1974. [Au.]

[15]Linda Nochlin, "Why Are There No Great Women Artists?" in *Women in Sexist Society*; Lise Vogel, "Fine Arts and Feminism: The Awakening Consciousness," *Feminist Studies* II (1974): 3–37; Helene Roberts, "The Inside, the Surface, the Mass: Some Recurring Images of Women," *Women's Studies* II (1974): 289–308. [Au.]

[16]*The Making of the English Working Class*, New York, 1973, p. 12. [Au.]

[17]Vineta Colby, *The Singular Anomaly: Women Novelists of the Nineteenth Century*, New York, 1970, p. 11. [Au.]

of two centuries, as well as most of the lucrative pot-boilers."[18] Patricia Meyer Spacks, in *The Female Imagination,* finds that "for readily discernible historical reasons women have characteristically concerned themselves with matters more or less peripheral to male concerns, or at least slightly skewed from them. The differences between traditional female preoccupations and roles and male ones make a difference in female writing."[19] Many other critics are beginning to agree that when we look at women writers collectively we can see an imaginative continuum, the recurrence of certain patterns, themes, problems, and images from generation to generation.

This book is an effort to describe the female literary tradition in the English novel from the generation of the Brontës to the present day, and to show how the development of this tradition is similar to the development of any literary subculture. Women have generally been regarded as "sociological chameleons," taking on the class, lifestyle, and culture of their male relatives. It can, however, be argued that women themselves have constituted a subculture within the framework of a larger society, and have been unified by values, conventions, experiences, and behaviors impinging on each individual. It is important to see the female literary tradition in these broad terms, in relation to the wider evolution of women's self-awareness and to the ways in which any minority group finds its direction of self-expression relative to a dominant society, because we cannot show a pattern of deliberate progress and accumulation. It is true, as Ellen Moers writes, that "women studied with a special closeness the works written by their own sex";[20] in terms of influences, borrowings, and affinities, the tradition is strongly marked. But it is also full of holes and hiatuses, because of what Germaine Greer calls the "phenomenon of the transience of female literary fame"; "almost uninterruptedly since the Interregnum, a small group of women have enjoyed dazzling literary prestige during their own lifetimes, only to vanish without trace from the records of posterity."[21] Thus each generation of women writers has found itself, in a sense, without a history, forced to rediscover the past anew, forging again and again the consciousness of their sex. Given this perpetual disruption, and also the self-hatred that has alienated women writers from a sense of collective identity, it does not seem possible to speak of a "movement."

I am also uncomfortable with the notion of a "female imagination." The theory of a female sensibility revealing itself in an imagery and form specific to women always runs dangerously close to reiterating the familiar stereotypes. It also suggests permanence, a deep, basic, and inevitable difference between male and female ways of perceiving the world. I think that, instead, the female literary tradition comes from the still-evolving relationships between women writers and their society. Moreover, the "female imagination" cannot be treated by literary historians as a romantic or Freudian abstraction. It is the product of a delicate network of influences operating in time, and it must be analyzed as it expresses itself, in language and in a fixed arrangement of words on a page, a form that itself is subject to a network of influences and conventions, including the operations of the marketplace. In this investigation of the English novel, I am intentionally looking, not at an innate sexual attitude, but at the ways in which the self-awareness of the woman writer has translated itself into a literary form in a specific place and time-span, how this self-awareness has changed and developed, and where it might lead.

I am therefore concerned with the professional writer who wants pay and publication, not with the diarist or letter-writer. This emphasis has required careful consideration of the novelists, as well as the novels, chosen for discussion. When we turn from the overview of the literary tradition to look at the individuals who composed it, a different but interrelated set of motives, drives, and sources becomes prominent. I have needed to ask why women began to write for money and how they negotiated the activity of writing within their families. What was their professional self-

---

[18]"Women's Lit: Profession and Tradition," *Columbia Forum* I (Fall 1972): 27. [Au.]

[19]Spacks, p. 7. [Au.]

[20]Moers, "Women's Lit," 28. [Au.]

[21]"Flying Pigs and Double Standards," *Times Literary Supplement* (July 26, 1974): 784. [Au.]

image? How was their work received, and what effects did criticism have upon them? What were their experiences as women, and how were these reflected in their books? What was their understanding of womanhood? What were their relationships to other women, to men, and to their readers? How did changes in women's status affect their lives and careers? And how did the vocation of writing itself change the women who committed themselves to it? In looking at literary subcultures, such as black, Jewish, Canadian, Anglo-Indian, or even American, we can see that they all go through three major phases. First, there is a prolonged phase of *imitation* of the prevailing modes of the dominant tradition, and *internalization* of its standards of art and its views on social roles. Second, there is a phase of *protest* against these standards and values, and *advocacy* of minority rights and values, including a demand for autonomy. Finally, there is a phase of *self-discovery*, a turning inward freed from some of the dependency of opposition, a search for identity.[22] An appropriate terminology for women writers is to call these stages, *Feminine, Feminist,* and *Female.* These are obviously not rigid categories, distinctly separable in time, to which individual writers can be assigned with perfect assurance. The phases overlap; there are feminist elements in feminine writing, and vice versa. One might also find all three phases in the career of a single novelist. Nonetheless, it seems useful to point to periods of crisis when a shift of literary values occurred. In this book I identify the Feminine phase as the period from the appearance of the male pseudonym in the 1840s to the death of George Eliot in 1880; the Feminist phase as 1880 to 1920, or the winning of the vote; and the Female phase as 1920 to the present, but entering a new stage of self-awareness about 1960.

It is important to understand the female subculture not only as what Cynthia Ozick calls "custodial"[23] — a set of opinions, prejudices, tastes, and values prescribed for a subordinate group to perpetuate its subordination — but also as a thriving and positive entity. Most discussions of women as a subculture have come from historians describing Jacksonian America, but they apply equally well to the situation of early Victorian England. According to Nancy Cott, "we can view women's group consciousness as a subculture uniquely divided against itself by ties to the dominant culture. While the ties to the dominant culture are the informing and restricting ones, they provoke within the subculture certain strengths as well as weaknesses, enduring values as well as accommodations."[24] The middle-class ideology of the proper sphere of womanhood, which developed in post-industrial England and America, prescribed a woman who would be a Perfect Lady, an Angel in the House, contentedly submissive to men, but strong in her inner purity and religiosity, queen in her own realm of the Home.[25] Many observers have pointed out that the first professional activities of Victorian women, as social reformers, nurses, governesses, and novelists, either were based in the home or were extensions of the feminine role as teacher, helper, and mother of mankind. In describing the American situation, two historians have seen a subculture emerging from the doctrine of sexual spheres:

> By "subculture" we mean simply "a habit of living" . . . of a minority group which is self-consciously distinct from the dominant activities, expectations, and values of a society. Historians have seen female church groups, reform associations, and philanthropic activity as expressions of this subculture in actual behavior, while a large and rich body of writing by and for women articulated the subculture impulses on the ideational level. Both behavior and thought point to child-rearing, religious activity,

[22]For helpful studies of literary subcultures, see Robert A. Bone, *The Negro Novel in America,* New York, 1958; and Northrop Frye, "Conclusion to *A Literary History of Canada,*" in *The Stubborn Structure: Essays on Criticism and Society,* Ithaca, 1970, pp. 278–312. [Au.]

[23]"Women and Creativity," p. 442. [Au.]

[24]Nancy F. Cott, introduction to *Roots of Bitterness,* New York, 1972, pp. 3–4. [Au.]

[25]For the best discussions of the Victorian feminine ideal, see Françoise Basch, "Contemporary Ideologies," in *Relative Creatures,* pp. 3–15; Walter E. Houghton, *The Victorian Frame of Mind,* New Haven, 1957, pp. 341–43; and Alexander Welsh's theory of the Angel in the House in *The City of Dickens,* London, 1971, pp. 164–95. [Au.]

education, home life, associationism, and female communality as components of women's subculture. Female friendships, strikingly intimate and deep in this period, formed the actual bonds.[26]

For women in England, the female subculture came first through a shared and increasingly secretive and ritualized physical experience. Puberty, menstruation, sexual initiation, pregnancy, childbirth, and menopause — the entire female sexual life cycle — constituted a habit of living that had to be concealed. Although these episodes could not be openly discussed or acknowledged, they were accompanied by elaborate rituals and lore, by external codes of fashion and etiquette, and by intense feelings of female solidarity.[27] Women writers were united by their roles as daughters, wives, and mothers; by the internalized doctrines of evangelicalism, with its suspicion of the imagination and its emphasis on duty; and by legal and economic constraints on their mobility. Sometimes they were united in a more immediate way, around a political cause. On the whole these are the implied unities of culture, rather than the active unities of consciousness.

From the beginning, however, women novelists' awareness of each other and of their female audience showed a kind of covert solidarity that sometimes amounted to a genteel conspiracy. Advocating sisterhood, Sarah Ellis, one of the most conservative writers of the first Victorian generation, asked: "What should we think of a community of slaves, who betrayed each other's interests? of a little band of shipwrecked mariners upon a friendless shore who were false to each other? of the inhabitants of a defenceless nation, who would not unite together in earnestness and good faith against a common enemy?"[28] Mrs.

Ellis felt the binding force of the minority experience for women strongly enough to hint, in the prefaces to her widely read treatises on English womanhood, that her female audience would both read the messages between her lines and refrain from betraying what they deciphered. As another conservative novelist, Dinah Mulock Craik, wrote, "The intricacies of female nature are incomprehensible except to a woman; and any biographer of real womanly feeling, if ever she discovered, would never dream of publishing them."[29] Few English women writers openly advocated the use of fiction as revenge against a patriarchal society (as did the American novelist Fanny Fern, for example), but many confessed to sentiments of "maternal feeling, sisterly affection, *esprit de corps*"[30] for their readers. Thus the clergyman's daughter, going to Mudie's for her three-decker novel by another clergyman's daughter, participated in a cultural exchange that had a special personal significance.

It is impossible to say when women began to write fiction. From about 1750 on, English women made steady inroads into the literary marketplace, mainly as novelists. As early as 1773, the *Monthly Review* noticed that "that branch of the literary trade" seemed "almost entirely engrossed by the ladies." J. M. S. Tompkins finds that most eighteenth-century epistolary novels were written by women; the Minerva Press published twice as many novels by women as by men; and Ian Watt simply says that the majority of all eighteenth-century novels came from the female pen.[31] At the same time, men were able to imitate, and even usurp, female experience. Oliver Goldsmith suspected that men were writing sentimental novels under female pseudo-

[26]Christine Stansell and Johnny Faragher, "Women and Their Families on the Overland Trail, 1842–1867," *Feminist Studies* II (1975): 152–53. For an overview of recent historical scholarship on the "two cultures," see Barbara Sicherman, "Review: American History," *Signs: Journal of Women in Culture and Society* I (Winter 1975): 470–84. [Au.]

[27]For a sociological account of patterns of behavior for Victorian women, see Leonore Davidoff, *The Best Circles: Society, Etiquette and the Season*, London, 1973, esp. pp. 48–58, 85–100. [Au.]

[28]Sarah Ellis, *The Daughters of England*, New York, 1844, ch. IX, p. 90. [Au.]

[29]Dinah M. Craik, "Literary Ghouls," *Studies from Life*, New York, n.d., p. 13. [Au.]

[30]Letter of October 6, 1851, in *Letters of E. Jewsbury to Jane Welsh Carlyle*, ed. Mrs. Alex Ireland, London, 1892, p. 426. For Fanny Fern, see Ann Douglas Wood, "The 'Scribbling Women' and Fanny Fern: Why Women Wrote," *American Quarterly* XXIII (Spring 1971): 1–24. [Au.]

[31]J. M. S. Tompkins, *The Popular Novel in England 1770–1800*, London, 1932, pp. 119–21; Dorothy Blakey, *The Minerva Press 1790–1820*, London, 1939; and Ian Watt, *The Rise of the Novel*, London, 1963, pp. 298–99. [Au.]

nyms, and men did write books on childcare, midwifery, housekeeping, and cooking.[32]

Early women writers' relationship to their professional role was uneasy. Eighteenth-century women novelists exploited a stereotype of helpless femininity to win chivalrous protection from male reviewers and to minimize their unwomanly self-assertion. In 1791 Elizabeth Inchbald prefaced *A Simple Story* with the lie that she was a poor invalid who had written a novel despite "the utmost detestation to the fatigue of inventing."[33] At the turn of the century, women evaded the issue of professional identity by publishing anonymously. In 1810 Mary Brunton explained in a letter to a friend why she preferred anonymity to taking credit for her novels:

> I would rather, as you well know, glide through the world unknown, than have (I will not call it *enjoy*) fame, however brilliant, to be pointed at, — to be noticed and commented upon — to be suspected of literary airs — to be shunned, as literary women are, by the more unpretending of my own sex; and abhorred as literary women are, by the pretending of the other! — my dear, I would sooner exhibit as a rope-dancer.[34]

Here again we need to remember the distinction between the novel as a form, and the professional role of the novelist. Many of the most consistent themes and images of the feminine novel, from the mysterious interiors of Gothic romance to the balancing of duty and self-fulfillment in domestic fiction, can be traced back to the late eighteenth century. Certainly nineteenth-century women novelists had some familiarity with Burney, Edgeworth, Radcliffe, and Austen, as well as with scores of lesser writers such as Inchbald and Holland. But almost no sense of communality and self-awareness is apparent among women writers before the 1840s, which Kathleen Tillotson sees as the decade in which the novel became the dominant form. Tillotson

points out that, despite the respectful attention paid by mid-Victorian critics to Jane Austen (attention that had some negative impact on Victorian women novelists), there appears to have been relatively little direct influence by Austen on Mrs. Gaskell, Harriet Martineau, the Brontës, and several minor writers.[35] Even George Eliot's debt to Austen has been much exaggerated by the concept of the Great Tradition.[36] The works of Mary Wollstonecraft were not widely read by the Victorians due to the scandals surrounding her life.

More important than the question of direct literary influence, however, is the difference between the social and professional worlds inhabited by the eighteenth- and nineteenth-century women. The early women writers refused to deal with a professional role, or had a negative orientation toward it. "What is my life?" lamented the poet Laetitia Landon. "One day of drudgery after another; difficulties incurred for others, which have ever pressed upon me beyond health, which every year, in one severe illness after another, is taxed beyond its strength; envy, malice, and all uncharitableness — these are the fruits of a successful literary career for a woman."[37] These women may have been less than sincere in their insistence that literary success brought them only suffering, but they were not able to see themselves as involved in a vocation that brought responsibilities as well as conflicts, and opportunities as well as burdens. Moreover, they did not see their writing as an aspect of their female experience, or as an expression of it.

Thus, in talking about the situation of the feminine novelists, I have begun with the women born after 1800, who began to publish fiction during the 1840s when the job of the novelist was becoming a recognizable profession. One of the many indications that this generation saw the will to write as a vocation in direct conflict with

[32]Myra Reynolds, *The Learned Lady in England 1650–1760*, New York, 1920, pp 89–91. [Au.]

[33]William McKee, *Elizabeth Inchbald, Novelist*, Washington, D.C., 1935, p. 20. [Au.]

[34]"Memoirs of the Life of Mrs. Mary Brunton by Her Husband," preface to *Emmeline*, Edinburgh, 1819, p. xxxvi. [Au.]

[35]Kathleen Tillotson, *Novels of the Eighteen-Forties*, London, 1956, pp. 142–45. [Au.]

[36]For a refutation of Leavis's view of Austen and Eliot, see Gross, *Rise and Fall of the Man of Letters*, pp. 302–03. [Au.]

[37]Quoted in S. C. Hall, *A Book of Memories of Great Men and Women of the Age*, London, 1877, p. 266. [Au.]

their status as women is the appearance of the male pseudonym. Like Eve's fig leaf, the male pseudonym signals the loss of innocence. In its radical understanding of the role-playing required by women's effort to participate in the mainstream of literary culture, the pseudonym is a strong marker of the historical shift.

There were three generations of nineteenth-century feminine novelists. The first, born between 1800 and 1820, included all the women who are identified with the Golden Age of the Victorian authoress: the Brontës, Mrs. Gaskell, Elizabeth Barrett Browning, Harriet Martineau, and George Eliot. The members of this group, whose coevals were Florence Nightingale, Mary Carpenter, Angela Burdett, and other pioneer professionals were what sociologists call "female role innovators"; they were breaking new ground and creating new possibilities. The second generation, born between 1820 and 1840, included Charlotte Yonge, Dinah Mulock Craik, Margaret Oliphant, and Elizabeth Lynn Linton; these women followed in the footsteps of the great, consolidating their gains, but were less dedicated and original. The third generation, born between 1840 and 1860, included sensation novelists and children's book writers. They seemed to cope effortlessly with the double roles of woman and professional, and to enjoy sexual fulfillment as well as literary success. Businesslike, unconventional, efficient, and productive, they moved into editorial and publishing positions as well as writing.

By the time the women of the first generation had entered upon their careers, there was already a sense of what the "feminine" novel meant in terms of genres. By the 1840s women writers had adopted a variety of popular genres, and were specializing in novels of fashionable life, education, religion, and community, which Vineta Colby subsumes under the heading "domestic realism." In all these novels, according to Inga-Stina Ewbank, "the central preoccupation . . . is with the woman as an influence on others within her domestic and social circle. It was in this preoccupation that the typical woman novelist of the 1840s found her proper sphere: in using the novel to demonstrate (by assumption rather than exploration of standards of woman-

liness) *woman's* proper sphere."[38] A double standard of literary criticism had also developed, as I show in Chapter 3, with a special set of terms and requirements for fiction by women.

There was a place for such fiction, but even the most conservative and devout women novelists, such as Charlotte Yonge and Dinah Craik, were aware that the "feminine" novel also stood for feebleness, ignorance, prudery, refinement, propriety, and sentimentality, while the feminine novelist was portrayed as vain, publicity-seeking, and self-assertive. At the same time that Victorian reviewers assumed that women readers and women writers were dictating the content of fiction, they deplored the pettiness and narrowness implied by a feminine value system. "Surely it is very questionable," wrote Fitzjames Stephen, "whether it is desirable that no novels should be written except those fit for young ladies to read."[39]

Victorian feminine novelists thus found themselves in a double bind. They felt humiliated by the condescension of male critics and spoke intensely of their desire to avoid special treatment and achieve genuine excellence, but they were deeply anxious about the possibility of appearing unwomanly. Part of the conflict came from the fact that, rather than confronting the values of their society, these women novelists were competing for its rewards. For women, as for other subcultures, literature became a symbol of achievement.

In the face of this dilemma, women novelists developed several strategies, both personal and artistic. Among the personal reactions was a persistent self-deprecation of themselves as women, sometimes expressed as humility, sometimes as coy assurance-seeking, and sometimes as the purest self-hatred. In a letter to John Blackwood, Mrs. Oliphant expressed doubt about "whether in your most manly and masculine of magazines a womanish story-teller like myself may not be-

[38]Inga-Stina Ewbank, *Their Proper Sphere: A Study of the Brontë Sisters as Early-Victorian Female Novelists*, London, 1966, p. 41. [Au.]
[39]*Saturday Review* IV (July 11, 1857): 40–41. See also David Masson, *British Novelists and Their Styles*, Cambridge, 1859, p. 134. [Au.]

come wearisome."[40] The novelists publicly proclaimed, and sincerely believed, their antifeminism. By working in the home, by preaching submission and self-sacrifice, and by denouncing female self-assertiveness, they worked to atone for their own will to write.

Vocation — the will to write — nonetheless required a genuine transcendence of female identity. Victorian women were not accustomed to *choosing* a vocation; womanhood was a vocation in itself. The evangelically inspired creed of work did affect women, even though it had not been primarily directed toward them. Like men, women were urged to "bear their part in the *work* of life."[41] Yet for men, the gospel of work satisfied both self-interest and the public interest. In pursuing their ambitions, they fulfilled social expectations.

For women, however, work meant labor for *others*. Work, in the sense of self-development, was in direct conflict with the subordination and repression inherent in the feminine ideal. The self-centeredness implicit in the act of writing made this career an especially threatening one; it required an engagement with feeling and a cultivation of the ego rather than its negation. The widely circulated treatises of Hannah More and Sarah Ellis translated the abstractions of "women's mission" into concrete programs of activity, which made writing appear selfish, unwomanly, and unchristian. "'What shall I do to gratify myself — to be admired — or to vary the tenor of my existence?'" are not, according to Mrs. Ellis, "questions which a woman of right feelings asks on first awakening to the avocations of the day." Instead she recommends visiting the sick, fixing breakfast for anyone setting on a journey in order to spare the servant, or general "devotion to the good of the whole family." "Who can believe," she asks fervently, "that days, months, and years spent in a continual course of thought and action similar to this, will not produce a powerful effect

upon the character?"[42] Of course it did; one notices first of all that feminine writers like Elizabeth Barrett, "Charlotte Elizabeth," Elizabeth M. Sewell, and Mrs. Ellis herself had to overcome deep-seated guilt about authorship. Many found it necessary to justify their work by recourse to some external stimulus or ideology. In their novels, the heroine's aspirations for a full, independent life are undermined, punished, or replaced by marriage.

Elizabeth Barrett Browning's *Aurora Leigh* (1857) is one of the few autobiographical discussions of feminine role conflict. Aurora's struggle to become an artist is complicated by the self-hatred in which she has been educated, by her internalized convictions of her weakness and narcissism, and by the gentle scorn of her suitor Romney. She defies him, however, and invokes divine authority to reject his proposal that she become his helpmeet:

> You misconceive the question like a man
> Who sees the woman as the complement
> Of his sex merely. You forget too much
> That every creature, female as the male,
> Stands single in responsible act and thought . . .
> I too have my vocation, — work to do,
> The heavens and earth have set me.
>
> (Book II, 460–66)

Aurora succeeds as a poet. But she marries Romney in the end, having learned that as a woman she cannot cope with the guilt of self-centered ambition. It is significant that Romney has been blinded in an accident before she marries him, not only because he has thereby received firsthand knowledge of being handicapped and can empathize with her, but also because he then needs her help and can provide her with suitably feminine work. When Aurora tells Romney that "No perfect artist is developed here / From any imperfect woman" (Book IX, 648–49) she means more than the perfection of love and motherhood; she means also the perfection of self-sacrifice. This conflict remains a significant one for English novelists up to the present; it is a major theme

[40]*Autobiography and Letters of Mrs. M. O. W. Oliphant,* ed. Mrs. Harry Cogshill, New York, 1899, p. 160. [Au.]

[41]"An Enquiry into the State of Girls' Fashionable Schools," *Fraser's* XXXI (1845): 703. [Au.]

[42]Sarah Ellis, *The Women of England,* New York, 1844, p. 9. [Au.]

for women novelists from Charlotte Brontë to Penelope Mortimer. Male novelists like Thackeray, who came from an elite class, also felt uncomfortable with the aggressive self-promotion of the novelist's career. As Donald Stone points out:

> Thackeray's ambivalent feelings towards Becky Sharp indicate the degree to which he attempted to suppress or make light of his own literary talents. The energies which make her (for a time) a social success are akin to those which made him a creative artist. In the hands of a major woman novelist, like Jane Austen or George Eliot, the destructive moral and social implications of Becky's behavior would have been defined more clearly and more urgently. Jane Austen's dissection of Lydia Bennet, and George Eliot's demolition of Rosamond Vincy, for example, indicate both how and why the defense of the status quo — insofar as women of the nineteenth century were concerned — was most earnestly and elaborately performed by women writers. Their heroines are hardly concerned with self-fulfillment in the modern sense of the term, and if they have severely limited possibilities in life it is because their authors saw great danger in, plus a higher alternative to, the practice of self-assertiveness.[43]

The dilemma is stated by George Eliot in *Romola* as the question of where "the duty of obedience ends and the duty of resistance begins."[44] Yet this was the question any Victorian woman with the will to write would have had to ask herself: what did God intend her to do with her life? Where did obedience to her father and husband end, and the responsibility of self-fulfillment become paramount? The problem of obedience and resistance that women had to solve in their own lives before they could begin to write crops up in their novels as the heroine's moral crisis. The forms that the crisis takes in feminine fiction are realistically mundane — should Margaret, in Mrs. Gaskell's *North and South,* lie to protect her brother? should Ethel May, in Charlotte Yonge's *Daisy Chain,* give up studying Greek to nurse her father? — but the

sources were profound, and were connected to the women novelists' sense of epic life. At the same time that they recognized the modesty of their own struggles, women writers recognized their heroism. "A new Theresa will hardly have the opportunity of reforming a conventual life," wrote George Eliot in *Middlemarch,* "any more than a new Antigone will spend her heroic piety in daring all for a brother's burial: the medium in which their ardent deeds took shape is forever gone. But we insignificant people with our daily words and acts are preparing the lives of many Dorotheas, some of which may present a far sadder sacrifice than that of the Dorothea whose story we know."[45]

The training of Victorian girls in repression, concealment, and self-censorship was deeply inhibiting, especially for those who wanted to write. As one novelist commented in 1860, "Women are greater dissemblers than men when they wish to conceal their own emotions. By habit, moral training, and modern education, they are obliged to do so. The very first lessons of infancy teach them to repress their feelings, control their very thoughts."[46] The verbal range permitted to English gentlewomen amounted almost to a special language. The verbal inhibitions that were part of the upbringing of a lady were reinforced by the critics' vigilance. "It is an immense loss," lamented Alice James, "to have all robust and sustaining expletives refined away from one."[47] "Coarseness" was the term Victorian readers used to rebuke unconventional language in women's literature. It could refer to the "damns" in *Jane Eyre,* the dialect in *Wuthering Heights,* the slang of Rhoda Broughton's heroines, the colloquialisms in *Aurora Leigh,* or more generally to the moral tone of a work, such as the "vein of perilous voluptuousness" one alert critic detected in *Adam Bede.*[48] John Keble cen-

[43]"Victorian Feminism and the Nineteenth-Century Novel," *Women's Studies* I (1972): 69. [Au.]

[44]*Romola,* New York, 1898, II, ch. XXIII, p. 157. [Au.]

[45]*Middlemarch,* ed. Gordon S. Haight, Boston, 1956, "Finale," p. 612. [Au.]

[46]Jane Vaughan Pinckney, *Tacita Tacit,* II, p. 276; quoted in Myron Brightfield, *Victorian England in Its Novels,* IV, Los Angeles, 1968, p. 27. [Au.]

[47]*The Diary of Alice James,* ed. Leon Edel, New York, 1934, p. 66. [Au.]

[48]*British Quarterly Review* XLV (1867): 164. On the term

sored Charlotte Yonge's fiction, taking the greatest care "that no hint of 'coarseness' should sully the purity of Charlotte's writings. Thus he would not allow Theodora in *Heartsease* to say that 'really she had a heart, though some people thought it was only a machine for pumping blood.' He also transformed the 'circle' of the setting sun into an 'orb' and a 'coxcomb' into a 'jackanapes.'"[49] While verbal force, wit, and originality in women was criticized, a bland and gelatinous prose won applause. "She writes as an English gentlewoman should write," the *North British Review* complimented Anne Marsh in 1849; "her pages are absolutely like green pastures."[50] Reduced to a pastoral flatness, deprived of a language in which to describe their bodies or the events of their bodies, denied the expression of pain as well as the expression of pleasure, women writers appeared deficient in passion.

It is easy to understand why many readers took the absence of expression for the absence of feeling. In "The False Morality of Lady Novelists," W. R. Greg argued that woman's sexual innocence would prevent her ever writing a great novel:

Many of the saddest and deepest truths in the strange science of sexual affection are to her mysteriously and mercifully veiled and can only be purchased at such a fearful cost that we cannot wish it otherwise. The inevitable consequence however is that in treating of that science she labours under all the disadvantages of partial study and superficial insight. She is describing a country of which she knows only the more frequented and the safer roads, with a few of the sweeter scenes and the prettier by-paths and more picturesque detours which be not far from the broad and beaten thoroughfares; while the rockier and loftier mountains, and more rugged tracts, the more sombre valleys, and the darker and more dangerous chasms, are never trodden by her feet, and scarcely ever dreamed of by her fancy.[51]

The results of restrictive education and intensive conditioning were taken as innate evidence of natural preference. In an ironic twist, many reviewers who had paternally barred the way to the sombre valleys, the darker chasms, and the more rugged tracts also blamed women for the emasculation of male prose, finding, like the *Prospective Review,* that the "writing of men is in danger of being marked" by "the delicacy and even fastidiousness of expression which is *natural* to educated women" (my italics).[52] When G. H. Lewes complained in 1852 that the literature of women was "too much a literature of imitation" and demanded that women should express "what they have really known, felt and suffered,"[53] he was asking for something that Victorian society had made impossible. Feminine novelists had been deprived of the language and the consciousness for such an enterprise, and obviously their deprivation extended beyond Victoria's reign and into the twentieth century. The delicacy and verbal fastidiousness of Virginia Woolf is an extension of this feminized language.

Florence Nightingale thought the effort of repression itself drained off women's creative energy. "Give us back our suffering," she demanded in *Cassandra* (1852), "for out of nothing comes nothing. But out of suffering may come the cure. Better have pain than paralysis."[54] It does sometimes seem as if feminine writers are metaphorically paralyzed, as Alice James was literally paralyzed, by refinement and restraint, but the repression in which the feminine novel was situated also forced women to find innovative and covert ways to dramatize the inner life, and led to a fiction that was intense, compact, symbolic, and profound. There is Charlotte Brontë's extraordinary subversion of the Gothic in *Jane Eyre,* in which the mad wife locked in the attic symbolizes the passionate and sexual

---

"coarseness," see Ewbank, *Their Proper Sphere,* pp. 46–47. [Au.]

[49]Margaret Mare and Alicia C. Percival, *Victorian Best-Seller: The World of Charlotte Yonge,* London, 1947, p. 133. [Au.]

[50]James Lorimer, "Noteworthy Novels," XI (1849): 257. [Au.]

[51]"The False Morality of Lady Novelists," *National Review* VII (1859): 149. [Au.]

[52]"Puseyite Novels," VI (1850): 498. [Au.]

[53]"The Lady Novelists," 132. [Au.]

[54]"Cassandra," in *The Cause,* ed. Ray Strachey, Port Washington, N.Y., 1969, p. 398. [Au.]

side of Jane's personality, an alter ego that her upbringing, her religion, and her society have commanded her to incarcerate. There is the crippled artist heroine of Dinah Craik's *Olive* (1850), who identifies with Byron, and whose deformity represents her very womanhood. There are the murderous little wives of Mary Braddon's sensation novels, golden-haired killers whose actions are a sardonic commentary on the real feelings of the Angel in the House.

Many of the fantasies of feminine novels are related to money, mobility, and power. Although feminine novelists punished assertive heroines, they dealt with personal ambition by projecting the ideology of success onto male characters, whose initiative, thrift, industry, and perseverance came straight from the woman author's experience. The "woman's man," discussed in Chapter 4, was often a more effective outlet for the "deviant" aspects of the author's personality than were her heroines, and thus male role-playing extended beyond the pseudonym to imaginative content.

Protest fiction represented another projection of female experience onto another group; it translated the felt pain and oppression of women into the championship of millworkers, child laborers, prostitutes, and slaves. Women were aware that protest fiction converted anger and frustration into an acceptable form of feminine and Christian expression. In the social novels of the 1840s and 1850s, and the problem novels of the 1860s and 1870s, women writers were pushing back the boundaries of their sphere, and presenting their profession as one that required not only freedom of language and thought, but also mobility and activity in the world. The sensation novelists of the 1870s, including Mary Braddon, Rhoda Broughton, and Florence Marryat, used this new freedom in a transitional literature that explored genuinely radical female protest against marriage and women's economic oppression, although still in the framework of feminine conventions that demanded the erring heroine's destruction.

From Jane Austen to George Eliot, the woman's novel had moved, despite its restrictions, in the direction of an all-inclusive female realism, a broad, socially informed exploration of the daily lives and values of women within the family and the community. By 1880, the three-decker had become flexible enough to accommodate many of the formerly unprintable aspects of female experience. Yet with the death of George Eliot and the appearance of a new generation of writers, the woman's novel moved into a Feminist phase, a confrontation with male society that elevated Victorian sexual stereotypes into a cult. The feminists challenged many of the restrictions on women's self-expression, denounced the gospel of self-sacrifice, attacked patriarchal religion, and constructed a theoretical model of female oppression, but their anger with society and their need for self-justification often led them away from realism into oversimplification, emotionalism, and fantasy. Making their fiction the vehicle for a dramatization of wronged womanhood, they demanded changes in the social and political systems that would grant women male privileges and require chastity and fidelity from men. The profound sense of injustice that the feminine novelists had represented as class struggle in their novels of factory life becomes an all-out war of the sexes in the novels of the feminists. Even their pseudonyms show their sense of feminist pride and of matriarchal mission to their sisters; one representative feminist called herself "Sarah Grand." In its extreme form, feminist literature advocated the sexual separatism of Amazon utopias and suffragette sisterhoods.

In the lives of the feminists, the bonds of the female subculture were particularly strong. The feminists were intensely devoted to each other and needed the support of close, emotional friendships with other women as well as the loving adulation of a female audience. In this generation, which mainly comprises women born between 1860 and 1880, one finds sympathetically attuned women writing in teams; Edith Somerville and Violet Martin were even said to have continued the collaboration beyond the grave.[55] Although they preached individualism,

---

[55]See Maurice Collis, *Somerville and Ross,* London, 1968, for an account of the careers of Edith Somerville and Violet Martin. After Martin's death in 1915, the "collaboration" continued through psychic communications. Katherine Bradley and Edith Cooper wrote under the name of "Mi-

their need for association led to a staggering number of clubs, activities, and causes, culminating in the militant groups and the almost terrifying collectivity of the suffrage movement. They glorified and idealized the womanly values of chastity and maternal love, and believed that those values must be forced upon a degenerate male society.

In their lives and in their books, most feminist writers expressed both an awareness of, and a revulsion from, sexuality. Like the feminine novelists, they projected many of their own experiences onto male characters, creating, for example, the Scarlet Pimpernels, "effeminate" fops by day and fearless heroes by night, semi-androgynous symbols of a generation in uneasy transition. To some degree these tactics were typical of the period in which they wrote; male novelists were creating "masculine" independent women who, as Donald Stone puts it, "could be used as a cover for those men who, for one reason or another, were anxious to proclaim their own standards and follow their own instincts."[56]

As the feminists themselves often seem neurotic and divided in their roles, less productive than earlier generations, and subject to paralyzing psychosomatic illnesses, so their fiction seems to break down in its form. In the 1890s the three-decker novel abruptly disappeared due to changes in its marketability, and women turned to short stories and fragments, which they called "dreams," "keynotes," and "fantasias." At the turn of the century came the purest examples of feminist literature, the novels, poems, and plays written as suffragette propaganda and distributed by the efficient and well-financed suffrage presses.

The feminist writers were not important artists. Yet in their insistence on exploring and defining womanhood, in their rejection of self-sacrifice, and even in their outspoken hostility to men, the feminist writers represented an important stage, a declaration of independence, in the female tradition. They did produce some interesting and original work, and they opened new subjects for other novelists. Sarah Grand's powerful studies of female psychology, George Egerton's bitter short stories, and Olive Schreiner's existential socialism were all best sellers in their own day and still hold attention. Through political campaigns for prostitutes and working women, and in the suffrage crusades, the feminists insisted on their right to use the male sexual vocabulary, and to use it forcefully and openly. The feminists also challenged the monopoly of male publishers and rebelled against the dictatorship of the male establishment. Men — John Chapman, John Blackwood, Henry Blackett, George Smith — had published the works of feminine novelists and had exerted direct and enormous power over their contents. Sarah Grand parodied the masculine critical hegemony by describing a literary journal she called the *Patriarch,* and feminist journalists, writing in their own magazines, argued against the judgments of the men of letters. In the 1860s the sensation novelists had begun to retain their copyrights, work with printers on a commission basis, and edit their own magazines. The feminists continued to expand this economic control of publishing outlets. Virginia Woolf, printing her own novels at the Hogarth Press, owed much of her independence to the feminists' insistence on the need for women writers to be free of patriarchal commercialism.

In its early stages feminist analysis was naive and incoherent, but by the turn of the century Mona Caird, Elizabeth Robins, and Olive Schreiner were producing cogent theories of women's relationship to work and production, to class structure, and to marriage and the family.[57] Robins and other members of the Women Writers Suffrage League were beginning to work out a theory of women's literature, making connections between the demands of the male publishing industry, the socialization of women, and the heroines, plots, conventions, and images of

---

chael Field"; the sisters Emily and Dorothea Gerard used the name "E. D. Gerard" for such joint efforts as *Beggar My Neighbor* (1882). [Au.]

[56]"Victorian Feminism and the Nineteenth-Century Novel," 79. [Au.]

[57]Mona Caird, *The Morality of Marriage,* London, 1897; Elizabeth Robins, *Way Stations,* London, 1913; Olive Schreiner, *Women and Labour,* London, 1911. [Au.]

women's fiction. Finally, the militant suffrage movement forced women writers to confront their own beliefs about women's rights, and in the process to reexamine their own self-hatred and inhibition.

English women (or at least those women who were over thirty, householders, the wives of householders, occupiers of property of £5 or more annual value, or university graduates) were given the franchise in 1918 by a government grateful for their patriotism during World War I.[58] Ironically, the death of many young male writers and poets during the war left English women writers with a poignant sense of carrying on a national literary tradition that had, at its heart, excluded them. Women felt a responsibility to continue, to take the men's place, but they also felt a pitiful lack of confidence. Alice Meynell's poem "A Father of Women" conveys some of the anxiety, as well as the guilt, of the survivors:

> Our father works in us,
> The daughters of his manhood. Not undone
> Is he, not wasted, though transmuted thus,
>     and though he left no son.

Meynell calls upon her father's spirit in the poem to arm her "delicate mind," give her "courage to die," and to crush in her nature "the ungenerous art of the inferior."

The literature of the last generation of Victorian women writers, born between 1880 and 1900, moved beyond feminism to a Female phase of courageous self-exploration, but it carried with it the double legacy of feminine self-hatred and feminist withdrawal. In their rejection of male society and masculine culture, feminist writers had retreated more and more toward a separatist literature of inner space. Psychologically rather than socially focussed, this literature sought refuge from the harsh realities and vicious practices of the male world. Its favorite symbol, the enclosed and secret room, had been a potent image in women's novels since *Jane Eyre*, but by the end of the century it came to be identified with the womb and with female conflict. In children's

books, such as Mrs. Molesworth's *The Tapestry Room* (1879) and Dinah Craik's *The Little Lame Prince* (1886), women writers had explored and extended these fantasies of enclosure. After 1900, in dozens of novels from Frances Hodgson Burnett's *A Secret Garden* (1911) to May Sinclair's *The Tree of Heaven* (1917), the secret room, the attic hideaway, the suffragette cell came to stand for a separate world, a flight from men and from adult sexuality.

The fiction of Dorothy Richardson, Katherine Mansfield, and Virginia Woolf created a deliberate female aesthetic, which transformed the feminine code of self-sacrifice into an annihilation of the narrative self, and applied the cultural analysis of the feminists to words, sentences, and structures of language in the novel. Their version of modernism was a determined response to the material culture of male Edwardian novelists like Arnold Bennett and H. G. Wells, but, like D. H. Lawrence, the female aestheticists saw the world as mystically and totally polarized by sex. For them, female sensibility took on a sacred quality, and its exercise became a holy, exhausting, and ultimately self-destructive rite, since woman's receptivity led inevitably to suicidal vulnerability.

Paradoxically, the more female this literature became in the formal and theoretical sense, the farther it moved from exploring the physical experience of women. Sexuality hovers on the fringes of the aestheticists' novels and stories, disguised, veiled, and denied. Androgyny, the sexual ethic of Bloomsbury and an important concept of the period, provided an escape from the confrontation with the body. Erotically charged and drenched with sexual symbolism, female aestheticism is nonetheless oddly sexless in its content. Again, "a room of one's own," with its insistence on artistic autonomy and its implied disengagement from social and sexual involvement, was a favorite image.

After the death of Virginia Woolf in 1941, the English women's novel seemed adrift. The harsh criticism of Bloomsbury, of female aestheticism, and especially of Virginia Woolf by writers for *Scrutiny* in the 1930s had pointed out the problems of disengagement. In her late writings, *The Years* (1937) and *Three Guineas* (1938), Woolf

[58]See Andrew Rosen, *Rise Up, Women!* London, 1974, p. 266. [Au.]

herself had tried to move in the direction of social realism. During the 1940s and 1950s, however, women writers, many of an older generation, continued to work in conservative modes untouched by either modernism or a sense of personal experiment. The works of such novelists as Rose Macaulay and Ivy Compton-Burnett are closely connected to a female tradition in their themes and awareness, but they seem to represent a passive rather than an active continuity. This passivity is one aspect of the larger situation of the postwar English novel. Adrian Mitchell describes "the disease of the British artist since 1945" as "a compulsion to stay small, to create perfect miniatures, to take no major risks."[59]

In the 1960s the female novel entered a new and dynamic phase, which has been strongly influenced in the past ten years by the energy of the international women's movement. The contemporary women's novel observes the traditional forms of nineteenth-century realism, but it also operates in the contexts of twentieth-century Freudian and Marxist analysis. In the fiction of Iris Murdoch, Muriel Spark, and Doris Lessing, and the younger writers Margaret Drabble, A. S. Byatt, and Beryl Bainbridge, we are beginning to see a renaissance in women's writing that responds to the demands of Lewes and Mill for an authentically female literature, providing "woman's view of life, woman's experience." In drawing upon two centuries of the female tradition, these novelists have been able to incorporate many of the strengths of the past with a new range of language and experience. Like the feminine novelists, they are concerned with the conflicts between art and love, between self-fulfillment and duty. They have insisted upon the right to use vocabularies previously reserved for male writers and to describe formerly taboo areas of female experience. For the first time anger and sexuality are accepted not only as attributes of realistic characters but also, as in Murdoch's *A Severed Head,* Lessing's *The Golden Notebook,* and A. S. Byatt's *The Game,* as sources of female creative power. Like the feminist novelists, contemporary writers are aware of their place in a political system and their connectedness to other women. Like the novelists of the female aesthetic, women novelists today, Lessing and Drabble particularly, see themselves as trying to unify the fragments of female experience through artistic vision, and they are concerned with the definition of autonomy for the woman writer. As the women's movement takes on cohesive force, and as feminist critics examine their literary tradition, contemporary women novelists will have to face the problems that black, ethnic, and Marxist writers have faced in the past: whether to devote themselves to the forging of female mythologies and epics, or to move beyond the female tradition into a seamless participation in the literary mainstream that might be regarded either as equality or assimilation.

Feminine, feminist, or female, the woman's novel has always had to struggle against the cultural and historical forces that relegated women's experience to the second rank. In trying to outline the female tradition, I have looked beyond the famous novelists who have been found worthy, to the lives and works of many women who have long been excluded from literary history. I have tried to discover how they felt about themselves and their books, what choices and sacrifices they made, and how their relationship to their profession and their tradition evolved. "What is commonly called literary history," writes Louise Bernikow, "is actually a record of choices. Which writers have survived their time and which have not depends upon who noticed them and chose to record the notice."[60] If some of the writers I notice seem to us to be Teresas and Antigones, struggling with their overwhelming sense of vocation and repression, many more will seem only Dorotheas, prim, mistaken, irreparably minor. And yet it is only by considering them all — Millicent Grogan as well as Virginia Woolf — that we can begin to record new choices in a new literary history, and to understand why, despite prejudice, despite guilt, despite inhibition, women began to write.

[59]Quoted in Bernard Bergonzi, *The Situation of the Novel,* London, 1972, p. 79. [Au.]

[60]*The World Split Open: Four Centuries of Women Poets in England and America, 1552–1950,* New York, 1974, p. 3. [Au.]

# Sandra Gilbert and
b. 1936

# Susan Gubar
b. 1944

*Sandra Gilbert and Susan Gubar are best known for their collaborative explorations of women's literary tradition. They have coauthored* The Madwoman in the Attic: The Woman Writer and the Nineteenth-Century Literary Imagination *(1979) and* The War of the Words *(1988), the first volume of* No Man's Land: The Place of the Woman Writer in the Twentieth Century. *They have also coedited* Shakespeare's Sisters: Feminist Essays on Women Poets *(1979) and* The Norton Anthology of Literature by Women *(1985), which provides canonical treatment of literature by women in English for college courses, and* The Female Imagination and the Modernist Aesthetic *(1986). Both Gilbert and Gubar were born in New York. Sandra Mortola Gilbert took a B.A. at Cornell (1957), an M.A. at New York University (1961), and a Ph.D. at Columbia (1968). She has taught in New York, New Jersey, Indiana, and California; she was an associate professor of English at the University of California-Davis from 1975 to 1985 and is now a professor of English at Princeton University. In addition to her scholarly study of D. H. Lawrence's poetry (1973), Gilbert has written poetry of her own, some of which is collected in* The Summer Kitchen *(1983) and* Emily's Bread *(1984). Susan David Gubar, professor of English at Indiana University-Bloomington, received her B.A. from City College of New York (1965), her M.A. from the University of Michigan (1968), and her Ph.D. from the University of Iowa (1972). She has also taught at the University of Illinois (1972–73) and at Tufts University (1982–83), and her academic honors include a Guggenheim fellowship (1983–84). Gubar has written numerous essays on eighteenth-century literature, science fiction and fantasy, and contemporary women's writing. "The Parables of the Cave" is the third chapter of* The Madwoman in the Attic.

## The Parables of the Cave

*"Next then," I said, "take the following parable of education and ignorance as a picture of the condition of our nature. Imagine mankind as dwelling in an underground cave . . .* — PLATO

*Where are the songs I used to know,*
*    Where are the notes I used to sing?*
*I have forgotten everything*
*    I used to know so long ago.*
— CHRISTINA ROSSETTI

*. . . there came upon me an overshadowing bright Cloud, and in the midst of it the figure of a Woman, most richly adorned with transparent Gold, her Hair hanging down, and her Face as the terrible Crystal for brightness [and] immediately this Voice came, saying, Behold I am God's Eternal Virgin-*

*Wisdom . . . I am to unseal the Treasures of God's deep Wisdom unto thee, and will be as Rebecca was unto Jacob, a true Natural Mother; for out of my Womb thou shalt be brought forth after the manner of a Spirit, Conceived and Born again.*
— JANE LEAD[1]

Although Plato does not seem to have thought much about this point, a cave is — as Freud pointed out — a female place, a womb-shaped enclosure, a house of earth, secret and often

[1] *Epigraphs: The Republic,* trans. W. H. D. Rouse (New York: Mentor, 1956), p. 312 (Book VII); "The Key-Note," *The Poetical Works of Christina G. Rossetti,* 2:11; *A Fountain of Gardens Watered by the River of Divine Pleasure,*

sacred.[2] To this shrine the initiate comes to hear the voice of darkness, the wisdom of inwardness. In this prison the slave is immured, the virgin sacrificed, the priestess abandoned. "We have put her living in the tomb!" Poe's paradigmatic exclamation of horror, with its shadow of solipsism, summarizes the Victorian shudder of disgust at the thought of cavern confrontations and the evils they might reveal — the suffocation, the "black bat airs," the vampirism, the chaos of what Victor Frankenstein calls "filthy creation." But despite its melodrama, Poe's remark summarizes too (even if unintentionally) the plight of the woman in patriarchal culture, the woman whose cave-shaped anatomy is her destiny. Not just, like Plato's cave-dweller, a prisoner of Nature, this woman is a prisoner of her own nature, a prisoner in the "grave cave" of immanence which she transforms into a vaporous Cave of Spleen.[3]

In this regard, an anecdote of Simone de Beauvoir's forms a sort of counter-parable to Plato's:

> I recall seeing in a primitive village of Tunisia a subterranean cavern in which four women were squatting: the old one-eyed and toothless wife, her face horribly devastated, was cooking dough on a small brazier in the midst of an acrid smoke; two wives somewhat younger, but almost as disfigured, were lulling children in their arms — one was giving suck; seated before a loom, a young idol magnificently decked out in silk, gold, and silver was knotting threads of wool. As I left this gloomy cave — kingdom of immanence, womb, and tomb — in the corridor leading upward toward the light of day I passed the male, dressed in white, well groomed, smiling, sunny. He was returning from the marketplace, where he had discussed world affairs with other men; he would pass some hours in this retreat of his at the heart of the vast universe to which he belonged, from which he was not separated. For the withered old women, for the young wife doomed to the same rapid decay, there was no universe other than the smoky cave, whence they emerged only at night, silent and veiled.[4]

Destroyed by traditional female activities — cooking, nursing, needling, knotting — which ought to have given them life as they themselves give life to men, the women of this underground harem are obviously buried in (and by) patriarchal definitions of their sexuality. Here is immanence with no hope of transcendence, nature seduced and betrayed by culture, enclosure without any possibility of escape. Or so it would seem.

Yet the womb-shaped cave is also the place of female power, the *umbilicus mundi*,[5] one of the great antechambers of the mysteries of transformation. As herself a kind of cave, every woman might seem to have the cave's metaphorical power of annihilation, the power — as de Beauvoir puts it elsewhere — of "night in the entrails of the earth," for "in many a legend," she notes, "we see the hero lost forever as he falls back into the maternal shadows — cave, abyss, hell."[6] At the same time, as herself a fated inhabitant of that earth-cave of immanence in which de Beauvoir's Tunisian women were trapped, every woman might seem to have metaphorical access to the dark knowledge buried in caves. Summarizing the characteristics of those female "great weavers" who determine destiny — Norns, Fates, priestesses of Demeter, prophetesses of Gaea[7] — Helen Diner points out that "all knowledge of Fate comes from the female depths; none of the surface powers knows it. Whoever wants to know about Fate must go down to the woman," meaning the Great Mother, the Weaver Woman who weaves "the world tap-

---

*and Springing Up in all Variety of Spiritual Plants . . .* (London, 1697–1701), 1:18. We are grateful to Catherine Smith for introducing us to the writings of Jane Lead. [Au.]

[2]Although see Helen Diner, *Mothers and Amazons: The First Feminine History of Culture* (New York: Anchor Books, 1973-reprint), for a comment on the parable of reincarnation at the end of *The Republic*: "Through Plato's earth gullet, roaring with birth, the souls rise and set, moving down when they come from Life and moving back up with a new destiny that they have been allotted" (p. 6). [Au.]

[3]Edgar Allan Poe, "The Fall of the House of Usher"; Sylvia Plath, "Nick and the Candlestick" ("black bat airs") and "Lady Lazarus" ("grave cave"), *Ariel*, pp. 6, 33. [Au.]

[4]De Beauvoir, *The Second Sex,* pp. 77–78. [Au]

[5]Navel of the world. The *omphalos* — Greek for navel — on Calypso's isle was the site of prophecy. [Ed.]

[6]De Beauvoir, p. 137. [Au.]

[7]Norns are the Norse version of the Fates; Demeter and Gaea are the Greek goddesses of the harvest and of the Earth. [Ed.]

estry out of genesis and demise" in her cave of power. Yet individual women are imprisoned in, not empowered by, such caves, like Blake's symbolic worms, "Weaving to Dreams the Sexual strife / And weeping over the Web of life."[8] How, therefore, does any woman — but especially a literary woman, who thinks in images — reconcile the cave's negative metaphoric potential with its positive mythic possibilities? Immobilized and half-blinded in Plato's cave, how does such a woman distinguish what she is from what she sees, her real creative essence from the unreal cutpaper shadows the cavern-master claims as reality?

In a fictionalized "Author's Introduction" to *The Last Man* (1826) Mary Shelley tells another story about a cave, a story which implicitly answers these questions and which, therefore, constitutes yet a third parable of the cave. In 1818, she begins, she and "a friend" visited what was said to be "the gloomy cavern of the Cumaean Sibyl." Entering a mysterious, almost inaccessible chamber, they found "piles of leaves, fragments of bark, and a white filmy substance resembling the inner part of the green hood which shelters the grain of the unripe Indian corn." At first, Shelley confesses, she and her male companion (Percy Shelley) were baffled by this discovery, but "At length, my friend . . . exclaimed 'This *is* the Sibyl's cave; these are sibylline leaves!'" Her account continues as follows.

On examination, we found that all the leaves, bark, and other substances were traced with written characters. What appeared to us more astonishing, was that these writings were expressed in various languages: some unknown to my companion . . . some . . . in modern dialects. . . . We could make out little by the dim light, but they seemed to contain prophecies, detailed relations of events but lately passed; names . . . and often exclamations of exultation or woe . . . were traced on their thin scant pages. . . . We made a hasty selection of such of the leaves, whose writing one, at least of us could understand, and then . . . bade adieu to the dim hypaethric cavern. . . . Since that period

. . . I have been employed in deciphering these sacred remains. . . . I present the public with my latest discoveries in the slight Sibylline pages. Scattered and unconnected as they were, I have been obliged to . . . model the work into a consistent form. But the main substance rests on the divine intuitions which the Cumaean damsel obtained from heaven.[9]

Every feature of this cave journey is significant, especially for the feminist critic who seeks to understand the meaning not just of male but also of female parables of the cave.

To begin with, the sad fact that not Mary Shelley but her male companion is able to recognize the Sibyl's cave and readily to decipher some of the difficult languages in which the sibylline leaves are written suggests the woman writer's own anxieties about her equivocal position in a patriarchal literary culture which often seems to her to enact strange rituals and speak in unknown tongues. The woman may *be* the cave, but — so Mary Shelley's hesitant response suggests — it is the man who knows the cave, who analyzes its meaning, who (like Plato) authors its primary parables, and who even interprets its language, as Gerard Manley Hopkins, that apostle of aesthetic virility,[10] was to do more than half a century after the publication of *The Last Man,* in his sonnet "Spelt from Sibyl's Leaves."

Yet the cave is a female space and it belonged to a female hierophant, the lost Sibyl, the prophetess who inscribed her "divine intuitions" on tender leaves and fragments of delicate bark. For Mary Shelley, therefore, it is intimately connected with both her own artistic authority and her own power of self-creation. A male poet or instructor may guide her to this place, but, as she herself realizes, she and she alone can effectively reconstruct the scattered truth of the Sibyl's leaves. Literally the daughter of a dead and dishonored mother — the powerful feminist Mary Wollstonecraft — Mary Shelley portrays

---

[8]Helen Diner, *Mothers and Amazons,* pp. 16–18. Blake, *For the Sexes: The Gates of Paradise* (from "The Keys . . . of the Gates," 15 & 16, lines 44–50). [Au.]

[9]Mary Shelley, "Author's Introduction" to *The Last Man* (Lincoln: University of Nebraska Press, 1965), pp. 1–4. [Au.]

[10]In an 1886 letter to his friend R. W. Dixon, Hopkins argues that "the male quality is the creative gift." [Ed.]

herself in this parable as figuratively the daughter of the vanished Sybil, the primordial prophetess who mythically conceived all women artists.

That the Sibyl's leaves are now scattered, fragmented, barely comprehensible is thus the central problem Shelley faces in her own art. Earlier in her introduction, she notes that finding the cave was a preliminary problem. She and her companion were misled and misdirected by native guides, she tells us; left alone in one chamber while the guides went for new torches, they "lost" their way in the darkness; ascending in the "wrong" direction, they accidentally stumbled upon the true cave. But the difficulty of this initial discovery merely foreshadows the difficulty of the crucial task of reconstruction, as Shelley shows. For just as the path to the Sibyl's cave has been forgotten, the coherent truth of her leaves has been shattered and scattered, the body of her art dismembered, and, like Anne Finch, she has become a sort of "Cypher," powerless and enigmatic.[11] But while the way to the cave can be "remembered" by accident, the whole meaning of the sibylline leaves can only be remembered through painstaking labor: translation, transcription, and stitchery, re-vision and re-creation.

The specifically sexual texture of these sibylline documents, these scattered leaves and leavings, adds to their profound importance for women. Working on leaves, bark, and "a white filmy substance," the Sibyl literally wrote, and wrote *upon,* the Book of Nature. She had, in other words, a goddess's power of maternal creativity, the sexual/artistic strength that is the female equivalent of the male potential for literary paternity. In her "dim hypaethric cavern" — a dim sea-cave that was nevertheless *open* to the sky — she received her "divine intuitions" through "an aperture" in the "arched dome-like roof" which "let in the light of heaven." On her "raised seat of stone, about the size of a Grecian couch," she *conceived* her art, inscribing it on

leaves and bark from the green world outside. And so fierce are her verses, so truthful her "poetic rhapsodies," that even in deciphering them Shelley exclaims that she feels herself "taken . . . out of a world, which has averted its once benignant face from me, to one glowing with imagination and power." For in recovering and reconstructing the Sibyl's scattered artistic/sexual energy, Shelley comes to recognize that she is discovering and creating — literally *de-ciphering* — her own creative power. "Sometimes I have thought," she modestly confesses, "that, obscure and chaotic as they are, [these translations from the Sibyl's leaves] owe their present form to me, their decipherer. As if we should give to another artist, the painted fragments which form the mosaic copy of Raphael's Transfiguration in St. Peter's; he would put them together in a form, whose mode would be fashioned by his own peculiar mind and talent."[12]

Given all these implications and overtones, it seems to us that the submerged message of Shelley's parable of the cave forms in itself a fourth parable in the series we have been discussing. This last parable is the story of the woman artist who enters the cavern of her own mind and finds there the scattered leaves not only of her own power but of the tradition which might have generated that power. The body of her precursor's art, and thus the body of her own art, lies in pieces around her, dismembered, dis-remembered, disintegrated. How can she remember it and become a member of it, join it and rejoin it, integrate it and in doing so achieve her own integrity, her own selfhood? Surrounded by the ruins of her own tradition, the leavings and unleavings of her spiritual mother's art, she feels — as we noted earlier — like someone suffering from amnesia. Not only did she fail to recognize — that is, to remember — the cavern itself, she no longer knows its languages, its messages, its forms. With Christina Rossetti, she wonders once again "Where are the songs I used to know, / Where are the notes I used to sing?" Bewildered by the incoherence of the fragments she confronts, she cannot help deciding that "I have

[11]In one of her poems, Anne Finch, Countess of Winchilsea, says that, beside three male poets, "we . . . but as Cyphers stand / T' increase your Numbers and to swell th' account / Of your delights which from our charms amount. . . ." [Ed.]

[12]Shelley, p. 4. [Au.]

forgotten everything / I used to know so long ago."

But it is possible, as Mary Shelley's introduction tells us, for the woman poet to reconstruct the shattered tradition that is her matrilineal heritage. Her trip into the cavern of her own mind, despite (or perhaps because of) its falls in darkness, its stumblings, its anxious wanderings, begins the process of re-membering. Even her dialogue with the Romantic poet who guides her (in Mary Shelley's version of the parable) proves useful, for, as Northrop Frye has argued, a revolutionary "mother-goddess myth" which allows power and dignity to women — a myth which is anti-hierarchical, a myth which would liberate the energy of all living creatures — "gained ground" in the Romantic period.[13] Finally, the sibylline messages themselves speak to her, and in speaking to her they both enable her to speak for herself and empower her to speak for the Sibyl. Going "down to the woman" of Fate whom Helen Diner describes, the woman writer recovers herself as a woman of art. Thus, where the traditional male hero makes his "night sea journey" to the center of the earth, the bottom of the mere, the belly of the whale, to slay or be slain by the dragons of darkness, the female artist makes her journey into what Adrienne Rich has called "the cratered night of female memory" to revitalize the darkness, to retrieve what has been lost, to regenerate, reconceive, and give birth.[14]

What she gives birth to is in a sense her own mother goddess and her own mother land. In this parable of the cave it is not the male god Osiris who has been torn apart but his sister, Isis, who has been dismembered and destroyed. Similarly, it is not the male poet Orpheus whose catastrophe we are confronting but his lost bride, Eurydice, whom we find abandoned in the labyrinthine caverns of Hades. Or to put the point another way, this parable suggests that (as the poet H. D. knew) the traditional figure of Isis in search of Osiris is really a figure of Isis in search of herself, and the betrayed Eurydice is really (like Virginia Woolf's "Judith Shakespeare"[15]) the woman poet who never arose from the prison of her "grave cave." Reconstructing Isis and Eurydice, then, the woman artist redefines and recovers the lost Atlantis of her literary heritage, the sunken continent whose wholeness once encompassed and explained all those figures on the horizon who now seem "odd," fragmentary, incomplete — the novelists historians call "singular anomalies," the poets critics call "poetesses," the revolutionary artists patriarchal poets see as "unsexed," monstrous, grotesque. Remembered by the community of which they are and were members, such figures gain their full authority, and their visions begin to seem like conceptions as powerful as the Sibyl's were. Emily Brontë's passionate A. G. A., Jane Lead's Sophia, H. D.'s *bona dea* all have a place in this risen Atlantis which is their mother country, and Jane Eyre's friendship for Diana and Mary Rivers, Aurora Leigh's love for her Italian mother land together with her dream of a new Jerusalem, Emily Dickinson's "mystic green" where women "live aloud," and George Eliot's concept of sisterhood — all these visions and re-visions help define the utopian boundaries of the resurrected continent.

That women have translated their yearnings for motherly or sisterly precursors into visions of such a land is as clear as it is certain that this metaphoric land, like the Sibyl's leaves and the woman writer's power, has been shattered and scattered. Emily Dickinson, a woman artist whose own carefully sewn together "packets" of poetry were — ironically enough — to be fragmented by male editors and female heirs, projected her yearning for this lost female home into the figure of a caged (and female) leopard. Her visionary nostalgia demonstrates that at times the memory of this Atlantis could be as painful for women writers as amnesia about it often was. "Civilization — spurns — the Leopard!" she noted, commenting that "Deserts — never rebuked her Satin — . . . [for] This was the Leopard's nature — Signor — / Need — a keeper — frown?" and adding, poignantly, that we should

---

[13]Northrop Frye, "The Revelation to Eve," in *Paradise Lost: A Tercentenary Tribute*, ed. Balachandra Rajan (Toronto: University of Toronto Press, 1969), p. 46. [Au.]

[14]Rich, "Re-Forming the Crystal," in *Poems: Selected and New*, p. 228. [Au.]

[15]See Woolf, p. 1078. [Ed.]

Pity — the Pard — that left her Asia —
Memories — of Palm —
Cannot be stifled — with Narcotic —
Nor suppressed — with Balm — [16]

Similarly, though she was ostensibly using the symbolism of traditional religion, Christina Rossetti described her pained yearning for a lost, visionary continent like Dickinson's "Asia" in a poem whose title — "Mother Country" — openly acknowledges the real subject:

Oh what is that country
    And where can it be
Not mine own country,
    But dearer far to me?

Yet mine own country,
    If I one day may see
Its spices and cedars,
    Its gold and ivory.

As I lie dreaming
    It rises, that land;
There rises before me
    Its green golden strand,
With the bowing cedars
    And the shining sand;
It sparkles and flashes
    Like a shaken brand. [17]

The ambiguities with which Rossetti describes her own relationship to this land ("Not mine own . . . But dearer far") reflect the uncertainty of the self-definition upon which her vision depends. Is a woman's *mother* country her "own"? Has Mary Shelley a "right" to the Sibyl's leaves? Through what structure of definitions and qualifications can the female artist claim her matrilineal heritage, her birthright of that power which, as Annie Gottlieb's dream asserted, is important to her *because of* her mother? Despite these implicit questions, Rossetti admits that "As I lie dreaming / It rises that land" — rises, significantly, glittering and flashing "like a shaken

brand," rises from "the cratered night of female memory," setting fire to the darkness, dispersing the shadows of the cavern, destroying the archaic structures which enclosed it in silence and gloom.

There is a sense in which, for us, this book is a dream of the rising of Christina Rossetti's "mother country." And there is a sense in which it is an attempt at reconstructing the Sibyl's leaves, leaves which haunt us with the possibility that if we can piece together their fragments the parts will form a whole that tells the story of the career of a single woman artist, a "mother of us all," as Gertrude Stein would put it, a woman whom patriarchal poetics dismembered and whom we have tried to remember. Detached from herself, silenced, subdued, this woman artist tried in the beginning, as we shall see, to write like an angel in the house of fiction: with Jane Austen and Maria Edgeworth, she concealed her own truth behind a decorous and ladylike facade, scattering her real wishes to the winds or translating them into incomprehensible hieroglyphics. But as time passed and her cave-prison became more constricted, more claustrophobic, she "fell" into the gothic/Satanic mode and, with the Brontës and Mary Shelley, she planned mad or monstrous escapes, then dizzily withdrew — with George Eliot and Emily Dickinson — from those open spaces where the scorching presence of the patriarchal sun, whom Dickinson called "the man of noon," emphasized her vulnerability. Since "Creation seemed a mighty Crack" to make her "visible," she took refuge again in the safety of the "dim hypaethric cavern" where she could be alone with herself, with a truth that was hers even in its fragmentation. [18]

Yet through all these stages of her history this mythic woman artist dreamed, like her sibylline ancestress, of a visionary future, a utopian land in which she could be whole and energetic. As tense with longing as the giant "korl woman," a metal sculpture the man named Wolfe carves from flesh-colored pig "refuse" in Rebecca Harding Davis's *Life in the Iron Mills*, she turned

---

[16] Dickinson, *Poems*, J. 492. See also J. 24 ("There is a morn by men unseen") for the metaphor of the "mystic green," and J. 486 ("I was the slightest in the House") for "I could not bear to live — aloud — / The Racket shamed me so — ." [Au.]

[17] *The Poetical Works of Christina G. Rossetti*, 1:116. [Au.]

[18] Dickinson, *Letters*, 1:210 ("man of noon"); J. 891 ("To my quick Ear the leaves conferred . . . Creation seemed a mighty Crack"). [Au.]

with a "wild, eager face," with "the mad, half-despairing gesture of drowning," toward her half-conscious imagination of that future. Eventually she was to realize, with Adrienne Rich, that she was "reading the Parable of the Cave / while living in the cave"; with Sylvia Plath she was to decide that "I am a miner" surrounded by "tears / The earthen womb / Exudes from its dead boredom"; and like Plath she was to hang her cave "with roses," transfiguring it — as the Sibyl did — with artful foliage.[19] But her vision of self-creation was consistently the same vision of connection and resurrection. Like the rebirth of the drowned Atlantans in Ursula Le Guin's utopian "The New Atlantis," this vision often began with an awakening in darkness, a dim awareness of "the whispering thunder from below," and a sense that even if "we could not answer, we knew because we heard, because we felt, because we wept, we knew that we were; and we remembered other voices."[20] Like Mary Shelley's piecing together of the Sybil's leaves, the vision often entailed a subversive transfiguration of those female arts to which de Beauvoir's cave-dwelling seamstresses were condemned into the powerful arts of the underground Weaver Woman, who uses her magical loom to weave a distinctively female "Tapestr[y] of Paradise."[21] And the fact that the cave is and was a place where such visions were possible is itself a sign of the power of the cave and a crucial message of the parable of the cave, a message to remind us that the cave is not just the place from which the past is retrieved but the place where the future is conceived, the "earthen womb" — or, as in Willa Cather's *My Antonia*, the "fruit cave" — from which the new land rises.[22]

Elizabeth Barrett Browning expressed this fi-nal point for the later nineteenth century, as if to carry Mary Shelley's allegorical narrative one step further. Describing a utopian island paradise in which all creatures are "glad and safe. . . . No guns nor springes in my dream," she populated this peaceful land with visionary poets who have withdrawn to a life in dim sea caves — "I repair / To live within the caves: / And near me two or three may dwell, / Whom dreams fantastic please as well," she wrote, and then described her paradise more specifically:

> Long winding caverns, glittering far
> Into a crystal distance!
> Through clefts of which, shall many a star
> Shine clear without resistance!
> And carry down its rays the smell
> Of flowers above invisible.[23]

Here, she declared, her poets — implicitly female or at least matriarchal rather than patriarchal, worshipers of the Romantic mother goddess Frye describes — would create their own literary tradition through a re-vision of the high themes their famous "masculinist" counterparts had celebrated.

> . . . often, by the joy without
> And in us overcome,
> We, through our musing, shall let float
> Such poems — sitting dumb —
> As Pindar might have writ if he
> Had tended sheep in Arcady;
> Or Aeschylus — the pleasant fields
> He died in, longer knowing;
> Or Homer, had men's sins and shields
> Been lost in Meles flowing;
> Or poet Plato, had the undim
> Unsetting Godlight broke on him.

Poet Plato revised by a shining woman of noon, a magical woman like Jane Lead's "Eternal Virgin-Wisdom," with "her Face as the terrible Crystal for brightness!" In a sense that re-vision is the major subject of our book, just as it was the theme of Barrett Browning's earnest, female prayer:

> Choose me the cave most worthy choice,
> To make a place for prayer,

[19]Rebecca Harding Davis, *Life in the Iron Mills, with a Biographical Interpretation by Tillie Olsen* (Old Westbury: Feminist Press Reprint, 1972), pp. 24, 32–33, 65; "Living in the Cave," *Adrienne Rich's Poetry*, p. 72; Plath, "Nick and the Candlestick," *Ariel*, pp. 33–34. [Au.]

[20]Ursula K. Le Guin, "The New Atlantis," in *The New Atlantis and Other Novellas of Science Fiction*, ed. Robert Silverberg (New York: Hawthorn, 1975), p. 75. [Au.]

[21]Dickinson, *Poems*, J. 278. [Au.]

[22]Willa Cather, *My Antonia* (Boston: Houghton Mifflin, 1918), pp. 337–39. [Au.]

[23]"An Island," *The Poetical Works of Elizabeth Barrett Browning*, pp. 332–35. [Au.]

And I will choose a praying voice
　　To pour our spirits there.

And the answer to Barrett Browning's prayer might have been given by the sibylline voice of

Jane Lead's Virgin-Wisdom, or Sophia, the true goddess of the cave: "for out of my Womb thou shalt be brought forth after the manner of a Spirit, Conceived and Born again."

# Annette Kolodny

b. 1941

*Annette Kolodny's career is an exemplary combination of feminist scholarship and political activism. Born and educated in New York City, she was briefly on the editorial staff at* Newsweek *(1962–63) before attending the University of California at Berkeley, where she took an M.A. (1965) and a Ph.D. (1969) in American literature. From 1969 to 1970 she taught at Yale before removing to Canada with her husband, who had been denied conscientious objector status and faced conscription. At the University of British Columbia from 1970 to 1974, Kolodny designed western Canada's first accredited, multidisciplinary women's studies program. Returning to the United States in 1974, Kolodny organized a women's studies program at the University of New Hampshire.* Her The Lay of the Land: Metaphor as Experience and History in American Life and Letters *appeared in 1975. Denied promotion and tenure at New Hampshire, Kolodny filed an anti-Semitism and sexism suit against the university and in 1980 was accorded a landmark out-of-court settlement, a portion of which she used to set up a legal fund and a task force against discrimination. Kolodny stayed in New Hampshire to work on* The Land Before Her: Fantasy and Experience of the American Frontiers, 1630–1860 *(published in 1984) before joining the faculty of the University of Maryland (1982–83) and then (in 1983) of Rensselaer Polytechnic Institute, where she is professor of literature. The third volume of her "Land" trilogy is in the works, as is* Dancing through the Minefield, *a social history of the new feminism. "A Map for Rereading: Gender and the Interpretation of Literary Texts" originally appeared in* New Literary History *11 (1980).*

# A Map for Rereading

## Gender and the Interpretation of Literary Texts

To a generation still in the process of divorcing itself from the New Critics' habit of bracketing off any text as an entity in itself, as though "it could be read, understood, and criticized entirely in its own terms,"[1] Harold Bloom has pro-

posed a dialectical theory of influence between poets and poets, as well as between poems and poems, which, in essence, does away with the static notion of a fixed or knowable text. As he argued in *A Map of Misreading* in 1975, "a poem is a response to a poem, as a poet is a response to a poet, or a person to his parent." Thus, for Bloom, "poems . . . are neither about 'subjects' nor about 'themselves.' They are necessarily about *other poems*."[2]

[1] Albert William Levi, *"De Interpretatione:* Cognition and Context in the History of Ideas," *Critical Inquiry* 3 (Fall 1976): 164. [Au.]

[2] Harold Bloom, *A Map of Misreading* (New York: Oxford

To read or to know a poem, according to Bloom, engages the reader in an attempt to map the psychodynamic relations by which the poet at hand has willfully misunderstood the work of some precursor (either single or composite) in order to correct, rewrite, or appropriate the prior poetic vision as his own. As first introduced in *The Anxiety of Influence* in 1973, the resultant "wholly different practical criticism" gives up "the failed enterprise of seeking to 'understand' any single poem as an entity in itself" and pursues instead "the quest of learning to read any poem as its poet's deliberate misinterpretation, *as a poet,* of a precursor poem or of poetry in general."[3] What one deciphers in the process of reading, then, is not any discrete entity but, rather, a complex relational event, "itself a synecdoche for a larger whole including other texts."[4] "Reading a text is necessarily the reading of a whole system of texts," Bloom explains in *Kabbalah and Criticism,* "and meaning is always wandering around between texts."[5]

To help purchase assent for this "wholly different practical criticism," Bloom asserted an identity between critics and poets as coequal participants in the same "belated and all-but-impossible act" of reading (which, as he hastens to explain in *A Map of Misreading,* "if strong is always a misreading"[6]). As it is a drama of epic proportions, in Bloom's terms, when the ephebe poet attempts to appropriate and then correct a precursor's meaning, so, too, for the critic, his own inevitable misreadings, or *misprisions,* are no less heroic — nor any the less creative.

"Poets' misinterpretations or poems" may be "more drastic than critics' misinterpretations or criticism," Bloom admits, but since he recognizes no such thing as "interpretations but only misinterpretations," all criticism is necessarily elevated to a species of "prose poetry."[7] The critic's performance, thereby, takes place as one more "act of misprision [which] displaces an earlier act of misprision"–presumably the poet's or perhaps that of a prior critic; and, in this sense, the critic participates in that same act of "defensive warfare" before his own critical forebears, or even before the poet himself, as the poet presumably enacted before his poetic father/precursor.[8] Their legacy, whether as poetry or as "prose poetry" criticism, consequently establishes the strong survivors of these psychic battles as figures whom others, in the future, will need to overcome in their turn: "A poet is strong because poets after him must work to evade him. A critic is strong if his readings similarly provoke other readings."[9] It is unquestionably Bloom's most brilliant rhetorical stroke, persuading not so much by virtue of the logic of his argument as by the pleasure his (intended and mostly male) readership will take in the discovery that their own activity replicates the psychic adventures of The Poet, every critic's *figura* of heroism.[10]

What is left out of account, however, is the fact that whether we speak of poets and critics "reading" texts or writers "reading" (and thereby recording for us) the world, we are calling attention to interpretative strategies that are learned,

---

University Press, 1975), p. 18. [Au.] See Bloom, p. 705. [Ed.]

[3] Harold Bloom, *The Anxiety of Influence: A Theory of Poetry* (New York: Oxford University Press, 1973), p. 43. [Au.]

[4] Harold Bloom, *Kabbalah and Criticism* (New York: Seabury Press, 1975), p. 106. This concept is further refined in his *Poetry and Repression: Revisionism from Blake to Stevens* (New Haven, Conn.: Yale University Press, 1976), p. 26, where Bloom describes poems as "defensive processes in constant change, which is to say that poems themselves are *acts of reading.* A poem is . . . a fierce, proleptic debate *with itself,* as well as with precursor poems." [Au.]

[5] Bloom, *Kabbalah and Criticism,* pp. 107–8. [Au.]

[6] Bloom, *Map of Misreading,* p. 3. [Au.]

[7] Bloom, *Anxiety of Influence,* pp. 94–95. [Au.]

[8] Bloom, *Kabbalah and Criticism,* pp. 125, 104, 108. [Au.]

[9] Ibid., p. 125; by way of example, and with a kind of Apollonian modesty, Bloom demonstrates his own propensities for misreading, placing himself amid the excellent company of those other Super Misreaders, Blake, Shelley, C. S. Lewis, Charles Williams, and T. S. Eliot (all of whom misread Milton's Satan), and only regrets "that the misreading of Blake and Shelley by Yeats is a lot stronger than the misreading of Blake and Shelley by Bloom" (pp. 125–26). [Au.]

[10] In *Poetry and Repression,* p. 18, Bloom explains that "by 'reading' I intend to mean the work both of poet and of critic, who themselves move from dialectic irony to synecdochal representation as they confront the text before them." [Au.]

historically determined, and thereby necessarily gender-inflected. As others have elsewhere questioned the adequacy of Bloom's paradigm of poetic influence to explain the production of poetry by women,[11] so now I propose to examine analogous limitations in his model for the reading — and hence critical — process (since both, after all, derive from his revisionist rendering of the Freudian family romance). To begin with, to locate that "meaning" which "is always wandering around between texts,"[12] Bloom assumes a community of readers (and, thereby, critics) who know that same "whole system of texts" within which the specific poet at hand has enacted his "misprision." The canonical sense of a shared and coherent literary tradition is therefore essential to the utility of Bloom's paradigm of literary influence as well as to his notions of reading (and misreading). "What happens if one tries to write, or to teach, or to think or even to read without the sense of a tradition?" Bloom asks in *A Map of Misreading*. "Why," as he himself well understands, "nothing at all happens, just nothing. You cannot write or teach or think or even read without imitation, and what you imitate is what another person has done, that person's writing or teaching or thinking or reading. Your relation to what informs that person *is* tradition, for tradition is influence that extends past one generation, a carrying-over of influence."[13]

So long as the poems and poets he chooses for scrutiny participate in the "continuity that began in the sixth century B.C. when Homer first became a schoolbook for the Greeks,"[14] Bloom

has a great deal to tell us about the carrying over of literary influence; where he must remain silent is where carrying over takes place among readers and writers who in fact have been, or at least have experienced themselves as, cut off and alien from that dominant tradition. Virginia Woolf made the distinction vividly over a half-century ago, in *A Room of One's Own,* when she described being barred entrance, because of her sex, to a "famous library" in which was housed, among others, a Milton manuscript. Cursing the "Oxbridge" edifice, "venerable and calm, with all its treasures safe locked within its breast," she returns to her room at the inn later that night, still pondering "how unpleasant it is to be locked out, and I thought how it is worse perhaps to be locked in; and, thinking of the safety and prosperity of the one sex and of the poverty and insecurity of the other and of the effect of tradition and of the lack of tradition upon the mind of a writer."[15] And, she might have added, on the mind of a reader as well. For while my main concern here is with reading (albeit largely and perhaps imperfectly defined), I think it worth noting that there exists an intimate interaction between readers and writers in and through which each defines for the other what s/he is about. "The effect . . . of the lack of tradition upon the mind of a writer" will communicate itself, in one way or another, to her readers; and, indeed, may respond to her readers' sense of exclusion from high (or highbrow) culture.

An American instance provides perhaps the best example. Delimited by the lack of formal or classical education, and constrained by the social and aesthetic norms of their day to conceptualizing authorship "as a profession rather than a calling, as work and not art,"[16] the vastly popular women novelists of the so-called feminine fifties often enough, and somewhat defensively, made a virtue of their sad necessities by invoking an audience of readers for whom aspirations to "lit-

---

[11]See, for example, Joanne Feit Diehl's attempt to adapt the Bloomian model to the psychodynamics of women's poetic production in "'Come Slowly — Eden': An Exploration of Women Poets and Their Muse," *Signs* 3 (Spring 1978): 572–87; and the objections to that adaptation raised by Lillian Faderman and Louise Bernikow in their Comments, *Signs* 4 (Fall 1978): 188–91 and 191–95, respectively. More recently, Sandra M. Gilbert and Susan Gubar have tried to correct the omission of women writers from Bloom's male-centered literary history in *The Madwoman in the Attic: The Woman Writer and the Nineteenth-Century Literary Imagination* (New Haven, Conn.: Yale University Press, 1979). [Au.] See Gilbert and Gubar, p. 1119. [Ed.]

[12]Bloom, *Kabbalah and Criticism*, pp. 107–8. [Au.]

[13]Bloom, *Map of Misreading*, p. 32. [Au.]

[14]Ibid., pp. 33–34. [Au.]

[15]Virginia Woolf, *A Room of One's Own* (1928; reprint ed., Baltimore: Penguin Books, 1972), pp. 9–10, 25–26. [Au.] See Woolf, p. 1078. [Ed.]

[16]Nina Baym, *Woman's Fiction: A Guide to Novels By and About Women in America, 1820–1870* (Ithaca, N.Y.: Cornell University Press, 1978), p. 32. [Au.]

erature" were as inappropriate as they were for the writer. As Nina Baym remarks in her recent study *Woman's Fiction,* "often the women deliberately and even proudly disavowed membership in an artistic fraternity." "'Mine is a story for the table and arm-chair under the reading lamp in the livingroom, and not for the library shelves,'" Baym quotes Marion Harland from the introduction to Harland's autobiography; and then, at greater length, Baym cites Fanny Fern's dedicatory pages to her novel *Rose Clark:*

> When the frost curtains the windows, when the wind whistles fiercely at the key-hole, when the bright fire glows, and the tea-tray is removed, and father in his slippered feet lolls in his arm-chair; and mother with her nimble needle "makes auld claes look amaist as weel as new," and grandmamma draws closer to the chimney-corner, and Tommy with his plate of chestnuts nestles contentedly at her feet; then let my unpretending story be read. For such an hour, for such an audience, was it written.
> Should any *dictionary on legs* rap inopportunely at the door for admittance, send him away to the groaning shelves of some musty library, where "literature" lies embalmed, with its stony eyes, fleshless joints, and ossified heart, in faultless preservation.[17]

If a bit overdone, prefaces like these nonetheless point up the self-consciousness with which writers like Fern and Harland perceived themselves as excluded from the dominant literary tradition and as writing for an audience of readers similarly excluded. To quote Baym again, these women "were expected to write specifically for their own sex and within the tradition of their woman's culture rather than within the Great Tradition. They never presented themselves as followers in the footsteps of Milton or Spenser."[18]

On the one hand, of course, increased literacy (if not substantially improved conditions of education) marked the generation of American women at midcentury, opening a vast market for a literature which would treat the contexts of their lives — the sewing circle rather than the whaling ship, the nursery instead of the lawyer's office — as functional symbols of the human condition.[19] On the other hand, while this vast new audience must certainly be credited with shaping the features of what then became popular women's fiction, it is also the case that the writers in their turn both responded to and helped to formulate their readers' tastes and habits. And both together, I would suggest, found this a means of accepting (or at least coping with) the barred entryway that was to distress Virginia Woolf so in the next century. But these facts of our literary history also suggest that from the 1850s on, in America at least, the meanings "wandering around between texts" were wandering around somewhat different groups of texts where male and female readers were concerned.[20] So that with the advent of women "who wished to be regarded as artists rather than careerists,"[21] toward the end of the nineteenth century, there arose the critical problem with which we are still plagued and which Bloom so determinedly ignores: the problem of reading any text as "a synecdoche for a larger whole including other texts" when that necessarily assumed "whole system of texts" in which it is embedded is foreign to one's reading knowledge.

The appearance of Kate Chopin's novel *The Awakening* in 1899, for example, perplexed readers familiar with her earlier (and intentionally "regional") short stories not so much because it turned away from themes or subject matter implicit in her earlier work, nor even less because it dealt with female sensuality and extramarital sexuality, but because her elaboration of those

[17]See ibid., pp. 32–33. [Au.]
[18]Ibid., p. 178. [Au.]

[19]I paraphrase rather freely here from some of Baym's acutely perceptive and highly suggestive remarks, ibid., p. 14. [Au.]
[20]The problem of audience is complicated by the fact that in nineteenth-century America distinct classes of so-called highbrow and lowbrow readers were emerging, cutting across sex and class lines; and, for each sex, distinctly separate "serious" and "popular" reading materials were also being marketed. Full discussion, however, is beyond the scope of this essay. In its stead, I direct the reader to Henry Nash Smith's clear and concise summation in the introductory chapter to his *Democracy and the Novel: Popular Resistance to Classic American Writers* (New York: Oxford University Press, 1978), pp. 1–15. [Au.]
[21]Baym, *Woman's Fiction,* p. 178. [Au.]

materials deviated radically from the accepted norms of women's fiction out of which her audience so largely derived its expectations. The nuances and consequences of passion and individual temperament, after all, fairly define the focus of most of her preceding fictions. "That the book is strong and that Miss Chopin has a keen knowledge of certain phases of feminine character will not be denied," wrote the anonymous reviewer for the *Chicago Times-Herald.* What marked an unacceptable "new departure" for this critic, then, was the impropriety of Chopin's focus on material previously edited out of the popular genteel novels by and about women which, somewhat inarticulately, s/he translated into the accusation that Chopin had entered "the overworked field of sex fiction."[22]

Charlotte Perkins Gilman's initial difficulty in seeing "The Yellow Wallpaper" into print repeated the problem, albeit in a somewhat different context: for her story located itself not as any deviation from a previous tradition of women's fiction but, instead, as a continuation of a genre popularized by Poe. And insofar as Americans had earlier learned to follow the fictive processes of aberrant perception and mental breakdown in *his* work, they should have provided Gilman, one would imagine, with a ready-made audience for *her* protagonist's progressively debilitating fantasies of entrapment and liberation. As they had entered popular fiction by the end of the nineteenth century, however, the linguistic markers for those processes were at once heavily male-gendered and highly idiosyncratic, having more to do with individual temperament than with social or cultural situations per se. As a result, it would appear that the reading strategies by which cracks in ancestral walls and suggestions of unchecked masculine willfulness were immediately noted as both symbolically and semantically relevant did not, for some reason, necessarily *carry over* to "the nursery at the top of the house" with its windows barred, nor even less to the forced submission of the woman who must "take great

pains to control myself" before her physician husband.[23]

A reader today seeking meaning in the way Harold Bloom outlines that process might note, of course, a fleeting resemblance between the upstairs chamber in Gilman — with its bed nailed to the floor, its windows barred, and metal rings fixed to the walls — and Poe's evocation of the dungeon chambers of Toledo; in fact, a credible argument might be made for reading "The Yellow Wallpaper" as Gilman's willful and purposeful misprision of "The Pit and the Pendulum." Both stories, after all, involve a sane mind entrapped in an insanity-inducing situation. Gilman's "message" might then be that the equivalent revolution by which the speaking voice of the Poe tale is released to both sanity and freedom is unavailable to her heroine. No *deus ex machina,* no General Lasalle triumphantly entering the city, no "outstretched arm" to prevent Gilman's protagonist from falling into her own internal "abyss" is conceivable, given the rules of the social context in which Gilman's narrative is embedded. When gender is taken into account, then, so this interpretation would run, Gilman is saying that the nature of the trap envisioned must be understood as qualitatively different, and so too the possible escape routes.

Contemporary readers of "The Yellow Wallpaper," however, were apparently unprepared to make such connections. Those fond of Poe could not easily transfer their sense of mental derangement to the mind of a comfortable middle-class wife and mother; and those for whom the woman in the home was a familiar literary character were hard pressed to comprehend so extreme an anatomy of the psychic price she paid. Horace Scudder, the editor of the *Atlantic Monthly* who first rejected the story, wrote only that "I could not forgive myself if I made others as miserable as I have made myself!" (Hedges, p. 40). And even William Dean Howells, who found the story "chilling" and admired it sufficiently to reprint it

[22]From "Books of the Day," *Chicago Times-Herald,* June 1, 1899, p. 9; excerpted in Kate Chopin, *The Awakening,* ed. Margaret Culley (New York: W. W. Norton, 1976), p. 149. [Au.]

[23]Charlotte Perkins Gilman, *The Yellow Wallpaper,* Afterword by Elaine R. Hedges (Old Westbury, N.Y.: Feminist Press, 1973), pp. 12, 11. Page references to this edition will henceforth be cited parenthetically in the text, with references to Hedges's excellent Afterword preceded by her name. [Au.]

in 1920, some twenty-eight years after its first publication (in the *New England Magazine* of May 1892), like most readers either failed to notice or neglected to report "the connection between the insanity and the sex, or sexual role, of the victim" (Hedges, p. 41). For readers at the turn of the century, then, that "meaning" which "is always wandering around between texts" had as yet failed to find connective pathways linking the fanciers of Poe to the devotees of popular women's fiction, or the shortcut between Gilman's short story and the myriad published feminist analyses of the ills of society (some of them written by Gilman herself). Without such connective contexts, Poe continued as a well-traveled road, while Gilman's story, lacking the possibility of further influence, became a literary dead end.

In one sense, by hinting at an audience of male readers as ill-equipped to follow the symbolic significance of the narrator's progressive breakdown as was her doctor-husband to diagnose properly the significance of his wife's fascination with the wallpaper's patternings; and by predicating a female readership as yet unprepared for texts which mirrored back, with symbolic exemplariness, certain patterns underlying their empirical reality, "The Yellow Wallpaper" anticipated its own reception. For insofar as writing and reading represent linguistically based interpretative strategies — the first for the recording of a reality (that has obviously, in a sense, already been "read") and the second for the deciphering of that recording (and thus also the further decoding of a prior imputed reality) — the wife's progressive descent into madness provides a kind of commentary upon, indeed is revealed in terms of, the sexual politics inherent in the manipulation of those strategies. We are presented at the outset with a protagonist who, ostensibly for her own good, is denied both activities and who, in the course of accommodating herself to that deprivation, comes more and more to experience her self as a text which can neither get read nor recorded.

In his doubly authoritative role as both husband and doctor, John not only appropriates the interpretative processes of reading — diagnosing his wife's illness and thereby selecting what may be understood of her "meaning"; reading to her rather than allowing her to read for herself — but, as well, he determines what may get written and hence communicated. For her part, the protagonist avers, she does not agree with her husband's ideas: "Personally, I believe that congenial work, with excitement and change, would do me good." But given the fact of her marriage to "a physician of high standing" who "assures friends and relatives that there is really nothing the matter with one but temporary nervous depression — a slight hysterical tendency — what is one to do?" she asks. Since her husband (and by extension the rest of the world) will not heed what she says of herself, she attempts instead to communicate it to "this . . . dead paper . . . a great relief to my mind." But John's insistent opposition gradually erodes even this outlet for her since, as she admits, "it *does* exhaust me a good deal — having to be so sly about it, or else meet with heavy opposition" (p. 10). At the sound of his approach, following upon her first attempt to describe "those sprawling flamboyant patterns" in the wallpaper, she declares, "There comes John, and I must put this away, — he hates to have me write a word" (p. 13).

Successively isolated from conversational exchanges, prohibited free access to pen and paper, and thus increasingly denied what Jean Ricardou has called "the local exercise of syntax and vocabulary,"[24] the protagonist of "The Yellow Wallpaper" experiences the extreme extrapolation of those linguistic tools to the processes of perception and response. In fact, it follows directly upon a sequence in which (1) she acknowledges that John's opposition to her writing has begun to make "the effort . . . greater than the relief"; (2) John refuses to let her "go and make a visit to Cousin Henry and Julia"; and (3) as a kind of punctuation mark to that denial, John carries her upstairs, "and laid me on the bed, and sat by me and read to me till it tired my head." It is after these events, I repeat, that the narrator first makes out the dim shape lurking "behind the outside pattern" in the wallpaper: "it is like a

[24]Jean Ricardou, "Composition Discomposed," trans. Erica Freiberg, *Critical Inquiry* 3 (Fall 1976): 90. [Au.]

woman stooping down and creeping" (pp. 21–22).

From that point on, the narrator progressively gives up the attempt to *record* her reality and instead begins to *read* it — as symbolically adumbrated in her compulsion to discover a consistent and coherent pattern amid "the sprawling outlines" of the wallpaper's apparently "pointless pattern" (pp. 20, 19). Selectively emphasizing one section of the pattern while repressing others, reorganizing and regrouping past impressions into newer, more fully realized configurations — as one might with any complex formal text — the speaking voice becomes obsessed with her quest for meaning, jealous even of her husband's or his sister's momentary interest in the paper. Having caught her sister-in-law "with her hand on it once," the narrator declares, "I know she was studying that pattern, and I am determined that nobody shall find it out but myself!" (p. 27). As the pattern changes with the changing light in the room, so too do her interpretations of it. And what is not quite so apparent by daylight becomes glaringly so at night: "At night in any kind of light, in twilight, candle light, lamplight, and worst of all by moonlight, it becomes bars! The outside pattern I mean, and the woman behind it is as plain as can be." "By daylight," in contrast (like the protagonist herself), "she is subdued, quiet" (p. 26).

As she becomes wholly taken up with the exercise of these interpretative strategies, so too, she claims, her life "is very much more exciting now than it used to be. You see I have something more to expect, to look forward to, to watch" (p. 27). What she is watching, of course, is her own psyche writ large; and the closer she comes to "reading" in the wallpaper the underlying if unacknowledged patterns of her real-life experience, the less frequent becomes that delicate oscillation between surrender to or involvement in and the more distanced observation of developing meaning. Slowly but surely the narrative voice ceases to distinguish itself from the woman in the wallpaper pattern, finally asserting that "I don't want anybody to get that woman out at night but myself" (p. 31), and concluding with a confusion of pronouns that merges into a grammatical statement of identity:

As soon as it was moonlight and that poor thing began to crawl and shake the pattern, I got up and ran to help her.

I pulled and *she* shook, and *I* shook and *she* pulled, and before morning *we* had peeled off yards of that paper. (p. 32; my italics)

She is, in a sense, now totally surrendered to what is quite literally her own text — or rather, her self as text. But in decoding its (or her) meaning, what she has succeeded in doing is discovering the symbolization of her own untenable and unacceptable reality. To escape that reality she attempts the destruction of the paper which seemingly encodes it: the pattern of bars entrapping the creeping woman. "'I've got out at last,' said I, 'in spite of you and Jane. I've pulled off most of the paper, so you can't put me back!'" (p. 36). Their paper pages may be torn and moldy (as is, in fact, the smelly wallpaper), but the meaning of texts is not so easily destroyed. Liberation here is liberation only into madness: for in decoding her own projections onto the paper, the protagonist has managed merely to reencode them once more, and now more firmly than ever, within.

With the last paragraphs of the story, John faints away — presumably in shock at his wife's now totally delusional state. He has repeatedly misdiagnosed, or misread, the heavily edited behavior with which his wife has presented herself to him; and never once has he divined what his wife sees in the wallpaper. But given his freedom to read (or, in this case, misread) books, people, and the world as he chooses, he is hardly forced to discover for himself so extreme a text. To exploit Bloom's often useful terminology once again, then, Gilman's story represents not so much an object for the recurrent misreadings, or misprisions, of readers and critics (though this, of course, continues to occur) as an exploration, within itself, of the gender-inflected interpretative strategies responsible for our mutual misreadings, and even horrific misprisions, across sex lines. If neither male nor female reading audiences were prepared to decode properly "The Yellow Wallpaper," even less, Gilman understood, were they prepared to comprehend one another.

It is unfortunate that Gilman's story was so

quickly relegated to the backwaters of our literary landscape because, coming as it did at the end of the nineteenth century, it spoke to a growing concern among American women who would be serious writers: it spoke, that is, to their strong sense of writing out of nondominant or subcultural traditions (both literary and nonliterary), coupled with an acute sensitivity to the fact that since women and men learn to read different worlds, different groups of texts are available to their reading and writing strategies. Had "The Yellow Wallpaper" been able to stand as a potential precursor for the generation of subsequent corrections and revisions, then, as in Bloom's paradigm, it might have made possible a form of fiction by women capable not only of commenting upon but even of overcoming that impasse. That it did not — nor did any other woman's fiction become canonical in the United States[25] — meant that, again and again, each woman who took up the pen had to confront anew her bleak premonition that, both as writers and as readers, women too easily became isolated islands of symbolic significance, available only to, and decipherable only by, one another.[26] If any Bloomian "meaning" wanders around between women's texts, therefore, it must be precisely this shared apprehension.

On the face of it such statements should appear nothing less than commonsensical, especially to those most recent theorists of reading who combine an increased attentiveness to the meaning-making role of the reader in the deciphering of texts with a recognition of the links between our "reading" of texts and our "reading"

of the world and one another. Among them, Bloom himself seems quite clearly to understand this when, in *Kabbalah and Criticism*, he declares: "That which you are, that only can you read."[27] Extrapolating from his description of the processes involved in the reading of literary texts to a larger comment on our ability to take in or decipher those around us, Wolfgang Iser has lately theorized that "we can only make someone else's thought into an absorbing theme for ourselves, provided the virtual background of our own personality can adapt to it."[28] Anticipating such pronouncements in almost everything they have been composing for over a hundred years now, the women who wrote fiction, most especially, translated these observations into the structures of their stories by invoking that single feature which critics like Iser and Bloom still manage so resolutely to ignore: and that is, the crucial importance of the *sex* of the "interpreter" in that process which Nelly Furman has called "the active attribution of significance to formal signifiers."[29] Antedating both Bloom and Iser by over fifty years, for example, Susan Keating Glaspell's 1917 short story "A Jury of Her Peers" explores the necessary (but generally ignored) gender marking which *must* constitute any definition of "peers" in the complex process of unraveling truth or meaning.[30]

The opening paragraph of Glaspell's story serves, essentially, to alert the reader to the significations to follow: Martha Hale, interrupted at her kitchen chores, must drop "everything right where it was" in order to hurry off with her husband and the others. As she does so, her eye makes "a scandalized sweep of her kitchen," noting with distress that "in no shape for leaving:

[25]The possible exception here is Harriet Beecher Stowe's *Uncle Tom's Cabin; or, Life Among the Lowly* (1852). [Au.]

[26]If, to some of the separatist advocates in our current wave of New Feminism, this sounds like a wholly acceptable, even happy circumstance, we must nonetheless understand that, for earlier generations of women artists, acceptance within male precincts conferred the mutually understood marks of success and, in some quarters, vitally needed access to publishing houses, serious critical attention, and even financial independence. That this was *not* the case for the writers of domestic fictions around the middle of the nineteenth century was a fortunate but anomalous circumstance. Insofar as our artist-mothers were separatist, therefore, it was the result of impinging cultural contexts and not (often) of their own choosing. [Au.]

[27]Bloom, *Kabbalah and Criticism*, p. 96. [Au.]

[28]Wolfgang Iser, *The Implied Reader: Patterns of Communication in Prose Fiction from Bunyan to Beckett* (Baltimore: John Hopkins University Press, 1974), p. 293. [Au.] See Iser in Ch. 7. [Ed.]

[29]Nelly Furman, "The Study of Women and Language: Comment on Vol. 3, No. 3," *Signs* 4 (Fall 1978): 184. [Au.]

[30]First published in *Every Week*, March 15, 1917, the story was then collected in *Best Short Stories of 1917*, ed. Edward O'Brien (London, 1917). My source for the text is Mary Anne Ferguson's *Images of Women in Literature* (Boston: Houghton Mifflin, 1973), pp. 370–85. [Au.]

her bread all ready for mixing, half the flour sifted and half unsifted." The point, of course, is that highly unusual circumstances demand this of her; "it was no ordinary thing that called her away." When she seats herself "in the big two-seated buggy" alongside her impatient farmer husband, the sheriff and his wife, and the country attorney, the story proper begins.

All five drive to a neighboring farm where a murder has been committed — the farmer strangled, his wife already arrested. The men intend to seek clues to the motive for the crime, while the women are, ostensibly, simply to gather together the few necessities, required by the wife incarcerated in the town jail. Immediately upon approaching the place, however, the very act of perception becomes sex-coded: the men look at the house only to talk "about what had happened," while the women note the geographical topography which makes it, repeatedly in the narrative, "a lonesome-looking place." Once inside, the men "go upstairs first — then out to the barn and around there" in their search for clues (even though the actual crime took place in the upstairs master bedroom), while the women are left to the kitchen and parlor. Convinced as they are of "the insignificance of kitchen things," the men cannot properly attend to what these might reveal and, instead, seek elsewhere for "a clue to the motive," so necessary if the county attorney is to make his case. Indeed, it is the peculiar irony of the story that although the men never question their attribution of guilt to Minnie Foster, they nonetheless cannot meaningfully interpret this farm wife's world — her kitchen and parlor. And, arrogantly certain that the women would not even "know a clue if they did come upon it," they thereby leave the discovery of the clues, and the consequent unraveling of the motive, to those who do, in fact, command the proper interpretative strategies.

Exploiting the information sketched into the opening, Glaspell has the neighbor, Mrs. Hale, and the sheriff's wife, Mrs. Peters, note, among the supposedly insignificant kitchen things, the unusual, and on a farm unlikely, remnants of kitchen chores left "half done," denoting an interruption of some serious nature. Additionally, where the men could discern no signs of "anger

— or sudden feeling" to substantiate a motive, the women comprehend the implications of some "fine, even sewing" gone suddenly awry, "as if she didn't know what she was about!" Finally, of course, the very drabness of the house, the miserliness of the husband to which it attests, the old and broken stove, the patchwork that has become Minnie Foster's wardrobe — all these make the women uncomfortably aware that to acknowledge fully the meaning of what they are seeing is "to get her own house to turn against her!" Discovery by discovery, they destroy the mounting evidence — evidence which the men, at any rate, cannot recognize as such; and, sealing the bond between them as conspirators in saving Minnie Foster, they hide from the men the canary with its neck broken, the penultimate clue to the strangling of a husband who had so systematically destroyed all life, beauty, and music in his wife's environment.

Opposing against one another male and female realms of meaning and activity — the barn and the kitchen — Glaspell's narrative not only invites a semiotic analysis but, indeed, performs that analysis for us. If the absent Minnie Foster is the "transmitter" or "sender" in this schema, then only the women are competent "receivers" or "readers" of her "message," since they alone share not only her context (the supposed insignificance of kitchen things) but, as a result, the conceptual patterns which make up her world. To those outside the shared systems of quilting and knotting, roller towels and bad stoves, with all their symbolic significations, these may appear trivial, even irrelevant to meaning; but to those within the system, they comprise the totality of the message: in this case, a reordering of who in fact has been murdered and, with that, what has constituted the real crime in the story.

For while the two women who visit Minnie Foster's house slowly but surely decipher the symbolic significance of her action — causing her husband's neck to be broken because he had earlier broken her canary's neck — the narrative itself functions, for the reader, as a further decoding of what that symbolic action says about itself. The essential crime in the story, we come to realize, has been the husband's inexorable strangulation, over the years, of Minnie Foster's spirit and personality; and the culpable criminality is the complicity of the women who had permitted the isolation and the loneliness to dominate Minnie Foster's existence: "'I wish I had come over to see Minnie Foster sometimes,'" declares her neighbor guiltily. "'I can see now — ' She did not put it into words."

> "I wish you'd seen Minnie Foster [says Mrs. Hale to the sheriff's wife] when she wore a white dress with blue ribbons, and stood up there in the choir and sang."
> The picture of that girl, the fact that she lived neighbor to that girl for twenty years, and had let her die for lack of life, was suddenly more than she could bear.
> "Oh, I *wish* I'd come over here once in a while!" she cried. "That was a crime! That was a crime! Who's going to punish that?"

The recognition is itself, of course, a kind of punishment. With it comes, as well, another recognition, as Mrs. Peters reveals experiences in her own life of analogous isolation, desperate loneliness, and brutality at the hands of a male. Finally they conclude: "We all go through the same things — it's all just a different kind of the same thing! If it weren't — why do you and I *understand?* Why do we *know* — what we know this minute?" By this point the narrative emphasis has shifted: to understand why it is that they know what they now know is for these women to recognize the profoundly sex-linked world of meaning which they inhabit; to discover how specialized is their ability to read that world is to discover anew their own shared isolation within it.

While neither the Gilman nor the Glaspell story necessarily excludes the male as reader — indeed, both in a way are directed specifically at educating him to become a better reader — they do nonetheless insist that, however inadvertently, he is a *different kind* of reader and that, where women are concerned, he is often an inadequate reader. In the first instance, because the husband cannot properly diagnose his wife or attend to her reality, the result is horrific: the wife descends into madness. In the second, because the men cannot even recognize as such the very clues for which they search, the ending is a happy one:

Minnie Foster is to be set free, no motive having been discovered by which to prosecute her. In both, however, the same point is being made: lacking familiarity with the women's imaginative universe, that universe within which their acts are signs,[31] the men in these stories can neither read nor comprehend the meanings of the women closest to them — and this in spite of the apparent sharing of a common language. It is, in short, a fictive rendering of the dilemma of the woman writer. For while we may all agree that in our daily conversational exchanges men and women speak more or less meaningfully and effectively with one another, thus fostering the illusion of a wholly shared common language, it is also the case that where figurative usage is invoked — that usage which often enough marks the highly specialized language of literature — it "can be inaccessible to all but those who share information about one another's knowledge, beliefs, intentions, and attitudes."[32] Symbolic representations, in other words, depend on a fund of shared recognitions and potential inference. For their intended impact to take hold in the reader's imagination, the author simply must, like Minnie Foster, be able to call upon a shared context with her audience; where she cannot, or dare not, she may revert to silence, to the imitation of male forms, or, like the narrator in "The Yellow Wallpaper," to total withdrawal and isolation into madness.

It may be objected of course, that I have somewhat stretched my argument so as to conflate (or perhaps confuse?) *all* interpretative strategies with language processes, specifically reading. But in each instance, it is the survival of the *woman as text* — Gilman's narrator and Glaspell's Minnie Foster — that is at stake; and the competence of her reading audience alone determines the outcome. Thus, in my view, both stories intentionally function as highly specialized language acts (called "literature") which examine

---

[31]I here paraphrase Clifford Geertz, *The Interpretation of Cultures* (New York: Basic Books, 1973), p. 13, and specifically direct the reader to the parable from Wittgenstein quoted on that same page. [Au.]

[32]Ted Cohen, "Metaphor and the Cultivation of Intimacy," *Critical Inquiry* 5 (Fall 1978): 78. [Au.]

the difficulty inherent in deciphering other highly specialized realms of meaning — in this case, women's conceptual and symbolic worlds. And further, the intended emphasis in each is the inaccessibility of female meaning to male interpretation.[33] The fact that in recent years each story has increasingly found its way into easily available textbooks, and hence into the women's-studies and American literature classrooms, to be read and enjoyed by teachers and students of both sexes, happily suggests that their fictive premises are attributable not so much to necessity as to contingency.[34] Men can, after all, learn to apprehend the meanings encoded in texts by and about women — just as women have learned to become sensitive readers of Shakespeare and Milton, Hemingway and Mailer.[35] Both stories function, in effect, as a prod to that very process by alerting the reader to the fundamental problem of "reading" correctly within cohabiting but differently structured conceptual worlds.

To take seriously the implications of such relearned reading strategies is to acknowledge that we are embarking upon a revisionist rereading of our entire literary inheritance and, in that process, demonstrating the full applicability of Bloom's second formula for canon formation,

"You are or become what you read."[36] To set ourselves the task of learning to read a wholly different set of texts will make of us different kinds of readers (and perhaps different kinds of people as well). But to set ourselves the task of doing this in a public way, on behalf of women's texts specifically, engages us — as the feminists among us have learned — in a challenge to the inevitable issue of "*authority* . . . in all questions of canon-formation."[37] It places us, in a sense, in a position analogous to that of the narrator of "The Yellow Wallpaper," bound, if we are to survive, to challenge the (accepted and generally male) authority who has traditionally wielded the power to determine what may be written and how it shall be read. It challenges fundamentally not only the shape of our canon of major American authors but, indeed, that very "continuity that began in the sixth century B.C. when Homer first became a schoolbook for the Greeks."[38]

It is no mere coincidence, therefore, that readers as diverse as Adrienne Rich and Harold Bloom have arrived by various routes at the conclusion that *re-vision* constitutes the key to an ongoing literary history. Whether functioning as ephebe poet or would-be critic, Bloom's reader, as "revisionist," "strives to *see* again, so as to esteem and *estimate* differently, so as then to *aim* 'correctively.'"[39] For Rich, "re-vision" entails "the act of looking back, of seeing with fresh eyes, of entering an old text from a new critical direction."[40] And each, as a result — though from different motives — strives to make the "literary tradition . . . the captive of the revisionary impulse."[41] What Rich and other feminist critics intended by that "re-visionism" has been the subject of this essay: not only would such revisionary rereading open new avenues for comprehending male texts but, as I have argued here, it would as well allow us to appreciate the variety

[33]It is significant, I think, that the stories do not suggest any difficulty for the women in apprehending the men's meanings. On the one hand this simply is not relevant to either plot; and on the other, since in each narrative the men clearly control the public realms of discourse, it would of course have been incumbent upon the women to learn to understand them. Though masters need not learn the language of their slaves, the reverse is never the case: for survival's sake, oppressed or subdominant groups always study the nuances of meaning and gesture in those who control them. [Au.]

[34]For example, Gilman's "The Yellow Wallpaper" may be found, in addition to the Feminist Press reprinting previously cited, in *The Oven Birds: American Women on Womanhood, 1820–1920*, ed. Gail Parker (Garden City, N.Y.: Doubleday, 1972), pp. 317–34; and Glaspell's "A Jury of Her Peers" is reprinted in *American Voices, American Women*, ed. Lee R. Edwards and Arlyn Diamond (New York: Avon Books, 1973), pp. 359–81. [Au.]

[35]That women may have paid a high psychological and emotional price for their ability to read men's texts is beyond the scope of this essay, but I enthusiastically direct the reader to Judith Fetterley's provocative study of the problem in *The Resisting Reader: A Feminist Approach to American Fiction* (Bloomington: University of Indiana Press, 1978). [Au.]

[36]Bloom, *Kabbalah and Criticism*, p. 96. [Au.]
[37]Ibid., p. 100. [Au.]
[38]Bloom, *Map of Misreading*, pp. 33–34. [Au.]
[39]Ibid., p. 4. [Au.]
[40]Adrienne Rich, "When We Dead Awaken: Writing as Re-Vision," *College English* 34 (October 1972): 18; reprinted in *Adrienne Rich's Poetry*, ed. Barbara Charlesworth Gelpi and Albert Gelpi (New York: W. W. Norton, 1975), p. 90. [Au.]
[41]Bloom, *Map of Misreading*, p. 36. [Au.]

of women's literary expression, enabling us to take it into serious account for perhaps the first time rather than, as we do now, writing it off as caprice or exception, the irregularity in an otherwise regular design. Looked at this way, feminist appeals to revisionary rereading, as opposed to Bloom's, offer us all a potential enhancing of our capacity to read the world, our literary texts, and even one another, anew.

To end where I began, then, Bloom's paradigm of poetic history, when applied to women, proves useful only in a negative sense: for by omitting the possibility of poet-mothers from his psychodynamic of literary influence (allowing the feminine only the role of muse — as composite whore and mother), Bloom effectively masks the fact of an *other* tradition entirely — that in which women taught one another how to read and write about and out of their own unique (and sometimes isolated) contexts. In so doing, however, he not only points up the ignorance informing our literary history as it is currently taught in the schools, but, as well, he pinpoints (however unwittingly) what must be done to change our skewed perceptions: all readers, male and female alike, must be taught first to recognize the existence of a significant body of writing by women in America and, second, they must be encouraged to learn how to read it within its own unique and informing contexts of meaning and symbol. *Re-visionary rereading,* if you will. No more must we impose on future generations of readers the inevitability of Norman Mailer's "terrible confession": "I have nothing to say about any of the talented women who write today. . . . I do not seem able to read them."[42] Nor should Bloom himself continue to suffer an inability to express useful "judgment upon . . . the 'literature of Women's Liberation.'"[43]

[42]Norman Mailer, "Evaluations — Quick and Expensive Comments on the Talent in the Room," collected in his *Advertisements for Myself* (New York: Berkley, 1966), pp. 434–35. [Au.]

[43]Bloom, *Map of Misreading,* p. 36. What precisely Bloom intends by the phrase is nowhere made clear; for the purposes of this essay, I have assumed that he is referring to the recently increased publication of new titles by women writers. [Au.]

# Deborah E. McDowell

b. 1951

*Deborah E. McDowell is one of the strong new voices of Afro-American literature and women's studies. Born in Birmingham, Alabama, McDowell received her B.A. from Tuskegee Institute (1972) and her M.A. (1974) and Ph.D. (1979) in American and Afro-American literature from Purdue University. She has taught at Colby College (1979–87), where she was tenured as associate professor of English, and since 1987, she has been associate professor of English at the University of Virginia. McDowell's publications include studies of the work of Alice Walker, Toni Morrison, Dorothy West, and Jesse Redmon Fauset, and she is the general editor of the Black Women Writers Series. Currently she is at work on* The Changing Same, *a study of generational connections among black women novelists. "New Directions for Black Feminist Criticism" is reprinted from* Black American Literature Forum *14 (1980).*

# New Directions for Black Feminist Criticism

"What is commonly called literary history," writes Louise Bernikow, "is actually a record of choices. Which writers have survived their times and which have not depends upon who noticed them and chose to record their notice."[1] Women writers have fallen victim to arbitrary selection. Their writings have been "patronized, slighted, and misunderstood by a cultural establishment operating according to male norms out of male perceptions."[2] Both literary history's "sins of omission" and literary criticism's inaccurate and partisan judgments of women writers have come under attack since the early 1970s by feminist critics.[3] To date, no one has formulated a precise or complete definition of feminist criticism, but since its inception, its theorists and practitioners have agreed that it is a "corrective, unmasking the omissions and distortions of the past — the errors of a literary critical tradition that arise from and reflect a culture created, perpetuated, and dominated by men."[4]

These early theorists and practitioners of feminist literary criticism were largely white females who, wittingly or not, perpetrated against the Black woman writer the same exclusive practices they so vehemently decried in white male scholars. Seeing the experiences of white women, particularly white middle-class women, as normative, white female scholars proceeded blindly to exclude the work of Black women writers from literary anthologies and critical studies. Among the most flagrant examples of this chauvinism is Patricia Meyer Spacks's *The Female Imagination*. In a weak defense of her book's exclusive focus on women in the Anglo-American literary tradition, Spacks quotes Phyllis Chesler (a white female psychologist): "I have no theory to offer of Third World female psychology in America. . . . As a white woman, I'm reluctant and unable to construct theories about experiences I haven't had."[5] But, as Alice Walker observes, "Spacks never lived in nineteenth-century Yorkshire, so why theorize about the Brontës?"[6]

Not only have Black women writers been "disenfranchised" from critical works by white women scholars on the "female tradition," but they have also been frequently excised from those on the Afro-American literary tradition by Black scholars, most of whom are males. For example, Robert Stepto's *From Behind the Veil: A Study of Afro-American Narrative* purports to be "a history . . . of the historical consciousness of an Afro-American art form — namely, the Afro-American written narrative."[7] Yet, Black women writers are conspicuously absent from the table of contents. Though Stepto does have a token two-page discussion of Zora Neale Hurston's *Their Eyes Were Watching God* in which he refers to it as a "seminal narrative in Afro-

---

[1]Louise Bernikow, *The World Split Open: Four Centuries of Women Poets in England and America, 1552–1950* (New York: Vintage Books, 1974), p. 3. [Au.]

[2]William Morgan, "Feminism and Literary Study: A Reply to Annette Kolodny," *Critical Inquiry* 2 (Summer 1976): B11. [Au.]

[3]The year 1970 was the beginning of the Modern Language Association's Commission on the Status of Women, which offered panels and workshops that were feminist in approach. [Au.]

[4]Statement by Barbara Desmarais quoted in Annis Pratt, "The New Feminist Criticisms: Exploring the History of the New Space," in *Beyond Intellectual Sexism: A New Woman, A New Reality,* ed. Joan I. Roberts (New York: David McKay, 1976), p. 176. [Au.]

[5]Patricia Meyer Spacks, *The Female Imagination* (New York: Avon Books, 1976), p. 5. Ellen Moers, *Literary Women: The Great Writers* (Garden City, N.Y.: Anchor Books, 1977) is another example of what Alice Walker terms "white female chauvinism." [Au.]

[6]Alice Walker, "One Child of One's Own — An Essay on Creativity," *Ms.*, August 1979, p. 50. [Au.]

[7]Robert Stepto, *From Behind the Veil: A Study of Afro-American Narrative* (Urbana: University of Illinois Press, 1979), p. x. Other sexist critical works include Donald B. Gibson, ed., *Five Black Writers* (New York: New York University Press, 1970), a collection of essays on Wright, Ellison, Baldwin, Hughes, and Leroi Jones, and Jean Wagner, *Black Poets of the United States: From Paul Laurence Dunbar to Langston Hughes,* trans. Kenneth Douglas (Urbana: University of Illinois Press, 1973). [Au.]

American letters,"[8] he did not feel that the novel merited its own chapter or the thorough analysis accorded the other works he discusses.

When Black women writers are neither ignored altogether nor merely given honorable mention, they are critically misunderstood and summarily dismissed. In *The Negro Novel in America,* for example, Robert Bone's reading of Jessie Fauset's novels is both partisan and superficial and might explain the reasons Fauset remains obscure. Bone argues that Fauset is the foremost member of the "Rear Guard" of writers "who lagged behind," clinging to established literary traditions. The "Rear Guard" drew their source material from the Negro middle class in their efforts "to orient Negro art toward white opinion," and "to apprise educated whites of the existence of respectable Negroes." Bone adds that Fauset's emphasis on the Black middle class results in novels that are "uniformly sophomoric, trivial and dull."[9]

While David Littlejohn praises Black fiction since 1940, he denigrates the work of Fauset and Nella Larsen. He maintains that "the newer writers are obviously writing as men, for men," and are avoiding the "very close and steamy" writing that is the result of "any subculture's taking itself too seriously, defining the world and its values exclusively in the terms of its own restrictive norms and concerns."[10] This "phallic criticism,"[11] to use Mary Ellmann's term, is based on masculine-centered values and definitions. It has dominated the criticism of Black women writers and has done much to guarantee that most would be, in Alice Walker's words, "casually pilloried and consigned to a sneering oblivion."[12]

Suffice it to say that the critical community has not favored Black women writers. The recognition among Black female critics and writers that white women, white men, and Black men consider their experiences as normative and Black women's experiences as deviant has given rise to Black feminist criticism. Much as in white feminist criticism, the critical postulates of Black women's literature are only skeletally defined. Although there is no concrete definition of Black feminist criticism, a handful of Black female scholars have begun the necessary enterprise of resurrecting forgotten Black women writers and revising misinformed critical opinions of them. Justifiably enraged by the critical establishment's neglect and mishandling of Black women writers, these critics are calling for, in the words of Barbara Smith, "nonhostile and perceptive analysis of works written by persons outside the 'mainstream' of white/male cultural rule."[13]

Despite the urgency and timeliness of the enterprise, however, no substantial body of Black feminist criticism — either in theory or practice — exists, a fact which might be explained partially by our limited access to and control of the media.[14] Another explanation for the paucity of Black feminist criticism, notes Barbara Smith, is the lack of a "developed body of Black feminist political theory whose assumptions could be used in the study of Black women's art."

Despite the strained circumstances under which Black feminist critics labor, a few committed Black female scholars have broken necessary ground. For the remainder of this essay I would like to focus on selected writings of Black feminist critics, discussing their strengths and weaknesses and suggesting new directions to-

[8]Stepto, *From Behind the Veil,* p. 166. [Au.]

[9]Robert Bone, *The Negro Novel in America* (1958; reprint ed., New Haven, Conn.: Yale University Press, 1972), pp. 97, 101. [Au.]

[10]David Littlejohn, *Black on White: A Critical Survey of Writing by American Negroes* (New York: Viking Press, 1966), pp. 48–49. [Au.]

[11]Ellmann's concept of "phallic criticism" is discussed in a chapter of the same name in her *Thinking about Women* (New York: Harcourt, Brace & World, 1968), pp. 28–54. [Au.]

[12]Introduction to *Zora Neale Hurston: A Literary Biography* by Robert Hemenway (Urbana: University of Illinois Press, 1976), p. xiv. Although Walker makes this observation

specifically about Hurston, it is one that can apply to a number of Black women writers. [Au.]

[13]Barbara Smith, "Toward a Black Feminist Criticism," pp. 168–85. [Au.]

[14]See Evelyn Hammonds, "Toward a Black Feminist Aesthetic," *Sojourner,* October 1980, p. 7, for a discussion of the limitations on Black feminist critics. She correctly points out that Black feminist critics "have no newspapers, no mass-marketed magazines or journals that are explicitly oriented toward the involvement of women of color in the feminist movement." [Au.]

ward which the criticism might move and pitfalls that it might avoid.

Unfortunately, Black feminist scholarship has been decidedly more practical than theoretical, and the theories developed thus far have often lacked sophistication and have been marred by slogans, rhetoric, and idealism. The articles that attempt to apply these theoretical tenets often lack precision and detail. These limitations are not without reason. As Dorin Schumacher observes, "the feminist critic has few philosophical shelters, pillars, or guideposts," and thus "feminist criticism is fraught with intellectual and professional risks, offering more opportunity for creativity, yet greater possibility of errors."[15]

The earliest theoretical statement on Black feminist criticism is Barbara Smith's "Toward a Black Feminist Criticism." Though its importance as a groundbreaking piece of scholarship cannot be denied, it suffers from lack of precision and detail. In justifying the need for a Black feminist aesthetic, Smith argues that "a Black feminist approach to literature that embodies the realization that the politics of sex as well as the politics of race and class are crucially interlocking factors in the works of Black women writers is an absolute necessity." Until such an approach exists, she continues, "we will not even know what these writers mean."

Smith points out that "thematically, stylistically, aesthetically, and conceptually Black women writers manifest common approaches to the act of creating literature as a direct result of the specific political, social, and economic experience they have been obliged to share." She offers, as an example, the incorporation of root-working, herbal medicine, conjure, and midwifery in the stories of Zora Neale Hurston, Margaret Walker, Toni Morrison, and Alice Walker. While these folk elements certainly do appear in the work of these writers, they also appear in the works of certain Black male writers, a fact that Smith omits. If Black women writers use these elements differently from Black male writers,

such a distinction must be made before one can effectively articulate the basis of a Black feminist aesthetic.

Smith maintains further that Zora Neale Hurston, Margaret Walker, Toni Morrison, and Alice Walker use a "specifically black female language to express their own and their characters' thoughts," but she fails to describe or to provide examples of this unique language. Of course, we have come recently to acknowledge that "many of our habits of language usage are sex-derived, sex-associated, and/or sex-distinctive," that "the ways in which men and women internalize and manipulate language" are undeniably sex-related.[16] But this realization in itself simply paves the way for further investigation that can begin by exploring some critical questions. For example, is there a monolithic Black female language? Do Black female high school dropouts, welfare mothers, college graduates, and Ph.D.s share a common language? Are there regional variations in this common language? Further, some Black male critics have tried to describe the uniquely "Black linguistic elegance"[17] that characterizes Black poetry. Are there noticeable differences between the languages of Black females and Black males? These and other questions must be addressed with precision if current feminist terminology is to function beyond mere critical jargon.

Smith turns from her discussion of the commonalities among Black women writers to describe the nature of her critical enterprise. "Black feminist criticism would by definition be highly innovative," she maintains. "Applied to a particular work [it] can overturn previous assumptions about [the work] and expose for the first time its actual dimensions." Smith then proceeds to demonstrate this critical postulate by interpreting

[16]Annette Kolodny, "The Feminist as Literary Critic," Critical Response, *Critical Inquiry* 2 (Summer 1976): 824–25. See also Cheris Kramer, Barrie Thorne, and Nancy Henley, "Perspectives on Language and Communication," *Signs* 3 (Spring 1978): 638–51, and Nelly Furman, "The Study of Women and Language: Comment on Vol. 3, no. 3," *Signs* 4 (Fall 1978): 152–85. [Au.]

[17]Stephen Henderson, *Understanding the New Black Poetry: Black Speech and Black Music as Poetic References* (New York: William Morrow, 1973), pp. 31–46. [Au.]

[15]Dorin Schumacher, "Subjectivities: A Theory of the Critical Process," in *Feminist Literary Criticism: Explorations in Theory,* ed. Josephine Donovan (Lexington: University Press of Kentucky, 1975), p. 34. [Au.]

Toni Morrison's *Sula* as a lesbian novel, an interpretation she believes is maintained in "the emotions expressed, in the definition of female character and in the way that the politics of heterosexuality are portrayed." Smith vacillates between arguing forthrightly for the validity of her interpretation and recanting or overqualifying it in a way that undercuts her own credibility.

According to Smith, "if in a woman writer's work a sentence refuses to do what it is supposed to do, if there are strong images of women and if there is a refusal to be linear, the result is innately lesbian literature." She adds, "because of Morrison's consistently critical stance toward the heterosexual institutions of male-female relationships, marriage, and the family," *Sula* works as a lesbian novel. This definition of lesbianism is vague and imprecise; it subsumes far more Black women writers, particularly contemporary ones, than not into the canon of Lesbian writers. For example, Jessie Fauset, Nella Larsen, and Zora Neale Hurston all criticize major socializing institutions, as do Gwendolyn Brooks, Alice Walker, and Toni Cade Bambara. Further, if we apply Smith's definition of lesbianism, there are probably a few Black male writers who qualify as well. All of this is to say that Smith has simultaneously oversimplified and obscured the issue of lesbianism. Obviously aware of the delicacy of her position, she interjects that "the very meaning of lesbianism is being expanded in literature." Unfortunately, her qualification does not strengthen her argument. One of the major tasks ahead of Black feminist critics who write from a lesbian perspective, then, is to define lesbianism and lesbian literature precisely. Until they can offer a definition which is not vacuous, their attempts to distinguish Black lesbian writers from those who are not will be hindered.[18]

Even as I call for firmer definitions of lesbianism and lesbian literature, I question whether a lesbian aesthetic is not finally a reductive approach to the study of Black women's literature which possibly ignores other equally important aspects of the literature. For example, reading *Sula* solely from a lesbian perspective overlooks the novel's density and complexity, its skillful blend of folklore, omens, and dreams, its metaphorical and symbolic richness. Although I do not quarrel with Smith's appeal for fresher, more innovative approaches to Black women's literature, I suspect that "innovative" analysis is pressed to the service of an individual political persuasion. One's personal and political presuppositions enter into one's critical judgments. Nevertheless, we should heed Annette Kolodny's warning for feminist critics to

> be wary of reading literature as though it were polemic. . . . If when using literary materials to make what is essentially a political point, we find ourselves virtually rewriting a text, ignoring certain aspects of plot or characterization, or over-simplifying the action to fit our "political" thesis, then we are neither practicing an honest criticism nor saying anything useful about the nature of art (or about the art of political persuasion, for that matter).[19]

Alerting feminist critics to the dangers of political ideology yoked with aesthetic judgment is not synonymous with denying that feminist criticism is a valid and necessary cultural and political enterprise. Indeed, it is both possible and useful to translate ideological positions into aesthetic ones, but if the criticism is to be responsible, the two must be balanced.

Because it is a cultural and political enterprise, feminist critics, in the main, believe that their criticism can effect social change. Smith certainly argues for socially relevant criticism in

[18]Some attempts have been made to define or at least discuss lesbianism. See Adrienne Rich's two essays, "It Is the Lesbian in Us . . ." and "The Meaning of Our Love for Woman Is What We Have," in *On Lies, Secrets and Silence* (New York: W. W. Norton, 1979), pp. 199–202 and 223–30, respectively. See also Bertha Harris's *"What We Mean to Say:* Notes Toward Defining the Nature of Lesbian Literature," *Heresies* 1 (Fall 1977): 5–8, and Blanche Cook's "'Women Alone Stir My Imagination': Lesbianism and the

Cultural Tradition," *Signs* 4 (Summer 1979): 718–39. Also, at least one bibliography of Black lesbian writers has been compiled. See Ann Allen Shockley's "The Black Lesbian in American Literature: An Overview," *Conditions: Five* 2 (Fall 1979): 133–42. [Au.]

[19]Annette Kolodny, "Some Notes on Defining a 'Feminist Literary Criticism,'" *Critical Inquiry* 2 (Fall 1975): 90. [Au.]

her conclusion that "Black feminist criticism would owe its existence to a Black feminist movement while at the same time contributing ideas that women in the movement could use." This is an exciting idea in itself, but we should ask: What ideas, specifically, would Black feminist criticism contribute to the movement? Further, even though the proposition of a fruitful relationship between political activism and the academy is an interesting (and necessary) one, I doubt its feasibility. I am not sure that either in theory or in practice Black feminist criticism will be able to alter significantly circumstances that have led to the oppression of Black women. Moreover, as Lillian Robinson pointedly remarks, there is no assurance that feminist aesthetics "will be productive of a vision of art or of social relations that is of the slightest use to the masses of women, or even one that acknowledges the existence and struggle of such women."[20] I agree with Robinson that "ideological criticism must take place in the context of a political movement that can put it to work. The revolution is simply not going to be made by literary journals."[21] I should say that I am not arguing a defeatist position with respect to the social and political uses to which feminist criticism can be put. Just as it is both possible and useful to translate ideological positions into aesthetic ones, it must likewise be possible and useful to translate aesthetic positions into the machinery for social change.

Despite the shortcomings of Smith's article, she raises critical issues on which Black feminist critics can build. There are many tasks ahead of these critics, not the least of which is to attempt to formulate some clear definitions of what Black feminist criticism is. I use the term here simply to refer to Black female critics who analyze the works of Black female writers from a feminist or political perspective. But the term can also apply to any criticism written by a Black woman regardless of her subject or perspective — a book

written by a male from a feminist or political perspective, a book written by a Black woman or about Black women authors in general, or any writings by women.[22]

In addition to defining the methodology, Black feminist critics need to determine the extent to which their criticism intersects with that of white feminist critics. Barbara Smith and others have rightfully challenged white women scholars to become more accountable to Black and Third World women writers, but will that require white women to use a different set of critical tools when studying Black women writers? Are white women's theories predicated upon culturally specific values and assumptions? Andrea Benton Rushing has attempted to answer these questions in her series of articles on images of Black women in literature. She maintains, for example, that critical categories of women, based on analyses of white women characters, are Euro-American in derivation and hence inappropriate to a consideration of Black women characters.[23] Such distinctions are necessary and, if held uniformly, can materially alter the shape of Black feminist scholarship.

Regardless of which theoretical framework Black feminist critics choose, they must have an informed handle on Black literature and Black culture in general. Such a grounding can give this scholarship more texture and completeness and perhaps prevent some of the problems that have had a vitiating effect on the criticism.

[20]Lillian S. Robinson, "Working Women Writing," *Sex, Class, and Culture* (Bloomington: Indiana University Press, 1978), p. 226. [Au.]

[21]Robinson, "The Critical Task," *Sex, Class, and Culture,* p. 52. [Au.]

[22]I am borrowing here from Kolodny, who makes similar statements in "Some Notes on Defining a 'Feminist Literary Criticism,'" p. 75. [Au.]

[23]Andrea Benton Rushing, "Images of Black Women in Afro-American Poetry," in *The Afro-American Woman: Struggles and Images,* ed. Sharon Harley and Rosalyn Terborg-Penn (Port Washington, N.Y.: Kennikat Press, 1978), pp. 74–84. She argues that few of the stereotypic traits which Mary Ellmann described in *Thinking about Women* "seem appropriate to Afro-American images of black women." See also her "Images of Black Women in Modern African Poetry: An Overview," in *Sturdy Black Bridges: Visions of Black Women in Literature,* ed. Roseann P. Bell et al. (New York: Anchor Books, 1979), pp. 18–24. Rushing argues similarly that Mary Ann Ferguson's categories of women (the submissive wife, the mother angel or "mom," the woman on a pedestal, for example) cannot be applied to Black women characters, whose cultural imperatives are different from white women's. [Au.]

This footing in Black history and culture serves as a basis for the study of the literature. Termed "contextual" by theoreticians, this approach is often frowned upon if not dismissed entirely by critics who insist exclusively upon textual and linguistic analysis. Its limitations notwithstanding, I firmly believe that the contextual approach to Black women's literature exposes the conditions under which literature is produced, published, and reviewed. This approach is not only useful but necessary to Black feminist critics.

To those working with Black women writers prior to 1940, the contextual approach is especially useful. In researching Jessie Fauset, Nella Larsen, and Zora Neale Hurston, for example, it is useful to determine what the prevalent attitudes about Black women were during the time that they wrote. There is much information in the Black "little" magazines published during the Harlem Renaissance. An examination of *The Messenger,* for instance, reveals that the dominant social attitudes about Black women were strikingly consistent with traditional middle-class expectations of women. *The Messenger* ran a monthly symposium for some time entitled "Negro Womanhood's Greatest Needs." While a few female contributors stressed the importance of women being equal to men socially, professionally, and economically, the majority emphasized that a woman's place was in the home. It was her duty "to cling to the home [since] great men and women evolve from the environment of the hearthstone."[24]

One of the most startling entries came from a woman who wrote:

The New Negro Woman, with her head erect and spirit undaunted, is resolutely marching forward, ever conscious of her historic and noble mission of doing her bit toward the liberation of her people in particular and the human race in general. Upon her shoulders rests the big task to create and keep alive, in the breast of black men, a holy and consuming passion to break with the slave traditions of the past; to spurn and overcome the fatal, insidious inferiority complex of the present, which . . . bobs up ever and anon, to arrest the progress of the New

Negro Manhood Movement; and to fight with increasing vigor, with dauntless courage, unrelenting zeal and intelligent vision for the attainment of the stature of a full man, a free race and a new world.[25]

Not only does the contributor charge the Black woman with a formidable task, but she also sees her solely in relation to Black men.

This information enhances our understanding of what Fauset, Larsen, and Hurston confronted in attempting to offer alternative images of Black women. Moreover, it helps to clarify certain textual problems and ambiguities of their work. Though Fauset and Hurston, for example, explored feminist concerns, they leaned toward ambivalence. Fauset especially is alternately forthright and cagey, radical and traditional, on issues that confront women. Her first novel, *There Is Confusion* (1924), is flawed by an unanticipated and abrupt reversal in characterization that brings the central female character more in line with a feminine norm. Similarly, in her last novel, *Seraph on the Swanee* (1948), Zora Neale Hurston depicts a female character who shows promise for growth and change, for a departure from the conventional expectations of womanhood, but who in the end apotheosizes marriage, motherhood, and domestic servitude.

These two examples alone clearly capture the tension between social pressure and artistic integrity which is felt, to some extent, by all women writers. As Tillie Olsen points out, the fear of reprisal from the publishing and critical arenas is a looming obstacle to the woman writer's coming into her own authentic voice. "Fear — the need to please, to be safe — in the literary realm too. Founded fear. Power is still in the hands of men. Power of validation, publication, approval, reputation. . . ."[26]

While insisting on the validity, usefulness, and necessity of contextual approaches to Black women's literature, the Black feminist critic must not ignore the importance of rigorous textual analysis. I am aware of many feminist critics' stubborn resistance to the critical methodology handed down by white men. Although the resis-

[24]*The Messenger* 9 (April 1927): 109. [Au.]

[25]*The Messenger* 5 (July 1923): 757. [Au.]
[26]Tillie Olsen, *Silences* (New York: Delacorte Press, 1978), p. 257. [Au.]

tance is certainly politically consistent and logical, I agree with Annette Kolodny that feminist criticism would be "shortsighted if it summarily rejected all the inherited tools of critical analysis simply because they are male and western." We should, rather, salvage what we find useful in past methodologies, reject what we do not, and, where necessary, move toward "inventing new methods of analysis."[27] Particularly useful is Lillian Robinson's suggestion that "a radical kind of textual criticism . . . could usefully study the way the texture of sentences, choice of metaphors, patterns of exposition and narrative relate to [feminist] ideology."[28]

This rigorous textual analysis involves, as Barbara Smith recommends, isolating as many thematic, stylistic, and linguistic commonalities among Black women writers as possible. Among contemporary Black female novelists, the thematic parallels are legion. In Alice Walker and Toni Morrison, for example, the theme of the thwarted female artist figures prominently.[29] Pauline Breedlove in Morrison's *The Bluest Eye,* for example, is obsessed with ordering things:

> Jars on shelves at canning, peach pits on the step, sticks, stones, leaves. . . . Whatever portable plurality she found, she organized into neat lines, according to their size, shape or gradations of color. . . . She missed without knowing what she missed — paints and crayons.[30]

Similarly, Eva Peace in *Sula* is forever ordering the pleats in her dress. And Sula's strange and destructive behavior is explained as "the consequence of an idle imagination."

Had she paints, clay, or knew the discipline of the dance, or strings; had she anything to engage her tremendous curiosity and her gift for metaphor, she might have exchanged the restlessness and preoccupation with whim for an activity that provided her with all she yearned for. And like any artist with no form, she became dangerous.[31]

Likewise, Meridian's mother in Alice Walker's novel *Meridian* makes artificial flowers and prayer pillows too small for kneeling.

The use of "clothing as iconography"[32] is central to writings by Black women. For example, in one of Jessie Fauset's early short stories, "The Sleeper Wakes" (1920), Amy, the protagonist, is associated with pink clothing (suggesting innocence and immaturity) while she is blinded by fairy-tale notions of love and marriage. However, after she declares her independence from her racist and sexist husband, Amy no longer wears pink. The imagery of clothing is abundant in Zora Neale Hurston's *Their Eyes Were Watching God* (1937). Janie's apron, her silks and satins, her head scarves, and finally her overalls all symbolize various stages of her journey from captivity to liberation. Finally, in Alice Walker's *Meridian,* Meridian's railroad cap and dungarees are emblems of her rejection of conventional images and expectations of womanhood.

A final theme that recurs in the novels of Black women writers is the motif of the journey. Though one can also find this same motif in the works of Black male writers, they do not use it in the same way as do Black female writers.[33] For example, the journey of the Black male character in works by Black men takes him underground. It is a "descent into the underworld,"[34] and is primarily political and social in its implications. Ralph Ellison's *Invisible Man,* Imamu Amiri Baraka's *The System of Dante's Hell,* and

---

[27]Kolodny, "Some Notes on Defining a 'Feminist Literary Criticism,'" p. 89. [Au.]

[28]Lillian S. Robinson, "Dwelling in Decencies: Radical Criticism and Feminist Perspectives," in *Feminist Criticism,* ed. Cheryl Brown and Karen Olsen (Metuchen, N.J.: Scarecrow Press, 1978), p. 34. [Au.]

[29]For a discussion of Toni Morrison's frustrated female artists see Renita Weems, "Artists Without Art Form: A Look at One Black Woman's World of Unrevered Black Women," *Conditions: Five* 2 (Fall 1979): 48–58. See also Alice Walker's classic essay, "In Search of Our Mothers' Gardens," *Ms.,* May 1974, for a discussion of Black women's creativity in general. [Au.]

[30]Toni Morrison, *The Bluest Eye* (New York: Pocket Books, 1970), pp. 88–89. [Au.]

[31]Toni Morrison, *Sula* (New York: Bantam Books, 1980), p. 105. [Au.]

[32]Kolodny, "Some Notes on Defining a "Feminist Literary Criticism,'" p. 86. [Au.]

[33]In an NEH Summer Seminar at Yale University in the summer of 1980, Carolyn Naylor of Santa Clara University suggested this to me. [Au.]

[34]For a discussion of this idea see Michael G. Cooke, "The Descent into the Underworld and Modern Black Fiction," *Iowa Review* 5 (Fall 1974): 72–90. [Au.]

Richard Wright's "The Man Who Lived Underground" exemplify this quest. The Black female's journey, on the other hand, though at times touching the political and social, is basically a personal and psychological journey. The female character in the works of Black women is in a state of becoming "part of an evolutionary spiral, moving from victimization to consciousness."[35] The heroines in Zora Neale Hurston's *Their Eyes Were Watching God,* in Alice Walker's *Meridian,* and in Toni Cade Bambara's *The Salt Eaters,* are emblematic of this distinction.

Even though isolating such thematic and imagistic commonalities should continue to be one of the Black feminist critic's most urgent tasks, she should beware of generalizing on the basis of too few examples. If one argues authoritatively for the existence of a Black female "conciousness" or "vision" or "literary tradition," one must be sure that the parallels found recur with enough consistency to support these generalizations. Further, Black feminist critics should not become obsessed in searching for common themes and images in Black women's works. As I pointed out earlier, investigating the question of "female" language is critical and may well be among the most challenging jobs awaiting the Black feminist critic. The growing body of research on gender-specific uses of language might aid these critics. In fact, wherever possible, feminist critics should draw on the scholarship of feminists in other disciplines.

An equally challenging and necessary task ahead of the Black feminist critic is a thoroughgoing examination of the works of Black male writers. In her introduction to *Midnight Birds,* Mary Helen Washington argues for the importance of giving Black women writers their due first:

Black women are searching for a specific language, specific symbols, specific images with which to record their lives, and, even though they can claim a rightful place in the Afro-American tradition and the feminist tradition of women writers, it is also clear that, for purposes of liberation, black women

writers will first insist on their own name, their own space.[36]

I likewise believe that the immediate concern of Black feminist critics must be to develop a fuller understanding of Black women writers who have not received the critical attention Black male writers have. Yet, I cannot advocate indefinitely such a separatist position, for the countless thematic, stylistic, and imagistic parallels between Black male and female writers must be examined. Black feminists critics should explore these parallels in an effort to determine the ways in which these commonalities are manifested differently in Black women's writing and the ways in which they coincide with writings by Black men.

Of course, there are feminist critics who are already examining Black male writers, but much of the scholarship has been limited to discussions of the negative images of Black women found in the works of these authors.[37] Although this scholarship served an important function in pioneering Black feminist critics, it has virtually run its course. Feminist critics run the risk of plunging their work into cliché and triviality if they continue merely to focus on how Black men treat Black women in literature. Hortense Spillers offers a more sophisticated approach to this issue in her discussion of the power of language and myth in female relations in James Baldwin's *If Beale Street Could Talk.* One of Spillers's most cogent points is that "woman-freedom, or its negation, is tied to the assertions of myth, or ways of sayings things."[38]

Black feminist criticism is a knotty issue, and while I have attempted to describe it, to call for clearer definitions of its methodology, to offer warnings of its limitations, I await the day when Black feminist criticism will expand to embrace other modes of critical inquiry. In other words,

[35]Mary Helen Washington, *Midnight Birds: Stories of Contemporary Black Women Writers* (Garden City, N.Y.: Anchor Books, 1980), p. 43. [Au.]

[36]Ibid., p. xvii. [Au.]

[37]See Saundra Towns, "The Black Woman as Whore: Genesis of the Myth," *The Black Position* 3 (1974): 39–59, and Sylvia Keady, "Richard Wright's Women Characters and Inequality," *Black American Literature Forum* 10 (1976): 124–28, for example. [Au.]

[38]Hortense Spillers, "The Politics of Intimacy: A Discussion," in Bell et al., eds., *Sturdy Black Bridges,* p. 88. [Au.]

I am philosophically opposed to what Annis Pratt calls "methodolatry." Wole Soyinka has offered one of the most cogent defenses against critical absolutism. He explains:

The danger which a literary ideology poses is the act of consecration — and of course excommunication. Thanks to the tendency of the modern consumer-mind to facilitate digestion by putting in strict categories what are essentially fluid operations of the creative mind upon social and natural phenomena, the formulation of a literary ideology tends to congeal sooner or later into instant capsules which, administered also to the writer, may end by asphyxiating the creative process.[39]

[39]Wole Soyinka, *Myth, Literature and the African World* (London: Cambridge University Press, 1976), p. 61. [Au.]

Whether Black feminist criticism will or should remain a separatist enterprise is a debatable point. Black feminist critics ought to move from this issue to consider the specific language of Black women's literature, to describe the ways Black women writers employ literary devices in a distinct way, and to compare the way Black women writers create their own mythic structures. If they focus on these and other pertinent issues, Black feminist critics will have laid the cornerstone for a sound, thorough articulation of the Black feminist aesthetic.

# Nina Baym

b. 1936

*Nina Baym's work has been instrumental in bringing about academic recognition of women's studies across the United States. Born in Princeton, New Jersey, Baym received her B.A. from Cornell University (1957) and her M.A. (1958) and Ph.D. (1963) in English from Harvard University. Since receiving her doctorate, Baym has taught English and American literature at the University of Illinois at Urbana-Champaign, where she became a full professor in 1972 and director of the School of Humanities in 1976. Baym has been a Guggenheim fellow (1975–76) and a fellow of the National Endowment for the Humanities (1982–83). She has served on the editorial boards of several major journals, including* American Quarterly, New England Quarterly, *and* American Literature, *and is an editor of* The Norton Anthology of American Literature. *Her publications include* The Shape of Hawthorne's Career *(1976),* Woman's Fiction: A Guide to Novels by and about Women in America (1820–1870) *(1978),* Nathaniel Hawthorne and His Mother *(1982), and* Novels, Readers, and Reviewers: Responses to Fiction in Antebellum America *(1984). "Melodramas of Beset Manhood" is reprinted from* American Quarterly 33 *(1981).*

# Melodramas of Beset Manhood

## How Theories of American Fiction Exclude Women Authors

This paper is about American literary criticism rather than American literature. It proceeds from the assumption that we never read American literature directly or freely, but always through the perspective allowed by theories. Theories account for the inclusion and exclusion of texts in anthologies, and theories account for the way we read them. My concern is with the fact that the theories controlling our reading of American literature have led to the exclusion of women authors from the canon.

Let me use my own practice as a case in point. In 1977 there was published a collection of essays on images of women in major British and American literature, to which I contributed.[1] The American field was divided chronologically among six critics, with four essays covering literature written prior to World War II. Taking seriously the charge that we were to focus only on the major figures, the four of us — working quite independently of each other — selected altogether only four women writers. Three of these were from the earliest period, a period which predates the novel: the poet Anne Bradstreet and the two diarists Mary Rowlandson and Sarah Kemble Knight. The fourth was Emily Dickinson. For the period between 1865 and 1940 no women were cited at all. The message that we — who were taking women as our subject — conveyed was clear: there have been almost no major women writers in America; the major novelists have all been men.

Now, when we wrote our essays we were not undertaking to reread all American literature and make our own decisions as to who the major authors were. That is the point: we accepted the going canon of major authors. As late as 1977, that canon did not include any women novelists. Yet, the critic who goes beyond what is accepted and tries to look at the totality of literary production in America quickly discovers that women authors have been active since the earliest days of settlement. Commercially and numerically they have probably dominated American literature since the middle of the nineteenth century. As long ago as 1854, Nathaniel Hawthorne complained to his publisher about the "damned mob of scribbling women" whose writings — he fondly imagined — were diverting the public from his own.

Names and figures help make this dominance clear. In the years between 1774 and 1799 — from the calling of the First Continental Congress to the close of the eighteenth century — a total of thirty-eight original works of fiction were published in this country.[2] Nine of these, appearing pseudonymously or anonymously, have not yet been attributed to any author. The remaining twenty-nine are the work of eighteen individuals, of whom four are women. One of these women, Susannah Rowson, wrote six of them, or more than a fifth of the total. Her most popular work, *Charlotte* (also known as *Charlotte Temple*), was printed three times in the decade it was published, nineteen times between 1800 and 1810, and eighty times by the middle of the nineteenth century. A novel by a second of the four women, Hannah Foster, was called *The Coquette* and had thirty editions by mid-nineteenth century. *Uncle Tom's Cabin,* by a woman, is probably the all-time biggest seller in American history. A woman, Mrs. E.D.E.N. Southworth, was probably the most widely read novelist in the nineteenth century. How is it possible for a critic or historian of American literature to leave these books, and these authors, out of the picture?

I see three partial explanations for the critical invisibility of the many active women authors in America. The first is simple bias. The critic does not like the idea of women as writers, does not believe that women can be writers, and hence does not see them even when they are right before his eyes. His theory or his standards may well be nonsexist but his practice is not. Certainly, an *a priori* resistance to recognizing women authors as serious writers has functioned powerfully in the mind-set of a number of influential critics. One can amusingly demonstrate the inconsistencies between standard and practice in such critics, show how their minds slip out of gear when they are confronted with a woman author. But this is only a partial explanation.

A second possibility is that, in fact, women have not written the kind of work that we call "excellent," for reasons that are connected with their gender although separable from it. This is a serious possibility. For example, suppose we required a dense texture of classical allusion in

[1]Marlene Springer, ed., *What Manner of Woman: Essays on English and American Life and Literature* (New York: New York University Press, 1977). [Au.]

[2]See Lyle H. Wright, *American Fiction: A Contribution Towards a Bibliography,* vol. 1, *1774–1850,* 2d ed. (San Marino, Calif.: Huntington Library Press, 1969). [Au.]

all works that we called excellent. Then, the restriction of a formal classical education to men would have the effect of restricting authorship of excellent literature to men. Women would not have written excellent literature because social conditions hindered them. The reason, though gender-connected, would not be gender per se.

The point here is that the notion of the artist, or of excellence, has efficacy in a given time and reflects social realities. The idea of "good" literature is not only a personal preference, it is also a cultural preference. We can all think of species of women's literature that do not aim in any way to achieve literary excellence as society defines it: for example, the "Harlequin Romances." Until recently, only a tiny proportion of literary women aspired to artistry and literary excellence in the terms defined by their own culture. There tended to be a sort of immediacy in the ambitions of literary women leading them to professionalism rather than artistry, by choice as well as by social pressure and opportunity. The gender-related restrictions were really operative, and the responsible critic cannot ignore them. But again, these restrictions are only partly explanatory.

There are, finally, I believe, gender-related restrictions that do not arise out of cultural realities contemporary with the writing woman, but out of later critical theories. These theories may follow naturally from cultural realities pertinent to their own time, but they impose their concerns anachronistically, after the fact, on an earlier period. If one accepts current theories of American literature, one accepts as a consequence — perhaps not deliberately but nevertheless inevitably — a literature that is essentially male. This is the partial explanation that I shall now develop.

Let us begin where the earliest theories of American literature begin, with the hypothesis that American literature is to be judged less by its form than by its content. Traditionally, one ascertains literary excellence by comparing a writer's work with standards of performance that have been established by earlier authors, where formal mastery and innovation are paramount. But from its historical beginnings, American literary criticism has assumed that literature pro-

duced in this nation would have to be groundbreaking, equal to the challenge of the new nation, and completely original. Therefore, it could not be judged by referring it back to earlier achievements. The earliest American literary critics began to talk about the "most American" work rather than the "best" work because they knew no way to find out the best other than by comparing American with British writing. Such a criticism struck them as both unfair and unpatriotic. We had thrown off the political shackles of England; it would not do for us to be servile in our literature. Until a tradition of American literature developed its own inherent forms, the early critic looked for a standard of Americanness rather than a standard of excellence. Inevitably, perhaps, it came to seem that the quality of "Americanness," whatever it might be, *constituted* literary excellence for American authors. Beginning as a nationalistic enterprise, American literary criticism and theory has retained a nationalist orientation to this day.

Of course, the idea of Americanness is even more vulnerable to subjectivity than the idea of the best. When they speak of "most American," critics seldom mean the statistically most representative or most typical, the most read or the most sold. They have some qualitative essence in mind, and frequently their work develops as an explanation of this idea of "American" rather than a description and evaluation of selected authors. The predictable recurrence of the term "America" or "American" in works of literary criticism treating a dozen or fewer authors indicates that the critic has chosen his authors on the basis of their conformity to his idea of what is truly American. For examples: *American Renaissance, The Romance in America, Symbolism and American Literature, Form and Fable in American Fiction, The American Adam, The American Novel and Its Tradition, The Place of Style in American Literature* (a subtitle), *The Poetics of American Fiction* (another subtitle). But an idea of what is American is no more than an idea, needing demonstration. The critic all too frequently ends up using his chosen authors as demonstrations of Americanness, arguing through them to his definition.

So Marius Bewley explains in *The Eccentric*

*Design* that "for the American artist there was no social surface responsive to his touch. The scene was crude, even beyond successful satire," but later, in a concluding chapter titled "The Americanness of the American Novel," he agrees that "this 'tradition' as I have set it up here has no room for the so-called realists and naturalists."[3] F. O. Matthiessen, whose *American Renaissance* enshrines five authors, explains that "the one common denominator of my five writers, uniting even Hawthorne and Whitman, was their devotion to the possibilities of democracy."[4] The jointly written *Literary History of the United States* proclaims in its "address to the reader" that American literary history "will be a history of the books of the great and the near-great writers in a literature which is most revealing when studied as a by-product of American experience."[5] And Joel Porte announces confidently in *The Romance in America* that "students of American literature . . . have provided a solid theoretical basis for establishing that the rise and growth of fiction in this country is dominated by our authors' conscious adherence to a tradition of non-realistic romance sharply at variance with the broadly novelistic mainstream of English writing. When there has been disagreement among recent critics as to the contours of American fiction, it has usually disputed, not the existence per se of a romance tradition, but rather the question of which authors, themes, and stylistic strategies *deserve* to be placed with certainty at the heart of that tradition" (emphasis added).[6]

Before he is through, the critic has had to insist that some works in America are much more American than others, and he is as busy excluding certain writers as "un-American" as he is including others. Such a proceeding in the political arena would be extremely suspect, but in criticism it has been the method of choice. Its final result goes far beyond the conclusion that only a handful of American works are very good. *That* statement is one we could agree with, since very good work is rare in any field. But it is odd indeed to argue that only a handful of American works are really American.[7]

Despite the theoretical room for an infinite number of definitions of Americanness, critics have generally agreed on it — although the shifting canon suggests that agreement may be a matter of fad rather than fixed objective qualities.[8] First, America as a nation must be the ultimate subject of the work. The author must be writing about aspects of experience and character that are American only, setting Americans off from other people and the country from other nations. The author must be writing his story specifically to display these aspects, to meditate on them, and to derive from them some generalizations and conclusions about "the" American experience. To Matthiessen the topic is the possibilities of democracy; Sacvan Bercovitch (in *The Puritan Origins of the American Self*) finds it in American identity. Such content excludes, at one extreme, stories about universals, aspects of experience common to people in a variety of times and places — mutability, mortality, love, childhood, family, betrayal, loss. Innocence versus experience is an admissible theme *only* if innocence is the essence of the American character, for example.

But at the other extreme, the call for an overview of America means that detailed, circumstantial portrayals of some aspect of American life are also, peculiarly, inappropriate: stories of wealthy New Yorkers, Yugoslavian immigrants, Southern rustics. Jay B. Hubbell rather ingratiatingly admits as much when he writes, "in both my teaching and my research I had a special interest in literature as a reflection of American life and thought. This circumstance may explain

[3] Marius Bewley, *The Eccentric Design: Form in the Classic American Novel* (New York: Columbia University Press, 1963), pp. 15, 291. [Au.]

[4] F. O. Matthiessen, *American Renaissance* (New York: Oxford University Press, 1941), p. ix. [Au.]

[5] Robert E. Spiller et al., eds., *Literary History of the United States* (New York: Macmillan, 1959), p. xix. [Au.]

[6] Joel Porte, *The Romance in America: Studies in Cooper, Poe, Hawthorne, Melville, and James* (Middletown, Conn.: Wesleyan University Press, 1969), p. ix. [Au.]

[7] A good essay on this topic is William C. Spengemann's "What Is American Literature?" *Centennial Review* 22 (Spring 1978): 119–38. [Au.]

[8] See Jay B. Hubbell, *Who Are the Major American Authors?* (Durham, N.C.: Duke University Press, 1972). [Au.]

in part why I found it difficult to appreciate the merits of the expatriates and why I was slow in doing justice to some of the New Critics. I was repelled by the sordid subject matter found in some of the novels written by Dreiser, Dos Passos, Faulkner, and some others."[9] Richard Poirier writes that "the books which in my view constitute a distinctive American tradition . . . resist within their pages forces of environment that otherwise dominate the world," and he distinguishes this kind from "the fiction of Mrs. Wharton, Dreiser, or Howells."[10] The *Literary History of the United States* explains that "historically, [Edith Wharton] is likely to survive as the memorialist of a dying aristocracy."[11] And so on. These exclusions abound in all the works which form the stable core of American literary criticism at this time.

Along with Matthiessen, the most influential exponent of this exclusive Americanness is Lionel Trilling, and his work has particular applicability because it concentrates on the novel form. Here is a famous passage from his 1940 essay, "Reality in America," in which Trilling is criticizing Vernon Parrington's selection of authors in *Main Currents in American Thought:*

> A culture is not a flow, nor even a confluence: the form of its existence is struggle — or at least debate — it is nothing if not a dialectic. And in any culture there are likely to be certain artists who contain a large part of the dialectic within themselves, their meaning and power lying in their contradictions: they contain within themselves, it may be said, the very essence of the culture. To throw out Poe because he cannot be conveniently fitted into a theory of American culture . . . to find his gloom to be merely personal and eccentric . . . as Hawthorne's was . . . to judge Melville's response to American life to be less noble than that of Bryant or of Greeley, to speak of Henry James as an escapist . . . this is not merely to be mistaken in aesthetic judgment. Rather it is to examine without attention and from the point of view of a limited and essen-

tially arrogant conception of reality the documents which are in some respects the most suggestive testimony to what America was and is, and of course to get no answer from them.[12]

Trilling's immediate purpose is to exclude Greeley and Bryant from the list of major authors and to include Poe, Melville, Hawthorne, and James. We probably share Trilling's aesthetic judgment. But note that he does not base his judgment on aesthetic grounds; indeed, he dismisses aesthetic judgment with the word "merely." He argues that Parrington has picked the wrong artists because he doesn't understand the culture. Culture is his real concern.

But what makes Trilling's notion of culture more valid than Parrington's? Trilling really has no argument; he resorts to such value-laden rhetoric as "a limited and essentially arrogant conception of reality" precisely because he cannot objectively establish his version of culture over Parrington's. For the moment, there are two significant conclusions to draw from this quotation. First, the disagreement is over the nature of our culture. Second, there is no disagreement over the value of literature — it is valued as a set of "documents" which provide "suggestive testimony to what America was and is."

One might think that an approach like this which is subjective, circular, and in some sense nonliterary or even antiliterary would not have had much effect. But clearly Trilling was simply carrying on a longstanding tradition of searching for cultural essence, and his essays gave the search a decided and influential direction toward the notion of cultural essence as some sort of tension. Trilling succeeded in getting rid of Bryant and Greeley, and his choice of authors is still dominant. They all turn out — and not by accident — to be white, middle-class, male, of Anglo-Saxon derivation or at least from an ancestry which had settled in this country before the big waves of immigration which began around the middle of the nineteenth century. In every case, however, the decision made by these men to become professional authors pushed them

[9]Ibid., pp. 335–36. [Au.]

[10]Richard Poirier, *A World Elsewhere: The Place of Style in American Literature* (New York: Oxford University Press, 1966), p. 5. [Au.]

[11]Spiller et al., *Literary History of the United States,* p. 1211. [Au.]

[12]Lionel Trilling, *The Liberal Imagination* (Garden City, N.Y.: Anchor Books, 1950), pp. 7–9. [Au.]

slightly to one side of the group to which they belonged. This slight alienation permitted them to belong, and yet not to belong, to the so-called "mainstream." These two aspects of their situation — their membership in the dominant middle-class white Anglo-Saxon group, and their modest alienation from it — defined their boundaries, enabling them to "contain within themselves" the "contradictions" that, in Trilling's view, constitute the "very essence of the culture." I will call the literature they produced, which Trilling assesses so highly, a "consensus criticism of the consensus."

This idea plainly excludes many groups but it might not seem necessarily to exclude women. In fact, nineteenth-century women authors were overwhelmingly white, middle-class, and Anglo-Saxon in origin. Something more than what is overtly stated by Trilling (and others cited below) is added to exclude them. What critics have done is to assume, for reasons shortly to be expounded, that the women writers invariably represented the consensus, rather than the criticism of it; to assume that their gender made them part of the consensus in a way that prevented them from partaking in the criticism. The presence of these women and their works is acknowledged in literary theory and history as an impediment and obstacle, that which the essential American literature had to criticize as its chief task.

So, in his lively and influential book of 1960, *Love and Death in the American Novel*, Leslie Fiedler describes women authors as creators of the "flagrantly bad best-seller" against which "our best fictionists" — all male — have had to struggle for "their integrity and their livelihoods."[13] And, in a 1978 reader's introduction to an edition of Charles Brockden Brown's *Wieland*, Sydney J. Krause and S. W. Reid write as follows:

> What it meant for Brown personally, and belles lettres in America historically, that he should have decided to write professionally is a story unto itself. Americans simply had no great appetite for serious literature in the early decades of the Republic —

certainly nothing of the sort with which they devoured . . . the ubiquitous melodramas of beset womanhood, "tales of truth," like Susanna Rowson's *Charlotte Temple* and Hannah Foster's *The Coquette*.[14]

There you see what has happened to the woman writer. She has entered literary history as the enemy. The phrase "tales of truth" is put in quotes by the critics, as though to cast doubt on the very notion that a "melodrama of beset womanhood" could be either true or important. At the same time, ironically, they are proposing for our serious consideration, as a candidate for intellectually engaging literature, a highly melodramatic novel with an improbable plot, inconsistent characterizations, and excesses of style that have posed tremendous problems for all students of Charles Brockden Brown. But by this strategy it becomes possible to begin major American fiction historically with male rather than female authors. The certainty here that stories about women could not contain the essence of American culture means that the matter of American experience is inherently male. And this makes it highly unlikely that American women would write fiction encompassing such experience. I would suggest that the theoretical model of a story which may become the vehicle of cultural essence is: "a melodrama of beset manhood." This melodrama is presented in a fiction which, as we will later see, can be taken as representative of the author's literary experience, his struggle for integrity and livelihood against flagrantly bad best-sellers written by women. Personally beset in a way that epitomizes the tensions of our culture, the male author produces his melodramatic testimony to our culture's essence — so the theory goes.

Remember that the search for cultural essence demands a relatively uncircumstantial kind of fiction, one which concentrates on national universals (if I may be pardoned the paradox). This search has identified a sort of nonrealistic narrative, a romance, a story free to catch an essential, idealized American character, to intensify

[13]Leslie Fiedler, *Love and Death in the American Novel* (New York: Criterion Books, 1960), p. 93. [Au.]

[14]Charles Brockden Brown, *Wieland*, ed. Sydney J. Krause and S. W. Reid (Kent, Ohio: Kent State University Press, 1978), p. xii. [Au.]

his essence and convey his experience in a way that ignores details of an actual social milieu. This nonrealistic or antisocial aspect of American fiction is noted — as a fault — by Trilling in a 1947 essay, "Manners, Morals, and the Novel." Curiously, Trilling here attacks the same group of writers he had rescued from Parrington in "Reality in America." But, never doubting that his selection represents "the" American authors, he goes ahead with the task that really interests him — criticizing the culture through its representative authors:

> The novel in America diverges from its classic [i.e., British] intention which . . . is the investigation of the problem of reality beginning in the social field. The fact is that American writers of genius have not turned their minds to society. Poe and Melville were quite apart from it; the reality they sought was only tangential to society. Hawthorne was acute when he insisted that he did not write novels but romances — he thus expressed his awareness of the lack of social texture in his work. . . . In America in the nineteenth century, Henry James was alone in knowing that to scale the moral and aesthetic heights in the novel one had to use the ladder of social observation.[15]

Within a few years after publication of Trilling's essay, a group of Americanists took its rather disapproving description of American novelists and found in this nonrealism or romanticism the essentially American quality they had been seeking. The idea of essential Americanness then developed in such influential works of criticism as *Virgin Land* by Henry Nash Smith (1950), *Symbolism and American Literature* by Charles Feidelson (1953), *The American Adam* by R. W. B. Lewis (1955), *The American Novel and Its Tradition* by Richard Chase (1957), and *Form and Fable in American Fiction* by Daniel G. Hoffman (1961). These works, and others like them, were of sufficiently high critical quality, and sufficiently like each other, to compel assent to the picture of American literature that they presented. They used sophisticated New Critical close-reading techniques to identify a myth of America which had nothing to do with the clas-

sical fictionist's task of chronicling probable people in recognizable social situations.

The myth narrates a confrontation of the American individual, the pure American self divorced from specific social circumstances, with the promise offered by the idea of America. This promise is the deeply romantic one that in this new land, untrammeled by history and social accident, a person will be able to achieve complete self-definition. Behind this promise is the assurance that individuals come before society, that they exist in some meaningful sense prior to, and apart from, societies in which they happen to find themselves. The myth also holds that, as something artificial and secondary to human nature, society exerts an unmitigatedly destructive pressure on individuality. To depict it at any length would be a waste of artistic time; and there is only one way to relate it to the individual — as an adversary.

One may believe all this and yet look in vain for a way to tell a believable story that could free the protagonist from society or offer the promise of such freedom, because nowhere on earth do individuals live apart from social groups. But in America, given the original reality of large tracts of wilderness, the idea seems less a fantasy, more possible in reality or at least more believable in literary treatment. Thus it is that the essential quality of America comes to reside in its unsettled wilderness and the opportunities that such a wilderness offers to the individual as the medium on which he may inscribe, unhindered, his own destiny and his own nature.

As the nineteenth century wore on, and settlements spread across the wilderness, the struggle of the individual against society became more and more central to the myth; where, let's say, Thoreau could leave in chapter 1 of *Walden*, Huckleberry Finn has still not made his break by the end of chapter 42 (the conclusion) of the book that bears his name. Yet one finds a struggle against society as early as the earliest Leatherstocking tale (*The Pioneers*, 1823). In a sense, this supposed promise of America has always been known to be delusory. Certainly by the twentieth century the myth has been transmuted into an avowedly hopeless quest for unencumbered space (*On the Road*), or the evocation of

---

[15]Trilling, *The Liberal Imagination*, p. 206. [Au.]

flight for its own sake *(Rabbit, Run* and *Henderson the Rain King),* or as pathetic acknowledgment of loss — for example, the close of *The Great Gatsby* where the narrator Nick Carraway summons up "the old island here that flowered once for Dutch sailors' eyes — a fresh, green breast of the new world . . . the last and greatest of all human dreams" where man is "face to face for the last time in history with something commensurate to his capacity for wonder."

We are all very familiar with this myth of America in its various fashionings, and owing to the selective vision that has presented this myth to us as the whole story, many of us are unaware of how much besides it has been created by literary Americans. Keeping our eyes on this myth, we need to ask whether anything about it puts it outside women's reach. In one sense, and on one level, the answer is no. The subject of this myth is supposed to stand for human nature, and if men and women share a common human nature, then all can respond to its values, its promises, and its frustrations. And in fact, as a teacher I find women students responsive to the myth insofar as its protagonist is concerned. It is true, of course, that in order to represent some kind of believable flight into the wilderness, one must select a protagonist with a certain believable mobility, and mobility has until recently been a male prerogative in our society. Nevertheless, relatively few men are actually mobile to the extent demanded by the story, and hence the story is really not much more vicarious, in this regard, for women than for men. The problem is thus not to be located in the protagonist or his gender per se; the problem is with the other participants in his story — the entrammeling society and the promising landscape. For both of these are depicted in unmistakably feminine terms, and this gives a sexual character to the protagonist's story which does, indeed, limit its applicability to women. And this sexual definition has melodramatic, misogynist implications.

In these stories, the encroaching, constricting, destroying society is represented with particular urgency in the figure of one or more women. There are several possible reasons why this might be so. It seems to be a fact of life that we all — women and men alike — experience social con-

ventions and responsibilities and obligations first in the persons of women, since women are entrusted by society with the task of rearing young children. Not until he reaches mid-adolescence does the male connect up with other males whose primary task is socialization; but at about this time — if he is heterosexual — his lovers and spouses become the agents of a permanent socialization and domestication. Thus, although women are not the source of social power, they are experienced as such. And although not all women are engaged in socializing the young, the young do not encounter women who are not. So from the point of view of the young man, the only kind of women who exist are entrappers and domesticators.

For heterosexual man, these socializing women are also the locus of powerful attraction. First, because everybody has social and conventional instincts: second, because his deepest emotional attachments are to women. This attraction gives urgency and depth to the protagonist's rejection of society. To do it, he must project onto the woman those attractions that he feels, and cast her in the melodramatic role of temptress, antagonist, obstacle — a character whose mission in life seems to be to ensnare him and deflect him from life's important purposes of self-discovery and self-assertion. (A Puritan would have said: from communion with Divinity.) As Richard Chase writes in *The American Novel and Its Tradition,* "The myth requires celibacy." It is partly against his own sexual urges that the male must struggle, and so he perceives the socializing and domesticating woman as a doubly powerful threat; for this reason, Chase goes on to state, neither Cooper nor "any other American novelist until the age of James and Edith Wharton" could imagine "a fully developed woman of sexual age."[16] Yet in making this statement, Chase is talking about his myth rather than Cooper's. (One should add that, for a homosexual male, the demands of society that he link himself for life to a woman make for a particularly misogynist version of this aspect of the American myth, for the hero is propelled not by a rejected attrac-

[16]Richard Chase, *The American Novel and Its Tradition* (Garden City, N.Y.: Anchor Books, 1957), pp. 55, 64. [Au.]

tion but by true revulsion.) Both heterosexual and homosexual versions of the myth cooperate with the hero's perceptions and validate the notion of woman as threat.

Such a portrayal of women is likely to be uncongenial, if not basically incomprehensible, to a woman. It is not likely that women will write books in which women play this part; and it is by no means the case that most novels by American men reproduce such a scheme. Even major male authors prominent in the canon have other ways of depicting women: for example, Cooper's *Pathfinder* and *The Pioneers,* Hemingway's *For Whom the Bell Tolls,* Fitzgerald's *The Beautiful and Damned.* The novels of Henry James and William Dean Howells pose a continual challenge to the masculinist bias of American critical theory. And in one work — *The Scarlet Letter* — a "fully developed woman of sexual age" who is the novel's protagonist has been admitted into the canon, but only by virtue of strenuous critical revisions of the text that remove Hester Prynne from the center of the novel and make her subordinate to Arthur Dimmesdale.

So Leslie Fiedler, in *Love and Death in the American Novel,* writes this of *The Scarlet Letter:*

> It is certainly true, in terms of the plot, that Chillingworth drives the minister toward confession and penance, while Hester would have lured him to evasion and flight. But this means, for all of Hawthorne's equivocations, that the eternal feminine does not draw us on toward grace, rather that the woman promises only madness and damnation. . . . [Hester] is the female temptress of Puritan mythology, but also, though sullied, the secular madonna of sentimental Protestantism.[17]

In the rhetorical "us" Fiedler presumes that all readers are men, that the novel is an act of communication among and about males. His characterization of Hester as one or another myth or image makes it impossible for the novel to be in any way about Hester as a human being. Giving the novel so highly specific a gender reference,

[17]Fiedler, *Love and Death in the American Novel,* p. 236. [Au.]

Fiedler makes it inaccessible to women and limits its reference to men in comparison to the issues that Hawthorne was treating in the story. Not the least of these issues was, precisely, the human reference of a woman's tale.

Amusingly, then, since he has produced this warped reading, Fiedler goes on to condemn the novel for its sexual immaturity. *The Scarlet Letter* is integrated into Fiedler's general exposure of the inadequacies of the American male — inadequacies which, as his treatment of Hester shows, he holds women responsible for. The melodrama here is not Hawthorne's but Fiedler's — the American critic's melodrama of beset manhood. Of course, women authors as major writers are notably and inevitably absent from Fiedler's chronicle.

In fact, many books by women — including such major authors as Edith Wharton, Ellen Glasgow, and Willa Cather — project a version of the particular myth we are speaking of but cast the main character as a woman. When a woman takes the central role, it follows naturally that the socializer and domesticator will be a man. This is the situation in *The Scarlet Letter.* Hester is beset by the male reigning oligarchy and by Dimmesdale, who passively tempts her and is responsible for fathering her child. Thereafter, Hester (as the myth requires) elects celibacy, as do many heroines in versions of this myth by women: Thea in Cather's *The Song of the Lark,* Dorinda in Glasgow's *Barren Ground,* Anna Leath in Wharton's *The Reef.* But what is written in the criticism about these celibate women? They are said to be untrue to the imperatives of their gender, which require marriage, childbearing, domesticity. Instead of being read as a woman's version of the myth, such novels are read as stories of the frustration of female nature. Stories of female frustration are not perceived as commenting on, or containing, the essence of our culture, and so we do not find them in the canon.

So the role of entrapper and impediment in the melodrama of beset manhood is reserved for women. Also, the role of the beckoning wilderness, the attractive landscape, is given a deeply feminine quality. Landscape is deeply imbued with female qualities, as society is; but where society is menacing and destructive, landscape is compliant and supportive. It has the attributes simultaneously of a virginal bride and a non-threatening mother; its female qualities are articulated with respect to a male angle of vision: what can nature do for me, asks the hero, what can it give me?

Of course, nature has been feminine and maternal from time immemorial, and Henry Nash Smith's *Virgin Land* picks up a timeless archetype in its title. The basic nature of the image leads one to forget about its potential for imbuing with sexual meanings any story in which it is used, and the gender implications of a female landscape have only recently begun to be studied. Recently, Annette Kolodny has studied the traditional canon from this approach.[18] She theorizes that the hero, fleeing a society that has been imagined as feminine, then imposes on nature some ideas of women which, no longer subject to the correcting influence of real-life experience, become more and more fantastic. The fantasies are infantile, concerned with power, mastery, and total gratification: the all-nurturing mother, the all-passive bride. Whether one accepts all the Freudian or Jungian implications of her argument, one cannot deny the way in which heroes of American myth turn to nature as sweetheart and nurture, anticipating the satisfaction of all desires through her and including among these the desires for mastery and power. A familiar passage that captures these ideas is one already quoted: Carraway's evocation of the "fresh green breast" of the New World. The fresh greenness is the virginity that offers itself to the sailors, but the breast promises maternal solace and delight. *The Great Gatsby* contains our two images of women: while Carraway evokes the impossible dream of a maternal landscape, he blames a non-maternal woman, the socialite Daisy, for her failure to satisfy Gatsby's desires. The true adversary, of course, is Tom Buchanan, but he is hidden, as it were, behind Daisy's skirts.

I have said that women are not likely to cast themselves as antagonists in a man's story; they are even less likely, I suggest, to cast themselves as virgin land. The lack of fit between their own experience and the fictional role assigned to them is even greater in the second instance than in the first. If women portray themselves as brides or mothers it will not be in terms of the mythic landscape. If a woman puts a female construction on nature — as she certainly must from time to time, given the archetypal female resonance of the image — she is likely to write of it as more active, or to stress its destruction or violation. On the other hand, she might adjust the heroic myth to her own psyche by making nature out to be male — as, for example, Willa Cather seems to do in *O Pioneers!* But a violated landscape or a male nature does not fit the essential American pattern as critics have defined it, and hence these literary images occur in an obscurity that criticism cannot see. Thus, one has an almost classic example of the double bind. When the woman writer creates a story that conforms to the expected myth, it is not recognized for what it is because of a superfluous sexual specialization in the myth as it is entertained in the critics' minds. (Needless to say, many male novelists also entertain this version of the myth, and do not find the masculinist bias with which they imbue it to be superfluous. It is possible that some of these novelists, especially those who write in an era in which literary criticism is a powerful influence, have formed their ideas from their reading in criticism.) But if she does not conform to the myth, she is understood to be writing minor or trivial literature.

Two remaining points can be treated much more briefly. The description of the artist and of the act of writing which emerges when the critic uses the basic American story as his starting point contains many attributes of the basic story itself. This description raises the exclusion of women to a more abstract, theoretical — and perhaps more pernicious — level. Fundamentally, the idea is that the artist writing a story of this essential American kind is engaging in a task very much like the one performed by his mythic hero. In effect, the artist writing his narrative is imi-

[18]Annette Kolodny, *The Lay of the Land: Metaphor As Experience and History in American Life and Letters* (Chapel Hill: University of North Carolina Press, 1975). [Au.]

tating the mythic encounter of hero and possibility in the safe confines of his study; or, reversing the temporal order, one might see the mythic encounter of hero and possibility as a projection of the artist's situation.

Although this idea is greatly in vogue at the moment, it has a history. Here, for example, is Richard Chase representing the activity of writing in metaphors of discovery and exploration, as though the writer were a hero in the landscape: "The American novel has usually seemed content to explore . . . the remarkable and in some ways unexampled territories of life in the New World and to reflect its anomalies and dilemmas. It has . . . wanted . . . to discover a new place and a new state of mind."[19] Richard Poirier takes the idea further:

> The most interesting American books are an image of the creation of America itself. . . . They carry the metaphoric burden of a great dream of freedom — of the expansion of national consciousness into the vast spaces of a continent and the absorption of those spaces into ourselves. . . . The classic American writers try through style temporarily to free the hero (and the reader) from systems, to free them from the pressures of time, biology, economics, and from the social forces which are ultimately the undoing of American heroes and quite often of their creators. . . . The strangeness of American fiction has . . . to do . . . with the environment [the novelist] tries to create for his hero, usually his surrogate.[20]

The implicit union of creator and protagonist is made specific and overt at the end of Poirier's passage here. The ideas of Poirier and Chase, and others like them, are summed up in an anthology called *Theories of American Literature,* edited by Donald M. Kartiganer and Malcolm A. Griffith. The editors write, "It is as if with each new work our writers feel they must invent again the complete world of a literary form." (Yet, the true subject is not what the writers feel, but what the critics think they feel.) "Such a condition of nearly absolute freedom to create has appeared to our authors both as possibility and liability, an utter openness suggesting limitless opportunity for the imagination, or an enormous vacancy in which they create from nothing. For some it has meant an opportunity to play Adam, to assume the role of an original namer of experience.[21] One can see in this passage the transference of the American myth from the Adamic hero *in* the story to the Adamic creator *of* the story, and the reinterpretation of the American myth as a metaphor for the American artist's situation.

This myth of artistic creation, assimilating the act of writing novels to the Adamic myth, imposes on artistic creation all the gender-based restrictions that we have already examined in that myth. The key to identifying an "Adamic writer" is the formal appearance, or, more precisely, the *informal* appearance, of his novel. The unconventionality is interpreted as a direct representation of the open-ended experience of exploring and taming the wilderness, as well as a rejection of "society" as it is incorporated in conventional literary forms. There is no place for a woman author in this scheme. Her roles in the drama of creation are those allotted to her in a male melodrama: either she is to be silent, like nature, or she is the creator of conventional works, the spokesperson of society. What she might do as an innovator in her own right is not to be perceived.

In recent years, some refinements of critical theory coming from the Yale and Johns Hopkins and Columbia schools have added a new variant to the idea of creation as a male province. I quote from a 1979 book entitled *Home as Found* by Eric Sundquist. The author takes the idea that in writing a novel the artist is really writing a narrative about himself and proposes this addition:

> Writing a narrative about oneself may represent an extremity of Oedipal usurpation or identification, a bizarre act of self fathering. . . . American authors have been particularly obsessed with *fathering* a tradition of their own, with becoming their "own sires." . . . The struggle . . . is central to the crisis of representation, and hence of style, that allows American authors to find in their own fantasies

---

[19]Chase, *American Novel,* p. 5. [Au.]
[20]Poirier, *A World Elsewhere,* pp. 3, 5, 9. [Au.]

[21]Donald M. Kartiganer and Malcolm A. Griffith, eds., *Theories of American Literature: The Critical Perspective* (New York: Macmillan, 1962), pp. 4–5. [Au.]

those of a nation and to make of those fantasies a compelling and instructive literature.[22]

These remarks derive clearly from the work of such critics as Harold Bloom, as any reader of recent critical theory will note. The point for our purpose is the facile translation of the verb "to author" into the verb "to father," with the profound gender restrictions of that translation unacknowledged. According to this formulation, insofar as the author writes about a character who is his surrogate — which, apparently, he always does — he is trying to become his own father.

We can scarcely deny that men think a good deal about, and are profoundly affected by, relations with their fathers. The theme of fathers and sons is perennial in world literature. Somewhat more spaciously, we recognize that intergenerational conflict, usually perceived from the point of view of the young, is a recurrent literary theme, especially in egalitarian cultures. Certainly, this idea involves the question of authority, and "authority" is a notion related to that of "the author." And there is some gender-specific significance involved since authority in most cultures that we know tends to be invested in adult males. But the theory has built from these useful and true observations to a restriction of literary creation to a sort of therapeutic act that can only be performed by men. If literature is the attempt to *father* oneself by the author, then every act of writing by a woman is both perverse and absurd. And, of course, it is bound to fail.

Since this particular theory of the act of writing is drawn from psychological assumptions that are not specific to American literature, it may be argued that there is no need to confine it to

American authors. In fact, Harold Bloom's *Anxiety of Influence,* defining literature as a struggle between fathers and sons, or the struggle of sons to escape from their fathers, is about British literature.[23] And so is Edward Said's book *Beginnings,* which chronicles the history of the nineteenth-century British novel as exemplification of what he calls "filiation." His discussion omits Jane Austen, George Eliot, all three Brontë sisters, Mrs. Gaskell, Mrs. Humphrey Ward — not a sign of a woman author is found in his treatment of Victorian fiction. The result is a revisionist approach to British fiction that recasts it in the accepted image of the American myth. Ironically, just at the time that feminist critics are discovering more and more important women, the critical theorists have seized upon a theory that allows the women less and less presence. This observation points up just how significantly the critic is engaged in the act of *creating* literature.

Ironically, then, one concludes that in pushing the theory of American fiction to this extreme, critics have "deconstructed" it by creating a tool with no particular American reference. In pursuit of the uniquely American, they have arrived at a place where Americanness has vanished into the depths of what is alleged to be the universal male psyche. The theory of American fiction has boiled down to the phrase in my title: a melodrama of beset manhood. What a reduction this is of the enormous variety of fiction written in this country, by both women and men! And, ironically, nothing could be further removed from Trilling's idea of the artist as embodiment of a culture. As in the working out of all theories, its weakest link has found it out and broken the chain.

---

[22]Eric J. Sundquist, *Home as Found: Authority and Genealogy in Nineteenth-Century American Literature* (Baltimore: Johns Hopkins University Press, 1979), pp. xviii–xix. [Au.]

[23]See Bloom in Ch. 2. [Ed.]

# 7

# READER-RESPONSE CRITICISM

*The literary work cannot be completely identical with the text, or with [the reader's] realization of the text, but in fact must lie halfway between the two.*

— WOLFGANG ISER

*Interpretive communities are made up of those who share interpretive strategies not for reading (in the conventional sense) but for writing texts, for constituting their properties and assigning their intentions.*

— STANLEY FISH

*It is . . . impossible to say from a text alone how people will respond to it. Only after we have understood how some specific individual responds, how the different parts of his individual personality re-create the different details of the text, can we begin to formulate general hypotheses about the way many or all readers respond. Only then — if then.*

— NORMAN N. HOLLAND

The critics grouped together here as reader-response theorists share a topic rather than a set of assumptions. They all have in common the conviction that the audience plays a vitally important role in shaping the literary experience and the desire to help to explain that role. But their interpretations of that role and their definitions of the literary experience vary enormously, in ways that dwarf the usual doctrinal distinctions even within diverse movements like Marxism or formalism.

Interest in the role of the reader goes back to the early classical period. Plato's Book X of *Republic* testifies to the philosopher's concern lest the audience be corrupted by texts that imitate falsely or concentrate the attention of the audience on unworthy matters; the *Ion,* while centrally involved with the question of creativity, suggests that the *enthousiasmós* the muse grants to the poet is transmitted, like magnetic force, through the performer to the spectator. In Aristotle's *Poetics,* tragedy is partially defined in terms of the emotional activity of the spectator, and the construction of the text is constantly subject to the question of how the audience will view the completed product. In Horace the audience becomes central. The chief criterion of excellence in the *Ars Poetica* is what will delight and instruct the reader or spectator, and the text is defined in operational terms as something whose language, incidents, and characters are to be judged as part of a literary (and in general, a cultural) scene. The legacy of Horace long endured; the rhetorical principle of criticism, based on an operational mode of thought, dominated Western literary criticism for nearly eighteen hundred years.

The displacement of the audience from the center of critical attention to its periphery is the result of romanticism, which exalted the genius of the author at the expense of the critic (who might be considered the reader's better-paid persona). Most nineteenth- and early twentieth-century criticism centered on the author, and even the shift toward formalism at midcentury displaced the creator only to focus attention on the text itself. The New Critics may have paid greatest attention to the intentional fallacy, since the tendency of the historical scholars they had displaced was to read for authorial meaning. But Wimsatt and Beardsley also wrote a companion piece, "The Affective Fallacy," to defend the autonomous text against the encroachment of critics (primarily I. A. Richards) who might attempt to define the text in terms of the emotions it aroused in a real audience. The autonomous text of the New Criticism expressed feelings and attitudes to an ideal audience, and no evidence of how actual readers had reacted to it could possibly budge the critics' theory. While the once-controversial and experimental works of high modernism (the fiction of Joyce and Woolf, the poetry of Yeats and Eliot) were becoming canonical texts in the first two decades after World War II, the New Criticism was establishing theoretical strictures valorizing the objective textual surface and cultivating the tactic of ignoring the audience.[1]

But like Plato's banishment of the poets, the exile of the audience could not be enforced for long. The return of the reader to center stage was encouraged by one of the Chicago Aristotelians, Wayne C. Booth, with *The Rhetoric of Fiction* (1961). Booth's innovative ideas fit within the prevailing formalism, but in the following decades, at least three other definably different modes of audience-centered criticism emerged. Within the structuralist movement, the audience became a central focus for theorists like Gerald Prince in addition to critics we have already discussed, like Gérard Genette, Jonathan Culler, and Umberto Eco (Ch. 4). A reader-oriented version of psychological criticism also developed, led by such theorists as David Bleich and Norman Holland. More recently, a phenomenological criticism of literature has arisen, which considers the reader as the performer of the text.

## RHETORICAL CRITICISM: BOOTH AND FISH

Probably the loosest of these groupings is the rhetorical approach, since it covers any perspective that treats the text as sending signals to the reader for interpretation. From Horace to Samuel Johnson, the principal variants in rhetorical theory have turned on two issues: the *object* communicated and the *character* of the audience

---

[1]During the New Critical ascendancy works of audience-oriented theory, like Louise Rosenblatt's *Literature as Exploration* (1938), led a buried life, valued by the education establishment and used in pedagogy but ignored by literary theorists.

addressed. On the first axis some critics, such as Dante, have emphasized the way literature communicates ethical and religious doctrine, while others, such as Horace, have concerned themselves chiefly with the pleasures enjoyed by the reader. On the other axis, critics such as Johnson have been concerned with what will be most generally pleasing to any audience, while others, such as Dryden, have assumed that texts are written to please and instruct a particular national group, or even a class within that group, and that the specific characteristics of the audience will dictate the rhetoric employed in the text. In a sense, the discrepancies in contemporary rhetorical criticism are most strongly marked along the axis of reader participation. The range runs from Wayne Booth, who emphasizes the way texts shape their audience into "proper" readers, to Susan Sontag, whose ideal condition would be the mutual transparency of text and reader, to Stanley Fish, who (in one phase of his work) views the text as essentially defined by the reader's mental experience of it.

Wayne Booth's approach is both the most traditionally formalistic of the audience-centered modes and the one that has achieved the most widespread recognition. So thoroughly have its methods been embraced by contemporary practical critics that some textbook writers have taken it for a form of the New Criticism. In fact, Booth, like his mentor R. S. Crane, opposed New Critical doctrine on fiction and wrote *The Rhetoric of Fiction* partly to refute the ideas of New Critics like Allen Tate and Caroline Gordon. The prevailing doctrines, derived from the theory and practice of Henry James, valorized realistic stories told through a "natural," objective narrative technique that avoided authorial commentary and other overt signals of the creator behind the tale. Booth's book made it clear that such "natural" techniques of modernism were no less artificial, no less rhetorical, than the direct address to the reader practiced by Fielding and Sterne.

The real question was not *whether* the novelist should use rhetoric — it was impossible to avoid doing so — but what sort of rhetoric to use. Each of the author's technical decisions would shape in a particular way the reader's evaluation of the characters and the action, making some effects easy and others impossible. The axioms that arise from Booth's theory are less simple than those implicit in the New Criticism. They suggest that a reader's emotional distance from the characters in a narrative depends not only on the characters' values and beliefs but on the distance from the reader at which the narrative technique places them. Even relatively vicious characters can become sympathetic if readers are granted access to their consciousness and distanced from that of their victims.

The impact of *The Rhetoric of Fiction* was immense, not only in the development of theory but also in altering the canon of fiction. The popularity of eighteenth-century novelists like Defoe, Fielding, and Sterne, long muted by the disapproval of the New Critics, recovered, in part owing to Booth's debunking of modernist premises. In addition, Booth's terminology — such as "implied author" for the formal location of authorial values within a text, or "unreliable narrator" for a narrator (either personified or not within the text) whose values (intellectual, aesthetic, or ethical) depart from those of the implied author — has become the standard vocabulary in fiction courses.

Like so many earlier rhetorical critics, Booth is a moralist concerned, as was Samuel Johnson in *The Rambler,* No. 4 (p. 225), with the ethics of fiction. To the extent that a novelist's choices shape an audience's sensibility, at least while the novel is being read, the author is morally manipulating the reader, and the question of whether or not such manipulation may have harmful aftereffects is bound to arise. In the last chapter of *The Rhetoric of Fiction,* Booth insists that the author's vision does indeed act on the reader, and that because the author is responsible for communicating this vision, the author whose signals are too subtle is at fault if the reader is led astray. This rather mild statement has been misconstrued as a blanket attack on modern and postmodern fiction, but its target was actually the art-for-art's-sake mentality that would divorce fiction from the society to which it is addressed. Booth's recent *The Company We Keep* (1988) clarifies his present views.

If Booth's reader is largely at the author's mercy, Stanley Fish places the reader on the judge's bench, interrogating the text. Fish began his career by advocating a method of interpretation that he called "affective stylistics," which could be seen as a special mode of the New Criticism. According to this method, the reader reads the text slowly, word by word, alive at each moment to the shifts in apparent position and direction. Texts that seemed to lead first to one conclusion, then another, Fish termed "self-consuming artifacts." The following passage from Sir Thomas Browne is an example:

> That Judas perished by hanging himself, there is no certainty in Scripture: though in one place it seems to affirm it, and by a doubtful word hath given occasion to translate it; yet in another place, in a more punctual description, it maketh it improbable, and seems to overthrow it.

Fish argues that Browne seems to commit himself to Judas's death by hanging up to the first comma, then gradually and *almost* entirely takes it all back: "The prose is continually opening, but then closing, on the possibility of verification in one direction or another."[2] (In a sense, this a variation on New Critic William Empson's sixth type of ambiguity, which turned on ambiguity of syntax.) But gradually Fish moved away from the idea that these features belonged primarily to the text, and insisted on their location within the reader. In effect, the text is not the words on the page but the minutely detailed performance they elicit from the reader.

"Interpreting the *Variorum*" begins with the latter view of the text, but it also marks the transition to Fish's theory of interpretive communities. The essay opens with a demonstration of affective stylistics and spells out some of the implications of locating the text within the reader. In the first part of the essay, Fish examines three Milton sonnets and discovers three difficult interpretive tangles that the combined wisdom of decades of Milton scholarship has been unable to untie. His conclusion is that the tangles are not merely an ineluctable part of the poems. The

---

[2]Stanley Fish, "Literature in the Reader," in *Is There a Text in This Class?* (Cambridge: Harvard University Press, 1980), p. 24.

reader's vacillations between one possibility and the next, the experience of the undecidability of the meaning of the sonnets, in fact constitutes their meaning.

Locating the text within the reader rather than in the words on the page is a bold procedure, since each reader is likely to come up with at least a slightly different "text." (Elsewhere, in *Self-Consuming Artifacts,* Fish blocks this procedure through an appeal to the "informed reader.") Fish is willing to concede that the text-within-the-reader is unstable, but he attempts to demonstrate, as do Derrida and his followers, that the "text-as-author's-words" is equally unstable, although he does not base this radical skepticism about meaning on the Derridean metaphysics of absence. Instead, for each posited location of meaning within the so-called hermeneutic circle, Fish casts doubt by pushing the point of anchor back, one step at a time — from the words to the conventions for reading the words to the linguistic rules themselves, and so forth. But Fish does not give the full proof, and his argument assumes that readers either can complete it for themselves or trust it can be done.[3]

Whether the reader is convinced of this is not important, however, since Fish finally accounts for the *relative* stability of readers' sense of canonical texts of literature by appealing to the idea of *interpretive communities*. Interpretive communities have tacitly agreed to certain principles of textual interpretation, which authors must recognize as they write their poems or plays or novels. (In legal circles Fish's theory is seen as one way of accounting for the relationship between statute law and the "community" of judges whose profession it is to interpret that law.) Fish does not attempt to describe in *Variorum* how an interpretive community is formed, or how, once constituted, its members change their minds and the way they read (and thereby create) texts. But he takes up these issues in the last four essays of *Is There a Text in This Class?* (1980), in which he develops the idea that the interpretive communities existing at any given time constitute systems of beliefs. New communities develop owing to gaps between existing systems (affective stylistics, for example, filled a gap produced by the New Critics' rejection of the audience), and they gain followers by appealing to the deeper, more fundamental beliefs of interpreters who previously were members of other communities. People change their interpretive communities as they discover conflicts between levels within their personal systems of belief; a conflict between a critic's formalist training and his or her social and historical interests, at a deeper level of belief, might be resolved, for example, by creating a new theory that would mediate between formalism and Marxism, or by joining a community based on a theorist (like Bakhtin) who had created such a mediating system.

---

[3]The "hermeneutic circle" (a vicious circle only when one is trying to think about it) refers to the difficulty of finding a stable point in the ascription of meaning to any text. Since any word has a large finite number of meanings, we are able to give a stable meaning to any word only from context, but the context itself consists of other words, with equally unstable meanings. Attempts to find a stable point by locating it in (for example) the speaker's intention, simply move the circularity elsewhere. See Ch. 9 on authorial intention for further discussion of the hermeneutic circle.

# THE STRUCTURALIST READER

The structuralist concern with the role of reader as the decoder of the text has already been discussed. In Chapter 4, Jonathan Culler's "Literary Competence" and Umberto Eco's "The Myth of Superman" present in theoretical and in practical terms how the central issues of semiotics have been applied to the audience. Culler argues that structuralism has been led astray by its long search for syntactic keys to authorial meaning and suggests that the movement would gain momentum if it concentrated its attention on the conventions that readers must learn and the procedures they must follow in interpreting the text. In a sense, this would dictate a search for rules and conventions. Eco's "The Myth of Superman" is a study of how certain of those conventions function in representing time within popular fiction — like comic books that must permit indefinite sequelae.

The most "rhetorical" structuralist analyst of the reader's role is Gerald Prince. In "Introduction to the Study of the Narratee," Prince, taking off from Wayne Booth's differentiation between *real* and *implied* authors, distinguishes between the *reader,* the human being who peruses the text, and the *narratee* (in French, *narrataire*), whom the narrator explicitly or implicitly addresses within the text.[4] The narratee also differs from the *ideal reader* ("one who would understand perfectly and would approve entirely the least of his words, the most subtle of his intentions") and from the *virtual reader,* "a certain type of reader" on whom the author bestows "certain qualities, faculties and inclinations according to his opinion of men in general . . . and according to the obligations he feels should be respected."[5]

Prince's narratee may be a very well-defined individual, like the "you" to whom Jean-Baptiste Clamence speaks in Albert Camus's *The Fall,* who is defined explicitly as a French lawyer on holiday in Amsterdam. Or the narratee may be defined only by class, like the middle-class lady or gentleman reading Balzac's *Père Goriot*: "You who hold this book with a white hand, you who settle back in a well-padded arm-chair." At other times, the narratee is defined by very subtle signals indeed, such as what has to be explained and what does not. (The narratee of Hemingway's *The Sun Also Rises* does not know what sort of drink Pernod is or the order of events in a bullfight.) The narratee's various functions are outlined by Prince:

> He constitutes a relay between the narrator and the reader, he helps establish the narrative framework, he serves to characterize the narrator, he emphasizes certain themes, he contributes to the development of the plot, he becomes the spokesman for the moral of the work.

What links Prince with Genette, Culler, and Eco, and with other semioticians like Michael Riffaterre is his confidence that the parameters of reading can be

---

[4]In *Poétique,* no. 14 (1973): 177–96.
[5]See also Peter Rabinowitz, "Truth in Fiction: A Re-examination of Audiences," *Critical Inquiry* 4 (Autumn 1977): 121–41.

specified and codified. But on this point, other structuralists, like Roland Barthes, have been less sure. In his late study, *The Pleasure of the Text* (1975), Barthes distinguishes between "*textes de plaisir*," those readerly texts whose order can be uncovered, and "*textes de jouissance*" or texts of bliss, those writerly texts, like the novels of Alain Robbe-Grillet, whose indefinite ambiguity frustrates the structuralist design.

## THE PSYCHOLOGY AND SOCIOLOGY OF THE AUDIENCE

In both the formalist-rhetorical and the semiotic-structuralist versions of reader-oriented criticism, the reader considered is generally the reader constructed within the tale: either the posited or implied reader for whom the rhetoric is contrived, or the narratee located explicitly, like a half-realized character, within the narrative framework. The psychological and sociological versions of reader-oriented criticism introduce a different reader, the *actual* reader whom Prince distinguishes from the objects of his concern. Critics like Norman Holland and David Bleich and some of the sociologists of literature leave the ideal reader behind in favor of the quivering and unpredictable individual reader and his or her genuine but subjective response. Shared by all these theories is a relaxed acceptance of a fact most of us have observed: The individual's response to literature is so conditioned by idiosyncratic differences between one reader and another that, after listening to a group of people discussing a text, we sometimes wonder whether they have all read the same words.

One of the earliest of the psychological theorists was Louise Rosenblatt, whose *Literature as Exploration* (1938) pioneered the notion of reading as a *transaction* between text and reader. Rosenblatt conceived of the reading process in this way:

> Through the medium of words, the text brings into the reader's consciousness certain concepts, certain sensuous experiences, certain images of things, people, actions, and scenes. The special meanings and, more particularly, the submerged associations that these words and images have for the individual reader will largely determine what the work communicates to *him*. The reader brings to the work personality traits, memories of past events, present needs and preoccupations, a particular mood of the moment, and a particular physical condition. These and many other elements in a never-to-be-duplicated combination determine his response to the peculiar contribution of the text.[6]

For Rosenblatt, each reading of a given text even by a single individual, will be different, not because the text is inexhaustible but because each time we read it we are at least slightly different people. Despite this seemingly free-wheeling attitude, Rosenblatt retains the sense that though our response to the work of art is inevitably subjective, some sorts of subjectivity are preferable to others. Minimally, a reader's response should be to what is in the text, not to what is projected onto the text. At one point Rosenblatt warns that "an undistorted vision of the work of art requires a consciousness of one's own preconceptions and prejudices

---

[6]Louise Rosenblatt, *Literature as Exploration* (rev. ed.; London: Heinemann, 1968), pp. 30–31.

concerning the situations presented in the work, in contrast to the basic attitudes toward life assumed in the text." While it is useful to know what sorts of distortions one is likely to perpetrate on situations in literature and in life (psychologists call this "reality-testing"), the implication of Rosenblatt's warning is that it is possible to achieve an "undistorted" view of a text — something equivalent to an objective interpretation.

Rosenblatt presents the reader's subjective response in terms of the common-sense psychology of prejudices and preoccupations; Norman Holland arrived at his reader-oriented criticism by way of orthodox Freudianism. His book *The Dynamics of Literary Response* (1968) presumed that the content of the text essentially determined the reader's response. Holland's text then had a manifest content (the story or poem, its events, its characters, its language, its form) and a latent content of primitive fantasy (oral aggression, anal withholding) hedged about and hidden by defenses (like symbolization or sublimation). In the reading transaction, the audience, in absorbing consciously the manifest content, would also be stimulated, under the table as it were, by the latent content, and the reader's own orality or anality would be gratified by the experience. In effect, the reader's experience would mirror the text's central fantasy and modes of defense.

As Holland explains in his introduction to *5 Readers Reading,* reprinted in this chapter, this model gradually began to seem less and less satisfactory as it became clearer that the actual responses of self-aware individuals differed a great deal more than this approach could explain. In Holland's new model, the text still possesses manifest and latent content, but instead of assuming that all individuals will react to this content in much the same way, Holland suggests not only that different types of reader will react in different ways, but that even people with similar obsessions may react differently according to their individual styles of coping. In "UNITY IDENTITY TEXT SELF," Holland claims that "any individual shapes the materials the literary work offers him . . . . to give him what he characteristically both wishes and fears, and . . . . he also constructs his characteristic way of achieving what he wishes and defeating what he fears."

As an example, Holland invites us to imagine three readers responding to *Hamlet,* all of whom share a love-hate relationship with authority figures. The one whose characteristic defense against authority figures is to establish "alternatives in response to their demands" might find in the play "dualisms, split characters, the interplay of multiple plots." The one who reacts by "establishing limits and qualifications on authority" might stress "irony and occasional farce, Osric, Polonius, the gravediggers." The one who reacts with total compliance would respond "by seeking out and accepting, totally, uncritically, with a gee-gosh, the authority of its author."[7]

Holland would reject Rosenblatt's notion that an "undistorted" view of a text is possible; for Holland the solid ground upon which interpretation may be based is that of the individual personality itself. Texts may come and go, but the self, the

[7]Norman Holland, "UNITY IDENTITY TEXT SELF," *PMLA* 90 (1975): 817–18.

personality style, the *identity theme* that determines the individual's repertory of fantasies and defense mechanisms remains remarkably constant over time. What Holland suggests is that to the extent that a work of art threatens the reader's identity theme, the reader recomposes the text so that it replicates this theme. In effect, Holland substitutes the unity of the self for the unity of art. He usually speaks of the self as though it were more objectively knowable than texts are. As Holland admits from time to time, however, we can know others' selves only through our own (and thus the issue of counter-transference between the reader of the text and the observer of that reader cannot be evaded). Furthermore, Holland's idea of the self — his notion that one's identity does not change as the result of life experience — is debatable. Whether the defensive reading of the text replicates precisely the self that began to read or whether the self is not at least slightly altered by the experience are questions that cannot be defined out of existence.

David Bleich's theory of reading is closer to social psychology than to orthodox Freudianism. Bleich places the reading of texts in a social setting — the classroom — where knowledge about art and life is synthesized by a group. For Bleich, the text is a symbolic object upon which readers act, and the reader's initial and private response to a text is totally subjective, including all sorts of idiosyncratic associations and feelings. Within the social setting of the classroom, the private response is "negotiated" into meaningful knowledge via the individual's sense of the group's purposes. In the course of articulating a response to a text under the social pressure of the group, the reader prunes away, or at least brackets off as private or irrelevant, those aspects of the response that may not apply to others or that are inconsistent with the aim of the class. The response to the text is generalized, placed within a context determined by the ideology of the group. Bleich feels that within the pedagogical setting, knowledge does not move from teacher to student but is constructed by students in accord with a sense of the group aim, which may be initially defined and articulated by a teacher. But Bleich's notions of reading apply beyond his posited pedagogical setting, since people often read or experience works of art within a social setting, with friends or family, and try to communicate a sense of the experience to others.

Any study of this process inevitably leads to the sociology of literature, a field in which one might expect the Marxists to have done a great deal of work. In practice, however, Marxist theorists have tended to shy away from empirical studies of the literary marketplace and how individuals and groups within social settings actually read texts. Two fine studies in literary sociology are Jeffrey Sammons's *Literary Sociology and Practical Criticism* (1977) and Janice Radway's *Reading the Romance: Women, Patriarchy, and Popular Literature* (1984). The former is a lucid overview of the major issues of literary sociology; the latter, a demonstration of what can be done in the field. Radway examines why women read popular romances, but instead of merely theorizing about the repressed American housewife and her need for escape, she uses interviews and questionnaires to study the responses of a community of romance readers. Radway's study is well grounded in reader-response theory, and her initial chapter presents an overview of literary reception.

A feminist approach to the reading process that is related to both Bleich and Radway is Elizabeth A. Flynn's "Gender and Reading" (1985), an empirical study of how male and female students responded to stories like Joyce's "Araby," Hemingway's "Hills Like White Elephants," and Woolf's "Kew Gardens." Flynn found that male students often had a great deal of difficulty in keeping the appropriate distance from a story that made them uncomfortable, such as "Araby" with its depiction of a love-obsessed boy. Males either got too close to the story, by inappropriately identifying with the protagonist, or kept their distance by attempting to dominate the situation, often by dismissing the story altogether (males tended more often than females to dismiss what they did not understand). In contrast, women tended to avoid both extremes in their reaction to "Hills Like White Elephants," a story that should be at least as upsetting to them. In fact, they generally tended to "arrive at meaningful interpretations of stories because they more frequently break free of the submissive entanglement in a text and evaluate characters and events with critical detachment." Flynn presents raw data with her conclusions so that it is possible to get some sense of her own detachment as a reader of her students' responses. But there are obviously a host of variables (such as the students' relative intelligence and reading experience as well as the ongoing attitude of the instructor) that are difficult to estimate.

## THE PHENOMENOLOGISTS

In effect, formalist/structuralist theories have staked out the reader within the text, while psycho/social theories have been based on the actual reader outside the text. To the extent that there can be a middle ground, it is occupied by the phenomenological approaches to literature, which focus on literature as it is experienced by the thinking subject, the "I" in the center of our conscious world. Two traditions occupy this territory — one represented by the French phenomenologists Jean-Paul Sartre and Georges Poulet, the other by the West German critics of the school of Constance, Wolfgang Iser and Hans Robert Jauss.

Although the late Jean-Paul Sartre has often been labeled a Marxist critic, his discussion of the role of the reader and the writer in *What Is Literature?* (1966) is thoroughly existentialist — and existentialism, as has often been observed, is the ethical and political branch of phenomenology. The reader of "Why Write?" (reprinted here) will find major similarities between it and the theories of Georges Poulet.

Poulet's discussion of the act of reading emphasizes the way reading transforms the book-as-object — the heavy, dead, material thing — into a subject, an intelligence, a mind to which we subordinate our own.

Whenever I read, I mentally pronounce an *I*, yet the *I* which I pronounce is not myself. This is true even when the hero of a novel is presented in the third person, and even when there is no hero and nothing but reflections or propositions. . . . Another *I*, who has replaced my own, and who will continue to do so as long as I read. . . . A second self takes over, a self which thinks and feels for me.[8]

[8]Georges Poulet, "Criticism and the Experience of Interiority," in Richard Macksey and Eugenio

For Poulet, the purpose of this abdication of the self is, paradoxically, the further realization of the self:

> The annexation of my consciousness by . . . the other which is the work . . . in no way implies that I am the victim of any deprivation of consciousness. Everything happens, on the contrary, as though, from the moment I become a prey to what I read, I begin to share the use of my consciousness with . . . the conscious subject ensconced at the heart of the work.

Poulet's characteristic images are close to those of Plato. The subjective consciousness of the text is *inbreathed* by the reader in a sort of passive inspiration, like the *enthousiasmós* of the *Ion* or the *Phaedrus*. For Iser and Jauss the relationship of author and reader is less like that of the demon and the human being it has possessed than of the composer and the performer of a piece of music, a metaphor that suggests a new kind of connection between writer and reader. For the formalists and structuralists, the reader is essentially determined by the text; Booth's novels "create" their ideal readers like a sculptor molding wax. Fish's interpretive communities create the text themselves; the author's words are an indeterminate framework to which the community brings the meaning. Psychological critics like Holland view the text as fantasy material with which the reader copes, as with a disturbing dream. But Iser and Jauss perceive in the text the mutual dependence — the creative collaboration — of composer and performer. Although the composer is clearly the primary genius whose intentions must be respected, without the performer, the composer would remain mute. Following the terminology of Roman Ingarden, Iser and Jauss speak of the text as being *concretized* by the reader: The vague and ideal word is in the reading process made flesh. The difference between Iser and Jauss is primarily one of perspective: Iser's interest is in the *act* of reading as it happens for each of us; Jauss's concern has been with the *history* of reading and the contribution a history of reception can make to the broader concerns of literary history.

For Iser, the reader's performative activity is called into play by the gaps (*Löcher*) that every text contains, since no text can be fully explicit about everything. In the process of reading, for example, we imagine what the hero and heroine look like in ways consistent with the descriptions we are given in the text; nevertheless, two readers' mental pictures of Tom Jones would be vastly different. (This, Iser says, is why film realizations of novels invariably make us say to ourselves, "That's not the way I pictured him.") But beyond filling in descriptions the text leaves indeterminate, the reader also imagines scenes the text leaves tacit, dialogue that is left unspoken, and so on. Furthermore, it is not just a matter of understanding and creating a full sense of illusion out of the words that are directly before the reader's eyes. In a novel, the reading process takes place within the flow of a narrative moving from a beginning through a middle to an end. As we

---

Donato, *The Structuralist Controversy: The Languages of Criticism and the Sciences of Man* (Baltimore: Johns Hopkins University Press, 1972), p. 56.

read a given sentence, we may be forced to revise our understanding of what we have already read and processed, or to form expectations of what will happen in the future, expectations that may be fulfilled or shattered. Underlying this process, and guiding it, are "two main structural components within the text: first, a repertoire of familiar literary patterns and recurrent literary themes, together with allusions to familiar social and historical contexts; and second, techniques or strategies used to set the familiar against the unfamiliar." The text in any mature work of art, in other words, depends on the reader's prior understanding of the themes and conventions of story-telling, but it works *against* those conventions as much as it employs them in order to *defamiliarize* the reader, who would otherwise be bored by a predictable text.

During the last two hundred years, according to Iser's *The Implied Reader,* these general principles have been worked out in the English novel in very different ways. The reader in the eighteenth century was "guided — directly or indirectly, through affirmation or through negation — toward a conception of human nature and of reality." The nineteenth-century reader, by contrast, "was not told what part he was to play. Instead he had to discover the fact that society had imposed a part on him, the object being for him eventually to take up a critical attitude toward this imposition." Readers of the Victorian novel, therefore, were nudged into making the correct discoveries for themselves. Both of these modes depend upon the reader's capacity for subscribing to the illusion provoked by the text. The twentieth-century novel, in contrast, insists on rupturing these illusions and calling attention to its own use of technique — all this in order

> to provoke the reader into establishing for himself the connections between perception and thought. . . . In this way he may then be given the chance of discovering himself, both in and through his constant involvement in "home-made" illusions and fictions.[9]

For Iser, the history of the novel is the history of the ways in which writers created gaps for their readers to fill, and to an extent, his ideas are easily assimilated to those of rhetorical critics like Wayne Booth. For Hans Robert Jauss, on the other hand, literary history is as much the history of the reader as of the canonized authors, or to be more accurate, of the relationship between writing and the reading public that consumes and stimulates its production. These ideas are based on the philosophy of Hans-Georg Gadamer, whose theories of interpretation turn on the positive contributions made by our prejudices. Normally, "prejudice" has a negative connotation when it refers to one cause of our injustice to others, but for Gadamer and his pupils, these prejudices (in German, *Vorurteilungen*) are what allow us to understand the changing world at all. Our preunderstandings give us a settled context, a *horizon of expectations,* against which we can place and evaluate the new. And our horizon of expectations is constantly changing as our life experience adds to and alters our framework of vision.

In literary terms, there is a dialogical relation between the text and the reading

---

[9]Wolfgang Iser, *The Implied Reader: Patterns of Communication in Prose Fiction from Bunyan to Beckett* (Baltimore: Johns Hopkins University Press, 1974), pp. xiii–xiv.

public. The public reads the text from within its current horizon of expectations — that set of cultural, ethical, and aesthetic norms current at any given moment — and attempts to bring the work within those horizons. For some works, like popular literature meant for instant consumption, there will be no problem in fitting the text into such a horizon, but other works may challenge the audience's horizon of expectations along one or more fronts. Such works may succeed in changing the preunderstanding of the reading public, or a substantial portion of it, as was the case with Flaubert's *Madame Bovary.* On the other hand, such works may fail to engage the audience entirely and may be forgotten; or, like Melville's *Moby-Dick,* they may be read, but their most individual qualities may be ignored because they cannot be assimilated to the preunderstanding of the day. Forgotten or misread works, however, may be rediscovered by a later audience, when the horizon of expectations has, so to speak, caught up with them. Change in the horizon is produced partly by literary texts themselves, whose success creates a market and stimulates imitation by other authors, and partly by changes in economic, social, and political conditions, which make ideas and relations within texts more or less attractive.

For Jauss the writing of literary history would require that we recreate the horizon of expectations of the reading public for any given period. This we can piece together, partly from the texts themselves, and partly from the public and private responses of various levels of the reading public: other authors, publishers, critics, and private consumers. Creating the materials out of which a literary history might be written would require both synchronic and diachronic studies. One might begin with a synchronic study, in effect taking a "snapshot" of the literary world at a given date (Jauss himself has done a study of the horizon of expectations in France in 1857, the year of *Madame Bovary* and of Baudelaire's *Fleurs du Mal*), and by comparing such "snapshots" at various dates, put together a sense of how these horizons changed over time. In addition, diachronic studies, like histories of the reception of a given text from its publication to the present day, would be a useful supplement to the snapshots.

These "time-lapse photos" would give a stronger sense of how literary opinion shifts over the centuries (Jauss has produced a study over time of the reception of Baudelaire's "Spleen" poems). The end product will take a long time to produce, given the sheer amount of research into the reception of texts the method requires. But the result proposed is a literary history that goes beyond the "scissors-and-paste" histories detailing the lives and works of those authors that are currently valued. The history Jauss envisions would allow us to understand the evolution of textual production in relation to the changes in the cultural scene that generated evolution, including many factors we currently ignore, such as those evanescent productions whose popularity in one age were a passport to obscurity in the next.

As one might expect, the Marxists were most offended by Jauss's insistence that literary history needed to be reformed in order to include the participation of the readers who made up the market for literature. One might have thought them the group most concerned with the influence of the individual in a mass society, yet Jauss's competition with them exposed their neglect of the group they theoretically most favored. In fact, the publication of "Literary History as a Challenge to Literary Theory" provoked a decade of quarreling between the reception theorists of Constance and the Marxists across the border in East Germany. In the 1980s, however, both parties have seen that what they have in common dwarfs their area of contention, and indeed, some post-Althusserian Marxists (like the British Tony Bennett) have proposed programs for revamping literary history using methods that closely resemble Jauss's proposals. In addition to these quarrels with the Marxists, Jauss's theories have also provoked a large number of scholars, not just in Germany but in England and North America as well, into undertaking reception studies, which are just beginning to produce the "snapshots" and "time-lapse photos" of the audience that will eventuate in the new literary history Jauss prophesied.

Interest in the reader is a late development in critical theory. As a topic for investigation, it has attracted each of the major schools of thought, from Marxism through structuralism and feminism to deconstruction. It is likely that, following its neglect in the wake of the "affective fallacy," critical understanding of the audience — in all its various manifestations — has changed more in the past twenty years than in the previous two thousand.

## Selected Bibliography

Altick, Richard. *The English Common Reader: A Social History of the Mass Reading Public, 1800–1900.* Chicago: University of Chicago Press, 1957.

Barthes, Roland. *The Pleasure of the Text.* New York: Hill and Wang, 1975.

Bleich, David. *Readings and Feelings: An Introduction to Subjective Criticism.* Urbana, Ill.: National Council of Teachers of English, 1975.

———. *Subjective Criticism.* Baltimore: Johns Hopkins University Press, 1978.

Booth, Stephen. *An Essay on Shakespeare's Sonnets.* New Haven: Yale University Press, 1969.

Booth, Wayne C. *The Rhetoric of Fiction.* Chicago: University of Chicago Press, 1961; second edition 1983.

———. *A Rhetoric of Irony.* Chicago: University of Chicago Press, 1974.

———. *The Company We Keep: Ethical Criticism and the Ethics of Reading.* Berkeley: University of California Press, 1988.

Cruse, Amy. *The Englishman and His Books in the Early Nineteenth Century.* London: George G. Harrap, 1930.

Culler, Jonathan. *Structuralist Poetics.* Ithaca: Cornell University Press, 1975.

Eco, Umberto. *The Role of the Reader: Explorations in the Semiotics of Texts.* Bloomington: Indiana University Press, 1979.

Escarpit, Robert. *Sociology of Literature.* Painesville, Ohio: Lake Erie College Press, 1965.

———. "The Sociology of Literature." *International Encyclopaedia of Social Science.* Vol. 9. New York: Macmillan, 1968, 417–25.

Fetterley, Judith. *The Resisting Reader: A Feminist Approach to American Fiction.* Bloomington: Indiana University Press, 1978.

Fish, Stanley. *Self-Consuming Artifacts: The Experience of Seventeenth-Century Literature.* Berkeley: University of California Press, 1972.

————. *Is There a Text in This Class? The Authority of Interpretive Communities*. Cambridge: Harvard University Press, 1980.

Flynn, Elizabeth A. "Gender and Reading." *College English* 45 (1983): 236–253.

Gadamer, Hans-Georg. *Truth and Method*. London: Sheed and Ward, 1975.

Hohendahl, Peter Uwe. "Introduction to Reception Aesthetics." *New German Critique* 10 (1977): 29–63.

Holland, Norman N. *The Dynamics of Literary Response*. New York: Oxford University Press, 1968.

————. *5 Readers Reading*. New Haven: Yale University Press, 1975.

Holub, Robert C. *Reception Theory: A Critical Introduction*. London: Methuen, 1984.

Ingarden, Roman. *The Cognition of the Literary Work of Art*. Evanston, Ill.: Northwestern University Press, 1973.

Iser, Wolfgang. *The Implied Reader: Patterns of Communication in Prose Fiction from Bunyan to Beckett*. Baltimore: Johns Hopkins University Press, 1974.

————. *The Act of Reading: A Theory of Aesthetic Response*. Baltimore: Johns Hopkins University Press, 1978.

Jauss, Hans Robert. "Literary History as a Challenge to Literary Theory." In *Toward an Aesthetics of Reception*, trans. Timothy Bahti, pp. 3–46. Minneapolis: University of Minnesota Press, 1982.

————. *Aesthetic Experience and Literary Hermeneutics*. Minneapolis: University of Minnesota Press, 1982.

————. "Theses on the Transition from the Aesthetics of Literary Works to a Theory of Aesthetic Experience." In *Interpretation of Narrative*, ed. Mario J. Valdès and Owen J. Miller, pp. 138–46. Toronto: University of Toronto Press, 1978.

Leavis, Q. D. *Fiction and the Reading Public*. London: Chatto and Windus, 1932.

Lesser, Simon O. *Fiction and the Unconscious*. Boston: Vintage, 1957.

Mailloux, Steven J. *Interpretive Conventions*. Ithaca: Cornell University Press, 1982.

Miles, David H. "Literary Sociology: Some Introductory Notes." *German Quarterly* 48 (January 1975): 20–45.

Miller, Owen J. "Reading as a Process of Reconstruction: A Critique of Recent Structuralist Formulations." In *Interpretation of Narrative*, ed. Mario J. Valdès and Owen J. Miller, pp. 19–27. Toronto: University of Toronto Press, 1978.

Naumann, Manfred. "Literary Production and Reception." *New Literary History* 8 (1976): 107–26.

Nelson, Cary. "Reading Criticism." *PMLA* 91 (1976): 801–15.

Poulet, Georges. "Criticism and the Experience of Interiority." In *The Structuralist Controversy: The Languages of Criticism and the Sciences of Man*, ed. Richard Macksey and Eugenio Donato. Baltimore: Johns Hopkins University Press, 1972.

Preston, John. *The Created Self: The Reader's Role in Eighteenth-Century Fiction*. New York: Barnes and Noble, 1970.

Prince, Gerald. "Introduction to the Study of the Narratee." *Poétique* 14 (1973): 177–96.

Rabinowitz, Peter. "Truth in Fiction: A Reexamination of Audiences." *Critical Inquiry* 4 (1977): 121–41.

————. *Before Reading*. Ithaca: Cornell University Press, 1987.

Radway, Janice A. *Reading the Romance: Women, Patriarchy, and Popular Literature*. Chapel Hill: University of North Carolina Press, 1984.

Reichert, John. *Making Sense of Literature*. Chicago: University of Chicago Press, 1977.

Richards, I. A. *Practical Criticism: A Study of Literary Judgment*. New York: Harcourt, Brace, 1935.

Richter, David. "The Reader as Ironic Victim." *Novel* 14, no. 2 (1981): 135–51.

―――. "The Reception of the Gothic Novel in the 1790's." In *The Idea of the Novel in the Eighteenth Century,* ed. Robert Uphaus. East Lansing, Mich.: Colleagues Press, 1988.

―――. "The Unguarded Prison: Reception Theory, Structural Marxism, and the Structure of Literary History." In *The Eighteenth Century: Theory and Interpretation,* forthcoming 1989.

―――. *The Reader, the Text, the Poem: The Transactional Theory of the Literary Work.* Carbondale: Southern Illinois University Press, 1978.

Rosenblatt, Louise. *Literature as Exploration.* 1938; New York: Modern Language Association, 1983.

Sammons, Jeffrey. *Literary Sociology and Practical Criticism.* Bloomington: Indiana University Press, 1977.

Sartre, Jean-Paul. *What Is Literature?* New York: Philosophical Library, 1966.

Schücking, L. L. *The Sociology of Literary Taste.* 3rd ed. Chicago: University of Chicago Press, 1966.

Suleiman, Susan, and Inge Crosman, eds. *The Reader in the Text: Essays on Audience and Interpretation.* Princeton: Princeton University Press, 1980.

Tompkins, Jane P., ed. *Reader-Response Criticism: From Formalism to Post-Structuralism.* Baltimore: Johns Hopkins University Press, 1980.

Weimann, Robert. "'Reception Aesthetics' and the Crisis of Literary History." *Clio* 5 (1975): 3–33.

Wellek, René. "Zur methodischen Aporie einen Rezeptions-geschichte." In *Geschichte: Ereignis und Erzählung,* ed. Reinhart Koselleck and Wolf-Dieter Stempel. Munich: Wilhelm Fink Verlag, 1973.

# Jean-Paul Sartre

1905–1980

*As a philosopher, novelist, dramatist, and essayist, Jean-Paul Sartre is indelibly associated with existentialism, the ethical and humanistic movement that developed from the phenomenological thought of Edmund Husserl and Martin Heidegger. Sartre was born in Paris and educated at the École Normale Supérieure, where he met his lifelong companion, Simone de Beauvoir (see Ch. 6). After graduating in 1929, Sartre taught for two decades at various lycées while adapting Husserlian phenomenology to the emotions and the imagination. Several shorter treatises culminated in his monumental* Being and Nothingness *(1943), whose title plays off* Being and Time, *the masterwork of Heidegger, with whom he had studied in Berlin. If Sartre's name became a household word, as those of his teachers did not, it was largely because Sartre presented his ideas accessibly in novels, such as* Nausea *(1938) and the* Roads to Freedom *trilogy (1945–49). His preferred mode (possibly because humanity expresses its nature best through action) was the drama, and successful plays like* The Flies *(1943),* No Exit *(1944),* Dirty Hands *(1948), and* The Condemned of Altona *(1959) won adherents to his ideas. After World War II (during which he served in the French army and was imprisoned until 1941), Sartre's principal interests were the politics of the Left and literary criticism. He produced studies of Baudelaire (1947) and Jean Genet (1952), leading to his dense and lengthy three-volume "total biography," from both Freudian and Marxist perspectives, of*

*Gustave Flaubert (L'Idiot de la famille, 1971–72). Sartre's theoretical view of literature, in which both phenomenological and Marxist themes predominate, is best seen in* What Is Literature? *(1949), from which "Why Write?" is reprinted here.*

# Why Write?

Each one has his reasons: for one, art is a flight; for another, a means of conquering. But one can flee into a hermitage, into madness, into death. One can conquer by arms. Why does it have to be *writing,* why does one have to manage his escapes and conquests by *writing*? Because, behind the various aims of authors, there is a deeper and more immediate choice which is common to all of us. We shall try to elucidate this choice, and we shall see whether it is not in the name of this very choice of writing that the engagement of writers must be required.

Each of our perceptions is accompanied by the consciousness that human reality is a "revealer," that is, it is through human reality that "there is" being, or, to put it differently, that man is the means by which things are manifested. It is our presence in the world which multiplies relations. It is we who set up a relationship between this tree and that bit of sky. Thanks to us, that star which has been dead for millennia, that quarter moon, and that dark river are disclosed in the unity of a landscape. It is the speed of our auto and our airplane which organizes the great masses of the earth. With each of our acts, the world reveals to us a new face. But, if we know that we are directors of being, we also know that we are not its producers. If we turn away from this landscape, it will sink back into its dark permanence. At least, it will sink back; there is no one mad enough to think that it is going to be annihilated. It is we who shall be annihilated, and the earth will remain in its lethargy until another consciousness comes along to awaken it. Thus, to our inner certainty of being "revealers" is added that of being inessential in relation to the thing revealed.

One of the chief motives of artistic creation is certainly the need of feeling that we are essential in relationship to the world. If I fix on canvas or in writing a certain aspect of the fields or the sea or a look on someone's face which I have disclosed, I am conscious of having produced them by condensing relationships, by introducing order where there was none, by imposing the unity of mind on the diversity of things. That is, I feel myself essential in relation to my creation. But this time it is the created object which escapes me; I can not reveal and produce at the same time. The creation becomes inessential in relation to the creative activity. First of all, even if it appears to others as definitive, the created object always seems to us in a state of suspension; we can always change this line, that shade, that word. Thus, it never *forces itself.* A novice painter asked his teacher, "When should I consider my painting finished?" And the teacher answered, "When you can look at it in amazement and say to yourself '*I'm* the one who did *that*!'"

Which amounts to saying "never." For it is virtually considering one's work with someone else's eyes and revealing what one has created. But it is self-evident that we are proportionally less conscious of the thing produced and more conscious of our productive activity. When it is a matter of pottery or carpentry, we work according to traditional norms, with tools whose usage is codified; it is Heidegger's famous "they" who are working with our hands. In this case, the result can seem to us sufficiently strange to preserve its objectivity in our eyes. But if we ourselves produce the rules of production, the measures, the criteria, and if our creative drive comes from the very depths of our heart, then we never find anything but ourselves in our work. It is we who have invented the laws by which we judge it. It is our history, our love, our gaiety that we recognize in it. Even if we should regard it without touching it any further, we never *receive* from it that gaiety or love. We put them

Translated by Bernard Frechtman.

into it. The results which we have obtained on canvas or paper never seem to us *objective*. We are too familiar with the processes of which they are the effects. These processes remain a subjective discovery; they are ourselves, our inspiration, our ruse, and when we seek to *perceive* our work, we create it again, we repeat mentally the operations which produced it; each of its aspects appears as a result. Thus, in the perception, the object is given as the essential thing and the subject as the inessential. The latter seeks essentiality in the creation and obtains it, but then it is the object which becomes the inessential.

This dialectic is nowhere more apparent than in the art of writing, for the literary object is a peculiar top which exists only in movement. To make it come into view a concrete act called reading is necessary, and it lasts only as long as this act can last. Beyond that, there are only black marks on paper. Now, the writer can not read what he writes, whereas the shoemaker can put on the shoes he has just made if they are his size, and the architect can live in the house he has built. In reading, one foresees; one waits. He foresees the end of the sentence, the following sentence, the next page. He waits for them to confirm or disappoint his foresights. The reading is composed of a host of hypotheses, of dreams followed by awakenings, of hopes and deceptions. Readers are always ahead of the sentence they are reading in a merely probable future which partly collapses and partly comes together in proportion as they progress, which withdraws from one page to the next and forms the moving horizon of the literary object. Without waiting, without a future, without ignorance, there is no objectivity.

Now the operation of writing involves an implicit quasi-reading which makes real reading impossible. When the words form under his pen, the author doubtless sees them, but he does not see them as the reader does, since he knows them before writing them down. The function of his gaze is not to reveal, by stroking them, the sleeping words which are waiting to be read, but to control the sketching of the signs. In short, it is a purely regulating mission, and the view before him reveals nothing except for slight slips of the pen. The writer neither foresees nor conjectures; he *projects*. It often happens that he awaits, as they say, the inspiration. But one does not wait for himself the way he waits for others. If he hesitates, he knows that the future is not made, that he himself is going to make it, and if he still does not know what is going to happen to his hero, that simply means that he has not thought about it, that he has not decided upon anything. The future is then a blank page, whereas the future of the reader is two hundred pages filled with words which separate him from the end. Thus, the writer meets everywhere only *his* knowledge, *his* will, *his* plans, in short, himself. He touches only his own subjectivity; the object he creates is out of reach; he does not create it *for himself*. If he rereads himself, it is already too late. The sentence will never quite be a thing in his eyes. He goes to the very limits of the subjective but without crossing it. He appreciates the effect of a touch, of an epigram, of a well-placed adjective, but it is the effect they will have on others. He can judge it, not feel it. Proust never discovered the homosexuality of Charlus, since he had decided upon it even before starting on his book. And if a day comes when the book takes on for its author a semblance of objectivity, it is that years have passed, that he has forgotten it, that its spirit is quite foreign to him, and doubtless he is no longer capable of writing it. This was the case with Rousseau when he reread the *Social Contract* at the end of his life.

Thus, it is not true that one writes for himself. That would be the worst blow. In projecting his emotions on paper, one barely manages to give them a languishing extension. The creative act is only an incomplete and abstract moment in the production of a work. If the author existed alone he would be able to write as much as he liked; the work as *object* would never see the light of day and he would either have to put down his pen or despair. But the operation of writing implies that of reading as its dialectical correlative and these two connected acts necessitate two distinct agents. It is the conjoint effort of author and reader which brings upon the scene that concrete and imaginary object which is the work of the mind. There is no art except for and by others.

Reading seems, in fact, to be the synthesis of

perception and creation.[1] It supposes the essentiality of both the subject and the object. The object is essential because it is strictly transcendent, because it imposes its own structures, and because one must wait for it and observe it; but the subject is also essential because it is required not only to disclose the object (that is, to make *there be* an object) but also so that this object might *be* (that is, to produce it). In a word, the reader is conscious of disclosing in creating, of creating by disclosing. In reality, it is not necessary to believe that reading is a mechanical operation and that signs make an impression upon him as light does on a photographic plate. If he is inattentive, tired, stupid, or thoughtless, most of the relations will escape him. He will never manage to "catch on" to the object (in the sense in which we see that fire "catches" or "doesn't catch"). He will draw some phrases out of the shadow, but they will seem to appear as random strokes. If he is at his best, he will project beyond the words a synthetic form, each phrase of which will be no more than a partial function: the "theme," the "subject," or the "meaning." Thus, from the very beginning, the meaning is no longer contained in the words, since it is he, on the contrary, who allows the signification of each of them to be understood; and the literary object, though realized *through* language, is never given *in* language. On the contrary, it is by nature a silence and an opponent of the word. In addition, the hundred thousand words aligned in a book can be read one by one so that the meaning of the work does not emerge. Nothing is accomplished if the reader does not put himself from the very beginning and almost without a guide at the height of this silence; if, in short, he does not invent it and does not then place there, and hold on to, the words and sentences which he awakens. And if I am told that it would be more fitting to call this operation a reinvention or a discovery, I shall answer that, first, such a reinvention would be as new and as original an act as the first invention. And, especially, when an object has never existed before,

there can be no question of reinventing it or discovering it. For if the silence about which I am speaking is really the goal at which the author is aiming, he has, at least, never been familiar with it; his silence is subjective and anterior to language. It is the absence of words, the undifferentiated and lived silence of inspiration, which the word will then particularize, whereas the silence produced by the reader is an object. And at the very interior of this object there are more silences — which the author does not tell. It is a question of silences which are so particular that they could not retain any meaning outside of the object which the reading causes to appear. However, it is these which give it its density and its particular face.

To say that they are unexpressed is hardly the word; for they are precisely the inexpressible. And that is why one does not come upon them at any definite moment in the reading; they are everywhere and nowhere. The quality of the marvelous in *The Wanderer* (*Le Grand Meaulnes*), the grandiosity of *Armance,* the degree of realism and truth of Kafka's mythology, these are never given. The reader must invent them all in a continual exceeding of the written thing. To be sure, the author guides him, but all he does is guide him. The landmarks he sets up are separated by the void. The reader must unite them; he must go beyond them. In short, reading is directed creation.

On the one hand, the literary object has no other substance than the reader's subjectivity; Raskolnikov's waiting is my waiting which I lend him. Without this impatience of the reader he would remain only a collection of signs. His hatred of the police magistrate who questions him is my hatred which has been solicited and wheedled out of me by signs, and the police magistrate himself would not exist without the hatred I have for him via Raskolnikov. That is what animates him, it is his very flesh.

But on the other hand, the words are there like traps to arouse our feelings and to reflect them toward us. Each word is a path of transcendence; it shapes our feelings, names them, and attributes them to an imaginary personage who takes it upon himself to live them for us and who has no other substance than these bor-

[1]The same is true in different degrees regarding the spectator's attitude before other works of art (paintings, symphonies, statues, etc.) [Au.]

rowed passions; he confers objects, perspectives, and a horizon upon them.

Thus, for the reader, all is to do and all is already done; the work exists only at the exact level of his capacities; while he reads and creates, he knows that he can always go further in his reading, can always create more profoundly, and thus the work seems to him as inexhaustible and opaque as things. We would readily reconcile that "rational intuition" which Kant reserved to divine Reason with this absolute production of qualities, which, to the extent that they emanate from our subjectivity, congeal before our eyes into impermeable objectivities.

Since the creation can find its fulfillment only in reading, since the artist must entrust to another the job of carrying out what he has begun, since it is only through the consciousness of the reader that he can regard himself as essential to his work, all literary work is an appeal. To write is to make an appeal to the reader that he lead into objective existence the revelation which I have undertaken by means of language. And if it should be asked *to what* the writer is appealing, the answer is simple. As the sufficient reason for the appearance of the aesthetic object is never found either in the book (where we find merely solicitations to produce the object) or in the author's mind, and as his subjectivity, which he cannot get away from, cannot give a reason for the act of leading into objectivity, the appearance of the work of art is a new event which cannot *be explained* by anterior data. And since this directed creation is an absolute beginning, it is therefore brought about by the freedom of the reader, and by what is purest in that freedom. Thus, the writer appeals to the reader's freedom to collaborate in the production of his work.

It will doubtless be said that all tools address themselves to our freedom since they are the instruments of a possible action, and that the work of art is not unique in that. And it is true that the tool is the congealed outline of an operation. But it remains on the level of the hypothetical imperative. I may use a hammer to nail up a case or to hit my neighbor over the head. Insofar as I consider it in itself, it is not an appeal to my freedom; it does not put me face to face with it; rather, it aims at using it by

substituting a set succession of traditional procedures for the free invention of means. The book does not serve my freedom; it requires it. Indeed, one cannot address himself to freedom as such by means of constraint, fascination, or entreaties. There is only one way of attaining it; first, by recognizing it, then, having confidence in it, and finally, requiring of it an act, an act in its own name, that is, in the name of the confidence that one brings to it.

Thus, the book is not, like the tool, a means for any end whatever; the end to which it offers itself is the reader's freedom. And the Kantian expression "finality without end"[2] seems to me quite inappropriate for designating the work of art. In fact, it implies that the aesthetic object presents only the appearance of a finality and is limited to soliciting the free and ordered play of the imagination. It forgets that the imagination of the spectator has not only a regulating function, but a constitutive one. It does not play; it is called upon to recompose the beautiful object beyond the traces left by the artist. The imagination can not revel in itself any more than can the other functions of the mind; it is always on the outside, always engaged in an enterprise. There would be finality without end if some object offered such a set ordering that it would lead us to suppose that it has one even though we can not ascribe one to it. By defining the beautiful in this way one can — and this is Kant's aim — liken the beauty of art to natural beauty, since a flower, for example, presents so much symmetry, such harmonious colors, and such regular curves, that one is immediately tempted to seek a finalist explanation for all these properties and to see them as just so many means at the disposal of an unknown end. But that is exactly the error. The beauty of nature is in no way comparable to that of art. The work of art *does not have* an end; there we agree with Kant. But the reason is that it is an end. The Kantian formula does not account for the appeal which resounds at the basis of each painting, each statue, each book. Kant believes that the work of art first exists as fact and that it is then seen. Whereas, it exists only

[2]*Zweckmässigkeit ohne Zweck,* purposiveness without purpose. See Kant, p. 248. [Ed.]

if one *looks* at it and if it is first pure appeal, pure exigence to exist. It is not an instrument whose existence is manifest and whose end is undetermined. It presents itself as a task to be discharged; from the very beginning it places itself on the level of the categorical imperative. You are perfectly free to leave that book on the table. But if you open it, you assume responsibility for it. For freedom is not experienced by its enjoying its free subjective functioning, but in a creative act required by an imperative. This absolute end, this imperative which is transcendent yet acquiesced in, which freedom itself adopts as its own, is what we call a value. The work of art is a value because it is an appeal.

If I appeal to my reader so that we may carry the enterprise which I have begun to a successful conclusion, it is self-evident that I consider him as a pure freedom, as an unconditioned activity; thus, in no case can I address myself to his passivity, that is, try to *affect* him, to communicate to him, from the very first, emotions of fear, desire, or anger. There are, doubtless, authors who concern themselves solely with arousing these emotions because they are foreseeable, manageable, and because they have at their disposal sure-fire means for provoking them. But it is also true that they are reproached for this kind of thing, as Euripides has been since antiquity because he had children appear on the stage. Freedom is alienated in the state of passion; it is abruptly engaged in partial enterprises; it loses sight of its task which is to produce an absolute end. And the book is no longer anything but a means for feeding hate or desire. The writer should not seek to *overwhelm;* otherwise he is in contradiction with himself; if he wishes to *make demands* he must propose only the task to be fulfilled. Hence, the character of pure presentation which appears essential to the work of art. The reader must be able to make a certain aesthetic withdrawal. This is what Gautier foolishly confused with "art for art's sake" and the Parnassians with the imperturbability of the artist. It is simply a matter of precaution, and Genet more justly calls it the author's politeness toward the reader. But that does not mean that the writer makes an appeal to some sort of abstract and conceptual freedom. One certainly creates the aesthetic object with feelings; if it is touching, it appears through our tears; if it is comic, it will be recognized by laughter. However, these feelings are of a particular kind. They have their origin in freedom; they are loaned. The belief which I accord the tale is freely assented to. It is a Passion, in the Christian sense of the word, that is, a freedom which resolutely puts itself into a state of passivity to obtain a certain transcendent effect by this sacrifice. The reader renders himself credulous; he descends into credulity which, though it ends by enclosing him like a dream, is at every moment conscious of being free. An effort is sometimes made to force the writer into this dilemma: "Either one believes in your story, and it is intolerable, or one does not believe in it, and it is ridiculous." But the argument is absurd because the characteristic of aesthetic consciousness is to be a belief by means of engagement, by oath, a belief sustained by fidelity to one's self and to the author, a perpetually renewed choice to believe. I can awaken at every moment, and I know it; but I do not want to; reading is a free dream. So that all feelings which are exacted on the basis of this imaginary belief are like particular modulations of my freedom. Far from absorbing or masking it, they are so many different ways it has chosen to reveal itself to itself. Raskolnikov, as I have said, would only be a shadow, without the mixture of repulsion and friendship which I feel for him and which makes him live. But, by a reversal which is the characteristic of the imaginary object, it is not his behavior which excites my indignation or esteem, but my indignation and esteem which give consistency and objectivity to his behavior. Thus, the reader's feelings are never dominated by the object, and as no external reality can condition them, they have their permanent source in freedom; that is, they are all generous — for I call a feeling generous which has its origin and its end in freedom. Thus, reading is an exercise in generosity, and what the writer requires of the reader is not the application of an abstract freedom but the gift of his whole person, with his passions, his prepossessions, his sympathies, his sexual temperament, and his scale of values.

Only this person will give himself generously; freedom goes through and through him and comes to transform the darkest masses of his sensibility. And as activity has rendered itself passive in order for it better to create the object, vice-versa, passivity becomes an act; the man who is reading has raised himself to the highest degree. That is why we see people who are known for their toughness shed tears at the recital of imaginary misfortunes; for the moment they have become what they would have been if they had not spent their lives hiding their freedom from themselves.

Thus, the author writes in order to address himself to the freedom of readers, and he requires it in order to make his work exist. But he does not stop there; he also requires that they return this confidence which he has given them, that they recognize his creative freedom, and that they in turn solicit it by a symmetrical and inverse appeal. Here there appears the other dialectical paradox of reading; the more we experience our freedom, the more we recognize that of the other; the more he demands of us, the more we demand of him.

When I am enchanted with a landscape, I know very well that it is not I who create it, but I also know that without me the relations which are established before my eyes among the trees, the foliage, the earth, and the grass would not exist at all. I know that I can give no reason for the appearance of finality which I discover in the assortment of hues and in the harmony of the forms and movements created by the wind. Yet, it exists; there it is before my eyes, and I can make *there be* being only if being already *is*. But even if I believe in God, I can not establish any passage, unless it be purely verbal, between the divine, universal solicitude and the particular spectacle which I am considering. To say that He made the landscape in order to charm me or that He made me the kind of person who is pleased by it is to take a question for an answer. Is the marriage of this blue and that green deliberate? How can I know? The idea of a universal providence is no guarantee of any particular intention, especially in the case under consideration, since the green of the grass is explained by biological laws, specific constants, and geographical determinism, while the reason for the blue of the water is accounted for by the depth of the river, the nature of the soil and the swiftness of the current. The assorting of the shades, if it is willed, can only be something *thrown into the bargain;* it is the meeting of two causal series, that is to say, at first sight, a fact of chance. At best, the finality remains problematic. All the relations we establish remain hypotheses; no end is proposed to us in the manner of an imperative, since none is expressly revealed as having been willed by a creator. Thus, our freedom is never *called forth* by natural beauty. Or rather, there is an appearance of order in the ensemble of the foliage, the forms, and the movements, hence, the illusion of a calling forth which seems to solicit this freedom and which disappears immediately when one regards it. Hardly have we begun to run our eyes over this arrangement, than the call disappears; we remain alone, free to tie up one color with another or with a third, to set up a relationship between the tree and the water or the tree and the sky, or the tree, the water and the sky. My freedom becomes caprice. To the extent that I establish new relationships, I remove myself further from the illusory objectivity which solicits me. I *muse* about certain motifs which are vaguely outlined by the things; the natural reality is no longer anything but a pretext for musing. Or, in that case, because I have deeply regretted that this arrangement which was momentarily perceived was not offered to me by somebody and consequently is not *real,* the result is that I fix my dream, that I transpose it to canvas or in writing. Thus, I interpose myself between the finality without end which appears in the natural spectacles and the gaze of other men. I transmit it to them. It becomes human by this transmission. Art here is a ceremony of the *gift* and the gift alone brings about the metamorphosis. It is something like the transmission of titles and powers in the matriarchate where the mother does not possess the names, but is the indispensable intermediary between uncle and nephew. Since I have captured this illusion in flight, since I lay it out for other men and have disengaged it and rethought it for them, they can consider it with confidence. It has become intentional. As for me, I remain, to be sure, at the border of the subjective and the objective without ever being able to contemplate the objective ordonnance which I transmit.

The reader, on the contrary, progresses in security. However far he may go, the author has gone farther. Whatever connections he may establish among the different parts of the book — among the chapters or the words — he has a guarantee, namely, that they have been expressly willed. As Descartes says, he can even pretend that there is a secret order among parts which seem to have no connection. The creator has preceded him along the way, and the most beautiful disorders are effects of art, that is, again order. Reading is induction, interpolation, extrapolation, and the basis of these activities rests on the reader's will, as for a long time it was believed that that of scientific induction rested on the divine will. A gentle force accompanies us and supports us from the first page to the last. That does not mean that we fathom the artist's intentions easily. They constitute, as we have said, the object of conjectures, and there is an *experience* of the reader; but these conjectures are supported by the great certainty we have that the beauties which appear in the book are never accidental. In nature, the tree and the sky harmonize only by chance; if, on the contrary, in the novel, the protagonists find themselves in a *certain* tower, in a *certain* prison, if they stroll in a *certain* garden, it is a matter both of the restitution of independent causal series (the character had a certain state of mind which was due to a succession of psychological and social events; on the other hand, he betook himself to a determined place and the layout of the city required him to cross a certain park) and of the expression of a deeper finality, for the park came into existence only *in order to* harmonize with a certain state of mind, to express it by means of things or to put it into relief by a vivid contrast, and the state of mind itself was conceived in connection with the landscape. Here it is causality which is appearance and which might be called "causality without cause," and it is the finality which is the profound reality. But if I can thus in all confidence put the order of ends under the order of causes, it is because by opening the book I am asserting that the object has its source in human freedom.

If I were to suspect the artist of having written out of passion and in passion, my confidence would immediately vanish, for it would serve no purpose to have supported the order of causes by the order of ends. The latter would be supported in its turn by a psychic causality and the work of art would end by re-entering the chain of determinism. Certainly I do not deny when I am reading that the author may be impassioned, nor even that he might have conceived the first plan of his work under the sway of passion. But his decision to write supposes that he withdraws somewhat from his feelings, in short, that he has transformed his emotions into free emotions as I do mine while reading him; that is, that he is in an attitude of generosity.

Thus, reading is a pact of generosity between author and reader. Each one trusts the other; each one counts on the other, demands of the other as much as he demands of himself. For this confidence is itself generosity. Nothing can force the author to believe that his reader will use his freedom; nothing can force the reader to believe that the author has used his. Both of them make a free decision. There is then established a dialectical going-and-coming; when I read, I make demands; if my demands are met, what I am then reading provokes me to demand more of the author, which means to demand of the author that he demand more of me. And, vice-versa, the author's demand is that I carry my demands to the highest pitch. Thus, my freedom, by revealing itself, reveals the freedom of the other.

It matters little whether the aesthetic object is the product of "realistic" art (or supposedly such) or "formal" art. At any rate, the natural relations are inverted; that tree on the first plane of the Cézanne painting first appears as the product of a causal chain. But the causality is an illusion; it will doubtless remain as a proposition as long as we look at the painting, but it will be supported by a deep finality; if the tree is placed in such a way, it is because the rest of the painting *requires* that this form and those colors be placed on the first plane. Thus, through the phenomenal causality, our gaze attains finality as the deep structure of the object, and, beyond finality, it attains human freedom as its source and original basis. Vermeer's realism is carried so far that at first it might be thought to be photographic. But if one considers the splendor of his texture, the pink and velvety glory of his little brick walls, the blue thickness of a branch of woodbine, the glazed darkness of his vestibules, the orange-colored flesh of his faces which are as polished as the stone of holy-water basins, one suddenly feels, in the pleasure that he experiences, that the finality is not so much in the forms or colors as in his material imagination. It is the very substance and temper of the things which here give the forms their reason for being. With this realist we are perhaps closest to absolute creation, since it is in the very passivity of the matter that we meet the unfathomable freedom of man.

The work is never limited to the painted, sculpted, or narrated object. Just as one perceives things only against the background of the world, so the objects represented by art appear against the background of the universe. On the background of the adventures of Fabrice[3] are the Italy of 1820, Austria, France, the sky and stars which the Abbé Blanis consults, and finally the whole earth. If the painter presents us with a field or a vase of flowers, his paintings are windows which are open on the whole world. We follow the red path which is buried among the wheat much farther than Van Gogh has painted it, among other wheat fields, under other clouds, to the river which empties into the sea, and we extend to infinity, to the other end of the world, the deep finality which supports the existence of the field and the earth. So that, through the various objects which it produces or reproduces, the creative act aims at a total renewal of the world. Each painting, each book, is a recovery of the totality of being. Each of them presents this totality to the freedom of the spectator. For this is quite the final goal of art: to recover this world by giving it to be seen as it is, but as if it had its source in human freedom. But, since what the author creates takes on objective reality only in the eyes of the spectator, this recovery is consecrated by the

ceremony of the spectacle — and particularly of reading. We are already in a better position to answer the question we raised a while ago: the writer chooses to appeal to the freedom of other men so that, by the reciprocal implications of their demands, they may readapt the totality of being to man and may again enclose the universe within man.

If we wish to go still further, we must bear in mind that the writer, like all other artists, aims at giving his reader a certain feeling that is customarily called aesthetic pleasure, and which I would very much rather call aesthetic joy, and that this feeling, when it appears, is a sign that the work is achieved. It is therefore fitting to examine it in the light of the preceding considerations. In effect, this joy, which is denied to the creator, insofar as he creates, becomes one with the aesthetic consciousness of the spectator, that is, in the case under consideration, of the reader. It is a complex feeling but one whose structures and condition are inseparable from one another. It is identical, at first, with the recognition of a transcendent and absolute end which, for a moment, suspends the utilitarian round of ends-means and means-ends,[4] that is, of an appeal or, what amounts to the same thing, of a value. And the positional consciousness which I take of this value is necessarily accompanied by the non-positional consciousness of my freedom, since my freedom is manifested to itself by a transcendent exigency. The recognition of freedom by itself is joy, but this structure of non-thetical consciousness implies another: since, in effect, reading is creation, my freedom does not only appear to itself as pure autonomy but as creative activity, that is, it is not limited to giving itself its own law but perceives itself as being constitutive of the object. It is on this level that the phenomenon specifically is manifested, that is, a creation wherein the created object is given *as object* to its creator. It is the sole case in which the creator gets any enjoyment out of the object he creates. And the word enjoyment which is applied to the positional consciousness of the

---

[3]In Stendhal's *Charterhouse of Parma* (1839). [Ed.]

[4]In *practical life* a means may be taken for an end as soon as one searches for it, and each end is revealed as a means of attaining another end. [Au.]

work read indicates sufficiently that we are in the presence of an essential structure of aesthetic joy. This positional enjoyment is accompanied by the non-positional consciousness of being essential in relation to an object perceived as essential. I shall call this aspect of aesthetic consciousness the feeling of security; it is this which stamps the strongest aesthetic emotions with a sovereign calm. It has its origin in the authentication of a strict harmony between subjectivity and objectivity. As, on the other hand, the aesthetic object is properly the world insofar as it is aimed at through the imaginary, aesthetic joy accompanies the positional consciousness that the world is a value, that is, a task proposed to human freedom. I shall call this the aesthetic modification of the human project, for, as usual, the world appears as the horizon of our situation, as the infinite distance which separates us from ourselves, as the synthetic totality of the given, as the undifferentiated ensemble of obstacles and implements — but never as a demand addressed to our freedom. Thus, aesthetic joy proceeds to this level of the consciousness which I take of recovering and internalizing that which is non-ego par excellence, since I transform the given into an imperative and the fact into a value. The world is *my task,* that is, the essential and freely accepted function of my freedom is to make that unique and absolute object which is the universe come into being in an unconditioned movement. And, thirdly, the preceding structures imply a pact between human freedoms, for, on the one hand, reading is a confident and exacting recognition of the freedom of the writer, and, on the other hand, aesthetic pleasure, as it is itself experienced in the form of a value, involves an absolute exigence in regard to others; every man, insofar as he is a freedom, feels the same pleasure in reading the same work. Thus, all mankind is present in its highest freedom; it sustains the being of a world which is both *its* world and the "external" world. In aesthetic joy the positional consciousness is an *image-making* consciousness of the world in its totality both as being and having to be, both as totally ours and totally foreign, and the more ours as it is the more foreign. The non-positional consciousness *really* envelops the harmonious totality of human freedoms insofar as it makes the object of a universal confidence and exigency.

To write is thus both to disclose the world and to offer it as a task to the generosity of the reader. It is to have recourse to the consciousness of others in order to make one's self be recognized as *essential* to the totality of being; it is to wish to live this essentiality by means of interposed persons; but, on the other hand, as the real world is revealed only by action, as one can feel himself in it only by exceeding it in order to change it, the novelist's universe would lack thickness if it were not discovered in a movement to transcend it. It has often been observed that an object in a story does not derive its density of existence from the number and length of the descriptions devoted to it, but from the complexity of its connections with the different characters. The more often the characters handle it, take it up, and put it down, in short, go beyond it toward their own ends, the more real will it appear. Thus, of the world of the novel, that is, the totality of men and things, we may say that in order for it to offer its maximum density the disclosure-creation by which the reader discovers it must also be an imaginary engagement in the action; in other words, the more disposed one is to change it, the more alive it will be. The error of realism has been to believe that the real reveals itself to contemplation, and that consequently one could draw an impartial picture of it. How could that be possible, since the very perception is partial, since by itself the naming is already a modification of the object? And how could the writer, who wants himself to be essential to this universe, want to be essential to the injustice which this universe comprehends? Yet, he must be; but if he accepts being the creator of injustices, it is in a movement which goes beyond them toward their abolition. As for me who read, if I create and keep alive an unjust world, I can not help making myself responsible for it. And the author's whole art is bent on obliging me to *create* what he *discloses,* therefore to compromise myself. So both of us bear the responsibility for the universe. And precisely because this universe is supported by the joint effort of our two freedoms, and because the author, with me as medium, has attempted to integrate it into the human, it must appear truly *in itself,* in its very marrow, as being shot through and through with a freedom which has taken human freedom as its end, and if it is not really the city of ends that it ought to be, it must at least be a stage along the way; in a word, it must be a becoming and it must always be considered and presented not as a crushing mass which weighs us down, but from the point of view of its going beyond toward that city of ends. However bad and hopeless the humanity which it paints may be, the work must have an air of generosity. Not, of course, that this generosity is to be expressed by means of edifying discourses and virtuous characters; it must not even be premeditated, and it is quite true that fine sentiments do not make fine books. But it must be the very warp and woof of the book, the stuff out of which the people and things are cut; whatever the subject, a sort of essential lightness must appear everywhere and remind us that the work is never a natural datum, but an *exigence* and a *gift.* And if I am given this world with its injustices, it is not so that I might contemplate them coldly, but that I might animate them with my indignation, that I might disclose them and create them with their nature as injustices, that is, as abuses to be suppressed. Thus, the writer's universe will only reveal itself in all its depth to the examination, the admiration, and the indignation of the reader; and the generous love is a promise to maintain, and the generous indignation is a promise to change, and the admiration a promise to imitate; although literature is one thing and morality a quite different one, at the heart of the aesthetic imperative we discern the moral imperative. For, since the one who writes recognizes, by the very fact that he takes the trouble to write, the freedom of his readers, and since the one who reads, by the mere fact of his opening the book, recognizes the freedom of the writer, the work of art, from whichever side you approach it, is an act of confidence in the freedom of men. And since readers, like the author, recognize this freedom only to demand that it manifest itself, the work can be defined as an imaginary presentation of the world insofar as it demands human freedom. The result of which is that there is no "gloomy literature," since, however dark may be the colors in which one paints the world, he paints it only so that free men may feel their freedom as they face it. Thus, there are only good and bad novels. The bad novel aims to please by flattering, whereas the good one is an exigence and an act of faith. But above all, the unique point of view from which the author can present the world to those freedoms whose concurrence he wishes to bring about is that of a world to be impregnated always with more freedom. It would be inconceivable that this unleashing of generosity provoked by the writer could be used to authorize an injustice, and that the reader could enjoy his freedom while reading a work which approves or accepts or simply abstains from condemning the subjection of man by man. One can imagine a good novel being written by an American Negro even if hatred of the whites were spread all over it, because it is the freedom of his race that he demands through this hatred. And, as he invites me to assume the attitude of generosity, the moment I feel myself a pure freedom I can not bear to identify myself with a race of oppressors. Thus, I require of all freedoms that they demand the liberation of colored people against the white race and against myself insofar as I am a part of it, but nobody can suppose for a moment that it is possible to write a good novel in praise of anti-Semitism.[5] For, the moment I feel that my freedom is indissolubly linked with that of all other men, it can not be demanded of me that I use it to approve the enslavement of a part of these men. Thus, whether he is an essayist, a pamphleteer, a satirist, or a novelist, whether he speaks only of individual passions or whether he attacks the social order, the writer, a free man addressing free men, has only one subject — freedom.

Hence, any attempt to enslave his readers threatens him in his very art. A blacksmith can

[5]This last remark may arouse some readers. If so, I'd like to know a single good novel whose express purpose was to serve oppression, a single good novel which has been written against Jews, negroes, workers, or colonial people. "But if there isn't any, that's no reason why someone may not write one some day." But you then admit that you are an abstract theoretician. You, not I. For it is in the name of your abstract conception of art that you assert the possibility of a fact which has never come into being, whereas I limit myself to proposing an explanation for a recognized fact. [Au.]

be affected by fascism in his life as a man, but not necessarily in his craft; a writer will be affected in both, and even more in his craft than in his life. I have seen writers, who before the war, called for fascism with all their hearts, smitten with sterility at the very moment when the Nazis were loading them with honors. I am thinking of Drieu la Rochelle in particular; he was mistaken, but he was sincere. He proved it. He had agreed to direct a Nazi-inspired review. The first few months he reprimanded, rebuked, and lectured his countrymen. No one answered him because no one was free to do so. He became irritated; he no longer *felt* his readers. He became more insistent, but no sign appeared to prove that he had been understood. No sign of hatred, nor of anger either; nothing. He seemed disoriented, the victim of a growing distress. He complained bitterly to the Germans. His articles had been superb; they became shrill. The moment arrived when he struck his breast; no echo, except among the bought journalists whom he despised. He handed in his resignation, withdrew it, again spoke, still in the desert. Finally, he kept still, gagged by the silence of others. He had demanded the enslavement of others, but in his crazy mind he must have imagined that it was voluntary, that it was still free. It came; the man in him congratulated himself mightily, but the writer could not bear it. While this was going on, others, who, happily, were in the majority, understood that the freedom of writing implies the freedom of the citizen. One does not write for slaves. The art of prose is bound up with the only regime in which prose has meaning, democracy. When one is threatened, the other is too. And it is not enough to defend them with the pen. A day comes when the pen is forced to stop, and the writer must then take up arms. Thus, however you might have come to it, whatever the opinions you might have professed, literature throws you into battle. Writing is a certain way of wanting freedom; once you have begun, you are engaged, willy-nilly.

Engaged in what? Defending freedom? That's easy to say. Is it a matter of acting as guardian of ideal values like Benda's clerk before the betrayal,[6] or is it concrete, everyday freedom which must be protected by our taking sides in political and social struggles? The question is tied up with another one, one very simple in appearance but which nobody ever asks himself: "For whom does one write?"

[6] The reference here is to Julien Benda's *La Trahison des clercs,* translated into English as *The Treason of the Intellectuals.* [Tr.]

# Wayne C. Booth

b. 1921

*His 1971 Quantrell Prize for undergraduate teaching at the University of Chicago is one indication that Wayne Clayson Booth has been the most effective teacher — in the most far-reaching sense — of the neo-Aristotelians. He was born in American Fork, Utah, and educated at Brigham Young University, where he received his B.A. in 1944. After serving in the infantry during World War II, Booth completed his M.A. and Ph.D. at the University of Chicago, where his mentor was R. S. Crane (see Ch. 3). He taught at Haverford and at Earlham College, where he became professor and chairman of the department of English before returning to a named chair at Chicago in 1962. Booth has received fellowships from the Ford Foundation (1952), the Guggenheim Foundation (1956–57 and 1969–70), and the National Endowment for the Humanities (1975–76). He served as dean of the college of the University of Chicago from 1964 to 1969, and as president of the Modern Language Association in 1982. Booth's meteoric success began with the publication of* The Rhetoric of Fiction *(1961; second ed., 1983)*, *which shifted from the formalism of Crane to the explicit consideration of the audience and the ways in which texts make the readers they require. Other works have included* A Rhetoric of Irony *(1974)*, Modern Dogma and the Rhetoric of Assent *(1974)*, *and his most ambitious work, a pluralistic guide to the variety of pluralisms,* Critical Understanding *(1979)*. The Company We Keep: Ethical Criticism and the Ethics of Reading *(1988) is a long-considered effort to clarify some of the controversy excited by Booth's hint, in* The Rhetoric of Fiction, *at the potentially injurious effects of narratives by Céline and Nabokov.*

# Control of Distance in Jane Austen's Emma

*Jane Austen was instinctive and charming. . . . For signal examples of what composition, distribution, arrangement can do, of how they intensify the life of a work of art, we have to go elsewhere.*
— HENRY JAMES

*A heroine whom no one but myself will much like.*
— JANE AUSTEN describing Emma

## SYMPATHY AND JUDGMENT IN "EMMA"

Henry James once described Jane Austen as an instinctive novelist whose effects, some of which are admittedly fine, can best be explained as "part of her unconsciousness." It is as if she "fell-a-musing" over her work-basket, he said, lapsed into "wool-gathering," and afterward picked up "her dropped stitches" as "little masterstrokes of imagination."[1] The amiable accusation has been

repeated in various forms, most recently as a claim that Jane Austen creates characters toward whom we cannot react as she consciously intends.[2]

Although we cannot hope to decide whether Jane Austen was entirely conscious of her own artistry, a careful look at the technique of any of her novels reveals a rather different picture from that of the unconscious spinster with her knitting needles. In *Emma* especially, where the chances for technical failure are great indeed, we find at work one of the unquestionable masters of the rhetoric of narration.

At the beginning of *Emma,* the young heroine has every requirement for deserved happiness but one. She has intelligence, wit, beauty, wealth, and position, and she has the love of those around her. Indeed, she thinks herself completely happy. The only threat to her happiness, a threat of which she is unaware, is herself: charming as she is, she can neither see her own excessive pride honestly nor resist imposing herself on the lives of others. She is deficient both in generosity and in self-knowledge. She discovers and corrects her faults only after she has almost ruined herself and her closest friends. But with the reform in her character, she is ready for marriage with the man she loves, the man who throughout

[1]"The Lesson of Balzac," *The Question of Our Speech* (Cambridge, 1905), p. 63. A fuller quotation can be found in R. W. Chapman's indispensable *Jane Austen: A Critical Bibliography* (Oxford, 1955). Some important Austen items published too late to be included by Chapman are: (1) Ian Watt, *The Rise of the Novel* (Berkeley, Calif., 1957); (2) Stuart M. Tave, review of Marvin Mudrick's *Jane Austen: Irony as Defense and Discovery* (Princeton, N.J., 1952) in *Philological Quarterly* 32 (July 1953): 256–57; (3) Andrew H. Wright, *Jane Austen's Novels: A Study in Structure* (London, 1953), pp. 36–82; (4) Christopher Gillie, "*Sense and Sensibility*: An Assessment," *Essays in Criticism* 9 (January 1959): 1–9, esp. 5–6; (5) Edgar F. Shannon, Jr., "*Emma*: Character and Construction," *PMLA* 71 (September 1956): 637–50. [Au.]

[2]See, for example, Mudrick, pp. 91, 165; Frank O'Connor, *The Mirror in the Roadway* (London, 1957), p. 30. [Au.]

the book has stood in the reader's mind for what she lacks.

It is clear that with a general plot of this kind Jane Austen gave herself difficulties of a high order. Though Emma's faults are comic, they constantly threaten to produce serious harm. Yet she must remain sympathetic or the reader will not wish for and delight sufficiently in her reform.

Obviously, the problem with a plot like this is to find some way to allow the reader to laugh at the mistakes committed by the heroine and at her punishment, without reducing the desire to see her reform and thus earn happiness. In *Tom Jones* this double attitude is achieved . . . partly through the invention of episodes producing sympathy and relieving any serious anxiety we might have, and partly through the direct and sympathetic commentary. In *Emma,* since most of the episodes must illustrate the heroine's faults and thus increase either our emotional distance or our anxiety, a different method is required. If we fail to see Emma's faults as revealed in the ironic texture from line to line, we cannot savor to the full the comedy as it is prepared for us. On the other hand, if we fail to love her, as Jane Austen herself predicted we would[3] — if we fail to love her more and more as the book progresses — we can neither hope for the conclusion, a happy and deserved marriage with Knightley following upon her reform, nor accept it as an honest one when it comes.[4] Any attempt to solve the problem by reducing either the love or the clear view of her faults would have been fatal.

[3]"A heroine whom no one but myself will much like" (James Edward Austen-Leigh, *Memoir of His Aunt* [London, 1870; Oxford, 1926], p. 157). [Au.]

[4]The best discussion of this problem is Reginald Farrer's "Jane Austen," *Quarterly Review* 228 (July 1917): 1–30; reprinted in William Heath's *Discussions of Jane Austen* (Boston, 1961). For one critic the book fails because the problem was never recognized by Jane Austen herself: Mr. E. N. Hayes, in what may well be the least sympathetic discussion of *Emma* yet written, explains the whole book as the author's failure to see Emma's faults. "Evidently Jane Austen wished to protect Emma . . . The author is therefore in the ambiguous position of both loving and scorning the heroine" ("'Emma': A Dissenting Opinion," *Nineteenth-Century Fiction* 4 [June 1949]: 18, 19). [Au.]

## SYMPATHY THROUGH CONTROL OF INSIDE VIEWS

The solution to the problem of maintaining sympathy despite almost crippling faults was primarily to use the heroine herself as a kind of narrator, though in third person, reporting on her own experience. So far as we know, Jane Austen never formulated any theory to cover her own practice; she invented no term like James's "central intelligence" or "lucid reflector" to describe her method of viewing the world of the book primarily through Emma's own eyes. We can thus never know for sure to what extent James's accusation of "unconsciousness" was right. But whether she was inclined to speculate about her method scarcely matters; her solution was clearly a brilliant one. By showing most of the story through Emma's eyes, the author insures that we shall travel with Emma rather than stand against her. It is not simply that Emma provides, in the unimpeachable evidence of her own conscience, proof that she has many redeeming qualities that do not appear on the surface; such evidence could be given with authorial commentary, though perhaps not with such force and conviction. Much more important, the sustained inside view leads the reader to hope for good fortune for the character with whom he travels, quite independently of the qualities revealed.

Seen from the outside, Emma would be an unpleasant person, unless, like Mr. Woodhouse and Knightley, we knew her well enough to infer her true worth. Though we might easily be led to laugh at her, we could never be made to laugh sympathetically. While the final unmasking of her faults and her humiliation would make artistic sense to an unsympathetic reader, her marriage with Knightley would become irrelevant if not meaningless. Unless we desire Emma's happiness and her reform which alone can make that happiness possible, a good third of this book will seem irredeemably dull.

Yet sympathetic laughter is never easily achieved. It is much easier to set up a separate fool for comic effects and to preserve your heroine for finer things. Sympathetic laughter is especially difficult with characters whose faults do not spring from sympathetic virtues. The grasping but witty Volpone can keep us on his side so long as his victims are more grasping and less witty than he, but as soon as the innocent victims, Celia and Bonario, come on stage, the quality of the humor changes; we no longer delight unambiguously in his triumphs. In contrast to this, the great sympathetic comic heroes often are comic largely because their faults, like Uncle Toby's sentimentality, spring from an excess of some virtue. Don Quixote's madness is partly caused by an excess of idealism, an excess of loving concern for the unfortunate. Every crazy gesture he makes gives further reason for loving the well-meaning old fool, and we can thus laugh at him in somewhat the same spirit in which we laugh at our own faults — in a benign, forgiving spirit. We may be contemptible for doing so; to persons without a sense of humor such laughter often seems a wicked escape. But self-love being what it is, we laugh at ourselves in a thoroughly forgiving way, and we laugh in the same way at Don Quixote: we are convinced that his heart, like ours, is in the right place.

Nothing in Emma's comic misunderstandings can serve for the same effect. Her faults are not excesses of virtue. She attempts to manipulate Harriet not from an excess of kindness but from a desire for power and admiration. She flirts with Frank Churchill out of vanity and irresponsibility. She mistreats Jane Fairfax because of Jane's *good* qualities. She abuses Miss Bates because of her own essential lack of "tenderness" and "good will."

We have only to think of what Emma's story would be if seen through Jane Fairfax's or Mrs. Elton's or Robert Martin's eyes to recognize how little our sympathy springs from any natural view, and to see how inescapable is the decision to use Emma's mind as a reflector of events — however beclouded her vision must be. To Jane Fairfax, who embodies throughout the book most of the values which Emma discovers only at the end, the early Emma is intolerable.

But Jane Austen never lets us forget that Emma is not what she might appear to be. For every section devoted to her misdeeds — and even they are seen for the most part through her own eyes — there is a section devoted to her self-reproach. We see her rudeness to poor fool-ish Miss Bates, and we see it vividly. But her remorse and act of penance in visiting Miss Bates after Knightley's rebuke are experienced even more vividly. We see her successive attempts to mislead Harriet, but we see at great length and in high color her self-castigation (Chs. 16, 17, 48). We see her boasting proudly that she does not need marriage, boasting almost as blatantly of her "resources" as does Mrs. Elton (Ch. 10). But we know her too intimately to take her conscious thoughts at face value. And we see her, thirty-eight chapters later, chastened to an admission of what we have known all along to be her true human need for love. "If all took place that might take place among the circle of her friends, Hartfield must be comparatively deserted; and she left to cheer her father with the spirits only of ruined happiness. The child to be born at Randalls must be a tie there even dearer than herself; and Mrs. Weston's heart and time would be occupied by it. . . . All that were good would be withdrawn" (Ch. 48).

Perhaps the most delightful effects from our sustained inside view of a very confused and very charming young woman come from her frequent thoughts about Knightley. She is basically right all along about his pre-eminent wisdom and virtue, and she is our chief authority for taking *his* authority so seriously. And yet in every thought about him she is misled. Knightley rebukes her; the reader knows that Knightley is in the right. But Emma?

> Emma made no answer, and tried to look cheerfully unconcerned, but was really feeling uncomfortable, and wanting him very much to be gone. She did not repeat what she had done; she still thought herself a better judge of such a point of female right and refinement than he could be; but yet she had a sort of habitual respect for his judgment in general, which made her dislike having it so loudly against her; and to have him sitting just opposite to her in angry state, was very disagreeable [Ch. 8].

Even more striking is the lack of self-knowledge shown when Mrs. Weston suggests that Knightley might marry Jane Fairfax.

> Her objections to Mr. Knightley's marrying did not in the least subside. She could see nothing but

evil in it. It would be a great disappointment to Mr. John Knightley [Knightley's brother]; consequently to Isabella. A real injury to the children — a most mortifying change, and material loss to them all; — a very great deduction from her father's daily comfort — and, as to herself, she could not at all endure the idea of Jane Fairfax at Donwell Abbey. A Mrs. Knightley for them all to give way to! — No, Mr. Knightley must never marry. Little Henry must remain the heir of Donwell [Ch. 26].

Self-deception could hardly be carried further, at least in a person of high intelligence and sensitivity.

Yet the effect of all this is what our tolerance for our own faults produces in our own lives. While only immature readers ever really identify with any character, losing all sense of distance and hence all chance of an artistic experience, our emotional reaction to every event concerning Emma tends to become like her own. When she feels anxiety or shame, we feel analogous emotions. Our modern awareness that such "feelings" are not identical with those we feel in our own lives in similar circumstances has tended to blind us to the fact that aesthetic form can be built out of patterned emotions as well as out of other materials. It is absurd to pretend that because our emotions and desires in responding to fiction are in a very real sense disinterested, they do not or should not exist. Jane Austen, in developing the sustained use of a sympathetic inside view, has mastered one of the most successful of all devices for inducing a parallel emotional response between the deficient heroine and the reader.

Sympathy for Emma can be heightened by withholding inside views of others as well as by granting them of her. The author knew, for example, that it would be fatal to grant any extended inside view of Jane Fairfax. The inadequacies of impressionistic criticism are nowhere revealed more clearly than in the suggestion often made about such minor characters that their authors would have liked to make them vivid but didn't know how.[5] Jane Austen knew perfectly

well how to make such a character vivid; Anne in *Persuasion* is a kind of Jane Fairfax turned into heroine. But in *Emma,* Emma must shine supreme. It is not only that the slightest glance inside Jane's mind would be fatal to all of the author's plans for mystification about Frank Churchill, though this is important. The major problem is that any extended view of her would reveal her as a more sympathetic person than Emma herself. Jane is superior to Emma in most respects except the stroke of good fortune that made Emma the heroine of the book. In matters of taste and ability, of head and of heart, she is Emma's superior, and Jane Austen, always in danger of losing our sympathy for Emma, cannot risk any degree of distraction. Jane could, it is true, be granted fewer virtues, and then made more vivid. But to do so would greatly weaken the force of Emma's mistakes of heart and head in her treatment of the almost faultless Jane.

## CONTROL OF JUDGMENT

But the very effectiveness of the rhetoric designed to produce sympathy might in itself lead to a serious misreading of the book. In reducing the emotional distance, the natural tendency is to reduce — willy-nilly — moral and intellectual distance as well. In reacting to Emma's faults from the inside out, as if they were our own, we may very well not only forgive them but overlook them.[6]

---

[5]A. C. Bradley, for example, once argued that Jane Austen intended Jane Fairfax to be as interesting throughout as she becomes at the end, but "the moralist in Jane Austen stood for once in her way. The secret engagement is, for her,

so serious an offence, that she is afraid to win our hearts for Jane until it has led to great unhappiness" ("Jane Austen," in *Essays and Studies, by Members of the English Association,* II [Oxford, 1911], 23). [Au.]

[6]I know of only one full-scale attempt to deal with the "tension between sympathy and judgment" in modern literature, Robert Langbaum's *The Poetry of Experience* (London, 1957). Langbaum argues that in the dramatic monologue, with which he is primarily concerned, the sympathy engendered by the direct portrayal of internal experience leads the reader to suspend his moral judgment. Thus, in reading Browning's portraits of moral degeneration — e.g., the duke in "My Last Duchess" or the monk in "Soliloquy of a Spanish Cloister" — our moral judgment is overwhelmed "because we prefer to participate in the duke's power and freedom, in his hard core of character fiercely loyal to itself. Moral judgment is in fact important as the thing to be suspended, as a measure of the price we pay for the privilege

There is, of course, no danger that readers who persist to the end will overlook Emma's serious mistakes; since she sees and reports those mistakes herself, everything becomes crystal clear at the end. The real danger inherent in the experiment is that readers will overlook the mistakes as they are committed and thus miss much of the comedy that depends on Emma's distorted view from page to page. If readers who dislike Emma cannot enjoy the preparation for the marriage to Knightley, readers who do not recognize her faults with absolute precision cannot enjoy the details of the preparation for the comic abasement which must precede that marriage.

It might be argued that there is no real problem, since the conventions of her time allowed for reliable commentary whenever it was needed to place Emma's faults precisely. But Jane Austen is not operating according to the conventions, most of which she had long since parodied and outgrown; her technique is determined by the needs of the novel she is writing. We can see this clearly by contrasting the manner of *Emma* with that of *Persuasion,* the next, and last-completed, work. In *Emma* there are many breaks in the point of view, because Emma's beclouded mind cannot do the whole job. In *Persuasion,* where the heroine's viewpoint is faulty only in her ignorance of Captain Wentworth's love, there are very few. Anne Elliot's consciousness is sufficient, as Emma's is not, for most of the needs of the novel which she dominates. Once the ethical and intellectual framework has been established by the narrator's introduction, we enter Anne's consciousness and remain bound to it much more rigorously than we are bound to Emma's. It is still true that whenever something must be shown that Anne's consciousness cannot show, we move to another center; but since her

consciousness can do much more for us than Emma's, there need be few departures from it.

The most notable shift for rhetorical purposes in *Persuasion* comes fairly early. When Anne first meets Captain Wentworth after their years of separation that follow her refusal to marry him, she is convinced that he is indifferent. The major movement of *Persuasion* is toward her final discovery that he still loves her; *her* suspense is thus strong and inevitable from the beginning. The reader, however, is likely to believe that Wentworth is still interested. All the conventions of art favor such a belief: the emphasis is clearly on Anne and her unhappiness; the lover has returned; we have only to wait, perhaps with some tedium, for the inevitable outcome. Anne learns (Ch. 7) that he has spoken of her as so altered "he should not have known her again!" "These were words which could not but dwell with her. Yet she soon began to rejoice that she had heard them. They were of sobering tendency; they allayed agitation; they composed, and consequently must make her happier." And suddenly we enter Wentworth's mind for one time only: "Frederick Wentworth had used such words, or something like them, but without an idea that they would be carried round to her. He had thought her wretchedly altered, and, in the first moment of appeal, had spoken as he felt. He had not forgiven Anne Elliot. She had used him ill" — and so he goes on, for five more paragraphs. The necessary point, the fact that Frederick believes himself to be indifferent, has been made, and it could not have been made without some kind of shift from Anne's consciousness.

At the end of the novel, we learn that Wentworth was himself deceived in this momentary inside view: "He had meant to forget her, and believed it to be done. He had imagined himself indifferent, when he had only been angry." We may want to protest against the earlier suppression as unfair, but we can hardly believe it to be what Miss Lascelles calls "an oversight."[7] It is deliberate manipulation of inside views in order to destroy our conventional security. We are thus made ready to go along with Anne in her long

---

of appreciating to the full this extraordinary man" (p. 83). While I think that Langbaum seriously underplays the extent to which moral judgment remains even after psychological vividness has done its work, and while he perhaps defines "morality" too narrowly when he excludes from it such things as power and freedom and fierce loyalty to one's own character, his book is a stimulating introduction to the problems raised by internal portraiture of flawed characters. [Au.]

[7]*Jane Austen and Her Art* (Oxford, 1939), p. 204. [Au.]

and painful road to the discovery that Frederick loves her after all.

The only other important breaks in the angle of vision of *Persuasion* come at the beginning and at the end. Chapter one is an excellent example of how a skilful novelist can, by the use of his own direct voice, accomplish in a few pages what even the best novelist must take chapters to do if he uses nothing but dramatized action. Again at the conclusion the author enters with a resounding reaffirmation that the Wentworth-Elliot marriage is as good a thing as we have felt it to be from the beginning.

> Who can be in doubt of what followed? When any two young people take it into their heads to marry, they are pretty sure by perseverance to carry their point, be they ever so poor, or ever so imprudent, or ever so little likely to be necessary to each other's ultimate comfort. This may be bad morality to conclude with, but I believe it to be truth; and if such parties succeed, how should a Captain Wentworth and an Anne Elliot, with the advantage of maturity of mind, consciousness of right, and one independent fortune between them, fail of bearing down every opposition?[8]

[8]It seems to be difficult for some modern critics, accustomed to ferreting values out from an impersonal or ironic context without the aid of the author's voice, to make use of reliable commentary like this when it is provided. Even a highly perceptive reader like Mark Schorer, for example, finds himself doing unnecessary acrobatics with the question of style, and particularly metaphor, as clues to the norms against which the author judges her characters. In reading *Persuasion,* he finds these clues among the metaphors "from commerce and property, the counting house and the inherited estate" with which it abounds ("Fiction and the Matrix of Analogy," *Kenyon Review* [Autumn 1949]: p. 540). No one would deny that the novel is packed with such metaphors, although Schorer is somewhat overingenious in marshaling to his cause certain dead metaphors that Austen could not have avoided without awkward circumlocution (esp. p. 542). But the crucial question surely is: What precisely are these metaphors of the countinghouse doing in the novel? Whose values are they supposed to reveal? Accustomed to reading modern fiction in which the novelist very likely provides no direct assistance in answering this question, Schorer leaves it really unanswered; at times he seems almost to imply that Jane Austen is unconsciously giving herself away in her use of them (e.g., p. 543).

But the novel is really very clear about it all. The introduction, coming directly from the wholly reliable narrator, establishes unequivocally and without "analogy" the conflict between the world of the Elliots, depending for its values on

Except for these few intrusions and one in Chapter 19, Anne's own mind is sufficient in *Persuasion,* but we can never rely completely on Emma. It is hardly surprising that Jane Austen has provided many correctives to insure our placing her errors with precision.

The chief corrective is Knightley. His commentary on Emma's errors is a natural expression of his love; he can tell the reader and Emma at the same time precisely how she is mistaken. Thus, nothing Knightley says can be beside the point. Each affirmation of a value, each accusation of error is in itself an action in the plot. When he rebukes Emma for manipulating Harriet, when he attacks her for superficiality and false pride, when he condemns her for gossiping and flirting with Frank Churchill, and finally when he attacks her for being "insolent" and "unfeeling" in her treatment of Miss Bates, we have Jane Austen's judgment on Emma, rendered dramatically. But it has come from someone who is essentially sympathetic toward Emma, so that his judgments against her are presumed to be temporary. His sympathy reinforces ours even as he criticizes, and her respect for his opinion, shown in her self-abasement after he has criticized, is one of our main reasons for expecting her to reform.

If Henry James had tried to write a novel about Emma, and had cogitated at length on the problem of getting her story told dramatically, he could not have done better than this. It is possible, of course, to think of *Emma* without Knightley as *raisonneur,* just as it is possible to think of *The Golden Bowl,* say, without the Assinghams as *ficelles* to reflect something not seen by the Prince or Princess. But Knightley, though he receives less independent space than the Assinghams and is almost never seen in an inside view, is clearly more useful for Jane Austen's purposes than any realistically limited *ficelle*

---

selfishness, stupidity, and pride — and the world of Anne, a world where "elegance of mind and sweetness of character" are the supreme values. The commercial values stressed by Schorer are only a selection from what is actually a rich group of evils. And Anne's own expressed views again and again provide direct guidance to the reader. [Au.]

could possibly be. By combining the role of commentator with the role of hero, Jane Austen has worked more economically than James, and though economy is as dangerous as any other criterion when applied universally, even James might have profited from a closer study of the economies that a character like Knightley can be made to achieve. It is as if James had dared to make one of the four main characters, say the Prince, into a thoroughly good, wise, perceptive man, a thoroughly clear rather than a partly confused "reflector."

Since Knightley is established early as completely reliable, we need no views of his secret thoughts. He has no secret thoughts, except for the unacknowledged depths of his love for Emma and his jealousy of Frank Churchill. The other main characters have more to hide, and Jane Austen moves in and out of minds with great freedom, choosing for her own purposes what to reveal and what to withhold. Always the seeming violation of consistency is in the consistent service of the particular needs of Emma's story. Sometimes a shift is made simply to direct our suspense, as when Mrs. Weston suggests a possible union of Emma and Frank Churchill, at the end of her conversation with Knightley about the harmful effects of Emma's friendship with Harriet (Ch. 5). "Part of her meaning was to conceal some favourite thoughts of her own and Mr. Weston's on the subject, as much as possible. There were wishes at Randalls respecting Emma's destiny, but it was not desirable to have them suspected."

One objection to this selective dipping into whatever mind best serves our immediate purposes is that it suggests mere trickery and inevitably spoils the illusion of reality. If Jane Austen can tell us what Mrs. Weston is thinking, why not what Frank Churchill and Jane Fairfax are thinking? Obviously, because she chooses to build a mystery, and to do so she must refuse, arbitrarily and obtrusively, to grant the privilege of an inside view to characters whose minds would reveal too much. But is not the mystery purchased at the price of shaking the reader's faith in Jane Austen's integrity? If she simply withholds until later what she might as well relate now — if her procedure is not dictated by the very nature of her materials — why should we take her seriously?

If a natural surface were required in all fiction, then this objection would hold. But if we want to read *Emma* in its own terms, the real question about these shifts cannot be answered by an easy appeal to general principles. Every author withholds until later what he "might as well" relate now. The question is always one of desired effects, and the choice of any one effect always bans innumerable other effects. There is, indeed, a question to be raised about the use of mystery in *Emma,* but the conflict is not between an abstract end that Jane Austen never worried about and a shoddy mystification that she allowed to betray her. The conflict is between two effects both of which she cares about a good deal. On the one hand she cares about maintaining some sense of mystery as long as she can. On the other, she works at all points to heighten the reader's sense of dramatic irony, usually in the form of a contrast between what Emma knows and what the reader knows.

As in most novels, whatever steps are taken to mystify inevitably decrease the dramatic irony, and, whenever dramatic irony is increased by telling the reader secrets the characters have not yet suspected, mystery is inevitably destroyed. The longer we are in doubt about Frank Churchill, the weaker our sense of ironic contrast between Emma's views and the truth. The sooner we see through Frank Churchill's secret plot, the greater our pleasure in observing Emma's innumerable misreadings of his behavior and the less interest we have in the mere mystery of the situation. And we all find that on second reading we discover new intensities of dramatic irony resulting from the complete loss of mystery; knowing what abysses of error Emma is preparing for herself, even those of us who may on first reading have deciphered nearly all the details of the Churchill mystery find additional ironies.

But it is obvious that these ironies could have been offered even on a first reading, if Jane Austen had been willing to sacrifice her mystery. A single phrase in her own name — "his secret engagement to Jane Fairfax" — or a short inside view of either of the lovers could have made us aware of every ironic touch.

The author must, then, choose whether to purchase mystery at the expense of irony. For many of us Jane Austen's choice here is perhaps the weakest aspect of this novel. It is a commonplace of our criticism that significant literature arouses suspense not about the "what" but about the "how." Mere mystification has been mastered by so many second-rate writers that her efforts at mystification seem second-rate.

But again we must ask whether criticism can be conducted effectively by balancing one abstract quality against another. Is there a norm of dramatic irony for all works, or even for all works of a given kind? Has anyone ever formulated a "law of first and second readings" that will tell us just how many of our pleasures on page one should depend on our knowledge of what happens on page the last? We quite properly ask that the books we call great be able to stand up under repeated reading, but we need not ask that they yield identical pleasures on each reading. The modern works whose authors pride themselves on the fact that they can never be read but only re-read may be very good indeed, but they are not made good by the fact that their secret pleasures can only be wrested from them by repeated readings.

In any case, even if one accepted the criticism of Jane Austen's efforts at mystification, the larger service of the inside views is clear: the crosslights thrown by other minds prevent our being blinded by Emma's radiance.

## THE RELIABLE NARRATOR AND THE NORMS OF "EMMA"

If mere intellectual clarity about Emma were the goal in this work, we should be forced to say that the manipulation of inside views and the extensive commentary of the reliable Knightley are more than is necessary. But for maximum intensity of the comedy and romance, even these are not enough. The "author herself" — not necessarily the real Jane Austen but an implied author, represented in this book by a reliable narrator — heightens the effects by directing our intellectual, moral, and emotional progress. She performs, of course, most of the functions described in Chapter 7. But her most important role

is to reinforce both aspects of the double vision that operates throughout the book: our inside view of Emma's worth and our objective view of her great faults.

The narrator opens *Emma* with a masterful simultaneous presentation of Emma and of the values against which she must be judged: "Emma Woodhouse, handsome, clever, and rich, with a comfortable home and happy disposition, seemed to unite some of the best blessings of existence; and had lived nearly twenty-one years in the world with very little to distress or vex her." This "seemed" is immediately reinforced by more directly stated reservations. "The real evils of Emma's situation were the power of having rather too much her own way, and a disposition to think a little too well of herself; these were the disadvantages which threatened alloy to her many enjoyments. The danger, however, was at present so unperceived, that they did not by any means rank as misfortunes with her."

None of this could have been said by Emma, and if shown through her consciousness, it could not be accepted, as it must be, without question. Like most of the first three chapters, it is nondramatic summary, building up, through the ostensible business of getting the characters introduced, to Emma's initial blunder with Harriet and Mr. Elton. Throughout these chapters, we learn much of what we must know from the narrator, but she turns over more and more of the job of summary to Emma as she feels more and more sure of our seeing precisely to what degree Emma is to be trusted. Whenever we leave the "real evils" we have been warned against in Emma, the narrator's and Emma's views coincide: we cannot tell which of them, for example, offers the judgment on Mr. Woodhouse that "his talents could not have recommended him at any time," or the judgment on Mr. Knightley that he is "a sensible man," "always welcome" at Hartfield, or even that "Mr. Knightley, in fact, was one of the few people who could see faults in Emma Woodhouse, and the only one who ever told her of them."

But there are times when Emma and her author are far apart, and the author's direct guidance aids the reader in his own break with Emma. The beautiful irony of the first description of

Harriet, given through Emma's eyes (Ch. 3) could no doubt be grasped intellectually by many readers without all of the preliminary commentary. But even for the most perceptive its effect is heightened, surely, by the sense of standing with the author and observing with her precisely how Emma's judgment is going astray. Perhaps more important, we ordinary, less perceptive readers have by now been raised to a level suited to grasp the ironies. Certainly, most readers would overlook some of the barbs directed against Emma if the novel began, as a serious modern novelist might well begin it, with this description:

> [Emma] was not struck by any thing remarkably clever in Miss Smith's conversation, but she found her altogether very engaging — not inconveniently shy, not unwilling to talk — and yet so far from pushing, shewing so proper and becoming a deference, seeming so pleasantly grateful for being admitted to Hartfield, and so artlessly impressed by the appearance of every thing in so superior a style to what she had been used to, that she must have good sense and deserve encouragement. Encouragement should be given. Those soft blue eyes . . . should not be wasted on the inferior society of Highbury. . . .

And so Emma goes on, giving herself away with every word, pouring out her sense of her own beneficence and general value. Harriet's past friends, "though very good sort of people, must be doing her harm." Without knowing them, Emma knows that they "must be coarse and unpolished, and very unfit to be the intimates of a girl who wanted only a little more knowledge and elegance to be quite perfect." And she concludes with a beautiful burst of egotism: "She would notice her; she would improve her; she would detach her from her bad acquaintance, and introduce her into good society; she would form her opinions and her manners. It would be an interesting, and certainly a very kind undertaking; highly becoming her own situation in life, her leisure, and powers." Even the most skilful reader might not easily plot an absolutely true course through these ironies without the prior direct assistance we have been given. Emma's views are not so outlandish that they could never have been held by a female novelist writing in her time. They cannot serve effectively as signs of her character unless they are clearly disavowed as signs of Jane Austen's views. Emma's unconscious catalogue of her egotistical uses for Harriet, given under the pretense of listing the services she will perform, is thus given its full force by being framed explicitly in a world of values which Emma herself cannot discover until the conclusion of the book.

The full importance of the author's direct imposition of an elaborate scale of norms can be seen by considering that conclusion. The sequence of events is a simple one: Emma's faults and mistakes are brought home to her in a rapid and humiliating chain of rebukes from Knightley and blows from hard fact. These blows to her self-esteem produce at last a genuine reform (for example, she brings herself to apologize to Miss Bates, something she could never have done earlier in the novel). The change in her character removes the only obstacle in the way of Knightley's proposal, and the marriage follows. "The wishes, the hopes, the confidence, the predictions of the small band of true friends who witnessed the ceremony, were fully answered in the perfect happiness of the union."

It may be that if we look at Emma and Knightley as real people, this ending will seem false. G. B. Stern laments, in *Speaking of Jane Austen*, "Oh, Miss Austen, it was not a good solution; it was a bad solution, an unhappy ending, could we see beyond the last pages of the book." Edmund Wilson predicts that Emma will find a new protégée like Harriet, since she has not been cured of her inclination to "infatuations with women." Marvin Mudrick even more emphatically rejects Jane Austen's explicit rhetoric; he believes that Emma is still a "confirmed exploiter," and for him the ending must be read as ironic.[9]

But it is precisely because this ending is neither life itself nor a simple bit of literary irony that it can serve so well to heighten our sense of a complete and indeed perfect resolution to all

[9]The first two quotations are from Wilson's "A Long Talk about Jane Austen," *A Literary Chronicle: 1920–1950* (New York, 1952). The third is from Mudrick, *Jane Austen*, p. 206. [Au.]

that has gone before. If we look at the values that have been realized in this marriage and compare them with those realized in conventional marriage plots, we see that Jane Austen means what she says: this will be a happy marriage because there is simply nothing left to make it anything less than perfectly happy. It fulfills every value embodied in the world of the book — with the possible exception that Emma may never learn to apply herself as she ought to her reading and her piano! It is a union of intelligence: of "reason," of "sense," of "judgment." It is a union of virtue: of "good will," of generosity, of unselfishness. It is a union of feeling: of "taste," "tenderness," "love," "beauty."[10]

In a general way, then, this plot offers us an experience superficially like that offered by most tragicomedy as well as by much of the cheapest popular art: we are made to desire certain good things for certain good characters, and then our desires are gratified. If we depended on general criteria derived from our justified boredom with such works, we should reject this one. But the critical difference lies in the precise quality of the values appealed to and the precise quality of the characters who violate or realize them. All of the cheap marriage plots in the world should not lead us to be embarrassed about our pleasure in Emma and Knightley's marriage. It is more than just the marriage: it is the *rightness* of *this* marriage, as a conclusion to all of the comic wrongness that has gone before. The good for Emma includes both her necessary reform and the resulting marriage. Marriage to an intelligent, amiable, good, and attractive man is the best thing that can happen to this heroine, and the

readers who do not experience it as such are, I am convinced, far from knowing what Jane Austen is about — whatever they may say about the "bitter spinster's" attitude toward marriage.

Our modern sensibilities are likely to be rasped by any such formulation. We do not ordinarily like to encounter perfect endings in our novels — even in the sense of "perfectedness" or completion, the sense obviously intended by Jane Austen. We refuse to accept it when we see it: witness the many attempts to deny Dostoevski's success with Alyosha and Father Zossima in *The Brothers Karamazov*. Many of us find it embarrassing to talk of emotions based on moral judgment at all, particularly when the emotions have any kind of affirmative cast. Emma herself is something of a "modern" in this regard throughout most of the book. Her self-deception about marriage is as great as about most other important matters. Emma boasts to Harriet of her indifference to marriage, at the same time unconsciously betraying her totally inadequate view of the sources of human happiness.

> If I know myself, Harriet, mine is an active, busy mind, with a great many independent resources; and I do not perceive why I should be more in want of employment at forty or fifty than one-and-twenty. Women's usual occupations of eye and hand and mind will be as open to me then, as they are now; or with no important variation. If I draw less, I shall read more; if I give up music, I shall take to carpet-work.

Emma at carpet-work! If she knows herself indeed.

> And as for objects of interest, objects for the affections, which is, in truth, the great point of inferiority, the want of which is really the great evil to be avoided in *not* marrying [a magnificent concession, this] I shall be very well off, with all the children of a sister I love so much, to care about. There will be enough of them, in all probability, to supply every sort of sensation that declining life can need. There will be enough for every hope and every fear; and though my attachment to none can equal that of a parent, it suits my ideas of comfort better than what is warmer and blinder. My nephews and nieces! — I shall often have a niece with me [Ch. 10].

[10]It has lately been fashionable to underplay the value of tenderness and good will in Jane Austen, in reaction to an earlier generation that overdid the picture of "gentle Jane." The trend seems to have begun in earnest with D. W. Harding's "Regulated Hatred: An Aspect of the Work of Jane Austen," *Scrutiny* 8 (March 1940): 346–62. While I do not feel as strongly aroused against this school of readers as does R. W. Chapman (see his *A Critical Bibliography*, p. 52, and his review of Mudrick's work in the *T. L. S.* [September 19, 1952]), it seems to me that another swing of the pendulum is called for: when Jane Austen praises the "relenting heart," she means that praise, though she is the same author who can lash the unrelenting heart with "regulated hatred." [Au.]

Without growing solemn about it — it is wonderfully comic — we can recognize that the humor springs here from very deep sources indeed. It can be fully enjoyed, in fact, only by the reader who has attained to a vision of human felicity far more profound than Emma's "comfort" and "want" and "need." It is a vision that includes not simply marriage, but a kind of loving converse not based, as is Emma's here, on whether the "loved" person will serve one's irreducible needs.

The comic effect of this repudiation of marriage is considerably increased by the fact that Emma always thinks of marriage for others as *their* highest good, and in fact unconsciously encourages her friend Harriet to fall in love with the very man she herself loves without knowing it. The delightful denouement is thus what we want not only because it is a supremely good thing for Emma, but because it is a supremely comic outcome of Emma's profound misunderstanding of herself and of the human condition. In the schematic language of Chapter 5, it satisfies both our practical desire for Emma's well-being and our appetite for the qualities proper to these artistic materials. It is thus a more resounding resolution than either of these elements separately could provide. The other major resolution of the work — Harriet's marriage with her farmer — reinforces this interpretation. Emma's sin against Harriet has been something far worse than the mere meddling of a busy-body. To destroy Harriet's chances for happiness — chances that depend entirely on her marriage — is as close to viciousness as any author could dare to take a heroine designed to be loved. We can laugh with Emma at this mistake (Ch. 54) only because Harriet's chance for happiness is restored.

Other values, like money, blood, and "consequence," are real enough in *Emma,* but only as they contribute to or are mastered by good taste, good judgment, and good morality. Money alone can make a Mrs. Churchill, but a man or woman "is silly to marry without it." Consequence untouched by sense can make a very inconsequential Mr. Woodhouse; untouched by sense or virtue it can make the much more contemptible Mr. and Miss Elliot of *Persuasion*. But it is a pleasant thing to have, and it does no harm unless, like the early Emma, one takes it too seriously. Charm and elegance without sufficient moral force can make a Frank Churchill; unschooled by morality it can lead to the baseness of Henry Crawford in *Mansfield Park* or of Wickham in *Pride and Prejudice*. Even the supreme virtues are inadequate in isolation: good will alone will make a comic Miss Bates or a Mr. Weston, judgment with insufficient good will a comic Mr. John Knightley, and so on.

I am willing to risk the commonplace in such a listing because it is only thus that the full force of Jane Austen's comprehensive view can be seen. There is clearly at work here a much more detailed ordering of values than any conventional public philosophy of her time could provide. Obviously, few readers in her own time, and far fewer in our own, have ever approached this novel in full and detailed agreement with the author's norms. But they were led to join her as they read, and so are we.

## EXPLICIT JUDGMENTS ON EMMA WOODHOUSE

We have said in passing almost enough of the other side of the coin — the judgment of particular actions as they relate to the general norms. But something must be said of the detailed "placing" of Emma, by direct commentary, in the hierarchy of values established by the novel. I must be convinced, for example, not only that tenderness for other people's feelings is an important trait but also that Emma's particular behavior violates the true standards of tenderness, if I am to savor to the full the episode of Emma's insult to Miss Bates and Knightley's reproach which follows. If I refuse to blame Emma, I may discover a kind of intellectual enjoyment in the episode, and I will probably think that any critic who talks of "belief" in tenderness as operating in such a context is taking things too seriously. But I can never enjoy the episode in its full intensity or grasp its formal coherence. Similarly, I must agree not only that to be dreadfully boring is a minor fault compared with the major virtue of "good will," but also that Miss Bates's exemplification of this fault and of this virtue entitle her to the respect which Emma denies. If I do not — while yet being able to laugh at Miss Bates — I can hardly understand, let alone enjoy, Emma's mistreatment of her.

But these negative judgments must be counteracted by a larger approval, and, as we would expect, the novel is full of direct apologies for Emma. Her chief fault, lack of good will or tenderness, must be read not only in relationship to the code of values provided by the book as a whole — a code which judges her as seriously deficient; it must also be judged in relationship to the harsh facts of the world around her, a world made up of human beings ranging in degree of selfishness and egotism from Knightley, who lapses from perfection when he tries to judge Frank Churchill, his rival, down to Mrs. Elton, who has most of Emma's faults and none of her virtues. In such a setting, Emma is easily forgiven. When she insults Miss Bates, for example, we remember that Miss Bates lives in a world where many others are insensitive and cruel. "Miss Bates, neither young, handsome, rich, nor married, stood in the very worst predicament in the world for having much of the public favour; and she had no intellectual superiority to make atonement to herself, or frighten those who might hate her, into outward respect." While it would be a mistake to see only this "regulated hatred" in Jane Austen's world, overlooking the tenderness and generosity, the hatred of viciousness is there, and there is enough vice in evidence to make Emma almost shine by comparison.

Often, Jane Austen makes this apology-by-comparison explicit. When Emma lies to Knightley about Harriet, very close to the end of the book, she is excused with a generalization about human nature: "Seldom, very seldom, does complete truth belong to any human disclosure; seldom can it happen that something is not a little disguised, or a little mistaken; but where, as in this case, though the conduct is mistaken, the feelings are not, it may not be very material. — Mr. Knightley could not impute to Emma a more relenting heart than she possessed, or a heart more disposed to accept of his."

## THE IMPLIED AUTHOR
## AS FRIEND AND GUIDE

With all of this said about the masterful use of the narrator in *Emma,* there remain some "intrusions" unaccounted for by strict service to the story itself. "What did she say?" the narrator asks, at the crucial moment in the major love scene. "Just what she ought, of course. A lady always does. — She said enough to show there need not be despair — and to invite him to say more himself." To some readers this has seemed to demonstrate the author's inability to write a love scene, since it sacrifices "the illusion of reality."[11] But who has ever read this far in *Emma* under the delusion that he is reading a realistic portrayal which is suddenly shattered by the unnatural appearance of the narrator? If the narrator's superabundant wit is destructive of the kind of illusion proper to this work, the novel has been ruined long before.

But we should now be in a position to see precisely why the narrator's wit is not in the least out of place at the emotional climax of the novel. We have seen how the inside views of the characters and the author's commentary have been used from the beginning to get the values straight and to keep them straight and to help direct our reactions to Emma. But we also see here a beautiful case of the dramatized author as friend and guide. "Jane Austen," like "Henry Fielding," is a paragon of wit, wisdom, and virtue. She does not talk about her qualities; unlike Fielding she does not in *Emma* call direct attention to her artistic skill. But we are seldom allowed to forget about her for all that. When we read this novel we accept her as representing everything we admire most. She is as generous and wise as Knightley; in fact, she is a shade more penetrating in her judgment. She is as subtle and witty as Emma would like to think herself. Without being sentimental she is in favor of tenderness. She is able to put an adequate but not excessive value on wealth and rank. She recognizes a fool when she sees one, but unlike Emma she knows that it is both immoral and foolish to be rude to fools.

[11]Edd Winfield Parks, "Exegesis in Austen's Novels," *The South Atlantic Quarterly* 2 (January 1952): 117. [Au.]

She is, in short, a perfect human being, within the concept of perfection established by the book she writes; she even recognizes that human perfection of the kind *she* exemplifies is not quite attainable in real life. The process of her domination is of course circular; her character establishes the values for us according to which her character is then found to be perfect. But this circularity does not affect the success of her endeavor; in fact it insures it.

Her "omniscience" is thus a much more remarkable thing than is ordinarily implied by the term. All good novelists know all about their characters — all that they need to know. And the question of how their narrators are to find out all that *they* need to know, the question of "authority," is a relatively simple one. The real choice is much more profound than this would imply. It is a choice of the moral, not merely the technical, angle of vision from which the story is to be told.

Unlike the central intelligences of James and his successors, "Jane Austen" has learned nothing at the end of the novel that she did not know at the beginning. She needed to learn nothing. She knew everything of importance already. We have been privileged to watch with her as she observes her favorite character climb from a considerably lower platform to join the exalted company of Knightley, "Jane Austen," and those of us readers who are wise enough, good enough,

and perceptive enough to belong up there too. As Katherine Mansfield says, "the truth is that every true admirer of the novels cherishes the happy thought that he alone — reading between the lines — has become the secret friend of their author."[12] Those who love "gentle Jane" as a secret friend may undervalue the irony and with those who see her in effect as the greatest of Shaw's heroines, flashing about her with the weapons of irony, may undervalue the emphasis on tenderness and good will. But only a very few can resist her.

The dramatic illusion of her presence as a character is thus fully as important as any other element in the story. When she intrudes, the illusion is not shattered. The only illusion we care about, the illusion of traveling intimately with a hardy little band of readers whose heads are screwed on tight and whose hearts are in the right place, is actually strengthened when we are refused the romantic love scene. Like the author herself, we don't care about the love scene. We can find love scenes in almost any novelist's works, but only here can we find a mind and heart that can give us clarity without oversimplification, sympathy and romance without sentimentality, and biting irony without cynicism.

[12]*Novels and Novelists*, ed. J. Middleton Murry (London, 1930), p. 304. [Au.]

# Hans Robert Jauss

b. 1921

*Hans Robert Jauss has been acknowledged the leader and principal theorist of the movement termed "reception aesthetics," which views literary history as formed, at least in part, by the readings and assessments that texts have received throughout the past. Jauss was born in 1921 and served on the Eastern front in the Waffen-SS throughout World War II. He completed his Ph.D. at the University of Heidelberg and taught there, and at Münster and Giessen, before joining the faculty at Constance, where he has been professor of Romance languages and literature since 1967. He has held visiting professorships at the Sorbonne, Columbia, Yale, Berkeley, and UCLA. Jauss's prodigious scholarly output (which also comprises over 75 articles, in addition to editions and translations) includes* Erinnerung in Marcel Prousts À la Recherche du temps perdu (Memory in Marcel Proust's Remembrance of Things Past, 1955); Untersuchungen zu mittelalterischen Tierdichtung (Researches *into Medieval Beast Literature, 1959); La génèse de la poésie allegorique française au Moyen-Age (The Origin of Medieval French Allegory, 1962); Literaturgeschichte als Provokation der Literatur-wissenschaft (Literary History as a Challenge to Literary Theory, 1967); Kleine Apologie der ästhetischen Erfahrung (Short Defense of Aesthetic Experience, 1972); Alternität und Modernität der mittelalterischen Literatur (Ancientness and Modernity in Medieval Literature, 1977); and Ästhe-tische Erfahrung und literarische Hermeneutik (Aesthetic Experience and Literary Hermeneutics, 1977). Jauss's major essays have been translated into English and are collected in Toward an Aesthetics of Reception (1978) and Aesthetic Experience and Literary Hermeneutics (1982). "Lit-erary History as a Challenge," excerpted here, was Jauss's inaugural lecture at Constance in 1967.*

# Literary History as a Challenge to Literary Theory

**V**[1]

In the question thus posed, I see the challenge to literary studies of taking up once again the problem of literary history, which was left un-resolved in the dispute between Marxist and For-malist methods. My attempt to bridge the gap between literature and history, between historical and aesthetic approaches, begins at the point at which both schools stop. Their methods conceive the *literary fact* within the closed circle of an aesthetics of production and of representation. In doing so, they deprive literature of a dimension that inalienably belongs to its aesthetic character as well as to its social function: the dimension of its reception and influence. Reader, listener, and spectator — in short, the factor of the au-dience — play an extremely limited role in both literary theories. Orthodox Marxist aesthetics treats the reader — if at all — no differently

from the author: it inquires about his social po-sition or seeks to recognize him in the structure of a represented society. The Formalist school needs the reader only as a perceiving subject who follows the directions in the text in order to dis-tinguish the [literary] form or discover the [lit-erary] procedure. It assumes that the reader has the theoretical understanding of the philologist who can reflect on the artistic devices, already knowing them; conversely, the Marxist school candidly equates the spontaneous experience of the reader with the scholarly interest of historical materialism, which would discover relationships between superstructure and basis in the literary work. However, as Walther Bulst has stated, "no text was ever written to be read and interpreted philologically by philologists,"[2] nor, may I add, historically by historians. Both methods lack the reader in his genuine role, a role as unalterable for aesthetic as for historical knowledge: as the

---

Translated by Timothy Bahti.

[1]In the first third of his essay, Jauss attempts to explain why "literary history has increasingly fallen into disrepute": Most literary history as written is merely the compilation of the lives and works of famous authors; it is unworthy of the name of history because it attempts no causal explanations of how events occurred as they did. Two schools of literary theory which have attempted to write genuine literary his-tory, the Marxists and the Russian Formalists, are each ham-strung by an inadequate conception of the literary work of art and a simplistic notion of how art operates within history. [Ed.]

[2]"Bedenken eines Philologen," *Studium generale* 7 (1954): 321–23. The new approach to literary tradition that R. Guiette has sought in a series of pioneering essays (partly in *Questions de littérature* [Ghent, 1960]), using his own method of combining aesthetic criticism with historical knowledge, corresponds almost literally to his (unpublished) axiom, "The greatest error of philologists is to believe that literature has been made for philologists." See also his "Eloge de la lecture," *Revue générale belge* (January 1966): 3–14. [Au.]

addressee for whom the literary work is primarily destined.

For even the critic who judges a new work, the writer who conceives of his work in light of positive or negative norms of an earlier work, and the literary historian who classifies a work in its tradition and explains it historically are first simply readers before their reflexive relationship to literature can become productive again. In the triangle of author, work, and public the last is no passive part, no chain of mere reactions, but rather itself an energy formative of history. The historical life of a literary work is unthinkable without the active participation of its addressees. For it is only through the process of its mediation that the work enters into the changing horizon-of-experience of a continuity in which the perpetual inversion occurs from simple reception to critical understanding, from passive to active reception, from recognized aesthetic norms to a new production that surpasses them. The historicity of literature as well as its communicative character presupposes a dialogical and at once processlike relationship between work, audience, and new work that can be conceived in the relations between message and receiver as well as between question and answer, problem and solution. The closed circle of production and of representation within which the methodology of literary studies has mainly moved in the past must therefore be opened to an aesthetics of reception and influence if the problem of comprehending the historical sequence of literary works as the coherence of literary history is to find a new solution.

The perspective of the aesthetics of reception mediates between passive reception and active understanding, experience formative of norms, and new production. If the history of literature is viewed in this way within the horizon of a dialogue between work and audience that forms a continuity, the opposition between its aesthetic and its historical aspects is also continually mediated. Thus the thread from the past appearance to the present experience of literature, which historicism had cut, is tied back together.

The relationship of literature and reader has aesthetic as well as historical implications. The aesthetic implication lies in the fact that the first reception of a work by the reader includes a test of its aesthetic value in comparison with works already read.[3] The obvious historical implication of this is that the understanding of the first reader will be sustained and enriched in a chain of receptions from generation to generation; in this way the historical significance of a work will be decided and its aesthetic value made evident. In this process of the history of reception, which the literary historian can only escape at the price of leaving unquestioned the presuppositions that guide his understanding and judgment, the reappropriation of past works occurs simultaneously with the perpetual mediation of past and present art and of traditional evaluation and current literary attempts. The merit of a literary history based on an aesthetics of reception will depend upon the extent to which it can take an active part in the ongoing totalization of the past through aesthetic experience. This demands on the one hand — in opposition to the objectivism of positivist literary history — a conscious attempt at the formation of a canon, which, on the other hand — in opposition to the classicism of the study of traditions — presupposes a critical revision if not destruction of the received literary canon. The criterion for the formation of such a canon and the ever necessary retelling of literary history is clearly set out by the aesthetics of reception. The step from the history of the reception of the individual work to the history of literature has to lead to seeing and representing the historical sequence of works as they determine and clarify the coherence of literature, to the extent that it is meaningful for us, as the prehistory of its present experience.[4]

---

[3]This thesis is one of the main points of the *Introduction à une esthétique de la littérature* by G. Picon (Paris, 1953); see esp. pp. 90 ff. [Au.]

[4]Correspondingly, Walter Benjamin (1931) formulated: "For it is not a question of representing the written works in relation to their time but of bringing to representation the time that knows them — that is our time — in the time when they originated. Thus literature becomes an organon of history and the task of literary history is to make it this — and not to make written works the material of history" (*Angelus Novus* [Frankfurt a.M., 1966], p. 456). [Au.]

From this premise, the question as to how literary history can today be methodologically grounded and written anew will be addressed in the following seven theses.

## VI

Thesis 1. A renewal of literary history demands the removal of the prejudices of historical objectivism and the grounding of the traditional aesthetics of production and representation in an aesthetics of reception and influence. The historicity of literature rests not on an organization of "literary facts" that is established *post factum*,[5] but rather on the preceding experience of the literary work by its readers.

R. G. Collingwood's postulate, posed in his critique of the prevailing ideology of objectivity in history — "History is nothing but the re-enactment of past thought in the historian's mind"[6] — is even more valid for literary history. For the positivistic view of history as the "objective" description of a series of events in an isolated past neglects the artistic character as well as the specific historicity of literature. A literary work is not an object that stands by itself and that offers the same view to each reader in each period.[7] It is not a monument that monologically reveals its timeless essence. It is much more like an orchestration that strikes ever new resonances among its readers and that frees the text from the material of the words and brings it to a contemporary existence: "words that must, at the same time that they speak to him, create an interlocutor capable of understanding them."[8] This dialogical

character of the literary work also establishes why philological understanding can exist only in a perpetual confrontation with the text, and cannot be allowed to be reduced to a knowledge of facts.[9] Philological understanding always remains related to interpretation that must set as its goal, along with learning about the object, the reflection on and description of the completion of this knowledge as a moment of new understanding.

History of literature is a process of aesthetic reception and production that takes place in the realization of literary texts on the part of the receptive reader, the reflective critic, and the author in his continuing productivity. The endlessly growing sum of literary "facts" that winds up in the conventional literary histories is merely left over from this process; it is only the collected and classified past and therefore not history at all, but pseudo-history. Anyone who considers a series of such literary facts as a piece of the history of literature confuses the eventful character of a work of art with that of historical matter-of-factness. The *Perceval* of Chrétien de Troyes, as a literary event, is not "historical" in the same sense as, for example, the Third Crusade, which was occurring at about the same time.[10] It is not a "fact" that could be explained as caused by a series of situational preconditions and motives, by the intent of a historical action

---

[5]After the fact. [Ed.]

[6]*The Idea of History* (New York and Oxford, 1956), p. 228. [Au.]

[7]Here I am following A. Nisin in his criticism of the latent Platonism of philological methods, that is, of their belief in the timeless substance of a literary work and in a timeless point of view of the reader: "For the work of art, if it cannot incarnate the essence of art, is also not an object which we can regard according to the Cartesian rule 'without putting anything of ourselves into it but what can apply indiscriminately to all objects'"; *La Littérature et le lecteur* (Paris, 1959), p. 57 (see also my review in *Archiv für das Studium der neueren Sprachen* 197 [1960]: 223–35). [Au.]

[8]Picon, *Introduction*, p. 34. This view of the dialogical

mode of being of a literary work of art is found in Malraux (*Les voix du silence*) as well as in Picon, Nisin, and Guiette — a tradition of literary aesthetics which is still alive in France and to which I am especially indebted; it finally goes back to a famous sentence in Valéry's poetics, "It is the execution of the poem which is the poem." [Au.]

[9]Peter Szondi, "Über philologische Erkenntnis," *Hölderlin-Studien* (Frankfurt a.M., 1967), rightly sees in this the decisive difference between literary and historical studies, p. 11: "No commentary, no stylistic examination of a poet should aim to give a description of the poem that could be taken by itself. Even the least critical reader will want to confront it with the poem and will not understand it until he has traced the claim back to the acts of knowledge whence they originated." Guiette says something very similar in "Eloge de la lecture" (see note 2). [Au.]

[10]Note also J. Storost (1960), who simply equates the historical event with the literary event ("A work of art is first of all an artistic act and hence historical like the Battle of Isos"). [Au.]

as it can be reconstructed, and by the necessary and secondary consequences of this deed. The historical context in which a literary work appears is not a factual, independent series of events that exists apart from an observer. *Perceval* becomes a literary event only for its reader, who reads this last work of Chrétien with a memory of his earlier works and who recognizes its individuality in comparison with these and other works that he already knows, so that he gains a new criterion for evaluating future works. In contrast to a political event, a literary event has no unavoidable consequences subsisting on their own that no succeeding generation can ever escape. A literary event can continue to have an effect only if those who come after it still or once again respond to it — if there are readers who again appropriate the past work of authors who want to imitate, outdo, or refute it. The coherence of literature as an event is primarily mediated in the horizon of expectations of the literary experience of contemporary and later readers, critics, and authors. Whether it is possible to comprehend and represent the history of literature in its unique historicity depends on whether this horizon of expectations can be objectified.

## VII

Thesis 2. The analysis of the literary experience of the reader avoids the threatening pitfalls of psychology if it describes the reception and the influence of a work within the objectifiable system of expectations that arises for each work in the historical moment of its appearance, from a pre-understanding of the genre, from the form and themes of already familiar works, and from the opposition between poetic and practical language.

My thesis opposes a widespread skepticism that doubts whether an analysis of aesthetic influence can approach the meaning of a work of art at all or can produce, at best, more than a simple sociology of taste. René Wellek in particular directs such doubts against the literary theory of I. A. Richards. Wellek argues that neither the

individual state of consciousness, since it is momentary and only personal, nor a collective state of consciousness, as Jan Mukařovský assumes the effect a work of art to be, can be determined by empirical means.[11] Roman Jakobson wanted to replace the "collective state of consciousness" by a "collective ideology" in the form of a system of norms that exists for each literary work as *langue* and that is actualized as *parole* by the receiver — although incompletely and never as a whole.[12] This theory, it is true, limits the subjectivity of the influence, but it still leaves open the question of which data can be used to comprehend the influence of a particular work on a certain public and to incorporate it into a system of norms. In the meantime there are empirical means that had never been thought of before — literary data that allow one to ascertain a specific disposition of the audience for each work (a disposition that precedes the psychological reaction as well as the subjective understanding of the individual reader). As in the case of every actual experience, the first literary experience of a previously unknown work also demands a "foreknowledge which is an element of the experience itself, and on the basis of which anything new that we come across is available to experience at all, i.e., as it were readable in a context of experience."[13]

A literary work, even when it appears to be new, does not present itself as something absolutely new in an informational vacuum, but predisposes its audience to a very specific kind of reception by announcements, overt and covert signals, familiar characteristics, or implicit allusions. It awakens memories of that which was already read, brings the reader to a specific emo-

[11]René Wellek, "The Theory of Literary History," in *Études dédiées au quatrième Congrès de linguistes — Travaux du Cercle Linguistique de Prague* (1936), p. 179. [Au.]

[12]In *Slovo a slovesnost*, I, p. 192, cited by Wellek (1936), pp. 179 ff. [Au.]

[13]G. Buck, *Lernen und Erfahrung* (Stuttgart, 1967), p. 56, who refers here to Husserl (*Erfahrung und Urteil*, esp. § 8) but who more broadly goes beyond Husserl in a determination of the negativity in the process of experience that is of significance for the horizontal structure of aesthetic experience (cf. note 56 below). [Au.]

tional attitude, and with its beginning arouses expectations for the "middle and end," which can then be maintained intact or altered, reoriented, or even fulfilled ironically in the course of the reading according to specific rules of the genre or type of text. The psychic process in the reception of a text is, in the primary horizon of aesthetic experience, by no means only an arbitrary series of merely subjective impressions, but rather the carrying out of specific instructions in a process of directed perception, which can be comprehended according to its constitutive motivations and triggering signals, and which also can be described by a textual linguistics. If, along with W. D. Stempel, one defines the initial horizon of expectations of a text as paradigmatic isotopy, which is transposed into an immanent syntagmatic horizon of expectations to the extent that the utterance grows, then the process of reception becomes describable in the expansion of a semiotic system that accomplishes itself between the development and the correction of a system.[14] A corresponding process of the continuous establishing and altering of horizons also determines the relationship of the individual text to the succession of texts that forms the genre. The new text evokes for the reader (listener) the horizon of expectations and rules familiar from earlier texts, which are then varied, corrected, altered, or even just reproduced. Variation and correction determine the scope, whereas alteration and reproduction determine the borders of a genre-structure.[15] The interpretative reception of a text always presupposes the context of experience of aesthetic perception: the question of the subjectivity of the interpretation and of the taste of different readers or levels of readers can be asked meaningfully only when one has first clarified which transsubjective horizon of understanding conditions the influence of the text.

The ideal cases of the objective capability of such literary-historical frames of reference are works that evoke the reader's horizon of expectations, formed by a convention of genre, style, or form, only in order to destroy it step by step — which by no means serves a critical purpose only, but can itself once again produce poetic effects. Thus Cervantes allows the horizon of expectations of the favorite old tales of knighthood to arise out of the reading of *Don Quixote*, which the adventure of his last knight then seriously parodies.[16] Thus Diderot, at the beginning of *Jacques le Fataliste*, evokes the horizon of expectations of the popular novelistic schema of the "journey" (with the fictive questions of the reader to the narrator) along with the (Aristotelian) convention of the romanesque fable and the providence unique to it, so that he can then provocatively oppose to the promised journey- and love-novel a completely unromanesque "vérité de l'histoire":[17] the bizarre reality and moral casuistry of the enclosed stories in which the truth of life continually denies the mendacious character of poetic fiction.[18] Thus Nerval in the *Chimères* cites, combines, and mixes a quintessence of well-known romantic and occult motifs to produce the horizon of expectations of a mythical metamorphosis of the world only in order to signify his renunciation of romantic poetry. The identifications and relationships of the mythic state that are familiar or disclosable to the reader dissolve into an unknown to the same degree as the attempted private myth of the lyrical "I" fails, the law of sufficient information is broken, and the obscurity that has become expressive itself gains a poetic function.[19]

There is also the possibility of objectifying the horizon of expectations in works that are histor-

[16]According to the interpretation of H. J. Neuschäfer, "Der Sinn der Parodie im Don Quijote," *Studia Romanica* 5 (Heidelberg, 1963). [Au.]

[17]Truth of history. [Ed.]

[18]According to the interpretation of Rainer Warning, "Illusion und Wirklichkeit in *Tristram Shandy* und *Jacques le Fataliste*," *Theorie und Geschichte der Literatur und der schönen Künste* 4 (Munich, 1965), esp. pp. 80 ff. [Au.]

[19]According to the interpretation of Karl Heinz Stierle, "Dunkelheit und Form in Gérard de Nervals 'Chimères,'" *Theorie und Geschichte der Literatur und der schönen Künste* 5 (Munich, 1967), esp. pp. 55 and 91. [Au.]

[14]Wolf Dieter Stempel, "Pour une description des genres littéraires," in *Actes du XIIe congrès international de linguistique Romane* (Bucharest, 1968), also in *Beiträge zur Textlinguistik*, ed. W. D. Stempel (Munich, 1970). [Au.]

[15]Here I can refer to my study, "Theory of Genres and Medieval Literature," Ch. 3 in this volume. [Au.] "This volume" is *Toward an Aesthetic of Reception*. [Ed.]

ically less sharply delineated. For the specific disposition toward a particular work that the author anticipates from the audience can also be arrived at, even if explicit signals are lacking, through three generally presupposed factors: first, through familiar norms or the immanent poetics of the genre; second, through the implicit relationships to familiar works of the literary-historical surroundings; and third, through the opposition between fiction and reality, between the poetic and the practical function of language, which is always available to the reflective reader during the reading as a possibility of comparison. The third factor includes the possibility that the reader of a new work can perceive it within the narrower horizon of literary expectations, as well as within the wider horizon of experience of life. I shall return to this horizontal structure, and its ability to be objectified by means of the hermeneutics of question and answer, in the discussion of the relationship between literature and lived praxis (see XII).

## VIII

Thesis 3. Reconstructed in this way, the horizon of expectations of a work allows one to determine its artistic character by the kind and the degree of its influence on a presupposed audience. If one characterizes as aesthetic distance the disparity between the given horizon of expectations and the appearance of a new work, whose reception can result in a "change of horizons" through negation of familiar experiences or through raising newly articulated experiences to the level of consciousness, then this aesthetic distance can be objectified historically along the spectrum of the audience's reactions and criticism's judgment (spontaneous success, rejection or shock, scattered approval, gradual or belated understanding).

The way in which a literary work, at the historical moment of its appearance, satisfies, surpasses, disappoints, or refutes the expectations of its first audience obviously provides a criterion for the determination of its aesthetic value. The distance between the horizon of expectations and the work, between the familiarity of previous aesthetic experience and the "horizontal change"[20] demanded by the reception of the new work, determines the artistic character of a literary work, according to an aesthetics of reception: to the degree that this distance decreases, and no turn toward the horizon of yet-unknown experience is demanded of the receiving consciousness, the closer the work comes to the sphere of "culinary" or entertainment art [Unterhaltungskunst].[21] This latter work can be characterized by an aesthetics of reception as not demanding any horizontal change, but rather as precisely fulfilling the expectations prescribed by a ruling standard of taste, in that it satisfies the desire for the reproduction of the familiarly beautiful; confirms familiar sentiments; sanctions wishful notions; makes unusual experiences enjoyable as "sensations"; or even raises moral problems, but only to "solve" them in an edifying manner as predecided questions.[22] If, conversely, the artistic character of a work is to be measured by the aesthetic distance with which it opposes the expectations of its first audience, then it follows that this distance, at first experienced as a pleasing or alienating new perspective, can disappear for later readers, to the extent that the original negativity of the work has become self-evident and has itself entered into the horizon of future aesthetic experience, as a henceforth familiar expectation. The classical character of the so-called masterworks especially belongs to this second horizontal change;[23] their beautiful form

[20]On this Husserlian concept, see Buck, *Lernen und Erfahrung*, pp. 64 ff. [Au.]

[21]"Culinary" art refers to popular literature that the public "eats up." [Ed.]

[22]Here I am incorporating results of the discussion of "kitsch," as a borderline phenomenon of the aesthetic, which took place during the third colloquium of the research group "Poetik und Hermeneutik" (now in the volume *Die nicht mehr schönen Künste — Grenzphänomene des Ästhetischen*, ed. H. R. Jauss [Munich, 1968]). For the "culinary" approach, which presupposes mere entertainment art, the same thing holds as for kitsch, namely, that here the "demands of the consumers are *a priori* satisfied" (P. Beylin), that "the fulfilled expectation becomes the norm of the product" (Wolfgang Iser), or that "its work, without having or solving a problem, presents the appearance of a solution to a problem" (M. Imdahl), pp. 651–67. [Au.]

[23]As also the epigonal; on this, see Boris Tomashevsky, in *Théorie de la littérature. Textes des formalistes russes*, ed.

that has become self-evident, and their seemingly unquestionable "eternal meaning" bring them, according to an aesthetics of reception, dangerously close to the irresistibly convincing and enjoyable "culinary" art, so that it requires a special effort to read them "against the grain" of the accustomed experience to catch sight of their artistic character once again (see section X).

The relationship between literature and audience includes more than the facts that every work has its own specific, historically and sociologically determinable audience, that every writer is dependent on the milieu, views, and ideology of his audience, and that literary success presupposes a book "which expresses what the group expects, a book which presents the group with its own image."[24] This objectivist determination of literary success according to the congruence of the work's intention with the expectations of a social group always leads literary sociology into a dilemma whenever later or ongoing influence is to be explained. Thus R. Escarpit wants to presuppose a "collective basis in space or time" for the "illusion of the lasting quality" of a writer, which in the case of Molière leads to an astonishing prognosis: "Molière is still young for the Frenchman of the twentieth century because his world still lives, and a sphere of culture, views, and language still binds us to him. . . . But the sphere becomes ever smaller, and Molière will age and die when the things which our culture still has in common with the France of Molière die" (p. 117). As if Molière had only mirrored the "mores of his time" and had only remained successful through this supposed intention! Where the congruence between

work and social group does not exist, or no longer exists, as for example with the reception of a work in a foreign language, Escarpit is able to help himself by inserting a "myth" in between: "myths that are invented by a later world for which the reality that they substitute for has become alien" (p. 111). As if all reception beyond the first, socially determined audience for a work were only a "distorted echo," only a result of "subjective myths," and did not itself have its objective a priori once again in the received work as the limit and possibility of later understanding! The sociology of literature does not view its object dialectically enough when it determines the circle of author, work, and audience so one-sidedly.[25] The determination is reversible: there are works that at the moment of their appearance are not yet directed at any specific audience, but that break through the familiar horizon of literary expectations so completely that an audience can only gradually develop for them.[26] When, then, the new horizon of expectations has achieved more general currency, the power of the altered aesthetic norm can be demonstrated in that the audience experiences formerly successful works as outmoded, and withdraws its appreciation. Only in view of such horizontal change does the analysis of literary influence achieve the dimension of a literary history of readers,[27] and do the

T. Todorov (Paris, 1965), p. 306, n. 53: "The appearance of a genius always equals a literary revolution which dethrones the dominant canon and gives power to processes subordinated until then. . . . The epigones repeat a worn-out combination of processes, and as original and revolutionary as it was, this combination becomes stereotypical and traditional. Thus the epigones kill, sometimes for a long time, the aptitude of their contemporaries to sense the aesthetic force of the examples they imitate: they discredit their masters." [Au.]

[24]R. Escarpit, *Das Buch und der Leser: Entwurf einer Literatursoziologie* (Cologne and Opladen, 1961; first, expanded German edition of *Sociologie de la littérature* [Paris, 1958]), p. 116. [Au.]

[25]K. H. Bender, "König und Vasall: Untersuchungen zur Chanson de Geste des XII. Jahrhunderts," *Studia Romanica* 13 (Heidelberg, 1967), shows what step is necessary to get beyond this one-sided determination. In this history of the early French epic, the apparent congruence of feudal society and epic ideality is represented as a process that is maintained through a continually changing discrepancy between "reality" and "ideology," that is, between the historical constellations of feudal conflicts and the poetic responses of the epics. [Au.]

[26]The incomparably more promising literary sociology of Erich Auerbach brought these aspects to light in the variety of epoch-making breaks in the relationship between author and reader; for this see the evaluation of Fritz Schalk in his edition of Auerbach's *Gesammelte Aufsätze zur romanischen Philologie* (Bern and Munich, 1967), pp. 11 ff. [Au.]

[27]See Harald Weinrich, "Für eine Literaturgeschichte des Lesers," *Merkur* 21 (November, 1967), an attempt arising from the same intent as mine, which, analogously to the way that the linguistics of the speaker, customary earlier, has been replaced by the linguistics of the listener, argues for a methodological consideration of the perspective of the reader in

statistical curves of the best-sellers provide historical knowledge.

A literary sensation from the year 1857 may serve as an example. Alongside Flaubert's *Madame Bovary,* which has since become world-famous, appeared his friend Feydeau's *Fanny,* today forgotten. Although Flaubert's novel brought with it a trial for offending public morals, *Madame Bovary* was at first overshadowed by Feydeau's novel: *Fanny* went through thirteen editions in one year, achieving a success the likes of which Paris had not experienced since Chateaubriand's *Atala.* Thematically considered, both novels met the expectations of a new audience that — in Baudelaire's analysis — had foresworn all romanticism, and despised great as well as naive passions equally:[28] they treated a trivial subject, infidelity in a bourgeois and provincial milieu. Both authors understood how to give to the conventional, ossified triangular relationship a sensational twist that went beyond the expected details of the erotic scenes. They put the worn-out theme of jealousy in a new light by reversing the expected relationship between the three classic roles: Feydeau has the youthful lover of the *femme de trente ans*[29] become jealous of his lover's husband despite his having already fulfilled his desires, and perishing over this agonizing situation; Flaubert gives the adulteries of the doctor's wife in the provinces — interpreted by Baudelaire as a sublime form of *dandysme* — the surprise ending that precisely the laughable figure of the cuckolded Charles Bovary takes on dignified traits at the end. In the official criticism of the time, one finds voices that reject *Fanny* as

well as *Madame Bovary* as a product of the new school of *réalisme,* which they reproach for denying everything ideal and attacking the ideas on which the social order of the Second Empire was founded.[30] The audience's horizon of expectations in 1857, here only vaguely sketched in, which did not expect anything great from the novel after Balzac's death,[31] explains the different success of the two novels only when the question of the effect of their narrative form is posed. Flaubert's formal innovation, his principle of "impersonal narration" (*impassibilité*) — attacked by Barbey d'Aurevilly with the comparison that if a story-telling machine could be cast of English steel it would function no differently than Monsieur Flaubert[32] — must have shocked the same audience that was offered the provocative contents of *Fanny* in the inviting tone of a confessional novel. It could also find incorporated in Feydeau's descriptions the modish ideals and suppressed desires of a stylish level of society,[33] and could delight without restraint in the lascivious central scene in which Fanny (without suspecting that her lover is watching from the balcony) seduces her husband — for the moral indignation was already diminished for them through the reaction of the unhappy wit-

---

[30]Cf. *ibid.,* p. 999, as well as the accusation, speech for the defense, and verdict of the *Bovary* trial in Flaubert, *Oeuvres,* Pléiade ed. (Paris, 1951), I, pp. 649–717, esp. p. 717; also about *Fanny,* E. Montégut, "Le roman intime de la littérature réaliste," *Revue des deux mondes* 18 (1858), pp. 196–213, esp. pp. 201 and 209 ff. [Au.]

[31]As Baudelaire declares, *Oeuvres complètes,* p. 996: "for since the disappearance of Balzac . . . all curiosity relative to the novel has been pacified and put to rest." [Au.]

[32]For these and other contemporary verdicts see H. R. Jauss, "Die beiden Fassungen von Flauberts *Education sentimentale,*" *Heidelberger Jahrbücher* 2 (1958), pp. 96–116, esp. p. 97. [Au.]

[33]On this, see the excellent analysis by the contemporary critic E. Montégut (see note 30 above), who explains in detail why the dream-world and the figures in Feydeau's novel are typical for the audience in the neighborhoods "between the Bourse and the boulevard Montmartre" (p. 209) that needs an "alcool poétique," enjoys "seeing their vulgar adventures of yesterday and their vulgar projects of tomorrow poeticized" (p. 210), and subscribes to an "idolatry of the material," by which Montégut understands the ingredients of the "dream factory" of 1858 — "a sort of sanctimonious admiration, almost devout, for furniture, wallpaper, dress, escapes like a perfume of patchouli from each of its pages" (p. 201). [Au.]

---

literary history and thereby most happily supports my aims. Weinrich shows above all how the empirical methods of literary sociology can be supplemented by the linguistic and literary interpretation of the role of the reader implicit in the work. [Au.]

[28]In *"Madame Bovary par Gustave Flaubert,"* Baudelaire, *Oeuvres complètes,* Pléiade ed. (Paris, 1951), p. 998: "The last years of Louise-Philippe witnessed the last explosions of a spirit still excitable by the play of the imagination; but the new novelist found himself faced with a completely worn-out society — worse than worn-out — stupified and gluttonous, with a horror only of fiction, and love only for possession." [Au.]

[29]Woman in her thirties. [Ed.]

ness. As *Madame Bovary,* however, became a worldwide success, when at first it was understood and appreciated as a turning-point in the history of the novel by only a small circle of connoisseurs, the audience of novel-readers that was formed by it came to sanction the new canon of expectations; this canon made Feydeau's weaknesses — his flowery style, his modish effects, his lyrical-confessional cliches — unbearable, and allowed *Fanny* to fade into yesterday's bestseller.

## IX

Thesis 4. The reconstruction of the horizon of expectations, in the face of which a work was created and received in the past, enables one on the other hand to pose questions that the text gave an answer to, and thereby to discover how the contemporary reader could have viewed and understood the work. This approach corrects the mostly unrecognized norms of a classicist or modernizing understanding of art, and avoids the circular recourse to a general "spirit of the age." It brings to view the hermeneutic difference between the former and the current understanding of a work; it raises to consciousness the history of its reception, which mediates both positions; and it thereby calls into question as a platonizing dogma of philological metaphysics the apparently self-evident claims that in the literary text, literature [Dichtung] is eternally present, and that its objective meaning, determined once and for all, is at all times immediately accessible to the interpreter.

The method of historical reception[34] is indis-

pensable for the understanding of literature from the distant past. When the author of a work is unknown, his intent undeclared, and his relationship to sources and models only indirectly accessible, the philological question of how the text is "properly" — that is, "from its intention and time" — to be understood can best be answered if one foregrounds it against those works that the author explicitly or implicitly presupposed his contemporary audience to know. The creator of the oldest branches of the *Roman de Renart,*[35] for example, assumes — as his prologue testifies — that his listeners know romances like the story of Troy and *Tristan,* heroic epics (*chansons de geste*), and verse fables (*fabliaux*), and that they are therefore curious about the "unprecedented war between the two barons, Renart and Ysengrin," which is to overshadow everything already known. The works and genres that are evoked are then all ironically touched on in the course of the narrative. From this horizontal change one can probably also explain the public success, reaching far beyond France, of this rapidly famous work that for the first time took a position opposed to all the long-reigning heroic and courtly poetry.[36]

Philological research long misunderstood the originally satiric intention of the medieval *Reineke Fuchs* and, along with it, the ironic-didactic meaning of the analogy between animal and human natures, because ever since Jacob Grimm it had remained trapped within the romantic notion of pure nature poetry and naive animal tales. Thus, to give yet a second example of modernizing norms, one could also rightly reproach French research into the epic since Bédier for living — unconsciously — by the criteria of Boileau's poetics, and judging a nonclassical literature by the norms of simplicity, harmony of part and whole, probability, and still others.[37]

[34]Examples of this method, which not only follow the success, fame, and influence of a writer through history but also examine the historical conditions and changes in understanding him, are rare. The following should be mentioned: G. F. Ford, *Dickens and His Readers* (Princeton, 1955); A. Nisin, *Les Oeuvres et les siècles* (Paris, 1960), which discusses "Virgile, Dante et nous," Ronsard, Corneille, Racine; E. Lämmert, "Zur Wirkungsgeschichte Eichendorffs in Deutschland," *Festschrift für Richard Alewyn,* ed. H. Singer and B. von Wiese (Cologne and Graz, 1967). The methodological problem of the step from the influence to the reception of a work was indicated most sharply by F. Vodička already in 1941 in his study "Die Problematik der Rezeption

von Nerudas Werk" (now in *Struktur vývoje* Prague, 1969) with the question of the changes in the work that are realized in its successive aesthetic perceptions. [Au.]

[35]Medieval French collection of beast-fables centering on Renart (the fox) and Ysengrin (the wolf). [Ed.]

[36]See H. R. Jauss, *Untersuchungen zur mittelalterlichen Tierdichtung* (Tübingen, 1959), esp. chap. IV A and D. [Au.]

[37]A. Vinaver, "A la recherche d'une poétique médiévale," *Cahiers de civilisation médiévale* 2 (1959), 1–16. [Au.]

The philological-critical method is obviously not protected by its historical objectivism from the interpreter who, supposedly bracketing himself, nonetheless raises his own aesthetic preconceptions to an unacknowledged norm and unreflectively modernizes the meaning of the past text. Whoever believes that the "timelessly true" meaning of a literary work must immediately, and simply through one's mere absorption in the text, disclose itself to the interpreter as if he had a standpoint outside of history and beyond all "errors" of his predecessors and of the historical reception — whoever believes this "conceals the involvement of the historical consciousness itself in the history of influence." He denies "those presuppositions — certainly not arbitrary but rather fundamental — that govern his own understanding," and can only feign an objectivity "that in truth depends upon the legitimacy of the questions asked."[38]

In *Truth and Method* Hans-Georg Gadamer, whose critique of historical objectivism I am assuming here, described the principle of the history of influence, which seeks to present the reality of history in understanding itself,[39] as an application of the logic of question and answer to the historical tradition. In a continuation of Collingwood's thesis that "one can understand a text only when one has understood the question to which it is an answer,"[40] Gadamer demonstrates that the reconstructed question can no longer stand within its original horizon because this historical horizon is always already enveloped within the horizon of the present: "Understanding is always the process of the fusion of these horizons that we suppose to exist by themselves."[41] The historical question cannot exist for itself; it must merge with the question "that the tradition is for us."[42] One thereby solves the question with

which René Wellek described the aporia[43] of literary judgment: should the philologist evaluate a literary work according to the perspective of the past, the standpoint of the present, or the "verdict of the ages"?[44] The actual standards of a past could be so narrow that their use would only make poorer a work that in the history of its influence had unfolded a rich semantic potential. The aesthetic judgment of the present would favor a canon of works that correspond to modern taste, but would unjustly evaluate all other works only because their function in their time is no longer evident. And the history of influence itself, as instructive as it might be, is an "authority open to the same objections as the authority of the author's contemporaries."[45] Wellek's conclusion — that there is no possibility of avoiding our own judgment; one must only make this judgment as objective as possible in that one does what every scholar does, namely, "isolate the object"[46] — is no solution to the aporia, but rather a relapse into objectivism. The "verdict of the ages" on a literary work is more than merely "the accumulated judgment of other readers, critics, viewers, and even professors";[47] it is the successive unfolding of the potential for meaning that is embedded in a work and actualized in the stages of its historical reception as it discloses itself to understanding judgment, so long as this faculty achieves in a controlled fashion the "fusion of horizons" in the encounter with the tradition.

The agreement between my attempt to establish a possible literary history on the basis of an aesthetics of reception and H.-G. Gadamer's principle of the history of influence nonetheless reaches its limit where Gadamer would like to elevate the concept of the classical to the status of prototype for all historical mediation of past with present. His definition, that "what we call 'classical' does not first require the overcoming of historical distance — for in its own constant

[38]Hans-Georg Gadamer, *Wahrheit und Methode — Grundzüge einer philosophischen Hermeneutik* (Tübingen, 1960), pp. 284–85; English edition as *Truth and Method: Fundamentals of a Philosophical Hermeneutics* (New York, 1975), p. 268. [Au.]
[39]*Ibid.*, p. 283; Eng., p. 267. [Au.]
[40]*Ibid.*, p. 352; Eng., p. 333. [Au.]
[41]*Ibid.*, p. 289; Eng., p. 273. [Au.]
[42]*Ibid.*, p. 356; Eng., p. 337. [Au.]

[43]Intractable paradox. [Ed.]
[44]Wellek, 1936, p. 184; *ibid.*, 1963, pp. 17–20. [Au.]
[45]*Ibid.*, p. 17. [Au.]
[46]*Ibid.* [Au.]
[47]*Ibid.* [Au.]

mediation it achieves this overcoming,"[48] falls out of the relationship of question and answer that is constitutive of all historical tradition. If classical is "what says something to the present as if it were actually said to it,"[49] then for the classical text one would not first seek the question to which it gives an answer. Doesn't the classical, which "signifies itself and interprets itself,"[50] merely describe the result of what I called the "second horizontal change": the unquestioned, self-evident character of the so-called "masterwork," which conceals its original negativity within the retrospective horizon of an exemplary tradition, and which necessitates our regaining the "right horizon of questioning" once again in the face of the confirmed classicism? Even with the classical work, the receiving consciousness is not relieved of the task of recognizing the "tensional relationship between the text and the present."[51] The concept of the classical that interprets itself, taken over from Hegel, must lead to a reversal of the historical relationship of question and answer,[52] and contradicts the principle of the history of influence that understanding is "not merely a reproductive, but always a productive attitude as well."[53]

This contradiction is evidently conditioned by Gadamer's holding fast to a concept of classical art that is not capable of serving as a general foundation for an aesthetics of reception beyond the period of its origination, namely, that of humanism. It is the concept of *mimesis,* understood as "recognition," as Gadamer demonstrates in his ontological explanation of the experience of art: "What one actually experiences in a work of art and what one is directed toward is rather how true it is, that is, to what extent one knows and recognizes something and oneself."[54] This concept of art can be validated for the humanist period of art, but not for its preceding medieval period and not at all for its succeeding period of our modernity, in which the aesthetics of mimesis has lost its obligatory character, along with the substantialist metaphysics ("knowledge of essence") that founded it. The epistemological significance of art does not, however, come to an end with this period-change, whence it becomes evident that art was in no way bound to the classical function of recognition.[55] The work of art can also mediate knowledge that does not fit into the Platonic schema if it anticipates paths of future experience, imagines as-yet-untested models of perception and behavior, or contains an answer to newly posed questions.[56] It is precisely concerning this virtual significance and productive function in the process of experience that the history of the influence of literature is abbreviated when one gathers the mediation of past art and the present under the concept of the *classical.* If, according to Gadamer, the classical *itself* is supposed to achieve the overcoming of historical distance through its constant mediation, it must, as a perspective of the hypostatized tradition, displace the insight that classical art at the time of its production did not yet appear "classical": rather, it could open up new ways of seeing things and perform new experiences that only in historical distance — in the recognition of what is now familiar — give rise to the appearance that a timeless truth expresses itself in the work of art.

The influence of even the great literary works of the past can be compared neither with a self-mediating event nor with an emanation: the tradition of art also presupposes a dialogical rela-

---

[48]*Wahrheit und Methode,* p. 274; Eng., p. 257. [Au.]

[49]*Ibid.* [Au.]

[50]*Ibid.* [Au.]

[51]*Ibid.,* p. 290; Eng., p. 273. [Au.]

[52]This reversal becomes obvious in the chapter "Die Logik von Frage und Antwort" (*ibid.,* pp. 351–60; Eng., pp. 333–41); see my "History of Art and Pragmatic History," § VII, included in this volume. [Au.]

[53]*Ibid.,* p. 280; Eng., p. 264. [Au.] For another critique of Gadamer's valorization of the "classical," see Barbara Herrnstein Smith in Ch. 8. [Ed.]

[54]*Ibid.,* p. 109; Eng., p. 102. [Au.]

[55]See *ibid.,* p. 110; Eng., p. 103. [Au.]

[56]This also follows from Formalist aesthetics and especially from Viktor Shklovsky's theory of "deautomatization"; cf. Victor Erlich's summary, *Russian Formalism,* p. 76: "As the 'twisted, deliberately impeded form' interposes artificial obstacles between the perceiving subject and the object perceived, the chain of habitual association and of automatic responses is broken: thus, we become able to *see* things instead of merely *recognizing* them." [Au.] See Shklovsky in Ch. 3. [Ed.]

tionship of the present to the past, according to which the past work can answer and "say something" to us only when the present observer has posed the question that draws it back out of its seclusion. When, in *Truth and Method,* understanding is conceived — analogous to Heidegger's "event of being" [*Seinsgeschehen*] — as "the placing of oneself within a process of tradition in which past and present are constantly mediated,"[57] the "productive moment which lies in understanding"[58] must be shortchanged. This productive function of progressive understanding, which necessarily also includes criticizing the tradition and forgetting it, shall in the following sections establish the basis for the project of a literary history according to an aesthetics of reception. This project must consider the historicity of literature in a threefold manner: diachronically in the interrelationships of the reception of literary works (see X), synchronically in the frame of reference of literature of the same moment, as well as in the sequence of such frames (see XI), and finally in the relationship of the immanent literary development to the general process of history (see XII).

## X

Thesis 5. The theory of the aesthetics of reception not only allows one to conceive the meaning and form of a literary work in the historical unfolding of its understanding. It also demands that one insert the individual work into its "literary series" to recognize its historical position and significance in the context of the experience of literature. In the step from a history of the reception of works to an eventful history of literature, the latter manifests itself as a process in which the passive reception is on the part of authors. Put another way, the next work can solve formal and moral problems left behind by the last work, and present new problems in turn.

How can the individual work, which positivistic literary history determined in a chronological series and thereby reduced to the status of a "fact," be brought back into its historical-sequential relationship and thereby once again be understood as an "event"? The theory of the Formalist school, as already mentioned, would solve this problem with its principle of "literary evolution," according to which the new work arises against the background of preceding or competing works, reaches the "high point" of a literary period as a successful form, is quickly reproduced and thereby increasingly automatized, until finally, when the next form has broken through, the former vegetates on as a used-up genre in the quotidian sphere of literature. If one were to analyze and describe a literary period according to this program — which to date has hardly been put into use[59] — one could expect a representation that would in various respects be superior to that of the conventional literary history. Instead of the works standing in closed series, themselves standing one after another and unconnected, at best framed by a sketch of general history — for example, the series of the works of an author, a particular school, or one kind of style, as well as the series of various genres — the Formalist method would relate the series to one another and *discover the evolutionary alternating relationship of functions and forms.*[60] The works that thereby stand out from, correspond to, or replace one another would appear as moments of a process that no longer needs to be construed as tending toward some end point, since as the *dialectical self-production of new forms* it requires no teleology. Seen in this way, the autonomous dynamics of literary evolution would furthermore eliminate the dilemma of the criteria of selection: the criterion here is the work as a new form in the literary

---

[57]*Wahrheit und Methode,* p. 275; Eng., p. 258. [Au.]
[58]*Ibid.,* p. 280; Eng., p. 264. [Au.]

[59]In the 1927 article, "Über literarische Evolution," by Yuri Tynyanov (in *Die literarischen Kunstmittel und die Evolution in der Literatur,* pp. 37–60), this program is most pregnantly presented. It was only partially fulfilled — as Yuri Striedter informed me — in the treatment of problems of structural change in the history of literary genres, as for example in the volume *Russkaja proza,* Voprosy poètiki 8 (Leningrad, 1926), or Y. Tynyanov, "Die Ode als rhetorische Gattung" (1922), now in *Texte der russischen Formalisten,* II, ed. J. Striedter (Munich, 1970). [Au.] See Tynyanov in Ch. 3. [Ed.]
[60]Y. Tynyanov, "Über literarische Evolution," p. 59. [Au.]

series, and not the self-reproduction of worn-out forms, artistic devices, and genres, which pass into the background until at a new moment in the evolution they are made "perceptible" once again. Finally, in the Formalist project of a literary history that understands itself as "evolution" and — contrary to the usual sense of this term — excludes any directional course, the historical character of a work becomes synonymous with literature's historical character: the "evolutionary" significance and characteristics of a literary phenomenon presuppose innovation as the decisive feature, just as a work of art is perceived against the background of other works of art.[61]

The Formalist theory of "literary evolution" is certainly one of the most significant attempts at a renovation of literary history. The recognition that historical changes also occur within a system in the field of literature, the attempted functionalization of literary development, and, not least of all, the theory of automatization — these are achievements that are to be held onto, even if the one-sided canonization of change requires a correction. Criticism has already displayed the weaknesses of the Formalist theory of evolution: mere opposition or aesthetic variation does not suffice to explain the growth of literature; the question of the direction of change of literary forms remains unanswerable; innovation for itself does not alone make up artistic character; and the connection between literary evolution and social change does not vanish from the face of the earth through its mere negation.[62] My thesis XII responds to the last question; the problematic of the remaining questions demands that the descriptive literary theory of the Formalists be opened up, through an aesthetics of reception, to the dimension of historical experience that must also include the historical standpoint of the present observer, that is, the literary historian.

The description of literary evolution as a ceaseless struggle between the new and the old, or as the alternation of the canonization and automatization of forms reduces the historical character of literature to the one-dimensional actuality of its changes and limits historical understanding to their perception. The alterations in the literary series nonetheless only become a historical sequence when the opposition of the old and new form also allows one to recognize their specific mediation. This mediation, which includes the step from the old to the new form in the interaction of work and recipient (audience, critic, new producer) as well as that of past event and successive reception, can be methodologically grasped in the formal and substantial problem "that each work of art, as the horizon of the 'solutions' which are possible after it, poses and leaves behind."[63] The mere description of the altered structure and the new artistic devices of a work does not necessarily lead to this problem, nor, therefore, back to its function in the historical series. To determine this, that is, to recognize the problem left behind to which the new work in the historical series is the answer, the interpreter must bring his own experience into play, since the past horizon of old and new forms, problems and solutions, is only recognizable in its further mediation, within the present horizon of the received work. Literary history as "literary evolution" presupposes the historical process of aesthetic reception and production up to the observer's present as the condition for the mediation of all formal oppositions or "differential qualities" ["Differenzqualitäten"].[64]

Founding "literary evolution" on an aesthetics of reception thus not only returns its lost direction insofar as the standpoint of the literary historian becomes the vanishing point — but not the goal!

61"A work of art will appear as a positive value when it regroups the structure of the preceding period, it will appear as a negative value if it takes over the structure without changing it." (Jan Mukařovský, cited by R. Wellek, 1963, pp. 48, 49.) [Au.]
62See. V. Erlich, *Russian Formalism*, pp. 254–57, R. Wellek, 1963, pp. 48 ff., and J. Striedter, *Texte der russischen Formalisten*, I, Introduction, § X. [Au.]

63Hans Blumenberg, in *Poetik und Hermeneutik* 3 (see note 22), p. 692. [Au.]
64According to V. Erlich, *Russian Formalism*, p. 252, this concept meant three things to the Formalists: "on the level of the representation of reality, *Differenzqualität* stood for the 'divergence' from the actual, i.e., for creative deformation. On the level of language it meant a departure from current linguistic usage. Finally, on the plane of literary dynamics, a . . . modification of the prevailing artistic norm." [Au.]

— of the process. It also opens to view the temporal depths of literary experience, in that it allows one to recognize the variable distance between the actual and the virtual significance of a literary work. This means that the artistic character of a work, whose semantic potential Formalism reduces to innovation as the single criterion of value, must in no way always be immediately perceptible within the horizon of its first appearance, let alone that it could then also already be exhausted in the pure opposition between the old and the new form. The distance between the actual first perception of a work and its virtual significance, or, put another way, the resistance that the new work poses to the expectations of its first audience, can be so great that it requires a long process of reception to gather in that which was unexpected and unusable within the first horizon. It can thereby happen that a virtual significance of the work remains long unrecognized until the "literary evolution," through the actualization of a newer form, reaches the horizon that now for the first time allows one to find access to the understanding of the misunderstood older form. Thus the obscure lyrics of Mallarmé and his school prepared the ground for the return to baroque poetry, long since unappreciated and therefore forgotten, and in particular for the philological reinterpretation and "rebirth" of Góngora. One can line up the examples of how a new literary form can reopen access to forgotten literature. These include the so-called "renaissances" — so called, because the word's meaning gives rise to the appearance of an automatic return, and often prevents one from recognizing that literary tradition can not transmit itself alone. That is, a literary past can return only when a new reception draws it back into the present, whether an altered aesthetic attitude willfully reaches back to reappropriate the past, or an unexpected light falls back on forgotten literature from the new moment of literary evolution, allowing something to be found that one previously could not have sought in it.[65]

The new is thus not only an *aesthetic* category. It is not absorbed into the factors of innovation, surprise, surpassing, rearrangement, or alienation, to which the Formalist theory assigned exclusive importance. The new also becomes a *historical* category when the diachronic analysis of literature is pushed further to ask which historical moments are really the ones that first make new that which is new in a literary phenomenon; to what degree this new element is already perceptible in the historical instant of its emergence; which distance, path, or detour of understanding were required for its realization in content; and whether the moment of its full actualization was so influential that it could alter the perspective on the old, and thereby the canonization of the literary past.[66] How the relationship of poetic theory to aesthetically productive praxis is represented in this light has already been discussed in another context.[67] The possibilities of the interaction between production and reception in the historical change of aesthetic attitudes are admittedly far from exhausted by these remarks. Here they should above all illustrate the dimension into which a diachronic view of literature leads when it would no longer be satisfied to consider a chronological series of literary facts as already the historical appearance of literature.

## XI

Thesis 6. The achievements made in linguistics through the distinction and methodological interrelation of diachronic and synchronic analysis are the occasion for overcoming the diachronic perspective — previously the only one practiced — in literary history as well. If the perspective of

[65]For the first possibility the (antiromantic) reevaluation of Boileau and of the classical *contrainte* poetics by Gide and Valéry can be introduced; for the second, the belated discovery of Hölderlin's hymns or Novalis's concept of future poetry (on the latter see H. R. Jauss in *Romanische Forschungen* 77 [1965], pp. 174–83). [Au.]

[66]Thus, since the reception of the "minor romantic" Nerval, whose *Chimères* only attracted attention under the influence of Mallarmé, the canonized "major romantics" Lamartine, Vigny, Musset, and a large part of the "rhetorical" lyrics of Victor Hugo have been increasingly forced into the background. [Au.]

[67]*Poetik und Hermeneutik* 2 (*Immanente Ästhetik — Ästhetische Reflexion*), ed. W. Iser (Munich, 1966), esp. pp. 395–418. [Au.]

the history of reception always bumps up against the functional connections between the understanding of new works and the significance of older ones when changes in aesthetic attitudes are considered, it must also be possible to take a synchronic cross-section of a moment in the development, to arrange the heterogeneous multiplicity of contemporaneous works in equivalent, opposing, and hierarchical structures, and thereby to discover an overarching system of relationships in the literature of a historical moment. From this the principle of representation of a new literary history could be developed, if further cross-sections diachronically before and after were so arranged as to articulate historically the change in literary structures in its epoch-making moments.

Siegfried Kracauer has most decisively questioned the primacy of the diachronic perspective in historiography. His study "Time and History"[68] disputes the claim of "General History" to render comprehensible events from all spheres of life within a homogeneous medium of chronological time as a unified process, consistent in each historical moment. This understanding of history, still standing under the influence of Hegel's concept of the "objective spirit," presupposes that everything that happens contemporaneously is equally informed by the significance of this moment, and it thereby conceals the actual noncontemporaneity of the contemporaneous.[69] For the multiplicity of events of one historical moment, which the universal historian believes can be understood as exponents of a

unified content, are de facto moments of entirely different time-curves, conditioned by the laws of their "special history,"[70] as becomes immediately evident in the discrepancies of the various "histories" of the arts, law, economics, politics, and so forth: "The shaped times of the diverse areas overshadow the uniform flow of time. Any historical period must therefore be imagined as a mixture of events which emerge at different moments of their own time."[71]

It is not in question here whether this state of affairs presupposes a primary inconsistency to history, so that the consistency of general history always only arises retrospectively from the unifying viewpoint and representation of the historian; or whether the radical doubt concerning "historical reason," which Kracauer extends from the pluralism of chronological and morphological courses of time to the fundamental antinomy of the general and the particular in history, in fact proves that universal history is philosophically illegitimate today. For the sphere of literature in any case, one can say that Kracauer's insights into the "coexistence of the contemporaneous and non-contemporaneous,"[72] far from leading historical knowledge into an aporia, rather make apparent the necessity and possibility of discovering the historical dimension of literary phenomena in synchronic cross-sections. For it follows from these insights that the chronological fiction of the moment that informs all contemporaneous phenomena corresponds as little to the historicity of literature as does the morphological fiction of a homogeneous literary series, in which all phenomena in their sequential order only follow immanent laws. The purely diachronic perspective,

[68]In *Zeugnisse — Theodor W. Adorno zum 60. Geburtstag* (Frankfurt a.M., 1963), pp. 50–64, and also in "General History and the Aesthetic Approach," *Poetik und Hermeneutik* 3. See also *History: The Last Things Before the Last* (New York, 1969), esp. chap. 6: "Ahasverus, or the Riddle of Time," pp. 139–63. [Au.]

[69]"First, in identifying history as a process in chronological time, we tacitly assume that our knowledge of the moment at which an event emerges from the flow of time will help us to account for its appearance. The date of an event is a value-laden fact. Accordingly, all events in the history of a people, a nation, or a civilization that take place at a given moment are supposed to occur then and there for reasons bound up, somehow, with that moment" (Kracauer, *History*, p. 141).[Au.]

[70]This concept goes back to H. Foccillon, *The Life of Forms in Art* (New York, 1948), and G. Kubler, *The Shape of Time: Remarks on the History of Things* (New Haven, 1962). [Au.]

[71]Kracauer, *History*, p. 53. [Au.]

[72]*Poetik und Hermeneutik* 3, p. 569. The formula of "the contemporaneity of the different," with which F. Sengle, "Aufgaben der heutigen Literaturgeschichtsschreibung," 1964, pp. 247 ff., refers to the same phenomenon, fails to grasp one dimension of the problem which becomes evident in his belief that this difficulty of literary history can be solved by simply combining comparative methods and modern interpretation ("that is, carrying out comparative interpretation on a broader basis," p. 249). [Au.]

however conclusively it might explain changes in, for example, the histories of genres according to the immanent logic of innovation and automatization, problem and solution, nonetheless only arrives at the properly historical dimension when it breaks through the morphological canon, to confront the work that is important in historical influence with the historically worn-out, conventional works of the genre, and at the same time does not ignore its relationship to the literary milieu in which it had to make its way alongside works of other genres.

The historicity of literature comes to light at the intersections of diachrony and synchrony. Thus it must also be possible to make the literary horizon of a specific historical moment comprehensible as that synchronic system in relation to which literature that appears contemporaneously could be received diachronically in relations of noncontemporaneity, and the work could be received as current or not, as modish, outdated, or perennial, as premature or belated.[73] For if, from the point of view of an aesthetics of production, literature that appears contemporaneously breaks down into a heterogeneous multiplicity of the noncontemporaneous, that is, of works informed by the various moments of the "shaped time" of their genre (as the seemingly present heavenly constellations move apart astronomically into points of the most different temporal distance), this multiplicity of literary phenomena nonetheless, when seen from the point of view of an aesthetics of reception, coalesces again for the audience that perceives them and relates them to one another as works of *its* present, in the unity of a common horizon of literary expectations, memories, and anticipations that establishes their significance.

Since each synchronic system must contain its past and its future as inseparable structural elements,[74] the synchronic cross-section of the literary production of a historical point in time necessarily implies further cross-sections that are diachronically before and after. Analogous to the history of language, constant and variable factors are thereby brought to light that can be localized as functions of a system. For literature as well is a kind of grammar or syntax, with relatively fixed relations of its own: the arrangement of the traditional and the uncanonized genres; modes of expression, kinds of style, and rhetorical figures; contrasted with this arrangement is the much more variable realm of a semantics: the literary subjects, archetypes, symbols, and metaphors. One can therefore seek to erect for literary history an analogy to that which Hans Blumenberg has postulated for the history of philosophy, elucidating it through examples of the change in periods and, in particular, the successional relationship of Christian theology and philosophy, and grounding it in his historical logic of question and answer: a "formal system of the explanation of the world . . . , within which structure the reshufflings can be localized which make up the process-like character of history up to the radicality of period-changes."[75] Once the substantialist notion of a self-reproducing literary tradition has been overcome through a functional explanation of the processlike relationships of production and reception, it must also be possible to recognize behind the *transformation* of literary forms and contents those *reshufflings* in a literary system of world-understanding that make the horizontal change in the process of aesthetic experience comprehensible.

From these premises one could develop the

[73]In 1960 Roman Jakobson also made this claim in a lecture that now constitutes chap. 11, "Linguistique et poétique," of his book, *Essais de linguistique générale* (Paris, 1963). Cf. p. 212: "Synchronic description envisages not only the literary production of a given period, but also that part of the literary tradition which has remained alive or been resuscitated in the period in question. . . . Historical poetics, exactly like the history of language, if it wants to be truly comprehensive, ought to be conceived as a superstructure built upon a series of successive synchronic descriptions." [Au.]

[74]Yuri Tynyanov and Roman Jakobson, "Probleme der Literatur- und Sprachforschung" (1928), now in *Kursbuch* 5 (Frankfurt a.M., 1966), p. 75: "The history of the system itself represents another system. Pure synchrony now proves to be illusory: each synchronic system has its past and its future as inseparable structural elements of this system." [Au.]

[75]First in "Epochenschwelle und Rezeption," *Philosophische Rundschau* 6 (1958), pp. 101 ff., most recently in *Die Legitimität der Neuzeit* (Frankfurt a.M., 1966); see esp. pp. 41 ff. [Au.]

principle of representation of a literary history that would neither have to follow the all too familiar high road of the traditional great books, nor have to lose itself in the lowlands of the sum-total of all texts that can no longer be historically articulated. The problem of selecting that which is important for a new history of literature can be solved with the help of the synchronic perspective in a manner that has not yet been attempted: a horizontal change in the historical process of "literary evolution" need not be pursued only throughout the web of all the diachronic facts and filiations, but can also be established in the altered remains of the synchronic literary system and read out of further cross-sectional analyses. In principle, a representation of literature in the historical succession of such systems would be possible through a series of arbitrary points of intersection between diachrony and synchrony. The historical dimension of literature, its eventful continuity that is lost in traditionalism as in positivism, can meanwhile be recovered only if the literary historian finds points of intersection and brings works to light that articulate the processlike character of "literary evolution" in its moments formative of history as well as its caesurae between periods. But neither statistics nor the subjective willfulness of the literary historian decides on this historical articulation, but rather the history of influence: that "which results from the event" and which from the perspective of the present constitutes the coherence of literature as the prehistory of its present manifestation.

## XII

Thesis 7. The task of literary history is thus only completed when literary production is not only represented synchronically and diachronically in the succession of its systems, but also seen as "special history" in its own unique relationship to "general history." This relationship does not end with the fact that a typified, idealized, satiric, or utopian image of social existence can be found in the literature of all times. The social function of literature manifests itself in its genuine possibility only where the literary experience of the reader enters into the horizon of expectations of

his lived praxis, preforms his understanding of the world, and thereby also has an effect on his social behavior.

The functional connection between literature and society is for the most part demonstrated in traditional literary sociology within the narrow boundaries of a method that has only superficially replaced the classical principle of *imitatio naturae* with the determination that literature is the representation of a pregiven reality, which therefore must elevate a concept of style conditioned by a particular period — the "realism" of the nineteenth century — to the status of the literary category par excellence. But even the literary "structuralism" now fashionable,[76] which appeals, often with dubious justification, to the archetypal criticism of Northrop Frye or to the structural anthropology of Claude Lévi-Strauss,[77] still remains quite dependent on this basically classicist aesthetics of representation with its schematizations of "reflection" [Wiederspiegelung] and "typification." By interpreting the findings of linguistic and literary structuralism as archaic anthropological constants disguised in literary myths — which it not infrequently manages only with the help of an obvious allegorization of the text[78] — it reduces on the one hand historical existence to the structures of an original social nature, on the other hand literature to this nature's mythic or symbolic expression. But with this viewpoint, it is precisely the eminently social, i.e., socially *formative* function of literature that is missed. Literary structuralism — as little as the Marxist and Formalist literary studies that came before it — does not inquire as to how literature "itself turns around to help inform . . . the idea of society which it presupposes" and has helped to inform the processlike character of his-

[76]N.B. This was composed in 1967. [Tr.]

[77]See Frye in Ch. 2 and Lévi-Strauss in Ch. 4. [Ed.]

[78]Lévi-Strauss himself testifies to this involuntarily but extremely impressively in his attempt to "interpret" with the help of his structural method a linguistic description of Baudelaire's poem "Les chats" provided by Roman Jakobson. See *L'Homme* 2 (1962), pp. 5–21; Eng. in *Structuralism*, ed. Jacques Ehrmann (Garden City, N.Y., 1971), a reprint of *Yale French Studies*, nos. 36–37 (1966). [Au.] See Jakobson and Lévi-Strauss in Ch. 4. [Ed.]

tory. With these words, Gerhard Hess formulated in his lecture on "The Image of Society in French Literature" (1954) the unsolved problem of a union of literary history and sociology, and then explained to what extent French literature, in the course of its modern development, could claim for itself to have first discovered certain law-governed characteristics of social existence.[79] To answer the question of the socially formative function of literature according to an aesthetics of reception exceeds the competence of the traditional aesthetics of representation. The attempt to close the gap between literary-historical and sociological research through the methods of an aesthetics of reception is made easier because the concept of the *horizon of expectations* that I introduced into literary-historical interpretation[80] also has played a role in the axiomatics of the social sciences since Karl Mannheim.[81] It likewise stands in the center of a methodological essay on "Natural Laws and Theoretical Systems" by Karl R. Popper, who would anchor the scientific formation of theory in the prescientific experience of lived praxis. Popper here develops the problem of observation from out of the presupposition of a "horizon of expectations," thereby offering a basis of comparison for my attempt to determine the specific achievement of literature in the general process of the formation of experience, and to delimit it vis-à-vis other forms of social behavior.[82]

According to Popper, progress in science has in common with prescientific experience the fact that each hypothesis, like each observation, always presupposes expectations, "namely those that constitute the horizon of expectations which first makes those observations significant and thereby grants them the status of observations."[83] For progress in science as for that in the experience of life, the most important moment is the "disappointment of expectations": "It resembles the experience of a blind person, who runs into an obstacle and thereby experiences its existence. Through the falsification of our assumptions we actually make contact with 'reality.' The refutation of our errors is the positive experience that we gain from reality."[84] This model certainly does not sufficiently explain the process of the scientific formation of theory,[85] and yet it can well illustrate the "productive meaning of negative experience" in lived praxis,[86] as well as shed a clearer light upon the specific function of literature in social existence. For the reader is privileged above the (hypothetical) nonreader because the reader — to stay with Popper's image — does not first have to bump into a new obstacle to gain a new experience of reality. The experience of reading can liberate one from adaptations, prejudices, and predicaments of a lived

---

[79]Now in *Gesellschaft — Literatur — Wissenschaft: Gesammelte Schriften 1938–1966*, eds. H. R. Jauss and C. Müller-Daehn (Munich, 1967), pp. 1–13, esp. pp. 2 and 4. [Au.]

[80]First in *Untersuchungen zur mittelalterlichen Tierdichtung*, see pp. 153, 180, 225, 271; further in *Archiv für das Studium der neueren Sprachen* 197 (1961), pp. 223–25. [Au.]

[81]Karl Mannheim, *Mensch und Gesellschaft in Zeitalter des Umbaus* (Darmstadt, 1958), pp. 212 ff. [Au.]

[82]In *Theorie und Realität*, ed. H. Albert (Tübingen, 1964), pp. 87–102. [Au.]

[83]*Ibid.*, p. 91. [Au.]

[84]*Ibid.*, p. 102. [Au.]

[85]Popper's example of the blind man does not distinguish between the two possibilities of a merely reactive behavior and an experimenting mode of action under specific hypotheses. If the second possibility characterizes reflected scientific behavior in distinction to the unreflected behavior in lived praxis, the researcher would be "creative" on his part, and thus to be placed above the "blind man" and more appropriately compared with the writer as a creator of new expectations. [Au.]

[86]G. Buck, *Lernen und Erfahrung*, pp. 70 ff. "[Negative experience] has its instructive effect not only by causing us to revise the context of our subsequent experience so that the new fits into the corrected unity of an objective meaning. . . . Not only is the object of the experience differently represented, but the experiencing consciousness itself reverses itself. The work of negative experience is one of becoming conscious of oneself. What one becomes conscious of are the motifs which have been guiding experience and which have remained unquestioned in this guiding function. Negative experience thus has primarily the character of self-experience, which frees one for a qualitatively new kind of experience." From these premises Buck developed the concept of a hermeneutics, which, as a "relationship of lived praxis that is guided by the highest interest of lived praxis — the agent's self-information," legitimizes the specific experience of the so-called humanities [Geisteswissenschaften] in contrast to the empiricism of the natural sciences. See his "Bildung durch Wissenschaft," in *Wissenschaft, Bildung und pädagogische Wirklichkeit* (Heidenheim, 1969), p. 24. [Au.]

praxis in that it compels one to a new perception of things. The horizon of expectations of literature distinguishes itself before the horizon of expectations of historical lived praxis in that it not only preserves actual experiences, but also anticipates unrealized possibility, broadens the limited space of social behavior for new desires, claims, and goals, and thereby opens paths of future experience.

The pre-orientation of our experience through the creative capability of literature rests not only on its artistic character, which by virtue of a new form helps one to break through the automatism of everyday perception. The new form of art is not only "perceived against the background of other art works and through association with them." In this famous sentence, which belongs to the core of the Formalist credo,[87] Victor Shklovsky remains correct only insofar as he turns against the prejudice of classicist aesthetics that defines the beautiful as *harmony of form and content* and accordingly reduces the new form to the secondary function of giving shape to a pre-given content. The new form, however, does not appear just "in order to relieve the old form that already is no longer artistic." It also can make possible a new perception of things by preforming the content of a new experience first brought to light in the form of literature. The relationship between literature and reader can actualize itself in the sensorial realm as an incitement to aesthetic perception as well as in the ethical realm as a summons to moral reflection.[88] The new literary work is received and judged against the background of other works of art as well as against the background of the everyday experience of life. Its social function in the ethical realm is to be grasped according to an aesthetics of reception in the same modalities of question and answer, problem and solution, under which it enters into the horizon of its historical influence.

How a new aesthetic form can have moral consequences at the same time, or, put another way, how it can have the greatest conceivable impact on a moral question, is demonstrated in an impressive manner by the case of *Madame Bovary,* as reflected in the trial that was instituted against the author Flaubert after the prepublication of the work in the *Révue de Paris* in 1857. The new literary form that compelled Flaubert's audience to an unfamiliar perception of the "well-thumbed fable" was the principle of impersonal (or uninvolved) narration, in conjunction with the artistic device of the so-called *style indirect libre,*[89] handled by Flaubert like a virtuoso and in a perspectively consequential manner. What is meant by this can be made clear with a quotation from the book, a description that the prosecuting attorney Pinard accused in his indictment as being immoral in the highest degree. In the novel it follows upon Emma's first "false step" and relates how she catches sight of herself in the mirror after her adultery:

> Seeing herself in the mirror she wondered at her face. Never had her eyes been so large, so black, or so deep. Something subtle spread about her being transfigured her.
> She repeated: "I have a lover! a lover!", delighting at the idea as at that of a second puberty that had come to her. So at last she was going to possess those joys of love, that fever of happiness of which she had despaired. She was entering upon something marvelous where all would be passion, ecstasy, delirium.

The prosecuting attorney took the last sentences for an objective depiction that included the judgment of the narrator and was upset over the "glorification of adultery" which he held to be even much more dangerous and immoral than the false

---

[87] Yuri Striedter has pointed out that in the diaries and examples from the prose of Leo Tolstoy to which Shklovsky referred in his first explanation of the procedure of "alienation," the purely aesthetic aspect was still bound up with an epistemological and ethical aspect. "Shklovsky was interested — in contrast to Tolstoy — above all in the artistic 'procedure' and not in the question of its ethical presuppositions and effects." (*Poetik und Hermeneutik* 2 [see note 67], pp. 288 ff.) [Au.] See Shklovsky in Ch. 3. [Ed.]

[88] Flaubert, *Oeuvres,* I, p. 657: "thus, as early as this first mistake, as early as this first fall, she glorified adultery, its poetry, its voluptuousness. Voilà, gentlemen, what for me is much more dangerous, much more immoral than the fall itself!" [Au.]

[89] The English term is "free indirect discourse." [Ed.]

step itself.[90] Yet Flaubert's accuser thereby succumbed to an error, as the defense immediately demonstrated. For the incriminating sentences are not any objective statement of the narrator's to which the reader can attribute belief, but rather a subjective opinion of the character, who is thereby to be characterized in her feelings that are formed according to novels. The artistic device consists in bringing forth a mostly inward discourse of the represented character without the signals of direct discourse ("So I am at last going to possess") or indirect discourse ("She said to herself that she was therefore at last going to possess"), with the effect that the reader himself has to decide whether he should take the sentence for a true declaration or understand it as an opinion characteristic of this character. Indeed, Emma Bovary is "judged, simply through a plain description of her existence, out of her own feelings."[91] This result of a modern stylistic analysis agrees exactly with the counterargument of the defense attorney Sénard, who emphasized that the disillusion began for Emma already from the second day onward: "The dénouement for morality is found in each line of the book"[92] (only that Sénard himself could not yet name the artistic device that was not yet recorded at this time!). The consternating effect of the formal innovations of Flaubert's narrative style became evident in the trial: the impersonal form of narration not only compelled his readers to perceive things differently — "photographically exact," according to the judgment of the time — but at the same time thrust them into an alienating uncertainty of judgment. Since the new artistic device broke through an old novelistic convention — the moral judgment of the represented characters that is always unequivocal and confirmed in the description — the novel was able to radicalize or to raise new questions of lived praxis, which during the proceedings caused the original occasion for the accusation — alleged lasciviousness — to recede wholly into the background. The question with which the defense went on its counterattack turned the reproach, that the novel provides nothing other than the "story of a provincial woman's adulteries," against the society: whether, then, the subtitle to Madame Bovary must not more properly read, "story of the education too often provided in the provinces."[93] But the question with which the prosecuting attorney's *réquisitoire* reaches its peak is nonetheless not yet thereby answered: "Who can condemn that woman in the book? No one. Such is the conclusion. In the book there is not a character who can condemn her. If you find a wise character there, if you find a single principle there by virtue of which the adultery might be stigmatized, I am in error."[94]

If in the novel none of the represented characters could break the staff across Emma Bovary, and if no moral principle can be found valid in whose name she would be condemnable, then is not the ruling "public opinion" and its basis in "religious feeling" at once called into question along with the "principle of marital fidelity"? Before what court could the case of Madame Bovary be brought if the formerly valid social norms — public opinion, religious sentiment, public morals, good manners — are no longer sufficient to reach a verdict in this case?[95] These open and implicit questions by no means indicate an aesthetic lack of understanding and moral philistinism on the part of the prosecuting attorney. Rather, it is much more that in them the unsuspected influence of a new art form comes to be expressed, which through a new *manière de voir les choses*[96] was able to jolt the reader of Madame Bovary out of the self-evident character of his moral judgment, and turned a predecided question of public morals back into an open problem. In the face of the vexation that Flaubert, thanks to the artistry of his impersonal style, did not offer any handhold with which to ban his novel on grounds of the author's immorality, the court to that extent acted consistently when it

[90]Erich Auerbach, *Mimesis: Dargestellte Wirklichkeit in der abendländischen Literatur* (Bern, 1946), p. 430; Eng., *Mimesis: The Representation of Reality in Western Literature*, trans. Willard R. Trask (Princeton, 1953), p. 485. [Au.]

[91]Flaubert, *Oeuvres*, I, p. 673. [Au.]

[92]*Ibid.*, p. 670. [Au.]

[93]*Ibid.*, p. 666. [Au.]

[94]Cf. *ibid.*, pp. 666–67. [Au.]

[95]*Ibid.*, p. 717. [Au.]

[96]Way of looking at things. [Ed.]

acquitted Flaubert as writer, but condemned the literary school that he was supposed to represent, but that in truth was the as yet unrecognized artistic device:

> Whereas it is not permitted, under the pretext of portraying character and local color, to reproduce in their errors the facts, utterances and gestures of the characters whom the author's mission it is to portray; that a like system, applied to works of the spirit as well as to productions of the fine arts, leads to a realism which would be the negation of the beautiful and the good, and which, giving birth to works equally offensive to the eye and to the spirit, would commit continual offences against public morals and good manners.[97]

Thus a literary work with an unfamiliar aesthetic form can break through the expectations of its readers and at the same time confront them with a question, the solution to which remains lacking for them in the religiously or officially sanctioned morals. Instead of further examples, let one only recall here that it was not first Bertolt Brecht, but rather already the Enlightenment that proclaimed the competitive relationship between literature and canonized morals, as Friedrich Schiller not least of all bears witness to when he expressly claims for the bourgeois drama: "The laws of the stage begin where the sphere of worldly laws end."[98] But the literary work can also — and in the history of literature this possibility characterizes the latest period of our modernity — reverse the relationship of question and answer and in the medium of art confront the reader with a new, "opaque" reality that no longer allows itself to be understood from a pre-

given horizon of expectations. Thus, for example, the latest genre of novels, the much-discussed *nouveau roman,* presents itself as a form of modern art that according to Edgar Wind's formulation, represents the paradoxical case "that the solution is given, but the problem is given up, so that the solution might be understood as a problem." Here the reader is excluded from the situation of the immediate audience and put in the position of an uninitiated third party who in the face of a reality still without significance must himself find the questions that will decode for him the perception of the world and the interpersonal problem toward which the answer of the literature is directed.

It follows from all of this that the specific achievement of literature in social existence is to be sought exactly where literature is not absorbed into the function of a *representational* art. If one looks at the moments in history when literary works toppled the taboos of the ruling morals or offered the reader new solutions for the moral casuistry of his lived praxis, which thereafter could be sanctioned by the consensus of all readers in the society, then a still-little-studied area of research opens itself up to the literary historian. The gap between literature and history, between aesthetic and historical knowledge, can be bridged if literary history does not simply describe the process of general history in the reflection of its works one more time, but rather when it discovers in the course of "literary evolution" that properly *socially formative* function that belongs to literature as it competes with other arts and social forces in the emancipation of mankind from its natural, religious, and social bonds.

If it is worthwhile for the literary scholar to jump over his ahistorical shadow for the sake of this task, then it might well also provide an answer to the question: toward what end and with what right can one today still — or again — study literary history?

---

[97]"Die Schaubühne als eine moralische Anstalt betrachtet," in *Schillers Sämtliche Werke,* Säkularausgabe, XI, p. 99. See also R. Koselleck, *Kritik und Krise* (Freiburg and Munich, 1959), pp. 82 ff.

[98]"Zur Systematik der künstlerischen Probleme," *Jahrbuch für Ästhetik* (1925), p. 440; for the application of this principle to works of art of the present, see M. Imdahl, *Poetik und Hermeneutik* 3, pp. 493–505, 663–64.

# Wolfgang Iser
## b. 1926

*Partly because his method involves critical analysis rather than historical scholarship and partly because he works on well-known British fiction, Wolfgang Iser is more familiar to North American critics than his phenomenologist colleague, Hans Robert Jauss. Iser was born in Marienberg, in what is now West Germany, in 1926, and received his Ph.D. from the University of Heidelberg in 1957. His published books include* Die Weltanschauungs Henry Fieldings (Henry Fielding's World View, *1952),* Walter Pater — Die Autonomie des Ästhetischen *(1960; translated as* Walter Pater: The Aesthetic Moment*),* Die Appelstruktur der Texte *(The Affective Structure of the Text, 1970), and* Spensers Arkadien: Fiktion und Geschichte in der Englische Renaissance, *(Spenser's Arcadia: Fiction and History in the English Renaissance, 1970). In North America, his most influential works are the two theoretical treatises based on the hermeneutics of Hans-Georg Gadamer and Roman Ingarden,* Der Implizite Leser *(1972; translated as* The Implied Reader*) and* Der Akte des Lesens *(1976; translated as* The Act of Reading*). Iser is professor of English literature at the University of Constance and permanent visiting professor at the University of California at Irvine.*

# The Reading Process: A Phenomenological Approach

## I

The phenomenological theory of art lays full stress on the idea that, in considering a literary work, one must take into account not only the actual text but also, and in equal measure, the actions involved in responding to that text. Thus Roman Ingarden confronts the structure of the literary text with the ways in which it can be *konkretisiert* (realized).[1] The text as such offers different "schematised views"[2] through which the subject matter of the work can come to light, but the actual bringing to light is an action of *Konkretisation*. If this is so, then the literary work has two poles, which we might call the artistic and the esthetic: the artistic refers to the text created by the author, and the esthetic to the realization accomplished by the reader. From this polarity it follows that the literary work cannot be completely identical with the text, or with the realization of the text, but in fact must lie halfway between the two. The work is more than the text, for the text only takes on life when it is realized, and furthermore the realization is by no means independent of the individual disposition of the reader — though this in turn is acted upon by the different patterns of the text. The convergence of text and reader brings the literary work into existence, and this convergence can never be precisely pinpointed, but must always remain virtual, as it is not to be identified either with the reality of the text or with the individual disposition of the reader.

It is the virtuality of the work that gives rise to its dynamic nature, and this in turn is the precondition for the effects that the work calls forth. As the reader uses the various perspectives offered him by the text in order to relate the patterns and the "schematised views" to one another, he sets the work in motion, and this very process results ultimately in the awakening of responses within himself. Thus, reading causes the literary work to unfold its inherently dynamic

[1]Cf. Roman Ingarden, *Vom Erkennen des literarischen Kunstwerks* (Tübingen, 1968), pp. 49 ff. [Au.]

[2]For a detailed discussion of this term see Roman Ingarden, *Das literarische Kunstwerk* (Tübingen, 1960), pp. 270 ff. [Au.]

character. That this is no new discovery is apparent from references made even in the early days of the novel. Laurence Sterne remarks in *Tristram Shandy:* ". . . no author, who understands the just boundaries of decorum and goodbreeding, would presume to think all: The truest respect which you can pay to the reader's understanding, is to halve this matter amicably, and leave him something to imagine, in his turn, as well as yourself. For my own part, I am eternally paying him compliments of this kind, and do all that lies in my power to keep his imagination as busy as my own."[3] Sterne's conception of a literary text is that it is something like an arena in which reader and author participate in a game of the imagination. If the reader were given the whole story, and there were nothing left for him to do, then his imagination would never enter the field, the result would be the boredom which inevitably arises when everything is laid out cut and dried before us. A literary text must therefore be conceived in such a way that it will engage the reader's imagination in the task of working things out for himself, for reading is only a pleasure when it is active and creative. In this process of creativity, the text may either not go far enough, or may go too far, so we may say that boredom and overstrain form the boundaries beyond which the reader will leave the field of play.

The extent to which the "unwritten" part of a text stimulates the reader's creative participation is brought out by an observation of Virginia Woolf's in her study of *Jane Austen:*

> Jane Austen is thus a mistress of much deeper emotion than appears upon the surface. She stimulates us to supply what is not there. What she offers is, apparently, a trifle, yet is composed of something that expands in the reader's mind and endows with the most enduring form of life scenes which are outwardly trivial. Always the stress is laid upon character. . . . The turns and twists of the dialogue keep us on the tenterhooks of suspense. Our attention is half upon the present moment, half upon the future. . . . Here, indeed, in

this unfinished and in the main inferior story, are all the elements of Jane Austen's greatness.[4]

The unwritten aspects of apparently trivial scenes and the unspoken dialogue within the "turns and twists" not only draw the reader into the action but also lead him to shade in the many outlines suggested by the given situations, so that these take on a reality of their own. But as the reader's imagination animates these "outlines," they in turn will influence the effect of the written part of the text. Thus begins a whole dynamic process: the written text imposes certain limits on its unwritten implications in order to prevent these from becoming too blurred and hazy, but at the same time these implications, worked out by the reader's imagination, set the given situation against a background which endows it with far greater significance than it might have seemed to possess on its own. In this way, trivial scenes suddenly take on the shape of an "enduring form of life." What constitutes this form is never named, let alone explained in the text, although in fact it is the end product of the interaction between text and reader.

## II

The question now arises as to how far such a process can be adequately described. For this purpose a phenomenological analysis recommends itself, especially since the somewhat sparse observations hitherto made of the psychology of reading tend mainly to be psychoanalytical, and so are restricted to the illustration of predetermined ideas concerning the unconscious. We shall, however, take a closer look later at some worthwhile psychological observations.

As a starting point for a phenomenological analysis we might examine the way in which sequent sentences act upon one another. This is of especial importance in literary texts in view of the fact that they do not correspond to any objective reality outside themselves. The world

---

[3]Laurence Sterne, *Tristram Shandy* (London, 1956), II, 11: 79. [Au.]

[4]Virginia Woolf, *The Common Reader,* First Series (London, 1957), p. 174. [Au.]

presented by literary texts is constructed out of what Ingarden has called *intentionale Satzkorrelate* (intentional sentence correlatives):

> Sentences link up in different ways to form more complex units of meaning that reveal a very varied structure giving rise to such entities as a short story, a novel, a dialogue, a drama, a scientific theory. . . . In the final analysis, there arises a particular world, with component parts determined in this way or that, and with all the variations that may occur within these parts — all this as a purely intentional correlative of a complex of sentences. If this complex finally forms a literary work, I call the whole sum of sequent intentional sentence correlatives the "world presented" in the work.[5]

This world, however, does not pass before the reader's eyes like a film. The sentences are "component parts" insofar as they make statements, claims, or observations, or convey information, and so establish various perspectives in the text. But they remain only "component parts" — they are not the sum total of the text itself. For the intentional correlatives disclose subtle connections which individually are less concrete than the statements, claims, and observations, even though these only take on their real meaningfulness through the interaction of their correlatives.

How is one to conceive the connection between the correlatives? It marks those points at which the reader is able to "climb aboard" the text. He has to accept certain given perspectives, but in doing so he inevitably causes them to interact. When Ingarden speaks of intentional sentence correlatives in literature, the statements made or information conveyed in the sentence are already in a certain sense qualified: the sentence does not consist solely of a statement — which, after all, would be absurd, as one can only make statements about things that exist — but aims at something beyond what it actually says. This is true of all sentences in literary works, and it is through the interaction of these sentences that their common aim is fulfilled. This is what gives them their own special quality in literary texts. In their capacity as statements,

observations, purveyors of information, etc., they are always indications of something that is to come, the structure of which is foreshadowed by their specific content.

They set in motion a process out of which emerges the actual content of the text itself. In describing man's inner consciousness of time, Husserl once remarked: "Every originally constructive process is inspired by pre-intentions, which construct and collect the seed of what is to come, as such, and bring it to fruition."[6] For this bringing to fruition, the literary text needs the reader's imagination, which gives shape to the interaction of correlatives foreshadowed in structure by the sequence of the sentences. Husserl's observation draws our attention to a point that plays a not insignificant part in the process of reading. The individual sentences not only work together to shade in what is to come; they also form an expectation in this regard. Husserl calls this expectation "preintentions." As this structure is characteristic of *all* sentence correlatives, the interaction of these correlatives will not be a fulfillment of the expectation so much as a continual modification of it.

For this reason, expectations are scarcely ever fulfilled in truly literary texts. If they were, then such texts would be confined to the individualization of a given expectation, and one would inevitably ask what such an intention was supposed to achieve. Strangely enough, we feel that any confirmative effect — such as we implicitly demand of expository texts, as we refer to the objects they are meant to present — is a defect in a literary text. For the more a text individualizes or confirms an expectation it has initially aroused, the more aware we become of its didactic purpose, so that at best we can only accept or reject the thesis forced upon us. More often than not, the very clarity of such texts will make us want to free ourselves from their clutches. But generally the sentence correlatives of literary texts do not develop in this rigid way, for the expectations they evoke tend to encroach on one

---

[5]Ingarden, *Vom Erkennen des literarischen Kunstwerks,* p. 29. [Au.]

[6]Edmund Husserl, *Zur Phänomenologie des inneren Zeitbewusstseins, Gesammelte Werke* (The Hague, 1966), 10:52. [Au.]

another in such a manner that they are continually modified as one reads. One might simplify by saying that each intentional sentence correlative opens up a particular horizon, which is modified, if not completely changed, by succeeding sentences. While these expectations arouse interest in what is to come, the subsequent modification of them will also have a retrospective effect on what has already been read. This may now take on a different significance from that which it had at the moment of reading.

Whatever we have read sinks into our memory and is foreshortened. It may later be evoked again and set against a different background with the result that the reader is enabled to develop hitherto unforeseeable connections. The memory evoked, however, can never reassume its original shape, for this would mean that memory and perception were identical, which is manifestly not so. The new background brings to light new aspects of what we had committed to memory; conversely these, in turn, shed their light on the new background, thus arousing more complex anticipations. Thus, the reader, in establishing these interrelationships between past, present and future, actually causes the text to reveal its potential multiplicity of connections. These connections are the product of the reader's mind working on the raw material of the text, though they are not the text itself — for this consists just of sentences, statements, information, etc.

This is why the reader often feels involved in events which, at the time of reading, seem real to him, even though in fact they are very far from his own reality. The fact that completely different readers can be differently affected by the "reality" of a particular text is ample evidence of the degree to which literary texts transform reading into a creative process that is far above mere perception of what is written. The literary text activates our own faculties, enabling us to recreate the world it presents. The product of this creative activity is what we might call the virtual dimension of the text, which endows it with its reality. This virtual dimension is not the text itself, nor is it the imagination of the reader: it is the coming together of text and imagination.

As we have seen, the activity of reading can be characterized as a sort of kaleidoscope of perspectives, preintentions, recollections. Every sentence contains a preview of the next and forms a kind of viewfinder for what is to come; and this in turn changes the "preview" and so becomes a "viewfinder" for what has been read. This whole process represents the fulfillment of the potential, unexpressed reality of the text, but it is to be seen only as a framework for a great variety of means by which the virtual dimension may be brought into being. The process of anticipation and retrospection itself does not by any means develop in a smooth flow. Ingarden has already drawn attention to this fact and ascribes a quite remarkable significance to it:

> Once we are immersed in the flow of *Satzdenken* (sentence-thought), we are ready, after completing the thought of one sentence, to think out the "continuation," also in the form of a sentence — and that is, in the form of a sentence that connects up with the sentence we have just thought through. In this way the process of reading goes effortlessly forward. But if by chance the following sentence has no tangible connection whatever with the sentence we have just thought through, there then comes a blockage in the stream of thought. This hiatus is linked with a more or less active surprise, or with indignation. This blockage must be overcome if the reading is to flow once more.[7]

The hiatus that blocks the flow of sentences is, in Ingarden's eyes, the product of chance, and is to be regarded as a flaw; this is typical of his adherence to the classical idea of art. If one regards the sentence sequence as a continual flow, this implies that the anticipation aroused by one sentence will generally be realized by the next, and the frustration of one's expectations will arouse feelings of exasperation. And yet literary texts are full of unexpected twists and turns, and frustration of expectations. Even in the simplest story there is bound to be some kind of blockage, if only because no tale can ever be told in its entirety. Indeed, it is only through inevitable omissions that a story gains its dynamism. Thus whenever the flow is interrupted and we are led off in unexpected directions, the opportunity is given to us to bring into play our

[7]Ingarden, *Vom Erkennen des literarischen Kunstwerks*, p. 32. [Au.]

own faculty for establishing connections — for filling in the gaps left by the text itself.[8]

These gaps have a different effect on the process of anticipation and retrospection, and thus on the "gestalt" of the virtual dimension, for they may be filled in different ways. For this reason, one text is potentially capable of several different realizations, and no reading can ever exhaust the full potential, for each individual reader will fill in the gaps in his own way, thereby excluding the various other possibilities; as he reads, he will make his own decision as to how the gap is to be filled. In this very act the dynamics of reading are revealed. By making his decision he implicitly acknowledges the inexhaustibility of the text; at the same time it is this very inexhaustibility that forces him to make his decision. With "traditional" texts this process was more or less unconscious, but modern texts frequently exploit it quite deliberately. They are often so fragmentary that one's attention is almost exclusively occupied with the search for connections between the fragments; the object of this is not to complicate the "spectrum" of connections, so much as to make us aware of the nature of our own capacity for providing links. In such cases, the text refers back directly to our own preconceptions — which are revealed by the act of interpretation that is a basic element of the reading process. With all literary texts, then, we may say that the reading process is selective, and the potential text is infinitely richer than any of its individual realizations. This is borne out by the fact that a second reading of a piece of literature often produces a different impression from the first. The reasons for this may lie in the reader's own change of circumstances, still, the text must be such as to allow this variation. On a second reading familiar occurrences now tend to appear in a new light and seem to be at times corrected, at times enriched.

In every text there is a potential time sequence which the reader must inevitably realize, as it is impossible to absorb even a short text in a single moment. Thus the reading process always involves viewing the text through a perspective that is continually on the move, linking up the different phases, and so constructing what we have called the virtual dimension. This dimension, of course, varies all the time we are reading. However, when we have finished the text, and read it again, clearly our extra knowledge will result in a different time sequence; we shall tend to establish connections by referring to our awareness of what is to come, and so certain aspects of the text will assume a significance we did not attach to them on a first reading, while others will recede into the background. It is a common enough experience for a person to say that on a second reading he noticed things he had missed when he read the book for the first time, but this is scarcely surprising in view of the fact that the second time he is looking at the text from a different perspective. The time sequence that he realized on his first reading cannot possibly be repeated on a second reading, and this unrepeatability is bound to result in modifications of his reading experience. This is not to say that the second reading is "truer" than the first — they are, quite simply, different: the reader establishes the virtual dimension of the text by realizing a new time sequence. Thus even on repeated viewings a text allows and, indeed, induces innovative reading.

In whatever way, and under whatever circumstances the reader may link the different phases of the text together, it will always be the process of anticipation and retrospection that leads to the formation of the virtual dimension, which in turn transforms the text into an experience for the reader. The way in which this experience comes about through a process of continual modification is closely akin to the way in which we gather experience in life. And thus the "reality" of the reading experience can illuminate basic patterns of real experience:

> We have the experience of a world, not understood as a system of relations which wholly determine each event, but as an open totality the synthesis of which is inexhaustible. . . . From the moment that experience — that is, the opening on to our *de facto* world — is recognized as the beginning of

[8]For a more detailed discussion of the function of "gaps" in literary texts see Wolfgang Iser, "Indeterminacy and the Reader's Response in Prose Fiction," *Aspects of Narrative* (English Institute Essays), ed. J. Hillis Miller (New York, 1971), pp. 1–45. [Au.]

knowledge, there is no longer any way of distinguishing a level of *a priori* truths and one of factual ones, what the world must necessarily be and what it actually is.[9]

The manner in which the reader experiences the text will reflect his own disposition, and in this respect the literary text acts as a kind of mirror; but at the same time, the reality which this process helps to create is one that will be *different* from his own (since, normally, we tend to be bored by texts that present us with things we already know perfectly well ourselves). Thus we have the apparently paradoxical situation in which the reader is forced to reveal aspects of himself in order to experience a reality which is different from his own. The impact this reality makes on him will depend largely on the extent to which he himself actively provides the unwritten part of the text, and yet in supplying all the missing links, he must think in terms of experiences different from his own; indeed, it is only by leaving behind the familiar world of his own experience that the reader can truly participate in the adventure the literary text offers him.

## III

We have seen that, during the process of reading, there is an active interweaving of anticipation and retrospection, which on a second reading may turn into a kind of advance retrospection. The impressions that arise as a result of this process will vary from individual to individual, but only within the limits imposed by the written as opposed to the unwritten text. In the same way, two people gazing at the night sky may both be looking at the same collection of stars, but one will see the image of a plough, and the other will make out a dipper. The "stars" in a literary text are fixed; the lines that join them are variable. The author of the text may, of course, exert plenty of influence on the reader's imagination — he has the whole panoply of narrative techniques at his disposal — but no author worth his salt will ever attempt to set the *whole* picture

before his reader's eyes. If he does, he will very quickly lose his reader, for it is only by activating the reader's imagination that the author can hope to involve him and so realize the intentions of his text.

Gilbert Ryle, in his analysis of imagination, asks: "How can a person fancy that he sees something, without realizing that he is not seeing it?" He answers as follows:

Seeing Helvellyn [the name of a mountain] in one's mind's eye does not entail, what seeing Helvellyn and seeing snapshots of Helvellyn entail, the having of visual sensations. It does involve the thought of having a view of Helvellyn and it is therefore a more sophisticated operation than that of having a view of Helvellyn. It is one utilization among others of the knowledge of how Helvellyn should look, or, in one sense of the verb, it is thinking how it should look. The expectations which are fulfilled in the recognition at sight of Helvellyn are not indeed fulfilled in picturing it, but the picturing of it is something like a rehearsal of getting them fulfilled. So far from picturing involving the having of faint sensations, or wraiths of sensations, it involves missing just what one would be due to get, if one were seeing the mountain.[10]

If one sees the mountain, then of course one can no longer imagine it, and so the act of picturing the mountain presupposes its absence. Similarly, with a literary text we can only picture things which are not there; the written part of the text gives us the knowledge, but it is the unwritten part that gives us the opportunity to picture things; indeed without the elements of indeterminacy, the gaps in the text, we should not be able to use our imagination.[11]

The truth of this observation is borne out by the experience many people have on seeing, for instance, the film of a novel. While reading *Tom Jones,* they may never have had a clear conception of what the hero actually looks like, but on seeing the film, some may say, "That's not how I imagined him." The point here is that the reader of *Tom Jones* is able to visualize the hero virtually for himself, and so his imagination senses

[9]M. Merleau-Ponty, *Phenomenology of Perception,* trans. Colin Smith (New York, 1962), pp. 219, 221. [Au.]

[10]Gilbert Ryle, *The Concept of Mind* (Harmondsworth, 1968), p. 255. [Au.]

[11]Cf. Iser, "Indeterminacy," pp. 11 ff., 42 ff. [Au.]

the vast number of possibilities; the moment these possibilities are narrowed down to one complete and immutable picture, the imagination is put out of action, and we feel we have somehow been cheated. This may perhaps be an oversimplification of the process, but it does illustrate plainly the vital richness of potential that arises out of the fact that the hero in the novel must be pictured and cannot be seen. With the novel the reader must use his imagination to synthesize the information given him, and so his perception is simultaneously richer and more private; with the film he is confined merely to physical perception, and so whatever he remembers of the world he had pictured is brutally cancelled out.

## IV

The "picturing" that is done by our imagination is only one of the activities through which we form the "gestalt" of a literary text. We have already discussed the process of anticipation and retrospection, and to this we must add the process of grouping together all the different aspects of a text to form the consistency that the reader will always be in search of. While expectations may be continually modified, and images continually expanded, the reader will still strive, even if unconsciously, to fit everything together in a consistent pattern. "In the reading of images, as in the hearing of speech, it is always hard to distinguish what is given to us from what we supplement in the process of projection which is triggered off by recognition . . . it is the guess of the beholder that tests the medley of forms and colours for coherent meaning, crystallizing it into shape when a consistent interpretation has been found."[12] By grouping together the written parts of the text, we enable them to interact, we observe the direction in which they are leading us, and we project onto them the consistency which we, as readers, require. This "gestalt" must inevitably be colored by our own characteristic selection process. For it is not given by the text itself; it arises from the meeting between the written text and the individual mind of the reader with its own particular history of experience, its own consciousness, its own outlook. The "gestalt" is not the true meaning of the text; at best it is a configurative meaning; ". . . comprehension is an individual act of seeing-things-together, and only that."[13] With a literary text such comprehension is inseparable from the reader's expectations, and where we have expectations, there too we have one of the most potent weapons in the writer's armory — illusion.

Whenever "consistent reading suggests itself . . . illusion takes over."[14] Illusion, says Northrop Frye, is "fixed or definable, and reality is best understood as its negation."[15] The "gestalt" of a text normally takes on (or, rather, is given) this fixed or definable outline, as this is essential to our own understanding, but on the other hand, if reading were to consist of nothing but an uninterrupted building up of illusions, it would be a suspect, if not downright dangerous, process: instead of bringing us into contact with reality, it would wean us away from realities. Of course, there is an element of "escapism" in all literature, resulting from this very creation of illusion, but there are some texts which offer nothing but a harmonious world, purified of all contradiction and deliberately excluding anything that might disturb the illusion once established, and these are the texts that we generally do not like to classify as literary. Women's magazines and the brasher forms of the detective story might be cited as examples.

However, even if an overdose of illusion may lead to triviality, this does not mean that the process of illusion-building should ideally be dispensed with altogether. On the contrary, even in texts that appear to resist the formation of illusion, thus drawing our attention to the cause of this resistance, we still need the abiding illusion that the resistance itself is the consistent pattern underlying the text. This is especially true of modern texts, in which it is the very precision of

[12]E. H. Gombrich, *Art and Illusion* (London, 1962), p. 204. [Au.]

[13]Louis O. Mink, "History and Fiction as Modes of Comprehension," *New Literary History* I (1970): 553. [Au.]

[14]Gombrich, *Art and Illusion*, p. 278. [Au.]

[15]Northrop Frye, *Anatomy of Criticism* (New York, 1967), pp. 169 f. [Au.]

the written details which increases the proportion of indeterminacy; one detail appears to contradict another, and so simultaneously stimulates and frustrates our desire to "picture," thus continually causing our imposed "gestalt" of the text to disintegrate. Without the formation of illusions, the unfamiliar world of the text would remain unfamiliar; through the illusions, the experience offered by the text becomes accessible to us, for it is only the illusion, on its different levels of consistency, that makes the experience "readable." If we cannot find (or impose) this consistency, sooner or later we will put the text down. The process is virtually hermeneutic. The text provokes certain expectations which in turn we project onto the text in such a way that we reduce the polysemantic possibilities to a single interpretation in keeping with the expectations aroused, thus extracting an individual, configurative meaning. The polysemantic nature of the text and the illusion-making of the reader are opposed factors. If the illusion were complete, the polysemantic nature would vanish; if the polysemantic nature were all-powerful, the illusion would be totally destroyed. Both extremes are conceivable, but in the individual literary text we always find some form of balance between the two conflicting tendencies. The formation of illusions, therefore, can never be total, but it is this very incompleteness that in fact gives it its productive value.

With regard to the experience of reading, Walter Pater once observed: "For to the grave reader words too are grave; and the ornamental word, the figure, the accessory form or colour or reference, is rarely content to die to thought precisely at the right moment, but will inevitably linger awhile, stirring a long 'brainwave' behind it of perhaps quite alien associations."[16] Even while the reader is seeking a consistent pattern in the text, he is also uncovering other impulses which cannot be immediately integrated or will even resist final integration. Thus the semantic possibilities of the text will always remain far richer than any configurative meaning formed while reading. But this impression is, of course, only to be gained through reading the text. Thus the configurative meaning can be nothing but a *pars pro toto*[17] fulfillment of the text, and yet this fulfillment gives rise to the very richness which it seeks to restrict, and indeed in some modern texts, our awareness of this richness takes precedence over any configurative meaning.

This fact has several consequences which, for the purpose of analysis, may be dealt with separately, though in the reading process they will all be working together. As we have seen, a consistent, configurative meaning is essential for the apprehension of an unfamiliar experience, which through the process of illusion-building we can incorporate in our own imaginative world. At the same time, this consistency conflicts with the many other possibilities of fulfillment it seeks to exclude, with the result that the configurative meaning is always accompanied by "alien associations" that do not fit in with the illusions formed. The first consequence, then, is the fact that in forming our illusions, we also produce at the same time a latent disturbance of these illusions. Strangely enough, this also applies to texts in which our expectations are actually fulfilled — though one would have thought that the fulfillment of expectations would help to complete the illusion. "Illusion wears off once the expectation is stepped up; we take it for granted and want more."[18]

The experiments in gestalt psychology referred to by Gombrich in *Art and Illusion* make one thing clear: ". . . though we may be intellectually aware of the fact that any given experience *must* be an illusion, we cannot, strictly speaking, watch ourselves having an illusion."[19] Now, if illusion were not a transitory state, this would mean that we could be, as it were, permanently caught up in it. And if reading were exclusively a matter of producing illusion — necessary though this is for the understanding of an unfamiliar experience — we should run the risk of falling victim to a gross deception. But it is

[16]Walter Pater, *Appreciations* (London, 1920), p. 18. [Au.]

[17]Partial. [Ed.]
[18]Gombrich, *Art and Illusion*, p. 54. [Au.]
[19]Ibid., p. 5. [Au.]

precisely during our reading that the transitory nature of the illusion is revealed to the full.

As the formation of illusions is constantly accompanied by "alien associations" which cannot be made consistent with the illusions, the reader constantly has to lift the restrictions he places on the "meaning" of the text. Since it is he who builds the illusions, he oscillates between involvement in and observation of those illusions; he opens himself to the unfamiliar world without being imprisoned in it. Through this process the reader moves into the presence of the fictional world and so experiences the realities of the text as they happen.

In the oscillation between consistency and "alien associations," between involvement in and observation of the illusion, the reader is bound to conduct his own balancing operation, and it is this that forms the esthetic experience offered by the literary text. However, if the reader were to achieve a balance, obviously he would then no longer be engaged in the process of establishing and disrupting consistency. And since it is this very process that gives rise to the balancing operation, we may say that the inherent nonachievement of balance is a prerequisite for the very dynamism of the operation. In seeking the balance we inevitably have to start out with certain expectations, the shattering of which is integral to the esthetic experience.

Furthermore, to say merely that "our expectations are satisfied" is to be guilty of another serious ambiguity. At first sight such a statement seems to deny the obvious fact that much of our enjoyment is derived from surprises, from betrayals of our expectations. The solution to this paradox is to find some ground for a distinction between "surprise" and "frustration." Roughly, the distinction can be made in terms of the effects which the two kinds of experiences have upon us. Frustration blocks or checks activity. It necessitates new orientation for our activity, if we are to escape the *cul de sac.* Consequently, we abandon the frustrating object and return to blind impulse activity. On the other hand, surprise merely causes a temporary cessation of the exploratory phase of the experience, and a recourse to intense contemplation and scrutiny. In the latter phase the surprising elements are seen in their connection with what has gone before, with the whole drift of the experience, and the enjoy-

ment of these values is then extremely intense. Finally, it appears that there must always be some degree of novelty or surprise in all these values if there is to be a progressive specification of the direction of the total act . . . and any aesthetic experience tends to exhibit a continuous interplay between "deductive" and "inductive" operations.[20]

It is this interplay between "deduction" and "induction" that gives rise to the configurative meaning of the text, and not the individual expectations, surprises, or frustrations arising from the different perspectives. Since this interplay obviously does not take place in the text itself, but can only come into being through the process of reading, we may conclude that this process formulates something that is unformulated in the text and yet represents its "intention." Thus, by reading we uncover the unformulated part of the text, and this very indeterminacy is the force that drives us to work out a configurative meaning while at the same time giving us the necessary degree of freedom to do so.

As we work out a consistent pattern in the text, we will find our "interpretation" threatened, as it were, by the presence of other possibilities of "interpretation," and so there arise new areas of indeterminacy (though we may only be dimly aware of them, if at all, as we are continually making "decisions" which will exclude them). In the course of a novel, for instance, we sometimes find that characters, events, and backgrounds seem to change their significance; what really happens is that the other "possibilities" begin to emerge more strongly, so that we become more directly aware of them. Indeed, it is this very shifting of perspectives that makes us feel that a novel is much more "true-to-life." Since it is we ourselves who establish the levels of interpretation and switch from one to another as we conduct our balancing operation, we ourselves impart to the text the dynamic lifelikeness which, in turn, enables us to absorb an unfamiliar experience into our personal world.

As we read, we oscillate to a greater or lesser degree between the building and the breaking of

[20]B. Ritchie, "The Formal Structure of the Aesthetic Object," in *The Problems of Aesthetics,* ed. Eliseo Vivas and Murray Krieger (New York, 1965), pp. 230 f. [Au.]

illusions. In a process of trial and error, we organize and reorganize the various data offered us by the text. These are the given factors, the fixed points on which we base our "interpretation," trying to fit them together in the way we think the author meant them to be fitted. "For to perceive, a beholder must *create* his own experience. And his creation must include relations comparable to those which the original producer underwent. They are not the same in any literal sense. But with the perceiver, as with the artist, there must be an ordering of the elements of the whole that is in form, although not in details, the same as the process of organization the creator of the work consciously experienced. Without an act of recreation the object is not perceived as a work of art."[21]

The act of recreation is not a smooth or continuous process, but one which, in its essence, relies on *interruptions* of the flow to render it efficacious. We look forward, we look back, we decide, we change our decisions, we form expectations, we are shocked by their nonfulfillment, we question, we muse, we accept, we reject; this is the dynamic process of recreation. This process is steered by two main structural components within the text: first, a repertoire of familiar literary patterns and recurrent literary themes, together with allusions to familiar social and historical contexts; second, techniques or strategies used to set the familiar against the unfamiliar. Elements of the repertoire are continually backgrounded or foregrounded with a resultant strategic overmagnification, trivialization, or even annihilation of the allusion. This defamiliarization of what the reader thought he recognized is bound to create a tension that will intensify his expectations as well as his distrust of those expectations. Similarly, we may be confronted by narrative techniques that establish links between things we find difficult to connect, so that we are forced to reconsider data we at first held to be perfectly straightforward. One need only mention the very simple trick, so often employed by novelists, whereby the author himself takes part in the narrative, thus establishing

perspectives which would not have arisen out of the mere narration of the events described. Wayne Booth once called this the technique of the "unreliable narrator,"[22] to show the extent to which a literary device can counter expectations arising out of the literary text. The figure of the narrator may act in permanent opposition to the impressions we might otherwise form. The question then arises as to whether this strategy, opposing the formation of illusions, may be integrated into a consistent pattern, lying, as it were, a level deeper than our original impressions. We may find that our narrator, by opposing us, in fact turns us against him and thereby strengthens the illusion he appears to be out to destroy; alternatively, we may be so much in doubt that we begin to question all the processes that lead us to make interpretative decisions. Whatever the cause may be, we will find ourselves subjected to this same interplay of illusion-forming and illusion-breaking that makes reading essentially a recreative process.

We might take, as a simple illustration of this complex process, the incident in Joyce's *Ulysses* in which Bloom's cigar alludes to Ulysses's spear. The context (Bloom's cigar) summons up a particular element of the repertoire (Ulysses's spear); the narrative technique relates them to one another as if they were identical. How are we to "organize" these divergent elements, which, through the very fact that they are put together, separate one element so clearly from the other? What are the prospects here for a consistent pattern? We might say that it is ironic — at least that is how many renowned Joyce readers have understood it.[23] In this case, irony would be the form of organization that integrates the material. But if this is so, what is the object of the irony? Ulysses's spear, or Bloom's cigar? The uncertainty surrounding this simple question already puts a strain on the consistency we have established and, indeed, begins to puncture it,

[21]John Dewey, *Art as Experience* (New York, 1958), p. 54. [Au.] See Dewey, p. 484. [Ed.]

[22]Cf. Wayne C. Booth, *The Rhetoric of Fiction* (Chicago, 1961), pp. 211 ff., 339 ff. [Au.]

[23]Richard Ellmann, "Ulysses: The Divine Nobody," in *Twelve Original Essays on Great English Novels*, ed. Charles Shapiro (Detroit, 1960), p. 247, classified this particular allusion as "mock-heroic." [Au.]

especially when other problems make themselves felt as regards the remarkable conjunction of spear and cigar. Various alternatives come to mind, but the variety alone is sufficient to leave one with the impression that the consistent pattern has been shattered. And even if, after all, one can still believe that irony holds the key to the mystery, this irony must be of a very strange nature; for the formulated text does not merely mean the opposite of what has been formulated. It may even mean something that cannot be formulated at all. The moment we try to impose a consistent pattern on the text, discrepancies are bound to arise. These are, as it were, the reverse side of the interpretative coin, an involuntary product of the process that creates discrepancies by trying to avoid them. And it is their very presence that draws us into the text, compelling us to conduct a creative examination not only of the text but also of ourselves.

This entanglement of the reader is, of course, vital to any kind of text, but in the literary text we have the strange situation that the reader cannot know what his participation actually entails. We know that we share in certain experiences, but we do not know what happens to us in the course of this process. This is why, when we have been particularly impressed by a book, we feel the need to talk about it; we do not want to get away from it by talking about it — we simply want to understand more clearly what it is in which we have been entangled. We have undergone an experience, and now we want to know consciously *what* we have experienced. Perhaps this is the prime usefulness of literary criticism — it helps to make conscious those aspects of the text which would otherwise remain concealed in the subconscious; it satisfies (or helps to satisfy) our desire to talk about what we have read.

The efficacy of a literary text is brought about by the apparent evocation and subsequent negation of the familiar. What at first seemed to be an affirmation of our assumptions leads to our own rejection of them, thus tending to prepare us for a re-orientation. And it is only when we have outstripped our preconceptions and left the shelter of the familiar that we are in a position to gather new experiences. As the literary text involves the reader in the formation of illusion and the simultaneous formation of the means whereby the illusion is punctured, reading reflects the process by which we gain experience. Once the reader is entangled, his own preconceptions are continually overtaken, so that the text becomes his "present" while his own ideas fade into the "past"; as soon as this happens he is open to the immediate experience of the text, which was impossible so long as his preconceptions were his "present."

## V

In our analysis of the reading process so far, we have observed three important aspects that form the basis of the relationship between reader and text: the process of anticipation and retrospection, the consequent unfolding of the text as a living event, and the resultant impression of lifelikeness.

Any "living event" must, to a greater or lesser degree, remain open. In reading, this obliges the reader to seek continually for consistency, because only then can he close up situations and comprehend the unfamiliar. But consistency-building is itself a living process in which one is constantly forced to make selective decisions — and these decisions in their turn give a reality to the possibilities which they exclude, insofar as they may take effect as a latent disturbance of the consistency established. This is what causes the reader to be entangled in the text-"gestalt" that he himself has produced.

Through this entanglement the reader is bound to open himself up to the workings of the text and so leave behind his own preconceptions. This gives him the chance to have an experience in the way George Bernard Shaw once described it: "You have learnt something. That always feels at first as if you had lost something."[24] Reading reflects the structure of experience to the extent that we must suspend the ideas and attitudes that shape our own personality before we can experience the unfamiliar world of the literary text. But during this process, something happens to us.

[24]G. B. Shaw, *Major Barbara* (London, 1964), p. 316. [Au.]

This "something" needs to be looked at in detail, especially as the incorporation of the unfamiliar into our own range of experience has been to a certain extent obscured by an idea very common in literary discussion: namely, that the process of absorbing the unfamiliar is labeled as the *identification* of the reader with what he reads. Often the term "identification" is used as if it were an explanation, whereas in actual fact it is nothing more than a description. What is normally meant by "identification" is the establishment of affinities between oneself and someone outside oneself — a familiar ground on which we are able to experience the unfamiliar. The author's aim, though, is to convey the experience and, above all, an attitude toward that experience. Consequently, "identification" is not an end in itself, but a stratagem by means of which the author stimulates attitudes in the reader.

This of course is not to deny that there does arise a form of participation as one reads; one is certainly drawn into the text in such a way that one has the feeling that there is no distance between oneself and the events described. This involvement is well summed up by the reaction of a critic to reading Charlotte Brontë's *Jane Eyre:* "We took up *Jane Eyre* one writer's evening, somewhat piqued at the extravagant commendations we had heard, and sternly resolved to be as critical as Croker. But as we read on we forgot both commendations and criticism, identified ourselves with Jane in all her troubles, and finally married Mr. Rochester about four in the morning."[25] The question is how and why did the critic identify himself with Jane?

In order to understand this "experience," it is well worth considering Georges Poulet's observations on the reading process. He says that books only take on their full existence in the reader.[26] It is true that they consist of ideas thought out by someone else, but in reading the reader becomes the subject that does the thinking. Thus there disappears the subject-object division that otherwise is a prerequisite for all knowledge and all observation, and the removal of this division puts reading in an apparently unique position as regards the possible absorption of new experiences. This may well be the reason why relations with the world of the literary text have so often been misinterpreted as identification. From the idea that in reading we must think the thoughts of someone else, Poulet draws the following conclusion: "Whatever I think is a part of *my* mental world. And yet here I am thinking a thought which manifestly belongs to another mental world, which is being thought in me just as though I did not exist. Already the notion is inconceivable and seems even more so if I reflect that, since every thought must have a subject to think it, this *thought* which is alien to me and yet in me, must also have in me a *subject* which is alien to me. . . . Whenever I read, I mentally pronounce an *I,* and yet the *I* which I pronounce is not myself."[27]

But for Poulet this idea is only part of the story. The strange subject that thinks the strange thought in the reader indicates the potential presence of the author, whose ideas can be "internalized" by the reader: "Such is the characteristic condition of every work which I summon back into existence by placing my consciousness at its disposal. I give it not only existence, but awareness of existence."[28] This would mean that consciousness forms the point at which author and reader converge, and at the same time it would result in the cessation of the temporary self-alienation that occurs to the reader when his consciousness brings to life the ideas formulated by the author. This process gives rise to a form of communication which, however, according to Poulet, is dependent on two conditions: the life-story of the author must be shut out of the work and the individual disposition of the reader must be shut out of the act of reading. Only then can the thoughts of the author take place subjectively in the reader, who thinks what he is not. It follows that the work itself must be thought of as a consciousness, because only in this way is there

---

[25]William George Clark, *Fraser's* (December, 1849): 692, quoted by Kathleen Tillotson, *Novels of the Eighteen-Forties* (Oxford, 1961), pp. 19 f. [Au.]

[26]Cf. Georges Poulet, "Phenomenology of Reading," *New Literary History* I (1969): 54. [Au.]

[27]Ibid., p. 56. [Au.]

[28]Ibid., p. 59. [Au.]

an adequate basis for the author-reader relationship — a relationship that can only come about through the negation of the author's own life-story and the reader's own disposition. This conclusion is actually drawn by Poulet when he describes the work as the self-presentation or materialization of consciousness: "And so I ought not to hesitate to recognize that so long as it is animated by this vital inbreathing inspired by the act of reading, a work of literature becomes (at the expense of the reader whose own life it suspends) a sort of human being, that it is a mind conscious of itself and constituting itself in me as the subject of its own objects."[29] Even though it is difficult to follow such a substantialist conception of the consciousness that constitutes itself in the literary work, there are, nevertheless, certain points in Poulet's argument that are worth holding onto. But they should be developed along somewhat different lines.

If reading removes the subject-object division that constitutes all perception, it follows that the reader will be "occupied" by the thoughts of the author, and these in their turn will cause the drawing of new "boundaries." Text and reader no longer confront each other as object and subject, but instead the "division" takes place within the reader himself. In thinking the thoughts of another, his own individuality temporarily recedes into the background, since it is supplanted by these alien thoughts, which now become the theme on which his attention is focussed. As we read, there occurs an artificial division of our personality, because we take as a theme for ourselves something that we are not. Consequently when reading we operate on different levels. For although we may be thinking the thoughts of someone else, what we are will not disappear completely — it will merely remain a more or less powerful virtual force. Thus, in reading there are these two levels — the alien "me" and the real, virtual "me" — which are never completely cut off from each other. Indeed, we can only make someone else's thoughts into an absorbing theme for ourselves, provided the virtual back-

ground of our own personality can adapt to it. Every text we read draws a different boundary within our personality, so that the virtual background (the real "me") will take on a different form, according to the theme of the text concerned. This is inevitable, if only for the fact that the relationship between alien theme and virtual background is what makes it possible for the unfamiliar to be understood.

In this context there is a revealing remark made by D. W. Harding, arguing against the idea of identification with what is read: "What is sometimes called wish-fulfilment in novels and plays can . . . more plausibly be described as wish-formulation or the definition of desires. The cultural levels at which it works may vary widely; the process is the same. . . . It seems nearer the truth . . . to say that fictions contribute to defining the reader's or spectator's values, and perhaps stimulating his desires, rather than to suppose that they gratify desire by some mechanism of vicarious experience."[30] In the act of reading, having to think something that we have not yet experienced does not mean only being in a position to conceive or even understand it; it also means that such acts of conception are possible and successful to the degree that they lead to something being formulated in us. For someone else's thoughts can only take a form in our consciousness if, in the process, our unformulated faculty for deciphering those thoughts is brought into play — a faculty which, in the act of deciphering, also formulates itself. Now since this formulation is carried out on terms set by someone else, whose thoughts are the theme of our reading, it follows that the formulation of our faculty for deciphering cannot be along our own lines of orientation.

Herein lies the dialectical structure of reading. The need to decipher gives us the chance to formulate our own deciphering capacity — i.e., we bring to the fore an element of our being of which we are not directly conscious. The production of the meaning of literary texts — which we discussed in connection with forming the

[29]Ibid. [Au.]

[30]D. W. Harding, "Psychological Processes in the Reading of Fiction," in *Aesthetics in the Modern World*, ed. Harold Osborne (London, 1968), pp. 313 f. [Au.]

"gestalt" of the text — does not merely entail the discovery of the unformulated, which can then be taken over by the active imagination of the reader; it also entails the possibility that we may formulate ourselves and so discover what had previously seemed to elude our consciousness. These are the ways in which reading literature gives us the chance to formulate the unformulated.

# Norman N. Holland

b. 1927

*An orthodox New Critic in his first book on Restoration comedy, Norman Holland is best known for his contributions to psychoanalytical and reader-response criticism. Holland was born in New York City and educated at the Massachusetts Institute of Technology (B.S., 1947) and at Harvard, where he received an LL.B. in 1950 and a Ph.D. in English in 1956. During the next ten years, Holland taught English at MIT while undergoing psychoanalytic training at the Boston Psychoanalytic Institute. One result of this dual endeavor was* Psychoanalysis and Shakespeare *(1966). In 1966 Holland moved to the State University of New York at Buffalo as professor and chairman of the English department. There he analyzed the theory underlying the literary techniques of his Shakespeare book in writing* The Dynamics of Literary Response *(1968), which claims that meaning is produced in a transaction between text and reader: the text manages the reader's defensive transformation of its informing fantasy. In 1970 Holland founded the Center for the Psychological Study of the Arts and served as director until 1979. During that decade, Holland's interests shifted from the text to the reader, influenced by Heinz Lichtenstein's notion of the "identity theme" by which the individual ego styles its response to threatening stimuli. Holland's reader-response criticism appears in works such as* Poems in Persons *(1973),* 5 Readers Reading *(1975),* Laughing *(1982), and* The I *(1985). Since 1983, Holland has been Millbauer Eminent Scholar and professor of English at the University of Florida, Gainesville. "The Question: Who Reads What How?" is from* 5 Readers Reading.

# The Question: Who Reads What How?

The story was William Faulkner's "A Rose for Emily," and its one description of Miss Emily as a young girl was as clear as a description could be. The narrator, apparently one of the townspeople, says: "We had long thought of them as a tableau, Miss Emily a slender figure in white in the background, her father a spraddled silhouette in the foreground, his back to her and clutching a horsewhip, the two of them framed by the back-flung front door." Faulkner has pictured the Griersons as exactly as a photographer would, but that precision quite disappears when the description passes over into the mind of a reader. It disappears even if the reader is as well trained and fairly experienced as the five students of English literature who are the subjects of this book. Sam, Saul, Shep, Sebastian, and Sandra (as I shall call them) all spoke about this "tableau."

Good-natured, easygoing, dapper Sam singled it out as virtually the first thing he wanted to talk about in the story: "The father was very domineering. One of the most striking [sic] images in the book is that of the townsfolk looking through the door as her father stands there with a horse-whip in his hands, feet spread apart and between or through him you see a picture of Emily standing in the background, and that pretty much sums up exactly the kind of relationship they had." Sam was stressing the father's dominance and, in doing so, was positioning the townspeople so that they could see Emily between her father's legs.

This was part of what he found highly romantic in the story. "The frailty and femininity that that evokes!" he sighed. "Just that one frail, 'slender figure in white,' just those words there really show us the Emily that was and the Emily that might have been." Yet, almost at the same moment he was responding to this lacy, feminine Emily, he could say, "The word 'tableau' is important. While they [the townspeople] may be envious and while they may be angry at the way that these people act, they yet need it, it seems, they in a way like to have it, much as one is terrified at the power of a god and yet needing him so much and, you know, sidling up to him and paying homage to him and in the same way I think Emily comes to function as this god symbol." A curious turnabout from frailty and femininity.

By contrast, Saul, a scholarly type, was circumspect. Sam, in his expansive way, trusted his memory, but Saul, when I asked him about that image, took out his copy of the story and read it over carefully to himself. "Ummm. I had remembered the word 'tableau,' and I had forgotten the rest of it. 'Horsewhip' there — rings — 'spraddled silhouette.' That seems right to me. That summarizes the relationship, I think. She's in the back in white, of course. I think of these white gowns in the plantation balls. The father a 'spraddled silhouette.' He's no longer stern and erect. He's spraddled across the door." Saul was seeing Emily's father exactly the opposite way from Sam, as a weakened, sprawled figure, at least until he read over to himself the sentence with the horsewhip in it again. "A horsewhip suggesting all sorts of nasty, sexual, sadistic overtones," but then he blurred that image. "Do they mean the horsewhip rather than his own stern demeanor? Or just the normal embodiment of his traditions suggests the decline like 'spraddled'

does? And then 'framed by the back-flung front door' just completes the tableau. It's a nice device. Faulkner makes that one work, too. That's a nice emblem." Well, maybe so, but Saul had so divided it up and dissolved it into questions and alternatives as to leave me quite puzzled about what he thought the thrust of the image finally was.

Shep presented himself as a rebel and radical, but his reading of the tableau seemed to me no more original or idiosyncratic than Saul's or Sam's. I read the passage to him, and he commented simply. "O.K. Protective image. That he's defending Southern womanhood, perhaps, and defending it in that same sort of mindless way that says, 'Well, now, we've got to defend it.'" He went on to decide that Southern womanhood might well have defended itself and then to make a suggestion quite opposite to "protective image." "You could, I suppose, as an alternative interpretation say that the horsewhip is something which he's also adept with indoors as well as outdoors, but I don't think so. Maybe there's overtones that Daddy is sadistic enough — horsewhips being pretty sadistic things to carry around when you're greeting people, you know — that Daddy is sadistic enough where he wouldn't mind taking a belt at Emily once in a while, but I don't think they're much more than overtones." In talking about the tableau as such, he talked only about Emily's father, and in this curiously alternative or opposed way. Earlier he had recalled Emily as a young woman (and the tableau is the only place she is so described): "I can see her as a very good-looking, dark-haired girl who had a penchant for wearing dark clothes." Again, I sense in his substituting dark for white a will opposing the text, although at the same time, Shep said he liked this story very much.

Sophisticated, sardonic, somewhat cynical, a lapsed Catholic with aspirations toward aristocracy, Sebastian did not discuss the tableau as such, although he clearly remembered it in typing Emily as "the aristocrat of the Southern town, whose father is the original superego with a horsewhip, beating off suitors." "He's denying her access to suitable sexual partners." Often, Sebastian tended to distance and type the characters this way and to flirt with the actual, physical details. Here he saw Miss Emily as "the aristocrat," her father as "the original superego," but converted the "suitors" to "sexual partners."

Sandra, the fifth reader, was a tall, very attractive woman, gentle and subdued in her manner. She liked the story intensely, had read it several times, and had even, in her freshman year, written a term paper on it. Yet she recalled the tableau oddly: "They said they always had this picture of him standing, you know, sitting in the door with a whip in his hand." As for Emily, "I see her as very young and dressed in white and standing up, I guess she's supposed to be standing up behind her father, who would probably be looking *very* cross, say, if someone had come to call on her. No doubt, she would have a certain amount — Possibly fearful, but probably more regretful because she's being, they even say, robbed of something at that point. . . . There would be a great amount of strain on her face because of her inability to do anything except just watch." Sandra saw the emotional overtones in the tableau in a more subtle, empathic way than the four male readers did, so that she, too, had her own version of the image.

Indeed, one can say that each of the readers had a different version of Emily and her father. He was standing, sitting; erect, sprawled; domineering, weakened; sadistic, protective, and so on — sometimes even to the same reader. Emily was dressed in white, as for a plantation ball, or black; frail, but godlike; fearful, but "the aristocrat." Some of these differences involve outright misreadings, but most do not. Conceivably, one could "teach" or coerce these five readers into consensus, but even so, whatever in each person's character originally colored his perception of the tableau would go on coloring his perception of every other element in the story. What is that something, that ineffable effect of personality on perception? That is the issue this book explores.

As the late Stanley Edgar Hyman once said, "Each reader poems his own poem." Yet we know very little — practically nothing — about such "poeming," about the way a reader recreates the literary experience in himself. Today's literary critics are expert in pointing out an essence for any literary work. Today's psychologists — particularly the psychoanalytic psychologists — are equally adept at conceptualizing the essential dynamics of individuals. Yet we do not know how literature and readers interact.

We can find out, if you and I apply to what Sam and the other readers said, a combination of the close reading literary critics have so skillfully developed in the last decades and psychological methods of reading from language to personality. We shall move slowly — sometimes we shall seem to go word by word — but once we have put psychoanalytic interpretation together with the literary critic's, we shall have established four principles that account for the way readers read to fit their personalities.

As of now, however, in the words of a recent book on the problem of literary response, "We know almost nothing about the process of reading and the interaction of man and book."[1] In a manner all too common in the world of belles-lettres, however, the "almost nothing" we know tends to become complexity piled upon complexity, language explained by more language, authorities resting on other authorities — a splendid disguise of abstractions much like the emperor's new clothes. "Scholars and critics," Walter Slatoff writes, "who would distinguish carefully between various sorts of Neo-Platonism, or examine in minute detail the structure of a chapter or the transmutations of a prevailing metaphor, or trace the full nuances of a topical allusion, will settle happily for mere labels like distance, involvement, identification,"[2] labels that not only suffer from vagueness but deceive, creating the illusion that they refer to some real reaction people in fact shared and the critic in fact observed.

This tradition — assuming a uniform response on the part of readers and audiences that the critic somehow knows and understands — goes back to Aristotle's concept of catharsis, and his notions about people's apparently fixed responses to details of wording. Or this tradition might even

[1] Walter J. Slatoff, *With Respect to Readers: Dimensions of Literary Response* (Ithaca and London: Cornell University Press, 1970), p. 188. [Au.]

[2] Ibid., p. 35. [Au.]

have originated in Plato's assertion that poetry debilitates. Although the Greeks observed the phenomena that they ascribed to audiences better than later theorists, the tradition flourished after them, reaching a peak with the "rules" of the lesser neoclassical critics. Early psychoanalytic writers on literature followed, rather uncritically, this collectivist view from the litterateurs. Thus we find Otto Rank defending his oedipal interpretations of myths because, "The people imagine the hero in this manner, investing him with their own infantile fantasies."[3] Freud himself assumed a collective response to *Oedipus Rex* in the letter of October 15, 1897, in which he reported to his confidant Fliess, "I have found love of the mother and jealousy of the father in my own case too, and now believe it to be a general phenomenon of early childhood." "If that is the case, the gripping power of *Oedipus Rex,* in spite of all the rational objections to the inexorable fate that the story presupposes, becomes intelligible." "Every member of the audience was once a budding Oedipus in phantasy, and this dream-fulfillment played out in reality causes everyone to recoil in horror, with the full measure of repression which separates his infantile from his present state."[4]

*Everyone* recoils? Freud himself avoided this fallacy when he studied jokes as a kind of mini-literature; they have a "frame" and a text with especially sensitive formal balances and a response. What would one think of a theory of jokes that always concluded, "and so you laugh" or "and so you don't laugh," regardless of whether you did or didn't in fact laugh? After all, someone might have heard the joke before; someone else might be depressed; a third person might have no sense of humor, and so on. Indeed, responses to jokes are so various that, for a time, researchers (at Yale) were exploring a "mirth response test," trying to sort personality types by observing which cartoons they found

funny.[5] Should we then postulate that responses to tragedy, something so infinitely more subtle than a cartoon, are fixed? No, and for some decades now we have, in fact, known the contrary.

It was in the 1920s that I. A. Richards asked his Cambridge undergraduates for the protocols that led to his ground-breaking *Practical Criticism.*[6] He asked his students "to comment freely in writing on" a series of poems, their authorship undisclosed. Richards found that these supposedly well-educated young Englishmen were evaluating very strangely indeed, misreading the plain sense of the poems, imposing cranky sets of preconceptions, responding in terms of stock sentimentalities, cynicisms, and other doctrines, as well as (perhaps) irrelevant memories. Richards, let us notice, was exploring his reader's conscious, verbalized responses to literature. Interested in education, he tended to concentrate on those parts of literary response that could be taught, and, indeed, his analysis of misreadings helped to reform, root and branch, the teaching of literature over the next four decades. Today, even among schoolchildren, one finds more sophisticated reading than Richards found among his jazz-age Cantabrigians.[7]

One would expect the giant entertainment corporations, with millions riding on each reel of celluloid, to have studied response far more carefully than impoverished English teachers could. But the published research in this field remains rather elementary.[8] There are many studies of

---

[5]Jacob Levine, "Response to Humor," *Scientific American* 194 (1956): 31–35. [Au.]

[6]I. A. Richards, *Practical Criticism: A Study of Literary Judgment* (New York: Harcourt, Brace, 1951). [Au.]

[7]James R. Squire, *The Responses of Adolescents While Reading Four Short Stories,* NCTE Research Report No. 2, 1964. James R. Wilson, *Responses of College Freshmen to Three Novels,* NCTE Research Report No. 7, 1966. Alan C. Purves with Victoria Rippere, *Elements of Writing about a Literary Work: A Study of Response to Literature,* NCTE Research Report No. 9, 1968. All published by National Council of Teachers of English, 508 South Sixth Street, Champaign, Illinois 61820. [Au.]

[8]Leo A. Handel, *Hollywood Looks at Its Audience: A Report of Film Audience Research* (Urbana: University of Illinois Press, 1950), particularly Chapters 11 and 12, provides an accurate sample of what is being published currently, although the work is twenty years old. [Au.]

---

[3]Otto Rank, *The Myth of the Birth of the Hero* (1914) (New York: Vintage Books, 1959), Chapter 3, p. 89n. [Au.]

[4]Marie Bonaparte, Anna Freud, Ernst Kris, eds., *The Origins of Psychoanalysis,* trans. Eric Mosbacher and James Strachey (New York: Basic Books, 1954), letter of October 15, 1897. [Au.]

effect, but they move casually back and forth between the transfer of information, the fulfillment of individuals' needs (for example, to escape), the impact on morality (typically delinquency), and immediate reactions of "like" and "dislike." Indeed, the industry has developed machines — the Lazarsfeld-Stanton program analyzer, the Cirlin Reactograph — with which an audience can indicate its fluctuating likes, dislikes, and indifferences. Of course, such a device cannot sort out variables — one cannot tell, for example, whether a member of the audience is disliking the whole movie or just the "bad guy" in it. In general, this one-dimensional quality carries over to the analysis of the content of films. The most sophisticated scheme I have seen only gets to issues like "Main story type," that is, "Is it a Western or a gangster movie?", "Marital status and changes of leads A, B, and C," "Sports (type and prominence)," or "Importance of part and characterization of unskilled labor." I understand that much research in this field is kept secret because of its commercial value. If what has been published is an accurate sample, there would seem to be little reason to do so.

Such simple categories show that a study of audience response demands at least one thing: some sensibly subtle way of analyzing the texts, both the text the artist creates and the text of what the audience says. I. A. Richards had that, with his marvelous sense of language, but his experience showed a second tool one must have to understand audiences. Without a psychology adequate to explain individual responses, one does not know what to do with them except pass judgment on them. "We rarely concern ourselves, for example," says Walter Slatoff, surveying the post-Richards critical scene, "with the problem of individual differences among readers. . . . On the few occasions we do entertain such questions we speak as though they were settled by reducing response to two categories — appropriate and inappropriate."[9] Thus, although Richards avowed a concern to maintain differences of opinion, he shifted the problem of evaluating poems to a much harsher dogmatism:

passing judgment on "the relative values of different states of mind, about varying forms, and degrees, of order in the personality."[10]

Had Richards had a usable psychology of individuals, he would have been able, presumably, to see how his protocols were reflecting personality at all levels, not just the teachable surface of consciousness. Indeed, David Bleich has recently done just that: shown how some of Richards's protocols reveal the unconscious themes his Cantabrigians were projecting into the texts as part of their response.[11] "It has become a matter of course that any item of human behavior shows a continuum of dynamic meaning, reaching from the surface through many layers of crust to the 'core'" — thus, Erik Erikson,[12] articulating with his customary eloquence one of the most basic and widely confirmed of psychoanalytic discoveries. Freud's earliest case histories showed it and so did this morning's experience in hundreds of clinics and consulting-rooms. I know, for example, how the style and subject and method of this book stem from very early experiences of my own and my whole present character, including various half-conscious wishes and fears. Although these unconscious and infantile sources are by no means the only ones, if so conscious an act as writing an experimental and theoretical book has strong buried components, I find it hard to believe that responding to a play, a movie, or a poem does not. And, of course, it does.

As the remainder of this book will show, readers respond to literature in terms of their own "lifestyle" (or "character" or "personality" or "identity"). By such terms, psychoanalytic writers mean an individual's characteristic way of dealing with the demands of outer and inner reality. Such a style will have grown through time from earliest infancy. It will also be what the individual brings with him to any new experi-

[9]Slatoff, *With Respect to Readers*, pp. 13–14. [Au.]

[10]Richards, *Practical Criticism*, pp. 347–49. [Au.]

[11]David Bleich, "The Determination of Literary Value," *Literature and Psychology* 17 (1967): 19–30. [Au.]

[12]Erik H. Erikson, "The Dream Specimen of Psychoanalysis," in Robert P. Knight and Cyrus R. Friedman, eds., *Psychoanalytic Psychiatry and Psychology,* Clinical and Theoretical Papers of the Austen Riggs Center, Vol. 1 (New York: Hallmark-Hubner Press, 1954), p. 140. [Au.]

ence, including the experience of literature. Each new experience develops the style, while the pre-existing style shapes each new experience. And this style can be described quite accurately (but not, of course, impersonally).

In short, psychoanalysis offers a powerful theory of individual responses to literature, and it has done so ever since Freud's 1905 study of jokes. (Interestingly, in that very early study, he also showed how social and economic factors would affect the pattern of inhibitions an individual brought to a joke and so affect his responses, but *indirectly*, as they filtered through his personality.) Other writers have extended this first psychoanalytic aesthetics, Freud's theory of jokes, to other genres and to literature generally.[13]

For the most part, however, psychoanalytic students of literature, like conventional literary critics, have looked not at the actual individual reading but at the text, the words-on-the-page. Then they have posited a response on the basis of the text. Thus, paradoxically, the psychology that more than any other deals closely and intensely with individuals — psychoanalytic psychology — has in this instance retreated from the living human being, the spirit, if you will, to the letter.

By contrast, conventional psychological literature offers hundreds of studies that deal with actual readers but that suffer from a lack of theory.[14] For example, physiological studies tell

how heart rate, the electrical resistance of the palm of the hand, or its sweat pattern, vary as subjects watch a movie. Indeed, an Italian experiment even investigated the differing ways identical and fraternal twins fidgeted![15] But I find it hard to believe a single variable such as pulse rate or fidget frequency could represent a complex, multivariant transaction like a response to a film.

Other studies resort to personality tests, but I think it is not much of an improvement over the physiological approach to be able to say that reading gruesome passages from Edgar Allan Poe increases the anxious and aggressive responses to inkblots. Much closer to the method of this book is the study in which judges were able to match viewers' open-ended comments on a movie to their Rorschach responses. Again, however, the experiment merely shows the correlation; it does not suggest an underlying mechanism, only that "individual differences in the perception of a motion picture are a function of global aspects of personality as elicited by the Rorschach."[16] Different personality tests lead to similarly vague conclusions: "Movie attendance is related in some instances to the central aspects of personality." A child's choices among stories "cohere with other observable characteristics of his personality."[17] Other studies claim to have shown that men watch the men in movies more than women do; that boys prefer adventure stories, while girls prefer stories about love, private life, and glamor; that children who are already

---

[13]Norman N. Holland, *The Dynamics of Literary Response* (New York: Oxford University Press, 1968). Robert Waelder, *Psychoanalytic Avenues to Art* (New York: International Universities Press, 1965). Ernst Kris, *Psychoanalytic Explorations in Art* (New York: International Universities Press, 1952). Simon O. Lesser, *Fiction and the Unconscious* (Boston: Beacon Press, 1957). Philip Weissman, *Creativity in the Theater: A Psychoanalytic Study* (New York: Dell Publishing Co., 1965). In addition to Freud's essays on *Jokes* (1905) and "The 'Uncanny'" (1919), see my attempt at a synthesis: "Freud on the Response," in Holland, *Psychoanalysis and Shakespeare* (New York: McGraw-Hill Book Co., 1966). [Au.]

[14]I am exceedingly grateful to Ms. Betty Jane Saik, Ms. Mary Z. Bartlett, and Mr. Stephen Gormey for assembling and helping me punch-card as complete an index of studies of response to the arts as *Psychological Abstracts* affords. It was after our own work, in 1972, that an excellent survey appeared by Alan C. Purves and Richard Beach, *Literature*

*and the Reader: Research in Response to Literature, Reading Interests, and the Teaching of Literature* (University of Illinois at Urbana-Champaign: National Council of Teachers of English, 1972). It supports our general conclusion that results are many but unsystematic. [Au.]

[15]When I am not using these studies substantively, I shall simply list them by author and *Psychological Abstracts (PA)* reference. Edward Opton, Jr., *PA* (1967): 5663. Jack Block, *PA* (1963): 7682. Richard C. Pillard et al., *PA* (1967): 6610. Luigi Gedda et al., *PA* (1956): 443. [Au.]

[16]Lutz von Rosenstiel, *PA* (1967): 4630. Marvin Spiegelman, "Effect of Personality on the Perception of a Motion Picture," *Journal of Projective Techniques* 19 (1955): 461–464. [Au.]

[17]E. M. Scott, *PA* (1958): 4129. G. Foulds, *PA* (1943): 994. [Au.]

pretty aggressive identify with different characters in a Western according to the degree of their pre-existing aggression, their sex, and the ending of the film.[18] No doubt, these studies (and hundreds more like them) follow out admirably the canons of experimental rigor. As a continuing line of research, however, they end most inconclusively, to judge, if nothing else, by the number of experimenters who turn to the same old issues over and over again. Instead of coherent research, one finds random observations. What these studies may have gained in rigor they certainly lack in theory.

One returns then to literary and psychoanalytic studies, weak in experiment but strong on theory. Not always, of course. I do not feel that my understanding of the differences in readers' responses is advanced by a literary critic's introducing an "*informed* reader" with (also italicized) "*literary* competence" or even a more generalized "reading self," who (or that) is roughly the critic's age, shares his ethnic background, "has experienced war, marriage, and the responsibility of children," and so on.[19] Some statements about response by literary and psychoanalytic folk do add more rigor and theory than these; some do suggest pervasive links between, on the one hand, the reader's personality (in depth) and his conscious reading skill and, on the other, his response. I am thinking of Morse Peckham's explanation of the effect of one's past aesthetic experiences on response, a theory supported by very detailed analyses from a variety of arts and corresponding to psychoanalytic notions of the role of the ego in art.[20] Similarly, child therapists like Lilli Peller and Kate Friedlaender have shown how children's stories reflect at a con-scious level the child's unconscious fantasies, and therefore how the age appropriate to the fantasy determines the age at which a child will like the story. They, too, are showing a theoretical basis for combining the detailed analysis of a story with the depth analysis of the response.[21]

Such studies, in effect, deal with classes of readers. Psychoanalysis, however, is par excellence the science of human individuality (if there can be a "science" of uniqueness), and we would expect it to be most interesting about literary response when it speaks about individuals. However, it must then necessarily give up repeatable experiments. For example, a group of experimenters, in projecting films for hospitalized psychiatric patients, found that the viewers interposed their individual defensive patterns between themselves and the film to keep the affect something they could tolerate. Hence, one could not assume that any given film would necessarily arouse certain feelings. Similarly, in an example of "poetry therapy," David V. Forrest showed how disturbed patients responded to the well-known lyric, "Western wind, when wilt thou blow," in terms of their several personality types, paranoid, schizoid, hysteric, and so on.[22] These papers suggest structures relating personality to response (through defense mechanisms or diagnostic categories that combine defense and level of fixation). They do not, however, take the further step: going beyond types and categories to examine the work of art, the response, and the responder in detail.

[18]Eleanor E. Maccoby et al., *PA* (1960): 4080. Paul I. Lyness, *PA* (1952): 7218. Robert S. Albert, *PA* (1959): 4603. [Au.]

[19]Stanley E. Fish, *Self-Consuming Artifacts: The Experience of Seventeenth-Century Literature* (Berkeley: University of California Press, 1972), p. 406. Slatoff, *With Respect to Readers*, pp. 55–56. [Au.]

[20]Morse Peckham, *Man's Rage for Chaos: Biology, Behavior, and the Arts* (New York: Chilton Books, 1965). See also my review article, "Psychoanalytic Criticism and Perceptual Psychology," *Literature and Psychology* 16 (1966): 81–92. [Au.]

[21]Lilli E. Peller, "Libidinal Phases, Ego Development, and Play," *The Psychoanalytic Study of the Child* 9 (1954): 178–98; "Reading and Daydreams in Latency; Boy-Girl Differences," *Journal of the American Psychoanalytic Association* 6 (1958): 57–70; "Daydreams and Children's Favorite Books: Psychoanalytic Comments," *The Psychoanalytic Study of the Child* 14 (1959): 414–33. Kate Friedlaender, "Children's Books and Their Function in Latency and Prepuberty," *American Imago* 3 (1942): 129–50. [Au.]

[22]Gordon Globus and Roy Shulman, "Considerations on Affective Response to Motion Pictures" (unpublished paper, Department of Psychiatry, Boston University School of Medicine); also cited in Holland, *Dynamics* (see note 13), pp. 94–95. David V. Forrest, "The Patient's Sense of the Poem: Affinities and Ambiguities," in Jack J. Leedy, ed., *Poetry Therapy: The Use of Poetry in the Treatment of Emotional Disorders* (Philadelphia: J. B. Lippincott Co., 1969), Chapter 20, pp. 231–59. [Au.]

One often finds analyses of the individual (but not the work) in case histories. Avery Weisman, for example, describes a rigid, obsessional man who could not face a sea captain's loss of authority in a movie and left the theater before the film's end. The whole setting — other patrons, streets, bodily sensations — seemed unreal to him: he had dealt with his guilt and anxiety by separating his intellectual processes of reality-testing from his conventional, pleasurable attachment to the dream world of the film. Edith Buxbaum, in a famous case, tells of a boy compulsively driven to read detective stories almost to the exclusion of any other activity. He was satisfying his aggressive wishes toward his mother by allying himself with the murderer. At the same time, he assuaged his guilt by feeling like the victim and also the detective. Thus his symptom served both defense and the gratification of instincts, and he became locked into it. Still more tragic was the patient of Gilbert J. Rose who committed suicide after witnessing a performance of Duerrenmatt's *The Visit:* he, like the hero of the play, felt himself the victim of a fantastically powerful bitch-goddess.[23]

Caroline Shrodes, however, has studied individual students' responses to particular literary works on the assumption that literary experience matches the therapeutic process: from identification and interaction with the work, to emotional catharsis, to insight into one's particular conflicts and relationships.[24] Less clinically, David Bleich in a growing series of moving and perceptive essays has analyzed the responses of ordinary readers, students usually, in order to elicit the unconscious themes of the text. In other words, he reverses the usual assumption of critics, that by analyzing the text one can understand the response; rather, he argues, by analyzing what readers find in it, one comes to understand the text.[25] And he is right to do so. To analyze the text in formal isolation as so many "words-on-a-page" (in the old formula of the New Criticism) is a highly artificial procedure. A literary text, after all, in an objective sense consists only of a certain configuration of specks of carbon black on dried wood pulp. When these marks become words, when those words become images or metaphors or characters or events, they do so because the reader plays the part of a prince to the sleeping beauty. He gives them life out of his own desires. When he does so, he brings his lifestyle to bear on the work. He mingles his unconscious loves and fears and adaptations with the words and images he synthesizes at a conscious level.

It is, therefore, quite impossible to say from a text alone how people will respond to it. Only after we have understood how some specific individual responds, how the different parts of his individual personality recreate the different details of the text, can we begin to formulate general hypotheses about the way many or all readers respond. Only then — if then.

At the same time, however, the reader is surely responding to *something*. The literary text may be only so many marks on a page — at most a matrix of psychological possibilities for its readers. Nevertheless only some possibilities, we would say, truly fit the matrix. One would not say, for example, that a reader of that sentence from "A Rose for Emily" who thought the "tableau" described an Eskimo was really responding to the story at all — only pursuing some mysterious inner exploration. In the basic question of this book, "Who reads what how?", there must be a "what," and our next task is to find out what it is.

[23]Avery D. Weisman, "Reality Sense and Reality Testing," *Behavioral Science* 3 (1958): 228–61. Edith Buxbaum, "The Role of Detective Stories in a Child Analysis," *Psychoanalytic Quarterly* 10 (1941): 373–81. Gilbert J. Rose, "Creative Imagination in Terms of Ego 'Core' and Boundaries," *International Journal of Psycho-Analysis* 45 (1964): 75–85. [Au.]

[24]Caroline Shrodes, "Bibliotherapy: An Application of Psychoanalytic Theory," *American Imago* 17 (1960): 311–19; "The Dynamics of Reading: Implications for Bibliotherapy," *ETC.: A Review of General Semantics* 18 (1961): 21–33. Both articles are based on her "Bibliotherapy: A Theoretical and Clinical Experimental Study" (Ph.D. dissertation, University of California, Berkeley, 1949). [Au.]

[25]David Bleich, "The Determination of Literary Value," *Literature and Psychology* 17 (1967): 19–30; "Emotional Origins of Literary Meaning," *College English* 31 (1969): 30–40; "Psychological Bases of Learning from Literature," *College English* 33 (1971): 32–45. [Au.]

# Stanley Fish

b. 1938

*The agent provocateur of contemporary literary theory, Stanley Fish was born in Providence, Rhode Island, and raised in Philadelphia. He received his A.B. at Penn (1959) and his A.M. and Ph.D. (1962) at Yale, which published his dissertation on John Skelton. Fish taught at Berkeley, becoming a full professor in 1974. In that year, Fish moved to Johns Hopkins as Kenan professor, and in 1986, as both professor of law and as chairman of the English department, to Duke University, where he has attracted a stellar group of theorists, including Fredric Jameson (Ch. 1) and Barbara Herrnstein Smith (Ch. 8). In his most recent metatheoretical work, Fish has attacked theory as pointless, impotent to constrain the will-to-power of interpretation, whereas formerly, he had restricted his rhetorical assaults to individual theorists like Wolfgang Iser or to fields like linguistics and stylistics. Fish's career as a gadfly began with his second book,* Surprised by Sin: The Reader in *Paradise Lost (1967), which transgressed with both feet the "affective fallacy" by which the New Criticism had eliminated the study of the audience. The object of Fish's concern has shifted from the implied reader immanent within the text in* Self-Consuming Artifacts: The Experience of Seventeenth-Century Literature *(1972), to the experience of actual readers and interpretive communities of readers in* Is There a Text in This Class? *(1980). "Interpreting the* Variorum," *the transitional essay in Fish's career, was included in a different form in* Is There a Text; *the original version, reprinted here, is from* Critical Inquiry 3 *(1977).*

## *Interpreting the* Variorum

### I

The first two volumes of the Milton *Variorum Commentary* have now appeared, and I find them endlessly fascinating. My interest, however, is not in the questions they manage to resolve (although these are many) but in the theoretical assumptions which are responsible for their occasional failures. These failures constitute a pattern, one in which a host of commentators — separated by as much as two hundred and seventy years but contemporaries in their shared concerns — are lined up on either side of an interpretive crux. Some of these are famous, even infamous: what is the two-handed engine in *Lycidas?* what is the meaning of Haemony in *Comus?* Others, like the identity of whoever or whatever comes to the window in *L'Allegro,* line 46, are only slightly less notorious. Still others are of interest largely to those who make editions: matters of pronoun referents, lexical ambiguities, punctuation. In each instance, however, the pattern is

consistent: every position taken is supported by wholly convincing evidence — in the case of *L'Allegro* and the coming to the window there is a persuasive champion for every proper noun within a radius of ten lines — and the editorial procedure always ends either in the graceful throwing up of hands, or in the recording of a disagreement between the two editors themselves. In short, these are problems that apparently cannot be solved, at least not by the methods traditionally brought to bear on them. What I would like to argue is that they are not *meant* to be solved, but to be experienced (they signify), and that consequently any procedure that attempts to determine which of a number of readings is correct will necessarily fail. What this means is that the commentators and editors have been asking the wrong questions and that a new set of questions based on new assumptions must be formulated. I would like at least to make a beginning in that direction by examining some of the points in dispute in Milton's sonnets. I choose the sonnets because they are brief and because one can move easily from them to the theoretical issues with which this paper is finally concerned.

Milton's twentieth sonnet — "Lawrence of virtuous father virtuous son" — has been the subject of relatively little commentary. In it the poet invites a friend to join him in some distinctly Horatian pleasures — a neat repast intermixed with conversation, wine, and song; a respite from labor all the more enjoyable because outside the earth is frozen and the day sullen. The only controversy the sonnet has inspired concerns its final two lines:

> Lawrence of virtuous father virtuous son,
>     Now that the fields are dank, and ways are mire,
>     Where shall we sometimes meet, and by the fire
>     Help waste a sullen day; what may be won
> From the hard season gaining; time will run
>     On smoother, till Favonius reinspire
>     The frozen earth; and clothe in fresh attire
>     The lily and rose, that neither sowed nor spun.
> What neat repast shall feast us, light and choice,
>     Of Attic taste, with wine, whence we may rise
>     To hear the lute well touched, or artful voice
> Warble immortal notes and Tuscan air?
>     He who of those delights can judge, and spare
>     To interpose them oft, is not unwise.[1]

The focus of the controversy is the word "spare," for which two readings have been proposed: leave time for and refrain from. Obviously the point is crucial if one is to resolve the sense of the lines. In one reading "those delights" are being recommended — he who can leave time for them is not unwise; in the other, they are the subject of a warning — he who knows when to refrain from them is not unwise. The proponents of the two interpretations cite as evidence both English and Latin syntax, various sources and analogues, Milton's "known attitudes" as they are found in his other writings, and the unambiguously expressed sentiments of the following sonnet on the same question. Surveying these arguments, A. S. P. Woodhouse roundly declares: "It is plain that all the honours rest with" the meaning "refrain from" or "forbear to." This declaration is followed immediately by a bracketed paragraph initialled D. B. for Douglas Bush, who, writing presumably after Woodhouse has died, begins "In spite of the array of scholarly names the case for 'forbear to' may be thought much weaker, and the case for 'spare time for' much stronger, than Woodhouse found them."[2] Bush then proceeds to review much of the evidence marshaled by Woodhouse and to draw from it exactly the opposite conclusion. If it does nothing else, this curious performance anticipates a point I shall make in a few moments: evidence brought to bear in the course of formalist analyses — that is, analyses generated by the assumption that meaning is embedded in the artifact — will always point in as many directions as there are interpreters; that is, not only will it prove something, it will prove anything.

It would appear then that we are back at square one, with a controversy that cannot be settled because the evidence is inconclusive. But what if that controversy is *itself* regarded as evidence, not of an ambiguity that must be removed, but of an ambiguity that readers have always experienced? What, in other words, if for the question "what does 'spare' mean?" we substitute the question "what does the fact that the meaning of 'spare' has always been an issue mean"? The advantage of this question is that it can be answered. Indeed it has already been answered by the readers who are cited in the *Variorum Commentary*. What the readers debate is the judgment the poem makes on the delights of recreation; what their debate indicates is that the judgment is blurred by a verb that can be made to participate in contradictory readings. (Thus the important thing about the evidence surveyed in the *Variorum* is not how it is marshaled, but that it could be marshaled at all, because it then becomes evidence of the equal availability of both interpretations.) In other words, the lines first generate a pressure for judgment — "he who of those delights can judge" — and then decline to

---

[1] All references are to *The Poems of John Milton*, ed. John Carey and Alastair Fowler (London, 1968). [Au.]

[2] *A Variorum Commentary on the Poems of John Milton*, vol. 2, pt. 2, ed. A. S. P. Woodhouse and Douglas Bush (New York, 1972), p. 475. [Au.]

deliver it; the pressure, however, still exists, and it is transferred from the words on the page to the reader (the reader is "he who"), who comes away from the poem not with a statement, but with a responsibility, the responsibility of deciding when and how often — if at all — to indulge in "those delights" (they remain delights in either case). This transferring of responsibility from the text to its readers is what the lines ask us to do — it is the essence of their experience — and in my terms it is therefore what the lines *mean*. It is a meaning the *Variorum* critics attest to even as they resist it, for what they are laboring so mightily to do by fixing the sense of the lines is to give the responsibility back. The text, however, will not accept it and remains determinedly evasive, even in its last two words, "not unwise." In their position these words confirm the impossibility of extracting from the poem a moral formula, for the assertion (certainly too strong a word) they complete is of the form, "He who does such and such, of him it cannot be said that he is unwise"; but of course neither can it be said that he is wise. Thus what Bush correctly terms the "defensive" "not unwise" operates to prevent us from attaching the label "wise" to any action, including *either* of the actions — leaving time for or refraining from — represented by the ambiguity of "spare." Not only is the pressure of judgment taken off the poem, it is taken off the activity the poem at first pretended to judge. The issue is finally not the moral status of "those delights" — they become in seventeenth-century terms "things indifferent" — but on the good or bad uses to which they can be put by readers who are left, as Milton always leaves them, to choose and manage by themselves.

Let us step back for a moment and see how far we've come. We began with an apparently insoluble problem and proceeded, not to solve it, but to make it signify; first by regarding it as evidence of an experience and then by specifying for that experience a meaning. Moreover, the configurations of that experience, when they are made available by a reader-oriented analysis, serve as a check against the endlessly inconclusive adducing of evidence which characterizes formalist analysis. That is to say, any determination of what "spare" means (in a positivist or

literal sense) is liable to be upset by the bringing forward of another analogue, or by a more complete computation of statistical frequencies, or by the discovery of new biographical information, or by anything else; but if we first determine that everything in the line before "spare" creates the expectation of an imminent judgment, then the ambiguity of "spare" can be assigned a significance in the context of that expectation. (It disappoints it and transfers the pressure of judgment to us.) That context is experiential, and it is within its contours and constraints that significances are established (both in the act of reading and in the analysis of that act). In formalist analyses the only constraints are the notoriously open-ended possibilities and combination of possibilities that emerge when one begins to consult dictionaries and grammars and histories; to consult dictionaries, grammars, and histories is to assume that meanings can be specified independently of the activity of reading; what the example of "spare" shows is that it is in and by that activity that meanings — experiential, not positivist — are created.

In other words, it is the structure of the reader's experience rather than any structures available on the page that should be the object of description. In the case of Sonnet XX, that experiential structure was uncovered when an examination of formal structures led to an impasse; and the pressure to remove that impasse led to the substitution of one set of questions for another. It will more often be the case that the pressure of a spectacular failure will be absent. The sins of formalist-positivist analysis are primarily sins of omission, not an inability to explain phenomena, but an inability to see that they are there because its assumptions make it inevitable that they will be overlooked or suppressed. Consider, for example, the concluding lines of another of Milton's sonnets, "Avenge O Lord thy slaughtered saints."

Avenge O Lord thy slaughtered saints, whose bones
   Lie scattered on the Alpine mountains cold,
   Even them who kept thy truth so pure of old
   When all our fathers worshipped stocks and stones,
Forget not: in thy book record their groans

Who were thy sheep and in their ancient fold
Slain by the bloody Piedmontese that rolled
Mother with infant down the rocks. Their moans
The vales redoubled to the hills, and they
To heaven. Their martyred blood and ashes sow
O'er all the Italian fields where still doth sway
The triple Tyrant: that from these may grow
A hundredfold, who having learnt thy way
Early may fly the Babylonian woe.

In this sonnet, the poet simultaneously petitions God and wonders aloud about the justice of allowing the faithful — "Even them who kept thy truth" — to be so brutally slaughtered. The note struck is alternately one of plea and complaint, and there is more than a hint that God is being called to account for what has happened to the Waldensians. It is generally agreed, however, that the note of complaint is less and less sounded and that the poem ends with an affirmation of faith in the ultimate operation of God's justice. In this reading, the final lines are taken to be saying something like this: From the blood of these martyred, O God, raise up a new and more numerous people, who, by virtue of an early education in thy law, will escape destruction by fleeing the Babylonian woe. Babylonian woe has been variously glossed;[3] but whatever it is taken to mean it is always read as part of a statement that specifies a set of conditions for the escaping of destruction or punishment; it is a warning to the reader as well as a petition to God. As a warning, however, it is oddly situated since the conditions it seems to specify were in fact met by the Waldensians, who of all men most followed God's laws. In other words, the details of their story would seem to undercut the affirmative moral the speaker proposes to draw from it. It is further undercut by a reading that is fleetingly available, although no one has acknowledged it because it is a function, not of the words on the page, but of the experience of the

reader. In that experience, line 13 will for a moment be accepted as a complete sense unit and the emphasis of the line will fall on "thy way" (a phrase that has received absolutely no attention in the commentaries). At this point "thy way" can refer only to the way in which God has dealt with the Waldensians. That is, "thy way" seems to pick up the note of outrage with which the poem began, and if we continue to so interpret it, the conclusion of the poem will be a grim one indeed: since by this example it appears that God rains down punishment indiscriminately, it would be best perhaps to withdraw from the arena of his service, and thereby hope at least to be safely out of the line of fire. This is not the conclusion we carry away, because as line 14 unfolds, another reading of "thy way" becomes available, a reading in which "early" qualifies "learnt" and refers to something the faithful should do (learn thy way at an early age) rather than to something God has failed to do (save the Waldensians). These two readings are answerable to the pulls exerted by the beginning and ending of the poem: the outrage expressed in the opening lines generates a pressure for an explanation, and the grimmer reading is answerable to that pressure (even if it is also disturbing); the ending of the poem, the forward and upward movement of lines 10–14, creates the expectation of an affirmation, and the second reading fulfills that expectation. The criticism shows that in the end we settle on the more optimistic reading — it feels better — but even so the other has been a part of our experience, and because it has been a part of our experience, it *means*. What it means is that while we may be able to extract from the poem a statement affirming God's justice, we are not allowed to forget the evidence (of things seen) that makes the extraction so difficult (both for the speaker and for us). It is a difficulty we experience in the act of reading, even though a criticism which takes no account of that act has, as we have seen, suppressed it.

[3]It is first of all a reference to the city of iniquity from which the Hebrews are urged to flee in Isaiah and Jeremiah. In Protestant polemics Babylon is identified with the Roman Church whose destruction is prophesied in the book of Revelation. And in some Puritan tracts, Babylon is the name for Augustine's earthly city, from which the faithful are to flee inwardly in order to escape the fate awaiting the unregenerate. See *Variorum Commentary*, pp. 440–41. [Au.]

## II

In each of the sonnets we have considered, the significant word or phrase occurs at a line break where a reader is invited to place it first in one and then in another structure of syntax and sense. This moment of hesitation, of semantic or syntactic slide, is crucial to the experience the verse provides, but, in a formalist analysis, that moment will disappear, either because it has been flattened out and made into an (insoluble) interpretive crux, or because it has been eliminated in the course of a procedure that is incapable of finding value in temporal phenomena. In the case of "When I consider how my light is spent," these two failures are combined.

> When I consider how my light is spent,
>     Ere half my days, in this dark world and wide,
>     And that one talent which is death to hide,
>     Lodged with me useless, though my soul more bent
> To serve therewith my maker, and present
>     My true account, lest he returning chide,
>     Doth God exact day-labour, light denied,
>     I fondly ask; but Patience to prevent
> That murmur, soon replies, God doth not need
>     Either man's work or his own gifts, who best
>     Bear his mild yoke, they serve him best, his state
> Is kingly. Thousands at his bidding speed
>     And post o'er land and ocean without rest:
>     They also serve who only stand and wait.

The interpretive crux once again concerns the final line: "They also serve who only stand and wait." For some this is an unqualified acceptance of God's will, while for others the note of affirmation is muted or even forced. The usual kinds of evidence are marshaled by the opposing parties, and the usual inconclusiveness is the result. There are some areas of agreement. "All the interpretations," Woodhouse remarks, "recognize that the sonnet commences from a mood of depression, frustration [and] impatience."[4] The object of impatience is a God who would first demand service and then take away the means of serving, and the oft noted allusion to the parable of the talents lends scriptural support to the accusation the poet is implicitly making: you have cast the wrong servant into unprofitable darkness. It has also been observed that the syntax and rhythm of these early lines, and especially of lines 6–8, are rough and uncertain; the speaker

is struggling with his agitated thoughts and he changes directions abruptly, with no regard for the line as a unit of sense. The poem, says one critic, "seems almost out of control."[5]

The question I would ask is "whose control?"; for what these formal descriptions point to (but do not acknowledge) is the extraordinary number of adjustments required of readers who would negotiate these lines. The first adjustment is the result of the expectations created by the second half of line 6 — "lest he returning chide." Since there is no full stop after "chide," it is natural to assume that this will be an introduction to reported speech, and to assume further that what will be reported is the poet's anticipation of the voice of God as it calls him, to an unfair accounting. This assumption does not survive line 7 — "Doth God exact day-labour, light denied" — which rather than chiding the poet for his inactivity seems to rebuke him for having expected that chiding. The accents are precisely those heard so often in the Old Testament when God answers a reluctant Gideon, or a disputatious Moses, or a self-justifying Job: do you presume to judge my ways or to appoint my motives? Do you think I would exact day labor, light denied? In other words, the poem seems to turn at this point from a questioning of God to a questioning of that questioning; or, rather, the reader turns from the one to the other in the act of revising his projection of what line 7 will say and do. As it turns out, however, that revision must itself be revised because it had been made within the assumption that what we are hearing is the voice of God. This assumption falls before the very next phrase "I fondly ask," which requires not one, but two adjustments. Since the speaker of line 7 is firmly identified as the poet, the line must be reinterpreted as a continuation of his complaint — Is that the way you operate, God, denying light, but exacting labor? — but even as that interpretation emerges, the poet withdraws from it by inserting the adverb "fondly," and once again the line slips out of the reader's control.

In a matter of seconds, then, line 7 has led

[4]*Variorum Commentary,* p. 469. [Au.]

[5]Ibid., p. 457. [Au.]

four experiential lives, one as we anticipate it, another as that anticipation is revised, a third when we retroactively identify its speaker, and a fourth when that speaker disclaims it. What changes in each of these lives is the status of the poet's murmurings — they are alternately expressed, rejected, reinstated, and qualified — and as the sequence ends, the reader is without a firm perspective on the question of record: does God deal justly with his servants?

A firm perspective appears to be provided by Patience, whose entrance into the poem, the critics tell us, gives it both argumentative and metrical stability. But in fact the presence of Patience in the poem finally assures its continuing instability by making it impossible to specify the degree to which the speaker approves, or even participates in, the affirmation of the final line: "They also serve who only stand and wait." We know that Patience to prevent the poet's murmur soon replies (not soon enough however to prevent the murmur from registering), but we do not know when that reply ends. Does Patience fall silent in line 12, after "kingly"? or at the conclusion of line 13? or not at all? Does the poet appropriate these lines or share them or simply listen to them, as we do? These questions are unanswerable, and it is because they remain unanswerable that the poem ends uncertainly. The uncertainty is not in the statement it makes — in isolation line 14 is unequivocal — but in our inability to assign that statement to either the poet or to Patience. Were the final line marked unambiguously for the poet, then we would receive it as a resolution of his earlier doubts; and were it marked for Patience, it would be a sign that those doubts were still very much in force. It is marked for neither, and therefore we are without the satisfaction that a firmly conclusive ending (in *any* direction) would have provided. In short, we leave the poem unsure, and our unsureness is the realization (in our experience) of the unsureness with which the affirmation of the final line is, or is not, made. (This unsureness also operates to actualize the two possible readings of "wait": wait in the sense of expecting, that is waiting for an opportunity to serve actively; or wait in the sense of waiting *in* service, a waiting that is itself fully satisfying because

the impulse to self-glorifying action has been stilled.)

The question debated in the *Variorum Commentary* is, how far from the mood of frustration and impatience does the poem finally move? The answer given by an experiential analysis is that you can't tell, and the fact that you can't tell is responsible for the uneasiness the poem has always inspired. It is that uneasiness which the critics inadvertently acknowledge when they argue about the force of the last line, but they are unable to make analytical use of what they acknowledge because they have no way of dealing with or even recognizing experiential (that is, temporal) structures. In fact, more than one editor has eliminated those structures by punctuating them out of existence: first by putting a full stop at the end of line 6 and thereby making it unlikely that the reader will assign line 7 to God (there will no longer be an expectation of reported speech), and then by supplying quotation marks for the sestet in order to remove any doubts one might have as to who is speaking. There is of course no warrant for these emendations, and in 1791 Thomas Warton had the grace and honesty to admit as much. "I have," he said, "introduced the turned commas both in the question and answer, not from any authority, but because they seem absolutely necessary to the sense."[6]

## III

Editorial practices like these are only the most obvious manifestations of the assumptions to which I stand opposed: the assumption that there *is* a sense, that it is embedded or encoded in the text, and that it can be taken in at a single glance. These assumptions are, in order, positivist, holistic, and spatial, and to have them is to be committed both to a goal and to a procedure. The goal is to settle on a meaning, and the procedure involves first stepping back from the text, and then putting together or otherwise calculating the discrete units of significance it contains. My

[6]*Poems Upon Several Occasions, English, Italian, And Latin, With Translations, By John Milton,* ed. Thomas Warton (London, 1791), p. 352. [Au.]

quarrel with this procedure (and with the assumptions that generate it) is that in the course of following it through the reader's activities are at once ignored and devalued. They are ignored because the text is taken to be self-sufficient — everything is *in* it — and they are devalued because when they are thought of at all, they are thought of as the disposable machinery of extraction. In the procedures I would urge, the reader's activities are at the center of attention, where they are regarded, not as leading to meaning, but as *having* meaning. The meaning they have is a consequence of their not being empty; for they include the making and revising of assumptions, the rendering and regretting of judgments, the coming to and abandoning of conclusions, the giving and withdrawing of approval, the specifying of causes, the asking of questions, the supplying of answers, the solving of puzzles. In a word, these activities are interpretive — rather than being preliminary to questions of value they are at every moment settling and resettling questions of value — and because they are interpretive, a description of them will also be, and without any additional step, an interpretation, not after the fact, but of the fact (of experiencing). It will be a description of a moving field of concerns, at once wholly present (not waiting for meaning, but constituting meaning) and continually in the act of reconstituting itself.

As a project such a description presents enormous difficulties, and there is hardly time to consider them here;[7] but it should be obvious from my brief examples how different it is from the positivist-formalist project. Everything depends on the temporal dimension, and as a consequence the notion of a mistake, at least as something to be avoided, disappears. In a sequence where a reader first structures the field he inhabits and then is asked to restructure it (by

[7]See my *Surprised by Sin: The Reader* in Paradise Lost (London and New York, 1967); *Self-consuming Artifacts: The Experience of Seventeenth-Century Literature* (Berkeley, 1972); "What Is Stylistics and Why Are They Saying Such Terrible Things About It?" in *Approaches to Poetics*, ed. Seymour Chatman (New York, 1973), pp. 109–52; "How Ordinary Is Ordinary Language?" in *New Literary History* 5 (Autumn 1973): 41–54; "Facts and Fictions: A Reply to Ralph Rader," *Critical Inquiry* 1 (June 1975): 883–91. [Au.]

changing an assignment of speaker or realigning attitudes and positions) there is no question of priority among his structurings; no one of them, even if it is the last, has privilege; each is equally legitimate, each equally the proper object of analysis, because each is equally an event in his experience.

The firm assertiveness of this paragraph only calls attention to the questions it avoids. Who is this reader? How can I presume to describe his experiences, and what do I say to readers who report that they do not have the experiences I describe? Let me answer these questions or rather make a beginning at answering them in the context of another example, this time from Milton's *Comus*. In line 46 of *Comus* we are introduced to the villain by way of a genealogy:

Bacchus that first from out the purple grape,
Crushed the sweet poison of misused wine.

In almost any edition of this poem, a footnote will tell you that Bacchus is the god of wine. Of course most readers already know that, and because they know it, they will be anticipating the appearance of "wine" long before they come upon it in the final position. Moreover, they will also be anticipating a negative judgment on it, in part because of the association of Bacchus with revelry and excess, and especially because the phrase "sweet poison" suggests that the judgment has already been made. At an early point then, we will have both filled in the form of the assertion and made a decision about its moral content. That decision is upset by the word "misused": for what "misused" asks us to do is transfer the pressure of judgment from wine (where we have already placed it) to the abusers of wine, and therefore when "wine" finally appears, we must declare it innocent of the charges we have ourselves made.

This, then, is the structure of the reader's experience — the transferring of a moral label from a thing to those who appropriate it. It is an experience that depends on a reader for whom the name Bacchus has precise and immediate associations; another reader, a reader for whom those associations are less precise will not have that experience because he will not have rushed to a conclusion in relation to which the word "misused" will stand as a challenge. Obviously I am discriminating between these two readers and between the two equally real experiences they will have. It is not a discrimination based simply on information, because what is important is not the information itself, but the action of the mind which its possession makes possible for one reader and impossible for the other. One might discriminate further between them by noting that the point at issue — whether value is a function of objects and actions or of intentions — is at the heart of the seventeenth-century debate over "things indifferent." A reader who is aware of that debate will not only *have* the experience I describe; he will recognize at the end of it that he has been asked to take a position on one side of a continuing controversy; and that recognition (also a part of his experience) will be part of the disposition with which he moves into the lines that follow.

It would be possible to continue with this profile of the optimal reader, but I would not get very far before someone would point out that what I am really describing is the intended reader, the reader whose education, opinions, concerns, linguistic competencies, etc. make him capable of having the experience the author wished to provide. I would not resist this characterization because it seems obvious that the efforts of readers are always efforts to discern and therefore to realize (in the sense of becoming) an author's intention. I would only object if that realization were conceived narrowly, as the single act of comprehending an author's purpose, rather than (as I would conceive it) as the succession of acts readers perform in the continuing assumption that they are dealing with intentional beings. In this view discerning an intention is no more or less than understanding, and understanding includes (is constituted by) all the activities which make up what I call the structure of the reader's experience. To describe that experience is therefore to describe the reader's efforts at understanding, and to describe the reader's efforts at understanding is to describe his realization (in two senses) of an author's intention. Or to put it another way, what my analyses amount to are descriptions of a succession of decisions made by readers about an author's intention; de-

cisions that are not limited to the specifying of purpose but include the specifying of every aspect of successively intended words; decisions that are precisely the shape, because they are the content, of the reader's activities.

Having said this, however, it would appear that I am open to two objections. The first is that the procedure is a circular one. I describe the experience of a reader who in his strategies is answerable to an author's intention, and I specify the author's intention by pointing to the strategies employed by that same reader. But this objection would have force only if it were possible to specify one independently of the other. What is being specified from either perspective are the conditions of utterance, of what could have been understood to have been meant by what was said. That is, intention and understanding are two ends of a conventional act, each of which necessarily stipulates (includes, defines, specifies) the other. To construct the profile of the informed or at-home reader is at the same time to characterize the author's intention and vice versa, because to do either is to specify the *contemporary* conditions of utterance, to identify, by becoming a member of, a community made up of those who share interpretive strategies.

The second objection is another version of the first: if the content of the reader's experience is the succession of acts he performs in search of an author's intentions, and if he performs those acts at the bidding of the text, does not the text then produce or contain everything — intention *and* experience — and have I not compromised my antiformalist position? This objection will have force only if the formal patterns of the text are assumed to exist independently of the reader's experience, for only then can priority be claimed for them. Indeed, the claims of independence and priority are one and the same; when they are separated it is so that they can give circular and illegitimate support to each other. The question "do formal features exist independently?" is usually answered by pointing to their priority: they are "in" the text before the reader comes to it. The question "are formal features prior?" is usually answered by pointing to their independent status: they are "in" the text before the reader comes to it. What looks like a step in an argument is actually the spectacle of an assertion supporting itself. It follows then that an attack of the independence of formal features will also be an attack on their priority (and vice versa), and I would like to mount such an attack in the context of two short passages from *Lycidas*.

The first passage (actually the second in the poem's sequence) begins at line 42:

The willows and the hazel copses green
Shall now no more be seen,
Fanning their joyous leaves to thy soft lays.

(ll. 42–44)

It is my thesis that the reader is always making sense (I intend "making" to have its literal force), and in the case of these lines the sense he makes will involve the assumption (and therefore the creation) of a completed assertion after the word "seen," to wit, the death of Lycidas has so affected the willows and the hazel copses green that, in sympathy, they will wither and die (will no more be seen by *anyone*). In other words at the end of line 43 the reader will have hazarded an interpretation, or performed an act of perceptual closure, or made a decision as to what is being asserted. I do not mean that he has done four things, but that he has done one thing the description of which might take any one of four forms — making sense, interpreting, performing perceptual closure, deciding about what is intended. (The importance of this point will become clear later.) Whatever he has done (that is, however we characterize it) he will undo it in the act of reading the next line; for here he discovers that his closure, or making of sense, was premature and that he must make a new one in which the relationship between man and nature is exactly the reverse of what was first assumed. The willows and the hazel copses green will in fact be seen, but they will not be seen by Lycidas. It is he who will be no more, while they go on as before, fanning their joyous leaves to someone else's soft lays (the whole of line 44 is now perceived as modifying and removing the absoluteness of "seen"). Nature is not sympathetic, but indifferent, and the notion of her sympathy is one of those "false surmises" that the poem is continually encouraging and then disallowing.

The previous sentence shows how easy it is to surrender to the bias of our critical language and begin to talk as if poems, not readers or interpreters, did things. Words like "encourage" and "disallow" (and others I have used in this paper) imply agents, and it is only "natural" to assign agency first to an author's intentions and then to the forms that assumedly embody them. What really happens, I think, is something quite different: rather than intention and its formal realization producing interpretation (the "normal" picture), interpretation creates intention and its formal realization by creating the conditions in which it becomes possible to pick them out. In other words, in the analysis of these lines from *Lycidas* I did what critics always do: I "saw" what my interpretive principles permitted or directed me to see, and then I turned around and attributed what I had "seen" to a text and an intention. What my principles direct me to "see" are readers performing acts; the points at which I find (or to be more precise, declare) those acts to have been performed become (by a sleight of hand) demarcations *in* the text; those demarcations are then available for the designation "formal features," and as formal features they can be (illegitimately) assigned the responsibility for producing the interpretation which in fact produced them. In this case, the demarcation my interpretation calls into being is placed at the end of line 42; but of course the end of that (or any other) line is worth noticing or pointing out only because my model *demands* (the word is not too strong) perceptual closures and therefore locations at which they occur; in that model this point will be one of those locations, although (1) it needn't have been (not every line ending occasions a closure) and (2) in another model, one that does not give value to the activities of readers, the possibility of its being one would not have arisen.

What I am suggesting is that formal units are always a function of the interpretative model one brings to bear; they are not "in" the text, and I would make the same argument for intentions. That is, intention is no more embodied "in" the text than are formal units; rather an intention, like a formal unit, is made when perceptual or interpretive closure is hazarded; it is verified by an interpretive act, and I would add, it is not verifiable in any other way. This last assertion is too large to be fully considered here, but I can sketch out the argumentative sequence I would follow were I to consider it: intention is known when and only when it is recognized; it is recognized as soon as you decide about it; you decide about it as soon as you make a sense; and you make a sense (or so my model claims) as soon as you can.

Let me tie up the threads of my argument with a final example from *Lycidas:*

> He must not float upon his wat'ry bier
> Unwept . . .                                    (ll. 13–14)

Here the reader's experience has much the same career as it does in lines 42–44: at the end of line 13 perceptual closure is hazarded, and a sense is made in which the line is taken to be a resolution bordering on a promise: that is, there is now an expectation that something will be done about this unfortunate situation, and the reader anticipates a call to action, perhaps even a program for the undertaking of a rescue mission. With "Unwept," however, that expectation and anticipation are disappointed, and the realization of that disappointment will be inseparable from the making of a new (and less comforting) sense: nothing will be done; Lycidas will continue to float upon his wat'ry bier, and the only action taken will be the lamenting of the fact that no action will be efficacious, including the actions of speaking and listening to this lament (which in line 15 will receive the meretricious and self-mocking designation "melodious tear"). Three "structures" come into view at precisely the same moment, the moment when the reader having resolved a sense unresolves it and makes a new one; that moment will also be the moment of picking out a formal pattern or unit, end of line/beginning of line, and it will also be the moment at which the reader having decided about the speaker's intention, about what is meant by what has been said, will make the decision again and in so doing will make another intention.

This, then, is my thesis: that the form of the reader's experience, formal units, and the structure of intention are one, that they come into view simultaneously, and that therefore the ques-

tions of priority and independence do not arise. What does arise is another question: what produces *them?* That is, if intention, form, and the shape of the reader's experience are simply different ways of referring to (different perspectives on) the same interpretive act, what is that act an interpretation *of?* I cannot answer that question, but neither, I would claim, can anyone else, although formalists try to answer it by pointing to patterns and claiming that they are available independently of (prior to) interpretation. These patterns vary according to the procedures that yield them: they may be statistical (number of two-syllable words per hundred words), grammatical (ratio of passive to active constructions, or of right-branching to left-branching sentences, or of anything else); but whatever they are I would argue that they do not lie innocently in the world but are themselves constituted by an interpretive act, even if, as is often the case, that act is unacknowledged. Of course, this is as true of my analyses as it is of anyone else's. In the examples offered here I appropriate the notion "line ending" and treat it as a fact of nature; and one might conclude that as a fact it is responsible for the reading experience I describe. The truth I think is exactly the reverse: line endings exist by virtue of perceptual strategies rather than the other way around. Historically, the strategy that we know as "reading (or hearing) poetry" has included paying attention to the line as a unit, but it is precisely that attention which has made the line as a unit (either of print or of aural duration) available. A reader so practiced in paying that attention that he regards the line as a brute fact rather than as a convention will have a great deal of difficulty with concrete poetry; if he overcomes that difficulty, it will not be because he has learned to ignore the line as a unit but because he will have acquired a new set of interpretive strategies (the strategies constitutive of "concrete poetry reading") in the context of which the line as a unit no longer exists. In short, what is noticed is what has been *made* noticeable, not by a clear and undistorting glass, but by an interpretive strategy.

This may be hard to see when the strategy has become so habitual that the forms it yields seem part of the world. We find it easy to assume that alliteration as an effect depends on a "fact" that exists independently of any interpretive "use" one might make of it, the fact that words in proximity begin with the same letter. But it takes only a moment's reflection to realize that the sameness, far from being natural, is enforced by an orthographic convention; that is to say, it is the product of an interpretation. Were we to substitute phonetic conventions for orthographic ones (a "reform" traditionally urged by purists), the supposedly "objective" basis for alliteration would disappear because a phonetic transcription would require that we distinguish between the initial sounds of those very words that enter into alliterative relationships; rather than conforming to those relationships the rules of spelling make them. One might reply that, since alliteration is an aural rather than a visual phenomenon when poetry is heard, we have unmediated access to the physical sounds themselves and hear "real" similarities. But phonological "facts" are no more uninterpreted (or less conventional) than the "facts" of orthography; the distinctive features that make articulation and reception possible are the product of a system of differences that must be *imposed* before it can be recognized; the patterns the ear hears (like the patterns the eye sees) are the patterns its perceptual habits make available.

One can extend this analysis forever, even to the "facts" of grammar. The history of linguistics is the history of competing paradigms each of which offers a different account of the constituents of language. Verbs, nouns, cleft sentences, transformations, deep and surface structures, semes, rhemes, tagmemes — now you see them, now you don't, depending on the descriptive apparatus you employ. The critic who confidently rests his analyses on the bedrock of syntactic descriptions is resting on an interpretation; the facts he points to are there, but only as a consequence of the interpretive (man-made) model that has called them into being.

The moral is clear: the choice is never between objectivity and interpretation but between an interpretation that is unacknowledged as such and an interpretation that is at least aware of itself. It is this awareness that I am claiming for myself, although in doing so I must give up the

claims implicitly made in the first part of this paper. There I argue that a bad (because spatial) model has suppressed what was really happening, but by my own declared principles the notion "really happening" is just one more interpretation.

## IV

It seems then that the price one pays for denying the priority of either forms or intentions is an inability to say how it is that one ever begins. Yet we do begin, and we continue, and because we do there arises an immediate counter-objection to the preceding pages. If interpretive acts are the source of forms rather than the other way around, why isn't it the case that readers are always performing the same acts or a random succession of forms? How, in short, does one explain these two "facts" of reading?: (1) the same reader will perform differently when reading two "different" (the word is in quotation marks because its status is precisely what is at issue) texts; and (2) different readers will perform similarly when reading the "same" (in quotes for the same reason) text. That is to say, both the stability of interpretation among readers and the variety of interpretation in the career of a single reader would seem to argue for the existence of something independent of and prior to interpretive acts, something which produces them. I will answer this challenge by asserting that both the stability and the variety are functions of interpretive strategies rather than of texts.

Let us suppose that I am reading *Lycidas*. What is it that I am doing? First of all, what I am not doing is "simply reading," an activity in which I do not believe because it implies the possibility of pure (that is, disinterested) perception. Rather, I am proceeding on the basis of (at least) two interpretive decisions: (1) that *Lycidas* is a pastoral and (2) that it was written by Milton. (I should add that the notions "pastoral" and "Milton" are also interpretations; that is they do not stand for a set of indisputable, objective facts; if they did, a great many books would not now be getting written.) Once these decisions have been made (and if I had not made these I would have made others, and they would be consequential in the same way), I am immediately predisposed to perform certain acts, to "find," by looking for, themes (the relationship between natural processes and the careers of men, the efficacy of poetry or of any other action), to confer significances (on flowers, streams, shepherds, pagan deities), to mark out "formal" units (the lament, the consolation, the turn, the affirmation of faith, etc.). My disposition to perform these acts (and others; the list is not meant to be exhaustive) constitutes a set of interpretive strategies, which, when they are put into execution, become the large act of reading. That is to say, interpretive strategies are not put into execution after reading (the pure act of perception in which I do not believe); they are the shape of reading, and because they are the shape of reading, they give texts their shape, making them rather than, as it is usually assumed, arising from them. Several important things follow from this account:

1. I did not have to execute this particular set of interpretive strategies because I did not have to make those particular interpretive (prereading) decisions. I could have decided, for example, that *Lycidas* was a text in which a set of fantasies and defenses find expression. These decisions would have entailed the assumption of another set of interpretive strategies (perhaps like that put forward by Norman Holland in *The Dynamics of Literary Response*) and the execution of that set would have made another text.

2. I could execute this same set of strategies when presented with texts that did not bear the title (again a notion which is itself an interpretation) *Lycidas, A Pastoral Monody*. . . . I could decide (it is a decision some have made) that *Adam Bede* is a pastoral written by an author who consciously modeled herself on Milton (still remembering that "pastoral" and "Milton" are interpretations, not facts in the public domain); or I could decide, as Empson did, that a great many things not usually considered pastoral were in fact to be so read; and either decision would give rise to a set of interpretive strategies, which, when put into action, would *write* the text I write when reading *Lycidas*. (Are you with me?)

3. A reader other than myself who, when presented with *Lycidas,* proceeds to put into ex-

ecution a set of interpretive strategies similar to mine (how he could do so is a question I will take up later), will perform the same (or at least a similar) succession of interpretive acts. He and I then might be tempted to say that we agree about the poem (thereby assuming that the poem exists independently of the acts either of us performs); but what we really would agree about is the way to write it.

4. A reader other than myself who, when presented with *Lycidas* (please keep in mind that the status of *Lycidas* is what is at issue), puts into execution a different set of interpretive strategies will perform a different succession of interpretive acts. (I am assuming, it is the article of my faith, that a reader will always execute some set of interpretive strategies and therefore perform some succession of interpretive acts.) One of us might then be tempted to complain to the other that we could not possibly be reading the same poem (literary criticism is full of such complaints) and he would be right; for each of us would be reading the poem he had made.

The large conclusion that follows from these four smaller ones is that the notions of the "same" or "different" texts are fictions. If I read *Lycidas* and *The Waste Land* differently (in fact I do not), it will not be because the formal structures of the two poems (to term them such is also an interpretive decision) call forth different interpretive strategies but because my predisposition to execute different interpretive strategies will *produce* different formal structures. That is, the two poems are different because I have decided that they will be. The proof of this is the possibility of doing the reverse (that is why point 2 is so important). That is to say, the answer to the question "why do different texts give rise to different sequences of interpretive acts?" is that *they don't have to,* an answer which implies strongly that "they" don't exist. Indeed it has always been possible to put into action interpretive strategies designed to make all texts one, or to put it more accurately, to be forever making the same text. Augustine urges just such a strategy, for example, in *On Christian Doctrine* where he delivers the "rule of faith" which is of course a rule of interpretation. It is dazzlingly simple: everything in the Scriptures, and indeed in the world when it is properly read, points to (bears the meaning of) God's love for us and our answering responsibility to love our fellow creatures for His sake. If only you should come upon something which does not at first seem to bear this meaning, that "does not literally pertain to virtuous behavior or to the truth of faith," you are then to take it "to be figurative" and proceed to scrutinize it "until an interpretation contributing to the reign of charity is produced." This then is both a stipulation of what meaning there is and a set of directions for finding it, which is of course a set of directions — of interpretive strategies — for making it, that is, for the endless reproduction of the same text. Whatever one may think of this interpretive program, its success and ease of execution are attested to by centuries of Christian exegesis. It is my contention that any interpretive program, any set of interpretive strategies, can have a similar success, although few have been as spectacularly successful at this one. (For some time now, for at least three hundred years, the most successful interpretive program has gone under the name "ordinary language.") In our own discipline programs with the same characteristic of always reproducing one text include psychoanalytic criticism, Robertsonianism (always threatening to extend its sway into later and later periods), numerology (a sameness based on the assumption of innumerable fixed differences).

The other challenging question — "why will different readers execute the same interpretive strategy when faced with the 'same' text?" — can be handled in the same way. The answer is again that *they don't have to,* and my evidence is the entire history of literary criticism. And again this answer implies that the notion "same text" is the product of the possession by two or more readers of similar interpretive strategies.

But why should this ever happen? Why should two or more readers ever agree, and why should regular, that is, habitual, differences in the career of a single reader ever occur? What is the explanation on the one hand of the stability of interpretation (at least among certain groups at certain times) and on the other of the orderly variety of interpretation if it is not the stability and variety of texts? The answer to all of these questions is

to be found in a notion that has been implicit in my argument, the notion of *interpretive communities*. Interpretive communities are made up of those who share interpretive strategies not for reading (in the conventional sense) but for writing texts, for constituting their properties and assigning their intentions. In other words these strategies exist prior to the act of reading and therefore determine the shape of what is read rather than, as is usually assumed, the other way around. If it is an article of faith in a particular community that there are a variety of texts, its members will boast a repertoire of strategies for making them. And if a community believes in the existence of only one text, then the single strategy its members employ will be forever writing it. The first community will accuse the members of the second of being reductive, and they in turn will call their accusers superficial. The assumption in each community will be that the other is not correctly perceiving the "true text," but the truth will be that each perceives the text (or texts) its interpretive strategies demand and call into being. This, then, is the explanation both for the stability of interpretation among different readers (they belong to the same community) and for the regularity with which a single reader will employ different interpretive strategies and thus make different texts (he belongs to different communities). It also explains why there are disagreements and why they can be debated in a principled way: not because of a stability in texts, but because of a stability in the makeup of interpretive communities and therefore in the opposing positions they make possible. Of course this stability is always temporary (unlike the longed for and timeless stability of the text). Interpretive communities grow larger and decline, and individuals move from one to another; thus while the alignments are not permanent, they are always there, providing just enough stability for the interpretive battles to go on, and just enough shift and slippage to assure that they will never be settled. The notion of interpretive communities thus stands between an impossible ideal and the fear which leads so many to maintain it. The ideal is of perfect agreement and it would require texts to have a status independent of interpretation. The fear is of interpretive anarchy, but it would only be realized if interpretation (text making) were completely random. It is the fragile but real consolidation of interpretive communities that allows us to talk to one another, but with no hope or fear of ever being able to stop.

In other words interpretive communities are no more stable than texts because interpretive strategies are not natural or universal, but *learned*. This does not mean that there is a point at which an individual has not yet learned any. The ability to interpret is not acquired; it is constitutive of being human. What is acquired are the ways of interpreting and those same ways can also be forgotten or supplanted, or complicated or dropped from favor ("no one reads that way anymore"). When any of these things happens, there is a corresponding change in texts, not because they are being read differently, but because they are being written differently.

The only stability, then, inheres in the fact (at least in my model) that interpretive strategies are always being deployed, and this means that communication is a much more chancy affair than we are accustomed to think it. For if there are no fixed texts, but only interpretive strategies making them; and if interpretive strategies are not natural, but learned (and are therefore unavailable to a finite description), what is it that utterers (speakers, authors, critics, me, you) do? In the old model utterers are in the business of handing over ready made or prefabricated meanings. These meanings are said to be encoded, and the code is assumed to be in the world independently of the individuals who are obliged to attach themselves to it (if they do not they run the danger of being declared deviant). In my model, however, meanings are not extracted but made and made not by encoded forms but by interpretive strategies that call forms into being. It follows then that what utterers do is give hearers and readers the opportunity to make meanings (and texts) by inviting them to put into execution

a set of strategies. It is presumed that the invitation will be recognized, and that presumption rests on a projection on the part of a speaker or author of the moves *he* would make if confronted by the sounds or marks he is uttering or setting down.

It would seem at first that this account of things simply reintroduces the old objection; for isn't this an admission that there is after all a formal encoding, not perhaps of meanings, but of the directions for making them, for executing interpretive strategies? The answer is that they will only *be* directions to those who already have the interpretive strategies in the first place. Rather than producing interpretive acts, they are the product of one. An author hazards his projection, not because of something "in" the marks, but because of something he assumes to be in his reader. The very existence of the "marks" is a function of an interpretive community, for they will be recognized (that is, made) only by its members. Those outside that community will be deploying a different set of interpretive strategies (interpretation cannot be withheld) and will therefore be making different marks.

So once again I have made the text disappear, but unfortunately the problems do not disappear with it. If everyone is continually executing interpretive strategies and in that act constituting texts, intentions, speakers, and authors, how can any one of us know whether or not he is a member of the same interpretive community as any other of us? The answer is that he can't, since any evidence brought forward to support the claim would itself be an interpretation (especially if the "other" were an author long dead). The only "proof" of membership is fellowship, the nod of recognition from someone in the same community, someone who says to you what neither of us could ever prove to a third party: "we know." I say it to you now, knowing full well that you will agree with me (that is, understand) only if you already agree with me.

# David Bleich

b. 1940

*David Bleich was born in New York City in 1940 and educated at the Massachusetts Institute of Technology and at New York University, where he received his Ph.D. in 1968. Since then Bleich has taught at Indiana University, where he is now full professor. Bleich is the author of articles on More's* Utopia *and James's* The Golden Bowl, *but his major work, which began to appear in the form of essays in* College English *in the late 1960s and early 1970s, is an ongoing study of the social psychology of the reading process. His pragmatic program for teaching students both about literature and about themselves was published as* Readings and Feelings *(1975); his theoretical discussion of the subjective and psychological character of the reading process appeared as* Subjective Criticism *(1978). His most recent book is* Utopia: The Psychology of a Cultural Fantasy *(1984).*

## Feelings about Literature

### INTRODUCTION: THE SUBJECTIVE ORIENTATION

Once a person has seen his responses in action in a general way and how they are constantly functioning, literature becomes less a subject he learns in school than a special opportunity to engage the emotions and thoughts foremost in his mind. Most people believe they know exactly what literature is; they believe they can recognize it when they see it even if they can't articulate a "definition." One of the results of exploring the feelings that arise in response to a single sentence written on the blackboard is that the assumed sense of what constitutes literature is called into question. The "itness" or objectivity of the actual phrase on the board loses its force. Norman Holland, in *The Dynamics of Literary Response*, performs a small experiment in order to demonstrate what is meant by "the willing suspension of disbelief." He quotes a prose passage that could pass for either history or literature and then asks his reader to examine the difference between what went on in his mind when he thought it was history versus what went on when he thought it was literature. Holland does not explore anyone's actual response, but he does report that he himself feels much more relaxed mentally when he reads the passage as literature. His conclusion is

that "it is the expectation we bring to the paragraph that determines the degree to which . . . we test it for the truth." While Holland's distinction between the search for truth and the search for relaxed pleasure is important, another finding, implicit in his experiment, is of particular interest to our discussion. That is, *it is the reader who determines whether a piece of writing is literature*. Sometimes, in practice, this mental act is not necessary because we believe it when we are told that a certain work is literature. But this only means that someone else decided it was literature, and we, by our own mental act, agreed that the previous act will also be our own. Our point is that a piece of writing *becomes* literature as a result of a subjective decision that it is literature. If you suspect that this may be a tautological point, just think of the Bible. Some read this book as if it were literature, some as if it were history, and some as if it were God's word. The only thing that all readers can agree on about the Bible is that it is a book. Obviously this is a rather trivial agreement, and the question of what the book is "essentially" is altogether determined by the individuals and groups of individuals who read the book and react to it.

To be sure, one does not spend much time thinking about whether a poem is a poem. The relevance of our private decision that it is a poem is that we are once again reminded that the essence of a symbolic work is not in its visible sensory structure or in its manifest semantic load but in its subjective re-creation by a reader and in his public presentation of that re-creation. We will explore this re-creation by dividing it into three phases — perception, affective response, and associative response.

## PERCEIVING THE WORK

In examining different modes of perception we will study an exercise frequently performed in introductory literature classes. We will study the work of seven students of a class that was asked to "say what the poem says" in their own prose. As a rule, exercises such as this, as well as the kind of investigations carried out by I. A. Richards in *Practical Criticism,* aim to point out *mistakes* in reading. This, of course, will not be our goal. Our aim, rather, will be to try to understand the patterns of perceptual emphasis in each reader and to suggest how these patterns will be relevant in understanding the reader's larger patterns of response and judgment. There are some who will say that retelling a poem in any other words but its own does some kind of violence to the poem. However, since we do not assume the inviolability of a poem beyond maintenance of the text, and since we further believe that the simple act of reading produces a subjective change in the text, we may reasonably assume that the prose presentation of a poem represents the reader's subjective perception of it.

A Drumlin Woodchuck

One thing has a shelving bank,
Another a rotting plank,
To give it cozier skies
And make up for its lack of size.

My own strategic retreat
Is where two rocks almost meet,
And still more secure and snug,
A two-door burrow I dug.

With those in mind at my back
I can sit forth exposed to attack
And one who shrewdly pretends
That he and the world are friends.

All we who prefer to live
Have a little whistle we give,

And flash, at the least alarm
We dive down under the farm.

We allow some time for guile
And don't come out for a while
Either to eat or drink.
We take occasion to think.

And if after the hunt goes past
And the double-barreled blast
(Like war and pestilence
And the loss of common sense),

If I can with confidence say
That still for another day,
Or even another year,
I will be there for you, my dear,

It will be because, though small
As measured against the All,
I have been so instinctively thorough
About my crevice and burrow.

Consider the following restatements of the poem.

A.   In order to feel secure, many animals find themselves a hiding place. Some choose a shelflike river bank, while others choose a piece of rotting timber. My own retreat is a burrow between two rocks which almost touch one another. I dug the burrow myself and made two entrances to it. I always know that there is a safe place just behind me, so I can sit out in the open and pretend as if I'm not afraid of anything. But when any of us hear the danger signal from the other animals, we each scurry to our own hiding places. Then we sit and wait, thinking about the games of life and death until the hunters pass by. I think of my shelter and my safety from day to day, and year to year, and I know that the tiny little hole that I have made so naturally is the only reason that I go on living.

B.   Small animals are constantly in danger; we depend on our instinct to keep alive. One safety measure is our homes — our nests or burrows. Some of us find niches and crannies in banks of earth, others build on rotten boards or other debris left by man. Since we're too small to stand up and fight man face to face, and our legs are too short to get away from dogs, we must hide to protect ourselves. We rely on our burrows for safety. We tunnel into the earth. Here, surrounded by the ground on all sides, we feel at home and safe.

For my own home, I chose a special spot. It is easily accessible in case of danger, yet hidden from normal view. Only I know that the two rocks that almost touch mark the path to my burrow. Besides being well hidden, my burrow itself goes far into the ground. The intricate tunnels keep me close and safe. If a dog does smell me out and finds my hole, and even if he's small enough to fit down, I can still escape — I've dug a secret rear exit for just such emergencies.

Knowing I've planned well and my burrow is a good retreat, I can go about my business in full view. I can pretend to be careless and nonchalant. But if danger is really imminent, the others and I have a signal — we give a shrill whistle as soon as any of us senses danger. When the warning sounds, we dive for our burrows — and safety. We do not come out — not for food or water or anything — until we are positive all danger is passed. Wisely, we wait.

And if after the dogs and hunters and noise of guns and whine of bullets have all died out, if I am again passed over and left alive, it is because (although I'm a small and insignificant creature of God's world) I planned my hideaway carefully and I am prepared for trouble.

C.     Everything on earth has some means, no matter how crude, of securing its comfort and protection. As for myself, I have cleverly devised a twofold plan of protection. My little retreat, in the first place, is well hidden by its natural surroundings; secondly, I have two entrances to the place, making an escape quite easy if necessary.

With the knowledge that I am secure against any danger presented by the world, I can appear to be brave by exposing myself to almost any danger. I know I am well protected, but other people don't and think me quite courageous.

Let me tell you about my strategy — mine and my friends who choose to live as I do. If any one of us detects danger, he warns the rest of us. We then retreat from the outside world and the danger, remaining secure and comfortable in our various burrows. We are smart enough to remain withdrawn until the danger is completely gone. We're really very clever about the whole thing.

Yet, when the danger passes, whatever it may have been — natural or manmade — if I am well and can hope to live a little longer, I owe it to one thing: my shrewdness. You see, I may be small in comparison with the rest of the world, but it's not my physical size that counts. Instead, it's my mental size, my capacity to be clever in living my life, that really adds up to something.

For accuracy, these are all rather good restatements. They speak in the speaker's voice and

they cover a significant part of the factual material in the original. If we so desired, we could say fairly easily that these three respondents perceived the poem "correctly." As we will see, however, this is not altogether true, and the mistakes and distortions in each restatement add up to a personal expression of style.

Response A is relatively spare and concentrates on the speaker's logic. Almost all of the particulars in the poem are omitted — the rotting plank, the farm, war and pestilence, the whistle, for example. More importantly, however, almost all of the important feelings are also omitted — coziness, security, confidence, shrewdness, alarm. The poem is restated as if it were a report. There is an emphasis on what the speaker knows about himself and his burrow. Such omissions do not necessarily represent inaccuracies of perception. On the contrary, they represent the perception of a particular train of thought — "this is a poem about the speaker's quiet understanding of how to remain safe and live long" — something *we have also seen* in the poem. For this reason, the restatement seems accurate. Even the brevity of the restatement should be taken as a representation of the brevity and concision of thought this respondent gets from the poem. We may say that this particular reader was disposed to selecting this logical, concise element in the poem as representing his own response. There does remain one further important omission in this restatement, made by the other two in this series as well, but we will return to it subsequently.

Response B differs significantly from A not simply in its more discursive presentation, but also in the fact that it inserts details that are not literally to be found in the poem. Such a restatement may seem more obviously revealing of subjective perception, but it is not in fact either more or less subjective. This respondent suggests a particular fear — of dogs — that is not found in the poem. Further, B explains that the speaker's fear of dogs comes from the fact that he thinks his legs are too short to escape from them. The dogs even may smell the speaker out of his hole, and they are accompanying a hunting party which poses the overall threat. B inserts other interesting details — she explains the burrows as another kind of nest; she says that some of the animals find "niches" in the banks of the earth and that homes are sometimes made in "other debris left by man." She then inserts the explicit fear of "fight[ing] man face to face," and adds that the safety of the burrow derives from its being "surrounded by ground on all sides." Then, the "almost touch[ing]" rocks "mark the path" to the burrow — which they do not do in the poem. The whole presentation of the dog smelling out the speaker is embellished by the thought that the dog may even be small enough to fit down the hole. Finally, the poem's "little whistle" is converted by B into a "shrill whistle." Our question is, Is there any pattern in these interesting additions to the poem? I think we may say that respondent B enlarged the poem in ways analogous to how respondent A narrowed its focus. B made the poem into a more dramatic experience. The speaker here is more conscious of his own weakness, of the fact that the threats are coming from particular sources of great strength. Man is in the picture prominently — accordingly, the need for safety is greater — "surrounded by ground on all sides." For the same reason, the little whistle becomes "shrill." Altogether, B "sees" the perilous elements in the story much more prominently than A and senses a more immediate, more precarious situation being recounted by the speaker. The added details, therefore, cannot be seen as "errors." They express an element in the poem on which I think many would agree: a sense in which the speaker is not all that logical and calm and is in fact involved in a rather important and crucial drama.

In contrast, C emphasizes the speaker's self-satisfaction with regard to his cleverness and employs a different set of insertions and exaggerations. We should immediately note that the word "clever" does not appear in this poem, even though it becomes an important element in C's restatement. The poem does mention shrewdness, guile, and confidence, but even so the emphasis placed by C on cleverness is an exaggeration. For example, C translates "my own strategic retreat" as "I have cleverly devised," thus inserting the element of self-congratulation where the original was less personal. In her second paragraph C attributes to the speaker a

thought about "other people," which also does not appear explicitly in the poem. C transfers the term "strategy" to the account of the contingency plan and then translates, "we allow some time for guile" (this refers presumably to expected deceit on the part of the threatening agency) as "we are smart enough to remain withdrawn." That is, the smartness mentioned in the poem is transferred to the speaker, and then C adds the additional superfluous comment, "We're really very clever about the whole thing." Finally, in her last paragraph, the speaker's profession of confidence and of instinctive thoroughness is translated as "my shrewdness," "my mental size," and "my capacity to be clever." Here again, the respondent transfers a word used earlier in the poem to a situation she later sees. This transference demonstrates how we allow a poem to create a mood in us: we automatically apply earlier images we had to later situations.

C's stress on mental capacity resembles A's restatement in that the stress is on the control or the victory of the speaker. The causes of the particular form these emphases take are personal. However, not only the exaggerations or additions are rooted in personal factors. The entire perception of the poem is so rooted, where the exaggerations serve as signals of these roots. There can be any number of reasons why these respondents picked out the things they did, but one of these reasons may be that none of the three cared to include in their perception a reference to the line, "I will be there for you, my dear," which suggests that the whole poem is an address to someone "dear" to the speaker, perhaps a lover. This is precisely the way two other respondents perceived this poem — completely informed by this one line:

D.  Hello Dear,
    As you probably know in this place of unrest, most of us need some sort of shelter of one kind or another to make our world a little more secure. It is a necessary precaution which the foolish ones refuse to realize to make up for our small stature. Several of my neighbors provided themselves with old rotten boards; a couple of others decided on the bank.
    However, I wish you could see my place that I finally found. I don't think anything else could beat

it. It is isolated in the woods between two rocks. For days, I have been working carving an entrance and an exit. I cannot tell you what a difference it makes just knowing that it is there. Sometimes when I get bored, I play this game. I sit on the outside, pretending I do not know that the hunter is there until the last second. I try to look very nonchalant like I am somehow above it all. I assume the air that everything is best in the best of all possible worlds. Yet, I cannot wait too long. I sure would hate to be a dead woodchuck. When I get too scared I whistle to calm myself, then I dash into my shelter. Since it is not easy to tell if I am still being hunted, I stay there for quite a long time devoting my time to contemplating the issues of the day.

I especially try to figure out why the hunter with the double-barreled shotgun is so quick to kill. I can never come up with any other solution than that he is evil, like war, disease, and madness.

All my confidence against danger rests in my burrow. If I keep alive from day to day or year to year, it is because I have equipped myself well. Now neither food nor drink seems to me more important. A refuge is the most important thing in the world, it is the only defense against humans that I know.

Well, remember I will always be here waiting for you.

Love, Me

E. God! You know, sometimes I get so fed up with people and the way they act and with the world and all its troubles that I just want to get away from it all. Kind of crawl into a hole like a groundhog does. I suppose a nice sloping hill I could hide behind or an old, rotted plank I could sort of crouch on would serve my purpose. But a hole's a little more secure, more snug somehow.

I don't know exactly what I'd do with my hole. I guess just sit around and wait till some unpleasant, personal something-or-other happened. Then I'd kind of jump into the hole head first and just sit. At first I'd think about apple pie or my first really nice kiss or some other nice-to-think-about thing. But I'd probably wind up thinking about what had driven me into my hole this time. I'd plan cunning deeds of how I could get back at my oppressors.

And then, after my moment of treacherous thoughts had passed, after I'd regained my common sense (the loss of which I would dutifully blame on the outside world, of course), I'd try to go back

to pleasant thoughts. And if I could do this, these thoughts would no longer be of pies and kisses, but they'd be thoughts of YOU, my dear.

I feel that if time and time again I can emerge from my hole a sound and whole member of this human race, this vast universe, and be there for YOU, if I can do this much, it is only because I have been so instinctively thorough about my crevice and burrow.

D's conception of the poem as a love note includes so many extra details that it does not pay to point them out individually. The overall sense of the note is the consciousness of intimate conversation, which D inserts *before* the actual text of the transcription, although in the poem one does not become aware of this intimacy until the end. For the first three respondents this end-placement seemed to diminish its importance, whereas D and E take the line as a defining characteristic. This demonstrates the sense in which the perception of the poem is a subjective reconstruction rather than a simple recording of facts. D also must have responded with a feeling of love, since that is what she makes explicit, in the final signature. Pursuant to this conception, D views the material of the poem almost as an invitation by the speaker to his beloved to join him in "my place that I finally found," while we observe that in the poem, the speaker makes no reference to having searched for and "finally found" the right place. While the dominant theme of personal security is retained in the note, it is portrayed on the one hand as "the only defense against humans that I know" and, on the other, as the means that allow the speaker to be "always" waiting for his beloved. This sense of eternity is likewise not found in the poem. While the phrase "defense against humans" is probably a simple sign of woodchuck identity, the context of the note also suggests it to be a defense against other people, which, in a standard critical interpretation of the poem as a comic allegory, would enter as a prominent fact, linked up with the allusion to war, pestilence, and common sense.

Interestingly, the warning whistle in the poem is altogether misinterpreted as being whistling "to calm myself." This error is part of the overall exaggerated sense of amorous privacy perceived by the respondent. Accordingly, the other animals alluded to in the opening of the poem become "neighbors" in this transcription, suggesting a community more intimate than a group of animals who merely suffer a common threat. This emphasis on private coziness and community completely replaces the speaker's prominent self-congratulation for his own cleverness, which so stood out for respondent C. The only such reference is to the "foolish ones" who do not realize what precautions they must take in order to make up for their small size. Even here, the thought of self-congratulation is minimized and in no way constitutes gloating over the others.

The distortion in respondent E's restatement reaches an even greater level of generality. Though the love theme appears, here toward the end and thus more like the poem, the feeling of interpersonal conversation transforms the literal sense of the poem directly into the allegorical, and the woodchuck's conversation is framed as a mere simile: "Kind of crawl into a hole like a groundhog does." Here again it is likely that the opening lines of E's restatement are taken from a response to material found toward the end of the poem — the speaker's analogy citing war, pestilence, and loss of common sense.[1] However, this transference emphasizes the human reality that E sees in the poem. To E, to her feelings, that is, the woodchuck imagery is ancillary or merely illustrative, as if there were no question at all in her mind that the human situation is primary. In the service of this certainty, a complete fabrication enters the restatement in the form of "apple pie or my first really nice kiss." Here too we see the influence of the perceptions of the end of the poem on the restatements of the beginning. In the third paragraph another important fabrication enters in the service of this primary perception: E attributes the loss of common sense to herself — or to the speaker — and declares the speaker's perception of this loss to be his projection onto the outside world. In the

poem, of course, as most readers agreed, the loss of common sense is definitely taking place in the world outside the woodchuck. This interpolation, therefore, suggests that the speaker felt a personal guilt in addition to his impatience with the troubles of the world. E then has the speaker conquer this guilt and reject the lesser thoughts of pies and kisses and return in capital letters to "YOU." Finally, E fabricates a transcendental vision of the whole affair, to "emerge . . . a sound and whole member of this human race, this vast universe, and be there for YOU. . . ."

Let me again stress that these distortions are not errors. Rather, they are personal embellishments of something which E perceived in the poem and which most professional critics would agree is there. In following instructions to write about what the poem says, E felt freest to present what she actually *felt* it to say. Many students, in commenting on their own transcriptions, said that they felt it was just not possible to relay all the feelings they thought were "in" the poem. E did not offer such an apology and we can surmise why: she added many details of her own, details that she sensed were there while reading. These, for her, were no less important than the "real" parts of the poem, which she distorted and exaggerated, since they were the source of her real feeling.

Consider now two final restatements which demonstrate yet different perceptual attitudes:

F.  It is strange and yet awe inspiring what the smarter of the human race can learn from the animal world.

The smaller species of animals seem to have a natural instinct for self-preservation. Some of them can use a shelving bank or a rotting plank as camouflage instead of immenseness for protection. A somewhat wiser animal, the woodchuck, uses his ability to burrow to fashion escape routes when danger approaches. He sits near these routes as if he were really exposed, ready to flee the moment the alarm is sounded by a lookout. He certainly isn't stupid enough to stick around and enter into a dangerous situation or even watch it, but waits in his refuge until all signs of danger pass — signs such as war, pestilence, or loss of common sense, common among man.

If man stays alive for another year, against the

---

[1] I call attention to the natural tendency of readers to see the work in terms of one overriding thought they perceive in the poem and then to reconstruct the poem according to this thought. . . . [Au.]

"dangers" he can create, it is only because he has built safeguards against danger, as the woodchuck builds burrows. Man too is small compared to the dangers surrounding him, but he too can learn to build crevices for protection.

G.    Everyone needs one place to which he can go for a little solitude, for a little security, from the anxieties that swirl around him. Maybe there is a need to really hide from danger, and maybe it is only a need to have a place to sit and think, to ponder over the dynamism around him. But either way, there is a need for a personal place to go. It follows that old adage: "A man's home is his castle." It implies privacy. It implies security. It hints that a man needs a place to call his own, to which he can retreat. In his own fortress, whether large or small, he can sit and watch, and think about what's "out there" and how it will affect him.

And it doesn't really matter where his retreat is, or how it is built. It need not be complicated and complex. Nor need it be elaborate. The security it affords is not in its design; it is the suitability that counts. One man might indeed need a castle. Another might find his "castle" in one small room. Yet another will find that perfect reflection can be found on a garden path — alone and undisturbed. It matters not where that castle is, or what it really looks like. It is the sense of security that is important, and when that security is felt, when a man can step back for a moment and take a look at the outside from the in, and yet have a feeling of assurance of his position, he has a real castle.

This personal place can be pretty important to a man. There are often certain danger signals that tell him it is time for a retreat into seclusion from the world around him. There is no one signal; every man has his own. For some it may take the form of tension, or anxiety. For others it may be an inability to understand or combat the forces that affect him. Real fear of something, too, can be the signal. Regardless of what that signal is, he knows it and hears it, and when he does, it's time to make haste for the retreat. Now is the occasion, and there is the place, to think and reflect. Let the others pass by the castle. It is time for him to turn and enter it.

He would be at no small disadvantage did he not have this place of retreat. But in it he has a sort of friend. His castle compensates for some things he may be lacking — immediate self-assurance, quickness in decision, and so on. But when he hears the danger signal and can take a step back

and pause, and look, at ease in the comfort and security of his castle, he is able to see things more clearly, to reason more logically. Without his refuge he might indeed be in real trouble. The castle might be thought of as a movie house. When he finds himself in trouble — real trouble — it is to his theater he goes and, alone, snaps on the projector. Here he can really focus in.

I place these two restatements in a religious or philosophical category, since their reflective moods contrast with the more emotional senses present in the other restatements. The important feature of these renditions is that one cannot locate a single line in the poem from which these can be said to "take off." The centers of emphasis here are on the interpretive abstraction itself. Respondent F views the poem as a homily on the human instinct for self-preservation and uses the woodchuck's situation as a kind of scriptural text for the homily. Even the presentation of this text is in the service of the homily. The characterization of the woodchuck as a "wiser animal" is the respondent's own interpolated detail, since the speaker of the poem does not in fact call himself wiser than the other animals. The restatement also shifts the poem from the first to the third person and without explicit notice says that the protagonist of the poem is mankind and not the woodchuck, a kind of shift which helps create the homiletic mood. The contrast between what is wise and what is "stupid" calls attention to what mankind "can learn" (a phrase used twice in the restatement) from the animals, rather than to an element in the woodchuck's personal sense of self-congratulation. Finally, in what is perhaps the one line used as a take-off point, F finds in the "war, pestilence, and the loss of common sense" proof that man is the subject here, since these are "common among man." This homiletic mood is what this respondent sees that the poem *actually says* and is not given as a reinterpretation. Again, this is not an error, but an important form of individuated perception created by the particular biases of the reader.

G's restatement is obviously the most radically distorted of all. In a case like this, there is very little doubt that the individual's preoccupations interfered with perception. Our question is, however, whether this is really an interference. All of the abstractions, which make almost no reference to the actual words of the poem, do in fact refer to particular parts of the poem, and G's restatement follows it just as the others do.

G creates his own theme — "a man's home is his castle" — and manipulates its specified meaning according to what he thinks he sees in the poem. The choice of possible refuges found in the poem, for example, is translated in G's second paragraph into his own set of choices — a "small room" or a "garden path." The overall mood of the restatement is reflective rather than homiletic, and the main thought of each paragraph is redundant. The first paragraph is the need itself; the second, the irrelevance of what form the castle is; the third, the nature of its importance; and the fourth, its use as a refuge. The only word in this restatement whose idea is taken from the poem is "signal," which the respondent enlarges considerably from its original use. In general G sees the poem in a metonymical relationship to a much larger reality: it is to him but a minor example of a major concern of his own life. While it is true that G does not say that this is his own concern, I cannot otherwise explain his elaborate effort to make his ideas clear. G is trying, harder than most of the respondents, to make clear what is in his own mind. The metaphorical nature of G's restatement demonstrates its personal nature, as well as G's own eagerness to take advantage of this assignment to express himself. Under normal circumstances, this respondent might be setting himself up for a torrent of criticism, with an invidious comparison between his work and that of, say, respondent A. From our standpoint, however, it is far more important to note that both G and A failed to take into account that one line, "I will be there for you, my dear."

Although one cannot say for sure, one can almost tell the reasons for the omission — in A's case, an excessive detachment from the poem, and in G's case, an excessive eagerness to appropriate the poem to some larger preoccupation of his own. The content of the line would bear this supposition out: it tells of a close relationship between the speaker and his hearer, and neither

respondent, for the reasons I have suggested, was able to perceive this relationship. Their own frames of mind at the time of reading did not allow this particular perception.

In class it is important to resist the temptation to criticize such restatements, and instead to emphasize two particular things. First, that each respondent does "see" something in the poem that everyone else can also see is "there." Second, that each person has a special way of seeing that something, which gives it its own personalized character, so that it could be called a "distortion." But this is just the word that should be avoided. This "distortion" is not that, but is instead an expression of personal style and concern. Each respondent should be alerted to his particular style of perception and should be urged to ask himself, Why do I think I saw the poem in just this way? Is there anything I know about myself that might explain this particular kind of perception? The respondent, in other words, should be asked to objectify himself deliberately, to look at his own work as an object in this disciplined context. The motive is created because *his own* work is the object of examination, while the whole question of a grade evaluation is rendered irrelevant.

The so-called "mistakes" are part of an individual's perceptual style, just as are the omissions, the exaggerations, and the superfluous material that almost everyone will insert. The purpose of having everyone resay the poem is not to see that prose can't say what verse can say, or even that another person can't say exactly what Frost said. These things should be so obvious that they are hardly worth spending time on. The purpose, rather, is to understand how and why each person sees differently. Most people do already know that each sees differently, but few are willing to look into the question of how and why this is the case.

## THE AFFECTIVE RESPONSE

The second level of feeling, so to speak, is an affective response. Here the respondent, more than just telling what he sees in the poem or what he thinks the poet says (though this kind of information inevitably is used), describes the actual affect he felt while reading the poem. Consider Robert Frost's "Away!" and two affective responses to it.

### Away!

Now I out walking
The world desert,
And my shoe and my stocking
Do me no hurt.

I leave behind
Good friends in town.
Let them get well-wined
And go lie down.

Don't think I leave
For the outer dark
Like Adam and Eve
Put out of the Park

Forget the myth.
There is no one I
Am put out with
Or put out by.

Unless I'm wrong
I but obey
The urge of a song:
I'm — bound — away!

And I may return
If dissatisfied
With what I learn
From having died.

H. Upon reading the first five stanzas of this poem, I felt an identification with the speaker. His sense of adventure and individualism pushed him out of the confines of ordinary existence and I admired his sense of freedom. It was like a compulsion to leave the familiar and find answers to searching questions among the unfamiliar. However, as I reached the last stanza and realized that the speaker's journey was one into death, I became sad. Since there is no physical return from death, the speaker could not relate his discoveries to anyone. Although death may be an adventure, it is not one to be shared with those left behind. Therefore, my feelings after reading the entire poem are somewhat uncertain since they would tend to sway two different directions if the poem was entirely as it seemed from the beginning or if it followed the same tone as the last stanza throughout.

I. "Away!" by Robert Frost makes me feel that the poet is a man who is free of those inhibitions that might make someone else feel guilty at leaving home for a simple change of scene. This feeling is a good one, because when I read this poem, I know how it would feel to be free of guilt in doing something unconventional — just to walk off to a new place. Frost has made his leaving of his friends to go to a new place very attractive; it seems that he is not relieved to be going, but that he is glad to be himself doing what he is doing. I felt, along with Frost, no regret at leaving because he has left no scores to settle, ahead or behind him, in his journey. This sense of freedom that I detect in the poem is hard to precisely define — I feel the urge to wander to new places with the poet; I want to share the satisfaction at having set out anew with a healthy satisfaction at what I am doing. That feeling of no regrets for anything done in the past that I find in the poem gives me a sense of continuity — there is no finality in what Frost is doing. The past, I feel, is not lost, but can be regained by coming back to it. But the poet is not unaware that change will occur; he is free of worrying that things won't be satisfactory; he just wants to wander around with himself and think for a while. Frost's wanting to do this, and having the courage to do it, even in a poem, evoked my admiration; it makes me glad that this sort of freedom exists; it made me feel good. And, I'm glad that Frost said that he had died by leaving this place, because leaving for somewhere else is probably all that death is, and no one ever said that he isn't free to come back. The freedom is the good feeling and the solidity of this poem.

These two responses represent two different degrees of affective involvement. Response H is about as rudimentary as one can get and still offer an affective report. There are only three personal statements of rather limited scope: "I felt an identification with the speaker," "I admired his sense of freedom," and "I became sad." In the first statement the feeling is hardly even named, though one might infer it from reading the poem. The second statement might help explain the first, though one wonders if admiration for someone else's sense of freedom amounts to an identification with that person. And the last statement shows a change of mood from a hopeful one to a depressed one. It is important to see these statements as interconnected. The identification with the speaker is actually an identification with what is perceived as the speaker's wish for freedom. For the respondent this wish is defeated by the last stanza, and so she is "sad" as a result of this relatively simple frustration. The affects reported by this respondent are not elaborated with further affect or analogy, but with a presumably rational explanation based on the facts of life and death. This response, therefore, is a kind of minimum. It is of course possible that H felt more deeply and complexly, but there is no way of telling this without further discussion from her. I offer it here to show just how limited an affective report can be and still reveal some of the process by which this affect can appear.

Restatement I, while still only naming feelings, does so in a much more specific and recognizably experiential form: "I know how it would feel to be free of guilt in doing something unconventional." This freedom from guilt develops in terms of a specific activity: "I feel the urge to wander to new places," "I want to share the satisfaction." So strong is this particular feeling of abandon, which leads to a similar admiration we found in restatement H, that the thought of death, even, is reduced in importance to "leaving for somewhere else." While there is a good deal of redundancy in this response, as in restatement G, there is an overall sense of its mood. This mood is not simply guiltlessness, abstractly or even behaviorally, but it derives from having found a kindred spirit in the poet. The respondent manufactures a relationship with him in order to express her feelings. It is not merely an identification, however, because the respondent says, "I feel the urge to wander to new places *with the poet*." It is actually an imaginary relationship, which gradually resolves itself into a discussion of that other person, the speaker/poet. There is an important piece of knowledge to be gained from this response: *the expression of affect naturally leads to its explanation in terms of relationship*.

Identification with a speaker or protagonist, present in both of these affective responses, is a rather common event in one's reading experience, perhaps the most basic event in our "getting into" a work of literature. In our responses, we observe it coming into play, unsolicited, as it were, as part of a natural expression of how we feel. It provides an important corroboration of

our principle of evaluating associative responses, as we will discuss shortly. In response I, the pleasure reported by the respondent is not guiltlessness by itself, but guiltlessness as the respondent imagines it to be so experienced by an important person, the poet. The thoughts of the poem gain a major additional importance through the respondent's having imagined them offered by a very important person. Think, for example, of the ordinary childhood situation where a child does something he thinks may be disapproved by his parent, like riding a bicycle on a dangerous street. But instead of disapproval, the parent says, "Oh, yes, I used to like to do that when I was young also." Together the act and the parent create a great positive affect in the child. Yet, it is the parent's words which are the key to producing the good feeling. Their action is the determining influence in the production of the affect associated with a particular experience, in the same way as peer group response so frequently validates all kinds of adolescent behavior that would never be tolerated in normal adult life.

Consider this principle now in the following affective response to Frost's "On Going Unnoticed."

### On Going Unnoticed

As vain to raise a voice as a sigh
In the tumult of free leaves on high.
What are you in the shadow of trees
Engaged up there with the light and breeze?

Less than the coral-root you know
That is content with the daylight low,
And has no leaves at all of its own;
Whose spotted flowers hang meanly down.

You grasp the bark by a rugged pleat,
And look up small from the forest's feet
The only leaf it drops goes wide,
Your name not written on either side.

You linger your little hour and are gone,
And still the woods sweep leafily on,
Not even missing the coral-root flower
You took as a trophy of the hour.

J.     When I hear the shrill whirr of a siren, an innate kind of fear drives me to the window to peer out at the passing ambulance. And as I see the flash of red and chrome speed by, a sadness mixes with my momentary fear. For a few brief minutes a stonelike tenseness hangs in my breast and throat.

Then the sight and sound are gone and so is the fearful sadness. Or when I read or hear that someone as young as me has died — although I do not even know the victim — I feel the same intense sadness. Again it is momentary. Quickly other, less significant details of everyday life subdue the feeling.

This same mixture of sadness and fear strikes me as I read Robert Frost's "On Going Unnoticed." I feel a hard knotted lump of something inside me as I read. No matter how many times I read it I have this same reaction — intense sadness, the kind of gloominess that comes quickly and lasts only a short time. This sadness is not the same kind that I feel when I think of my dying father. It is rather the same unhappiness I feel every time I discover something not really close to me alone, but something universal, that I dislike but can't change.

Perhaps because I have had the same thoughts before myself, but always shoved them out of my mind, my first feeling is that Frost is right. Also like the ambulance or the unexpected death of a young person, the reading of this poem fills me with fear. I feel that the poet is correct, and I am suddenly reminded that it could, at any time, be me who rushes headlong into some unknown extinction, only to be "unnoticed." "On Going Unnoticed" hits me with a powerful blow at the time I read it and for the few minutes I think about it afterward. Then ambiguously when the book is closed I convince myself that some other you may "linger your little hour and be gone," but not me.

Yet the truth is that I still feel, without any great mass of data for proof, that Frost is right. And in the future when I come across this idea that man is "less than the coral-root," that the "forest" will not miss him, or even remember his name when he leaves, the sadness and fear will be there. It will again be momentary, but it will be there.

Finally as I read the poem I feel it is important because it is true. Although it will return, this feeling too is short lived. I can easily dismiss it and plunge into the more insignificant thoughts and actions that make up my life.

We cannot deny, at the outset, that J is especially articulate and that such a special skill or fluency in language might here be the source of that "something extra" not found in the other responses. Without exploring the issue in great depth, however, I will only say that my experience has been that "verbal skill" is not an independent talent, and that it is not possible for us teachers to distinguish between this skill and a person's strong desire to express himself. I have seen many students with lesser vocabulary and fluency compose equally vivid and powerful statements.

We observe in the opening paragraph the almost automatic impulse to explain the affect in detail and with more than one example. While these analogies may be classified as associations, they are more important as ways to help the reader recreate that feeling than as means for determining what aspect of the personality is involved. That is the basic functional difference between an affective analogy and an associative analogy. The analogies themselves involve others — the victim in the ambulance or the peer who has died — the speaker's relationship to these people being purely subjective. Nevertheless, these human elements in the analogies take us one step further toward the level of associative analogy involving important relationships.

In the second paragraph we actually do see an important associative analogy, though it is presented rather obliquely. The "intense sadness" described by J "is not the same kind that I feel when I think of my dying father." There must obviously be an important truth in J's manifest denial. I take it, however, that the sad thoughts of her dying father are constant and nagging rather than intense and transient. More fundamentally, however, the denial only covers up the real analogy, which aims to express the feeling that some very important part of her emotional investment in life is threatened by both her dying father and the intense sadnesses described in the opening paragraph. The remainder of the response does reveal this analogy. What J terms "something universal" turns out to be something very personal indeed. In the third paragraph we observe the by-now-familiar habit of the reader's assuming a certain intimacy with the poet/speaker. J observes that the "poet is correct" "perhaps because I have had the same thoughts before myself." That is, the poet is "correct" because he feels the way I do. The way J particularly feels, we now learn, is that she herself feels she may "linger [her] little hour and be gone," just like the ambulance victim, the dead peer, or the dying father. J then expresses this very personal feeling in the "universal" sense she mentioned earlier — that it is "man," the species, rather than her, the individual, who is "less than the coral-root." By the end of the response, J emphasizes the "truth" of this feeling rather than its depth or intensity. Even for this articulate and responsive young woman, the intense and important personal feeling must be justified by its truth or universality and is not allowed to stand by itself, even though it is very plain both to us and to her that the foundation of this truth or correctness lies in the fact that she was willing and able to make it apply to her own life.

In spite of the complexity of the foregoing response, its analysis led to a more complex understanding of it as a feeling, a personal sense of mortality which, though transient, is real in all of us. Indirectly, the personality of the respondent is manifest in such a response, but it is really only the quality and terms of a single affect which we know about in any detail. The response demonstrates the multiplicity of directions in which even a single, though important, affect may be elaborated and, in an important sense, "explained" by the different sorts of analogies brought to bear. The opening portions of the response show some kind of mystery regarding what the respondent actually feels about "going unnoticed," and it is not until the concluding portions of the response that we discover how important a feeling she really has, and how many aspects of her previous experience are stimulated by the affect derived from a single poetic experience. If we limit the discussion of emotional response to affect alone, this response represents about the furthest we can go. Nevertheless, it is clear from this response that the pursuit of one's affective reaction naturally and automatically leads to the study of an associative response.

## THE ASSOCIATIVE RESPONSE

### Mending Wall

Something there is that doesn't love a wall,
That sends the frozen-ground-swell under it,
And spills the upper boulders in the sun;
And makes gaps even two can pass abreast.
The work of hunters is another thing:
I have come after them and made repair
Where they have left not one stone on a stone,
But they would have the rabbit out of hiding,
To please the yelping dogs. The gaps I mean,
No one has seen them made or heard them made,
But at spring mending-time we find them there.
I let my neighbor know beyond the hill;
And on a day we meet to walk the line
And set the wall between us once again.
We keep the wall between us as we go.
To each the boulders that have fallen to each.
And some are loaves and some so nearly balls
We have to use a spell to make them balance;
"Stay where you are until our backs are turned!"
We wear our fingers rough with handling them.
Oh, just another kind of outdoor game.
One on a side. It comes to little more:
There where it is we do not need the wall:
He is all pine and I am apple orchard.
My apple trees will never get across
And eat the cones under his pines, I tell him.
He only says, "Good fences make good neighbors."
Spring is the mischief in me, and I wonder
If I could put a notion in his head:
"*Why* do they make good neighbors? Isn't it
Where there are cows? But here there are no cows.
Before I built a wall I'd ask to know
What I was walling in or walling out,
And to whom I was like to give offense.
Something there is that doesn't love a wall,
That wants it down." I could say "Elves" to him,
But it's not elves exactly, and I'd rather
He said it for himself. I see him there
Bringing a stone grasped firmly by the top
In each hand, like an old-stone savage armed.
He moves in darkness as it seems to me,
Not of woods only and the shade of trees.
He will not go behind his father's saying,
And he likes having thought of it so well
He says again, "Good fences make good neighbors."

1 K. "Something there is that doesn't love a wall." I remember when I was young and how I was always sent to my room for punishment of something I had done wrong. I hated being sent to my room, not in the beginning, of course, because I always thought I'd get even with my Mom and show her that I could have a lot of fun in there. As the hours went by, though, I usually ran out of things to do and therefore I would always try to think of a good story to tell sweet ole Dad about how mean Mom had been to me. I just hated those four blank walls; I guess that's because I saw them so often.

2     . . . The gaps I mean,
         No one has seen them made or heard them
         made,
         But at spring mending-time we find them there.

This reminds me of the making-up time with my boyfriend. At times I can see us drifting apart from one another, having little spats over a trivial subject. This drifting apart usually is not completely revealed until after the climactic fight, when we tell each other how rotten the other one is and also the long list of faults he has. But after the big fight, usually about a week, he comes over and we laugh about the stupidity of the fight. Making up or "mending" our disputes and troubles were fun. I guess its because things go so well for awhile after the fight. We're each very nice to each other.

3     Another thing along the same line that this quote reminds me of is how my boyfriend and I appreciate each other more and get along so much better when we do not see each other very often or when we are a considerable distance apart. We seem to enjoy each other's company much more and have a fewer number of fights. I feel that sometimes it's better not to be around someone you care about a lot, because if you're around them all the time you tend to pick out all their faults. Of course, its usually because you picture this person as being perfect and that is usually what you try to expect from them instead of overlooking these faults.

4     And on a day we meet to walk the line
         And set the wall between us once again.

This brings back the memories of the neighborhood gang fights. It wasn't really a "gang fight" like in the movies or on television shows, but what I mean by a gang fight is a whole group of kids would get together and decide that they weren't going to play with one certain person. Of course, every once in a while that poor creature ended up being yourself, and that was when it was really bad. It always seemed like there was only one person that never got "ganged-up" against and that was my neighbor. I guess you could call her the "brains" of the mob. She was really a troublemaker, the more I look back at the situation. Well, anyway, whenever it was my turn to be hated, I always got my notice when Carol started drawing "the property line." The funniest part of this whole situation was that her mother always got into the fight. The line always went "you better kept off of my property or I'll call the poleece" — her mother had a French accent. It was really ridiculous! They even set up a guard duty to make sure I wouldn't cross their property — all the kids in the neighborhood took a different shift. Thank goodness for public sidewalks and streets! These fights or gang-ups happened about once every two months to the same person. Usually after about a week of the whole deal, Carol would come over and dumb ole me or whoever the fight was against would, of course, get "buddy-buddy" with her and then was the shift of the scene to some other poor soul. These fights seemed to follow a cycle; I'm only glad that summer vacations last only three months! To look back at the good old days really makes you see the stupidity of it all, but what is funnier is to see the young neighborhood kids today holding the same "gang fights" with the "property line" disputes.

5     To each the boulders that have fallen to each.
         And some are loaves and some so nearly balls
         We have to use a spell to make them balance:
         "Stay where you are until our backs are turned!"

The camping days of my life and the experiences were horrible when they occurred but funny to talk about afterwards. The words "boulders" and "balls" remind me of the overnight camp-out in the woods. At camp we had what was called a "family" — half boys and half girls with a couple of counselors. Well, my "family" slept out in the woods one evening. In preparing for the evening, the boys were to rig up a tarp for us (the girls) to sleep under. They did a beautiful job of rigging the tarp, making sure that it was up securely by placing big logs on it in key spots where they would supposedly not get loose and drop. Well, at least that was the main idea, but during the middle of the night one of these logs worked itself loose and fell — directly onto my head. Now, you can see probably very well how the words "boulder" and "balls" remind me of this experience. It was quite a surprise to be awakened during the middle of the night with a thump on the head which left a beautiful bump! In fact it was rather upsetting, especially when you are supposed to have a tarp over your head for protection! At first, of course — considering the time of night — I had no idea about what was happening, but immediately afterwards I did manage to become both upset and scared. It was like "Chicken Little" and "the sky is falling" story. I kept thinking that it was a dream; the only thing that could make me think different was the evidence on my forehead — the bump.

6     He is all pine and I am apple orchard

My apple trees will never get across
And eat the cones under his pines,

When I came across this line in the poem it
brought back memories of when a group of us
would always try to sneak over to the apple orchard
behind my house and steal apples. It probably
sounds stupid, but sometimes I thought it was fun
to get caught picking the apples, because when we
ran to get away from the old woman who was
chasing us, we could think of a real juicy story of
how we managed to sneak away with Mrs. Larsen's
apples while she tried to run after us and catch us.
Sometimes we used to have wars in the trees. We
would climb up in the trees — one row for each
side, to make sure that we wouldn't hit our own
players — and throw apples at each other. What a
riot! Sometimes we managed to catch one of our
foes off guard and off balance and knock them
right out of the tree with only one "little" apple.
One thing we were lucky about when we had these
wars was that no one got hurt, especially when
they got knocked out of the trees. That part made
the game a little better.

7    Before I built a wall I'd ask to know
What I was walling in or walling out,
And to whom I was like to give offense

The three lines above remind me of mental
blocks. Sometimes when I am walking outside, my
mind drifts off into some world or on something I
need to get done. This is all I am concentrating on,
and this is what gets me in a lot of trouble with
my friends because when they pass me and speak
to me, they usually receive no reply because I
usually don't hear or see them. The next time I see
them they tell me how stuck-up I am because I
don't speak to them while passing on the street. In
short, to try to apply this problem with the above,
I build a wall which closes out my friends sometimes which then gives them an offensive feeling
toward me.

8    Another instance of about the same type of
situation is walling out your friends from activities
that you are in or walling out the concern for their
feelings and the possibility of hurting them in this
way which could possibly result in ill-feelings towards you.

9    Through this poem, memories of good and bad
times of my childhood were brought back. One
experience, in particular, was the "property line"
affair. This seems to show the foolishness of walls
or lines separating people — it can cause ill feelings, and sometimes walls are built to stop per-

sisting quarrels. The "Berlin Wall," for instance,
was built to keep the East Berliners from going
over to the better life plus it walled out the possible
chance of jealousy of seeing how well the others
are living.

10    This wall could also mean the wall of racial
prejudice and narrow-mindedness of so many people. The United States especially is having many
problems with civil rights. There are so many
whites and colored people that are so narrow-
minded that these are the ones that usually cause
the riots and killings. Another point to bring in is
that so many people do things without thinking
about them first, such as the colored trying to get
their rights and the ways they go about getting
them. Many whites, in the treating of the civil
rights problems, only follow present behavior lines
of their fathers. They do not try to think things out
for themselves to see if they can find an answer to
their problems, but all they do is just go by the
ways and rules of their predecessors. The line that
I am going to quote can show more exactly what I
mean by racial prejudice and narrow-minded people.

He moves in darkness as it seems to me,
Not of woods only and the shade of trees.

K's response is almost all association. There
are numerous thoughts, in the usual sense, and
numerous affects present, though these are always connected with the associations rather than
directly to the poem. The authenticity of the
response is documented by the fluency of the
associations, their conversational presentation,
their line-by-line sequence, and most importantly, by the single theme they present. This
theme, however, is not manifest, but I will try
to show that it is prominent in the response and
that it provides a far stronger sense of the reader's
experience and relationship with the poem than
any of the affective responses we have just studied. I will also note that this response is an
excellent example of the use of important interpersonal relationships. Each association is characterized by either an interpersonal or group experience, and the response culminates with
thoughts on political and social situations which
K finds analogous to the more personal material
she has discussed.

While the response is organized so that each
association seems to be to particular lines, this

is not altogether the case: the association is usually to a part of a line or to a word or specific image. It will become clear how these apparent disjunctions add up to a surprisingly unified response.

One behavioral schema dominates the response. Let us call it, "K, the victim." In paragraph 1 she is sent to her room by her mother. In paragraph 4 she is the frequent victim of the neighborhood ringleader-bully, whose mother partakes in the bullying. In paragraph 5 a log falls on her head. In paragraph 6 she is the victim of Mrs. Larsen's wrath, for picking her apples. Paragraph 7 finds her friends chewing her out for being "stuck-up." In paragraph 9 she speaks of victimization by the Berlin wall, and in the last paragraph, she speaks of the various kinds of victims resulting from the struggle for equal rights.

We may say that this theme expands as the response proceeds. K begins with a mother-daughter scene, goes through a boyfriend-girl-friend episode and commentary, then into various kinds of groups until, at the end, she reaches public life. One can all too easily describe this expansion as "growth of social awareness." While this may be part of what is happening, it is certainly not the whole story. Beginning in paragraph 6, the central point of the victim stories changes. There, for the first time, K openly names her own aggression as the cause: "A group of us would always try to sneak over to the apple orchard behind my house and steal apples." I note for future reference that this important change takes place in response to a part of the poem which affirms the separateness of the apple orchards and the pines. The poem's statement of stasis provokes K into revealing the key personal fact that her own aggression may have played a part in her victimizations. The line acts as a kind of invitation to K to "step over" the peaceful situation. This she does by bringing out a tale of her own aggression in what heretofore has been a series of personal complaints.

Clearly, K reports these events as if the theft and the deliberate fun in getting caught were only a game, and Mrs. Larsen is portrayed as a kind of villain who interferes with children's play. In fact, she is made a villain to begin with in order to create the game of stealing apples. Theft is not the only interesting aspect to this game: "Sometimes we used to have wars in the trees," in which, obviously, K was an active participant, some of the pleasures of which included "catching one of our foes off guard and off balance and knocking them right out of the tree with only one 'little' apple." The whole activity was, metaphorically, "a riot." There is very little doubt, however, that this is all kid stuff and simply came to mind with the poetic use of the term "apple orchard."

In the light of K's remarks in paragraphs 9 and 10, however, this association is not only kid stuff. There, where she is trying to find an overview for all the associations she has presented, she cites the "property line" affair as the outstanding association, no doubt because it was the most personally painful of the various things she remembered. Instead of mentioning this pain again, she calls such lines or walls "foolishness." She then rises above not only her own pain but political reality as well by tearing down the Berlin wall as a similar foolishness. This international allusion, however, relates as much to the "war" waged between the trees in paragraph 6 as it does to the property line disputes. In paragraph 7, moreover, K describes how she erects her own "wall": "I built a wall which closes out my friends sometimes which then gives them an offensive feeling toward me." There is reason to believe, in other words, that in addition to being a victim, K does harbor a private guilt over being the aggressor and the wallbuilder, a guilt overcome by the moralistic disquisition against walls.

Her last paragraph is most revealing in this regard. Again there is a moralistic declaration against the narrow-mindedness of racially prejudiced people. To her, it is *both* white and "colored people" whose narrow-mindedness "usually causes riots and killings." She then singles out "the colored" (with the "people" now missing from the phrase) as using means "to get their rights" "without thinking about [these means] first." Finally, though it is far from clear, K's last quotation suggests an ironic identification of narrow-mindedness with "darkness." The poem itself nowhere alludes to a "color" question, but K's allusion to it combines interestingly with that final quotation to make it rather clear that she is a member of the white majority, complete with its color-coded imagery about knowledge and ignorance, good and evil, light and darkness. And this majority is suspiciously similar to the gang and its ringleader that selected her for its periodic assaults.

In addition to this mild suggestion that K takes some pride in or takes refuge in being on the stronger side, another theme running counter to the victim's sentiments appears in paragraphs 2 and 3, where she is discussing her relationship with her boyfriend. Ostensibly, paragraph 2 shows the association to be about "spring mending-time," with the analogy to mending a relationship. However, paragraph 3 casts a different light on things. K reports that she and her boyfriend "get along so much better when we do not see each other very often or when we are a considerable distance apart." This is not an uncommon situation, especially in relationships between younger people. However, I think there is a connection between K's value of separateness here, her "mental blocks" in paragraph 7 where she mentally separates herself from her friends passing her on the street, and the ever so faint value of racial separateness in paragraph 10. We should also note in this regard that when she was sent to her room alone, as she reports in paragraph 1, "I always thought . . . that I could have a lot of fun in there," but that she had to finally call on "sweet ole Dad" to bail her out.

In pointing out possible counterthemes to what I am calling the "main theme" in the response, I am underscoring the emotional dialectic that takes place in this, and, as I have come to see, in almost every response. That is, there are always certain patterns of conscious assertion, while there are other, less obvious patterns that reveal another side to the assertions. It is quite obvious that such a dialectic does not take place consciously, since the respondent only picks out things in the poem, seemingly at random, which strike important emotional chords. In this response I think the dialectic amounts to the following situation: "I surely don't like being a victim so much, yet I seem to have a distinct sympathy with or perhaps envy of the victimizer. This is something of a problem for me, so perhaps it is best just to withdraw to my own room or mind, where this is no longer a problem." This "withdrawal" takes place in the final paragraphs in her discussion of the narrow-mindedness of both sides of the equal rights dispute. This is of course a very familiar pattern, often found in public life in the name of reason and compromise, but which, if viewed from a personal basis, avoids the problems of commitment and obviates the risks of getting involved and taking a stand.

K views the poem as being about walls, if we are to judge from her more reflective discussion at the end of the response and from the kinds of things in the poem to which she responded. Her overall sympathy is with a speaker who she takes to be, so to speak, against walls. While she agrees in paragraph 1 that she in fact "doesn't love a wall," she subsequently offers associations of pleasures in crossing walls surreptitiously, and even of building them herself, as in paragraphs 3 and 7. Ultimately, it turns out, she "doesn't love a wall," but not because they are intrinsically a bad thing. Rather, she would prefer not to cope with their meaning and function, good or bad, and she takes comfort in the speaker's own judgment that people who think that "good fences make good neighbors" "move in darkness."

K, like most of the other respondents we have studied, identifies with the speaker, though she doesn't say so directly. Instead, due to the associative nature of her response, she uses the homiletic pronouncements in the poem as documentation for her views. As a critical posture, this is not new, since we are almost forced to "play along" with the speaker. But numerous critical discussions of this poem in class have shown that one need not sympathize or identify with this speaker. Some student almost always asks, "Well, if this guy doesn't like walls, why does he take the initiative: 'I let my neighbor know beyond the hill'?" At this point the whole problem of the interesting relationship between the speaker and his neighbor is exposed. A whole range of new perceptions of the poem appears, and attention moves away from walls to the speaker's attitude toward his neighbor, and toward whoever is listening to him in the poem.

The other, more personal and psychological theme is also implicit in K's response. It surfaces in academic criticism as the theme of "tradition," and is based on the speaker's remark that the neighbor "will not go behind his father's saying." To be sure, the theme of tradition is only inferred from the fact that the neighbor is old and that, according to the speaker, he says what his father said. From these meager facts the neighbor is billed as an establishmentarian dogmatist, played off against the man of enlightened ideas, the speaker. The personal basis of this theme of "tradition" does appear in K's associations, in paragraphs 1, 4, and 6. I am referring to K's reported confrontations with her mother, her neighbor's mother, and Mrs. Larsen. The encounter with the latter ended in success, while those with the former two ended only in humiliation. It is a rather common need of a child, and then especially an adolescent (which K was at the time of this response) to test and defeat the authority of the parents' generation, and usually of the parents themselves. It is because this important personal impulse is at work in K's response that she finds support in the speaker's judgment that his neighbor "moves in darkness." In terms of this particular theme, K's response develops *from* punishment at the hands of her mother, to humiliation at the hands of her neighbor's mother, to a childish victory over Mrs. Larsen, and finally, if figuratively, to a kind of moral victory over the older neighbor in the poem. K appropriates this latter victory to help enunciate her own resentment of the "dark" and "stupid" behavior of her own neighbor, and perhaps of her mother, an even more intimate "neighbor." The presence of this theme in her response helps explain K's own sense of personal enlightenment about political and social affairs, and the expression of such enlightenment in these latter terms provides an acceptable justification for her presentation of such personal material.

This is not a scheme that K cooked up for just this occasion. Rather, it is a relatively common psychological habit of people to shift the discussion to such large terms when they sense that the time has come to dissolve the personal issue altogether, without either stopping the conversation abruptly or drawing a conclusion from the personal issue in its own terms. Such a homiletic windup is an exhortation to oneself, really, framed as if it were a general reflection and a vague exhortation to others.

We should now recognize this habit as the one with which we began our discussion of the elementary presentation of feelings above. At even the simplest level, instead of saying "I like so and so," we say "so and so is nice." In the poem, the speaker criticizes the neighbor, instead of reporting his own irritation. And then K appropriates the common habit. The habit of objectification is fundamental in human mental functioning, and no one does without it. Our point here is that we can observe its subjective function, especially so in these associative responses. There will come a point in almost anyone's response when some form of objectification will come to the rescue to depersonalize the response. Professional criticism, framed as it always is in objective terms, is an institutional form of this universal psychological habit. Beyond a certain point it is assumed feelings cannot be discussed — they are inimical to truth. We now see here in the case of literary response and judgment that truth is not a viable goal, and that we must understand the habit of objectification in its subjective origin.

The associative response, therefore, is the most complex but the most useful form of expressing feelings about literature. It reveals perception, affect, associations, relationships, and finally a patterned presentation of all of these in a way that demonstrates how they are organized in that particular person. Most of all, the associative response shows most clearly that each individual reworks a poem according to the demands of his personality at the time of reading. Some responses show very vividly the effect of the respondent's *current* preoccupations: these preoccupations are frequently a subject of the associations. While this may be true in the foregoing response, it is definitely not clear. But in each response, we may be sure that it in some way represents a combination of the aggregate self-image, and the self-image at the time of reading. My guess is that the boyfriend material and the rebellion material in K's response does represent current preoccupation, for K is an adolescent, where such preoccupations are expectable. If one goes through the steps of understanding perception and affect, the logic of studying associations becomes clear and an experimental basis is formed for the study of the larger process of critical judgment.

# Elizabeth A. Flynn

b. 1944

*One of the major empirical researchers into questions of gender and the reading process, Elizabeth A. Flynn was born in Jersey City and raised in Ramsey, New Jersey. She received her B.A. degree from Pace University in New York in 1966, and her M.A. and Ph.D. from Ohio State University in 1969 and 1977. Flynn has taught at Ohio State and at Antioch College; since 1979 she has been associate professor, head of the Humanities Department, and director of the Institute for Research on Language and Learning at Michigan Technological University. Flynn is the author of over a dozen essays and monographs on reading issues but is best known as editor (with Patrocinio Schweickart) of the collection of feminist reader-response criticism* Gender and Reading *(1986), to which she contributed the title essay. Reprinted here, it originally appeared in* College English *45 (1983).*

## Gender and Reading

Recent scholarship on the relationship between gender and reading has arisen primarily from two different sources: reading research that examines the behavior of elementary and high school students, and feminist literary criticism that analyzes literary texts from a reader-oriented perspective. Reading researchers have contributed empirical data on gender-related similarities and differences among developing readers, and feminist literary critics have contributed descriptive studies of the ways in which texts shape responses along gender lines. We know very little, though, about the reading patterns of relatively mature male and female readers. In an attempt to extend the studies of reading researchers to include college-age students and to bring an empirical orientation to the reader-oriented work of feminist critics, I conducted an exploratory study designed to examine the interpretive strategies of college freshmen in their responses to three frequently anthologized short stories, James Joyce's "Araby," Ernest Hemingway's "Hills Like White Elephants," and Virginia Woolf's "Kew Gardens." The twenty-six women and twenty-six men who comprised my sample were enrolled in a freshman composition course taught at Michigan Technological University in 1980. Students in seven sections of composition wrote responses to the stories during three different class sessions. They were told that a wide range of responses was possible, including summarizing the stories, analyzing them, or relating them to their own experiences. (See the Appendix for a description of the course, the students, and the assignments.)

My analysis of the data was informed by a conception of the reading process which assumes that reading involves a confrontation between self and "other." The self, the reader, encounters the "other," the text, and the nature of that confrontation depends on the background of the reader as well as on the text. Text and reader are necessarily foreign to each other in some ways, and so the exchange between them involves an imbalance, what Wolfgang Iser calls "asymmetry" or "contingency." Georges Poulet emphasizes this imbalance in his description of the reading process. He writes, "Since every thought must have a subject to think it, this thought, which is alien to me and yet in me, must also have a subject which is alien to me. It all happens, then, as though reading were the act by which a thought managed to bestow itself within me with a subject not myself."[1] The reader allows the foreign object to "bestow itself" within his or her mind, and so self and other coexist, for a time.

What Poulet does not emphasize is that the coexistence of reader and text can take a number of different forms. The reader can resist the alien thought or subject and so remain essentially unchanged by the reading experience. In this case the reader dominates the text. Or the reader can allow the alien thought to become such a powerful presence that the self is replaced by the other and so is effaced. In this case the text dominates the reader. Either the reader resists the text and so deprives it of its force, or the text overpowers the reader and so eliminates the reader's powers of discernment. A third possibility, however, is that self and other, reader and text, interact in such a way that the reader learns from the experience without losing critical distance; reader and text interact with a degree of mutuality. Foreignness is reduced, though not eliminated. Self and other remain distinct and so create a kind of dialogue.[2]

The dominant pole is characterized by detachment, observation from a distance. The reader imposes a previously established structure on the text and in so doing silences it. Memory dominates over experience, past over present. Readers who dominate texts become complacent or bored because the possibility for learning has been greatly reduced. Judgment is based on previously established norms rather than on empathetic engagement with and critical evaluation of the new material encountered. The reader absents the text. A response to Joyce's "Araby" illustrates this strategy of domination. The student wrote enthusiastically about his encounter with the text, but there is little evidence that a pattern of meaning was created as a result of that encounter.

The beauty that one comes away with from reading "Araby" is the feeling. When I read this story I could almost say I was there. I was able to relate some of my past experiences with what James Joyce used for setting. The general feeling of the street, and the buildings gazing at one another are all related to past experiences. I am able to say that, "Hey, I was on a street just like that." And when I can put my personal experience to work the story becomes loaded with color.

The adjectives that are used throughout the story are very descriptive. The garden was not just a garden, but it was a wild garden. I am able to picture a wild garden; however, a wild garden may be one thing to you and another to me, but it makes no difference to the net effect.[3]

The student's positive attitude toward the reading experience suggests that subsequent readings of the story will result in meaningful interaction. This first reading, however, has not moved the student very far beyond himself. The text activated his imagination, and so he remembered

---

[1] Wolfgang Iser, *The Act of Reading: A Theory of Aesthetic Response* (Baltimore: Johns Hopkins University Press, 1978), p. 167; Georges Poulet, "Criticism and the Experience of Interiority," trans. Catherine and Richard Macksey, in *Reader-Response Criticism: From Formalism to Post-Structuralism*, ed. Jane P. Tompkins (Baltimore: Johns Hopkins University Press, 1980), p. 44. [Au.] See Iser, p. 1219. [Ed.]

[2] These categories were also suggested by Tzvetan Todorov's discussion of the Spanish conquest of the Indians in his course "The Conquest of America," taught at the School of Criticism and Theory, Northwestern University, June/July 1981. Professor Todorov argued that individual Spaniards assimilated Indian culture into their own and in so doing destroyed it, identified so strongly with Indian culture that they lost their European identity, or engaged in dialogical interaction with the Indians. [Au.]

[3] Distracting errors in punctuation and spelling have been corrected in this and other response statements. [Au.]

streets and gardens from his own past. He has not yet put those images to use in comprehending the story, however. He makes no reference to the plot of "Araby" or even to its protagonist.

The submissive pole, in contrast, is characterized by too much involvement. The reader is entangled in the events of the story and is unable to step back, to observe with a critical eye. Instead of boredom the reader experiences anxiety. The text is overwhelming, unwilling to yield a consistent pattern of meaning. A response to "Araby" written by another student illustrates this submissive stance.

> "Araby" is another story that has great inner meaning. Each paragraph has some meaning; for example, the first paragraph has some deep inner meaning about what the houses represent. The second paragraph is the same way, in the deep meaning sense, but talks about some dead priest's home and what was found in the back yard. And every paragraph in between, right up to the last one, has something to be interpreted. I would start to interpret them if I could, but I can't make much sense out of the whole thing.
>
> In describing the story, it starts out with a street description of some old homes. The story then goes to some boys playing in the street, and then to a specific boy and what is happening to him as he, apparently, falls in love with a neighbor girl. The narrator tells about all the little things the boy is doing when falling in love like gazing under the window blind until she comes out and walking behind her when she is walking to school. And then his first time talking to her.

This student was so close to the textual details that he could make no sense of them; he brought little of his past experiences to bear on the text and so could gain no critical distance from it. He summarized the plot of the story in hope that some meaning would emerge. For him the text is a reservoir of hidden meanings rather than a system of signs to be acted on. Like the author of the previous response, this student will no doubt interact with the text more meaningfully in subsequent readings of the story. Right now, however, he is so overwhelmed by the text that he is unable to assign meaning to it.

These two responses are potentially interactive but are so far from revealing meaningful engagement with the text that they represent minimal communication. Productive interaction involves the active participation of the reader in the construction of meaning. Readers formulate hypotheses as they encounter the signs of the text, and those hypotheses are constantly being altered as new information is processed. Iser in *The Act of Reading* explains the process as follows: "The reader's communication with the text is a dynamic process of self-correction, as he formulates signifieds which he must then continually modify" (p. 67). As the reader's perspective shifts, so do the signs in the text, so that they are constantly taking on different patterns of significance. The reader's energies are expended attempting to find a consistent pattern of meaning from among the seemingly incompatible stimuli, and meaning is finally achieved only when tensions are resolved. Iser calls this resolution a closed gestalt. Signs no longer appear unrelated or contradictory but, rather, form a meaningful whole.

Within the category of interaction, then, we have levels of engagement with the text. A reader may be at an early stage of the interactive process and so unable to resolve the conflicting patterns that phantasmagorically emerge and recede during the act of reading. Characters, images, events, take on importance and then shrink into insignificance as the reader gropes toward meaning. Evaluations of textual details shift until the reader reconciles conflicting elements and achieves a balance between detachment and involvement.

Productive interaction, then, necessitates the stance of a detached observer who is empathetic but who does not identify with the characters or the situation depicted in a literary work. Comprehension is attained when the reader achieves a balance between empathy and judgment by maintaining a balance of detachment and involvement. Too much detachment often results in too much judgment and hence in domination of the text; too much involvement often results in too much sympathy and hence in domination by the text. However, when the reader is able to integrate past experience with the experience created by the text through critical evaluation of the interwoven signs encountered in the process of reading, comprehension is achieved and learning takes place. Iser describes the effect of productive interaction as follows:

> The new experience emerges from the restructuring of the one we have stored, and this restructuring is what gives the new experience its form. But what actually happens during this process can again only be experienced when past feelings, views, and values have been evoked and then made to merge with the new experience. The old conditions the form of the new, and the new selectively restructures the old. The reader's reception of the text is not based on identifying two different experiences (old versus new), but on the interaction between the two. (p. 132)

Past and present are synthesized into a new experience. The reader is transformed, renewed.

The following response statement reveals features of the interactive process. The discussion of "Araby" is clearly an initial reaction, but it nevertheless suggests that the student achieved a balance of detachment and involvement in reading the story.

> "Araby" by James Joyce is a very complicated story for as short as it is. He uses many symbols in this story. Religion is mentioned several times and through his use of this, it seems that the boy in the story imagines himself to be a crusader. He has a very high opinion of himself. When Mangan's sister asks him to buy her something at the bazaar he feels as if he is on a crusade for her. Joyce mentions a chalice and speaks of prayers and praises all concerned with this girl. The boy in the story treats the girl as an idol or a god. I think he fears touching her not only because he admires her so but also because it will make her appear more human. She might not appear so glorious in his eyes.
>
> The boy places entirely too much importance on going to the bazaar. He can hardly wait until Saturday comes and when it does he is even more impatient waiting for his uncle. It's like he's living his life to do this one thing, buy the girl something at the bazaar (Araby). When he gets to Araby he rushes in and soon realizes everything is above his price range. He becomes angry and disappointed, realizing that all along he had been fooling himself. He was too filled with self-importance and his sense of purpose to realize what might happen.

This student interacted with the text in the sense that she not only described the plot of the story, she also assessed the character of the boy and evaluated his behavior. She took the stance of an understanding and yet detached observer who seemed to understand what motivated the boy's behavior yet did not judge him overharshly. Like the narrator of the story — the young man who reflected on his childhood experiences — the student observed the boy from a distance and so came to understand him and hence to understand the text. She created a consistent pattern of meaning and resolved the tension between the unselfconscious and deluded young boy and the more knowing, more judgmental narrator.

My analysis of the responses to "Araby," "Hills Like White Elephants," and "Kew Gardens" revealed, not surprisingly, that the preponderance of responses by both women and men were submissive. Because students were encountering the stories for the first time, they had difficulty stepping back from the texts in order to interpret them. Response statements contained attempts at interaction with the stories — partial explanations of characters or events, questions, tentative hypotheses. But they also contained expressions of frustration, uncertainty, puzzlement. Most students struggled to move from entanglement in the text to interaction with it. They wanted to comprehend the stories but had not yet been successful in doing so. A response written by a woman student is typical of the majority of the responses in the sample.

> This story ["Araby"] left me in the fog. Even though I read it over and over it still seems like I missed something in it.
>
> It starts off describing a street then it tells of a house. In this house lives a boy and his aunt and uncle. The author goes on and tells you about the street the children play on and also about the girl the boy likes.
>
> The boy sort of worships her; he never talks to her, he just admires her from a distance. One day she finally does talk to him. He was so shocked he didn't know what he said to her. She asked him if he was going to Araby (bazaar). He said he would try to go, and if he did he'd bring something back for her.
>
> When he got home he asked if he could go. His

aunt and uncle said yes (in a way, but they really didn't give their final approval). So the day of the bazaar he waited all day for his uncle (work?), who didn't get home until late; finally when he did get home his uncle said he could go.

At the end he goes to the bazaar and the English girl asked if she could help him in a rude manner.

All I know is that he was Irish Catholic.

The reliance on plot summary, the expression of frustration, and the uncertainty are characteristic of statements written by students who have not yet arrived at a satisfying interpretation of a text. Actions are related but not evaluated. Events are retold but not deciphered.

On the periphery of these seemingly amorphous and indistinguishable responses to the three short stories, though, were statements that revealed distinct patterns of response along gender lines. Some differences between the responses of some women and men students did emerge. A pattern of dominance was evident in some of the men's responses, especially in statements based on "Araby" and "Hills Like White Elephants," but no such pattern was evident in responses written by women. Also, more women than men were able to resolve the tensions in the stories and form a consistent pattern of meaning.

Differences between the men's and women's statements were most pronounced in "Araby." The predicament of a young boy losing his sense of perspective because of his infatuation with his friend's older sister seemed to evoke extremes of rejection or identification in some of the men students, responses that interfered with their understanding of the story.

With the exception of the dominant response quoted above and the response of a male student who effaced the text by fragmenting it into disconnected examples of metaphoric personification, the male students who displayed a tendency toward domination of the text did so because they judged characters without empathizing with them or because they detached themselves from the emotional content of the text. One male student, for instance, rejected the text in its entirety and in so doing dominated it.

This story seemed to be about a deranged person that is in love with a degradable woman. The author seems to fill in the story with descriptive words,

because he realizes the events of the story are boring.

The story was written in such a way that no one would know what was happening, so that he could be thought of as a good writer. . . . In this case, since no one knows what he's talking about many ideas about what is hidden in the story will be made up and therefore he will be thought of as a good writer (even though he thought of B.S. in the first place).

This student's way of dealing with the difficulty of the text was to dismiss it. The response is characteristically dominant in that it defends one-way projection as an appropriate reading strategy and thereby renders the text voiceless.

Four other male students were overly judgmental in their treatment of Mangan's sister, a response that distracted them from a central concern of the story, the boy's solipsistic infatuation. Three male students saw the girl as manipulating the boy for her own ends. One described the boy as having been "used" by the girl. Another described the girl as "just using him." Another remarked that the girl was "just playing him along." The fourth male student described the girl as "ignoring" the boy and equated her with the woman at the bazaar who was abrupt with him. The student wrote, "He had been ignored by the lady in the booth just like he had been ignored by the girl he was in love with, or were they the same people?"

The dominant reader is often a detached reader; the text is not engaged, and so the reader feels little empathy for the central characters. In three of the responses written by male students. the protagonist was treated with detachment, and so his experience was kept at a safe distance. One male student called the protagonist a "little guy"; another described the events portrayed in the story as "some guy's fantasy"; still another endowed the narrator with the name "Jack" and referred to him as a "young kid." If the boy is simply a "little guy," then his experiences are insignificant, and the conflict described in the story need not be taken seriously. The tone of the response statement written by the student who named the protagonist "Jack" is complacent, matter-of-fact.

This is a story about a young kid who is in love

with his friend's sister. The boy and his friend love to tease his sister by hiding in the shadows at night when she would call her brother in for tea.

Jack was madly in love with this girl and went totally out of his way just to see her but not speak to her. He used to peep out the window and watch for her to leave for school and would chase after her. He would always walk behind her until it came time to part in different ways and then he would speed up and pass her.

Jack would never hardly speak to her until she spoke to him first. She asked him if he was going to the bazaar Araby because it was going to be excellent. He went completely out of his way to see Araby because he said if he went he would bring her something.

He was at the bazaar and was looking for something to buy her but this crabby lady drove him away and that made him very mad.

The response trivializes the boy's situation. The student's account suggests that the boy's frustration is externally induced, and it omits mention of the discovery the boy makes about himself.

These dominant responses suggest that these male readers were uncomfortable with "Araby," either because they found it too difficult or because its focus on male infatuation disturbed them. These responses account for fewer than half of the men's responses, however. An even greater number of male students had difficulty comprehending the story because they were too involved in the text, sometimes because they identified with the protagonist too strongly and were unable to distance themselves from him. These submissive responses almost always revealed an inability on the part of the reader to deal with the ending of the story. The conclusion of "Araby" brings together the narrator's perspective and the young boy's perspective so that the reader will recognize the extent to which the boy's fantasies isolated him from his family and peers. Very few male students responded to the resonating finale, though, often because they were unable to recognize the boy's limitations.

A few male students expressed dissatisfaction with the ending of the story. One wrote, "In judging this story, I really didn't think it was very good. I didn't like the way the author ended the story." Another responded, "The story just ended." A third suggested changing the ending

to a happier one. The one male student who gave a fairly full account of the conclusion nevertheless failed to recognize the significance of the boy's judgment upon himself, partially because he identified with the boy too strongly. His response reads:

James Joyce uses imagery and symbolism to illustrate the feelings which a young boy goes through when he is infatuated with a girl. Joyce says that the boy would sleep at her door waiting to see her. He would follow her to school thinking about her as he walked behind her. "Her name was like a summons to all his foolish blood."

The young boy's feelings were not understood by the older generation who were callous to his words. They considered the bazaar to be a small happening, when it was actually a big event in the boy's eyes.

The boy finally does arrive at the bazaar but does not find things as he wanted them to be. He is shaken from the fantasy world by the absence of the girl. This anguish he feels because of the loss of the fantasy world is illustrated by the symbolistic sentence, "Gazing up into the darkness I saw myself as a creature driven and derided by vanity, and my eyes burned with anguish and anger." The protective coating was lifted and the bright light shown into his unprepared eyes causing them to burn and redden.

Joyce tells the story of a young boy's growing up through these imaginative symbols and images. These images tell the story in a vivid, alive manner.

The student clearly identified with the boy's experience and sympathized with him. He also recognized that the boy is "shaken from his fantasy world" and that the experience at the bazaar removes him of his "protective coating." His focus on the girl's absence, however, interfered with his comprehension of the boy's final judgment on himself. According to this student's account, the boy's epiphany results from a feeling of loss rather than a recognition of his own self-delusion.

That other male students identified with the boy is evident in their response statements. One, for instance, wrote, "It was easy to relate to the narrator's boyish infatuation with an older girl, since I can recall having similar experiences." His identification was not accompanied by comprehension of the story, however. He admitted,

"I couldn't grasp the central thought in the story." Since a resolution of the tensions in "Araby" necessitates some understanding of the ending of the story and thus some detachment from the boy's situation, such close identification no doubt interfered with the student's ability to create a consistent pattern of meaning. Four other male students mentioned that they could relate to the boy's experience, and they, too, had difficulty interpreting the story. Only two women students mentioned that they could relate to the boy's experience. Their responses suggest that their identification with the boy was also a distraction, though not to the extent that it was for the men. Both mentioned that the boy felt anger or humiliation at the end of the story, but neither gave a full explanation for the boy's feelings.

The women students in the sample were, for the most part, better able to achieve a balance between detachment and involvement in reading "Araby." No women students judged Mangan's sister overharshly, and none referred to the protagonist as a "little guy" or a "young kid." Many recognized the boy's limitations and yet regarded his experience as significant. And although the majority of responses by women students were submissive in that they revealed entanglement in the text, eleven women were successful in making sense of the story, usually because they came to a satisfying interpretation of its ending. One female student wrote, "After being tempted many times the boy finally realizes that he cannot survive in the world of vanity, and that he must return to the real world. The world that is filled with illusions that people put forward to make everything look nicer." Another woman observed, "He realized here that he had been driven there by his vain love for this girl as stated in the last paragraph." Another accounted for the ending as follows: "I think he had come to realize how foolishly he had acted. This realization embarrassed him, so he turned it to anger at himself." Another female student described the boy's unsuccessful visit to the bazaar and concluded, "He gave up and left; thinking of himself as a person driven by vanity." Another wrote, "In the end, I think he realizes how foolish his feelings have been. In the darkness of the bazaar, he sees things in a new way. He realizes he just has a crush on this girl and she will never feel anything for him." Most of these accounts employ the word *vanity* and make specific reference to the last line of the text.

The concerns in "Hills Like White Elephants" are quite different from those of "Araby," and yet the students' responses followed a pattern similar to that found in the responses to Joyce's story. Some men dominated the text, though this strategy was not evident in the responses of the women. The majority of responses were submissive, but more women students were able to resolve the tensions in the story than were men students. Once again, men students were often closer to the extremes of domination or submission, and the women were often closer to the interactive center.

"Hills Like White Elephants" focuses on a conversation between an American man and a young woman called Jig as they await a train that will take them to Madrid, where Jig will have an abortion. The conversation is tense because Jig is being pressured into going through with the operation yet is resistant because she feels the child would bring some stability and meaning to the couple's relationship. The conflict is resolved through the young woman's denial of her feelings and the man's assertion of his will. This is a story, then, about female vulnerability and defeat. The imagery suggests that the woman's position is life-affirming and that renewal is possible only through her victory over the man. The ending of the story, though, suggests that she is powerless to change the nature of the relationship.

Surprisingly, only one student, a male, was overly judgmental in his reaction to the story. We might expect that college freshmen would be moralistic in their responses to an unmarried couple contemplating an abortion. He wrote, "In the story the man wants the girl to get an abortion. This man seems to know an awful lot about the operation so it must not be the first time he did it to a girl. The fact that he had so many hotel tags on his luggage indicates that he has only one thing on his mind." Other indications of domination by male students suggested rejection of the text because of its difficulty, or detachment from it rather than harsh judgment of the characters. The male student who found the protagonists of "Araby" to be "deranged" and "degradable" also rejected "Hills Like White Elephants," but his response suggests that he was bothered not by the immorality of the protagonists but by the difficulty of the text.

> The story stank. It was boring and didn't end with any main idea. It ended like a dream; it exists and has a hidden reason for happening. The hidden reason isn't worth finding out because it is small in comparison to the time it takes to search for it. A dream is enjoyable, but after being known it is thrown in the trash and forgotten forever.

This student seems once again to be reacting so strongly because he was unable to comprehend the text. He didn't understand the ending of the story, and he experienced the text as dreamlike because it seemed to defy coherent analysis. The student emphasized the imbalance between the value of the message contained in the story and the amount of energy required to extract that message. Perhaps he did not understand the nature of the conflict well enough to come to some evaluation of it.

Another dominant response by another male student also emphasized the difficulty of the story. He wrote:

> My impression of the story was that it wasn't a story at all. It was just a short conversation between two people. The story consisted of just a couple of pages filled with quotes.
>
> Another reason I didn't like it was it left the reader blind. The story just starts right up and doesn't tell anything about who the people are or about what is going on. I had to read through the story a couple of times just to figure out what they were talking about. Nothing was said right out in the open about getting an abortion.
>
> All I have to say [is] it was short and different.

This student, too, rejected the story because he could not understand it. The text, for him, was "just a couple of pages filled with quotes."

The student who referred to the narrator of "Araby" as "Jack" and who detached himself from the boy's plight responded in a similar way to "Hills Like White Elephants." Once again he revealed an inability to empathize with the pro-

tagonists, and once again he trivialized the conflict being described. In the concluding paragraph of his response he wrote, "Finally after a lot of nagging she asked if he would do anything for her and he said yes. She then gave him the pretty please bit with a dozen pleases and asked him to quit bugging her and finish his drink." The student's use of slang expressions suggests that he did not take the interchange between the two seriously.

The male students, on the whole, revealed less self-involvement in "Hills Like White Elephants" than they did in "Araby." Fewer felt the need to dominate it, and there is less evidence of identification with the male protagonist. None of the male students, understandably, indicated that they had had a comparable experience to the one described in the story. They nevertheless had difficulty resolving its seemingly discordant elements, often because they were unable to make connections between the setting and the conversation between the man and the young woman.

Five of the twenty-six men in the sample discussed the relationship between setting and theme in analyzing the story. The remaining male students either ignored the setting or expressed frustration in attempting to interpret it. One male student wrote, "The 'Hills Like White Elephants' could find little meaning in my interpretation of the story. I know that this symbol holds the key to the understanding of the conflict in the story but my imagination didn't quite cut through the story so I could see the meaning." Another responded, "I'm having a hard time trying to figure out what the hills represent." These male students, and numerous female students as well, were unable to recognize that the setting establishes a dichotomy between fertility and infertility, which provides an indirect commentary on the man's desire for the abortion and the woman's reluctance to go through with it, so the students were unable to recognize the significance of the man's defeat of the woman at the end of the story. The effect of this inability to make sense of the ending was an inability to evaluate the conversation between the man and the woman and so to recognize that the woman has been defeated. One male student, for instance, accounted for the ending as follows: "She says she's fine. She seems to be scared because of the unwanted operation. The heat and tension have caused them to argue. When the entire event is over, the relationship will be much better." Another male student said, "The story just seems to be about two people who travel a lot, are in love, and are now troubled with a pregnancy." In neither response is there an evaluation of the respective positions of the two protagonists. The students are too close to the events of the story to see that two different approaches to life are being displayed and judged.

One male student successfully integrated setting and characterization in his response.

Hemingway's "Hills Like White Elephants" relates the conversation between an American couple in Spain as they await a train to ride to the city for an abortion operation. The girl is hesitant about having the abortion, and comments on various aspects of their present surroundings and their past relationship to convey this to the man. She sees the cool white hills, trees, and river across the valley as symbolizing the beauty and meaning a child could bring to their life, whereas the treeless landscape, the rail station, and the bar equate with the barren, transient life they have known to this point.

The man loves the girl, but tries to convince her that their life is happiest when they are alone together; the prospect of a child has brought unhappiness. He does not want to assume fatherhood and its responsibilities; he does not want to share her.

Another male student made reference to the sterility/fertility dichotomy in the setting and concluded, "The girl gazes longingly at the hills almost as if she wishes she was surrounded by this fertile, rather than the dry, sterile area." His response statement made no reference, however, to the conflict between the two characters or to the man's final domination. One male student saw a connection between the phrase "hills like white elephants" and an abortion, since a "white elephant" refers to something gotten rid of, as does an abortion. He also wrote, "The part of the skin of the hills may have something to do with the skin of the child after the abortion." Neither association, however, led him toward a satisfying interpretation of the story, and he concluded his response with a digression: "Something that just occurred to me is that the sun was shining brightly on the hills, giving them an appearance of being white. Could this possibly have meant the son of God shining down on the dead child and taking its soul to heaven? The white being the brillance of Jesus on the child?" Another male student made a connection between the white hills and the abortion but did not use the insight to evaluate the characters or their conflict, but found instead that "the story is trying to make us aware of the complex problem and feelings about abortion." This student concluded that "the argument between the two main characters is unresolved at the end of the story." Another male student referred to a different aspect of the setting, the train station, and decided, "The significance of the train station is that this whole ordeal can be carried right out of their lives afterwards and forgotten. The easy way out!" This account minimizes the significance of the resonating decision made at the end and implies that the choice will have few emotional ramifications.

These responses are typical of other submissive responses by male students in that they demonstrate a lack of critical distance. Often the male students in the sample portrayed the conflict as an argument between two equals which remains unresolved at the end of the story. Or the men's responses indicated that they were unaware of the man's domination or the woman's powerlessness. The women's responses were also predominantly submissive and also demonstrated a lack of critical distance. More women than men related setting to theme, however, and more women seemed able to gain enough distance from the two characters to judge their situation.

Although we might expect that women students would react to "Hills Like White Elephants" the way some men reacted to "Araby" — by identifying with the same-sex protagonist and thereby losing critical perspective — this tendency was present but not pronounced in the response statements. A woman student who digressed in her response about the problems of "pregnancy before marriage" and who mentioned the example of a close friend who consulted her for advice did not come to a very precise critical assessment of the couple. She wrote, "Something had changed their lives. They were no longer happy; they had fallen into a rut." And another woman student who projected onto Jig her own delight in the purity and innocence of babies made no reference to the conflict between the two characters and said nothing of Jig's defeat at the end of the story. In both cases, it would seem, a preoccupation with the pregnancy distracted the students from the central focus of the story, the interaction between the characters.

More frequently, however, sympathy for Jig was accompanied by discernment of the limitations of the two characters. One woman student, for instance, empathized with the female character and yet revealed an awareness of her weakness.

Ernest Hemingway's "Hills Like White Elephants" is a unique story. In it, there is a conflict going on between what may be man and wife or may be two lovers. The story takes place in a train station located near a river with mountains in the background. The mountains are a representative of the conflict. The girl believes that together they can have everything; however he disagrees. The actual conflict in the story is whether she should have an abortion or not. She is unsure but is willing to do it because of her love. He wants her to have the abortion because all he needs is her.

This story could have been written today. Abortion often causes conflicts. The men like represented in the story don't always realize the many side effects which the woman experiences. They try to say that there are none, physical or mental, but there are. In the story, the girl doesn't care much about herself. She cares more for her lover/husband.

Typically, in the end, the male's dominant views have come through. She agrees to have the abortion, and says that there is nothing wrong. Unfortunately this relationship will probably end because conflicts are not resolved. To have a meaningful relationship, they must be more open.

Although the student clearly sympathized with the female character, she was able to gain enough distance to see that Jig is incapable of asserting herself and of making her wishes known. The student was also aware of the man's domination of the woman and of the lack of communication between the two. And unlike a number of students who made no evaluation of the positions of the two characters, this student recognized that Jig's defeat is unfortunate. Another woman student was even more emphatic in her assessment of the two characters. She observed, "The woman is childlike and submissive wanting what the man wants and on the whole the relationship suggests shallowness and a sense of being naive (especially the woman seems to be naive)." A third woman student expressed a similar attitude. She wrote, "I get the distinct feeling that the girl is young and doesn't have too much mind of her own. She is very undecided in her decision of keeping the baby or not. The man is pressuring her to have the operation and gives reasons for it."

Other women students used the setting as a touchstone for evaluating the characters in the story. One woman, for instance, saw the couple's discussion of the hills as a commentary on their approaches to life. She responded, "When the girl says the hills are like white elephants, the man says he never saw a white elephant. This seems to be saying that the man has no imagination. He just goes through life drinking beer and talking." Another woman took Jig's attitude toward the hills to be a reflection of her attitude toward her child.

During the course of the story her feelings change about the child. She states that the hills no longer remind her of white elephants, which leads you to believe that she is no longer sure about the abortion. It is obvious that the man is pressuring her to get the operation because he says that he will love her more if she gets it. She is torn both ways because she wants the baby, but if she keeps it she'll probably lose the man; and in order to keep the man she must give up the baby.

Another student mentioned Jig's looking across the field and seeing a cloud drift past. This gesture, and Jig's comment, "And we could have everything and every day we make it more impossible," revealed to the student that Jig wants to have the child and that the man's resistance to her desire is a reflection of his unwillingness to take on the responsibilities of fatherhood. Another woman student discussed Jig's confusion in terms of the title of the story. She said, "In my opinion the girl didn't know what to do at first so the baby was the white elephant but toward the end it seems she felt the operation was the white elephant. But she was still all confused not knowing which way to go." Another woman student used the setting to determine the author's attitude toward the abortion. She said, "The sombre tone and lifeless setting help to convey the type of operation. For example, the countryside is described as treeless and extremely hot. From this we can infer that the operation was not a pleasant one, but rather sad and unwanted. This idea is supported even more by the tone of the conversation." Two other women students used the setting to decipher character and theme. One thought Jig's reference to the hills looking like white elephants revealed her preoccupation with her unborn child. Another interpreted her comment that the hills look like skin to mean "although they look perfect and pure on the surface, there is something beneath the skin, some substance. This is how she imagines her relationship is: perhaps once clean and pure on the top, but underneath it all there seems to be nothing to bind them together."

The responses to "Kew Gardens" did not follow the pattern of the responses to the other two stories in that there was little evidence of domination of the text. Although both men and women students had difficulty comprehending the story, their frustrations did not take the form of aggression. It was as if the text, which deals explicitly with the rejuvenating powers of nature, had had the effect on the students that the garden had on the individuals who passed through it: it soothed and calmed otherwise anxious souls. The male student who found both "Araby" and "Hills Like White Elephants" to be boring and meaningless seemed to be pacified by "Kew Gardens."

> The story was slow-moving, about a park. The people in the park were all going about their business while the insects were going about theirs, in their own world. It was like going to a park and resting on the ground, relaxing and seeing an ant just walking on the ground. The park itself was completely peaceful to you, and you see the ant and he seems without a worry, but then you remember he is in his own world and doesn't even know you exist.

Instead of resisting the text, the student placed himself within it. Domination became acceptance. Other male students who rejected or resisted the other stories seemed to be similarly drawn into the world of "Kew Gardens." The student who trivialized both "Araby" and "Hills Like White Elephants" took the events in "Kew Gardens" much more seriously. The student who reduced "Araby" to a series of unrelated figures of speech made an attempt to interpret "Kew Gardens" by identifying a common characteristic of the people who passed through the garden, their tendency to reflect on their past.

The preponderance of responses to "Kew Gardens" like the responses to the other two stories, were submissive in that students had difficulty stepping back from the events of the story and finding a pattern of meaning. Responses included unassimilated plot summaries, hypotheses about the meaning of the text which accounted for only a fragment of the textual details, and expressions of frustration or confusion. As in the responses to the other two stories, however, more women were able to evaluate the disparate elements in the text and shape them into a meaningful pattern, one that involved empathetic judgment. Four male students and nine female students formulated statements that revealed a consistent pattern of meaning. The women's responses, however, tended to be more sharply focused.

One male student interpreted the story as follows:

> In the short story, "Kew Gardens," Virginia Woolf contrasts the unity and orderliness of nature with the apparent aimlessness of humanity. She describes the beauty of a flower bed, with all the different colored flowers joining together to produce a sense of unity and purpose, and then describes various persons as they stroll through the garden, each with his or her own thoughts and meaningless actions.
>
> Virginia Woolf shows how humans are wrapped up in their own world. We hurry about, busily attending to our own seemingly important affairs, and show little thought or concern for others around us. Instead of unity we practice individuality. We see, but we are blind to anyone and anything around us that does not directly benefit us.

Three other male students recognized that Woolf

contrasts the human order with the natural order. One student wrote, "Woolf seems to be telling us that nature is actually a controlling force on man, not the other way around as usually is thought." Another wrote, "The human values weren't worth much compared to the easy-going life found in the garden. Descriptions of the people were vague and they all seemed to fade away into the hot atmosphere. This seemed to show they were fading away from nature back to the world of work." Another student wrote, "Through the detailed description of nature, the author relates nature's ingredients to human experiences. It seems throughout the essay that these human experiences are just another breeze, meaning that although many have gone by, many more are to come, and that many of these experiences aren't as important as the people think they are."

Nine women students expressed similar themes, often focusing, however, more sharply on the limitations of the people described in the story. One student wrote: "We listen to the human voices and see how ridiculous the conversations are. If the garden is left in silence it seems to live. But as soon as some person starts talking the garden is silent. The snail doesn't move. The voices cause everything to freeze. Once the people are gone the garden comes to life." Another observed, "It seems the author, Virginia Woolf, feels that nature is above mankind in the story. She gives the insects the ability to think and to possess goals. The humans walk about aimlessly and searching for something. What they are searching for I get the feeling they don't really know." Another wrote:

Now the people themselves seemed to have influence over what takes place in (the) garden, but it was as if the garden had some sort of control over their past lives. It was as if the garden seemed to hide important mistakes that the people who came through the garden had made. The lives of the people seemed to change after they left the garden, almost as if they had just reached a turning point in their lives. It seems as if the flowers and the insects are an audience for the players: the players being all of the people that come into the garden, and they all seem to be putting an act on for each other.

These four male students and nine female students focused on the constancy of nature in contrast with the inconstancy of humanity. The women students, however, were more critical of the characters in the story: their conversations are "ridiculous"; they are searching for something but do not know what; the people are "putting on an act" for each other. Other responses by women students also indicated critical detachment. One woman wrote, "The garden, which all the people pass, is a symbol of nature's stability. The people who pass represent the unpredictable human race. The first couple that passes shows how people are never really satisfied with what they have. The small family seemed disjointed and unhappy. When the disoriented old man went by, the reader was aware of the kind of self-destruction one can induce." Another wrote, "Man's separation is shown through the disjointed conversation of the characters. They all have their own thoughts and show little concern for anyone else's thoughts. This is true of all three groups that pass the flower bed." Another wrote, "The people didn't seem to really relate to their surroundings; instead they allowed their thoughts to take them elsewhere. They chose to dive into the past and just leave the garden behind."

The conclusions that can be drawn from the analysis of the responses to the three stories must necessarily be tentative because of the size and nature of the sample. In order to make conclusive assertions about the relationship between gender and reading we need to look at a large number of response statements, at the responses of women and men readers from a variety of backgrounds, and at responses to numerous kinds of texts at various stages in the reading process. The study does suggest, however, that male students sometimes react to disturbing stories by rejecting them or by dominating them, a strategy, it seems, that women do not often employ. The study also suggests that women more often arrive at meaningful interpretations of stories because they more frequently break free of the submissive entanglement in a text and evaluate characters and events with critical detachment. My own informal observations of student readers bear out these contentions. I have noticed, for instance, that some male students react unempathetically to literature about vulnerable women characters such as Sylvia Plath's *The Bell Jar* and Margaret Atwood's *Surfacing*, and judge the protagonists "insane" or "crazy." I have also observed that women are often receptive to texts in that they attempt to understand them before making a judgment on them.

If further research supports my central contention, then we may find that women are considerably more confident and competent readers than they are speakers. Research on the relationship between gender and speaking indicates that men are assertive speakers who dominate conversations but that women are hesitant and deferential in speaking to others. Robin Lakoff in *Language and Women's Place,* for instance, argues that women are tentative and cautious in their speech; men are authoritative, coercive. She observed that men more frequently use forceful intensifiers such as the superlative *very,* whereas women use less forceful intensifiers such as *so* and *such.* She also found that women tend to use questions when declaratives would be more appropriate and to use modals and hedges to express uncertainty more than men do.[4]

Pamela Fishman's research essentially supports Lakoff's contention that women lack power in speech settings. In order to determine how women and men interact in conversation, Fishman placed tape recorders in the homes of three couples and then analyzed their topics of conversation. Fishman found that men dominated the conversations, either by ignoring topics initiated by their partner or by developing topics they themselves initiated. Fishman writes:

> We have seen that, at least among intimates in their homes, women raise many more topics than men. They do so because their topics often fail. They fail because the men don't work interactionally to develop them, whereas the women usually do work at developing topics raised by men. Thus, the definition of what are appropriate or inappropriate topics for a conversation are the man's choice. What part of the world a couple orients to is in his

control, not hers. Men control topics as much, if not more, by veto as by a positive effort.[5]

Reading is a silent, private activity and so perhaps affords women a degree of protection not present when they speak. Quite possibly the hedging and tentativeness of women's speech are transformed into useful interpretive strategies — receptivity and yet critical assessment of the text — in the act of reading. A willingness to listen, a sensitivity to emotional nuance, an ability to empathize with and yet judge, may be disadvantages in speech but advantages in reading. We may come to discover that women have interpretive powers that have not been sufficiently appreciated.

## APPENDIX

The twenty-six women and twenty-six men were enrolled in one of the seven sections of freshman composition taught by two male colleagues and myself in the spring quarter, 1980. Students wrote responses to the three stories during the first twenty minutes of the first class period in which the story was to be discussed. This structure insured that responses would be relatively free of the influence of the instructor or other classmates. Eleven women and eleven men in the sample who were enrolled in sections taught by one of the instructors read "Hills Like White Elephants" during week two, "Kew Gardens" during week three, and "Araby" during week ten of a ten-week quarter. The remaining fifteen women and fifteen men studied "Hills Like White Elephants" in week five, "Araby" in week eight, and "Kew Gardens" in week nine. Students knew that response statements would count toward their grade (responses to nine stories would constitute 15 percent of their grade) and that they would receive full credit if their responses indicated they had read the stories carefully. Instructors provided little feedback on the responses, and students did not know their statements would

[4]Robin Lakoff, *Language and Women's Place* (New York: Harper and Row, 1975), pp. 142–43. [Au.]

[5]Pamela Fishman, "What Do Couples Talk About When They're Alone?" in *Women's Language and Style,* ed. Douglass Butturff and Edmund L. Epstein (Akron, Ohio: E. L. Epstein, 1978), p. 21. [Au.]

be used for research purposes until the end of the term.

Students had the benefit of study questions that followed each story in the Norton anthology. They sometimes made reference to the questions in their responses, especially in discussing "Hills Like White Elephants," since a question indicated to them that Jig and the man were discussing an abortion.

Students who comprised the sample were fairly representative of the 1979–80 freshman class as a whole. The women in the sample had a mean score of 20.5 on their ACT composite score, compared to a mean score of 21.7 for all freshman women at Michigan Tech who entered the university in 1979. The men in the sample had a mean score of 19.04 on the English ACT, compared to a mean score for all freshman men at Michigan Tech of 19.8 (Mean scores for the sample were based on ACT scores of only 24 women and 24 men, as scores were not available for two women and two men.) These scores indicate that both in the sample and in the freshman class as a whole, women had somewhat higher verbal abilities, at least as measured by the ACT. Students in the sample were representative of Michigan Tech freshmen in other ways, as well. All but two men and one woman were 18 or 19 years old. Twenty-four of the twenty-six men were majoring in a field related to science, engineering, or math; the remaining two were majoring in business administration. Eighteen of the women were majoring in a field related to science, engineering, or math; the remaining eight were majoring in nursing (three), business administration (four), or social sciences (one). None of the students was majoring in humanities.

The selection of students was complicated by the fact that Michigan Tech is a predominantly male institution: in 1979–80, men outnumbered women 4 to 1. The ratio of men to women in the 1979–80 freshman class was 3 to 1, but the ratio in the seven sections of composition which served as a source for the sample was even higher (3.5 to 1), since a number of women students generally place into honors sections. I had originally intended to include forty women and forty men in the sample, but found I had responses to the three stories from only twenty-six women after I eliminated students not taking the course in sequence. The twenty-six men were selected from the data pool at random.

# 8

# ISSUE UNDER DEBATE: THE CANON

*I think there is a substance that prevails, however powerful the agents of change, that* King Lear, *underlying a thousand dispositions, subsists in change, prevails, by being patient of interpretation.*
— FRANK KERMODE

*When the value of a work is seen as unquestionable, those of its features that would, in a noncanonical work, be found alienating — for example, technically crude, philosophically naive, or narrowly topical — will be glozed over or backgrounded. . . . For example, incidents or sentiments of brutality, bigotry, and racial, sexual or national chauvinism . . . will be repressed or rationalized.*
— BARBARA HERRNSTEIN SMITH

*Canon-formation is not literary history. They are . . . dialectically opposed critical functions. When we practice literary history, we are relating works to a wider context, to other works, to aspects of the author's personal history or of a broader socio-political history . . . and so on. Yet when we . . . "elect" a canon of great works of art, we are removing those works from their historical context, and inserting them in an imaginary pantheon that we assume will last forever. A canonical text possesses, we believe, an authority . . . a value and a meaning that survives its contextual origins and the "test of time."*
— TREVOR ROSS

Which texts shall be accepted into the canon and which shall be relegated to the apocrypha? This was the question that both the compilers of the Masoretic text of the Old Testament in the first and second centuries and the patristic fathers establishing the New Testament in the third century had to answer. In those days, the books of Daniel and Esther were accepted into the canon, while the prophecies of Baruch ben Sirach and the chronicles of the Maccabees were exiled to the apocrypha; the gospels of Matthew and Luke were given canonical authority while the gospel of Nicodemus was discarded. Today, the equivalent question concerns a less well codified canon of texts: the major works of imaginative literature. While everyone knows that the canon of major Western writers includes Homer, Dante, Shakespeare, Molière, Tolstoy, . . . and so on down the list, below that level the consensus dissolves into controversy, and it is less clear who will survive and who will perish, whose reputation is beyond question and whose is vulnerable to challenge.

The one undeniable truth is that most works of the imagination do perish. Robert Escarpit, the French sociologist of literature, estimated that no more than one book in two hundred is read — read by a genuine public, that is, beyond the occasional burrower in libraries — ten years after its publication. Fewer still last twenty years or thirty; almost none survive a century. A century was the measure Samuel Johnson used to define a classic. In the preface to his 1763 edition of Shakespeare (p. 229), he explained that since the plays had survived a century — nearly a hundred and fifty years, in fact — and had lost their topical interest, they seemed meant for all time and might be criticized judicially against the other classics of drama that had also outlasted their age. It should hardly be surprising that "instant classics" — works that seem upon publication to be destined for a long life — most often surprise us by their premature decease: Thomas Wolfe was a great novelist in the 1930s but is almost unread today; even a recent biography (1987) failed to touch off a Wolfe revival.

But even long survival carries no guarantee of indefinite tenure. An important group of American poets, including John Greenleaf Whittier, Henry Wadsworth Longfellow, Sidney Lanier, and James Russell Lowell, were classics to the generation of Americans who entered school before World War II but are virtually unknown to the generation of Americans entering school today. Textbooks that once enshrined them as classics no longer have room for them. The same is true for English literature. Not long ago, the poetry of Walter Scott was thought worthy of memorization; today readers have little time even for his prose. Poets like Matthew Prior and George Crabbe, novelists like Elizabeth Manley, Robert Bage, and Charles Reade, and playwrights like Arthur Pinero have all dropped in esteem to near the vanishing point. Their works are out of print, exiled from most of the newest school anthologies, and can only be found in better university libraries and used bookshops. A glance through older catalogues of the Modern Library in America or the Everyman's Library or World's Classics editions in England confirms the difference between the canon of an earlier day and that of our own.

Survival is a risky business. The lists of required reading a culture prescribes for its educated elite have to be tailored to the short span of a human life. Like nature, therefore, literature has an ecology that forbids unlimited expansion; when something is added, something else must go. In a sense, the debate over the canon began when poets realized that they were competing for fame not merely with their coevals but with all of their predecessors. Hence Horace's remark, "I hate it when a book is condemned, not for being bad but for being new," which has been echoed by poet-critics for centuries thereafter.[1] But the contemporary debate over the canon is not entirely parallel with the poets' long-standing complaint that there cannot be room on Parnassus for everyone. The new interest is not in the *facts* of literary ecology but in the *process* by which certain texts achieve canonical status,

[1]Horace, *Epistles* II.1. 76–77.

particularly the relationship between literary value and the more sordid matters of literary economics and politics.

The debate over the canon has evolved, like the canon itself. As late as the mid-nineteenth century, in essays like Sainte-Beuve's "What Is a Classic?" (1850; reprinted in this chapter) or Arnold's "The Study of Poetry" (see Part I), literary value was assumed ultimately to be a function of human nature. "A true classic," says Sainte-Beuve,

> is an author who has enriched the human spirit, who has truly increased its treasure, who has caused it to take a step forward, who has discovered some unequivocal moral truth or laid fresh hold on some eternal passion in that heart where all seemed known and explored; who has conveyed his thought, his observation, or his discovery in whatever form, only let it be liberal and grand, choice and judicious, intrinsically wholesome and seemly; who has spoken to all men in a style of his own which at the same time turns out to be every man's style, a style which is new without neologism, at once new and old, easily contemporaneous with every age.

Arnold appeals to "the best that has been thought and said" as though it could be true for all time. T. S. Eliot speaks of the "tradition" as an "eternal order" — a club to which new members, agreeable to the charter founders, are always welcome (see Eliot's essay in Part I). For such critics, though beauty is necessarily subjective — not the object's possession of a quantum of Platonic essence but a conformity or relation between the object of art and human nature — quality is in effect absolute because human nature is presumed constant. The ecology of literature is seen as a winnowing process: Time destroys the worst and leaves the best, and time will do this, apparently, without any help from literary critics. Absolutists are operating nowadays as well. Hans-Georg Gadamer, the mentor of the reception theorists Iser and Jauss, defends the classic as "a truly historical category, a consciousness of something enduring, of significance that cannot be lost and is independent of all the circumstances of time." Like Hegel, who understood the classic as "that which signifies itself and hence also interprets itself," Gadamer feels that the timelessness of the classic is in itself "a mode of historical being."[2]

On the other side are the relativists who believe that literary quality is a function of the current interests of the reading public; each public revises the short list drawn up by publics of the past to accord with its own cultural needs. This is the perspective of Jane Tompkins's *Sensational Designs: The Cultural Work of American Fiction, 1790–1860* (1985), which suggests that imaginative texts are admired in a society to the extent that they meet its cultural needs. Thus, Susan Warner's didactic *The Wide Wide World* (1850) was immensely popular in its day because its sentimental melodrama defined cultural stereotypes in an intelligible way for a public adrift because of rapid social change.

Novels like *The Wide Wide World* are of undoubted historical interest, and certainly writers like Warner (and Harriet Beecher Stowe) more closely defined

---

[2]Hans-Georg Gadamer, *Truth and Method* (New York: Continuum Press, 1982), p. 256–57.

the interests and tastes of the American public of their time than did writers like Hawthorne or Melville, Emerson or Thoreau. But Tompkins wishes to go further. She denigrates Hawthorne's early survival as due primarily to his connections in New England editorial and publishing circles, which kept his works alive through biographies and new editions for twenty years after his death. Tompkins recognizes that no conspiracy of editors could have kept Hawthorne before the public for a hundred and thirty years, but she does not allow his fame since the 1870s to result from his classical timelessness. Rather, she claims, each generation of readers has *redefined* Hawthorne's greatness according to its own terms, and therefore nothing intrinsic to the author's work has preserved his reputation. The "classic" Hawthorne thus splinters, in this analysis, into different facets, each of which has, for assorted social, political, economic, and cultural reasons, been the darling of successive interpretive communities and interest groups.

Tompkins's analysis of Hawthorne translates the concept of aesthetic quality into ideology. Her ultimate end is to show how cultural politics may alter the literary canon — how feminists may displace Hawthorne and Melville in favor of currently neglected writers like Warner and Stowe.[3] But critics have long tried to influence the canon, and it is difficult to know how far they have ever succeeded. Jeremy Collier's "Short View of the Profanity . . . of the English Stage" (1698) is sometimes credited with having cleaned up the nastiness of Restoration comedy, although recent stage historians have suggested that the most offensive plays were written in the 1670s and that the stage had been cleaning up its own act for two decades before Collier wrote. And despite the prestige of Samuel Johnson, the "Great Cham of Literature" in eighteenth-century England, his preference for Richardson over Fielding ("a barren rascal") has not been echoed by succeeding generations.

Perhaps the closest equivalent to a Johnson in our own day was F. R. Leavis. It is hard to think of a twentieth-century critic of greater moral weight and prestige. Unlike Sainte-Beuve, Leavis conceived of literature as a manifestation of culture and of culture itself as something molded by the forces of history. This may be how one must treat his claim, in Chapter 1 of *The Great Tradition*, that "the great novelists are Jane Austen, George Eliot, Henry James, and Joseph Conrad" (with D. H. Lawrence included as an addendum). For this sociocultural savant, the novel was a genre designed to speak of man and society, of the individual and his consciousness, against the backdrop of the social forces that shaped them and

[3]Like Barbara Herrnstein Smith's "Contingencies of Value" in this chapter, Tompkins assumes that aesthetic approbation simply mirrors the political and cultural interests of a dominant class, which then uses the literary canon as a way of inculcating its values — a vicious canonical circle, parallel to the hermeneutic circle discussed in Ch. 9. While interests clearly play their part in literary evaluation and in canon-formation, the unresolved question is whether this part is played solely by those interests that hinge on class or gender or ethnicity, or whether interests broader in their application and longer-ranging in their goals also play a serious role. One of the best-considered attempts to widen the canonical circle is Charles Altieri, "The Idea and Ideal of a Literary Canon," in Robert Von Hallberg, ed., *Canons* (Chicago: University of Chicago Press, 1983), pp. 41–64.

conflicted with them. For this reason, the greatest novelists were those for whom these issues were paramount. Mere humorists like Fielding and Sterne in the eighteenth century, or Thackeray in the nineteenth, need not apply. At the same time, contemporary modernists like Woolf and Joyce — for whom society did not exist as a separable force but as something implicit within individual consciousness — did not appeal to Leavis. As a result, his list of favorites, while certainly enshrined in today's canon, seems quirky rather than inexorably ordained, a quirkiness that to later eyes seems a common characteristic of all lists drawn up by magisterial critics.

If magisterial critics like Johnson, Arnold, Eliot, and Leavis cannot dictate the canon, then who does? Perhaps it is a mistake to look to individuals; perhaps institutional factors should be explored, as Barbara Herrnstein Smith has done in "Contingencies of Value." To begin with, it seems clear that social change produces audiences with new and varied interests. The politics of feminism over the past twenty years has sparked a growth of interest in previously neglected female authors.[4] But although it appears that society has changed rapidly over the past half-century, the canon has not. Strong conservative forces (including the very *idea* of a canon) are operating to keep the canon constant. Institutional education is arguably the strongest of these conservative forces. The most widely read texts are those read in schools, where teachers are likely to teach the texts that were valued during their own education. Furthermore, some texts may survive precisely because they are useful to educators: Xenophon's *Memorabilia* may have endured not because of its intellectual quality but because it was a perfect vehicle for teaching children the principles of Greek syntax; and some poems may be extant today because they are perfect examples of prosody or symbolism.

Also to be considered are other classes of people who are responsible for altering the literary canon. Since education is an important conservative force, those who compile textbooks and anthologies function, more and more self-consciously these days, as both the preservers and the reshapers of a tradition. Today the editors of anthologies are indeed tastemakers, but given the institutional framework of publishing, their individual tastes are seldom any more decisive than those of the magisterial critics. When an editor compiles a list of texts to be included in a book, the editor's voice does not sing solo. The project editor assigned by the publisher will make suggestions for inclusion and exclusion, and after these are assimilated, the list will be sent out to a number of experts who will express their own preferences. Meanwhile, editors have their own institutional reasons for repressing the quirks of personal taste. Most of them want their books to sell, and they will do so only if they provide what the teachers who assign textbooks want.

In this process we can identify initiators (the authors of texts), mediators (editors, publishers, marketers, teachers), and ultimately, consumers. This structure also exists for trade books, although here, book reviewers (and the editors who give prominence to certain books and not to others, who assign books to reviewers

<hr>

[4]See Ch. 6, "Feminist Literary Criticism," pp. 1068–69.

likely to be friendly or hostile) have an important mediating role. In the nineteenth century, the editors of magazines determined which novels would be serialized — an important determinant of sales and reputation, while the heads of circulating libraries (and some of these, like Mudie's, were large and influential) could often make or break reputations by including authors on or excluding authors from their lists. All these mediators between author and reader operate under capitalism: They may indulge their personal taste, but at the risk that the market may disagree and put them out of business.

These factors, along with others, are cited in Smith's essay, which makes the best possible case for relativism. Smith feels that the evaluation of a work is not influenced by any absolute quality it possesses but by whether or not it meets the cultural needs of a public. (For Smith, "aesthetic value" is an aspect of economics, broadly conceived.) As society changes, the work takes one of two trajectories: downward to oblivion or upward toward canonical status. Smith recognizes that even canonical works can "always move into a trajectory of extinction" under unfavorable circumstances. But canonical status works to protect a text from this path because "features that would, in a noncanonical work, be found alienating . . . technically crude, philosophically naive, or narrowly topical — will be glozed over or backgrounded." If a work is bigoted or chauvinistic, "there will be a tendency among humanistic scholars and academic critics to 'save the text' by transferring the locus of its interest to more formal or structural features."

Smith's paradigm of the relationship between a culture and its canon is also fascinating on the question of how the generic categorization of cultural objects follows from society's changing interests and purposes. An illuminating example of these dynamic relations in action can be found in Houston Baker's "Generational Shifts and the Recent Criticism of Afro-American Literature," reprinted in this chapter. Here Baker shows, from an explicitly Marxist perspective, how shifts in the class interests of three "generations" of critics of Afro-American literature have changed not only the language of criticism but also their evaluations of the primary texts of that tradition.

It is obvious that the middle ground between canonical absolutism and relativism will be difficult to defend philosophically; at the same time, many critics have found it hard to believe firmly in either extreme. The indubitable fact that once-canonized texts can disappear into oblivion undermines any idea of absolute quality. Yet, despite Smith's arguments, the fact that Homer and Shakespeare have been revered over the centuries seems to be the result of more than accident or the inertia of literary institutions. A psychological explanation of this may be found in Kant's notion that the judgment of taste is subjective but absolute, that the disinterested apprehension of beauty we experience makes us *feel* (whatever our empirical knowledge to the contrary) that everyone ought to agree with us, that our judgment is true for everyone and for all time. (See Kant's essay, p. 248.)

Few critics have mediated between absolution and relativism with the deftness of Frank Kermode. In *The Classic,* excerpted here, Kermode accepts the relativist position in principle but also holds that "the survival of the classic" depends on its having "a surplus of the signifier" — what might be called the sort of very rich economy that lends it use and value in a large variety of cultural systems. Classics like *King Lear* or *Wuthering Heights* "must always signify more than is needed by any one interpreter or any one generation of interpreters." By richness texts endure: Ripeness is all.

## Selected Bibliography

Altieri, Charles. *Act and Quality*. Amherst: University of Massachusetts Press, 1981.

Baym, Nina. "Melodramas of Beset Manhood." *American Quarterly* 33 (1981): 123–39.

Beardsley, Monroe C. *Aesthetics: Problems in the Philosophy of Criticism*. New York: Hackett, 1981.

Eliot, T. S. *What Is a Classic?* London: Faber, 1945.

Ellis, John. *The Theory of Literary Criticism*. Berkeley: University of California Press, 1974.

Escarpit, Robert. *Sociology of Literature*. London: Cass, 1971.

Fiedler, Leslie A., and Houston A. Baker, Jr., eds. *English Literature: Opening Up the Canon*. Baltimore: Johns Hopkins University Press, 1981.

Fowler, Alistair. "Genre and the Literary Canon." *New Literary History* 11 (1979): 97–119.

Gadamer, Hans-Georg. *Truth and Method*. New York: Continuum Press, 1982.

Hirsch, E. D. *The Aims of Interpretation*. Chicago: University of Chicago Press, 1976.

Hume, David. "Of the Standard of Taste." In *Four Dissertations*. London: A. Millar, 1757.

Kant, Immanuel. *Critique of Judgment*. Trans. J. H. Bernard. New York: Hafner, 1966.

Kermode, Frank. *The Classic*. Cambridge: Harvard University Press, 1983.

Krieger, Murray. "Literary Analysis and Evaluation — and the Ambidextrous Critic." In *Criticism: Speculative and Analytical Essays*, ed. L. S. Dembo. Madison: University of Wisconsin Press, 1968.

Leavis, Frank Raymond. *Revaluation: Tradition and Development in English Poetry*. New York: New York University Press, 1963.

Reichert, John. *Making Sense of Literature*. Chicago: University of Chicago Press, 1977.

Richards, I. A. *Principles of Literary Criticism*. 1924; New York: Harcourt Brace, 1961.

Robinson, Lillian. "Treason Our Text: Feminist Challenges to the Literary Canon." *Tulsa Studies in Women's Literature* 2 (1983): 83–98.

Sammons, Jeffrey. *Literary Sociology and Practical Criticism*. Bloomington: Indiana University Press, 1977.

Segers, Rien T. *The Evaluation of Literary Texts*. Lisse: 1978.

Strelka, Joseph. *Problems of Literary Evaluation*. University Park: Pennsylvania State University Press, 1969.

Von Hallberg, Robert, ed. *Canons*. Chicago: University of Chicago Press, 1983.

# Charles-Augustin Sainte-Beuve
## 1804–1869

*The most celebrated European literary critic of his age, Charles-Augustin Sainte-Beuve was born at Boulogne-sur-Mer. His mother, widowed before her son was born, managed to have him educated in Paris, where he elected to study medicine. Concurrently with his scientific studies, Sainte-Beuve immersed himself in French literature and history, and ultimately his love of literature determined his career. During his college years Sainte-Beuve contributed literary essays to journals; in 1827, one of his reviews caught the eye of Victor Hugo. Under the influence of Hugo and fellow romantic writers (as well as the poetry of Wordsworth and Coleridge), Sainte-Beuve wrote a novel,* Volupté *(1834) and three volumes of poetry — the small success of which confirmed that his true genius was as a critic. Throughout the 1830s he wrote a series of character sketches of literary figures for the* Revue des Deux Mondes *and the* Revue de Paris; *these "portraits," a genre he made his own, established his reputation. In 1836 Sainte-Beuve joined a commission on French literary history and in 1837 became visiting professor at the Academy of Lausanne. His lectures on seventeenth-century Jansenism evolved into the history* Port-Royal *(1840–48), one of his greatest successes. During the* Port-Royal *years, Sainte-Beuve was appointed the librarian at the French Institute's Mazarine Library (1840) and elected to the French Academy (1844). In 1849 he began a weekly column of literary essays for the* Constitutionnel, *"Causeries du lundi," which made him famous throughout Europe. These "Monday Discourses" ran for twenty years; collected, they fill twenty-eight volumes. Perhaps the pinnacle of his achievement occurred in 1865, when Sainte-Beuve, the man of letters, was nominated for senator. "What Is a Classic?" was first published in 1850.*

# What Is a Classic?

This is a delicate question, and one of which a good many different solutions might have been given at different periods and seasons. A clever man has this day propounded it to me, and even if I cannot solve it, I want at least to try to examine and discuss it before our readers, were it only to induce them to reply to it themselves, and if I can, clear up their ideas and mine upon it. And why should not one occasionally venture to treat in criticism of some of those subjects which are not personal, in which not someone, but something, is spoken of, and which our neighbors the English have so successfully made into a complete branch, under the modest title of essays? It is true that, in order to treat of such subjects, which are always in a measure abstract and moral, one must speak in a calm atmosphere, be sure of one's own attention and that of others, and seize one of those quarters of an hour of silence, moderation, and leisure, which are seldom granted to our beloved France, and which her brilliant genius bears with impatience, even when she is wishing to be good, and has given up making revolutions.

Translated by A. J. Butler.

A classic, according to the usual definition, is an author of past times, already hallowed by general admiration, who is an authority in his own style. The word *classic*, taken in this sense, begins to appear among the Romans. With them the *classici*, properly so called, were not all the citizens of the different classes, but only those of the highest class, who possessed, at least, an income of a certain fixed figure. All those who had a lower income were known by the appellation of *infra classem*, below *the* class properly so called. For example, we find the word *classicus* used by Aulus Gellius[1] and applied to writers: a writer of worth and mark is *classicus assiduusque scriptor*, a writer who counts, who has some possessions under the sun, and who is not confounded with the proletariat crowd. Such an expression presupposes an age sufficiently advanced for a criticism and classification, as it were, of literature to have come into existence.

For the moderns, the true and only classics were, in the first instance, naturally the ancients. The Greeks, who by rare good fortune had — a

[1]Aulus Gellius, Roman scholar and antiquarian of the second century A.D. [Ed.]

happy relief to their intellect — no other classics than themselves, were at first the sole classics of the Romans, who spent much trouble and ingenuity on imitating them. They in their turn, after the fine ages of their literature, after Cicero and Virgil, had their own classics, and they became almost exclusively the classics of the centuries which succeeded. The Middle Ages, which, though not as ignorant as might be thought of Latin antiquity, were wanting in the sense of proportion and taste, confused the ranks and orders. Ovid was put on a better footing than Homer, and Boethius appeared to be a classic at least equal to Plato. The "new birth" of literature in the fifteenth and sixteenth centuries came to clear up this long confusion, and then only was admiration graduated. The real classic authors of the twofold antiquity stood out for the future on a luminous background, and formed two harmonious groups on their two eminences.

Meanwhile, modern literature had been born, and some of the more precocious members of it, like the Italian, already had their own fashion of antiquity. Dante had appeared, and his posterity had lost no time in saluting him as a classic. Italian poetry may have retreated greatly since then, but when she has desired, she has already recovered and always retained some impulse, some reverberation, from this high origin. It is of no slight importance for poetry thus to take its point of departure, its classic source in a lofty place — rather, for example, to descend from a Dante than to issue laboriously from a Malherbe.[2]

Modern Italy had her classics, and Spain had every right to believe she was also in possession of hers, when France still had hers to seek. Indeed, a few writers of talent endowed with originality and exceptional raciness, a few brilliant efforts isolated and without successors, shattered immediately and needing always to be begun afresh, do not suffice to confer upon a nation the solid and imposing basis of literary wealth. That idea of a *classic* implies in itself something which has sequence and solidity, which forms a whole and makes a tradition, something which has "composition," is handed on to posterity and

lasts. It was only after the brilliant years of Louis XIV that the nation felt with a thrill of pride that this happiness had come to it. All voices then told it to Louis XIV with flattery, exaggeration, and emphasis, and yet with a certain perception of truth. Then appeared a singular and quaint inconsistency: the men who were most in love with the wonders of that age of Louis the Great, and who went so far as to sacrifice all the ancients to the moderns, those men, of whom Perrault was the chief, tended to exalt and consecrate those very men whom they found the most ardent and contradictory adversaries. Boileau defended and supported the ancients with anger against Perrault, who cried up the moderns, that is to say Corneille, Molière, Pascal, and the eminent men of his century, including Boileau as one of the first. The good La Fontaine, when he took Doctor Huet's part in the quarrel, did not perceive that he himself, in spite of his oversight, was in his turn on the eve of waking up to find himself a classic.

An instance is the best definition: France possessed her century of Louis XIV, and could consider it at a little distance; she knew what it was to be classic better than by any reasoning. The eighteenth century, till its upheaval, added to this idea by a few fine works due to its four great men. Read Voltaire's *Siècle de Louis XIV*, Montesquieu's *La Grandeur et la Décadence des Romains*, Buffon's *Époques de Nature*, the *Vicaire Savoyard*, and the fine pages of meditations and descriptions of nature by Jean Jacques,[3] and say whether the eighteenth century in its memorable past has not known how to reconcile tradition with independence and liberty of development. But at the beginning of this century and under the Empire, in presence of the first attempts of a decidedly novel and somewhat daring literature, the idea of a classic among some refractory minds, influenced more by vexation than by severity, contracted and shrank strangely. The first dictionary of the Academy (1694) simply defined a classic author as "an ancient author, highly approved, who is an authority in the subject he treats of." The dictionary of the Academy of

---

[2]François de Malherbe (1555–1628), French poet known for precision of technique and poverty of imagination. [Ed.]

[3]Rousseau (1712–78). [Ed.]

1835 urges this definition much more closely, and makes it exact and even narrow instead of, as it was, somewhat vague. It defines classic authors as "those who have become *models* in any language," and, in the articles which follow, these expressions — *models, rules* established for composition and style, *strict rules* of the art to which you must *conform* — are continually recurring. This definition of the *classic* has evidently been made by our respectable precursors of the Academy, in presence and in sight of what was then called the *romantic*, that is to say, in sight of the enemy. It seems to me that the time ought now to have come to renounce these restricting and timid definitions and to widen their spirit.

A true classic, as I should like to hear it defined, is an author who has enriched the human mind, who has really augmented its treasures, who has made it take one more step forward, who has discovered some unequivocal moral truth, or has once more seized hold of some eternal passion in that heart where all seemed known and explored; who has rendered his thought, his observation, or his discovery under no matter what form, but broad and large, refined, sensible, sane, and beautiful in itself; who has spoken to all in a style of his own which yet belongs to all the world, in a style which is new without neologisms, new and ancient, easily contemporaneous with every age.

Such a classic may have been revolutionary for a moment, or at least may have seemed to be, but he is not so; he has not, in the first instance, fallen upon everything around him; he has overthrown only what was in his way so as quickly to replace the balance in favor of order and beauty.

You can, if you will, set down some names under this definition, which I would purposely make grand and compendious, or in one word, generous. I should place there first the Corneille of *Polyeucte*, of *Cinna*, of *Les Horaces*. I should place there Molière, the most complete and the richest genius we have had in French.

"Molière is so great," said Goethe (that king of criticism),

> that he surprises us afresh every time we read him. He is a man who stands alone; his plays verge on

the tragic, and no one has had the courage to imitate them. His *Avare*, where the vice destroys all affection between father and son, is one of the most sublime of works, and dramatic in the highest degree. Every action in a play for the stage must be important in itself and tend towards a still greater event. *Tartuffe* is a model in this respect. What a setting out of the subject is the first scene! Everything is highly significant from the beginning, and makes you anticipate something still more important. The outset of any similar play of Lessing's which may be cited is very fine; but that of *Tartuffe* is unique. It is the greatest thing of the kind. . . . Every year I read a play of Molière's, just as from time to time I gaze at some engraving after the old Italian masters.[4]

I do not pretend to say that this definition of a classic which I have just given does not go somewhat beyond the idea one generally forms for oneself under that name. It is especially made to comprise conditions of order, wisdom, moderation, and reasonableness, which prevail over and contain all others. Having occasion to praise M. Royer-Collard, M. de Rémusat said: "If he gets from our classics a pure taste, appropriate terms, variety of phrase, a careful attention in suiting expression to thought, to himself alone he owes the character which he gives to it all." One sees here that the part allotted to classic qualities seems rather to depend on selection and nicety of meaning, to an ornate and restrained style, and that, too, is the general opinion. In this sense the classics, properly so called, would be writers of the second rank — correct, sensible, elegant, always clear, expressing themselves with a passion not devoid of nobility, and a power kept slightly in reserve. Marie-Joseph Chénier has traced the poetic spirit of these temperate and accomplished writers in these lines, where he shows himself their apt disciple:

> C'est le bon sens, la raison qui fait tout,
> Vertu, génie, esprit, talent et goût.
> Qu'est-ce vertu? Raison mise en pratique;
> Talent? Raison produite avec éclat;
> Esprit? Raison qui finement s'exprime;

[4] From the *Conversations with Eckermann* (1836–48) [Ed.]

Le goût n'est rien qu'un bon sens delicat;
Et le génie est la raison sublime.[5]

In writing these lines he was evidently thinking of Pope, Despréaux,[6] and Horace, the master of them all. The real essence of this theory, which makes imagination and even feeling subordinate to reason, and of which Scaliger, perhaps, struck the first note among modern writers, is, strictly speaking, the *Latin* theory, and this has also for a long time been the French theory. It has some truth in it if it is only used in the right place, if that word *reason* is not misused; but it is evident that it is misused, and that if reason, for instance, can be confused with poetic genius and their union results in a moral epistle, it cannot be the same thing as that genius which we find so varied and so diversely creative in expressing the passions of the drama or the epic. Where will you find reason in the fourth book of the *Aeneid*, and in the ecstasies of Dido? Where will you find it in the madness of Phaedra? Be this as it may, the spirit which has prompted this theory tends to place in the first rank of the classics those writers who have governed their inspiration rather than those who have given themselves more up to it, to place Virgil there more certainly than Homer, Racine more than Corneille. The masterpiece which this theory loves to quote, and which does indeed unite every condition of prudence, strength, progressive daring, moral elevation and greatness, is *Athalie*. In Turenne,[7] in his last two campaigns, and Racine in *Athalie*, we have the great examples of what wise and prudent men can do when they come into possession of the full maturity of their genius, and enter upon their crowning exploits.

Buffon, in his *Discourse on Style*, in which he insists on that oneness of plan, arrangement, and execution which is the stamp of really classic work, has said:

> Every subject is one only; and *however spacious it may be it can be comprised in a single treatise.* Interruptions, pauses, and sections should only be used when different subjects are treated of, or when, having to speak of great, complicated, or incongruous matters, the march of genius finds itself impeded by the multiplicity of the obstacles in its way and constrained by the requirements of the circumstances; otherwise a great number of divisions, far from making a work more solid, destroy its unity; the book seems clearer at first sight, but the author's intention remains obscure.

And he continues his criticism, having in his mind Montesquieu's *l'Esprit des Lois*, a book excellent at bottom, but all cut up into segments, into which the illustrious author, worn out before the end, could not breathe all his spirit, nor even to some extent arrange all his matter. Yet I find it hard to believe that Buffon was not thinking in the same place by way of contrast of Bossuet's *Discours sur l'Histoire Universelle*, a subject, indeed, both vast and single, and which the great author has yet been able to comprise in one solitary treatise. Let anyone open the first edition of 1681, before the division into chapters which was introduced later, and which has passed from the margin into the text and cut it up; everything is there unfolded in one sequence and almost at one breath, and one would say that the orator has here done like the Nature of whom Buffon writes, that he *has worked on an eternal plan and has nowhere deviated from it,* so far does he seem to have penetrated into the intimacy of the counsels of Providence.

*Athalie* and the *Discours sur l'Histoire Universelle*, such are the highest masterpieces which the strict classic theory can offer alike to its friends and its enemies. Yet in spite of all the admirable simplicity and majesty with which these unique productions are executed, we should like for the practical purposes of art to extend this idea a little, and to show that there is room for enlarging it without going so far as to relax

---

[5]"It is good sense, reason, that accomplishes everything: virtue, genius, wit, talent, and taste. What is virtue? Reason put into practice. Talent? Reason produced with glitter. Wit? Reason which expresses itself precisely. Taste is nothing but delicate good sense, and genius is sublime reason." Marie-Joseph Chénier (1764–1811), poet and tragedian, was the brother of the guillotined romantic poet André Chénier. [Ed.]

[6]The French critic Nicolas Boileau (1636–1711), neo-classical poet and critic, author of the influential *L'Art poétique* (1674). [Ed.]

[7]Turenne (1611–75) was commander-in-chief under Louis XIV; his final campaigns in the third Dutch war (1672–75) were marked by brilliant tactical moves against superior forces. [Ed.]

it. Goethe, whom I like to quote on such a subject, says:

> I call all *healthy* work classic, all *unhealthy* work romantic. The poem of the *Nibelungen* is for me as classic as Homer; both are healthy and vigorous. It is not because they are new that the works of the day are romantic, but because they are weak, sickly, or diseased. It is not because they are old that the works of past times are classic, but because they are energetic, fresh, and healthy. If we were to consider the romantic and the classic from these two points of view, we should soon all be agreed.[8]

And, indeed, I should like every free mind to travel round the world and give itself up to the contemplation of the different literatures in their primitive vigor and their infinite variety before marking down and fixing its ideas on this subject. What would such a mind see? First of all a Homer, the father of the classic world, but himself less certainly a single and very distinct individual than the vast and living expression of an active period and a semibarbarous civilization. To make a classic properly so called of him, it has been necessary to attribute to him a design, a plan, literary intentions, qualities of criticism and urbanity as an afterthought, of which he would certainly never have dreamt in the overflowing development of his natural inspiration. And whom do we see beside him? Imposing and venerable men of antiquity it is true, such as Aeschylus or Sophocles, but all mutilated, and standing there only to represent to us the wreck of themselves, all that remains of many others doubtless as worthy as they to survive, who have perished forever beneath the ill-treatment of the ages. This thought alone might teach a man of well-balanced mind not to look at literature as a whole, even classic literature, with too simple and too limited a view, and he may learn from it that that exact and well-proportioned order which has had so much force since, has been introduced only artificially into our admiration of the past.

And how would it be when we enter the modern world? The greatest names we perceive at the outset of literature are those which most

shock and disturb certain restricted ideas of the beautiful and the fitting which it has been thought desirable to convey in poetry. Is Shakespeare a classic, for instance? Yes, he is so today, for England and for the world; but in the time of Pope he was not. Pope and his friends were the only classics in the full sense; they seemed to become so indubitably the day after their death. Today they are still classics and they deserve to be; but they are only in the second rank, and there they may be seen forever, surpassed and kept in their place by him who has again his place on the topmost skyline.

In shall certainly not be the one to speak evil of Pope or of his excellent followers, especially when they are as sweet and natural as Goldsmith; next to the greatest, these, between writers and poets, are perhaps the best fitted for imparting charm to life. One day, when Lord Bolingbroke was writing to Dr. Swift, Pope put a postscript to the letter, in which he said: "I imagine that if we three were to spend even three years together, the result might be some advantage to our century." No, we must never speak lightly of those who have had the right to say such things of themselves without boasting, and it would be much better to envy the favored and fortunate ages when men of talent could suggest such unions, which were not then chimerical. These ages, whether we call them by the name of Louis XIV or of Queen Anne, are the only really classic ages, using the word in its limited sense, the only ones which offer a propitious climate and shelter to perfected talent. We here, in our disconnected period, are but too well aware of it, when talents possibly equal to theirs have got lost and dissipated through the uncertain ties and hardships of the times. Anyway, let us apportion to each kind of greatness its due influence and superiority. The true master genius triumphs over those difficulties which wreck others; Dante, Shakespeare, and Milton knew how to attain to their supremacy and to produce their imperishable works in spite of obstacles, persecutions, and storms. The opinions of Byron about Pope have been the subject of much discussion, and an attempt has been made to explain that kind of contradiction which has led the singer of *Don Juan* and of *Childe Harold* to extol the purely

[8]From *Conversations with Eckermann*. [Ed.]

classic school, and declare it to be the only good one, while he himself took so different a course. Goethe has once more said the right word about this, when remarks that Byron, so great in the outburst and spring of his poetry, yet feared Shakespeare, who is more capable than he of creating and putting life into his characters. He would have liked to deny him; he was irked by that unselfish superiority; he felt that he could never comfortably display himself beside him. He has never renounced Pope because he did not fear him; he well knew that Pope was a *wall* beside him.

If the school of Pope had kept the supremacy, and a kind of honorary empire over the past, as Byron wished, Byron would have been the first and only one of his kind; the erection of Pope as that wall hid Shakespeare's great form from sight, whereas, while Shakespeare reigns and dominates in all his height, Byron is only second.

We in France had no great classic before the era of Louis XIV; we lacked Dantes and Shakespeares, those original authorities to which one returns sooner or later in the days of emancipation. We have had only, as it were, the rough drafts of great poets, such as Mathurin Régnier and Rabelais, without any ideal, without the passion and the gravity which give consecration. Montaigne was a sort of classic before his time, of the Horatian breed, but one who, for want of worthy surroundings, abandoned himself like a strayed child to all the libertine fancies of his pen and his humor. The result is that we have earned less than any other nation the right to claim loudly one day, through our author-ancestors, our literary liberties and charters, and that it has been a still greater difficulty to us to work out our freedom and remain classic. Yet, with Molière and La Fontaine among our classics of the great era, there is sufficient cause for refusing no rights of legitimacy to any who will make the venture with knowledge.

The important thing now seems to me to be to preserve the notion and the cult, and at the same time to widen it. There is no recipe for making classics: this point must sooner or later be clearly recognized. To think that by imitating certain qualities of purity, of sobriety, of correctness and elegance, quite independently even of character and the divine spark, you will become a classic, to think that after Racine the father there is room for Racine the son; an estimable and melancholy role which is the worst thing in poetry. Yet more: it is not a good thing to appear too quickly and right off, to one's contemporaries, as a pure classic; see how faint the color looks at a distance of twenty-five years! How many there are of these precocious classics who do not last and are only ephemeral! You turn round one morning and are surprised to find them no longer standing behind you. They have only been there, in the gay phrase of Madame de Sévigné, as a breakfast for the sun. With regard to classics the most spontaneous are still the best and the greatest: ask those virile geniuses who are really born immortal and who flourish perpetually, whether it is not so. Apparently the least classic of the four poets of Louis XIV was Molière; he was applauded then far more than he was esteemed; people enjoyed him without knowing his value. After him the least classic seemed to be La Fontaine; and see what came of it — for both of them — two centuries later. Far before Boileau, before even Racine, are they not today unanimously recognized as the most fruitful writers, the richest as regards the characteristics of universal morality?

After all, we need really sacrifice nothing — depreciate nothing. The temple of taste, I quite believe, needs rebuilding; but in rebuilding it, it is merely a question of making it greater, and of letting it become the Pantheon of all the nobility of mankind — of all those who have had a notable and lasting share in increasing the sum of the pleasures and possessions of the mind. As for me, who would in no sense pretend (as is evident) to be the architect or director of such a temple, I will confine myself to expressing some wishes — competing for the specification, as it were. Above all, I would exclude no one worthy to enter, and I would give everyone the place due to him, from Shakespeare, the most unfettered of creative geniuses and unconsciously the greatest of the classics, to Andrieux, the very last of the classics in miniature. "In my Father's house are many mansions."[9] Let that be no less

[9]Gospel of John 14:3. [Ed.]

true of the kingdom of the beautiful here than of the kingdom of heaven above. Homer always and everywhere would be the first in it, the most like a god; but behind him, like the attendant train of the three kings of the East, would follow those three grand poets, those three Homers long ignored by us, who also themselves have made grand and admirable epics, the Hindu poets Valmiki and Vyasa, and the Persian Firdousi.[10] In the realm of taste, it is a good thing to know, at least, that such men exist, and not to split up the human race. Having paid this homage to what it is sufficient to perceive and recognize, we would quit our own boundaries no more, and we would divert our eyes with a thousand splendid or agreeable sights, and rejoice in a thousand various and surprising meetings; yet their apparent confusion would never be wanting in concord and harmony. The most ancient of sages and poets — those who have put human morality into maxims and have chanted it in plainsong — would converse with each other in rare suave speech, and would not be surprised to understand each other at the very first word. Solon, Hesiod, Theognis, Job, Solomon, and why not Confucius himself? would greet the most ingenious modern authors, La Rochefoucauld or La Bruyère, who would say to each other as they listened to them: "They knew all that we know, and we have found nothing new by bringing experience up to date." On the hill most in sight, with the most easy slopes, Virgil surrounded by Menander, Tibullus, Terence, Fénelon, would abandon himself with them to converse full of charm and a sacred enchantment; his gentle face would beam with radiance and the hue of modesty, as on that day when, entering the Roman theater just as they had been reciting his verses, he saw the entire assembly rise in front of him by a simultaneous movement and pay him the same homage as to Augustus himself. Not far from him, and regretting to be separated from so dear a friend, Horace would preside in his turn (so far as a poet and sage so keen of wit can be said to preside) over the group of the poets of civic life and of those who have known how to talk as well as sing — Pope and

Despréaux, the one grown less irritable and the other less censorious. That true poet, Montaigne, would be there with them, and his presence would completely remove all appearance of a literary academy from this charming corner. La Fontaine would forget himself there, and, henceforth less flighty, would be content to remain. Voltaire would pass by, but he would not have the patience to stop, though at the same time delighting in it. On the same hill as Virgil, a little lower down, Xenophon would be seen with an unaffected look very little like a captain, but of a kind to make him rather resemble a priest of the Muses. He would gather around him the Attic minds of every language and of every country — Addison, Pellisson, Vauvenargues, all who feel the value of suave expression, exquisite simplicity, and a sweet, though not unadorned, carelessness. In the center of the place three great men would often like to meet before the portico of the principal temple (for there would be several within the enclosure), and if those be together, there would not be a fourth, however great, to whom it would occur to take part in their intercourse or their silence, so great would appear their beauty, their grand proportions, and that perfection of harmony which has only once been seen when first the world was young. Their three names have become the ideal of all art — Plato, Sophocles, and Demosthenes. And, moreover, having duly honored these demigods, do you not see yonder a numerous and familiar crowd of excellent spirits, who always prefer to follow Cervantes, Molière — the practical painters from the life — those indulgent friends who are still the first of benefactors, who seize the whole man with laughter, pour out experience for him in mirth, and are aware of the powerful influence of rational, hearty, lawful joy? I will not here go on any longer with this description, which would occupy a whole book if it were complete. Be sure that the Middle Ages and Dante would fill some of the sacred heights; Italy would wholly unfold herself like a garden at the feet of the singer of Paradise; Boccaccio and Aristotle would disport themselves there, and Tasso would find once more the orange groves of Sorrento. In short, the different nations would have each a special nook kept for it, but the

---

[10]Valmiki is the author of the epic *Ramayana*, Vyasa of the *Mahabharata*, Firdousi of the *Shah Nameh*. [Ed.]

authors would delight in coming out of it, and as they walk about they would recognize, where least they expect it, their brothers or their masters. Lucretius, for instance, would love to discuss with Milton the origin of the world and the disentanglement of chaos; but as they argue each after his manner, they will but agree about the divine representations of poetry and nature.

These are our classics; everybody's imagination can complete the sketch, and even choose his favorite group for himself. For there must be a choice, and the first condition of taste when all has been surveyed is not to roam ceaselessly, but once for all to stay with a settled opinion. Nothing palls on the mind so much and is so injurious to taste as ceaseless roamings; the poetic spirit is not the Wandering Jew. Notwithstanding all this, my concluding advice when I speak of choosing and of forming an opinion is not to imitate even those who please us the most among our masters in the past. Let us be satisfied with feeling them, with interpreting them, with admiring them, and for ourselves, latecomers that we are, let us try at least to be ourselves. Let us make our choice with our own proper instincts. Let us have the sincerity and naturalness of our own thoughts, our own feelings — that always is possible. Let us add to it what is more difficult, a high aim, an impetus towards some lofty ideal; and while we speak our own language and submit to the conditions of the age in which we are placed, and from which we draw alike our strength and our failings, let us ask ourselves from time to time, while we lift our brows towards the hills and fasten our eyes on the group of reverend beings: "What would they say of us?"

But why do we speak continually of being an author, of writing? An age, perchance, is coming when there will be no more writing. Happy are those who read and read again, who can obey their free inclinations in their reading! There comes a period in life when, our wanderings all finished and our experiences all acquired, there is no keener pleasure than to study and deepen the things we know, to relish what we taste, just as when you behold again and again the people you love; purest delight of the mature mind and taste. It is then that this word *classic* assumes its true meaning, and is defined by the irresistible and discerning choice of every man of taste. Taste has now been created, it is formed and defined; the right meaning is now achieved if we are to have it at all. There is no longer any time to try about, nor any wish to make further discoveries. You stand by your friends, by those who have been proved by a long connection. Old wine, old books, old friends. You say to yourself like Voltaire in those delightful lines:

Jouissons, écrivons, vivons, mon cher Horace!
. . .
J'ai vécu plus que toi: mes vers dureront moins:
Mais, au bord du tombeau, je mettrai tous mes
  soins
A suivre les leçons de ta philosophie,
A mépriser la mort en savourant la vie,
A lire tes écrits pleins de grâce et de sens,
Comme on boit d'un vin vieux qui rajeunit les
  sens.[11]

Finally, be it Horace or another, whoever the author is that we prefer, and that gives us back our own thoughts in full richness and maturity, we shall at any rate beg from one of these good and ancient spirits a perpetual entertainment, an unwavering friendship which will never fail us, and that habitual impression of serenity and sweetness, which reconciles us, who so often need it, to mankind and to ourselves.

[11]"Let us play, write, live, my dear Horace! . . . I have lived longer than you but my verse will survive less long; but, on the edge of the grave, I take all possible care to follow the lessons of your philosophy, to despise death while savoring life, to read your writings, full of grace and of sense, the way one drinks an old wine that rejuvenates the senses." [Ed.]

# F. R. Leavis

## 1895–1978

*Frank Raymond Leavis, a critic of firm standards and implacable moralism, was born in Cambridge, England, and was educated there at the Perse School. Leavis survived his tenure as an ambulance bearer on the Western Front in World War I to become a lecturer at Emmanuel College in 1925. He moved on to Downing College in 1932, where he was elected to a fellowship in 1936. He and his wife, the former Queenie Dorothy Roth, were the founding editors of* Scrutiny *(1932–53), a quarterly journal of criticism that potently advanced their critical principles. Leavis retired from Downing College in 1962 to serve as a visiting professor of English at a number of universities, including those of York (1965–68), Wales (1969), and Bristol (1970). He received numerous honorary degrees, and in the year of his death was made a Companion of Honour. It has been said that Leavis's early critical interest was in poetry* (New Bearings in English Poetry: A Study of the Contemporary Situation *[1932];* Revaluation: Tradition and Development in English Poetry *[1936])* and that his later interest was in the novel *(The Great Tradition: Jane Austen, George Eliot, Henry James, Joseph Conrad [1948]; D. H. Lawrence, Novelist [1955]; Anna Karenina and Other Essays [1968]; Dickens the Novelist [1971; with Q. D. Leavis]). But this generalization does not take into account his continuing preoccupation with criticism itself* (The Common Pursuit *[1952])* and with questions of teaching and the university *(Education and the University: A Sketch for an "English" School [1943]; Literature in Our Time and the University [1969; based on the Clark Lectures of 1965]; The Living Principle: "English" as a Discipline of Thought [1975]). The following selection is from the first chapter of the revised edition of* The Great Tradition *(1960).*

## From *The Great Tradition*

> *. . . not dogmatically but deliberately . . .*
> — JOHNSON, *Preface to Shakespeare*

The great English novelists are Jane Austen, George Eliot, Henry James, and Joseph Conrad — to stop for the moment at that comparatively safe point in history. Since Jane Austen, for special reasons, needs to be studied at considerable length, I confine myself in this book to the last three. Critics have found me narrow, and I have no doubt that my opening proposition, whatever I may say to explain and justify it, will be adduced in reinforcement of their strictures. It passes as fact (in spite of the printed evidence) that I pronounced Milton negligible, dismiss "the Romantics," and hold that, since Donne, there is no poet we need bother about except Hopkins and Eliot. The view, I suppose, will be as confidently attributed to me that, except Jane Austen, George Eliot, James, and Conrad, there are no novelists in English worth reading.

The only way to escape misrepresentation is never to commit oneself to any critical judgment that makes an impact — that is, never to *say* anything. I still, however, think that the best way to promote profitable discussion is to be as clear as possible with oneself about what one sees and judges, to try and establish the essential discriminations in the given field of interest, and to state them as clearly as one can (for disagreement, if necessary). And it seems to me that in the field of fiction some challenging discriminations are very much called for; the field is so large and offers such insidious temptations to complacent confusions of judgment and to critical indolence. It is of the field of fiction belonging to Literature that I am thinking, and I am thinking in particular of the present vogue of the Victorian age. Trollope, Charlotte Yonge, Mrs. Gaskell, Wilkie Collins, Charles Reade, Charles and Henry Kingsley, Marryat, Shorthouse[1] — one after another the minor novelists of that period are being commended to our attention, written up, and publicized by broadcast, and there is a marked tendency to suggest that they not only have various kinds of interest to offer but that they are living classics. (Are not they all in the literary histories?) There are Jane Austen, Mrs. Gaskell, Scott, "the Brontës,"[2] Dickens, Thackeray, George Eliot, Trollope, and so on, all, one gathers, classical novelists.

It is necessary to insist, then, that there are important distinctions to be made, and that far from all of the names in the literary histories really belong to the realm of significant creative achievement. And as a recall to a due sense of differences it is well to start by distinguishing the few really great — the major novelists who count in the same way as the major poets, in the sense that they not only change the possibilities of the art for practitioners and readers, but that they are significant in terms of the human awareness they promote; awareness of the possibilities of life.[3]

[1]The novelist who has not been revived is Disraeli. Yet, though he is not one of the great novelists, he is so alive and intelligent as to deserve permanent currency, at any rate in the trilogy Coningsby, Sybil and Tancred: his own interests as expressed in these books — the interests of a supremely intelligent politician who has a sociologist's understanding of civilization and its movement in his time — are so mature. [Au.]

[2]See note, "The Brontës," [p. 1306]. [Au.]

[3]Characteristic of the confusion I am contending against is the fashion (for which the responsibility seems to go back to Virginia Woolf and Mr. E. M. Forster) of talking of Moll Flanders as a "great novel." Defoe was a remarkable writer, but all that need be said about him as a novelist was said by Leslie Stephen in Hours in a Library (First Series). He made no pretension to practising the novelist's art, and matters little as an influence. In fact, the only influence that need be noted is that represented by the use made of him in the nineteen-twenties by the practitioners of the fantastic conte (or pseudo-moral fable) with its empty pretence of significance.

Associated with this use of Defoe is the use that was made in much the same milieu of Sterne, in whose irresponsible (and nasty) trifling, regarded as in some way extraordinarily significant and mature, was found a sanction for attributing value to other trifling.

The use of Bunyan by T. F. Powys is quite another matter.

To insist on the pre-eminent few in this way is not to be indifferent to tradition; on the contrary, it is the way towards understanding what tradition is. "Tradition," of course, is a term with many forces — and often very little at all. There is a habit nowadays of suggesting that there is a tradition of "the English Novel," and that all that can be said of the tradition (that being its peculiarity) is that "the English Novel" can be anything you like. To distinguish the major novelists in the spirit proposed is to form a more useful idea of tradition (and to recognize that the conventionally established view of the past of English fiction needs to be drastically revised). It is in terms of the major novelists, those significant in the way suggested, that tradition, in any serious sense, has its significance.

To be important historically is not, of course, to be necessarily one of the significant few. Fielding deserves the place of importance given him in the literary histories, but he hasn't the kind of classical distinction we are also invited to credit him with. He is important not because he leads to Mr. J. B. Priestley but because he leads to Jane Austen, to appreciate whose distinction is to feel that life isn't long enough to permit of one's giving much time to Fielding or any to Mr. Priestley.

Fielding made Jane Austen possible by opening the central tradition of English fiction. In fact, to say that the English novel began with him is as reasonable as such propositions ever are. He completed the work begun by The Tatler and The Spectator, in the pages of which we see the drama turning into the novel — that this development should occur by way of journalism

It is a mark of the genuine nature of Mr. Powys's creative gift (his work seems to me not to have had due recognition) that he has been able to achieve a kind of traditional relation to Bunyan — especially, of course, in Mr. Weston's Good Wine. Otherwise there is little that can be said with confidence about Bunyan as an influence. And yet we know him to have been for two centuries one of the most frequented of all classics, and in such a way that he counts immeasurably in the English-speaking consciousness. It is, perhaps, worth saying that his influence would tend strongly to reinforce the un-Flaubertian quality of the line of English classical fiction . . . as well as to co-operate with the Jonsonian tradition of morally significant typicality in characters. [Au.]

being in the natural course of things. To the art of presenting character and *mœurs*[4] learnt in that school (he himself, before he became a novelist, was both playwright and periodical essayist) he joined a narrative habit the nature of which is sufficiently indicated by his own phrase, "comic epic in prose." That the eighteenth century, which hadn't much lively reading to choose from, but had much leisure, should have found *Tom Jones* exhilarating is not surprising; nor is it that Scott, and Coleridge, should have been able to give that work superlative praise. Standards are formed in comparison, and what opportunities had they for that? But the conventional talk about the "perfect construction" of *Tom Jones* (the late Hugh Walpole brought it out triumphantly and you may hear it in almost any course of lectures on "the English Novel") is absurd. There can't be subtlety of organization without richer matter to organize, and subtler interests, than Fielding has to offer. He is credited with range and variety and it is true that some episodes take place in the country and some in Town, some in the churchyard and some in the inn, some on the high-road and some in the bed-chamber, and so on. But we haven't to read a very large proportion of *Tom Jones* in order to discover the limits of the essential interests it has to offer us. Fielding's attitudes, and his concern with human nature, are simple, and not such as to produce an effect of anything but monotony (on a mind, that is, demanding more than external action) when exhibited at the length of an "epic in prose." What he *can* do appears to best advantage in *Joseph Andrews. Jonathan Wild*, with its famous irony, seem to me mere hobbledehoydom (much as one applauds the determination to explode the gangster-hero), and by *Amelia* Fielding has gone soft.

We all know that if we want a more inward interest it is to Richardson we must go. And there is more to be said for Johnson's preference, and his emphatic way of expressing it at Fielding's expense, than is generally recognized. Richardson's strength in the analysis of emotional and moral states is in any case a matter of common

acceptance; and *Clarissa* is a really impressive work. But it's no use pretending that Richardson can ever be made a current classic again. The substance of interest that he too has to offer is in its own way extremely limited in range and variety, and the demand he makes on the reader's time is in proportion — and absolutely — so immense as to be found, in general, prohibitive (though I don't know that I wouldn't sooner read through again *Clarissa* than *A la recherche du temps perdu*). But we can understand well enough why his reputation and influence should have been so great throughout Europe; and his immediately relevant historical importance is plain: he too is a major fact in the background of Jane Austen.

The social gap between them was too wide, however, for his work to be usable by her directly: the more he tries to deal with ladies and gentlemen, the more immitigably vulgar he is. It was Fanny Burney who, by transposing him into educated life, made it possible for Jane Austen to absorb what he had to teach her. Here we have one of the important lines of English literary history — Richardson–Fanny Burney–Jane Austen. It is important because Jane Austen is one of the truly great writers, and herself a major fact in the background of other great writers. Not that Fanny Burney is the only other novelist who counts in her formation; she read all there was to read, and took all that was useful to her — which wasn't only lessons.[5] In fact, Jane Austen, in her indebtedness to others, provides an exceptionally illuminating study of the nature of originality, and she exemplifies beautifully the relations of "the individual talent" to tradition. If the influences bearing on her hadn't comprised something fairly to be called tradition she couldn't have found herself and her true direction; but her relation to tradition is a creative one. She not only makes tradition for those coming after, but her achievement has for us a retroactive effect: as we look back beyond her we see in what goes before, and see because of her, potentialities and significances brought out in

[4]Manners. [Ed.]

[5]For the relation of Jane Austen to other writers see the essay by Q. D. Leavis, "A Critical Theory of Jane Austen's Writings," in *Scrutiny* 10, no. 1. [Au.]

such a way that, for us, she creates the tradition we see leading down to her. Her work, like the work of all great creative writers, gives a meaning to the past.[6]

The great novelists in that tradition are all very much concerned with "form"; they are all very original technically, having turned their genius to the working out of their own appropriate methods and procedures. But the peculiar quality of their preoccupation with "form" may be brought out by a contrasting reference to Flaubert. Reviewing Thomas Mann's *Der Tod in Venedig*, D. H. Lawrence[7] adduces Flaubert as figuring to the world the "will of the writer to be greater than and undisputed lord over the stuff he writes." This attitude in art, as Lawrence points out, is indicative of an attitude in life — or towards life. Flaubert, he comments, "stood away from life as from a leprosy." For the later Aesthetic writers, who, in general, represent in a weak kind of way the attitude that Flaubert maintained with a perverse heroism, "form" and "style" are ends to be sought for themselves, and the chief preoccupation is with elaborating a beautiful style to apply to the chosen subject. There is George Moore, who in the best circles, I gather (from a distance), is still held to be among the very greatest masters of prose, though — I give my own limited experience for what it is worth — it is very hard to find an admirer who, being pressed, will lay his hand on his heart and swear he has read one of the "beautiful" novels through. "The novelist's problem is to evolve an orderly composition which is also a convincing picture of life" — this is the way an admirer of George Moore sees it. Lord David Cecil, attributing this way to Jane Austen, and crediting her with a superiority over George Eliot in "satisfying the rival claims of life and art," explains this superiority, we gather, by a freedom from moral preoccupations that he supposes her

to enjoy. (George Eliot, he tells us, was a Puritan, and earnestly bent on instruction.)[8]

As a matter of fact, when we examine the formal perfection of *Emma*, we find that it can be appreciated only in terms of the moral preoccupations that characterize the novelist's peculiar interest in life. Those who suppose it to be an "aesthetic matter," a beauty of "composition" that is combined, miraculously, with "truth to life," can give no adequate reason for the view that *Emma* is a great novel, and no intelligent account of its perfection of form. It is in the same way true of the other great English novelists that their interest in their art gives them the opposite of an affinity with Pater and George Moore; it is, brought to an intense focus, an unusually developed interest in life. For, far from having anything of Flaubert's disgust or disdain or boredom, they are all distinguished by a vital capacity for experience, a kind of reverent openness before life, and a marked moral intensity.

It might be commented that what I have said of Jane Austen and her successors is only what can be said of any novelist of unqualified greatness. That is true. But there *is* — and this is the point — an English tradition, and these great classics of English fiction belong to it; a tradition that, in the talk about "creating characters" and "creating worlds," and the appreciation of Trollope and Mrs. Gaskell and Thackeray and Meredith and Hardy and Virginia Woolf, appears to go unrecognized. It is not merely that we have no Flaubert (and I hope I haven't seemed to suggest that a Flaubert is no more worth having than a George Moore). Positively, there is a continuity from Jane Austen. It is not for nothing that George Eliot admired her work profoundly, and wrote one of the earliest appreciations of it to be published. The writer whose intellectual weight and moral earnestness strike some critics as her handicap certainly saw in Jane Austen something more than an ideal contemporary of

---

[6]In the next four paragraphs, omitted here, Leavis discusses other critics who have seen the central tradition of the English novel beginning with Austen. [Ed.]

[7]D. H. Lawrence, *Phoenix: The Posthumous Papers of D. H. Lawrence* (London: Heinemann, 1936), p. 308. [Au.]

[8]She is a moralist and a highbrow, the two handicaps going together. "Her humour is less affected by her intellectual approach. Jokes, thank heaven, need not be instructive." — Lord David Cecil, *Early Victorian Novelists: Essays in Revaluation* (London: Constable, 1934), p. 299. [Au.]

Lytton Strachey.[9] What one great original artist learns from another, whose genius and problems are necessarily very different, is the hardest kind of "influence" to define, even when we see it to have been of the profoundest importance. The obvious manifestation of influence is to be seen in this kind of passage:

> A little daily embroidery had been a constant element in Mrs. Transome's life; that soothing occupation of taking stitches to produce what neither she nor any one else wanted, was then the resource of many a well-born and unhappy woman.

> In short, he felt himself to be in love in the right place, and was ready to endure a great deal of predominance, which, after all, a man could always put down when he liked. Sir James had no idea that he should ever like to put down the predominance of this handsome girl, in whose cleverness he delighted. Why not? A man's mind — what there is of it — has always the advantage of being masculine, — as the smallest birch-tree is of a higher kind than the most soaring palm — and even his ignorance is of a sounder quality. Sir James might not have originated this estimate; but a kind Providence furnishes the limpest personality with a little gum or starch in the form of tradition.[10]

The kind of irony here is plainly akin to Jane Austen's — though it is characteristic enough of George Eliot; what she found was readily assimilated to her own needs. In Jane Austen herself the irony has a serious background, and is no mere display of "civilization." George Eliot wouldn't have been interested in it if she hadn't perceived its full significance — its relation to the essential moral interest offered by Jane Austen's art. And here we come to the profoundest kind of influence, that which is not manifested in likeness. One of the supreme debts one great writer can owe another is the realization of unlikeness (there is, of course, no significant unlikeness without the common concern — and the common seriousness of concern — with essential human issues). One way of putting the difference between George Eliot and the Trollopes whom we are invited to consider along with her is to say that she was capable of understanding Jane Austen's greatness and capable of learning from her. And except for Jane Austen there was no novelist to learn from — none whose work had any bearing on her own essential problems as a novelist.[11]

Is there no name later than Conrad's to be included in the great tradition? There is, I am convinced, one: D. H. Lawrence. Lawrence, in the English language, was the great genius of our time (I mean the age, or climatic phase, following Conrad's). It would be difficult to separate the novelist off for consideration, but it was in the novel that he committed himself to the hardest and most sustained creative labour, and he was, as a novelist, the representative of vital and significant development. He might, he has shown conclusively, have gone on writing novels with the kind of "character creation" and psychology that the conventional cultivated reader immediately appreciates — novels that demanded no unfamiliar effort of approach. He might — if his genius had let him. In nothing is the genius more manifest than in the way in which, after the great success — and *succès d'estime*[12] — of *Sons and Lovers* he gives up that mode and devotes himself to the exhausting toil of working out the new things, the developments, that as the highly conscious and intelligent servant of life he saw to be necessary. Writing to Edward Garnett of the work that was to become *Women in Love* he says: "It is *very* different from *Sons and Lovers*: written in another language almost. I shall be sorry if you don't like it, but am prepared. I shan't write in the same manner as *Sons and Lovers* again, I

---

[9]It is perhaps worth insisting that Peacock is more than that too. He is not at all in the same class as the Norman Douglas of *South Wind* and *They Went*. In his ironical treatment of contemporary society and civilization he is seriously applying serious standards, so that his books, which are obviously not novels in the same sense as Jane Austen's, have a permanent life as light reading — indefinitely rereadable — for minds with mature interests. [Au.]

[10]The passages are from *Middlemarch*. [Ed.]

[11]In the next passage, omitted here, Leavis continues to trace the line of development and influence through Henry James and Joseph Conrad and to discuss why Dickens, though a "great genius," is not a stimulus to an "adult mind." [Ed.]

[12]Recognition. [Ed.]

think — in that hard, violent style full of sensation and presentation."[13]

Describing at length what he is trying to do he says:

> You mustn't look in my novel for the old stable *ego* of the character. There is another *ego*, according to whose action the individual is unrecognizable, and passes through, as it were, allotropic states which it needs a deeper sense than any we've been used to exercise, to discover are states of the same single radically unchanged element. (Like as diamond and coal are the same pure simple element of carbon. The ordinary novel would trace the history of the diamond — but I say, "Diamond, what! This is carbon." And my diamond might be coal or soot, and my theme is carbon.) You must not say my novel is shaky — it is not perfect, because I am not expert in what I want to do. But it is the real thing, say what you like. And I shall get my reception, if not now, then before long. Again I say, don't look for the development of the novel to follow the lines of certain characters: the characters fall into the form of some other rhythmic form, as when one draws a fiddle-bow across a fine tray delicately sanded, the sand takes lines unknown.[14]

He is a most daring and radical innovator in "form," method, technique. And his innovations and experiments are dictated by the most serious and urgent kind of interest in life. This is the spirit of it:

> Do you know Cassandra in Aeschylus and Homer? She is one of the world's great figures, and what the Greeks and Agamemnon did to her is symbolic of what mankind has done to her since — raped and despoiled her, to their own ruin. It is not your brain that you must trust to, nor your will — but to that fundamental pathetic faculty for receiving the hidden waves that come from the depths of life, and for transferring them to the unreceptive world. It is something which happens below the consciousness, and below the range of the will — it is something which is unrecognizable and frustrated and destroyed.[15]

It is a spirit that, for all the unlikeness, relates Lawrence closely to George Eliot.[16] He writes, again, to Edward Garnett:[17]

> You see — you tell me I am half a Frenchman and one-eighth a Cockney. But that isn't it. I have very often the vulgarity and disagreeableness of the common people, as you say Cockney, and I may be a Frenchman. But primarily I am a passionately religious man, and my novels must be written from the depth of my religious experience. That I must keep to, because I can only work like that. And my Cockneyism and commonness are only when the deep feeling doesn't find its way out, and a sort of jeer comes instead, and sentimentality and purplism. But you should see the religious, earnest, suffering man in me first, and then the flippant or common things after. Mrs. Garnett says I have no true nobility — with all my cleverness and charm. But that is not true. It is there, in spite of all the littlenesses and commonnesses.

It is this spirit, by virtue of which he can truly say that what he writes must be written from the depth of his religious experience, that makes him, in my opinion, so much more significant in relation to the past and future, so much more truly creative as a technical inventor, an innovator, a master of language, than James Joyce. I know that Mr. T. S. Eliot has found in Joyce's work something that recommends Joyce to him as positively religious in tendency (see *After Strange Gods*). But it seems plain to me that there is no organic principle determining, informing, and controlling into a vital whole, the elaborate analogical structure, the extraordinary variety of technical devices, the attempts at an exhaustive rendering of consciousness, for which *Ulysses* is remarkable, and which got it accepted by a cosmopolitan literary world as a new start. It is rather, I think, a dead end, or at least a pointer to disintegration — a view strengthened by Joyce's own development (for I think it significant and appropriate that *Work in Progress — Finnegans Wake*, as it became — should have engaged the interest of the inventor of Basic English).

It is true that we can point to the influence of Joyce in a line of writers to which there is no

[13]*The Letters of D. H. Lawrence*, ed. Aldous Huxley (London: Heinemann, 1934), p. 172. [Au.]

[14]*Letters*, p. 198. [Au.]

[15]*Letters*, p. 232. [Au.]

[16]*Letters*, p. 190. [Au.]

[17]Lawrence too has been called a Puritan. [Au.]

parallel issuing from Lawrence. But I find here further confirmation of my view. For I think that in these writers, in whom a regrettable (if minor) strain of Mr. Eliot's influence seems to me to join with that of Joyce, we have, insofar as we have anything significant, the wrong kind of reaction against liberal idealism.[18] I have in mind writers in whom Mr. Eliot has expressed an interest in strongly favourable terms: Djuna Barnes of *Nightwood*, Henry Miller, Lawrence Durrell of *The Black Book*. In these writers — at any rate in the last two (and the first seems to me insignificant) — the spirit of what we are offered affects me as being essentially a desire, in Laurentian phrase, to "do dirt" on life. It seems to me important that one should, in all modesty, bear one's witness in these matters. "One must speak for life and growth, amid all this mass of destruction and disintegration."[19] This is Lawrence, and it is the spirit of all his work. It is the spirit of the originality that gives his novels their disconcerting quality, and gives them the significance of works of genius.

I am not contending that he isn't, as a novelist, open to a great deal of criticism, or that his achievement is as a whole satisfactory (the potentiality being what it was). He wrote his later books far too hurriedly. But I know from experience that it is far too easy to conclude that his very aim and intention condemned him to artistic unsatisfactoriness. I am thinking in particular of two books at which he worked very hard, and in which he developed his disconcertingly original interests and approaches — *The Rainbow* and *Women in Love*. Reread, they seem to me astonishing works of genius, and very much more largely successful than they did when I read them

(say) fifteen years ago. I still think that *The Rainbow* doesn't build up sufficiently into a whole. But I shouldn't be quick to offer my criticism of *Women in Love*, being pretty sure that I should in any case have once more to convict myself of stupidity and habit-blindness on later rereading. And after these novels there comes, written, perhaps, with an ease earned by this hard work done, a large body of short stories and *nouvelles* that are as indubitably successful works of genius as any the world has to show.

I have, then, given my hostages. What I think and judge I have stated as responsibly and clearly as I can. Jane Austen, George Eliot, Henry James, Conrad, and D. H. Lawrence: the great tradition of the English novel is *there*.

## NOTE: "THE BRONTËS"

It is tempting to retort that there is only one Brontë. Actually, Charlotte, though claiming no part in the great line of English fiction (it is significant that she couldn't see why any value should be attached to Jane Austen), has a permanent interest of a minor kind. She had a remarkable talent that enabled her to do something firsthand and new in the rendering of personal experience, above all in *Villette*.

The genius, of course, was Emily. I have said nothing about *Wuthering Heights* because that astonishing work seems to me a kind of sport. It may, all the same, very well have had some influence of an essentially undetectable kind: she broke completely, and in the most challenging way, both with the Scott tradition that imposed on the novelist a romantic resolution of his themes, and with the tradition coming down from the eighteenth century that demanded a plane-mirror reflection of the surface of "real" life. Out of her a minor tradition comes, to which belongs, most notably, *The House with the Green Shutters*.

[18]See D. H. Lawrence's *Fantasia of the Unconscious*, especially Ch. XI. [Au.]

[19]*The Letters of D. H. Lawrence*, p. 256. [Au.]

# Frank Kermode

b. 1919

*John Frank Kermode — Renaissance scholar, student of modernism, theorist of narrative — was born on the Isle of Man in the United Kingdom. An eclectic critic of exploratory temperament, Kermode took his B.A. at Liverpool University in 1940, but his M.A. waited until 1947 while he served six years in the Royal Navy. He has held appointments at many English schools, notably at the University of Manchester (1958–65), the University of London (1967–74), and King's College, where he has been King Edward VII Professor of English since 1974. He has also been a visiting professor at a number of American institutions, including Harvard University (1961, 1977–78), Bryn Mawr (1965), and Princeton (1970). He belongs to the elite Royal Society of Literature (fellow), British Academy (fellow), American Academy of Arts and Sciences (honorary member), and L'Ordre des Arts et des Sciences (officer). Kermode has edited books on the English pastoral, Shakespeare, Milton, Donne, Spenser, the metaphysical poets, and T. S. Eliot. His own works include studies of Shakespeare (1963, 1964, 1965), Donne (1957), and Wallace Stevens (1960; revised 1967), as well as* Romantic Image *(1957),* Sense of an Ending *(1967),* Continuities *(1968),* Novel and Narrative *(1972),* The Classic *(1975),* The Genesis of Secrecy *(1979),* The Art of Telling *(1983), and* Forms of Attention *(1985). More recently, with Robert Alter he has collaboratively edited* The Literary Guide to the Bible *(1987). The selection is the fifth chapter of* The Classic.

# From *The Classic*

Horace provided a rule of thumb, sensible so far as it goes, when he said: *est vetus atque probus, centum qui perficit annos*; he did not know the word "classic" in the literary sense, but Pope was right to put it into his imitation of Horace's line:

Who lasts a century can have no flaw,
I hold that Wit a Classic, good in law.[1]

What they leave out is any account of the temporal agencies of survival, the most important of which is a more or less continuous chorus of voices asserting the value of the classic; and of course they say nothing about the difficulties that arise in consequence of periodic changes in language, generic expectation, ideology, and so forth. The imperialist view of the classic accommodates all these. . . . It does so by modification of the basic model (renovations, translations, and the like) and by other means we can broadly call allegorical. But ultimately it rests on the notion of a moment privileged, timeless yet capable of contemporaneity with all others, a classic in which all lesser classics participate. If we were to think of theirs as a scientific theory we should reject it either as we reject Ptolemaic astronomy (because discrepancies between the model and observational data require too many new rules — epicycles, *translationes* — for the model itself to remain credible; a new model is required) or more simply because it is not, as Popper would say, testable.[2] It is easy to see that such criteria have no relevance. And yet such models change, by other and perhaps obscurer laws. We are less able to rest easy with the imperial model in its purity.

A new model would require us in the first

---

[1] *Ep.*, II, i, 39; *Imitations of Horace*, 1st Ep. of 2nd Book, 55–56. [Au.]

[2] In *The Logic of Scientific Discovery* (1959), Sir Karl Popper (b. 1902) held that hypotheses need not be derived inductively from raw data so long as they were testable and could be confirmed or falsified by the facts. [Ed.]

place to abandon the notion of the absolute classic and consider, more simply, the Horatian case, the text which continues to be read several generations after it was written. A classic, then, is a book that is read a long time after it was written; one might want to qualify this by adding "without institutional constraint," "by the competent" and perhaps other rules. Once we made this new start we can see some of the problems in quite a different light. *Translationes* become transitions from a past to a present system of beliefs, language, generic expectations; renovations become very specific attempts to establish the relevance of a document which has had a good chance of losing it. The *querelle*[3] persists, but with major changes in the historiographical assumptions of the two sides.

These are some of the topics I have to consider in this last chapter. There are others, all related to the ones I have mentioned; the most important is the extreme variety of response characteristic of the modern reading of the classic. But I daresay it is best to approach these questions by way of a single familiar text; and I have chosen *Wuthering Heights* for what I take to be good reasons. It meets the requirement that it is read in a generation far separated from the one it was presented to; and it has other less obvious advantages. It happens that I had not read the novel for many years; furthermore, although I could not be unaware that it had suffered a good deal of interpretation, and had been the centre of quarrels, I had also omitted to read any of this secondary material. These chances put me in a position unfamiliar to the teacher of literature; I could consider my own response to a classic more or less untrammelled by too frequent reading, and by knowledge of what it had proved possible, or become customary, to say about it. This strikes me as a happy situation, though some may call it shameful. Anyway, it is the best way I can think of to arrive at some general conclusions about the classic, though I daresay those conclusions will sound more like a programme

for research than a true ending to this briefer exercise.

I begin, then, with a partial reading of *Wuthering Heights* which represents a straightforward encounter between a competent modern reader (the notion of competence is, I think, essential however much you may think this demonstration falls short of it) and a classic text. However, in assuming this role, I could not avoid noticing some remarks that are not in the novel at all, but in Charlotte Brontë's Biographical Notice of her sisters, in which she singles out a contemporary critic as the only one who got her sister's book right. "Too often," she says, "do reviewers remind us of the mob of Astrologers, Chaldeans and Soothsayers gathered before the 'writing on the wall,' and unable to read the characters or make known the interpretation." One, however, has accurately read "the Mene, Mene, Tekel, Upharsin[4] of an original mind" and "can say with confidence, 'This is the interpretation thereof.' " This latterday Daniel was Sidney Dobell, but a modern reader who looks him up in the hope of coming upon what would after all be a very valuable piece of information is likely to be disappointed. Very few would dream of doing so; most would mistrust the critic for whom such claims were made, or the book which lent itself to them. Few would believe that such an interpretation exists, however frequently the critics produce new "keys." For we don't think of the novel as a code, or a nut, that can be broken; which contains or refers to a meaning all will agree upon if it can once be presented *en clair*.[5] We need little persuasion to believe that a good novel is not a message at all. We assume in principle the rightness of the plurality of interpretations to which I now, in ignorance of all the others, but reasonably confident that I won't repeat them, now contribute.

When Lockwood first visits Wuthering Heights he notices, among otherwise irrelevant decorations carved above the door, the date *1500* and the name *Hareton Earnshaw*. It is quite clear that everybody read and reads this (on p. 2) as a

[3]The quarrel between the devotees of the ancients and the moderns was a critical topic of the late seventeenth century. See, for example, Dryden, p. 163. [Ed.]

[4]The mystical and prophetic words inscribed by the spectral hand during Belshazzar's feast. [Ed.]

[5]In clear (said of a transmission not in cipher). [Ed.]

sort of promise of something else to come. It is part of what is nowadays called a "hermeneutic code"; something that promises, and perhaps after some delay provides, explanation.[6] There is, of course, likely to be some measure of peripeteia[7] or trick; you would be surprised if the explanation were not, in some way, surprising, or at any rate, at this stage unpredictable. And so it proves. The expectations aroused by these inscriptions are strictly *generic*; you must know things of this kind before you can entertain expectations of the sort I mention. Genre in this sense is what Leonard Meyer (writing of music) calls "an internalized probability system."[8] Such a system could, but perhaps shouldn't, be thought of as constituting some sort of contract between reader and writer. Either way, the inscriptions can be seen as something other than simple elements in a series of one damned thing after another, or even of events relative to a story as such. They reduce the range of probabilities, reduce randomness, and are expected to recur. There will be "feedback." This may not extinguish all the informational possibilities in the original stimulus, which may be, and in this case is, obscurer than we thought, "higher," as the information theorists say, "in entropy."[9] The narrative is more than merely a lengthy delay, after which a true descendant of Hareton Earnshaw reoccupies the ancestral house; though there is little delay before we hear about him, and can make a guess if we want.

When Hareton is first discussed, Nelly Dean rather oddly describes him as "the late Mrs. Linton's nephew." Why not "the late Mr. Earnshaw's son"? It is only in the previous sentence that we have first heard the name Linton, when the family of that name is mentioned as having previously occupied Thrushcross Grange. Perhaps we are to wonder how Mrs. Linton came

to have a nephew named Earnshaw. At any rate, Nelly's obliquity thus serves to associate Hareton, in a hazy way, with the house on which his name is *not* carved, and with a family no longer in evidence. Only later do we discover that he is in the direct Earnshaw line, in fact, as Nelly says, "the last of them." So begins the provision of information which both fulfils and qualifies the early "hermeneutic" promise; because, of course, Hareton, his inheritance restored, goes to live at the Grange. The two principal characters remaining at the end are Mr. and Mrs. Hareton Earnshaw. The other names, which have intruded on Earnshaw — Linton and Heathcliff — are extinct. In between there have been significant recursions to the original inscription — in Chapter 20 Hareton cannot read it; in 24 he can read the name but not the date.

We could say, I suppose, that this so far tells us nothing about *Wuthering Heights* that couldn't, with appropriate changes, be said of most novels. All of them contain the equivalent of such inscriptions; indeed all writing is a sort of inscription, cut memorably into the uncaused flux of event; and inscriptions of the kind I am talking about are interesting secondary clues about the nature of the writing in which they occur. They draw attention to the literariness of what we are reading, indicate that the story is a story, perhaps with beneficial effects on our normal powers of perception; above all they distinguish a *literary* system which has no constant relation to readers with interests and expectations altered by long passages of time. Or, to put it another way, Emily Brontë's contemporaries operated different probability systems from ours, and might well ignore whatever in a text did not comply with their generic expectations, dismissing the rest somehow — by skipping, by accusations of bad craftsmanship, inexperience, or the like. In short, their internalized probability systems survive them in altered and less stringent forms; we can read more of the text than they could, and of course read it differently. In fact, the only works we value enough to call classic are those which, and they demonstrate by surviving, are complex and indeterminate enough to allow us our necessary pluralities. That "Mene, Mene, Tekel, Upharsin" has now many interpre-

---

[6]The idea of the "hermeneutic code" is proposed by Roland Barthes in *S/Z*. See the introduction to Poststructuralism, Ch. 5. [Ed.]

[7]Reversal. [Ed.]

[8]Leonard B. Meyer, *Music, the Arts and Ideas*, 1967, p. 8 (speaking of musical styles). [Au.]

[9]Entropy is the measure of the degree of randomness in a thermodynamic system, and by extension, of noise in an informational system. [Ed.]

tations. It is in the nature of works of art to be open, in so far as they are "good"; though it is in the nature of authors, and of readers, to close them.

The openness of *Wuthering Heights* might be somewhat more extensively illustrated by an inquiry into the passage describing Lockwood's bad night at the house, when, on his second visit, he was cut off from Thrushcross Grange by a storm. He is given an odd sort of bed in a bedroom-within-a-bedroom; Catherine Earnshaw slept in it and later Heathcliff would die in it. Both the bed and the lattice are subjects of very elaborate "play"; but I want rather to consider the inscriptions Lockwood examines before retiring. There is writing on the wall, or on the ledge by his bed: it "was nothing but a name repeated in all kinds of characters, large and small — *Catherine Earnshaw*, here and there varied to *Catherine Heathcliff*, and then again to *Catherine Linton*." When he closes his eyes Lockwood is assailed by white letters "which started from the dark, as vivid as spectres — the air swarmed with Catherines." He has no idea whatever to whom these names belong, yet the expression "nothing but a name" seems to suggest that they all belong to one person. Waking from a doze he finds the name *Catherine Earnshaw* inscribed in a book his candle has scorched.

It is true that Lockwood has earlier met a Mrs. Heathcliff, and got into a tangle about who she was, taking first Heathcliff and then Hareton Earnshaw for her husband, as indeed, we discover she, in a different sense, had also done or was to do. For she had a merely apparent kinship relation with Heathcliff — bearing his name as the wife of his impotent son and having to tolerate his ironic claim to fatherhood — as a prelude to the restoration of her true name, Earnshaw; it is her mother's story reversed. But Lockwood was not told her first name. Soon he is to encounter a ghost called Catherine Linton; but if the scribbled names signify one person he and we are obviously going to have to wait to find out who it is. Soon we learn that Mrs. Heathcliff is Heathcliff's daughter-in-law, *née* Catherine Linton, and obviously not the ghost. Later it becomes evident that the scratcher must have been Catherine Earnshaw, later Linton, a girl

long dead who might well have been Catherine Heathcliff, but wasn't.

When you have processed all the information you have been waiting for you see the point of the order of the scribbled names, as Lockwood gives them: *Catherine Earnshaw, Catherine Heathcliff, Catherine Linton*. Read from left to right they recapitulate Catherine Earnshaw's story; read from right to left, the story of her daughter, Catherine Linton. The names Catherine and Earnshaw begin and end the narrative. Of course some of the events needed to complete this pattern had not occurred when Lockwood slept in the little bedroom; indeed the marriage of Hareton and Catherine is still in the future when the novel ends. Still, this is an account of the movement of the book: away from Earnshaw and back, like the movement of the house itself. And all the movement must be *through* Heathcliff.

Charlotte Brontë remarks, from her own experience, that the writer says more than he knows, and was emphatic that this was so with Emily. "Having formed these beings, she did not know what she had done." Of course this strikes us as no more than common sense; though Charlotte chooses to attribute it to Emily's ignorance of the world. A narrative is not a transcription of something pre-existent. And this is precisely the situation represented by Lockwood's play with the names he does not understand, his constituting, out of many scribbles, a rebus for the plot of the novel he's in. The situation indicates the kind of work we must do when a narrative opens itself to us, and contains information in excess of what generic probability requires.

Consider the names again; of course they reflect the isolation of the society under consideration, but still it is remarkable that in a story whose principal characters all marry there are effectively only three surnames, all of which each Catherine assumes. Furthermore, the Earnshaw family makes do with only three Christian names, Catherine, Hindley, Hareton. Heathcliff is a family name also, but parsimoniously, serving as both Christian name and surname; always lacking one or the other, he wears his name as an indication of his difference, and this persists after death since his tombstone is inscribed with the one word *Heathcliff*. Like Frances, briefly the wife of Hindley, he is simply a sort of interruption in the Earnshaw system.

Heathcliff is then as it were between names, as between families (he is the door through which Earnshaw passes into Linton, and out again to Earnshaw). He is often introduced, as if characteristically, standing outside, or entering, or leaving, a door. He is in and out of the Earnshaw family simultaneously; servant and child of the family (like Hareton, whom he puts in the same position, he helps to indicate the archaic nature of the house's society, the lack of sharp social division, which is not characteristic of the Grange). His origins are equally betwixt and between: the gutter or the royal origin imagined for him by Nelly; prince or pauper, American or Lascar,[10] child of God or devil. This betweenness persists, I think: Heathcliff, for instance, fluctuates between poverty and riches; also between virility and impotence. To Catherine he is between brother and lover; he slept with her as a child, and again in death, but not between latency and extinction. He has much force, yet fathers an exceptionally puny child. Domestic yet savage like the dogs, bleak yet full of fire like the house, he bestrides the great opposites: love and death (the necrophiliac confession), culture and nature ("half-civilized ferocity") in a posture that certainly cannot be explained by any generic formula ("Byronic" or "Gothic").

He stands also between a past and a future; when his force expires the old Earnshaw family moves into the future associated with the civilized Grange, where the insane authoritarianism of the Heights is a thing of the past, where there are cultivated distinctions between gentle and simple — a new world in the more civil south. It was the Grange that first separated Heathcliff from Catherine, so that Earnshaws might eventually live there. Of the children — Hareton, Cathy, and Linton — none physically resembles Heathcliff; the first two have Catherine's eyes (33) and the other is, as his first name implies, a Linton. Cathy's two cousin-marriages, constituting an endogamous route to the civilized ex-

ogamy of the south — are the consequence of Heathcliff's standing between Earnshaw and Linton, north and south; earlier he had involuntarily saved the life of the baby Hareton. His ghost and Catherine's, at the end, are of interest only to the superstitious, the indigenous now to be dispossessed by a more rational culture.

If we look, once more, at Lockwood's inscriptions, we may read them thus [see Figure 1].

Earnshaws persist, but they must eventually do so within the Linton culture. Catherine burns up in her transit from left to right. The quasi-Earnshaw union of Heathcliff and Isabella leaves the younger Cathy an easier passage; she has only to get through Linton Heathcliff, who is replaced by Hareton Earnshaw, Hareton has suffered part of Heathcliff's fate, moved, as it were, from Earnshaw to Heathcliff, and replaced him as son-servant, as gratuitously cruel; but he is the last of the Earnshaws, and Cathy can both restore to him the house on which his name is carved, and take him on the now smooth path to Thrushcross Grange.

Novels, even this one, were read in houses more like the Grange than the Heights, as the emphasis on the ferocious piety of the Earnshaw library suggests. The order of the novel is a civilized order; it presupposes a reader in the midst of an educated family and habituated to novel reading; a reader, moreover, who believes in the possibility of effective ethical choices. And because this is the case, the author can allow herself to meet his proper expectations without imposing on the text or on him absolute generic control. She need not, that is, know all that she is saying. She can, in all manner of ways, invite the reader to collaborate, leave to him the supply of meaning where the text is indeterminate or discontinuous, where explanations are required to fill narrative lacunae.

Instances of this are provided by some of the dreams in the book.[11] Lockwood's brief dream

---

[10]East Indian. [Ed.]

[11]My subsequent reading in *Wuthering Heights* criticism (which has certainly substantiated my vague sense that there was a lot of it about) has taught me that the carved names, and Lockwood's dreams, have attracted earlier comment. Dorothy Van Ghent's distinguished essay asks why Lockwood, of all people, should experience such a dream as that

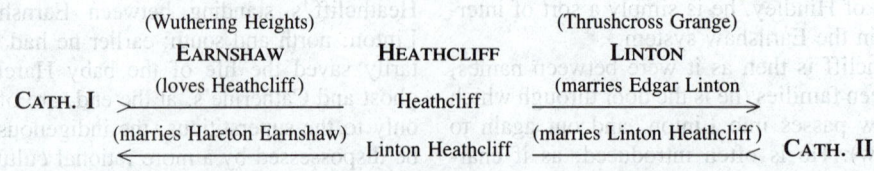

Figure I. Heathcliff stands between Earnshaw and Linton as having Earnshaw origins but marrying Isabella Linton. He could also be represented as moving from left to right and right to left — into the Linton column, and then back to the Earnshaw when he usurps the hereditary position of Hareton. Hareton himself might be represented as having first been forced out of the Earnshaw column into the intermediate position when Heathcliff reduces him to a position resembling the one he himself started from, a savage and inferior member of the family. But he returns to the Earnshaw column with Cath. II. Finally they move together (without passing through the intermediate position, which has been abolished) from left to right, from Wuthering Heights to Thrushcross Grange.

of the spectral letters is followed by another about an interminable sermon, which develops from hints about Joseph in Catherine's Bible. The purport of this dream is obscure. The

of the ghost-child, and decides that the nature of the dreamer — "a man who has shut out the powers of darkness" — is what gives force to our sense of powers "existing autonomously" both without and within. (*The English Novel: Form and Function*, 1953.) Ronald E. Fine suggests that the dreams are "spasms of realism" and that Emily Brontë arranged the story to fit them, or as he says, lets the dreams generate the story. He emphasizes their sexual significance, and the structural relations between them, explained by the generative force of a basic dream of two lovers seeking to be reunited ("Lockwood's Dream and the Key to *Wuthering Heights*," *Nineteenth Century Fiction* 24, 1969–70, 16–30). Ingeborg Nixon suggests that "the names must have been written by Catherine after her first visit to Thrushcross Grange as a child . . . but they form a silent summary of the whole tragic dilemma"; they indicate three possibilities for Catherine, who of course chooses *Linton*. This is to give the inscriptions the most limited possible "hermeneutic" sense, reading them back into a possible chronology and ignoring their larger function as literary or defamiliarizing signs ("A note on the Pattern of *Wuthering Heights*," *English Studies* 44, 1964). Cecil W. Davies notices that "Heathcliff" is an Earnshaw name, and argues that this makes him "in a real, though nonlegal sense, a true inheritor of Wuthering Heights" ("A Reading of *Wuthering Heights*," *Essays in Criticism* 19, 1969). Doubtless C. P. Sanger's justly celebrated essay ("The Structure of *Wuthering Heights*" [1926]) is partly responsible for the general desire to fit everything that can be fitted into legal and chronological schemes; but the effect is often to miss half the point. All these essays are reprinted, in whole or in part, in the Penguin Critical Anthology, *Emily Brontë*,

preacher Jabes Branderham takes a hint from his text and expands the seven deadly sins into seventy times seven plus one. It is when he reaches the last section that Lockwood's patience runs out, and he protests, with his own allusion to the Bible: "He shall return no more to his house, neither shall his place know him any more." Dreams in stories are usually given a measure of oneiric ambiguity, but stay fairly close to the narrative line, or if not, convey information otherwise useful; but this one does not appear to do so, except in so far as that text may bear obscurely and incorrectly on the question of where Hareton will end up. It is, however, given a naturalistic explanation: the rapping of the preacher on the pulpit is a dream version of the rapping of the fir tree on the window.

Lockwood once more falls asleep, but dreams again, and "if possible, still more disagreeably than before." Once more he hears the fir-bough, and rises to silence it; he breaks the window and finds himself clutching the cold hand of a child who calls herself Catherine Linton.

He speaks of this as a dream, indeed he ascribes to it "the intense horror of nightmare," and

ed. J.-P. Petit, 1973. Other collections include one by Miriam Allott in the Macmillan Casebook series (1970), Thomas A. Vogler's *Twentieth-Century Interpretations of "Wuthering Heights"* (1965), and William A. Sale's Norton edition (1963). [Au.]

ISSUE UNDER DEBATE: THE CANON

the blood that runs down into the bedclothes may be explained by his having cut his hand as he broke the glass; but he does not say so, attributing it to his own cruelty in rubbing the child's wrist on the pane; and Heathcliff immediately makes it obvious that of the two choices the text has so far allowed us the more acceptable is that Lockwood was not dreaming at all.

So we cannot dismiss this dream as "Gothic" ornament or commentary, or even as the kind of dream Lockwood has just had, in which the same fir-bough produced a comically extended dream-explanation of its presence. There remain all manner of puzzles: why is the visitant a child and, if a child, why Catherine *Linton*? The explanation, that this name got into Lockwood's dream from a scribble in the Bible is one even he finds hard to accept. He hovers between an explanation involving "ghosts and goblins," and the simpler one of nightmare; though he has no more doubt than Heathcliff that "it" — the child — was trying to enter. For good measure he is greeted, on going downstairs, by a cat, a brindled cat, with its echo of Shakespearian witchcraft.

It seems plain, then, that the dream is not simply a transformation of the narrative, a commentary on another level, but an integral part of it. The Branderham dream is, in a sense, a trick, suggesting a measure of rationality in the earlier dream which we might want to transfer to the later experience, as Lockwood partly does. When we see that there is a considerable conflict in the clues as to how we should read the second tapping and relate it to the first we grow aware of further contrasts between the two, for the first is a comic treatment of 491 specific and resistible sins for which Lockwood is about to be punished by exile from his home, and the second is a more horrible spectral invasion of the womb-like or tomb-like room in which he is housed. There are doubtless many other observations to be made; it is not a question of deciding which is the single right reading, but of dealing, as reader, with a series of indeterminacies which the text will not resolve.

Nelly Dean refuses to listen to Catherine's dream, one of those which went through and through her "like wine through water"; and of those dreams we hear nothing save this account of their power. "We're dismal enough without conjuring up ghosts and visions to perplex us," says Nelly — another speaking silence in the text, for it is implied that we are here denied relevant information. But she herself suffers a dream or vision. After Heathcliff's return she finds herself at the signpost: engraved in its sandstone — with all the permanence that Hareton's name has on the house — are "Wuthering Heights" to the north, "Gimmerton" to the east, and "Thrushcross Grange" to the south. Soft south, harsh north, and the rough civility of the market town (something like that of Nelly herself) in between. As before, these inscriptions provoke a dream apparition, a vision of Hindley as a child. Fearing that he has come to harm, she rushes to the Heights and again sees the spectral child, but it turns out to be Hareton, Hindley's son. His appearance betwixt and between the Heights and the Grange was proleptic;[12] now he is back at the Heights, a stone in his hand, threatening his old nurse, rejecting the Grange. And as Hindley turned into Hareton, so Hareton turns into Heathcliff, for the figure that appears in the doorway is Heathcliff.

This is very like a real dream in its transformations and displacements. It has no simple narrative function whatever, and an abridgement might leave it out. But the confusion of generations, and the double usurpation of Hindley by his son and Heathcliff, all three of them variants of the incivility of the Heights, gives a new relation to the agents, and qualifies our sense of all narrative explanations offered in the text. For it is worth remarking that no naturalistic explanation of Nelly's experience is offered; in this it is unlike the treatment of the later vision, when the little boy sees the ghost of Heathcliff and "a woman," a passage which is a preparation for further ambiguities in the ending. Dreams, visions, ghosts — the whole pneumatology[13] of the book is only indeterminately related to the "natural" narrative. And this serves to muddle routine "single" readings, to confound explanation and expectation, and to make necessary a full recognition of the intrinsic plurality of the text.

[12]Anticipatory. [Ed.]
[13]Theory of spirits. [Ed.]

Would it be reasonable to say this: that the mingling of generic opposites — daylight and dream narratives — creates a need, which we must supply, for something that will mediate between them? If so, we can go on to argue that the text in our response to it is a provision of such mediators, between life and death, the barbaric and the civilized, family and sexual relations. The principal instrument of mediation may well be Heathcliff: neither inside nor out, neither wholly master nor wholly servant, the husband who is no husband, the brother who is no brother, the father who abuses his changeling child, the cousin without kin. And that the chain of narrators serve to mediate between the barbarism of the story and the civility of the reader — making the text itself an intermediate term between archaic and modern — must surely have been pointed out.

What we must not forget, however, is that it is in the completion of the text by the reader that these adjustments are made; and each reader will make them differently. Plurality is here not a prescription but a fact. There is so much that is blurred and tentative, incapable of decisive explanation; however we set about our reading, with a sociological or a pneumatological, a cultural or a narrative code uppermost in our minds, we must fall into division and discrepancy; the doors of communication are sometimes locked, sometimes open, and Heathcliff may be astride the threshold, opening, closing, breaking. And it is surely evident that the possibilities of interpretation increase as time goes on. The constraints of a period culture dissolve, generic presumptions which concealed gaps disappear, and we now see that the book, as James thought novels should, truly "glories in a gap," a hermeneutic gap in which the reader's imagination must operate, so that he speaks continuously in the text. For these reasons the rebus — *Catherine Earnshaw, Catherine Heathcliff, Catherine Linton* — has exemplary significance. It is a riddle that the text answers only silently; for example it will neither urge nor forbid you to remember that it resembles the riddle of the Sphinx — what manner of person exists in these three forms? — to which the single acceptable and probable answer involves incest and ruin.

I have not found it possible to speak of *Wuthering Heights* in this light without, from time to time, hinting — in a word here, or a trick of procedure there — at the new French criticism.[14] I am glad to acknowledge this affinity, but it also seems important to dissent from the opinion that such "classic" texts as this — and the French will call them so, but with pejorative intent — are essentially naïve, and become in a measure plural only by accident. The number of choices is simply too large; it is impossible that even two competent readers should agree on an authorized naïve version. It is because texts are so naïve that they can become classics. It is true, as I have said, that time opens them up; if readers were immortal the classic would be much closer to changelessness; their deaths do, in an important sense, liberate the texts. But to attribute the entire *potential* of plurality to that cause (or to the wisdom and cunning of later readers) is to fall into a mistake. The "Catherines" of Lockwood's inscriptions may not have been attended to, but there they were in the text, just as ambiguous and plural as they are now. What happens is that methods of repairing such indeterminacy change; and, as Wolfgang Iser's neat formula has it, "the repair of indeterminacy" is what gives rise "to the generation of meaning."[15]

Having meditated thus on *Wuthering Heights* I passed to the second part of my enterprise and began to read what people have been saying about the book. I discovered without surprise that no two readers saw it exactly alike; some seemed foolish and some clever, but whether they were of the party that claims to elucidate Emily Brontë's intention, or libertarians whose purpose is to astonish us, all were different. This secondary material is voluminous, but any hesitation I might have had about selecting from it was ended when I came upon an essay which in its mature authority dwarfs all the others: Q. D. Leavis's "A Fresh Approach to *Wuthering Heights*."[16]

[14]Kermode refers to both structuralism and poststructuralism. [Ed.]

[15]"Indeterminacy and the Reader's Response," in *Aspects of Narrative*, ed. J. Hillis Miller, 1971, 42. [Au.]

[16]F. R. Leavis and Q. D. Leavis, *Lectures in America*, 1969, 83–152. [Au.]

Long-meditated, rich in insights, this work has a sober force that nothing I say could, or is intended to, diminish. Mrs. Leavis remarks at the outset that merely to *assert* the classic status of such a book as *Wuthering Heights* is useless; that the task is not to be accomplished by ignoring "recalcitrant elements" or providing sophistical explanations of them. One has to show "the nature of its success"; and this, she at once proposes, means giving up some parts of the text. "Of course, in general one attempts to achieve a reading of a text which includes all its elements, but here I believe we must be satisfied with being able to account for some of them and concentrate on what remains." And she decides that Emily Brontë through inexperience, and trying to do too much, leaves in the final version vestiges of earlier creations, "unregenerate writing," which is discordant with the true "realistic novel" we should attend to.

She speaks of an earlier version deriving from *King Lear*, with Heathcliff as an Edmund figure, and attributes to this layer some contrived and unconvincing scenes of cruelty. Another layer is the fairy-story, Heathcliff as the prince transformed into a beast; another is the Romantic incest-story: Heathcliff as brother-lover; and nearer the surface, a sociological novel, of which she has no difficulty in providing, with material from the text, a skilful account. These vestiges explain some of the incongruities and inconsistencies of the novel — for example, the ambiguity of the Catherine-Heathcliff relationship — and have the effect of obscuring its "human centrality." To summarize a long and substantial argument, this real novel, which we come upon clearly when the rest is cut away, is founded on the contrast between the two Catherines, the one willing her own destruction, the other educated by experience and avoiding the same fate. Not only does this cast a new light on such characters as Joseph and Nelly Dean as representatives of a culture that, as well as severity, inculcates a kind of natural piety, but [it] enables us to see Emily Brontë as "a true novelist . . . whose material was real life and whose concern was to promote a fine awareness of human relations and the problem of maturity." And we can't see this unless we reject a good deal of the text as belonging more to "self-indulgent story" than to the "responsible piece of work" Emily was eventually able to perform. Heathcliff we are to regard as "merely a convenience"; in a striking comparison with Dostoevsky's Stavrogin, Mrs. Leavis argues that he is "enigmatic . . . only by reason of his creator's indecision," and that to find reasons for thinking otherwise is "misguided critical industry." By the same token the famous passages about Catherine's love for Heathcliff are dismissed as rhetorical excesses, obstacles to the "real novel enacted so richly for us to grasp in all its complexity."[17]

Now it seems very clear to me that the "real novel" Mrs. Leavis describes *is* there, in the text. It is also clear that she is aware of the danger in her own procedures, for she explains how easy it would be to account for *Wuthering Heights* as a sociological novel by discarding certain elements and concentrating on others, which, she says, would be "misconceiving the novel and slighting it." What she will not admit is that there is a sense in which all these versions are not only present but have a claim on our attention. She creates a hierarchy of elements, and does so by a peculiar archaeology of her own, for there is no *evidence* that the novel existed in the earlier forms which are supposed to have left vestiges in the only text we have, and there is no reason why the kind of speculation and conjecture on which her historical argument depends could not be practised with equal right by proponents of quite other theories. Nor can I explain why it seemed to her that the only way to establish hers as the central reading of the book was to explain the rest away; for there, after all, the others *are*. Digging and carbon-dating simply have no equivalents here; there is no way of distinguishing old signs from new; among readings which attend to the text it cannot be argued that one attends to a truer text than all the others.

It is true that "a fine awareness of human relations," and a certain maturity, may be pos-

[17]For a different approach to Mrs. Leavis's reading see D. Donoghue, "Emily Brontë: On the Latitude of Interpretation," *Harvard English Studies* I, ed. M. W. Bloomfield, 1970; reprinted in *Emily Brontë*, ed. J.-P. Petit, 1973, 296–314, 316. [Au.]

tulated as classic characteristics; Eliot found them in Virgil. But it is also true that the coexistence in a single text of plurality of significances from which, in the nature of human attentiveness, every reader misses some — and, in the nature of human individuality, prefers one — is, empirically, a requirement and a distinguishing feature of the survivor, *centum qui perficit annos*. All those little critics, each with his piece to say about *King Lear* or *Wuthering Heights*, may be touched by a venal professional despair, but at least their numbers and their variety serve to testify to the plurality of the documents on which they swarm; and though they may lack authority, sometimes perhaps even sense, many of them do point to what is *there* and ought not to be wished away.

A recognition of this plurality relieves us of the necessity of a *Wuthering Heights* without a Heathcliff, just as it does of a *Wuthering Heights* that "really" ends with the death of Catherine, or for that matter an *Aeneid* which breaks off, as some of the moral allegorists would perhaps have liked it to, at the end of Book VI. A reading such as that with which I began Chapter I is of course extremely selective, but it has the negative virtue that it does not excommunicate from the text the material it does not employ; indeed, it assumes that it is one of the very large number of readings that may be generated from the text of the novel. They will of course overlap, as mine in some small measure does with that of Mrs. Leavis.

And this brings me to the point: Mrs. Leavis's reading is privileged; what conforms with it is complex, what does not is confused; and presumably all others would be more or less wrong, in so far as they treated the rejected portions as proper objects of attention. On the other hand, the view I propose does not in any way require me to reject Mrs. Leavis's insights. It supposes that the reader's share in the novel is not so much a matter of knowing, by heroic efforts of intelligence and divination, what Emily Brontë really meant — knowing it, quite in the manner of Schleiermacher, better than she did — as of responding creatively to indeterminacies of meaning inherent in the text and possibly enlarged by the agency of time.

We are entering, as you see, a familiar zone of dispute. Mrs. Leavis is rightly concerned with what is "timeless" in the classic, but for her this involves the detection and rejection of what exists, it seems to her irrelevantly or even damagingly, in the aspect of time. She is left, in the end, with something that, in her view, has not changed between the first writing and her reading. I, on the other hand, claimed to be reading a text that might well signify differently to different generations, and different persons within those generations. It is a less attractive view, I see; an encouragement to foolishness, a stick that might be used, quite illicitly as it happens, to beat history, and sever our communications with the dead. But it happens that I set a high value on these, and wish to preserve them. I think there is a substance that prevails, however powerful the agents of change; that *King Lear*, underlying a thousand dispositions, subsists in change, prevails, by being patient of interpretation; that my *Wuthering Heights*, sketchy and provocative as it is, relates as disposition to essence quite as surely as if I had tried to argue that it was Emily Brontë's authorized version, or rather what she intended and could not perfectly execute.

This "tolerance to a wide variety of readings" is attacked, with considerable determination, by E. D. Hirsch, committed as he is to the doctrine that the object of interpretation is the verbal meaning of the author; I think he would be against me in all details of the present argument. For example, he says quite firmly that interpretations must be judged entire, that they stand or fall as wholes; so that he could not choose, as I do, both to accept Mrs. Leavis's "realist" reading and to reject her treatment of Heathcliff.[18] But as I said in Chapter 2, Hirsch makes a mistake when he allows that the "determinations" (*bestimmungen*) of literary texts are more constrained than those of legal texts; and a further difficulty arises over his too sharp distinction between criticism and interpretation. In any case he does not convince me that tolerance in these matters represents "abject intellectual surrender";

[18]*Validity in Interpretation*, 168. [Au.] See Hirsch in Ch. 9. [Ed.]

and I was cheered to find him in a more eirenic[19] mood in his later paper. He is surely right to allow, in the matter of meaning, some element of personal preference; the "best meaning" is not uniform for all.

This being so one sees why it is thought possible, in theory at any rate, to practise what is called "literary science" as distinct from criticism or interpretation: to consider the structure of a text as a system of signifiers, as in some sense "empty," as what, by the intervention of the reader, takes on many possible significances.[20] To put this in a different way, one may speak of the text as a system of signifiers which always shows a surplus after meeting any particular restricted reading. It was Lévi-Strauss who first spoke of a "surplus of signifier" in relation to shamanism, meaning that the patient is cured because the symbols and rituals of the doctor offer him not a specific cure but rather a language "by means of which unexpressed, and otherwise inexpressible, psychic states can be immediately expressed."[21] Lévi-Strauss goes on to make an elaborate comparison with modern psychoanalysis. But as Fredric Jameson remarks, the importance of the concept lies rather in its claim for the priority of the signifier over the signified: a change which itself seems to have offered a shamanistic opportunity for the expression of thoughts formerly repressed.[22]

The consequences for literary texts are much too large for me to enter on here; among them, of course, is the by-passing of all the old arguments about "intention." And even if we may hesitate to accept the semiological method in its entirety we can allow, I think, for the intuitive rightness of its rules about plurality. The gap between text and meaning, in which the reader operates, is always present and always different in extent.[23] It is true that authors try, or used to try, to close it; curiously enough, Barthes reserves the term "classic" for texts in which they more or less succeed, thus limiting plurality and offering the reader, save as accident prevents him, merely a product, a consumable. In fact what Barthes calls "modern" is very close to what I am calling "classic," and what he calls "classic" is very close to what I call "dead."

There is, in much of the debate on these matters, a quality of outrageousness, of the *outré*, and there is no reason why this should not be taken into account. We should, however, recall that in any *querelle* it is the modern that is going to display it most palpably. The prime modern instance is the row between Raymond Picard and Roland Barthes, which followed the publication of Barthes's *Racine* in 1963. The title of Picard's brisk pamphlet puts the point of the quarrel with a familiar emphasis: *Nouvelle Critique ou nouvelle imposture?* (1965), and it contrives to make Barthes sound like the critic, deplored by all though read by few, who said that Nelly Dean stood for Evil. Barthes makes of the violent but modest drama of Racine something unrestrainedly sexual; if the text doesn't fit his theory he effects a "transformation"; he uses neologisms to give scientific dignity to absurdities, and makes of the work under consideration "an involuntary rebus, interesting only for what it doesn't say."[24]

Barthes's reply is splendidly polemic; the old criticism takes for granted its ideology to the degree that it is unconscious of it; its vocabulary is that of a schoolgirl (specifically, Proust's Gisèle, Albertine's friend) seventy-five years ago. But the world has changed; if the history of philosophy and the history of history have been transformed, how can that of literature remain constant? Specifically the old criticism is the victim of a disease he calls *asymbolie*; any use of language that exceeds a narrow rationalism is

---

[19]Tending to or productive of peace. [Ed.]

[20]F. Jameson, *The Prison-House of Language*, 1972, 195, compares the Frege-Carnap distinction between *Sinn* (unchanging formal organization) and *Bedeutung* (the changing significance given to the text by successive generations of readers). [Au.]

[21]*Structural Anthropology*, 1968, 198. [Au.]

[22]Jameson, 1972, 196. [Au.] See Jameson on the return of the repressed in *Lord Jim* in Ch. 1. [Ed.]

[23]". . . commentaries or interpretations are generated out of an ontological lack in the text itself . . . a text can have no ultimate meaning . . . the process of interpretation . . . is properly an infinite one" (Jameson, 176, paraphrasing Jacques Derrida).

[24]Picard, 135. [Au.]

beyond its understanding. But the moment one begins to consider a work as it is in itself, symbolic reading becomes unavoidable. You may be able to show that the reader has made his rules wrong or applied them wrongly, but errors of this kind do not invalidate the principle. And in the second more theoretical part of this very notable document Barthes explains that in his usage a symbol is not an image but a plurality of senses; the text will have many, not through the infirmity of readers who know less history than Professor Picard, but in its very nature as a structure of signifiers. "L'oeuvre propose, l'homme dispose."[25] Multiplicity of readings must result from the work's "constitutive ambiguity," an expression Barthes borrows from Jakobson. And if that ambiguity itself does not exclude from the work the authority of its writer, then death will do so: "By erasing the author's signature, death establishes the truth of the work, which is an enigma."[26]

I have suggested that the death of readers is equally important, as a solvent of generic constraints. However much we know about history we cannot restore a situation in which a particular set of arbitrary rules of a probability system is taken for granted, internalized. To this extent I am firmly on Barthes's side in the dispute; and I have found much interest in his later attempts — which don't, however, command anything like total agreement — to describe the transcoding operations by which, in contemplating the classic, we filter out what can now be perceived as mere ideological deposits and contemplate the limited plurality that remains.[27]

Barthes denies the charge that on his view of the reading process one can say absolutely anything one likes about the work in question; but he is actually much less interested in defining constraints than in asserting liberties. There are some suggestive figures in his recent book Le

Plaisir du texte (1973), from which we gather that authorial presence is somehow a ghostly necessity, like a dummy at bridge, or the shadow without which Die Frau ohne Schatten[28] must remain sterile; and these are hints that diachrony, a knowledge of transient dispositions, may be necessary even to the nouvelle critique competently practised. Such restrictions on criticism à outrance[29] can perhaps only be formulated in terms of a theory of competence and performance analogous to that of linguistics.

Though I am more than half-persuaded (largely by Dr. Jonathan Culler)[30] that such a theory could be constructed, I am certainly not to speak of it now. I will suffice to say that in so far as it is thought possible to teach people to read the classics it is assumed that knowledge of them is progressive. The nature of that knowledge is, however, as Barthes suggests, subject to change. Secularization multiplies the world's structures of probability, as the sociologists of religion tell us, and "this plurality of religious legitimations is internalized in consciousness as a plurality of possibilities between which one may choose."[31] It is this pluralism that, on the long view, denies the authoritative or authoritarian reading that insists on its identity with the intention of the author, or on its agreement with the readings of his contemporaries; or rather, it has opened up the possibilities, exploited most aggressively by the structuralists and semiologists, of regarding the text as the permanent locus of change; as something of which the permanence no longer legitimately suggests the presence and permanence of what it appears to designate.

I notice in a very recent book on The Early Virgil — though it is by no means a Formalist

[25]"The work proposes, man disposes," Barthes's variant on the proverbial "Man proposes, God disposes." [Ed.]

Critique et Vérité, 1966, 52–53. [Au.]

ural code" of S/Z (1970) serves some of the ... s. Leavis's archaeological categories, though ... to retain the period elements that he drops.

[28]The Woman without a Shadow, opera by Richard Strauss with libretto by Hugo von Hofmannsthal, about a dyer's wife who sells her shadow — and with it her hope of posterity — to a princess. [Ed.]

[29]Beyond measure. [Ed.]

[30]See Culler, "Literary Competence," in Ch. 4. [Ed.]

[31]P. L. Berger, "Secularization and the Problem of Plausibility," extracted from The Sacred Canopy (1967) in Sociological Perspectives, ed. K. Thompson and J. Tunstall, 1971, 446–59; developing the thesis of Berger and T. Luckmann, The Social Construction of Reality, 1976. [Au.]

or Structuralist study — what seems a characteristic modern swerve in the interpretation of the Fourth Eclogue; the author believes that the *puer*[32] is the poem itself, that the prophecy relates to a new golden age of poetry, an age which the Eclogue itself inaugurates; and this, like the author's remarks on the self-reflexiveness of the whole series of eclogues, seems modern, for it insists in some measure on the literariness of the work, its declared independence of the support of external reference. Even the arithmological elements in its construction serve to confirm it in this peculiar status.[33] And we see how sharply this form of poetic isolation differs from the privileged status accorded the Eclogue by the "imperialist" critics of my first chapter: there would be, for Mr. Berg, no question of Christian prophecy in the Eclogue — there is not even any question of a reference to some recent or impending political event involving Antony or Octavius or Pollio himself. By the same token no interpretation of Virgil which depends on the assumption, in however sophisticated a form it may be presented, that his *imperium* was to be transformed into the Christian Empire, his key words — *amor, fatum, pietas, labor*[34] — given their full significance in an eternal pattern of which he could speak without actual knowledge, would be acceptable to this kind of criticism. When we say now that the writer speaks more than he knows we are merely using an archaism; what we mean is that the text is under the absolute control of no thinking subject, or that it is not a message from one mind to another.

The classic, we may say, has been secularized by a process which recognizes its status as a literary text; and that process inevitably pluralized it, or rather forced us to recognize its inherent plurality. We have changed our views on change. We may accept, in some form, the view proposed by Michel Foucault, that our period-discourse is controlled by certain unconscious constraints, which make it possible for us to think in some ways to the exclusion of others.[35] However subtle we may be at reconstructing the constraints of past *epistèmes*, we cannot ordinarily move outside the tacit system of our own; it follows that except by extraordinary acts of divination we must remain out of close touch with the probability systems that operated for the first readers of the *Aeneid* or of *Wuthering Heights*. And even if one argues, as I do, that there is clearly less epistemic discontinuity than Foucault's crisis-philosophy proposes, it seems plausible enough that earlier assumptions about continuity were too naïve. The survival of the classic must therefore depend upon its possession of a surplus of signifier; as in *King Lear* or *Wuthering Heights* this may expose them to the charge of confusion, for they must always signify more than is needed by any one interpreter or any one generation of interpreters. We may recall that, rather in the manner of Mrs. Leavis discarding Heathcliff, George Orwell would have liked *King Lear* better without the Gloucester plot, and with Lear having only one wicked daughter — "quite enough," he said.

If, finally, we compare this sketch of a modern version of the classic with the imperial classic that occupied me earlier, we see on the one hand that the modern view is necessarily tolerant of change and plurality whereas the older, regarding most forms of pluralism as heretical, holds fast to the time-transcending idea of Empire. Yet the new approach, though it could be said to secularize the old in an almost Feuerbachian way, may do so in a sense which preserves it in a form acceptable to changed probability systems. For what was thought of as beyond time, as the angels, or the *majestas populi Romani*,[36] or the *imperium* were beyond time, inhabiting a fictive perpetuity, is now beyond time in a more human sense; it is here, frankly vernacular, and inhabiting the world where alone, we might say with Wordsworth, we find our happiness — our felicitous readings — or not at all. The language of the new Mercury may strike us as harsh after the songs of Apollo; but the work he contemplates

---

[32]The boy in *Eclogue* 4:8, whose birth Virgil prophesies will usher in a new golden age. [Ed.]

[33]William Berg, *The Early Virgil*, 1973. [Au.]

[34]Love, fate, piety, work. [Ed.]

[35]See the introduction to Poststructuralism and Foucault, "What Is an Author?", both in Ch. 5. [Ed.]

[36]Majesty of the Roman people. [Ed.]

stands there, in all its native plurality, liberated not extinguished by death, the death of writer and reader, unaffected by time yet offering itself to be read under our particular temporal disposition. "The work proposes; man disposes." Barthes's point depends upon our recalling that the proverb originally made God the disposer.

The implication remains that the classic is an essence available to us under our dispositions, in the aspect of time. So the image of the imperial classic, beyond time, beyond vernacular corruption and change, had perhaps, after all, a measure of authenticity; all we need do is bring it down to earth.

# Barbara Herrnstein Smith

## b. 1932

*Barbara Herrnstein Smith is a scholar of aesthetics, literary theory, and linguistic theory. Born in New York City, Smith took her B.A. (1954), M.A. (1955), and Ph.D. (1965) in English and American literature at Brandeis University in Massachusetts. She has been an instructor at the Sanz School of Languages in Washington, D.C. (1956–57), a member of the literature faculty at Bennington College (1962–74), and a professor at the University of Pennsylvania (1974–87), where in 1979 she was named director of the Center for the Study of Art and Symbolic Behavior, and in 1980 University Professor of English and communications. Smith has been a fellow of (1970–71) and a consultant for (1974) the National Endowment of the Humanities as well as a Guggenheim fellow (1977–78) and a chair of the Modern Language Association (1987–88). Currently she is a professor at Duke University in a department that includes other renowned literary theorists, such as Fredric Jameson (see Ch. 1) and Stanley Fish (Ch. 7). Most of Smith's publications have been academic articles. Her books include* Poetic Closure: A Study of How Poems End, *which won the Christian Gauss Award and the Explicator Award for 1968, and* On the Margins of Discourse: The Relation of Literature to Language *(1978). "Contingencies of Value" is from* Critical Inquiry 10 *(1983).*

# Contingencies of Value

## 1. THE EXILE OF EVALUATION

It is a curious feature of literary studies in America that one of the most venerable, central, theoretically significant, and pragmatically inescapable set of problems relating to literature has not been a subject of serious inquiry for the past fifty years. I refer here to the fact not merely that the study of literary evaluation has been, as we might say, "neglected," but that the entire problematic of value and evaluation has been evaded and explicitly exiled by the literary academy. It is clear, for example, that there has been no broad and sustained investigation of literary evaluation that could compare to the constant and recently intensified attention devoted to every aspect of

literary *interpretation*. The past decades have witnessed an extraordinary proliferation of theories, approaches, movements, and entire disciplines focused on interpretive criticism, among them (to recite a familiar litany) New Criticism, structuralism, psychoanalytic criticism, reader-response criticism, reception aesthetics, speech-act theory, deconstructionism, communications theory, semiotics, and hermeneutics. At the same time, however, aside from a number of scattered and secondary essays by theorists and critics who are usually otherwise occupied,[1] no one in par-

---

[1] The most recent of these include E. D. Hirsch, Jr., *The Aims of Interpretation* (Chicago, 1976), esp. the essays

ticular has been concerned with questions of literacy value and evaluation, and such questions regularly go begging — and, of course, begged — even among those whose inquiries into other matters are most rigorous, substantial, and sophisticated.

Reasons for the specific disparity of attention are not hard to locate. One is the obvious attachment of problems of interpretation and meaning to the more general preoccupation with language that has dominated the entire century and probably, as well, the fact that disciplines such as linguistics and the philosophy of language are more accessible to literary scholars than the corresponding disciplines, especially economics and sociology, that are more broadly concerned with the nature of value and evaluative behavior. The reasons for the general neglect and exile, however, are more complex, reflecting, among other things, the fact that literary studies in America, from the time of its inception as an institutionalized academic discipline, has been shaped by two conflicting and mutually compromising intellectual traditions and ideologies, namely — or roughly namely — positivistic philological scholarship and humanistic pedagogy. That is, while professors of literature have sought to claim for their activities the rigor, objectivity, cognitive substantiality, and progress associated with science and the empirical disciplines, they have also attempted to remain faithful to the essentially conservative and didactic mission of humanistic studies: to honor and preserve the culture's traditionally esteemed objects — in this case, its canonized texts — and to illuminate and transmit the traditional cultural values presumably embodied in them. One consequence or manifestation of this conflict has been the continuous absorption of "literary theory" in America with institutional debates over the proper methods and objectives of the academic *study* of literature and, with respect to the topic at hand, the drastic confinement of its concern with literary evaluation to debates over the cognitive status of evaluative criticism and its proper place, if any, in the discipline.

A bit of history will be helpful here. In accord with the traditional empiricist doctrine of a fundamental split or discontinuity between fact and value (or description and evaluation, or knowledge and judgment), it was possible to regard the emerging distinction within literary studies between "scholarship" and "criticism" as a reasonable division of labor. Thus, the scholar who devoted himself to locating and assembling the historical and philological facts necessary to edit and annotate the works of, say, Bartholomew Griffin might remark that, although Griffin was no doubt a less fashionable poet than such contemporaries as Spenser and Shakespeare, the serious and responsible scholar must go about his work in a serious and responsible manner, leaving questions of literary merit "to the critics." The gesture that accompanied the remark, however, was likely to signal not professional deference but intellectual condescension; for the presumably evenhanded distribution of the intellectual responsibilities of literary study — the determination of facts to the scholar and value to the critic — depended on an always questionable and increasingly questioned set of assumptions: namely, that literary value was a determinate property of texts and that the critic, by virtue of certain innate and acquired capacities (taste, sensibility, etc., which could be seen as counterparts to the scholar's industry and erudition), was someone specifically equipped to discriminate it.

The magisterial mode of literary evaluation that issued from this set of assumptions (and which, in Anglo-American criticism, characteristically reproduced itself after the image — and in the voice — of Dr. Johnson and also of such latter-day "master-critics" as Matthew Arnold and T. S. Eliot) was practiced most notably by F. R. Leavis in England and, in America, per-

"Evaluation as Knowledge" (1968) and "Privileged Criteria in Evaluation" (1969); Murray Krieger, "Literary Analysis and Evaluation — and the Ambidextrous Critic," in *Criticism: Speculative and Analytic Essays*, ed. L. S. Dembo (Madison, Wis., 1968); a number of brief essays by Anglo-American as well as continental European theorists in *Problems of Literary Evaluation*, ed. Joseph Strelka (University Park, Pa., and London, 1969); and the chapters on value and evaluation in John Ellis, *The Theory of Literary Criticism* (Berkeley and Los Angeles, 1974), John Reichert, *Making Sense of Literature* (Chicago, 1977), and Jeffrey Sammons, *Literary Sociology and Practical Criticism* (Bloomington, Ind., and London, 1977). All of them either participate directly in the self-justifying academic debates outlined below or are haunted by them into equivocation. [Au.]

haps most egregiously, by Yvor Winters.[2] Its reaches and a taste of its once familiar flavor can be recalled in this passage from Leavis' *Revaluation*:

There are, of course, discriminations to be made: Tennyson, for instance, is a much better poet than any of the pre-Raphaelites. And Christina Rossetti deserves to be set apart from them and credited with her own thin and limited but very notable distinction. . . . . There is, too, Emily Brontë, who has hardly yet had full justice as a poet. I will record, without offering it as a checked and deliberated judgment, the remembered impression that her *Cold in the earth* is the finest poem in the nineteenth-century part of *The Oxford Book of English Verse*.[3]

Such unabashed "debaucheries of judiciousness" (as Northrop Frye would later characterize them)[4] were, however, increasingly seen as embarrassments to the discipline, and the practice of evaluative criticism became more defensive, at least partly in response to the renewed and updated authority given to axiological skepticism.

In the thirties and forties, a number of prominent philosophers, among them A. J. Ayer and Rudolph Carnap, began to argue that value judgments are not merely distinct from empirically verifiable statements of fact but vacuous pseudostatements, at best suasive and commendatory, at worst simply the emotive expressions of personal sentiment, and in any case neither reflecting nor producing genuine knowledge.[5] For the positivistic literary scholar, such arguments reinforced his impression that the work of his critical colleague was the intellectually insubstantial activity of a dilettante, while the true discipline of literary studies was exhibited in his own labors, in which he had always sought to achieve a rigor and objectivity as free as possible from the contamination of value ascription. In the institutional struggles that ensued, various maneuvers were developed to secure for "criticism" not only a central place in the discipline but also an intellectual status equal in respectability to that of empirical science and what was commonly referred to as "serious scholarship."

One obvious tactic, still favored in many quarters of the literary academy, was to invoke the humanistic mission of literary studies and turn the fact-value split against the scholars' claim of centrality. Thus Winters would maintain that while science was value-neutral — or, as he put it, "amoral" — literary studies had moral responsibilities. The function of historical scholarship and philology was, accordingly, ancillary: specifically, it was "to lay the groundwork for criticism," while the important job was, precisely, to evaluate literature.[6] For Winters, this meant to declare, forthrightly and unequivocally, what was good and bad literature (which was to say, "moral" or "decadent" literature), and he did not hesitate, himself, to rank-order not only poets and poems but also literary genres, verse forms, and entire centuries.

Winters had a genius for unequivocality that was imitated but never matched by his numerous followers. In any case, a more common tactic, exemplified by a number of the New Critics, was to devise some formulation of critical activity that bridged the fact-value split or at least unobtrusively edged the two sides together. Thus, in 1951, W. K. Wimsatt, Jr., in an important essay titled "Explication as Criticism," observed that it was necessary to find "an escape between the two extremes of sheer affectivism and sheer scientific neutralism" and attempted to demonstrate how evaluation could be assimilated into the typical New Critical production of increasingly exquisite explications and fine-grained analyses: "But then, finally, it is possible to conceive and produce instances where explication in the neutral sense is so integrated with special and local value intimations that it rises from neutral-

[2]See Johnson, "Preface to Shakespeare," p. 229; Arnold, "The Study of Poetry," p. 396; Eliot, "Tradition and the Individual Talent," p. 466; Leavis, *The Great Tradition*, earlier in this chapter. [Ed.]

[3]F. R. Leavis, *Revaluation: Tradition and Development in English Poetry* (London, 1936; New York, 1963), pp. 5–6. [Au.]

[4]See Frye, "The Archetypes of Literature," in Ch. 2. [Ed.]

[5]See esp. A. J. Ayer, *Language, Truth, and Logic* (London, 1936). [Au.]

[6]Yvor Winters, *The Function of Criticism* (Denver, 1957), p. 17 [Au.]

ity gradually and convincingly to the point of total judgment."[7]

It may be recalled here that Wimsatt's attempt to expose "the affective fallacy" was directed largely at the "psychological theory of value" developed by I. A. Richards in the twenties, which Wimsatt charged with amounting to subjectivism and leading to impressionism and relativism. Richards' theory was, however, in effect an updated rehearsal of the eighteenth-century empiricist-normative account and, like the latter, designed to *rebut* axiological skepticism.[8] An adequate theory of criticism, Richards wrote, must be able to answer such questions as "What gives the experience of reading a certain poem its value?" and "Why is one opinion about works of art not as good as another?";[9] and while the first of these questions no doubt seemed to Wimsatt altogether different from what, for him, would have been the more proper question of what gives *the poem itself* its value, the second of them makes Richards' normative objectives quite clear. Indeed, he consistently put his psycho-neurological account of value in the service of canonical judgments and repeatedly translated it into versions of evaluative absolutism and objectivism. Thus, the remarkable chapter on "Badness in Poetry" in *Principles of Literary Criticism* concludes its excruciating examination of the failure of a sonnet by Ella Wheeler Wilcox to produce a "high level of organization" of "adequate [neural] impulses" with Richards' observation that, although "those who enjoy [the sonnet] certainly seem to enjoy it to a high degree," nevertheless, with good and bad poetry, as with brandy and beer, the "actual universal preference of those who have tried both fairly is the same as superiority in value of one over the other. Keats, by universal qualified opinion, is a more

efficient poet than Wilcox, and that is the same as saying his works are more valuable."[10] The invocation of an "actual" universality coupled with such question-begging hedges as "fairly" and "qualified" is, as we shall see, characteristic of traditional empiricist-normative accounts. It was not, one suspects, its alleged relativism that made Richards' theory so unabsorbable by the literary academy but rather the raw jargon and unedifying physiology that attended it.

The boldest move in the midcentury effort to give disciplinary respectability and cognitive substance to criticism was, of course, Frye's call upon it to redefine itself as a project that banished evaluation altogether. In his "Polemical Introduction" to the *Anatomy of Criticism*, Frye insisted that, if criticism was ever to become a "field of genuine learning" (significantly exemplified by "chemistry or philology"), it would have to "snip . . . off and throw . . . away" that part that had "no organic connection with [it]," — namely, evaluation.[11] For Frye, the shifting assessments and rank-orderings made by critics were not only a noncumulative accumulation of subjective judgments but also irrelevant to "real criticism," since he believed, echoing and endorsing Eliot, that "the existing monuments of literature form an ideal order among themselves." "This," Frye commented, "is criticism, and very fundamental criticism. Much of this book attempts to annotate it" (*AC*, p. 18).

In what proved to be a memorable passage, he derided "all the literary chit-chat which makes the reputations of poets boom and crash in an imaginary stock-exchange," and observed:

This sort of thing cannot be part of any systematic study, for a systematic study can only progress: whatever dithers or vacillates or reacts is merely leisure-class gossip. The history of taste is no more a part of the *structure* of criticism than the Huxley-Wilberforce debate is a part of the structure of biological science. (*AC*, p. 18)

In view of Frye's Platonic conception of litera-

[7]W. K. Wimsatt, Jr., *The Verbal Icon* (Louisville, Ky., 1954), p. 250. [Au.]

[8]See the discussion of David Hume [pp. 212–22]. [Au.] Axiology is the study of norms or values. [Ed.]

[9]I. A. Richards, *Principles of Literary Criticism* (1924; London, 1960), pp. 5–6. "The two pillars upon which a theory of criticism must rest," Richards declared, "are an account of value and an account of communication" (p. 25). It was, of course, the latter that subsequently became the overriding concern of critical theory. [Au.]

[10]Ibid., p. 206. [Au.]

[11]Northrop Frye, *Anatomy of Criticism: Four Essays* (Princeton, N.J., 1957), pp. 18, 19; all further references to this work, abbreviated *AC*, will be included in the text. [Au.]

ture and positivistic conception of science, it is not surprising that he failed to recognize that his analogy here cuts both ways. For not only could the Huxley-Wilberforce debate be seen as very much a part of the "structure" of biological science (which, like that of any other science, including any science of literature, is by no means independent of its own intellectual, social, and institutional history), but, since the "order" of "the existing monuments of literature" is the distinctly sublunary product of, among other things, evaluative practices, any truly systematic study of literature would sooner or later have to include a study of *those practices*. In other words, the structure of criticism cannot be so readily disengaged from the history of taste because they are mutually implicating and incorporating.

Joining as it did both an appeal to scientific objectivity and a humanistic conception of literature, while at the same time extending the promise of a high calling and bright future to a project pursued in the name of "criticism," Frye's effort to banish evaluation from literary study was remarkably effective — at least to the extent of haunting a generation of literary scholars, critics, and teachers, many of whom are still inclined to apologize for making overt value judgments, as if for some temporary intellectual or moral lapse.[12] It was hardly the last word on the subject, however, and as late as 1968 we find E. D. Hirsch, Jr., attempting to rehabilitate the cognitive status of evaluative criticism in an essay significantly titled "Evaluation as Knowledge." In the essay, Hirsch argues that the value judgment of a literary work, when properly directed to the work itself and not to a "distorted version of it," closely coordinated with a correct interpretation of its objective meaning and rationally justified with reference to a specific criteria, *does* constitute a genuine proposition and, therefore, like a "pure description," does "qualify as objective knowledge."[13] Since just about every concept engaged by Hirsch's argument is at issue in contemporary epistemology and critical theory, it is not surprising that it did not settle the question of the intellectual status of evaluative criticism — for Hirsch or anyone else.[14]

The debate over the proper place of evaluation in literary studies remains unresolved and is, I believe, unresolvable in the terms in which it has been formulated. Meanwhile, although evaluative criticism remains intellectually suspect, it certainly continues to be practiced as a magisterial privilege in the classrooms of the literary academy and granted admission to its journals as long as it comes under cover of other presumably more objective types of literary study, such as historical description, textual analysis, or explication. At the same time, however, the fact that literary evaluation is not merely an aspect of formal academic criticism but a complex set of social and cultural activities central to the very nature of literature has been obscured, and an entire domain that is properly the object of theoretical, historical, and empirical exploration has been lost to serious inquiry.

Although I confine my comments here primarily to the American literary academy and to Anglo-American critical theory, the situation — and its intellectual and institutional history — has not been altogether different in continental Europe. The dominance of language- and interpretation-centered theories, movements, and approaches, for example, is clearly international, and versions of the positivist/humanist conflict

---

[12]It should be recalled that, like many others (e.g., Hirsch [see n. 14 below]), Frye continued to maintain that *interpretive* criticism could lay claim to objectivity. See his remarks in a paper delivered in 1967: "The fundamental critical act . . . is the act of recognition, seeing what is there, as distinguished from merely seeing in a Narcissus mirror of our own experience and social and moral prejudice. . . . When a critic interprets, he is talking about his poet; when he evaluates, he is talking about himself" ("Value Judgements," in *Criticism: Speculative and Analytic Essays*, p. 39). [Au.]

[13]Hirsch, *The Aims of Interpretation*, p. 108. See also n. 43 below, for Hirsch's neo-Kantian formulation. [Au.]

[14]In a recent unpublished essay, "Literary Value: The Short History of a Modern Confusion" (1980), Hirsch argues that, although literary *meaning* is determinate, literary value is not. With respect to the latter, however, he concludes that "there are some stable principles" — namely, ethical ones — "that escape the chaos of purely personal relativity" (p. 22). As will be seen in the analysis below, "personal relativity" neither produces chaos nor is in itself chaotic. The escape route of ethical principles and other appeals to higher goods are discussed below. [Au.]

have shaped the development of literary studies in Europe as well. Certain exceptions are, however, instructive. When, in the twenties and thirties, East European theorists also sought to transform literary studies into a progressive, systematic science, the problematic of value and evaluation was not excluded from the project. For example, the historically variable functions of texts and the interrelations among canonical and noncanonical works and other cultural products and activities were recognized and documented by, among others, Jurij Tynjanov and Mikhail Bakhtin; and Jan Mukařovský's explorations of the general question of aesthetic value were both original and substantial.[15] Also, studies in the sociology of literature, especially in France and Germany, and the project of reception aesthetics have concerned themselves with aspects of literary evaluation.[16] It should also be noted, however, that the study of value and evaluation remained relatively undeveloped in the later work of formalists and structuralists,[17] while Marxist literary theory has only recently begun to move from minimal revisions of orthodox aesthetic axiology toward a radical reformulation.[18]

It may be added that, although the theoretical perspective, conceptual structures, and analytic techniques developed by Jacques Derrida are potentially of great interest here (especially in conjunction with the renewed attention to Nietzsche), their radical axiological implications remain largely unexplored,[19] and, insofar as it has been appropriated by American critical theory, deconstruction has been put almost entirely in the service of antihermeneutics, which is to say that it has been absorbed by our preemptive occupation with interpretive criticism. Recent moves toward opening the question of value and evaluation in the American literary academy have come primarily from those who have sought to subject its canon to dramatic revaluation, notably feminist critics. Although their efforts have been significant to that end, they have not, however, amounted as yet to the articulation of a well-developed noncanonical theory of value and evaluation.

One of the major effects of prohibiting or inhibiting explicit evaluation is to forestall the exhibition and obviate the possible acknowledgment of divergent systems of value and thus to ratify, by default, established evaluative authority. It is worth noting that in none of the debates of the forties and fifties was the traditional academic canon itself questioned, and that where evaluative authority was not ringingly affirmed, asserted, or self-justified, it was simply assumed. Thus Frye himself could speak almost in one breath of the need to "get rid of . . . all casual, sentimental, and prejudiced value-judgments" as "the first step in developing a genuine poetics" and of "the masterpieces of literature" which are

[15]See Jurij Tynjanov, "On Literary Evolution" (Moscow, 1927), trans. Ladislav Matejka and Krystyna Pomorska, in *Readings in Russian Poetics*, ed. Matejka and Pomorska (Cambridge, Mass., 1971); Mikhail Bakhtin, *Rabelais and His World* (Moscow, 1965), trans. Helene Iswolsky (Cambridge, Mass., 1968); and Jan Mukařovský, *Aesthetic Norm, Function, and Value as Social Facts* (Prague, 1934), trans. Mark E. Suino (Ann Arbor, Mich., 1970). [Au.] See Tynyanov, in Ch. 3. [Ed.]

[16]For surveys and discussions, see Sammons, *Literary Sociology and Practical Criticism*, and Rien T. Segers, *The Evaluation of Literary Texts: An Experimental Investigation into the Rationalization of Value Judgments with Reference to Semiotics and Esthetics of Reception* (Lisse, 1978). For a recent study of considerable interest, see Jacques Leenhardt and Pierre Józsa, *Lire la lecture: Essai du sociologie de la lecture* (Paris, 1982). [Au.]

[17]It is not mentioned as such, e.g., in Jonathan Culler's *Structuralist Poetics: Structuralism, Linguistics, and the Study of Literature* (Ithaca, N.Y., 1975). [Au.]

[18]See, e.g., the thoroughly equivocal discussions of "objective value" in Stefan Morawski, *Inquiries into Fundamentals of Aesthetics* (Cambridge, Mass., and London, 1974), and the revalorization of the standard Eng. Lit. canon in Althusserian terms in Terry Eagleton, *Criticism and Ideology: A Study in Marxist Literary Theory* (London, 1976). pp. 162–87. For other discussions of this point, see Hans Robert Jauss,

"The Idealist Embarrassment: Observations on Marxist Aesthetics," *New Literary History* 7 (Autumn 1975): 191–208; Raymond Williams, *Marxism and Literature* (Oxford, 1977), esp. pp. 45–54 and 151–57; Tony Bennett, *Formalism and Marxism* (London, 1979), esp. pp. 172–75; and Peter Widdowson, " 'Literary Value' and the Reconstruction of Criticism," *Literature and History* 6 (1980): 138–50. See also n. 35 below. [Au.] See Jauss in Ch. 7. [Ed.]

[19]See, however, Arkady Plotnitsky, "Constraints of the Unbound: Transformation, Value, and Literary Interpretation" (Ph.D. diss., University of Pennsylvania, 1982), for an extensive and sophisticated effort along such lines. [Au.]

"the materials of literary criticism" (*AC*, pp. 18, 15). The identity of those masterpieces, it seemed, could be taken for granted or followed more or less automatically from the "direct value-judgement of informed good taste" or "certain literary values . . . fully established by critical experience" (*AC*, pp. 27, 20).

In a passage of particular interest, Frye wrote:

> Comparative estimates of value are really inferences, most valid when silent ones, from critical practice. . . . The critic will find soon, and constantly, that Milton is a more rewarding and suggestive poet to work with than Blackmore. But the more obvious this becomes, the less time he will want to waste belaboring the point. (*AC*, p. 25)

In addition to the noteworthy correlation of validity with silence (comparable, to some extent, to Wimsatt's discreet "intimations" of value), two other aspects of Frye's remarks here repay some attention. First, in claiming that it is altogether obvious that Milton, rather than Blackmore, is "a more rewarding and suggestive poet [for the critic] to work with," Frye begged the question of *what kind of work* the critic would be doing. For surely if one were concerned with a question such as the relation of canonical and noncanonical texts in the system of literary value in eighteenth-century England, one would find Blackmore just as rewarding and suggestive *to work with* as Milton. Both here and in his repeated insistence that the "material" of criticism must be "the masterpieces of literature" (he refers also to "a feeling we have all had: that the study of mediocre works of art remains a random and peripheral form of critical experience" [*AC*, p. 17]), Frye exhibits a severely limited conception of the potential domain of literary study and of the sort of problems and phenomena with which it could or should deal. In this conceptual and methodological confinement, however (which betrays the conservative force of the ideology of traditional humanism even in the laboratories of the new progressive poetics), he has been joined by just about every other member of the Anglo-American literary academy during the past fifty years.

The second point of interest in Frye's remarks is his significant conjoining of Milton with Blackmore as an illustration of the sort of comparative estimate that is so obvious as not to need belaboring. Blackmore, we recall, was the author of an ambitious epic poem, *The Creation*, notable in literary history primarily as the occasion of some faint praise from Dr. Johnson and otherwise as a topos of literary disvalue; its function — indeed, one might say, its *value* — has been to stand as an instance of bad poetry. This handy conjunction, however (and similar ones, such as Shakespeare and Edgar Guest, John Keats and Joyce Kilmer, T. S. Eliot and Ella Wheeler Wilcox, that occur repeatedly in the debates outlined above), evades the more difficult and consequential questions of judgment posed by genuine evaluative diversity and conflict: questions that are posed, for example, by specific claims of value made for noncanonical works (such as modern texts, especially highly innovative ones, and such culturally exotic works as oral or tribal literature, popular literature, and "ethnic" literature) and also by judgments of literary value made by or on behalf of what might be called noncanonical or culturally exotic audiences (such as all those readers who are not now students, critics, or professors of literature and perhaps never were and never will be within the academy or on its outskirts).

The evasion is dramatized when conflicts of judgment arising from fundamental and perhaps irreconcilable diversity of interest are exhibited in currently charged political contexts. A specific example will illustrate my point here. In 1977 a study of Langston Hughes's poetry was published by Onwuchekwa Jemie, a Nigerian-born, American-educated poet and critic, at that time associate professor of English and Afro-American literature at the University of Minnesota. In one section of his study, Jemie discusses Hughes's poetic cycle, "Madame," in relation to Eliot's "The Love Song of J. Alfred Prufrock" and Ezra Pound's "Hugh Selwyn Mauberley," comparing various formal and thematic aspects of the three works. He observes, for example, that each of them is "consistent in language, tone and attitude with the socio-psychological milieu which it explores: the ghetto dialect and sassy humor [in Hughes's work], the cynical polished talk of literary London [in Pound's], and the bookish ruminations of Prufrock's active mind in inactive body"; he then concludes pointedly: "In short, to fault one poem for not being more like the other, for not dealing with the matter and in the manner of the other, is to err in judgment."[20] Soon after its publication, a reviewer of Jemie's book in the London *Times Literary Supplement* took it very much to task for, among other things, its "painfully irrelevant comparisons," citing the passage quoted above.[21] And, a few weeks later, there appeared in *TLS* an extraordinary letter to the editor from Chinweizu, himself a Nigerian-born, American-educated writer and critic. Responding to the review and particularly to the phrase, "painfully irrelevant comparisons," he shot back:

> Painful to whom? Irrelevant to whom? To idolators of white genius? Who says that Shakespeare, Aristophanes, Dante, Milton, Dostoevsky, Joyce, Pound, Sartre, Eliot, etc. are the last word in literary achievement, unequalled anywhere? . . . The point of these comparisons is not to thrust a black face among these local idols of Europe which, to our grave injury, have been bloated into "universality"; rather it is to help heave them out of our way, clear them from our skies by making clear . . . that we have, among our own, the equals and betters of these chaps. . . . In this day and age, British preferences do not count in the Black World. As Langston Hughes himself put it half a century ago: "If white people are pleased, we are glad. If they are not, it doesn't matter."[22]

This brief case history in the problem of literary evaluation illustrates, among other things, what genuine evaluative conflict sounds like. (It also illustrates that, contrary to Frye's assertion, the history of taste is not "a history where there

are no facts" [*AC*, p. 18], though we have barely begun to recognize either how to chronicle its episodes and shape its narrative or its significance not only for "the structure of criticism" but also for the structure of "literature.") I would suggest that it is, also among other things, the very possibility of that sound that is being evaded in Anglo-American literary studies and, furthermore, that when the sound reaches the intensity that we hear in Chinweizu's letter, the literary academy has no way to acknowledge it except, perhaps, in the language of counteroutrage.[23]

It is clear that, with respect to the central pragmatic issues as well as theoretical problems of literary value and evaluation, American critical theory has simply painted itself out of the picture. Beguiled by the humanist's fantasy of transcendence, endurance, and universality, it has been unable to acknowledge the most fundamental character of literary value, which is its mutability and diversity. And, at the same time, magnetized by the goals and ideology of a naive scientism, distracted by the arid concerns of philosophic axiology, obsessed by a misplaced quest for "objectivity," and confined in its very conception of literary studies by the narrow intellectual traditions and professional allegiances of the literary academy, it has foreclosed from its own domain the possibility of investigating the dynamics of that mutability and understanding the nature of that diversity.

The type of investigation I have in mind here would seek neither to establish normative "criteria," devise presumptively objective evaluative procedures, nor discover grounds for the "justification" of critical judgments or practices. It would not, in short, be a literary axiology or, in effect, the counterpart for evaluative criticism of what a literary hermeneutics offers to be for interpretive criticism. It would seek, rather, to clarify the nature of literary — and, more broadly,

---

[20]Onwuchekwa Jemie, *Langston Hughes: An Introduction to the Poetry* (New York, 1976), p. 184. [Au.]

[21]C. W. B. Bigsby, "Hand in Hand with the Blues," *Times Literary Supplement*, 17 June 1977, p. 734. [Au.]

[22]Chinweizu, letter to the editor, *Times Literary Supplement*, 15 July 1977, p. 871. [Au.] The reader who examines the full text of both Bigsby's review and Chinweizu's letter will wonder whether this is a quarrel over "literary evaluation" or over turf between black and white literary critics. In a sentence omitted by Smith, for example, Chinweizu says, "Any *bête blanche* intruder into the affairs of a "Burnt Cork" is free to submit his preferences, but he is not likely to get them filled." [Ed.]

[23]Thus Sammons, in his embattled book, writes of "the elements . . . in the canon of great literature" to which we should be attentive so that, faced with charges of elitism, "we will not have to stand mute before claims that inarticulateness, ignorance, occult mumbling, and loutishness are just as good as fine literature" (*Literary Sociology and Practical Criticism*, p. 134). [Au.]

aesthetic — value in conjunction with a more general rethinking of the concept of value; to explore the multiple forms and functions of literary evaluation, institutional as well as individual, in relation to the circumstantial constraints and conditions to which they are responsive; to chronicle "the history of taste" in relation to a general model of historical evaluative dynamics and specific local conditions; and to describe and account for the various phenomena and activities that appear to be involved in literary and aesthetic evaluation in relation to our more general understanding — as it is and as it develops — of human culture and behavior.

The sort of inquiry suggested here (which obviously could not be pursued within the confines of literary study or critical theory as they are presently conceived and demarcated) might be expected to make its accounts internally consistent, externally connectable, and amenable to continuous extension and refinement; for it is thus that the theoretical power and productivity of those accounts would be served and secured. This is not, however, to imagine a monolithic intellectual project that would offer to yield an ultimately comprehensive, unified, and objective account of its subject; for to imagine it thus would, of course, be to repeat, only on a grander scale, elements of the raw positivism and naive scientism that were, in part, responsible for both the exile of evaluation and the confinements of modern critical theory. What is desirable, rather, is an inquiry pursued with the recognition that, like any other intellectual enterprise, it would consist, at any given time, of a set of heterogeneous projects; that the conceptual structures and methodological practices adopted in those projects would themselves be historically and otherwise contingent (reflecting, among other things, prevailing or currently interesting conceptual structures and methods in related areas of inquiry); that whatever other value the descriptions and accounts produced by any of those projects might and undoubtedly would have (as indices of twentieth-century thought, for example, to future historians), their specific value as descriptions and accounts would be a function of how well they made intelligible the phenomena within their domain to whoever, at whatever time and

from whatever perspective, had an interest in them; and that its pursuit would be shaped by — that is, energized and transformed in response to — those interests, and its descriptions and accounts continuously and variously interpreted and employed in accord with them.[24]

The discussion that follows is designed to suggest a theoretical framework for such an inquiry.[25]

## 2. THE ECONOMICS OF LITERARY AND AESTHETIC VALUE

All value is radically contingent, being neither an inherent property of objects nor an arbitrary projection of subjects but, rather, the product of the dynamics of an economic system. It is readily granted, of course, that it is in relation to a system of that sort that commodities such as gold, bread, and paperback editions of *Moby-Dick* acquire the value indicated by their market prices. It is traditional, however, both in economic and aesthetic theory as well as in informal discourse, to distinguish sharply between the value of an entity in that sense (that is, its "exchange-value") and some other type of value that may be referred to as its utility (or "use-value") or, especially with respect to so-called "nonutilitarian" objects such as artworks or works of literature, as its "intrinsic value." Thus, it might be said that whereas the fluctuating price of a particular paperback edition of *Moby-Dick* is a function of such variables as supply and demand, production and distribution costs, and the publisher's calculation of corporate profits, these factors do not affect the value of *Moby-Dick* as experienced by an individual reader or its intrinsic value as a work of literature. These distinctions, however, are not as clear-cut as may appear.

Like its price in the marketplace, the value of

24See Gonzalo Munévar, *Radical Knowledge: A Philosophical Inquiry into the Nature and Limits of Science* (Indianapolis, 1981), for an elaboration of a "performance model" of scientific activity along the lines implied here. [Au.]

25For a companion piece to the present essay, see my "Fixed Marks and Variable Constancies: A Parable of Literary Value," *Poetics Today* 1 (Autumn 1979): 7–31. [Au.]

an entity to an individual subject is *also* the product of the dynamics of an economic system, specifically the personal economy constituted by the subject's needs, interests, and resources — biological, psychological, material, and experiential. Like any other economy, moreover, this too is a continuously fluctuating or shifting system, for our individual needs, interests, and resources are themselves functions of our continuously changing states in relation to an environment that may be relatively stable but is never absolutely fixed. The two systems are, it may be noted, not only analogous but also interactive and interdependent; for part of our environment *is* the market economy, and, conversely, the market economy is comprised, in part, of the diverse personal economies of individual producers, distributors, consumers, and so forth.

The traditional discourse of value — including a number of terms I have used here, such as "subject," "object," "needs," "interests," and, indeed, "value" itself — reflects an arbitrary arresting, segmentation, and hypostasization of the continuous process of our interactions with our environments — or what could also be described as the continuous interplay among multiple configurable systems. It is difficult to devise (and would be, perhaps, impossible to sustain) a truly Heraclitean discourse that did not reflect such conceptual operations, but we may recognize that, insofar as such terms project images of discrete acts, agents, and entities, fixed attributes, unidirectional forces, and simple causal and temporal relationships, they obscure the dynamics of value and reinforce dubious concepts of noncontingency — that is, concepts such as "intrinsic," "objective," "absolute," "universal," and "transcendent." It is necessary, therefore, to emphasize a number of other interactive relationships and forms of interdependence that are fragmented by our language and commonly ignored in critical theory and aesthetic axiology.

First, as I have already suggested, a subject's experience of an entity is always a function of his or her personal economy: that is, the specific "existence" of an object or event, its integrity, coherence, and boundaries, the category of entities to which it "belongs" and its specific "features," "qualities," or "properties" are all the variable products of the subject's engagement with his or her environment under a particular set of conditions. Not only is an entity always experienced under more or less different conditions, but the various experiences do not yield a simple cumulative (corrected, improved, deeper, more thorough, or complete) knowledge of the entity because they are not additive. Rather, each experience of an entity frames it in a different role and constitutes it as a different configuration, with different "properties" foregrounded and repressed. Moreover, the subject's experiences of an entity are not discrete or, strictly speaking, successive, because recollection and anticipation always overlay perception and the units of what we call "experience" themselves vary and overlap.

Second, what we speak of as a subject's "needs," "interests," and "purposes" are not only always changing (and it may be noted here that a subject's "self" — or that on behalf of which s/he may be said to act with "self-interest" — is also variable, being multiply reconstituted in terms of different roles and relationships), but they are also not altogether independent of or prior to the entities that satisfy or implement them; that is, entities also produce the needs and interests they satisfy and evoke the purposes they implement. Moreover, because our purposes are continuously transformed and redirected by the objects we produce in the very process of implementing them, and because of the complex interrelations among human needs, technological production, and cultural practices, there is a continuous process of mutual modification between our desires and our universe.[26]

[26]Some aspects of this process are discussed by Pierre Bourdieu in "La Métamorphose des goûts," *Questions de sociologie* (Paris, 1980), pp. 161–72. The more general interrelations among human "needs and wants," cultural practices, and economic production have been examined by Marshall Sahlins in *Culture and Practical Reason* (Chicago, 1976), Mary Douglas in *The World of Goods* (New York, 1979), and Jean Baudrillard in *For a Critique of the Political Economy of the Sign* (Paris, 1972), trans. Charles Levin (St. Louis, 1981). Although Baudrillard's critical analysis of the concept of "use-value" — and, with it, of "sign value" — is of considerable interest for a semiotics of the marketplace, his effort to develop, "as a basis for the practical overthrow of political economy" (p. 122), a theory of a value "beyond

Of particular significance for the value of "works of art" and "literature" is the interactive relation between the *classification* of an entity and the functions it is expected or desired to perform. In perceiving an object or artifact in terms of some category — as, for example, "a clock," "a dictionary," "a doorstop," "a curio" — we implicitly isolate and foreground certain of its possible functions and typically refer its value to the extent to which it performs those functions more or less effectively. But the relation between function and classification also operates in reverse: thus, under conditions that produce the "need" for a door-stopping object or an "interest" in Victorian artifacts, certain properties and possible functions of various objects in the neighborhood will be foregrounded, and both the classification and value of those objects will follow accordingly. As we commonly put it, one will "realize" the value of the dictionary *as a* doorstop or "appreciate" the value of the clock *as a* curio.[27] (The mutually defining relations among classification, function, and value are nicely exhibited in the *OED*'s definition of "curio" as "an object of art, piece of bric-à-brac, etc., valued as a curiosity," which is, of course, something like — and no less accurate than — defining "clock" as "an object valued as a clock.") It may be noted here that human beings have evolved as distinctly opportunistic creatures and that our survival, both as individuals and as a species, continues to be enhanced by our ability and inclination to reclassify objects and to "realize" and "appreciate" novel and alternate functions for them — which is also to "misuse" them and to fail to respect their presumed purposes and conventional generic classifications.

The various forms of interdependence emphasized here have considerable bearing on what may be recognized as the economics of literary

and aesthetic value. The traditional — idealist, humanist, genteel — tendency to isolate or protect certain aspects of life and culture, among them works of art and literature, from consideration in economic terms has had the effect of mystifying the nature — or, more accurately, the dynamics — of their value. In view of the arbitrariness of the exclusion, it is not surprising that the languages of aesthetics and economics nevertheless tend to drift toward each other and that their segregation must be constantly patrolled.[28] (Thus, an aesthetician deplores a pun on "appreciation" appearing in an article on art investment and warns of the dangers of confusing "the uniqueness of a painting that gives it scarcity value . . . with its unique value as a work of art.")[29] To those for whom terms such as "utility," "effectiveness," and "function" suggest gross pragmatic instrumentality, crass material desires, and the satisfaction of animal needs, a concept such as use-value will be seen as irrelevant to or clearly to be distinguished from aesthetic value. There is, however, no good reason to confine the domain of the utilitarian to objects that serve only immediate, specific, and unexalted ends or, for that matter, to assume that the value of artworks has altogether nothing to do with pragmatic instrumentality or animal needs.[30] The recurrent impulse or effort to define aesthetic

[28]The magnetism or recurrent mutually metaphoric relation between economic and aesthetic — especially literary — discourse is documented and discussed by Marc Shell in *The Economy of Literature* (Baltimore, 1978) and Kurt Heinzelman in *The Economics of the Imagination* (Amherst, Mass., 1980). [Au.]

[29]Andrew Harrison, *Making and Thinking* (Indianapolis, 1978), p. 100. [Au.]

[30]See George J. Stigler and Gary S. Becker, "De gustibus non est disputandum," *American Economics Review* 67 (March 1977): 76–90, for an ingenious and influential attempt (at the opposite extreme, perhaps, of Baudrillard's [see n. 26 above]) to demonstrate that differences and changes of behavior (including aesthetic behavior) that appear to be matters of "taste" and, as such, beyond explanation in economic terms can be accounted for (*a*) as functions of subtle forms of "price" and "income" and (*b*) on the usual (utilitarian) assumption that we always behave, all things considered, so as to maximize utility. As Stigler and Becker acknowledge, recent experimental studies of "choice behavior" in human (and other) subjects suggest that this latter assumption itself requires modification. [Au.]

value" (created out of what he calls "symbolic exchange") is less successful, partly because of its utopian anthropology and partly because the value in question does not escape economic accounting. [Au.]

[27]For an excellent analysis of the relation between classification and value, see Michael Thompson, *Rubbish Theory: The Creation and Destruction of Value* (Oxford, 1979), esp. pp. 13–56. [Au.]

value by contradistinction to all forms of utility or as the negation of all other nameable sources of interest or forms of value — hedonic, practical, sentimental, ornamental, historical, ideological, and so forth — is, in effect, to define it out of existence; for when all such particular utilities, interests, and sources of value have been subtracted, nothing remains. Or, to put this in other terms: the "essential value" of an artwork consists of everything from which it is usually distinguished.

To be sure, various candidates have been proposed for a pure, nonutilitarian, interest-free, and, in effect, value-free source of aesthetic value, such as the eliciting of "intrinsically rewarding" intellectual, sensory, or perceptual activities, or Kant's "free play of the cognitive faculties." A strict accounting of any of these seemingly gratuitous activities, however, would bring us sooner or later to their biological utility and/or survival value (and indeed to something very much like "animal needs"). For although we may be individually motivated to engage in them "for their own sake" (which is to say, for the sake of the gratifications they provide), our doing so apparently yields a long-term profit in enhanced cognitive development, behavioral flexibility, and thus biological fitness, and our general tendency to do so is in all likelihood the product of evolutionary mechanisms.[31] Moreover, as I have pointed out elsewhere, the occasioning of such activities (or "experiences") is not confined to "works of art" and therefore cannot, without circularity, be said to constitute the defining "aesthetic function" of the objects so labeled.[32] More generally, it may be observed that since there are no functions performed by artworks that may be specified as unique to them and also no way to distinguish the "rewards" provided by the art-related experiences or behavior from those provided by innumerable other kinds of experience and behavior, any distinctions drawn between "aesthetic" and "non- (or extra-) aesthetic" value are fundamentally problematic.[33]

Suggestions of the radically contingent nature of aesthetic value are commonly countered by evidence of apparent noncontingent value: for example, the endurance of certain classic canonical works (the invocation of Homer being a topos of the critical tradition) and, if not quite Pope's "gen'ral chorus of mankind," then at least the convergent sentiments of people of education and discrimination. Certainly any theory of aesthetic value must be able to account for continuity, stability, and apparent consensus as well as for drift, shift, and diversity. The tendency throughout formal aesthetic axiology has been to explain the constancies and convergences by the inherent qualities of the objects and/or some set of presumed human universals and to explain the variabilities and divergences by the errors, defects, and biases of individual subjects. The classic development of this account is found in Hume's essay, *Of the Standard of Taste*, where the "catholic and universal beauty" is seen to be the result of

[t]he relation which nature has placed between the form and the sentiment. . . . We shall be able to ascertain its influence . . . from the durable admiration which attends those works that have survived all the caprices of mode and fashion, all the mistakes of ignorance and envy.

The same Homer who pleased at Athens two thousand years ago, is still admired at Paris and London. All the changes of climate, government, religion and language have not been able to obscure his glory. . . .

It appears then, that amidst all the variety and caprice of taste, there are certain general principles of approbation and blame, whose influence a care-

---

[31]See Robert Fagen, *Animal Play Behavior* (Oxford, 1981), pp. 248–358, for an extensive analysis of "intrinsically rewarding" physical activities and an account of the evolutionary mechanisms that apparently produce and sustain them. [Au.]

[32]See the related discussion of "cognitive play" in my *On the Margins of Discourse: The Relation of Literature to Language* (Chicago, 1978), pp. 116–24. [Au.]

[33]Monroe Beardsley's "instrumentalist" (that is, utilitarian) theory of aesthetic value (*Aesthetics: Problems in the Philosophy of Criticism* [New York, 1958], pp. 524–76) and Mukařovský's otherwise quite subtle exploration of these questions (see n. 15, above) do not altogether escape the confinements and circularities of formalist conceptions of, respectively, "aesthetic experience" and "aesthetic function." [Au.]

ful eye may trace in all the operations of the mind. Some particular forms or qualities, from the original structure of the internal fabric are calculated to please, and others to displease; and if they fail of their effect in any particular instance, it is from some apparent defect or imperfection in the organ.

Many and frequent are the defects . . . which prevent or weaken the influence of those general principles.[34]

The essay continues by enumerating and elaborating these defects, introducing the familiar catalog (already given vivid expression in, among other places, Pope's *Essay on Criticism*: "Of all the causes which conspire to blind / Man's erring judgment and misguide the mind") with an analogy, also a commonplace of the tradition, between "the perfect beauty," as agreed upon by men "in a sound state of the organ," and "the true and real colors" of objects as they appear "in daylight to the eye of a man in health."[35]

The following is a more recent statement of the traditional view:

False judgments and intuitions of an object can only be corrected if there is a correct and permanently valid intuition of an object. . . . The relativity of value judgments merely proves that subjective judgments are conjoined with the person, that mistaken judgments — of which there is no dearth in the history of literature — are always the fault of the person.

. . . Just as the universal validity of a mathematical proposition does not necessarily imply that everyone can understand it, "but merely that every-

one who understands it must agree with it," so the universal validity of aesthetic value does not necessarily mean that evidence of it is felt by everyone. Aesthetic values demand an adequate attitude, a trained or reliably functioning organ. Moreover, the fact that the history of literature contains, albeit tacitly, a firm gradation of valuable works of art is an indication that values transcend historicity.

. . . The value-feeling organ must not be encumbered with prejudgments, pre-feelings, or arbitrarily formed opinions if it wishes to address itself adequately to the object, a process that is by no means always easy, . . . for the human being is in part — an external but not uninfluential part — a historical creature, embedded in a whole cluster of behavior compulsions that stem from his environment.[36]

This conflation of, among others, Hume, Kant, Nicolai Hartmann, and Roman Ingarden is remarkable only in making particularly flagrant the logical incoherence of the standard account, whether in its empiricist, idealist, or phenomenological guise.

Given a more sophisticated formulation, Hume's belief that the individual experience of "beauty" can be related to "forms" and "qualities" that gratify human beings "naturally" by virtue of certain physiological structures and psychological mechanisms is probably not altogether without foundation.[37] Taken as a ground for the justification of normative claims, however, and transformed accordingly into a model of standards-and-deviations, it obliged him (as it did and does many others) to interpret as so many instances of individual pathology what are, rather, the variable products of the interaction between, on the one hand, certain *relatively* uniform innate structures, mechanisms, and tendencies and, on the other, innumerable cultural and contextual variables as well as other individual variables — the latter including particulars of personal history, temperament, age, and so forth.

[34]David Hume, *"Of the Standard of Taste" and Other Essays*, ed. John W. Lenz (Indianapolis, 1965), pp. 8–10. [Au.] See Hume, p. 212. [Ed.]

[35]Ibid., p. 10. At the conclusion of the essay, Hume almost — but not quite — reinstalls the very *de gustibus* argument that the standard of taste was presumably designed to answer: "But where there is such a diversity in the internal frame or external situation as is entirely blameless on both sides, . . . a certain degree of diversity of judgment is unavoidable and we seek in vain a standard by which we can reconcile the contrary sentiments" (pp. 19–20). Of course, the qualification ("as is entirely blameless on both sides") that keeps this from being a total turnabout also introduces a new normative consideration (how to determine whether or not — or to what extent — something "in the internal frame or external situation" is *blamable*) and thus moves again toward the type of potentially infinite regress into which all axiologies typically tumble. [Au.]

[36]Walter Hinderer, "Literary Value Judgments and Value Cognition," trans. Leila Vannewitz, in *Problems of Literary Evaluation*, pp. 58–59. [Au.]

[37]The discipline of "empirical aesthetics" has been developed out of precisely such a belief. For a recent survey and discussion of its findings, see Hans and Shulamith Kreitler, *Psychology of the Arts* (Durham, N.C., 1972). See also n. 50 below. [Au.]

What produces evaluative consensus, such as it is, is not the healthy functioning of universal organs but the playing out of the *same* dynamics and variable contingencies that produce evaluative divergences.

Although value is always subject-relative, not all value is equally subject-variable. Within a particular community, the tastes and preferences of subjects — that is, their tendency to find more satisfaction of a particular kind in one rather than another of some array of comparable items and to select among them accordingly — will be conspicuously *divergent* (or indeed idiosyncratic) to the extent that the satisfactions in question are themselves functions of types of needs, interests, and resources that (*a*) vary individually along a wide spectrum, (*b*) are especially resistant, if not altogether intractable, to cultural channeling, and/or (*c*) are especially responsive to circumstantial context. Conversely, their tastes and preferences will tend to be similar to the extent that the satisfactions in question are functions of types of needs, interests, and resources that (*a*) vary individually within a narrow spectrum, (*b*) are especially tractable to cultural channeling, and (*c*) remain fairly stable under a variety of conditions.

Insofar as satisfactions ("aesthetic" or any other: erotic, for example) with regard to some array of objects are functions of needs, interests, and resources of the first kind, preferences for those objects will appear "subjective," "eccentric," "stubborn," and "capricious." Insofar as they are functions of the second, preferences will seem so obvious, "natural," and "rational" as not to appear to be matters of taste at all. Indeed, it is precisely under the latter conditions that the value of particular objects will appear to be inherent, that distinctions or gradations of value among them will appear to reduce to differences in the properties or qualities of the objects themselves, and that explicit judgments of their value will appear to be objective. In short, here as elsewhere, a coincidence of contingencies among individual subjects will be interpreted by those subjects as noncontingency.

Because we are dealing here not with two opposed sets of discrete determinants but with the possibility of widely differing specifications for a large number of complexly interacting variables, we may expect to find a continuous exhibition of every degree of divergence and convergence among the subjects in a particular community over the course of its history, depending in each instance on the extent of the disparity and uniformity of each of the relevant contingencies *and* on the strength of various social practices and cultural institutions that control the exhibition of extreme "deviance."[38] It may be noted that the latter — that is, the normative mechanisms within a community that suppress divergence and tend to obscure as well as deny the contingency of value — will always have, as their counterpart, a *counter*mechanism that permits a recognition of that contingency and a more or less genial acknowledgement of the inevitability of divergence: hence the ineradicability, in spite of the efforts of establishment axiology, of what might be called folk-relativism: "Chacun à son goût"; "De gustibus . . .";[39] "One man's meat is another's poison"; and so forth.

The prevailing structure of tastes and preferences (and the consequent illusion of a consensus based on objective value) will always be implicitly threatened or directly challenged by the divergent tastes and preferences of some subjects within the community (for example, those not yet adequately acculturated, such as the young, and others with "uncultivated" tastes, such as provincials and social upstarts) as well as by most subjects outside it or, more significantly, on its *periphery* and who thus have occasion to interact with its members (for example, exotic visitors, immigrants, colonials, and members of various minority or marginalized groups). Consequently, institutions of evaluative authority will be called upon repeatedly to devise arguments and procedures that validate the community's established tastes and preferences, thereby warding off bar-

---

[38]See Morse Peckham, *Explanation and Power: The Control of Human Behavior* (New York, 1979), for an account of deviance (or what he calls "the delta effect") as the product of the relation between cultural practices and the randomness of behavior and, more generally, for a highly original discussion of the processes and institutions of cultural channeling. [Au.]

[39]Each to his own taste; about tastes [there is no disputing]. . . . [Ed.]

barism and the constant apparition of an imminent collapse of standards and also justifying the exercise of their own normative authority. In Hume's words, "It is natural to seek a Standard of Taste; a rule by which the various sentiments of men may be reconciled; at least a decision afforded confirming one sentiment and denying another" — the usefulness of such a rule to the latter end being illustrated in the essay by that memorable vignette of the barbarian in the drawing room who "would assert an equality of genius and elegance between Ogilby and Milton or Bunyan and Addison" and what ensues: "Though there may be found *persons* who give preference to the former authors, *no one* pays attention to such taste; and *we* pronounce without scruple the sentiment of these pretended critics to be absurd and ridiculous."[40] The sequence emphasized here is no less telling than the embarrassment of the argument by the examples.

Both informally, as in the drawing rooms of men of cultivation and discrimination or the classrooms of the literary academy, and formally, as in Hume's essay and throughout the central tradition of Western critical theory, the validation commonly takes the form of privileging absolutely — that is, "standard"-izing — the particular contingencies that govern the preferences of the members of the group and discounting or, as suggested above, pathologizing all other contingencies.[41] Thus it will be assumed or maintained: (*a*) that the particular *functions* they expect and desire the class of objects in question (for example, "works of art" or "literature") to perform are their intrinsic or proper functions, all other expected, desired, or emergent functions being inappropriate, irrelevant, extrinsic, abuses of the true nature of those objects or violations of their authorially intended or generically intrinsic purposes; (*b*) that the particular *conditions* (circum-

stantial, technological, institutional, and so forth) under which the members of the group typically interact with those objects are suitable, standard, or necessary for their proper appreciation, all other conditions being irregular, unsuitable, substandard, or outlandish; and, perhaps most significantly, (*c*) that the particular *subjects* who compose the members of the group are of sound mind and body, duly trained and informed, and generally competent, all other subjects being defective, deficient, or deprived — suffering from crudenesses of sensibility, diseases and distortions of perception, weaknesses of character, impoverishment of background-and-education, cultural or historical biases, ideological or personal prejudices, and/or undeveloped, corrupted, or jaded tastes.

With regard to this last point (*c*), we may recall here the familiar specifications of the "ideal critic" as one who, in addition to possessing various exemplary natural endowments and cultural competencies, has, through exacting feats of self-liberation, freed himself of all forms of particularity and individuality, all special interests (or, as in Kant, all interests whatsoever), and thus of all bias — which is to say, one who is "free" of everything in relation to which any experience or judgment of value occurs. (In these respects, the ideal critic of aesthetic axiology is the exact counterpart of the "ideal reader" of literary hermeneutics.)

We may also note, with regard to the first point (*a*), that the privileging of a particular set of functions for artworks or works of literature may be (and often is) itself justified on the grounds that the performance of such functions serves some higher individual, social, or transcendent good, such as the psychic health of the reader, the brotherhood of mankind, the glorification of God, the project of human emancipation, or the survival of Western civilization. Any selection from among these alternate and to some extent mutually exclusive higher goods, however, would itself require justification in terms of some yet *higher* good, and there is no absolute stopping point for this theoretically infinite regress of judgments and justifications. This is not to say that certain functions of artworks do not serve higher — or at least more general compre-

[40]Hume, *"Of the Standard of Taste,"* pp. 5, 7. [Au.]

[41]Communities are of all sizes and so are drawing rooms; the provincials, colonials, and marginalized groups mentioned above (including the young), insofar as they constitute social communities, may also be expected to have prevailing structures of tastes and preferences and to control them in the same ways as do more obviously "establishment" groups. Folk-relativism is neither confined to the folk nor always exhibited by them. [Au.]

hensive, or longer-range — goods better than others. It is to say, however, that our selection among higher goods, like our selection among any array of goods, will always be contingent.

## 3. THE MULTIPLE FORMS, FUNCTIONS, AND CONTEXTS OF EVALUATIVE BEHAVIOR

It follows from the conception of value outlined here that evaluations are not discrete acts or episodes punctuating experience but indistinguishable from the very processes of acting and experiencing themselves. In other words, for a responsive creature, to exist is to evaluate. We are always calculating how things "figure" for us — always pricing them, so to speak, in relation to the total economy of our personal universe. Throughout our lives, we perform a continuous succession of rapid-fire cost-benefit analyses, estimating the probable "worthwhileness" of alternate courses of action in relation to our always limited resources of time and energy, assessing, reassessing, and classifying entities with respect to their probable capacity to satisfy our current needs and desires and to serve our emergent interests and long-range plans and purposes. We tend to become most conscious of our own evaluative behavior when the need to select among an array of alternate "goods" and/or to resolve an internal "contest of sentiments" moves us to specifically verbal or other symbolic forms of cost accounting: thus we draw up our lists of pros and cons, lose sleep, and bore our friends by overtly rehearsing our options, estimating the risks and probable outcomes of various actions, and so forth. Most of these calculations, however, are performed intuitively and inarticulately, and many of them are so recurrent that the habitual arithmetic becomes part of our personality and comprises the very style of our being and behavior, forming what we may call our principles or tastes — and what others may call our biases and prejudices.

I have been speaking up to this point of the evaluations we make for ourselves. As social creatures, however, we also evaluate for one another through various kinds of individual acts and also through various institutional practices. The long-standing preoccupation of aesthetic axiology with the logical form and cognitive substance of verbal "value judgments" and, in particular, with debates over their "validity," "truth-value," and "verifiability," has obscured the operation and significance of institutional and other less overt forms of evaluation. It has also deflected attention from the social contexts, functions, and consequences of all forms of aesthetic and literary evaluation, including their complex productive relation to literary and aesthetic value. Although I am more concerned here with the latter questions and shall return to them below, some comments on *explicit* aesthetic judgments (and on certain familiar axiological perplexities regarding them) are in order.

Evaluations are among the most fundamental forms of social communication and probably among the most primitive benefits of social interaction. (Animals — insects and birds as well as mammals — evaluate *for* one another, that is, signal to other members of their group the "quality" of a food supply or territory by some form of specialized overt behavior.)[42] We not only produce but also solicit and seek out both "expressions of personal sentiment" and "objective judgments of value" because, although neither will (for nothing can) give us "knowledge" of *the* value of an object, both may let us know other things we could find useful. For example, other people's reports of how well certain objects have gratified them, though "mere expressions of subjective likes and dislikes," may nevertheless be useful to us if we ourselves have produced those objects or if — as lovers, say, or parents or potential associates — we have an independently motivated interest in the current states, specific responses, or general structure of tastes and preferences of those people. Also, an assertion that some object (for example, some artwork) is good, great, bad, or middling can, no matter how magisterially delivered or with what

[42]To the extent that such forms of behavior are under the control of innate mechanisms that respond directly to — or, in effect, "register" — the conditions in question, they are not, strictly speaking, verbal or symbolic. For this reason, such evaluations may be "objective" in a way that, for better or worse, no human value judgment can be. [Au.]

attendant claims or convictions of absoluteness, usually be unpacked as a judgment of its *contingent* value: specifically, as the evaluator's observation and/or estimate of how well that object, relative to others of the same implied category, has performed and/or is likely to perform certain particular (though taken-for-granted) functions for some particular (though only implicitly defined) set of subjects under some particular (unspecified but assumed) set or range of conditions. Any evaluation, therefore, is "cognitively substantial" in the sense of being potentially informative about *something*. The actual interest of that information, however, and hence the value of that evaluation to *us* (and "we" are always heterogeneous) will vary, depending on, among other things, the extent to which we have any interest in the object evaluated, believe that we take for granted the same taken-for-granted functions and assume the same assumed conditions, and also think that we (or others whose interests are of interest to us) are among that implicitly defined set of subjects — or, of course, the extent to which we have an interest in the evaluator's sentiments by reason of our independently motivated interest in him or her.

In view of the centrality of the question in post-Kantian aesthetic axiology, it may be noted that if the set of relevant subjects implied by an evaluation is not contextually defined or otherwise indicated, it will usually be appropriately taken to consist of the evaluator himself and all others whom s/he believes are *like* himself or herself in the pertinent respects. Of course, some evaluators believe that *all* other people are — or should be — like themselves in the pertinent respects: hence, apparently, the curious and distracting notion that every aesthetic judgment "claims universal subjective validity."[43] The fa-

miliar subjectivist/objectivist controversy is commonly seen to turn on whether, in making an aesthetic judgment, I speak "for myself *alone*" or "for *everyone*." A consideration of the social functions of such judgments, however, suggests that, if such a formulation is wanted at all, it should be that, in making aesthetic judgments, I tend to speak "for myself *and some others*."

We may also consider here what is thought to be the suspect propositional status of value judgments as distinguished from and compared to that of so-called factual statements and the consequent demotion of the former to the status of "pseudostatements." There is, of course, no way for us to be certain that someone's reports of his or her personal likes or dislikes are sincere, or that the estimates and observations offered are the estimates and observations actually made. Like all other utterances, value judgments are context-dependent and shaped by the relation of the speaker to his or her audience and by the structure of interests that sustains the verbal transaction between them. (In effect, there is no such thing as an honest opinion.) For this reason, we will always interpret (supplement and discount) evaluations in the light of other knowledge we have of the evaluator (or think we have: there is no absolute end to this regress, though in practice we do the best we can), including our sense — on whatever grounds — of the possibility of flattery or other kinds of deception: the evaluator may be the author's personal friend or professional rival, s/he may not want to hurt the cook's feelings, s/he may want to recommend himself or herself by creating the impression that s/he shares our tastes, and so forth. In all these respects, however, value judgments are no different from any other kind of utterance, and neither their reliability nor their "validity" as "prop-

---

[43]Kant's tortured attempt, which occupies most of *The Critique of Judgment*, to ground such a claim on the possibility of a cognition of pure aesthetic value (that is, "beauty") produced by nothing but the free operation of universal cognitive faculties has been recently revived and supplemented by Hirsch's attempt to ground it on the possibility of "correct interpretation," specifically the "re-cognition" of that "universally valid cognition of a work . . . constituted by the kind of subjective stance adopted in its creation" (*The Aims of Interpretation*, pp. 105–6). For a recent and very thorough

examination of *The Critique of Judgment*, see Paul Guyer, *Kant and the Claims of Taste* (Cambridge, Mass., and London, 1979); for a thoroughly irreverent examination of it, see Jacques Derrida, "Economimesis," trans. Richard Klein, *Diacritics* 2 (Summer 1981): 3–25. [Au.] See Kant p. 248. Smith apparently understands Kant as claiming that the judgment of taste is universal in fact rather than in its subjective aspect. See the introduction to Kant, p. 244. [Ed.]

ositions" is any more (or any less) compromised by these possibilities than that of any other type of verbal behavior, from someone's saying (or otherwise implying) that s/he has a headache to his or her solemn report of the measurement of a scientific instrument.

There is a tenacious conviction among those who argue these questions that unless one judgment can be said or shown to be more "valid" than another, then all judgments must be "equal" or "equally valid." Indeed, it is the horror or apparent absurdity of such egalitarianism that commonly gives force to the charge that "relativism" produces social chaos or is a logically untenable position. While the radical contingency of all value certainly does imply that no value judgment can be more valid than another in the sense of being a more accurate statement of *the* value of an object (for the latter concept then becomes vacuous), it does not follow that all value judgments are equal or equally valid. On the contrary, what does follow is that the concept of "validity" is *inappropriate* with regard to evaluations and that there is no nontrivial parameter with respect to which they *could* be "equal." This is not to say that no evaluations can be better or worse than others. What must be emphasized, however, is that the value — the "goodness" or "badness" — of an evaluation, like that of anything else (including any other type of utterance), is *itself* contingent, and thus a matter not of its abstract "truth-value" but of how well it performs various desired/able functions for the various people who may at any time be concretely involved with it. In the case of an aesthetic evaluation, these people will always include the evaluator, who will have his or her own particular interest in the various effects of the judgments s/he produces, and may also include anyone from the artist to a potential publisher or patron, various current or future audiences of the work, and perhaps someone who just likes to know what's going on and what other people think is going on. Each of them will have his or her own interest in the evaluation, and it will be better or worse for each of them in relation to a different set of desired/able functions. What all this suggests is that the obsessive debates over the cognitive substance, logical status, and "truth-value" of aes-

thetic judgments are not only unresolvable in the terms given but, strictly speaking, pointless.

As was indicated above, the value of an explicit verbal evaluation — that is, its utility to those who produce and receive it — will, like that of any other type of utterance, always be a function of specific features of the various transactions of which it may be a part, including the relevant interests of the speaker and any of those who, at any time, become members of his or her de facto audience. It follows that the value of a value judgment may also be quite minimal or negative. For example, depending on specific (and readily imaginable) contextual features, an aesthetic judgment may be excruciatingly *uninteresting* to the listener or elicited from the speaker at considerable expense to himself or herself. Also, aesthetic judgments, like any other use of language, may be intimidating, coercive, and otherwise socially and politically oppressive. If they are so, however, it is not because of any characteristic frailty of their propositional status (and "justifying" them — that is, giving a show of justice to their claims of objectivity or universal validity — will not eliminate the oppression) but, once again, because of the nature of the transactions of which they are a part, particularly the social or political relationship between the evaluator and his or her audience (professor and student, for example, or censor and citizen) and the structure of power that governs that relationship.[44] We may return now from the discussion of individual overt value judgments to the more general consideration of evaluative behavior, normative institutions, and the social mechanisms by which literary and aesthetic value are produced.

## 4. THE CULTURAL RE-PRODUCTION OF VALUE

We do not move about in a raw universe. Not only are the objects we encounter always to some extent pre-interpreted and preclassified for us by

[44]I discuss these and related aspects of verbal transactions in *On the Margins of Discourse*, pp. 15–24 and 82–106, and in "Narrative Versions, Narrative Theories," *Critical Inquiry* 7 (Autumn 1980): 225–26 and 231–36. [Au.]

our particular cultures and languages, but also pre-evaluated, bearing the marks and signs of their prior valuings and evaluations by our fellow creatures. Indeed, preclassification is itself a form of pre-evaluation, for the labels or category names under which we encounter objects not only, as we suggested earlier, foreground certain of their possible functions but also operate as signs — in effect, as culturally certified endorsements — of their more or less effective performance of those functions.

Like all other objects, works of art and literature bear the marks of their own evaluational history, signs of value that acquire their force by virtue of various social and cultural practices and, in this case, certain highly specialized and elaborated institutions. The labels "art" and "literature" are, of course, commonly signs of membership in distinctly honorific categories. The particular functions that may be endorsed by these labels, however, are, unlike those of "doorstops" and "clocks," neither narrowly confined nor readily specifiable but, on the contrary, exceptionally heterogeneous, mutable, and elusive. To the extent — always limited — that the relation between these labels and a particular set of expected and desired functions is stabilized within a community, it is largely through the normative activities of various institutions: most significantly, the literary and aesthetic academy which, among other things, develops pedagogic and other acculturative mechanisms directed at maintaining at least (and, commonly, at most) a *sub*population of the community whose members "appreciate the value" of works of art and literature "as such." That is, by providing them with "necessary backgrounds," teaching them "appropriate skills," "cultivating their interests," and, generally, "developing their tastes," the academy produces generation after generation of subjects for whom the objects and texts thus labeled do indeed perform the functions thus privileged, thereby insuring the continuity of mutually defining canonical works, canonical functions, and canonical audiences.[45]

It will be instructive at this point to consider the very beginning of a work's valuational history, namely, its initial evaluation by the artist (here, the author); for it is not only a prefiguration of all the subsequent acts of evaluation of which the work will become the subject but also a model or paradigm of all evaluative activity generally. I refer here not merely to that ultimate gesture of authorial judgment that must exhibit itself negatively — that is, in the author's either letting the work stand or ripping it up — but to the thousand individual acts of approval and rejection, preference and assessment, trial and revision that constitute the entire process of literary composition. The work we receive is not so much the achieved consummation of that process as its enforced abandonment: "abandonment" not because the author's techniques are inadequate to his or her goals but because the goals themselves are inevitably multiple, mixed, mutually competing, and thus mutually constraining, and also because they are inevitably unstable, changing their nature and relative potency and priority during the very course of composition. The completed work is thus always, in a sense, a temporary truce among contending forces, achieved at the point of exhaustion, that is, the literal depletion of the author's current resources or, given the most fundamental principle of the economics of existence, at the point when the author simply has something else — more worthwhile — to do: when, in other words, the time and energy s/he would have to give to further tinkering, testing, and adjustment are no longer compensated for by an adequately rewarding sense of continuing interest in the process or increased satisfaction in the product.

It is for comparable reasons that we, as readers of the work, will later let our own experience of it stand: not because we have fully "appreciated" the work, not because we have exhausted all its possible sources of interest and hence of value, but because we, too, ultimately have something else — more worthwhile — to do. The reader's experience of the work is pre-

---

[45]Pierre Macherey and Etienne Balibar analyze some aspects of this process in "Literature as an Ideological Form:

Some Marxist Propositions," trans. James Kavanagh, *Praxis* 5 (1981): 43–58. [Au.]

figured — that is, both calculated and pre-enacted — by the author in other ways as well: for, in selecting this word, adjusting that turn of phrase, preferring this rhyme to that, the author is all the while testing the local and global effectiveness of each decision by impersonating in advance his or her various presumptive audiences, who thereby themselves participate in shaping the work they will later read. Every literary work — and, more generally, artwork — is thus the product of a complex evaluative feedback loop that embraces not only the ever-shifting economy of the artist's own interests and resources as they evolve during and in reaction to the process of composition, but also all the shifting economies of his or her assumed and imagined audiences, including those who do not yet exist but whose emergent interests, variable conditions of encounter, and rival sources of gratification the artist will attempt to predict — or will intuitively surmise — and to which, among other things, his or her own sense of the fittingness of each decision will be responsive.[46]

But this also describes all the other diverse forms of evaluation by which the work will be subsequently marked and its value reproduced and transmitted: that is, the innumerable implicit acts of evaluation performed by those who, as may happen, publish the work, purchase, preserve, display, quote, cite, translate, perform, allude to, and imitate it; the more explicit but casual judgments made, debated, and negotiated in informal contexts by readers and by all those others in whose personal economies the work, in some way, "figures"; and the highly specialized institutionalized forms of evaluation exhibited in the more or less professional activities of scholars, teachers, and academic or journalistic critics — not only their full-dress reviews and explicit rank-orderings, evaluations, and revaluations, but also such activities as the awarding of literary prizes, the commissioning and publishing of articles about certain works, the compiling of anthologies, the writing of introductions, the construction of department curricula, and the drawing up of class reading lists. All these forms of evaluation, whether overt or covert, verbal or inarticulate, and whether performed by the common reader, professional reviewer, big-time bookseller, or small-town librarian, have functions and effects that are significant in the production and maintenance or destruction of literary value, both reflecting and contributing to the various economies in relation to which a work acquires value. And each of the evaluative acts mentioned, like those of the author, represents a set of individual economic decisions, an ajudication among competing claims for limited resources of time, space, energy, attention — or, of course, money — and also, insofar as the evaluation is a socially responsive act or part of a social transaction, a set of surmises, assumptions, or predictions regarding the personal economies of other people.

Although, as I have emphasized, the evaluation of texts is not confined to the formal critical judgments issued within the rooms of the literary academy or upon the pages of its associated publications, the activities of the academy certainly figure significantly in the production of literary value. For example, the repeated inclusion of a particular work in literary anthologies not only promotes the value of that work but goes some distance toward creating its value, as does also its repeated appearance on reading lists or its frequent citation or quotation by professors, scholars, and academic critics. For all these acts, at the least, have the effect of drawing the work into the orbit of attention of a population of potential readers; and, by making it more accessible to the interests of those readers (while, as indicated above, at the same time shaping and supplying the very interests in relation to which they will experience the work), they make it more likely both that the work will be experienced at all and also that it will be experienced as valuable.

The converse side to this process is well known. Those who are in positions to edit anthologies and prepare reading lists are obviously those who occupy positions of some cultural

[46]See Howard Becker, *Art Worlds* (Berkeley, Los Angeles, and London, 1982), pp. 198–209, for a description of some of the specific constraints that shape both the process and its termination and, more generally, for a useful account of the ways in which artworks are produced by "social networks." [Au.]

power; and their acts of evaluation — represented in what they exclude as well as in what they include — constitute not merely recommendations of value but, for the reasons just mentioned, also determinants of value. Moreover, since they will usually exclude not only what they take to be inferior literature but also what they take to be nonliterary, subliterary, or paraliterary, their selections not only imply certain "criteria" of literary value, which may in fact be made explicit, but, more significantly, they produce and maintain certain definitions of "literature" and, thereby, certain assumptions about the desired and expected functions of the texts so classified and about the interests of their appropriate audiences, all of which are usually not explicit and, for that reason, less likely to be questioned, challenged, or even noticed. Thus the privileging power of evaluative authority may be very great, even when it is manifested inarticulately.[47] The academic activities described here, however, are only a small part of the complex process of literary canonization.

When we consider the cultural re-production of value on a larger time scale, the model of evaluative dynamics outlined above suggests that the "survival" or "endurance" of a text — and, it may be, its achievement of high canonical status not only as a "work of literature" but as a "classic" — is the product neither of the objectively (in the Marxist sense) conspiratorial force of establishment institutions nor of the continuous appreciation of the timeless virtues of a fixed object by succeeding generations of isolated readers, but, rather, of a series of continuous interactions among a variably constituted object, emergent conditions, and mechanisms of cultural selection and transmission. These interactions are, in certain respects, analogous to those by virtue of which biological species evolve and

survive and also analogous to those through which artistic choices evolve and are found fit or fitting by the individual artist. The operation of these cultural-historical dynamics may be briefly indicated here in quite general terms.

At a given time and under the contemporary conditions of available materials, technology, and techniques, a particular object — let us say a verbal artifact or text — may perform certain desired/able functions quite well for some set of subjects. It will do so by virtue of certain of its "properties" as they have been specifically constituted — framed, foregrounded, and configured — by those subjects under those conditions and in accord with their particular needs, interests, and resources — and also perhaps largely as prefigured by the artist who, as described earlier, in the very process of producing the work and continuously evaluating its fitness and adjusting it accordingly, will have multiply and variably constituted it. Two points implied by this description need emphasis here. One is that the value of a work — that is, its effectiveness in performing desired/able functions for some set of subjects — is not independent of authorial design, labor, and skill. The second, however, is that what may be spoken of as the "properties" of the work — its "structure," "features," "qualities," and, of course, its "meanings" — are not fixed, given, or inherent in the work "itself" but are at every point the variable products of some subject's interaction with it. (It is thus never "the *same* Homer.") To the extent that any aspect of a work is recurrently constituted in similar ways by various subjects at various times, it will be because the subjects who do the constituting, *including the author*, are themselves similar, not only in being human creatures and in occupying a particular universe that may be, for them, in many respects recurrent or relatively continuous and stable, but also in inheriting from one another, through mechanisms of cultural transmission, certain ways of interacting with that universe, including certain ways of interacting with texts and "works of literature."

An object or artifact that performs certain desired/able functions particularly well at a given time for some community of subjects, being perhaps not only "fit" but exemplary — that is, "the

[47]For a well-documented illustration of the point, see Nina Baym, "Melodramas of Beset Manhood: How Theories of American Fiction Exclude Women Authors," *American Quarterly* 33 (Summer 1981): 125–39. In addition to anthologies, Baym mentions historical studies, psychological and sociological theories of literary production, and particular methods of literary interpretation. [Au.] See Baym in Ch. 6. [Ed.]

best of its kind" — under those conditions, will have an immediate survival advantage; for, relative to (or in competition with) other comparable objects or artifacts available at that time, it will not only be better protected from physical deterioration but will also be more frequently used or widely exhibited and, if it is a text or verbal artifact, more frequently read or recited, copied or reprinted, translated, imitated, cited, and commented upon — in short, culturally reproduced — and thus will be more readily available to perform those or other functions for other subjects at a subsequent time.

Two possible trajectories ensue:

1. If, on the one hand, under the changing and emergent conditions of that subsequent time, the functions for which the text was earlier valued are no longer desired/able or if, in competition with comparable works (including, now, those newly produced with newly available materials and techniques), it no longer performs those original functions particularly well, it will, accordingly, be less well maintained and less frequently cited and recited so that its visibility as well as interest will fade, and it will survive, if at all, simply as a physical relic. It may, of course, be subsequently valued specifically *as a* relic (for its archeological or "historical" interest), in which case it *will* be performing desired/able functions and pursue the trajectory described below. It may also be subsequently "rediscovered" as an "unjustly neglected masterpiece," either when the functions it had originally performed are again desired/able or, what is more likely, when different of its properties and possible functions become foregrounded by a new set of subjects with emergent interests and purposes.

2. If, on the other hand, under changing conditions and in competition with newly produced and other re-produced works, it continues to perform *some* desired/able functions particularly well, even if not the same ones for which it was initially valued (and, accordingly, by virtue of *other* newly foregrounded or differently framed or configured properties — including, once again, emergent "meanings"), it will continue to be cited and recited, continue to be visible and

available to succeeding generations of subjects, and thus continue to be culturally re-produced. A work that has in this way survived for some time can always move into a trajectory of extinction through the sudden emergence or gradual conjunction of unfavorable conditions of the kind described above under (1). There are, however, a number of reasons why, once it has achieved canonical status, it will be more secured from that risk.

First, when the value of a work is seen as unquestionable, those of its features that would, in a noncanonical work, be found alienating — for example, technically crude, philosophically naive, or narrowly topical — will be glozed over or backgrounded. In particular, features that conflict intolerably with the interests and ideologies of subsequent subjects (and, in the West, with those generally benign "humanistic" values for which canonical works are commonly celebrated) — for example, incidents or sentiments of brutality, bigotry, and racial, sexual, or national chauvinism — will be repressed or rationalized, and there will be a tendency among humanistic scholars and academic critics to "save the text" by transferring the locus of its interest to more formal or structural features and/or allegorizing its potentially alienating ideology to some more general ("universal") level where it becomes more tolerable and also more readily interpretable in terms of contemporary ideologies. Thus we make texts timeless by suppressing their temporality. (It may be added that to those scholars and critics for whom those features are not only palatable but for whom the value of the canonical works consist precisely in their "embodying" and "preserving" such "traditional values," the transfer of the locus of value to formal properties will be seen as a descent into formalism and "aestheticism," and the tendency to allegorize it too generally or to interpret it too readily in terms of "modern values" will be seen not as saving the text but as betraying it.)

Second, in addition to whatever various and perhaps continuously differing functions a work performs for succeeding generations of individual subjects, it will also begin to perform certain characteristic cultural functions by virtue of the very fact that it *has* endured — that is, the functions of a canonical work as such — and will be valued and preserved accordingly: as a witness to lost innocence, former glory, and/or apparently persistent communal interests and "values" and thus a banner of communal identity; as a reservoir of images, archetypes, and topoi — characters and episodes, passages and verbal tags — repeatedly invoked and recurrently applied to new situations and circumstances; and as a stylistic and generic exemplar that will energize the production of subsequent works and texts (upon which the latter will be modeled and by which, as a normative "touchstone," they will be measured). It these ways, the canonical work begins increasingly not merely to survive within but to shape and create the culture in which its value is produced and transmitted and, for that very reason, to perpetuate the conditions of its own flourishing. Nothing endures like endurance.

To the extent that we develop within and are formed by a culture that is itself constituted in part *by* canonical texts, it is not surprising that those texts seem, as Hans-Georg Gadamer puts it, to "speak" to us "directly" and even "specially":

> The classical is what is preserved precisely because it signifies and interprets itself; [that is,] that which speaks in such a way that it is not a statement about what is past, as mere testimony to something that needs to be interpreted, but says something to the present as if it were said specially to us. . . . This is just what the word "classical" means, that the duration of the power of a work to speak directly is fundamentally unlimited.[48]

It is hardly, however, as Gadamer implies here, because such texts are uniquely self-mediated or unmediated and hence not needful of interpretation but, rather, because they have already been so thoroughly mediated — evaluated as well as interpreted — for us by the very culture and cultural institutions through which they have been preserved and by which we ourselves have been formed.

What is commonly referred to as "the test of time" (Gadamer, for example, characterizes "the classical" as "a notable mode of 'being historical,' that historical process of preservation that through the constant proving of itself sets before us something that is true")[49] is not, as the figure implies, an impersonal and impartial mechanism; for the cultural institutions through which it operates (schools, libraries, theaters, museums, publishing and printing houses, editorial boards, prize-awarding commissions, state censors, etc.) are, of course, all managed by persons (who, by definition, are those with cultural power and commonly other forms of power as well), and, since the texts that are selected and preserved by "time" will always tend to be those which "fit" (and, indeed, have often been *designed* to fit) their characteristic needs, interests, resources, and purposes, that testing mechanism has its own built-in partialities accumulated in and thus *intensified by* time. For example, the characteristic resources of the culturally dominant members of a community include access to specific training and the opportunity and occasion to develop not only competence in a large number of cultural codes but also a large number of diverse (or "cosmopolitan") interests. The works that are differentially re-produced, therefore, will often be those that gratify the exercise of such competencies and engage interests of that kind: specifically, works that are structurally complex and, in the technical sense, information-rich — and which, by virtue of those very qualities, are especially amenable to multiple reconfiguration, more likely to enter into relation with the emergent interests of various subjects, and thus more readily adaptable to emergent conditions.[50] Also,

48Hans-Georg Gadamer, *Truth and Method*, trans. Sheed and Ward, Ltd. (New York, 1982), pp. 257–58. [Au.] For a very different refutation of Gadamer, see Jauss in Ch. 7. [Ed.]

49Ibid., p. 255. [Au.]

50Structural complexity and information-richness are, of course, subject-relative as "qualities" and also experientially subject-variable; that is, we apparently differ individually in our tolerance for complexity in various sensory/perceptual modes and in our competence in processing information in different codes, so that what is interestingly complex and engagingly information-rich to one subject may be intolerably chaotic to another. See Gerda Smets, *Aesthetic Judgment and Arousal* (Louvain, 1973), and Sven Sandström, *A Common Taste in Art: An Experimental Attempt* (Lund, 1977), for two recent studies relevant to the point. Its relation to the general problem of aesthetic and literary value, itself a very complex

as is often remarked, since those with cultural power tend to be members of socially, economically, and politically established classes (or to serve them and identify their own interests with theirs), the texts that survive will tend to be those that appear to reflect and reinforce establishment ideologies. However much canonical works may be seen to "question" secular vanities such as wealth, social position, and political power, "remind" their readers of more elevated values and virtues, and oblige them to "confront" such hard truths and harsh realities as their own mortality and the hidden griefs of obscure people, they would not be found to please long and well if they were seen to undercut establishment interests *radically* or to subvert the ideologies that support them *effectively*. (Construing them to the latter ends, of course, is one of the characteristic ways in which those with antiestablishment interests participate in the cultural re-production of canonical texts and thus in their endurance as well.)

It is clear that the needs, interests, and purposes of culturally and otherwise dominant members of a community do not exclusively or totally determine which works survive. The antiquity and longevity of domestic proverbs, popular tales, children's verbal games, and the entire phenomenon of what we call "folklore," which occurs through the same or corresponding mechanisms of cultural selection and re-production as those described above specifically for "texts," demonstrate that the "endurance" of a verbal artifact (if not its achievement of *academic* canonical status as a "work of literature" — many folkloric works do, however, perform all the functions described above as characteristic of canonical works *as such*) may be more or less independent of institutions controlled by those with political power. Moreover, the interests and purposes of the latter must always operate in interaction with non- or antiestablishment interests and purposes as well as with various other contingencies and "accidents of time" over which they have limited, if any, control, from the burning of libraries to political and social revolutions, religious iconoclasms, and shifts of dominance among entire languages and cultures.

As the preceding discussion suggests, the value of a literary work is continuously produced and re-produced by the very acts of implicit and explicit evaluation that are frequently invoked as "reflecting" its value and therefore as being evidence of it. In other words, what are commonly taken to be the *signs* of literary value are, in effect, also its *springs*. The endurance of a classic canonical author such as Homer, then, owes not to the alleged transcultural or universal value of his works but, on the contrary, to the continuity of their circulation in a particular culture. Repeatedly cited and recited, translated, taught and imitated, and thoroughly enmeshed in the network of intertextuality that continuously *constitutes* the high culture of the orthodoxly educated population of the West (and the Western-educated population of the rest of the world), that highly variable entity we refer to as "Homer" recurrently enters our experience in relation to a large number and variety of our interests and thus can perform a large number of various functions for us and obviously has performed them for many of us over a good bit of the history of our culture. It is well to recall, however, that there are many people in the world who are not — or are not yet, or choose not to be — among the orthodoxly educated population of the West: people who do not encounter Western classics at all or who encounter them under cultural and institutional conditions very different from those of American and European college professors and their students. The fact that Homer, Dante, and Shakespeare do not figure significantly in the personal economies of these people, do not perform individual or social functions that gratify their interests, *do not have value for them*, might properly be taken as qualifying the claims of transcendent universal value made for such works. As we know, however, it is routinely taken instead as evidence or confirmation of the cultural deficiency — or, more piously, "deprivation" — of such people. The fact that other verbal artifacts (not necessarily "works of literature" or even "texts") and other objects and

---

matter, cannot be pursued here but is discussed briefly in *On the Margins of Discourse*, pp. 116–24.

events (not necessarily "works of art" or even artifacts) have performed and do perform for them the various functions that Homer, Dante, and Shakespeare perform for us and, moreover, that the possibility of performing the totality of such functions is always distributed over the totality of texts, artifacts, objects, and events — a possibility continuously realized and thus a value continuously "appreciated" — commonly cannot be grasped or acknowledged by the custodians of the Western canon.

# Houston A. Baker, Jr.
b. 1943

*The work of Houston A. Baker, Jr., aims to determine the aesthetics of an Afro-American literary tradition, which he believes must be based on criteria that are different from those underlying Anglo-American tradition. Born in Kentucky, Baker received a B.A. in English from Howard University in 1965, and an M.A. (1966) and Ph.D. (1968) from the University of California, Los Angeles. He has taught at Yale (1968–69) and the University of Virginia (1970–73), where he became a full professor in 1973. Since 1974, Baker has been a professor at the University of Pennsylvania. He served as director of the Afro-American Studies Program (1974–77), and in 1982 he was appointed Albert M. Greenfield Professor of Human Relations. He has held visiting professorships at Cornell University (1977) and at Haverford College (1983–85). Baker has received a Guggenheim fellowship (1978–79), a National Humanities Center fellowship (1982–83), and a Rockefeller Minority Group fellowship (1982–83). In addition to his collections of poetry and edited books, Baker has also published a number of critical and theoretical studies, including* Long Black Song: Essays in Black American Literature and Culture *(1972);* A Many-Colored Coat of Dreams: The Poetry of Countee Cullen *(1974);* The Journey Back: Issues in Black Literature and Criticism *(1980);* Blues, Ideology, and Afro-American Literature: A Vernacular Theory *(1984); and* Modernism and the Harlem Renaissance *(1987). "Generational Shifts and the Recent Criticism of Afro-American Literature" is from the Spring 1981 issue of* Black American Literature Forum.

# Generational Shifts and the Recent Criticism of Afro-American Literature

**I**

There exist any number of possible ways to describe changes that have occurred in Afro-American literary criticism during the past four decades. If one assumes a philosophical orientation, one can trace a movement from democratic pluralism ("integrationist poetics") through romantic Marxism (the "Black Aesthetic") to a version of Aristotelian metaphysics (the "Reconstruction of Instruction"). From another perspective, one can describe the ascendant class interests that have characterized Afro-America since World War II, forcing scholars, in one instance, to assess Afro-American expressive culture at a mass level and, in another instance, to engage in a kind of critical "professionalism" that seems contrary to mass interests. One can survey, on yet another level, transformations in the recent criticism of Afro-American literature from a perspective in the philosophy of science; from this vantage point, one can explore conceptual, or "paradigm," changes that have marked the critical enterprise in recent years. These various levels of analysis can be combined, I think, in the notion of the "generational shift."

A "generational shift" can be defined as an ideologically motivated movement overseen by young or newly-emergent intellectuals who are dedicated to refuting the work of their intellectual predecessors and to establishing a new framework of intellectual inquiry. The affective component of such shifts is described by Lewis Feuer: "Every birth or revival of an ideology is borne by a new generational wave: in its experience, each such new intellectual generation feels everything is being born anew, that the past is meaningless, or irrelevant, or nonexistent."[1] The new generation's break with the past is normally signaled by its adoption of what the philosopher of science Thomas S. Kuhn (to whose work I shall return later) designates a new "paradigm"; i.e., a new set of guiding assumptions that unifies the intellectual community.[2]

In the recent criticism of Afro-American literature, there have been two distinct generational shifts. Both have involved ideological and aesthetic reorientations, and both have been accompanied by shifts in literary-critical and literary-theoretical paradigms. The first such shift occurred during the mid-1960s. It led to the displacement of what might be described as integrationist poetics and gave birth to a new object of scholarly investigation.

## II

The dominant critical perspective on Afro-American literature during the late 1950s and early 1960s might be called the poetics of integrationism. Richard Wright's essay "The Literature of the Negro in the United States," which appears in his 1957 collection entitled *White Man, Listen!*, offers an illustration of integrationist poetics.[3] Wright optimistically predicts that Afro-American literature may soon be indistinguishable from the mainstream of American arts and letters. The basis for his optimism is the Supreme Court's decision in *Brown* vs. *Topeka Board of Education* (1954), in which the Court ruled that the doctrine "separate but equal" was inherently unequal. According to Wright, this ruling ensures a future "equality" in the experiences of black and white Americans, and this equality of *social* experience will translate in the literary domain as a homogeneity of *represented* experience (pp. 103–105). When Afro-American writers have achieved such equality and homogeneity, they will stand at one with the majority culture — in a relationship that Wright terms "entity" (p. 72).

But the foregoing stipulations apply only to what Wright calls the "Narcissistic Level" — i.e., the self-consciously literate level — of Afro-American culture (pp. 84–85). At the folk, or mass, level the relationship between Afro-American and the majority culture has always been one of "identity" (as in "the black person's quest for identity"), or separateness (p. 72). And though Wright argues that the self-consciously literate products of Afro-America that signify a division between cultures (e.g., "protest" poems and novels) may disappear relatively quickly under the influence of the Brown decision, he is not so optimistic with regard to the "Forms of Things Unknown" (p. 83) — i.e., the expressive products of the black American masses. For blues, jazz, work songs, and verbal forms such as folktales, boasts, toasts, and dozens are func-

---

[1]Lewis S. Feuer, *Ideology and Ideologists* (Oxford: Basil Blackwell, 1975). p. 70. Professor Chester Fontenot was kind enough to remind me that T. S. Eliot's "Tradition and the Individual Talent" and Harold Bloom's *The Anxiety of Influence* also offer approaches to questions of the relationships between old and new generations of intellectuals or writers. [Au.] See Eliot, p. 466, and Bloom, p. 705. [Ed.]

[2]Thomas S. Kuhn, *The Structure of Scientific Revolutions* (Chicago: University of Chicago Press, 1970). [Au.]

[3]Richard Wright, "The Literature of the Negro in the United States," in *White Man, Listen!* (Garden City, NY: Anchor Books, 1964), pp. 69–105. All citations from Wright's essay refer to this edition and are hereafter marked by page numbers in parentheses. [Au.]

tions of the black masses' relationship of "identity" with the mainstream culture. They signal, that is to say, *an absence of equality* and represent a *sensualization* of the masses' ongoing suffering (p. 83). They are, according to Wright, improvisational forms filled "with a content wrung from a bleak and barren environment, an environment that stung, crushed, all but killed" (p. 84). Only when the "Forms of Things Unknown" have disappeared altogether, or when conditions have been realized that enable them to be raised to a level of self-conscious art, will one be able to argue that an egalitarian ideal has been achieved in American life and art. The only course leading to such a positive goal, Wright implies, is momentous social action like that represented by the 1954 Supreme Court decision.

Hence, the black spokesman who champions a poetics of integrationism is constantly in search of social indicators (such as the Brown decision) that signal a democratic pluralism in American life. The implicit goal of this philosophical orientation is a raceless, classless community of men and women living in perfect harmony (p. 105). The integrationist critic, as Wright demonstrates, founds his predictions of a future, homogeneous body of American creative expression on such social *evidence* as the Emancipation Proclamation, Constitutional amendments, Supreme Court decisions, or any one of many other documented claims that suggest that America is moving toward a pluralistic ideal. The tone that such critics adopt is always one of optimism.

Arthur P. Davis offers a striking example of an Afro-American critic who has repeatedly sought to discover evidence to support his arguments that a oneness of all Americans and a harmonious merger of disparate forms of American creative expression are impending American social realities. What seems implicit in Davis's critical formulations is a call for Afro-American writers to speed the emergence of such realities by offering genuine, *artistic* contributions to the kind of classless, raceless literature that he and other integrationist critics assume will carry the future. An injunction of this type can be inferred, for example, from the 1941 "Introduction" to *The Negro Caravan*, the influential anthology of Afro-American expression that Davis coedited with Sterling Brown and Ulysses Lee:

The editors . . . do not believe that the expression "Negro literature" is an accurate one, and in spite of its convenient brevity, they have avoided using it. "Negro literature" has no application if it means *structural peculiarity*, or a Negro school of writing. The Negro writes in the forms evolved in English and American literature. . . . The editors consider Negro writers to be American writers, and literature by American Negroes to be a segment of American literature. . . . The chief cause for objection to the term is that "Negro literature" is too easily placed by certain critics, white and Negro, in an alcove apart. The next step is a double standard of judgment, which is dangerous for the future of Negro writers.[4] (my italics)

In the 1950s and 1960s, Davis continued to champion the poetics implicit in such earlier work as *The Negro Caravan*. His essay "Integration and Race Literature," which he presented to the first conference of Afro-American writers sponsored by the American Society of African Culture in 1959, states:

The course of Negro American literature has been highlighted by a series of social and political crises over the Negro's position in America. The Abolition Movement, the Civil War, Reconstruction, World War I, and the riot-lynching period of the twenties all radically influenced Negro writing. Each crisis in turn produced a new tradition in our literature; and as each crisis has passed, the Negro writer has dropped the social tradition which the occasion demanded and moved towards the mainstream of American literature. The integration controversy is another crisis, and from it we hope that the Negro will move permanently into full participation in American life — social, economic, political, and literary.[5]

The stirring drama implied here of black writers finding their way through various "little" traditions to the glory of the "great" mainstream is a function of Davis's solid faith in American pluralistic ideals. He regards history and society from a specific philosophical and ideological stand-

[4]Brown, Davis, and Lee, eds., *The Negro Caravan* (New York: Dryden Press, 1941; Arno repr. 1969), p. 7. All citations from the work refer to this edition and are hereafter marked by page numbers in parentheses. [Au.]

[5]In *The American Negro Writer And His Roots, Selected Papers From The First Conference of Negro Writers, March, 1959* (New York: American Society of African Culture, 1960), pp. 39–40. [Au.]

point: Afro-Americans and their expressive traditions, like other minority cultures, have always moved unceasingly toward a unity with American majority culture. He thus predicts — like Wright — the eventual disappearance of social conditions that produce literary works of art that are identifiable (in terms of "structural peculiarity") as "Negro" or "Afro-American" literature.

Wright and Davis represent a generation whose philosophy, ideology, and attendant poetics support the vanishing of Afro-American literature qua *Afro-American* literature. I shall examine this proposition at greater length in the next section. At this point, I simply want to suggest that the consequences of this generational position for literary-critical axiology can be inferred from the "Introduction" to *The Negro Caravan*. The editors of that work assert: "They [Afro-American writers] must ask that their books be judged as books, without sentimental allowances. In their own defense they must demand a single standard of criticism" (p. 7). This assertion suggests that black writers should construct their works in ways that make them acceptable in the sight of those who mold a "single standard of criticism" in America. These standard bearers were for many years, however, a small, exclusive community of individuals labelled by black spokesmen of the sixties as the "white, literary-critical establishment." And only a poetics buttressed by a philosophical viewpoint that augured the eventual unification of *all* talented creative men and women as judges could have prompted such able spokesmen as Wright, Brown, and Davis to consider that works of Afro-American literature and verbal art be subjected to a "single standard" of American literary-critical judgment.

## III

The generational shift that displaced the integrationist poetics just described brought forth a group of intellectuals most clearly distinguished from its predecessors by its different ideological and philosophical posture vis-à-vis American egalitarian ideals. After the arrests, bombings, and assassinations that comprised the white South's reaction to non-violent, direct-action protests by hundreds of thousands of civil rights

workers from the late fifties to the mid-sixties, it was difficult for even the most committed optimist to feel that integration was an impending American social reality.[6] Rather than searching for documentary evidence and the indelible faith necessary to argue for an undemonstrated American egalitarianism, the emerging generation set itself the task of analyzing the nature, aims, ends, and arts of those hundreds of thousands of their own people who were assaulting America's manifest structures of exclusion.

The Afro-American masses demonstrated through their violent acts ("urban riots") in Harlem, Watts, and other communities throughout the nation that they were intent on black social and political sovereignty in America. Their acts signaled the birth of a new ideology, one that received its proper name in 1966,[7] when Stokely Carmichael designated it "Black Power":

[Black Power] is a call for black people in this country to unite, to recognize their heritage, to build a sense of community. It is a call for black people to begin to define their own goals, to lead their own organizations and to support those organizations. It is a call to reject the racist institutions and values of [American] society.[8]

This definition, drawn from Carmichael and Charles Hamilton's work entitled *Black Power*, expresses a clear imperative for Afro-Americans to focus their social efforts and political vision on their *own* self-interests. This particularity of Black Power — its sharp emphasis on the immediate concerns of Afro-Americans themselves — was a direct counterthrust by an emergent generation to the call for a general, raceless, classless community of men and women central to an earlier integrationist framework. The community that was of interest to the emergent gen-

<hr />

[6]For historical details on the events of this period, the reader may wish to consult John Hope Franklin, "A Brief History," in *The Black American Reference Book*, ed. Mabel M. Smythe (Englewood Cliffs, N.J.: Prentice-Hall, 1976), pp. 1–89. [Au.]

[7]The phrase was originally uttered as part of a call-and-response chant between Carmichael and his audience during the course of a several-day protest march in Mississippi. [Au.]

[8]From Stokely Carmichael and Charles V. Hamilton, *Black Power: The Politics of Liberation in America* (New York: Vintage, 1967), pp. 43–44. [Au.]

eration was not a future generation of integrated Americans, but rather a present, vibrant group of men and women who constituted the heart of Afro-America. The Afro-American masses became, in the late sixties and early seventies, both subject and audience for the utterances of black political spokesmen moved by a new ideology.

The poetics accompanying the new ideological orientation were first suggested by Amiri Baraka (LeRoi Jones) in an address entitled "The Myth of a 'Negro Literature,'" which he presented to the American Society of African Culture in 1962:

> Where is the Negro-ness of a literature written in imitation of the meanest of social intelligences to be found in American culture, i.e., the white middle class? How can it even begin to express the emotional predicament of black Western man? Such a literature, even if its "characters" *are* black, takes on the emotional barrenness of its model, and the blackness of the characters is like the blackness of Al Jolson, an unconvincing device. It is like using black checkers instead of white. They are still checkers.[9]

At the self-consciously literate level of Afro-American expression, the passage implies, black spokesmen have deserted the genuine emotional referents and the authentic experiential categories of black life in America. The homogeneity between their representations of experience and those of the white mainstream are a cause for disgust rather than an occasion for rejoicing. Finally, the quoted passage implies that the enervating merger of black and white expression at the "Narcissistic" level (to use Wright's phrase) of Afro-American life is a result of the black writer's acceptance of a "single standard of criticism" molded by white America. Baraka, thus, inverts the literary-critical optimism and axiology of an earlier generation, rejecting entirely the notion that "Negro Literature" should not stand apart as a unique body of expression. It is precisely the desertion by black writers of those aspects of Afro-American life that foster the

uniqueness and authenticity of black expression that Baraka condemns most severely in his essay.

But where, then, does one discover in Afro-America genuine reflections of the true emotional referents and experiential categories of black life if not in its self-consciously literate works of art? Like the more avowedly political spokesmen of his day, Baraka turned to the world of the masses, and there he discovered the "forms of things unknown" (Wright's designation for black, folk expressive forms):

> Negro music alone, because it drew its strengths and beauties out of the depth of the black man's soul, and because to a large extent its traditions could be carried on by the lowest classes of Negroes, has been able to survive the constant and willful dilutions of the black middle class. Blues and jazz have been the only consistent exhibitors of "Negritude" in formal American culture simply because the bearers of its tradition maintained their essential identities as Negroes; in no other art (and I will persist in calling Negro music Art) has this been possible. (p. 107)

In this statement, Baraka seems to parallel the Richard Wright of an earlier generation. But while Wright felt that the disappearance of the "forms of things unknown" would signal a positive stage in the integration of American life and art, Baraka established the Harlem Black Arts Repertory Theatre/School in 1965 as an enterprise devoted to the continuance, development, and strengthening of the "coon shout," blues, jazz, holler, and other expressive forms of the "lowest classes of Negroes."[10] He, and other artists who contributed to the establishment of the school, felt that the perpetuation of such forms would help give birth to a new black nation. Larry Neal, who worked with Baraka during the mid-sixties, delineates both the complementarity of the Black Arts and Black Power movements and the affective component of a generational shift in his often-quoted essay "The Black Arts Movement":

[9] In *Home, Social Essays* (New York: Morrow, 1966), p. 110. All citations of the essay refer to this edition and are hereafter marked by page numbers in parentheses. [Au.]

[10] For an account of this enterprise, the reader may consult Theodore R. Hudson, *From LeRoi Jones to Amiri Baraka: The Literary Works* (Durham, N.C.: Duke University Press, 1973), pp. 20–25. [Au.]

Black Art is the aesthetic and spiritual sister of the Black Power concept. As such, it envisions an art that speaks directly to the needs and aspirations of Black America. In order to perform this task, the Black Arts Movement proposes a radical reordering of the western cultural aesthetic. It proposes a separate symbolism, mythology, critique, and iconology.[11]

The Black Arts Movement, therefore, like its ideological counterpart Black Power, was concerned with the articulation of experiences (and the satisfaction of audience demands) that found their essential character among the black urban masses. The guiding assumption of the movement was that if a literary-critical investigator looked to the characteristic musical and verbal forms of the masses, he would discover unique aspects of Afro-American creative expression — aspects of form and performance — that lay closest to the veritable emotional referents and experiential categories of Afro-American culture. The result of such critical investigations, according to Neal and other spokesmen such as Baraka and Addison Gayle, Jr. (to name but three prominent advocates for the Black Arts), would be the discovery of a "Black Aesthetic" — i.e., a distinctive code for the creation and evaluation of black art. From an assumed "structural peculiarity" of Afro-American expressive culture, the emergent generation of intellectuals proceeded to assert a *sui generis* tradition of Afro-American art and a unique "standard of criticism" suitable for its elucidation.

Stephen Henderson's essay entitled "The Forms of Things Unknown," which stands as the introduction to his anthology *Understanding the New Black Poetry*, offers one of the most suggestive illustrations of this discovery process at work.[12] Henderson's formulations mark a high point in the first generational shift in the recent criticism of Afro-American literature because he is a spokesman *par excellence* for what emerged

from his generation as a new object of literary-critical and literary-theoretical investigation. Before turning to the specifics of his arguments, however, I want to focus for a moment on the work of Thomas Kuhn to clarify what I mean by a "new object" of investigation.

## IV

In his work *The Structure of Scientific Revolutions*, Kuhn sets out to define the nature of a scientific "revolution," or shift in the fundamental ways in which the scientific community perceives and accounts for phenomena. He first postulates that the guiding construct in the practice of normal science is what he defines as the "paradigm"; i.e., a constellation of "beliefs, values, techniques and so on shared by the members of a given community."[13] He further defines a paradigm as the "universally recognized scientific achievements that for a time provide model problems and solutions to a community of practitioners [of normal science]" (p. viii). A paradigm, thus, sets the parameters of scholarly investigation, constraining both the boundaries of an investigator's perception and the degree of legitimacy attributed to various problems and methodologies. A forceful example of a scientific revolution and its enabling paradigm shift was the displacement of geocentrism by a Copernican cosmology. Kuhn writes: "The Copernicans who denied its traditional title 'planet' to the sun were not only learning what 'planet' meant or what the sun was. Instead, they were changing the meaning of 'planet' so that it could continue to make useful distinctions in a world where all celestial bodies, not just the sun, were seen differently from the way they had been seen before" (pp. 128–29).

The effects of this kind of paradigmatic shift on the assumptions and higher-order rules of a scholarly community are additionally clarified when Kuhn says:

Led by a new paradigm, scientists adopt new in-

[11]In *The Black Aesthetic*, ed. Addison Gayle, Jr. (New York: Doubleday, 1971), p. 272. [Au.]

[12]*Understanding the New Black Poetry: Black Speech and Black Music as Poetic References* (New York: Morrow, 1973), pp. 1–69. All citations refer to this edition and are hereafter marked by page numbers in parentheses. [Au.]

[13]Kuhn, *Structure* (Chicago: University of Chicago Press, 1970), p. 175. All citations refer to this edition and are hereafter marked by page numbers in parentheses. [Au.]

struments and look in new places. Even more important, during revolutions scientists see new and different things when looking with familiar instruments in places they have looked before. It is rather as if the professional community had been suddenly transported to another planet where *familiar objects are seen in a different light and are joined by unfamiliar ones as well . . .* paradigm changes . . . cause scientists to see the world of their research-engagement differently. In so far as their only recourse to that world is through what they see and do, we may want to say that after a revolution scientists are responding to a different world. (my italics, p. 111)

Kuhn cites as an experimental instance of such changes in perception the classic work of George M. Stratton. Stratton fitted his subjects with goggles that contained inverting lenses. Initially, these subjects saw the world upside down and existed in a state of extreme disorientation. Eventually, though, their entire visual field flipped over, and:

> Thereafter, objects are again seen as they had been before the goggles were put on. The assimilation of a previously anomalous visual field . . . reacted upon and changed the field itself. Literally as well as metaphorically . . . [the subject] accustomed to inverting lenses . . . [underwent] *a revolutionary transformation of vision.* (my italics, p. 112)

In terms of the present discussion of Afro-American literary criticism, I want to suggest that Stephen Henderson and other Afro-American intellectuals of his generation fomented a change in the perceptual field of Afro-American literary study that amounted, finally, to a "revolutionary transformation" of literary-critical and literary-theoretical vision vis-à-vis black expressive culture. Before the mid-sixties scholars were led by an integrationist paradigm that permitted them to perceive as "literature" or "art" only those Afro-American expressive works that approached or conformed to the "single standard of criticism" advocated by the editors of *The Negro Caravan*. In adopting such a "standard," an integrationist poetics bound its perceptual field and constrained its domain of legitimate investigative problems to Afro-American expressive objects and events that came nearest this standard. Under the old paradigm, therefore, a scholar could not *see* that

"Negro music" qua "*Negro* music" or "Negro Poetry" qua "*Negro* poetry" constituted *art*. For "Negro-ness" was viewed by the old paradigm as a condition (a set of properties of "structural peculiarities") that excluded such a phenomenon as "*Negro* poetry" from the artworld.[14] The integrationists held it as a first law that *art* was an American area of achievement in which race and class did not comprise significant variables. To discover, assert, or label the "Negro-ness" or "Blackness" of an expressive work as a fundamental condition of its "artistic-ness" was, thus, for the new generation to "flip over" the integrationist field of vision. And this revised perceptual orientation is precisely what Henderson and his contemporaries achieved. Their efforts made it possible for literary-critical and literary-theoretical investigators to see "familiar objects" in a different light and to include previously "unfamiliar" objects in an expanded (and sharply modified) American artworld. In "The Forms of Things Unknown," Henderson masterfully outlines the hypotheses, boundaries, and legitimate problems of the new paradigmatic framework called the "Black Aesthetic."

## V

Henderson's assumption is that in literature there exists "such a commodity as 'blackness' " (p. 3). He further argues that this "commodity" should be most easily located in poetry "since poetry is the most concentrated and the most allusive of the verbal arts" (p. 3). Implicit in these statements is Henderson's claim that an enabling condition for art (and particularly for "poetry") in Afro-American culture is the possession of *blackness* by an expressive object or event. The ontological status — the very condition of being — of *Afro-American* poetic expression is, in fact, a function of this commodity of blackness. The

---

[14]In "The Artworld," in *Philosophy Looks at the Arts*, ed. Joseph Margolis (Philadelphia: Temple University Press, 1978), pp. 132–45, Arthur Danto writes, "terrain is constituted artistic in virtue of artistic theories, so that one use of theories, in addition to helping us discriminate art from the rest, consists in making art possible." The *theoretical* constraints of the integrationist paradigm excluded "Negro" expressive works from the American, literary artworld. [Au.]

most legitimate paradigmatic question that a literary-critical investigator or a literary theorist can pose, therefore, is: In what place and by what means does the commodity "blackness" achieve form and substance?

The title of Henderson's essay suggests the answer he provides to this question. He states that blackness must be defined, at a *structural* level of expressive objects and events, as an "interior dynamism" that derives its force from the "inner life" of the Afro-American folk (pp. 5–6). And he is quite explicit that what he intends by "inner life" is, in fact, the constellation of cultural values and beliefs that characterizes what the philosopher Albert Hofstadter calls a "reference public." Hofstadter writes:

> Predication of "good" . . . tends to lose meaningful direction when the public whose valuations are considered in judging the object is not specified. I do not see how we can hope to speak sensibly about the aesthetic goodness of objects unless we think of them in the context of reception and valuation by persons, the so-called "context of consumption." Properties by virtue of which we value objects aesthetically — e.g., beauty, grace, charm, the tragic, the comic, balance, proportion, expressive symbolism, verisimilitude, propriety — always require some reference to the apprehending and valuing person. . . . Any public taken as the public referred to in a normative esthetic judgment I shall call the judgment's *reference public*. The reference public is the group whose appreciations or valuations are used as data on which to base the judgment. It is the group to which universality of appeal may or may not appertain.[15]

Henderson says that the existence of black poetry is a function of a black audience's concurrence that a particular verbal performance (whether written or oral) by some person of "known Black African ancestry" is, in fact, po-

[15] Albert Hofstadter, "On the Grounds of Aesthetic Judgment," in *Contemporary Aesthetics*, ed. Matthew Lipman (Boston: Allyn and Bacon, 1973), pp. 473–74. In both the concept "artworld" and "reference public," I have interpreted the Black Aesthetic as an institutional theory of art. For a recent critique of such theories, the reader may consult Marx W. Wartofsky, "Art, Artworlds, and Ideology," *Journal of Aesthetics and Art Criticism* 38 (1980); 239–47. In contrast to the "institutional" dimensions of the Black Aesthetic are its idealistic assumptions. [Au.]

etry (p. 7). The array of values and beliefs — the cultural codes — that allows a black reference public to make such a normative judgment constitutes the inner life of the folk. "Inner life," then — on the assumption that the operative codes of a culture are historically conditioned and are maintained at a level of interacting cultural systems — is translated as "ethnic roots." Questions of the ontology and valuation of a black poem, according to Henderson, "cannot be resolved without considering the ethnic roots of Black poetry, which I insist are ultimately understood only by Black people themselves" (pp. 7–8). What he seeks to establish, or to support, with this claim, I think, is a kind of cultural holism — an interconnectedness (temporally determined) of a cultural discourse — that can only be successfully apprehended through a set of theoretical concepts and critical categories arrived at by in-depth investigation of the fundamental expressive manifestations of a culture.

In order to achieve such apprehension, the literary investigator (like the cultural anthropologist) must go to the best available informants; i.e., to natives of the culture, or to the "reference public." "One must not consider the poem in isolation," writes Henderson, "but in relationship to the reader/audience, and the reader to the wider context of the phenomenon which we call, for the sake of convenience, the Black Experience" (p. 62). His tone approximates even more closely that of cultural anthropology in the following stipulations on literary-critical axiology:

> . . . the recognition of Blackness in poetry is a value judgment which on certain levels and in certain instances, notably in matters of meanings that go beyond questions of structure and theme, must rest upon one's immersion in the totality of the Black Experience. It means that the ultimate criteria for critical evaluation must be found in the sources of the creation, that is, in the Black Community itself. (pp. 65–66)

The notion that a conditioning cultural holism is a necessary consideration in the investigation of a culture's works of verbal art receives yet another designation that has anthropological parallels when Henderson talks of a "Soul Field." Field theory in anthropology stresses the continuous nature of conceptual structures that make up various areas, or "fields," of a culture, e.g., kinship or color terms and their attendant *connotations* or *sense*. For Henderson, the "Soul Field" of Afro-American culture is "the complex galaxy of personal, social, institutional, historical, religious, and mythical meanings that affect everything we say or do as Black people sharing a common heritage" (p. 41). In this definition, "meanings" is the operative term, and it situates the author's designation of "field" decisively within the realm of semantics. Henderson's "Soul Field" is, thus, similar to J. Trier's *Sinnfeld*, or conceptual field; i.e., the area of a culture's linguistic system that contains the encyclopedia or mappings of various "senses" of lexical items drawn from the same culture's *Wortfeld*, or lexicon.[16]

The theoretical concepts and critical categories for analyzing black poetry that Henderson sets forth in "The Forms of Things Unknown" are coextensive with the case he makes for the holism and continuity of Afro-American culture. His three major categories are theme, structure, and saturation. And in dividing each category into analytic subsets, he never loses sight of the "inner life" of the folk, or that interconnected "field" of uniquely black meanings and values that he postulates as the essential determinants of these subsets. He, thus, seeks to ensure a relationship of identity between his own critical categories and the "real," experiential categories of Afro-American life. For example, he identifies "theme" with what he perceives as the *actual* guiding concern of the collective, evolving consciousness of Afro-American.

He finds that the most significant concern of that consciousness has always been "the idea of liberation" (p. 18) and suggests that the "old word, 'freedom,' " might be substituted for this phrase to denote the overriding theme (i.e., that which is "being spoken of") of Afro-American expressive culture. Hence, a "real" lexical category ("freedom") and its complex conceptual mappings in Afro-American culture are identified as one subject of the critical category "theme."

[16]For reflections on field theory and on the work of Trier, see John Lyons, *Semantics*, I (Cambridge: Cambridge University Press, 1977), pp. 250–61. [Au.]

Similarly, the *actual* speech and music of Afro-American culture and their various forms, techniques, devices, nuances, rules, and so on are identified as fundamental structural referents in the continuum of black expressive culture:

> Structurally speaking . . . whenever Black poetry is most distinctively and effectively *Black*, it derives its form from two basic sources, Black speech and Black music. . . . By Black speech I mean the speech of the majority of Black people in this country. . . . This includes the techniques and timbres of the sermon and other forms of oratory, the dozens, the rap, the signifying, and the oral folktale. . . . By Black music I mean essentially the vast fluid body of Black song — spirituals, shouts, jubilees, gospel songs, field cries, blues, pop songs by Blacks, and, in addition, jazz (by whatever name one calls it) and non-jazz by Black composers who *consciously or unconsciously* draw upon the Black musical tradition. (pp. 30–31)

Here, Henderson effectively delineates a continuum of Afro-American verbal and musical expressive behavior that begins with everyday speech and popular music and extends to works of "high art."

Finally, "saturation" is a category in harmony with the assumed uniqueness of both the Afro-American *Sinnfeld* and *Wortfeld*. For Henderson insists that "saturation" is a perceptual category that has to do with a distinctive semantics:

> Certain words and constructions [e.g., *rock, jelly, jook*] seem to carry an inordinate charge of emotional and psychological weight [in Afro-American culture], so that whenever they are used they set all kinds of bells ringing, all kinds of synapses snapping, on all kinds of levels. . . . I call such words 'mascon' words. . . . to mean *a massive concentration of Black experiential energy* which powerfully affects the meaning of Black speech, Black song, and Black poetry — if one, indeed, has to make such distinctions. (p. 43)

From an assumed "particularity," wholeness, and continuity of Afro-American culture — characteristics that manifest themselves most clearly among the Afro-American folk or masses — Henderson, thus, moves to the articulation of theoretical concepts and critical categories that provide what he calls "a way of speaking about all kinds of Black poetry despite the kinds of questions that can be raised" (p. 10). He proposes, in short, a theory to account for the continuity — the unity in theme, structure, and semantics — of black speech, music, and poetry (both oral and written). He refuses, from the outset, to follow a traditional literary-critical path; i.e., predicating this continuity on history or chronology alone. Instead, he observes the contemporary scene in Afro-American poetry (i.e., the state of the art of black poetry in the 1960s and early 1970s) and realizes that the oral tradition of the urban masses is the dominant force shaping the work of Afro-American poets. From this modern instantiation of the reciprocity between expressive folk culture and self-conscious, literary expression, he proposes that *all* black "poetic" expression can be understood in terms of such a reciprocal pattern. "Understanding" the "new black poetry" in its relationship to black urban folk culture, therefore, provides direction and definition in the larger enterprise of understanding the artistic codes — or the cultural system that is "art" — in black American culture. A comprehension of the "forms of things unknown" and the cultural anthropological assumptions that it presupposes lead to the discovery of a unique artistic tradition, one embodying peculiar themes, structures, and meanings.

The "Black Aesthetic" signaled for Henderson and his contemporaries the codes that determine this tradition as well as the theoretical standpoint (one marked by appropriate categories) that would enable one to see, to "speak about," this tradition. And like all new paradigms, the "Black Aesthetic" had distinctive perceptual and semantic ramifications. It changed the meaning of both "black" and "aesthetic" in the American literary-critical universe of discourse so that these terms could continue to make "useful distinctions" in a world where works of Afro-American expressive art had come to be seen quite differently from the manner in which they were viewed by an older integrationist paradigm.

# VI

Earlier, I referred to the philosophical orientation of the Black Aesthetic as romantic Marxism. Having discussed Henderson's work, perhaps I can now clarify this designation. For me, the fact that the aesthetics of the Black Arts movement

were idealistically centered in the imagination of the black critical observer makes them "romantic."[17] This critical centrality of the Afro-American mind is illustrated by Henderson's assumption that "Blackness" is not a theoretical reification, but a reality, accessible only to those who can "imagine" in uniquely black ways. From this perspective, the word "understanding" in the title of his anthology is a sign for spiritual journey in which what the *black* imagination seizes upon as *black* must be *black*, whether it existed before or not.

The notion of a "reference public" gives way, therefore, at a lower level of the Black Aesthetic's argument, to a kind of impressionistic chauvinism. For it is, finally, *only* the black imagination that can experience blackness, in poetry, or in life. As a result, the creative and critical framework suggested by Henderson resembles, at times, a closed circle:

> . . . for one who is totally immersed, as it were, or saturated in the Black Experience the slightest formulation of the typical or true-to-life [Black] experience, whether positive or negative, is enough to bring on at least subliminal recognition [or of the "formulation" of the experience as "Black"]. . . . I have tried to postulate a concept that would be useful in talking about what Black people feel is their distinctiveness, without being presumptuous enough to attempt a description or definition of it. This quality or condition of Black awareness I call *saturation*. I intend it as a sign, like the mathematical symbol *infinity*, or the term "Soul." It allows us to talk about the thing [a "distinctive" feeling of "Blackness"], even to some extent to use it, though we can't, thank God! ultimately abstract and analyze it: it must be experienced. (pp. 63, 68)

"Saturation" also gives way, then, at a lower level of the argument to cultural xenophobia. Rather than an indicator for a *sui generis* semantics, it becomes a mysterious trait of consciousness. In "Saturation: Progress Report on a Theory of Black Poetry," an article that appeared two

[17]I have discussed the romantic idealism of the Black Aesthetic in "The Black Spokesman as Critic: Reflections on the Black Aesthetic," the fifth chapter of my book entitled *The Journey Back: Issues in Black Literature and Criticism* (Chicago: University of Chicago Press, 1980), pp. 132–43. [Au.]

years after his anthology, Henderson comments on the critical reactions that his romantic specifications evoked:

> Some people — critics, white and Black — have difficulty with this last standard [i.e., the critical standard of "intuition" for judging the successful rendering of "Black poetic structure"]. They call it mysterious, mystical, chauvinistic, and even (in a slightly different context) a "curious metaphysical argument" (Saunders Redding). I call it *saturation*. I authenticate it from personal experience. To those critics I say: Remember Keats did the same, proving poetic experience by his pulse and the "holiness of the imagination."[18]

But if Henderson's romanticism led him to chauvinistically posit an "intuitive sense," a "condition" of "Blackness" that can only be grasped by the "saturated" or "immersed" black imagination, it also led him to suggest the kind of higher-order, cultural-anthropological argument that I have extrapolated from his work and discussed in the preceding section. I think the romanticism of Henderson and his contemporaries — like that of romantics gone before who believed they were compelled to "create a system or be enslav'd by another Man's" — lay in their metaphysical rebelliousness, their willingness to postulate a positive and distinctive category of existence ("Blackness") and then to read the universe in terms of that category.[19] The predication of such a category was not only a radical political act designed to effect the liberation struggles of Afro-America, but also a bold critical act designed to break the interpretive monopoly on Afro-American expressive culture that had been held from time immemorial by a white, literary-critical establishment that set a "single standard of criticism":

> If the critic is half worth his salt, then he would attempt to describe what occurs in the poem and to *explain* — to the extent that it is possible —

how the "action" takes place, i.e., how the elements of the work interact with one another to produce its effect. And if one of those elements is "Blackness" — as value, as theme, or as structure, especially the latter — then he is remiss in his duty if he does not attempt to deal with it in some logical, orderly manner.[20]

Given Henderson's arguments for the black person's own intuitive sense of experience as the only valid guide to the recognition of "Blackness" as an "element," it seems unlikely that many white critics would prove "worth their salt" vis-à-vis Afro-American literature and criticism. And there is a kind of implicit antinomianism in the following assertion from his essay "The Question of Form and Judgment in Contemporary Black American Poetry: 1962–1977": "Historically, the question of what constitutes a Black poem or how to judge one does not really come to a head until the 1960s and the promulgation of the Black Aesthetic in literature and the other arts. In a special sense . . . 'Black' poetry was invented in the 1960s along with the radicalization of the word 'Black' and the emergence of the Black Power philosophy."[21] Here, the faith that postulated "Blackness" as a distinctive category of existence is seen as the generative source of a new art, politics, and criticism nullifying the interpretive authority of a white, critical orthodoxy.

The rebelliousness that seemed to close the circle of Afro-American criticism to white participants, however, was not only romantic, it was also Marxist. Henderson and his contemporaries attempted to base their arguments for an Afro-American intuitive sense of "Blackness" on the notion that such a sense was a function of the continuity of Afro-American culture. The distinctive cultural circumstances that comprised the material bases of Afro-American culture — i.e., the means and instrumentalities of production, distribution, and consumption that marked the

---

[18]Stephen Henderson, "Saturation: Progress Report on a Theory of Black Poetry," *Black World* 24 (1975); 14. [Au.]

[19]The words on the creation of system are, of course, those of William Blake's Los, drawn from *Jerusalem*. Los, like the Black Aestheticians, also refused at points to "reason" or "compare," feeling that the imperative "business" was "to create." [Au.]

[20]Henderson, "Saturation," p. 9. [Au.]

[21]Henderson, "The Question of Form," in *A Dark and Sudden Beauty: Two Essays in Black American Poetry by George Kent and Stephen Henderson*, ed. Houston A. Baker, Jr. (Philadelphia: Afro-American Studies Program of the University of Pennsylvania, 1977), p. 24. [Au.]

formation and growth of an African culture in America — were always seen by spokesmen for the Black Aesthetic as determinants of a *consciousness* that was distinctively "Black." And the most accurate reflection of the economics of slavery (and their subsequent forms) in the American economy was held to take place at a mass or folk level. Hence, the expressive forms of black folk consciousness were defined by Black Aestheticians as underdetermined by material circumstances that vary within a narrow range. To take up such forms is to find oneself involved with the "authentic" or basic (as in the "material base") categories of Afro-American existence. "Culture determines consciousness" became a watchword for the Black Aesthetic, and by "culture" its spokesmen meant a complex of material and expressive components that could only be discovered at a mass level of Afro-American experience. It was their emphasis on this level — an emphasis motivated by a paradoxical desire to ground an idealistic rebelliousness in a materialist reading of history — that led to a deepened scholarly interest during the sixties and early seventies in both Afro-American folklore and other black expressive forms that had long been (in Henderson's words) "under siege" by "white critical condescension and snobbery, and more recently, outright pathological ignorance and fear."[22] And through their investigation of the "forms of things unknown" in recent years, some white critics were able to reenter the critical circle.[23] They reentered, however, not as superordinate authorities, but as serious scholars working in harmony with some of the fundamental postulates of the Black Aesthetic.

There is also a more clichéd sense in which the Black Aesthetic was Marxist, and it finds its best illustration in the insistence by spokesmen for the new paradigm that expressive culture has a "social function." Black Aestheticians were quick to assert that works of verbal art have direct effects in the solution of social problems and in the shaping of social consciousness. The prescriptive formulations of a spokesman like Ron Karenga demonstrate this aspect of the Black Aesthetic: "All black art, irregardless of any technical requirements, must have three basic characteristics which make it revolutionary. In brief, it must be functional, collective and committing."[24] Like Mao Tse-Tung, whom he is paraphrasing, Karenga and other spokesmen for the Black Arts felt that poems and novels could (and *should*) be designed to move audiences to revolutionary action.

It should be clear at this point that there were blatant weaknesses in the critical framework that actually accompanied the postulates of the Black Aesthetic. Too often in their attempts to locate the parameters of Afro-American culture, spokesmen for the new paradigm settled instead for a romantically conceived domain of "race." And their claims to have achieved a scholarly consensus on "culture" sometimes revealed themselves as functions of a defensive chauvinism on the part of the spokesmen who had gained the limelight. What is encouraging, though, in any evaluation of the Afro-American intellectual milieu during the later stages of the Black Arts movement is that Black Aesthetic spokesmen *themselves* first pointed out (and suggested ways beyond) such critical and theoretical weaknesses.

In his essay "The Black Contribution to American Letters: The Writer as Activist — 1960 and After," Larry Neal identifies the Black Aesthetic's interest in an African past and in African-American folklore as a species of Herderian nationalism and goes on to say: "Nationalism, wherever it occurs in the modern world, must legitimize itself by evoking the muse of history. This is an especially necessary step where the nation or group feels that its social oppression is inextricably bound up with the destruction of its traditional culture and with the suppression of that culture's achievements in the intellectual sphere.[25] A social group's reaction in such na-

[22]Henderson, "Question of Form," p. 32. [Au.]

[23]I have in mind Robert E. Hemenway, author of the superb scholarly effort *Zora Neale Hurston: A Literary Biography* (Urbana: University of Illinois Press, 1977) and Lawrence W. Levine, author of the important book *Black Culture and Black Consciousness: Afro-American Folk Thought From Slavery to Freedom* (New York: Oxford University Press, 1977). [Au.]

[24]"Black Cultural Nationalism," in *The Black Aesthetic*, p. 33. [Au.]

[25]Neal, "The Black Contribution to American Letters: Part

tionalistic instances, according to Neal, is understandably (though also, regrettably) one of total introspection — i.e., drawing in unto itself and labeling the historically oppressive culture as "the enemy" (p. 782). A fear of the destruction of Afro-American culture by an "aggressive and alien" West, for example, prompted Black Aesthetic spokesmen to think only in racial terms and to speak only in "strident" tones as a means of defending their culture against what they perceived as threats from the West. Such a strategy, however, in Neal's view, represents a confusion of politics and art, an undesirable conflation of the "public" domain of social activism and the "private" field of language reserved for artistic creation and literary-theoretical investigation.

Such a response is, in his estimation, finally a form of distorted "Marxist literary theory in which the concept of race is substituted for the Marxist idea of class" (p. 783). The attempt to apply the "ideology of race to artistic creation" (p. 784), he says, is simply a contemporary manifestation of Afro-American literature's (and, by implication, literary criticism's) historical dilemma:

The historical problem of black literature is that it has in a sense been perpetually hamstrung by its need to address itself to the question of racism in America. Unlike black music, it has rarely been allowed to exist on its own terms, but rather [has] been utilized as a means of public relations in the struggle for human rights. Literature can indeed make excellent propaganda, but through propaganda alone the black writer can never perform the highest function of his art: that of revealing to man his most enduring human possibilities and limitations. (p. 784)

In order to perform the "highest function" of artistic creation and criticism the black spokesman must concentrate his attention and efforts on "method" — on "form, structure, and genre" — rather than on "experience" or "content" (pp.

783–84). Neal, therefore, who called in the sixties for a literature and a criticism that spoke "directly to the needs and aspirations of black people," ends his later essay by calling for a creativity that projects "the accumulated weight of the world's aesthetic, intellectual, and historical experience" as a function of its mastery of "form." His revised formalist position leads not only to a condemnation of the critical weaknesses of former allies in the Black Aesthetic camp, but also to a valorization of the theoretical formulations of such celebrated "Western" theoreticians as Northrop Frye and Kenneth Burke (pp. 783–84).

A new order of literary-critical and literary-theoretical thought — one that sought to situate the higher-order rules of the Black Aesthetic within a contemporary universe of literary-theoretical discourse — was signaled during the mid-seventies not only by Neal's essay, but also by symposia and conferences on the Black Arts that occurred throughout the United States.[26] It was at one such symposium that Henderson presented his essay "The Question of Form and Judgement," which I have previously cited.[27] Like Neal, Henderson is drawn to a more formalist critique in his 1977 essay. For example, he implicitly rejects an intuitive "saturation" in favor of a more empirical approach to literary study: "in criticism, intuition, though vital, is not enough. The canons, the categories, the dynamics must be as clear and reasoned as possible. These must rest on a sound empirical base" (p. 36). This "sound empirical base" is, in the final

---

[26]I have in mind the conferences of black writers sponsored by the Howard University Institute for the Arts and the Humanities. Also important, I think, were the symposia held at the University of Pennsylvania in 1975 and 1977. Proceedings of these national gatherings can be found in *The Image of Black Folk in American Literature* (Washington, D.C.: Howard University Institute for the Arts and the Humanities, 1976) and in *Reading Black: Essays in the Criticism of African, Caribbean, and Afro-American Literature* (Ithaca, N.Y.: Cornell University, Africana Studies and Research Center, Monograph Series No. 4, 1976). [Au.]

[27]The symposium was entitled "The Function of Black American Poetry, 1760–1977," and it was sponsored by the Afro-American Studies Program at the University of Pennsylvania, March 24–26, 1977. Selected proceedings of this symposium appeared in *A Dark and Sudden Beauty*. [Au.]

II, The Writer as Activist — 1960 and After," in *The Black American Reference Book*, ed. Mabel M. Smythe (Englewood Cliffs, N.J.: Prentice-Hall, 1976), pp. 781–82. All citations refer to this edition and are hereafter marked by page numbers in parentheses. [Au.]

analysis, a *data base* acquired through the kind of cultural-anthropological investigation that I suggested when discussing "The Forms of Things Unknown." "Black poetry," Henderson continues, "can and should be judged by the same standards that any other poetry is judged by — by those standards which validly arise out of the culture" (p. 33). And the primary and secondary sources that he takes up in his 1977 discussion indicate that he has a very clear notion of "culture" as a category in literary study.

I think it would be incorrect to assert that the mid- and later-seventies witnessed a total revisionism on the part of former advocates for the Black Aesthetic. It seems fair, however, to say that some early spokesmen had by this time begun to point out weaknesses of the structure they had raised on the ideological foundations of Black Power. The defensive inwardness of the Black Aesthetic — its manifest appeal to a radically conditioned, revolutionary, and intuitive standard of critical judgment — made the new paradigm an ideal instrument of vision for those who wished to usher into the world new and *sui generis* Afro-American objects of investigation. Ultimately, though, such introspection could not answer the kinds of theoretical questions occasioned by the entry of these objects into the world. In a sense, the Afro-American literary-critical investigator had been given — through a bold act of the critical imagination — a unique literary tradition but no distinctive theoretical vocabulary with which to discuss this tradition. He had been given linguistic forms of power and beauty, but the language meted out by Karenga and others of his ilk was, sometimes, little more than a curse. A new paradigm (one coextensive with a contemporary universe whose participants were attempting to formulate adequate, theoretical ways of discussing art) was in order.

## VII

Discussing the manner of progression of a new philosophical posture born of a generational shift, Feuer comments:

> . . . from its point of origin with an insurgent generational group, the new emotional standpoint, the

new perspective, the new imagery, the new metaphors and idioms spread to the more conventional sections of their own generation, then to their slightly older opponents and their relative elders. Thus, by the time that conservative Americans spoke of themselves as "pragmatic," and virtually every American politician defined himself as a "pragmatist," the word "pragmatist" had become a cliché, and its span as a movement was done. A new insurgent generation would perforce have to explore novel emotions, images, and idioms in order to define its own independent character, its own "revolutionary" aims against the elders.[28]

One might substitute "Black Aesthetic" and "Black Aesthetician" for the implied "pragmatism" and the explicit "pragmatist" of the foregoing remarks. For by the end of the 1970s, the notion of a uniquely Afro-American field of aesthetic experience marked by unique works of verbal and literary art had become a commonplace in American literary criticism. The philosophical tenets that supported early manifestations of this notion, however, had been discredited by the failure of revolutionary black social and political groups to achieve their desired ends. "Black Power," that is to say, as a motivating philosophy for the Black Aesthetic, was deemed an ideological failure by the mid-seventies because it had failed to give birth to a sovereign Afro-American state within the United States. Hence, those who adopted fundamental postulates of the Black Aesthetic as givens in the late seventies did so without a corresponding acceptance of its initial philosophical buttresses.

The "imagery" of a new and resplendent nation of Afro-Americans invested with Black Power, like the "emotional standpoint" which insisted that this hypothetical nation should have a collective and functional literature and criticism, gave way in the late seventies to a new idiom. In defining its independent character, a new group of intellectuals found it *de rigueur* to separate the language of criticism from the vocabulary of political ideology. Their supporting philosophical posture for this separation was a dualism predicated on a distinction between "literary" and "extraliterary" realms of human be-

[28]Feuer, *Ideology and Ideologists*, p. 57. [Au.]

havior. Their proclaimed mission was to "reconstruct" the pedagogy and study of Afro-American literature so that it would reflect the most advanced thinking of a contemporary universe of literary-theoretical discourse. This goal was similar in some respects to the revisionist efforts of Neal and Henderson discussed in the preceding section. Like their immediate forerunners, the "reconstructionists" were interested in establishing a sound theoretical framework for the future study of Afro-American literature. In their attempts to achieve this goal, however, some spokesmen for the new generation (whose work I shall discuss shortly) were hampered by a literary-critical "professionalism" that was a function of their emergent class interests.

At the outset of the present essay, I implied that the notion "generational shifts" was sufficient to offer some account of the "ascendant class interests that have characterized Afro-America since World War II." The emergence of a mass, black audience, which was so important for the Black Power and Black Arts movements, was the first instance that I had in mind.[29] But the vertical mobility of Afro-Americans prompted by black political activism during the sixties and early seventies also resulted in the emergence during the 1970s of what has been called a "new black middle class."[30] The opening

of the doors, personnel rosters, and coffers of the white academy to minority groups effected by the radical politics of the past two decades provided the conditions of possibility for the appearance of Afro-American critics who have adopted postures, standards, and vocabularies of their white compeers. The disappearance of a mass black audience for both literary-critical and revolutionary-political discourse brought about by the billions of dollars and countless man-hours spent to suppress the American radical left in recent years has been ironically accompanied, therefore, by the emergence of Afro-American spokesmen whose class status (new, black middle-class) and privileges are, in fact, contingent upon their adherence to accepted (i.e., white) standards of their profession. Bernard Anderson's reflections on the situation of black corporate middle-managers who assumed positions in the late sixties and early seventies serve as well to describe the situation of a new group of Afro-American literary critics:

As pioneers in a career-development process, these [black] managers face challenges and uncertainties unknown to most white managers. Many feel an extra responsibility to maintain high performance levels, and most recognize an environment of competition that will tolerate only slight failure. . . . Some black middle managers feel the need to conform to a value system alien to the experience of most black Americans but essential for success in professional management.[31]

[29] I have discussed this phenomenon at length in *The Journey Back*, pp. 126–31. [Au.]

[30] It is difficult to date the first, contemporary usage of this term. Ben J. Wattenberg and Richard Scammon's article entitled "Black Progress and Liberal Rhetoric" (*Commentary*, April 1973, pp. 35–44), which proclaimed that 52 percent of Black Americans could be defined as "middle class," certainly gave life to ongoing attempts to define what E. Franklin Frazier designated the "Black Bourgeoisie" in his seminal study *Black Bourgeoisie* (1957). The special issue of *Ebony* magazine entitled "The Black Middle Class" (August 1973) seems to have been prompted as much by the necessity to answer Wattenberg and Scammon as by a desire to "update" Frazier at a time when (between 1960 and 1970) the number of blacks employed in professional and technical operations had increased by 131 percent and the number of blacks in the clerical force had grown by 121 percent. Some of the major investigative issues that are signalled by the employment of the term "new black middle class" are addressed by William Julius Wilson in his study *The Declining Significance of Race: Blacks and Changing American Institutions* (Chicago: University of Chicago Press, 1978). In

1979 and 1980, the Afro-American Studies Program of the University of Pennsylvania took up the issues raised by Wilson and by the concept of a "new black middle class" in its annual spring symposia. The proceedings of those symposia can be found in: *The Declining Significance of Race?: A Dialogue Among Black and White Social Scientists*, ed. Joseph R. Washington, Jr. (Philadelphia: Afro-American Studies Program of the University of Pennsylvania, 1979) and *Dilemmas of the New Black Middle Class*, ed. Joseph R. Washington, Jr., in manuscript. Essentially, the term "new black middle class" seems to denote a stratum of Afro-American professionals whose education, occupations, and income place them on a level near that of their similarly-employed white counterparts. [Au.]

[31] Quoted from William Julius Wilson, "The Declining Significance of Race: Myth or Reality," in *The Declining Significance of Race?* ed. Joseph R. Washington, Jr., p. 15. [Au.]

One result of a class-oriented professionalism among Afro-American literary critics has been a sometimes uncritical imposition upon Afro-American culture of literary theories borrowed from prominent white scholars.

When such borrowings have occurred among the generation that displaced the Black Aesthetic, the outcome has sometimes been disastrous for the course of Afro-American literary study. For instead of developing the mode of analysis suggested by the higher-order arguments of a previous generation, the emergent generation has chosen to distinguish Afro-American literature as an autonomous cultural domain and to criticize it in terms "alien" to the implied cultural-anthropological approach of the Black Aesthetic. Rather than attempting to assess the merits of the Black Aesthetic's methodological assumptions, that is to say, the new generation has adopted the "professional" assumptions (and attendant jargon) that mark the world of white academic literary critics. A positive outcome to the emergent generation's endeavors has been a strong and continuing emphasis on the necessity for an adequate theoretical framework for the study of Afro-American literature. The negative results of their efforts have been an unfortunate burdening of the universe of discourse surrounding Afro-American culture with meaningless jargon and the articulation of a variety of lamentably confused utterances on language, literature, and culture. The emergent generation is fundamentally correct, I feel, in its call for serious literary study of Afro-American literature. But it is misguided, I believe, in its wholesale adoption of terminology and implicit assumptions of white, "professional" critics. A view of essays by principal spokesmen for the new theoretical prospect will serve to clarify these judgments. The essays appear in the handbook of the new generation entitled *Afro-American Literature: The Reconstruction of Instruction* (1979).[32]

Edited by Dexter Fisher and Robert B. Stepto,

*Afro-American Literature* "grew out of the lectures and course design workshops of the 1977 Modern Language Association/National Endowment for the Humanities Summer Seminar on Afro-American Literature" (p. 1). The volume sets forth basic tenets of a new paradigm. The guiding assumption — i.e., that a literature known as "Afro-American" exists in the world — is stated as follows by Stepto in his "Introduction": "[Afro-American] literature fills bookstore shelves and, increasingly, the stacks of libraries; symposia and seminars on the literature are regularly held; prominent contemporary black writers give scores of readings; and so the question of the literature's existence, at this juncture in literary studies, is not at issue" (p. 1). The second, fundamental assumption — i.e., that literature consists in "written art" (p. 3) — is implied by Stepto later in the same "Introduction" when he is describing the unit of *Afro-American Literature* devoted to "Afro-American folklore *and* Afro-American literature as well as Afro-American folklore *in* Afro-American literature" (pp. 3–4). According to the editor, folklore can be transformed into a "written art" that may, in turn, comprise "fiction" (p. 4). Further, he suggests that the "folk" roots of a work like Frederick Douglass's *Narrative of the Life of Frederick Douglass* are to be distinguished from its "literary roots" (p. 5). The condition signaled by "written" seems at first glance, therefore, a necessary one for "literary" and "literature" in Stepto's thinking.

There is, however, some indication in the "Introduction" that the new generation does not wish to confine its definition of the "literary" exclusively to what is "written." At the midpoint of his opening remarks, Stepto asserts that there are "discrete literary texts that are inherently interdisciplinary (e.g., blues) and often multigeneric (dialect voicings in all written art forms)" (p. 3). If "blues" and "dialect voicings" constitute, respectively, a literary text and a genre, then it would appear to follow that *any distinctly Afro-American expressive form* (not merely *written* ones) can be encompassed by the "literary" domain. The boundaries of the new generation's theoretical inquiries, therefore, can apparently be expanded at will to include whatever seems dis-

[32]Dexter Fisher and Robert B. Stepto, eds., *Afro-American Literature: The Reconstruction of Instruction* (New York: Modern Language Association of America, 1979). All citations refer to this edition and are hereafter marked by page numbers in parentheses. [Au.]

tinctly expressive in Afro-America. Stepto suggests, for example, that "a methodology for an integrated study of *Afro-American folklore* and literature" (my italics, p. 4) should form part of the scholar-teacher's tools. And he goes on to propose that there are "various ways in which an instructor . . . can present *a collection of art forms* and still respond to the literary qualities of many of those forms in the course of the presentation" (my italics, p. 3). On one hand, then, the new prospect implies a rejection of modes of inquiry that are sociological in character or that seek to explore ranges of experience lying beyond the transactions of an exclusive sphere of written art: "central . . . to this volume as a whole" is a rejection of "extraliterary values, ideas, and pedagogical constructions that have plagued the teaching of . . . [Afro-American] literature" (p. 2). On the other hand, the new prospect attempts to preserve a concern for the "forms of things unknown" (e.g., blues) by reading them under the aspect of a Procrustean definition of "literary." Similarly, it attempts to maintain certain manifestations of Afro-American ordinary discourse (e.g., dialect voicings) as legitimate areas of study by reading them as literary genre. Finally, the new prospect, as defined by Stepto, implies that the entire realm of the Afro-American arts can be subsumed by the "literary" since any collection of black art forms can be explicated in terms of its "literary qualities." Such qualities, under the terms of the new prospect, take on the character of sacrosanct, cultural universals (a point to which I shall return shortly).

Kuhn points out that a paradigmatic shift in a community's conception of the physical world results in "the whole conceptual web whose strands are space, time, matter, force and so on" being shifted and "laid down again on nature whole" (p. 149). While the earlier Black Aesthetic was concerned to determine how the commodity of "blackness" shaped the Afro-American artistic domain, the emergent theoretical prospect attempts to discover how the qualities of a "literary" domain shape Afro-American life as a whole. There is, thus, a movement from the whole of culture to the part signaled by the most recent generational shift in Afro-American literary criticism. For what the new group seeks to

specify is a new "literary" conceptual scheme for apprehending Afro-American culture. This project constitutes its main theoretical goal. Two of *Afro-American Literature*'s most important essays — Stepto's "Teaching Afro-American Literature: Survey or Tradition: The Reconstruction of Instruction" and Henry Louis Gates, Jr.'s "Preface to Blackness: Text and Pretext" — are devoted to this goal.

Stepto's basic premise in "Teaching Afro-American Literature" is that the typical (i.e., normative) teacher of Afro-American literature is a harried, irresponsible pedagogue ignorant of the "inner" workings of the Afro-American literary domain. It follows from this proposition that pedagogy surrounding the literature must be reconstructed on a sound basis by someone familiar with the "myriad cultural metaphors," "coded structures," and "poetic rhetoric" of Afro-America (p. 9). Stepto asserts that only a person who has learned *to read* the discrete literary texts of Afro-America in ways that ensure a proximity and "intimacy, with writers and texts outside the normal boundaries of nonliterary structures" (p. 16) can achieve this required familiarity. According to the author, moreover, it is a specific form of "literacy" — of proficient reading — that leads to the reconstruction of instruction.

Understandably, given the author's earlier claims, this literacy is not based on a comprehension or study of "extraliterary" structures. Its epistemological foundation is, instead, the instructor's apprehension and comprehension of what Stepto calls the "Afro-American canonical story or pregeneric myth, the particular historicity of the Afro-American literary tradition, and the Afro-American landscape or *genius loci*" (p. 18). This "pregeneric myth," according to Stepto, is "the quest for freedom *and* literacy" (p. 18), and he further asserts that the myth is an "aesthetic and rhetorical principle" that can serve as the basis for constructing a proper course in Afro-American literature (p. 17). The Afro-American "pregeneric myth" is, therefore, (at one and the same instant) somehow a prelinguistic reality, a quest, and a pedagogical discovery principle.

It is at this point in Stepto's specifications that what I earlier referred to as an "unfortunate burdening" of the universe of discourse surrounding Afro-American culture with jargon becomes apparent. For the author's formulations on a "pregeneric myth" reflect his metaphysical learnings far more clearly than they project a desirable methodological competence. They signal, in fact, what I called at the outset of this essay a "version of Aristotelian metaphysics." Stepto's pregeneric myth has the character of prime matter capable of assuming an unceasing variety of forms. Just as for Aristotle "the elements are the simplest physical things, and within them the distinction of matter and form can only be made by an abstraction of thought,"[33] so for Stepto the pregeneric myth is *informed matter* that serves as the core and essence of that which is "literary" in Afro-America. It is the substance out of which all black expression molds itself: "The quest for freedom and literacy is found in every major text . . ." (p. 18). Further: "If an Afro-American literary tradition exists, it does so not because there is a sizeable chronology of authors and texts but because those authors and texts seek collectively their own literary forms — their own admixture of genre — bound historically and linguistically to a shared pregeneric myth" (p. 19).

A simplified statement of the conceptual scheme implied by Stepto's notion of cultural evolution would be: The various *structures* of a culture derive from the informed matter of myth. The principal difficulty with this notion is that the author fails to make clear the mode of being of a "myth" that is not only *pregeneric*, but also, it would seem, *prelinguistic*. "Nonliterary structures," Stepto tells us, evolve "almost exclusively from freedom myths devoid of linguistic properties" (p. 18). Such structures, we are further told, "speak rarely to questions of freedom *and* literacy" (p. 18). The question one must pose in light of such assertions is: Are "nonliterary

structures" indeed devoid of linguistic properties? If so, then "literacy" and "freedom" can scarcely function as dependent variables in a single, generative myth. For under conditions of mutual inclusiveness (where the variables are, *ab initio*, functions of one another) the structures generated from the myth could not logically be devoid of that which is essential to literacy; i.e., *linguistic properties*. It is important to note, for example, that the "nonliterary" structure known as the *African Methodist Episcopal Church* preserves in its name, and particularly in the linguistic sign "African," a marker of the structure's cultural origin and orientation. And it is difficult to imagine the kind of cognition that would be required to summon to consciousness *cultural structures* devoid of all linguistic properties such as a name, a written history, or a controlling interest in the semantic field of a culture's language. But, perhaps, what Stepto actually meant to suggest by his statement was that "freedom myths" are devoid of linguistic properties. Under this interpretation of his statement, however, one would have to adopt a philosophically idealistic conception of myth that seems contrary to the larger enterprise of the reconstructionists. For Stepto insists that the "reconstruction" of Afro-American literary instruction is contingent upon the discoverability through "literacy" (a process of *linguistic* transaction) of the Afro-American pregeneric myth. And how could such a goal be achieved if myths existed only as *prelinguistic*, philosophical ideals? In sum, Stepto seems to have adopted a critical rhetoric that plays him false. Having assumed some intrinsic merit and inherent clarity in the notion "pregeneric myth," he fails to analytically delineate the mode of existence of such a myth or to clarify the manner in which it is capable of generating two *distinct kinds* of cultural structures.

One sign of the problematical status of this myth in Stepto's formulations is the apparent "agentlessness" of its operations. According to the author, the pregeneric myth is simply "set in motion" (p. 20), and one can observe its "motion through both chronological and linguistic time" (p. 19). Yet, the efficacy of motion suggested here seems to have no historically based community of agents or agencies for its origination

[33]Sir David Ross, *Aristotle* (London: Methuen, 1923), pp. 73–74. "Prime" matter is unlike "secondary matter" since the latter can not only "exist apart" (e.g., "tissues" may or may not be combined into organs) but can also be severed in reality (i.e., organs may be broken up into their component tissues). It is the inseparability of "form" and "matter" where Stepto is concerned (his "myth" is both structured and structuring) that gives his pregeneric myth the character of "prime" or "informed" matter (See Ross, p. 71). [Au.]

or perpetuation. The myth and its operations, therefore, are finally reduced in Stepto's thinking to an aberrant version of Aristotle's "unmoved mover." For Aristotle specifies that the force which moves the "first heaven" has "no contingency; it is not subject even to minimal change (spatial motion in a circle), since that is what it originates."[34] Stepto, however, wants both to posit an "unmoved" substance as his pregeneric myth *and* to claim that this myth *moves* as "literary history." In fact, he designates the shape of its literary-historical movement as a circle — a "magic circle" or *temenos* — representing one kind of ideal harmony, or perfection of motion.

At this point in his description, Stepto (not surprisingly) feels compelled to illustrate his formulations with examples drawn from the Afro-American literary tradition. He first asserts that the phrase "the black belt" is one of Afro-America's metaphors for the *genius loci* (a term borrowed from Geoffrey Hartman signifying "spirit of place") that resides within the interior of the "magic circle" previously mentioned (p. 20). Employing this metaphor, the late-nineteenth-century founder and president of Tuskegee Institute, Booker T. Washington, wrote:

> So far as I can learn the term was first used to designate a part of the country which was distinguished by the colour of the soil. The part of the country possessing this thick, dark soil was, of course, the part of the south where the slaves were more profitable, and consequently they were taken there in the largest numbers. Later, and especially since the war, the term seems to be used wholly in a political sense — that is, to designate the counties where the black people out number the white.[35]

Stepto feels that this description comprises an act

---

[34]*Metaphysics*, in *Aristotle's Metaphysics*, ed. John Warrington (London: J. M. Dent, 1956), p. 346. When Aristotle discusses "The Prime Mover" in one of the books of the *Metaphysics*, he sets forth what according to Sir David Ross is his only "systemic essay in theology" (Warrington, p. 331). Stepto, in adducing the agentless operation of his pregeneric myth, is on similar theological ground, attempting to find something that is "eternal, substance, and actuality" (Warrington, p. 345) to move the great sphere of Afro-American literary lights. [Au.]

[35]Quoted from *Afro-American Literature*, pp. 20–21. [Au.]

of disingenuity on Washington's part. However, when he proceeds to demonstrate that Washington's statement is a "literary offense" (something akin to a sin of shallowness in the reading of metaphor) vis-à-vis the metaphor "the black belt," Stepto does not summon logical, rhetorical, or linguistic criteria. In condemning Washington for describing only geological and political dimensions of the black belt rather than historical and symbolic dimensions, Stepto summons "extraliterary" criteria, insisting that the turn-of-the-century black leader's "offense" was committed in order to insure his success in soliciting philanthropic funds for Tuskegee. The author of *Up From Slavery*, in Stepto's view, merely glossed the metaphor "the black belt" in order to keep his white, potential benefactors happy.

We, thus, find ourselves thrust into the historical dust and heat of turn-of-the-century white philanthropy in America. And what Stepto calls a "geographical metaphor" (i.e., "the black belt") becomes, in his own reading, simply a sign for one American region where such philanthropy had its greatest impact. Contrary to his earlier injunction, therefore, Stepto allows a "nonliterary structure" to become central to his own "reading of art" (p. 20). He assumes, however, that he has achieved his interpretation of Washington solely on the basis of his own "literacy" in regard to the black leader's employment of metaphor. He further assumes that when he contrasts W. E. B. Du Bois's employment of "the black belt" with Washington's usage that he is engaged in a purely "literary" act of "reading within tradition" (p. 21). But if the "tradition" that he has in mind requires a comprehension of turn-of-the-century white philanthropy where Washington is concerned, then surely Stepto does his reader a disservice when he fails to reveal that Du Bois's "rhetorical journey into the soul of a race" (p. 21) in fact curtailed white philanthropy to Atlanta University, cost Du Bois his teaching position at the same university, and led the author of *The Souls of Black Folk* to an even deeper engagement with the metaphor "the black belt."

In his attempt to maintain the exclusively "literary" affiliations of a pregeneric myth and its operations, Stepto introduces historical and so-

---

ciological structures into his reading only where they will not seem to conflict dramatically with his claim that all necessary keys for literacy in the tradition generated by the pregeneric myth are linguistically situated within the texts of black authors themselves. Such reading is, at best, an exercise in the positing of cultural metaphors followed by attempts to fit such metaphors into a needlessly narrow framework of interpretation. Yet, Stepto asserts "it is reading of this sort that our instructor's new pedagogy should both emulate and promote" (p. 21).

Rather than offering additional examples of such reading, Stepto turns to a consideration of what one early-twentieth-century critic called the relationship between "tradition and the individual talent."[36] For Stepto, this relationship is described as the tension between "Genius and *genius loci*" and between *temenos* and *genius loci*. And the mediation between these facets of Afro-American culture constitutes what the author calls "modal improvisation." Although his borrowed terminology is almost hopelessly confusing here, what Stepto seems to suggest is that the Afro-American literature instructor must engage in "literate" communion with the inner dynamics of the region of Afro-America comprised by a pregeneric myth and its myriad forms and operations. The instructor's pedagogical "genius" consists in his ability to comprehend the "eternal landscape" (p. 22) that is the pregeneric myth — i.e., the sacred domain of the "literary" in Afro-American culture.

An "eternal landscape" (without beginning or end and agentless in its creation and motions) is but another means of denoting for Stepto what he describes earlier in his essay as the "various dimensions of literacy achieved within the *deeper recesses* of the art form" (my italics, p. 13). At another point in "Teaching Afro-American Literature," the author speaks of an *"immersion in* the multiple images and landscapes of metaphor" (my italics, p. 15). This cumulative employment of images of a sacred interiority seems to suggest that Stepto believes there is an inner sanctum of pregeneric, mythic, literary "intimacy" resident in works of Afro-American art. Further, he seems to feel that entrance to this sanctum can be gained only by the initiated. One might posit, therefore, that what is presented by "Teaching Afro-American Literature" is a scheme of mystical literacy that finally comprises what might be called a *theology of literacy*. For the "conceptual web" laid upon Afro-America by Stepto's essay asserts the primacy and sacredness among cultural activities of the literary-critical and literary-theoretical enterprise. The argument of the essay is, in the end, a religious interpretation *manqué*, complete with an unmoved mover, a priestly class of "literate" initiates, and an eternal landscape of cultural metaphor that can be obtained by those who are free of literary "offense." And the "qualities" that derive from such a landscape (since they are coextensive with the generation of cultural structure) operate as "universals."

The articulation of such a literary-critical orthodoxy is scarcely a new departure in the history of literary criticism. In his "General Introduction" to *The English Poets* published in 1880, Matthew Arnold wrote: "More and more mankind will discover that we have to turn to poetry to interpret life for us, to console us, to sustain us. Without poetry, our science will appear incomplete; and most of what now passes for religion and philosophy will be replaced by poetry."[37] As a function of this conceptualization of the "higher uses" of poetry, Arnold confidently proclaimed: "In poetry, which is thought and art in one, it is the glory, the eternal honour, that charlatanism shall have no entrance; that this noble sphere be kept inviolate and inviolable" (p. 3). Stepto's assumption that his "reconstructed" scheme for teaching Afro-American literature may "nurture literacy in the academy" (p. 23) is

[36]T. S. Eliot, "Tradition and the Individual Talent," in *Selected Essays* (New York: Harcourt, Brace, 1950), pp. 3–11. According to Eliot, the poet can not know what valuable poetic "work" is to be done "unless he lives in what is not merely the present, but the present moment of the past, unless he is conscious, not of what is dead, but of what is already living" (p. 11). [Au.] See Eliot, p. 466. [Ed.]

[37]Matthew Arnold, "The Study of Poetry," in *The Works of Matthew Arnold*, IV (New York: AMS Press, 1970), p. 2. All citations refer to this edition and are hereafter marked by page numbers in parentheses. [Au.] See Arnold, p. 379. [Ed.]

certainly akin to Arnold's formulations on the exalted mission of poetry. And his zeal in preserving "inviolate" the sacred domain of the literary surely constitutes a modern, Arnoldian instance of a theology of literacy. As a function of his zeal, Stepto condemns with fierce self-righteousness any pedagogical contextualization of Afro-American literature that might lead a student to ascribe to, say, a Langston Hughes poem, a use-value, or meaning, in opposition to the kind of linguistic and rhetorical values made available by the reconstruction of instruction.

The author of "Teaching Afro-American Literature" emerges as a person incapable of acknowledging that the decision to investigate the material bases of the society that provided enabling conditions for Hughes's metaphors is a sound literary-theoretical decision. Semantic and pragmatic considerations of metaphor suggest that the information communicated by metaphor is hardly localized in a given image on a given page (or, exclusively within the confines of a "magical" literary circle). Rather, the communication process is a function of myriad factors; e.g., a native speaker's ability to recognize ungrammatical sentences, the vast store of encyclopedic knowledge constituting a speech community's common knowledge of objects and concepts, relevant information supplied by the verbal context of a specific metaphoric text, and, finally, the relevant knowledge brought to bear by an "introjecting" listener or reader.[38] Conceived under these terms, metaphoric communication may actually be more fittingly comprehended by an investigation of the material bases of society than by an initiate's passage "from metaphor to metaphor and from image to image of the same metaphor in order to locate the Afro-American *genius loci*" (p. 21). Hughes is, perhaps, more comprehensible, for example, within

the framework of Afro-American verbal and musical *performance* than within the borrowed framework for the description of *written* inscriptions of cultural metaphor adduced by Stepto. Only a full investigation of Afro-American metaphor — an analysis based on the best theoretical models available — will enable a student to decide.

The zeal that forced Stepto to adopt a narrow, "literary" conception of metaphor should not be totally condemned. For it is correct (and fair) to point out that a kind of sacred crusade did seem in order by the mid-seventies to modify or "reconstruct" the instruction and study of Afro-American literature that were not then based on sound theoretical foundations. While I do not think the type of mediocre instruction and misguided criticism that Stepto describes were, in fact, as prevalent as he assumes, I do feel that there were enough charlatans about in the mid-seventies to justify renewed vigilance and effort. But though one comes away from "Teaching Afro-American Literature" with a fine sense of these villains, one does not depart the essay (or others in *Afro-American Literature*) with a sense that reconstructionists are either broad-minded or well-informed in their preachments. In fact, I think the instructor who seeks to model his course on the formulations of Stepto might find himself as nonplused as the critic who attempts to pattern his investigative strategies on the model implicit in Gates's "Preface to Blackness: Text and Pretext."

Just as Stepto's work begins with the assumption that the pedagogy surrounding Afro-American literature rests on a mistake, so Gates's essay commences with the notion that the criticism of Afro-American literature (prior to 1975) rested upon a mistake. This mistake, according to Gates, consisted in the assumption by past critics that a "determining formal relation" exists between "literature" and "social institutions."

The idea of a determining formal relation between literature and social institutions does not in itself explain the sense of urgency that has, at least since the publication in 1760 of *A Narrative of the Uncommon Sufferings and Surprising Deliverance of Briton Hammon, a Negro Man*, characterized

---

[38]These "factors" are treated in detail by Samuel R. Levin in *The Semantics of Metaphor* (Baltimore: The Johns Hopkins University Press, 1977) and by Robert Rogers in *Metaphor: A Psychoanalytic View* (Berkeley: University of California Press, 1978). Additional theoretical discussion of metaphor can be found in the stimulating issue of *Critical Inquiry* 5 (Autumn 1978) devoted to the subject. [Au.]

nearly the whole of Afro-American writing. This idea has often encouraged a posture that belabors the social and documentary status of black art, and indeed the earliest discrete examples of written discourse by slave and ex-slave came under a scrutiny not primarily literary. (p. 44)

For Gates, "social institutions" is an omnibus category equivalent to Stepto's "nonliterary structures." Such institutions include: the philosophical musings of the Enlightenment on the "African Mind," eighteenth-century debates concerning the African's place in the great chain of being, the politics of abolitionism, or (more recently) the economics, politics, and sociology of the Afro-American liberation struggle in the twentieth century. Gates contends that Afro-American literature has repeatedly been interpreted and evaluated according to criteria derived from such "institutions."

As a case in point, he surveys the critical response that marked the publication of Phillis Wheatley's *Poems on Various Subjects, Religious and Moral*, discovering that "almost immediately after its publication in London in 1773," the black Boston poet's collection became "the international antislavery movement's most salient argument for the African's innate mental equality" (p. 46). Gates goes on to point out that "literally scores of public figures" provided prefatory signatures, polemical reviews, or "authenticating" remarks dedicated to proving that Wheatley's verse was (or was not, as the case may be) truly the product of an African imagination. Such responses were useless in the office of criticism, however, because "virtually no one," according to Gates, "discusses . . . [Wheatley's collection] as poetry" (p. 46). Hence: "The documentary status of black art assumed priority over mere literary judgment; criticism rehearsed content to justify one notion of origins or another" (p. 46).

Thomas Jefferson's condemnation (on "extraliterary" grounds) of Wheatley and of the black eighteenth-century epistler Ignatius Sancho set an influential model for the discussion of Afro-American literature that, in Gates's view, "exerted a prescriptive influence over the criticism of the writings of blacks for the next 150 years"

(p. 46). Jefferson's recourse to philosophical, political, religious, economic and other cultural systems for descriptive and evaluative terms in which to discuss black writing was, in short, a *mistake* that has been replicated through the decades by both white and Afro-American commentators. William Dean Howells, the writers of the Harlem Renaissance, and, most recently, according to Gates, spokesmen for the Black Aesthetic have repeated the critical offense of Jefferson. They have assumed that there is, in fact, a determining formal relation between literature and other cultural institutions and that various dimensions of these other institutions constitute areas of knowledge relevant to literary criticism. Gates says, "No," in thunder, to such assumptions. For as he reviews the "prefaces" affixed to various Afro-American texts through the decades, he finds no useful criteria for the practice of literary criticism. He discovers only introductory remarks that are "pretexts" for discussing African humanity, or for displaying "artifacts of the sable mind" (p. 49), or for chronicling the prefacer's own "attitude toward being black in white America" (p. 65).

Like Larry Neal,[39] Gates concludes that such "pretexts" and the lamentable critical situation that they imply are functions of the powerful influence of "race" as a variable in all spheres of American intellectual endeavor related to Afro-America. And like Neal, he states that racial considerations have been substituted for "class" as a category in the thinking of those who have attempted to criticize Afro-American literature, resulting in what he calls "race and superstructure" criticism: "blacks borrowed whole the Marxist notion of base and superstructure and made of it, if you will, race and superstructure" (p. 56). Gates also believes that Afro-American creative writers have fallen prey to the mode of thought that marks "race and superstructure" criticism. For these writers have shaped their work on polemical, documentary lines designed to prove the equality of Afro-Americans or to argue

[39]I refer to Neal's "The Black Contribution to American Letters," which I discussed in an earlier section of this essay. [Au.]

a case for their humanity. And in the process, they have neglected the "literary" engagement that results in true art.

What, then, is the path that leads beyond the critical and creative failings of the past? According to Gates, it lies in a semiotic understanding of literature as a "system" of signs that stand in an "arbitrary" relationship to social reality (pp. 64–68). Having drawn a semiotic circle around literature, however, he moves rapidly to disclaim the notion that literature as a "system" is radically distinct from other domains of culture:

> It is not, of course, that literature is unrelated to culture, to other disciplines, or even to other arts; it is not that words and usage somehow exist in a vacuum or that the literary work of art occupies an ideal or reified, privileged status, the province of some elite cult of culture. It is just that the literary work of art is a system of signs that may be decoded with various methods, all of which assume the fundamental unity of form and content and all of which demand close reading. (p. 64)

The epistemology on which the description rests is stated as follows:

> . . . perceptions of reality are in no sense absolute; reality is a function of our senses. Writers present models of reality, rather than a description of it, though obviously the two may be related variously. In fact, fiction often contributes to cognition by providing models that highlight the nature of things precisely by their failure to coincide with it. Such certainly is the case in science fiction. (p. 66)

The semiotic notion of literature and culture implied by Gates seems to combine empiricism (reality as a "function of our senses") with an ontology of the sign that suggests that signs are somehow "natural" or "inherent" to human beings. For if "reality" is, indeed, a function of our senses, then observation and study of these physiological capacities should yield some comprehension of a subject's "reality." In truth, however, it is not these physiological processes in themselves that interest Gates, but rather the operation of such processes under the conditions of "models" of cognition, which, of course, is a very different thing. For if one begins not with the senses, but with cognition, then one is required to ask: How are "models" of cognition

conceived, articulated, and transmitted in human cultures? Certainly, one of the obvious answers here is *not* that human beings are endowed at birth with a "system of signs," but rather that *models of cognition are conceived in, articulated through, and transmitted by language.* And like other systems of culture, language *is* a "social institution." Hence, if cognitive "models" of "fiction" differ from those of other spheres of human behavior, they do not do so because fiction is somehow discontinuous with social institutions. In fact, it is the attempt to understand the coextensiveness of language *as a social institution* and literature *as a system within it* that constitutes what is, perhaps, the defining process of literary-theoretical study in our day.

When, therefore, Gates proposes metaphysical and behavioral models that suggest that a literature, or even a single text (p. 67), exists as a structured "world" ("a system of signs") that can be comprehended without reference to "social institutions," he seems misguided in his claims and only vaguely aware of recent developments in literary study, symbolic anthropology, linguistics, the psychology of perception, and other related areas of intellectual inquiry. He seems, in fact, to have adopted, without qualification, a theory of the literary sign (of the "word" in a literary text) that presupposes a privileged status for the creative writer: "The black writer is the point of consciousness of his language" (p. 67). What this assertion means to Gates is that a writer is more capable than others in society of producing a "complex structure of meanings" — a linguistic structure that (presumably) corresponds more closely than those produced by non-writers — to the organizing principles by which a group's world view operates in consciousness (p. 67).

One might be at a loss to understand how a writer can achieve this end unless he is fully aware of language *as a social institution* and of the relationship that language bears to other institutions that create, shape, maintain, and transmit a society's "organizing principles." Surely, Gates does not mean to suggest that the mind of the writer is an autonomous semantic domain where complex structures are conceived and maintained "non-linguistically." On the other hand, if such structures of meaning are, in fact, "complex" *because* they are linguistically maintained, then so, too, are similar structures that are conceived by non-writers.

That is to say, Gates renders but small service to the office of theoretical distinction when he states that "a poem is above all atemporal and must cohere at a symbolic level, if it coheres at all" (p. 60), or when he posits that "literature approaches its richest development when its 'presentational symbolism' (as opposed by Susanne Langer to its 'literal discourse') cannot be reduced to the form of a literal proposition" (p. 66). The reason such sober generalities contribute little to our understanding of literature, of course, is that Gates provides no just notion of the nature of "literal discourse," failing to admit both its social-institutional status and its fundamental existence as a symbolic system. On what basis, then, except a somewhat naive belief in the explanatory power of semiotics can he suggest a radical disjunction between literature and other modes of linguistic behavior in a culture? The critic who attempted to pattern his work on Gates's model would find himself confronted by a theory of language, literature, and culture that suggests that "literary" meanings are conceived in a nonsocial, noninstitutional manner by the "point of consciousness" of a language and are maintained and transmitted in an agentless fashion within a closed circle of "intertextuality" (p. 68). It does seem, therefore, that despite his disclaimer, Gates feels that "literature is unrelated to culture." For culture consists in the interplay of various human symbolic systems, an interplay that is essential to the production and comprehension of meaning. Gates's independent literary domain, which produces meanings from some mysteriously nonsocial, noninstitutional medium, bears no relationship to such a process.

One reason Gates fails to articulate an adequate theory of literary semantics in his essay, I think, is that he allots an inordinate amount of space to the castigation of his critical forebears. And his attacks are often restatements of shortcomings that his predecessors had recognized and discussed by the later seventies. Yet Gates provides elaborate detail in, for example, his analysis of the Black Aesthetic.

Among the many charges that he levels against Stephen Henderson, Addison Gayle, Jr., and the present author is the accusation that the spokesmen for a Black Aesthetic assumed they could "achieve an intimate knowledge of a literary text by recreating it from the inside: Critical thought must become the thought criticized" (p. 66). Though Gates employs familiar terminology here,[40] what he seems to object to in the work of Black Aesthetic spokesmen is their treatment of the text as subject. He levels the charge, in short, that these spokesmen postulated a tautological, literary-critical circle, assuming that the thought of an Afro-American literary text was "black thought" and, hence, could be "rethought" only by a black critic. And while there is some merit in this charge (as Henderson's and Neal's previously mentioned reconsiderations of their initial critical postures make clear), it is scarcely true, as Gates argues, that Black Aestheticians did nothing in their work but reiterate presuppositions about "black thought" and then interpret Afro-American writing in accord with the entailments of such presuppositions. For the insular vision that would have resulted from this strategy would not have enabled Black Aestheticians to discuss and interpret Afro-American verbal behavior in the holistic ways conceived by Henderson, Neal, Gayle, and the present author. Spokesmen for the Black Aesthetic seldom conceived of the "text" as a *closed* enterprise. Instead, they normally thought (at the higher level of their arguments) of the text as an occasion for transactions between writer and reader, between performer and audience. And far from insisting that the written text is, in itself, a repository of inviolable "black thought" to be preserved at all costs, they called for the "destruction of the text" — for an open-endedness of performance and response that created conditions of possibility for the emergence of both new

---

[40]Gérard Genette defines the text as "subject" in *Figures* (Paris: Editions du Seuil, 1966). Georges Poulet and Paul Ricoeur have also entered reflections on the process whereby "critical thought *becomes* the thought criticized." The quotation here is from Maria Corti's *An Introduction to Literary Semiotics* (Bloomington: Indiana University Press, 1978), p. 43. [Au.]

meanings and new strategies of verbal transaction.[41] True, such spokesmen never saw the text as discontinuous with its social origins, but then they also never conceived of these "origins" as somehow divorced from the semantics of the metaphorical instances represented in black "artistic" texts. In short, they never thought of culture under the terms of a semiotic analysis that restricted its formulations to the literary domain alone.

On the other hand, they were certainly never so innocent as Gates would have one believe. Their semantics were never so crude as to permit them to accept the notion that the words of a literary text stand in a one-to-one relationship to the "things" of Afro-American culture. In fact, they were so intent on discovering the full dimensions of the artistic "word" that they attempted to situate its various manifestations within a continuum of verbal behavior in Afro-American culture as a whole. Further, they sought to understand this continuum within the complex webs of interacting cultural systems that ultimately gave meaning to such words.

Rather than a referential semantics, therefore, what was implicit in the higher-order arguments of Black Aesthetic spokesmen (as I have attempted to demonstrate in my earlier discussions) was an anthropological approach to Afro-American art. I think, in fact, that Gates recognizes this and is, finally, unwilling to accept the kind of critical responsibilities signaled by such an enterprise. For though he spends a great deal of energy arguing with Henderson's and my own assumptions on Afro-American culture, he refuses (not without some disingenuity) to acknowledge our *actual readings of Afro-American texts*. The reason for this refusal, I think, is that our readings bring together, in what one hopes are useful ways, our knowledge of various social institutions, or cultural systems (including language), in our attempts to reveal the *sui generis* character of Afro-American artistic texts. Gates's formulations, however, imply an ideal critic whose readings would summon knowledge *only* from the literary system of Afro-America. The semantics endorsed by his ideal critic would *not* be those of a culture. They would constitute, instead, the specially consecrated meanings of an intertextual world of "written art."

The emphasis on "close reading" (p. 64) in Gates's formulations, therefore, might justifiably be designated a call for a "closed" reading of selected Afro-American written texts. In fact, the author implies that the very defining criteria of a culture may be extrapolated from selected written, literary texts rather than vice-versa (p. 62). For example, if any Afro-American literary artist has entertained the notion of "frontier," then Gates feels the notion must have defining force in Afro-American culture (pp. 63–64). Only by ignoring the mass level of Afro-America and holding up the "message" of literary works of art by Ralph Ellison and Ishmael Reed as "normative" utterances in Afro-American culture can Gates support such a claim. His claim is, thus, a function of the privileged status he grants to the writer and the elitist status that he bestows on "literary uses of language" (p. 62).

But if it is true that scholarly investigations of an Afro-American expressive tradition must begin at a mass level — at the level of the "forms of things unknown" — then Gates's claim that the notion of "frontier" has defining force in Afro-America would have to be supported by the testimony of, say, the blues, work songs, or early folktales of Afro-America. And I think that an emphasis on frontier, in the sense intended by Frederick Jackson Turner, is scarcely to be discerned in these cultural manifests.

Gates, however, is interested only in what *writers* (as "points of consciousness") have to say, and he seems to feel no obligation to turn to Afro-American folklore. In fact, when he comments on Henderson's formulations on Afro-American folk language, or vernacular, he reveals not only a lack of interest in folk processes, but also some profound misconceptions about the nature of Afro-American language.

Henderson attempts to establish a verbal and

---

[41] I have discussed the concept of "the destruction of the text" in *The Journey Back*, pp. 127–28. In his essay "And Shine Swam On," which serves as the "Afterword" for the anthology *Black Fire*, ed. Larry Neal and LeRoi Jones (New York: Morrow, 1968), Neal says that true Afro-American poetry lies in verbal and musical performance, not in *written* texts: "The text could be destroyed and no one would be hurt in the least by it" (p. 653). [Au.]

musical continuum of expressive behavior in Afro-American culture as an analytical category. In this process, he encounters certain verbal items that seem to claim (through usage) expansive territory in the Afro-American "sign field." Gates mistakenly assumes that Henderson is setting such items (e.g., "jook," "jelly") apart from a canon of "ordinary" usage as "poetic discourse." This assumption is a function of Gates's critical methodology, which is predicated on a distinction between ordinary and poetic discourse. And the assumption compels him to cast aspersions on the originality of Henderson's work by asserting that "practical critics" since the 1920s (p. 61) have been engaged in actions similar to those of the Black Aesthetic spokesman.

The fault here is that Gates fails to recognize that Henderson is *not* seeking to isolate a lexicon of Afro-American "poetic" usages, nor to demonstrate how such usages "superimpose" a "grammar" (Gates's notion) on "nonliterary discourse" (p. 61). Henderson is concerned, instead, to demonstrate that Afro-American ordinary discourse is, in fact, continuous with Afro-American artistic discourse and that an investigation of the black oral tradition would finally concern itself not simply with a lexicon, but also with a "grammar" adequate to describe the syntax and phonology of *all* Afro-American speech.

Gates is incapable of understanding this notion, however, because he believes that the artistic domain is unrelated to ordinary, "social" modes of behavior. Hence, he is enamored of the written, literary work, suggesting that a mere dictionary of black "poetic" words and their "specific signification" would lead to an understanding of how "Black English" departs from "general usage" (p. 61). This view of language is coextensive with his views of literature and culture. For it concentrates solely on words as "artistic" words and ignores the complexities of the syntax and phonology that give resonance to such words. "A literary text," Gates writes, "is a linguistic event; its explication must be an activity of close textual analysis" (p. 68).

It is not, however, the "text" that constitutes an "event" (if by this Gates means a process of linguistic transaction). It is rather the reading or performance by human beings of a kind of score, or graphemic record, if you will, that constitutes *the event* and, in the process, produces (or reproduces) the meaningful text. And the observer or critic who wishes to "analyze" such a text must have a knowledge of far more than the mere words of the performers. He should, it seems to me, have some theoretically adequate notions of the entire array of cultural forces which shape the performers' or readers' cognition and allow them to actualize the text as an instance of a distinctive cultural semantics. Gates has no such notions to bring to bear. And his later essay in *Afro-American Literature* entitled "Dis and Dat: Dialect and the Descent" reveals some confusion on issues of both language and culture.

Briefly, we are told by Gates that "culture is imprisoned in a linguistic contour that no longer matches . . . the changing landscape of fact" (p. 92). This appears a mild form of Whorfianism[42] until one asks: How do "facts" achieve a nonlinguistic existence? The answer is that *they do not achieve such an existence*. Placed in proper perspective, Gates's statement simply means that different communities of speakers of the same language have differential access to "modern" ideas. But in his efforts to preserve language apart from other social institutions, Gates ignores agents or speakers until he wishes to add further mystery and distinctiveness to his own conceptions of language. When he finally comes to reflect on speakers, he invokes the notion of "privacy," insisting that lying and remaining silent both offer instances of the employment of a "personal" thesaurus by a speaker (p. 93). Now, this conception stands in contrast to Gates's earlier Whorfianism.[43] And, to my knowledge, it

[42]By "Whorfianism" I mean the scholarly position assumed by Benjamin Lee Whorf. Whorf, in his studies of the Hopi Indians, emphasized the interpenetration of language and reality; the worldview of the Hopi, according to Whorf, is coded into their language. Hence, language and worldview are coextensive (mild Whorfianism) or coterminous (strong Whorfianism), and this makes for a kind of linguistic determinism in human affairs. For a more detailed view of Whorf's thought, consult *Language, Thought and Reality*, ed. John B. Carroll, a collection of Whorf's essays published by the MIT Press in 1956. [Au.]

[43]Instead of language determining worldview, the individ-

possesses little support in the literature of linguistic or semiotics.

The notions that Gates advocates presuppose uniquely "personal" meanings for lexical items that form part of a culture's "public discourse." But what is unique, or personal, about these items is surely their difference from public discourse; their very identity, that is to say, is a function of public discourse. Further, the ability to use such lexical items to lie, or to misinform, scarcely constitutes an argument for privacy. Umberto Eco, for example, writes:

> A sign is everything which can be taken as significantly substituting for something else. This something else does not necessarily have to exist or to actually be somewhere at the moment in which a sign stands for it. Thus *semiotics is in principle the discipline studying everything which can be used in order to lie.* If something cannot be used to tell a lie, conversely it cannot be used to tell the truth: it cannot in fact be used "to tell" at all.[44]

The *word*, in short, becomes a sign by being able *to tell*, and unless Gates means to propose the idealistic notion that each human mind generates its own system of meaningful, nonpublic signs, it is difficult to understand how he conceives of sign usage in lying as an instance of "private" usage of language. His goal in "Dis and Dat" (an unfortunate choice of lexical items for his title since the phonological feature *d* for *th* is not unique to Black English Vernacular, but rather can be found in other non-standard language varieties) is to define Afro-American "dialect" as a kind of "private," subconscious code signifying a "hermetic closed world" (p. 94). The problem with this very suggestive notion, however, is that Gates not only seems to misunderstand the issue of privacy in language and philosophy, but also seems to fail to comprehend the nature of Black English Vernacular as a natural language.

He bases his understanding of this language on a nineteenth-century magazine article by a writer named James A. Harrison, who asserted that "the poetic and multiform messages which nature sends him [the Afro-American] through his auditory nerve" are reproduced, in words, by the Afro-American (p. 95). Gates takes Harrison's claims seriously, assuming that there is a fundamental physiological difference between the linguistic behavior of Afro-Americans and other human beings: "One did not believe one's eyes, were one black; one believed [presumably on the basis of the Afro-American's direct auditory contact with nature] . . . one's ears" (p. 109). On the basis of such problematical linguistic and cultural assumptions as the foregoing, Gates proposes that Black English Vernacular was essentially musical, poetical, spoken discourse generated by means other than those employed to generate standard English and maintained by Afro-Americans as a code of symbolic inversion.

There are reasons for studying the process of symbolic, linguistic inversion in Afro-American culture, and, indeed, for studying the relationship between the tonal characteristics of African languages (which is what both Harrison and Gates have in mind when they say "musical") in relationship to Afro-American speech. Such study, however, should not be grounded on the assertions of Wole Soyinka, Derek Walcott, or James A. Harrison (Gates's sources). It should be a matter of careful, holistic cultural analysis that summons as evidence a large, historical body of informed comment and scholarship on Black English Vernacular. A beginning has been made in this direction by Henderson in his previously mentioned essay "The Question of Form and Judgment," which commences with the assumption that a discussion of Afro-American poetry (whether written in "dialect" or in standard English) must be based on sound historical notions of Black English Vernacular resulting from detailed research.[45]

---

ual worldview (under the aspect of "privacy") determines, or fashions, its own peculiar language. [Au.]

[44]Umberto Eco, *A Theory of Semiotics* (Bloomington: Indiana University Press, 1976), pp. 6–7. [Au.]

[45]This is not, however, an injunction to regard Henderson as an expert on Black English Vernacular as a subject of study *in itself.* For such expert testimony one must turn to the work of Geneva Smitherman, William Labov, and others. A good beginning, of course, is Lorenzo Turner's pioneering study *Africanisms in the Gullah Dialect.* [Au.]

Neither Gates nor Stepto, who are the principal spokesmen for the new theoretical prospect in *Afro-American Literature*, has undertaken the detailed research in various domains of Afro-American culture that leads to adequate theoretical formulations. Stepto's stipulations on the ontology of a pregeneric myth from which all Afro-American cultural "structures" originate are just as problematical as Gates's notions of a generative, artistic "point of consciousness" whose "literary uses of language" are independent of "social institutions." The narrowness of Stepto's conception of the "literary" forces him to adopt "nonliterary" criteria in his reading of *Up From Slavery*. And the instability of Gates's views of language and culture forces him to relinquish his advocacy for a synchronic, close reading of literary utterances when he comes to discuss Afro-American dialect poetry. Social institutions, and far more than "literary" criteria, are implied when he asserts:

> When using a word we wake into resonance, as it were, its entire previous history. A text is embedded in specific historical time; it has what linguists call a diachronic structure. To read fully is to restore all that one can of immediacies of value and intent in which speech actually occurs. (p. 114)

Here, contextualization, rethinking the "intent" of the speaker, and "institutional" considerations are all advocated in a way that hardly seems opposed to the critical strategies of the Black Aesthetic.

To concentrate exclusively on the shortcomings and contradictions of Stepto and Gates, however, is to minimize their achievements. For both writers have suggested, in stimulating ways, that Afro-American literature can be incorporated into a contemporary universe of literary-theoretical discourse. True, the terms on which they propose incorporation amount in one instance to a theology of literacy and, in another, to a mysterious semiotics of literary consciousness. Nonetheless, the very act of proposing that a sound, theoretical orientation toward an Afro-American literary tradition is necessary constitutes a logical second step after the paradigmatic establishment of that tradition by the Black Aesthetic.

Furthermore, Stepto and Gates are both better critics than theoreticians. Hence, they provide interpretations of texts that are, at times, quite striking. (Gates's reflections on structuralism and his structuralist reading of the *Narrative of the Life of Frederick Douglass* are quite provocative.) In addition, neither is so imprisoned by his theoretical claims that he refuses to acknowledge the claims of radically competing theories. For example, the essay by Sherley Anne Williams entitled "The Blues Roots of Contemporary Afro-American Poetry" (pp. 72–87) that appears in *Afro-American Literature* is based on the work of Henderson and stands in direct contrast in its methodology to the stipulations on written, non-institutional, literary art adduced by Stepto and Gates. And although Robert Hemenway, in his fine essay on Zora Neale Hurston's relationship to Afro-American folk processes (pp. 122–52), makes a gallant attempt to join the camp of Stepto and Gates, his work finally suggests the type of linguistic, expressive continuum implied by Henderson rather than the segmented model of Gates. Finally, Robert O'Meally's brilliant essay on Frederick Douglass's *Narrative* (pp. 192–211) is antithetical at every turn to Stepto's notion that critical "literacy" is a function of the reader's understanding of written "metaphor," or inscribed instances of "poetic rhetoric *in isolatio*" (p. 9). For it is O'Meally's agile contextualizing of Douglass's work within the continuum of Afro-American verbal behavior that enables him to provide a reading of the work that suggests "intertextual" possibilities that are far more engaging than those suggested by Stepto's own reading of the *Narrative* (pp. 178–91).

In his editorial capacity, therefore, Stepto has rendered a service to the scholarly community by refusing to allow his theory of the "literary" to foreclose the inclusion of essays that contradict, or sharply qualify, his own explicit claims. Unfortunately, he and his coeditor did not work as effectively in their choice of course designs — the models of "reconstructed" instruction toward which the whole of *Afro-American Literature* is directed (if we are to believe the volume's title). Briefly, the section entitled "Afro-American Literature Course Designs" reflects all of the theoretical confusions that have been surveyed heretofore. There are models for courses based on weak distinctions between "literary" and "socio-historical" principles (p. 237); the assumption that literature is an "act of language" (p. 234); the notion that the "oral tradition is . . . a language with a grammar, a syntax, and standards of eloquence of its own" (p. 237); the idea that folk forms are "literary" genres (p. 246); and, finally, the assumption that "interdisciplinary" status can be achieved merely by bringing together different forms of art rather than by summoning methods and models from an array of intellectual disciplines (pp. 250–55). The concluding course designs, thus, capture the novelty and promise, as well as the shortcomings, of the new theoretical prospect. The types of distinctions, concerns, and endeavors they suggest are, indeed, significant for the future study of Afro-American literature and verbal art. What they lack — i.e., sound theories of ordinary and literary discourse, an adequate theory of semantics, and a comprehensive theory of reading — will, one hopes, be provided in time by scholars of Afro-American literature who are as persuaded as the reconstructionists that the Afro-American literary tradition can, indeed, withstand sharp critical scrutiny and can survive (as a subject of study) the limitations of early attempts at its literary-theoretical comprehension.

## VIII

In *Ideology and Utopia*, Karl Mannheim writes:

> To-day we have arrived at the point where we can see clearly that there are differences in modes of thought, not only in different historical periods but also in different cultures. Slowly it dawns upon us that not only does the content of thought change but also its categorical structure. Only very recently has it become possible to investigate the hypothesis that, in the past as well as the present, the dominant modes of thought are supplanted by new categories when the social basis of the group of which these thought-forms are characteristic disintegrates or is transformed under the impact of social change.[46]

The generational shifts discussed in the preceding pages attest the accuracy of Mannheim's observation. The notion of "generational shift," as I have defined it, begins with the assumption that changes in the "categorical structure" of thought are coextensive with social change. The literary-theoretical goal of an analysis deriving from the concept of generational shifts is a "systematic and total formulation" of problems of Afro-American literary study. For only by investigating the guiding assumptions (the "categories" of thought, as it were) of recent Afro-American literary criticism can one gain a sense of the virtues and limitations of what have stood during the past four decades as opposing generational paradigms. What emerges from such an investigation is, first, a realization of the socially and generationally conditioned selectivity, or partiality, of such paradigms. They can be as meetly defined by their exclusions as by their manifest content. The quasi-political rhetoric of the Black Aesthetic seems to compete (at its weakest points) with the quasi-religious and semiotic jargon of the reconstructionists for a kind of flawed critical ascendancy.

Yet what also emerges from an investigation of generational shifts in recent Afro-American literary criticism is the sense that this criticism has progressed during the past forty years to a point where some "systematic" formulation of theoretical problems is possible. The extremism and shortsightedness of recent generations have been counterbalanced, that is to say, by their serious dedication to the analysis of an object that did not even exist in the world prior to the mid-sixties. The perceptual reorientations of recent generations have served as enabling conditions for a "mode of thought" that takes the theoretical investigation of a unique tradition of *Afro-American literature* as a normative enterprise.

Given the foregoing discussion, it is perhaps clear that my own preference where such theoretical investigation is concerned is the kind of

***

[46]*Ideology and Utopia: An Introduction to the Sociology of Knowledge* (New York: Harcourt, Brace, 1936), pp. 82–83. My reading in "ideology" and the "sociology of knowl-

edge" prompted this essay on generational shifts. It seemed appropriate to situate the discussion within its proper ambit as a means of concluding. [Au.]

holistic, cultural-anthropological approach that is implicit in the work of Henderson and other spokesmen for the Black Aesthetic. This does not mean, however, that I seek to minimize the importance of the necessary and forceful call that the reconstructionists have issued for serious literary-theoretical endeavors on the part of Afro-Americanists. Still, I am persuaded that at this juncture in the progress of critical generations the theoretical prospect that I call the "anthropology of art" is the most realistic and fruitful approach to the future study of Afro-American literature and culture.[47] The guiding assumption of the anthropology of art is coextensive with the basic tenets of the Black Aesthetic insofar as both prospects assert that works of Afro-American literature and verbal art can not be adequately understood unless they are contextualized within the interdependent systems of Afro-American culture. But the anthropology of art *departs from both the Black Aesthetic and the reconstructionist prospects in its assumption that art can not be studied without serious attention to the methods and models of many disciplines*. The contextual-

ization of a work of literary or verbal art, from the perspective of the anthropology of art, is an "interdisciplinary" enterprise in the most contemporary sense of that word. Rather than ignoring (or denigrating) the research and insights of scholars in the natural, social, and behavioral sciences, the anthropology of art views such efforts as positive, rational attempts to comprehend the full dimensions of human behavior. And such efforts serve the literary-theoretical investigator as guides and contributions to an understanding of the symbolic dimensions of human behavior that comprise Afro-American literature and verbal art.

In his essay "Ideology as a Cultural System," Clifford Geertz writes: "The sociology of knowledge ought to be called the sociology of meaning, for what is socially determined is not the nature of conception but the vehicles of conception."[48] I think the anthropology of art stands today not only as a "vehicle of conception" rich in theoretical possibilities, but also as a "categorical structure" that may signal a next generational shift in the criticism of Afro-American literature.

---

[47]In *The Journey Back: Issues in Black Literature and Criticism*, I discuss the assumptions and methodology of this approach to literary study. [Au.]

[48]In *The Interpretation of Cultures: Selected Essays by Clifford Geertz* (New York: Basic Books, 1973), p. 212. [Au.]

# 9

# ISSUE UNDER DEBATE: AUTHORIAL INTENTION

*The poem is not the critic's own and not the author's (it is detached from the author at birth and goes about the world beyond his power to intend about it or control it). The poem belongs to the public. It is embodied in language, the peculiar possession of the public.*

— WILLIAM K. WIMSATT AND MONROE C. BEARDSLEY

*In ["The Intentional Fallacy"] the position was taken . . . that the text, being public, means what the speech community takes it to mean. This position is, in an ethical sense, right . . . : if the author has bungled so badly that his utterance will be misconstrued, then it serves him right when people misunderstand him. However, put in linguistic terms, the position becomes unsatisfactory.*

— E. D. HIRSCH

*I am not suggesting that a literary work has only one possible reading. . . . What I am suggesting is that a theory of interpretation must account for the fact that we do draw a distinction between a possible and a correct interpretation, even if we may not agree in any given case what the correct reading is.*

— P. D. JUHL

*As long as one thinks that a position on intention (either for or against) makes a difference in achieving valid interpretations, the ideal of theory itself is saved. Theory wins. But as soon as we recognize that there are no theoretical choices to be made, then the point of theory vanishes. Theory loses.*

— STEVEN KNAPP AND WALTER BENN MICHAELS

Unlike the issue of the canon, the debate over authorial intention and its relation to literary meaning is quite new. For most of the first two thousand years of literary theory, texts were naively assumed to be the product of the intention of the author, and simple readers and sophisticated critics alike spoke fearlessly about what, for example, Pope had meant to say in his "Epistle to Arbuthnot." Poets were attacked for their ideas and defended themselves, unaware that the *I* of the poem might represent anyone unconnected with themselves. Up through the nineteenth century, narrative poems and dramatic monologues were popular literary forms, and no one seems to have experienced any problems in distinguishing between characters meant to represent their authors (like the *I* of "Tintern Abbey") and those who represented an Other (like the Duke in "My Last Duchess").

With the emergence of both modernism and the New Criticism, however, the picture grew more complicated. The most prestigious products of modernism, like T. S. Eliot's "Love Song of J. Alfred Prufrock" or James Joyce's *Portrait of the Artist as a Young Man,* portrayed characters whose relationship to the author was strangely ambiguous, for they were treated with an ironic detachment that might betoken affection or scorn or some unpredictable combination of attitudes. Poets like William Butler Yeats spoke of the characters in their poems as "masks," and Ezra Pound called one of his volumes *Personae,* after the Greek word for the mask that both hid the tragic actor and amplified his voice.

These modernist innovations, which created an intensely but impersonally dramatic poetry and fiction, were, in effect, "read back" through the centuries of literary history by the New Critics, who claimed that the speaker in "Epistle to Arbuthnot" was not Pope but "Pope," a dramatic character created by the poet of the same name. Eventually, this critical practice and others like it prevailed and were codified in "The Intentional Fallacy" (1946), by William K. Wimsatt and Monroe Beardsley.

In 1946, Wimsatt and Beardsley were addressing a critical scene very different from today's, one in which the principal research of the university professor was historical scholarship rather than interpretation. In this context, "The Intentional Fallacy" was one of the major implements by which hegemony passed from literary history to interpretive criticism, for it called into question — successfully, at the time — some of the philosophical bases underlying historical research. Philologists presumed that the meaning of the text depended principally on the intention of the author and that research into the author's life and works — letters and papers, the literary, social, and political scene — was necessary to glean the best possible sense of those intentions. Wimsatt and Beardsley set historical scholars a simple dilemma: If authorial intentions had been successfully embodied in a text, then textual meaning — available through the public conventions of language — would yield all the critic needed. But if this were so, then what would external evidence add to knowledge? If a poem plainly meant A, then what would be the status of (say) a letter by the author claiming that B was intended? Would the letter be more reliable than the text? What if the author had lied or had a change of heart between writing the letter and writing the poem?

But the issue is not just of the reliability of evidence. Historical scholars might be able to discover whether authors had read poems to which their own seemed to allude, but finding the truth would not guarantee its relevance. If an allusion makes sense — if it fits into the formal pattern of the poem — then it functions in the poem whether or not the author intended it. If an allusion makes no sense within that formal pattern, then its presence would make no more difference to the critical act of interpretation than would an ink blot on the manuscript. As Wimsatt and Beardsley suggest, one might consult the oracle, T. S. Eliot himself, and ask if he had been thinking of Donne's "Song" when he wrote line 124 of "Prufrock," but his answer would have only biographical, not critical, significance.

In the twenty years following Wimsatt and Beardsley's essay, the textual autonomy of the New Criticism overshadowed literary scholarship. And when the intentional fallacy was combined with the doctrine that literary works operate by paradox and ambiguity, the result was a growing mass of critical interpretation, much of which would probably appall the authors of the texts. On the one hand, interpretation was governed by public norms of language rather than by a sense of what the author probably intended; on the other hand, literary language was assumed to be intrinsically paradoxical and ambiguous. Since even incomplete dictionaries provide dozens of meanings for even the simplest terms, the number of possible interpretations of a brief lyric poem could be enormous, while really difficult texts, like James's *The Turn of the Screw*, could acquire hundreds of cabalistic commentaries.

By 1967, the stage was set for the next swing of the pendulum, when E. D. Hirsch, in *Validity in Interpretation*, attacked the intentional fallacy on its own philosophical grounds.[1] In effect, Wimsatt and Beardsley had insisted that literature be read according to the public norms of language. Hirsch does not dispute this; he merely points out that because of the variety of possible usages, meaning as a *shared type* is totally indeterminate. Hirsch claims that when there are two interpretations of a given text, both of which are equally consistent with those public norms (and by this point, many texts had accumulated a host of such interpretations), the only objective basis for deciding between them is by referring to authorial intention. Hirsch concedes that many poems are intentionally ambiguous. But the ambiguities that are not *willed* — that are the product of the multiple potential uses of verbal tokens — are irrelevant. If meaning is an affair of consciousness, it must be willed, and when one has the choice between an author's will and his critic's will, between the author's intended meaning and a critic's interpretation, one must choose the author's meaning. There are an indefinite number of critics but only one author. Without privileging authorial meaning, modern philology would perforce descend to the state of Babel.

If interpretation were to become purely a matter of finding the original and authoritative meaning bestowed by the author, it might seem that critics would be out of work. In fact, this need not happen. Hirsch differentiates between what the philosopher Edmund Husserl calls the inner and the outer horizon of textual meaning, and what philosopher Gottlob Frege calls *Sinn* and *Bedeutung*, "meaning" and "significance" — "meaning in" a text and "meaning to or for" an interpreter. For Hirsch, the author's intended meaning is constant, but its significance changes over time. The words of Homer's *Iliad* have the same meaning they had over two and a half millennia ago, but clearly their significance has changed. Twentieth-century critics like Simone Weil have used their experience of World War II and

---

[1] The year 1967 was also the beginning of the end for the "affective fallacy." In that year Norman Holland's *Dynamics of Literary Response* and Stanley Fish's *Surprised by Sin*, major works that insistently defined texts through the principle of audience response, were published.

the Nazi occupation of Europe to deepen readers' appreciation of Homer's epic, but Homer is clearly not talking about World War II; this area belongs to significance, not meaning. We understand the meaning of a satire like Jonathan Swift's "A Modest Proposal" through a consideration of the oppressed state of Ireland in 1729; its significance, however, extends to the modern world. The meaning must remain constant as the significance changes; otherwise, it would hardly make sense to say that a text's significance has altered. If its central meaning were not the same, we should not be calling it the same text.[2]

Hirsch concedes that we cannot always agree on authorial meaning. Not all ambiguities and conflicts of interpretation (on the level of meaning) can be cleared up by reference to the author's letters or diaries and other historical documents. Nevertheless, what we are seeking is a historical fact — the act of authorial intention — and no piece of evidence that bears on it can be ruled out of court by formalist theory. Each interpreter must present the best possible evidence, and the community of scholars must judge between them. In "Objective Interpretation," Hirsch attempts to adjudicate between conflicting interpretations of Wordsworth's "A slumber did my spirit seal" by F. W. Bateson and Cleanth Brooks and shows that though Brooks's interpretation is plausible according to the norms of language, and though it might even be the sort of thing you or I might mean to say, it would not as likely be what someone with the peculiar beliefs of William Wordsworth (particularly his belief in pantheism) would have meant. Bateson's interpretation, though less plausible on its face, less likely to have been intended by the average person, is for that very reason more authentically Wordsworthian.

Since an entire industry had emerged that produced ever more novel and unexpected interpretations of the canonical texts, it is not surprising that Hirsch's demonstration of the need to choose authorial interpretation or descend to chaos did not end the matter. Hirsch's ideas were debated back and forth in the pages of the literary journals. The most complete, careful, and lucid treatment of the issue was produced by the philosopher P. D. Juhl in *Interpretation* (1980).

Juhl essentially concurs with Hirsch's conclusions rather than with those of Wimsatt and Beardsley, but in the process he is forced to dismiss or disprove a great many of Hirsch's theoretical presumptions. Juhl agrees with Hirsch's claim that *meaning* had to mean *authorial meaning* or the game would be lost. But he does not accept the claim that authorial meaning has to be privileged over any rival meanings to avoid the chaos that might result if it was not. Juhl was particularly scornful of the idea that one must privilege authorial meaning or risk losing all objective basis for discriminating between one interpretation of a text and another. If settling conflicts were the only issue, mere priority would serve, or a tribunal of critics could pass final judgment on the readings of texts. According to Juhl, we should give authorial meaning privileged status in trying to discriminate between

---

[2]Since 1967, Hirsch has changed his mind somewhat about the boundaries between meaning and significance. See "Meaning and Significance Reinterpreted," *Critical Inquiry* 11 (1984): 202–25 and the reply by James L. Battersby and James Phelan, "Meaning as Concept and as Extension: Some Problems," *Critical Inquiry* 12(1986): 605–15.

rival interpretations of a text because texts are speech acts, like all our other utterances in the course of a lifetime, and we interpret poems and novels by exactly the same rules: by examining the language — and any other signs we can find — for evidence of the speaker's intention. Juhl's rejection of the anti-intentionalist position of Wimsatt and Beardsley rests on the speech-act theory of John Searle and H. P. Grice and turns on the difference between a *sentence* and an *utterance*.

Wimsatt and Beardsley had rightly claimed that a sentence such as "I like my secretary better than my wife" can, by the public norms of language, be ambiguous; it can mean either that the speaker prefers his secretary to his wife, or that he likes his secretary better than his wife does. To find out which, we could ask the speaker. For Beardsley and Wimsatt, finding out that he meant the latter would clear up the question of intention, but it would leave the sentence as ambiguous as before. Juhl agrees that the *sentence* is and must always remain ambiguous, but he insists that once the speaker has made his intention clear, his previous *utterance* of that sentence has now become an unambiguous speech act. And utterances are what count. Someone else might easily have used the words of "A slumber did my spirit seal" to mean precisely what Brooks claimed the poem meant; but the question of literary interpretation is not what those sentences *might* have meant but what Wordsworth's utterance of those sentences *did* mean. On the evidence, Juhl agrees that Bateson was closer than Brooks to expressing what Wordsworth meant by that utterance as a speech act. In the final chapter of *Interpretation,* reprinted here, Juhl sets out to explain why, though literary works have one and only one correct interpretation (one *meaning* in Hirsch's sense), critics are unlikely to agree on that interpretation, and why such texts are likely to be construed in a number of mutually incompatible ways.

Juhl's book did not end the matter any more than Hirsch's did. The latest turn of the screw is provided by Steven Knapp and Walter Benn Michaels in "Against Theory" (1982). Knapp and Michaels's target is not just Hirsch and Juhl, or even the defense of authorial meaning; it is *theory* itself, defined as "the attempt to govern interpretations of particular texts by appealing to an account of interpretation in general." Their argument — that theory is futile — falls into two parts: First, they attack what they call the ontological side of theory for

> imagining a mode of language devoid of intention. . . . This strange ontological project is always in the service of an epistemological goal. That goal is . . . the governance of interpretive practice by some larger and more principled account. . . . If the ontological project of theory has been to imagine a condition of language before intention, its epistemological project has been to imagine a condition of knowledge before interpretation.[3]

Then they mount an epistemological attack on theory, which seems to refute Stanley Fish's argument about the controlling force of the reader's beliefs in interpretation. But far from disagreeing with Fish, Knapp and Michaels argue that Fish did not go far enough. They challenge Fish's own beliefs and their influence

[3]*Against Theory,* p. 1433.

on his theory about the role of beliefs, and in effect, they accuse Fish of trying to argue the necessity of prior beliefs from a position that locates him outside and above that necessity.[4] But all theory, not just that of Fish, would be a target for this argument, which is an extension of Fish's final comment in "Interpreting the *Variorum*" (Ch. 7): "You will agree with me only if you already agree with me." We will find an interpretation, or a theory of interpretation, persuasive if it agrees with our previous beliefs and unpersuasive if it does not. But if this is so, then there is no point to theory, since far from constraining interpretation, it appeals only to those who are already convinced.

In the first part of their argument, which is most directly relevant to this discussion, Knapp and Michaels make a similar sort of case against the ideas about authorial intention of Hirsch, Juhl, and Paul de Man — in effect, accusing them of separating things that cannot be separated and later joining them. Hirsch, for example, treats language and intention as if they were different things, although language would not even be recognized as language without the prior assumption of intention. Similarly, Juhl first treats language and speech acts as separable, then joins them, when in fact any piece of language will automatically be interpreted as a speech act. In contrast, poststructuralists like de Man feel that meaning can exist in the absence of intention. As Knapp and Michaels state,

> The issue in both cases is the presence or absence of intention: the positive theorist [Hirsch and Juhl] adds intention; the negative theorist subtracts it. In our view, however, the relation between meaning and intention, or, in slightly different terms, between language and speech acts is such that intention can neither be added to nor subtracted from language because language consists of speech acts which are also always intentional. Since language has intention already built into it, no recommendation about what to do with intention has any bearing on the question of how to interpret any utterance or text.[5]

What they are suggesting is that Hirsch and Juhl are arguing over a nonproblem, a conclusion that might be more tenable if the literary scene had not witnessed so much vituperative controversy over that very nonproblem during the forty years between "The Intentional Fallacy" and "Against Theory." In fact, what Hirsch and Juhl had been trying to do was to put authorial intent and meaning, or language and speech act, back together again; they were certainly not artificially separating them as an academic exercise.

If Knapp and Michaels's ontological argument seems poorly motivated, there is still the epistemological argument that the theories of Hirsch and Juhl constitute beliefs about meaning and intention, which no one is constrained to accept. As

---

[4]Fish would surely admit that when he talks about *texts* he is as precommitted to interpretation by prior belief as anyone else. His argument about the necessity of beliefs is on the *metacritical* level (talk about how we talk) and not on the critical level. For Knapp and Michaels, this is a distinction without a difference.

[5]*Against Theory,* p. 24. "Against Theory 2: Hermeneutics and Deconstruction" [*Critical Inquiry* 14 (1987): 49–68] advances even more extreme views — that meaning is determined solely by intention and not by linguistic convention at all. One is tempted to ask, with Wittgenstein (*Philosophical Investigations,* I, 38): "Can I say 'bububu' and mean 'If it doesn't rain I shall go for a walk'? — It is only in a language that I can mean something by something."

Knapp and Michaels argue, positing that literary texts are speech acts or that meaning is different from significance will solve the problems of literary interpretation only if it reinforces previously held beliefs about meaning or speech acts or interpretation. For them, there is no exit: Nothing can be solved by attacking the problem at a higher level of discourse. We have beliefs, beliefs about beliefs, beliefs about beliefs about beliefs, beliefs all the way up. No direct refutation is possible, for no matter what one says, Knapp and Michaels can reply, "So you believe. . . ." What the reader of "Against Theory" will have to decide in the long run is whether belief systems are as hermetically sealed against persuasion as they imply, or whether it is possible, on the contrary, to get outside one's own belief system long enough to see what it looks like, to try other systems, to change one's mind.

Those who accept the arguments in "Against Theory" as valid also have to decide just how much of the "project" of critical theory is vitiated by such arguments — how much of the critical theory contained in this anthology, from Plato to Juhl, conforms to Knapp and Michaels's notions of what that "project" is. As Adena Rosmarin wrote in one of the many rebuttals that "Against Theory" generated,

> intention and belief have been and are central to certain theoretical arguments . . . but they are by no means central to all. Many have thought that literary meaning is grounded in or, what is the same, explained by what it imitates. Such mimetic objects include not only authorial intention but also ideas, actions, "general nature," the feelings or imagination of the poet, and mental and natural processes. Others have thought that literary meaning is explained by its internal structures, or by the activity of reading, or by convention systems. Unless Plato, Plotinus, Aristotle, Johnson, Wordsworth, Shelley, Coleridge, Holland, Iser, and Culler . . . are to be seen as not doing theory, then arguing against "theory in general" by arguing against intention and belief must be less than persuasive.[6]

If "Against Theory" proposes an argument that, even if accepted at face value, would not fulfill its claims to destroy the rationale of literary theory in general, why did it generate the sort of interest it did? Why was it published by a major critical journal, and why did that journal devote over a hundred pages in subsequent issues to a dozen rebuttals or defenses of its reasoning or its premises? Perhaps "Against Theory" should be seen, as Plato saw his dialogues, less as a piece of philosophy than as an *occasion* for philosophy. Whatever its merit in itself, the essay generated and continues to generate a great deal of light as theorists from all quarters, in arguing against its rebarbative propositions, learned what theory is and where they themselves stand. "Against Theory," like many poems, is valuable because of what it brings out in its readers. But in another sense, the significance of "Against Theory" is sociological as well as philosophical. "Against Theory" was written at the right time, when "theory" had become the most prestigious of academic specialties and a suitable target for a pinprick. And it was not merely a

[6]Adena Rosmarin, "The Theory of 'Against Theory,'" in *Against Theory*, p. 83.

lot of grumbling by one of the many scholars who wish theory would go away, but a *theorist's* antitheoretical essay — and therefore part of a tradition. As W. J. T. Mitchell points out, "the antitheoretical polemic is one of the characteristic gestures of theoretical discourse: the philosophy of science has Paul Feyerabend's *Against Method*; Marxist criticism has E. P. Thompson's *Poverty of Theory*."[7] "Against Theory," whatever one thinks of it, was at least inevitable.

## Selected Bibliography

Austin, J. L. *How to Do Things with Words*. Cambridge: Harvard University Press, 1962.

Beardsley, Monroe C. "The Limits of Critical Interpretation." In *Art and Philosophy: A Symposium*. New York: New York University Press, 1966.

Booth, Wayne C. *A Rhetoric of Irony*. Chicago: University of Chicago Press, 1974.

Cavell, Stanley. "Aesthetic Problems of Modern Philosophy." In *Must We Mean What We Say?* New York: Charles Scribner's Sons, 1969.

Child, Arthur. *Interpretation: A General Theory*. Berkeley: University of California Press, 1965.

Cioffi, F. "Intention and Interpretation in Criticism." In *Collected Papers on Aesthetics*. Oxford: Blackwell, 1965.

Davis, Walter A. *The Act of Interpretation: A Critique of Literary Reason*. Chicago: University of Chicago Press, 1978.

De Molina, David Newton. *On Literary Intention: Critical Essays*. Edinburgh: Edinburgh University Press, 1976.

Eaton, Marcia M. "Good and Correct Interpretations of Literature." *Journal of Aesthetics and Art Criticism* 29 (1970): 227–33.

Ellis, John M. *Theory of Literary Criticism: A Logical Analysis*. Berkeley: University of California Press, 1974.

Freedman, Ralph. "Intentionality and the Literary Object." In *Directions for Criticism: Structuralism and Its Alternatives,* ed. Murray Krieger and L. S. Dembo. Madison: University of Wisconsin Press, 1976.

Frege, Gottlob. "On Sense and Reference." In *Philosophical Writings of Gottlob Frege*. Oxford: Blackwell, 1952.

Gadamer, Hans-Georg. *Truth and Method*. New York: Continuum Press, 1982.

Grice, H. P. "Utterer's Meaning and Intentions." *Philosophical Review* 78 (1969): 147–77.

Hampshire, Stuart. "On Referring and Intending." In *Freedom of Mind*. Princeton: Princeton University Press, 1971.

Hancher, Michael. "Three Kinds of Intention." *Modern Language Notes* 87 (1972): 827–51.

Hempel, Carl G., and Paul Oppenheim. "The Logic of Explanation." In *Readings in the Philosophy of Science*, ed. Herbert Feigl and May Brodbeck. New York: Appleton-Century-Crofts, 1953.

Hirsch, E. D. *Validity in Interpretation*. New Haven: Yale University Press, 1967.

Hungerland, I. C. *Poetic Discourse*. Berkeley: University of California Press, 1958.

Ingarden, Roman. *The Literary Work of Art: An Investigation on the Borderlines of Ontol-*

---

[7]See W. J. T. Mitchell, ed., *Against Theory: Literary Studies and the New Pragmatism* (Chicago: University of Chicago Press, 1985), p. 2.

*ogy, Logic, and Theory of Literature*. Evanston, Ill.: Northwestern University Press, 1973.

Juhl, P. D. *Interpretation: An Essay in the Philosophy of Literary Criticism*. Princeton: Princeton University Press, 1980.

Kermode, Frank. "Can We Say Absolutely Anything We Like?" In *Art, Politics, and Will: Essays in Honor of Lionel Trilling*. New York: Basic Books, 1977.

Kuhns, Richard. "Semantics for Literary Languages." *New Literary History* 4 (1972): 91–105.

Lohner, Edgar. "The Intrinsic Method: Some Limitations." In *The Disciplines of Criticism*, ed. Peter Demetz et al. New Haven: Yale University Press, 1968.

Meiland, Jack W. *The Nature of Intention*. London: Methuen, 1970.

Mitchell, W. J. T., ed. *Against Theory: Literary Studies and the New Pragmatism*. Chicago: University of Chicago Press, 1985.

Palmer, Richard E. *Hermeneutics: Interpretation Theory in Schleiermacher, Dilthey, Heidegger, and Gadamer*. Evanston, Ill.: Northwestern University Press, 1969.

Pratt, Mary Louise. *Toward a Speech Act Theory of Literary Discourse*. Bloomington: Indiana University Press, 1977.

Reichert, John F. "Description and Interpretation in Literary Criticism." *Journal of Aesthetics and Art Criticism* 27 (1969): 281–92.

Searle, John R. "The Logical Status of Fictional Discourse." *New Literary History* 6 (1974): 319–32.

Strawson, Peter F. "Intention and Convention in Speech Acts." In *The Philosophy of Language*, ed. John R. Searle. London: Oxford University Press, 1971.

Weitz, Morris. *Problems in Aesthetics*. New York: Macmillan, 1970.

Wimsatt, William K., and Monroe C. Beardsley. "The Intentional Fallacy." In *The Verbal Icon: Studies in the Meaning of Poetry*. Lexington: University Press of Kentucky, 1954.

Wittgenstein, Ludwig. *Philosophical Investigations*. New York: Macmillan, 1968.

# W. K. Wimsatt and

1907–1975

# Monroe C. Beardsley

1915–1985

*Of the three important essays on which W. K. Wimsatt and Monroe C. Beardsley collaborated, "The Intentional Fallacy" (1946) is probably the most celebrated. The premier heresy hunter among the New Critics, William Kurtz Wimsatt was born in Washington, D.C., and educated at Georgetown University and at Yale, where he took his Ph.D. in 1939 and taught until his death. Yale published his dissertation,* The Prose Style of Samuel Johnson, *in 1941. In addition to other works on Samuel Johnson and Alexander Pope, Wimsatt is also the author of* The Verbal Icon *(1954),* Literary Criticism: A Short History *(with Cleanth Brooks, 1957),* Hateful Contraries *(1965), and* The Day of the Leopards *(1976), a bitter response to contemporary trends in life and letters. Wimsatt argued for a "tensional" criticism that would avoid the intentional, affective, genetic, and stylistic "fallacies." Like Shelley, he found the value of poetry in its mystical incarnation, through metaphor, of relations and connections within reality. The formalist aesthetician Monroe Curtis Beardsley was born in Bridgeport, Connecticut, and educated at Yale (B.A., 1936; Ph.D., 1939). He taught philosophy there before moving on to Mt. Holyoke College (1944–46), Swarthmore College (1947–69), and finally Temple University. Beardsley's books include* Aesthetics from Classical Greece to the Present *(1966),* Aesthetic Inquiry *(1967), and* The Possibility of Criticism *(1970). The text of "The Intentional Fallacy" is taken from the version reprinted in* The Verbal Icon.

# The Intentional Fallacy

## I

The claim of the author's "intention" upon the critic's judgment has been challenged in a number of recent discussions, notably in the debate entitled *The Personal Heresy,* between Professors Lewis and Tillyard. But it seems doubtful if this claim and most of its romantic corollaries are as yet subject to any widespread questioning. The present writers, in a short article entitled "Intention" for a *Dictionary*[1] of literary criticism, raised the issue but were unable to pursue its implications at any length. We argued that the design or intention of the author is neither available nor desirable as a standard for judging the success of a work of literary art, and it seems to us that this is a principle which goes deep into some differences in the history of critical attitudes. It is a principle which accepted or rejected points to the polar opposites of classical "imitation" and romantic expression. It entails many specific truths about inspiration, authenticity, biography, literary history and scholarship, and about some trends of contemporary poetry, especially its allusiveness. There is hardly a problem of literary criticism in which the critic's approach will not be qualified by his view of "intention."

"Intention," as we shall use the term, corresponds to *what he intended* in a formula which more or less explicitly has had wide acceptance. "In order to judge the poet's performance, we must know *what he intended.*" Intention is design or plan in the author's mind. Intention has ob-

vious affinities for the author's attitude toward his work, the way he felt, what made him write.

We begin our discussion with a series of propositions summarized and abstracted to a degree where they seem to us axiomatic.

1. A poem does not come into existence by accident. The words of a poem, as Professor Stoll has remarked, come out of a head, not out of a hat. Yet to insist on the designing intellect as a *cause* of a poem is not to grant the design or intention as a *standard* by which the critic is to judge the worth of the poet's performance.

2. One must ask how a critic expects to get an answer to the question about intention. How is he to find out what the poet tried to do? If the poet succeeded in doing it, then the poem itself shows what he was trying to do. And if the poet did not succeed, then the poem is not adequate evidence, and the critic must go outside the poem — for evidence of an intention that did not become effective in the poem. "Only one *caveat* must be borne in mind," says an eminent intentionalist[2] in a moment when his theory repudiates itself; "the poet's aim must be judged at the moment of the creative act, that is to say, by the art of the poem itself."

3. Judging a poem is like judging a pudding or a machine. One demands that it work. It is only because an artifact works that we infer the intention of an artificer. "A poem should not mean but be."[3] A poem can *be* only through its *meaning* — since its medium is words — yet it

[1]*Dictionary of World Literature,* ed. Joseph T. Shipley (New York, 1942), pp. 326–29. [Au.]

[2]J. E. Spingarn, "The New Criticism," in *Criticism in America* (New York, 1924), pp. 24–25. [Au.]
[3]Archibald MacLeish in "Ars Poetica." [Ed.]

*is*, simply *is*, in the sense that we have no excuse for inquiring what part is intended or meant. Poetry is a feat of style by which a complex of meaning is handled all at once. Poetry succeeds because all or most of what is said or implied is relevant; what is irrelevant has been excluded, like lumps from pudding and "bugs" from machinery. In this respect poetry differs from practical messages, which are successful if and only if we correctly infer the intention. They are more abstract than poetry.

4. The meaning of a poem may certainly be a personal one, in the sense that a poem expresses a personality or state of soul rather than a physical object like an apple. But even a short lyric poem is dramatic, the response of a speaker (no matter how abstractly conceived) to a situation (no matter how universalized). We ought to impute the thoughts and attitudes of the poem immediately to the dramatic *speaker,* and if to the author at all, only by an act of biographical inference.

5. There is a sense in which an author, by revision, may better achieve his original intention. But it is a very abstract sense. He intended to write a better work, or a better work of a certain kind, and now has done it. But it follows that his former concrete intention was not his intention. "He's the man we were in search of, that's true," says Hardy's rustic constable, "and yet he's not the man we were in search of. For the man we were in search of was not the man we wanted."

"Is not a critic," asks Professor Stoll, "a judge, who does not explore his own consciousness, but determines the author's meaning or intention, as if the poem were a will, a contract, or the constitution? The poem is not the critic's own." He has accurately diagnosed two forms of irresponsibility, one of which he prefers. Our view is yet different. The poem is not the critic's own and not the author's (it is detached from the author at birth and goes about the world beyond his power to intend about it or control it). The poem belongs to the public. It is embodied in language, the peculiar possession of the public, and it is about the human being, an object of public knowledge. What is said about the poem

is subject to the same scrutiny as any statement in linguistics or in the general science of psychology.

A critic of our *Dictionary* article, Ananda K. Coomaraswamy, has argued[4] that there are two kinds of inquiry about a work of art: (1) whether the artist achieved his intentions; (2) whether the work of art "ought ever to have been undertaken at all" and so "whether it is worth preserving." Number (2), Coomaraswamy maintains, is not "criticism of any work of art *qua* work of art," but is rather moral criticism; number (1) is artistic criticism. But we maintain that (2) need not be moral criticism: that there is another way of deciding whether works of art are worth preserving and whether, in a sense, they "ought" to have been undertaken, and this is the way of objective criticism of works of art as such, the way which enables us to distinguish between a skillful murder and a skillful poem. A skillful murder is an example which Coomaraswamy uses, and in his system the difference between the murder and the poem is simply a "moral" one, not an "artistic" one, since each if carried out according to plan is "artistically" successful. We maintain that (2) is an inquiry of more worth than (1), and since (2) and not (1) is capable of distinguishing poetry from murder, the name "artistic criticism" is properly given to (2).

## II

It is not so much a historical statement as a definition to say that the intentional fallacy is a romantic one. When a rhetorician of the first century A.D. writes: "Sublimity is the echo of a great soul," or when he tells us that "Homer enters into the sublime actions of his heroes" and "shares the full inspiration of the combat," we shall not be surprised to find this rhetorician considered as a distant harbinger of romanticism and greeted in the warmest terms by Saintsbury.[5] One may wish to argue whether Longinus should be

[4]Ananda K. Coomaraswamy, "Intention," in *American Bookman* I (1944), pp. 41–48. [Au.]

[5]The rhetorician is Longinus; see "On the Sublime," p. 80. [Ed.]

called romantic, but there can hardly be a doubt that in one important way he is.

Goethe's three questions for "constructive criticism" are "What did the author set out to do? Was his plan reasonable and sensible, and how far did he succeed in carrying it out?" If one leaves out the middle question, one has in effect the system of Croce — the culmination and crowning philosophic expression of romanticism. The beautiful is the successful intuition-expression, and the ugly is the unsuccessful; the intuition or private part of art is *the* aesthetic fact, and the medium or public part is not the subject of aesthetic at all.[6]

> The Madonna of Cimabue is still in the Church of Santa Maria Novella; but does she speak to the visitor of to-day as to the Florentines of the thirteenth century?

> *Historical interpretation* labours . . . to reintegrate in us the psychological conditions which have changed in the course of history. It . . . enables us to see a work of art (a physical object) as its *author saw it* in the moment of production.[7]

The first italics are Croce's, the second ours. The upshot of Croce's system is an ambiguous emphasis on history. With such passages as a point of departure a critic may write a nice analysis of the meaning or "spirit" of a play by Shakespeare or Corneille — a process that involves close historical study but remains aesthetic criticism — or he may, with equal plausibility, produce an essay in sociology, biography, or other kinds of nonaesthetic history.

## III

> I went to the poets; tragic, dithyrambic, and all sorts. . . . I took them some of the most elaborate passages in their own writings, and asked what was

the meaning of them. . . . Will you believe me? . . . there is hardly a person present who would not have talked better about their poetry than they did themselves. Then I knew that not by wisdom do poets write poetry, but by a sort of genius and inspiration.[8]

That reiterated mistrust of the poets which we hear from Socrates may have been part of a rigorously ascetic view in which we hardly wish to participate, yet Plato's Socrates saw a truth about the poetic mind which the world no longer commonly sees — so much criticism, and that the most inspirational and most affectionately remembered, has proceeded from the poets themselves.

Certainly the poets have had something to say that the critic and professor could not say; their message has been more exciting: that poetry should come as naturally as leaves to a tree, that poetry is the lava of the imagination, or that it is emotion recollected in tranquillity. But it is necessary that we realize the character and authority of such testimony. There is only a fine shade of difference between such expressions and a kind of earnest advice that authors often give. Thus Edward Young, Carlyle, Walter Pater:

> I know two golden rules from *ethics,* which are no less golden in *Composition,* than in life. 1. *Know thyself;* 2dly, *Reverence thyself.*

> This is the grand secret for finding readers and retaining them: let him who would move and convince others, be first moved and convinced himself. Horace's rule, *Si vis me flere,* is applicable in a wider sense than the literal one. To every poet, to every writer, we might say: Be true, if you would be believed.

> Truth! there can be no merit, no craft at all, without that. And further, all beauty is in the long run only *fineness* of truth, or what we call expression, the finer accommodation of speech to that vision within.

And Housman's little handbook to the poetic mind yields this illustration:

> Having drunk a pint of beer at luncheon — beer is

[6]See Croce, "Aesthetica in Nuce," p. 449. [Ed.]
[7]It is true that Croce himself in his *Ariosto, Shakespeare and Corneille* (London, 1920), chap. 7, "The Practical Personality and the Poetical Personality," and in his *Defense of Poetry* (Oxford, 1933), p. 24, and elsewhere, early and late, has delivered telling attacks on emotive geneticism, but the main drive of the *Aesthetic* is surely toward a kind of cognitive intentionalism. [Au.]

[8]From the *Apology.* [Ed.]

a sedative to the brain, and my afternoons are the least intellectual portion of my life — I would go out for a walk of two or three hours. As I went along, thinking of nothing in particular, only looking at things around me and following the progress of the seasons, there would flow into my mind, with sudden and unaccountable emotion, sometimes a line or two of verse, sometimes a whole stanza at once.

This is the logical terminus of the series already quoted. Here is a confession of how poems were written which would do as a definition of poetry just as well as "emotion recollected in tranquillity" — and which the young poet might equally well take to heart as a practical rule. Drink a pint of beer, relax, go walking, think on nothing in particular, look at things, surrender yourself to yourself, search for the truth in your own soul, listen to the sound of your own inside voice, discover and express the *vraie vérité*.[9]

It is probably true that all this is excellent advice for poets. The young imagination fired by Wordsworth and Carlyle is probably closer to the verge of producing a poem than the mind of the student who has been sobered by Aristotle or Richards. The art of inspiring poets, or at least of inciting something like poetry in young persons, has probably gone further in our day than ever before. Books of creative writing such as those issued from the Lincoln School are interesting evidence of what a child can do.[10] All this, however, would appear to belong to an art separate from criticism — to a psychological discipline, a system of self-development, a yoga, which the young poet perhaps does well to notice, but which is something different from the public art of evaluating poems.

Coleridge and Arnold were better critics than

most poets have been, and if the critical tendency dried up the poetry in Arnold and perhaps in Coleridge, it is not inconsistent with our argument, which is that judgment of poems is different from the art of producing them. Coleridge has given us the classic "anodyne" story, and tells what he can about the genesis of a poem which he calls "psychological curiosity," but his definitions of poetry and of the poetic quality "imagination" are to be found elsewhere and in quite other terms.

It would be convenient if the passwords of the intentional school, "sincerity," "fidelity," "spontaneity," "authenticity," "genuineness," "originality," could be equated with the terms such as "integrity," "relevance," "unity," "function," "maturity," "subtlety," "adequacy," and other more precise terms of evaluation — in short, if "expression" always meant aesthetic achievement. But this is not so.

"Aesthetic" art, says Professor Curt Ducasse, an ingenious theorist of expression, is the conscious objectification of feelings, in which an intrinsic part is the critical moment. The artist corrects the objectification when it is not adequate. But this may mean that the earlier attempt was not successful in objectifying the self, or "it may also mean that it was a successful objectification of a self which, when it confronted us clearly, we disowned and repudiated in favor of another."[11] What is the standard by which we disown or accept the self? Professor Ducasse does not say. Whatever it may be, however, this standard is an element in the definition of art which will not reduce to terms of objectification. The evaluation of the work of art remains public; the work is measured against something outside the author.

## IV

There is criticism of poetry and there is author psychology, which when applied to the present or future takes the form of inspirational promotion; but author psychology can be historical too, and then we have literary biography, a legitimate

---

[9]True truth. [Ed.]

[10]See Hughes Mearns, *Creative Youth* (Garden City, 1925), esp. pp. 10, 27–29. The technique of inspiring poems has apparently been outdone more recently by the study of inspiration in successful poets and other artists. See, for instance, Rosamond E. M. Harding, *An Anatomy of Inspiration* (Cambridge, 1940); Julius Portnoy, *A Psychology of Art Creation* (Philadelphia, 1942); Rudolf Arnheim and others, *Poets at Work* (New York, 1947); Phyllis Bartlett, *Poems in Process* (New York, 1951); Brewster Ghiselin (ed.), *The Creative Process: A Symposium* (Berkeley and Los Angeles, 1952). [Au.]

[11]Curt Ducasse, *The Philosophy of Art* (New York, 1929), p. 116. [Au.]

and attractive study in itself, one approach, as Professor Tillyard would argue, to personality, the poem being only a parallel approach. Certainly it need not be with a derogatory purpose that one points out personal studies, as distinct from poetic studies, in the realm of literary scholarship. Yet there is danger of confusing personal and poetic studies; and there is the fault of writing the personal as if it were poetic.

There is a difference between internal and external evidence for the meaning of a poem. And the paradox is only verbal and superficial that what is (1) internal is also public: it is discovered through the semantics and syntax of a poem, through our habitual knowledge of the language, through grammars, dictionaries, and all the literature which is the source of dictionaries, in general through all that makes a language and culture; while what is (2) external is private or idiosyncratic; not a part of the work as a linguistic fact: it consists of revelations (in journals, for example, or letters or reported conversations) about how or why the poet wrote the poem — to what lady, while sitting on what lawn, or at the death of what friend or brother. There is (3) an intermediate kind of evidence about the character of the author or about private or semiprivate meanings attached to words or topics by an author or by a coterie of which he is a member. The meaning of words is the history of words, and the biography of an author, his use of a word, and the associations which the word had for *him,* are part of the word's history and meaning.[12] But the three types of evidence, especially (2) and (3), shade into one another so subtly that it is not always easy to draw a line between examples, and hence arises the difficulty for criticism. The use of biographical evidence need not involve intentionalism, because while it may be evidence of what the author intended, it may also be evidence of the meaning of his words and the dramatic character of his utterance. On the other hand, it may not be all this. And a critic who is concerned with evidence of type (1) and moderately with that of type (3) will in the long run produce a different sort of comment from that of the critic who is concerned with (2) and with (3) where it shades into (2).

The whole glittering parade of Professor Lowes's *Road to Xanadu,* for instance, runs along the border between types (2) and (3) or boldly traverses the romantic region of (2). "'Kubla Khan,'" says Professor Lowes, "is the fabric of a vision, but every image that rose up in its weaving had passed that way before. And it would seem that there is nothing haphazard or fortuitous in their return." This is not quite clear — not even when Professor Lowes explains that there were clusters of associations, like hooked atoms, which were drawn into complex relation with other clusters in the deep well of Coleridge's memory, and which then coalesced and issued forth as poems. If there was nothing "haphazard or fortuitous" in the way the images returned to the surface, that may mean (1) that Coleridge could not produce what he did not have, that he was limited in his creation by what he had read or otherwise experienced, or (2) that having received certain clusters of associations, he was bound to return them in just the way he did, and that the value of the poem may be described in terms of the experiences on which he had to draw. The latter pair of propositions (a sort of Hartleyan associationism which Coleridge himself repudiated in the *Biographia*) may not be assented to. There were certainly other combinations, other poems, worse or better, that might have been written by men who had read Bartram and Purchas and Bruce and Milton. And this will be true no matter how many times we are able to add to the brilliant complex of Coleridge's reading. In certain flourishes (such as the sentence we have quoted) and in chapter headings like "The Shaping Spirit," "The Magical Synthesis," "Imagination Creatrix," it may be that Professor Lowes pretends to say more about the actual poems than he does. There is a certain deceptive variation in these fancy chapter titles; one expects to pass on to a new stage in the argument, and one finds — more and more sources, more and more about "the streamy nature of association."[13]

---

[12] And the history of words *after* a poem is written may contribute meanings which if relevant to the original pattern should not be ruled out by a scruple about intention. [Au.]

[13] Chaps. 8, "The Pattern," and 16, "The Known and

"Wohin der Weg?" quotes Professor Lowes for the motto of his book. "Kein Weg! Ins Unbetretene."[14] Precisely because the way is *unbetreten,* we should say, it leads away from the poem. Bartram's *Travels* contains a good deal of the history of certain words and of certain romantic Floridian conceptions that appear in "Kubla Khan." And a good deal of that history has passed and was then passing into the very stuff of our language. Perhaps a person who has read Bartram appreciates the poem more than one who has not. Or, by looking up the vocabulary of "Kubla Khan" in the *Oxford English Dictionary,* or by reading some of the other books there quoted, a person may know the poem better. But it would seem to pertain little to the poem to know that *Coleridge* had read Bartram. There is a gross body of life, of sensory and mental experience, which lies behind and in some sense causes every poem, but can never be and need not be known in the verbal and hence intellectual composition which is the poem. For all the objects of our manifold experience, for every unity, there is an action of the mind which cuts off roots, melts away context — or indeed we should never have objects or ideas or anything to talk about.

It is probable that there is nothing in Professor Lowes's vast book which could detract from anyone's appreciation of either *The Ancient Mariner* or "Kubla Khan." We next present a case where preoccupation with evidence of type (3) has gone so far as to distort a critic's view of a poem (yet a case not so obvious as those that abound in our critical journals).

In a well known poem by John Donne[15] appears this quatrain:

Moving of th' earth brings harmes and feares,
  Men reckon what it did and meant,
But trepidation of the spheares,
  Though greater farre, is innocent.

A recent critic in an elaborate treatment of Donne's learning has written of this quatrain as follows:

> He touches the emotional pulse of the situation by a skillful allusion to the new and the old astronomy. . . . Of the new astronomy, the "moving of the earth" is the most radical principle; of the old, the "trepidation of the spheres" is the motion of the greatest complexity. . . . The poet must exhort his love to quietness and calm upon his departure; and for this purpose the figure based upon the latter motion (trepidation), long absorbed into the traditional astronomy, fittingly suggests the tension of the moment without arousing the "harmes and feares" implicit in the figure of the moving earth.[16]

The argument is plausible and rests on a well substantiated thesis that Donne was deeply interested in the new astronomy and its repercussions in the theological realm. In various works Donne shows his familiarity with Kepler's *De Stella Nova,* with Galileo's *Siderius Nuncius,* with William Gilbert's *De Magnete,* and with Clavius's commentary on the *De Sphaera* of Sacrobosco. He refers to the new science in his Sermon at Paul's Cross and in a letter to Sir Henry Goodyer. In *The First Anniversary* he says the "new philosophy calls all in doubt." In the *Elegy on Prince Henry* he says that the "least moving of the center" makes "the world to shake."

It is difficult to answer argument like this, and impossible to answer it with evidence of like nature. There is no reason why Donne might not have written a stanza in which the two kinds of celestial motion stood for two sorts of emotion at parting. And if we become full of astronomical ideas and see Donne only against the background of the new science, we may believe that he did. But the text itself remains to be dealt with, the analyzable vehicle of a complicated metaphor. And one may observe: (1) that the movement of the earth according to the Copernican theory is a celestial motion, smooth and regular, and while it might cause religious or philosophic fears, it could not be associated with the crudity and earthiness of the kind of commotion which the speaker in the poem wishes to discourage; (2) that there is another moving of the earth, an

---

Familiar Landscape," will be found of most help to the student of the poem. [Au.]

[14] Goethe: "Whither leads the road? No road! Into the untraveled." [Ed.]

[15] "A Valediction, Forbidding Mourning." [Ed.]

[16] Charles M. Coffin, *John Donne and the New Philosophy* (New York, 1927), pp. 97–98. [Au.]

earthquake, which has just these qualities and is to be associated with the tear-floods and sigh-tempests of the second stanza of the poem; (3) that "trepidation" is an appropriate opposite of earthquake, because each is a shaking or vibratory motion; and "trepidation of the spheres" is "greater far" than an earthquake, but not much greater (if two such motions can be compared as to greatness) than the annual motion of the earth; (4) that reckoning what it "did and meant" shows that the event has passed, like an earthquake, not like the incessant celestial movement of the earth. Perhaps a knowledge of Donne's interest in the new science may add another shade of meaning, an overtone to the stanza in question, though to say even this runs against the words. To make the geocentric and heliocentric antithesis the core of the metaphor is to disregard the English language, to prefer private evidence to public, external to internal.

## V

If the distinction between kinds of evidence has implications for the historical critic, it has them no less for the contemporary poet and his critic. Or, since every rule for a poet is but another side of a judgment by a critic, and since the past is the realm of the scholar and critic, and the future and present that of the poet and the critical leaders of taste, we may say that the problems arising in literary scholarship from the intentional fallacy are matched by others which arise in the world of progressive experiment.

The question of "allusiveness," for example, as acutely posed by the poetry of Eliot, is certainly one where a false judgment is likely to involve the intentional fallacy. The frequency and depth of literary allusion in the poetry of Eliot and others has driven so many in pursuit of full meanings to the *Golden Bough* and the Elizabethan drama that it has become a kind of commonplace to suppose that we do not know what a poet means unless we have traced him in his reading — a supposition redolent with intentional implications. The stand taken by F. O. Matthiessen is a sound one and partially forestalls the difficulty.

If one reads these lines with an attentive ear and is sensitive to their sudden shifts in movement, the contrast between the actual Thames and the idealized vision of it during an age before it flowed through a megalopolis is sharply conveyed by that movement itself, whether or not one recognizes the refrain to be from Spenser.

Eliot's allusions work when we know them — and to a great extent even when we do not know them, through their suggestive power.

But sometimes we find allusions supported by notes, and it is a nice question whether the notes function more as guides to send us where we may be educated, or more as indications in themselves about the character of the allusions. "Nearly everything of importance . . . that is apposite to an appreciation of 'The Waste Land,'" writes Matthiessen of Miss Weston's book,[17] "has been incorporated into the structure of the poem itself, or into Eliot's Notes." And with such an admission it may begin to appear that it would not much matter if Eliot invented his sources (as Sir Walter Scott invented chapter epigraphs from "old plays" and "anonymous" authors, or as Coleridge wrote marginal glosses for *The Ancient Mariner*). Allusions to Dante, Webster, Marvell, or Baudelaire doubtless gain something because these writers existed, but it is doubtful whether the same can be said for an allusion to an obscure Elizabethan:

> The sound of horns and motors, which shall bring
> Sweeney to Mrs. Porter in the spring.

"Cf. Day, *Parliament of Bees:*" says Eliot,

> When of a sudden, listening, you shall hear,
> A noise of horns and hunting, which shall bring
> Actaeon to Diana in the spring,
> Where all shall see her naked skin.

The irony is completed by the quotation itself; had Eliot, as is quite conceivable, composed these lines to furnish his own background, there would be no loss of validity. The conviction may grow as one reads Eliot's next note: "I do not know the origin of the ballad from which these lines are taken: it was reported to me from Syd-

[17]Jessie Weston's *From Ritual to Romance* (1920), an influence on *The Waste Land*. [Ed.]

ney, Australia." The important word in this note — on Mrs. Porter and her daughter who washed their feet in soda water — is "ballad." And if one should feel from the lines themselves their "ballad" quality, there would be little need for the note. Ultimately, the inquiry must focus on the integrity of such notes as parts of the poem, for where they constitute special information about the meaning of phrases in the poem, they ought to be subject to the same scrutiny as any of the other words in which it is written. Matthiessen believes that notes were the price Eliot "had to pay in order to avoid what he would have considered muffling the energy of his poem by extended connecting links in the text itself." But it may be questioned whether the notes and the need for them are not equally muffling. F. W. Bateson has plausibly argued that Tennyson's "The Sailor Boy" would be better if half the stanzas were omitted, and the best versions of ballads like "Sir Patrick Spens" owe their power to the very audacity with which the minstrel has taken for granted the story upon which he comments. What then if a poet finds he cannot take so much for granted in a more recondite context and rather than write informatively, supplies notes? It can be said in favor of this plan that at least the notes do not pretend to be dramatic, as they would if written in verse. On the other hand, the notes may look like unassimilated material lying loose beside the poem, necessary for the meaning of the verbal symbol, but not integrated, so that the symbol stands incomplete.

We mean to suggest by the above analysis that whereas notes tend to seem to justify themselves as external indexes to the author's *intention,* yet they ought to be judged like any other parts of a composition (verbal arrangement special to a particular context), and when so judged their reality as parts of the poem, or their imaginative integration with the rest of the poem, may come into question. Matthiessen, for instance, sees that Eliot's titles for poems and his epigraphs are informative apparatus, like the notes. But while he is worried by some of the notes and thinks that Eliot "appears to be mocking himself for writing the note at the same time that he wants to convey something by it," Matthiessen believes

that the "device" of epigraphs "is not at all open to the objection of not being sufficiently structural." "The *intention,*" he says, "is to enable the poet to secure a condensed expression in the poem itself." "In each case the epigraph is *designed* to form an integral part of the effect of the poem." And Eliot himself, in his notes, has justified his poetic practice in terms of intention.

> The Hanged Man, a member of the traditional pack, fits my purpose in two ways: because he is associated in my mind with the Hanged God of Frazer, and because I associate him with the hooded figure in the passage of the disciples to Emmaus in Part V. . . . . The man with Three Staves (an authentic member of the Tarot pack) I associate, quite arbitrarily, with the Fisher King himself.

And perhaps he is to be taken more seriously here, when off guard in a note, than when in his Norton Lectures he comments on the difficulty of saying what a poem means and adds playfully that he thinks of prefixing to a second edition of *Ash Wednesday* some lines from *Don Juan:*

> I don't pretend that I quite understand
> My own meaning when I would be *very* fine;
> But the fact is that I have nothing planned
> Unless it were to be a moment merry.

If Eliot and other contemporary poets have any characteristic fault, it may be in *planning* too much.

Allusiveness in poetry is one of several critical issues by which we have illustrated the more abstract issue of intentionalism, but it may be for today the most important illustration. As a poetic practice allusiveness would appear to be in some recent poems an extreme corollary of the romantic intentionalist assumption, and as a critical issue it challenges and brings to light in a special way the basic premise of intentionalism. The following instance from the poetry of Eliot may serve to epitomize the practical implications of what we have been saying. In Eliot's "Love Song of J. Alfred Prufrock," toward the end, occurs the line: "I have heard the mermaids singing, each to each," and this bears a certain resemblance to a line in a Song by John Donne, "Teach me to heare Mermaides singing," so that for the reader acquainted to a certain degree with Donne's poetry, the critical question arises: Is Eliot's line an allusion to Donne's? Is Prufrock thinking about Donne? Is Eliot thinking about Donne? We suggest that there are two radically different ways of looking for an answer to this question. There is (1) the way of poetic analysis and exegesis, which inquires whether it makes any sense if Eliot-Prufrock *is* thinking about Donne. In an earlier part of the poem, when Prufrock asks, "Would it have been worth while, . . . To have squeezed the universe into a ball," his words take half their sadness and irony from certain energetic and passionate lines of Marvell "To His Coy Mistress." But the exegetical inquirer may wonder whether mermaids considered as "strange sights" (to hear them is in Donne's poem analogous to getting with child a mandrake root) have much to do with Prufrock's mermaids, which seem to be symbols of romance and dynamism, and which incidentally have literary authentication, if they need it, in a line of a sonnet by Gérard de Nerval. This method of inquiry may lead to the conclusion that the given resemblance between Eliot and Donne is without significance and is better not thought of, or the method may have the disadvantage of providing no certain conclusion. Nevertheless, we submit that this is the true and objective way of criticism, as contrasted to what the very uncertainty of exegesis might tempt a second kind of critic to undertake: (2) the way of biographical or genetic inquiry, in which, taking advantage of the fact that Eliot is still alive, and in the spirit of a man who would settle a bet, the critic writes to Eliot and asks what he meant, or if he had Donne in mind. We shall not here weigh the probabilities — whether Eliot would answer that he meant nothing at all, had nothing at all in mind — a sufficiently good answer to such a question — or in an unguarded moment might furnish a clear and, within its limits, irrefutable answer. Our point is that such an answer to such an inquiry would have nothing to do with the poem "Prufrock"; it would not be a critical inquiry. Critical inquiries, unlike bets, are not settled in this way. Critical inquiries are not settled by consulting the oracle.

# E. D. Hirsch, Jr.
b. 1928

*As a scholar of romanticism and a theorist on interpretation, rhetoric and composition, and cultural literacy, Eric Donald Hirsch has stressed the necessity of understanding the type to know the token. Born in Memphis, Hirsch was educated at Cornell (B.A., 1950). After serving in the navy during the Korean War, Hirsch completed his Ph.D. at Yale University in 1957 and taught there for ten years; during that time he published his dissertation,* Wordsworth and Schelling: A Typological Study of Romanticism *(1960), and* Innocence and Experience: An Introduction to Blake *(1964). In 1966 he became a full professor at the University of Virginia, and the following year published* Validity in Interpretation *(1967). Dedicated "to William K. Wimsatt and R. S. Crane," this study of hermeneutics has been credited with breaching the formalist wall around the text erected by the New Criticism. The key idea, derived from Husserl, is that many of the potential ambiguities of language can be cleared up by knowing what genre a text belongs to and what sort of thing an author is likely to mean — which reestablished the philosophical rationale for the relevance of authorial intention and historical and biographical detail to textual meaning. In later works like* The Aims of Interpretation *(1976) and* The Philosophy of Composition *(1977), Hirsch broadened his conservative typology to include literary interpretation and rhetoric, even as the critical scene had moved past him and in other directions. In his best-selling* Cultural Literacy *(1987), which takes up elementary- and secondary-school issues, he argues for the social value of a cultural common ground over and above basic skills. "Objective Interpretation," later appended to* Validity in Interpretation, *originally appeared in* PMLA *75 (1960).*

# Objective Interpretation

The fact that the term "criticism" has now come to designate all commentary on textual meaning reflects a general acceptance of the doctrine that description and evaluation are inseparable in literary study. In any serious confrontation of literature it would be futile, of course, to attempt a rigorous banishment of all evaluative judgment, but this fact does not give us the license to misunderstand or misinterpret our texts. It does not entitle us to use the text as the basis for an exercise in "creativity" or to submit as serious textual commentary a disguised argument for a particular ethical, cultural, or aesthetic viewpoint. Nor is criticism's chief concern — the present relevance of a text — a strictly necessary aspect of textual commentary. That same kind of theory which argues the inseparability of description and evaluation also argues that a text's meaning is simply its meaning "to us, today." Both kinds of argument support the idea that interpretation is criticism and vice versa. But there is clearly a sense in which we can neither evaluate a text nor determine what it means "to us, today" until we have correctly apprehended what it means. Understanding (and therefore interpretation, in the strict sense of the word) is both logically and psychologically prior to what is generally called criticism. It is true that this distinction between understanding and evaluation cannot always show itself in the finished work of criticism — nor, perhaps, should it — but a general grasp and acceptance of the distinction might help correct some of the most serious faults of current criticism (its subjectivism and relativism) and might even make it plausible to think of literary study as a corporate enterprise and a progressive discipline.

No one would deny, of course, that the more important issue is not the status of literary study as a discipline but the vitality of literature — especially of older literature — in the world at large. The critic is right to think that the text should speak to us. The point which needs to be grasped clearly by the critic is that a text cannot be made to speak to us until what it says has been understood. This is not an argument in favor of historicism as against criticism — it is simply a brute ontological fact. Textual meaning is not a naked given like a physical object. The text is first of all a conventional representation like a musical score, and what the score represents may be construed correctly or incorrectly. The literary text (in spite of the semimystical claims made for its uniqueness) does not have a special ontological status which somehow absolves the reader from the demands universally imposed by all linguistic texts of every description. Nothing, that is, can give a conventional representation the status of an immediate given. The text of a poem, for example, has to be construed by the critic before it becomes a poem for him. Then it is, no doubt, an artifact with special characteristics. But before the critic construes the poem it is no artifact for him at all, and if he construes it wrongly, he will subsequently be talking about the wrong artifact, not the one represented by the text. If criticism is to be objective in any significant sense, it must be founded on a self-critical construction of textual meaning, which is to say, on objective interpretation.

The distinction I am drawing between interpretation and criticism was one of the central principles in the now vestigial science of hermeneutics. August Boeckh, for example, divided the theoretical part of his *Encyclopädie* into two sections, one devoted to *Interpretation* (*Hermeneutik*) and the other to *Kritik*. Boeckh's discussion of this distinction is illuminating: interpretation is the construction of textual meaning as such; it explicates (*legt aus*) those meanings, and only those meanings, which the text explicitly or implicitly represents. Criticism, on the other hand, builds on the results of interpretation; it confronts textual meaning not as such, but as a component within a larger context. Boeckh defined it as "that philological function through which a text is understood not simply in its own terms and for its own sake, but in order to establish a relationship with something else, in such a way that the goal is a knowledge of this relationship."[1] Boeckh's definition is useful in emphasizing that interpretation and criticism confront two quite distinct "objects," for this is the fundamental distinction between the two activities. The object of interpretation is textual meaning in and for itself and may be called the *meaning* of the text. The object of criticism, on the other hand, is that meaning in its bearing on something else (standards of value, present concerns, etc.), and this object may therefore be called the *significance* of the text.

The distinction between the meaning and the significance of a text was first clearly made by Frege in his article "Über Sinn und Bedeutung," where he demonstrated that although the meanings of two texts may be different, their referent or truth-value may be identical.[2] For example, the statement, "Scott is the author of *Waverley*," is true and yet the meaning of "Scott" is different from that of "the author of *Waverley*." The *Sinn* of each is different, but the *Bedeutung* (or one aspect of *Bedeutung* — the designatum of "Scott" and "author of *Waverley*") is the same. Frege considered only cases where different *Sinne* have an identical *Bedeutung*, but it is also true that the same *Sinn* may, in the course of time, have different *Bedeutungen*. For example, the sentence, "There is a unicorn in the garden," is prima facie false. But suppose the statement were made when there *was* a unicorn in the garden (as happened in Thurber's imaginative world); the statement would be true; its relevance would have shifted. But true or false, the meaning of the proposition would remain the same, for unless its *meaning* remained self-identical, we would have nothing to label true or false. Frege's distinction, now widely accepted by logicians, is a special case of Husserl's general distinction between the inner and outer horizons of any meaning. In section A I shall try to clarify Husserl's concept and to show how it applies to the problems of textual study and especially to the basic assumptions of textual interpretation.

My purpose is primarily constructive rather than polemical. I would not willingly argue that interpretation should be practiced in strict separation from criticism. I shall ignore criticism simply in order to confront the special problems involved in construing the meaning or *Sinn* of a text. For most of my notions I disclaim any originality. My aim is to revive some forgotten insights of literary study and to apply to the theory of interpretation certain other insights from linguistics and philosophy. For although the analytical movement in criticism has permanently advanced the cause of intrinsic literary study, it has not yet paid enough attention to the problem of establishing norms and limits in interpretation. If I display any argumentative intent, it is not, therefore, against the analytical movement, which I approve, but only against certain modern theories which hamper the establishment of normative principles in interpretation and which thereby encourage the subjectivism and individualism which have for many students discredited the analytical movement. By normative principles I mean those notions which concern the nature of a correct interpretation. When the critic clearly conceives what a correct interpretation is in principle, he possesses a guiding idea against which he can measure his construction. Without such a guiding idea, self-critical or objective interpretation is hardly possible. Current theory, however, fails to provide such a principle. The most influential and representative statement of modern theory is *Theory of Literature* by Wellek and Warren, a book to which I owe much. I ungratefully select it (especially

[1]August Boeckh, *Encyclopädie und Methodologie der philologischen Wissenschaften* (1886), p. 170. [Au.]

[2]Gottlob Frege, "Über Sinn und Bedeutung," *Zeitschrift für Philosophie und philosophische Kritik, 100* (1892). The article has been translated, and one English version may be found in H. Feigl and W. Sellars, *Readings in Philosophical Analysis* (New York, 1949). [Au.]

Chap. 12) as a target of attack, both because it is so influential and because I need a specific, concrete example of the sort of theory which requires amendment.[3]

## THE TWO HORIZONS OF TEXTUAL MEANING

The metaphorical doctrine that a text leads a life of its own is used by modern theorists to express the idea that textual meaning changes in the course of time.[4] This theory of a changing meaning serves to support the fusion of interpretation and criticism and, at the same time, the idea that present relevance forms the basis for textual commentary. But the view should not remain unchallenged, since if it were correct, there could be no objective knowledge about texts. Any statement about textual meaning could be valid only for the moment, and even this temporary validity could not be tested, since there would be no permanent norms on which validating judgments could be based. While the "life" theory does serve to explain and sanction the fact that different ages tend to interpret texts differently, and while it emphasizes the importance of a text's present relevance, it overlooks the fact that such a view undercuts *all* criticism, even the sort which emphasizes present relevance. If the view were correct, criticism would not only lack permanent validity, but could not even claim current validity by the time it got into print. Both the text's meaning and the tenor of the age would have altered. The "life" theory really masks the idea that the reader construes his own, new meaning instead of that represented by the text.

The "life" theory thus implicitly places the principle of change squarely where it belongs, that is, not in textual meaning as such, but in changing generations of readers. According to Wellek, for example, the meaning of the text changes as it passes "through the minds of its readers, critics, and fellow artists."[5] Now when even a few of the norms which determine a text's

meaning are allotted to readers and made dependent on their attitudes and concerns, it is evident that textual meaning must change. But is it proper to make textual meaning dependent upon the reader's own cultural givens? It may be granted that these givens change in the course of time, but does this imply that textual meaning itself changes? As soon as the reader's outlook is permitted to determine what a text means, we have not simply a changing meaning but quite possibly as many meanings as readers.

Against such a reductio ad absurdum, the proponent of the current theory points out that in a given age many readers will agree in their construction of a text and will unanimously repudiate the accepted interpretation of a former age. For the sake of fair-mindedness, this presumed unanimity may be granted, but must it be explained by arguing that the text's meaning has changed? Recalling Frege's distinction between *Sinn* and *Bedeutung,* the change could be explained by saying that the meaning of the text has remained the same, while the significance of that meaning has shifted.[6] Contemporary readers will frequently share similar cultural givens and will therefore agree about what the text means to them. But might it not be the case that they agree about the text's meaning "to them" because they have first understood its meaning? If textual meaning itself could change, contemporary readers would lack a basis for agreement or disagreement. No one would bother seriously to discuss such a protean object. The significance of textual meaning has no foundation and no objectivity unless meaning itself is unchanging. To fuse meaning and significance, or interpretation and criticism, by the conception of an autonomous, living, changing meaning does not really free the reader from the shackles of historicism; it simply destroys the basis both for any agreement among readers and for any objective study whatever.

The dilemma created by the fusion of *Sinn* and *Bedeutung* in current theory is exhibited as soon as the theorist attempts to explain how norms can be preserved in textual study. The

[3]René Wellek and Austin Warren, *Theory of Literature* (1956). Ch. 12 is by Wellek. [Au.]
[4]See, for example, ibid., p. 31. [Au.]
[5]Ibid., p. 144. [Au.]

[6]It could also be explained, of course, by saying that certain generations of readers tend to misunderstand certain texts. [Au.]

explanation becomes openly self-contradictory: "It could be scarcely denied that there is [in textual meaning] a substantial *identity* of 'structure' which has remained the *same* throughout the ages. This *structure* however, is dynamic: it *changes* throughout the process of history while passing through the minds of its readers, critics, and fellow artists."[7] First the "structure" is self-identical; then it changes! What is given in one breath is taken away in the next. Although it is a matter of common experience that a text appears different to us than it appeared to a former age, and although we remain deeply convinced that there *are* permanent norms in textual study, we cannot properly explain the facts by equating or fusing what changes with what remains the same. We must distinguish the two and give each its due.

A couplet from Marvell, used by Wellek to suggest how meaning changes, will illustrate my point:[8]

My vegetable love should grow
Vaster than empires and more slow.

Wellek grants that "vegetable" here probably means more or less what we nowadays express by "vegetative," but he goes on to suggest that we cannot avoid associating the modern connotation of "vegetable" (what it means "to us"). Furthermore, he suggests that this enrichment of meaning may even be desirable. No doubt, the associated meaning *is* here desirable (since it supports the mood of the poem), but Wellek could not even make his point unless we could distinguish between what "vegetable" probably means as used in the text and what it commonly means to us. Simply to discuss the issue is to admit that Marvell's poem probably does not imply the modern connotation, for if we could not separate the sense of "vegetative" from the notion of an "erotic cabbage," we could not talk about the difficulty of making the separation. One need not argue that the delight we may take in such new meanings must be ignored. On the contrary, once we have self-critically understood

the text, there is little reason to exclude valuable or pleasant associations which enhance its significance. However, it is essential to exclude these associations in the process of interpretation, that is, in the process of understanding what a text means. The way out of the theoretical dilemma is to perceive that the meaning of a text does not change and that the modern, different connotation of a word like "vegetable" belongs, if it is to be entertained at all, to the constantly changing significance of a text's meaning.

It is in the light of the distinction between meaning and significance that critical theories like T. S. Eliot's need to be viewed.[9] Eliot, like other modern critics, insists that the meaning of a literary work changes in the course of time, but, in contrast to Wellek, instead of locating the principle of change directly in the changing outlooks of readers, Eliot locates it in a changing literary tradition. In his view, the literary tradition is a "simultaneous" (as opposed to temporal) order of literary texts which is constantly rearranging itself as new literary works appear on the public scene. Whenever a new work appears it causes a rearrangement of the tradition as a whole, and this brings about an alteration in the meaning of each component literary text. For example, when Shakespeare's *Troilus* entered the tradition, it altered not only the meaning of Chaucer's *Troilus,* but also, to some degree, the meaning of every other text in the literary tradition.

If the changes in meaning Eliot speaks of are considered to be changes in significance, then his conception is perfectly sound. And indeed, by definition, Eliot is speaking of significance rather than meaning, since he is considering the work in relation to a larger realm, as a component rather than a world in itself. It goes without saying that the character of a component considered as such changes whenever the larger realm of which it is a part changes. A red object will appear to have different color qualities when viewed against differently colored backgrounds. The same is true of textual meaning. But the meaning of the text (its *Sinn*) does not change any more than the hue and saturation of the red

[7]Wellek and Warren, p. 144. My italics. [Au.]

[8]Ibid., pp. 166–67. [Au.] The couplet is from "To His Coy Mistress." [Ed.]

[9]Eliot, "Tradition and the Individual Talent." [Au.] See Eliot, p. 466. [Ed.]

object changes when seen against different backgrounds. Yet the analogy with colored objects is only partial: I can look at a red pencil against a green blotting pad and perceive the pencil's color in that special context without knowing the hue and saturation of either pencil or blotter. But textual meaning is a construction, not a naked given like a red object, and I cannot relate textual meaning to a larger realm until I have construed it. Before I can judge just how the changed tradition has altered the significance of a text, I must understand its meaning or *Sinn*.

This permanent meaning is, and can be, nothing other than the author's meaning. There have been, of course, several other definitions of textual meaning — what the author's contemporaries would ideally have construed, what the ideal present-day reader construes, what the norms of language permit the text to mean, what the best critics conceive to be the best meaning, and so on. In support of these other candidates, various aesthetic and psychological objections have been aimed at the author; first, his meaning, being conditioned by history and culture, is too confined and simple; second, it remains, in any case, inaccessible to us because we live in another age, or because his mental processes are private, or because he himself did not know what he meant. Instead of attempting to meet each of these objections separately, I shall attempt to describe the general principle for answering all of them and, in doing so, to clarify further the distinction between meaning and significance. The aim of my exposition will be to confirm that the author's meaning, as represented by his text, is unchanging and reproducible. My problem will be to show that, although textual meaning is *determined* by the psychic acts of an author and realized by those of a reader, textual meaning itself must not be *identified* with the author's or reader's psychic acts as such. To make this crucial point, I shall find it useful to draw upon Husserl's analysis of verbal meaning.

In his chief work, *Logische Untersuchungen*, Husserl sought, among other things, to avoid an identification of verbal meaning with the psychic acts of speaker or listener, author or reader, but to do this he did not adopt a strict, Platonic idealism by which meanings have an actual existence apart from meaning experiences. Instead, he affirmed the objectivity of meaning by analyzing the observable relationship between it and those very mental processes in which it is actualized, for in meaning experiences themselves, the objectivity and constancy of meaning are confirmed.

Husserl's point may be grasped by an example from visual experience.[10] When I look at a box, then close my eyes, and then reopen them, I can perceive in this second view the identical box I saw before. Yet, although I perceive the same box, the two acts of seeing are distinctly different — in this case, temporally different. The same sort of result is obtained when I alter my acts of seeing spatially. If I go to another side of the room or stand on a chair, what I actually "see" alters with my change in perspective, and yet I still "perceive" the identical box; I still understand that the *object* of my seeing is the same. Furthermore, if I leave the room and simply recall the box in memory, I still understand that the *object* I remember is identical with the object I saw. For if I did not understand that, how could I insist that I was remembering? The examples are paradigmatic: All events of consciousness, not simply those involving visual perception and memory, are characterized by the mind's ability to make modally and temporally different *acts* of awareness refer to the same *object* of awareness. An object for the mind remains the same even though what is "going on in the mind" is not the same. The mind's object therefore may not be equated with psychic processes as such; the mental object is self-identical over against a plurality of mental acts.[11]

The relation between an act of awareness and its object Husserl calls "intention," using the

[10]Most of my illustrations in this section are visual rather than verbal since the former may be more easily grasped. If, at this stage, I were to choose verbal examples I would have to interpret the examples before making my point. I discuss a literary text in sections B and C. The example of a box was suggested to me by Helmut Kuhn, "The Phenomenological Concept of 'Horizon,'" in *Philosophical Essays in Memory of Edmund Husserl,* ed. Marvin Farber (Cambridge, Mass., 1940). [Au.]

[11]See Aaron Gurwitsch, "On the Intentionality of Consciousness," in *Philosophical Essays,* ed. Farber. [Au.]

term in its traditional philosophical sense, which is much broader than that of "purpose" and is roughly equivalent to "awareness." (When I employ the word subsequently, I shall be using it in Husserl's sense.)[12] This term is useful for distinguishing the components of a meaning experience. For example, when I "intend" a box, there are at least three distinguishable aspects of that event. First, there is the object as perceived by me; second, there is the act by which I perceive the object; and finally, there is (for physical things) the object which exists independently of my perceptual act. The first two aspects of the event Husserl calls "intentional object" and "intentional act" respectively. Husserl's point, then, is that *different* intentional acts (on different occasions) "intend" an *identical* intentional object.

The general term for all intentional objects is meaning. Verbal meaning is simply a special kind of intentional object, and like any other one, it remains self-identical over against the many different acts which "intend" it. But the noteworthy feature of verbal meaning is its suprapersonal character. It is not an intentional object for simply one person, but for many — potentially for all persons. Verbal meaning is, by definition, *that aspect of a speaker's "intention" which, under linguistic conventions, may be shared by others*. Anything not sharable in this sense does not belong to the verbal intention or verbal meaning. Thus, when I say, "The air is crisp," I may be thinking, among other things, "I should have eaten less at supper," and "Crisp air reminds me of my childhood in Vermont," and so on. In certain types of utterance such unspoken accompaniments to meaning may be sharable, but in general they are not, and therefore they do not generally belong to verbal meaning. The nonverbal aspects of the speaker's intention Husserl calls "experience" and the verbal ones "content." However, by content he does not mean simply intellectual content, but all those aspects of the intention — cognitive, emotive, phonetic (and in writing, even visual) — which may be conveyed to others by the linguistic means employed.[13]

Husserl's analysis (in my brief exposition) makes the following points then: Verbal meaning, being an intentional object, is unchanging, that is, it may be reproduced by different intentional acts and remains self-identical through all these reproductions. Verbal meaning is the sharable content of the speaker's intentional object. Since this meaning is both unchanging and interpersonal, it may be reproduced by the mental acts of different persons. Husserl's view is thus essentially historical, for even though he insists that verbal meaning is unchanging, he also insists that any particular verbal utterance, written or spoken, is historically determined. That is to say, the meaning is determined once and for all by the character of the speaker's intention.[14]

Husserl's views provide an excellent context for discussing the central problems of interpretation. Once we define verbal meaning as the content of the author's intention (which for brevity's sake I shall call simply the author's "verbal intention"), the problem for the interpreter is quite clear: he must distinguish those meanings which belong to that verbal intention from those which do not belong. This problem may be rephrased, of course, in a way that nearly everyone will accept: the interpreter has to distinguish what a text implies from what it does not imply; he must give the text its full due, but he must also preserve norms and limits. For hermeneutic theory, the problem is to find a *principle* for judging whether various possible implications should or should not be admitted.

I describe the problem in terms of implication, since, for practical purposes, it lies at the heart

---

[12]Although Husserl's term is a standard philosophical one for which there is no adequate substitute, students of literature may unwittingly associate it with the intentional fallacy. The two uses of the word are, however, quite distinct. As used by literary critics the term refers to a purpose which may or may not be realized by a writer. As used by Husserl the term refers to a process of consciousness. Thus in the literary usage, which involves problems of rhetoric, it is possible to speak of an unfulfilled intention, while in Husserl's usage such a locution would be meaningless. [Au.]

[13]Edmund Husserl, *Logische Untersuchungen. Zweiter Band. Untersuchungen zur Phänomenologie und Theorie der Erkenntnis. I Teil* (2d ed. Halle, 1913), pp. 96–97. [Au.]

[14]Ibid., p. 91. [Au.]

of the matter. Generally, the explicit meanings of a text can be construed to the satisfaction of most readers; the problems arise in determining inexplicit or "unsaid" meanings. If, for example, I announce, "I have a headache," there is no difficulty in construing what I "say," but there may be great difficulty in construing implications like "I desire sympathy" or "I have a right not to engage in distasteful work." Such implications may belong to my verbal meaning, or they may not belong. This is usually the area where the interpreter needs a guiding principle.

It is often said that implications must be determined by referring to the context of the utterance, which, for ordinary statements like "I have a headache," means the concrete situation in which the utterance occurs. In the case of written texts, however, context generally means verbal context: the explicit meanings which surround the problematical passage. But these explicit meanings alone do not exhaust what we mean by context when we educe implications. The surrounding explicit meanings provide us with a sense of the whole meaning, and it is from this sense of the whole that we decide what the problematical passage implies. We do not ask simply, "Does this implication belong with these other explicit meanings?" but rather, "Does this implication belong with these other meanings *within a particular sort of total meaning?*" For example, we cannot determine whether "root" belongs with or implies "bark" unless we know that the total meaning is "tree" and not "grass." The ground for educing implications is a sense of the whole meaning, and this is an indispensable aspect of what we mean by context.

Previously I defined the whole meaning of an utterance as the author's verbal intention. Does this mean that the principle for admitting or excluding implications must be to ask, "Did the author have in mind such an implication?" If that is the principle, all hope for objective interpretation must be abandoned, since in most cases it is impossible (even for the author himself) to determine precisely what he was thinking of at the time or times he composed his text. But this is clearly not the correct principle. When I say, "I have a headache," I may indeed imply, "I would like some sympathy," and yet I might not

have been explicitly conscious of such an implication. The first step, then, in discovering a principle for admitting and excluding implications is to perceive the fundamental distinction between the author's verbal intention and the meanings of which he was explicitly conscious. Here again, Husserl's rejection of psychologism is useful. The author's verbal intention (his total verbal meaning) may be likened to my "intention" of a box. Normally, when I perceive a box, I am explicitly conscious of only three sides, and yet I assert with full confidence (although I might be wrong) that I "intend" a box, an object with *six* sides. Those three unseen sides belong to my "intention" in precisely the same way that the unconscious implications of an utterance belong to the author's intention. They belong to the intention taken as a whole.

Most, if not all, meaning experiences or intentions are occasions in which the whole meaning is not explicitly present to consciousness. But how are we to define the manner in which these unconscious meanings are implicitly present? In Husserl's analysis, they are present in the form of a "horizon," which may be defined as a system of typical expectations and probabilities.[15] "Horizon" is thus an essential aspect of what we usually call context. It is an inexplicit sense of the whole, derived from the explicit meanings present to consciousness. Thus, my view of three surfaces, presented in a familiar and typically box-like way, has a horizon of typical continuations; or, to put it another way, my "intention" of a whole box defines the horizon for my view of three visible sides. The same sort of relationship holds between the explicit and implicit meanings in a verbal intention. The explicit meanings are components in a total meaning which is bounded by a horizon. Of the manifold typical continuations within this horizon the author is not and cannot be explicitly conscious, nor would it be a particularly significant task to determine just which components of his meaning the author *was* thinking of. But it is of the utmost importance to determine the horizon which de-

[15]See Edmund Husserl, *Erfahrung und Urteil,* ed. L. Landgrebe (Hamburg, 1948), pp. 26–36, and Kuhn, "The Phenomenological Concept of 'Horizon.'" [Au.]

fines the author's intention as a whole, for it is only with reference to this horizon, or sense of the whole, that the interpreter may distinguish those implications which are typical and proper components of the meaning from those which are not.

The interpreter's aim, then, is to posit the author's horizon and carefully exclude his own accidental associations. A word like "vegetable," for example, had a meaning horizon in Marvell's language which is evidently somewhat different from the horizon it has in contemporary English. This is the linguistic horizon of the word, and it strictly bounds its possible implications. But all of these possible implications do not necessarily belong within the horizon of the particular utterance. What the word implies in the particular usage must be determined by asking, "Which implications are typical components of the whole meaning under consideration?" By analogy, when three surfaces are presented to me in a special way, I must know the typical continuations of the surfaces. If I have never encountered a box before, I might think that the unseen surfaces were concave or irregular, or I might simply think there are other sides but have no idea what they are like. The probability that I am right in the way I educe implications depends upon my familiarity with the type of meaning I consider.

That is the reason, of course, that the genre concept is so important in textual study. By classifying the text as belonging to a particular genre, the interpreter automatically posits a general horizon for its meaning. The genre provides a sense of the whole, a notion of typical meaning components. Thus, before we interpret a text, we often classify it as casual conversation, lyric poem, military command, scientific prose, occasional verse, novel, epic, and so on. In a similar way, I have to classify the object I see as a box, a sphere, a tree, and so on before I can deduce the character of its unseen or inexplicit components. But these generic classifications are simply preliminary indications. They give only a rough notion of the horizon for a particular meaning. The aim of interpretation is to specify the horizon as far as possible. Thus, the object I see is not simply a box but a cigarette carton,

and not simply that but a carton for a particular brand of cigarettes. If a paint mixer or dyer wants to specify a particular patch of color, he is not content to call it blue; he calls it Williamsburg Blue. The example of a color patch is paradigmatic for all particular verbal meanings. They are not simply *kinds* of meanings, nor are they single meanings corresponding to individual intentional acts (Williamsburg Blue is not simply an individual patch of color); they are *typical* meanings, particular yet reproducible, and the typical *components* of such meanings are similarly specific. The interpreter's job is to specify the text's horizon as far as he is able, and this means, ultimately, that he must familiarize himself with the typical meanings of the author's mental and experiential world.

The importance of the horizon concept is that it defines in principle the norms and limits which bound the meaning represented by the text. But, at the same time, the concept frees the interpreter from the constricting and impossible task of discovering what the author was explicitly thinking of. Thus, by defining textual meaning as the author's meaning, the interpreter does not, as it is so often argued, impoverish meaning; he simply excludes what does not belong to it. For example, if I say, "My car ran out of gas," I imply, typically, "The engine stopped running." Whether I also imply "Life is ironical" depends on the generality of my intention. Some linguistic utterances, many literary works among them, have an extremely broad horizon which at some points may touch the boundaries of man's intellectual cosmos. But whether this is the case is not a matter for a priori discussion; the decision must be based on a knowledgeable inference as to the particular intention being considered.

*Within* the horizon of a text's meaning, however, the process of explication is unlimited. In this respect Dryden was right; no text is ever fully explicated. For example, if I undertook to interpret my "intention" of a box, I could make explicit unlimited implications which I did not notice in my original intention. I could educe not only the three unseen sides, but also the fact that the surfaces of the box contain twenty-four right angles, that the area of two adjoining sides is less than half the total surface area, and so on.

And if someone asked me whether such meanings were implicit in my intention of a box, I must answer affirmatively. In the case of linguistic meanings, where the horizon defines a much more complex intentional object, such determinations are far more difficult to make. But the probability of an interpreter's inference may be judged by two criteria alone — the accuracy with which he has sensed the horizon of the whole and the typicality of such a meaning within such a whole. Insofar as the inference meets these criteria, it is truly an explication of textual meaning. It simply renders explicit that which was, consciously or unconsciously, in the author's intention.

The horizon which grounds and sanctions inferences about textual meaning is the "inner horizon" of the text. It is permanent and self-identical. Beyond this inner horizon any meaning has an "outer horizon"; that is to say, any meaning has relationships to other meanings; it is always a component in larger realms. This outer horizon is the domain of criticism. But this outer horizon is not only unlimited, it is also changing since the world itself changes. In general, criticism stakes out only a portion of this outer horizon as its peculiar object. Thus, for example, Eliot partitioned off that aspect of the text's outer horizon which is defined by the simultaneous order of literary texts. The simultaneous order at a given point in time is therefore the inner horizon of the meaning Eliot is investigating, and this inner horizon is just as definite, atemporal, and objective as the inner horizon which bounds textual meaning. However, the critic, like the interpreter, must construe correctly the components of his inner horizon, and one major component is textual meaning itself. The critic must first accurately interpret the text. He need not perform a detailed explication, but he needs to achieve (and validate) that clear and specific sense of the whole meaning which makes detailed explication possible.

## DETERMINATENESS OF TEXTUAL MEANING

In the previous section I defined textual meaning as the verbal intention of the author, and this argues implicitly that hermeneutics must stress a reconstruction of the author's aims and attitudes in order to evolve guides and norms for construing the meaning of his text. It is frequently argued, however, that textual meaning has nothing to do with the author's mind but only with his verbal achievement, that the object of interpretation is not the author but his text. This plausible argument assumes, of course, that the text automatically has a meaning simply because it represents an unalterable sequence of words. It assumes that the meaning of a word sequence is directly imposed by the public norms of language, that the text as a "piece of language" is a public object whose character is defined by public norms.[16] This view is in one respect sound, since textual meaning must conform to public norms if it is in any sense to be verbal (i.e., sharable) meaning; on no account may the interpreter permit his probing into the author's mind to raise private associations (experience) to the level of public implications (content).

However, this basically sound argument remains one-sided, for even though verbal meaning must conform to public linguistic norms (these are highly tolerant, of course), no mere sequence of words can represent an actual verbal meaning with reference to public norms alone. Referred to these alone, the text's meaning remains indeterminate. This is true even of the simplest declarative sentence like "My car ran out of gas" (did my Pullman dash from a cloud of Argon?). The fact that no one would radically misinterpret such a sentence simply indicates that its frequency is high enough to give its usual meaning the apparent status of an immediate given. But this apparent immediacy obscures a complex process of adjudications among meaning possibilities. Under the public norms of language alone no such adjudications can occur, since the array of possibilities presents a face of blank indifference. The array of possibilities only begins to become a more selective system of *probabilities* when, instead of confronting merely a word sequence, we also posit a speaker who very likely means something. Then and only then does the most usual sense of the word sequence become

[16]The phrase, "piece of language," comes from the first paragraph of Empson's *Seven Types of Ambiguity*. It is typical of the critical school Empson founded. [Au.]

the most probable or "obvious" sense. The point holds true a fortiori, of course, when we confront less obvious word sequences like those found in poetry. A careful exposition of this point may be found in the first volume of Cassirer's *Philosophy of Symbolic Forms,* which is largely devoted to a demonstration that verbal meaning arises from the "reciprocal determination" of public linguistic possibilities and subjective specifications of those possibilities.[17] Just as language constitutes and colors subjectivity, so does subjectivity color language. The author's or speaker's subjective act is formally necessary to verbal meaning, and any theory which tries to dispense with the author as specifier of meaning by asserting that textual meaning is purely objectively determined finds itself chasing will-o'-the-wisps. The burden of this section is, then, an attack on the view that a text is a "piece of language" and a defense of the notion that a text represents the determinate verbal meaning of an author.

One of the consequences arising from the view that a text is a piece of language — a purely public object — is the impossibility of defining in principle the nature of a correct interpretation. This is the same impasse which results from the theory that a text leads a life of its own, and, indeed, the two notions are corollaries since any "piece of language" must have a changing meaning when the changing public norms of language are viewed as the only ones which determine the sense of the text. It is therefore not surprising to find that Wellek subscribes implicitly to the text-as-language theory. The text is viewed as representing not a determinate meaning, but rather a system of meaning potentials specified not by a meaner but by the vital potency of language itself. Wellek acutely perceives the danger of the view:

> Thus the system of norms is growing and changing and will remain, in some sense, always incompletely and imperfectly realized. But this dynamic

conception does not mean mere subjectivism and relativism. All the different points of view are by no means equally right. It will always be possible to determine which point of view grasps the subject most thoroughly and deeply. A hierarchy of viewpoints, a criticism of the grasp of norms, is implied in the concept of the adequacy of interpretation.[18]

The danger of the view is, of course, precisely that it opens the door to subjectivism and relativism, since linguistic norms may be invoked to support any verbally possible meaning. Furthermore, it is not clear how one may criticize a grasp of norms which will not stand still.

Wellek's brief comment on the problem involved in defining and testing correctness in interpretation is representative of a widespread conviction among literary critics that the most correct interpretation is the most "inclusive" one. Indeed, the view is so widely accepted that Wellek did not need to defend his version of it (which he calls "Perspectivism") at length. The notion behind the theory is reflected by such phrases as "always incompletely and imperfectly realized" and "grasps the subject most thoroughly." This notion is simply that no single interpretation can exhaust the rich system of meaning potentialities represented by the text. Hence, every plausible reading which remains within public linguistic norms is a correct reading so far as it goes, but each reading is inevitably partial since it cannot realize all the potentialities of the text. The guiding principle in criticism, therefore, is that of the inclusive interpretation. The most "adequate" construction is the one which gives the fullest coherent account of all the text's potential meanings.[19]

Inclusivism is desirable as a position which induces a readiness to consider the results of others, but, aside from promoting an estimable tolerance, it has little theoretical value. Although its aim is to reconcile different plausible readings

---

[17]Vol. 1, *Language* (New Haven, 1953). It is ironic that Cassirer's work should be used to support the notion that a text speaks for itself. The realm of language is autonomous for Cassirer only in the sense that it follows an independent development which is reciprocally determined by objective *and* subjective factors. See pp. 69, 178, 213, 249–50, and passim. [Au.]

[18]Wellek and Warren, *Theory of Literature,* p. 144. [Au.]

[19]Every interpretation is necessarily incomplete in the sense that it fails to explicate all a text's implications. But this kind of incomplete interpretation may still carry an absolutely correct system of emphases and an accurate sense of the whole meaning. This kind of incompleteness is radically different from that postulated by the inclusivists, for whom a sense of the whole means a grasp of the various possible meanings which a text can plausibly represent. [Au.]

in an ideal, comprehensive interpretation, it cannot, in fact, either reconcile different readings or choose between them. As a normative ideal, or principle of correctness, it is useless. This point may be illustrated by citing two expert readings of a well-known poem by Wordsworth. I shall first quote the poem and then quote excerpts from two published exegeses to demonstrate the kind of impasse which inclusivism always provokes when it attempts to reconcile interpretation and, incidentally, to demonstrate the very kind of interpretive problem which calls for a guiding principle:

A slumber did my spirit seal;
    I had no human fears:
She seemed a thing that could not feel
    The touch of earthly years.

No motion has she now, no force;
    She neither hears nor sees;
Rolled round in earth's diurnal course,
    With rocks, and stones, and trees.

Here are excerpts from two commentaries on the final lines of the poem; the first is by Cleanth Brooks, the second by F. W. Bateson:

[The poet] attempts to suggest something of the lover's agonized shock at the loved one's present lack of motion — of his response to her utter and horrible inertness. . . . Part of the effect, of course, resides in the fact that a dead lifelessness is suggested more sharply by an object's being whirled about by something else than by an image of the object in repose. But there are other matters which are at work here: the sense of the girl's falling back into the clutter of things, companioned by things chained like a tree to one particular spot, or by things completely inanimate like rocks and stones. . . . [She] is caught up helplessly into the empty whirl of the earth which measures and makes time. She is touched by and held by earthly time in its most powerful and horrible image.

The final impression the poem leaves is not of two contrasting moods, but of a single mood mounting to a climax in the pantheistic magnificence of the last two lines. . . . The vague living-Lucy of this poem is opposed to the grander dead-Lucy who has become involved in the sublime processes of nature. We put the poem down satisfied, because its last two lines succeed in effecting a reconciliation between the two philosophies or social attitudes.

Lucy is actually more alive now that she is dead, because she is now a part of the life of Nature, and not just a human "thing."[20]

If we grant, as I think we must, that both the cited interpretations are permitted by the text, the problem for the inclusivist is to reconcile the two readings.

Three modes of reconciliation are available to the inclusivist: (1) Brooks's reading includes Bateson's; it shows that any affirmative suggestions in the poem are negated by the bitterly ironical portrayal of the inert girl being whirled around by what Bateson calls the "sublime processes of Nature." (2) Bateson's reading includes Brooks's; the ironic contrast between the active, seemingly immortal girl and the passive, inert, dead girl is overcome by a final unqualified affirmation of immortality. (3) Each of the readings is partially right, but they must be fused to supplement one another. The very fact that the critics differ suggests that the meaning is essentially ambiguous. The emotion expressed is ambivalent and comprises both bitter regret and affirmation. The third mode of reconciliation is the one most often employed and is probably, in this case, the most satisfactory. A fourth type of resolution, which would insist that Brooks is right and Bateson wrong (or vice versa), is not available to the inclusivist, since the text, as language, renders both readings plausible.

Close examination, however, reveals that none of the three modes of argument manages to reconcile or fuse the two different readings. Mode 1, for example, insists that Brooks's reading comprehends Bateson's, but although it is conceivable that Brooks implies all the meanings which Bateson has perceived, Brooks also implies a pattern of emphasis which cannot be reconciled with Bateson's reading. While Bateson construes a primary emphasis on life and affirmation, Brooks emphasizes deadness and inertness. No amount of manipulation can reconcile these divergent emphases, since one pattern of

[20]Cleanth Brooks, "Irony as a Principle of Structure," in *Literary Opinion in America*, ed. M. D. Zabel (2d ed. New York, 1951), p. 736; F. W. Bateson, *English Poetry: A Critical Introduction* (London, 1950), pp. 33, 80–81. [Au.] For Brooks, see Ch. 3. [Ed.]

emphasis irrevocably excludes other patterns, and, since emphasis is always crucial to meaning, the two constructions of meaning rigorously exclude one another. Precisely the same strictures hold, of course, for the argument that Bateson's reading comprehends that of Brooks. Nor can mode 3 escape with impunity. Although it seems to preserve a stress both on negation and on affirmation, thereby coalescing the two readings, it actually excludes both readings and labels them not simply partial, but wrong. For if the poem gives equal stress to bitter irony and to affirmation, then any construction which places a primary stress on either meaning is simply incorrect.

The general principle implied by my analysis is very simple. The submeanings of a text are not blocks which can be brought together additively. Since verbal (and any other) meaning is a *structure* of component meanings, interpretation has not done its job when it simply enumerates what the component meanings are. The interpreter must also determine their probable structure and particularly their structure of emphases. Relative emphasis is not only crucial to meaning (perhaps it is the most crucial and problematical element of all), it is also highly restrictive; it excludes alternatives. It may be asserted as a general rule that whenever a reader confronts two interpretations which impose different emphases on similar meaning components, at least one of the interpretations must be wrong. They cannot be reconciled.

By insisting that verbal meaning always exhibits a determinate structure of emphases, I do not, however, imply that a poem or any other text must be unambiguous. It is perfectly possible, for example, that Wordsworth's poem ambiguously implies both bitter irony and positive affirmation. Such complex emotions are commonly expressed in poetry, but if that is the kind of meaning the text represents, Brooks and Bateson would be wrong to emphasize one emotion at the expense of the other. Ambiguity or, for that matter, vagueness is not the same as indeterminateness. This is the crux of the issue. To say that verbal meaning is determinate is not to exclude complexities of meaning but only to insist that a text's meaning is what it is and not a

hundred other things. Taken in this sense, a vague or ambiguous text is just as determinate as a logical proposition; it means what it means and nothing else. This is true even if one argues that a text could display shifting emphases like those magic squares which first seem to jut out and then to jut in. With texts of this character (if any exist), one need only say that the emphases shift and must not, therefore, be construed statically. And static construction would simply be wrong. The fundamental flaw in the "theory of the most inclusive interpretation" is that it overlooks the problem of emphasis. Since different patterns of emphasis exclude one another, inclusivism is neither a genuine norm nor an adequate guiding principle for establishing an interpretation.

Aside from the fact that inclusivism cannot do its appointed job, there are more fundamental reasons for rejecting it and all other interpretive ideals based on the conception that a text represents a system of meaning possibilities. No one would deny that for the interpreter the text is at first the source of numerous possible interpretations. The very nature of language is such that a particular sequence of words can represent several different meanings (that is why public norms alone are insufficient in textual interpretation). But to say that a text *might* represent several structures of meaning does not imply that it does in fact represent all the meanings which a particular word sequence can legally convey. Is there not an obvious distinction between what a text might mean and what it does mean? According to accepted linguistic theory, it is far more accurate to say that a written composition is not a mere locus of verbal possibilities, but a record (made possible by the invention of writing) of a verbal actuality. The interpreter's job is to reconstruct a determinate actual meaning, not a mere system of possibilities. Indeed, if the text represented a system of possibilities, interpretation would be impossible, since no actual reading could correspond to a mere system of possibilities. Furthermore, if the text is conceived to represent all the *actual* structures of meaning permissible within the public norms of language, then no single construction (with its exclusivist pattern of emphases) could be correct, and any legitimate construction would be just as incorrect as any other. When a text is conceived as a piece of language, a familiar and all too common anarchy follows. But, aside form its unfortunate consequences, the theory contradicts a widely accepted principle in linguistics. I refer to Saussure's distinction between *langue* and *parole*.

Saussure defined *langue* as the system of linguistic possibilities shared by a speech community at a given point in time.[21] This system of possibilities contains two distinguishable levels. The first consists of habits, engrams, prohibitions, and the like derived from past linguistic usage; these are the "virtualities" of the *langue*. Based on these virtualities, there are, in addition, sharable meaning possibilities which have never before been actualized; these are the "potentialities." The two types of meaning possibilities taken together constitute the *langue* which the speech community draws upon. But this system of possibilities must be distinguished from the actual verbal utterances of individuals who draw upon it. These actual utterances are called *paroles;* they are uses of language and actualize some (but never all) of the meaning possibilities constituting the *langue*.

Saussure's distinction pinpoints the issue: does a text represent a segment of *langue* (as modern theorists hold) or a *parole?* A simple test suffices to provide the answer. If the text is composed of sentences, it represents *parole,* which is to say, the determinate verbal meaning of a member of the speech community. *Langue* contains words and sentence-forming principles, but it contains no sentences. It may be represented in writing only by isolated words in disconnection (*Wörter* as opposed to *Worte*). A *parole,* on the other hand, is always composed of sentences, an assertion corroborated by the firmly established principle that the sentence is the funda-

mental unit of speech.[22] Of course, there are numerous elliptical and one-word sentences, but wherever it can be correctly inferred that a text represents sentences and not simply isolated words, it may also be inferred that the text represents *parole,* which is to say, actual, determinate verbal meaning.

The point is nicely illustrated in a dictionary definition. The letters in boldface at the head of the definition represent the word as *langue,* with all its rich meaning possibilities. But under one of the subheadings, in an illustrative sentence, those same letters represent the word as *parole,* as a particular, selective actualization from *langue.* In yet another illustrative sentence, under another subheading, the very same word represents a different selective actualization. Of course, many sentences, especially those found in poetry, actualize far more possibilities than illustrative sentences in a dictionary. Any pun, for example, realizes simultaneously at least two divergent meaning possibilities. But the pun is nevertheless an actualization from *langue* and not a mere system of meaning possibilities.

The *langue-parole* distinction, besides affirming the determinateness of textual meaning, also clarifies the special problems posed by revised and interpolated texts. With a revised text, composed over a long period of time (*Faust,* for example), how are we to construe the unrevised portions? Should we assume that they still mean what they meant originally or that they took on a new meaning when the rest of the text was altered or expanded? With compiled or interpolated texts, like many books of the Bible, should we assume that sentences from varied provenances retain their original meanings or that these heterogeneous elements have become integral components of a new total meaning? In terms of Saussure's distinction, the question becomes: should we consider the text to represent a compilation of divers *paroles* or a new unitary *parole* "respoken" by the new author or editor? I submit that there can be no definitive answer to the question, except in relation to a specific scholarly or aesthetic purpose, for in reality the question

[21]This is the "synchronic" as opposed to the "diachronic" sense of the term. See Ferdinand de Saussure, *Cours de linguistique générale* (Paris, 1931). Useful discussions may be found in Stephen Ullman, *The Principles of Semantics* (Glasgow, 1951), and W. v. Wartburg, *Einführung in die Problematik und Methodik der Sprachwissenschaft* (Halle, 1943). [Au.] See the introduction to Ch. 4, Structuralism and Semiotics. [Ed.]

[22]See, for example, Cassirer, *Symbolic Forms,* Vol. 1, *Language,* p. 304. [Au.]

is not, "How are we to interpret the text?" but, "*Which* text are we to interpret?" Is it to be the heterogeneous compilation of past *paroles,* each to be separately considered, or the new, homogeneous *parole?* Both may be represented by the written score. The only problem is to choose, and having chosen, rigorously to refrain from confusing or in any way identifying the two quite different and separate "texts" with one another. Without solving any concrete problems, then, Saussure's distinction nevertheless confirms the critic's right in most cases to regard his text as representing a single *parole.*

Another problem which Saussure's distinction clarifies is that posed by the bungled text, where the author aimed to convey a meaning which his words do not convey to others in the speech community. One sometimes confronts the problem in a freshman essay. In such a case, the question is, does the text mean what the author wanted it to mean or does it mean what the speech community at large takes it to mean? Much attention has been devoted to this problem ever since the publication in 1946 of Wimsatt's and Beardsley's essay on "The Intentional Fallacy."[23] In that essay the position was taken (albeit modified by certain qualifications) that the text, being public, means what the speech community takes it to mean. This position is, in an ethical sense, right (and language, being social, has a strong ethical aspect): if the author has bungled so badly that his utterance will be misconstrued, then it serves him right when people misunderstand him. However, put in linguistic terms, the position becomes unsatisfactory. It implies that the meaning represented by the text is not the *parole* of an author, but rather the *parole* of the speech community. But since only individuals utter *paroles,* a *parole* of the speech community is a nonexistent, or what the Germans call an *Unding.* A text can represent only the *parole* of a speaker or author, which is another way of saying that meaning requires a meaner.

However, it is not necessary that an author's text represent the *parole* he desired to convey. It is frequently the case, when an author has bun-

gled, that his text represents no *parole* at all. Indeed, there are but two alternatives: either the text represents the author's verbal meaning or it represents no determinate verbal meaning at all. Sometimes, of course, it is impossible to detect that the author has bungled, and in that case, even though his text does not represent verbal meaning, we shall go on misconstruing the text as though it did, and no one will be the wiser. But with most bungles we are aware of a disjunction between the author's words and his probable meaning. Eliot, for example, chided Poe for saying "My most immemorial year," when Poe "meant" his most *memorable* year.[24] We all agree that Poe did not mean what speakers of English generally mean by the word "immemorial" — and so the word cannot have the usual meaning. (An author cannot mean what he does not mean.) The only question, then, is: does the word mean more or less what we convey by "never to be forgotten" or does it mean nothing at all? Has Poe so violated linguistic norms that we must deny his utterance verbal meaning or content?

The question probably cannot be answered by fiat, but since Poe's meaning is generally understood, and since the single criterion for verbal meaning is communicability, I am inclined to describe Poe's meaning as verbal.[25] I tend to side with the Poes and Malaprops of the world, for the norms of language remain far more tolerant than dictionaries and critics like Eliot suggest. On the other hand, every member of the speech community, and especially the critic, has a duty to avoid and condemn sloppiness and needless ambiguity in the use of language, simply in order to preserve the effectiveness of the *langue* itself. Moreover, there must be a dividing line between verbal meanings and those meanings which we

[23]See p. 1383. [Ed.]

[24]T. S. Eliot, "From Poe to Valéry," *Hudson Review* 2 (1949): 232. [Au.]
[25]The word is, in fact, quite effective. It conveys the sense of "memorable" by the component "memorial," and the sense of "never to be forgotten" by the negative prefix. The difference between this and jabberwocky words is that it appears to be a standard word occurring in a context of standard words. Perhaps Eliot is right to scold Poe, but he cannot properly insist that the word lacks a determinate verbal meaning. [Au.]

half-divine by a supra-linguistic exercise of imagination. There must be a dividing line between Poe's successful disregard of normal usage and the incommunicable word sequences of a bad freshman essay. However, that dividing line is not between the author's meaning and the reader's, but rather between the author's *parole* and no *parole* at all.

Of course, theoretical principles cannot directly solve the interpreter's problem. It is one thing to insist that a text represents the determinate verbal meaning of an author, but it is quite another to discover what that meaning is. The very same text could represent numerous different *paroles,* as any ironic sentence discloses ("That's a *bright* idea?" or "That's a bright *idea!*"). But it should be of some practical consequence for the interpreter to know that he does have a precisely defined task, namely, to discover the author's meaning. It is therefore not only sound but necessary for the interpreter to inquire, "What in all probability did the author mean? Is the pattern of emphases I construe the author's pattern?" But it is both incorrect and futile to inquire, "What does the language of the text say?" That question can have no determinate answer.

## VERIFICATION

Since the meaning represented by a text is that of another, the interpreter can never be certain that his reading is correct. He knows furthermore that the norms of *langue* by themselves are far too broad to specify the particular meanings and emphases represented by the text, that these particular meanings were specified by particular kinds of subjective acts on the part of the author, and that these acts, as such, remain inaccessible.[26] A less self-critical reader, on the other hand, approaches solipsism if he assumes that the text represents a perspicuous meaning simply because it represents an unalterable sequence of words. For if this perspicuous meaning is not verified in some way, it will simply be the inter-

preter's own meaning, exhibiting the connotations and emphases which he himself imposes. Of course, the reader must realize verbal meaning by his own subjective acts (no one can do that for him), but if he remembers that his job is to construe the author's meaning, he will attempt to exclude his own predispositions and to impose those of the author. However, no one can establish another's meaning with certainty. The interpreter's goal is simply this — to show that a given reading is more probable than others. In hermeneutics, verification is a process of establishing relative probabilities.

To establish a reading as probable it is first necessary to show, with reference to the norms of language, that it is possible. This is the criterion of *legitimacy:* the reading must be permissible within the public norms of the *langue* in which the text was composed. The second criterion is that of *correspondence:* the reading must account for each linguistic component in the text. Whenever a reading arbitrarily ignores linguistic components or inadequately accounts for them, the reading may be presumed improbable. The third criterion is that of *generic appropriateness:* if the text follows the conventions of a scientific essay, for example, it is inappropriate to construe the kind of allusive meaning found in casual conversation.[27] When these three preliminary criteria have been satisfied, there remains a fourth criterion which gives significance to all the rest, the criterion of plausibility or *coherence.* The three preliminary norms usually permit several readings, and this is by definition the case when a text is problematical. Faced with alternatives, the interpreter chooses the reading which best meets the criterion of coherence. Indeed, even when the text is not problematical, coherence remains the decisive criterion, since the meaning is "obvious" only because it "makes sense." I wish, therefore, to focus attention on the criterion of coherence and shall take for granted the demands of legitimacy, correspondence, and generic appropriateness. I shall try to show that verification by the criterion of coherence, and

[26]To recall Husserl's point, a particular verbal meaning depends on a particular species of intentional act, not on a single, irreproducible act. [Au.]

[27]This third criterion is, however, highly presumptive, since the interpreter may easily mistake the text's genre. [Au.]

ultimately, therefore, verification in general, implies a reconstruction of relevant aspects in the author's outlook. My point may be summarized in the paradox that objectivity in textual interpretation requires explicit reference to the speaker's subjectivity.

The paradox reflects the peculiar nature of coherence, which is not an absolute but a dependent quality. The laws of coherence are variable; they depend upon the nature of the total meaning under consideration. Two meanings ("dark" and "bright," for example) which cohere in one context may not cohere in another.[28] "Dark with excessive bright" makes excellent sense in *Paradise Lost,* but if a reader found the phrase in a textbook on plant pathology, he would assume that he confronted a misprint for "dark with excessive blight." Coherence depends on the context, and it is helpful to recall our definition of context: it is a sense of the whole meaning, constituted of explicit partial meanings plus a horizon of expectations and probabilities. One meaning coheres with another because it is typical or probable with reference to the whole (coherence is thus the first cousin of implication). The criterion of coherence can be invoked only with reference to a particular context, and this context may be inferred only by positing the author's horizon, his disposition toward a particular type of meaning. This conclusion requires elaboration.

The fact that coherence is a dependent quality leads to an unavoidable circularity in the process of interpretation. The interpreter posits meanings for the words and word sequences he confronts, and, at the same time, he has to posit a whole meaning or context in reference to which the submeanings cohere with one another. The procedure is thoroughly circular; the context is derived from the submeanings and the submeanings are specified and rendered coherent with reference to the context. This circularity makes it very difficult to convince a reader to alter his construction, as every teacher knows. Many a self-willed student continues to insist that his reading is just

as plausible as his instructor's, and, very often, the student is justified; his reading does make good sense. Often, the only thing at fault with the student's reading is that it is probably wrong, not that it is incoherent. The student persists in his opinion precisely because his construction *is* coherent and self-sustaining. In such a case he is wrong because he has misconstrued the context or sense of the whole. In this respect, the student's hardheadedness is not different from that of all self-convinced interpreters. Our readings are too plausible to be relinquished. If we have a distorted sense of the text's whole meaning, the harder we look at it the more certainly we shall find our distorted construction confirmed.

Since the quality of coherence depends upon the context inferred, there is no absolute standard of coherence by which we can adjudicate between different coherent readings. Verification by coherence implies therefore a verification of the grounds on which the reading is coherent. *It is necessary to establish that the context invoked is the most probable context.* Only then, in relation to an established context, can we judge that one reading is more coherent than another. Ultimately, therefore, we have to posit the most probable horizon for the text, and it is possible to do this only if we posit the author's typical outlook, the typical associations and expectations which form in part the context of his utterance. This is not only the one way we can test the relative coherence of a reading, but it is also the only way to avoid pure circularity in making sense of the text.

An essential task in the process of verification is, therefore, a deliberate reconstruction of the author's subjective stance to the extent that this stance is relevant to the text at hand.[29] The im-

[28]Exceptions to this are the syncategorematic meanings (color and extension, for example) which cohere by necessity regardless of the context. [Au.]

[29]The reader may feel that I have telescoped a number of steps here. The author's verbal meaning or verbal intention is the object of complex intentional acts. To reproduce this meaning it is necessary for the interpreter to engage in intentional acts belonging to the same species as those of the author. (Two different intentional acts belong to the same species when they "intend" the same intentional object.) That is why the issue of "stance" arises. The interpreter needs to adopt sympathetically the author's stance (his disposition to engage in particular kinds of intentional acts) so that he can "intend" with some degree of probability the same intentional

portance of such psychological reconstruction may be exemplified in adjudicating between different readings of Wordsworth's "A Slumber Did My Spirit Seal." The interpretations of Brooks and Bateson, different as they are, remain equally coherent and self-sustaining. The implications which Brooks construes cohere beautifully with the explicit meanings of the poem within the context which Brooks adumbrates. The same may be said of Bateson's reading. The best way to show that one reading is more plausible and coherent than the other is to show that one context is more probable than the other. The problem of adjudicating between Bateson and Brooks is therefore, implicitly, the problem every interpreter must face when he tries to verify his reading. He must establish the most probable context.

Now when the *homme moyen sensuel*[30] confronts bereavement such as that which Wordsworth's poem explicitly presents, he adumbrates, typically, a horizon including sorrow and inconsolability. These are for him components in the very meaning of bereavement. Sorrow and inconsolability cannot fail to be associated with death when the loved one, formerly so active and alive, is imagined as lying in the earth, helpless, dumb, inert, insentient. And since there is no hint of life in Heaven but only of bodily death, the comforts of Christianity lie beyond the poem's horizon. Affirmations too deep for tears, like those Bateson insists on, simply do not cohere with the poem's explicit meanings; they do not belong to the context. Brooks's reading, therefore, with its emphasis on inconsolability and bitter irony, is clearly justified not only by the text but by reference to universal human attitudes and feelings.

However, the trouble with such a reading is apparent to most Wordsworthians. The poet is not an *homme moyen sensuel;* his characteristic attitudes are somewhat pantheistic. Instead of regarding rocks and stones and trees merely as

inert objects, he probably regarded them in 1799 as deeply alive, as part of the immortal life of nature. Physical death he felt to be a return to the source of life, a new kind of participation in nature's "revolving immortality." From everything we know of Wordsworth's typical attitudes during the period in which he composed the poem, inconsolability and bitter irony do not belong in its horizon. I think, however, that Bateson overstates his case and that he fails to emphasize properly the negative implications in the poem ("No motion has she now, no force"). He overlooks the poet's reticence, his distinct unwillingness to express any unqualified evaluation of his experience. Bateson, I would say, has not paid enough attention to the criterion of correspondence. Nevertheless, in spite of this, and in spite of the apparent implausibility of Bateson's reading, it remains, I think, somewhat more probable than that of Brooks. His procedure is also more objective. Even if he had botched his job thoroughly and had produced a less probable reading than that of Brooks, his method would remain fundamentally sound. Instead of projecting his own attitudes (Bateson is presumably not a pantheist) and instead of positing a "universal matrix" of human attitudes (there is none), he has tried to reconstruct the author's probable attitudes so far as these are relevant in specifying the poem's meaning. It is still possible, of course, that Brooks is right and Bateson wrong. A poet's typical attitudes do not always apply to a particular poem, although Wordsworth is, in a given period, more consistent than most poets. Be that as it may, we shall never be certain what any writer means, and since Bateson grounds his interpretation in a conscious construction of the poet's outlook, his reading must be deemed the more probable one until the uncovering of some presently unknown data makes a different construction of the poet's stance appear more valid.

Bateson's procedure is appropriate to all texts, including anonymous ones. On the surface, it would seem impossible to invoke the author's probable outlook when the author remains unknown, but in this limiting case the interpreter simply makes his psychological reconstruction on the basis of fewer data. Even with anonymous texts it is crucial to posit not simply some author

---

objects as the author. This is especially clear in the case of *implicit* verbal meaning, where the interpreter's realization of the author's stance determines the text's horizon. [Au.]

[30]Average sensible man. [Ed.]

or other, but a particular subjective stance in reference to which the construed context is rendered probable. That is why it is important to date anonymous texts. The interpreter needs all the clues he can muster with regard not only to the text's *langue* and genre, but also to the cultural and personal attitudes the author might be expected to bring to bear in specifying his verbal meanings. In this sense, all texts, including anonymous ones, are "attributed." The objective interpreter simply tries to make his attribution explicit, so that the grounds for his reading are frankly acknowledged. This opens the way to progressive accuracy in interpretation, since it is possible then to test the assumptions behind a reading as well as the coherence of the reading itself.

The fact that anonymous texts may be successfully interpreted does not, however, lead to the conclusion that all texts should be treated as anonymous ones, that they should, so to say, speak for themselves. I have already argued that no text speaks for itself and that every construed text is necessarily attributed. These points suggest strongly that it is unsound to insist on deriving all inferences from the text itself. When we date an anonymous text, for example, we apply knowledge gained from a wide variety of sources which we correlate with data derived from the text. This extrinsic data is not, however, read into the text. On the contrary, it is used to verify that which we read out of it. The extrinsic information has ultimately a purely verificative function.

The same thing is true of information relating to the author's subjective stance. No matter what the source of this information may be, whether it be the text alone or the text in conjunction with other data, this information is extrinsic to verbal meaning as such. Strictly speaking, the author's subjective stance is not part of his verbal meaning even when he explicitly discusses his feelings and attitudes. This is Husserl's point again. The intentional object represented by a text is different from the intentional acts which realize it. When the interpreter posits the author's stance he sympathetically reenacts the author's intentional acts, but although this imaginative act is necessary for realizing meaning, it must be distinguished from meaning as such. In no sense does the text represent the author's subjective stance: the interpreter simply adopts a stance in order to make sense of the text, and, if he is self-critical, he tries to verify his interpretation by showing his adopted stance to be, in all probability, the author's.

Of course, the text at hand is the safest source of clues to the author's outlook, since men do adopt different attitudes on different occasions. However, even though the text itself should be the primary source of clues and must always be the final authority, the interpreter should make an effort to go beyond his text wherever possible, since this is the only way he can avoid a vicious circularity. The harder one looks at a text from an incorrect stance, the more convincing the incorrect construction becomes. Inferences about the author's stance are sometimes difficult to make even when all relevant data are brought to bear, and it is self-defeating to make the inferential process more difficult than it need be. Since these inferences are ultimately extrinsic, there is no virtue in deriving them from the text alone. One must not confuse the result of a construction (the interpreter's understanding of the text's *Sinn*) with the *process* of construction or with a validation of that process. The *Sinn* must be represented by and limited by the text alone, but the processes of construction and validation involve psychological reconstruction and should therefore be based on all the data available.

Not only the criterion of coherence but all the other criteria used in verifying interpretations must be applied with reference to a psychological reconstruction. The criterion of legitimacy, for example, must be related to a speaking subject, since it is the author's *langue*, as an internal possession, and not the interpreter's which defines the range of meaning possibilities a text can represent. The criterion of correspondence has force only because we presume that the author meant something by each of the linguistic components he employed, and the criterion of generic appropriateness is relevant only so far as generic conventions are possessed and accepted by the author. The fact that these criteria all refer ultimately to a psychological construction is hardly surprising when we recall that to verify a text is simply to establish that the author probably meant what we construe his text to mean. The interpreter's primary task is to reproduce in himself the author's "logic," his attitudes, his cultural givens, in short, his world. Even though the process of verification is highly complex and difficult, the ultimate verification principle is very simple — the imaginative reconstruction of the speaking subject.[31]

The speaking subject is not, however, identical with the subjectivity of the author as an actual historical person; it corresponds, rather, to a very limited and special aspect of the author's total subjectivity; it is, so to speak, that "part" of the author which specifies or determines verbal meaning.[32] This distinction is quite apparent in the case of a lie. When I wish to deceive, my secret awareness that I am lying is irrelevant to the verbal meaning of my utterance. The only correct interpretation of my lie is, paradoxically, to view it as being a true statement, since this is the only correct construction of my verbal intention. Indeed, it is only when my listener has *understood* my meaning (presented as true) that he can *judge* it to be a lie. Since I adopted a truth-telling stance, the verbal meaning of my utterance would be precisely the same, whether I was deliberately lying or suffering from the erroneous conviction that my statement was true. In other words, an author may adopt a stance which differs from his deepest attitudes in the same way that an interpreter must almost always adopt a stance different from his own.[33] But for the process of interpretation, the author's private experiences are irrelevant. The only relevant aspect of subjectivity is that which determines verbal meaning or, in Husserl's terms, content.

In a sense all poets are, of course, liars, and to some extent all speakers are, but the deliberate lie, spoken to deceive, is a borderline case. In most verbal utterances, the speaker's public stance is not totally foreign to his private attitudes. Even in those cases where the speaker deliberately assumes a role, this mimetic stance is usually not the final determinant of his meaning. In a play, for example, the total meaning of an utterance is not the intentional object of the dramatic character; that meaning is simply a component in the more complex intention of the dramatist. The speaker himself is spoken. The best description of these receding levels of subjectivity was provided by the scholastic philosophers in their distinction between "first intention," "second intention," and so on. Irony, for example, always entails a comprehension of two contrasting stances (intentional levels) by a third and final complex intention. The speaking subject may be defined as the final and most comprehensive level of awareness determinative of verbal meaning. In the case of a lie, the speaking subject assumes that he tells the truth, while the actual subject retains a private awareness of his deception. Similarly, many speakers retain in their isolated privacy a self-conscious awareness of their verbal meaning, an awareness which may agree or disagree, approve or disapprove, but which does not participate in determining their verbal meaning. To interpretation, this level of awareness is as irrelevant as it is inaccessible. In construing and verifying verbal meaning, only the speaking subject counts.

A separate exposition would be required to discuss the problems of psychological reconstruction. I have here simply tried to forestall the current objections to extrinsic biographical and historical information by pointing, on the one hand, to the exigencies of verification and, on the

[31]Here I purposefully display my sympathies with Dilthey's concepts, *Sichhineinfühlen* and *Verstehen*. In fact, my whole argument may be regarded as an attempt to ground some of Dilthey's hermeneutic principles in Husserl's epistemology and Saussure's linguistics. [Au.]

[32]Spranger aptly calls this the "cultural subject." See Eduard Spranger, "Zur Theorie des Verstehens und zur geisteswissenschaftlichen Psychologie," in *Festschrift Johannes Volkelt zum 70. Geburtstag* (Munich, 1918), p. 369. It should be clear that I am here in essential agreement with the American anti-intentionalists (term used in the ordinary sense). I think they are right to exclude private associations from verbal meaning. But it is of some practical consequence to insist that verbal meaning is that aspect of an author's meaning which is interpersonally communi*cable*. This implies that his verbal meaning is that which, under linguistic norms, one *can* understand, even if one must sometimes work hard to do so. [Au.]

[33]Bally calls this "dédoublement de la personalité." See his *Linguistique générale et linguistique française*, p. 37. [Au.]

the other, to the distinction between a speaking subject and a "biographical" person. I shall be satisfied if this part of my discussion, incomplete as it must be, will help revive the half-forgotten truism that interpretation is the construction of *another's* meaning. A slight shift in the way we speak about texts would be highly salutary. It is natural to speak not of what a text says, but of what an author means, and this more natural locution is the more accurate one. Furthermore, to speak in this way implies a readiness (not notably apparent in recent criticism) to put forth a wholehearted and self-critical effort at the primary level of criticism — the level of understanding.

# P. D. Juhl

b. 1946

*One of the most lucid recent theorists on the problems of meaning and intention in aesthetic contexts, P. D. Juhl was born in Hamburg, West Germany, in 1946. Educated at Columbia, he received his B.A. in 1969 and his Ph.D. in both German and philosophy only two years later. Juhl taught at Kenyon College and the University of Florida before being appointed to an associate professorship at Princeton University in 1976. Juhl has published articles in* Modern Language Notes *and* Critical Inquiry *as well as in collections such as* The Uses of Criticism *and Hans Robert Jauss's series,* Poetik und Hermeneutik. *The essay reprinted here is from his book,* Interpretation *(1980).*

# *Does a Literary Work Have One and Only One Correct Interpretation?*

## 1. INTRODUCTION

Edmund Wilson has claimed that the governess in Henry James's *The Turn of the Screw* "is a neurotic case of sex repression, and that the ghosts are not real ghosts but hallucinations of the governess."[1] Alexander Jones, on the other hand, insists that the ghosts are not hallucinations of the governess but are in fact quite real.[2] Christine Brooke-Rose has taken yet another view; she maintains that the question whether the ghosts are real or are hallucinations is left open.[3] If one

of these statements about *The Turn of the Screw* is true, does it follow that the other two are false? Or could all three be true? Or if not true, at least acceptable? Could the ghosts be both real and mere hallucinations of the governess?

The existence of divergent interpretations such as these raises the general issue of whether a literary work has one and only one correct reading or whether it usually has several correct, acceptable or admissible readings. Can we in principle determine the correct interpretation of a work, or is it not just in fact but logically — that is, in virtue of our concept of a literary work or of its meaning — impossible to find such a reading? Is the idea that one of the possible readings of a work is correct unintelligible?

Many structuralists reject the notion of literature as communication, representation, or expression. Interpretation, on this view, "is not a

[1] Edmund Wilson, "The Ambiguity of Henry James," in *A Casebook on Henry James's "The Turn of the Screw"* ed. Gerald Willen (New York: Crowell, 1960), p. 115. [Au.]

[2] Alexander E. Jones, "Point of View in *The Turn of the Screw*," *ibid.*, pp. 316f. [Au.]

[3] Christine Brooke-Rose, "The Squirm of the True: A Structural Analysis of Henry James's *The Turn of the Screw*," *PTL* 1 (1976): 513. [Au.]

matter of recovering some meaning which lies behind the work and serves as a centre governing its structure; it is rather an attempt to participate in and observe the play of possible meanings to which the text gives access."[4] Although interpretation — at least on the moderate view defended by Culler — is governed by rules or conventions, they impose only relatively loose constraints on what a text can mean and hence allow a variety of different, equally acceptable interpretations of any given work. It is not difficult to see that, on this view, one cannot speak of "the correct interpretation" of a text; nor can one say of an interpretation or an interpretive statement that it is true, inasmuch as the admissible interpretations of a given work may be incompatible.

Similarly, Joseph Margolis has maintained that "given the goal of interpretation, we do not understand that an admissible account necessarily precludes all others incompatible with itself."[5] Hence it would appear that the proper model of confirmation in literary interpretation is not truth and falsity, but rather plausibility and implausibility: "where his effort is interpretive, we cannot judge the critic's remarks to be simply true or false, accurate or inaccurate, but only that his interpretation . . . is 'plausible,' 'reasonable,' 'admissible,' 'indefensible,' 'not impossible,' and the like."[6]

The same holds true if we believe with Iser that the meaning of a text depends on the reader's creativity and imagination in filling in the so-called gaps in the text — in filling in, that is,

what is left open or unspecified in a text.[7] For if these gaps can be filled in a number of different, equally legitimate and possibly inconsistent ways, then again one could not say of an interpretive statement that it is true or that a certain interpretation is the correct reading of the text.

In the following, I shall present a few considerations in support of the view that a literary work has one and only one correct interpretation.

[4]Jonathan Culler, *Structuralist Poetics* (Ithaca: Cornell University Press, 1975), p. 247. [Au.]

[5]Joseph Margolis, *The Language of Art and Art Criticism* (Detroit: Wayne State University Press, 1965), p. 92. See also his "Works of Art are Physically Embodied and Culturally Emergent Entities," in *Culture and Art,* ed. Lars Aagaard-Mogensen (Atlantic Highlands, N.J.: Humanities Press, 1976), p. 40, and "Three Problems in Aesthetics," in *Art and Philosophy,* ed. Sidney Hook (New York: New York University Press, 1966), p. 266. [Au.]

[6]Margolis, *The Language of Art and Art Criticism,* p. 76. For a lucid and persuasive discussion of Margolis's claims, see Annette Barnes, "Half an Hour before Breakfast," *Journal of Aesthetics and Art Criticism* 34 (1975): 261–71. [Au.]

[7]Wolfgang Iser, *The Implied Reader* (Baltimore: Johns Hopkins University Press, 1974), pp. 279ff. See also his essay, "The Reality of Fiction," *New Literary History* 6 (1975): 35.

The view that a literary work has more than one "correct" interpretation has also been defended by, among others, Umberto Eco, *Das offene Kunstwerk* [Translation of *Opera aperta*] (Frankfurt: Suhrkamp, 1973), pp. 8, 11, 29f., 31, 37f., 56–59, et passim; Stuart Hampshire, "Types of Interpretation," in Hook (ed.), *Art and Philosophy,* pp. 101–108; Tzvetan Todorov, "How to Read?" in *The Poetics of Prose* (Ithaca: Cornell University Press, 1977), pp. 238–89; Paul Ricoeur, "The Model of the Text," *New Literary History* 5 (1973), pp. 103, 107f.; Alan Tormey, *The Concept of Expression* (Princeton: Princeton University Press, 1971), pp. 134–41; John F. Reichert, "Description and Interpretation in Literary Criticism," *Journal of Aesthetics and Art Criticism* 28 (1969): 290; Uwe Japp, *Hermeneutik* (Munich: Fink, 1977), pp. 46–58; András Horn, *Das Literarische* (Berlin: De Gruyter, 1978), pp. 37, 79–83; Barbara Herrnstein Smith, *On the Margins of Discourse* (Chicago: University of Chicago Press, 1978), pp. 38f., 74f., 124, and 137–54; and Robert J. Matthews, "Describing and Interpreting a Work of Art," *Journal of Aesthetics and Art Criticism* 36 (1977): 5–14. Matthews's argument for the claim that literary interpretations are typically neither true nor false (p. 13) rests on two crucial premises: (1) that a necessary condition for a person to be "able to interpret *x* . . . [is that he] *not* be in a position to know whether the statements constituting the interpretation are true of *x*" (p. 9); and (2) that external evidence is irrelevant (p. 12). He defends only the first premise, however. For a critical discussion of Matthews's claims, see Michael Hancher, "Describing and Interpreting Speech Acts," *Journal of Aesthetics and Art Criticism* 36 (1978), pp. 483–85.

That a literary work does not have one and only one correct reading also follows from C. L. Stevenson's theory, according to which interpretive claims are normative statements about how a text ought to be read ("On the Reasons That Can Be Given for the Interpretation of a Poem," in Margolis (ed.), *Philosophy Looks at the Arts* [New York: Charles Scribner's Sons, 1962], pp. 121–39). See also Arthur Child, *Interpretation* (Berkeley: University of California Press, 1965), pp. 125ff., and Frank Kermode's interesting essay "Can We Say Absolutely Anything We Like?", in *Art, Politics and Will,* ed. Quentin Anderson et al. (New York: Basic Books, 1977), pp. 159–72. [Au.]

## 2. MULTIPLICITY OF MEANING AND INCOMPATIBLE INTERPRETATIONS

Let us look a little more closely at the claim that there is not in principle one and only one correct interpretation of a literary work or that such interpretations are neither true nor false. Jonathan Culler has claimed that we "cannot ask [a theory of literature] to account for the 'correct' meaning of a work since we manifestly do not believe that for each work there is a single correct reading. . . . Indeed, the striking facts that do require explanation are how it is that a work can have a variety of meanings, but not just any meaning whatsoever. . . ."[8]

In order to clarify the issue, it will be useful to distinguish between two possible senses of the claim that a work can have a variety of meanings.

It may mean that a literary work usually suggests several different ideas, that it evokes or conveys a variety of different attitudes or feelings. For example, one might want to say that Wordsworth's poem "A slumber did my spirit seal" does not just convey, as Cleanth Brooks has maintained, "the lover's agonized shock"[9] at the death of the beloved, nor just a sense of pantheistic affirmation of "the grander dead-Lucy" who "is now a part of the life of Nature, and not just a human 'thing,'"[10] as F. W. Bateson has contended. Rather, one might want to say that the poem conveys both agonized shock and a sense of affirmation. In this sense of the claim that a work can have a variety of meanings, it is perfectly consistent with the assumption that there is in principle one and only one correct interpretation of a work. If the various meanings of a work are logically compatible, then the corresponding interpretive statements can all be true.[11]

Alternatively, the claim may be that a literary work can have a variety of mutually *incompatible* meanings. For instance, one might want to allow that the following interpretations of Wordsworth's poem are *jointly* acceptable: (a) that the poem conveys "the lover's agonized shock" at the death of the beloved and is not a pantheistic affirmation of "the grander dead-Lucy" who has become part of the life of nature; (b) that the poem does indeed celebrate "the grander dead-Lucy who has become involved in the sublime processes of nature"[12] and does not express grief or inconsolability; (c) that the poem is neither just an expression of the lover's agonized shock nor just a pantheistic celebration of the dead Lucy, but suggests both the lover's agony and affirmation.

In other words, in the second sense of the claim that a work can have a variety of meanings, it may be "true" both that the poem expresses pantheistic affirmation and that it does not express pantheistic affirmation. This is an example of Margolis's principle of tolerance, that incompatible interpretations of a literary work can be jointly defended as plausible.[13] This interpretation of the claim, unlike the first, is indeed inconsistent with the assumption that there is one and only one correct reading of a work and hence with the assumption that literary interpretations are true or false.

It is important not to confuse the claim that a work may have a variety of logically incompatible meanings with another one which, unlike

---

[8]*Structuralist Poetics*, p. 122. [Au.]

[9]See Brooks, "Irony as a Principle of Structure," in Ch. 3. [Ed.]

[10]F. W. Bateson, *English Poetry: A Critical Introduction* (London: Longmans Green, 1966), p. 59. [Au.]

[11]Accordingly, I do not deny, of course, that a literary work may, in a sense, have several correct interpretations. For if a work has several correct interpretations, they must (if I am right) be logically compatible. Consequently, they will be *partial* interpretations of the work or interpretations of one or another of its different aspects. And these various

(correct) partial interpretations — since they must be logically compatible — can be combined into one (comprehensive) interpretation of the work. It is important to notice, however, that when critics offer different interpretations of a given work, those interpretations are *in fact* usually incompatible. See Hirsch's excellent discussion, *Validity in Interpretation* (New Haven: Yale University Press, 1967), pp. 227–30, and also pp. 128–32. [Au.] See Hirsch, earlier in this chapter. [Ed.]

[12]Bateson, *English Poetry*, p. 59. [Au.]

[13]Margolis, *The Language of Art and Art Criticism*, pp. 91f. See also John Hospers, "Implied Truths in Literature," in *Art and Philosophy*, ed. William Kennick (New York: St. Martin's Press, 1964), pp. 320–21. [Au.]

Margolis's principle of tolerance, is uncontroversial: namely, that for many works a variety of logically incompatible interpretations have been offered. For it does not follow from this that a literary work cannot have one and only one correct interpretation. It is *prima facie* quite conceivable that of the incompatible interpretations provided for a work only one is correct. Thus Culler and Margolis are not just saying that literary works are frequently construed in a number of incompatible ways. Rather, they are claiming that incompatible interpretations may be "true" of the same work or, to put it another way, that we would be prepared to allow that if a work has a certain meaning *x*, it might also have another meaning *y* which is logically incompatible with *x*.

When confronted with two incompatible interpretations of a work, we could do several things: (1) We could say that each is (separately) plausible and the available evidence does not allow us to decide between them. (2) Or we could choose one and try to defend it and attempt to show that the other reading is inadequate or "incorrect." (3) Or we could modify the two interpretations so as to make them compatible and say, as in the case of Wordsworth's poem "A slumber did my spirit seal," for example, that it expresses both the lover's agonized shock at the death of the beloved and pantheistic affirmation. (This would be to opt for a third interpretation distinct from, and incompatible with, either of the original readings.)

But it would be very peculiar to say of Wordsworth's poem that it expresses the lover's grief and inconsolability *and* that it does *not* express the lover's grief and inconsolability but rather pantheistic affirmation. There is no evidence that in practice critics or other readers would be prepared to allow that logically incompatible readings could be jointly true. Nor does it help here, as Annette Barnes has pointed out,[14] to shift from

truth to plausibility and to say that while logically incompatible readings cannot be jointly true, they can be jointly plausible. The conjunction "the work means *x* and it does not mean *x*, but *y*" can no more be plausible than it can be true. If critics did allow logically incompatible readings to be jointly true or plausible, we would be forced to speak of different works corresponding to the various incompatible meanings of a given text.

But even if logically incompatible readings of a work cannot be jointly true or plausible, they may be *separately* plausible. Even if Wordsworth's poem cannot both express the lover's agonized shock and not express it, the reading according to which it expresses the lover's agonized shock may be just as plausible as the reading according to which it does not express this, but rather pantheistic affirmation. That any given work have at least two separately plausible readings is not quite sufficient, however, for a work not to have one and only one correct reading. We must also not in principle be able to say more than that a reading is plausible. Thus we can alternatively construe the claim that a work has several incompatible meanings as follows. For any given work there are several incompatible readings each of which is separately plausible and none of which can in principle be shown to be significantly more likely to be correct than any of the others.[15]

[14]"Half an Hour Before Breakfast," pp. 264f., 269. On logically incompatible interpretations, see also Shlomith Rimmon's clear and helpful discussion in *The Concept of Ambiguity* (Chicago: University of Chicago Press, 1976), pp. 7–11, 14, 17. [Au.]

[15]Although this interpretation of the thesis that a work usually has several (incompatible) meanings precludes the possibility that there is one and only one correct reading of a work, it does not allow us, strictly speaking, to say that a work *has* several (incompatible) meanings. All we can say of a work now is "it *could* mean *x* and it *could* mean *y*, not *x*." One might object that since it is in principle impossible to say more than that the work *could* mean *x*, in the sense that *x* is a plausible, admissible, or acceptable reading, to say that the work could mean *x* is to say that it means *x* or that the work *has* the meaning *x*. But this would be to miss the point. It is not because we cannot say of any reading that it is correct, as opposed to being plausible or admissible, it is because a work cannot both mean *x* and not mean *x* that we cannot say it *has* the meaning *x* if a reading according to which the work does not mean *x* is also plausible or admissible. [Au.]

## 3. POSSIBLE READINGS AND CRITICAL CHOICES

The conception of the meaning of a literary work which underlies the view that a literary work may have several or many logically incompatible meanings seems to be something like this. An interpretation of a literary work is analogous to a statement about the meaning of a word or sentence in a particular language; it is in important respects like a statement about the meaning of the word "man" in English, for example, or about the meaning of, say, the English sentence "He almost killed the dragon" in abstraction from its use by a speaker on a particular occasion. Culler, for instance, writes:

> The meaning of a sentence, one might say, is not a form or an essence, present at the moment of its production and lying behind it as a truth to be recovered, but the series of developments to which it gives rise, as determined by past and future relations between words and the conventions of semiotic systems. . . .[16]

> The written word is an object in its own right.[17]

> Interpretation is . . . an attempt to participate in and observe the play of possible meanings to which the text gives access.[18]

> The sign has a life of its own which is not governed by any *arché* or *telos*, origin or final cause, and

the conventions which govern its use in particular types of discourse are epiphenomena: they are themselves transitory cultural products.[19]

Of course, Culler does not want to go quite as far as Derrida or Kristeva; for he insists that "at any one time the production of meaning in a culture is governed by conventions."[20] The main differences between the meaning of a sentence (*in abstracto*) in a given language and the meaning of a literary work would seem to be these: the sentences of a natural language are not typically ambiguous in as many ways as are literary works; and the relevant conventions differ inasmuch as there is a special set of rules for the interpretation of literature (in addition to the semantic and syntactic rules of ordinary language) whose mastery constitutes literary competence.[21]

In this and the following section I shall try to show that this model, even if it is modified in certain respects, fails to account adequately for some central facts about the interpretation of literary works. These facts provide strong evidence that a literary work has one and only one correct reading. They support the view that the meaning of a literary work (rather than being like the meaning of a sentence (*in abstracto*) is like the meaning of a person's *utterance* of a sentence in a certain context — that is, like the meaning of a speech act.[22]

Consider the sentence

Cary saw the girl laughing at John.

Provided we know that the sentence is ambiguous and in what ways it is so, it would not make sense to say, in specifying the meaning of this sentence in English, that it just means

(i) Cary saw the girl as she (the girl) was laughing at John.

---

[16]*Structuralist Poetics*, p. 132. See also pp. 123–24. [Au.]

[17]*Ibid.*, p. 133. [Au.]

[18]*Ibid.*, p. 247. See also Smith, *On the Margins of Discourse*, pp. 51ff., 59, 69f., 74f., 124, and Siegfried Schmidt, *Elemente einer Textpoetik* (Munich: Bayerischer Schulbuch-Verlag, 1974), p. 87. Schmidt holds (pp. 41ff.), however, that a work can have only logically compatible meanings which must be capable of being integrated into a coherent whole ("Textgesamtgestalt"). But see also Schmidt, "Text und Bedeutung" in Schmidt (ed.), *Text, Bedeutung, Ästhetik* (Munich: Bayerischer Schulbuch-Verlag, 1970), p. 49. [Au.]

Ricoeur claims that although a text will have several meanings, "the kind of 'plurivocity' which belongs to texts as texts is something other than the polysemy of individual words in ordinary language and the ambiguity of individual sentences" ("The Model of the Text," p. 107). This is no doubt true. But since the ambiguity of individual words or sentences is used here only as an analogy, the objections raised below apply to Ricoeur's thesis as well. [Au.]

[19]Culler, *Structuralist Poetics*, p. 248. [Au.]

[20]*Ibid.*, p. 249. [Au.]

[21]See *ibid.*, pp. 113–30, *et passim*. [Au.]

[22]For a detailed and illuminating application of speech act theory to literature, see Mary Louise Pratt, *Toward a Speech Act Theory of Literary Discourse* (Bloomington: Indiana University Press, 1977). See also Michael Hancher's critical appraisal of the book in "Beyond a Speech Act Theory of Literary Discourse," *Modern Language Notes* 97 (1977): 1081–98. [Au.]

or that it just means

(ii) Cary saw the girl who is laughing at John.

In other words, under these circumstances it would not make sense to *choose* one of the linguistically possible readings of the sentence and say that it means (i), not (ii), or vice versa. On the other hand, if we are interpreting a person's utterance of the sentence on some particular occasion, then it would make sense to choose one of its possible readings even if we cannot in fact tell whether the utterance means (i) or (ii) or possibly both.

Consider now the following poem:

The shooting of the hunters she heard;
But to pity it moved her not.

It has at least three possible readings:

(1) She heard the hunters shooting (at animals or people), but she had no pity for the victims.

(2) She heard the hunters being shot but did not pity them.

(3) She heard the hunters shooting at someone or something, and she heard the hunters being shot (at), but did not pity either.

If the meaning of a literary work is like the meaning of a sentence *in abstracto,* then we should have to say that the poem means (1), (2), and (3). But it would not make sense to decide between these readings, just as it would not make sense, in specifying the meaning of the sentence "Cary saw the girl laughing at John," to choose one of its possible readings and to say it means (i) and not (ii). If someone did say this, we would be inclined to think either that he does not know that the sentence is ambiguous or that he is talking, not about the sentence, but about an utterance of the sentence on some particular occasion. In other words, on the model we are considering, it would be *unintelligible* to suppose that the poem could, for example, mean (1) and not also (2) and (3).

If we look at the practice of literary interpretation, however, we find that critics do in fact choose between the possible readings of a given text. For example, each of the three readings of the poem by Wordsworth mentioned above is, as far as the linguistic rules of English as well as Culler's conventions of literary interpretation are concerned, a possible reading of the text. Nevertheless, most of the critics who have offered an interpretation of the poem have chosen one of its possible readings and have claimed that it is the most probable interpretation, whereas the other possible readings which they have considered are incorrect, improbable, or implausible.

Of course, we do not always choose between the various possible readings of a work. Sometimes a critic will say of a particular work that it could mean so-and-so or that it could equally well mean such-and-such. But in saying this, a critic is not implying that it would not make sense to choose one of the possible readings; rather, he is saying that the evidence we possess is not sufficient to allow us to determine which of the possible readings is most probably correct.[23] Similarly, even if we believe that a particular work is ambiguous in the sense that the textual evidence provides more or less equal support for two or more interpretations, it would not be unintelligible to suppose that only one of the readings in question is correct.

A good example is R. S. Crane's interpretation of the fourth book of *Gulliver's Travels.* Crane believes that there is nothing in the text which would allow us to decide between the reading of the fourth Voyage as presenting a radically pessimistic picture of man and the reading according to which human nature is portrayed as not altogether hopeless.[24] Yet he does not go on to suggest that therefore it would be unintelligible to suppose that only one of the two interpretations might be correct. Rather, he proceeds to argue that the former interpretation is more likely to be correct.

Of course, he does so on the basis of "external" evidence of what Swift intended to convey. But then the anti-intentionalist needs to explain

[23]See Monroe C. Beardsley, *The Possibility of Criticism* (Detroit: Wayne State University Press, 1970), p. 44. [Au.]
[24]R. S. Crane, "The Houyhnhnms, the Yahoos, and the History of Ideas," in *Reason and the Imagination: Studies in the History of Ideas, 1600–1800,* ed. J. A. Mazzeo (New York: Columbia University Press, 1962), pp. 234ff., 237ff., 243f. [Au.]

how Crane and the vast majority of other critics could be so utterly misguided in their interpretative *practice* as to suppose that what they were offering in producing evidence of the author's intention is evidence of what the text means. Surely, the task of a theory of interpretation is to account for the most central aspects of critical practice, such as the kinds of evidence which the vast majority of critics implicitly accept as relevant, the kinds of things critics do in trying to establish that a work means so-and-so, and the kinds of inferences they draw from the fact or the assumption that a certain interpretation is "correct." Now, on the anti-intentionalist thesis, it is difficult to see how standard interpretive practice could be explained except as being the result of an enormous conceptual confusion. What I am referring to here are not metacritical pronouncements about the nature of literary interpretation, but rather the facts of actual interpretive practice and its implicit assumptions. And it is precisely these facts and assumptions that a theory of interpretation needs to account for.[25]

I have claimed that critics commonly choose between the possible readings of a text and say that it means this rather than that; they do so, as we have seen, at least occasionally even if they believe that on the basis of the textual evidence several interpretations are equally possible or plausible. Consequently, it would appear to be intelligible to suppose that only one of the possible readings of a given text is correct.

## 4. CRITICAL DISAGREEMENTS AND ACCEPTABLE READINGS

On the view that the meaning of a literary work is like the meaning of an ambiguous sentence *in abstracto,* it is difficult to account for the fact that in interpreting a work we usually choose one of its possible readings. This could be explained, however, on something like the following hypothesis.[26]

In order to be possible, plausible, or admissible, an interpretation of a literary work must satisfy linguistic constraints, certain requirements of textual coherence, and general rules or conventions of literary interpretation (such as Culler's). For any given work there are usually several readings which meet these conditions. Our concept of a literary work or of its meaning is such that there are no further constraints which an interpretation must or could satisfy in order to qualify for the more restrictive status of being true rather than merely plausible or admissible. That it is plausible or admissible is the most that could be said of an interpretation. So far the hypothesis introduces nothing new.

We now assume further that a critic may impose additional restrictions corresponding to his interests or his purpose in reading a work. He may, for example, want to read it in the way the author's contemporaries construed it; he may want to interpret it as a study in abnormal psychology; or he may want to give a Freudian or an existentialist reading; and so on. But since no such supplementary restriction is derivable from our concept of the meaning of a work, the fact that only one of the admissible readings of a given text satisfies a certain additional restriction of this sort does not make the interpretation in question correct. The most one might be able to establish is that a certain interpretation is "the correct — reading" of a particular text, where the blank is filled in by a suitable specification of the additional restriction imposed. But that an interpretation is the correct — reading of a work does not imply, of course, that it is the correct reading of the work. Nor does it have any bearing on the (objective) plausibility of that reading relative to other admissible interpretations of the work.

[25]See on this point Stanley Cavell, "A Matter of Meaning It," in *Must We Mean What We Say?* (New York: Scribners, 1969), p. 227. See also Colin Lyas, "Personal Qualities and the Intentional Fallacy," in *Philosophy and the Arts* 6 (1973): 199, 209. [Au.]

[26]For some suggestions along these lines, see Joseph Margolis, "Critics and Literature," *British Journal of Aesthetics* 11 (1971): 378; I. C. Hungerland, "The Concept of Intention in Art Criticism," *Journal of Philosophy* 52 (1955): 738ff., and *Poetic Discourse* (Berkeley: University of California Press, 1958), pp. 168–71, 175; and Marcia M. Eaton, "Good and Correct Interpretations of Literature," *Journal of Aesthetics and Art Criticism* 29 (1970–71): 231. [Au.]

The fact that in interpreting a work we usually make a choice between its possible readings could then be explained by assuming that when we do so, we have imposed further restrictions of this kind corresponding to our interests. There is another problem, however, which this hypothesis cannot eliminate so easily.

If a literary work has a variety of plausible or "acceptable"[27] readings, then we should expect that the critics who have examined a particular text *agree* that the various (incompatible) interpretations, which are "acceptable" according to the model, are indeed acceptable interpretations of the text. But such agreement is extremely rare. It is not just that critics do not agree on an interpretation. That, as we have seen, could be accommodated by the view that for any work there is a variety of plausible or acceptable readings — namely, if the critics in question simply preferred, for whatever reason, different interpretations of the set of "acceptable" readings but did not deny that the other readings are (objectively) equally "correct" or acceptable. It is the fact that they do almost invariably deny this which is difficult for this thesis to explain.

I have suggested in section 2 that critics are not prepared to allow that logically incompatible readings of a given work could be *jointly* plausible or acceptable. The point here is that although critics do allow that logically incompatible readings could be separately acceptable, they do not agree in most cases which reading or readings of a particular work *are* separately acceptable. In particular, they deny as a rule that readings incompatible with their own are also (separately) acceptable. It is important to notice that the crucial test of this claim is not whether a critic is prepared to assert that certain readings incompatible with his own might also be (separately) acceptable, but rather whether *when actually confronted* with readings incompatible with his own, he is in fact willing to concede that those readings are equally acceptable.

Culler, for example, maintains that "the claim is not that competent readers would agree on an interpretation but only that certain expectations about poetry and ways of reading guide the interpretive process and impose severe limitations on the set of acceptable or plausible readings."[28] But if the fact that competent readers hold different interpretations of the same text shows that it has several equally "correct," plausible, or acceptable readings, then what is it that these readers are disagreeing about when each of them denies that the others' interpretations are acceptable?

Let us consider a parallel in ordinary discourse.

The sentence

The boys are lying about the house.

is ambiguous and hence has more than one correct reading. Competent speakers of English will recognize at least two different interpretations of this sentence *in abstracto*:

(1) The boys are lying around in the house.
(2) The boys are not telling the truth about the house.

Now suppose that competent speakers of English disagreed about whether the proper reading of the sentence is (1) or (2). In that case, one could not expect a grammar of English simply to assign two readings to the sentence without qualification. Rather, the two readings would have to be marked as relative to certain dialects, so as to exhibit the fact that the sentence is not ambiguous in either of the relevant dialects. Thus, on the face of it, if a literary work has several "correct" or acceptable interpretations, one would expect that competent critics are in agreement about this, as competent speakers are in the case of a sentence which has several readings.

If we are to retain the view that for every work there is a variety of equally "correct" or acceptable interpretations, then we need to account for the fact that competent critics nevertheless disagree about which of those "correct" or acceptable interpretations is indeed correct. The explanation suggested by the hypothetical example of a disagreement over the proper reading of the sentence "The boys are lying about

---

[27]Culler, *Structuralist Poetics*, pp. 124f., 127. [Au.]

[28]*Ibid.*, p. 127. [Au.]

the house" would seem to be implausible in the case of a literary parallel. For it would be difficult to show, for example, that the dispute about Wordsworth's poem is rooted in the different dialects of the critics involved. Furthermore, if this were the right explanation, the controversy could be expected to dissolve as soon as the critics became aware of this.

Nor can disagreements about the meaning of a work be explained by assuming that usually each of the participants in a dispute has imposed a different supplementary restriction corresponding to his interests or purpose in interpreting the work. For, on the hypothesis sketched at the beginning of this section, such further restrictions have no bearing on the question whether a certain reading is or is not acceptable. Hence each of the critics could be expected to agree that the other readings are (objectively) equally acceptable. Nevertheless, a disagreement about the meaning of a work could be due to the fact that each critic has imposed a different supplementary restriction — if, for example, each has tacitly assumed that the others have imposed the same supplementary restriction. But this should become obvious fairly quickly in the course of the dispute. One would therefore expect the critics to acknowledge that each of their readings is "correct" given the corresponding supplementary restrictions. Hence the dispute should dissolve.

One might argue, however, that disagreements about which reading or readings are acceptable could be explained as follows. Let us assume that the acceptability of a reading is determined in the way postulated by the above hypothesis so that any given work will have several acceptable readings. Nonetheless, in practice critics might generally impose one further restriction, say, correspondence to the author's intention. Thus a reading that is acceptable might be regarded as unacceptable by the critics who conform to the general practice. Disputes about the meaning of a work could then be explained as disputes about what the author intended.

But, by hypothesis, any given work has some acceptable readings other than the one which the author intended. Suppose then that a critic refuses to adopt this restriction and chooses one of the acceptable readings of a particular work

which does not correspond to what the author intended. One would expect, on the hypothesis under consideration, that critics who, in conformity to the general practice, reject that reading as unacceptable would nevertheless admit that it is acceptable, provided one does not adopt the author's intention as a supplementary restriction. The problem, however, is that as a rule critics are not prepared to relativize in this way their claim that a certain reading is unacceptable. What they are claiming in rejecting a reading as unacceptable is that it fails to account (or account adequately) for certain facts which *any* interpretation must (satisfactorily) account for, regardless of what supplementary restriction a critic may decide to impose.

I am not suggesting that a literary work has only one possible reading. Clearly, for virtually any work there are a number of possible and perhaps plausible interpretations; and this is brought out by the fact that critics who disagree about the meaning of a given work will generally, or can be gotten to, admit that the interpretations with which they take issue and reject are nonetheless in some sense possible or have a certain plausibility. What I am suggesting is that a theory of interpretation must account for the fact that we do draw a distinction between a possible and a correct interpretation, even if we may not agree in any given case what the correct reading is.[29]

Critics who propose and defend an interpretation of a work do not usually claim merely that their reading is possible or plausible; rather, they typically claim implicitly, if not explicitly, that it is more likely to be correct than the various other interpretations which they have considered in determining what the text means.[30] Conse-

---

[29]Culler's use of the terms "possible," "plausible," and "acceptable" in characterizing "correct" interpretations (*ibid.*, pp. 243, 124, 127f., 120) blurs this distinction — not surprisingly, since he believes no such distinction can be drawn. (See also e.g. Hampshire, "Types of Interpretation," p. 108, and Margolis, *The Language of Art and Art Criticism*, p. 76.)

[30]This conclusion is confirmed by a series of empirical studies of literary interpretations conducted by Savigny, *Argumentation in der Literaturwissenschaft* (Munich: Beck, 1976); Grewendorf, *Argumentation und Interpretation: Wissenschaftstheoretische Untersuchungen am Beispiel germanistischer Lyrikinterpretationen* (Kronberg: Scriptor, 1975);

quently, although a literary work usually has several possible or even plausible readings, there is strong evidence that it has one and only one correct interpretation.

The facts I have presented here do not constitute conclusive evidence, however, since it remains conceivable that we should be mistaken in drawing a distinction between a possible or plausible and a correct interpretation of a work.[31] If it turned out to be in principle impossible to determine which of the possible or plausible readings of a work is correct, then we might have to assume that this distinction is illusory. I shall argue in section 9 below, however, that the relevant facts can be adequately explained without assuming that it is in principle impossible to determine the correct interpretation of a work.[32]

## 9. WHY ARE THERE SEVERAL INTERPRETATIONS FOR MOST LITERARY WORKS?

If a literary work has one and only one correct interpretation, then we must account for the fact that most works which have received any atten-

and Georg Meggle and Manfred Beetz, *Interpretationstheorie und Interpretationspraxis* (Kronberg: Scriptor, 1976). See esp. Savigny, p. 41, and Grewendorf, p. 80. For a list of the interpretations analyzed, see Savigny, pp. 9–12.

In claiming that a particular interpretation is more likely to be correct than various alternative readings, a critic is not necessarily, nor typically, claiming "finality" for the interpretation in question. See Hampshire, "Types of Interpretation," p. 108; also Monroe C. Beardsley, "The Limits of Critical Interpretation," in Hook, ed., *Art and Philosophy*, pp. 73–74. [Au.]

[31]For a parallel in ethics, see J. L. Mackie, *Ethics*, pp. 34–35. [Au.]

[32]In the section that follows, omitted here, Juhl attempts to demonstrate that literary critics presume in practice that there is only one correct interpretation of a literary text. The fact that critics cite parallel passages from other texts by the same author, for example, works as evidence for an interpretation only if literary texts are speech acts and the author's intention is relevant to the text's meaning. Juhl then attempts to refute arguments that support the idea of multiple correct interpretations, by citing the need we have to reread texts and the many reinterpretations that works have received throughout history; Juhl claims that rereading may have psychological rather than hermeneutic significance, and that reinterpretation often (though not always) involves changes in the significance (*Bedeutung*) of a text, rather than in its meaning (*Sinn*). [Ed.]

tion have been interpreted in a number of different (incompatible) ways. (The interpretations in question here are statements about the meaning of a work, not about its significance.) It might seem that this could be more readily explained on the assumption that a work has many (incompatible) meanings. I shall try to show that we can account for this quite as easily on the view that a literary work has one and only one correct interpretation.

If we look at the various interpretations of Henry James's *The Turn of the Screw*, for example, it is undeniable that there is some evidence for each of them. One might be inclined to say that all or most of the readings can account in a more or less plausible way for the central features of the text. This may be to admit more than the facts warrant, however; for it is not clear that the critics who have offered interpretations of the work, or for that matter critics who are thoroughly familiar with it but who have not committed themselves to a particular reading, would be prepared to accept this claim. But we can say at least this much. Given the available evidence, there are several interpretations none of which can, in such a way as to command general assent, be shown to be correct or to be incorrect. The relevant facts allow more than one reading.

Now this is no more surprising on the assumption that a work has one and only one correct interpretation than on the view that it has a variety of meanings. For to say that a work has one correct reading is not to say that we can *in fact* determine what the correct reading is. It is to say rather that it is intelligible to suppose that an interpretation is not just plausible but correct, that although a certain reading may be plausible given the evidence we possess, it could nevertheless turn out to be wrong. It is to say that we can imagine what it would be like for an interpretation to be correct or incorrect. The discovery of evidence which would show beyond reasonable doubt that a certain reading of *King Lear*, for example, is correct, and all other interpretations wrong, is no doubt highly unlikely. But from the fact that such evidence is not forthcoming, it does not follow that there could not in principle be such evidence. Nor does this assumption provide a more satisfactory explanation of the fact that a literary work can usually be construed in a variety of ways. This can be explained quite adequately on the assumption that although it is in principle possible to determine the correct reading of a given work, we do as a matter of fact lack the necessary evidence.

Whether a work means this or that frequently depends on precisely what associations certain words have in a particular passage; it depends on the significance of a gesture, an image, of an obscure antithesis or parallel, on the implications of a metaphor or the symbolic import of certain objects. It depends on the explanation of a character's actions, on his motives, attitudes, feelings. It depends on the narrator's reliability — the extent, that is, to which the narrator's beliefs, feelings, attitudes, and the like provide the proper frame of reference for interpreting the work.[33] Is the work to be taken as expressing or suggesting the narrator's beliefs, or does it call them into question? Does the narrator distort events? Is the governess in *The Turn of the Screw,* for example, suffering from delusions, or can we generally trust her reports?

Given questions such as these, it is not surprising that even where we know a great deal about the period and the author of a certain work, such evidence should leave considerable room for disagreement. Facts — when we have them — about the author's knowledge, beliefs, idiolect, and such usually provide only inconclusive evidence for the significance of certain images, for example, or the explanation of a character's action. Even explicit declarations of intention, as I have suggested earlier, do not constitute incontrovertible evidence.[34] In some cases, we do not have enough evidence to say, for instance, what the precise associations of a word in a given passage or line are; in others, we have a great deal of evidence, but it conflicts, different sets of facts supporting different conclusions.[35]

Hence, on the view that a literary work is a speech act, one could not in practice expect facts about the author and the period of a certain work to rule out more than some of the readings which might conceivably be proposed or which purely "internal" considerations might appear to allow.

Furthermore, given inconclusive evidence about what the author intended to convey by having a character commit suicide or murder, for example, our own beliefs about such matters come to play a much larger role. Because a certain view of the situation seems clearly right to us, it is often difficult to believe that the author could have thought otherwise. Thus when the evidence is inadequate, it is often easy to convince oneself that the author "must have" meant a certain passage in the way that our own beliefs would require.

That literary works are interpreted in a variety of ways is also in part due to the fact that literary interpretations satisfy two different demands. An interpretation is logically tied, as I have argued, to what we take to be the author's intention and hence must tell us what the author was up to in writing a particular work. It can usually be expected to answer a further demand as well. It does so, however, not in virtue of our concept of what it is for a work to mean so-and-so, but rather in virtue of its social function. We read literary works because they satisfy certain of our interests, needs, or values. We therefore expect an interpretation to show us, among other things, that and how a work does so; we expect it to tell us why a work is worth reading.[36] Now when the relevant facts allow a number of different assumptions about what the author intended, it is not surprising that, as a result of this demand, critics should make different choices. When it is difficult to tell objectively whether there is more

---

[33]See Wayne C. Booth's discussion of some of the problems of interpreting impersonal narrative in *The Rhetoric of Fiction* (Chicago: University of Chicago Press, 1961), pp. 311–74. [Au.]

[34]See A. J. Close, "Don Quixote and the 'Intentionalist Fallacy,'" in *On Literary Intention,* ed. David Newton de Molina (Edinburgh: Edinburgh University Press, 1976), pp. 180–81. [Au.]

[35]For some examples and a detailed discussion of some of the difficulties involved in reaching a decision in such

cases, see Hirsch, *Validity in Interpretation,* pp. 181–98. [Au.]

[36]Frequently, this demand is satisfied in the way I have suggested in considering the inexhaustibility of literary works, namely, in terms of the relation between the meaning of a work and our problems and concerns. But the meaning of a work, as opposed to its significance, may of course also answer many different interests; whether it can continue to do so depends on the readings which the available evidence allows. [Au.]

evidence for one or another of a certain set of readings, it is easy to persuade oneself that the more relevant, interesting, or aesthetically more satisfying reading is at least as plausible as any of the alternatives.[37] This also explains why aesthetic considerations occasionally have some appeal.

I have suggested in Chapter 4 that an interpretation is an explanation of a complex human action. If this is true, then one cannot expect questions of interpretation to be decidable in quite as straightforward a way as matters of description. It does not follow, however, that such explanations cannot in principle be shown to be true or false. If explanations of complex actions in other areas of life are correct or incorrect, then it is implausible to suppose that literary interpretations are not. There is a good deal of persistent disagreement in the interpretation of the major philosophical works, for example. Yet, I take it, one would not want to say that, therefore, such interpretations are not true or false. That there are more disagreements over literary works is no reason to suppose that literary interpretations differ in this respect from interpretations of philosophical texts; nor is it surprising in view of the kinds of considerations involved in determining what a literary work means and the lack of sufficient evidence of the appropriate sort.[38]

I have tried to show that we need not assume that a literary work usually has a variety of logically incompatible meanings in order to account for the fact that for most literary works a variety of logically incompatible interpretations have been offered. Why, then, say that a literary work has several or many meanings?

Those who hold this view usually claim either that external evidence is irrelevant or that, though relevant in some sense, it is always and necessarily compatible with more than one reading of the text and, in particular, with more than one of the readings which the "internal" evidence permits. Here is an example. Pierre Menard's *Don Quixote*[39] (let us assume that he completed the work), written in the early twentieth century, has a different meaning from Cervantes' *Don Quixote*, although the two are textually identical. This shows that external evidence is relevant in the sense that it can rule out certain interpretations permitted by the text. But, one might argue, although the assumption that *Don Quixote* was written in the twentieth century would rule out various readings of the text, it would also make room for several new ones. This is true, no doubt, inasmuch as all we have done is to transpose *Don Quixote* from the seventeenth to the twentieth century. There is no reason to suppose, however, that more restrictive assumptions about the author could not rule out all but one interpretation of the text. If the meaning of a work is logically tied to the author's intention, as I have argued in Chapters III to VI, or what a work expresses is linked to the author's beliefs in the way suggested in Chapter VII, then there is good reason to believe that any interpretation of a given text can in principle be shown to be correct or incorrect.[40]

I want to emphasize that this thesis does not

---

[37]See on this point Alastair Fowler's pertinent remarks ("Intention Floreat," in de Molina, p. 253): "An interpretation faithful to every proportion of the original, but lacking in relevance or interest, would be of little use. The bearing of this truth on habits of construction is incalculable. How often do we unconsciously meet the choice between falsifying the construct or neglecting the work? It is repugnant to admit that we are temporarily or permanently incapable of receiving anything from what nevertheless was once a great work. But this may often be so." [Au.]

[38]For detailed analyses and discussions of interpretive controversies, see Meggle and Beetz, *Interpretationstheorie und Interpretationspraxis*. On the reasons why it may seem that confirming an interpretation involves the "hermeneutic circle," see Wolfgang Stegmüller, "Der sogenannte Zirkel des Verstehens," *Natur und Geschichte: X. Deutscher Kongress für Philosophie* (Hamburg: Felix Meiner Verlag, 1973), pp. 21–46, and Hirsch, *Validity in Interpretation*, pp. 164–68.

On the question whether interpretations of people's behavior in ordinary life are true or false, see Jonathan Glover, "Introduction," in Glover, ed., *Philosophy of Mind* (Oxford:

Oxford University Press, 1976), pp. 1–3; and, on the status of psychoanalytic interpretations, see B. A. Farrell, "The Criteria for a Psycho-Analytic Interpretation," in Glover (ed.), pp. 15–34. [Au.]

[39]In Jorge Luis Borges's story, "Pierre Menard, Author of the *Quixote*," the obsessed title character recreates Cervantes's novel so thoroughly as to become its "author." [Ed.]

[40]For a detailed defense of this view see Juhl, *Interpretation*, Appendix. [Au.]

reduce or eliminate multiplicity of meaning in the usual sense. It is perfectly consistent with this view that the various elements of a work should suggest or express a number of different ideas, attitudes, feelings, and so on, that the words of a poem should have multiple associations and connections, and that a work as a whole should convey a variety of things. What I am denying is that a work can have logically incompatible meanings in the sense that it could both express the idea that man is doomed to destroy himself, for example, and not express this, or that it is in principle impossible to determine which of these readings, if any, is correct.

Nor am I claiming that we can in fact resolve any significant number of interpretive controversies. The reason is that we lack the necessary evidence to rule out more than a few of the possible readings of most works. Also, as even a cursory glance at the critical literature about virtually any text will show, critics are generally aware of a great deal of external evidence and use it quite freely to support one interpretation or to cast doubt on another. It is possible, of course, that on occasion someone should discover further evidence which shows a particular reading to be wrong beyond reasonable doubt. But the discovery of such evidence for all but one interpretation of any given text is unlikely. Nevertheless, as long as it is in principle possible that there should be such evidence, a work will have one and only one correct interpretation.

## 10. CONCLUSION

I have given a few arguments for the claim that a literary work has one and only one correct interpretation. If it does, then a work cannot have logically incompatible meanings. It is consistent with this claim, however, both (a) that a work may express or convey a number of different things, and (b) that literary works are typically construed in a variety of logically incompatible ways.

1. I have argued that on the assumption that a literary work has a number of logically incompatible meanings, it is difficult to account for several central facts which are easily explained on the view that a work has one and only one correct interpretation: (i) Critics are not prepared in practice to allow that logically incompatible readings can be jointly plausible or acceptable. (ii) Critics usually choose one of the possible readings of a text; at least occasionally, a critic will do so even if he believes that on the basis of the textual evidence several readings are equally plausible or acceptable. Hence it appears to be intelligible to suppose that only one of the possible readings of a work is correct. (iii) Critics generally do not agree about which readings of a particular work are or are not acceptable. In particular, a critic will typically deny in practice that readings incompatible with his are also (separately) acceptable. Furthermore, a critic who defends a certain interpretation of a work does not as a rule claim merely that his interpretation is possible or plausible, but rather that of all the alternative readings he has considered, it is the most likely to be correct.

2. I have presented further evidence in support of the claim that the meaning of a literary work is not like the meaning of an ambiguous sentence *in abstracto,* but rather like the meaning of a person's utterance or speech act: (i) Parallel passages in works by the same author always carry greater weight than parallel passages in the works of other authors. As we have seen, even structuralist critics, who might be expected to reject arguments involving an appeal to the author's intention, tacitly accept this rule. (ii) I have also considered an interpretation which Culler cites to illustrate his claim about the difference between understanding the words and sentences of which a poem consists and understanding a poem. The interpretation certainly appears to imply that the work is a speech act. Culler gives no reason for thinking otherwise. In fact, his "rule of significance," according to which a poem should be read as expressing some significant attitude toward man or his relation to the universe, ensures that a poem is, or is construed as, a speech act. But if a work is a speech act, then it cannot have logically incompatible meanings, and it would appear to be possible in principle to determine whether a certain reading is or is not correct.

3. Finally, I have dealt with three consider-

ations which might appear to support the view that a literary work has many meanings: the survival of such works, their inexhaustibility, and the fact that they are usually construed in a variety of ways. I have tried to show that we can adequately account for these facts without abandoning the assumption that a work has one and only one correct interpretation.

# Steven Knapp and

b. 1951

# Walter Benn Michaels

b. 1948

*Steven Knapp and Walter Benn Michaels are generally considered the point men of what W. J. T. Mitchell has labeled "the new pragmatism," an antitheoretical movement originating in the philosophy of Richard Rorty and the metatheoretical speculations of Stanley Fish. Knapp is associate professor of English at the University of California at Berkeley; he is the author, among other works, of* Personification and the Sublime: Milton to Coleridge *(1985). Michaels is professor of English at Berkeley; he is the editor of* Glyph 8 *(1981), coeditor (with Donald E. Pease) of* The American Renaissance Reconsidered *(1985), and author of the essays that comprise* The Gold Standard and the Logic of Naturalism *(forthcoming). In addition to "Against Theory," Knapp and Michaels have collaborated on "Against Theory 2: Hermeneutics and Deconstruction,"* Critical Inquiry *14 (1987): 49–68.*

# *Against Theory*

I

By "theory" we mean a special project in literary criticism: the attempt to govern interpretations of particular texts by appealing to an account of interpretation in general. The term is sometimes applied to literary subjects with no direct bearing on the interpretation of individual works, such as narratology, stylistics, and prosody. Despite their generality, however, these subjects seem to us essentially empirical, and our argument against theory will not apply to them.

Contemporary theory has taken two forms. Some theorists have sought to ground the reading of literary texts in methods designed to guarantee the objectivity and validity of interpretations. Others, impressed by the inability of such procedures to produce agreement among interpreters, have translated that failure into an alternative mode of theory that denies the possibility of correct interpretation. Our aim here is not to choose between these two alternatives but rather to show that both rest on a single mistake, a mistake that is central to the notion of theory per se. The object of our critique is not a particular way of doing theory but the idea of doing theory at all.

Theory attempts to solve — or to celebrate the impossibility of solving — a set of familiar problems: the function of authorial intention, the status of literary language, the role of interpretive assumptions, and so on. We will not attempt to solve these problems, nor will we be concerned with tracing their history or surveying the range of arguments they have stimulated. In our view, the mistake on which all critical theory rests has been to imagine that these problems are real. In fact, we will claim such problems only seem real — and theory itself only seems possible or relevant — when theorists fail to recognize the fundamental inseparability of the elements involved.

The clearest example of the tendency to generate theoretical problems by splitting apart terms that are in fact inseparable is the persistent debate over the relation between authorial intention and the meaning of texts. Some theorists have claimed that valid interpretations can only be obtained through an appeal to authorial intentions. This assumption is shared by theorists who, denying the possibility of recovering authorial intentions, also deny the possibility of valid interpretations. But once it is seen that the meaning of a text is simply identical to the author's intended meaning, the project of *grounding* meaning in intention becomes incoherent. Since the project itself is incoherent, it can neither succeed nor fail; hence both theoretical attitudes toward intention are irrelevant. The mistake made by theorists has been to imagine the possibility or desirability of moving from one term (the author's intended meaning) to a second term (the text's meaning), when actually the two terms are the same. One can neither succeed nor fail in deriving one term from the other, since to have one is already to have them both.

In the following two sections we will try to show in detail how theoretical accounts of intention always go wrong. In the fourth section we will undertake a similar analysis of an influential account of the role interpretive assumptions or beliefs play in the practice of literary criticism. The issues of belief and intention are, we think, central to the theoretical enterprise; our discussion of them is thus directed not only against specific theoretical arguments but against theory in general. Our examples are meant to represent the central mechanism of all theoretical arguments, and our treatment of them is meant to indicate that all such arguments will fail and fail in the same way. If we are right, then the whole enterprise of critical theory is misguided and should be abandoned.

## 2. MEANING AND INTENTION

The fact that what a text means is what its author intends is clearly stated by E. D. Hirsch when he writes that the meaning of a text "is, and can be, nothing other than the author's meaning" and "is determined once and for all by the character of the speaker's intention."[1] Having defined meaning as the author's intended meaning, Hirsch goes on to argue that all literary interpretation "must stress a reconstruction of the author's aims and attitudes in order to evolve guides and norms for construing the meaning of his text." Although these guides and norms cannot guarantee the correctness of any particular reading — nothing can — they nevertheless constitute, he claims, a "fundamentally sound" and "objective" method of interpretation (pp. 224, 240).

What seems odd about Hirsch's formulation is the transition from definition to method. He begins by defining textual meaning as the author's intended meaning and then suggests that the best way to find textual meaning is to look for authorial intention. But if meaning and intended meaning are already the same, it's hard to see how looking for one provides an objective method — or any sort of method — for looking for the other; looking for one just *is* looking for the other. The recognition that what a text means and what its author intends it to mean are identical should entail the further recognition that any appeal from one to the other is useless. And yet, as we have already begun to see, Hirsch thinks the opposite; he believes that identifying meaning with the expression of intention has the supreme theoretical usefulness of providing an objective method of choosing among alternative interpretations.

Hirsch, however, has failed to understand the force of his own formulation. In one moment he

[1]E. D. Hirsch, Jr., *Validity in Interpretation* (New Haven, Conn., 1967), pp. 216, 219. Our remarks on Hirsch are in some ways parallel to criticisms offered by P. D. Juhl in the second chapter of his *Interpretation: An Essay in the Philosophy of Literary Criticism* (Princeton, N. J., 1980). Juhl's position will be discussed in the next section. All further citations to these works will be included in the text. [Au.] See Hirsch and Juhl, both in this chapter. [Ed.]

identifies meaning and intended meaning; in the next moment he splits them apart. This mistake is clearly visible in his polemic against formalist critics who deny the importance of intention altogether. His argument against these critics ends up invoking their account of meaning at the expense of his own. Formalists, in Hirsch's summary, conceive the text as a "'piece of language,'" a "public object whose character is defined by public norms." The problem with this account, according to Hirsch, is that "no mere sequence of words can represent an actual verbal meaning with reference to public norms alone. Referred to these alone, the text's meaning remains indeterminate." Hirsch's example, "My car ran out of gas," is, as he notes, susceptible to an indeterminate range of interpretations. There are no public norms which will help us decide whether the sentence means that my automobile lacks fuel or "my Pullman dash[ed] from a cloud of Argon." Only by assigning a particular intention to the words "My car ran out of gas" does one arrive at a determinate interpretation. Or, as Hirsch himself puts it, "The array of possibilities only begins to become a more selective system of *probabilities* when, instead of confronting merely a word sequence, we also posit a speaker who very likely means something" (p. 225).[2]

This argument seems consistent with Hirsch's equation of meaning and intended meaning, until one realizes that Hirsch is imagining a moment of interpretation before intention is present. This is the moment at which the text's meaning "remains indeterminate," before such indeterminacy is cleared up by the *addition* of authorial intention. But if meaning and intention really are inseparable, then it makes no sense to think of intention as an ingredient that needs to be added; it must be present from the start. The issue of determinacy or indeterminacy is irrelevant. Hirsch thinks it's relevant because he thinks, correctly, that the movement from indeterminacy to determinacy involves the addition of information, but he also thinks, incorrectly, that

adding information amounts to adding intention. Since intention is already present, the only thing added, in the movement from indeterminacy to determinacy, is information *about* the intention, not the intention itself. For a sentence like "My car ran out of gas" even to be recognizable as a sentence, we must already have posited a speaker and hence an intention. Pinning down an interpretation of the sentence will not involve adding a speaker but deciding among a range of possible speakers. Knowing that the speaker inhabits a planet with an atmosphere of inert gases and on which the primary means of transportation is railroad will give one interpretation; knowing that the speaker is an earthling who owns a Ford will give another. But even if we have none of this information, as soon as we attempt to interpret at all we are already committed to a characterization of the speaker as a speaker of language. We know, in other words, that the speaker intends to speak; otherwise we wouldn't be interpreting. In this latter case, we have less information about the speaker than in the other two (where we at least knew the speaker's planetary origin), but the relative lack of information has nothing to do with the presence or absence of intention.

This mistake no doubt accounts for Hirsch's peculiar habit of calling the proper object of interpretation the "author's meaning" and, in later writings, distinguishing between it and the "reader's meaning."[3] The choice between these two kinds of meaning becomes, for Hirsch, an ethical imperative as well as an "operational" necessity. But if all meaning is always the author's meaning, then the alternative is an empty one, and there is no choice, ethical or operational, to be made. Since theory is designed to help us make such choices, all theoretical arguments on the issue of authorial intention must at some point accept the premises of anti-intentionalist accounts of meaning. In debates about intention, the movement of imagining intentionless meaning constitutes the theoretical movement itself. From the standpoint of an argument against critical theory, then, the only important question

---

[2] The phrase "piece of language" goes back, Hirsch notes, to the opening paragraph of William Empson's *Seven Types of Ambiguity,* 3rd ed. (New York, 1955). [Au.]

[3] See Hirsch, *The Aims of Interpretation* (Chicago, 1976), p. 8. [Au.]

about intention is whether there can in fact be intentionless meanings. If our argument against theory is to succeed, the answer to this question must be no.

The claim that all meanings are intentional is not, of course, an unfamiliar one in contemporary philosophy of language. John Searle, for example, asserts that "there is no getting away from intentionality," and he and others have advanced arguments to support this claim.[4] Our purpose here is not to add another such argument but to show how radically counterintuitive the alternative would be. We can begin to get a sense of this simply by noticing how difficult it is to imagine a case of intentionless meaning.

Suppose that you're walking along a beach and you come upon a curious sequence of squiggles in the sand. You step back a few paces and notice that they spell out the following words.

A slumber did my spirit seal;
  I had no human fears;
She seemed a thing that could not feel
  The touch of earthly years.[5]

This would seem to be a good case of intentionless meaning: you recognize the writing as writing, you understand what the words mean, you may even even identify them as constituting a rhymed poetic stanza — and all this without knowing anything about the author and indeed without needing to connect the words to any notion of an author at all. You can do all these things without thinking of anyone's intention. But now suppose that, as you stand gazing at this pattern in the sand, a wave washes up and recedes, leaving in its wake (written below what you now realize was only the first stanza) the following words:

No motion has she now, no force;
  She neither hears nor sees;
Rolled round in earth's diurnal course,
  With rocks, and stones, and trees.

[4] John R. Searle, "Reiterating the Differences: A Reply to Derrida," *Glyph* 1 (1977): 202. [Au.]

[5] Wordsworth's lyric has been a standard example in theoretical arguments since its adoption by Hirsch; see *Validity in Interpretation*, pp. 227–30 and 238–40. [Au.] See Hirsch and Juhl, both in this chapter. [Ed.]

One might ask whether the question of intention still seems as irrelevant as it did seconds before. You will now, we suspect, feel compelled to explain what you have just seen. Are these marks mere accidents, produced by the mechanical operation of the waves on the sand (through some subtle and unprecedented process of erosion, percolation, etc.)? Or is the sea alive and striving to express its pantheistic faith? Or has Wordsworth, since his death, become a sort of genius of the shore who inhabits the waves and periodically inscribes on the sand his elegiac sentiments? You might go on extending the list of explanations indefinitely, but you would find, we think, that all the explanations fall into two categories. You will either be ascribing these marks to some agent capable of intentions (the living sea, the haunting Wordsworth, etc.), or you will count them as nonintentional effects of mechanical processes (erosion, percolation, etc.). But in the second case — where the marks now seem to be accidents — will they still seem to be words?

Clearly not. They will merely seem to *resemble* words. You will be amazed, perhaps, that such an astonishing coincidence could occur. Of course, you would have been no less amazed had you decided that the sea or the ghost of Wordsworth was responsible. But it's essential to recognize that in the two cases your amazement would have two entirely different sources. In one case, you would be amazed by the identity of the author — who would have thought that the sea can write poetry? In the other case, however, in which you accept the hypothesis of natural accident, you're amazed to discover that what you thought was poetry turns out not to be poetry at all. It isn't poetry because it isn't language; that's what it means to call it an accident. As long as you thought the marks were poetry, you were assuming their intentional character. You had no idea who the author was, and this may have tricked you into thinking that positing an author was irrelevant to your ability to read the stanza. But in fact you had, without realizing it, already posited an author. It was only with the mysterious arrival of the second stanza that your tacit assumption (e.g., someone writing with a stick) was challenged and you realized that you had made one. Only now, when positing an author seems impossible, do you genuinely imagine the marks as authorless. But to deprive them of an author is to convert them into accidental likenesses of language. They are not, after all, an example of intentionless meaning; as soon as they become intentionless they become meaningless as well.

The arrival of the second stanza made clear that what had seemed to be an example of intentionless language was either not intentionless or not language. The question was whether the marks counted as language; what determined the answer was a decision as to whether or not they were the product of an intentional agent. If our example has seemed farfetched, it is only because there is seldom occasion in our culture to wonder whether the *sea* is an intentional agent. But there *are* cases where the question of intentional agency might be an important and difficult one. Can computers speak? Arguments over this question reproduce exactly the terms of our example. Since computers are machines, the issue of whether they can speak seems to hinge on the possibility of intentionless language. But our example shows that there is no such thing as intentionless language; the only real issue is whether computers are capable of intentions. However this issue may be decided — and our example offers no help in deciding it — the decision will not rest on a theory of meaning but on a judgment as to whether computers can be intentional agents. This is not to deny that a great deal — morally, legally, and politically — might depend on such judgments. But no degree of practical importance will give these judgments theoretical force.

The difference between theoretical principle and practical or empirical judgments can be clarified by one last glance at the case of the wave poem. Suppose, having seen the second stanza wash up on the beach, you have decided that the "poem" is really an accidental effect of erosion, percolation, and so on and therefore not language at all. What would it now take to change your mind? No theoretical argument will make a difference. But suppose you notice, rising out of the sea some distance from the shore, a small submarine, out of which clamber a half dozen figures in white lab coats. One of them trains his binoculars on the beach and shouts triumphantly, "It worked! It worked! Let's go down and try it again." Presumably, you will now once again change your mind, not because you have a new account of language, meaning, or intention but because you now have new evidence of an author. The question of authorship is and always was an empirical question; it has now received a new empirical answer. The theoretical temptation is to imagine that such empirical questions must, or should, have theoretical answers.

Even a philosopher as committed to the intentional status of language as Searle succumbs to this temptation to think that intention is a theoretical issue. After insisting, in the passage cited earlier, on the inescapability of intention, he goes on to say that "in serious literal speech the sentences are precisely the realizations of the intentions" and that "there need be no *gulf* at all between the illocutionary intention and its expression."[6] The point, however, is not that there *need* be no gulf between intention and the meaning of its expression but that there *can* be no gulf. Not only in serious literal speech but in *all* speech what is intended and what is meant are identical. In separating the two Searle imagines the possibility of expression without intention and so, like Hirsch, misses the point of his own claim that when it comes to language "there is no getting away from intentionality." Missing this point, and hence imagining the possibility of two different *kinds* of meaning, is more than a theoretical mistake; it is the sort of mistake that makes theory possible. It makes theory possible because it creates the illusion of a choice between alternative methods of interpreting.[7]

[6]Searle, "Reiterating," p. 202. [Au.]

[7]In conversation with the authors, Hirsch mentioned the case of a well-known critic and theorist who was persuaded by new evidence that his former reading of a poem was mistaken but who, nevertheless, professed to like his original reading better than what he now admitted was the author's intention. Hirsch meant this example to show the importance of choosing intention over some other interpretive criterion. But the critic in Hirsch's anecdote was not choosing among separate methods of interpretation; he was simply preferring his mistake. Such a preference is surely irrelevant to the theory of interpretation; it might affect what one does *with*

To be a theorist is only to think that there is such a choice. In this respect intentionalists and anti-intentionalists are the same. They are also the same in another respect: neither can really escape intention. But this doesn't mean the intentionalists win, since what intentionalists want is a guide to valid interpretation; what they get, however, is simply a description of what everyone always does. In practical terms, then, the stakes in the battle over intention are extremely low — in fact, they don't exist. Hence it doesn't matter who wins. In theoretical terms, however, the stakes are extremely high, and it still doesn't matter who wins. The stakes are high because they amount to the existence of theory itself; it doesn't matter who wins because as long as one thinks that a position on intention (either for or against) makes a difference in achieving valid interpretations, the ideal of theory itself is saved. Theory wins. But as soon as we recognize that there are no theoretical choices to be made, then the point of theory vanishes. Theory loses.[8]

---

an interpretation, but it has no effect on how one *gets* an interpretation.

[8]The arguments presented here against theoretical treatments of intention at the local utterance level would apply, virtually unaltered, to accounts of larger-scale intentions elsewhere in Hirsch; they would apply as well to the theoretical proposals of such writers as M. H. Abrams, Wayne C. Booth, R. S. Crane, and Ralph W. Rader — all associated, directly or indirectly, with the Chicago School. Despite variations of approach and emphasis, these writers tend to agree that critical debates about the meaning of a particular passage ought to be resolved through reference to the broader structural intentions informing the work in which the passage appears. Local meanings, in this view, should be deduced from hypothetical constructions of intentions implicit, for example, in an author's choice of genre; these interpretive hypotheses should in turn be confirmed or falsified by their success or failure in explaining the work's details. But this procedure would have methodological force only if the large-scale intentions were different in theoretical status from the local meanings they are supposed to constrain. We would argue, however, that all local meanings are always intentional and that structural choices and local utterances are therefore related to intention in exactly the same fashion. While an interpreter's sense of one might determine his sense of the other, neither is available to interpretation — or amenable to interpretive agreement — in a specially objective way. (Whether interpretations of intention at any level are best conceived as hypotheses is another, though a related, question.) [Au.] See Booth in Ch. 7; Crane in Ch. 3; and Rader, also in Ch. 3. [Ed.]

## 3. LANGUAGE AND SPEECH ACTS

We have argued that what a text means and what its author intends it to mean are identical and that their identity robs intention of any theoretical interest. A similar account of the relation between meaning and intention has recently been advanced by P. D. Juhl. According to Juhl, "there is a logical connection between statements about the meaning of a literary work and statements about the author's intention such that a statement about the meaning of a work *is* a statement about the author's intention." Juhl criticizes Hirsch, as we do, for believing that critics "*ought to* . . . try to ascertain the author's intention," when in fact, Juhl argues, "they are necessarily doing so already" (*Interpretation*, p. 12). But for Juhl, these claims serve in no way to discredit theory; rather, they themselves constitute a theory that "makes us aware of what we as critics or readers are doing in interpreting literature" and, more crucially, "provides the basis for a principled acceptance or rejection of an interpretation of a literary work" (p. 10). How is it that Juhl derives a theory from arguments which seem to us to make theory impossible?

What makes this question particularly intriguing is the fact that Juhl's strategy for demonstrating the centrality of intention is apparently identical to ours; it consists "in contrasting statements about the meaning of a literary work created by a person with statements about the meaning of a text produced by chance, such as a computer poem" (p. 13).[9] But Juhl's treatment of examples like our wave poem reveals that his sense of the relation between language and intention is after all radically different from ours. Like Hirsch, but at a further level of abstraction, Juhl ends up imagining the possibility of language prior to and independent of intention and thus conceiving intention as something that must be added to language to make it work. Like Hirsch, and like theorists in general, Juhl thinks that intention is

[9]In fact, Juhl employs the same poem we do — Wordsworth's "A Slumber Did My Spirit Seal" — in his own treatment of accidental "language" (*Interpretation*, pp. 70–82). The device of contrasting intentional speech acts with marks produced by chance is a familiar one in speech-act theory. [Au.]

a matter of choice. But where Hirsch recommends that we choose intention to adjudicate among interpretations, Juhl thinks no recommendation is necessary — not because we need never choose intention but only because our concept of a literary work is such that to read literature is already to have chosen intention.

Discussing the case of a "poem" produced by chance ("marks on [a] rock" or "a computer poem"), Juhl points out that there is "something odd about *interpreting* [such a] 'text.'" However one might understand this text, one could not understand it as a representation of "the meaning of a particular utterance." We agree with this — if it implies that the random marks mean nothing, are not language, and therefore cannot be interpreted at all. But for Juhl the implications are different. He thinks that one *can* interpret the random marks, though only in the somewhat specialized sense "in which we might be said to 'interpret' a sentence when we explain its meaning to a foreigner, by explaining to him what the individual words mean, how they function in the sentence, and thus how the sentence *could* be used or what it *could* be used to express or convey" (pp. 84–86).

Our point is that marks produced by chance are not words at all but only resemble them. For Juhl, the marks remain words, but words detached from the intentions that would make them utterances. Thus he can argue that when a "parrot utters the words 'Water is pouring down from the sky,'" one can understand that "the words mean 'It is raining'" but deny that the "'parrot *said* that it is raining'" (p. 109).[10] It is clear that, for Juhl, the words continue to mean even when devoid of intention. They mean "*in abstracto*" and thus constitute the condition of language prior to the addition of intention, that is, prior to "a speaker's utterance or speech act." In literary interpretation, this condition of language is never operative because, Juhl claims, "our notion of the meaning of a literary work" is "like our no-

tion of the meaning of a person's speech act," not "like our notion of the meaning of a word in a language" (p. 41).[11]

Implicit in Juhl's whole treatment of meaning and intention is the distinction made here between language and speech acts. This distinction makes possible a methodological prescription as strong as Hirsch's, if more general: when confronted with a piece of language, read it as a speech act. The prescriptive force of Juhl's argument is obscured by the fact that he has pushed the moment of decision one step back. Whereas Hirsch thinks we have to add intention to *literature* in order to determine what a text means, Juhl thinks that adding intentions to *language* gives us speech acts (such as literary works) whose meaning is already determinate. Juhl recognizes that as soon as we think of a piece of language as literature, we already regard it as a speech act and hence the product of intention; his prescription tells us how to get from language in general to a specific utterance, such as a literary work.[12]

But this prescription only makes sense if its two terms (language and speech acts) are not already inseparable in the same way that meaning and intention are. Juhl is right of course to claim that marks without intention are not speech acts, since the essence of a speech act is its intentional character. But we have demonstrated that marks without intention are not language either. Only by failing to see that linguistic meaning is always identical to expressed intention can Juhl imagine

[10]Juhl briefly acknowledges the strangeness of the sort of distinction he makes here when he asks whether words produced by chance could even be called "words" (*Interpretation*, p. 84). But he drops the question as abruptly as he raises it. [Au.]

[11]For additional remarks on meaning "*in abstracto*," see Juhl, *Interpretation*, pp. 25 n, 55–57, 203, 223, 238, 288–89. [Au.]

[12]Juhl's motives are, in fact, not far from Hirsch's. For both theorists, meaning *in abstracto* is indeterminate or ambiguous ("indeterminate" for Hirsch, "ambiguous" for Juhl); both appeal to intention in order to achieve determinate or particular meanings or, as Juhl says, to "disambiguate" the text (*Interpretation*, p. 97). This theoretical interest in the problem of indeterminacy derives in part from the widespread notion that words and sentences have a range of "linguistically possible" meanings, the ones recorded in dictionaries and grammar books. But a dictionary is an index of frequent usages in particular speech acts — not a matrix of abstract, pre-intentional possibilities. (For Hirsch's terminological distinction between ambiguity and indeterminacy, see *Validity in Interpretation*, p. 230.) [Au.]

language without speech acts. To recognize the identity of language and speech acts is to realize that Juhl's prescription — when confronted with language, read it as a speech act — can mean nothing more than: when confronted with language, read it as language.

For Hirsch and Juhl, the goal of theory is to provide an objectively valid method of literary interpretation. To make method possible, both are forced to imagine intentionless meanings or, in more general terms, to imagine a separation between language and speech acts.[13] The method then consists in adding speech acts to language; speech acts bring with them the particular intentions that allow interpreters to clear up the ambiguities intrinsic to language as such. But this separation of language and speech acts need not be used to establish an interpretive method; it can in fact be used to do just the opposite. For a theorist like Paul de Man, the priority of language to speech acts suggests that all attempts to arrive at determinate meanings by adding intentions amount to a violation of the genuine condition of language. If theory in its positive or methodological mode rests on the choice of speech acts over language, theory in its negative or antimethodological mode tries to preserve what it takes to be the purity of language from the distortion of speech acts.

The negative theorist's hostility to method depends on a particular account of language, most powerfully articulated in de Man's "The Purloined Ribbon." The essay concerns what de Man sees as a crucial episode in Rousseau's *Confessions,* in which Rousseau attempts to interpret, and thereby to justify, a particularly incriminating speech act. While working as a servant, he had stolen a ribbon from his employers. When accused of the theft, he blamed it on a fellow servant, Marion. In the passage that interests de Man, Rousseau is thus concerned with two crimes, the theft itself and the far more heinous act of excusing himself by accusing an innocent girl. This second act, the naming of Marion, is the one that especially needs justifying.

Rousseau offers several excuses, each an explanation of what he meant by naming Marion. But the explanation that intrigues de Man is the surprising one that Rousseau perhaps meant nothing at all when he said "Marion." He was merely uttering the first sound that occurred to him: "Rousseau was making whatever noise happened to come into his head; he was saying nothing at all."[14] Hence, de Man argues, "In the spirit of the text, one should resist all temptation to give any significance whatever to the sound 'Marion.'" The claim that "Marion" was meaningless gives Rousseau his best defense: "For it is only if . . . . the utterance of the sound 'Marion' is truly without any conceivable motive that the total arbitrariness of the action becomes the most effective, the most efficaciously performative excuse of all" (p. 37). Why? Because, "if the essential non-signification of the statement had been properly interpreted, if Rousseau's accusers had realized that Marion's name was 'le premier objet qui s'offrit,' they would have understood his lack of guilt as well as Marion's innocence" (p. 40).

But de Man is less interested in the efficacy of the "excuse" than he is in what it reveals about the fundamental nature of language. The fact that the sound "Marion" can mean nothing reminds us that language consists of inherently meaningless sounds to which one adds meanings — in other words, that the relation between signifier and signified is arbitrary. Why does de Man think this apparently uncontroversial description of language has any theoretical interest? The recognition that the material condition of language

[13] This distinction, in one form or another, is common among speech-act theorists. H. P. Grice, for example, distinguishes between "locutions of the form 'U (utterer) meant that . . .'" and "locutions of the form 'X (utterance-type) means . . . ,'" characterizing the first as "occasion-meaning" and the second as "applied timeless meaning" (H. P. Grice, "Utterer's Meaning, Sentence-Meaning, and Word-Meaning," in *The Philosophy of Language,* ed. Searle [London, 1971], pp. 54–56). And Searle, citing Wittgenstein ("Say 'it's cold here' and *mean* 'it's warm here'"), distinguishes between meaning as a "matter of intention" and meaning as a "matter of convention" (*Speech Acts* [Cambridge, 1969], p. 45). [Au.]

[14] Paul de Man, "The Purloined Ribbon," *Glyph* 1 (1977): 39; all further citations to this work will be included in the text. [Au.] A parallel point — the discrepancy between the grammatical form of an utterance and its rhetorical intention — can be found in de Man, in Ch. 5. [Ed.]

is inherently meaningless has no theoretical force in itself. But de Man thinks that the material condition of language is not simply meaningless but is also already "linguistic," that is, sounds are signifiers even before meanings (signifieds) are added to them. As a collection of "pure signifier[s]," in themselves "devoid of meaning and function," language is primarily a meaningless structure to which meanings are secondarily (and in de Man's view illegitimately) added (p. 32). Thus, according to de Man, Rousseau's accusers mistakenly added a meaning to the signifier "Marion" — hearing a speech act where they should have heard only language. This separation of language and speech act is the precondition for de Man's version of the theoretical choice.

De Man's separation of language and speech acts rests on a mistake. It is of course true that sounds in themselves are meaningless. It is also true that sounds become signifiers when they function in language. But it is not true that sounds in themselves are signifiers; they become signifiers only when they acquire meanings, and when they lose their meanings they stop being signifiers. De Man's mistake is to think that the sound "Marion" remains a signifier even when emptied of all meaning.[15] The fact is that the meaningless noise "Marion" only *resembles* the signifier "Marion," just as accidentally uttering the sound "Marion" only *resembles* the speech act of naming Marion. De Man recognizes that the accidental emission of the sound "Marion" is not a speech act (indeed, that's the point of the example), but he fails to recognize that it's not language either. What reduces the signifier to noise and the speech act to an accident is the absence of intention. Conceiving linguistic activity as the accidental emission of phonemes, de Man arrives at a vision of "the absolute randomness of language, prior to any figuration or meaning": "There can be no use of language which is

[15]Another, perhaps more usual, way of reaching this notion of the pure signifier is by observing that one signifier can be attached to many different meanings and concluding from this that the signifier has an identity of its own, independent of meaning in general. But the conclusion doesn't follow. Far from attaining its true identity when unrelated to any meaning, a signifier in this condition merely ceases to be a signifier. [Au.]

not, within a certain perspective thus radically formal, i.e., mechanical, no matter how deeply this aspect may be concealed by aesthetic, formalistic delusions" (pp. 44, 41).

By conceiving language as essentially random and mechanical, de Man gives a new response to the dilemma of the wave poem and suggests a fuller account of why that dilemma is central to theory in general. Our earlier discussion of the wave poem was intended to show how counterintuitive it is to separate language and intention. When the second stanza washed up on the beach, even the theorist should have been ready to admit that the poem was not a poem because the marks were not language. But our subsequent discussions of Juhl and de Man have revealed that theory precisely depends on not making this admission. For Juhl, the accidental marks remain language, but language *in abstracto* and hence inherently ambiguous. The wave poem thus presents a positive theorist like Juhl with a choice between the multiple meanings of intentionless marks and the determinate meaning of an intentional speech act. Since the point of positive theory is to ground the practice of determining particular meanings, the positive theorist chooses to read the marks as an intentional act. But when a negative theorist like de Man encounters the second (accidental) stanza, it presents him with a slightly different version of the same choice. For de Man the marks are not multiply meaningful but essentially meaningless, and the choice is not between one intentional meaning and many intentionless meanings but between intentional meaning and no meaning at all. Since, in de Man's view, all imputations of meaning are equally groundless, the positive theorist's choice of intention seems to him pointless. In apparent hostility to interpretive method, the negative theorist chooses the meaningless marks. But the negative theorist's choice in fact provides him with a positive methodology, a methodology that grounds the practice of interpretation in the single decisive truth about language. The truth about language is its accidental and mechanical nature: any text, "properly interpreted," will reveal its "essential nonsignification" (p. 40). For both Juhl and de Man, proper interpretation depends upon following a methodological prescription. Juhl's prescription is: when confronted with language, read it as a speech act. De Man's prescription is: when confronted with what seems to be a speech act, read it as language.

The wave poem, as encountered by a theorist, presents a choice between two kinds of meaning or, what comes to the same thing, two kinds of language. The issue in both cases is the presence or absence of intention; the positive theorist adds intention, the negative theorist subtracts it.[16] In our view, however, the relation between meaning and intention or, in slightly different terms, between language and speech acts is such that intention can neither be added nor subtracted. Intention cannot be added to or subtracted from meaning because meanings are always intentional; intention cannot be added to or subtracted from language because language consists of speech acts, which are also always intentional. Since language has intention already built into it, no recommendation about what to do with intention has any bearing on the question of how to interpret any utterance or text. For the non-theorist, the only question raised by the wave poem is not *how* to interpret but whether to interpret. Either the marks are a poem and hence a speech act, or they are not a poem and just happen to resemble a speech act. But once this empirical question is decided, no further judgments — and therefore no theoretical judgments — about the status of intention can be made.

## 4. THEORY AND PRACTICE

Our argument so far has concerned what might be called the ontological side of theory — its peculiar claims about the nature of its object. We have suggested that those claims always take the form of generating a difference where none in fact exists, by imagining a mode of language devoid of intention — devoid, that is, of what makes it language and distinguishes it from accidental or mechanical noises and marks. But we have also tried to show that this strange ontological project is more than a spontaneous anomaly; it is always in the service of an epistemological goal. That goal is the goal of method, the governance of interpretive practice by some larger and more principled account. Indeed, theoretical controversy in the Anglo-American tradition has more often taken the form of arguments about the epistemological situation of the interpreter than about the ontological status of the text. If the ontological project of theory has been to imagine a condition of language before intention, its epistemological project has been to imagine a condition of knowledge before interpretation.

The aim of theory's epistemological project is to base interpretation on a direct encounter with its object, an encounter undistorted by the influence of the interpreter's particular beliefs. Several writers have demonstrated the impossibility of escaping beliefs at any stage of interpretation and have concluded that theory's epistemological goal is therefore unattainable. Some have gone on to argue that the unattainability of an epistemologically neutral stance not only undermines the claims of method but prevents us from ever getting any correct interpretations. For these writers the attack on method thus has important practical consequences for literary criticism, albeit negative ones.[17]

But in discussing theory from the ontological side, we have tried to suggest that the impossibility of method has no practical consequences, positive or negative. And the same conclusion has been reached from the epistemological side

---

[16]At least this is true of the present generation of theorists. For earlier theorists such as W. K. Wimsatt and Monroe C. Beardsley, the objective meanings sought by positive theory were to be acquired precisely by *subtracting* intention and relying on the formal rules and public norms of language. This, of course, is the view they urge in "The Intentional Fallacy" (*The Verbal Icon: Studies in the Meaning of Poetry* [Lexington, Ky., 1954], pp. 3–18. [Au.] See Wimsatt and Beardsley, earlier in this chapter. [Ed.]

[17]Negative theory rests on the perception of what de Man calls "an insurmountable obstacle in the way of any reading or understanding" (*Allegories of Reading* [New Haven, Conn., 1979], p. 131). Some theorists (e.g., David Bleich and Norman Holland) understand this obstacle as the reader's subjectivity. Others (like de Man himself and J. Hillis Miller) understand it as the aporia between constative and performative language, between demonstration and persuasion. In all cases, however, the negative theorist is committed to the view that interpretation is, as Jonathan Culler says, "necessary error" (*The Pursuit of Signs* [Ithaca, N.Y., 1981], p. 14). [Au.] See Holland and Bleich, both in Ch. 7. [Ed.]

by the strongest critic of theoretical attempts to escape belief, Stanley Fish. In his last essay in *Is There a Text in This Class?*, Fish confronts the "final question" raised by his critique of method, namely, "what implications it has for the practice of literary criticism." His answer is, "none whatsoever":

> That is, it does not follow from what I have been saying that you should go out and do literary criticism in a certain way or refrain from doing it in other ways. The reason for this is that the position I have been presenting is not one that you (or anyone else) could live by. Its thesis is that whatever seems to you to be obvious and inescapable is only so within some institutional or conventional structure, and that means that you can never operate outside some such structure, even if you are persuaded by the thesis. As soon as you descend from theoretical reasoning about your assumptions, you will once again inhabit them and you will inhabit them without any reservations whatsoever; so that when you are called on to talk about Milton or Wordsworth or Yeats, you will do so from within whatever beliefs you hold about these authors.[18]

At the heart of this passage is the familiar distinction between "theoretical reasoning" and the "assumptions" or "beliefs" that inform the concrete "practice of literary criticism." Where most theorists affirm the practical importance of their theories, Fish's originality lies in his denial that his theory has any practical consequences whatsoever. But once theory gives up all claims to affect practice, what is there left for theory to do? Or, since Fish's point is that there is nothing left for theory to *do*, what is there left for theory to *be*? Understood in these terms, Fish's work displays the theoretical impulse in its purest form. Stripped of the methodological project either to ground or to undermine practice, theory continues to imagine a position outside it. While this retreat to a position outside practice looks like theory's last desperate attempt to save itself, it is really, as we hope to show, the founding gesture of all theoretical argument.

[18]Stanley Fish, *Is There a Text in This Class? The Authority of Interpretive Communities* (Cambridge, Mass., 1980), p. 370; all further citations to this work will be included in the text. [Au.] Also see the conclusion of Fish, "Interpreting the *Variorum*," pp. 1252–53. [Ed.]

Fish's attack on method begins with an account of belief that is in our view correct. The account's two central features are, first, the recognition that beliefs cannot be grounded in some deeper condition of knowledge and, second, the further recognition that this impossibility does not in any way weaken their claims to be true. "If one believes what one believes," Fish writes, "then one believes that what one believes is *true*, and conversely, one believes that what one doesn't believe is not true" (p. 361). Since one can neither escape one's beliefs nor escape the sense that they are true, Fish rejects both the claims of method and the claims of skepticism. Methodologists and skeptics maintain that the validity of beliefs depends on their being grounded in a condition of knowledge prior to and independent of belief; they differ only about whether this is possible. The virtue of Fish's account is that it shows why an insistence on the inescapability of belief is in no way inimical to the ordinary notions of truth and falsehood implicit in our sense of what knowledge is. The character of belief is precisely what gives us those notions in the first place; having beliefs just *is* being committed to the truth of what one believes and the falsehood of what one doesn't believe. But to say all this is, as Fish asserts, to offer no practical help or hindrance to the task of acquiring true beliefs. We can no more get true beliefs by looking for knowledge than we can get an author's meaning by looking for his or her intention, and for the same reason: knowledge and true belief are the same.

So far, this argument seems to us flawless. But Fish, as it turns out, fails to recognize the force of his own discussion of belief, and this failure is what makes him a theorist. It commits him, ultimately, to the ideal of knowledge implicit in all epistemological versions of theory, and it leads him to affirm, after all, the methodological value of his theoretical stance. Fish's departure from his account of belief shows up most vividly in his response to charges that his arguments lead to historical relativism. The fear of relativism is a fear that the abandonment of method must make all inquiry pointless. But, Fish rightly says, inquiry never seems pointless; our present beliefs about an object always seem better than any previous beliefs about the same object: "In other words, the idea of progress is inevitable, not, however, because there *is* a progress in the sense of a clearer and clearer sight of an independent object but because the *feeling* of having progressed is an inevitable consequence of the firmness with which we hold our beliefs" (pp. 361–62).

As an account of the inevitable psychology of belief, this is irreproachable. But when he later turns from the general issue of intellectual progress to the particular case of progress in literary criticism, Fish makes clear that he thinks our psychological assurance is unfounded. Our present beliefs only *seem* better than earlier ones; they never really *are*. And, indeed, the discovery of this truth about our beliefs gives us, Fish thinks, a new understanding of the history of literary criticism and a new sense of how to go about studying it. According to what Fish calls the "old model" for making sense of the history of criticism, the work of critics "like Sidney, Dryden, Pope, Coleridge, Arnold" could only be seen as "the record of the rather dismal performances of men . . . who simply did not understand literature and literary values as well as we do." But Fish's new model enables us to "regard those performances not as unsuccessful attempts to approximate our own but as extensions of a literary culture whose assumptions were *not inferior but merely different*" (pp. 367–68; our emphasis).

To imagine that we can see the beliefs we hold as no better than but "merely different" from opposing beliefs held by others is to imagine a position from which we can see our beliefs without really believing them. To be in this position would be to see the truth about beliefs without actually having any — to know without believing. In the moment in which he imagines this condition of knowledge outside belief, Fish has forgotten the point of his own earlier identification of knowledge and true belief.

Once a theorist has reached this vision of knowledge, there are two epistemological ways to go: realism and idealism. A realist thinks that theory allows us to stand outside our beliefs in a neutral encounter with the objects of interpretation; an idealist thinks that theory allows us to stand outside our beliefs in a neutral encounter with our beliefs themselves. The issue in both cases is the relation between objects and beliefs. For the realist, the object exists independent of beliefs, and knowledge requires that we shed our beliefs in a disinterested quest for the object. For the idealist, who insists that we can never shed our beliefs, knowledge means recognizing the role beliefs play in *constituting* their objects. Fish, with his commitment to the primacy of beliefs, chooses idealism: "objects," he thinks, "are made and not found"; interpretation "is not the art of construing but the art of constructing" (pp. 331, 327). Once he arrives at epistemological idealism, Fish's methodological payoff immediately follows. Knowing that "interpreters do not decode poems" but "make them," "we are free to consider the various forms the literary institution has taken and to uncover the interpretative strategies by which its canons have been produced and understood" (pp. 327, 368). By thinking of the critic as an idealist instead of a realist, Fish is able to place literary criticism at the very center of all literary practice:

No longer is the critic the humble servant of texts whose glories exist independently of anything he might do; it is what he does, within the constraints embedded in the literary institution, that brings texts into being and makes them available for analysis and appreciation. The practice of literary criticism is not something one must apologize for; it is absolutely essential not only to the maintenance of, but to the very production of, the objects of its attention. (p. 368)

We began this section by noting that Fish, like us, thinks that no general account of belief can have practical consequences. But, as we have just seen, *his* account turns out to have consequences after all. Why, then, is Fish led both to assert that his argument has no practical consequences and to proclaim its importance in providing a new model for critical practice? The answer is that, despite his explicit disclaimers, he thinks a true account of belief must be a *theory* about belief, whereas we think a true account of belief can only be a *belief* about belief.[19] The

[19]Fish calls his account a "general or metacritical belief"

difference between these two senses of what it means to have a true account of something is the difference between theory and the kind of pragmatist argument we are presenting here. These two kinds of positions conceive their inconsequentiality in two utterly different ways. A belief about the nature of beliefs is inconsequential because it merely tells you what beliefs are, not whether they are true or false in particular or in general. From this point of view, knowing the truth about belief will no more help you in acquiring true beliefs than knowing that meaning is intentional will help you find correct meanings. This is not in the least to say that you can't have true beliefs, only that you can't get them by having a good account of what beliefs are.

Fish's *theory* about beliefs, on the other hand, strives to achieve inconsequentiality by standing outside all the practical commitments that belief entails. It is perfectly true that one can achieve inconsequentiality by going outside beliefs but only because, as Fish himself insists, to be outside beliefs is to be nowhere at all. But of course Fish doesn't think that his theory about beliefs leaves him nowhere at all; he thinks instead that it gives him a way of arriving at truth, not by choosing some beliefs over others but by choosing beliefless knowledge over all beliefs. The truth of knowledge, according to Fish, is that no beliefs are, in the long run, truer than others; all beliefs, in the long run, are equal. But, as we have noted, it is only from the standpoint of a theory about belief which is not itself a belief that this truth can be seen. Hence the descent from "theoretical reasoning" about our beliefs to the actual practice of believing — from neutrality to commitment — demands that we forget the truth theory has told us. Unlike the ordinary methodologist, Fish wants to repudiate the attempt to derive practice from theory, insisting that the world of practice must be founded not on theoretical truth but on the repression of theoretical truth. But the sense that practice can only

(*Is There a Text in This Class?* p. 359; cf. pp. 368–70). [Au.]

begin with the repression of theory already amounts to a methodological prescription: when confronted with beliefs, forget that they are not really true. This prescription gives Fish everything theory always wants: knowledge of the truth-value of beliefs and instructions on what to do with them.[20]

We can now see why Fish, in the first passage quoted, says that his position is "not one that you (or anyone else) could live by . . . even if you [were] persuaded" by it. Theory, he thinks, can have no practical consequences; it cannot be lived because theory and practice — the truth about belief and belief itself — can never in principle be united. In our view, however, the only relevant truth about belief is that you can't go outside it, and, far from being unlivable, this is a truth you can't help but live. It has no practical consequences not because it can never be *united* with practice but because it can never be *separated* from practice.

The theoretical impulse, as we have described it, always involves the attempt to separate things that should not be separated: on the ontological side, meaning from intention, language from speech acts; on the epistemological side, knowledge from true belief. Our point has been that the separated terms are in fact inseparable. It is tempting to end by saying that theory and practice too are inseparable. But this would be a mistake. Not because theory and practice (unlike the other terms) really are separate but because theory is nothing else but the attempt to escape practice. Meaning is just another name for expressed intention, knowledge just another name for true belief, but theory is not just another name for practice. It is the name for all the ways people have tried to stand outside practice in order to govern practice from without. Our thesis has been that no one can reach a position outside practice, that theorists should stop trying, and that the theoretical enterprise should therefore come to an end.

[20]In one respect Fish's prescription is unusual: it separates the two theoretical goals of grounding practice and reaching objective truth. It tells us what is true and how to behave — but not how to behave in order to find out what is true. [Au.]

# Alternative Contents

Acknowledgments (*continued from page iv*)

Walter Benjamin, "The Work of Art in the Age of Mechanical Reproduction," from *Illuminations* by Walter Benjamin, copyright © 1955 by Suhrkamp Verlag, Frankfurt a.M.; English translation © 1968 by Harcourt Brace Jovanovich, Inc. Reprinted by permission of Harcourt Brace Jovanovich, Inc.

David Bleich, "Feelings about Literature," from *Readings and Feelings: An Introduction to Subjective Criticism* by David Bleich. Copyright © 1975 by the National Council of Teachers of English. Reprinted by permission of the publisher.

Harold Bloom, "A Meditation upon Priority," from *The Anxiety of Influence: A Theory of Poetry* by Harold Bloom. Copyright © 1973 by Oxford University Press, Inc. Reprinted by permission.

Giovanni Boccaccio, "The Definition of Poetry," from *Boccaccio on Poetry*, translated by Charles G. Osgood. Copyright © 1956 by Macmillan Publishing Company. Reprinted with permission of Macmillan.

Wayne C. Booth, "Control of Distance in Jane Austen's *Emma*," from *The Rhetoric of Fiction* by Wayne C. Booth. Copyright © 1961, 1983 by the University of Chicago. Reprinted by permission of the author and the University of Chicago Press.

Cleanth Brooks, "Irony as a Principle of Structure," from *Literary Opinion in America*, edited by Morton Dauwen Zabel. Reprinted by permission of the author.

Peter Brooks, "Freud's Masterplot: Questions of Narrative," from *Yale French Studies* 55/56 (1977). Copyright © 1977 by Yale University Press. Reprinted by permission of the publisher.

Kenneth Burke, "Literature as Equipment for Living," from *The Philosophy of Literary Form*, 3rd ed. rev., by Kenneth Burke. Copyright © 1973 by the Regents of the University of California. Reprinted by permission of the University of California Press. "Symbolic Action in a Poem by Keats," from *A Grammar of Motives* by Kenneth Burke. Copyright © 1969 Kenneth Burke. Reprinted by permission of the University of California Press.

Hélène Cixous, "The Laugh of the Medusa," translated by Keith Cohen and Paula Cohen, reprinted from *Signs* 1 (1976) by permission of the translators and the University of Chicago Press.

R. S. Crane, "Toward a More Adequate Criticism of Poetic Structure," from *The Languages of Criticism and the Structure of Poetry* by R. S. Crane. Copyright © 1953 by the University of Toronto Press. Reprinted by permission of the University of Chicago Press.

Benedetto Croce, "Aesthetica in Nuce," from *Philosophy, Poetry, History: An Anthology of Essays* by Benedetto Croce, translated by Cecil Sprigge (1966). Reprinted by permission of Oxford University Press.

Jonathan Culler, "Literary Competence," reprinted from *Structuralist Poetics: Structuralism, Linguistics, and the Study of Literature*, © Jonathan Culler 1975. Used by permission of the publishers, Cornell University Press and Routledge and Kegan Paul, Ltd.

Paul de Man, "Semiology and Rhetoric," from *Diacritics* 3:3 (Fall 1973). Reprinted by permission of the Johns Hopkins University Press.

Jacques Derrida, "Structure, Sign, and Play in the Discourse of the Human Sciences," from *The Structuralist Controversy: The Languages of Criticism and the Science of Man*, edited by Richard Macksey and Eugenio Donato, published by the Johns Hopkins University Press. Reprinted by permission of the publisher. "The Purloined Letter," from *The Purveyor of Truth* in *Yale French Studies* 52 (1975). Copyright © 1975 by Yale University Press. Reprinted by permission of the author and the publisher.

John Dewey, "The Act of Expression," from *Art as Experience* by John Dewey. Copyright © 1934 by John Dewey; renewed. Reprinted by permission of the Putnam Publishing Group.

Emily Dickinson, lines from "Civilization — spurns — the Leopard!" reprinted by permission of the publishers and the Trustees of Amherst College from *The Poems of Emily Dickinson*, edited by Thomas H. Johnson. Cambridge, Mass.: The Belknap Press of Harvard University Press. Copyright 1951, © 1955, 1979, 1983 by the President and Fellows of Harvard College.

Umberto Eco, "The Myth of Superman," translated by Natalie Chilton from *The Role of the Reader: Explorations in the Semiotics of Texts* by Umberto Eco. Copyright © 1979 by Umberto Eco. Reprinted by permission of Indiana University Press.

T. S. Eliot, "Tradition and the Individual Talent," from *Selected Essays* by T. S. Eliot. Copyright © 1950 by Harcourt Brace Jovanovich, Inc.; renewed 1978 by Esme Valerie Eliot. Reprinted by permission of Faber and Faber Ltd. and Harcourt Brace Jovanovich, Inc.

Stanley Fish, "Interpreting the *Variorum*," from *Critical Inquiry* 2. Copyright © 1976 by the University of Chicago. Reprinted by permission of the author and the University of Chicago Press.

Elizabeth Flynn, "Gender and Reading," from *College English* 45. Copyright © 1983 by the National Council of Teachers of English. Reprinted with permission.

Michel Foucault, "What Is an Author?" from *Textual Strategies: Perspectives in Post-Structuralist Criticism*, edited by Josue Harari, published by Cornell University Press. Copyright © 1979 Cornell University Press. Reprinted by permission of the Société Française de Philosophie and Cornell University Press.

Sigmund Freud, "Creative Writers and Daydreaming," from *Collected Papers*, vol. 4, by Sigmund Freud. Authorized translation under the supervision of Joan Riviere. Published by Basic Books, Inc., by arrangement with Sigmund Freud Copyrights Ltd., the Institute of Psycho-Analysis, and the Hogarth Press for permission to quote from *The Standard Edition of the Complete Psychological Works of Sigmund Freud* translated and edited by James Strachey. Reprinted by permission.

Robert Frost, "A Drumlin Woodchuck," "Away!" "On Being Unnoticed," and "Mending Wall," from *The Poetry of Robert Frost*, edited by Edward Connery Lathem. Copyright © 1969 by Holt, Rinehart and Winston, Inc. Copy-

Art. Copyright © 1957 Susanne K. Langer; copyright renewed © 1985 Leonard Langer. Reprinted with the permission of Charles Scribner's Sons.

F. R. Leavis, excerpts from *The Great Tradition* by F. R. Leavis. Copyright © 1960 by F. R. Leavis. Reprinted by permission of New York University Press, Chatto and Windus, Ltd., and the executors of the estate of F. R. Leavis.

Claude Lévi-Strauss, "The Structural Study of Myth," from *Structural Anthropology* by Claude Lévi-Strauss. Copyright © 1963 by Basic Books, Inc. Reprinted by permission of Basic Books, Inc., Publishers.

Georg Lukács, "The Ideology of Modernism," from *Realism in Our Time: Literature and the Class Struggle* by Georg Lukács. Translated from the German by John and Necke Mander. Copyright © 1962 by Merlin Press, Ltd. Reprinted by permission of Merlin Press, Ltd., and of Harper & Row, Publishers, Inc.

Karl Marx, "Consciousness Derived from Material Conditions," from *The German Ideology*. Reprinted by permission of International Publishers Co., New York.

Deborah E. McDowell, "New Directions for Black Feminist Criticism," reprinted from *Black American Literature Forum* 14:4 (Winter 1980). Copyright © 1980 by Indiana State University.

Jan Mukařovský, "Standard Language and Poetic Language," from *A Prague School Reader on Esthetics, Literary Structure, and Style*, translated by Paul L. Garvin. Reprinted by permission of Georgetown University Press.

Friedrich Nietzsche, excerpts from *The Birth of Tragedy*. Translated by Francis Golffing. Translation copyright © 1956 by Doubleday and Company, Inc. Reprinted by permission of the publisher.

Plato, *Ion*, reprinted from *Plato: Phaedrus, Ion, Gorgias, and Symposium, with Passages from the Republic and Laws*, translated by Lane Cooper. Copyright © 1938 by Lane Cooper. Reprinted by permission of Cornell University Press.

Plotinus, "On the Intellectual Beauty," reprinted by permission of Faber and Faber Ltd. from *Plotinus: The Enneads*, 3rd ed., edited by B. S. Page, translated by Stephen Mackenna.

Vladimir Propp, "The Morphology of the Folktale," from *Readings in Russian Poetics*, edited and translated by Ladislaw Matejka and Krystyna Pomorska, published by MIT Press. Copyright 1978. Reprinted by permission of the publisher.

Marcel Proust, "Meditation on Time and Memory" from *Remembrance of Things Past, Volume Three: The Captive, The Fugitive, and Time Regained* by Marcel Proust, translated by C. K. Scott Moncrieff, Terence Kilmartin, and Andreas Mayor. Translation copyright © 1981 by Random House and Chatto and Windus. Reprinted by permission of Random House, Inc., and Chatto and Windus.

Ralph Rader, "Defoe, Richardson, Joyce, and the Concept of Form in the Novel," from *Autobiography, Biography, and the Novel*, published by the William Andrews Clark Memorial Library. Copyright © 1973 Ralph Rader. Reprinted by permission of the author.

I. A. Richards, "Beliefs and Poetry," and "The Two Uses of Language," from *Principles of Literary Criticism* by I. A. Richards. Reprinted by permission of Harcourt Brace Jovanovich, Inc.

Pierre de Ronsard, "A Brief on the Art of French Poetry" by Pierre de Ronsard, translated by James Harry Smith, reprinted from *The Great Critics*, compiled and edited by James Harry Smith and Edd Winfield Parks, with the permission of W. W. Norton & Company, Inc. Copyright 1932, 1939, 1951 and renewed 1967 by James Harry Smith and Edd Winfield Parks.

Edward W. Said, "The Text, the World, the Critic," from *Textual Strategies: Perspectives in Post-Structuralist Criticism*, edited by Josue Harari, published by Cornell University Press. Copyright © 1979 Cornell University Press. Reprinted by permission of the publisher.

Jean-Paul Sartre, "Why Write?" from *What Is Literature?* by Jean-Paul Sartre, translated by Bernard Frechtman. Reprinted by permission of the Philosophical Library, Publishers.

Friedrich von Schiller, from "On Naive and Sentimental Poetry," from *Two Essays by Friedrich von Schiller*, translated by Julius A. Elias. Copyright © 1966 by the Frederick Ungar Publishing Company. Reprinted by permission of the publisher.

Victor Shklovsky, "Art as Technique," reprinted from *Russian Formalist Criticism: Four Essays*, translated and with an introduction by Lee T. Lemon and Marion J. Reis by permission of the University of Nebraska Press. Copyright © 1965 by the University of Nebraska Press.

Elaine Showalter, from *A Literature of Their Own: British Women Novelists from Brontë to Lessing* by Elaine Showalter. Copyright © 1977 by Princeton University Press. Excerpt reprinted with permission of Princeton University Press.

Barbara Herrnstein Smith, "Contingencies of Value," from *Critical Inquiry* 10 (1984). Copyright © 1984 by the University of Chicago. Reprinted by permission of the author and the University of Chicago Press.

Susan Sontag, "Against Interpretation," from *A Susan Sontag Reader* by Susan Sontag. Copyright 1963, 1964, 1966, 1967, 1968, 1969, 1973, 1974, 1975, 1977, 1978, 1980, 1982 by Susan Sontag. Reprinted by permission of Farrar, Straus and Giroux, Inc.

Madame de Staël, "Essay on Fiction," from *Madame de Staël on Politics, Literature, and National Characteristics*, translated by Morroe Berger. Reprinted by permission of the estate of Paula Berger.

Tzvetan Todorov, "A Structural Analysis of Literature: The Tales of Henry James," from *Structuralism: An Introduction*, Wolfson College Lectures 1972, edited by David Robey (1973). Reprinted by permission of Oxford University Press.

Leo Tolstoy, Chapter 16 from *What Is Art?* by Leo Tolstoy, translated by Aylmer Maude (1930). Reprinted by permission of the Oxford University Press.

Lionel Trilling, "The Meaning of a Literary Idea," from *The Liberal Imagination* by Lionel Trilling. Reproduced by permission of the estate of Lionel Trilling.

Yuri Tynyanov, "On Literary Evolution," from *Readings in*

# Index

Andrewes, Lancelot, 464
Androgyny, 1072; in Cixous, 1073, 1097; in Kristeva, 999; in
    Showalter, 1070, 1117; in Woolf, 1070
Anima, in Jung, 644, 669, 670, 672, 673, 675, 676
Animus, in Jung, 644, 669, 670, 672, 673, 675
Anthropology, 1006; in Baker, 1351, 1373; in Frye, 680, 681,
    683; in Lévi-Strauss, 869
Anticipation, in Fish, 1245, 1246, 1249; in Iser, 1223–1225, 1229;
    in Barbara Herrnstein Smith, 1329
Antonioni, Michelangelo, 549
Anxiety of authorship, in Gilbert and Gubar, 1071, 1121
Anxiety of influence, in Bloom, 644, 707, 708, 1127; in Dryden,
    192; in Eliot, 465; in Gilbert and Gubar, 644
Apollinaire, Guillaume, 854, 895
Apollo, in Nietzsche, 405, 406, 408, 410, 414
Apollonius, 100
Aporia, 950; in de Man, 1433; in Derrida, 974; in Jameson, 628,
    634
Apparition, in Langer, 535–538
Approaches, critical, 9
Apuleius, 155
Aquinas, St. Thomas, 118, 122
Aragon, Louis, 993
Arché-écriture, in Derrida, 945
Archetype, 5; in Baym, 1155; in Eco, 931; in Frye, 680, 681,
    683, 685; in Jung, 644, 665, 669–673, 676, 870; in Plotinus,
    110, 113, 116; in Barbara Herrnstein Smith, 1342
Archilochus, 30, 31, 69, 87, 89, 100, 411, 412, 896
Architectonic, in Sidney, 132, 139
Architecture, in Benjamin, 587; in Hegel, 344, 352, 353, 355
Arendt, Hannah, 1050
Ariosto, Ludovico, 215, 334, 458, 651; Orlando Furioso, 137,
    335, 338
Aristophanes, 44, 104, 166, 169, 170, 172, 186, 1327
Aristotle, 1, 4, 6, 8, 12–14, 17, 38–40, 42, 66, 67, 71, 79, 98,
    131, 132, 154, 156, 161, 162, 166, 167, 169, 170, 171, 175,
    189, 191, 192, 200, 220, 224, 234, 244, 291, 312, 344, 370,
    379, 506, 522, 531, 532, 545, 588, 598, 626, 630, 679, 687,
    703, 712, 725, 731, 732, 809, 811, 813, 814, 896, 930, 981,
    985, 1008, 1234, 1298, 1380, 1386; materialism of, 38; Meta-
    physics, 119, 121, 808, 1361, 1362; Nicomachean Ethics, 143;
    Poetics, 42–65, 125, 129, 137, 138, 142, 144, 147, 148, 152,
    161, 167, 176, 236, 379, 401, 415, 710, 711, 713, 772, 776,
    807, 818, 822, 850, 890, 895, 896, 931, 1038, 1158; Politics,
    41; problematic method, 38; Rhetoric, 56
Arnheim, Rudolf, 579, 580, 584
Arnold, Matthew, 1, 80, 518, 519, 708, 734, 826, 1321, 1386,
    1435; biography, 379; Culture and Anarchy, 379; "Dover
    Beach," 801; elitism, 380; Essays in Criticism, 379;
    "The Function of Criticism at the Present Time," 382–396;
    holistic criticism, 380; "The Study of Poetry," 396–402, 1287,
    1363
Arrian, 84
Art, in Arnold, 379; in Benjamin, 572, 574, 577, 583; in Bocca-
    cio, 124; in Coleridge, 310; in Crane, 809, 824; in Croce,
    448, 451, 453, 456; in Derrida, 946; in Dewey, 485, 489, 498;
    in Dryden, 179, 187; in Emerson, 359, 368; in Freud, 640,
    651; in Frye, 677; in Hegel, 343, 345–351, 353, 354; in Hor-
    ace, 76; in Hume, 217; in James, 424, 428; in Samuel John-
    son, 228, 236; in Jung, 645, 656, 660; in Kant, 244–246, 262,
    268; in Longinus, 79–81, 83, 101; in Marx, 570, 571; in
    Marxist criticism, 555, 556; in Nietzsche, 404, 405, 413, 414;
    in Plato, 31, 210; in Plotinus, 4, 107–109, 116; in Pope, 198,
    200–202, 203; in Potebnya, 723; in Proust, 474, 478–480, 482;
    in Ronsard, 126, 127; in Schiller, 275; in Shklovsky, 738; in
    Sidney, 133, 143, 154; in de Staël, 280; in Todorov, 911, 912;
    in Tolstoy, 437–440, 444

Artaud, Antonin, 543
Articulation, in Fish, 1250
Artist, 1, 2, 7; in Baym, 1155–1157; in Croce, 453; in Eliot, 466;
    in Emerson, 359; in Freud, 640; in Frye, 679; in James, 426,
    433; in Jung, 663, 666; in Kant, 247; in Langer, 532; in
    Longinus, 80; in Nietzsche, 407; in Plotinus, 107, 109, 112;
    in Proust, 476, 478, 480; in Sartre, 1177; in Sidney, 133; in
    Tolstoy, 436; see also Author, Poet
Ashbery, John, 708
Associationism, 300, 301
Associative response, in Bleich, 1256, 1263, 1265, 1267, 1269,
    1270
Assumptions, critical, 6; in Crane, 816; in Knapp and Michaels,
    1425
Atget, Eugène-August, 577
Attitude, in Richards, 774
Atwood, Margaret, Surfacing, 1283
Auden, W. H., 680
Audience, 2, 3, 5–8, 10, 1158; and affective fallacy, 1376; char-
    acter of, 1159; in Aristotle, 7, 51, 53, 55, 1158; in Baker,
    1351, 1367; in Bakhtin, 725; in Benjamin, 574, 575, 577, 579,
    583, 585; in Bleich, 1159, 1166; in Booth, 1160, 1161, 1168;
    in Croce, 447; in Culler, 1159, 1163; in Dante, 1160; in
    Dewey, 485, 486; in Dryden, 162, 170, 174, 177–182, 186,
    193, 1160; in Eco, 1159, 1163; in Fish, 1160, 1168; in Flynn,
    1166; in Freud, 641, 642, 655, 656; in Genette, 1159; in
    Greenblatt, 1059, 1061; in Holland, 1159, 1165, 1168, 1236;
    in Horace, 66, 67, 70, 72, 76, 1158, 1160; in Hume, 209, 218,
    220, 246; in Iser, 1168; in James, 424; in Jauss, 1168, 1171,
    1198, 1199, 1203, 1204; in Samuel Johnson, 224, 226, 233,
    236, 237, 239, 241, 1160; in Kant, 246; in Kolodny, 1066,
    1135; in Langer, 532; in Longinus, 79, 80, 83, 91; in New
    Criticism, 727, 1159; in Nietzsche, 413; in Plato, 33, 1158;
    in Poulet, 1167, 1168; in Proust, 477, 480; in rhetorical the-
    ory, 5; in Richards, 1159; in Ronsard, 129; in Rosenblatt,
    1164, 1165; in Said, 1023; in Barbara Herrnstein Smith, 1336,
    1339; in Sontag, 1160; in de Staël, 281; in structuralism, 1159,
    1163; in Tolstoy, 436; national, 5, 181; universal, 5; see also
    Reader
Auerbach, Erich, 1204, 1217
Augustine, St., 118, 788, 1251, 1252
Aura, in Benjamin, 558, 574, 575, 579, 581, 589
Austen, Jane, 433, 828, 840, 1064, 1071, 1080–1082, 1085, 1103,
    1105, 1110, 1115, 1124, 1157, 1221, 1288, 1300, 1302, 1303,
    1306; Emma, 808, 823, 1185–1198; Mansfield Park, 814,
    1195; Persuasion, 814, 1188–1190, 1195; Pride and Preju-
    dice, 814, 826
Austin, J. L., 725, 1013
Authenticity, in Benjamin, 573–575, in Lukács, 607
Author, 2, 8; in Burke, 501; in Coleridge, 309; in de Man, 1020;
    in Foucault, 952, 978–985, 987, 988, 995; in Freud, 641; in
    Hirsch, 1396, 1397, 1399, 1405; in James, 425; in Jauss, 1200;
    in Juhl, 1419; in Knapp and Michaels, 1428; in Kristeva, 995,
    996, 1004; in Longinus, 79; in neo-Aristotelianism, 734; in
    Poe, 372; in Rader, 838; in Barbara Herrnstein Smith, 1340;
    in de Staël, 280; in Todorov, 913; in Tynyanov, 754; in
    Wimsatt and Beardsley, 1384, 1387; see also Poet
Author-function, in Foucault, 982–985, 987, 988; in Kristeva,
    1004
Authoritative discourse, in Bakhtin, 783–785, 789
Authority, 1285; in Barthes, 1318; in Baym, 1157; in Benjamin,
    582; in Cixous, 1102; in Derrida, 946; in Foucault, 952; in
    Gilbert and Gubar, 1121; in Greenblatt, 1062; in Hirsch,
    1409; in Barbara Johnson, 1038, 1043, 1049, 1053–1056; in
    Kermode, 1316; in Said, 1031; in Sainte-Beuve, 1292; in
    Barbara Herrnstein Smith, 1325, 1333
Autobiography, in Rader, 833–835, 840

Automatization, 1210; in Jauss, 1213; in Mukařovský, 851, 861, 862; in Tynyanov, 751; *see also* Defamiliarization

Autonomous complex, in Jung, 662–664

Autonomy, in Greenblatt, 1058; in neo-Aristotelianism, 733; in New Criticism, 733; in Rader, 734

Avenarius, Richard, 740

Awareness, in F. R. Leavis, 1301; in Q. D. Leavis, 1316

Axiology, in Baker, 1348, 1351; in Barbara Herrnstein Smith, 1323, 1327, 1329, 1331, 1335

Ayer, A. J., 949, 1322

Babbitt, Irving, 463

Bach, Johann Sebastian, 245, 443

Bachelard, Gaston, 1020

Bacon, Francis, 315, 316, 325, 326, 336, 339, 534, 981

Bage, Robert, 1286

Bainbridge, Beryl, 1118

Baker, Ernest, 1104

Baker, Houston A., Jr., 1290; biography, 1344; "Generational Shifts and the Recent Criticism of Afro-American Literature," **1344–1373**

Bakhtin, Mikhail, 79, 80, 724; 898, 953, 954, 990, 994, 995, 1003, 1162; biography, 780–781; collaborations with Medvedev and Voloshinov, 724; *Discourse in the Novel*, **781–791**; practical criticism, 725; *Problems of Dostoevsky's Poetics*, **791–798**

Balance, in Cleanth Brooks, 804

Baldwin, James, 1138, 1145

Balibar, Étienne, 1338

Balzac, Honoré de, 563, 604, 621, 894, 897, 899, 982, 1010, 1086, 1205; *La Peau de chagrin*, 717; *Père Goriot*, 1163

Bambara, Toni Cade, 1141, 1145

Baraka, Amiri (LeRoi Jones), 1138, 1344, 1348, 1349

Barbauld, Anna Laetitia, 1068

Barnes, Djuna, 1306

Barth, John, 942

Barthes, Roland, 543, 550, 645, 711, 713, 720, 850, 854, 918, 921, 924, 927, 947, 950, 1013, 1321; biography, 1005; "From Work to Text," **1006–1010**; *Pleasure of the Text*, 1164; *S/Z*, 948, 1309

Base (*Grundlage*), in Marx, 561, 569, 572, 591; *see also* Superstructure

Bataille, Georges, 1007

Bate, Walter Jackson, 706

Bateson, Frederick W., 1377, 1378, 1390, 1402, 1408, 1413

Battersby, James L., 1377

Batyushkov, Konstantin Nikolaievich, 755

Baudelaire, Charles, 370, 558, 684, 694, 697, 700, 702, 704, 853, 878–889, 972, 974, 1170, 1205, 1214, 1389

Baudrillard, Jean, 1329, 1330

Baym, Nina, 1068, 1128, 1069; biography, 1146; "Melodramas of Beset Manhood," **1146–1157**, 1340

Beardsley, Monroe C., 1015, 1159, 1331, 1377, 1378, 1416, 1433; biography, 1383; "The Intentional Fallacy," **1383–1391**

Beaumont, Francis, 175, 185, 286; *The Faithful Shepherdess*, 193

Beaumont, Francis, and John Fletcher, *Philaster*, 185

Beauty, 80; as ideal form, 4; in Aristotle, 390, 397; in Arnold, 390, 397; in Benjamin, 575; in Croce, 447, 448, 453, 457; in Dryden, 178; in Emerson, 359–361, 366, 369; in Hegel, 345, 355, 356; in Horace, 70; in Hume, 210, 212, 214, 215, 217, 218, 220; in James, 433; in Kant, 244–246, 248–259, 266, 343, 1177; in Keats, 317, 318; in Nietzsche, 411; in Plotinus, 4, 107–110, 113–115, 117; in Poe, 371, 373; in Pope, 200, 202; in Richards, 771, 773, 779; in Sartre, 1177; in Shelley, 338; in Sidney, 150, 156; in Tolstoy, 443; in Wordsworth, 292

Beauvoir, Simone de, 1064, 1065, 1072, 1120, 1125; biography, 1087; "Myths: Of Women in Five Authors," **1087–1089**; *The Second Sex*, 1087

Beckett, Samuel, 548, 601, 604, 605, 611, 978

Becoming, in Plato, 13

*Bedeutung*, 1376, 1393, 1394; *see also* Significance

Beethoven, Ludwig van, 436, 444, 574

Behaviorism, 299

Behn, Aphra, 1064

Being, in Derrida, 960, 969; in Heidegger, 961; in Barbara Johnson, 1040; in Plato, 13; in Plotinus, 111, 112, 114; in Sartre, 1174

Beliefs, in Baker, 1351; in Booth, 1160; in Fish, 1378, 1379, 1434; in Hirsch, 1379; in Barbara Johnson, 1049; in Juhl, 1379, 1421; in Kermode, 1308; in Knapp and Michaels, 1379, 1380, 1425, 1433–1436; in Richards, 772, 776, 777, 780

Belinsky, Vissarion, 593, 722

Bellow, Saul, *Henderson the Rain King*, 1153

Bely, Andrey, 722, 739, 740

Benda, Julien, 1184

Benedict, Ruth, *Patterns of Culture*, 684

Benjamin, Walter, 543, 550, 558–560, 607, 609–611, 712, 716, 954, 1199; biography, 571; "The Work of Art in the Age of Mechanical Reproduction," 558, **571–588**

Benn, Gottfried, 601, 602, 605, 606, 611

Bennett, Arnold, 1117

Bennett, Tony, 723, 1171, 1325

Benveniste, Émile, 630, 692, 693, 856, 870, 888, 896, 897

Bercovitch, Sacvan, 1149

Bergman, Ingmar, 548, 549

Bergonzi, Bernard, 1104

Bergson, Henri, 472, 526, 607, 632

Berkeley, George, 300

Besant, Walter, 422, 423–428, 430

Bewley, Marius, 1148

Bialostosky, Don, 731

Bigsby, C. W. B., 1327

Black Aesthetic, 1365, 1373; and cultural xenophobia, 1353; as romantic Marxism, 1353; in Baraka, 1349; in decline, 1357; in Henderson, 1353; undermined by failure of Black Power, 1357

Black Arts, as aesthetic of Black Power, 1348

Black English Vernacular, in Gates, 1370

Black female chauvinism, in McDowell, 1145

Black female thematics, in McDowell, 1144

Black feminist criticism, 1139; in McDowell, 1139; in Barbara Smith, 1139

Black male chauvinism, in Bone, 1139; in Littlejohn, 1139; in Stepto, 1138

Blackmore, Richard, 205, 1326

Blackmur, Richard P., 516, 726, 729, 807, 916, 1036

Blackness, in Henderson, 1350

Blake, William, 524, 539, 706, 1121, 1127, 1354; "The Sunflower," 919

Blanchot, Maurice, 916

Blazons, in Kristeva, 1000, 1001

Bleich, David, 642, 1164, 1236, 1239, 1433; biography, 1254; "Feelings about Literature," **1254–1271**

Bloom, Harold, 637, 643, 919, 949, 1070, 1126–1129, 1133, 1136, 1157; *The Anxiety of Influence*, 1345; biography, 705; "A Meditation upon Priority," **705–710**

Blues, in Baker, 1345, 1359, 1368

Blues aesthetic, in Baraka, 1348

Boccaccio, Giovanni, 119, 134, 212, 222, 335, 336, 904, 1298; biography, 122; *Decameron*, 122, 746, 898; "The Definition of Poetry," **123–124**

Bodkin, Maud, 645

Boeckh, August, 1392, 1393

Deus ex machina, in Aristotle, 53; in Horace, 71

Dewey, John, 13, 14, 109, 1228; "The Act of Expression," **486–499**; aesthetics, 485; biography, 484; influence, 484

Diachronic, in Hirsch, 1404; in Jauss, 1209, 1211–1214; in Kermode, 1318; *see also* Synchronic

Dialect, in Mukařovský, 861; in Ronsard, 128

Dialectic, as method, 14; in Bleich, 1269; in Burke, 511; in Culler, 926; in Derrida, 944, 946, 947, 1035; in Hegel 342–345; in Iser, 1231; in Lacan, 647, 648; in Lukács, 597; in Marxist criticism, 558, 561; in Nietzsche, 414; in Said, 1028, 1034; in Sartre, 1175; in Trilling, 521

Dialectical materialism, in Marx, 554, 556, 561, 591

Dialogism, 14; in Bakhtin, 725, 726, 782, 786, 788, 789, 791, 799, 989, 994; in Jauss, 1169, 1199, 1200, 1208; in Kristeva, 953, 995

Dickens, Charles, 371, 372, 422, 433, 441, 442, 550, 828, 1086, 1301, 1304; *A Christmas Carol*, 436; *David Copperfield*, 838; *Great Expectations*, 719; *Hard Times*, 485

Dickinson, Emily, 706, 1071, 1123, 1124, 1147

Diction, in Aristotle, 39, 46, 47, 56, 62; in Arnold, 401; in Coleridge, 312; in Crane, 815, 820; in Dryden, 181; in Genette, 896; in Samuel Johnson, 235; in Longinus, 80, 81, 83, 87; in Ronsard, 130; in Sidney, 156; in Wordsworth, 283, 284, 289, 293, 294, 311; *see also* Language

Didacticism, in Croce, 452, in James, 432, in Samuel Johnson, 223, 224, in de Staël, 278, in Tolstoy, 434; *see also* Ethics and literature

Didactic literature, in Crane, 811–813

Diderot, Denis, *Jacques le Fataliste*, 1202

Difference, in de Man, 1015; in Derrida, 961, 962; in Fish, 1250; in Barbara Johnson, 1041; in Kristeva, 992; in Lacan, 695; in Todorov, 710; in Tynyanov, 753

*Différence*, in Derrida, 970

Dilthey, Wilhelm, 1410

Diogenes Laertius, 980

Dionysius of Halicarnassus, 207

Dionysos, 33, 107; in Nietzsche, 405, 407, 408, 410, 412, 415, 418

Discourse, 12, 14, 1032; in Aristotle, 57; in Bakhtin, 782, 786, 788–790, 794, 798, 799; in Culler, 918, 921, 928; in Derrida, 962, 967; in Eco, 855; in Foucault, 951–953, 981, 982, 985, 987, 988, 1032; in Genette, 856, 893, 896–898; in Kolodny, 1136; in Kristeva, 953, 995, 1003, 1005; in operationalism, 13; in Ricoeur, 1023; in Said, 953

Discursivity, in Foucault, 985, 986

Disinterestedness, in Arnold, 389, 391, 392, 396; in Booth, 1188; in Hume, 218; in Kant, 245, 248, 249, 251, 252, 1290; in Nietzsche, 411

Displacement, 1313; in Freud, 647, 652; in Lacan, 687

Disraeli, Benjamin, 1301

Dissociation of sensibility, in Eliot, 464

Distance, in Booth, 1160, 1186, 1188; in Flynn, 1273, 1279

Distortion, in Bleich, 1260

Dithyramb, in Aristotle, 42, 43; in Nietzsche, 411

Division of labor, in Marx, 567

Döblin, Alfred, 600

Dobrolyubov, Nikolai, 722

Dollimore, Jonathan, 954

Dominance, in Flynn, 1275, 1278

Dominant, in Derrida, 944; in Kolodny, 1128, 1133; in Mukařovský, 851, 862, 863; in Showalter, 1108; in Tynyanov, 753

Domination, in Flynn, 1272, 1273, 1275, 1277, 1279, 1281

Donne, John, 173, 286, 464, 465, 508, 589, 678, 727, 803, 804, 805, 1300, 1376, 1388–1391

Donoghue, Denis, 1316

Doolittle, Hilda (H. D.), 1123

Dos Passos, John, 520, 527–529, 600, 1150

Dostoevsky, Fyodor, 403, 441, 594, 606, 630, 636, 725, 748, 785, 787, 791, 1327; *The Brothers Karamazov*, 526, 814, 1194; *The Double*, 795; *The Idiot*, 797; *Notes from Underground*, 791–798; *The Possessed*, 1316

Double-voicedness, in Bakhtin, 725, 783, 784, 787, 789, 790

Doubles, in Derrida, 976

Douglas, Norman, 1304

Drabble, Margaret, 1118

Drama, 79, 160, 326; in Coleridge, 314; in Crane, 814, 815; in Dryden, 165, 174; in Hegel, 344; in Samuel Johnson, 231, 233, 237; in Nietzsche, 404; in Schiller, 277; in Shelley, 329, 330; in Sontag, 549; in Wordsworth, 293

Dramatic ratio, in Burke, 507

Dreams, as wish fulfillment, 5; in Freud, 404, 638, 640, 653, 713; in Jung, 645, 670, 675; in Kermode, 1312, 1313; in Nietzsche, 404, 406, 409, 412

Dreiser, Theodore, 519, 557, 1150

Dreyer, Carl, 580

Dreyfus, Alfred, 472, 476

Drives, in Freud, 638, 715

Dryden, John, 5, 6, 80, 197, 205, 223, 236, 278, 286, 464, 588, 1308, 1399, 1435; "Absalom and Achitophel," 812; "Alexander's Feast," 204; biography, 160; "Essay of Dramatic Poesy," 133, **163–196**; *Fables*, 207

Du Bellay, Jean, 125

Du Bois, W. E. B., 1362

Ducasse, Curt, 1386

Duck, Stephen, 616

Dürrenmatt, Friedrich, *The Visit*, 1239

Duhamel, Georges, 585

Dumas, Alexandre, 433, 451, 1010; *The Three Musketeers*, 931

Durkheim, Emile, 869

Durrell, Lawrence, 1306

*Dynamis*, in Aristotle, 7; in Crane, 819; *see also* Effect

Eagleton, Terry, 553, 562, 563, 728, 1325

Eberhart, Richard, 706

Eco, Umberto, 855, 1370, 1412; biography, 929; "The Myth of Superman," **929–941**

Economics, in Marx, 554; in Marxist criticism, 561, 563

Economics and literature, 1287; in Barbara Herrnstein Smith, 1328–1330, 1335, 1338

*Écriture*, in Foucault, 952

*Écriture féminine* 1064; in Cixous, 1091–1093, 1095–1097, 1099; in Woolf, 1065

Edgeworth, Maria, 1110, 1124

Education, in Dewey, 484, 485

Effect, in Crane, 817; in Poe, 370–373, 375; in Rader, 838; in rhetorical theories, 7

Effects of poetry, in Pope, 202; in Sidney, 134, 139, 141, 144

Egerton, George, 1116

Ego, 642; in Croce, 458; in Freud, 639, 640, 654, 655, 703; in Jung, 662, 666–669, 673; in Lacan, 621, 648, 701; in Lawrence, 1305

Ego ideal, in Freud, 692

Eichenbaum, Boris, 752, 1004

*Eidolon* (image), in Plato, 4

*Eidos* (shaping form), in Crane, 818, 820, 821; in Derrida, 961; in neo-Aristotelianism, 731

*Ekstasis*, 79; in Coleridge, 313; in Jung, 665; in Longinus, 102; in Nietzsche, 407; in Pope, 202; in Schopenhauer, 407

Elegy, 498; in Dante, 121; in Ronsard, 127; in Sidney, 145

Eliot, George (Mary Ann Evans), 432, 828, 1029, 1030, 1064, 1080, 1081, 1083, 1086, 1103–1106, 1110, 1111, 1113, 1115, 1123, 1124, 1157, 1288, 1300, 1301, 1303, 1306; *Adam Bede*, 436, 1113, 1251; *Middlemarch*, 1304

Eliot, T. S., 8, 441, 519, 520, 522–525, 532, 539, 549, 589, 594, 601, 602, 678, 706, 722, 726, 727, 801, 1034, 1127, 1159, 1287, 1300, 1305, 1306, 1321, 1323, 1326, 1327, 1363, 1375, 1389, 1390, 1395, 1405; biography, 463; *The Cocktail Party*, 463; criticism, 464; *Four Quartets*, 463; "The Love Song of J. Alfred Prufrock," 842; modernism, 463, 464; *Murder in the Cathedral*, 463; *Prufrock and Other Observations*, 463; "Tradition and the Individual Talent," 464, **466–471**, 645, 727, 1345; *The Waste Land*, 463, 1251
Ellis, Sarah, 1109, 1112
Ellison, Ralph, 1138, 1144, 1368
Ellmann, Mary, 1064–1066, 1105, 1139, 1142
Ellmann, Richard, 837, 839, 841, 845
Emergent form, in Rader, 828
Emerson, Ralph Waldo, 377, 708; biography, 357; *Essays*, 357; idealism, 357, 358; metaphysics, 357; "The Poet," **358–369**
Emotion, in Aristotle, 54; in Bleich, 1254; in Booth, 1188; in Crane, 816; in Dewey, 490–493, 495; in Eliot, 469, 470; in Freud, 651; in Jung, 657; in Langer, 531, 536; in Proust, 479; in Richards, 774; in Sartre, 1180; in Shelley, 324; in Trilling, 521; in Wordsworth, 295; *see also* Feelings
Empathy, in Flynn, 1273
Empedocles, 43, 709, 896
Empiricism, in Aristotle, 39; in Crane, 732; in Dewey, 485; in Lévi-Strauss, 946
Empson, William, 119, 500, 716, 726, 729, 769, 927, 1161, 1426; *Seven Types of Ambiguity*, 925
Ending, in Peter Brooks, 712, 713, 716, 718, 720; in Barbara Johnson, 1038; in Rader, 831; *see also* Denouement
Engels, Friedrich, 555, 565, 591, 592, 1032
Enlightenment, 278, 484, 706, in de Staël, 279
Entanglement, in Flynn, 1274, 1277
*Enthousiasmós*, 20, 32; in Boccaccio, 122; in Plato, 33, 37; in Wordsworth, 291; *see also* Inspiration
Epic, 79, 322, 326, 570; in Aristotle, 42, 45, 55, 59, 60, 64, 65; in Arnold, 399, 400; in Bakhtin, 795; in Benjamin, 587; in Crane, 813, 815; in Dryden, 166, 174; in Frye, 680; in Genette, 890; in Hegel, 344; in Hume, 219; in Jauss, 1206; in Kristeva, 991, 997; in Lukács, 597; in Nietzsche, 412; in Plato, 891; in Propp, 759, 764; in Schiller, 273, 277; in Sidney, 147
Epictetus, 788
Epicurus, 220
*Epistemé*, in Derrida, 959, 960, 969; in Foucault, 951, 952, 954, 979; in Jameson, 630; in Kermode, 1319; in Lévi-Strauss, 966
Epistemological project, in Knapp and Michaels, 1378, 1433
Epistemology, in Plato, 20
Erasmus, 148, 208
Erikson, Erik, 1106, 1236
Erlich, Victor, 722
Escarpit, Robert, 1204, 1286
Eschenbach, Wolfram von, *Parsifal*, 935
Essential structure, in Cleanth Brooks, 728
Estrangement, in Benjamin, 580
Ethics, 13; in Bakhtin, 785; in Hume, 213, 214; in James, 421, 424; in Jung, 669; in Kant, 245, 251, 256; in Sidney, 137, 139, 142; in Tolstoy, 438; in Wordsworth, 295
Ethics and literature, in Booth, 1161, 1188, 1194, 1196, 1197; in Crane, 826; in Dante, 121; in Dewey, 492; in Fish, 1243; in Flynn, 1277, 1278; in Hegel, 345, 346; in Hume, 210, 212, 221; in James, 432, 433; in Jameson, 635; in Jauss, 1217; in Barbara Johnson, 1040, 1047; in Samuel Johnson, 226, 227, 234; in Kermode, 1312; in Leavis, 1303; in Lukács, 606; in Nietzsche, 418; in Pope, 206; in Proust, 480; in Sartre, 1183; in Shelley, 329, 339; in Shklovsky, 1216; in Barbara Herrnstein Smith, 1324; in de Staël, 279–282; in Tolstoy, 434, 439–

441; in Wimsatt and Beardsley, 1384; in Winters, 1322; in Wordsworth, 287, 298; *see also* Didacticism
Euripides, 32, 51, 55, 56, 59, 62, 90, 91, 104, 151, 155, 167, 169, 172, 231, 328, 404, 414, 415, 774, 1178; *Bacchae*, 91, 412; *Electra*, 106; *Iphigenia at Aulis*, 53, 54; *Iphigenia at Tauris*, 50, 52–54, 90; *Medea*, 52, 53, 64, 171; *Orestes*, 52, 53, 64, 90, 91
Evaluation, in Bakhtin, 793, 796; in Baym, 1148; in Booth, 1160; in Croce, 461; in feminist criticism, 1325; in Flynn, 1272, 1278, 1280; in formalism, 1325; in Frye, 1323, 1324; in Hirsch, 1392; in Hume, 1331; in James, 429; in Jauss, 1199; in Mukařovský, 865, 866; in Richards, 1323; in Said, 1035; in Barbara Herrnstein Smith, 1320, 1321, 1324, 1327, 1328, 1335, 1338; in Structuralism, 1325; in Tolstoy, 435, 445; in Wimsatt, 1322; institutions in, 1340; *see also* Taste, Value
Evidence, external, 1375, 1377, 1387, 1389, 1409, 1412, 1416, 1422, 1423, 1428; in Juhl, 1417, 1420, 1421, 1423; internal, 1375, 1378, 1387, 1389, 1422, 1423
Evolution, in Baker, 1361; in Hegel, 348, 356; in Jauss, 1209, 1210, 1214; in Russian formalism, 1209, 1210; in Tynyanov, 748, 749, 752–756
Ewbank, Inga-Stina, 1111, 1113
Exchange-value, in Barbara Herrnstein Smith, 1328
Exhibition value, in Benjamin, 576, 577
Existentialism, 630–632; in Sartre, 1167
Expectation, in Fish, 1243–1246, 1249; in Iser, 1222, 1225, 1227; in Jauss, 1202
Experience, in Dewey, 486–488, 490; in Fish, 1243, 1244; in Hume, 211, 214, 217, 219; in Husserl, 1397; in Iser, 1225–1231; in Kant, 258; in Barbara Herrnstein Smith, 1329
Explication, in New Criticism, 726, 728
Expression, 8, 545, 1386; in Baker, 1348, 1349, 1353; in Bakhtin, 795; in Bleich, 1261, 1263; in Boccaccio, 123; in Crane, 813; in Croce, 447, 451, 453, 454–456, 459, 460, 462, 1385; in Dewey, 109, 485, 488–491, 493, 496–498; in Dryden, 164; in Eliot, 466; in Emerson, 359, 365; in Foucault, 979, 984; in Genette, 890; in Hegel, 349–351; in Hume, 215; in James, 427, 428, 431; in Barbara Johnson, 1047; in Juhl, 1411; in Jung, 661; in Knapp and Michaels, 1425, 1428; in Kolodny, 1137; in Langer, 531, 532, 535; in Longinus, 109; in Mukařovský, 867; in Plotinus, 113; in Poe, 495; in Pope, 203; in Proust, 474, 482; in Schiller, 275; in Showalter, 1114; in Todorov, 910; in Tolstoy, 436, 444; in Wimsatt and Beardsley, 1383, 1386; in Woolf, 1086
Expressive criticism, in Wordsworth, 283
Expressive form, in Langer, 531, 537, 538, 541
Expressiveness, in Longinus, 98
Extraversion, in Jung, 661

Fable, 630; in Samuel Johnson, 236; in Shklovsky, 742; in Sidney, 152
*Fabula*, 170, 710; in Peter Brooks, 713, 715, 716, 718; in Shklovsky, 723–724; *see also* Plot, *Sjužet*, Story
Facsimile; in Derrida, 976, 977
Fact vs. value, in Barbara Herrnstein Smith, 1321–1323
Fairy tale, in Propp, 756–769
Fallacy. *See* Affective fallacy, Intentional fallacy, etc.
Fame, in Horace, 74; in Longinus, 89
Fancy, in Coleridge, 301, 303, 306, 310, 311; in Dryden, 164, 189, 190, 196; in Emerson, 359; in Samuel Johnson, 224, 230, 237; in Sidney, 150; in Wordsworth, 284
Fanon, Frantz, *The Wretched of the Earth*, 1033
Fantasies, 9
Fantastic, in Todorov, 906, 907
Fantasy, in Flynn, 1276; in Freud, 651–653, 656; in Holland, 1165; in Jung, 665; in Rader, 830, 832; in Schiller, 274; in Showalter, 1114, 1115

Frye, Northrop, 1, 5, 119, 637, 644, 732, 811, 850, 854, 922, 923, 1031, 1034, 1108, 1123, 1125, 1214, 1225, 1322, 1323, 1325–1327, 1356; *Anatomy of Criticism*, 645, 677; "The Archetypes of Literature," **677–685**; biography, 677; *Fables of Identity*, 677
Functions, in Propp, 757
Furman, Nelly, 1133

Gadamer, Hans-Georg, 1169, 1207, 1208, 1342; *Truth and Method*, 1287
Galileo Galilei, 38, 986, 988, 1388
Gallop, Jane, 1075
Gance, Abel, 574, 578
Gaps (*Löcher*), in Iser, 1224, 1225; in Kermode, 1314
Garth, Samuel, 207
Gasché, Rodolphe, 949
Gaskell, Elizabeth, 1110, 1111, 1113, 1157, 1301, 1303
Gates, Henry Louis, 1360, 1364, 1366, 1367, 1371
Gayle, Addison, Jr., 1349, 1367
Geertz, Clifford, 954, 1135, 1373
Gellert, Christian Fürchtegott, 413
Gender, 1, 1063; in Baym, 1148, 1154, 1155; in Flynn, 1271, 1274, 1275, 1277, 1282; in Kolodny, 1128, 1130, 1132, 1133, 1135, 1137; in Kristeva, 999, 1000; *see also* Feminist literary criticism
Gender and creativity, in Woolf, 1082
Gender and history, in Woolf, 1079, 1080
Gender and language, in Dante, 121; in Lakoff, 1067; in McDowell, 1140
Gender and race, 1074
General action model, in Rader, 829, 832
General nature, in Samuel Johnson, 224, 229, 230, 232, 284; in Wordsworth, 292
Generational shifts, in Baker, 1345, 1347, 1349, 1357, 1372, 1373
Generic appropriateness, in Hirsch, 1406, 1409; *see also* Genre
Generosity, in Sartre, 1180, 1182, 1183
Genêt, Jean, 716, 1009, 1097, 1178
Genetic structuralism, 560; *see also* Goldmann, Lucien
Genette, Gérard, 720, 855, 857, 898, 919, 965, 1013, 1014, 1090, 1159, 1163, 1367; biography, 890; *Figures*, 711; "Frontiers of Narrative," **890–899**
Genius, 2, 198, 1159; in Arnold, 384; in Benjamin, 572; in Boccaccio, 124; in Coleridge, 302, 304, 305, 310, 311; in Derrida, 946; in Dryden, 166, 173, 185, 196; in Emerson, 359–361, 364, 369; in Foucault, 988; in Horace, 67, 76; in Hume, 210, 215, 218–220; in James, 426; in Samuel Johnson, 229, 240; in Kant, 246, 247, 268, 270; in Leavis, 1304, 1306; in Longinus, 83, 85, 99–101, 105; in Nietzsche, 413; in Plotinus, 108; in Pope, 197–200; in Proust, 476; in Rader, 842; in Sainte-Beuve, 1295, 1296; in Schiller, 273; in Sidney, 133, 154; in Sontag, 548; in de Staël, 280; in Woolf, 1079, 1083–1085
Genre, 161; in Aristotle, 39, 42, 45, 67, 379; in Baker, 1359, 1360; in Bakhtin, 726; in Barthes, 1006; in Crane, 733, 814, 823; in Croce, 448, 458; in Culler, 920, 922, 928; in Dante, 120, 121; in Dryden, 181; in Foucault, 978; in Frye, 645, 680, 732; in Genette, 894; in Greenblatt, 1058, 1059; in Hegel, 344; in Hirsch, 1399, 1406, 1409; in Horace, 67, 69; in Hume, 221; in Jauss, 1202, 1203, 1206, 1213, 1218; in Samuel Johnson, 224, 232, 233; in Kermode, 1307–1309, 1312, 1314; in Knapp and Michaels, 1429; in Kolodny, 1130; in Kristeva, 989, 1003; in Lacan, 690; in Langer, 531; in Lukács, 608; in Mukařovský, 864; in neo-Aristotelianism, 732; in New Criticism, 728; in Nietzsche, 414; in Plato, 891; in Propp, 764; in Said, 1031; in Schiller, 273; in Showalter, 1111; in Sidney, 132, 133, 138, 139, 145; in Barbara Herrnstein Smith, 1330; in de Staël, 279; in Todorov, 906–908; in Tynyanov, 750,

753; genre theories, 5; *see also* individual genres, including Comedy, Epic, Tragedy, etc.
Gibbon, Edward, 278, 336, 424, 1086
Gide, André, 520, 601, 611, 627, 1211; *The Counterfeiters*, 611
Gilbert, Sandra, 644; biography, 1119; *The Madwoman in the Attic*, 1069, 1070; "The Parables of the Cave," **1119–1126**
Gilbert, Stuart, 841, 843, 845
Gilbert, W. S., 1104
Gilman, Charlotte Perkins, 1066, 1068, 1130, 1135, 1136
Giovanni, Nikki, 1074
Glasgow, Ellen, *Barren Ground*, 1154
Glaspell, Susan Keating, 1066, 1133, 1135; "A Jury of Her Peers," 1134–1136
Gnostics, 107
Godard, Jean-Luc, 549
Gödel, Kurt, 945
Godwin, William, 321, 371, 372
Goethe, Johann Wolfgang von, 272–274, 278, 282, 384–386, 392, 445, 460, 516, 592, 914, 1016, 1294, 1296, 1297, 1385, 1388; *Faust*, 453, 574, 661, 662; *Iphigenia on Tauris*, 390; *The Sorrows of Young Werther*, 273, 275, 719, 795
Gogol, Nikolai, 442, 738, 744, 748, 784; *The Nose*, 723
Golden, Leon, 41
Goldmann, Lucien, 559–561, 563, 989
Goldsmith, Oliver, 612, 618, 620, 1109, 1296; *The Vicar of Wakefield*, 733
Gombrich, Ernst, 1225, 1226
Goncourt, Edmond de, 431, 472; *Chérie*, 431
Góngora, 1211
Gordon, Caroline, 1160
Gorgias, 18
Gorky, Maxim, 593, 747
Gothic novel, 370, 451; in Foucault, 985; in Showalter, 1110; in Wordsworth, 288
Graff, Gerald, 8
Gramsci, Antonio, 560
Grand, Sarah, 1116
Gray, Thomas, 283, 289, 612; "Elegy in a Country Churchyard," 800, 802, 821, 822
Greenblatt, Stephen, 953, 954; biography, 1057; Introduction to *The Power of Forms in the English Renaissance*, **1057–1059**; "*King Lear* and Harsnett's 'Devil-Fiction,'" **1060–1062**; *see also* New Historicism
Greer, Germaine, 1107
Greg, W. R., 1114
Greimas, A. J., 621, 628, 711, 948, 1013
Grice, H. P., 1378, 1431
Griffin, Bartholomew, 1321
Griffith, D. W., 549
*Grundlage*, in Marx, 554; *see also* Base
Gubar, Susan, 644, 1069, 1070; biography, 1119; *The Madwoman in the Attic*, 1069, 1070; "The Parables of the Cave," **1119–1126**
Guest, Edgar, 1326
Gynocritics, in Showalter, 1064

Habermas, Jurgen, 626
*Hamartia* (tragic flaw), in Aristotle, 40, 51
Hammett, Dashiell, 516, 899
Hamsun, Knut, *Hunger*, 745
Happiness, in Kant, 250
Hardy, Thomas, 800, 1303; *Return of the Native*, 644
Harris, Bertha, 1141
Harris, James "Hermes," 9
Harris, Zellig, 647
Harsnett, Samuel, 1060, 1061
Hartman, Geoffrey, 1, 707, 708, 949, 1362

Hartmann, Nicolai, 1332
Hauptmann, Gerhard, 664
Hawthorne, Nathaniel, 429, 529, 530, 641, 1147, 1150, 1154, 1288; *The Scarlet Letter*, 1154
Haydon, Benjamin, 320
Hazlitt, Thomas, 317
Hegel, Georg Wilhelm Friedrich, 13, 274, 446–448, 484, 525, 538, 554, 561, 576, 590, 596, 599, 602, 633, 899, 943, 946, 947, 1002, 1208, 1212, 1287; *Aesthetics*, 342, 435; biography, 341; dialectic, 343; holistic thought, 342; *Logic*, 341; *Phenomenology of Spirit*, 341, 342, 646; *Philosophy of Art*, **345–356**, 579; *Philosophy of Right*, 341
Hegemony, in Williams, 560, 561
Heidegger, Martin, 599, 602, 605, 606, 609, 631, 632, 687, 693, 704, 936, 943, 946, 947, 955, 961, 962, 1174, 1208
Heilbrun, Carolyn, 1105
Heilman, Robert B., 726, 729–731, 821
Heine, Heinrich, 754
Hemenway, Robert E., 1355, 1371
Heminges, John, 233
Hemingway, Ernest, 520, 527, 528, 801, 899, 1136; *For Whom the Bell Tolls*, 1154; "Hills Like White Elephants," 1271, 1277; "The Killers," 813; *The Sun Also Rises*, 1163
Henderson, Stephen, 1349–1352, 1354, 1356, 1358, 1367, 1370, 1373
Henley, Nancy, 1140
Heraclitus, 359, 418, 470, 1329
Herbert, George, 464
Herder, Johann Gottfried von, 590
Hermeneutic circle, 1162; in Hirsch, 1407; in Juhl, 1422
Hermeneutic code, in Barthes, 711
Hermeneutics, 1320; in Bakhtin, 781; in Barthes, 1007; in Hirsch, 1392, 1397, 1400, 1406; in Jauss, 1203; in Barbara Herrnstein Smith, 1334; in Sontag, 547, 550; *see also* Interpretation
Hernadi, Paul, 9, 12
Herodotus, 48, 82, 89, 93–95, 97, 98, 102, 104, 135, 142, 327
Hesiod, 24, 30, 31, 84, 89, 126, 134, 158, 438, 896, 1298
Heteroglossia, in Bakhtin, 725, 790; *see also* Dialogism
Hicks, Granville, 556, 563
Hill, Christopher, *Milton and the English Revolution*, 553
Hinderer, Walter, 1332
Hirsch, E. D., Jr., 805, 1316, 1320, 1324, 1376, 1377, 1413, 1421, 1425–1430; biography, 1391–1392; "Objective Interpretation," **1392–1411**
Historicism, 722, 954; in Dryden, 166; in Hirsch, 1394; in Jauss, 1199; in Tynyanov, 749
Historicity, in Baker, 1360; in Derrida, 969; in Heidegger, 599; in Jauss, 1199–1201, 1209, 1212; in Lukács, 608
History, 6, 8, 79; as text, 8, 14; in Althusser, 561; in Aristotle, 40, 48; in Baker, 1353, 1355; in Barthes, 1006, 1008, 1010, 1317; in Bloom, 705; in Cixous, 1096; in Coleridge, 302, 309; in Crane, 826; in Croce, 451, 1385; in Derrida, 960, 962, 969; in Dryden, 176; in Foucault, 951, 978, 980; in Frye, 677; in Greenblatt, 1058; in Hegel, 343, 356; in Horace, 70; in Hume, 219; in Jameson, 625, 632, 634, 635; in Jauss, 1207, 1209, 1212; in Barbara Johnson, 1051, 1052; in Samuel Johnson, 227, 233, 236, 238; in Kermode, 1316, 1318; in Kristeva, 990; in Leavis, 1288; in Lukács, 606; in Marx, 568; in Marxist criticism, 554, 561; in McDowell, 1143; in New Criticism, 728; in Rader, 828; in Said, 1024, 1025, 1033, 1036; in Schiller, 274; in Shelley, 322, 327; in Sidney, 132, 134, 135, 137, 139–143, 147, 155; in Barbara Herrnstein Smith, 1338; in de Staël, 278, 280, 281; in Tolstoy, 438; in Trilling, 527; in Williams, 619; in Wordsworth, 292
History and literature, in Arnold, 384–386, 397–399; in Bakhtin, 726; in Benjamin, 574, 585, 588; in Bloom, 705, 708; in Croce,

461, 462; in Eliot, 465, 467; in Frye, 681; in Greenblatt, 954; in Iser, 1169; in Jameson, 631, 633, 635; in Jauss, 1210; in Samuel Johnson, 590; in Kolodny, 1128; in Lukács, 599, 603; in McDowell, 1143; in Said, 953; in Shelley, 322, 323, 332, 333, 335; in Showalter, 1117; in Taine, 590, 591; in Wilson, 593, 596; in Woolf, 1085
Hjelmslev, Louis, 621
Hobbes, Thomas, 13, 534
Hoffman, Daniel G., 1152
Hoffmann, E. T. A., 1094; "The Sandman," 640
Hofmannsthal, Hugo von, 599, 608, 1318
Hofstadter, Albert, 1351
Hölderlin, Friedrich, 341, 1020, 1211
Holland, Norman N., 635, 642, 720, 1164, 1165, 1251, 1254, 1380, 1433; biography, 1232; *Dynamics of Literary Response*, 1376; *5 Readers Reading*, 1165, 1232; "The Question: Who Reads What How?" **1232–1239**
Homer, 20, 23, 24, 28, 30–32, 34, 35, 43, 44, 48, 56, 60, 61, 63, 69, 70, 75, 76, 82, 84, 89, 96, 100, 101, 122, 126, 134, 138, 147, 151, 155, 158, 160, 174, 186, 198, 200, 205, 207, 212, 213, 215, 230, 239, 242, 273, 276, 305, 322, 327, 328, 339, 360, 361, 368, 369, 382, 409, 411, 438, 467, 546, 590, 591, 602, 606, 891, 894, 981, 985, 1128, 1285, 1290, 1293, 1295, 1296, 1305, 1331, 1340, 1343; *Iliad*, 53, 57, 60, 65, 84–87, 90, 127, 379, 400, 1376, 1377; *Margites*, 45; *Odyssey*, 51, 53, 55, 59–62, 65, 84, 86, 93, 97, 106, 127, 141, 176, 685
Homologies, in Goldmann, 560; in Williams, 560; *see also* Structures of feeling
Hooker, Richard, 316, 317
Hopkins, Gerard Manley, 708, 1027, 1028, 1031, 1036, 1121, 1300
Horace, 5, 7, 79, 129, 130, 132, 142, 148, 158, 161, 162, 166, 169–171, 173, 178, 197, 199, 207, 208, 211, 220, 223, 273, 332, 339, 340, 725, 1078, 1079, 1159, 1295, 1307, 1385; *The Art of Poetry*, 66, 67, **68–77**, 121, 125, 129, 134, 138, 141, 155, 161, 167, 173, 176, 188, 193, 201, 225, 451, 452; biography, 66; *Epistles*, 146, 147, 165, 175, 176, 187, 193, 199, 226, 1286; *Satires*, 151, 174
Horizon of expectations, 1211; in Gadamer, 1169; in Hirsch, 1398, 1399, 1407; in Husserl, 1376, 1393, 1398; in Jauss, 1169, 1170, 1201, 1202, 1204, 1206, 1207, 1213, 1216, 1218; in Popper, 1215; in Sartre, 1182
Horkheimer, Max, 626
Horney, Karen, 1106
Housman, A. E., 800, 1385
Howard, Sir Robert, 160
Howe, Irving, 518, 557
Howells, William Dean, 1130, 1150, 1154, 1365
Hughes, Langston, 1138, 1326, 1327, 1364
Hugo, Victor, 441, 1211; *Les Misérables*, 931; *Notre-Dame de Paris*, 904
Hulme, T. E., 496, 722
Humanism, and poststructuralism, 955
Human nature, 1287, 1332; and evaluation, 1287; in Arnold, 390; in Crane, 826; in Dewey, 498; in Hume, 211, 215, 217; in Samuel Johnson, 241, 242; in Lukács, 601; in Nietzsche, 403; in Shelley, 327, 334; in Barbara Herrnstein Smith, 1332; in Wordsworth, 286, 291, 292
Humboldt, Wilhelm von, 273
Hume, David, 5, 198, 245, 246, 300, 336, 1323, 1331, 1332, 1334; biography, 209; "Of the Standard of Taste," 209–212, **212–222**, 1331; skepticism, 209; *Treatise of Human Nature*, 209
Humor, in Dryden, 166, 180, 185–187, 192; in Hume, 220; in Keats, 320; in Shelley, 330
Hurston, Zora Neale, 1074, 1138, 1139, 1141, 1143, 1145, 1355, 1371

1180; in Tynyanov, 753; in Wimsatt and Beardsley, 1383, 1384, 1387, 1390

Intentional fallacy, 838, 1397; in Burke, 501; in New Criticism, 1376; in Wimsatt and Beardsley, 1384, 1405

Intentionality, 1427

Interaction, in Flynn, 1273, 1274

Interests, in Barbara Herrnstein Smith, 1328, 1329, 1331, 1333, 1334, 1335–1343; in Juhl, 1417–1419, 1421

Internally persuasive discourse, in Bakhtin, 783, 785–787

Interpretation, 1159, 1375; constraints on, 1376, 1379, 1393, 1399, 1418, 1424; in Aquinas, 118; in Barthes, 711, 1007; in Bleich, 1259, 1260; in Crane, 818, 823; in Culler, 918, 919, 921, 922, 925, 927–929, 1412, ; 1415, 1417, 1418; in de Man, 1011, 1014, 1017; in Derrida, 970, 973; in Eco, 855; in Fish, 1161, 1162, 1241, 1242, 1245, 1247–1250, 1252, 1378; in Flynn, 1275, 1277, 1278; in Foucault, 980; in Freud, 593, 641; in Frye, 645, 685; in Greenblatt, 1059; in Hirsch, 1316, 1376, 1377, 1392–1395, 1397–1399, 1401, 1402, 1403, 1408, 1410, 1411; in Holland, 1234; in Iser, 1224, 1227; in Jakobson and Lévi-Strauss, 886; in Jameson, 562, 627; in Jauss, 1202; in Barbara Johnson, 1047, 1048; in Juhl, 1378, 1411, 1413–1423; in Kermode, 1308, 1314, 1316, 1317; in Knapp and Michaels, 1378, 1379, 1424, 1426, 1428, 1431, 1433, 1435; in Kolodny, 1130–1132, 1136; in Lévi-Strauss, 875; in McKeon, 12; in New Criticism, 728, 729; in Nietzsche, 961; in Rader, 837; in Richards, 778; in Said, 1024, 1027; in Barbara Herrnstein Smith, 1321; in Sontag, 544, 546–550; in structuralism, 854, 857; in Wellek, 1401; in Wilson, 588; in Wimsatt and Beardsley, 1375; see also Hermeneutics

Interpretive communities, in Fish, 1161, 1252, 1253; in Tompkins, 1288

Interpretive crux, in Fish, 1241, 1245

Interpretive strategies, in Fish, 1249–1253; in Flynn, 1271, 1275, 1282

Intertextuality, in Barthes, 1008; in Gates, 1367; in Kristeva, 989, 990; in Barbara Herrnstein Smith, 1343; see also Heteroglossia

Intoxication, in Nietzsche, 406, 407

Intrinsic value, in Barbara Herrnstein Smith, 1328; see also Evaluation, Value

Introversion, in Jung, 661

Intuition, in Baker, 1354; in Croce, 447, 450, 454–455, 459, 460, 1385; in Joyce, 839; in Kant, 247, 249, 259, 261, 264, 266, 269, 271; in Keats, 317; in Mukařovský, 866, 867; in Nietzsche, 418; in Plotinus, 107; in Rader, 837; in Wordsworth, 292

Invention, 128; in Boccaccio, 123; in Ronsard, 125; in Sidney, 137; see also Creativity

Involvement, in Flynn, 1273, 1274

Irigaray, Luce, 646, 1072, 1073

Irony, 544, 839, 1127; in Booth, 1191–1193; in Cleanth Brooks, 729, 800–806; in Hirsch, 1410; in Iser, 1229; in Jameson, 633; in Barbara Johnson, 1041, 1049, 1052; in Leavis, 1302, 1304; in New Criticism, 722; in Plato, 18, 20; in Rader, 836, 837, 840, 841; in Robert Penn Warren, 728

Iser, Wolfgang, 1133, 1167, 1272, 1273, 1314, 1380, 1412; biography, 1219; "The Reading Process: A Phenomenological Approach," **1219–1232**

Iteration, in Derrida, 945, 970; in Eco, 936, 938; in Barbara Johnson, 1038; see also Repetition

Ivanov, Vyacheslav, 739, 747

Jacobus, Mary, 1071, 1075

Jakobson, Roman, 717, 722, 724, 850–854, 857, 869, 1012, 1013, 1213, 1214, 1318; biography, 877–878; "Charles Baudelaire's 'Les Chats,'" **878–889**

James, Alice, 1113, 1114

James, Henry, 463, 484, 519, 522, 529, 530, 630, 633, 837, 840, 855, 900–917, 1114, 1150, 1154, 1160, 1185, 1190, 1191, 1197, 1288, 1300, 1304, 1306; biography, 420; expressive criticism, 421; theories of fiction, 420, 421; Works: "The Altar of the Dead," 910, 911, 913; "The Art of Fiction," **422–433**; "The Author of 'Beltraffio,'" 912; The Beast in the Jungle, 916, 917; "The Beldonald Holbein," 903; "The Birthplace," 913, 914; "Brooksmith," 903; "In the Cage," 902–904; An International Episode, 431; "Maud-Evelyn," 909; The Portrait of a Lady, 811; "Sir Dominick Ferrand," 901, 903, 909, 913; "Sir Edmund Orme," 905, 906, 908, 909; "The Death of the Lion," 912; "The Figure in the Carpet," 902, 915, 916; "The Friends of the Friends," 908; "The Private Life," 912, 913, 915; "The Pupil," 903; "The Real Thing," 911, 912; "The Tone of Time," 913; The Turn of the Screw, 905, 907, 908, 1411, 1420; "The Velvet Glove," 914

James, William, 484, 494, 740, 892

Jameson, Fredric, 553, 562, 563, 648, 954, 1240, 1317, 1319; biography, 620–621; The Political Unconscious, 562, 621, **621–636**; The Prison House of Language, 621

Jarrell, Randall, "Eighth Air Force," 805–806

Jarry, Alfred, 585

Jauss, Hans Robert, 1167, 1325, 1342, 1411; biography, 1197–1198; "Literary History as a Challenge to Literary Theory," **1198–1218**

Jazz, in Baker, 1345, 1352

Jefferson, Thomas, 1365

Jemie, Onwuchekwa, 1326, 1327

Jerome, St., 983

Jews, 79, 85

Johnson, Barbara, 950, 1063; biography, 1036–1037; "Melville's Fist: The Execution of Billy Budd," **1037–1056**

Johnson, Samuel, 5, 6, 209, 278, 282–284, 296, 297, 384, 423, 588, 590, 593, 613, 620, 723, 1086, 1159, 1161, 1288, 1321, 1326, 1380; biography, 223; Irene, 384; Lives of the Poets, 384, 497; moralism of, 224; "Preface to Shakespeare," 133, **229–243**, 380, 553; The Rambler, **225–228**; Rasselas, **228–229**; rhetorical principles, 223; tragic vision, 225; universalizing perspective, 224

Jones, Alexander, 1411

Jones, Ernest, Hamlet and Oedipus, 641

Jones, LeRoi. See Baraka, Amiri

Jonson, Ben, 160, 162, 169, 175, 180, 185, 189, 190, 192, 194, 196, 240, 465, 588, 1033, 1301; Works: The Alchemist, 180, 182, 812; Bartholomew Fair, 180; Catiline, 177, 183; Epicoene, 180, 182, 184, 186–188; Every Man in His Humour, 185; Every Man out of His Humour, 203; Magnetic Lady, 179; Sad Shepherd, 193; Sejanus, 177; Timber, or Discoveries, 168; Volpone, 182, 812, 1187

Jouissance, in Barthes, 948, 1010, 1164

Joyce, James, 421, 520, 525, 598, 599, 601, 604, 611, 684, 828, 829, 835, 837, 838, 844, 898, 935, 1159, 1289, 1305, 1306, 1327, 1375; "Araby," 1271, 1272, 1274, 1276; Dubliners, 843; Finnegans Wake, 695, 845; Portrait of the Artist as a Young Man, 828, 837, 839–841, 1033; Stephen Hero, 841; Ulysses, 597, 813, 837, 841, 844–846, 1096, 1228

Judgment, 12, 190; in Arnold, 396; in Baker, 1365; in Bakhtin, 793, 797; in Baym, 1148; in Bleich, 1270, 1271; in Booth, 840, 1188, 1190; in Crane, 810, 811, 823–825; in Croce, 461; in Dryden, 172, 183, 185, 187, 190, 193; in Eliot, 467; in Fish, 1243; in Flynn, 1272, 1276, 1278, 1281, 1283; in Frye, 678; in Hume, 211, 213, 214, 217, 219; in Barbara Johnson, 1051–1054, 1056; in Samuel Johnson, 230; in Jung, 658; in Kant, 244, 246, 248–258, 260, 261, 263, 266, 267; in Knapp and Michaels, 1428; in Leavis, 1300; in McDowell, 1141; in Pope, 199, 200, 201, 204, 206; in Rader, 833, 840; in Said, 1035; in Barbara Herrnstein Smith, 1336, 1337; in Wimsatt and Beardsley, 1386

*Letters of a Portuguese Nun*, 282

Lévi-Strauss, Claude, 13, 14, 621, 629, 647, 686, 694, 697, 702, 711, 722, 756, 850, 852, 853, 856, 946, 961, 963, 964, 989, 991, 1214, 1317; biography, 868–869; method, 872; "Charles Baudelaire's 'Les Chats,'" **878–890**; "The Structural Study of Myth," **869–877**

Levin, Richard, 814

Levin, Samuel R., 1364

Levine, Lawrence W., 1355

Lewes, George Henry, 1103, 1104, 1118

Lewis, C. S., 1127

Lewis, R. W. B., 1152

Lewis, Sinclair, *Babbitt*, 515

Lewis, Wyndham, 841

Lexicon, in Mukařovský, 862

Liberalism, in Trilling, 520

Libido, in Freud, 638, 644, 646, 651; in Frye, 684

Lichtenstein, Heinz, 1232

Lindenberger, Herbert, 954

Linguistics, in Lévi-Strauss, 850

Linton, Eliza Lynn, 1111

Literary competence, in Culler, 918, 920

Literary ecology, and the canon, 1287; in Barbara Herrnstein Smith, 1340

Literary economy, in Aristotle, 64; *see also* Economics and literature

Literary history, 553, 1138, 1375; in Bakhtin, 785, 789; in Baym, 1147, 1151; in Crane, 810; in Frye, 680, 683; in Gilbert and Gubar, 1128; in Greenblatt, 1058; in Iser, 1169; in Jauss, 1168, 1197–1199, 1209, 1212, 1213, 1218; in Kolodny, 1129, 1136; in Kristeva, 993; in Leavis, 1301; in Rader, 836, 838; in Russian formalism, 1210; in Said, 1027; in Shklovsky, 748; in Showalter, 1105, 1106, 1110, 1118; in Tynyanov, 748, 749, 755; in Wimsatt and Beardsley, 1383; *see also* History, History and literature

Literary pragmatics, in Bakhtin, 725

Literary sociology, in Jauss, 1204, 1214; in Sammons, 1325; *see also* Society and literature

Literary system, in Culler, 918–922, 928

Literature, in Arnold, 379, 384, 397; in Barthes, 1007; in Bleich, 1254; in Burke, 501, 514, 516; in Culler, 918; in de Man, 1011, 1021; in Eliot, 588; in Foucault, 952, 982; in Freud, 642; in Frye, 677; in Genette, 890; in Greenblatt, 1060; in Samuel Johnson, 239; in Kristeva, 1002; in Leavis, 1300; in Marxist criticism, 555; in Proust, 481, 482; in Russian formalism, 724; in Trilling, 519, 520; in Williams, 619

Livy, 142, 327

Locke, John, 299, 300, 336, 534; *Essay Concerning Human Understanding*, 299

Logocentrism, in Derrida, 1073

Longfellow, Henry Wadsworth, 1286

Longinus, 78, 207, 734, 826, 827, 1384; identity of, 78; influence of, 80; method of, 79; *On the Sublime*, **80–106**, 125

Lowell, James Russell, 1286

Lowes, John Livingston, 1387

Lucan, 328, 335; *Pharsalia*, 238

Lucretius, 138, 332, 335, 406, 693, 1299

Lukács, Georg, 553, 556, 559, 563, 631, 635, 719, 1035, 1036; biography, 596–597; *History and Class Consciousness*, 596; "The Ideology of Modernism," 557, **597–611**; *Theory of the Novel*, 627, 629

Lyric, 79, 596; as drama, 1384; in Bakhtin, 795; in Cleanth Brooks, 802; in Crane, 810, 813, 814, 822, 824; in Croce, 458; in Culler, 854; in Dryden, 166; in Genette, 896; in Hegel, 344; in Joyce, 839; in Poe, 374; in Ronsard, 128; in Schiller, 277; in Sidney, 150, 156; in Wordsworth, 293; *see also* Poem

Lyrical intuition, in Croce, 447, 448, 450, 485, 728

Lysias, 18

Macaulay, Rose, 1118

Macaulay, Thomas Babington, 424

Macherey, Pierre, 562, 1338

Machiavelli, Niccolo, 13, 330; *Clitia*, 221

Maclean, Norman, 731, 813, 820

MacLeish, Archibald, 593, 1383

Maecenas, 66

Magnitude, in Aristotle, 47, 48, 60, 61, 65, 713; in Kant, 263–266; in Plotinus, 110; in Poe, 373

Mailer, Norman, 1066, 1136

Male chauvinism, in Baym, 1147

Malherbe, François de, 1293

Mallarmé, Stéphane, 576, 866, 895, 918, 1009, 1211

Malory, Sir Thomas, *Morte D'Arthur*, 239, 645

Malraux, André, 1089

Man, Paul de. *See* de Man, Paul

Mandeville, Thomas, 617

Manifest content, in Freud, 547, 640; in Holland, 1165

Manley, Elizabeth, 1286

Mann, Thomas, 547, 598, 602, 604, 1303; *Doctor Faustus*, 608; *Lotte in Weimar*, 597

Mannheim, Karl, 1372

Mansfield, Katherine, 1117, 1197

Mapping of literary theory, in Abrams, 3, 8, 12, 14; in Crane, 9, 12; in Friedman, 9, 12; in Frye, 645; in Hernadi, 9, 12; in McKeon, 12, 13

Margolis, Joseph, 1412

Marlowe, Christopher, 465, 707

Marryat, Captain, 1301

Marryat, Florence, 1115

Marsh, Robert C., 731

Martial, 164, 169

Martin, Violet, 1115

Martineau, Harriet, 1110, 1111

Marvell, Andrew, 685, 802, 804, 1376, 1389, 1391, 1395, 1399; "To His Coy Mistress," 821

Marx, Karl, 5, 8, 343, 500, 446, 447, 518, 553, 554, 561, 571, 572, 591, 985, 1032, 1118, 1290; biography, 565; *Capital*, 565; *Communist Manifesto*, 565; *Critique of Political Economy*, 555, 565, **569–571**; *The German Ideology*, **565–569**; socialist revolutionary, 556

Marxist criticism, 14, 446, 518, **553–636**, 986, 1006, 1006, 1162, 1166, 1167, 1171, 1198, 1344; and feminism, 1075; as political movement, 556; in Baker, 1353–1355; in Henderson, 1354; in Kristeva, 953

Mask, in Jung, 644; in Pound, 1375; in Yeats, 1375

Massinger, Philip, 464, 465

Materialism, in Aristotle, 4

Material of art, in Plotinus, 109

Mathesius, Vilem, 851

Matter, in Crane, 807, 809, 817; in Rader, 830

Matthiessen, F. O., 1149, 1389, 1390

Maupassant, Guy de, 442, 901

Mayakovsky, Vladimir, 593, 754

McCarthy, Mary, 588

McCoy, Richard, 954

McDowell, Deborah, 1074; biography, 1137; "New Directions for Black Feminist Criticism," **1138–1146**

McGann, Jerome, 954

McKeon, Richard, 12, 14, 731

Meaning, 1377, 1393; in Croce, 1385; in Culler, 918; in de Man, 1432; in Eliot, 1395; in Hirsch, 1376, 1378, 1392–1398, 1400, 1403, 1405, 1406, 1411; in Husserl, 1396; in Juhl, 1377, 1415, 1417, 1420, 1421, 1430; in Kermode, 1308; in Knapp and

129; in Stepto, 1360–1362; in structuralism, 852; in Wagner, 404; in Weber, 625

Mytheme, in Lévi-Strauss, 850, 853, 872, 873, 966

Nabokov, Vladimir, 942

Naive, 318; in Kermode, 1314; in Schiller, 273, 274, 276, 277, 409, 661, 684; *see also* Sentimental

Narcissism, in Jung, 658

*Narrataire. See* Narratee

Narratee, 1163, 1164; in Derrida, 972; in Prince, 1163

Narrative, 891; in Aristotle, 60, 891; in Barthes, 948; in Peter Brooks, 644, 710–713, 716, 720; in Crane, 814; in Derrida, 971; in Dryden, 168, 177, 179; in Eco, 855, 930–932, 934, 938, 939; in Frye, 645, 682; in Genette, 856, 890, 892, 893–895, 897–899; in James, 428; in Jameson, 621, 623, 628, 629, 635; in Samuel Johnson, 235; in Kermode, 1309, 1311, 1313; in Kristeva, 994, 997, 1003, 1004; in Lacan, 688; in Longinus, 96; in Lukács, 597; in Plato, 891; in Poe, 371; in Rader, 840; in Schiller, 277; in Sidney, 149; in Todorov, 901, 904; *see also* Fiction, Novel

Narratology, 857; in Peter Brooks, 710

Narrator, in Booth, 1192, 1196; in Derrida, 971, 973, 976; in Juhl, 1421

Naturalism, in Dewey, 484; in Lukács, 603, 606, 610

Nature, 612; in Baym, 1155, 1156; in Benjamin, 575; in Boccaccio, 124; in Coleridge, 305, 310, 316; in Crane, 824; in Croce, 447; in Derrida, 946; in Dewey, 498; in Dryden, 166, 169, 170, 172, 176, 189–191, 194; in Emerson, 359, 360, 362, 365; in Hegel, 342, 345, 347, 350; in Horace, 70, 76; in Hume, 215, 220; in Barbara Johnson, 1046, 1051, 1053; in Samuel Johnson, 224, 226, 228, 230, 232, 233, 238, 239, 241; in Jung, 674; in Kant, 245, 246, 250, 261, 262, 264–269, 271; in Kermode, 1312; in Lévi-Strauss, 946, 963, 964; in Longinus, 81, 101, 103, 105; in Nietzsche, 407, 409; in Plato, 210; in Plotinus, 108–110, 112, 116; in Pope, 198, 199, 200–204, 205, 207; in Proust, 478; in Richards, 780; in Schiller, 273–276; in Sidney, 137, 144; in de Staël, 278, 281; in Williams, 612–616, 618–620; in Wordsworth, 287, 288, 291–293, 295

Neal, Larry, 1348, 1349, 1355, 1358, 1365, 1367, 1368

Negative capability, in Eliot, 468; in Keats, 317, 318, 320; in Trilling, 529

Neo-Aristotelianism, 7, 721, 724, 728, 730–734, **807–846**; aesthetics, 731; disputes with New Criticism, 731; later generations, 731; origins, 731; pluralism, 734; positivism of, 732

Neoplatonism, 17; in Plotinus, 107

Nerval, Gérard de, 1202, 1211, 1391

Neurosis, in Freud, 657

New Criticism, 7, 8, 503, 519, 533, 544, 721, 722, 724, 726–730, 769, 811, 857, 949, 1011, 1058, 1126, 1152, 1160, 1239, 1320, 1391; and authorial intention, 1375; decline and fall, 730; disdain of professionalism, 730

New Historicism, 953, 954, 1057; in Greenblatt, 1058, 1059

Newman, John Henry, 1086

New pragmatism, 1424

Newton, Isaac, 160, 178, 986, 986

Newton, Judith Lowder, 1075

*Nibelungenlied*, 1296

Nietzsche, Friedrich, 546, 624, 626, 628, 631, 658, 706, 707, 943, 946, 947, 951, 955, 961, 962, 970, 980, 1014, 1015, 1019, 1020, 1099, 1325; biography, 403; *The Birth of Tragedy from the Spirit of Music*, 403, **405–419**; central theme, 403; *The Genealogy of Morals*, 706, 1031; philosophical style, 403; *Thus Spake Zarathustra*, 403, 661, 662; *The Will to Power*, 1031

Nightingale, Florence, 1082, 1111, 1114

Nochlin, Linda, 1106

*Nom-du-Père*, in Lacan, 647, 648

Noumena, in Kant, 300

Novalis (Friedrich von Hardenberg), 1211

Novel, in Bakhtin, 781, 784, 787; in Peter Brooks, 720; in Coleridge, 309; in Crane, 812; in Culler, 920; in Eco, 931; in Foucault, 985; in Genette, 890, 895, 898, 899; in Iser, 1222; in James, 421–423, 425, 427, 428, 431, 433; in Kermode, 1308, 1312; in Kristeva, 990, 992, 995–997, 1000, 1002, 1004, 1005; in Leavis, 1304–1306; in Nietzsche, 414; in Propp, 764; in Proust, 477; in Rader, 828; in Showalter, 1107, 1110; in de Staël, 278, 280; in Todorov, 911; in Tolstoy, 443; in Tynyanov, 751; in Wordsworth, 288; *see also* Fiction, Narrative

Objectification, in Bleich, 1270

Objective correlative, in Eliot, 463–465, 532, 727

Objectivity, in Hirsch, 1376, 1407; in Husserl, 1396; in Barbara Herrnstein Smith, 1322, 1337; *see also* Subjectivity

Objects of imitation, in Aristotle, 43

Oedipus complex, in Bloom, 644, 707, 708; in Freud, 639, 641; in Lacan, 686, 690; in Lévi-Strauss, 876

Ogden, C. K., 769

Ogilby, John, 214

Ohmann, Richard, 8, 905, 1014

Oliphant, Margaret, 1111, 1112

Olmi, Ermanno, 549

Olsen, Tillie, 1143

Olson, Elder, 46, 731, 813

O'Meally, Robert, 1371

O'Neill, Eugene, 520, 527–529

Ontological project, in Knapp and Michaels, 1378, 1433

Opera, in Nietzsche, 415–418

OPOYAZ, 722, 724, 737, 748

Oral phase, in Freud, 638, 646

Order, in Horace, 69; in Ronsard, 128

Organic form, 7, 921; in Cleanth Brooks, 800, 805; in Coleridge, 302, 303, 305; in Emerson, 365; in James, 431; in Longinus, 103; *see also* Form

Originality, 1386; in Baym, 1148; in Bloom, 706, 708; in Coleridge, 305; in Eliot, 467, 468; in Emerson, 369; in Foucault, 988; in Freud, 655; in Jauss, 1201; in Kant, 271; in Lévi-Strauss, 871; in Leavis, 1302, 1303, 1306; in New Criticism, 728; in Poe, 372, 375, 376; in Russian formalism, 1211; in Said, 1023; in Todorov, 910

Orrery, Roger Boyle, Earl of, 193

Orwell, George, 636, 1319; *Nineteen Eighty-Four*, 812

Otway, Thomas, *The Orphan*, 814

Over-Soul, in Emerson, 357, 358

Overdetermination, 9; in Althusser, 623

Ovid, 148, 154, 158, 173, 174, 190, 196, 211, 220, 332, 1078

Ovsyaniko-Kulikovsky, Dmitri, 738, 740

Ozick, Cynthia, 1105, 1108

Ozu, Yasuhiro, 550

Painting, 7; in Benjamin, 587; in Croce, 450; in Foucault, 985; in Frye, 681; in Hegel, 344, 354, 355; in Kant, 269; in Langer, 536, 541, 542; in Plotinus, 107; in Sontag, 548; in Tolstoy, 442, 444; in Wordsworth, 290

Parable, 141; in Gilbert and Gubar, 1122, 1123; *see also* Fable

Paradigm, 6; in Baker, 1350, 1355, 1359, 1372; in Kuhn, 1345, 1349, 1350

Paradigmata, in Lacan, 647; in structuralism, 848, 849; in Todorov, 711, 1013; *see also* Syntagmata

Paradox, 544; in Cleanth Brooks, 729, 1376

Paraphrasable content, in Cleanth Brooks, 728

Parapraxis, in Freud, 638, 643

Parmenides, 896

Parody, in Bakhtin, 787

Radway, Janice, 1166
Rahv, Philip, 518, 557
Raleigh, Sir Walter, 802
Rank, Otto, 1235
Ransom, John Crowe, 501, 726, 727–730
Raphael, 579
Reade, Charles, 1286, 1301
Reader, 1158, 1159; actual, 1163, 1164; and gender, 2; ideal, 8, 1163; implied, 1164; social, 1166; virtual, 1163; in Baker, 1351, 1367; in Bakhtin, 786; in Barthes, 711, 948, 1006, 1009; in Benjamin, 581; in Bleich, 1255, 1258, 1260; in Booth, 1188, 1191, 1193; in Peter Brooks, 720; in Burke, 515; in Culler, 920, 922–924, 926; in de Man, 1020; in Eco, 855, 930, 935, 936, 938, 939; in Fish, 1161, 1162, 1244–1247, 1249, 1253, 1378; in Flynn, 1273; in Frye, 685; in Genette, 856, 898; in Hirsch, 1394, 1396; in Holland, 1232, 1239; in Hume, 209, 211; in Iser, 1221, 1222, 1225, 1227, 1229, 1232; in Jakobson and Lévi-Strauss, 888; in Jauss, 1198, 1200, 1202, 1206, 1216; in Barbara Johnson, 1041, 1055; in Samuel Johnson, 237; in Kermode, 1309, 1312, 1314, 1317, 1321; in Kolodny, 1066, 1129, 1133, 1135; in Kristeva, 996; in Langer, 536; in Mukařovský, 862; in neo-Aristotelianism, 731, 734; in New Criticism, 727; in Rader, 830, 835, 841, 846; in Richards, 726; in Said, 1034; in Sartre, 1176, 1178, 1180; in Sontag, 543, 544; in de Staël, 280; in structuralism, 1163; in Todorov, 906, 908; in Wordsworth, 284, 295–297; see also Audience
Reader-response criticism, **1158–1285**
Reading, as activity or process, 8; in Barthes, 1006, 1009; in Bloom, 1127; in Culler, 920, 922–924; in Fetterley, 1067; in Fish, 1243, 1244, 1248, 1251; in Flynn, 1067, 1271; in Holland, 1234; in Iser, 1224, 1229, 1232, 1274; in Jauss, 1216; in Barbara Johnson, 1040, 1041, 1049, 1051; in Kermode, 1308; in Kolodny, 1066, 1128, 1131; in Poulet, 1272; in Sartre, 1175, 1177, 1178, 1180
Real, in Lacan, 647, 695, 1006; see also Imaginary, Symbolic
Realism, 829; in Booth, 1196; in Burke, 515; in James, 421, 423, 424, 427; in Jameson, 635; in Jauss, 1214; in Samuel Johnson, 225; in Knapp and Michaels, 1435; in Kristeva, 993; in Lukács, 557, 597, 598, 600, 604, 606, 608, 611; in Mukařovský, 864; in Proust, 474, 476; in Rader, 828, 832; in Sartre, 1182; in Showalter, 1115, 1118
Realism-plot-judgment form, in Rader, 828, 829, 837, 838; see also Action model, Pseudofactual form, Simular form
Reality, in Benjamin, 582; in Croce, 451; in Freud, 652; in James, 426; in Lukács, 603; in Propp, 758, 766; in Proust, 474, 477
Reality principle, in Freud, 638
Reality-testing, in Holland, 1239
Realization, in Iser, 1220
Reason, in Crane, 811; in Croce, 447; in Kant, 250, 251, 256, 264; in Plato, 26, 27; in Pope, 201; in Schiller, 277; in Shelley, 321, 323; in de Staël, 279
Reception, 1320; in Benjamin, 579, 584, 587, 588; in Fish, 1250; in Jauss, 1170, 1198–1202, 1204, 1206, 1210, 1211, 1213; in Kant, 246; in Kolodny, 1131; in Radway, 1166; in Said, 1023; in Sontag, 543
Receptivity, in Flynn, 1283
Recognition, in Aristotle, 49, 50, 53, 60, 712; in Barthes, 712; in Peter Brooks, 718, 719; in Dryden, 170
Reconstructionism (mode of Afro-American poetics), in Baker, 1358–1361, 1364, 1373
Redding, Saunders, 1354
Reed, Ishmael, 1368
Reference, in Richards, 770–772, 774; in Ricoeur, 1023; see also Bedeutung, Significance
Referentiality, in Richards, 726
Reflection, in Lukács, 557, 558, in Marxist criticism, 557, 558

Reichenbach, Hans, 932
Reification, in Jameson, 635
Relations of production, in Marx, 567–570; in Marxist criticism, 558, 560
Relativism, in Barbara Herrnstein Smith, 1337
Religion, 13; in Arnold, 392, 393, 397; in Frye, 684; in Hegel, 342, 346; in New Criticism, 728; in Propp, 760; in Richards, 771; in Allen Tate, 529; in Tolstoy, 434, 441
Rembrandt, 210, 482, 574, 575
Renaissance, 125, 126, 131, 133, 160, 197, 417, 439, 458, 460, 575, 584, 587, 706, 727, 814, 815, 953, 992, 993, 1058, 1060
Renan, Ernest, 1031
Renoir, Jean, 550
Repertoire, in Fish, 1252; in Iser, 1228
Repetition, in Peter Brooks, 713, 714, 718; in Freud, 715, 716; in Jameson, 633; in Lévi-Strauss, 877; in Wordsworth, 707
Repetition compulsion, 714; in Freud, 642, 643, 715, 718; in Lacan, 687, 690, 698
Representation, 1127, 1430; in Aristotle, 545, 891; in Baker, 1348; in Bakhtin, 781–784, 786, 790; in Benjamin, 580, 582; in Peter Brooks, 714; in Coleridge, 312; in Crane, 812, 813, 819, 820, 824; in Croce, 453; in Culler, 919; in de Man, 1017; in Derrida, 972; in Freud, 651; in Frye, 682; in Genette, 890, 892, 893, 896, 899; in Greenblatt, 1058, 1062; in Hegel, 348, 355; in Hirsch, 1392; in James, 423; in Jameson, 621, 631; in Jauss, 1198–1200, 1209, 1212, 1214; in Samuel Johnson, 224, 230, 236, 242; in Juhl, 1411; in Kant, 248, 249, 251, 252, 255, 256, 259, 262, 263, 268, 271, 300; in Kolodny, 1135; in Kristeva, 993, 995, 1004; in Rader, 838, 844; in Ronsard, 128; in Russian formalism, 723; in Schiller, 276, 277; in Shelley, 325; in Todorov, 903; see also Imitation
Repression, 642; in Freud, 638, 643, 653, 659, 717; in Barbara Johnson, 1043–1045, 1055; in Jung, 658; in Lacan, 646, 647, 687; in Showalter, 1113, 1114
Response, in Bakhtin, 793; in Bleich, 1263, 1264, 1270; in Flynn, 1275, 1282; in Holland, 1234, 1235, 1238; in Kermode, 1308; in Rader, 828; in Richards, 1235
Retrospection, in Iser, 1223–1225, 1229
Return of the repressed, in Peter Brooks, 714, 719; in Cixous, 1097; in Jameson, 1317; in Lacan, 701
Reversal, in Aristotle, 49, 50, 56, 60; in Dryden, 170; in Barbara Johnson, 1040; in Kermode, 1309
Revolution, critical, 6, 8, 14; political, 569; scientific, 6
Reynolds, Sir Joshua, 297
Rhetoric, 79, 220; in Aristotle, 47; in Bakhtin, 790; in Boccaccio, 123, 124; in Booth, 1160, 1185, 1188; in Croce, 459; in Culler, 922; in de Man, 1013–1015, 1020; in Hume, 214, 219; in Kant, 269; in Ronsard, 125, 128; in Sidney, 137, 157; in Trilling, 525
Rhetorical criticism, 6, 1159; in Hume, 209; in Samuel Johnson, 223; in Wordsworth, 283
Rhyme, in Peter Brooks, 644, 714; in Coleridge, 302; in Dryden, 162, 179, 189, 190, 192, 195, 196; in Jakobson and Lévi-Strauss, 880, 881, 883, 886; in Langer, 536; in Pope, 206; in Ronsard, 130; in Sidney, 154, 158
Rhythm, in Poe, 375; in Shklovsky, 747, 748; in Tynyanov, 750, 752; see also Meter
Ricardou, Jean, 1131
Rich, Adrienne, 1075, 1123, 1125, 1136, 1141
Richards, I. A., 533, 726–729, 801, 807, 1159, 1201, 1235, 1236, 1256, 1323, 1386; biography, 769; *Principles of Literary Criticism*, **769–780**
Richardson, Dorothy, 1117
Richardson, Juliet, 1075
Richardson, Samuel, 280, 833, 836, 838, 1288, 1302; *Clarissa*, 295, 832, 1030; *Pamela*, 828–832
Richter, David, 853

667, 670, 672, 675, 676; in Lacan, 646–648, 700; in Trilling, 526, 528
Undecidability, in Fish, 1162; in Jameson, 629
Understanding, in Coleridge, 310, 313; in Hume, 214, 219; in Kant, 248, 259, 261, 265, 270, 271; in Schiller, 273, 274
Unity, 236, 921, 1386; in Aristotle, 47, 48, 60, 64; in Bakhtin, 781; in Coleridge, 310; in Crane, 807, 823; in Dewey, 492; in Foucault, 984; in Frye, 679; in Hegel, 348, 350, 353; in Horace, 71; in Kant, 267; in Mukařovský, 863; in neo-Aristotelianism, 732; in Plotinus, 107, 109, 112, 114; in Poe, 373; in Sainte-Beuve, 1295; in Schiller, 275, 277
Unity of action, in Aristotle, 161; in Dryden, 161, 167, 168, 175, 177, 181, 182, 186; in Samuel Johnson, 236, 238; in Sidney, 133
Unity of place, in Corneille, 161; in Dryden, 161, 167–169, 175, 183, 186; in Samuel Johnson, 236–238; in Sidney, 133, 154
Unity of time, in Aristotle, 45, 46, 161; in Corneille, 161; in Dryden, 161, 167, 168, 175, 183, 186; in Samuel Johnson, 224, 236–238; in Sidney, 133, 154, 155
Universality, in Aristotle, 49; in Samuel Johnson, 224; in Kant, 245, 252–255, 261; in Sidney, 142; in Barbara Herrnstein Smith, 1336
University, as factor in artistic change, 7
Unreliable narrator, in Booth, 1160
Updike, John, *Rabbit, Run*, 1153
Use-value, in Baker, 1364; in Barbara Herrnstein Smith, 1328, 1330
Utility, in Kant, 245
Utterance, in Juhl, 1415, 1416, 1423; in Knapp and Michaels, 1429, 1433

Valentinus, 708, 709
Valéry, Paul, 572, 573, 584, 623, 890, 920, 1012, 1200, 1211
Valmiki, 1298
Value, 1287; in Aristotle, 892; in Booth, 1160, 1194–1196; in Crane, 824, 825; in Dryden, 167; in Hirsch, 1324; in Jameson, 625, 626; in Jauss, 1203; in Samuel Johnson, 229; in Plato, 26, 892; in Rader, 828, 846; in Sidney, 147; in Barbara Herrnstein Smith, 1321, 1322, 1327–1330, 1335, 1342; in Tolstoy, 435; in Tynyanov, 748; *see also* Evaluation, Judgment, Taste
Van Gogh, Vincent, 493, 494, 1181
Velasquez, Diego, 245
Velleius Paterculus, 167, 169, 170, 180
Verification, in Hirsch, 1406, 1407, 1410
Verisimilitude, in Coleridge, 313; in Croce, 451; in Dryden, 168, 169, 171, 178, 182, 189; in Hume, 219; in Iser, 1229; in Jameson, 621; in Samuel Johnson, 231, 236; in Lacan, 691; in Rader, 835; in Ronsard, 128; in de Staël, 279, 281
Vermeer, Jan, 482, 1181
Verne, Jules, 562, 894
Verse, 139; in Dryden, 166, 176; in Samuel Johnson, 242; in Sidney, 148; in Wordsworth, 286; *see also* Prose, Prosody
Veselovsky, Alexander, 723, 740
Vico, Giambattista, 322, 590, 592, 706, 708, 1036
Vida, Marco Girolamo, 208
Villon, François, 380, 860
Virgil, 66, 122, 129, 130, 137, 138, 148, 154, 158–160, 165, 169, 173, 174, 186, 191, 198, 199, 200, 208, 220, 273, 309, 332, 339, 340, 417, 996, 1078, 1079, 1293, 1295, 1298, 1319; *Aeneid*, 127, 136, 141, 142, 144, 153, 204, 238, 379, 449, 451; *Eclogues*, 145, 185, 189, 395; *Georgics*, 192
Virtual object, in Iser, 1223, 1224; in Langer, 537
Voltaire, 232, 233, 238, 240, 305, 336, 386, 394, 452, 1293, 1298, 1299; *Candide*, 280, 703
Vulgar Marxism, 556, 557, 563; *see also* Marxist criticism
Vyasa, 1298

Wagner, Richard, 404, 418, 457; *Die Meistersinger*, 406; *Parsifal*, 405; *Tristan und Isolde*, 404, 505
Walcott, Derek, 1370
Walker, Alice, 1074, 1138–1141, 1144, 1145
Waller, Edmund, 166, 203
Walsh, William, 208
Ward, Mrs. Humphrey, 1157
Warner, Susan, 1287
Warren, Austin, 519, 523, 726, 1393–1395
Warren, Robert Penn, 525, 726, 729, 731, 799
Washington, Booker T., 1362
Washington, Mary Helen, 1145
Watson, L. Grant, 1037
Watt, Ian, 828–830, 832, 835, 1109
Watteau, Jean Antoine, 478
Wattenberg, Ben, 1358
Weaver, Raymond, 1037
Weber, Max, 624, 625
Webster, John, 1389; *The Duchess of Malfi*, 814
Weil, Simone, 1376
Wellek, René, 519, 523, 525, 726, 727, 1201, 1207, 1393–1395, 1401
Wells, H. G., 1117
Welsh, Alexander, 1108
West, Benjamin, 320
Weston, Jessie, 1389
Wharton, Edith, 1150, 1153, 1154
Wheatley, Phillis, 1074, 1365
White, Gilbert, of Selborne, 616
White, Hayden, 954
White female chauvinism, in Moers, 1138; in Spacks, 1138
Whitehead, Alfred North, 17, 532
Whitman, Walt, 550, 706, 708, 778
Whittier, John Greenleaf, 1286
Whorf, Benjamin Lee, 538, 1369
Wilcox, Ella Wheeler, 1323, 1326
Wilde, Oscar, 705, 706, 1027–1031, 1036
Will, in Coleridge, 301, 306, 310; in Dewey, 494; in Hirsch, 1376; in Jung, 661, 665, 668; in Nietzsche, 403, 404, 413; in Plotinus, 115; in Schiller, 273; in Schopenhauer, 403; in Shelley, 337
Williams, Charles, 1127
Williams, Raymond, 556, 560–563, 612, 954, 1325; biography, 611–612; *The Country and the City*, 560, 612, **612–620**; *The English Novel*, 634; *Keywords: A Vocabulary of Culture and Society*, 555; *Marxism and Literature*, 612
Williams, Tennessee, *A Streetcar Named Desire*, 548
Williams, William Carlos, 706; "The Dance," 853
Willing suspension of disbelief, in Coleridge, 307
Will to power, in Nietzsche, 403; in Said, 1034
Wilson, Edmund, 518, 539, 553, 557, 1193, 1411; biography, 588; "The Historical Interpretation of Literature," **589–596**; *The Triple Thinkers*, 588
Wilson, J. Dover, 1058, 1059
Wilson, William Julius, 1358
Wimsatt, William K., Jr., 500, 727, 731, 799, 1015, 1159, 1322, 1323, 1326, 1375, 1378, 1391, 1433; biography, 1382; "The Intentional Fallacy," **1383–1391**
Winckelmann, Johann Joachim, 245
Winters, Yvor, 726, 1322
Wish-fulfillment, in Freud, 653, 654, 713; in Rader, 830
Wit, in Dryden, 164, 165, 167, 169, 172, 173, 175, 182, 185, 186, 187, 193; in Samuel Johnson, 242; in Keats, 320; in Pope, 198, 199, 200–208; in Schiller, 275; in Shelley, 330; in Sidney, 148, 150, 153, 154
Withers, George, 165
Withim, Philip, 1037, 1050